HEBREW – ENGLISH EDITION OF
THE BABYLONIAN TALMUD

SEDER KODASHIM

ZEBAHIM

תלמוד בבלי

מסכת

זבחים

עם פירוש רש״י ותוספות

ובצירוף תִרגום ופירוש והערות באנגלית

על ידי

אהרן מרדכי פרידמאן ז״ל

בעריכת

יחזקאל (איזידור) אפשטין ז״ל

דפוס שונצין

שנת להחזיר העטרה ליושנה לפ״ק

לונדון

HEBREW-ENGLISH EDITION OF
THE BABYLONIAN TALMUD

ZEBAHIM

TRANSLATED INTO ENGLISH
WITH NOTES, GLOSSARY AND INDICES BY
RABBI DR. H. FREEDMAN, B.A., Ph.D.

UNDER THE EDITORSHIP OF
RABBI DR. I. EPSTEIN, B.A., PH.D., D. LITT.

LONDON
THE SONCINO PRESS
1988

0-900689-93-5

PUBLISHERS' NOTE

This HEBREW-ENGLISH EDITION of THE SONCINO TALMUD is being published to facilitate the easier reference to the original text by scholars and students.

The Soncino Press is privileged to be able to include the Novellae of Rabbi Moshe Feinstein o.b.m., on Tractate Zebahim (© Copyright 1973 Judaica Press Ltd), and we wish to thank Judaica Press Ltd. for permission to include this original material.

The Publishers wish to express their sincere thanks to Rabbi Dr. A. Melinek, B.A., Ph.D., for his painstaking care in examining the texts and making the necessary corrections for the preparation of these Tractates.

It has been necessary to duplicate some of the original Hebrew-Aramaic pages in this Tractate where the text has been of such length as to require more than one page of English translation.

נדפס בדפוס האחים גרויס
Printed in U.S.A. GROSS BROS. Printing Co. Inc.
3125 SUMMIT AVENUE, UNION CITY, NJ 07087
Tel. (201) 865-4606 • (212) 594-7757

EPILOGUE

BY

THE VERY REV. THE CHIEF RABBI

ISRAEL BRODIE

With the appearance of the volumes of the Order Ḳodashim the great enterprise of the Soncino English translation of the Babylonian Talmud is at last completed and fulfilled. On the shelves of reference libraries in this country and in other lands now stands a monumental work of many volumes attractively set up and printed. Students of basic Rabbinic literature can now gratefully welcome an apparatus which takes an honourable place among the aids which are indispensable for the understanding and appreciation of the actual text of the Talmud. Fifteen years ago the appearance of the first eight volumes of the unabridged English translation was hailed with satisfaction by professional scholars and reviewers. They remarked on the general accuracy of the translation, the brief and valuable notes added to the text, as well as the indices of Biblical references and subject matter at the end of each Tractate. The pattern of the early volumes has been retained throughout the years and that despite technical difficulties and the hazards, interruptions and uncertainties of the war period. The indefatigable Mr. Jacob Davidson, Governing Director of the Soncino Press must be congratulated for his tenacity and determination to see the work through to its successful end. The erudite Editor, Rabbi Dr. I. Epstein, now Principal of Jews' College, and his goodly company of collaborators responsible for the translation and notes have demonstrated a high standard in scholarship which adds prestige to Anglo-Jewry.

My predecessor Joseph Herman Hertz ז״ל had the pleasure of writing an admirable and comprehensive Foreword to the whole work which is printed in the volume Baba Ḳamma, which began the series of translations. It now falls to my lot to write this Epilogue to the last volumes.

The Foreword and the introductions to the Orders and Tractates deal adequately with the structure of the Talmud, its contents, its redaction, its study and its identification with the life and fate of the people of Israel. My contribution will confine itself to an appraisal of the work as a whole in the light of the contemporary Jewish situation. Accessibility to the discipline of Torah-study has from the earliest times been the right and prerogative of every Jew. It is a continuous study to be pursued throughout life. It is a study, the neglect of which, neither the distractions of poverty or the surfeit of riches can excuse, nor the very building of the Holy Temple in Jerusalem, justify. Bible, Mishnah and Talmud have formed the three main basic categories of the Torah discipline. Whereas, however, most students might cope with Bible and Mishnah, the Talmud was reserved for the few—'one in a thousand'—prepared to spend earnest laborious days and nights in its study and investigation. That has been the experience of the generations. It remains true to-day and painfully so. The last decades have witnessed the disappearance of the great centres of Rabbinic learning in Eastern Europe. Renowned teachers, famed for their piety and vast erudition were delivered to the slaughter, they and their hundreds of innocent and devoted disciples. Thousands of scrolls of the Law and precious Rabbinic works were desecrated and given over to fire and destruction. The centres of Jewish *Wissenschaft* in Germany and Austria which had produced great giants of scientific scholarship, whose labours were devoted to historical, linguistic and archaeological problems of the Bible, Talmud and Jewish literature generally, have ceased. The population of European Jewry has been greatly reduced while Jewish learning in the traditional sense leads but a precarious existence. On the other hand, one must pay respect to the heroic efforts which, with some assistance from American and British Jewries, have enabled some Yeshivot to be opened and maintained in some of the surviving communities and Displaced Persons' camps. But to all intents and as far as one can interpret the trend of events, it is principally to the State of Israel and the Jewries in English-speaking countries that one has to turn to provide space for the roots of the 'Tree of Life' to be strongly and firmly planted. In other words, it has been decreed that the continuity and maintenance of Jewish spiritual values as expressed in Literature and Life shall become the responsibility and concern mainly of Israel and the hegemony of the English-speaking communities of the Golah. In Israel providentially the Torah has found safe and—we trust—permanent lodgment.

But it is equally the historic task and opportunity of the 'remnant' outside the Holy Land to encourage and increase the study of the Torah for 'its own sake', and for its practical bearing on our lives. The Sacred Scriptures as well as Rabbinic literature in Talmud and Midrash embody a civilisation whose influence pervades and explains many of the phenomena of Jewish existence. The right understanding and interpretation of the fundamental sources must become the chief preoccupation of teachers and students everywhere. In this connection the English translation of the Talmud is particularly important. English is now the vernacular of more than half of the Jewish population of the world. Not everyone—not even one in a thousand—has access to the original—sometimes difficult and intractable—texts of our sources. Nor can a translation however perfect ever replace the original. Nevertheless the earnest Jewish cultured reader who is unfamiliar with the original can read and study a translation which introduces him to a world of thought, feeling and content which will repay the painstaking efforts and concentration demanded. On the other hand, the Talmud student who makes use of a reliable translation which has the crowning merit of general accuracy and important explanatory notes, will find much that will be helpful to him in his attempts to elucidate the texts. The Talmud, despite wilful misunderstanding and vilification of prejudiced detractors, belongs to the few great works of world culture—its encyclopaedic variety is now more broadly accessible to the non-Jewish scholar. My last word to all those concerned with the Soncino Talmud is in the form of a blessing attributed to Moses when he beheld the completed tabernacle of the wilderness 'May it be the will of Heaven that the Divine Presence rest upon the work of your hands'.

ISRAEL BRODIE

INTRODUCTION TO *SEDER ḲODASHIM*

BY

THE EDITOR

GENERAL CHARACTER AND CONTENTS

The Hebrew term *Ḳodashim* means Holy Things. This term, in the Biblical context, applies to the sacrifices, the Temple and its appurtenances, as well as its officiating priests; and it is with these holy things, places and persons that the Seder Ḳodashim is mainly concerned. Its position between *Neziḳin* (Torts) and *Ṭohoroth* (Clean-
a nesses) is determined, according to Maimonides,[1] by the sequence in which the laws dealt with in these three orders appear in the Bible.[2] This Seder contains also the Tractate Ḥullin which, although it treats of non-holy things, is included because the rules it prescribes regarding the slaughter of animals and birds, and their ritual fitness for use, constitute an integral part of the law of Holiness[3] of which, as will be seen, the sacrificial cult was designed as vehicle of the highest religious expression.

The 'Order' comprises eleven tractates[4] arranged in the separate printed editions of the Mishnah in the following sequence:

ZEBAḤIM (Animal-offerings): Regulates the procedure for the offering of animal-sacrifices through its various stages, and lays down the conditions which render them acceptable or otherwise. 14 Chapters.

MENAḤOTH (Meal-offerings): Prescribes the rules regarding the preparation and presentation of meal- and drink-offerings; the bringing of the sheaf of barley (Lev. XXIII, 10); the two loaves (Lev. XXIII, 17); and the shewbread (Lev. XXIV, 5). 13 Chapters.

ḤULLIN (Non-holy): Prescribes the rules for the slaughtering of animals and birds for normal consumption, and treats of the whole body of the dietary laws. 12 Chapters.

BEKOROTH (Firstlings): Deals with the laws concerning the first-born of men, animals, laid down in Ex. XIII, 12-13, Num. XVIII, 15-17, and Deut. XV, 19-23, and the tithing of cattle (Lev. XXVII, 32-33). 9 Chapters.

'ARAKIN (Estimations): Gives the rules for determining the amount which must be paid in fulfilment of a vow to dedicate to the Temple the 'market-value' or 'worth' of a person or a thing according to Lev. XXVII, 2-27; and sets forth the laws relating to the Jubilee year (Lev. XXV, 8ff). 9 Chapters.

TEMURAH (Substitution): Sets forth the rules governing the substitution of one offering for another in accordance with the law prescribed in Lev. XXVII, 10. 7 Chapters.

KERITHOTH (Excisions): Deals with offences which carry with them the penalty of *Kareth* (v. Glos.), if committed wilfully, and of a sin-offering if committed in error; and discusses the cases in which an 'unconditional' or a 'suspensive guilt-offering' is due. 6 Chapters.

ME'ILAH (Trespass): Treats of the laws of Sacrilege or making unlawful use of consecrated things, in accordance with Lev. V, 15—16. 6 Chapters.

b TAMID[1] (the Continual [Offering]): Describes the Temple service, in connection with the daily morning and evening sacrifice, prescribed in Ex. XXIX, 38-41, and Num. XXVIII, 2-8. 7 Chapters.

MIDDOTH (Dimensions): Contains the measurements and descriptions of the Temple, its courts, gates and halls and the Altar, and includes an account of the service of the priestly watches in the Temple. 5 Chapters.

ḲINNIM ([Bird-]nests): Gives the regulations for the offering of birds prescribed in expiation of certain offences and certain conditions of uncleanness (see Lev. I, 14; V, 7 and XII, 8) and discusses the case in which birds belonging to different persons or to different offerings have become mixed up with one another. 3 Chapters.

This sequence is also followed in the six volume edition of Seder Ḳodashim in which the tractates appear as follows:

Vol. I Zebaḥim.

Vol. II Menaḥoth.

Vols. III and IV Ḥullin.

Vol. V Bekoroth and 'Arakin.

Vol. VI Temurah, Kerithoth, Me'ilah, Tamid, Middoth and Ḳinnim.

For the edition de luxe it was found necessary to publish the 'Order' in 9 volumes.

Of the eleven tractates that constitute the 'Order', all, except Middoth and Ḳinnim, have Gemara in the Babylonian version of
c the Talmud.[1] No Gemara is extant in the Palestinian version. Maimonides, however, speaks of the existence of a Palestine Gemara to Ḳodashim.[2] That this 'Order' was a subject of study in the Palestinian no less than in Babylonian schools is seen from the many statements contained in the Babylonian Gemara emanating from Palestinian Amoraim. There are indeed few pages in the Babylonian Gemara on Ḳodashim in which Palestinian Amoraim do not figure in discussions relevant to the 'Order'. The only conclusion to be arrived at is that there was once a Palestinian Gemara to Ḳodashim but that it has been lost to us as have many other literary products of the past.[3]

The Gemara on the 'Order' Ḳodashim is a testimony to the strong interest which the teachers of the Palestinian and Babylonian schools continued to take in the sacrificial cult even after its cessation with the destruction of the Temple. This interest was more than merely historical and academic. It was based on strictly practical considerations. There were in fact two motives that kept alive the study of the Seder Ḳodashim even after its laws had fallen into disuse. One sprang from the unquenchable hope that the Temple would sooner or later be rebuilt, involving the restoration of the sacrificial cult, so that the knowledge of its laws would once again become essential. The other was the belief that the study of the sacrificial laws could serve as a surrogate for the Temple cult and was no less efficacious
d than the actual offering of the sacrifice itself.[1] These motives lay behind the unceasing intellectual activity that centred round the Seder Ḳodashim throughout the intervening centuries to the present day, and which has crystallised itself in a mass of commentaries on the 'Order'; and in our own times the conviction that has seized many minds that we are witnessing the *Athḥalta di-Geulah* ('beginning of the redemption') has led to the assiduous study of Seder Ḳodashim in many of the higher schools of learning in the Holy Land.

a (1) *Introduction to Seder Zera'im.* (2) *Neziḳin* has its basis in Exodus; *Ḳodashim*, in Leviticus I-X; *Ṭohoroth*, in Leviticus XI-XV. For another explanation, see Z. Frankel, *Darke ha-Mishneh*, p. 262. (3) For the place of the dietary laws in the Jewish scheme of Holiness, see I. Epstein, *The Jewish Way of Life*, pp. 161-164. (4) According to all editions of the Mishnah, with the exception of the Riva di Trento 1559 edition in which Hullin and Bekoroth appear in Ṭohoroth.

b (1) In the Naples 1492 edition Middoth is placed before Tamid.

c (1) In Tamid only chapters 1, 2, 4 have Gemara. (2) See Maimonides, *loc. cit.* Whether he had ever seen it, is very doubtful, since he is not known to have made citation of it anywhere. (3) The Palestine Gemara on Ḳodashim, claimed to have been discovered by Solomon Leb Friedländer and of which he published several tractates under the title *Talmud Yerushalmi Seder Ḳodashim* (Szinervaralja 1907-8), has been proved a forgery. See H. L. Strack, *Introduction to the Talmud and Midrash* (English ed.), Philadelphia, 1931, pp. 68 and 266, n. 16.

d (1) See e.g. Men. 110*a*; Ta'an. 27*b*; Midrash Ex. Rab. XXXVIII; Midrash, Lev. Rab. IX.

THE CONCEPTION OF SACRIFICES IN RABBINIC TEACHING

The sacrificial laws of the Torah, discussed and elaborated in this 'Order', are interspersed throughout the Pentateuch, but the main collection of them is to be found in the Book of Leviticus. The sacrifices set forth were varied in character. There were obligatory sacrifices, and there were voluntary sacrifices. There were collective sacrifices brought in the name of the entire community: the early morning and afternoon sacrifices, and the additional sacrifices on Sabbaths, New Moons, Festivals, and the Day of Atonement; and there were besides individual sacrifices. Some sacrifices were honorific in character and were offered in worship or as an expression of homage to God; others were piacular and were brought in expiation of sin; others again were tributary and presented in recognition of God as bestower of the gifts of Nature. To the honorific belong the peace-offering (*shelem*, plur. *shelamim*), the thank-offering (*todah*), and the burnt-offering (*'olah*). The sin-offering (*haṭṭath*) and guilt-offering (*asham*) belong to the piacular; and included in the tributary are the firstlings (*bekoroth*) and the cattle tithes (*ma'aser behemah*).[2]

The sacrificial material was drawn from the animal and vegetable kingdoms. The animal sacrifice came from the herd or flock and in some cases from among birds. The vegetable offerings (*minḥah*) consisted either of plain unbaked flour, baked cakes, or parched corn. There were in addition liquid offerings (*nesakim*) brought in conjunction with sacrifices, and there was also an incense-offering (*keṭoreth*) compounded of several odoriferous vegetable products.

The sacrifices involved a series of acts of which the sprinkling of the blood was the most important in the case of animal sacrifices, and the burning of the handful (*Komeẓ*) in the case of vegetable offerings.

The origin of sacrifices is wrapped in obscurity. Many widely differing theories have been propounded in explanation, but all are highly conjectural. All that can be said with certainty is that sacrifices are found to have formed a universal element of worship from the earliest times, and that there are traces among the precursors of Israel of sacrificial practices anterior to those instituted in the Torah. This admission does not detract from the claim of the sacrificial laws of the Torah to divine origin, any more than the fact that religious belief did not begin with the Sinaitic Revelation affects the validity of the Religion of Israel. On the contrary, the universality and antiquity of sacrifices only serve to testify to a deep-rooted sacrificial instinct in the human heart which seeks to respond to the claims of God upon man, and which like all other instincts needs correcting, purifying and directing.

The need for a reconciliation of man with the higher power on whom his welfare depends lies after all at the heart of all religion. Religious consciousness has been defined by William James as consisting in a sense (*a*) of uneasiness 'that there is *something wrong about us* as we naturally stand', and (*b*) of a solution for that uneasiness — of a sense 'that we are *saved from the wrongness* by making proper
a connection with the higher powers'.[1] In mythology and polytheism the gods are filled with envy, anger and hatred, and sacrifices are brought in order to effect a reconciliation and re-establish connection with them. But the God of Israel can be angry only on account of injustice, and cannot be reconciled otherwise than by the doing justly, loving mercy, and walking humbly with Him. It was therefore essential to transform the crude ideas and desires concerning man's approach to God by filling them with a spiritual-ethical content; and it was for securing this end that the sacrifices instituted in the Torah were designed as a most effective means.

How were the sacrifices prescribed in the Torah to serve this purpose? In considering the Jewish sacrificial system, we are impressed by two unique features which characterise it. First, sacrifices were ordained exclusively for ritual or religious sins, and not for social sins.[2] Second, no sacrifice could be offered in expiation of the deliberate transgressions but only for such offences as had been committed in error or under constraint.[3] These two reservations, which have no parallel in other sacrificial systems, affect the whole quality of the sacrifices of the Torah. Not the needs of God are the sacrifices intended to satisfy, but the needs of man.[4] They are no longer conceived as gifts to an offended Deity in appeasement of its anger, or in reparation for a wrong done to fellowman. Their aim is essentially man's spiritual regeneration and perfection. They are designed, in all their parts, to foster in the mind of the worshipper
b a sense of the awfulness of ritual sin,[1] in that it creates an estrangement alike between man and God and between man and man.

The grave view which the Bible takes of ritual sins is bound up with the significance of the ritual law. It is almost a truism that the ritual law of the Torah has for its purpose the religious and moral perfection of man. Have not the sages of the Talmud already declared that the precepts have been given only to ennoble mankind?[2] This is true of the negative religious precepts no less than of the positive ones. Both sets of precepts have one common aim — the perfection of man. While the positive precepts have been ordained for the cultivation of virtue and for the promotion of those finer qualities which distinguish the truly religious and ethical being, the negative precepts are designed to combat vice and suppress other evil tendencies, and instincts that stand athwart man's strivings towards perfection.[3]

Thus conceived, the ritual law is charged with a moral and religious dynamism capable of transforming the individual and, through the individual, the society of which he forms a unit. The disregard of a ritual precept is accordingly no longer a private affair; in so far as it lowers man's moral fibre and his power of resistance to evil, every ritual offence is in a sense a social offence. Viewed in this light, the insistence of the Torah on the need of sacrifices in expiation of ritual sin becomes readily intelligible. The purpose is twofold. They serve to bring home to the offender the seriousness of ritual sins even if committed unwillingly, and at the same time they guard him from lapsing through force of habit into wilful transgression.

This appreciation of the sacrificial laws of the Torah has already been stressed by Maimonides in Book III, Chapter 46 of his *Guide*,

(2) The Paschal Lamb seems also to have belonged to the tributary, the lamb being offered vicariously by the household in recognition of God's deliverance of the houses of Israel in Egypt. See Ex. XII, 27. It is not without significance that the Paschal Lamb is often bracketed with the firstlings and cattle tithe, and that, except for what concerns their consumption, they are governed by the same sacrificial regulations. See Zeb. 56*b*.

a (1) *Varieties of Religious Experience*, p. 508. (2) The guilt-offering entailed by the social offences enumerated in Lev. V, 21ff, was required only if the offender had denied his guilt on oath, his offering being in expiation of his sin against God rather than his fellow. As for the sin he had committed against his fellow, 'even if he were to bring all the "rams of Nebaioth" (Isaiah, LX, 7) in the world, he would not be forgiven until he obtains pardon from his fellow' (B.K. 92*a*); see also Yoma 85*b*. (3) The wrongs enumerated in Lev. V, 21ff (see previous note), for which even wilful offenders were to bring a guilt-offering, contained in them a certain element of constraint which brought them into the category of unwilful offences. The man who, for example, denied that he had misappropriated the property of his fellow and, on being adjured, takes a false oath, may have done so because he lacked the moral courage to admit his guilt after having once tried to conceal it; cf. Aaron ha-Levi, *Sefer ha-Ḥinnuk*, Precept 123, with reference to the 'oath of testimony', for which the offering prescribed (Lev. V, 1ff) applies to 'witting' as well as 'unwitting' cases. Otherwise for deliberate offences, unless the penalty is committed to an earthly tribunal, repentance secures divine forgiveness. See Yoma 86*a*, and Tosefta, Yom ha-Kippurim V (Zuckermandel's ed.), p. 190. (4) Cf. Midrash Num. Rab. XXI, 16-17, and Pesikta Rabbathi (ed. Friedmann) p. 80*a*.

b (1) The term 'ritual' is used throughout in a comprehensive sense, and denotes all the religious precepts of the Torah concerning the relations between man and God. (2) Midrash Gen. Rab. XLIV, 1. (3) See I. Epstein *op. cit.* p. 161.

which is devoted to the application of this idea to various offerings. 'Do not consider this', he writes, 'a weak argument, for it is the object of all these ceremonies to impress on the mind of every sinner and transgressor the necessity of continually remembering and mentioning his sin'. 'When this theory', he continues, 'has been well established in the minds of people they must certainly be led by it to consider disobedience to God as a disgraceful thing. Every-
a one will thus be careful that he should not sin'.[1]

This explanation of sacrifices by Maimonides will appear contradictory to the view advanced by him in the thirty-second chapter of the same book where he regards the institution as a concession to a people still hankering after the idolatrous practices of their environment and age. 'It was in accordance with the wisdom and plan of God,' he declares, 'that He did not command us to discontinue all these manners of service; for to obey such a commandment would have been contrary to the nature of man who generally cleaves to that which he is used. It would in these days have made the same impression as a prophet would make at present if he called to the service of God and told us in His name that we should not pray to Him nor fast, nor seek His help in time of trouble, that we should serve Him in thought and not by any action.'[2]

No part of Maimonides' *Guide* has aroused more controversy than his theory regarding sacrifices. Most outspoken and unsparing among his critics was Naḥmanides, who prefers to see in sacrifices a moral symbolism founded on a psychological analysis of conduct.[3] His staunchest defender is Abrabanel,[4] who quotes a Midrash in support of the Maimonidean view. In reality, both the critics and the defenders of Maimonides misconstrued his attitude to the problem. To obtain a full insight into Maimonides' interpretation of sacrifices, it is not sufficient to limit our study to one particular chapter in his *Guide*. We must of necessity extend our investigation to other parts of his work and include in our survey his great *Halachic* masterpiece, the *Mishneh Torah*, where he presents to us the independent Jewish view which his philosophic speculations and critical enquiries served to confirm and strengthen.

Turning to the *Mishneh Torah*, we find Maimonides adopting an entirely different attitude. Sacrifices, he there declares, belong to the class of divine commandments designated as *ḥukkim* (statutes), for which no reason is ascertainable (*Me'ilah*, VIII, 8). This assertion, sufficiently categorical, appears in turn to be modified in his *Guide*, Book III, 26, where he distinguishes between the sacrificial institution in itself and its detailed rules: sacrifices in general have a reason, but no reason can be given for its details.

Thus, we see Maimonides adopting four distinct attitudes in regard to sacrifices which, summarised, are as follows:

(1) Sacrifices have no reason (*Mishneh Torah, Me'ilah* VIII, 8).

(2) Sacrifices are a concession to the idolatrous propensities of the early Israelites (*Guide* III, 32).

(3) Sacrifices are designed as prevention of sin and as consequent safeguard of the ritual Law (*Guide* III, 46).

(4) Sacrifices have a reason in general, but not as to their detailed rules (*Guide*, III, 26).

These apparent clashings and crossings of Maimonides' views have their explanation, it is here submitted, in the distinction which must be drawn between voluntary sacrifices and obligatory sacrifices.

Obligatory sacrifices have been ordained by God. They form accordingly an integral part of revealed religion. Their reason may be unknown. But the fact that God had commanded them imparts to them a spiritual and moral quality making for human perfection; and this may be after all the best explanation that can be given for them. Voluntary sacrifices on the other hand have not been enjoined by God. They cannot therefore lay claim to the elevating tendency inherent in divine commands; and in consequence would not have been included in the Torah, but for some definite purpose, which must be understandable and clear to the human mind.

This distinction between obligatory and voluntary sacrifices accounts for the difference of Maimonides' approach to the problem in the *Mishneh Torah* and his *Guide*, III, 32. A careful reading of that Chapter in his *Guide*, where he traces the root of sacrifices to idolatrous instincts makes it evident that Maimonides was concerned there only with *voluntary* sacrifices. Honorific in character, voluntary sacrifices would be brought only as tokens of worship and homage. As such they were under the best of circumstances inferior to
b prayer which is the 'service of the heart'.[1] But that is not all. Through their idolatrous origin and by their very nature, voluntary sacrifices were not without lurking dangers. Unlimited in number, and unattended by confession and the repentance which are fundamental to expiatory offerings, or by the mental preparation that is inseparable from other obligatory offerings, voluntary sacrifices were liable to become a source of inner injury to righteous life. The reality of this danger was exemplified in later Jewish history; and it was against the abuse of this type of sacrifices that the prophets launched their scathing denunciations.[2] Yet far from being suppressed by the Torah, they received, paradoxically enough, divine approval. The only feasible explanation, in the opinion of Maimonides, was that they were to be considered in the light of a concession, because of their inestimable value as a road through which primitive Israel could travel, albeit slowly and gradually, from idolatrous superstition to the highest service of the one and only God.

But whatever perils voluntary sacrifices might involve, there were no such dangers lurking in obligatory sacrifices ordained by
c God.[1] They could accordingly, irrespective of their reason, serve as means to righteous life. The difficulty, however, of finding a rational explanation for them gave them the character of statutory laws; and it is with reference to obligatory offerings therefore that Maimonides asserts in his Code that they belong to the *ḥukkim* of the Torah.[2]

Obligatory offerings form also, as is to be seen from the context, the subject of discussion in the *Guide*, Book III, 46, where Maimonides ascribes to them a practical motive — the prevention of sin. This is not inconsistent with his classification in the *Mishneh Torah* of the obligatory sacrifices among the *ḥukkim*. Even *ḥukkim*, it is well to remember have, according to Maimonides, a cause and serve a practical purpose, though their reason is not so evident nor their object so generally clear as those of other precepts[3]. There is therefore in Maimonides' attempts to present a *rationale* of obligatory offerings nothing incompatible with his assertion of their statutory

a (1) Friedländer's translation, pp. 364-5. (2) *Op. cit.* p. 322. (3) See Naḥmanides' commentary on the Pentateuch, Leviticus, I, 9. (4) In the preface to his commentary on Leviticus; see *infra*, p. xxix.

b (1) Ta an *2a*; see also Midrash Tanḥuma, *Wa yera*, 1. (2) Cf. also David Kimḥi on Jer. VII, 23. This is an important distinction which, strange to say, appears to have been overlooked by all those writers who deal with the attitude of the prophets to the sacrifices. Yet it is fundamental and must be taken into consideration before we can speak of an antagonism of the prophets to the sacrifical cult. In fact a reference to the prophetic utterances, cited by the critical school in support of their views on the problem, i.e. I Sam. XV, 22; Hosea VI, 6; Amos V, 21ff; Isaiah I, 11ff; Micah VI, 6ff; Jeremiah VII, 21ff, shows that they are all concerned with voluntary sacrifices. This is a subject which deserves to be treated at length, but space here forbids a full discussion. The literature on the problem of the attitude of the prophets to sacrifices is too extensive to be listed. Among the most recent, however, might be mentioned H. H. Rowley, *The Re-discovery of the Old Testament* (1946); and to go back earlier, J. Hoschander, *The Priests and Prophets* (1938).

c (1) All obligatory sacrifices, public and private (except the few tributary ones), were piacular or had at least in them a piacular element. See Sheb. *2a-b*, and Tosefta Menahoth, X 12. See also G. F. Moore, *Judaism*, I. p. 497 and III, p. 151-2. (2) In support of his view that the sacrifices belong to the *ḥukkim*, Maimonides in his Code *(loc. cit.)* quotes a dictum 'By the merit of the sacrifices the world stands'. Thi; dictum is but an extension of the idea mentioned in Ta'an. *27a* where this is said in his reference to the *Ma'amadoth*, the attendances at the Daily Offering which is the obligatory offering *par excellence*. (3) *Guide*, III, 29.

character. While the *modus operandi* for the effectiveness of the sacrificial rites must elude natural explanation, it is still possible to detect in them certain aspects, the value of which is discernable by the human mind.

Actually, however, Maimonides' treatment of obligatory sacrifices in his *Guide*, III, 46, while accounting for the main outlines, leaves much of the detailed rules unexplained. This is in conformity with his insistence in III, 26, of the same work that details call for no explanation, as they have been ordained for no other purpose than as tests for man's obedience. Details, he argues, are a necessary part of the structure of anything 'which can receive different forms, but receives one of them'. 'Those who therefore trouble themselves to find a cause for any of these detailed rules are in my eyes void of sense.' 'You ask,' he continues by way of illustration, 'why must a lamb be sacrificed and not a ram, and the same question would be asked why a ram had been commanded instead of a lamb . . . the same is to be said as to the question why were seven lambs sacrificed and not eight; the same question might have been asked if they were eight, ten or twenty lambs, so long as some definite number of
a lambs were sacrificed.'[1] This does not mean to imply that the details are altogether arbitrary. They may be arbitrary as far as man is concerned. Having been given as tests of obedience one set of details could have served the same purpose as well as any other. But they are certainly not arbitrary as far as the divine law-giver is concerned. They have in the words of Maimonides been 'dictated by his will'. They have their source in the will of God and as such can admit nothing of the fortuitous or adventitious.

What Maimonides means to convey, in deprecating all attempts to discover a reason for the details, is that their value is derived not from their content but from the fact that they are grounded in the will of God. All that matters here is that they have been ordained by God, and this is sufficient to compel their observance. This may appear a blind, irrational attitude running counter to the whole trend of Maimonidean thought. The fact, rejoins Maimonides, is that in whatever we do in life we cannot avoid making our decision in favour of one of many possible forms without necessarily having to rationalise about our choice.[2] As against the details, however, stand the commandments in themselves. These have their source, according to Maimonides, in the wisdom of God. As such they have a definite purpose. This purpose, as he conceives it, is primarily educative. Their aim is the highest perfection of man — intellectual and moral. They are designed to infuse right knowledge, inculcate truths and train man to righteous life and action. They cannot, however, produce these effects unless the ideals and principles they enshrine are properly understood. The explanation of them thus becomes an important religious need and duty; and in regard to sacrifices in particular the appreciation of their significances and meaning, as far as their general character is concerned, constitutes an integral part of their fulfilment.

Thus the varying interpretations of sacrifices given by Maimonides, far from conflicting with each other, supplement and complement each other. Voluntary sacrifices are a concession to the hankering after ancient idolatrous forms and practices of worship. Obligatory sacrifices belong to the *ḥukkim*, the reason for which though not so evident, it is proper for man to investigate. This, however, applies to the laws in their broad outline, but not to the details, for which no explanation need be sought, except that they were prescribed as mere tests of obedience.

This somewhat lengthy exposition of Maimonides' views on sacrifices may appear to be out of place in an Introduction to a Talmudic 'Order'. It is, however, included here because it presents the classical rabbinic tradition from which Maimonides, despite foreign guidance and system, never departed. Essentially rabbinic
b is the idea of the statutory character of obligatory sacrifices.[1] 'The sacrificial institutions,' writes Moore 'were an integral part of revealed religion and had the obligation of statutory law. It was not for the interpreters of the law to narrow their scope or substract from their authority. Nor was it of any practical concern to enquire why the divine law-giver had ordained thus and not otherwise or indeed ordained them at all. It was enough that he had enjoined upon Israel the observance of them.'[2] Likewise rabbinic in origin is the theory as to the idolatrous associations of voluntary sacrifices, being found in a Midrash which, as already mentioned, Abrabanel[3] cites in his support. Commenting on the verse, *What man soever there be of the house of Israel that killeth an ox . . . and hath not brought it unto the door of the Tent of Meeting... he hath shed blood* (Lev. XVII, 3), R. Phinehas in the name of R. Levi says: The matter may be compared to the case of a king's son who thought he could do what
c he liked and habitually ate the flesh of *nebeloth*[1] and *terefoth*.[1] Said the king: 'I will have him always at my own table, and he will automatically be hedged round.' Similarly, because Israel were passionate followers after idolatry in Egypt and used to bring their sacrifices to the satyrs, the Holy One, blessed be He, said: 'Let them offer their sacrifice at all times in the Tent of Meeting and they will be separated from idolatry, etc.'[2] The words, 'let them offer their sacrifices at all times' make it evident that the reference is to voluntary sacrifices since obligatory sacrifices were strictly circumscribed in point of time and circumstance. Nor is the practical motive of sacrifices advanced by Maimonides absent from rabbinic thought. 'What,' says the Midrash, 'is the meaning of the words *'he offered it up for a burnt-offering instead of his son'* (Gen. XXII, 13)? At every sacrificial act Abraham performed with the ram, he prayed, 'May it be Thy will that this service be regarded as if I performed it with my son, as if he had been slaughtered, as if his blood had been sprinkled, and as if he had been made ashes.'[3] Here we have a significance ascribed by the Rabbis to sacrifices which is but a vivid formulation of the practical motive given by Maimonides. It was also a Midrashic dictum to which Maimonides appealed in support of his view that the details of the sacrifices have been given to serve only as tests of obedience.[4]

But whatever theory the Rabbis of the Talmud may have held as to the sacrificial cult, there is little doubt that they had an appreciation of its fundamentally educational value. This is shown by the designation *Ḥokmah* which they came to give to this 'Order'. *Ḥokmah* means wisdom; and wisdom in the Jewish conception was not theoretical but practical. It was not an intellectual pursuit, but essentially a religious ethic. Through this designation, the Talmudic conception of the sacrifices as educative becomes unmistakably clear. Their object was conceived of as being to instil in the heart of the devotee that wisdom whose mainspring and motive was the 'fear of the Lord', and to which the observance of the ritual law was designed as an aid.

a (1) Friedländer, *op. cit.* pp. 311, 312. (2) This is how the difficult chapter in the *Guide* (III, 26) is to be understood. While rejecting the view of those theologians who, following the Mohammedan Ashariyah (see *Guide* III, 17), hold that the commandments have no object at all and that they had been dictated only by the will of God, Maimonides accepts their position as far as the detailed rules are concerned. His assertion that the details have no ulterior object can only mean that they have their source in the will of God. A similar notion that the commandments have no reason is found in Ber. 33*b*. See Maimonides *Guide*, III, 48; and I. Epstein, *Judaism of Tradition*, pp. 42-43.

b (1) See *supra* p. xxvii, n. 2. (2) G. F. Moore *op. cit.* I, 504. (3) See *supra*, p. xxiv.

c (1) V. Glos. (2) Midrash Lev. Rab. XXIII, 5. See D. Hoffmann, *Leviticus*, p. 88, and W. Bacher, *Die Aggada der palästinensischen Amoräer*, II, p. 316. (3) Midrash quoted by Baḥya b. Asher in his commentary on the Pentateuch, Lev. I, 9. For the various versions of this Midrash, see M. Kasher, *Torah Shelemah*, III (2), p. 903. (4) *Guide*, III, 26. 'What difference does it make to God whether a beast is killed by cutting the neck in front or in the back? Surely the commandments are only intended as a means of trying man' (Midrash Gen. Rab. XLIV, 1). This Midrashic dictum is generally understood in the sense that the commandments are educative, ennobling in character, see *supra* p. xxiii. Maimonides evidently gave the Midrash a different interpretation, and while not accepting the illustration drawn from slaughtering, as the rules of slaughtering have in his view a definite educative value, he applies the Midrashic principles to sacrifices.

The observance of the ritual law which the sacrificial cult inspired made it a vehicle of Holiness of the highest expression.
a Whatever its root meaning, *Ḳodesh*,[1] the Hebrew term for Holiness, denotes both that which pertains to God and that which is recognised to be the character of God. This character has from the earliest days in Jewish teaching been associated with ideals of righteousness. The pursuit of Holiness involved for man a self-surrender to God accompanied by a resolve to make the divine pattern of righteousness his own. This is the Holiness which the sacrificial cult was divinely designed to foster. Its contribution to Holiness was both of a negative and positive character. On the negative side, by safeguarding the observance of the ritual law, the sacrifices served to strengthen what the Torah regarded as the only available defences against the forces inimical to Holiness. On the positive side, through the confession and repentance which accompanied them, as well as the solemnity of their setting, the sacrifices helped to draw man near to God in close communion than which there is no greater power making for Holiness.

The view of the sacrifices outlined above has much bearing on the question of their restoration in the future — a restoration which Maimonides in his *Mishneh Torah* includes among the tenets of tra-
b ditional Judaism.[1] Here, too, the distinction may have to be drawn between voluntary offerings and obligatory offerings. In fact the prayers for the restoration of sacrifices that figure so largely in our Liturgy are specifically restricted to obligatory sacrifices. Granted that with the disappearance of the passion for idol worship' (*yiẓra di abodah zarah*)[2] there could be little, if any, religious value in the restoration of voluntary offerings; it is otherwise with obligatory offerings. As a safeguard for the observance of the ritual law, the obligatory sacrifices have lost none of their validity. The sickness and distress of the modern world is derived in the last resort from the lack of correspondence between man's moral progress and his intellectual and scientific achievements. Indeed, the terrific power of evil at the command of man leads a modern writer, Lewis Mumford,[3] to advocate a moral tightening by the introduction of all kinds of inhibitions and renunciations in order to train man in the habit of that inner check and self-restraint so essential to human survival. But surely no humanly contrived restrictions and restraints can take the place of those divinely ordained in the ritual law of the Torah. Thus do the grim and tragic experiences of our time only serve to confirm the attitude of traditional Judaism to the ritual law as an indispensable aid to moral law; and the restoration of the obligatory offerings in the days to come[4] can only serve to strengthen and safeguard the ritual law for the regeneration and perfection of Israel and, through Israel, of the whole of humanity. Well, then, may the disciple of the Law in delving into the intricacies of the Seder Ḳodashim re-echo, in no narrow spirit, the words of that ancient prayer, 'May it be Thy will that the Temple be rebuilt speedily in our days and grant us our portion in Thy Law.'[5]

METHOD AND SCOPE

TEXT. The Text used for this edition is in the main that of the Wilna Romm Edition. Note has, however, been taken of the most important variants of manuscript and printed editions some of which have been adopted in the main body of the translation, the reason for such preference being generally explained or indicated in the Notes. All the censored passages appear either in the text or in the Notes.

TRANSLATION. The translation aims at reproducing in clear and lucid English the central meaning of the original text. It is true some translators will be found to have been less literal than others, but in checking and controlling *every line* of the work, the Editor has endeavoured not to lose sight of the main aim of the translation. Words and passages not occurring in the original are placed in square brackets.

NOTES. The main purpose of these is to elucidate the translation by making clear the course of the arguments, explaining allusions and technical expressions, thus providing a running commentary on the text. With this in view resort has been made to the standard Hebrew commentators, Rashi, the Tosafists, Asheri, Alfasi, Maimonides, Maharsha, the glosses of BaḤ, Rashal,
c Strashun, the Wilna Gaon, etc.[1] Advantage has also been taken of the results of modern scholarship, such as represented by the names of Graetz, Bacher, Weiss, Halevy, Levy, Kohut, Jastrow, Obermeyer, Klein, Büchler and Krauss, and—happily still with us—Ginzberg and Herford among others, in dealing with matters of general cultural interest with which the Talmud teems—historical, geographical, archaeological, philiological and social.

GLOSSARY AND INDICES. Each tractate is equipped with a Glossary wherein recurring technical terms are fully explained, thus obviating the necessity of explaining them afresh each time they appear in the text. To this have been added a Scriptural Index and a General Index of contents.

In the presentation of the tractates the following principles have also been adopted:

(i) The Mishnah and the words of the Mishnah recurring and commented upon in the Gemara are printed in capitals.

(ii) תנן introducing a Mishnah cited in the Gemara, is rendered 'we have learnt'.

(iii) תניא introducing a Baraitha, is rendered 'it has been (or was) taught'.

(iv) תנו רבנן introducing a Tannaitic teaching, is rendered 'Our Rabbis taught'.

(v) Where an Amora cites a Tannaitic teaching the word 'learnt' is used, e.g., תני רב יוסף, 'R. Joseph learnt'.

(vi) The word tanna designating a teacher of the Amoraic period (v. Glos.) is written with a small 't'.

(vii) A distinction is made between . . . הלכה כ referring to a Tannaitic ruling and . . . . הלכתא כ which refers to the ruling of an Amora, the former being rendered 'the *halachah* is . . .' and the latter, 'the law is . . .'

(viii) R. stands either for Rabbi designating a Palestinian teacher or Rab designating a Babylonian teacher, except in the case of the frequently recurring Rab Judah where the title 'Rab' has been written in full to distinguish him from the Tanna of the same name.

(ix) רחמנא, lit., 'The Merciful One', has been rendered 'the Divine Law' in cases where the literal rendering may appear somewhat incongruous to the English ear.

(x) Biblical verses appear in italics except for the emphasized word or words in the quotation which appear in Roman characters.

(xi) No particular English version of the Bible is followed, as the Talmud has its own method of exegesis and its own way of understanding Biblical verses which it cites. Where, however, there is a radical departure from the English versions, the rendering of a recognized English version is indicated in the Notes. References to chapter and verse are those of the Massoretic Hebrew text.

a (1) Either (i) 'bright', or (ii) 'separation'; see N.H. Snaith, *The Distinctive Ideas of the Old Testament*, pp. 26ff.

b (1) See Maimonides, *Yad, Melakim*, XI, 1. (2) See Sanh. 64*a*. (3) *Programme for Survival*, pp. 60ff. (4) The enormous legal difficulties involved in the restoration of sacrifices within our present social and political framework places the whole question outside the realm of practical *halachah*. Compare A. I. Kook, *Mishpaṭ Kohen*, Responsa, 89ff. (5) Aboth, V 23.

c (1) These names are referred to more fully in the list of Abbreviations at the end of each tractate.

(xii) Any answer to a question is preceded by a dash (—), except where the question and the answer form part of one and the same argument.

(xiii) Inverted commas are used sparingly, that is, where they are deemed essential or in dialogues.

(xiv) The archaic second person 'thou', 'thee' etc. is employed only in *Haggadic* passages or where it is necessary to distinguish it from the plural 'you', 'yours', etc.

(xv) The usual English spelling is retained in proper names in vogue like Simeon, Isaac, Akiba, as well as in words like *halachah, Shechinah, shechitah,* etc. which have almost passed into the English language. The transliteration employed for other Hebrew words is given at the end of each tractate.

(xvi) It might also be pointed out for the benefit of the student that the recurring phrases 'Come and hear:' and 'An objection was raised:' or 'He objected:' introduce Tannaitic teachings, the two latter in contradiction, the former either in support or contradiction of a particular view expressed by an Amora.

CONCLUSION

For technical reasons this set of six volumes, comprising the fifth of the six 'Orders' of the Talmud, appears last, and with its publication the Soncino edition of the Babylonian Talmud is brought to completion. The moment has thus arrived for bidding farewell to a task which has absorbed the best energies of myself and a number of fellow-workers for over fifteen years. Surveying this monumental work, all those who had a share in its production may well, in no spirit of boastfulness, congratulate themselves on an achievement which promises to be of abiding value. This translation of the Talmud with its accompanying expository and cultural notes makes accessible for the first time to the English-reading student that part of the heritage of Israel to which more than to anything else, the Jewish people owes its preservation, and from which humanity as a whole has drawn no little sustenance for its religious and moral life. To bring the knowledge of this ancient treasure to many to whom it has hitherto been *terra incognita*, and thus enable it more and more to exert its potent and benign influence, has been the aim of this undertaking, the successful conclusion of which is itself the best reward for the faithful toil bestowed upon it.

Those of us who have been associated with this publication from the beginning to the end cannot better express our gratitude for being privileged to witness this consummation than in the age-honoured formula of thanksgiving:

תם ונשלם שבח לבורא עולם

FINISHED AND COMPLETED:
PRAISE TO THE CREATOR OF THE UNIVERSE

All who have taken part can thank God that to them has been granted the opportunity to apply their powers, whether great or small, to a work which should serve to communicate abroad the religious faith and wordly wisdom enshrined in the pages of the Talmud, for the inspiration and guidance of this generation and the generations to come.

This, too, is a fitting occasion for the Editor to pay the warmest of tributes to the several translators and other contributors for all the learning and industry they brought to bear on their work, as well as the skill with which they discharged the respective tasks committed to them. Where each one gave of his best, it would be invidious to single out names. Special mention must however be made of Mr Maurice Simon, M.A. for his helpfulness in many directions, especially in the matter of style and diction, and to Mr Eli Cashdan, M.A. for his careful attention to proofs and other valuable assistance. Thanks are also due to my wife for 'looking well after the ways of her household', and thus making it possible for me to engage in this work.

The driving force behind this gigantic work was of course Mr. J. Davidson, the Governing Director of the Soncino Press. His was the vision that inspired it, the energy that produced it, and the courage that enabled him to carry it through to the end, notwithstanding difficulties and obstacles that at times seemed insurmountable. Jewish learning has long been under a deep obligation to Mr. Davidson for his fine publications, but the debt owed to him for the splendid array of beautiful volumes that comprise the Soncino edition of the complete Babylonian Talmud in English passes all calculation.

And now to conclude on a more personal note, I tender my humble thanks to Almighty God for having granted me life and strength to perform this most exacting and strenuous task, and to witness its completion. May it be His will that these volumes should help to spread the knowledge of His Torah among an ever-growing circle of disciples, and to foster an appreciation of Jewish teachings in an ever-increasing measure in English-speaking Jewries and beyond.

With this prayer I take leave of my editorial task, a task which covered the whole of the Talmud, commonly known as *Shass*. It is a solemn occasion which, in accordance with Jewish custom, calls for a celebration. Such a celebration would be marked by the recital of what is called a *Hadran*, in which the hope is expressed that the ending of the study of the Talmud shall prove but the prelude to a new beginning. This is the note on which, I feel, all those who have contributed to the preparation of this version of the Babylonian Talmud would like this work to conclude. And so in response to their wishes and the promptings of my own heart, I say *au revoir* to this Talmudic work, to the accompaniment, in an abbreviated form, of the traditional *Hadran:*

הדרן עלך שיתא סדרי תלמוד והדרך עלי

May it be Thy will, O Lord our God, that Thy Torah be our occupation in this world and be with us in the world to come . . .

Make pleasant, we beseech Thee, O Lord our God, the words of Thy Torah in our mouth and in the mouth of Thy people, so that we all with our offspring and the offspring of the offspring of Thy people, the House of Israel, may all know Thy Name and learn Thy Torah for its own sake . . .

We give thanks before Thee, O Lord our God, and the God of our ancestors, that Thou hast set our portion with those that sit in the House of Study and not with those (idlers) who sit at streetcorners . . .

May it be Thy will, O Lord our God, even as Thou hast helped to complete Seder Ķodashim and the whole of Six Sedarim of the Talmud, so to help us to begin other books and to complete them, to learn, to teach, to heed, to do and to fulfil in love all the words of instruction in Thy Torah . . . and may there be fulfilled in us (the promise): *When thou walkest it shall lead thee; when thou liest down it shall watch over thee; and when thou awakest it shall talk with thee* (Proverbs, VI, 22).

For by me thy days shall be multiplied, and thy years of life shall be increased (Proverbs, IX, 11). *Length of days is in its right hand; in its left are riches and honours* (Proverbs, III, 16). *The Lord will give strength unto His people; the Lord will bless His people with peace.* (Psalms, XXIX, 11).

Amen.

I. EPSTEIN

Jews' College, London.
13th Nisan, 5708.
22nd April, 1948.

INTRODUCTION

Zebaḥim (Animal Sacrifices) is the first Tractate of Ḳodashim, the fifth of the six 'Orders' (Sedarim) which constitute the Talmud. Its older name, Sheḥitath Ḳodashim (the Slaughtering of Consecrated animals) is found on 45*a* and in B.M. 109*b*; while in the Tosefta it is called Korbanoth (Sacrifices). It consists of fourteen chapters.

With the destruction of the Temple and the consequent abolition of sacrifices, the subject matter of this Tractate became obsolete. Nevertheless, the intense love and reverence for the Temple, which found expression in the name Beth 'Olamim, the Eternal House, even after it was laid waste, ensured the continuance of the study of the sacrifices which was equivalent to offering them. Possibly, indeed, this belief had grown up among the Babylonian Jews even while the Temple stood in all its glory, on account of their own inability to travel all that distance to Jerusalem to sacrifice.[1] It is worth noting that children commenced their Biblical studies with the Book of Leviticus, which dealt with sacrifices (Lev. Rab. VII. 3). On the other hand, amongst the earlier *amoraim*, interest in this subject waned, and the Talmud (Ber. 20*a*) relates that the generation of Rab concentrated upon (or confined itself to) the study of the first four 'Orders', which were of practical importance in their daily lives, but neglected the remaining two. Curiously enough, there was a revival of interest amongst the *later amoraim*, and the Tractate before us shews how meticulously they studied this subject down to its minutest details, just as though the sacrificial system was still being carried on with all its ceremonial. Graetz (*Gesch*. IV. 320) maintains that Rab Judah, an earlier *amora* and a disciple of Rab, studied these laws privately only. Weiss (*Dor*. III. 186-7) points out that there are forty-six laws on this subject recorded by Rab Judah in the name of Rab. It is unlikely that he stated these laws *privately*, but must have done so publicly in the Academy, where they would certainly give rise to discussion and study. He maintains, however, that this generation made no attempt to discover *new* laws, whereas the later generation of *amoraim* extended their investigations to hypotheses and suppositions not hitherto dealt with and the laws that would govern them.

The following is a brief *resumé* of its contents:

CHAPTER I: the validity or otherwise of sacrifices offered under a designation other than their own.

CHAPTERS II and III treat of irregularities arising either because the men who officiated were unfit, or in the carrying out of the sacrificial rites, or in the intentions expressed during the performance of these rites.

CHAPTER IV continues the same subject, and in the latter half deals particularly with *piggul*.

CHAPTER V and VI give an account of the place where the animal sacrifices and bird sacrifices and meal-offerings were offered, how their blood was sprinkled, and the laws governing their consumption. This is logically followed in CHAPTER VII by a discussion of irregularities in the rites of bird sacrifices.

CHAPTER VIII: The mingling of different animals before they are sacrificed, and of their limbs or blood after they are offered.

CHAPTER IX: What is sanctified by the altar, in the sense that if wrongly placed thereon, it must nevertheless not be removed; what is sanctified by the Service Vessels in similar circumstances.

CHAPTER X deals with the order of precedence of various sacrifices over one another.

CHAPTER XI: What must be washed when stained by blood of sacrifices; the laws governing the flesh boiled in the Service Vessels.

CHAPTER XII: Which priests had the right to share in the sacrifices, and what rights the priests in general possess in them.

CHAPTER XIII deals with offences in sacrificing elsewhere than at the legitimate sanctuary, and CHAPTER XIV continues this subject, and also gives a historical account of public and private sanctuaries and altars (*bamoth*).

A peculiarity worth noting in this Tractate is the number of Mishnahs from CHAPTER IX and onwards which gives the Biblical sources of the law and the method of exegesis by which the laws are deduced. Such are found on Folios 83*a*, 85*b*, 89*a*, 92*a*, 98*b*, 103*a*, and 112*a*.

There is very little *Aggadah* in this Tractate. Of interest are the passages which relate how the site of the Temple was chosen (54*b*); the symbolic interpretation of sacrificial rites (88*b*); the sublime expression of resignation to and confidence in God's will: 'even though He slay many of thee, do thou keep silent' — a passage doubtlessly evoked by the many persecutions of the Jewish people (115*b*); the historical data on the duration of the various sanctuaries at Gilgal, Nob and Gibeon, and Shiloh, before the Temple was built (118*b*); the panic which seized the heathen kings when God revealed His law to Israel, and their song acclaiming His Kingship (116*a*) — aptly allegorising the final triumph of true religion in its irreconcilable conflict with heathenism.

H. FREEDMAN

The indices of this Tractate have been compiled by Dr Judah J. Slotki, M.A.

(1) V. Weiss, *Dor*, III, p. 231 (Ed. New York—Berlin, 1924).

PREFATORY NOTE BY THE EDITOR

The Editor desires to state that the translation of the several Tractates, and the notes thereon, are the work of the individual contributors and that he has not attempted to secure general uniformity in style or mode of rendering. He has, nevertheless, revised and supplemented, at his own discretion, their interpretation and elucidation of the original text, and has himself added the footnotes in square brackets containing alternative explanations and matter of historical and geographical interest.

ISIDORE EPSTEIN

תלמוד בבלי

מסכת

זבחים

CHAPTER I

MISHNAH. [2*a*] ALL SACRIFICES SLAUGHTERED NOT IN
a THEIR OWN NAME[1] ARE VALID,[2] SAVE THAT THEY DO NOT FREE THEIR OWNERS OF THEIR OBLIGATION,[3] WITH THE EXCEPTION OF THE PASSOVER-OFFERING AND THE SIN-OFFERING.[4] [THIS HOLDS GOOD OF] A PASSOVER-OFFERING IN ITS PROPER TIME;[5] AND A SIN-OFFERING AT ALL TIMES. R. ELIEZER SAID: ALSO THE GUILT-OFFERING [IS INVALID], [AND THE LAW HOLDS GOOD OF] A PASSOVER-OFFERING IN ITS PROPER TIME, AND A SIN-OFFERING AND A GUILT-OFFERING AT ALL TIMES. R. ELIEZER ARGUED: THE SIN-OFFERING COMES ON ACCOUNT OF SIN, AND THE GUILT-OFFERING COMES ON ACCOUNT OF SIN: AS A SIN-OFFERING [SLAUGHTERED] NOT IN ITS OWN NAME IS INVALID, SO IS THE GUILT-OFFERING INVALID [SLAUGHTERED] NOT IN ITS OWN NAME. JOSE B. ḤONI SAID: [SACRIFICES] SLAUGHTERED IN THE NAME OF A PASSOVER-OFFERING OR A SIN-OFFERING ARE INVALID. SIMEON THE BROTHER OF 'AZARIAH[6] SAID: IF ONE SLAUGHTERED THEM UNDER A HIGHER DESIGNATION THAN THEIR OWN THEY ARE VALID; UNDER A LOWER DESIGNATION THAN THEIR OWN, THEY ARE INVALID. HOW SO? IF ONE SLAUGHTERED MOST SACRED SACRIFICES UNDER THE DESIGNATION OF LESSER SACRIFICES,[7] THEY ARE INVALID; IF ONE SLAUGHTERED LESSER SACRIFICES UNDER THE DESIGNATION OF MOST SACRED SACRIFICES, THEY ARE VALID. IF ONE SLAUGHTERED A FIRSTLING OR TITHE IN THE NAME
b OF A PEACE-OFFERING,[1] IT IS VALID; IF ONE SLAUGHTERED A PEACE-OFFERING IN THE NAME OF A FIRSTLING OR TITHE, IT IS INVALID.

GEMARA. Why must [the Tanna] teach, SAVE THAT THEY DO NOT FREE [THEIR OWNERS OF THEIR OBLIGATION]; let him teach, 'and they do not free their owners of their obligation?'[2] —He informs us this: they merely do not free their owners of their obligation, yet they retain their [original] sanctity, and no alteration therein is permitted, in accordance with Raba's dictum. For Raba said: If a burnt-offering was slaughtered under a different designation, its blood must not be sprinkled under a different designation.[3]

If you wish, I can say [this follows] from reason, and if you wish I can say, from Scripture. If you wish, I can say [this follows] from reason: because he made an alteration therein [once], is he to go on making alterations therein?[4] And if you wish, I can say [it follows] from Scripture: *That which is gone out of thy lips thou shalt observe and do; according as thou hast vowed a freewill-offering unto the Lord thy God* etc.:[5]

a (1) I.e. under a different designation. E.g., a burnt-offering slaughtered as a peace-offering. (2) They count as a sacrifice, and all their rites, such as sprinkling the blood, burning the *emurim* (v. Glos), and eating the flesh, must be performed. (3) If the owner vowed e.g., a burnt-offering, this sacrifice does not free him of his obligation and he must bring another. (4) These are altogether invalid; hence they must be burnt (not on the altar), and the usual rites may not be performed. (5) *Sc.* from midday on the eve of Passover until nightfall. (6) Soṭah 21*a*. (7) Sacrifices were divided into two categories: (i) Most sacred; these included the sin-offering, meal-offering, burnt-offering and guilt-offering; and (ii) Lesser sacrifices e.g., the peace-offering, Passover-offering and the thanksoffering.

b (1) The sanctity of the former is lower, v. *infra* 89*a*. (2) Which is more in keeping with the terse style of the Mishnah. (3) But as the blood of a burnt-offering. (4) Obviously not—one wrong does not authorise another! (5) Deut. XXIII, 24.

כל הזבחים שנזבחו שלא לשמן. שנשחט עולה לשם שלמים: כשרים. לזרוק דמן ולהקטיר אימוריהם ולאכול את הנאכלין אע"פ שמצותן לשוחטן לשמן כדיליף בגמ': אלא שלא עלו וכו'. וצריך להביא אחר לחובתו או לנדרו וישחטו לשמו: חוץ מן הפסח והחטאת. שהן פסולין לגמרי ויליף לה בגמ': *הפסח בזמנו. [פסול] שלא לשמו כל זמן שחיטתו דהיינו מחצות היום של ערב פסח עד הערב אבל קודם לכן ואחר מכאן קיימא לן (לקמן דף ז:) דפסח בשאר ימות השנה [שלמים] הוא וכל דינו כשלמים ואמרינן לעיל דשאר זבחים כשרין שלא לשמן ובגמ' יליף לה מקראי: אף האשם. כדמפרש טעמא ואזיל: הנשחטין לשם פסח. כל שאר זבחים שנזבחו בי"ד בניסן לשם פסח או שנזבחו לשם חטאת בכל זמן פסולין כי היכי דאינהו פסולין לשם אחרים ובגמרא יליף טעמא דאחרים לשם פסח בברייתא: שמעון אחי עזריה. על שם שעזריה עסק בפרקמטיא וסיפק צרכי שמעון אחיו בשעה שהיה עוסק בתורה והתנו ביניהן שיהא חלק לעזריה בשכר תלמודו של שמעון כדאמרי' בסוטה (דף כא.) אם יתן איש את כל הון ביתו וגו' לא כשמעון אחי עזריה לפיכך נקרא על שמו שלמד על ידו: שחטן. לשאר זבחים לשם גבוה מהן כשרין כדמפרש ואזיל ובגמרא (לקמן דף יא:) יליף לה ומפרש להאי כשרין אי כשרין [ועלו] קאמר ובתרתי *פליגי אי כשרין ולא עלו קאמר ובגבוה ובנמוך הוא דפליגי: לשם נמוך מהן פסולין. לגמרי: בכור ומעשר בהמה נמוכין משלמים כדאמרינן בפ' כל התדיר (לקמן דף פט.) מפני שהשלמים טעונין מתן ארבע סמיכה ונסכים ותנופת חזה ושוק: **גמ'** למה לי למיתני אלא. להאריך בלשונו ליתני ולא עלו לבעלים כו' לשון קצרה כדקיימא לן (פסחים דף ג:) לעולם ישנה אדם לתלמידו דרך קצרה: הא קמ"ל. שאין בהם שום ירידה אלא אותה לבדו: אבל בקדושתייהו קיימי ואסור לשנויי בהו. תו שינויא אחרינא לעבוד אחת משאר עבודות לכתחילה שלא לשמה: מיהו אם עבר ושינה כשר: משום דשני בה. חדא זימנא לישני בה כל הני וניזיל:

תורה אור

כל

*הזבחים א*שנזבחו שלא לשמן כשרים א] אלא שלא עלו לבעלים לשם חובה °חוץ מן הפסח והחטאת ב] הפסח בזמנו והחטאת בכל זמן רבי אליעזר אומר אף האשם הפסח בזמנו והחטאת והאשם בכל זמן אמר רבי אליעזר החטאת באה על חטא והאשם בא על חטא מה חטאת פסולה שלא לשמה אף האשם פסול שלא לשמו *יוסי בן חוני אומר הנשחטין לשם פסח ולשם חטאת פסולין שמעון אחי עזריה אומר שחטן לשם גבוה מהן כשרין לשם נמוך מהן פסולין כיצד קדשי קדשים ששחטן לשם קדשים קלים פסולין קדשים קלים ששחטן לשם קדשי קדשים כשרין הבכור והמעשר ששחטן לשם שלמים כשרין שלמים ששחטן לשם בכור ולשם מעשר פסולין: **גמ'** *למה לי למיתנא ג] אלא שלא עלו ליתני ולא עלו לבעלים לשם חובה הא קמ"ל לבעלים הוא דלא עלו לשם חובה אבל בקדושתייהו קיימי ואסור לשנויי בהו וכדרבא *דאמר רבא בעולה ששחטה שלא לשמה אסור לזרוק דמה שלא לשמה *איבעית אימא סברא איבעית אימא קרא איבעית אימא סברא משום דשני בה כל הני לישני בה וליזיל איבעית אימא קרא °מוצא שפתיך תשמור ועשית כאשר נדרת לה' אלהיך נדבה וגו' *האי נדבה נדר

דברים כג

כל הזבחים שנזבחו כו'. עבודה קמייתא נקט והוא הדין קבלה והולכה וזריקה כדקתני סיפא (לקמן ד' יג.) ושינוי קודש שייך בהנך ארבע עבודות כגון עולה לשם שלמים אבל שינוי בעלים לא שייך אלא בזריקה כגון שוחט או מקבל או מוליך קרבן ראובן ע"מ לזרוק דמו לשם שמעון כדמוכח לקמן בפירקין (דף י.) וצריך לדקדק מנא ליה להש"ס שינוי בעלים דקבעי לקמן בפרקין (דף ד.) מנא לן דבעינן זביחה לשמה כו' והדר קאמר אשכחנא שינוי קודש שינוי בעלים מנא לן משמע דאמתניתין קאי וכולה מתניתין לא מישתמעא כלל שינוי בעלים דלישנא דלשמן משמע לאפוקי שינוי קודש וכולה מתניתין לא נקיט אלא שינוי קודש דקתני נמי בסיפא (שם דף יג.) כיצד לשמן ושלא לשמן לשם פסח לשם שלמים ונראה דסמך אמתניתין דלקמן פרק בית שמאי (דף מו:) דתנן לשם ששה דברים הזבח נזבח לשם זבח לשם זובח וכן פירש בקונטרס בגמ' וא"ת אי אההיא קאי א"כ הוה ליה לפרושי נמי מנא לן לשם השם לשם אישים [לשם ריח] לשם ניחוח וי"ל דלא אתי לפרושי אלא בהני דכשירין ולא עלו לשם חובה אבל הנך כשירין ומרצין ועלו לשם חובה כמו שאפרש ועוד י"ל דשלא לשמן דמתניתין משמע בין שינוי קודש בין שינוי בעלים כמו ברייתא דרבי שמעון קמלה שלא לשמה דמוקי ריש פ"ק דמנחות (דף ב:) בשינוי בעלים ולהכי *נמי [לא פריך] בפירקין דהנך ארבעה דברים מנא לן דלא מיירי בהן במתני' ומיהו רבה חוקא מוקי לה בשינוי בעלים אבל רבא ורב אשי לא מוקמי לה הכי התם ואם תאמר והא בפרק בית שמאי (לקמן דף מו:) דריש להו מדכתיב עולה אשה ריח ניחוח לה' עולה לשם עולה והיינו שינוי קודש ובפירקין בגמ' (לקמן דף ד.) דריש שינוי קודש מקרא אחרינא ויש לומר דקרא דהתם בהקטרת אימורים והכא בעבודת הדם ואע"ג דקתני לשם ו' דברים הזבח נזבח הוא הדין הזבח נקטר דהא קרא דמייתי התם בהקטרה מיירי ומ"מ שפיר דריש מקרא דהתם זביחה לשם ו' דברים מדאיתקש אל שם זבח דלשם זבח דהיינו שינוי קודש הוי בין בעבודת דם [כדיליף] מקראי דפירקין בין בהקטרה [כדיליף] מקרא דהתם ה"ה שאר *חמשה דברים יהו בזביחה כמו בהקטרה ומיהו הא לא מצינן למילף מהיקישא דנימא ולא עלו לשם חובה ואיכא מרצה *בכל (מקום) הנך ו' דברים דההוא קרא כתיב בהקטרת אימורים והוא עצמו שלא הוקטרו אימורים כשר ולקמן דמייתי קרא לשם זבח דהיינו שינוי קודש לא מייתי נמי קרא לשם זובח דהיינו שינוי בעלים *משום דהנהו ו' דברים לא שייך לפרש בשעת הקטרה דבשעת הקטרה לא משכחת לשם זובח דשינוי בעלים ליתיה אלא בשוחט ע"מ לזרוק או מקבל ומוליך ע"מ לזרוק כדמוכח בפירקין (לקמן ד' ח.) ובשעת הקטרה כבר נזרק הדם ואם כן מהיכא תיתי הקטרה לשם זובח דבההוא קרא לעולה אשה ריח ניחוח לא כתיב ומעבודת דם לא אתי דעבודת דם גופיה ליתיה אלא בע"מ לזרוק כדפרישית והשתא זביחה לשם ששה דברים והקטרה לשם חמשה אי נמי הא דקאמר זביחה לשם ששה דברים לא שחישב בשעת שחיטה לשם ו' דברים אלא כלומר הזבח נעשה לשם ו' דברים וכל אחת בשעתה °ובפ' המפקיד (ב"מ דף מג:) פירשתי הא דמחשבה פוסלת בקדשים אי בדיבור הזבח נעשה [שלא] לשמה או אפילו במחשבה: **הפסח** בזמנו. אבל שלא בזמנו לא ואפי' שוחטו לשם עולה ואפילו למ"ד בעי עקירה מ"מ הוי שלמים כדדרשינן ואם מן הצאן קרבנו לזבח שלמים כל דשחיט ליה שלמים ליהוי לקמן בפירקין (דף ח:): **החטאת** באה על חטא והאשם בא על החטא. איכא חטאת ואשם נמי דאין באין על חטא כגון חטאת יולדת ואשם מצורע אלא משום דרובא אתו על חטא משוו להו אהדדי: **לשם** גבוה מהן כשירין. בגמרא* מיבעי לן אי בעי למימר כשירין ומרצין ופליגי בתרתי או כשירין ואין מרצין ולא פליגי אלא בחדא [משמע דלא מספקא אלא בחדא] כגון *בגבוה אבל בנמוך פשיטא ליה דפסולין לגמרי קאמר ותימה מנא ליה דילמא פסול ולא עלו קאמר דאשכחן [בברייתא] כי האי גוונא דתניא לקמן (דף ז.) שלמים ששחטן לשם תודה פסולין והיינו פסולין ולא עלו ולא פסולין לגמרי ויש לומר משום דדרשינן טעמא דשמעתא בגמרא (שם דף יא:) מדכתיב ולא יחללו את קדשי בני ישראל אשר ירימו במעבס [מהם] אין מחללין בנמוך מהם מחללין וחילול משמע פסול גמור ואע"ג דדרשינן בגמרא* קדשים מחללין קדשים ואין חולין מחללין קדשים ולא מיפסלו שאר קדשים שלא לשמן מכל מקום שייך בהן חילול משום פסח וחטאת דמיפסלו *ועוד יש לדקדק מגופה דמתניתין הבכור והמעשר ששחטן לשם שלמים כשירין משום דהוי לשם גבוה דאי לשם נמוך מיפסלי והיינו לענין פסול גמור דבבכור ובמעשר לא שייך לא עלו לבעלים לשם חובה: **ואסור** לשנויי. יש מקומות שהתנא [אינו] חושש לאשמעינן חידוש זה ובפרק התכלת (מנחות דף מח:) גבי שאר שלמי נזיר וגבי אשם נזיר ואשם מצורע דקתני כשירין ולא עלו ולא קתני אלא: **קרי** ליה נדר וקרי ליה נדבה. משמע הכא דכל היכא דכתיב נדר נדר דוקא נדבה נדבה דוקא וכן בפרק קמא דר"ה (דף ו.) לענין בל תאחר ואפילו לר"מ בפ"ק דחולין (דף ב.) דדריש טוב אשר לא תדור טוב מזה ומזה שאינו נודר כל עיקר אלמא קרי לנדבה נדר שאני הכא דדריש מדשני קרא בדיבוריה א"נ בחולין דריש דכיון דחייש קרא לתקלה לא שנא נדר לא שנא נדבה דבתרוייהו איכא למיחש אי נמי משום דנדר נפקא לן מקרא דכי תחדל לנדור ש"מ דטוב אשר לא תדור לנדבה אתא:

ואם

מסורת הש"ס:
וגי' רש"ק בשם ס"י הפסח בזמנו כל זמן כו' ומוחק כל הני תיבות
מנחות ד: ידים פ"ד מ"ב
פסחים עג: ע"ש
מנחות ב.
נ"א פליגי בגבוה ונמוך או כשירין ולא עלו קאמר ובנמוך הוא כו'
[לקמן ז:]
[ברכות ד: וש"נ]
לקמן ד: מנחות ב.
נ"א ד' נ"ק נ"א מכל
נ"א משום דשינוי בעלים לא שייך כו' נ"ק בשם ס"י
לקמן יא:
נ"א בנמוך
לקמן ג:
נ"ע דלקמן בגמרא רוצה לדייק כן ממלת כשירין המי דילמא הא כדאיתא כו' וא"כ מפסולים יוכל לדחות ג"כ

עין משפט נר מצוה:
א א מיי' פט"ו מהל' פסה"מ הל' א סמג לאוין שלג:
ב ב מיי' שם הל"ג:

גליון הש"ס

מתני' חוץ מן הפסח. עיין מנחות דף מח ע"ב תוס' ד"ה כבשי: תוס' ד"ה כל וכו' ובפ' המפקיד פירשתי. עיין לקמן דף ד' ע"ב תוס' ד"ה מחשבה ודף מא ע"ב רש"י ד"ה כגון שנתן ובמנחות דף ב ע"ב רש"י ד"ה אבל מחשבה דמינכרא ובפסחים דף סא ע"א תוס' ד"ה ר"מ סבר ובחולין דף לט ע"א תוס' ד"ה אלא זביחה:

וגי' רש"ק מהי פריך בפירקין כו' מנא לן דהא מיירי בהן כו' וגי' רש"ק ולהכי נמי לא מפרש בפירקין הנך ס'

שיטה מקובצת
(כתב יד)

הגהות נפלאות אסיפות לרבינו בצלאל אשכנזי ז"ל מתוך גפ"ת כ"י שהי' לפניו. וגם חדושים ושיטות הראשונים ז"ל שקבצן וכתבן על גליון הש"ס שלו ד' ווינציאה הפ"ב.

א] אלא שלא עלו כו'. וצריך להביא אחר לחובתו או לנדרו כפי' בקונטרס ודוקא נדר שהוא חייב באחריותו אבל נדבה אם שחטו שלא לשמה אין צריך להביא אחר דהא אפי' אם נאבד אינו חייב באחריותו. תוס' הר"פ:
ב] הפסח בזמנו. פסול שלא לשמו כל זמן שחיטתו דהיינו מחצות היום של ערב פסח עד הערב אבל קודם זמנו ואחר זמנו קי"ל דהוי שלמים דפסח בשאר ימות השנה שלמים הוי וכל דינו כשלמים וא"כ כי שחטו נמי לשם עולה או לשם קרבן אחר כשר הוא ודינו כשלמים כדקיי"ל כל הזבחים שנזבחו שלא לשמן כשרים ומ"מ קודם זמנו ולאחר זמנו אינם שוים דאחר זמנו לא בעי עקירה ואפי' שחטו סתם כשר ואפי' שחטו לשם פסח בפירוש כשר ושלמי' לשם פסח קשחים כדאמרי' במס' חולין בפ' השוחט אבל קודם זמנו אם שחטו סתם פסול כיון דסתמא לשם פסח קאי לכך בעי עקירה שיעקרנו בפירוש משם פסח לשם אחר וא"ת מאי איריא דפסח בזמנו דפסול שלא לשמו אפי' קודם זמנו נמי דהא אם שחטו קודם זמנו לשם פסח או סתמא נמי פסול אע"ג דדינו להיות כשלמים די"ל דהתם לאו משום דשלא לשמו הוא דמיפסל אלא משום דקודם זמנו שם פסח עליו לגמרי כיון דלפסח קאי וכי שחיט ליה לשם פסח או סתמא הו"ל פסח ששחטו קודם חצות דמיפסל משום דבין הערבים אמר רחמנא ושנה הכתוב לעכב חד בפ' החדש הזה לכם וחד בפ' ויעשו בני ישראל את הפסח במועדו ואע"ג דאיכא קראי בגמרא נמי דקודם זמנו הוי שלמים היינו דוקא ע"י עקירה כדדריש ליה בגמרא ע"י כלל ופרט וכלל ואף למאי דמסיק לובה ריבויא הוא מ"מ ממעים לשמו כמו שאפרש בגמרא בעז"ה והילכך קודם זמנו לעולם שם פסח עליו עד דעקר ליה שם פסח לשם שלמים ולכך מיפסל לשם פסח או סתמא מטעם פסח ששחטו קודם חצות כדפי' רש"י אבל שחטו לאחר הפסח לשם אחר הוי שלמים כיון דנפק ליה משם פסח ואפי' שחטו לשם עולה דהשתא הוי שלא לשמו אפ"ה כשר דמידי דהוה אזבחים דכשרין שלא לשמן לא משכחת שלא לשמו פסול בפסח אלא בזמנו דוקא ותדע דפסח ששחט קודם זמנו לשם פסח לאו משום שינוי קודש הוא דמיפסל דהא נמי אם שחטו סתמא פסול וכל הזבחים דפסולין משום שינוי קודש כששחטן שלא לשמן אם שחטן סתמא כשרים כדמוכח בגמרא תוס' מו"ך: ג] אלא כלומר משמע שיש בו כשרות אחר שלא וכו' אבל בקדושתייהו קיימי פי' בשם קדושה ראשונה דעדיין שם הראשון עליהם ואסור לשנויי בהו גם מכאן ואילך תוס' מו"ך:

אלא

נדר הוא אלא אם כמה שנדרת עשית יהא נדר ואם לא נדבה יהא ונדבה מי שרי לשנויי בה אמר ליה רבינא לרב פפא לא הוית גבן באורתא בתחומא בי הרמך דרמי רבא מילי מעלייתא אהדדי ושני להו מאי מילי מעלייתא תנן כל הזבחים שנזבחו שלא לשמן כו' טעמא דשלא לשמן הא סתמא עלו נמי לבעלים לשם חובה אלמא סתמא נמי כלשמן דמי ורמינהי *כל הגט שנכתב שלא לשם אשה פסול וסתמא נמי פסול ושני זבחים בסתם לשמן עומדין אשה בסתמא לאו לגירושין עומדת וזבחים בסתמא כשירין מנלן אילימא מהא דתנן כל הזבחים שנזבחו שלא לשמן כו' ולא קתני שלא נזבחו לשמן גבי גט נמי הקתני כל הגט שנכתב שלא לשם אשה פסול ולא קתני שלא נכתב לשם אשה פסול אלא מהא א] (א) *דתנן כיצד לשמן ושלא לשמן לשם פסח ולשם שלמים טעמא דאמר לשם פסח ולשם שלמים הא לשם פסח וסתמא כשר אלמא סתמן כלשמן דמי דילמא שאני התם דאמר °כל העושה על דעת ראשונה הוא עושה אלא מסיפא שלא לשמן ולשמן לשם שלמים ולשם פסח טעמא דאמר לשם שלמים ולשם פסח הא סתמא ולשם פסח כשר דילמא שאני התם דאמר *יוכיח סופו על תחילתו אי נמי אידי דתנא לשמן ושלא לשמן תנא נמי שלא לשמן ולשמן אלא מהא *לשם ששה דברים הזבח נזבח לשם זבח לשם זובח לשם (ב) שם לשם אשים לשם ריח לשם ניחוח והחטאת והאשם לשם חטא א"ר יוסי אף מי שלא היה בלבו לשם אחת מכל אלו כשר שתנאי בית דין הוא אתנו בית דין דלא לימא לשמו דילמא אתי למימר שלא לשמו ואי סלקא דעתך סתמא פסול קיימי בית דין ומתני מילתא דמיפסיל ביה וגבי גט דסתמא פסול מנלן אילימא מהא דתנן *היה עובר בשוק ושמע (ג) סופרים מקרין איש פלוני גירש פלונית ממקום פלוני ואמר זה שמי וזה שם אשתי פסול לגרש בו דילמא כדרב פפא דאמר *רב פפא הכא בסופרים העשויין להתלמד עסקינן ולא איכתוב לשום כריתות כלל אלא מהא

יתר

נדר הוא. דהא כאשר נדרת כתיב ויש חילוק בין נדר לנדבה נדר דאמר הרי עלי ונדבה הרי זו: אם כמה שנדרת עשית. שעבד עבודותיה לשמה: יהא נדר. ויעלה זה לנדרך: ואם לאו יהא לנדבה. כאילו התנדבת לזה נדבה אחרת ולא לשם הראשונה: ונדבה מי שרי לשנויי בה. וכיון דרחמנא קרייה נדבה מי שרי לשנויי בה הא אמרינן בפ' שני (לקמן ד' כט:) אסור לחשב בקדשים ויליף מקרא דלא יחשב והכי מידרש קרא אם מוצא שפתיך תשמור ועשית אז יהיה נדר אשר נדרת ואם לאו נדבה: (מפי השמועה במנחות עד כאן): לא הוית גבן באורתא בתחומא. כלומר חבל על שלא היית אמש בשבת אצלנו בתוך התחום שתוכל לבא לבית המדרש ולשמוע: בי הרמך. שם מקום: ושני להו. ופירקן: שלא לשמן. משמע דעקר שמייהו בהדיא: שלא לשם אשה. האשה הזאת שנכתב לשום אחרת ששמה כשם זו פסול דכתיב וכתב לה לשמה: וסתמא נמי פסול. כגון אם כתבו הסופר [סתם] לשם לאה שיהא מזומן לכשיבא אדם אלנו ששמו ושם אשתו (שוין) כן ויתננו לו ולקמן מפרש מנלן ממתני' דסתם פסול: ושני. ותריץ רבא גופיה דרמינהו אהדדי: בסתמן לשמן עומדין. הילכך כל כמה דלא עקר שמייהו בהדיא הוו לשמן: מנלן. *ממתני' היכי שמע ליה רבא דתיקשה ליה: שנזבחו שלא לשמן. משמע דעקר שמן מהן: שלא נזבחו לשמן. משמע שלא הזכיר שמן עלייהו דהייט סתמא: שנכתב שלא לשם אשה זו. משמע שנכתב לשם אחרת בפירוש: כיצד לשמן כו'. מתני' היא: לשם פסח ולשם שלמים. כך חישב עליו: הא לשם פסח וסתמא. שלא חישב אחריו לשם שלמים כשר ואע"ג דסוף שחיטה סתמא אישתחיט: אלמא סתמן כלשמן דמי. דאי כשלא לשמן דמי הויא ליה כאילו אמר לשם פסח ולשם שלמים: על דעת [ראשונה. אבל] היכא דשחטיה כוליה סתמא אימא לך דפסול: הא סתמא [ולשם] פסח. תחילה שחטה סתם וסופה לשם פסח כשר ולא מיפסיל משום תחילתה אלמא סתמא כלשמן: א"נ איידי כו'. כלומר לעולם לא תידוק מיניה הא סתמא ולשם פסח כשר דלעולם אימא לך פסול דסתמא כשלא לשמו והאי דקתני לשם שלמים איידי דפריש בלשמן ולא לשמן לשם שלמים דהתם דווקא הוא דאילו סתמא הוי כשר דעל דעת ראשונה הוא עושה פריש נמי תנא דמתני' בשלא לשמו ולשמו לשם שלמים ולשם פסח ולאו דווקא דה"ה לסתמא ולשם פסח דמיפסל בתחילת שחיטה: לשם ששה דברים. משנה בפרק ב"ש ומקראי יליף להו: לשם זבח. לשם מה שהוקדש: לשם זובח. שיתכפר בו בעליו ולא שיתכפר בו אחר: לשם (ד) שם. (לנחת רוח) להקב"ה שאמר (*ונעשה רצונו): לשם אשים. להקטירם ולא לעשותם צלי על המזבח קרבונ"ש בלע"ז: לשם ריח. לאפוקי איברים שצלאן והעלן דשוב אין בהן ריח והכי מפרש להו התם: לשם ניחוח. לשם הנחת רוח להקב"ה שאמר ונעשה רצונו: שלא היה בלבו. לשמו אלא סתם ולא הזכיר אחד מאלה: שתנאי בית דין הוא. שישחטו סתם ולא יזכירו בשחיטתן לשמו כדמפרש טעמא ואזיל אתנו ב"ד דלא לימא לשמן כו': וגבי גט דסתמא פסול מנא ליה. כלומר היכי שמע ליה רבא ממתני' דגיטין דפסול דפיקשה ליה ורמינהי אהדדי: מקרין. את התלמידין שמלמדין אותן לכתוב טופסי גיטין: דלא איכתוב לשם כריתות כלל. אבל היכא דאיכתב ג] לשם כריתות שיהא מזומן לו לכשיזדמן לו *מגרש ששמו ושם אשתו ג] שוין בו כשר ונמלך

ואם לאו יהא נדבה. אע"ג דבפ"ק דר"ה (דף ו.) דריש ליה לענין בל תאחר דלא שייך לאחר שחיטה הכא דריש מפשטיה דקרא דמשמע דקרי ליה לנדר נדבה: **זבחים** בסתם לשמן הן עומדין. ואינו פסול עד שיכוין שלא לשמן [וא"ת בפ"ק דחולין (דף יב:) בעי ר"י אי קטן יש לו מחשבה וכו' ופי' בקונטרס כגון בשחיטת קדשים דיליף בריש זבחים דבעי לשמה ושחט קטן עולה לשמה מי הוי כוונה או לא הא משמע הכא דמסתמא נמי כשר ואינו פסול עד שיכוין שלא לשמן] וי"ל דסתמא דקטן גרע דאין לו דעת להבין שהן קדשים וסבור שהן חולין והוה ליה מתעסק ופסול כדאמר בפרק בית שמאי (לקמן דף מו:) לשם חולין כשירין משום חולין פסולה והאי קטן אפילו אומר יודע אני שהן קדשים ולשמן אני מתכוין מיבעיא לן אי כוונתו כוונה או דילמא לא מהני אם אין מעשיו מוכיחין: **סתם** אשה לאו לגירושין עומדת. ואפי' זינתה תחת בעלה מכל מקום לאו להתגרש בגט זה עומדת וגם אם לא ירצה הבעל לא יגרשנה *אלא שלא תשמש ומתוך הא מילתא מיתרצא מה שמקשים בסוף פרק שני דגיטין (דף כג.) דאמר עובד כוכבים אדעתא דנפשיה עביד ואינו כשר לכתוב את הגט ובפ' שני דעבודה זרה (דף כו:) אמרי' ימול ארמאי ואל ימול כותי משום דכותי מתכוין לשם הר גריזים [והתם נמי] בעינן לשמה כדדרשינן (שם דף כז.) מלה' המול (ימול) ואפי' הכי מכשרינן ארמאי דיש לחלק בין גט למילה כמו שמחלק כאן בין זבחים לגט *הא סתמא פסול משום דסתם אשה לאו לגירושין קיימא ולכך נמי [בעובד כוכבים] פסול אע"ג דעביד סתם אבל מילה סתמא לשמה קיימא כמו זבחים הילכך עובד כוכבים כשר אע"ג דעביד סתם: **הא** לשם פסח וסתמא כשר. פי' בקונטרס ד] דסוף שחיטה סתמא אישתחיט ותימה כיון דאמר בתחילת שחיטה לשם פסח *וכי כל שעה יש לו לדבר עד שיגמר שחיטתו ונראה לפרש דבשתי עבודות איירי כגון דשחיט לשם פסח וקיבל סתם ומיהו בפרק תמיד נשחט (פסחים דף נט:) מיבעי לן אי בעבודה אחת תנן או בשתי עבודות ועבודה אחת היינו כדפירש הקונטרס ויש ליישב דאפילו אם תימצי לומר לשם פסח וסתמא פסול [אפ"ה] אין צריך לדבר כל שעה אלא שבתחילת שחיטה יאמר שעושה כל השחיטה לשם שחיטת פסח: **אתנו** בית דין דלא לימא לשמה דילמא אתי למימר שלא לשמה. בשמעתא קמייתא דגיטין (דף ג.) דמפרש דלכך לא תיקנו לומר בפני נכתב לשמה למ"ד לפי שאין בקיאין לשמה משום דאי מפסת ליה לדיבורא אתי למיגזייה לא הוי מצי למימר דילמא אתי למימר שלא לשמה דמי הוא שוטה כל כך שנותן גט לאשה זו שנכתב לשמה והוא אומר שלשם אחרת נכתב אבל אדם השוחט קרבן פעמים שטועה וסבור שהוא קרבן אחר וכן המקבל ומוליך וזורק: *) **קיימי** בית דין ומתני כו'. יש תימה למה לו להאריך כל זה הא בהדיא אמר סתמא כשר ונראה לפרש דמי שלא היה בלבו היינו שלא אמר בהדיא לשם אחד ה] מכל אלו אבל חישב בלבו למה שדינו להיות הא סתמא פסול **) להכי [דייק] מתנאי בית דין וכי מתנו בית דין דלא לימא בהדיא ובמחשבה סגי ושמא אתי לידי פסול שלא יחשב כלל וישחוט סתמא ויפסל: **בסופרים** העשויין להתלמד עסקינן. ואפילו למאן דאמר בפרק קמא דעירובין (דף יג.) גבי מגילת סוטה דמוחקין אותה מן התורה אף על גב דבעינן לשמה ואף על גב דתורה

*) עיין צ"ק **) ועי' רש"ק

עין משפט נר מצוה

ג א מיי' פ"ד מהל' מעה"ק הלכה י ועיין רש"ק:

ד ב ג ד מיי' פ"ג מהל' גירושין הל"ה סמג עשין נ טוש"ע אה"ע סי' קלא סעיף א:

הגהות הב"ח

(א) גמ' אלא מהא כיצד לשמן כצ"ל ותיבת דתנן נמחק: (ב) שם לשם השם: (ג) שם ושמע קול סופרים מקרין איש פלוני מגרש את פלוני': (ד) רש"י ד"ה לשם השם לנחת רוח להקב"ה שאמר ונעשה רצונו. נ"ב לא"ו היינו לשם ניחוח וכן מבואר לקמן דף מו ע"ב ור"ל שהוא שוחט לשם הקב"ה וממילא הוא נחת רוח כו' מה שא"כ לשם ניחוח שצריך לשחוט עבור נחת רוח וק"ל:

גליון הש"ס

גמ' כל העושה על דעת ראשונה. לקמן דף מא ע"ב שבת דף לא ע"א: תום' ד"ה סתם וכו' אלא שלא תשמש. עיין בתשובת הר"ם אלשקר סי' פה:

נ"א דהתם

נ"א ולא נ' בסוף שחיטה לשם פסח

שיטה מקובצת

א] אלא מהא כיצד לשמן כו' וא"ת והמקשה מאי ס"ד וכי תעלה על דעתך דלעולם יעמוד ויאמר לשם פסח וי"ם דאה"נ דבכל עבודה ועבודה יש לו לפרש לשם פסח והשתא לפי' זה הוי פי' דמתני' דלשמו ושלא לשמו בשתי עבודות כמו בשחיטה וקבלה ששחט לשם פסח וקבל לשם שלמים ולא נהירא דע"כ דלשמו ושלא לשמו דמתני' ר"ל הכל בעבודה אחת כדפ"ה לקמן דאי בשתי עבודות היינו רישא הפסח והחטאת ששחטו שלא לשמו וקבל והלך וזרק שלא לשמו דאו או קאמר כדפ"ה לקמן דליכא למימר דעשה כל העבודות שלא לשמן דלמה לי כולי האי בחדא סגי אלא ע"כ או או קאמר וא"כ סיפא דקתני לשמו ושלא לשמו ר"ל בעבודה אחת ששחט לשם פסח ולשם שלמים וא"כ הדרא קושיא לדוכתיה וי"ל דמשחיטה פריך דמשמע ליה לשמו ושלא לשמו בשחיטה ששחט סימן ראשון לשם פסח ושני לשם שלמים ולהכי דייק הא לשם פסח וסתמא כשר אלמא סתמא כלשמו דמי דאי כשלא לשמו דמי נהי דאין צריך לעמוד ולומר לשם פסח מ"מ בכל סימן וסימן היה לו להזכיר לשם פסח. תוס' שוך: ב] דאיכתב ליה לשם אשתו: ג] כן כשר ותיבות שוין בו נמחק: ד] בקונטרס פי' וכו' ותוס' שוך תירצו דמשחיטה פריך דמשמע ליה לשמו ושלא לשמו בשחיטה ששחט סימן אחד לשם פסח וסימן ב' לשם שלמים ולכך דייק הא לשם פסח וסתמא כשר אלמא סתמא כלשמן דמי דאי כשלא לשמן דמי נהי דא"צ לזבוח לעולם לשם פסח מ"מ בכל סימן וסימן היה לו להזכיר לשם פסח ע"כ: ה] לשם אחד והא דקאמר ר"י שלא היה בלבו היינו שלא היה ניכר וידוע לשומעין אם היה בלבו לכך והיינו (דשני) [דשחט] בשתיקה כלומר שלא נדר בשפתיו מה שחשב בלבו והא דפריך בגמרא ואי ב"ד סתמא פסול קיימי ב"ד ומתני' מילתא דמיפסל ביה. ה"פ מילתא שיבא לידי פסול דהיינו ע"י שתיקה דמתוך שישתוק אולי ישכח ולא יכוין גם בלבו ומיפסל א' סתמא פסול דיותר יבא שלא יחשוב בלל כשהוא מחשב בלבו מאם לטעות ולומר שלא לשמו אם הוא אומר לשמו בפירוש. תוס' שוך:

מסורת הש"ס

גיטין כד

לקמן יג. פסחים נט.

ג"י הב"ק היכא שמעינן ממתניתין דסתמא כשר ותיקשי ליה לרבא

[גיטין סו. נדרים סב. חולין לט:]

לקמן מו:

גיטין כד.

[שם:]

ס"א ל"ג

ס"א ונעשה רצונו

ר"א לגרש לאמי

is this a freewill-offering—[2b] surely it is a vow?[6] The meaning however is this: if you have acted in accordance with your vow,[7] let it be the fulfilment of your vow; but if not, let it count as
a a freewill-offering.[1] Now as a freewill-offering is it permitted to make a change in it?[2]

Rabina said to R. Papa: You were not with us in the evening within the Sabbath limit of Be Harmack,[3] when Raba pointed out a contradiction in two important laws, and then reconciled them. What are these important laws?—We learnt: ALL SACRIFICES SLAUGHTERED NOT IN THEIR OWN NAME etc. Thus it is only when they are slaughtered for another purpose; but if no purpose is defined, they even acquit their owners of their obligation, which proves that an undefined purpose is the same as its own purpose [defined]. But the following contradicts it: 'Every *Geṭ*[4] which was written not in the name of the woman [for whom it is intended][5] is invalid;[6] and [in point of fact if it is written with] an undefined purpose it is also invalid?[7] And he answered it: Sacrifices, where no purpose is defined, stand [to be slaughtered] for their own purpose;[8] whereas a woman, if nothing is defined, does not stand to be divorced.

Now, how do we know that sacrifices slaughtered with undefined purpose are valid? Shall we say, because we learned: ALL SACRIFICES SLAUGHTERED NOT IN THEIR OWN NAME etc., while he [the Tanna] does not teach, 'which were not slaughtered under their own designation'. But surely in the case of the *Geṭ* too, he also teaches: Every *Geṭ* which was written not in the name of the woman, is invalid, and does not teach, 'which was not written in the name of the woman is invalid'!—Rather, it follows from what we learned: How is 'in its own name and not in its own name' meant? In the name of the Passover-offering and in the name of a
b peace-offering.[1] Thus it is [invalid] only because he stated[2] 'in the name of the Passover-offering and in the name of a peace-offering' but, [if he slaughtered it] in the name of the Passover-offering and [sprinkled its blood] with undefined purpose, it is fit; which proves that with purpose undefined it is as in its own name![3]—Perhaps it is different there, because one may argue: Whoever does anything, does it with the original [expressed] intention!—Rather, it follows from the second clause: [How is] 'not in its own name and in its own name' [meant]? In the name of a peace-offering [first] and [then] in the name of the Passover-offering. Thus it is [invalid] only because he stated,[2] 'In the name of a peace-offering and in the name of the Passover-offering'; but [if he slaughtered it] without a defined purpose [and sprinkled the blood] in the name of the Passover-offering, it is valid![3]—Perhaps it is different there, because we say: the end illumines the beginning.[4] Alternatively, [perhaps] because he teaches 'in its own name and not in its own name' [in the first clause], he also teaches 'not in its own name and in its own name' [in the second clause]![5] Rather, it follows from this: A sacrifice is slaughtered for the sake of six things: For the sake of the sacrifice, for the sake of the sacrificer, for the sake of the Divine Name, for the sake of fire-offerings, for the sake of a savour, for the sake of pleasing, and a sin-offering and a guilt-offering for the sake of sin.[6] R. Jose said: Even if one did not have any of these
c purposes in his heart, it is valid, because it is a regulation[1] of the Beth din.[2] Thus the Beth din made a regulation that one should not state its purpose, lest he come to state a different purpose. Now if you think that an undefined purpose [renders] it invalid, would the Beth din arise and make a regulation which would invalidate it?[3]

Now how do we know in the case of a *Geṭ* that an undefined purpose [renders] it invalid? Shall we say from what we learned: If one was passing through the street and heard the voice of scribes dictating: 'So-and-so divorced So-and-so of such a place,'[4] whereupon he exclaimed, 'That is my name and my wife's name,' it [the *Geṭ* so written] is invalid for divorcing therewith![5]—Yet perhaps that is [to be explained] as [did] R. Papa. For R. Papa said: We are discussing scribes engaged in practising, so that it was not written for the purpose of divorcement at all![6]—Rather [it

(6) *As thou hast vowed* implies that we are treating of a vow; while *a freewill-offering* applies to a *nedabah* (a freewill-offering). When one vows, 'Behold, I undertake to bring a sacrifice,' it is technically called a vow; if one declares, 'Behold, this animal be for a sacrifice,' it is a freewill-offering. In the first case, if he subsequently dedicates an animal in pursuance of his vow, and it is lost before it is sacrificed, he must bring another. In the latter case, should the animal be lost or become unfit, his obligation is at an end. (7) I.e., you have slaughtered it in the name of the sacrifice which you actually vowed.
a (1) *Additional* to the vow originally made. (2) Of course not. Hence, though it was slaughtered for a different purpose, its other rites must still be performed for the right purpose. (3) To be able to visit us at the schoolhouse. — He was referring to the Sabbath. Be Harmack is in the vicinity of Pumbeditha; Obermeyer, *Die Landschaft Babylonian* p. 124. (4) Deed of Divorce. (5) Of course a name must be written in the *Geṭ*; but even if this particular woman's name is written, yet without having her in mind, so that the fact of the name being identical is a pure coincidence, the *Geṭ* is unfit. (6) Giṭ. 24a. (7) Hence an undefined purpose is the same as a *wrongful* purpose. (8) This may be assumed.
b (1) I.e. he slaughtered the paschal sacrifice in the name of a Passover-offering as required but sprinkled the blood in the name of a peace-offering. V. *infra* 13a. (2) Not necessarily, as mere wrongful intention is effective. (3) Which proves that where the purpose is undefined the sacrifice is valid. (4) Hence since the end (sprinkling) was in the name of the Passover-offering, we assume the beginning (the slaughtering) to have been likewise. (5) For the sake of parallelism. Yet actually if he slaughters it without a defined purpose, it may be invalid. (6) He who offers the sacrifice must have these in mind (or express them): (i) the particular sacrifice it is intended to be; (ii) the person for whom it is sacrificed; (iii) that it is sacrificed in honour of the Divine Name; (iv) with the intention of burning the *emurim* on the altar, not merely roasting it; (v) and (vi) with the intention that it shall provide a pleasing savour to God (v.e.g., Lev. III, 5—*niḥoaḥ*, translated there 'sweet', is rendered 'pleasing').
c (1) Lit., 'stipulation'. (2) That one should not define its purpose—the name of the sacrifice for which it is offered, *infra* 46b. (3) Surely not. This then proves Raba's first point. (4) They were teaching pupils to write a *Geṭ*, and had selected the names at random. (5) Giṭ. 24a. (6) But if a scribe writes a *Geṭ* for the purpose of divorce, selecting names at random, perhaps it is valid.

follows] from this: [3a] Even more; If he wrote [a *Geṭ*] to divorce his wife and then changed his mind; then a fellow-citizen met him and said to him 'My name is the same as yours, and my wife's name is the same as your's, it [the *Geṭ*] is invalid for divorcing therewith![6]—Yet perhaps it is different there, because it had been designated for that particular person's divorce![7]—Rather, from the following: Even more: If he had two wives of the same name, and he wrote [a *Geṭ*] to divorce the elder therewith, he cannot divorce the younger with it.[8]—Perhaps it is different there, as it had been designated for that particular wife's divorce! — Rather, from the following: Even more: If he said to the writer, 'Write it and I will then divorce whichever I desire,' it is invalid for divorcing therewith![8]—Perhaps it is different there, because selection is not retrospective![9]—Rather, from this: He who writes formulas of
a *Giṭṭin*[1] must leave blanks for the name of the husband, and the name of the wife, the names of the witnesses, and the date.[2] Rab Judah said in Samuel's name: He must also leave a blank for [the passage], 'Behold, thou art permitted unto all men'.

He [Raba] pointed out a further contradiction. Did then Rab Judah say in Rab's name: If one slaughtered a sin-offering under the designation of a burnt-offering, it is invalid; [if one slaughtered it] under the designation of *ḥullin*,[3] it is valid? This proves that its own kind destroys it, while a different kind does not destroy it.[4] But the following contradicts it: 'Every *Geṭ* written not in the name of the woman [for whom it is intended] is invalid',[5] and [in point of fact] even [if written] in the name of a Gentile woman it is still invalid.[6] And he answered: In the case of a *Geṭ*, disregard the Gentile woman altogether,[7] [and] it is then [written] without defined purpose, which is invalid.[8] But as for sacrifices, disregard the *ḥullin*,[9] [and] it is [a sacrifice slaughtered] without defined purpose, which is valid.[10]

He pointed out another contradiction. Did then Rab Judah say in Rab's name: If one slaughtered a sin-offering under the designation of a burnt-offering, it is invalid; [if he slaughtered it] under the designation of *ḥullin* it is valid? This proves that its own kind destroys it, while a different kind does not destroy it. But it was taught: [*And every earthen vessel into*] *whose inside* [*any of them falleth, whatsoever is in it shall be unclean, and it ye shall break*][11] but not the
b inside of the inside, and even a non-earthen vessel[1] saves it.[2] And he answered it: They [the Rabbis] treated *ḥullin* in respect to consecrated animals as a partition in respect to an oven. Just as a partition in respect to an oven has no effect at all, so *ḥullin* in respect to consecrated animals has no effect at all. For we learned: If an oven is partitioned with boards or curtains, and a reptile is found in one compartment, the whole is unclean. If a defective receptacle,[3] which is stuffed with straw, is lowered into the air-space of an oven, and a reptile is in it, the oven becomes unclean; if a reptile is in the oven the foodstuffs in it [the receptacle] become unclean;[4] while R. Eliezer declares it clean. Said R. Eliezer: It follows *a fortiori*: If it protects in the case of a corpse, which is stringent,[5] shall it not protect it in the case of an earthen vessel[6] which is less stringent?

(7) And for no other. (8) Giṭ. 24*b*. (9) His subsequent intention has no retrospective validity in the sense that it is regarded as though he had intended it thus in the first place, and so it is still possible that he had first intended it for the other, and therefore it is invalid.

a (1) Plural of *Geṭ*. He writes them to have them ready whenever the occasion arises. (2) Then he can fill them in as required. But he cannot fill them in in the first place, though writing them for the express purpose of divorce, and then find persons with the same name (Giṭ. 26*a*). This proves that they must be written expressly for persons who are to use them. (3) V. Glos.—i.e., not as a sacrifice at all. (4) A sin-offering and a burnt-offering are of the same kind—both are sacred, and by substituting the name of the latter for that of the former, he destroys its validity. But *ḥullin*, being non-sacred, is of a different kind, as it were, and does not harm it. (5) Giṭ. 24*a*. (6) Now a Gentile woman belongs to a different category, in that the law of *Geṭ* does not apply to her at all, and yet she destroys the validity of the *Geṭ*. (7) Regard the *Geṭ* as though it had not been written for her. (8) Since it must be written expressly for a particular woman. (9) Viz., that it was slaughtered as *ḥullin*. (10) V. *supra* 2*b*. (11) Lev. XI, 33.

b (1) Lit., 'a vessel of rinsing.' This is the technical designation of all non-earthen vessels, because they can be purified from ritual uncleaness in a ritual bath (*mikweh*). (2) If a reptile (*sherez*) falls inside an earthen utensil containing eatables, even without touching them, they become unclean. On this the comment is made: only if it falls inside, but not into the inside of the inside. Thus: if a utensil containing eatables is lying in an earthen oven (ancient ovens were open on top), with its mouth protuding above the top of the oven, and a reptile falls into the oven, the foodstuffs remain clean, as the inside of the utensil is regarded as the 'inside of the inside,' of an oven. This holds good not only when the inner utensil too is an earthen one, but even if it is non-earthen. The difference between the two is this: an earthen vessel is defiled only if the reptile falls *inside*, whereas a non-earthen vessel is defiled even if the reptile touches it on the outside. Now a non-earthen vessel is really of a different kind, since it differs in law, and yet it protects the foodstuffs in it from defilement, acting as interposition between the foodstuffs and the vessel in the oven. Thus a different kind too can 'destroy' the status of the food as being 'inside' the oven and gives it the status of being 'inside the inside'. (3) Lit. 'a beehive (shaped receptacle)'. (4) Thus the receptacle, not being of the same kind as the oven, does not destroy the status of the food as being in the air-space of the oven. If the receptacle were whole it would protect the eatables, as above. Since it is not whole, however, it lacks the status of a utensil; and this is so *even* if it is stuffed with straw as a repair. (5) If this partition were in a room containing a corpse, it would suffice to protect the foodstuffs from defilement, though the contaminating powers of a corpse are far greater than those of a reptile in an oven. (6) As in the case of the oven.

*יתר על כן *כתב לגרש את אשתו ונמלך מצאו בן עירו ואמר לו שמי כשמך ושם אשתי כשם אשתך פסול לגרש בו דילמא שאני התם דאינתיק ליה לשם גירושין דההוא אלא מהא *יתר על כן *יש לו שתי נשים ששמותיהן שוות כתב לגרש את הגדולה לא יגרש בו את הקטנה דילמא שאני התם דאינתיק ליה לשם גירושין דההיא אלא מהא יתר על כן *אמר ללבלר כתוב ולאיזה שארצה אגרש פסול לגרש בו דילמא שאני התם דאין ברירה אלא מהא *הכותב טופסי גיטין צריך שיניח מקום האיש ומקום האשה *ומקום העדים ומקום הזמן ואמר רב יהודה אמר שמואל אף צריך שיניח מקום הרי את מותרת לכל אדם: תו רמי מילתא אחריתי מי *אמר רב יהודה אמר רב חטאת ששחטה לשם עולה פסולה *שחטה לשם חולין כשירה אלמא דמינה מחריב בה דלאו מינה לא מחריב בה ורמינהי כל הגט שנכתב שלא לשם אשה פסול א] ואפי' לשם עובדת כוכבים נמי פסול ושני גט דל עובדת כוכבים מיניה הוה ליה סתמא וסתמא פסול קדשים דל חולין מינייהו הוה ליה סתמא וסתמא כשירים ורמא מילתא אחריתי מי אמר רב יהודה אמר רב חטאת ששחטה לשם עולה פסולה שחטה לשם חולין כשירה אלמא דמינה מחריב בה דלא מינה לא מחריב בה והתניא *°תוכו ולא תוך תוכו ואפי' כלי שטף מציל ושני עשו חולין אצל קדשים כמחיצה אצל תנור מה מחיצה אצל תנור לא מהניא ליה כלל אף חולין אצל קדשים לא מהניא ליה כלל *דתנן תנור שחצצו בנסרים או ביריעות ונמצא שרץ במקום אחד הכל טמא *כוורת שהיא פחותה ופקוקה בקש ומשולשלת לאויר התנור שרץ בתוכה התנור טמא שרץ בתנור אוכלין שבתוכה טמאין ורבי אליעזר מטהר אמר רבי אליעזר קל וחומר אם הציל במת החמור לא תציל בכלי חרס הקל אמרו לו לא

אם

ונמלך. שלא יגרשנה : דילמא שאני התם. דלאו סתמא הוא אלא שלא לשמה ממש : דאינתיק. מאחר כל האנשים והנשים [לשם] גירושין של זה ושל זו : אלא מהא. דעדיפא מקמייתא דהכא חד גברא הוא : דאין ברירה. וגריעה מסתמא דשמא בשעה שנכתב לא היה בדעתו של בעל לזו ואינתק לשם האחרת : הכותב טופסי גיטין. שיהו מזומנין לו טופס לשון טפוס מול"ל בלע"ז : מקום הרי את כו'. דהו עיקר גופו אלמא סתמא פסול ואף על גב דאיכתב לשם כריתות לכשיזדמן לו : תו רמי מילתא אחריתי. אדרבינא ורב פפא קאי דקאמר ב] דרמי רבא אהדדי ושנינהו : דרב יהודה אמר רב. לקמן בפרק בית שמאי (דף מו:) : לשם חולין כשירה. קס"ד סברא דידיה היא כדמפרש דמינה מחריב בה דבר שהוא מינו מועיל ג] בו לעקור את שמו : דלאו מינה. כגון חולין שאינו מין קדשים לא מחריב בה ואין שמו נתפס על הזבח לעקור שמו ממנו : פסול. לגרש בו אשה אחרת : ואפי' לשם עובדת כוכבים. דהא שלא לשם האשה קתני דמשמע שלא לשם אשה זו אלא לשום אשה אחרת כל דהו ואע"ג דעובדת כוכבים לאו בת גירושין היא מהניא לפסול אלמא דלאו מינה ד] [מחריב] בה : דל עובדת כוכבים מיניה. ואימא נמי דלאו מינה לא מחריב בה אפילו הכי פסול דהוה ליה סתמא דמיהו לאו לשם אשה זו נכתב : דל חולין מינייהו. כדסבירא לן דלא חייל ולא מחריב ביה דלא מיניה הוא הוו להו שחוטין סתם ואמרן לעיל סתמא כשירה : תוכו. ה] כל כלי חרש וגו' (ויקרא יא) ולא תוך תוכו כלי המונח בתנור ופיו למעלה מן פי התנור ואוכלין ומשקין בתוכו ושרץ בתנור אוכלין שבכלים טהורין והכי אמרינן בת"כ אבל היה פיו בתוך התנור תוכו קרינן ביה : ואפי' כלי שטף מציל. כלומר לא מיבעיא כלי חרס המונח בתנור דמציל על האוכלין שבתוכו דהא תוך תוכו הוא וכלי גופיה ליכא למימר דמיטמא ו] באויר ויטמא אוכלין שבו דאין כלי חרס מיטמא מגבו אלא אפי' כלי שטף שמיטמא מגבו הכא טהור ומציל דאמר [בפ' קמא דפסחים] (דף כ:) אוכלין ז] מיטמאים מאויר כלי חרס ואין כלי מיטמא מאויר כלי חרס ומדקתני כלי שטף מציל אלמא דלאו מיניה חיין ביה ח] [ומבטל את שם תוכו] הכא נמי ליחול שם חולין וליפסל : ושני *הכא עשו חולין אצל קדשים כו'. כלומר לעולם דלאו מינה לאו מחריב ביה וכלי שטף אצל כלי חרס מיניה הוא דהא מנא והא מנא אבל חולין אצל קדשים הוי דלאו מיניה כמחילה אצל תנור דאמרינן ביה לקמן דלא מהניא ביה להיות חציצה בין שרץ לאוכלין כדאמרן דלאו מיניה לא מחריב בה : שחצצו בנסרים. שעשה מחיצה באמצעו וחלקו עד למעלה מפיו הכל טמא אפילו אוכלין שבעבר השני של מחיצה : כוורת שהיא פחותה. גרסינן בטהרות ולהכי נקט פחותה דלאו כלי הוא (א) דאי הואי שלימה הוה מצלת על אוכלין שבתוכה כדאמרן ט] אפי' כלי שטף מציל אבל השתא דלאו כלי הוא הויא כמחילה בעלמא : ופקוקה בקש. רבותא נקט דאע"ג דפקוקה פחיתתה בקש לא הוי כלי ואפי' פיה למעלה מפי י] תנור לא מצלת על אוכלין שבתוכה : ומשולשלת. תלויה : אוכלין שבתוכה טמאים. והיינו דאמרן דלא מינה כגון מחילה לא מחריב בה לבטל שם תוכו ממנו :

אם

דתורה להתלמד עבידא כדקאמר התם לענין גט מודה כדפרישית שם ובפ"ב דגיטין (דף כ.) וס"ת נמי פסלינן [בגט] בפ"ב דגיטין (דף יט:) כדמוכח בעובדא דההוא גברא דעל לבי כנישתא שקל ספר תורה ויהב לדביתהו : כתב לגרש את אשתו ונמלך כו'. תימה מה ענין זה אלא סתם ויש לומר יא] דס"ד כיון דנמלך אם כן מסתמא כתבו מתחילה שאם יחזור בו יגרש מי שירצה : הכותב טופסי גיטין כו'. כל הנך משניות בפ' כל הגט (גיטין דף כו.) ותימה דלא קתני בהך יתר על כן דעל כרחין יתר הוא דמכל הנך קמייתא לא מצי למידק סתמא פסול אלא מהך ויש לומר דמשום דאמר לבלר דקתני ברישא *דהך יתר כמו כן *דדייקינן מזאת [סתמא] ודייקינן מינה אין ברירה* וקשה לה"ר יצחק דפ"ק דפסחים (דף יד.) תנן הוסיף ר"ע אף ע"ג דלמאן דמוקי מילתא דר' חנינא בולד [וולד] הטומאה דרבנן לא שמעינן לה ממילתיה דר' עקיבא דמיירי בפסולא [דאורייתא] מיהו יש לומר *אע"ג דקתני הוסיף אי לא הוה תני ליה לא הוה *[קמשמע לן] מידי : ואמר רב יהודה אמר שמואל אף צריך שיניח כו'. איצטריך לאיתויי דרב יהודה משום דמינה דייקינן בגיטין דאתיא כרבי אלעזר דאמר עדי מסירה כרתי דקי"ל כוותיה ואיכא דמוקי לה התם כר"מ ומפרש מפני התקנה משום קטטה ולדידיה ליכא למידק מינה סתמא פסול יב] : ואפילו לשם עובדת כוכבים נמי פסול. מדקתני שנכתב שלא לשם אשה דמשמע (על) [כל] נשים בכלל ולא דמי לשלא לשמן דכל הזבחים דלא אמרינן אפי' חולין בכלל דהתם איכא לפרושי שנזבחו שלא לשם זבח זה אלא לשם זבח אחר : ורמינהו תוכו ולא תוך תוכו ואפי' כלי שטף מציל. מפרש בקונטרס שרץ באוירו ואוכלין בפנימי לא מיבעיא כלי חרס דאין מיטמא מגבו אלא אפי' כלי שטף דמיטמא מגבו אין אוכלין שבתוכו יג] [טמאים] שגם כלי שטף אינו מקבל טומאה מאויר כלי חרס כדאמר בפ' קמא דפסחים (דף כ:) אוכלין מקבלין טומאה מאויר כלי חרס ואין כלים מקבלים טומאה מאויר כלי חרס וקשה לפירושו דאם כן מה חידוש יותר בכלי שטף מכלי חרס ועוד דאיכא חידוש יותר בכלי חרס כגון אם שרץ באויר כלי חרס פנימי ואוכלין בכלי חרס חיצון יד] טהורין אע"פ שהפנימי טמא טו] ונראה לפרש דכל רבותא של כלי שטף היינו משום דלאו מינה הוא וס"ד דלא מחריב בה וטמא קמ"ל טז] [ודוקא בכלי שטף שאינו מינו היה טמא אי לאו קרא] אבל תוך תוכו שהכל הוא של חרס מינו פשיטא שהוא טהור בלא פסוק דתוך דוקא אמר רחמנא וכן מוכח לקמן דכלי שטף דוקא איצטריך קרא דפריך ומי אמר רבא חטאת ששחטה על מי שמחוייב עולה כשירה אלמא לאו מינה לא מחריב בה והתניא תוכו ולא תוך תוכו ואפי' כלי שטף מציל ומשני ארבעה תוכו כתיבי חד תוכו ולא תוך תוכו פי' אפי' לא כתב אלא תוך הוה מיעטנא כלי חרס פנימי שאין אוכלין שבתוכו מקבלין טומאה ע"י שרץ שבחיצון שהרי אין השרץ תוכו ודוקא כלי חרס פנימי דהוי דומיא דידיה מעיטנא דמינה מחריב בה ואוקן להכי כתב וי"ו של תוכו למימר דאפי' לאו מינה כגון כלי שטף *מחריב בה ומציל יז] ותימה אמאי לא שני במתניתין נמי הכי שאני התם דאמר קרא תוכו ולא תוך תוכו ולא איצטריך אלא לכלי שטף וי"ל דעדיפא משני הכא דקאי על חטאת לשם חולין כשירה ועל זה תירץ עשו חולין אצל קדשים דאינן מינם כלל ולכך לא מחריב בה כמחילה אצל תנור יח] כמו מחילה וכמו כוורת הקש פחותה שאינה כלי כלל ואינה מצלת כלל אבל כלי שטף קרוי מינו קצת שיש לו שם כלי עליו ולכך מחריב ומציל אבל לקמן קאי על חטאת ששחטה לשם מחוייב עולה כשירה דאע"ג שהוא קדשים קרוי אינו מינו ולא מחריב בה ועל זה פריך מאי שנא מכלי שטף שהוא כלי ואינו מינו ומחריב ועל זה צריך לתרץ משום קרא תוכו ולא תוך תוכו אבל לא מצי לתרץ עשוהו כמחילה אצל תנור דההוא אינו כלי כלל והשתא הכא ולקמן מתרץ דומה בדומה (ודוקא בכלי שטף שאינו מינו היה טמא אי לאו קרא אבל תוך יט] שהכל חרס טהור בלא פסוק דחד תוך אמר רחמנא) :

שכן

ה א מיי' פ"ג מהל' גירושין הל"ע טוש"ע אה"ע סי' קלא סעי' ב
ו ב מיי' שם הל"ג טוש"ע שם סעי' ג :
ז ג מיי' שם הל"ד טוש"ע שם סעי' ד :
ח ד מיי' פ"ג מהל' גירושין הל"ז :
ט ה מיי' פט"ו מהל' פסה"מ הל"ד :
י ו מיי' פי"ד מהל' כלים הל' ח ט :
יא ז מיי' שם הל"ז :
יב ח מיי' שם הל"א :

כ"א דדייקין מזאת דדייקין מינה כו' [וע"ע תוס' גיטין כד: סד"ה יתר מכן]

כ"א אפי' הכי קתני הוסיף דאי לא כו' נ"ק [רש"ק כי קשה ליה]

[גיטין כד.]
[שם:]
גיטין כו. ע"ש
[לקמן מו:]
חולין כה.
כלים פ"ח מ"א
תוספתא ב"ק דכלים פ"ו
ס"א
ל"ג

שיטה מקובצת

א] ואפי' לשם נויה נמי פסול. דהלשון משמע שלא לשם אותה אשה ותימה דמתניתין נמי נידוק הכי שנזבחו שלא לשמן ואפי' לשם חולין נמי לא עלו וכ"ת משום דמתני' מפרש בהדיא בסיפא שלא לשמן היינו לשם שלמים גבי לשמו ושלא לשמו גבי גיטין נמי מפרש בהדיא ונמלך ומצאו בן עירו וכו' דאין זה לשם נויה וי"ל דודאי אי הוה תני במתניתין שלא לשם זבח כי ההיא דקתני שלא לשם אשה אז היה משתמע הכי אבל השתא דקתני שנזבחו שלא לשמן משמע שפיר שלא לשם זבח זה אלא לשם זבח אחר . תוס' סוך : ב] דקאמר ליה מילי דרמי : ג] תיבת בו נמחק : ד] דלאו מינה נמי מחריב בה : ה] של כלי חרס ותיבות כלומ' נמחק : ו] דמיטמא מאויר אות ב' נמחק : ז] אוכלין ומשקין מיטמאים : ח] ביה לבטל את שם תוכו : ט] כדאמרן דאפי' כלי : י] מפי התנור לא : יא] דס"ד כיון שהוא בעיר מי ששמו כשמו אם כן היה דעת הסופר שאם ימלך זה לגרש בו יגרש אחר ועוד כיון דמצאו בן עירו מיד ואמר לו שמו כשמי אלמא קטטה ביניהם מקודם לכן ולכך כתב לו הסופר סתמא גם לצרכו.הכי הוה ס"ד ודחי ליה מ"מ אנתיק . תוס' סוך : יב] סתמא פסול והס"ד פי' שאם יכתבו שם האשה תבא אשה מן השוק שיהיה שמה כך ותהיה סבורה שבעלה צוה לגרש ויבא לידי קטטה בין איש לאשתו ולכך אתינן מילתא דרב יהודה דמוקי לה כר"א דבעי כתיבה לשמה מדאצטריך גם להניח הרי את מותרת לכל אדם דמשום קטטה לא שייך לומר . תוס' סוך : יג] שבתוכו מטאין שגם : יד] חיצון טהורים אע"פ : טו] טמא דהוי רבותא טפי מבכלי שטף דאינו מקבל טומאה מאויר ונראה: טז] תיבות ודוקא בבלי כו' עד לאו קרא נמחק: יז] ומציל וא"ת הא קיי"ל כל דבר המקבל טומאה אינו חוצץ בפני הטומאה וי"ל משום דגלי קרא דאין הכלים מטמאין מאויר כ"ח כדאיתא בפ"ח דכלים משנה ד' וקשה דסוף סוף הדרא קושיא לדוכתיה כיון דאין כלים שבעולם מטמא מאויר כ"ח א"כ מה לי כ"ח ומה לי כלי (עץ) [שטף] לעולם כו' ומאי אפילו ונראה דלא מבעיא כ"ח דמינה הוא אלא אף כלי שטף דלאו מינה הוא ומחריב בה ובקונטר' נמי פי' כך בסוף ההלכה גבי ד' תוכו כתיב כו' ופי' שם אלא בא ללמד על כלי שטף שאף הוא מציל דלא תימא דלאו מינה לא מחריב וא"ת לישני הכא ד' תוכו כתיב כדמשני לקמן וי"ל דמ"מ קשיא לילף מינייהו לענין לשמה דלאו מינה מחריב בה כגון חולין כו' כמו לענין תוך תוכו ומשני עשו חולין אצל קדשים כמחיצה אצל תנור כלומר ליכא לדמויי כלל חולין לכלי שטף דכלי שטף חשיב שפיר מינה כיון דאידי ואידי כלי הוא אלא למחיצה דמיא ולאו מצלא משום דלאו מינה הוא וחולין אצל קדשים לא שנא. ולישנא עשו חולין אצל קדשים מוכח קצת דמעיקרא הוי בעי למילף חולין מיתורא דתוך תוכו דכלי שטף. אבל ליכא לשנויי דהשתא לא ידע מיתורא דד' תוכו כתיבי כדמשני לקמן שהרי בסמוך בסוף סוגיין משמע שידע ליה ליתורא דקאמר דהכא נמי לייתי תוכו ליפשט מק"ו כמו שפי' שם בקונטרס. והא ליכא למימר דשפיר ידע יתורא דתוך תוכו לגבי כ"ח דהוי מינה ולאו לגבי כלי שטף דלאו מינה הוא ודוי ס"ד דהא דקאמר אפי' כלי שטף מסברא קאמר והשתא פריך שפיר גם זה אינו כדמוכח בפי' הקונטרס גבי ד' תוכו כתיב דכל עיקר היתור לא איצטריך לכ"ח לכך נראה דעדיפא א) כו' וא"ת אמאי לא משני כדלעיל גבי גט דל עובדת כוכבים מינה כו' נהי דלאו מינה לא מחריב ב) שניה תוך תוכו והוי סתמא מ"מ תוכו ולא תוך תוכו ולכך מציל וי"ל (דאפ"ה) [דאם] אינו חשוב תוך תוכו סתמא א"כ הוי בכלל תוכו וכן משמע לישנא דברייתא דקאמר ולא תוך תוכו ואפילו כלי שטף דמשמע [דממיעוטא] תוך תוכו מציל בכלי שטף הוא מטעם יתור כדפי' תוס' סוך : יח] תיבות כמו מחיצה נמחק : יט] אבל תוך תוכו שבכלי חרס טהור כו' דחד תוכו אמר :

א) כוון לדברי התוס' בד"ה ורמינהו דכתבו שם וי"ל דעדיפא משני הכא וכו'. ב) נראה דל"ל לא מחריב לבטל שם תוכו מ"מ הוי סתמא ולא הוי בכלל תוכו ולכך מציל.

הגהות הב"ח

(א) רש"י ד"ה כוורת וכו' דלאו כלי הוא וכמחילה כ"ל ודאי הוא :

גליון הש"ס

תוס' ד"ה הכותב וכו' דהך יתר כמו כן. פי' נסורי אבן חגיגה ד' כג ע"ב ד"ה וקתני :

אם הציל במת חמור שכן א] חלוקה באוהלין תציל בכלי חרש הקל ג] שאין חלוקין *באוהלין התינח לרבנן לרבי אליעזר מאי איכא למימר ר' אליעזר קל וחומר קאמר אי הכי ג] *התם נמי לימא קל וחומר קדשים מחללין קו"שים חולין לא כל שכן אלא ד] טעמא דרב כרבי ס] אלעזר *דאמר רבי אלעזר מאי טעמא דרב °ולא יחללו את קדשי בני ישראל ו] את אשר ירימו לה' קדשים מחללין קדשים ואין חולין מחללין קדשים אלמא אתא קרא אפקיה מקל וחומר ז] הכא נמי ליתי תוכו לפקיה מק"ו האי תוכו מיבעי ליה לאוכלין שגיבלן בטיט והכניסן לאויר תנור סד"א הואיל ובנגיעה לא מטמא באוירו נמי לא מטמו [קמ"ל] ח] ורבנן הנך לא צריכי קרא: רב יוסף בר אמי רמי שינוי קודש אשינוי בעלים ומשני מי אמר *רב חטאת ששחטה לשם חטאת כשירה לשם עולה פסולה אלמא דלאו מינה מחריב בה דמינה לא מחריב בה והאמר רב *חטאת ששחטה על מי שמחוייב חטאת פסולה על מי שמחוייב עולה כשרה אלמא דבר מינה מחריב בה דלאו מינה לא מחריב בה ומשני *התם °וישחט אותה לחטאת אמר רחמנא והרי חטאת לשם חטאת נשחטה *הכא וכפר עליו כתיב *ולא על חבירו °חבירו דומיא דידיה שמחוייב כפרה (א) כמותה רב חביבא רמי שינוי בעלים אתוך תוכו ומשני ומי אמר רב חטאת ששחטה על מי שמחוייב [חטאת פסולה על מי שמחוייב] עולה כשירה אלמא דמינה מחריב בה (ב) לאו מינה לא מחריב בה והתניא תוכו ולא תוך תוכו אפילו כלי שטף מציל ומשני ס] *ארבעה תוכו כתיבי (תוכו) תוך תוכו תוך תוכו חד לגופיה וחד לגזירה שוה חד תוכו של זה ולא תוכו של אחר אידך תוכו ולא תוך תוכו ואפילו בלי שטף מציל: מנלן

שכן חולקין אוהלים. פי' בקונטרס שכן דרך בני אדם לחלוק אהלים במחילה הילכך אהל אחרינא הוא אבל תנור אין דרך לחלקו משמע לפירושו דפליגי אף בתנור שחללו בנסרים או בירעות ובתורת כהנים משמע דבכוורת פתוחה ופקוקה ומשולשלת לאויר תנור דוקא פליגי ולא כשחללו בנסרים וטעמא משום דכוורת שיש לה ד' מחילות חיילא דדמי לכלי ולכך מטהר אבל מחילה אחת בתנור מודה ר' אליעזר דלא חיילא וטמא והכי איתא בפרשת ויהי ביום השמיני גבי תוכו ולא תוך תוכו כילד חבית שנתנה בתנור ופיה למעלה מן התנור כו' מיכן אמרו כוורת שהיא פתוחה כו' ור' אליעזר אומר מצלת אמר ר' אליעזר אם הצילה במת חמור לא תציל בכלי חרס הקל אמרו לו אם הצילה במת חמור מקום שהמחילה מצלת תציל בכלי חרס הקל שאין כז] מחילה מצלת משמע דשכן חולקים אהלים דאמרו לו דמתניתין הייט נמי פירושו דאמרו לו דתורת כהנים לכך נראה לרבינו הקדוש לפרש הכי אם הציל כוורת פתוחה ופקוקה באהל המת שכן חולקין אהלים פירוש שכן מחילה אחת המפסקת מצלת תאמר בכלי חרס שתחת כוורת שאין חולקין אהלים פי' שמחילה אחת המפסקת בתנור אינה חוצצת אלמא בתנור שחללו לא פליגי והא דמסיים בתורת כהנים בתר הכי כח] וקתני בלשון שמופתיטו שאמר לו ר' יוחנן בן נורי [אם הציל אוהלים מיד אוהלים במת כט] חמור שכן חולקים אוהלים יצילו אוהלים מיד ל] אוהלים בשרץ שכן אין חולקים כלי חרס אמר רבי יוסי אמרתי לר' יוחנן בן נורי] תמיה אני אם קיבל ממך רבי אליעזר תשובה מפני שהוא הגדון פירש לא] ר"ש שגם שם פליג ר' אליעזר ועל זה נ"ע ונראה לי ברוך גם מהכא משמע לב] בפירוש דחולקים אהלים דקאמר ר' יוחנן בן נורי לג] היינו מחילה של תנור ועל זה אמר לו רבי יוסי הלא גם שם פליג רבי אליעזר והשתא פירכא דאמרו לו ופירכא דר' יוחנן בן נורי הכל אחד אלא דמר אמר בהאי לישנא ומר אמר בהאי לישנא ואין להפך לד] הגירסא כמו שיש א) [מקלת ספר] בתורת כהנים ולגרום באמרו לו שכן חולקים אהלים ולפרש כפי' ר"ש ועל ר' יוחנן בן נורי נגרום שכן מחילה מצלת ועל זה יתיישב ר' יוסי שאומר הלא הוא הגדון אין לומר כן שהרי בתוספתא דמסכת כלים לה] ב) מוכחא כי ליכא מילתא דאמרו לו כלל כי אם דברי ר' יוחנן בן נורי שכן חולקין אהלים ועלה א"ר יוסי הלא הוא הגדון והתם אין לשנות הגירסא כיון דאמרו לו לא איירי התם ש"מ דחולקין אהלים הוי פירושן לו] גבי כלי חרס מחילה המפסקת בתנור כמו פירכא דמחילה [מצלת] דאמרו לו שניהן סוברין שרבי אליעזר לז] מודה [במחילה] גבי תנור ועל זה אמר ר' יוסי הוא הגדון גם שם פליג ר"א. ברו"ך:

לח] **הכא** נמי נימא קל וחומר קדשים מחללין קדשים כו'. יש תימה דעד השתא אסיקנא איפכא מתוך הסברא דאדרבה בשביל שהם קדשים ומינה לכך מחריב בה אבל חולין דלאו בר מינה לא מחריב ונראה לפרש דעביד קל וחומר משום דמה קדשים שאין מחללין כגון בשוחט חטאת סתם וכסבור שהיא עולה דכשירה ואפ"ה מחללין קדשים בשוחט לשם עולה חולין שמחללין כגון בכסבור שהן חולין דאמר בסוף בית שמאי (לקמן דף מו:) משום חולין פסולה לא כל שכן שמחללין קדשים בשוחטן לשם חולין: **לא** יחללו את קדשי בני ישראל. אע"ג דהאי קרא כתיב בטבל ובתרומה כדמוכח לקמן (דף יא:) בגמרא דשמעון אחי עזריה דילמא קדשי מיותר קדרים דהוה מצי למיכתב ולא יחללו את אשר ירימו:

א) נ"ע טעות סופר ב) נ"ל מוכחא דליכא מילתא כו' נ"ק מה

אם הציל. המחילה במת החמור באהל המת שהמחילה מפסקת [ומה]ין] וכלים שמעבר השני טהורין דכתיב (במדבר יט) כל אשר באהל יטמא והני לאו בההוא אהל ניניהו : שכן חולקין. דרך בני אדם לחלוק אוהלין במחילה הלכך אהל אחרינא הוא : תציל בכלי חרס. יא] [בתמיה שאין חולקין כלי חרס] במחילות הלכך תוכו קרינא ביה : התינח לרבנן. דאמרי מחילה לא מצלא איתא לדרב דאמר דלאו מיניה לא מחריב ביה : אלא לר' אליעזר מאי איכא למימר. לימא דרב תנאי היא : ר' אליעזר קל וחומר קאמר. לעולם בעלמא ר' אליעזר כרב סבירא ליה כגון חולין וקדשים אבל לענין מחילה מקל וחומר יליף כיון דבמת החמור מצלא קל וחומר לכלי חרס הקל שהשרץ קל מן המת: הכי גרסינן אלא טעמא דרב כר' יב] אלעזר ולא יחללו את קדשי הכי דריש ליה אין יג] דבר אחר מחלל את קדשי בני ישראל וגזירת הכתוב היא : ופרכינן אלמא לר' אלעזר דבעית לאוקמה לדרב אליביה אתא קרא דלא יחללו ואפקיה מק"ו דהוה לן למידרש קדשים מחללין קדשים יד] כו' : ה"נ ליתי תוכו. קרא יתירא דדרשינן לקמן תוכו ולא תוך תוכו טו] (וקאמרת מקרא למידק למידרש תוכו ולא תוך תוכו) וקאמרת מסברא דלא ממעט אלא תוך כלי אחר אבל מחילה דלאו בת מיניה לית ליה לאיתרוביה אי לאו משום קל וחומר ואמאי אמרת קל וחומר ליתי תוכו וליפקיה דמדמעט תוך תוכו מכלל דתוכו לעולם טמא דאי מחילה טז] (*בעלמא) מצלא למה לי קרא למעוטי תוך תוכו השתא תוכו מציל תוך תוכו מבעיא והאי שבעבר המחילה תוכו הוא לרב דהאמרת דלאו מיניה לא מחריב ביה : אמר לך ר' אלעזר האי תוכו דאתי למעוטי תוך תוכו ובעית למידק מיניה מחילה לא מצלא : מיבעי ליה לאוכלין שגיבלן . וחיפן בטיט סביב שאין השרץ יכול ליגע בהן והכניסן לאויר התנור והני הוא דאיתרבו לטומאה מדרשא דלא תוך תוכו הוא כדקאמרת תוך תוכו הוא דמציל אבל הקפת טיט לא מיחרבא ביה לבטולי שם תוכו יז] *דלאו מיניה כה"ג לא מחריב ביה דס"ד אמינא הואיל וא"א להם ליטמא במגע שרץ לא נטמאו נמי מתורת אויר כלי חרס *קמ"ל מיסופא יח] דלא תוך תוכו הוא (דאמר) דלא מטמא אבל הני מיטמו ומיהו מחילה אע"ג דלאו מיניה הוא אתא ק"ו ורבייה לאיתרובי ביה : ורבנן יט] הני. אוכלין לא צריכי קרא הך וי"ו יתירא דדריש לקמן למעוטי תוך תוכו ואיתרבו הנך כ] [דלאו] מיניה ניניהו לא אילטריך קרא לרבוייניהו דהני מתוך נפקי דהא בתוך ניניהו ומהיכא תיתי לך לטהרינהו והא דקאמר הואיל ובנגיעה לא מטמאו לאו איריא היא לטהרינהו מדין אויר : שינוי קודש. חטאת לשם עולה : שינוי בעלים. חטאת ראובן כא] ששחט לשם שמעון להתכפר בה שמעון דקי"ל [לקמן] דפסולה דכתיב לכפר עליו כב] ולא על חבירו : חטאת ששחטה לשם חטאת. חטאת חלב ששחטה לשם חטאת דם והא מילתא לקמן בפירקין (דף ז.) : והאמר רב. בשינוי בעלים חטאת ראובן ששחטה להתכפר בה שמעון אם שמעון מחוייב חטאת כג] (הוה) פסולה אבל אם מחוייב עולה ולא חטאת כשרה אלמא לאו מיניה לאו מחריב ביה : התם. כד] שינוי קודש נפקא לן [לפסולא מושחט] אותה לחטאת שתהא שחיטה לשם חטאת וכאן הרי חטאת לשם חטאת נשחטה: הכא. בשינוי בעלים פסולה נפקא לן מעליו ולא על חבירו והילכך חבירו דומיא דידיה דבר מיניה הוא דמחריב ביה לבטולי שמיה : ארבעה תוכו כתיבי. כילד תוכו תרי זימני ודרוש תוך ודרוש תוכו דהוה מצי למיכתב אל תוך וכתיב תוכו למיעוטא וכן בחבירו : חד לגופיה. שיטמא [*אוכלין] מאוירן : וחד לג"ש. שיטמא שרץ את הכלי ואע"פ שלא נגע כה] כו' כדיליף ליה בהכל שוחטין (חולין דף כד:) נאמר תוכו ליטמא ונאמר תוכו לטמא : ולא תוכו של אחר. למעוטי כלי שטף מטומאת אויר אא"כ נגע : וחד תוכו ולא תוך תוכו. כדפרישית לעיל וע"כ עיקר קרא לכלי שטף אתא דאי למעוטי כלי חרס שבתוך התנור ופיו למעלה מפי התנור שיציל על האוכלין שבתוכו למה לי וי"ו יתירא למעוטי לכתוב כל אשר כו] [בתוך] יטמא ומהיכא תיתי לטמויי אוכלים שבפנימי הא לאו תוכו ניניהו אלא ללמד על כלי שטף שאף הוא יציל דלא תימא דלאו מיניה לאו מחריב ביה הילכך גזירת הכתוב היא : ומנלן

א] שכן חולקין אהלים (תיבות חלוקה באוהלין נמחק) משמע שכן חילוק מחיצה מועילה (באהלים) [באוהל המת] להציל תאמר בכ"ח דלא וקשה דהוא הדין והיא התשובה דבמחיצה נמי פליגי כדפרש"י אלא נראה כפרש"י ז"ל שכן חולקין אהלים כלומר שכן דרך בני אדם לחלוק אהלים כו' וא"ת וכי בדרך בני אדם תליא מילת' ור"י מפרש דאה"נ דכי אמר רחמנא כל אשר באהל יטמא ולא מה שבאהל (אחרים) [אחר] זהו לפי דרך בני אדם. וא"ת התינח דליכא למילף שרץ ממת כדאמרי' שכן חולקים אהלים אבל כוורת פקוקה המצלת במת מטעם צמיד פתיל ולא מטעם מחיצה א"כ נילף שרץ ממת מק"ו ואמאי פליגי רבנן בכוורת וי"ל דכיון דלענין מחיצה נדחה הק"ו דשרץ ממת תו ליכא למילף בכוורת דאיכא למפרך מה למת שכן מחיצה מצלת כך יש לפרש לפי שיטת הקונטרס דפי' דרבנן פליגי בין בכוורת בין במחיצה מיהו קשה דבת"כ משמע דר"א בר פלוגתיהו דרבנן לא פליג במחיצה דקתני במלתייהו דרבנן אמרו לו אם הצילה במת החמור שכן מחיצה מצלת כו' משמע דבמחיצה כ"ע מודו דלא מצלא בכ"ח לכך נ"ל דאה"נ דבמחיצה מדו כ"ע ושכן חולקין אהלים ר"ל שכן מועיל חילוק אהלים דמצלת מחיצה גבי מת מה שאין כן בשרץ דכ"ע מודו דהיינו כי הא דת"כ וק"ו דר"א ה"ק אם הצילה במת החמור מטע' מוקף צמיד פתיל זאכוורת קאי דוקא ותימה לר"א מחיצה נמה ניליף מהאי דינא ק"ו ממת לשרץ וצ"ל דפשיטא ליה דליכא למילף מחיצה מק"ו לפי שדרך בני אדם להלוק אהלים כמו שפי' רבינו יחיאל נ"ע זה תירוץ טכל לומר מבחוץ. תוס' סוך: ב] שאין חולקין בכלי חרס תיבות חלוקין באהלין נמחק: ג] אי הכי. התם תיבת הכא נמחק: ד] אלא היינו טעמא. וגרסינן אלא משום דהשתא לאצריכנא להא שינויי דלעיל דעשו חולין כמחיצה דאפילו באת לדמות חולין לכלי שטף מ"מ ניחא משום דגבי חולין אצל קדשים גלי קרא ולכך לא ילפינן מהתם ומהאי טעמא ניחא בין לר"א ובין לרבנן. תוס' סוך. ה] כרבי אלעאי תיבת אלעזר נמחק: ו] תיבות את אשר ירימו לה' נמחק: ז] עי' בהשמטות בסוף המסכת: ח] ורבנן הנך לא צריכי קרא פ"ה האי וי"ו יתירא דדריש לקמן למעוטי תוך תוכו ואתרבו הנך (מיניה דתוכו נינהו) [אוכלין שגבלן בטים] לא איצטרי' [קרא לרבויינהו] דהני מתיך נפקי דהא בתוך נינהו ואי משום דאמרת הואיל ובנגיעה לא מטמא לאו [איריא] היא דאין לדמות נגיעה לאויר הילכך הא דאיצטריך תוך תוכו לגלויי דתוכו טמא אפי' בהפסקה היינו להפסקה דמחיצה וכוורת לאפוקי מק"ו דר"א וא"ת לרבנן למה לי האי טעמא תיפוק ליה דאינהו פרכי ליה (לקמן) לר' לדבריך נמי דאית לך הק"ו ליתי ח) תוכו בשביל אוכלין שגבלן בטיט והנך לא צריכי קרא. תוס' סוך:ט] עי' בהשמטות בסוף המסכת: י] מפסקת דכלים שמעבר: יא] בתמיה שאין חולקין כלי הרס: יב] בר' אלעאי תיבת אלעזר נמחק: יג] תיבת ג) דבר נמחק מחלל רק: יד] קדשים חולין לא כ"ש הס"ד ותיבת כו' עד תיבת וקאמרת נמחק: טו] תיבת בעלמא או הג"א תיבת מעליא נמחק: יז] דלא דוקא תוך תוכו אבל הני והשאר נמחק: יט] ורבנן הנך אוכלין: כ] הנך אוכלין שגבלן בטיט ולא איצטריך ותיבות דלאו מיניה נינהו נמחק: כא] (ראובן) שנשחט להתכפר בה ותיבות ששחט לשם עליו ולא: כג] חטאת הוא פסולה: כד] בשינוי קודש דפסולה נפקא לן מושחט אותה: כה] נגע בו ותיבת כו' נמחק: כו] אשר בתוך יטמא: כז] שאין המחיצה מצלת: כח] תיבת וקתני נמחק: כט] מיד אהלים באהל השרץ שכן אין: ל] פירש רבי תיבות ר"ש ל"ש ונמחק: לא] [illegible] תיבות של תנור נמחק: לב] משמע דפי' אות ב' נמחק: לג] דהיינו מחיצה מצלת תיבות של תנור נמחק: לד] להפך הגירסא כמו שיש במעט [illegible] לה] תיבות מוכחא כי נמחק: לו] הוי פירושן דמפסקת ומצלת כמו. והשאר נמחק: לז] אלעזר מודה גבי אות ה' נמחק ותיבת במחיצה ל"ש: לח] מה"ד התם נמי ותיבת הכא נמחק:

א) נראה דצ"ל ליתי תוכו ומפיק מק"ו דבשביל אוכלין וכו'. ב) אולי צ"ל אין חולין מחלל את קדשי בני ישראל רק קדשים ותיבת דבר נמחק.

נ"א בכלי חרס

נ"ל הבא

לקמן מו:

ויקרא כב

הגהות הב"ח
(א) גמ' שמחוייב כפרה כמותו : (ב) שם דלאו מינה לא :

[לקמן ז. איתא רבא וכצ"ל ועי' זבחים ס: ומנחות ג : ותוס' זבחים ז. ד"ה אמר רבה]

רס"ק מ"ז

[שם]

נ"א הכא

שם ד

לקמן ז:. ח. פסחים סב.
נ"א מעליא ומלא

ויקרא ד

חולין כב.

נ"א דלאו סב"א מחריב

ס"א קמ"ל מישופא דוקא תוך תוכו הוא פי' אבל הני מיטמו

גליון הש"ס
גמ' חבירו דומיא דידיה. עיין חולין דף לב ע"א תוס' ד"ה אבל :

וגי' ז"ק אוכלין וחשקן שגבלן

Not so, they replied: [3b] if it protects in the case of a corpse,
a which is stringent, that is because it is divided into tents;[1] shall it therefore protect in the case of earthen vessels which are less stringent but which are not divided into tents?[2] Now this is well according to the Rabbis.[3] But what can be said on R. Eliezer's view?[4]—R. Eliezer argues *a fortiori*.[5] If so, here too we can argue *a fortiori*: if sacred animals profane sacred animals, how much more does *ḥullin*![6]—Rather, Rab's reason is in accordance with R. Eleazar.[7] For R. Eleazar said: What is Rab's reason? *And they shall not profane the holy things of the children of Israel, which they set apart unto the Lord*:[8] holy things profane holy things, but *ḥullin* does not profane holy things.[9] This proves that a Scriptural text comes and nullifies the argument *a fortiori*; then here too, let the text '*its inside*' come and nullify the argument *a fortiori*?[10]—This text, '*its inside*', is required in respect of foodstuffs pasted round with clay and placed within the air-space of an oven. You might think,
b since they cannot be defiled by contact,[1] they cannot be defiled through its air-space either. Hence [the deduction] informs us that it is not so.[2] And the Rabbis?—[They argue,] No text is necessary in respect of these [foodstuffs].[3]

R. Joseph b. Ammi pointed out a contradiction between change [of intention] in respect of sanctity and change [of intention] in respect of owners,[4] and answered it. Did then Rab say: If one slaughters a sin-offering [for one offence] as a sin-offering [for another offence],[5] it is fit; as a burnt-offering, it is unfit? This then proves that another kind destroys it, whereas its own kind does not destroy it. Yet surely Rab said: If a sin-offering is slaughtered on behalf of one who is liable to a sin-offering,[6] it is unfit; on behalf of one who is liable to a burnt-offering, it is fit. This proves that a person of the same category as the offender destroys it, whereas one of a different category does not destroy it? And he answered: In the former case, the Divine Law states, *And he shall kill it for a sin-offering*,[7] and lo, a sin-offering has been slaughtered as a sin-offering. But in the latter case it is written, *and the priest shall make atonement for him*,[8] [which intimates,] '*for* him', but not for his fellow, and 'his fellow' implies one like himself, who stands in need of atonement just as he does.[9]

R. Ḥabibi shewed a contradiction between the law of change [of intention] in respect of owners and that of the inside of the inside, and then answered it. Did then Rab say: If a sin-offering is slaughtered on behalf of one who is liable to a sin-offering, it is unfit; on behalf of one who is liable to a burnt-offering, it is fit? This then proves that its own kind destroys it, whereas a different kind does not destroy it. Yet surely it was taught: '*Its inside*', but not the inside of it inside, and even a non-earthen vessel protects
c it?[1] And he answered: '*Its inside*' is written four times, 'the inside [*tok*]', 'its inside [*toko*]; 'the inside' [*tok*], '*its* inside [*toko*]';[2] one is required for its essential law;[3] another for a *gezerah shawah*;[4] a third [intimates] the inside of this, but not the inside of another;[5] and finally [to teach]: Its inside, but not the inside of its inside, and even a non-earthen vessel protects.[6]

a (1) A single partition across a room is sufficient to divide it into two rooms, and if a corpse is in one, eatables or utensils in the other are not contaminated. Hence it is right that even a defective receptacle should have the same effect. (2) I.e., a partition placed in an earthen vessel (*sc.* an oven) does not divide it into separate compartments (here designated 'tents'), as stated *supra 3a*: therefore a defective receptacle cannot do so either; so Tosaf. Rashi explains more simply: if it protects . . . into tents — i.e., it is quite usual to partition off a room into two, therefore a partition converts it into two separate tents. But it is not usual to partition an oven: hence the partition cannot affect its status. On this interpretation it appears that R. Eliezer holds that a partition does affect it, protecting the foodstuffs from contamination. In that case they differ not only in respect to a defective receptacle, but also in respect to the partitioning of an oven by a board or curtain. (3) The view that the defective receptacle (or, a partition) does not protect agrees with Rab's statement that what is not of its own kind does not 'destroy' it. (4) According to him a different kind too apparently 'destroys' it: is then Rab's ruling a matter of dispute between the Rabbis and R. Eliezer? (5) Generally he agrees with Rab, but in this particular case he rules differently, because of his argument. (6) When one kills a sin-offering as a burnt-offering, he is still killing it as something sacred, and yet you say it is unfit. How much more should it be unfit when he kills it as *ḥullin*, which is not sacred at all! (7) Not because a different kind does not 'destroy' it, but because a Scriptural text teaches this law. Sh. M. emends: R. Elai. (8) Lev. XXII, 15. (9) Tosaf. suggests that '*the holy things*' is superfluous, being understood from the context, and is therefore employed for this deduction. (10) From this text, '*its inside*,' it is deduced *supra a*, but not 'the inside of the inside', which is explained as meaning the inside of a second vessel within the first. Now from this it is deduced *a fortiori* that a *partition* does not destroy the unity of an oven (v. *supra a*), for if it did, a text would surely not be necessary for teaching that another vessel within the first protects its contents.

b (1) For a '*creeping thing*' cannot touch them. (2) The food is defiled. This is learnt from the deduction, its '*inside*', but not 'the inside of its 'inside', whence it follows that a partition does not protect; and it is in respect of a partition of this nature, viz., clay pasted round food, that this conclusion is drawn. (3) For they are obviously 'inside' of the oven. (4) I.e. between wrongful intention in respect of the sacrifice and that in respect of the owner thereof; e.g., he offered the sacrifice under the name of one who was not its owner. (5) Its owner had incurred the liability on account of a particular offence, whereas in slaughtering it he (or the priest) intended it as a sin-offering for some other offence. (6) But who is not the owner of this particular sacrifice. (7) Lev. IV, 33. (8) Ibid. 26, 31, 35. (9) For otherwise he cannot be called 'his fellow' in this respect. Hence the exclusion of his fellow applies only to such a case.

c (1) Cf. *supra 3a* n. b 1. (2) V. Lev. XI, 33, where *toko* (lit, 'its inside') is repeated twice, though in each case *tok* ('inside') would suffice. Each *tok* (which could have been written) is interpreted; further, each addition, '*toko*', is likewise interpreted, which gives four in all. (3) Viz., that any food or drink within it is defiled through the reptile (*sherez*) entering its air-space. (4) V. Glos. Teaching that the dead reptile defiles the *utensil* too, through entering its air-space, even without touching it; v. Ḥul. 24b. (5) Only an earthen vessel thus becomes unclean through its air-space without actual contact, but not a non-earthen vessel. (6) Hence this is a specially decreed law and stands by itself; therefore its principle cannot be applied to sacrifices.

[4a] How do we know that the slaughtering must be in its own name? Because Scripture says, *And if his offering be a zebaḥ slaughtering of peace-offerings:*[7] [this teaches] that its slaughtering must be in the name of a peace-offering. But perhaps that is their name?[8]—Since it is written, *He that offereth the blood of the peace-offerings*[9] and [he] *that dasheth the blood of the peace-offerings [against the altar]*,[10] and '*zebaḥ*' is not written,[11] whereas here '*zebaḥ*' is written, you may infer from it that the slaughtering must be in the name of a peace-offering.

We have thus learned [it of] slaughtering; how do we know
a [it of] the other [sacrificial] services?[1] And if you say, let us learn them from slaughtering [by analogy], then it may be objected: as for slaughtering, the reason is because it disqualifies in the case of a Passover-sacrifice [if done] on behalf of those who cannot eat it.[2]—Rather Scripture says, *He that offereth the blood of the peace-offerings*[3] which teaches that the reception [of its blood] must be in the name of peace-offerings. Then let the Divine Law state it of the reception [of the blood], whence the slaughtering [too] could be derived?—[That is not done] because [the analogy] can be refuted. As for the reception [of the blood], the reason is because it is unfit [if done] by a lay-Israelite or a woman.[4] We have thus learned [it of] slaughtering and receiving; how do we know [it of] sprinkling? And if you answer, let us learn it from the former [by analogy, then it may be argued]: As for the former, the reason is because they require the north,[5] and are practised in the case of the inner sin-offerings!—Rather, Scripture says, '*He that dasheth the blood of the peace-offerings!*' [which teaches] that the sprinkling [dashing] must be in the name of peace-offerings. Then let the Divine Law write it in respect to sprinkling, whence the others could be derived?—[That is impossible] because [the analogy] can be refuted: as for sprinkling, that is because a lay-Israelite is liable to death on its account.[6]

We have thus found it of all [rites]; whence do we know [it] of carrying? And if you say, let us learn it from all the others, [then it may be argued]: As for all the others, that is because they are rites which cannot be dispensed with; will you say the same of carrying,
b which can be dispensed with?[1]—Rather, Scripture says, *And the priest shall bring near*[2] *the whole ... to the altar*,[3] and a Master said: This refers to the *carrying* of the limbs to the [altar] ascent; while it was also taught, [*And Aaron's sons ...*] *shall present* [*the blood*]:[4] this refers to the *receiving* of the blood. Now, Scripture expresses this by a term denoting carrying[5] in order to teach that carrying cannot be excluded from the scope of receiving.[6]

Now we have thus found [it] of change [of intention] in respect of sanctity;[7] whence do we know it of change [of intention] in respect of owner?—Said R. Phinehas the son of R. Ammi: Scripture says, *And the flesh of the slaughtering of his peace-offerings for thanksgiving* etc.,[8] [which teaches] that the slaughtering must be in the name of a thanksoffering; now since this is superfluous for change in respect of sanctity, for that is deduced from the other text, transfer its teaching to change in respect of owners.[9] But is that the purpose of this verse? Surely it is required for what was taught. [Viz.,] '*And the flesh of the zebaḥ [slaughtering] of his peace-offerings for thanksgiving*': Abba Ḥanin said on R. Eliezer's authority: This comes to teach that if a thanksoffering is slaughtered in the name of a peace-offering, it is valid; if a peace-offering is slaughtered in the name of a thanksoffering, it is invalid.[10] What is the difference between these two cases?—A thanksoffering is designated a peace-offering, but a peace-offering is not designated a thanksoffering![11]—
c We state [our deduction] from the word '*slaughtering*'.[1] Yet it is still needed [thus]: How do we know [it of] a sin-offering and a guilt-offering?[2] From the word 'slaughtering'.[3]—If so,[4] let Scripture write, *And the flesh of his peace-offerings* for thanksgiving slaughtering [*shall be eaten* etc.][5] why state, *the slaughtering [of his peace-offerings for thanksgiving]*?[6] So that both laws may be inferred from it.

We have thus found [it of] slaughtering; whence do we know [it of] other services?[7] And if you say, Let us learn [them] from slaughtering, [then it may be objected]: as for slaughtering, the reason is because it disqualifies in the case of a Passover-offering, [when it is done] for the sake of those who cannot eat it!—'Slaughtering' is stated in reference to change [of intention] in respect of sanctity, and 'slaughtering' is stated in reference to change [of intention] in respect of owner; as in the case of the slaughtering stated in reference to change in respect of sanctity, you do not differentiate between slaughtering and other services, so also in the case of the slaughtering which stated in reference to change of owners, you must not differentiate between slaughtering and other rites. This can be refuted: as for change in respect of sanctity, [that is] because its disqualification is intrinsic,[8] and it is [operative] in respect of the four services,[9] and it is [operative] after death,[10] and it is [operative] in the case of the community as

(7) Lev. III, 1. So literally. E.V. 'sacrifice of peace-offerings'. (8) Perhaps the Heb. *zebaḥ* simply means 'sacrifice', as E.V., the name of the offering being the sacrifice of peace-offerings, and thus it has no bearing on the question of slaughtering. (9) Lev. VII, 33. (10) Ibid. 14. (11) It does not say, 'He that offereth the blood of the '*zebaḥ*' of the peace-offerings.'

a (1) Receiving the blood, carrying it to the part of the altar where it is to be sprinkled, and the actual sprinkling, count as separate services. (2) E.g., on behalf of aged and infirm, who cannot eat. But if the blood is sprinkled on their behalf, the offering is not unfit; and similarly in the case of any other of the services performed on their behalf. (3) The Rabbis refer this to the receiving of the blood. (4) It must be done by a priest. The slaughtering however may be done by a lay-Israelite too, and therefore, but for the text which teaches otherwise, I might think that it need not be done specifically in the name of that particular sacrifice. (5) They must both be done at the north side of the altar. (6) If he performs it. But the slaughtering may be done by a non priest; while the receiving and carrying, though forbidden to a non priest, do not involve death. By 'death' is meant death at the hands of heaven, not capital punishment.

b (1) If the animal is killed at the very spot where the blood is to be sprinkled. (2) *We-hikrib*; E.V. 'offer'. (3) Lev. I, 13. (4) Ibid. 5. (5) The same Heb. word, *hikrib* here explained to mean the receiving of the blood, is interpreted as *carrying* (the limbs) in the other verse. (6) I.e., receiving includes carrying, and the law of one applies to the other. (7) I.e., that a particular sacrifice must not be offered in the name of a different sacrifice. (8) Ibid. VII, 15. (9) This is a principle of Talmudic exegesis: where a verse is superfluous in respect of the subject upon which it directly bears, its teaching is to be transferred to another, analagous subject. (10) 'Valid' and 'invalid' mean that the bringer has discharged or not discharged his obligations respectively. (11) 'Peace-offering' is a wider term, which includes but is not included in the term 'thanksoffering'.—Thus the verse is required for a different purpose.

c (1) Whereas the other teaching is deduced from the phrase '*his peace-offerings for thanksgiving*'. (2) That their flesh too may be eaten only on the day when they are sacrificed and the following night, as that text is interpreted in respect of thanksgiving. (3) Which term includes other sacrifices. (4) If that is the only teaching of that verse. (5) Thus '*zebaḥ*' would be written *immediately* in connection with eating. (6) Bringing 'slaughtering' into connection with the sacrifice rather than with the eating. (7) *Sc.* that they must not be performed in the name of any but their true owner. (8) I.e., an illegitimate intention is expressed in respect to the sacrifice itself. (9) An illegitimate intention in respect of any service disqualifies it (according to the terms of the Mishnah). But change in respect of owner is a disqualification only for sprinkling, which constitutes the principal rite of atonement, either at that rite itself, or by expressing an intention at the slaughtering or any other service that the sprinkling shall be for a different owner. (10) If the owner dies, his son must bring it, and if he slaughters it for a different purpose it is invalid.

ומנלן דבעינן זביחה לשמה · לכתחילה דאי ממולא שפתיך לא מיפרשי ביה* עבודות: ממאי דלענין שחיטה יג] קרוי זבח [דלמא] היינו שמייהו · זבח שלמים ולא נאמר זבח משום שחיטה: מה לזביחה שכן יד] פוסלת שלא לשם אוכלין בפסח · שאם שחטו שלא לאוכלין כגון לחולה ולזקן שאין יכולין לאכול כזית פסול ואפילו הן בעליו דכתיב איש לפי אכלו אכילה בכזית ושאר עבודות לא פסלי שלא לאוכלין דכתיב תכוסו ותניא (פסחים דף סא·) רבי אומר לשון סורסי הוא זה כאדם האומר לחבירו כוס לי טלה זה והכי אמרינן בפסחים (דף עח:) דאין (מחשבה) *אוכלין בזריקה: המקריב · קבלה הוא דתניא והקריבו טו] זה קבלת הדם: שכן פסולה בזר · לאפוקי שחיטה שכשירה בזר כדלקמן בפרק שלישי (דף לב·) שחיטה וקבלה טעונות לפון בפ' איזהו מקומן (לקמן דף מח·) יליף להו מקראי: וישנן בחטאות הפנימיות · אבל זריקת מזבח החיצון לית בהו: זריקה זר חייב עליה מיתה · אבל שחיטה כשרה בזר וקבלה והולכה אע"פ שפסולה בזר אין חייב עליה מיתה כדאמרי' בסדר יומא (דף כד·) ארבעה עבודות זר חייב עליהם מיתה זריקה והקטרה וניסוך המים והיין דכתיב גבי והזר הקרב יומת ועבדתם עבודת מתנה ודרשינן עבודת מתנה ולא עבודת סילוק ועבדתם עבודה תמה ולא עבודה שיש אחריה עבודה והני כולהו יש אחריהם עבודה: מכולהו · במה הצד השוה שבהן שהן עבודה וצריכה לשמה אף אני אביא הולכה: הולכה אפשר לבטלה · שאם רצה שוחט בצד המזבח וזורק כדתניא במתניתין (לקמן דף יג.) : והקריבו זו קבלת הדם · ושחט את בן הבקר והקריבו בני אהרן הכהנים זו קבלה דהא בתר שחיטה כתיב *ולא אפשר לאוקומיה בהולכה ואף על גב דלשון הולכה הוא כדחזינן בהולכת אברים דכתיב ביה הקרבה ולשון הולכה היא: טז] ה"ג ואפקיה רחמנא קבלה בלשון הולכה למימרא דהולכה לא תפקה מכלל קבלה: שינוי בעלים מנלן · שצריך לשוחטו על מנת שיתכפרו בו בעליו ולא שיתכפר בו אחר דקתני לקמן (דף מו:) לשם ששה דברים הזבח נזבח לשם זובח יז] מנלן דבעינן לשם זובח: זבח תודת שלמיו · שתהא זביחתו לשם תודה: כשרה · ועלו לשם חובה: פסולה · כלומר לא עלו לשם חובה: תודה קרויה שלמים · כדכתיב תודת שלמיו כמו חטאת הקהל (ויקרא ד) תורת משה עבדי (מלאכי ג) : אנן מזבח תודה קאמרי' · דרשא דידן יח]ואבא חנן מתודת שלמיו: חטאת ואשם מנין · בת"כ קתני לה גבי האי קרא ובשר זבח תודת שלמיו ביום קרבנו יאכל למדנו לתודה שנאכלת ליום ולילה: חטאת ואשם מנין · ת"ל זבח : א"כ · דלהך דרשא לחודיה אתא לרבות חטאת ואשם שתהא אכילתו ליום ולילה יט] לכתוב לזבח לבסוף לגבי אכילה : לא חלקת · דהא כולהו איתרבו לעיל : שכן פסולו בגופו · לקמן מפרש לה ואזיל : וישנו בד' עבודות · שאם שחט שלא לשמו או קיבל והלך וזרק שלא לשמו אע"פ שלא חישב כ] אלא על השחיטה שלא לשמו פסול כדרבינן להו לעיל אבל שינוי בעלים לא שייך אלא בזריקה דהא דרבינן שחיטה לפסול בשינוי בעלים אינו אלא כגון ששחט על מנת לזרוק להתכפר בו אחר אבל שחט שלא לשם בעליו ולא הזכיר על מנת לזרוק אין זו מחשבה דשנוי בעלים לא שייך בקרבן אלא להתכפר בו וכפרה בזריקה היא והכי אמרי' לקמן בפרקין (דף י·) שאם אמר הריני שוחט לשם פלוני כשר שחטו על מנת לזרוק לשם פלוני פסול וכן לענין קבלה והולכה לא שייך שינוי בעלים אא"כ חישב לקבל על מנת לזרוק לשם אחר : וישנו לאחר מיתה · המפריש קרבנו ומת והיורש מקריבו שייך בו שינוי קדש אבל לא שינוי בעלים שהרי מתו בעליו:וישנו בצבור · אבל שנוי בעלים לא שייך בקרבן צבור שהרי הכל בעליו:

תורה אור

א] מנלן *דבעינן זביחה לשמה דאמר קרא (ויקרא ג) °ואם זבח שלמים קרבנו שתהא זביחה לשם [שלמים] ודילמא היינו שמייהו *מדכתיב (ז) °המקריב את דם השלמים °הזורק את דם השלמים ולא כתיב זבח והכא כתיב זבח שמע מינה שתהא זביחה לשם שלמים אשכחן זביחה שאר עבודות מנלן וכי תימא לילף מזביחה ג] *מה לזביחה שכן (א) נפסלה שלא לשם אוכלין בפסח אלא אמר קרא המקריב את דם השלמים שתהא קבלה לשם שלמים ולכתוב רחמנא בקבלה ולילף שחיטה מינה משום דאיכא למיפרך מה לקבלה שכן פסולה בזר ג] ואשה אשכחן שחיטה וקבלה זריקה מנלן וכי תימא לילף (ב) מהני מה להני שכן טעונות צפון וישנן בחטאות הפנימיות אלא אמר קרא הזורק את דם השלמים שתהא זריקה לשם שלמים ולכתוב רחמנא בזריקה ולילף מינה משום דאיכא למיפרך מה לזריקה שכן חייב עליה זר מיתה אשכחן כולהו הולכה מנלן וכי תימא לילף מכולהו מה לכולהו שכן עבודה שאי אפשר לבטלה תאמר בהולכה שאפשר לבטלה אלא אמר קרא °*והקריב ד] את הכל המזבחה *ואמר מר זו הולכת אברים לכבש ותניא ה] °והקריבו *זו קבלת הדם ו] (ג) ואפיק רחמנא בלשון הולכה למימרא דהולכה לא תפקה מכלל קבלה ז] ואשכחן שנוי קודש שנוי בעלים מנלן אמר רב פנחס בריה דרב אמי אמר קרא °ובשר זבח תודת שלמיו שתהא זביחה לשם תודה אם אינו ענין לשינוי קודש דנפקא לן מהתם תנהו ענין לשינוי בעלים והאי להכי הוא דאתא הא מיבעי ליה *לכדתניא ובשר זבח תודת שלמיו אבא חנין אומר משום רבי אליעזר בא ללמד תודה ששחטה לשם שלמים כשרה שלמים ששחטן לשם תודה פסולה מה הפרש בין זה לזה תודה קרויה שלמים ואין שלמים קרויה תודה אנן מזבח ח] קאמרינן ואכתי מיבעי ליה חטאת ואשם מנין תלמוד לומר זבח אם כן ט] נכתוב קרא ובשר תודת שלמיו י] [זבח] מאי זבח שמע מינה תרתי אשכחן זביחה שאר עבודות מנלן וכי תימא לילף מזביחה מה לזביחה שכן פוסל שלא לשם אוכלין בפסח נאמרה זביחה בשינוי קודש ונאמרה זביחה בשינוי בעלים מה זביחה האמורה בשינוי קודש לא חלקת בין זביחה לשאר עבודות אף זביחה האמורה בשינוי בעלים לא תחלק בהן בין זביחה לשאר עבודות איכא למיפרך *מה לשינוי קודש (פסחים ס:) יא] שכן (ד) פסולה בגופה וישנו בארבע עבודות יב] וישנו לאחר מיתה וישנו *בציבור כביחיד

ואע"ג

מה לזביחה שכן פוסל שלא לשם אוכלין בפסח · וא"ת זריקה נמי תפסול מק"ו דשחיטה שאינו פוסל בשינוי בעלים אלא על מנת לזרוק ופוסלת על מנת שלא לשם אוכלין ק"ו זריקה שפוסלת בזורק שלא לשם בעלים שתפסול שלא לשם אוכלין וי"ל דאיכא למיפרך מה לזביחה שכן טעונה לפון וישנה בחטאות הפנימיות מיהו אכתי לא קמא ליה הך פירכא עד בסמוך לכך י"ל דהכא לא יליף מזביחה אלא קבלה והולכה · ברו"ך · ועוד נראה דבפ' תמיד נשחט (פסחים דף סא·) ממעט שאר עבודות שלא[פסול]לשם אוכלין: מה לזריקה שכן חייב עליה זר כו' · וא"ת ונילף קבלה והולכה משחיטה וזריקה וי"ל מה להנך שכן חייבין בחוץ כדלקמן בשמעתין: דהולכה לא תפקה מכלל קבלה · וזריקה לא אתיא מכולהו שישנן בחטאות הפנימיות: בא ללמד תודה ששחטה לשם שלמים כשרה · תימה דבסוף כל הפסולין (לקמן דף נו·) דרשי' מיניה מנין לרבות שלמי נזיר ושלמי פסח ת"ל שלמיו פי' דנאכלין ליום ולילה וי"ל דהתם דריש מדכתביה גבי אכילה: ש"מ תרתי · וא"ת ואימא כוליה [להכי] הוא דאתא שתהא זביחה לשם תודה וי"ל דאיכא לרבויי חטאת ואשם מדכתיב *ביה אכילה :

וישנן לאחר מיתה · אבל שינוי בעלים אינן לאחר מיתה בפסחים (דף סא·) הקשה רבינו (דלמא מאחר) דשיעבודא לאו דאורייתא כמו כן אין שינוי קודש לאחר מיתה דמאי נפקא מינה דלא עלו לשם חובה הא לא מחייבי יורשין להביא אחר דפלוגתא היא בקדושין בפ"ק (דף יג:) גבי האשה שהביאה חטאתה ומתה יביאו יורשין עולתה דקאמר שמואל והוא שהפרישתה מחיים *ורב אשי אמר אפי' שלא הפרישתה מחיים והל"ל הכא למ"ד שיעבודא [לאו] דאורייתא שאין שנוי קודש לאחר מיתה *תרתי מיהא דווקא ויש לומר דנפקא מינה אם הפריש שתי שלמים או שתי עולות לאחריות ופירש שאם אחת מתה או אבודה השניה תהיה קריבה עולה כדין הראשונה ואם קרבה הראשונה כתקונה השניה תהיה חולין וכי מתו בעלים ועשה יורש אחת שלא לשמה הרי היא כאילו נאבדה וקרבה שניה תחתיה ואם עשה הראשונה כתיקנה או השניה חולין אבל אם לא פירש כלום אלא סתם הפריש שתים *לאחריות או אפילו נעשית הראשונה כתיקנה הוי שניה רועה ודמיה קרבי עולה כמו גבי מפריש שתי חטאות לאחריות כדאיתא לקמן (דף יא:) מותר חטאת קרב עולה *)והכי נמי האי בהפריש שתי שלמים או שתי עולות לאחריות ועי"ל דלאחר מיתה הוי [איסור] בשינוי קודש כשמשנהו אבל ליכא איסורא בשינוי בעלים כיון דליכא בעלים מיהו אכתי לא ידע דרשא דמולא שפתיך דמינה נפקא איסור לשינוי קודש מדמייתי לה בסמוך · הגה"ה : וישנן בציבור · משא"כ בשינוי בעלים דאם שחט **)לשמו התמיד הרי הוא בעליו ואפי' לשם עובד כוכבים לא מיפסיל דבעינן חבירו דומיא דידיה מחוייב כפרה כמותו · ברו"ך :

*) ונראה נמי דהכא **) נ"א לשם יחיד

מחשבה

רב

נ"א עבודה לשמו

רש"מ וג"א דאין מחשבת אוכלין בזריקה ולא בקבלה והולכה בשחיטה כצ"ל

הגהות הב"ח
(א) גמ' מה לזביחה שכן פסולה שלא לשם: (ב) שם זריקה מנ"ל וכ"ת לילף מהני כיב ע"ל דף ע"א: (ג) שם ואפקיה רחמנא לקבלה בלשון הולכה: (ד) שם מה לשינוי קודש שכן פסולו בגופו ויכו':

[עירובין קו. יומא כז. מנחות י: חגיגה יא. פסחים סה: לקמן יד: ודף כד: לה.]

[עמ"ש תוס' יומא כז. ד"ה והקריבו וכו' על פירש"י הכא]

לקמן ז.

יג א ב מיי' פ"ד מהל' מעה"ק הל' ו ופי"ג מהלכות פסה"מ הל' ל'
יד ג מיי' פט"ו מהל' פסה"מ הלכה ה:

נ"א לא ס"ד מדכתיב כו'

[לקמן קי.]

[נ"ל גבי]

נ"א דלמ"ד

[נ"ל והקריב הכהן את הכל והקטיר]

לקמן יג. [קדושין נג: חגיגה יא.]

[נ"ל ורב אשי]

גי' נ"ק חדא

נ"א בשלמים או עולות הפריש שתים

שיטה מקובצת
א] מנלן דבעינן זביחה [לשמה] פי' הקונטרס ואי ממוצא שפתיך תשמור לא מפרשי כלל בד' עבודות של דם וקשה דהא ועשית כתיב בהאי קרא דמוצא שפתיך ועשית משמע [בעבודת] הדם וכן קשה הא דאמר תלמודא גבי לא ידענא במאי דפי' לא ידענא במאי אמר הא אמר רחמנא מוצא שפתיך תשמור ועשית וי"ל פי' שלא ישנה ממוצא שפתיו ודלמא לאו לענין לשמה משתעי קרא (וה"ה דאף) ואף כי ישנה באחת במחשבה שלא לשמה מקרי, שפיר מוצא שפתיך כיון דבשאר עבודות לא שינה · ת' מהר"פ: ב]עי' בהשמטות בסוף המסכת: ג] תיבת ואשה נמחק: ד]והקריב הכהן את הכל : ה] עי' בהשמטות בסוףהמסכת: ו] הדם והולכה היא ואפקיה · ה"נ ואפקיה רחמנא בלשון הולכה למימרא כו' פי' לשון הולכה היא כמו שמוכיח מקרא דוהקריב הכהן את הכל המזבחה ואמת הוא דע"כ זו קבלת הדם כדפי' ואפקיה רחמנא בלשון הולכה כלומר למה אפקיה רחמנא בלשון הולכה כיון שהוא קבלה למימרא דלא תפקיה כו' ויש להקשות נילף זריקה משחיטה וקבלה והולכה ולישתוק מזריקה דמאי פרכת שכן טעונה צפון הולכה לא בעי צפון וי"ל דמ"מ איכא למיפרך שכן ישנן בחטאות הפנימיות דהולכה נמי הוי בחטאות הפנימיות שהיה מוליך את הדם עד להיכל ועד לפרכת · תוס' שוך : ז] עי' בהשמטות בסוף המסכת : ח] מזבח תודת קאמרינן : ט] אם כן לכתוב קרא תודת שלמיו זבח ללמד על חטאת (ושלמים) [ואשם] שנאכלין ליום ולילה ומדאקדמיה זבח לתודה ש"מ זבח לשם תודה · וא"ת ואימא כוליה לזביחה לשם תודה הוא דאתא ומנלן לרבות חטאת ואשם (הנאכל) [דנאכל] ליום ולילה ויש לומר מדכתביה להאי קרא גבי אכילה שמע מינה לרבות נמי חטאת ואשם לאכול יום ולילה · תוס' שוך : י] שלמיו זבח מאי זבח תודת שלמיו שמע מינה : יא] שכן פסולו בגופו וישנן בד' עבודות משא"כ בשינוי בעלים וא"ת והלא לקמן מוכח מקראי פסול בכל ד' עבודות בשינוי בעלים ותירץ בקונטרס דאינו אלא בשוחט ע"מ לזרוק בשינוי בעלים או מקבל ע"מ כו' ויש להקשות דהלא אנו באים ללמוד דלא חלקת בין שינוי בעלים לשינוי קודש וא"כ ניתא כמו דבשינוי קודש מיפסל בכל ד' העבודות [אפי' אם לא חישב] ע"מ לזרוק כן שינוי בעלים נמי ולפי' דאחד ששחט לשם בעליו ולא הזכיר ע"מ לזרוק אין זו מחשבה דשם בעלים לא שייך בקרבן אלא להתכפר בו וכפרה בזריקה והשתא ניחא שפיר דאין למילף משינוי קודש כי אם עבודות דשייכא בה מחשבת שינוי בעלים ובשחיטה וקבלה והולכה לא שייכא מחשבת שינוי אלא א"כ דחשב ע"מ לזרוק· תוס' שוך : יב] וישנו לאחר מיתה · פי' (המקריב)[המפריש] קרבנו ומת היורש מקריבו ושייך בו שינוי קודש ולא שינוי בעלים דאין בעלים לאחר מיתה דקדק ריב"א דהכא אתיא כמ"ד שעבודא דאורייתא דלמ"ד שעבודא לאו דאורייתא אפי' משינוי קודש לא יביאו יורשין אחר (מיתה) וא"כ שינוי קודש נמי אינו (אלא) לאחר מיתה ואומר רבי דאתיא נמי כמ"ד שעבודא לאו דאורייתא ואפ"ה ישנו שינוי קודש לאחר מיתה כגון שהפריש שתי (חטאית) [שלמים או עולות] לאחריות וכשמשנה בזה לא יעלה זה לשם חובה וצריך להקריב השני· תוס' שוך: יג] שחיטה וזריקה קאי זבח ותיבת קרוי נמחק : יד] שכן נפסלת שלא לשם כו' שחטו שלא לשם אוכלין כגון : טו] זו קבלת : טז] היא הס"ד ומה"ד והולכה היא ה"ג ואפקיה רחמנא לקבלה : יז] תיבות מנלן דבעינן לשם זובח נמחק : יח] דידן ודאבא חנן : יט] לכתבינהו לזבח : כ] חישב ע"מ לזרוק שלא לשמו (תיבות אלא על השחיטה נמחק) ס"א אלא על השחיטה או על הקבלה והולכה שלא לשמה פסול כדרבינן להו לעיל :

ואע"ג דתרתי לאו דוקא תרתי מיהא דוקא מאי שנא שינוי בעלים דלא הוי פסולו בגופו מחשבה בעלמא שינוי קודש נמי מחשבה בעלמא הוא אלא כיון דאחשבה פסלה ה"נ כיון דאחשבה פסלה ולרב פנחס בריה דרב מרי *דאמר יש שינוי בעלים לאחר מיתה תרתי מיהא איכא למיפרך אלא אמר רב א] אשי אמר קרא °ונרצה לו לכפר עליו *ולא על חבירו והאי להכי הוא דאתא האי מיבעי ליה לכדתניא *ונרצה לו לכפר עליו ב]רבי שמעון אומר את שעליו חייב באחריותו ואת שאינו עליו אינו חייב באחריותו ג] ואמר רב יצחק בר אבדימי מאי טעמא כיון דאמר עלי כמאן דטעון ליה אכתפיה דמי רב אשי מונרצה לו לכפר קאמר: אשכחן זביחה וזריקה קבלה מנלן וכי תימא לילף מזביחה וזריקה מה לזביחה וזריקה שכן עבודה שחייבין עליה בחוץ אלא אמר ד] רב אשי אתיא מאיל נזיר דכתיב °ואת האיל יעשה זבח שלמים *שתהא עשייתו לשם שלמים ואם אינו ענין לשינוי קודש דנפקא ליה מהתם תנהו ענין לשינוי בעלים אמר ליה רב אחא בר אבא לרבא אימא יעשה כלל זבח פרט כלל ופרט אין בכלל אלא מה שבפרט זביחה אין מידי אחרינא לא אי כתיב יעשה שלמים זבח כדקאמרת השתא דכתיב יעשה זבח שלמים הוה ליה כלל שאינו (א) מלא וכל כלל שאינו מלא אין דנין אותו בכלל ופרט רבינא אמר לעולם דנין ולה' חזר וכלל אמר ליה רב אחא (ב) מדיפתי לרבינא והא לא דמי כללא קמא לכללא בתרא כללא קמא מרבה עשיות ותו לא כללא בתרא כל לה' ואפילו שפיכת שירים והקטרת אימורין *הא תנא דבי רבי ישמעאל ה] בכללי ופרטי (ג) דריש כי האי גוונא כלל ופרט וכלל אי אתה דן אלא כעין הפרט מה הפרט מפורש עבודה ובעינן לשמן אף כל עבודה ובעינן לשמן אי מה הפרט מפורש עבודה וחייבין עליה בחוץ אף כל עבודה וחייבין עליה בחוץ שחיטה וזריקה אין קבלה והולכה לא אי נמי מה הפרט מפורש דבר הטעון צפון וישנו בחטאות (ד) הפנימיות אף כל הטעון צפון וישנו בחטאות הפנימיות שחיטה וקבלה אין זריקה לא איכא למימר הכי ואיכא למימר הכי *שקולין הן ויבאו שניהן לישנא אחרינא ו] וחדא חדא תיקו במילתא איבעית אימא זריקה ז] מדרב אשי נפקא אשכחן איל נזיר שאר שלמים מנלן וכי תימא נילף מאיל נזיר מה לאיל נזיר שכן יש ח] עמהן דמים אחרים א"כ נכתוב ט] *שלמי מאי שלמים לרבות כל שלמים אשכחן שלמים שאר כל קדשים מנלן וכי תימא נילף משלמים מה לשלמים שכן טעונין סמיכה ונסכים ותנופת חזה ושוק אלא אמר קרא °זאת התורה לעולה ולמנחה ולחטאת ולאשם ולמילואים ולזבח השלמים היקישן הכתוב לשלמים מה שלמים בין שינוי קודש בין שינוי בעלים בעינן לשמה אף כל בין שינוי קודש בין שינוי בעלים בעינן לשמה י] אימא היכא דשחיט להו שלא לשמה ליפסלו אמר קרא °מוצא שפתיך תשמור ועשית כאשר נדרת וגו' *האי נדבה נדר הוא יא] [אלא] אם כמה שנדרת עשית יהא נדר ואם לאו יהא נדבה ואיצטריך מוצא שפתיך ואיצטריך זאת התורה דאי כתב רחמנא מוצא (ה) יב](הוה אמינא) לא

רש"י

יג] ולאע"ג דתרתי לאו דוקא תרתי דוקא · *לאע"ג דמותבינן ארבעה יד] פרכי איכא תרתי שאינן עיקר כדמפרש ואזיל : תרתי מיהא דוקא · והשתא מפרש אמאי תרתי לאו דוקא : ולרב פנחס כו' · ולקמן בשילהי שמעתין אזלה לה הך פירכא דלאחר מיתה : לכפר עליו · היינו זריקה אלמא זריקה לשם בעלים בעיא : את שעליו · כגון נדר דאמר הרי עלי עולה חייב באחריותו אם הפריש בהמה לנדרו אם מתה או נגנבה דהכי משמע אותו שעליו יקריב אותו ונרצה לו ועד שיקריבנו לא נרצה ולא נפטר : את שאינו עליו · כגון דאמר הרי זו עולה : מונרצה לו טו] לכפר קאמר · דהכי משמע לו לכפר ולא טז] לחבירו : שכן עבודה שחייבין עליה בחוץ · יז] דכתיב (ויקרא יז) אשר ישחט מחוץ למחנה וזורק נמי מרבינן ליה לקמן בפ' השוחט (דף קז·) דם שפך לרבות הזורק תאמר בקבלה והולכה שאין חייבין עליה בחוץ דתנן בפ' בתרא (שם קיב:) והעולק והבולל כו' והמקבל דמים בחוץ פטור : יעשה כלל · שיהו כל עשיותיו לשם שלמים : זבח פרט · שחיטה הוא דבעי לשמה : אי כתיב יעשה שלמים זבח כדקאמרת · דמשמע כללא שיהו עשייתו יח] שלמים : השתא דכתיב יעשה זבח שלמים · לא גמר הכלל את דבריו ולא נשלם להשמיעו על מה הוזכרו כאן העשיות יט] עד שבא זבח והפסיק את הדבר : כלל שאינו מלא · כ] ולא נתמלא דבריו להשלים · מלא פרדאשביי"ן בלע"ז : לה' · יעשה זבח שלמים לה' : כא] עשייתו · עבודות המיוחדות שחיטה וזריקה קבלה והולכה : שפיכת שירים · שנשפכין שירי הדם ליסוד כב] [אחר] שנתן ארבע מתנות ואינן מעכבין כפרה : הא תנא דבי רבי ישמעאל כו' · בשילהי אלו טריפות (חולין דף סו·) גבי פרשת חגבים : איכא למימר הכי · עבודה וחייבין עליה בחוץ ואתיא לה זריקה : ואיכא למימר הכי · עבודה שטעונה צפון ואתיא לה קבלה : שקולין הן · המדות שוות והי מינייהו מפקת אי דרשת הא אנא דרישנא לאידך הלכך יבאו שניהם והולכה על כרחך לא תפקה מכלל קבלה : מדרב אשי · מונרצה לו לכפר וכלל ופרט לאיתויי קבלה דאי לזריקה לא איצטריך : שכן יש עמו דמים אחרים · שבאין עמו חטאת ועולה : אשכחן שלמים · בין בשינוי קודש בין בשינוי בעלים : שכן טעונין כו' · ושאר זבחים יש מהן שאין טעונים סמיכה ולא נסכים כגון בכור ומעשר ופסח ויש מהן שאין טעונין נסכים כגון חטאת ואשם כג] וכולן אין אחד שיהא טעון חזה ושוק : ליפסלו · שהרי לא נעשו כהלכתן ואין זריקתן מתרת בשרן לאכילה : ואיצטריך · למיכתב זאת התורה למיגמר משלמים ולא תימא ממוצא שפתיך נפקא דלכתחילה בעינן לשמה : לא

תוספות

מחשבה בעלמא · ואפי' יהא צריך דיבור כיון דליכא מעשה הוי כמחשבה בעלמא ויש תימה דהכא משוי להו וכפ' תמיד נשחט (פסחים סב:) משמע שיש חילוק דמפרש מה בין כד] לשמן לשלא לשמן לאוכליו ושלא לאוכליו זה פסולו בגופו וזה אין פסולו בגופו וי"ל דכיון דלא מיפסיל אלא מפני שאין יכול לאכול כזית כגון לשם חולה וזקן [א] חשיב ספי פסולו בקודש מחמת דבר אחר כיון דאם היה יכול לאכול היה כשר וקשה דעל כרחין שלא למנוין ולערלים ולטמאין צריך לומר דלא חשיבי פסולן בגופו כי היכי דלא תיקשי לן נמי מה בין לשמן ושלא לשמן למנוין ושלא למנוין למולין ולערלים לטמאין ולטהורים וי"ל דשינוי בעלים חשבינן פסולו בגופו משום דתלוי [ג] בזריקה כה] (בכפרה) ושם בעלים [על הכפרה] אבל שלא לאוכלין ושלא למנויין תלוי בשחיטה ואין שם בעלים על השחיטה אי נמי שלא לאוכלין כו] [ושלא למנויין] יכול לקיים מחשבתו בהיתר [באותן] שיהיו מנויין עליו כז] אם אינם חולים וזקנים אבל שלא לשמה אינו יכול לקיימו לכך קרוי פסולו בגופו :

הגה"ה ה"ג במגילה (דף ח·) מאי [משמע] אמר רב יצחק בר אבדימי : רב אשי כח] (אמר) מונרצה לו קאמר · תימה למה לי קרא לשינוי בעלים בזריקה הא אפי' שאר עבודות לא מיפסלי אלא בחושב על מנת לזרוק כ"ש זורק כט] *עצמו [דבעינן] שם בעלים :

שכן עבודה וחייבים ל] · פירוש עבודה שחייבין עליה בחוץ :

שקולים הם ויבאו שניהם · אע"ג דהכא תרתי והכא חדא חשיב להו שקולין והקשה הרב רבי חיים דהשתא משמע דהיכא דלא ידע הי מינייהו לרבוי מרבי תרוייהו וכן בריש ב"ק (דף ג·) דמרבי מושלח שן ורגל משום דשקולין הן וכן בפ"ק דערכין (דף ד:) גבי נפשות ואיש בפרק כל האסורים (תמורה דף כח:) ופרק שור שנגח ארבעה וה' (ב"ק דף מ:) דרשינן מן הבהמה להוציא את הרובע ומן הצאן להוציא את הנוגח וקאמר מפני שיש ברובע מה שאין בנוגח ויש בנוגח מה שאין ברובע הוצרך לומר רובע והוצרך לומר נוגח ותירץ דהיכא דאיכא משמעות בריבויי מרבינן כל השקולים כי הכא דזבח משמע לרבויי כעין זביחה כל שהיא עבודה וכן ושלח יש במשמע רגל ושן ונפשות נמי משמע הכל אבל מן לא משמע למעוטי שניהם *) :

אימא היכא דשחיט שלא לשמן ליפסלו · תימה הא בכל דוכתא בעינן בקדשים לא] [שינה] לעכב והכא לא שינה וי"ל דפריך משינוי קודש דאיכא תרי קראי ואמרי' לעיל אם אינו ענין לשינוי קודש תנהו ענין לשינוי בעלים ופריך לב] דהשתא אימר תרוייהו בשינוי קודש ולעכב וקשה מאי משני אמר קרא מוצא שפתיך דלמא האי קרא לאו לשינוי בעלים דלא אשכחן שינה בהן הכתוב ולא קשה מידי דמוצא שפתיך לא משמע שינוי בעלים · [הג"ה] [ג]ונראה דפריך מכח סברא כעין קושיא דר"ל לג] דלקמיה דאימא דליפסלו כיון דאמרת דלא עלו לשם חובה או נימא דיעלו דאם כשרין הן ירצו ואם אין מרצין למה באין לד] [ומיהו] לא דמי דר"ש לקיש פריך יהו כשרין גמורין כמו שאר קדשים דלא שנה לעכב לה] *בו ליפסלו והכא לא הוה ליה למיפרך שלא לשמה ליפסלו אלא הוה ליה למימר וליתכשרו ויעלו לחובה כשאר קדשים

*) [וע' שיטות תוס' ב"ק מ: ד"ה ויש]

שיטה מקובצת

א] רב אמי תיבת אשי נמחק : ב] רבי שמעון אומר את שעליו חייב כו' · ודייק ממשמעות דקרא ונרצה לו לכפר עליו אימתי נרצה לו כשהוא לכפר ואז לא יביא אחר הא אם לא כיפר יביא אחר ואימתי אני אומר שיביא אחר לכפר כשאמר עליו שאז עליו אחריות · תוס' טוך ותוס' ר"פ : ג] באחריותו מאי משמע אמר רב יצחק : ד] אמר רבא ותיבות רב אשי נמחק : ה] ישמעאל הוא דדריש כללי ופרטי כי האי גוונא : ו] אחרינא שקול הוא וכל חדא וחדא תיקו אמילתיה אב"א : ז] מדרב אשי נפקי · כלומר והולכה לא תפקית (מהולכה) [מכלל קבלה] וזריקה אתיא מדרב אשי ונרצה לו לכפר וא"ת למה לי קרא למיפסל שינוי בעלים בזריקה (או)[הא] מקבל ע"מ לזרוק שלא לשם בעלים [פסול] כדפ"ח לעיל א"כ כ"ש זורק עצמו וי"ל [דהת"א] דגזירת הכתוב הוא ובעינן זורק ע"מ להקטיר או ע"מ לשפוך שירים דלעולם בעינן ב' עבודות בענין [שלא לשם בעלים דהא חזינן] דשחיטה וקבלה דלא מהניא כי אם [במחשב מעבודה לעבודה] הוא א)דכותיה אשכחן גבי פיגול דאינו [מפגל כי אם] במחשב מעבודה לעבודה' תוס' טוך : ח] יש עמו דמים : ט] נכתוב שלמיו מאי : י] אימא היכא דשחיט להו שלא לשמה ליפסלו' פי' בתוס' אע"ג דלא שינה הכתוב לעכב מ"מ ליפסלו מסברא כיון דשינה בלשמן כאילו חסר העבודה ששינה בה [וא"ת הא] מדשינה הכתוב לעכב בחטאת ש"מ היכא שלא שינה הכתוב דאינו פסול ותירצו בתוס' דאדרבה הייתי אומר אם [שינה בכל] הקרבנות לפיסולא מהיקשא דחטאת דאתקש כולהו לחטאת בהיקשא דזאת התורה וכ"ת א"כ הייתי מקשה פסח למה לי דשינה [לפסול] תיפוק ליה מהיקשא דחטאת י"ל כיון דפסח לא הוי בהדיא כתוב בההוא ענינא (דמשום ביום) [דמביום] צוותו נפקא כדאמרינן לקמן (דף ז ע"ב) הייתי אמר [illegible]

ואיכא דבעי לפי מאי דסברא ור"ל דהיינו לפי מאי דמפרש בכל הקרבנות ממוצא כו' לכך אצטריך שינה לעכב דלא תילף הכשרה בפסח וחטאת [מהיקשא] דשלמים · תוס' הר"פ : יא] הוא אלא : יב] מוצא שפתיך הוה אמינא : יג] ה"ג ואע"ג דתרתי לאו דוקא תרתי מיהו דוקא · דמהגי ארבעה תיבת דמותבינן נמחק : יד] פירכא איכא : טו] תיבת לכפר נמחק : טז] לכפר ולא על חבירו תס"ד : יז] בחוץ כלומר שכן עבודה חשובה להתחייב עליה בחוץ דכתיב : יח] עשייתו לשם שלמים : יט] תיבת עד נמחק : כ] מלא לא אות ו' נמחק : כא] מה"ד עשיות' עבודות המיוחדות שחיטה : כב] ליסוד אחר : כג] ואשם ואין בכולן שיהא אות ו' ותיבת אחד נמחק : כד] בין לשמו לשלא לשמו : כה] תיבות בכפרה ושם בעלים נמחק : כו] תיבות ושלא למנוין ל"ש : כז] עליו מי שאינן תיבות אם אינם נמחק : כח] תיבת אמר נמחק : כט] עצמו שלא לשם בעלים (תיבת דבעינן נמחק) : ל] בעינן ב' עבודות בענין זה [כמו] בשחיטה וקבלה דלא מהניא בהם (ע"מ) [כ"א] בע"מ דכותיה אשכחן בפיגול (דאי לא) [דלא] מפגל כי אם במחשב מעבודה לעבודה : לא] בקדשים שינה : לב] ופריך השתא אימא דתרוייהו בשינוי קודש ומיהו קשה דמאי משני : לג] דר"ל דלקמן : לד] באין ולא נראה דריש ל"ש ותיבות לא דמי נמחק : לה] לעכב או ליפסלו דהכא · תיבת בו נמחק :

א] אולי צ"ל וסו"ל דזריקה נמי דכוותיה הוא ודכוותיה אשכחן וכו' :

הגהות צ"ק [א] חשיב ספי פסולו מחמת דבר אחר כו' [ב] בזריקה ועיקר כפרה בזריקה ושם בעלים על הזריקה כו' כצ"ע : [ג] ואין נראה לומר דפריך כו' :

ג"א לאע"ג דמסכי ארבעה דפרכינן איכא סי' צ"ק

לקמן ז: ע"ש פסחים סא. ע"ש

[לעיל ג: וש"נ]

מגילה ח.

הגהות הב"ח

(א) גמרא כלל שאינו מלא נ"ב לישנא דקרא בכסף מלא : (ב) שם א"ל רב אחא מדיפתי נ"ב ע"ל דף ח ע"ב : (ג) שם בכללי ופרטי [illegible] (ד) שם [illegible] (ה) שם [illegible]

לקמן ח: [ב"ק סד. שבועות ה. כריתות כב.]

גליון הש"ס

גמ' שתהא עשייתו לשם שלמים · עי' מנחות דף מז ע"א תוס' ד"ה מחשבה [illegible]

[מיר נח: ב"ק ג. ערכין ה:]

צ"ל שלמיו מאי שלמים [illegible]

ויקרא ז

דברים כג [לעיל ג. מנחות ב.]

[צ"ל ליפסלו ו-ע"ס"ס]

a in the case of an individual.[1] [4b] Now although two [of these refutations] are not exact,[2] two at all events are! (For how is change in respect of owner different, that it is not an intrinsic disqualification? [Surely] because it is a mere intention![3] Then change in respect of sanctity too is a mere intention! But what you must say is that since he intended it [for a wrongful purpose], he disqualified it; then here too,[4] since he intended it [for a different owner], he disqualified it.[5] Furthermore, according to R. Phinehas the son of R. Mari who maintained: Change in respect of owner does operate after death,[6] on two points at least you can refute it.) —Rather, said R. Ashi, Scripture says, *And it shall be accepted for him to make atonement for him,*[7] [implying,] but not for his fellow.[8] But does it come for this purpose? Surely it is required for what was taught: *And it shall be accepted for him to make atonement for him:* R. Simeon said: Where [the sacrifice] is [a liability] upon him, he is responsible for its loss; where it is not [a liability] upon him, he is not responsible for its loss.[9] And R. Isaac b. Abdimi said: What is the reason? Since he declared, '[I take] upon myself [to bring an offering],' it is as though he carried it on his shoulder![10]—R. Ashi makes his deduction from *'and it shall be accepted for him to make*
b *atonement'*.[1]

We have now learned [it of] slaughtering and sprinkling: how do we know [it of] the receiving [of the blood]? And if you say, let us learn it from slaughtering and sprinkling, [it can be objected]: as for slaughtering and sprinkling, the reason is because [each is] a service which involves culpability [if performed] without [the Temple court]![2]—Rather said R. Ashi: It is deduced from the nazirite's ram. For it is written, *And he shall offer the ram for a slaughtering of peace-offerings,*[3] [which teaches] that it must be offered specifically as a peace-offering. Now since this teaching is superfluous regarding change in respect of sanctity, as that is deduced from the other text, apply its teaching to change in respect of owner. R. Aḥa b. Abba said to Raba: Let us say, *'he shall offer'* is a general proposition:[4] *'slaughtering'* is a particularization: now [where we have] a general proposition followed by a particularization, [the rule is] the general proposition includes only what is contained in the particularization; hence slaughtering is so,[5] but every other service is not so?—If [Scripture] wrote, 'He shall offer a peace-offering as a slaughtering,' it would be as you say. Since however it writes, *'he shall offer for a slaughtering of peace-offerings,'* it is an incomplete general proposition,[6] and an incomplete general proposition is not treated as a case of a general proposition followed by a particularization. Rabina said: In truth we do treat it as such, but *'unto the Lord'*[7] is another general proposition.[8] R. Aḥa of Difti said to Rabina: But the first generalization is dissimilar from the last generalization, for the first includes [sacrificial] *acts* but nothing more, whereas the last one implies everything that is *'unto the Lord'*, even the pouring
c out of the residue [of the blood] and the burning of the *emurim*?[1]—

a (1) A public sacrifice, just like a private sacrifice, is disqualified if offered for another purpose. (2) As it proceeds to explain. (3) Nothing wrong is actually done to the sacrifice. (4) Viz., in respect of wrongful ownership. (5) Thus both can be regarded as intrisic or non-intrinsic disqualifications. (6) As a disqualification. The bracketed passage explains the two points in which they are not really different. (7) Lev. I, 4. (8) This proves that the 'sprinkling' which effects the atonement must be performed in the name of its owner. (9) If a man declares, 'I vow an animal for a sacrifice,' he thereby undertakes a liability. If he subsequently sets aside an animal and it dies or is lost before it is sacrificed, he must replace it. But if he declared, 'I vow *this* animal for a sacrifice,' he accepted no liability beyond that animal, and if it dies his obligation ceases. R. Simeon deduces it from the verse quoted, which he renders and interprets thus: *And it shall be accepted for him:* When is it accepted for him? When its effect is to *make atonement* in which case he does not bring another. Hence if it did not make atonement, he must bring another. And when must he bring another in order to make atonement (i.e. to be quit of his obligation)? When he declared it a liability *'upon him'* (E.V. *for him*). Sh. M. (10) As though he had it in his care all the time, and until it is actually sacrificed his vow is not fulfilled. Thus the verse is required for a different purpose.

b (1) Which implies: it must be *'for him to make atonement,'* but not for another to make atonement. Whereas R. Simeon's deduction is from *'upon him'** as stated in end of n. 9, p. 14. (2) But there is no culpability if the other two services (receiving and carrying of the blood) are done outside their legitimate boundaries. (3) Num. VI, 17. (4) *'He shall offer* (lit. 'do')' is a term embracing all services, while 'slaughtering' is a particular one. (5) I.e., the deduction made regarding change in respect of owner applies to slaughtering. (6) *'He shall offer'* obviously requires the completion of *'peace-offerings'* before we know to what it refers at all; 'slaughtering' however interposes, and therefore it is only an incomplete generalization. (7) The continuation of this verse. (8) For it implies any service performed *'unto the Lord.'* Thus we have a general proposition followed by a particularization and followed again by a general proposition. The exegetical rule then is that the general proposition includes all things similar to the particularization, and thus the other services are included.

c (1) Whereas only the four services under discussion are sacrificial acts.

◁ *For the continuation of the English translation of this page see overleaf.*

*See Corrigenda.

ואע"ג דתרתי לאו דוקא תרתי מיהא דוקא מאי שנא שינוי בעלים דלא הוי פסולו בגופו מחשבה בעלמא שינוי קודש נמי מחשבה בעלמא הוא אלא כיון דאחשבה פסלה ה"נ כיון דאחשבה פסלה ולרב פנחס בריה דרב מרי *דאמר יש שינוי בעלים לאחר מיתה תרתי מיהא איכא למיפרך אלא אמר רב א] אשי אמר קרא °ונרצה לו לכפר עליו (ויקרא א) *ולא על חבירו והאי להכי הוא דאתא האי מיבעי ליה לכדתניא *ונרצה לו לכפר עליו ב]רבי שמעון אומר את שעליו חייב באחריותו ואת שאינו עליו אינו חייב באחריותו ג] ואמר רב יצחק בר אבדימי מאי טעמא כיון דאמר עלי כמאן דטעון ליה אכתפיה דמי רב אשי מונרצה לו לכפר קאמר: אשכחן זביחה וזריקה קבלה והולכה מנלן וכי תימא לילף מזביחה וזריקה מה לזביחה וזריקה שכן עבודה שחייבין עליה בחוץ אלא אמר ד] רב אשי אתיא מאיל נזיר דכתיב °ואת האיל יעשה (במדבר ו) זבח שלמים *שתהא עשייתו לשם שלמים ואם אינו ענין לשינוי קודש דנפקא ליה מהתם תנהו ענין לשינוי בעלים אמר ליה רב אחא בר אבא לרבא אימא יעשה כלל זבח פרט כלל ופרט אין בכלל אלא מה שבפרט זביחה אין מידי אחרינא לא אי כתיב יעשה שלמים זבח כדקאמרת השתא דכתיב יעשה זבח שלמים הוה ליה כלל שאינו (א) מלא וכל כלל שאינו מלא אין דנין אותו בכלל ופרט רבינא אמר לעולם דנין ולה' חזר וכלל אמר ליה רב אחא (ב) מדיפתי לרבינא והא לא דמי כללא קמא לכללא בתרא כללא קמא מרבה עשיות ותו לא כללא בתרא כל לה' ואפילו שפיכת שיריים והקטרת אימורין *הא תנא דבי רבי ישמעאל ה] בכללי ופרטי (ג) דריש כי האי גוונא כלל ופרט וכלל אי אתה דן אלא כעין הפרט מה הפרט מפורש עבודה ובעינן לשמן אף כל עבודה ובעינן לשמן אי מה הפרט מפורש עבודה וחייבין עליה בחוץ אף כל עבודה וחייבין עליה בחוץ שחיטה וזריקה אין קבלה והולכה לא אי נמי מה הפרט מפורש דבר הטעון צפון וישנו בחטאות (ד) הפנימיות אף כל הטעון צפון וישנו בחטאות הפנימיות שחיטה וקבלה אין זריקה לא איכא למימר הכי ואיכא למימר הכי *שקולין הן ויבאו שניהן לישנא אחרינא ו] וחדא חדא תיקו במילתא איבעית אימא זריקה ז] מדרב אשי נפקא אשכחן איל נזיר שאר שלמים מנלן וכי תימא נילף מאיל נזיר מה לאיל נזיר שכן יש ח] עמהן דמים אחרים א"כ נכתוב ט] *שלמי מאי שלמים לרבות כל שלמים אשכחן שלמים שאר כל קדשים מנלן וכי תימא נילף משלמים מה לשלמים שכן טעונין סמיכה ונסכים ותנופת חזה ושוק אלא אמר קרא °זאת התורה לעולה ולמנחה ולחטאת (ויקרא ז) ולאשם ולמילואים ולזבח השלמים היקישן הכתוב לשלמים מה שלמים בין שינוי קודש בין שינוי בעלים בעינן לשמה אף כל בין שינוי קודש בין שינוי בעלים בעינן לשמה י] אימא היכא דשחיט להו שלא לשמה ליפסלו אמר קרא °מוצא שפתיך תשמור ועשית כאשר נדרת וגו' (דברים כג) *האי נדבה נדר הוא יא] (רש"ק) [אלא] אם כמה שנדרת עשית יהא נדר ואם לאו יהא נדבה ואיצטריך מוצא שפתיך ואיצטריך זאת התורה דאי כתב רחמנא מוצא (ה) יב] (הוה אמינא) לא

[לעיל ב. מנחות ב.]
נ"ל שלמיו מאי שלמים ס' רש"ק [וכ"ה בילקוט] פ' ויקרא

רש"י

יג] ואע"ג דתרתי לאו דוקא תרתי דוקא · *אע"ג דמותבינן ארבעה יד] פרכי איכא תרתי שאין עיקר כדמפרש ואזיל: תרתי מיהא דוקא · והשתא מפרש אמאי תרתי לאו דוקא: ולרב פנחס כו' · ולקמן בשילהי שמעתין אזלא לה הך פירכא דלאחר מיתה: לכפר עליו · היינו זריקה אלמא זריקה לשם בעלים בעיא: את שעליו · כגון נדר דאמר הרי עלי עולה חייב באחריותו אם הפריש בהמה לנדרו אם מתה או נגנבה דהכי משמע אותו שעליו יקריב אותו ונרצה לו ועד שיקריבנו לא נרצה ולא נפטר: את שאינו עליו · כגון דאמר הרי זו עולה: מונרצה לו טו] לכפר קאמר · דהכי משמע לו לכפר ולא טז] לחבירו: שכן עבודה שחייבין עליה בחוץ · יז] דכתיב (ויקרא יז) אשר ישחט מחוץ למחנה וזורק נמי מרבינן ליה לקמן בפ' השוחט (דף קז·) דם שפך לרבות הזורק תאמר בקבלה והולכה שאין חייבין עליה בחוץ דתנן בפ' בתרא (שם קיב:) והיוצק והבולל כו' והמקבל דמים בחוץ פטור: יעשה כלל · שיהו כל עשיותיו לשם שלמים: זבח פרט · שחיטה הוא דבעי לשמה: אי כתיב יעשה שלמים זבח כדקאמרת · דמשמע כללא שיהו עשייתו יח] שלמים: השתא דכתיב יעשה זבח שלמים · לא גמר הכלל את דבריו ולא נשלם להשמיעו על מה הוזכרו כאן העשיות יט] עד שבא זבח והפסיק את הדבר: כלל שאינו מלא · כ] ולא נתמלא דבריו להשלים · מלא פרדאשבי"ן בלע"ז: לה' · יעשה זבח שלמים לה': כא] עשייתו · עבודות המיוחדות שחיטה וזריקה קבלה והולכה: שפיכת שירים · שנשפכין שירי הדם ליסוד כב] [אחר] שנתן ארבע מתנות ואין מעכבין כפרה: הא תנא דבי רבי ישמעאל כו' · בשילהי אלו טריפות (חולין דף סו·) גבי פרשת חגבים: איכא למימר הכי · עבודה וחייבין עליה בחוץ ואתיא לה זריקה: ואיכא למימר הכי · עבודה שטעונה צפון ואתיא לה קבלה: שקולין הן · המדות שוות והי מינייהו מפקת אי דרשת הא תנא דריסנא לאידך הלכך יבאו שניהם והולכה על כרחך לא תפקה מכלל קבלה: מדרב אשי · מונרצה לו לכפר וכלל ופרט לאיתויי קבלה דאי לזריקה לא איצטריך: שכן יש עמו דמים אחרים · שבאין עמו חטאת ועולה: אשכחן שלמים · בין בשינוי קודש בין בשינוי בעלים: שכן טעונין כו' · ושאר זבחים יש מהן שאין טעונים סמיכה ולא נסכים כגון בכור ומעשר ופסח ויש מהן שאין טעונין נסכים כגון חטאת ואשם כג] ובכולן אין אחד שיהא טעון חזה ושוק: ליפסלו · שהרי לא נעשו כהלכתן ואין זריקתן מתרת בשרן לאכילה: ואיצטריך · למיכתב זאת התורה למיגמר משלמים ולא תימא ממוצא שפתיך נפקא דלכתחילה בעינן לשמה: לא

תוספות

מחשבה בעלמא · ואפי' יהא צריך דיבור כיון דליכא מעשה הוי כמחשבה בעלמא ויש תימה דהכא משוי להו וכפ' תמיד נשחט (פסחים סב:) משמע שיש חילוק דמפרש מה בין כד] לשמן לשלא לשמן לאוכליו ושלא לאוכליו זה פסולו בגופו וזה אין פסולו בגופו וי"ל דכיון דלא מיפסיל אלא מפני שאין יכול לאכול כזית כגון לשם חולה וזקן [א] חשיב טפי פסולו בקודש מחמת דבר אחר כיון דאם היה יכול לאכול היה כשר וקשה דעל כרחין שלא למנוין ולערלים ולטמאין צריך לומר דלא חשיבי פסולן בגופו כי היכי דלא תיקשי לן נמי מה בין לשמן ושלא לשמן למנוין ושלא למנוין למולין ולערלים לטמאין ולטהורים וי"ל דשינוי בעלים חשבינן פסולו בגופו משום דתלוי [ב] בזריקה כה] (בכפרה) ושם בעלים [על הכפרה] אבל שלא לאוכלין ושלא למנויין תלוי בשחיטה ואין שם בעלים על השחיטה אי נמי שלא לאוכלין כו] [ושלא למנויין] יכול לקיים מחשבתו בהיתר [באותן] שיהיו מנויין עליו כז] אם איכא חולים וזקנים אבל שלא לשמה אינו יכול לקיימו לכך קרוי פסולו בגופו:

הגה"ה ה"ג במגילה (דף ח·) מאי [משמע] אמר רב יצחק בר אבדימי: רב אשי כח] (אמר) מונרצה לו קאמר · תימה למה לי קרא לשינוי בעלים בזריקה הא אפי' שאר עבודות לא מיפסלי אלא בשוחט על מנת לזרוק כ"ש זורק כט] *עצמו [דבעינן] שם בעלים:

(הג"ה נמצא בתוס' ישנים בכת"י)

שכן עבודה וחייבים ל] · פירוש עבודה שחייבין עליה בחוץ:

שקולים הם ויבאו שניהם · אע"ג דהכא תרתי והכא חדא חשיב להו שקולין והקשה הרב רבי חיים דהשתא משמע דהיכא דלא ידע הי מינייהו לרבויי מרבי תרוייהו וכן בריש ב"ק (דף ג·) דמרבי מושלח שן ורגל משום דשקולין הן וכן בפ"ק דערכין (דף ד:) גבי נפשות ואילו בפרק כל האסורים (תמורה דף כח:) ופרק שור שנגח ארבעה וה' (ב"ק דף מ:) דרשינן מן הבהמה להוציא את הרובע ומן הצאן להוציא את הנוגח וקאמר מפני שיש ברובע מה שאין בנוגח ויש בנוגח מה שאין ברובע הוצרך לומר רובע והוצרך לומר נוגח ותירץ דהיכא דאיכא משמעות בריבוי מרבינן כל השקולים כי הכא דזבח משמע לרבויי כעין זביחה כל שהיא עבודה וכן ושלח יש במשמע רגל ושן ונפשות נמי משמע הכל אבל מן לא משמע למעוטי שניהם *):

אימא היכא דשחיט שלא לשמן ליפסלו · תימה הא בכל דוכתא בעינן בקדשים לא] [שינה] לעכב והכא לא שינה וי"ל דפריך משינוי קודש דאיכא תרי קראי ואמרי' לעיל אם אינו ענין לשינוי קודש תנהו ענין לשינוי בעלים ופריך לב] דהשתא אימר תרוייהו בשינוי קודש ולעכב וקשה מאי משני אמר קרא מוצא שפתיך דלמא ההוא קרא אתא לשינוי בעלים דלא אשכחן ששינה בהן הכתוב ולא קשה מידי דמוצא שפתיך לא משמע שינוי בעלים · [הג"ה] [ג]ונראה דפריך מכח סברא כעין קושיא דר"ל לג] דלקמיה דאימא דליפסלו כיון דאמרת דלא עלו לשם חובה או נימא דיעלו דאם כשרין קן ירצו ואם אין מרצין למה באין לד] [ומיהו] לא דמי דריש לקיש פריך יהו כשרין גמורין כמו שאר קדשים דלא שנה לעכב לה] *בו ליפסלו והכא לא הוה ליה למיפרך שלא לשמה ליפסלו אלא הוה ליה למימר וליתכשרו ויעלו לחובה כשאר קדשים

*) [ועי' היטב תוס' ב"ק מ: ד"ה ויש]

שיטה מקובצת

א] רב אשי תיבת אשי נמחק: ב] רבי שמעון אומר את שעליו חייב כו' · ודייק ממשמעות דקרא ונרצה לו לכפר עליו איכתי נרצה לו כשהוא לכפר ואז לא יביא אחר הא אם לא כיפר יביא אחר ואימתי אני אומר שיביא אחר לכפר כשאמר עליו שאז עליו אחריות · תוס' חוץ ותוס' ר"פ: ג] באחריותו מאי משמע אמר רב יצחק: ד] אמר רבא ותיבות רב אשי נמחק: ה] ישמעאל הוא דדריש כללי ופרטי כי האי גוונא: ו] אחרינא שקול הוא וכל חדא וחדא תיקו אמילתיה אב"א: ז] מדרב אשי נפקי · כלומר והולכה לא תפקיה (מהולכה) [מכלל קבלה] וזריקה אתיא מדרב אשי ונרצה לו לכפר וא"ת למה לי קרא למיפסל שינוי בעלים בזריקה (או)[הא] מקבל ע"מ לזרוק שלא לשםבעלים[פסול]כדפ"ח לעיל א"כ כ"ש זורק עצמו וי"ל [דהו"א] דגזירת הכתוב הוא ובעינן זורק ע"מ להקטיר או ע"מ לשפוך שירים דלעולם בעינן ב' עבודות בענין [שלא לשם בעלים דהא חזינן] דשחיטה וקבלה דלא מהניא כי אם [במחשב מעבודה לעבודה] הוא א)רכותיה אשכחן גבי פיגול דאינו [מפגל כי אם] במחשב מעבודה לעבודה · תוס' חוץ: ח] יש עמו דמים: ט] נכתוב שלמיו מאי: י] אימא היכא דשחיט להו שלא לשמה ליפסלו · פי' בתוס' אע"ג דלא שינה הכתוב לעכב מ"מ ליפסלו מסברא כיון דשינה בלשמן כאילו חסר העבודה ששינה בה [וא"ת הא] מדשינה הכתוב לעכב בחטאת ש"מ היכא שלא שינה הכתוב דאינו פסול ותירצו בתוס' דאדרבה הייתי אומר אם [שינה בכל] הקרבנות לפיסולא מהיקשא דחטאת דאתקש כולהו לחטאת בהיקשא דזאת התורה וכ"ת א"כ הייתי מקשה פסח למה לי דשינה [לפסול] תיפוק ליה מהיקשא דחטאת י"ל כיון דפסח לא הוי בהדיא כתוב בהתוא ענינא (דמשום ביום) [דמביום] צוותו נפקא כדאמרינן לקמן (דף ז ע"ב) הייתי אומר [דלאו להכי אתא] דה"נ הוה ס"ד תלמודא לקמן וי"מ דמכח מה ראית פריך כלומר בפסח וחטאת נמי לא שינה בהם הכתוב וליכא אלא חד קרא [דבעינן לשמה והא] דמוכח עיכובא היינו משום דילפינן פסח וחטאת לשמה למצוה מהיקשא דשלמים א"כ קרא דלשמה דכתיב גבי פסח [וחטאת לעכב] אתא כיון דלמצוה [ילפי' מהיקשא]דשלמים ופריך הכא הכי [מנא לי] למיקם קרא [דגבי] פסח וחטאת לעיכובא [והא דכתיב]הכא גבי [שלמים למצוה] איפוך אנא [דהא] דכתיב גבי [פסח וחטאת למצוה] וקרא [דכתיב] גבי שלמים לעיכובא [אכן] אינו נראה [דמשמע] דפריך (מהיכא) [הכא] דשלא לשמה בכל [הקרבנות] לפסול לכן נראה כרפי' וא"ת לפי מה דפי' שסברא הוא [אף] בלא שינה הכתוב דחסר בעבודה א"כ למה שינה הכתוב בפסח וחטאת תיפוק ליה מהאי סברא דפרישנא וי"ל דהיינו לפי מה דמכשירין בכל הקרבנות ממוצא כו' לכך אצטריך שינה לעכב דלא תילף הכשרה בפסח וחטאת [מהיקשא] דשלמים · תוס' הר"פ: יא] הוא אלא: יב] מוצא שפתיך הוה אמינא: יג] ה"ג ואע"ג דתרתי לאו דוקא תרתי מיהו דוקא אע"ג דמהני ארבעה תיבת דמותבינן נמחק: יד] פירכא איכא: טו] תיבת לכפר נמחק: טז] לכפר ולא על חבירו הס"ד: יז] בחוץ כלומר שכן עבודה חשובה להתחייב עליה בחוץ דכתיב: יח] עשייתו לשם שלמים: יט] תיבת עד נמחק: כ] מלא לא אות ו' נמחק: כא] מה"ד עשיות' עבודות המיוחדים שחיטה: כב] ליסוד אחר: כג] ואשם ואין בכולן שיהא אות ו' ותיבות אין אחד נמחק: כד] בין לשמו לשלא לשמו לאוכליו: כה] תיבות בכפרה ושם בעלים נמחק: כו] תיבות ושלא למנויין ל"ש: כז] עליו מי שאינן תיבות אם אינם נמחק: כח] תיבת אמר נמחק: כט] עצמו שלא לשם בעלים(תיבת דבעינן נמחק)וגזירת הכתוב הוא דבעינן זורק ע"מ להקטיר או ע"מ לשפוך [שירים דלעולם] בעינן ב' עבודות בענין זה [כמו] בשחיטה וקבלה דלא מהניא בהם (ע"מ) [כ"א] בע"מ דרכותיה אשכחן בפיגול (דאי לא) [דלא] מפגל [כי אם] במחשב מעבודה לעבודה · תוס' הר"פ: ל] וחייבין עליה פירוש בחוץ: לא] בקדשים שינה: לב] ופריך השתא אימא דתרוייהו בשינוי קודש ומיהו קשה דמאי משני: לג] דר"ל דלקמן: לד] באין ולא נראה דריש לקיש תיבת מיהו ל"ש ותיבות לא דמי נמחק: לה] לעכב או ליפסלו דהכא · תיבת בו נמחק:

א) אולי צ"ל וסו"א הזריקה נמי דכוותיה סוף ודכוותיה אשכחן וכו':

הגהות צ"ק [א] חשיב טפי פסולו מחמת דבר אחר כו': [ב] בזריקה ועיקר כפרה בזריקה ושם בעלים על הזריקה כו' כנ"ל: [ג] ואין נראה לומר דפריך כו':

מסורת הש"ס

נ"א אע"ג דמסבי ארבעה דפרכינן איכא ס' נ"ק
לקמן ז: ע"ש פסחים סא. ע"ש
[לעיל ג: וש"נ]
מגילה ח.
לקמן ה: [ב"ק סד. שבועות סו. כריתות כב.]
[מיר נח: ב"ק ג. ערכין ד.]

הגהות הב"ח

גליון הש"ס

[ג"ל לא ליפסלו וכ"ה בכת"י]

אם

Continuation of translation from previous page as indicated by ◁

Behold the Tanna of the School of R. Ishmael[2] [even] in the case of a general proposition and particularization of this nature applies the rule that in a general proposition followed by a particularization and followed again by a general proposition you must be guided by the particularization: just as that is explicitly a [sacrificial] service,[3] and we require rightful intention, so in the case of every [sacrificial] service we require rightful intention. If so, [you may argue:] just as the particularization is explicitly a service which involves culpability [if it is performed] without [its legitimate boundaries], so is every service [included] which involves culpability [if performed] without; hence slaughtering and sprinkling are indeed included, but not receiving and carrying? Or [you may argue]: as the particularization is explicitly something that must be done at the north [side of the altar] and is operative in the case of the inner sin-offerings, so all [services] which must be done at the north and are operative in the case of the inner sin-offerings [are included]; hence slaughtering and receiving are indeed included, but not sprinkling?—You can argue in this way or in that way; they are equally balanced, and so both [arguments] are admissible.[4] (Another version: Each argument stands.) Alternatively, I can say, sprinkling follows from R. Ashi's deduction.[5]

We have thus found [it true of] the nazirite's ram; how do we know [it of] the other peace-offerings? And if you say, Let us learn them from the nazirite's ram, [it can be argued:] As for the d nazirite's ram, the reason is because other sacrifices[1] accompany it.[2]—If so,[3] Scripture should write, [*And he shall offer the ram for* . . .] *his peace-offerings*;[4] why state, [for] *peace-offerings*?—In order to include all peace-offerings.

We have thus found [it true of] peace-offerings; how do we know [it of] other sacrifices? And if you say, Let us learn them from peace-offerings, [it can be argued:] As for peace-offerings, the reason is because they require laying [of hands], libations, and the waving of the breast and shoulder![5] Rather, Scripture says, *This is the law of the burnt-offering, of the meal-offering, and of the sin-offering, and of the guilt-offering, and of the consecration-offering, and of the sacrifice of peace-offerings*;[6] thus Scripture assimilates them to peace-offerings. Just as we require peace-offerings [to be offered] for their own sake, [thus forbidding] both change in respect of sanctity and change in respect of owner, so do we require all [sacrifices to be offered] for their own sake, [thus forbidding] both change in respect of sanctity and change in respect of owner.

Let us say that if one slaughtered them in a different name they are invalid?—Scripture says, *That which is gone out of thy lips thou shalt observe and do; as thou has vowed a nedabah* [freewill-offering] etc.:[7] is this a freewill-offering—surely it is a vow? The meaning however is this: if you acted in accordance with your vow, let it be [the fulfilment of your] vow; but if not, let it count as a freewill-offering.[8]

Now [both texts viz.,] '*that which is gone out of thy lips*' and '*this is the law*' etc., are required.[9] For if the Divine Law wrote, '*that which*

(2) Who formulated thirteen rules of exegesis, including this one. (3) *Sc.* slaughtering. (4) Since one approach includes slaughtering and sprinkling, and the other includes slaughtering and receiving, you must admit both, since neither is stronger than the other. Carrying too is then included, for it is really a part of the act of receiving. (5) *Supra*, from the verse '*and it shall be accepted for him*' etc.; hence the present deduction must be in respect of receiving.

d (1) Lit., 'blood'. (2) And it is natural that one cannot be sacrificed in the name of one person and a second in the name of another, when all are for the same person. The other sacrifices are the sin-offering and the burnt-offering. (3) If the deduction of the verse were intended to be confined to this particular sacrifice. (4) V. marginal gloss. (5) But no other sacrifices require all these, and consequently they may be offered under another designation either in respect of sanctity or of ownership. (6) Lev. VII, 37. (7) Deut. XXIII, 24. (8) V. *supra*. Since it counts as a freewill-offering, it is obviously valid. (9) One might argue that the text, '*that which* .... *lips*' etc. itself proves that a sacrifice must in the first place at least be offered for its own sake. Hence the Talmud proceeds to shew that that is not so.

is gone out of thy lips' [only], I would say, [5a] I do not know to what
a this refers,[1] therefore the Divine Law wrote *'this is the law'* etc. While if the Divine Law wrote *'this is the law'* [only], I would say that they become invalid;[2] therefore the Divine Law wrote, *'that which is gone out of thy lips'* etc.

Resh Lakish lay face downward[3] in the Beth Hammidrash, and raised a difficulty: If they are valid, let them be accepted;[4] while if they are not accepted,[5] for what purpose do they come?[6]—Said R. Eleazar to him: We find that those [sacrifices] which come after the death [of their owners] are valid, yet they are not accepted.[7] For we learnt: If a woman brought her sin-offering [after child-birth] and then died, her heirs must bring her burnt-offering; [if she brought] her burnt-offering, her heirs do not bring her sin-offering.[8] I agree in the case of a burnt-offering,[9] he replied, since it comes after death;[10] but in the case of a guilt-offering which does not come after death,[11] whence do we know [that it is valid]?[12]—He replied, Lo, [support to] your contention is [available] close at hand: R. ELIEZER SAYS, ALSO THE GUILT-OFFERING [IS INVALID].[13] Thereupon he exclaimed: Is this he who is spoken of as a great man? I speak to you of an explicit Mishnah, and you answer me with R. Eliezer's view![14] Rather, said Resh Lakish: I will find a solution myself: *'That which is gone out of thy lips* etc:' is this a freewill-
b offering—surely it is a vow,[1] etc. as above.[2]

R. Zera and R. Isaac b. Abba were sitting, and Abaye sat with them. They sat and debated: Resh Lakish had a difficulty about the guilt-offering, which does not come after death, and he adduced an exegesis on *'that which goeth out of thy lips'*. Yet say, That which may come as a vow or as a freewill-offering must be brought[3] but do not propitiate,[4] but a guilt-offering is not to be brought at all?[5] Said Abaye to them: Resh Lakish solved [the difficulty] from the following text: *And he shall kill it for a sin-offering:*[6] only *it* [when slaughtered] in its own name is valid and [when slaughtered] not in its own name is invalid;[7] but other sacrifices [slaughtered] not in their own name are valid. You might think then that they are 'accepted'. Therefore it states, *'that which goeth out of thy lips'*.[8] Then say, That which comes as a vow or a freewill-offering must be brought but is not 'accepted', whereas a guilt-offering is even 'accepted' too?[9]—Said Abaye: You cannot maintain that a guilt-offering is [in such circumstances] accepted, [as the reverse follows] from a burnt-offering, *a fortiori*: if a burnt-offering, whose purpose is not to make atonement, is not 'accepted,[10] then how much more is a guilt-offering, whose purpose is to make atonement, not 'accepted'. As for a burnt-offering [you might argue], the reason [that it is not 'accepted'] is because it is altogether burnt! Then let peace-offerings prove it.[11] As for peace-offerings, [you might argue] [they are not 'accepted'] because they require libations and the waving of the breast and shoulder. Then let a burnt-offering prove
c it.[1] And thus the argument revolves: the characteristic of the former is not that of the latter and the characteristic of the latter is not that of the former. The factor common to both is that they are holy [sacrifices], and if slaughtered not in their own names they are valid, yet not 'accepted', so also do I adduce the guilt-offering which is holy, hence if one slaughters it not in its name it is valid and not accepted. [No:] The factor common to both [it may be argued] is that they are [also] brought as public offerings![2]—Then

a (1) I would not know that Scripture refers at all to the offering of a sacrifice for a purpose other than its own. (2) If not offered for their own sake. (3) Lit. 'on his stomach.' He was very stout, v. Giṭ. 47a. (4) I.e., let their owners be regarded as having fulfilled their obligations. (5) If they do not acquit their owners. (6) Why are they valid? At this stage he did not know that their validity is deduced from Scripture. (7) I.e., they do not propitiate. (8) Because in the latter case, it is a sin-offering whose owner died (the passage treats of the case where she dedicated both animals before her death) before it was offered, and it is a traditional law that such is not sacrificed but left to die.—Yet the burnt-offering is offered, though no propitiation is required on behalf of a dead woman. The present case is similar. (9) That even if it is killed for a different purpose, it must still be offered (i.e., the remaining rites must be carried out). (10) The same therefore applies to peace-offerings and other sacrifices which come after death. (11) A guilt-offering is not brought after the death of the owner, but is left to pasture. (12) Since the Tanna of the Mishnah mentions as exceptions only the paschal-offering and sin-offering. (13) *Sc.* it is invalid—presumably because it does not come after death. (14) My difficulty concerns the law stated *anonymously* in the Mishnah, which presumably is authoritative, and it is not enough to answer me that according to *R. Eliezer* there is no difficulty.

b (1) Resh Lakish had not known of this when he raised the difficulty, and arrived at this exegesis independently. (2) V. *supra* 2b. (3) I.e. if slaughtered not in its own name, the other sacrificial rites in connection with it must be performed. (4) I.e., the vow is not thereby fulfilled, since it was not brought in its proper name. (5) The sacrifice in such circumstances being considered invalid. (6) Lev. IV, 33. (7) Altogether, and therefore we cannot proceed with the remaining rites. (8) Teaching that it does not propitiate as the offering for which it was originally intended. (9) So that another sacrifice is not required. (10) If slaughtered not under its own name. (11) Which are not altogether burnt, yet are not 'accepted'.

c (1) Which does not require these. (2) The daily burnt-offering and the lambs of peace-offerings offered on Pentecost were public offerings. But no guilt-offering was ever a public offering.

גמרא

לא ידע במאי כתב רחמנא זאת התורה ואי כתב רחמנא זאת התורה הוה אמינא ליפסלו כתב רחמנא מוצא שפתיך רמי ריש לקיש על מעוהי בי מדרשא ומקשי א] אם כשרים הם ירצו ואם אין מרצין למה באין אמר לו ר' *אליעזר מצינו בבאין לאחר מיתה שהן כשרין ואין מרצין דתנן **האשה שהביאה חטאתה ומתה יביאו יורשין עולתה עולתה ומתה לא יביאו יורשין חטאתה א"ל מודינא לך בעולה דאתיא לאחר מיתה אשם דלא אתי לאחר מיתה מנלן א"ל הרי מחלוקתך בצידו רבי אליעזר אומר אף האשם אמר זהו שאומרין עליו אדם גדול הוא קאמינא אנא משנה שלימה ואת אמרת לי ר' אליעזר אלא אמר ריש לקיש אפתח אנא פתחא לנפשאי °מוצא שפתיך וגו' האי נדבה נדר הוא כו' כדלעיל יתיב רבי זירא ורבי יצחק בר אבא ויתיב אביי גבייהו ויתבי וקאמרי קשיא ליה לריש לקיש אשם דלא אתי לאחר מיתה ונסיב לה תלמודא מוצא שפתיך ג] אימא הבא בנדר ובנדבה לייתי ולא לירצי אשם לא לייתי כלל אמר להו אביי ריש לקיש מהכא פתח °ושחט אותה לחטאת אותה לשמה כשרה שלא לשמה פסולה הא שאר קדשים שלא לשמן כשירין ג] יכול ירצו ת"ל מוצא שפתיך ואימא הבא בנדר ונדבה לייתי ולא לירצי אשם ד] (נמי) ארצויי נמי לירצי אמר אביי אשם דמירצי לא מצית אמרת קל וחומר מעולה ומה עולה שאינה מכפרת אינה מרצה אשם שמכפר אינו דין שאינו מרצה מה לעולה שכן כליל שלמים יוכיחו מה לשלמים שכן טעונין ה] נסכין ותנופת חזה ושוק °עולה תוכיח *וחזר הדין לא ראי זה כראי זה ולא ראי זה כראי זה הצד השוה שבהן שהן קדשים ושחטן שלא לשמן כשירין ואין מרצין אף אני אביא אשם שהוא קודש ושחטו שלא לשמו כשר ואינו מרצה מה להצד השוה שבהן שכן ישנו בציבור תודה תוכיח

מה

רש"י

לא ידעינן במאי · קאמר רחמנא מוצא שפתיך תשמור והא לא כתיב בהדי' בהאי קרא עבודות לשמן ודלמא לאו בלשמן משתעי קרא כתב רחמנא זאת התורה למילף משלמים דמפרשה בהו לשמן : ו] הכי גרסי' רמי ריש לקיש על מעוהי · שוכב על בטנו פניו ז] (*על) כלפי קרקע : למה הן באין · ואכתי לא ח] קמא ליה טעמא דמתני' דילפינן ממוצא שפתיך : ואין מרצין · שאין כפרה למתים ואף אתה אל תתמה על אלו : האשה · יולדת : ט] לא יביאו יורשין חטאתה · דהויא לה חטאת שמתו בעליה והלכתא גמירי לה דלמיתה אזלה י] : מודינא לך בעולה · שאם שחטה שלא יא] לשמן שתתקרב אע"פ שאינה מרצה הואיל ומצינו שבאה לאחר מיתה ואינה מרצה וה"ה לשלמים ושאר קרבנות חוץ מחטאת (א) *ואשם מיהו דלא אתי לאחר מיתה דקי"ל (תמורה דף יח.) דכל שבחטאת מתה באשם רועה מנא לן דקרב שלא לשמן הואיל ואינו מרצה דלא אפיק תנא דמתני' אלא פסח וחטאת : מחלוקתך יב] · *וסייעתך דאיכא רבי אליעזר דקאי כוותך : משנה שלימה · סתם מתני' דלא פסל אלא חטאת (ב) : פתחא לנפשאי · מנלן (ג) דקרבי : יתיב רבי זירא וכו' · וקמתמה אפירוקיה דר"ל : וקשיא ליה לריש לקיש אשם · אמאי קרב שלא לשמו שלא לרצות הא לא אתי לאחר מיתה : ונסיב יג] תלמודא · כלומר נסיב קרא לתלמודא דמילתיה : אימא הבא בנדר ונדבה · כדמשמע קרא לייתו ולא לירצו כו' : ריש לקיש מהכא פתח · לה (ד) (מהכא) לא נפקא ליה ממוצא שפתיך דליקרב אלא דלא לירצי והקרבתו מהאי קרא יליף ושחט אותה לחטאת אותה מיעוטא הוא אותה הוא דבעינן לשמה ואי לא פסולה כדילפינן לקמן הא שאר קדשים כו' : ארצויי נמי לירצו · כיון דנפקא לן הקרבתן מאותה : אינה מרצה · כדאמר אם לאו יהא נדבה : אשם שמכפר · על לאוין האמורים בשבועת הפקדון והקדש ושפחה חרופה : שכן טעונים נסכים · ולא גרס סמיכה דאשם נמי טעון סמיכה : שלמים ישנו בצבור · כבשי עצרת :

הקים

תוספות

קדשים שלא שנה לעכב כל כמה דאכתי לא ידע קרא דמוצא שפתיך ואי פריך ליפסלו דנגמר מחטאת יד] *[ופסח] בהיקישא דזאת התורה כדפרישית בסמוך אי במה מצינו איכא למיפרך שכן כרת ואי בהקישא דזאת התורה א"כ ליכתוב חדא או טו] לחטאת גרידא או פסח גרידא ואי נאמר דבכל דוכתא דמצרכינן שנה לעכב הייט מהכא טז] [מדכתיב] מוצא שפתיך וגו' א"כ אתי שפיר הא דפריך וליפסלו כו' · ע"כ הג"ה :

הג"ה מצינו בבאין לאחר מיתה שכשרין ואין מרצין · וא"ת מי דמי הני לא עלו אבל באין לאחר מיתה עלו לגמרי לשם חובה דלמ"ד שיעבודא דאורייתא אם היה הקרבן נפסל היו היורשין זקוקין להביא אחר ואפילו למ"ד לאו דאורייתא אם הפריש שניהם לאחריות אם נפסל הראשון חייבין להקריב את השני נמצא דבאין לאחר מיתה מרצין לענין שעולין לשם חובה משא"כ בשינוי קודש וי"ל דמ"מ דמיא קצת להדדי לענין דאין מרצין ריצוי גמור דאין כפרה למת ולאו בר חיוב הבאה הוא אלא *שנתחייב מחיים ובשינוי קודש ובעלים נמי אין רצוי גמור וא"ת ומה ראיה מייתי מבאין לאחר מיתה אטו מי ילפינן מינה בכל מקום שלא שנה הכתוב דאינו אלא למצוה דנימא כשרין ולא עלו וי"ל דדוקא שנוי קודש ושנוי בעלים יז] דוקא מדמי דהוי באין לאחר מיתה שאין לו בעלים וכמו שלשם כשר ואינו מרצה כמו כן כאן ששינה אותו מבעליו והוי כאין לו בעלים יח] :

עולתה ומתה לא יביאו יורשין חטאתה · משמע *אבל אם היתה יט] יכולה להביא חטאתה אחר *עולתה עלתה לה עולתה לשם עולה וכן משמע בתורת כהנים בפרשת אשה כי תזריע שאם הביאה עולתה תחילה תביא חטאתה ממין עולתה וכן במס' קינים (ספ"ב) ותימה דבפרק תמיד נשחט (פסחים דף נט.) אמרי' זה בנין אב שכל חטאות קודמות לעולת כ] העוף אפי' חטאת העוף לעולת בהמה ואפי' דיעבד קאמר דפסול מדמשני שאני עולת מצורע דרחמנא אמר והעלה שהעלה כבר והייט דיעבד דלכתחילה חטאת קודמת כדכתיב בהדיא בקרא כא] ש"מ דבעלמא דיעבד לא ותירץ ה"ר חיים דה"ה דבעלמא כשר דיעבד והא דבעי קרא במצורע משום דכתיב ביה הוויה זאת תהיה בהוויתו יהא דמשמע עיכובא כדאמר פ"ק דמנחות (דף ה·) ונראה לי דילפי' חטאת ועולה של יולדת מחטאת ועולה של מצורע דגילה הכתוב דאם עשה עולה תחלה כשירה מוהעלה כדאיתא בפ' תמיד נשחט (פסחים נט·) ואי לא קרא דוהעלה דמכשר היה פוסל בכל מקום מטעם דיש מחוסר זמן לבו ביום שאמר הכתוב להקריב חטאת קודם לעולה אפי' בעלמא דליכא תהיה דמשמע עיכובא תדע דתניא בפ"ק דמנחות (דף ה·) הקדיש חטאתו לאשמו לא יהא אחד ממרס בדמו אלא תצא לבית השריפה וקאמר הא דמיפסיל לאו משום תהיה דהא לא קאי אשחיטה משום דלאו עבודה היא אלא מטעם דיש מחוסר זמן לבו ביום שאמר הכתוב להקדיש אשם תחילה וזה הטעם למה לא יהיה גבי חטאת ועולה בעלמא ולכך איצטריך והעלה במצורע להכשיר וגמרינן מיניה בעלמא (פסחים דף נט.) להכשיר אם הקדיש עולה לחטאת אבל לא גמרינן מיניה בחטאת ואשם כי אם קרבנות כמותם · ברוך : **לא** יביאו יורשין חטאתה · הגירסא משובשת בתורת כהנים ופירשתי במנחות בפ"ק (דף ד:) : **אשם** דלא אתא לאחר מיתה מנא לן · תימה כיון דעולה ושלמים ניחא ליה נילף אשם מינייהו בהיקישא דזאת התורה ולמה לי מוצא שפתיך וי"ל דאדרבה הוה אמינא איפכא דנילף שאר קדשים מאשם דלא אתו כלל : **אשם** לא ניתי כלל · תימה הא לא איצטריך מוצא שפתיך כלל אלא לאשם דלשאר קדשים אתו מסברא כדאמרינן דלא צריכי קרא דהא אתו לאחר מיתה וי"ל דהשתא הדר ביה מההוא טעמא דאע"ג דאמר ליה מודינא לך בעולה לא היה אומר כן אלא מתוך דוחק : **הא** שאר כל הקדשים אפילו שלא לשמן כשירין · ואם תאמר *ל"ל אותה הא מדצריכי קראי לעכב בפסח וחטאת מכלל דשאר קדשים כשרין וכי תימא נילף מינייהו מה להנך שכן כרת ובהיקישא דזאת התורה נמי לא אתו דא"כ לא ליכתוב עיכובא אלא באחד בפסח או בחטאת ואידך לייתו מהיקשא : **מה** לשלמים שכן טעונין נסכים · לא גרסינן סמיכה דאשם נמי טעון סמיכה כדאמר לקמן בפירקין (דף יא·) וה"ר חיים פירש דמשום אשם מצורע מלי למינקט סמיכה למ"ד בריש כל הפסולים (לקמן דף לג·) כב] סמיכה לאו דאורייתא : **תודה** כג] יוכיח · אע"ג דאשכחן עולה שבאה בנדבת ציבור שמקיילין בהן את המזבח (תודה) ושלמים לא אתו בנדבת ציבור דהא ממעטינן להו בתורת כהנים בפרשת ואם מן הצאן קרבנו לזבח שלמים :

חטאת

עין משפט נר מצוה

כ"א ופסח וקטס כופרין בסמוך

כט א מיי' פ"ה מהל' מחוסרי כפרה הל' יג:

מנחות ד: קדושין יב: קינין סוף פ"ב

נ"א שנתחייב הקרבן מחוייב ז"ק

אבל אם היתה חיה יכולה כו' ז"ק

עולתה ועולתה לה כו'

[קדושין ס: כה. וש"נ]

מסורת הש"ס

נ"א למטה ז"ק

נ"ל אליעזר

ס"א מיהו אשם דלא אתי כו'

ס"א מחלוקת המסייעתך

הגהות הב"ח

(א) רש"י ד"ה מודינא וכו' חוץ מחטאת ופסח מיהו אשם דלא אתי: (ב) ד"ה משנה וכו' חטאת ופסח הס"ד: (ג) ד"ה פתחא וכו' דקרב כבר ואות י' נמחק: (ד) ד"ה ר"ל מהכא פתח לה פתחא לא נפקא:

גליון הש"ס

גמ' א"ל ר"א מצינו · ע' מ"ס דף ע"ב תוס' ד"ה ור"א: שם עולה תוכיח · תמוה לי הא גם עולה לריכה נסכים ואי דעולת עוף יוכית א"כ איך פרכינן עלה מה לעולה שיש בציבור הא עולת עוף אינה בציבור ולכך נראה דס"ס שלמים ונסכים ולריך עיון :

ע' רש"י [פמ"ש בס"ד לקמן מה: על הגליון כתוס' ד"ה ואתא]

ז"ק מ"ט

שיטה מקובצת

א] אם כשרים הם ירצו כו' · עיקר הקושיא דרשב"ל בא מהא דקאמר אם אינם מרצים למה באים כדמשמע מניין וזהו כעין קושיא דלעיל שהקשה [אימא היכא] דשחיט להו שלא לשמה ליפסלו ומיהו קשה למה לא הקשה בפשיטות כמו לעיל ונראה דרשב"ל היה עושה עצמו כאילו היה [מסופק אם קרא] לעכב או למצוה והיה קשה לו ממה נפשך אי כשרים הם ונאמר דהנך קראי דלשמה למצוה בעלמא נינהו לכך הם כשרים א"כ ירצו [כיון] דלמצוה בעלמא נינהו לענין כשרות הקרבנות ה"נ נימא לענין ריצוי ואם אינם מרצים למה באים כלומר ואם נפשך [לומר] לעכב אע"ג שלא שינה בו הכתוב כדפי' לעיל ולכך אין מרצין למה באים כי היכי דקראי אתו לעכב לענין ריצוי [הכי נמי נימא לענין כשרות הקרבן דהא] עיקר [סכה ממה נפשך] אתא לאקשויי כך פי' מורי שי' תוס' הר"פ : ב] עי' בהשמטות בסוף המסכת : ג] עי' בהשמטות בסוף המסכת : ד] אשם ארצוי נמי לירצו (תיבת נמי נמחק) אין להקשות דלעיל מקשה אשם לא לייתי כלל דמסברא יש לנו לפסול באשם [יותר] משאר קרבנות והכא מקשה מסברא יש להכשיר באשם [יותר] משאר קרבנות וי"ל דלעיל לא היה יודע מדרשא דאותה ויש לפסול מסברא באשם יותר משאר קרבנות ממה מצינו בחטאת אבל עתה דאנו יודעים [מדרשא דאותה אף] דיכולים לפסול באשם כיון דאשם בא לכפר ולא שייך ביה ואם לאו יהא נדבה י"ל דאין להכשירו לחצאין וכי גלי קרא באשם אותה לגמרי אכשרי אפי' לרצות ולכפר : ה] שכן טעונין סמיכה · לא גרסינן סמיכה דאשם נמי טעון סמיכה כדנפקא לן לקמן [דף יא ע"א] מכהטאת וכאשם [ואפשר] דגרסי' [משום] אשם מצורע שאינו טעון סמיכה ואם תאמר אי מיירי באשם מצורע הא אשם מצורע טעון נסכים ומאי מקשה שכן טעונין סמיכה ונסכים [וי"ל דהכי פריך מה לשלמים] שכן כולן טעונין סמיכה ונסכים אבל אין כל האשמות טעונין סמיכה ונסכים ותימה מאי קאמר [עולה תוכיח] הא בעולה כתיב ופשך וי"ל דר"ל [עולת העוף וא"ת] מאי פריך בסמוך שכן ישנן בצבור כביחיד והלא עולת העוף אינה באה בצבור וי"ל דמ"מ פריך משם עולה שישנו בצבור [דעל מה מצינו אף] פרכא כל דהו פרכינן · תוס' פוך : ו] תיבות הכי גרסינן נמחק : ז] תיבות על נמחק : ח] לא קיימי : ט] יולדת הס"ד ומה"ד יביאו יורשיה עולתה דשעבודא דאורייתא הס"ד : י] אולה · א) ובעם זה מועיל דוקא היכא דמעכב הריצוי חיסרון בעלים כגו הכא אבל בהרבה מקומות כשירין ומוצין : יא] שלא לשמה שתקריב : יב] פולוקתך מחלוקת המסייעתך : יג] ונסיב לה : יד] מחטאת ומפסח דאי במה מצינו איכא למיפרך : טו] או חטאת אות ל' נמחק : טז] מדכא מדאיצטריך מוצא : יז] ושנוי בעלים דהוי שינוי בעלים כבאין לאחר : יח] בעלים ושינוי קודש נמי יליף משינוי בעלים הס"ד : יט] היתה חיה : כ] תיבת העוף נמחק : כא] בקרא ואחר ישחט את העולה ש"מ דבעלמא אפילו דיעבד : כב] הפסולים סמיכת אשם מצורע : כג] תודה תוכיח :

א) כוונתו בזה לתרץ מה שהקשו התוס' ד"ה הג"ה וא"ת ומה ראי' וכו' ודו"ק:

עין משפט
נר מצוה

טז א מיי' פ"ד מהל' פסה"מ הלכה טו:
יז ב מיי' פי"ד מהלכות מעה"ק הל' ג:
גי' צ"ק קדשים הס"ד ואח"כ מה"ד חטאת
יח ג מיי' שם הל' ב:
יט ד מיי' פ"א מהלכות תמורה הל' ה:

מסורת הש"ס

תורה אור

מה לתודה שכן טעונה לחם עולה ושלמים יוכיחו וחזר הדין לא ראי זה כראי זה ולא ראי זה כראי זה הצד השוה שבהן שהן קדשים ושחטן שלא לשמן כשר ואינו מרצה אף אני אביא אשם שהוא קדש ושחטו שלא לשמו כשר ואינו מרצה מה להצד השוה שבהן שהן א] באין בנדר ובנדבה אלא אמר רבא זאת התורה וגו' הקישו הכתוב לשלמים מה שלמים שהן קדשים ושחטן שלא לשמן כשרים ואין מרצין אף אני אביא אשם שהוא קודש כו' ב]מאי חזית דאקשת לשלמים אקיש לחטאת הא מיעט רחמנא אותה (סימן הג"ש *בש"ר) יתיב רב הונא ורב נחמן ויתיב רב ששת גבייהו ויתבי וקאמרי ג]קשיא ליה לריש לקיש אשם דלא אתי לאחר מיתה לימא ליה ר"א אשם נמי אתי לאחר מיתה אמר להו רב ששת אשם למאי קרב למותרו חטאת נמי מיקרב קרבה מותרה חטאת אף ע"ג דקרבה מותרה מיעט רחמנא הוא *אשם נמי כתיב ביה הוא ההוא לאחר הקטרת אימורים הוא דכתיב *כדתניא אבל אשם לא נאמר בו הוא אלא לאחר הקטרת אימורין והוא עצמו ד] אם לא (א) הקטירו אימורין כשר ואלא הוא למה לי לכדרב הונא אמר רב *דאמר רב הונא אמר רב אשם שניתק [א]לרעיה ושחטו סתם כשר ניתק אין לא ניתק לא מאי טעמא אמר קרא הוא בהווייתו יהא יתבי רב נחמן ורב ששת ויתיב רב אדא בר מתנה גבייהו ויתבי וקאמרי הא דקאמר רבי אלעזר מצינו בבאין לאחר מיתה שהן כשרין ואין מרצין לימא ליה ריש לקיש הנהו נמי לייתו ולירצו אמר להן רב אדא בר מתנה יולדת אם היא ילדה בניה מי ילדו מתקיף לה רב ה]אסי ומאן לימא לן דאי איכא כמה עשה גבה לא מיתכפרא וכיון דכי איכא כמה עשה גבה מיכפרא יורשיה נמי מיכפר למימרא דקניא להו והאמר רבי יוחנן [ב]הניח מנחה לשני בניו ומת קריבה [ג]ואין בו שותפות ואי ס"ד קניא להו ו] °נפש אמר רחמנא ולא קניא להו והאמר ר' יוחנן [ד]הניח בהמה לשני בניו ומת קריבה ואין ממירין בה אי אמרת בשלמא קניא להו היינו דאין ממירין בה דהויא להו ז] כשותפין ושותפין

ר"ה שלמה יצחק

ויקר' ג

חטאת נמי מיקרב קרבה מותרה · ואפי' הכי פסולה שלא לשמה כיון דאינה באה לאחר מיתה לשם חטאת כי אם לשם עולה אשם נמי כיון דאינו קרב להדיא לשם אשם אלא לשם עולה לא דמי לשאר קדשים* : [ומקשה] חטאת אע"ג דקרב מותרה מיעט רחמנא הוא למסקנא זו משמע שעומד מוקשה דלימא ליה ר' אליעזר אשם נמי כו' נ"ל דגרס וחטאת בוי"ו וכל זה מדברי רב ששת וה"פ וחטאת אע"ג דקרב מותרה מיעט רחמנא הוא שלא תכשירנה מדאתיא לאחר מיתה כמו מחיים ומשום הכי איצטריך לריש לקיש לעיל אותה והא דפריך אשם נמי כתיב ביה הוא לאו לסתור דבריו של רב ששת קאתי אלא הכי קאמר היכי ממעטת ליה מפסול שלא לשמן מאותה הא כתיב בה הוא יט]לפוסלן :

מיעט רחמנא היא · בכמה מקומות משמע דמדכתיב היא בחטאת נפקא לן עיכובא דלקמן בגמ' (דף י:) דרבי אליעזר אומר אף האשם כ] א"ל ר' יהושע חטאת נאמר בה היא בשחיטה[וכו'] ובפ"ק דמנחות (דף ד·) כא] חטאת טעמא מאי דכתיב בה היא ותימה דלקמן בפירקין (דף ז:) כב] *גמרא חוץ מן הפסח והחטאת ויליף לה מקראי אחריני וה"ר חיים מפרש דצריכי תרי קראי חד לחטאת ששחטה לשם עולה וחד לחטאת חלב ששחטה לשם חטאת נזיר ומצורע אע"ג דכולן שמן חטאת מ"מ פסולה כיון דאינן באין לכפר דינן כמו עולות כדאמרינן לקמן ולא דמי לחטאת חלב ששחטה לשם חטאת [דם] דכשרה וקצת קשה מהא דפריך בריש מנחות (דף ג:) גבי חטאת חלב לשם חטאת נזיר ומצורע ליתכפר דכתיב זאת תורת ומאי פירכא והלא גלי קרא דכתיב בה היא ונראה דאיצטריך היא גבי חטאת לגלויי אמנחת חוטא *ואמנחת קנאות כג]ואשמה דכתב בה היא וכמו בפסח (והיינו) דאמר לקמן גבי פסח אלא הוא למה לי לכדתניא כל מקום שנאמר בו הוא כו' ורבינו *ש"י מוחקו משום דליתיה בברייתא דלקמן ובחגס מחק דשמא היא ברייתא בתוספתא ומיהו קצת תימה אמאי צריך תרי כד] קראי חד לחטאת וחד כה] לפסח וה"ר יצחק מפרש חד לחטאת נקבה דלא אתי מותרה גופה עולה אלא תרעה עד שהסתאב ויביא בדמיה עולה ולהכי פסולה בשנוי קודש וחד בשעיר נשיא דהוי זכר ומותרו גופיה הוי עולה כי הפריש שתים לאחריות ואימא דלא ליפסול בשלא לשמן ויש שום צריכותא דלא מלינן למילף חד מחבריה דאי הוי כתיב בנשיא בדידיה סגי וצ"ע :

[אולי צ"ל נש"ד]

צ"ל אמר נ"ק

גי' הצ"ק ואמנחת קנאות דמעכבי דכתיב בה נמי היא ועי"ל דהיא דחטאת אתיא לגלויי אהוא דאשם דלא מעכב כהוא דפסח והייט דאמר לקמן כו' כצ"ל ועי' בתוס' במנחות דף ד ע"א תוספות ד"ה חטאת

הגה"ה ניתק אין לא ניתק לא אמר קרא הוא בהווייתו יהא · משמע הכא דניתק לרעייה דאורייתא ותימה דבפסחים בסוף אלו דברים (דף עג·) משמע דהוי דרבנן דמפרש התם דוקא שחטו סתם דיעבד אבל לכתחלה לא גזירה לאחר כפרה אטו לפני כפרה ולא קאמר גזירה לאחר ניתוק אטו קודם ניתוק וי"ל דה"פ בהווייתו יהא קודם כפרה הלכך כו] *אבל כפרה נמי בעי ניתוק גזירה אטו לפני כפרה [נ"א מנחה] ור"ת לא גריס כאן ניתק אין לא ניתק לא כז] וכן בפ"ק דמנחות (דף ד·) לאחר ולקמן ליתיה בפ' פרת חטאת (קטו:) ולא בתמורה פ' ואלו קדשים כח] (דף יח.) ובא לפרש טעם למה הוא כשר כיון דגמירי דבאשם רועה ומפרש משום דכתיב הוא דמשמע בהווייתו יהא פירוש בהווייתו מה שסופו להיות דהיינו עולה שסופו עומד לכך כשיסתאב ויפלו דמיו לנדבה °ואין לחוש אי קאי קרא אהלכתא כט] דכי האי גוונא אשכחן בפ' הלוקח עובר פרתו (בכורות דף טז·) דאיצטריך קרא ואיצטריך הלכתא והשתא הא דנקט בכל דוכתא כל שבחטאת מתה באשם רועה לא נקט רעיה אלא לפי שתיקנוה חכמים וכי גמירי כל שבחטאת מתה באשם קרב עולה דרעיה דרבנן היא:

נפש אמר רחמנא · ומשמע דמנפש קדריש וכן בסוף המנחות והנסכים (מנחות קד:) קתני הכל באין בשותפות חוץ ממנחה דכתיב נפש ותימה דבתורת כהנים דריש נפש ולא ציבור קרבנו ולא שותפין ונראה דרישא דקרא מייתי בכל מקום : *ולא קניא להו והאמר רבי יוחנן · עיין נ"ק דרבי יוחנן אדרבי יוחנן הוי מצי לאקשויי :

הקיש הכתוב · אשם לשלמים ואין משיבין על ההיקש: אקיש לחטאת · דפסול : קשיא ליה לריש לקיש אשם משום דלא אתי לאחר מיתה לימא ליה ר' אליעזר אשם נמי אתי לאחר מיתה · ח] שאשם שמתו בעליו רועה ודמיו נופלין לקיץ המזבח : למותרו · שדמיו נופלין לנדבה כדפרישית : חטאת נמי · מותרו נדבה הוא כגון הפריש שתי חטאות לאחריות מתכפר באחת מהן והשניה תרעה (יומא סה·) והיא קריבה לאחר מיתת בעלים שהרי נתכפר בחבירתה בחייו ואין זו חטאת שמתו בעליה אלמא אתיא חטאת לאחר מיתה ואפי' הכי פסולה שלא לשמה ואשם נמי ליפסול: מיעט רחמנא הוא · בשעיר נשיא כתיב בשחיטתו (ויקרא ד) ושחט אותו במקום אשר ישחט את העולה לפני ה' חטאת הוא שישחטנו לשם חטאת ואם לאו פסול דהוא משמע בהווייתו יהא אם בהווייתו ט] יהא כשר ואם לאו פסול ומינה ילפי' פסול דחטאת לקמן בפרקין (דף י:) : אשם נמי כתיב ביה אשם הוא · בצו את אהרן (ג) י] והקטירו המזבח אשה לה' אשם הוא בזמן שהוא לשם אשם כשר ואם לאו פסול : ההוא לאחר הקטרת אימורין (ג) · דלא ילפינן מיניה כדתניא לקמן בפ"ק אבל אשם לא נאמר בו הוא אלא לאחר הקטרת אימורין וליכא למימר בהקטרה יא] דמבעי לשמו לעכב דהוא עצמו שלא הוקטרו יב] אימורין כשר דאין כפרה אלא בדם ואע"ג דכתיב באשם קדש קדשים הוא[ג] (ויקרא ו) קודם שחיטה לא ילפינן מיניה דלא משמע לשמו אלא כשכתוב הוא עם שם הקרבן כגון חטאת הוא אשם הוא והיכא דכתיב גבי אחת מעבודת הדם : שניתק לרעייה · שמתו בעליו או שנתכפרו באחר וניתק מדין אשם לרעייה שאמרו לו ב"ד יד] הוציאו וירעה : ושחטו סתם כשר · לעולה הואיל וסופו לקיץ המזבח שהוא עולה : ניתק אין · דמיעקר שם אשם מיניה משנמסר לרועה וקם סתמיה לעולה לא ניתק לא הוי סתמיה לעולה דאמר קרא אשם הוא בהווייתו יהא טו] : הנהו נמי לייתו ולירצו · אורשים : יולדת · עולת יולדת דאייתי ראיה מיניה יביאו יורשים עולתה מאי לייתו ולירצו היכא אם היא ילדה כו' : מאן לימא דאי איכא כמה עשה גבה · דיולדת דלא מיכפרא עולתה עלייהו אם טז] הביאה מחיים עולה מכפרת על עשה ועל לא תעשה שניתק לעשה דתניא גבי עולת נדבה בת"כ (ד) ונרצה לו מלמד שהמקום מרוצה לו ועל מה המקום מרוצה לו אם תאמר דברים שחייבין עליהם מיתת ב"ד מיתה בידי שמים כרת (בידי שמים) מלקות ארבעים חטאות יז] אשמות הרי עונשן אמור הא אין עולה באה אלא על עשה ועל לא תעשה שניתק לעשה : למימרא דקני להו · ליורשין בהמת קרבן אביהן דקפרכת תכפר עלייהו : אין בה משום שותפות · דאמרינן בהמנחות והנסכים (מנחות קד:) הכל בא בשותפות לא חילק הכתוב אלא מנחה שנאמר בו נפש: ה"ג [נפש] אמר רחמנא · ונפש כי תקריב קרבן מנחה וגו' (ויקרא ב) : דאין ממירין בה · אם המיר יח] אינו תמורה : ושותפין

אחד

הגהות הב"ח

(א) גמ' והוא עצמו אם לא הוקטרו אימוריו כשר ואלא הוא: (ב) רש"י ד"ה אשם נמי וכו' והקטיר אותם הכהן המזבחה אשה לה': (ג) ד"ה ההוא וכו' אימורין הוא דכתיב דלא וכו' וליכא למימר בהקטרת אימורין דבעי לשמו וכו' אימוריו כשר: (ד) ד"ה מאן לימא וכו' בת"כ נ"ב פרשה ג' פ"ד:

[מנחות ד.]

לקמן ז: י: [מנחות ד.]

לקמן קיב. קטו: פסחים ענ. נזיר כה: ע"ש מנחות ד. תמורה יח.

גליון הש"ס

תוס' ד"ה הג"ה וכו' ואין לחוש אי קאי קרא אהלכתא · עי' מיר דף סא ע"ב תוס' ד"ה ואימא · ונע"ק :

שיטה מקובצת

א] באין בנדר ובנדבה' ולעיל אעולה [לא פריך האי פירכא]לפי דעדיפא [פריך שכן כליל] א"נ דהוי פירכא כ"ד משום דבאה בנדר ונדבה איכא נמי קולא [במה שהיא כשרה] ואינה מכפרת [ובחד] מחד לא פרכינן פירכא כל דהו [ופרכא כל דהו] מיהו הוי ולא לגמרי כי [פרכא כל דהו כמו] תורת הזמה לא פריך בב"מ' תוס' טוך: אלא אמר רבא זאת כו' הלכך מכח היקשא דזאת לא מצית למימר דאשם לייתי ולירצי דהא איתקש לשלמים אבל גבי פירכא קמייתא דהוי פריך אשם לא לייתי כלל לא מצי לשנויי מהאי היקשא דהכא דאדרבה דהו"א ליקשינן לחטאת כדפריך הכא דעדיין לא הי' יודע דרשא דאותה ומיהו קשה לייתי לעיל מהאי היקשא דשלמים [וכי פריך] ליה ליקשי לחטאת יתרץ ליה מאותה כדעבד השתא אלא נראה דמעיקרא דהוי פריך אשם לא לייתי כלל מכח דכיון דלא שייך ביה סברא דאם לאו יהא נדבה מסתבר לדמויי לחטאת הוא כיון דשניהם באים לכפרה ואפי' בלא היקשא והלכך לא אתיא הך היקשא דשלמים ומפקא מהך סברא כיון דכשרות [לא ידעינן] באשם לכך אייתי אותה להכשיר אשם ולאפקא מהאי סברא ואכתי קשה אשם ארצויי נמי לירצי ועל אותה קושיא שייך שפיר להביא היקשא דשלמים [כיון דאפיקתיה] מהך סברא דמדמינן ליה לחטאת כך נראה למורי ואע"ג דגם עתה סברא הוא דכיון דכשר ירצה כדפי' לעיל דאין לומר דכשר להצאין [כיון דבא] לכפרה דלא שייך ביה ואם לאו יהא נדבה אפ"ה אמרי' השתא דמפקינן מהיקשא דשלמים לומר שאינו מרצה דמ"מ כבר יצא [לתרץ על]עיקר [הקושיא דלא לייתי כלל לפרכא] דכיון דבא לכפר כחטאת הלכך אמרינן היקשא משלמים : ב] מאי חזית כו' אאשם פריך דלא פריך אשר קרבנות [דהא בהו כתיב] מוצא שפתיך ואם כמו שנדרת כו' : ג] וקאמרי קא קשיא : ד] עצמו שלא הוקטרו אימורין : ה] רב אסי תיבת אסי נמחק : ו] אמר רחמנא נפש ולא : ז] להו דשותפין אות כ' נמחק: ח]מיתה דקי"ל כל שבחטאת מתה באשם רועה: ט]בהווייתו הוא יהא: י]והקטיר אותם הכהן המזבחה : יא]בהקטרה דנבעי לשמו : יב] אימוריו כשר : יג] הוא · גליון וא"ת הא כתיב כחטאת כאשם הוא ולגבי עבודות כתבי וי"ל דלא הוי מיעוט כיון דכתיב האשם הוא ולא כתב אשם הוא כמו חטאת הוא בלא ה' ועוד דאיצטריך לומר האשם היא דמעין צפון והוי כאילו לא כתיב בה הוא ע"כ: יד] ב"ד הוציאוהו : טו] יהא והווייתו אשם ואין אשם בא בנדבה הס"ד : טז] אם הביאתה: יז] חטאות ואשמות : יח] המיר בה : יט] הוא דמשמע פסול ונהי [דאותה בא] לסתור היקשא מ"מ לא בא לסתור מה שכתוב בהדיא ולא לסתור דברי רב ששת פריך אלא פריך לפי המסקנא היאך מכשירין משעם אותה הא כתיב הוא לפוסלן ומשני האי הוא בתר הקטרה: כ] האשם אמרינן אמר לו ר' יהושע : כא] דמנחות אמרינן : כב] בפירקין בגמ' דחוק : כג] קנאות דכתב בהו הוא כמו בחטאת וכמו בפסח ותיבת ואשמה ל"ש תמחק : כד] תרי הוא תיבת קראי נמחק : כה] וחד בפסח אות ל' נמחק : כו] הילכך לאחר ופרה ותיבת איכא נמחק : כז] לא ובפ"ק תיבת וכן ל"ש ונמחק : כח] קדשים אלא גרסי' אשם פי' שמתו בעליו או שנתכפר באחר ושחטה סתם כשר לעולה הוא בהווייתו יהא עלה כיון שמתו בעליו אי שנתכפרו באחר וכ"ת והלא גמירי דבאשם : כט] אהילכתא לפי' ר"ת דפריא דהלכה נישנית כל שבחטאת מתה באשם (עולה) [רועה] :

let the thanksgiving-offering prove it.[3] [5b] As for the thanksgiving-offering [it is not 'accepted'] because it requires loaves [as an accompaniment]![4] Then let the burnt-offering and peace-offerings prove it. And thus the argument revolves: the characteristic of the one is not that of the other, and that of the other is not that of the first. The factor common to all is that they are holy [sacrifices], and if one slaughters them not in their own name, they are valid and are not accepted; so also do I adduce the guilt-offering which is holy, and hence if one slaughters it not in its name it is valid and is not accepted. [No] the factor common to them all [it may be asked] is that they come as a vow or as a freewill-offering!—Rather said Raba: [Scripture saith,] '*This is the law* etc.,' thus Scripture assimilated it [the guilt-offering] to peace-offerings. As the peace-offerings are holy [sacrifices], and if slaughtered not in their own name are valid and are not accepted, so do I adduce the guilt-offering too which is holy etc. What reason do you see to assimilate it to peace-offerings: assimilate it to the sin-offering?[5]—Surely the Divine Law expressed a limitation [in the word] '*it*'.[6]

[Mnemonic: *HaGeSH BaSaR*][7] R. Huna and R. Naḥman were sitting, and R. Shesheth sat with them. They sat and said: Now Resh Lakish had experienced a difficulty, what about the guilt-
a offering which does not come after death?[1] But R. Eleazar could have answered him that the guilt-offering too comes after death?[2] —Said R. Shesheth to them: In what way is a guilt-offering brought? As a remainder![3] Then the remainder of a sin-offering too is indeed offered.[4] [This, however, is no argument;] in the case of a sin-offering though the remainder thereof is offered, yet the Divine Law expressed a limitation in the word 'it' [*hu*]![5]—But in connection with the guilt-offering too *hu* [it] is written?[6]—That is written after the burning of the *emurim*, as it was taught: But in the case of a guilt-offering, '*it is*' [*hu*] is stated only *after* the burning of the *emurim*, and in fact if the *emurim* are not burnt at all it [the offering] is valid.[7] Then what is the purpose of '*it*'?—For R. Huna's teaching in Rab's name. For R. Huna said in the name of Rab: If a guilt-offering was transferred to pasture and one then slaughtered it without a defined purpose, it is valid.[8] Thus, if it was transferred, it is so, but if it was not transferred, it is not so. What is the reason? Scripture says, '*it is*', intimating, it must be in its essential form.[9]

R. Naḥman and R. Shesheth sat, and R. Adda b. Mattenah sat with them. Now they sat and debated: Now as to what R. Eleazar said: 'We find in the case of sacrifices that come after the death [of their owners] that they are valid, yet are not accepted', let
b Resh Lakish say to him, Let these too come and be accepted?[1]—Said R. Adda b. Mattenah to them: As for [the offering of] a woman after confinement, if she gave birth, did her children give birth?[2] To this R. Assi demurred: Yet who is to say if she had been guilty of [the neglect of] many affirmative precepts she would not be atoned for?[3] And since she would be forgiven if she had been guilty of neglecting affirmative precepts, then her heirs too may thus be atoned for![4]—Are we then to say that they [the heirs] acquire it?[5] But surely R. Joḥanan said: If one leaves a meal-offering to his two sons and dies, it is offered, and the law of partnership does not apply to it.[6] If however you think that they acquire a title to it, surely the Divine Law saith, *And when a soul* [*bringeth a meal-offering*]![7] Will you then say that they do not acquire it? Surely R. Joḥanan said: If one leaves an animal [dedicated for a sacrifice] to his two sons, and dies, it is offered, but they cannot effect substitution with it.[8] Now it is well if you say that they acquire it; for that reason they cannot effect substitution with

(3) Which was likewise never a public offering, yet conformed to the same law as the others. (4) V. Lev. VII, 12. (5) Which is mentioned in the same verse. (6) As *supra a*. (7) The object of this mnemonic, which means 'bring near flesh' is not clear. D.S. emends into *HaNeSH NaSHaD*, consisting of key letters of the names of the Amoraim in the two paragraphs that follow.

a (1) *Supra 5a*. (2) For when its owner dies, it is left to graze until it contracts a blemish, whereupon it is sold and the money spent on a sacrifice, viz., a burnt-offering. (3) As explained in preceding note. (4) E.g., if a man sets aside *two* animals for his sin-offering, in case one is lost the other should be available. When the first is subsequently offered, the second is treated as a guilt-offering whose owner died. Thus a sin-offering too may be brought after death, and yet if it is sacrificed for a different purpose it is invalid; then a guilt-offering too should be invalid, and this justifies Resh Lakish's difficulty. (5) Lev. IV, 24 (referring to the sin-offering, brought '*when a ruler sinneth*'): *And he shall . . . kill it . . . before the Lord; it is a sin-offering*. This emphatic *hu* ('it is') implies that it must be brought as such, and if offered as a different sacrifice, it is invalid. (6) Lev. VII, 5: *And the priest shall make them smoke on the altar for an offering made by fire unto the Lord: it is* (hu) *a guilt-offering*. (7) I.e., we cannot say that it teaches that if the *emurim* are burnt in the name of a different sacrifice this offering is invalid, since the sacrifice is fit even if the *emurim* are not burnt at all. (8) If it was slaughtered (in the Temple court) before it became blemished, it is valid as a burnt-offering, since that would eventually have been brought from its proceeds (v. note 2). The flesh is then burnt on the altar, while the hide belongs to the priest. (9) Hence unless it was formally transferred to grazing on the instructions of the Beth din, it is not valid as a burnt-offering if it was slaughtered without a defined purpose.

b (1) For the heirs. (2) They do not need the sacrifice. (3) Through the burnt-offering necessitated by childbirth. Burnt-offerings make atonement for the violation of positive precepts and negative precepts which are technically regarded as having been transformed into positive precepts. I.e., where the violation of a negative precept necessitates the performance of a positive one: e.g., the violation of '*Thou shalt not rob*' (Lev. XIX, 13) necessitates the performance of the positive precept, '*he shall restore that which he took by robbery*' (ib. V, 23) —Thus this burnt-offering would serve another purpose too. (4) If they were guilty of the same. (5) And it becomes their own, so that it can make atonement for them. (6) All sacrifices may be brought in partnership, except a meal-offering. Here this does not apply. (7) Lev. II, 1.—So literally; E.V. *and when any one*. From this word '*a soul*' the Talmud deduces that it can be brought by one person only. But if heirs acquire a title to their father's sacrifices, this meal-offering has now two owners. (8) When a person dedicates an animal for a sacrifice, he must not propose another as a substitute; if he does, both are sacred (Lev. XXVII, 33). This is called effecting substitution. Here this does not apply, so that if they declare a substitute for it, it does not become sacred.

it, because they become partners, [6a] and partners cannot effect substitution. But if you say that they do not acquire it, let them indeed even effect substitution?—There it is different, because Scripture saith, *'And if he change it at all,'* which is to include the
a heir;[1] and [the same verse teaches,] one can change, but not two.[2] To this R. Jacob of Nehar Peḳod demurred: If so, when it is written, *And if a man will redeem ought*[3] in connection with tithe, which is also to include the heir, will you say there too, One can redeem, but not two?—Tithe is different, because as far as their father too is concerned it [redemption] can be done in partnership.[4] R. Assi said to R. Ashi: Now from this itself [you may argue]: It is well if you agree that they acquire it, for that reason one [heir] at least can effect substitution.[5] But if you say that they do not acquire it, how can he effect substitution? Surely R. Abbahu said in R. Joḥanan's name: He who sanctifies [the animal] must add the fifth, whilst only he for whom atonement is made can effect substitution;[6] and he who gives *terumah* of his own for another man's produce, the goodwill is his![7]—It does not effect a fixed [absolute] atonement, but it does make a floating atonement.[8]

The question was asked: Do they make atonement in respect of
b the purpose for which they came, or do they not make atonement?[1] Said R. Shisha the son of R. Idi: Reason asserts that it does not make atonement; for if you think that it does, what is the purpose of a second [sacrifice]? What then: [do you maintain]; it does not make atonement? Why then is it offered?[2]—Said R. Ashi: This is the difficulty felt by R. Shisha the son of R. Idi: It is well if you say that it does not make atonement; [for though slaughtered] for a different purpose, yet it comes in virtue of [having been dedicated for] its true purpose,[3] while the second [sacrifice] comes to make atonement. But if you say that it has made atonement, what is the purpose of the second?

The question was asked: Does it [a burnt-offering] make atonement[4] for [the violation of] a positive precept [committed] after the separation [of the animal], or not? Do we say, it is analogous to a sin-offering: just as a sin-offering [makes atonement] only for [the sins committed] before separation, but not for [those committed] after separation, so here too [it makes atonement] only for [the sins committed] before separation, but not for [those committed] after separation. Or, perhaps, it is unlike a sin-offering, for a separate sin-offering is incurred for each sin, whereas here, since it makes atonement if he had been guilty of [violating] many positive precepts,[5] it may also make atonement for positive precepts [neglected] after separation?—Come and hear: *And he shall lay [his hand upon the head of the burnt-offering]; and it shall be accepted [for him to make atonement for him]*;[6] does then the laying [of hands] make atonement? Surely atonement can be made only with the blood, as it says, *For it is the blood that maketh atonement by*
c *reason of the life!*[1] What then is taught by the verse, *And he shall lay . . . and it shall be accepted . . . to make atonement?*—[To teach] that if he treated [the laying of hands] as the residue of the precept,[2] Scripture regards him as though he did not make atonement, and yet he did make atonement. Now what is meant by 'he did not make atonement' and he did make atonement'? Surely, 'he did make atonement' [means] in respect of positive precepts [neglected] before the separation [of the animal], while 'he did not make atonement' in respect of the positive precept of laying [of hands], because it is a positive precept [neglected] after separation?[3]—Said Raba: You speak of the precept of laying [the hand]? There it is different, because as long as he has not yet slaughtered, he is subject to the injunction 'Arise and lay [hands]';[4] when then is it a [neglected] positive precept? After the slaughtering; and in respect of [a precept neglected] after the slaughtering no question arises.[5] R. Huna b. Judah said to Raba: Perhaps it means, 'It did

a (1) The emphatic *'at all'* is expressed in Hebrew by the doubling of the verb, and this doubling is interpreted as an extension including the heir. (2) Since it is couched in the singular. (3) Lev. XXVII, 31. (4) If the produce belonged to partners in the first place, they could tithe and redeem the tithe in partnership. Hence the same applies to a man's heirs. (5) If he is the only heir. (6) If A dedicates an animal for B's sacrifice, and it subsequently receives a blemish and must be redeemed, then if A, who sanctified it, redeems it himself, he must add a fifth to its value, but not if B redeems it (this is deduced from Lev. XXVII, 15). Again, only B effects substitution, but not A. Since then the heir does effect substitution, he is obviously regarded as in the place of B, hence its owner. (7) I.e., he (*sc.* the man who gives it) can give it to any priest he desires. If money is offered for the *terumah* to be given to a particular priest, that money belongs to him. (8) I.e., it does not make an absolute atonement for the heir as though he were its absolute owner; therefore in the case of a meal-offering, though there are two heirs, they still offer it. But the heir has, as it were, a light floating right of atonement in it (i.e., he has some slight rights of ownership in it), and therefore he can effect substitution.

b (1) When a sacrifice is killed for a purpose other than its own, its owner has not fulfilled his obligation. Nevertheless the question arises where this was brought in order to make atonement for a certain sin, whether the owner can regard it as having made that atonement, or not. It makes no practical difference, save that the owner may feel himself forgiven even before he offers the second sacrifice. (2) Why do we proceed with the sacrificial rites e.g. sprinkling, if it does not make atonement in any case? (3) Originally it was dedicated for its rightful purpose. This hallows it, and so even when it is killed for a different purpose it retains its sanctity, and therefore the other sacrificial rites must be proceeded with. (4) On the atoning effect of a burnt-offering V. *supra* 5*b* n. b 3. (5) One burnt-offering makes atonement for all. (6) Lev. I, 4.

c (1) Lev. XVII, 11. (2) I.e., as something unimportant, and so neglected it altogether. (3) Which solves the question propounded. (4) Hence *before* he slaughtered he cannot be said to have violated it. (5) It certainly does not make atonement for such (though further on R. Jeremiah asks even in respect of such too), and the question is only in respect of precepts neglected after the separation of the animal, but before it is slaughtered.

תורה אור

*ושותפין לא מצו ממירין אלא אי אמרת לא קניא להו א] אמורי נמי לימרו שאני התם *דאמר קרא °אם המר ימיר ^{ויקרא כז} ^ילרבות את היורש אחד ממיר ואין שנים ממירין מתקיף לה רב יעקב מנהר פקוד אלא מעתה גבי מעשר דכתיב °ואם גאל יגאל ^{שם} *לרבות ^יאת היורש הכי נמי אחד גואל ואין שנים גואלין שאני מעשר דגבי אבוהון נמי איתיה בשותפות אמר ליה רב אסי לרב אשי ומינה אי אמרת בשלמא קניא להו היינו דחד מיהא מימר אלא אי אמרת לא קניא להו היכי מימר והאמר רבי אבהו אמר ר' יוחנן *המקדיש מוסיף חומש ^יומתכפר עושה תמורה ^יוהתורם משלו על של חבירו טובת הנאה שלו מקיבעא לא מכפרא מקופיא מכפרא: איבעיא להו כיפרו על מה שבאו או לא כיפרו אמר רב (א) ששת בריה דרב אידי מסתברא דלא כיפרו דאי סלקא דעתך כיפרו שני למה הוא בא ואלא מאי לא כיפרו למה הוא קרב אמר רב אשי רב שישא בריה דרב אידי הכי קא קשיא ליה אי אמרת בשלמא לא כיפרו שלא לשמו מכח לשמו קאתי ושני (ב) למה הוא בא לכפר אלא ג] אי אמרת כיפרו שני למה הוא בא: איבעיא להו אעשה *דלאחר הפרשה מכפרא או לא מכפרא מי אמרינן מידי דהוה אחטאת מה חטאת דקודם הפרשה אין דלאחר הפרשה לא אף הכא נמי דקודם הפרשה אין לאחר הפרשה לא או דלמא לא דמיא לחטאת דחטאת על כל חטא וחטא בעי לאיתויי חדא חטאת והכא כיון (ג) דאיכא כמה עשה גביה מכפרא אעשה דלאחר הפרשה נמי מכפרא תא ^{שם ה}שמע* °וסמך ונרצה (ד) וכי סמיכה מכפרת ^{שם יז}והלא אין כפרה אלא בדם שנאמר °כי הדם הוא בנפש יכפר אלא מה תלמוד לומר וסמך ונרצה לכפר ג] ^ישאם עשאה לסמיכה שירי מצוה מעלה עליו הכתוב כאילו לא כיפר וכיפר (ה) ד] מאי לאו דכיפר עשה דקודם הפרשה לא כיפר אעשה דסמיכה דהוה ליה עשה דלאחר הפרשה אמר רבא עשה דסמיכה קאמרת שאני התם דכל כמה דלא שחיט בעמוד וסמוך קאי אימת (ו) קא הוי עשה לאחר שחיטה לאחר שחיטה לא קא מיבעיא לן א"ל רב הונא בר יהודה לרבא אימא כיפר גברא לא

רש"י

ושותפין לא מצו ממירין: דתניא הכל ממירין [חוץ מן השותפים] לפי שכל הפרשה כולה נאמרה בלשון יחיד כמו לא יחליפנו ולא ימיר אותו ואם המר ימיר אחד מימר ולא שנים ממירין: שאני התם · אע"ג דלא קניא להו גזירת הכתוב הוא דשני יורשין אין ממירין זבח שהפריש אביהן: אחד ממיר · דהא דיורש ממיר בקרבן אביו מהכא נפקא לן אם המר לרבות את היורש דהוה מצי למיכתב אם ימר והכא נמי בלשון יחיד כתביה: אם ס] יגאל איש ממעשרו לרבות יורש · שמוסיף חומש ופודה את מעשר אביו: איתיה בשותפות · דלא אשכחן דמימעט שותפין מפדיון מעשר שני ותמורה היינו טעמא משום דכל הפרשה נאמרה בלשון יחיד: המקדיש מוסיף חומש כו' · אדם שנדר קרבן והפרישו חבירו משלו להתכפר בו הנודר והומם ובא לחללו אם המפריש מחללו מוסיף חומש ואם המתכפר מחללו אינו מוסיף חומש דתלייה רחמנא לחומש במקדיש דכתיב (ויקרא כז) ואם המקדיש יגאל את ביתו ויסף חמישיתו ואם גאל יגאל את השדה [המקדיש אותו]: ומתכפר עושה תמורה · דאיהו הוה בעלים דידיה ובמסכת תמורה יליף טעמא בפ"ק: והתורם · תרומה משלו על הכרי של חבירו טובת הנאה של מפריש הוא בידו לתתה ו] לכהן שירצה ואם בא ישראל ואמר לו הילך סלע זו ותן תרומתך לבן בתי כהן אותה ז] סלע טובת הנאה של מפריש הוא ויליף התם טעמא ח] את כל מעשר תבואתך ונתת (דברים כו) מי שהפרישה מתבואתו בידו לתתה: ומשני מקיבעא לא מכפרא מקופיא מכפרא · ט] כפרה קבועה שיהא יורש בעליו ממש אין להן הלכך גבי מנחה כשרה ליקרב דלאו י] *דשותפין היא אבל כפרה קופיא וצפה ממילא יש להן בו והלכך ממיר: קופיא לשון צף כמו (חגיגה טז:) אקפו ידייכו וכמו (מלכים ב ו) ויצף הברזל תרגום וקפא ברזלא ויש לו יא] דומה במסכת יומא (דף טז:): כיפרו על מה שבאו · קדשים שנזבחו שלא לשמן יב] יקרבו ותנן לא עלו לשם חובה וצריך להביא אחר מיהו מבעיא יג] ליה אם כפרו על החטא שהופרשו עליו ונפקא מיניה שלא ידאג מן היסורין בינתיים: אמר רב אשי רב שישא בריה דרב אידי · דיליף יד] לא כיפרו מדבעי לאיתויי שני: הכי טו] קשיא ליה · בהבאת שני טפי מהקרבת ראשון: אי אמרת בשלמא לא כיפרו · אפילו הכי מיקרב טז] קרבי דשלא לשמו מכח לשמו קאתי דמתחילתו לשמו הוקדש ושני בא לכפר על החטא כגון אם עולה היא מכפרת על עשה או אם אשם הוא יכפר על אשמו: אעשה דלאחר הפרשה כו' · אסתם יז] עולה קאי שנזבחו לשמן: אחטאת · דלא מכפרא יח] אלא שגגת כרת דקודם הפרשה דכתיב או הודע אליו חטאתו וגו' (ויקרא ד): כיון דהאי איכא כמה עשה גביה מכפרא · שהרי לא חייב הכתוב (ז) להביאו יט] שתחייב על כל עשה ועשה אלא דורון בעלמא כ] וכתיב ונרצה לו מלמד שנתרצה להקדוש ברוך הוא (בת"כ פ' ויקרא) אלמא כולן נתכפרו: שירי מצוה · שלא נחשבה בעיניו ולא עשאה: כאילו לא כיפר וכיפר · כלומר אף על פי כן כיפר: מאי כיפר ומאי לא כיפר (ח) לאו כיפר עשה קמא דקודם הפרשה ולא כיפר עשה דסמיכה דהוה ליה לאחר הפרשה: בעמוד וסמוך קאי · ואכתי כל כמה דלא שחטיה לא עבר עליה: כיפר גברא · על כל עשה שבידו וניצל מן היסורין כא]: לא

תוספות

אחד מימר ולא שנים ממירין · משמע דלרבי יוחנן יורש מימר ותימה דבפ' מי שהוציאוהו (עירובין מו:) קאמר רבי יוחנן רבי מאיר ורבי יהודה הלכה כרבי יהודה ובריש תמורה (דף ב·) וערכין (דף ג·) פליגי בה רבי מאיר ורבי יהודה וקאמר רבי יהודה יורש אינו מימר וי"ל משום דר' יוחנן אית ליה הלכה כסתם משנה ובריש תמורה וערכין אומר הכל ממירין לאתויי יורש: **מתכפר** עושה תמורה · והא דתניא בפ' קמא דתמורה (דף ט·) לא יחליפנו בשל אחרים הא מפרש התם כגון דאמר מריה דבהמה דהקדש כל הרוצה להמיר בבהמתו ימיר: **מקופיא** מכפרא · תימה דבפ' קמא דתמורה (דף י·) ילפינן דמתכפר עושה תמורה מנזיר והיא כפרה קבועה היא וי"ל דלא יליף מנזיר אלא דמפריש אינו מימר אבל מתכפר עושה תמורה אפי' מקופיא וא"ת דיורש בקופיא גרידא כב] קרי מתכפר ומימר וכי הוו שנים יורשים מיקרו שותפין ולא ממירין והא ביומא פרק הוציאו לו (דף נ:) קבעי בפר כה"ג שאחיו הכהנים מתכפרים אי בקביעותא מתכפרין והוו שותפין ולא מצי ממיר או מקופיא מתכפרין וכולו של כהן גדול ומצי מימר דיחיד הוא אלמא לא חשיב מתכפר כשהוא מקופיא מדכהן גדול מימר ולא מיקרו שותפין מה שאחיו מתכפרין בו בקופיא וי"ל כג] דבשמעתא שניהם היורשין הוו מקופיא לכך מיקרו שותפין ולא ממירין אבל התם כיון דאיכא השתא בהאי קרבן כפרת כהן גדול דקביעא לא חשיבא לגביה אחיו כמו שותפין על ידי כפרת קופיא: **דאי** ס"ד כיפרו שני למה הוא בא · תימה כמה קרבנות אדם מתנדב ומביא זה אחר זה מיד אע"פ שכיפר הראשון שנעשה לשמו וי"ל דפריך שני למה חייב להביא ואם תאמר מאי קאמר שני למה הוא בא דלמא קאתי לכפר אמחשבה דשלא לשמן דחשיב עשה לאחר שחיטה כמו סמיכה דבסמוך ומיהו כד] יש לומר דמחשבה תלויה בעובד וקרבן לא מכפר אלא על בעליה ונראה דמאשם קדייק שאינו בא נדבה: **אלא** מאי לא כיפרו למה הוא קרב · ל"ע דהיינו קשיא דריש לקיש דאם כשירין הם ירצו ואם אינן מרצין למה הן באין: **או** דלמא לא דמיא לחטאת · תימה דנפשוט ממתני' דפ"ק דשבועות (דף ב:) דאפי' לר' שמעון דלית ליה (שם יא:) לב בית דין מתנה עליהן שעיר שלא קרב כה] עליו ברגל זה יקרב ברגל אחר אע"פ שמרגל שעברו נתכפרו כבר אטומאת מקדש וקדשיו דקודם הפרשה כו] דקאתי האי שעיר מכפר אטומאה שאחר כך ויש לומר כיון שאבד וקרב אחר תחתיו איגלאי מילתא שלא היתה הפרשתן הפרשה עד רגל אחר דשחטי ליה: **והלא** אין כפרה אלא בדם · כז] בפרק תמיד נשחט (פסחים נט:) אמרי' כל כמה דלא אכלי כהנים בשר לא מצי מכפר דכתיב ואכלו אותם אשר כופר בהם מלמד שהכהנים אוכלין בשר ובעלים מתכפרים כח] אבל מכל מקום עיקר כפרה אינה אלא בדם: **לאחר** שחיטה לא קא מיבעיא לן · בסוף הסוגיא בעי רבי ירמיה אפילו לאחר שחיטה: לא

עין משפט נר מצוה

כ א מיי' פ"א מהל' תמורה הלכה א·

כא ב מיי' שם הלכה ה:

כב ג מיי' פ"ז מהלכות ערכין הלכה ב ופ"ה מהל' מעשר שני הלכה א:

כג ד מיי' פ"ז מהלכות ערכין הלכה ד:

כד ה מיי' פ"א מהלכות תמורה הלכה ד:

כה ו מיי' פ"ד מהלכות [תרומות] הלכה ב:

כו ז מיי' פ"ג מהלכות מעה"ק הלכה יב:

מסורת הש"ס

תמורה ב:

ת"כ פרשה בחקותי

יומא נ: תמורה י. נדרים לו:

נ"א תל שותפין אהא

יומא ה: מנחות צג:

[עי' תוספות שבת עב. ד"ה כי אתא]

הגהות הב"ח

(א) גמ' אמר רב שישא בריה דר' אידי מסתברא: (ב) שם מכח לשמו קאתי ושני הוא כצ"ל ותיבת למה נמחק: (ג) שם והכא כיון דהאי איכא כמה: (ד) שם ת"ש וסמך ונרצה לו לכפר עליו וכי סמיכה: (ה) שם כאילו לא כיפר וכיפר מאי כיפר ומאי לא כיפר מאי לאו: (ו) שם אימת הוי כצ"ל ותיבת קא נמחק: (ז) רש"י ד"ה כיון דאי וכו' לא חייב הכתוב להמביאם שיתחייבו וכו' בעלמא הס"ד ואח"כ מ"ה וסמך ונרצה לו לכפר עליו מלמד וכו' אלמא כולן נתכפר: (ח) ד"ה מאי כיפר וכו' כיפר מאי לאו:

שיטה מקובצת

א] להו מסורי אות א' נמחק: ב] אי אמרת כיפרו שני למה הוא בא· תימה מאי פריך הא גלי קרא ואם לאו יהא נדבה למדנו שלא עלו לשם חובה וצריך להביא אחר וצ"ל דה"ק למה הוא בא [על מה מכפר מה] שלא כיפר הראשון ומיבעיא באשם דאי בעולה ושלמים מאי בעי ליה שני למה בא הלא הוא בא בנדבה והלא אדם מתנדב שלמים ועולה כמה שירצה וא"ת לפי מה שפרש"י דכפרו כדי להגין עליו מן היסורין מאי פריך למה הוא בא) להגין עליו מן היסורים וי"ל דה"פ כיון דכפרו עליו להגין מן היסורין שני למה הוא מביא: איבעי' להו אעשה דלאחר הפרשה מכפרא· אעולה קא בעי דמכפרת על עשה כדפרש"י לעיל · תוס' סוף: ג] לכפר לומר לך שאם: ד] וכיפר מאי כיפר מאי לא כיפר: ה] אם גאל יגאל: ו] לתתה לכל כהן אות ל' נמחק: ז] תיבת סלע נמחק: ח] טעמא מדכתיב את: ט] מכפרא כלומר כפרה קבועה שהוא קא קשיא ליה בהקרבת שני

התורש: י] דלא הל שותפין אהא וכן לענין מרצין ס"א וכן לענין; שאלתא דרב אשי לעיל: יא] ויש לו דמיון במסכת: יב] וקרבו אות י' נמחק: יג] מבעיא לן: יד] דיליף שלא: טו] הכי קא קשיא ליה בהקרבת שני [ספי] מתקרבת: טז] מקרב קרב אות י' נמחק· יז] אסתם עולות: יח] דלא מכפרא אלא על שגגת: יט] להביאו שתחייבנו: כ] בעלמא הוא וכתיב ונרצה לו מלמד שנתרצה מכל להקב"ה: כא] וניצל מן היסורין· גליון פי' אפי' לאחר הפרשה: כב] גרידא קאמרת הכא דמתכפר ומימר: כג] וי"ל ס"א דשאני התם לפי [שהוא מקבעא] לכהן הגדול ולכן [גם] כפרה דכהנים [דקופיא לא חשיבא] אבל הכא דמת [זה שהיה לו] כפרה דקבעא [לכן דקופיא חשיבא]: כד] ומיהו בזה: כה] תיבת עליו נמחק: כו] וקאתי אות ד' נמחק: כז] בדם ואע"ג דבפרק: כח] תיבת אבל נמחק:

א) מלה דל"ל יומא דבא שמני ג"כ לעגין מן היסורים·

כו א מיי' פ"ד מהלכות מחוסרי כפרה הלכה ג :

כח ב מיי' פי"ב מהלכות פסולי המוקדשין הלכה ו :

[במשנה איתא מן השמן וסיים קרא דכתיב בפרשת מצורע יד פסוק כט והנותר מן השמן אשר על כף וגו' לכפר עליו לפני ה' וכן העתיקו הילקוט ודע דלעיל בקרא יח כתיב והנותר בשמן אשר על כף וגו' וכפר עליו הכהן לפני ה']

לא כיפר קמי שמיא מי לא *תנן °והנותר *בשמן אשר על כף (א) וגו' לכפר עליו לפני ה' *אם נתן כיפר ואם לא נתן לא כיפר דברי ר"ע ר' יוחנן א] [בן נורי] אומר שירי מצוה הן בין ניתן בין שלא ניתן כיפר ומעלין עליו כאילו לא כיפר מאי כאילו לא כיפר אילימא דמבעי (ב) לאיתויי קרבן אחרינא האמרת בין ניתן בין לא ניתן כיפר אלא כיפר גברא לא כיפר קמי שמיא הכא נמי כיפר כו' התם נמי כיפר מתן בהונות ב] לא כיפר מתנות הראש ת"ש ר' שמעון אומר *כבשי עצרת למה הן באין כבשי עצרת שלמים נינהו אלא שעירי עצרת למה הן באין על טומאת מקדש וקדשיו נזרק דמו של ראשון שני למה קרב על טומאה שאורעה בין זה לזה אמור מעתה ראויין היו ישראל להקריב קרבנותיהן בכל עת ובכל שעה אלא שחיסך הכתוב ג] והא הכא דעשה דלאחר הפרשה (ג) וקא מכפרא אי דאפרשינהו בבת אחת הכי נמי הכא במאי עסקינן דאפרשינהו בזה אחר זה ד] וליקו ולימא ליה לקרא דכי כתיבא בזה אחר זה כתיבא אמר רב פפא קרבנות צבור קאמרת ג'שאני קרבנות צבור דלב בית דין קמתנה עליהן כדרב יהודה אמר שמואל *דאמר רב יהודה אמר שמואל קרבנות צבור ה] סכין מושכתן למה שהן אמר ליה רב יוסף בריה דרב ו] שמואל לרב פפא *ומי אית ליה לרבי שמעון לב בית דין מתנה עליהן *והאמר רב אידי בר אבין אמר רב עמרם אמר רבי יצחק אמר רבי יוחנן תמידין שלא הוצרכו לצבור לדברי

תורה אור ויקרא יד

לא כיפר מתנות הראש · פי' בקונט' ויביא לוג אחר ויתן מתנות הראש ולר' עקיבא צריך להתחיל בבהונות ותימה דבסוף הוציאו לו (יומא דף סא·) משמע דלכולי עלמא אין מתנות הראש מעכבות ואפילו נשפך הלוג דפליגי התם ר"א ור"ש ורבנן בנתן מקצת מתנות שבבהונות ונשפך הלוג וקתני סיפא גמר מתנות שבבהונות ונשפך הלוג דברי הכל מתנות שבראש אינן מעכבות טז] כלל דאין צריך להביא אחר דבעינן אחר אי אפשר לפרש וזהו דלא כתנאי דהכא וי"ל דלר' יוחנן בן נורי נמי אין מעכבות כלל ואין צריך לעשותן ומעיקרא ס"ד לא כיפר קמי שמיא אפילו מה שעשה כבר כגון מתנות בהונות עצמן אע"פ שנתנן אין בהן ריצוי גמור לפי שחיסר מתנות הראש אע"ג דלא מעכבי כמו שאמר לעיל שקרבן שעשה לא כיפר קמי שמיא בשביל סמיכה שלא עשה אע"ג דלא מעכבא והדר מסיק יז] ומתן בהונות שכבר עשה כיפר לגמרי שיש בהן ריצוי גמור אבל מתנות הראש לא כיפר קמי שמיא ואין צריך לעשותן דכתיב והנותר וגו' וכן הקרבן כשר וכיפר על כל עשה שקודם לכן אבל סמיכה לא כיפר דהויא לאחר הפרשה עד שיביא קרבן אחר אבל קשה על זה דלא הוי ליה לתרץ רק התם כתיב והנותר וגבי סמיכה לא כתיב והנותר וי"ל דהתם ה"פ מתנות הראש לא מעכבי דכיון שקיבל מדם האשם ומן השמן על הבהונות אינו קרוי עוד מחוסר כפורים אלא מותר לאכול בקדשים וליכנס למקדש דמתן שמן נמי קרוי קרבן כדאמר פרק בית שמאי (לקמן מד:) לכל קרבנם לרבות לוג שמן של מצורע ולכן לכל הפחות *צריך ליתן על הבהונות קודס שיהא מותר בקדשים · ברוך :

ולכן לכל הפחות א"צ ליתן על הראש קודם כו' צ"ק

וליקו ולימא ליה לקרא דכי כתיבא בזה אחר זה כתיבא · הא לא פריך דלימא ליה לקרא שלא חייב להביא שנים אלא כשהפריש בזה אחר זה אבל הפריש שנים בבת אחת יח] [אינו חייב] שזו אינו קושיא דאפי' הפריש שנים בבת אחת נהי כשקרב האחד לא מהני השני שהופרש עמו מכל מקום יכול יט] להפריש אחר כן ולהקריב ומועיל דלעולם חייבה תורה להביא שנים אלא הכי פריך דאטו מי לימא ליה לקרא כ] דכי משתעי [שצריך להקריב ב' דוקא *כשמפריש בזה אחר זה וקשה ליפרך נמי דאטו מי לימא ליה לקרא דכי משתעי] ע"י לב ב"ד ונראה דבלאו קרא הוה קשיא ליה משעירי עצרת שעושין כל שנה שדוחק הוא להעמידם ולומר שהיו מפרישין אותן בזה אחר זה : סכין מושכתן למה שהן · בסוף פרק קמא דשבועות (דף יב:) אמרינן דשמואל סבר להא דר' יוחנן כא] דהתם ובסמוך מייתי לה (ה) אמר רבי יוחנן תמידין שלא הוצרכו לצבור לדברי ר"ש אין נפדין תמימים פירוש אלא מקילין בגופן את המזבח כדקאמר התם לר' שמעון ופי' שם בקונט' דשמואל סבר לה להא דאמר רבי יוחנן כב] לדברי ר"ש אין נפדין תמימים ומקילין בהן את המזבח דאמר שמואל סכין מושכתן למה שהן פי' סכין כג] השוחטן סתם מושכתן לקרבן שהופרשו מתחילה כד] כגון עולת תמיד לעולת קיץ אע"פ שאין זה אותו קרבן כיון דמעיקרא עולה והשתא עולה והשתא קשה מאי מייתי התם תניא נמי הכי מברייתא הלא ממתני' דהתם הוה ליה לאיתויי ועוד דבהדיא מוכח בשמעתין דמילתיה דשמואל דווקא כרבנן דפליגי עליה דרבי שמעון דאית להו לב בית דין מתנה עליהן ויש פירושים ברש"י שמוגה בהן נראה בעיני דלא גרסינן הא דשמואל הכא דהא בפרק קמא דשבועות מוקמינן לה אליבא דמאן דלית ליה לב בית דין מתנה עליהן וזהו דוחק למחוק כל מילתיה דשמואל מן הספרים ועוד נראה שדברי הקונטרס סותרים זה את זה שפירש סכין מושכתן למה שהן ראויין ועומדין כגון תמידין שלא הוצרכו לצבור שנקחו מתרומה ישנה והגיע אחד בניסן מקילין בהן את המזבח ואף על גב דלשם תמידין נלקחו ולא לשם עולות נדבת צבור הואיל ולא חזו תו לציבור קרבי למאי דחזו משום דלב בית דין מתנה עליהן אם הוצרכו הוצרכו ואם לאו יקיצו בהן אלמא לפירושו לא מהני תנאי בית דין למיקרב תו לתמידין ואחר כך פירש לדברי חכמים נפדין תמימים דאית להו לב בית דין מתנה עליהן להכשירן לתמידי שנה הבאה שאם לא הוצרכו יהיו לדמיהן שיפדו אותן ממעות חולין בלא מום ויוליאום לחולין ויפלו דמיהן למותר תרומה ואחר כך יקחו אותן מתרומה חדשה ויוכשרו לתמידים ונראה כפירוש הערוך* וזה לשונו סכין מושכתן למה שהן פירוש למה שהן אם תמידין אם מוספין סכין מושכתן להיות כן אבל טרם שמושכתן הסכין אין לומר איזה תמיד ואיזה מוספין אלא תלויין ועומדין בתנאי לב בית דין שכך מתנה עליהן לב בית דין אף על פי שהמרו שהן תמידין אם ירצו להקריבן לשם זבח אחר רשאין לפי שבזמן שמשך כה] הסכין לשקיטת התמיד הרי הוא תמיד ובזמן שמשך זה הסכין לשל מוסף הרי הוא מוסף וזה סייעתא לר' יוחנן [דאמר] שאם לא הוצרכו להן [אליבא דרבנן] נפדין תמימים שלא משכתן סכין (ו) לעולם והשתא להאי פירושא לא גרסינן תניא נמי הכי דמילתא דשמואל כרבנן אלא גרסי' תניא מודה ר' שמעון כו' וטעמא

[כערך משך]

לא כיפר קמי שמיא · נגאת רוח לקונו דלא עבד מצוה מן המובחר : אם נתן · שיריים על ראש מצורע כיפר ז] כו' דכפרה אמתנות הראש כתיבא : שירי מצוה הן · דכתיב והנותר הלכך הוי כשפיכת שירי הדם דחטאת דלא מעכבי כדלקמן (דף נב·): לא כיפר מתנות הראש · ויביא לוג אחר ויתן מתנות הראש ולר' עקיבא צריך שיתחיל בבהונות : כבשי עצרת שלמים נינהו · והיכי תנא סיפא דמילתיה על טומאת מקדש וקדשיו והלא חובה ללחם הן באין להתיר את החדש במקדש למנחות ולבכורים : שעירי עצרת · גבי עצרת כתיבי שני שעירים חד בתורת כהנים ועשיתם שעיר עזים אחד לחטאת וחד בחומש הפקודים למוספין וקיימא לן במסכת שבועות (דף ב·) שעירי הרגלים באין על טומאת מקדש וקדשיו שאין בה ידיעה לא בתחילה ולא בסוף : שני למה קרב · והלא ראשון כיפר ח] לטומאה שלפניו : בין זה לזה · קס"ד בין הקרבתו של זה להקרבתו של זה : [ראויים היו ישראל כו' · דכל שעה] בספק חוטאין קיימי : אלא שחיסך הכתוב · ט] *חסך מעוטותיהם ולא דקדק אחריהם לפי שחס על ממונם וחבירו במסכת מנחות (דף עו:) מפני החיסחון ומפרש מאי מפני החיסחון התורה חסה על ממונם של ישראל : והא הכא · דטומאה שאירעה בין זה לזה עשה דלאחר הפרשה הוא שהרי מאתמול אופרשו וקתני דשני מכפר טומאת מקדש וקדשיו עשה נמי הוא דכתיב וישלחו מן המחנה וגו' (במדבר ה) : אי דאפרשינהו בבת אחת הכי נמי · דלא מכפר שני אמידי ואין צריך י] לבא : הכא במאי עסקינן · דהוצרך שני לבא יא] דאפרשינן בזה אחר זה והאי שאורעה בין זה לזה דקתני שאורעה אתמול בין הפרשתו של זה להפרשתו של זה ולעולם אעשה דלאחר הפרשה לא מכפר : וליקום ולימא ליה כו' · בתמיה אפשר שלא בא הכתוב אלא לכך והלא בכל שנה הצריכו יב] שנים : לב בית דין · יג] (העם) העוסקין בצרכי צבור מתנה עליהן שאפי' יפרישו הכהנים בבת אחת לא תהא הפרשת האחרון הפרשה עד סמוך להקרבתו כדי שיהא ראוי שני זה לבא על טומאה שאורעה בינתיים : קרבנות צבור סכין · השוחטן מושכתן למה שהן ראויים ועומדין ואפילו לא ידע השוחט מה הן יד] (או) כגון תמידין שלא הוצרכו לצבור שניקחו מתרומה ישנה והגיע אחד בניסן שמצוה להביא מן החדש כדאמרינן בראש השנה (דף ז·) שוחטן וכשרין לקיץ המזבח כדין שאר מותר תרומת כסף הנשאר בקופות טו] התרומה כשמגיע אחד בניסן שמקיילין בו את המזבח ואע"ג דלשם תמידין נלקחו ולא לשם עולת נדבת צבור כגון קיץ המזבח הואיל ולא חזו לתמידין קרבי למאי דחזו משום דלב ב"ד מתנה עליהן אם (ד) הוצרכו ואם לאו יקייצו בהן את המזבח ונראה בעיני דלא דלא גרסי לה להא דשמואל הכא דהא מוקמינן ליה בפ"ק דשבועות (דף יב:) אליבא דמאן דלית ליה לב בית דין מתנה עליהן :

גיטין פ"ד משנה ·

תוספתא דשבועות פ"א

ג"א חסך על מעוטותיהם ולא כו' ג"ק

שבועות יב:

מנחות עו:

[שבועות יא: מנחות שם]

הגהות הב"ח

(א) גמ' על כף וגו' וכפר עליו הכהן לפני ה' אם נתן : (ב) שם דמיבעי ליה לאיתויי : (ג) שם דלאחר הפרשה הוא וקא: (ד) רש"י ד"ה קרבנות וכו' אם הוצרכו הוצרכו ואם לאו : (ה) תוס' ד"ה סכין וכו' מייתי לה להא דאמר ר' יוחנן : (ו) בא"ד שלא משכתן סכין מעולם וכו':

צ"ל כשמפריש בזה אחר זה ומשני דקרא משתעי ע"י לב ב"ד כו' רש"ק

שיטה מקובצת

א] יוחנן בן נורי : ב] לא כיפר מתנות הראש' פי' הקונטרס ויביא לוג אחר כו' ולא נהירא דהא אמרינן בפ' הוציאו לו (דף ס"א) נשפך הלוג אחר שנגמר מתנותיו של בהונות דברי הכל מתנות הראש לא מעכבות [אלא נראה] דמעיקרא (הקשה) [פירש] כיפר גברא להגין מן היסורין לא כיפר קמי שמיא שלא עשה מן המובחר ודחי [דהא] לא מקרי לא כיפר בשביל כך [אלא כיפר מתן בהונות לא כיפר] מתנות הראש קמי שמיא ולא עשה בהם נחת רוח ליוצרו אבל להביא לוג אחר לכ"ע לא צריך : ג] והא הכא דעשה דלאחר הפרשה הוא · פ"ה

[דטומאה שארעה בין זה כו' וקשה] מ"מ מאי פשיט אבעייתו הוא בעי מדבר שאין בו כרת ופשיט ליה מכרת וי"ל דהוא פשיט מכ"ש מדקאמר שהוא מכפר בדבר שיש בו כרת כ"ש [בדבר שאין בו כי אם עשה לבדו] מ"מ קשה דתפשוט כמו כן בחטאת דעשה דלאחר הפרשה מכפרת ולעיל משמע דפשיטא ליה בחטאת [לא] מהני' ועוד קשה דכרת ולאו איכא נמי הכא דכתיב ולא יטמאו את מחניהם וכתיב את מקדש ה' טמא ונכרתה תו' גבי קדשים בטומאת הגוף (כרת איכא) אבל עשה ליכא כלל לכך נראה למורי דפריך משעירי עצרת אעשה דעולה דיש לספק לזה כמו לזה דטעמא מאי מספקא לן בעולה משום [דבא] על עשה טבא שעירי עצרת נמי מכפרת על טומאת מקדש וקדשיו שארעה בין רגל לרגל שעבר ושעירי הרגלים מכפרים על אין בה ידיעה לא בתחלה ולא בסוף והא דקאמר אעשה דלאחר הפרשה לאו דוקא אלא כלומר כמו עשה דעולה כדפי' תוס' הר"ש ז"ל: ד] וליקו ולימא לקרא כי כתיב בזה כו' לא מיירי קרא כי אם שהפריש שניהם בזה אחר זה אבל אם הפרישם בבת אחת אין צריך להקריב השני כך פרש"י וקשה דגם אם הפרישם בבת אחת יניח השני ויפריש אחר [ויקרבנו] וא"כ מיירי שפיר בכל ענין שיביא אותם שני שעירים אף כשהפרישם בבת אחת א) תוס' טוך: ה] עי' בהשמטות בסוף המסכת: ו] דרב שמעיה תיבת שמואל נמחק: ז] כיפר ואם לא נתן לא כיפר תיבת כו' נמחק: ח] כיפר על מה שלפניו ותיבת לטומאה ל"ש ונמחק : ט] חשך הכתוב על עונותם: י] להביא אחר תיבת לבא נמחק: יא] דאפרשינהו: יב] הצריכו הכתוב: יג] תיבת העם נמחק : יד] תיבת או נמחק: טו] בקופות של תרומה אות ה' נמחק : טז] מעכבות והעין זה קתני התם גבי מתנות של פר ושעיר של יוה"כ והיינו דאינן מעכבות כלל : יז] מסיק דמתן אות ו' נמחק : יח] בבת אחת אינו חייב 'אלא אחת : יט] יכול להביא השני שהפריש ולהפריש אחר אחר כך ולהקריבו: כ] לקרא דשנים שחייבה [תורה] לאותן שהופרשו [שלא] בבת אחת יש תימה אי קא מהני לב ב"ד דאטו מי לימא קרא דכי : כא] יוחנן דאמר התם ובסמוך מייתי לה תמידין והיבות אמר ר' יוחנן נמחק : כב] יוחנן דלדברי : כג] סכין השוחטת סתם : כד] מתחילה לכך : כה] שמשך זה הסכין של תמיד הרי ותיבת לשחיטת ואות ה' נמחק :

א) וכתוס' ד"ה וליקו כתבו ליישב זה ·

make atonement'—for the person, [6b] 'and it did not make atonement' before Heaven?[6] Did we not learn: *And the rest of the oil that is in the priest's hand he shall put upon the head of him that is to be cleansed; and the priest shall make atonement for him before the Lord;*[7] if he put [it], he made atonement; while if he did not put [it], he did not make atonement—this is the view of R. Akiba. R. Joḥanan b. Nuri said: It is but the residue of a precept,[8] therefore whether he did put [it on his head] or he did not, he made atonement, yet we regard him as though he did not make atonement. What is meant by 'as though he did not make atonement'? Shall we say, that he must bring another sacrifice? But you say, 'Whether he did put or he did not put, he made atonement'! Hence it must mean, 'It made atonement'—for the person, 'yet it did not make atonement'—before Heaven. Then here too [it may mean that] 'it did make atonement etc'!—[No:] there too it means that 'he made atone-
a ment'—in respect of putting it on the thumbs,[1] but 'he did not make atonement'—in respect of the putting it on the head.[2]

Come and hear: R. Simeon said: For what purpose are the [sacrificial] lambs of Pentecost brought?[3] [Surely] the lambs of Pentecost are peace-offerings![4] Rather the question is: For what purpose are the two he-goats of Pentecost brought?[5]—[To make atonement] for the defilement of the Temple and its holy things.[6] Now once the blood of the first has been sprinkled, for what purpose is the second offered?[7] [To make atonement] for uncleanness which [may have] occurred in the interval between the two. From this it follows that Israel should have been perpetually[8] engaged in offering their sacrifices,[9] but that Scripture spared them.[10] Now in this case it is a positive command [violated] *after* the separation [of the animals],[11] yet it makes atonement!—[No:] If they were separated at the same time, that indeed would be so;[12] but the circumstances are that they were separated one after the other.[13] Are we then to arise and assert that the written law of Scripture [that *two* are brought] holds good only [when they are separated]
b one after the other?[1]—Said R. Papa: Do you speak of *public* sacrifices? Public sacrifices are different, because the Beth din tacitly stipulates concerning them,[2] in accordance with Rab Judah's diction in Samuel's name. For Rab Judah said in Samuel's name: The knife draws them to their legitimate purpose.[3] Said R. Joseph the son of R. Samuel to R. Papa: Does then R. Simeon accept the thesis that the Beth din makes a tacit stipulation? Surely R. Idi b. Abin said in the name of R. 'Amram in the name of R. Isaac in the name of R. Joḥanan: Daily burnt-offerings which are not required

(6) I.e., it has technically made atonement, the laying of the hands not being absolutely indispensable, yet not satisfactorily, in the proper way. On this interpretation it has nothing to do with the question when these precepts were violated. (7) Lev. XIV, 18. (8) Since Scripture refers to this oil as '*the rest*'; hence it is not indispensable.

a (1) V. Lev. XIV, 14. (2) Therefore more oil must be brought for that purpose. But whereas R. Joḥanan b. Nuri holds that it is sufficient now for the oil to be put on his head, R. Akiba rules that it must also be put again on his thumbs. (3) Lev. XXIII, 18; Num. XXVIII, 27. (4) Whose purpose is to permit the use of the new wheat for meal-offerings and first-fruits. (5) V. Lev. XXIII, 19 and Num. XXVIII, 30. (6) I.e., for the sin of entering the Temple or eating the flesh of sacrifices whilst unclean. (7) Seeing that atonement has already been made with the first. The essence of atonement was the sprinkling of the blood. (8) Lit., 'at every time and every moment'. (9) For this possibility is always before us; thus, immediately the blood of the *second* has been sprinkled, a third ought to be brought, and so on. (10) For the strain and obligation would be too great. (11) They were separated the previous day. The injunction against entering the Sanctuary lies in the passage: *Command the children of Israel, that they put out of the camp ... whosoever is unclean by the dead* (Num. V, 2). Since this is expressed affirmatively, it ranks as a *positive* command. (12) The second would *not* make atonement for anything not atoned for by the first, and so it would have no purpose. (13) And the second makes atonement for the defilement which occurred in the interval on the eve of the Festival between the separations.

b (1) That is hardly feasible! (2) That no matter when they are actually separated, the last is to be regarded as though separated *immediately* prior to its being offered, and therefore it makes atonement up to that very moment. (3) If an animal is slaughtered as a public sacrifice, yet for a purpose other than for which they had been originally intended the knife, as it were, automatically dedicates it to a legitimate purpose, and the sacrifice is valid. The reason is that Beth din is regarded as tacitly stipulating their purpose (v. Shebu. 12b), and so the same holds good here too.

for the community[4] [7a] cannot be redeemed, according to R. Simeon's view, as long as they are unblemished, while on the view of the Sages they can be redeemed while unblemished.[5] Moreover,[6] surely R. Jeremiah asked R. Zera: If the blood of the Pentecostal he-goats was received in two basins,[7] and the blood of one was
a sprinkled, what is the purpose of the second?[1] [To which he replied:] On account of defilement that occurred between the sprinkling [of the blood] of the one and that of the other. Thus he is in doubt only in respect of [the violation of] a positive command after the *slaughtering*, but he does not ask in respect of [the violation of] a positive command after the *separating* [of the animal]![2]—[No:] Perhaps his question is hypothetical.[3]

It was taught: If one slaughtered a thanksoffering in the name of his fellow's thanksoffering,[4]—Rabbah ruled: It is valid;[5] while R. Ḥisda said: It is invalid. Rabbah ruled, 'It is valid', [because] a thanksoffering has been slaughtered as a thanksoffering. R. Ḥisda said, 'It is invalid', because it must be slaughtered in the name of *his* peace-offering.[6] Rabbah said: Whence do I know it? Because it was taught: *And the flesh of his peace-offerings for thanksgiving shall be eaten on the day of his offering*:[7] Abba Ḥanin said on R. Eliezer's authority: This comes to teach that if a thanksoffering is slaughtered in the name of a peace-offering, it is valid; if a peace-offering is slaughtered in the name of a thanksoffering, it is invalid. What is the difference between these two cases? A thanksoffering is designated a peace-offering, but a peace-offering is not designated a thanksoffering.[8] Thus a peace-offering [slaughtered] as a thanksoffering is invalid, whence it follows that a thanksoffering [slaughtered] as a [different] thanksoffering is valid. Surely that means, [even in the name] of his fellow's [thanksoffering].[9] No: only [when brought in the name of] his own.[10] But what if it is [in the name of] his fellow's: it is invalid? Then instead of teaching, 'if a *peace-offering* is slaughtered in the name of a *thanksoffering*, it is invalid', let him teach, 'if a *thanksoffering* [is slaughtered in the name of] a *thanksoffering* [of a different class, it is invalid], and how much more so a peace-offering in the name of a thanksoffering?—He wishes to teach of a peace-offering [slaughtered] in the name of *his own* thanks-
b offering.[1] You might argue, Since a thanksoffering is designated a peace-offering, a peace-offering too is designated a thanksoffering, and when he kills it [the former] in the name of the thanksoffering, it should be valid. Therefore he informs us [that it is not so].

Raba said: If one slaughters a sin-offering [for one offence] as a sin-offering [for another offence], it is valid; as a burnt-offering, it is invalid.[2] What is the reason? The Divine Law saith, *And he shall kill it for a sin-offering*,[3] and lo, a sin-offering has been slaughtered for a sin-offering; [while from the same verse we learn that if it is slaughtered] for a burnt-offering, it is invalid.[4]

Raba also said: If one slaughters a sin-offering on behalf of [another] person who is liable to a sin-offering, it is invalid; on behalf of one who is liable to a burnt-offering, it is valid. What is the reason?—[*And the priest*] *shall make atonement for him*,[5] but not for his fellow, and 'his fellow' implies one like himself, being in need of atonement as he is.[6]

Raba also said: If one slaughters a sin-offering on behalf of a person who is not liable in respect of anything at all,[7] it is invalid, because there is not a single Israelite who is not liable in respect of an affirmative precept; and Raba said: A sin-offering makes atonement for those who are liable in respect of an affirmative precept, *a fortiori*: seeing that it makes atonement for those who are liable to *kareth*, how much the more for those who are liable in respect of an affirmative precept![8] Shall we then say that it belongs to the same category?[9] But surely Raba said: If one slaughters a sin-offering on behalf of [another] person who is liable to a sin-offering, it is invalid; on behalf of a person who is liable to a burnt-offering,

(4) 'Not required' means here not fit as such. There was an annual levy of one *shekel* for the public sacrifices, which was to be paid not later than the first of Nisan. From that date the statutory public sacrifices had to be purchased from the new funds, and not from the old. If animals however were purchased with the old funds, they were offered as extra public sacrifices (if it happened at any time that there was a paucity of private sacrifices), but not as the statutory public sacrifices, such as the daily burnt-offering. (5) For we assume a tacit stipulation of the Beth din that it be permitted to redeem them even while unblemished (normally this is forbidden) and thus, becoming *ḥullin*, they can be purchased with the new *shekels* and then be offered as daily burnt-offerings. R. Simeon however rejects this assumption, and therefore holds that they cannot be redeemed but must be offered as extra public sacrifices. (6) Even assuming that the Biblical text itself might be explained as referring to the case where the two goats were separated one after the other. (7) They were both killed at the same time.
a (1) According to R. Simeon, since no defilement could occur in the interval, as they were killed simultaneously. (2) Presumably R. Jeremiah was certain that according to R. Simeon it does make atonement in that case. (3) He may be in doubt about the latter too, but his question is this: on the hypothesis that R. Simeon holds that it does make atonement in the latter case, how is it in the former one? (4) A and B each brought one, and A's offering was killed for the purpose for which B's was brought. (5) He has done his duty, and does not bring another. (6) Cf. Lev. VII, 15: *And the flesh of* his *peace-offerings for thanksgiving*. (7) Ibid. (8) *Supra* 4a. (9) Belonging to a different class. (10) Even if he killed it for a different *reason*. E.g., he brought a thanksoffering for being freed from prison, but declared it to be on account of having made a sea-journey in safety. Here, though the reason is different, yet both belong to the same category, and therefore it is valid.
b (1) Where he was to bring both. (2) V. *Supra* 3b. (3) Lev. IV, 33. (4) V. *infra* 7b. (5) Ibid 26, 31, 35. (6) V. *Supra* 3b. (7) Actually specifying thus. (8) Hence it is the same as though he had slaughtered it on behalf of another person who is liable to a sin-offering. (9) I.e., that sins of omission fall into the same category as offences entailing a sin-offering.

לדברי ר' שמעון אין נפדין תמימים *לדברי חכמים °נפדין תמימין ועוד הא בעא מיניה ר' ירמיה מר' זירא שעירי עצרת שקבל דמן בשני כוסות ונזרק דמו של ראשון שני למה הוא א] בא על טומאה שאורעה בין [זריקה של] זה לזה (נזרק דמו של שני למה הוא קריבין) עד כאן לא מיבעיא ליה אלא עשה דלאחר שחיטה אבל עשה דלאחר הפרשה לא קא מיבעיא ליה דלמא אם תימצי לומר קאמר: איתמר תודה ששחטה לשם תודת חבירו ב] (כשרה) רבה אמר כשרה רב חסדא אמר פסולה רבה אמר כשרה תודה לשם תודה נשחטה רב חסדא אמר פסולה (א) ג] לשום שלמים דידיה ד] נשחטה בעינן אמר רבה מנא אמינא לה *דתניא °ובשר זבח תודת שלמיו ביום הקריבו את זבחו וגו' אבא חנין אמר משום ר' אליעזר בא ללמד °תודה ששחטה לשם שלמים כשרה שלמים שנשחטו לשם תודה פסולים ומה הפרש בין זה לזה °תודה קרויה שלמים ואין שלמים קרויין תודה שלמים לשם תודה פסולה הא תודה לשם תודה כשרה מאי לאו דחבריה לא דידיה אבל דחבריה מאי פסולה אדתני שלמים ה] לשם תודה פסולה ליתני תודה לשם תודה וכ"ש שלמים לשם תודה שלמים לשם תודה דידיה איצטריך ליה סלקא דעתך אמינא מדתודה קרויה שלמים שלמים נמי קרויין תודה וכי שחיט להו לשם תודה ליכשרו קא משמע לן: אמר *רבא °חטאת ששחטה לשם חטאת כשירה לשם עולה ו] פסולה מאי טעמא °ושחט אותה לחטאת אמר רחמנא והרי חטאת לשם חטאת נשחטה לשם עולה פסולה ואמר רבא *חטאת ששחטה על מי שמחוייב חטאת פסולה °על מי שמחוייב עולה כשרה מאי טעמא וכפר עליו *עליו ולא על חבירו חבירו דומיא דידיה במחוייב כפרה כמותו ואמר רבא *חטאת °ששחטה ז] על מי שאינו מחוייב כלום פסולה שאין לך אדם בישראל שאינו מחוייב עשה ואמר רבא חטאת מכפרת על חייבי עשה מק"ו על חייבי כריתות מכפרת על חייבי עשה לא כל שכן למימרא דבת מינה היא והאמר רבא חטאת ששחטה על מי שמחוייב חטאת פסולה ח] על מי שמחוייב עולה כשרה מקיבעא

לדברי רבי שמעון אין נפדין תמימין · דהכי גמר לה רבי יוחנן מרביה דפליגי בה רבי שמעון ורבנן לרבי שמעון לית ליה לב ב"ד מתנה עליהן ט] להכשירן לתמידי שנה הבאה [לומר] אם הוצרכו הוצרכו ואם לאו יהא קדושים לדמיהן שיפדו אותן ממעות חולין בלא מום ויוציאם לחול ויפלו דמיהם למותר תרומה ואחר כך יחזרו ויקחו אותם מתרומה חדשה י] ויוכשרו לתמידין ולדברי חכמים נפדין תמימים דאית להו לב בית דין מתנה עליהן תנאי זה אלמא לית ליה לרבי שמעון לב בית דין מתנה עליהן יא] (בהן) דאי אית ליה יוכשרו לתמידין ולא יקיילו יב] *אלא לית [ליה לב ב"ד מתנה] כך שמעתי בשבועות: ועוד · אי נמי בעית למימר דקרא דחיק ומוקי אנפשיה כשהפרישן בזה אחר זה ובטומאה דערב יום טוב קאמר מי מלית למימר דכי קתני שאירעה בין זה לזה בהפרשה קאמר והא בעא מיניה כו': בשתי כוסות · יג] נשחטין כאחד ואין שהות לאורועי טומאה בין שחיטתיהן ונזרק דמו של ראשון שני למהקרב לר' שמעון הרי אין יד] טומאה בין זה לזה ואמר ליה לטומאה שאורעה בין זריקתו של זה לזריקתו של זה: ע"כ לא מיבעיא טו] כו' · אפילו לרבי ירמיה לא טז] מתמה אלא אי מכפר אעשה דלאחר שחיטתו אי לא מכלל דפשיטא ליה דבין זה לזה דקאמר רבי שמעון בטומאת י"ט קאמר יז] בין שחיטתו של זה לשחיטתו של יח] זה: דלמא אם תמצא לומר קאמר · דלמא תרוייהו קמיבעיא ליה והכי קמיבעיא ליה האי בין זה לזה דקאמר רבי שמעון קודם הפרשה קאי או לאחר הפרשה קאי ואם תימצי לומר יט] אחר הפרשה נמי קאי קודם שחיטה או אפילו לאחר שחיטה עד זריקה ואהדר ליה איהו אפילו עד זריקה כ] ודלמא לא קיימא לן כר' זירא ולא איפשיטא בעיין: תודה ששחטה לשם תודת חבירו · לא ששחטה ע"מ שיתכפר בה מי שאינו בעליה* כא] ואין זה שינוי בעלים *אלא שינוי קודש שהיתה לראובן תודה ולשמעון תודה אחרת ושחט את תודתו של זה לשם תודתו של זה כב] *[וה"ה] בשוחט חטאת חלב לשם חטאת דם: כשרה · ועולה לבעלים דאפי' שינוי קדש אין כאן: פסולה · כג] לא עלתה לבעלים דשינוי קדש הוא: לשם שלמים דידיה בעינן · דכתיב זבח תודת שלמיו והאי דאיפלוג בתודה משום דמינה מייתי רבה סייעתא למילתיה מדאבא חנן ומיהו ה"ה לשאר זבחים: כשרה · עלתה לבעלים: פסולין · לא עלו: לא דידיה · כד] ואע"פ שלא באו על הודייה אחת דארבעה צריכין להודות כדאמרינן בברכות (דף נד:) וכתיב בהו (תהלים קז) ויזבחו זבחי תודה ושחט תודה בשעת עלייתו מן הים לשם תודה שהפריש על יציאתו מבית האסורין כה]: חטאת ששחטה לשם חטאת · כגון חטאת חלב שנשחטה לשם חטאת דם: כשרה · ועלתה לו: פסולה · פסולה לגמרי כדתנן חוץ מן הפסח והחטאת: על מי שמחוייב חטאת · בשינוי בעלים על מנת לזרוק דמה לשם חבירו המחוייב חטאת כמותו: שאינו מחוייב עשה · שלא עבר כו] עשה ובעשה שייך למימר חטאת כדמפרש ואזיל: ואמר רבא חטאת מכפרת על חייבי עשה · הלכך מחוייב כפרה כמותו הוא: למימרא · דעשה בת מינה דחטאת היא: והאמר רבא כו' על מי שמחוייב עולה כשרה · כז] אלמא לאו מיניה הוא דהא כח] עבירות עשה בידו שהפריש עולה עליהן: מקיבעא

וטעמא משום דכהן לכפר על [טומאת] מקדש וקדשיו (ב) כמתניתין דהתם ובברייתא. חידש טפי ממתניתין והא דקתני שתחלתו לא בא אלא לכפר על מזבח החיצון לאפוקי שעיר הפנימי דבעינן תרתי טומאת. מקדש ומזבח החיצון ואף על גב דמשמע התם דאי כט] לא משום גזירה (ג) הוי מקילין בגופן אפי' במותר חטאות הפנימיות הייט משום דהכי גמירי דמותר חטאות לבור לעולה ורבינו חננאל מפרש כפירוש הערוך וגריס התם תניא נמי הכי *וקאי אמילתא דרבי יוחנן דאמר דלרבי שמעון מקילין בהן בגופן הואיל ומעיקרא עולה והשתא עולה אבל לא במותר חטאת כו' ותימה אמאי נטר עד לסוף דלעיל הוה ליה לאתויי:

דלמא אם תימצי לומר קאמר · ורבי זירא נמי שהשיב נמי לרבי ירמיה על טומאה שאירעה בין זו לזו כמו כן אם תימצי לומר קאמר וקושיא ראשונה ומי אית ליה לרבי שמעון לב בית דין מתנה לא חש לתרץ דאיכא למימר דאפרשינהו בזה אחר זה ולית חושש בקושיא דליקו ולימא ליה לקרא כו' *ועוד דהיכא דלית ליה תקנתא ברעייה אית ליה לרבי שמעון לב בית דין מתנה כדמוכח במנחות פ' התודה (עט:) ומיהו האמוכח דהיכא דאית ליה תקנתא ברעייה לית ליה לב בית דין מתנה וכאן אית ליה תקנתא ברעייה:

תודה ששחטה לשם תודת חבירו ל] כשרה · ועולה לשם חובה משום שטי בעלים לא מיפסלא דאין שינוי בעלים אלא (א"כ) בזריקה ורב חסדא אמר פסולה פירוש לא עלתה לשם חובה משום דאי שינוי קודש כשאמר תודת פלוני לשם תודה אחרת של פלוני אבל אמר תודה זו לשם פלוני כשרה גמורה לפי שהוא שינוי בעלים בשחיטה *דכשירה גמורה:

הגה"ה רב חסדא אמר פסולה · נראה דוקא בתודה פליג משום דכתיב לא] בהן קרא שלמיו ובקונטרס פירש דהוא הדין בשאר קרבנות:

אמר רבא חטאת ששחטה לשם חטאת כשרה · פירש רבינו תם *דרבה כרב חסדא ס"ל דהא דרבה אידחי וטעמא דתודה משום *שלמים משמע דר"ל דאיירי ששחטה לשם חטאת חבירו ונראה דלאו בהכי מיירי מדלא קאמר בהדיא חבירו אלא מיירי בחטאת חלב לשם חטאת דם לב] כדאמר רבא לקמן בפירקין (דף ט:) חטאת חלב ששחטה לשם חטאת דם לשם חטאת עבודת כוכבים כשרה לשם חטאת נזיר לשם חטאת מצורע פסולה הני עולות נינהו ואם תאמר ותרתי *דרבה למה לי ויש לומר דהך דהכא נקט לאשמועינן דשינוי קודש איפכא משינוי בעלים אע"ג דרבא לא פירש הפסוקים כדבריו מדאמר בריש פירקין (לעיל דף ג:) דרב יוסף בר אמי רמי שינוי קודש *) לג] ומשני [והא] דלקמן נקט לחלק בחטאות וגם משום בעיא דאחר כך דבעי רבא חטאת חלב ששחטה לשם חטאת דטומאת מקדש וקדשיו מהו:

חטאת ששחטה על מי שמחוייב עולה כשרה · וכגון שלא הפרישה עדיין דאי הפרישה הוה ליה כעל מי שאינו מחוייב כלום אם תימצי לומר דלא מכפרא אעשה דלאחר הפרשה דמסתמא עולה יביא ויכפר על הכל א"נ דאמר הרי עלי עולה דכשיפרישנה יכפר על כל עשה שעבר:

על מי שאינו מחוייב כלום פסולה · **) אי דגרסינן בהא מימרא עולה דגבי עולה נמי כתיב לכפר עליו דאי גרסינן הכא חטאת ל"ל אידך מילתא דרבא דחטאת מכפרת על חייבי עשה מהכא שמעינן לה:

על חייבי עשה לא כל שכן · מהאי קל וחומר הוה לן למימר דאפילו מקיבעא מכפרא אלא דאינה מכפרא הואיל ועיקרא למילתא אחריתי קאתיא ואהני קל וחומר לקופיא: עולה

*) נ"ל אשינוי בעלים **) נ"א אית דגרסי ל"ק

כט א מיי' פ"ד מהל' שקלים הלכה יא:
ל ב מיי' פט"ו מהלכות פסה"מ הלכה יג:
לא ג מיי' שם הלכה ז:
לב ד מיי' שם הלכה ח:
לג ה מיי' שם הלכה ט והלכה יד:

וקאי אמילתא דרב שמואל בר יצחק דאמר דלר"ש דוקא תמידין מקילין בהם כו'

גירסת הצ"ק ועוד היכא דלית ליה תקנתא בקיץ המזבח איכא לר"ש לב ב"ד מתנה ומיהו הא מוכח במנחות בפ' התודה דהיכא דאית ליה תקנתא ברעייה וכו' כצ"ל

שנוי בעלים בשחיטה הס"ד

[לעיל ג:] [נ"ל דרבא] [לעיל ג: ה. לקמן ח: פסחים סב:] [נ"ל שלמיו דידיה]

שבועות י: | מהרש"ק מ"ז | ולא יקייצו אלא לייתו בדמיהן נ"ק | [לעיל ד.] | ויקרא ז | [לעיל ג: איתא רב] | ויקרא ד

וגי' הצ"ק בעליה הוא שינוי בעלים אלא דאיירי בשינוי קודש כו' כצ"ל

תודתו של זה הס"ד ואח"כ ד"ה כשרה ועולה לבעלים דאפי' ש"ק אין כאן דהוי כשוחט חטאת חלב לשם חטאת דם הס"ד ואח"כ ד"ה פסולה כו'

הגהות הב"ח

(א) גמ' רב חסדא אמר פסולה נשחטה לשם שלמים דידיה בעינן: (ב) תוס' ד"ה (כדף קודם) סכינכו' מקדש וקדשיו דתני במתני' התם ובברייתא חידש טפי ממתניתין דקתני כצ"ל ותיבת והא נמחק: (ג) שם דאי לאו משום גזרה אטו לפני כפרה הוו מקילין:

גליון הש"ס

גמ' תודה קרויה שלמים· כעין זה מנחות דף טו ע"א ועיין לקמן דף סג ע"ב תוס' ד"ה מנחה ובמנחות דף ע"ב תוס' ד"ה מדאפקעינהו: שם חטאת ששחטה לשם חטאת כשרה· עיין נזיר דף כז ע"ב תוס' ד"ה שהרי:

שיטה מקובצת

א] הוא קרב על טומאה שארעה בין זה לזה עד כאן לא מיבעיא כו' והשאר נמחק: ב] תיבת כשרה נמחק: ג] לשם שלמים: ד] תיבת נשחטה נמחק: ה] שלמים דידיה לשם: ו] עולה ודאי פסולה: ז] על מי שאינו מחויב כלום פסולה דהוי שפיר מחויב כפרה כמותה כדמפרש ואזיל ואמר רבא כו' ולפרושי מלתא קמייתא אתא: ח] על מי שמחויב עולה כשרה' אלמא לאו מינה הוא והא הכא עבירות עשה בידו שהפריש עולה עליה ומשני מקיבעא לא מכפרא כו' כך פי' הקונטרס ומ"מ קשה היאך פשיטא ליה לרבא דפסול והא לקמן מספקא ליה לרבא אפי' על חטאת חלב ששחטה על מי שמחוייב חטאת דטומאת מקדש וקדשיו דשמא לא הוי מחוייב כפרה כמותו לפי שאינה קבועה כמותה כ"ש על מי שאינו מחוייב כלום לכך נ"ל דגרסי' עולה ששחטה על מי שאינו מחוייב כו' דגבי עולה הוא דכתיב וכיפר עליה הכהן ואמר רבא חטאת כו' ועלה פריך למימרא דבת מינה היא ולא בעי לשנויי דלכך כי שחטה על מי שמחוייב עולה כשרה משום דלא גרע מטומאת מקדש וקדשיו משום דלא בעי למיפשט בעיא דרבא דלקמן ולכך משני משום דמקיבעא לא מכפרי תוס' שוך: ט] עליהן להכשיר: י] חדשה ויתכשרו לתמידין זה לא נאמר אלא יעשה מהן קיץ למזבח: יא] תיבת בהן ל"ש ונמחק: יב] יקייצו בהן אלא ברמיהן כך שמעתי בשבועות והשאר ל"ש ונמחק: יג] ששחטן תיבת נשחטין נמחק: יד] אין כאן טומאה: טו] מבעיא כלומר: טז] לא מבעיא תיבת מתמה נמחק: יז] קאמר שהייתה: יח] של האחר והיינו עשה דלאחר הפרשה הס"ד: יט] לומר לאחר: כ] זריקה ס"א ואין למיפשט בעיין מתשובת ר' זירא [דאפשר] דהשיב באת"ל [דאת"ל] דאינו מכפר על עשה דלאחר הפרשה כמו [כן שעירי עצרת דמכפרין] על טומאת מקדש וקדשיו [ליכא למבעיא על טומאה שבין] שחיטה לשחיטה [דהא דהשיב] רבי זירא על [הבעיא] דלעיל דאמר [על טומאה שאירעה] לאחר שחיטת הראשון לא למיפשט האבעיא דאבעיא לן דודאי ר' זירא לא פליג ארבא [דסבר דליכא למיפשט האבעיא אלא] דהשיב באת"ל הואיל והוא שאל באת"ל [דמכפר אעשה דלאחר הפרשה אם עד אחר שחיטה] או עד זריקה כו': כא] בעליה ס"א לפי שזהו שינוי בעלים והכא בשינוי קודש איירי: כב] זה ס"א ולא שיתכפר בה אחר אלא בשחט כו' תיבות וה"ה ל"ש ונמחק: כג] פסולה אין פסולה ממש אלא לא: כד] דידיה וקכ"ל אע"פ: כה] האסורין כיון דדידיה נינהו הס"ד: כו] על עשה: כז] כשרה ועולה מכפרת אעשה: כח] דהא הכא עבירות כו' עליה הס"ד: כט] דאי לאו משום: ל] רבה אמר כשרה: לא] דכתיב בה: לב] דם כדפי' בקונטרס: לג] קודש אשינוי בעלים ועוד דהא ס"א והא דלקמן:

מקיבעא לא מכפרא מקופיא מכפרא *ואמר רבא עולה ששחטה שלא לשמה אסור לזרוק דמה שלא לשמה איבעית אימא קרא איבעית אימא סברא איבעית אימא קרא °מוצא שפתיך תשמור וגו׳ איבעית אימא סברא משום דשני בה כו׳ כדריש (א) פירקא ואמר רבא עולה הבאה לאחר מיתה שחטה בשינוי קודש פסולה *בשינוי בעלים כשרה דאין בעלים לאחר מיתה *ורב פנחס בריה דרב אמי אמר יש בעלים לאחר מיתה אמר ליה רב אשי לרב פנחס בריה דרב אמי דוקא קאמר מר יש בעלים לאחר מיתה ובעי לאיתויי עולה אחריתי או דלמא דאי איכא כמה עשה גביה מכפרא א״ל דוקא קאמינא ואמר רבא עולה דורון היא היכי דמי אי דליכא תשובה °זבח רשעים תועבה ואי דאיכא תשובה א] *והתניא ב׳עבר על מצות עשה ושב לא זז משם עד שמוחלים לו אלא ש״מ דורון הוא (חטא״ת ע״ל מ״י מכפ״ר עול״ה לאח״ר דורו״ן סימ״ן) תניא נמי הכי א״ר שמעון חטאת למה באה לכפר אלא ג׳למה באה לפני עולה *לפרקליט שנכנס ב] [ריצה פרקליט נכנס] דורון אחריו: חוץ מן ד׳הפסח ה׳והחטאת כו׳: פסח מנלן דכתיב °שמור את חדש האביב ועשית פסח שיהו כל עשיותיו לשם פסח ג] אשכחן שינוי קודש שינוי בעלים מנלן דכתיב °ואמרתם זבח פסח הוא שתהא זביחה לשם פסח אם אינו ענין לשינוי קודש תנהו ענין לשינוי בעלים אשכחן למצוה לעכב מנלן אמר קרא °וזבחת פסח לה׳ אלהיך וגו׳ מתקיף לה רב ספרא האי וזבחת להכי הוא דאתא האי מיבעי ליה לכדרב נחמן דאמר רב נחמן אמר רבה בר אבוה מנין *) למותר ו׳פסח שקרב שלמים שנאמר °וזבחת פסח לה׳ אלהיך צאן ובקר והלא אין פסח בא אלא מן הכבשים ומן העזים ד] מכאן למותר הפסח שיהא לדבר הבא מן הצאן ומן הבקר ומאי נידהו שלמים אלא אמר רב ספרא וזבחת פסח לכדרב נחמן שמור את חדש האביב (ב) למצוה בשינוי קודש ואמרתם זבח פסח ה] בשינוי בעלים למצוה הוא לעכב בין הכא והכא ואשכחן זביחה שאר עבודות מנלן הואיל *וגלי גלי רב אשי אמר הואיל וגלי גלי לא אמרינן אלא [עבודות] מנלן דכתיב °זאת התורה לעולה ולמנחה וגו׳ ותניא °ביום צותו את בני ישראל להקריב את קרבניהם זה בכור ומעשר ופסח הקישו הכתוב לשלמים מה שלמים בין שינוי קודש בין שינוי בעלים בעינן למצוה אף כל בין שינוי קודש בין שינוי בעלים למצוה *וכשלמים מה שלמים בין זביחה בין שאר עבודות לא חלקת בהן למצוה אף פסח לא תחלוק בו בין זביחה לשאר עבודות לעכב ו] (משום שנאמר הוא בזביחה אינו אלא לעכב) אלא הוא למה לי (ג) כדתניא ז] נאמר בפסח הוא בשחיטה לעכב *אבל אשם לא נאמר בו הוא אלא לאחר הקטרת אימורין והוא עצמו שלא הוקטרו אימוריו כשר: חטאת מנלן דכתיב °ושחט אותה לחטאת שתהא שחיטה לשם חטאת אשכחן שחיטה קבלה מנלן דכתיב ולקח

*) פסחים ע: מנחות פג: [לקמן ט.]

עולה דורון היא · אע״ג דאעשה מכפרת יותר מחטאת דהא מכפרא מקיבעא: ריצה פרקליט · אע״ג דאיכא עולת יולדת ומצורע וכזיר דלא מייתי קרבן אלא לאישתרויי בקדשים כדאמר בפרק בתרא דכריתות (דף כו·) *ואפילו הם חטאתם קודמת לעולה דלא חלקה תורה:

מקיבעא לא מכפרא · חטאת עשה: מקופיא מכפרא · הלכך על מי שמחוייב עולה כשרה ח] כיון [דהפריש] עולה שייכי כולהו עשה שבידו לעולה ותו לא שייך חטאת גביה אבל מי שלא הפריש כלום ועבירות עשה בידו שייך חטאת גביה דאילו הוה מתחייב חטאת מכפר עשה מקופיא הלכך חייל שמיה אחטאתו שנשחטה לשמו לפוסלה: לאחר מיתה · שמת בעליה והקריבה היורש: פסולה · לא עלתה (ד) ׳וצריך היורש להביא אחרת: יש בעלים · שהיורש הוא בעליה: דוקא קאמר מר · *אי פליגי אדרבא ובעי לאתויי אחריתי או דלמא דאי איכא כמה עשה גביה ט] דיורש מכפרא אם לא שינה בה ומיהו היכא דשני לא בעי לאיתויי אחריתי דהא איהו לא נדר מידי: עולה דורון היא · אינה באה לכפר על עשה כפרה ממש אלא אחר שכפרה התשובה על העשה היא באה להקבלת פנים כאדם שסרח במלך וריצהו ע״י פרקליטין וכשבא להקביל פניו מביא דורון בידו: היכי דמי · כלומר י] היכי דמי שתהא באה לכפרה: אי דליכא תשובה · אעבירות עשה שבידו: זבח רשעים תועבה · פסוקיהוא במשלי (כא): למה באה לפני עולה · כל מקום שמביא חטאת ועולה חטאת קודם כדיליף לקמן בפרק כל התדיר (דף פט:): פרקליט · מליץ טוב: פסח מנלן (ה) · בין למצוה בין לעכב יא] דקס״ד לא אתי לן כשאר זבחים משלמים דלא כתיב בההוא קרא דזאת התורה דאיתרבי כל הזבחים מיניה למצוה: מותר הפסח · שאבד יב] *ונתכפר באחר ונמצא הראשון: לדבר הבא מן הצאן ומן הבקר · הייט שלמים שהן באין מכל צאן ומכל בקר בין זכרים בין נקבות מה שאין כן בשאר זבחים שהוקבעו או בזכר או בנקבה עולה ואשם הוקבעו בזכרים חטאת הוקבע בנקבות והוקבע בזכרים כגון שעיר נשיא אינו בא יג] בנקבה: למצוה בשינוי קודש· יד] בכולהו עשיות ילפינן מיניה דהא כתיב ועשית הוא טו] · משמע פסח הוא בהוייתו לשמו כשר שלא לשמו פסול: טז] דהכא והכא · בשינוי קודש ובשינוי בעלים דהוא משמע אתרוייהו כשהוא עשוי כמצותו משמע: ואשכחן זביחה · בשינוי [קודש ובשינוי] בעלים: ביום צותו · יז] סמוך לזאת התורה ודרשינן סמוכין ביום צותו להקריב את קרבניהם לרבות קרבנות שלא הוזכרו במקרא בענין שלמעלה: אף כל כו׳ · הלכך (ו) מצוה בפסח ילפינן משלמים דרבינן להו לעיל לשינוי קודש ולשינוי בעלים (ועשית פסח לעכב בכל עשיותיו בשינוי קדש ואמרתם זבח פסח לעכב בזביחה בשינוי בעלים): וכשלמים · כלומ׳ כיון דגלי קרא עכובא בזביחה ילפינן שאר עבודות לעכובא מהיקשא דמצוה כשלמים מה שלמים כו׳: הכי גרסי׳ אלא הוא למה לי לכדתניא יח] [וכו׳] אבל אשם לא נאמר כו׳ ול״ג כל מקום שנאמר יט] בזביחה (ז) איט· אלא לעכב דהך ברייתא לקמן היא בפירקין בדינא ר׳ אליעזר ורבי יהושע ול״ג ליה: לכדתניא · כלומר לגלויי על הוא דגבי אשם דלא ילפינן פסול מיניה כדמהדר ליה רבי יהושע לר׳ אליעזר לקמן בפירקין (דף י:) שהיה דורש אשם הוא לשמו כשר שלא לשמו פסול וקא מהדר ליה רבי יהושע פסח נאמר בו הוא בשחיטה לפיכך שלא לשמו פסול אבל אשם כו׳:

ואמרתם זבח פסח הוא׳ קרא כתיב ברישא ושמור את חודש האביב הוה ליה לאוקומי כ] [בשינוי בעלים] באם אינו ענין אלא משום דכייל בה כל עבודות דכתיב ועשית פסח כא] [דמשמע] מסתמא כל עשיות הלכך מוקי ליה לשינוי קודש כב]: וזבחת פסח · בסוף התודה (מנחות פב·) דריש לה במשנה לדבר שבחובה [שיהא באה מן החולין] והתם בגמרא כג] נמי מייתי דרשא דהכא: ומאי ניהו שלמים · דעולה ליכא למימר דאינה באה מכל צאן ובקר כדפי׳ בקונטרס דאינה באה נקבה ועוד איכא לקמן תלתא קראי וההוא דאם כבש מוכח בהדיא דהוי שלמים ועוד דדוחין קדשים קלים אצל קדשים קלים ולא אצל קדשי קדשים כדלקמן (דף ט·): וזבחת פסח לכדרב נחמן · בסיפרי פרשת עשר תעשר דריש כולהו בשנוי קודש והכי איתא התם *וזבחת אין לי אלא זביחה שאר עבודות מנין כד] ואשינוי [קודש] קאי ת״ל ועשית יכול אף הקטר חלבו ת״ל וזבחת ואין זה בסוגיא שלנו: הוא לעכב בין הכא בין הכא · בשינוי קודש בכל עבודות בשינוי בעלים בזביחה אע״ג דהוא בזביחה כתיב כה] בפרשת בא אל פרעה וקרא דועשית בפרשת ראה אנכי מכל מקום משמע הוא בהוייתו כשהוא עשוי כמצותו כדפי׳ בקונטרס והשתא הא דקאמר אשכחן זביחה שאר עבודות מנא לן אשינוי בעלים קאי עוד יש לפרש דבין בשינוי קודש בין בשינוי בעלים קבעי מנא לן לעכב דהוא קאי דוקא אזביחה ומדאפקיה רחמנא לשינוי בעלים בלשון שינוי קודש אית לן לאוקומי כו] הא דזביחה לעכב בין בשינוי בעלים בין בשינוי קודש ושינויא דהואיל וגלי גלי לא ניחא להאי פירושא כמו לפירוש קמא: מה שלמים בין בזביחה בין בשאר עבודות לא חלקת בהן · *וא״ת כיון דכתיב ועשית פסח לעכב בשינוי קודש בכל עשיות לשתוק קרא כז] מזביחה ותיתי משלמים דמה שלמים לא חלקת בין בשינוי קודש לשינוי בעלים למצוה אף לפסח לא תחלוק לעכב: אלא הוא למה לי · לקמן בפרק בית שמאי (דף לז:) ובפסחים פרק מי שהיה טמא (דף צז·) דריש הוא דפסח למעוטי תמורת פסח ותרי הוא כתיבי ובפסחים בסוף תמיד נשחט (דף סג:) דריש רבי אליעזר מהוא דפסח לא הוא כשר לשם אחרים ולא אחרים כשרין לשמו ורבי אליעזר לטעמיה דאית ליה עכובא באשם ולא מוקי ליה למימר אבל אשם לא נאמר בו הוא כו׳: כל מקום שנאמר הוא בזביחה · פירש בקונטרס ולא גרסינן ליה משום דליתיה בברייתא דלקמן ואין למחוק בשביל כך הספרים דאפשר שהיא בברייתא בשום מקום בתוספתא כח]:
זריקה

[לעיל ב:]
נ״א לאפלוגי אדרבא וכס״ד ל״ק
[לעיל ד: פ״ש פסחים סא. ע״ש]
יומא פו׳ [שבועות יג:]
[גי׳ הערוך לפרקליט שנכנס לרצות רצה פרקליט ונכנס דורון מליצי ריעי [איוב טז] תרגום פרקליטי חברוי]
נ״א וקרב אחר
[עי׳ לקמן יז: מנחות נג: מ״ק ז:]
ס״א ל״ג
ס״א הלכך למצוה משלמים והנך קראי אם אינו ענין למצות דנפקא לן מהתם תנהו ענין לעכב.
לעיל ה: ולקמן י׳: [מנחות ד׳:]

הגהות הב״ח

(א) גמ׳ כדריש פירקא נ״ב דף ב׳ סוף ע״א: (ב) שם חדש האביב ועשית למצוה: (ג) שם למה לי לכדתניא פסח נאמר בו הוא בשחיטה: (ד) רש״י ד״ה פסולה לא עלתה לו וצריך: (ה) ד״ה פסח מנלן דכתיב ועשית בין למצוה: (ו) ד״ה אף כל וכו׳ הלכך למצוה בפסח ילפינן משלמים והני קראי דרבינן: (ז) ד״ה הכי גרסינן ובו בזביחה הוא לעכב וכו׳ ורבי יהושע הס״ד ותיבות ל״ג ליה נמחק:

לד א מיי׳ פט״ו מהל׳ פסה״מ הלכה טו:
נ״ל אפי׳ הכי חטאתם כו׳ ל״ק
לה ב מיי׳ פ״ח מהל׳ תשובה הלכה ד:
לו ג סמג עשין רעו
לז ד מיי׳ פט״ו מהלכות פסה״מ הלכה יא והלכה יא:
לח ה מיי׳ שם הלכה ט והלכה ד
לט ו מיי׳ פ״ד מהלכות קרבן פסח הלכה י:
נ״ל וזבחת פסח שתהא שחיטתו לשם פסח שחטו שלא לשמו פסול אין לי אלא זביחה כו׳ ל״ק

שיטה מקובצת

א] תשובה למה לי עולה והתניא: ב] שנכנס לרצות ריצה פרקליט נכנס: ג] אשכחן שינוי קודש [אא״ה כאן חסר שורה שלימה והתחלה ועוד משורה שניה כמה תיבות רק הענין מובן להמעיין] כדמוכח בסמוך וא״ת למצוה תיפוק ליה מהיקשא דשלמים דהא כתיב בהדיא בקרא [illegible] ד] אלא מכאן: ה] פסח בשינוי בעלים הוא לעכב: ו] לעכב הלכך [illegible] משלמים והנך קראי אם אינו ענין למצוה דנפקא לה מהתם תנהו ענין לעכב ותיבות משום שנאמר הוא בזביחה אינו אלא לעכב נמחק: ז] תיבות נאמר בפסח הוא בשחיטה לעכב נמחק: ח] כשרה דכיון שהפריש ל״ש ונמחק: ט] גביה דהורש: י] כלומר היכי דמי (לעכבא): יא] בשינוי בעלים: יב] שאבד הפסח: יג] בא נקבה הס״ד: יד] קודש וכולהו: טו] הוא ס״א הוא לעכב בין הכא ובין הכא כלומר בין בשינוי קודש ובין בשינוי בעלים דפסח הוא משמע בהוייתו יהא לשמו כשר שלא לשמו פסול והוא תרוייהו הוייות משמע כלומר כשהוא עשוי כמצוותן: טז] מה״ד הבא והכא: יז] צוותו כו׳: יח] תיבת וכו׳ נמחק: יט] שנאמר הוא בזביחה אינו בא אלא: כ] לאוקמי בשינוי בעלים: כא] פסח דמשתמע כל ותיבת מסתמא נמחק: כב] קודש ז״ל תוס׳ הר״פ וי״ל דאותו פסוק דועשית משתמע שינוי קודש דמשמע כל עשיותיו דפסח ואיזה שינוי דפוסל בכל עבודות שינוי קודש הוא דשינוי בעלים אינו בד׳ עבודות כי אם ע״מ לזרוק: כג] בגמרא מייתי נמי הא דהכא ותיבת דרשא ל״ש ונמחק: כד] תיבות ואשינוי קודש ל״ש ונמחק ותיבת קאי ג״כ נמחק: כה] עי׳ בהשמטות בסוף המסכת: כו] הוא דזביחה: כז] קרא כואמרתם זבח פסח ותיתי תיבת מזביחה ל״ש ונמחק: כח] בתוספתא או בת״כ הס״ד:

א) מלת דל״ע בשינוי קודש ובשינוי בעלים דקס״ד וכו׳ ·

a it is valid?[1] [7b]—It [a sin-offering] does not make a fixed atonement but it does make a floating atonement.[2]

Raba also said: If a burnt-offering was killed for a different purpose, its blood must not be sprinkled for a different purpose. This follows either from Scripture or by reason. If you will, it is [deduced from] a text: *That which is gone out of thy lips thou shalt observe*, etc.[3] Alternatively, it is logical: because he has made an alteration therein, etc. as stated at the beginning of this chapter.[4]

Raba also said: If a burnt-offering is brought after [the] death [of its owner], and is slaughtered under a changed sanctity,[5] it is invalid;[6] but [if it is slaughtered] with a change in respect of ownership,[7] it is valid, for there is no ownership after death. But R. Phinehas the son of R. Ammi maintained: There is ownership after death.[8] R. Ashi asked R. Phinehas the son of R. Ammi: Do you particularly maintain that there is ownership after death, and so he [the heir] must bring another burnt-offering;[9] or perhaps, if he [the heir] has violated many affirmative precepts, it makes
b atonement for him?[1] I maintain it particularly, he answered him.

Raba said further: A burnt-offering is a votive gift.[2] For how is it possible?[3] If there is no repentance, then *the sacrifice of the wicked is an abomination!*[4] While if there is repentance, surely it was taught: If one violated an affirmative precept and repented, he does not stir thence until he is forgiven.[5] Hence it follows that it is a votive gift.

(Mnemonic: For whom does a sin-offering atone? A burnt-offering after a votive gift.)[6] It was taught likewise. R. Simeon said: For what purpose does a sin-offering come?—[You ask,] 'for what purpose does a sin-offering come?' Surely in order to make atonement!—Rather, [the question is:] Why does it come before the burnt-offering?[7] [Because it is] like an intercessor who enters [to appease the King]: When the intercessor has appeased [him], the gift follows.[8]

WITH THE EXCEPTION OF THE PASSOVER-OFFERING AND THE SIN-OFFERING. How do we know it of the Passover-offering?—Because it is written, *Observe the month of Abib, and prepare the Passover-offering*;[9] [this intimates] that all its preparations must be in the name of the Passover-offering. We have thus found [that] change in respect of sanctity [disqualifies it]; how do we know [the same of] change in respect of owner?—Because it says, *Then ye shall say: It is the slaughtering of the Lord's Passover*,[10] [which teaches] that the 'slaughtering' must be done in the name of the Passover-offering. Now since this teaching is redundant in respect of change in respect of sanctity,[11] apply the teaching to change in respect of owner. We have thus found it as a regulation;[12] how do we know
c that it is indispensable?[1]—Scripture saith, *And thou shalt sacrifice the Passover-offering unto the Lord thy God*.[2] To this R. Safra demurred: Does this [passage], '*And thou shalt sacrifice* etc.' come for this purpose: Surely it is required for R. Naḥman's dictum? For R. Naḥman said in Rabbah b. Abbuha's name: How do we know that the left-over of a Passover-offering is brought as a peace-offering?[3] Because it is said, '*And thou shalt sacrifice the Passover-offering unto the Lord thy God, of the flock and of the herd*.' Now surely the Passover-offering comes only from lambs or from goats?[4] Hence we learn that the left-over of the Passover-offering is to be [utilised] for something which comes from the flock and from the herd; and what is it? A peace-offering.—Rather, said R. Safra: '*And thou shalt sacrifice the Passover-offering*' [is required] for R. Naḥman's dictum; '*Observe the month of Abib*' [is required] for the regulation in respect of changed sanctity; '*Then ye shall say: [It is] the slaughtering of the Lord's Passover*' [is required] for the regulation relating to change in respect of owner; '*it is*'[5] teaches that it is indispensable, both in the former and in the latter cases.[6]

Now we have thus found [it in the case of] slaughtering: how do we know [it of] the other services?—Since it was revealed [in the one], it was [also] revealed [in the others].[7] R. Ashi said: We do not argue, 'Since it was revealed, it was revealed'. How then do we know it of [the other] services?—Because it is written, *This is the law of the burnt-offering, of the meal-offering, [and of the sin-offering, and of the guilt-offering, and of the consecration-offering, and of the sacrifice*
d *of peace-offerings*].[1] Now it was taught: *In the day that He commanded the children of Israel to present their offerings*[2] refers to the firstling, tithe, and Passover-offering. Thus Scripture assimilates it [the Passover-offering] to the peace-offering: as [in the case of the] peace-offering we require as a regulation [that there shall not be] either change in respect of sanctity or change in respect of owner, so in the case of all [these] do we require as a regulation [that there shall not be] either change in respect of sanctity or change in respect of owner. Again, it is like the peace-offering [in this respect]: As you do not differentiate in the peace-offering between slaughtering and the other services in respect of the regulation, so must you not differentiate in the case of the Passover-sacrifice between slaughtering and the other services in respect of indispensability.[3] Then in that case, what is the purpose of '*it is*'?—For what was taught: As for the Passover-offering, '*it is*' is stated there to teach indispensability as far as slaughtering is concerned; whereas in the case of a guilt-offering '*it is*' is stated only after the burning of the *emurim*, and in fact if the *emurim* are not burnt at all, it [the offering] is valid.[4]

How do we know it of the sin-offering?[5]—Because it is written, *And he shall kill it for a sin-offering*,[6] which intimates that it must be killed for the sake of a sin-offering. We have thus found [it of] slaughtering; how do we know [it of] receiving [the blood]?—Be-

a (1) Now a burnt-offering atones for sins of omission. But if these fall into the same category as offences entailing a sin-offering, then just as the latter is invalid when slaughtered on behalf of another who is liable to a sin-offering, so should it be invalid when slaughtered on behalf of another who is liable to a burnt-offering, for 'his fellow' *is* then like himself (V. *supra*). (2) Cf. *supra* 6a. A sin-offering does not make atonement for the omission of positive precepts when it is directly dedicated for that purpose only, but only when it is dedicated for sins which entail a sin-offering, but whose owner has *also* been guilty of sins of omission. Since it does not atone for sins of omission standing by themselves, one who is in need of a burnt-offering (on account of sins of omission) is not 'his fellow' similar to 'himself', and therefore if a sin-offering is slaughtered on behalf of such, it is valid, provided that one had already vowed a burnt-offering, which covers all his sins of omission, so that a sin-offering is quite superfluous as far as he is concerned. But if he had not vowed a burnt-offering, a sin-offering has a certain relation to him in so far that if he was liable to a sin-offering too, this would make atonement for the sins of omission also. Hence he is sufficiently similar to his fellow to invalidate his fellow's sin-offering slaughtered on his behalf. (3) Deut. XXIII, 24. (4) *Supra* 2a. (5) I.e., as a different sacrifice, e.g., a peace-offering. (6) And another must be brought before the deceased is deemed to have fulfilled his vow. (7) For a different person (8) V *Supra* 4b. (9) As in n. 6.

b (1) For the heir is the owner. (2) It does not actually atone for sins of omission, but after one has repented this comes as a gift of appeasement, as it were. (3) For it to make atonement in actuality. (4) Prov. XXI, 27. (5) I.e., he is undoubtedly forgiven even without a sacrifice. (6) A string of words so arranged as to facilitate the remembering of the subjects discussed hereunder. (7) When one has to bring both, the sin-offering takes precedence; *infra* 89b. (8) Thus the sin-offering is the intercessor and the burnt-offering follows as a gift. (9) Deut. XVI, 1. (10) Ex. XII, 27. (11) As that has been derived from Deut. XVI, 1. (12) I.e., these verses teach that the Passover-offering must be sacrificed specifically as such and for its registered owner.

c (1) In the sense that it is otherwise disqualified. (2) Deut. XVI, 2. This too has the same teaching as XVI, 1. Since however it is superfluous in that case, it must intimate that this regulation is indispensable. (3) E.g., if an animal dedicated for a Passover-sacrifice was lost, whereupon its owners registered for another animal, and then the first was found after the second was sacrificed. Or again, if a sum of money was dedicated to buy a paschal lamb, but it was not all expended; then too the surplus must be used for a peace-offering. (4) But not from the herd, which means the larger cattle. (5) Heb. '*hu*'. This is regarded as superfluous and hence interpreted as emphasizing the regulation to the extent of making it indispensable. (6) A change either in respect of sanctity or owner invalidates the paschal sacrifice. (7) I.e., they follow automatically.

d (1) Lev. VII. 37. (2) Ibid. 38. (3) What is indispensable for slaughtering is also indispensable for the other services.—Here follows a short passage in the original which the commentaries delete. (4) V. *Supra* 5b. (5) That if not slaughtered for its own sake it is invalid. (6) Lev. IV, 33.

cause it is written, [8a] *And the priest shall take of the blood of the sin-offering,*[7] which intimates that receiving must be for the sake of a sin-offering. We have thus found [it of] slaughtering and receiving: How do we know it of sprinkling?—Because Scripture saith, *And the priest shall make atonement for him through his sin-offering,*[8] [which teaches] that atonement must be [made] for the sake of the sin-offering.[9] We have thus found [the law relating to] change in respect of sanctity; how do we know it of change in respect of owner?—Scripture saith: [*And the priest shall make atonement*] *for him*, implying for him, but not for his fellow. We have thus found it as a regulation: how do we know that it is indispensable?—As R. Huna the son of R. Joshua said [elsewhere; Scripture saith,] *'his sin-offering'*, [where] *'sin-offering'* [alone would suffice]: so here too, [Scripture
a saith,] *his sin-offering* [where] *sin-offering* [alone would suffice].[1] We have thus found the regulation relating to change in respect of sanctity, and [a prohibition of] change in respect of owner at the sprinkling, this being both a regulation and indispensable. How do we know that it is indispensable [in the case of all services][2] as far as change in respect of sanctity is concerned; and that [the prohibition of] change in respect of ownership at the other services is both a regulation and indispensable?—Said R. Jonah: It is inferred from a nazirite's sin-offering, for it is written, *And the priest shall bring them before the Lord, and shall prepare his sin-offering, and his burnt-offering:*[3] [this intimates] that all its preparations [*sc.* the services] must be for the sake of a sin-offering. We have thus found it regarding change in respect of sanctity; how do we know change in respect of owner?[4]—Said R. Huna son of R. Joshua: [Scripture saith,] *'his sin-offering'*, [where] *'sin-offering'* [alone would suffice]. To this Rabina demurred: If so, how do you interpret [the superfluous] *'his burnt-offering'* [where] *'burnt-offering'* [alone would suffice]? (But according to Rabina, how does he interpret [the apparently superfluous] *'his meal-offering'*, *'his drink-offering'*, where *'meal-offering'*, *'drink-offering'* [alone would suffice]?[5]—He requires those [for the following deduction]: Their meal-offering and their drink-offering [intimates] at night; their meal-offering and their drink-offering, even on the next day.)[6] But how do you interpret [the superfluous] *his burnt-offering* [where] *burnt-offering* [alone would suffice]? Furthermore, can they[7] be learnt from each other? The sin-offering
b of forbidden fat[1] cannot be learnt from a nazirite's sin-offering, since the latter is accompanied by another sacrifice.[2] [On the other hand] a nazirite's sin-offering cannot be learnt from the sin-offering of forbidden fat, since the latter is a case of *kareth*![3]—Rather, said Raba: We infer it from a leper's sin-offering, for it is written, *And the priest shall prepare*[4] *the sin-offering,*[5] which teaches that all its preparations [services] must be for the sake of a sin-offering. Thus we have found [the law relating to] change in respect of sanctity; how does he know it of change in respect of owner?—Scripture saith, *And* [*he shall*] *make atonement for him that is to be cleansed:*[5] [this intimates,] for this [man] who is to be cleansed, but not for his fellow who is to be cleansed.

Yet [the question] still [remains]: Can they be learnt from each other? The sin-offering of forbidden fat cannot be learnt from the leper's sin-offering, since the latter is accompanied by another sacrifice. [On the other hand] a leper's sin-offering cannot be learnt from the sin-offering of forbidden fat, since the latter is a case of *kareth*!—One cannot be learnt from one, but one can be learnt from two.[6] But in the case of which should it not be written? [Shall we say,] Let the Divine law not write it in the case of the sin-offering of forbidden fat, and let it be deduced from these others? [Then I can argue that] the reason in the case of these others is that another sacrifice accompanies them! [If we say,] Let the Divine law not write it in the case of the nazirite's sin-offering and let it be deduced from these others: [I can argue that] the reason in the case of these others is that no absolution [revocation] is possible![7] [If I say,] Let the Divine law not write it in the case of the leper's sin-offering, and let it be deduced from these others: [then I can argue that] the reason in the case of these others is that
c they do not come in poverty![1] — Rather, Scripture saith, *This is the law of the burnt-offering, of the meal-offering, and of the sin-offering . . .* [*and of the sacrifice of peace-offerings*]:[2] thus the Writ assimilated it [the sin-offering] to the peace-offering. As in the case of peace-offerings both change in respect of sanctity and change in respect of name [are prohibited, for] we require [that the services be performed] for their own [*sc.* that of the peace-offerings'] sake, this being a regulation;[3] so in the case of the sin-offering both change in respect of sanctity and change in respect of name [are prohibited, for] we require [that the services be performed] for their own sake, this being a regulation. Therefore the regulation is deduced from a peace-offering, while these other verses[4] teach that it is indispensable. Again, we have found [this of] the sin-offering

(7) Ibid. 34. (8) Ibid. 35. This is apparently the Talmudic rendering of the verse. (9) Atonement consists in essence of the sprinkling.—Carrying the blood to the side of the Altar where it is sprinkled is included in receiving (Rashi).

a (1) The emphasis implicit in *'his'* intimates indispensability. (2) Sh. M. deletes bracketed words. (3) Num. VI, 16. (4) A passage follows here in the original which the commentaries delete. (5) *'His meal-offering'* and *'his drink-offering'* (or rather 'their') occur quite frequently; why does Rabina ask only about *'his burnt-offering'* and not about these? (6) V. *infra* 84a. (7) *Sc.* different kinds of sin-offerings.

b (1) This is the technical designation of all sin-offerings brought on account of actual sin, in contrast e.g., to a nazirite's sin-offering, which is not really brought through sin at all. (2) Lit., 'other blood'. (3) A sin-offering is brought for the unwitting transgression of an injunction which, if deliberately violated, entails *kareth* (v. Glos). (4) E.V. 'offer'. (5) Lev. XIV, 19. (6) For Scripture need not have intimated the teaching in the case of all those.—This answer implies that one intimation at least is superfluous. (7) A nazirite can be absolved of his vow altogether, and then his sacrificial obligations automatically expire. But in no circumstances can the other two be freed of their obligations.

c (1) If a leper is too poor he can bring a bird instead of an animal for a sin-offering (V. Lev. XIV, 21-22). But this leniency is not permitted in the case of the other two. (2) Lev. VII, 37. (3) But not, however, indispensable to the extent that a peace-offering is invalid if offered as a different sacrifice. (4) Quoted above, teaching that change of name and of sanctity are forbidden, which are now superfluous.

ולקח הכהן מדם החטאת שתהא קבלה לשם חטאת ואשכחן שחיטה וקבלה זריקה מנלן א] דאמר קרא °וכפר עליו הכהן מחטאתו שתהא כפרה לשם חטאת אשכחן שנוי קדש שנוי בעלים מנלן אמר קרא עליו *עליו ולא על חבירו אשכחן למצוה לעכב מנלן כדאמר רב הונא בריה דרב יהושע חטאת חטאתו הכא נמי חטאת חטאתו אשכחן מצוה בשנוי קדש וזריקה בשנוי בעלים בין למצוה בין לעכב לעכב ב] בכל עבודות בשנוי קדש ג] ובשאר עבודות בשנוי בעלים בין למצוה בין לעכב מנלן אמר ר' יונה אתיא מחטאת נזיר דכתיב °והקריב הכהן לפני ה' ד] ועשה את חטאתו ואת עולתו שיהו כל עשיותיו לשם חטאת ה] אשכחן שנוי קדש שנוי בעלים מנלן (א) ו] (אם אינו ענין לשנוי קדש תניהו ענין לשנוי בעלים אשכחן למצוה לעכב מנלן) אמר רב הונא ז] [בריה דר"י] חטאת חטאתו מתקיף לה רבינא אלא מעתה עולת עולתו מאי דרשת ביה ולרבינא מנחת מנחתו נסך נסכו מאי דרשת בהו ח] ההוא *מבעי ליה מנחתם ונסכיהם בלילה מנחתם ונסכיהם אפי' למחר אלא עולת עולתו מאי דרשת (ב) בהו ותו מי גמרי מהדדי חטאת חלב מחטאת נזיר לא גמרה שכן יש עמה דמים אחרים חטאת נזיר מחטאת חלב לא גמרה שכן כרת ט] אלא אמר רבא אתיא מחטאת מצורע דכתיב °ועשה הכהן את החטאת שיהו כל עשיותיו לשם חטאת ואשכחן שנוי קדש שנוי בעלים מנליה אמר קרא °וכפר על המטהר וגו' על המטהר זה ולא על המטהר חבירו ואכתי מי ילפא מהדדי חטאת חלב מחטאת מצורע לא ילפא שכן יש עמה דמים אחרים חטאת מצורע מחטאת חלב לא גמרה שכן כרת י] מחדא לא אתיא תיתי חדא מתרתי בהי לא לכתוב [לא לכתוב] רחמנא בחטאת חלב ותיתי מהנך מה להנך שכן יש עמהם דמים אחרים לא לכתוב רחמנא בחטאת נזיר ותיתי מהנך מה להנך שכן אין להן שאלה לא לכתוב רחמנא בחטאת מצורע ותיתי מהנך מה להנך שכן אין באין בדלות אלא אמר קרא °זאת התורה לעולה ולמנחה וגו' הקישו הכתוב לשלמים מה שלמים בין שנוי קדש בין שנוי בעלים בעינן לשמן למצוה אף חטאת בין שנוי קדש בין שנוי בעלים בעינן לשמן למצוה הילכך מצוה משלמים והנך קראי לעכב ואשכחן חטאת חלב דכתיב בה לחטאת חטאת

רש"י

ולקח הכהן. לשון קבלה הוא: וכפר. היינו בזריקה הלכה לא אצטריך קרא דבכלל קבלה יא] היא מתרביא ליה: אשכחן למצוה כו'. ואי קשיא מצוה מהיקשא דזאת התורה משלמים אתיא כשאר כל הזבחים אין הכי נמי ומסקנא מהתם יליף לה לקמיה ומעיקרא סוא דמהדרינן דנכתבו כולהו בגופיה: כדאמר רב הונא כו'. לקמן בשמעתין: חטאתו. וכפר עליו הכהן מחטאתו (כשזרק דמו לשמו חטאת חטאתו) מדהוה ליה למכתב מחטאת וכתיב וי"ו יתירא למדרש בה לשם בעלים: אשכחן מצוה בשנוי קדש. בכל עבודות וזריקה אשכחן בה מצוה ועכוב בשנוי בעלים דהאי מחטאתו יב] נמי בזריקה כתיב שהיא הכפרה: לעכב בכל עבודות בשנוי קדש. שלא למדנו לאחד מהן ושאר עבודות לבד מזריקה בשנוי בעלים בין למצוה בין לעכב מנלן: שיהו כל עשיותיו לשם חטאת. ולמצוה לא אצטריך קרא דהא נפקא לן משאר חטאות והאי לעכובא: [ה"ג בס"א] אשכחן שנוי קדש שנוי בעלים מנלן: אמר רב הונא כו'. גבי נזיר כתיב ועשה את חטאתו ואת עולתו יג] הרי למצוה וכשלמים מה שלמים לא חלקת בהן בין זריקה לשאר עבודות בשנוי בעלים למצוה אף חטאת לא תחלק בין זריקה לשאר עבודות לעכב הרי לך מצוה ועכוב בין בשנוי קדש בין בשנוי בעלים כך נ"ל וכן יש לפרש גבי חטאת מצורע לקמן כ"ל: ולרבינא. דלא קשיא ליה אלא עולת עולתו מנחתו ונסכו דכתיבי נמי גבי נזיר אמאי לא קשיא ליה: ההוא מיבעי ליה. כי היכי דדרשינן לכל מנחתם *ונסכיהם יד] בלילה ואפי' למחר שיוכשרו טו] לבא למחר (ג) לבא בלילה טז] הכי נמי דרשינן להאי ועשה את מנחתו יז] כל זמן שיעשנו הוא קרוי מנחתו ונסכו של זה אע"פ שלא קרבו עם זבחו: מי גמרי. שאר חטאות וחטאת נזיר מהדדי דתמצי לומר חד למצוה וחד לעכב סתם חטאת קרי חטאת חלב משום דשכיחא טפי: שכן כרת. מכפרת על חייבי כרת אלמא לא גמרי מהדדי וכיון דלא גמרי מהדדי תרווייהו למצוה אצטריכו: ואשכחן שנוי קדש. ולעכב דהא נפקא לן מצוה לעיל בשאר חטאות: וכפר על המטהר. סיפיה דועשה הכהן את החטאת הוא יח] ועל המטהר אכולהו עשיות קאי: ותיתי מהנך. נזיר ומצורע: שאלה. נזיר נשאל לחכם ועוקר נזירתו ופטור מן הקרבן: שכן אין באין בדלות גרסינן. שאין יט] *חטאות יורדות בעניות להביא עוף: והנך קראי לעכב. וכשלמים מה שלמים לא חלקת בהן למצוה אף חטאת לא תחלוק בו לעכב וכיון דכתיב עכובא בזריקה אתיא להו כ] לכולהו עבודות בהך דרשא מהיקשא דשלמים: אשכחן חטאת חלב דכתיב ביה לחטאת. ושחט אותה לחטאת בסתם חטאת כתיב (ד) כא] אם נפש כי תחטא וגו': חטאת

תוספות

זריקה מנלן מוכפר עליו הכהן מחטאתו. הרבה יש תימה דהני קראי דשחיטה וקבלה ושחט אותה לחטאת ולקח הכהן כתיבי בסתם חטאת כגון חטאת חלב בפרשת ויקרא גבי כשבה והאי קרא דוכפר עליו הכהן מחטאתו כתיב בחטאת דשמיעת קול וביטוי שפתים אבל בחטאת חלב לא כתיב מחטאתו אלא על חטאתו כתיב ובתורת כהנים באותה פרשה עצמה דחטאת חלב דריש מקרא דמחטאתו אע"ג דלא כתיב בההיא פרשתא וזהו תימה דשביק קרא דעל חטאתו דכתיב בההיא פרשתא ושמא משום דעל חטאתו לאחר הקטרת אימורים הוא דכתיב אבל תימה דלקמן משמע דכל הני קראי דהכא בחטאת חלב כתיבי דקאמר אשכחנא חטאת חלב כב] אבל חטאת דשמיעת קול וביטוי שפתים מנא לן וי"ל דהכי קאמר לקמן אשכחנא חטאת חלב עכובא שחיטה וקבלה בשנוי קדש ושאר עבודות נילף כדאמר לעיל מה שלמים לא חלקת בין זביחה לשאר עבודות למצוה אף כאן לא תחלוק לעכב וקבלה נמי לא הוצרך לכתוב אבל שמיעת קול מנא לן דאע"ג דכתיב ביה וכפר עליו מחטאתו ודרשינן לעיל לשם חטאת היינו שנוי קדש בזריקה ולא חלקת לא נימא בזריקה לפי שהיא עיקר כפרה ושנוי בעלים בחטאת חלב נגמר משמיעת קול דליכא פירכא וי"מ דמחטאתו דקאמר היינו בשעיר נשיא דכתיב ביה נמי מחטאתו כג] וקאי גם אחטאת חלב וקשה דכתיב לאחר הקטרת אימורים נראה לי. ברו"ך. ועוד כ"ל דלא הוה מצי למדרש מוכפר על חטאתו אשר חטא דכתיב בחטאת חלב משום דהכי קאמר על פשעו אשר חטא כד] *) (ולא בשמיעת קול מיירי בחטאת קרבנו) ולא כה] משעיר נשיא דכתיב מחטאתו ונסלח לו והיינו מפשעו וחטאתו שלו ונסלח לו אבל בשמיעת קול לא כתיב כו] זה ולא זו אלא מחטאתו היינו מקרבנו. ברו"ך:

וזריקה בשנוי בעלים בין למצוה בין לעכב. תימה דמהאי קרא כז] וכפר עליו הכהן מחטאתו דרשינן תרווייהו זריקה בשנוי קדש ושנוי בעלים ואם כן מחטאת חטאתו תיפוק ליה נמי עכובא בשנוי קדש כמו בשנוי בעלים דאתרווייהו קאי:

ועשה את חטאתו שיהו כל עשיותיו לשם חטאת אשכחנא שנוי קדש שנוי בעלים מנ"ל אמר רב הונא בריה דרב יהושע חטאת חטאתו. כך גירסת הקונטרס ולגירסא זו מוקי ברישא לעכב בשנוי קדש קודם שנעמיד למצוה בשנוי בעלים באם אינו ענין ואינו משמע כן בכולי פירקא לעיל גבי שלמים ופסח דקאמר אשכחנא שנוי קדש שנוי בעלים מנא לן ומוקי ברישא בשנוי בעלים באם אינו ענין קודם שיעמיד קרא לעכב. ומיהו י"ל דשאני הכא דכבר אשכחנא קרא לזריקה בשנוי בעלים ואית ספרים דגרסי אם אינו ענין לשנוי קדש דנפקא ליה מהתם תניהו ענין לשנוי בעלים אשכחנא למצוה לעכב מנא לן אמר רב הונא בריה דרב יהושע חטאת חטאתו ולגירסא זו לא צריכין תו לקרא דלעיל בזריקה וניחא נמי הא דגרסינן לעיל כדאמר רב הונא בריה דרב יהושע חטאת חטאתו דמשמע דעיקר מילתא לא אתמר אההיא והיינו משום דלבסוף לא קיימא:

מנחתם ונסכיהם בלילה מנחתם ונסכיהם אפי' למחר. לאו מהאי קרא [קדריש]:

הילכך מצוה משלמים והנך קראי לעכב. וא"ת למה לי למכתב בכולהו לכתוב כח] *בהך ואינך כולהו אתו מדכתיב זאת תורת החטאת תורה אחת לכל החטאות כדלקמן בשמעתא דמבוג ויש לומר דבמסקנא לא

*) מהרש"ק מ"ז ויש למחוק ב' תיבות בשמיעת קול וכצ"ל ולא מיירי בחטאת כו' ועיין חלופי גרסאות

שיטה מקובצת

א] (שנאמר) [דאמר קרא] וכפר עליו הכהן. גבי חטאת דשמיעת הקול כתיב (ויקרא ה') תימה אמאי שביק קרא דוכפר עליו הכהן על חטאתו אשר חטא דכתיב גבי חטאת חלב או מוכפר עליו הכהן מחטאתו דכתיב גבי שעיר נשיא וי"ל דההוא בחטאת קא מיירי ולא בקרבן חטאת [דוכפר] על חטאתו אשר חטא [לא מיירי] בקרבן א): ב] תיבות בכל עבודות ל"ש ונמחק: ג] ולשאר עבודות אות ב' נמחק: ד] ה"ג רש"י ועשה כו' שיהו כל עשיותיו לשם חטאת ואם אינו ענין למצוה לשינוי קודש [דהא] נפקא מהתם תנהו ענין לעכב בשינוי קודש אשכחן שינוי קודש בין למצוה בין לעכב שינוי בעלים בין למצוה בין לעכב מנלן אמר רב הונא אתיא חטאת חטאתו [דמשמע שינוי בעלים למצוה] וכיון דגלי גלי ומשתמע בין למצוה ובין לעכב. וקשה דמיד דשמעינן שינוי קודש למצוה הוי לן לאהדורי שינוי בעלים למצוה ולאהדורי [אח"כ] אשינוי קודש לעכב כי כך שיטת התלמוד בכל הסוגיא לאוקמי מצוה בשינוי בעלים קודם שנדע עיכובא בשינוי קודש לכך נראה [דגרסי' אם] אינו ענין בשינוי קודש דנפקא לן מהתם תנהו ענין בשינוי בעלים אשכחן למצוה בין בשינוי קודש בין בשינוי בעלים לעכב מנלן בין בשינוי קודש בין בשינוי בעלים אמר רב הונא אתיא חטאת חטאתו דמשמע לעכב בשינוי בעלים ונפקא לעכב בשינוי קודש ב) הכי דחטאת חטאתו לא משמע אלא בשינוי בעלים דוקא הואיל ופשטא דקרא משתמע שינוי קודש הוי מוקמינן ליה בשינוי בעלים ואם אינו ענין קרא דחטאת קאי אשינוי בעלים וכ"ש בשינוי קודש [דחטאת] חטאתו משמע לעכב וקאי אתרוייהו: ה] חטאת ואשכחן: ו] תיבות אם אינו ענין כו' לעכב מנלן נמחק: ז] רב הונא בריה דרב יהושע: ח] עיין בהשמטות בסוף המסכת: ט] אלא אמר רבא אתיא וכו' אשכחן שינוי קודש בין למצוה בין לעכב שינוי בעלים מנלן בשאר עבודות בין למצוה בין לעכב כך פי' רש"י ולא נהירא דחדא דקודם היה לנו להעמיד הפסוק בשינוי בעלים למצוה משינוי קודש לעכב כמו שהקשיתי לעיל ועוד דמה הרויח רבא למימר (חטאת) [אתיא מחטאת] מצורע הלא חטאת נזיר לא סלקינן מינה אלא מכח הני פירכא מה לחטאת נזיר שכן יש עמהם דמים אחרים והוא חושש ומביא עמו חטאת מצורע דשייך למיפרך הכי לכן נראה לפרש דאינו חוזר מקרא דנזיר רק מחטאת חטאתו משום קושיא דרבינא אבל לא חשש לאידך קושיא (דאי) [דמי] גמרי מהדדי וה"ק אלא אמר רבא מקראי

מסורת הש"ס

ויקרא ד · שם · במדבר ו · ויקרא יד · שם · שם ז

[לעיל ג: ד: ז. פסחים סב.]

רש"ק

רש"ק מ"ז

לקמן פד. תמורה יד. מנחות מד:[נב. תענית ב:]

נ"א ונסכיהם גבי קרבנות החג אפי' בלילה כו'

[צ"ל חטאות חלב ונזיר]

צ"ל כחד צ"ק

הגהות הב"ח

(א) גמ' שינוי בעלים מנלן (אם אינו ענין וכו' מנלן) תא"מ ונ"ב רש"י לא גרס ליה אלא ה"ג אשכחן שינוי קדש שינוי בעלים מנלן אמר רב הונא כו': (ב) שם עולתו מאי דרשת ביה ותו: (ג) רש"י ד"ה ההוא וכו' למחר או לבא: (ד) ד"ה אשכחן וכו' כתיב ואם נפש אחת תחטא:

דלעיל ידעינן שינוי קודש ושינוי בעלים למצוה ולעכב נפקא לן בשינוי קודש מועשה את החטאת והילכך פריך שפיר אשכחן שינוי קודש לעכב שינוי בעלים מנלן ומשני דכתיב וכפר על המטהר ולא על המטהר חבירו וקאי אכל עשיותיו כדכתיב ברישא דקרא ועשה כדפי' בקונטרס: י] כרת. חדא מחדא: יא] קבלה רבינן ליה תיבות היא מתרביא נמחק: יב] תיבת נמי נמחק: יג] מתיבות הרי למצוה כו' עד סוף הדבור נמחק: יד] ונסכיהם הכתובים בקרבנות החג מנחתם ונסכיהם: טו] תיבות לבא למחר נמחק: טז] בלילה ולבא למחר: יז] מנחתו דכתיב גבי נזיר: יח] הוא על המטהר ואכולהו עשיות: יט] שאין חטאותם: כ] כולהו אות ל' נמחק: כא] תיבת אם נמחק: כב] חלב ג) אכל אות ב' נמחק: כג] מחטאתו (ונבי) [וגלי] תיבת וקאי ל"ש ותיבת גם נמחק: כד] מתיבת ולא כו' עד תיבת קרבנו נמחק: כה] ולא בשעיר נשיא דהא כתיב מחטאתו: כו] לא כתיב לא זה: כז] קרא דוכיפר: כח] לכתוב בחד ואינך תיבת בהך ל"ש ונמחק:

א) והא דלא מייתי מקרא דשעיר נשיא (ויקרא ד') עי' בתוס' בסוד"ה אריקה בכם י"מ. ב) נראה דצ"ל אף דחטאת חטאתו לא משמע וכו' משתמע שינוי קודש רק דמוקמינן ליה בשינוי בעלים באם אינו ענין וכו' וקרא דחטאת וכו'. ג) אולי צ"ל חלב כו' חטאת תיבת א"ל נמחק.

כ א מיי' פט"ו מהל' פסה"מ הלכה יב:
כא ב מיי' שם הל"א:

תורה אור

חטאת דעבודת כוכבים (א) א] דשמיעת הקול ובטוי שפתים וטומאת מקדש וקדשיו דלא כתיב בהו מנלן חטאת דעבודת כוכבים אתיא מחטאת חלב שכן כרת כמותה והנך כולהי אתיין במה הצד: תנו רבנן פסח בזמנו לשמו כשר שלא לשמו פסול ב] *ובשאר ימות השנה לשמו פסול *שלא לשמו כשר (של"ו קבאיצ"ן ממה"ר בצ"א ב"א סימן) מנא הני מילי אמר אבוה דשמואל אמר קרא ג] °ואם מן הצאן קרבנו לזבח שלמים לה' דבר הבא מן הצאן יהא לזבח שלמים (ב) אימא שלמים אין מידי אחרינא לא אמר רבי אילא א"ר יוחנן לזבח לרבות כל זבח אימא (ג) כל דשחיט ד] להוי כמותה אי הוה כתיב לשלמים וזבח כדקאמרת השתא דכתיב לזבח שלמים לכל דשחיט ליה שלמים להוי אימא לזבח כלל שלמים פרט כלל ופרט אין בכלל אלא מה שבפרט שלמים אין מידי אחרינא לא לה' הדר וכלל מתקיף לה ר' יעקב מנהר פקוד הא לא דמי (ד) כללא בתרא לכללא קמא כללא קמא מרבי' זבחים ותו לא כללא בתרא לה' כל דלה' ואפי' ה] לעופות ואפי' למנחות הא *תנא דבי רבי ישמעאל ו] בכללי ופרטי (ה) דריש כי האי גוונא כלל ופרט וכלל אי אתה דן אלא כעין הפרט מה הפרט מפורש שהוא שלא לשמו וכשר אף כל שהוא שלא לשמו וכשר אי מה הפרט מפורש דבר הבא בנדר ובנדבה אף כל הבא בנדר ובנדבה עולה ושלמים אין חטאת ואשם לא ז] אלא לזבח רבויא הוא אימא לכל דשחיט ליה להוי כוותיה א"ר אבין

דוחין

חטאת דעבודת כוכבים. דכתיב בפ' שלח לך ולא כתיב בהאי ענייגא וכן חטאת דשמיעת הקול לא כתיב בההוא ענייגא דההוא ענייגא בחטאת דשגגת כרת קיימא כדילפינן בהוריות (דף ב.): שמיעת הקול. שבועת העדות ושמעה קול אלה (שמיעת ח] הקול) ושבועת ביטוי וטומאת מקדש וקדשיו בחד ענייגא כתיבי בקרבן עולה ויורד ט] ושמעה קול אלה או נפש כי תשבע לבטא או נפש אשר תגע וגו' ומוקמא לה במסכת שבועות בטומאת מקדש וקדשיו: אתיין במה הצד. מחטאת חלב וחטאת נזיר ומצורע דכי פרכת מה לחטאת חלב שכן כרת חטאת נזיר ומצורע יוכיחו מה לחטאת נזיר ומצורע שכן יש עמהן דמים אחרים חטאת חלב תוכיח הצד השוה שבהן י] כו' אף אני אביא חטאת דשמיעת הקול ומחטאת חלב וחדא מהני לא אתיא דאי מחטאת חלב וחטאת נזיר איכא למיפרך מה להצד השוה שבהן שכן אינן באין בדלות תאמר בשבועת ביטוי שהיא בעולה ויורד אי מחטאת חלב וחטאת מצורע איכא למיפרך מה להצד השוה שבהן שכן אינן בשאלה תאמר בשבועה שישנה בשאלה: שלא לשמו פסול. כדאמרי' (לעיל דף ז:): בשאר ימות השנה לשמו פסול יא]. כדאמרי' במס' פסחים (דף סא.) שחטו קודם חצות פסול דכתיב בין הערבים וכמה פעמים שנה הכתוב בקביעות זמנו בי"ד בין הערבים: שלא לשמו כשר. כדמפרש ואזיל: מנהני מילי. דבשאר ימות השנה שלא לשמו כשר: ואם מן הצאן קרבנו כו'. (ו) לאו קרא יתירא קא דריש אלא יב] משמעותא דקרא משמע ליה הכי ואם יג] דבר הבא מן הצאן (ז) דהייט פסח שאינו בא אלא מן הצאן היה קרבנו הרי הוא לזבח שלמים ועל כרחך שלא בזמנו קאמר דאי בזמנו הא ילפינן ליה לעיל דפסול: ואימא שלמים אין כו'. שחטו לשם שלמים ליתכשר אבל שחטו לשם עולה ליפסיל וברייתא קתני שלא לשמו כשר ואפילו שחטו לשם עולה או לשם חטאת: לזבח. קרא יתירא הוא דמצי למכתב לשלמים: אימא לכל דשחיט להוי כוותיה. יד] שחטו לשם עולה יהא עולה דהא אתרבי ליה כל זבח: ה"ג אי הוה כתיב לשלמים וזבח כדקא אמרת. דאי כתב הכי הוה משמע יהא כשלמים או כשאר זבח: השתא דכתיב לזבח שלמים. הכי משמע לכל זבח שיזבחנו לשמו שלמים יהיה: ואימא לזבח כלל כו'. אמאי דריש להאי זבח שלמים הכי דרוש הכי דבר הבא מן הצאן יהא לכל הזבחים כלל שכשר שלא לשמו כי הדר כתב שלמים פרט שלא הכשרתיו בעקירת שמו אלא א"כ שחטו לשלמים אבל שחטו לשם זבח אחר פסול: ואפי' טו] לעופות. שחטו לשם (ח) חטאת עוף: אף כל שהוא שלא לשמו. ילא לשמו: חטאת ואשם לא. שחטו לשם חטאת ואשם יהא פסול אפילו לשלמים: אלא לזבח רבויא הוא. אינו לשון כלל ולא דרשי' ליה בכלל ופרט שאין כללות ופרטות באין מרבוי לשון אלא ממשמעות המקראות וכגון (ב"ק דף סג.) בכל אשר תאוה נפשך כלל (ט) וכן מן הבהמה כלל בקר וצאן פרט אבל לזבח שלמים שתי תיבות דבוקות הן כאילו כתיב לזבח טז] השלמים וקרא יתירא בעלמא הוא דהוה מצי למכתב יז] לשלמים וכל מקרא של לשון ייתור אינו לכלל ופרט אלא לרבות וכמאן דכתיב לשלמים וזבח דמי דאיתרבו ליה כל הזבחים:

דוחין

לא קאי ואע"ג דבפרק דם חטאת (לקמן דף צג.) תנן יח] תורה אחת לכל החטאות הייט במילתא דכתיבא התם אשר יזה מדמה על הבגד ומיהו איכא דאית ליה הך סברא לר' שמעון בריש מסכת מנחות (דף ג:) וא"ת למה לי למכתב בחטאת חלב עכובא בכל עבודות לכתוב בחדא ונימא מה שלמים לא חלקת יט] למצוה אף חטאת לא תחלוק כדקאמר לעיל וי"ל דכי האי גוונא זמנין דטרח ליה קרא וכתב א"כ אתי לדרשא אחריתא וא"ת מנא לן בחטאת נזיר עכובא בשנוי בעלים ויש לומר מחטאת חטאתו אע"ג דלעיל לא קאי עיקר פירכא *סמיך אותו מי גמירי מהדדי:

חטאת דעבודת כוכבים אתיא מחטאת חלב שכן כרת כמותה. יש ספרים שכתוב בהן חטאת דעבודת כוכבים וטומאת מקדש וקדשיו ואינו נראה דאע"ג דכרת כמותה מכל מקום איכא למיפרך מה לחטאת חלב שכן אינה באה בדלות כדפרכינן לעיל גבי חטאת מצורע:

שמיעת קול. *דלא כתיב לחטאתו גבי עבודה מנלן עכובא אבל כתיב לחטאת על דברים אחרים ואין בכך כלום:

כ] (*ה"ג) **הנך** כולהו אתיין במה הצד כא]. הקשה רבינו תם מה להנך שכן אין באין בדלי דלות תאמר בהנך ותירץ כיון דדלי דלות גופיה פסולה שלא לשמה כב] הייט מנחת חוטא דפסולה שלא לשמה כדתנן בריש מנחות (דף ב.) ומפיק לן מדכתיב כי חטאת היא אין סברא שמה שבאין בדלי דלות יגרום להם בעשירות להיות כשירין שלא לשמן כיון שהדלי דלות עצמן פסול וקשה א"כ לעיל דפריך גבי מצורע מה להנך שכן אינן באין בדלות תאמר במצורע מאי קושיא והלא דלות כג] הייט חטאת העוף וחטאת העוף פסולה שלא לשמה כדתנן בפרק קדשי קדשים (לקמן דף סד:) ומפיק ליה בתורת כהנים מחטאת היא וכיון דפסולה בדלות היאך יש לה לגרום בעשירות הכשר שלא לשמה כד] ואם תאמר והא בחטאת חלב למדה משלמים בהיקש למצוה והיכי ילפי' שאר חטאות במה הצד הא בעיא היא לקמן פרק איזהו מקומן (דף נ.) אי דבר הלמד בהיקש חוזר ומלמד בבנין אב לאו פירכא היא כלל דכולהו חטאות נמי ילפי' למצוה משלמים ולעכב הוא דילפינן בשאר חטאות מהנך דכתיב עכובא בגופייהו ואם תאמר וחטאות הצבור כגון שעירי ראשי חדשים ומועדות מנלן הא לא אתו במה הצד דמה להנך שכן שנוי בעלים פוסל בהן מה שאין כן בקרבן צבור כדאמר לעיל (דף ד.) דשנוי בעלים ליתא בצבור כביחיד אע"ג דלא שייך שנוי בעלים בצבור מ"מ פירכא טובה היא כדאשכחן בפ"ק דקדושין (דף ה:) מה לכסף שכן פודין בו הקדשות ומעשר שני תאמר בחופה וכן פרק החובל (ב"ק דף פח.) מה לאשה שאינה במילה ועוד קשה חטאות פנימיות לרבי שמעון דאמר כל שאינו על מזבח החיצון אין בו משום פיגול איכא למיפרך מה להנך שכן פיגול פוסל בהן תאמר בחטאות הפנימיות ויש לומר דבפר העלם דבר של צבור כתיב חטאת הקהל היא ודרים מינה בת"כ שפסול שלא לשמו אם כן אשכחן צבור וגם פנימי לעכב ולמצוה ילפינן משלמים:

הגה"ה בשאר ימות השנה לשמו פסול. הייט קודם הפסח דבעי עקירה או כגון דנדחו בעלים לפסח שני אבל אח"כ לא דפסח בשאר ימות השנה שלמים ושלמים לשם פסח קשחיט כה] כדאמר בפ' תמיד נשחט (פסחים דף סד.) ובפ' שני דחולין (דף ל.) ומיהו איכא למ"ד בסוף אלו דברים (פסחים דף עג:) דבעי עקירה:

לשמו פסול (*כתוב) בקונטרס דלא חזו כו] למילתייהו ורבינו ש"י הגיה כדאמר בפסחים (דף סא.) שחטו קודם חצות פסול שנאמר בין הערבים וכמה פעמים שנה הכתוב. בקביעות זמנו בארבעה עשר בין הערבים וסוגיא דהש"ס נמי משמע לקמן בגמרא *) כז] הפסח ששחטו שחרית דמבין הערבים נפיק ואין לומר דנפיק מדדרשינן הכא לזבח שלמים שצריך שיעקרנו לזבח שלמים דדילמא הני מילי למצוה אבל לעכב לא:

ואם מן הצאן קרבנו. פי' בקונטרס לאו קרא יתירא דריש אלא ממשמעות דקרא משמע ליה הכי וזהו תימה דאי לא כח] מייתי קרא יתירא מנא ליה לאוקומי בפסח ונראה דמייתורא דריש דלא הוה צריך למכתב לזבח השלמים דאשלמים קאי [ועי"ל] דבסמוך דריש כשב לרבות פסח לאליה ופירש רבינו ש"י דמיותר דמדכתיב בתר הכי בשלמים ואם מן העז קרבנו מכלל דעד השתא איירי בכשב וה"נ י"ל מדכתיב לעיל אם מן הבקר קרבנו מכלל דהכא בצאן מיירי אם כן (י) הצאן מיותר הוא למותר פסח. ברוך:

אי הוה כתב לזבח השלמים כדקאמרת. הוה ליה למימר אי הוה כתב כט] לזבח כדקאמרת דשלמים לא צריך כלל:

אלא לזבח רבויא הוא. משמע ליה לגמרא שהוא רבויא כדאמר *(ב"ק דף סג.) בכל כללא כל רבויא דמשמע ליה לחלק בין כל לבכל הילכך לא דרשינן ליה בכללא ופרטא אלא בריבה ומיעט ובקונטרס האריך בפירושו:

גי' רש"ק סמיך אמי גמירי מהדדי וגי' צ"ק לא קאי אעיקר פירכא סמיך דמי גמירי כו'

גי' צ"ק דלא כתיב על חטאתו גבי עבודה מנלן עכובא אבל כתיב על חטאתו כו'

נ"א הגה"ה

לעיל ד: ב"ק סד. חולין סו. [כריתות כח.]

הגהות הב"ח

(א) גמ' חטאת דע"ז ודשמיעת: (ב) שם ואימא שלמים: (ג) שם אימא לכל דשחיט: (ד) שם לא דמי כללא כ"ב ע"ל דף ד ע"ב: (ה) שם בכללי ופרטי כי האי גוונא דריש כלל: (ו) רש"י ד"ה ואם מן וכו' לאו קרא יתירא. נ"ב כלומר השתא דקס"ד דדריש ליה מכלל ופרט לזבח לאו ייתורא הוא עד דמסיק אלא לזבח ריבויא כו' וכמו שפירש בקונטרס גופיה לשם אבל מודה הקונטרס דמן הצאן ייתורא הוא דאתי לפסח וכדכתבו התוס': (ז) בא"ד דהייט פסח. נ"ב ושלא לשמו נפקא לן מדכתיב מן הצאן קרבנו כלומר ששחט הפסח לשם קרבנו שהוא מחוייב להקריב כגון עולה כו' דהייט שלא לשמו: (ח) ד"ה ואפי' וכו' לשם עולת עוף: (ט) ד"ה אלא לזבח וכו' נפשך כלל כו' וכן וכו' מקרא של ייתור לשון אינו: (י) תוס' ד"ה ואם וכו' א"כ מן הצאן:

שיטה מקובצת

א] ושמיעת אות ד' נמחק: ב] ובשאר ימות השנה לשמו פסול. דלא חזי למידי והתם בפסח שני פריך (שלא) לשמו פסול שלמים לשם פסח קשחיט ומשני לא נצרכא אלא לקודם זמנו דבעי עקירה לכ"ע והילכך קתני פסול כל כמה דלא עקריה ולפסח עצמו לא (הוי) [חזי] דהא שינה בין הערבים לעכב. תוס' טוך: [אא"ה בגמרא שלנו שבדפוס לא נמצא ועי' תוס' ד"ה טעמא שלא לשמו גירסת ר"ת עכ"ה]: ג] ואם מן הצאן. זה לשון הר"פ ואם מן הצאן פי' בקונטרס לאו קרא יתירא כו' ולא נראה דהא כתיב באותה פרשה או זכר או נקבה ופסח אינו בא אלא זכר ועוד דכולה פרשה לא איירי אלא בשלמים והילכך איצטריך קרא לפרושי דין מן שלמים כמו ואם מן הבקר ואם לאו קרא יתירא מנ"ל לאוקמי בפסח ולכך נראה דמייתורא דקרא דריש דהא בתר כן כתיב אם כשב אם עז וא"כ למאי איצטריך ואם מן הצאן דכתיב ברישא דקרא הלא בכלל כשב ועז הוא אלא ש"מ מייתורא הוא לפסח לדרוש דבר הבא מן הצאן יהיה לזבח שלמים. תוס' טוך: ד] דשחיט ליה להוי: ה] ואפילו עופות ואפי' מנחות: ו] ישמעאל הוא דדריש בכללי: ז] עי' בהשמטות בסוף המסכת: ח] שמיעת קול אות ה' נמחק: ט] ויורד שמיעת קול ושמעה קול אלה שבועת ביטוי או כו': י] שבהן שהן חטאות וצריכין לשמה בין בשינוי קודש ובין בשינוי בעלים אף: יא] פסול. דלא חזי למלתיה: יב] אלא ממשמעותא: יג] ואם מדבר: יד] כוותיה. ואם שחטו: טו] ואפילו עופות: טז] לזבח של שלמים אות ה' נמחק:

*) [דף יא:]

גי' צ"ק כדאמרי' בב"ק דמחלק בין כל לבכל הילכך כללא ובכל רבויא ה"נ משמע ליה לחלק בין זבח ובין לזבח הילכך לא כו' וכ"ה בת"י

יז] למכתב וכן לשלמים כל מקרא: יח] תנן בהדיא: יט] חלקת לעכב אף: כ] הג"ה ותיבות ה"ג נמחק: כא] הצד. משלשתן כך פרש"י והדין עמו דהרי מנזיר ומצורע לא אתיא דאיכא למיפרך שכן יש עמהם דמים אחרים ואי מחטאת חלב כו' עד בשאלה וא"ת והשתא נמי דאתיא משלשתן איכא למיפרך מה להנך כו' ותירץ ר"ת דמה שבאים בדלי דלות לא מהני להכשירם שלא לשמה דדלי דלות מאי ניהו עשירית האיפה והיא פסולה שלא לשמה כדכתיב עשירית האיפה היא דמשמע היא לשמה כשירה שלא לשמה פסולה וא"ת כו': כב] לשמה דהיינו: כג] דלות במצורע היינו: כד] לשמה וי"ל דהואיל דאין כל הקרבנות הבאים בדלות פסול בשלא לשמו דהא איכא עולת העוף משום הכי פריך שפיר. תו' ר"פ ותוס' טוך: כה] קשחיט. ס"א למאן דאית ליה לא בעי עקירה גליון: כו] דלא חזי למילתיה: כז] בגמרא דהפסח: כח] לא מייתורא דקרא מנא ליה לאוקמי בפסח כיון דבשלמים כתיב. גליון: כט] כתב לשלמים וזבח:

of forbidden fat, where *for a sin-offering* is written;[5] [8b] how do we know [it of] the sin-offerings of idolatry, hearing a voice, swearing clearly with the lips and the defilement of the Sanctuary and its sacred objects, where [*'for a sin-offering'*] is not written?[6]—The sin-offering of idolatry is inferred from the sin-offering of forbidden fat, since it entails *kareth*, just as the latter does. While all the others are inferred [by analogy] through a common characteristic.[7]

a Our Rabbis taught: The Passover-offering, in its season,[1] [if slaughtered] in its own name, is valid; if not [slaughtered] in its own name, it is invalid. During the rest of the year, [if slaughtered] in its own name, it is invalid; if not [slaughtered] in its own name, it is valid.[2] (Mnemonic: *ShaLeW, KaB'AYZaN, MeMaHeR, BeZa, BA.*) Whence do we know it?—Said Samuel's father: Scripture saith, *And if his offering for a sacrifice of peace-offerings unto the Lord be of the flock*:[3] [this teaches that] whatever comes of the flock is to be for a sacrifice of peace-offerings.[4] Then say, [if sacrificed as] a peace-offering, it is [valid]; but [if sacrificed as] anything else, it is not valid?[5] Said R. Ela in R. Johanan's name: *'For a sacrifice'* includes every sacrifice.[6] Then say, For whatever purpose it is slaughtered, let it be such?[7]—If it were written, 'for peace-offering and a sacrifice', [it would be] as you say; since however it is written, *'for a sacrifice of peace-offerings'*, [its implication is,] for whatever purpose it is slaughtered, let it be a peace-offering. Yet say, *'for a sacrifice'* is a generalization, while *'of peace-offerings'* is a particularization; now [in the case of] a generalization and a particularization, the generalization includes only what is contained in the particularization; [hence if it is sacrificed as] a peace-offering, it is [valid], but [if it is offered as] anything else, it is not [valid]?—*'Unto the Lord'* is again a generalization.[8] To this R. Jacob of Nehar Pekod demurred: But the last generalization is dissimilar from the first, [for] the first generalization includes sacrifices but nothing else, whereas the last generalization, *'unto the Lord'*, implies what-
b ever is the Lord's, even [if he slaughtered it] for fowl-[offerings],[1] and even for meal-offerings?—This is in accordance with the Tanna of the School of R. Ishmael who applies the rule to a generalization and a particularization of this nature, [and maintains that even in such a case, where you have] a generalization, a particularization and a generalization [in this sequence,] you must be guided by the particularization: as the particularization is explicitly something that is not in its own name, and it is valid,[2] so whatever that is not in its own name is valid. Then [say:] as the particularization is explicitly something which can come as a vow or a freewill-offering,[3] so everything which can come as a vow or as a freewill-offering [is included]; [hence, if he slaughters the Passover-offering out of its season as] a burnt-offering or as a peace-offering it is [valid], [but if he slaughters it then as] a sin-offering or a guilt-offering, it is not [valid]!—Rather, *'For a sacrifice'* is an extension.[4] Then say, for

(5) In Lev. IV, 33. The passage deals with an offering brought for sins other than those which the Talmud proceeds to enumerate. (6) The sin-offering of idolatry: *And when ye shall err, and not observe all these commandments* etc.; *and if one person sin through error* etc. (Num. XV, 22, 27). The Talmud relates this to idolatry in ignorance. The text: *And if any one sin, in that* he heareth the voice *of adjuration* etc. ... or *if any one touch an unclean thing* (and then, according to the Rabbinic interpretation, enters the Sanctuary or eats sacred food) ... or *if any one swears clearly with his lips* etc. (Lev. V, 1—4). (7) They are inferred by analogy through the feature common to the sin-offering of forbidden fat, that of a nazirite, and that of a leper. The only feature they have in common is that they are sin-offerings, and both change in respect of sanctity and change in respect of owner disqualify them. Therefore the others here enumerated, which have the same feature, viz., that they are sin-offerings, are likewise disqualified by change of sanctity or change of owner.

a (1) The time for killing it is from midday on the fourteenth of Nisan until nightfall. (2) This refers to an animal dedicated for a Passover-offering which was lost when it was required and found later. It is then to be sacrificed as a peace-offering. (3) Lev. III, 6. (4) Since a Passover-offering comes of the flock it is included in this deduction. Further, that can only mean after its season, for it has already been deduced *supra* that if it is offered for anything but itself in its season it is invalid. (5) Whereas it is simply stated, 'if not slaughtered in its own name, it is valid', which implies that it is valid if sacrificed as *any* offering. (6) For these words (one word in the original) are superfluous, hence they are interpreted as an extension. (7) E.g., if it is slaughtered as a burnt-offering, it is a burnt-offering.—Actually it is a peace-offering under all circumstances. (8) In such cases the generalization includes everything that is similar to the particularization; hence, anything that comes of the flock.

b (1) I.e., if he slaughtered it as the sin-offering of a bird. (2) As explained above. (3) Both are votive offerings. A vow is technically where one vows to bring a sacrifice, without specifying the animal at the time; a freewill-offering is a vow to bring a particular animal for an offering. (4) Rashi: it is not interpreted under the rule of generalization etc., but as an extension, in which case even cases not similar to itself are included. The rule of generalization etc., is applied only where the *natural sense* of the passage yields a generalization and a particularization, without anything in the text being superfluous. Here, however, *'for a sacrifice of peace-offerings'* is regarded as altogether superfluous, and therefore it is held to be an extension.

whatever it is slaughtered, let it be such![5]—Said Rabin: [9a] We transfer sacrifices which are eaten to sacrifices which are eaten, but do not transfer sacrifices which are eaten to sacrifices which are not eaten.[6] Are then a sin-offering and a guilt-offering not eaten?—[Say] rather, we transfer sacrifices which are eaten by all to sacrifices which are eaten by all, but do not transfer sacrifices which
a are eaten by all to sacrifices which are not eaten by all.[1] R. Jose son of R. Abin said: We transfer sacrifices of lesser sanctity to sacrifices of lesser sanctity, but do not transfer sacrifices of lesser sanctity to sacrifices of higher sanctity.[2] To this R. Isaac son of R. Sabarin demurred: Then say that if one slaughtered it as tithe, let it be tithe;[3] and in respect of what law would that be? That it should not require a drink-offering; and that the penalty of flagellation should be incurred by one who violates the injunction, *It shall not be redeemed?*[4]—Scripture saith, *The tenth shall be holy,*[5] [which implies,] this one [the tenth] can be tithe, but no other can be tithe. [Again,] say that if one slaughtered it as a firstling, let it be as a firstling: in respect of which law? That it should not require a drink-offering; or that it should be given to the priests?—As for a firstling too, similarity of law with tithe is deduced from the fact that 'passing' is written in both cases.[6] Say that if one slaughtered it as a substitute,[7] let it be a substitute: in respect of which law? To be flagellated on its account;[8] or alternatively, that in respect thereof we should be guilty of, '*it shall not be redeemed*'?[9]—Said Mar Zuṭra the son of R. Naḥman: Scripture saith, *Then both it and that for which it is changed shall be* [*holy*], [which implies;] This is a substitute but no other is a substitute.[10] And say that if one slaughters is as a thanksoffering, let it be a thanksoffering: in respect of what law? That it may re-
b quire [the addition of] loaves.[1]—Can there be a case where the Passover-offering itself does not require loaves, yet its remainder does require loaves! If so, then now too [you may argue:] Can there be a case where the Passover-offering itself does not require a drink-offering [to accompany it], yet its remainder requires a drink-offering?—This is our argument: Can there be a case where the remainder of the thanksoffering itself requires no loaves, yet the remainder of that which was converted into a thanksoffering[2] shall require loaves!

To this[3] R. Yemar the son of R. Hillel demurred: And whence [does it follow] that it is written in reference to the remainder of a Passover-offering: perhaps it is written of the remainder of a guilt-offering?[4]—Said Raba, Scripture saith: '*And if his offering for a sacrifice of peace-offerings be of the flock*',[5] [which implies that it refers to] that for which the whole flock is equally fit.[6] To this R. Abin b. Ḥiyya—others say, R. Abin b. Kahana—demurred: Everywhere else you say that '*of*' is a limitation, yet here '*of*' is an extension?[7]—Said R. Mani: Here too '*of*' is a limitation, [teaching] that it cannot be two years old nor a female.[8] R. Ḥana of Baghdad demurred: Can you say that this text is written in reference to the Passover-remainder; surely since it states, *If* [*he bring*] *a lamb* [*for his offering*] . . . *And if* [*his offering be*] *a goat,*[9] it follows that it does
c *not* refer to a Passover remainder?[1]—That is required for what was taught: '[*If he bring*] *a lamb*': this is to include the Passover-offering, in respect of its fat tail.[2] When it is stated, 'If [*he bring*] *a lamb*', it is to include a Passover-offering more than a year old,[3] and a peace-offering which comes in virtue of a Passover-offering[4] in respect of all the regulations of peace-offerings, [viz.,] that they require laying on [of the hands],[5] drink-offerings, and the waving of the breast and shoulder. [Again,] when it states, '*and if* [*his offering be*] *a goat*',[6] it breaks across the subject [and] teaches that a goat does not require [the burning of the] fat tail [on the altar].[7] But is that[8] deduced from this? Surely it is deduced from [the verse quoted by] Samuel's father? For Samuel's father said: *And if his offering for a sacrifice of peace-offerings unto the Lord be of the flock*[9] [teaches that] whatever comes of the flock must be for a sacrifice of peace-offerings.[10]—But still, this is deduced from [the verse quoted by] R. Naḥman in the name of Rabbah b. Abbuhah. For R. Naḥman said in Rabbah b. Abbuha's name: How do we know that a Passover remainder is brought as a peace-offering? Because it says, *And thou shalt sacrifice the Passover-offering unto the Lord thy God, of the flock and of the herd.*[11] Yet surely the Passover-offering comes only from lambs or from goats? From this [we learn] that the Pass-over-remainder must be [utilised] for something which comes from
d the flock and from the herd; and what is it? A peace-offering.[1]

(5) As above. (6) The animal dedicated for a Passover-offering was in the first place consecrated as a sacrifice which is eaten. Now that it cannot be offered for what it was originally intended, it is transferred to a peace-offering, which is eaten, and not to a burnt-offering, which cannot be eaten.

a (1) The Passover-offering and peace-offering are eaten by all, whereas the sin-offering and the guilt-offering are eaten by male priests only. (2) These are fully discussed in Ch. V. (3) For that too is a sacrifice of lesser sanctity. (4) Lev. XXVII, 33. The Talmud (Bek. 32*b*) interprets this to mean that it may not be sold; hence if one does sell it, he is liable to flagellation, which is the penalty for the violation of a negative command. (5) Ibid. 32. (6) Tithe: *Whatsoever passeth under the rod* (ibid); Firstling: *All that openeth the womb thou shalt cause to pass* (E.V. *Set apart*—the same root is used in both texts) *to the Lord* (Ex. XIII, 12). The employment of the same word in both cases teaches that they are similar in law. Therefore since this Passover-offering cannot be transferred to tithe, it cannot be transferred to a firstling either. (7) Lev. XXVII, 33: *Neither shall he change it; and if he change it at all, then both it and that for which it is changed shall be holy; it shall not be redeemed.* From this it is learnt that if one consecrates an animal to substitute another consecrated animal, both are holy, the second having the same sanctity as the first. (8) For having violated the injunction, *Neither shall he change it.* (9) Sh. M. deletes. (10) I.e., only if one consecrates a non-sacred animal (*ḥullin*, v. Glos) as a substitute does the law apply, but not when one consecrates as a substitute an animal which had already been consecrated earlier, as is the case of this lost Passover-offering.

b (1) V. Lev. VII, 12 seq. (2) Lit., 'the remainder of that which comes thereto (*sc.* the thanksoffering) from the world.'—Thus here we are treating of the remainder of a Passover-offering which it is proposed shall rank as a thanksoffering if slaughtered as such. (3) *Sc.* the interpretation of the verse Lev. III, 6 quoted *supra* 8*b*, q.v. (4) Since a guilt-offering too was a ram without blemish from the flock, and might not come from the herd. (5) Lev. III, 6. (6) I.e., sheep and goats too, whereas the guilt-offering must be a ram. (7) If you interpret *of the flock* as intimating that *all* animals included in the term 'flock' are meant. (8) By relating the verse to a Passover-offering remainder you exclude a two years old animal and a female. (V. Ex. XII, 5). (9) Lev. III, 7, 12.

c (1) This verse must simply refer to an ordinary peace-offering; for if it referred to a Passover remainder, it is obviously a lamb or a goat (V. Ex. XII, 5), and it need not be stated. (2) The fat tail of all other sacrifices is explicitly counted in the *emurim* (q.v. Glos) which are burnt on the altar (V. Lev. III, 9; VII, 3). The burning of the *emurim* is not mentioned at all in connection with the Passover, however, but deduced from elsewhere; consequently a verse is required to teach that the fat tail too is included. (3) I.e., dedicated as a Passover-offering, and consequently unfit for its purpose (V. Ex. XII, 5). (4) E.g., the substitute of a Passover-offering; or where the owner of a Passover-offering registered for a different animal, so that the first is a Passover remainder: both are sacrificed as peace-offerings. (5) V. Lev. III, 2. (6) Ibid. 12. (7) '*And if*' is regarded as a disjunctive, teaching that the provisions that apply to a lamb do not apply to a goat, unless expressly stated. The fat tail is mentioned in connection with the former (V. 9) but not the latter. (8) *Sc.* that a Passover-offering more than a year old, which is therefore a Passover remainder, is sacrificed as a peace-offering. (9) Lev. III, 6. (10) *Supra* 8*b*, q.v. (11) Deut. XVI, 2.

d (1) *Supra* 7*b*. Hence if you object that the law under discussion is deducted in accordance with the teaching of Samuel's father, it can be counter-objected that it follows from the verse last quoted.

דוחין קדשים הנאכלים אצל קדשים הנאכלין ואין דוחין קדשים הנאכלין אצל קדשים שאינן נאכלין אטו חטאת ואשם מי לא מיתאכלי אלא דוחין קדשים הנאכלין לכל אדם אצל קדשים הנאכלין לכל אדם ואין דוחין קדשים הנאכלין לכל אדם אצל קדשים שאין נאכלין לכל אדם רבי יוסי ברבי אבין אמר דוחין קדשים קלים אצל קדשים קלים ואין דוחין קדשים קלים אצל קדשי קדשים מתקיף לה רב יצחק ברבי א] סבריו אימא שחטיה לשם מעשר ליהוי מעשר למאי הילכתא דלא ליבעי נסכים ב] ולמלקא עליה ג] (בלא ימכר) °בלא יגאל אמר קרא °העשירי יהיה קודש זה מעשר ואין אחר מעשר אימא שחטיה לשם בכור ליהוי כבכור למאי הילכתא דלא ליבעי נסכים ד] אי נמי דליתביה לכהנים בכור נמי עברה *עברה ממעשר גמר ואימא שחטיה לשם תמורה ליהוי תמורה למאי הילכתא למלקא עליה ה] אי נמי למיקם עליה °בלא ימכר ולא יגאל אמר מר זוטרא בריה דרב נחמן אמר קרא °והיה הוא ותמורתו זו ו] תמורה ואין אחר תמורה ואימא שחטיה לשם תודה ליהוי כי תודה למאי הילכתא להטעינו לחם מי איכא מידי דפסח גופיה לא בעי לחם ומותרו בעי לחם אי הכי השתא נמי מי איכא מידי דפסח גופיה לא בעי נסכים ומותרו בעי נסכים אנן הכי קאמרינן מי איכא מידי דמותר תודה עצמה לא בעי לחם ואילו מותר דאתיא ז] להו מעלמא בעיא לחם מתקיף לה רב ח] [יימר] בריה דרב הילל וממאי דבמותר פסח כתיב דילמא במותר אשם כתיב אמר רבא אמר קרא °ואם מן הצאן קרבנו לזבח שלמים דבר השוה בכל (א) הצאן מתקיף לה ר' אבין בר חייא ואיתימא ר' אבין בר כהנא בכל אתר את אמרת מן להוציא וכאן מן לרבות אמר ר' מני הכא נמי מן להוציא דלא אתי בן שתי שנים ולא אתי (ב) בנקיבה מתקיף לה רב חנא בגדתאה ומי מצית אמרת דכי כתיב האי במותר פסח כתיב ט] והא מדכתיב °אם כשב (ג) °אם עז מכלל דלאו במותר פסח כתיב ההוא מיבעי ליה *לכדתניא (ד) כבש לרבות את הפסח לאליה כשהוא אומר אם כבש לרבות *פסח שעיברה י] שנתה ושלמים הבאים מחמת פסח לכל מצות שלמים שיטענו סמיכה ונסכים ותנופת חזה ושוק כשהוא אומר (ה) אם עז הפסיק הענין לימד °על העז שאינה טעונה אליה והא מהכא נפקא מדאבוה דשמואל נפקא דאמר אבוה דשמואל ואם מן הצאן קרבנו לזבח שלמים דבר הבא מן הצאן יהא לזבח שלמים *ואכתי מדרב נחמן אמר רבה בר אבוה נפקא *דאמר רב נחמן אמר רבה בר אבוה מנין למותר פסח שקרב שלמים שנאמר °וזבחת פסח לה' אלהיך צאן ובקר והלא אין פסח בא אלא מן הכבשים ומן העזים אלא מכאן למותר הפסח שיהא לדבר הבא מן הצאן ומן הבקר ומאי נידו שלמים יא] אלא תלתא קראי כתיבי
חד

תורה אור: ויקרא כז | שם | שם | שם | שם ג | שם | שם | דברים טז

רש"י

דוחין קדשים הנאכלין. פסח זה מתחלה הוקדש לשם קרבן הנאכל הילכך דוחין אותו אצל שלמים שהן נאכלין ולא אצל עולה (ו): שאין נאכלין לכל אדם. אלא לזכרי כהונה: ליהוי מעשר. דהא קדשים קלים הוא. בכור ומעשר אין טעונין נסכים בפרק שתי מדות (מנחות דף צ:): במעשר בהמה כתיב יהיה קודש לא יגאל ודרשינן בבכורות בפרק כל פסולי המוקדשין (דף לב:) דהאי לא יגאל לא ימכר הוא: עברה עברה. בבכור כתיב (שמות יג) והעברת כל פטר רחם ובמעשר כתיב כל אשר יעבור תחת השבט (ויקרא כז): למילקא עלה. משום לא יחליפנו: זו תמורה. (ז) ממש יב] שהעומדת כשהיא חולין אצל בהמת קדשים והמיר יג] הוא דהויא תמורה: ואין אחר. זבח (ח) יד] ראשון ששחטו לשם תמורה: ומותרו בעי נסכים. דהא אמרת שלמים ניהוי טו]: דמותר תודה עצמה. כגון הפריש תודתו ואבדה והפריש אחרת ונמצאת הראשונה אין השניה טעונה לחם כדאמרי' בפ' התודה (מנחות דף עט:) טז] זבח התודה טעון לחם ולא ולדה ולא תמורתה ולא חליפתה טעונין לחם: ומותר דאתי לה מעלמא. תודה שבאה ממותר פסח: דילמא במותר אשם כתיב. האי ואם מן הצאן דאשם נמי איל תמים מן הצאן הוא ואינו בא מן הבקר: בכל צאן. בכבשים ועזים כגון פסח לאפוקי אשם דאינו בא מן העזים: בכל אתר את אמר. בכל מקום אתה אומר מן להוציא הוא כגון מן הבהמה להוציא רובע ונרבע מן הבקר להוציא את הנעבד מן הצאן להוציא את המוקצה (ב"ק דף מ:): וכאן אתה אומר מן לרבות. דקאמרת יז] [מן הצאן] פסח משמע שבא מכל צאן: ה"נ. כי מוקמינן לה בפסח מן להוציא הוא דלא אתי בן שתי שנים ולא אתי נקיבה ומיהו הצאן מכל מין צאן משמע בין כבשים בין עזים ומיעוטא דמן לנקיבות אתא: ה"ג דלא אתי בן שתי שנים ולא אתי נקיבה: והא מדכתיב אם כבש (ט) אם עז מכלל דלאו במותר הפסח הוא דכתיב. אלא בשלמים גרידי וה"ק אם נדר להביא מן הצאן יביא איזה שירצה או כבש או עז דאי במותר הפסח כתיב למה לי אם כבש אם עז פשיטא דמכבשים ומעזים הוא בא דהא בגופיה כתיב מן הכבשים ומן העזים (שמות יב): לכדתניא כו'. לחלק ביניהם ולפרש הילכותיהן לומר (י) שהכבש טעון אליה למזבח והעז אין אלייתו בכלל אימורים: כבש. קרא יתירא הוא דכיון דכתיב יח] [מעיקרא ואם מן הצאן וכתיב] בתריה ואם עז מכלל דעד השתא בכבש איירי דאין לך מן הצאן אלא שני מינין: לאליה. שתהא יט] קריבה עם אימורין כנגד הכליות ולמטה דכתיב לעומת העצה יסירנה מקום שהכליות יועצות: שלמים הבאין מחמת פסח. חגיגת ארבעה עשר כדאמרי' בפסחים (דף סט:): והא מהכא נפקא. דפסח שעברה שנתו קרב שלמים והלא זה הוא מותר הפסח והא ילפת לה לעיל מדאבוה דשמואל: ומאי ניהו שלמים. דבאין מכל צאן ובקר בין זכרים ובין נקיבות:
עיברה

תוספות

דוחין קדשים קלים. נראה דבין ר' יוסי בר' אבין ורבי אבין איכא בינייהו בכור דלרבי אבין ליכא למיפרך מבכור דאין נאכל לכל אדם: דלא ליבעי נסכים. הוה מצי למימר דלא ליבעי תנופת חזה ושוק: כ] למאי נפקא מינה למילקא עליה בלא יגאל. תימה היכי לקי אחר שחיטה כא] אלא יגאל הא אמרינן בבכורות בפרק כל פסולי המוקדשין (דף לב:) דלאחר שחיטה מדרבנן: העשירי זה מעשר. אכתי דרשינן מינה (ב"מ דף ו.) עשירי ודאי ולא עשירי ספק: אי נמי דליתביה לכהנים. הוה מצי למימר נמי דלא בעי סמיכה כדדרשינן בת"כ וסמך ידו על ראש קרבנו ולא בכור ומעשר ופסח (מנחות דף צג:): דילמא במותר אשם כתיב. תימה הא כתיב הכא לזבח השלמים ואילו מותר אשם קרב עולה כב] וי"ל דהאי דכתיב לזבח השלמים לאו שיהיה לזבח השלמים אלא שיעקור שם אשם ממנו לשוחטו לשם שלמים או לשם זבח אחר כדדרשינן ליה (לעיל דף ח:) בכלל ופרט ולעולם קרב עולה ואתא קרא למימר דבעי עקירה: ושלמים הבאין מחמת פסח לכל מצות שלמים. פי' בקונטרס חגיגת ארבעה עשר וכן לקמן סוף כל הפסולים (דף לו.) גבי תודה שנאכלת ליום ולילה מנין לרבות שלמי נזיר ושלמי פסח ת"ל שלמיו ופי' בקונטרס שלמי פסח חגיגת י"ד וקשה דבפסחים באלו דברים (דף ע:) דריש מקרא בהדיא דחגיגת י"ד נאכלת לשני ימים ולילה אחד כג] [ובת"כ בפ' בשר זבח תודת שלמיו מרבי חגיגת י"ד לשני ימים ולילה אחד] ושלמים הבאין מחמתו ליום ולילה ונראה דודאי שלמי פסח דכל הפסולין (שם) היינו מותר הפסח כד] כי ההוא דת"כ ובפסחים פ' האשה (דף פט.) גבי חמשה שנתערבו עורות פסחיהם דקאמר וניתי מותר הפסח דנאכל ליום ולילה ובפ"ק דר"ה (דף ה.) קרי למותר הפסח שלמי פסח לחשיב פסח לבל תאחר ופריך פסח זימנא קביעא ליה כו' ומשני מאי פסח שלמי פסח סד"א הואיל ומחמת פסח קאתו ועל כרחיה לאו היינו חגיגת י"ד דכיון דקתני פסח לא שביק מותר הפסח דמיקרי פסח טפי דהיינו פסח ממש ומוקי לה בחגיגת י"ד ושלמים הבאין מחמת הפסח דשמעתין נמי היינו מותר הפסח אע"ג דכבר תנא פסח שעיברה שנתו האי שלמי פסח הוי לא עיברה שנתו כה] ולא זמנו *) או עיברה זמנו ולא שנתו אע"ג דמקרא אחרינא נפקי הכי רגילות התנא כמו (ב"מ דף ל.) והתעלמת דדריש פעמים שמתעלם כגון זקן ואינה לפי כבודו וכהן והוא בבית הקברות כו] [ושלו מרובה משל חבירו אע"ג] דקרא לא אתי אלא לזקן ואינה לפי כבודו ובפ' מי שהיה טמא (פסחים דף צו:) פי' בקונטרס דהיינו תמורת פסח עצמו ואע"ג דדרשינן התם הוא קרב ואין תמורתו קריבה הא מוכח התם דכל היכא דפסח קרב גם תמורתו קריבה ולקמן פרק ב"ש (דף לז.) בתחלתו כז] נדקדק וכן משמע דפריך מותר הפסח ליהוי תודה למאי כח] להטעינו לחם מי איכא מידי כו' ולימא להוית נאכל ליום ולילה כמו תודה אלא ש"מ מותר פסח נמי בלאו הכי נאכלים ליום ולילה דהיינו שלמי פסח. נ"ל ברו"ך:
חד

*) גי' רש"ק או עיברה זמנו ושנתו אע"ג כו'

עין משפט נר מצוה

מב א מיי' פ"ד מהל' קרבן פסח הל"ז:
מג ב מיי' פ"א מהל' מעש"ק הל"ח:

שיטה מקובצת

א] ברבי סברין: ב] נסכים ולמלקא. ס"א ולמיקם עליה בלא (ימכר) [יגאל] תימה דהא [בפ' כל פסולי המוקדשים] ילפינן לה מתמורה מה תמורה מחיים אף [מעשר] מחיים וכי [עביד] פסח לשם מעשר אחר שחיטה הוא [ואינו עובר] עליו משום לא יגאל ואומר ריב"א דמכי שחיט [ליה] אתעקר משם פסח [ועדיין] הוא חי ואית ביה בלא יגאל כדאמרי' [יבמות דף קכ וגיטין דף ע] שחט שנים או רוב שנים הרי הוא כחי לכל דבריו. תוס' סוף: ג] תיבות בלא ימכר נמחק: ד] נסכים א"נ למיקם עליה בלא ימכר ובלא יגאל אי נמי כו': ה] תיבות א"נ למיקם עליה בלא ימכר ולא יגאל נמחק: ו] זו בתמורה: ז] דאתיא לה: ח] רב יימר: ט] והא מדכתיב אם כשב. פ"ה דאי במותר הפסח כו' וקשה לפי' שני דפי' לעיל דמייתורא דקרא קא דריש שפיר א"צטריך אם כבש אם עז לגופיה לריבה ומיעט וריבה דכתיב גבי שלמים דאין מקרא יוצא מידי פשוטו והילכך איצטריך משום שלמים שאם נדר מן הצאן יביא מה שירצה או כבש או עז [ועוד] דלעיל היה לו להקשות זאת הקושיא לכך פי' הר"ם דהא אתקפתא להא דאמר דבר הבא מן הצאן דבר השוה בכל צאן וה"ק · אא"ב במותר אשם איירי קרא ומאי מן הצאן מקצת צאן ניחא דא"צטריך אם כבש אם עז לגופיה לשלמים לומר שבאים מן הצאן שהרי מן הצאן ליכא למילף דהא הצאן לא משמע כי אם מקצת צאן דשייך באשם אלא אי אמרת קרא מיירי במותר הפסח ור"ל דבר הבא מכל צאן יהיה לזבח שלמים הא שלמים אקרי פסח ופסח ידעינן שפיר מקרא אחרינא שבא מכבש ועז דכתיב מן הכבשים ומן העזים תקחו וא"כ או כבש או עז למה לי אלא ש"מ דלא במותר פסח כתיב: י] שעיברה שנתו: יא] אלא תלתא קראי כתיבי. (פי') חד לקודם זמנו ונראה לפרש דקרא דלעיל ואם מן הצאן מיירי בקודם זמנו ולהכי בעי עקירה כדפי' לעיל לשמו פסול מכעין הפרט או מריבה ומיעט אבל אינך קראי מיירי לאחר זמנו ולא משתמע מינייהו דבעי עקירה אלא משתמע מינייהו דלגמרי הוו שלמים בלא עקירה ולמאן דאמר דלאחר זמנו נמי בעי עקירה אע"ג דלא מוכח מקראי מ"מ יליף לה מקודם זמנו וא"ת מאי פריך והא מרבא נפקא מהתם נפקא מן הצאן דבר הבא בכל צאן דמיירי קודם זמנו לעברה שנתו דאיירי לאחר זמנו וי"ל דעיקר [קושיא] מההיא דמייתי דוזבחת פסח צאן ובקר אההיא דעברה שנתו דמיירי לאחר זמנו אבל מההיא דמן הצאן דמיירי קודם זמנו לא פריך דשפיר היה יודע דמיירי התם בקודם זמנו מדבעי עקירה ואגב דמצריך להו מצריך נמי קרא דמן הצאן כך נראה למורי. סוף: יב] שהעמדה: יג] והמיר בה הוא: יד] זבח אחר תיבת ראשון נמחק ס"א תיבת זבח אינו: טו] ניהוי ושלמים בעי סמיכה ונסכים הס"ד: טז] תיבת זבח נמחק: יז] דקאמרת מן הצאן: יח] מעיקרא ואם מן הצאן וכתיב: יט] שתהא אליתו קריבה עם אימוריו כנגד: כ] מה"ד ולמלקא ותיבות למאי נפקא מינה נמחק: כא] שחיטה על לא אות א' נמחק: כב] עולה לפר"ת או רועה לפרש"י כדאמרי' כל שבחטאת מתה באשם רועה וי"ל דאתא קרא לפרושי הוא דאמרי' באשם רועה היינו קודם עקירה ששחטו סתמא אבל אם עקר אותו אשם בשעת שחיטה אשמעינן קרא דהוי שלמים. תוס' סוף: כג] אחד ובת"כ בפרשת בשר זבח תודת שלמיו מרבי חגיגת י"ד לשני ימים ולילה אחד: כד] הפסח אמנם ריב"א מפרש כפרש"י דבמותר פסח לא איירי א"כ היינו עברה שנתו: כה] עיברה שנתו וזמנו תיבת ולא ל"ש ונמחק: כו] ואבידתו מרובה תיבות ושלו משל חבירו ואע"ג ל"ש ונמחק: כז] בתחלתו מדקדק כן וכן משמע עוד לעיל דפריך: כח] למאי הלכתא:
חד

מסורת הש"ס

[לקמן לז: מעילה יג. תמורה ה:]
פסחים עו: לז. מנחות פב.
כמו וליטעמיך
[לעיל ז: מנחות פג. פסחים ע:]

הגהות הב"ח

(א) גמ' השוה בכל צאן כצ"ל ואות ה' נמחק: (ב) שם ולא אתי נקבה כצ"ל ואות ב' נמחק: (ג) שם מדכתיב אם כשב ואם עז: (ד) שם לכדתניא כשב לרבות: (ה) שם כשהוא אומר ואם עז: (ו) רש"י ד"ה דוחין וכו' אצל עולה שאין נאכל הס"ד: (ז) ד"ה זו תמורה תמורה ממש: (ח) ד"ה ואין אחר זבח אחר ששחטו: (ט) ד"ה והא מדכתיב וכו' ואם עז וכו' במותר פסח הוא וכו' במותר פסח כתיב למה לי אם כשב אם: (י) ד"ה לכדתניא וכו' לומר שהכשב טעון וכו' אימורין הס"ד ואח"כ מ"ה כשב יתורא וכו' השתא בכשב איירי:

*חד א] לעיברה זמנו ועיברה שנתו וחד לעיברה זמנו ולא שנתו וחד ללא עיברה לא זמנו ולא שנתו וצריכי דאי כתב רחמנא חד הוה אמינא (א) היכא ב] דעיברה שנתו וזמנו דאידחי מפסח לגמרי אבל עיברה זמנו ולא שנתו דחזי לפסח שני אימא לא ואי כתב רחמנא הני תרתי משום דאידחי להו ממילתייהו אבל היכא דלא עבר לא זמנו ולא שנתו דחזי לפסח אימא לא צריכי: אמר רב משמיה דמבוג חטאת ששחטה לשום חטאת נחשון כשירה דאמר קרא °זאת תורת החטאת *תורה אחת לכל החטאות יתיב רבא וקאמר לה להא שמעתא איתיביה רב משרשיא לרבא רבי שמעון אומר *כל המנחות שנקמצו שלא לשמן כשירות ועלו לבעלים לשום חובה לפי שאין המנחות דומות לזבחים שהקומץ מחבת לשם מרחשת מעשיה מוכיחין עליה שהיא מחבת חריבה לשם בלולה מעשיה מוכיחין שהיא חריבה אבל בזבחים אינו כן שחיטה אחת לכולן קבלה אחת לכולן ג] זריקה אחת לכולן טעמא דמעשיה מוכיחין הא אין מעשיה מוכיחין לא אמאי לימא °זאת תורת המנחה *תורה אחת לכל המנחות אלא אי איתמר הכי איתמר אמר רב משמיה דמבוג חטאת ששחטה על מנת שיתכפר בה נחשון כשירה *אין כפרה למתים ולימא מת בעלמא הא קמ"ל טעמא דמת הא ד] דחי דומיא דנחשון פסולה ומאי ניהו חטאת נזיר וחטאת מצורע ה] הני עולות נינהו אלא אי איתמר הכי איתמר אמר רב משמיה דמבוג חטאת ששחטה על ו] שמחוייב חטאת כנחשון (ב) כשירה חטאת נחשון עולה היא ז] איכא דאמר אמר רב משמיה דמבוג חטאת ששחטה (ג) לשם חטאת נחשון פסולה חטאת נחשון ח] עולה היא ולימא חטאת נזיר וחטאת מצורע עיקר חטאת נקט *אמר ט] *רב חטאת חלב ששחטה לשם חטאת דם לשם חטאת עבודת כוכבים כשירה לשם חטאת נזיר לשם חטאת מצורע פסולה הני עולות נינהו בעי רבא חטאת חלב ששחטה לשם חטאת דטומאת מקדש וקדשיו מהו מי אמרינן כרת כמותה או דילמא אין קבוע כמותה י] *רב אחא בריה דרבא מתני כולהו לפסולא מ"ט °ושחט אותה לחטאת לשם אותה חטאת א"ל רב אשי לרב אחא בריה דרבא יא] [בעיא דרבא] היכי מתניתו לה אמר ליה אנן בשינוי בעלים מתנינן לה יב] [והכי מתנינן לה] אמר רבא חטאת חלב ששחטה על מי שמחוייב חטאת דם וחטאת עבודת כוכבים פסולה על מי שמחוייב חטאת נזיר וחטאת מצורע כשירה יג] ובעיין לה הכי בעי רבא חטאת חלב ששחטה על מי שמחוייב חטאת דטומאת מקדש וקדשיו מהו מי אמרי' כרת כמותה או יד] דילמא אין קבוע כמותה תיקו: *איתמר שחטה לשמה לזרוק דמה שלא לשמה רבי יוחנן אמר פסולה וריש לקיש אמר כשירה ר' יוחנן אמר פסולה מחשבין מעבודה לעבודה וילפינן ממחשבת פיגול ור"ל אמר כשירה אין מחשבין מעבודה לעבודה ולא ילפינן ממחשבת פיגול ואזדו לטעמייהו דאיתמר השוחט

רש"י

טו] עיברה זמנו. זמן שחיטת הפסח: לא זמנו ולא שנתו. טז] ואם שחטו קודם הפסח לשם שלמים כשר ואע"ג דחזי לפסח ראשון: ממילתייהו. מפסח ראשון: משמיה דמבוג. שם מקום: חטאת ששחטה לשם חטאת נחשון. שעיר יז] חטאת [דחנוכת] הנשיאים: כשרה. ולא הויא שינוי קדש דלא אמרי' חטאת נחשון כיון דלדורון אתי ולא לכפרה על חטא הרי היא (ד) יח] כשחיטה לשם עולה וכ"ש דשינוי בעלים לא הוי דלא שחטה להתכפר בה נחשון: ועלו לבעלים. ר"ש פליג אמנחות ומודה בזבחים: מחבת ומרחשת. שני כלים שבהם מטגנים את המנחות שכל המנחות היו יט] עשר עשר חלות מחבת לפה ומעשיה קשים (ה) כ] מתוך שהכלי צף מעשיה מתפשטין והאור שורף את השמן מרחשת עמוקה ומעשיה רוחשין ורכין שאין האור שורף את השמן וכשמניח אדם אצבעו עליה נראה כמו כא] רוחשת: חריבה. מנחת חוטא שאין בה שמן דכתיב (ויקרא ה) לא ישים עליה שמן: מעשיה מוכיחין. דמחשבה הניכרת שהיא שקר סבר ר"ש דלא מהניא: שחיטה אחת לכולן. וכי שחיט עולה לשם חטאת ליכא הכירא דמשקר הילכך מהניא כב] מחשבה כ"ך שמעתי במנחו"ת: טעמא כו'. אלמא אפי' לרבי שמעון דמהדר (ו) להכשירא לא יליף מזאת תורה וכ"ש דמדרבנן קשיא לך דאמרי אף במנחות לא עלו אלמא לא דרשי כג] תורה להכי ולרבא דאמר לעיל (דף ז.) חטאת חלב ששחטה לשם חטאת דם כשירה ליכא למיפרך מינה דהתם כיון דכי הדדי נינהו דתרוייהו חטאת סתמא שמייהו וכפרת שתיהן שוה על הכרת אין שם שינוי קודש והרי חטאת לשם חטאת נשחטה ואילו מנחת מחבת ומנחת מרחשת אין שמותיהן שוין זו שמה לבדה וזו שמה לבדה אלא לרב קשיא דהא לשם חטאת נחשון שינוי גמור הוא שהרי היא כעולה וקאמר כשרה משום תורת כד] חטאת: אלא אי איתמר. דרב הכי איתמר ובשינוי בעלים איתמר: שיתכפר בה (ז). היינו שינוי בעלים: שאין כפרה למתים. הילכך לא קרינא ביה במחוייב כפרה כמותו: הא חי. אם שחטה בשינוי בעלים לשם אדם חי: דומיא דנחשון. שמחוייב חטאת שאינה על חטא הדומה לשעיר נחשון כגון חטאת נזיר ומצורע הבאות להכשיר פסולה: ופרכינן הני עולות נינהו. ואנן כה] קים לן לעיל (דף ז.) חטאת ששחטה על מי שמחוייב עולה כשירה והני כעולה דמו כו]: פשיטא ל"ג: עיקר חטאת נקט. שורש החטאת שהיא היתה חטאת יחיד ראשונה כז]: לשם חטאת עבודת כוכבים. רבותא נקט אע"ג דלא דמיא לשאר חטאות שהן בכבשה או שעירה והיא איכא כשירה בכבשה אלא בשעירה כח]: בעיא דרבא היכי מתניתו לה. (ח) וכיון דאמרת דרבא בכולהו פסיל ואפילו חטאת חלב לשם חטאת דם כ"ש לשם חטאת דטומאת מקדש וקדשיו: מי אמרינן כרת כמותה. והוה ליה מחוייב כפרה כמותו וקרינן ביה עליו ולא על חבירו וחבירו דומיא דידיה או דילמא (ט) כו' דאין קבוע כמותו שבא בעולה ויורד: שחטה לשמה. שלא חישב על השחיטה אלא על הזריקה חישב בשעת שחיטה דהיינו מעבודה לעבודה: מחשבין מעבודה לעבודה. כלומר מחשבה מועלת מעבודה לעבודה במחשבת שלא לשמו: כט] דילפינן ממחשבת פיגול. דמהניא ביה *הכי דתנן בפרק שני (לקמן דף כז:) השוחט את הזבח על מנת לזרוק דמו למחר פיגול: אין מחשבין מעבודה לעבודה. בשלא לשמו דלא ילפינן לה מפיגול דהתם עיקר מחשבתו המביאה לידי פיגול זו היא ל] שיחשוב בעבודה זו לעשות עבודה אחרת מן אחת העבודות להאכיל לאדם או למזבח חוץ לזמנו וזריקה אכילת מזבח היא והוא הדין לא] אם חישב על הקטרת החלב שאינה מן לב] עבודות הילכך לא דמיא לשלא לשמו:

תוספות

חד לעיברה שנתו וזמנו. ה"ה שנתו בלא זמנו ואע"פ שבשעה שהקדישו לא היה ראוי לפסח דכשיגיע זמנו תעבור שנתו דאפי' לג] מפריש נקיבה לפסחו או זכר בן שתי שנים תורת שלמים עליו כדתנן במי שהיה טמא (פסחים דף צז:) ירעה עד שיסתאב וימכר ויביא בדמיו שלמים: איתיביה רב משרשיא לרבא כו'. לד] תימה מאי קושיא הא רבא הוא דמפרש טעמא דר"ש בריש מנחות (דף ג:) מזאת תורת ואומר ר"ת דהכא גרסי' רבה ורבה לטעמיה דמשני התם כאן בשינוי קודש כאן בשינוי בעלים ועוד י"ל דאפי' גרסינן רבא רוצה ליישב דברי רב לכולהו אמוראי דהתם ולפי' ר"ת קשה דנראה דרב משרשיא תלמידו של רבא היה ולא של רבה ועוד י"ל שרוצה רבא ליישב דברי רב משמיה דמבוג אפי' כרבנן דפליגי עליה דר"ש דלית להו זאת תורת ורב משרשיא כשהקשה לו מר"ש היה יכול להקשות ממתני' דמנחות אלא ניחא ליה למיפרך מברייתא דאפי' לר"ש דמכשיר לא מזאת תורת מכשיר וכן משמע מפי' הקונטרס ואע"ג דבפ' דם חטאת (לקמן דף צג.) דרשינן תורה אחת לכל החטאות ליכא מאן דפליג היינו במידי דכתיבא בהדיא בחטאת גופה דרשינן ליה לכ"ע כגון לה] הני דפרק דם חטאת אבל שינוי קודש לא כתב בחטאת ובריש איזהו מקומן (לקמן דף מח.) דדריש תורה אחת לכל האשמות וקאמר הניחא למאן דאית ליה תורת אלא למאן דלית ליה תורת היינו לר"ש ולרבנן לו] בריש מנחות (דף ג:) לרבא: לשם חטאת נזיר לשם חטאת מצורע. לעיל (דף ז.) איכא שמעתא אחריתי לז] *דרב דמחלק בין שוחט [לשם חטאת] לשוחט לשם עולה ושם פירשתי תרתי דרבא למה לי: ושחט אותה לחטאת. לעיל בפירקין *דרשינן ליה למילתא אחריתי ושמא הכא דריש מדלא כתיב ושחט לחטאת אותה: על מי שמחוייב חטאת דטומאת מקדש וקדשיו מהו. *מיהו גרע ממי שאינו מחוייב כלום: מחשבין מעבודה לעבודה. כדאמר כגון משחיטה לזריקה לח] (כמו שינוי בעלים) אבל משחיטה לקבלה לא דהא מפיגול יליף לה וק"ו לט] דרב אשי דיליף משינוי בעלים*) לא הוי אלא משחיטה לזריקה כמו שינוי בעלי'

*) נ"א נמי לא הוי כו' נ"ק ותימה

עין משפט נר מצוה

מד א מיי' פט"ו מהל' פסה"מ הל"ט:
מה ב מיי' שם הל"ו.
מו ג ד מיי' שם הל"ו:
מז ה מיי' שם הל"י:

שיטה מקובצת

א] חד לעברה זמנו ועברה שנתו וחד לעברה זמנו כו' ללא עברה: ב] היכא דעברת כו' אבל עברה: ג] זריקה אחת לכולן כו'. ולא אמר הולכה אחת לכולן משום דר"ש היא דמכשיר בהילוך משום דהוי עבודה דאפשר לבטלה והא דקאמר זריקה אחת לכולן ואע"ג דיש ניתנין במתן ד' ויש ניתנין במתן אחת הוא אין מעשיה מוכיחין דהא קי"ל כל הניתנין במתן ד' שנתנן במתן אחת כיפר. תוס' סוף: ד] הא חי דומיא: ה] הני עולות נינהו. ואין זו שינוי בעלים דלא פסלינן שינוי בעלים אלא א"כ שינה למחוייב כפרה כמותו וכיון דעולה לאו לכפרה אתא א"כ אין מחוייב כפרה כמותו. סוף: ו] על מי שמחוייב: ז] עולה היא ס"א ולאו בר מינה ואינו שינוי בעלים: ח] נחשון כעולה הוא. אות י' נמחק: ט] אמר רבא: י] כמותה תיקו: יא] דרבא בעיא דרבא: יב] לה והכי מתנינן לה אמר רבא: יג] כשירה דהני עולות נינהו (והוי) [ולא הוי] שינוי בעלים דלאו מינה ובעיין: יד] דילמא אין קבוע כמותה. הקשה הר"ר יחיאל מפאריז תיפשוט ליה מדידיה דלא בעי קבוע כמותה דאי בעי (לעיל) אמאי איצטריך [לעיל לומר] הני עולות נינהו תיפוק ליה דחטאת מצורע אינו קבוע כמותה וי"ל דאיצטריך להאי טעמא דעולות נינהו משום חטאת דשמיעות הקול וביטוי שפתים פי' דשוחט חטאת דשמיעת קול על מי שמחוייב חטאת נזיר או חטאת מצורע דעתה אין קבוע יותר מזה. תוס' סוף: טו] עברה: טז] אם: יז] שעיר חנוכת הנשיאים: יח] (כשחיטה) כשחוטה (ס"א כשירה): יט] היו באות עשר: כ] קשים שמתוך שהכלי: כא] כמו שרוחש הס"ד: כב] מהניא מחשבתו הס"ד והשאר נמחק: כג] דרשי זאת תורת: כד] תורת החטא': כה] ואנן קיימא לן: כו] דמו וי"מ הני עולה נינהו ושינוי קודש הוא ופשיט' דפסולה. גליון: כז] ראשונה וי"מ חטאת ראשונה (שמצינו שלא בא) [שלא מצינו שבא] על חטאת נקט: כח] בשעירה והוי כשינוי קודש אפ"ה כיון דכרת כמותו מין חטאת חד הוי. גליון: כט] מה"ד דילפינן ממחשבת כו' ביה כה"ג דתנן תיבת הכי נמחק: ל] היא שיחשב אות ו' נמחק ס"א שיחשב בשעת מאחת העבודות להאכיל כו': לא] הדין נמי: לב] העבודות: לג] דאפי' הפריש נקבה: לד] כו' טעמא דמעשיה מוכיחי' כו' לא אמר תורה

מסורת הש"ס

מנחות סב:
[מנחות ג:]
תוספתא דמנחות רפ"ק מנחות ג: מט.
[מנחות ג.]
[נ"ל רבא וכן משמע בתוס' דף ז. ד"ה אמר רבא ע"ש]
דמהניא ביה דתנן ס'

הגהות הב"ח

(א) גמ' הוה אמינא ה"מ היכא דעיברה: (ב) שם כנחשון כשרה חטאת. נ"ב פי' דהכי הוי דינא בשינוי בעלים: (ג) שם לשם חטאת נחשון פסולה. נ"ב פי' דהכי הוי דינא בשינוי קדש: (ד) רש"י ד"ה כשרה וכו' הרי היא כנשחטה לשם: (ה) ד"ה מחבת וכו' דמתוך: (ו) ד"ה טעמא וכו' להכשירה לא יליף מזאת התורה: (ז) ד"ה שיתכפר בה נחשון היינו שינוי בעלים הס"ד ואח"כ מ"ה אין וכו' במחוייב כפרה. נ"ב ע"ל תחילת דף ד' ודף ז' סוף ע"א: (ח) ד"ה בעיא וכו' דכיון: (ט) ד"ה מי אמרי' וכו' או דילמא אין כצ"ל ותיבת כו' נמחק:

רבא מכח קושיא זו וטעמא משום דמעשיה מוכיחים וקשה מידי הוא טעמא אלא לרבא ורבא קאמר התם דלאו משום מעשיה מוכיחים אלא משום זאת תורת כו'. תוס' סוף: לה] כגון האי דפרק דם חטאת. דאתא דא"כ לכתוב ושחט לאותה חטאת ח"א גליון: לו] ולרבנן דריש מנחות: לז] אחריתי דרבא דמחלק בין שוחט לשם חטאת לשוחט: לח] תיבות כמו שינוי בעלים נמחק: לט] וק"ו נמי דרב אשי:

In fact, however, three texts are written: [9b] One refers to [an animal] whose time [for slaughtering] is overpassed and whose year has passed;[2] another [is required] for [an animal] whose time [for slaughtering] is overpassed but whose year is not passed; and the third is required for an animal neither whose time [for slaughtering] nor whose year is passed.[3] Now [all three texts] are necessary. For if the Divine Law wrote one text [only], I would say that it applies only [to an animal] whose year is passed and also its time [for slaughtering], since it is completely disqualified from a Passover-offering. But if its time [for slaughtering] is passed but not its year, I would say that it is not [valid, if slaughtered as a peace-offering], since it is eligible for the second Passover.[4] While if the Divine Law stated these two, [I would argue that they are valid if slaughtered as a peace-offering] because they have been disqualified from their own purpose.[5] But if neither its time [for slaughtering] nor its year has passed, so that it is eligible for the [first] Passover, I would say that it is not so. Hence [all three texts] are necessary.

Rab said in Mabog's name: If one slaughtered a sin-offering as the sin-offering of Nahshon[6] it is valid, for Scripture saith, *This is the law of the sin-offering*,[7] [which teaches that] there is one law for all sin-offerings.[8] Raba sat and reported this discussion, whereupon R. Mesharshia raised an objection to Raba: R. Simeon said: All meal-offerings whose fistfuls were taken under a different desig-
a nation[1] are valid and acquit their owners of their obligation, because meal-offerings are dissimilar from [blood] sacrifices. For when one takes a fistful of a griddle [meal-offering] in the name of a stewing-pan [meal-offering], its preparation proves that it is a griddle [meal-offering].[2] [If one takes a fistful of] a dry meal-offering[3] in the name of [a meal-offering] mingled [with oil],[4] its preparation proves that it is a dry [meal-offering]. But in the case of [animal] sacrifices it is not so, for there is the same slaughtering for all, the same receiving for all, [and] the same sprinkling for all.[5] Thus it is only because its preparation proves its nature; hence if its preparation did not prove its nature, this would not be so. Yet why? let us say [that] *This is the law of the meal-offering*[6] [intimates that] there is one law for all meal-offerings?—Rather if stated, it was thus stated: Rab said in Mabog's name: If one slaughtered a sin-offering in order that Nahshon might be forgiven through it, it is valid, [for] no atonement [is required] for the dead.[7] Then let him speak of any dead person?—He informs us this: The reason [that it is valid] is that he [Nahshon] is dead. Hence [if one slaughtered it] for a living person similar to Nahshon, it is invalid. And who are meant? [Those who are liable to] a nazirite's sin-offering or a leper's sin-offering.[8] But these are [as] burnt-offerings?[9]—Rather if stated, it was thus stated: Rab said in Mabog's name: If one slaughters a sin-offering for a [wrong] person who is liable to a sin-offering such as Nahshon's, it is valid, [for] Nahshon's sin-offering was [as] a burnt-offering.

Others state that Rab said in Mabog's name: If one slaughters a sin-offering in the name of Nahshon's sin-offering, it is invalid, for Nahshon's sin-offering is [as] a burnt-offering. Now let him state a
b nazirite's sin-offering or a leper's sin-offering?[1]—He mentions the original sin-offering [of that nature].[2]

Raba[3] said: If one slaughters a sin-offering of forbidden fat in the name of a sin-offering of blood [or] in the name of a sin-offering for idolatry, it is valid. [If one slaughters it] in the name of a nazirite's sin-offering or a leper's sin-offering, it is invalid, [for] these are [in fact] burnt-offerings.[4] Raba asked: If one slaughters a sin-offering of forbidden fat in the name of a sin-offering on account of the defilement of the Sanctuary and its sacred flesh, what is the law? Do we say, [the latter entails] *kareth*,[5] just as the former;[6] or perhaps the latter is not fixed like itself?[7] R. Aha son of Raba recited all these cases as invalid. What is the reason?—*And he shall kill it for a sin-offering*[8] [intimates that it must be killed] for the sake of *that* sin-offering.[9] Said R. Ashi to R. Aha the son of Raba: How then do you recite Raba's question?[10]—We recite it in reference to change in respect of owner, he answered him, and we recite it thus: Raba said: If one slaughters a sin-offering of forbidden fat on behalf of a [wrong] person who is liable to a sin-offering for blood or a sin-offering for idolatry, it is invalid; [but if he slaughters it] on behalf of a person who is liable to a nazirite's sin-offering or a leper's sin-offering, it is valid. And as for the question, this is what Raba asked: If one slaughters a sin-offering of forbidden fat on behalf of a person who is liable to a sin-offering on account of the defilement of the sanctuary and its sacred flesh, what is the law?
c Do we say, [the latter entails] *kareth* like itself;[1] or perhaps the latter is not fixed like itself?[2] The question stands over.

It was stated: If one slaughtered it for its own sake with the intention of sprinkling its blood for the sake of something else,[3] R. Johanan said: It is invalid; while Resh Lakish said: It is valid. R. Johanan said [that] it is invalid [because] an [effective] intention can be expressed at one service in respect to another service,[4] and we learn [by analogy] from the intention of *piggul*.[5] While Resh Lakish said [that] it is valid, [because] an [effective] intention cannot be expressed at one service in respect to another, and we do not learn from the intention of *piggul*. Now they are consistent

(2) I.e., it was lost until it was too late for slaughtering as a Passover-offering, and is also more than a year old. (3) I.e., if it is slaughtered before Passover as a peace-offering it is valid, though it was eligible for a Passover-offering. (4) V. Num. IX, 9 seq. (5) Which was to be slaughtered at the first Passover. (6) Which Nahshon, the prince of the tribe of Judah, brought at the dedication of the altar; V. Num. VII, 12 seq. (7) Lev. VI, 18. (8) They all stand in the same category. Hence although Nahshon's sin-offering was not on account of sin at all, yet by slaughtering an ordinary sin-offering as such one is not deemed to have changed its purpose, and therefore it is valid.

a (1) V. Lev. II, 2. The priest, in taking the fistful, declared that he took it for the sake of a different type of meal-offering. (2) His declaration is manifestly untrue and of no account, since one can see what meal-offering it is.—For the various types of meal-offerings mentioned here V. Lev. II, 4 seq. (3) Which is brought on account of sin, v. Lev. V, 11*f*. (4) Which was not brought on account of sin, v. Lev. II, 1 seq. (5) In these acts there is nothing to indicate the nature of the sacrifice. Consequently a false declaration is effective to invalidate them. (6) Lev. VI, 7. (7) A sin-offering slaughtered for a wrong person is invalid, provided that he is likewise liable to a sin-offering. This condition is obviously unfulfilled here: hence the sacrifice is valid. (8) Which are not brought on account of sin at all, just as Nashhon's sin-offering was not on account of sin. (9) Rashi: A nazirite's sin-offering is the same as a burnt-offering, since it is not brought on account of sin, and it is stated *supra 7a* that if one slaughters a sin-offering in the name of a different person who is liable to a burnt-offering, it is valid. Sh. M. cites a reverse interpretation: These are as burnt-offerings; hence his action is tantamount to slaughtering a sin-offering as a burnt-offering, which is *obviously* invalid. What then does Rab inform us?

b (1) Since that is in fact what he means to imply by 'Nahshons' sin-offering'. (2) Nahshon was the first to bring a sin-offering which was not for sin. Hence his is mentioned as an example of all sin-offerings of that nature (Sh. M.). (3) So amended in margin and Sh. M.; cur. edd. Rab. (4) As above. But in the first clause the others too are on account of sin. (5) V. Glos. (6) Hence it is valid. (7) For if the transgressor is too poor he can bring two birds instead of an animal, which is not permitted in the case of the former. (8) Lev. IV, 33. (9) Not in the name of any other. (10) When is Raba in doubt?

c (1) Hence it is invalid. (2) Hence it is valid. (3) Declaring this intention at the time of slaughtering. (4) It is effective to render the animal unfit. (5) V. Glos. There this is certainly the case; v. *infra 27b*.

with their views. For it was stated: [10a] If one slaughters an animal with the express intention of sprinkling its blood or burning its fat to an idol, — R. Joḥanan said: It is forbidden [for any use],[6] [for] an [effective] intention can be expressed at one service in respect to another service, and we learn 'without' from 'within'.[7] Resh Laḳish rules that it is permitted,[8] for an [effective] intention cannot be expressed at one service in respect of another service, and we do not learn 'without' from 'within'. [Now these are both necessary.] For if we were informed [of their views] in the latter case, I might argue that Resh Laḳish rules [thus only] in this instance, yet he agrees with R. Joḥanan [that] 'within' [is learnt] from 'within'.[9] While if we were informed [of their views] in the former instance, I might argue that R. Joḥanan rules [thus only] there, yet he agrees with Resh Laḳish in the present case.[10] Thus both are required.

a When R. Dimi came,[1] he said: R. Jeremiah raised an objection in support of R. Joḥanan, while R. Ela [did so] in support of Resh Laḳish. R. Jeremiah in support of R. Joḥanan: If it is valid where one says, 'Behold, I slaughter after its time [for slaughtering],'[2] yet it is invalid if one slaughters it with the intention of sprinkling the blood after time; then seeing that it is invalid if he declares, 'Behold, I slaughter for the sake of something else,' is it not logical that it is invalid if one slaughters it with the intention of sprinkling the blood for the sake of something else? To this Raba b. Ahilai demurred: As for [intending to sprinkle its blood] after time, the reason [that this invalidates it even at the slaughtering] is that it entails *kareth*![3] Rather said Raba b. Ahilai, This is his argument: If it is valid where one says, 'Behold, I slaughter [this sacrifice] without its precincts,'[4] yet it is invalid when one slaughters it with the intention of sprinkling its blood without its precincts; then seeing that it is invalid when he declares, 'Behold, I slaughter for the sake of something else,' is it not logical that it is invalid if one slaughters it with the intention of sprinkling the blood for the sake of something else? To this R. Ashi demurred: As for [its unfitness when one intends sprinkling the blood] without its precincts, the reason is because it operates [as a disqualification] in the case of all sacrifices. Will you say that the same applies in the case of an intention for the sake of a different sacrifice, which does not operate [thus] save in the case of a Passover-offering and a sin-offering? Rather said R. Ashi, This is how he argues: If it is valid where one says, 'Behold, I slaughter [this sacrifice] in the name of so-and-so,'[5] yet it is invalid [if one declares his intention] to sprinkle its blood for the sake of so-and-so; then seeing that when he declares, 'Behold, I slaughter [it] for the sake of something else,' it is
b invalid,[1] is it not logical that it is invalid if he slaughters it with the intention of sprinkling the blood for the sake of something else?

R. Ela [raised an objection] in support of Resh Laḳish: Let it not be stated in the case of sprinkling[2] and it could be inferred *a minori* from slaughtering and receiving;[3] then for what purpose did the Divine Law state [it]? To teach that you cannot [effectively] express an intention in respect of one service at a [previous] service.[4] To this R. Papa demurred: Yet perhaps [its purpose is on the contrary to intimate] that you can express an intention in respect of one service at a [previous] service? — If so, let Scripture be silent about it, and infer it by R. Ashi's *a minori* argument. And the other?[5] — Refute [the argument] thus: as for those [slaughtering and receiving], the reason may be that they require the north[6] and are present at the inner sin-offerings. And the other?[7] — Now, at all events, we are discussing peace-offerings.[8]

It was stated: If one slaughters it in its own name with the intention of sprinkling its blood for the sake of something else, — R. Naḥman says: It is invalid; Rabbah says: It is valid. But Rabbah retracted on account of R. Ashi's *a minori* argument.

R. ELIEZER SAID: THE GUILT-OFFERING TOO. It was taught: R. Eliezer said: A sin-offering comes on account of sin, and a guilt-offering comes on account of sin: just as a sin-offering [slaughtered] under a different designation is invalid, so is a guilt-offering invalid [if slaughtered] under a different designation. Said R. Joshua to him: That is not so. If you say [thus] of the sin-offering, [the reason
c is] because its blood is [sprinkled] above [the scarlet line].[1] Said R. Eliezer to him: Let the Passover-offering prove it: though its blood is [sprinkled] below, yet if one slaughters it for the sake of something else it is invalid. As for the Passover-offering, replied R. Joshua, the reason is that it has a fixed time. Said R. Eliezer to him: Then let

(6) Even if he did not eventually sprinkle it thus. (7) Idolatrous sprinkling of the blood etc. is naturally done without the Temple, while the illegitimate action of *piggul* is done within the Temple. (8) If he did not eventually sprinkle it idolatrously. (9) *Sc.* if one slaughters a sacrifice with the intention of sprinkling its blood in the name of a different sacrifice, his illegitimate intention is in respect of something that is done within, and therefore we learn by analogy from *piggul* that his intention is effective. (10) By reversing the argument.

a (1) From Palestine to Babylon. R. Dimi and Rabin were two Palestinian *amoraim* who travelled between the Palestinian and the Babylonian academies to transmit the teachings of one to the other. (2) Since whenever he slaughters it, that is the time. (3) This illegitimate intention renders the flesh *piggul immediately*, so that if one eats it even *within* the permitted time he is liable to *kareth*. Since it is so strict, it is natural that an illegitimate intention in respect of one service expressed at an earlier service is effective. (4) For his declaration cannot negative the fact that he is slaughtering it *within* its precincts. (5) For change of name is a disqualification at the sprinkling, but not at the slaughtering.

b (1) Viz., in the case of a Passover-offering and a sin-offering. (2) That an intention for a different sacrifice disqualifies it. (3) If slaughtering for the sake of a different sacrifice disqualifies, though it is valid when done by a *zar* (lay-Israelite), how much the more sprinkling, which may not be performed by a *zar*. And if you answer that slaughtering may be more stringent because a Passover-offering slaughtered for others than those enrolled for it is invalid; then let receiving prove it, where this disqualification does not operate. (4) I.e., the illegitimate intention in respect of sprinkling must be expressed at the sprinkling. (5) R. Joḥanan: How does he rebut this argument? (6) They are performed at the north side of the altar. (7) Resh Laḳish: how does he rebut this argument? (8) Which are not slaughtered at the north nor on the inner altar. Hence the argument does not apply.

c (1) The blood of some sacrifices was sprinkled on the upper half of the altar, and the blood of other sacrifices was sprinkled on the lower half; a scarlet line on the altar demarcated them. — The fact that the blood of the sin-offering was sprinkled above that line may be the reason for greater stringency.

*השוחט את הבהמה לעבודת כוכבים לזרוק דמה לעבודת כוכבים ולהקטיר חלבה לעבודת כוכבים ר' יוחנן אמר אסורה מחשבין מעבודה לעבודה וילפינן חוץ מפנים ריש לקיש אמר מותרת אין מחשבין מעבודה לעבודה ולא ילפינן חוץ מפנים *ואי אשמעינן בהא בהא אמר ריש לקיש אבל פנים מפנים אימא מודי ליה לרבי יוחנן ואי אשמעינן הא בהא קאמר רבי יוחנן אבל בההיא אימא מודי ליה לריש לקיש צריכי כי אתא רב דימי אמר מתיב רב ירמיה לסיועיה לרבי יוחנן ורבי אילא לסיועיה לריש לקיש רב ירמיה לסיועיה לרבי יוחנן ומה במקום שאם אמר הריני שוחט חוץ לזמנו שהוא כשר שחטו על מנת לזרוק דמו חוץ לזמנו פסול מקום שאם אמר הריני שוחט שלא לשמו פסול שחטו על מנת לזרוק דמו שלא לשמו אינו דין שיהא פסול מתקיף לה רבא בר אהילאי מה לחוץ לזמנו (א)*שכן כרת אלא אמר רבא בר אהילאי הכי קאמר ומה מקום שאם אמר הריני שוחט חוץ למקומו שהוא כשר שחטו על מנת לזרוק דמו חוץ למקומו פסול מקום שאם אמר הריני שוחט שלא לשמו שהוא פסול [שחטו ע"מ] לזרוק דמו שלא לשמו אינו דין שיהא פסול מתקיף לה רב אשי מה לחוץ למקומו שכן נוהג בכל הזבחים תאמר בשלא לשמו שאינו נוהג אלא בפסח וחטאת אלא אמר רב אשי הכי קאמר ומה במקום שאם אמר הריני שוחט לשם פלוני שהוא כשר לזרוק דמו (שלא לשמו) לשם פלוני פסול מקום שאם אמר הריני שוחט שלא (ב)לשמן שהוא פסול [שחטו ע"מ] לזרוק דמן שלא לשמן אינו דין שיהא פסול רבי אילא לסיועיה לריש לקיש לא תאמר בזריקה ותיתי מק"ו מבינייא משחיטה וקבלה למאי הלכתא כתב רחמנא לומר דאין מחשבין מעבודה לעבודה מתקיף לה רב פפא ודלמא דמחשבין מעבודה לעבודה אם כן לשתוק קרא מיניה ותיתי מקל וחומר דרב אשי ואידך פריך הכי מה להנך שכן טעונות צפון וישנן בחטאות הפנימיות ואידך השתא מיהא בשלמים קיימין איתמר שחטה לשמה לזרוק דמה שלא לשמה רב נחמן אמר פסולה רבה אמר כשרה והדר ביה רבה לגבי רב נחמן מק"ו דרב אשי:

רבי אליעזר אומר אף (את) האשם: תניא *אמר ר' אליעזר חטאת באה על חטא ואשם בא על חטא מה חטאת שלא לשמה פסולה אף אשם שלא לשמו פסול אמר לו רבי יהושע לא אם אמרת בחטאת שכן דמה למעלה אמר לו רבי אליעזר פסח יוכיח שדמו למטה ושחטו שלא לשמו פסול אמר לו רבי יהושע מה לפסח שכן זמנו קבוע אמר לו רבי אליעזר חטאת תוכיח אמר לו רבי יהושע

הוזרני

רש"י

השוחט את הבהמה. של חולין (ג) לעבודת כוכבים אסורה בהנאה כדין זבחי מתים וזבחי מתים ילפינן (ע"ז דף כט:) שם שם מעגלה ערופה: לזרוק דמה לעבודת כוכבים. (ועבודת) השחיטה לא נעשית לשם עבודת כוכבים אלא בשעת שחיטה חישב י] לעבוד הזריקה לשם עבודת כוכבים ולא זרק: מחשבין מעבודה לעבודה. מחשבה היא לענין זבחי מתים יא] ליאסר בהנאה: דילפינן. עבודת כוכבים שהיא חוץ ממחשבת פיגול שהוא פנים: מותרת. לאכילה: אין מחשבין מעבודה לעבודה. ואינה אסורה אלא אם כן שחט לעבודת כוכבים שבשחיטתה עבד עבודת כוכבים או זרק יב] לעבודת כוכבים: פנים מפנים. מחשבת שלא לשמו מפיגול: הריני שוחט חוץ לזמנו. ולא חישב על מנת לאכול ולא על מנת לזרוק או להקטיר אלא על השחיטה חישב סתם חוץ לזמנה כשר דלאו מחשבה היא יג]*דאין זמן אלא באכילת אדם (ד) ומזבח יד](דזהו) פיגול: שכן כרת. האוכל פיגול אפי' לאלתר חייב כרת הואיל וחמור מהניא ביה מעבודה לעבודה: הריני שוחטו חוץ למקומו. שלא חישב לא על אכילה ולא על זריקה אלא(ה)טו]אמר הריני שוחט חוץ למקומו כשר דהא חזינן דבמקומו הוא שוחטו ועוד דבאכילת אדם או מזבח תלה רחמנא לחוץ למקומו וחוץ לזמנו דכתיב ואם האכל יאכל וגו' וילפינן חוץ למקומו וחוץ לזמנו מהאי קרא לקמן (דף יג.): על מנת לזרוק דמו חוץ למקומו (ו)טז]כו' פסול. (בפרק שני) והשתא ליכא למפרך שכן כרת שאין חייבין כרת על אכילתן כדתניא לקמן [בפרק שני] (דף כח.): שחט לשם פלוני כשר. דאין שינוי בעלים חל על השחיטה דלא שייך שם בעלים אלא על הכפרה והיינו דאמרן לעיל (דף ד.) דשינוי בעלים איתו בד' עבודות: לא תאמר בזריקה. מחשבין שלא לשמו דרבינן ליה(ז)לעיל יז] בכולהו עבודות: משחיטה וקבלה. ומה שחיטה שכשרה בזר פסולה בשלא לשמה זריקה לא כל שכן יח] כי פרכת מה לשחיטה שכן פוסלת שלא לשם אוכלין בפסח קבלה תוכיח: דאין מחשבין מעבודה לעבודה. אלא בשעת זריקה גופה בעי מיחשב: ודלמא. להכי כתביה לאשמועינן רבותא דמחשבין מעבודה לעבודה יט] [שלא] בשעת זריקה גופה בעי מחשב דאפי' לא חישב על הזריקה בשעתה אלא בשעת שחיטה הויא מחשבה: אם כן. דמחשבין אתא לאשמועינן לשתוק קרא מיניה ותיתי דמחשבין מקל וחומר דרב אשי כדאמרן ומה אם במקום שאם אמר הריני שוחט לשם פלוני כו': ואידך. רבי יוחנן פריך הכי דלא נפקא לן זריקה מקל וחומר דקבלה ושחיטה: מה להנך כו'. הלכך לאו קרא יתירא הוא דניליף מיניה דאין מחשבין: השתא מיהת בשלמים קיימינן. דבשלמים כתיבא מחשבה שלא לשמו כ] הלכך מצי למילף זריקה משחיטה וקבלה וליכא למיפרך לצפון דשלמים לא בעי צפון וליתנהו פנימיות: שכן דמה למעלה. מחוט הסיקרא דתנן במס' מדות (פ"ג מ"א) חוט הסיקרא חוגרת באמצע להבדיל בין דמים עליונים לדמים התחתונים ויליף לקמן (דף נג.) מן והיתה הרשת עד חצי המזבח התורה נתנה מחילה להבדיל וחטאת בהמה כא] נעשית למעלה דכתיב בה (ויקרא ד) על קרנות וכן עולת העוף כדלקמן (דף סד:) ושאר זבחים שלא פירש בהן נעשין למטה דכתיב בהו מזבח ולא כתיב בהו קרנות וכוליה מזבח ליכא למימר כב] דהוה מקומן שהרי תורה נתנה מחילה:

תוספות

ותימה דלקמן (דף יג.) דפריך וקבלה מי פסלה ט' ומשני כאן במחשבת שלא לשמן כאן במחשבת פיגול אמאי לא משני אידי ואידי במחשבת שלא לשמן וקבלה כג] לא עשה בה מחשבה כמעשה כגון בשוחט על מנת לקבל שלא לשמן ובזריקה כד] (לא) עשה בה מחשבה כמעשה ונראה לי דלקמן מיירי שחישב בעבודה עצמה אם קבל [לגמור הקבלה] שלא לשמן פסול ואם קבל [לגמור] חוץ לזמנו כשר ואם זרק לגמור הזריקה חוץ לזמנו פסול וכן מקטיר לגמור ההקטרה למחר דהוה פסול אי לאו דמעטיה קרא לקמן משום דאין מעכבת כפרה אבל ליכא לפרושי לקמן מחשבת פיגול דלא פסלה בקבלה כגון שוחט על מנת לקבל כה] דמן חוץ לזמנו דבשלא לשמן נמי לא פסלה דמעבודה לעבודה ילפינן מפיגול *(ואי) במקבל על מנת לזרוק חוץ לזמנו הוה פיגול אלא כדפרשינן בחישב בעבודה עצמה. ברו"ך *ובלאו הכי תימה דהוי מצי למימר קבלה לא עשה בה מחשבה כמעשה לענין שינוי בעלים:

ריש לקיש אמר מותרת. מודה ר"ל דחייב מיתה כדאמרינן בפרק ארבע מיתות (סנהדרין סא.) מידי דהוה אמשתחוה להר דהר מותר כו] ועובדו בסייף ושחיטת מומר לא חשיב כדפי' בפ"ק דחולין (דף יד.) גבי שוחט בשבת ואין לתמוה והיאך נהרג דילמא מימלך ולא זריק לעבודת כוכבים כדאמר בפרק ד' מיתות (סנהדרין סא.) כז] דניסת שאמר אלך אעבוד פטור דמימלך ולא עביד דהכא ודאי לא מימלך כיון דעבד מעשה ששחט על מנת לזרוק ועוד הכא אפילו ידוע ודאי שלא יזרוק חשיב עובד עבודת כוכבים בשחיטה [זו] כששוחט ע"מ לזרוק:

מקום שאם אמר הריני שוחט שלא לשמן כו'. וא"ת שוחט שלא לשם אוכלין בפסח יוכיח דשוחט שלא לשם אוכלין פסול ושוחט ע"מ לזרוק שלא לשם אוכלין כשר ויש לומר דלא דמי כח] התם דזורק עצמו שלא לשם אוכלין כשר:

לא תאמר בזריקה ותיתי בק"ו משחיטה וקבלה. תימה כט] אמאי לא פריך שכן טעונות צפון וישנן בחטאות הפנימיות וכ"ת משום דבשלמים ל] קיימא אם כן מאי צריך למילף מבינייא ניליף בק"ו לא] מקבלה שאין חייבין עליה בחוץ ואפילו הכי פסלה בה מחשבה ועוד למה לי קרא בזריקה לשינוי בעלים דדרשי' לכפר עליו תיתי מבינייא משחיטה וקבלה ועוד קשה אמאי אין מחשבת אוכלין בפסח בזריקה תיתי בק"ו משחיטה שכשירה בזר כיון דלא פרכינן מלפון וחטאות הפנימיות ומיהו דילמא לב] (תכוסו) מיעוטא הוא ואע"ג לג] דשלא למטיין דהייט שינוי בעלים כתיב נמי לד] [א] (תכוסו) ולא ממעטי זריקה לא דמי (עיין פסחים דף סא.):

והדר ביה לה] רבה לגבי דרב נחמן מקל וחומר דרב אשי. לו] [הייט] [ג]לרבנן דאליבא דר' שמעון ליכא קל וחומר דאיכא למיפרך מה לשינוי בעלים שכן נוהג במנחות תאמר בשינוי קודש שאינו נוהג במנחות לרבי שמעון (מנחות דף ב:):

חטאת

מסורת הש"ס (גליון)

נ"א לעשות

ע"ז לד: סנהדרין ס: חולין לט.

נ"א וצריכי דאי

נ"א משום שלא עשה כלום דהא בזמנו שחט וגי' הצ"ק דאין מחשבת הזמן פוסלת אלא באכילת אדם או מזבח הס"ד

[תוספתא ריש פ"א]

הגהות הב"ח

(א) גמ' שכן כרת. נ"ב עיין פרק כיצד הרגל דף כה בתד"ה אי לא: (ב) שם שלא לשמו שהוא פסול לזרוק דמו שלא לשמו אינו דין: (ג) רש"י ד"ה השוחט את הבהמה של חולין לזרוק דמה לעבודת כוכבים ועבודת השחיטה וכו' ולא זרק הס"ד ואח"כ מ"ה אסורה בהנאה וכו' ערופה הס"ד ואח"כ מ"ה מחשבין: (ד) ד"ה הריני וכו' ומזבח הס"ד ותיבת פיגול נמחק: (ה) ד"ה הריני שוחטו חוץ למקומו וכו' אלא כך אמר וכו' רחמנא חוץ למקומו: (ו) ד"ה על מנת וכו' למקומו פסול כצ"ל ותיבת כו' נמחק: (ז) ד"ה לא תאמר וכו' לעיל. נ"ב דף ד ע"א וע"ש:

עין משפט נר מצוה

מח א מיי' פ"ב מהל' שחיטה הלכה ט סמג עשין כג טוש"ע יו"ד סימן ד סעיף א:

מט ב מיי' שם הלכה טו:

עי' בחלופי גרסאות

עיין צ"ק

[עי' תוס' ב"ק כה. ד"ס אי לא]

שיטה מקובצת

א] ריש לקיש אמר מותרת. ונראה לפרש דמ"מ חייב סקילה ואע"פ שהבהמה מותרת דכה"ג אמרי' [בפרק ארבע מיתות בית דין] וא"ת היאך הבהמה מותרת הרי שחיטת מומר היא וי"ל דמשום פעם אחת לא מיקרי מומר [הואיל ולא הורגל בכך] דכה"ג אמרינן בחולין גבי השוחט בשבת דאסורה לאותו יום הא למחר מותר וצריך לומר [דלא מתסר משום דעבר באקראי] בעלמא הואיל ולא הורגל בכך וא"ת אמאי יהרג כו' א) וי"ל דהתם שאני דאינו עושה שום מעשה. לשון תוס' טוך: ב] מפנים וצריכי דאי: ג] ריש לקיש ובספר ישן כתוב אבל חוץ מפנים אימא מודי ליה לר' יוחנן (ופי') דאי אשמועינן בהא בהשוחט לשמו בהא אמר ריש לקיש דכשירה דלא ילפינן לשמו מפיגול אבל חוץ מפנים אימא מודי לר"י דאסורה מחמת חומרא דעבודת כוכבים: ד] לזרוק דמו שלא לשמו אינו דין שיהא פסול [וא"ת שוחט שלא לשם] אוכליו דפסח יוכיח דבשחיטה שלא לאוכליו פסול וכו' ה"נ בשלא לשמו וי"ל דאיכא למימר בשוחט ע"מ לזרוק דמו שלא לשמו דין שיהא פסול כדין אם חישב בזריקה עצמה שלא לשמה דהשתא ליכא למימר שלא לשם אוכליו יוכיח שכשר בשוחט ע"מ לזרוק דשאני שלא לאוכליו דפסח כיון דבזריקה עצמה אינה נפסלת כשזורק שלא לאוכליו כדפי' בריש פירקין. תוס' טוך: ה] פסול שחטו על מנת לזרוק: ו] תיבות שלא לשמו נמחק: ז] שלא לשמו פסול שחטו ע"מ לזרוק דמו שלא לשמו: ח] השתא מיהא בשלמים קיימינן וקש' דמשהיטה להודיה ניליף זריקה

ולימא למיפרך מה לשחיטה שכן נפסלת שלא לאוכליו בפסח דהשתא מיהא בשלמים [קיימינן] ואמר מורי דמ"מ פרכינן שפיר שלא לאוכליו וה"ק השתא מיהא בשלמים קיימינן ולא פרכינן פירכא דצפון דהוי בקדשי קדשים לשלמים דהם קדשים קלים אבל מדבר שהוא כפסח שהן קדשים קלים כשלמים פרכינן שפיר לגבי שלמים. תוס' מהר"פ: ט] פסולה רבא אמר כשרה והדר ביה רבא לגבי ר"נ: י] חישב לעשות הזריקה: יא] ליאסר: יב] זרק דמה: יג] היא ס"א משום דלא עשה כלום דהא בזמנה שחיט: יד] ומזבח הס"ד ומה"ד פסול פיגול ותיבת דזהו ל"ש ונמחק: טו] אלא כך אמר הריני שוחט לחוץ למקומו: טז] תיבת כו' נמחק: יז] לעיל לכולהו אות ב' נמחק: יח] שכן וכו': יט] מעבודה לעבודה דאפילו לא הישב והשאר נמחק: כ] לשמו דכתיב הזורק את דם השלמים שתהא זריקה לשם שלמים: כא] בהמה ניתנת תיבת נעשית נמחק: כב] למימר דהוי אות ה' נמחק: כג] וקבלה דלא: כד] תיבת לא נמחק: כה] לקבל דמו: כו] והעיבדו: כז] מיתות דמסית שאמר: כח] דמי דשאני התם: כט] מאן דלא פריך ס"א מאי דס"ד השתא דלא כו': ל] דבשלמים קיימינן תיבות א"כ ל"ש ונמחק: לא] מקבלה ומה קבלה שאם אמר הריני שוחט ע"מ לקבל חוץ לזמנו כשר כדאמרינן לקמן דבעינן שיחשב באכילת אדם [או] באכילת מזבח קבל שלא לשמו פסול זריקה לא כ"ש ר"ל דאה"נ אלא דלא סגיא ליה דלא כתיב שחיטה דשחיטה גופיה לא אתי מינייהו משום דשחיטה כשרה בזר. תוס' טוך: לב] דלמא תכוסו: לג] ואע"ג דגבי שלא אות ד' נמחק: לד] נמי תכוסו: לה] ביה רבא אות ה' נמחק: לו] לרבה אליבא דר"ש ותיבת היינו ל"ש ונמחק:

הגהות צ"ק

[א] בהכות ולא ממעטי זריקה דלא דמי: [ג] לרבה אליבא דר"ש ליכא ק"ו כצ"ל ור"ל לרבה דמתרץ הסוגיא בפ"ק דמנחות דגבי ר"ש דלא סתרי אהדדי דבפ"ק ס"ל דצ"ו ובפ"ב ס"ל דלא עלו לפ"ז איכא למיפרך מה לש"ב כו':

א) כוונתם לדברי התוספות בד"ה ר"ל שכתבו ואין לתמוה וכו'.

נא ב מיי' פ"ט מהלכות מעשה הקרבנות הל' ו:

[ד"ה מעטע] [תיבת מצורע מיותר כי במצורע כתיב כחטאת כאשם (ויקרא יד) אכן בפ"ו (ויקרא ז פ"ז) כתוב כחטאת כאשם ועי' רש"י מנחות כח. ד"ה היקש דחטאת ואשם וכו'] *ג"ש דעונו עונו מחטאת כו' צ"ק

תורה אור

חוזרני חלילה חזר רבי אליעזר ודנו דין אחר חטאת נאמר בה *היא א] בשחיטה היא לשמה כשירה שלא לשמה פסולה ופסח נאמר בו הוא ב] בזביחה הוא לשמו כשר שלא לשמו פסול אף אשם נאמר בו הוא הוא לשמו כשר שלא לשמו פסול אמר לו רבי יהושע חטאת נאמר בה היא בשחיטה היא לשמה כשרה שלא לשמה פסולה פסח נאמר בו הוא בזביחה הוא לשמו כשר שלא לשמו פסול אבל *אשם לא נאמר בו הוא אלא לאחר הקטרת אימורין והוא עצמו שלא הוקטרו אימורין כשר אמר לו *ר' אליעזר הרי ג] אומר °כחטאת כאשם ד] מה חטאת שלא לשמו פסול אף אשם שלא לשמו פסול אמר מר אמר לו ר' יהושע חוזרני חלילה ה] ולמיהדר דינא ולייתי במה הצד משום דאיכא למיפרך מה להצד השוה שבהן שכן יש בהן (א) צד כרת אמר ו] לו ר' יהושע לא אם אמרת בחטאת שכן דמה למעלה ולימא ליה לא אם אמרת בחטאת שכן נכנס דמה לפני ולפנים בחטאות החיצונות קאמרינן שאם נכנס דמה ז] [לפני] ולפנים פסולה אית ליה לרבי אליעזר אף האשם (ב) שכן מכפרת על חייבי כריתות מחטאת דשמיעת הקול ח] שכן טעונה ארבע מתנות *כרבי ישמעאל דאמר כל הדמים טעונה ארבע מתנות (שכן טעונה) על ארבע קרנות וליטעמיך האיכא אצבע ט] *האיכא קרן האיכא חודה אלא *חד מתרי תלת טעמי נקט אמר מר אמר לו ר' יהושע לא אם אמרת י] לימא ליה רבי אליעזר אשם נמי דמו למעלה אמר אביי יא] *אשם דמו למעלה לא מצית אמרת ק"ו יב] מעולה ומה עולה שהיא כליל דמה למטה אשם שאינו כליל לא כל שכן מה לעולה שכן אינה מכפרת חטאת העוף תוכיח מה לחטאת העוף שכן אינה מין זבח עולה תוכיח לא ראי זה כראי זה ולא ראי זה כראי זה הצד השוה שבהן שהן קדשי קדשים יג] ודמן למטה אף אני אביא אשם שהוא קודש קדשים ודמו למטה א"ל רבא מפרזקיא לרב אשי ולפרוך מה להצד השוה שבהן שכן אין להן קצבה תאמר באשם שיש לו קצבה אלא היינו טעמא דרבי אליעזר דאמר קרא °הכהן המחטא אותה אותה דמה למעלה °ואין דמו של אחר למעלה אי הכי *חטאת נמי נימא אותה לשמה כשרה שלא לשמה פסולה הא שאר זבחים בין לשמן בין שלא לשמן כשרין °ההוא אותה לאו דוקא דהא שייר פסח הכא נמי לאו דוקא דהא שייר עולת העוף בזביחה מיהא לא שייר מידי ואי בעית אימא הא מני רבי אלעזר ברבי שמעון היא דאמר האי מקום לחוד והאי מקום לחוד *דתניא דמים התחתונים ניתנין מחוט הסיקרא ולמטה והעליונים מחוט הסיקרא ולמעלה אמר רבי אלעזר ברבי שמעון במה דברים אמורים בעולת העוף אבל בחטאת בהמה היא עצמה אין נעשה אלא על גופה של קרן: *תנן התם שהיה רבי עקיבא אומר כל דמים שנכנסו יד] להיכל לכפר פסולים וחכמים אומרים חטאת בלבד רבי אליעזר אומר אף האשם שנאמר כחטאת כאשם בשלמא רבי אליעזר כדקאמר טעמא אלא רבנן מאי (ג) טעמא אמר רבא אשם נכנס דמו לפנים פסול לא מצית °אמרת קל וחומר מעולה מה עולה

ויקרא ו

חוזרני חלילה · ולא יקום הדין ולקמן פריך וניהדר דינא וניתי במה הצד: נאמר בה היא טו] בשחיטה · שעיר נשיא: הרי הוא אומר כו' · ואין משיבין על ההיקש ולקמן בסוף שמעתא מפרש טעמייהו טז]*דרבנן דסמכי אהיקשא אחרינא והך היקשא דרשינן לגופא אחריתי: יז]תיתי במה הצד · דפסח וחטאת נאכלין (ליום ולילה) אף אני אביא אשם: צד כרת · חטאת באה על שגגת כרת ופסח חייבים עליו כרת טהור שלא היה בדרך רחוקה: שכן נכנס דמה לפני ולפנים · כגון ביום הכפורים: בחטאות החיצונות קאמרינן · במתני' יח] דפסולה ואע"ג דלא עיילי לפנים ומינייהו יליף ר' אליעזר: שאם נכנס דמה לפנים פסול · פירכא היא וה"ק ולימא ליה מה לחטאת החיצונה שכן אם נכנס דמה לפנים פסולה דכתיב (ויקרא ו) וכל חטאת אשר יובא מדמה כו' תאמר באשם דלא מיפסיל בהכי: אית ליה לרבי אליעזר אף יט] באשם שנכנס דמו לפנים פסול לקמן בשמעתין: ולימא ליה ר' יהושע מה לחטאת שכן מכפרת על חייבי כריתות: מחטאת דשמיעת קול · יליף רבי אליעזר דאינה באה על כרת: ולימא ליה שכן טעונה ארבע מתנות · תאמר באשם כ] שאינו טעון אלא שתי מתנות שהן ד': כר' ישמעאל כו' · באיזהו מקומן (לקמן נג:) נאמר כאן סביב בעולה ואשם ונאמר להלן סביב בחטאת [המילואים] מה להלן פיסוק ארבע מתנות דהא ד' (ד)מתנות כתיבי בה ואי אפשר לשתי קרנות בבת אחת אף כאן פיסוק ד' מתנות כא] באותה מתנה שנותן לקרן שהוא כשתים צריך לפסוק לצפונה של קרן ולמזרחה של קרן: ולימא ליה שכן טעונין ד' מתנות על ד' קרנות · מה שאין כן באשם דר' ישמעאל גופיה לא בעי בשאר זבחים אלא ד' מתנות בשתי קרנות דקתני כב] בדר' ישמעאל אי מה להלן ארבע מתנות כג] [על ארבע קרנות] אף כאן כו' אמרת עולה טעונה יסוד וקרן מזרחית דרומית לא היה לה יסוד: וליטעמיך · טובא הוה ליה לרבי יהושע למיפרך דהא איכא קרן ואצבע וחודה שחטאת טעונה ליתן מתנותיה באצבע כנגד חודה של (ה) קרן כד] אבן של אמה על אמה ברום אמה בד' מקצעות המזבח מה שאין כן בשאר הדמים דאפילו עולת העוף שהיא למעלה מחוט הסיקרא כדלקמן אינה צריכה להגביה כ"כ ולתת על הקרן ממש אלא שתהא למעלה מן החוט כל שהוא כדתניא לקמן (דף סד.) עשאה למטה מרגליו אפי' אמה כשרה ואין שום זבח טעון כה] מתנות אצבע אלא זורק מן הכלי אל קיר *המזבח למקצעותיו השנים והדם מתפשט לצפון ולמערב ואין מתנתו כנגד חודה במשך מלמעלה למטה כחטאת שצריכה כנגד חודה לקמן באיזהו מקומן (דף נג.): ולימא ליה רבי אליעזר אשם נמי דמו למעלה · דהא רבי אליעזר מקיש אשם לחטאת: חטאת העוף · דמה למטה לקמן בפרק קדשי קדשים (דף סד.): אינה מין זבח · אלא מין מליקה: אין להן קצבה · לדמיהן ואשם יש לו קצבה לדמיו בכסף שקלים: המחטא אותה · הזורק דמה ובחטאת כתיב ומיעט אותה בחטאת למעוטי שאר קדשים ממקום מתן דמו של חטאת: אי הכי · בשחיטת חטאת נמי כתיב (ו) אותה לחטאת ומיעוטא הוא כו] ולידרשה ר' אליעזר למעוטי אשם מפסול שלא לשמו: שייר עולת העוף · שהיא למעלה דילפינן לקמן (דף סה.) מומלק והקטיר מה הקטרה בראשו של מזבח אף מליקה בראשו של מזבח: בזביחה כז] לא שייר מידי · (ז) אדבר שהוא זבח לא שייר כלום שכל הזבחים נמעטו שלא יהא כח] דמו למעלה ועולת העוף לאו שיורא הוא דאינו זבח כמותו: הא מני · דלא חשיב עולת העוף שיור רבי אלעזר בר' שמעון היא: דאמר האי מקום · דחטאת בהמה לחוד ודעולת העוף לחוד אע"פ ששניהם למעלה אין מקומן שוה הלכך במיעוטא כט] חטאת ליכא שיור: במה דברים אמורים · דעליונים לא קביע להו מקום אלא ל] שיהא מן החוט ולמעלה: בעולת העוף אבל חטאת בהמה אינה נעשית אלא בגופה של קרן · האבן של אמה על אמה שבראש לא] מזבח שכל למטה מן הקרנות פסולה ואף על פי שהיא למעלה מן החוט ארבע אמות: כל דמים החיצונים שנכנסו להיכל לכפר פסולין ואף על גב דלא כתיב אלא וכל חטאת אשר יובא מדמה וגו' מרבה רבי עקיבא קדשי קדשים וקדשים קלים מריבויא דכל וכל לב] לקמן בכל הזבחים שנתערבו (דף פב.): אלא לרבנן מאי טעמייהו · הא ודאי איתקש אשם לחטאת:

עולה

חטאת נאמר בה היא · בכמה מקומות משמע דמדכתיב היא נפקא לן עכובא ותימה דלעיל נפקא לן מקראי אחרינא ולעיל (דף ה.:) פירשתי: הרי הוא אומר כחטאת כאשם · באשם *מצורע כתיב והוה מצי למילף אשם מחטאת *)בגזירה שוה לג]דעון עון מחטאת דשמיעת קול דהא למותרת כדבה גמירי לד] ואין ג"ש למחצה כדאמר בריש מנחות (דף ד.) אלא אי לאו היקשא לה] הוה ממעט אשם מאותה: מה להצד השוה שבהן שכן צד כרת · ואע"ג דאשם תלוי נמי בא על כרת אינו בא לכפר אלא להגן ולכי מתיידע מייתי חטאת וה"נ הוה מצי למימר °שכן באין בצבור: מחטאת דשמיעת הקול · וליכא למיפרך מה לפסח חטאת שכן כרת דהא מחדא לא פרכינן כל דהו: ומה עולה שהיא כליל כו' · תימה כיון דאתי האי ק"ו ומפיק מהיקשא אם כן תהא עולה פסולה שלא לשמה ק"ו מחטאת שאינה כליל וכי תימא מה לחטאת שכן מכפרת פסח יוכיח ומיהו כיון דכתיב אותה בחטאת לא קשה · ותימה (ח) לסברתו דעביד קל וחומר מעולה שהיא כליל שלא לשמו נמי ליכשר באשם לו] והו לימא חטאת יוכיח: הג"ה כל דמים שנכנסו להיכל לכפר פסולים · לא דמי להא דאמר לז] (לקמן דף סג. ומנחות דף ח. ושם) לח] *[שלמים ששחטן] בהיכל כשירות לא יהא טפל חמור מן העיקר דהני מילי היכא דכתיב אל פתח אהל מועד שתלה לט] הכשירו בהיכל:

אשם

דאיכא למיפרך מה [לעולה שכן] אינה מכפרת דאיכא למימר חטאת העוף תוכיח כיון דגם חטאת העוף שלא לשמו פסול כדאיתא פרק קדשי קדשים דף סו. ע"ב בפרש"י ע"ש ותו ליכא שום יוכיח:

גליון הש"ס

גמ' ואין דמו של אחר למעלה · עי' לקמן דף נג ע"ב תוס' ד"ה מה לכאן: שם ההוא אותה לאו דוקא · עיין לקמן דף נה ע"א תוס' ד"ה מה חטאת: שם אמרת ק"ו · עי' ב"מ דף קטו ע"א תוס' ד"ה ואידך: תוס' ד"ה מה וכו' שכן באין בצבור · כדלקמן דף יג ע"א:

ועי' בהגהות גרסאות נ"י מנחות שנקמצו ועיין נ"ק

נ"א דרבי יהושע

נאמר בה היא לשמה כשרה שלא לשמה פסולה ופסח נאמר בו הוא לשמו כשר שלא לשמו פסול כו' נ"א גי' רש"י והשאר יש מחוק

[לעיל ה: ו: מנחות ד.]

[מנחות ח. לקמן קטו.]

[לקמן נג: לד:]

[פי' תוספות לקמן נג: ד"ה וקרן]

[לקמן ג. נה יבמות מה: ושנ]

נ"א בשחיטה חטאת

לקמן נג.

לקמן פט:

הגהות הב"ח

(א) גמ' צד כרת נ"ב ע"ל תחלת דף יג: (ב) שם אף האשם ולימא ליה שכן מכפרת וכו' מחטאת דשמיעת הקול ולימא ליה שכן וכו' שכן טעונה ארבע מתנות על ארבע קרנות: (ג) שם רבנן מאי טעמייהו אמר רבא: (ד) רש"י ד"ה כרבי ישמעאל וכו' דהא ד' קרנות כתיבי ביה ואי אפשר לד' קרנות בבת אחת: (ה) ד"ה וליטעמיך וכו' כנגד חודה של קרן קרן אבן: (ו) ד"ה אי הכי וכו' כתיב ושחט אותה: (ז) ד"ה בזביחה וכו' כדנ"ג: (ח) תוס' ד"ה ומה עולה וכו' ותימה לסברתו נ"ב ואין להקשות

שיטה מקובצת

א] תיבת בשחיטה נמחק: ב] תיבת בזביחה נמחק: ג] הרי הוא אומר כחטאת כאשם פ"ה דהיקשא הוא וכו' וא"ת והלא אין היקש למחצה וי"ל דשאני הכא דמיעט רחמנא אותה אותה שלא לשמה פסול אבל אחרת לא כדאמרינן לעיל וא"ת רבי אליעזר מאי דריש האי אותה וי"ל דדריש אותה כרב אחא דמתני כולהו לפסול לעיל מאותה וכוליה קרא להכי הוא דאתא · תוס' סוך: ד] מה חטאת שלא לשמה פסול · פי' כמו חטאת ששחטה שלא לשמה וא"ת והלא בגופיה דחטאת לא כתיב פסול שלא לשמה למצוה [אלא דילפינן משלמים] וא"כ הוי למד מן הלמד בקדשים וי"ל דלמצוה לא צריך דסמיך לזאת תורת דאיתקש (מנחות) לכולהו ולא צריכא לן באשם אלא לעיכובא ועיכובא דחטאת כתיבא ואין זה למד מן הלמד · תוס' סוך: ה] חלילה וליהדר אות מ' נמחק: ו] אמר מר אמר לו: ז] דמה לפני ולפנים: ח] מחטאת דשמיעת הקול יליף פי' דליכא בה כרת וא"ת א"כ מאי פריך לעיל שיש בהן צד כרת וי"ל דס"ם שם חטאת איכא כרת וא"ת א"כ השתא נמי מאי משני ס"ם שם חטאת מכפרת על חייבי כריתות משא"כ באשם וי"ל דשם חטאת פירכא כל דהו ועל מה הצד פרכינן פירכא כל דהו אבל על חדא מחדא לא פרכינן פירכא כל דהו: ט] האיכא קרן האיכא חודה · לאו דוקא דבעינן חודה וקרן דלמאן דאית ליה חודה לא בעי קרן ולמאן דאית ליה קרן לא בעי חודה אלא למר כדאית ליה ולמר כדאית ליה וקרן לא הוי בכלל פירכא דלעיל דקאמר שכן דמה למעלה דהא עולת העוף דמה למעלה מחוט הסיקרא ולא בעי קרן כדפי' בקונטרס · תוס' סוך: י] אמרת בחטאת כו': יא] עיין בהשמטות בסוף המסכת: יב] מעולה וא"ת שלא לשמה נמי ליתכשר לר"א באשם מק"ו דעולה ומה עולה שהיא כליל לאישים כשר בשלא לשמו אשם דאינו כליל כו' דאיכא למיפרך (הבא) [הכי] מה לעולה שאינה מכפרת וליכא [למימר] חטאת העוף [תוכיח] דחטאת העוף פסול שלא לשמו · תוס' סוך: יג] קדשי קדשים ודמו למטה: יד] שנכנסו לכפר להיכל: טו] היא בשחיטת אות ה' נמחק: טז] דרבנן ס"א טעמיה דר' יהושע דסמיך כו': יז] כה"ד ותיתי במה הצד מפסח וחטאת דנאכלין: יח] במתניתין דפסולות: יט] אף האשם אות ב' נמחק: כ] באשם ארבע מתנות אינו טעון: כא] מתנות דאותה מתנה אות ב' נמחק: כב] דקתני התם: כג] מתנות על ארבע קרנות: כד] קרן נמשך מלמעלה ולמטה והקרן היה אבן: כה] תיבת מתנות נמחק: כו] הוא ולידרשיה: כז] בזביחה מיהא: כח] יהא דמן אות ו' נמחק: כט] זריקת דם: ל] אלא שיהו: לא] שבראש המזבח: לב] וכל כדלקמן: לג] שוה דעונו ותיבות עון עון ל"ש: לד] גמירי בריש מנחות ואין ג"ש וכו' תיבות כדאמר בריש מנחות נמחק: לה] עיין בהשמטות בסוף המסכת: לו] באשם וי"ל דהו ליכא למימר חטאת העוף יוכיח: לז] דאמר בפ"ק דמנחות עיין תוספות ד"ה מנחה שנקמצה: לח] שלמים ששחטו: לט] שתלה הכתוב באהל מועד הס"ד:

the sin-offering prove it. R. Joshua replied: [10*b*] I am moving in a circle.[2] R. Eliezer then drew another analogy. In the case of a sin-offering it says, *It is* [*a sin-offering*],[3] [which intimates that if it is slaughtered] for its own sake it is valid, and if it [is] not [slaughtered] for its own sake it is invalid;[4] [Again] in the case of a Passover-offering it says, *It is* [*the sacrifice of the Lord's Passover*],[5] [which likewise intimates,] for its own sake it is valid, and if not for its own sake, it is invalid; [then] in the case of a guilt-offering too it says, *It is* [*a guilt-offering*],[6] [hence this too intimates,] for its own sake it is valid, while if not for its own sake, it is invalid. Said R. Joshua to him: '*It is*' is stated of the sin-offering in connection with the slaughtering, [and so] '*it is*' [intimates], for its own sake it is valid, and if not for its own sake, it is invalid. [Again] '*it is*' is stated of the Passover-offering in connection with the sacrificing,[7] [and here too] '*it is*' [intimates,] for its own sake it is valid, while if it is not for its own sake, it is invalid. But as for the guilt-offering, '*it is*' is stated of it only *after* the burning of the *emurim* [is prescribed], and yet if the *emurim* were not burnt at all it is valid.[8] Said R. Eliezer to him: Lo, it says, *As is the sin-offering, so is the guilt-offering*:[9] [hence] as the sin-offering is invalid if not [slaughtered] for its own sake, so is the guilt-offering invalid if not [slaughtered] for its own sake.

The Master said: 'R. Joshua said to him: I am moving in a circle.' Yet let the argument revolve and the inference be made from the
a feature common to both.[1]—[That argument is not employed] because it can be refuted: the feature common to both is that there is an aspect of *kareth* in them.[2]

The Master said:[3] 'R. Joshua said to him: That is not so. If you say [thus] of the sin-offering, [the reason is] because its blood [is sprinkled] above [the scarlet line].' Yet let him [rather] say to him: That is not so. If you say [thus] of the sin-offering, [the reason is] because its blood enters the innermost shrine?[4]—We are discussing the outer sin-offerings.[5] [Yet let him say: The reason is] because if its blood enters the innermost shrine it is invalid?—R. Eliezer holds that the guilt-offering too [is invalid in that case]. [Let him say to him: The reason is] because it makes atonement for those who are liable to *kareth*?—[R. Eliezer draws his analogy] from the sin-offering incurred through hearing a voice.[6] [Let him say to him: The reason is] because it [the blood] requires four applications?—[R. Eliezer holds] as R. Ishmael, who maintains: All blood[7] requires four applications. [Yet let him say: The reason is because the blood requires four applications] on the four horns [of the altar]?[8]—Now according to your reasoning, surely there are [the distinctions of] the finger, the horn, and the point?[9] Rather [the fact is that] he [R. Joshua] mentions [but] one of two or three reasons [distinctions].

The Master said: 'Said R. Joshua to him: That is not so. If you say' etc. Let R. Eliezer answer him: The blood of a guilt-offering
b too is [sprinkled] above [the scarlet line]?[1]—Said Abaye: You cannot say that the blood of a guilt-offering is [sprinkled] above, [as the reverse may be inferred] from a burnt-offering, *a fortiori*: if the blood of a burnt-offering, which is completely burnt, is [sprinkled] below, how much the more [is this true of] a guilt-offering, which is not completely burnt. As for a burnt-offering, the reason is because it does not make atonement! Let the bird sin-offering prove it.[2] As for a bird sin-offering, the reason is because it is not a species that is slaughtered![3] Then let a burnt-offering prove it. Thus the peculiarity of the one is not the peculiarity of the other, and that of the other is not the same as the peculiarity of the first: the feature common to both is that they are sacrifices of the higher sanctity,[4] and their blood is [sprinkled] below: so will I adduce a guilt-offering too, that [since] it is of the higher sanctity, its blood is [sprinkled] below. Raba of Parzakia[5] said to R. Ashi: But let him refute [it thus]: The feature common to both is that [their value] is unfixed; will you then say [the same of] a guilt-offering, which has a fixed [value]?[6] Rather this is R. Eliezer's reason,[7] viz., because Scripture saith, *The priest that offereth* it *for a sin-offering*:[8] ['*it*' requires] its blood [to be sprinkled] above, but the blood of no other [sacrifice] is [sprinkled] above. If so, let us say with respect to [the slaughtering of] the sin-offering too, [only] *it* is valid [when slaughtered] in its own name but invalid when not [slaughtered] in its own name, whereas other sacrifices are valid whether in their
c own name or not in their own name?[1]—That '*it*' is not meant particularly, since it disregards the Passover-offering.[2] Then here too it is not meant particularly, since it disregards the bird burnt-offering?[3]—At all events nothing which is slaughtered is omitted.[4] Alternatively, this agrees with R. Eleazar son of R. Simeon, who maintained: [The blood of] the one is [sprinkled] in a separate place, and [that of] the other is [sprinkled] in a separate place.[5] For it was taught: The lower blood is applied below the scarlet line, while the upper [blood is applied] above the scarlet line.[6] Said R. Simeon b. Eleazar: This holds good only of the bird burnt-offering; but in the case of the animal sin-offering its [blood] is applied essentially on the very horn [of the altar].[7]

We learnt elsewhere:[8] For R. Akiba maintained: All blood which entered the *Hekal*[9] to make atonement is unfit; but the Sages rule: The sin-offering alone [is unfit].[10] R. Eliezer said: The guilt-offering too [is thus], for it says, *As is the sin-offering, so is the guilt-offering*.[11] As for R. Eliezer, it is well, his reason being as stated. But what is the reason of the Rabbis?—Said Raba: [They argue that] you cannot say that if the blood of the guilt-offering enters within it is unfit, [for the reverse follows] from the burnt-offering,

(2) This way of arguing leads nowhere. (3) Lev. IV, 24. (4) *It is* implies emphasis: it must be slaughtered as a sin-offering and nothing else. (5) Ex. XII, 27. (6) Lev. VII, 5. (7) Likewise the slaughtering. (8) Obviously then '*it is*' cannot have the same implication here. V. *supra* 5*b*. (9) Lev. VII, 7.

a (1) Lit. from 'what is the side' (which they have in common)? V. *Supra a* bottom; the feature common to both the sin-offering and the Passover-offering is that they may be eaten one night only. The guilt-offering shares this feature, and therefore it also, like the other two, should be invalid if slaughtered for a different purpose. (2) The sin-offering is brought on account of an unwitting offence which if wilful is punishable by *kareth*. The neglect to bring the Passover-offering by one who is not unclean or on a distant journey is likewise punishable by *kareth* (Num. IX, 13). (3) Emended text (Sh. M.). (4) In the case of the sin-offering of the Day of Atonement. (5) Those which do not enter the innermost shrine — i.e., all save that of the Day of Atonement. (6) V. Lev. V, 1*ff*. This does not involve *kareth*. (7) The blood of *all* sacrifices. (8) Whereas even R. Ishmael admits that the blood of the guilt-offering is not sprinkled on the *four* horns, but only on two. (9) The blood of the sin-offering must be applied with the finger on the point (i.e., the top) of the horn, whereas the blood of other sacrifices is not applied actually on the top. —The point is: If one is seeking distinctions, there are many other than that drawn by R. Joshua.

b (1) For R. Eliezer likens the guilt-offering to the sin-offering. (2) Its blood is sprinkled below, though it does make atonement. (3) The bird-offering was not slaughtered, its neck being wrung (Lev. I, 15). (4) V. *Supra* 2*a* n. a 7. (5) Farausag, in the vicinity of Be Dura, one of the four districts in the middle of which Baghdad was built; v. Obermeyer, *Landschaft*, pp. 268-9. (6) V. Lev. V, 15 *seq*. (7) For holding that the blood of a guilt-offering is sprinkled below. (8) Lev. VI, 19. The Heb. אותה המחטא is understood to mean he who sprinkles its blood in accordance with its law as a sin-offering, viz., above the scarlet line.

c (1) Since the unfitness of a sin-offering when not killed for its own sake is deduced from, *And he shall kill it for a sin-offering* (Lev. IV, 33). Then R. Eliezer should regard the '*it*' here too as a limitation and not apply the same law to the guilt-offering. (2) To which the same law applies, as was shewn *supra* 7*b*. (3) Whose blood too is sprinkled above; *infra* 65*a*. (4) The limitation of '*it*' applies to all slaughtered sacrifices. (5) Though the blood of both the sin-offering and the bird burnt-offering is sprinkled above the scarlet line, yet each has a different place. Therefore the limitation of '*it*' in respect to the sprinkling of the blood has no exception at all. (6) At any point above it.—'Lower' and 'upper' mean that which is applied below and that which is applied above respectively. (7) And not merely anywhere above the line. (8) *Infra* 81*b*. (9) The hall containing the golden altar etc., contrad. to the Holy of Holies (Jast.). (10) When Moses rebuked Aaron for not eating the flesh of the sin-offering on the day of his consecration, he said to him: *Behold, the blood of it was not brought into the sanctuary within; ye should certainly have eaten it* (Lev. X, 18; v. also ib. VI, 23). This proves that if it had been brought '*within*' Aaron would have been right, for the sacrifice would have thereby become unfit. Now the passage actually refers to a sin-offering: R. Akiba holds that its implication extends to all other sacrifices too, while the Rabbis confine it to the sin-offering. (11) Lev. VII, 7.

a fortiori. If [11*a*] the burnt-offering is fit when its blood enters within, though it is entirely burnt, how much the more is the guilt-offering [fit], seeing that it is not entirely burnt. [But it may be asked:] As for the burnt-offering, [the reason is] because it does not make a atonement?—Let a sinner's meal-offering prove it.[1] (Yet he should rather say: Let the sin-offering of a bird prove it?[2]—The sin-offering of a bird is the subject of a question by R. Abin.)[3] As for a sinner's meal-offering,[4] [the reason is] because it is not of the species that is slaughtered?[5] Let the burnt-offering prove it. And thus the argument revolves, the peculiarity of the one not being that of the other, while the peculiarity of the latter is not that of the former: the feature common to both is that they are sacrifices of the higher sanctity, and when their blood enters within they are fit; so too will I adduce the guilt-offering which is a sacrifice of the higher sanctity, and if its blood enters within it is fit. Raba of Barnesh[6] said to R. Ashi: Yet let him refute [it thus]: The feature common to both is that they have no fixed [value]; will you say [the same of] the guilt-offering, which has a fixed [value]? Rather this is the Rabbis' reason, viz., because Scripture saith, [*And no sin-offering whereof any of*] *its blood* [*is brought into the tent of meeting . . . shall be eaten; it shall be burnt with fire*]:[7] [this intimates] the blood of this [sacrifice], but not the blood of another [sacrifice]. And the other?[8] —'*Its blood*' [implies,] but not its flesh.[9] And the other?[10]—[Scripture writes,] '*its blood*' [where] 'blood' [would suffice].[11] And the other?—He does not interpret 'blood', '*its blood*' [as having a particular significance].

It is well according to the Rabbis who maintain that if one slaughters a guilt-offering under a different designation it is valid: for that reason a meal-offering is likened to a sin-offering and to a guilt-offering. For it was taught, R. Simeon said: [It is written,] b *It is most holy, as the sin-offering, and as the guilt-offering*:[1] a sinner's meal-offering is like a sin-offering, therefore if its fistful [of flour] is taken under a different designation, it is invalid;[2] a votive meal-offering is like a guilt-offering, therefore if he [the priest] takes its fistful under a different designation, it is valid. But according to R. Eliezer, in respect of which law is a meal-offering likened to a sin-offering and a guilt-offering?—In respect of the other [ruling] of R. Simeon. For it was taught: [If the fistful was carried to the altar] not in a service-vessel,[3] it is invalid; but R. Simeon declares it valid.[4] Now Rab Judah son of R. Ḥiyya said, What is R. Simeon's reason?—Scripture saith, '*It is most holy, as the sin-offering, and as the guilt-offering*': [this teaches:] If he [the priest] comes to perform its service with his hand, he does so with his right hand, as in the case of the sin-offering; [if he comes] to perform the service with a vessel, he may do so with his left hand, as in the case of the guilt-offering.[5] Now R. Simeon utilises this verse for both purposes?[6] —The essential purpose of the text is to teach the dictum of Rab

a (1) This makes atonement, yet if it enters within it remains fit, for the disqualification is stated in reference to the entering of *blood* only. (2) This would provide a better analogy, as it is a blood-sacrifice just as the other sacrifices under consideration. (3) Whether it is unfit when its blood enters within (*infra* 92*b*). The objection and answer are parenthetical, and now the Talmud returns to its discussion. (4) Emended text (BaḤ); omitting, and let him refute', of cur. edd. (5) It is not a blood-sacrifice. (6) A town in the vicinity of Matha Meḥasia, a suburb of Sura (Obermeyer, *op. cit.* pp. 296-7). (7) Lev. VI, 23. (8) R. Eliezer: how does he explain '*its blood*'? (9) If its flesh is taken '*into the tent of meeting*', into the inner sanctuary, it is not disqualified. (10) The Rabbis: how do they know this? (11) Hence '*its*' excludes that of other sacrifices, while '*blood*' excludes the flesh of the same sacrifice.

b (1) Lev. VI, 10. This refers to the meal-offering, and since it is likened to two other sacrifices, R. Simeon deduces that one kind of meal-offering is like a sin-offering, while another is like a guilt-offering, as explained in the text. (2) The taking of the fistful of the meal-offering and its burning on the altar are the equivalent of the sprinkling of the blood of an animal sacrifice. (3) A service-vessel is one that has been sanctified for use in the Temple in connection with the sacrificial service. (4) If the priest carried it in his hand to the altar. (5) This being R. Simeon's view. Others hold that the service of all sacrifices must be done with the right hand (*infra* 24*b*). (6) He had made two distinct deductions from the same verse.

◁ *For the continuation of the English translation of this page see overleaf*

עולה שהיא כליל נכנס דמה לפנים כשרה אשם שאינו כליל לא כ"ש מה לעולה שכן אינה מכפרת מנחת חוטא תוכיח ולימא חטאת העוף תוכיח חטאת העוף *בעיא דרבי אבין היא (א) ולפרוך מה למנחת חוטא שכן אינה מין זבח עולה תוכיח *וחזר הדין לא ראי זה כראי זה ולא ראי זה כראי זה הצד השוה שבהן שהן קדשי קדשים א] ונכנס (*דמן) נ"א לפנים כשרין אף אני אביא אשם שהוא קודש קדשים ונכנס דמו לפנים כשר אמר ליה רבא מברניש לרב אשי ולפרוך מה להצד השוה שבהן שכן אין להן קצבה תאמר באשם שיש לו קצבה אלא היינו טעמייהו דרבנן דאמר קרא דמה דמה של זו ולא דמה של אחר ואידך *דמה ולא בשרה ואידך דם דמה ואידך דם דמה לא דריש בשלמא לרבנן דאמרי אשם ששחטו שלא לשמו כשר היינו דאיתקש מנחה לחטאת מנחה לאשם *דתניא רבי שמעון אומר °קדש קדשים היא כחטאת וכאשם א מנחת חוטא הרי היא כחטאת לפיכך קמצה שלא לשמה פסולה מנחת נדבה הרי היא כאשם לפיכך קמצה שלא לשמה כשרה אלא לרבי אליעזר למאי הלכתא איתקש מנחה לחטאת ומנחה לאשם לכי אידך דרבי שמעון *דתנן ב שלא בכלי שרת פסולה ורבי שמעון מכשיר *ואמר רב יהודה בריה דרבי חייא מ"ט דר"ש אמר קרא קדש קדשים היא כחטאת וכאשם בא לעבודה ביד עובדה בימין כחטאת (ב) בכלי עובדה בשמאל כאשם ור"ש האי קרא מפיק ליה להכי ומפיק ליה להכי עיקר קרא לכדרב יהודה בריה דרבי חייא הוא דאתא ומנחת חוטא דפסולה שלא (ג) לשמה ב] [טעמא אחרינא הוא] חטאת טעמא מאי דכתיב בה היא מנחת חוטא נמי כתיב בה היא ג] ולרבנן למאי הלכתא איתקש אשם לחטאת לומר לך מה חטאת טעונה סמיכה אף אשם טעון סמיכה : יוסף בן חוני אומר הנשחטין כו' : א"ר יוחנן יוסף בן חוני ורבי אליעזר אמרו דבר אחד רבה אמר באחרים לשם חטאת פליגי (ד) דתניא *הפסח שעברה שנתו ושחטו בזמנו לשמו וכן השוחט אחרים לשם פסח בזמנו רבי אליעזר פוסל ורבי יהושע ג מכשיר א"ר יהושע אם בשאר ימות השנה שאינו כשר לשמו אחרים כשרים לשמו בזמנו שהוא כשר לשמו אינו דין שיכשרו אחרים לשמו אמר לו רבי אליעזר או חילוף הדברים ומה אם בשאר ימות השנה שאינו כשר לשמו כשר הוא לשם אחרים בזמנו שהוא כשר לשמו אינו דין שיוכשר לשם אחרים ויוכשר פסח בארבעה עשר שלא לשמו וכך אתה אומר מה לי הוכשרו אחרים בשאר ימות השנה לשמו שכן הוא כשר לשם אחרים ויוכשרו אחרים בזמנו לשמו שכן הוא פסול לשם אחרים אמר לו רבי יהושע אם כן ד] הורעתה כח פסח ונתת כח בשלמים חזר רבי אליעזר ודנו דין אחר מצינו מותר פסח בא שלמים ואין מותר שלמים בא פסח ומה פסח שמותרו בא שלמים שחטו בזמנו לשום שלמים פסול שלמים שאין מותרו בא פסח אם שחטם לשם פסח בזמנו אינו דין שיהו פסולין

אמר

אשם שאינו כליל לא כל שכן · לא שייך למימר חטאת תוכיח דאיכא למימר מה לחטאת שכן דמה למעלה ושכן לד כרת ושכן באה בגבור : **מנחת** חוטא הרי היא כחטאת · אין זה למד מלמד דאע"ג דחטאת ילפינן למלוה משלמים לעיל מכל מקום עכובא *בגופיה כתיבי ומנחת נדבה כאשם לאו משום דמאשם ילפא כא] למלוה דמנחה גופה איתקש לשלמים כאשם אלא למימרא דלא הוי כחטאת : *"**בא** לעובדה ביד עובדה בימין כחטאת · דכתיב בה אצבע דילפינן מגזירה שוה ממצורע דאצבע הוי ימין וא"ת הלא איבעיא לן פרק איזהו מקומן (לקמן דף נ.) אי ילפינן היקש מג"ש ואי מצורע חולין כב] [הוא] הוה אתי שפיר כג] *[ולא] קשה למ"ד דבעי למד קדש ומלמד קודש פרק איזהו מקומן (גם זה שם) : כד] **הכי** גרסינן עיקר קרא לכדרב' יהודה בריה דרבי חייא הוא כו' · תימה דברים מנחות (דף ב:) משמע דאידך דרשא עיקר דפריך אביי מכדי מחשבה דפסיל רחמנא היקשא הוא*: **הורעתה** כח פסח ונתת כח בשלמים · דבזמנו שלמים פסח לשם שלמים כשר ואילו בזמן הפסח שלמים לשם פסח פסולים והלא יש פסוק בפסח לפסול שלא לשמו ואילו בשלמים אין פסוק :

אמר

עולה נכנס דמה לפנים כשרה · בין לרבנן בין לרבי אליעזר דלא פ] דרשינן כל וכל והיקשא נמי ליכא הכא : מנחת חוטא · דקרבן עולה ויורד דשמיעת הקול : הוכיח · שמכפרת ואם נכנסה לפנים כשירה דלא פסל הכתוב אלא דם : ונימא חטאת העוף תוכיח · והכי שפיר טפי שהוא ממיני דמים וראויה להוכיח על מיני דמים : חטאת העוף בעיא דר' אבין היא · היכא דהכניס דמה לפנים בצוארה שאין לדמה קבלה ומיבעיא ליה בפ' דם חטאת (לקמן לב:) אם נפסלה בכך או לא ולא איפשיטא לה : דמה · אשר יובא מדמה : ולא בשרה · שאם נכנס בשרה להיכל אינה נפסלת : דם דמה לא דריש · דכיון דלא מצי למיכתב וכל חטאת אשר יובא אל אהל מועד דאיצטריך למיכתב דם למעוטי בשר אורחיה דקרא למיכתב מדמה : קדש קדשים היא כחטאת וכאשם ו] · במנחה הוא דכתיב וקא א"ר שמעון מדקא מקיש מנחות לחטאת ואשם להכי מקיש ז] [לשניהם לומר לך דיש מהם כחטאת ויש מהם כאשם] שתהא מנחת חוטא כחטאת דלא לשמה פסולה ומנחת נדבה כאשם דכשר שלא לשמו : אלא לרבי אליעזר · כיון דחטאת ואשם כי הדדי נינהו למאי הלכתא איתקש לתרווייהו : שלא בכלי שרת · שלא קדש הקומץ בכלי שרת פסולה שהמנחות הוקשו לזבחים ליטעון ארבע עבודות קמיצה כנגד שחיטה מתן קומץ בכלי שרת כנגד קבלת הדם הולכה כנגד הולכה הקטרה כנגד זריקה : ור"ש מכשיר · אם הוליכו בידו בקומצו עד המזבח והקטירו : כחטאת וכאשם · להכי איתקש מנחה לחטאת ולאשם שאינן שוין בהלכותיהן לומר לך : בא לעובדה · ח] *בהלכות והקטרות ביד שלא בכלי : עובדה בימין · שהקומץ בה כזריקת דם חטאת שהיא ביד באצבע ובימין דכתיב בחטאת ולקח הכהן מדם החטאת באצבעו ונתן וגו' ודרשינן לקמן בפ"ב (דף כד·) באצבעו ונתן שלא תהא נתינה אלא בימין דכל מקום שנאמר אצבע וכהונה אינו אלא ימין : בא לעובדה בכלי · רשאי לעובדה בשמאל להוליך הכלי שקדשה בתוכו בשמאלו למזבח וליתן בשמאלו מן הכלי על האשים כזריקת דם אשם שהוא מן הכלי למזבח שאינה בנתינת אצבע דלא כתיב אצבע אלא בחטאת וכשרה בשמאל לר"ש ט] בכל הזבחים חוץ מחטאת י] דאמרינן לקמן בפרק שני (שם:) זרק בשמאל פסול ור"ש מכשיר חוץ מחטאת משום דרבי שמעון תרתי בעי אצבע וכהונה דגמרינן ממצורע דכתיב ביה אצבע וכהונה וימין וטבל הכהן באצבעו הימנית וזריקת כל הזבחים לא כתיב בו אצבע אלא כהונה חוץ מחטאת : מנחת חוטא כתיב בה (ה) כי חטאת היא · גבי שמיעת הקול בויקרא : ולרבנן · דפליגי עליה דר' אליעזר במתני' למאי הלכתא כו' : חטאת כתיב בה (ויקרא ד) וסמך ידו על ראש החטאת : אמרו דבר אחד · דרבי אליעזר נמי פסיל באחרים הנשחטים לשם פסח בזמנו ולשם חטאת כל ימות השנה ומברייתא דלקמן דייק לה רבי יוחנן : ורבה אמר באחרים לשם חטאת פליגי · יוסף בן חוני ורבי אליעזר (ו) יא] ולא פסיל רבי אליעזר אלא באחרים לשם פסח אבל באחרים לשם חטאת מכשיר כדתניא כו' ובין רבה ובין ר' יוחנן דייקי מילתייהו מהא מתני' ובמסקנא בעינא לפרושי דיוקייהו : הפסח שעברה שנתו · דהו לא חזי לפסח סתמיה שלמים כדרבינן לעיל (דף ח:) מקראי : ושחטו בזמנו לשמו · דהוה ליה שוחט שלמים לשם פסח : וכן השוחט · אחד מכל הזבחים לשם פסח בזמנו : אם בשאר ימות השנה שאינו כשר לשמו · כדילפינן לה במסכת פסחים (דף סא·) שחטו קודם חצות פסול שנאמר בין הערבים וכמה פעמים שנה הכתוב לעכב יב] קביעות זמנו בי"ד בין הערבים : אחרים כשרים לשמו · דרבי אליעזר מודה בו דלא פליג אלא בזמנו כדתנן בהדיא אבל כל ימות השנה אין שם שחיטת פסח חל על קרבן אחר : אמר לו לרבי אליעזר או חילוף · · יג] אם ק"ו אתה בא לדרוש יכול אני להחליפו בענין אחר ולומר דבר שאינו ולהכשיר פסח בזמנו שלא לשמו : ויוכשר פסח בי"ד שלא לשמו · ובדין הזה יד] אתה יכול להכשיר פסח בזמנו שלא לשמו : וכן אתה אומר · בתמיה התדרוש ק"ו טו] ויתכשרו : מה לי הוכשרו אחרים כו' · טז] ק"ו שדרשת יש עליו תשובה : מה לי הוכשרו אחרים כו' יוכשרו אחרים כו' · בתמיה ומהכא דייק רבי יוחנן למילתיה ואמר דכי היכי דפסיל רבי אליעזר באחרים לשם פסח פסיל יז] באחרים לשם חטאת דהא טעמו דרבי אליעזר משום דהוא פסול לשם אחרים יח] וה"נ בחטאת איתא ורבה דייק מסיפא שחזר רבי אליעזר מדין זה ודנו בדין אחר ומודה דאחרים לשם חטאת כשרים : א"כ · אם אתה פוסל אחרים לשמו בזמנו יט] הורעת פסח ונתת כח בשלמים שכל השנה שהיא זמן שלמים פסח הנשחט (ז) לשמו כשר והיום שהוא זמן פסח כל שלמים הנשחטין לשמו פסולין נמצאת מחשבת (ח) כ] שלו *גדול כח בשלמים מפסח וקרא אשכחן דאחמור בפסח מבשלמים דכתיב ביה הוא ובכל הזבחים הכשיר שלא לשמן :

נא א מיי' פט"ו מהלכות פסה"מ הלכה ב :

נב ב מיי' פי"ב שם הלכה ו :

גי' צ"ק בגופים כתיב הס"ד ואח"כ מה"ד מנחת נדבה כו'

נג ג מיי' פט"ו שם הלכה יב :

פי' בחילופי גירסאות

גי' הצ"ק ומ"מ קשה למ"ד דלא בעי כו'

[עיין במנחות ב: נד"ה מכדי מחשבה כו' לא קשיא מידי ע"ש]

[לקמן לב:]

[קדושין כה: וש"נ]

[לקמן סג.]

מנחות ב:

שם כו.

נ"ל בהולכה הקטרה צ"ק

פסחים סב: תוספתא דפסחים פ"ד

ר"א גרוע

שיטה מקובצת

א] קדשים ונכנסו לפנים תיבת דמן נמחק : ב] לשמה טעמא אחרינא הוא : ג] מנחת חוטא נמי כתיב בה היא · תימה לרבנן דר"ש דאמרי קדשה שלא בכלי שרת פסולה למאי הלכתא איתקש מנחת חוטא לחטאת ואשם אי משום פסול שלא לשמו במנחת חוטא תיפוק ליה שהיא כדאמרינן ואי משום כשרות דמנחת נדבת (לימא דאיתקש מנחת נדבה לאשם כדאמרי' לעיל) לשתוק מיני' ומזאת תורת העולה נפקא הואיל ותורת שלמים עליו כדפי' וכ"ת דאיצטריך היקשא לומר דמה חטאת טעון ימין (אני) [אף] קמיצה בעי ימין תיפוק ליה דבפ"ק דמנחות מייתי תרי קראי חד לקומץ וחד לקידוש קומץ ואי משום עבודת ימין לחוד (בא לעובדה בימין כחטאת עובדה בימין) הא אית להו לרבנן (קדשה שלא בכלי שרת פסולה) דכל מקום שנאמר אצבע או כהונה אינה אלא ימין וי"ל דאיצטריך הקישא כדדרשינן [בחולין דף כא ולקמן דף צח] מה חטאת אינה באה אלא מן החולין ובידו הימנית (אי מה חטאת פסולה שלא לשמה אף כל המנחות פסולות בשלא לשמה ת"ל כאשם) [אא"ה בחולין דף כ"א ולקמן דף צ"ח ע"א ובמנחות דף פ"ג ע"א ליתא להאי סיומא ואולי היה כך גירסתם או

הגהות הב"ח

(א) גמ' בעיא דרבי אבין היא מה כצ"ל ותיבת ולפרוך נמחק : (ב) שם בימין כחטאת בא לעובדה בכלי עובדה : (ג) שם שלא לשמה ה"ט חטאת טעמא מאי : (ד) שם כדתניא הפסח : (ה) רש"י ד"ה מנחת חוטא כתיב בה חטאת כצ"ל ותיבת כי נמחק : (ו) ד"ה ורבה וכו' בן חוני ור' אליעזר ר"א לא פסיל אלא : (ז) ד"ה א"כ אם וכו' הנשחט לשמו נ"ב פי' לשם שלמים : (ח) בא"ד נמצאת מחשבת שלא לשמו גדול כחו בשלמים מבפסח :

שהוא מדברי התוס' דרבנן בעי להאי כחטאת וכאשם להכי עכ"ה] ובידו הימנית דנקט לאו דוקא דהא עיק' דרשא כדנפקא לן במנחות דבעי ימין אלא אגב אינו בא אלא מן החולין נקט לה תוס' סוך : ד] עי' **בהשמטות** בסוף המסכת : ה] דרשי אות נ' נמחק : ו] וכאשם יש מהם שהוא כחטאת ויש מהם כאשם האי קרא במנחה: ז] מקיש לה שתהא מנחת חוטא והשאר ל"ש ונמחק : ח] עבודת הקטרה ביד : ט] לר"ש **כדאמרי' בפ' שני** [דף כד] בכל · ס"א מתיבת בכל עד תיבות משום דר"ש אינו : י] תיבות דאמרינן לקמן בפ' שני ל"ש ונמחק : יא] אליעזר דלא : יב] לעכב בקביעות : יג] חילוף כלומר אם : יד] הוד **אני יכול תיבת אתה נמחק** : טו] ויתכשרו ס"א ותכשירו שלא לשמו דלא תדרוש [ק"ו] זה כמו דלא תדרוש האחר שיש עליו כו' : טז] אחרים כו' ועוד ק"ו : יז] פסח פסיל נמי באחרים : יח] אחרים והאי דין **נמי בחטאת איתא ורבה** דייק מסיפא דהדר ר"א : יט] הורעתה כח : כ] מחשבת שלא לשמו גדול כח בשלמים מבפסח : כא] ילפא דאשם גופיה לא ידעינן דכשר אלא מהיקשא וא"ת תיפוק [ליה] הכשר [מזאת **תורת**] **דאיתקש** [כל המנחות] כולהו לשלמים וי"ל דלכך בא זה הפסוק לאשמועינן דאין מנחת נדבה כחטאת אלא הרי הוא כאשם תוס' סוך : כב] חולין הוי תיבת הוא ל"ש : כג] שפיר [ומיהו עדיין] קשה למ"ד דלא בעי למד קודש ומלמד קודש כדפריך בפרק איזהו מקומן עכ"ה : כד] תיבות הכי גרסינן נמחק :

Continuation of translation from previous page as indicated by ◁

Judah the son of R. Ḥiyya, while that a sinner's meal-offering is invalid when [the priest does] not [take its fistful] for its own sake is [based] on a different reason. [Thus:] what is the reason of a sin-offering?7 Because *'it is'* is written in connection therewith; then in connection with a sinner's meal-offering too *'it is'* is written. Now according to the Rabbis, in respect of which law is a guilt-offering likened to a sin-offering?—To teach you: as a sin-offering requires laying on [of hands], so does a guilt-offering require laying on [of hands].

JOSEPH b. ḤONI SAID: SACRIFICES SLAUGHTERED [IN THE NAME OF A PASSOVER-OFFERING OR A SIN-OFFERING ARE INVALID]. R. Joḥanan said: Joseph b. Ḥoni and R. Eliezer said the
c same thing.[1] Rabbah said: They disagree in respect of others slaughtered in the name of a sin-offering. For it was taught: A Paschal lamb which has passed its year,[2] and he [its owner] slaughtered it in its season,[3] for its own purpose;[4] and similarly, when a man slaughters other [sacrifices] as a Passover-offering in its season,—R. Eliezer disqualifies them;[5] while R. Joshua declares them valid. Said R. Joshua: If during the rest of the year, when it is not valid [if slaughtered] in its own name, yet others [slaughtered] in its name are valid;[6] then is it not logical that in its season, when it is valid [if slaughtered] in its own name, others [slaughtered] in its name are valid? Said R. Eliezer to him: Yet perhaps the argument is to be reversed? If it is valid [when slaughtered] during the rest of the year in the name of another sacrifice,[7] though it is not valid [if slaughtered then] in its own name; is it not logical that it should be valid [when slaughtered] in its season in the name of another sacrifice, seeing that it is valid [if slaughtered, then] in its own name; and thus a Passover-offering [slaughtered] on the fourteenth [of
d Nisan] under a different designation should be valid.[1] Now, would you say thus? [But in point of fact your *a minori* argument can be refuted thus:] As for others being valid during the rest of the year [when slaughtered] in its [*sc.* the Passover-offering's] name, that is because it is valid [when slaughtered then] in the name of other [sacrifices]; should then others [slaughtered] in its season[2] in its name be valid, seeing that it [the Passover-offering] is invalid [if slaughtered then] in the name of others?[3] Said R. Joshua to him: If so, you lessen the strength of the Passover-offering and increase the strength of the peace-offering?[4] Subsequently R. Eliezer proposed a different argument: We find that a Passover remainder[5] comes as a peace-offering, whereas a peace-offering remainder does not come as a Passover-offering. Now if the Passover-offering, whose remainder comes as a peace-offering, is [nevertheless] unfit if one slaughters it in its season as a peace-offering; is it not logical that the peace-offering is unfit if slaughtered in the name of a Passover-offering in its season, seeing that its remainder does not come

(7) That it is invalid when not slaughtered for its own sake.
c (1) R. Eliezer too holds that other sacrifices slaughtered as a Passover-offering in its time or as a sin-offering at any time are invalid. R. Joḥanan deduces this anon. (2) It became a year old on the first of Nisan, and was then set aside for the Passover sacrifice. Since a year is the extreme limit for such (V. Ex. XII, 5: *a male of the first year*), it automatically stands to be a peace-offering, being unfit for its original purpose. (3) I.e., on the eve of Passover. (4) *Sc.* as a Passover-offering. Thus he slaughtered a peace-offering as a Passover sacrifice. (5) He infers this *a minori*: If an animal set aside for the Passover-offering is disqualified when slaughtered in its season (on the eve of Passover) as a peace-offering, though if left until after Passover it *must* be offered as such; then how much the more is a peace-offering disqualified if slaughtered on the eve of Passover as a Passover-offering, seeing that if left over and not brought as a peace-offering at the time appointed for same it cannot be brought as a Passover-offering on Passover eve. (6) For all sacrifices except the Passover-offering and the sin-offering are valid when slaughtered for a different purpose (*supra* 2a). (7) *Sc.* a peace-offering.

d (1) Which however is obviously wrong. Hence by a *reductio ad absurdum* the deduction *a minori* is shewn to be inadmissible. (2) On the eve of Passover. (3) Surely not. From this R. Joḥanan deduces that just as R. Eliezer declares others unfit when slaughtered in the name of the Passover-offering, so are they unfit when slaughtered in the name of a sin-offering. For R. Eliezer's reason, as seen here, is because it (the Passover-offering) is unfit when slaughtered in the name of a different sacrifice, and this same holds good of the sin-offering too. (4) For at the proper season for peace-offerings (i.e., during the rest of the year) the Passover-offering if slaughtered as a peace-offering is fit; whereas at the season of the Passover-offering (on Passover eve) a peace-offering slaughtered in the name of a Passover-offering is unfit! Yet in fact while Scripture insists that the Passover-offering must be killed in its own name (V. *supra* 7b), there is no such insistence with respect to the peace-offering.—'Weaken' and 'strengthen' mean to weaken and strengthen the necessity for (or, the insistence on) slaughtering these sacrifices for nought but their own sake. (5) If an animal was dedicated for a Passover-offering, lost and refound after Passover.

עולה שהיא כליל נכנס דמה לפנים כשרה אשם שאינו כליל לא כ"ש מה לעולה שכן אינה מכפרת מנחת חוטא תוכיח ולימא חטאת העוף תוכיח חטאת העוף *בעיא דרבי אבין היא (א) ולפרוך מה למנחת חוטא שכן אינה מין זבח עולה תוכיח *וחזר הדין לא ראי זה כראי זה ולא ראי זה כראי זה הצד השוה שבהן שהן קדשי קדשים א] ונכנס (*דמן) לפנים כשרין אף אני אביא אשם שהוא קודש קדשים ונכנס דמו לפנים כשר אמר ליה רבא מברניש לרב אשי ולפרוך מה להצד השוה שבהן שכן אין להן קצבה תאמר באשם שיש לו קצבה אלא היינו טעמייהו דרבנן דאמר קרא דמה דמה של זו ולא דמה של אחר ואידך *דמה ולא בשרה ואידך דם דמה ואידך דם דמה לא דריש בשלמא לרבנן דאמרי אשם ששחטו שלא לשמו כשר היינו דאיתקש מנחה לחטאת מנחה לאשם *דתניא רבי שמעון אומר °קדש קדשים היא כחטאת וכאשם *מנחת חוטא הרי היא כחטאת לפיכך קמצה שלא לשמה פסולה מנחת נדבה הרי היא כאשם לפיכך קמצה שלא לשמה כשרה אלא לרבי אליעזר למאי הלכתא איתקש מנחה לחטאת ומנחה לאשם לכי אידך דרבי שמעון *דתנן ב שלא בכלי שרת פסולה ורבי שמעון מכשיר *ואמר רב יהודה בריה דרבי חייא מ"ט דר"ש אמר קרא קדש קדשים היא כחטאת וכאשם בא לעובדה ביד עובדה בימין כחטאת (ב) בכלי עובדה בשמאל כאשם ור"ש האי קרא מפיק ליה להכי ומפיק ליה להכי עיקר קרא לכדרב יהודה בריה דרבי חייא הוא דאתא ומנחת חוטא דפסולה שלא (ג) לשמה ב] [טעמא אחרינא הוא] חטאת טעמא מאי דכתיב בה היא מנחת חוטא נמי כתיב בה היא ג] ולרבנן למאי הלכתא איתקש אשם לחטאת לומר לך מה חטאת טעונה סמיכה אף אשם טעון סמיכה: יוסף בן חוני אומר הנשחטין כו': א"ר יוחנן יוסף בן חוני ורבי אליעזר אמרו דבר אחד רבה אמר באחרים לשם חטאת פליגי (ד) דתניא *הפסח שעברה שנתו ושחטו בזמנו לשמו וכן השוחט אחרים לשם פסח בזמנו רבי אליעזר פוסל ורבי יהושע ג מכשיר א"ר יהושע אם בשאר ימות השנה שאינו כשר לשמו אחרים כשרים לשמו בזמנו שהוא כשר לשמו אינו דין שיכשרו אחרים לשמו אמר לו רבי אליעזר או חילוף הדברים ומה אם בשאר ימות השנה שאינו כשר לשמו כשר הוא לשם אחרים בזמנו שהוא כשר לשמו אינו דין שיוכשר לשם אחרים ויוכשר פסח בארבעה עשר שלא לשמו וכך אתה אומר מה לי הוכשרו אחרים בשאר ימות השנה לשמו שכן הוא כשר לשם אחרים ויוכשרו אחרים בזמנו לשמו שכן הוא פסול לשם אחרים אמר לו רבי יהושע אם כן ד] הורעתה כח פסח ונתת כח בשלמים חזר רבי אליעזר ודנו דין אחר מצינו מותר פסח בא שלמים ואין מותר שלמים בא פסח ומה פסח שמותרו בא שלמים שחטו בזמנו לשום שלמים פסול שלמים שאין מותרי בא פסח אם שחטם לשם פסח בזמנו אינו דין שיהו פסולין

אמר

רש"י

עולה נכנס דמה לפנים כשרה · בין לרבנן בין לרבי אליעזר דלא ה] דרשינן כל וכל והיקשא נמי ליכא הכא: מנחת חוטא · דקרבן עולה ויורד דשמיעת הקול: תוכיח · שמכפרת ואם נכנסה לפנים כשירה דלא פסל הכתוב אלא דם: ונימא חטאת העוף תוכיח · והכי שפיר טפי שהוא ממיני דמים ורלויה להוכיח על מיני דמים: חטאת העוף בעיא דר' אבין היא · היכא דהכניס דמה לפנים בלוארה שאין לדמה קבלה ומיבעיא ליה בפ' דם חטאת (לקמן צב:) אם נפסלה בכך או לא ולא איפשיטא לה: דמה · אשר יובא מדמה: ולא בשרה · שאם נכנס בשרה להיכל אינה נפסלת: דם דמה לא דריש · דכיון דלא מצי למיכתב וכל חטאת אשר יובא אל אהל מועד דאיצטריך למיכתב דם למעוטי בשר אורחיה דקרא למיכתב מדמה: קדש קדשים היא כחטאת וכאשם ו] · במנחה הוא דכתיב וקא א"ר שמעון מדקא מקיש מנחות לחטאת ואשם להכי מקיש ז] [לשניהם לומר לך דיש מהם כחטאת ויש מהם כאשם] שתהא מנחת חוטא כחטאת דלא לשמה פסולה ומנחת נדבה כאשם דכשר שלא לשמו: אלא לרבי אליעזר · כיון דחטאת ואשם כי הדדי נינהו למאי הלכתא איתקש לתרווייהו: שלא בכלי שרת · שלא קדש הקומץ בכלי שרת פסולה שהמנחות הוקשו לזבחים ליטעון ארבע עבודות קמילה כנגד שחיטה מתן קומץ בכלי שרת כנגד קבלת הדם הולכה כנגד הולכה הקטרה כנגד זריקה: ור"ש מכשיר · אם הוליכו בידו בקומצו עד המזבח והקטירו: כחטאת וכאשם · להכי איתקש מנחה לחטאת ולאשם שאינן שוין בהלכותיהן לומר לך: בא לעובדה · ח] *בהלכות והקטרות ביד שלא בכלי: עובדה בימין · שהקומץ בה כזריקת דם חטאת שהיא ביד באצבע ובימין דכתיב בחטאת ולקח הכהן מדם החטאת באצבעו ונתן וגו' ודרשינן לקמן בפ"ב (דף כד·) באצבעו ונתן שלא תהא נתינה אלא בימין דכל מקום שנאמר אצבע וכהונה אינו אלא ימין: בא לעובדה בכלי · ראשי לעובדה בשמאל להוליך הכלי שקדשה בתוכו בשמאלו למזבח וליתן בשמאלו מן הכלי על האשים כזריקת דם אשם שהוא מן הכלי למזבח שאינה בנתינת אצבע דלא כתיב אצבע אלא בחטאת וכשרה בשמאל לר"ש ט] בכל הזבחים חוץ מחטאת י] דאמרינן לקמן בפרק שני (שם:) זרק בשמאל פסול ור"ש מכשיר חוץ מחטאת משום דרבי שמעון תרתי בעי אצבע וכהונה דגמרינן ממצורע דכתיב ביה אצבע וכהונה וימין וטבל הכהן באצבעו הימנית ובזריקת כל הזבחים לא כתיב בו אצבע אלא כהונה חוץ מחטאת: מנחת חוטא כתיב בה (ה) כי חטאת היא · גבי שמיעת הקול בויקרא: ולרבנן · דפליגי עליה דר' אליעזר במתני' למאי הלכתא כו': חטאת כתיב בה (ויקרא ד) וסמך ידו על ראש החטאת: אמרו דבר אחד · דרבי אליעזר נמי פסיל באחרים הנשחטים לשם פסח בזמנו ולשם חטאת כל ימות השנה ומברייתא דלקמן דייק לה רבי יוחנן: ורבה אמר באחרים לשם חטאת פליגי · יוסף בן חוני ורבי אליעזר (ו) יא] ולא פסיל רבי אליעזר אלא באחרים לשם פסח אבל באחרים לשם חטאת מכשיר כדתניא כו' ובין רבה ובין ר' יוחנן דייקי מילתייהו מהא מתני' ובמסקנא בעינא לפרושי דיוקייהו: הפסח שעברה שנתו · דתו לא חזי לפסח סתמיה שלמים כדדרשינן לעיל (דף ח:) מקראי: ושחטו בזמנו לשמו · דהוה ליה שוחט שלמים לשם פסח: וכן השוחט · אחד מכל הזבחים לשם פסח בזמנו: אם בשאר ימות השנה שאינו כשר לשמו · כדילפינן לה במסכת פסחים (דף סא·) שחטו קודם חצות פסול שנאמר בין הערבים וכמה פעמים שנה הכתוב לעכב יב] קביעות זמנו בי"ד בין הערבים: אחרים כשרים לשמו · דרבי אליעזר מודה בו דלא פליג אלא בזמנו כדתנן בהדיא אבל כל ימות השנה אין שם שחיטת פסח חל על קרבן אחר: אמר לו רבי אליעזר או חילוף ·· יג] אם ק"ו אתה בא לדרוש יכול אני להחליפו בענין אחר ולומר דבר שאינו ולהכשיר פסח בזמנו שלא לשמו: ויוכשר פסח בי"ד שלא לשמו · ובדין הזה יד] אתה יכול להכשיר פסח בזמנו שלא לשמו: וכן אתה אומר · בתמיה התדרוש ק"ו טו] ויתכשרו: מה לי הוכשרו אחרים כו' · טז] ק"ו שדרשת יש עליו תשובה: מה לי הוכשרו אחרים כו' יוכשרו אחרים כו' · בתמיה ומהכא דייק רבי יוחנן למילתיה ואמר דכי היכי דפסיל רבי אליעזר באחרים לשם פסח פסיל יז] באחרים לשם חטאת דהא טעמו דרבי אליעזר משום דהוא פסול לשם אחרים יח] וה"נ בחטאת איתא ורבה דייק מסיפא שחזר רבי אליעזר מדין זה ודנו בדין אחר ומודה דאחרים לשם חטאת כשרים: א"כ · אם אתה פוסל אחרים לשמו בזמנו יט] הורעת פסח ונתת כח בשלמים שכל השנה שהיא זמן שלמים פכח הנשחט (ז) לשמו כשר והיום שהוא זמן פסח כל שלמים הנשחטין לשמו פסולין נמצאת מחשבת (ח) כ] שלו *גדול כח בשלמים מפסח וקרא אשכחן דאחמור בפסח מבשלמים דכתיב ביה הוא ובכל הזבחים הכשיר שלא לשמן:

אמר

תוספות

אשם שאינו כליל לא כל שכן · לא שייך למימר חטאת תוכיח דאיכא למימר מה לחטאת שכן דמה למעלה ושכן לד כרת ושכן באה בלבור: **מנחת** חוטא הרי היא כחטאת · אין זה למד מלמד דאע"ג דחטאת ילפינן למנוה משלמים לעיל מכל מקום עבודה *בגופיה כתיבי ומנחת נדבה כאשם לאו משום דמאשם ילפא כא] למנוה דמנחה גופה איתקש לשלמים כאשם אלא למימרא דלא הוי כחטאת: *בא **לעובדה** ביד עובדה בימין כחטאת · דכתיב בה אצבע דילפינן מגזירה שוה ממצורע דאצבע הוי ימין וא"ת הלא איבעיא לן פרק איזהו מקומן (לקמן דף נ.) אי ילפינן היקש מג"ש ואי מצורע חולין כב] [הוא] הוה אתי שפיר כג] *[ולא] קשה למ"ד דבעי למד קדש ומלמד קודש פרק איזהו מקומן (גם זה שם): כד] **הכי** גרסינן עיקר קרא לכדר' יהודה בריה דרבי חייא הוא כו' · תימה דבריש מנחות (דף ב:) משמע דאידך דרשא עיקר דפריך אביי מכדי מחשבה דפסיל רחמנא היקישא הוא*: **הורעתה** כח פסח ונתת כח בשלמים · דבזמן שלמים פסח לשם שלמים כשר ואילו בזמן הפסח שלמים לשם פסח פסולים והלא יש פסוק בפסח לפסול שלא לשמו ואילו בשלמים אין פסוק:

אמר

תורה אור: וייקרא ו · ויקרא ז

עין משפט נר מצוה

נא א מיי' פט"ו מהלכות פסה"מ הלכה כ:

נב ב מיי' פי"ח שם הלכה ו:

גי' צ"ק בגופיה כתיבי כו"ד ואח"כ מס"ד מנחת נדבה כו'

נג ג מיי' פ"ו שם הלכה יג:

עי' בתוספות גירסאות

גי' צ"ק ומ"מ קשה למ"ד דלא בעי כו'

[עיין במנחות ב: בד"ה מכדי מחשבה כו' לא קשיא מידי ע"ש]

מסורת הש"ס

[לקמן צב:]

[קדושין כה: וש"נ]

[לקמן סב.]

מנחות ב:

שם כו.

צ"ל בהולכה הקטרה צ"ק

פסחים סב: תוספתא דפסחים פ"ד

ר"א גרוע

הגהות הב"ח

(א) גמ' בעיא דרבי אבין היא מה כצ"ל ותיבת ולפרוך נמחק: (ב) שם בימין כחטאת בא לעובדה בכלי עובדה: (ג) שם שלא לשמה ה"ט חטאת טעמא מאי: (ד) שם כדתניא הפסח: (ה) רש"י ד"ה מנחת חוטא כתיב בה חטאת כצ"ל ותיבת כי נמחק: (ו) ד"ה ורבה וכו' בן חוני ור' אליעזר ר"א לא פסיל אלא: (ז) ד"ה א"כ אם וכו' כגשחט לשמו כ"ב פי' לשם שלמים: (ח) בא"ד נמלאת מחשבת שלא לשמה גדול כח בשלמים מפסח:

שיטה מקובצת

א] קדשים ונכנסו לפנים תיבת דמן נמחק: ב] לשמה טעמא אחרינא הוא: ג] מנחת חוטא נמי כתיב בה היא · תימה לרבנן דר"ש דאמרי קדשה שלא בכלי שרת פסולה למאי הלכתא איתקש מנחת חוטא לחטאת ואשם אי משום פסול שלא לשמו במנחת חוטא תיפוק ליה מהיא כדאמרינן ואי משום כשרות דמנחת נדבה (לימא דאיתקש מנחת נדבה לאשם כדאמרי' לעיל) לשתוק מיני' וזאת תורת העולה נפקא הואיל ותורת שלמים עליו כדפי' וכ"ת דאיצטריך היקשא לומר דמה חטאת טעון ימין (אנו) [אף] קמיצה בעי ימין תיפוק ליה דבפ"ק דמנחות מייתי תרי קראי חד לקומץ וחד לקידוש קומץ ואי משום עבודת ימין לחוד (בא לעובדה בימין כחטאת עובדה ביטין) הא אית להו לרבנן (קדשה שלא בכלי שרת פסולה) דכל מקום שנאמר אצבע או כהונה אינה אלא ימין וי"ל דאיצטריך הקישא כדדרשינן [בחולין דף כא ולקמן דף צח] מה חטאת אינה באה אלא מן החולין ובידו הימנית (אי מה חטאת פסולה שלא לשמה אף כל המנחות פסולות בשלא לשמה ת"ל כאשם) [אא"ה בחולין דף כ"א ולקמן דף צ"ה ע"א ובמנחות דף פ"ג ע"א ליתא להאי סיומא ואולי היה כך גירסתם אי

שתוא מדברי התוס' דרבנן בעי להאי כחטאת וכאשם להכי עכ"ה] ובידו הימנית דנקט לאו דוקא דהא עיק' דרשא כדנפקא לן במנחות דבעי ימין אלא אגב אינו בא אלא מן החולין נקט לה תוס' סוך : ד] עי' בהשמטות בסוף המסכת : ה] דרשי אות נ' נמחק : ו] וכאשם יש מהם שהוא כחטאת ויש מהם שהוא כאשם האי קרא במנחה: ז] מקיש לה שתהא מנחת חוטא והשאר ל"ש ונמחק : ח] עבודת הקטרה ביד : ט] לר"ש כדאמרי' בפ' שני [דף כד] בכל · ס"א מתיבת בכל עד תיבות משום דר"ש אינו : י] תיבות דאמרינן לקמן בפ' שני ל"ש ונמחק : יא] אליעזר דלא : יב] לעכב בקביעות : יג] חילוף כלומר אם : יד] הזה אני יכול תיבת אתה נמחק : טו] ויתכשרו ס"א ותכשירו שלא לשמו דלא תדרוש [ק"ו] זה כמו דלא תדרוש האחר שיש עליו כו' : טז] אחרים כו' ועוד ק"ו : יז] פסח פסיל נמי באחרים : יח] אחרים והאי דין נמי בחטאת איתא ורבה דייק מסיפא דהדר ר"א : יט] הורעתה כח : כ] מחשבת שלא לשמו גדול כח בשלמים מבפסח : כא] ילפא דאשם גופיה לא ידעינן דכשר אלא מהיקשא וא"ת תיפוק [ליה] הכשר [מזאת] תורת דאיתקש [כל המנחות] כולהו לשלמים וי"ל דלכך בא זה הפסוק לאשמועינן דאין מנחת נדבה כחטאת אלא הרי הוא כאשם תוס' סוך : כב] חולין הוי תיבת הוא ל"ש : כג] שפיר [ומיהו עדיין] קשה למ"ד דלא בעי למד קודש ומלמד קודש כדפריך בפרק איזהו מקומן עכ"ה : כד] תיבות הכי גרסינן נמחק :

עין משפט
נר מצוה

נ"א כו' כלומר וא"כ

נ"א דמותר חטאת כו' כמו מדינא דמותר כו' נ"ק [ד"ה שאני התם]

נד א מיי' פ"י מהלכות מאכלות אסורות הלכה יט :

נה ב מיי' פט"ו מהל' פסה"מ הלכה יא :

נו ג מיי' פ"ג מהלכות תמידין הלכה יא :

ג"י' נ"ק ולא אמרו דבר ט'

אמר לו רבי יהושע מצינו מותר חטאת בא עולה ואין מותר עולה בא חטאת ומה חטאת שמותרה בא עולה שחטה לשם עולה פסולה עולה שאין מותרה בא חטאת שחטה לשם חטאת אינו דין שתהא פסולה אמר לו רבי אליעזר לא אם אמרת בחטאת שכן כשרה לשמה כל השנה כולה תאמר בפסח שאינו כשר לשמו אלא בזמנו הואיל והוא פסול לשמו דין הוא שיפסלו אחרים לשמו: שמעון אחי עזריה אומר כו': רב אשי מתני משמיה דרבי יוחנן ורב אחא בריה דרבא מתני משמיה דרבי ינאי מאי טעמא דשמעון אחי עזריה דאמר קרא (ויקרא כב) °ולא יחללו את קדשי בני ישראל את אשר ירימו לה' במורם מהן אין מתחללין בנמוך מהם מתחללין והאי להכי הוא דאתא והא מיבעי ליה לכדשמואל *דאמר שמואל *מנין לאוכל את הטבל שהוא במיתה שנאמר ולא יחללו את קדשי בני ישראל את אשר ירימו לה' בעתידים לתרום הכתוב מדבר אם כן לכתוב קרא אשר הורמו א] מאי אשר ירימו שמע מיניה תרתי: בעי רבי זירא (א) כשרין ואין מרצין וכי פליג בחדא פליג או דלמא כשרין ומרצין ב] ובתרתי פליגי אמר אביי ואיתימא רבי זריקא תא שמע הבכור והמעשר ששחטן לשם שלמים כשרים שלמים ששחטן לשם בכור או לשם מעשר פסולין ואי ס"ד כשרין ומרצין בכור בר ריצויי הוא אלא כשרין ואין מרצין ג] ומדסיפא כשרין ואין מרצין רישא נמי כשרין ואין מרצין מידי איריא הא כדאיתא והא כדאיתא אלא מאי קמ"ל גבוה ונמוך קמ"ל תנינא כיצד קדשי קדשים ששחטן לשם קדשים קלים כו' מהו דתימא קדשי קדשים וקדשים קלים הוא דאיכא גבוה ונמוך אבל קלים וקלים לא הא נמי תנינא *שלמים קודמים את הבכור מפני שהן טעונין מתן ארבע וסמיכה ונסכים ותנופת חזה ושוק הא עיקר ההיא אגררא נסבה: **מתני'** *הפסח ששחטו (ב) שחרית בארבעה עשר שלא לשמו רבי יהושע מכשיר כאילו נשחט בשלשה עשר בן בתירא פוסל כאילו נשחט בין הערבים *) אמר שמעון בן עזאי מקובל אני מפי שבעים ושנים זקן ביום שהושיבו את *) רבי אליעזר ד] בישיבה שכל הזבחים (ג) הנאכלין שנזבחו שלא לשמן כשרין אלא שלא עלו לבעלים משום חובה חוץ מן הפסח ומן החטאת ולא הוסיף בן עזאי אלא העולה ולא הודו לו חכמים: **גמ'** *אמר רבי אלעזר אמר רבי אושעיא מכשיר היה בן בתירא בפסח ששחטו שחרית בארבעה עשר לשמו דכוליה יומא זמניה הוא ומאי כאילו איידי דאמר רבי יהושע כאילו אמר איהו נמי כאילו אי הכי אדמיפלגי בשלא לשמו ליפלגו בלשמו אי איפלגו בלשמו הוה אמינא אבל בשלא לשמו מודי רבי יהושע לבן בתירא הואיל ומקצתו ראוי קא משמע לן והכתיב (שמות יב) °בין הערבים אמר עולא בריה דרב עילאי בין שני ערבים תמיד דכתיב ביה (שם כט) °בין הערבים הכי נמי דכולי יומא כשר התם מדכתיב (שם) °את הכבש ה] *אחד תעשה בבקר מכלל דבין הערבים בין הערבים ממש (ד) אימא חד בבקר אידך כוליה יומא אחד בבקר ולא שנים בבקר נרות דכתיב (שם) °בין הערבים הכי נמי דכולי יומא כשר שאני התם דכתיב (שם כז) °מערב ועד בקר *ותניא °מערב ועד בקר תן לה מדתה שתהא דולקת והולכת מערב ועד בקר דבר אחר ו] אין לך עבודה כשרה מערב ועד בקר אלא זו בלבד קטורת דכתיב בה (שם ל) °בין הערבים הכי נמי דכולי יומא כשר שאני קטרת דאיתקש

*) ידים פ"ד מ"ב **) [נ"ל ר' אלעזר בן עזריה וכ"א במשנה שבמשניות]

רש"י

אמר לו רבי יהושע מצינו מותר חטאת בא עולה · כדתניא בתמורה (דף כג:) זה מדרש דרש יהוידע הכהן כל דבר שבא ממותר חטאת וממותר אשם ילקח בהן עולה לקיץ המזבח והיכי דמי מותר חטאת כגון הפריש מעות לחטאתו וניתותרו אי נמי מפריש שתי חטאות לאחריות דקי"ל בתמורה (דף כב·) מתכפר באחת מהן והשניה תרעה : ומה חטאת שמותרה כו' · ואם ק"ו כזה אתה דורש יש לך לפסול עולה לשם חטאת ומהכא דייק רבה מילתיה לעיל מדלא אהדר ליה רבי אליעזר הכא נמי פסילנא בנשחטין לשם חטאת: שכן כשרה לשמה כל השנה · לפיכך עולה הנשחטת לשם חטאת כשרה: ולא יחללו את קדשי · אין ז] (כאן) חילול כשירימו אותם לשם גבוה מהם : בעתידין לתרום · דהיינו טבל דכתיב ירימו דבר העתיד ומסיים ח] בהא בסנהדרין פרק אלו הן הנשרפין גמר (ה) חילול מתרומה דכתיב בה ומתו בו כי יחללוהו : א"כ · דלכר"ש אחי עזריה לחודיה אתא לכתוב ולא יחללו אשר הורמו מ"ש לשון עתיד דנקט ש"מ למידרש ביה נמי הא: בעי רבי זירא · לשם גבוה מהן כשרים דקתני כשרין ואין מרצין קאמר כת"ק ולא פליג אלא בנמוך דקאמר פסולים לגמרי : ובתרתי פליגי · לשם גבוה מכשיר לגמרי ובנמוך פסיל לגמרי ואילו רבנן בתרווייהו ט] מכשירים ואין מרצין קאמרי : ת"ש · מדקא מפרש מילתיה ונקיט בכור ומעשר דלא לרצויי אתו ש"מ כשרין ואין מרצין קאמר : ומדסיפא · הבכור והמעשר ששחטן לשם שלמים כשרים ואין מרצין (ו) רישא קדשים קלים ששחטן לשם קדשי קדשים נמי כשרין ואין מרצין קאמר : הא כדאיתא כו' · כשרין דקתני גבי בכור כשרין למילתייהו קאמר י] [*וכשרים נמי דקתני גבי קדשי קדשים למילתייהו קאמר] ואפי' לרצות לשם חובה: אלא מאי קמשמע לן · האי דנקט הבכור והמעשר אי לאו לגלויי עלה דרישא נקט לה ולמימר דכשרין ואין מרצין קאמר : גבוה ונמוך קמשמע לן · בתמיה וכי אתא לפרושי לן היכי דמי יא] נמוך לשם גבוה : תנינא · ברישא דמילתא: הא נמי תנינא · לקמן בפרק כל התדיר (דף פט·) דבכור נמוך משלמים : שלמים קודמין את הבכור· אם שניהם עומדים לישחט בעזרה ולהקריב: שהן טעונים מתן ארבע · שתי מתנות שהן ארבע ובכור במתנה אחת כדתנן באיזהו מקומן (לקמן נו:) סמיכה ונסכים ליתנהו בבכור כדילפינן במנחות בפרק שתי מדות (דף צ:) : הא עיקר · שנשנית תחילה לצורך לאשמועינן גבי פסול שלא לשמו דאיכא בקדשים קלים גבוה ונמוך : ההיא · דכל התדיר אגררא יב] נסבה שנה שם את הקודמים זה לזה ונקט נמי האי בהדייהו אע"ג דכבר תנייה הכא : **מתני'** רבי יהושע מכשיר · דפסח בשאר ימות השנה חשיב ליה : בן בתירא פוסל · בגמרא מפרש להו : שבעים ושנים זקן · בגמרא מפרש אמאי לא תנא זקנים : כל הזבחים הנאכלין · אבל עולה לא : לא הוסיף בן עזאי · על דברי חכמים לפסול חוץ מפסח ומחטאת אלא העולה : **גמ'** מכשיר היה בן בתירא בפסח ששחטו שחרית לשמו · (ז) והוה ליה זמנו לפיכך פסול שלא לשמו כדאמר פסח בזמנו שלא לשמו פסול : ומאי כאילו · נשחט בין הערבים והאמרת דכולא יומא בין הערבים קרי ליה מדקמכשרת ליה שחרית וקרא כתיב בין הערבים אלמא סבירא ליה בין ערב של אמש לערב של אחריו יג] כדמפרשינן ליה לקמיה דהיינו מעלות השחר שפסק ליל של אמש עד שתשקע החמה ומאי כאילו הא הוא גופיה בין הערבים (ח) : ליפלגו בלשמו · ולימא יד] [פסח ששחטו בי"ד שחרית] ר' יהושע פוסל ובן בתירא מכשיר : אבל בשלא לשמו מודה רבי יהושע · דאע"ג דשחרית לאו זימניה הוא פסול הואיל ומקצתו של יום ראוי לשמו קמ"ל : והא כתיב בין הערבים · לרבי אושעיא פריך היכי מצי למימר פסח זמנו שחרית : בין שני ערבים · מעלות השחר עד שקיעת החמה דהיינו בין סוף ערב דאתמול טו] ותחילת ערב דאורתא : ואימא חד בבקר · את הראשון לא ישהא יותר מחצות והשני כל היום זמנו דלא שחרית ולא ערבית כדכתיב בין הערבים טז] דמפרשת ליה כל יומא : ולא שנים בבקר · הלכך על כרחך צריך להשהות השני עד הערב : מדתה · חצי לוג לכל נר ונר כך שיערו חכמים לילי תקופת טבת שלא תכבה כל הלילה ובתמוז ובניסן ובתשרי אם תדליק שליש היום לא איכפת לן יז] : אין לך עבודה · מעבודות שהן אמורות ביום כגון עבודות הדם יח] *וקמצו וקטרת שכשרין מהדלקת נרות ואילך שזו מאוחרת לכולן : דאיתקש

תוספות

אמר ר' אליעזר לא אם אמרת בחטאת · יט] *דין הוא שאחרים כשרים לשמו [וקשה] כהי דלא דמי לפסח מ"מ ק"ו איכא וא"כ כ] [תימא] יפסלו נמי מהאי דינא *מותר חטאת בא עולה כמו דינא דמותר פסח בא שלמים וי"ל דאעיקר טעמו סמיך כא] כדאיתא בפסחים (דף סג:*) וצ"ל דהא לא אם אמרת דקאמר רבי אליעזר לדברי רבי יהושע קאמר אליבא דרבי יוחנן כב] ורבינו תם מצא בספר ישן ברישא דשמעתא כג] רבה אמר באחרים לשם חטאת כד] ומצא ובאחרים בוי"ו ורבה לא בא אלא לפרש דברי רבי יוחנן ור' יוחנן עצמו מודה דבאחרים לשם חטאת פליגי *ולא אמרו דבר אחד אלא כה] באחרים לשם פסח : **הג"ה** אי איפלוג בלשמו כו' · ותימה השתא נמי דפליגי בשלא לשמו אני יכול לטעות כו] כר"י לבן בתירא שיפסול י"ד לשמו שחרית ולפרש טעמו משום דמקצתו ראוי וי"ל דמזה אינו חושש משום דשום תנא לא מכשיר פסח שחרית אלא כז] זה: **הג"ה** אחד בבקר ולא שנים בבקר בעלמא

שיטה מקובצת

א] מאי אשר ירימו כו' וא"ת ואימא כולה קרא לכדשמואל הוא דאתא כדמשמע מאשר ירימו וי"ל דא"כ לכתוב קרא ולא יחללו את אשר ירימו לה' את קדשי בני ישראל ל"ל ש"מ [דבא] לומר במורם מהם כו' וא"ת אכתי איצטריך לדרשא דלעיל ולא יחללו את קדשי בני ישראל קדשים מחללים קדשים ואין חולין מחללין קדשים וי"ל דא"כ לימא קרא ולא יחללו קודש מאי קדשים ש"מ דדרשינן נמי הא: תרתי · ס"א ואימא כולה להכי הוא דאתא א"כ לימא קרא הרימו מאי ירימו : ב] ובתרתי פליגי [דלשם גבוה לת"ק] כשרים ולא עלו ולהאי תנא נמי עלו ופליג נמי (מסיפא) [בסיפא] דקתני פסולים דמשמע פסולים לגמרי ולת"ק כשרים ולא עלו וא"ת מי הוקיקו למימר [דפליג] (מסיפא) [בסיפא] ודלמא לא פליגי אלא (מרישא) [ברישא] דקתני כשרים דמשמע כשרים ומרצים אבל (מסיפא) [בסיפא] לא פליג כלל והא דקתני פסולים ר"ל דלא פסולים [לגמרי אלא] כמו פסולים דגבי תודה כדפרש"י לעיל [דף ז' ע"א] ונראה כיון דנפקא ליה מחילול משמע דפסולים לגמרי עי"ל דזה ליכא למימר דא"כ עלו [ולא עלו] מבעיא (כדהתם) לשנות וא"ת א"כ [ה"נ] ברישא דקאמר כשרים ור"ל דמרצין (כשרין ומרצין) ואמאי קאמר כשרין אלא עלו מבעיא ליה [למימר] וי"ל איידי דתני סיפא פסולים [דהוי] פסולים לגמרי קאמר ברישא כשרים : ג] ומדסיפא · פי' וכ"ת אדפשים מסיפא דכשרין ואין מרצין [תפשוט] מרישא דכשרין ומרצין לכן אמר מדסיפא כשרין ואין מרצין כו' וק"ל : ד] אליעזר בן עזריה: ה] האחד תעשה: ו] אחר מערב עד בקר אין לך : ז] אין כאן : ח] ומסיים לה בסנהדרין תיבת בהא נמחק : ט] בתרווייהו כשרים אות מ' נמחק : י] קאמר וכשרים דקתני גבי קדשים קלים כשרים למילתייהו קאמר ותיבת נמי ל"ש: יא] תיבות נמוך נמחק: יב] אגררא' אגב גררא נסבא: יג] אחריו כדמפרש לה לקמיה: יד] ולימא הפסח ששחט בשחרית לשמו ר' יהושע: טו] דאתמול לתחילת ערב: טז] הערבים כדמפרשת ליה כל יומא הס"ד ומה"ד האחד בבקר ולא שנים בבקר: יז] לן מיהו בירושלמי מפרש דביומי ניסן ותשרי הוו עושין פתילות עבות לפי שיעור הלילות · תוס' : יח] הדם ס"א היום וקמיצה וקטורת שכשרה מהדלקת: יט] בחטאת כו' ולפיכך דין הוא שאחרים כשרים לשמו וקשה : כ] וא"כ נימא תיבת תימא ל"ש ונמחק : כא] סמיך אקרא דכתיב זבח פסח הוא כדאיתא בפסחים בפ' תמיד נשחט : כב] עי' בהשמטות בסוף המסכת : כג] דשמעתא ורבה : כד] תיבות ומצא ובאחרים נמחק : כה] אלא מאחרים לשם פסח ע"כ : כו] לטעות בדברי בן בתירא ותיבת כר"י ואות ל' נמחק : כז] אלא הוא ולית הלכתא כוותיה הלכך ליכא למיחש דלמא אתי לטעוי בדבריו הס"ד ותיבת זה נמחק :

מסורת הש"ס

רס"ק פ"ט

נ"א א"כ דלדרשת ר"ש כו' נ"ק בשם ס"י

סנהדרין פג· פ"ש

[לקמן פט·]

תוספתא דפסחים

ג"י' רש"ק וכ"א נ"ג וכל"ל קאמר ולא אלו

[פסחים כתי ושם איתא א"ר אושעיא א"ר אלעזר]

[נ"ל האחד]

יומא טו: פסחים נט. מנחות פט·

הגהות הב"ח

(א) גמ' בעי רבי זירא כשרין · נ"ב והא דפשיטא ליה בנמוך פסולין לגמרי היינו מכח דיוקא דקרא ולא יחללו את קדשי כשרים מהן אין מחללין הא בנמוך מהן מחללין והיינו פסול לגמרי : (ב) שם במשנה בשחרית בי"ד : (ג) שם הנאכלים : (ד) שם ואימא חד : (ה) רש"י ד"ה בעתידין וכו' חילול חילול מתרומה: (ו) ד"ה ומדסיפא וכו' ואין מרצין קאמר רישא: (ז) ד"ה מכשיר וכו' דהוה ליה : (ח) ד"ה ומאי וכו' הערבים הוא הס"ד :

נ"ל וקמצו של מנחה וקטרת וכו' סס"ד

as a Passover-offering? [11b] Said R. Joshua to him: We find that a sin-offering remainder comes as a burnt-offering,[6] but a burnt-offering remainder does not come as a sin-offering. Now if the sin-offering is unfit when slaughtered as a burnt-offering, though its remainder comes as a burnt-offering; is it not logical that a burnt-offering slaughtered as a sin-offering is unfit, seeing that its remainder
a does not come as a sin-offering?[1] Not so, replied R. Eliezer to him. If you speak of a sin-offering, the reason [that a burnt-offering slaughtered in its name is fit] is because it [the sin-offering] is fit [when slaughtered] in its own name throughout the year. Will you say the same of a Passover-offering which is fit [when slaughtered] in its own name only in its season? Since then that itself is unfit [when slaughtered] in its own name [during the rest of the year], it is logical that others slaughtered in its name [during the rest of the year] are unfit.

SIMEON THE BROTHER OF AZARIAH SAID etc. R. Ashi recited the following in R. Joḥanan's name, and R. Aḥa son of Raba recited it in R. Jannai's name: What is the reason of Simeon the brother of Azariah? Because Scripture saith, *And they shall not profane the holy things of the children of Israel, which they shall exalt unto the Lord*:[2] [this teaches that] they are not profaned [rendered unfit] through what is superior [higher] than themselves, but they are profaned through what is inferior to themselves.[3] But does this text come for this purpose? Surely it is required for Samuel's dictum! For Samuel said: Whence do we know that he who eats *ṭebel*[4] is liable to death? From the verse, *And they shall not profane the holy things of the children of Israel, which they shall exalt unto the Lord*: the Writ refers to that which is yet to be exalted.[5]—If so,[6] Scripture should write, 'which *were* exalted [offered]': why state, '*which*
b *they* shall *exalt*'? Hence infer both from this.[1]

R. Zera asked: Are they valid yet do not propitiate, and so he disagrees in one only; or are they valid and propitiate, and he disagrees in both?[2]—Said Abaye—others maintain, R. Zeriḳa,—Come and hear: IF ONE SLAUGHTERED A FIRSTLING OR TITHE IN THE NAME OF A PEACE-OFFERING, IT IS VALID; IF ONE SLAUGHTERED A PEACE-OFFERING AS A FIRSTLING OR TITHE, IT IS INVALID. Now if you think that [he means that] they are valid and propitiate, is propitiation applicable to a firstling?[3] Hence they are valid and do not propitiate, and since the second clause [means that] they are valid and do not propitiate, [in] the first clause too they are valid and do not propitiate. But what argument is this? The one is according to its nature, and the other is according to its nature.[4] Then what does he inform us?[5] [The principle governing] a higher and lower sanctity![6] Surely we learnt it: HOW SO? IF ONE SLAUGHTERED MOST SACRED SACRIFICES UNDER THE DESIGNATION OF LESSER SACRIFICES etc. — You might say, Only in the most sacred sacrifices and the lesser sacrifices is there higher and lower, but not where both are lesser sacrifices. [Hence we are informed that it is not so.] But we learnt this too: The peace-offering takes precedence over the firstling,

(6) Tem. 23b.
a (1) Yet in fact it is not unfit, which shews that an *ad majus* argument from the law of a remainder is inadmissible. As R. Eliezer does not answer that in his view it is indeed unfit, Rabbah deduces that he admits that other sacrifices slaughtered as sin-offerings are fit. (2) Lev. XXII, 15. (3) Rendering: *they shall not profane the holy things* (*sc.* the sacrifices) when they *exalt* them, i.e., when they offer them as a sacrifice whose sanctity is higher than their own. (4) V. Glos. (5) I.e., offered. The verb ירימו is imperfect (*which they* shall *exalt*) and hence refers to '*holy things*', which includes *terumah* (q.v. Glos.), which are *yet* to be separated from the produce, so that it is all *ṭebel*.—For the liability to death (at the hands of Heaven) v. Sanh. 83a. (6) That the text teaches the former dictum of Simeon the brother of Azariah only.
b (1) The root word 'exalt' teaches the former, and the future tense teaches the latter. (2) Does Simeon the brother of Azariah mean that when slaughtered in the name of a higher sacrifice they are fit, yet do not propitiate, i.e., they do not acquit their owner of their obligation; but if slaughtered in the name of a lower sacrifice they are completely unfit? In that case he agrees with the first Tanna as far as the former instance is concerned, and disagrees only in respect of the latter. Or does he mean in the former instance that they also propitiate? If so, he disagrees with the first Tanna in respect of the former too, the first Tanna holding that they do *not* propitiate. (3) Surely not! (4) Where there is no question of propitiation it means that they are valid but do not propitiate. But where propitiation does apply (*sc.* in the first clause) they may propitiate too. (5) By the second clause. (6) Is that the only purpose of this second clause dealing with the firstling etc.?

◁ *For the continuation of the English translation of this page see overleaf.*

עין משפט
נר מצוה

נ"א כו' כלומר וא"כ

נ"א דמותר חטאת כו' כמו מדינא דמותר כו' צ"ק

[ד"ה שאני התם]

נד א מיי' פ"י מהלכות מאכלות אסורות הלכה יט :

נה ב מיי' פט"ו מהל' פסה"מ הלכה יא :

נו ג מיי' פ"ג מהלכות תמידין הלכה יא :

ג' צ"ק ולא אמרו דבר ס'

אמר ר' אליעזר לא אם אמרת בחטאת · יט] *דין הוא שאחרים כשרים לשמו [וקשה] נהי דלא דמי לפסח מ"מ ק"ו איכא וא"כ כ] [תימא] יפסלו נמי מהאי דינא *מותר חטאת בא עולה כמו דינא דמותר פסח בא שלמים וי"ל דאעיקר טעמו סמיך כא] כדאיתא בפסחים (דף סג:*) וי"ל דהא לא אם אמרת דקאמר רבי אליעזר לדברי רבי יהושע קאמר אליבא דרבי יוחנן כב] ורביט תם מלא בספר ישן ברישא דשמעתא כג] רבה אמר באחרים לשם חטאת כד] ומנא ובאחרים בוי"ו ורבה לא בא אלא לפרש דברי רבי יוחנן ור' יוחנן עצמו מודה דבאחרים לשם חטאת פליגי *ולא אמר אמרו דבר אחד אלא כה] באחרים לשם פסח : **הג"ה** אי איפלוג בלשמן כו' · ותימה השתא נמי דפליגי בשלא לשמן אני יכול לטעות כו] כר"י לבן בתירא שיפסול י"ד לשמו שחרית ולפרש טעמו משום דמקצתו ראוי וי"ל דמזה אינו חושש משום דשום תנא לא מכשיר פסח שחרית אלא כז] זה: **הג"ה** אחד בבקר ולא שנים בבקר· בעלמא

אמר לו רבי יהושע מצינו מותר חטאת בא עולה ואין מותר עולה בא חטאת ומה חטאת שמותרה בא עולה שחטה לשם עולה פסולה עולה שאין מותרה בא חטאת שחטה לשם חטאת אינו דין שתהא פסולה אמר לו רבי אליעזר לא אם אמרת בחטאת שכן כשרה לשמה כל השנה כולה תאמר בפסח שאינו כשר לשמו אלא בזמנו הואיל והוא פסול לשמו דין הוא שיפסלו אחרים לשמו : שמעון אחי עזריה אומר כו' : רב אשי מתני משמיה דרבי יוחנן ורב אחא בריה דרבא מתני משמיה דרבי ינאי מאי טעמא דשמעון אחי עזריה דאמר קרא °ולא יחללו את קדשי בני ישראל את אשר ירימו לה' במורם מהן אין מתחללין בנמוך מהם מתחללין והאי להכי הוא דאתא והא מיבעי ליה לכדשמואל *דאמר שמואל *מנין לאוכל את הטבל שהוא במיתה שנאמר ולא יחללו את קדשי בני ישראל את אשר ירימו לה' בעתידים לתרום הכתוב מדבר אם כן לכתוב קרא אשר הורמו א] מאי אשר ירימו שמע מיניה תרתי : בעי רבי זירא (א) כשרין ואין מרצין וכי פליג בחדא פליג או דלמא כשרין ומרצין ב] ובתרתי פליגי אמר אביי ואיתימא רבי זריקא תא שמע הבכור והמעשר ששחטן לשם שלמים כשרים שלמים ששחטן לשם בכור או לשם מעשר פסולין ואי ס"ד כשרין ומרצין בכור בר ריצויי הוא אלא כשרין ואין מרצין ג] ומדסיפא כשרין ואין מרצין רישא נמי כשרין ואין מרצין מידי איריא הא כדאיתא והא כדאיתא אלא מאי קמ"ל גבוה ונמוך קמ"ל תנינא כיצד קדשי קדשים ששחטן לשם קדשים קלים כו' מהו דתימא קדשי קדשים וקדשים קלים הוא דאיכא גבוה ונמוך אבל קלים וקלים לא הא נמי תנינא *שלמים קודמים את הבכור מפני שהן טעונין מתן ארבע וסמיכה ונסכים ותנופת חזה ושוק הא עיקר ההיא אגררא נסבה : **מתני'** *הפסח ששחטו (ב) שחרית בארבעה עשר שלא לשמו רבי יהושע מכשיר כאילו נשחט בשלשה עשר בן בתירא פוסל כאילו נשחט בין הערבים *) אמר שמעון בן עזאי מקובל אני מפי שבעים ושנים זקן ביום שהושיבו את *) רבי אליעזר ד] בישיבה שכל הזבחים (ג) הנאכלין שנזבחו שלא לשמן כשרין אלא שלא עלו לבעלים משום חובה חוץ מן הפסח ומן החטאת ולא הוסיף בן עזאי אלא העולה ולא הודו לו חכמים : **גמ'** *אמר רבי אלעזר אמר רבי אושעיא מכשיר היה בן בתירא בפסח ששחטו שחרית בארבעה עשר לשמו דכוליה יומא זמניה הוא ומאי כאילו איידי דאמר רבי יהושע כאילו אמר איהו נמי כאילו אי הכי אדמיפלגי בשלא לשמו ליפלגו בלשמו אי איפלגו בלשמו הוה אמינא אבל בשלא לשמו מודי רבי יהושע לבן בתירא הואיל ומקצתו ראוי קא משמע לן והכתיב °בין הערבים אמר עולא בריה דרב עילאי בין שני ערבים תמיד דכתיב ביה °בין הערבים הכי נמי דכולי יומא כשר התם מדכתיב °את הכבש ה] *אחד תעשה בבקר מכלל דבין הערבים בין הערבים ממש (ד) אימא חד בבקר אידך כוליה יומא אחד בבקר ולא שנים בבקר נרות דכתיב °בין הערבים הכי נמי דכולי יומא כשר שאני התם דכתיב מערב ועד בקר *ותניא °מערב ועד בקר ‎׳תן לה מדתה שתהא דולקת והולכת מערב ועד בקר דבר אחר ו] אין לך עבודה כשרה מערב ועד בקר אלא זו בלבד קטורת דכתיב בה °בין הערבים הכי נמי דכולי יומא כשר שאני קטרת דאיתקש

*) ידים פ"ד מ"ב **) [נ"ל ר' אלעזר בן עזריה וכ"א במשנה שבמשניות]

תורה אור: ויקרא כב · שמות יב · שם כט · שם · שם · כז · שם ל

אמר לו רבי יהושע מליט מותר חטאת בא עולה · כדתניא בתמורה (דף כג:) זה מדרש דרש יהוידע הכהן כל דבר שבא ממותר חטאת וממותר אשם ילקח בהן עולה לקיץ המזבח והיכי דמי מותר חטאת כגון הפריש מעות לחטאתו וניתותרו אי נמי מפריש שתי חטאות לאחריות דקי"ל בתמורה (דף כד·) מתכפר באחת מהן והשניה תרעה : ומה חטאת שמותרה כו' · ואם ק"ו כזה אתה דורש יש לך לפסול עולה לשם חטאת ומהכא דייק רבה מילתיה לעיל מדלא אהדר ליה רבי אליעזר אנא נמי פסילנא בנשחטין לשם חטאת : שכן כשרה לשמה כל השנה · לפיכך עולה הנשחטת לשם חטאת כשרה : ולא יחללו את קדשי · אין ז] (כאן) חילול כשירימו אותם לשם גבוה מהם : בעתידין לתרום · דהיינו טבל דכתיב ירימו דבר העתיד ומסיים ח] בהא בסנהדרין פרק אלו הן הנשרפין גמר (ה) חילול מתרומה דכתיב בה ומתו בו כי יחללוהו : *א"כ · דלכר"ש אחי עזריה לחודיה אתא לכתוב ולא יחללו אשר הורמו מ"ש לשון עתיד דנקט ש"מ למידרש ביה נמי הא : בעי רבי זירא · לשום גבוה מהן כשרים דקתני כשרין ואין מרצין קאמר כת"ק ולא פליג אלא בנמוך דקאמר פסולים לגמרי : ובתרתי פליגי · לשם גבוה מכשיר לגמרי ובנמוך פסיל לגמרי ואילו רבנן בתרווייהו ט] מכשירים ואין מרצין קאמרי : ת"ש · מדקא מפרש מילתיה ונקיט בכור ומעשר דלא לרצויי אתו ש"מ כשרין ואין מרצין קאמר : ומדסיפא · הבכור והמעשר ששחטן לשם שלמים כשרים ואין מרצין (ו) רישא קדשים קלים ששחטן לשם קדשי קדשים נמי כשרין ואין מרצין קאמר : הא כדאיתא כו' · כשרין דקתני גבי בכור כשרין למילתייהו קאמר י] [*וכשרים נמי דקתני גבי קדשי קדשים למילתייהו קאמר] ואפי' לרצות לשם חובה : אלא מאי קמשמע לן · האי דנקט הבכור והמעשר אי לאו לגלויי עלה דרישא נקט לה ולמימר דכשרין ואין מרצין קאמר : גבוה ונמוך קמשמע לן · בתמיה וכי אתא לפרושי לן היכי דמי יא] נמוך לשם גבוה : תנינא · ברישא דמילתא : הא נמי תנינא · לקמן בפרק כל התדיר (דף פט·) דבכור נמוך משלמים : שלמים קודמין את הבכור· אם שניהם עומדים לישחט בעזרה ולהקריב: שהן טעונים מתן ארבע · שתי מתנות שהן ארבע ובכור במתנה אחת כדתנן באיזהו מקומן (לקמן נו:) סמיכה ונסכים ליתנהו בבכור כדילפינן במנחות בפרק שתי מדות (דף צ:) : הא עיקר · שנשנית תחילה לצורך לאשמועינן גבי פסול שלא לשמו דאיכא בקדשים קלים גבוה ונמוך : ההיא · דכל התדיר אגררא יב] נסבה ששנה שם את הקודמים זה לזה ונקט נמי האי בהדייהו אע"ג דכבר תנייה הכא : **מתני'** רבי יהושע מכשיר · דפסח בשאר ימות השנה חשיב ליה : בן בתירא פוסל · בגמרא מפרש להו : שבעים ושנים זקן · בגמרא מפרש אמאי לא תנא זקנים : כל הזבחים הנאכלין · אבל עולה לא : לא הוסיף בן עזאי · על דברי חכמים לפסול חוץ מפסח ומחטאת אלא העולה : **גמ'** מכשיר היה בן בתירא בפסח ששחטו שחרית לשמו · (ז) והוא ליה זמנו לפיכך פסול שלא לשמו כדאמר פסח בזמנו שלא לשמו פסול : ומאי כאילו · נשחט בין הערבים והאמרת דכולא יומא בין הערבים קרי ליה מדקמכשרת ליה שחרית וקרא כתיב בין הערבים אלמא סבירא ליה בין ערב של אמש לערב של אחריו יג] כדמפרשינן ליה לקמיה דהיינו משעלה השחר שפסק ליל של אמש עד שתשקע החמה ומאי כאילו הא הוא גופיה בין הערבים (ח) : ליפלגו בלשמו · ולימא יד] [פסח ששחטו בי"ד שחרית] ר' יהושע פוסל ובן בתירא מכשיר : אבל בשלא לשמו מודה רבי יהושע · דאע"ג דשחרית לאו זימניה הוא פסול הואיל ומקצתו של יום ראוי לשמו קמ"ל : והא כתיב בין הערבים · לרבי אושעיא פריך היכי מצי למימר פסח זמנו שחרית : בין שני ערבים · מעלות השחר עד שקיעת החמה דהייט בין סוף ערב דאתמול טו] ותחילת ערב דאורתא : ואימא חד בבקר · את הראשון לא ישהא יותר מחצות והשני כל היום זמנו ורלה שחרית רלה ערבית כדכתיב בין הערבים טז] דמפרשת ליה כל יומא : ולא שנים בבקר · הלכך על כרחך צריך להשהות השני עד הערב : מדתה · חצי לוג לכל נר ונר כך שיערו חכמים לילי תקופת טבת שלא תכבה כל הלילה ובתמוז ובניסן ובתשרי אם תדליק שליש היום לא איכפת לן יז] : אין לך עבודה · מעבודות שהן אמורות ביום כגון עבודות הדם יח] *וקמצו וקטרת שכשרין מהדלקת נרות ואילך שזו מאוחרת לכנן : דאיתקש

מסורת הש"ס

רש"ק מ"ע

נ"א א"כ דלדרשה ר"ש כו' צ"ק בשם ס"ש

סנהדרין פג' ע"ש

[לקמן פט']

תוספתא דפסחים

ג' רש"ק וג"א נ"ג וכו"ל קאמר ולפ"ע אלו

[פסחים כח' ושם איתא א"ר אושעיא א"ר אלעזר]

[צ"ע האחר]

יומא סו' פסחים נט. מנחות פט'

הגהות הב"ח

(א) גמ' בעי רבי זירא כשרין · נ"ב והא דפשיטא ליה בנמוך פסולין לגמרי היינו מכח דיוקא דקרא ולא יחללו את קדשי במורם מהן אין מתחללין הא בנמוך מהן מתחללין והיינו פסול לגמרי : (ב) שם במשנה בשחרית בי"ד : (ג) שם הנאכלים : (ד) שם ואימא חד : (ה) רש"י ד"ה בעתידין וכו' חילול מתרומה: (ו) ד"ה ומדסיפא וכו' ואין מרלין קאמר רישא: (ז) ד"ה מכשיר וכו' דהוה ליה : (ח) ד"ה ומאי וכו' הערבים הוא הס"ד :

נ"ל וקמצו של מנחה וקטרת וכו' ס"א

שיטה מקובצת
א] מאי אשר ירימו כו' · וא"ת ואימא כולה קרא לכדשמואל הוא דאתא כדמשמע מאשר ירימו וי"ל דא"כ לכתוב קרא ולא יחללו את אשר ירימו לה' את קדשי בני ישראל ל"ל ש"מ[דבא] לומר במורם מהם כו' וא"ת אכתי איצטריך לדרשא דלעיל ולא יחללו את קדשי בני ישראל קדשים מחללים קדשים ואין חולין מחללין קדשים וי"ל דא"כ לימא קרא ולא יחללו קודש מאי קדשים ש"מ דדרשינן נמי הא : תרתי · ס"א ואימא כולה להכי הוא דאתא א"כ לימא קרא הרימו מאי ירימו : ב] ובתרתי פליגי · [דלשם גבוה לת"ק] כשרים ולא עלו ולהאי תנא נמי עלו ופליג נמי (מסיפא) [בסיפא] דקתני פסולים דמשמע פסולים לגמרי ולת"ק כשרים ולא עלו וא"ת מי הזקיקו למימר [דפליג] (מסיפא) [בסיפא] ודלמא לא פליגי אלא (מרישא) [ברישא] דקתני כשרים דמשמע כשרים ומרצים אבל (מסיפא) [בסיפא] לא פליג כלל והא דקתני פסולים ר"ל דלא פסולים [לגמרי אלא] כמו פסולים דגבי תודה כדפרש"י לעיל [דף ז' ע"א] ונראה כיון דנפקא ליה מחילול משמע דפסולים לגמרי ע"ל דזה ליכא למימר דא"כ עלו [ולא עלו] מבעיא (כדהתם) לשנות וא"ת א"כ [ה"נ] ברישא דקאמר כשרים ור"ל דמרצין (כשרין ומרצין) ואמאי קאמר כשרין אלא עלו מבעיא ליה [למימר] וי"ל איידי דתני סיפא פסולים [דהוי] פסולים לגמרי קאמר ברישא כשרים : ג] ומדסיפא · פי' ובית ארפשים מסיפא דכשרין ואין מרצין מרישא דכשרין ומרצין לכן אמר מדסיפא כשרין ואין מרצין וכו' וק"ל : ד] אליעזר בן עזריה : ה] האחד תעשה : ו] אחר עד בקר אין לך : ז] אין כאן : ח] וסמים לה בסנהדרין תיבת בהא נמחק : ט] בתרוייהו כשרים את מ' נמחק :

י] קאמר וכשרים דקתני גבי קדשים קלים כשרים למילתייהו קאמר ותיבת נמי ל"ש: יא] תיבות נמוך נמחק : יב] אגררא' אגב גררא נסבא : יג] אחריו כדמפרש לה לקמיה: יד] ולימא הפסח ששחט בשחרית לשמו ר' יהושע: טו] דאתמול לתחילת ערב : טז] הערבים כדמפרשת ליה כל יומא הס"ד ומה"ד האחד בבקר ולא שנים בבקר: יז] לן מיהו בירושלמי מפרש דביומי ניסן ותשרי הוו עושין פתילות עבות לפי שיעור הלילות · תוס' : יח] הדם ס"א היום וקמיצה וקטורת שכשרה מהדלקת : יט] בחטאת כו' ולפיכך דין הוא שאחרים כשרים לשמו וקשה : כ] וא"כ נימא תיבת תימא ל"ש ונמחק : כא] סמיך אקרא דכתיב זבח פסח הוא בהוייתו יהא כדאיתא בפסחים בפ' תמיד נשחט : כב] עי' בהשמטות בסוף המסכת : כג] דשמעתא ורבה : כד] תיבות ומנא ובאחרים נמחק : כה] אלא מאחרים לשם פסח ע"כ : כו] לטעות בדברי בן בתירא ותיבת כר"י ואות ל' נמחק : כז] אלא הוא ולית הלכתא כוותיה הלכך ליכא למיחש דלמא אתי למטעי בדבריו הס"ד ותיבת זה נמחק :

Continuation of translation from previous page as indicated by ◁

because the former requires four [blood-] sprinklings, laying on [of hands], drink-offerings, and the waving of the breast and the c shoulder?[1]—The present passage[2] is the main source, while in the other it is taught incidentally.[3]

MISHNAH. IF ONE SLAUGHTERS THE PASSOVER-OFFERING ON THE MORNING OF THE FOURTEENTH [OF NISAN] UNDER A DIFFERENT DESIGNATION, R. JOSHUA DECLARES IT VALID, JUST AS IF IT HAD BEEN SLAUGHTERED ON THE THIRTEENTH; BEN BATHYRA DECLARES IT INVALID, AS IF IT HAD BEEN SLAUGHTERED IN THE AFTERNOON.[4] SAID SIMEON B. 'AZZAI: I HAVE A TRADITION FROM THE MOUTH OF SEVENTY-TWO ELDER[S][5] ON THE DAY THAT R. ELEAZAR [SON OF AZARIAH][6] WAS APPOINTED TO THE ACADEMY,[7] THAT ALL SACRIFICES WHICH ARE EATEN,[8] THOUGH SLAUGHTERED UNDER A DIFFERENT DESIGNATION ARE VALID, SAVE THAT THEIR OWNERS HAVE NOT DISCHARGED THEIR OBLIGATION, EXCEPT THE PASSOVER-OFFERING AND THE SIN-OFFERING. THUS THE SON OF 'AZZAI ADDED[9] ONLY THE BURNT-OFFERING, BUT THE SAGES DID NOT AGREE WITH HIM.

GEMARA. R. Eleazar said in R. Oshaia's name: Ben Bathyra declared fit a Passover-offering which one slaughtered in its own name on the morning of the fourteenth, because [he holds that] the *whole* day is its season.[10] Then what does AS IF [etc.] mean?[11]—Because R. Joshua states AS IF,[12] he too says, AS IF. If so, instead of disputing where it is [slaughtered] under a different designation, d let them dispute where it is [slaughtered] in its own name?[1]—If they differed where it is [slaughtered] in its own name, I would say that R. Joshua agrees with Ben Bathyra [that it is invalid] when [slaughtered] under a different designation, since part of it [the day] is fit [eligible]. Hence he informs us [that it is not so].

But surely it is written, *At dusk*?[2]—Said 'Ulla the son of R. Ila'i: [That means,] Between two evenings.[3] Then [will you say] that the *whole* day is fit for the daily offering too, seeing that *at dusk*[4] is written in connection therewith?—There, since it is written, *'The one lamb thou shalt offer in the morning'*, it follows that *'at dusk'* is meant literally. Yet say, One [*must* be offered] in the morning, while the other [*may* be offered] the whole day?—[Scripture prescribes] *one* for the morning and not two for the morning. Again, will you say that the whole day is fit for [the lighting of] the lamps, since *'at dusk'* is written in connection therewith?[5]—There it is different, because it is written, [*to burn*] *from evening to morning*,[6] and it was taught: *'From evening to morning'*: Furnish it with its [requisite] measure, so that it may burn from evening to morning. Another interpretation: You have no other [service] valid from evening to morning save this alone.

Now [will you say] in the case of incense too, where *'at dusk'* is written,[7] that the whole day is fit [for the burning thereof]?—

c (1) V. *Infra* 89a. It takes precedence because its sanctity is higher. (2) *Sc.* our Mishnah. (3) As part of the order of precedence observed in *all* sacrifices. Yet the main source of the ruling that the peace-offering enjoys a higher sanctity than the firstling is our own Mishnah. (4) V. Mishnah 2a. (5) The Gemara discusses *infra* why the text uses the singular. (6) Emended text. (7) As its head. V. Ber. 27b. (8) This excludes the burnt-offering. (9) As being unfit. (10) And not the afternoon only. For that very reason he declares it invalid when not slaughtered for its own sake. (11) Seeing that if the *whole* day is the season, there is no point in saying AS IF IT HAD BEEN SLAUGHTERED IN THE AFTERNOON. (12) On his view it is pertinent, since he holds that only the afternoon is its season.

d (1) According to Ben Bathyra it is valid, while in R. Joshua's view it is invalid. (2) Ex. XII, 6. How then can R. Oshaia maintain that the whole day is the proper time? (3) This being the literal meaning of the Hebrew בין הערבים. I.e., between the evening of the fourteenth (which he counts as until dawn) and the evening of the fifteenth, hence the whole *day* of the fourteenth. (4) Ibid. XXIX, 39. (5) Ibid. XXX, 8. (6) Ibid. XXVII, 21. (7) Ibid. XXX, 8,—the same text as that quoted for the lamps.

Incense is different, [12a] because it is likened to lamps.[8]

But there too it is written, *There thou shalt sacrifice the Passover-offering* at even [*ba-'ereb*]?[9]—That comes to teach deferment. For it was taught: Let that in connection with which *ba-'ereb* [at even] and *ben ha-'arbayim* [between the evenings][10] are said be deferred after that in connection with which *ben ha-'arbayim* alone is said.[11] Now can there be a case where if he slaughtered it in the morning you say that it is its proper time, yet when afternoon arrives you
a say that it should be deferred?[1]—Yes, for surely R. Joḥanan said: The *halachah* is that one must recite the *minḥah* [afternoon] service and then recite the additional service.[2]

Now, what is the purpose of '*ben ha-'arbayim*' [at dusk] written in connection with incense and lamps?[3] Furthermore, [it was taught:][4] Rabbi rebutted the words of R. Joshua on Ben Bathyra's view: That is not so.[5] If you speak of the thirteenth, where no part of it is fit, will you speak [thus] of the fourteenth, where part of it is fit? Now if this is correct,[6] then the *whole* of it is fit![7]—Rather said R. Joḥanan: Ben Bathyra declared unfit a Passover-offering which one slaughtered in the morning of the fourteenth, whether in its own or in a different name, since part of it is fit [for the slaughtering].[8] R. Abbahu sneered at this view: If so, how is it possible on Ben Bathyra's ruling for a Passover-offering to be fit?[9] If one separates it now, it is rejected *ab initio;* while if one separated it yesterday, it was eligible and rejected![10]—Rather said R. Abbahu:
b It must be [that he separated it] after midday.[1] Abaye said: You may even say [that one separates it] in the morning, [because the disqualification of] prematureness does not apply to the same day.[2] R. Papa said: You may even say [that one separates it] the [previous] evening:[3] prematureness does not apply to the night. For R. Ishmael taught: On the night of the eighth day it enters the fold to be tithed.[4] And [this is] in accordance with R. Aftoriḳi. For R. Aftoriḳi pointed out a contradiction. It is written, *Then it shall be seven days under its dam;*[5] hence on the [following] night it is eligible. Yet it is written, *But from the eighth* day *and thenceforth it may be accepted* [*for an offering*],[5] whence it follows that it was not eligible the [previous] evening. How is this [to be reconciled]? The night for sanctification and the day for acceptance.[6]

R. Zera asked R. Abbahu: Must we say that R. Joḥanan holds that live animals can be [permanently] rejected?[7]—Even so, replied he. For R. Joḥanan said: [With regard to] an animal belonging to two partners; if one [of them] dedicates half, and then purchases [the other] half and dedicates it, it is holy, yet cannot be offered up;[8] and it establishes [the sanctity of] a substitute,[9] and
c the substitute is as itself.[1] This proves three things: that live animals may be rendered [permanently] rejected;[2] that which is rejected

(8) Since 'at dusk' refers to both, as stated in the preceding note. (9) Deut. XVI, 6. (10) E.V. *at dusk.* (11) In connection with the Passover-offering both expressions are used (Ex. XII, 6; Deut. XVI, 6), while in connection with the daily-offering one only is stated (Num. XXVIII, 4). Hence the former is sacrificed after the latter.

a (1) Until after the afternoon daily offering. (2) On the Sabbath, festivals and New Moon there are three services, the morning service, the additional service and the afternoon service in that order (beside the evening service, which is recited the previous evening). The additional service must commence before the time of the afternoon service, which is from half an hour after noon until dusk. If one had not recited it by then, he must give precedence to the afternoon service. This is exactly analogous to our own case. (3) Since its meaning must be elucidated through another text (*supra* 11*b*). (4) In objection to R. Oshaia. (5) *Sc.* that it is as though it was slaughtered on the thirteenth. (6) That Ben Bathyra holds that the *whole* of the fourteenth is the proper time. (7) And not only part! (8) If slaughtered in its own name, it is invalid because the proper time is the afternoon. If not in its own name, it is invalid because part of that day is the proper time for it, and hence the law on 2*a* applies. (9) Even if it is slaughtered at the proper time (in the afternoon of the fourteenth) and in its own name. (10) If one separates the animal for a Passover-offering on the *morning* of the fourteenth, it is fit for nothing at all then, neither for a Passover-offering nor for a peace-offering. Thus from the very beginning it is ineligible (technically 'rejected'), and R. Joḥanan holds *infra* that in such circumstances it can never be eligible again, even if conditions subsequently alter. Again, if one separated it the *previous* day, it was then eligible for a peace-offering, but on the following morning it was 'rejected' (became ineligible), and in the view of all Rabbis it then remains permanently rejected.

b (1) When it is actually eligible.—The answer is obvious, and R. Abbahu's objection is probably only rhetorical, as a means of expressing the opinion that according to Ben Bathyra as interpreted by R. Joḥanan the animal cannot be separated for the Passover-offering until the afternoon. (2) Where an animal becomes eligible for a particular purpose during the day, the earlier part of the same day is not regarded as premature, in the sense discussed here. (3) Which is also the fourteenth of Nisan. (4) An animal cannot be sacrificed before it is eight days old, and for the same reason when animals are to be tithed it does not enter the fold for the purpose. Yet if the tithing is taking place on the night of the eight day (it will be eight days old the next day) it does enter. This proves that prematureness does not apply to the night. (5) Lev. XXII, 27. (6) It can be sanctified on the night of the eighth but not 'accepted', i.e., sacrificed, until the following day. (7) V. following notes. For otherwise you need not answer that one separates it after midday. (8) Since it was not fit for offering originally, as the half belonging to the other partner was as yet secular. Hence it must now be sold, and an animal purchased with the money and sacrificed. (9) The reference is to Lev. XXVII, 33: *neither shall he change it* (a consecrated animal): *and if he change it, then both it and the change thereof shall be holy.* Thus here, if one substitutes another animal for this one, the substitute too is holy.

c (1) It may not be sacrificed, but must be sold. (2) As here: the animal having been rendered ineligible when dedicated, since half remained secular, it remains so even when the other half too is dedicated. There is an opposing view that only a dead animal can become permanently ineligible, V. Yoma 64*a*.

דאיתקש לנרות התם נמי כתיב שם תזבח את הפסח בערב ההוא ליאוחר דבר הוא דאתא א] *דתניא יאוחר דבר שנאמר בו בערב ובין הערבים לדבר שלא נאמר בו אלא בין הערבים בלבד ומי איכא מידי דאילו שחיט ליה מצפרא אמרת זימניה הוא וכי מטי בין הערבים אמרת יאוחר דבר אין *דהא"ר יוחנן ב] *הלכה מתפלל של מנחה ואח"כ מתפלל של מוספין ובין הערבים דכתיב גבי קטרת ונרות למה לי ועוד ג] *השיב רבי תחת בן בתירא לדברי רבי יהושע לא אם אמרת בשלשה עשר שאין מקצתו ראוי תאמר בארבעה עשר שמקצתו ראוי ד] ואם איתא כולו ראוי הוא אלא א"ר יוחנן פוסל היה בן בתירא בפסח ששחטו בארבעה עשר שחרית בין לשמו בין שלא לשמו ה] הואיל ומקצתו ראוי מגדף בה רבי אבהו א"כ פסח כשר לבן בתירא היכי משכחת לה אי דאפרשיה האידנא דחוי מעיקרו הוא ואי ו] דאפרשינהו מאתמול נראה ונדחה הוא אלא אמר רבי אבהו תהא לאחר חצות אביי אמר אפילו תימא מצפרא *אין מחוסר זמן לבו ביום רב פפא אמר אפילו תימא מאורתא* לילה אין מחוסר זמן דתני דבי ז] ר' ישמעאל ליל שמיני נכנס לדיר להתעשר וכדרבי אפטוריקי *דרבי אפטוריקי רמי כתיב °והיה שבעת ימים תחת אמו הא לילה חזי וכתיב °ומיום השמיני והלאה ירצה הא לילה לא חזי הא כיצד ח] לילה לקדושה ויום להרצאה ט] א"ל רבי זירא לרבי אבהו לימא קסבר רבי יוחנן בעלי חיים נדחין אמר ליה אין *דא"ר יוחנן בהמה של שני שותפין הקדיש חציה וחזר ולקח חציה והקדישה קדושה ואינה קריבה ועושה תמורה ותמורתה כיוצא בה *ושמע מינה תלת שמע מינה בעלי חיים נדחין וש"מ דחוי מעיקרא הוה דחוי י] וש"מ

יש

תורה אור: דברים טז · ויקרא כב · שם

רש"י

דאיתקש לנרות · ובהעלות אהרן וגו' והיינו בין הערבים דקטורת: יאוחר דבר · יאוחר פסח לתמיד דאע"ג דכולה יומא זמניה אי שהייה עד זמן שחיטת התמיד תמיד קודם לו: אין דהא"ר יוחנן · במסכת ברכות: יא] הלכה · כדברי האומר היו לפניו ב' תפלות אחת של מנחה ואחת של מוספין ששהא ולא התפלל של מוספין עד יב] זמן חבירתה משהינן לה: ובין הערבים דכתיב גבי קטורת ונרות למה לי · הואיל ומיניה לא הוי משמע לן בין הערבים ממש ומבעי לן קרא יג] אחריני לפרושי: ועוד · תני בתוספתא תיובתא לר' אושעיא דקתני השיב רבי תחת בן בתירא כו': לדברי ר' יהושע · דאמר כאילו נשחט בי"ג: שאין מקצתו ראוי · לשמו הלכך לא קרינן ביה פסח בזמנו אלמא יד] דרבי דס"ל כבן בתירא ומשום דמקצתו ראוי לשמו הוא דקאמר טעמיה: ואם איתא · דבן בתירא טו] שחרית מכשר לשמו כולו ראוי לשמו הוא: מגדף בה · בהא דרבי יוחנן: א"כ · דבין לשמו ובין שלא לשמו פסול: פסח כשר · בזמנו לשמו לבן בתירא: היכי משכחת לה אי דאפרשיה האידנא · בי"ד טז] בשחרית: דחוי מעיקרא הוא · דבשעת הפרשה לא חזי למידי ושמעינן ליה לר' יוחנן דאמר יז] דחוי מעיקרא הוי דחוי לגמרי שלא יח] להירצות עוד: ואי דאפרשיה מאתמול נראה ונדחה הוא · דכי אפרשיה חזי להקריבו שלא לשמו וכי מטיא י"ד שחרית לא חזי למידי ונראה ונדחה שוב אינו חוזר ונראה לדברי הכל בשלמא לרבנן פסח אינו נדחה כלל או מלשמו או משלא לשמו דעד זמן שחיטתו חזי לשלמים ובזמנו חזי לפסח אלא לבן בתירא דחוי הוא: תהא לאחר חצות · משכחת לה פסח כשר לבן בתירא במפריש לאחר חצות דהיינו זמן שחיטתו וחזי לשמו: אפי' תימא מצפרא · ואין כאן דחוי מעיקרו הואיל וראוי היום אין כאן חסרון זמן ראייתו: ליל שמיני נכנס · הולד יט] להתעשר וקיימא לן בבכורות בפרק מעשר בהמה (דף מ·) מחוסר זמן אינו נכנס לדיר להתעשר כ]: הא לילה · ליל שמיני חזי ולא הוי מחוסר זמן: לקדושה · ראוי להקדישו ואע"ג דלא חזי לילה להקרבה קאמרינן דמקדיש ליה אלמא לילה אין מחוסר זמן הואיל ומחר יהיה ראוי: לימא קסבר ר' יוחנן כו' · מדאיצטריך לן לשנויי אליביה במפריש לאחר חצות דאי לא שמיע לך מיניה בעלי חיים נדחים ראוי להפרישו לעולם דדלמא אין דחוי אלא בשחוטין כגון מת המשתלח כא] ישפך הדם במס' יומא (דף סג·): הקדיש חציה · אחד מהם: ועושה תמורה · דהא אינה דשותפין: (א) ואינה קריבה · הואיל ובתחילת הקדשה לא נראה להקריב דחציה היתה חולין ודחוי מעיקרו הוא הלכך אינה קריבה עוד ותרעה ולוקחין בדמיה אחרת:

תוספות

בעלמא דרשינן אחד כב] מן המיוחד שבעדרו (מגילה דף כח·):

ובין הערבים דכתיב בקטורת ונרות למה לי · בין הערבים דתמיד ניחא ליה כג] לכדאמר בריש תמיד נשחט (פסחים דף נח·) דזימניה מכי ינטו צללי ערב:

ואם איתא כוליה ראוי הוא · ולא מלי לתרץ דנקט מקצתו ראוי משום רבי יהושע משום דהכי פריך מנא ליה לר' אושעיא דבן בתירא מכשיר פסח שחרית אי משום דפסול שלא לשמו דלמא טעמא משום דמקצתו ראוי דהא חזינן הכא דטעם טוב הוא אבל לדברי ר' אושעיא דאינו תופסו לטעם טוב א"כ מאי פריך רבי לרבי יהושע הלא בכולו ראוי הוא תליא מילתא כד]:

הג"ה אי דאפרשיה האידנא דחוי מעיקרא הוא · דלא דמי למחוסר כפורים כה] דלא חשיב דחוי קודם הבאת קרבנו דאין זמנו עד שיטהר ויטבול אבל האי לא חזי לפסח ושלמים אע"פ שהיה זמן שלמים כו]:

רב פפא אמר אפילו תימא מאורתא לילה אין מחוסר זמן · כז] בריש מנחות (דף ה·) משמע דרב פפא ס"ל יש מחוסר זמן לבו ביום וצריך לחלק בין מחוסר זמן דהכא להתם כח]:

לילה אין מחוסר זמן · וכן משמע בברייתא ובחגיגה (דף ט:) לרבי יוחנן וכן במנחות פרק שתי הלחם (דף ק·) ובנזיר (יח:) וביומא פרק אמר להם הממונה (דף כט:):

לילה לקדושה כט] יום להרצאה · א) הקשה ל] הרב רבי יוסף דבתמורה (דף י·) משמע דאם במעי תמימה קדוש דקדושה חלה אעובר במעי אמו והילך קדוש בין לבר פדא בין לר' יוחנן והא לילה לקדושה דוקא אבל קודם לכן לא לא]:

יום להרצאה · תימה תיפוק לי מביום צוותו ולמה לי דכתיב לב] ביום השמיני וי"ל דאי לא כתיב אלא והיה שבעת ימים תחת אמו הוה אמינא אם שחט בלילה אם עלו לא ירדו והשתא קמשמע לן דהוי מחוסר זמן ותרד לג] [אפילו לר"ש] דאין פסולו בקודש ובפ' בתרא (לקמן קיב:) נמי לד] תנן מחוסר זמן ששחטו בחוץ אינו בכרת דאם עלו לא ירדו מוכח התם דקרי מתקבל לפתח אהל מועד וחייב כרת בחוץ לה] ולר"י דאמר (לקמן דף פד·) בשחיטת לילה אם עלה לו] תרד י"ל למ"ד בפרק בתרא (שם קכ·) אין לילה בבמה השתא שהוא מחוסר זמן אם שחטו לז] לילה אחר שביעי פסול אף בבמה וקשה למאן דאמר יש פסול לילה בבמה יש לומר דמודה אף ר"י דבבמה שחיטת לילה לא תרד לח]:

הג"ה קדושה ואינה קריבה · לא דמי לרגלה של זו עולה דתמכר לצורכי עולה (תמורה דף יא:) דהתם אינה דחויה כיון דבידו לקדשה:

ש"מ בעלי חיים נדחין · וא"ת מאי קמ"ל ר' יוחנן מתני' היא בפ' מי שהיה טמא (פסחים לז:) המפריש נקבה לפסחו כו' ואמרי' עלה בגמ' (נח·) ש"מ תלת וכי תימא משום דאיכא פלוגתא דתנאי בבעלי חיים נדחין בפ' שני שעירי (יומא דף סד·) ואשמעינן ר' יוחנן דבעלי חיים נדחין הא א"ר יוחנן חדא זימנא וי"ל דמפריש נקבה דחייה בידים ואפי' לט] [רב] מודה התם דבעלי חיים נדחין ומיהו קשה מאכל חלב והמיר דתו דהוי דחייה בידים ועוד דהוי נראה ונדחה ולמה ליה לרבי יוחנן לאשמועינן וצריך לדקדק בכל הנך מימרות דר' יוחנן הנך תלת דבעלי חיים נדחים ובשני מקומות דפליגי רב ור' יוחנן בההיא דבפרק שני שעירי ובההיא דלקמן פ' קדשי קדשים (דף סו·) גבי מזבח שנפגם*:

ושמע מינה יש דיחוי בדמים · פי' בקונט' בדבר שאין בו אלא קדושת דמים מ] *לא תימא שאין דחוי מעיקרא (אין בו) אלא בקדושת הגוף וא"ת א"כ דחוי מעיקרא ודחוי בדמים הכל אחד דכל דחוי מעיקרא אין בו אלא קדושת דמים מא] וי"ל דמשכחת לה בקבל דם בכלי שיש בו מים דראשון ראשון דחוי מב] וחזר ונהפך למראה דם ובפ' התערובת (לקמן דף עח·) אמרי' דדם לתוך מים ראשון ראשון בטל ולענין כיסוי אינו כן דאין דחוי אלא מצות וה"ר חיים מפרש יש דחוי בדמים שדוחה תמורה שלא לקרב מג] *ואמרי' כאן דאין קדושה אלא לדמים לא אלימא להתפיס התמורה לדחותה מקדושתה לעשותה כיוצא בה וכפי' זה משמע מתוך גירסת הספרים דכריתות דגרסי' התם (דף כח·) כך ש"מ בעלי חיים נדחין דקתני ואינה קריבה וש"מ קדושת דמים מדחה דקתני ותמורתה כיוצא בה וש"מ יש דחוי בדמים דקתני קדושה למאי לדמים ודאי מעיקרו לא קתני התם ומיהו ה"ר חיים גרים דחוי מעיקרו ולא גרים יש דחוי בדמים וכן יש כמה ספרים ולפי' קשה מההיא דמפריש נקבה לפסחו דלא קאמר התם תמורתה כיוצא בה ואמרי' עלה יש דחוי בדמים וקמד] בפ' בתרא דכריתות (דף כח·) דקאמר ר' אלעזר אמר ר' אושעיא מסמא מקדם עביד שהפריש קן לכבשתו והעני כו' דקאמר ש"מ תלת ולא שייכא תמורה מה] [דאין תמורה בעופות] ורבינו ש"י פי' בתשובה כמו שפי' מו] וכתב דבר זה למדתי פירושו ממס' כריתות דגרסי' התם בלשון זה ש"מ קדושת דמים מדחה כלומר ש"מ אפי' מז] שלא קידשה מתחילה להקרבת גופו אלא מח] קדושת דמים כגון הקדיש חציה וחציה שני חולין מט] והכי נמי פרשינן ליה יש דיחוי בדמים כגון נקבה לפסחו לא חזיא גופא לפסח אלא לדמיה וכי אקדשה לדמים אקדשה ואידי דדחויה היא דלא חזיא לאקרובי גופא לדבר שהוקדשה לה אמרי' מדחה מלקרב

א) פי' בתמורה י ע"ב שתירצו ת"ל וי"ל דקודם שנולד מצי מקדיש ליה ומייתי לה בבכורות מקרא עכ"ל הש"ק

עין משפט נר מצוה

נז א מיי' פ"ג מהלכות תפלה הלכה יא סמג עשין יט טוש"ע א"ח סי' רפו סעיף ד:

נח ב מיי' פט"ו מהל' פסה"מ הלכה יב:

נט ג עי' כ"מ פ"ו מהל' בכורות הלכה יד:

ס ד ה מיי' פט"ו מהל' מעה"ק הל' ד ופסק דקריבה ודלא כר"י:

שיטה מקובצת

א] דאתא כדתניא: ב] עי' בהשמטות בסוף המסכת: ג] ועוד תניא: ד] עי' בהשמטות בסוף המסכת: ה] לשמו לשמו דבעי בין הערבים שלא לשמו הואיל: ו] דאפרשיה: ז] דתני דבי ר' ישמעאל נ"א דבי שמואל: ח] לילה לקדושה' אבל קודם ליל שמיני אינו קדוש ותימה דאמרינן בתמורה דעובר קדוש במעי אמו וי"ל דשאני התם דחלה קדושה [אגב אמו] אבל אם הקדישו קדושת הפה אינו ראוי להל' עד [ליל] שמיני · א"נ במעי אמו אינו ראוי להקרבה ורחמנא לא פסלי' משום מחוסר זמן אלא כשנולד וראוי הוא להקריבו רחמנא פסליה משום מחוסר זמן (דקאמר) [דכתיב] אשר יולד אלמא בלידה תליא מילתא: ט] ויום להרצאה' וא"ת תיפוק ליה מביום צוותו להקריב ביומאתא מקריב ואי אתה מקריב בלילה ולמה [לי] ביום השמיני וי"ל דאיצטריך לר"ש דאמר [אם שחטום] בלילה אם עלו לא ירדו קמ"ל דהכא אם עלו ירדו דלא הוי פסולו בקדש · לשון תוס' פו"ך: י] וש"מ יש דחוי בדמים · י"ס גורסים וש"מ קדושת דמים נדחה והיא היא וי"ס דקדושת דמים מדחה התמורה לענין דאינה קריבה וליתא דבפרק בתרא (דתמורה) [דכריתות דף כח·] קאמר הני תלת גבי עוף ובגבי עוף לא שייך תמורה ואע"ג דכולהו ש"מ דקאמר הכא משניות הן קאמר ש"מ כלומר דהלכה כך תוס' אחרות: יא] ברכות דהלכה והר"א: יב] עד זמן המנחה מתפלל של מנחה אע"ג דזמן המוספין קודם כיון דשהי עד זמן: יג] קרא אחרינא אות י' נמחק: יד] אלמא רבי אות ד' נמחק: טו] דבן בתירא מכשיר שחרית: טז] בי"ד שחרית הס"ד: יז] דאמר לקמן: יח] להירצות ס"א להראות: יט] הולד לדיר להתעשר: כ] להתעשר א"כ ש"מ דליל ח' לאו מחוסר זמן הוא הס"ד: כא] המשתלח ישפך ס"א ונשפך: כב] תיבת מן נמחק: כג] דאיצטריך לכדאמר: כד] מילתא ע"כ: כה] כפורים קודם הבאתם דהוי דחוי באמצע דהתם לא חשיב: כו] שלמים ודאי כה"ג דיחוי מעיקרא הוא הס"ד: כז] זמן בבכורות ובריש: כח] להתם דהתם מיירי בעבודות שוקדים עבודת ערבית לעבודת שחרית אבל הכא מיירי בהפריש הס"ד: כט] תיבות יום להרצאה נמחק: ל] הקשה' עי' בתוס' פרק בתרא (דף קיד): לא] לא וי"ל דלא שייך מחוסר זמן אלא כשנולד כדכתיב שור או כשב וגו' כדמשמע בפ' כיצד מעריכין דיליף לה מקדיש בכור במעי אמו ולא מטעם ליה קרא אלא כשנולד הא במעי אמו קדיש ולא שייך ביה מחוסר זמן · תו"א: לב] ביום השמיני וי"ל דאי לא כתב אלא והיה (שמונת) [שבעת] ימים תחת אמו (הוה) [הוא] גזירת הכתוב דהוי בלילה נלין: לג] ותרד אפי' לר"ש משמע דאם עלה ירד דאין: לד] נמי דתנן מחוסר זמן כו' אינו בכרת ואי עלה לא ירד הא מוכח: לה] בחוץ ומיהו קשה לר"י דאמר: לו] עלה לא ירד ע"כ: לז] שוחט בלילה: לח] תרד ע"כ: לט] ואפי' רב: מ] קדושת דמים ולא תימא שאין דחוי מעיקרא פוסל תיבות ואין בו נמחק: מא] דמים דחויין מצינו דהוי מעיקרא בקדוש קדושת הגוף בקבל: מב] דחוי ואפי' חזר ונהפך: מג] לקרב ולא אמרינן: מד] וכן התם פרק בתרא (דף כח): מה] תמורה (בעופות) ל"ש ונמחק: מו] שפי' כאן: מז] ואפי' דבר שלא קדש: מח] אלא לקדושת: מט] חולין דחוי הוא מלהקריב גופו בתחילה הקדישו ואינו קרב לעולם הואיל תרוה ידחה ולא נימא אי דחוי פקרשים אלא בדבר הקדוש לגופו תורה מקריב אבל קדושת דמים לא לימא בו תורת דחוי ואי אתא לו שעת הכשר נקרבה כמו הכא דחזר ולקח חציה והכא נמי הכא פרישנא ליה:

הגהות הב"ח

(א) רש"י ד"ה ואינה וכו' קודם ד"ה ועושה:

מסורת הש"ס

פסחים נט. · לקמן לה. ברכות כח. · [תוספתא פסחים פ"ד] · מנחות ה. [יומא סג:] · חגיגה ט: וש"נ · חולין פא. · קדושין ז. תמורה כו. [כריתות כז.] · פסחים לח. יומא סד. כריתות כח: [תמורה כו: קדושין ז: לקמן נט: עג:] · [עי' תוספות יומא סד: ד"ה בריית'] · ול"מ שאין דחוי אלא כו' נ"ק · א"ל כיון דאין קדושה נ"ק

תורה אור

יש דחוי בדמים *אמר עולא אמר רבי יוחנן *אכל חלב והפריש קרבן והמיר דת וחזר בו הואיל ונדחה ידחה איתמר נמי אמר ר' ירמיה אמר רבי אבהו אמר רבי יוחנן *אכל חלב והפריש קרבן ונשתטה וחזר ונשתפה הואיל ונדחה ידחה וצריכי דאי אשמעינן קמייתא משום דהוא דחי נפשיה בידים אבל הכא דממילא אידחי א] כישן דמי ואי אשמעינן הכא משום דאין בידו לחזור אבל הכא דיש בידו לחזור אימא לא צריכא בעי רבי ירמיה אכל חלב והפריש קרבן והורו בית דין שחלב מותר וחזרו בהן מהו מי הוי דחוי או לא הוי דחוי אמר ליה ההוא סבא כי ב] פתח רבי יוחנן בדחויין מהא פתח מאי טעמא התם גברא אידחי קרבן לא אידחי הכא קרבן נמי אידחי: אמר שמעון בן עזאי מקובלני מפי שבעים ושנים זקן כו': למה לי למתנא שבעים ושנים זקן דכולהו בחדא ג] שיטתא הוו קיימי: לא הוסיף בן עזאי אלא העולה: אמר רב הונא מאי טעמא דבן עזאי °עולה (ויקרא) הוא אשה ריח ניחוח לה' היא לשמה כשרה שלא לשמה פסולה אשם נמי כתיב ביה הוא ההוא לאחר הקטרת אימורים הוא דכתיב האי נמי לאחר הקטרת אימורים הוא דכתיב תרי הוא כתיבי גבי אשם *נמי תרי הוא כתיבי אלא ד] בן עזאי בקל וחומר מייתי לה ומה חטאת שאינה כליל שחטה שלא לשמה פסולה עולה שהיא כליל לא כל שכן מה לחטאת שכן מכפרת פסח יוכיח מה לפסח שכן זמנו קבוע חטאת תוכיח *וחזר הדין לא ראי זה כראי זה ולא ראי זה כראי זה הצד השוה שבהן שהן קדשים ושחטן שלא לשמן פסול אף אני אביא עולה שהיא קדשים ושחטה שלא לשמה פסולה *מה להצד השוה שבהן שיש בהן צד כרת בן עזאי צד

יש דחוי בדמים · יש תורת דחוי בקדושת דמים אע"פ שאינה קדושת הגוף כגון הכא ה] שהקדיש חליה (א) לא קדשה אלא לדמיה שהרי אין לו חלק ו] [אלא] בחליה ואין קדושה ראויה לפשוט בכולה על פיו ואפי' הכי שייך בה דחוי ותדחה עולמית ולא אמרי' לא אלימא קדושת דמים ליפסל משום דחוי: לישנא אחרינא יש דחוי בשביל הדמים שלא פרע לקנות חליה של חבירו שלא היתה קנויה לו כשהקדישה שעדיין לא קנה חליה משל חבירו ואינ"ו נרא"ה למור"י: והמיר דת · נדחה מקרבן ז] בהכל שוחטין (חולין דף ה:) מעם הארץ פרט למומר: ונשתטה · נדחה דבעינן דעת במסכת ערכין בפ' האומר משקלי עלי (דף כא·): נשתפה · שקט משעמומו ח] כגון על הר נשפה (ישעיה יג) דמתרגם על טורא שליא: הורו ב"ד שחלב מותר · נדחה ט] לו דאילו עבר השתא לאו בר קרבן הוא דאמרינן בהוריות (דף ג:) יחיד שעשה בהוראת ב"ד פטור: מהא פתח · ודורש בו שידחה: התם · גבי מומר ושוטה גברא אידחי מקרבן קרבן לא אידחי תורת חטאת זאת לא נדחית מישראל מן הכשרין אבל הכא תורת קרבן זה נדחית מן הכל: למה לי למיתני זקן · ליתני זקנים: בחדא י] · בישיבה אחת היו יושבין וכולן היו כאיש אחד: לאחר הקטרת אימורין כתיב · וליכא למידרשיה לעיכובא יא] *דעלמו שלא הוקטרו אימוריו כשר והאי הוא דרשינן *למילתא אחריתי: תרי הוא כתיבי · ואם אין השני ענין לאחר הקטרה דהא כתיב חד תנהו ענין לעבודת דם ולפסול בשלא יב] לשמן · חד הוא כתיב באיל עולה של מילואים בואתה תצוה וחד הוא כתיב בויקרא גבי עולת בן לאן: אשם נמי תרי (אשם) הוא יג] כתיבי · חד בצו את אהרן אחר הקטרה וחד בויקרא אשם הוא אשם לה' ואע"ג דליכא חד מינייהו דכתיב גבי עבודת דם מן האחד באשם אינו ענין לכך כדאמרת בעולה:

לד

מלקרב לעולם *אפילו לאחר פסח דכל מותר הפסח הוי שלמים ונקיבה לשלמים מיחזא חזיא דקתני מתני' דמיה לשלמים אבל איהי גופה לא אלמא אלימא קדושת דמים למיסלומר בה תורת דחוי ולא אשכחינן תנאי דפליגי בהא מילתא מיהו בהא מילתא טובא אתא לאשמועינן יד] ורבינו חננאל מפרש יש דיחוי בדמים כלומר טו] דדמים דחוים (והדיחוי בדמים) שלא יקריב מן הדמים קרבנו שהיה בדעתו להפריש כמו יש דחוי בדמים דמי שהיה טמא (פסחים דף צח·) דתנן התם גבי מפריש נקבה לפסחו ירעה עד שיסתאב וימכר ויביא בדמיו שלמים ור"ש נמי פי' כן התם יש דחוי בדמים אפילו הדמים דחויין שאין מביאין מהן פסח שהיה דעתו כן בשעת הפרשה מיהו אינו כן אלא טז] מביא מן הדמים פסח כדתניא פ' בתרא דכריתות (דף כח·) המפריש נקבה לפסחו ירעה עד שיסתאב ותימכר ויביא בדמיה פסח ומתוך כך ברייתא רבינו שמואל מוחק בפרק מי שהיה טמא (פסחים דף צח.) שלמים וגרים יביא בדמיה פסח אמנם אין גירסא זו נכונה דאם כן היכי קאמר בגמרא ש"מ יש דחוי מעיקרו יז] [ויש] דחוי בדמים [ובעלי] חיים נדחין הלא כי נמי בעלמא אין דחוי אין יכול להקדיש איהי גופה פסח שהרי נקבה היא ובפסח כתיב זכר תמים בן שנה א"כ על כרחך התם פ' מי שהיה טמא גרסי' שלמים ור"ת אומר דאין למחוק הספרים דבאלו קדשים אמרי' המפריש נקבה לפסחו תרעה ויביא בדמיה פסח נשתיירה אחר הפסח תרעה עד שתסתאב וימכר ויביא בדמיה שלמים ומתני' דמי שהיה טמא בכה"ג מיירי בנשתיירה אחר הפסח ופירוש של יש דחוי בדמים הוי יש דיחוי בדבר שאין בו רק קדושת דמים ולא קדושת הגוף ול"ע בההיא דכריתות יח] א"ר אלעזר א"ר אושעיא מטמא מקדש עשיר כו' ומתיב רב עוקבא המפריש נקבה לפסחו יט] תרעה ילדה זכר ירעה ויביא בדמיו פסח כו' ר"ש אומר הוא עצמו יקרב פסח ומשני כ] כי אמרינן לרבנן ור"ש ס"ל דבע"ח אין נדחין דתניא מת אחד מהם מביא חבירו שלא בהגרלה דברי ר"ש והשתא מאי ס"ד מעיקרא דפריך מר"ש לסיועי' מרבנן וי"ל כא] דת"ק נמי מודה דבע"ח אין נדחין והא דקאמר ירעה טעמא כרבי אלעזר דתמורה פ' אלו קדשים (דף יח:) דתנן המפריש נקבה לעולה וילדה זכר ירעה רבי אליעזר אומר אף הוא עצמו יקרב עולה ומפרש בגמרא דגבי מפריש נקבה לפסחו וילדה זכר לא הוה א"ר אליעזר הוא עצמו יקרב פסח דגמירי למקום שהמותר הולך שם הולד הולך ולפני הפסח דאימיה קדשה לדמי פסח שלא היה יכול להמתין עד שתלד הזכר ויקריבנו פסח ולכך ולד נמי לדמי פסח אע"ג דקסבר בע"ח אין נדחים ומיהו קשה אדפריך ליה מברייתא דכריתות לסייעיה מת"ק דרבי אליעזר דתמורה דאית ליה בעלי חיים נדחין דקאמרי במפריש נקבה לעולה וילדה זכר ירעה וממתניתין דפסחים כב] ופלוגתא דתנאי ביומא (דף סד:) ועוד קשה היכי מייתי מההיא דמת אחד מהם דאית ליה לר"ש כג] דאין נדחין דלמא שאני התם דלא דחייה בידים ועוד קשה היכי מייתי מההיא דרבי אליעזר דפשיטא ליה כד] התם דבעלי חיים נידחים ולעיל מבעיא ליה התם בכריתות (דף כז·) ובתמורה פירשתי *לפני רבינו דחידושא דרבי יוחנן הוי אע"ג דבידו לתקן וליקח חליה השני וכן כה] רבי אלעזר אמר רבי אושעיא פ' בתרא דכריתות בידו להפקיר נכסיו והוי עני והוה ראוי הקן שהפריש ומיהו אין בידו כ"כ כמו נפגם המזבח כו] *בריש פ' קדשי קדשים (לקמן דף נט·) דחוי מעיקרו הוא וכשר כז] [והכא] לכ"ע משמע דכשר דבידו לתקן כדאיתא פרק לולב הגזול (סוכה דף לג·) ולכך נמי נקט רבי יוחנן אכל חלב והפריש קרבן והמיר דתו וחזר שידחה דהוה ליה נראה ונדחה ולא נקט שהפריש קרבן לאחר שהמיר דתו דההוא כשר כיון דבידו לתקן בקל כמו נפגם המזבח וגם דחוי מעיקרו דכשר ובכריתות פ' בתרא דפריך לר' אושעיא מר' שמעון ולא מייתי ליה סייעתא מרבנן משום דעד כאן לא פליגי רבנן ואמרי שנדחה משום דאין בידו לתקן כלל בשעת הקדש שהיא נקבה לפסחו אבל היכא שבידו לתקן קצת כגון מטמא מקדש עשיר שהפריש קן דאי בעי מפקר נכסיה מודה דלא הוי דיחוי כל זה פי' רבינו הקדוש זצוק"ל וקשה כח] לי על זה מאי פריך לעיל אי אפרשיה מגפרא דחוי מעיקרו הוא הלא בידו להשהותו עד חלות כמו כט] הקדיש חובות בגלגל דכשירין בשילה פרק אחרון (לקמן קיח·) וכן ל] אותו ואת בנו: וש"מ דחוי מעיקרו הוי דחוי · תימה דגבי לא] הדם אמרינן פ' לולב הגזול (סוכה דף לג:) היכא לב] (דאשכחן) דאסור מערב יו"ט דדחוי מעיקרא לא הוי דחוי וי"ל דשאני התם דבידו לתקנו תדע דגבי לג] לולב שנקטם ראשו [מעי"ט] ועלתה בו תמרה [בי"ט] מיבעיא ליה אי יש דחוי אי לאו לד] [ולא] פשטינן לה מהא משום דנקטם אין בידו לתקנו וא"ת מ"ט דר' יוחנן דאמר דחוי מעיקרו הוי דחוי לילף ממחוסר זמן דלא הוי דחוי כדאמר בפ' שני שעירי (יומא דף סד·) וי"ל דשאני מחוסר זמן דחוזר לה] [ונראה] ממילא וא"ת אמאי איצטריך לרבי יוחנן מיעוטא דמום בם הגי הוא דכי עבר לו] מומם ירצו *הא כל הדחויים אם עבר מומם לא ירצו הואיל ונידחו אידחו הא לז] מום עובר לא ילפינן [דלדחי] דלא הוי דחוי דהתם ממילא הוי וי"ל דהיכא מום דאינו עובר אלא על ידי רפואה: הכא קרבן אידחי · וגרע מדאידחי גברא והא דמשמע איפכא בהוריות פ' בתרא (דף יא·) גבי נשיאות מהו שתפסיק לא דמי דהתם לא אידחי קרבן מן החלב שאכל דעדיין הוא חייב קרבן ור"ת פירש לח] איפכא דגבי הורו ב"ד לא היה *דחוי דגברא אידחי שאינו יודע אם פטור אם לאו קרבן לא אידחי דאי לא דהתירו ב"ד היה קרב ונמלא שלא היה דחוי אלא ע"י טעותו אבל הכא אפילו קרבן נמי אידחי דכיון שהוא שוטה או מומר פטור הוא לכולי עלמא: בן עזאי בק"ו מייתי לה. אף ע"ג דפסול שלא לט] לשמן מוליאו מידי פגול דבעינן שיהיו כל מתירים בכשרות לא דמיא להא דאמר בפ"ק *דפסחים (דף יא) כל דין שתחילתו להחמיר וסופו להקל אינו דין תימה ובן עזאי אי דריש אותה לשמה כשרה שלא לשמה פסולה הא שאר קדשים כו' קל וחומר מאי אהני ליה *ואי לא דריש א"כ אשם ליעכב מהיקישא דכחטאת וכאשם: מה להצד השוה שבהן שכן יש בהן צד כרת · תימה ולר"א דפסל חטאת ואשם ליפסול נמי עולה ותיתי מחטאת ואשם [ופסח] וי"ל דשייך קצת צד כרת באשם משום דאיכא אשם תלוי ומיהו לא שייך כמו בחטאת ופסח כדמוכח לעיל:

עין משפט נר מצוה

ר"א ואתי פסח אע"ג דכל מותר פסחת כו' מיהו טובא אתי לאשמועי' כו' צ"ק

סא א ב מיי' פ"ג מהל' שגגות הלכה ם ודלא כר"י:

שיטה מקובצת

א] אידחי אימא כישן: ב] כי הוה פתח' זה לשון תלמיד הר"פ ונראה לר"ת כי הוה פתח ר' יוחנן כו' לפי שהיה תופסו לחידוש לפי שהוא דחוי גרוע יותר משאר דחויין ולכך פריך מ"מ כלומר למה ומשני הכא גבי אכל חלב והורו ב"ד גברא אדחי כלומר נהי דגברא אדחי מיהו הקרבן עצמו לא אידחי שהרי טעו ב"ד אבל גבי אכל חלב כו' קרבן נמי אידחי והכל יודעים דקרבן שוטה ומומר לאו כלום הם דובח רשעים תועבה ע"כ· כי הוה פתח [בהא פתח] פרש"י בדיחוי גדול יותר מתני דלעיל ולפיכך פתח ביה לפי שהיה (לו) פשוט [לו] יותר · ופריך מ"מ הוי דחוי טפי ומשני התם גברא אידחי פי' גבי אכל חלב והפריש קרבן והמיר אבל הכא גבי הורו ב"ד שהחלב מותר תורת קרבן נמי אידחי והסברא הפוכה דמעיקרא הוי מספקא ליה (מאכל) [באכל] חלב והורו ב"ד יותר מתני דלעיל והשתא פשיטא ליה דדחוי גדול הוא מתני דלעיל ור"ת פי' דת"ק כי פתח ר"י כו' שהי' תופסו לחידוש טפי שהוא דיחוי גרוע יותר משאר דיחויין לפיכך פתח ביה כדאמרי' בעלמא מילתא דאתיא מדרשא חביבא ליה ולכך פריך מ"מ כלומר למה גרע משאר דיחוין דלעיל ומשני כו' כמו שכתוב בתוס' תלמיד הר"פ לעיל · תוס' פ"ק: ג] בחדא שעתא: ד] בן עזאי כו' · תימה למאי דס"ד השתא דק"ו ימור הוא הא דפסל בן עזאי בעולה מסה נפשך אי דריש אותה אפי' עולה נמי אימעוט ואי לא דריש אותה אפי' אשם נמי לירבי מהיקשא דחטאת ואשם וי"ל דלעולם דריש אותה ואפ"ה לא אימעוט עולה דלהכי אתני ק"ו וא"ת אם כן באשם נמי יפסול דהא לא גרע היקשא מק"ו וכמו דק"ו מפיק ליה ממשמעותיה ה"נ התיקש וי"ל דמוקי ליה היקשא דלעיל דכחטאת וכאשם כדמוקי להו רבנן מה חטאת טעונה סמיכה אף אשם טעון סמיכה ומיהו קשה לר"א דאית ליה היקשא לאשם כדאמר לעיל לייתי עולה משלשתן מפסח וחטאת ואשם דליכא למיפרך כדפריך לעיל מה להצד השוה שבהן שכן יש בהן צד כרת דאשם לית ביה צד כרת כדמפורש לעיל ותירץ מורי כיון דאשם תלוי בא להגין על ספק כרת צד כרת קרינן ביה אך פסח וחטאת [יותר חשיבא] הלכך לעיל פריך שפיר מה לפסח וחטאת שיש בהן צד כרת יותר מבאשם דאע"ג דפירכא כל דהו היא אחרא מתרתי פרכינן וכן הכא פרכינן פירכא שיש בו צד כרת יותר מבעולה דבעולה לא שייך כרת כלל: ה] הכא כשהקדיש חציה לא הקדישה: ו] חלק אלא: ז] מקרבן כדתניא: ח] משעמומו כמו תיבת כגון נמחק: ט] נדחה הוא תיבת לו נמחק: י] בחדא שעתא: יא] לעיכובא דהוא עצמו שלא: יב] לשמה חד: יג] הוא דכתיב: יד] לאשמועינן עכ"ל ורבי': טו] כלומר שלא והשאר נמחק: טז] אלא יביא: יז] מעיקרו ויש דחוי בדמים ובעלי חיים נדחין הלא כי נמי אמרינן בעלמא אין דיחוי אין יכול: יח] דכריתות דא"ד: יט] וילדה תיבת תרעה נמחק: כ] ומשני אמרי דבי ר' אושעיא כי אמרינן לרבנן דר"ש ס"ל: כא] וי"ל דס"ד דת"ק: כב] דפסחים ומפלוגתא: כג] לר"ש בעלי חיים אינן נדחים תיבת דאין ל"ש ונמחק: כד] תיבת התם נמחק: כה] וכן דר': כו] המזבח דפריך: כז] וכשר לכ"ע ושמעינן דכשר כל היכא דבידו תיבות והכא ושמע ל"ש ונמחק: כח] וקשה · עי' [תוס'] לקמן (דף נט ע"א) [ד"ה עד שלא נבנה המזבח]: כט] כמו שהקדיש חובות בגלגל דכשרין בשילה כדאיתא פרק: ל] וכן המקדיש אותו לאחר שחישת בנו ע"כ הצ"ה: לא] דגבי מיעוט הדם: לב] תיבת דאשכחן נמחק: לג] דגבי נקטם ראשו: לד] לאו ולא איפשטיה ליה אלא מהא: לה] דחזור ונראה: לו] עבר מומם ירצו הא כל הדחוים לא ירצו תיבות אם עבר מומם נמחק: לז] ממום שחיה עובר לא ילפינן ותיבת דלדחי ל"ש: לח] ור"ת פי' כאן איפכא כו' לא חיו א) דחוי: לט] שלא לשמו מוציאו כו' שיהיו כל מתיריו בכשרות:

א) אולי צ"ל לא חיו מקרבן דחוי הנבדל כו' ·

מסורת הש"ס

צ"ק

סנהדרין מו. הוריות יא. כריתות ד

[סנהדרין שם נדרים לו:]

הגהות הב"ח

(א) רש"י ד"ה יש דחוי וכו' דלא קדשה וכו' אין לו חלק בחליה של חבירו ואין:

צ"ל דעלמו שלא כו' ס"א

[לעיל ס:]

[עי' בתוספות ב"ב קיג: ד"ה תרוייהו נמי]

[קדושין סו: כא. וש"נ]

[לעיל ז:]

וכתמורה פירשתי ולרבינו פי' · צ"ק

צ"ל דפריך וכ"ס בפי'

הא כל הדחוים כו' ונדחו נדחו הא ממום עובר לא ילפינן כו' צ"ק

כ"א אלא דיחוי כו' צ"ק

[צ"ל פ' שני דפסחים כח:]

ואי לא דריש א"כ אשם נמי לא לעכב כו' צ"ק

ab initio is rejected;[3] and [12b] that rejection applies to monetary sanctity.[4]

'Ulla said in R. Joḥanan's name: If one ate *ḥeleb*[5] and set aside a sacrifice,[6] then apostatized, yet subsequently retracted, since it was [once] rejected,[7] it remains rejected. It was stated likewise: R. Jeremiah said in R. Abbahu's name in R. Joḥanan's name: If a man ate *ḥeleb*, set aside an offering, became insane, and then regained his sanity, since it [the offering] was [once] rejected, it remains so.[8] Now both rulings are necessary. For had he informed us of the first only, [you might have said that] the reason is that he made himself ineligible [to offer a sacrifice] with his own hands; but in the latter case where he was involuntarily disqualified, he is [merely] as one who fell asleep.[9] Again, had he informed us the latter case only, you might argue that the reason is because his recovery is not dependent on himself; but in the former case [apostasy] it is not so, since it lies with him to retract. Thus both are required.

R. Jeremiah asked: If one ate *ḥeleb*, set aside a sacrifice, then the Beth din[10] ruled that *ḥeleb* is permitted, yet subsequently they retracted, what is the law? Does this constitute [permanent]
a rejection[1] or does it not constitute [permanent] rejection? Said a certain old man to him: When R. Joḥanan commenced [his rulings] on rejected [sacrifices], he commenced with this very case.[2] What is the reason? There[3] the *person* was disqualified, but the sacrifice was not rejected[4]; whereas here the *sacrifice* too became rejected.[5]

SAID SIMEON THE SON OF 'AZZAI: I HAVE A TRADITION FROM THE MOUTH OF SEVENTY-TWO ELDER[S], etc. Why does he state, SEVENTY-TWO ELDER[S]?[6]—Because they all held this view unanimously.[7]

BEN 'AZZAI ADDED ONLY THE BURNT-OFFERING. R. Huna said: What is Ben 'Azzai's reason?—*It is a burnt-offering, an offering made by fire, of a sweet savour unto the Lord*:[8] *'it is'* implies that [when it is slaughtered] in its own name it is valid; when not in its own name, it is invalid. But *'it is'* is written in the case of the guilt-offering too?—That is written after the burning of the *emurim*.[9] But in this case too it is written after the burning of the *emurim*?—*'It is'* is written twice [in connection with the burnt-offering].[10] Yet *'it is'* is written twice in the case of the guilt-offering too?[11]—Rather, Ben 'Azzai infers it *a fortiori*: If a sin-offering is invalid when one slaughters it under a different designation, though it is not entirely burnt, how much the more is a burnt-offering [invalid in such circumstances], seeing that it is entirely burnt. As for the sin-offering, [it may be argued] the reason is that it makes atonement! Then let the Passover-offering prove it. As for the Passover-offering, the reason is because its time [for slaughtering] is fixed! Then let the sin-offering prove it. And thus the argument revolves: the feature peculiar to the one is not that peculiar to the other, and the feature peculiar to the other is not that peculiar to the first. Their common characteristic is that they are sacred sacrifices, and if one slaughters them under a different designation they are invalid; so will I adduce the burnt-offering too, which is a sacred sacrifice, and if one slaughters it for a different purpose, it is invalid. [No:] their common feature is that

(3) This animal was not eligible for dedication by a single partner from the very outset. (4) This animal was sanctified from the very outset only for its value. i.e., that the money for which it would be sold should be expended for a sacrifice; nevertheless it becomes permanently ineligible for the altar. This excludes the possible view that only an animal that was fit in the first place to be dedicated to the altar can be rendered permanently ineligible. (5) Forbidden fat. V. Glos. (6) For atonement, v. Lev. IV, 27-28. (7) For sacrifices are not accepted from apostates, cf. Ḥul. 5*b*. (8) An insane person cannot offer. (9) When he had to sacrifice. This gap in his intelligent consciousness does not of course permanently disqualify him. (10) V. Glos.

a (1) For when they ruled that *ḥeleb* is permitted, the sacrifice became rejected, since a sin-offering can be brought only when one is liable. (2) Teaching that it is permanently rejected. (3) In the cases of apostasy and insanity. (4) The animal separated still belonged to the category of sin-offerings, save that its owner was not fit to bring it. (5) Hence it follows *a minori* that it remains rejected. (6) In the singular. (7) Sh. M. emends: they were all present at the same sitting (when they stated this). This apparently is Rashi's reading too. (8) Lev. I, 17. (9) V. *supra*, 5*b* for notes. (10) The one already quoted, and the other in Ex. XXIX, 18. Though there too it is after the burning of the *emurim*, yet since its teaching is unnecessary in that respect, as one text is sufficient for that, you must apply its teaching as intimating that when not slaughtered in its own name it is unfit. (11) Lev. V, 19 and VII, 5.

a an aspect of *kareth* is involved in them![1]—Ben 'Azzai [13*a*] does not admit the refutation of *kareth*.[2] Then let him adduce the guilt-offering too?[3]—The feature common to both is that they apply to the whole community as to an individual.[4] Alternatively he does admit the refutation of *kareth*, but Ben 'Azzai had a tradition.[5] And when R. Huna said [that he inferred it] *a fortiori*, he said this only in order to sharpen his disciples.[6]

MISHNAH. IF ONE SLAUGHTERED THE PASSOVER-OFFERING OR THE SIN-OFFERING NOT IN THEIR OWN NAME, [AND] HE RECEIVED [THE BLOOD], WENT [WITH IT], AND SPRINKLED [IT] NOT IN THEIR OWN NAME, OR IN THEIR OWN NAME AND NOT IN THEIR OWN NAME, OR NOT IN THEIR OWN NAME AND IN THEIR OWN NAME,[7] THEY ARE DISQUALIFIED. HOW IS 'IN THEIR OWN NAME AND NOT IN THEIR OWN NAME' MEANT? — IN THE NAME OF THE PASSOVER-SACRIFICE [FIRST] AND [THEN] IN THE NAME OF A PEACE-OFFERING. 'NOT IN THEIR OWN NAME AND IN THEIR OWN NAME' [MEANS] IN THE NAME OF A PEACE-OFFERING [FIRST] AND [THEN] IN THE NAME OF THE PASSOVER-OFFERING. FOR A SACRIFICE CAN BE DISQUALIFIED AT [ANY ONE OF] THE FOUR SERVICES: SLAUGHTERING, RECEIVING, CARRYING AND SPRINKLING. R. SIMEON DECLARES IT VALID IN THE CARRYING, BECAUSE HE ARGUED: [THE SACRIFICE] IS IMPOSSIBLE WITHOUT SLAUGHTERING, WITHOUT RECEIVING AND WITHOUT SPRINKLING, BUT IT IS POSSIBLE WITHOUT CARRYING. [HOW SO]? ONE SLAUGHTERS IT AT THE SIDE OF THE ALTAR AND SPRIN-
b KLES [FORTHWITH].[1] R. ELIEZER SAID: IF ONE GOES WHERE HE NEEDS TO GO, AN [ILLEGITIMATE] INTENTION DISQUALIFIES [IT]; WHERE HE NEED NOT GO, AN [ILLEGITIMATE] INTENTION DOES NOT DISQUALIFY [IT].[2]

GEMARA. Does then receiving disqualify? Surely it was taught: *And they shall present*:[3] this refers to the receiving of the blood. You say, This refers to the receiving of the blood: yet perhaps it is not so, but rather it means the sprinkling? When it says, *And they shall dash [the blood]*,[4] lo, sprinkling is stated, hence to what can I apply, '*And they shall present*'? It must refer to the receiving of the blood. *Aaron's sons, the priests*[4] [teaches] that [these services] must be performed by a legitimate priest[5] [robed] in priestly vestments.[6] Said R. Akiba: How do we know that receiving must be performed by none but a legitimate priest [robed] in priestly vestments? '*Aaron's sons*' is stated here, while elsewhere it says, *These are the*
c *names of the sons of Aaron, the priests that were anointed*:[1] as there it refers to legitimate priest[s] [robed] in priestly vestments,[2] so here too it means by a legitimate priest [robed] in priestly vestments. R. Tarfon observed: May I lose my sons if I have not heard a distinction made between receiving and sprinkling, yet I cannot explain [what it is]! Said R. Akiba: I will explain it. In the case of receiving intention was not made tantamount to action, whereas in the case of sprinkling intention was made tantamount to action.[3] [Again] if one received [the blood] without [its proper precincts], he is not liable to *kareth*, whereas if one sprinkles [it] without, he is punished with *kareth*. If unfit men received it,[4] they are not liable on its account, if unfit men sprinkled it, they are liable on its account. Said R. Tarfon to him, By the [Temple] service! You have[not] deviated to the right or the left![5] I heard [it] yet could not explain it, whereas you investigate it and agree with [my] tradition. In these words he addressed him: 'Akiba! whoever departs from thee is as though he departed from life!'—Said Raba: There is no difficulty: the one refers to an intention of *piggul*,[6] while the other [our Mishnah] refers to an intention for the sake of something else. This too may be proved, because it teaches, FOR A SACRIFICE CAN BE DISQUALIFIED, but it does not teach, 'For a sacrifice becomes *piggul*'. This proves it.

Now, does not an intention of *piggul* disqualify it [the sacrifice] at the receiving? Surely it was taught: You might think that an intention [of *piggul*] is effective only at the sprinkling; whence do we know to include slaughtering and receiving? From the text, *And if any of the flesh of the sacrifice of his peace-offerings be at all eaten on the third day, it shall not be accepted . . . it shall be an abhorred thing*
d [*piggul*];[1] Scripture treats of the services which lead to eating.[2] You might think that I also include the pouring out of the residue [of the blood] and the burning of the *emurim*; therefore it states, . . . *on the third day, it shall not be accepted, neither shall it be imputed unto him that offereth it*.[3] Now sprinkling was included in the general statement,[4] and why was it singled out? That an analogy therewith might be drawn, intimating: as sprinkling is a service and is indispensable for atonement, so every [act which is a] service and is indispensable for atonement [is included]; thus the pouring out of the residue and the burning of the *emurim* are excluded, since

a (1) V. *supra* 10*b* n. a 2. (2) Because it does not feature in the same way in both of them. For the sin-offering is brought for a sin of *commission* which involves *kareth*, whereas it is the *omission* to bring the Passover-offering that entails *kareth*. (3) That it is invalid when slaughtered under a different designation, by the same analogy. V. *supra* 10*b*, where the analogy is proposed but rejected because *kareth* is not involved in the guilt-offering. Since, however, Ben Azzai does not admit that this is a refutation, the analogy stands. (4) A sin-offering may be incurred by the whole community, just as by an individual, v. Lev. IV. The Passover-offering too, though brought by individuals, is a communal (public) sacrifice, since the whole community must bring one (Yoma 51*a*). But a guilt-offering is never brought by the whole community. (5) In respect of the burnt-offering, as stated in the Mishnah. Hence he does not infer it *a fortiori* at all. (6) Challenging them, as it were, to find the fallacy in his statement. (7) I.e., one of the services was for its own sake and another was for a different purpose, in the order stated.

b (1) Where it is straightway sprinkled. Since then the blood may not be carried at all, the sacrifice cannot be disqualified if it is carried for a different purpose. (2) The Gemara discusses this. (3) Lev. I, 5. (4) Ibid. (5) Which excludes one of profaned birth, e.g., the issue of a divorced woman, and one suffering from a physical blemish or defect; v. Lev. XXI, 7, 17. (6) Lit., 'service vessels' (here, robes). 'The *priests*' implies that they must be vested as priests.

c (1) Num. III, 3. (2) Legitimate, since Nadab and Abihu, Eleazar and Ithamar, Aaron's sons, are enumerated (v. 2). 'Robed in priestly vestments' is deduced from the end of the verse: *whom he consecrated to minister in the priest's office*; cf. Lev. XXI, 10: *and that is consecrated to put on the garments*. (3) The reference is to *illegitimate* intention and action. An illegitimate intention is now assumed to mean an intention to receive the blood in the name of a different sacrifice or to eat of its flesh after the permitted time, which would render it *piggul* (q.v. Glos.). Thus an illegitimate intention at the receiving of the blood does not disqualify, which contradicts the view in the Mishnah. — The difficulty is answered at the end of the discussion. (4) E.g., lay Israelites or intoxicated priests. (5) You have stated exactly what I heard, but had forgotten. (6) Such an intention does not disqualify at the receiving.

d (1) Lev. VII, 18. (2) I.e. which permit the consumption of the flesh; these include receiving. (3) '*Accepted*' is understood to refer to the sprinkling, which makes the sacrifice acceptable. (4) I.e., as one of the services which 'lead to eating'.

צד כרת לא פריך אשם נמי לייתי אשם פריך מה להצד השוה שבהן שכן ישנן בצבור כביחיד ואיבעית אימא צד כרת נמי פריך ובן עזאי גמרא גמיר לה והא דקאמר רב הונא קל וחומר לא אמרה אלא *לחדד בה תלמידיו:

מתני' *א*הפסח והחטאת ששחטן שלא לשמן קבל והלך וזרק שלא לשמן או ב לשמן ושלא לשמן או שלא לשמן ולשמן פסולים כיצד לשמן ושלא לשמן לשם פסח ולשם שלמים שלא לשמן ולשמן לשם שלמים ולשם פסח ג שהזבח נפסל בארבעה דברים בשחיטה ובקבול ד ובהילוך ובזריקה רבי שמעון מכשיר בהילוך *שהיה א] אומר אי אפשר שלא בשחיטה ושלא בקבלה ושלא בזריקה אבל אפשר בלא הילוך שוחט בצד המזבח וזורק רבי (א) *אליעזר אומר המהלך במקום שהוא צריך להלך מחשבה פוסלת במקום שאינו צריך להלך אין מחשבה פוסלת:

גמ' וקבלה מי פסלה ב] *והתניא °והקריבו זו קבלת הדם ג] אתה אומר קבלת הדם או אינו אלא זריקה כשהוא אומר וזרקו הרי זריקה אמור הא מה אני מקיים והקריבו זו קבלת הדם בני אהרן הכהנים ה שתהא בכהן כשר ובכלי שרת *אמר רבי עקיבא מנין לקבלה שלא תהא ד] [אלא] בכהן כשר ובכלי שרת נאמר כאן בני אהרן ונאמר להלן °אלה שמות בני אהרן הכהנים המשוחים מה להלן בכהן כשר ובכלי שרת אף כאן בכהן כשר ובכלי שרת אמר רבי טרפון *אקפח את בניי אם לא שמעתי ה] להבחין הפרש בין קבלה לזריקה ואין לי לפרש אמר רבי עקיבא אני אפרש קבלה לא עשה בה מחשבה כמעשה זריקה עשה בה מחשבה כמעשה ו קבלו בחוץ אינו חייב כרת ז זרקו בחוץ ענוש כרת ח קבלוהו פסולין אין חייבין עליו ט זרקוהו פסולין חייבין עליו אמר לו רבי טרפון העבודה ו] *את הטית ימין ושמאל אני שמעתי ואין לי לפרש אתה דורש ומסכים לשמועה בלשון הזה אמר לו *עקיבא כל הפורש ממך כפורש מחייו אמר רבא לא קשיא ז] כאן במחשבת פיגול כאן במחשבת שלא לשמה דיקא נמי דקתני י שהזבח נפסל ולא קתני מתפגל ש"מ: ומחשבת פיגול לא פסלה בקבלה והתניא יכול לא תהא מחשבה מועלת אלא בזריקה בלבד מנין לרבות שחיטה כ וקבלה ת"ל °ואם האכל ל יאכל מבשר זבח שלמיו ח] *(פיגול הוא) לא ירצה בדברים המביאין לידי אכילה הכתוב מדבר יכול שאני מרבה אף שפיכת שירים *והקטרת אימורין ת"ל ט] °ביום השלישי לא ירצה י] המקריב אותו לא יחשב זריקה בכלל היתה ולמה יצתה להקיש אליה לומר לך מה זריקה מיוחדת שהיא עבודה יא] (ומכפרת) ומעכבת כפרה אף כל יב] עבודה ומעכבת כפרה ° יצאו שפיכת שירים והקטרת אימורין שאין מעכבין את הכפרה אלא

תורה אור

רש"י

צד כרת לא פריך. לפי שאינו שוה בשניהם דחטאת אינו ענוש כרת על הבאתו אלא שעל שגגת כרת הוא בא ופסח ענוש כרת על הבאתו: אשם נמי לייתי. לפסול יג] בשלא לשמו מבנין אב כדאמר רבי אליעזר לעיל (דף י:) דקא"ל רבי יהושע חוזרני חלילה ופרכינן וליהדר דינא ולייתי במה הצד וסליקנא להך אתקפתא משום דאיכא למיפרך מה להצד השוה שבהן שכן יש בהן צד כרת. ומשני לבן עזאי אשם מפירכא אחריתא מסלק ליה דלא לייתי בבנין אב דפריך מה להצד השוה שבהן שישנו בצבור פסח קרי ליה קרבן צבור כדאמרן בסדר יומא בפ' הוציאו לו (דף נא.) משום דאתי בכינופיא: גמרא גמיר לה. מפי ע"ב זקנים כדתנן: לחדד יד] תלמידיו. שיקשו לו תשובה עליו א"כ שיתנו לבם להיות חריפין לדרוש קלים וחמורים מאיליהן כבן עזאי טו]: **מתני'** וקבל והלך וזרק כו'. או או קתני קבל או הלך או זרק (ב): או לשמו ושלא לשמו. שחישב בעבודה אחת לשמו ושלא לשמו: אבל אפשר בלא הילוך. הלכך לא חשיבא למיפסל: המהלך במקום שהוא צריך להוליך. הולכה זו מחשבה פוסלת בה אם חישב בה שלא לשמה ובגמ' מפרש למילתי' מאי צריך ומאי אין צריך: **גמ'** והקריבו. דכתיב בעולה ושחט את בן הבקר והקריבו בני אהרן טז] את הדם זו קבלת הדם וללמד שצריך לקבלו בכלי: אתה אומר כו' או אינו אלא (ג) יז] לזריקה. דהא לשון הקרבה למזבח הוא כדכתיב לכהן המקריב אותה וגו' והאי נמי בהקרבה למזבח משתעי דהיינו זריקה אבל קבלה *לא צריך [כלי] מאהל מועד ואילך: כשהוא אומר כו' זו קבלת הדם. כדאשכחן קבלה בעולת סיני (שמות כד) ויקח משה חצי הדם וישם באגנות ואע"ג דהקרבה לשון הולכה היא כדאמרן לעיל (דף ז.) והקריב הכהן את הכל זו הולכת אברים לכבש הכא כיון דזימנין יח] הולכה ליתיה כלל כמו השוחט בצד המזבח לא כתב לה קרא ואקבלה הוא יט] דאכתביה והיכא דאיצטריכא הולכה נפקא לן דהויא עבודה מדאפקא רחמנא לקבלה בלשון הולכה: בכהן כשר. לאפוקי חללים ובעלי מומין: ובכלי שרת. שיהו מלובשים בגדי כהונה כ] דכהנים משמע (הכהנים) בכיהונם (לקמן דף יח:) והיינו בגדי כהונה וכל היכא דקתני נמי בכהן כשר ובכלי שרת בבגדי כהונה קאמר: אמר רבי עקיבא. ר' עקיבא לא משמע ליה מהכא דאיכא למימר בני אהרן כל שהן והכהנים בכיהונם לא משמע ליה כא]: מה להלן בכהנים כשרין. הכתוב מדבר דהא אלעזר ואיתמר כב] כתיבי ובכלי שרת נמי הכתוב מדבר דכתיב אשר מלא את ידם והיינו לשון רבוי בגדי כהונה דכתיב (ויקרא כא) ומלא את ידו ללבוש את הבגדים וכתיב נמי ובגדי הקדש אשר לאהרן יהיו לבניו אחריו למשחה בהם ולמלא בם את ידם (שמות כט): כג] להבחין הפרש כו'. ואתה עושה את הקבלה כשאר עבודות: ואין לי לפרש. איני יודע לפרש מה הפרש שמעתי ביניהן: לא עשה בה מחשבה כמעשה. השתא סלקא כד] דעתך (ד) הא דקאמר אין מחשבה פוסלת בשבילה אם חישב בה חוץ לזמנו או שלא לשמו אלמא לא פסלה בקבלה כה]: קבלו בחוץ אינו חייב כרת. דשחיטה היא דכתיב כו] לחובא [ואל פתח אהל מועד] וזריקה נפקא מדם א) יחשב לקמן בפרק השוחט (דף קז.): קבלו פסולין. זרים ושאר חייבי מיתות כגון שתויי יין והדומה להם: אין חייבין עליו. מיתה דבעיא עבודה תמה שאין אחריה עבודה בסדר יומא (דף כד.) ובפרק בתרא דהכא (דף קיב:) נמי תנן אין בהם משום זרות ולא משום טומאה ולא משום מחוסר בגדים כו': אתה דורש. מאליך ומסכים למה ששמעתי: מחשבת פיגול. דחוץ לזמנו לא פסלה בקבלה: דיקא נמי. [דתנא] דמתניתין לא איירי במחשבת פיגול: אלא בזריקה. במחשב בשעת זריקה ע"מ לאכול מזבחו ביום השלישי כדכתיב בקרא דמחשבת פיגול המקריב אותו לא יחשב ילפינן מיניה בפ"ב (לקמן כט.) במחשב בשעת הקרבה לאכול מזבחו ביום השלישי הכתוב מדבר כז] [והקרבה] היינו זריקה: בדברים המביאים. את הקרבן לידי היתר אכילה הכתוב מדבר: אף שפיכת שירים. אם שפך שירי הדם ליסוד על מנת לאכול בשר חוץ לזמנו או אם הקטיר אימורין במחשבה זו: לא ירצה. היינו זריקה שהיא מרצה כח]: בכלל היתה. בכלל הדברים המביאין לידי אכילה: שאין מעכבין. שירים אין מעכבין כדתניא באיזהו מקומן (לקמן דף נב.) יכול יעכבנו תלמוד לומר ואת כל הדם ישפך נתקו הכתוב ועשאו שירי מצוה כו' הקטרת אימורין לא מעכבין כפרה דכתיב כט] הדם הוא בנפש יכפר: *לא קשיא הא. *דקתני לעיל מחשבה קבלה לא פסלה בפיגול לא כשחישב בשעת קבלה על אכילת בשר אלא במחשב בשעת שחיטה על מנת לקבל דם למחר ל] דאילו זריקה כהאי גוונא עשה בה מחשבה כמעשה אם שחט על מנת לזרוק דם למחר פיגול דהיינו אכילת מזבח (ה) (ואי נמי) דאיתרבי בהדיא אפי' שפיכת שירים לקמן: הא דאמר ס'. לא] והאי דקתני מנין לרבות שחיטה וקבלה לב] (ו) מחשב בשעת קבלה על מנת לשפוך שירים או אחת משאר האכילות לג] קאמרי: ושפיכת שירים לא פסלה בהו מחשבה. דקתני לעיל יכול שאני מרבה אף שפיכת שירים: אלא באכילת בשר. בשחישב לאכול בשר חוץ לזמנו: מנין לרבות שפיכת שירים. וכל שכן תחלת זריקה: לא

א) [ע"ש כי הוא טעם ר"י אמנם טעמא דר"ש מאו זכה]

תוספות

אתה אומר זו קבלת הדם כו'. לעיל (דף ד.) פי' בקונט' דמוקמינן והקריבו בקבלה ולא בהולכה משום דוהקריבו נאמר מיד אחר שחיטה וקבלה היא עבודה ראשונה שאחר שחיטה ולפירושו קשה היכי בעי למימר הכא או אינו אלא זריקה אלא נראה דמוקמי' לה בקבלה או בזריקה לפי שהן עבודות חשובות שאי אפשר לבטלן מה שאין כן בהולכה*:

בכהן כשר ובכלי שרת. פירש בקונטרס כלי שרת בגדי כהונה וקשה דהא נפקא לקמן בפרק שני (דף יז:) מקרא דאין בגדיהם עליהן אין כהונה עליהן והוו להו זרים ואפילו בעבודה דלא מעכבא כפרה ויש לומר דאי לאו גזרה שוה דהכא הוה אמרינן מה שהקפידה תורה אמחוסר בגדים היינו היכא דכתיבי בגדים אבל היכא דלא כתיבי בגדים לא וגבי נתינת אש וסידור איברים לא הוה בעינא בגדים מכהן בכיהונו אלא מדגלי רחמנא גבי קבלה גזרה שוה ילפינן בכל דוכתא דהכהן הוי בכיהונו:

דיקא נמי דקתני שהזבח נפסל. במסקנא לא חיישינן להאי דיקא דבקבלה נמי איכא פסול פיגול

פיגול הוא לא ירצה נמחק : ט] תיבות ביום השלישי א) לא ירצה ל"ש : י] המקריב אותו לא ירצה היינו זריקה שמרצה . תוס' הר"ש : יא] תיבת ומכפרת נמחק : יב] כל שהוא עבודה : יג] לפסול שלא אות ב' נמחק :
יד] לחדד בה תלמידיו : טו] כבן עזאי . ס"א אינו : טז] אהרן הכהנים : יז] אלא זריקה אות ל' נמחק : יח] דזמנין דהולכה : יט] הוא דכתביה אות א' נמחק : כ] בגדי כהונה הכהנים משמע בבידונם : כא] ליה והספא
ליה מסתבר אחר כך : כב] ואיתמר התם : כג] תיבת להבחין נמחק : כד] סלקא דעתי' דקאמר אין כו' בשבילה אדם שחישב בה : כה] בקבלת מחשבה שלא לשמו הס"ד : כו] דכתיב בחוץ לחובא : כז] מדבר
והקרבה והיינו זריקה כדמסיים בדברים והד"א : כח] מרצה ס"א אינו וה"ג בת"כ ת"ל המקריב אותו ול"ג לא ירצה : כט] דכתיב כי הדם : ל] למחר ולכך לא פסלה דבעינן מחשב בעבודה לאכילת אדם או לאכילת מזבח
ואילו זריקה נמי אתרבי אות ד' נמחק : לא] כו' והא אות י' נמחק : לב] וקבלה זהו במחשב : לג] האכילות למחר קאמר הס"ד :
א) נראה דל"ל תיבות ביום השלישי ל"ש : י] לא ירצה המקריב אותו היינו זריקה במרצה .

עין משפט נר מצוה

סב א מיי' פט"ו מהל' פסה"מ הל' א ד יא:
סג ב מיי' פי"ג שם הלכה א:
סד ג מיי' שם הלכה ד ופט"ו שם הלכה א ופ"ד מהל' מעה"ק הל' י:
[ועי' תוס' יומא כז. ד"ה והקריבו]
סה ד מיי' פי"ג מהל' פסה"מ הלכה ט:
סו ה מיי' פ"ס מהלכות מעשה הקרבנות הל' א ופ"א מהל' פסולי המוקדשין הלכה כב:
סז ו מיי' פי"ט מהל' מעה"ק הלכה ו:
סח ז מיי' שם הלכה ג:
סט ח מיי' פ"ט מהלכות ביאת מקדש הל' ב:
ע ט מיי' שם הל' ג:
עא י מיי' פי"ג מהל' פסה"מ הלכה ג:

שיטה מקובצת

א] שהיה ר' שמעון: ב] פסלה במחשבה: ג] (הדם אתה אומר קבלת הדם או): ד] אלא בכהן: ה] תיבת להבחין נמחק: ו] העבודה אם הטית: ז] לא קשיא הא דקתני לעיל דמחשבה לא פסיל בפיגול לא כשחישב בשעת קבלה על אכילת בשר אלא כשחישב בשעת שחיטה על מנת לקבל דמו למחר [לא] פסלה דבעינן מחשב בעבודה לאכילת אדם או אכילת מזבח ואילו זריקה כה"ג עשה מחשבה כמעשה אם שחט על מנת לזרוק דם למחר פיגול דהיינו אכילת מזבח כפ"ה ותימה למורי למה איצטריך לדחוק וליתן חילוק בין פיגול ושלא לשמו לוקמא כולה בשלא לשמו ובענין דשוחט ע"מ לקבל שלא לשמו כשר והיינו לא עשה בו מחשבה כמעשה ומתני' איירי במחשב בקבלה עצמה אבל בזורק עשה בו מחשבה כמעשה דשוחט ע"מ לזרוק דמו שלא לשמו פסול וי"ל דהא תינח לר"י אבל לר"ל מאי איכא למימר דקאמ' לעיל אף בשוחט ע"מ לזרוק דמו שלא לשמו כשר דאין מחשבין מעבודה לעבודה ומ"מ קשה לוקמא בשינוי בעלים דאף ר"ל מודה דשוחט ע"מ לזרוק בשינוי בעלים פסול ושוחט ע"מ לקבל בשינוי בעלים כשר [וי"ל] דלא מצי לאוקמא בשינוי בעלים דא"כ תקשה לך הלשון דקאמר לא עשה בו מחשבה כמעשה משמע הא אם עשה בה [מעשה] [שקבל הדם] בשינוי בעלים פסול וזה אינו דאפי' קבל בשינוי בעלים נמי כשר כדהוכחנו לעיל דלא שייך שינוי בעלים רק בזריקה אבל אי מיירי בפיגול ניחא דקתני לא עשה בה מחשבת כמעשה דאם היה מקבל חוץ לזמנו או חוץ למקומו פסול מיהא הוי תוס' שנץ: ח] תיבות

[ברכות נג:]
פסחים נט:
[נ"ל שהיה רבי שמעון אומר כ"ה במשנה שבמשניות]
נ"ל אלעזר
חגיגה יא. לעיל ד. [קדושין נו:]
[תוס' פ"א]
שבת יז. קטו.
עיין חלופי גרסאות [נ"ל שלא כך היתה בתוספתא]
[קדושין סו:]
נ"א ביום השלישי
[ובת"כ תני' והקטרת אימורין ת"ל המקריב אותו וכו']

הגהות הב"ח

(א) במשנה ר' אלעזר בר"ש אומר המהלך: (ב) רש"י ד"ה וקבל וכו' או זרק שלא לשמו או לשמו כצ"ל והד"א: (ג) ד"ה אתה וכו' אלא זריקה דהא: (ד) ד"ה לא עשה וכו' סלקא דעתך דהכי קאמר: (ה) ד"ה לא קשיא וכו' אכילת מזבח ואי נמי אפילו שיריים דאיתרבי בהדיא לקמן: (ו) ד"ה הא דאמר וכו' במחשב:

גליון הש"ס

גמ' יצאו שפיכת שיריים. לקמן דף נט ע"א:

שייך לע"ב
*נ"א הא דקתני לעיל מחשבה לא פסלה בקבלה לא כשחישב כו'

אלא לא קשיא °הא דאמר הריני א] [שוחט] ע"מ לקבל דמה למחר הא דאמר הריני מקבל דמה על מנת לשפוך שירים למחר א"ל ההוא מרבנן לרבא ושפיכת שירים והקטרת אימורין לא פסלה בהו מחשבה ב] *והתנן יכול לא תהא מחשבה מועלת אלא באכילת בשר מנין לרבות שפיכת שירים והקטרת אימורים ת"ל °ואם האכל יאכל *בשתי אכילות הכתוב מדבר אחת אכילת אדם ואחת אכילת מזבח לא קשיא הא דאמר [א]הריני זורק על מנת לשפוך שירים למחר הא דאמר הריני [ב]שופך שירים על מנת להקטיר אימורין למחר: א"ר יהודה בריה דרבי חייא שמעתי [ג]שטבילת אצבע מפגלת בחטאת פנימית ג] שמעה אילפא אמרה קמיה ד] (א) דרב פדא אמר כלום למדנו פיגול אלא משלמים מה שלמים אין טבילת אצבע מפגלת בהן אף חטאת אין טבילת אצבע מפגלת בה[ו]קוכי הכל משלמים ה] (ב) למדו אי מה שלמים שלא לשמן אין מוציא מידי פיגול אף חטאת שלא לשמה אין מוציא מידי פיגול אלא מאי אית לך למימר מרבויא דקראי קאתיא ו] [ה"נ מרבויא דקרא קאתי] אמר ריב"ל בעליה זו שמעתי ז] שטבילת אצבע מפגלת תהי בה רשב"ל (ג) כלום למדו פיגול אלא משלמים מה שלמים אין טבילת אצבע מפגלת ח] בהן אף חטאת אין טבילת אצבע מפגלת בה[ו]קוכי הכל משלמים למדו אי מה שלמים שלא לשמן אין מוציא מידי פיגול אף חטאת שלא לשמה אין מוציא מידי פיגול אמר רבי יוסי ברבי חנינא ט] אין הכל משלמים למדו הואיל וחוץ למקומו פוסל בשלמים ושלא לשמו פוסל בחטאת מה חוץ למקומו הפוסל בשלמים מוציא מידי פיגול אף שלא לשמו הפוסל בחטאת מוציאה מידי פיגול א"ר ירמיה מצדה תברא מה לחוץ למקומו הפוסל בשלמים שכן נוהג בכל הזבחים תאמר בשלא לשמו שאינו נוהג אלא בפסח וחטאת בלבד אלא מאי אית לך למימר דבר הפוסל בהן מוציאם מידי פיגול דבר המעכב בהן מביאן לידי פיגול הכא נמי דבר הפוסל בה מוציא מידי פיגול דבר המעכב בה מביאה לידי פיגול אמר רב מרי אף אנן נמי תנינא *זה הכלל [ד]כל הקומץ ונותן בכלי והמוליך והמקטיר בשלמא קומץ היינו שוחט מוליך היינו מוליך מקטיר נמי היינו זורק אלא נותן בכלי מאי ניהו אילימא דדמי לקבלה מי דמי התם ממילא הכא איהו קא שקיל ורמי י] אלא כיון דלא סגי דלא יהיב *על כרחיה עבודה חשובה היא ה"נ כיון דלא סגי דלא עביד לה על כרחי' היינו הולכה לא לעולם דדמי לקבלה ודקאמרת הכא ממילא התם איהו קא שקיל ויהיב כיון דאידי ואידי מתן כלי הוא מה לי ממילא מה לי קא שקיל ויהיב לימא כתנאי דתני חדא טבילת אצבע מפגלת בחטאת ותניא אידך לא מפגלת ולא מתפגלת מאי לאו תנאי היא יא] לא הא רבנן הא רבי שמעון אי רבי שמעון מאי איריא טבילת אצבע האמר

כל

לא קשיא הא. דקמרבי שפיכת שירים כגון דאמר הריני זורק או אחת משאר עבודות על מנת לשפוך שירים למחר שהרי חישב להאכיל את המזבח חוץ לזמנו: והא. דמעטינהו לעיל כגון דאמר הריני שופך שירים כו' כללא דמילתא בעינן מחשבה בשעת עבודה על יב] אכילת אדם או למזבח הלכך חישב בשעת שפיכת שיריים על אכילת בשר לא כלום היא דלא הואי מחשבה בשעת עבודה: שמעתי מרבותי שטבילת אצבע. האמור בחטאות הפנימיות וטבל הכהן אצבעו וגו' (ויקרא ד) מפגלת בחטאת אם טבל ע"מ להקטיר אימורים למחר: כלום למדנו פיגול. בחטאת אלא משלמים דעיקר פיגול בשלמים כתיב ואם האכל יאכל ושלמים אין בהן טבילת אצבע שכל הדמים בזריקה מן הכלי למזבח חוץ מן החטאת שהיא במתנת אצבע: ופרכינן יג] וכי הכל משלמים למדו. (ד) דין פיגול בכל הזבחים יד] כדינו בשלמים: אי מה שלמים אין שלא לשמו מוציאו מידי פיגול. אם שחט במחשבת חוץ לזמנו וקבל טו] והוליך שלא לשמן לא יצאו מידי פיגולן שהרי אין שלא לשמו פוסל בשלמים והוה ליה קרב המתיר כמצותו בפיגול בלא פסול מחשבה אחרת: אף חטאת. אע"פ שלא לשמו פסול בה לא תוציאנה מידי פיגול ואנן תנן בפ"ב (לקמן דף כט:) הפסח והחטאת ששחטן חוץ לזמנו וקבל והלך וזרק שלא לשמו זהו שלא קרב המתיר כמצותו ואינה פיגול ליענש כרת על אכילתו כדילפינן בפ"ב (שם דף כח:) מקרא כהרצאת כשר כך הרצאת פיגול שיקרבו כל מתירין דהיינו ארבע עבודות בלא פסול מחשבה אחרת: אלא מאי אית לך למימר מרבויא דקרא קאתי. כל הזבחים לפיגול בת"כ ולא משלמים למדו הלכך כל חד וחד מאי דפסיל טז] מוציאו מידי פיגול וכן לענין הבאתו לידי פיגול כל חד וחד מאי דכתיב ביה דהוי עבודה מביאו לידי פיגול: הכי גרסינן שטבילת אצבע מפגלת יז]: אין הכל משלמים למדו. ודקשיא לך בחטאת היאך שלא לשמו מוציאה מידי פיגול: הואיל וחוץ יח] למקומה כו'. מחשבת ע"מ יט] לאוכלו חוץ למחיצת אכילתו דהיינו בכל העיר וחוץ לעיר הוי חוץ למקומו פוסל בשלמים (ה) בהדיא מרבינן לה לפסולא בפ"ב אלא שאין בו כרת: מוליא מידי פיגול. כדילפינן בפ"ב שכל כ] מחשבת פסול מוציאתו מידי פיגול: מלדה תברא. תשובתה בצדה אם מחוץ למקומו אתה לומד לשלא לשמו ולהעמיד פיגול על עבודות הטהנות בשלמים ותו לא אלא שמוציאתה מידי פיגול תלמד בחטאת שלא לשמו מחוץ למקומו כא] דשלמים יש להשיב מה לחוץ למקומו כב] דין הוא שיוציא מידי פיגול שהרי כג] פסול וחמור לנהוג בכל הזבחים תאמר כו': אלא מאי אית לך למימר. אם באת לומר הכל משלמים למדו מה יש לך (ו) טעם כד] בשלא לשמו המוציא חטאת מידי פיגול כך יש לך לומר שלמים דבר הפוסל בהו כגון חוץ למקומו מוציאן מידי פיגול: ודבר המעכב בהו. כגון ד' עבודות הדם כה] מביאין לידי פיגול: הכא נמי. אף חטאת דבר הפוסל בה כגון שלא לשמה מוציאה ודבר המעכב בה כל הכתוב בעבודת דמה וטבילת אצבע בכלל (ז): אף אנן נמי תנינא. דטבילת אצבע מפגלת דתנן במנחות כל הקומץ כו] בכל ד' עבודות [אם] חישב על מנת לאכול שיריים או להקטיר קומץ למחר פיגול: בשלמא קומץ. מפגל דהיינו כשוחט שמוליא דם שהוא חלק גבוה *מן הבשר כז] [והבשר] שיריים הם אף זה הפריש קומץ מתוך שיריים וכן שאר ב' עבודות כח] א) דמפגל מהיקישא דהוקש מנחה לזבח דכתיב זאת התורה ואמר לקמן (דף נח.) כט] דהך היקישא מה שלמים מפגל ומתפגלין אף כל מפגלין ומתפגלין: התם ממילא. טפל הדם בכלי הכא קא שקיל בידיה ורמי: אלא כיון דלא סגי דלא יהיב. קומץ לכלי לקדשו בתוס כדאמרינן לעיל (דף יח.) שלא בכלי שרת פסולה ואמרינן טעמא במסכת סוטה בפרק שני (דף יד:) מידי דהוה אדם ל] לאו אע"ג דקדישתיה סכין בטוחר בהמה הדר בעי לקבוליה וקדושיה בכלי זימנא אחריתי קומץ נמי אע"ג דקדשה מנחה כולה בכלי בעי לקדושי קומץ זימנא אחריתי הלכך עבודה חשובה היא ומפגלה הכי נמי בטבילת אצבע כיון דלא סגי כו' היינו הולכה שמוליך הדם באצבעו (ח) לקרבן למזבח: לעולם דדמי לקבלה. הלכך אתיא בהיקישא דאיתקוש מנחות לשלמים דהא איתרבי קבלה בשלמים לפגל כדאמרי' לעיל ומתן כלי במנחה כקבלה בדם אבל טבילת אצבע לא איתרבאי ולא תיפשוט לא]: לא מפגלת. אם טבל על מנת להקטיר אימורין למחר: ולא מתפגלת. אם שחט [או קבל] ע"מ לטבול אצבע למחר: מאי לאו תנאי היא. דמר חשיב לה הולכה ומר לא חשיב לה הולכה: לא. דכ"ע הולכה היא והא דקתני אינה מפגלת רבי שמעון היא דאמר במתניתין הולכה לא מפגלא כדתנן ורבי שמעון מכשיר בהילוך:

כל

א) נ"ל דהא נ"ק

ויש לפרש במסקנא דנקט לשון פסול דאיירי בשלא לשמן דהוי בכל ד' עבודות ומיהו אשכחן דיקא דלא קאי לבסוף גבי כל הניסוס דמים באחר (קדושין דף כח:)*: **על** מנת לשפוך שירים למחר. ל"ע בפרק קמא דמעילה (דף ז.) דמיבעיא לן חישב לנשפכין מהו ופי' רבינו דהתם מיירי שנשפך מן הכלי על הרצפה ומיבעיא ליה אם מוליך אותו מקבלת דם הנשאר בכלי על מנת לזרוק מאותן נשפכין חוץ לזמנו שהרי ראויין לאוספן או דלמא כיון דבכוס איתיה דם וההוא דעל הרצפה הולך לאיבוד לא פסלה בהו*: **הג"ה** תהי בה ריש לקיש כלום למדנו אלא משלמים. תימה הא ריש לקיש גופיה קאמר לקמן (יד.) מודה רבי שמעון בהולכת (אברים) חטאות הפנימיות: **אי** מה שלמים כו'. זה אין שייך לומר דמחשבת יום שני לא יפסול בחטאת כמו בשלמים דפשיטא דבכל חד אזלינן בתר חוץ לזמנו דידיה: **אלא** מאי אית לך למימר דבר הפוסל בהן כו'. השתא מסיק דמסברא יש לנו לומר כן דדבר הפוסל מוליא מידי פיגול ודבר המעכב בה מביא לידי פיגול כמו בשלמים ואין שייך להקשות שכן נוהג בכל הזבחים: **זה** הכלל כל הקומץ ונותן בכלי. בהגשה אין פיגול דקמילה כנגד שחיטה ואין לו פיגול קודם שחיטה:

מודה

עב א מיי' פי"ג מהל' פסה"מ הל' ב ופי"ח שם הלכה ו:

עג ב מיי' פי"ג שם הלכה ז:

[ועי' תוס' מעילה ז. ד"ה חושב]

עד ג מיי' פי"ג שם הלכה ג:

עה ד מיי' פי"ג שם הלכה ו:

[ועי' ב"מ מה: ועי' מ"ש על לידון]

שיטה מקובצת
א] הריני שוחט ע"מ לקבל דמו למחר: ב] מחשבה והתניא יכול: ג] פנימית. ס"א אינו: ד] קמיה דבר פדא אמר ליה: ה] משלמים למדנו: ו] קאתיא ה"נ מרבויא דקרא קאתיא: ז] שמעתי מרבי רש"י גרים שטבילת אצבע מפגלת ול"נ מפגלת אצבע פירוש ר"ל כך אם חשב בשעת זריקה ע"מ לטבול למחר [מפגלת] הטבילה וזה אינו דאין זה מחשב בעבודה לאכילת אדם או למזבח. מהר"פ: ח] מפגלת בה אות ן' נמחק: ט] אין הכל משלמים למדנו פרש"י ודקשיא לך כו' תימה אמאי לא אמרינן כמו כן הואיל וטבילת אצבע מעכבת בחטאת והולכה מעכבת בשלמים מה עבודה המעכבת בשלמים (המביאה) [מביאה] לידי פגול אף טבילה המעכבת בחטאת הפנימית (המביאה) [מביאה] לידי פגול [וי"ל] טבילת אצבע לא שייך כלל בשלמים אבל שלא לשמו דשייך קצת בשלמים לענין דאין מרצין שפיר ילפינן זה מזה. מהר"פ: י] אלא כיון דלא סגי. פ"ה כיון דלא סגי (איהו) כו' עד למזבח וא"ת א"כ מאי טעמא בחטאות חיצונות נמי ליפסיל טבילת אצבע דלא סגי כו' ועוד קשה דבהקומץ זוטא אמר ר' ינאי הולכת בזר פסולה משום דכיון דלא סגי דלא עביד עבודה חשובה היא והכי דחי האי טעמא במסקנא ואמר הר"ם (דמשני)[דמרשני] בדיבוריה קרא לכתוב בפנימית וטבל ובחיצונית לא כתיב וטבל אלא ולקח ש"מ דלא אמרינן הך טעמא דכיון דלא סגי גבי חיצוניות וכן למסקנא לכך לא אמרינן הך סברא דלא סגי משום דא"כ אמאי כתיב בפנימית ולא כתיב בחיצוניות הא שייך האי טעמא אף בחיצוניות אלא ודאי האי סברא דלא סגי אע"ג דהוי בעלמא הבא ליתא וניחא הכל: יא] לא הא רבנן כו'. כלומר בין למר ובין למר הולכה היא אלא הא רבנן והא ר"ש כלומר הא ר"ש דהולכה לא פסלא במחשבה וה"ה טבילת אצבע נמי אע"ג דטעמא דר"ש בהולכה משום דאפשר לבטלה והכא בטבילת אצבע אי אפשר לבטלה מ"מ כיון דלא חשיבא טבילת אצבע עבודה רק מטעם הולכה לא יפסל בה טפי מחשבה מהולכה. כך נראה למורי מהר"ש ז"ל: יב] דבר שהוא אכילת: יג] וכי נמי: יד] הזבחים כדינן של שלמים הס"ד: טו] וקבל או הלך שלא לשמו לא יצאו: טז] דפסול ביה: יז] מפגלת ול"ג מפגלת אצבע: יח] וחוץ למקומו: יט] לאכול ממנו חוץ: כ] שכל מחשבה פסולה מוציאתו: כא] למקומו דבשלמים: כב] למקומו דשלמים: כג] שהרי פסולו: כד] טעם לומר בשלא: כה] הדם מביאו לידי: כו] הקומץ כו': כז] הבשר שהן שירים אף זה ותיבות והבשר תם ל"ש ונמחק: כח] עבודות מפגלים מהיקישא: כט] לקמן בהך היקישא: ל] אדם דם לאו: לא] התשום מנאי אי טבילת אצבע הוי כהולכה או לא הס"ד:

תורה אור
ויקר' ז

[נ"ל והתניא]

[לקמן כח: מנחות יז. חולין פה:]

הגהות הב"ח
(א) גמ' קמיה דבר פדא: (ב) שם משלמים למדנו אי מה: (ג) שם כלום למדנו כצ"ל וכן בכל העמוד: (ד) רש"י ד"ה ופרכינן וכו' למדנו וכי דין: (ה) ד"ה הואיל וכו' דבהדיא: (ו) ד"ה אלא וכו' מה יש לך לומר טעם: (ז) ד"ה הכא נמי וכו' בכלל מביאה הס"ד: (ח) ד"ה אלא כיון וכו' לקרבו למזבח:

גליון הש"ס
גמ' הא דאמר. עיין לעיל דף ט ע"ב תוס' ד"ה מחשבין:

מנחות יב.

נ"א על כרחין הייט קבלה עבודה חשובה

these are not indispensable for atonement![5] [13*b*]—There is no difficulty:[6] In the one case it means that he declared, 'Lo, I slaughter [this sacrifice] with the intention of receiving its blood to-morrow'; while in the other case it means that he declared, 'Lo, I receive the blood with the intention of pouring out its residue to-morrow'.[7]

One of the Rabbis said to Raba: Now does not intention disqualify at the pouring out of the residue and the burning of the *emurim*? Yet surely it was taught: You might think that intention is effective only in connection with the eating of the flesh. Whence do we know to include the pouring out of the residue and the burning of the *emurim*? From the text, *And if* [*any of the flesh . . .*] *be at all eaten* [*on the third day . . . it shall be an abhorred thing*]:[8] Scripture refers to two eatings, viz., eating by man and eating by the altar.[9] There is no difficulty: In the one case he declares, 'Lo, I sprinkle [the blood] with the intention of pouring out the residue
a to-morrow';[1] in the other he declares, 'Lo, I pour out the residue with the intention of burning the *emurim* to-morrow.'[2]

R. Judah the son of R. Ḥiyya said: I have heard that the dipping of the finger [in the blood][3] renders [a sacrifice] *piggul* in the case of an inner sin-offering.[4] Ilfa heard this and reported it before Bar Padda. Said he: Do we learn *piggul* from ought else but from a peace-offering?[5] Then as the dipping of the finger does not render a peace-offering *piggul*,[6] so in the case of a sin-offering too, the dipping of the finger does not render *piggul*. But do we really learn everything from a peace-offering? If so, [then reason thus:] as [a service] in the name of a different sacrifice does not free a peace-offering from *piggul*, so [a service] in the name of a different sacrifice does not free a sin-offering from *piggul*.[7] What then can you say?
b That it is deduced from the extension implied in Scriptural texts;[1] and so here too it is deduced from the extension implied in the Scriptural texts.[2]

R. Joshua b. Levi said: In this upper chamber I heard that the dipping of the finger renders *piggul*. Thereat R. Simeon b. Laḳish wondered: Do we learn *piggul* from ought else but from the peace-offering? Then as the dipping of the finger does not render the peace-offering *piggul*, so in the case of the sin-offering too, the dipping of the finger does not render it *piggul*. But do we then really learn everything from the peace-offering? If so, [then reason thus:] as [a service] in the name of a different sacrifice does not free a peace-offering from *piggul*, so [a service] in the name of a different sacrifice does not free a sin-offering from *piggul*?—Said R. Jose b. Ḥanina: Yes, indeed, we really learn everything from the peace-offering: since [the intention to consume it] without its precincts disqualifies a peace-offering, while [performing a service] for the sake of something else disqualifies a sin-offering, then as [the intention to consume it] without its precincts, which disqualifies the peace-offering, frees it from *piggul*, so [performing a service] for the sake of something else, which disqualifies the sin-offering, frees it from *piggul*. R. Jeremiah observed: The refutation [of this analogy] is at its side.[3] As for [the intention of consuming it] without its precincts, which disqualifies a peace-offering, [it frees it from *piggul*] because it operates [as a disqualification] in all sacrifices; will you say [the same of performing a service] for the sake of something else, which operates in the case of the Passover-offering and the sin-offering only? Rather, what must you say?[4] That that which disqualifies it [a peace-offering] frees it from *piggul*, while that which is indispen-
c sable for it renders it *piggul*;[1] so here too that which disqualifies it [the sin-offering] frees it from *piggul*, while that which is indispensable to it[2] renders it *piggul*.[3]

R. Mari said, We too have learned likewise: This is the general principle: Whoever takes the fistful [of the meal-offering], places it in the utensil, carries it [to the altar] or burns it [thereon] [renders it *piggul*].[4] Now as for *taking* the fistful, it is well [that this effects *piggul*, as] it corresponds to slaughtering; carrying [the fistful] corresponds to carrying [the blood]; burning [it] corresponds to sprinkling. But to what does putting [the fistful] into a utensil correspond? Shall we say that it is similar to receiving: is it then similar? There it is automatic,[5] whereas here he takes it himself and places it [in the utensil]. But since you cannot dispense with placing it [in the utensil],[6] you must say that it is an important service;[7] so here too, since one cannot dispense with it[8] you must say that it is [part of] carrying [the blood to the altar]!—No: in truth it is similar to receiving, and as to your objection: There it is automatic whereas here he takes it himself and places it [in the utensil, the answer is:] since both are [instances of] placing in a utensil, what does it matter whether it is automatic or whether he personally takes and places it [there]?

Shall we say that it is a controversy of Tannaim?[9] For one [Baraitha] taught: The dipping of the finger renders a sin-offering *piggul*; while another taught: It does not effect *piggul*, nor does it become *piggul*.[10] Surely then it is a controversy of Tannaim!—No:
d one agrees with our Rabbis and the other agrees with R. Simeon.[1] If R. Simeon, why particularly the dipping of the finger? Surely he

(5) Hence the intention of *piggul* at the reception of the blood does disqualify it. (6) So Rashi. Cur. edd.: 'Rather (answer thus)'. (7) Both may be styled intentions of *piggul* at the receiving of the blood, yet they are obviously different intentions; the former does not disqualify the sacrifice, whereas the latter does. (8) The emphatic '*be at all eaten*' is expressed in the original by doubling the verb, which in Talmudic exegesis denotes extension. (9) Sprinkling the blood and pouring out its residue at the foot of the altar are regarded as the eating of the altar. Thus in connection with these too, an illegitimate intention renders the sacrifice *piggul*, which contradicts the previous statement.

a (1) Then the sacrifice becomes *piggul*, since it was his intention to give the altar its food on the morrow, which is after its appointed time. (2) This does not render it *piggul*, since the wrongful intention was not at one of the four services. (3) V. Lev. IV, 6: *And the priest shall dip his finger in the blood, and sprinkle of the blood* etc. (4) One sacrificed at the inner altar. If he dipped his finger in the blood with the intention of burning the *emurim* the next day, the sacrifice becomes *piggul*. (5) The law of *piggul* is expressly written only in connection with the peace-offering, whence we extend the law to other sacrifices. (6) Since there is no dipping of the finger in the case of a peace-offering, the blood being dashed on the altar direct from the utensil. Since it is not a statutory service, it cannot render the sacrifice *piggul* even if it is done. (7) It is stated *infra* 28*b* that if a sacrifice is slaughtered with the intention of consuming it after its prescribed period, which renders it *piggul*, it remains *piggul* only if the subsequent services (receiving, carrying and sprinkling), which are technically designated the *mattirin* (q.v. Glos) are performed without any other intention which would disqualify it in any case. Now if one slaughtered a peace-offering with the intention of consuming it after its prescribed period, thus rendering it *piggul*, and then performed the subsequent services in the name of a different sacrifice, it remains *piggul*, since this change of name does not disqualify a peace-offering. A sin-offering in like circumstances ceases to be *piggul*, since change of name does disqualify it. (Though the flesh of course remains forbidden, it is not forbidden as *piggul*, so that eating it does not render one liable to *kareth*.) But if *piggul* of other sacrifices were completely analogous to *piggul* of a peace-offering, as Bar Padda's objection implies, then the sin-offering too should not be free from *piggul*.

b (1) The extension of *piggul* to other sacrifices is effected not by analogy with the peace-offering, but from extending particles in the text; hence the conditions of *freeing* it from *piggul* need not be the same. By the same reasoning the conditions for *making* it *piggul* need not be the same. (2) Hence though there is no *piggul* at the dipping of the finger in the case of the peace-offering, there is in the case of the sin-offering. (3) Obvious and inherent. (4) If you insist on retaining a complete analogy with the sin-offering.

c (1) If performed with a *piggul* intention. (2) Which excludes the dipping of the finger. (3) Thus the analogy is complete in its *principles*, though the detailed application of these principles varies according to the individual laws of the various sacrifices. (4) If he performs one of these services with the intention of consuming the rest or burning the fistful on the morrow.—The burning of the fistful corresponds to the sprinkling of the blood of an animal sacrifice. (5) It naturally drops into the basin. (6) I.e., it is a necessary part of the service. (7) It is a definite service in that an illegitimate intention thereat effects *piggul*. (8) *Sc.* the dipping of the finger. (9) Whether it is analogous to *receiving* the blood or to *carrying* the blood. (10) It does not effect *piggul*, if the priest dipped his finger with the intention of burning the *emurim* the next day; and it does not become *piggul*, if he slaughtered or received the blood with the intention of dipping the finger on the morrow.

d (1) All agree that it is part of carrying, but the ruling that it does not render it *piggul* is in accordance with R. Simeon in our Mishnah that there can be no *piggul* at the carrying.

said, [14*a*] Whatever is not [offered] on the outer altar, like the peace-offering, is not subject to *piggul*?[2]—Rather, both agree with the Rabbis,[3] yet there is no difficulty: the one refers to outer sin-offerings, while the other refers to the inner sin-offerings.[4] As for the outer sin-offerings, it is obvious, since 'and he shall dip' is not written in connection therewith?—It is necessary [to teach it]: One might argue, since *'and he shall take'* is written,[5] and if an ape came and placed [the blood] thereon [his finger], he [the priest] must take it again, it is as though 'and he shall dip' were written.[6] Therefore he informs us that for that very reason 'and he shall dip' is not written, so that it may imply the one and imply the other.[7]

R. SIMEON DECLARES IT FIT IN THE CARRYING. R. Simeon b. Laḳish said: R. Simeon agrees that an [illegitimate] intention disqualifies at the carrying [of the blood of] the inner sin-offerings, because it is a service which cannot be omitted.[8] But R. Simeon said: Whatever is not [offered] on the outer altar, like the peace-offering, does not entail liability on account of *piggul*?[9]—Said R. Joseph son of R. Ḥanina: He agrees that it disqualifies it,[10] *a minori*: If [offering] for the sake of something else disqualifies a sin-offering, though it is valid in the case of a peace-offering; is it not logical that [the intention of consuming it] after time disqualifies a sin-offering,
a seeing that it disqualifies in the case of a peace-offering?[1]

We have thus found [that the intention of consuming it] after time [disqualifies it]. How do we know that [the intention to eat it] without its precincts [disqualifies]?[2] If [you would learn it] from after time [by analogy], [you may refute it:] as for after time, that is because [it involves] *kareth*.[3] If from [sacrificing] for the sake of something else, that is because it operates at the *bamah*?[4]—Where does [sacrificing] for the sake of something else operate [as a disqualification]? [You must say] in the case of the Passover-offering and the sin-offering; and the Passover-offering and the sin-offering were not sacrificed at the *bamah*![5] Alternatively, it is a Scriptural analogy, [for *And if any of the flesh of the sacrifice of his peace-offerings be at all eaten*] *on the third* [*day*][6] refers to [the disqualification of] after time, while *it shall be an abhorred thing* [piggul][7] [refers to the intention of eating it] without its precincts.[8]

Raba said: If you will say that R. Simeon agrees with his son, who maintained, Between the *ulam*[9] and the altar is north, [R. Simeon will then hold that] an [illegitimate] intention is effective in the case of the carrying [of the blood] of inner sin-offerings only from within the entrance of the *ulam*.[10] And if you will say that [R. Simeon] agrees with R. Judah who maintained: The [whole of the] inner part of the Temple court is sanctified; [he will then hold that] an [illegitimate] intention is effective during the passage of the removal of the incense dishes only from the entrance of the *hekal*
b and without.[1] Again, if you will say that he holds that the sanctity of the *hekal* and that of the *ulam* is one, [then] an [illegitimate] intention is effective only from the entrance of the *ulam* and without.[2] And if you will say that within the entrance is as within [the *hekal*]; then an [illegitimate] intention is not effective even for one step save within the stretching out of his [one's] hand.[3] But if you will say that he holds that carrying without [using] the foot is not called carrying, then an [illegitimate] intention is not effective at all.

Abaye said to R. Ḥisda's *amora*:[4] Ask R. Ḥisda, what of carrying by a lay-Israelite [*zar*]?—It is valid, he replied, and a Scriptural text supports me: *And they killed the Passover lamb, and the priests dashed* [*the blood, which they received*] *of their hand, and the Levites*

(2) While we are now discussing the inner sin-offerings. (3) Who maintain that there is *piggul* at the carrying of the blood. (4) In the former case the dipping of the finger does not effect *piggul*, because Scripture does not say that the priest must dip his finger in the blood, but merely that he must take of the blood with his finger, which taking means the receiving of the blood (cf. *infra* 48*a*). (5) Lev. IV, 30. (6) Since we interpret *'he shall take'* in the sense that he must *personally* take the blood from the utensil, which is impossible without dipping his finger into it. (7) By not saying 'and he shall dip' Scripture intimates that the dipping is not a service on a par with the other services, and so it is not subject to *piggul*. At the same time *'and he shall take'* definitely implies that the priest *personally* must do this, which is in fact dipping. (8) Because it is unusual to slaughter it in the *hekal* (the inner sanctuary). Hence it is slaughtered in the Temple court and the blood carried to the horns of the inner altar in the *hekal*. Consequently R. Simeon's argument in the Mishnah does not apply here. (9) For eating its flesh. (10) Though one does not incur *kareth*, which is the penalty for eating *piggul*.

a (1) It will disqualify both the outer and the inner sin-offerings. (2) In the case of the inner sin-offerings. (3) V. *supra* n. 9. (4) V. Glos. Slaughtering for a different purpose is a disqualification of a sacrifice offered on a private *bamah*, when such was permitted. But slaughtering it without its precincts did not disqualify. (5) For only votive sacrifices were offered at the *bamah*, which excludes these two. Hence the refutation falls to the ground. (6) Lev. VII, 18. (7) Ibid. (8) Scripture, by including them both in the same verse, assimilates them to each other and makes the same law apply to both. In such a case the analogy cannot be rebutted even when there is a point of dissimilarity. (9) Lit., 'porch', 'entrance', 'hall'. The hall leading to the interior of the Temple. (10) A sin-offering must be slaughtered in the north (*infra* Ch. V.). Now it is possible for R. Simeon to agree with his son (*infra* 20*a*) that the northern part of the Temple court (*'azarah*) between the *ulam* and the altar, though actually to the west of the altar, and therefore one cannot apply to it the Scriptural injunction, *And he shall kill it on the side of the altar northward before the Lord* (Lev. I, 11), is nevertheless 'north' in respect of sacrifices of the higher sanctity. The reason for his view in the Mishnah on 13*a* is that he holds an illegitimate intention expressed during the passage of the blood from the place of slaughtering to the *ulam* is disregarded, since this passage could altogether have been avoided by slaughtering at the entrance of the *ulam*. But if he agreed with R. Jose that the sacrifice must be slaughtered actually between the northern side of the altar and the northern wall of the Temple court, the passage of the blood would be an indispensable service, and therefore an illegitimate intention during that passage would disqualify it.

b (1) The *hekal* is the 'Holy', the hall containing the golden altar etc., contrad. to the Holy of Holies (Jast.). The reference is to the burning of the shewbread incense, in virtue of which the shewbread was permitted to be eaten, in the same way as the sprinkling of the blood permits the flesh of the sacrifice; consequently it is on a par therewith and the same law applies to both. Now, if R. Simeon holds that the whole of the inner part of the Temple court is sanctified, so that the incense can be burnt there and not necessarily at the altar only, it follows that its carriage to the altar is not an essential act, and therefore an illegitimate intention does not render the shewbread *piggul*. (2) I.e., only at the five cubits of the thickness of the wall of the *ulam*. For the intention is not effective within the *ulam* itself, since that is as the inner part, nor is it effective without the entrance, since the shewbread incense can be burnt there. (3) He stands at the entrance of the *ulam* and stretches out his hand to the pavement; an illegitimate intention during that action is effective. (4) V. Glos.

*כל שאינו על מזבח החיצון כשלמים אין בו משום פיגול אלא הא והא רבנן ולא קשיא כאן בחטאות החיצונות כאן בחטאות הפנימיות חטאות החיצונות פשיטא (א) א] לא כתיב בהו וטבל אצטריך סלקא דעתך אמינא הואיל וכתיב ולקח ואי אתי קוף רמי להו אידיה בעי למישקל זימנא אחריתי (ב) כמאן דכתיב וטבל דמי [קמ"ל] ב] להכי לא כתיב וטבל דמשמע הכי ומשמע הכי: רבי שמעון מכשיר בהילוך: א"ר שמעון בן לקיש ג] מודה רבי שמעון בהולכת חטאות הפנימיות שמחשבה פוסלת בהו הואיל ועבודה ד] שאין יכול לבטלה והאמר *רבי שמעון כל שאינו על מזבח החיצון כשלמים אין חייבין עליו משום פיגול ה] א"ר (ג) יוסי ברבי חנינא מודה היה לפסול מקל וחומר ומה שלא לשמן שהוכשרו בשלמים פסול בחטאת חוץ לזמנו שפוסל בשלמים אינו דין שיפסול בחטאות (ד) ו] ואשכחן חוץ לזמנו חוץ למקומו מנלן אי מחוץ לזמנו מה לחוץ לזמנו שכן כרת אי משלא (ה) לשמה שכן נוהג בבמה ז] (חוב) שלא לשמן במאי נוהג בפסח וחטאת פסח וחטאת בבמה לא ח] קרבו ואיבעית אימא הקישא הוא *שלישי זה חוץ לזמנו פיגול ט] [זה] חוץ למקומו אמר רבא אם תימצי לומר ר' שמעון סבר לה כבריה דאמר *בין האולם ולמזבח צפון אין מחשבה מועלת בהולכת חטאות הפנימיות אלא מפתח אולם ולפנים ואם תמצי לומר סבר לה כרבי יהודה דאמר תוך עזרה מקדש אין מחשבה מועלת בהולכת סילוק בזיכין אלא מפתח היכל ולחוץ ואם תמצי לומר *סבר קדושת היכל ואולם חדא היא אין מחשבה מועלת אלא מפתח אולם ולחוץ ואם תמצי לומר תוך הפתח כלפנים אין מחשבה מועלת אפילו פסיעה אחת אלא בכדי הושטת ידו ואם תמצי לומר סבר הולכה שלא ברגל לא שמה הולכה אין מחשבה מועלת כלל: *א"ל *אביי לאמוריה דרב חסדא בעי י] מיניה מרב חסדא הולכה בזר מהו א"ל כשרה ומקרא מסייעני °וישחטו את הפסח ויזרקו הכהנים יא] את הדם מידם והלוים מפשיטים מתיב רב ששת *זר *ואונן

שיכור

רש"י

כל קרבן שאינו על מזבח החיצון כשלמים. שלמדנו מהם פיגול לכל הזבחים אין בו משום פיגול לקמן בפרק בית שמאי (דף מג.) : בחטאות החיצונות. איכא מפגלת דלא כתיב בהו וטבל אלא ולקח הכהן מדם החטאת באצבעו והיא לקיחה קבלה היא ומינה ילפינן קבלה לקמן באיזהו מקומן (דף מח.) : אילטריכא מהו דתימא הואיל וכתיב ולקח. דמשמע הוא בעצמו יקח : ואי אתי קוף ורמי להו אידיה. על אצבעו בעי מיהדר ומשקל אלמא ולקח נמי יב] אאצבעו קאי שיטבול אצבעו אימא כמאן דכתיב וטבל דמי : להכי לא יג] כתביה טבילה. בהדיא אלא כתב קבלה יד] ומדסמכיה אאצבעו וכתן הוא דיליף לטבול אצבעו שצריך ליקח בעצמו ולטבול דמשמע הכי דלא תהא טבילת אצבע טו] עבודה חשובה בהן לפגל מדלא אחשבה קרא להצריכה בפירוש ומשמע הכי שצריכה היא לטבול טז] בחטאות (ו) החיצונה ולא דלישקל קוף ולירמייה לדם על האצבע דבעינן לקיחת אצבע מעליותא דולקח נמי אאצבע קאי : שאי אפשר לבטלה. *דלאו אורח ארעא לשחוט בהיכל ועל כרחו הוא שוחטו בעזרה ומוליכה בהיכל לקרנות מזבח פנימי ולהזאת פרוכת : כל שאינו. כל קרבן שאין מתן דמו על מזבח החיצון לאפוקי חטאות הפנימיות וקס"ד דה"ה לפסול יז] דשלא לשמו : מודה יח] הוא לפסול. נהי דאין בהן פיגול להתחייב כרת על אכילתו אבל מודה הוא דמחשבה חוץ לזמנו פוסלתו מק"ו והכי נמי הוה מצי לתרוצי ליה אכן במחשבה שלא לשמו קיימינא דפסלה בהו אלא דבעי רבי יוסי בר' חנינא לאשמועינן דמחשבת חוץ לזמנו פסלה בהו לר"ש : חוץ לזמנו הפוסל בשלמים כו'. ומיהו כרת לא נפקא לן בו מינה דהא ק"ו מכח שלא לשמו אתי ודיו להבא מן הדין להיות כנדון : חוץ למקומו מנא לן. דהא חוץ למקומו נמי בשלמים כתיב ומינייהו גמרינן לכל הזבחים ולר' שמעון דלא גמר מינייהו אלא חיצונות כמותן מנ"ל דפסלה בפנימיות : אי מחוץ לזמנו. במה מצינו : אי משלא לשמו. ובק"ו כדלעיל: שכן נוהג בבמה. יט] [בקרבן במת יחיד בשעת היתר הבמות שהרי שינוי קדש הוא תאמר בחוץ למקומו דלא שאין מחילה בבמה] וכל הבקעה מקומו עד סוף העולם : ומשני שלא לשמו במאי נוהג. באיזה קרבן אתה מולא פסולו בפסח וחטאת והני בבמה לא קרבי דתנן לקמן (דף קיז.) כל הנידר ונידב קרב בבמה ושאינו נידר ונידב אינו קרב בבמה : ואיבעית אימא. חוץ למקומו מחוץ לזמנו אתי ולא פרכינן שכן כרת דהיקשא הוא דאיתקש חוץ למקומו לחוץ לזמנו בפ' שני (לקמן דף כח.) בקרא אחרינא דאמרינן אם האכל יאכל ביום השלישי זה מחשבת חוץ לזמנו לא יחשב לו פיגול יהיה קרא יתירא הוא לאתויי חוץ למקומו וכיון דאיתקוש גמרינן מהדדי ואין משיבין על ההיקש : אמר רבא את"ל ר' שמעון סבר לה כבריה דאמר. לקמן בפ' שני (דף כ.) : בין האולם למזבח צפון. חלק לפוני שבעזרה שבין האולם ולמזבח אע"ג דלא קרינן ביה על ירך המזבח לפונה דהא במערבו של מזבח הוא הוי צפון לענין שחיטת קדשי קדשים : אין מחשבה מועלת כ] בחטאות הפנימיות. אפילו לפסול : אלא מפתח האולם ולפנים. שאם חישב בהולכת הדם ממקום כא] שחיטתו עד האולם איכא מחשבה שהרי אפשר לבטל הולכה זו לשחוט אצל פתח האולם אבל אי סבר כרבי יוסי דפליג אדרבי אלעזר בר' שמעון ואומר אין צפון אלא כנגד המזבח מקיר כב] המזבח לפוני עד כותל העזרה לפונית הויא לה עבודה שאין יכול לבטלה דהא חטאת טעונה צפון לשחיטתה דכתיב במקום אשר תשחט העולה וגו' ולפון בעולה כתיב : ואת"ל. ר' שמעון סבר לה כר' יהודה דאמר לקמן בפ' קדשי קדשים (דף נט.) תוך עזרה מקדש כל רצפת העזרה בין האולם ולמזבח מקודשת להקטיר חלבים כמזבח עצמו דכתיב ביום ההוא קדש המלך את תוך החצר ותניא לקמן דברים ככתבן דברי ר' יהודה : אין מחשבה מועלת. לר' שמעון בהולכת בזיכי לחם הפנים שהן מתירין את הלחם כדם המתיר את הבשר וכקומץ המתיר את השיריים והלחם מתפגל במחשבת עבודת הבזיכים הואיל והן מתירין כג] *)רבי שמעון אי כרבי יהודה סבר לה אין מחשבת הולכה מועלת בה לפסול אלא מפתח היכל ולחוץ משהגיע לפתח היכל עד שמגיע ליציאת אולם לרצפת העזרה שלפניו דבכל ההיכל לא מהגיא מחשבה שהרי כל ההיכל כשר להושיב שם שלחן לסדר עליו עד הפתח ואולם כי עזרה כד] סבירא לן ומן האולם ולחוץ נמי לא מהגיא מחשבה בהולכה שהרי אפשר להקטירו על רצפת העזרה מיד אם ירצה נמצאת הולכתו עד המזבח שלא לצורך : ה"ג ואת"ל סבר רבי שמעון קדושת אולם והיכל חדא היא אין מחשבה מועלת אלא מפתח אולם ולחוץ. כלומר ה' אמות של עובי כותל פתחו של אולם דבכל חללו של אולם לא מהגיא דכפנים דמי וחוץ לפתח לא מהגיא דאפשר להקטיר שם : ואת"ל סבר כה] לה תוך פתח האולם כלפנים אין מחשבה מועלת אפילו פסיעה שלימה אלא בכדי הושטת ידו. עומד בפתח האולם ומושיט ידו לרצפה הייט הולכה ומהגיא בה מחשבה: הכי גרסינן ואם תמלי לומר הולכה שלא ברגל לא שמה הולכה אין מחשבה מועלת כלל. דהא הושטת ידו הולכה שלא ברגל היא: ויזרקו הכהנים את הדם מידם. [מידם] של שוחטין משמע כו] ושוחטין זרים נינהו ואשמועינן קרא שהזרים לוקחין אותו מיד המקבל ומוליכין אותו כז] לזרוק:

שיטור

*) נ"א ואי ר"ש כר' יהודה סבר כו' נ"ק

תוספות

מודה היה לפסול מקל וחומר. מכאן מתרצים ההיא דפ' הנזקין (גיטין דף נד: ושם) דקאמר ר' יוסי כהן גדול ביום הכפורים יוכיח דכי אמר פיגול מהימן ור' יוסי סבירא ליה כר"ש בפ' הקומץ זוטא (מנחות דף יד.) דאין פיגול אלא בדבר הנעשה על מזבח החיצון ולמאי דאמר הכא דמודה הוא לפסול ניחא דפיגול לאו דוקא ועוד יש לפרש הייני שלא לשמה ולא נהירא : ומה שלא לשמן כו'. תימה מה לשלא לשמן שכן נוהג בד' עבודות תאמר בחוץ לזמנו שאינו נוהג אלא בזריקה וכי האי גוונא פריך לעיל (דף ז.) כח] *(מה לחוץ לזמנו שכן כרת) ויש לומר דאי הוה פריך הכי הוה עביד ק"ו ומשני בעלים כט] *דהוי כפיגל בזריקה ומיהו קשה מה לשנוי בעלים שכן פוסל בזביחה בפסח ל] *או בזריקה לחודיה וי"ל דשלא לשמן יוכיח וילפינן במה הצד משנוי קדש ושנוי בעלים לא] : הג"ה תוך עזרה מקדש. טעמא דרבי יהודה לקמן בפרק קדשי קדשים (דף נט.) וצריך לדקדק לר' יהודה כיון דעזרה מקדש *היכי משכחת לה בפסולין דאם ירדו לא יעלו וי"ל דמשכחת לה [באותם] דירדו בלשכה או באולם או על גבי דף *ועדיף מאויר דאמר פ"ב (לקמן כו.) תלה ושחט פסול א"נ שחט על הרצפה ואח"כ נתן על הדף דהשתא ירדו *ול"ע דלקמן (דף קג.) מבעיא להו ירדו מהו שיעלו [וי"ל דשחט על הרצפה ואח"כ נתן על הדף] ועוד יש לומר דמודה רבי יהודה בדמים לקמן דבעי מזבח והדם לא עלה ברצפה ותו דלשון אם עלו דנקט הייט לדינא דקודם דאתא דוד וקדיש רצפה וקודם בנין שלמה. הג"ה לב]:

שיכור

עין משפט נר מצוה

עו א מיי' פ"ט מהל' ביאת מקדש הל' א ב והלכה טו ופ"ה מהלכות פסה"מ הלכה כו סמג לאוין שם:

עז ב מיי' פ"ט מהל' ביאת מקדש הל' טו ופ"ב הלכה ו סמג לאוין שנ:

עיין בסוף המסכתא שנדפס בשם הרב הגאון המפורסם הג"ד דמדינת פפלאן שמיישב בטוב טעם שאין מהכרח למחוק הג"ה זו

*דלא הוי פיגול אלא בזריקה נ"ק

דלא עדיף מאויר נ"ק

ע' רש"ק והתוס' גרסתו רש"ק

שיטה מקובצת

א] פשיטא דלא: ב] להכי לא כתיב וטבל כו'. וא"ת והיאך ס"ד לומר דלכתוב וטבל ולשתוק מולקח והא אצטריך לקמן לומר שתהא קבלה לשם חטאת וגם דקבלה טעונה צפון וי"ל דה"ק לכתוב תרתי וטבל עם ולקח : ג] מודה ר"ש כו'. פרש"י דלאו אורח כו' וקשה דאמרינן לקמן שלמים ששחטן בהיכל כשרים וכו' משום שלא יהא טפל חמור מן העיקר ולא פסלינן משום דלאו אורח ארעא ועוד דאמרינן התם עובד אדם עבודת רבו במקום רבו משמע דשפיר הוי אורח ארעא לכך נראה למורי דטעמא משום דחטאת טעונה צפון ובהיכל לא הוי צפון דאפילו למ"ד בין האולם ולמזבח קרוי צפון מודה דמבית החליפות ואילך לא הוי צפון וכ"ש בהיכל עצמו שמחיצות ההיכל מפסקת : ד] שאי אפשר לבטלה (ותיבות שאין יכול נמחק) והאמר ר' שמעון וכו'. וקס"ד דפסול שלא לשמו נמי ליתנהו בה יכ"ש פסול דחוץ לזמנו דלא יליף כלל משלמים ולכך פריך לריש לקיש ומשני דמודה לפסול אף חוץ לזמנו מק"ו ושלא לשמו אית ליה דמודה בה ר"ש וה"ה דהוי מצי למימר אנן בשלא לשמו קיימינן [ולא] בפיגול אלא דרוצה לתרץ לדבריו דאף בחוץ לזמנו דקפריך ליה מודה ר"ש דאף הוא פסול : ס] א"ר יוסי בר' חנינא. ע' תוס'

מסורת הש"ס

[לקמן מג. מו: שבועות ז.]

[לקמן מג. מו: שבועות ז.]

ס"א ל"ג

[לקמן כח.]

רש"ק

[גם כ. יומא נו.]

[לקמן נח: נט. עירובין ב. יומא מד:]

יומא מט.

נ"א רב ששת

גם

רש"ק

נ"ק

הגהות הב"ח

(א) גמ' פשיטא הא לא כתיב: (ב) שם זימנא אחריתי אימא כמאן: (ג) שם אמר רבי יוסף בר' חנינא מודה הוא לפסול וכו' שלא לשמו: (ד) שם אשכחן כצ"ל ואות ו' נמחק: (ה) שם אי משלא לשמו וכו' לשמו כמאי: (ו) רש"י ד"ה להכי לא וכו' בחטאות הפנימיות ולא דלישקול:

גליון הש"ס

רש"י ד"ה שא"א לבטלה דלאו אורח ארעא. ע' לקמן סג ע"א תוס' ד"ה שכן: תוס' ד"ה ומה וכו' או בזריקה לחודיה. סייעו דבש"ב פוסל בזורק לשם אחרים אבל בפיגול אינו פוסל אלא במחשב ע"מ לאכול או להקטיר למחר אבל לא בזורק בשביל מחר. אבל קשה דמה תירצו דשלא לשמן יוכיח הא בשלא לשמן ג"כ הכי הוא דפוסל בזורק לשם עולה וא"כ פרכינן מה לסכך שפוסלים בזריקה לחודה. אח"ז מצאתי שעמד בזה בצ"ק ותירוצו אינו מובן ע"ש : ד"ה כגב"ס וכו'. היכי משכחת לה בפסולים דאם ירדו לא יעלו. ע' לקמן פז ע"א תוס' ד"ה כגס ומנחות נז ע"ב תוס' ד"ה כגס :

לקמן (דף קד ע"ב) : ו] אשכחן אות ו' נמחק : ז] בבמה שלא לשמו : ח] לא קרבי ואבעית אימא הקישא הוא . עיין תוס' מנחות (דף עט ע"א) : ט] פיגול זה חוץ למקומו : י] בעי מיניה . פי' שא"ל לאמורא שישאל מרב חסדא : יא] תיבות את הדם נמחק : יב] נמי אאצבע אות ו' נמחק : יג] לא כתב ביה טבילה : יד] ומדסמכי אצבעו אונתן הוא דיליף לטבילת אצבע : טו] אצבע חשובה עבודה : טז] לטבול בחטאות : יז] לפסול בשלא : יח] מודה היה לפסול נהי כו' כרת על אכילתן אבל מודה הוא דמחשבת חוץ : יט] בבמה בקרבן במת יחיד בשעת היתר במות שהרי שינוי קודש תאמר בחוץ למקומו דלא שאין מודעות בבמה וכל הבקעה : כ] מועלת בהולכת חטאות הפנימיות : כא] ממקום שחיטה ועד האולם : כב] מקיר המזבח הצפוני : כג] מתירין ור"ש : כד] עזרה סבירא לן ס"א לא חשיב : כה] תיבת לה נמחק : כו] משמע השוחטין זרים : כז] המקבל ומוליכין אותו [illegible]

[illegible]

תורה אור

*שיכור יובעל מום בקבלה בהולכה בזריקה פסול יוכן יושב דוכן שמאל תיובתא והא רב חסדא קרא קאמר א] הדעביד מעשה אצטבא רבה ורב יוסף דאמרי תרוייהו הולכה בזר מחלוקת ר' שמעון ורבנן רבי שמעון דאמר עבודה שאפשר לבטלה לאו עבודה היא כשרה בזר לרבנן ופסולה א"ל אביי ב] והא שחיטה דעבודה שא"א לבטלה וכשרה בזר א"ל *שחיטה לאו עבודה היא ולא *והאמר ר' זירא אמר רב ישחיטת פרה בזר פסולה ואמר רב (א) עלה ג] אלעזר וחוקה כתיב בה שאני פרה *דקדשי בדק הבית היא ולאו כל דכן הוא קדשי בדק הבית הויא עבודה קדשי מזבח לאו עבודה היא אמר רב שישא בריה דרב אידי מידי דהוה אמראות נגעים דלאו עבודה היא ובעיא כהונה והרי הולכת אברים לכבש דעבודה שאפשר לבטלה היא חופסולה בזר דכתי' °והקרי' הכהן את הכל [והקטיר] המזבחה (ויקרא א) *ואמר מר זו הולכת אברים לכבש היכא *דגלי גלי והיכא דלא גלי לא גלי ולאו כל דכן הוא ומה הולכת אברים לכבש דלא מעכבא כפרה בעיא כהונה הולכת דם דמעכבא כפרה [לא כ"ש] (מיבעיא) *איתמר ד] [נמי] אמר עולא א"ר אלעזר הולכה בזר פסולה אפילו לרבי שמעון איבעיא להו *הולכה שלא ברגל שמה הולכה או לא שמה הולכה ת"ש וכן יושב וכן שמאל פסול הא עומד דומיא דיושב כשר דלמא יושב דקשייף מישף עומד דומיא דיושב ה] דנייד פורתא ת"ש *שחט ישראל וקבל הכהן נתנו לחבירו וחבירו לחבירו התם נמי *דנייד פורתא ומאי קמ"ל °ברוב עם הדרת מלך (משלי יד) ת"ש *קבל הכשר ונתן לפסול יחזיר לכשר אימא יחזור הכשר ויקבלה איתמר אמר עולא א"ר יוחנן יהולכה שלא ברגל לא שמה הולכה
אפשר

רש"י

שיכור. היינו שתוי יין ו]: מעשה אילטבא. עומדין במקומן הזר אצל הכהן המקבל והכהן שהוא לו ואוחזו עד שבא הזורק ונוטלו מידו ואין הזר ז] מקרבן לצד המזבח לא בהולכת רגל ולא בהושטת יד אלא כאילטבא זו שמניחין כלי עליה: והא שחיטה כו'. אלמא טעם לא בהא תלי וליכא למיפשט לרבנן דמשום דסבירא להו דהולכה אי אפשר ח] *לבטל א"כ בשחיטה דאי אפשר לבטל תיפסל בזר והא שחיטה בזר כשרה: ומשני שחיטה לאו עבודה היא. מדאתכשרו בה כל הפסולים אבל מידי דהוי עבודה ואי אפשר לבטלה פסול בזר: ואמר רב עלה. לפרושי ט] למילתיה מאי טעם פסולה דכתיב בשחיטתה ונתתם אותה אל אלעזר הכהן ושחט וכתיב בה בפרה חוקה וכל היכא דכתיב חוקה עכובא: שאני פרה. י] וחילוק טעם זה אינו מטעם עבודה דהא אינה קדושת מזבח אלא קדושת דמים בעלמא כקדשי בדק הבית ועל כרחך טעם הפוסל בה לאו משום תורת עבודה אלא גזירת הכתוב בעלמא היא אבל בקדשי מזבח דשייכי בהן יא] עבודות לא חשיבא להיות עבודה: הולכת אברים אפשר לבטלה. שאם רצה מפשיט ומנתח אצל המזבח: היכא דגלי גלי. הולכת אברים דגלי בהן כהן בעינן כהן אבל הולכת הדם דלא גלי בהו כהן לרבי שמעון יב] דאפשר לבטלה לא בעי כהן: אפילו לר' שמעון. דאע"ג דאמר ר' שמעון לא פסל בה מחשבה משום דאין היתר הקרבן תלוי בה ולא קרינא בה דברים המביאים לידי אכילה אבל עבודה הוי ליפסל בזר: שמה הולכה. (ב) ופסלה בה מחשבה לרבנן או אם עשאה זר פסולה: או לא שמה הולכה. ולא פסלה מחשבה: וכן כהן יושב. קתני *דפסול בהולכה יג] (ג) [הא עומד] דאינו מוליך אלא בהושטת יד דומיא דיושב כשר אלמא שמה הולכה: דשייף מישף. שמגרר עצמו לצד המזבח שייף משפשף בקרקע שייף מגרר כמו שייף ליה מישחא (שבת דף י:) שף אחת ובועט שתים (מנחות דף עו.) פדיי"ר ודכוותה דוק מיניה בעומד דכשרה דנייד פורתא בשפשוף רגלים: ת"ש דתנן בסדר הפסח שחט ישראל כו'. כן היה דרכן לעשות: נתנו לחבירו. דקתני התם הכהנים עומדים שורות שורות: יחזיר לכשר. שנתנו לו ואשמעינן יד] תרתי בה חדא דלא מיפסל במאי דאפסקיה פסול (ד) ואשמעינן טו] בה דהולכה זו שעשה הכשר שלא ברגל שהושיט לפסול שהיה עומד בצד המזבח לא נעשית בהכשר ולא שמה הולכה דקתני יחזירנה למי שנתנה לו טז] ואי הולכה שלא ברגל שמה הולכה אמאי יחזירנה לאחור יבא כשר ויטלנה מידו לצד המזבח יז] וזה לא יושיטנה לו אלא דמעשה אצטבא בעלמא עביד: אימא יחזור כשר. לצד המזבח ויקבלנו יטלנו מיד הפסול דהולכת (ה) כשר קמא כשרה: לא שמה הולכה. ואינה כשרה להוליכה כן ואין מחשבה מפגלת בה:
אפשר

תוספות

שיכור. פירש בקונטרס שתוי יין ולא משמע כן בפרק מומין אלו פסולין באדם (בכורות דף מה:) אלא שיכור בשאר דברים המשכרים יח] *ודלא כר' יהודה דאמר מחלי עבודה מיהו שיכור דתנן התם ודאי לא הוי שתוי יין כדפרי' התם בהדי מומין דמחלי עבודה בעי למיחשבה אבל שיכור דהכא פשטיה משמע שתוי יין והא כדאיתא והא כדאיתא ולכולי עלמא מחלל לעבודה כדפריך התם בפשיטות אחולי מיחל עבודה הוא*: והא שחיטה שאי אפשר לבטלה וכשרה. פרש"י אלמא לאו באפשר לבטלה תלי ואת אמרת לרבנן פסול ותימה דמאי פירכא לרבנן ודאי לא בהא תלי והא דפסלי בהולכה משום דמקבלה ואילך מצות כהונה אלא פריך דמכשיר לר' שמעון משום דאפשר לבטל הא לא תלי בהא מדמכשר זר בשחיטה אע"ג דאי אפשר לבטלה ובסמוך דפריך מהולכת אברים לרבי שמעון פריך וכן יט] דמייתי אמר ר' אלעזר הולכה בזר פסולה כ] לרבי שמעון: הג"ה שחיטה לאו עבודה היא. פירש בקונטרס מדאתכשרו בה כל הפסולים ואי אפשר לומר כן כא] דאהכשר זר גופה מייתי לה כב] [הכא] ובפ"ק דמנחות (דף ו:) ומיהו יש ליישב פירושו דכיון דבשום מקום לא בעי כהן בשחיטה לאו עבודה היא ולהכי פריך עלה מפרה וה"ר יעקב דאורליינ"ש מפרש לאו עבודה היא לפי שעוה בחולין ובקדשים א"כ לאו מטעם עבודה נוה המקום שחיטה ולי נראה לאו עבודה היא מדמכשרינן לקמן בפ' שני (דף כו.) עומד בדרום והושיט ידו לצפון ושחט בקדשי קדשים ובמקבל פסול דדרשינן אותו בצפון ולא שוחט בצפון אבל כג] מקבל בצפון ובשלמים מכשירין עומד בחוץ והושיט ידו לפנים ושחט ואם קבל קבלתו פסולה דדרשינן בפ' כל הפסולין (לקמן דף לב:) בן הבקר לפני ה' ולא שוחט לפני ה' אבל קבל קבלתו פסולה משום דכתיב לעמוד לפני ה' לשרתו אלמא כל שירות לפני ה' ש"מ כד] מדמכשיר רחמנא עומד בחוץ והושיט ידו לפנים ושחט מכלל דשחיטה כה] לאו עבודה היא ועוד מדאמר בההיא שמעתא בפ"ב (דף כו.) כו] נתלה ושחט שחיטתו כשרה דשחיטה על ירך אמר רחמנא ולא שוחט על ירך (אמר רחמנא) אלמא דשחיטה לאו עבודה היא דאי עבודה היא לא הוה מכשר רחמנא בכי האי גוונא דהא כז] נתלה וקבל אמרינן דקבלתו פסולה משום דאין דרך שירות בכך ומדפריך הכא ובפ' חטאת העוף (לקמן דף סח:) ובפ"ק דמנחות (דף ו:) מפרה דאמר רב שחיטת פרה בזר פסולה משמע קצת כפי' הקונטרס מיהו גם לפי מה שפירשתי יש ליישבו אבל קשה לי לפירושו דא"כ לשמעון התימני דבעי פרק כל הפסולין (לקמן דף לב:) שיהא כח] ידיו של שוחט לפנים מן הנשחט הויא שחיטה עבודה א): שאני פרה דקדשי בדק הבית היא. בפ"ק דחולין (דף יא.) פירשתי ב): והרי הולכת אברים לכבש דאפשר לבטלה ופסולה בזר דכתיב והקריב הכהן את הכל המזבחה ואמר מר כו' כט] שאני הכא דגלי קרא. הקשה ה"ר אליהו מאברוויקא הקדוש דבפ"ב דיומא (דף כז.*) אמרינן מדאצטריך למכתב כהן בהולכת אברים לכבש פי' לגופיה לא אצטריך אלא לגלות דהולכת עלים למזבח לא בעי כהן ומדאצטריך מעוט להולכת עלים א"כ סידור ב' גזרי עלים בעי כהונה ל] ג) (בלאו קרא מטעם) וא"כ רבי שמעון דבעי ב' כהנים התם (דף כו:) לשני גזרי עלים מנא ליה דהא כהן דכתב גבי הולכת אברים אצטריך לגופיה משום דאפשר לבטלה וי"ל דרבי שמעון לטעמיה דאמר התם (דף מה.) הצאת אליתא לא צריך למכתב ביה כהן דוכי תעלה על דעתך שזר קרב למזבח וא"כ רבי שמעון ע"כ שני גזרי עלים בעו כהונה בלא קרא מטעמא דוכי תעלה על דעתך כו' דכמו דלית ליה במפוחא לית ליה אפשר להו בזריקה אבל לרבנן אית להו בזריקה כמו דאית להו במפוחא וכהן דגבי הולכת אברים לגופיה לא אצטריך דהא לית לא] טעמא דאפשר לבטלה אלא לגלות על שני גזרי עלים דבעי כהונה ובפ' הקומץ רבה (מנחות דף כ.) לב] אמר לא מלח כהן אלא זר פריך וכי תעלה על דעתך שזר קרב יש לומר דאפילו לרבנן דאית להו במפוחא וזריקה פריך שאין יכולין למלוח בטוב על ידי זריקה: לג] (כל זה בהג"ה דאיבעיא להו) ד) איבעיא להו הולכה שלא ברגל שמה הולכה או לא. פרש"י לפסול בה מחשבה וגם בזר דאי שמה הולכה מחשבה שלא לשמו או פיגול פוסלת בה ואי לא שמה הולכה לד] אינה קרויה עבודה וצריך להחזיר המזרק אחריו ולעשות הולכה ברגל וגם אם עשאה זר או יושב אין בכך כלום ויכול לתקנה לה] בכהן [בהולכת רגל] דכהן או אם זר מוליך [בהולכת רגל] פסולה [ואינו] יכול לתקנה בכהן להחזירה ולהוליכה כהן וקאמר ת"ש וכן יושב פסול הא עומד דומיא דיושב שאינו זז ממקומו כשר אלמא הויא הולכה ועשה עבודה כתקנה ולכך נמי כי עשאה מיושב פסול דכתיב לעמוד לשרת אבל מיושב פסול לא מצי מוכח דהויא הולכה עבודה בלאו דיוקא [משום] דדלמא לאו עבודה היא ויושב פסול היינו כי לא תקנה ולא החזיר הדם לאחוריו לעשות הולכה אחרת:
הולכה

א) [ע' תוס' יומא מב. ד"ה שחיטה שכתבו ישוב על זה] ב) [ע"ע תוס' ע"ז כג: ד"ה אלא מעתה] ג) רש"קמ"ז ד) ע' נ"ק שמהפך הגי' של תוס'

עין משפט נר מצוה

נ"י סל"ק וכר"י דאמר ובכ"מ לרבי יהודה
עח א מיי' פ"א מהל' ביאת מקדש הל' א ופ"ה שם הלכה טו סמג לאוין ש:
[וע' היטב תוס' בכורות מה: ד"ה ובשאר]
עט ב מיי' שם פ"ו הל' א ופ"ט הלכה טו:
פ ג מיי' פ"ב שם הלכה ת ופ"ט הל' טו:
[לקמן סח: יומא מב. מנחות ה: ו:]
פא ד מיי' פ"ב שם הל' יח ופ"ט הלכה טו ופ"ד מהל' עבודת יוה"כ הלכה א:
פב ה מיי' פ"א מהל' פסה"מ הלכה כו:
פג ו מיי' פ"א מהלכות פרה הלכה ב ופ"ד הלכה יז:
[עי' לעיל ז: מנחות נב: מ"ק ז:]
פד ח מיי' פ"א מהל' פסה"מ הלכה כב:
ל"א קשיא
פה ט מיי' פ"א מהל' קרבן פסח הל' יד:
פו כ מיי' פ"א מהלכות פסה"מ הלכה כג:

מסורת הש"ס

ל"א לבטל ותיפסל בזר א"כ כו' נ"ק
יומא מב. ע"ש מנחות ה: לקמן סח:
[יומא מב. וש"נ]
לעיל ד. לקמן כד: לה. פסחים סה: חגיגה יא. [יומא כז. מנחות י.]
מנחות יג:
גי' הל"ק דפסול הא אינו יושב ואינו מוליך אלא בהושטת יד כו' כצ"ל
[לקמן לב.]
[שם ד"ה הולכת]

הגהות הב"ח

(א) גמ' ואמר רב עלה אלעזר וחוקה: (ב) רש"י ד"ה שמה וכו' פסלה בה מחשבה: (ג) ד"ה וכן וכו' דפסול בהולכה והא יושב אינו מוליך: (ד) ד"ה יחזיר וכו' פסול אידך לאשמעינן וכו' דאי הולכה: (ה) ד"ה אימא וכו' דכשר קמא:

שיטה מקובצת

א] קאמר דעבידי: ב] והא שחיטה. פ"ה נהי דרבנן עבדו אשר כשא שאפשר פ"מ לא פסלה זר בהולכה שהרי יש עבודה שאי אפשר כגון שחיטה ומכשרה בזר אלמא טעמא דלאו הא בהא תליא ולא נהירא דשאני הכא דגלי קרא. ועוד קשה דבסמוך פריך לר"ש מהולכת אברים והא לא פריך לר"ש לכך נראה דה"פ איך יכשיר ר"ש בהולכה שאמר משום דאפשר לבטלה הוא והא אין הדבר תלוי בזה דהא שחיטה דאי אפשר לבטלה וכשרה בזר א"כ היינו טעמא דגלי קרא בקבלה ואילך מצות כהונה ופסולין בזר בכל ענין בין אפשר ובין לא אפשר ועוקר קבלה בזר פסולה ואפילו לר"ש [בהולכה] (דלא [פסל בהולכה] לר"ש) דפסלה (הא"ל) דאפשר לבטלה דשאני לשמו כמחשבה פיגול דחזי כשחיטה ואם האכל רבנן דברים המביאין לידי אכילה הלכך כיון דאפשר הקרבן תלוי בהולכה (לזר) [לא] פסלה בה מחשבה באם פ"ס עבודה היא ופסולה בזר: ג] עלה ס"א מאי טעמא: ד] איתמר נמי: ה] דנייד פורתא.

שיטה מקובצת

מהר"ם: כב] הבא ובפ"ק: כג] אבל המקבל: כד] ש"מ מדאכשר: כה] דשחיטה. ס"א מכלל דשאר שחיטות לאו: שירות וגו': כו] דנתלה: כז] דהא דנתלה: כח] שיהא ידי השוחט לפנים: כט] ואמר מר כו' ומשני דשאני: ל] תיבות בלאו קרא מטעם נמחק: לא] לית להו: לב] רבה דאמר: לג] תיבות כל זה כהגה דאיבעיא להו נמחק: לד] הולכה אינה כו'. זה לשון תלמיד הר"פ הולכה שלא ברגל לענין דפסלה בה מחשבה לרבנן או אם עשה זר פסולה כך פי' הקונטרס ולא נהירא דמאי בעי אם פסל בה מחשבה ופשיט ליה מדקאמר הא עומד דומיא דיושב לפשוט ליה תא מפשיטות המשנה דפסלה יושב אלמא הולכה שלא ברגל הולכה וחשיבא עבודה היא דאי לאו עבודה היא אמאי מיפסלא ביושב לכ"נ דלענין דמפסל בה מחשבה פשיט ליה דפסולה דאי שמה הולכה א"כ איפסלא במחשבה ואי לא שמה הולכה אם כן הוי הולכה כמי שאינו וצריך לחזור ולעשותה אלא לענין לחזור ולעשות קא בעי והכי קאמר הולכה שלא ברגל שמה הולכה לענין שלא חסר עבודת הולכה ואינו צריך לחזור ולעשותה או לא שמה הולכה והוי כמש חיסר עבודת הולכה ואפילו אם עמד כהן צריך לחזור ולעשותה הלכך פשיט ליה מדיוקא דעומד דומיא דיושב כשר אלמא דשמה הולכה דאי לא שמה הולכה היאך עומד דומיא דיושב כשר הרי חסר עבודה ע"כ: לה] הכהן בהושטת יד דכהן ואי שמה עבודה אם זר מוליך בהושטת יד פסולה ואינו יכול כו' תיבות בהולכת רגל או בהולכת רגל נמחק:

ד] דנייד פורתא. [ותימה] אי אמרת בשלמא דלא נייד אשמועינן דהולכה שלא ברגל שמ"ה הולכה אלא אי אמרת דנייד מאי אשמועינן. הר"פ: ו] יין לקמן בפ"ב יליף מקראי דכל הפסולין מחללין העבודה חוץ מן השתויה: ז] חוץ מקרבו: ח] אפשר לבטלה דא"כ: ט] לפרושי טעמא למלתא מאי טעם פסולה דכתיב אלעזר בשחיטתה: י] פרה חילוק: יא] בהן עבודה לא את ו' ת' נמחק: יב] שמעון דלא משוי אפשר לבטלה כאי אשר: יג] בהולכה הא יושב אינו מוליך אלא בהושטת יד ולא פסול אלא משום יושב דבעינן לעמוד ולשרת הא עומד ומוליך ותיבות דאינו אלא ל"ש ונמחק: יד] ואשמועינן בה תרתי חדא: טו] תיבת בה נמחק: טז] לא צריך שיחזיר לכשר שנתנה לו ואי: יז] המזבח וזר לא: יח] המשכרים לר"י תיבת ודלא נמחק: יט] כן נראה: כ] פסולה אפילו: כא] כן והרי בהולכה נמי על זה אנו דנין דלתכשר [בזר] ויש ליישב פי' הקונטרס לאו עבודה דלא מצינו בשום מקום דהקפידה תורה להצריך בה כהן הלכך אע"ג דאי אפשר לבטלה עשויה בזר פריך והרי שחיטת פרה דבעינן כהונה אלמא עבודה היא ואפ"ה כשרה בזר בשאר קדשים.

a *flayed them.*[1] R. Shesheth objected: A *zar*, an *onen*,[2] [14b] one who is intoxicated and one who is [physically] blemished are unfit to receive [the blood], carry [it] and sprinkle [it], and the same applies to one who is sitting and to [the performance of these by] the left hand. This is indeed a refutation! But R. Ḥisda quotes a text?—It means that he [the *zar*] served as a [mere] post.[3]

Rabbah and R. Joseph both maintained: Carriage by a *zar* is a [subject of] controversy between R. Simeon and the Rabbis. [According to] R. Simeon who says that a [Temple] service which can be dispensed with is not a service, [carriage] by a *zar* is valid. But according to the Rabbis it is invalid. Said Abaye to them: But slaughtering is a service which cannot be dispensed with, and yet it is valid [when done] by a *zar*?—Slaughtering is not a service, he replied.[4] Is it not? Surely R. Zera said in Rab's name: The slaughtering of the [red] heifer by a *zar* is invalid; and R. Papa[5] observed thereon: [The reason is because] *'Eleazar'* and *'Statute'* are written in connection with it.[6]—The [red] heifer is different, because it is of the holy things of the Temple repair.[7] But does it not follow *a fortiori*: it is a service in the case of the holy objects of the Temple repair, yet it is not a service in the case of holy objects dedicated to the altar![8]—Said R. Shisha the son of R. Idi: Let it be analogous to the inspection of [leprous] plagues, which is not a b service, and yet requires the priesthood.[1]

Yet the carrying of the limbs to the ascent[2] is a service which can be dispensed with,[3] and yet it is invalid [when done] by a *zar*, for it is written, *And the* priest *shall offer* [bring near] *the whole, and make it smoke* [burn it] *upon the altar*,[4] and a Master said: This refers to the carrying of the limbs to the ascent?—Where [Scripture] has revealed [that a priest is required], it has revealed [it], but where [Scripture] has not revealed [it], it has not.[5] But does not [the reverse] follow *a fortiori*: if the carrying of the limbs to the ascent requires the priesthood, though it is not indispensable to atonement,[6] how much the more [does] the carrying of the blood [require a priest], seeing that it is indispensable to atonement![7]

It was stated likewise: 'Ulla said in R. Eleazar's name: Carriage by a *zar* is invalid even according to R. Simeon.

It was asked: Is carriage without [moving] the foot[8] called carriage[9] or not?—Come and hear: And the same applies to one who is sitting and to [the performance of these by] the left hand, [which renders it] invalid. Hence standing similar to sitting[10] is valid!—[No:] perhaps sitting means that he drags himself along, [and then] standing similar to sitting means that he moves slightly.

Come and hear: A [lay-] Israelite slaughtered [the Passover-offering] and a priest received [the blood]; he handed it to his colleague, and his colleague to his colleague![11]—There too it means that they [the priests] moved slightly. Then what does he c [the Tanna] inform us?[1]—That *in the multitude of people is the king's glory*.[2]

Come and hear: If a fit person received [the blood] and handed it to an unfit one, the latter must return it to the fit one![3]—Say, the fit person must go round and take it.[4]

It was stated: 'Ulla said in R. Joḥanan's name: Carriage with-

a (1) II Chron. XXXV, 11. Thus the priests were only required for the sprinkling, but the blood was brought to them (which is the carrying) by those who slaughtered the sacrifice, these being *zarim*. (2) V. Glos. (3) On which the blood was placed. A priest received the blood and gave it to the *zar*, who held it until another priest took it from him and carried it to the altar. Thus the *zar* did not carry it himself but was completely passive. (4) Rashi: Since it may be done by all who are otherwise unfit to perform the sacrificial service. (5) Emended text (BaḤ). (6) Num. XIX, 2 *seq.*: *This is the* statute *of the law which the Lord hath commanded, saying: Speak unto the children of Israel, that they bring thee a red heifer . . . and ye shall give her unto* Eleazar *the priest . . . and he shall* slaughter *her* (this is the literal translation, not as E.V.) *before his face*. Thus the text specifies that Eleazar, viz., a priest, must slaughter, and by referring to it as a *'statute'* intimates that this is indispensable. This proves that slaughtering is a service. (7) This is the technical term for all objects dedicated to the Temple which cannot be sacrificed. (8) Surely if it is a service in the former case it is all the more so in the latter.

b (1) And likewise with the red heifer, being of the holy things of the Temple repair, the slaughtering thereof is not deemed in the category of Temple services, and the requirement of a priest is a special feature of the ritual connected therewith. (2) The inclined ascent leading to the altar.—These limbs were carried there for burning. (3) By slaughtering the sacrifice near the altar, and burning the limbs on the spot. (4) Lev. I, 13. (5) Hence according to R. Simeon the carrying of the blood to the altar may not require a priest, notwithstanding that the carrying of the limbs does. (6) Even if the limbs are not burnt at all the purpose of the sacrifice is achieved. (7) *Var. lec.* add: this is indeed a difficulty. (8) When the blood is merely transferred by hand. (9) So that an illegitimate intention will disqualify the sacrifice, on the view of the Rabbis; and likewise if it is performed by a *zar*. (10) Viz., standing without moving. (11) This is a description of the sacrifice of the Passover. The priests stood in rows, passing the blood from one to another, until it reached the altar for sprinkling. Thus the blood was carried without the priests moving their feet.

c (1) In stating that the priests were drawn up in rows. (2) Prov. XIV, 28. (3) Hence carrying without using the feet does not count at all. For otherwise the unfit might simply be regarded as a post on which the fit person had placed the blood, and it would not be necessary for the former to *return* it to the latter, but simply for another *fit* person to come and take it. (4) He must go to the other side of the unfit and take it from him. In that case his first carriage definitely counts.

out [moving] the foot is not called carriage. [15*a*] [Now the question arises:] Can this be repaired or can it not be repaired?[5]—Come and hear: If a fit person received [the blood] and handed it to an unfit one, the latter must return it to the fit one. Now, granted that the fit person receives it back, yet if you think that it cannot be repaired, it has [already] been made invalid. [This does not prove anything:] do you think that the lay-Israelite[6] stood within? No: it means that the lay-Israelite stood without.[7] It was stated: 'Ulla said in R. Joḥanan's name: Carriage without [moving] the foot is invalid. This proves that it cannot be repaired.

R. Naḥman raised an objection to 'Ulla: If [the blood] was spilled from the vessel on to the pavement, and one [a priest] collected it, it is valid?[8]—The circumstances here are that [the
a blood] had run outward.[1] Would it run without [only] and not enter within?[2]—[It fell] on sloping ground.[3] Alternatively, [it fell] into a depression.[4] Another alternative is that it [the blood] was thick.[5] But does the Tanna trouble to teach us all these![6] Moreover, instead of teaching in another chapter, 'If it was spilt on to the ground[7] and [the priest] collected it, it is unfit'[8]; let him [the Tanna] draw a distinction in that very case,[9] thus: When does this hold good? [Only] if [the blood] ran without; but if it entered within, it is unfit? This is indeed a refutation.

It was stated: Carriage without moving the foot is [the subject of] a controversy between R. Simeon and the Rabbis.[10] In the case of a long carriage all agree that it is unfit; they disagree only in respect of a short carriage.[11] This was ridiculed in the West [Eretz Israel][12]: if so, as for [the law that] an [illegitimate] intention[13] disqualifies a sin-offering of a bird, how is this possible according to R. Simeon? if [the priest] expressed this intention *before* the blood issued, it is nothing;[14] if *after* the blood has issued, then surely the precept has already been performed?[15]—What difficulty is this? perhaps [the priest expressed his intention] between the issuing [of the blood] and its reaching the altar? For surely R. Jeremiah asked R. Zera: What if one was sprinkling, and the sprinkler's hand was cut off before the blood reached the altar air-space? And he answered him, It is invalid. What is the reason? Because it is essential that 'he shall sprinkle' and 'he shall put' [of the blood upon the
b horns of the altar].[1]

When R. Papa and R. Huna the son of R. Joshua came from [the academy] they stated: This was the [point of their] derision: Do they not differ about a long passage? Surely they differ precisely in respect of a long passage?[2] Rather, all agree that it is not invalid in the case of a short passage;[3] they differ in the case of a long passage.

If a *zar* carried [the blood],[4] whereupon a priest returned it and then carried it [himself], — the sons of R. Ḥiyya and R. Jannai disagree. One maintains that it is valid, while the other holds that it is invalid; the former holding that it can be repaired,[5] while the latter holds that it cannot be repaired. If a priest carried [the blood] but returned it and then a *zar* carried it [to the altar] again,—said R. Simi b. Ashi: He who declares it valid [in the previous case], holds [here] that it is invalid; while he who declares it invalid [there], holds [here] that it is valid.[6] Raba said: Even he who declares it invalid [in the previous case], holds that it is invalid

(5) Do we regard the carriage as simply having been omitted, in which case the blood can be taken back and the carriage performed; or do we regard the carriage as having been performed improperly, thus disqualifying the blood permanently, so that it cannot be repaired, and the sacrifice is consequently invalid? (6) The unfit person. (7) Further away from the altar, not nearer to it. Hence the blood had been handed *backward*, and that certainly does not constitute carriage at all, and it can be repaired. The question under discussion, however, is whether a wrongly performed service can be repaired. (8) Since it had been originally received in a vessel. Now, he assumed that the blood had run down toward the altar, so that we have a form of carriage without the foot, yet this can be repaired by collecting it.

a (1) Away from the altar. (2) Nearer the altar. Surely the blood would run in all directions! (3) Sloping away from the altar. (4) Where it could not run at all in any direction. (5) Semi-solid, and so could not run. (6) Would he state a law that holds good in such exceptional circumstances only? (7) Directly from the animal's throat. (8) *Infra* 25*a*. (9) I.e., where it was spilt from the vessel. (10) R. Simeon does not regard carriage as a service at all (v. Mishnah 13*a*); hence however it is done it cannot disqualify the sacrifice. The Rabbis, however, do regard it as a service, and therefore if done improperly the sacrifice is disqualified. (11) I.e., when the animal is slaughtered so near the altar that the priest merely stretches out his hand and sprinkles the blood without walking at all. (12) V. Sanh. 17*b*. (13) At the sprinkling. (14) For the bird is killed near the altar and its blood made to spurt against the altar direct from the bird. This act of making it spurt constitutes a short carriage, during which, on the present hypothesis, there can be no disqualification, according to R. Simeon. (15) This assumes that immediately the blood spurts from the neck, even before it reaches the altar, the precept has been performed.

b (1) Cf. Lev. IV, 6-7. The priest must both 'sprinkle' the blood and 'put' it on the altar, i.e., see that it actually reaches the altar; consequently, until it actually reaches the altar the service is still being performed, and therefore if the priest's hand is cut off just then, we have a service performed by a priest with a physical blemish, which is invalid (v. Lev. XXI, 17 *seq*.). By the same reasoning, an illegitimate intention during the passage of the blood to the altar may disqualify it.—This argument is unrefuted, and therefore the view that the controversy refers to a short passage may be correct. (2) Since R. Simeon states that it is *possible* without walking (12*a*), he obviously refers to a case where walking is, in fact, done. (3) *Var. lec.*, that it *is* invalid (BaḤ). (4) Actually walking in doing so. (5) *Sc.* the invalidity of the *zar's* action. (6) For the former makes the status of the last person who carries it the determining factor, while the latter reverses it.

אפשר לתקנה או לא אפשר לתקנה ת"ש קבל הכשר ונתן לפסול יחזיר לכשר א] ונהי נמי דיחזור הכשר ויקבלנו אי סלקא דעתך לא אפשר לתקנה איפסלא לה מי סברת דקאי זר גואי לא דקאי זר בראי איתמר אמר עולא אמר ר' יוחנן הולכה שלא ברגל פסולה ב] אלמא *לא אפשר לתקנה איתיביה רב נחמן לעולא *נשפך מן הכלי על הרצפה ואספו כשר הכא במאי עסקינן כשיצא לחוץ לבראי נפיק לגואי לא עייל במקום מדרון איבעית אימא בגומא ואיבעית אימא בסמיכא °ואיכפל תנא לאשמועינן כל הני ועוד אדתני באידך פירקין *נשפך על הרצפה' ואספו פסול ליפלוג בדידיה במה דברים אמורים כשיצא לחוץ אבל נכנס לפנים פסול תיובתא אתמר הולכה שלא ברגל מחלוקת ר"ש ורבנן ג] בהולכה רבתי דכולי עלמא לא פליגי דפסולה כי פליגי בהולכה זוטרתי מחכו עלה במערבא אלא חטאת העוף ד] דפסולה בה מחשבה לר"ש היכי משכחת לה אי דחשיב עלה מקמי דליפוק דם לא כלום היא ואי בתר דנפק דם ה] איתעבידא ליה מצותו מאי קושיא דלמא מדפריש (א) ועד דמטא למזבח דהא בעא מיניה רבי ירמיה מרבי זירא היה מזה ונקטעה ידו של מזה עד שלא הגיע דם לאויר המזבח מהו וא"ל ו] [°פסולה מ"ט] והזה ונתן בעינן כי אתו רב פפא ורב הונא בריה דרב יהושע מבי רב אמרי היינו תוכא ובהולכה רבתי לא פליגי ז] והא כי פליגי בהולכה רבתי פליגי *אלא בהולכה זוטרתי כולי עלמא לא פליגי (ג) דלא פסלה ח] כי פליגי בהולכה רבתי הוליכו זר והחזירו כהן וחזר והוליכו פליגי בה בני רבי חייא ור' ינאי חד אמר כשר וחד אמר °פסול מר סבר אפשר לתקנה ומר סבר לא אפשר לתקנה הוליכו כהן והחזירו וחזר והוליכו זר אמר רב שימי בר אשי לדברי המכשיר ט] פסול לדברי הפוסל מכשיר רבא אמר אף לדברי הפוסל °פסול מאי טעמא דהא צריך לאמטוייה

הדרן עלך כל הזבחים

אפשר לתקנה. בין שעשאה זר בין שעשאה כהן (ג) אמרינן י] דאין הולכה ופסולה דהא נעשית שלא כהלכתה מיהו יש לה תקנה להחזירה לאחוריה ולחזור להוליך ברגל או אין לה תקנה: יחזיר לכשר. אלמא אפשר לתקנה: ונהי נמי כו'. כלומר ואי נמי מפרשת לה (ד) *דככשר יא] ראשון [שיוליך] לצד המזבח קאמר וכל שכן דשמעת יב] דהולכת כשר קמא דהואי שלא ברגל כשרה היא יג] מכל מקום ש"מ דכשרה ע"י תקנה: איפסלא. בהולכת כשר יד] ראשונה: מי סברת דקאי זר גואי. לצד המזבח שהקריב הראשון טו] בהושטתו לצד המזבח: דקאי זר בראי. (ה) וכשר שהושיטה לו הרחיקה מן המזבח הלכך לאו הולכה הואי לפסול *וכי פשטינן יחזור כשר ויטלט וזר מעשה אילטבא הוא דעבד דליכא הושטת יד המקרבתו למזבח: טז] פסלה. ואפילו עשאה כהן פוסלת הדם והויא דפסחים בדניידי וכדשנינן: נשפך מן הכלי על הרצפה ואספו כשר. הואיל ונתקבל בכלי משנה היא בפ' שלישי בכל הפסולים קס"ד כשנשפך (ו) ונתפשט ברצפה נתקרב לצד המזבח יז] וקתני כשר והוי נמי דאמרת דלריך להחזירו לאחוריו ולחזור יח] ולהוליך ברגל מ"מ בתקנתא סגי לה: כשילא לחוץ. כשנשפך לא נתפשט לצד המזבח אלא נתפשט להלן מן המזבח ונתרחק: ופרכינן לבראי נפיק לגואי לא עייל. בתמיה וכי אפשר לדם ללול שישפך ולא יתפשט לכל לדדין: במקום מדרון. יט] ומשופע חוץ למזבח: בגומא. שעומד במקומו ולא נתפשט: אי נמי בסמיכא. דם עבה וקרוב לקרוש: באידך פירקין. בפ' שני: נשפך על הרצפה. מלואר בהמה ולא נתקבל (ז) בכלי: לפלוג בדידיה. בהאי דפרק שלישי דאיירי בקבלת כלי נפלוג בה חילוק לפסול שפעמים שאף מן הכלי לרצפה פסול כ] אלא מדלא אשכח פסול אלא מלואר בהמה ש"מ נשפך מן הכלי לא שנא נפק לבראי ול"ש עייל לגואי כשר: תיובתא. דעולא: מחלוקת ר' שמעון ורבנן. דמתני' היא אי הויא עבודה אי לא לרבי שמעון כא] לא הויא עבודה דהא קתני מתני' ר' שמעון מכשיר בהילוך דלא פסל בה מחשבה בהולכה שלא ברגל כב] ומשום דלאו הולכה היא: בהולכה רבתי כו'. מסקנא היא למילתיה דקמפרש ואומר דכי פליגי ר"ש ורבנן (בהולכה זוטרתא) כג] [בהולכה זוטרתא פליגי ששחט בלד המזבח וזרק דהיינו שלא ברגל אבל בהולכה רבתי דהיינו ברגל לא פליגי ולקמן מותיב לה ממתניתין דשמעינן מינה דבשוחט נמי רחוק מן המזבח מכשיר רבי שמעון מדקתני שאם רלה שוחט בלד המזבח וזורק: מחכו עליה במערבא. [מחייכו עליה] דהאי שמעתא דמוקי טעמא דר"ש בהולכה זוטרתא] ולמימר דלאו הולכה היא ואע"פ שאי אפשר לבטלה לא לאו עבודה היא: אלא חטאת העוף. דקיימא לן בפ' קדשי קדשים (לקמן דף סה.) דפסל בה מחשבה בהזאת דמה כד] שהוא עיקר עבודתה דכתיב שם והזה מדם החטאת על קיר וגו' שאוחזה בגופה ומתיז דמה לקיר והך התזה הולכה זוטרתי היא וכיון דטעמא דר"ש משום דהולכה זוטרא לא פסל בה כה] מחשבה היכי *פסל בהך: אי דחשיב עליה מקמי דליפוק דם. דהיינו בהתזתה: הא אמרת כו] לא כלום היא. דהא הולכה זוטרתי היא: ואי כז] בתר שנעקר הדם. וניתז מן הצואר חשיב: הא איתעבידא מצותיה. דקס"ד מכי נפק דם גמרה לה עבודת הזאתה ואע"ג דלא מטא דם למזבח אא"ב בהולכה רבתי פליגי וטעמא דר"ש משום דאפשר לבטלה הוא הא דחטאת כח] אי אפשר לבטלה אלא אי אמרת (ח) משום טעם דלאו הולכה היא ובשלא ברגל פליגי היכי פסלה בהך הלא אין כאן מחשבה אלא בהולכה שלא ברגל ולר' יוחנן דאמר לעיל הולכה שלא ברגל לא שמה הולכה כט] [ולא פסיל בה מחשבה] ליכא למיפרך מהא דכי אמר ר' יוחנן ל] הולכה רבתי קאמר שאין דרכה בכך אבל השוחט בלד המזבח כו' וכן חטאת העוף שנמלקת אלל המזבח עיקר הולכתה בכך ומודה בה רבי יוחנן: לא] ומאי קושיא דלמא מדפריש. דם דפסק לה הולכה מתחלת הזאה ושנה להזאה עד דמטי למזבח וחיילא עלה המחשבה: דהא בעא מיניה כו' היה מזה. בחטאת העוף או בחטאות הפנימיות: מהו. מי הויא עבודה בבעל מום ופסולה או לא דאיכא למימר מכי פריש דם גמרה לה: וא"ל פסולה לב] מ"ט והזה. דחטאת העוף או דחטאות הפנימיות דכתיב בהן הזאה והזה ונתן בעינן הזאה דומיא דנתן דגבי הדדי כתיבי והזה מן הדם וגו' ונתן הכהן מן הדם על קרנות וגו' אלמא ישנה להזאה עד שיגיע למזבח: היינו תוכא. הא דמחכו במערבא משום דקשיא להו הכי: ובהולכה רבתי לא פליגי והא כי פליגי כו'. דהא לג] *דקתני אפשר שלא בהילוך ש"מ בהילוך עסקינן וטעם משום שאפשר לבטלה הוא *והא מיהא לא ביטל: אלא בהולכה זוטרתי כ"ע לא פליגי דפסולה גרסינן וטעמא משום דא"א לבטל ומאן דגריס דלא פסלה טעמא משום דלאו כלום היא ואין שם הולכה עליה אלא כולה לורך זריקה היא והא לא הוה בדעתיה למחשב אזריקה אלא אהולכה ולא חשיב מידי ופסול דחטאת העוף כדאוקי מדפריש ועד דמטא למזבח ומשום מחשבת הזאה ולא משום מחשבת הולכה: הוליכו זר. ברגל והחזירו כהן שהעבודה עליו מוטלת וחזר *והוליכו כשר והא דתניא לעיל זר ואונן בהולכה פסול כשלא הוחזרה: אפשר לתקנה. להולכת פסול ולא דמיא לשאר עבודות דאילו שחיטה וקבלה וזריקה מאחר שנעשו בפסול אי אפשר לחזור ולעשותן בהכשר וא"ת קבלה נמי יש לתקן כגון שלא קבל הפסול כל הדם ויכול כשר לחזור ולקבל ההיא ודאי כשרה לד] ובפ' שלישי (לקמן דף לג.) תנן לה אם יש דם הנפש יחזור הכשר ויקבל וכן בזריקה: הכי גרסינן הוליכו כהן והחזירו וחזר והוליכו זר: אמר רב שימי לדברי המכשיר. בהוליכו זר והחזירו כהן וחזר והוליכו: פוסל. לה] *כיון דהתם מ"ט מכשיר דאזיל בתר בתרייתא ה"נ זיל בתר בתרייתא: לדברי הפוסל לו]. דאזיל בתר הולכה קמייתא מכשיר *כיון דאזיל בתר קמייתא (ס): אף לדברי הפוסל [שם] פוסל כאן דהא לריך לאמטוייה לז] [מאחר שנתרחק לריך לחזור ולהביאו ללד מזבח נמלא דהולכה אחרונה לנורך ככל ההולכות]:

הולכה שלא ברגל מחלוקת ר"ש ורבנן. יש מפרש פירוש אחר אבל פירוש הקונטרס עיקר: חטאת העוף דפסלה [הזאה] היכי משכחת לה. כיון דמכשיר ר"ש בהולכה שלא ברגל אלא ודאי אפכא מסתברא ותלוי הדבר *באפשר לבטלה דרחוק מן המזבח הולכה זו [אפשר לבטלה] דאי בעי הוה שחיט בצד המזבח ולא פסלה בה מחשב' אבל שחט קרוב למזבח דהולכה זו של הושטת יד לא אפשר לבטלה פסלה בה מחשבה והכי בחטאת העוף פסלה מחשבה בהזאה מכי נפיק עד דמטא למזבח דלא אפשר לבטל דבר זה אבל לאידך דלא תליא באפשר ולא אפשר אלא הולכה שלא ברגל לא חשיבא והוי כאילו איתעביד אם כן בחטאת העוף נמי כאילו אתעביד מלותו ומשני דרחמנא *מחשבה זו מחשבה שלימה. ברו"ך:

אלא חטאת העוף דפסלה בה מחשבה היכי משכחת לה. אי אמרת בשלמא בהולכה (*שלא ברגל) פליגי אבל בזוטרתי דלא אפשר לבטלה פסלה מחשבה משכחת לה מיקמי דתיפוק דם משום דדם הנתון בצואר כנתון בכלי שרת ולא דמי לבעיא דרבי אבין בריש דם חטאת (לקמן דף לב:) דאיבעיא ליה אי צואר ככלי שרת אי לא אבל אי בזוטרתי לא פסלה לר' שמעון היכי משכחת לה אבל מכל זריקה דעלמא לא קשיא ליה לח] אי מיקמי דליפוק דם מן הכלי לאו כלום הוא ואי בתר דנפק הא איתעביד ליה מצותו משום לט] [דמדמפריש] ליה עד דמטא לא איתעביד מצותו מ] אבל בהזאה סד"א דלא צריך מזבח מידי דהוה אהזאה דפרוכת ובין הבדים דהויא הזאה אע"פ שלא נגע* מא]. הגה"ה:

טו א מיי' פ"א מהל' פסה"מ הלכה כו:
גי' הש"ק באפשר לבטלה הולכה זו דרחוק מן המזבח דאי בעי הוי שחט בצד המזבח לא פסלה כצ"ל
טח ב מיי' פ"ב שם הלכה ז:
טט ג ד מיי' שם פ"א הלכה כו:
מחשבה להולכה זו עבודה שלימה הס"ד וכצ"ל ש"ק
נ"א רבתי

שיטה מקובצת

א] עי' בהשמטות בסוף המס': ב] עי' בהשמטות בסוף המסכת: ג] עי' בהשמטות בסוף המס': ד] העוף דפסיל: ה] הא איתעבידא מצותו. תימה תיקשי ליה אכל זריקה היכא פסלא בה מחשבה אי מקמי כו' ואומר השר מקוצי דהתם משעה שמנענע הדם בכלי לצאת הוי תחילת התחלת זריקה מקמי דליפוק דם מן הכלי וניכר לעינים שהדם מנענע ורוצה לצאת אבל הדם שבצואר העוף אינו נראה לעינים ועד שיצא לחוץ לא הוי התחלת הזאה ועוד תירץ ריב"א דבזריקת דמים בעלמא ידע שפיר דפסלה בה מחשבה מדפריש דם עד דמטי למזבח אבל הזאת חטאת העוף סד"א מדפריש גמרה לה עבודת הזאה מידי דהוה אהזאת פרוכת כו'. מהר"ם: ו] וא"ל פסולה מ"ט: ז] והא כי פליגי כו' וא"ת מאי פריך והלא כבר תירצנו לעיל זאת הקושיא דמיירי דאיכא הולכה מעט וי"ל דמ"מ פריך שפיר הכא דפשט המשנה משמע דמיירי בשוחט רחוק מן המזבח: אלא בהולכה זוטרתי כו' א) וטעמא משום דלא אפשר לבטלה וגם דרכה בכך והשתא ניחא דבחטאת העוף פסלה בה מחשבה משום דהוי כהולכה זוטרתי ולא הוצרכו לשנוייא דלעיל. מהר"ם: ח] כי פליגי בהולכה רבתי. דלרבי שמעון לא פסלה כיון דאפשר [לבטלה] דשוחט בצד המזב' וזורק דאותה סברא דהשתא מיהא כיון ששחט ברחוק למזבח אי אפשר לבטלה לא ס"ל וקשה לריב"א דלעיל קאמר גבי טבילת אצבע דהוי כהולכת זוטרתי קאמר ר"ש דלא מפגלא אע"ג דלא אפשר לבטלה טבילת אצבע לכך נראה כגירסא אחרת אלא בהולכה זוטרתי כ"ע לא פליגי דלא פסלה משום דלאו כלום ואין שם הולכה עליה ופסולה דהזאת העוף מדפריש עד דמטא למזבח ומטעם מחשבת הזאה ולא מטעם מחשבת הולכה

בי' הש"ק דככשר אחר של צד המזבח קאמר והולכת כשר קמא דהואי שלא ברגל כשרה היא מ"מ ש"מ דכשירה ע"י תקנה כצ"ל
לקמן לג.

הגהות הב"ח

(א) גמ' מדפריש דם ועד דמטא: (ב) שם לא פליגי (דלא פסלה) תא"מ ונ"ב ס"א דפסלה: (ג) רש"י ד"ה אפשר וכו' כהן דאמרת דאינה הולכה: (ד) ד"ה ונהי וכו' ואי נמי מפרשת לה דלכשר אחד של צד המזבח קאמר דיחזור וכשר דשמעת מינה דהולכת כשר: (ה) ד"ה דקאי וכו' הכשר: (ו) ד"ה כשפך וכו' נתפשט ברלפה ונתקרב: (ז) ד"ה נשפך וכו' בכלי פסול הס"ד: (ח) ד"ה הא איתעבידא וכו' אי אמרת טעמא דר"ש משום דלאו הולכה: (ט) ד"ה לדברי הפוסל וכו' בתר קמייתא ה"נ זיל בתר קמייתא הס"ד:

[ע' משנה למלך פ"א מהל' פסה"מ ה' כג ופ' י"א הלכה א]

גליון הש"ס

גמ' ואיכפל תנא. שבת ס ע"א:

רש"ק
ז"ק
נ"א פסול בה כאן ז"ק
ז"ק
ז"ק
יחזור לכשר ז"ק
ז"ק
ז"ק
רש"ק

וא"ת ס"ם תקשי מרבנן דקאמרי לעיל דטבילת אצבע מפגלא דהוי הולכה זוטרתי והיכי קאמר הכא דברי הכל לא פסלה וי"ל דלעיל היינו למאי דבעי' למימר דהולכה (שדרכו) [שלא]בתל (כבעין דלעיל דשייתי מעומד דומיא דיושב) דשמה הולכה הלכך כ"ש הולכה ופסולה בה מחשבה אבל הכא דמסקינן דהולכה שלא ברגל לא שמיה הולכה ה"ה בהולכה זוטרתי. מהר"ם: ט] המכשיר פוסל: י] אמרינן דאינו הולכה: יא] דבכשר אחר שלצד המזבח תיבת שיוליך ל"ש: יב] דשמעת מינה: יג] היא וא"כ מכל מקום: יד] כשר ראשון הס"ד: טו] הראשון את הדם בהושטתו: טז] פסולה: יז] המזבח קצת וקתני: יח] ולחזור ולהוליכו ברגל: יט] מדרון במשופע חוץ: כ] פסול וליתני הכי בד"א דאם נתן בכלי כשר כשיצא לחוץ אבל נכנס לפנים פסול: כא] שמעון לאו עבודה היא דהא תיבת הוי ל"ש ונמחק: כב] ברגל קאמר ומשום: כג] ומיהו פליגי ששחט בצד המזבח וזורק דהיינו שלא ברגל אבל בהולכה רבתי דהיינו ברגל לא פליג ולקמן מותיב ליה ממתניתין דשמעינן מינה דבשוחט רחוק מן המזבח נמי מכשיר ר"ש מדקתני שאם ירצה שוחט [illegible]

א) סיום תי' זו חמאת כתוס' סד"ה חטאת העוף.

לאמטוייה אמר ליה א] רב ירמיה לרב אשי הכי אמר רב ירמיה מדיפתי הא צריך לאמטוייה מחלוקת רבי (א) אליעזר ורבנן דתנן ר"א אומר המהלך במקום שצריך להלך מחשבה פוסלת מקום שאין צריך להלך אין מחשבה פוסלת ואמר רבא הכל מודים קבלו בחוץ והכניסו בפנים זהו הילוך שצריך להלך קבלו בפנים והוציאו לחוץ זהו הילוך שאין צריך להלך *לא נחלקו ב] אלא כשהכניסו וחזר והוציאו *מר סבר הא צריך לאמטוייה ומ"ס לאו כהילוך הצריך לעבודה דמי איתיביה אביי ר"א אומר המהלך מקום שצריך להלך מחשבה פוסלת כיצד קבלו ג] בחוץ והכניסו לפנים זהו הילוך שצריך להלך קבלו בפנים והוציאו לחוץ זהו הילוך שאין צריך לילך ד] והא חזר והכניסו הילוך שצריך להלך הוא א"ל *אי תניא תניא ה]:

הדרן עלך כל הזבחים

כל *הזבחים (ב) ו] שקבלו דמן [א]זר [ב]אונן [ג]טבול יום ז] *[ד]ומחוסר כפורים [ה]ומחוסר בגדים [ו]שלא רחץ ידים ורגלים *[ז]ערל [ח]טמא [ט]יושב *)[י]עומד על גבי כלים על גבי בהמה *על גבי רגלי חברו ח] פסל *[כ]קבל בשמאל פסל ר"ש מכשיר: **גמ'** זר מנלן דתני לוי °דבר אל אהרן ואל בניו לאמר ט] וינזרו מקדשי בני ישראל וגו' י] בני ישראל למעוטי מאי אילימא למעוטי נשים קרבן נשים בטומאה קרב אלא למעוטי עובדי כוכבים השתא ציץ לא מרצה דאמר מר *ובעובדי כוכבים בין בשוגג בין במזיד לא הורצה בטומאה קרב אלא הכי קאמר וינזרו מקדשי בני ישראל ולא יחללו *דבי רבי ישמעאל תנא יא] אתיא בק"ו מבעל מום (ג) מה בעל מום שאוכל אם עבד חילל

°ויקרא כב

*) יומא כח.

רש"י

הא צריך לאמטוייה. דקאמרת לאחשובה עבודה מהאי יב] טעם מחלוקת ר' אליעזר ורבנן (ד) במתני': בחוץ. להלן מן המזבח והכניסו בפנים יג] לצד המזבח: והוליכו לחוץ. כלומר ריחקו מן המזבח הנך חוץ ופנים כולהו בעזרה: הא צריך לאמטוייה. יד] לכשיחזור ויקריבנו לצד המזבח אם תהא אותה הולכה במחשבה פסולה טו]: לאו כהילוך הצריך לעבודה דמי. הואיל ושלא לצורך הוליכו על חנם הוצרך לחזור ולהכניסו: אי תניא. דמודה בה ר' אליעזר תניא ואין מחלוקת בין ר"א לת"ק אלא טז] אר"ש אבוה קאי ופליג:

הדרן עלך כל הזבחים

כל הזבחים. אונן. כל זמן שלא נקבר המת: טבול יום. דשרץ ודמת יז] ושאר טומאות שלא הוצרכו לקרבן: מחוסר כפורים. זב ומצורע שטבלו והעריב שמשן ולא הביאו כפרתן: מחוסר בגדים. כהן גדול שישנם בפחות משמונה וכהן הדיוט בפחות מד': ושלא רחץ ידים ורגלים. מן הכיור: ערל. כהן שמתו אחיו מחמת מילה: יושב או עומד על גבי כלים. שיש חציצה בין רגליו לרצפה וכולהו יליף בגמ' דפסלי בעבודה: **גמ'** וינזרו מקדשי וגו'. גבי מקריבים בטומאה כתיב דסמיך ליה כל איש אשר יקרב מכל זרעכם: (למעוטי מאי) בני ישראל למעוטי מאי. קרבן של מי הוא ממעט מלהזהיר כהנים על הטומאה: אילימא למעוטי בנות ישראל. קרבן נשים שלא הוזהרו כהנים מלהקריבו בטומאה: קרבן נשים בטומאה קרב. בתמיה וכי יש כח יח] בקרבן נשים לדחות הטומאה: אלא למעוטי קרבן עובדי כוכבים. עובד כוכבים ששלח עולתו יט] כדתניא בהכל שוחטין (חולין דף יג:) איש איש לרבות את העובדי כוכבים שנודרים נדרים ונדבות כישראל: השתא ציץ לא מרצה. על טומאת עולין שבקרבנו כגון נטמא הדם או החלב כדרך שמרצה על של ישראל: דאמר מר. במנחות בהקומץ רבה (דף כה.): לא הורצה. דכתיב לרצון להם ולא לעובדי כוכבים: בטומאת הגוף יהא קרב. בתמיה והלא כ] [אפילו] אל קרבן יחיד דישראל לא נדחת: אלא הכי קאמר וינזרו מקדשי. יתרחקו כא] בטומאה מכל קדשים: בני ישראל לא יחללו. והזרים אף הם ינזרו כדי שלא יחללום לימד על זר שעבד שחילל את הקדשים ופסלם: בעל מום שאוכל. את קדשי קדשים דכתיב (ויקרא כא) מקדשי הקדשים ומן הקדשים יאכל: אם עבד חילל. דכתיב כב] מום בו ולא יחלל את מקדשי (שם):

תוספות

זר ואונן. הא דלא תנא בעל מום ושתויי יין *ופרועי ראש משום דכתיב בהן חילול בהדיא*: **טבול** יום. אע"כ תני טמא וזו ואין צריך לומר זו קתני ומשום דאיכא תרי קראי תני תרוייהו והא דלא תני טמא ברישא דניחא ליה למיתני טמא בהדי ערל כדאשכחן בפרק הערל (יבמות דף ע.) ובחגיגה (דף ד:) ועוד איכא תנא דמרבי ליה לערל כי טמא ומיהו סוגיא דגמ' דלא כוותיה מדמצרכי ליה תרי קראי וכי תימא דאצטריך לערל בקרבן לצבור דאילו טמא שרי כג] דהא כי מרבי *ר"ע לערל כי טמא היינו כד] *בזב ומצורע דמההוא קרא דריש דכתיב איש איש מזרע אהרן והוא צרוע או זב ואותה טומאה לא הותרה בצבור:

אלא למעוטי עובדי כוכבים השתא צין לא מרצה. הקשה הרב רבי יום טוב דהכא משמע דהאי בני ישראל לא אתא למעוטי עובדי כוכבים ולקמן אמרינן בפ' ב"ש (דף מה.) קדשי עובדי כוכבים אין חייבין עליהם משום טמא דילפינן חילול מטומאה ובטומאה כתיב בני ישראל ולא עובדי כוכבים ואין לומר דמבני ישראל דכתיב גבי אכילת קודש בטומאה קדרים שזהו פסוק שני לו בפרשת אמור אל הכהנים דלא משמע הכי בתורת כהנים ובריש תמורה (דף ג.) דמייתי התם בהדיא קרא דוינזרו ועוד דגבי וינזרו כתיב חילול ולא גבי אכילת קודש בטומאה וי"ל דקרא דוינזרו מיירי בכל שימוש בין בכהן טמא ששימש בין בזר ששימש וגם איירי בכל טומאה בין באכילת קדשים בטומאה בין בטמא ששימש ופשיטא ליה דלמעוטי קדשי עובדי כוכבים מאכילה בטומאה לחודיה לא אתא דמבני ישראל דכתיב בתריה גבי אכילה בטומאה נפקא ואתא למידרש זר מבני ישראל ולא יחללו כה] ובאכילת טומאה דכתיב הכא לאשמועינן כו] דכתיב ביה חילול לאגמורי אנותר וא"ת א"כ במכות (דף יד:) ובשבועות (דף ז.) ובפרק הערל (יבמות דף עה.) אמאי דחק ר' יוחנן כז] אזהרה לאכילת קודש בטומאה תיפוק לן מהכא ויש לומר משום דהאי קרא הוי לאו שבכללות דאתא נמי לטמא ששימש מיהו קשה בפרק אלו הן הנשרפין (סנהדרין דף פג.) דיליף טמא ששימש במיתה מחילול חילול מתרומה ופריך לילף חילול חילול מנותר דבכרת ולא במיתה ומשני חילול דרבים עדיף ולא יחללו מלא יחללו אבל נותר כתיב כי את קדש ה' חילל בל' יחיד והשתא אכתי הוה ליה למילף מאכילת טומאה דבכרת דבהאי קרא גופיה ועוד כיון דמחד קרא נפקי נקים קדשי חילול דשימוש לחילול דאכילה *ועוד דלקמן שילהי פ' בית שמאי (דף מו.) אמרינן ולא יחללו בשני חלולין הכתוב מדבר אחד פסול נותר ואחד פסול טומאה ומקשי אהדדי אם כן בנותר נמי איכא חילול דרבים ולא יחללו ומתו בו כי יחללוהו ופריך נילף כרת מחילול דנותר דכתיב גבי כרת כי את קדש ה' חלל ונכרתה ולכך משני היינו חילול דיחיד אבל לא יחללו דקרא דוינזרו אע"ג דמיירי בטמא שאכל וגם בנותר *ההוא חילול לא כתיב עונש בהדיה. ז"ה עיקר ברו"ך. ועוד י"ל דבהאי קרא דלא יחללו משמע טמא ששימש וזר ששימש ואכילת קודש ונותר ולא ידעינן להי מינייהו נקים אי לזר דבמיתה או לאכילת קודש ונותר דבכרת לכך צריך ג"ש ומיהא קשה לתנא דבי ר' ישמעאל דלא נפקא לן זר מהאי קרא ועוד קשה *אדנפקא לן ליה בעל מום ששימש במיתה מטמא ששימש נילף מאכילת קודש דבכרת וחילול דרבים וקשה לרבינו זצ"ל דלקמן דיליף דאין חייבין על קדשי עובדי כוכבים על עון דנותר דיליף מחילול חילול דטומאה דכתיב בני ישראל ולא עובדי כוכבים הלא ההוא קרא גופיה בנותר מישתעי כדתני לוי בשני חילולין הכתוב מדבר ועוד קשה לי כח] מנלן ללוי דדריש שני חילולין חילול נותר וחילול טומאה הלא לוי גופיה בשמעתין מוקי לקרא בשני חילולין אחריני חילול טומאה וחילול זרות וי"ל כיון דטומאה וזרות כתיב בקרא אפילו לא כתיב אלא חד חילול ממילא הוה קאי אתרוייהו ותימה לי הא אצטריך חילול לשון רבים לאגמורי מיתה בטמא ששימש פרק הנשרפין (סנהדרין דף פג.). ברו"ך:

אתיא בקל וחומר מבעל מום. מיושב שאוכל לא מצי למילף דמה ליושב שכן פסול לעדות כדקאמר בסמוך וממחוסר בגדים ושלא רחוץ ידים ורגלים נמי דהני לא פסלי אלא מטעם זרות כט] אבל קשה דנילף בק"ו משתויי יין (דלקמן) ופרועי ראש (ועומד על גבי כלים) [וי"ל] דלא קשיא מידי משתויי יין דלקמן מפיק שתויי יין דחילל מחוקה חוקה ממחוסר בגדים ומחוסר בגדים לא נפקא לן דחילל אלא מטעם דזרות וזר אכתי לא קמ"ל וגם מפרועי ראש לא קשיא מידי דשילהי פרק שני דסנהדרין (דף כב:) אמרינן דפרועי ראש למיתה גמירי אבל למיחל לא גמירי ואפילו למאן דאמר התם דמחלל היינו משום דאיתקש לשתויי יין דמחלי מטעם זרות ול"ע אמאי לא יליף מק"ו דיושב דאינו במיתה וגם זר דאיתו במיתה בקבלה לפי שאינה עבודה תמה ומחללי כל שכן פרועי ראש דבמיתה דמחללי. ברו"ך:

זר

עין משפט נר מצוה

ופרועי ראש נמחק נ"ק [ועי' היטב תוס' מנחות ו. ד"ה שקמצן]

א א מיי' פ"ט מהל' ביאת מקדש הלכה א:

ב ב מיי' פ"ב שם הלכה ו ז:

ג ג מיי' פ"ד שם הל' ד:

ד ד מיי' פ"ה מהל' ביאת מקדש הלכה ה:

[ביבמות חגיגה שם]

ה ה מיי' פ"י מהלכות כלי מקדש הלכה ד:

ו ו מיי' פ"ה מהלכות ביאת מקדש הל' א:

ז ז מיי' פ"ו שם הל' ח:

ח ח מיי' פ"ד שם הל' א:

ט ט י מיי' פ"ה שם הלכה יז:

י כ מיי' שם הלכה יח:

שיטה מקובצת

[illegible]

הגהות הב"ח

[illegible]

מסורת הש"ס

[illegible]

וי"ל דאיירי בטמא שרץ שהוא ראשון ואינו מטמא את הכלי ולא חשיב בעל מום ושתויי יין משום דכתיב בהו חילול בהדיא בעל מום דכתיב לא יגש ולא יחלל ושתויי יין [illegible]

[illegible]

[here too]. What is the reason?—Because he is bound [15b] to bring it up.[7]

a R. Jeremiah[1] said to R. Ashi, This is what R. Jeremiah of Difti[2] said: [The validity of the argument,] 'Surely he is bound to bring it up', is disputed by R. Eliezer and the Rabbis. For we learned: R. ELIEZER SAID: IF ONE GOES WHERE HE NEEDS TO GO, AN [ILLEGITIMATE] INTENTION DISQUALIFIES IT; [IF HE GOES] WHERE HE NEED NOT GO, AN [ILLEGITIMATE] INTENTION DOES NOT DISQUALIFY IT. Whereon Raba commented: All agree that if [the priest] received [the blood] without and carried it within,[3] that is a necessary walk. If he received [it] within and carried it without, it is an unnecessary walk.[4] They disagree only where he brought it within and then carried it without again: One Master holds, But he must surely bring it up [to the altar;][5] while the other Master holds: This is not the same as a carriage required for the service.[6] Abaye refuted him: R. Eliezer said: If one goes where he must go, an [illegitimate] intention disqualifies it. How so? If he received it without and brought it within, it is a necessary walk. If he received it within and carried it without, it is an unnecessary walk. Whence,[7] if he carried it within again, it is a necessary walk? — Said he [Raba] to him: If it was taught, it was taught.[8]

CHAPTER II

MISHNAH. ALL SACRIFICES WHOSE BLOOD WAS b CAUGHT BY A ZAR, AN ONEN, A ṬEBUL YOM,[1] ONE LACKING SACRIFICIAL ATONEMENT,[2] ONE LACKING [PRIESTLY] VESTMENTS, ONE WHO HAD NOT WASHED HIS HANDS AND FEET,[3] AN UNCIRCUMCISED [PRIEST], AN UNCLEAN [PRIEST], ONE WHO WAS SITTING, ONE STANDING ON UTENSILS[4] OR ON AN ANIMAL OR ON HIS FELLOW'S FEET, ARE DISQUALIFIED. IF [THE PRIEST] CAUGHT [THE BLOOD] WITH HIS LEFT HAND, IT IS DISQUALIFIED. R. SIMEON DECLARES IT VALID.[5]

GEMARA. How do we know [that] a *zar* [disqualifies the sacrifice if he receives the blood]?—Because Levi taught: [Scripture says,] *Speak unto Aaron and to his sons, that they separate themselves from the holy things of the children of Israel* etc.[6] What does '*the children* [*sons*] *of Israel*' exclude? Shall we say that it excludes [the sacrifice of] women? Can women's sacrifice be offered in uncleanness?[7] Again, is it to exclude [the sacrifices of] heathens? seeing that [even] the headplate does not propitiate, for a Master c said: But in the case of [the sacrifices of] heathens, whether [done][1] in ignorance or deliberately, propitiation is not effected,[2] can these [actually] be offered in uncleanness! Hence this is what [Scripture] means: *that they separate themselves from the holy things of the children of Israel, and that they* [the children of Israel] *profane not* [*My holy name*].[3]

The School of R. Ishmael taught: [That a *zar* disqualifies the sacrifice] is inferred *a minori* from [a priest] with a blemish: if [a priest] with a blemish, who may eat [of the sacrifice], profanes

(7) Since in fact the blood was taken away from the altar, it *must* be brought back. This becomes a service, and is therefore disqualified by a *zar*.

a (1) Sh. M. reads: Rabina. (2) Obermeyer, *op. cit.* p. 197 conjectures that this is identical with Dibtha, in the neighbourhood of Wasit, north of Harpania. (3) I.e., he received it at some distance from the altar and brought it up to the altar. (4) During the course of which an illegitimate intention does *not* disqualify the sacrifice, on all views. (5) Hence an illegitimate intention even during this *second* passage to the altar disqualifies it. (6) Since there was no need in the first place to take it away from the altar. Hence an illegitimate intention during that passage does not disqualify it. (7) Sh. M. deletes. (8) I must accept it.

b (1) V. Glos. for these terms. (2) A priest who became unclean through the dead was sprinkled with the ashes of the red heifer mixed with water; then he took a ritual bath; and on the eighth day of his uncleanness he offered a sacrifice, which made atonement for him. Similarly, a leper and a *zab* (q.v. Glos.) took a ritual bath on becoming clean, and offered a sacrifice the following day. In all these cases they are regarded as 'lacking atonement' after their ritual bath and before they offer their sacrifice. (3) At the laver; v. Ex. XXX, 18 *seq*. (4) I.e., not directly on the pavement. (5) In the law concerning the last case. (6) Lev. XXII, 2. This prohibits the priest from officiating whilst unclean (see following verses). Hence the phrase '*the children*' (or, 'sons', which may be the meaning of the Heb. בני) apparently implies a limitation: only from the sacrifices of '*the children of Israel*' must they hold aloof when they are unclean, but not from other sacrifices. (7) Surely not.

c (1) I.e., offered in an unclean state. (2) V. *infra* 45*b*. (3) Since '*the children of Israel*' cannot be a limitation, it is interpreted as an additional subject of '*separate*': the children of Israel (i.e., *zarim*) too must separate themselves from the sacrifices, as otherwise they profane God's name, by disqualifying the sacrifice.

[it] when he officiates,[4] [16a] is it not logical that a *zar*, who may not eat,[5] profanes [the sacrifice] by officiating? [No:] as for [a priest] with a blemish, the reason may be because in his case the man who offers [officiates] is treated on a par with what is offered![6] Then let an unclean [priest] prove it.[7] As for an unclean [priest], the reason is that he defiles [the flesh of the sacrifice]! Then let one with a blemish prove it. And thus the argument revolves, the distinguishing feature of one not being that of the other, and the distinguishing feature of the other not being that of the first. The feature common to both is that they are admonished [not to officiate], and if they do officiate, they profane [the sacrifice]; so will I also adduce a *zar*, who is [likewise] admonished, that if he officiates, he profanes.

How do we know that he is admonished? If from, *'that they separate themselves'*,[8] surely profanation is written in its very context![9]—Rather, from [the text] *But a common man* [zar] *shall not draw nigh unto you.*[10] But the [argument] can be refuted: the feature common to both is that they were not permitted at the
a high places![1]—Do not say, 'Let an unclean [priest] prove it', but say, 'Let an *onen* prove it'.[2] As for an *onen*, [the reason is] because he is forbidden [to partake of] the Second tithe![3] Then let a [priest] with a blemish prove it.[4] And thus the argument revolves, the distinguishing feature of one is not that of the other [and *vice versa*]; the feature common to both is that they are forbidden etc. But here too let us refute [the argument]: the feature common to both is that they were not permitted at the high places? To this R. Sama the son of Raba demurred: And who is to tell us that an *onen* was forbidden at the high places; perhaps he was permitted at the high places?[5]

R. Mesharshia said: It is inferred *a minori* from [a priest who] sits. If one who is sitting profanes [the sacrifice] if he officiates, though he may eat [thereof when sitting]; is it not logical that a *zar*, who may not eat, profanes [it] if he officiates? As for one who is sitting, the reason may be because he is unfit to testify![6]—[The inference is] from a scholar who is sitting.[7] [Then refute it thus:] As for the general interdict[8] of one who sits, the reason may be because such is unfit to testify![9]—One does not refute by a general interdict.[10] And should you say that you can refute [thus], [then say that] it is inferred from one who sits and one of these others.[11] And how do we know that one who is sitting is fit
b at the high place?[1]—Scripture saith, To stand *before* the Lord, *to minister to Him*:[2] before the Lord [one must stand], but not at the high place.[3]

ONEN. How do we know it? — Because it is written, *Neither shall he go out of the Sanctuary, and he shall not profane [the Sanctuary of his God]*:[4] hence if another [priest, when an *onen*,] does not go out, he does profane [it]. R. Eleazar said, [it is inferred] from this verse: *Behold, have* they *offered [their sin-offering and burnt-offering this day before the Lord]*?[5] It was *I* who offered. Hence it follows that had *'they'* offered, it would rightly have been burnt.[6] Now, why does not R. Eleazar draw [the inference] from [the text] *'Neither shall he go out of the Sanctuary'*? — He can answer you: Is it then written, but if another goes out, he does profane it?[7] And the other; why does he not draw [the inference] from [the text] *'Behold, have they offered'*? — He holds that it was burnt on account of uncleanness.[8]

The school of R. Ishmael taught: It is inferred *a minori* from a

(4) V. Lev. XXI, 22*f*. (5) The flesh of the most sacred sacrifices, such as a sin-offering. (6) A blemish disqualifies a priest from offering the sacrifice, just as it disqualifies an animal from being sacrificed. (7) He may not officiate; but an animal cannot become unclean while alive, to render it unfit for a sacrifice. He too disqualifies a sacrifice by officiating. (8) As on 15*b*. (9) Why infer it *a minori*? (10) Num. XVIII, 4.

a (1) Before the Temple was built sacrifices were offered at the *bamoth* or high places (v. *infra* 112*a*). A priest with a blemish and an unclean priest might not officiate, as in the Temple, but a *zar* could do so. (2) He could officiate at the high places, yet if he officiated in the Temple he disqualified the sacrifice. (3) V. Deut. XXVI, 14. (4) Who is not so forbidden. (5) This objection is left unanswered. Hence the argument by inference from a priest with a blemish cannot be sustained. (6) A witness may not sit when giving his testimony. Of course, this has nothing to do with sacrifices, but in order to refute an argument based on an inference *a minori* it is sufficient to shew that the premise is subject to a particular restriction from which the other is free. (7) He was permitted to testify sitting. (8) Lit. 'name'. (9) I.e., we find that sitting disqualifies one (though not all) from testifying, but we never find a *zar* disqualified from testifying. (10) In the abstract, but rather from the actual person. Since then the argument is based on a scholar who sits, it remains unrefuted. (11) An *onen*, an unclean priest, or a priest with a blemish.

b (1) For otherwise this inference too can be refuted as above. (2) Deut. X, 8. (3) *'Before the Lord'* is understood to mean in the Temple. (4) Lev. XXI, 12. This refers to a High Priest when an *onen*: he must remain in the sanctuary (for sacrificing), and is assured that he will not profane, i.e., disqualify the sacrifices at which he officiates. (5) Ibid. X, 19. (6) A he-goat was sacrificed as a sin-offering on the eighth day of Aaron's consecration (v. Lev. VIII, 33-IX, 3). On that same day Aaron's sons, Nadab and Abihu, died (Ibid. X, 1-2), and the he-goat, instead of being eaten, was burnt. Moses was angry, and enquired whether the reason was that Aaron's other sons, Eleazar and Ithamar, had officiated in their bereavement, to which Aaron replied as in the text. R. Eleazar's interpretation of the text as a rhetorical question does not agree with E.V., which makes it a positive statement. His reason is because if it were a positive statement it is superfluous, as Aaron should simply have answered, 'Behold, there have befallen one such things as these this day,' as he goes on to say, and which was the real cause of the burning of the sacrifice. (7) Surely not. Possibly an ordinary priest too does not disqualify the sacrifice, yet Scripture specifically states that a High Priest does not disqualify it, lest it be thought that precisely because his sanctity is greater he does disqualify it. (8) V. *infra* 101*a*. Hence the passage has nothing to do with bereavement.

זר שאינו אוכל אינו דין שאם עבד חילל מה לבעל מום שכן עשה בו קרב כמקריב טמא יוכיח מה לטמא שכן מטמא בעל מום יוכיח *וחזר הדין לא ראי זה כראי זה ולא ראי זה כראי זה הצד השוה שבהן שמוזהרין ואם עבדו חיללו אף אני אביא זר שהוא מוזהר ואם עבד חילל א] מנלן דמוזהר אי מוינזרו חילול בגופיה כתיב ביה אלא °מוזר לא יקרב אליכם איכא למיפרך מה להצד השוה שבהן שכן לא הותרו בבמה לא תימא טמא יוכיח אלא אימא אונן יוכיח מה לאונן שכן אסור במעשר [בעל מום] יוכיח *וחזר הדין לא ראי זה כראי זה ג] הצד השוה שבהן שמוזהרין כו' ה"נ לפרוך מה להצד השוה שבהן שכן לא הותרו בבמה מתקיף לה רב סמא בריה דרבא ג] ומאן לימא לן דאונן אסור בבמה דלמא שרי בבמה רב משרשיא אמר אתיא ק"ו מיושב (א) מה יושב שאוכל אם עבד חילל זר שאינו אוכל אינו דין שאם עבד חילל ד] מה ליושב שכן פסול לעדות מיושב ת"ח מה לשם יושב שכן פסול לעדות שם יושב לא פריך ואם ת"ל פריך אתיא מיושב ומחדא מהנך ויושב דכשר בבמה מנלן אמר קרא °לעמוד לפני ה' לשרתו לפני ה' ולא לפני במה: אונן ה] מנלן דכתיב °ומן המקדש לא יצא ולא יחלל הא אחר שלא יצא חילל ו] רבי אלעזר אמר מהכא °הן הקריבו אני הקרבתי מכלל דאי אינהו אקריב שפיר אישתרוף ורבי אלעזר מאי טעמא לא אמר מומן המקדש לא יצא אמר לך מי כתיב הא אחר שלא יצא חילל ואידך מ"ט לא אמר מהן הקריבו קסברי ז] *מפני טומאה נשרפה דבי רבי ישמעאל תנא אתיא בק"ו מבעל מום ומה בעל

רש"י

זר שאינו אוכל· בקדשי קדשים: שכן עשה בו קרב כמקריב· המום פוסל בקרבן כדרך שפוסל בכהן: טמא יוכיח· שלא עשה בו קרב כמקריב שאין בהמה מקבלת טומאה מחיים כשם שהכהן טמא מחיים וכתיב וינזרו ולא יחללו אלמא טמא שעבד חילל: שמוזהרין· שלא לעבוד טמא מוינזרו בעל מום מולא יגש: היכא מוזהר· זר: אי נימא מוינזרו· ח] דרשת ליה להאי קרא בני ישראל להזהיר זרים כדאמר לעיל: חילול בגופיה כתיב· וק"ו למה לך: ה"נ מה להצד כו' שכן לא הותרה בבמה· בבמת יחיד ט] (בבמה) בשעת היתר הבמות דתנן בפ' בתרא (לקמן קיג·) הזמן והנותר והטמא שוין בזה ובזה ובברייתא י] תניא (ב) עלה דברים שוותה במה קטנה לבמה גדולה דם מתיר ומפגל ומומין תאמר בזר שכשר בבמה כדתנן התם אלו דברים שבין במה גדולה לבמה קטנה וקתני התם כיהון ובגדי שרת וקראי נמי יא] מוכחי בגדעון ומנוח ושמואל שהקריבו בבמה: אונן· ילפינן לקמן מקראי אם עבד חילל: שכן אסור במעשר· דכתיב לא אכלתי באוני (דברים כו): אונן מוזהר שלא יעבוד· דכתיב בכהן גדול ומן המקדש לא יצא ולא יחלל הא אחר שלא יצא חילל: דלמא שרי בבמה· דגבי אונן כתיב ומן המקדש: יושב אם עבד חילל· לקמן ילפינן לה בפירקין (כג:): שכן פסול לעדות· דאמרי' במס' שבועות (דף ל·) ועמדו שני האנשים בעדים הכתוב מדבר: ומשני מיושב תלמיד חכם· יב] *הכא מייתי לה דכשר לעדות כדאמרי' התם (שם) שבית דין חולקים לו כבוד ומושיבים אותו: יג] [שם יושב]· מליט שם יושב בעלמא שפסול לעדות משום שם יושב תאמר בשם זר שאינו נפסל לעדות משום שם זרות: שם יושב לא פריך· הואיל והווא יושב ת"ח דמייתי מיניה לק"ו כשר לעדות: ומחד מהנך· אונן או טמא או בעל מום: ויושב דכשר בבמה מנא לן· דלא נפרך שכן לא הותרו בבמה דהא מדשבקיה רב משרשיא לקל וחומר דלעיל דאונן וטמא ובעל מום ונקט יושב משום יד] הני פירכי שבקיה דלא משכחת היתר בבמה בהדיא לחד מינייהו הכא מגליה: לעמוד לפני ה'· במקדש הוא דבעי' עמידה: אונן מנלן· דפסול כדקתני מתני': ומן המקדש וגו'· לעיל מיניה כתיב לאביו ולאמו לא יטמא ובכהן גדול משתעי וסמיך ליה ומן המקדש וגו' כלומר אף ביום שמתו אביו ואמו אין צריך לצאת מן המקדש אלא עומד ומקריב ולא יחלל שאין הקדשים מתחללין בכך הא הדיוט שלא יצא ועבד חילל: הן הקריבו· הן היום הקריבו וגו' מתשובתו של אהרן אתה לומד מה אמר לו משה מדוע לא אכלתם כו' שמא בניך הקריבוה באנינות א) שהיו אוננים על נדב ואביהוא טו] *ופסלתיה ולכך נשרפה אמר לו אהרן וכי הן הקריבו והלא הדיוטות הן ופסולין לעבודה אני הקרבתי שאמרת לי ועשה את קרבן העם וגו' ואני כהן גדול ומקריב אונן מכלל דאי אינהו אקרוב דשפיר אשתרוף ולא היה משה אומר להם מדוע לא אכלתם: מי כתיב הא אחר כו'· דלמא אחר נמי לא חילל ובדידיה אילטריך ליה למישרייה דלא תימא מתוך טז] חשובו וקדושתו יתירה הוא פסול אונן: קסבר מפני טומאה· שנגע בה נשרפה ולא הוזכר שם אנינות לענין הקרבה והן (ג) הקריבו ה"ק הן היום הלא עדיין יום הוא *והייתי אסורין בקדשים לאכול עד הערב יז] ומתוך כך אירע בה טומאה באונס ואיכא תנאי דפליגי לקמן (דף קא·) בהא חד אמר מפני טומאה נשרפה וחד אמר מפני אנינות נשרפה שלא היו יכולין לאוכלה אפילו לערב דקסבר אנינות לילה נמי אסור ואפילו נקבר המת ולפי שלא היו לה אוכלין נשרפה וכדר' יוחנן בן ברוקה דאמר בפסחים (דף פב·) גבי נטמאו בעלים של פסח אף זה ישרף מיד שאין לו אוכלין ואין טעון עבור צורה: שאינו

א) עי' נ"ק ועי' ברמב"ן בחומש פרשת שמיני

תוספות

זר שאינו אוכל כו'· ואין לומר דטמא בקרבן צבור וכהן גדול אונן יח] יוכיח שאינן אוכלין ועובדים דמה להנך שכן אינן מוזהרים תאמר בזר דמוזהר: מה לטמא שכן מטמא· לא מצי למיפרך שכן עשה בו קריבים כמקריבים [כדפי' בקונטרס]:

אף אני אביא זר שמוזהר כו'· לכך צריך לטעמא דאזהרה משום דלא תימא טמא בקרבן צבור וכהן גדול אונן יוכיח כדפרישית ומהאי טעמא נמי צריך לקמן בערל הלכתא גמירי לה דלא אתי בק"ו:

היכן מוזהר· תימה נימא מוהקריבו בני אהרן דדרשי' (לקמן דף נג·) מקבלה ואילך מצות כהונה מיהא עדיפא יט] משני להו גמור מוכל זר לא יקרב:

הג"ה דלמא שרי בבמה· והאי דלא חשיב אונן לקמן בסוף מכילתין (דף קיג·) בדברים שבין במה גדולה לבמה קטנה כדחשיב כיהון ובגדי שרת דילמא תנא ושייר דשייר נמי יושב:

ומה יושב שאוכל· כגון במורם מקדשים כ] ובכור:

מה ליושב שכן פסול לעדות· צריך ליזהר שלא לדון ע"פ עדות דמיושב ובגט אשה צריך ליזהר יותר ושמא דיעבד אין לחוש דאמר בירושלמי פרק ד' מיתות גבי מברך את השם והדיינין שומדין על רגליהם מיכן לדיינין שקבלו עדות מעומד שדנין על פי עדותן ומשמע התם דכי היכי דאין עכובא בישיבת הדיינין אע"פ שיש להם לישב מן התורה ה"נ אין עכובא בעמידת העדים אע"פ שיש להם לעמוד מן התורה הקשה ה"ר אפרים כהן גזלן יהא פסול לעבודה קל וחומר מבעל מום שכשר לעדות ואם עבד חילל ולייתי מבעל מום ומחד מהנך ולאו קושיא היא דכיון דגזלן אינו מוזהר לא אתי מינייהו כדפרישית לעיל:

מיושב תלמיד חכם· א"כ הא דאמרי' (שבועות דף ל:) דתלמיד חכם לא ליזל לאסהודי לקמיה דזוטר מיניה לאו משום דצריך לעמוד אלא משום זילותא דהא אי אזיל לאסהודי (מכנפשיה) מעיד מיושב ותו דאמרינן בפרק שבועת העדות (שם) הני מילי לממונא אבל לאיסורא ילך להעיד אין חכמה ואין תבונה לנגד ה' ותימה בסנהדרין (יט·) דאמרו לו ינאי עמוד על רגליך ויעידו בך והא מלך עדיף מתלמיד חכם דמלך אין יכול למחול על כבודו ותלמיד חכם יכול למחול וי"ל דלא דמי דטעמא דמחיל תלמיד חכם משום דתורה דידיה היא אבל מלך כתיב שתהא אימתו עליך אין זה שלו אלא של אחרים ואין יכול למחול זה ולגבי מצות יכול למחול דאם מוחל על כבודו כא] בשביל כך לא יניח שלא תהא אימתו עליך ועוד יש לומר דעובדא דינאי דיני נפשות הוה ובדיני נפשות אפילו תלמיד חכם עומד ואם תאמר היכי גמר מיושב תלמיד חכם מה ליושב תלמיד חכם שכן פסול לחליצה דחליצה בעי מעומד כדאמר שילהי מצות חליצה (יבמות קו·) בתי עמודי וטעמא משום דכתיב ועמד ואמר ומיהו כב] טעמא על כרחין דחליצה מעומד לאו משום ועמד ואמר דמי כתיב ויעמד ויאמר כדדייק פ' בתרא דמועד קטן (דף כא·) גבי קריעה אלמא טעמא משום דהוי כמו דין ויטול תלמיד חכם לישב כג] ובדיעבד אם חלצה מיושב כשרה תדע דהא תניא חלצה בין עומד בין יושב בין מוטה כשרה ואי מקרא דועמד ואמר בעינן מעומד אם כן ליהוי עכובא מקרא דככה אלא מטעם דין הוי כדפרישית ובספרי דריש עומד מקרא דועמד ואמר אסמכתא הוא כד] א): הגה"ה ואם תאמר. מה ליושב שכן אסור בעזרה כדאמר (יומא דף כה·) אין ישיבה בעזרה אלא למלכי בית דוד ושמא איט מן התורה תדע דאי דאורייתא אמאי צריך קרא לקמן (דף כג:) ליושב למצוה תיפוק ליה דאפילו כה] בלאו עבודה אין ישיבה ב) ומיהו איצטריך קרא לעובד בהשתחוואה):

קסבר מפני טומאה נשרפה· הוה מצי למימר כדבסמוך לתנא דבי רבי ישמעאל דקסבר מפני אנינות נשרפה והן הקריבו כו] אתי לאזהרה שאמר

שיטה מקובצת

א] חילל היכן מוותר אילימא מוינזרו: ב] זה כו' הצד: ג] ומאן לימא לן כו'· דכתיב ומן המקדש לא יצא ולא יחלל ודייקינן הא אחר שלא יצא חלל ודוקא במקדש כדקאמר קרא אבל בבמה לא וא"ת והיכי ס"ד הכי דאונן אסור בבמה והא מן המקדש כתיב בקרא וי"ל דס"ל משום רבותא דכה"ג נקטיה דלא יצא אפילו מן המקדש אבל לעולם ה"ה בבמה וא"ת והא מדלא תני ליה לקמן גבי חילוק דבמה גדולה לקטנה אלמא אסור בבמה וי"ל דתנא ושייר וכ"ת מאי שייר דהאי שייר שייר יושב· מהר"פ: ד] מה ליושבא) משמע מהכא דיושב פסול לעדות וא"כ צריך כו' עד עדותן כו' דכי היכי דאין כו' עד התורה כיון דמחד קרא נפקא לכך י"ל דפריך הכא מה ליושב שכן פסול לעדות לכתחלה· מהר"פ: ה] אונן (סנהדרין דף פד ע"א): ו] חילל וא"ת מאי קאמר אם איתא דאחר נמי לא חילל הוי ליה למכתב גבי כהן הדיוט ולא גבי כה"ג וי"ל דאי כתביה גבי כהן הדיוט הוי אמינא הא כה"ג אם עבד חילל דמתוך חשיבות הוא נפסל כך

בעל מום שאוכל אם עבד חילל אונן שאין אוכל אינו דין שאם עבד חילל מה לבעל מום שכן עשה בו קריבין כמקריבין זר יוכיח מה לזר שכן אין לו תקנה בעל מום יוכיח *וחזר הדין לא ראי זה כראי זה ולא ראי זה כראי זה הצד השוה שבהן שהן מוזהרין ואם עבדו חיללו אף אני אביא אונן שמוזהר ואם עבד חילל היכן מוזהר אילימא מומן המקדש לא יצא חילול בגופיה כתיב ביה אלא °מהן הקריבו וקסבר א] *מפני אנינות נשרפה איכא למפרך מה להצד השוה שבהן ב] שכן לא הותרה מכללו טמא יוכיח מה לטמא שכן מטמא הנך יוכיחו וחזר הדין כו' הצד השוה שבהן שמוזהרין כו' ולפרוך מה להצד השוה שבהן שכן לא הותרו מכללן אצל כהן גדול בקרבן יחיד שם טומאה מיהא אישתראי רב משרשיא אמר ג] אתיא בקל וחומר מיושב ומה יושב שאוכל אם עבד חילל אונן שאינו אוכל אינו דין שאם עבד חילל מה ליושב שכן פסול לעדות מיושב תלמיד חכם מה לשם יושב שכן פסול לעדות שם יושב לא פריך ואם תימצי לומר פריך אתיא מיושב ומחדא מהנך: אונן פסול: אמר ד] רבא לא שנו אלא בקרבן יחיד ה] אבל בקרבן צבור מרצה קל וחומר מטומאה (א) מה טומאה שלא הותרה מכללה אצל כהן גדול בקרבן יחיד הותרה אצל הדיוט בקרבן צבור אנינות שהותרה מכללה אצל כהן גדול בקרבן יחיד אינו דין שהותרה אצל כהן הדיוט בקרבן ציבור מתקיף לה רבא בר אהילאי לא תותר אנינות אצל כהן גדול בקרבן יחיד מקל וחומר ומה טומאה שהותרה אצל כהן הדיוט בצבור לא הותרה אצל כהן גדול בקרבן יחיד אנינות שלא הותרה אצל כהן הדיוט בקרבן צבור אינו דין שלא תותר אצל כהן גדול בקרבן יחיד ותותר טומאה אצל כ"ג בקרבן יחיד מק"ו ומה אנינות שלא הותר אצל כהן הדיוט בקרבן צבור הותרה אצל כהן גדול בקרבן יחיד טומאה שהותרה אצל כהן הדיוט בקרבן צבור אינו דין שהותרה אצל כ"ג בקרבן יחיד ולא תותר טומאה אצל כהן הדיוט בקרבן צבור מקל וחומר ומה אנינות שהותרה אצל כ"ג בקרבן יחיד לא הותרה אצל כהן הדיוט בקרבן צבור טומאה שלא הותרה אצל כהן גדול בקרבן יחיד אינו דין שלא תותר בכהן הדיוט בקרבן צבור (ולא תותר ולא תותר אני נות וטומאה טומאה יחיד ויחיד ציבור סימן) אלא

שאינו אוכל · דכתיב לא אכלתי באוני : [אין לו תקנה] · ואונן יש לו תקנה למחר : בעל מום · יש לו תקנה כשיעבור מומו : חילול בגופיה כתיב · כיון דדייקת הא אחר שלא יצא ו] ק"ו תו למה לך : וקסבר מפני אנינות נשרפה · שלא היו לו אוכלין וכדפרישית וכשאמרו לו מפני אנינות שרפתוה טעה כסבור שהקריבוה אוננים ואמר להם שמא באנינות הקריבוה ומיהו חילול לא יליף ר' ישמעאל מיניה דהי לאו ז] (קרא אחרינא) הוה אמינא האי דאמר להו שמא באנינות הקרבתם אותו לאו למימרא דאי עביד הכי שפיר אשתרוף אלא כשאמרו לו מפני אנינות שרפטוה אמר להם שמא עברתם על האזהרה והקרבתם ח] אוננין ואמר לו אהרן וכי הן הקריבו דאסורים להקריב אוננין אני הקרבתי שאין אנינות פוסל בי : לא הותרו מכללן · זר ובעל מום מכלל איסורן שנאסרו במקדש לא הותרו אצל שום קרבן ולא אצל שום אדם תאמר באונן שהותר מכללו אצל כהן גדול : טמא יוכיח · שהותר מכללו אצל קרבן צבור דכתיב במועדו ואפילו בטומאה ואם עבד בקרבן יחיד חילל : ולפרוך מה להצד השוה · שבשלשתן שכן לא הותרו בקרבן יחיד אפי' אצל כ"ג אבל אונן הותר : שם טומאה מיהא הא אישתראי · כגון בצבור הלכך לאו פירכא היא ואי קשיא למה לי למימר טמא יוכיח בזר נמי משכחת לה דהותר שם זרות בבמה אין זה הותר מכללו שהרי לא נאסר שם מעולם אבל אונן הותר מכללו שהרי נאסר במקדש אצל כהן [הדיוט] : מתקיף לה רבא בר אהילאי יט] אדרבא פריך דפשיטא ליה דטומאה לא הותרה לכהן גדול בקרבן יחיד מדלא אשכחן דאישתראי אלא בצבור ופשיטא ליה דהותרה בצבור אפילו אצל כהן הדיוט מדאישתראי סתמא ופשיטא ליה דאנינות הותרה אפילו בקרבן יחיד אצל כהן גדול מדאשתראי סתמא ובאיסור אנינות אצל כהן הדיוט בא לחלק על ידי ק"ו ולומר לא נאסר אלא ביחיד ולא אמרי' סתמא איתסר אם במה שלא חלקו הכתובים אתה בא לחלק על ידי קל וחומר אמאי פשיטא לך בהנך דלעיל יש לך לדרוש קל וחומר חילוף ולהחליף את כולן י] : לא תותר אנינות אצל כהן גדול ביחיד · וכי שרייה בצבור שרייה : מק"ו ומה טומאה שהותרה כו' · דהא סתמא אישתרי : לא הותרה כו' · דהא לא אשכחן דאישתראי ביחיד דלא כתיב במועדו אלא בצבור אנינות כו' : ותותר טומאה כו' · כלומר אי נמי דריש הכי ותותר טומאה אצל כ"ג יא] ביחיד ואוקי איסורא בכהן הדיוט : ולא תותר טומאה אצל כהן הדיוט כו' · כלומר א"כ החליף ודרוש בו כמלא מסולק מכולן ולא אל תחלוק במה שלא פירשו לך הכתובים : דאיכא

שאמר להם משה שמא עברתם על איסור הקרבת אנינות וטעיתם מחמת כך לשורפו ומיהו לא יתול כדפי' בקונטרס בסמוך וסוגיא זו יג] לא כחד מהנך תנאי דפ' טבול יום (לקמן קא·) ואין לתמוה על זה *דהנהו תנאי דרשי קראי דהתם לפי האמת דקי"ל דאונן מחיל עבודה מקרא אחרינא אבל אי לאו דנפקא לן מקרא אחרינא מהתם לא הוה שמעינן דהוה דרישנא לקרא כי הכא וכדמפרש ליה בקונטרס :

והיכן מוזהר כו' אלא מהן הקריבו וקסבר מפני אנינות נשרפה · שלא היו* יד] אוכלין כל היום ולילה שאחרי כן ולמחרתו יהיה טו] [נותר] ונשרף בו ביום בלא עבור צורה דקסבר אנינות לילה נמי אסור ואפי' נקבר המת וכשאמר לו אהרן מפני אנינות נשרפה טעה משה שלא הבין מפני אנינות דקאמר אהרן שזהו שלא היו ראויין לאכול מחמת אנינותם אלא טז] קסבר שהקריבו אוננים ואמר להו משה שמא יז] באנינות הקרבתוה ומיהו חילול לא יליף ר' ישמעאל מיניה דאי לאו קרא אחרינא הוה אמינא דכי נמי יח] דאמר להם באנינות אקרבתוה לא למימר דאי עבוד הכי שפיר אשתרוף אלא כשאמרו לו מפני אנינות שרפטוה אמר להם שמא עברתם על אזהרה והקרבתם אוננים ואמר יט] אהרן וכי הן הקריבו כך פי' בקונט' וקצת צריך להוסיף על פירושו דכשאמר להם שמא עברתם על אזהרה והקרבתם אוננים כ] רוצה לומר וטעיתם לשורפה על כך כא] דאי לאו הכי מה ענין זה אצל כב] (זה) שריפה ועל זה השיב אהרן הן הקריבו אני הקרבתי ומפני אנינות שאמרתי לא מפני הקרבתם באנינות אלא מפני שלא יכולנו לאכול מפני אנינותינו וא"ת בפ' כיצד צולין (פסחים פב·) ולקמן בפרק התערובת (דף פג·) דדרשינן חטאת שנכנס דמה לפנים פסולה מהן לא הובא את דמה כג] היכי דריש ליה דלמא הכי קאמר ליה שמא כד] טעית לשורפה מפני שנכנס דמה לפנים וי"ל דלא דמי דלמה היה לו להזכיר למשה הנך פסולין דיוצא ונכנס דמה לפנים דבשלמא גבי אנינות היה סבור שמא טעה לפי שאמר לו אהרן מפני אנינות נשרפה וה"ר חיים תירץ דאנינות לא אמר לו משה בפירוש אלא מתוך תשובתו של אהרן אבל הן לא הובא את דמה אמר משה בפי' משמע בהדיא דאם הובא שפיר אישתרוף : **שכן** לא הותרו מכללן · פירש בקונטרס וזר דהותר בבמה אין זה הותר מכללו שהרי לא נאסר שם מעולם והקשה ה"ר חיים דבהקומץ רבה (מנחות כה·) קרי כה] עון יולא הותר מכללו כו] בבמה ותירץ דשאני גבי לין דכתיב לרצון להם בכל מקום שמרצה ועוד י"ל דאפילו מיקרי הותר מכללו מ"מ פרכינן הכא שפיר שכן לא הותרו מכללן במקום שנאסרו : **שם** טומאה מיהא אישתראי · וא"ת מה להנך זר בעל מום שכן במיתה תאמר באונן וכו' וי"ל דסבר לה כרבנן דאמרי (סנהדרין פג·) בעל מום ששימש באזהרה ולא כרבי [דאמר] במיתה וא"ת מה להנך שכן פסולין בפרה בעל מום זר וטמא תאמר באונן (לקמן דף יז:) וי"ל טבול יום יוכיח : **אתיא** בק"ו מיושב · תימה מה ליושב שכן לא הותר מכללו : **אבל** בקרבן צבור מרצה · תימה הרי חטאת דאהרן דהיינו שעיר דר"ח דקיימא לן פרק טבול יום (לקמן קא·) ובשמעתין דאם הקריבוה באנינות פסולה וי"ל כיון דלא ילפינן אלא מטומאה דינו כטומאה דאינו מרצה אלא כז] באימורין אבל הקרבן אינו נאכל ועוד דבלאו הכי סתר ליה שפיר להאי ק"ו : **ומה** טומאה · תימה אי אנינות לילה דאורייתא איכא למיפרך מה לטומאה שכן הותרה בפסח הבא בטומאה באכילה תאמר באנינות שלא הותר : **ולא** תותר אנינות כו' · תימה מה לטומאה שכן מטמא כח] ויש לומר דאינו ק"ו גמור אלא סתירת דברים כט] : *)**כל** חדא וחדא תיקום בדוכתיה ל] ל"ע פ"ק דחולין (דף כג:) גבי ק"ו דכשר בתורים פסול בבני יונה וגבי כשר שבפרה פסול בעגלה (שם כג:) וגבי ויהיו כל הכלים מקבלין טומאה מאויר ומק"ו (שם כה·) ובפר' ואלו מנחות (מנחות עה·) גבי חלות ורקיקים ובפר' כל המנחות (שם דף סג:) גבי שלמי יחיד שטעונין סמיכה ובפ' השוכר את הפועלים (ב"מ פח:) גבי שור אוכל במחובר ובפרק כיצד הרגל (ב"ק כה:) דקאמר ותהא שן חייבת ברשות הרבים מק"ו ובפ"ק דקדושין (דף יד.) ותהא יבמה יוצאה בגט מקל וחומר ובנזיר פרק שלשה מינין (דף מד·) גבי **) טמא כמיטמא ובסוף יש מותרות (יבמות פז:) דנעשה מתים כחיים מק"ו צריך לדקדק בכולן אמאי לא אמר כל חדא וחדא תיקום בדוכתיה ושמא שאני הכא משום דהני

*) שייך לדף שאחר זה **) נ"ל מטמא נ"ק

[נ"ל ק"ו]

[קדושין כא. וש"נ]

[לקמן קא. פסחים פב:]

דהנהו תנאי דהתם דרשי קראי לפי האמת דקי"ל דאונן מחיל עבודה וילפינן מקרא אחרינא כו' אחרינא מהך קרא לא הוה כו' נ"ק

נ"א שלא היו יכולין לאכול כל היום ולילה שאחריו עד למחרתו והיו שורפין בו ביום כו' נ"ק

שיטה מקובצת

א] מפני אנינות נשרפה· וא"ת חילול נמי בגופיה כתיבא כדאמר לעיל הא אקריבו אינהו שפיר אשתרוף [וי"ל דאי] לאו קרא אחרינא הוי אמינא הא דאמר להו שמא באנינות הקרבתם אותה לאו למימרא דאי עבדי הכי שפיר אשתרוף כו' כפ"ה וא"ת בפרק התערובת כו' וי"ל דלא דמי לאנינות א) [דלא] אמר משה בפירוש אלא מתוך תשובתו של אהרן כדפי' אבל הן לא הובא את דמה כתוב בפירוש משמע בהדיא הא אם הובא שפיר אשתרוף · תוספות בסגנון אחר : ב] שכן לא הותרה מכללו וא"ת הרי הותר מכללו בבמה וי"ל דהואיל ושם לא נאסר מעולם אין זה הותר מכללו דמכללו משמע ממקום שנאסר וכפ"ה והקשה הר"ר חיים כהן כו' וי"ל דה"פ מה לזר שכן לא הותר בבמת צבור תאמר באונן שכן הותר מכללן בבמת צבור · מהר"פ : ג] אתיא בקל וחומר מיושב · לא בא רב משרשיא לחלוק על דברי דבי רבי ישמעאל שהוא תנא אלא תנא דבי רבי ישמעאל אמר דבריו בקיצור אתיא מקל וחומר ולא יותר ופי' התלמוד לעיל מבעל מום ואונן ורב משרשיא פי' מיושב ויש לתמוה על הסוגיא דלעיל אמר לתנא דבי ר' ישמעאל קאתי זר מאונן ובעל מום דקאמר אונן יוכיח אלמא פשיטא ליה אונן מחלל יותר מזר והכא פשיט אונן מבעל מום וזר (אלא) [אלמא] פשיט ליה דזר מחלל יותר מאונן ואמר מורי דתנא דלעיל מיירי לפי אותה שיטה דקים לן דאונן מחלל עבודה מקרא דהן הקריבו או מן המקדש כו' הא אחר שלא יצא כו' אבל זר לא נפקא לן מינזרו דלא מיירי כלל בזרות אלא בטומאה והכא איירי לפי אותה שיטה דזר מחלל עבודה מינזרו ולא נפקא לן אונן לא מהן הקריבו ולא מן המקדש לא יצא· מהר"פ· אתיא מיושב כו' וא"ת מה ליושב שכן לא הותר מכללו במקדש אצל כה"ג בקרבן יחיד תאמר באונן כו' וי"ל דהוי פירכא כל דהו ופירכא כל דהו לא פרכינן על חדא מחדא ומיהו לבסוף דקאמר אתיא מיושב וחד מהנך קשה דאיכא למיפרך מה להצד השוה שבהן שכן לא הותר מכללן במקדש וי"ל

הגהות הב"ח

(א) גמרא ומה טומאה :

שיטה מקובצת

כהנים שלא היו אוננים היו מותרים לאכול אף על פי שהאוננים הקריבוה כיון דקרבן צבור הוה וחילול עבודה דאונן נפקא ליה לרבא מלא יחלל וסבירא ליה דאנינות לילה לאו דאורייתא והיינו [הן] היום כדפי' לעיל ותדע דאי קסבר אנינות לילה דאורייתא א"כ היכא יליף דתותר אנינות מטומאה הא איכא למיפרך מה לטומאה שכן הותר מכללו אצל אכילת פסחים · מהר"פ: ו] יצא חילול ק"ו: ז] לאו ק"ו ותיבות קרא אחרינא נמחק : ח] אוננין גליון כלומר טעיתם לשורפה על כך ואין בו · אלא אזהרה : ט] אהילאי אדרבה פריך : י] כולן ודרוש לא והדר"א : יא] כה"ג בקרבן יחיד ואוקי : יב] אלא לא תחלוק : יג] דלא כחד : יד] היו לה אוכלין : טו] יהיה נשרף בו ביום ולכן ישרף בלא עבור צורה : טז] קסבר מפני אנינות נשרפה שלא היו לה אוכלין וקסבר אנינות לילה דאורייתא מיהו לא יליף חילול ר' ישמעאל מיניה דאי לאו קרא אחרינא כו' · לשון מהר"פ : יז] שמא אקרבתוה באנינות ופסלתוה ומיהו חילול: יח] נמי אמר להם שמא: יט] ואמר לו אהרן וכי הן הקריבו דאסורים להקריב אוננים אני שאני כה"ג הקרבתים שאין אנינות פוסלת בי כך: כ] אוננים היה רוצה לומר משה שמא טעיתם לשורפה : כא] עיין בהשמטות בסוף המסכת: כב] תיבת זה נמחק : כג] דמה דמשמע הא אם הובאה דמה פסולה והיכי דריש ליה דלמא : כד] שמא עברת על האזהרה וטעית : כה] היבת עון נמחק : כו] מכללו לפי שהותר בבמה : כז] אלא

(נמשך) דשם טומאה מיהא אישתראי ונליף מיושב ומטמא · מהר"פ : ד] אמר רבה אות א' נמחק : ה] אבל בקרבן צבור מרצה טומאה הא מדכתיב הן היום הקריבו משמע אי אקרבוה שפיר אשתרוף והתם קרבן צבור הוי וי"ל דנהי דמרצה מ"מ אינו נאכל דדיו לבא מן הדין [להיות] כנדון דמטומאה גמרינן לה והתם אינו נאכל אע"ג דמרצה ומיהו קשה דלא דמי לטומאה דהתם הא דאינו נאכל היינו משום דנטמא הבשר כשנוגע בה הלכך אע"ג דמרצה הבשר (טמאה) [טמא] אבל באנינות לא שייך למימר הכי לכך נראה דרבא סבר דבאנינות נשרפה ומה שלא אכלוה היום מפני שהיו אוננים ולא היו להם אוכלים אבל ודאי אם היה שם האימורין אבל : כח] מטמא ועוד הרבה איכא למיפרך על אלו קלים וחמורים : כט] דברים בעלמא הס"ד : ל] בדוכתיה' כלומר אם באתם לחלק בכתובים ולומר דלא מיירי בכל ענין א"כ תעשה קלים וחמורים להוציא מהם דברים שאינם אלא ודאי אין להוציא ולגרוע על המפורש בכתובים והא דשרי רחמנא אונן [בכה"ג] אין לחלק בין קרבן צבור בין קרבן יחיד וכשאסר רחמנא אונן כהן הדיוט בכל ענין אסרו בין בקרבן יחיד בין בקרבן צבור וקרבן צבור דשרי רחמנא [בטומאה] בין בכהן גדול ובין בכהן הדיוט וכשאסר רחמנא קרבן יחיד בטומאה בין בכהן גדול ובין בכהן הדיוט כל חד וחד בדוכתיה · מהר"פ :
חדא

(א) והוא תירוץ של ה"ר חיים בתוספות סוד"ס וסיכן

[priest] with a blemish. If [16b] a [priest] with a blemish, who does eat [thereof], profanes [it] if he officiates, it is surely logical that an *onen*, who may not eat thereof, profanes it by his officiating. In the case of a [priest] with a blemish, the reason may be because they who sacrifice are regarded the same as those which are sacri-
a ficed![1] Then let a *zar* prove it. As for a *zar*, the reason may be because there is no remedy for him![2] Then let a [priest] with a blemish prove it.[3] And thus the argument revolves: the feature peculiar to one is not that of the other, and the feature which characterises the other is not that of the first. The feature common to both is that they are admonished [not to officiate], and if they do officiate, they profane it. So do I adduce an *onen* too who is admonished, and if he officiates, he profanes it. Now, where is he admonished? Shall we say, in the text, *'Neither shall he go out of the Sanctuary'*? Surely profanation is written in that very context![4]—Rather, [it is inferred] from [the text], *'Behold, have they offered'*, and he [the school of R. Ishmael] holds that it was burnt on account of bereavement.[5] This argument may be refuted: As for the feature common to both, it is that there is no exception to the general interdict![6] Then let an unclean [priest] prove it.[7] As for an unclean [priest], the reason is that he defiles [the flesh]! Then let the others prove it. And thus the argument revolves etc. The feature common to both is that they are admonished etc. Yet let us refute it [thus]: As for their common feature, it is that there is no exception to the general [interdict] in favour of a High Priest in the case of a private sacrifice?[8]—The interdict[9] of uncleanness is nevertheless raised.[10]

R. Mesharshia said: It is inferred *a minori* from [a priest] who sits: if a priest, who eats sitting, profanes [the sacrifice] if he officiates whilst sitting, it is surely logical that an *onen*, who may not eat [thereof], profanes [the sacrifice] by his officiating. As for one who sits, the reason may be because he is unfit to testify?—[The argument is] from a scholar who sits. [Then refute it thus:] As for the interdict of sitting, that may be because such is unfit to testify?—One does not refute from the [general] interdict of sitting. And should you say that you can refute thus, [say that] it is inferred from one who sits and one of
b these others.[1]

[ALL SACRIFICES WHOSE BLOOD WAS CAUGHT BY...] AN ONEN... ARE DISQUALIFIED. Rabbah[2] said: They learned this only of a private sacrifice, but in the case of a public sacrifice[3] it is accepted,[4] [this being inferred] from uncleanness, *a minori*: if the general interdict of uncleanness was not raised in favour of a High Priest in the case of a private sacrifice, yet it was permitted to an ordinary priest in the case of a public sacrifice; then bereavement, whose general interdict was raised in favour of a High Priest in the case of a private sacrifice, is surely permitted to an ordinary priest in the case of a public sacrifice. To this Raba b. Ahilai demurred: Let [the interdict of] bereavement *not* be raised in favour of a High Priest in the case of a private sacrifice, *a minori*: if [the interdict of] uncleanness was not raised in favour of a High Priest in the case of a private sacrifice, though it was raised for an ordinary priest in the case of a public sacrifice; is it not logical that [the interdict of] bereavement, which was not raised for an ordinary priest in the case of a public sacrifice, shall not be raised for a High Priest in the case of a private sacrifice? [Or, argue thus:] Let uncleanness be permitted to a High Priest in the case of a private sacrifice, *a minori*: if bereavement, which is not permitted to an ordinary priest in the case of a public sacrifice, is permitted to a High Priest in the case of a private sacrifice; is it not logical that uncleanness, which is permitted to an ordinary priest in the case of a public sacrifice, is permitted to a High Priest in the case of a private sacrifice? Again, [argue thus:] let uncleanness not be permitted to an ordinary priest in the case of a public sacrifice, *a minori*: If bereavement is not permitted to an ordinary priest in the case of a public sacrifice, though it is permitted to a High Priest in the case of a private sacrifice; then uncleanness, which is not permitted to a High Priest in the case of a private sacrifice, is surely not permitted
c to an ordinary priest in the case of a public sacrifice? [Mnemonic:[1] Let it not be permitted; let it not be permitted; bereavement and uncleanness, private sacrifice; private sacrifice; public sacrifice.][2]

a (1) V. *supra* 16a n. 6. (2) Under no circumstances can he become fit to officiate. An *onen* however, will be fit on the next day. (3) He may become whole again. (4) If it is so interpreted as to make it bear upon an ordinary priest, there is no need for the inference *a minori*. (5) Nevertheless the text itself does not prove that if an *onen* officiates the sacrifice is disqualified, as Moses may have meant: Perhaps you transgressed the law by sacrificing it in bereavement, and having done so, you mistakenly thought that it is now disqualified (Rashi, as elaborated by Tosaf.). (6) Lit., 'it was not permitted out of its general rule'. There is no exception to the general law that a *zar* and a blemished priest may not officiate; but a High Priest is excepted from the law interdicting an *onen* to officiate. (7) There is an exception in his case, for if the majority of the people are unclean on the eve of Passover, they offer the Paschal lamb in their unclean state. (8) As opposed to a communal sacrifice. The Passover-offering is accounted as the latter, since the whole nation had to offer one. (9) Lit., 'name'. (10) There is an exception to the general interdict of uncleanness, viz., in the case of the Paschal offering.

b (1) Cf. *supra a* for notes. (2) Text as emended by Sh. M. Cur. edd. Raba. (3) One offered on behalf of the whole community. (4) This is the technical term to denote that it is made valid (generally, in virtue of the headplate *worn* by the High Priest).

c (1) For the various arguments just adduced. (2) The point of all these objections is this: if the Scriptural law can be qualified by logical arguments, these can easily be reversed and precisely the opposite conclusions drawn.

[17a] But you can refute it thus, and you can refute it thus;[3] [therefore] let each one remain in its place.[4]

ṬEBUL YOM. Whence do we know it?—For it was taught, R. Simai said: Where is the allusion that if a *ṭebul yom* officiates he profanes [the sacrifice]? In the text, *They* [the priests] *shall be holy . . . and not profane:*[5] since this cannot refer to an unclean [priest], for [his prohibition] is deduced from, *That they separate themselves,*[6] apply it to a *ṭebul yom.*[7] Say, apply it to the making of a baldness and the shaving off of the corners of the beard?[8]—Since a *ṭebul yom* is liable to death for officiating (and how do we know that? because we deduce [similarity of law] from the use of 'profanation'
a here and in the case of *terumah,*)[1] [it follows that] he who is unfit [to partake of] *terumah* profanes the service [of sacrifice], whereas he who is not unfit [to partake of] *terumah* does not profane the service.

Rabbah said: Why must the Divine Law enumerate an unclean priest, a *ṭebul yom,* and one who lacks atonement?[2]—They are all necessary. For had the Divine Law written [the law for] an unclean priest [only, I would say that he disqualifies the sacrifice] because he defiles.[3] [If the law were written] with reference to a *ṭebul yom,* one who lacks atonement could not be derived from it, seeing that [the former] is disqualified [to partake] of *terumah.*[4] [If it were written] with reference to one who lacks atonement, a *ṭebul yom* could not be learnt from it, seeing that [the former] lacks a [positive] act.[5]

Now, [one] cannot be derived from one [other], [but] let one be derived from two?[6]—In which should the Divine Law not write [this ruling]? Should it not write [it] with respect to one who lacks atonement, so that it might be inferred from the others, [it might be argued]: as for the others, [their peculiar feature is] that they are disqualified [to partake of] *terumah.* Rather, let not the Divine Law write it of a *ṭebul yom,* which could be inferred from the others. For how will you refute [the analogy]: as for these others,
b [the reason is that] they are wanting in a [positive] act?[1] [This would be no refutation] for after all, its[2] uncleanness is but slight![3]

(3) You can argue either way. (4) Assume each law to be without exceptions. Thus, when Scripture permits bereavement to a High Priest, it applies to both private and public sacrifices, while it is forbidden to an ordinary priest likewise in the case of both. Again, when uncleanness is forbidden in the case of a private sacrifice, the interdict applies to the High Priest also; on the other hand, when it is permitted in the case of public sacrifices, that applies to an ordinary priest too. (5) Lev. XXI, 6. The passage treats of defilement, among other things. (6) Ibid. XXII, 2; that verse forbids an unclean priest to officiate. (7) As intimating that he too must not officiate, and if he does, he 'profanes', i.e., disqualifies the sacrifice. (8) Which is mentioned in the preceding verse, ibid. XXI, 5. Perhaps Scripture teaches that a priest who transgresses these interdicts 'profanes' (disqualifies) a sacrifice if he officiates.

a (1) V. Glos. The allusion is to Lev. XXII, 9: *They shall therefore keep My charge,* (this refers to *terumah,* as the whole passage shews) *lest they bear sin for it, and die therein, if they profane it.* Since 'profanation' (i.e., defilement) is punishable by death there, the same holds good here. It also follows conversely that the present passage can apply only to such as 'profane' *terumah.*—By 'death' is meant death at the hands of heaven, not actually capital punishment by man. (2) These are similar to one another, and therefore only one need be mentioned, and the others would follow by analogy. (3) Either the flesh of the sacrifice, or another person by contact. (4) Which the latter is not. (5) Viz., the offering of a sacrifice. But a *ṭebul yom* merely has to wait for sunset. (6) Let Scripture write the law with reference to two of these, and the third could be derived by analogy.

b (1) The unclean priest must take a ritual bath. (2) Reading as Rashi, which is preferable to cur. edd. 'their'. (3) The uncleanness of one who lacks atonement is slighter than that of a *ṭebul yom,* since the latter must still wait for sunset, but not the former. Hence the question remains, why must Scripture indicate the law for all three?

אלא איכא למיפרך הכי ואיכא למיפרך הכי °כל א] חדא וחדא תיקו בדוכתיה: טבול יום: מנלן *דתניא רבי סימאי אומר רמז לטבול
ויקרא כא
יום שאם עבד חילל מנין ת״ל °קדושים יהיו ולא יחללו אם אינו ענין לטמא דנפיק ב]
שם כב
°מוינזרו תנהו ענין לטבול יום אימא תנהו ענין לקורח קרחה ולמשחית פאת זקן טבול יום דאם עבד במיתה מנא לן דגמר חילול חילול מתרומה ג] *דפסיל בתרומה מחיל עבודה דלא פסיל בתרומה לא מחיל עבודה אמר רבה למה לי דכתב רחמנא טמא וטבול יום ומחוסר כפורים צריכי דאי כתב רחמנא טמא שכן מטמא בטבול יום מחוסר כפורים לא אתי מיניה שכן ד] פסול בתרומה במחוסר כפורים טבול יום לא אתי מיניה שכן מחוסר מעשה מחדא לא אתי תיתי חדא מתרתי בהי לא לכתוב רחמנא לא לכתוב במחוסר כפורים ותיתי מהנך מה להנך שכן ה] פסולים בתרומה אלא לא לכתוב רחמנא בטבול יום ותיתי מהנך דמאי פרכת מה להנך שכן מחוסרים מעשה ו] סוף סוף קלישא לה טומאתן
קסבר

ז] דאיכא למיפרך הכי כו׳ · *יש לדון (א) כו׳ ויש להחליף ולא נדע איזה נדרוש הלכך כל חדא תיקו בדוכתה ככתיבתה סתם כשהותרה אניעת לכ״ג סתם בין ביחיד בין בצבור הותרה וכשנאסרה להדיוט בין ביחיד בין בצבור נאסרה וכשהותרה טומאה בצבור הותרה אף לכהן הדיוט וכשנאסרה בקרבן יחיד נאסרה אף לכ״ג: קדושים יהיו · גבי טומאה כתיב באמור ולא יחללו וגו׳ כי את אשי ה׳ לחם וגו׳ בחילול קדשים הכתוב מדבר: דנפקא ליה מוינזרו · דכתיב ביה חילול: ח] וכימא תנהו ענין וכו׳ · דמינייהו סליק לא יקרחו קרחה וסמיך ליה קדושים יהיו: אלא לא גרס: ט] טבול יום דאם עבד במיתה · י] שיטיא הוא כלומר לא מלית *למיתני תנהו ענין לקורח קרחה דמיתה גבי טבול יום שעבד יא] ילפינן לה בסנהדרין באלו הן הנשרפין (דף פג:) יב] וגמר חילול חילול מתרומה ומחילול דהאי קרא יליף לה נאמר כאן חילול ונאמר בטמא וטבול יום שאכלו תרומה חילול ומתו בו כי יחללוהו מה להלן במיתה כו׳ והלכך הואיל והאי קרא לג״ש מתרומה אתא ולא מפרש ביה במאי קאי לא תתנהו ענין אלא לפסולין לתרומה יג] דילפי׳ מיניה דפסול בתרומה מחיל עבודה יד] כו׳: למה לי דכתב רחמנא טמא וטבול יום כו׳ · אטמא לא קמיבעיא ליה דאי לאו כתב טמא לא הוה אתי לן חד מנייהו שיחלל עבודה דהא טבול יום בהם איתו ענין לטמא טו] ילפינן ואי לא הוה כתב טמא בוינזרו הוה אוקימנא לקדושים יהיו בטמא וכן מחוסר כפורים נמי לא כתב טז] בה חילול אלא מדאיקרי טמא ילפינן ליה לקמן (ב) וכי מיבעי ליה לרבה טבול יום ומחוסר כפורים קמיבעיא יז]: במחוסר כפורים טבול יום לא אתי מיניה שכן מחוסר מעשה· הבאת קרבן תאמר בטבול יום שאינו מחוסר יח] הבאת קרבן ושימשא ממילא ערבא בטמא ליכא למימר דלא אתיא מיני׳ דהא איהו נמי מחוסר טבילה ועוד דטמא לא קמיבעיא ליה מדלא קאמר בסיפא דמילתא לא לכתוב טמא ותיתי מהנך דתו לא הוה ליה לשניי עלה מידי: קלישא ליה טומאתו · דמחוסר כפורים יט] שהרי העריב שמשו ואו ליכא פירכא דמה כ] הלד דהוה ליה חד מינייהו נמי שאינו מחוסר מעשה:
קסבר

דהני ק״ו סתרי אהדדי מה שאין כן בהנהו כא] והטעם כמו שפירש בקונט׳ משום דנכתבו הכתובים סתם דכשהותרה אניעת לכ״ג סתם בין ביחיד בין בצבור הותרה וכשנאסרה להדיוט בין ביחיד בין בצבור נאסרה וכשהותרה טומאה לצבור הותרה אף לכהן הדיוט וכשנאסרה בקרבן יחיד נאסרה אף לכ״ג ואם במה שלא חלקן הכתובים נדון לחלק על ידי ק״ו אמאי פשיטא בהאי טפי מבהאי דיש לדרוש חלוף ולהחליף את כולן הלכך אמרינן כל חדא וחדא תיקום בדוכתיה כב]*: **טבול** יום מנא לן · תימה תיפוק לי מדכתיב גבי טבול יום ובא השמש וטהר מכלל שהוא טמא כדדריש לקמן מחוסר כפורים מדכתיב וטהרה מכלל שהיא טמאה כג] ותירץ ה״ר חיים דגבי טבול יום איכא למידרש וטהר טהר יומא כד] כדדרשינן בשמעתא קמייתא דברכות (דף ב:) אבל וטהרה לא שייך למידרש הכי ואע״ג דבפ׳ הערל (יבמות עד:) דרשי׳ וטהרה כה] לטבולת יום ארוך ההיא מחוסרת כפרה היא ועל ידי מכלל שהיא טמאה לא אתי מיניה טבול יום גרידא ומיהו קשה דאיכא קרא אחרינא בקדשים לא יאכל עד אשר יטהר דמוקמינן בפרק הערל (שם) בזב בעל שתי ראיות דלאו בר קרבן הוא ולענין תרומה וכימא מכלל שהוא טמא ויש לומר דרבי סימאי דדריש הכא טבול יום מקרא אחרינא *סבר לה כתנא כו] [דפליג התם אתנא] דבי רבי ישמעאל דמוקי ליה התם בזב בעל שלש ראיות ומאי עד אשר יטהר עד דמייתי כפרה ומיהו קשה דגבי כז] נגיעת כלי כתיב במים יובא וטמא עד הערב וטהר כח] [מכלל שהוא טמא] וצריך לומר דאי לאו קרא דר׳ סימאי דהכא דדריש טבול יום מולא יחללו לא הוה דרשינן מחוסר כפרה מוטהרה מכלל שהיא טמאה ולא טבול יום מוטהר מכלל שהוא טמא משום דקלישא טומאתייהו אבל מכיון דאשכחן קרא בהדיא לטבול יום ואע״ג דקלישא טומאתיה תו דרשינן שפיר מוטהרה מחוסר כפרה כט] ותימה במים יובא וטמא הלא מפורש בהדיא ל] לטבול יום דאיקרי טמא וי״ל דצריך קרא גבי עבודה לא] דלא יחללו דשמעתין וגבי אכילת תרומה וקדשים קרא אחרינא בפרק הערל (שם) ולא ילפינן מהדדי אבל וטהרה דכתיב גבי יולדת לב] דרשינן מיניה מחוסר כפורים דאסור בקדשים פרק הערל וגבי דמחלל עבודה לקמן בפרקין דאשה כשרה לשחוט קדשים כדתנן ריש כל הפסולין א״כ שייך בה חילול עבודה ותימה דגבי זב וזבה ובעל קרי ושכבת זרע כתיבי כמה פעמים ורחץ במים וטמא עד הערב אלמא טבול יום איקרי טמא בין לעבודה בין לקדשים דקראי סתמא כתיבי ואיקרי טמא לכל מילי ועוד קשה דבפ׳ שלשה מינין (נזיר מה·) ובפ׳ אלו הן הגולין (מכות דף ח:) אמרינן טמא יהיה לרבות טבול יום עוד טומאתו בו לרבות מחוסר כפורים לענין ביאת מקדש והשתא ל״ל קרא הא איקרי טמא לענין עבודה ולאכילת קדשים וכי תימה דלא נילף ביאת מקדש מנייהו (ועוד) קשה שהרי קרא דורחץ במים וטמא עד הערב סתמא כתיב דטבול יום איקרי טמא לכל מילי ואפי׳ לביאת מקדש ועוד תימה כיון דדרשי׳ טבול יום מטמא יהיה למה איצטריך תו עוד טומאתו למחוסר כפורים תיפוק לי מוכפר עליה הכהן וטהרה כדדרשינן לקמן בפירקין מכלל שהיא טמאה לענין עבודה ובפ׳ הערל (יבמות דף עד:) לענין אכילת קדשים נדרוש נמי לענין ביאת מקדש דקרא בכל מילי מיירי שהיא טמאה קודם כפרה *ואין לתרץ נמי דאי לאו אלא חד רבויא הוה מוקמינא ליה במחוסר כפורים משום דמחוסר מעשה ולא בטבול יום משום דשמשא ממילא ערבא דאם כן הוה ליה למימר איפכא טמא יהיה לרבות מחוסר כפורים עוד טומאתו בו לרבות טבול יום ונראה לתרץ דלענין ביאת מקדש לא הוה דרישנא מחוסר כפורים מוטהרה מכלל שהיא טמאה משום דכרת דטומאת מקדש כתיב איש אשר יטמא ולא יתחטא דמיירי בטומאת מת אבל מחוסר כפרה דלא שייך במת לא ליהוי בכרת* ועוד י״ל דצריך קרא לרבות טבול יום לג] [משום דכרת דטומאת מקדש כתיב ולא יתחטא] דמשמע אבל נתחטא שהזה ושנה וטבל דלאו מחוסר מעשה הוא כגון טבול יום לא הוי בכרת ומהני טעמי אתי שפיר דליכא למימר למה לי קרא הא איתקש קדש למקדש דהא קרא דביאת מקדש מיבעי לפטורא וקרא ובא השמש וטהר איצטריך משום דכתיב בשרץ דקיל טפי מנדה ושכבת זרע לד]: **הג״ה** ולמאי דפרישית דמוטהרה מכלל שהיא טמאה לא הוה מרבינן מחוסר כפורים אי לאו דאשכחן טבול יום מקרא דרבי סימאי קלת קשה הא דקאמר בסמוך דאי כתב רחמנא במחוסר כפורים טבול יום לא אתי מיניה הא לא אתי לן מחוסר כפורים אי לאו דאשכחנא קרא בטבול יום לה] וי״ל שרוצה לומר אי כתב רחמנא מחוסר כפורים בפירוש וכי האי גוונא לו] בפרק הולד (יבמות דף כג·) גבי שפחה ונכרית ומיהו קשה אי להאי אתיא א״כ ניכתוב רחמנא טבול יום ומחוסר כפורים בהדיא ולא ליכתוב טמא וי״ל דכיון דלא לז] משכחת לריכותא בהני לא חש לדקדק: **רמז** לטבול יום שאם עבד חילל מנין · הוה מצי למילף מיושב או מבעל מום וחד מהנך: **דגמר** חילול חילול מתרומה · הקשה ה״ר חיים כיון דטבול יום יליף מתרומה אם כן טבול יום שאכל תרומה יהא במיתה ובפ׳ הנשרפין (סנהדרין פג·) לא חשיב טבול יום וטמא הוא הדין א״כ כי היכי דממעטי התם (דף פד·) רבנן בעל מום שימש מדכתיב בו ולא בעל מום ה״ה ומתו בו דכתיב בתרומה בו ולא בטבול יום ומיהו טמא שימש אין למעט מדכתיב בו דלהכי אהני ג״ש דחילול חילול וכן טבול יום ששימש נמי הוי במיתה כדאיתא הכא והתם והיינו טעמא דדמי לטמא טפי מבעל מום ונראה דה״ה לתרומה דלא ממעטינן טבול יום וכן פירש בקונטרס בהדיא דטבול יום שאכל תרומה במיתה ויש ליתן טעם דלא חשיב ליה התם משום דטמא וטבול יום מחד קרא נפקי דהכי כתיבי קראי בפרשת אמור אל הכהנים ובא השמש וטהר ואחר יאכל מן הקדשים וגו׳ והדר כתיב ולא ישאו עליו חטא ומתו בו כי יחללוהו וקלת תימה היכי יליף התם בסנהדרין מחוסר כפורים ששימש במיתה משום דאיקרי טמא וטמא ילפינן חילול חילול מתרומה לח] נימא דפסול בתרומה במיתה ודלא פסול בתרומה לא כדאמרינן הכא דפסול בתרומה מחיל עבודה כו׳ ויש לומר כיון דמחיל עבודה לט] *מטעמא דנפקא לן מוינזרו ולא יחללו כל דאיקרי טמא מ] [סברא היא דגמרינן] בגזירה שוה דחילול חילול מתרומה פרק הנשרפין דהוי במיתה אע״ג דטהור לתרומה:
קסבר

מסורת הש״ס:
נ״ל כלומר יש לדרוש ולהחליף ולא נדע כו׳ צ״ק
סנהדרין פג:
נס״י למיתניה ענין
נס״י ליתא
עי׳ בחדושי מהרש״א בסנהדרין שם ועיין צ״ק
עיין צ״ק נ״ל
נ״ל נטמא

הגהות הב״ח
(א) רש״י ד״ה דאיכא וכו׳ יש לדון כך ויש: (ב) ד״ה למה לי וכו׳ לקמן דף יט ע״ב וכי מיבעי וכו׳ קמיבעיא נ״ב ס״ד:

עין משפט נר מצוה
יא א מיי׳ פ״ב מהלכות ביאת מקדש הלכה ו:
[ועי׳ היטב תוס׳ מנחות סב: ד״ה ויהיו זכחי ותוס׳ מנחות נט. ד״ה ונתת ותוס׳ חולין כג: ד״ה ותהא]
[עי׳ תוס׳ לקמן כח: ד״ה מחשבה]
גי׳ צ״ק סבר דאידך תנא דבי ר״י ומוקי ליה כו׳

שיטה מקובצת
א] חדא וחדא · עיין מנחות (דף נט ע״א) תוס׳ [ד״ה ונתת] (ודף סב ע״ב) תוס׳ [ד״ה ויהיו]: ב] דנפיק לן מוינזרו: ג] דפסיל בתרומה כו׳· תימה הרי טבול יום דלא פסול בתרומת ומחיל העבודה וי״ל דלא קאמר דכל דלא פסיל לא מחיל העבודה דאה״נ דאם נוכל להוכיח מפסוק דמחלל עבודה שפיר ניחא אע״ג דלא פסיל בתרומה אבל הכא ה״ק לא ידעינן במאי מיירי קרא רק באם אינו ענין הלכך לית לן לאוקמי ולא יחלל רק במאן דפסיל בתרומה כיון דנפקא לן שוה שבא באם אינו ענין זה במיתה מחילול חילול דתרומה ולא בקורח קרחה דלא פסיל בתרומה ואע״ג דלא סליק[אלא] מיניה׳ ה״נ למה לי דכתב רחמנא טבול יום ומחוסר כפורים ול״ג טמא דאי לא כתיב טמא כו׳ · מהר״פ: ד] פוסל בתרומה: ה] שכן פוסלים בתרומה: ו] סוף סוף קלישא כו׳ ותימה דלעיל קאמר במחוסר כפורים טבול יום לא אתי מיניה שכן מחוסר מעשה ואמאי לא קאמר דמ״מ קלישא ליה טומאתו דמחוסר כפורים דהכי קאמר ליה השתא אע״ג דמן הצד הוא כ״ש חדא מהדא וי״ל דלא דמי לעיל גבי מחוסר כפורים ר״ל מחוסר מעשה שמחוסר כפרה (מהו) [מה] שאינו כן בטבול יום אבל הכא מחוסר מעשה דקאמר אינו ר״ל מחוסר כפרה דהא טמא לאו מחוסר כפרה הוא כגון טמא שרץ וטמא מת ומגע דוב אלא ר״ל שכן מחוסר מעשה יותר מטבול יום דשמשא ממילא ערבא הלכך קאמר שפיר דקלישא טומאתו דמחוסר כפורים כיון שטבל והעריב שמשו לא מקרי מחוסר מעשה אלא מחוסר כפרה מיקרי וטמא לאו מחוסר כפרה הוא הלכך לא שייך למפרך מידי · מהר״פ ז״ל: ז] מה״ד איכא למיפרך הכי כו׳ יש לדון וכן יש תיבת כו׳ נמחק: ח] מה״ד אימא: ט] לא גרס וה״ג טבול יום: י] ושניא הוא כלומר לא מצית לאוקמי באם אינו ענין: יא] שעבד מינה ילפינן: יב] הנשרפין דגמר אות ו׳ נמחק: יג] לתרומה היינו טבול יום דילפינן: יד] עבודה ומינה דלא פסיל בתרומה לא מחיל עבודה הס״ד ותיבת כו׳ נמחק: טו] לטמא הוא דילפינן: טז] כתב ביה: יז] קמבעיא ליה הס״ד ומה״ד ה״ג במחוסר: יח] מחוסר מעשה דשמשא ממילא ערבא וטמא ליכא: יט] כפורים לענין קדשים: כ] דמה להצד דהו״ל חד מינייהו שאינו: כא] שהטעם כאן כמו: כב] בדוכתיה ככתיבתה סתם הס״ד: כג] טמאה עד השתא ותירץ: כד] יומא ולא קאי וטהר אגברא כדדרשינן: כה] וטהרה לטבול יום שהיא טבולת יום ארוך כו׳ כפרה נמי היא: כו] כתנא קמא דפליג התם אתנא דבי: כז] נגיעת כלי · ס״א תרומה בכלי: כח] וטהר · לשון הר״פ מכלל שהוא טמא אלמא דטבול יום איקרי טמא וי״ל דאי לאו קרא דרבי סימאי דדריש הכי דטבול יום אקרי טמא לא נפקא ליה דאיכא למימר דקלישא טומאתיה לענין שלא יחלל העבודה וכ״ת והלא מחוסר כפרה נפקא לן דמחלל עבודה מוטהרה מכלל שהיא טמאה ולא אמרינן דקלישא טומאה ו״ל דלאחר דגלי לן ר׳ סימאי מקרא דלא יחללו דטבול יום מחלל עבודה אע״ג דקלישא כו׳ ע״כ: כט] מתיבת ותימה עד סוף הדבור מוקף חצי לבנה שהוא הג״ה: ל] בהדיא דטבול יום אקרי טמא: לא] עבודה ולא יחללו: לב] יולדת דדרשינן: לג] טבול יום משום דטמא הנכנס למקדש כתוב בטומאת מת ולא יתחטא דמשמע: לד] ורע ע״כ הג״ה: לה] בטבול יום דמחלל וי״ל: לו] גוונא איכא בפרק: לז] דלא אשכחנא צריכותא לא תיבת בהני נמחק: לח] מתרומה ליתא: לט] תיבת מטעמא נמחק: מ] טמא סברא דגמרינן מתרומה דהוי תיובת בג״ש דחילול חילול פרק הנשרפין נמחק:

קסבר *מחוסר כפורים דזב כזב דמי א] ומחוסר כפורים דזב כזב דמי תנאי היא *דתניא שרפה אונן ומחוסר כפורים א כשרה יוסף הבבלי אומר אונן כשרה מחוסר כפורים פסולה מאי לאו בהא קמיפלגי מר סבר מחוסר כפורים דזב כזב דמי ומר סבר ג לאו כזב דמי לא דכולי עלמא כזב דמי והכא בהא קמיפלגי דכתיב °והזה הטהור *מכלל שהוא טמא ג לימד על טבול יום שכשר בפרה מר סבר טומאה דכל התורה כולה °ומר סבר טומאה דהך פרשה הלכך (א) אונן וטבול יום דטמא שרץ דקילי אתו בקל וחומר מטבול יום דמת אבל מחוסר כפורים דזב דחמיר שכן טומאה יוצאה עליו מגופו לא: מחוסר בגדים: מנלן *אמר רבי אבוה אמר רבי יוחנן ומטו בה משמיה דרבי אלעזר ברבי שמעון דאמר קרא °וחגרת אותם אבנט אהרן ובניו וחבשת להם מגבעות והיתה להם כהונה לחקת עולם ד בזמן שבגדיהם עליהם כהונתם עליהם אין בגדיהם עליהם אין כהונתם עליהם והא מהכא נפקא מהתם נפקא דתניא מנין לשתויי יין ה שאם עבד חילל תלמוד לומר °יין ושכר אל תשת וגו' °ולהבדיל בין הקודש ובין החול מחוסר בגדים ושלא רחוץ ידים ורגלים מנין

תלמוד

(במדבר יט) (שמות כט) (ויקרא י) (שם)

תורה אור

רש"י

קסבר · רבה דדרשה להאי שמעתא למימר דכולהו צריכי: מחוסר כפורים דזב כזב · ה"ה למצורע אלא חד מנייהו נקט מחוסר כפורים דזב כזב דמי לענין קדשים שלא הותר אללו ב] הוה ליה כאילו לא טבל ואם אכלו חייב כרת או אם נגע בהו ג] טמאן למנות בהן ראשון ושני לכך לא קלשה טומאה אצל קדשים כלל: שרפה אונן כו' · בפרה אדומה קאי: כשרה · דקדשי בדק הבית היא ואין אונן (ב) אסור בה דלא כתיבי הנך קראי אלא בקדשי מזבח: כזב דמי · והוה ליה טמא וקרא כתיב איש טהור: לאו כזב דמי · וה"ל כטבול יום דקיימא ד] [לן] דכשר בפרה: לא דכ"ע כזב דמי ה] ולענין שאר קדשים שטבול יום אסור בהו ו] הוה מחוסר כפורים דזב חמור מטבול יום דשאר טומאות שאין טעונות כפרה: והכא · גבי פרה בהאי קרא קמיפלגי והזה הטהור על הטמא טהור כל דהוא משמע דהא קרא יתירא הוא דכתיב לעיל מיניה ולקח אזוב וטבל במים איש טהור והוה ליה למכתב והזה על הטמא לימד על טבול יום שכשר בפרה דאשכחן טבול יום דאיקרי טהור למעשר דכתיב ורחץ במים וטהר: מר סבר טומאה דכל התורה · ת"ק סבר האי טבול יום דאכשר בה קרא אטבול יום דכל הטומאות שבתורה ז] קאי ואף טבול יום דזב שהוא מחוסר כפורים: טומאה דאותה פרשה · והיינו דמת טבול יום דטומאת מת אכשר בה הלכך טבול יום של שאר טומאות דמגע ומשא כגון שרץ ונבילה (ג) ומגע ח] [זב] אתי להכשירא מטבול יום דמת מק"ו ומה טבול יום [דמת] דטומאת שבעה כשר טבול יום דטומאת ערב לא כ"ש אבל מחוסר כפורים ט] כו': והיתה להם · הלבישה הזאת (ד) לכהונה אלמא כהונתן תלויה בבגדיהן ואי לא הוו להו זרים ובזר אשכחן דמחיל עבודה: ובין החול · עבודה שאתה עובד בשכרות קרויה חול: חוקה

תוספות

קסבר רבה מחוסר כפורים דזב כזב דמי · הכי נמי אית ליה פרק שני דכריתות (דף י·) ופירש בקונט' לענין קדשים שלא הותר י] אכלן הוה ליה כאילו לא טבל ואם אכלן חייב כרת או אם נגע בהן טמאן למנות בהן ראשון ושני וקשה לפירושו דאם כן למ"ד לאו כזב דמי לית ביה כרת ובריש מסכת כלים תנן בהדיא דמחוסר כפורים שנכנס למקדש *חייב יא] דתנן עזרת ישראל מקודשת ממנה שאין מחוסר כפורים נכנס לשם וחייב חטאת וכן בההיא דפרק אלו הן הגולין (מכות דף ח:) ושלשה מינין (נזיר מה·) טמא יהיה לרבות טבול יום עוד טומאתו בו לרבות מחוסר כפורים ובהקומץ רבה (מנחות דף כז:) מחוסר כפרה שנכנס לפנים ממחיצתו לעזרה בשוגג חייב חטאת במזיד ענוש כרת ואיתקש קודש למקדש בהערל (יבמות עה.) ובמכות (דף יד·) ובשבועות (דף ז·) ודוחק לומר דכל הני אתיין כמאן דאמר מחוסר כפורים דזב כזב דמי ועוד דבההיא סוגיא דנזיר יב] וטמא יהיה לרבות טבול יום דכ"ע מחוסר כפורים דזב לאו כזב דמי ואפילו הכי מרבה התם כרת למקדש במחוסר כפורים ומיהו פלוגתא דאמוראי יג] איכא ריש פ' כל הפסולין (לקמן לג:) אית דאמרי הא דאיתקש קודש למקדש היינו אפילו לכרת דביאה במקצת יד] שמה ביאה כמו נגיעה ואית דאמרי לענין מלקות דוקא איתמר ומוקי לה בכל קדש לא תגע אזהרה לנוגע לקודש דליכא אלא לאו אע"ג דאל המקדש לא תבא הוי בכרת ועוד מה שפי' בקונטרס לענין למנות בו ראשון ושני לקדש *תימה הלא טבול יום אין מונין בו ראשון ושני *לטומאתםו [וכ"ש מחוסר כפורים] ועוד הא תנן במסכת מעילה (דף ח·) חטאת העוף כו' הוכשר ליפסל בטבול יום ובמחוסר כפורים ודייק בגמ' ליפסל אין לטמויי לא ורבינו תם היה אומר דלא נקט פסול במחוסר כפורים אלא אגב טבול יום והקשה לו הרב רבינו חיים מהא דבסוטה פרק כשם (ד' כט·) אמרי' מנין לרביעי בקודש שהוא פסול ומה מחוסר כפורים שמותר בתרומה פסול בקודש משמע פסול אין טמא לא ועוד אי מונין בו ראשון ושני א"כ יעשה רביעי חמישי בקודש מק"ו ומיהו יש לומר בזה דחמישי אין ללמוד דמן הדין הוה למימר דיו כתרומה אי לאו משום דמפרך ק"ו ודי לנו במעלה אחת יותר מתרומה שיעשה רביעי ומיהו עוד קשה מהא דתנן בפ' בתרא דנדה (דף עא:) היושבת על דם טוהר (היתה) מערה מים לפסח חזרו לומר הרי היא כמגע טמא מת לקדשים ומוקי לה בגמ' כאבא שאול דאמר טבול יום תחלה לקודש משמע אבל לרבנן לא טו] ודוחק לומר דכולהו ההיא דמעילה ודסוטה ורבנן דאבא שאול סברי כמ"ד מחוסר כפורים דזב לאו כזב דמי °ומפרש הרב ר' חיים דנפקא מינה *לענין פסח הבא בטומאה דתנן (פסחים דף עה:) לא יאכלו ממנו זבין וזבות דלמ"ד מחוסר כפורים דזב כזב דמי אין שוחטין וזורקין עליו דלא איתשראי בצבור אלא טמא מת וה"ה טמא שרץ דאין טומאה יוצאה מגופו בק"ו ממת כדאיתא לקמן ומ"ד לאו כזב דמי שוחטין והכי מוכח בהדיא בפרק שני דכריתות (דף י·) ועוד דנפקא מינה לענין טומאה דחוייה בצבור יז] (לקמן דף לג:): **שרפה** אונן ומחוסר כפורים כשרה · פי' בקונט' דפרה קדשי בדק הבית היא וקשה דמ"מ אית בה כל פסולין שבקרבן כגון יח] שלא לשמה דאמר בהקומץ רבה (מנחות כז:) ושבע הזאות שבפרה שעשאן שלא לשמן פסולות ונפקא לן בסיפרי משום דחטאת קרייה רחמנא ומהאי טעמא נמי אמרינן בפ"ק דחולין (דף יא·) דטרפות פוסל בה ונראה דהיינו טעמא יט] הכא משום דטבול יום כשר בפרה ואתי אונן ומחוסר כפורים בק"ו מטבול יום שאסור בנגיעת תרומה ומותר בפרה כ] ולמ"ד מחוסר כפורים דזב כזב דמי לא אתי בק"ו דמה לטבול יום דמת שמותר לאכול בפסח הבא בטומאה מה שאין כן *במחוסר כפורים והאי כא] דטבול יום כשר מן התורה אפשר דמדרבנן פסול דהא אמרינן דאפי' בגדי אוכלי קודש מדרס לחטאת כל שכן טבול יום והא כב] [דאמרי' במסכת פרה (פ"ג) מטמאין היו כהן השורף את הפרה להוציא מלבן של צדוקים שאמרו] במעורבי שמש היתה נעשית לאו היינו טבול יום ממש אלא אחיו הכהנים היו מניחין ידיהם על ראשו ומאותה נגיעה היה טבול יום כדתניא בתוספתא ואיכא כג] בהו היכרא לצדוקים ועוד יש לפרש דטבול יום ממש היה כשר בה והא דבגדי אוכלי קודש מדרס לחטאת משום היסח הדעת דשאר טומאות: **והזה** הטהור · ואף על גב דהזאת מי חטאת כשרה בזר ושרפה כד] פסול מכל מקום יליף שרפה מהזאה: **אונן** וטבול יום של טמא שרץ דקילי אתו מק"ו מטבול יום דמת · ואין להקשות מה לטבול יום שכן מותר במעשר מה שאין כן באונן דמנגיעה ילפינן כדאמר בפ' הערל (יבמות עב:) ערל שהזה הזאתו כשרה מידי דהוה אטבול יום שאע"פ שאסור בתרומה כשר בפרה ופריך מה לטבול יום שכן מותר במעשר ומשני אטו אנן לאכילה קאמרינן לנגיעה קאמרינן ומה טבול יום שאסור בנגיעה דתרומה מותר בפרה ערל שמותר בנגיעה דתרומה אינו דין שמותר בפרה וה"נ ילפינן אונן וא"ת מחוסר כפורים ובעל מום יוכיחו שמותרין בתרומה ואסורין בפרה אף אני אביא ערל ואונן ומיהו אאונן לא קשיא דמה להנך שכן לא הותרו מכללן תאמר באונן שהותר מכללו אלא כ"ג אבל אערל קשה כה] ונראה לי דמה למחוסר כפורים שאסור ליגע בקדשים אבל ערל ואונן מותרין אבל מבעל מום קשה · ברו"ך · ועוד מה לטבול יום שכן אינו מחוסר מעשה תאמר בערל: *אין בגדיהם עליהן אין כהונתן עליהם · מהכא ילפינן מיתה בפרק הנשרפין (סנהדרין דף פג:) דקאמר אין בגדיהם עליהם הוו להו זרים ואמר מר זר ששימש במיתה והקשה הרב רבי יעקב מאורלינש והא מיתה כתיבא בהדיא בפרשת ואתה תצוה ותירץ דאף על גב דכולהו בגדים כתיבי התם מכל מקום מיתה אמכנסיים דוקא כתיבא כדמשמע פשטא דקרא וקרא דוחגרת דכתיב בפרשה שאחריה דדרשינן מינה דאין בגדיהם עליהם אין כהונתן עליהם איצטריך לשאר בגדים ומיניה לא הוה ילפינן מכנסיים דמכנסיים לא כתיבי התם ועוד יש לומר דקרא דוחגרת צריך לחילול עבודה דמקרי זר* · ברו"ך:

תלמוד

עין משפט נר מצוה

יב א מיי' פ"ד מהל' פרה אדומה הלכה יד:

יג ב מיי' פ"ג מהלכות ביאת מקדש הלכה ט וע"ש בכ"מ ופי"ח מהל' פסה"מ הלכה יד:

נ"ל בכרת ל"ק

יד ג מיי' פ"א מהלכות פרה אדומה הלכה יג:

טו ד מיי' פ"י מהלכות כלי המקדש הלכה ד:

טז ה מיי' פ"א מהל' ביאת מקדש הל' ח:

פי' צ"ק נ"א

נ"א לתרומס

גירסת צ"ק במחוסר כפורים הס"ד ואח"כ מה"ד דטבול יום כשר בפרה האי ע"י דכשר כו'

מסורת הש"ס

[כריתות י· עיין שם]

יבמות עד תוספתא דפרה פ"ג

צ"ק

יומא מג: יבמות עג.

סנהדרין פג:

נ"א לענין פסח הבא בטומאה דתנן פסח הבא בטומאה לא יאכלו ממנו זבין וזבות דלמ"ד כו' כזב דמי גם מחוסר כפורים לא יאכלו ממנו דלא איתשראי בצבור כו' ולמ"ד לאו כזב דמי יאכלו ממנו והכי מוכח בהדיא כו' צ"ק וע"ש

[עיין לקמן כד בתוספות ריש עמוד א']

[וע"ע תוס' סנהדרין פג· ד"ה אין]

הגהות הב"ח

(א) גמ' דהך פרשה הלכך טבול יום דנבלה וטמא שרץ דקילי כצ"ל: (ב) רש"י ד"ה כשרה וכו' ואין אונן ומחוסר כפורים אסור בה: (ג) ד"ה טומאה וכו' ונבלה אתו כצ"ל ותיבת ומגע נמחק: (ד) ד"ה והיתה וכו' כהונה כצ"ע ואות ל' נמחק:

גליון הש"ס

גמ' ומ"ס טומאה דהך פרשה · עיין יומא דף ו ע"א תוס' ד"ה ריצ"ב: תוס' ד"ה קסבר וכו' ומפרש הר"ר חיים · עי' יבמות דף ז ע"ב תוד"ס ר"א:

שיטה מקובצת

א] דמי לימא מחוסר אות ו' נמחק: ב] אצלו והוה ליה: ג] בהו פימאן: ד] דקיימא לן: ה] דמי לענין שאר: ו] הוי מחוסר: ז] שבתורה קאמר ותיבת קאי נמחק: ח] ומגע הזב: ט] תיבת וכו' נמחק: י] הותר אצלו דהוה ליה: יא] חייב כרת: יב] דנזיר טמא יהיה: יג] דאמוראים היא ותיבת איכא ל"ש:

יד] במקצת נתנו: טו] לטומאה וכ"ש מחוסר כפורים ועוד הא תנן במסכת מעילה פרק שני חטאת: טז] לא אלמא טבול יום דיולדת לא מנינן בו ראשון ושני וכ"ש מחוסר כפורים: יז] בצבור דאם הן טמאי מתים עושין בטומאה ואם הם זבים נדחין לשני: יח] כגון שרפה שלא: יט] טעמא' ס"א משום דילפינן מק"ו דטבול יום פסול בתרומה כשר בפרה כדבסמוך כ"ש אונן כו': כ] בפרה כ"ש אונן ומחוסר כפורים: כא] והאי ס"א ושמא אע"ג דטבול כו': כב] והא דאמרינן במסכת פרה בפ"ג וממאין היו את הכהן השורף את הפרה מפני הצדוקין שלא יהיו אומרין: כג] ואיכא בהכי: כד] ושרפה בזר: כה] מתיבת ונראה לי עד תיבת ברוך מוקף בחצי לבנה:

[17b]—He holds that a *zab* lacking atonement is as a *zab*.[4]

Now, whether a *zab* lacking atonement is as a *zab*, is dependent on Tannaim. For it was taught: If an *onen* or one lacking atonement burns it,[5] it is fit.[6] Joseph the Babylonian said: If an *onen* [burns it], it is fit, [but] if one who lacks atonement burns it, it is unfit. Now surely they disagree in this: one Master holds that a *zab* lacking atonement is as a *zab*,[7] while the other Master holds that he is not as a *zab*![8]—No. All agree that he is as a *zab*, but here they disagree in the following: For it is written, *And the clean person shall sprinkle upon the unclean*,[9] whence it follows that he is unclean, thus teaching that a *ṭebul yom* is fit [to officiate] at the [red] heifer.[10] Now, one Master holds: This applies to every form of uncleanness mentioned in the Torah;[11] while the other Master holds that it applies to the uncleanness dealt with in this chapter only.[12] Therefore an *onen* and a *ṭebul yom* rendered [originally] unclean through
a a [dead] reptile,[1] who are less stringent, are derived *a minori* from a *ṭebul yom* rendered [originally] unclean through a dead body. But a *zab* who lacks atonement is not [thus derived], since he is more stringent, as his uncleanness proceeds from his own body.

ONE LACKING THE [PRIESTLY] VESTMENTS. Whence do we know it?—Said R. Abbahu in R. Joḥanan's name, and some derive ultimately [the teaching] from R. Eleazar the son of R. Simeon: Because Scripture saith, *And thou shalt gird them with girdles, Aaron and his sons, and bind head-tires on them; and they shall have the priesthood by a perpetual statute*:[2] When wearing their [appointed] garments, they are invested with their priesthood; when not wearing their garments, they are not invested with their priesthood. Now, is this derived from the verse quoted? surely it is derived from elsewhere? For it was taught: How do we know that if one who had drunk wine officiates, he profanes [the sacrifices]? Because it is written, *Drink no wine nor strong wine . . . that ye may put difference between the holy and the profane*.[3] How do we know [the same of] one who lacks [priestly] vestments and [of] one who had not

(4) Until he brings his sacrifice, not only must he not partake of the flesh of sacrifices, but he even incurs *kareth* for doing so, just as a *zab* who has not had his ritual bath at all. Similary, he defiles the flesh just as a *zab* does. (Rashi. Tosaf explains it differently.) Hence his uncleanness is not less at all. — Though a *zab* is mentioned, the same applies to a leper too. (5) *Sc.* the red heifer, v. Num. XIX. (6) Because the red heifer does not possess the sanctity of a sacrifice, but only of anything which is dedicated for general Temple use, technically called 'the sacred objects of the Temple repair'. An *onen* and one lacking atonement are disqualified to officiate at real sacrifices only. (7) Hence his service is unfit, because Scripture specifies '*a man that is clean*' (v. 9). (8) Hence he is clean. (9) Ibid. 19. (10) '*The clean person*' is superfluous, as the preceding verse states '*and a clean person shall take hyssop*' etc. The repetition is understood to indicate that even if his cleanness is not absolute, but relative only, he is fit, and we do find in Lev. XIV, 8 that a *ṭebul yom* is designated 'clean': *And he shall bathe himself in water and be clean*. (11) Including a *ṭebul yom* who had been a *zab*. He still lacks atonement, and thus Scripture teaches that although such is unfit elsewhere, an exception is made in the case of the red heifer. (12) Viz., that caused by contact with a dead body.

a (1) BaḤ. emends omitting *onen*: therefore a *ṭebul yom* rendered (originally) unclean through a *sherez* or through carrion. (2) Ex. XXIX, 9. (3) Lev. X, 9f. This is interpreted as meaning that the officiating of such profanes, i.e., invalidates the sacrifice.

washed his hands and feet? [18a] Because *'statute'* is written in connection with each, to serve as a *gezerah shawah*![4]—If [it were derived] from that verse, I would argue that it applies [only] to a service for which a *zar* is liable to death; but as for a service for which a *zar* is not liable to death, I would say that it is not so,[5] hence we are informed [that it is not so].

We have thus found [it in the case of] one who lacks [priestly]
a vestments; how do we know it of one who has drunk wine?[1]—We deduce it from the word *'statute'* [written here and] in the case of one who lacks vestments. But the Tanna deduces it from the text, *That ye may put a difference* etc.?—That is before he has established the *gezerah shawah*. But the Tanna learns [the law for] one who lacks vestments from that of one who drank wine?[2]—This is what he means: How do we know that no distinction is drawn between one who lacks vestments and one who drank wine or who did not wash his hands and feet? Because *'statute'* is written in respect of each, to serve as a *gezerah shawah*.[3] Then what is the need of *'that ye may put difference'* etc.?[4]—To teach the practice of Rab. For Rab would not appoint an interpreter from one Festival day to the next, on account of drinking.[5]

But still, is it deduced from this text? surely it is deduced from elsewhere, viz., *And the sons of Aaron* the priest *shall put [fire upon the altar]*,[6] [which implies,] in his priestly state;[7] this teaches that if a High Priest donned the vestments of an ordinary priest and officiated, his service is unfit?—If [we made the deduction] from the earlier text, I would argue that it applies only to a service which is essential for atonement, but not to a service which is not essential
b for atonement.[1]

But still, is it deduced from this text? surely it is deduced from elsewhere, viz., *And Aaron's sons*, the priests, *shall lay the pieces* etc.[2] [which intimates,] *'the priests'* in *their* priestly state, whence we learn that if an ordinary priest donned the vestments of a High Priest and officiated, his service is unfit?—If [we made the deduction] from the earlier text, I would argue that it applies only to an insufficiency [of vestments],[3] but not to an excess. Therefore it [the present text] informs us [that it is not so].

Our Rabbis taught: If [the priestly vestments] trailed [on the floor], or did not reach [the floor] or were threadbare, and [the priest] officiated [in them], his service is valid. But if he put on two pairs of breeches, two girdles, or if one [garment] was wanting, or if there was one too many, or if he had a plaster on a wound in

(4) V. Glos.—In the present context: *it shall be a* statute *for ever*; the verse for one lacking atonement has been quoted in the text; the washing of the hands and feet: *And it shall be a statute for ever to them* (Ex. XXX, 21).—The use of the same word in connection with all three teaches that the same law applies to all. (5) Scripture says, *Drink no wine ... when ye go into the tent of meeting, that ye die not.* The Talmud interprets this as referring to a service which if performed by those unfit to do so involves death, viz., sprinkling the blood, burning the fats, and making the libations of water or wine. Now, the *conditions* of the various disqualifications, such as officiating without priestly vestments or without having washed the hands and feet, are deduced from those of a *zar*: where a *zar* incurs a penalty, officiating without vestments, etc. incurs a penalty. Hence as far as the present verse is concerned, since death is mentioned, I would think that the sacrifice is disqualified only where the death penalty is incurred.

a (1) That he disqualifies the sacrifice even by officiating in a service for which he does not incur the death penalty. (2) Not *vice versa*, as here. (3) But in fact the law of one who has drunk wine is learned from that of one who lacks vestments. (4) Since we learn by a *gezerah shawah* that one who drank wine 'profanes' (disqualifies) the sacrifice, this text adds nothing. (5) The Rabbis gave their public addresses, in the course of which they taught the law, through the medium of an interpreter. Now, once Rab had ushered in the festival and had partaken of the meal, eating and drinking, he would not appoint an interpreter, i.e., he would not give such an address, until the following day, when the effect of the wine would have worn off. He learnt this from the present verse, *'that ye may put a difference between the holy and the profane'*, which he interpreted to mean that one must not drink before he comes to teach the law, whereby the difference between the holy and the profane is taught. (6) Lev. I, 7. (7) Wearing the priestly vestments.

b (1) Such as putting the fire upon the altar. Hence *'the priest'* teaches that even for this service he must be in his priestly state.—Though the difficulty was apparently why the *former* verse was required, the answer shows that the real difficulty was why Scripture added *'the priest'* in the verse now quoted. (2) Lev. I, 8. (3) E.g., if a High Priest wears the vestments of an ordinary priest.

תלמוד לומר °חוקה °חוקה לגזירה שוה אי מהתם הוה אמינא הני מילי עבודה דזר חייב עליה מיתה אבל עבודה דאין זר חייב עליה מיתה אימא לא קמ"ל אשכחן מחוסר בגדים שתויי יין מנלן אתיא חוקה חוקה ממחוסר בגדים והא תנא א] ולהבדיל בין וגו' קא נסיב לה מקמי ב] דליקום גזירה שוה והא תנא מחוסר בגדים הוא דקא יליף משתויי יין ה"ק מנין שלא (א) ג] נחלקו בין מחוסר בגדים לשתויי יין ושלא רחוץ ידים ורגלים תלמוד לומר חוקה חוקה לגזירה שוה אלא להבדיל למה לי לכדרב *דרב לא מוקים אמורא עליה מיומא טבא לחבריה משום שכרות אכתי מהכא נפקא מהתם נפקא °ונתנו בני אהרן הכהן בכיהונו [א]לימד על כהן גדול שלבש בגדי כהן הדיוט ועבד עבודתו פסולה אי מהתם הוה אמינא ה"מ עבודה דמעכבא כפרה ד] אבל עבודה דלא מעכבא כפרה לא ואכתי מהכא נפקא מהתם נפקא °וערכו בני אהרן הכהנים את הנתחים וגו' הכהנים בכיהונן [ב]מכאן לכהן הדיוט שלבש בגדי כהן גדול ועבד עבודתו פסולה אי מהתם הוה אמינא הני מילי חיסור ה] אבל ייתור לא קמ"ל: *תנו רבנן היו מרושלין מסולקין משוחקים ועבד עבודתו כשירה [ג]לבש שני מכנסים שני אבנטים חסר אחת יתר אחת או שהיתה לו רטיה על ו] מכת בשרו תחת בגדו *או שהיו מטושטשין

תורה אור: ויקרא י · שמות כט · ויקרא א · שם

רש"י

חוקה חוקה. בשתויי יין ז] [כתיב] חוקת עולם [ובמחוסר] בגדים כתיב כהונה לחוקת עולם וברחילת יד ורגל כתיב והיתה להם (ב) לחוקת עולם: אי מהתם. משתויי יין הוה אמינא ח] ה"מ דמחלי עבודה [במחוסר בגדים] בעבודה שהזר חייב עליה מיתה כדכתיב בההוא קרא בבואכם אל אהל מועד ולא תמותו בעבודה שיש בה חיוב מיתה לפסולים הכתוב מדבר ואינה אלא ט] ארבע עבודות זריקה והקטרה וניסוך המים והיין כדילפינן בפ"ב י] בסדר יומא (דף כד.) ועבדתם עבודת מתנה וגו' והזר הקרב יומת עבודת מתנה ולא עבודת סילוק ועבדתם עבודה תמה ולא עבודה שיש אחריה עבודה כגון קבלה והולכה וקמילה וכל חיוב מיתות יא] בפסולי עבודה מזרות גמרינן כדתנן בפ' בתרא (לקמן קיב:) הקומץ והבולל והיוצק והמקבל דמים וכו' ואין בהם לא משום זרות ולא משום טומאה ולא משום מחוסר בגדים ולא משום שלא רחץ ידים ורגלים אלמא מזר גמרינן: אבל עבודה שאין זר חייב עליה מיתה אימא לא. מחלי לה מחוסר בגדים להכי כתב והיתה להם (ג) לכהונת עולם לשויינהו זרים כשאין בגדיהם עליהם ובזר אשכחן חילול ולא חלק בין עבודה שיש בה מיתה לעבודה שאין בה מיתה יב]: אשכחן מחוסר בגדים. בכל העבודות: שתויי יין מנלן. דפסלי עבודה שאין הזר חייב עליה מיתה: והא תנא מלהבדיל קנסיב לה. לשתויי יין ולא גמר מגזירה שוה ואכן ניקו וניפלוג עלה למילף מקרא אחרינא: הכי מילי מקמי דתיקו ליה גזירה שוה. לא הוה ליה למילף שתויי יג] יין אלא מלהבדיל ובמסקנא (ד) אידכר ליה גזירה שוה ותנא (ליה) שבקיה לאורחיה קמייתא ונקט גזירה שוה *למילף יד] משתויי יין מחוסר בגדים: והא תנא. נקטיה לגזירה שוה מחוסר בגדים הוא דיליפנא משתויי יין ולא שבקיה לאורחיה: והכי קאמר מנין שלא טו] נחלקו כו'. לעולם לא למילף מחוסר בגדים משתויי יין אתא אלא למילף שתויי יין ממחוסר בגדים והכי קאמר למדו לעבודות של מיתה שמתחללות בשיכרות מנין שלא טז] נחלוק בין מחוסר בגדים לשתויי יין דכי היכי דמחוסר בגדים כל עבודותיו פסולות אף שתויי יין ושלא רחץ כן תלמוד לומר חוקה חוקה: אלא (ה) יז] בין החול למה לי. הואיל ולא ילפינן מינה חילול לעבודה: לא מוקים אמורא עליה. למידרש (ו) בפירקין: מיומא טבא לחבריה. משעה שאכל ושתה ועשה יום טוב עד למחר דהכי משמע קרא יין ושכר אל תשת בבואכם וגו' וכן בשעה שאתה בא להבדיל ולהורות בין דבר קדושה לדבר חול אל תהי שכרות: מהכא נפקא. מחוסר בגדים: מהתם נפקא. אפתי קרא אחרינא כתיב ולמאי יח] איצטריך הכהן הכא גבי ונתנו בני אהרן הכהן אש לאשמועינן מחוסר בגדים: בכיהונו. בשעה שהוא מלובש בגדיו נקרא אהרן הכהן ולא כשהוא לבוש בגדי הדיוט: אי מהתם. מוהיתה להם כהונה הוי מוקמינא ליה [במחוסר] היא בעבודה המעכבת כפרה אבל נתינת אש של הדיוט דמצוה בעלמא היא שהרי יש שם אש שירדה מן השמים אימא לא תיבעי בגדים קא משמע לן ונתנו בני אהרן הכהן אש כ] להכי כתב הכא חסרון בגדים למילף [דאף בעבודה שאינה מחוסר כפרה] דאי עבד אהרן בבגדי הדיוט לאו שפיר עבד והא ליכא למיפרך לימא האי *ולא תיבעי ההוא דהכא לאו בגדים כתיבי ואי לאו כא] דכתב והיתה להם כהונה [אלא וחגרת אותם אבנט] דשמעינן כהונה תלויה בבגדים לא הוה ידעינן הכהן בכיהונו מאי היא: הכהנים. אבני קאי דהוו הדיוטים: בכיהונן. ברצוין להן שנתלית כהונתן בהן: אי מהתם. מוהיתה להם כהונה: כב] [חיסור. כגון כה"ג בבגדי כהן הדיוט: אבל ייתור. כגון כהן הדיוט בבגדי כה"ג]: מרושלין. נגררין בקרקע: מסולקין. מן הקרקע מתוך שהם קצרים: משוחקים. ישנים: כשרין. ואע"ג דכתיב מדו בד שתהא כמדתו מצוה בעלמא היא ולא לעכב: חיסר אחת. כג] מכל הבגדים: ייתר אחת. הוסיף עליהם שום בגד בעולם: רטייה. אספלנית"א שחוצץ בין בשרו לבגד דבעינן ילבש על בשרו:

*) ס"א ולא תיבעי ההוא קרא דוהיתה להם כהונה דהכא לאו כו'

מטושטשין

תוספות

תלמוד לומר חוקה חוקה לגזירה שוה. מכאן אומר ר"ת דהא דאמרינן במנחות (דף יט.) כל מקום שנאמר תורה וחוקה אינו אלא לעכב לאו חד טעמא נינהו דחוקה מגזירה שוה ותורה ממשמעות*: **אתיא** חוקה חוקה ממחוסר בגדים. בפ' הנשרפין (סנהדרין דף פד.) אמרינן דאונן באזהרה דכתיב ומן המקדש לא יצא ולא יחלל הא אחר שלא יצא חילל ולא ילפי' שיהא במיתה [בג"ש] חילול חילול מתרומה משום דחילול בגופיה לא כתיב מכללא [דכ"ג] הוא דקאתי הוי דבר הבא מן הכלל וכל דבר הבא מן הכלל אין דנין אותו בגזירה שוה וקשה מהך דשמעתין דהא כד] אין בגדיהם עליהם אין כהונתן עליהן אינו כתיב בפי' וילפינן חוקה חוקה ממחוסרי בגדים וכן בכל הנך דכתיב ולא יחללו דדייקינן הא עבד חיללו וילפינן מיתה חילול חילול מתרומה ובתורם מן הרעה על היפה דלא ילפינן דלהוי במיתה בגזירה שוה דחטא חטא תירץ ה"ר יעקב מאורליינ"ש משום דהוי דבר הבא מן הכלל כה] [וצריך לחלק אמאי הוי דבר שבכלל] טפי מהני ותימה לי דבפ' הנשרפין (שם פג:) בעי שתויי יין ושלא רחוץ ידים ורגלים במיתה מנא לן וקאמר דבגופייהו כתיב בהו מיתה בהדיא והשתא למה לי למיכתב מיתה תיפוק ליה מגזרה שוה דחוקה חוקה ממחוסר בגדים כדילפינן חילול בהו מהתם מיהו לקמן בפירקין (דף כב.) אמרינן דהוו שלשה כתובין הבאין כאחד ואין מלמדין מחוסר בגדים ושתויי יין ושלא רחוץ ידים והשתא אתי שפיר גם קושיית ה"ר יעקב דהשתא בשלשתן כתיב מיתה מיותר למימר בהני (זרים) דווקא דמקריין זרים בגזירה שוה דחוקה איכא מיתה אבל יושב אע"ג דקרוי זר אינו במיתה אבל שאר פסולין כגון ערל ואונן לא איצטריך קרא למעוטינהו ממיתה כיון דלא איקרו זרים. ברו"ך: כו] חוזרני לומר דקושית ה"ר יעקב קיימת דהא למ"ד נמי דבעי' שלשה כתובין הבאין כאחד ליכא מיותר כי אם השנים ואחד הוי לגופיה וא"כ תרי קראי במחוסר בגדים למה ובתרווייהו כתיב חקה [א] ומיהו וחגרת דדרשינן מינה חוקת עולם אצטריך משום חילול דאע"ג דממילא שמעינן מדאיקרי כז] [זר מ"מ] זר במכנסים לא כתיב ולעולם בפרשה דלעיל קאי מיתה אכולהו בגדים כח]: **הג"ה** כהן גדול שלבש בגדי כהן הדיוט ועבד עבודתו פסולה. ואם תאמר הא דאמר רבי יוסי כט] (יומא דף יב:) שני אינו ראוי לא לכהן גדול ולא לכהן הדיוט כהן גדול משום איבה כהן הדיוט משום מעלין בקודש ולא מורידין מדקאמר משום איבה משמע דמן הדין כהן גדול הוא וא"כ כהן הדיוט תיפוק ליה משום מחוסר בגדים ואין לפרש דלאחר מיתת הראשון קאמר דלא הוי כהן גדול משום איבה דהא מודה ר' יוסי (שם יג.) דאם מת ראשון שני חוזר לעבודתו ויש לומר דכהן גדול ל] נתמנה לעבודתו בפה ומסתלק בפה [ב](ובפ' קמא דיומא לא](דף יב) דריש ליה מקרא ובירושלמי) ומסתברא שהדבר תלוי במלך ואחיו הכהני' כמו שמצינו בפ' הבא על יבמתו (יבמות סא.) ביהושע בן גמלא דאוקמיה ינאי מלכא ואמרינן לב] בירושלמי ובפ"ק דיומא (דף יב:) ובתוספתא (דיומא פ"א) ביוסף בן אלם מצפורי שאירע פסול בכה"ג ושימש תחתיו וכשיצא אמר למלך אדוני המלך פר ושעיר *שקרבו היום משל מי [משלי או משל כה"ג א"ל המלך לא דייך ששימשת שעה א' לפני מי שאמר והיה העולם] כו' וידע לג] שהוסר מן הכהונה:

*) נ"ל שקרבין

מסולקין

עין משפט נר מצוה

יז א מיי' פ"י מהלכות כלי המקדש הל' ד:
יח ב ג מיי' שם הל' ה:
[ע' תוס' מנחות יט. ד"ה תורה ותוס' חולין כח. ד"ה אמר]

מסורת הש"ס

ביצה ד. כריתות יג: [מס' סופרים פ' יח הל"ד]
תוספתא דמנחות פ"א
פסחים סה: [לקמן לה.]
צ"ל למילף שתויי יין ממחוסר בגדים

הגהות הב"ח

(א) גמ' מנין שלא נחלוק בין מחוסר: (ב) רש"י ד"ה חוקה וכו' להם חק עולם: (ג) ד"ה אבל עבודה וכו' וכתיב והיתה להם כהונה לחוקת עולם: (ד) ד"ה הכי מילי וכו' ממחוסר בגדים: (ה) ד"ה אלא ולהבדיל בין קודש ובין החול למה: (ו) ד"ה לא נכוי בפירקים:

שיטה מקובצת

הכא דהוי להו זרים בלא בגדי כהונה וי"ל דכי איצטריך גז"ש משום כהן כשר הוא דאיצטריך. ואם תאמר מאחר דאיצטריך גז"ש משום כהן כשר למה לי קרא דהכא והיתה (לכהן כהונת) [להם כהונה לחקת] עולם לומר דהוו להו זרים תיפוק ליה לר"ע משום דאין גז"ש למחצה וי"ל דמגז"ש לא הוי ידעינן חילול עבודה רק אזהרה בעלמא להכי איצטריך (הכי) [הכא] למדרש דהוי להו זרים ומחללין עבודה: אבל [עבודה] דלא מעכבא כפרה לא. פ"ה אימא לא תיבעי בגדים כלומר אפילו לכתחילה קמ"ל ונתנו בני אהרן לומר דאי עביד במחוסר בגדים לא שפיר עביד כלומר צריך שיהא לבוש בגדיו בנתינת אש לכתחילה והא דקתני עבודתו פסולה לאו דוקא דהא כיון דלא מעכבא כפרה לא שייך בה חילול עבודה אלא כלומר לא שפיר עביד: ה] אבל ייתור אימא לא וא"ת ולעיל גבי כה"ג שלבש בגדי [כהן] הדיוט אמאי לא משני אי מהתם הוי אמינא דמחוסר בגדים לגמרי אבל כי לבש בגדי כהן הדיוט לא כדמשני הכא וי"ל דלא מצינו למימר הכי דהא דאמר לעיל וחגרת אותם אבנט אהרן ובניו והיתה [להם] כהונה [לחוקת] עולם משמע דגם אהרן שהיה כה"ג אם לא היה כל בגדיו עליו דהיינו שמונה בגדים אין כהונתו עליו דכיון דקרא מיירי באהרן ובניו איית לן למימר הכי: ז"ל: ו] תיבת מכת נמחק: ז] יין כתיב חוקת עולם ובבגדים: ח] אמינא הא דמחוסר בגדים מחלי עבודה ותיבות במחוסר בגדים ל"ש ונמחק: ט] בארבע: י] דסדר: יא] דפסולי: יב] מיתה. הגהת הר"ש ז"ל וא"ת וליכתוב האי קרא דבגדיהם עליהם ולישתוק מלהבדיל בין הקודש ובין החול דלמסקנא ניחא שם ע"כ: יג] [שתויי יין]:

שיטה מקובצת

א] תנא מלהבדיל: ב] מקמי דתיקום ליה גזרה: ג] שלא נחלק: ד] אבל עבודה דלא מעכבא כפרה לא. פ"ה כגון נתינת אש דמצוה בעלמא כו' [ולא] רצה לפרש משום דכל עיקר נתינת אש אינו אלא הויא לצורך הקטרה (והקפרה) [הקטרה] לא משום דאיכא הקטרת קומץ דמעכבא שמתיר המנחה ואת"ה מ"מ לישתוק מקרא דבגדיהם עליהם דכיון דחזינן במעכבא כ"ש במעכבא וי"ל דאי לאו קרא דבגדיהם הוה דרשינן מינה דכי אין בגדיהם עליהן הוי להו זרים לא הוי דרשינן הכא מכהונן הכהן בכיהונו לענין שיהו בגדים דבלא בגדים לא שייך בכיהונו להכי איצטריך והיתה כו' בעלמא דבכל מקום דכתיב כהן דרשינן בכיהונו כמ"ש מהו קשה לעיל בפ"ק אמאי איצטריך והקריבו כהנים גבי קבלה לומר (בכיהונו) [בכהן ובכלי] שרת תיפוק ליה מאין בגדיהן כדדרשינן הכא דהוו להו זרים וי"ל דאי הוי כתיב בני אהרן ולא הכהנים הוי אמינא דלא קפיד קרא אכהנים בכיהונו והא דאמר הכא הוה להו זרים הו"א ה"מ במקום שכתוב כהן דמשמע שהתפקיד בכיהונו והילכך איצטריך לומר כהן בכיהונו וא"ת א"כ מאי פריך הכא הא מהתם נפקא [ולמה] ליה נתינת אש למכתב הכהנים לישני כדפי' וי"ל דשאני הכא דהאי ונתנו בני אהרן כתיב אחר קרא דוהקריבו ואם כן ידעינן שפיר בלא הכהנים דבעי בכיהונם כמו בקבלה דכיון דכתיב בה קמייתא גלי בעבודה שאחרי כן. ומיהו קשה לר"ע למה לי גז"ש דבני אהרן לעיל (דף י"ג ע"א) לכהן ולכלי שרת פי' בגדי כהונה תיפוק ליה מדכתיב הכהנים בעינן בגדי כהונה כדאמרינן

יד] למילף שתויי יין ממחוסר: טו] שלא נחלק כו' לעולם לאו למילף: טז] שלא נחלק: יז] אלא להבדיל בין הקודש ובין: יח] איצטריך האי [הכהן]: יט] ליה להההיא: כ] אש על המזבח להכי כתיב: כא] לאו כתיב: כב] כהונה הס"ד ומה"ד חיסור כגון כה"ג בבגדי הדיוט הס"ד ויתור כהן הדיוט בבגדי כה"ג: כג] חיסר אחת מן הבגדים: כד] דהא דאין בגדיהם עליהם אינו כתוב בפירוש כו' והשאר נמחק: כה] הכלל וצריך לחלק אמאי הוי דבר הבא מן הכלל: כו] מתיבת חוזרני עד סוף הדיבור צ"ל מוקף בחצאי לבנות והיא הגהה: כז] מדאיקרי זר מ"מ זר במכנסים: כח] בגדים עכ"ל הגהה: כט] יוסי בפ"ק דיומא ובהוריות פ' בתרא ותיבת שני נמחק: ל] גדול נתמנה לעבודה בפה: לא] ובפ"ק דיומא בירושלמי: לב] ואמרינן בתוספתא כו' והשאר נמחק: לג] וידע שהוסיף אות ו' נמחק:

הגהות צ"ק [א] ומיהו וחגרת דדרשינן מינה אין בגדיהם עליהם אין כהונתם עליהם איצטריך משום חילול דאע"ג דממילא שמעינן נמי מיתה מדאיקרי זר מיהו לא כתיב ולעולם בפרשה כו': [ב] צ"ל נמחק וכו"ל וממסתלק בפה וכירושלמי דריש ליה מקרא ומסתברא כו':

תורה אור

"מטושטשין או א] מקורעין ועבד עבודתו פסולה אמר רב יהודה אמר שמואל מרושלין כשרין מסולקין פסולין והתניא מסולקין כשרין אמר רמי בר חמא לא קשיא כאן שסילקן על ידי אבנט כאן דליתנהו מעיקרא כלל רב אמר ב'אחד זה ואחד זה פסולין: רב הונא איקלע לארגיזא רמאליה בר אושפיזכניה מי אמר שמואל מרושלין כשרין ומסולקין פסולין והתניא מסולקין כשרין א"ל בר מינה דההיא דשנייה רמי בר חמא אלא לרב קשיא וכי תימא מאי מרושלין מסולקין על ידי אבנט ג] 'ואבנט מיגז אגיז אלא מסולקין קשיא אמר רבי זירא רב חדא תני ד'מרושלין שסילקן ע"י אבנט כשרין אמר ר' ירמיה מדיפתי מרושלין שלא סילקן תנאי היא *דתניא °על ארבע כנפות כסותך ארבע ה'ולא שלש או אינו אלא ארבע ולא חמש כשהוא אומר °אשר תכסה בה ו'הרי בעלת חמש אמור הא מה אני מקיים ארבע ולא שלש ומה ראית לרבות בעלת חמש ולהוציא בעלת שלש מרבה אני בעלת חמש שיש בכלל חמש ארבע ומוציא אני בעלת שלש שאין בכלל שלש ארבע ותניא אידך על ארבע כנפות כסותך ארבע ולא שלש ארבע ולא חמש מאי לאו בהא קמיפלגי דמר סבר יתר כמאן דאיתיה דמי ומר סבר כמאן דליתיה דמי לא דכ"ע כמאן דאיתיה דמי ושאני הכא דרבי רחמנא אשר תכסה בה ואידך האי אשר תכסה בה מאי עביד ליה מיבעי ליה לכדתניא °וראיתם אותו *פרט ז'לכסות לילה או אינו אלא פרט לכסות סומא כשהוא אומר אשר תכסה בה ח'הרי כסות סומא אמור הא מה אני מקיים וראיתם אותו פרט לכסות לילה ומה ראית לרבות כסות סומא ולהוציא כסות לילה מרבה אני כסות סומא שישנה בראיה אצל אחרים ומוציא אני כסות לילה שאינה בראיה אצל אחרים ג] [ואידך נפקא ליה מאשר ואידך *אשר לא דריש]: תנו רבנן ט'בד שיהו של בוץ י'בד שיהו חדשים כ'בד שיהו שזורים ל'בד שיהו חוטן כפול ששה בד שלא ילבש של חול עמהן א"ל אביי לרב יוסף בשלמא שיהו של בוץ הא קמ"ל בוץ אין מידי אחרינא לא אלא בד שיהו חדשים אין שחקין לא והתניא משוחקין כשרים אמר ליה וליטעמיך בד שיהו חוטן כפול ששה בד חד חד לחודיה משמע אלא הכי קאמר בגדים שנאמר בהן בד צריכין שיהו של בוץ חדשים שזורין שיהא חוטן כפול ששה יש מהן למצוה יש מהן לעכב *ממאי דהאי בד כתנא הוא אמר ד] רבי יוסף ברבי חנינא דבר העולה מן הקרקע בד בבד אימא עמרא עמרא מיפצל כיתנא נמי מיפצל על ידי לקותא מיפציל רבינא אמר מהכא °פארי פשתים יהיו על ראשם ה] [ומכנסי פשתים יהיו על מתניהם לא יחגרו ביזע] א"ל רב אשי לרבינא והא עד דאתא יחזקאל מנלן ולטעמיך הא *דאמר רב חסדא דבר זה מתורת משה רבינו לא למדנו מדברי יחזקאל בן בוזי למדנו °כל בן נכר ערל לב וערל בשר לא יבא אל מקדשי *(לשרתני) עד שבא יחזקאל מנלן אלא גמרא גמירי לה ו] ואתא יחזקאל ואסמכיה אקרא הכא נמי גמרא גמירי לה כו' מאי °לא יחגרו ביזע אמר אביי מ'לא יחגרו במקום שמזיעין כדתניא כשהם חוגרין אין חוגרין לא למטה ממתניהן ולא למעלה מאציליהן אלא כנגד

(דברים כב) (שם) (במדבר טו) (יחזקאל מד) (שם) (שם)

רש"י

מטושטשין. בטיט: מקורעין. ואפילו הן חדשים דלאו בגד (א) ז] הוא הראוי לעבודה דבעינן לכבוד ולתפארת: כאן שסילקן ע"י אבנט. תשקורליי"ר בלע"ז כדרך שהנשים עושות כשרין דהא איתנהו: אחד זה ואחד זה. אחד מרושלין ואחד מסולקין יותר מדאי שלא על ידי אבנט: והתניא. בברייתא דלעיל: אלא לרב קשיא. מרושלין: וכ"ת מאי מרושלין. דמכשר תנא כגון שסילקן עד למדתו על ידי אבנט וקמכשר ליה תנא דקסבר אבנט מיגז ח] אגיז כלומר כל סלוק שע"י אבנט הוה ליה כחותך וטול היתר שבהן ומכשירו: אלא מסולקין קשיא. דקתני כשרין וסתם מסולקין גבוהין מן הקרקע למעלה מרגליו משמע ולרב ליכא לאוקומא כגון שסילקן ע"י אבנט ט] כדתרצה שמואל דהא על כרחיך י] לרב דשני דסילוק אבנט מיגז יא] אגיז והשתא הוו כולהו כקצרים מעיקרא: רב חדא תני. להנך מרושלין ומסולקין דברייתא בחדא מילתא תני להו מרושלין שסילק רישולן ע"י אבנט עד כדי מדתו כשרין אבל מסולקין יותר מדאי פסולין אפילו ע"י אבנט: ולא שלש. לימד על טלית של בת שלש כנפות שפטורה מן הציצית והיכי דמי כגון שעיגל אחת מד' כנפיה: בת חמש. כגון שחתך מעט מן הכנף ולא עיגל שני מורשי קרנתא (ב) יב] ממקום חתך דנעשה כשתי כנפות: הרי בעלת חמש אמור. לחיוב דריבויא הוא: מר סבר. מאן דפטר בעלת חמש סבר לא אמרינן יתר כמאן דליתיה דמי אלא כמאן דאיתיה הוא ולא קרינן לה בת ארבע ומאן דמחייב ס"ל יתר כמאן דליתיה דמי להאי חמישי וגבי מרושלין נמי לא הוי ייתור בגדים: פרט לכסות לילה. *טלית העשויה לכסות לילה פטורה מן הציצית: שישנה בראיה כו'. וקרינן ביה וראיתם אותו: בד. יג] (ג) שהוא מן בוץ כדמפרש לקמן ממשמעותא: חדשים. כשעת שהיו יד] בבדי פשתן: שיהו שזורים וחוטן כפול ששה. ולקמן פריך והא בד לחודיה משמע כמו לבדו: שלא ילבש של חול עמהם. דמשמע לבדו ילבש: וליטעמיך. דילפת טו] לה *ממשמעותא (ד) מקראי חוטן כפול ששה טז] מנא ליה: דברים שנאמר בהן בד צריכין כו' יש מהן למצוה. חדשים יז] לכוי דלאו ממשמעותא אתי ויש מהן לעכב בוץ ושזורים וחוטן כפול ששה בוץ כדמפרש ואזיל דבר העולה מן הקרקע בד בבד שזורים כיון דבד הייטו בוץ ובעלמא קרי ליה שש משזר וחוטן כפול ששה כדאמרינן בסדר יומא (דף עא:) יח] וילפינן בסדר יומא מקראי דברים שנאמר בהן שש חוטן כפול ששה ויליף ליה לעיכובא: העולה מן הקרקע בד בבד. קנה יחידי מכל יט] *גיזעי ואין ב' קנים עולים מגזע אחד: ואימא עמרא. שאף הצמר עולה מן הבהמה בד בבד נימא נימא לבדה: מיפציל. הנימא מתפצלת ומתחלקת לשנים על גבי בהמה מאליה: כיתנא נמי מיפציל. לפני טוויתו כותשים הגבעול והוא נחלק לנימין הרבה: אגב לקותא. שמכין אותו וחובטים אותו בעץ או בגלגל הוא נכתש ונחלק: ומכנסי פשתים יהיו וגו'. ובעלמא כ] הרי הוא אומר ומכנסי בד ש"מ בד הייטו פשתים: דבר זה. כא] קאמר לה לקמן (דף כב:) אמתני' דקתני ערל מחלל עבודה: בן נכר. שנתנכרו מעשיו מחמת ערלת לבו שהוא ערל לב רשע: וערל בשר. שמתו אחיו מחמת מילה לא יבא אל מקדשי ולקמן (דף כב:) יליף בה חילול בהדיא: במקום שמזיעין. במקום שהבשר נכפל על הבשר ומתחמם ומזיע: כשהן חוגרין. אבנטיהם בשעת עבודה: למטה ממתניהם. מקום שנכפל ונופל שומן הבטן על הקילבוסת שקורין אנק"א: ולא למעלה מאציליהן. למעלה כב] מנגד מרפקן שקורא קו"דא לפי ששם *היד שוכב תמיד על הצלעות ומזיע:

תוספות

מסולקין כשרין. הא דתניא בפ' תמיד נשחט (פסחים סה:) מדו בד כמדתו פי' הקונטרס דהייטו למצוה ולא לעכב: ואידך אשר לא דריש. משמע הכא דאיכא דמרבה כסות דסומא ולא מרבה בעלת חמש ומקשה ר"ת דבפ' התכלת (מנחות דף מג.) גבי פלוגתא דר' שמעון מרבי התם רבי שמעון כסות סומא מאשר תכסה ובעלת חמש מאשר ולאו פירכא היא דההיא סוגיא כמאן דמרבי הכא בעלת חמש ומיהו קשה כג] אההיא דמנחות* ולקמן בפ' בית שמאי (דף מ.) אמרינן דר"ש אשר לא דריש ויש לומר דהכי אמרינן אשר כי האי לא דריש וטובא איכא כי האי גוונא בפ' קמא דבכורות (דף ו:) דדריש ר"ש את הגמל ובפ"ק דמנחות (דף יא:) לא דריש את: והתניא משוחקין כשרין. תימה דביומא (דף יב:) דרשינן מה ת"ל ילבש לרבות את השחקין ואמאי לריך רבוי*: ואימא עמרא. ה"ר אפרים היה מדקדק דקנבוס דתנן שילהי כלאים שמותר עם למר אין זה מה שאנו קורין קנב"א בלע"ז מדלא פריך ואימא קנבוס שעולה בד בבד והיה אומר דקנבוס הוא כד] פשתן ואסור עם הצמר משום כלאים כה] והשיב לו רבינו חיים כהן דהאי דלא פריך ואימא קנבוס משום דבגדי כהונה אי אפשר להיות אלא מצמר ופשתים *דכל בגדים האמורים בתורה סתם הייטו צמר ופשתים כו] ועוד דכל קנבוס איטו עולה בד בבד דפירש בקונטרס בד בבד קנה יחידי מכל גרעין ואין שני קנים עולים מגרעין אחד ואפשר דקנבוס איטו כן אלא כז] כמו חיטין שכמה שבלין עולין מחיטה אחת*:

עין משפט נר מצוה

יט א ב ג ד מיי' פ"ח מהלכות כלי המקדש הלכה ד:

כ ה ו מיי' פ"ג מהלכות ציצית הלכה ג סמג עשין כו טוש"ע א"ח סי' י' סעיף א:

כא ז ח מיי' שם הל' ז סמג שם טוש"ע א"ח סימן יז סעיף א וסימן יח סעיף א:

נ"ל דלקמן נ"ק

כב ט מיי' פ"ח מהלכות כלי המקדש הל' יג:

כג י מיי' שם הל' ד:

כד כ ל מיי' שם הל' יד:

כה מ מיי' פ"י שם הלכה כ:

[ע' תוס' יומא יב: ד"ה ילבש]

נ"א דכל בגדים האמורים בתורה סתם הייטו למר ופשתים לתנא דבי רבי ישמעאל וגם לרבנן דתנא דבי ר"י לא קשה מידי לפי מה דפי' קונטרס ט' כן הוא בס"א

[וע"ע תוס' יומא עא: ד"ה ואימא וכו']

שיטה מקובצת

א] מקורעין. פ"ה דלאו בגד הראוי הוא דבעינן לכבוד ולתפארת ולקמן גבי יש מהן למצוה פ"ה כגון חדשים דמשום נוי הוא וצ"ל דלא מלתפארת נפיק ליה דא"כ הו"ל לעכב כמו מקורעין דהכא כיון דממשמעות דקרא נפקית ליה אלא ודאי ר"ל משום הידור מצוה (כגון) כשאר מצות דעלמא דמלתפארת לא ממעטינן כי אם בגד שאינו ראוי כמו שמבואר בלשונו: ב] אלמא אבנט מיגז גאיז: ג] אחרים. ס"א ואידך מאשר דריש ואידך אשר לא דריש: ד] ר' יוסי: ה] ראשם ומכנסי פשתים יהיו על מתניהם לא יחגרו ביזע: ו] לה ס"א ואסמכוה רבנן אקרא: ז] בגד הראוי הוא לעבודה: ח] מיגז גאיז: ט] כדתרץ לשמואל נ"א דכיון דאמרינן דאבנט מיגז גאיז א"כ כשסילק ע"י אבנט יותר מכדינם הוו פסולים משום דאבנט מיגז גייז להו מה דסילק כמאן דליתנהו מעיקרא כלל: י] דהא ע"כ שני לרב ס"א דבמרושלין דברייתא כשרישלן ע"י אבנט אם כן ש"מ דמסולקים דברייתא לאו דסילק ע"י אבנט הוא אלא בקצרים מעיקרא וקתני כשרים: יא] מיגז גאיז: יב] קרנתא דמקום: יג] בד שיהו של בוץ כדמפרש: יד] בבד פשתן: טו] דילפת ליה: טז] ששה מי משמע ליה מקראי חס"ד ומה"ד בגדים שנאמר בהן בד: יז] חדשים למצוה: יח] כדאמרינן בסדר יומא דילפינן מקראי דברים כו' כפול ששה ויליף לה: יט] מכל גרעין ותיבת גזעי נמחק: כ] ובעלמא קרי להו מכנסי בד: כא] זה לקמן קאמר לה: כב] ומכנגד מרפקן כו' ששם הזרוע שוכב תמיד: כג] קשה אחדדי ותיבת אההיא ל"ש ונמחק: כד] הוא מין: כה] כלאים ושלח לר"ת תשובות מלאות שערות שתלש מזקנו על מנהג העולם מרוב צער: כו] ופשתים לתנא דבי ר' ישמעאל וגם לרבנן דתנא דבי ר' ישמעאל לא קשה מידי לפום מאי דפירש בקונטרס. ותיבות ועוד דכל קנבוס אינו עולה בד בבד נמחק: כז] אלא. ס"א כמה קנים יוצאים מגרעין אחד כמו:

מסורת הש"ס

מנחות מג:

מנחות שם. שבת כה:

[לקמן מ. מנחות מג:]

נ"א ממשמעותיה דקרא חוטן כפול ששה מי משמע ליה מקרא ספ"ד נ"ש

[יומא עא:]

[לקמן כב: מ"ק ס.] יומא עא: תענית יז: סנהדרין כב: ודף פג:

ליתא בקרא

נ"א גרעין

נ"א הזרוע

הגהות הב"ח

(א) רש"י ד"ה מקורעין וכו' בגד הראוי הוא דבעינן: (ב) ד"ה בת חמש וכו' דמקום: (ג) ד"ה בד שיהו מין בוץ: (ד) ד"ה וליטעמיך וכו' מקרא כו' ליס ספ"ד ואח"כ מ"ה בגדים שנאמר:

גליון הש"ס

רש"י ד"ה פרט לכסות וכו' טלית העשויה. וכ"כ רש"י שבת דף כה ע"ב ד"ה לכסות ועי' מנחות דף מ ע"ב ברש"י ד"ה ס"ג:

his flesh, or if [his garments] were [18*b*] besmeared or torn, and he officiated, his service is invalid. Rab Judah said in Samuel's name: Trailing [garments] are fit; [garments which] do not reach [the pavement] are unfit. But it was taught, If they do not reach [the ground] they are fit?—Said Rami b. Ḥama, There is no difficulty: The latter means where he hitches them up by the girdle;[4] the former, where from the very outset they are not long enough.[5] Rab said: Either [garments] are invalid.

R. Huna visited Argiza.[6] His host's son put a difficulty to him: Did then Samuel say, Trailing [garments] are fit, while those which do not reach [the ground] are unfit? but it was taught, If they do not reach [the ground] they are fit?—Said he to him, Disregard that, for Rami b. Ḥama has answered it. But the difficulty is according to Rab. And should you answer, What is meant by 'trailing'? Those which are hitched up by the girdle, for the girdle
a cuts off [the length],[1] but then there is a difficulty about garments which do not reach?—Said R. Zera, Rab learns [both clauses as one]: Trailing [garments] which are hitched up by a girdle are fit.

R. Jeremiah of Difti said: As to trailing [garments] which he did not lift up, there is a controversy of Tannaim. For it was taught: [*Thou shalt make thee twisted cords*] *upon the four corners of thy covering*:[2] '*four*' [intimates,] but not three.[3] Yet perhaps that is not so, but rather, '*four*' [intimates,] but not five?[4] When it says, *Wherewith thou coverest thyself*[5] a five-cornered [garment] is alluded to.[6] Hence, how can I interpret '*four*'? as intimating four but not three. Now, why do you include a five-cornered garment and exclude a three cornered one? I include a five-cornered one, because five includes four, and I exclude a three-cornered one, because three does not include four. Now, another [Baraitha] taught: '*Upon the four corners of thy covering*': four but not three, four but not five. Surely, they disagree in this: one Master holds: The additional [corner] is counted as existent;[7] while the other Master holds: It is as non-existent?[8]—No: all agree that it is as existent, but here it is different, because Scripture includes [a five-cornered garment in the phrase,] '*Wherewith thou coverest thyself*'.

And the other? how does he utilise this phrase, '*Wherewith thou coverest thyself*'?—He requires it for what was taught: '*That ye may*
b *look upon it*':[1] this excludes night attire.[2] Yet perhaps that is not so, but rather it excludes a blind man's garment? When it says, '*wherewith thou coverest thyself*', lo, a blind man's garment is alluded to. Hence, how can I interpret, '*that ye may look upon it*'? As excluding night attire. Now, why do you include a blind man's garment and exclude a night garment? I include a blind man's garment because it can be seen by others, while I exclude night attire, because it is not seen by others. And the other?[3]—He deduces it from '*wherewith*'.[4] And the other?—He does not interpret '*wherewith*' [as having a separate significance].

Our Rabbis taught: [*And the priest shall put on his garment of*] bad:[5] this teaches that they [his garments] must be of linen; '*bad*' implies that they must be new; '*bad*' implies that they must be of twisted thread; '*bad*' implies that the thread must be sixfold; '*bad*' implies that secular garments must not be worn with them. Abaye said to R. Joseph: As for saying, '"*bad*" implies that they must be of linen,' it is well, for he informs us this: only of linen, but not of anything else. But when he says, '"*bad*" implies that they must be new,' [does it mean] only new but not threadbare? Surely it was taught: Threadbare [garments] are fit!—Said he to him: And according to your reasoning, [when he says] '"*bad*" implies that the thread must be sixfold,' [yet surely] '*bad*' implies each [thread] separately?[6] Rather, this is what he means: the garments which it is stated are to be '*bad*', must be of linen, new, of twisted thread, and of six-fold thread: Some of these [provisions] are recommendations [only], while others are indispensable.

How do you know that '*bad*' means flax [linen]?—Said R. Joseph son of R. Ḥanina: [It connotes] that which comes up from the ground in separate stalks.[7] Say that it means wool?[8]—Wool splits.[9] But flax too splits?[10]—It splits through beating.[11] Rabina said, [It is deduced] from the following: *They shall have linen tires upon their heads, and shall have linen breeches upon their loins; they shall*
c *not gird themselves with* [*anything that causes*] *sweat* [bayaza'].[1] Said R. Ashi to Rabina: Then how did we know this before Ezekiel came?—Then according to your reasoning, when R. Ḥisda said: We did not learn this[2] from the Torah of Moses our Teacher, but we learnt it from Ezekiel the son of Buzi: *No alien, uncircumcised in heart and uncircumcised in flesh* [*shall enter into My sanctuary*]:[3] whence did we know it until Ezekiel came? But indeed it was a tradition, and Ezekiel came and gave it a support in Scripture; so this too was a tradition etc.

What does '*they shall not gird themselves with* [*anything that causes*] *sweat*' mean?[4]—Said Abaye: They shall not gird themselves in the place where they sweat.[5] As it was taught: When they gird themselves, they must do so neither below their loins nor above their

(4) But they are long enough to reach the ground. (5) Lit., 'they are not present at all'. (6) Obermeyer *op. cit.* p. 144 conjectures that this was a place in the district of Be Ketil by the 'Jewish Canal' which branched out of the left bank of the Tigris and ran parallel to it. He suggests however in note 1 a.l. that ארגיזא is an error here for חרתא דארגיז, Hira in the south of Babylon, which fell within R. Huna's jurisdiction, whereas Argiza was in the distant north, and he had no connection with same.

a (1) Only then does the Tanna of the Baraitha rule that they are fit, but not if they are actually trailing on the ground. (2) Deut. XXII, 12. (3) A garment of three corners only, the fourth being rounded, so that it is not a corner, is exempt. (4) E.g., if one corner is cut away, leaving two in its stead. (5) Ibid. (6) For this is really superfluous and therefore interpreted as an extension, to include garments with more than four corners. (7) Hence it is not four-cornered, and therefore exempt. (8) And the same principle would apply to priestly garments that trail: one holds that the superfluous length is as non-existent, and so they are fit; while the other maintains that they are as existent, and therefore unfit.

b (1) Num. XV, 39. This refers to a fringed garment. (2) Which is not looked upon. (3) Who utilises '*wherewith thou coverest thyself*' to include a five-cornered garment: whence does he learn the present law? (4) Which he regards as an extension. (5) E.V. '*linen*'. Lev. VI, 3 *et passim*. (6) *Bad* is derived from *badad*, to be alone, separate. (7) Where two stalks do not come out of one root. (8) For each thread grows separately on the sheep's back. (9) On the animal the threads split up. (10) Before it is woven into linen. (11) But not naturally of its own accord.

c (1) Ezek. XLIV, 18. (2) That an uncircumcised priest disqualifies the service, *infra* 22*b*. (3) Ibid. 9. (4) The Heb. *bayaza'* is connected with *ze'ah*, (sweat), but its exact meaning in this verse is not clear. (5) Where flesh folds over flesh and causes perspiration.

elbows,[6] but [19a] [in the place] corresponding to their elbows.[7]

R. Ashi said: Ḥanna b. Nathana told me, I was once standing before King Izgedar;[8] my girdle lay high up, whereupon he pulled it down, observing to me, It is written of you, [*And ye shall be unto Me*] *a kingdom of priests and a holy nation.*[9] When I came before Amemar he said to me: The text, *'And kings shall be thy foster-fathers'*[10] has been fulfilled in you.

We learnt elsewhere: If a priest has a wound on his finger, he may wind a reed about it in the Temple, but not in the Country.[11] But if his purpose is to squeeze out blood, it is forbidden in both places.[12] R. Judah the son of R. Ḥiyya said: They learnt this only a of a reed, but a small belt[1] constitutes an excess garment.[2] But R. Joḥanan said: They ruled [that] excess garments [disqualify] only [when they are worn] where garments are worn; but if not where garments are worn, they are not an excess. Yet deduce [that it disqualifies] on account of an interposition?[3]—It is on his left hand,[4] [or even on the right], but not in the place of service.[5] Now this disagrees with Raba, for Raba said in R. Ḥisda's name: In the place of garments even a single thread interposes; but [what is] not in the place of garments, if three [fingerbreadths] square, it interposes; if less than this, it does not interpose. Now he certainly disagrees with R. Joḥanan;[6] but are we to say that he disagrees with R. Judah the son of R. Ḥiyya?[7]—[No:] a small belt is different, because it is of [some] account.[8]

Another version states it thus: R. Judah the son of R. Ḥiyya said: They learnt this only of a reed, but a small belt interposes. While R. Joḥanan maintained: They said [that] interposition [disqualifies even] when less than three square only in the place of garments; but if not where garments are worn, then if it is three square it interposes; if less, it does not interpose: and that is identical with Raba['s ruling] in R. Ḥisda's name. Shall we say that he [Raba] disagrees with R. Judah the son of R. Ḥiyya?—[No, for] a small belt is different, since it is of [some] account. Now according to R. Joḥanan, why particularly [specify] a reed? let him mention a small belt?—He informs us *en passant* that a reed heals.

Raba asked: What if a wind entered through his garment?[9] Do we require [the garment to be] *on* his flesh, which [condition] is now absent; or perhaps, this is the normal mode of wearing? Further, is vermin an interposition? There is no question where it is dead, for it certainly interposes. But what if it is alive? Do we say, Since it moves to and fro, it is natural, and does not interpose; or perhaps it does interpose, since he objects to it? Does earth b interpose?—Earth certainly interposes![1]—Rather [the question is] what about dust of earth? Does [the space between the sleeves and] the armpit interpose?[2] do we require [it to be] on his flesh, which [condition] is absent; or perhaps this is the normal mode of wearing? What if he thrust his hand into his bosom? does his body[3] interpose or not? Does a thread interpose?—A thread certainly interposes—Rather [the question is] what about a hanging thread.[4] Mar the son of R. Ashi asked: What if one's hair entered beneath his garment?[5] is his hair as [part of] his body, or is it not as his body? R. Zera asked: Do the *tefillin*[6] interpose? There is no question on the view that night is not the time for *tefillin*,[7] for since they interpose at night,[8] they interpose by day too. The question is raised only on the view that night is the time for *tefillin*. What then? Does a precept which is incumbent upon the body interpose or not? Now this question travelled about until it reached R. Ammi. Said he to him [the questioner]: We have an explicit teaching that *tefillin* interpose. An objection is raised: Priests engaged in their [sacrificial] service, Levites on their dais[9] and Israelites during their *ma'amad*[10] are exempt from prayer[11] and *tefillin*. Surely that means that if they do put them on, they do not interpose?—No: [it means that] if they do put them on, they do interpose. If so, [can you say,] they are exempt? Surely he should state, they are *forbidden* [to don them]?—Since there are the Levites and the Israelites, of whom he cannot teach, 'they are c forbidden,'[1] he therefore teaches, They are exempt. But it was taught: If he put them on, they do not interpose?—There is no difficulty; one refers to [the *tefillin* of] the hand,[2] the other to that of the head. Wherein does that of the hand differ? because it is written, [*And the priest shall put on his linen garment, and his linen breeches*] *shall he put upon his flesh*,[3] which implies that nothing may interpose between it and his flesh; then with respect to that of the head too it is written, *And thou shalt set the mitre upon his head?*[4]—It was taught: His hair was visible between the headplate and the

(6) As these hung naturally down. (7) Where these naturally touch the body. (8) Or, Yezdyird, a Persian king. (9) Ex. XIX, 6. Hence you must wear your girdle like priests, and not so high. (10) Isa. XLIX, 23. (11) This is a technical designation for all places outside the Temple.—The reference is to the Sabbath, when the Rabbis forbade healing. Nevertheless they permitted this in the Temple when the priest is officiating at the sacrifice, as it is indecorous for his wound to be exposed then. (12) The act constitutes making a wound, which is forbidden.

a (1) Used as a bandage. (2) Which is forbidden, *supra* 18a. (3) Nothing may interpose between the priest's hand and the sacrifice, when he has to handle it. (4) Which he does not use for the purpose. (5) Not on the part of the hand which he needs for service. (6) For R. Joḥanan holds that it never interposes save in the place of garments. (7) For he rules that a small belt is an interposition, and this is less than three fingerbreadths square. (8) A rag less than that size is of no account, whereas a belt, being made up into an article, is of some account. (9) And blew it away from immediate contact with his body.

b (1) Surely there cannot be a question about this. (2) If the garment is loosely cut with broad sleeves. (3) I.e., the hand, which now comes between the body and the garment. (4) Hanging from the garment itself. (5) If the hair of the head grew so long that it fell within the garment. (6) V. Glos. (7) I.e., that there is no obligation to wear these at night. The reference is to Deut. VI, 8 and it is disputed in 'Erub. 96a whether this applies to night as well as to daytime. (8) As there is no need to wear them then, they are definitely superfluous, and so constitute an interposition. (9) Engaged in singing the Temple hymns. (10) A body of Israelites, representing the people, stood (ma'amad—*'amad* standing) in the Temple court during the sacrificing of the daily burnt-offering (v. Ta'an. 26a). (11) The 'Eighteen Benedictions' which were recited daily, and which constituted the Prayer *par excellence*.

c (1) For they are certainly *permitted* to put them on, since they do not officiate at the actual sacrificing. (2) That interposes. (3) Lev. VI, 3. (4) Ex. XXIX, 6.

כנגד אצילי ידיהן אמר רב אשי אמר לי הונא בר נתן זימנא חדא הוה קאימנא קמיה דאיזגדר מלכא והוה מדלי לי המיינאי ותיתייה ניהליה ואמר לי °ממלכת כהנים וגוי קדוש כתיב בכו כי אתאי קמיה דאמימר א"ל אקיים בך °והיו מלכים אומניך: *תנן התם [א]כהן שלקה באצבעו [א] כורך עליה גמי במקדש [ב]אבל לא במדינה ואם להוציא ממנה דם כאן וכאן אסור *אמר ר' יהודה בריה דרבי חייא לא שנו אלא גמי אבל צילצול קטן הוי יתור בגדים ורבי יוחנן אמר לא אמרו יתור בגדים אלא במקום בגדים אבל שלא במקום בגדים לא הוי יתור (א) [ב] ותיפוק ליה משום חציצה בשמאל א"נ שלא במקום עבודה ופליגא דרבא [ג] דאמר רבא אמר רב חסדא [ג]במקום בגדים אפי' נימא אחת חוצצת [ד]שלא במקום בגדים שלש על שלש [ד] חוצצות פחות מכאן אינן חוצצות אדרבי יוחנן ודאי פליגא אדר' יהודה בריה דרבי חייא מי לימא דפליגא [ה]שאני צילצול קטן דחשיב לישנא אחרינא אמרי לה אמר ר' יהודה בריה דרבי חייא לא שנו אלא גמי אבל צילצול קטן חוצץ ורבי יוחנן אמר לא אמרו חציצה בפחות משלש על שלש אלא במקום בגדים אבל שלא במקום בגדים שלש על שלש חוצצות [ה] פחות מיכן אינה חוצצת והיינו דרבא אמר רב חסדא לימא פליגא אדר' יהודה בריה דרבי חייא שאני צילצול קטן דחשיב ולר' יוחנן מאי איריא גמי לשמועינן צילצול קטן (ב) מילתא אגב אורחיה קמ"ל דגמי מסי בעי רבא [ו]נכנסה לו רוח בבגדו מהו על בשרו בעינן והא ליכא או דלמא דרך לבישה בכך [ז]כינה מהו שתחוץ [ח]מתה לא תבעי לך דודאי חייצא חיה מאי מי אמרינן כיון דאתא ואזלא רביתא היא ולא חייצא או דלמא כיון דקפיד עלה חייצא עפר מהו שיחוץ [ט]עפר ודאי חייץ אלא [י]אבק עפר מהו [כ]בית השחי מהו שיחוץ על בשרו בעינן והא ליכא או דלמא דרך לבישה בכך [ל]הכניס ידו לתוך חיקו מהו גופו מי חייץ או לא נימא מהו שתחוץ נימא ודאי חייצא אלא [מ]נימא מדולדלת מהו בעי מר בר רב אשי [נ]יצא שערו בבגדו מהו *שערו כגופו דמי או לאו כגופו דמי בעי רבי זירא תפילין מהו שיחוצו אליבא דמאן דאמר *) לילה לאו זמן תפילין הוא לא תבעי לך כיון דלילה חייצי יום נמי חייצי כי תיבעי לך למ"ד לילה זמן תפילין מאי מצוה דגופיה חייץ או לא חייץ איגלגל מילתא ומטא לקמיה דרבי אמי א"ל תלמוד ערוך הוא בידינו תפילין חוצצות מיתיבי [ס]כהנים בעבודתן ולוים בדוכנן וישראל במעמדן פטורין מן התפלה ומן התפילין מאי לאו אם הניחן אינן חוצצות לא אם הניחן חוצצות א"ה פטורים אסורים מיבעי ליה כיון דאיכא לוים וישראל דלא מתנו ליה אסור משום הכי תנא פטורין והתניא אם הניחן אינן חוצצות לא קשיא [ע]הא דיד הא דראש מאי שנא דיד דכתיב °ילבש על בשרו שלא יהא דבר חוצץ בינו לבשרו דראש נמי כתיב °ושמת המצנפת על ראשו **) תנא [פ]שערו היה נראה בין ציץ למצנפת ***) ששם

*) [עירובין צו' מנחות לו:] **) [ערכין ג:] ***) [שס.]

שמות יט | ישעיה מט | ויקרא ו | שמות כט | נזיר נט. (marginal references)

רש"י

כנגד אצילי [ו] ידיהם · על צלעותיהן כנגד המרפק: איזגדר מלכא · כך שמו ומלך פרס היה: והוה מדלי המיינאי ותיתייה ניהליה · אבנטו היה גבוה חגור מלמעלה מכנגד אצילי ידיו והפשיטו למטה כדי לנאותו: אמר ממלכת כהנים כתיב בכו · וצריכין אתם לנהוג עצמכם בתפארת של כהנים דכתיב בהו לא יחגרו ביזע: כורך עליה גמי · בשעת עבודה שגמי הוא (ג) שתרפא שם מכתו ואע"ג דגמי מסי מכה וכל דבר שיש בו משום רפואה אסור משום שבות גזירה שמא ישחוק סמנים ה"מ במדינה אבל במקדש לא גזרו משום שבות: ואם להוציא דם · *שמתכוין לכך: כאן וכאן אסור · דחבורה הוא ואיסור דאורייתא: צילצול · בגדי"ל: אבל שלא במקום בגדים · כגון אצבע: ותיפוק לי משום דחוצץ · בין ידו לעבודה ואסור דבעינן ולקח הכהן שתהא קבלה בעצמו של כהן והיכי שרי (ד) ר' יוחנן: בשמאל · שאינה כשרה לעבודה: שלא במקום עבודה · כגון [ז] *על גב היד: ופליגא דרבא · אדרבי יוחנן: שלש על שלש חוצצות · כלומר הוי ייתור בגדים ואיידי דנקט [ח] בנימא אחת במקום בגדים לישנא דחציצה דשייכא בה נקט נמי במסקנא לישנא דחציצה: ודאי פליגא · דהא אמר [שלא במקום בגדים] (ה) לא הוי ייתור בגדים ואפי' שלש על שלש במשמע: מי לימא דפליגא · דאיהו אמר צילצול קטן חוצץ ורבא אמר פחות משלש לא [ט] חוצץ: דחשיב · לפי שעשוי לנוי והוי בגד: *ל"א אמרי לה [י] כו' · בדר' יהודה בר' חייא לא פליגי לישני דחוצץ נמי דקאמר משום ייתור בגדים [יא] הוא דלא שייכא (ו) למימר חציצה שלא במקום בגדים ושלא במקום עבודה דאי במקום עבודה אפי' נימא חייצא ובדר' יוחנן הוא *דפליגי לישני: לימא [יב] פליג · דרבא אדר' יהודה *דאילו רבי יוחנן פשיטא לן דפליג עליה ואפילו צילצול קטן מכשר דהא עלה קמהדר ופליג אלא דרבא דאיתמר (ז) (עלה) בעלמא מי לימא פליג אדרבי יהודה דנימא דרבא אפי' צילצול קטן מכשר שלא במקום בגדים: ולר' יוחנן · [יג] דקאמר אפי' צילצול לא חייץ מאי איריא דנקט תנא דמתני' גמי לשמועינן צילצול לא הוי ייתור וכל שכן גמי: דגמי מסי · (ח) רופא המכה ואפ"ה מותר דאין שבות במקדש דכולה מסכתא באיסור שבת איירי ועיקר משום שבות נקט לה ומשנה זו בעירובין וכן כולה הך סוגיא התם היא: נכנסה לו רוח בבגדו · והבדילתו מבשרו בשעת עבודה: רביתא היא · הרי היא כבשרו: כיון דקפיד עלה · דברצונו לא תהא בבשרו: אבק עפר · דק [יד] ואינו מרגיש בו: בית השחי מהו שיחוץ · אויר בית השחי כגון [טו] בתי זרועותיו של חלוקו שהוא רחב ואינו נוגע בבית השחי מהו שיחוץ וצריך שיהו בתי זרועותיו דחוקים ונוגעין בבשר: גופו · ידו שהיא גופו: נימא · משמע דאתיא מעלמא: נימא מדולדלת · מן הבגד (ט) [טז] מגוררין ותחובה בו קצת אלא שנתקה מעיקרא: יצא שערו · מראשו למטה עד שנכנס בין כתונת [יז] לבשרו מהו את"ל ידו לא חייצא שערו מאי: מהו שיחוצו · למיהוי ייתור בגדים: אליבא דמ"ד · בפרק בתרא דעירובין (דף צו') ובהקומץ רבה (מנחות לו:): לא תבעי לך · דודאי חייצי כדמפרש טעמא כיון דבעבודות לילה [יח] חיילין דהא לא מצוה הוה דניהוי כגופיה משום חביבותא דמצות: [יט] דיום נמי חיילי · דאל"כ מלינו [כ] עבודות לילה חמיר מעבודות יום והן קלים מהן: ולוים בדוכנן · לשיר: ישראל במעמדן · על כל משמר ומשמר היה מעמד של ישראל בירושלים שבאין ועומדין בעזרה בשעת התמיד והן שלוחי כל ישראל לעמוד על קרבנן דכתיב תשמרו להקריב לי במועדו שתהא שמירתכם עליו בשעת הקרבתו במסכת תענית (דף כו'): פטורין מן התפלה · (שאין יכולין לכוין): ומן התפילין · דקיימא לן (סוכה דף כה') העוסק במצוה פטור מן המצוה: דלא מיתני ליה אסורין · שאין יכול לשעת בהן איסור: דיד · חוצצות דהוא בין בגד לבשר: דראש · אין חוצצות כדמפרש ואזיל: שערו · של כהן גדול שהיה נראה בין ציץ שעל מצחו למצנפת שבגובה ראשו:

תוספות

כורך עליה גמי במקדש אבל לא במדינה · פי' בקונט' גמי מרפא ואסור משום שחיקת סמנים ונראה לפרש גזירה אטו להוציא דם וכן בכל הנהו (דעירובין (דף קג·) יש לפרש טעמא) דאסירי במדינה משום איסורא דקתני בתר הכי כאן וכאן אסור ומיהו בירושלמי משמע דטעמא משום שחיקת סמנין דמסיק פרק כל כתבי הקודש גבי רבי שלקה באצבעו בשבת ונתן עליה ספוג יבש וקשר עליה גמי מבחוץ וקאמר התם דלמדנו [כא] דספוג איט מרפא אלא משמר גמי לפי שהוא מן המוכן ובסמוך נמי קאמר קא משמע לן דגמי מסי משמע דהיינו טעמא דאבל לא במדינה: **מאי** איריא גמי לשמועינן צילצול קטן [כב] · תימה הא איצטריך לאשמועינן גמי משום אבל לא במדינה דטעמא דשחיקת סמנים לא שייך בצילצול דהא לא מסי וי"ל דמ"מ הוה ליה לאשמועינן צילצול דהוי חידוש גדול יותר דלא הוי ייתור בגדים מלאשמועינן איסור של גמי במדינה ומשני דקמ"ל דגמי מסי משום לשון חכמים מרפא: **תפלין** מהו שיחוצו · פירש בקונטרס למיהוי ייתור בגדים ואי אפשר לומר כן דהא קאמר [כג] לימוד ערוך דתפילין חוצצות ובשל יד איירי דבשל ראש הא אמרינן בסמוך דאין חוצצות ואי משום ייתור בגדים אפי' דראש נמי ומיהו למאן דאמר לעיל לא אמרו ייתור בגדים אלא במקום בגדים אבל שלא במקום בגדים לא ניחא דשל יד הוי במקום בגדים ולא של ראש [כד] ומשום חציצה ממש נראה טפי [כה] כדדריש בסמוך על בשרו שלא יהא דבר חוצץ מיהו הא דתניא אינן חוצצות ואוקמינן לה בשל ראש לא הוי שום חידוש שלא [כו] יהא חציצה כי אם שאינן [משום] ייתור בגדים אם לא דתאמר דקמ"ל דשערו היה נראה א"כ קמ"ל דלא חציצי תחת פתילי הציץ: וחוקה

עין משפט נר מצוה

כו א מיי' פ"י מהלכות כלי המקדש הלכה ז:
כז ב מיי' פ"א מהלכות שבת הלכה כה סמג לאוין סה טוש"ע א"ח סימן שכח סעיף כד בהגה:
כח ג מיי' פ"י מהלכות כלי המקדש הלכה ה:
כט ד ה מיי' שם הלכה ח:
ל ו ז מיי' שם הלכה ז:
עירובין קג:
לא ח מיי' שם הלכה ו:
לב י כ ל מ נ מיי' שם הלכה ז:
לג ס מיי' פ"ד מהלכות תפילין הלכה יג:
לד ע מיי' פ"י מהלכות כלי המקדש הלכה ו:
לה פ מיי' שם הלכה ג:

מסורת הש"ס

רש"ל שמהדקה בגמי כדי שתוציא דמה
[עירובין קג: כל הענין]
רש"ל פ"ג יד או ע"ג אצבע
גי' ס"ק נ"א אמר ר"י כו' בדר' יהודה בר' חייא לא פליגי לישנא אחרינא דחוצץ כמי כו'
גי' ס"ק דפליגי לישנא אחרינא
רש"ל דאילו לדר' פשיטא לן דלא פליג

שיטה מקובצת

א] כורך עליה גמי במקדש אבל לא במדינה פ"ה גמי מרפא ואסור משום שחיקת סמנים וקשה דא"כ כי פריך לקמן א"כ מאי שנא גמי דנקט לישני ליה משום אבל לא במדינה נקט וי"ל דגמי אינו מסי וטעמא דאמרינן אבל לא במדינה משום גזירת שמא יוציא דם ומעתה ניחא הא דאמר לקמן דגמי לאו דוקא קאמר כלומר א) שהוא מתכוין להוציא דסג)דבכל דוכתי הוי טעמא דאבל לא במדינה כמו איסורא דסיפא אבל בירושלמי משמע כפרש"י כו' עד רבי ומ"מ י"ל דספוג רחב ואינו מוציא דם כל כך כמו גמי שהוא דק · לשון מהר"פ: ב] יתור בגדים ותיפוק ליה כו' א"נ בימין שלא: ג] דרבא אמר רב חסדא דאמר: ד] שלש חוצצת פחות מכאן אינן חוצצות: ה] פחות משלש על שלש תיבת מיכן ל"ש ונמחק והיינו דרבא אמר רב חסדא ג) בעלמא מספקא ליה לתלמוד אי הא דקאמר פחות מג' אינה חוצצת מיירי אף בצלצול קטן או שמא חלוק צלצול דחשיב · מהר"פ:ו] (אצילי ידיהם אות ו' נמחק): ז] כגון גב היד: ח] דנקט ס"א בגדים חוצצין נקט נמי הכא לשון חציצה: ט] לא חייץ הס"ד: י] לה אמר רב יהודה כו' לא בא לשנות כלל דברי רב יהודה אלא בא לשנות דברי רבי יוחנן מזה דנהי דקאמר אבל צלצול קטן חוצץ מטעם ייתור בגדים קאמר דהציצה לא שייך כלל שלא במקום בגדים ועוד דהא ודאי מיירי שלא במקום עבודה דאי במקום עבודה הא ודאי לא שרינן וכיון דמיירי שלא במקום עבודה לא שייך חציצה ואיידי דבעי למינקט בדברי ר' יוחנן חציצה נקט נמי (הכי) [הכא] לשון חציצה:כך היא נוסחת רש"י של מהר"פ: יא] הוא (וחציצה)[דחציצה] לא שייכא למימר שלא במקום בגדים: יב] לימא דרבא פליג אדרב יהודה כו' דהא עליה קמהדר כו' דאתמר בעלמא:יג] יוחנן דאמר אפילו צלצול כו' נמי לשמועינן צלצול: יד] דק מאד: טו] בית יד תיבת זרועו נמחק: טז] הבגד ועודה תחובה בו קצת: יז] לבשרו וקשה לרב"א דהוי ליה למימר נכנס שערו לכן פי' שיער בית השחי ובית הערוה קאמר שיצא לחוץ ונפל על בטנו וחוצץ בין בגדיו וכה"ג איתא (בבכורות) [בברכות כג'] מהר"פ: יח] לילה חייצי דהא לאו אות ן' נמחק: יט] מה"ד ביום נמי: כ] מצינו חמור עבודת לילה: כא] דלמדנו ממנו ג' דברים דספוג אינו מרפא אלא משמר וגמי מרפא ואי משום הוצאות דם היאך היה עושה זה רבי ותיבות לפי שהוא מן המוכן ל"ש: כב] קטן דלא הוי ייתור בגדים וכ"ש גמי לפי' שני דפי' לעיל ומשני דמילתא אגב אורחא קמ"ל דגמי מסי ולשון חכמים מרפא כלומר שאין זו החידוש דלא נזרינן שמא יוציא דם במקדש ובקונט' פי' קמ"ל דגמי מסי כו' לשון מהר"פ: כג] קאמר בסמוך תלמוד ערוך בידינו דתפילין חוצצת ובשל יד איירי דאי של ראש: כד] ראש ס"א ומיהו טפי נראה לפרש דמשום חציצה ממש קא בעי: כה] טפי לפרש: כו] תהא חציצה כו':

הגהות הב"ח

(א) גמ' לא הוי ייתור בגדים ותיפוק וכו' א"נ בימין ושלא במקום עבודה: (ב) שם צילצול קטן אגב אורחיה כצ"ל ותיבת מילתא ליתא: (ג) רש"י ד"ה כורך וכו' שתירפא שם: (ד) ד"ה ותיפוק לי וכו' והיכי שרי לרבי יוחנן · נ"ב בעירובין לא מפרש לה אר"י והכא דקדייק דאר"י קאי [משמע דאצילצול] קאי דשרי ר"י ולא אגמי וי"ל דאפשר [דלרבי יהודה בר' חייא מיירי מתניתין] דוקא לגבי מכה ולא הוה חציצה [אבל לר' יוחנן] דאמר שלא במקום בגדים לא הוי ייתור [בגדים משמע דשרי] בכל מקום לזה פריך ותיפוק ליה משום חציצה ולאסור ודו"ק: (ה) ד"ה ודאי וכו' אמר דלא: (ו) ד"ה ל"א אמרי לה וכו' דלא שייכא חציצה כצ"ל ותיבת למימר נמחק: (ז) ד"ה לימא וכו' דאיתמר לה בעלמא: (ח) ד"ה דגמי מסי מרפא מכה: (ט) ד"ה נימא וכו' מגוררת:

א) נראה דצ"ל לאו דוקא קאמר וכזה נימא נמי דהוי דומיא דסיפא ואם להוציא דם כאן וכאן אסור כלומר שהוא מתכוין · ב) ר"ל דבכל המשניות שנשנו שם בעירובין אחר זה דאבל לא במדינה · ג) נראה דצריך לומר לימא פליגי וכו' וע"ז כתב מספקא ליה וכו' ·

ששם (א) מניחין תפילין: מחוסר כיפורים מנלן אמר רב הונא אמר קרא °וכפר עליה הכהן וטהרה *טהרה מכלל שהיא טמאה: ושלא רחוץ ידים ורגלים: אתיא חוקה חוקה ממחוסר בגדים: ת"ר **כהן גדול שלא טבל ושלא קידש בין בגד לבגד ובין עבודה לעבודה ועבד עבודתו כשרה ואחד כהן גדול ואחד כהן הדיוט שלא קידש ידיו ורגליו שחרית ועבד עבודתו פסולה א"ל רב אסי לרבי יוחנן מכדי *חמש טבילות ועשרה קדושין דאורייתא וחוקה כתיב בהו ליעכבו א"ל אמר קרא °ולבשם לבישה מעכבת ואין דבר אחר מעכב צהבו פניו *אמר ליה וי"ו אאופתא כתבי לך א] אי הכי דצפרא נמי אמר חזקיה אמר קרא °והיתה להם חק עולם לו ולזרעו לדורותם ב] דבר המעכב בזרעו מעכב בו דבר שאינו מעכב בזרעו אין מעכב בו רבי יונתן אמר מהכא °ורחצו ממנו משה ואהרן ובניו דבר המעכב בבניו מעכב בו דבר שאינו מעכב בבניו אין מעכב בו רבי יונתן מ"ט לא אמר מדחזקיה אמר לך ההוא לדורות הוא דכתיב ואידך מ"ט לא אמר מהאי מיבעי ליה לכדרבי יוסי ברבי חנינא *דאמר רבי יוסי ברבי חנינא כל כיור *שאין בו כדי לקדש ארבעה כהנים ממנו אין מקדשין בו שנאמר ורחצו ממנו ג] משה ואהרן ובניו: ת"ר כיצד מצות קידוש ה"מניח ידו הימנית על גבי רגלו הימנית וידו השמאלית על גבי רגלו השמאלית ומקדש רבי יוסי ברבי יהודה אומר מניח שתי ידיו זו על גב זו ועל גבי שתי רגליו זו על גבי זו ומקדש אמרו לו הפלגתה אי אפשר לעשות כן שפיר קאמרי ליה אמר רב יוסף וחבירו מסייעו מאי בינייהו אמר אביי ד] עמידה מן הצד איכא בינייהו א"ל רב סמא בריה דרב אשי לרבינא וליתיב מיתב ולקדש אמר קרא °לשרת ושירות מעומד הוא: ת"ר וקידש ידיו ורגליו ביום אין צריך לקדש בלילה ובלילה צריך לקדש ביום דברי רבי שהיה רבי אומר לינה מועלת בקידוש ידים ורגלים רבי אלעזר ברבי שמעון אומר אין לינה מועלת בקידוש ידים ורגלים תניא אידך *היה "עומד ומקריב על גבי מזבח כל הלילה ה] לאורה טעון קידוש ידים ורגלים דברי רבי רבי אלעזר בר"ש אומר כיון שקידש ידיו ורגליו מתחילת עבודה אפילו מיכן ועד עשרה ימים ואינו צריך לקדש וצריכא דאי אשמעינן קמייתא בההיא קאמר רבי דפסק ליה מעבודה לעבודה אבל בהא דלא פסק ליה אימא מודי ליה רבי לרבי אלעזר ברבי שמעון ואי אשמעינן בהא בהא קאמר רבי אלעזר ברבי שמעון אבל בהא אימא מודי ליה לרבי צריכא מאי טעמא דרבי דכתיב °בגשתם מ"ט דרבי אלעזר בר"ש דכתיב °בבואם ואידך נמי הא כתיב בבואם אי כתיב בגשתם ולא כתיב בבואם הוה אמינא על כל גישה וגישה כתב רחמנא בבואם ואידך נמי הא כתיב בגשתם אי כתיב בבואם ולא כתיב בגשתם °הוה אמינא אפילו אביאה ריקנית אביאה ריקנית הא כתיב לשרת אלא בגשתם מיבעי ליה לכדרב אחא בר יעקב *דאמר רב אחא בר יעקב הכל מודים בקידוש שני כשהוא לבוש מקדש דאמר קרא או בגשתם מי שאינו מחוסר אלא גישה בלבד יצא זה שמחוסר לבישה וגישה °להקטיר אשה למה לי מהו

רש"י

ששם מניח תפילין · הלכך ליכא חלילה ותנא דאילטריך לאשמועינן אם הניחן אין חוללות משום ייתור בגדים הוא דאילטריך ו] לאשמועינן דלאו בגד הוא: מכלל שהיא טמאה · עד עכשיו וטמא כתיב ביה וינזרו ולא יחללו: אתיא חוקה חוקה · מה להלן אם עבד חילל אף כאן אם עבד חילל: כהן גדול כו' · כגון בחמש עבודות של יום הכפורים דילפינן בסדר יומא (דף לב·) שהוא משנה מבגדי זהב לבגדי לבן ומבגדי לבן לבגדי זהב וצריך לכל חילוף טבילה ושני קידושין מן המקרא אם לא טבל ולא קידש עבודתו כשרה: שחרית · בין ביום הכפורים בין בכל השנה עבודתו פסולה כדילפינן חוקה חוקה ממחוסר בגדים: דאורייתא · דכתיב ורחץ את בשרו במים ולבשם והתם יליף לכולה מילתא: וחוקה כתיב בהו · לאחר שגמר כל הפרשה כתיב והיתה להם לחוקת עולם בחדש השביעי בעשור וגו': אמר קרא ולבשם · שינה הכתוב בלבישה לעכב דכתיב ילבש ולבשם ולהכי כתיב ז] הכא עכובא למעוטי עכובא דחוקה דלא קיימא אהאי קרא דאיירי ברחילה ולבישה אלא אשאר ח] (שני) דברים האמורים בפרשה: ואין דבר אחר · ט] בפסוק זה מעכב: צהבו פניו · של ר' אסי מפני שמחה כסבור טעם הגון שמע: וי"ו אאופתא כתיבי לך · כתבתי לך וי"ו על הבקעת אות שאין ניכרת י] בה מפני שורות הבקעת שמפסיקות בה הפסקות הרבה לשון אחר השורות עצמו קרי להו ווי"ן שדומין לה כלומר אין זה טעם דהיכא לאקשויי א"כ אפילו קדוש של שחרית יא] [של יוה"כ] נמי לא לעכב ביה דהא אימעוט ביום הכפורים מולבשם: והיתה להם (ב) לחק עולם · בקידוש כתיב: בזרעו · בכהנים הדיוטים דהיינו קידוש שבשעת כניסה שנוהג בכל הכהנים מעכבא יב] באהרן ביום הכפורים דהא חוקה כתיב: לדורות הוא דכתיב · אזהרה לנהוג חוקה זו לזרעו אחריו ולאו להיקשא אתא: שאין בו · שאין מחזיק מים כשיעור ארבע קידושין: *משה ואהרן · תרין ובניו תרין שאף משה כהן היה בשבעת ימי המילואים ואע"ג דלא כהנו בבת אחת מיהו קרא להכי מידרים: מניח ידיו כו' · דבעינן ידיו ורגליו (ג) יג] כאחד ירחצו כדכתיב קרא: הפלגתה · דברים ממדת כל אדם דאי אפשר לו שלא יפול: אמר רב יוסף · הא דרבי יוסי ברבי יהודה כשחבירו מסייעו מחזיק בו שלא יפול: מאי בינייהו · במאי פליגי: עמידה מן הצד · כגון זו שאינו בלא סיוע לרבנן לא הויא עמידה ואנן עמידה בעינן כדמפרש לקמן: אמר קרא לשרת · או בגשתם אל המזבח לשרת איתקש קידוש לשירות: (ד) אינו צריך לקדש בלילה · אם לא יצא ולא הסיח דעתו: צריך לקדש ביום · כדמסיים מילתיה שהלינה פוסלת בקידוש ועמוד השחר הוא העושה לינה לקמן בפרק המזבח מקדש (דף פז·): מתחילת עבודה · כשהתחיל לעבוד עבודות *הללו ולא הסיח שוב דעתו יד] *[עד עשרה ימים ובלבד שיהא עומד ועובד]: דפסק ליה מן העבודה · אלא שלא הסיח דעתו דלא תני בה היה עומד ומקריב כי הכא: דכתיב בגשתם · טו] וגישה דשחרית גישה אחריתי היא שהרי יש כאן מערכה חדשה: דכתיב בבואם · והרי [זה] לא יצא: טז] אבל גישה וגישה · ואפי' שתיהן בו ביום: אביאה ריקנית · נכנס שלא לעבוד: דרב אחא בר יעקב · בסדר יומא: הכל מודים · ר"מ ורבנן דפליגי *בקידוש שלפני כל טבילה של יז] טבילות [כ"ג רבנן אמרי] קידש ידיו ורגליו ופשט רבי מאיר אומר פשט קידש ידיו ורגליו מודים הם בקידוש של אחר טבילה שלובש הבגדים שהוא מחליף ואחר כך מקדש ואינו מקדש כשהוא ערום דכתיב בגשתם ירחצו מי שאינו מחוסר אחר קידוש אלא גישה: להקטיר אשה · דכתיב גבי קידוש למה לי פשיטא דבעיא קידוש דהא גישת מזבח היא: מהו

תוספות

וחוקה כתיב בהו ליעכבו · אפי' למאן דאמר (יומא דף ס·) דלא כתיבא חוקה אלא יח] [בדברים הנעשים] בבגדי לבן בפנים לכל הפחות קידוש דהוי בין בגדי זהב לבגדי לבן ליעכב דלורך פנים כפנים כדאמר שילהי הוליאו לו (שם דף ס:) דקטרת שחפנה קודם שחיטת הפר פסולה דלורך פנים כפנים דמי: **אי** הכי דלפרא נמי · *תימה מאי קושיא כיון דהוי במיתה אתי בקל וחומר מיושב שאינו במיתה ואם עבד חילל וכי תימא מה ליושב כו' ונילף מיושב וחד מהנך ועוד דשם יושב לא פריך ואמאי חשיב ליה וי"ו אאופתא:

וחבירו מסייעו יט] במסכת תמיד (דף כח· פרק א מ"ד) משמע *דאותו [שהיה הולך לתרומת הדשן] היה כ] מהלך יחידי וההיא פליגא או היה שם דבר שהיה מסייעו:

עמידה מן הצד איכא בינייהו · לרבנן לא שמיה עמידה מן הצד ונראה כא] כשקורין בתורה שלא לסמוך משום דאמר (רבי) במגילה פרק הקורא את המגילה עומד (דף כא·) דבתורה בעי עמידה ובירושלמי נמי אמרינן דאסור לסמוך משום דכשם שניתנה באימה כך נוהגין אותה באימה:

וליתב מיתיב וליקדש · לאו ישיבה ממש קאמר דאין ישיבה בעזרה אלא סמיכה*:

אלא כב] האי בגשתם מיבעי ליה לכדרב אחא בר יעקב · אף על גב דביומא משמע דרבי נמי אית ליה דרב אחא בר יעקב כג] דקסבר דתרתי שמע מינה: מיתיבי

עין משפט נר מצוה

לו א מיי' פ"ה מהלכות ביאת מקדש הלכה ז ופ"ב מהלכות עבודת יוה"כ הלכה ג:

לז ב מיי' פ"ה מהלכות ביאת מקדש הלכה טז:

עיין ש"ק

לח ג מיי' שם הלכה ג:

לט ד ה מיי' שם הלכה ח:

גי' הש"ק דאותו שהלך לתרום המזבח היה מהלך יחידי והיה מקדש ידיו ורגליו ההיא פליגא או היה שום דבר כו' כצ"ל

מסורת הש"ס

[יבמות עד: סנהדרין פג:]

יומא לב: תוספתא דמנחות פ"א ע"ש תוספתא דיומא פ"א

[יומא יט: לא: עא:]

חולין עז:

פסחים נ: תוספתא דמנחות פ"א תוספתא דיומא פ"א

יומא לב:

מגילה ז"ק *פ"א

[ופי' היטב בתוס' דיומא כה: ד"ה אין ישיבה]

לקמן כה:

הגהות הב"ח

(א) גמ' ששם מניח תפילין: (ב) רש"י ד"ה והיתה להם חק עולם: (ג) ד"ה מניח וכו' כאחת כדכתיב קרא ירחצו הס"ד: (ד) ד"ה אינו · נ"ב ע"ל בדף כ ע"ב:

נ"א שאין מחזיק כדי: רש"ק

גליון הש"ס

גמ' הוה אמינא אפילו אביאה ריקנית · עיין סנהדרין דף פג ע"א תוס' ד"ה ולא משום טומאה:

גי' הש"ק בקידוש שלפני כל טבילה וטבילה דרבנן סברי קידש ידיו וכו' כצ"ל ועיין במסכת יומא דף לב ע"ב

שיטה מקובצת

א] אי הכי דצפרא נמי ואפשר דצפרא מרבינן מג"ש דמחוסר בגדים א"כ מיעט דולבשם לאו דוקא מאותו דצפרא כמו כן לא יהיה דוקא מן האחריני · מהר"פ: ב] דבר המעכב בזרעו כגון תמיד של שחרית שבכל יום שנוהג בכהנים הדיוטים אבל עבודת יה"כ שאינו נוהג אלא בכה"ג אין מעכב בו: ג] משה ואהרן ובניו · אע"ג דמשה היה לוי מ"מ היה משמש בז' ימי המילואים וא"ת ליבעי שיתא דד' בנים היו לאהרן וי"ל דכבר מתו נדב ואביהוא וא"ת והרי ארבע נמי לא שימשו ביום אחד דבז' ימי המילואים ששימש משה לא שימש אהרן ואח"כ ששימש אהרן שוב לא שימש משה ואפ"ה קחשיב להו ד' כמו כן ליבעי שיתא אע"פ שנדב ואביהוא לא שימשו וי"ל דמיעוט בניו שנים והר"ם תירץ דבשמיני למילואים נמי שימש משה שמה שהובחרה העבודה באהרן כדכתיב קרב אל המזבח היינו דוקא עבודת היום כגון עגל וכבש ושאר עבודות דשייכי (לשמיני) (לשמינית)[ליום השמיני של] ימי המילואים אבל עבודות שהיו עושין בכל יום כגון תמידין וקטורת זה עשה משה כדכתיב ויהי באחד לחודש הוקם המשכן ואח"כ כתיב ויעל את העולה אלמא משמע מי (שהוקם) [שהקים] את המשכן דהיינו משה העלה את העולה ובאותו יום שהוקם את המשכן היה שמיני למילואים ונטל עשר עטרות. מהר"פ: ד] עמידה מן הצד כו' וא"כ צריך ליזהר בכל מקום שצריך עמידה כגון בתפילה והקורא בתורה שלא יסמוך כדאיתא בירושלמי כו' ור' יחיאל מפריש היה אומר דדוקא שלא היה יכול לעמוד בלי סמיכה לא שמה עמידה אבל היכא שהיה יכול לעמוד בלי סמיכה אף כי עושה סמיכה שמה עמידה וטורי אומר אם הוא סומך כל כך בחוזק שאם תנטל הדבר שהוא סומך עליו יפול לא שמה עמידה ואם לאו שמה עמידה · מהר"פ: ה] לאורה · גליון פי' לעמוד השחר: ו] לאשמועינן ולפי' השני שפי' לעיל מטעם חציצה צריך לפרש דהיא נופא קמ"ל דשערו היה נראה (שום) (וליכא משום) חציצה ומהכא משמע שהיה הציץ נתון על גובה הראש ולא על מצחו ממש דשל כהן הדיוט קורין ליה מגבעות אלא משום דשל כה"ג היתה קטנה לפי שהיה מניח הציץ על שערו אבל של כהן הדיוט היתה גדולה וטכסה כל הראש ואע"ג דביומא קרי לשל הדיוט מצנפת לשון חכמים לחוד ולשון תורה לחוד · מהר"פ: ז] ולהכי כתיב עכובא הכא למעוטי ולומר דעכובא דחוקה לא קיימא: ח] תיבת שני נמחק: ט] שבפסוק זה: י] תיבת בה נמחק: יא] שחרית של יה"כ: יב] מעכבא בו: יג] ורגליו בחדא רחיצה כדכתיב בקרא הס"ד: יד] דעתו עד עשרה ימים ובלבד שיהא עומד ועובד: טו] בגישתם וגישת שחרית גישה: טז] מה"ד על כל גישה וגישה: יז] של ה' [טבילות] ותיבת כה"ג רבנן אמרי ל"ש תמחק: יח] אלא בדברים הנעשים: יט] מסייעו לקדש: כ] הולך יחידי ושמא ההיא פליגא: כא] ונראה דצריך להזהיר בשעה שקורין בתורה: כב] תיבת האי נמחק: כג] יעקב קסבר את ד' נמחק:

mitre, [19*b*] and there he laid the *tefillin*.[5]

ONE LACKING IN SACRIFICIAL ATONEMENT. Whence do we know it?—Said R. Huna, Scripture saith, *And the priest shall make atonement for her, and she shall be clean*:[6] *'She shall be clean'* proves that she is unclean [before atonement is made for her].[7]

AND ONE WHO HAD NOT WASHED HIS HANDS OR HIS FEET. [The implication of] *'statute'* is derived from *'statute'* written in connection with one who lacked his priestly vestments.[8]

Our Rabbis taught: If a High Priest did not perform immersion or did not sanctify [himself][9] between the changing of robes and between the services,[10] and he officiated, his service is valid. But the service of both a High Priest or an ordinary priest who officiated without the sanctification at daybreak of their hands and feet is invalid. Said R. Assi to R. Joḥanan: Consider: The five immersions and the ten sanctifications[11] are scriptural, and *'statute'*
a is written in connection with them; then let them be indispensable?[1] —Said he to him: Scripture saith, *And put them on*:[2] the putting on [of the priestly vestments] is indispensable, but nothing else is indispensable.[3] [At that] his face lit up.[4] Said he to him: I have written you a *waw* on a tree-trunk:[5] [for] if that is so, [the sanctifications] of the morning[6] too [should not be indispensable]!—Said Hezekiah, Scripture saith, *And it shall be a statute for ever to them, even to him and to his seed throughout their generations*:[7] that which is indispensable for *'his seed'* is indispensable for himself, and that which is not indispensable for *'his seed'* is not indispensable for himself.[8] R. Jonathan said, He deduced it from this: *That Moses and Aaron and his sons might wash their hands and their feet thereat*:[9] that which is indispensable in the case of his sons is indispensable in his own case; while that which is not indispensable in the case of his sons is not indispensable in his own case. Why does R. Jonathan not deduce it from the text quoted by Hezekiah?—He can answer you: That is written [to shew that the law holds good] for all generations.[10] And the other? why did he not deduce it from this text?—He requires it for R. Jose son of R. Ḥanina's [ruling]. For R. Jose son of R. Ḥanina said: You may not wash in a laver which does not contain sufficient [water] for the sanctifications of four priests, for it says, *That Moses and Aaron and his sons might wash their hands and their feet thereat*.[11]

Our Rabbis taught: How is the precept of 'sanctification' [fulfilled]? [The priest] places his right hand on his right foot and
b his left hand on his left foot, and sanctifies them.[1] R. Jose son of Judah said: He places his both hands on each other and on his two feet lying on each other, and sanctifies them. Said they to him: You have made it too hard, for it is impossible to do it thus. Surely they speak rightly to him?—Said R. Joseph: His colleague assists him.[2] Wherein do they differ?—Said Abaye: They disagree in respect of standing by being supported.[3] Said R. Sima the son of R. Ashi to Rabina: And let him indeed sit and perform his sanctifications?—Scripture saith, [*And thou shalt anoint Aaron and his sons, and sanctify them*,] *that they may minister*,[4] and the ministration must be done standing.[5]

Our Rabbis taught: If [the priest] sanctified his hands and feet by day, he need not sanctify [them] at night; [if he sanctified them] at night, he must sanctify [them] by day. This is Rabbi's view, for Rabbi maintained: The passing of the night is effective in respect of the sanctification of hands and feet.[6] R. Eleazar son of R. Simeon said: The passing of the night is not effective in respect of the sanctification of hands and feet. Another [Baraitha] taught: If [a priest] was standing and offering [the fats] on the altar throughout the night, at dawn he needs sanctification of hands and feet: this is Rabbi's view. R. Eleazar son of R. Simeon said: Since he sanctified his hands and feet at the beginning of the service, he need not sanctify [them again] even for ten days.[7] Now, both are necessary. For if we were informed of the first [Baraitha], [I would argue that] Rabbi ruled thus only there, [the circumstances being]
c that there had been an interval between one service and another;[1] but here that there was no interval, I would say that Rabbi agrees with R. Eleazar son of R. Simeon. While if we were informed of the latter [Baraitha], I would argue that here only does R. Eleazar son of R. Simeon rule thus, but in the former he agrees with Rabbi. Hence they are both necessary.

What is Rabbi's reason?—Because it is written, *When they approach* [*the altar to minister*].[2] What is R. Eleazar son of R. Simeon's reason?—Because it is written, *When they enter* [*into the tent of meeting, they shall wash with water*].[3] And the other too? surely it is written, *When they enter*!—If *'when they approach'* were written and not *'when they enter'* I would say that for every single approach [sanctification is necessary];[4] therefore the Divine Law wrote, *'when they enter.'* And the other too? surely it is written, *'when they approach'*!—If *'when they enter'* were written and not *'when they approach'*, I would say that [they must wash] even for a mere entrance.[5] 'For a mere entrance'! surely it is written, *'to minister'*?—Rather, *'when they approach'* is required for R. Aḥa son of Jacob's [ruling]. For R. Aḥa son of Jacob said: All agree with respect to the second 'sanctification,' that [the priest] performs this sanctification when he is clothed,[6] for Scripture saith, *'or when they approach'*: he who lacks nothing but the approach [washes his hands and feet]; hence he who has yet to clothe himself and then approach is excluded. What is the purpose of, *to cause an offering made by fire*

(5) Thus the *tefillin* did not actually interpose. (6) Lev. XII, 8. (7) Although she had already performed her ritual ablutions. Thus Scripture designates even such as unclean, and he is disqualified in the same way as an unclean priest is disqualified. (8) V. *supra* 17*b*, 18*a*. (9) This is the technical designation for washing the hands and feet at the laver. (10) On the Day of Atonement the High Priest performed five services, in the course of which he changed his robes several times. Each change was to be preceded by *ṭebillah* (immersion) and sanctification; v. Yoma 32*a*. (11) Five for the hand and five for the feet.

a (1) So that the service should be invalid. (2) Lev. XVI, 4. (3) The verse reads: *He shall put on the holy linen tunic, and he shall have the linen breeches . . . and shall be girded with the linen girdle, and with the linen mitre shall he be attired . . . and he shall bathe his flesh in water, and put them on*. Thus *'put them on'* is emphasized by being repeated in the verse, to teach that that only is indispensable, but the other thing mentioned, viz., bathing, is not indispensable. (4) R. Assi was very pleased with the answer. (5) On which, owing to its rough lined surface the letter is not visible. This is an idiom for idle talk. (6) On the Day of Atonement. (7) Ex. XXX, 21. (8) *'His seed'* denotes an ordinary priest, while *'statute'* implies indispensability, as stated above. Hence the sanctification of the morning which is normally indispensable for an ordinary priest is indispensable for a High Priest on the Day of Atonement. (9) Ex. XL, 31. (10) But not to provide an analogy. (11) *'His sons'* implies at least two; hence it must be big enough for four.

b (1) So that he washes his hands and feet simultaneously, by pouring water on each pair with his fore hand. (2) So that he does not fall. (3) Lit., 'a standing from the side'. The priest must stand when performing these ablutions, and if R. Jose b. R. Judah's method is adopted, he can stand only by being supported. He holds that that is sufficient, while the first Tanna holds that that is not called standing. (4) Ex. XXX, 30. (5) *'Sanctify them'* is interpreted as in the present discussion. Thus the ablutions are made analogous to ministrations, and as the latter must be done standing, the former too must be done standing. (6) As soon as one night passes, the previous sanctification ceases to count. (7) As long as he is continuously engaged thus.

c (1) For in the first Baraitha it is not stated that the priest was actually engaged in officiating all night. (2) Ex. XXX, 20. Each time the priest 'approaches' the altar he must wash his hands. At daybreak there is a new approach since the altar has to be freshly arranged with new wood; therefore he must wash his hands again. (3) Ibid. As long as he is engaged on the sacrifices there is no new entry. (4) Even in the same day. (5) Without officiating. (6) The changing of the garments by the High Priest on the Day of Atonement was preceded by immersion, and the immersion was preceded and followed by 'sanctification'. All agree that the second 'sanctification' is done *after* the priest has donned the robes into which he was to change, v. Yoma 32*b*.

to smoke?[7] [20a]—You might say: This [sanctification] is required only for a service which is indispensable to atonement, but not for a service which is not indispensable to atonement; hence [this
a clause] informs us otherwise.[1]

When R. Dimi came,[2] he said in R. Joḥanan's name: Ilfa asked: On the view that the passing of the night is of no effect in respect of the sanctification of hands and feet, does the water of the laver become unfit?[3] Do we say: For what purpose is this [water]? for the sanctification of hands and feet; but the sanctification of hands and feet itself is not nullified by the passing of the night. Or perhaps, since [the water] is sanctified in a service vessel, it becomes unfit? When Rabin came, he said in R. Jeremiah's name, who reported R. Ammi's statement in R. Joḥanan's name: Ilfa subsequently resolved [this problem]: there is the same controversy about the one as about the other. Said R. Isaac b. Bisna to him:[4] Rabbi, do you say thus? Thus did R. Ammi[5] say, reporting R. Joḥanan in Ilfa's name: If the laver was not lowered [into the well] in the evening,[6] [the priest] performs his sanctifications in it for the service of the night,[7] but on the morrow he does not perform his ablutions. Now we questioned this: 'on the morrow he does not perform his ablutions' because he does not need [further] sanctification; or perhaps [the water] has become unfit through the passing of the night?[8] Now, we could not resolve this, and yet to the Master it is clear?—Come and hear: Ben Kaṭṭin made twelve spouts for the laver; he also made wheels [pulleys] for the laver, so that its water should not become unfit through the passing of the night.[9] Surely this is [even] according to R. Eleazar son of R. Simeon?[10]—No: it represents Rabbi's view. Yet surely, since the first clause is according to R. Eleazar son of R. Simeon, the second clause too is according to R. Eleazar son of R. Simeon. For the first clause
b teaches: [The High Priest then] came to his bullock,[1] which bullock stood between the *ulam* [porch][2] and the altar, its head toward the south and its face toward the west,[3] while the priest stood in the east and faced west. Now, whom do you know to maintain that between the *ulam* and the altar was north?[4] R. Eleazar son of R. Simeon. For it was taught: What is the north? From the northern wall of the altar to the northern wall of the Temple court and the whole of the space opposite the altar is north: that is R. Jose son of R. Judah's view. R. Eleazar son of R. Simeon added the space between the *ulam* and the altar.[5] Rabbi adds the place where the priests and lay-Israelites tread. But all agree that the place on the inside of the knives chamber[6] is unfit![7]—Now, is it reasonable that [the first Baraitha] represents R. Eleazar son of R. Simeon's view and not Rabbi's? Seeing that Rabbi goes further than R. Jose son of R. Judah, does he not go further than R. Eleazar son of R. Simeon's [definition]?[8]—This is what we mean: If you think that it agrees with Rabbi, let him station it in the place where the feet of the priests and the lay-Israelites tread!—What then? it is according to R. Eleazar son of R. Simeon? Then let him station it [in the space] from the northern wall of the altar to the northern wall of the Temple court? What then must you answer? [that it was placed in the position indicated] on account of the High Priest's fatigue;[9] so on this view too,[10] it was on account of the High Priest's weakness.

R. Joḥanan said: If [the priest] sanctified his hands and feet for
c the removal of the ashes,[1] he need not sanctify [them again] on the morrow,[2] because he has already done so at the beginning of the service. According to whom? if according to Rabbi, surely he said that the passing of the night renders it null! if according to R. Eleazar son of R. Simeon, surely he said, He need not sanctify himself [again] even for ten days!—Said Abaye: In truth it is according to Rabbi, and [the nullifying effect of] the passing of the night is [merely] Rabbinical, and he admits that the passing of the night does not nullify from cock-crow until morning. Raba said: In truth it agrees with R. Eleazar son of R. Simeon, but R. Joḥanan accepted his view [only] in respect of the beginning of the service, but not in respect of the end of the service.[3]

An objection is raised: When his brother priests saw him descend,[4] they quickly ran and sanctified their hands and feet at

(7) Ibid. That too is enumerated as one of the purposes for which the priest must wash. But it is surely obvious, as it is included in the clause, '*when they approach the altar to minister*'.

a (1) For '*to cause an offering made by fire to smoke*' refers to the burning of the limbs on the altar, and that is not really essential to the efficacy or validity of the sacrifice. (2) V. 10a n. a 1. (3) After the passing of the night. (4) To R. Jeremiah. (5) *Var. lec.* R. Assi. (6) Thereby leaving its water unchanged. (7) Such as the burning of the fats and the other parts of animals sacrificed during the day. (8) So that he *may not* perform his ablutions thereat. (9) He attached it to pulleys whereby it was lowered into the well in the evening and drawn up in the morning, which made the water fresh, being now accounted as part of the well water. (10) Which shews that the water is unfit even though the priest would not require further 'sanctification'.

b (1) To make confession of sins over it.—This was on the Day of Atonement. (2) The hall leading to the interior of the Temple. (3) It stood between north and south, and the face was made to turn toward the west. (4) Of the Temple. For immediately after making confession he sacrificed the animal on the spot, and that had to be done in the north. (5) This agrees with the first clause of the Baraitha now being discussed, whence it is deduced that the Baraitha is according to R. Eleazar b. R. Simeon. (6) Where the knives were kept. (7) V. Yoma (Sonc. ed.) 35b, and notes. (8) Surely he does; hence the first Baraitha describing the bullock's position may well be according to him. (9) Owing to his heavy duties on this day we spare him as much labour as possible. Therefore the bullock was stationed near the *Hekal* (the inner court), to save him carrying the blood a long way. (10) That it agrees with Rabbi.

c (1) The day's service commenced at cockcrow (before dawn) with the removal of a shovelful of ashes from the altar, which was placed at the east side of the slope leading to the altar. (2) I.e., at daybreak, the earlier period still belonging to night. (3) Here the sanctification was performed at the beginning of the day's service, in such a case R. Joḥanan rules as R. Eleazar b. R. Simeon. But if it is performed in the evening for the burning of the fats, which is the end of the previous day's service, he needs fresh 'sanctification' on the morrow. (4) With the shovelful of ash.

מהו דתימא א] הני מילי עבודה דמעכבא כפרה אבל עבודה דלא מעכבא כפרה לא קמ"ל כי אתא רב דימי אמר רבי יוחנן בעי אילפא לדברי האומר אין לינה מועלת בקידוש ידים ורגלים מי כיור מהו שיפסלו מי אמרינן הני למאי לקידוש ידים ורגלים קידוש ידים ורגלים גופייהו לא ג] פסול בהו לינה או דלמא כיון ג] דקדוש להו בכלי שרת מיפסלי כי אתא רבין אמר רבי ירמיה אמר רבי אמי אמר ר' יוחנן הדר פשיט אילפא כמחלוקת בזו כך מחלוקת בזו אמר לפניו ר' יצחק בר ביסנא רבי אתה אומר כן ד] *אלא הכי* אמר (א) ר' אסי אמר ר' יוחנן [משמיה דאילפא] כיור שלא שקעו מבערב מקדש ממנו לעבודת לילה ולמחר אינו מקדש והוינן בה ה] למחר אינו מקדש דלא צריך לקדוש או דלמא איפסלו בלינה ולא פשיט לן ומרקא פשיט ליה מיפשיט ת"ש *בן קטין עשה שנים עשר דד לכיור אף הוא עשה מוכני לכיור שלא יהיו מימיו נפסלין בלינה מאי לאו רבי אלעזר ברבי שמעון היא לא רבי היא והא מדרישא רבי אלעזר ברבי שמעון סיפא נמי רבי אלעזר ברבי שמעון דקתני רישא *בא לו אצל פרו (ב) ופר היה עומד בין האולם ולמזבח ראשו לדרום ופניו למערב והכהן עומד במזרח ופניו למערב מאן שמעת ליה דאמר בין האולם ולמזבח צפון רבי אלעזר ברבי שמעון *דתניא איזהו צפון מקיר מזבח צפוני ועד כותל עזרה צפוני וכנגד כל המזבח כולו צפון דברי *רבי יוסי ברבי יהודה רבי אלעזר ברבי שמעון מוסיף *אף בין האולם ולמזבח רבי מוסיף אף מקום דריסת רגלי הכהנים ומקום דריסת רגלי ישראל אבל מן ההליפות ולפנים הכל מודים שפסול ותסברא רבי אלעזר ברבי שמעון היא ולא רבי ו] *[השתא רבי] אדרבי יוסי ברבי יהודה מוסיף אדרבי אלעזר בר' שמעון לא מוסיף אנן הכי קאמרינן אי ס"ד רבי היא לוקמה במקום דריסת רגלי כהנים ובמקום דריסת רגלי ישראל אלא מאי רבי אלעזר ברבי שמעון היא לוקמה מקיר מזבח צפוני עד כותל עזרה צפוני אלא מאי אית לך למימר משום חולשא דכהן גדול הכא נמי משום חולשא דכהן גדול: *אמר רבי יוחנן קידש ידיו ורגליו לתרומת הדשן למחר אינו צריך לקדש שכבר קידש מתחילת עבודה למאן אי לרבי האמר פסלה לינה אי לרבי אלעזר בר"ש האמר ז] אין צריך לקדש אפי' מיכן ועד עשרה ימים אמר אביי לעולם לרבי ולינה דרבנן היא ומודי ח] דמקרות הגבר ועד צפרא לא פסלה לינה רבא אמר לעולם רבי אלעזר ברבי שמעון ט] [היא וראה ר"י דבריו] בתחילת עבודה ולא בסוף עבודה מיתיבי *ראוהו אחיו הכהנים שירד והן רצו ובאו מיהרו וקידשו ידיהם ורגליהם מן הכיור בשלמא

מהו דתימא ה"מ · דבעינן קידוש שחרית בעבודה דמעכבת כפרה כגון דם וקמילה אבל כל הקטרת אימורין דלא מעכבא אימא לא תיבעי קידוש: מהו שיפסלו · בלינה אם לא שקעה *בבור י] *(בני הגולה) דאמרי' בסדר יומא (דף לז·) דמשקע להו: או דילמא כיון יא] דקדוש (ג) בכלי שרת איפסלו · דלא דמי לקידוש ידים שהמים ניגבו ואין לינה על מי לחול: ה"ג כי אתא רבין אמר ר' ול"ג ת"ש (ד): אמר לפניו רבי יצחק בר ביסנא · לפני ר' (ה) אמי וטולה רבין אמר לה: שלא שקעו · בבור: לעבודת לילה · להקטיר חלבים: והוינן בה · קמיה דרבי (ו) *אסי ולא יב] פשטו לן: דלא צריך לקדושי · וכרבי אלעזר בר' שמעון דלא פסל לינה בקידוש או דילמא אין ראויות לקדש יג] דאיפסלו להו בלינה ואפי' לר' אלעזר דאי לרבי יד] ליכא למיבעי *אין צריך דהא אפילו בקידוש פסל: ולא פשטו ר' (ז) *אסי הך בעיא למימר דאין צריך לקדש קאמר ולא לפו סלה בלינה כדקאמרת כמחלוקת בזו כך מחלוקת בזו ומר פשיט מיפשט דלר' אלעזר לא פסלה בלינה: שנים עשר דד · שמוציאין מימיו ואמרינן בסדר יומא שיהו שנים עשר כהנים העסוקים בתמיד מקדשים בבת אחת: מוכני · מפרש התם טו] גלגלים שמעלין אותו בגלגלין מן הבור שחרית שלא יהא מימיו נפסלים בלינה לפיכך משקעין אותו ערבית בבור שיהו מימיו מחוברים למי המעין ובטלה טז] ליכתן: מאי לאו · אפילו ר' אלעזר קאמר לה דאף על גב דפליג בקידוש שניגב מודה יז] במים: בא לו · כהן יח] אצל פרו להתוודות עליו ביום הכיפורים יט] דכתיב וכפר בעדו וגו' (ויקרא טז): ראשו לדרום ופניו למערב · *) מצפון לדרום היה עומד ופניו למערב והתם מפרש לה בעוקם את ראשו והתם פריך לוקמיה להדיא ממזרח למערב ומשנינן לה: והכהן עומד · אחוריו למזרח המזבח ופניו למערב כלפי ההיכל: ואמרינן טעמא התם:

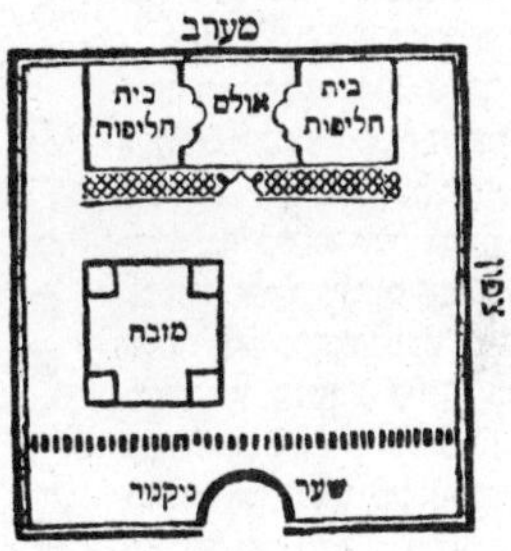

מיתיבי ראוהו אחיו הכהנים כו' · למאי דס"ד נה] דלא מיירי בכהני חדתי יש תימה דלא פריך מרישא דתני נו] קידוש בתורם את הדשן ויש לומר דפשיטא דההיא דתרומת הדשן הוי בכהני חדתי *וקצת קשה דלמאי ס"ד *דלא הוו חדתי דבמתניתין דתמיד (דף לג.) משמע דכולהו הוו חדתי שהעזרה היתה ננעלת והם היו בחוץ ממקום שהיו ישנים שם בבית נז] המוקד [הג"ה ויש לומר דסלקא דעתיה דמאן דלא פסיל בלינה לא פסיל בהיסח הדעת ומאן דפסיל בהאי פסיל בהאי והני כהני הוה לאו היסח הדעת שהיו ישנים בבית המוקד · ע"כ הג"ה]: יליהה

מאן שמעת ליה [דאמר] כו' · דקתני בפירקא דבתריה (דף מג:) שחטו וקיבל כ] במזרק את דמו סמוך לוידויו מיד אלמא בין האולם ולמזבח לפון הוא לשחיטת קדשי קדשים דהא פר חטאת הוא: כנגד כל המזבח · כנגד לפונו ולא מן המזבח והלאה לא לצד מזרח ולא לצד מערב ואע"פ שהוא בחצי חלק כא] עזרה הלפוני לאו כשר הוא לשחיטת חטאת דבעינן על ירך המזבח וליכא: ר' אלעזר מוסיף אף בין האולם ולמזבח · שהוא מערבו של מזבח ובלבד שיהא כב] (כל) חלק לפונו של עזרה אבל מזרחו של מזבח לצד שער נקנור שבו נכנסין לעזרה לא מכשר אפי' חלק לפוני דקילא קדושתיה דהוא מקום דריסת ישראל וכהנים י"א אמה מקום דריסת ישראל מן השער ולפנים וי"א אמה כג] עד לצד המזבח מקום של *דריסת רגלי הכהנים: רבי מוסיף · אף לפון שבאותן עשרים ושתים אמה של צד מזרח שהן דריסת ישראל וכהנים: ה"ג אבל מן החליפות ולפנים הכל מודים שפסול **) ומיהו בית כד] חליפות האולם עודף רוחבו על רוחב ההיכל ט"ו אמה לצפון וט"ו לדרום והוא נקרא בית החליפות כה] שהיה בכותל האולם מאחריו חלוטת שהכהנים מלניעין שם את סכיניהם [וסכין קרי חילוף בלשון ערבי] הכי תנן לה במסכת מדות ואשמועי' דמאחורי האולם לאו לפון הוא לשחיטת קדשי קדשים דכיון דלא מתחזי מזבח התם לא קרינן כו] על ירך אע"ג דמכשרינן ליה לקמן (דף כו·) לשחיטת קדשים קלים לקדשי קדשים פסול: ותסברא דר' אלעזר היא ולא רבי · דלא מודה רבי בבין האולם ולמזבח דליהוי לפון: כז] השתא רבי כו' · האי מוסיף דקתני אדר' יוסי קאי אדר' אלעזר לא קאי והא [ע"כ] אדר' אלעזר [נמי] אמרה למילתיה כח] דעל כרחך כיון דמכשר מקום קדושה קלה לשחוט שם מקום קדושה חמורה לכ"ש: אנן הכי קאמרי' · הא (ח) דשקליה ליה מרבי לאו משום דרבי לא מכשיר בין האולם ולמזבח לשחיטת חטאת אלא הכי קשיא לן כיון דרבי נמי מכשיר (לפון) לצפון שבמזרח למה לו לשוחטו אלל האולם לוקמיה בצפון המזרחי סמוך לכניסתן לעזרה דהא לאו אורח ארעא לאקרובי להיכל: אלא מאי ר"א היא · ומשום דלא מכשר מקום דריסת ישראל וכהנים כט] ושחיטת חטאת ממטי ליה להתם אכתי תקשה לך דהוה מצי לאוקמי מקיר מזבח לפוני עד כותל עזרה לפוני דהאי לפון לדברי הכל: אלא מאי אית לך למימר · עליה: משום חולשה דכ"ג · שכל עבודות ל] (פנים) של יום הכיפורים עליו ותש כחו להכי ממטינן ליה להתם לפי שהוא צריך להכניס דמו להיכל ולהזות ולא יכבד עליו משוי המזרק והדם: ה"נ · כי מוקמת ליה כרבי הא טעמא איכא: תרומת הדשן · דכתיב והרים את הדשן בכל בקר היה נוטל לא] מחתה מן הגחלים המאוכלות הפנימיות ויורד ונותנה במזרחו של כבש בדרומו של מזבח כדכתיב ושמו אלל המזבח ושם היה נבלע במקומו והיא היתה בכל יום ראשונה לכל העבודות: מתחילת עבודה · שזו תחילת עבודת יום לב] הוא: הא אמרת פסלה לינה · ולינה בעמוד השחר תליא דכתיב עד בקר: הא אמר מכאן ועד י' ימים · ואת תלית טעמא משום דקדיש בתחלת עבודת יום זה: ולינה דרבנן · לינה זו שתועיל בקידוש שאין המים בפניו מדרבנן הוא דגזור בה שלא תזלזל בלינה ומודה רבי שכשהעלו לכיור מן הבור מקרות הגבר שהוא זמן תרומת הדשן כדאמרינן בפרק קמא דיומא (דף כ·) דמשום האי פורתא לא פסלה לינה בקידוש דלא מסקי אינשי אדעתייהו לג] דדמי כמה שקידש ביום: וראה רבי יוחנן דבריו · של ר' אלעזר נכונים במקדש ידיו בתחלת עבודת היום דלא פסל בה לינה ולא במי שקידש בלילה להקטיר חלבים שהוא סוף עבודת יום אתמול: ראוהו אחיו שירד · משנה היא במסכת תמיד (פרק ב מ"א) בתורם את הדשן שירד מן המזבח והמחתה של תרומת הדשן בידו: מיהרו וקידשו כו' · להוציא את הדשן שבמקום המערכה או לכלכן להפוח שבאמלע המזבח והכי תנן בה התם החלו מעלין באפר על גבי התפוח וקא סלקא דעתך בכהנים שעבדו כל הלילה קאי ומקודשי ידים ורגלים היו וצריכין לחזור ולקדש עכשיו לד] *שתמשך עבודה זו עד היום ויפסל קידוש הלילה בלינת עמוד השחר *ויועיל להם קידוש זה של אחר קרות הגבר: בשלמא

*) בין לפון ודרום נ"ק   **) נ"ל ומהו נ"ק

פוסלת בקידוש ידים ורגלים ובלינת מי כיור לא איירי מידי ולא ידעינן מאי קסבר בהן: או דלמא איפסלא בהו בלינה ואין ראוי לקדש קאמר דאיפסלא בהו בלינה ואפילו לר"א דאמר דאין לינה מועלת בקידוש מודה דמיפסלא בהו לינת דאי לרבי לא אצטריך דמילתא דפשיטא היא דלרבי מי כיור נפסלים בלינה והשתא בקידוש ידים

הרשן הוי בכהני חדתי לפי שע"י פיים היתה נעשית ותחלת עבודה היא אבל שאר כהני...
יהא בהם אחד שאינו חדש שעוסק באברים שלא נתעכל כל הלילה: לז] המוקד · ונראה ד...
בלינה לא פסיל בהאי היסח הדעת ומאן דפסיל בהאי פסיל בהאי והני כהני הוי להו היסח הדעת שהו...

עין משפט
נר מצוה

מ א מיי' פ"ג מהלכות בית הבחירה הל' יח:
מא ב מיי' שם ופ"ה מהל' ביאת מקדש הל' יח:
פי' נ"ק
*בכסיפא דלא נ"ק
מב ג מיי' פ"ד מהל' עבודת יוה"כ הל' א:
בהג"ה ז בכע"ב לא מקומה ועיין בחלופי גרסאות
מג ד ה מיי' פ"ה מהל' בית הבחירה הלכה טו טז:
מד ו מיי' פ"ה מהל' ביאת מקדש הל' ה:
מה ז מיי' פ"ב מהל' תמידין הלכה יג:
לקמן כה.

שיטה מקובצת

ידים פסיל לינה במים לא כ"ש אלא ע"כ לר"א איצטריך ולא פשיט רב אסי כו' עד לא פסלה בהו לינה [כפ"ה] וקשה דלרבי נמי איצטריך ליה שפיר לומר דמקדש ממנו לעבודת הלילה דהא איכא למ"ד לקמן דאינו מקדש לעבודת לילה כלל ועוד קשה דמאי קאמר דלא צריך לקדושי ולא נפשום מידי אי מודה במי כיור אי לא והא מדקתני מקדש ממנו לעבודת לילה משמע הא לעבודת היום אינו מקדש אלמא פסלה בה לינה במי כיור לכך נראה לר"י דודא' פשיטא דסבר דלינה פסלה במי כיור מדקתני לעבודת לילה אבל לעבודת היום לא אלא קא בעי אי היינו לרבי או לרבי אלעזר דאי אמרינן אינו צריך לקדש א"כ היינו ר"א ופשטינן דלינה פוסלת במי כיור לר"א ואי אמרינן דפסיל בהו לינה א"כ היינו שפיר כרבי ולא מצינו למיפשט מיניה מידי דהא שמעינן דלעבודת לילה מיהו מקדש כדפי' ולא אמרי' איפסלו כמתירים · מהר"ם: ו] רבי אלא רבי אדרבי [יוסי] ותיבת השתא ל"ש: ז] האמר אפילו מכאן ועד עשרה ימים אין צריך לקדש: ח] ומודי רבי: ט] שמעון [היא וראה ר' יוחנן דבריו של ר' אלעזר: י] בכור הגולה: יא] דקדיש: יב] ולא פשיט: יג] לקדש קאמר: יד] תיבות ליכא למיבעי ל"ש ונמחק: טו] התם גלגל שמעלין כו' שלא יהו מימיו: טז] ובטלה קדושתן הס"ד: יז] מודה [הוא במים: יח] כהן גדול: יט] כדכתיב: כ] וקבל דמו במזרק סמוך לוידויו מיד: כא] חלק העזרה: כב] שיהא בחלק צפוני: כג] אמה עוד: כד] בית החליפות: כה] החליפות ששם בכותל: כו] קרינן ביה: כז] צפון הס"ד ומה"ד אדר"א בר שמעון בתמיה הס"ד: כח] למילתיה וע"כ כיון כו' קדושה קלה כ"ש מקום קדושה חמורה הס"ד: כט] וכהנים לשחיטת: ל] עבודות של היום עליו: לא] נוטל במחתה: לב] יום הבא הס"ד ומה"ד הא אמר פסלה לינה: לג] ארעתייהו ודמי כמי שקידש: לד] שמא תמשך: לה] דס"ד השתא: לו] קידש ידיו ורגליו מן הכיור ותורם את הדשן וי"ל דפשיטא ליה דהדוא תרומת כהנים ס"ד שא"א שלא

בכור סגולה נ"ק
*נ"א בגלגל
נ"ל אמי כס"ד וכשלא יש למחוק נ"ק
בי' נ"ק הא אמר רבי אמי אמר ר"י כו'
[נ"ל אי צריך]
נ"ל ר' אמי נ"ק
יומא כה: לז. תוספתא דיומא פ"ב
[שם ויומא לה:]
יומא לו.
[לקמן נג.]
[לעיל יח.]
נ"ל אלא רבי נ"ק
[לקמן כה:] יומא כב. כו: ע"ש

שיטה מקובצת

א] הני מילי עבודה דמעכבא כו' תימה דהא לא החוץ [ידים ורגלים] גמרינן חוקה חוקה ממחוסר בגדים ובמחוסר בגדים כתיב קראי לחלל בין מעכבא ובין לא מעכבא ואומר מירי דהא דילפינן חוקה חוקה ממחוסר בגדים היינו לענין היכא דצריך קידוש שיחלל אם לא קידש אבל קשה היכא מצי למעוטי הקטרה מקדוש הא כתיב (ורחצו) [ירחצו] מים ולא (תמותו) [ימתו] הא אם לא (תרחצו תמותו) [ירחצו ימתו] וע"כ בהקטרה מיירי דעבודה תמה היא דהא מוכח התם ביומא דליכא מיתה לא בזר ולא בכל הפסולים אלא באותה עבודה שהיא עבודה תמה [ואם כן] משתמע (ספי) דבעי קידוש בהקטרה [טפי] משאר עבודות ונראה לי דלעולם הייתי ממעט הקטרה מקידוש משום דכתיב ולשרת דדוקא עבודה המעכבא כפרה הוי בכלל [ולא עבודה דלא מעכבא כפרה] (הוא למעט הקטרה) ואע"ג דכתיב ולא (תמותו) [ימותו] דמשמע דמיירי בהקטרה שהיא עבודה תמה לא מוקמינן ליה בהקטרה הואיל ולא מעכבא [כפרה] אלא בזריקה ולהקטרת קומץ דמעכבא כפרה ועבודה תמה הן קמ"ל להקטיר אשה לרבות כל עבודות לקידוש אף דלא מעכבא· מהר"ם: ב] לא פסיל: ג] דקדיש: ד] תיבת אלא נמחק: ה] למחר אינו מקדש דלא צריך לקידושי ומני ר"א [היא] דאמר אין לינה

(א) גמ' הכי אמר ר' אמי: (ב) שם אצל פרו ופרו: (ג) רש"י ד"ה או דלמא כיון דקדוש להו בכלי: (ד) ד"ה ה"ג כי וכו' ת"ש דאמר הס"ד: (ה) ד"ה אמר לפניו וכו' לפני ר' ירמיה וטולה רבין אמר לה שלא: (ו) ד"ה והוינן וכו' דר' אמי ולא: (ז) ד"ה ולא פשט ר' אמי הך: (ח) ד"ה אנן הכי קאמרינן הא דקשיא לן מרבי לאו משום:

גליון הש"ס גמרא
אי לרבי האמר פסלה לינה. עיין זבחים דף קיב ע"ב תוספות ד"ה ילא:

עין משפט נר מצוה

מו א מיי' פ"ה מהלכות ביאת מקדש הלכה ו:

מז ב מיי' שם הלכה ה:

נ"י בס"ק מיניה וס"ד דמאן דלא פסיל בלינה פסיל בהיסח הדעת אבל משום קידוש כלי כו' ליתא שם ובאמת בסוכה נ. ד"ה ואי לא מייתי אלא האי דפ"ק דמנחות

דבלל בחוץ ולא משום יוצא רש"ק · וגי' הנ"ק אלא משום עבודה בחוץ אבל משום יוצאה לא וכפ' התכלת גבי שתי הלחם נמי משמע דלא כו' והג"ה או כפול כאן ושייך לעיל

מח ג מיי' שם הל' י:

מט ה מיי' שם הל' יא:

נ ו ז מיי' שם הל' ה:

נא ח מיי' שם הלכה ו:

אחרינא לא נ"ק

יומא כה. [מנחות ק.]

ובפי' שלפנינו שם לא פי' כלום ואפשר שכך היה בגירסא לפני התוספות

נ"ל דדייק פ' שתי הלחם אמרת ליפתן כו' נ"ק

גמרא

בשלמא לאביי דמוקים לה כרבי ומודי רבי דמקרות הגבר עד צפרא לא פסלה לינה הא מני רבי היא אלא לרבא דמוקים לה כרבי אלעזר ברבי שמעון אבל לרבי מקרות הגבר עד צפרא פסלה לינה הא מני אי רבי א] פסלה לינה אי רבי אלעזר בר"ש הא אמר אפי' מיכן ועד עשרה ימים אינו צריך לקדש לעולם כרבי אלעזר ברבי שמעון והכא במאי עסקינן בכהני חדתי: איבעיא להו יציאה מהו שתועיל בקידוש ידים ורגלים אם תימצי לומר לינה לא פסלה דלא פריש אבל יציאה דפריש אסוחי מסח דעתיה או דלמא כיון דבידו לחזור לא מסח ת"ש קידש ידיו ורגליו ונטמאו מטבילן ואין צריך לקדש יצאו הרי הן בקדושתן יצאו ידיו לא קמיבעיא לן כי קמיבעיא לן יצא כל גופו מאי ת"ש *שלא רחוץ ידים ורגלים *מקדש בכלי שרת בפנים קידש בכלי שרת בחוץ או בכלי חול בפנים *או שטבל במי מערה ועבד עבודתו פסולה טעמא דקידש בכלי שרת בחוץ הא קידש בפנים ויצא עבודתו כשירה דלמא קידש בכלי שרת בחוץ היכי דמי כגון דאפיק ידיו לבר וקידש (הא קידש בפנים ויצא דאפיק ידיה לבר ב] כשירה) אבל יצא כל גופו תיבעי לך א"ל רב זביד לרב פפא ת"ש יצא חוץ ג] למחיצת חומת העזרה אם לשהות טעון טבילה אם לפי שעה טעון קידוש ידים ורגלים א"ל הכא במאי עסקינן כגון שיצא להסך רגליו ולהטיל ד] מים הא בהדיא קתני לה *כל המיסך רגליו טעון טבילה וכל המטיל מים טעון קידוש ידים ורגלים תני והדר מפרש ת"ש פרה רבי חייא בר יוסף אמר מקדש בכלי שרת בפנים ויוצא ורבי יוחנן אמר אפי' בחוץ ואפי' בכלי חול ואפי' במקידה של חרס אמר רב פפא שאני פרה הואיל וכל מעשיה בחוץ לא פסלה בה יציאה אי הכי למה לי דמקדש כעין עבודה *פנים איבעיא להו טומאה מהו שתועיל לקידוש ידים ורגלים אם תימצי לומר יציאה לא פסלה דגברא חזי אבל הכא דגברא לא חזי אסוחי מסח דעתיה או דלמא כיון דהדר חזי ה] [דק ליה] ולא מסח דעתיה ת"ש קידש ידיו ורגליו ונטמאו מטבילן ואין צריך לקדש נטמאו ידיו לא מיבעיא לן [כי ו] מיבעיא לן] נטמא כל גופו תיפוק לי כיון דבעי למעבד הערב שמש אסוחי מסח דעתיה כגון דאיטמי סמוך לשקיעת החמה ת"ש פרה רבי חייא ברבי יוסף אמר מקדש בכלי שרת בפנים ויוצא ורבי יוחנן אמר אפילו בחוץ ואפילו בכלי חול ואפילו במקידה של חרס

רש"י

בשלמא לאביי דמוקי לה · להא דר' יוחנן כרבי ומודה רבי דמקרות הגבר ועד לפרא לא פסלה לינה בקידוש הא מני (א) נמי דקתני דקידוש זה לא יפסל בעמוד השחר אבל קידוש הלילה יפסל רבי היא : אלא לרבא כו' הא מני · שמלריכין קידוש על קידוש ומתיר קידוש השני בקרות הגבר : אי רבי הא אמר פסלה לינה · אף בזה שבקרות הגבר : ואי ר' אלעזר · אף הראשון לא יפסל ושני זה למה : בכהני חדתי · שלא שימשו בלילה ולא היו רחוצי ידים ורגלים : יציאה · חוץ לעזרה מהו שתועיל כדרך שפוסל בכל הקדשים שקדשו בכלי שרת שאם יצאו נפסלין ביוצא : דלא פריש · (ב) לא נבדל ז] מעבודה : ונטמאו · הידים בדבר שאין טומאתו מן התורה שיטמא גופו אלא בפיגול או בנותר ששנינו בפסחי' (דף קכ:) שמטמאים את הידים : מטבילין · את הידים ח] לבדן : יצאו ידיו · שהושיטן לחוץ : מקדש בכלי שרת · או כיור או כלי שרת אחר דמרבינן לקמן בשמעתין כל כלי שרת לקידוש : בפנים · שהרי ט] הוקבעו לו מקום בעזרה דכתיב ונתת את הכיור וגו' והתם כתיב ורחצו ממנו : בכלי חול פסול · דרחצו ממנו כתיב וכי איתרבו שאר כלים לקמן דומיא דידיה איתרבו : או שטבל במי מערה · שהן כשרין לטבילה וה"ה למים חיים אלא שרוב טבילות במים מכונסין י] : עבודתו פסולה · ולא אמרי' טבילה דבר חשוב הוא ומהני' ליה במקום קידוש : הא קידש בפנים ויצא יא] כשרין · דאי ס"ד פסולה השתא קידש בפנים ויצא פסולה קידש בחוץ מיבעיא וכי יש יציאה גדולה מזו : ומשני דילמא קידש בחוץ · דאילטריך ליה לתנא למיתני *דפסולה : כגון דאפיק ידיה לבר · וגופיה בפנים וקידש דאילו קידש בפנים והוציא ידיו תניא לעיל הרי הן בקדושתן אבל יצא גופו לא תידוק מינה : אם (ג) יב] לשהות טעון טבילה · קס"ד משום היסח הדעת : הכא במאי עסקינן · דקתני אם לשהות טעון טבילה : שילא להסך רגליו · לגדולים ודכוותיה סיפא דקתני אם לפי שעה טעון קידוש שילא להטיל מים דאמרינן בסדר יומא (דף ל·) מלוה לשפשף בידו ניצוצות שעל גבי רגליו שלא יראה ככרות שפכה לפיכך צריך לקדש ידיו ורגליו : בהדיא קתני לה · בסיפא דההיא : פרה · בעבודת פרה אדומה יג] שהיה חוץ לירושלים בהר המשחה : ויולא · אלמא לא פסל יציאה בקידוש ידים ורגלים : יד] כעין עבודה · שינוי' הוא : טומאה · קס"ד טו] נטמאו ידיו ולא גופו קמיבעיא ליה: את"ל יציאה לא פסלה · התם הוא משום דגברא חזי לחזור וליכנס לא מסח דעתיה ולא מיפסל קידוש בהיסח הדעת : או דלמא כיון דהדר חזי · על ידי *)הטבילה **)דק ליה מדקדק (ד) טז] בקדושין ונזהר מליגע ידיו בדבר טינוף ולא מסח דעתיה :

*) הטבילה הס"ד והא"כ מ"ה דק ליה כו' נ"ק **) נ"א דקיל

והא

מי

תוספות

יציאה מהו שתועיל בקידוש ידים ורגלים · פירש בקונטרס כדרך שפוסלת בכל הקדשים שקדשו בכלי שאם יצאו נפסלין ביוצא ואי אפשר לומר כן אלא כדמפרש טעמא משום דכיון דפריש אסוחי מסח דעתיה *מיניה דמשום קידוש כלי לא מיפסל ביוצא במידי שלא נעשה בו עבודה עדיין כדמוכח בפ"ק דמנחות (דף ט·) ובפ' התודה (שם דף עח) *דאמר בללה חוץ לחומת העזרה רבי יוחנן אמר פסולה ור"ש לקיש אמר כשרה אלמא *לרבי יוחנן לא פסיל אלא משום יז] *(דס"ד דמאן דלא פסיל בלינה לא פסיל בה היסח הדעת ומאן דפסיל פסיל בהאי והני כהני הוו להו היסח הדעת שהיו ישנים בבית המוקד · הג"ה) עבודה בחוץ אבל משום יציאה לא יח] [וכן משמע] בפרק התכלת (שם מז·) גבי שתי הלחם דלא קדוש ליפסל ביוצא אלא בשחיטת הזבח אע"ג דכבר נתקדש בכלי דרבי סבירא ליה דתנור מקדש בפרק רבי ישמעאל (שם עב:) ומיהו יש לדחות דבאין עם הזבח שאני דהא נסכים הבאין עם הזבח לא מיפסלי בלינה כי אם בשחיטת הזבח כדאמר זעירי בפרק התודה (שם עט.) ואילו באין בפני עצמן תנן קדשו בכלי נפסלין בלינה ויש עוד ראיה יט] מהא דתנן במעילה פרק ב' (דף ט·) גבי מנחות ושתי הלחם קרמו בתנור הוכשרו ליפסל במחוסר כיפורים ובלינה כ] אבל יוצא לא קתני ואע"ג דגבי עופות וזבחים הוה מצי למיתני יוצא אגב כא] *אחרים לא תני אגב שתי הלחם ולחם הפנים ומנחות כב] והא דאמר בפרק כל שעה (פסחים לו·) גבי לישה דמנחות נהי דבזריזין ליתא במקום זריזין איתא אורחא דמילתא נקט שדרך לעשותם במקום זריזין יהא דאמר פרק המזבח מקדש (לקמן פה) כלי שרת אין מקדשין ליקרב אבל מקדשין ליפסל היינו בטבול יום ובמחוסר כיפורים ובלינה אבל לא ביוצא ול"ע *מה שפירש בקונטרס פ' שתי מדות (מנחות פז:) גבי שלחן אבל מקדשין ליפסל בלינה וביוצא ולקמן בסוף המזבח מקדש (דף פח·) פירש בקונט' אבל מקדשין ליפסל ביוצא אם יצא חוץ לקלעים או נגע בו טבול יום והא כג] *דאמר פרק שתי הלחם (מנחות נה:) [א' שתי הלחם וא'] לחם הפנים לישתן ועריכתן בחוץ אלמא מדת יבש לא נתקדשה וכן בסוף כל המנחות באות מצה (שם סג·) דריש ר"ש תנור תנור שתי פעמים שתהא אפייתן בתנור ושיהא הקדשן בתנור ופריך והתנן ר"ש אומר לעולם הוי רגיל לומר שתי הלחם ולחם הפנים כשרות בעזרה וכשירות בבית פאגי לאו משום דאי נתקדשה הוה מיפסלא ביוצא אלא משום דדבר מכוער להוציא לחוץ לאחר שנתקדשה ואם תאמר וכיון דבקדושת כלי לא מיפסלא ביוצא מנחת כהנים ותביתי כ"ג דלית בהו קמילה אימתי מיפסלי ביוצא ושמא בלותן מועיל קידוש כלי כד] ומהאי טעמא יתכן פי' הקונט' דהכא :

קידש בכלי שרת בחוץ כו' · כה] תימה דמשמע הא הכניס בכלי שרת בפנים וקידש עבודתו כשרה אלמא לא מיפסלא ביציאת המים כו] וי"ל דלא שייך היסח הדעת במים כמו בידים ועוד דאין כלי מקדש ליפסל ביוצא אלא בפנים *)כדמשמע בההיא דסוכה (דף נ·) דפריך וניתי במקודשת ועוד כדפירשנו כז] דאין כלי מקדש ליפסל ביוצא עד שנעשית מצותו והיינו הקידוש כמו מנחה עד שעת קמילה כח] ולכן מיבעיא ליה בקידוש ידים ורגלים טפי מבמים:

כל המטיל מים בעי קידוש ידים ורגלים · תימה דתיפשוט מהכא דאין יציאה מועלת דמשמע כט] הא בחנם לא פסלה יציאה וי"ל דודאי אי נפיק בשעת עבודה לא מיפסל בהכי כיון דאין שוהא אלא מעט :

*) ועיין נ"ק

מסורת הש"ס

תוספתא דמנחות פ"א

נ"ל כיצד וכ"ה בתוספ' שם

[לקמן כה.]

דפסולה כגון כו' הס"ד נ"ק

נ"א בעינן

שיטה מקובצת

א] רבי הא אמר פסלה: ב] לבר עבודתו כשרה: ג] חוץ לחומת העזרה: ד] ולהטיל מים: ה] חזי דק ליה : ו] כי קא מבעיא לן: ז] נבדל מן העבודה: ח] הידים לבד הס"ד: ט] שהרי הוקבע לו : י] מכונסין וקמ"ל דעבודתו פסולה והד"א : יא] ויצא כשרה : יב] לשהות: יג] אדומה שהיתה : יד] ורגלים הס"ד ומה"ד למה לי דמקדש · לקדש בכלי חול ובכלי שרת למה לי דמקדש הס"ד : טו] קס"ד שנטמאו : טז] מדקדק בקידושו : יז] מתיבת דס"ד עד תיבת עבודה שייך לע"א ותיבת הג"ה נמחק : יח] לא וכן משמע : יט] ראיה וכן משמע בפ"ב דמעילה גבי מנחות כו' עד לא קתני ויש דוחין ראיה זו שהרי גבי חטאת קתני ומועלין בהן משהוקדשו (קדישו בכלי) [נמלקו] הוכשרו לפסול בטבול יום ולא קתני יוצא אע"ג דאמת הוא דמיפסל ביוצא ומיהו מ"מ יש להביא ראיה מדלא תניא במנחות ש"מ דלא פסלה בהו קדושת כלי ליפסל ביוצא דאי אמרת בשלמא במנחות דוקא איכא למימר אגב דלא תניא במנחות לא תניא בחטאת אע"ג דמיפסלא ביוצא אלא אי מיפסלא ביוצא אמאי משייר הכא והכא אלא ודאי קדושת כלי לא מהני ליפסל ביוצא: כ] ובלינה ואילו יוצא: כא] אגב אחרינך: כב] ומנחות אלא אי פסלא ביוצא במנחות אמאי משייר ליה הכא והכא' מהר"פ : כג] והא דדייק פרק שתי הלחם אמרת לישתן ועריפתן : כד] כלי · כדאמרינן בפ"ב דמעילה ושאין לו מתירין משיקדש בכלי : כה] תימה הכא משמע הא הכנים הכלי שרת בפנים כו' אלמא לא פסלא יציאה במים וכ"ש בקידוש דהא לעיל איבעיא לן לר' אלעזר בר' שמעון דאמר אין לינה מועלת בקידוש אם מועלת במי כיור : כו] וי"ל כו' וא"ת מ"מ דייקינן מיניה דווקא דקידש בחוץ אבל (הכנים) [הוציא] הכלי והמים (מבחוץ) [לחוץ] וחזור והכניסו וקידש מבפנים שפיר דמי אלמא לא פסיל יציאה בפנים וכ"ש קידוש דהא לעיל מבעיא לן לר' אלעזר דאמר אין לינה פוסלת בקידוש אם מועלת במי כיור וי"ל דשאני יוצא לפי שקדושת הכלי לא מהני ליפסל ביוצא כדמוכח בפ"ק דמנחות דאמרינן בללה חוץ לחומה כשרה ור' יוחנן פוסל כו' כמו שכתבו התוס' לעיל והא דקא בעי הכא אי יציאה פסלה בקידוש אי לא משום היסח הדעת הוא אבל במים לא שייך טעם זה וקשה דהטעם של היסח הדעת לא איצטרך אלא לר"א אבל לרבי דאמר לינה פוסלת פסלה נמי יציאה בקידוש כמו לינה בלא טעמא דהיסח הדעת מדקאמר בבעיא דלעיל ואת"ל דלא פסלה משום דלא פירש אבל יציאה דפירש אסוחי מסח דעתיה אלא למ"ד לינה לא פסלא ואם כן תימה השתא אמאי פסול יוצא מטעם קדושת כלי הא (הוכרחנו) [הוכחנו] דקדושת כלי לא מהניא למפסיל ביוצא כדפרישנא וי"ל דודאי בקידוש ידים ורגלים מהני הקידוש ליפסל ביוצא משום דכיון דקידש ונעשית מצותו מהניא קדושה בכלי שרת ליפסל ביוצא מידי דהוי אמנחה לאחר קמיצה שפסולה ביוצא אבל מי כיור לא פסלא ביוצא כדמשמע מדיוקא כדפרשינן משום דעדיין לא נעשית מצותו שלא נעשה מהם עדיין קידוש ידים ועוד יש לפרש דודאי במי כיור מהני קידוש כלי ליפסל מיד ביוצא כמו במנחות שאינן נקמצות והא דמשמע הכא מדיוקא דאם הכנים בפנים וקידש כשר היינו משום דקדשינהו בחוץ לא מיפסלא ביוצא עד דקלטינהו מחיצות כדמוכח בסוכה · עכ"ה מהר"פ : כז] כדפרשנו לעיל : כח] קמיצה ולהכי מבע"ל : כט] דמשמע דוקא משום הטלת מים הא בחנם כו' וי"ל דנוכל לאוקמי בשעת עבודה דודאי אי נפיק כו' אלא מעט כיון דעסיק בעבודה לא מסח דעתיה וכי קא מבעיא לן בין עבודה לעבודה אבל אין לאוקמי באמצע העבודה דזה לא תמצא שיצא לשהות זמן מרובה בתוך העבודה :

תיבת

הגהות הב"ח (א) רש"י ד"ה בשלמא וכו' הא מני רבי היא דקתני וכו' יפסל הס"ד : (ב) ד"ה דלא פריש לא נבדל: נ"ב ותימה דלעיל דף יט ע"ב מבואר בבריתא דר"ש פליג אף באינו מקריב רק בלא יצא ממקדש אינו פוסל בלינה ולא פריש דכאן היינו לא פריש ממקדש וק"ל ול"ע : (ג) ד"ה אם לשהות טעון : (ד) ד"ה א"ד כו' מדקדק בקידוש ונזהר :

גליון הש"ס גמרא ת"ש פרה · עיין פ"ד דפרה משנה א בהרע"ב ותוס' יו"ט :

the laver.[5] [20b] Now it is well according to Abaye who interprets it [R. Joḥanan's ruling] as agreeing with Rabbi, for Rabbi admits that the passing of the night does not nullify [in the interval between] cockcrow and morning; for this will then be according to Rabbi. But according to Raba, who interprets it as agreeing with R. Eleazar son of R. Simeon [only], but in Rabbi's opinion the passing of the night nullifies [even] from cockcrow until morning, with whom does this agree? If with Rabbi, then the passing of the night nullifies it; if with R. Eleazar son of R. Simeon, surely he said that he does not need sanctification even for ten days?—In truth, it agrees with R. Eleazar son of R. Simeon, the reference
a being to fresh priests.[1]

It was asked: Is going out [of the Temple court] effective [to invalidate] sanctification of hands and feet?[2] If you say that the passing of the night does not invalidate [it], that is because [the priest] did not cease [officiating], but since he ceases when he goes out, he turns his mind away from it;[3] or perhaps since it rests with him to go back, he does not turn his mind away from it?—Come and hear: If he sanctified his hands and feet and they were defiled,[4] he immerses them,[5] but he need not sanctify [them].[6] If they [his hands and feet] went out [from the Temple court],[7] they retain their sanctity!—If [only] his hands went out we are not in doubt; our doubt is where his whole body went out; what [is the law then]?—Come and hear: He whose hands or feet are unwashed must sanctify them at a service vessel within.[8] If he sanctified [them] in a service vessel without, or in an unconsecrated vessel within; or if he immersed in the water of a pit,[9] and officiated, his service is invalid.[10] Thus it is only because he sanctified [his hands] from a service vessel without; but if he sanctified [them] within and then went out, his [subsequent] service is valid![11]—[No:] Perhaps what is meant by 'he sanctified [them] in a service vessel without'? That e.g. he stretched his hands without and sanctified them;[12] but if his whole body went out, you may [certainly] be in doubt. Said R. Zebid to R. Papa, Come and hear: If [the priest] went without the barrier of the wall of the Temple court, if [it was his intention] to tarry there, he needs immersion; if for a short while, he needs sanctification of hands and feet!—Said he to him: That means where he went out to ease himself at nature's call. But that is explicitly taught: He who eases himself needs immersion, and he who answers nature's call requires sanctification of hands and feet?—
b He [first] teaches [the general law] and then defines it.[1]

Come and hear: [For the services in connection with the red] heifer, R. Ḥiyya b. Joseph said: [The priest] must sanctify [himself] from a service vessel within and then go out;[2] whereas R. Joḥanan maintained: [He can sanctify himself] even without [the Temple], even in a profane vessel, even in a fire pot!—Said R. Papa, The [red] heifer is different; since all its services are without, going out does not disqualify it. If so, why must he sanctify [himself at all]?—We want it to be done like the services within.

It was asked: Is uncleanness effective in respect of sanctification of hands and feet?[3] If you say that going out does not invalidate [sanctification], that may be because the person remains fit; but here that the person is no longer fit [for service] he turns his mind from it.[4] Or perhaps, since he will be fit again, he is careful and does not turn his mind away from it?—Come and hear: If [the priest] sanctified his hands and his feet and they became unclean, he must immerse them, but need not [re-]sanctify them!—Where his *hands* [only] became unclean, we do not ask; our question is where his whole body was defiled. 'His whole body'! surely I may deduce that he will turn his mind away from it, since he must wait for the setting of the sun?[5]—[The question arises where] e.g. he became unclean just before sunset! Come and hear: [For the service in connection with the red] heifer, R. Ḥiyya b. Joseph said: [The priest] must sanctify [himself] from a service vessel within and then go out; whereas R. Joḥanan maintained: [He can sanctify himself] even without the Temple, even in a profane vessel, even in a firepot.

(5) In order to remove the ash and make room for the fresh pile of wood (the first priest removed only one shovelful).

a (1) Who had not been ministering earlier in the night. (2) To make it necessary to repeat it. (3) Therefore he must repeat his lustrations when he returns. (4) With an uncleanness which defiles them only, but not the whole body. (5) Immersion in a ritual bath (מקוה). (6) In the laver. (7) The priest stood at the entrance and thrust his hands and feet without. (8) Sanctification might be done either at the laver or from any service vessel v. *infra*; 'within' means within the Temple court. (9) Though normally this cleanses. (10) Immersion, even of the whole body, does not count as sanctification. (11) For if that too were invalid, this law is superfluous, since he is standing without at the very moment of lustrations. (12) Whilst standing within. Only then is it necessary to state this law.

b (1) The Tanna first states the law about going out, and then defines the cases to which this law applies. (2) The burning of the red heifer and the gathering of its ashes and mixing it with water, which are the services here referred to, were done outside Jerusalem. (3) It is now assumed that the question is: if the priest's hands became unclean, without the rest of his body, must he re-sanctify them? (4) Which nullifies sanctification. (5) He does not become clean even after immersion until sunset.

[21a] Now in the case of the [red] heifer we defile him, for we learnt: They used to defile the priest who was to burn the heifer and then make him immerse, in order to combat the opinion of the Saddu-
a cees,[1] who maintained: It[s service] was performed [only] by [priests] who had experienced sunset![2] This proves that uncleanness does not invalidate it.[3]—The [red] heifer is different, since a *ṭebul yom* is not unfit for it. If so, why must he sanctify himself [at all]?—Because we want it similar to the [usual sacrificial] service.

It was asked: Can [the priest] sanctify his hands and feet *in* the laver?[4] [Do we argue,] the Divine Law states, [*And Aaron and his sons shall wash . . .*] *thereat*,[5] but not *in* it; or perhaps it means even in it?—Said R. Naḥman son of Isaac, Come and hear: Or if he immersed in the water of a pit and officiates, his service is invalid. Hence [if he used] the water of the laver in a similar way to the water of a pit[6] and officiated, his service is valid?—No: it is particularly necessary for him [the Tanna] to teach about the water of a pit, lest you say: If he can bathe his whole body therein,[7] how much the more his hands and feet.[8]

R. Ḥiyya son of Joseph said: The water of the laver becomes unfit for the *mattirin*, as the *mattirin* [themselves], and for the [burning of the] limbs, as the limbs [themselves]. R. Ḥisda maintained: Even for the *mattirin* they become unfit only at dawn, as the limbs.[9] While R. Joḥanan maintained: Once the laver is sunk,[10]
b it may not be drawn up again.[1] Does this mean that it is not even fit for a night service?[2] Surely R. Assi said, reporting R. Joḥanan in Ilfa's name: If the laver was not sunk [into the pit] before evening, [the priest] may sanctify [himself] thereat for a night service, but he may not sanctify [himself] thereat on the morrow?—What is meant by 'it may not be drawn up'? for a day service; but it is indeed fit for a night service. If so, this is identical with R. Ḥiyya b.

a (1) V. Sanh. (Sonc. ed.) 52*b* n. 2. (2) I.e., by priests upon whom the sun had set after their immersion, as in the case of the sacrificial service in general. The Rabbis however held that immediately after immersion (when he is called a *ṭebul yom* v. Glos) a priest was fit for the burning of the red heifer. V. Parah III, 7. (3) *Sc.* the sanctification. (4) By actually putting his hands and feet into it. (5) Ex. XXX, 19. The Heb. means literally, from it. (6) I.e., putting his hands and feet *in* the laver. (7) If unclean, and such bathing constitutes valid immersion and makes him clean. (8) But it is still possible that if he used the water of the laver in the *same* way, putting his hands and feet *into* it, his sanctification is invalid. (9) The *mattirin* (q.v. Glos) are the sprinkling of the blood of animal sacrifices, and the burning of the fistful of meal of the meal-offerings; they are so called because they enable the sacrifices to be eaten or make them fit for the altar, and they must be done before sunset of the day on which the sacrifices are brought. Now the laver was sunk every day in a pit (v. *supra* 20*a*); if this laver was not sunk into it before sunset, its water is unfit on the morrow for 'sanctification' where the priest wishes to perform a *mattir*, just as the blood and the fistful of meal themselves become unfit for their purpose at sunset. Again, the limbs of the sacrifice must be burned before dawn of the day following its offering; if the laver is not sunk into the pit before dawn, its water is unfit for 'sanctification' on the following day for the service of burning the limbs. That is R. Ḥiyya b. Joseph's view. R. Ḥisda maintains that for the sprinkling of the blood too the water is unfit only if the laver was not sunk in the pit by dawn. (10) Into the pit at sunset.

b (1) Until dawn. It is now assumed that he means that even if a priest wishes to burn limbs during the night the laver cannot be drawn up, as this would render its water unfit. (2) Viz., burning the limbs.

נב א מיי' פ"ה מהלכות פרה הלכה יד :

נג ב מיי' פ"ה מהלכות ביאת מקדש הלכה יג :

חגיגה כג: צ"ש יומא ג. פרה פ"ג מ"ז ע"ש

תורה אור

והא פרה דטמויי מטמינן ליה דתנן *[א]מטמאין היו הכהן השורף את הפרה ומטבילין אותו להוציא מלבן של צדוקין שהיו אומרים במעורבי שמש היתה נעשית ש"מ לא פסלה בה [א] (מחשבת) טומאה שאני פרה הואיל [ב] דטבול יום לא פסיל בה אי הכי למה לי דמקדש כעין עבודה [בעינן] איבעיא להו מהו לקדש ידיו [ג] [ורגליו] בכיור °ממנו אמר רחמנא ולא בתוכו או דלמא אפילו בתוכו אמר רב נחמן בר יצחק תא שמע *או שטבל [לעיל כ:] במי מערה ועבד עבודתו פסולה הא מי כיור דומיא דמי מערה ועבד עבודתו כשרה [ב]לא מי מערה איצטריכא ליה שלא תאמר כל גופו טובל בהן ידיו ורגליו לא כל שכן אמר רבי חייא בר יוסף מי כיור נפסלין למתירין כמתירין [ד] לאברים כאברים רב חסדא אמר אף למתירין אין נפסלין אלא בעמוד השחר כאברין [ה] ורבי יוחנן אמר כיור כיון ששקעו שוב אין מעלהו למימרא דלעבודת לילה נמי לאחזי *והאמר רבי אסי אמר רבי יוחנן משמיה [לקמן ו:] דאילפא כיור שלא שקעו מבערב מקדש ממנו לעבודת לילה ולמחר אינו מקדש מאי אינו מעלהו נמי דקאמר לעבודת יום אבל לעבודת לילה חזי [אי הכי] היינו דרבי חייא בר יוסף איכא

שמות ל

והא פרה דטמויי מטמאינן ליה. אחר קידוש זה [ו] כדתנן ט' וטבילה זו בהר המשחה היתה והכי תנן לה במסכת פרה (פ"ג מ"ז) ואחר טבילתו מיד הוא מסדר מערכתה ושורפה אלמא אחר הקידוש הזה היתה וש"מ לא פסלה [ז] לה טומאה י"ש חסרו"ן בספרי"ס ונראה לי הגירסא הכי שאני פרה הואיל וטבול יום כשר בה [ח] טומאה לא פסלה בקידושין שלה: אי הכי למה לי דמקדש. הואיל ואין קידוש כשאר (א) קידוש עבודה: בכיור. שיכניס ידיו ורגליו בתוכו: הא כיור דומיא דמערה. והיכי דמי כגון שנכנס לתוכו: מי מערה אילטריך ליה. כלומר לעולם דכוותיה בכיור נמי פסול והאי דנקט מי מערה אילטריך סד"א הואיל וטבילה מעלייתא היא עדיפא היא מכיור שהן שאובין וקידוש אין כאן וטבילה אין כאן אבל הכא טבילה איכא קמשמע לן: ה"ג אמר רבי חייא בר יוסף מי כיור נפסלין למתירין כמתירין לאברים כאברים ורב חסדא אמר אף למתירין אין נפסלין אלא בעמוד השחר כאברים: מי כיור. לפי זמן [ט] עבודה שהקידוש צריך לה הוי זמן מימיו ליפסל אם עבודת [מתיר הוא כגון עבודת] דם או קמצים שנפסלים בבא הלילה עליהם כדאמרי' באיזהו מקומן (לקמן דף נו.) מנין לדם שנפסל בשקיעת החמה וכו' מי כיור נפסלין בשקיעת החמה אם לא נשקע הכיור בבור לפני שקיעת החמה נפסלים מימיו לקדש עוד [י] מהם לצורך עבודת יום מחר אפי' שיקעו קודם עמוד השחר העושה לינה בכל מקום אינו מועיל לו שלפי עבודתו הוא חשובו וכן אם שקעו לפני שקיעת החמה והעלהו בלילה מכיון שמלאו הלילה שעה אחת חוץ לבור נפסלו מימיו לעבודת היום: לאברים כאברים. לקדש מהן לעבודת הקטר חלבים נפסלין בעמוד השחר כמו [יא] שאברים נפסלין בלינת עמוד השחר כדכתיב עד בקר אבל כל הלילה כשרין לקדש מהן לעבודת [א] לילה [יב] ואם שיקעו קודם עמוד השחר מעט כשרין מימיו לקידוש עבודת [היום: אף] למתירין כו' כאברים. כשם שאין האברים נפסלין אלא בעמוד השחר אף כל [יג] לינות אין פוסלות בשום קדושה אלא בעמוד השחר: ור' יוחנן אמר כיור כיון ששקעו. בבור כדרך מלותו סמוך לשקיעת החמה: שוב אין מעלהו. כל הלילה וקס"ד דאפי' לעבודת הלילה [יד] קאמר ר' יוחנן דמיפסל בה העלאתו ואתרוייהו פליג: לעבודת לילה. הקטר חלבים: ולמחר אינו מקדש. קס"ד דאסור לקדש הימנו קאמר שנפסל בשקיעת החמה לעבודת יום אלמא כולה כרבי חייא סבירא ליה: מאי אינו מעלהו נמי דקאמר. רבי יוחנן לעיל לעבודת יום משום פסול עבודת יום קאמר לה שלא יפסלו מימיו לעבודת יום וקא סלקא דעתך השתא [ב] שהעלאת הלילה תפסלם לעבודת [טו] מתיר כר' חייא: אי הכי היינו דרבי חייא. [ג] מאי אינו מעלהו דקאמר רבי יוחנן עלה דר' חייא ודרב חסדא מאי אתא למימר הא רבי חייא נמי ה"ק:

מי כיור נפסלין למתירין כמתירין. פי' לדם וקומץ נפסלים מימיו בשקיעת [טז] [החמה] כמו שהמתירין נפסלין בשקיעת החמה כדאמר באיזהו מקומן (לקמן דף נו.): **כיור** כיון ששקעו אין מעלהו. למאי דס"ד השתא דהעלאת לילה [יז] פוסלן לכל עבודות יש תימה דתיקשי ליה כמה משניות דמסכת תמיד (דף כח.) שהיה מקדש לתרומת הדשן ואחיו הכהנים שהיו מקדשים כמו כן בלילה ומיהו איכא לאוקמינהו כר' אלעזר בר"ש וכמאן דפסיט לעיל כמחלוקת בזו כך מחלוקת בזו [יח] והא כרבי אבל קשה אכתי היאך היו עושין תרומת הדשן לרבי וי"ל בכהנים ישנים שניעורו כל הלילה ואין צריכין לקדש ומתני' דיומא (דף כב.) דמוכחא שהיה תרומת הדשן בכהני חדתי דקאמר עלה דלכך לא [יט] הוה פייס בתחילה בתרומת הדשן משום אונס שינה כר' אלעזר בר"ש אי נמי י"ל שהיה להם מים בכלי שרת אחר כדי קידוש של תרומת הדשן ועוד יש לומר דמקידוש תרומת הדשן לא קשיא מידי דפסול עבודת לילה דרבנן ויש עוד טעם להכשיר בתרומת הדשן טפי [ד] מבכולה לילה כדפירש בקונטרס בסמוך עוד יש לומר דניחא ליה למיפרך מדר' יוחנן אדר"י טפי ממתניתין דתמיד משום דאיכא לדחויי דסבירא ליה למתני' דמקרות הגבר עד לפרא לא פסלה לינה אפי' במים אע"ג דסוגיא דשמעתין ודאי לאו הכי סבירא ולהאי פירוש ניחא השתא דלא מצי לאקשויי מברייתא דלעיל דפליגי בה רבי ורבי אלעזר בר"ש דקתני קידש בלילה צריך לקדש ביום דמשמע הא בלילה מיחזי חזי: **כיור** כיון ששקעו. פירוש האי דמהני שיקוע למים היינו קודם שנפסלו דלאחר שנפסלו אמרי' בפ' כל שעה (פסחים דף לד:) דאין זריעה להקדש: **כיור** שלא שקעו. השתא ס"ד דלאו דוקא [כ] אלא אפילו שקעו מעלהו [ומקדש] לעבודת לילה אלא רבותא נקט הכי אע"פ שלא היה משוקע [כא] בשקיעת החמה כשר לעבודת לילה אבל לבסוף דמשני ומסיק דאיכא בינייהו גזירת שיקוע ניחא דנקט שלא שקעו דאם איתא דשקעו אין מעלהו עד תרומת הדשן: **מאי** אין מעלהו דקאמר לעבודת היום. פי' שיהא כשר לקדש לענין שיועיל לו קידוש לעבודת יום כגון קומץ ודם אבל לעבודת לילה כגון לאיברים חזי ופריך היינו דר' חייא בר' יוסף ומשני איכא בינייהו גזרת שיקוע כלומר [כב] לר"י אסור להעלותו גזירה שמא יפשע ולא יחזור וישקיענו דר' יוחנן אית ליה גזירת שיקוע ולהכי נקט שלא שקעו דאם שקעו לא יעלהו עד תרומת הדשן דלמא פשע אבל אם לא שקעו או שקעו והעלהו מקדש ממנו ור' חייא בר יוסף לא גזר וסבירא ליה דמעלהו כל שעה שירצה ולא חיישינן דלמא פשע וא"ת ולמה היו משקעין אותו כלל בערב [כג] היה להם להמתין עד סמוך לעמוד השחר [ה] כיון שהיו יכולין [כד] [להעלות] כל הלילה לקדש לאברים וי"ל (דלמא) לא רצו להמתין זמן שיקועו עד סמוך לזמן פסולו דלמא פשע ולא משקע ליה בעמוד השחר וה"ה שהיו יכולין לקבוע זמן שיקוע בתחילת הלילה או באמצעה [כה] *) דכדי שיהא זכור בעמוד השחר אלא לפי שהוא זמן פסול מתירים של דם וקומץ קבעו זמנו בערב ולר' יוחנן אע"פ שעל [כו] כרחן יש להן להעלותן לתרומת הדשן לא דמי כדפי' בקונטרס [לקמן וז"ל] דלא סגיא ליה בלאו קידוש זה שזכה לפיים של תרומת הדשן ולגזירת שיקוע ליכא למיחש דכיון שמלאו שקוע והעלהו ועכשיו הגיע זמן הסמוך לפסולו לא פשע [כז] ליה והדר משקע ליה ולא דמי למעלהו בלילה שמניחו לקדש כהנים הבאין תמיד להקטיר ואתי למיפשע וא"ת ויפסול מימיו ומה בכך והא השתא נמי כשמשקעו בעמוד השחר וחוזר ומעלהו ביום לא היה יכול לקדש במימיו למתירין דכבר נפסלו ולא מהני להו זריעה אלא לאברים היה יכול לקדש ומי הוא שוטה שיכול לקדש ביום קידוש גמור שיועיל לכל העבודות והוא עומד ומקדש קידוש שאינו מועיל אלא לאברים וי"ל דכיון [כח] דקידש להו המים בכלי שרת מצוה לשומרן כשאר קדשים שלא יפסלו כדפי' בקונטרס בהך דשמעתין אי נמי כדי שלא יבואו [כט] לידי נותר ויטמאו את הידים וכשמעלין את הכיור ביום היו מערין מימיו בכלי שרת דפעמים שמקדשין הרבה כהנים בכל דדין ומי שיש לו לקדש לאברים מקדש מן המים שבכלי שרת ושנים עשר כהנים [ו] שהיו מקדשין בבת אחת מן הכיור לצורך התמיד אף על פי שהיה פייס של תמיד קודם ע"ה כדמוכח במסכת תמיד (פ"א) מ"מ לא היו מקדשין בלילה עד שהיה יום ומעלין הכיור ונותנים מימיו בכלי שרת וממלאין אותו מים חדשים ומקדשים מהם שהרי היה זורק דם התמיד ונפסלו מימיו למתירין ולא מהני להו זריעה [ל] והא דפסלה להו לינה במים בכולה שמעתין היינו כרבי ולא כרבי אלעזר בר"ש למאי דפסיט אילפא לעיל כמחלוקת בזו כך מחלוקת בזו [וכולהו אמוראי דלעיל מודו דלכל הפחות ספיקא הוי והכא מפשט פשט ועוד צריך לומר דהא דאמר אביי לעיל דמקרות הגבר עד לפרא לא פסלה לינה היינו קידוש אבל במים פוסלת [לא] והאי דפסלה נמי לינה במים אינו אלא מדרבנן דכיון דלא פסיל בקידוש לא פסיל במים דהכל [אחד] כדאמר לעיל כמחלוקת בזו כך מחלוקת בזו] ורבינו פי' בענין אחר וזה לשונו ומאי אינו מעלהו דקאמר משום חשש עבודת היום שאם יעלהו לעבודת לילה קודם תרומת הדשן יהיו סבורים העולם [לב] שמשקעין אותו בשקיעת החמה שלא יפסלו המים למתרין וקודם השחר שלא יפסלו לאברים [לג] ויבא לקדש ממנו למחר למתירין אף על פי שלא היה משוקע כל

*) נ"ל ונלבד שיהא זכור כו'

שיטה מקובצת

א] תיבת מחשבת נמחק: ב] הואיל וטבול יום כשר בה לא פסיל בה טומאה בקידוש שלה א"ה: ג] ידיו ורגליו בכיור: ד] לאברים כאברים. וא"ת והיכא דשקעו בעמוד השחר למה נפסלו אף למתירין אע"ג דנפסלים בלינה תועיל שקיעה מטעם זריעה מידי דהוי אמים שנטמאו דאמרי' משיקן במקוה ומהורין אלמא אמרי' דזריעתן מטהרתן וי"ל דאין זריעה להקדש וא"ת ולר' חייא בר יוסף הלא היו מי כיור נפסלין למתירין בהעלאתו לצורך תרומת הדשן בלילה וי"ל דאה"נ דכבר נפסלו בהעלאתו לצורך תרומת הדשן ובאותן המים לא היה מועיל הקידוש כי אם לאברים וא"ת ממה היו מקדשין למתירין למחר וי"ל דלמחר היו נותנין אותן מים שנפסלו בכלי שרת אחר וחוזר ושוקע הכיור בבור וממלאין מים חדשים למתירין וא"כ הא (דתניא) [דתנן] אף הוא (היה עושה) [עשה] מוכני לכיור פי' כדי לחזור ולשקעו בבור בעמוד השחר לא היה מועיל אותו שיקוע כי אם לקדש אותן כהנים [שנתעסקו בהקטרת] אברים וא"ת כיון דמ"מ היה צריך לחזור ולמלאות מים חדשים למתירין כדפי' א"כ לאחר תרומת הדשן למה היו משקעין אותו כלל כיון דאותו שיקוע לא היה מועיל למתירין ולפסול אף לאברים ומיד לאחר עמוד השחר ישאבו מים חדשים לצורך מתירין ולצורך אברים וי"ל דמשום הכי לא עביד הכי שאין מביאין קדשים לבית הפסול או פעמים שמתעסקין הרבה כהנים כו'. מהר"פ: ה] עי' בהשמטות בסוף המסכ': ו] זה הס"ד ומה"ד דתנן: ז] לא פסלה בה: ח] בה לא פסיל בה טומאה בקידוש שלה הס"ד: ט] זמן העבודה שהקידוש כו' אם עבודת מתיר הוא כגון עבודת דם: י] מהם לצורך עבודת יום מחר ואפי' שוקעו: יא] כמו שהאברים: יב] לילה אבל אם היו משוקעים כל הלילה והעלן בעמוד השחר נפסלים בכך אף לאברים הס"ד ומה"ד אף למתירין כו' ואם שיקעו: יג] כל לינה אין פוסלת אלא בעמוד השחר כי הטעם שהמים נפסלין בלינה אינו אלא מטעם קדושת הכלי ודי לנו ליתן פסול לינה כדין שאר דברים הנקדשים בכלי שרת: יד] הלילה. היינו אברים ופדרים קאמר ר"י ומפסל בהעלותו דס"ל דלאברים כמתירין תדרך שיהא משוקע כל הלילה ואתרוייהו: טו] לעבודת מחר כר"ח: טז] בשקיעת החמה: יז] לילה פוסלת: יח] בזו. ורבי יוחנן סבר לה כרבי אבל קשה וכו' לשון מהר"פ בטה היו מקדשין בתרומת הדשן והיכא משכחת לה תרומת הדשן לרבי כו' עד ולדידיה המוכני שעשה לכיור לא היה בשביל שלא יפסלו מימיו אלא כדי להשמיע את הקול כדמסיק בסוף שמעתין ואע"ג דאכתי לא ידעינן טעמא דקלא היינו דוקא בשעה שיקיע בראשון דקאמר שלא היו משקעין אותו עד תרומת הדשן והוא היה סבר דבשיקוע לא הוי קלא אבל השתא נאמר לראב"ש שהיה משוקע עד תרומת הדשן והיו מעלין אותו לקדש ממנו ושקיעה משום קלא דהעזרה כי

שיטה מקובצת

היכי דלשמעו כהנים וליתו וא"ת כיון דאמרי לאברים כמתירין תיפסל הקידוש בשקיעת החמה כמו להמים לרבי מידי דהוי אלינה דפוסל בקידוש כמו במים וי"ל דלפי פי' ר' יחיאל מפרש ניחא פי' דלאברים כמתירין דאינו אלא מטעם גזירה דיש לתמוה מה טעם עבדו אברים כמתירין וכי עדיפי דם קידוש עבודת אברים טפי מאברים גופייהו אלא אין זה מן הדין אלא משום דגזורין לצורך אברים אטו לצורך מתירין דאי שרית לקדש ממנו לאחר לצורך אברים כי העלהו בלילה ושקעו בעמוד השחר אתי לקדש ממנו לצורך מתירין ואע"ג דבאברים גופייהו לא גזרינן אטו מתירין התם היינו טעמא דודאי לא אתי למטעי להשוות מתירין לאברים לענין לילה דויל קרי בי רב הוא גבי אברים [כתיב] על מוקדה על המזבח כל הלילה וגבי מתירין כתיב ביום צוותו אבל גבי מים של קידוש שפיר אתי לאחלופי כמי' והשתא נמי ניחא דדוקא במים שייך למיגזר כדפי' אבל בקידוש גופיה לא שייך למיגזר לאותו קידוש שמבעוד יום שנפסל בשקיעת החמה למתירין ומ"מ כשר הוא לאברים דלאמי ניחוש לה אי משום שלא יעשה עבודת מתירין באותו קידוש קודם לינת עמוד השחר הא מתירין בלילה ליכא ואי לאחר כבר פסול ליה אותו קידוש בלינת עמוד השחר אף לאברים אבל בקידוש שייך בהך שיקוע איכא למיגזר שפיר מן יעשה לאחר בין אברים [בין] מתירין בקידוש שקדשו ממנו במים ששקע בעמוד השחר ולכך אסור המים אף לאברים של לילה דאי לאו הא לא קיימא הא מ"מ קשה [א] (אי אסורו) שקעו ממנו אלא דלעיל דקתני בשילחי קידש בלילה כו' עד היה א"כ מעולה בלילה וי"ל דניחא ליה להקשות דר"א אדר' ולמסקנא ניחא שפיר דאשאר עושה אברים כמתירין ועי"ל דמיירי כשקידש בכלי שרת ולכך חזי לעבודת לילה אבל הכא מיירי במי כיור. וכ"ת היא גופיה תיקשי לך מ"ט כלי שרת מפי' מי כיור [דלפי'] מה שפי' שאין זה אלא מטעם גזירה ניחא דדוקא במי כיור איכא למיגזר הא משום הא כדפי' לפי' שהרגילין כולם קדשו ממנו אבל כלי שרת שאין רגילות לקדש ממנו לא רצו למיגזר השתא להכי שוב וכל לומר דלרבי קידוש דתרומת הדשן היה בכלי שרת דלא גזרו כדפי' לא

נצפרך בכהני עתיקי ע"כ : יט] לא היה : כ] דלאו דוקא שלא שקעו אלא אפילו שקעו מעלה : כא] משוקע קודם : כב] כלומר אי שקעו אסור ותיבות לר"י ל"ש ונמחק : כג] בערב ולא עד סמוך : כד] שהיו יכולין כל הלילה לקדש לאברים וי"ל דלא רצו : כה] באמצעה בכ : כז] פשע ביה והדר משקע כו' לקדש כל כהנים כו' למיפשע עכ"ל וא"ת : כח] דכיון דק : כט] יבואו ויטמאו את : ל] זריעה והאי דפסלא בהו לינה : לא] פוסלת ומאי דפסלה נמי מדרבנן הוין דלא פסיל בקידוש לא פסיל במים דהכל אחד כדאמרי לעיל כמחלוקת בזו : שלכך משקעין : לג] לאברים ויבואו :

א) נראה דנ"ל ומ"מ קבה אם

הגהות צ"ק [א] לילה הס"ד ואח"כ ד"ה אף למתירין כו' בעמוד השחר ואם שיקעו קודם עמוד השחר מטעם כשרים מימיו לקידוש שיהא ישלין כל הלילה : [ו] זה :

הגהות הב"ח (א) רש"י ד"ה אי הכי וכו' כשאר קידוש הס"ד ואח"כ מ"כ ותשני כעין עבודה :

נד א מיי' פ"ס מהל' ביאת מקדש הל' יג :

נה ב מיי' שם הל' יא :

תורה אור

א] איכא בינייהו גזירת שיקוע *והאמר רבי יוחנן קידש ידיו לתרומת הדשן למחר אין צריך לקדש שכבר קידש מתחילת עבודה ב] בשלמא לרבא דמוקים להא כרבי אלעזר ברבי שמעון הא כרבי ג] אלא לאביי דמוקים לה כרבי קשיא דרבי אדרבי מאי שנא התם דמשקע ליה ומאי שנא הכא דלא משקע ליה ד] דמסלק ליה והדר משקע ליה ה] אי הכי למחר אינו מקדש [*אמאי אין צריך לקדש] ו] למימרא דלמתירין מיחזא חזי היינו דרב חסדא איכא בינייהו מצות שיקוע מיתיבי *לא היו רואין אותו ולא שומעין את קולו עד ששומעים קול של עץ שעשה בן קטין מוכני לכיור והן אומרים הגיע [עת] קידוש ידים ורגלים מן הכיור מאי לאו דמסלק ליה אלמא משקע ליה ז] לא דמשקע ליה אי דמשקע ליה מי משתמע קליה משקע ליה בגילגלא לישנא אחרינא דמשקע ליה בחומרתיה כי היכי דלישתמע קליה ולשמעי וליתי והא הוה *גביני כרוז בי תרי היכרי הוו עבדי דשמע מהאי אתי ושמע מהאי אתי: גופא *אמר רבי יוסי ברבי חנינא כל °כיור שאין בו כדי לקדש ארבעה כהנים ממנו אין מקדשין בו שנאמר °ורחצו ממנו משה ואהרן ובניו וגו' מיתיבי °כל הכלי' מקדשין בין שיש בהן רביעי' בין

רש"ק | תמיד כח. | יומא כ: | [לעיל יט:] | שמו' מ

כל הלילה רק בשקיעת החמה ובעמוד השחר והיינו גזירת שיקוע דקאמר בסמוך דגזרינן שיהא משוקע כל הלילה עד תרומת הדשן כדי שידעו העולם שלא שקעוהו מבעוד יום כי אם להיות זכורים על ידי כך שיקוע דסוף כל הלילה כג] שכשמלאוהו משוקע בשעת תרומת הדשן יחזרוהו וישקעוהו קודם היום כי אם יעלוהו לאחר שקיעת החמה יש לגזור שמא יאמרו כד] שלהכשירו לעבודת מתירין למחר שיקעוהו בשקיעת החמה וכשר למתירין אף על פי שיעלהו לאחר שקיעת החמה ופריך אי הכי היינו דרבי חייא ברבי יוסף שפוסל למתירין בשקיעת החמה כי לרב חסדא שאינו פוסל למתירין אלא בעמוד השחר לא איכפת לן במה שיכשירום למחר למתירין כי בשיקוע דעמוד השחר מתכשר אפי' למתירים ומשני איכא בינייהו גזירת שיקוע דרבי יוחנן גזר [ו] להשהותו בשיקוע משום שיקוע דשקיעת החמה שאנו צריכין אז לשקעו כדי להזכיר שיקוע דסוף הלילה שלא יאמרו שאינו להזכיר אלא להכשיר למתירין ולכך צריך להשהותו עד תרומת הדשן כדפרישית ורבי חייא בר יוסף לא גזר [ז] והא"ר יוחנן קידש ידיו לתרומת כו' בשלמא לרבא דמוקי ליה להיא כרבי אלעזר בר' שמעון הא כרבי *) איכא למימר דסבירא ליה לרבא דלרבי אלעזר ברבי שמעון לא פסלה לינה במי כיור כמאן דאמר לעיל כמחלוקת בזו כך מחלוקת בזו ולא כההיא דלא פשיט ליה לעיל ולמחר אינו מקדש דבמילתיה דאילפא אינו צריך לקדש קאמר כרבי אלעזר ברבי שמעון ולא קאי אמי כיור לפוסלם למחר כי כשרים הם לרבי אלעזר בר"ש אלא לאביי דמוקי לה כרבי קשיא דרבי אדרבי דמאי שנא בהא דכיון דשקעו שוב אינו מעלהו דמצריך לשקעו כדי להזכיר שישקעוהו בסוף הלילה ומאי שנא בהא דקאמר דכבר קידש מתחילת עבודה דמשמע דתרומת הדשן תחלת עבודת היום שמשם ואילך עסוקים בעבודת היום בלא הפסק וכל שעה מקדש ועובד כל הבא לעבוד משם ואילך משמע דלא משקע ליה אחר שהעלהו לתרומת הדשן שאם כן יש הפסק בדבר ומשני הא דקרי ליה תחילת עבודה לאו משום דלא משקע ליה דודאי מסלק ליה והדר משקע ליה וקלת יש תימה בין לפי' זה בין לפירוש אחר לישנא דמסלק ליה דהא כמי היה יודע דמסלק ליה ואין קשה לו אלא משיקוע (דבתרא) מאי שנא הכא דמשקע ליה ומאי שנא התם דלא משקע ליה : **אי** משקע ליה . שהיה למעלה וכרב חסדא כה] ומורידין לבור הלא אין קולו נשמע וא"ת לישני דנשמע קולו דקתני היינו בהעלותו וי"ל היינו [ח] כו] דקא אמר דמשקע ליה בגלגלא (כגון) לבור והקול שנשמע היינו בהוליאו מן הבור ומעלהו ואי בעית אימא דמשקע [ט] בחומרתיה דהיה בגלגלא אף השיקוע כדי להשמיע קול הרבה בהורידו ובהעלותו : **הגה"ה** איכא בינייהו גזירת שיקוע . פירש רש"י משקעו בערב שלא ישכח לשקעו בעמוד השחר אבל לילה אינו פוסלו כלל לעבודת דם למחר אם משקעו בעמוד השחר ולרבי חייא לילה פוסלו וקשה אם כן איכא בינייהו טובא דלרבי יוחנן לילה אינה פוסלת ולרבי חייא פוסלת ועוד דליפרך מיד הייני דרב חסדא ועוד דבסמוך פריך מכח למחר אינו צריך לקדש אלמא למתירין חזי היינו דרב חסדא משמע דבלאו ההיא דלמחר וכו' לא הוה מצי למפרך מידי לכך נראה לי גזירת שיקוע ואם לא שיקעו יהא פסול מדרבנן לעבודת דם משום כז] לילה אפילו שקעו בעמוד השחר ולר' חייא יהא פסול מן התורה ולכך פריך למחר אינו צריך לקדש אלמא אפילו מדרבנן כשרה לעבודת דם ואין לילה פוסלן ואם כן היינו דרב חסדא וקאמר איכא בינייהו מצות שיקוע . ברו"ך :

*) דאיכא דס"ל דלראב"ש לא פסלה לינה אפילו במי כיור

איכא בינייהו גזירת שיקוע . כלומר הא דאוקים אין מעלהו דרבי יוחנן משום פסול עבודת יום לא כדקס"ד שיהא הלילה פוסלו לעבודת היום כרבי חייא אלא שמא לא יחזור וישקעו ונמלא עמוד השחר פוסלו לעבודת מחר [א] ולעולם (אם שקעו קודם עמוד השחר כשר) והיינו דלא נקט רבי יוחנן לישנא דפסולה אלא לשון איסור העלאה שלא יגרמו להן ליפסל דכיון דקדש להו בכלי שרת מלוה לשמרן כשאר קדשים ומיהו בהעלאה לא מיפסיל ולקמן פריך היינו דרב חסדא דאמר לילה לא פסיל אלא עמוד השחר פוסל ורבי חייא לא אסר ליה להעלותו משום גזירת שיקוע אלא ח] דבהעלותו נפסל מיד לעבודת מתיר הלכך נקט לשון נפסלין : והאמר רבי יוחנן כו'. אלמא (א) אמר שמעלהו לקדש לתרומת הדשן ט] ולא הצריך לחזור ולשקעו ובשלמא העלאתו לא קשיא לן דלא סגי י] בלאו קידוש זה שזכה לפיים של תרומת הדשן ולגזירת שיקוע ליכא למיחש דכיון שמלאו משוקע והעלהו ועכשיו הגיע הזמן הסמוך לפסולו לא פשע ביה והדר משקע ליה ולא דמי למעלהו בלילה שמניחו לקדש בו כהנים הבאים תמיד להקטיר ואתי למיפשע ביה אלא הא קשיא יא] לך דלא איירי בה רבי יוחנן במלות שיקוע וגימא דניסקעיה : בשלמא לרבא דמוקי . לעיל הא מילתא דר' יוחנן אליבא דרבי אלעזר דאמר אין לינה מועלת בקידוש איכא למימר דמשום הכי לא חש יב] לשיקוע דקסבר רבי אלעזר דבמי כיור גופייהו נמי לא פסלה [ב] לינה : הא. דאמר ר' יוחנן לעיל אין מעלהו : כרבי. אמרה דאמר לינה מועלת בקידוש וכל שכן במי כיור : אלא לאביי. יג] דאוקים לעיל כרבי קשיא דרבי אדרבי לעיל א"ר יוחנן אליבא דרבי לגזירת שיקוע חייש [ג] והכא נמי נשקעיה והכא ליכא למיתלי טעמא במודה רבי דמקרות הגבר עד לפרא לא פסלה לינה דבשלמא גבי קידוש דפסול לינה דידיה דרבנן שהרי אין המים בעולם הוא דאיכא למימר הכי אבל מי כיור דהוו קמן וקדושת כלי עליהם ולינה דידהו דאורייתא עמוד השחר הוא דגרים ליה : מאי שנא התם דמשקע ליה . כלומר מאי שנא גבי אין מעלהו דחש לגזירת יד] שיקוע ומ"ש כו' : דמסלק ליה והדר משקע ליה . לאחר קידוש תרומת הדשן ורבי יוחנן הוא דלא איירי בתקנת מי כיור אלא בהלכות קידוש לאשמועינן דמודי רבי מקרות הגבר עד לפרא לא פסלה לינה : הכי גרסי' אי הכי למחר אינו מקדש אין צריך לקדש היינו דרב חסדא כו'. אי הכי דלר' יוחנן אוקמא דלילה לא פסל ולמחר אינו מקדש [ד] בתמיה : אמאי. א"ר יוחנן משמיה דאילפא מקדש ממנו לעבודת לילה ולמחר אינו מקדש דשמעי' מיניה דמשום דלא שיקעו טו] בערב קא פסל להו קידוש מחר : ומשני אין צריך לקדש. קאמר דכיון שקידש לעבודת לילה אין צריך טז] למחר ואשמעי' דאין לינה מועלת בקידוש וכדרבי אלעזר : היינו דרב חסדא. השתא יז] דאוקמא אין מעלהו דר' יוחנן משום פסול עמוד השחר אבל לילה לא פסיל הייט דרב חסדא : איכא בינייהו מלות שיקוע. לר' יוחנן מלות שיקוע מבערב כדי שימלאהו משוקע בקידוש תרומת הדשן ויהא נזכר לחזור ולשקעו והייט דקאמר (ב) כיון ששקעו אלמא מבערב הוא משקע ליה ולרב חסדא לא החמירו בו כל כך ואין מלות שיקועו אלא סמוך לזמן פסולו קודם עמוד השחר : לא היו רואין אותו כו'. יח] [במי שזכה] בתרומת הדשן קמיירי במסכת תמיד כשהיה נכנס לעזרה לקדש ידיו ורגליו לא היה מכנים בידו לא נר ולא אבוקה אלא מהלך לאור המערכה ולא היו רואין אותו אחיו יט] [הכהנים] שהיו בבית מוקד עד ששומעין כו' : והן אומרים הגיע. לכיור מזרזין את עלמן להיות נכונים להעלות אפר לתפוח לאחר שירד זה מן המזבח כדתנן לעיל גבי ראוהו אחיו הכהנים שירד : מאי לאו . האי שמיעת קול העץ דקתני כ] דסליק ליה לכיור מן הבור אלמא משוקע הוה וקשיא ליה לרב חסדא דאמר לא משקע ליה עד לפרא: לא דמשקע כא]. השתא : מי משתמע קליה. הלא אין מוכני לריך לשוקעו אלא להעלותו אבל שיקועו משלשלו לבור והוא טפל מאליו : ומשני דמשקע ליה בגלגלא. כי היכי דלישתמע קליה וישמעו [ה] הכהנים הישנים בעיר וניתו לפיים דתנן במסכת תמיד (פרק ג מ"ח) מיריחו היו שומעין את קול העץ שעשה כו' : בחומרתיה . גלגלא : והא כב] גביני כרוז. שהיה מכריז עמדו הכהנים לעבודתכם ולוים לדוכנכם וישראל למעמדכם : גביני . שם האיש : בי תרי היכרי הוו עבדי. שתי היכרות עושין לדבר: כל הכלים מקדשים. מים שנתקדשו בהן לקדש את הידים ורגלים : בין

שיטה מקובצת

א] איכא בינייהו גזירת שיקוע . לכאורה משמע דה"פ דלעולם ר"י סבר כר' חייא בר יוסף דלמתירין כו' אלא דר"י מחמיר וגזר להעלותו אף לאברים בלילה שמא ישכח לחזור ולשקוע למחר ונמצא עמוד השחר פסלו למחר אף לאברים ויביאו קדשים לבית הפסול אבל אי העלוהו או שלא שקעו בשקיעת החמה מקדש הימנו לעבודת הלילה אבל ר' חייא בר יוסף לא גזר כלל ומ"מ היה מעלהו שפיר לתרומת הדשן ולא חיישינן שמא ישכח לחזור ולשקוע כיון (שהתם) [שהוא] תחילת עבודת היום ומצאוהו משוקע וסמוך לפסולו לא אתי למפשע וקשה למורי דהיאך נאמר שיסבור ר"י למתירין כמתירין כו' כיון דלא משמע ולא מוכח מתוך דבריו דכי נמי אמרינן דסבר למתירין כאברים איכא למגזר שפיר גזירת שיקוע לכך נראה כפ"ה דאה"נ דהשתא נאמר דר"י סבר כרב חסדא דלמתירין כאברים והאי אין מעלהו לעבודת היום דקאמר ר"י לאו משום פסול שיהא הלילה פוסלו לעבודת היום כר' חייא דלמתירין כמתירין דהא סבר ר"י דלמתירין כאברים אלא משום שמא ישכח לחזור ולשקע כדפי' ולהכי נקט אין מעלהו ולא לישנא דפסול דלא אסר רק להעלותו שלא יגרם להם לפסול ומצוה לשומרם כשאר קדשים אבל לעולם אם העלם ושוקעם בעמוד השחר לא מיפסל אף למתירין ומ"מ קשה חדא דכל זה חסר מן הספר שבא לשנות הפי' דאין מעלהו לעבודת היום כמו שהי' סובר המקשה ועוד מיד הוי ליה למיפרך היינו דרב חסדא ועוד מדמקשה לקמן אי הכי היינו דרב חסדא מכלל דעד השתא לא אסיק אדעתיה דהיינו רב חסדא ועוד מאי דחיק לומר איכא בינייהו גזירת שיקוע והלא הרבה איכא בינייהו דלר"י מתירין כאברים ולר' חייא אברים כאברים ומתירין כמתירין ועוד קשה לכל הפירושים מאי שנא הכא דגרסינן גזירת שיקוע ולקמן גרסינן מצות שיקוע והכל אחד הוא לכך נראה כפי' ראשון דאינו מעלהו לעבודת היום שלא יפסול למתירין לר"י כר' חייא דמתירין כמתירין אלא דמוסיף הוא על ר' חייא גזירת שיקוע פי' כיון דלמתירין כמתירין אסור להעלותו כלל בלילה שאם הי' מעלהו כלל לאברים למחר נפיק מיניה חורבא דכיון [דמעלהו] בעמוד השחר ויעשה קידוש לאברים אתי לאכשרינהו נמי למתירין וכ"ת מ"מ גזרינן הכי י"ל משום דהרואים אותו משוקע בעמוד השחר יאמרו משוקע היה כל הלילה וחזי אף למתירין [ונפיק] מיניה חורבא לכך אינו מעלהו כלל וחשתא ניחא דמוכח שפיר ממילתיה מדקאמר שוב אינו מעלהו דאית ליה למתירין כמתירין ומהאי טעמא נפיק מיניה חורבא דאי סבירא ליה לאברים כאברים איזה חורבא נפיק אבל ודאי בדיעבד אם העלהו בלילה וקדשו לאברים מהני הקידוש גם השתא ניחא נמי האי דנקט לשון גזירת כיון דמשום שמא יבא לידי חורבא הוא וי"מ דהטעם [הוא] שאם היה מעלהו למחר לאחר שיקוע ויקדשו לאברים אתי לקדושי אף למתירין משום דאמרי כשם ששיקוע עמוד השחר מועיל לאברים אע"ג דפסול לינה עמוד השחר פוסל בו ושוב לא [תיפסל] בלינה מאחר ששקעו כמו כן כששיקעו בשקיעת החמה הפוסל במתירין שוב לא תפסל בלינה אף כי העלהו בלילה אבל עתה דמצרכינן שיקוע תו ליכא למיגזר והאי פי' לא נהירא דאיך ישעו בזה שידעו ששקיעת החמה גופיה אינו אלא משום פסול לילה וכ"ש דפסול לילה גופיה פוסלתן למתירין למה משקע ליה הרי מיד יבאו אחיו הכהנים שיהו צריכין להעלותו כדי לקדש ידיהן א[לא ודאי היה משקע] כדי להשמיע קול. סליק שמעתתא דמי כיור. מהר"פ ז"ל : ח] אלא דבהעלאתו : ט] הד[שן אין צריך לחזור :] י] סגי ליה בלא קידוש : יא] קשיא לן דלא כו' שיקוע. ס"א ולא אמר לאחר תרומת הדשן חוזר [ומשקעו : יב] לא חש] למיתני והחזר ומשקעו דקסבר : יג] לאביי דאוקמא לעיל כרבי כו' אליבא דרבי דחייש לגז[ירת שיקוע והכא לא] אמר דנשקעיה והכא ליכא למימר דטעמא דמודה רבי דמקרות כו' לא פסלה בה לינה : [יד] לגזירת שיקוע :] טו] שיקעו מבערב : טז] אין צריך לקדש למחר : יז] השתא דאוקמת : יח] כו' . במי שוכה : [יט] הכהנים שהיו] בבית המוקד : כ] דקתני דמסלק : כא] דמשקעי ליה : כב] והא הוה : כג] דסוף כל [הלילה שכשמצאוהו :] כד] יאמרו שלא הכשירו לעבודת מתירין למחר אלא כששקעוהו : כה] חסדא ומורידו : כו] [דקאמר . ס"א משקע] ליה בגלגל לבור : כז] משום לינה אפילו :

שיטה מקובצת

ולא ימעו כלל בזה אלא ודאי הטעות כדפי' שלא יאמרו דכל הלילה היה משוקע דלא חזו להעלאת שהיתה בלילה ויכשירו אף למתירין והיינו דקאמר אינו מעלהו לעבודת היום דהיינו מתירין אבל לעבודת הלילה אם עבר והעלהו כר' חייא בר יוסף כו' ולאברים ותרומת הדשן איכא למימר דמשכחת לה בכהני עתיקי. מהר"פ ז"ל : ב] עי' בהשמטות בסוף המסכת : ג] עי' בהשמטות בסוף המסכ': ד] עי' בהשמטות בסוף המסכת: ה] עי' בהשמטות בסוף המסכת : ו] ה"ג למימרא דלמתירין נמי מיחזא חזי היינו דרב חסדא איכא בינייהו מצות שיקוע. כלומר נהי דלית ליה לר"י גזירת שיקוע כדפי' מ"מ אית ליה מצות שיקוע שמצוה להשהותו בשיקוע כל הלילה עד זמן תרומת הדשן ולרב חסדא לית ליה מצות שיקוע ולכאורה נראה דלרב חסדא לא היה משקע כלל [עד] לאחר תרומת הדשן וזה קשה מדקאמר ר"י כיון ששקעו בשקיעת החמה משמע דשיקוע בשקיעת החמה דבר פשוט הוא לכו"ע לכך נראה דרב חסדא מודה דצריך לשקע בשקיעת החמה ולא פליג אר"י אלא מהעלאו' לילה דר"י סבר כיון ששקעו שוב אינו מעלהו כל הלילה עד תרומת הדשן ורב חסדא סבר דאע"ג דצריך לשקע בשקיעת החמה מ"מ מעלהו בלילה לאברים ופדרים ואין צריך להשהותו בשיקוע עד תרומת הדשן וכ"ת ולמה להם אותו שיקוע דשקיעת החמה כיון דלמתירין כאברים וי"ל דכל זה אינו אלא כי אם שעל ידי כך יהי' זכור משיקוע של עמוד השחר ובהא פליגי דרב חסדא סבר דדי לו בשיקוע של שקיעת החמה כדי להוכיח משיקוע של עמוד השחר ור"י סבר דלא יזכור משיקוע של עמוד השחר אם אינו מוצאו משוקע בשעת תרומת הדשן ולכך נמי קבעו אותו שיקוע בשקיעת החמה שהיא שעה מסויימת ולא קבעוהו בחצי הלילה או בשלישית הלילה דדלמא אתי למינשייהו ולא יזכור לשקע כלל גם בשיקוע [עמוד השחר לאחר] תרומת הדשן והא דקאמר איכא בינייהו מצות שיקוע ר"ל איכא בינייהו אם מצוה להשהותו משוקע כל הלילה עד תרומת הדשן. מהר"פ : ז] לא דמשקע ליה. פ"ה משום לינה

לעיל כ. [וש"נ]

Joseph ['s view]? [21b]—They disagree as to a preventive measure in respect of sinking [the laver].[3] But surely R. Joḥanan said: If [the priest] sanctified his hands for the removal of the ashes, he need not sanctify [them again] on the morrow, because he has already sanctified [them] at the beginning of the service.[4] According to Raba who explains that this agrees with R. Eleazar son of R. Simeon, it is well: this [the present ruling] agrees with Rabbi.[5] But according to Abaye who explains that it agrees with Rabbi, Rabbi is selfcontradictory, [for] why must he lower it there.[6]
a whereas here he must not lower it?—It means that he raises it[1] and then lowers it again.[2] If so, 'on the morrow he does not sanctify'—why so?[3] [The meaning is] that he *need* not sanctify,[4] which is to say that [the previous sanctification] is indeed fit for the *mattirin*. Then it is the same as R. Ḥisda['s ruling]?[5]—They disagree in respect of the regulation of lowering.[6]

An objection is raised: They neither saw him nor heard him until they heard the sound of the wood of the machine which Ben Kaṭṭin made for the laver, and then they exclaimed, 'It is time to sanctify hands and feet at the laver'.[7] Surely it means that he raised it,[8] and which proves that it was sunk [earlier]?—No: it means that he lowered it [now].[9] If he lowered it, would the sound be heard?[10]—He lowered it by the wheel.[11] Another version: He lowered it by means of its stone,[12] in order that the sound of it should be heard, so that they [the priests] might hear it and come. But there
b was Gebini the crier?[1]—They made two alarms; some heard the one and came, whilst others heard the other and came.

The [above] text [stated]: 'R. Jose son of R. Ḥanina said: You may not wash in a laver which does not contain sufficient [water] for the sanctification of four priests, for it says, *That Moses and Aaron and his sons wash their hands and their feet thereat*'.[2] An objection is raised: All vessels sanctify,[3] whether they contain a *rebi'ith*[4]

(3) When R. Joḥanan rules that the laver must not be brought up for a service the following day, it is not because its water is unfit if it is not in the pit during any part of the night, but as a preventive measure, lest it is not lowered again before dawn, which would disqualify it. Hence R. Joḥanan does not say that the water is unfit, but merely that the laver must not be brought up. (4) V. *supra* 20a. Thus the laver is drawn up before dawn, and R. Joḥanan does not add that it must be lowered again immediately before dawn. (5) Who maintains that the passing of the night nullifies the previous sanctification, and all the more will it disqualify the water of the laver itself. (6) I.e., why does he fear there that if he brings it up he will not lower it again.

a (1) In the morning for the removal of the ashes. (2) Although R. Joḥanan does not mention it, that is merely because he is discussing the sanctification of hands and not the regulations of the laver. (3) Now that you explain that according to R. Joḥanan the night does not disqualify, why cannot he sanctify his hands on the morrow? (4) Because he has already sanctified his hands for the night service. Thus he informs us that the passing of the night does not nullify the sanctification, this being in agreement with R. Eleazar. (5) Now that you say that he does not bring it up because dawn is a disqualification, but that the night itself does not disqualify, R. Joḥanan's view is identical with R. Ḥisda's. (6) In R. Joḥanan's opinion it must be done in the evening, so that when the priest comes to clean the ashes in the morning he will find it so, and thus remember to lower it again immediately before dawn. But R. Ḥisda holds that this is unnecessary, and it is sufficient to lower it just before dawn. (7) When the priest who was to remove the ashes entered the Temple court to sanctify his hands and feet, he did not carry a light with him, but walked by the light of the altar fire. His fellow-priests in the adjoining chamber therefore neither saw nor heard him, until they heard the sound of the machine drawing up the laver from the pit, and then they knew that they themselves must prepare for the next service. (8) From the pit. Hence until then it was *in* the pit, which contradicts R. Ḥisda's view that it was not lowered until dawn. (9) They heard the sound of it being lowered. (10) The wheel was unnecessary for this, as one could simply unfasten the rope by which it was held up, whereupon it would fall automatically. (11) Though it was unnecessary, precisely in order that he might be heard. (12) A stone used as a wheel or pulley.

b (1) Who apprised the priests and others every morning when it was time for them to get up; v. Yoma 19b. (2) V. *supra* 19b. (3) The water placed in them, so that this water can be used by the priests for sanctifying their hands and feet. (4) V. Glos.

[22a] or they do not contain a *rebi'ith*,[5] provided they are service vessels?—Said R. Adda b. Aḥa:[6] This means where one bales out from it.[7] But the Divine Law saith, *'Thereat'*?[8]—*They should wash*[9] is to include any service vessel.[10] If so, then a profane vessel too [should be fit]?—Said Abaye: You cannot say [that] a profane vessel [is fit], this being deduced from its base, *a fortiori*: If its base, which was anointed together with it [the laver], does not sanctify [the water poured into it],[11] is it not logical that a profane vessel, which was not anointed with it, does not sanctify?

And how do we know [that] its base [does not sanctify]? Because it was taught: R. Judah said: You might think that the base sanctifies, just as the laver sanctifies; therefore it says, *Thou shalt also make a laver of brass, and the base thereof of brass.*[12] I have made it alike in respect of brass, but not in respect of anything else. Mar Zuṭra the son of R. Mari said to Rabina: As for its base, [it does not sanctify] because it is not made for its inside [to be used]; will you say [the same of] a profane vessel, which is made for its inside?[13] Rather, *'thereat'* excludes a profane vessel. If so, [it excludes] a service vessel too?—Surely the Divine Law included [it by writing] *'they should wash'*. And what [reason] do you see [for this
a choice]?[1]—The one [a service vessel] needs anointing like itself [the laver], while the other does not need anointing like itself.

Resh Laḳish said: Whatever can make up [the prescribed quantity of] the water of a *miḳweh*,[2] makes up the water of the laver;[3] but it does not make up to a *rebi'ith*.[4] What does this exclude? Shall we say, it excludes miry [liquid] clay?[5] then how is it meant? If a cow would bend and drink thereof,[6] it is [fit] even for a *rebi'ith* too;[7] while if a cow would not bend and drink thereof, it cannot make up even [the quantity of] a *miḳweh* too! Again, if it is to exclude red insects,[8] [these are permitted] even in the mass,[9] for surely it was taught: R. Simeon b. Gamaliel said: You may perform immersion in whatever originates in the water; while R. Isaac b. Abdimi said: You may perform immersion in the eye of a fish![10]—Said R. Papa: It excludes the case where one added a *se'ah* and took out a *se'ah*. For we learnt: If a *miḳweh* had exactly forty *se'ah*, and one added a *se'ah* and took out a *se'ah*, it is fit. And Rab Judah b. Shila said in R. Assi's name in R. Joḥanan's name: Up to the greater part thereof.[11] R. Papa said: If one cut out a *rebi'ith* therein,
b one may bathe needles and hooks,[1] since it is derived from a valid *miḳweh*.[2]

R. Jeremiah said in the name of Resh Laḳish: The water of a *miḳweh* is fit for the water of the laver.[3] Are we to say that it [the water of the laver] need not be 'living' water? Surely it was taught: [*But its inwards and its legs shall he wash*] *with water*,[4] but not with wine; *'with water,'* but not with a mixture;[5] *'with water'* includes any water,[6] and all the more [does it include] the water of the laver. Now what does 'and all the more the water of the laver' imply? Surely that it is 'living' water?[7]—No: it means, which is holy.[8] Is then its holiness an advantage? Surely the school of Samuel taught:

(5) In that case it is certainly insufficient for four priests. (6) Sh. M. emends: Ahabah. (7) Tosaf.: the priest takes up water from the laver with a small vessel. This need not contain a *rebi'ith*, but the laver must contain the larger quantity. Rashi translates and explains differently. (8) Rashi: which implies that one must wash from the *laver* only. Tosaf.: which implies that any other vessel used must be of the same size as the laver. (9) Ex. XL, 32. (10) *'They should wash'* is superfluous, and is therefore regarded as an extension. (11) To be used for this purpose.—This implies that the base itself could hold water. (12) Ibid. XXX, 18 (13) Surely not.

a (1) For excluding the one and including the other; why not reverse it? (2) V. Glos. A *miḳweh* must contain not less than forty *se'ahs* water. Yet if it is short of this quantity, it can be made up with other liquids, as enumerated in Miḳ. VII, 1 q.v. (3) If it contains insufficient for the lustrations of four priests. (4) Which is required for the ordinary washing of the hands before eating food. (5) Reading *narok*, as in Suk. 19b *et passim*. Edd. have here *nadok*, which Rashi translates, thin clay, such that can be poured from one vessel into another. (6) If it is so loose that its presence in water would not deter a cow from drinking it. (7) If the *rebi'ith* is partly made up of such miry clay, it is sufficient and valid for the ritual washing of the hands. (8) Which originate in the water. (9) Even if the whole *miḳweh* consists of these, it is fit, whereas Resh Laḳish permits them only to make up the prescribed quantity. (10) A huge fish whose eye had dissolved in its socket. (11) Any liquid other than water can sometimes make up the quantity and sometimes not. Thus: if the *miḳweh* contains thirty nine *se'ahs* and another is added of a different liquid, it is not valid. But if it contains forty, and then a different liquid is added and a *se'ah* of water is removed, it remains fit. For it was fit without the added *se'ah*, and this *se'ah* becomes null (loses its identity) in the rest, and so the *miḳweh* remains fit. Rab Judah says that it remains fit even if in this way one removes up to (but not including) the greater part of the water. But if one has a *rebi'ith* of water, adds a little of another liquid, and then removes the same quantity, it is not fit, because a *rebi'ith* is too little for the other liquid to lose its identity in it.

b (1) If one cuts out a little hollow in the side of a full-sized *miḳweh* and the water flows into it, you may purify these small objects in it, even though it is not freely joined to the larger *miḳweh*. (2) Lit., 'Since it comes from the fitness of a *miḳweh*'. (3) Though the former is not 'living' (i.e. running) water, it may be drawn into the laver. (4) Lev. I, 9. (5) Two parts water and one part wine. (6) Even non-running. (7) For that is apparently its only superiority, and so the passage does not refer to the actual water of the laver, but means any living water. (8) I.e., all the more is the water of the laver (actual) fit, seeing that it is holy.

בין שאין בהן רביעית ובלבד שיהו כלי שרת אמר רב אדא בר א] אחא *בקודח בתוכו והא ממנו אמר רחמנא ירחצו ב'לרבות כלי שרת אי הכי כלי חול נמי אמר אביי כלי חול לא מצית אמרת מקל וחומר מכנו ומה כנו שנמשח עמו אינו מקדש כלי חול שאינו נמשח עמו אינו דין שאינו מקדש וכנו מנלן דתניא ר' יהודה אומר יכול יהא כנו מקדש כדרך שהכיור מקדש תלמוד לומר °ועשית כיור נחשת וכנו נחשת לנחשת הקשתיו ולא לדבר אחר אמר ליה מר זוטרא בריה דרב מרי לרבינא מה לכנו שאין עשוי לתוכו תאמר בכלי חול שעשוי לתוכו אלא ממנו ג'למעוטי כלי חול אי הכי כלי שרת נמי הא רבי רחמנא ירחצו ומה ראית זה טעון משיחה כמוהו וזה אין טעון משיחה כמוהו: אמר ריש לקיש ד'כל המשלים למי מקוה משלים למי כיור לרביעית אינו משלים למעוטי מאי אילימא למעוטי טיט *הנדוק היכי דמי ה'אי דפרה שוחה ושותה ממנו אפי' לרביעית נמי ואי אין פרה שוחה ושותה ממנו אפילו למקוה נמי אין משלים ג] אלא למעוטי יבחושין אדומין אפילו בעינייהו נמי דהא תניא רשב"ג אומר ו'כל שתחילת ברייתו מן המים מטבילין בו ג] ואמר רב יצחק בר אבדימי ז'מטבילין בעינו של דג אמר רב פפא ח'למעוטי נתן סאה ונטל סאה *דתנן °מקוה שיש בו מ' סאה מכוונות נתן סאה ונטל סאה הרי זה כשר ואמר רב יהודה בר שילא אמר רב אסי א"ר יוחנן ט'עד רובו אמר רב פפא אםקדח בו רביעית מטבילין בו מחטין וצינוריות הואיל ומהכשירא דמקוה אתיא א"ר ירמיה אמר ריש לקיש מי מקוה כשירים למי כיור למימרא דלא מים חיים נינהו והתניא °במים *י'ולא ביין במים ולא במזוג במים לרבות שאר מים וק"ו למי כיור מאי ק"ו למי כיור לאו דמים חיים נינהו לא ד] (לקדוש) דקדיש וקדישי מעליותא היא והא תנא ה] *רבי שמואל מים שאין להם שם לווי יצאו

רש"י

בין שאין בהן רביעית. הלוג מים ואע"ג ו] *דליכא שיעורא (א) גבי נטילת ידים לגבי קידוש לא בעינן שיעור: בקודח (ב) בתוכו. קודח דופנו של כיור ותוחב בתוכו כלי קטן ומקלחו לחוץ ויונק מימי הכיור ומוליא ז] *אבל באפיה נפשיה בעינן שיעור ארבעה כהנים: והא ממנו כתיב. אמתני' פריך דאמר כל כלי שרת ראויין הם לקדש ח]: ירחצו. ובקרבתם אל המזבח ירחצו קרא יתירא הוא האי ירחצו דהא כתיב לעיל מיניה ורחצו ממנו וסמיך ליה בבואם אל אהל מועד ובקרבתם אל המזבח לא לכתוב ירחצו דהא אורחצו הסמוך קאי: שנמשח עמו. ונתקדש במשיחתו כמותו אינו מקדש ידים ורגלים: לנחושת הקשתיו. לא בהיקשא יליף לה אלא כלומר [דימיתיו לכיור] להיות של נחשת הכן כמו הכיור (דימיתיו לכיור): ולא לדבר אחר. לא היקשתי שניהם בפסוק אחד ללמוד שאר דברים ולומר שכנו מקדש כמותו דמדאיצטריך למיכתב נחשת גבי כנו זימנא אחריתי שמע מינה לאו לאקשינהו בעי דאי איתקוש נחשת נמי ניתי בהיקשא אלא שמע מינה למאי ט] דדמיא פריש בהדיא ולמאי דלא פריש לא דמיא: לנחשת. לענין נחשת י] הקשתיו: הקשתיו. דימיתיו: כל המשלים למקוה. במסכת מקואות (פ"ז מ"א) תנן יש מעלין ולא פוסלין מעלין משלימין לארבעים סאה והתם יא] מפרש להו: משלים למי כיור. לשיעור ד' כהנים: לרביעית. של נטילת ידים אינו משלים: למעוטי מאי. אתא דאין משלים לרביעית: אילימא למעוטי טיט הנדוק. שהוא מן המעלין את המקוה כדקתני התם: נדוק. יב] דק שראוי להריקו מכלי אל כלי: אי דפרה שוחה ושותה ממנו. שאינו עב ליפסל משתיית בהמה: אפי' לרביעית נמי. דכל זמן יג] *שנפסלו משתיית בהמה בין בכלי בין בקרקע פסולין הא לא נפסלו כשרין: אפי' למקוה נמי לא. דלא נדוק הוא: יבחושין אדומין. כמין יתושין בלא כנפים כדרך שגדל בשולי חביות של יין שלנו מבחוץ יבחושים דקין אף הן נבראים מן המים: אפי' בעינייהו נמי. אם כל המקוה נעשה מהן כשר וריש לקיש נקט ליטנא דהשלמה: בעינו של דג. דג גדול שנימוק שומן עינו בחורו: למעוטי נתן סאה ונטל סאה. למעוטי הנך מינים דתנן בהן לגבי מקוה פעמים מעלין ופעמים אין מעלין מי פירות וכל משקה שאינו מים ותמד משהחמיץ וקתני התם פעמים מעלין פעמים אין מעלין כילד מקוה שיש בו ל"ט סאין ונפלה יד] סאה מהן לתוכ' לא העלתהו פירוש לא השלימתהו ואף לא פסלתו פעמים דמעלין כילד היו בתוכו ארבעים סאה מכוונות נתן סאה מאלו המינים ונטל סאה אחר הנתינה כשר דבטלו להנך קמאי במקוה השלם הילכך כי חזר ונטל לא מיפסיל נמלא שהמקוה הזה נשלם על ידיהם לכשנטל סאה ודכוותיה בנטילת ידים לא משלמי שאם היתה טו] בו רביעית מים ונתן ממינים הללו לתוכו רובע רביעית ונטל כנגדם פסולה דלא חשיבא שיעור טז] זוטרא דרביעית לבטולינהו: עד רובו. אם עירב בו ממינין הללו עד רובו של מקוה ולא רובו בכלל ע"י נתינת ונטילת סאה כשר: אם קדח רביעית. בדופן המקוה והמים נמשכין שם ואף על פי שנתמעטו המים ואין מעורבין מי המקוה באותה קדיחה: מטבילין בו מחטין כו'. ליצוריות מזלגות קטנות של טווי זהב: מי מקוה. אף על פי שאינן חיין: כשרים. להשאיב הכיור יז] בתוכו למלאות מהן ולתת לתוכו: למימרא. דלא בעי מים חיים: והתניא. בת"כ והקרב והכרעים ירחץ במים ולא במזוג מים ויין מזוגים יחד שני חלקי מים ואחד יין: שאר מים. ואפילו מכונסין: מאי קל וחומר למי כיור לאו יח] [למימרא דמים חיים ניהו. וה"ק ק"ו] למים חיים הראויין לכיור שכשירין לרחילת קרבי קדשים: לא דקדשי. ומי כיור ממש קא יליף בק"ו שרוחלין במימיו קרבים וק"ו שלהן דקדשי הוא: והא תנא דבי שמואל. לא ידענא אהיכא קאי ומיהו שמעינן מינה דהיכא דכתיב מים סתמא אין מי כיור כשרין נו: יכול לרבות שאר מים] *) יכול שאני מרבה אף מי תותין תלמוד לומר מים מים שאין להם שם לווי יצאו מי תותים שיש להם שם לווי **):

תוספות

בין שאין בהן רביעית. למאי דקס"ד בלא קודח יש תימה דגרע מנטילת ידים ויש לומר דנטילת ידים נמי כשיש בו רביעית טפלין אפילו לשנים והכא בדהוה ביה רביעית מעיקרא: והא ממנו אמר רחמנא. פי' בקונטרס דאמתניתין יט] (פריך) דאמר כל כלי שרת ראוין לקדש פריך וקשה תיקשה ליה מתניתין [דיומא] (דף מג:) דקתני דכהן גדול מקדש בקיתון של זהב ונראה דקאי אהא דשני בקודח מתוכו כ] [ופריך] והא ממנו אמר רחמנא דאין לקדש אפי' קודח אלא אם כן יהא כמוהו שיהא בו כשיעור: קודח מתוכו. פי' שנוטל כא] ממימיו בכלי קטן וכשירה לקדש כיון דבאין מכלי גדול וכה"ג לקמן אם קדח בו רביעית מטבילין בו מחטים וצנוריות כב] דמהכשירות דמקוה אתו ובקונטרס לא פירש כן: ק"ן מכנו. משמע שיש לו תוך ועשוי כמין תיבה פרולה למעלה והכיור יושב עליו כג] *ורבי' פי' כעין יורה כפוייה על פיה ונפחתו כד] שוליה: לרביעית אינו משלים. פי' בקונטרס לרביעית לנטילת ידים וקלת כה] תימה והיה נראה לפרש לרביעית היינו להטביל מחטין וצנוריות דבהכי מיירי בסוף שמעתא ומיהו נראה כפירוש הקונט' דבימי ר"ל כבר בטלו רביעית דמקוה כדמוכח בנזיר בפרק שלשה מינים (דף לח.): למעוטי טיט *הנדוק. אע"ג דמשלים למי מקוה אין מטבילין בו כדאמר בפרק קמא דסוכה (דף יט.) גבי אויר מלטרף ואין ישינים תחתיו ופריך מי איכא מידי דאיהו לא חזי ומלטרף וקאמר טיט הנדוק יוכיח ולא כמו שפירש שם בקונטרס דאע"ג דמשלים כדתנן במסכת מקואות פ"ז אלו מעלין ולא פוסלין מי השלג והברד וטיט הנדוק מכל מקום אם עשה מקוה שלם מטיט הנדוק לא עלתה לו טבילה דלפירושו אין זה יוכיח דטיט הנדוק בשעה שהוא משלים חזי לטבילה ולא דמי כו] [לאויר] דאין ישינים תחתיו אפי' בשעה שהוא משלים לפיכך נראה [דטיט הנדוק נמי] אפי' בשעה שמלטרף אין מטבילין בו והכי תנן במסכת מקואות פ"ב (מ"י) מקוה שיש בו מ' סאה כז] וטיט רבי אליעזר אומר מטבילין במים ואין מטבילין בטיט רבי יהושע אומר בטיט ובמים באיזה טיט אמרו בטיט שהמים לפין על גביו ואם היו המים מלד אחד מודה רבי יהושע שמטבילין במים ואין מטבילין בטיט באיזה טיט אמרו בטיט שהקנה יורד מאליו כח] בתוכו דברי רבי מאיר רבי יהודה אומר מקום שאין קנה המדה עומד אבא כט] אליעזר [בן דילאי] אומר מקום שהמשקולת יורדת רבי אליעזר אומר היורד בפי חבית רבי שמעון אומר ל] היורד בשפופרת הנוד רבי אליעזר ברבי לדוק אומר הנמדד בלוג והיינו טיט הנדוק דסוכה (דף יט:) דאמר יוכיח לא] [דכשהטיט מלד א' מלטרף לכ"ע ואין מטבילין בו]: אפילו לרביעית. כאן פי' בקונטרס דאמרינן פרק כל הבשר (חולין דף קו.) מים שנפסלו משתיית בהמה בין בכלים בין בקרקע פסולין הא לא נפסלו כשירים ואינו כן דהתם תניא בהדיא בקרקע כשירים ופליגי התם באפסקא בבת בירתא אבל במקומן כשירין לכולי עלמא ואפי' מקוה והא דקאמר הכא אי אין פרה שוחה ושותה ממנו אפילו למקוה נמי אינו משלים לא קשיא מידי דהתם במים צלולים מיירי בלא טיט אלא שהם סרוחים ונפסלו משתיית בהמה והכא מיירי בנוים עבים שנפסלו על ידי טיט המעורב בהן ויש תימה מנא ליה האי שיעורא דכל הני תנאי דמסכת מקואות (פ"ב) לא מיירו בשתיית פרה לב]: נתן סאה כשר. במי פירות מיירי כדפי' פרק הערל (יבמות דף פב:) אבל מים שאובין אפי' כל היום כולו לג] [כשר דראשון ראשון בטל] ויש תימה דגבי קרב וכרעים דרשינן במים ולא במזוג והכא גבי לד] *כיור כתיב במים ומכשרינן במזוג: והא תנא *רבי שמואל. פי' בקונטרס לא ידענא אהיכא קאי ומיהו בתורת כהנים תניא לה] [והקרב והכרעים ירחץ במים ולא ביין ולא במזוג במים לרבות שאר מים] *) יכול שאני מרבה אף מי תותין תלמוד לומר מים מים שאין להם שם לווי יצאו מי תותים שיש להם שם לווי **):

*) [בת"כ שלפנינו לא נמצא עדיין] **) [ע' בהרא"ש ריש פי"ד דנגעים ד"ה מים חיים כו' ושמא אכך מתניא וכו' ע"ש דגם בת"כ שהעתיק בזה"ל מים חיים ולא מלוחים ולא פושרים ולא המכזבים וכו' לא נמצא עדיין בת"כ שלפנינו]

עין משפט נר מצוה

נו א מיי' פ"ה מהל' ביאת מקדש הל' יא בהשגה וסמג עשין קעה:

נז ב ג מיי' שם הל"ט:

נח ד מיי' שם הלי"ב:

נט ה מיי' שם ומיי' פ"ח מהל' מקוואות הל"ט סמג עשין רמח טוש"ע או"ח סי' קס סעי' ט:

ס ו ז מיי' שם הלכה יא טוש"ע יו"ד סי' רא סעי' לג וטוש"ע או"ח סי' קס סעי' י:

סא ח מיי' פ"ז שם הלכה ו:

סב ט י מיי' פ"ד שם הלכה ז טוש"ע יו"ד סי' רא סעי' כד:

סג כ מיי' פ"ו מהל' מעה"ק הל"ץ:

שיטה מקובצת

א] בר אהבה תיבת אחא נמחק: ב] אלא למעוטי. פי' קושיא היא ותירוצא דקושיא זו מיתרצא לקמי' אמר רב פפא למעוטי נתן סאה וכו' וק"ל: ג] ואמר. וא"ת והלא שלג וברד משלימין למקוה אבל בעינייהו לא וי"ל דשלג וברד אין תחילתו מן המים הילכך לא מהני בהו בעינייהו וברד היינו גרילא ולא גרילילא. תו"א: ד] תיבת לקדוש נמחק: ה] תנא. דבי תיבת ר' ל"ש: ו] ואע"ג. דבעינן שיעורא: ז] ומוציא. ס"א ואותו כלי אינו מחזיק רביעית אבל הכיור עצמו בעינן: ח] לקדש. והא ממנו כתיב דמשמע דוקא ממש מן הכיור: ט] למאי. דדמי: י] נחשת. הס"ד ומה"ד הקשתיו. דימיתיו הס"ד: יא] מפרש. מאן נינהו הס"ד: יב] נדוק רך שראוי: יג] זמן. שלא נפסלו משתית בהמה ולא נעשה בהם מלאכה כשרים לידים דהכי תנן התם ומייתי לה בפ' כל הבשר מים שנפסלו משתית בהמה: יד] (ונפלה) [ונפל] (בה) סאה תיבת מהן נמחק: טו] תיבת בו נמחק: טז] שיעור. זוטרתא: יז] הכיור. לתוכו או למלאות: יח] לאו. למימרא דמים חיים נינהו בתמיה וה"ק ק"ו: יט] דאמתניתין פריך דאמר כל כלי ראוין לקדש וקשה תקשה ליה מתניתין דיומא: כ] מתוכו. אבל לעולם ידע שפיר דאם יש שיעור בכלי שרת דמקדשין בו כמו בכיור אבל קשיא ליה למאי דשני בקודח מתוכו דמשמע דלית בהכשיעור וסש"ה פריך: כא] ממימיו לשון הר"פ פרש"י שנוקב בכיור נקב מצדו ומדבקין שם כלי אחד קטן שמקלח מים לקדש ולא נהירא דפשיטא דהוי כמו כיור גופיה ומאי פריך ממנו אמר רחמנא. לכן נראה שנוטל אותו בכלי קטן ונותן אותו תוך הכיור ונוטל מימיו ומקדש בו וכה"ג כשרים לקדש כיון דמכלי גדול קא אתי וכה"ג כו': כב] דמהכשירא: כג] ורבינו. ש"י פי' בחומש: כד] שולים. גליון ולא נראה רא"ב לא היה יכול לקדש ממנו. תו' מהר"פ: כה] וקצת היה נראה לפרש: כו] דמי. לאויר: כז] סאה. טיט ומים: כח] תיבת בתוכו נמחק: כט] אלעזר בן דולעי: ל] ר"ש אומר הנכנס בשפופרת: לא] יוכיח. דכשהטיט מצד אחד מצטרף לכ"ע ואין מטבילין בו. לב] פרה. גליון ונראה התם דלא איירי אלא לענין הטבלה במים מפליג בין קנה יורד ואינך חילוקים כדמפרש התם אבל הכא איירי בהטבלה בטיט עצמו ובקנה יורד עצמו איכא לאפלוגי ולא משכחת ליה אלא בין שוחה ושותה הפרה לאין שוחה ושותה. תו' חיצוניות: לג] כולו. כשר דראשון ראשון בטל: לד] גבי טבילה ותיבת כיור ל"ש ונמחק: לה] תניא. כה"ג:

הגהות הב"ח

(א) רש"י ד"ה בין וכו' לגבי נטילה: (ב) ד"ה בקודח מתוכו כצ"ל וכן בגמרא.

מסורת הש"ס

כ"ה דנפיק

ר"ה ולאותו הכלי אינו צריך להחזיק רביעית אבל בכיור עצמו בעינן שיעור ד' כהנים

ז"ק

ז"ק מ"ז

[בסוכה יח: ובן ברים פ"ז דמקוואות אי' הגדוק ברי"ש וכן בפירוש הרמב"ם והרכב מכרעטורה והתוי"ט גרסו כולם פירש"י בסוכה יט: הגדוק שראוי להוריקו מכלי אל כלי וכו' ולע"ק בפרש"י דסכה ד"ה נדוק]

יבמות פב: מקוואות פ"ז משנה ב

נ"א שלא נפסלו משתיית בהמה כשרין לידים כדאית' בפ' כל הבשר מים שנפסלו כו'

[תורת כהנים]

[צ"ל דבי]

רש"ק

עין משפט נר מצוה

מד א מיי' פ"ה מהל' ביאת מקדש הלי"ב :
מה ב מיי' פ"ד שם הלכה ט : [עיין לעיל במשנה טו:]
מו ג ד מיי' פ"ב שם הלכה יב :
[וע"ע תוס' חגיגה ד: ד"ה דמרבה]
עיין בחילופי גירסאות

גמרא

יצאו מי כיור שיש להם שם לווי אלא לאו דראויין למי כיור אלמא מים חיים נינהו תנאי היא *דאמר ר' יוחנן מי כיור ר' ישמעאל אומר מי מעין הן וחכמים אומרים [א]שאר מימות הן : ערל : מנלן *אמר רב חסדא דבר זה מתורת משה רבינו לא למדנו מדברי יחזקאל בן בוזי למדנו °כל בן נכר ערל לב וערל בשר לא יבא אל מקדשי (לשרתני) ומנלן דמחלי עבודה דכתיב °בהביאכם א] (את) בני נכר ערלי לב וערלי בשר להיות במקדשי לחלל את ביתי : תנו רבנן בן נכר ב] יכול בן נכר ממש תלמוד לומר ערל לב אם כן מה תלמוד לומר בן נכר שנתנכרו מעשיו לאביו שבשמים ואין לי אלא ערל לב ערל בשר מנין תלמוד לומר וערל בשר *וצריכי דאי כתב רחמנא ערל בשר משום דמאיס אבל ערל לב דלא מאיס אימא לא ואי אשמעינן ערל לב משום דאין לבו לשמים אבל ערל בשר דלבו לשמים אימא לא צריכי : טמא פסול : אמרו זקני דרום לא שנו אלא טמא שרץ אבל טמא מת ג] מתוך שמרצה בציבור מרצה נמי ביחיד אי הכי טמא שרץ נמי ליתי בקל וחומר מטמא מת מה טמא מת שטעון הזאה שלישי ושביעי מרצה טמא שרץ שאינו טעון הזאה ג' ושביעי אינו דין שמרצה קסברי זקני דרום מכפרין כמתכפרין מה מתכפרין [ב]טמא מת אין טמא שרץ לא אף מכפרין טמא מת אין טמא שרץ לא מאי קסברי אי קסברי *אין שוחטין וזורקין על טמא שרץ אמאי לא עבדי ציבור בטומאה הא כל שביחיד נדחה ציבור עבדי בטומאה אלא קסברי שוחטין וזורקין על טמא שרץ אמר עולא תקע להו (א) ר"ל לדרומאי וכי איזה כח מרובה כח מכפרין או כח מתכפרין הוי אומר כח מתכפרין ומה במקום [ג]שנטמאו בעלים בשרץ ד] משלחין קרבנותיהן כהן שנטמא בשרץ אינו מרצה ה] מקום שנטמאו בעלים במת [ד]שאין משלחין קרבנותיהן כהן שנטמא במת אינו דין שאינו מרצה ו] קסברי זקני דרום טמא מת [נמי] משלח קרבנותיו והכתיב °איש איש כי יהיה טמא ועשה פסח בחדש השני וגו' למצוה והא כתיב °איש לפי

תורה אור: יחזקאל מד | שם | במדבר ט | שמות יב

רש"י

יכול בן נכר ממש . עובד כוכבים : תלמוד לומר ערל לב . אינו נפסל אלא מחמת ערלות לבו אלמא בכהן קאמר : שנתנכרו מעשיו . נחשבים לנכרים למקום : ערל בשר . והוא צדיק מנין : טמא פסול . דתנן במתני' ז] טמא מחלל עבודה ועל כרחיך בקרבן יחיד קאמר דאילו קרבן צבור קרב בטומאה : מתוך שמרצה בצבור . לכתחילה : מרצה ביחיד . דיעבד על ידי ח] שהציץ מרצה עליו והאי דבטומאת מת פשיטא לן דכתיב במועדו ואפי' בטומאה משמע בין ט] שכהן (נמי) טמא בין שהצבור טמאין ומדגלי בדוכתא אחריתי גבי טומאת בעלים דכי אישתראי טומאה בצבור במת אישתראי דכתיב איש (ב) כי יהיה טמא לנפש ילפינן מינה איש נדחה ואין צבור נדחין אף גבי כהן המרצה נמי במת אישתראי : אי הכי ל"ג : טמא שרץ נמי ליתי בקל וחומר . דמרצה בצבור לכתחילה בק"ו מטמא מת : קסברי זקני דרום . דאמרי מת דווקא: מכפרין כמתכפרין. כשהותרה טומאה בצבור שניהם היו במשמע הכהן והצבור דהא י] ממועדו נפקא לן (פסחים דף עז.) הילכך כהן כציבור מה כשהותרה טומאה אצל רוב צבור שנטמאו טמא מת הותר ולא טמא שרץ יא] [אף כשהותר לכהן בקרבן צבור מת הותר ולא שרץ] : מאי קסברי . זקני דרום דפשיטא להו דלא הותרה טומאת שרץ אצל רוב צבור ותיתי בקל וחומר : אי קסברי אין שוחטין וזורקין . את הפסח על יחיד טמא שרץ יב] ואף ע"ג דיכול לטבול ולאכול לערב ואיכא למ"ד בפסחים (דף צ:) [דס"ל] הכי ויליף לה מאיש איש כי יהיה טמא לנפש ואפילו חל שביעי שלו ערב הפסח במשמע דהוה ליה כטמא שרץ יג] : אמאי לא עבדי ציבור בטומאה הא כל שביחיד נדחה צבור עבדי בטומאה. דאיש ולא ציבור קאמר רחמנא : אלא סברי (ג) יד] לן כמ"ד התם שוחטין וזורקין על טמא שרץ . הואיל וחזי לאורתא הילכך צבור טמאי שרץ אף הן לא הותר להן ליכנס לעזרה טמאין אלא ישלחו קרבנותיהם לעזרה טו] ויקריבוהו כהנים טהורין ויטבלו ויאכלו לערב דלא הותרה להם טומאה אלא במקום שאילו לא הותרה היו נדחין הילכך טמא מת שאינו מותר לאכול לערב טז] הותר להן אבל טומאת שרץ לא ואין כאן ק"ו שהרי יכולין לעשותו בטהרה : תקע להו . צעק להם קול גדול : איזה כח מרובה . לדחות את הטומאה : הוי אומר כח מתכפרין . כדמפרש ואזיל (ד) שהיחיד טמא שרץ משלח קרבנו לעזרה כדקאמריתו שוחטין וזורקין על טמא שרץ והכהן המרצה בו אם נטמא בשרץ פסול לו כדמוקמיתו מתני' דקתני טמא פסול בטמא שרץ : מקום שאם נטמאו בעלים כו' . יחיד שנטמא במת אין משלח פסחו לעזרה לשחוט עליו יז] [אלא נדחה לפסח שני] כדכתיב איש איש כי יהיה וגו' ואע"ג דכחו מרובה משל כהן אצל שרץ : כהן שנטמא במת אינו דין שאינו מרצה. שהרי כחו רע משל בעלים אצל שרץ ואמאי אמרי זקני דרום מרצה ביחיד מגו דמרצה בצבור : טמא מת נמי . יחיד טמא מת נמי משלח קרבנותיו כלומר אם שילח פסחו לעזרה ושחטו וזרקו עליו פטור מלעשות פסח שני ואף על פי שלא יאכל יח] ממנו דקסברי אכילת פסחים לא מעכבת ומיהו לכתחילה אמר רחמנא (ה) נדחה לפסח שני וצבור עבדי בטומאה הילכך כהן המכפר בקרבן יחיד מתוך שמרצה [בצבור] לכתחילה מרצה ביחיד דיעבד : והכתיב איש איש וגו' ועשה פסח בחדש השני . אלמא מידחי : לפי הכא

תוספות

יצאו מי כיור שיש להם שם לווי . הא דאמרינן בסוכה (דף יג.) ובחולין (דף סב:) כל שנשתנה שמו קודם מתן תורה ובאה תורה והקפידה עליו זהו שם לווי לא קשיא מידי דכך שמו מי כיור בשעת מתן תורה : *ערל . מפרש *רבינו שלמה יט] בכל מקום שמתו אחיו מחמת מילה ור"ת מפרש דמומר לערלות וקרי ליה לבו לשמים לפי שאינו עושה אלא מדאגת צער המילה ובריש הערל (יבמות דף ע.) פירשתי*: משום דאין לבו לשמים. אפילו שב בשעת עבודה אמרינן בסוף מנחות (דף קט.) דאין קרבנו ריח ניחוח ואע"ג דהשתא לבו לשמים מתחילה לא היה לבו *לשמים : אבל טמא מת . פירוש קודם שביעי מרצה אפי' בקרבן יחיד על ידי ציץ מתוך שמרצה בלא ציץ והא דאמר עון הקדשים ולא עון מקדישים מוקמינן להו בטומאת שרץ וכן כל טומאת מת דשמעתין היינו קודם שביעי שלו אבל בשביעי היינו כמו טמא שרץ דאינו מרצה ביחיד לפי ששוחטין וזורקין עליו וגם אינו מרצה בצבור טמא מת בשביעי [נמי] לפי שיכולין לעשות ע"י שלוחין טהורים ולאורתא מצו אכלי הפסח בטהרה . ברוך : אי הכי טמא שרץ נמי . בקונטרס לא גרס אי הכי כ] דאפי' לית לן מתוך שמרצה כו' מצי לאקשויי הך פירכא טמא שרץ לירצי בצבור מקל וחומר מטמא מת ויש ליישב אי הכי דקאמרת מתוך שמרצה וכו' וילפת יחיד בדיעבד מצבור לכתחילה א"כ טמא שרץ נמי לירצי ביחיד דהא מרצה הוא בציבור מק"ו דטמא מת אבל אי לאו מתוך לא הוה קשיא מידי דאמינא דמתני' דפסלה טמא איירי בין בטמא מת בין בטמא שרץ ועוד יש לפרש כי נמי אמרינן מתוך הוה לכו לאוקמי מתני' בזב ומצורע מי שטומאה יוצאת מגופו אבל טמא מת ושרץ לא דמרצו ביחיד בדיעבד הואיל ומרצו בצבור לכתחילה ושרץ מקל וחומר ומשני טמא שרץ אינו מרצה בציבור לכתחילה שהרי מכפרין כמתכפרין ובמתכפרין טמאי שרץ אינן עושים פסח בטומאה שהרי שוחטין וזורקין על טמא שרץ וכל שאין היחיד נדחה אין צבור עושין בטומאה אלא שולחין שלוחיהן הטהורים ועושים פסחיהן בשבילם וא"כ איכא למיפרך מה לטמא מת שכן מרצה בצבור מה שאין כן בטמא שרץ : [הגה"ה] . ורבינו תם גרס אי הכי ומפרש דבמועדו אפי' בטומאה היינו בין במת בין בשרץ בין דפסח בין דתמיד והא דקאמרי זקני דרום לא שנו אלא טמא שרץ אבל טמא מת מתוך שמרצה בצבור איירי בריצוי של אכילה בטומאה כלומר מתוך שמרצה ריצוי גדול שנאכל בטומאת בעלים במת מרצה נמי ביחיד ששימש בטומאת מת אבל טמא שרץ נהי דיש לו ריצוי בצבור כגון היכא דנטמאו הכהנים או הסכינים בשרץ דעבדי בטומאה דבמועדו אמר רחמנא ואפילו בטומאה וכל שביחיד נדחה בצבור עבדי בטומאה מ"מ אין לו ריצוי גדול כמו מת ואילו נטמאו צבור בשרץ כא] אין להם לאכול בטומאה כמו שאמר לבסוף ופריך אי הכי טמא שרץ נמי כיון דאמרת דבטומאת מת מרצה ביחיד מטעם דמרצה בצבור דאכלי בטומאת מת א"כ טמא שרץ נמי בקרבן יחיד לירצי מקל וחומר מטמא מת כב] דיחיד ומשני קסברי זקני דרום מכפרין פירוש דיחיד כמתכפרין דטמא מת אין טמא שרץ לא *) ואם תאמר ומנ"ל דבמועדו איירי אף בטומאת שרץ אי ממשמעותא דמועדו אם כן אפילו זב ומצורע אי מקל וחומר דמת שטעון שלישי ושביעי מה לטומאת מת שכן אישתראי לאכול בטומאת בעלים תאמר בשרץ דאם נטמאו בעלים בשרץ לא אכלי כג] [ויש לומר דהאי דלא אכלי] לאו משום חומר דשרץ אלא משום דשוחטין וזורקין עליו [ולא] איפטר ליה מפסח וכה"ג במת בשביעי שלו אם היו רוב צבור טמאים בשביעי שיכולים ליטהר לערב לא הוו אכלי בטומאה וקשה לפירוש ר"ת כי היכי דאמר מכפרין כמתכפרים כד] [למעוטי טומאת שרץ דלא לירצי ביחיד] הכי נמי נימא בציבור ודווקא טמא מת ולא טמא שרץ ואי משום דאתי קל וחומר ומפיק מהיקשא הכא

*) עיין ל"ק בדיבור זה שהאריך

שיטה מקובצת

א] תיבת את נמחק : ב] יכול בן נכר ממש . תימה תיפוק ליה שהוא זר וי"ל דשמא פסול דזרות לא שייך אלא מבני ישראל . ת"א : ג] עי' בהשמטות בסוף המסכת : ד] בשרץ . שמשלחין : ה] מקום שנטמאו בעלים במת כו' . וקשה דמה לשרץ שאינו מרצה בצבור כלל לפ"ה תאמר במת שמרצה בצבור ואף לפר"ת איכא למיפרך מה לשרץ שכן אינו מרצה לענין אכילת בעלים בטומאה כדפי' לעיל תאמר במת שכן מרצה לענין אכילת בעלים בטומאה נמי ואומר הר"ם דאין זה ק"ו אלא סתירת דברים בעלמא על מה שאמרו זקני דרום דלענין מכפרים בטמא מת אין חילוק בין צבור ליחיד ואע"ג דלענין מתכפרים יש חילוק בין צבור ליחיד כדפרישית וע"ז פריך דאדרבה יש לי לדון ק"ו אחר דמשמע דאיכא הרצאה לבעלים יותר מלגבי כהן שהרי גרע טפי מבעלים דבעלים משלחין קרבנותיהן וכהן לא מרצה וא"כ כ"ש שיש לנו לומר דגריעותא שהוא בבעלים דטמא מת שאינו משלח שיהיה בכהן שנטמא במת שלא ירצה ולהשוות כהן לבעלים לענין מת ביחיד וכמו דבעלים יש חילוק בין צבור ליחיד כמו כן בכהנים נחלק בין צבור ליחיד כיון דבשרץ הורע כח כהן מכח בעלים וא"כ בקל יש לנו לומר דלא אמרינן מתוך . הר"פ : ו] קסברי [זקני דרום] טמא מת נמי כו' וא"כ הו"ל אינו נדחה ביחיד וכל שאינו נדחה ביחיד אין צבור מביא (טומאה) [בטומאה] כדאמרי' בפסח שני וא"ת א"כ טומא' דהורצה במת היכי משכחת לה וי"ל כיון דאם בא יחיד לימלך אמרינן ליה תמתין עד פסח שני כדמסיק הכא למצוה (נדחה) [קרינא] שפיר [נדחה] (קרינא) כיון דאינו מרצה לכתחילה : ז] קאי . כלומר דקתני במתני' ותיבת דתנן ל"ש ונמחק: ח] ידי . הציץ שמרצה : ט] בין . שהכהן : י] מבמועדו : יא] שרץ . אף כשהותר לכהן בקרבן צבור מת הותר ולא שרץ : יב] שרץ. ונדחה לפסח שני ואע"ג כו' לערב . דאיכא מ"ד בפסחים : יג] שרץ . שאינו מחוסר אלא טבילה והזאה ויכול ליטהר כדי לאכול הפסח בלילה והכי משמע קרא דכתיב ולא יכלו לעשות הפסח ביום ההוא דמשמע הא למחר יכולין לעשותו . הס"ד : יד] להו. כמ"ד : טו] לעזרה. ויקריבו : טז] לערב . אם אינו בשביעי שלו הותר : יז] עליו. אלא נדחה לפסח שני : יח] יאכל. היינו דקסברי אכילת פסחים לא מעכבי ומיהו כו' רחמנא . יחיד נדחה לפסח שני וצבור עבדי בטומאה כו' שמרצה . בצבור לכתחלה : יט] שלמה . ז"ל : כ] מתיבות דאפילו כו' עד תיבות משא"כ בטמא שרץ מוקף חצי לבנה ואח"כ צ"ל ע"כ הג"ה: כא] בשרץ . אינו נאכל בטומאה: כב] מטמא מת . בקרבן : כג] לא אכלי. וי"ל דהאי דלא אכלי בצבור לאו : כד] כמתכפרים למעוטי טמא שרץ דלא לירצי ביחיד ה"נ נימא בצבור דמכפר בצבור כמתכפר בצבור ולא "הא כהן מרצה בצבור בטומאת שרץ ולא ידחה במועדו אלא דוקא טמא :

הגהות הב"ח

(א) גמ' תקע להו (ר"ל) [ריש לקיש] תא"מ וכ"ב סלא ריש גלותא : (ב) רש"י ד"ה מרצה וכו' דכתיב איש איש : (ג) ד"ה אלא סברי לה כמ"ד : (ד) ד"ה הוי אומר כח וכו' ואזיל ומה במקום שנטמאו וכו' שביחיד טמא : (ה) ד"ה טמא מת וכו' אמר רחמנא יחיד נדחה :

מסורת הש"ס: סוטה טז. | לעיל יח: [וש"נ] | פסחים עז. יבמות עח. | צ"פ | [פסחים סט. וש"נ]

[Only] water which has no special name [is fit],[9] [22*b*] which excludes the water of the laver, which has a special name.[10] Hence it surely means such as is *fit* for the water of the laver,[11] which proves that it must be 'living' water?–It is a controversy of Tannaim. For R. Joḥanan said: As for the laver,—R. Ishmael said: It is the water of a spring;[12] While the Sages maintain: It may be ordinary water.

AN UNCIRCUMCISED [PRIEST]. Whence do we know it?— Said R. Ḥisda: We did not learn this from the Torah of Moses our Teacher, but from the words of Ezekiel the son of Buzi: *No alien, uncircumcised in heart and uncircumcised in flesh, shall enter into My*
a *sanctuary.*[1] And how do we know that they profane the service?[2]— Because it is written, *In that ye have brought in aliens, uncircumcised in heart and uncircumcised in flesh, to be in My sanctuary,* to profane it, *even My house, [when ye offer My bread, the fat and the blood].*[3]

Our Rabbis taught: [It says,] *Alien*: you might think that this means literally an alien; therefore Scripture teaches, *uncircumcised in heart.* If so, why does Scripture call him *'alien'*? Because his actions are alien to his Father in Heaven.[4] Now, I know only [that] the 'uncircumcised in heart'[5] [invalidates the sacrifice]; how do I know that the uncircumcised in flesh [does likewise]? Because the text states, *'and uncircumcised in flesh.'* And they are both necessary. For if the Divine Law wrote [that] one uncircumcised in flesh [is disqualified], I would say that the reason is because he is repulsive; but an 'uncircumcised in heart' is not repulsive, and so he is not disqualified. And if we were informed about an 'uncircumcised in heart', I would say that the reason is that his heart is not toward Heaven, but [as for] an 'uncircumcised in flesh', whose heart is toward Heaven,[6] he is not [disqualified]. Thus both are necessary.

AN UNCLEAN [PRIEST] . . . IS DISQUALIFIED. The Elders of the South said: They learnt this only of [a priest] unclean through a reptile, but [as for] one unclean through a corpse, since [the headplate] propitiates in the case of a public sacrifice, it propitiates in the case of a private sacrifice.[7] If so, let it be deduced from one unclean through a corpse, *a fortiori,* [that] one unclean through a reptile too [does not invalidate the sacrifice]: if [the headplate] propitiates [in the case of] one unclean through a corpse, who must be besprinkled on the third and on the seventh [days of his
b defilement],[1] surely [it] propitiates [in the case of] one unclean through a reptile, who need not be besprinkled on the third and on the seventh [days]?—The Elders of the South hold that those who make atonement [the priests] are like those for whom atonement is made [the people]: as in the case of those for whom atonement is made, if they are unclean through a corpse [the headplate] does [propitiate], but if they are unclean through a reptile [it does] not,[2] so are those who make atonement: one unclean through a corpse is [included in the propitiatory effect of the headplate], whereas one unclean through a reptile is not [included]. What do they [these Elders] hold? If they hold, you may not slaughter [the Passover] and sprinkle [its blood] on behalf of one who is unclean through a reptile,[3] why may the community not sacrifice in uncleanness: surely [it is a principle that] wherever an individual is relegated [to the second Passover], the community celebrates it in uncleanness? Rather, they hold that you do slaughter and sprinkle on behalf of him who is unclean through a reptile.

'Ulla said: Resh Lakish[4] criticised the southern scholars: Now, whose power is greater, the power of those who make atonement, or the power of those for whom atonement is made? Surely, the power of those for whom atonement is made.[5] Then if a priest who was unclean through a reptile cannot propitiate [officiate], though where the owners were defiled by a reptile they can send their sacrifices [to the Temple]; is it not logical that a priest who was defiled by a corpse should not be able to propitiate, seeing that if the owners were defiled by a corpse they cannot send their
c sacrifices?[1]—The Elders of the south hold: One who is unclean through a corpse can also send his sacrifices.[2] But it is written, *If any man of you . . . shall be unclean [by reason of a dead body] . . . yet he shall keep the Passover [unto the Lord] in the second month [on the fourteenth day at dusk they shall keep it]*?[3]—That is a recommendation.[4]

(9) For the washing of the sacrificial parts. (10) It is not called simply water, but the water of the laver. (11) But not the actual water of the laver. (12) I.e., running water.

a (1) Ezek. XLIV, 9. (2) I.e., make the sacrifice unfit. (3) Ibid. 6. (4) They estrange him from God. (5) An apostate. (6) For this is understood to refer to one whose brothers died through circumcision, so that he fears the operation, but would otherwise have it performed. (7) V. Ex. XXVIII, 36-38: *And thou shalt make a plate of pure gold . . . and it shall be upon Aaron's forehead, and Aaron shall bear the iniquity committed in the holy things . . . and it shall always be upon his forehead, that they may be accepted before the Lord.* According to the Rabbis, this means that in virtue of the headplate a public sacrifice is *'accepted'*, i.e., valid, even if the whole congregation or all the officiating priests are unclean, and indeed must be offered at the very outset in such conditions, as the public sacrifice may not be postponed. This is technically called propitiating (making acceptable). The matter is further explained in the text.

b (1) V. Num. XIX, 19. (2) I.e., only when the whole or the majority of the nation is unclean through a corpse must the public sacrifice be brought. (3) If an individual is unclean through a reptile and has not performed *ṭebillah* (q.v. Glos.), though he can do so and be clean in the evening, nevertheless the Passover may not be slaughtered on his behalf, and he must postpone his sacrifice for the second Passover. There is an opposing view in Pes. 90*b*. (4) The original is ר״ל and it is not clear what it stands for. BaḤ. suggests, Resh Galutha, the Head of the Exile. (5) As the text proceeds to shew: the owner of a sacrifice can send it to the Temple even when he is unclean through a reptile, whereas a priest cannot officiate in like circumstances.

c (1) Because they will be unfit to partake of it in the evening.—Though sacrifices in general are mentioned, much of the present discussion refers more particularly to the Passover. (2) E.g., he was registered for a particular Passover-offering (this could be sacrificed only on behalf of people specially registered for it) and became unclean through a corpse: if he sent the sacrifice and had it slaughtered, he does not celebrate the second Passover a month later, though he cannot partake of the first. (3) Num. IX, 10 f. Thus he is relegated to the second month. (4) Scripture orders him to be relegated. Yet if he does have it slaughtered at the first, he has fulfilled his obligation.

But it is written, *According to every man's* [23a] *eating*?[5]—That [too] is [only] a recommendation. Yet is it not indispensable?[6] Surely it was taught: [*Then shall he and his neighbour next unto him take one*] *according to the number of* [be-miksath] *the souls*:[7] this teaches that the Paschal lamb is not slaughtered save for those who are registered [numbered] for it. You might think that if he slaughtered it for those who were not registered for it, he should be as one who violates the precept, yet it is fit. Therefore it is stated, *Ye shall make your count* [takosu]:[7] it is reiterated, to teach that it is indispensable; and eaters are assimilated to registered [persons]![8]—The Elders of the south do not assimilate [them].[9] Yet even if they do not assimilate [them], there is still the same refutation: If a priest who was defiled by a reptile cannot propitiate, though if the owners were defiled by a reptile they can send their sacrifices *at the very outset*; is it not logical that a priest who was defiled through a corpse should not be able to propitiate, seeing that if the owners were defiled through a corpse they cannot send their sacrifices
a *at the very outset*?[1]

An objection is raised: [If the blood of a Passover-offering is sprinkled, and then it became known that it was unclean, the headplate propitiates; if the person became unclean, the headplate does not propitiate;] because they [the Sages] ruled: [In the case of] a nazirite one who sacrifices the Passover-offering, the headplate propitiates for the uncleanness of the blood, but the headplate does not propitiate for the uncleanness of the person. With what [was the person defiled]? Shall we say, With the uncleanness of a reptile? surely you maintain [that] you may slaughter [the Passover-offering] and sprinkle [its blood] on behalf of one who is unclean through a reptile! Hence it must refer to defilement by a corpse, yet it teaches, 'The headplate does not propitiate', which proves that if the owners were defiled, they cannot send their sacrifices![2]—No: if the owners were defiled through a corpse, that would indeed be so.[3] But the meaning here is that the *priest* was defiled by a reptile. If so, consider the last clause: If he was defiled with the 'uncleanness of the deep',[4] the headplate propitiates.[5] But surely R. Ḥiyya taught: They [the Sages] spoke of the 'uncleanness of the deep' in respect of a corpse alone. What does this exclude? Surely it excludes the 'uncleanness of the deep' caused by a reptile?—No: it excludes the 'uncleanness of the deep' of gonorrhoea.[6]

Again, as to what Rami b. Ḥama asked: As to the priest who propitiates with their sacrifices, is the 'uncleanness of the deep' permitted to him, or is the 'uncleanness of the deep' not permitted
b to him?[1] You may solve that the 'uncleanness of the deep' is permitted to him, for here we are treating of the priest?[2]—Rami b. Ḥama certainly disagrees [with the Elders of the south].[3]

Come and hear:[4] *And Aaron shall bear the iniquity of the holy*

(5) Ex. XII, 4. This implies that he must be fit to partake thereof. (6) In the sense that the sacrifice offered in contravention of this law does not count at all, and the man must bring the second Passover. (7) Ibid. 4. (8) Just as the sacrifice is unfit if slaughtered for those who are not registered for it, so is it unfit if slaughtered on behalf of men who cannot partake of it, for the eaters are coupled with the registered persons in the same verse. (9) Since only '*number*' is repeated, but not '*eating*'.

a (1) For the Elders of the south merely maintain that if they *sent* their sacrifices and had them slaughtered, they do not bring a second Passover. But they must of course admit that they must not send them in the first place.—The objection remains unanswered. (2) In the sense that even if they do, they must still bring the second Passover. (3) The headplate would propitiate. (4) This is a technical term denoting the hidden uncleanness of a corpse which is now discovered for the first time. E.g., if he was in a house and it is subsequently learned that a corpse had been there; v. Pesaḥim 80*b*. (5) And he is not liable to a second offering. This is a traditional law. (6) A *zab* (gonorrhoeist) is unclean seven days, and the Passover-offering may not be offered on his behalf. Now, if the eve of Passover marks the seventh day of his uncleanness, he is in a state of doubt: if he does not discharge on that day, he will be clean in the evening; if he does discharge, he becomes unclean for a further seven days. Thus he too is unclean with the 'uncleanness of the deep', and R. Ḥiyya teaches that the headplate does not propitiate in his case.

b (1) If the priest who offers the Passover sacrifice or the sacrifices of a nazirite on behalf of their owners was defiled with the 'uncleanness of the deep', does the headplate propitiate, so that the sacrifices are valid, or not? (2) On the interpretation of the Elders of the south. (3) He must interpret the Mishnah as referring to the uncleanness of the owners. (4) This is a refutation of Rami b. Ḥama.

עין משפט נר מצוה

סז א מיי' פ"ב מהל' קרבן פסח הל"ח :
סח ב ג מיי' פ"ד מהל' קרבן פסח הל"ב וכ"ז שם הל"ב ופ"ד מהל' ביאת מקדש הל' ו וכ"ז מהל' נזירות הל' טו :
סט ד מיי' פ"ז מהל' נזירות הל"ח :

גמרא

לפי אכלו למצוה ולעכובי לא *והתניא °במכסת נפשות מלמד "שאין הפסח נשחט אלא למנוייו שחטו שלא למנוייו יכול יהא כעובר על המצוה א] תלמוד לומר תכוסו הכתוב *שנה עליו לעכב ואיתקש אוכלין למנויין זקני דרום לא מקשי ב] וכי לא מקשי נמי (א) מהא נמי אית להו פירכא ומה במקום שנטמאו בעלים בשרץ שמשלחין קרבנותיהם לכתחילה כהן שנטמא בשרץ אינו מרצה ג] מקום שנטמאו בעלים במת שאין משלחין קרבנותיהן לכתחילה כהן שנטמא במת אינו דין שאינו מרצה מיתיבי *"מפני שאמרו נזיר ועושה פסח הציץ מרצה על טומאת דם ואין הציץ מרצה על טומאת הגוף ד] במאי אילימא בטומאת שרץ האמרת שוחטין וזורקין על *טומאת שרץ אלא טומאת מת וקתני אין הציץ מרצה אלמא נטמאו בעלים במת אין משלחין קרבנותיהם לא אי דאיטמו בעלים במת ה"נ הכא במאי עסקינן כגון שנטמא כהן בשרץ אי הכי ה] אימא סיפא "נטמא טומאת התהום הציץ מרצה הא תני רבי חייא *לא "אמרו טומאת התהום אלא למת בלבד למת ו] למעוטי מאי לאו למעוטי טומאת התהום דשרץ לא למעוטי טומאת התהום דזיבה ואלא הא *דבעי רמי בר חמא כהן המרצה בקרבנותיהם הותרה לו טומא' התהום או לא ז] הותרה לו טומאת התהום תפשוט דטומאת התהום הותרה לו דהא הכא בכהן קיימינא דרמי בר חמא ודאי פליגי תא שמע °ונשא אהרן את עון הקדשי' *וכי איזהו עון נושא אם

שמות יב | ויקרא כח | ל"ל אבא

* פסחים טז: יומא ז. מנחות כה.

רש"י

לפי אכלו . הראוי לאכילה תכוסו עליו דהיינו שחיטה : במכסת . לשון מנין כמו מכסת ערכך (ויקרא כז) : ואיתקש אוכלין למניין . מה מנויין מעכבי אף אוכלים מעכבי שאם שחטו לטמאים ולערלים ח] ולחולה וזקן שאין יכולין לאכול כזית פסול ואפי' הן מנויין דהא לפי אכלו בהאי קרא כתיב ט] לגבי מניין : וכי לא מקשי נמי . וסברי טמא מת משלח קרבנותיו בדיעבד אית להו הך פירכא גופא דפרכינן לעיל אמילתייהו י] דמוקמינן מתניתין בכהן טמא שרץ אבל כהן טמא מת הציץ מרצה דהא מודה מיהא דלכתחילה אמר רחמנא טמא מת ידחה לשני וטמא שרץ אמרינן לעיל דשוחטין עליו לכתחילה : ומה במקום כו' בעלים . יחיד : מיתיבי . לזקני דרום : מפני שאמרו . משנה היא בכילד צולין (פסחים דף פ:) שהנזיר ועושה פסח כו' קס"ד יא] האי טומאת הגוף בבעלים קאמר ולהכי נקט נזיר ועושה פסח דאילו שאר קרבנות אין טומאת בעלים פסול בהן אבל עושה פסח אכילתו מעכבא ונזיר נמי כשנטמא במת סותר נזירותו וצריך לחזור ולמנות כדכתיב (במדבר ו) וכי ימות מת עליו וגו' ואין ראוי לקרבנות תגלחתו עד שיטהר ויביא תחילה קרבנות (ב) נזירותיב] טומאתו שתי תורים ואשם . וימנה את נזירתו ואחר כך יביא קרבנות נזירות טהרה וקתני אין הציץ מרצה בדיעבד: אלמא נטמאו כו' . כלומר אם שלח קרבנו ושחטו וזרקו עליו לא נפטר מפסח שני : הכי נמי . דמרצה ציץ : כגון שנטמא כהן בשרץ . כדתנן טמא פסול ואוקימנא בשרץ ותנן נזיר ועושה פסח וה"ה לכל קרבנות יחיד והא דנקט הני משום סיפא נקט דבעי מיתני נטמא טומאת התהום הרי זה מרצה וכי גמירי היתר טומאת התהום בנזיר ועושה פסח גמירי לה בכילד צולין וטומאת התהום טומאת ספק והתם מפרש איזוהי טומאת התהום כו' והילכתא גמירי לה דהותרה בנזיר ועושה פסח כדאמרי' בכילד צולין (פסחים דף פ:) : לא אמרו . דהותרה טומאת התהום בנזיר ועושה פסח אלא בטומאת המת בלבד : מאי לאו למעוטי טומאת התהום דשרץ . דלא הותרה ומק"ו לא אתיא שאין דנין ק"ו מהלכה : טומאת התהום דזיבה . כגון ראה בין השמשות ספק כולה מן היום או כולה מן הלילה ואין כאן אלא ראייה אחת ספק חציה מן היום וחציה מן הלילה והוי לה כשתי ראיות דזב מטמא בימים ובראיות והך טומאת התהום הוא דממעט משום דתמירא דיוצאה עליו מגופו : דבעי רמי בר חמא . בכילד צולין : כהן המרצה בקרבנותיהן . של נזיר ועושה פסח הותרה לו טומאת התהום אם נטמא בה : יג] והא הכא בכהן אוקמא לה . לרישא דקתני אין הציץ מרצה על טומאת הגוף ועלה קתני נטמא טומאת התהום הרי זה מרצה : יד] דרמי בר חמא פליג הוא . אדזקני דרום הוא מוקים להאי בטומאת בעלים וסבירא (ג) דאין יחיד טמא מת משלח קרבנותיו דאכילת פסחים מעכב : תא שמע . תיובתא לרמי בר חמא : ונשא אהרן . בציץ כתיב : את עון הקדשים . פסול קרבנות ירצה בציץ : אם

תוספות

הכא נמי לייתי ק"ו ליפוק מהיקשא ועוד קשה היכי יליף טמא שרץ דיחיד בק"ו מטמא מת דיחיד הא טמא טו] גופיה דיחיד יליף על ידי מתוך וכי האי גוונא חשיב בבנין אב בפרק איזהו מקומן (לקמן דף נא.) דקאמר לן בדם כשר הואיל ולן טז] כשר באימורין ודבר הלמד בבנין אב אינו חוזר ומלמד בקל וחומר וי"ל דבעיא היא באיזהו מקומן והכא אם יז] נאמר דילפי' קאמר ועוד י"ל דהאי מתוך אינו בבנין אב דאי הוי בבנין אב א"כ יאכל ביחיד כבציבור : **זקני** דרום לא מקשי . וזקני דרום תנאי הוו ופליגי אמתני' דתמיד נשחט (פסחים דף סא.) דתנן השוחט לערלים ולטמאים פסול יח] אי נמי סבירא להו כר' נתן ולית להו הא דקאמר הש"ס יט] בכילד צולין (שם דף עח:) דמודה ר' נתן היכא דגברא לא חזי : **מפני** שאמרו נזיר ועושה פסח . אע"ג כ] דפרשי' זקני דרום תנאי היא אפירכא דסיפא סמיך דנטמא טומאת התהום מרצה [א] (דכולי עלמא אית כא] להון טומאת התהום מרצה) דהילכתא גמירי לה כדאיתא פרק כילד צולין (פסחים פ:) וכן ברייתא דר' חייא לא אמרו טומאת התהום אלא למת בלבד דפליך מינה התם לרבי יוסי : **אלא** בטומאת מת כב] בבעלים וקתני אין הציץ מרצה . וקשיא לזקני דרום דאמרו איש איש למצוה : **לא** למעוטי טומאת התהום דזיבה . וא"ת מ"מ קשיא ברייתא דר' חייא דלא אמרו טומאת התהום אלא למת בלבד הא כג] איטמי כהן טומאה ידועה לא מרצי ותירץ ה"ר חיים דמיירי במת בשביעי והוי כטומאת שרץ דשוחטין וזורקין ולא מרצי משום דמכפרין כמתכפרין והשתא חמיר בשביעי דלא מרצי וטמא מת בראשון מרצי והיינו טעמא דבשביעי יכול לעשות בטהרה על ידי שליח וחזי למיכל לאורתא אבל בראשון לא אפשר לתקנו ולעשותו בטהרה לכך בדיעבד כשר ומיירי ברייתא דר' חייא כד] [בטומאת התהום דאי איטמי] כהן בטומאת ודאי של שרץ או במת בשביעי שלו אינו מרצה ביחיד אפי' בדיעבד (שהרי אינו מרצה בציבור בתמיד) דהא מכפרין כמתכפרין וציבור טמאי שרץ או בשביעי של מת לא עבדי בטומאה אלא שולחים קרבנותיהם על ידי טהורין כיון דחזו לאורתא אבל בטומאת התהום מרצה כהן ביחיד אבל בבעלים לא מתוקמא ברייתא דר' חייא דכיון דשוחטין וזורקין על טמאי שרץ ושולחים קרבנותיהם ביד טהורים איזה ריצוי ציץ שייך וגם טומאת התהום נמי לא שריא להו למיעבד אינהו גופייהו כיון דשוחטין וזורקין עליהן ומצו למיעבד ע"י טהורין ועוד יש לפרש דמיירי בכהן שקיבל הדם בטומאת התהום דמת שמרצה לכתחילה לזרוק ולא מהדרי' אטהורין אפי' איכא כהן טהור הא טומאה ידועה לא מרצה לכתחילה אלא מהדרינן אטהורין דטומאה דחויה היא בציבור וכי האי גוונא צריך לפרש בפרק כילד צולין (שם פא.) דבעי התם כהן המרצה בתמיד הותרה לו טומאת התהום או לא הותרה ומאי קמיבעיא ליה הא קיימא לן במועדו אפי' בטומאה אלא אי יכול לזרוק בטומאה לכתחילה קמיבעיא ליה כדפרישית ואפי' איכא טהורין : **טומאת** התהום דזיבה . פ"ה כגון ראה בין השמשות כה] של י"ג ספק כולה מן היום או מן הלילה ואין כאן אלא ראייה אחת ספק חציה מן היום וחציה מן הלילה ויש כאן שתי ראיות דזב מטמא בימים ובראיות וקשה דבפרק כילד צולין (ג"ז שם) לא מני משכח לרבי יוסי טומאת התהום כו] ולימא כי האי גוונא ונראה לי ברו"ך דבעינן שהספק לא יהא נודע עד לאחר שחיטה [ב] ואם אמרו לו לאחר שחיטה ראית בין השמשות סוף יום שלשה עשר הא בעינן כז] טומאת התהום שלא יהא אחד מכיר בסוף העולם לכך בעי התם בשלמא לרבנן משכחת לה דשחטו על זב בשביעי שלו דשוחטין וזורקין על טמא שרץ ואח"כ ראה וסותר אבל לר' יוסי דאמר מקצת היום ככולו ומכאן ולהבא מטמא ולא סתר מידי כח] [היכי משכחת ליה] ורבינו הקשה לימא שראה לפני שחיטה ושחטו עליו וחזר הזב וראה שניה דסתר אפי' לר' יוסי וצריך למנות שבעה דזב תלוי בראיות וליכא לא תחילת היום בטהרה ולא סוף היום ולדידי אתי שפיר דכיון דראה בצפרא מיד היה ספק אולי יראה עוד כט] ביום והוי כנודע הספק קודם ל] שחיטה ורבינו מתרץ בזה דכיון דראייה ראשונה אינה מטמאה במשא א"כ מועיל לו מה ששחטו וזרקו עליו אע"ג דראייה שנייה מצטרפת לראשונה לחייבו מנין שבעה מכל מקום לעולם היה קרוי טמא שרץ בשעת עשיית הקרבן וגם אחר כן לא פקע שמו ויצא ידי פסחו וקשה [ג] על לא] פירושו משמעתין *) (כהן המרצה [ד] בציבור היא) וי"ל כגון שראה אחת בי"ג וטבל והעריב שמשו ושחט למחר הפסח ואחרי כן ראה שנייה ומצטרפת ואין זה קרוי נודע הספק קודם שחיטה כיון שטהור גמור בשעת שחיטה וליכא למימר אולי יראה [ה] לשני ימים ומצטרפין דלר' יוסי אינה מצטרפת לראשונה . ברו"ך :

*) רש"ק מ"ז

אם

מסורת הש"ס

פסחים סא. עח: ע"ש

[פסחים סא. עח: יומא לג: נב: יבמות מ. שבועות יד. מנחות יט:]

פסחים פ: תוספתא דפסחים פ"ו תוספתא דנזיר פ"ו תוספתא דמנחות פ"ק

נזיר סג. [פסחים פ: פא:]

פסחים פ:

הגהות הב"ח

(א) גמ' לא מקשי נמי מיהא לית כצ"ל ותיבת נמי נמחק : (ב) רש"י ד"ה מפני וכו' קרבנות נזיר טמא שתי תורים : (ג) ד"ה דרמי וכו' וסבירא ליה דאין :

שיטה מקובצת

א] המצוה . וכשר : ב] מקשי . אמר רב אשי וכי לא מקשי נמי אית להו פירכא: ג] מקום שנטמאו בעלים במת כו' תימה דדיו לבא מן הדין להיות כנדון בסוף דינא מה בעלים לכתחלה לא מרצה אבל בדיעבד מרצה אף כהן בדיעבד מרצה והשתא לא קשה מידי דהא דמרצה ביחיד דקאמרי דיעבד דוקא קאמרי וי"ל דלפי מה שפי' הר"מ ניחא דפי' דלא בא משום ילפותא גמור כי אם לסתור סברת דזקני דרום הילכך לא שייך למימר לא דיו ולא שום פירכא כיון דאין זה אלא סתירת דברים בעלמא . לשון מהר"פ : ד] במאי אילימא בטומאת שרץ כו' תימה היאך מתוקמא בטומאת שרץ הלא נזיר אינו מעכב מלשלח קרבנותיו בשביל טומאת שרץ דבנזיר כתיב וכי ימות מת עליו בפתע פתאום וכו' [סותר] ומביא קרבן טומאה אבל בטומא' שרץ אינו סותר ומביא קרבן טומאה וי"ל דטומאת שרץ דקאמר ר"ל כעין טומאת שרץ כגון טמא מת בשביעי שלו וא"ת והלא לא שייך שביעי [בקרבני נזירות] ששחטו עליו בשביעי שלו שהרי הוא סותר כל נזירתו ואינו מביא קרבן תגלחתו עד שימנה כל נזירתו שלאחריה מביא קרבן טומאה ואח"כ מונה כל נזירתו בטהרה ומביא קרבן תגלחתו [והרי] כבר עבר הרבה ימים דלא הוי שביעי שלו וליכא למימר קרבן נזירתו דלטומאה קאמר שמביא אשם ושתי תורים וקאמר אם מביא בשביעי שלו דאינו נפטר דאין לו להביאם [אלא ביום] שמיני הא ודאי ליתא דאין אכילתו מעכבת בקרבנות מידי דהוה אשאר קרבנות שאין אכילה פוסלת רק בפסח ונזירות טהרה דגלי קרא ונראה דמשכחת שביעי בנזיר כגון שנטמא לאחר (מלא) [מלאות] שמונה בנזירתו ונטמא קודם הבאת קרבנותיו דאינו סותר אלא מונה ז' ימים (ונאכל) ומביא קרבן תגלחת דטהרתו בשמיני ועל זה [אמר] אם הביא בשביעי דאין הציץ מרצה ובעי' טהרת בעלים בנזיר כמו בפסח . מהר"פ : ה] אימא סיפא כו' ואי אמרת דרישא דמתניתין בנטמא בשרץ היכא קאמר בסיפא נטמא כו' פי' בשרץ והא תנא ר' חייא כו' . הר"פ : ו] למעוטי.פי' וא"כ היכא תני סיפא נטמא טומאת התהום הציץ מרצה דבע"כ היינו טומאת התהום דשרץ דהא רישא וסיפא בחד גוונא היא [הג"ה] וקשה לי על זה דהא אוקמינן

שיטה מקובצת

מילתא דר' חייא במת ובשרץ א"כ הוי שפיר דומיא דרישא וגם התלמוד מתחילה לא היה מקשה לאו למעוטי טומאת התהום (דשרץ אלמא) [דשרץ אלא] משום דא"כ לא מתוקמא (דשרץ) [רישא] בטומא' שרץ דלא הוי רישא דומיא דסיפא ומשלא [ליכא] למעוטי טומאת תהום דזיבה אבל מתני' מתוקמא שפיר בשרץ והוי רישא דומיא דסיפא אבל מה שהקשה רבינו פרץ ז"ל דלא הוי רישא דומיא דסיפא לא קשיא דאין לחוש מן הדיוק אם יהיה סותר (דריש כלל) [הרישא] כשנאמרו למעוטי טומאת התהום דזיבה תעמיד אותו בבעלים שזהו הדיוק אין לחוש אם [לא] יהיה דומיא דרישא נ"ל ברוך: ז] לא . תפשוט דהותרה לו דהא הכא והשאר נמחק : ח] ולחולה ולזקן: ט] כתיב . גבי : י] אמלתייהו . דאוקמי' : יא] קס"ד . דהאי אין הציץ מרצה על טומאת: יב] טומאה שהם שתי תורים : יג] בה. מה"ד דהא הכא : יד] דרמב"ח פליג אדזקני דרום דהוי מוקים להיא כו': טו] טמא. מת: טז] ולן . באימורין כשר : יז] אם תמצא לומר דילפינן : יח] עי' בהשמטות בסוף המסכת : יט] הש"ס . בפרק כיצד צולין : כ] אע"ג . דפרשי : כא] אית להו טומאת התהום כו' כדאיתא בפרק כיצד צולין וכן ברייתא דר"ח דלא אמרו כו' התם לרבי יוסי . דף פ"א : כב] מת . דבעלים: כג] הא טומאת ידועה לא מרצי : כד] ומיירי ברייתא דר"ח בכהן בטומאת ודאי (והשאר נמחק) כו' בשביעי שלו ואינו מרצה: כה] תיבות של י"ג נמחק : כו] התהום . דזיבה ונימא כי האי גוונא . ונראה לי דבעינן ותיבת ברוך נמחק : כז] בעינן . בטומאת : כח] מידי . היכא משכחת לה ורבינו הקשה לימא דראה לפני : כט] עוד . בו ביום : ל] שחיטה. וזה לשון הרב רבינו פרץ ז"ל פי' רש"י ז"ל כגון ראה בין השמשות כו' עד וזב מטמא בראיות כבימים ושתים לטומאת שבעה כדאמרי' שתים לטומאה ושלשה לקרבן דלענין כהן מקריב איירי בשמעתין ול"נ דטומאת התהום משמע דלבסוף נתברר הדבר ובכה"ג לא נתברר הדבר יותר מבתחילה בשעת טומאה אלא נ"ל כדמפרש התם כגון בשביעי שלו ולאחר שהביא קרבנותיו של נזירות ראה וסתר זהו טומאת התהום שנתברר לבסוף אבל בשעת שהביאו קרבנותיהן נזיר ועושה פסח לא היה יודע אם יראה יומים ומיירי ע"כ בבעלים דאי בכהן לא היה נכנס בעזרה אם היה זב ואפי' בעל ב' ראיות דהא מחוסר הערב שמש וכ"ש בזב בעל (שתי) [שלש] ראיות דהא מחוסר כפרה וא"כ אפילו קודם שראה איך היה נכנס מתחלה [בעזרה] להקריב קרבנות (בעזרה) והך דר' חייא לא הוי דומיא דרישא דהא אוקמינא רישא בכהן שנטמא והך דר' חייא איירי בבעלים ואל תתמה על זה דהא בלאו הכי נמי לא הוי דומיא דרישא ממש דהא אוקמינא רישא בטומאת שרץ ומילתא דרבי חייא איירי [במת] והתם אפי' בדיעבד אין הציץ מרצה ובמילתא דר' חייא הוי אפי' לכתחילה כך פי' מורי [ע"כ] : לא] על . פירושנו דשמעתין בכהן המרצה בצבור איירי וי"ל :

אילימא

הגהות צ"ק [א] מיטס אלו מן דכולי עד מרלה נמחק : [ב] ואפילו אמר לו לאחר שחיטה ראיתי כפ"ש של י"ג הא כו' : [ג] וקשה על פירושי : [ד] כ"ל כנגור דהא לא הותרה טומאת שרץ : [ה] כ' ימים :

אם עון פיגול הרי כבר נאמר °לא יחשב אם עון נותר הרי כבר נאמר °לא ירצה *הא אינו נושא אלא עון טומאה שהותרה מכללה בצבור מאי טומאה א] אילימא (א) מטומאת שרץ היכא אישתרי אלא טומאת מת ולאו כגון שנטמאו בעלים במת אלמא נטמאו בעלים במת משלחין קרבנותיהן ובמאי אי בנזיר °וכי ימות מת עליו אמר רחמנא אלא לעושה פסח (ולאו כגון שנטמאו בעלים במת) לעולם בשרץ ושם טומאה בעולם ואיכא דדייק ומייתי הכי עון הקדשים אין עון מקדישין לא ב] מאי טומאה אילימא טומאת שרץ מי אישתריא בציבור אלא לאו טומאת מת ועון קדשים אין ג] עון מקדישים לא לעולם טומאת שרץ ושם טומאה בעולם: יושב: מנלן *אמר רבא אמר רב ד] נחמן אמר קרא °לעמוד לשרת לעמידה בחרתיו ולא לישיבה ת"ר °לעמוד לשרת א) מצוה כשהוא *אומר °העומדים ב) שנה עליו הכתוב לעכב א"ל רבא לרב נחמן מכדי יושב כזר דמי ומחיל עבודה אימא מה זר במיתה אף יושב במיתה אלמה *תניא אבל ערל אונן יושב אינן במיתה אלא באזהרה משום דהוי מחוסר בגדים ושלא רחוץ ידים ורגלים ה] שני כתובין הבאין כאחד וכל

א) [ע' תוס' לעיל פז. סד"ה מיושב] ב) [פסחים סה. וש"נ]

רש"י

אם עון פיגול הרי כבר נאמר לא ירצה ואם עון נותר הרי כבר נאמר לא יחשב. ה"ג לה בת"כ וכן הגמרא בכל מקום וה"ק איזה פסול קרבן ו] מרצה הוא אם עון פיגול דמחשבת חוץ למקומו דאיקרי פיגול כדאמר לקמן בפירקין (דף כח.) פיגול הוא לא ירצה אם אינו לענין חוץ לזמנו תניהו לענין חוץ למקומו הרי כבר נאמר לא ירצה: אם עון נותר. פסול מחשבת נותר שחישב לאוכלו לאחר שנעשה נותר דהייט מחשבת חוץ לזמנו: הרי כבר נאמר המקריב אותו לא יחשב. והאי קרא בחוץ לזמנו מיתוקמא בפירקין ובספרים שלנו גירסא זו משובשת בכ"מ בהש"ס ומחליפין המקראות ולאותה הגירסא איך יכול לפרש נותר זה במחשבת חוץ לזמנו והפיגול במחשבת חוץ למקומו דלא יחשב בחוץ לזמנו כתיב וצריך אתה לפרש נותר ממש ואי אפשר לומר כן שאין הקרבן שקרבו מתיריו בהכשר ז] נפסל מלרצות ולעלות לשם חובה אם הותיר ממנו ח]: הא אינו נושא כו'. ט] הא כלומר *הנה מצינו שאינו נושא אלא עון הטומאה ויש טעם לדבר ליתן י] נשיאת פסול קדשים זה על טומאה הואיל ומצינו לה היתר אחר שהותרה מכללה בצבור לכתחילה הילכך יחיד שלא הותרה אצלו יבא הציץ וירצה בדיעבד: אילימא טומאת שרץ. יא] מתוקמא בכהן או בבעלים ולמימר דהאי דשוחט וזורק על טמא שרץ ציץ הוא דמרצה: היכא אישתראי. בצבור כיון דאין יחיד נדחה לצבור לא עבדי בטומאה: לאו כגון שנטמאו בעלים במת. בתמיה ומי לא מיירי בטומאת בעלים וקתני משלחין: וכי ימות מת עליו אמר רחמנא. יב] דטמא ראש נזרו וסותר ואין ראוי לקרבנות טהרה עד שיעברו ימי טומאה ויביא כפרת טומאת נזירותו שתי תורים ואשם וימנה וישלים ויביא קרבנות תגלחתו: אלא בעושה פסח. וש"מ טמא מת משלח פסחו וקשיא לרמי בר חמא: לעולם. טומאת שרץ קאמרינן (ב) יג] מהכא דציץ מרצה לשחוט ולזרוק על טמא שרץ ודקשיא לך היכא אישתראי בכן: ושם טומאה בעולם. אשכחן דאישתראי יד] בכן וטעמא גדול בהו להטיל ריצוי ציץ על טומאת שרץ: ואיכא דדייק. לישנא דקראי טו] ומייתינא להך תיובתא דברייתא לזקני דרום וסייעתא לרמי בר חמא: עון. מקדישים לא. טומאת הגוף בין דכהנים בין דבעלים לא מרצה במאי טומאה קאי דקא ממעט טומאת הגוף: אילימא טומאת שרץ. ונוקמא זקני דרום בכהן דאילו גוף דבעלים לא בעי ציץ שהרי אין נוגע בו בטומאה ולאורתא בטהרה אכיל ליה: היכא אישתראי בצבור. הא כיון דאית להו שוחטין וזורקין על טמא שרץ ויחיד אין נדחה לצבור לא עבדי בטומאה: אלא לאו טומאת מת. טז] *) שאינו משלח קרבנות ולא כהן טמא מת מרצה בקרבן יחיד: לעולם בטומאת שרץ. קאי וקממעט כהן טמא שרץ מלרצות יז] כדאוקמי זקני דרום פסול דמתניתין אטמא שרץ וטומאת בעלים אין צריכין ציץ שהרי קרבן בטהרה קרב ודקשיא לך היכא אישתראי בצבור שום טומאה בעולם אישתראי בהו: לעמוד לשרת. רישיה דקרא כי בו בחר ה' אלהיך מכל שבטיך יח] לעמוד [א] לשרת וגו': יט] לא לישיבה. א) וכיון דלא נבחרו הוו להו זרים וזר מחיל עבודה: העומדים שם. *) [לעיל מיניה כתיב] ושרת ככל אחיו הלוים וגו': [אימא מה זר וכו'. וניגמר במה מצינו בזר שמחיל עבודה וחייב מיתה אף יושב שמחלל עבודה במיתה]:

*ס"א אלמא אין טמא מת משלח קרבנות מהרש"ק *) נ"ל רישיה דקרא רש"ק שני

תוספות

אם עון פיגול הרי כבר נאמר לא ירצה ואם עון נותר הרי כבר נאמר לא יחשב. כך כ] פי' הקונטרס משום דאמרי' לקמן בפירקין (דף כח.) דאיסור רבה דחוץ לזמנו שהוא בכרת מקרא רבה ופרשה רבה בצו את אהרן ואיסורא זוטא דחוץ למקומו דליכא כרת מקרא זוטא ופרשתא זוטא בפרשת קדושים תהיו והביא ראייה מתורת כהנים ורבינו תם מקיים גירסת הספרים דגרסינן איפכא בפיגול לא יחשב ובנותר לא ירצה דלקמן בפירקין מסקינן דתרווייהו [ב] מקרא אחרינא נפקי דכתיב ביה לא ירצה ולא יחשב ומה שנזכר פיגול קודם לנותר אף ע"ג דבקרא כתיב כא] נותר ברישא דהיינו חוץ לזמנו משום דלשון פיגול כתיב בקרא בהדיא: אם עון נותר הרי כבר נאמר כו'. לאו נותר ממש [קאמר] כדאמרי' לקמן בפירקין (דף כט.) לאחר שהוכשר יפסל אלא במחשבת נותר דהיינו מחשב לאוכלו חוץ לזמנו: הא אינו נושא אלא עון טומאה שהותרה מכללה. וא"ת תיפוק לי דלא משכחת מידי דמיתוקם ביה קרא אלא בטומאה ואומר רבינו תם משום דכתיב גבי ציץ לרצון להם דמשמע דבר שהוא לרצון במקום אחר ולהכי דחיק לאשכוחי הותר מכללן מכל הני דפריך מינייהו (במנחות דף כה.) יוצא ושמאל ובעל מום כב] [וא"ת (א"כ) נותר ופיגול היכן הותרו מכללן דאיצטריך ליה לא ירצה ולא יחשב ואומר רבינו תם דפיגול הותר מכללו בבמה דלא שייך שם מחשבת חוץ למקומו והא דפריך בהקומץ רבה (מנחות דף כה.) אימא עון יוצא שהותר מכללו בבמה כג] אמר קרא לרצון להם לפני ה' עון דלפני ה' אין עון דיוצא לא חוץ למקומו חשיב שפיר לפני ה' שהמחשבה בפנים ואין לומר דבבמה לא קרינן ליה הותר מכללו כיון דהכשירו בכך כדקאמר התם גבי שמאל דכיון דאסור בפנים אין זה קרוי הכשירו בכך ונותר כדי נסבה ואגב פיגול נקט נותר הואיל ומשכח ביה קרא אע"ג דלא צריך אי נמי נותר הותר מכללו בראשו של מזבח דאיכא למאן דאמר אין לינה מועלת בראשו של מזבח בריש תמיד נשחט (פסחים ד' נט.) ובפ' המזבח מקדש (לקמן ד' פז.) ומיהו פלוגתא דאמוראי היא וקשיא [ג] למ"ד [דאית ליה] לינה מועלת מהך ברייתא ונראה דנותר יש ללמדו עון עון מריצוי ציץ ופגול נמי מלינן למילף כד] ואפי' לא משכחת בהו הותר מכללן ולרצון להם איכא לאוקמי כדדרשי' בפ' הבא על יבמתו (יבמות דף ס:) כה] [להם לרצון ולא לפורענות] אבל לעובדי כוכבים אפי' לפורענות ועוד י"ל דנותר הותר מכללו במנחת כהנים ומנחת כהן משיח וקומץ וכל דבר שאין לו מתירים כו] אין חייבים עליהן משום פיגול כדתנן פ' ב"ש (לקמן דף מג:) ואפי' פסולא נמי נראה דליכא מדאמר לעיל בסוף פ"ק (דף יד.) דמודה ר' שמעון בהולכת חטאות הפנימיות ופריך והא"ר שמעון כל שאינו על מזבח החיצון אין חייבין עליו משום פגול ומשני מודה ר' שמעון דפסול מק"ו ומה שלא לשמו הכשר בשלמים פסול בחטאת חוץ לזמנו הפסול בשלמים אינו דין שיפסל בחטאת משמע דאי לאו ק"ו כז] הוה אמינא דאפי' פסולא ליכא א"כ במנחת כהנים ובמנחת נסכים דליכא ק"ו דלא מיפסל בזו שלא לשמן ליכא פסולא כלל אלמא אשכחן נותר דהותר מכללו לגמרי: לאו כגון שנטמאו בעלים במת. תימה מאי קשיא ליה לוקמה בטומאת הדם שנטמא הדם הציץ מרצה דגבי טומאת דם מייתי לה בכולי הש"ס (לקמן מה.) דדם שנטמא וזרקו בשוגג הורצה ותנן נמי בפסחים (דף עח:) נטמא כח] *הדם והבשר קיים זורק הדם וי"ל דס"ל להאי לישנא דלית ליה למימר דנשא עון טומאה אלא בכי האי גוונא שהותרה בצבור דהיינו בטומאת בעלים דהותרה לאכול בטומאת הגוף למאי דלא מסיק אדעתיה השתא עון קדשים ולא עון מקדישים: אי נימא טומאת שרץ בבעלים היכא אישתראי. דאי סבר שוחטין וזורקין על טמא שרץ וכן טמא מת בשביעי שלו דחשיב כטמא שרץ הא לא עבדי צבור בטומאה כיון דאין יחיד נדחה לצבור נמי לא עבדי בטומאה אלא עושין שליח לשחוט בעטורס כיון דאיכא אכלי לאורתא ואי סבר אין שוחטין וזורקין על טמא שרץ דהשתא לצבור עבדי בטומאה א"כ אין הציץ מרצה על היחיד דהא אין שוחטין וזורקין עליו כט] אלא נטמאו בעלים במת וקודם שביעי מרצה ליחיד שהביא פסחו וסייעתא לזקני דרום דאמרי איש איש למנוה וקשה מאי פריך היכא אישתראי לוקמה בכהן שנטמא בשרץ דמרצה בצבור מק"ו דלעיל לרמי בר חמא דלית ליה כמו זקני דרום מכפרים כמתכפרין ועוד כי משני לעולם בשרץ ושם טומאה בעולם הא כיון דשוחטין וזורקין על טמא שרץ א"כ ריצוי ציץ ל"ל הא קרב בטהרה כדפירש רבינו שלמה בסמוך ואי סבר אין שוחטין על טמא שרץ א"כ לא יועיל ציץ *כדפירש לעיל אי בשרץ היכא אישתראי וי"ל דמעיקרא בעי לאוקמה בטומאת בעלים בשרץ והוה מצי למפרך ל"ל ריצוי ציץ אלא שפיר פריך היכא אישתראי וכי משני לעולם בשרץ רוצה לומר ולא בטומאת בעלים אלא בטומאת כהן גרידא וכ"ש בטומאת מת וסבר רמי בר חמא טומאת מת מרצה בכהן ביחיד וקצת קשה דלא ה"ל למימר שם טומאה בעולם משמע דטומאת מת בצבור קאמר והלא טומאת שרץ נמי הותרה לכהן מק"ו דלעיל אלא משום דעיקר היתר לצבור בטומאת מת כתיבא להכי נקט ליה. ברו"ך: אימא מה זר במיתה אף יושב במיתה. פי' בקונטרס דניגמר במה מצינו מה זר מחלל עבודה וחייב מיתה אף יושב שמחלל עבודה במיתה וקשה דגבי ערל ואונן נמי היה לן להקשות כמו כן דליהוי במיתה מבנין ל] אב ונראה דפריך משום דדרשי' לעמידה בחרתיו ולא לישיבה שלא בחר בכהנים יושבים אלא נחשבים כמו ישראלים זרים לכך מחלל עבודה לא] כזר [ומש"ה גם במיתה להוי כזר] ומשני משום דהוי מחוסר בגדים ושלא רחוץ ידים ורגלים לב] [שני כתובים הבאים כאחד דבמחוסר בגדים כתיב ביה מיתה ולא ישאו עון ומתו ובשלא רחוץ ידים ורגלים] נמי כתיב ביה מיתה ולא ימותו ובחנם נכתבה. דהא ילפי' חוקה לגזירה שוה אלא למימרא דלא ילפי' מיתה מהא דקרי' רחמנא זר וניחא השתא דהלא

א) מדברי התוס' ד"ה אימא מה זר נראה דצריך למחוק מן וכיון עד מחיל עבודה וס"א ה"ג ולא לישיבה ומהכא נפיק לן אזהרה בסנהדרין (דף פג.) גבי לא הן השרפין לעיכוב כדקתני לקמן העומדים שם לשרת כו' אבל

ד] א) רב. הונא אמר רב: ס] שני כתובין. פ"ה וה"ה כו' אלא משום דמחוסר בגדים כו' שייך למיפרך דטעם דידהו לא הוי משום פיסול זר ומשני: נג] ורגלים. שני באחד ולפי מה שפרשתי [לעיל בהא] דמטעם זרות פסלינן ליושב כמו כן מחוסר בגדים ושלא דמחוסר בגדים פסול מטעם זרות וכתיב ביה מיתה בפרשת ואתה תצוה ולא ימותו ושלא

א) נראה דלא גרים כלל אמר רבא רק רב הונא אמר רב.

עין משפט נר מצוה

ע א מיי' פ"ד מהל' ביאת מקדש הל"ו ופ"א מהל' פסה"מ הל' לד ופי"א הלכה יט:

עא ב מיי' פ"ו מהל' ביאת מקדש הל"ח:

עב ג מיי' פ"ע שם הל"ח:

עג ד מיי' פ"ה שם הל' יז:

מסורת הש"ס

רש"ק מוחק זה

שיטה מקובצת

א] אילימא טומאת שרץ. פ"ה ותוקמא בין בכהן בין בבעלים ולא דק דבכהן לא מצי לאוקמי שהרי לזקני דרום אמרי' לעיל דטומאת שרץ לא מרצי כלל ומתני' דפסלא טמא היינו טמא [שרץ דמחלל] העבודה וא"כ איך קאמר דציץ מרצה אלא דוקא בבעלים מוקמינן ליה והא שוחטין וזורקין על טמא שרץ היינו על ידי ריצוי דציץ: היכא אישתראי. בצבור. [וא"ת] מאי פריך הא כהן טמא שרץ הותר בצבור לכ"ע לפר"ת ולפ"ה נמי מרצה כהן טמא שרץ בצבור למאן דפליג אזקני דרום והכי קיימינן לאותבי לרמי בר חמא דפליג אזקני דרום [וי"ל] דדייק מגופיה דהך ברייתא דמשמע דבאותו ענין שהותר בצבור ציץ מרצה ביחיד וא"כ לאו בכהן שנטמא בשרץ איירי דהא לא מרצי ביחיד לכ"ע כדפי' גבי שוחטין וזורקין על טמא שרץ כיון דאמר שהציץ מרצה ביחיד הוי ליה יחיד אינו נדחה וכל שביחיד אינו נדחה צבור לא עבדי בטומאה הילכך פריך שפיר היכא אישתראי היתר גמור לאכול בטומאה דלרצון להם משמע היתר גמור באכילה לכ"ע כדפי': ב] מאי טומאה. פי' איזה טומאת יחיד נושא אילימא טומאת שרץ כו' [אלא לאו] טומאת [מת] ואשכחן דאשתראי בצבור דכתיב איש איש כי יהיה טמא לנפש איש נדחה לפסח שני ואין צבור נדחה לפסח שני אלא עושין בטומאה [מאי] לאו שנטמאו בעלים [בטומאת מת] וקתני ונשא דציץ מרצה אלמא נטמאו בעלים במת משלחין קרבנותיהן. מהר"ם: אי נימא טומאת שרץ. פ"ה ונוקמא זקני דרום בכהן כו' עד אכיל ליה. ותימה למה שינה לשונו דלעיל אמר דנוקמא בכהן או בבעלים ועוד דבכל שמעתין קאמר דהא דשוחטין וזורקין ע"י ריצוי דציץ וכאן פי' בלא ציץ ונראה לי דזה דחוק לרש"י דכי דייקינן עון קדשים עון מקדישים לא וקאמר אי נימא מטומאת שרץ משמע דאי מוקמית לה בטומאת שרץ לא קשה מידי וזה תימה דאדרבה דקשיא לזקני דרום דאינהו סברי דשוחטין וזורקין על טמא שרץ ולכך הוצרך לפרש רבותי דדרשת עון מקדישים לא אית להו לזקני דרום שוחטין וזורקין מסברא בלא שום קרא. ברוך: ג] עון מקדישים לא. טומאת הגוף בין דכהן בין דבעלים לא מרצי וא"ת מעיקרא ללשון ראשון איך [היה המקשה] אסיק אדעתין מהא דכתיב עון הקדשים דמשמע עון הקדשים ולא עון המקדישים ונראה לפרש דמעיקרא היה סבור מדקתני אלא עון טומאה שהותרה מכללה בצבור הותרה ביחיד ובצבור הותר אף לענין בעלים וכמו כן ביחיד הילכך הוי פריך רמי בר חמא. מהר"פ: ד] א) רב. וזה דוחק דכ"ש באים כאחד ולפי'

רחוץ רגלים פסול מטעם זרות ומה דלא נקיט זר ונקט הני דתנינן דלא ילפינן מיתה [בהם] אפי' היכא דידעינן [דפסולם משום] זרות כגון יושב אי לא כתיב מיתה בגופייהו וכגון מחוסר בגדים ושלא רחוץ רגלים אע"ג (דפסלינהו) [דפסולייהו] משום זרות לא הוו בהו מיתה אי לאו דכתיב בגופייהו ומתוך כך ניחא הא דקשה דלמה איצטריך למכתב מיתה בגופייהו תיפוק ליה משום (דפסלינהו) [דפסולייהו] מטעם זרות ובזרות כתיב מיתה והילכך ניחא משום דכל עיקר מיתה שנכתבה בגופייהו היינו לאשמועינן בעלמא דהנך דפסלי מטעם זרות ליכא בהו חיוב מיתה כיון דלא כתיב בגופייהו מהר"ם: ו] קרבן. הוא מרצה: ז] בהכשר. חוזר ונפסל: ח] ממנו. כדאמרי' לקמן בתר דהוכשר יפסול: ט] תיבת הא נמחק: י] ליתן. נשיאות: יא] ותוקמא בכהן: יב] רחמנא. דטומאה סותר ראש: יג] קאמרי'. הכא: יד] דאישתראי בהו ושעמא גדול הוא את ו' ותיבת בהו נמחק: טו] דקראי. ומייתי הך תיובתא: טז] מת. אלמא (לא) [אין] טמא מת משלח: יז] מלרצות. כדאוקמה: יח] שבטיך. וגו' הס"ד: יט] לא לישיבה. מהכא נפקא לן אזהרה בסנהדרין באלו הן הנשרפין ועיכוב כדקתני לקמן כשהוא אומר העומדים ככל אחיו הלוים וגו' הס"ד ומה"ד אימא מה זר במיתה אף יושב במיתה. ולינמור במה מצינו בזר שמיחל העבודה וחייב מיתה אף יושב שמחלל העבודה במיתה. הס"ד: כ] כך גרים הקונטרס: כא] כתיב. ברישא חוץ לזמנו: כב] מום. וא"ת נותר ותיבות א"כ נמחק: כג] בבמה. ומשני: כד] למילף. הכי: כה] להם לרצון ולא לפורעניות: כו] מתירין. ואין: כז] ק"ו. הוה אמינא: כח] נטמא. החלב: כט] עליו. אלמא נטמאו: ל] אב. וי"ל דאה"נ דהוי"ל מעל ואונן והד מתרי פירכא נקט ודוחק: לא] כזר. הילכך פריך שפיר אימא מה זר כו' הואיל ויושב פסיל ליה מטעם זרות א"כ אף במיתה להוי כזר אבל ערל ואונן לא. שני כתובים הבאים כאחד יומתו ושלא רחוץ ידים ורגלים.

הגהות צ"ק [א] לשרת כו' וגו' ולא לישיבה וכיון דלא נבחרו ה"ל זרים וזר מחיל עבודה כדילפינן מושרת ככל אחיו הלוים העומדים שם הס"ד וכצ"ל: [ב] נ"ל מקרא אחרינא: [ג] נ"א למ"ד דליכה מועלת כו':

הגהות הב"ח (א) גמ' אילימא טומאה כצ"ל ואות מ"ס נמחק: (ב) רש"י ד"ה לעולם וכו' קאמרינן הכא כצ"ל ואות מ"ס נמחק:

גליון הש"ס גמ' לעמוד לשרת מצוה. עיין לעיל דף טו ע"א תוס' ד"ה מיושב:

things:[5] now, what iniquity does he bear? [23*b*] If the iniquity of *piggul*,[6] surely it is already said, *it shall not be accepted*?[7] If the iniquity of *nothar*,[8] surely it is already said, *neither shall it be imputed* [*unto him that offereth it*]?[9] Hence he bears nought but the iniquity of defilement, which is inoperative,[10] in opposition to its general rule, in the case of a community.[11] Now which uncleanness [is meant]? if we say, the uncleanness of a reptile, where has that been waived?[12] Hence it must mean uncleanness through a corpse, which proves that if the owners become unclean through a corpse they send their sacrifices. And of whom [is this said]? If of a nazirite, the Divine Law saith, *And if any man die very suddenly beside him*, etc![13] Hence it can only refer to one who is offering the Paschal lamb!—In truth it refers to [the uncleanness of] a reptile, yet uncleanness elsewhere [was waived].[14]

a Others make this deduction:[1] [The headplate makes atonement] only for the iniquity of the holy things, but not for the iniquity of those who hallow them.[2] Which uncleanness [is meant]? If we say, the uncleanness of a reptile? is then that inoperative in the case of a community? Hence it must surely be the uncleanness of a corpse, and yet only the iniquity of the holy things [is atoned for], but not the iniquity of those who hallow them?—No: in truth it means uncleanness through a reptile, yet uncleanness elsewhere [is waived].

[A PRIEST] SITTING. Whence do we know it?—Said Raba in R. Naḥman's name: Scripture saith, [*For the Lord thy God hath chosen him*—the priest—*out of all thy tribes*,] to stand *to minister* [*in the name of the Lord*]:[3] I have chosen him to stand, but not to sit.

Our Rabbis taught: '*To stand to minister*' is a recommendation;[4] when it says [further], *who* stand [*there before the Lord*],[5] the Writ has repeated it, to make [standing] indispensable. Raba said to R. Naḥman: Consider: one sitting is as a *zar*,[6] and profanes the service; then let us say: just as a *zar* is liable to death,[7] so is one who sits liable to death. Why then was it taught: But an uncircumcised [priest], an *onen*, and one sitting are not liable to death but are merely under an injunction [not to officiate]? — Because [a priest] lacking the [priestly] vestments and one whose hands

(5) Ex. XXVIII, 38. '*Shall bear*' means shall make atonement for, i.e., shall make a sacrifice valid in spite of certain irregularities. (6) V. Glos. (7) Lev. XIX, 7. (8) V. Glos. (9) Ib. VII, 18. Text as emended by Rashi on the basis of Torath Kohanim. The edd. reverse the proof-texts, and Tosaf. defends their reading. (10) Lit., 'permitted'. (11) If the whole community or the majority thereof is unclean, they sacrifice the Passover-offering in the first month, as usual, and are not relegated to the second month as an individual would be. (12) In favour of a community—Scripture speaks only of uncleanness through a corpse. (13) Num. VI, 9. Scripture proceeds to say that he must then bring certain sacrifices and re-commence his period of naziriteship, at the conclusion of which he brings the prescribed sacrifices on the shaving of his head. Thus whilst unclean he cannot bring the latter. (14) Though the Scriptural permission to a community applies only to uncleanness through a corpse, yet since we find that *same* form of uncleanness is inoperative, it is logical to say that the propitiating powers of the headplate hold good in the case of uncleanness through a reptile.

a (1) Which supports Rami b. Ḥama and refutes the Elders of the south. (2) I.e., only when the sacrifice itself is defiled, but not when its owners or the priests—'those who hallow them'—are unclean. This is deduced direct from Scripture, which speaks only of the '*holy things*'. (3) Deut. XVIII, 5. (4) I.e., this text alone would merely indicate that it is *preferable* that the priest shall stand. (5) Ibid. XVIII, 7. (6) For since he has not been chosen 'to sit', he is then like a *zar* (a lay-Israelite) who has not been chosen. (7) For officiating.

and feet are not washed are two laws which come as one,[8] [24a]
a and two laws that come as one do not illumine [other cases].[1] And on the view that they do illumine [other cases], one who has drunk wine is a third case, and [when] three [laws come as one] all agree that they do not illumine [other cases].

ONE STANDING ON UTENSILS OR ON AN ANIMAL OR ON HIS FELLOW'S FEET, [THE SACRIFICES] ARE INVALID. Whence do we know it?—For the school of R. Ishmael taught: Since the pavement sanctifies[2] and the service vessels sanctify;[3] just as with the service vessels nothing may interpose between him [the priest] and the service vessels;[4] so with the pavement nothing must interpose between him and the pavement.

Now they are all necessary.[5] For if we were informed about vessels, I would argue that [standing on them disqualifies] because they are not flesh, but in the case of an animal, which is flesh, [standing on it does] not [disqualify]. And if we were informed about an animal, [the reason is] because it is not human, but as for his fellow, who is human, I would say [that standing on his feet does] not [disqualify]. Hence [they are all] necessary.

It was taught: R. Eliezer said: If one foot is on the utensil and the other on the pavement, one foot on the stone and the other on the pavement, we consider: wherever if the stone or the utensil be removed, he can stand on the other foot, his service is valid; if not, his service is invalid. R. Ammi asked: What if a [paving] stone become loosened and he stood on it?[6] If it is not his intention to fit it [in the pavement] there is no question, for it certainly interposes;[7] the question arises where it is his intention to fit it in: what then? Since it is his intention to fit it in, it is as though [already] fitted; or perhaps [we say], Now at all events it is separate? Rabbah
b Zuṭi[1] stated the question thus: R. Ammi asked: What if the stone became uprooted,[2] and he stood in its place? What is the question? [This:] When David sanctified [it], did he sanctify the upper pavement [only], or perhaps he sanctified [it] right to the nethermost soil?[3] Then let him ask about the whole of the Temple court?[4] —In truth, he is certain that he sanctified it to the nethermost soil, but this is his question: Is this a natural way of service,[5] or is it not a natural way of service? The question stands.

IF [THE PRIEST] RECEIVED [THE BLOOD] IN HIS LEFT HAND, IT IS DISQUALIFIED; R. SIMEON DECLARES IT FIT. Our Rabbis taught: [*And the priest shall take of the blood of the sin-offering with his finger, and put it upon the horns of the altar*]:[6] '*with his finger he shall take*': this teaches that receiving must be done with the right hand; '*with his finger he shall put*': this teaches that applying [the blood on the altar] must be done with the right hand.[7] Said R. Simeon: Is then 'hand' stated in connection with receiving? Rather, [interpret it thus:] '*with his finger he shall put*' teaches that the application must be with the right; [and] since 'hand' is not stated in connection with receiving, if he received [it] with his left [hand], it is fit.[8] Now as for R. Simeon, what will you? if he admits the *gezerah shawah*,[9] what does it matter if 'hand' is not written in connection with receiving?[10] While if he does not admit the *gezerah shawah*, what if 'hand' were written in connection with receiving? —Said Rab Judah: In truth, he does not admit the *gezerah shawah*, and this is what he means: Is then '*right hand*' stated in connection with receiving? Since then '*right hand*' is not stated in connection with receiving, if he received [it] with the left hand, [the service] is fit. Said Rabbah to him: If so, [the same applies] even to the
c application [of the blood on the altar] too?[1] Moreover, does not R. Simeon accept the *gezerah shawah*? Surely it was taught, R. Simeon said: Wherever 'hand' is stated, it refers to the right only; [wherever] 'finger' [is stated], it refers to the right only?—Rather said Raba: In truth he admits the *gezerah shawah*, and this is what he says: Is then 'hand' stated in connection with receiving? Since not 'hand' but 'finger' is written, and [the blood] cannot be received with the finger,[2] therefore if he received it with the left [hand], it is fit. Said R. Sama the son of R. Ashi to Rabina: But it is possible to make a handle at the edge of the bowl[3] and receive

(8) I.e., to teach the same thing. They too profane the service, and it is stated in Sanh. 83a that they are liable to death, and the same analogy might be drawn from each, viz., that those who profane the service are liable to death.

a (1) For otherwise only one should be mentioned, and by analogy the other as well as all analogous cases, would be included. (2) The priest, in that he may sacrifice there only, and not elsewhere. But v. next note. (3) The blood that is caught in them. This is the reading of cur. edd. Sh. M. offers an alternative reading, which is preferable: since the pavement is sanctified, and the service vessels are sanctified. (4) When he takes one for receiving the blood, nothing must be on his hands, e.g., gloves. (5) The enumeration of vessels, an animal, and his fellow's feet. (6) So that it moves about. (7) It is not accounted part of the pavement.

b (1) Lit., 'the small.' (2) Entirely leaving the earth beneath it exposed. (3) Lit., 'the soil of the deep'. (4) What if the pavement is removed and the priests stand on the earth beneath? (5) To stand on the earth beneath the paving stone. (6) Lev. IV, 25. (7) '*Finger*' stands between 'take' and 'put' in the text, and so the Rabbis apply it to both; and it is stated below that 'finger' always means that of the right hand. (8) It is now assumed that R. Simeon agrees that 'hand' means the right, but not 'finger'. (9) Whereby it is deduced that '*hand*' in connection with sacrifices means the right. The *gezerah shawah* is from a leper, where both '*hand*' and '*finger*' are written. (10) 'Finger' is however written both here and in connection with a leper; and there it is definitely the right.

c (1) Since *right* hand is not stated there either. (2) The receiving vessel cannot be held by a finger only. Hence 'finger', which denotes the right one, must refer to the applying of the blood, but not to the receiving. (3) In which the blood is caught.

וכל שני כתובים הבאין כאחד אין מלמדין ולמאן דאמר מלמדין [א] שתויי יין הוה ליה שלישי ושלשה [ב] לד"ה אין מלמדין: עומד על גבי כלים על גבי בהמה על גבי רגלי חבירו פסול: מנלן דתנא דבי רבי ישמעאל הואיל ורצפה מקדשת וכלי שרת מקדשים מה כלי שרת לא יהא דבר חוצץ בינו לבין כלי שרת אף רצפה לא יהא דבר חוצץ בינו לבין הרצפה וצריכא דאי אשמעינן כלי משום דלאו מינא דבשר [ג] נינהו אבל בהמה דמינא דבשר הוא אימא לא ואי אשמעינן בהמה דלא מינא דאדם הוא אבל חבירו דאדם הוא אימא לא צריכא *תניא רבי אליעזר אומר רגלו אחת על הכלי ורגלו אחת על הרצפה רגלו אחת על האבן ורגלו אחת על הרצפה רואין כל שאילו [ד] ינטל הכלי ותנטל האבן יכול לעמוד על רגלו אחת ויעבוד עבודתו כשירה ואם לאו עבודתו פסולה בעי רבי אמי נדלדלה האבן ועמד עליה מהו היכא דאין דעתו לחברה לא תיבעי לך דודאי חייצא כי תיבעי לך דדעתו לחברה מאי כיון דדעתו לחברה כמה דמחבר' דמיא או דילמא השתא מיהא הא תלישא רבה זוטי בעי לה הכי בעי רבי אמי נעקרה האבן ועמד במקומה מהו מאי קא מיבעיא ליה כי קדיש דוד רצפה עליונה קדיש או דילמא עד לארעית דתהומא קדיש ותיבעי ליה כל העזרה כולה לעולם פשיטא ליה דעד ארעית דתהומא קדיש והכי קמיבעיא ליה דרך שירות בכך או אין דרך שירות בכך תיקו: קיבל בשמאל פסול ור"ש מכשיר: ת"ר *באצבע ולקח *מלמד שלא תהא קבלה אלא בימין °באצבע ונתן מלמד שלא תהא נתינה אלא בימין אמר ר"ש וכי נאמרה יד בקבלה אלא באצבעו ונתן שלא תהא נתינה אלא בימין הואיל ולא נאמרה יד בקבלה קיבל בשמאל כשר ור"ש ממה נפשך אי אית ליה גזירה שוה כי לא נאמרה יד בקבלה מאי הוי ואי לית ליה גזירה שוה כי נאמרה יד בקבלה מאי הוי אמר רב יהודה לעולם לית ליה גזירה שוה והכי קאמר וכי נאמר יד ימין בקבלה הואיל ולא נאמר יד ימין בקבלה קבל בשמאל כשר א"ל רבה א"ה אפילו נתינה נמי ועוד וכי לית ליה לר"ש ג"ש *והתניא ר"ש אומר כל מקום שנאמר יד אינה אלא ימין אצבע אינה אלא ימין אלא אמר רבא לעולם אית ליה ג"ש והכי קאמר וכי נאמרה יד בקבלה הואיל ולא נאמר' יד בקבלה אלא אצבע ואי אפשר לקבלה באצבע קיבל בשמאל כשר אמר ליה רב סמא בריה דרב אשי לרבינא איפשר דעביד ליה אזן לשפת מזרק ומקבל (א) בה אלא אמר אביי

במקרא

ויקרא ד

רש"י

*שני כתובין הבאין כאחד. ה] דבתרוייהו כתיב קראי למיתה בסנהדרין באלו הן הנשרפין וטובא קשיא לי בגוה חדא דמה לו ללמוד מהן הא מיתה בגופה כתיב דכיון דזר הוא והזר הקרב יומת דהא מחוסר בגדים נמי הכי ילפינן ליה בסנהדרין אין בגדיהן עליהן אין כהונתן עליהן והוו להו זרים ועוד א"כ חילול עבודה לא נילף מיניה דבחילול נמי קראי טובא איכא: הואיל ו] ורצפה מקדשת. לעמוד לשרת שהרי דוד קידשה בשתי תודות ובשיר של פגעים כדאמרינן לקמן בשמעתין כי קדיש דוד כו': וכלי שרת מקדשין. כדכתיב וימשחם ויקדש אותם (במדבר ז): לא יהא דבר חוצץ בין כהן לכלי שרת. בקבלת הדם כדכתיב ולקח הכהן (ויקרא ד) שתהא לקיחה בעצמו של כהן: וצריכא. למיתני במתני' חצילת כלים ובהמה ורגל חבירו לפי הסדר שנשנו בה: דלאו מינא דבשר אדם הוא. וכיון דאינו ממין אדם כלל הוי מין בשאינו מינו וחוצץ: רגלו אחת על האבן. שמוטלת על הרצפה ואינה מן הרצפה: נידלדלה. *אבן אחת ז] מאבניה מקביעותה ומתנענעת ברצפה: נידלדלה. לכאן ולכאן: נעקרה. לגמרי והגומא נראית שם ועמד בגומא ועבד: כי קדיש דוד. ח] שהיה מקדש אותה בשתי תודות ובשיר של פגעים כדתנן במס' שבועות (דף יד. טו:): תיבעי ליה כל העזרה כולה. שנטלה רצפה שלה: דרך שירות בכך. מי הוי אורח ארעא ומיקרי שירות או לא: באצבעו ולקח. דכתיב ולקח הכהן מדם החטאת באצבעו ונתן על קרנות הטילו הכתוב לאצבע בין קבלה לזריקה ט] דורשהו לפניו ולאחריו לומר שלא יהיו אלא בימין דילפינן לקמן בשמעתין כל מקום שנאמר אצבע אינו אלא ימין: וכי נאמרה יד בקבלה. קס"ד דאם נאמרה בה יד הוה ר"ש מודה בה אבל באצבע לא יליף בה ימין לקמן בעי לה ומשנינן לה: אלא באצבעו ונתן כו'. בהא מודינא לך דזריקת חטאת בעיא ימין: ור"ש. דאמר אי הוה כתיב בה יד הוה יליף לה ימין ומאצבע לא יליף: ממה נפשך אי אית ליה ג"ש י]. דילפינן יד יד דקמיצה ממצורע דכתיב ביה על בהן ידו הימנית אף כל מקום שנאמר יא] יד אינה אלא ימין: כי לא נאמר יד בקבלה מאי הוי. הרי נאמר בה אצבעו ונילף אצבע אצבע נמי מהתם דכתיב במצורע וטבל הכהן את אצבעו הימנית: יב] ה"ג לעולם לית ליה ג"ש וה"ק וכי נאמר יד ימנית כו': אלא אמר רבא לעולם אית ליה ג"ש וה"ק וכי נאמר יג] בה יד בקבלה. אי הוה כתב יד שהיה ראויה לאחוז בכלי ולקבל הדם *הוא יד] איכא למידרש נמי אקבלה והואיל ולא נאמר כאן יד אלא אצבע ואי אפשר לקבל דם בכלי באצבע לבדה ע"כ משום נתינה הוא דכתיב טו] בה שהוא ראוי לה ולא משום קבלה נמצא שאף אצבע לא נאמר בו לפיכך קיבל בשמאל כשר: אוזן. כמו שעושים לכדים של חרס שקורין מאניק"ו: ומקבל ביה. בההוא אוזן מקבל את הדם באצבע שתוחב אצבעו לתוכה ועושה את המזרק ומקבל:

נדרש

תוספות

זר הוי קרא שלישי וא"כ ליהוו שלשה כתובין הבאין כאחד ולמאי דפרישית אתי שפיר דמיתה דמחוסר בגדים לא טז] מיתורא אלא משום דאשכחן דזר הוי במיתה ולכך אמרינן דלא ילפינן מיתה מהא דקרייה רחמנא זר *ולפירוש הקונטרס דיליף מבינייא קשה דהוה ליה שלשה כתובים הבאין כאחד ובקונטרס פירש וה"ה נמי דמצי למימר משום דהוי זר ושלא רחוץ ידים ורגלים שני כתובים הבאין כאחד דהא מחוסר בגדים גופיה לא כתיבא ביה מיתה אלא משום דזר הוא וחדא מינייהו נקט ואי איפשר לומר כן דבהדיא אשכחן מיתה במחוסר בגדים בפרשת ואתה תצוה ומיהו פירוש הקונטרס על כרחין עיקר דבסנהדרין סוף פרק הנשרפין (דף פג: ושם ד"ה אין) יליף בהדיא מחוסר בגדים במיתה משום דהוו להו זרים דאין בגדיהם עליהם אין כהונתן עליהן ומיתה דכתיבא בפרשת ואתה תצוה מפרש ה"ר יעקב מאורלינש דבמכנסים כתיב וקרא דוחגרת דדריש מיניה ברים פירקין בסנהדרין אין בגדיהם עליהם אין כהונתן עליהם והוו להו זרים אילטריך לשאר בגדים ומיניה לא הוה ילפינן מכנסים דלא כתיבא בההיא פרשתא ומיהו למאן דמרבי ביומא (דף ה:) מכנסיים מוזה הדבר [וי"ו מוסיף על ענין ראשון] קשה מיתה דכתב רחמנא גבי מכנסים למה לי ועוד קשה לפירוש הקונטרס דליהוי זר ומכנסים ושלא רחוץ שלשה כתובים:

הואיל ורצפה מקדשת. דוד קידשה כדפירש בקונטרס ואע"ג דשלמה בנה הבית דוד קידשה כדאמר לקמן בשמעתא כי קדיש דוד וכו' ובירושלמי דפרק ב' דשבועות אמרינן דוד זה מלך גד זה נביא יז] ומה שפירש בקונטרס שקידשה בשתי תודות ובשיר אינו כן דעזרה אינה מקדשה בשתי תודות אלא בשירי מנחה כדאיתא בשבועות (דף טו.) יח]:

הואיל ורצפה מקדשת. פירוש דמקדשת האדם לעבוד עבודה שם דאינו יכול לעבוד במקום אחר וכלי שרת פירוש בגדי כהונה מקדשין האדם לעבוד עבודה מה כלי שרת לא יהא דבר חוצץ בינו לבין כלי שרת דהא כתיב על בשרו כדאמרינן לעיל (דף יט.) ובגדי כהונה קרי להו כלי שרת כדאמר לעיל (דף יג.) שתהא בכהן כשר ובכלי שרת ובקונטרס פי' שבכלי שרת ממש שלא יהא דבר חוצץ בין כהן לכלי שרת יט] בקבלת הדם כדכתיב ולקח הכהן שתהא לקיחה בעצמו של כהן ואם תאמר מדחשיב ליה הכא חצילה ולעיל נמי דפריך ותיפוק לי משום חצילה וגבי ההוא דכריך ידיה בשיראי (פסחים דף מ.) אלמא לקיחה ע"י ד"א לא שמה לקיחה ובפ' לולב הגזול (סוכה דף לז.) קאמר רבא דלקיחה ע"י דבר אחר שמה לקיחה ויש לומר דהתם (ב) כ] [לא] מיירי כגון דכריך ידיה בסודר וטטל לולב דהא ודאי לא הוי לקיחה אלא דצריך ליה ללולב בסודרא וטטלו ובאותו ענין מייתי רבא ראיה מאזוב וכן צריך לומר מתוך שמעתא דהתם *דקאמר רבא גופיה מין במינו אינו חוצץ הא בשאינו מינו חוצץ ואמאי והא לקיחה ע"י דבר אחר שמה לקיחה ושמא חד מינייהו רבה ולמאי דפרישית ניחא דכי צריך ליה ללולב בסודר אף על פי שאינו חיבור גמור האי כמו בית יד ולהכי חשיב ליה לקיחה וקצת קשה מההיא דיומא (דף נח.) דקאמר הניח מזרק בתוך מזרק מהו מאי קא מיבעיא ליה הא כי האי גוונא הויא לקיחה על ידי ד"א שמה לקיחה דליהוי חילון בית יד לפנימי ויש לומר דלאי אחיז ליה חילון בדופניו שמטלטל הפנימי על ידו הכי נמי דהויא לקיחה מטעם בית יד אלא הכא במאי עסקינן כגון שנושא החילון מתחתיו דלא מהני כלל לפנימי *):

*) [וע"ע תוס' פסחים מ. ד"ה דכריך ותוס' יומא נח. ד"ה מין ותוס' סוכה לז. ד"ה כי היכי]

במקרא

מסורת הש"ס

נ"א שני כתובין הבאין כאחד כו' דתרוייהו מחלי עבודה וכתיב בהו מיתה בסנהדרין וה"ה דהוה מצי למימר דהוי זר ושלא רחוץ ידים ורגלים שני כתובין הבאין כאחד דהא מחוסר בגדים לא כתיב ביה מיתה אלא משום דזר הוא וחדא מינייהו נקט

שבת נג:

נ"א אבן אחת מאבני הרצפה מקביעותה ומתנענעת לכאן ולכאן רש"ק

[ע' תוס' יומא נג: ד"ה שתא]

מנחות י.

נ"ל הוי

הגהות הב"ח

(א) גמ' ומקבל ביה אלא: (ב) תוס' ד"ה הואיל וכו' וי"ל דהתם מיירי כגון דכריך לולב בסודרא ונטל בסודר בידו דהוא ודאי לא הוי לקיחה אלא היכא דכריך ליה ללולב:

עין משפט נר מצוה

עד א מיי' פ"ב מהל' ביאת מקדש הל' ח.

עה ב מיי' שם הל"ט

נ"א ולפירוש הקונטרס דיליף כמה מלינו קשה כו' וגי' רש"ק ולפירוש הקונטרס דיליף מחדא וכו'

עו ג מיי' פ"א מהל' ביאת מקדש הל' יב:

[מנחות יט. ע"ש]

שיטה מקובצת

א] מלמדין מאי איכא למימר הא איכא שתויי יין נמי והוי: ב] ושלשה כתובים הבאים כאחד: ג] תיבת נינהו נמחק: ד] שאילו נטל הכלי ותנטל האבן ויכול לעמוד: ה] דבתרווייהו. ס"א מחלי עבודה וכתיב בהו מיתה כדאיתא בסנהדרין וה"ה נמי דהוי מצי למימר משום דהוי זר ושלא רחוץ ידים ורגלים שני כתובים הבאים כאחד דהא מחוסר בגדים גופיה לא כתיב ביה מיתה אלא משום דזר הוא וחדא מינייהו נקיט: ו] ורצפה. מקודשת ס"א מקדשת האדם לעבוד עבודה שם דאינו יכול לעבוד במקום אחר ויש גורסין הואיל ורצפה מקודשת כלומר לעמוד כו': ז] אחת מאבני הריצפ' מקביעות' ומנענעת לכאן ולכאן הס"ד ומה"ד נעקרה: ח] שהיו מקדשין אותה בשתי תודות: ט] לזריקה ולדורשו: י] ג"ש דלקמן: יא] שנאמר בו: יב] (הימנית) לעולם לית ליה ג"ש גרסי' ותיבות ה"ג נמחק: יג] תיבת בה נמחק:

יד] הוא דאיכא: טו] דכתיב. (ביד שהשבו)[ביה שהוא]: טז] לא מיתרא אלא משום כו' ולפירוש הקונטרס דיליף מבנין אב קשה: יז] נביא. אבל מה: יח] בשבועות. וי"מ הואיל והד"א: יט] שרת. בשעת קבלת הדם כדכתיב כו' וא"ת מ"ש דהשיב ליה כו' וגבי ההוא נמי דכריך ידו בשיראי. בשילהי מקום שנהגו: כ] דהתם לא מיירי כו' ללולב בסודרא ונטל שני ראשי הסודר ובאותו ענין:

*במקרא נדרש לפניו ולאחריו קמיפלגי אמר אביי הא דרבי אלעזר ברבי שמעון מפקא מדאבוה ומפקא מדרבנן דתניא רבי אלעזר ברבי שמעון אומר כל מקום שנאמר אצבע בקבלה שינה בקבלה פסול בנתינה כשר וכל מקום שנאמר אצבע בנתינה שינה בנתינה פסול בקבלה כשר והיכן נאמר אצבע בנתינה דכתיב °ולקחת מדם הפר ונתת על קרנות המזבח באצבעך וקסבר *מקרא נדרש לפניו ולא לפני פניו (א) א] ולאחריו: *אמר רבה בר בר חנה אמר ב] רבי יוחנן כל מקום שנאמר אצבע וכהונה אינה אלא ימין קא סלקא דעתין תרתי בעינן כדכתיב °ולקח הכהן מדם החטאת באצבעו ויליף ממצורע דכתי' °וטבל הכהן את אצבעו הימנית ג] והרי קמיצה דלא כתיב בה אלא כהונה *ותנן [א]קמץ בשמאל פסול ד] אלא אמר רבא או אצבע או כהונה א"ל אביי *הרי הולכת אברים לכבש דכתיב בהו כהונה דכתיב °והקריב הכהן את הכל [והקטיר] המזבחה ואמר מר זו הולכת אברים לכבש *ותנן [ב]הרגל של ימין בשמאלו ובית עורה לחוץ ה] [כי אמרינן] או אצבע או כהונה בדבר המעכב כפרה דומיא דמצורע והרי קבלה ו] דכתב בהו כהונה ודבר המעכב בכפרה הוא ותנן קבל בשמאל פסול ור"ש מכשיר ר"ש תרתי בעי מי בעי ר"ש תרתי והתניא רבי שמעון אומר כל מקום שנאמר יד אינו אלא ימין אצבע אינו אלא ימין אצבע לא בעיא כהונה כהונה בעיא אצבע ואלא כהן למה לי ז] בכיהונו והרי זריקה דלא כתב בהו אלא כהונה ותנן זרק בשמאל פסול ולא פליג רבי שמעון אמר אביי פליג בברייתא דתניא קיבל בשמאל פסול ורבי שמעון מכשיר זרק בשמאל פסול ורבי שמעון מכשיר אלא הא *דאמר רבא °יד יד לקמיצה רגל רגל לחליצה אזן אזן לרציעה למה לי מדרבה בר בר חנה נפקא חד לקומץ וחד לקידוש קומץ ולר"ש

שמות כט | ויקרא ד | שם יד | שם א

רש"י

נדרש (ב). ר"ש סבר ח] מקרא נדרש לאחריו ולא לפניו הילכך אצבע אונתן דכתיב בתריה קאי ולא אולקח דכתיב לקמיה ורבנן סברי מקרא נדרש לפניו ולאחריו: מפקא מדאבוה. מוצאת מכלל דברי אביו ומכלל דברי חכמים: כל מקום שנאמר אצבע בקבלה. תורה אור ולא בנתינה כגון האי קרא דלעיל דר' אלעזר בר"ש דריש אצבע אולקח דהיינו לפניו ולא אונתן: שינה בקבלה. שקיבל בשמאל (ג) וקאמר לך במקום שנכתב שם תתננו ולא ט] במה שלא נכתב בו: ולקחת מדם הפר. בפר המילואים כתיב: ולא לפני פניו. דלא דריש להאי באצבע דמילואים אולקחת ולא לאחריו דלא דריש להאי באצבעו דחטאת יחיד (ויקרא ד) אונתן והיינו פליג אדאבוה דאבוה סבר לאחריו ולא לפניו ואדרבנן דאינהו סברי בין לפניו בין לאחריו: וכהונה. כגון הכהן או הכהנים: תרתי בעינן. אצבע וכהונה כגון האי קרא דכתיב גבי זריקת חטאת ולקח הכהן מדם החטאת באצבעו וקאמר י] רבי יוחנן דהכא ימין בעי דגמר ממצורע עשיר דכתיב ביה אצבע וכהונה ומפרש יא] ביה ימנית: הרגל של ימין. נושא ביד שמאל לכבש משום דרגל ימין יב] קרבה תחילה עם הראש כדקיימא לן בפ"ב דסדר יומא (דף כה.) והילכך מוליך הראש בימין שהוא חשוב והרגל בשמאל: ובית עורה לחוץ. כלפי העם ומקום החתך כלפי המוליך דהכי שפיר שלא יראה החתך: המעכב כפרה. דומיא דהזאה של מצורע יג] כגון קמיצה אבל הולכת איברים דלא מעכבא כפרה דהוא עצמו שלא הוקטרו אימורין כשר לא בעיא ימין: קבלה כתב בה כהונה. דכתיב יד] והקריבו בני אהרן הכהנים ואמר מר זו קבלת הדם: ואלא כהן למה לי. בקבלה הא כתיב בני אהרן טו] אי לאו לאגמורי אימין אתא: בכיהונו. בבגדי כהונה: זרק בשמאל פסול ור"ש מכשיר. אשאר כל הזבחים (ד) דלא כתב בהו אצבע אלא וזרקו הכהנים אבל בזריקת חטאת מודה ר"ש כדאמר לעיל באצבעו ונתן שלא תהא נתינה אלא בימין: ואלא הא דאמר רבא. במנחות בפ"ק (דף י.) יד יד לקמיצה בפרשת מצורע עשיר כתיב על תנוך אזן הימנית ועל בהן ידו הימנית ועל בהן רגלו הימנית וקרא יתירא הוא כדמפרש התם וקאמר רבא יד דמצורע אתי לג"ש למיגמר יד דקמיצה מינה שתהא בימין והיכא טז] כתב יד בקמיצה וימלא כפו ממנה: לחליצה. שתהא בימין: למה לי. יד בקמיצה: מדרבה בר בר חנה נפקא. דהא כהונה כתיב יז]: לקידוש קומץ. בכלי שרת שיהא בימין שיאחז הכלי שהוא מקדש בו בידו הימנית:

תוספות

במקרא נדרש לפניו ולאחריו קמיפלגי. הא דפליגי אמוראי בפרק השואל (ב"מ דף צה.) במקרא נדרש לפניו ולא לפני פניו ופריך ממתני' דהשואל לא מצי למימר דההיא ר"ש דלא דריש קרא לפניו דהתם הוי מטעמא דהוי"ו מוסיף על ענין ראשון ומודה ר"ש כדאמר בהקומץ רבה (מנחות דף יט.) היינו טעמא דר"ש והביא וי"ו מוסיף על ענין ראשון וגבי ולקח ונתן לא אמרינן וי"ו *מוסיף על ענין ראשון וא"כ נילף קבלה מנתינה בימין כדפי' התם בקונטרס דאצבעו הפסיק הענין בין ולקח לונתן יח] ופ' קמא דקדושין (דף טו:) משמע דכולי עלמא יט] דרשינן מקרא לפניו בלא וי"ו מוסיף כ] על ענין [וא"כ איכא] למילף קבלה מנתינה דפריך ונקיש מזוזה לתלמוד תורה ובפ"ק דראש השנה (דף ט:) דרשי כולי עלמא מקרא לפניו ובלפני פניו ולאחריו פליגי ובסמוך קשה טפי דקאמר רבי אלעזר בר"ש כל מקום שנא' אצבע בנתינה שינה בנתינה פסול בקבלה כשר כגון ולקחת מדם הפר ונתת על קרנות המזבח באצבעך וקסבר מקרא נדרש לפניו ולא לפני פניו כא] ולאחריו נימא וי"ו מוסיף על ענין ראשון ושמא רבי אלעזר בר"ש לית ליה וי"ו מוסיף א"כ לא דרשינן וי"ו מוסיף כדי לדרוש המקרא לפני פניו: **והרי** זריקה ותנן זרק בשמאל פסול. אפילו בשאר זבחים ולא פליג ר"ש אמר אביי פליג בברייתא ופרש"י זרק בשמאל בשאר קרבנות אבל בחטאת מודה ר"ש דבעי ימין כדאיתא בברייתא לעיל והקשה הרב ר' יעקב מאורליינש מאי קושיא ואמאי כב] פליג ר"ש בברייתא נהי דלא כתב אלא כהונה מ"מ אתיא מהיקשא דזאת התורה דאמר לקמן סוף דם חטאת (דף צח.) ובמנחות סוף התודה (דף פג.) מה חטאת אינה באה אלא מן החולין וביום ובידו הימנית אף כל וכו' ופריך ידו הימנית מדרבה בר בר חנה נפקא דכל מקום שנאמר אצבע וכהונה אינה אלא ימין ומשני כדי נסבה אי נמי סבר לה כר"ש דכהונה בעיא אצבע משמע בהדיא דר"ש יליף שאר קרבנות כג] מחטאת והשיב לו ר"ת דלא גרסינן והרי זריקה דאינה משנה בשום מקום אלא גרסינן והרי מליקה ומשנה היא לקמן בפרק חטאת העוף (דף סח.) דתנן כל הפסולין שמלקו מליקתן פסולה ואין מטמאין בגדים אבית הבליעה מלק בשמאל או בלילה כד] כו' והש"ס הביאה בקוצר שכן דרך הש"ס לקצר כמה משניות והסופרים טעו וכתבו במקום מליקה זריקה ועופות לא אתו בהיקשא דזאת התורה אבל זריקה בשאר קרבנות פסל שפיר בשמאל דיליף בהיקשא דזאת התורה כדמשמע שילהי דם חטאת (לקמן דף צח.) ובסמוך נמי גרסינן בברייתא מלק בשמאל פסול ור"ש מכשיר ועוד אומר ר"ת דאפילו גרסינן זרק מליט למימר דההוא תנא דזאת התורה דמפיק ימין מחטאת סבר לה כר"ש דכהונה בעיא אצבע אבל ר"ש לא סבר לה כוותיה כה] למילף ימין בזריקה בשאר קרבנות מחטאת משום דזריקה לא ילפינן מהזאה וקשה על זה מעיקרא כי פריך והרי זריקה דלא פליג ר"ש כו] דילמא היינו משום דיליף מהיקשא ויש לומר דעדיפא משני פליג בברייתא וקשה לפר"ת דאפילו גרס בברייתא מלק על כרחיך אמת הוא דמכשיר ר"ש זריקה בשמאל כדמוכח בסמוך ובפ"ק (לעיל דף יח.) דאמר ומאי טעמא דר"ש בא לעובדה בכלי עובדה בשמאל כאשם והיינו בזריקת אשם כז] דבקבלה לא איירי דאפי' חטאת נמי לא בעי ימין בקבלה לר"ש דאמר לעיל וכי נאמרה יד בקבלה (לר"ש) כו' וצריך לתרץ דהאי תנא סבר לה סותיה בחדא ואם תאמר לפירוש רבינו תם נמי דגרסינן מלק הא מליקה נפקא לן בפ"ק דחולין (דף כב.) ימין אפילו לר"ש מדכתיב ואת השני יעשה עולה כמשפט דרשינן *כמשפט חטאת בהמה כח] דאינה באה אלא מן החולין וביום ובידו הימנית והתם נמי פריך ימנית מדרבה בר בר חנה נפקא ומשני כר"ש דכהונה בעיא אצבע וי"ל דמליקה שהיא כנגד שחיטה לא נפקא והתם בהזאה מיירי דבעיא ימין אבל מהיקשא לא ילפינן עופות מחטאת בהמה ולכך איצטריך נמי כמשפט התם א"נ ההוא תנא סבר כתנא דפליג עליה דר"ש לעיל ופוסל קבלה בשמאל משום דמקרא נדרש לפניו ולאחריו ומוקי אצבעו דכתיב גבי חטאת גם על קבלה ולדידהו ילפינן שפיר מליקה בימין מחטאת דקבלה לא שייך למילף דליתיה בעוף וילפינן מליקה אבל ר"ש דאמר קבל בשמאל כשר ולית ליה ימין בחטאת בהמה אלא בהזאה לחודה בעולת העוף

עז א מיי' פי"א מהל' פסה"מ הל"ב:
עח ב מיי' פ"ו מהל' מעה"ק הלי"א:

נ"א מוסיף על ענין ראשון למילף קבלה כו' צ"ק

שיטה מקובצת
א] פניו ולא לאחריו: ב] אמר ריש לקיש כל מקום: ג] והרי קמיצה כו' וא"ת ולישני הכא דשאני קמיצה דכתיב בה יד וילפינן יד יד לקמיצה כדאמר בסמוך אבל בעלמא בעינא כהונה ואצבע וי"ל דמקידוש קומץ בכלי שרת פריך דהתם ליכא ג"ש דיד יד ואפ"ה אמרינן קמץ בשמאל פסול וסמיך אברייתא דמנחות דפסל בקומץ ובקידוש קומץ: ד] תיבת אלא נמחק: ה] לחוץ כי אמרינן: ו] דכתיב בה כהונה: ז] לי בכיהונו: ח] דמקרא נדרש: ט] במקום שלא: י] וקאמר ריש לקיש דהכא: יא] ומפרש בה: יב] ימין קרב: יג] מצורע או כגון: יד] דכתיב בה: טו] הא כתיב בני אהרן וא"כ אמאי כתיב ביה כהן (הא) [אי] כו': טז] והיכא כתיב: יז] כתיב בה: יח] לונתן ובפ"ק: יט] עלמא דרשי מקרא: כ] מתיבת על עד תיבת דפריך נמחק: כא] ולא לאחריו: כב] ואמאי משני אביי דפליג ר"ש כו' דלא כתיב בה אלא כהונה כו' דאמר לקמן בסוף דם חטאת: כג] מחטאת. דכי היכא דמתן דם דידיה חוי בימין דכתיב ביה אצבע ה"ה בשאר קרבנות: כד] כו'. ואם היתה המליקה כשירה פשיטא דאינו מטמא אבית הבליעה ולא חשבינן ליה פסולו בקודש הר"ש: כה] כוותיה ולא יליף ימין: כו] ר"ש. מאי קשיא ליה דלמא כו' משני דפליג וקשה לפר"ת: כז] אשם שהיא בשמאל דבקבלה לא איירי כו' לר"ש כדקאמר לעיל וכי נאמרה יד בקבלה וצריך לתרץ כו' כוותיה. ס"א [סבר לה] כר"ש ור"ש לא סבר ליה כוותיה: כח] בהמה מה חטאת בהמה דאינה באה כו' והתם נמי פריך ידו הימנית מדרבה בר בר חנה כו' בעי אצבע. גליון מהיקשא דזאת התורה נפקא כמאן דאית ליה היקשא בפ"ק דחולין ובריש מנחות. ע"כ:

[שבת לב: וש"נ]
[שבת לב: וש"נ]
לקמן לח. מנחות י. [כל הסוגיא עד סופו] סג. חולין כב.
מנחות ו. י.
שם ולעיל יד: ושע"נ חגיגה יא.
תמיד לא: [מנחות י. יומא מח:]
מנחות י.
צ"ק
צ"ל כמשפט חטאת בהמה מה חטאת בהמה אינה כו' צ"ק

הגהות הב"ח
(א) גמ' ולא לפני פניו ולא לאחריו: (ב) רש"י ד"ה נדרש לפניו ולאחריו קמפלגי ר"ש סבר: (ג) ד"ה שינה וכו' בשמאל פסל וקאמר: (ד) ד"ה זרק וכו' כל הזבחים קאי דלא:

גליון הש"ס
גמ' יד יד לקמיצה. עיין לקמן סג. ע"ב תוס' ד"ה מה חטאת בכה"ג:

[the blood]?[4]—Rather said Abaye: [24b] They disagree [on the question] whether a text is to be interpreted with what precedes and with what follows it.[5]

Abaye said: The following [teaching] of R. Eleazar son of R. Simeon disagrees with his father's and with the Rabbis'. For it was taught, R. Eleazar son of R. Simeon said: Wherever 'finger' is stated in connection with receiving,[6] if [the priest] varied the reception [of the blood],[7] it is unfit; if the application, it is fit. And wherever 'finger' is stated in connection with the application, if he varied the application, it is unfit; if the reception, it is fit. And where is 'finger' stated in connection with the application?—For it is written, *And thou shalt take of the blood of the bullock, and put it upon the horns of the altar with thy finger;*[8] and he holds: A text is interpreted with its precedent, but not with its ante-precedent, nor with what follows it.

a Rabbah b. Bar Ḥanah said in R. Joḥanan's name:[1] Wherever 'finger' and 'priesthood' are stated, they refer to the right only. It was assumed that we require both, as it is written, *And the* priest *shall take of the blood of the sin-offering with his* finger;[2] and it is learnt from a leper, where it is written, *And the priest shall dip his right finger.*[3] But surely 'priesthood' alone is written in connection with the taking of the fistful [of flour] yet we learnt: If [the priest] took the handful with his left [hand], is it unfit?—Said Raba: [He meant] *either* 'finger' *or* 'priesthood'. Said Abaye to him: Yet 'priesthood' is written in connection with the carrying of the limbs to the [altar] ascent, as it is written, *And the priest shall offer the whole, and make it smoke on the altar,*[4] and a master said: This refers to the carrying of the limbs to the ascent; yet we learnt: [The priest carries] the right foot [of the sacrifice] in his left hand with the inside of the skin outward?—When do we say [that] either 'finger' or 'priesthood' [implies the right], only in respect of [a service] which is indispensable to atonement, as in the case of a leper.[5] But priesthood is written in connection with receiving, which is indispensable to atonement, yet we learnt: IF HE RECEIVED [THE BLOOD] WITH HIS LEFT HAND, IT IS UNFIT; BUT R. SIMEON DECLARES IT FIT?—R. Simeon requires both.[6] Does then R. Simeon require both? Surely it was taught, R. Simeon said: Wherever 'hand' is stated, it refers to the right only; [wherever] 'finger' [is stated], it refers to the right only?—[Where] 'finger' [is stated] he does not require 'priesthood', [but] where 'priesthood' [is stated], he does require 'finger'. Then what is the purpose of 'priesthood'?[7] [To teach that they must be] in their priestly state.[8]

But 'priesthood' alone is written in connection with sprinkling, yet we learnt: IF HE SPRINKLED WITH HIS LEFT HAND, IT IS UNFIT, and R. Simeon does not disagree?—Said Abaye: He does disagree in a Baraitha, for it was taught: If [the priest] received with his left hand, it is unfit; but R. Simeon declares it fit. If he sprinkled with his left hand, it is unfit; but R. Simeon declares it fit.

Then as to what Raba said, [We draw an analogy of] 'hand' 'hand' in respect of taking the fistful; 'foot', 'foot', in respect of *haliẓah*;
b 'ear' 'ear' in respect of boring [the ear].[1]—Why is this necessary [in respect of the fistful], seeing that it can be deduced from Rabbah b. Bar Ḥanah's [exegesis]?—One [is required] for the *taking* of the

(4) Holding it with the finger only. (5) Simultaneously. R. Simeon holds that a text can be interpreted only with what follows; hence 'finger' refers to *'and he shall put'*, but not to *'and he shall take'*, which precedes. While the Rabbis hold that it goes with both. (6) As in the present case. He holds that *'finger'* here refers to the preceding *'and he shall take'*, as its literal meaning does imply. (7) Receiving it with the left hand. (8) Ex. XXIX, 12.

a (1) Sh. M. reads: in the name of Resh Lakish. (2) Lev. IV, 25. (3) Ibid. XIV, 16. (4) Ibid. I, 13. (5) Whereas even if the limbs are not burnt at all, the efficacy of the sacrifice is unaffected. (6) 'Finger' and 'priesthood'. (7) In connection with receiving, seeing that it is already written that this must be done by the sons of Aaron. (8) In their priestly vestments.

b (1) V. Men. 9b and 10a. Raba refers to Lev. XIV, 14, which deals with a leper's purification: *And the priest shall take of the blood of the guilt-offering, and the priest shall put it upon the tip of the* right ear *of him that is to be cleansed, and upon the thumb of his* right hand, *and upon the great toe of his* right foot. Raba teaches that the *'right'* is mentioned in these cases in order to teach that when *'hand'*, *'foot'* and *'ear'* are written in connection with the taking of the fistful, the ceremony of *ḥaliẓah* (q.v. Glos; v. also Deut. XXV, 9) and the boring of the ear of a slave who refuses to accept his freedom (v. Ex. XXI, 5f) respectively, the right is meant in each case.

fistful, and the other for the *sanctification* of the fistful.[2] [25a] But according to R. Simeon, who does not require the sanctification of the fistful [at all], or on the view that R. Simeon does indeed require the sanctification of the fistful, yet he certainly holds that it is fit if done with the left,[3] what is the purpose of Raba's [analogy of] 'hand', 'hand'? If in respect of the actual taking of the fistful, that is deduced from Rab Judah the son of R. Ḥiyya's [teaching]. For Rab Judah the son of R. Ḥiyya said, What is R. Simeon's reason? Scripture saith, *It is most holy, as the sin-offering, and as the guilt-offering:*[4] [this teaches:] If [the priest] comes to perform its service with his hand, he does so with the right hand, as in the case of a sin-offering; [if he comes] to perform the service with a vessel, he may do so with the left hand, as in the case of the guilt-offering?[5] —It is necessary only in respect of [a priest] who takes the fistful of a sinner's meal-offering: You might think, since R. Simeon said, [The reason is] that his sacrifice should not be adorned,[6] let it be fit too even if [the priest] takes the fistful with his left hand. Therefore [the text] informs us [that it is not so].

MISHNAH. IF THE BLOOD WAS POURED OUT ON TO THE
a PAVEMENT[1] AND [THE PRIEST] COLLECTED IT, IT IS UNFIT.

GEMARA. Our Rabbis taught: *And the anointed priest shall take of the blood of the bullock:*[2] [this means,] of the life blood, but not of the blood of the skin or of the draining blood;[3] '*of the blood of the bullock*' [implies,] he is to receive the blood [direct] from the bullock.[4] For if you think that '*of the blood of the bullock*' [is meant literally] as it is written, [viz.,] of *the blood* [indicating] even a portion of the blood [only], surely Rab said: He who slaughters [the sacrifice] must receive *all* the blood of the bullock, for it says, *And all the remaining blood of the bullock shall he pour out.*[5] Hence '*from the blood of the bullock*' means, he is to receive the blood [direct] from the bullock; for [the author of this exegesis] holds: You subtract, add, and interpret.[6]

The [above] text [stated]: Rab said: He who slaughters [the sacrifice] must receive all the blood of the bullock, for it says, '*And* all *the remaining blood of the bullock shall he pour out*'. But surely this is written of the remainder [of the blood]?[7]—Since it is inapplicable to the remainder, for *all* the blood is not available [at the time],[8] apply it to receiving.

Rab Judah said in Samuel's name: He who slaughters must raise the knife upwards,[9] for it is said, '*And he shall take of the blood of the bullock,*' but not of the blood of the bullock plus something else. And with what does he wipe the knife?—Said Abaye: With the
b edge of the bowl,[1] as it is written, *Wipers* [cleaners] *of gold.*[2]

R. Ḥisda said in the name of R. Jeremiah b. Abba: He who

(2) The fistful was sanctified by being placed in a service vessel. We now learn that while this is done the vessel must be held in the right hand. (3) For it is no worse than sprinkling, and in fact corresponds to it. (4) Lev. VI, 10. (5) V. *supra* 11a. (6) A sinner's meal-offering has no oil or incense, and R. Simeon states the reason because it is unfitting that a sinner's offering should be given the same adornment as another sacrifice.

a (1) Straight from the animal's neck. (2) Lev. IV, 5. (3) The life blood is the first blood that gushes out; the draining blood is that which follows. (4) And not permit it to pour on to the pavement first; if he does, it is unfit. (5) Ibid. 7. (6) You may subtract a letter from one word and add it to another, where the context warrants it, and then interpret the text in accordance with this alteration. Thus here the partitive מ ('of' or 'from') is removed from מדם blood, and added to הפר the bullock, so that it reads: and he shall take the (not, of the) blood from the bullock. (7) It refers to the pouring out of the remainder, and not to receiving at all. (8) As some of it has already been sprinkled on the horns of the altar. (9) So that none of the blood on the knife runs into the bowl.

b (1) Taking care that the blood does not flow into it. (2) Ezra I, 10; E.V. *bowls of gold*. Abaye connects the Heb. *kefore* with *kapper*, to wipe away (whence its general meaning of to atone or forgive).

ולר"ש דלא בעי קידוש קומץ ולמאן דאמר לר"ש נמי בעי קידוש קומץ בשמאל אכשורי מכשר יד יד דרבא למה לי אי לקמיצה עצמה א] מדרב יהודה בריה דרבי חייא נפקא *דאמר ר"י בריה דרביחייא מאי טעמא דרבי שמעון [דאמר קרא] °קודש קדשי' היא כחטאת וכאשם בא לעובודה ביד עובדה בימין כחטאת בא לעובדה בכלי עובדה בשמאל כאשם לא נצרכא ב] [אלא] לקומץ מנחת חוטא סד"א *הואיל ואמר ר"ש *שלא יהא קרבנו מהודר כי קמץ לה בשמאל נמי תיתכשר קא משמע לן: **מתני'** *א*נשפך הדם על הרצפה ואספו פסול: **גמ'** תנו רבנן °ולקח הכהן המשיח מדם הפר מדם הנפש ולא מדם העור ולא מדם התמצית מדם הפר דם מהפר יקבלנו דאי סלקא דעתך מדם הפר כדכתיב מדם ואפילו מקצת דם *והאמר רב (א) ג] השוחט צריך שיקבל את *כל דמו של פר שנאמר °ואת כל *דמו ישפוך אלא מדם הפר דם מהפר יקבלנו וקסבר *גורעין ומוסיפין ודורשין גופא אמר רב יהודה אמר רב השוחט צריך שיקבל את כל דמו של פר שנאמר °ואת כל דם הפר ישפך והא בשיריים כתיב אם אינו ענין לשיריים דהא ליתיה לכוליה דם תנידו ענין (ב) ד] בקבלה אמר רב יהודה אמר שמואל השוחט צריך שיגביה סכין למעלה שנאמר °ולקח מדם הפר ולא מדם הפר ודבר אחר ודם סכין במאי מקנח ליה אמר אביי *בשפת מזרק כדכתיב °כפורי זהב אמר רב חסדא אמר רב ירמיה בר אבא השוחט צריך שיתן ורידין

ולרבי שמעון דלא בעי קידוש קומץ. כדאמר בהקומץ רבה (מנחות דף כו.) שלא בכלי שרת פסולה ורבי שמעון מכשיר: ולמ"ד נמי ר"ש בעי קידוש קומץ. דאיכא אמוראי דפליגי התם במילתיה דר"ש ואיכא למ"ד הכל מודים בקומץ שטעון קידוש וכי קאמר *ר"ש כשרה בהקטרה קאמר אם נטלו מתוך כלי שרת לאחר שקידשו והקטירו בידו: בשמאל אכשורי מכשר. לקדש דלא עדיף קידוש הקומץ מקבלת הדם דמכשר לה רבי שמעון בשמאל: אי לקמיצה גופה. שתהא בימין דלר"ש לא נפקא ליה מוקמן הכהן דהא ה] אמרו לעיל דבעינן לרבי שמעון אצבע מדר' יהודה נפקא: מאי טעמא דר' שמעון. דמכשר הקטרת קומץ שלא בכלי אם ו] העלן למזבח בידו אמר קרא במנחה קדש קדשים הוא (ג) להכי איתקש מנחה לחטאת ואשם לומר לך בא לעבודה ביד עובדה בימין כחטאת שזריקת דמה ז] בימין במתן אצבע ולא בכלי ובעיא ימין דכתיב בה אצבע וכהונה: בא לעבודה בכלי עובדה בשמאל כאשם. שזריקה בכלי (ד) והיא כשרה בשמאל לר"ש כדאמר לעיל זרק בשמאל פסול ור' שמעון מכשיר אלמא אי בעי ביד עביד אי בכלי עביד וממילא נפקא קמילה בימין דהא עבודת יד היא ולא עבודת כלי: לקומץ דמנחת חוטא. שתהא קמילתו בימין (ה): דהואיל וא"ר שמעון. בפ"ק דמנחות (דף ו.) בדין הוא שתהא מנחת חוטא טעונה שמן ולבונה שלא יהא חוטא נשכר ומפני מה לא הטעינה שלא יהא קרבנו מהודר ח] סד"א קמילת שמאל תתכשר בה קמ"ל יד יד דרבא כולה שמעתי' במנחות: **מתני'** נשפך על הרצפה. מצואר בהמה שלא נתקבל בכלי: **גמ'** מהפר יקבלנו. שאם נשפך מן הצואר על הרצפה ואספו פסול שהרי לא נתקבל מהפר* דאי ס"ד דהאי מ"ם דכתיבא במדם דרשינן ליה כדכתיב דמשמע מקצת הדם יקבל והאמר רב ט] כו': גורעין. אות מתיבה זו ומוסיפין אותה על חבירתה ודורשים י] *כר"ש בסדר יומא: יא] בשפיכת שיריים כתיב. ולא בקבלה: דהא ליתיה לכוליה דם. שכבר ניתן ממנו על הקרנות: סכין למעלה. שלא יפול יב] דם הסכין על המזרק: ודבר אחר. סכין: בשפת מזרק. ולא יג] לתוכו: כפורי זהב. קרי למזרקין בספר עזרא על שם קיטוח כדאמר במסכת חולין (דף ח:) אי איכא בליתא דפריכא למכפריה א"נ ובעי לכפורי ידיה בההוא גברא גבי נירון קיסר (גיטין דף נו.): צריך שיתן ורידין

הטוף נמי לא יד] הוה בעי ימין במליקה אלא בהזאה דווקא וא"ת וכיון דר' שמעון פליג במליקה א"כ מתני' דפרק חטאת העוף (לקמן דף סח.) דמלק בשמאל כו' לא אתיא כרבי שמעון טו] והא על כרחין כרבי שמעון אתיא מדקתני סיפא או בלילה אינו מטמא בגדים אבית הבליעה ומפרש טעמא משום דכל שפסולו בקדש אינו מטמא בגדים אבית הבליעה ומפרש בגמרא דכיון דהך שחיטה מתרת את האיסור פי' שאם עלה לא ירד והיינו כרבי שמעון דלרבי יהודה נשחטה בלילה תרד דממעט לה מזאת היא העולה בפירקין וי"ל דההוא תנא סבר לה כוותיה בחדא ופליג עליה בחדא אי נמי אפי' רבי יהודה מודה בעופות דלא ירדו משום טז] לילה דכיון דהוה פסולן בקודש דלא כתיב שלשה מיעוטי אלא בבהמה וא"ת דבריש מזבח מקדש (לקמן דף פג:) מפקי רבי עקיבא ורבי יוסי הגלילי מעולה וכבשים דמזבח מקדש את הראוי לו ומאן דדריש מכבשים פוסל הרבה בעוף יותר מבבהמה וי"ל דרבי יהודה סבר כמאן דדריש מעולה ולא מהכבשים או משאר דרשות דהתם ורבינו שמואל מיישב גירסת הספרים ומפרש והרי זריקה דלא כתיב אלא כהונה ותנן זרק בשמאל פסל ולא פליג רבי שמעון דמכיון דתנן יז] כל הזבחים שקיבל בשמאל פסל כל שכן זריקה שהיא עיקר כפרה ולא פליג רבי שמעון כי אם על קבלה ואי הוה פליג אזריקה הוה ליה לאשמועינן כח דהיתירא דמכשיר ר' שמעון בזריקה וכ"ש בקבלה יח] ול"ע אי יט] מצי לפרש הכי לשון ותנן זרק בשמאל פסל כ] *והא דאמרי' בפרק כל הפסולין (לקמן דף לג.) קבל בימין ונתן בשמאל יחזור לימין והיינו משום הזריקה דבעי ימין דאי משום הולכה* כא] מפני מה הא לא כתיב בה אצבע ואמאי פסל ותו דרבי שמעון הוה ליה לפלוגי ולהכשיר משום דעבודה שאפשר לבטלה הוא כב] ושמא לכתחילה קאמר יחזור לימין שלא יעשה זריקה בשמאל אבל בדיעבד זרק בשמאל כשר כג] א"נ משום הולכה נמי קאמר דלכתחילה יחזור לימין אבל בדיעבד כשר *א"נ מיירי בחטאת דמודה ר' שמעון דבעי ימין בזריקה וא"ת וכיון דילפינן אצבע דחטאת בגזירה שוה מאצבע דמצורע דהויא בימין היכי ילפינן ימין בשאר קרבנות מחטאת בהיקישא דזאת התורה הא פלוגתא דאמוראי היא בריש איזהו מקומן (לקמן דף נ.) אי דבר הלמד מגזירה שוה חוזר ומלמד בהיקש או לא ונראה מתוך כך דכל שכן דניחא הכא טפי דהכי פריך והרי זריקה דלא כתיב בה אצבע ולא פליג ר' שמעון ואע"ג דדרשי' ימין מהיקישא דחטאת הניחא למאן דאמר דבר הלמד בגזירה שוה חוזר ומלמד בהיקש אלא למאן דאמר אין חוזר ומלמד בהיקש אמאי לא פליג ר' שמעון והשתא הא דמשני כד] בפ"ק דחולין (דף כב.) סבר לה כרבי שמעון דכהונה בעיא אצבע היינו כמאן דאמר חוזר ומלמד בהיקישא כה] *אבל רבי שמעון דמכשר בברייתא הכא שמאל בזריקה לא בעי למילף ימין בהיקישא דזאת התורה מחטאת דסבר דזריקה מהזאה לא ילפינן ואידך שינויא דמשני בפרק התודה (מנחות דף פג.) כדי נסבה הוי כמאן דאמר אין חוזר ומלמד בהיקישא ומיהו בפרק קמא דחולין (דף כב.) לית שינויא דכדי נסבה אבל בסוף דם חטאת (לקמן דף לח.) משני תרוייהו ומיהו אפשר דהכא מודו כולי עלמא דחוזר ומלמד בהיקישא כיון דמצורע כו] חול דהוא מלמד ראשון ותירוץ זה אנו צריכין בסמוך [דדריש] בא לעובדה ביד עובדה בימין כחטאת והיינו היקש וחטאת גופיה מגזירה שוה דמצורע ילפינן לה ואם תאמר מאי פריך והרי זריקה דלא כתיב אצבע אלא כהונה ופסולה ולא פליג רבי שמעון כז] [מת"ק] נמי הוה ליה למיפרך אמאי פסל שהרי בחטאת בעי אצבע בברייתא כדאמר באצבעו ולקח וגם אמרו דתנא קמא סבר מקרא נדרש לפניו אבל מכהונה לא יליף ואי פסול בזריקת שמאל בשאר קרבנות מהיקישא דזאת התורה א"כ מאי פריך כח] מר' שמעון ונראה לי דמדרבנן לא הוה בעי למיפרך דהוה מצי למימר דטעמא דרבנן לאו משום דאצבע נדרש לפניו וברייתא דתני באצבעו ולקח לדברי ר' שמעון נקטיה וטעמא דרבנן דפסלי שמאל בקבלה משום דכתיב ולקח הכהן מן הדם וסברי רבנן כהונה לא בעיא אצבע וכן משמע פרק דם חטאת (לקמן דף לח.) דפריך ימין מדרבה בר בר חנה נפקא ומשני ימין כדי נסבה ואיבעית אימא כר' שמעון דאמר כהונה בעיא אצבע מכלל דלרבנן כהונה לא בעיא אצבע ולכך הוצרך לשניי כדי נסבה כט] ולרבנן דכתיב בהו בזריקה בשאר קרבנות כהן משמע ימין ולא צריך למילף מאצבע דחטאת. ל] ברו"ך:

גורעין ומוסיפין ודורשין. לא שייך למיפרך סכינא חריפא אפסקא קראי אלא כשמחסר תיבה אחת כי ההיא דיש טחלין (ב"ב דף קיא:) ואם תאמר תיפוק לי מדממעטינן דם סכין כל שכן שעל הרצפה ויש לומר דדילמא דם סכין גרע משום דנתקבלה בפסול אי נמי אי לאו טעמא דגורעין ומוסיפין ודורשין הוה אמינא דמדם הפר ודבר אחר אתא למעוטי שעל הרצפה אבל דסכין שפיר דמי:

בשפת מזרק. לא] [פירש"י] בחוץ ולא שיפול [לתוכו פי'] בתוך המזרק דאם כן הוה ליה דבר אחר [ואין להקשות] דגבי הזאה דפרה אמרינן גמר להזות מקנח לב] ידיו בגופה של פרה בפרק קמא דמנחות (דף ז:) אבל הכא לא מקנח ליה לסכין בגופה של פרה לפי שאז היה הסכין מלא נימין ולא היה עוד נאה לשחוט ומיהו בההיא שמעתא גופה גבי פרה אמרינן בשלמא ידו מקנח לה בגופה של פרה אלא אצבעו במאי מקנח אמר אביי בשפת מזרק והשתא ידו נמי ליקנח בשפת מזרק

עט א מיי' פ"א מהל' פסולי המוקדשין הלכה כג:
פ ב ג ד ה מיי' פ"ד מהל' מעשה"ק הל"א:

כ"א ר"ש שלא בכלי שרת כשירה בהקטרה כו' כצ"ל

לעיל יח. וש"נ

[מנחות ו.]

יומא מח. לעיל טו. מכר במנחות כו:

[יומא מח. ע"ש טו: ע"ש דליתא והאמר רב יהודה השוחט צריך שיקבל וכו']

יומא מח. [בכורות מד:] כ"ב קיא:

[לקמן נג: מנחות ז:]

[סוטה טו. מנחות יז:]

[ע' תוס' לקמן לה: ד"ה למעוטי]

[נ"ל דם הפר ישפך וכ"ה בסמוך וביומא מח.]

נ"א דבפרק כל הפסולין תנן קיבלו בימין כו'

נ"א מ"מ קשה הא לא כתיב כו' כצ"ל

נ"א ואינו

נ"א כך שמעתי

ואידך שנויא דמשני כו' כצ"ל ומתיבת אבל ר"ש כו' עד לא ילפינן שייך לסוף הדבור נ"ק

הגהות הב"ח

(א) גמ' והאמר רב יהודה אמר רב השוחט צריך: (ב) שם תניהו ענין לקבלה: (ג) רש"י ד"ה מאי טעמא וכו' קדשים הוא לאשם ולחטאת לכך איתקש: (ד) ד"ה בא לעבודה וכו' בכלי וכו' שזריקה בכלי: (ה) ד"ה לקומץ וכו' בימין כו' ס"א דהואיל כצ"ל והד"א:

שיטה מקובצת

א] מדרב יהודה. האי סוגיא אליבא דמ"ד דבר הלמד בג"ש חוזר ומלמד [בהיקש] ולעיל דקאמר ולא פליג ר"ש [מקשה] אליבא דמ"ד אין חוזר ומלמד דרוצה ליישב אליבא דכ"ע תר"פ: ב] לא נצרכא. אלא: ג] והאמר. רב יהודה אמר רב: ד] ענין לקבלה: ה] דהא. אמרי' לעיל כו' אצבע וכהונה (בעי) מדר' יהודה ב"ר חייא [נפקא]: ו] אם. העלו למזבח כו' קדש קדשים הוא. כחטאת וכאשם לחכי: ז] דמה. ביד ימין במתן: ח] מהודר. אימא קמיצת ותיבות סד"א ל"ש ונמחק: ט] רב יהודה א"ר: י] ודורשין. כך שמעתי ותיבות כר"ש נמחק: יא] מה"ד והא בשפיכת: יב] יפול מן הסכין: יג] ולא לתוכו הס"ד: יד] לא בעי ימין כו' וא"ת כיון: טו] שמעון. והיכי מצי למימר הכי: טז] משום. בלילה דכיון כו' דלא כתיב

גבי פליקה מיעוטי: יז] תיבות כל הזבחים נמחק: יח] בקבלה. דאינו עבודה כל כך ואע"ג דאכתי קשה ניליף מחטאת. הניחא למ"ד כו' אמאי לא פליג ר"ש דמסברא יש ליישב מילתיה דר"ש אליבא דכ"ע. לשון מהר"פ: יט] אי מצינו לפרש כו' גירסת הספרים הכי ותיבת לשון ל"ש ונמחק: כ] פסל דבפ' כל כו' ותיבות והא דאמרי' ל"ש ונמחק: כא] הולכה. מכל מקום הא לא ותיבות מפני מה ל"ש: כב] הוא. כי היכא דהוה מכשיר לעיל בשילהי פ"ק הולכה בזר אי לאו משום דיליף מק"ו: כג] כשר. או משום: כד] דמשני. בשילהי דם חטאת ותיבות בפ"ק דחולין נמחק: כה] בהקישא ואידך שנויא כו' והשאר בס"א אינו: כו] דמצורע. חולין דהוא כו' בסמוך דדריש בא: כז] שמעון. את"ק דר"ש דלעיל נמי הוה ליה כו' וגם אמרי' דת"ק: כח] פריך. לר"ש: כט] נסבה. דכהן ותיבת ולרבנן נמחק: ל] דחטאת: הס"ד ומתחיל הדבור חד לקידוש קומץ. אע"ג דקידוש קומץ במקום קבלה הוא ... מדרבה בר בר חנה קידוש קומץ לא אתיא מהיקשא דזאת התורה: כי קמץ לה נמי בשמאל נמי תיתכשר' אע"ג דמחטאת ילפינן לה דשייך טעמא דשלא יהא קרבנו מהודר בפ"ק דמנחות: תו"ה: לא] מזרק. פי' משיפול בחוץ ולאו משיפול בתוך המזרק: לב] מקנח. ידו:

פא א מיי' פ"ד מהל' מעה"ק הל"ט :
פב ב מיי' פ"ו מהל' פרה אדומה הל"ח :
פג ג מיי' פ"ד מהל' מעה"ק הל"ח :
פד ד מיי' פ"ט מהל' מקואות הלכה טו סמג עשין מח טוש"ע יו"ד סי' רא סעיף יא :
פה ה מיי' פ"א מהל' פסה"מ הל' כט :
פו ו מיי' שם הל' ל :
פז ז מיי' פ"א מהל' מעשה הקרבנות הל"ג :
פח ח מיי' פ"א מהל' פסה"מ הל' טו :

ורידין לתוך הכלי איתמר נמי אמר רב אסי אמר רבי יוחנן ורידין צריך שיראו אויר כלי בעא מיניה רבי אסי מרבי יוחנן היה מקבל ונפחתו שולי מזרק עד שלא הגיע דם לאויר א] מהו *אויר שאין סופו לנוח כמונח דמי או *לא כמונח דמי אמר ליה תניתוה חבית שמונחת תחת הזינוק מים שבתוכה ושבחוצה לה פסולין צירף פיה לזינוק מים שבתוכה פסולין ושבחוצה לה כשירין האי מאי בעי מיניה אויר שאין סופו לנוח וקא פשט ליה אויר שסופו לנוח תרתי קא בעי מיניה אם תימצי לומר אויר שאין סופו לנוח לאו כמונח דמי אויר שסופו לנוח מאי רב יוסף מתני הכי רב כהנא מתני חבית בעא מיניה ופשט ליה חבית רבה מתני חבית בעא מיניה ופשט ליה מזרק אי אתה מודה במזרק שאי איפשר לו בלא זינוק *תנן התם בנתן ידו או רגלו או עלי ירקות כדי שיעברו מים לחבית פסולין עלי קנים ועלי אגוזים ב] כשירה זה הכלל דבר המקבל טומאה פסולין דבר שאינו מקבל טומאה כשירין מנא הני מילי דאמר רבי יוחנן משום רבי יוסי בר אבא אמר קרא °אך מעין (ויקרא יא) ובור מקוה מים יהיה טהור הוייתן על ידי טהרה תהא אמר רבי *חייא אמר רבי יוחנן זאת אומרת גאויר כלי ככלי דמי א"ל רבי זירא לרבי חייא בר אבא ודילמא בשותת א"ל *תרדא כדי שיעברו מים לחבית תנן ואמר רבי חייא בר אבא אמר רבי יוחנן מעדותו של רבי צדוק נישנית משנה זו *דתנן העיד רבי צדוק דעל הזוחלין שקילחן ג] בעלי אגוזין שהן כשירין זה היה מעשה באוהלייא ובא מעשה לפני חכמים בלשכת הגזית ד] והכשירו *אמר רבי זירא אמר רבי (א) ההצורם אזן הפר ואח"כ קיבל דמו פסול שנאמר °ולקח מדם הפר (ויקרא ד) פר שהיה כבר אשכחן קדשי קדשים קדשים קלים מנלן אמר רבא תניא °שה (שמות יב) תמים זכר בן שנה שיהא תמים ובן שנה בשעת שחיטה בקבלה בהולכה בזריקה מנין ת"ל יהיה כל הוויותי' לא יהיו אלא תם ובן שנה איתיביה אביי *רבי יהושע אומר וכל הזבחים שבתורה שנשתייר מהן כזית בשר או כזית חלב זורק את הדם °תרגומא אבן שנה ומי איכא מידי דבשעת שחיטה בן שנה בשעת הולכה וזריקה בן שתים אמר רבא °זזאת אומרת ה] שעות פוסלות בקדשים אמר רבי אמי אמר רבי אלעזר חהיא בפנים ורגליה בחוץ חתך ואח"כ שחט כשירה

שחט

ורידין לתוך כלי. ו] דכיון קבלה מהפר שפיר והאי תוך לאו דווקא דהא לא אפשר אלא על אוירו של תוך כלי : שולי מזרק. קרקעיתו פיני"ו בלע"ז : עד שלא הגיע דם לאויר מזרק. לבין דופני ז] מזרק בעוד הדם למעלה מהן ומיהו על כנגד אוירו הן דהא ורידין רואים אויר ח] כלי [בעינן] : אויר שאין סופו לנוח. כגון האי שעתידים שוליו ליפול עד שלא ינוח דם לתוכו כמונח דמי והוה ליה כמי שנתקבל ט] ונשפך דכשר לאוספו או לא כמונח דמי והוה ליה כנשפך מן הצואר לרצפה דפסול וכשהגיע דם לאויר דופנותיו עד שלא נפחתו שוליו לא מיבעיא ליה דמשנכנס לתוכן הויא קבלה : חבית שמונח תחת הזינוק. כנור המקלח מים מהר זקוף והקילוח מקלח למרחוק ונופל לחבית וחבית זו אינה מונחת שם לשם קידוש מי חטאת י] : מים שבתוכה ושבחוצה לה פסולין יא]. כלומר שלא יתן כלי לתוך אוירה ויאחזנו בידו לקבל בו הקילוח לקידוש יב] ואף לא חוצה לה למעלה מאוגניה כנגד אוירה דכיון שהגיעו מים כנגד אוירה הרי הן כמונחים בתוכה *ופסק להו חיותייהו ואנן מים חיים אל כלי יג] בעינן לקדוש אלמא אויר כמונח דמי ולקמיה פריך האי אויר שסופו לנוח הוא : צירף פיה לזינוק. שאין אויר מפסיק בין פיה לזינוק : שבתוכה. כלומר שבאו לתוך אויר דופנותיה פסולים : שבחוצה לה. אע"פ שכנגד אוירה (ב) כשירין שעדיין לא פירשו מן הצינור ואפי' אויר אין כאן : וקא פשיט ליה אויר שסופו לנוח הוא. כגון הא דקתני רישא שבחוצה לה פסולין דילמא האי דחשיב ליה כמונח משום דראוי היה לנוח שהרי חבית זו שלימה וראוי היה לנוח אי לא שבא זה וקלט אבל נפחתו שולי מזרק לא היה עתיד יד] ראוי לנוח : תרתי בעא מיניה. ופשט ליה חדא מינייהו : חבית בעא מיניה. לא הוה שמיעא ליה הא מתניתין ובעא מיניה חבית שמונחת תחת הזינוק מים שבחוצה טו] [לה] כנגד אוירה מהו לקלוט אותן למי חטאת ופשט ליה מהא מתני' דפסולין: ופשט ליה מזרק. לא ולמד מקבלת דם : אי אתה מודה במזרק שאי איפשר לו בלא זינוק. כששוחט על אויר הכלי אין הדם שותת טז] במקומו אלא מקלח לרוחב הכלי עד להלן ואי אויר שסופו לנוח לאו כמונח דמי נמצא כשהוא יורד לכלי מן האויר הוא בא ולא מן הפר והתורה אמרה דם מהפר יקבלנו *וגבי חבית נמי אויר שסופו לנוח הוא וכמונח דמי ופסולין : נתן ידו או רגלו. קילוח היורד מהר מעוקם שמשפע ועולה ואין הקילוח יורד לחבית ונתן ידו למעלה יז] מראש הצנור [לעשות כעין מרזב] כדי שיעברו המים דרך ידו לחבית של קידוש : וכן עלי ירקות. הראויין לאכילה ומקבלין טומאה יח] : פסולין. [המים] כדיליף לקמיה : הוייתן. של מים המטהרים ע"י טהרה תהא כשאתה מהווה אותם להיות מקוה או קדוש הוי מהווה אותם על ידי דבר שאין מקבל טומאה : זאת אומרת אויר כלי ככלי דמי יט]. מדקתני נתן ידו כו' פסל דהא אין המים שותתין כ] מידו לכלי בשתיתה אלא בהעברה כשיוצאין מידו מקלחין להם על פני רחב פי החבית ואפי' הכי פסול אלמא משילאו מידו לקלח על פני אויר הוה ליה כאילו שתתו מידו לכלי שהרי ידו על כנגד שפת הכלי מונחת ומשילאו מידו מקלחים באו כנגד אוירו דאי לאו ככלי דמי אמאי פסול הלא מן האויר באין לו והוה ליה כנותן ידו בצינור משוך מן הקילוח עשר אמות : דילמא בשותת. מידו לכלי ולא באו מן האויר : תרדא. שוטה בהול : שיעברו תנן. והעברה בקילוח משמע : הצורם. אקרני"ר דהוי מום דתנן (בכורות דף לז.) נפגמה אזנו גבי מום : ואחר כך קיבל דמו. דהוה כא] ביה מום בין שחיטה לקבלה : שהיה כבר. צריך שיהא שלם בשעת קבלה כבשעת שחיטה : אשכחן קדשי קדשים. כב] דהאי בפר (*העלם דבר של צבור) כתיב : בשעת שחיטה. דכתיב (שמות יב) תכוסו על השה דהיינו שחיטה וסמיך ליה שה תמים וגו' : שנשתייר מהן. בשעת זריקה כג] *אם נטמא כל הבשר והחלב או שאבד לא יזרוק רבי יהושע לטעמיה דדריש ועשית עולותיך הבשר והדם אם אין בשר אין דם *במנחות (דף ט) קתני מיהא זורק ואין לך בעל מום גדול מזה קשיא לרבא דאמר בעינן תם בשעת זריקה אבל לרבי זירא לא קשיא כד] דהא לא בעי תם אלא בשחיטה וקבלה : תרגומא אבן שנה. אביי אמר ליה לרבא תרגמה אבן שנה כה] למתניתך דבעי כל הוויותיו *בשעת שחיטה אבן שנה קאי דסליק מיניה בן שנה יהיה כל הווייתו יהיה בן שנה אבל אם נכנס בשנה שניה בין שחיטה לזריקה פסול דשעות פוסלות בקדשים כו] כדפירש ואזיל אבל תם לא תילף מיניה דהאי יהיה לאו אתמים קאי וקבלה בקדשים קלים בתמימות הואיל וגלי בקדשי קדשים גלי : שעות פוסלות בקדשים. דשנה האמורה בקדשים קיימא לן בפרק יוצא דופן במסכת נדה (דף מז:) דאין מונין לה מתשרי כשאר ראשי שנים אלא מיום שנולד מעת לעת לשנה הבאה וילפינן לה מקרא דכתיב בהו בן שנתו שנתו שלו ולא (ג) שנתו של מנין עולם ואשמעינן הכא דלא תימא מיום ליום הוא דבעינן ולא משגח לשעה אלא אף משגח לשעה שאם נולד בניסן בי"ד ובט' שעות ושחטו לשנה הבאה בי"ד בניסן בט' שעות אסור לזרוק דמו בעשירית שכבר עברה שנתו : הוא בפנים. בעזרה : חתך. כז] רגליה ואחר כך שחט כשרה שלא נתערב דם פסול יוצא עם דם שבמזרק שנתקבל בו הדם ולקמיה פריך הא שויה בעלת מום : *שחט ואחר כך חתך פסולה. כח] שמשנשחטה נפסל דם הרגלים ביוצא וכל דמי בהמה יונקים זה מזה ועלה ויצא דרך בית שחיטה ונתערב בדם המזרק ופסלו :

ה"ג

מזרק נראה לפי שצריך לשרוף לטוליה דם אבל אצבעו לא אפשר לקנח בגוף הפרה שהיה מזה בהר המשחה אל נכח פני אהל מועד וכי בין כל הזאה והזאה ירד מן ההר לקנח ידיו בגוף הפרה אי נמי כדפי' בקונטרס לקמן בפרק דם חטאת (דף צג:) שלא יתלכלך אצבעו בנימין בין ההזאות דהכי נמי חיישינן לנימין בפ' כל כתבי (שבת דף קכז:) גבי מפשיטין את הפסח עד החזה וכן נראה דשחיטתה והזייתה במקום אחד היו כדאיתא בפרק פרת חטאת (לקמן דף קיג.) וכן במסכת מדות (דף לה.) תנן כל הכתלים שהיו שם גבוהין עשרים אמה חוץ מכותל מזרחי שכהן השורף רואה פתחו של היכל בשעת הזייה* . ע"כ :

זאת אומרת אויר כלי ככלי דמי. מהכא הוה מצי למיפשט לעיל ול"ע פרק המזבח מקדש (לקמן דף פז:) גבי אויר כבש ככבש דמי :

קדשים קלים מנין. ותימה דלעיל גבי מדם הפר [ולא מדם הטור] לא קאמר קדשים קלים מנין וי"ל לומר דכיון דגלי הכא ה"ה התם :

שחט

[וע' תוס' מנחות ז: ד"ה אלא]

גליון הש"ס

גמ' תרגומא אבן שנה. ע' יומא דף מט ע"ב תוס' ד"ה שאני : שם אלא אומרת שעות פוסלות. ע' טורי אבן ר"ה דף ט ע"ב ד"ה פחות מל' יום: רש"י ד"ה מים שבתוכה ושבחוצה לה וכו' ופסק לה חיותייהו. עיין בר"ש פ"ט מ"ג דפרה :

[ב"ק קה: ב"מ כ: כריתות יח: וע' בכל המקומות מה שפירש"י אבן בערוך ערך תרד גרס תררא ופי' שוטה מוליד ריר]

שיטה מקובצת

א] לאויר מזרק. פי' קודם שהגיע לאויר המחיצות המזרק שאם לא נפחתו עד שהיה כנגד המחיצות פשיטא דכמונח דמי : ב] אגוזים. כשירין : ג] שקילחן. בעלין : ד] הגזית. והכשירוהו : ה] שעות פוסלות בקדשים. הקשה הר"ר אליעזר משאנז למה לי למעוטי שנת עולם תיפוק ליה דאי מנינן בקדשים משנת עולם דהיינו תשרי א"כ לעולם לא תמצא תמידין של ר"ה קריבין דהא לכל הפחות בעינן שיהיה שמנה ימים קודם ר"ה ומיד שנכנס הוא בתשרי בן שתי שנים הוא ותמיד בן שנה בעינן ועוד קשה דמנלן דשעות פוסלות בקדשים ואי משנתו שלו ולא שנת של עולם הא בערכין איצטריך קראי חד למעוטי שנת עולם וחד למימר דמנינן מעת לעת ותירץ דקושיא חדא מתרץ לחברתה דע"כ שנתו לא איצטריך למעוטי שנת עולם דמתמיד נפקא דא"כ לא תמצא תמיד כשר כדפי' אלא איצטריך משום מעת לעת ולומר דשעות פוסלות בקדשים: מהר"פ: ו] כלי. דלתחזי קבלה: ז] דופני המזרק: ח] אויר הכלי הס"ד : ט] שנתקבל. בכלי ונשפך : י] חטאת. ובמי חטאת בעינן שיהו שאובין לשם מי חטאת הס"ד : יא] פסולין לא מבעיא שבתוכה שכבר ירדו בתוך החבית אלא אפי' שבחוצה לה פסולין : יב] לקידוש דכיון שהגיעו כו' והשאר בס"א אינו : יג] כלי של קידוש בעינן : יד] וראוי לנוח : טו] שבחוצה. לה : טז] שותת ממקומו אלא מקלח כו' ואי אמרת שסופו לנוח : יז] למעלה. בראש הצינור לעשות כעין מרזב : יח] טומאה : הס"ד ומה"ד [כדי שיעברו מים] לחבית. האי חבית מיירי כשנתנה שם לשם מי חטאת : מלשון הר"פ פירש"י שלפניו פסולין המים : יט] דמי. ש"מ אויר כלי ככלי דמי שהרי על עובי שפת הכלי מונחת ואין המים שותתין ונופלים מידו לכלי כדמסיק [כדי שיעברו] דמשמע כשיצאו המים מידו הם מקלחין להלן ורחוק מידו קצת על פני אויר רחוק הכלי ואח"כ נופלים בכלי וכיון שהם מקלחין א"כ הקילוח גבוה קצת למעלה [באויר] שכנגד המחיצות לכל הפחות כשיעור עובי ידו ואותו אויר שהוא קצת למעלה מן האויר שכנגד המחיצות קורא אויר כלי הילכך ש"מ אויר כלי ככלי דמי ומים שיוציא [מידו והולכים] באויר הכלי כדפי' הרי הם כמתחים תוך הכלי ומאז חשובה נתינת מים אל הכלי שהזכיר הכתוב גבי מי חטאת דכתיב ונתן מים חיים אל כלי ולכך לא [חשיבא] נתינת מים לכלי ע"י טהרה שהרי ידו מקבלת טומאה דאי אויר כלי לאו ככלי דמי ואינו חשוב נתינת כלי עד שיגיעו המים לאויר שתוך המחיצות א"כ אמאי פסול הא מן האויר באים המים לכלי והווייתו בכלי ע"י טהרה מן האויר ואע"ג דלסוף סוף באים דרך אויר לכלי מ"מ יש הפסקת אויר בין ידו לנתינת הכלי וכיון שהווייתו תוך [הכלי] ע"י טהרה אין לחוש במה שעברו דרך ידו שמקבלת טומאה דהא לא פסלינן אלא נתן ידו ותלו כדי שיעברו המים לחבית אבל אם הביא ידו תוך הצינור ורחוק קצת מן הקילוח והיו עוברים דרך ידו ליכא חששא כיון שהווייתו ע"י טהרה בכלי של קידוש : מלשון הר"פ פירש"י שלפניו : כ] שותתין ונופלין מידו לכלי כו' מקלחין להלן על פני רוחב פי החבית : כא] דהוה ליה מום : כב] קדשים דהא גבי פר העלם כו' : כג] זריקה. אבל אם : כד] לא קשיא דהוא : כה] למתניתין דמשמע דבעי כל הוויותיו כשעת שחיטה כו' דסליק מיניה וה"ק בן שנת יהיו הווייתו יהיו בן שנה כו' : כו] בקדשים. כדמפרש ואזיל כו' אתמים קאי וא"ת קדשים קלים בתמימות דבעינא תם בשעת קבלה והולכה מנלן וי"ל כיון דגלי לן קרא דבעינן תם משעת שחיטה משה תמים בקדשים קלים גבי קבלה ה"ה [בהולכה] דבעינן תם כמו בקדשי קדשים והולכה לא תפקיה מכלל קבלה כך מביא הר"פ לשון רש"י : כז] תתך הרגלים : כח] שמשנשחטה. פ"א לפי שקודם שנשחטה נפסל הרגלים כו' :

תיבות

[ב"מ יב. קב.]

הגהות הב"ח

(א) גמ' אמר ר' זירא אמר ר' יוחנן הצורם : (ב) רש"י ד"ה שבחוצה וכו' אוירה הן כשרין : (ג) ד"ה שעות וכו' ולא שנה של מנין עולם :

פרה פ"ו מ"ד

[נ"ל ר' חייא בר אבא]

[עדיות פ"ז מ"ד]

בכורות לז: ע"ש [לקמן כו. ע"ש]

[בכורות שם] תוספתא דזבחים פ"ד תוספתא דפסחים פ"ו פסחים עט. מנחות ט. כו. מעילה טו. [לקמן קט.]

נ"ל אלא ע"כ אויר שסופו לנוח כמונח דמי וגבי חבית כו' נ"ק

[נ"ל כהן משיח וכ"כ רש"י בכורות לט:] אבל אם נטמא נ"ק [נ"ל לקמן קד. ופסחים עז.]

[נ"ל כשעת]

שייך לדף כו.

slaughters must let [25b] [the blood of] the jugular veins[3] run [straight] into the vessel. It was stated likewise: R. Assi said in R. Joḥanan's name: The jugular veins must see the air-space of the vessel.[4] R. Assi asked R. Joḥanan: What if one was receiving, and the bottom of the bowl split before the blood reached the air-space? is [an object in] the air, where it will not eventually come to rest, regarded as at rest, or not?[5]—Said he to him, We have learnt it: If a barrel lies beneath a spout, the water inside it and outside it is unfit; if one joined its mouth to the spout, the water inside it is fit, and the water outside it is unfit.[6] How now! He asked him about [an object in] the air, where it will *not* eventually come to rest, and he answered him about [an object in] the air
a where it *will* eventually come to rest?[1]—He asked him two [questions]: should you say that [an object in] the air where it will not eventually come to rest is *not* regarded as at rest, how about [an object in] the air where it will eventually come to rest?[2] That is how R. Joseph recited it. R. Kahana recited it that he asked him about a barrel,[3] and he answered him about a barrel. Rabbah recited it that he asked him about a barrel, and he solved [it] for him [from the case of] a bowl; [arguing thus,] do you not agree that in the case of the bowl, sprinkling [of blood] is unavoidable?[4]

We learnt elsewhere: If one places [there] one's hand or foot or vegetables leaves, in order that the water should flow into the barrel, it [the water] is unfit.[5] [If one placed there] leaves of canes or leaves of nuts, it is fit. This is the general rule: [If the water is conducted into the barrel by means of] anything which can become unclean, it is unfit; [by means of] anything which cannot become unclean, it is fit.[6] How do we know it?—Because R. Joḥanan said on the authority of R. Jose b. Abba: Scripture saith, *Nevertheless a fountain or a cistern wherein is a gathering of water shall be clean*:[7] its existence must be [effected] through purity.[8] R. Ḥiyya said in R. Joḥanan's name: This proves that the air-space of a vessel is as the vessel [itself].[9] Said R. Zera to R. Ḥiyya b. Abba: But perhaps it refers to a direct run [into the barrel]?—Fool! replied he: we
b learnt, 'So that the water shall flow into the barrel.'[1] R. Ḥiyya b. Abba also said in R. Joḥanan's name: This Mishnah was taught on the testimony of R. Zadok. For we learnt: R. Zadok testified[2] that running water which is assembled by means of nut leaves is fit. There was such a case in Ahaliyya,[3] which was referred to the Sages in the Chamber of Hewn Stone,[4] and they declared it fit.

R. Zera said in the name of Rab:[5] If [the priest] slits the [sacrificial] bullock's ear and then receives its blood,[6] it is unfit, for it is said: *And [the anointed priest] shall take of the blood of the bullock*:[7] [this implies:] the bullock as it was before.[8] We have thus found [this law true of] sacrifices of higher sanctity;[9] how do we know [it of] sacrifices of lower sanctity?—Said Raba, It was taught: *Your lamb shall be without blemish, a male of the first year*:[10] [this teaches] that it must be without a blemish and a year old when it is slaughtered. How do we know [that it must be likewise] at the receiving [of the blood], the carrying, and the sprinkling? Because it says, '*it shall be*', [teaching that] at all its stages [as a sacrifice] it must be without blemish and a year old.

Abaye raised an objection to him: R. Joshua said: [In the case of] all sacrifices prescribed in the Torah whereof as much as an olive of flesh or fat remained,[11] [the priest] sprinkles the blood?—Relate this to [the provision that it must be] a year old.[12] Yet is it possible
c for it to be a year old at the slaughtering, yet two years old[1] at the carrying and sprinkling?—Said Raba: This proves that [even] hours disqualify in the case of sacrifices.[2]

R. Ammi said in R. Eleazar's name: [In the case of the animal] being within [the Temple court] while its legs were without, if

(3) Lit. 'must place the jugular veins'. (4) I.e., they must be directly over the receiving vessel, so that the blood pours straight into it. (5) Here the blood is over the air-space of the receiving vessel. Yet it will not remain in the vessel when it falls into it. Do we nevertheless regard that blood as though it had actually been caught in the vessel and then spilled, in which case it can be collected and is fit, or as though it had poured from the animal's throat on to the ground, so that it is unfit? (6) This treats of the water which was mixed with the ashes of the red heifer for lustration: this had to be 'living' (i.e., running) water, v. Num. XIX, 17: *And for the unclean they shall take of the ashes of the burning of the purification from sin, and running* (lit., 'living') *water shall be put thereto in a vessel*. In the present case water is running down a spout or channel, and below that spout, and at some distance from it, lies a barrel, which was not placed there in order to receive the water. If one now takes a vessel and holds it within the air-space of the barrel, or above the mouth of the barrel ('outside') and catches that water, it is unfit, because had it been permitted to come to rest in the barrel it would have ceased to be running water; and so now too it lacks that status. Again, if the mouth of the barrel is flush with the spout, and one holds the vessel inside its air-space, the water thus gathered is unfit. If however one holds the vessel immediately beneath the spout, the water thus collected is fit, because it never entered the air-space within the barrel. (In general, in order for the water to be fit it must be collected directly as it runs in a service vessel specially placed there for that purpose.)—From this passage we see that once an object enters the air-space it is regarded as at rest.

a (1) The water would normally enter the barrel and remain there. (2) And he solved for him the latter question. (3) Viz., this very law that has just been stated, of which he was ignorant. (4) Some of the blood must spout through the air into the bowl. Now if an object in the air is not regarded as already at rest, then the blood has entered the bowl and not directly from the animal's throat but from the air, and should be unfit. (5) Water was running down from a hillside, and one placed his hand etc. in order to direct it into a barrel, which had been placed there for the purpose of collecting the water. The water so collected is unfit for lustration; v. Parah VI, 4. (6) A person's hand can become unclean; similarly vegetable leaves, if they are edible. (7) Lev. XI, 36. (8) Water must be collected for ritual cleansing purposes through an object which is itself clean, i.e., which cannot become unclean. (9) When the water flows over the hand, it does not fall directly into the barrel but first spreads out over the air-space above it. If that air-space were not as the barrel itself, the water would be regarded as falling from the *air* into the barrel, not from the hand, and so would be fit.

b (1) The Hebrew does not imply to fall directly into it. (2) V. 'Ed. (Sonc. ed.) VII 4. (3) Horowitz, *Palestine*, p. 22, identifies it with Bait Ilu, near Jerusalem. (4) In the inner court of the Temple, where the great Sanhedrim sat. V. also *J.E.* XII, 576. (5) So Bek. 39b. Cur. edd. Rabbi. (6) From the throat, in the usual way. He slit the ear immediately after slaughtering it, so that between the slaughtering and the reception of the blood it was a blemished animal. (7) Lev. IV, 5. (8) It must be in the same state when the priest receives the blood as it was before, viz., unblemished. (9) Such as the sin-offering, to which this text refers. (10) Ex. XII, 5. This refers to the Passover-offering, which was a sacrifice of lower sanctity. (11) By the time of sprinkling, the rest having been lost or defiled. There can be no greater blemish than this. (12) At all its stages as a sacrifice it must be a year old, but it need not be without a blemish at all its stages.

c (1) I.e., more than a year old. (2) The age of a sacrifice is calculated exactly from the moment of birth, and even the least excess ('hours' means any short period, even minutes) disqualifies the animal. Thus it may reach the age limit at the moment of slaughtering and exceed it a moment afterwards.

he cut off its legs and then slaughtered it, it is fit;[3] [26a] if he slaughtered and then cut off [the legs], it is unfit.[4] 'If he cut off [the legs] and then slaughtered [it], it is fit'? Surely he offers a blemished animal!—Say rather: If he cut off [the legs] and then received [the blood], it is fit; if he received [the blood] and then cut off [the legs], it is unfit. 'If he cut off [the legs] and then received [the blood] it is fit'? Surely R. Zera said: If one slits the ear of a firstling[5] and then receives its blood, it is unfit, because it says, *'And he shall take of the blood of the bullock'*, [implying,] the bullock as it was originally!—Said R. Ḥisda in Abimi's name: He cuts the limb as far as the bone.[6] 'If he received [the blood] and then cut, it is unfit': from this you may infer that the blood which is absorbed in the limbs is blood?[7]—[No:] perhaps [the unfitness is] on account of the fattiness.[8] Then you may infer from this that if the flesh of sacrifices of lower sanctity passes out [from the Temple court]
a before the sprinkling of the blood, it is unfit?[1]—[No:] perhaps [R. Ammi in R. Eleazar's name] referred to sacrifices of higher sanctity.

Our Rabbis taught: Sacrifices of higher sanctity are slaughtered on the north [side of the Temple court], and their blood is received on the north in service vessels. If he stood in the south, stretched out his hand to the north and slaughtered, his slaughtering is valid; if he [thus] received [the blood], his reception is invalid. If he projected his head and the greater part of his body [into the north side],[2] it is as though he had entered [the north] entirely. If [the animal] struggled and passed over into the south[3] and then returned, it is fit.[4] Sacrifices of lower sanctity are slaughtered [anywhere] within [the Temple court], and their blood is received in a service vessel within. If he stood without and stretched his hand within and slaughtered, his slaughtering is valid; if he received [the blood thus], his reception is invalid. If he projected his head and the greater part of his body within, he is not regarded as having entered. If it struggled[3] and went without and returned, it is unfit. This proves that sacrifices of lower sanctity whose flesh went without before the sprinkling of the blood are unfit!—[No:] perhaps this refers to the fat-tail, the lobe above the liver, and the two kidneys.[5]

Samuel's father asked Samuel: What if it [the animal] is within, while its feet are without?[6]—It is written, *Even that they may bring them unto the Lord*,[7] he replied, [which intimates] that the whole of it must be within. What if one suspended[8] [the animal] and slaughtered it? It is valid, he replied. You have erred, he observed, for the slaughtering must be *'on the side'* [*of the altar*] [9] which provi-
b sion is unfulfilled.[1] What if [the slaughterer] was suspended and slaughtered [thus]?[2]—It is invalid, he replied.[3] You have erred, said he; the slaughtering must be *'on the side'* but the slaughterer need not be *'on the side'*. What if he suspended himself and received [the blood]? It is valid, he replied.[4] You have erred, observed he, for such is not the way of service.[5] What if he suspended [the sacrifice][6] and received [the blood]?—It is invalid, he answered. You have erred, he retorted: slaughtering must be *'on the side'*, but receiving need not be *'on the side'*.

Abaye said: In the case of sacrifices of higher sanctity[7] they are all invalid, except where he suspended himself and slaughtered.[8] In the case of sacrifices of lower sanctity, they are all valid, except where he suspended himself and received [the blood].[9] Said Raba: Why do you say that if he suspended [the animal] and received the blood it is valid in the case of sacrifices of lower sanctity? [Presumably] because the air-space of within is as within! Then in the case of sacrifices of higher sanctity too, the air-space of the north is as the north?—Rather said Raba: In the case of sacrifices of both higher and lower sanctity they are [all] valid, except in the case of sacrifices of higher sanctity, where he suspended [the animal] and slaughtered it,[10] and in the cases of sacrifices of both higher and lower sanctity, where he suspended himself and received [the blood].

R. Jeremiah asked R. Zera: What if he [the priest] is within and his locks [of hair] are without?—Said he to him, Have you not said that *'even that they may bring them unto the Lord'* intimates that the whole of it [the animal] must come within? So here too, *when*
c *they go in unto the tent of meeting*[1] intimates, that the *whole* of him must enter the tent of meeting.

MISHNAH. IF [THE PRIEST] APPLIED IT [THE BLOOD] ON THE ASCENT,[2] [OR ON THE ALTAR, BUT] NOT OVER AGAINST ITS BASE;[3] IF HE APPLIED [THE BLOOD] WHICH SHOULD BE APPLIED BELOW [THE SCARLET LINE] ABOVE [IT], OR THAT WHICH SHOULD BE APPLIED ABOVE, BELOW;[4] OR THAT WHICH SHOULD BE APPLIED WITHIN [HE APPLIED] WITHOUT, OR WHAT SHOULD BE APPLIED WITHOUT [HE APPLIED] WITHIN,[5] IT IS UNFIT, BUT DOES NOT INVOLVE KARETH.[6]

(3) If the blood of a sacrifice passes without the Temple court before it is sprinkled, it is unfit. In this case, if one cut off the legs first, the blood that passed out (*sc.* that contained in the legs) did not mingle with that which remained within. (4) Because immediately it is slaughtered the blood of the legs is unfit (v. preceding note), and this is naturally mingled with the rest of the blood. (5) Which was offered as a sacrifice. On 25*b* the text has 'bullock' instead of 'firstling'. (6) This does not constitute a blemish, and at the same time the cut prevents the blood below it, which is without the Temple court, from ascending and mingling with the blood above, which is within. (7) So that *kareth* (q.v. Glos.) is incurred for its consumption. For if it did not rank as blood whilst absorbed in the limb (cf. Ḥul. 113*a*), it could not disqualify the other blood which is received and sprinkled. (8) Which is absorbed in the blood. This fattiness counts as flesh, and it ascends and mingles with the blood which pours out from the neck and thus disqualifies it.

a (1) Though it would certainly be carried out *after* the sprinkling, since it may be eaten anywhere in Jerusalem. (2) He was standing almost in the middle of the court, on its south side, but so near to the line dividing north and south that he could easily stretch over to the other side. (3) After being slaughtered. (4) Because the disqualification of going out applies only to going out of the Temple. (5) These were burnt on the altar, and therefore although part of sacrifices of lower sanctity they ranked as sacrifices of higher sanctity. (6) May it be slaughtered thus at the outset? (7) Lev. XVII, 5. (8) In the air-space of the Temple court. (9) Ibid. I, 11.

b (1) *'On the side'* implies on the ground. (2) The animal being on the ground. (3) Thinking that the two were analogous. (4) Again thinking it analogous to the former. (5) But slaughtering is not really part of the (priestly) service, since it may be performed by a *zar*. (6) After having slaughtered it. (7) In connection with which *'on the side'* is stated. (8) Because *'on the side'* is written of the animal, but not of the slaughterer. Again, the blood must be received in the north, and he holds that the air-space of the north is not the north itself. Hence if he suspended himself and received the blood it is invalid. (9) Here neither 'north' nor *'on the side'* is mentioned. Therefore only the exception is invalid, because that is not the way of service. (10) For the reason stated above.

c (1) Ex. XXVIII, 43. (2) Leading to the altar, instead of on the altar. (3) The blood was to be sprinkled over against the base of the altar, which means on a side provided with a foundation. This excludes the south-east corner, which had no base (*infra* 53*a*). (4) A scarlet line ran round the sides of the altar: some blood was to be applied above, and some below. (5) 'Within' means on the inner altar; 'without', on the outer altar. (6) For the eating of its flesh.

מסורת הש"ס

נ"ל ס"ג חתך ואחר כך שחט כשרה בעלת מוס קמקריב כו' ס"י

נ"א ודם נפסל ביוצא בין בקדשים קלים ובין בקדשי קדשים וג"מ שחייב כרת על אכילתו דאי לאו דם הוא ובשר נמי לא הוי אהיכא כו'

[לקמן נג:]

[שבועות כח:]

נ"א אבל גבי הכנסת צפון לא בעינן כולו דהא בעזרה הוא

עין משפט נר מצוה

פט א ב מיי' פ"א מהל' פסה"מ הלכה טו :

צ ג מיי' שם הלכה ז :

צא ד מיי' שם הל' ח :

צב ה מיי' שם הל' ט :

צג ו מיי' שם הלכה י :

צד ז ח מיי' שם הל' יא :

[לעיל כה: ע"ש בכורות לט: ע"ש]

נ"א הפר [וכ"ה בתוס' יומא נ. ד"ה ואת]

צה ט מיי' שם הל' יב :

צו י מיי' שם הלכה יג :

צז כ מיי' שם הל' יד :

צח ל מיי' שם הל' יז :

צט מ נ מיי' שם הלכה יז וע"ש בכ"מ :

ק ס מיי' שם הלכה יט :

קא ע מיי' שם הל' יב :

קב פ מיי' פ"ב שם הלכה י :

נ"א בפיגול ונותר וטמא משום דלא מפסל ביוצא ומיהו קשה

תורה אור

שחט ואחר כך חתך פסולה חתך ואח"כ שחט כשרה בעל מום קא מקריב אלא אימא א)[חתך ואח"כ קיבל כשרה] קיבל ואח"כ חתך פסולה (א) חתך ואח"כ קיבל כשרה והא *א"ר זירא הצורם אזן ב) *בבכור ואח"כ קיבל דמו פסול שנאמר ולקח מדם הפר פר שהיה כבר א"ר חסדא אמר אבימי ג) חותך באבר עד שמגיע לעצם קיבל ואח"כ חתך פסולה שמעת מינה דם המובלע באברים דם הוא דלמא משום שמנונית שמעת מינה בשר קדשים קלים שיצא לפני זריקת דם פסול דלמא בקדשי קדשים ת"ר קדשי קדשים שחיטתן בצפון וקיבול דמן בכלי שרת בצפון עמד בדרום והושיט ידו לצפון ושחט שחיטתו כשרה קיבל קבלתו פסולה הכנים ראשו ורובו כאילו נכנס כולו *פרכסה ויצתה לדרום וחזרה כשרה קדשים קלים שחיטתן בפנים וקיבול דמן בכלי שרת בפנים עמד בחוץ והכנים ידו לפנים ושחט שחיטתו כשרה קיבל קבלתו פסולה הכנים ראשו ורובו כאילו לא נכנס פרכסה ויצתה לחוץ וחזרה פסולה שמע מינה בשר קדשים קלים שיצא לפני זריקת ד) דמים פסולים דילמא באליה ויותרת הכבד ושתי כליות בעא מיניה אבוה דשמואל משמואל היא בפנים ורגליה בחוץ מהו א"ל כתיב והביאום לה' עד שתהא כולה לפנים תלה ושחט מהו א"ל כשרה א"ל *איתבשת בעינן שחיטה על ירך וליכא נתלה ושחט מהו אמר ליה פסולה אמר ליה איתבשת שחיטה על ירך ולא שוחט על ירך נתלה וקבל מהו אמר ליה כשרה אמר ליה איתבשת אין דרך שירות בכך תלה וקיבל מהו אמר ליה פסולה אמר ליה איתבשת שחיטה על ירך ולא קבלה על ירך אמר אביי בקדשי קדשים כולן פסולות בר מנתלה ושחט בקדשים קלים כולן כשרות בר מן נתלה וקיבל אמר רבא מאי שנא תלה וקיבל בקדשים קלים דכשרה דאויר פנים כפנים דמי בקדשי קדשים נמי אויר צפון כצפון דמי אלא אמר רבא בין בקדשי קדשים בין בקדשים קלים כשרות בר מן תלה ושחט בקדשי קדשים נתלה וקיבל בין בקדשי קדשים בין בקדשים קלים בעא מיניה רבי ירמיה מרבי זירא הוא בפנים וציציתו בחוץ מהו אמר ליה לאו אמרת והביאום לה' עד שתבא כולה לפנים הכא נמי בבואם אל אהל מועד עד שיבא כולו לאהל מועד:

מתני' נתנו על גבי הכבש שלא כנגד היסוד נתן את הניתנין למטה למעלה ואת הניתנין למעלה למטה ואת הניתנין בפנים בחוץ ואת הניתנין בחוץ בפנים פסול ואין בו כרת:

גמ'

שחט ואח"כ חתך פסולה · דדם פסול לא בטל ברוב כדמוכח פ' התערובת (לקמן דף עט:) יח) דגזרי' גזירה במקדש : **חתך** ואח"כ שחט כשרה · ובסמוך דקאמר והביאום כתיב שתהא כולה לפנים הייט לכתחלה ע"כ : **שמע** מינה דם המובלע באברים דם הוא · פי' בקונט' ונפקא מינה שחייבין כרת על אכילתו ואי אפשר לומר כן דהא קי"ל בכריתות (דף כא:) דדם האברים בלאו ואין לפרש דמיירי הכא להתחייב עליו משום דם קודש שנפרש מן האבר דפשיטא דשרי באכילה כדפירשנו בחולין (דף יד·*) מכמה ראיות ונראה לפרש דאיירי הכא ליפסל ביוצא ואפי' למ"ד אין יוצא בבשר יט) בקדשים קלים הייט משום דסופה לצאת אי נמי לענין דאין מועלין בו ואין חייבין עליו משום פיגול או לענין דם חטאת שניתז על הבגד : **דילמא** באליה ויותרת הכבד · וא"ת מ"מ תיפשוט דאימורי קדשים קלים שיצאו לפני זריקה פסולין ולקמן בפרק כל התדיר (דף פט:) רוצה לומר דכשרין וי"ל דמכאן אין ראיה דדלמא כר' אליעזר ס"ל דפסיל כ) ביוצא התם (תוספית) דא"ר אליעזר אימורי קדשים כא) שיצאו לפני זריקה פסולים ביוצא ואין חייבין עליהן משום פיגול וכו' אבל רבי עקיבא מחייב *וקשה לרב פפא דאמר התם בדעיילינהו לגואי בשעת זריקה לא פליגי פירוש דאינם פסולין הלא הכא קאמר פסולה וליכא לפרושי הכא דהזרה לאחר זריקה דדומיא דלעיל בכשרה הוי דמיירי בחזרה קודם קבלה וי"ל דה"פ עיילינהו לגואי לא פליגי פירוש דודאי חייבין עליהם משום פיגול דזריקה מועלת לחייב משום פיגול על יוצא כי האי דלפני זריקה והיה לפנים בשעת זריקה אבל מכל מקום נפסל ביוצא לכולי עלמא כדאיתא במתניתין כי פליגי בעיילינהו בתר זריקה אי חייבין משום פיגול דהא עיילינהו או לאו כב) :

*ה"ג ה) שחט ואחר כך חתך פסולה בעלת מום קמקריב אלא אימא חתך ואחר כך קיבל · שחתכו בין שחיטה לקבלה כשרה : והא"ר זירא הצורם כו' · אלמא המום פוסל בקבלה : ומשני אמר רב חסדא אמר אבימי חותך באבר עד שמגיע לעצם · דלאו מום הוא והדם מעוכב ע"י חתיכה ו) מלעלות וליכנס לפנים : קבל ואחר כך חתך פסולה · מילתיה דרבי אלעזר הדר ונקיט כמו אמר מר : ש"מ דם המובלע באברים דם הוא ז) *וכרת נמי לחייב דאי לא הוי דם אהיכא חייל פסול יוצא אמיא בעלמא : דלמא משום שמנונית · דחזיא לאכילה וחשיבי כבשר לא יפסולי ביוצא כדכתיב (שמות כב) ובשר בשדה טריפה ומיבלע בדם הרגל ונפקא דרך בית שחיטה ופסלה לה לדם שבמזרק : ש"מ בשר קדשים קלים שיצא מן העזרה לפני זריקה פסול · ואע"פ שסופו לצאת אחר זריקה ולהיות נאכל בכל העיר השתא מיהא לא מטא זמניה ותיהוי הך דרב אמי אמר ר' אלעזר ח) דלא כדרבי יוחנן דמכשר ליה לקמן בפר' כל התדיר (דף פט:): דלמא· כי אמרה ט) רבי [אמי אמר ר' אלעזר] : בקדשי קדשים · אמר דמיפסל לפני זריקה ביוצא לדברי הכל שאין סופו לצאת : וקיבול דמן בכלי שרת בצפון · לקמן ילפינן לה באיזהו מקומן (דף מט·) דכמך קבלה לשחיטה : עמד · בחלק דרומי של עזרה סמוך לאמצעה : הושיט ידו לצפון ושחט שחיטתו כשרה · לקמן ילפינן לה אותו בצפון ואין השוחט בצפון אבל המקבל צריך להיות בצפון הלכך קיבל קבלתו פסולה : הכניס ראשו ורובו · בצפון וקיבל כאילו נכנס כולו כדקי"ל בכל התורה רובו ככולו : פרכסה · לאחר שחיטה ויצאה לדרום וחזרה כשרה דאין פסול יוצא י) אלא מתוך המחיצות והאי וחזרה לאו דוקא אלא איידי דבעי למיתני סיפא גבי פנים וחוץ וחזרה לאשמועינן רבותא דאע"ג דחזרה פסולה תנא רישא נמי וחזרה : שחיטתן בפנים יא) · דכתיב (ויקרא ג) בשלמים ושחטו פתח אהל מועד דהייט תוך העזרה : וקיבול דמן בכלי שרת בפנים · קבלה בפנים נפקא לן מלעמוד לפני ה' לשרתו (דברים י) אלמא כל שירות לפני ה' הוא: עמד בחוץ והושיט ידו בפנים ושחט שחיטתו כשרה · לקמן בפרק כל הפסולין (דף לב:) ילפי' לה בן הבקר לפני ה' ולא השוחט לפני ה' : קבל קבלתו פסולה · כדפרישית: הכניס ראשו ורובו כאילו לא נכנס · כדילפינן לקמן במתניתין בבואם אל אהל מועד עד שיבא כולו וגבי עזרה יב) דכתיב יעמוד לפני ה' בעי נמי כולו דכיון דגלי בחדא גלי בכולהו והכי אמר במתניתין* : פרכסה · לאחר שחיטה ויצאה לחוץ וחזרה פסולה דאיפסלא ביוצא כדגמרי' פסול יוצא בפסחים בכילד צולין (דף פב·) מהן לא הובא את דמה אל הקודש פנימה (ויקרא י) ומבשר בשדה טריפה (שמות כב) : דילמא · הא דקתני פסולה באליה ויותרת ט' דאימורין נינהו ואימורי קדשים קלים קדשי קדשים הן : היא בפנים כו' מהו · לשוחטה לכתחילה יג) : תלה · הבהמה באויר העזרה : על ירך · משמע יד) אגלו : נתלה · השוחט באויר העזרה מהו : אמר ליה פסולה · מיניה קגמר לה דשמע דקא"ל תלה ושחט פסול וסבר ה"ה לנתלה : אמר ליה כשרה · כדאמר ליה לנתלה ושחט : טו) [א"ל פסולה · מיניה גמר כדאמר ליה בתלה ושחט ובנתלה וקבל וסבר ה"ה לתלה וקיבל] : בקדשי קדשים · דכתיב בהו על ירך : כולן פסולין בר מן נתלה ושחט · דבשוחט לא כתיב ירך אלא בנשחט כדכתיב אותו על ירך אבל תלה וקבל פסולה דאויר צפון לאו כצפון דמי ובעינן קבלה בצפון כדגמרי' באיזהו מקומן (לקמן מט·) ואף על גב דלא כתיב ירך בקבלה צפון מיהא כתיב בה : בקדשים קלים · טז) לא כתיב בהו על ירך ולא כתיב בהו צפון כולן כשרים בר מנתלה וקבל דאין דרך שירות בכך : דאויר פנים כפנים דמי · דהא על כרחך פנים יז) מיהו כתיב בהו ומודית דאויר פנים כפנים : אם כן בקדשי קדשים · אמאי פלגת אדאבוה דשמואל בתלה וקבל לימא נמי אויר צפון כצפון דמי : אלא אמר רבא · כולה כאבוה דשמואל קאמר לה אלא דאבוה דשמואל לא איירי בקדשים קלים : בר מן תלה ושחט בקדשי קדשים · דבעינן על ירך אבל בקדשים קלים דלא כתיב על ירך כשרה תלה וקבל כשר בכולן דדרך שירות בכך ואויר צפון כצפון דמי ובקבלה לא כתיב על ירך : ונתלה וקבל בין בקדשים כו' · נמי פסול דקבלה שירות היא ואין דרך שירות בכך אבל נתלה ושחט כשרה דשחיטה לאו שירות היא ועל ירך נמי לאו בשוחט כתיב אלא בבהמה : ציציתו · ציצית ראשו דהייט שערו : **מתני'** נתנו · למתן דמו : על גבי הכבש · שאינו מקום מתן דמים או במזבח שלא כנגד היסוד וילפינן לקמן דעולה טעונה מתן דמים כנגד היסוד שהיא יסוד המזבח למטה ממתן דמה למעוטי קרן מזרחית דרומית דלא הוה לה יסוד כדאמרינן באיזהו מקומן (לקמן דף נג:) : למטה · מחוט הסיקרא : ואין בו כרת · אין באכילתו כרת ובגמרא מפרש למאי איצטריך למתנייה :

גמ'

שיטה מקובצת

א] תיבות חתך ואח"כ קיבל כשרה נמחק : ב] אזן הפר : ג] חותך באבר עד שמגיע לעצם והשתא לא הוי בעל מום דאין נעשה בעל מום [עד] שמגיע לעצם וא"ע א"כ אמאי הדר ביה מהא דקאמר חתך ואח"כ שחט וי"ל דמ"מ מום עובר הוי קודם שיגיע נמי לעצם ולא מצי מקריב ליה עד שיעבור המום אבל בקבלה לא הוי פסול מום עובר וקרינא ביה שפיר (מום) [מדם הפר] שהיה כו כבר כך פי' מורי' הר"פ: ד] דמים פסול : ה] ה"ג חתך ואח"כ שחט כשרה: ו] חתיכה זו מלעלות וליכנס לפנים והשתא אפילו חתך ואח"כ שחט כשרה והאי דלא אמר אלא לפי שלא אמרו [אמורא] בתירוץ ראשון: גליון: ז] הוא ודם נפסל ביוצא בין בקדשי קדשים בין בקדשים קלים ונ"מ שחייב עליו כרת על אכילתו דאי לאו דם הוא ובשר נמי לא הוי אהיכא: ח] אלעזר פליגא אדרבי יוחנן : ט] רב אמי אמר רבי אלעזר : י] יוצא בתיך המחיצות והאי וחזרה לאו דוקא דמאי מהניא חזרה בצפון ודרום והא לאו יוצא הוא : יא] בפנים בעזרה : יב] עזרה נמי דכתיב לעמוד לפני ה' דבעינן נמי כולו דכתיב כו' והכי אמר בשמעתין אבל לגבי הכנסות צפון לא בעינן כולו שהרי הוא עומד בעזרה הס"ד: יג] לכתחלה ולעיל דקאמר חתך ואח"כ שחט כשרה היינו בדיעבד : יד] אצלה כלומר שיהא אצלה בקרקע : טו] ושחם הס"ד ומה"ד אין דרך שירות בכך וקבלה שירות הוא הס"ד ומה"ד תלה הבהמה וקבל הדם מהו הס"ד ומה"ד א"ל פסולה כדקאמרת לי בתלה ושחט הס"ד : טז] קלים דלא : יז] פנים מיהא : יח] התערובת בההיא שמעתתא דנזורינן : יט] בבשר קדשים קלים : כ] דפסיל התם ביוצא הג"ה ותיבת תוספת נמחק : כא] קדשים קלים שיצאו כו' מחייב מיהו קשה : כב] לאו ברוך עכ"ח :

הגהות הב"ח

(א) גמ' אלא אימא חתך ואח"כ קיבל כשרה קיבל ואח"כ חתך פסולה והא אמר וכו' אזן הפר ואח"כ:

שמואל

גמ' אמר שמואל א] פסול בשר *אבל בעלים נתכפרו מאי טעמא דאמר קרא °ואני נתתיו לכם על המזבח לכפר כיון שהגיע דם למזבח נתכפרו בעלים אי הכי בשר נמי אמר קרא לכפר °לכפרה נתתיו ולא לדבר אחר אלמא קסבר ב שלא במקומו כמקומו דמי תנן באידך פירקין *נתנו על הכבש שלא כנגד היסוד נתן את הניתנין למטה למעלה ואת הניתנין למעלה למטה ואת הניתנין בפנים בחוץ ואת הניתנין בחוץ בפנים אם יש דם הנפש יחזור הכשר ויקבל ואי ב] ס"ד שלא במקומו כמקומו למה לי יחזור הכשר ויקבל וכי תימא להתיר בשר באכילה מי איכא זריקה דלא מכפרת ושריא בשר באכילה אי דיהביה כשר ה"נ ג הכא במאי עסקינן דיהביה פסול ולידהוי דחוי *דתנן וכולן שקיבלו חוץ לזמנו וחוץ למקומו אם יש דם הנפש יחזור הכשר ויקבל קיבלו אין זרקו לא מ"ט לאו משום דהוי דחוי לא משום דפסיל במחשבה אי הכי קבלה נמי ועוד מי פסלה מחשבה *והאמר רבא ד אין מחשבה מועלת אלא במי שראוי לעבודה ובדבר הראוי לעבודה ג] ובמקום הראוי לעבודה לא תימא זרקו לא אלא אימא שחטו לא מאי קמ"ל דפסלה מחשבה תנינא *לפיכך הן פוסלין במחשבה הא קמ"ל ה דמקבלה ואילך לא פסלה מחשבה מ"ט כדרבא מיתיבי *חישב ליתן את הניתנין למעלה למטה למטה למעלה לאלתר כשר ד] (למחר פסול) חזר וחישב חוץ

ויקרא יז | מנחות לב. | רפ"ק מ"ז

גמ' אמר שמואל פסול · דקתני מתני' אבשר קאי אבל בעלים נתכפרו: על המזבח. (א) כל המזבח שוה לענין כפרה: לכפרה נתתיו ה] · הקשיתי (ב)כל מקומות המזבח שוין ולא לדבר אחר שתהא זריקה חשובה להתיר בה בשר דזריקה הוא דשריא לה דכתיב ודם זבחיך ישפך והדר והבשר תאכל (דברים יב): יחזור הכשר ויקבל · יחזור כהן הכשר לקבלה ויקבל כדי מתן (ג) ו] מן הבהמה ויחזור ויתן במקומו וקס"ד השתא דעד השתא בכהן כשר נמי איירי והאי הכשר דקתני כדי נסבה: למה לי יחזור · הלא נתכפרו: וכי תימא להתיר בשר באכילה · דזריקה הוא דשריא לה: ומי איכא זריקה דלא מיכפרא · כגון הך בתרייתא דלאו לכפרה אתיא דהא איכפר בקמייתא: אי דיהביה · שלא במקומו כהן כשר הכי נמי דלא בעי יחזור ויקבל: הכא במאי עסקינן דיהביה פסול · והא דקתני נתנו על גבי הכבש ארישא קאי דקתני כל הפסולים ששחטו כו' וכולן שקיבלו את הדם כו' ועלה קאי נתנו על גבי הכבש כו' בפ"ג: וליהוי דחוי · כיון דאמרי' שלא במקומו כמקומו דמי ובלבד שיהא במזבח כי יהביה פסול ז] הויא לה זריקה פסולה כאילו נתנו פסול במקומו וניהוי כל הדם דחוי ולא תיהוי ליה תו תקנתא: דהא תנן · בההיא: וכולן שקבלו · את הדם ואפסולין קאי שקבלו את הדם במחשבת אכילת בשר חוץ לזמנו או חוץ למקומו: אם יש דם הנפש · עוד בצואר בהמה יחזור הכשר ויקבל מן הדם ויתן שלא במחשבה וכשר דמחשבה דחשיב עלה קמא לא ח]נפסל דכיון דאינו ראוי לעבודה אין מחשבתו מחשבה: קבלו אין · הוא דאית ליה תקנתא *ט]: מאי טעמא לאו משום · דזריקה פסולה מבויא ליה דחוי משום דגמר י] כפרתו: לא · הא דדייקינן זרקו לא יא] משום דמיפסיל במחשבה דהא בעושה מחשבה קיימינא ודכוותה דייקינן זרקו לא: א"ה · דמחשבת פסולין פסלה מקבלה שקיבל במחשבה ליפסיל ועוד מי פסל (ד) יב] במחשבת כהן פסול: במי שראוי לעבודה · כהן כשר: ובדבר הראוי לעבודה · מנחת חטים לאפוקי מנחת יג] [העומר שהיא של] שעורים דלא חייל עלה פגול ליענש כרת באכילתה: ובמקום הראוי לעבודה · לאפוקי נפגם המזבח הכי מפורש במנחות (דף ה:): לא תימא זרקו לא · דודאי איכא תקנתא ואפי' זרקו פסול במחשבה: אלא אימא שחטו לא · שאם שחטו פסול במחשבה תו ליכא תקנתא דכיון דכל הפסולין כשירין לשחוט יד]פוסלין (ה) מחשבתן: תנינא · בההיא משנה גופה כל הפסולין ששחטו שחיטתן כשרה לפיכך · הן (ו)פסולין במחשבה: הא קמ"ל · הא דקתני וכולן שקיבלו את הדם כו' טו] [אע"ג] דבשחיטה תנן פוסלין במחשבה אבל בקבלה ומקבלה ואילך לא פסלי ולא למידק מיניה זרקו לא דה"ה לזרקו אלא קיימתא דכולהו נקט דכיון דפסול אינו ראוי לה לא פסלה מחשבתו: כדרבא · דאמר אין מחשבה מועלת אלא בראוי לעבודה: חישב · כהן כשר: ליתן את הניתנין כו' · ששחט או קיבל או הוליך על מנת לזרוק הזריקה שלא במקומו: לאלתר כשר · אם חישב על מנת לזרוק שלא במקומו היום כשר (ז) ואי נמי זריקה פסולה היא ונמצא שעבד שאר העבודות על מנת לזרוק את הדם בפסול כשר הוא בזריקה הוגנת במקומו כדאמרינן במשנה כל הפסולין (לקמן לו:) אין המחשבה פוסלת אלא חוץ לזמנו וחוץ למקומו ופסח וחטאת שלא לשמן: חזר וחישב · בעבודה שניה על מנת לאוכלו חוץ למקומו פסול ואין חייבין כרת על אכילתו:

תורה אור

אמר שמואל טז] פסול בשר אבל בעלים נתכפרו · נראה דקאי אניתנין למעלה שנתנן למטה ולמטה שנתנן למעלה אבל אניתנין על גבי הכבש לא קאי דהא כולי עלמא מודו יז] בשלא במקומו דלאו כמקומו דמי אע"ג דבפ' המזבח מקדש (לקמן פז·) מרבה כבש כמזבח לענין קידוש דאם עלו לא ירדו ובפ' כל המנחות (מנחות נז:) לענין הקטרה דהמעלה מכולן ע"ג הכבש לר' יוחנן חייב מ"מ לענין דמים לא מליטו בשום מקום כבש כמזבח דלקמן בפ' קדשי קדשים (דף סב:) גבי עולה וגבי חטאת ממעטינן מדכתיב קיר המזבח ולא קיר הכבש ועל כרחין שמואל לאו אכולה יח] *מילתיה קאי דניתנין בפנים שנתנן בחוץ ובחוץ שנתנו בפנים לכ"ע לאו כמקומן דמי כדמוכח פ' כל הפסולין לקמן בסופו (דף לה:) דא"ר יהודה חישב להניח דמו למחר פסול דכבר מחשבה כמעשה ופריך (שם לו·) וליפלוג בשיפא על ניתנין למטה שחשב ליתנן למעלה שיהא פסול ומשני קסבר ר' יהודה שלא במקומו כמקומו דמי יט]*(תוספות)והשתא אנותי הדר פריך וליפלוג ר' יהודה בנתנן הניתנין בפנים בחוץ ובחוץ בפנים אלמא *דהני [לכ"ע] שלא במקומו כ]מיקרי (ע"כ) ומיהו לקמן פירש בקונטרס דמהניתנין בחוץ שחישב ליתן בפנים דוקא קמקשי דהתם ודאי אי הוה יהיב חטאת חיצונה בפנים מיפסלא דכתיב וכל חטאת אשר יובא וגו' אבל מחישב ליתן הניתנין בפנים בחוץ לא פריך וכן *מוכיח מדקמשני קסבר רבי יהודה בעינן מקום כא] שהוא משולש בדם ובבשר ובאימורים פירוש דגבי מחשבת חוץ למקומו כתיב שלישי ודרשינן ביהא אותו כב] (שלישי) חוץ למקומו משולש בדם ובשר ואימורים שהיה מותר בו דהייט חוץ לעזרה ממש שבשעת היתר הבמות נשתלש בכל אלה (תוספות).והותר שם לאפוקי פנים שלא הותרו מעולם ליכנס בלשתן דדם חטאת אסור דכתיב וכל חטאת אשר יובא מדמה וכן האימורין כתיב ועולה לא יעלו עליו (ע"כ) והניתנין בפנים שנתנן בחוץ לא שייך האי שינויא ומיהו מליטו למימר דבעי' נמי שיהא המחשבה במקום משולש תדע דאי כג] לאו הכי למ"ד שלא במקומו לאו כמקומו דמי מאי הוה משני מבפנים אחוץ מיהו ר' יהודה אית ליה כמקומו דמי ונראה (תוס') ור' יוחנן דאמר בסמוך שלא במקומו לאו כמקומו דמי הייטו דוקא לרבנן אבל לר' יהודה אית ליה כמקומו דמי אפי' לר' יוחנן כדמשני פרק כל הפסולין (גם זה שם) על ניתנין למעלה למטה ולמטה למעלה וה"ה דסבר כן בניתנים בפנים שנתנן בחוץ והתם לא פריך אלא מניתנים בחוץ שנתנן בפנים דוקא כדפי' רש"י משום דנפסל בשעה כד] שהובא בהיכל וא"כ מלי שמואל קאי אכולהו אבל לא מלי למימר כמקומו דמי על בחוץ שנתנו לפנים· שנפסל בביאתו בהיכל קודם שנתנן על מזבח הזהב (ע"כ): (הגה"ה) ועוד נראה דעל כרחין כבש נמי כמקומו דמי מדלא פריך לקמן דליפלוג ר' יהודה אחישב ליתנו על גבי כבש וכי תימא משום דיאספנו ואין כאן בית מיחוש כה] מחשבה דהרי בחשב לשפוך מן הכלי על הרצפה יאספנו לכ"ע הא לקמן אמרי' דלר' יהודה לא יאספנו היכא דקלטי' מזבח וא"כ מהאי טעמא לא יאספנו מעל גבי כבש דכבש מקדש פסולין כמזבח ומיהו כיון דפרישית לעיל דלענין דמים לא הוי כבש כמזבח לא קלטיה ויאספנו ומיהו על כרחיך אכבש נמי קאי שמואל דלקמן בשמעתין פריך' יוחנן אי שלא במקומו לאו כמקומו דמי א"כ זריקתו אינה כלום ליהוי כנשפך מן הכלי על הרצפה ויאספנו משמע לשמואל ולר"ש לקיש דאמרי שלא במקומו כמקומו דמי ניחא והאי לדידהו נמי תיקשי מניתנין על גבי הכבש ומניתנין בפנים שנתנן בחוץ כו] אבל על ניתנין בחוץ שנתנן בפנים דמודו כולהו דשלא כמקומו דמי לא שייך למיפרך האי (לדידהו נמי תיקשי מניתנין על גבי כבש ומניתנים בפנים בחוץ תוס') פסול נימא יאספנו שהרי בלא ניתנין על מזבח הזהב כבר נפסל בביאתו בהיכל ואפי' נשפך שם לא יהא כשר כז] לאספנו · ע"כ הג"ה: לכפרה נתתיו ולא לדבר אחר · בעלמא (לקמן דף מו·) דרשינן לכפרה נתתיו ולא למעילה: ואי שלא במקומו כמקומו דמי למה לי יחזור הכשר ויקבל · תימה דלקמן בפ' התערובת (דף עט:) תנן הניתנין למטה שנתערבו בניתנין למעלה ר' אליעזר אומר יתן למעלה ורואה אני את *הניתנין למטה כאילו הן מים ויחזור ויתן למטה והשתא אמאי יחזור ויתן למטה הרי כבר נתכפר וי"ל כיון דאית ליה לשם כפרת התחתון ומיהו קשה לרבנן דלית להו רואין ומשמע התם דלרבנן יחזור ויתן למטה דקתני נתן *למעלה ולא נמלך (כשר) : הכא במאי עסקינן דיהביה פסול · כט] תימה אם כן אפילו נתן במקומו נמי וי"ל דהאי פסול היינו טמא דאיירי ביה לעיל ל] ואי יהביה במקומו כולי עלמא מודי דהוי דחוי ולא יחזור כשר ויקבל כדאמר בפ"ק דמעילה (דף ה:) דאין לך עושה שירים ופסול אלא טמא הואיל ומרצה בקרבן ציבור וחוץ לזמנו וחוץ למקומו הואיל ומרצה לפיגולו לא]: ואי

קנ א ב ג מיי' פ"ב מהלכות פסה"מ הלכה י ועי"ש:

קד ד ה מיי' פ"ד מהל' פסה"מ הלכה ג:

נ"א מתניתין

נ"א ופריך הו וליפלוג בניתנין בפנים שנתנו בחוץ והשתא כו'

דבהני שלא במקומן מודה כו' צ"ק

שיטה מקובצת

א] שמואל בשר פסול : ב] ואי [ס"ד] שלא במקומו כו' · וקשה דמשמע דאי לאו כמקומו דמי ניהא שפיר ואיך ניהא) הא דקתני פסול אפילו פסיל נמי לא להוי והלא ממש כמי שלא עשה כלום כיון דשלא כמקומו דמי וי"ל דמ"מ פסול הוא משום מחשבת הינוח וכר"י דאמר מחשב ע"מ להניחו עד למחר פסול הואיל ואם הניח עד למחר פסול וא"ת א"כ לאלתר נמי אמאי כשר אי כשלא כמקומו דמי ליפסל משום מחשבת חוץ למקומו ר"ל דכיון דגלי קרא במחשבת חוץ למקומו דבעינן מקום משולש כדמוכח לקמן מקראי א"כ לא מיפסיל משום מחשבת הינוח ואע"ג דאם נתנו כמו שחשב פסול הוי : ג] ובמקום הראוי לעבודה פי' כגון שנפגם המזבח וא"ת תיפוק ליה משום דאינו ראוי והוי ליה כאילו מחשב לזרוק על הרצפה ולא פסלה בה מחשבה וי"ל דקמ"ל דאע"ג דבר הקטרה הוא כדמוכח לקמן לגבי קומץ הואיל ואינו ראוי לשאר עבודות לא פסיל בהו : ד] תיבות (מחשבה) למחר פסול נמחק : ה] נתתיו לכפרה : ו] מתן דם : ז] פסול דהוי : ח] מיפסל : ט] תקנתא הא זרקו הנך פסולים לא תני בהו תקנתא משום דבזריקה הוי הכפרה ואז משוי ליה דיחוי כדפי' : י] דגמר לה : יא] לא לאו משום דהוי דחוי אלא משום דמיפסיל במחשבה קיימינא : יב] פסול מחשבת כהן : יג] מנחת העומר שהיא של שעורי' כו' באכילתה דאינה ראויה אלא לעבודה זו בלבד (דדבר החדש) [אא"ה בכאן כתב על הגליון צ"ל האסור ול"נ דכך צ"ל] [דהדש דבר אסור הוא וכתיב ממשקה ישראל ה"א אע"ג דמנחת קנאות באה מן השעורים התם קמח הכא סולת : יד] לשחוט פסלי מחשבתן: טו] כו' דאע"ג

לקמן נג. | ג"ז שם | מנחות ה: | לקמן לא: | לקמן נג:

נ"א הא זרקו פסולין לא אית ליה תו תקנתא

הגהות הב"ח

(א) רש"י ד"ה על המזבח לכפר כו': (ב) ד"ה לכפרה נתתיו וכו' דכל: (ג) ד"ה יחזור וכו' כדי מתן דמו מן הבהמה: (ד) ד"ה א"ה דמחשבת וכו' מי פסל מחשבה בכהן פסול: (ה) ד"ה אלא וכו' במחשבתן: (ו) ד"ה תנינא וכו' הן פוסלין במחשבה: (ז) ד"ה לאלתר וכו' ואי נמי וכו' במשנה דכל:

גליון הש"ס

גמ' אבל בעלים נתכפרו. עי' לקמן דף כב ע"ב ובתוס' שם ד"ה אותה: שם לכפרה נתתיו. עיין לקמן דף לח ע"א תוספות ד"ה וכיפר:

נ"א ל"ג ומהרש"ק מוחק מן מניתנין עד נימא

[במשנה שם איתא ורואה אני את הניתנים למעלה כאילו כו']

ס"א למעלה ולא נמלך אלו ואלו מודים שיחזור ויתן למטה

טז] שמואל בשר פסול : יז] דשלא במקומו : יח] אכולה מתני' : יט] תיבת תוספת נמחק : כ] במקומו הוי ומיהו ותיבות מיקרי ע"כ נמחק : כא] מקום שיהא : כב] שיהא אותו חוץ למקומו כו' ואימורים דהיינו חוץ כו' בכל אלה והותר שם (והשאר נמחק) : כג] דאי לא תימא הכי [ז"ל תוס' רי"ד] דאי לא תימא הכי אם כן מצינו למימר כפי' הקונטרס דמהוץ (בפנים) [אבפנים] קא פריך אבל (מחוץ בפנים) [מבפנים אבחוץ] לא דכמקומו דמי ושמואל נמי קאי אכולהו ועוד דע"כ כבש נמי כמקומו דמי [ע"כ] : כד] בשעה דהובא בהיכל : כה] מחשבת פסיל דהרי הוא כחשב לשפוך כו' על הרצפה דיאספנו : כו] מתיבת אבל כו' עד תיבת פסול נמחק : כז] כשר שיאספנו : כח] כמכופר דלא יהיב : כט] פסול תימה פסול מאן דכר שמיה ופ"ה דקאי ארישא דקתני כו' ותימה א"כ אמאי קתני הניתנים למטה שנתנם למעלה אפילו : ל] לעיל דאית ליה ריצוי בקרבן צבור הלכך אי יהביה במקומו כו' דהוי דחוי כל הדם ולא יחזור הכשר ויקבל : לא] לפיגולו אבל השתא ששינה את מקומו דאיכא דחוי [אחר] דחוי דהוי טמא ושלא במקומו וכיון דתרי דחוי הוי אינו עושה שירים ואע"ג דדחוי אחד [וכל] שהזריקה עשויה יותר בהכשר היא פוסלת שאר הדם (ואינו) ועושה שירים ופריך ולהוי דחוי כיון דאצרת שלא במקומו כמקומו ובלבד שיהא במזבח כי יהבי פסול הוי ליה זריקת פסול לחוד בשביל שנתנה פסול ואין כאן [אלא חד] דיחוי והוי ממש כאילו נתנו פסול במקומו דהוי ליה דיחוי ולית ליה תקנתיה :

א) נראה דר"ל דתקשה הברייתא שהביא הש"ס בסמוך דאם חישב ליתן וכו' לאלתר כשר למחר פסול ואמאי קשה דהא לקמן בגמ' ד' מחק הא דלמחר פסול וצ"ע

[26b] *GEMARA*. Samuel said: It is the flesh that is unfit, but its owners are forgiven.[7] What is the reason?—Because Scripture saith, *And I have given it to you upon the altar to make atonement*:[8] once the blood has reached the altar, the owners are forgiven. If so, the flesh too [should be fit]?—Scripture saith, '*to make atonement*': I have given it for atonement, but not for any other purpose.[9]

Now this proves that he holds that [when blood is] not [applied] in its [proper] place, it is as [though applied] in its [proper] place.[10] Now we learned in another chapter: If [the priest] applied it [the blood] on the ascent, [or on the altar, but] not over against its base; if he applied [the blood] which should be applied below [the scarlet line] above [it], or that which should be applied above, below; or that which should be applied within [he applied] without, or what should be applied without [he applied] within: then if
a life-blood[1] is still available, a fit [priest] must receive [it] a second time.[2] Now if you maintain that [when blood is] not [applied] in its [proper place], it is as though [applied] in its [proper] place, why must a fit [priest] receive [it] again? And should you answer, In order to permit the flesh for consumption; is there a sprinkling which makes no atonement yet permits the consumption of the flesh?[3]—Had a fit [priest] applied it [in the first place], that would indeed be so;[4] the circumstances here are that an unfit [priest] applied it [in the first place].[5] But let it constitute [complete] rejection.[6] For we learnt: But if any of these[7] received [the blood, intending to consume the flesh] after time or without bounds, and the life blood is [still] available, a fit [priest] must receive [it] a second time.[8] Thus, only if they received [the blood with that intention], but not if they sprinkled [it thus];[9] what is the reason? is it not because this effects [complete] rejection?—No: the reason is because it became unfit through an [illegitimate] intention. If so, [the same should apply to] receiving? Moreover, does an [illegitimate] intention[10] disqualify it? Surely Raba said: An [illegitimate] intention is without effect save [when purposed] by one who is fit for the service and in connection with that which is fit for the service,[11] and in a place fit for the service![12]—Do not say, but not if they sprinkled it [thus]; 'say rather, but not if they
b slaughtered it [thus]?[1] What does he inform us? that an [illegitimate] intention disqualifies? But we have learnt it: Therefore they[2] invalidate [the sacrifice] by an [illegitimate] intention [purposed at slaughtering]?[3]—This is what we are informed,[4] viz., that from receiving and onwards intention [on the part of an unfit priest] does not invalidate. What is the reason? As [that stated] by Raba.

An objection is raised: If [the priest] intends applying [the blood] which should be applied above [the line] below [it], [or what should be applied] below, above, immediately,[5] it is valid.[6] If he

(7) They have fulfilled their obligation, and do not bring another offering. (8) Lev. XVII, 11. (9) Only in respect of atonement does Scripture intimate that the application of the blood on any part of the altar (since 'altar' is not further localised) is efficacious. But the fitness of the flesh is governed by its own peculiar laws. (10) As far as the fitness of the flesh for consumption is concerned.

a (1) The first blood which gushes out as the animal is slaughtered. (2) For re-sprinkling, v. *infra* 32a. (3) For this second sprinkling does not make atonement, since that was already effected by the first. (4) No further application would be necessary. (5) Hence the second application is needed even for making atonement. (6) Since blood not applied in its proper place is as though applied in its proper place, then if an unfit priest does this it is as though he applied it in the proper place, which it is now assumed definitely invalidates the sacrifice, and it cannot be repaired. (7) *Sc.* all who are unfit for any reason. (8) *Infra* 32a. (9) In which case there would be no remedy. (10) On the part of an unfit priest. (11) E.g., a meal-offering of wheat. This excludes the meal-offering of barley brought in connection with the '*omer* (q.v. Glos.), since barley was unfit for other meal-offerings. (12) This excludes the case where the altar itself was mutilated.

b (1) Because since even unfit priests are fit to slaughter (as are lay-Israelites too), their illegitimate intention disqualifies. (2) Persons unfit to slaughter. (3) *Infra* 31b. (4) By stating 'if any of these *received* the blood etc.' (5) He intended applying it thus in the wrong place on the day of slaughtering, which is the proper time. (6) If he eventually sprinkled the blood in the right place, for this illegitimate intention does not disqualify, v. Mishnah *infra* 36a.

subsequently intended [27a] [to consume it] without bounds, it is invalid, but does not involve *kareth*;[7] [if he intended consuming it] after time, it is invalid, and entails *kareth*. [If he intended sprinkling the blood in the wrong place] on the morrow, it is invalid; if he subsequently intended [to consume it] without bounds or after time, it is invalid, and does not involve *kareth*.[8] Now if you say that [blood] not [applied] in its [proper] place [on the altar] is as [though applied] in its [proper] place, is this [merely] invalid? Surely it is *piggul*![9]—Said Mar Zuṭra: Sprinkling which permits the consumption of the flesh can render [it] *piggul*; sprinkling which does not permit the consumption of the flesh[10] does not render [it] *piggul*.[11]

R. Ashi said to Mar Zuṭra: Whence do you know this? [Assuredly] because it is written, *And if any of the flesh of his peace-offerings be at all eaten on the third day . . . it shall be* piggul *[an abhorred thing, and*
a *the soul that eateth of it shall bear his iniquity:]*[1] [thus *kareth* is incurred] only where *piggul* causes [the prohibition of the flesh], which excludes this case,[2] where not *piggul* causes it but a different interdict is the cause. If so,[3] it should not be disqualified either?—Said R. Naḥman b. Isaac: It is analogous to the intention of leaving [the blood] until the morrow, this being in accordance with R. Judah.[4]

Resh Laḳish said: In truth, [the Mishnah means] UNFIT literally,[5] and [blood] not [applied] in its [proper] place is as [though applied in] its [proper] place,[6] yet there is no difficulty:[7] in one case he applied it in silence; in the other he applied it with an expressed intention.[8] We learnt: If he intended applying above [the line] what should be applied below [it], or below what should be applied above [etc.] as far as 'It is analogous to the intention of leaving [the blood] until the morrow, this being in accordance with R. Judah.'[9]

R. Joḥanan said: Both cases[10] are where he sprinkles it in silence, and the wrong place is not as the right place; but the one is where life-blood is [still] available, while the other is where life-blood is not available.

We learnt: IT IS UNFIT, BUT DOES NOT INVOLVE KARETH. As for Resh Laḳish, it is well: he rightly teaches, IT IS UNFIT, BUT
b DOES NOT INVOLVE KARETH.[1] But according to R. Joḥanan, why teach that it DOES NOT INVOLVE KARETH?[2] This is a difficulty. And according to Samuel, what is meant by IT DOES NOT INVOLVE KARETH?[3]—This is what [the Tanna] means: If he sprinkled [it thus] with an [illegitimate] intention, IT IS UNFIT, BUT DOES NOT INVOLVE KARETH.

Now as for R. Joḥanan, if the wrong place [on the altar] is not as the right place,[4] let it be as though [the blood] had been spillt from the [service] vessel on to the pavement, and so let him collect it?[5]—He agrees with the view that it must not be gathered. For R. Isaac b. Joseph said in R. Joḥanan's name: All agree, if [the priest] sprinkled the blood above which should be sprinkled above, or below which should be sprinkled below, but not in accordance with the regulations,[6] that he must not re-gather it.[7] They disagree only where he sprinkled below what should be sprinkled above, or above what should be sprinkled below: there R. Jose holds, He must not re-gather it; while R. Simeon maintains,

(7) For eating it. (8) Since it was already invalid through the first, a second illegitimate intention does not render it *piggul*. (9) How can you say that if he intended applying it in the wrong place on the morrow it is only invalid? On the present hypothesis it is the same as though he had intended applying it in the *right* place on the morrow, and that should render it *piggul*. For the sprinkling of the blood on the altar constitutes, as it were, the altar's consumption, and just as an intention to consume the flesh after time makes it *piggul*, so should a similar intention to sprinkle the blood make it *piggul*! (10) Where the blood is not sprinkled in its proper place. (11) And, as Samuel stated, if the blood is not sprinkled on the proper place on the altar the flesh may not be eaten, though the sacrifice has made atonement.

a (1) Lev. VII, 18; *'shall bear his iniquity'* implies *kareth*. (2) *Sc.* where the blood is not sprinkled in the proper place. (3) That it does not constitute sprinkling in respect of an illegitimate intention. (4) Who holds that the sacrifice then becomes invalid (*infra* 36a). In intending to sprinkle the blood in the wrong place on the morrow, he has also tacitly expressed his intention of leaving the blood until the morrow. (5) Not only is the flesh unfit, but the whole sacrifice is invalid. He thus disagrees with Samuel. (6) In this he agrees with Samuel. (7) Caused by the text quoted by Samuel. (8) The text adduced by Samuel, which intimates that the owners are forgiven, holds good where the priest sprinkled the blood in the wrong place, with no unlawful intention attending the sprinkling. While the Mishnah which states UNFIT, implying that the owners are not forgiven either, holds good where in addition to sprinkling it in the wrong place he intended consuming the flesh after time; and the Mishnah thus teaches that in such a case the sacrifice is unfit, but not *piggul*, since the sprinkling which was not in its proper place did not permit the consumption of the flesh. (9) All the objections raised against Samuel are raised against Resh Laḳish, since he too holds that the wrong place is as the right place. (10) Our Mishnah which simply states that it is unfit, and the Mishnah in the next chapter, quoted *supra* 26b, which teaches that the blood must be re-sprinkled.

b (1) He explains the Mishnah as referring to one who expressed an illegitimate intention. Therefore the Tanna must teach that *kareth* is not incurred in spite of this illegitimate intention. (2) It is obvious that he does not incur *kareth* simply for sprinkling the blood in a wrong place. (3) For he too explains the Mishnah as referring to where the priest is silent. (4) So that it does not count as sprinkling at all. (5) And re-sprinkle. (6) E.g., with his left hand or with an illegitimate intention. (7) For re-sprinkling. For since it was sprinkled in the proper place, there can be no further sprinkling

תורה אור

*חוץ למקומו פסול ואין בו כרת חוץ לזמנו פיגול וחייבין עליו כרת [ג]למחר פסול חזר וחישב בין חוץ לזמנו בין חוץ למקומו פסול ואין בו כרת ואי שלא במקומו כמקומו דמי האי פסול פיגול הוא אמר מר זוטרא [ז]זריקה דשריא בשר באכילה מייתא לידי פיגול זריקה דלא שריא בשר באכילה לא מייתא לידי פיגול א"ל רב אשי למר זוטרא מנא לך הא א] דכתיב °ואם האכל יאכל מבשר זבח שלמיו פיגול יהיה מי שפיגולו גרם לו יצא זה שאין פיגולו גרם לו אלא איסור דבר אחר גרם לו ב] אי הכי איפסולי נמי לא ליפסל אמר רב נחמן בר יצחק מידי דהוה אמחשבת הינוח ואליבא *דרבי יהודה ג] ריש לקיש אמר לעולם פסול ממש ושלא במקומו כמקומו דמי ולא קשיא כאן שנתן בשתיקה כאן שנתן באמירה ד] תנן חישב ליתן את הניתנין למטה למעלה למעלה למטה ה] עד מידי דהוה אמחשבת הינוח ואליבא דרבי יהודה ו] כו' רבי יוחנן אמר אידי ואידי שנתן בשתיקה ושלא במקומו לאו כמקומו דמי והא דאיכא דם הנפש הא דליכא דם הנפש תנן פסול ואין בו כרת בשלמא לריש לקיש היינו דקתני פסול ואין בו כרת אלא לרבי יוחנן מאי אין בו כרת קשיא ולשמואל מאי אין בו כרת ה"ק אם נתן במחשבה פסול ואין בו כרת ורבי יוחנן אי שלא במקומו לאו כמקומו דמי ליהוי כי נשפך מן הכלי על הרצפה ויאספנו סבר לה כמ"ד לא יאספנו דאמר רב יצחק בר יוסף א"ר יוחנן הכל מודים בניתנין למעלה שנתנן למטה שנתנן למטה שלא כמצותן לא יאספנו לא נחלקו אלא בניתנין למעלה שנתנן למטה שנתנן למעלה שרבי *יוסי אומר ז] לא יאספנו ורבי שמעון אומר יאספנו ומשנתינו

(ויקרא ז)

רש"י

חוץ לזמנו פיגול וחייבין עליו כרת · שהרי קרבו מתיריו דהכי תנן במתני' (לקמן כט:) חוץ למקומו פסול חוץ לזמנו פיגול שהרי קרבו מתיריו מהן ח] פיגול מהן שתיקה ואין כאן פסול מחשבה אחרת להוציאו מיד פיגול : למחר פסול · אבל אם הותה מחשבה שחישב בעבודה ראשונה ליתן את הניתנין למטה למעלה חישב לזרוק אותה זריקה למחר פסול כדמוקמינן לקמן מידי דהוה אמחשבת הינוח שהרי שחט ע"מ להניח דמו למחר פסול ורבי יהודה היא דפסיל ליה בפ"ג (לקמן לה:) : חזר וחישב · בעבודה שניה בין חוץ לזמנו בין חוץ למקומו פסול ואין בו כרת דהא איפסיל ליה במחשבה קמייתא ותו לא חייל עליה פיגול דלא קרבו כל מתיריו : ואי שלא במקומו · דמזבח כמקומו דמי : האי פסול · בתמיה אמאי קרי ליה פסול להאי דחישב ליתן שלא במקומו למחר פיגול הוא שהרי חישב בשחיטה ע"מ לזרוק דמו למחר דהיא אכילת מזבח *אלא ט] לאו כמקומו דמי ולא חשיבא אכילה: זריקה דשריא בשר באכילה כו' · כגון במקום מתן הדם מייתי לידי פיגול בין שחישב בה ע"מ להקטיר אימורים למחר בין שחישב בשחיטה לזרוק למחר י] : זריקה דלא שריא בשר באכילה · יא] אי הוה עביד לה בזמנה כגון זריקה שלא במקומו לא מייתי לידי פיגול בין שחישב בה ע"מ להקטיר אימורים למחר בין שחישב בשחיטה למיעבד הך זריקה למחר לא מייתי לידי פיגול : פיגול יהיה · והנפש האוכלת וגו' : מי שפיגולו גורם · שלא יאכל הוא דקאי בעונש תחת יצא בשר שנזרק הדם שלא במקומו דאיסור זריקה שלא במקומו גרם לו שלא יאכל הלכך אין חייבין על פיגולו כרת ונפקא לן מהכא דאי חישב בזריקה שלא במקומו ע"מ לאכול או להקטיר למחר לא הויא מחשבת זריקה לענין פיגול ומינה כי חישב בשחיטה ע"מ לעשות זריקה זו חוץ לזמנו לא הויא מחשבה בזריקה המפגלת : אי הכי · דלא הויא זריקה לענין מחשבה איפסולי נמי לא נפסול : אמחשבת הינוח · דהא חשיב מיהא להניחו למחר: ואליבא דר' יהודה · לקמן בפ' כל הפסולין (דף לה:) תנן להניח מדמו למחר כשר ור' יהודה פוסל: וריש לקיש אמר כו' · אמתניתין קאי ופליג אדשמואל : לעולם פסול ממש · דלא תני תנא פסול אבשר לחודיה אי לא פריש בהדיא ומתני' פסול לגמרי קאמר שאף בעלים לא נתכפרו: ושלא במקומו · כשמואל סבירא ליה דכמקומו דמי לענין כפרה ולא להתיר באכילה כדדריש ליה שמואל לקרא דלעיל ואני נתתיו לכם וגו' ולא קשיא יב] אמתני' : כאן שנתן בשתיקה · דרשא דקרא דמשמע בעלים נתכפרו כשנתן יג] בשלא במקומו בשתיקה ומתני' דקתני פסול בנתן במחשבת לאכול בשר חוץ לזמנו ואשמעינן דפסול ואין בו כרת דמחשבת זריקה זו מחשבה הוא לפסול דכמקומו דמי ולא לפגל דזריקה דלא שריא בשר באכילה לא מייתי לידי פיגול: תנן כו' · כל הנך תיובתא דאותבי' יד] לשמואל מותבי' נמי לריש לקיש דהא כוותיה סבירא ליה דשלא במקומו כמקומו דמי : ורבי יוחנן אמר אידי ואידי · מתניתין דקתני פסול וליכא תקנתא ומתניתין דכל הפסולים דתני תקנתא שנתן בשתיקה : בשלמא לריש לקיש · דאוקי מתני' כשנתן במחשבה איצטריך למיתני אין בו כרת לאשמועינן דאע"ג דחשיב בהך זריקה חוץ לזמנו אינו פיגול וכדאמרן (א) טו] דלא שריא בשר באכילה לא מייתי לידי פיגול : אלא לרבי יוחנן · דמוקי בשתיקה והאי טז] פסול משום דלא במקומו הוא פשיטא דאין בו כרת קשיא : ולשמואל מאי אין בו כרת · דהיא נמי מוקי לה בשתיקה : הכי קאמר ואם נתן במחשבה · דחוץ לזמנו פסול ואין בו כרת ואיצטריך לאשמועינן יז] אע"ג דלענין כפרה כמקומו דמי מחשבת פיגול לא חיילא הואיל ולא שריא בשר באכילה אבל לרבי יוחנן לא מצי לשנויי הכי דכיון דאשמעינן תנא דידן פסול ומשום דשלא במקומו (הוא אלמא) לאו כמקומו דמי פשיטא דאם נתן במחשבה לא הויא מחשבה דהוי כאילו נתנו על הרצפה דלא קרבו כל מתיריו : ורבי יוחנן · כיון דלאו זריקה הוא כלל ניהוי כמי שנשפך מן הכלי על הרצפה ויאספנו ואפי' ליכא דם הנפש אחריתא אמאי פסול יח] יאסוף את זה מן המזבח ויחזור ויתננו במקומו בשלמא לשמואל ולריש לקיש כיון דזריקה היא לכפרה אידחי ליה מלאספו שהרי כיפר אלא לר' יוחנן יאספנו : סבר לה · תנא דמתניתין: כמ"ד לא יאספנו · יט] כיון דהגיע למזבח ואע"ג דשלא כהילכתו הוא קלטיה מזבח לאפוקי מתורת כפרה אחריתי : הכל מודים בניתנין למעלה שנתנן למטה שלא כמצוותן · כגון במחשבה או בשמאל : שלא יאספנו · לחזור וליתנו כמצותו דכיון דניתן במקומו אזדא ליה תורת זריקה מיניה : לא נחלקו · הנך תנאי דבעינן למימר כ] שרבי יוסי אומר לא יאספנו ואף על גב דלאו כמקומו דמי : ורבי שמעון אומר י' · וע"כ ליכא למימר דטעמא

תוספות

ואי שלא במקומו כמקומו דמי כו' · תימה ואי לאו כמקומו דמי לאלתר אמאי כשר וי"ל דהוה מצי למימר וליטעמיך והשתא ניחא הא דקאמר לקמן בסוף כל הפסולין (דף לו.) ר' יהודה לטעמיה דקאמר שלא במקומו כמקומו דמי ופירש שם בקונטרס דשמעינן ליה כא] *דהכא בברייתא דמוקמינן כוותיה בשמעתין (תוספות) ומנא ליה לקמן דר' יהודה סובר כן בעלמא דקאמר ר' יהודה לטעמיה אי *ברייתא דשמעתין דלמא סוברת דלאו כמקומו דמי אלא דסמיך אהא דקתני לאלתר כשר א"כ על כרחין כמקומו דמי וסיפא דלמחר פסולה אתיא כרבי יהודה כמו מחשבת הינוח (ע"כ) : **יצא** זה שאין פיגולו גרם לו · וא"ת אמאי איצטריך לקמן (דף כט:) לא יחשב לומר שמחשבות מוציאות זו מזו תיפוק ליה מהכא מי שפיגולו גרם לו יצא זה שאין פיגולו גרם לו כב] ועוד קשה לרבא דמסיק בסוף פ"ק דמנחות (דף יג·) לדברי האומר שירים שחסרו בין קמיצה להקטרה מקטיר קומץ עליהן וקיי"ל דאותן שירים אסורים באכילה *דמהניא להו הקטרה למיקבעינהו בפיגול ולאפוקי מידי מעילה וי"ל דהא דמיתסר באכילה אין מחמת כג] מיעוט ההקטרה של קומץ הלכך לא ממעטי' ליה מאם האכל יאכל כד] מי שפיגולו גרם לו משמע דאי לא הוי המחשבה הוי הזריקה מעלייתא ומשתריא בשר יצא זה שאין פיגולו גרם לו דאפי' לא הוי המחשבה לא הויא זריקה מעלייתא דהא לא שריא בשר *באכילה (תוספות) וי"ל דמי שפיגולו גרם לו משמע באותה עבודה עצמה דאי לא הויא מחשבה הויא הזריקה מעלייתא ומשתריא בשר באכילה יצא זה שנתן למטה למעלה שאין פיגולו גרם לו ואפילו לא הויא המחשבה לא הויא זה זריקה מעלייתא דהא לא שרייא בשר באכילה אבל אם שחט חטאת שלא לשמה או במחשבת חוץ למקומו והדם קיבל או זרק חוץ לזמנו סד"א ליהוי פיגול ובכרת דכיון דבאותה עבודה דפיגול ליכא מחשבה אחרת קמ"ל לא יחשב אי נמי אימא הני מילי כי נפסל תחלה לא הדר תו מיקבע בפיגול בעבודה שאחריה אבל כי נקבע בפיגול בעבודה כה] אחת ובעבודה שניה שאחריה חשב שלא במקומו לא פקע שם כרת מיניה קמ"ל לא יחשב וקשה לר' יהודה דאזיל בתר מחשבה שקדמה כדתנן בפירקין כו] ולאלתר דכשר במסקנא אתיא כרבי יהודה דסבר שלא במקומו כמקומו דמי ותימה כיון דמחשבה כמעשה לרבי יהודה *א"כ לאלתר כשר היינו בעלים נתכפרו אבל בשר פסול כדאמר שמואל לעיל וא"כ חזר וחישב חוץ לזמנו בעבודה שניה אמאי פיגול להתחייב כרת הא זריקה דלא שריא בשר באכילה לא מייתי לידי פיגול כמו בסיפא למחר פסול ולא פיגול מהאי טעמא ונראה כז] דר' יהודה לא עביד מחשבה כמעשה אלא היכא דבמעשה פסול גמור ולא נתכפרו בעלים ואם כן לאלתר כשר היינו כשר גמור ושריא בשר באכילה דאי לאו הכי ליפלוג בניתנין למעלה למטה שיהא פסול בשר באכילה כמו במעשה · ברוך ע"כ : **אלא** דבר אחר גרם לו · והקשה ה"ר חיים מידי דבר אחר כתיב כדאמר בבבא קמא (דף כה·) מי שקרויו גרם לו יצא זה שאין קרויו גרם לו אלא דבר אחר גרם לו ופריך מידי דבר אחר כתיב וי"ל דסמיך אקרא דלא יחשב לא יערב בו מחשבות אחרות אע"ג דלריכי תרוייהו מ"מ סברא הוא שדבר אחר *יגרום לו כח] [פיסול להפקיע מידי פיגול] כיון דאשכחן מחשבות שמוציאים זו את זו אי נמי קרא יתירא קדרים הכא והא דאמר פרק גיד הנשה (חולין קא·) מי שגידו אסור ובשרו מותר יצא זה שגידו ובשרו אסור לא דמיא להכא : **וריש** לקיש אמר כו' · אע"ג דלריש לקיש לריכי לשטויי כדרבא ובפ"ק דמנחות (דף ה:) משמע דלא סבר ליה כוותיה בדבר הראוי לעבודה מ"מ באיך סבר ליה כוותיה שפיר :

לאו

עין משפט נר מצוה

קה א מיי' פט"ו מהל' פסה"מ הלכה ב :

קו ב ג מיי' שם הל' ו :

מסורת הש"ס

נ"א אלא לאו דלאו כמקומו כו'

[לקמן לה:]

נ"א מברייתא נ"ק

ומהניא נ"ק

נ"א באכילה ומי שפיגולו כו' כצ"ל והשאר נמחק נ"ק

יש מהפכים הגירסא מר"י לר"ש ור"ש מקיים הגירסא

[לקמן לו.]

הגהות הב"ח

(א) רש"י ד"ה בשלמא וכו' וכדאמרן זריקה דלא שריא :

שיטה מקובצת

א] הא א"ל דכתיב : ב] אי הכי איפסולי כו'' תימה מאי אמרת בשלמא איכא הכא הא אפילו אי אמרינן לאו כמקומו דמי קשיא אמאי למחר פסול אי לאו משום מחשבת הינוח ותירץ השר מקוצי דה"ק אי אמרת בשלמא לאו כמקומו דמי ניחא דלמחר פסול משום מחשבת הינוח משום דליכא אכילת מזבח אבל השתא דאמרינן כמקומו דמי והוי שפיר אכילת מזבח ומ"מ גלי קרא אם האכל יאכל דליכא פיגול אם כן יש לנו לומר דמעטיה קרא לגמרי דאף מחשבת הינוח לא הוי כיון דלאו במקומו הוא דחישב ומשני דלהכי לא מהני קרא להוציאו ממחשבת הינוח' תו"ח : ג] ר"ל (אומר) [אמר לעולם] פסול ממש' כלומר הא מתני' דקתני פסול פסול לגמרי משמע אף לענין שלא נתכפרו בעלים ושלא במקומו כמקומו דמי ודרשינן שפיר כיון שהגיע דם לאויר המזבח נתכפרו הבעלים ולא קשיא מן המקרא דמשמע כמקומו דמי ובמתני' אמרינן פסול ממש דמתני' מיירי (במחשבת) [במחשבה] שנתן (במחשבת) [במחשבה] לאכול בשר חוץ לזמנו והויא מחשבה לפסול· דכמקומו דמי והלכך הוי פסול לגמרי ומ"מ אין בו כרת דזריקה דלא שריא בשר באכילה לא מייתא לידי פיגול ואפ"ה פסול מידי דהוה אמחשבת הינוח כך שיטת הקונטרס והא דנקט לאכול בשר חוץ לזמנו לא דק דהא אם הניח הבשר עד למחר לא מיפסלא קרבן ומחשבה בדם לא מצינן למימר דהא כיון דכמקומו דמי לא מיפסל אם הניח שאר הדם למחר ולא מצי למינקט) מחשבת אימורין עד למחר דפסול מיהא מדרבנן הוא דאומר רבינו פרק דאיכא לאוקמי במחשב ע"מ לשפוך שירים למחר ואע"ג דשירים לא מעכבי מ"מ איכא למימר (איכא) דנזרינן אטו להניח דם: ד] באמירה במחשבה תנן הניתנין והשאר נמחק : ה] למטה כו' עד ס"א כל הני תיובתא ושנינן כדשנינן: ו] תיבת כו' נמחק : ז] שר' יוסי אומר יאספנו ור"ש אומר לא יאספנו : ח] מהן בפיגול ומהן בשתיקה : ט] אלא ש"מ לאו : י] למחר דזריקה דשריא בשר באכילה אי הוי עביד לה בזמנה מיתי לידי פיגול הס"ד : יא] כי עביד כו' ותיבות אי הוה ל"ש ונמחק : יב] ולא קשיא קרא : יג] כשנתן שלא במקומו כו' בנתן הניתנין למעלה למטה במחשבה : יד] דאותבינן לעיל: טו] וכדאמרן דכיון: טז] והאי דתני פסול : יז] לאשמועינן דאע"ג : יח] יאסף מן המזבח : יט] לא יאספנו דכיון : כ] למימר קמן הס"ד ומה"ד אלא שר' יוסי אומר יאספנו ור"ש אומר לא יאספנו ותיבות ור"ש אומר כו' נמחק : כא] ליה בברייתא דהכא : כב] לו לשון הר"פ וי"ל דאי לא כתיב לא יחשב [הוא] במחשבה בעלמא לא ואי כתיב לא יחשב הוא"א דוקא התם [הוא דאינו פסול] לגמרי [שפיר] מכפר אבל הכא דפסול לגמרי (שיכפר) איכא לא [יכפר] קמ"ל : כג] מחמת גריעות הזריקה ולא מחמת גריעות ההקטרה : כד] דמי שפיגולו : כה] בעבודה ראשונה ובעבודה : כו] כדתנן בפרקין הס"ד ומה"ד לאלתר כשר והוא דבור בפני עצמו ושייך לדף כו ע"ב : כז] ונראה לי : כח] לו פיסול להפקיע מידי פיגול ואין זה אלא גילוי מילתא בעלמא דכיון דאשכחן :

א) אולי צ"ל ולא מני למנקט כך במחשב באימורין דא"ס הניח האימורין עד למחר פסול דרבנן מיהא הוי ועי' היטב בתוספות לקמן (דף לו) ד"ה שיאכלנהו · ב) אולי צ"ל דוקא התם דפסיל לגמרי פסול מעילה מידי פיגול אבל הכא דאינו פסיל לגמרי דהא מכפר אימא דאינו מוציא מידי פיגול קמ"ל :

ומשנתינו כדברי האומר לא יאספנו ורב חסדא אמר אבימי הכל מודין בניתנין למטה שנתנן למעלה שלא יאספנו וכל שכן בניתנין למעלה שנתנן למטה הואיל ודמים העליונים למטה הן באין לא נחלקו אלא בניתנין לפנים שנתנן בחוץ *בחוץ שנתנן לפנים שר' יוסי אומר יאספנו ור"ש אומר לא יאספנו אמר רב נחמן בר יצחק אף אנן נמי תנינא *רבי יהודה אומר °זאת היא העולה הרי אלו *מיעוטין [א]פרט לנשחטה בלילה ושנשפך דמה ושיצא דמה חוץ לקלעים אם עלתה תרד ר"ש אומר עולה אין לי אלא עולה כשרה מנין לרבות שנשחטה בלילה ושנשפך דמה ושיצא דמה חוץ לקלעים [ב]והלן והיוצא והטמא ושנשחט חוץ לזמנו וחוץ למקומו ושקיבלו פסולין וזרקו את דמה והניתנין למעלה שנתנן למטה והניתנין למטה שנתנן למעלה והניתנין בפנים שנתנן בחוץ והניתנין בחוץ שנתנן בפנים והפסח והחטאת ששחטן שלא לשמן מנין ת"ל תורת העולה ריבה תורה אחת לכל העולין שאם עלו לא ירדו יכול שאני מרבה אף הרובע והנרבע והמוקצה והנעבד והאתנן והמחיר והכלאים והטריפה ויוצא דופן ת"ל זאת ומה ראית לרבות את אלו ולהוציא את אלו א] *מרבה אני את אלו שהיה פסולן בקודש ומוציא אני את אלו שלא היה פסולן בקודש קתני מיהא הניתנין למטה שנתנן למעלה ולמעלה שנתנן למטה ולא פליג רבי יהודה מ"ט לאו משום דקלטיה מזבח ושמע מינה לא יאספנו א"ר ב] *אליעזר [ג]מזבח הפנימי מקדש פסולין מאי קמ"ל תנינא הניתנין בפנים כו' אי מהתם הוה אמינא ה"מ דם דחזי ליה אבל קומץ דלא חזי ליה אימא לא קמ"ל מיתיבי קטרת זרה שעלה לגבי מזבח תרד שאין לך מקדש פסולין אלא מזבח החיצון בראוי לו חיצון אין פנימי לא תריץ הכי [ד]קטרת זרה שעלתה למזבח החיצון תרד שאין מזבח החיצון מקדש פסולין אלא הראוי לו והפנימי בין ראוי לו בין שאין ראוי לו מאי טעמא האי רצפה ג] והאי כלי שרת:

מתני' [ה]השוחט את הזבח לזרוק דמו בחוץ או מקצת דמו בחוץ להקטיר אימוריו בחוץ או מקצת אימוריו בחוץ לאכול בשרו בחוץ או כזית מבשרו בחוץ או לאכול כזית מעור האליה בחוץ [ו]פסול ואין בו כרת לזרוק דמו למחר מקצת דמו למחר להקטיר אימוריו למחר או מקצת אימוריו למחר לאכול בשרו למחר או כזית מבשרו למחר או לאכול כזית מעור האליה למחר [ז]פיגול [ח]וחייבין עליו כרת:

גמ' סברוה [ט]עור אליה כאליה

תורה אור: ויקרא ו

רש"י

דטעמא ד] דר' יוסי משום דס"ל דשלא במקומו כמקומו דמי דאם כן אדמיפלגי באסיפה ליפלגי בכפרה ונימא רבי יוסי כיפר ור' שמעון לא כיפר אלא לרבי יוסי נמי לאו כמקומו דמי ואפ"ה לא יאספנו ומשניתינו כדברי האומר לא יאספנו ומשום הכי תנא פסול במתני'*: ורב חסדא אמר אבימי הכל מודים· ר' יוסי ור"ש: בניתנין למטה שנתנן למעלה שלא יאספנו · דהואיל וניתן במזבח הראוי לו לא הוי כנשפך על הרצפה דקלטיה מזבח לאפוקי מכלל זריקה במקום אחר : וכל שכן בניתנין למעלה שנתנן למטה · דקרובה היא למתנה גמורה שהרי דמים העליונים למטה הן שותתין ויורדין הלכך האי דם סופו לירד למטה היה ראוי וכי יהביה למטה *קלטיה מזבח מלאוספו ולחזור וליתנו למעלה : שרבי יוסי אומר יאספנו · דכיון דלמזבח זה לא היה ראוי לא קלטיה כלל : ורבי שמעון אומר לא יאספנו · שהרי לשם מזבח היה ראוי והרי בא לשום מזבח : אף אנן נמי תנינא · דאיתיה לדר' יוחנן דאמר דאיכא דאית ליה לא יאספנו ואע"ג דשלא במקומו לאו כמקומו דמי לענין כפרה לענין אסיפה ה] מיהו קלטיה מזבח : זאת היא העולה · הרי אלו ג' מעוטין לפי שבא המקרא הזה ללמדנו על הפסולין ו] למזבח שעלו דלא ירדו דילפינן מעולה על מוקדה על המזבח כל הלילה משעלה על מוקדה תהא שם כל הלילה לפיכך מיעט לך בו ג' ז] [מעוטין למעט בו ג'] פסולין: זאת· היא מיעוטא זאת ולא אחרת היא הוי מיעוטא ה"א דהעולה הוי מיעוטא כלומר העולה המיוחדת ולא כולן : פרט לנשפך דמה ולשנשחטה בלילה ושילא דמה · אבל שאר פסולין אם עלו לא ירדו ולקמן בפרק המזבח מקדש (דף פד:) מפרש טעמא דרבי יהודה דמרבי שאר פסולין ומפיק הנך : אין לי אלא עולה כשרה · תהא על מוקדה כל הלילה עד הבקר : והלן · שלן בשרה חוץ למזבח : והיוצא · שיצא בשרה : והטמא ושנשחט · ע"מ להקטיר חוץ לזמנו כו' : מנין · שכיון שעלו לא ירדו : רובע ונרבע · על פי עד אחד שמותר להדיוט ואסור לגבוה ונפקי לן מקראי במסכת תמורה בפ' כל האסורין (דף כח·) : וכן מוקצה ונעבד וטריפה · מוקצה שהקצהו לתקרובת עבודת כוכבים : נעבד · שהשתחוה לבהמה : כלאים · שור או כשב פרט לכלאים כי יולד פרט ליוצא דופן (חולין דף לח:) : מאי ראית · אחר שריבה הכתוב ומיעט ולא פירש לך הכתוב מה ריבה ומה מיעט : אמרת· ומעצמך מרבה אני את אלו שהיה פסולן בקדש משבאו לעזרה נפסלו : קתני מיהת כו'· ולא פליג רבי יהודה לשווינהו כנשפך על הרצפה ונימא ירדו כדאמר ר' יהודה פרט לנשפך דמה ואלמא לאו כנשפך דמה קחשיב ליה : מאי טעמא לאו משום דקלטיה מזבח· לקדושי ושמע מינה לענין אסיפה לא יאספנו והא ליכא למימר משום דקסבר שלא במקומו כמקומו דמי ומשום דכיפרה הוא דהא דומיא דשאר זריקות פסולות קתני ליה ומדרבי שמעון הייט טעמא דלא מייתי ליה ח] דאיכא למימר טעמא דרבי שמעון משום דתורת העולה ריבה ואפילו נשפך דמה נמי קאמר דלא ירדו : מקדש פסולין · שאם עלו לא ירדו ואף על גב דלא כתיב קרא אלא בחילון : תנינא הניתנין בחוץ שנתנן בפנים לא ירדו · אבריהם ממזבח ולא פליג ר' יהודה מאי לאו דקלטיה פנימי לדם זה ט] שניתנו עליו ואע"פ שנפסל בכניסתו להיכל משום וכל חטאת אשר יובא מדמה (ויקרא ו) א)הוה ליה כנשפך דמה : הני מילי דם · י] שפסול הוא דמקדש הואיל וחזי ליה דם בעלמא כגון דמים הפנימיים : אבל קומץ דלא חזי יא] כלל · דכתיב (שמות ל) לא תעלו עליו קטרת זרה ועולה ומנחה אימא אם עלה עליו ירד קמ"ל : קטרת זרה · קטרת נדבה שלא התיר הכתוב אלא קטרת של ציבור שחרית וערבית : שעלתה לגבי מזבח · קסלקא דעתך דבמזבח הקטרת קאי : בראוי לו · לאפוקי קמצים שלא קידשו בכלי הכי מפרש לקמן בפרק המזבח (דף פג:) : האי רצפה · יב] בבנין אבנים שלא נמשח לפיכך אין קדושתו בזה חמורה : והאי כלי שרת · ונמשח עם המשכן : **מתני'** את הזבח · שלמים או שאר הנאכלין : פסול ואין בו כרת · והאוכלו ואפילו בחוץ אין ענוש כרת : לאכול את בשרו למחר · ליכא לאוקומה בשלמים אלא בתודה יג] וחטאת ואשם דאילו בשלמים מחר זמנו הוא אבל לזרוק דמו או להקטיר אימוריו אפילו בשלמים הוי למחר חוץ לזמנו : פיגול וחייבין עליו כרת · האוכלו אפילו בזמנו ענוש כרת ובגמרא יליף לה : **גמ'**

א) נ"א לא הוה ·

תוספות

לאו משום דקלטיה מזבח וש"מ לא יאספנו · פי' בקונטרס יד] והא ליכא למימר משום דסבר שלא במקומו כמקומו דמי ומשום דכיפרה הוא דהא דומיא דשאר זריקות פסולות קתני לה וקשה דהא בסוף כל הפסולין (לקמן נו.) מסקינן דר' יהודה אית ליה שלא במקומו כמקומו דמי טו] ונראה לפרש דהאי דקא"ר יהודה כמקומו דמי לא לענין דנתכפר אלא לענין מחשבה דווקא הוי כמקומו דכיון דמהניא הזריקה לענין דאם עלו לא ירדו מהניא נמי שלא לפסול במחשבה ולכך טז] מיד לאלתר כשר ומיהו קשה דא"כ בתר דשני כמקומו דמי מאי קפריך התם מחישב ליתן הניתנין בחוץ בפנים ובפנים בחוץ הא התם נמי קלטי' מזבח דאם עלו לא ירדו וה"ר יוסף מפרש דהכי מייתי סייעתא מ"ט לאו משום דקלטיה מזבח דאפי' בפנים וחוץ קאמר רבי יהודה דקלטיה מזבח אע"ג דפני' ודחוץ לכ"ע לאו כמקומו ואפי' הכי קאמר רבי יהודה דקלטיה מזבח לענין דאם עלו לא ירדו הכי נמי קלטיה מזבח לענין דלא יאספנו ומיהו לא יתכן פי' זה למאי דפרישי' לעיל דמאן דאית ליה כמקומו דמי אפי' בפנים וחוץ קאמר מדפריך לר' יוחנן ואי שלא במקומו לאו כמקומו להוי כנשפך מן הכלי ויאספנו ולשמואל ולריש לקיש לא פריך (תוספות) ורבי חיים בה"ר מרדכי מפ' דמוכח יז] מנתנו בחוץ שנתנו בפנים דלכולי עלמא לאו כמקומו דמי ואין זריקתו כלום לפי שנפסל מקודם שנכנס להיכל וכהי דאין תקנה באסיפה לפי שנפסל קודם הזריקה כ"ש דהוה לן למימר דהוי כנשפך הדם מן הכוס על הרצפה דאמר ר' יהודה תרד דכל זבח שלא נזרק כלל אם עלו אימורין ירדו לר' יהודה ואפי' הכי אמר דקלטיה המזבח לזריקתו ואמרינן לא ירדו ה"ה בניתנין למטה למעלה דאמר ר' יוחנן דלא כמקומו דמי ולא כיפר כלל דנימא דמהניא הזריקה וקלטיה מזבח שלא יאספנו עוד להועיל זריקה אחרת · ברו"ך ע"כ: **האי** רצפה והאי כלי שרת· ועדיף יח] מכלי שרת דלא מקדשי פסולין ליקרב ומזבח מקדש :

אמר

עין משפט נר מצוה

קז א מיי' פ"ג מהל' פסה"מ הלכה ו :

קח ב מיי' שם הל' ז :

קט ג ד מיי' שם הלכה יח

קי ה מיי' פי"ד מהל' פסה"מ הלכה י :

קיא ו ז מיי' פי"ג מהלכות פסה"מ הלכה א ופט"ז הל' א :

עיין ל"ק דקאמר האי דבחוץ ונתן בפנים הוא טעות גמור דהי אך שייך לומר יאספנו הלא כבר איפסלא קודם הזריקה בביאתו בהיכל כמ"ש תוס' לעיל כו: בד"ה אמר שמואל וצ"ע

קיב ח מיי' פי"ח מהל' פסה"מ הלכה ו :

קיג ט מיי' פי"ד מהל' פסה"מ הלכה ז :

מסורת הש"ס

ע"כ שייך לע"א

נדה מ. ע"ש לקמן פד. הוריות ב:

קלטי' מזבח לאפוקי מלאוספו כו' כצ"ל ז"ק

נ"א אחר שריבה הכתוב ומיעט מרבה אני כו' ז"ק

[נ"ל אלעזר]

שיטה מקובצת

א] אלו אחר שריבה הכתוב ומיעט אמרת מרבה אני את כו' ומוציא אני את אלו שאין פסולן בקודש· פי' רובע ונרבע ופרש"י דאותם פסולים קודם שבאו לעזרה ולא נהירא דהא פסיק ותני רובע ומי לא עסקינן [דנרבע] [דרבע] אחר שבא לעזרה לכ"נ לפרש שהיה פסולן בקודש דיש הכשר במקום אחר בקודש וה"ש שלא לשמו יש לו הכשר בשלמים בפנים שנתנם בחוץ [יש לו הכשר] כל אחר כמשפטו ושקבלו פסולים פי' טמא בצבור (והלן בבמה) והלן בדם שכן כשר באברים (באברים משום בשר) והיוצא (בבמה טמא פי') [דמה] הוקלקלים [שכן כשר] בבמה ושנשחט בלילה משום אברים ופדרין דקריבין בלילה [אך משנשפך] דמה קשיא וי"ל כיון דשחיטה שהיא עבודה ראשונה עשויה בהכשר הכשר במקום אחר קרינא ביה וה"ה לכולם שייך טעם זה משום הכשר שחיטה אבל [בנשחט] בלילה צריך לומר משום אברים ופדרים: ב] אמר ר' מזבח הפנימי מקדש פסולים· שאם עלו לא ירדו ואע"ג דלא כתיב קרא אלא בחיצון: ג] והאי כלי שרת· אע"ג דאמרינן כלי שרת אינו מקדש אלא הראוי לו הכא שאני דאית בה תרתי שהוא מזבח וכלי שרת הלכך מקדש פסולים ליקרב הקשה הר"ר שמואל מאיברא וכי יפה כח מתנת פסולן הא בכשרים לא מקדש דכתיב מנחה ונסך לא תסכו עליו וכיון דנסכים לא (רמו) [מקרבי] עליה היאך יקדש פסולים להקריב עליו וי"ל דקרא לכתחלה אבל דיעבד יקדש עוד תירץ דהא דמקדש פסולים דוקא ירדו דודאי מעל מזבח הפנימי אלא לומר שאם עלו אחר כן על מזבח החיצון שלא ירדו ומיירי בקמצים שלא קדשו בכלי שלא קדשו שהעלה על מזבח הפנימי ואח"כ העלה על מזבח החיצון ומזה [מיירי למה] שהמזבח הפנימי מקדשם דאי לאו דמזבח הפנימי מקדשם מזבח החיצון לא היה מקדשם דאינו מקדש כי אם הראוי לו [ופי'] הראוי לו (הוי) [היינו] דנתקדשו בכלי והלכך מיירי כמו כן שלא נתקדשו דאי נתקדשו בכלי דל מהכא מזבח הפנימי מזבח החיצון מקדשם ת"ח: ד] דטעמא דר"ש משום דס"ל כו' ונימא ר' יוסי לא כיפר ורבי שמעון כיפר אלא לר' שמעון נמי לא : ה] אסיפה מיהא : ו] הפסולין שעלו למזבח דלא : ז] ג' מיעוטין למעט ג' פסולין הס"ד ומה"ד זאת' הרי מיעוט: ח] דלא כיפר כלל דאיכא: ט] זה שניתן: י] דם פסול: יא] דלא חזיא ליה כלל: יב] רצפה בנין אבנים ואין קדושתו חמורה כזה שהוא כלי שרת המטלטל הס"ד: יג] בתודה ובחטאת: יד] בקונטרס דאי לאו קלטיה מזבח הו"ל כנשפך דמה דפליג ר' יהודה והא: טו] דמי וא"כ מאי מייתי הכא לכך נ"ל הא דמייתי הכא מזבח ולעיל לר"י דוקא פריך דלשמואל לא קשיא אפילו מבחוץ שנתנם בפנים דמאי פרכת ליהוי כנשפך ויאספנו הואיל ולאו כמקומו דמי לכ"ע [דהא] גלי קרא בהדיא דלא יאספנו דכתיב וכל אשר יובא מדמה אל אהל מועד באש תשרף [אבל הכא] מוכח שפיר מדקלטיה מזבח ש"מ לא יאספנו ומינה שמעינן גם בנתן למעלה ולמטה למ"ד לאו כמקומו דמי דליכא למימר דשאני חוץ בפנים דגלי קרא אבל חטאת [מנ"ל] דנהי דגלי לענין דלא כיפר ואין לו תקנה כי [אם באחרת] מ"מ לענין קליטת מזבח דלא ירדו שייך למילף מחוץ [שאם עלה לא ירד] כגון למעלה ולמטה למ"ד שלא במקומו לאו כמקומו דמי וכיון דקלטה מזבח לענין דלא ירדו ממילא שמעינן דלא יאספו תדע מדפליג ר"י גבי ניתז דמה מן הצואר על הרצפה ואמר התם ירדו וגבי חוץ בפנים מודה דלא ירדו' לשון מהר"פ ז"ל: טז] תיבת מיד נמחק : יז] מהניתנין בחוץ שנתן בפנים דלכולי עלמא: יח] ועדיף משאר כלי שרת :

א) נ"ל דלא גלי קרא שפיר אמרינן דכמקומו דמי ·

סייעתא

שיטה מקובצת

סייעתא [מהא דקלטיה] מזבח משום דאפבנים וחוץ קאמר ר' דאם עלו לא ירדו ואע"ג דמפנים לחוץ לכ"ע לאו כמקומו דמי כדמשמע בסוף כל הפסולים ומיהו קשה לעיל כי פריך לר"י דאמר לאו כמקומו דמי כנשפך כו' אמאי [לא] קשה כמו כן לשמואל מתן [הניתנים] בפנים בחוץ דקתני במתני' [דפסול] דהא דפנים לחוץ לכ"ע לאו כמקומו דמי ושמא מר"י [illegible] להקשות משום דלר"י [illegible] [illegible] השירים ואיבעית אימא טעמא משום דגלי קרא דכל חטאת אשר יובא מדמה וגו' אבל בניתנים בפנים שנתנם בחוץ א)לא דנימא כמקומו דמי והשתא ניחא הכל דהכא מוכח דלא יאספנו מן בחוץ שנתנם בפנים דהתם ודאי [לאו] כמקומו דמי ואפ"ה קתני ר"י לא יאספנו אלמא משום דקלטיה

הא

He must re-gather it; [27*b*] and our Mishnah agrees with the view that he must not re-gather it. But R. Ḥisda said in Abimi's name: All agree, if he sprinkled below what should be sprinkled above, that he does not re-gather it, and all the more if he sprinkled above what should be sprinkled below, since the blood above runs down a below.[1] They disagree only where he sprinkled without what should be sprinkled within, or within what should be sprinkled without.[2] R. Jose holds, He must not re-gather it, and R. Simeon rules: He must re-gather it.

R. Naḥman b. Isaac said: We have also learnt to the same effect. R. Judah said: [*This is the law of the burnt-offering:*] *it is that which goeth up* [*on its firewood upon the altar all night unto the morning*]:[3] here you have three limitations: it excludes [an animal] slaughtered at night; it excludes [an animal] whose blood was spilt; and it excludes [an animal] whose blood was carried out beyond the hangings: if any one [of these] ascended [the altar], it descends.[4] R. Simeon said: 'Burnt-offering': I only know [this] of a fit burnt-offering;[5] whence do I know to include one which was slaughtered at night, or whose blood was spilt, or whose blood passed without the hangings, or who[se flesh] spent the night [away from the altar], or who[se flesh] went out, or the unclean, or which was slaughtered [with the intention of burning its flesh] after time or without bounds, or whose blood was received and sprinkled by unfit [priests]; or whose blood was applied below [the scarlet line] when it should have been applied above, or above when it should have been applied below, or without when it should have been applied within, or within when it should have been applied without; or a Passover-offering or a sin-offering which one slaughtered for a different purpose,[6]—whence do we know [to include all these]? From the phrase, '*the law of the burnt-offering,*' which intimates one law for all burnt-offerings, [viz.,:] that if they ascended, they do not descend. You might think that I include also a *roba'* and a *nirba'*,[7] one set aside [for an idolatrous sacrifice] or worshipped; b a [harlot's] hire or the price [of a dog],[1] or a hybrid, or a *trefah*, or an animal calved through the cesarean section? The text however states '*it is that*'.[2] And why do you include the former and exclude the latter? I include the former, because their disqualification arose in the sanctuary, while I exclude the latter whose disqualification did not arise in the sanctuary. At all events, he teaches [the cases where] one sprinkled below what should be sprinkled above, or above what should be sprinkled below, and R. Judah does not disagree. What is the reason? Is it not because the altar has received it?[3] which proves that one cannot re-gather it.

R. Eleazar said: The inner altar sanctifies the unfit.[4] What does he inform us: We have learnt it: 'that which should be applied within' etc.?—If [I drew my information] from there [only], I would say that it applies only to blood, which is eligible for it;[5] but [if one threw] the fistful [of flour on the inner altar], which is not eligible for it at all,[6] I would say that it is not so. Hence he informs us [otherwise].[7]

An objection is raised: If strange incense[8] ascended the altar, it must descend, because only the outer altar sanctifies the unfit, in the case of such as are [otherwise] eligible for it.[9] Thus, only the outer one, but not the inner one?—Answer it thus: If strange incense ascended the altar, it must descend, for the outer altar does not sanctify the unfit save in the case of what is [otherwise] eligible for it; but the inner [altar sanctifies] both what is eligible and what is not eligible for it. What is the reason? One [the outer altar] is [but as the] pavement,[10] while the other [the inner altar] is a service vessel.[11]

MISHNAH. IF ONE SLAUGHTERS THE SACRIFICE [INTENDING] TO SPRINKLE ITS BLOOD WITHOUT, OR PART OF c ITS BLOOD WITHOUT; TO BURN ITS EMURIM[1] OR PART OF ITS EMURIM WITHOUT; TO EAT ITS FLESH OR AS MUCH AS AN OLIVE OF ITS FLESH WITHOUT, OR TO EAT AS MUCH AS AN OLIVE OF THE SKIN OF THE FAT-TAIL[2] WITHOUT, IT IS UNFIT, AND DOES NOT INVOLVE KARETH.[3] [IF HE SLAUGHTERS IT, INTENDING] TO SPRINKLE ITS BLOOD OR PART OF ITS BLOOD ON THE MORROW, TO BURN ITS EMURIM OR PART OF ITS EMURIM ON THE MORROW, TO EAT ITS FLESH OR AS MUCH AS AN OLIVE OF ITS FLESH ON THE MORROW, OR TO EAT AS MUCH AS AN OLIVE OF THE SKIN OF ITS FAT-TAIL ON THE MORROW, IT IS PIGGUL, AND INVOLVES KARETH.[4]

GEMARA. Now it was thought that the skin of the fat-tail

a (1) In any case; hence it is almost as though he sprinkled it below. (2) 'Within' and 'without' means on the inner and the outer altars respectively. (3) Lev. VI, 2. (4) From the passage, '*which goeth up on its firewood upon the altar all night*' the Rabbis deduce that once it ascends the altar it must not be taken down all night. But the three words in Hebrew which are rendered '*it is that which goeth up*' are really superfluous, and therefore are interpreted as excluding three cases, as enumerated in the text, from the operation of this law. (5) That if it goes up, it does not descend. (6) *Sc.* as burnt-offerings. (7) A male animal and a female animal respectively used for bestiality.

b (1) Referring to Deut. XXIII, 19: *Thou shalt not bring the hire of a harlot, or the price of a dog, into the house of the Lord thy God for any vow.* (2) Heb. *zoth*, a limitation excluding these. (3) And thus sanctified it, in the sense that it cannot be collected for re-sprinkling. (4) That if they ascend, they do not descend, though the Scriptural text refers only to the outer altar. (5) For some blood, though that particular blood should not have been applied there. (6) Flour is never burnt on the inner altar. (7) That flour is not removed. (8) The incense of a private and votive meal-offering. Scripture permits incense only at public sacrifices. (9) V. *infra* 83*b*. (10) It is an immoveable unanointed erection of stone. (11) It was moveable, and consecrated by anointing, like all other service vessels. Therefore its sanctity and sanctifying powers are greater.

c (1) V. Glos. (2) V. Gemara. (3) Even if one actually eats it without. (4) Even if one eats it in the proper time.

[28a] is as the fat-tail:[5] [then the difficulty arises:] surely he intends for man what is for the altar's consumption?[6]—Said Samuel, The author of this is R. Eliezer, who maintains that you can intend [with effect] for human consumption what is meant for the altar's consumption, and for the altar's consumption what is meant for human consumption.[7] For we learnt: If one slaughters a sacrifice [intending] to eat what is not normally eaten,[8] or to burn [on the altar] what is not normally burnt, it is fit;[9] but R. Eliezer invalidates [the sacrifice].[10] How have you explained it? as agreeing with R. Eliezer? Then consider the sequel:[11] This is the general rule: Whoever slaughters, receives, carries, and sprinkles [intending] to eat what is normally eaten or to burn [on the altar] what is normally burnt [after time etc.] . . .: thus, only what is normally eaten, but not what is not normally eaten, which agrees with the Rabbis. Thus the first clause agrees with R. Eliezer and the final clause with the Rabbis?—Even so, he answered him.

a R. Huna said: The skin of the fat-tail is not as the fat-tail.[1] Rabbah observed, What is R. Huna's reason?—*The fat thereof* [is] *the fat-tail* [*entire*],[2] but not the skin of the fat-tail.

R. Ḥisda said: In truth, the skin of the fat-tail is as the fat-tail, but we treat here [in the Mishnah] of the fat-tail of a goat.[3]

Now, all these [scholars] did not say as Samuel, [because] they would not make the first clause agree with R. Eliezer and the second clause with the Rabbis. They did not say as R. Huna, because they hold that the skin of the fat-tail is as the fat-tail. [But] why do they not say as R. Ḥisda?—Because what does [the Tanna of the Mishnah] inform us [on this view]? [Presumably] that the skin of the fat-tail is as the fat-tail![4] Surely we have learnt it: The skin of the following is as their flesh: the skin under the fat-tail?[5] And R. Ḥisda?[6]—It is necessary: You might think that only in respect of uncleanness does it combine, because it is soft;[7] but as for here, I would say [Scripture writes] [*Even all the hallowed things of the children of Israel unto thee have I given them*] *for a consecrated portion*,[8] which means, as a symbol of greatness, [so that they must be eaten] just as kings eat; and kings do not eat thus.[9] [Hence] I would say [that it is] not [as the flesh]; therefore he informs us [that it is].

An objection is raised: If one slaughters a burnt-offering [in-
b tending] to burn[1] as much as an olive of the skin under the fat-tail out of bounds, it is invalid, but does not involve *kareth*; after time, it is *piggul*, and involves *kareth*. Eleazar b. Judah of Avlas said on the authority of R. Jacob, and thus also did R. Simeon b. Judah of Kefar 'Iccum say on the authority of R. Simeon: The skin of the legs of small cattle, the skin of the head of a young calf, and the skin under the fat-tail, and all cases which the Sages enumerated of the skin being the same as the flesh, which includes the skin of the pudenda: [if he intended eating or burning these] out of bounds [the sacrifice] is invalid, and does not involve *kareth*; after time, it is *piggul*, and involves *kareth*.[2] Thus [this is taught] only [of] the burnt-offering,[3] but not [of] a sacrifice.[4] As for R. Huna, it is well; it is right that he specifies a burnt-offering.[5] But according to R. Ḥisda,[6] why does he particularly teach 'burnt-offering': let him teach 'sacrifice'?—R. Ḥisda can answer you: I can explain this as referring to the fat-tail of a goat;[7] alternatively I can answer: Read 'sacrifice'.[8]

IT IS UNFIT, AND DOES NOT INVOLVE KARETH etc. Whence do we know it?—Said Samuel: Two texts are written. What are they?—Said Rabbah: [*And if any of the flesh of the sacrifice of his peace-offerings be at all eaten*] *on the third day*: this refers to [an intention of eating the flesh] after time; *it shall be* piggul [*an abhorred thing*] refers to [an intention of eating the flesh] out of bounds;
c *and the soul that eateth of it* [*shall bear his iniquity*:][1] [only] one [involves *kareth*], but not two,[2] viz., after time, and excluding out of bounds. Yet say that '*and the soul that eateth of it*' refers to out of bounds, and excludes after time?—It is logical that after time is graver, since [Scripture] commences with it. On the contrary, out of bounds is more likely [to be meant] since it is near it?[3]—Rather said Abaye: When R. Isaac b. Abdimi came,[4] he said: Rabbah[5] relies on what a Tanna taught, [Viz.;] When Scripture mentions the 'third [day]' in the pericope '*Ye shall be holy*',[6] which need not be stated, since it has already been said, *And if any of the*

(5) Even in respect of burning on the altar, so that in the case of lamb peace-offerings, the skin of the fat-tail, just as the fat-tail itself, is burnt on the altar '*entire*' (v. Lev. III, 9). (6) Which intention should not count at all. (7) I.e., the intention counts. (8) E.g., the *emurim*, which are burnt on the altar. He intended eating these after time or out of bounds. (9) Because such an illegitimate intention concerning time or place does not count, seeing that the things could not be eaten or burnt at all. (10) *Infra* 35a. (11) The end of the present Mishnah, *infra* 29b.
a (1) It is eaten, and not burnt on the altar. The difficulty therefore does not arise. (2) Lev. III, 9. (3) Which was not burnt on the altar; v. *supra* 9a. (4) If the Mishnah treats of the fat-tail of a lamb, then on Samuel's interpretation we are informed that you can intend for human consumption what is meant for the altar's consumption; while on R. Huna's interpretation the Tanna informs us that the skin of the fat-tail is *not* as the fat-tail. But if it treats of the fat-tail of a goat, then the only thing that the Tanna can inform us is that its skin is regarded as itself in the sense that it is edible, because it is soft, and therefore counts as ordinary flesh. (5) There must be at least as much as an olive of flesh before it can be defiled, and at least as much as the size of an egg before it can defile as *nebelah* (carrion, v. Lev. XI, 39f). If there is less than these standards, it can be made up by the skin under the fat-tail (Ḥul. 122a). Thus this teaches that this skin is as the fat-tail itself, and so the present teaching on R. Ḥisda's interpretation is superfluous. (6) How does he answer this? (7) And edible. (8) Num. XVIII, 8. (9) Though the skin is edible yet kings would not eat it.
b (1) Heb. להקטיר which generally refers to the burning of these parts (the *emurim*) which are always burnt on the altar, even in the case of peace-offerings. (2) V. Ḥul. (Sonc. ed.) 132a, q.v. notes. (3) Only there does an illegitimate intention in respect of the skin of the fat-tail disqualify the sacrifice, since the whole sacrifice is burnt. (4) Unspecified, which would include peace-offerings. (5) According to R. Huna, Scripture definitely teaches that the skin of the fat-tail is not counted as *emurim*. But there is no such teaching in respect of a burnt-offering: hence the present ruling can apply to a burnt-offering but not to other sacrifices. (6) Who maintains that the skin of the fat-tail of all sacrifices is burnt along with it as *emurim*. (7) In which case the reference is to an intention of *eating* it out of bounds or after time, not to burning it on the altar. (8) Instead of burnt-offering.
c (1) Lev. VII, 18; '*shall bear his iniquity*' means that he incurs *kareth*. (2) This follows from the sing. '*it*'. (3) The word *mimennu*, ('of it'), is in immediate proximity to the word *piggul*, which on the present exegesis extends the law to eating out of bounds. (4) From Palestine to Babylon. (5) Emended text. Printed edd: Rab. (6) This is the name of the pericope or weekly reading commencing with Lev. XIX, 1. The verse alluded to is: *And if it* (the flesh of a sacrifice) *be eaten at all on the* third day, *it is* piggul (*a vile thing*); *it shall not be accepted*.

כאליה דמי והא קא מחשב מאכילת מזבח לאדם אמר שמואל א] הא מני *ר' אליעזר היא דאמר מחשבין מאכילת מזבח לאכילת אדם ומאכילת אדם לאכילת מזבח *דתנן השוחט את הזבח לאכול דבר שאין דרכו לאכול להקטיר דבר שאין דרכו להקטיר כשר ור"א פוסל במאי אוקימתא כר"א אימא סיפא *זה הכלל כל השוחט והמקבל והמוליך והזורק לאכול דבר שדרכו לאכול ולהקטיר דבר שדרכו להקטיר דבר שדרכו לאכול אין שאין דרכו לאכול לא אתאן לרבנן רישא ר' אליעזר וסיפא רבנן אמר ליה אין ב] רב הונא אמר עור אליה לאו כאליה דמי אמר ג] רבא מ"ט דרב הונא °חלבו האליה ולא עור האליה רב חסדא אמר לעולם עור האליה כאליה דמי והכא במאי עסקינן באליה של גדי כולהו כשמואל לא אמרי רישא ר"א וסיפא רבנן לא מוקמי כרב הונא לא אמרי עור אליה כאליה דמי קא משמע להו כרב חסדא מאי טעמא לא אמרי מאי קמ"ל עור אליה כאליה דמי ד] תנינא *ואלו שעורותיהן כבשרן *עור שתחת האליה ורב חסדא איצטריך סד"א ה"מ לענין טומאה דרכיך מצטרף אבל הכא אימא °למשחה *לגדולה כדרך שהמלכים אוכלין ולא עבידי מלכים דאכלי הכי אימא לא קמ"ל מיתיבי *השוחט את העולה להקטיר כזית מעור שתחת האליה חוץ למקומו פסול ואין בו כרת חוץ לזמנו פיגול וחייבין עליו כרת אלעזר בן יהודה איש אבלי' אומר משום רבי יעקב וכן היה רבי שמעון בן יהודה איש כפר עיכוס אומר משום ר' שמעון אחד עור בית הפרסות בהמה דקה ואחד עור הראש של עגל הרך ואחד עור שתחת האליה וכל שמנו חכמים גבי טומאה ואלו שעורותיהן כבשרן להביא עור של בית הבושת חוץ למקומו פסול ואין בו כרת חוץ לזמנו פיגול וחייבין עליו כרת עולה אין אבל זבח לא בשלמא לרב הונא היינו דקתני עולה אלא לרב חסדא מאי איריא דתני עולה ליתני זבח אמר לך רב חסדא איבעית אימא באליה של גדי ואיבעית אימא תני זבח: פסול ואין בו כרת כו': מנה"מ אמר שמואל תרי קראי כתיבי מאי היא אמר רבה °שלישי *זהו חוץ לזמנו פיגול זהו חוץ למקומו והנפש האוכלת ממנו אחד ולא שנים ח] זהו חוץ לזמנו ולמעוטי חוץ למקומו ואימא והנפש האוכלת ממנו זהו חוץ למקומו ולמעוטי חוץ לזמנו מסתברא חוץ לזמנו עדיף דפתח ביה אדרבה חוץ למקומו עדיף דסמיך ליה אלא אמר אביי כי אתא רב יצחק בר אבדימי ו] *[אמר רב] סמיך אדתני תנא כשהוא אומר שלישי בפרשת קדושים תהיו שאין ת"ל שהרי כבר נאמר °ואם האכל יאכל מבשר זבח (א) ז] השלמים ביום השלישי אם

רש"י

כאליה דמי. ואפילו לענין הקטרה ובשלמי כבש שאלייתו קריבה נמי העור ח] קרב כי היכי דלענין אכילה חשיב ליה בשר לענין מצות הקטרתו נמי בשר הוא וקתני מתני' דכי שחיט שלמים לאכול עור האליה בחוץ או למחר הויא מחשבה ואע"ג דחישב מאכילת מזבח לאדם: רבי אליעזר היא. לקמן בפ' כל הפסולים (דף לה.): לאכול דבר שאין דרכו לאכול. כגון אימורים או חוץ לזמנו או חוץ למקומו: ולהקטיר. חוץ לזמנו או חוץ למקומו: דבר שאין דרכו להקטיר. כגון בשר: לאכול דבר שדרכו לאכול. בשר: שדרכו להקטיר. אימורין אבל אם חישב להקטיר בשר למחר או לאכול אימורין למחר כשר שאין מחשבין מאכילת אדם למזבח ומאכילת מזבח לאדם: לאו כאליה דמי. לענין מצות הקטרתו הוא דמעטיה קרא כדמפרש *רבה חלבו האליה תמימה גבי הקטרת אליה כתיב ופריש בהדיא חלב ולא עור: והכא במאי עסקינן. מתני' דחשיב ליה אכילת אדם באליה של גדי שאינה קריבה כדאמרן בפ"ק (לעיל דף ט.) לימד על העז שאינה טעונה אליה: מאי קמ"ל. תנא דמתני' אי באליה של גדי קאי אי אמרת בשלמא בשל כבש קמ"ל לשמואל דמחשבין מאכילת אדם ט] למזבח ומאכילת מזבח לאכילת אדם כרבי אליעזר ולרב הונא דמוקי לה כרבנן אשמעינן תנא דידן דעור אליה לאו כאליה דמי להקטירו אלא לרב חסדא למה לי למתנייה אי לאשמועינן דעור אליה לענין אכילת אדם כאליה דמי וכי חשיב עליה לאוכלו למחר כאילו חישב על כזית מבשרו הואיל ורכיך וחזי לאכילה: תנינא. בשחיטת חולין: ואלו שעורותיהן כבשרן. לטמא טומאת נבילות וקחשיב עור האליה: מצטרף. לטמא טומאת אוכלין בכביצה או טומאת נבילות בכזית: אבל הכא. לענין קדשים כתיב גבי מתנות כהונה לכל קדשי בני ישראל לך נתתים למשחה (במדבר יח) והיינו לגדולה כדמתרגמינן לרבו ללמד שיהו אוכלין אותן דרך אכילת מלכים המשוחים ולא עבידי מלכים דאכלי עור אימא לא תהא מחשבה י]: עגל הרך. מפרש בהעור והרוטב כל שנתו: להביא עור בית הבושת. של נקבה וזה לבדו יש לך להביא עוד אלא קדשים מכל השנויים שם: יא] עור בית הפרסות. מן הארכובה ולמטה: חוץ למקומו. אם שחט ע"מ לאכול מאחת מאלו חוץ למקומו: עולה אין. גבי עולה הוא דתנא מחשבת הקטרת עור יב] אליה דפסלה: אבל זבח. סתמא לא קתני שמע מינה אין מחשבת הקטרה מועלת בעור האליה בשאר זבחים: לרב הונא. דאמר בהדיא מעטיה קרא גבי אליה דנהוי אימורין אבל גבי עולה לא אימעיט דכתיב הנתחים ועור האליה בשר הוא: אלא לרב חסדא. דאמר גבי אליית אימורין עור נמי קרב ליתני זבח סתמא: איבעית אימא. הך מתני' נמי באליה של גדי ולא מיתני ליה זבח באליה במחשבת הקטרה אלא במחשבת אכילת אדם כי מתני' מנהני מילי. דמחשבת יג] *חוץ לזמנו וחוץ למקומו פוסלת וענוש כרת באכילה זאת שחישב עליו חוץ לזמנו: תרי קראי כתיבי. חד חוץ לזמנו וחד חוץ למקומו: שלישי. אם האכל יאכל מבשר זבח (ב) יד] השלמים ביום השלישי (ויקרא ז) ומוקי' ליה תנא לקמן במחשב בשעת עבודה לאכול מזבחו ביום השלישי הכתוב מדבר: זה חוץ לזמנו. דשלישי חוץ לזמן אכילת שלמים הוא: פגול. דכתיב בסיפיה דקרא פגול יהיה קרא יתירא הוא לרבות חוץ למקומו ומסתברא דלמחשבת חוץ למקומו מוקמינן לה ולא למחשבת שאר פסלות כגון לשפוך דמו טו] [על הרצפה או] ע"מ לערבו בדם הפסולין דדמי לחוץ לזמנו קמרבי בהאי קרא וחוץ למחילה דמי לחוץ לזמן: ממנו. משמע דלא קאי אשוכה תשא דנפקא לן מיניה כרת אלא אחד מינייהו דאחד משמע ולא שנים מדלא כתיב האוכלת ולשתוק טז]: למעוטי. דממנו מיעוטא הוא: עדיף. לאוקומי כרת עליה: דסמיך ליה. דהאי ממנו סמוך לפגול יהיה דמרבינן ביה חוץ למקומו: כשהוא אומר שלישי. בפרשת קדושים תהיו קרא זוטא ואם האכל יאכל ביום השלישי פגול הוא לא ירצה (ויקרא יט): תנהו לחוץ למקומו. דבאוכל ממש ביום השלישי ליכא לאוקמא דהא כתיב לא ירצה ואמרינן לקמן (דף כט.) וכי אחר שהוכשר יחזור ויפסל אלא על כרחך במחשב בשעת עבודה ע"מ כן קאמר: אם

תוספות

אמר שמואל הא מני ר' אליעזר היא. וסבר לה כההוא תנא דאמר בריש הקומץ רבה (מנחות דף יז.) דלר' אליעזר הוי בכרת ולא סבר לה כרבי ירמיה דמוקי בסוף פירקין (דף לא:) סיפא כרבי אליעזר דלא תיקשי רישא וסיפא כר' אליעזר ומליעתא כרבנן וא"ת לרבי אליעזר מאי איריא עור האליה אפילו אליה נמי וכי לאשמועינן יז] עור האליה כבשר תנינא ואלו שעורותיהן כבשרן כדפריך בסמוך וי"ל כיון דעיקרה אתא לאשמועינן כר' אליעזר אין לחוש אי אגב אורחיה אשמועינן דעור כבשר אע"ג דתנינא יח] דאשכחן בשמעתא קמייתא דברכות (דף ב.) דפריך וליתני לאת הכוכבים ומשני מילתא אגב אורחיה קמ"ל דכפרה לא מעכבא אע"ג דתנינא במסכת נגעים (פ' י"ד מ"ג) העריב שמשו אוכל בתרומה הביא כפרתו אוכל בקדשים*:

תנינא אלו שעורותיהן כבשרן. הקשה ה"ר יעקב מאורלייניש טובא קמ"ל דבפ' העור והרוטב (חולין דף קכב:) אמרינן אל תקניטני שבלשון יחיד אני שונה אותה גבי עור הראש של עגל הרך דפליגי רבנן משום דסופו *להקשות ועור האליה הוי לכ"ע כבשר ועוד קשה היכי דייק מעור הראש דיחידאה היא מברייתא דאלעזר בן יהודה יט] *הא פשיטא לן מדפריך תנינא הא *קחשיב עור האליה דהוי לכולי עלמא כבשר:

להביא עור של בית הבושת. פי' בקונטרס וזה לבדו יש לך עוד להביא אלא קדשים מכל השנויים שם. ותימה הא איכא נמי עור השליל ופי' בקונטרס בחולין (דף ט.) דלא חשיב שליל משום דאינו נוהג בעולה ותימה והרי כ] בית הבושת דאין נוהג בעולה ונראה דלא קתני שליל משום דאמר פרק כל הפסולין (לקמן דף לה.) דפיגל בשליל לא נתפגל הזבח כא] ולא קאמר להביא כב] אלא *דבר שאינו לגמרי בעולה ומשום דמיירי ברייתא בעולה לא תנא בית הבושת בהדיא וקאמר להביא*:

בשלמא לרב הונא היינו דקתני עולה. תימה דבתוספתא קתני זבח וי"ל דרב הונא הוה מוקי לה כרבי אליעזר דאמר מחשבין מאכילת מזבח לאדם:

אלא לרב חסדא מאי איריא דקתני עולה ליתני זבח. לשמואל לא מקשה כג] למה לי למיתני עולה ליתני זבח דלאו תני זבח הוה מוקמינן ליה כרבי אליעזר: מסתברא

תורה אור: °חלבו האליה — ויקרא ג | °למשחה — במדבר יח | °שלישי — ויקרא ז | °ואם האכל — שם

מסורת הש"ס: לקמן לה: | לקמן לה. | לקמן כט: | ע"ל רבא | חולין נה: קכב. נדה נה. | [לקמן לה. סוטה טו. חולין קלב.] | [תוספתא פ"ב ע"ש חולין כה:] | [לעיל יד.] | [דלא גרסינן אמר רבה מוכח כמה דוכתי עיין יבמות ג. ובתוספות שם ד"ה אמר ובחולין קי. ובתו' שם ד"ה איכא דמוכח כן לאנשי אחר העיון בכל הכהו תוספות הכל מוכח דגם אמר רב לא היה גרסינן ע"ש] | נ"א חוץ לזמנו פוסלת וענוש כרת עליו וחוץ למקומו פוסלת ואין בו כרת

הגהות הב"ח

(א) גמ' מבשר זבח שלמיו ביום השלישי: (ב) רש"י ד"ה שלישי וכו' זבח שלמיו ביום:

עין משפט נר מצוה: קיד א מיי' פ"א מהל' שאר אבות הטומאה הלכה ט: | [וע"ע תוס' מנחות עג. ד"ה הכל ביתר ביאור] | להקשות וקמ"ל הכא דעור כו' כצ"ל וכ"ה בכ"י צ"ק | נ"ל הא קתני עור האליה ופשיטא לן מדפריך תנינא דהוי לכולי עלמא כבשר | נ"א דבר שהוא פיגול לגמרי כשלמים | [וע' תוס' חולין ט ד"ה ולהביא]

שיטה מקובצת

א] הא מני ר' אליעזר היא. וא"ת א"כ מאי איריא עור האליה אפי' האליה עצמה נמי ואי לאשמועינן דעור האליה כאליה דמי תנינא ואלו שעורותיהן כבשרן כדפריך בסמוך ונראה לפרש הואיל ועיקר בבא אתא לאשמועינן כר"א אגב אורחיה אשמועינן דעור האליה כאליה דמי אע"ג דשמעינן לה במקום אחר. תו"ח: ב] אין רישא ר' אליעזר וסיפא רבנן: ג] אמר רבה: ד] תנינ' ואלו שעורותיהן כבשרן. הקשה הר"ר יעקב מאורליינש מ"יתא מאותה משנה הא אמרינן בחולין אל תקניטני בלשון יחיד (שונה) אני [שונה] אותה וי"ל דהא דקאמר התם דהוי כיחידאה קאי על עור הראש של עגל הרך דפליגי רבנן עליה משום שסופה להקשות אבל עור האליה לכ"ע הוי כבשר. תו"ח: ה] שנים איזה זה: ו] אבדימי אמר רבה: ז] זבח שלמיו: ח] העור נמי קרב: ט] אדם לאכילת מזבח ומאכילת: י] מחשבה הס"ד ומה"ד עור בית הפרסות בהמה דקה מן הארכובה ולמטה הס"ד ומה"ד עגל הרך: יא] ד"ה עור בית כו' ולמטה נמחק: יב] עור האליה: יג] דמחשבת ס"א [חוץ לזמנו] פוסלת וענוש כרת באכילתו ואת שחישב עליו חוץ למקומו פוסלת ואין בו כרת. זו גירסת הר"פ ברש"י שלו: יד] זבח שלמיו: טו] דמו על הרצפה או ע"מ כו' הפסולין דמסברא דומיא דשלישי דהיינו חוץ לזמנו: טז] ולשתוק ולמעוטי אתא והד"א: יז] לאשמועינן דעור: יח] דתנינא כדאשכחן בריש יבמות ובשמעתא קמייתא: יט] תיבות הא פשיטא לן מדפריך תנינא נמחק: כ] והרי חשיב בית: כא] הזבח והואיל ולא הוי פיגול לגמרי כשלמים שיריה אבל בית הבושת דינו ממש כשלמים דאם נתפגל בית הבושת נתפגל הזבח. מהר"פ: כב] להביא א) דבר שאינו לגמרי בשלמים ומשום דמיירי בעולה: כג] מקשה דלמה לי:

א) אולי צ"ל להביא אלא דבר שהוא פיגול לגמרי כשלמים וכו' וכ"ה בכ"י צ"ק.

קטו א ב מיי' פי"ג מהלכות פסה"מ הל' ג סמג לאוין שנ :
קטז ג מיי' פי"ח מהל' פסה"מ הלכה טז :
קיז ד מיי' פי"ג מהל' פסה"מ הלכה ג :

אם אינו ענין לחוץ לזמנו תנהו לענין חוץ למקומו ומיעט רחמנא גבי נותר ואוכליו עונו ישא למעוטי חוץ למקומו ואימא ואוכליו עונו ישא זהו חוץ למקומו א] ולמעוטי נותר מכרת ב] מסתברא נותר הוה ליה לאוקמי בכרת למגמר עון עון לחוץ לזמנו דדמי ליה בז"ב אדרבה חוץ למקומו הוה ליה לאוקמי בכרת למגמר עון עון לחוץ לזמנו דדמי ליה במקד"ש אלא אמר רבי יוחנן *תני זבדי בר לוי אתיא קודש קודש כתיב הכא (א) את קדש ה' חילל ונכרתה וכתיב התם ושרפת את הנותר באש ג] וגו' מה להלן נותר אף כאן נותר ומיעט רחמנא גבי נותר ואוכליו עונו ישא למעוטי חוץ למקומו מכרת ומאי חזית דקרא אריכא בחוץ לזמנו ושלישי דפרשת קדושים תהיו חוץ למקומו איפוך אנא מסתברא אריכא בחוץ לזמנו דגמר עון עון מנותר דדמי ליה בז"ב אדרבה אריכא בחוץ למקומו ושלישי דקדושים תהיו בחוץ לזמנו משום דדמי ליה סמכיה וקא ממעט ליה אלא אמר רבא ד] כולהו מקרא אריכא אתיין דכתיב האכל יאכל **בשתי אכילות הכתוב מדבר אחד אכילת אדם ואחד אכילת מזבח מבשר זבח שלמיו *מה שלמים מפגלין ומתפגלין אף כל מפגלין ומתפגלין בשלישי זה חוץ לזמנו לא ירצה *כהרצאת כשר כן הרצאת פסול ומה הרצאת כשר עד שיקריבו כל מתיריו אף הרצאת פסול עד שיקריבו כל מתיריו המקריב בהקרבה הוא נפסל ואינו נפסל בשלישי אותו בזבח הכתוב מדבר ואינו מדבר ה] בכהן לא יחשב
לא

תורה אור: ויקרא יט | שם | שמות כט | ויקרא ז

אם אינו ענין לענין מחשבת חוץ לזמנו תנהו לענין חוץ למקומו. ופיגול דקרא אריכא דנו את אהרן לא תידרשיה לחוץ למקומו אלא טוליה קרא בחוץ לזמנו הלכך ממנו אחוץ לזמנו קאי וכ"ת הכא נמי כרת כתיב דסמיך ליה ואוכליו עונו ישא וגו' ההוא בנותר ממש מיתוקם כדמפרש ואזיל וכדי שלא תאמר שניהם במשמע מיעט רחמנא ואוכליו דהיינו מיעוטא מדלא כתיב והאוכל למעוטי חוץ למקומו דלעיל מיניה : ואימא ואוכליו עונו ישא אחוץ למקומו. דסליק מיניה קאי וכדי שלא תאמר אין מקרא יוצא מידי פשוטו ואף נותר במשמע והכי דבלא ירצה ליתא אבל בכרת איתיה להכי מיעט ואוכליו דמשמע אחד ולא שנים למעט נותר מכרת : ה"ג מסתברא נותר אית לך לאוקומי בכרת למיגמר עון עון לחוץ לזמנו ו] דדמי ליה בז"ב אדרבה חוץ למקומו הוה ליה לאוקומי בכרת ז] דמיגמר עון עון לחוץ לזמנו דדמי ליה במקד"ש. והכי פירושא נותר הוה ליה לאוקומי בכרת ח] דמיגמר עון עון כו' שמלמד כרת על חוץ לזמנו שאין כרת מפורש בו אלא נשיאות עון אמורה בו ולימד מכאן בגזירה שוה דהכא כתיב נשיאות עון ומפרש כרת הלכך אי מוקמת ליה להאי ט] בנותר איכא למילפיה לג"ש שפיר דדמו אהדדי בשני דברים הללו ששניהן נפסלים בזמן זה בזמן ממש וזה במחשבת זמן ושניהם נוהגים בבמה כדתנן בפרק בתרא י](לקמן דף קיג.) דכי פרכת ונילף עון עון מטומאת בשר דכתיב ונשא אהרן את עון הקדשים מה להלן לאו ולא כרת אף כאן לאו ולא כרת אמרינן מנותר הוה ליה למילף יא] דדמי ליה בז"ב אבל אי מוקמת ליה להאי כרת בחוץ למקומו כי גמרת ליה חוץ לזמנו מיניה בג"ש ופרכינן ליה ונילף עון עון מטומאה ליכא לתרוצי מחוץ למקומו הוה ליה למילף דדמי ליה בז"ב דהא אין פסולו בזמן ואינו נוהג בבמת יחיד שאין שם מחילות יב] : במקד"ש. מ' מחשבה ק' קלת ד' דם ש' שלישי חוץ לזמנו וחוץ למקומו שניהם פסולין במחשבה ואם חישב במקלתו נפסל כולו ושניהם נפסלין בעבודת הדם ובשניהם נאמר שלישי לאפוקי טומאה דאינה פסול מחשבה ואם נטמא מקלתו לא נטמא כולו וישנה לאחר זריקת דמים ולא נאמר בו שלישי יתירא אבל בחוץ לזמנו וחוץ למקומו שלישי מיותר לג"ש דלעיל דבכל חד מינייהו כתיב והנותר ביום השלישי באש ישרף וסמיך ליה ואם האכל יאכל ולא בעי למכתב שלישי : אתיא קודש קודש. דהאי ואוכליו בנותר כתיב : קרא אריכא. ואם האכל יאכל דנו את אהרן אריכא הוא : איפוך אנא. ואימא דאריכא בחוץ למקומו וכתיב ביה נשיאות עון ושלישי דקדושים תהיו חוץ לזמנו ואימעוט מכרת : מסתברא אריכא בחוץ לזמנו. דכיון דלא פריש ביה כרת בהדיא אלא בג"ש דעון עון מנותר יליף מסתברא דדמי מדדמי יליף דדמי ליה בז"ב דאי יג] מוקמן ליה בחוץ למקומו תו לא יליף כרת מנותר דלא דמי ליה במידי : אדרבה. מסתברא משום דדמי ליה חוץ לזמנו לנותר סמכיה לנותר וקא ממעט ליה מאוכליו דלא תימא משום דדמי ליה ניגמר מיניה : כולהו מקרא אריכא אתיין. זה לחיוב וזה לפטור כדיליף ליה רבה בריש שמעתין : בשתי אכילות כו'. שמחשבת שתיהן פוסלת דהא לקמן במחשבה מוקי ליה תנא ולא באוכל ביום השלישי : אחד אכילת אדם כו'. דלא שנא חישב לאכול למחר ל"ש חישב להקטיר אימורין למחר פגול : מבשר זבח שלמיו. הקיש זבחים לשלמים מה שלמים יש בהן מפגלין ויש בהם יד] מתפגלין שהדם הוא המפגל והבשר והאימורין המתפגלין : אף כל. שיש בו מפגלין ומתפגלין פיגול נוהג בו יצאו מנחת כהנים ומנחת כהן משיח ומנחת נסכים שהם מתירין את עצמם ואין בהם שירים להתפגל מחמת עבודות מתיריהם שאין פיגול נוהג בהן : לא ירצה טו] המקריב. משמע (ב) אזריקה לא תהא זריקה זו מרצה שמע מינה דעד שיזרק הדם מחשבת פיגול תלויה ועומדת נזרק הדם הוקבע הפיגול לא נזרק הדם כגון שנשפך בטל הפיגול דכתיב ביה הרצאה כדכתיב גבי כשר : מה הרצאת כשר. לא קרי ליה הרצאה אלא בזריקה שהוא סוף ארבע עבודות המתירות אף פיגול אינו קבוע עד שיזרק הדם שהיא סוף כל מתיריו : בהקרבה הוא נפסל. השתא יליף (ג) טז] (פסול) דבמחשבה הכתוב מדבר שמחשב בשעת הקרבה לאוכלו בשלישי : ואינו נפסל בשלישי. אם בהקרבה לא חישב ע"מ כן ואכל ממנו בשלישי אין הקרבן נפסל למפרע דהכי מידריש לא ירצה המקריב לא תהא זריקתו מרצה אם ע"מ כן הקריבו : אותו בזבח הוא מדבר ואינו מדבר בזובח. כלומר (ד) ושלא תאמר דהאי המקריב לאו להכי הוא דאתא אלא לומר לך שהכהן המקריבו לא יחשב עוד בכהונה ויפסל מלכהן לכך נאמר אותו הזבח בלא יחשב ואין הכהן בלא יחשב :
לא

מסתברא נותר אית לן לאוקומי בכרת למיגמר עון עון לחוץ לזמנו דדמי ליה בז"ב. פי' בקונטרס אי מוקמת ליה להאי יז] בנותר איכא למילפיה לגזירה שוה שפיר דדמו אהדדי בשני דברים הללו ששניהם נפסלים בזמן זה בזמן ממש וזה במחשבת זמן ושניהם נוהגין בבמה כדתנן בפ' בתרא (לקמן דף קיג.) יח] וכי פרכת ונילף עון עון דטומאת בשר דכתיב ונשא אהרן את עון הקדשים מה להלן לאו ולא כרת אף כאן לאו ולא כרת אמרינן מנותר הוה ליה למילף דדמי ליה בז"ב אבל אי מוקמת להאי כרת לחוץ למקומו כי גמרת [ליה] חוץ [לזמנו] מיניה בגזירה שוה ופרכת ליה ונילף עון עון מטומאה ליכא לתרוצי מחוץ למקומו הוה ליה למילף דדמי [ליה] בז"ב דהא אין יט] נפסלים בזמן ואינו נוהג בבמת יחיד שאין שם מחילות (עד כאן לשונו) ופירוש זה תימה גדול דמה סברא היא זו ומנין לנו דנוקי קרא בנותר כדי ללמוד ממנו חוץ לזמנו מעון כ] כדי שלא נלמוד מטומאה ועוד הא לענין במה שוה נמי נותר לטומאת בשר כדאמרינן בסוף מכילתין (גם זה שם) אבל *הפיגול והנותר והטמא שוין כא] זה בזה וכן טמא שימש ליכא למימר דהוא נמי לא הותר בבמה כדאמר לעיל מה להלד השוה שבהן שכן לא כב] הותרו בבמה ועוד כשמקשה אדרבה חוץ למקומו הוה ליה לאוקומי כו' דדמי במקד"ש בלאו כג] דומיא דמקד"ש אית לן למילף חוץ לזמנו מחוץ למקומו טפי מטומאה כדאמרינן בפ' בית שמאי (לקמן דף מה:) שכן הותר לין טהור כד] (*בקרא) חוץ לזמנו וחוץ למקומו לא הותרו מכללם ואין לין מרצה ושניהם טהורין ושניהם כה] [לא] עשה קרב כמקריב מה שאין כן בטומאה דמאי דחוץ למקומו הותר מכללו בבמה אין זה קרוי הותר כו] מכללו על כן נראה לפרש דגזירה שוה זו ניתנה בסיני למילף עון עון הנך קראי דהכא זה מזה ולכך מסתברא לן לאוקומי טפי בנותר מבחוץ למקומו משום דדמי לחוץ לזמנו בז"ב דאית לן לאוקומי קרא במילתא שיהיו דומין זה לזה מה שאנו למידין בגזירה שוה ולא משום שלא נלמוד מטומאה כדפירש כז] [רש"י] ופריך אדרבה חוץ למקומו דמי ליה במקד"ש וכי האי גוונא הויא סוגיא דלעיל בריש פירקין (דף יז.) דפסיל בתרומה מחיל עבודה דלא פסיל בתרומה לא מחיל עבודה וא"ת דמוקמינן קרא בדדמי טפי לג"ש טומאת בשר תיהוי בכרת בג"ש דעון עון וי"ל דממעט כח] ליה קרא מכרת כדאמר לקמן פרק ב"ש (דף מג:) וטומאתו עליו מי שטומאתו פורחת ממנו כט] (יוצא עליו מגופו) יצאת טומאת בשר שאין טומאה פורחת ממנו : **ואיפוך** אנא. תימה ל] הא כתיב קרא שלישי והא דמוקמינן ליה בחוץ למקומו באם אינו ענין לחוץ לזמנו מוקמינן ליה בחוץ למקומו א"כ קרא קמא לא] היינו קרא אריכא אית לן לאוקומי בחוץ לזמנו לב] ודוחק לומר דסבר המקשה אין מוקדם ומאוחר בתורה : **מה** שלמים מפגלין ומתפגלין. תימה מהיקישא דזאת התורה נפקא לן לקמן בפ' דם חטאת (דף לח.) ובמנחות פרק התודה (דף פג.) וכמה דרשות דרשינן מהאי היקישא אע"ג דנפקי מקראי אחריני :
למקום

נ"ל הזמן

[נ"ל בזמן קרב]

[עי' כריתות ה.]

[לעיל יג: מנחות יז חולין פא:]

לקמן לח. מנחות פג.

[לקמן מב: מנחות טז:]

הגהות הב"ח

(א) גמ' כתיב הכא כי את וכו' את הנותר באש כי קדש הוא מה להלן : (ב) רש"י ד"ה לא ירצה וכו' משמע דאזריקה קאי לא : (ג) ד"ה בהקרבה וכו' יליף דבפסול מחשבה : (ד) ד"ה אותו וכו' כלומר שלא כצ"ל ואות ו' נמחק :

שיטה מקובצת

א] ולמעוטי נותר מכרת. פ"ה דס"ד דאית ביה כרת מדכתיב [ונכרתה הנפש] והנפש ההיא גבי פיגול דנהי דע"כ לא איירי בנותר מדכתיב לא ירצה מ"מ אין מקרא יוצא מידי פשוטו והייתי אומר דהכרת קאי אנותר ולא ירצה אחוץ למקומו לכך אצטריך ואוכליו למעוטי נותר מכרת. מהר"פ : ב] מסתברא כו' פרש"י כו' ולא נהירא חדא דכל זה מבחוץ בא דאמרינן דלא תקשי מטומאה דהוי ליה לפרש בהדיא ועוד היכי מצי למילף מטומאה התם איכא פירכא דלא מצי למילף ועוד הא אמרינן לקמן הפיגול והנותר והטמא שוה בזה ובזה פי' בבמה גדולה ובבמה קטנה ונראה לפרש א) כו'. לשון הר"פ : ג] וגו' לא יאכל כי קדש הוא : ד] אלא אמר רבא כו' כל זה שהב"א רבא לא אצטריך לן לבעיין אלא מפרש הוא כל הפסוק : ה] מדבר בזובח ותיבת בכהן נמחק : ו] לזמנו לענוש כרת : ז] בכרת למגמר עון : ח] בכרת למגמר עון : ט] להאי כרת : י] בתרא וכ"ת למה איצטריך טעם זה דדמי ליה בז"ב איצטריך דכי מוקמת : יא] למילף מפי דדמי : יב] מחיצות ואין ראוי לומר ביה חוץ למקומו : יג] דאי מוקמת אות ז' נמחק : יד] בהם שהם מתפגלין שהדם כו' והאימורין הם המתפגלין הס"ד : טו] ירצה משמע ותיבת המקריב נמחק : טז] יליף דבפסול מחשבה : יז] להאי כרת בנותר איכא למילפה בג"ש שפיר : יח] בתרא דכי פרכת : יט] אין פסולו בזמן : כ] מעון ולא נלמוד : כא] שוין בזה ובזה וכן טמא ששימש נמי ליכא : כב] לא הותר : כג] בלאו טעמא ותיבת דומיא נמחק : כד] טהור בזמן קרב דחוץ לזמנו : כה] ושניהם לא : כו] הותר בבמה ותיבת מכללו נמחק : כז] כדפי' ו ש"י : כח] תיבת ליה נמחק : כט] תיבות יוצא עליו מגופו נמחק : ל] תימה דהא כתיב בקרא : לא] קמא דהיינו : לב] לזמנו דמסברא קרא קמא לעולם בחוץ לזמנו :

א) ר"ל ונראה לפרש כמו שכתבו התוס' בד"ה מסתברא ונראה לפרש דג"ש זו ניתנה וכו'.

flesh of his sacrifices be at all eaten on the third day etc.; [28b]—if it is superfluous in respect of after time, apply it to out of bounds,[7] and the Divine Law expresses a limitation in connection with *nothar*:[8] *But every one that eateth* it *shall bear his iniquity*,[1] which excludes [eating or intending to eat] out of bounds. Yet say that '*but every one that eateth* it *shall bear his iniquity*' refers to out of bounds, and thus excludes *nothar* from *kareth*?—It is logical that *nothar* must be made to involve *kareth*, so that the meaning of '*iniquity*', where it refers to [the intention of] eating after time, may be learned by analogy, since it is similar thereto in respect of *ZaB*.[9] On the contrary, [eating] without bounds should be made to involve *kareth*, so that the meaning of '*iniquity*', where it refers to [the intention of] eating after time, may be learned by analogy, since it
a is similar thereto in respect of MiḲDaSH?[1] Rather said R. Joḥanan, Zabdi b. Levi taught: *Ḳodesh* is learned from *ḳodesh*. Here is written, *Because he hath profaned the* ḳodesh [*holy thing*] *of the Lord;*
b *and that soul shall be cut off from the people*;[1] and it is written elsewhere, [*And if aught of the flesh of the consecration, or of the bread, remain unto the morning,*] *then thou shalt burn the nothar* [*remainder*] *with fire; it shall not be eaten, because it is* ḳodesh [*holy*]:[2] just as there, [*ḳodesh* is connected with] *nothar*, so here too [it is connected with] *nothar*, and the Divine Law expresses a limitation in connection with *nothar*: *But every one that eateth* it *shall bear his iniquity*, which excludes without bounds from *kareth*. And why do you interpret the long text[3] as referring to after time, and '*third*' in the pericope '*Ye shall be holy*' as referring to without bounds; perhaps I may reverse it?[4]—It is logical that the long text refers to after time, since the meaning of '*iniquity*' is learned by analogy from *nothar*, and [after time] is similar thereto in respect of *ZaB*. On the contrary, [say that] the long text refers to without bounds, and 'third' in '*Ye shall be holy*' refers to after time: because it is similar thereto [Scripture] places it close by and excludes it?[5]—Rather said Raba: The whole is deduced from the long text. For it is written, '[*But if any of the flesh be*] *at all eaten*':[6] Scripture refers to two eatings, viz., eating by man and eating by the altar.[7] '*Of the sacrifice of his peace-offerings*': as [parts of] the peace-offering render *piggul*, and parts are rendered *piggul*, so [in sacrifices where there are parts which] render *piggul* and [parts which] are made *piggul* [the law of *piggul* applies].[8] '*Third*' means after time. '*It shall not be accepted*': as the acceptance of the valid [sacrifice], so is the acceptance of the invalid. And as the acceptance of the valid necessitates that all its *mattirin* be offered, so does the acceptance
c of the invalid necessitate that all its *mattirin* be offered.[1] '*Him that offereth*': it becomes unfit in offering, but does not become unfit through [being eaten on] the third [day].[2] '*It*': Scripture speaks

(7) While *piggul* mentioned in Lev. VII, 18 will definitely refer to the intention of eating after time, to which the whole verse is now understood to refer. (8) V. Glos. (9) *ZaB* is a mnemonic, standing for *zeman*, (time) and *bamah*, (high place).—In both texts, viz., Lev. VII, 18 and Lev. XIX, 8 Scripture states that he who eats it '*shall bear his iniquity*'; the meaning of '*iniquity* is further clarified in the latter text by the addition, '*and that soul shall be cut off from his people*', i.e., *kareth*. Now, on the present exegesis this latter verse may refer either to *nothar* or to eating without bounds, while the former text (Lev. VII, 18) definitely refers to the eating of the flesh before it is actually *nothar* and *within* bounds, after the illegitimate intention of eating it after time. Now, if the punishment of *kareth* in Lev. XIX, 8 is made to refer to *nothar* (owing to the word '*it*' it can only refer to *one*), then we can argue that '*iniquity*' in VII, 18 too means *kareth*, by analogy with '*iniquity*' in Lev. XIX, 8. And the reason for drawing this analogy is that the two are alike in two respects: (i) Both are defects arising through time, *nothar* being the case where he actually eats the flesh after time, and Lev. VII, 18 refers to the illegitimate intention of eating after time. (ii) Both were forbidden not only in the Temple, but also in the High Places used before the Temple was built. For but for this similarity, the meaning of '*iniquity*' in VII, 18 might be deduced from Ex. XXVIII, 38: *And Aaron shall bear the iniquity committed in the holy things*. There '*iniquity*' refers to sacrificing in a state of uncleanness, which is forbidden by a negative injunction, but does not involve *kareth*. and so if an analogy were drawn with this verse, one would say that in Lev. VII, 18 too there is no *kareth*. But if Lev. XIX, 8 is made to refer to eating without bounds, this second analogy might indeed be drawn, since it lacks the two points of similarity, (a private sacrifice offered at a high place might be eaten anywhere) and accordingly nothing will indicate that '*iniquity*' means *kareth*. So Rashi. Tosaf. explains that there was already a tradition that the meaning of '*iniquity*' must be deduced by drawing an analogy between Lev. VII, 18 and XIX, 8, and not with Ex. XXVIII, 38. But for that very reason it is logical to make Lev. XIX, 8 refer to *nothar*, so as to justify the analogy through the two points of similarity.

a (1) *M* = *Maḥshabah* (intention); *Ḳ* = *Ḳeẓath* (a part or portion); *D* = *Dam* (blood), and *SH* = *SHelishi* (third). (i) Both after time and without bounds invalidate the sacrifice by mere intention. (ii) In both cases the illegitimate intention even in respect of a portion of the flesh only disqualifies. (iii) Both disqualify only if expressed during the service in connection with the blood (sprinkling) but not after. And finally (iv) the 'third' day is mentioned in connection with both. Uncleanness is dissimilar in respect of all these: (i) The flesh does not become unclean merely through the intention of defiling it. (ii) If a portion of the flesh is defiled, the rest remains clean. (iii) The flesh can be defiled *after* the sprinkling of the blood. And finally (iv) 'third' is not stated in connection with it *as a superfluous word*. But it is mentioned redundantly in connection with the others, as shewn above, so that an analogy (*gezerah shawah*) might be drawn.

b (1) Lev. XIX, 8. (2) Ex. XXIX, 34. (3) *Sc.* Lev. VII, 18. (4) And '*third*' in Lev. XIX, 7 refers to after time, and it is that which is excluded from *kareth*. (5) Because the intention to eat after time is similar to eating *nothar*, Scripture couples them, and expresses a limitation to shew that no *kareth* is involved, as otherwise we would think that *kareth* is involved in the former because it is similar to *nothar*. (6) Lev. VII, 18. (7) V. *supra* 13b.—The exegesis of the whole verse is irrelevant here, but as Raba quotes it he interprets the whole (Sh. M.). (8) The blood of the peace-offering is the vehicle through which *piggul* is effected, viz., if an illegitimate intention is expressed during one of the services connected with the blood, the flesh and the *emurim* are thereby rendered *piggul*. Just as this is so in the case of the peace-offering, so does the law of *piggul* operate in the case of all sacrifices of which the same can be said. This excludes the meal-offerings of priests and of the anointed priest and of the drink-offerings.—He treats the word 'sacrifice' in the text as alluding to other sacrifices too, which are thus assimilated to peace-offerings, since they are coupled with them.

c (1) He understands '*it shall not be accepted*', to refer to the sprinkling of the blood, which is the last of the *mattirin*, i.e., the services which make the sacrifice 'accepted',—valid. Thus he renders: this sprinkling shall not be accepted (valid), which implies that the sacrifice does not become *piggul* until the sprinkling, and if e.g., the blood is spilt and not sprinkled, the sacrifice is not *piggul*. The acceptance of the invalid means the stamping of the sacrifice as *piggul*, and this does not take place unless the *mattirin* are offered, as explained. (2) Here he deduces that the sacrifice becomes *piggul* through an illegitimate intention, thus: the sacrifice becomes unfit only when he is actually offering it, viz., by then intending to eat thereof on the third day. But if he had no illegitimate intention at the actual offering, yet ate thereof on the third day, it does not become *piggul* retrospectively.

of the sacrifice, and not of the priest.[3] *'It shall not be imputed'*: [29*a*] other intentions must not be mingled therein.[4] *'An abhorred thing* [piggul]': this refers to [the intention of eating it] without bounds.[5] *'It shall be'*: this teaches that they combine with each other.[6] *'And the soul that eateth of it'*: one, but not two; and which is it? [the intention of eating it] after time, for the meaning of *'iniquity'* is learnt from *nothar*, since it is similar to it in *ZaB*.[7]

R. Papa said to Raba: According to you, how do you interpret *'third'* in the pericope, *'Ye shall be holy'*?[8]—That is needed to teach [that the illegitimate intention must concern] a place which has a threefold function, viz., in respect of the blood, the flesh,
a and the *emurim*.[1] But I may deduce that from the earlier text, viz., *'And if* [it] *be at all eaten'*, since the Divine Law expresses it by the word *'third'*?[2]—Said R. Ashi: I reported this discussion before R. Mattenah, whereupon he answered me: If [I deduced it] from there, I would say: *'Third'* is a particularization, and *'piggul'* is a generalisation,[3] and so the generalisation becomes an addition to the particularization, and therefore other places are included too. Hence [the text in *'Ye shall be holy'*] informs us [that it is not so].

Our Rabbis taught: *'And if any of the flesh of the sacrifice of his peace-offerings be at all eaten* [*on the third day*]': R. Eliezer said: Incline your ear to hear: Scripture speaks of one who *intends* eating of his sacrifice on the third day. Yet perhaps that is not so, but rather [Scripture speaks] of one who *eats* of his sacrifice on the third day? You can answer: After it has become fit, shall it then become unfit?[4] Said R. Akiba to him: Behold, we find that a *zab* and a *zabah* and a woman 'who watches from day to day' are presumed to be clean, yet since they have a discharge they undo [their cleanness];[5] hence you too need not wonder at this, that after [the sacrifice] has become fit it then becomes unfit. Said he to him: Lo, it says, '[*unto him*] *that offereth*', [intimating that] it becomes unfit at the offering, but it does not become unfit on the third [day]. Yet perhaps that is not so, but it says, *'him that offereth'*, meaning the
b *priest* who offers it?[1] When it says *'it'*, [Scripture] speaks of the sacrifice, and does not speak of the priest. Ben 'Azzai said: Why is *'it'* stated? Because it is said, [*When thou shalt vow a vow unto the Lord thy God,*] *thou shalt not delay to pay it*:[2] You might think that also he who delays [the fulfilment of] his vow incurs [the sentence] *'it shall not be accepted'*: therefore it says, *'it'*: *'it'* [piggul] is subject to *'it shall not be accepted'*, but he who delays his vow is not subject to *'it shall not be accepted'*. Others[3] say: *'it shall not be imputed'* [teaches that] it becomes unfit through imputation [illegal intention], but does not become unfit through [being eaten on] the third [day]. Now, how does Ben 'Azzai know that Scripture speaks of the sacrifice and not of the priest?[4]—I can say that he deduces it from [the exegesis of] the 'Others'.[5] Alternatively, I can say [that he knows this] because it is written, [*it*] *shall not be accepted*, and '[*it*] *shall not be accepted*' can only apply to the sacrifice.[6]

Now Ben 'Azzai [deduces]: *'it'* is subject to *'it shall not be accepted'*, but he who delays [the payment of] his vow is not subject to *'it shall not be accepted'*: [but] is this deduced from the present text? Surely it is deduced from [the text cited by] 'Others'? For it was taught: Others say: You might think that a firstling which passed

(3) *Var. lec.* the sacrificer.—Scripture does not mean that the priest is henceforth unfit to officiate, but that the *sacrifice* is unfit. Without this *'it'* the text might mean: he that offereth (viz., the priest) shall not be accepted, i.e., shall henceforth be disqualified to officiate. (4) The animal is *piggul* only if this, *sc.* to eat it after time, was his only intention. But if he also expressed another which would disqualify the sacrifice without rendering it *piggul*, this intention negatives the other; cf. Mishnah on 27*b* and *infra b*. (5) Since the intention of eating it after time has already been dealt with. (6) He understands *'it shall be'* to intimate that both these illegitimate intentions rank as one and combine. Thus, if he intended eating half as much as an olive after time and half as much as an olive without bounds (the standard of disqualification is an olive) the intentions combine to invalidate the sacrifice. (7) V. notes *supra* 28*b*. (8) For it is unnecessary in respect of after time, as stated *supra* 28*a* and *b*, while on Raba's present exegesis it is also irrelevant in respect of without bounds.

a (1) It is disqualified only if he intends to eat it in a place where the blood is sprinkled, the flesh is eaten, and the *emurim* (q.v. Glos.) are burnt, e.g., without the Temple court. This excludes an intention to partake thereof in the *hekal*, since the flesh is not eaten, nor are the *emurim* burnt there. So Rashi. Tosaf. gives several other explanations. (2) *'Third'* intimates after time, and in the same verse without bounds is hinted at too, as already explained. Hence 'third' here can have that same significance as is now attributed to it in the pericope *'Ye shall be holy'*. (3) I.e., *'third'* indicates a place with that threefold function, while *piggul* is a general term denoting all places. (4) Surely not. If it was sacrificed with the proper intention, and so was fit, surely it cannot become retrospectively unfit because he eats it on the third day. (5) When a *zab* or a *zabah* (q.v. Glos.) cease to discharge, they must count seven consecutive clean days without any discharge. During this period they are presumed to be clean, yet a discharge within the seven days undoes the days which have already passed and they become *retrospectively* unclean for that time too, and they must count seven days anew. Similarly, according to Biblical law a *niddah* (q.v. Glos.) can cleanse herself seven days after her menstrual flow commenced. During the following eleven days, which are called the eleven days between the menses, she cannot become a *niddah* again, it being axiomatic that a discharge of blood in that period is not a sign of *niddah*, but *may* be symptomatic of gonorrhoea. A discharge on one or two days within the eleven renders her unclean for that period only, and if she has a ritual bath (*tebillah*) the following morning she is clean. Yet if she has another discharge on the same day after the ritual bath, she is retrospectively unclean for the whole day, and *retrospectively* defiles any human beings or utensils with which she came into contact. Should she experience *three* discharges on three consecutive days within that period she becomes unclean as a *zabah*; hence on the first and the second days she is called 'one who watches from day to day', to see whether she will be unclean for those days only, or as a *zabah*.

b (1) He is henceforth unfit to officiate. (2) Deut. XXIII, 22. (3) 'Others' often refers to R. Meir, Hor. 13*b*. (4) Seeing that he utilises *'it'* for a different purpose. (5) Since according to them *'it shall not be imputed'* is necessary to teach that there is no unfitness through the sacrifice being eaten on the third day, Scripture obviously does not refer to the unfitness of the priest, for if it did, how could I think that he is unfit? Not he has done wrong but the eater. (6) The Hebrew is not applicable to a priest.

עין משפט
נר מצוה

קיח א מיי' פי"ד מהל' מעס"ק הלכה טו סמג לאוין שלא:

לא יערב בו מחשבות אחרות פיגול זה חוץ למקומו יהיה מלמד שמצטרפין זה עם זה והנפש האוכלת ממנו אחד ולא שנים ואיזה זה חוץ לזמנו דגמר עון עון מנותר דדמי ליה בז"ב אמר ליה רב פפא לרבא לדידך שלישי דפרשת קדושים תהיו מאי דרשת ביה ההוא מיבעי ליה *למקום שיהא משולש בדם בבשר ובאימורין תיפוק לי מקרא קמא אם האכל יאכל מדאפקיה רחמנא בלשון שלישי אמר רב אשי אמריתה לשמעתא קמיה דרב מתנה א"ל אי מהתם הוה אמינא שלישי פרט פיגול כלל ונעשה כלל מוסף על הפרט ואיתרבו ויקרא ז שאר מקומות קא משמע לן ת"ר °ואם האכל יאכל מבשר זבח שלמיו אמר רבי אליעזר כוף אזנך לשמוע במחשב לאכול מזבחו ביום השלישי הכתוב מדבר או אינו אלא באוכל מזבחו ליום שלישי אמרת א] אחר שהוא כשר יחזור ויפסל אמר לו רבי עקיבא הן מצינו בזב וזבה ושומרת יום כנגד יום שהן בחזקת טהרה וכיון שראו סתרו אף אתה אל תתמה על זה שאע"פ שהוכשר שיחזור ויפסל אמר ב] ליה הרי הוא אומר המקריב בשעת הקרבה הוא נפסל ואינו נפסל בשלישי ג] או אינו אומר המקריב אלא זה כהן המקריב כשהוא אומר אותו בזבח הוא מדבר ואינו מדבר בכהן *בן עזאי אומר אותו מה ת"ל לפי שנא' °לא תאחר דברים כג לשלמו יכול אף מאחר נדרו בלא ירצה ת"ל אותו אותו בלא ירצה *ואין המאחר נדרו בלא ירצה אחרים אומרים לא יחשב במחשבה הוא נפסל ואינו נפסל בשלישי ובן עזאי דבזבח הכתוב מדבר ואינו ד] בכהן מנא ליה אי בעית אימא נפקא ליה מדאחרים ואיבעית אימא מדכתיב לא ה] *ירצו ולא ירצה זיבחא הוא ובן עזאי אותו בלא ירצה ואין מאחר נדרו בלא ירצה מהכא נפקא מדאחרים נפקא *דתניא אחרים אומרים יכול יהא בכור שעיברה שנתו כפסולי

רש"י

לא יערב בו מחשבות אחרות. מכאן למחשבות שמוליאות זו מזו שמחשבת פסול מוליאה מידי פיגול כדתנא מתני' כילד לא קרב המתיר כמלותו כו': יהיה. עשאן הכתוב לחוץ למקומו ולחוץ לזמנו הויה אחת מלמד שמלטרפין חלאי שיעוריהן לפסול את הקרבן כדתנן במתני' לאכול כחלי זית בחוץ כחלי זית למחר פסול: דדמי ליה בז"ב ולא (א) שבקיה חוץ לזמנו דדמי לנותר דאתיא ג"ש מיניה ועגמר חוץ למקומו דלא דמי לנותר במידי והא דלא שנייה רבה בריש שמעתא הכי כי פרכינן אדרבה חוץ למקומו עדיף דסמיך ליה משום דאכתי לא קמה ליה ג"ש דתני לוי בר זבדי ו] דכרת בנותר כתיב דנימא דנשיאות עון דגבי מחשבה בדדמי לנותר משתעי הואיל ומינה גמר: שיהא משולש כו'. ולימד על מחשבת חוץ למקומו שאינה מועלת אלא או בקדשי קדשים שחישב עליהם לאוכלם חוץ לעזרה או בקדשים קלים לאוכלם חוץ לעיר פרט למחשב (ב) לאכול בהיכל דלא פסיל דבעינן ז] שחישב על מקום המשולש: בדם בבשר ואימורין. היינו חוץ לעזרה בשעת היתר הבמות לאפוקי היכל שאין בו הקטרת אימורין ולא אכילת בשר: תיפוק לי מקרא קמא. מדאפקיה רחמנא בלשון שלישי לחוץ לזמנו וכתיב בההוא קרא חוץ למקומו: שלישי פרט. מקום משולש ולא פנים: מאחר שהוכשר. בעבודת דמו ח] כתקונו: בזב וזבה. שפסקו והתחילו למנות ימי ספורן ומנו ד' או ה' ימים ואם ראו סתרו כל מניינם כדאמרינן במס' נדה (דף סז:) ואחר תטהר אחר אחר לכולן שלא תהא טומאה מפסקת ט] בהן: ושומרת יום כנגד יום. הרואה תוך אחד עשר יום שבין נדה לנדה וטבלה למחר י] שחרית הרי היא טהורה דמקצת היום ככולו וטבילתה ביום ואם תראה היום סתרה טהרתה ואדם וכלים שנגעו בהן היום טמאין למפרע כדתנן בפ"ב דנדה (דף עב.) ושוין ברואה תוך אחד עשר יום כו' וטבלה ביום של אחריו ושמשה הרי זו תרבות רעה ומגעה ובעילתה תלויין וזו היא תלייתן אם תראה היום יהיו טמאין למפרע וחייבין בקרבן: הרי הוא אומר המקריב. (ג) בהקרבה נפסל והכי מידרש לא ירצה המקריב אין הקרבתו מרצה: אלא זה כהן המקריב. ואמר לך הכתוב שלא יהא כשר יא] לכהונה ושמע מינה תרתי שעת הקרבה ופסול (ד) יב] כהן: אותו. דא"כ ליכתוב המקריב לא יחשב השתא דכתיב אותו הזבח בלא יחשב ואין המקריב בלא יחשב: במחשבה הוא נפסל. (ה) זה מפורש מן הראשון דהמקריב לא משמע להו שעת הקרבה עד דגמר קרא למילתיה ואמר המקריב אותו לא יחשב במחשבה זאת דהאי לא יחשב יג] לדרשא הוא דהא כתיב לא ירצה: נפקא ליה מדאחרים. מדאיצטריך קרא למימר ואינו נפסל בשלישי שמע מינה בזבח הכתוב מדבר דאי בזובח למה יפסל בשלישי הלא הוא לא חטא כי אם האוכל: מדכתיב לישנא דלא ירצה ולא ירצה זיבחא הוא. דאין לשון לא ירצה נופל בפסול כהן: שעיברה שנתו. וזהו איחור דכתיב לפני ה' תאכלנו שנה בשנה:

תוספות

למקום שיהא משולש בדם ובבשר ואימורים. פירש בקונטרס פרט למחשב לאכול בהיכל דלא פסול דבעינן יד] שחישב על מקום המשולש בדם ובשר ואימורים דהיינו חוץ לעזרה בשעת היתר הבמות לאפוקי היכל שאין בו הקטרת אימורים ולא אכילת בשר ובזה לא דק בקונטרס דאכילת בשר מלי משכחת בהיכל כדאמר לקמן (דף סא.) שאם הקיפו עובדי כוכבים את כל העזרה שכהנים נכנסים בהיכל ואוכלין שם ק"ק ועוד קשה לפירוש הקונטרס מאי קפריך תיפוק לי מקרא קמא מדאפקיה רחמנא בלשון שלישי הא האי שלישי לאו בחוץ למקומו כתיב אלא בחוץ לזמנו ומקום משולש לא שייך בחוץ לזמנו אלא בחוץ למקומו ועוד דקתני *הוה אמינא שלישי פרט רש"ק הא האי שלישי בחוץ לזמנו טו] [כתיב ופיגול] במקום משולש כתיב ויש מפרשים דמקום משולש הייט דלא פסלה מחשבה אלא במזבח החילון שנשתן כשירין בו לאפוקי מזבח הפנימי שאין טתנין בו רק דם וזה אי אפשר דמתנות הפנימיות פלוגתא דר' שמעון ורבנן דרבנן מחייבין בפיגולן כרת וכן ר"מ ורבנן סברי בפ' בית שמאי (לקמן דף מב:) גבי ארבעים ושלש של יום הכיפורים ולעיל בפ"ק (דף יג:) גבי טבילת אלבע בחטאות הפנימיות דאמרינן דפסול מק"ו טז] ואמר נמי בגיטין (דף נד:) כהן גדול ביום הכפורי' יוכיח דכי אומר פגול מהימן ובמקום שאינו משולש אפילו פסול ליכא כדמוכח לקמן בפ' כל הפסולים (דף לו.) וי"מ דמקום משולש הייט דבעינן שיעמוד יז] *המחשבה במקום משולש פרט לעומד חוץ בעזרה ושוחט בסכין ארוכה ולפירוש זה יח] קשה ממתנות הפנימיות דלאו מקום משולש הוא והוי פיגול (תוספות) ויש לומר חוץ לעזרה אין שלשתן כשרין שהרי דם ואימורין נפסלין שם אבל היכל יש דם שלא נפסל שם כגון דם פנימי ואימורין אם הכניסן שם לא נפסלו בכך מיהו אין נראה דשלהי כל הפסולין (לקמן דף לו.) קאמר מחשב לניתנין בחוץ שנתנו בפנים דאינו פסול משום דאינו מקום משולש הג"ה ע"כ והרב ר' יום טוב מפרש דמקום משולש הייט שיחשוב לזרוק במקום שדם ובשר ואימורין פסולין כגון מחשב לזרוק יט] קדשים קלים חוץ לירושלים אבל מחשב לזרוק בירושלים לא דאין שום פסול בבשר וקדשי קדשים אפילו בירושלים ליון דבזה כ] *המקום שלשתן פסולין שם ולהאי פירושא ניחא הא דקשיא לן לעיל אברייתא דחישב ליתן את הניתנין למטה למעלה למטה לאלתר כשר דמשמע דאי שלא במקומו לאו כמקומו דמי ניחא ויתיישב לפי' זה משום דלאו מקום משולש הוא ומיהו קשה כא] אם כן למחר פסול אמאי לאו מקום משולש הוא וכי תימא מידי דהוי אמחשבת היטח ואליבא דר' יהודה הא משמע לעיל דלא לריך להאי טעמא אלא לאחי דמסקינן שלא במקומו כמקומו דמי וי"מ דשלישי בחוץ לזמנו איירי ובעינן שיחשוב לזרוק ליום שלשתן פסולין אפילו לאכול הבשר הייט ליום שלישי דאם חישב לזרוק דם שלמים למחר לא פיגל עד שיהא משולש באכילה דהייט לשלשה ימים והוא הדין בקדשי קדשים לזרוק דמן למחר כב] פיגול דזמן אכילתו נמי למחר אלא דקרא בשלמים כתיב דזמנו ליום שלישי והכי קאמר ההוא מיבעי ליה למקום משולש דאם חישב לזרוק דם שלמים בחוץ ליום הג' פיגל אבל קודם השלישי לא פיגל והא דאמר בפ' איזהו מקומן (לקמן דף נו:) דקדשים הנאכלין ליום ולילה מחשבים בדמן משתשקע החמה ההוא כמאן דלית ליה מקום משולש דפלוגתא דתנאי היא בפ' כל הפסולין (לקמן דף לו:) ופי' זה לא יתכן כלל דכולה שמעתא כג] מיירי במקום שיהא משולש: **וכיון** שראו סתרו. פי' הקונטרס דזב וזבה שפסקו והתחילו למנות ימי ספורן ומנו ארבעה או חמשה ימים וקשה דאין זה קרוי חזקת טהרה כד] אלא נראה דמיירי בשביעי שלהן לאחר שטבלו (תוספות) דזב וזבה טבילתן ביום ואם טבלו בשביעי ואחר כך נגעו בטהרות או שמשו וראו לאח"כ (או) קודם הערב שמש טמאים למפרע ואם המתינה לשמש עד הלילה ואח"כ ראתה אינה טמאה אלא מכאן ולהבא (הג"ה ע"כ) ומיהו כה] רבי יוסי דאמר פ' כילד לולין (פסחים דף פא.) דלא מטמא למפרע לא יתכן: **ואין** מאחר נדרו בלא ירצה. יש תימה דלמה לן קרא דמהיכא תיתי לן דהוי בלא ירצה דאיצטריך קרא כו] דלא ירצה למעוטיה: **נפקא** לן מדאחרים. תימה הא רבי אליעזר נמי דריש שאינו נפסל בשלישי ואפילו הכי לריך פסוק שאין כז] כהן נפסל וי"ל דרבי אליעזר כיון דלא דריש לא יחשב לומר במחשבה הוא נפסל

ה"א שלישי פרט למקום משולש הא האי שלישי בחוץ לזמנו כתיב כצ"ל וכ"ה בס"י נ"ק

[נ"ל ממחשב]

שיטה מקובצת

א] אמרת מאחר שהוכשר יחזור: ב] אמר לו הרי הוא אומר המקריב בהקרבה ותיבת בשעת נמחק: ג] או אינו [אומר המקריב] אלא [זה] כהן המקריב. פ"ה האי או אינו אינו כמו כל או אינו שבתלמוד דאינו ר"ל או אינו דכולה לכהן הוא דאתא ולא למידרש דאין הקרבן נפסל בשלישי (בשלישי) אלא בשעת הקרבה ובהא קאמר דהכהן לא ירצה אצל זה דמה פשע הכהן במה שהותירו לאכלו אלא ודאי המקריב משמע בשעת הקרבה כלומר דאם חישב בשעת הקרבה (גם) הזובח והכהן לא ירצה והכי משמע קרא משמע בהקרבה הוא נפסל בשלישי וכמו כן משמע נמי דמיירי בכהן שחישב מדכתיב מחשבה בלשון המקריב משמע דקאי נמי [אכהן] דליכא למימר דכוליה לכהן הוא דאתא דאין לו לפסול במה שהותירו כיון דלא פשע. העתקת לשון רש"י של מהר"פ ז"ל: ד] ואינו מדבר בכהן: ה] לא ירצה: ו] זבדי דאשמועינן דכרת: ז] דבעינן שיחשב: ח] כתקנן הס"ד: ט] מפסקת ביניהם הס"ד: י] למחר ס"א ביום של אחריו: יא] כשר עוד לכהונה: יב] כהן דאי אכהן קאי ע"כ מהקרבה קאמר והאי או אינו משונה מכל או אינו שבתלמוד שפירושו או אינו בא לדרשא זו אלא לדרשא אחרת והכא אי אפשר לומר כן דלמה הכהן נפסל אם אכלו הבעלים מבשר זבח ביום השלישי אלא ע"כ במחשבת הכהן הוא עצמו נפסל וגם הזבח נפסל מדכתיב והנפש האוכלת ממנו עונה תשא: יג] יחשב יתירה הוא לדרשא דהא: יד] דבעינן שיחשב: טו] בחוץ לזמנו כתיב. וי"מ והשאר נמחק: טז] מקו"ו ואמרינן נמי בגיטין בהניזקין כה"ג ביוה"כ כו' אמר פיגול: יז] שיעמד המחשב: יח] זה נמי קשה ממתנות כו' הוא ולא יהא פיגול. הג"ה. וי"ל: יט] לזרוק דם קדשים: כ] הקרבן שלשתן כו' ניחא. לשון מהר"פ דגבי חוץ לזמנו [מתוקם] זמן משולש כגון חטאת שחישב למחר שאינו [ראוי] אף לאכילת בשר [ע"כ]: כא] קשה דאם כן למחר אמאי פסול הא לאו מקום: כב] למחר פיגל דזמן אכילתן לאו למחר אלא דקרא בשלמים כתיב כו' בחוץ לזמנו ליום הג' פיגל אבל: כג] שמעתא לא מיירי אלא במקום: כד] טהרה עד שימנו ז' ימים לשון הר"פ ז"ל וי"ל שמנה שבעת ימים אבל לא גמר היום דמקצת היום ככולו: כה] ומיהו לרבי יוסי: כו] קרא למעוטי חס"ד גליון וי"ל דסד"א שיפסל באיחור חטאתו כמו באיחור זמן גופו כמו קרבן הבא כבש והביאו לאחר שנתו: כז] שאין הכהן נפסל כדקאמר או אינו:

הגהות הב"ח

(א) רש"י ד"ה דדמי וכו' ולא שבקינן לחוץ וכו' ונגמר לחוץ וכו' שנייה רבה: (ב) ד"ה שיהא משולש וכו' לאוכלן בהיכל דלאו פסול הוא דבעינן: (ג) ד"ה הרי הוא אומר המקריב בשעת הקרבה: (ד) ד"ה אלא זה וכו' כהן הס"ד ואח"כ מ"ה כשהוא אומר אותו: (ה) ד"ה במחשבה הוא נפסל מקרא זה וכו' לדרשה הוא דהאי דהא:

[לקמן לו. פג:]

ר"ס ו.

נ"ל ירצה

שם פ: תמורה כח: [תוספתא סנהדרין פ"ג]

כפסולי המוקדשין ויפסל ת"ל °ואכלת לפני ה' אלהיך מעשר דגנך א] וגו' מקיש בכור למעשר מה מעשר אינו נפסל משנה לחבירתה *אף בכור אינו נפסל משנה לחבירתה איצטריך סלקא דעתך אמינא הני מילי בכור דלאו בר הרצאה הוא אבל קדשים דבני הרצאה נינהו אימא לא לירצו קמ"ל ואכתי מהתם נפקא °והיה בך חטא ולא בקרבנך חטא (א) ב] ובן עזאי ההוא מבעי ליה והיה בך חטא ולא באשתך חטא סלקא דעתך אמינא הואיל ואמר *רבי אלעזר ואיתימא רבי יוחנן אין אשתו של אדם מתה אא"כ ג] מבקשין ממנו ממון ואין לו שנאמר °אם אין לך לשלם למה יקח משכבך מתחתיך בהאי עון דבל תאחר נמי מתה קמ"ל: אחרים אומרים ד] במחשבה הוא נפסל ואינו נפסל בשלישי ורבי אליעזר ה] לא יחשב מאי עביד ליה מיבעי ליהלכדרבי ינאי דאמר רבי ינאי מנין למחשבות שמוציאות זו מזו שנאמר לא יחשב לא יערב בו מחשבות ו] אחרות ורב מרי מתני אמר רבי ינאי מנין למחשב בקדשים שהוא לוקה ת"ל °לא יחשב א"ל רב אשי לרב מרי לאו שאין בו מעשה הוא וכל לאו שאין בו מעשה אין לוקין עליו אמר ליה רבי יהודה היא *דאמר לאו שאין בו מעשה לוקין עליו: **מתני'** *זה הכלל ב"כל השוחט והמקבל והמהלך והזורק לאכול דבר שדרכו לאכול ולהקטיר דבר שדרכו להקטיר ז] כזית חוץ למקומו פסול ואין בו כרת חוץ לזמנו פגול וחייבין עליו כרת ובלבד שיקריב המתיר כמצותו כיצד קרב המתיר כמצותו שחט בשתיקה קבל והלך וזרק חוץ לזמנו ח] או ששחט חוץ לזמנו וקבל והלך וזרק בשתיקה או ששחט וקבל והלך וזרק חוץ לזמנו זהו שמקריב המתיר כמצותו כיצד לא קרב המתיר כמצותו שחט חוץ למקומו קבל והלך וזרק חוץ לזמנו או ששחט חוץ לזמנו קבל והלך וזרק חוץ למקומו או ששחט וקבל והלך וזרק חוץ למקומו ט] (ולזמנו) הפסח והחטאת ששחטן שלא לשמן וקבל והלך וזרק חוץ לזמנו או ששחט חוץ לזמנו קיבל והלך וזרק שלא לשמן או ששחט וקבל והלך וזרק י] דמן שלא לשמן זהו שלא קרב המתיר כמצותו *ד"לאכול כזית בחוץ כזית למחר כזית למחר כזית בחוץ כחצי זית בחוץ כחצי זית למחר כחצי זית למחר כחצי זית בחוץ פסול ואין בו כרת אמר רבי יהודה זה הכלל כל שמחשבת הזמן קדמה למחשבת המקום פגול וחייבין עליו כרת ואם מחשבת המקום קדמה למחשבת הזמן פסול ואין בו כרת *וחכמים אומרים ה"זה וזה פסול ואין בו כרת *)לאכול 'כחצי זית להקטיר כחצי כזית כשר שאין אכילה והקטרה מצטרפין: **גמ'** אמר אילפא *מחלוקת בשתי עבודות אבל בעבודה אחת דברי הכל עירוב מחשבות הוי ורבי יוחנן אמר אף בעבודה אחת מחלוקת בשלמא לאילפא מדרישא בשתי עבודות סיפא נמי בשתי עבודות אלא לרבי יוחנן רישא בשתי עבודות וסיפא בעבודה אחת אין

*)מנחות יז. [וש"נ]

מעילה ד.

כפסולי המוקדשין. כאילו נפל בו מום: מה מעשר אינו נפסל משנה לחבירתה. שהרי בשלישי יא] זמן ביעור לבער כל המעשרות מן הבית ולהתוודות כדכתיב מקצה שלש שנים תוציא (דברים יד): דלאו בר הרצאה הוא. אינו בא לכפר אבל קדשים כגון עולה שמכפרת על עשה ושלמים שמביאין לדורון ליתן שלום בין ישראל לאביהם שבשמים ואימא הואיל ואיחרו יב] *פסול בעבודה הוא ולא לירצו קא משמע לן: ולא בקרבנך חטא. שאם איחרו אינו נפסל והיה בך חטא סיפיה דקרא דלא תאחר לשלמו *הוא: הא אוקימנא במס' (ב)ר"ה: מבקשין ממנו יג]. ממונו שגזל: משכבך. אשתו: שמוציאות זו מזו. מחשבת פסול מוציאה מיד פיגול: לא יד] יחשב. קרי ביה (ג) לא יחשב להזהיר כהנים על כך: רבי יהודה היא. במס' שבועות (דף ג:) והנותר ממנו עד בקר באש תשרפו בא הכתוב ליתן עשה אחר לא תעשה לומר שאין לוקין עליו דטעמא דבא הכתוב הא לא בא הכתוב לוקה המותיר ואע"ג דאין בו מעשה: **מתני'** זה הכלל כל השוחט ומקבל כו'. או זו או זו: לאכול דבר שדרכו לאכול. בשר: או להקטיר דבר שדרכו להקטיר. אימורין כדילפינן לעיל דשתי אכילות מפגלות ובלבד דליחשיב עלייהו להאכילו למחר לראוי להן אימורין למזבח בשר לאדם: ובלבד שיקריב המתיר כמצותו. טו] הדם הוא המתיר כמצותו שלא יהיה בו פסול אחר אם יש בו פסול מחשבה אחרת יצא מידי פיגול כדילפינן לעיל דמחשבות מוציאות זו מזו: הפסח והחטאת ששחטן שלא לשמן. מוציאן מידי פיגול אבל שאר זבחים אין שלא לשמן מוציאן מידי פיגול דהא כשרים הן שלא לשמן: לאכול כזית בחוץ כזית למחר. היינו הך דאמרן אלא דרישא איירי בב' עבודות וכאן בעבודה אחת ששחט על מנת לאכול כזית למחר טז] כזית בחוץ ולמאן דמוקי לה בגמרא להא נמי בשתי עבודות משום כחצי זית נקט לה לאשמועינן דמצטרפין זה עם זה: רבי יהודה אומר כו'. אכולה מתני' פליג דלית ליה מחשבות מוציאות זו מזו אלא אם כן קדם פסולו לפיגולו דתו לא קרינן ביה כהרצאת כשר ובעבודה אחת נמי פליג דאית ליה תפוס לשון ראשון: לאכול כחצי זית ולהקטיר כחצי זית. ושניהם חוץ לזמנו או חוץ למקומו כשר שאין אכילה והקטרה מצטרפין לפוסלו דהכא ליכא שיעורא והכא ליכא שיעורא: **גמ'** בשתי עבודות. דהא דתני סיפא כזית למחר כזית בחוץ דפליג ר' יהודה עלה בשתי עבודות מיירי כי רישא ששחט על מנת לאכול כזית למחר וקבל על מנת לאכול כזית בחוץ ההא הוא דפליג רבי יהודה שהרי הוקבע בפיגול והו לא אתא מחשבת פסול ומפקע לה אבל בעבודה אחת אפילו ר' יהודה מודה דלא הוקבע בפיגול במחשבה מעורבת: אף בעבודה אחת מחלוקת. דאית ליה לר' יהודה תפוס לשון ראשון: מדרישא בשתי עבודות. דקתני בהדיא כילד לא קרב המתיר כמצותו שחט חוץ לזמנו וקבל והלך יז] חוץ למקומו: סיפא נמי. כזית למחר כזית בחוץ דפליגי בה ר' יהודה ורבנן: בשתי עבודות. קא מיירי והאי דהדר נקיט ליה לאשמועינן צירוף כחצי זית דלא אשמועינן ברישא: אין

נפסל איכא למימר יח] שהוא לשון חשיבות ואתא למימר שאף הכהן נפסל אי לאו דמעטיה קרא בהדיא אבל בן עזאי דדריש לא יחשב לשון מחשבה יט] ממילא שמעינן דלאו בכהן מיירי: **אלא** אם כן מבקשין ממנו ממון ואין לו. פי' בקונטרס ממון שגזל ונראה דמיירי בנדר כדאמר בפ' שני דשבת (דף לב:) דבעון נדרים אשתו של אדם מתה שנאמר למה יקח משכבך מתחתיך והא דדריש הכא בך חטא ולא באשתך חטא מיירי במשלם אחר כן אלא שעבר על בל תאחר:

מחלוקת בשתי עבודות. פי' בקונטרס כגון שחיטה והולכה והא דקאמר בתר הכי מדרישא בשתי עבודות סיפא נמי בשתי עבודות פי' בקונטרס דהאי דהדר נקיט ליה לאשמועינן צירוף בחצי זית דלא אשמועינן ברישא וזהו כ] דוחק והיה נראה לפרש שתי עבודות כי ההוא דפ"ק דמעילה (דף ד.) דמפרש סימן ראשון חוץ לזמנו וסימן שני חוץ למקומו כעין שתי עבודות ועבודה אחת היינו סימן אחד. וצריך לומר לפירוש זה דאילפא ס"ל ישנה לשחיטה מתחילה ועד סוף ומפגלין בחצי מתיר כא] דאי אינה לשחיטה אלא לבסוף כך (יש) לי מחשב בשני סימנים כמו מחשב בסימן אחד כיון דאין המחשבה חלה אלא בגמר רוב שחיטה אבל ר' יוחנן יכול לסבור כאביי דאמר בלחלות מודה רבי מאיר דתרווייהו חיילי דלא שייך ביה הקדמה אבל כזית למחר כזית בחוץ אפילו בסימן אחד פליגי ושייך ביה הקדמה בתחילת סימן ובסופו ולקמן דאמר אביי סימן ראשון וסימן שני נקט דבר המסויים ואליבא דאילפא אבל לר' יוחנן הוי מצי למנקט בסימן אחד בתחילתו ובסופו דהא ר' יוחנן סבר ישנה לשחיטה מתחילה ועד סוף פ' השוחט (חולין כט:) כב] א"כ סובר הכא בסימן אחד נמי מחלוקת ויכול לסבור ר' יוחנן נמי כרבא כג] בלחלות נמי פליגי וכל שכן בסימן אחד דפליג דשייך ביה הקדמה דסבר רבי יוחנן ישנה לשחיטה מתחילה ועד סוף. הג"ה:

אמר

עין משפט נר מצוה

קיט א מיי' פ"א מהל' בכורות הלכה יג:

קכ ב מיי' פי"ד מהל' פסה"מ הלכה ח:

קכא ג מיי' פט"ז מהל' פסה"מ הל' א:

קכב ד ה מיי' שם הלכה ב:

קכג ו מיי' פי"ד מהל' פסה"מ הלכה י:

מסורת הש"ס

דברים יד

ר"ה כה בעבירה [ר"ה ו.]

גי' ז"קטוא והכי אוקימנא במס' ר"ה וכל"ל והר"א

ס"פ כנמזו

שבת לב:

משלי כב

סנהדרין כב. ר"ס ו.

יבמ"ן מ"ש

ויקרא ז

מכות יז. [לעיל כח.]

[ב"מ נא. סנהדרין סג. שבועות ג: תמורה ג.] מכות ד: טז. כ:

[מנחות יב. לקמן סט.]

[נ"ע חכמים היינו ת"ק וכן בסקא תח"ע וכנ"ל ולמ"ש תוספות מנחות יב. ד"ה וחכמים וכו' ע"ש יש ליישב]

הגהות הב"ח

(א) גמ' ולא בקרבנך חטא הא אוקימנא לבן עזאי ההוא: (ב) רש"י ד"ה הא וכו' ר"ה הס"ד ואח"כ מ"ה מבקשין ממנו ממון: (ג) ד"ה לא יחשב קרי ביה לא יְחַשֵּׁב:

שיטה מקובצת

א] דגנך ובכורות בקרך: ב] חטא הא מוקמינן והיה בך כו' והשאר ל"ש: ג] מבקשים פי' כלומר מבקשים ממנו ואומר שאין לו שהכל משועבדים לכתובת אשתו והיא אומרת גם כן שאין לו. גליון בגמ' ישנה: ד] אומרים לא יחשב במחשבה: ה] אליעזר האי לא: ו] תיבת אחרות נמחק: ז] תיבת כזית נמחק: ח] או ששחט כו' פי' או או קתני אם עשה אחד מאלה ע"מ לאכול חוץ למקומו וכל השלשה חוץ לזמנו לא קרב המתיר כמצותו וכן פי' רש"י ז"ל במנחות בפ"ק (דף י"ב ע"א) על משנה הקומץ את המנחה לאכול שיריה בחוץ כו' שהיא דומה למשנה זאת. גליון: ט] תיבת ולזמנו נמחק: י] תיבת דמן נמחק: יא] זמן הביעור: יב] ואיחרו בא בעבירה: יג] ממנו ממון: יד] לא יְחַשֵּׁב קרי ביה לא יְחַשֵּׁב: טו] דמתיר הדם הס"ד ימה"ד כמצותו שלא יהיה בו פסול אחר אבל אם יש: טז] למחר וכזית בחוץ: יז] וקבל והלך וזרק חוץ: יח] למימר לא יחשב הוא לשון חשיבות לשון הר"פ ז"ל והילכך אע"ג דבזבח מיירי לומר שיהא נפסל מ"מ מדכתיב המקריב הייתי אומר שאף הכהן נפסל אי לאו דמעטיה קרא בהדיא אבל בן עזאי כו': יט] מחשבה ולומר דבמחשבה אינו נפסל מסילא: כ] דוחק. לשון מהר"פ דליפליג בחדא וישמיענו דמצטרפין ולמה לי תרי בבא לכך נראה דמיירי בב' עבודות מ"ש ברישא ובסיפא מיירי בעבודה אחת כעין ב' עבודות כגון בין סימן לסימן ולא נהירא חדא דבמעילה מוקי לה בסימן ראשון לסימן שני וע"ק דקאמר אח"כ מיד מדרישא בשתי עבודות וקשה תרתי בשתי עבודות למה לי ואי לאשמועינן צירוף דחצי חצי מ"מ הו"ל למיפרך [לימא הך] רישא (ומימרא)[ולימרא](דרב) [דרבי] יהודה פליג עליה לחדא לכך נ"ל דהכל בשחיטה איירי בעבודה אחת כעין שתי עבודות קאמר כדאמרינן במעילה בפ"ק בסימן ראשון לסימן שני וקסבר ישנה לשחיטה מתחילה ועד סוף ומפגלין בחצי מתיר וא"כ חלה שפיר הפיגול בסימן ראשון כמי בעבודה שלימה והשתא סיפא אשמועינן דכת"ג חשיב שתי עבודות [ע"כ] ונראה לפרש. ותיבת והיה נמחק: כא] מתיבת דאי כו' עד סוף הדבור מוקף בחצי לבנה: כב] השוחט וגם סובר ותיבות א"כ נמחק: כג] כרבא דאמר.

a its [first] year[1] is [29b] as dedicated animals rendered unfit,[2] and so unfit; therefore it says, *And thou shalt eat before the Lord thy God . . . the tithe of thy corn . . . and the firstlings of thy herd and of thy flock;*[3] the firstling is assimilated to tithe: as tithe does not become unfit through [being kept] from one year until the following, so the firstling does not become unfit through [being kept] from one year until the next?—It is necessary: You might think that this holds good only of a firstling, which is not subject to acceptance,[4] but [other] sacrifices which are subject to acceptance, I would say that they are not 'accepted'.[5] Hence ['*it*'] informs us [that it is not so].

Yet still it is deduced from elsewhere [viz.,] [*Thou shalt not delay to pay it . . .*] *and it will be sin in thee,* [which teaches,] but it will not be sin in thy offering?[6]—But we have interpreted this according to Ben 'Azzai[7] [as teaching] '*and it will be sin in* thee', but it will not be sin in thy wife. For you might think that I can argue, Since R. Eleazar—others state, R. Joḥanan—said: A man's wife does not die save when money is demanded from him and he lacks it,[8] for it says, *If thou hast not wherewith to pay, why should he take away thy bed from under thee?*[9] she also dies on account of this sin of [violating the injunction] '*Thou shalt not delay*'; [hence Scripture] informs us [that it is not so].

'Others say, "*It shall not be imputed*" [teaches that] it becomes invalid through imputation [intention], but it does not become invalid through [being eaten on] the third day.' Now, how does R. Eliezer utilise this [text], '*it shall not be imputed*'?—He needs it for the teaching of R. Jannai. For R. Jannai said: How do we know that [illegal] intentions negative each other? Because it says, '*it shall not be imputed*', [which means,] other [illegal] intentions shall
b not be mingled therewith.[1] R. Mari recited it [thus]: R. Jannai said: How do we know that he who purposes an [illegitimate] intention in respect of sacrifices is flagellated?[2] Because it says, *Lo yeḥasheb.*[3] Said R. Ashi to R. Mari: But it is a negative injunction not involving an action,[4] and one is not flagellated on account of a negative injunction which does not involve action?—This is according to R. Judah, he replied, who maintained: One is flagellated on account of a negative injunction which does not involve action.

MISHNAH. THIS IS THE GENERAL RULE: HE WHO SLAUGHTERS OR RECEIVES [THE BLOOD], OR CARRIES [IT] OR SPRINKLES [IT], [INTENDING] TO EAT AS MUCH AS AN OLIVE OF THAT WHICH IS NORMALLY EATEN OR TO BURN [ON THE ALTAR] AS MUCH AS AN OLIVE OF THAT WHICH IS NORMALLY BURNT WITHOUT BOUNDS, [THE SACRIFICE] IS INVALID, BUT IT DOES NOT INVOLVE KARETH; [INTENDING TO EAT OR BURN] AFTER TIME, IT IS PIGGUL AND INVOLVES KARETH, PROVIDED THAT THE MATTIR[5] IS OFFERED IN ACCORDANCE WITH THE LAW.[6] HOW IS THE MATTIR OFFERED IN ACCORDANCE WITH THE LAW [APART FROM THAT]? IF ONE SLAUGHTERED IN SILENCE, AND RECEIVED, OR SPRINKLED, [INTENDING TO EAT THE FLESH] AFTER TIME; OR IF ONE SLAUGHTERED [INTENDING TO EAT] AFTER TIME, AND RECEIVED, WENT AND SPRINKLED IN SILENCE; OR IF ONE SLAUGHTERED, AND RECEIVED, WENT, AND SPRINKLED [INTENDING TO EAT] AFTER TIME; THAT IS OFFERING THE MATTIR IN ACCORDANCE WITH THE LAW. HOW IS THE MATTIR NOT OFFERED IN ACCORDANCE WITH THE LAW? IF ONE SLAUGHTERED [INTENDING TO EAT] WITHOUT BOUNDS, [AND] RECEIVED, WENT, AND SPRINKLED [WITH THE INTENTION OF EATING] AFTER TIME; OR IF ONE SLAUGHTERED [INTENDING TO EAT] AFTER TIME, [AND] RECEIVED, WENT, AND SPRINKLED [INTENDING TO EAT] WITHOUT BOUNDS; OR IF ONE SLAUGHTERED, RECEIVED, WENT, AND SPRINKLED [INTENDING TO EAT] WITHOUT BOUNDS; IF ONE SLAUGHTERED THE PASSOVER-OFFERING
c OR THE SIN-OFFERING FOR THE SAKE OF SOMETHING ELSE,[1] AND RECEIVED, WENT, AND SPRINKLED [INTENDING TO EAT THEM] AFTER TIME; OR IF ONE SLAUGHTERED [THEM, INTENDING TO EAT THEM] AFTER TIME, [AND] RECEIVED, WENT, AND SPRINKLED FOR THE SAKE OF SOMETHING ELSE; OR IF ONE SLAUGHTERED, RECEIVED, WENT, AND SPRINKLED FOR THE SAKE OF SOMETHING ELSE; IN THESE CASES THE MATTIR WAS NOT OFFERED IN ACCORDANCE WITH THE LAW.[2] [IF ONE INTENDED] TO EAT AS MUCH AS AN OLIVE WITHOUT BOUNDS [AND] AS MUCH AS AN OLIVE ON THE MORROW, [OR] AS MUCH AS AN OLIVE ON THE MORROW [AND] AS MUCH AS AN OLIVE WITHOUT BOUNDS;[3] HALF AS MUCH AS AN OLIVE WITHOUT BOUNDS [AND] HALF AS MUCH AS AN OLIVE ON THE MORROW; HALF AS MUCH AS AN OLIVE ON THE MORROW [AND] HALF AS MUCH AS AN OLIVE WITHOUT BOUNDS, [THE SACRIFICE] IS UNFIT, AND DOES NOT INVOLVE KARETH.[4] SAID R. JUDAH, THIS IS THE GENERAL RULE: WHERE THE INTENTION OF TIME PRECEDES THE INTENTION OF PLACE, [THE SACRIFICE] IS PIGGUL, AND INVOLVES KARETH; BUT IF THE INTENTION OF PLACE PRECEDES THE INTENTION OF TIME, IT IS UNFIT AND DOES NOT INVOLVE KARETH.[5] BUT
d THE SAGES MAINTAIN: IN BOTH CASES[1] [THE SACRIFICE] IS UNFIT AND DOES NOT INVOLVE KARETH. [IF ONE INTENDS] TO EAT HALF AS MUCH AS AN OLIVE [WITHOUT BOUNDS OR AFTER TIME] [AND] TO BURN HALF AS MUCH AS AN OLIVE [SIMILARLY], IT IS FIT, FOR EATING AND BURNING DO NOT COMBINE.[2]

GEMARA. Ilfa said: The controversy is in respect of two services, but in the case of one service all agree that it constitutes a mingling of intentions.[3] But R. Joḥanan maintained: The controversy is in respect of a single service too. As for Ilfa, it is well: since the first clause treats of two services,[4] the second clause too[5] treats of two services. But according to R. Joḥanan, the first clause treats of two services and the second clause of one service?

a (1) The firstling must be sacrificed within its first year. If it is not, its owner transgresses the injunction, *Thou shalt not delay.* (2) Through a blemish. (3) Deut. XIV, 23. (4) The firstling does not come to make atonement, and therefore is not subject to 'acceptance'. (5) If delayed, i.e., that the vower has not duly fulfilled his vow and must bring another sacrifice. (6) I.e., the offering does not become invalid. (7) Emended text. (8) The money which he robbed. (9) Prov. XXII, 27; '*thy bed*' is understood to mean 'thy wife'.
b (1) V. *supra a* top. (2) As are all who violate a negative injunction. (3) *It shall not be imputed.* But with a different vowelling this reads *lo yaḥshob*, he (the priest) shall not intend (to eat it after time), and thus this becomes a negative injunction. (4) Talking is not considered an action. (5) The enabler, i.e., the blood, through the sprinkling of which the sacrifice may be eaten. (6) I.e., that no other illegitimate intention is expressed.

c (1) As different sacrifices, whereby they are invalid, *supra 2a*. (2) In all these cases there was an illegitimate intention which invalidated the sacrifice in addition to that which would render it *piggul*. Hence it is not *piggul* but only invalid, as already stated. (3) The intentions being in that order. (4) For the same reason as before. (5) R. Judah holds that an invalidating intention does not negative a *piggul* intention if the latter is expressed first.
d (1) Whatever the order. (2) In intention. (3) Even R. Judah agrees that where both intentions are expressed at the same service, the sacrifice is not *piggul* but merely unfit, even if the *piggul* intention preceded. (4) As it is explicitly taught: IF ONE SLAUGHTERED [INTENDING TO EAT] AFTER TIME AND RECEIVED THE BLOOD ETC. WITHOUT BOUNDS. (5) *Sc.* IF ONE SLAUGHTERED INTENDING TO EAT AS MUCH AS AN OLIVE ON THE MORROW AND AS MUCH AS AN OLIVE WITHOUT BOUNDS.

[30a]—Even so: the first clause treats of two services, while the second clause can refer to either one service or two services.

We learnt: SAID R. JUDAH: THIS IS THE GENERAL RULE: IF THE INTENTION OF TIME PRECEDED THE INTENTION OF PLACE, IT IS PIGGUL, AND INVOLVES KARETH. As for R. Joḥanan, it is well: hence he teaches, THIS IS THE GENERAL RULE.[6] But according to Ilfa, what is the implication of THIS IS THE GENERAL RULE?—That is indeed a difficulty.

We learnt elsewhere: [If one declares,] 'This [animal] be a substitute for a burnt-offering, a substitute for a peace-offering,' it is a substitute for a burnt-offering [only]: this is R. Meir's view. Said R. Jose: If such was his original intention,[7] since it is impossible to pronounce both designations simultaneously, his declarations a are valid.[1] But if, having declared, 'This [animal] be a substitute for a burnt-offering,' he declared as an afterthought, 'This be a substitute for a peace-offering,' it is a burnt-offering. It was asked: What if [one declares,] 'This [animal] be a substitute for a burnt-offering and a peace-offering,' [or] '[This animal be a substitute for] half [a burnt-offering] and half [a peace-offering]'? Said Abaye: Here R. Meir certainly agrees [with R. Jose]. Raba said: There is still the controversy. Raba said to Abaye: According to you who maintain that here R. Meir certainly agrees, Yet lo! slaughtering is analogous to half and half, yet they disagree?[2]—Said he to him: Do you think that *shechitah* counts only at the end? [No:] *Shechitah* counts from the beginning until the end, and our Mishnah means that he declared [that he cut] one organ [intending to eat the flesh] after time and the second organ [intending to eat it] without bounds.[3]

b Yet surely *kemiẓah*[1] is analogous to halves, yet they disagree?[2]—There too it means that he burnt a fistful of the meal-offering [with the intention of eating] after time and a fistful of the frankincense [intending to eat] without bounds. Yet they disagree in respect of the fistful of a sinner's meal-offering, where there is no frankincense?—They do not disagree there. R. Ashi said: If you should say that they do disagree, they disagree in the steps.[3]

R. Shimi b. Ashi recited [the passage] as Abaye; R. Huna b. Nathan recited [it] as Raba. When R. Dimi came,[4] he said: R. Meir stated [his ruling] in accordance with the thesis of R. Judah, who maintained: Regard the first expression. For we learnt: R. JUDAH SAID, THIS IS THE GENERAL RULE: IF THE INTENTION OF TIME PRECEDED THE INTENTION OF PLACE, IT IS PIGGUL,

(6) This phrase is always regarded as including something not explicitly stated; according to R. Joḥanan then it includes the case of both intentions being expressed at one service. (7) To declare it a substitute for both.

a (1) V. Lev. XXVII, 33: *He shall not inquire whether it be good or bad, neither shall he change it; and if he change it at all, then both it and that for which it is changed shall be holy*. This is interpreted as meaning that if an animal is dedicated for a particular sacrifice, e.g., a peace-offering, and then a second is substituted for it, both are holy, the second having exactly the same holiness as the first. Now R. Meir rules that if he declares it a substitute for two consecrated animals in succession, only the first declaration is valid, and the second is disregarded. But R. Jose maintains that if the second statement was not added as an afterthought but was part of the original intention, the whole is valid. Consequently, the animal is put out to graze until it receives a blemish, when it must be sold, and the money expended half for a burnt-offering and half for a peace-offering. (2) When one slaughters the sacrifice with the intention of eating as much as an olive without bounds and as much as an olive after time, the second intention is not an afterthought cancelling the first, since both are possible; yet R. Judah regards the first statement only. This is analogous to making an animal a substitute for half a burnt-offering and half a peace-offering, for here too both are possible. Now R. Meir who regards the first statement only in substitution agrees with R. Judah in our Mishnah, and therefore in the declaration in question too he should regard the first statement only. (3) *Shechitah* consists of cutting across the two organs of the throat, viz., the windpipe and the gullet. Here R. Judah disagrees, because he regards them as two separate statements; but in a statement of 'halves' R. Judah (and R. Meir) would agree that the whole counts as one statement and that both parts are regarded. V. also Pes. (Sonc. ed.) 63a n. 3.

b (1) V. Glos. (2) If the priest takes the fistful of the meal-offering for burning on the altar while expressing the intention of eating as much as an olive after time and as much as an olive without bounds. There is the same controversy in Men. 12a between R. Judah and the Sages as here. (3) As the priest took one step while carrying the fistful to the altar he declared his intention of partaking of the offering without bounds, and as he took another step, his intention of partaking thereof after time. Hence here also we have two separate statements. (4) From Palestine to Babylon.

אין רישא בשתי עבודות סיפא בין בעבודה אחת בין בשתי עבודות: תנן אמר רבי יהודה זה הכלל אם מחשבת הזמן קדמה למחשבת המקום פיגול וחייבין עליו כרת בשלמא לרבי יוחנן היינו דקתני זה הכלל א] אלא לאילפא מאי זה הכלל קשיא: *תנן התם הרי זו תמורת עולה תמורת שלמים הרי זו תמורת עולה דברי רבי מאיר אמר רבי יוסי *אם לכך נתכוון תחילה הואיל ואי אפשר להוציא שתי שמות כאחת דבריו קיימין ואם משאמר הרי זו תמורת עולה (א) ב] ונמלך ואמר הרי זו תמורת שלמים הרי זו עולה איבעיא להו הרי זו ג] תמורת עולה ושלמים מהו ד] לחצות מהו אמר אביי בהא ודאי מודה רבי מאיר רבא אמר עדיין היא מחלוקת אמר ה] רבא לאביי לדידך דאמרת בהא ודאי מודה רבי מאיר ו] הרי שחיטה דלכי לחצות דמי ופליגי אמר ליה *מי סברת אינה לשחיטה אלא לבסוף ישנה לשחיטה מתחילה ועד סוף ומשנתינו דאמר סימן ראשון חוץ לזמנו סימן שני חוץ למקומו הרי קמיצה ז] דלכי לחצות דמי *ופליגי ח] התם נמי ט] שהקטיר קומץ מנחה חוץ לזמנו י] *קומץ לבונה חוץ למקומו הרי קומץ דמנחת חוטא דליכא לבונה בהדיה ופליגי לא פליגי אמר רב *אשי אם תימצי לומר פליגי פליגי בפסיעות רב שימי בר אשי מתני כדאביי רב הונא בר נתן מתני כדרבא כי אתא רב דימי אמר רבי מאיר בשיטת רבי יהודה אמרה דאמר תפוס לשון ראשון דתנן אמר רבי יהודה זה הכלל אם מחשבת הזמן קדמה את מחשבת המקום פיגול וחייבין עליו כרת אמר

רש"י

אין רישא בשתי עבודות · דהא מפרש בהדיא סיפא איכא לאוקמא בתרווייהו פליגי : היינו דקתני זה הכלל · לאיתויי עבודה אחת : תנן התם · במסכת תמורה : הרי זו תמורת עולה תמורת שלמים · שהעמיד בהמת חולין אצל שתים אחת עולה ואחת שלמים ואמר הרי זו תמורת עולה תמורת שלמים הרי זו תמורת עולה תפוס לשון ראשון ואין קדושה חלה על קדושה : הואיל ואי אפשר לקרות שתי שמות כאחת · והולכך להקדיש זה אחר זה : דבריו קיימין · ותרעה יא] ותימכר ויביא בדמי חציה עולה ובדמי חציה שלמים וכן מפרש בתמורה : ה"ג איבעיא להו הרי זו תמורת עולה ושלמים מהו · מי אמרי' הא דפליג ר' מאיר ואמר תפוס לשון ראשון משום דאמר יב] תמורת תמורת תרי זימני והוה ליה כנמלך אבל הכא דאמר תמורת עולה ושלמים חד דיבורא הוא ותרווייהו חיילי או דלמא תפוס לשון ראשון לעולם ופשטה קדושת עולה בכולה ותו לא אתו שלמים וחיילי : לחצות מהו · את"ל יג] פשטה קדושת עולה בכולה אמר הרי יד] (זו) בהמה זו לחצות לעולה ושלמים מאי הא' טו] חד דיבורא הוא ואין זה חל בלא זה או דלמא כיון דפשטה פלגא פשטה בכולה ולא אתו שלמים וחיילי : והרי שחיטה · דקתני מתני' לאכול כזית למחר כזית בחוץ : דכי לחצות דמי · דלאו מיהדר אימלוכי טז] שהרי כמה זיתים יש בהו חד דיבורא הוא ופליגי וקא"ר יהודה תפוס לשון ראשון ור' מאיר דתמורה בשיטת רבי יהודה דמתניתין קאי דאמרינן בשמעתין ר"מ בשיטת רבי יהודה אמרה : אמר ליה מי סברת אינה לשחיטה אלא לבסוף · יז] דלהוי הך תרתי מחשבות (ב) בסוף שחיטה יח] וחד דיבורא הוא ואפי' הכי נימא ר' יהודה תפוס לשון ראשון : ישנה לשחיטה מתחילה ועד סוף · וכי היכי דמהניא מחשבה בסוף יט] מהניא בתחילתה ומתוקמא מתני' כגון דאמר כ] שחיטת סימן ראשון חוץ לזמנו ובשחיטת סימן שני חוץ למקומו ואית ליה לרבי יהודה מפגלים בחצי מתיר דהיינו חד סימן ותרי דבורי נינהו ואיפגל ליה מדבורא קדמאה אבל לחצות לחד דבור הוא מודי כא] (ומהכא שמעינן דרבא אליבא דר"מ סבירא ליה אינה לשחיטה אלא בסוף מדליף עדיין היא מחלוקת *ממתני' והיינו דאמר בתמיד נשחט (פסחים דף סג·) נימא קסברי אחרים אין לשחיטה אלא לבסוף וכדרבא דאמר רבא עדיין היא מחלוקת (ג) ממתני' דתמורת עולה ושלמים כלחצות דאחרים היינו רבי מאיר ורבא מוקי דלרבי מאיר אינה לשחיטה אלא לבסוף) : הרי קמיצה · דפליגי רבי יהודה ורבנן בה בפרק קמא דמנחות (דף יב·) כי מחשב לאכול כזית למחר כזית בחוץ כו' : דכי לחצות דמי · דחד דיבורא הוא וזיתים הרבה יש ולאו מיהדר אימלוכי הוא והכא ליכא לפלוגי בהרי דבורי כדפלגא בשחיטה בב' סימנין : דאמר קומץ כב] מנחה כו' · שהמנחה יש לה שני מתירין הקומץ והלבונה וכי פליגי רבי יהודה ורבנן לאו בקמיצה פליגי דאין קמיצה בלבונה אלא בהקטרה פליגי כג] שהיא עבודה בכל אחת ואחת וכגון שהקטיר קומץ כד] מנחה על מנת לאכול כזית למחר *וקומץ כה] לבונה על מנת לאכול כזית בחוץ ואית ליה לרבי יהודה מפגלין בחצי מתיר וכיון כו] דהיינו תרי דבורי נינהו מקמא איפגלא לה אבל בקמיצה דחד מתיר הוא לא פליג רבי יהודה : מנחת חוטא · מטמא מקדש או שמיעת הקול מביא מנחה בדלי דלות דכתיב לא יתן עליה לבונה (ויקרא ה) : פליגי בפסיעות · ובמחשבת הולכה דאמר בפסיעה ראשונה חוץ לזמנו ובפסיעה שניה אמר חוץ למקומו דהוו להו תרי דבורי : מתני כדאביי · תני מתנייתא כדאביי דבלחצות מודי רבי מאיר : מתני כדרבא · תני מתנייתא כדרבא דבלחצות נמי פליג רבי מאיר :

תוספות

אמר רבי יוסי אם לכך נתכוון מתחילה · פרק מרובה (ב"ק דף עג:) אמרינן תרי תוך כדי דיבור הוו חד כדי שאילת רב לתלמיד דזוטר וחד כדי שאילת תלמיד לרב דנפיש ותוך כדי דיבור קטן מודה רבי יוסי דמועיל דיבורו והכי קאמר אם אמר תמורת שלמים בתוך כדי דיבור קטן של תמורת עולה דהשתא דומה כט] דנתכוון מתחילה לכך ואפי' עומד וצוח שלא נתכוון הואיל ואי אפשר · להוציא שתי שמות כאחת דבריו קיימין ונמלך קרי ליה תוך כדי דיבור גדול כשאמרו לאחר כדי דיבור קטן שדומה לנמלך ואפי' אומר שנתכוון מתחלה לשניהם לא אמר כלום : דבריו קיימים · וא"ת והא אמרינן בפ"ב דקדושין (דף נ:) ובעירובין פרק מי שהוציאוהו (דף נ·) כח] ובפ' נערה המאורסה (נדרים סט:) כל שאינו בזה אחר זה כט] בבת אחת אינו וי"ל דכיון *דמשכחת בזה אחר זה כגון דאמר חציה לדמי עולה וחציה לדמי שלמים ואפילו בקדושת הגוף משכחת לה כגון בבהמה של שני שותפין ועוד דכל שאינו בזה אחר זה בבת אחת אינו מיירי בדבר שאי אתה יכול לקיים את שניהם שסותרים זה את זה כגון מקדש אשה ובתה דהי מינייהו מפקת וכן קיים ליכי ומופר ליכי דנדרים וכן ארבע אמות דעירובין (דף מח:) אבל הכא מקיימי תרווייהו וכן בפרק השולח בגיטין (דף מב·) הכותב כל נכסיו לשני עבדיו קנו ומשחררין זה את זה ולא אמרינן כל שאינו בזה אחר זה אפי' בבת אחת אינו משום דהתם בזה אחר זה א"א לקיים את שניהם דבזה אחר זה קמא קני נפשיה וקני חבריה ובתרא לא קני כלל אבל בבת אחת אפשר לקיים את שניהם ואמרי' קנו ומשחררין זה את זה והא דאמרינן בפ"ק דקדושין (דף ז:) חלייך בחצי פרוטה וחלייך בחצי פרוטה דאינה מקודשת וקמבעיא ליה שני חלייך בפרוטה מהו לא שייך למימר תפשוט מדרבה דאמר כל שאינו בזה אחר זה אפי' בבת אחת אינו דכל שאינו בזה אחר זה מיירי בדבר שאין השני יכול לחול מחמת שחל הראשון תחלה כגון שתי אחיות ושתי תרומות ושתי מעשרות הלכך בבת אחת אינו משום דהי מינייהו ל] מפקת אבל גבי קדושין בזה אחר זה אינו לא זה ולא זה אבל בבת אחת תפסי תרווייהו והא דאמר בסוף פ"ק דמנחות (דף יא·) היכי דמי ריבה שמנה כגון שהפריש לה שני לוגין ומשמע קצת מתוך הסוגיא שיש בהן קדושת הגוף וגבי חסר לבונתה לא] דדייק התם הא יתר כשרה [והתניא יתר פסולה] ומפרשי שם כגון שהפריש לה שני קמצים ואכשרה קאי לב] כדפרישית התם והשתא היכי קדשי הא אמרי' כל שאינו בזה אחר זה בבת אחת אינו ונראה לפרש כגון דאמר יקדש קומץ אחד מתוך שני קמצים כדאמר בפרק התודה (שם עח:) ובפ"ב דקדושין (דף נא·) גבי תודה שנשחטה על שמונים חלות הכל מודים היכא דאמר ליקדשו מ' מתוך שמונים דקדשי: לחצות מהו · פי' בקונט' דאמר הרי בהמה זו לחצותה לעולה לג] ושלמים ואין זה דומה לחציה עולה וחציה שלמים דפליגי בהדיא לד] א) בתמורה (דף כו·) ובפרק כיצד מערימין (דף נט) אבל בפ' תמיד נשחט (פסחים סג·) לא דקדק בקונטרס שהביא הך דשמעתין ופי' לחצות כגון דאמר חציה תמורת עולה וחציה תמורת שלמים ור"ח מפרש לחצות כגון דאמר לחצי היום תיהוי עולה ושלמים א"כ עולה ושלמים תהוי לחצי ב) היום : אמר אביי בהא ודאי מודה ר"מ · ופריך והרי שחיטה דכי לחצות דמי דכיון דאינה לשחיטה אלא לבסוף לה] ג) היכי הוציא שני הדיבורים קודם שיהא סוף שחיטה ד) והוי כאילו אמר לו] לבסוף שחיטה יהא כזית חוץ לזמנו וכזית חוצה) למקומו לז]: [סימן ראשון חוץ לזמנו·] ודווקא סימן אחד דהוי דבר המסויים ומפגלין בחצי מתיר אבל אם אמר מקצת ראשון · חוץ לזמנו ומקצת שני חוץ למקומו לא הוי פיגול אע"ג דמפגלין בחצי מתיר כיון דלא הוי דבר המסוים ולא דמי לפסיעות וא"ת דמשמע הכא דרבא סבירא ליה אינה לשחיטה אלא לבסוף והיינו כריש לקיש דפרק שני דחולין (דף כט:) ושמעינן ליה לרבא בפרק החולץ (יבמות לו·) דבכולי הש"ס הלכתא כרבי יוחנן לגבי ר"ל בר מתלת ויש לומר דשאני לח] הכא מדקאמר לה ר"ל משמיה דלוי סבא ויש לתמוה רבא דפריך ליה לאביי וס"ד דס"ל אינה לשחיטה אלא לבסוף תיקשי ליה לט] מתני' דהקדים מולים לערלים כשר ערלים למולים פסול הרי בסוף שחיטה חל דיבור ראשון ולא שני דאי הוו חיילי תרווייהו הא קיימא לן דמקצת ערלה לא פסלה : והרי קמיצה דכי לחצות דמי ופליגי · תימה דלא פריך ממליקה דחטאת העוף דפליגי מ] דחטאת העוף הכשירו בסימן אחד וליכא שני מתירין ויש לומר דאיכא שני מתירין כגון מפרקת וסימן אחד :

א) [נ"ל בתמורה בפרק כילד מערימין כי הוא פרק שם] ב) היום אמר אביי כו' הד"א נ"ק ג) נ"א וכי הוליא ד) נ"א הוי כאילו נ"ק ה) למקומו ומשני ישנה לשחיטה מתחלה ועד סוף ודאמר סימן ראשון כו' והוזקא סימן שלם דהוי דבר כו' והד"א כצ"ל נ"ק

עין משפט נר מצוה

קכד א מיי' פ"ד מהל' תמורה הלכה ד:

כ"א דמשכחת להלאן כגון דאמר כו' נ"ק וכ"ה סגירסא הכרא"ש המס' נדרים דף סט ע"ב ע"ש

מסורת הש"ס

ב"ק עג: תמורה כה: נדרים סט:

פסחים סג. חולין כט: וש"נ

מנחות יב.

נ"א קורס

נ"א אמי

ר"א וקורט

הגהות הב"ח

(א) גמ' ואם משאמר הרי זו תמורת עולה ונמלך: (ב) רש"י ד"ה אמר ליה מי וכו' תרתי מחשבות כל חד בסוף שחיטה וחד: (ג) ד"ה ישנה וכו' במתניתין דתמורה:

גי' בכ"ק בתמורת עולה ושלמים כו' להלות ממתני' כו' עדיין היא מחלוקת ואחרים היינו כו' וכ' בס'

שיטה מקובצת

א] אלא לאילפא מאי זה הכלל · דליכא למימר דנקים ליה לכלל משום עבודה כעין שתי עבודות כיון דאינו מראה טעם חדש אבל לר"י ניחא דמראה לנו טעם חדש דאמרי' תפוס לשון ראשון ובעבודה אחת נמי וא"כ הכלל דקאמר ר"י בכל ענין הוא אמת דהיכא דמחשבת הזמן קדמה הוי פיגול משום דתפוס לשון ראשון אבל לאילפא לא הוי כלל היכי דהוי עירוב מחשבות אפילו קדמה מחשבת הזמן וא"כ מאי זה הכלל : ב] נמלך ואמר : ג] עי' בהשמטות בסוף המסכת : ד] לחצות מהו פי' הקונטרס כו' עד לכך פי' ר"ח דה"ק לחצות היום תהיה בהמה זו עולה והציה תמורת שלמים מהו · פי' מי אמרינן דדוקא כי אמר תמורת עולה ושלמים לחלות הקדושה א"כ דעתו שיחול מיד הקדושה מיד שהוציא הדבור וא"כ כיון שהקדיש עולה פשטה עליה [קדושת עולה] בכולה אבל כי אמר לחצות היום (יחצו) [יחולו] שניהם אפי' כי אמר שלמים מ"מ אין דעתו שתחול הקדושה [אלא] עד אותה שעה ממש וא"כ אין לאחת הקדמה להברתה שלות הקדושה עליה כבר יצא הדבור מפיו גם דבור שני דשלמים וא"כ תרוייהו חיילי נכתב בגליון על דברי התוספות כד"ה לחצות ·

ברגע אחד ולא שייך כאן טעמא דתפוס לשון ראשון או דלמא מ"מ איכא למימר שדעתו היה שיחולו הקדושה כדרך סדר דבורו וע"כ שייך כמו כן תפוס לשון ראשון · מהר"פ ז"ל : ה] אמר ליה רבא : ו] עיין בהשמטות בסוף המסכת: ז] קמיצה דכי : ח] התם נמי כגון דאמר קומץ דמנחה כו' · פ"ה בשעה שהקטיר קומץ [מנחה ע"מ לאכול כזית למחר וקומץ] הלבונה אמר חוץ למקומו ולא מיירי בקמיצה כי אם בהקטרה דיש שני מתירין קומץ ולבונה ולא מצי לשנויי גבי מנחת חוטא כגון שהקטיר חצי קומץ חוץ לזמנו וחצי קומץ חוץ למקומו דכיון דלא הוי מסויים לא מהני אפילו למ"ד מפגלין בחצי מתיר וא"ת מ"ש מחטאת העוף (משום) דאין בו אלא סימן אחד אמרינן דשייך ביה תפוס לשון ראשון למ"ד מפגלין בחצי מתיר וי"ל דכיון (דרוב בני אדם חולקין) [דחולקין] עמו המפרקת הוי ליה כשני סימנים · מהר"פ ז"ל : ט] תיבת שהקטיר נמחק: י] וקומץ דלבונה: יא] ותרעה עד שיסתאב ותימכר : יב] תמורה תמורה תרי : יג] את"ל בתמורת עולה ושלמים פשטה : יד] הרי בהמה זו לחצותה לעולה ולשלמים: טו] האי ודאי חד : טז] אימלוכי הוא שהרי : יז] דניהוי הנך תרתי : יח] שחיטה יחד וחד : יט] בסוף שחיטה מהניא : כ] דאמר בשחיטת סימן : כא] מתיבת ומהכא עד תיבות הרי קמיצה נמחק : כב] קומץ דמנחה : כג] שהיא · ס"א שנוהגת בשניהם וכגון שהקטיר: כד] קומץ המנחה : כה] וקומץ הלבונה : כו] דהני תרי: כז] דומה לנתכוון: כח] ובנדרים פ' נערה: כט] זה אפילו בב"א אינו וי"ל דהכא משכחת' ותיבת דכיון ואות ד' נמחק : ל] מינייהו מייתת והי מינייהו מפקת : לא] לבונתה נמי דייק התם : לב] קאי כדמוכח התם ותיבת כדפרישית נמחק : לג] לעולה ולשלמים : לד] בתמורה בפרק כיצד מערימים דהתם שמא מתחלה לא היה דעתו אלא לעולה אבל הכא כיון דאמר בלשון (זה) לחצות ודאי לתרוייהו איכוין מידו אם כן צריך להגיה הספרים לחצותה ובכל הספרים גרסינן לחצות ור"ח כו' · לשון הר"פ ז"ל : לה] לבסוף הרי הוציא תיבת היכי נמחק : לו] אמר לסוף אות ב' נמחק : לז] למקומו דדמי להצות היום ומסיק ישנה לשחיטה מתחלה ועד סוף ומיירי דאמר שתהא סימן ראשון כו' והד"א : לח] התם תיבת הכא נמחק : לט] ליה דמתני' בפרק תמיד נשחט דהקדים : מ] דפליגי וחטאת כו' אות ד' נמחק :

והא

אמר ליה אביי והא א] רבה בר בר חנה א"ר יוחנן כי מגעת להו ב] רבי מאיר ורבי יוסי בהדי הדדי לא פליגי ולא פליגי והא מיפלג פליגי א"ל פליגי במאי דפליגי ולא פליגי במאי דלא פליגי דאמר *רבי יצחק בר יוסף א"ר יוחנן הכל מודים היכא דאמר תחול זו ואחר כך (אמר) תחול זו דברי הכל לא חיילא לא תחול זו אלא א"כ חלה זו דברי הכל חיילא כי פליגי דאמר תמורת עולה תמורת שלמים רבי מאיר סבר ג] מדהוה ליה למימר תמורת עולה ושלמים ואמר תמורת עולה תמורת שלמים שמע מינה מיהדר קא הדר ביה ד] ור' יוסי אי אמר תמורת עולה ושלמים הוה אמינא פלגא תמורת עולה ופלגא תמורת שלמים להכי אמר תמורת עולה תמורת שלמים למימרא דכולה עולה וכולה שלמים הויא אמר ליה הוא אמר לא פליגי ואנא אמינא פליגי אמר עולא ואיתימא רב אושעיא *אפשר ידעין חברין בבלאה כזית כזית תנן או כזית וכזית תנן כזית כזית תנן אבל כזית וכזית דברי הכל עירוב מחשבות הוי או דלמא *כזית וכזית תנן דלרבי יהודה פרטא הוי וכל שכן כזית כזית תא שמע דבעא מיניה לוי מרבי חישב ה] לאכול כזית למחר בחוץ מהו א"ל *זו שאילה עירוב מחשבות הוי אמר לפניו רבי שמעון ברבי לא משנתינו היא לאכול כזית בחוץ כזית למחר כזית למחר כזית בחוץ כחצי זית בחוץ כחצי זית למחר כחצי זית למחר כחצי זית בחוץ פסול ואין בו כרת הא אידך עירוב מחשבות הוי א"ל הוא ו] שאל בי דבר חכמה ואת אמרת משנתינו לדידך דאתניתך תרתי לא קשיא לך לדידיה דלא אתניתיה אלא חדא ושמעינהו לרבנן דקא גרסי תרתי ז] וסבר דידי דווקא ודידהו עירוב מחשבות הוי או דלמא דידהו דווקא ולדידי שיורי שייר לי ומדשייר לי לדידי הא שייר להו לדידהו נמי בהך והי אתנייה אילימא כזית ח] וכזית אתנייה האי לאו שיורא הוא אלא כזית כזית אתנייה ותיבעי ליה כזית וכזית סבר *איבעי מיניה חדא דשמענא תרתי דאי בעינא כזית וכזית הא ניחא אי אמר לי כללא כ"ש כזית למחר בחוץ אלא אי אמר לי פרטא אכתי כזית למחר בחוץ קא מיבעיא לי אי הכי השתא נמי התינח אי אמר ליה כזית למחר בחוץ פרטא כ"ש כזית וכזית אלא אי א"ל כללא אכתי כזית וכזית מיבעי ליה ט] אם כן מרתח רתח השתא

אמר ליה אביי והאמר רבה בר בר חנה כו' · כו] לתרווייהו לית להו תפוס לשון ראשון כדמפרש לקמן והלכך רבי מאיר דתמורה בשחיטה לא כרבי יהודה סבירא ליה כז] דשחיטה הויא כמו לחלות דאמר אביי דמודה רבי מאיר ולא כרבי יהודה ותימה דמאי מקשי ליה רבה לאביי לעיל והרי שחיטה דכי לחלות דמי ופליגי הלא ר' יהודה ודאי הוא דאית ליה תפוס לשון ראשון אבל רבי מאיר לא דלית ליה לאביי רבי מאיר בשיטת רבי יהודה אלא מדאמר *תמורה כו' שמע מינה מהדר קהדר ביה ואפילו אמר מתחלה נתכוונתי לומר שניהם לא מהימנינן ליה : כזית כזית תנן אבל כזית וכזית דברי הכל עירוב מחשבות הוי · מכאן הגי"ה רבינו תם הספרים דגרסינן בשבועות בסוף שבועת הפקדון (דף לח·) דלא לך לא לך איט חייב אלא אחת דכללא הוי ואיט לא לך ולא לך חייב על כל אחת ואחת דהוי פרטא והכא משמע איפכא דטפי הוי עירוב מחשבות כזית וכזית מכזית כזית וכן משמע התם בירושלמי דמדמי שאילת שלום בגט ללא לך ולא לך וגבי שאילת שלום אמרינן בגיטין (דף פז·) שאילו פסול ושאילו כשר · ברוך : *קשה לי מלמחר בחוץ דאמר רבי מודה רבי יהודה בעירוב מחשבות והייט כמו לחלות ולעיל דאמר רבה כח] דלחלות פליגי ומייתי ראיה לאביי משחיטה דרבי יהודה ומאי ראיה הא רבי יהודה מודה ועוד דסבר רבא אינה לשחיטה אלא לבסוף וכיון דאין המחשבה חלה עד משהו אחרון כך שוה כזית למחר כזית בחוץ כמו כזית למחר כט]וכזית בחוץ ופליגי לרבא ועוד תמורת עולה ושלמים דפליגי לרבא · ברו"ך : א"כ מרתח רתח · שלא היה לו להניח כזית וכזית ולשאל מכזית למחר בחוץ דמשמע דמדשבקיה דפשיטא ליה דפרטא הוא:

ויקן

כי מגעת להו · אם תרצה לקרב את דבריהם קרובים הם להיות שוים דתרווייהו לית להו תפוס לשון ראשון כדמפרש לקמיה והלכך אפילו רבי מאיר דתמורה בשחיטה לא סבר לה כר' יהודה : ול"פ · בתמיה : והא שמעי' להו דפליגי ואמר ליה פליגי במאי דפליגי· כדמפרש ואזיל: ול"פ במאי דלא פליגי · והאי ל"פ דקאמר הכי קאמר ל"פ בתפוס לשון ראשון י] אלא בדעתיה דגברא בהוכחת דיבורו על מחשבתו אבל תרווייהו אית להו דבתר כוונתו אזלינן : הכל מודים היכא דאמר תחול תמורת עולה ואח"כ תחול תמורת שלמים דברי הכל לא חיילא·דאין קדושה חלה על(א)קדושה: חיילא · הואיל ונתכוון לכך ותרעה ויהא דמי חציה עולה ודמי חציה שלמים : מיהדר קהדר ביה · ולחזור אי אפשר יא] : ורבי יוסי · אמר לך האי גברא לא מיהדר קהדר אלא לכך נתכוון וסבר אי אמינא יב] (תורת) תמורת עולה ושלמים משתמע פלגא עולה פלגא שלמים וקדושה ואינה קריבה דאי אפשר להקריב לחצאין אימא תמורת עולה תמורת שלמים כי היכי דתפשוט קדושת עולה בכולה וקדושת שלמים בכולה וטעי דסבר השתא קרבה הלכך לתרווייהו איכוין ודבריו קיימין ותימכר : ה"ג להכי אמר תמורת עולה תמורת שלמים למימרא דכולה עולה כולה שלמים · וכ"ך קבלת"י בתמור"ה שמעינן מיהא מדרבה בר בר חנה דהיכא דאמר תמורת עולה ושלמים מודה רבי מאיר אלמא לאו כרבי יהודה סבירא ליה דמתני' להא דמיא דלכך נתכוון תחלה והא דאמר כזית כזית תרי זימני משום דבעא למיחשב בשני זיתים ועל כרחך לאו מיהדר הוא דכמה זתים יש בה: אמר ליה· רב דימי לאביי ומדרבה בר בר חנה מותבת לי איהו אמר לא פליגי ואנא אמינא פליגי אף באומר תמורת עולה ושלמים שנתכוון לשניהם אית ליה לרבי מאיר תפוס לשון ראשון כר' יהודה : כזית כזית תנן · דלרבי יהודה הוי פרטא וכשתי מחשבות ניהו ואפילו בעבודה אחת ותפוס לשון ראשון אבל כזית וכזית דחד דבורא הוא עירוב מחשבות ואיט פגול : ת"ש · דכזית וכזית תנן וכ"ש כזית כזית: דבעא מיניה לוי מרבי כזית למחר בחוץ · חישב על זית יג] לאכלו למחר חוץ למקומו לר' יהודה מהו מי אמרי' בהא יד]מודי רבי יהודה (ב) והדא מחשבה מעורבת היא דההוא גופיה דקחשיב לאכול למחר טו] חשיב בחוץ וכחדא אכילה או דלמא תפוס לשון ראשון לעולם : זו שאילה · בניחותא שאילה גדולה שאלת : עירוב מחשבות הוי · אפי' לר' יהודה : לא משנתינו היא זו · ואמאי קלסת ליה הא מתניתין היא דעירוב מחשבות הוי מדנקט פלוגתייהו בכזית למחר כזית בחוץ דהוי שתי אכילות בהא הוא דפליג ר' יהודה הא כזית למחר בחוץ דבחדא אכילה טז] קחשיב לאוכלו למחר חוץ למקומו מודי : הוא שאלני דבר חכמה · לפום מאי דאתניתיה : לדידך יז] (ג) הוא דאתניתך במתניתין תרתי · לך יח] שניתים במחלוקותם דבין בכזית כזית בין בכזית וכזית פליגי : לא קשיא לך · דאמרת מדהתנינן הך תרתי ולא תנן הך שמע מינה בהא מודי רבי יהודה : לדידיה דלא אתניתיה אלא חדא : ללוי שלא שניתי לו במחלוקותם אלא אחת מהם ולקמן מפרש דכזית אתנייה : יט] ושמעינהו להו לרבנן · דבי מדרשא אחר הלמידי דקא (ד) גרסינן תרתי כמו ששניתי לך ולא ידע לוי אם מעצמם הוסיפוה או אני שניתיה להם ומשום הכי מספקא ליה הך שלישי דסבר הי דוקא כ] משנתו או משנתיהם : דידי דוקא · דבכזית כזית הוא דפליגי ודידהו דכזית וכזית עירוב מחשבות הוי ולא קבלוה מרבי אלא הם טעו והוסיפוה וכ"ש כזית למחר בחוץ האי עירוב מחשבות או דלמא דידהו דוקא ומפיו שמעוה ולדידי שורי שייר לי ולא שנאה ולעולם אף בה נחלקו ואע"פ שלא היה לי ללומדה כא] מלא ששנה לי: וכי היכי דשייר לי· הך דכזית וכזית שייר להו נמי הך דכזית למחר בחוץ ולא שנאה להם ולעולם אף בה נחלקו הילכך דבר חכמה שאל : והי אתנייה · דלא הוה ליה למילף הך מיניה : אילימא כזית וכזית אתנייה · ולרבי יהודה פרטא הוי האי לאו שיורא הוא דממילא מצי למילף דכל שכן כזית כזית וכיון דלא שייר ליה מידי הוי ליה למשמע דאי בהא דכזית למחר בחוץ נמי איפלוג הוה מתני לה ניהליה ודווקא אתנייה כב] בדהאך הוא דפליגי אבל בהא מודה רבי יהודה : אלא כזית כזית אתנייה · דלא הוה ליה למילף מינה ההיא דכזית *כזית וכי שמעינהו לרבנן דתנו לה איסתפק ליה אי אתנינהו רבי לדידהו ולדידיה שייריה אי לדידיה דווקא אתנייה ואינהו כג] הא דאוספוה : ותיבעי ליה כזית וכזית · האיל ומספקא ליה אי רבי אתנינהו כד] לה אי לא: ה"ג הניחא אי אמר לי כללא כל שכן כזית למחר בחוץ אלא כה] אמר לי פרטא אכתי כזית למחר בחוץ תיבעי לי אי הכי השתא נמי האיתא אי א"ל כזית למחר בחוץ פרטא כל שכן כזית וכזית אלא אי א"ל כללא אכתי כזית וכזית מיבעיא ליה א"כ מירתח רתח השתא כזית וכזית כללא כזית למחר בחוץ מיבעיא : א"כ מירתח קא רתח · כלומר הכי סבר לוי איבעי מיניה הך דאישמע מיניה תרתי דאי אמר לי בה פרטא כ"ש כזית וכזית דתרי אכילות ניהו ואיכא לפלוגינהו בתרי דיבורי ואי אמר לי כללא בניחותא בלא רתיחה אישמע מיניה דהך הוא דהוי כללא אבל כזית וכזית פרטא וכדאתנינהו לרבנן דאם סבירא ליה בכזית וכזית נמי כללא מירתח רתח ומהדר לי בריתחא מאי

ר"ה תמורת עולה תמורת שלמים כו' סס"ד ואח"כ מה"ד ש"ת

[תמורה כו. ע"ש]

[נ"א מתחיל הדיבור עירוב מחשבות הוי קשה לי כו'] נ"ק

[פסחים פט: גיטין פח: חולין מס.]

שבועות לח. קדושין מג.

[לקמן לב: ב"ק קטו.]

[שבועות לט קדושין מג] [חולין נג.]

נ"ל וגדים ע"ק

שיטה מקובצת

א] והא אמר רבה כו': ב] להו לר"מ: ג] מדהוה ליה למימר כו' ואע"ג דתוך כדי דבור יכול לחזור ודאי אי הוי חזר ביה רשאי אבל הכא דנמלך [והוי] כמו דאמר תחול זו ואח"כ תחול זו דלא חיילא · מהר"פ : ד] עיין בהשמטות בסוף המסכת: ה] לאכול כזית למחר בחוץ מהו א"ל [זו שאילה] עירוב מחשבות הוי תימה דכיון (דכזית) [דבחד כזית] קא מחשב הויא ליה כתמורת עולה ותמורת שלמים דאמרי' לעיל תפוס לשון ראשון ובחדא מילתא קא מחשב וי"ל דלא דמי דהתם אי אפשר לקיים שניהם דאין קדושה חלה על קדושה והלכך אמרינן תפוס לשון ראשון אבל למחר בחוץ בידו לעשות איסור זה וכיון דיכול לעשות כן תפסה המחשבה בשניהם והוי עירוב מחשבה · כפ"ה מהר"פ : ו] הוא שאלני דבר ותיבת בי נמחק : ז] תרתי מספקא ליה ואמר דידי ותיבת וסבר נמחק: ח] וכזית אתנייה דלרבי יהודה פרטי הוי כ"ש כזית כזית אלא כו' ותיבות האי לאו שיורא הוא ל"ש : ט] אם כן מירתח קרתח כו' וקשה דמהכא משמע דשייך ריתחא אף כשדעת השואל להחמיר שהיה סבור דכזית וכזית חוי פיגול והוי פרטא וכרת [וקרתח] להורות לו שהוא כללא וליכא חיוב כרת ובפרק אלו טרפות גבי נעקרה הצלע והוליא פ"ה דלא שייך ריתחא אלא כשטעה השואל להקל בהוראה א) ועוד קשה דלבעי סיניה כזית וכזית ואי אמר ליה פרטא ש"מ דכזית למחר בחוץ כללא דאי הוי פרטא א"כ מירתח קא רתח השתא כזית למחר בחוץ פרטא כזית וכזית מבעיא וי"ל דהכא לאו איסור והיתר הוא דלהוי שייך ריתחא להוציא השואל מטעותו אלא קרתח לפי שמעצמו היה לו להבין מדאתנייה במתניתין כזית כזית דהוי פרטא משמע כזית וכזית הוי כללא מדלא אתנייה נמי בהדי כזית כזית וכזית אבל אי בעי מיניה כזית וכזית וא"ל פרטא אכתי כזית למחר בחוץ מספקא דשמא הוי כללא ב) כי למה יכעוס (עמו) [עליו] אם בשביל שלא שנה לו במשנה כזית למחר בחוץ מש"ה משמע דהוי כללא דדוקא כזית כזית הוי פרטא הא כזית למחר בחוץ הוי כללא ועוד הרי אפילו כזית וכזית לא שנה לו שהוא פרטא וכן משמע מתוך פ"ה ולפי מה שפי' הר"ר יהודה מקורביל שם ניחא דמרתח קרתח היכא שמבין מתוך השואל שאין דעתו לשאול לו השאילה שניה הלכך דרך השואלים לשאול תחלה כזית וכזית ואח"כ כזית למחר בחוץ אבל אי הוי שואל מתחלה מכזית למחר בחוץ או יבין שאין בדעתו לשאול כלל מכזית וכזית וטועה הוא בכזית וכזית ולכך אינה שואלה שאם היה דעתו לשאלה שהיה מסופק ממנה היה שואל תחלה ממנה וקא רתח להוציאו מטעותו' מהר"פ: י] ראשון דכולהו לית להו תפוס לשון ראשון אלא: יא] אי אפשר · גליון משום דאין מוציא דבריו לבטלה הלכך הויא תמורת עולה פירוש ולא שלא יוכל לחזור מדבורו הראשון דקא מהדר הדר ביה בתוך כדי דבור אלא כלומר שהוא כנמלך וכמ"ד תחול זו ואח"כ תחול זו ע"כ: יב] תיבת תורת נמחק: יג] זית אחד לאכלו : יד] מודה ר' יהודה דחדא מחשבה: טו] למחר חישב בחוץ : טז] אכילה היא קחשיב לאוכלו : יז] לדידך דאתנייתך ותיבת הוא נמחק : יח] לך ששניתי : יט] ושמעינהו לוי לרבנן ותיבת להו נמחק : כ] דוקא משנתי או משנתם הס"ד : כא] ללומדה מצד ששנה ותיבת מצד נמחק: כב] אתנייה דבהך: כג] ואינהו הוא: כד] אתנינהו ליה: כה] אלא אי אמר : כו] כו' משמע דתרווייהו לית: כז] מתיבת דשחיטה כו' עד תיבת ותימה דמאי כו' בס"א אינו: כח] רבא דבלחצות : כט] תיבת וכזית ל"ש ונמחק :

א) לכאורה נראה דהכא ג"כ קולא לענין תשלום אם אכל בשוגג דאם אינו חייב כרת הוי חולין בעזרה · ב) נראה דנ"ל דשמא הוי ג"כ פרטא כי למה יכעוס עליו דשמא כשבילו כו' משמע ליה דהוי ·

הגהות · הב"ח

(א) רש"י ד"ה הכל וכו' קדושה כס"ד ואח"כ מ"ה ד"ה חיילא : (ב) ד"ה דבעא מיניה וכו' דחדא מחשבה : (ג) ד"ה לדידך דאתניתך כצ"ל ותיבת הוא נמחק : (ד) ד"ה ושמעינהו וכו' דקא גרסי תרתי :

AND INVOLVES KARETH. [30b] Said Abaye to him: Yet surely Rabbah b. Bar Ḥanah said in R. Joḥanan's name: When you bring R. Meir and R. Jose together, [you find that] they do not disagree.[5] But do they not disagree? Surely they do disagree?—They disagree in what they disagree, he answered him, and they do not disagree in what they do not disagree.[6] For R. Isaac b. Joseph said in R. Joḥanan's name: All agree that if he declared 'Let this [sanctity] fall upon the animal and after that let that [sanctity] fall upon it,' [the latter] does not fall upon it.[7] 'Let this [sanctity] not fall upon it unless the other falls upon it [too],' all
a agree that [the latter] does not fall upon it.[1] They disagree only where he declares, '[Let this animal be] a substitute for a burnt-offering, a substitute for a peace-offering.' R. Meir holds: Since he should have said, 'A substitute for a burnt-offering *and* a peace-offering,'[2] but said [instead], 'A substitute for a burnt-offering, a substitute for a peace-offering,' you may infer that he has indeed retracted.[3] And R. Jose?[4]—Had he declared, 'A substitute for a burnt-offering and a peace-offering,' I might have interpreted it, Half as a substitute for a burnt-offering and half as a substitute for a peace-offering;[5] therefore he declared, 'A substitute for a burnt-offering, a substitute for a peace-offering,' to intimate that the *whole* should be a burnt-offering and the whole should be a peace-offering![6]—Said he [R. Dimi] to him [Abaye]: He [Rabbah b. Bar Ḥanah] said that they do not disagree, but I maintain that they do disagree.[7]

'Ulla—others state, R. Oshaia—said: Perhaps our Babylonian colleagues know whether we learnt, 'As much as an olive... as much as an olive'; or did we learn, 'As much as an olive . . . *and* as much as an olive'?[8] [The point of the question is this:] Did we learn, 'As much as an olive . . . as much as an olive,'[9] but [if he declared,] '. . . As much as an olive . . . *and* as much as an olive,'
b all agree that it constitutes a mingling of intentions.[1] Or perhaps we learnt '. . . as much as an olive . . . *and* as much as an olive,' and this, in R. Judah's opinion, constitutes a detailed enumeration,[2] and all the more [if he declared] '. . . as much as an olive . . . as much as an olive?'—Come and hear, for Levi asked Rabbi: What if he intended eating as much as an olive on the morrow [after time] without bounds? Said he to him: That is indeed a question: it constitutes a mingling of intentions.[3] Thereupon R. Simeon b. Rabbi observed, Is this not [taught in] our Mishnah: [IF HE INTENDED] TO EAT AS MUCH AS AN OLIVE WITHOUT, AS MUCH AS AN OLIVE ON THE MORROW; [OR] AS MUCH AS AN OLIVE ON THE MORROW, AS MUCH AS AN OLIVE WITHOUT; [OR] HALF AS MUCH AS AN OLIVE WITHOUT, HALF AS MUCH AS AN OLIVE ON THE MORROW; [OR] HALF AS MUCH AS AN OLIVE ON THE MORROW, HALF AS MUCH AS AN OLIVE WITHOUT: IT IS INVALID, AND DOES NOT INVOLVE KARETH. Hence it follows that the other case[4] constitutes a mingling of intentions.[5] Nevertheless he asked me a profound question, he replied, though you say that it is [implied in] our Mishnah. Since I taught *you* both [cases], you find no difficulty.[6] But him I taught only one,[7] while he heard that the Rabbis read *both* versions [in the Mishnah]. Hence his doubt: was my teaching exact,[8] whereas their [additional case] constitutes a mingling of intentions;[9] or perhaps their [version]
c is exact,[1] whilst I had simply omitted [one case when I taught him], and just as I had omitted this instance, so had they omitted the other instance.[2] Now, which [case] did he teach him? If we say [that] he taught him: '. . . as much as an olive . . . *and* as much as an olive,' [surely] that is not an omission![3] Hence he taught him, 'As much as an olive . . . as much as an olive.'[4] Then let him ask about 'as much as an olive . . . *and* as much as an olive'?[5]—He reasoned: I will ask him one case from which I may infer both. For if I ask about 'as much as an olive . . . *and* as much as an olive,' it is well if he answers me that it is a comprehensive statement,[6] then all the more is it so [in the case of] 'as much as an olive on the morrow without'; but if he answers me that it is a detailed enumeration, then I will still have the question about 'as much as an olive on the morrow without'. If so, [the same objection can be urged] now too: it is well if he answered him that 'as much as an olive on the morrow without' constitutes a detailed enumeration, then all the more is it so in the case of 'as much as an olive and as much as an olive'. But if he answered him that it is a comprehensive statement, he would still have the question: [what about] 'as much as an olive and as much as an olive'?—If so, he [Rabbi] would have shewn asperity:

(5) For, as shewn anon, both reject the view that only the first statement is regarded. That being so, R. Meir's ruling on substitution does *not* agree with R. Judah in our Mishnah. (6) They disagree only in the case cited, where their controversy is explicitly stated. But they do not disagree on the general question whether a man's first statement only is to be regarded, for they both hold that a man's complete intention must be taken into account, the point at issue being what is his intention. (7) If he declared, 'Let the sanctity of this animal, dedicated for a burnt-offering, fall upon this one as its substitute, and then let the sanctity of the other dedicated for a peace-offering fall upon it', it is not seized with the sanctity of the second, for sanctity cannot fall upon an animal which already possesses it.

a (1) Since he obviously intended the animal to assume both sanctities simultaneously. (2) If he intended both. (3) Having declared it a substitute for the one, he retracted and made it a substitute for the other. But retraction is not permitted, and therefore it retains the first sanctity only. (4) Does he not allow this argument? (5) In which case it could not be sacrificed at all. (6) Erroneously thinking that then the animal itself could be offered (presumably, as whichever sacrifice he desired, when he actually came to sacrifice it).—Thus on the present interpretation R. Meir too does not disagree with R. Jose that you cannot regard only a man's first statement, which contradicts R. Dimi. (7) Precisely on the point whether a man's first statement only is to be regarded. (8) In the Mishnah, did the man state, 'I declare my intention to eat as much as an olive without bounds, as much as an olive after time', or, '. . . *and* as much as an olive after time'? (9) R. Judah regards this as two distinct (and to some extent self-contradictory) intentions, since they are not joined by 'and'.

b (1) Hence it is not *piggul*. (2) Each is a separate statement, and there is no mingling of intentions. Hence R. Judah regards the first only. (3) Even in R. Judah's opinion. (4) Viz., where he declares both intentions in respect of the *same* piece. (5) Why praise it then as a question worthy of asking? (6) I taught you both versions, viz., that he declares, 'as much as an olive . . . as much as an olive'; or 'as much . . . *and* as much', etc., and the controversy of R. Judah and the Rabbis applies to both. Hence, since the Mishnah teaches these, and not a twofold declaration in respect of the *same* piece, you rightly deduce that there obviously even R. Judah admits that we have a mingling of intentions. (7) Which one is explained anon. (8) Viz., that the controversy applies to one case only. (9) In my opinion, so that they read this into the Mishnah incorrectly. If so, a twofold declaration in respect of the *same* piece certainly constitutes a mingling of intentions.

c (1) The controversy applies to both. (2) Viz., two declarations in respect of the same piece. Hence he was right to raise the question. (3) For the case of 'as much as an olive . . . *as* much as an olive' follows *a fortiori*. If R. Judah holds that we have a detailed enumeration and no mingling of intentions even when the priest uses the copulative, how much more so when his statements are disjoined. Hence he would have understood that this too is included, but *only* this and no other, so that a twofold declaration in respect of the same piece would *certainly* be a mingling of intentions, and there would be no room for his question. (4) Only on this assumption is there room for his question. This proves that the reading in the Mishnah is 'as much as an olive . . . as much' etc. (5) According to the explanation above he was in doubt about that too. (6) *Sc.* it is a mingling of intentions.

[31a] seeing that 'as much as an olive and as much as an olive' is a comprehensive statement, is there a question about 'as much as an olive on the morrow without'![7]

It was stated: [If one declares, 'I will eat] half [as much as] an olive after time, half an olive without bounds, and half as much as an olive after time,'—Said Raba: 'Then the *piggul* awaked as one a asleep'.[1] But R. Hamnuna maintained: This constitutes a mingling of intentions.[2] Raba said: Whence do I say it?—Because we learnt: If one combines as much as an egg of an edible of first degree with as much as an egg of an edible of second degree, [the combination] ranks as first degree. If one separates them, each ranks as second degree.[3] But if one re-combined them, [the mixture] ranks as first degree. Whence [does this follow]?—Because the second clause teaches: If each falls separately on a loaf of *terumah*, they render it unfit; if they both fall [on it] simultaneously, they render it second degree.[4] But R. Hamnuna argues: There you had the requisite standard;[5] but here the standard is absent.[6]

R. Hamnuna said: Whence do I say it?—Because we learnt: An edible which was defiled by a principal degree of uncleanness, b and [one] which was defiled by a derivative of uncleanness[1] combine with each other to defile according to the lesser of the two.[2] Surely that means even if [the standard quantity] is subsequently made up?[3]—[No:] perhaps [this holds good only] when one does not make up [the standard].

When R. Dimi came, he said: [When one declares his intention of eating] half an olive without bounds and half an olive after time and [another] half an olive after time,—Bar Ḳappara taught: It is *piggul*, [because the declaration in respect of] half an olive is of no effect as against [that in respect of] an olive.[4] When Rabin came, he said: [If one declares his intention of eating] half as much as an olive after time and [another] half an olive after time and half an olive without bounds,—Bar Ḳappara taught: It is *piggul*, [because the declaration in respect of] half an olive is of no effect as against [that of] an olive.[5] R. Ashi recited it thus: [If one declares his intention to eat] half an olive after time, and an olive, half without bounds and half after time,[6]—Bar Ḳappara taught: It is *piggul*, [because the declaration in respect of] half an olive is of no effect as against [that of] an olive.[7]

R. Jannai said: If one intended dogs to eat it on the morrow, it is *piggul*, because it is written, *And the dogs shall eat Jezebel in the* c *portion of Jezreel.*[1] To this R. Ammi demurred: If so, if he intended fire to eat it on the morrow, is that too *piggul*, since it is written, *A fire not blown by man shall* eat [*consume*] *him?*[2] And should you say, That indeed is so,—surely we learnt, [IF HE INTENDED] TO EAT HALF AS MUCH AS AN OLIVE [ILLEGITIMATELY] AND TO BURN HALF AS MUCH AS AN OLIVE [ILLEGITIMATELY], IT IS FIT, BECAUSE EATING AND BURNING DO NOT COMBINE?—If he expressed [his intention] in terms of eating, that indeed would be so;[3] here [in the Mishnah] however he expressed it in terms of burning: [hence they do not combine,] because the term eating is one thing and the term burning is another.

R. Assi[4] asked: What if he intended as much as an olive to be eaten [illegitimately] by two men? Do we go by his intention, and there is the standard [of disqualification]; or do we go by the eaters, and there is not the standard?—Said Abaye, Come and hear: [IF HE INTENDED] TO EAT HALF AS MUCH AS AN OLIVE AND TO BURN HALF AS MUCH AS AN OLIVE [ILLEGITIMATELY], IT IS FIT, BECAUSE EATING AND BURNING DO NOT COMBINE.

(7) I.e., Rabbi would have replied with asperity, 'Why, even the former case is a mingling of intentions; how much more so that which you ask'.

a (1) Cf. Ps. LXXVIII, 65.—The first half, on finding as it were the last half, awakes from its slumber and combines with it. Thus he intends to eat as much as an olive after time; this renders it *piggul* and cannot be undone by the intention of eating *half* as much as an olive without bounds. (2) Hence it is not *piggul*. (3) A man who becomes unclean through contact with a corpse, and a *shereẓ* ('creeping thing') rank as principal (*ab*, lit., 'father') degree of uncleanness, and if a foodstuff comes into contact with them, it becomes unclean in the first degree; if that in turn comes into contact with another foodstuff, the latter is unclean in the second degree. The minimum standard of foodstuffs to defile is as much as an egg. Now, the first combination contains the standard quantity for defilement, and that in the first degree; hence the whole ranks as such. But if one divides the whole, each part contains less than the standard in the first degree; hence each part is second degree. (4) In *ḥullin* (non-sacred food) there is nothing below second degree, so that if second degree food touches *ḥullin*, the latter remains clean. In *terumah* (q.v. Glos.) there is a third degree, but it goes no further, and the *terumah* is then called unfit, but not unclean, since it cannot defile other *terumah*. Now, if each of these separated masses falls on *terumah* consecutively, the *terumah* is disqualified only, since neither mass contains as much of first degree to render it second. But if they both fall on it together, as much as an egg of first degree has touched it at the same moment, and therefore the *terumah* becomes *unclean* in the second degree, so that it can render other *terumah* unfit. This proves that the firsts in each combine, and the same is true here. (5) In the first place there was one mass of the requisite standard; therefore the two masses recombine. (6) There was never the complete standard by itself to render it *piggul*.

b (1) 'Derivative' is another name for first degree. (2) If each contains only half the standard. Thus the combination disqualifies *terumah* (rendering it third), but does not defile it (i.e., it does not render it second). (3) Even if one adds a first degree edible to make up to the size of an egg, yet since the combination is only a second, that portion thereof which is first does not re-awake to combine with the addition. (4) Since the two *piggul* intentions (viz., to eat after time) were consecutive. (5) But only in this case. In the former case, however, when he declares his intention to eat half an olive without bounds and half an olive after time, these two intentions immediately combine, and his subsequent declaration that he will eat half an olive after time cannot upset the previous combination; hence it is not *piggul*. Thus we have a controversy between R. Dimi and Rabin as to Bar Ḳappara's teaching. (6) Thus combining the latter two in his declaration. (7) This goes further than R. Dimi's view. For here he actually combined the latter two intentions, and yet they are separated and the two intentions concerning after time recombined.

c (1) II Kings IX, 10. This proves that eating by dogs is designated eating. (2) Job XX, 26. (3) They would combine. (4) Emended text. Cur. edd: Ashi.

תורה אור

השתא כזית וכזית כללא כזית למחר בחוץ מיבעיא א] (לישנא אחרינא כזית למחר בחוץ פרטא כזית ב] כזית מיבעיא) איתמר חצי זית חוץ לזמנו חצי זית חוץ למקומו וחצי זית חוץ לזמנו אמר רבא א ויקץ כישן הפיגול ורב המנונא אמר עירוב מחשבות הוי אמר רבא מנא אמינא לה דתנן* ב כביצה אוכל ראשון וכביצה אוכל שני שבללן זה בזה ראשון חלקן זה שני וזה שני הא חזר ועירבן ראשון הוי ממאי מדקתני סיפא *ג נפל זה ג] בעצמו וזה בעצמו על ככר של תרומה פסלוה נפלו שניהן כאחת עשאוה שניה ורב המנונא אמר התם איכא שיעורא הכא ליכא שיעורא אמר רב המנונא מנא אמינא לה דתנן *ד האוכל שנטמא באב הטומאה ושנטמא בולד הטומאה מצטרפין זה עם זה לטמא בקל ד] שבשניהם מאי לאו אע"ג דהדר מלייה דלמא דלא הדר מלייה ה] כי אתא רב דימי אמר חצי זית חוץ למקומו וחצי זית חוץ לזמנו וחצי זית חוץ לזמנו תני בר קפרא פיגול אין חצי זית מועיל במקום כזית כי אתא רבין אמר חצי זית חוץ לזמנו וחצי זית חוץ לזמנו וחצי זית חוץ למקומו תני בר קפרא פיגול אין חצי זית מועיל במקום כזית רב אשי מתני הכי ה חצי זית חוץ לזמנו וכזית חציו חוץ למקומו וחציו חוץ לזמנו תני בר קפרא פיגול אין חצי זית מועיל במקום כזית אמר רבי ינאי ו] ו חישב שיאכלוהו כלבים למחר פיגול דכתיב °ואת איזבל יאכלו הכלבים בחלק יזרעאל (מלכים ב ט) מתקיף לה רבי אמי ז] אלא מעתה ז חישב שתאכלהו אש למחר דכתיב °תאכלהו אש לא נופח (איוב כ) ה"נ דפיגול וכי תימא הכי נמי והתנן לאכול כחצי זית ולהקטיר *חצי כזית כשר שאין אכילה והקטרה מצטרפין ח אי דאפקה בלשון אכילה ח] ה"נ הכא במאי עסקינן דאפקה בלשון הקטרה דלשון אכילה לחוד ולשון הקטרה לחוד בעי ט] *רב אשי חישב לאכול כזית בשני בני אדם מהו בתר מחשבה אזלינן י] דאיכא שיעורא או בתר אוכלין אזלינן וליכא שיעורא אמר אביי ת"ש לאכול כחצי זית ולהקטיר כחצי זית כשר שאין אכילה והקטרה מצטרפין

הא

רש"י

מאי תיבעי לך השתא כזית וכזית הוה לך למידק דהוי כללא מדלא אתניתא אלא כזית כזית לפרטא הא כזית וכזית כללא כזית למחר בחוץ מיבעיא לך ובעיין איפשיט דבעינן לעיל כזית כזית תנן או כזית וכזית תנן ש"מ דכזית וכזית תנן ומהכא אמרינן בגמ' דהאומר לחבירו בקדושין (דף מז·) ובגמרא דשבועת הפקדון (שבועות לח·) רבי היא דאמר ל"ש כזית כזית ל"ש כזית וכזית פרטא הוי : לישנא אחרינא יא] [לא] גרסינן : ויקץ כישן (א) פיגול · כיון שמלא חצי יב] זית ראשון חצי זית אחרון שהוא מינו ניעור משנתו ומבטלו *שנצטרף עם יג] חוץ למקומו לפסול ולא לפגל וחוזר מצטרף עם זה לפגל ובטל לו חצי זית דחוץ למקומו מלהוציא מידי פיגול דאין חצי זית מועיל במקום כזית ולא אמרי' כבר נצטרף עם שאצלו לפסול ולא יחזור ויפרד ממנו : עירוב מחשבות הוי · מכיון שנצטרף שוב לא יד] יפרד: ראשון · התערובות הזה תורת ראשון עליו לעשות מגעו שני דהא איכא שיעורא דראשון בגוויה ליתן טומאה: חלקן זה שני וזה שני · שהרי בכל אחד חצי שיעור דראשון וחצי שיעור דשני ותנן לקמן בשמעתא ראשון ושני מצטרפין לטמא בקל שבשניהם: הא חזר ועירבן ראשון · כדמסיים ואזיל מגופא דמתני' אלמא כשחזר ומצא את מינו ניעור מצירוף דשאינו מינו : נפל זה טו] בעצמו וזה בעצמו · כשנסתלק הראשון כנפל חבירו עליה טז] פסלה ולא טימאה ליעשות שניה שכשנפל האחד לא היה בו כביצה ראשון וכשנפל חבירו כבר נסתלק זה : נפלו שניהם כאחד · וה"ה בזה אחר זה אם נפל השני בעוד הראשון עליה שניהם כאחד קרי ליה : עשאוה שניה · אלמא הדרי ומצטרפי ראשון בזה ושבזה : התם איכא שיעורא · מעיקרא יז] שלם הוא ונחלק הלכך כשחזר ועירבו חזר שמו עליו : אבל הכא מעיקרא חצי זית פגול וחצי זית פסול לא נקרא שם פגול עליו כי אם שם פסול הלכך כי הדר אתי חצי יח] [זית] דזמן לא פקע שם פסול למיחל שם פגול : ה"ג האוכל חצי ביצה שנטמא באב הטומאה יט] וחצי ביצה אחרת שנטמא בולד הטומאה מצטרפין כ] זה עם זה לטמא בקל שבשניהם מאי לאו אף על גב דהדר מלייה לא דלא הדר מלייה : לטמא בקל שבשניהם · אם נגע בתרומה פסלה ולא טמאה דליכא כשיעור מן הראשון מאי לאו אפי' חזר והשלים מאוכל ראשון אחר על זה עד שהיה בו כביצה אוכל ראשון כא] דאינו עושה עוד ראשון הואיל ולא היה בו מעולם שיעור קודם שנתערב עם אוכל שני אלמא כי לא הוי ביה שיעורא מעיקרא אין חוזר וניעור וא"ת אי (ב) כב] בלא הוי ביה שיעורא מעיקרא היאך קיבל טומאה מאב הטומאה מתחילתו תשובה לדבריך שהאוכל מקבל טומאה בכל שהוא אבל לטמא אחרים צריך כביצה ובריית' שלימה כג] בת"כ כל אשר בתוכה יטמא מכל האוכל מלמד שמטמא בכל שהוא יכול יטמא אחרים בכל שהוא ת"ל אשר יאכל דהיינו כביצה כדאמרי' בפ"ח דיומא (דף פ·) אוכל הנאכל בבת אחת ושיערו חכמים אין בית הבליעה מחזיק יותר מכביצת תרנגולת : ה"ג בדרב דימי חצי זית חוץ למקומו וחצי זית חוץ לזמנו וחצי זית חוץ לזמנו תנא בר קפרא כו' · דכיון דהוי להו הנך תרי דזמן גבי הדדי מצטרפי ולא אמרינן מכי כד] חשיב אחצי זית דזמן קמא נצטרף עם חצי זית דמקום שקדמו דהא כה] דאמרת (לעיל כט·) יהיה מלמד שמצטרפין (ג) היכא דליכא מינו לצרופי בהדיה : כי אתא רבין אמר · לאו הכי תני בר קפרא דכיון שקדמו חצי זית דמקום אתי חצי זית קמא דזמן ואיצטריף כו] ושוב אין חוזר וניעור אלא הכי תנא חצי זית חוץ לזמנו וחצי זית חוץ לזמנו וחצי זית חוץ למקומו פיגול אין חצי זית דמקום מועיל לבטל זמן דהוי כזית : רב אשי כו' · כרבא סבירא ליה דאמר לעיל ויקץ כישן הפיגול ואפילו אפסקיה במחשבת מקום ועדיפא דרב אשי מדרבא דאשמעינן רבותא כז] אע"ג דאחשבינהו לזמן ומקום בחד דבורא וצירפן בשפתיו לכזית אחד ואפ"ה מצטרף למינו : יאכלו הכלבים · אלמא שמיה אכילה : אלא מעתה חישב · על הבשר כח] לאכול באש הדיוט למחר : הכי נמי דהוי פיגול : וכי תימא הכי נמי והא אנן תנן · דאפי' אש כט] גבוה במידי דחזי לה ואורחה לא מצטרפא אם חישבה עם אכילת אדם ואע"ג דאכילה שמה אלמא לא מדמי אכילות להדדי דכל חדא וחדא למילתיה הוא דהויא אכילה : בתר אוכלין · שניס האוכלין את הזית :

הא

תוספות

ויקץ כישן הפיגול · לא שייך הכא מצא מין את מינו וניעור ל] : עירוב מחשבות הוי · לא] שאין הפסול מניח הפיגול ליפרד מעליו לב] : הא חזר ועירבן ראשון הוי · תימה מה ענין זה אצל זה דגבי קרבן כשאמר חצי זית חוץ למקומו וחצי זית חוץ לזמנו הרי כבר נפסל הקרבן ואינו חוזר ונעשה פיגול אבל חצי ביצה ראשון וחצי ביצה שני שנתערבו דנעשה שני אין הטעם לפי שנתבטל חצי ביצה הראשון אלא משום דאין לו כח לטמאות לג] בפני עצמו הלכך כשיצטרף עמו חצי ביצה ראשון למה לא יהא ראשון : נפלו שניהם כאחד עשאוה שניה · למ"ד יש נוגע חוזר ונוגע : התם איכא שיעורא · פי' בקונט' מעיקרא שיעור שלם הוה ונחלק הלכך כשחזר וערבו שמו חזר עליו אבל הכא מעיקרא חצי זית פיגול וחצי זית פסול לא נקרא שם פיגול עליו כי אם שם פסול הלכך כי הדר אתי חצי זית דזמן לא פקע שם פסול למיחל שם פיגול ולפירוש זה הוה ליה למימר התם הוה ביה שיעורא הכא לא הוה ביה שיעורא ומפרש ר"ת לד] איכא שיעורא שיש מן השני כשיעור לפיכך מניח לו לראשון להפרד מעליו לה] והלך לו להתחבר אצל ראשון אחר הכא ליכא שיעורא מן הפסול ואין מניח לו לפיגול להפרד מעליו : אמר רב המנונא מנא אמינא לה דתנן האוכל שנטמא באב הטומאה · שהיה בו כביצה ושנטמא בולד הטומאה שהיה בו כמו כן כביצה מצטרפין זה עם זה אם יש חצי ביצה מן הראשון וחצי ביצה מן השני מצטרפין לטמא בקל שבשניהם מאי לאו אע"ג דהדר מלייה שלקח מן הראשון ושם עליו אלמא כיון דליכא שיעורא מן השני אין מניח לו לראשון להפרד מעליו לילך לו אצל ראשון חבירו ומשני דלמא דלא הדר מלייה ואין לדמות זה לטומאה שבטלה לו] חזרה וניעורה דהכא לא בטלה והכא טעמא משום דאין לז] להפרד ממנו ולפי' רבינו תם שפירשתי לא צריכא למה שפירש בקונטרס דאוכל מקבל טומאה בכל שהוא והארכתי בפרק המצניע [שבת דף צא· ד"ה אי לענין] : חישב שיאכלוהו כלבים למחר פיגול · בסוף כל הפסולין (לקמן דף לו·) אמרינן דחישב שיאכלוהו טמאים לא הוי פיגול וצריך לפרש טעם אמאי גרע מאכילת כלבים א) : ואת איזבל יאכלו הכלבים · לח] הא פשיטא ליה דשייכא ליה גבי בהמה בדבר הראוי לה כדכתיב תהיה כל תבואתך לאכול אלא מאכילת בשר מייתי ראיה לט] : דכתיב תאכלהו אש לא נופח · תימה דלא מייתי קרא דאם האכל יאכל דבשתי אכילות הכתוב מדבר אחת אכילת אדם ואחת אכילת מזבח (לעיל יג:) וכתיב (ויקרא ו) אשר תאכל האש את העולה וי"ל דאש דגבוה פשיטא ליה דשמה אכילה מ] ובכל מקום אין אכילה והקטרה מצטרפין ב) אבל השתא דאמרת דכל אכילות אש שמה אכילה קשיא ליה אמאי אין מצטרפין : שאין אכילה והקטרה מצטרפין · מרישא הוה מא] מצינא למידק דקתני להקטיר דבר שדרכו להקטיר הא דבר שאין דרכו להקטיר לא אלמא אכילת אש לא שמה אכילה :

הא

א) [לקמן לו: ד"ה שיאכלוהו כו' כתבו הטעם ע"ש] ב) [עיין תוספות מנחות יז: ד"ה דלא שנא וכו' התעוררת רב בסוגיא דהכא]

עין משפט נר מצוה

קכה א מיי' פט"ז מהל' פסה"מ הלכה ד :

קכו ב ג מיי' פ"ד מהל' טומאת אוכלין הלכה יג :

קכז ד מיי' שם הלכה יב :

קכח ה מיי' פט"ז מהל' פסה"מ הלכה ד :

קכט ו ז ח מיי' פי"ד מהלכות פסה"מ הלכה י :

מסורת הש"ס

הש"ק מ"ז וכל"ק מקיימו

כ"א ואינו מצטרף

טהרות פ"א מ"ה

נ"ש שם

נ"ש שם מעילה יז:

בחצי זית נ"ק

נ"נ רב אסי

שיטה מקובצת

א] מתיבת לישנא עד תיבת איתמר לא גריס רש"י : ב] כזית כזית מיבעיא בס"י כזית וכזית מיבעיא : ג] זה לעצמו וזה לעצמו : ד] שבשניהם מאי לאו אע"ג דהדר מלייה' פ"ה לפי שיטתו אפי' כו' אבל קשה לר"ת על הא דפי' דאוכלים מקבלים טומאה בכל שהוא מהא דאמרינן באהלות (פי"ג מ"ה) אלו ממעטין בחלון וחשיב פחות מכביצה אוכלים ואי מקבלים טומאה היאך חוצצין (דקיי"ל) [דהא קיי"ל] דכל דבר המקבל טומאה אינו חוצץ בפני הטומאה ולפי' ניחא דלעולם הוו בו כשיעור מעיקרא [עד] שנטמא באב הטומאה שחלקן ועירבן עד חצי ביצה מ"מ מייתי שפיר א) דכי הדר מלייה שלקח חצי ביצה מן הראשון ושם עם השני דליכא שיעורא כיון דהשני אין מניחו לראשון להפרד ממנו ולילך לו אצל הראשון חבירו ודחי דלא הדר מלייה' לשון הר"פ ז"ל : ה] כי אתא רב דימי כו' · כרב המנונא ס"ל מיהו הכא דהוה תני דדמי גבי אהדדי מצטרפין ולא אמרינן מכי חשיב אחצי זית זמן קמא מצטרף בהדי חצי זית חוץ שקדמו דכתיב יהיה מלמד שמצטרף דה"פ כי ליכא זמן בהדיה לאצטרופי ורבין אמר דלאו להכי תני בר קפרא דגם בענין זה אינו חוזר וניעור דכיון שהפסול נקבע בחצי זית דזמן קמא אלא להכי תני חצי זית חוץ לזמנו [וחצי זית חוץ לזמנו] וחצי זית חוץ למקומו כו' · מהר"פ ז"ל : ו] חישב שיאכלוהו כלבים כו' וא"ת והלא בפ' כל הפסולים כו' וי"ל דשאני טמאים שפוסלים ב) קודם אכילה בנגיעה ואע"פ שיטול חבירו לתוכו בבית הבליעה שלו אין דרך אכילה בכך וריב"א פי' דלקמן אינו בא רק לדחות ראייתו של רבא שהביא לרב חסדא אבל דברי רב חסדא לא נדחו ועוד דשיאכלוהו טמאים אין זה בידו הלכך לא הוי מחשבה והוי כאילו לא אמר כלום אבל אכילת כלבים הויא בידו' מהר"פ ז"ל : ז] אלא מעתה חישב כו' · פ"ה דאף בשל הדיוט היה לו להיות פיגול כו' אבל תימה דגבי מזבח נמי אשכחן אכילה דכתיב בפיגול גופיה ואם האכל כו' עד אין ג) מצטרפין ואפי' כי מפקה להקטרה בלשון אכילה (דהא)[דלא] מקרייא אכילה לפי שאין אכילה לגבוה אלא אכילת אש אבל השתא (כי)[כו' אמאי] אין מצטרפין · דהא גם הקטרה לא פקע ממנה שם אכילת אש כמו בהדיוט ומשני דהיינו [טעמא] לפי שהלשון חלוק דהקטרת אש לא שמה אכילה · מהר"פ ז"ל : ח] הכי נמי · גליון דהוי פיגול ומצטרף הב"ע כלומר מתניתין דאין אכילה והקטרה מצטרף טיירי דאפקה כו' ע"כ : ט] בעי רבא תיבות רב אשי נמחק : י] והא איכא : יא] לא גרסינן : יב] חצי הזית ראשון את חצי הזית אחרון : יג] עם של חוץ : יד] לא יעיר הס"ד : טו] זה לעצמו וזה לעצמו : טז] עליה פסלה ולא טימאוה לעשות אות י' נמחק : יז] מעיקרא שיעור שלם : יח] חצי זית : יט] [ושנטמא בולד] תיבות וחצי ביצה אחרת נמחק : כ] מצטרפין' גליון כלומר וחצי ביצה נגע בולד הטומאה : כא] אוכל ראשון קאמר דאינו נעשה עוד : כב] אי בדלא הוה ביה : כג] שלימה היא בתו"כ : כד] מכי אחשיב : כה] דהא דאמרינן יהיה מלמד שמצטרפין ה"מ היכא דליכא מינו לאצטרופי בהדיה : כו] ואיצטריף בהדיה ושיב : כז] ואע"ג דאחשבינהו : כח] הבשר להאכילה תיבת לאכול נמחק : כט] אש דגבוה במידי כו' לא מצטרפא עם מחשבת אכילת אדם : ל] וניעור דמחשבות הויין : לא] פר"ת שאין : לב] מעליו ממנו הס"ד : לג] לטמאות אחרים : לד] ר"ת התם : לה] מעליו וילך לו : לו] שבטלה וחזרה : לז] דאין מניחו להפרד : לח] הכלבים הא דלא מייתי ראיה מקרא דולבהמתך ולחיה אשר בארצך תהיה כל תבואתה לאכול דהא פשיטא ליה דשייכא אכילה גבי בהמה : לט] ראיה דסד"א דגבי כלבים לאו אכילה היא : מ] אכילה ומכל מקום : מא] הוה מצי למידק :

הא

א) נראה דצ"ל דמאי לאו אע"ג דהדר מלייה וכו' השני כיון דליכא בשני שיעורא אין מניחו וכו' · ב) וכן תי' התוס' לקמן דף לו ע"ב ד"ה שיאכלוהו · ג) נראה דצ"ל עד אין אכילה והקטרה מצטרפין וכוונתו לדברי התוספות כד"ה דכתיב ·

הגהות הב"ח

(א) רש"י ד"ה ויקץ כישן הפיגול וכו' ומבטלו לצירוף שמצרף וכו' וחוזר ומצרף : (ב) ד"ה לטמא וכו' וא"ת אי דלא וכו' כהוכו : (ג) ד"ה ה"ג וכו' מלמד שמצטרפין היינו דוקא היכא :

א]הא לאכול ולאכול דומיא דלאכול ולהקטיר והיכי דמי בשני בני אדם מצטרף *ש"מ בעי רבא חישב לאכול כזית ביתר מכדי אכילת פרס מהו לאכילת גבוה מדמינן ליה או לאכילת הדיוט מדמינן ליה אמר אביי ת"ש לאכול כחצי זית ולהקטיר כחצי זית כשר שאין אכילה והקטרה מצטרפין טעמא דלאכול ולהקטיר הא לאכול ולאכול ג]מצטרף והא הקטרה ביותר מכדי אכילת פרס הוא דלמא בהיסק גדול: לאכול כחצי זית ולהקטיר כחצי זית כשר ג] : *טעמא דלאכול ולהקטיר הא לאכול ולאכול דבר שאין דרכו לאכול מצטרף הא קתני רישא לאכול ד]את שדרכו לאכול (מצטרף) את שדרכו לאכול אין שאין דרכו לא אמר רבי ירמיה הא מני *רבי אליעזר היא דאמר מחשבין מאכילת אדם לאכילת מזבח ומאכילת מזבח לאכילת אדם *דתנן השוחט את הזבח לאכול דבר שאין דרכו לאכול ולהקטיר דבר שאין דרכו להקטיר כשר ורבי אליעזר פוסל אביי אמר אפי' תימא רבנן ולא תימא הא לאכול ולאכול דבר שאין דרכו לאכול אלא אימא הא לאכול ולאכול דבר שדרכו לאכול מאי קמ"ל אי דבר שדרכו לאכול קמ"ל מרישא ש"מ כחצי זית בחוץ כחצי זית למחר פסול *(הא כחצי זית למחר ה] *פיגול אלא) אי לאכול ולהקטיר מדוקיא דרישא ש"מ לאכול דבר שדרכו לאכול אין שאין דרכו לאכול לא השתא ומה לאכול ולאכול דבר שאין דרכו לאכול לא מצטרף לאכול ולהקטיר מיבעי לאכול ולהקטיר איצטריך ס"ד אמינא התם הוא דלאו כי אורחיה קא מחשב אבל הכא דבהאי כי אורחיה ובהאי כי אורחיה אימא ליצטרף קא משמע לן:

הדרן עלך כל הזבחים שקבלו דמן

כל *יהפסולין ששחטו שחיטתן כשרה שהשחיטה כשרה בזרים ובנשים ובעבדים ובטמאים ואפילו בקדשי קדשים ובלבד שלא יהיו טמאים נוגעין בבשר *דלפיכך הן פוסלין במחשבה וכולן

הא לאכול ולאכול דומיא דלאכול ולהקטיר מצטרף · וא"ת דלמא לעולם לא יד] יצטרף ואתא למידק דלאכול ולאכול בחד גברא מצטרף ואפי' ביתר מכדי אכילת פרס וכן בתר הכי דדייק אביי דלאכול ולאכול ביתר מכדי אכילת פרס מצטרף מדקתני לאכול ולהקטיר דלמא אתא למידק דלאכול ולאכול בשני בנ"א מצטרף ויש לומר דדייק מדתלי טעמא שאין הקטרה ואכילה מצטרפין משום דהאי אכילה והאי הקטרה הא אי חשיבא הקטרה כאכילה הוה מצטרף טו] (אי חשיבא הקטרה) אע"ג דהוי כעין שני בני אדם וביתר מכדי אכילת פרס: **ביתר** מכדי אכילת פרס מהו · וא"ת נוכח מדתנן חצי זית בחוץ חצי זית למחר פסול וי"ל דדלמא בלהקטיר אע"ג דרישא קתני לאכול כזית בחוץ כזית למחר שמא בבא דחצי זית מיירי בלהקטיר דווקא: **ומאי** קמ"ל אי לאכול ולאכול טז] שדרכן לאכול כו' · תימה טובא קמ"ל כדדייק אביי גופיה לעיל לאכול ולאכול בשני בני אדם וביתר מכדי אכילת פרס:

הדרן עלך כל הזבחים שקבלו דמן

כל הפסולין ששחטו: **שהשחיטה** כשרה בנשים · בגמרא מוכח דנשים שוחטות אפי' לכתחילה יז]*הא דתנן ששחטו דיעבד משום דבעי למיתני טמאים דלכתחילה לא ולא קאמר משום דבעי למיתני נשים דקתני ברישא יח] מכן תשובה למה שכתבו בהלכות א"י דנשים לא ישחטו מפני שדעתן קלה ועוד כתוב בהן שחט ולא בירך וערום ששחט שחיטה פסולה ונראה שהם אומרות בעלמא שהיה אומר אותו החכם יט] שכתב הלכות ארץ ישראל: **ובטמאים** · מפרש בגמרא דלכתחילה אין שוחטין שמא יגעו בבשר ואע"ג דדם קדשים איט מכשיר חיבת הקודש מכשרת או כשהעבירה בנהר ועדיין משקה טופח עליה כדאמר בפ"ק דפסחים (דף כ:) וא"ת תיפוק ליה דלמא אתיא לאימשוכי בפנים כ] ואפי' טהור גמור לבן זומא דאמר (יומא ל.) הנכנס למקדש טעון טבילה כא] אין יכול לשחוט בסכין ארוכה דלמא אתי לאמשוכי כב] כדאמר בפ' אמר להם הממונה (שם דף לא.) וי"ל דבטהור שייך למיגזר טפי דלמא אתי לאימשוכי אבל טמא מיזהר זהיר ומידכר ומשום הכי לא נקט נמי שמא יכניס ידו לפנים אע"ג דאיכא איסורא כג] למאן דאמר (לקמן לב:) ביאה במקצת שמה ביאה ומיהו איכא למימר דנקט טעמא דהוי לכולי עלמא והקשה ה"ר אפרים כד] והיאך במוקדשין שוחט דאע"ג דמוקי לה בגמ' בסכין ארוכה איך יתכן שיהא כל כך ארוכה כה] מהר הבית עד עזרת ישראל כדתנן במסכת כלים (פ"א מ"ח) החיל מקודש כו] מהר הבית שאין עובדי כוכבים וטמאי מתים נכנסין לשם עזרת נשים מקודשת כז]הימנה שאין טבול יום נכנס לשם ואפי' כח] אי האי סוגיא בטמא שרץ ומותר ליכנס בחיל מ"מ עזרת נשים ארוכה קל"ה אמה*) והיאך יתכן שתהא סכין ארוכה כל כך כט] וי"ל דהיכא דנטמא בעזרת נשים לא החמירו

*)[מדות פ"ב מ"ב]

הא לאכול ולאכול · לשניס דומיא דלאכול ולהקטיר שאין זית שלם לאוכל אחד מצטרף: ביתר מכדי אכילת פרס · לשהות בין תחילת אכילתו לסופה יותר מכדי אכילת פרס דאיטו גבי כל איסורים שבתורה קיימא לן דלא הויא אכילה הכא מאי: לאכילת גבוה מדמינן לה · דהא איתקוש לענין מחשבה אכילת גבוה ואכילת אדם בהדי הדדי ואכילת גבוה אף ביותר מכדי אכילת פרס היא פעמים שאיט ממהר לשרוף: ה"ג ו] לאסל ולאכול דומיא דלהקטיר מצטרף · והיכי דמי יותר מכדי אכילת פרס לאכול חצי זית ולחזור ולאכול חצי זית ובין זה לזה יותר מכדי אכילת פרס דומיא דהקטרה מצטרף: דלמא · האי להקטיר דקתני בהיסק גדול קאמר ודכוותה דוקא לאכול ולאכול דמצטרף: ה"ג מתני' לאכול כחצי זית כו' טעמא דלאכול ולהקטיר כו' דבר שאין דרכו לאכול כי האי להקטיר דמתני' דקמיירי (הא) באימורים: הא קתני רישא זה הכלל כל השוחט והמקבל לאכול דבר שדרכו לאכול כו' · אלמא מאכילת ז] מזבח לאדם לאו מחשבה היא: הא מני הך סיפא · דאיצטריך למיתני אין אכילה והקטרה מצטרפין רבי אליעזר היא: לאכול דבר שאין דרכו לאכול · ח][דהייט] אימורין וחישב עליו חוץ למקומו או חוץ לזמנו: אלא אימא הא לאכול ולאכול דבר שדרכו לאכול · הכי דוק מיניה אכילה והקטרה אין מצטרפין לפגל ט] הא לאכול ולאכול דבר שדרכו לאכול מצטרף ואע"ג דחשיב לתלאין: ומאי קמ"ל· הך סיפא אי לאו למידק מיניה הא לאכול ולאכול דבר שאין דרכו לאכול דומיא דלהקטיר י] מאי קמשמע לן למה לי למתני אי לאכול ולאכול דבר שדרכו לאכול קא משמע לן כדקאמרת דמחשבת תלאין מצטרפת מרישא שמעת מינה: ואי לאכול ולהקטיר · כלומר ואי היא גופה קא אתא לאשמועינן דאין אכילה והקטרה מצטרפת ולאו לדיוקא דילה אתאי: מדיוקא דרישא שמע מינה · דקתני לאכול דבר שדרכו לאכול הויא מחשבה אבל לאכול דבר שאין דרכו לאכול לא הוי מחשבה ש"מ דאם חישב לאכול חצי זית בשר וחצי זית יא] אימורים לא מצטרפי וכל שכן לאכול חצי זית בשר ולהקטיר חצי זית אימורין דלא מצטרפי יב]: השתא ומה לאכול ולאכול לא מצטרפי · בשר ואימורים לאכול ולהקטיר מיבעיא: יג] התם · כי חישב לאכול אימורים הוא דלא מצטרף בהדי אכילת בשר משום דלאו כי אורחיה קמחשב אבל לאכול בשר ולהקטיר אימורין דבהאי כי אורחיה קמחשב כו' קמ"ל:

הדרן עלך כל הזבחים שקבלו דמן

כל הפסולין ששחטו שחיטתן כשרה · כדיליף בגמ': ובטמאים · בטמא שרץ קאמר שאינו מטמא כלי דלאו אב הטומאה הוא או בטמא מת וכגון שבדק קרומית של קנה ושחט בה אבל בסכין לא שהוא מטמא את הסכין והסכין מטמא את (א) הבשר וכגון דעביד סכין אריכא ושחיט: לפיכך הן פוסלין · את הקרבן במחשבה אם שחטוהו (ב) במחשבה הואיל וראויין לעבודה זו מחשבתן מחשבה וסלן

מצטרפי דהשתא ומה הוא דבור אחד : יג] מבעיא הס"ד ומה"ד לאכול ולהקטיר איצטריך פי' לעולם לגופיה ורבנן היא כדאמרן ואע"ג דמדוקיא שמעינן לה איצטריך סד"א התם כי כו' : יד] לא מצטרף : טו] תיבות או

חשיבה הקטרה נמחק : טז] ולאכול דבר שדרכו לאכול : יז] דמפרש דהוא דתנן : יח] ברישא מכאן תשובה : יט] החכם מדעתו : כ] דאפילו טהור : כא] טבילה איבעיא לן בפרק אמר להם הממונה אי יכול לשחוט בסכין

ארוכה אי לא דלמא : כב] תיבות כדאמר בפרק אמר להם הממונה נמחק : כג] איסורא דאורייתא למאן : כד] אפרים וטמא היאך שוחט במוקדשין דאע"ג : כה] ארוכה מעזרת נשים עד כו' ותיבות מהר הבית נמחק :

כו] מקדש ממנו שאין תיבות מהר הבית נמחק : כז] מקודשת ממנו תיבת חיסנה נמחק : כח] ואפילו הוי האי טמא טבול יום והלא עזרת נשים כו' והשאר נמחק : כט] וי"ל דמיירי בטמא מת שאסור

מן התורה ליכנס במחנה לויה ואפילו מת עצמו כדכתיב ויקח משה את עצמות יוסף עמו ודרשינן עמו במחיצתו וכיון שאינו אסור אלא מדרבנן לא גזור וכ"ש בטומאה שאירעה בפנים דליכא איסור שהייה אי

שמא מיירי בזהתר הבמות · לשון מהר"ם ז"ל :

א) כוונתם לדברי התוס' בד"ה כל ·

אם

עין משפט נר מצוה

קל א ב מיי' פי"ד מהלכות פסה"מ הלכה י :

א ג מיי' פ"א מהלכות פסה"מ הלכה א ופ"ט מהלכות ביאת מקדש הל' ו ופ"ס מהלכות מעה"ק הלכה א :

ב ד מיי' פי"ד מהלכות פסה"מ הלכה ב ·

ג"ק מ"ו

[צ"ל מדקאמר הא דתנן כו']

נ"א נ"ג

נ"א וכחצי זית למחר

שיטה מקובצת

א] הא לאכול ולאכול כו'· א) ואם תאמר כו' וי"ל דסברא הוא כיון שיש לדקדק כל הני רבותות אית ליה דדייקינן כל [מה] דאפשר לדייק דאם לא בא כי אם לדקדק הא ביתר מכדי אכילת פרס מצטרף ליתני לאכול בשני בני אדם דלא מצטרף וכ"ש לאכול ולהקטיר וכן אם לא בא כי אם לדקדק הא בשני בני אדם מצטרף ליתני לאכול באדם אחד ביותר מכדי אכילת פרס דלא מצטרף וכ"ש אכילה והקטרה · מהר"ם ז"ל : ב] ולאכול דומיא דלהקטיר מצטרף והא הקטרה דביותר מכדי : ג] כשר כו' : ד] לאכול דבר שדרכו לאכול דבר שדרכו תיבות את מצטרף נמחק : ה] למחר וכחצי זית למחר פיגול אי תיבת אלא נמחק : ו] ה"ג הא לאכול : ז] מאכילת אדם למזבח ומאכילת מזבח: ח]לאכול אימורין אין דרכו לאכול וחישב ותיבת דהיינו ל"ש ונמחק: ט]לפגל אבל אכילה ואכילה מצטרפין לפגל מתיבת הא עד תיבות ואף על גב ל"ש ונמחק : י] תיבות מאי קמשמע לן נמחק: יא]וזית אימורין למחר לא מצטרפי : יב] דלא

מנחות יב: כל הסוגיא

[לעיל כח.]

לקמן לס. [לעיל כח.]

חולין כג

לעיל טו:

הגהות הב"ח

(א) רש"י ד"ה ובטמאים וכו' את הבשר הס"ד ואח"כ מ"ה ובלבד שלא יהיו טמאים נוגעין בבשר וכגון דעביד סכין : (ב) ד"ה לפיכך וכו' שחטוהו במחשבה חוץ לזמנו וחוץ למקומו הואיל וראויין :

[31b] Hence if he intended to eat [half as much as an olive] and to *eat* [half as much as an olive] in a way similar to [the intention of] eating and burning,—and how is that possible? [that the two half olives] should be eaten by *two* men,—they would combine. This proves it.

Raba asked: What if he intended to eat as much as an olive within more than the time required for eating half [a loaf]?[5] Do we compare this to the eating of the All-High,[6] or do we liken it to human eating?—Said Abaye, Come and hear: [IF HE INTENDED] EATING HALF AS MUCH AS AN OLIVE AND BURNING HALF AS MUCH AS AN OLIVE, IT IS FIT, BECAUSE EATING AND BURNING DO NOT COMBINE. Thus only eating and burning; but eating and eating in a way similar to eating and burning combine, though
a burning requires more than the time for eating half [a loaf]![1]—[No:] perhaps it means in a big fire.[2]

[IF HE INTENDED] TO EAT HALF AS MUCH AS AN OLIVE AND TO BURN HALF AS MUCH AS AN OLIVE IT IS FIT. Thus only to eat and to burn; but [if he intended] to eat [what is fit for eating] and to eat what is not fit for eating[3] they combine. Yet surely the first clause teaches: [IF HE INTENDS] TO EAT WHAT IS NORMALLY EATEN [IT IS UNFIT]. Hence, only what is normally eaten, but not what is not normally eaten?—Said R. Jeremiah, This[4] is in accordance with R. Eliezer, who maintained [that] you can intend [with effect] for the altar's consumption what is meant for human consumption and for human consumption what is meant for the altar's consumption. For we learnt: If one slaughters the sacrifice [intending] to eat what is not normally eaten or to burn [on the altar] what is not normally burnt, it is fit; but R. Eliezer invalidates [it].[5] Abaye said: You may even say that it is according to the Rabbis; but do not deduce: But [if he intends] to eat [what is fit for eating] and to eat what is not normally eaten [it is fit]; deduce rather: But [if he intends] to eat [what is normally eaten] and to eat what is normally eaten[6] [it is invalid]. [Then] what does [the Tanna] inform us? If he informs us [the law concerning] what is normally eaten,[7] you can infer this from the first clause: [IF HE INTENDS TO EAT] HALF AS MUCH AS AN OLIVE WITHOUT, HALF AS MUCH AS AN OLIVE ON THE MORROW, [HIS INTENTIONS] COMBINE. If [he informs us about intending] to eat and to burn,[8] you can infer this by deduction from the first clause, [viz.,] only [if he intends] to eat what is normally eaten, but not [if he intends to eat] what is not normally eaten. Then seeing that [intentions] to eat [what is normally eaten] and *to eat* what is not normally eaten do not combine, is it necessary [to teach about
b intentions] to eat and to burn [that they do not combine]?[1]—He needs [to teach about intending] to eat and to burn. For you might argue, Only there[2] [do they not combine], because his intention is not normal; but here, where [his intentions in respect of] each are normal,[3] I would say that they combine. Hence he informs us [otherwise].

CHAPTER III

c *MISHNAH.* ALL UNFIT PERSONS[1] WHO SLAUGHTERED, THEIR SLAUGHTERING IS VALID, FOR SLAUGHTERING IS VALID [EVEN WHEN PERFORMED] BY LAY-ISRAELITES [ZARIM], AND BY WOMEN, AND BY SLAVES, AND BY UNCLEAN, EVEN IN THE CASE OF SACRIFICES OF HIGHER SANCTITY, PROVIDED THAT UNCLEAN [PERSONS] DO NOT TOUCH THE FLESH; THEREFORE THEY[2] INVALIDATE [THE SACRIFICE] BY

(5) A loaf is the size of eight (according to Maim. six) eggs, and half a loaf constitutes the average meal. The eating of forbidden food in general is punishable only if as much as an olive thereof, which is the standard for punishment, is eaten in the time of an average meal. (6) *Sc.* the consumption of the *emurim* on the altar. Naturally, this sometimes requires more time than the human standard, and therefore if this comparison is made his intention counts

a (1) Emended text (Rashi). 'Eating and eating' means an intention to eat half as much as an olive and another intention to eat half as much as an olive. (2) Where it will be quickly consumed. (3) For what he would burn (the *emurim*) is not fit for eating. (4) The final clause. (5) V. *supra* 28a for notes. In view of R. Eliezer's opinion it is necessary to state here that intentions in respect of eating and burning (human consumption and the altar's consumption) do not combine. (6) I.e., two intentions in respect of two half standards. (7) Viz., that they combine. (8) That they do not combine. I.e., if the law is taught for its own sake, and not for the sake of a deduction.

b (1) Surely not. (2) When he intends to eat what is normally eaten and to eat what is not normally eaten. (3) He intends to eat what is eaten, and to burn what is burnt, though not in the right time or place.

c (1) As enumerated in the Mishnah *supra* 15b. (2) These unfit persons. (3) V. *supra* 26a for notes.

AN [ILLEGITIMATE] INTENTION. [32a] BUT IF ANY OF THESE RECEIVED THE BLOOD [INTENDING TO EAT THE FLESH OR BURN THE EMURIM] AFTER TIME OR WITHOUT BOUNDS AND LIFE-BLOOD IS [STILL] AVAILABLE, A FIT [PRIEST] MUST RECEIVE [IT] A SECOND TIME. IF A FIT PERSON RECEIVED [THE BLOOD] AND GAVE [IT] TO AN UNFIT ONE, HE MUST RETURN IT TO THE FIT ONE. IF HE RECEIVED [THE BLOOD] IN HIS RIGHT HAND AND TRANSFERRED [IT] TO HIS LEFT, HE MUST RE-TRANSFER IT TO HIS RIGHT. IF HE RECEIVED [IT] IN A SACRED VESSEL AND POURED IT [THENCE] INTO A SECULAR [NON-SACRED] VESSEL, HE MUST RETURN IT TO THE SACRED VESSEL. IF IT SPILT FROM THE VESSEL ON TO THE PAVEMENT AND ONE COLLECTED IT, IT IS FIT. IF [THE PRIEST] APPLIED IT ON THE ASCENT [OR ON THE ALTAR], [BUT] NOT OVER AGAINST ITS BASE; [OR] IF HE APPLIED WHAT SHOULD BE APPLIED BELOW [THE SCARLET LINE] ABOVE [IT], OR WHAT SHOULD BE APPLIED ABOVE, BELOW; OR WHAT SHOULD BE APPLIED WITHIN [HE APPLIED] WITHOUT, OR WHAT SHOULD BE APPLIED WITHOUT, WITHIN[3] AND LIFE-BLOOD IS [STILL] AVAILABLE, A FIT [PRIEST] MUST RECEIVE [BLOOD] ANEW.

GEMARA. 'WHO SLAUGHTERED' [implies] only if done, but
a not at the very outset.[1] But the following contradicts it: *And he shall slaughter:*[2] [this teaches that] slaughtering by a *zar* is valid,[3] for slaughtering by *zarim*, women, slaves, and unclean persons is valid, even in the case of most sacred sacrifices. Yet perhaps that is not so, but rather [it must be done] by priests? You can answer: Whence do you come [to propose this]? From the fact that it is said, *And thou and thy sons with thee shall keep the priesthood in everything that pertaineth to the altar,*[4] you might think that this applies to *shechitah* too. Therefore Scripture states, *And he shall kill the bullock before the Lord; and Aaron's sons, the priests, shall present the blood:*[5] from receiving onwards priesthood is prescribed, which teaches that *shechitah* by any person is valid![6]—The truth is that it [may be performed] even at the very outset too, but because [the Tanna] wishes to include unclean, who may not [slaughter] in the first place lest they touch the flesh,[7] he states, WHO SLAUGHTERED.

Is then [the slaughtering by] an unclean person well if it was done? The following, however, contradicts it: *And he shall lay [his hands upon the head of the burnt-offering . . .] and he shall kill the bullock [before the Lord]:*[8] as 'laying' must be [done] by clean [persons only], so must *shechitah* [be done] by clean [persons only]?—That is [only] a Rabbinical law.[9] Why does 'laying' differ? because it is written, *before the Lord?*[10] Yet surely *'before the Lord'* is written of *shechitah* too?—It is possible to make a long knife and slaughter.[11] But in the case of 'laying' too, he can project his hands [into the
b Temple court] and lay?[1]—He holds that partial entry is designated entry.[2]

R. Ḥisda recited it reversely: *And he shall lay . . . and he shall kill:* as *shechitah* requires clean persons, so 'laying' requires clean persons. Why does *shechitah* differ? because it is written, *'before the Lord'?*

a (1) I.e., if they slaughtered, it is valid; but we do not permit them to slaughter in the first place. (2) Lev. I, 5. (3) Since Scripture does not specify a priest. (4) Num. XVIII, 7. (5) Lev. I, 5. (6) This implies at the very outset. (7) And defile it. (8) Ibid. I, 4 f. (9) By Scriptural law, however, *shechitah* may be done in the first place by unclean persons; hence their *shechitah* is valid, if performed, even by Rabbinical law. The exegesis is therefore to be understood as a mere support to the law, and not as its source. (10) In the text just quoted. Since *shechitah* must be *'before the Lord'* i.e., in the Temple court, 'laying' too must be done there, as *shechitah* immediately follows it. Hence unclean are excluded, since they may not enter the Temple court. (11) The sacrifice, which is within, while he stands without.

b (1) While his body is without. (2) Even if his hands only enter the Temple court, it is as though he entered it entirely.

עין משפט
נר מצוה

ג א מיי' פ"ד מהלכות פסה"מ הלכה כ :
ד ב מיי' פ"א מהלכות פסה"מ הלכה כו :
ה ג ד מיי' שם הלכה כד ופי"א שם הל' כ:
ו ה מיי' שם פ"א הלכה כה :
ז ו מיי' פ"ג מהלכות פסה"מ הלכה י :
ח ז מיי' פ"א מהלכות פסה"מ הלכה א :
ט ח ט מיי' פ"ג מהל' מעס"ק הלכה יא :

*א] וכולן שקיבלו את הדם חוץ לזמנו וחוץ למקומו אם יש דם הנפש יחזור הכשר ויקבל *ב] קיבל הכשר ונתן לפסול יחזור לכשר ד] קיבל בימינו ונתן לשמאלו יחזור לימינו ה] קיבל בכלי קדש ונתן לכלי חול יחזור לכלי קדש *ו] נשפך מן הכלי על הרצפה ואספו כשר *ז] נתנו על גבי הכבש שלא כנגד היסוד נתן את הניתנין למטה למעלן ואת הניתנין למעלן למטה ואת הניתנין בפנים בחוץ ואת הניתנין בחוץ בפנים א] אם יש דם הנפש יחזור הכשר ויקבל: **גמ'** ב] שחטו דיעבד אין לכתחלה לא ורמינהו *ושחט שחיטה בזר כשרה שהשחיטה כשרה בזרים ובנשים ובעבדים ובטמאים ואפילו בקדשי קדשים או אינו אלא בכהנים אמרת וכי מאין באתה מכלל שנאמר °ואתה ובניך אתך תשמרו את כהונתכם לכל דבר המזבח יכול אף בשחיטה ת"ל °ושחט את בן הבקר לפני ה' ג] *והקריבו וגו' מקבלה ואילך *מצות כהונה לימד על השחיטה שכשרה בכל אדם הוא הדין דאפי' לכתחילה נמי ומשום דקא בעי למיתנא טמאים דלכתחילה לא גזירה שמא יגעו בבשר תנא ששחטו וטמא דיעבד שפיר דמי ורמינהו *וסמך ושחט מה סמיכה בטהורים אף שחיטה בטהורים ח] מדרבנן מ"ש סמיכה ט] דכתיב לפני ה' שחיטה נמי הכתיב לפני ה' אפשר דעביד סכין ארוכה ושחיט סמיכה נמי אפשר דמעייל ידיה וסמיך קסבר *ביאה במקצת שמה ביאה רב חסדא מתני איפכא וסמך ושחט מה שחיטה בטהורין אף סמיכה בטהורין מאי שנא שחיטה דכתיב לפני ה' סמיכה

(במדבר יח) (ויקרא א)

וכולן · הפסולין : שקיבלו הדם · על מנת לאכול ד] ולהקטיר חוץ לזמנו או חוץ למקומו : אם יש דם הנפש · עוד בבהמה יחזור הכשר ויקבל ויזרוק הכשר שאין מחשבתן של אלו פוסלתן בקבלה לפי שאין ראויין לה ואין מחשבה פוסלת אלא במי שראוי לעבודה דכתיב המקריב אותו לא יחשב (ויקרא ז) בראוי להקרבה הכתוב מדבר : יחזור לכשר · דלא מיפסיל בהכי ובפרק ה] [ראשון] (דף יד:) שנינן לה למאן דאית ליה הולכה שלא ברגל שמה הולכה למר כדאית ליה ולאידך כדאית ליה: נתנו ו]· הפסול על גבי הכבש או שלא כנגד היסוד כו': יחזור הכשר ויקבל · אי סבירא ז] לן דפסול עושה שיריים אשמעינן האי תנא דשלא במקומו לאו כמקומו דמי לפיכך לא עשאן שיריים ואי סבירא ליה דשלא במקומו כמקומו דמי והויא לה זריקה גמורה באדם פסול אשמעינן דאין פסול עושה שיריים : **גמ'** ה"ג ורמינהו ושחט שחיטה בזר כשרה מדלא כתיב ושחט הכהן : וכי מאין באת · לומר שצריכה כהונה והלא לא נאמר בה כהן והקריבו הכהנים · ומדכתיב בקבלה כהונה ובשחיטה לא כתיב לימד על השחיטה שכשרה בזר : מה סמיכה בטהורים · כדמפרש לקמיה : מדרבנן · שמא יגעו בבשר : מאי שנא סמיכה · דבטהורים מדאורייתא : דכתיב לפני ה' · ושחט

החמירו עליו לנאת כמו שמפרש רבינו תם משום דקשיא ליה דהתם אסר ליה לטבול יום ליכנס בעזרת נשים משום דסמוך למחנה ח] [שכינה] ואמרינן נמי בגמ' שחידשו דברים ואמרו טבול יום אל יכנס למחנה לויה פירוש לא בכל מחנה לויה ט] דמפתח הר הבית עד שער ניקנור מחנה לויה כדתנא בתוספתא ובסיפרי ובפרק בתרא דמכילתין (דף קטז:) ובכלים (פ"א מ"ח) משמע דשרי בכולהו חוץ מעזרת נשים ואפי' טבול יום דזבין וזבות אלא במחנה לויה כגון עזרת נשים דסמוך למחנה שכינה קאמר ובמסכת תמיד משמע דשרי בכל מחנה לויה גבי בית המוקד שזקני בית אב ישנים שם וקתני י] כשאירע קרי לאחד מהן הולך וטובל וחוזר לאחיו הכהנים עד שהשערים נפתחין והולך לו ואין לך סמוך למחנה שכינה יותר מבית המוקד שחציה בקודש וחציה בחול ובסוטה פרק היה נוטל (דף כ:) יא] (הא) דקתני והם אומרים הוליאוה שלא תטמא העזרה ופריך עלה מהא דדרשינן דטמא מת מותר ליכנס במחנה לויה ואפי' מת עצמו כדכתיב ויקח משה את עצמות יוסף עמו עמו במחילתו ואי דרבנן אסור מאי קושיא ומתוך כך מחלק רבינו תם דלא גזור היכא דנטמא בעזרה ומורי מתרץ דבעזרת נשים החמירו יותר מאחר מקומות אע"פ שסמוכים ממש למחנה יב] לויה לפי שהוא מקום כניסה ויליאה לכל אדם יותר שדרך שם נכנסין לעזרת ישראל דרך שער נקנור שהוא שער העליון המשמש הכניסה והיליאה והא דפריך בסוטה על מה שאמר הוליאוה משום דקתני הוליאוה תרי זימני דמשמע שהיו נבהלים להוליאה וממהרין מאד ואי לאו דאיכא איסורא דאורייתא לא היו דוחקין כל כך למהר והא דאמר בפרק אלו הן הנשרפין (סנהדרין דף פא:) כהן המשמש בטומאה אין אחיו הכהנים מביאין אותו לב"ד אלא מוליאין אותו חוץ לעזרה ומפלעין את מוחו בגיזרין לאו דווקא חוץ לעזרת ישראל אלא אף חוץ לעזרת נשים וחוץ לחיל וכי ה"ג נמי הוי ההיא דסוטה דקתני שלא תטמא העזרה יג] והיו זקוקין להוליאה אף חוץ לחיל להר הבית דהא מפרש טעמא התם שמא תפרוס נדה וא"ת וכיון דטבול יום מותר בשאר העזרה כדפרישית אמאי אילטריך לו למצורע בערב הפסח לדחות עשה ילך בשאר הלשכות ויכניס שם ידיו לבהונות וי"ל דלא אפשר משום דכתיב פתח אהל מועד והייט בשער נקנור שהוא מכוון כנגדו ומיהו בקדשי קדשים לא אפשר ליה לטמא לשחוט בלידי העזרה [דשחיטתן] בלפון ולא משכחת פתח מכוון לגד הלפון כדמוכח בגמ' למ"ד מרחק לפון דפריך וליעבד פשפש ומשני הכל בכתב ולפירוש רבינו תם נמי דמפרש דנטמא בעזרת נשים לא גזור מ"מ למ"ד מרחק לפון יד] ושחיט בסכין ארוכה עשרים ושתים אמה ואין לחוש בכך [הא דקאמר] דשחיטה כשירה בדיעבד ושמא יגעו בבשר נקט משום קדשים קלים וה"ר אפרים היה מפרש דמשכחת לה דשחיט טמא דרך גגין ועליות דלא נתקדשו ובסכין ארוכה למ"ד ביאה במקלת שמה ביאה שאין יכול להכנים שם ידו ומיהו התינח בקדשים קלים שיכול לתלות הבהמה ולשחטה אבל בקדשי קדשים לא אפשר דבעינן שחיטה על ירך כדאמר לעיל בפרק שני (דף כו·) אם לא נאמר דעביד טו] בסכין ארוכה מן העליה והגג עד הרלפה ולהאי פירושא לא תקשי לו מיניה ממלורע שיכנים ידיו לבהונות דרך גגין ועליות ולא אילטריך לדחות עשה דהיאך יעלה לגגין דרך הר הבית והחיל: **ת"ל** והקריבו מקבלה ואילך מלות כהונה· ואם תאמר תיפוק ליה מהיקשא דסמיכה ושחיטה דמה סמיכה בזרים אף שחיטה בזרים כדדריש ר"ש בריש הקומץ רבה (מנחות יט·) וי"ל דאי לאו דרשא דהכא הוה ממעטינן שחיטה מדכתיב תשמרו את כהונתכם דמשמע אפי' שחיטה בכלל ואע"ג דאילטריך לן לעיל ספ"ק (דף יג·) והקריבו בני אהרן הכהנים לגז"ש שתהא בכהן כשר ובכלי שרת מ"מ דריש מיניה שפיר מקבלה ואילך מלות כהונה : **מאי** שנא סמיכה דבטהורים דכתיב לפני ה' · פי' בקונטרס דהייט מדכתיב ושחט את בן הבקר לפני ה' וכיון דבעינן תיכף לסמיכה שחיטה אין סמיכה מבחוץ ושחיטה מבפנים אלא אף הסמיכה מבפנים ואין טמא נכנס לעזרה והקשה הרב רבי יעקב דאורליינ"ש דבפ' בתרא (דף*) משמע דכתיב בסמיכה גופה לפני ה' דקאמר דאין סמיכה בבמה משום דכתיב לפני ה' ואי לא כתב בה לפני ה' אלא מקרא דשחיטה הא שחיטה גופה ישנה בבמה והתם פירש בקונטרס דהייט קרא דכתיב בפר כהן משיח לפני ה' וסמך ומיהו לקמן בשמעתין (דף לג.) משמע כפירוש הקונט' דהכא דפריך למאן דאמר תיכף לסמיכה שחיטה לאו דאורייתא מדתניא וסמך ושחט מה סמיכה בטהורים אף שחיטה בטהורים ואי אמרת לאו דאורייתא בטמאין נמי משכחת לה משמע בהדיא דלא ידעינן סמיכה לפני ה' אלא משום דתיכף לסמיכה שחיטה וצריך לדחוק ההוא דלקמן דפ' בתרא (גם זה שם) ומיהו יש ליישב ההיא דלקמן בשמעתין משום טז] דההיא סוגיא כמאן דאמר ביאה במקלת לאו שמה ביאה דאי משום לפני ה' אפשר דמעייל ידיה וסמיך אבל אי אמרת תיכף לסמיכה שחיטה לא אפשר יז] דמרחק לפון מיהו וסמך ושחט דכתיב גבי עולה דטעונה לפון דריש בתורת כהנים בפרשת ויקרא מה סמיכה בטהורים אף שחיטה בטהורים ובהדיא דריש התם מקרא דלעיל דכתיב יקריב אותו לרצונו לפני ה' וסמך יח] מדכתיב ממש וסמך אבל לפני ה' דריש לפני ה' ולא כפי' הקונטרס דפרק בתרא דדריש לה מקרא אחרינא דפר כהן משיח תדע דמפר כהן משיח היכי מלי למילף שאר סמיכות לפני ה' יט] שאני התם דקדושה חמורה היא חטאות הפנימיות :
ורבי

שיטה מקובצת
א] אם יש דם הנפש כו'· האי תנא אי ס"ל דפסול עושה שיריים א"כ צריך לפרש דחוץ למקומו לאו כמקומו דמי ולכך יחזור הכשר ויקבל ואי ס"ל כמקומו דמי (אינו) צריך לפרש [אינו] עושה שיריים· כפ"ה ואגב חורפיה לא דק דמאן דאית ליה לאו כמקומו דמי לא קאי אפסול כלל כדמוכח לעיל מידו ודאי (כמ"ד) [למ"ד] כמקומו דמי ע"כ אפסול קאי וא"ת א"כ מאי איבעי ליה לר"ל מר"י אי פסול עושה שיריים אי לא והא אית ליה לר"ל לעיל כמקומו דמי וא"כ תפשוט מהא דפסול אינו עושה שיריים וי"ל דאיכא למימר משום דדוקא שנתנו למעלה או למטה אבל אם נתנו בהכשירו לא יחזור הכשר ויקבל ומיהו קשה דא"כ תפשוט דפסול עושה שיריים מדנקט פסול [שנתן שלא בהכשירו] משמע משום פסול לחוד עושה שיריים לכך נ"ל כדפי' לעיל בפ' קבלה דאי קאי אפסול היינו אפסא דבהא מיהא כ"ע מודו דעושה שיריים הואיל ומרצה בצבור כדאיתא במעילה [עי' תוס' דף כו ע"ב ד"ה סבר כ"ע עכ"ס]:
ב] ששחטו דיעבד :
ג] והקריבו הכהנים וגו' מקבלה ואילך מצות כהונה·תימה תיפוק ליה מהיקשא דסמיכה לשחיטה כדדריש ר"ש בפ' הקומץ רבה וי"ל דאי לאו דרשא דהכא הוי ממעטינן שחיטה נמי בכלל כהונה מדכתי' כהונתכם ואף על גב דאיצטרך בפ"ק והקריבו בני אהרן הכהנים לג"ש שתהא בכהן כשר ובכלי שרת מ"מ דריש נמי מקבלה ואילך מצות כהונה· מהר"פ: ד] לאכול או להקטיר חוץ :
ה] ראשון מפרש לה :
ו] נתנו פסול זה על גבי:
ז] סבירא ליה דפסול :
ח] שכינה אמרי':ט] לויה קאמר דמפתח הר הבית כו' מחנה לויה כדתניא:
י] וקתני אירע קרי לאחד כו' וחוזר ויושב אצל אחיו הכהנים וכו' נפתחין יוצא והולך לו:

יא] נטל אותו דקתני כו' תטמא העזרה פריך עלה : יב] למחנה שכינה לפי : יג] שהרי היו זקוקין להוציאה אף חוץ להר הבית כו' מותר בשארי צידי העזרה כדפרישית כו' למצורע שחל שמיני שלו בערב הפסח כו' ידיו לבהונות ויקיים את שחיטתו ה"ל : יד] צפון הוי שחוט בסכין : טו] דעביד סכין ארוכה מן כו' תוקפו ממצורע שיכניס כו' דהיאך יעלה לגגין ועליות אם לא דרך הר הבית : טז] משום דההיא סוגיא : יז] דמרחק לפון ועלה כתיב דמשונה צפון ועלה דריש בת"כ בפ' ויקרא: יח] ה' וסמך ולא : יט] ה' דלמא שאני התם דקדושה החטאות הפנימיות חמורה היא הס"ד

[לעיל כו:] [לעיל יד:] [יומא מח. לעיל מו.] [לעיל כו.] [יומא כו.] [ז"ל והקריבו בני אהרן הכהנים וגו'] [ברכות לא: וש"נ] [לקמן לג:] [יומא לא.] [רש"ק] [וע"ע תוספות חולין כ: ד"ה שמא יגע] [קינה: וע"ש ברש"י ד"ה לפני ה' וסמך לרצונו לפני ה' וסמך ליה וסמך את ידו ויקרא א]

סמיכה נמי כתיב לפני ה' אפשר דמעייל ידיה וסמיך שחיטה נמי אפשר דעביד סכין ארוכה ושחיט הא מני שמעון התימני היא דתניא ושחט את בן הבקר לפני ה' א] ולא השוחט לפני ה' שמעון התימני אומר מנין שיהיו ידיו של שוחט לפנים מן הנשחט ת"ל ושחט את בן הבקר לפני ה' שוחט את בן הבקר יהא ב] לפני ה' אמר עולא אמר ריש לקיש *טמא שהכניס ידו לפנים לוקה שנאמר °בכל קדש לא תגע ג] וגו' מקיש ביאה לנגיעה מה נגיעה במקצת שמה נגיעה °אף *ביאה °במקצת שמה ביאה איתיביה רב הושעיא לעולא *[ב]מצורע שחל שמיני שלו להיות בערב הפסח וראה קרי בו ביום וטבל אמרו חכמים אע"פ שאין טבול יום אחר נכנס זה נכנס ד] מוטב יבוא עשה שיש בו כרת וידחה עשה שאין בו כרת *ורבי יוחנן אמר דבר תורה אפי' עשה אין בו שנאמר °ויעמד יהושפט בקהל יהודה וירושלם בבית ה' לפני החצר החדשה מאי חצר החדשה ה] אמר ר' יוחנן שחידשו בה דברים (הרבה) ואמרו *[ג]טבול יום אל יכנס למחנה לויה ואי אמרת ביאה במקצת שמה ביאה היכי מעייל ידיה (א) בבהונות אידי ואידי עשה שיש בו כרת הוא א"ל *מטונך שאני מצורע הואיל והותר לצרעתו הותר לקיריו אמר רב יוסף קסבר עולא רובן זבים ונעשו טמאי מתים הואיל והותרו לטומאתן הותרו לזיבתן אמר ליה אביי מי דמי טומאה אישתראי זיבה לא אישתראי (ב) אמר ליה דלמא הכי קאמר מר רובן טמאי מתים ונעשו זבים הואיל והותרו לטומאתן הותרו לזיבתן אמר ליה אין (ג) ואכתי לא דמי מצורע היתירא הוא הואיל ואישתרי אישתרי טומאה דחויה היא להא אידחאי להא לא אידחאי אמר ליה רבא אדרבה איפכא מסתברא מצורע היתירא הוא להא אישתראי ולהא לא אישתראי טומאה דחויה הוא מה לי חד דחויא מה לי שתי דחיות

מכלל

תורה אור: ויקרא יב · ד"ה ב כ

רש"י

ושחט את בן הבקר לפני ה' וכיון דבעינן תיכף לסמיכה שחיטה אין סמיכה מבחוץ ושחיטה מבפנים אלא אף הסמיכה בפנים ואין טמא נכנס לעזרה: ואין השוחט לפני ה'· שאם רגלו עומד חוץ לעזרה ושוחט בסכין ארוכה: לפנים מן הנשחט· לפנים מן הבהמה: ה"ג שוחט את בן הבקר יהיה לפני ה': [מה] נגיעה · סתם במקצת היא: שחל שמיני שלו . והיה לו היום ליכנס להר הבית לחלל שער נקנור שלא נתקדש להכניס ידיו לבהונות וראה קרי ובעל קרי אין נכנס להר הבית כדאמרי' באלו דברים (פסחים דף סז:) זב וכל זב לרבות בעל קרי שמשתלח חוץ לשתי מחנות כדאמרינן התם: אע"פ שאין טבול יום אחר · של טומאת קרי נכנס להר הבית דקסבר טבול יום דזב כזב דמי ו] זה נכנס ומכניס ידיו לעזרה ליתן מדם האשם ומלוג השמן על בהונותיו כדי שיטהר לאכול פסחו לערב והוא ישלחנו לעזרה היום לשחוט ולזרוק עליו אבל הוא לא יכנס לעזרה ז] (ושוחט בסכין ארוכה) דטבול יום שנכנס לעזרה בכרת כדאמרי' בהקומץ רבה (מנחות כז:): מוטב יבוא עשה· של פסח: שיש בו כרת וידחה עשה· דשילוח טמאים מהר הבית שאין בו כרת שאין ענוש כרת אלא מחומת העזרה ולפנים: אפי' עשה אין בו · בהר הבית לגבי טבול יום דקסבר טבול יום דזב לאו כזב דמי: *נכח החצר החדשה · הר הבית שחידשו בה בהלכותיה: אידי ואידי · עשה של כרת טבול יום לגבי עזרה בכרת הוא והא קא מעייל ח] לעזרה שהרי אי אפשר להוציא דם האשם לחלל השער דמיפסל ביוצא: מטונך · ממשאך ט] שבאתה עלי להכביד אכביד עליך ממצורע השיבות שגזירת הכתוב היא אלא שהותרה לו ביאה במקצת שהרי מחוסר כיפורים הוא והוא מכניס ידיו לבהונות: הואיל והותרה · ביאה י] מקצת לצרעתו: הותרה · אף לטבול יום של קרי שלו: אמר רב יוסף · שמע מינה מדעולא דאמר הואיל ואישתרי להא אישתרי להא: רובן · של ציבור זבין בפסח ולא נדחית טומאת זיבה אלא נעשו טמאי מתים בו ביום הואיל והותרו לטומאת המת שנדחה אצלן הותרו יא] לזיבתן: טומאה אישתראי · שבאה אחרונה זיבה ראשונה עומדת במקומה ולא דמי למצורע דהתם איכא למימר מיגו דקמייתא לא הוי אסירא ליה בתרייתא לא חמירא לך מקמייתא שהרי טמא היה ומותר אבל הכא כי הוה זיבה גרידתא הוו אסירי השתא דאיתוספא טומאה עלייהו *אישתרו להו: הואיל והותרו לטומאתן · הקודמת אינן נאסרין מחמת האחרונה שהרי אף הראשונה טומאה של כרת היתה והיו מותרים היום: היתירא הואי · בהיתר גמור יב] גלה עליו תורה ביאה במקצת:

טומאה

תוספות

ורבי יוחנן אמר דבר תורה אפי' עשה אין בו · לפרושי ברייתא קאתי ולאו לאיפלוגי דר' יוחנן לאו תנא הוא כדמוכח בפ"ק דכתובות (דף ח·) גבי חתנים מן המנין ומשני רב תנא ופליג ואר' יוחנן לא משני הכי תדע דאי דאורייתא אם כן היה לנו לאסור מפתח הר הבית שכל זה מחנה לויה כדאיתא בסוף מכילתין (דף קטז:) ובהדיא תנן במס' כלים (פ"א מ"ח) עזרת נשים מקודשת הימנו שאין טבול יום נכנס לשם אבל בהר הבית ובחיל מותר יג] ותני נמי בתמיד (דף כו·) דבא וישב לו אצל אחיו הכהנים ומיהו מתוך פירכות הללו מיתרצא פירכא קמייתא דאע"ג דר' יוחנן לאו תנא הוא דלמא סבר לה כמתני' דתמיד יד] וכלים ולמאי דפירש בקונט' טעמא דברייתא דאין טבול יום של טומאת קרי נכנס להר הבית משום דקסבר טבול יום דזב כזב דמי ואמרינן פ' אלו דברים (פסחים סז:) זב וכל זב לרבות בעל קרי ור' יוחנן דאמר אפילו עשה אין בו משום דקסבר טבול יום דזב לאו כזב דמי אתי שפיר דפלוגתא דתנאי היא טו] ואיכא למ"ד טבול יום דזב לאו כזב דמי ומיהו קשה דאי קסבר האי תנא טבול יום דזב כזב דמי אם כן איכא לאו דלא יטמאו את מחניהם ואין עשה דוחה את לא תעשה ועשה ועוד קשה מדאמרינן פרק ג' מינין (נזיר דף מה·) טמא יהיה לרבות טבול יום עוד טומאתו בו לרבות מחוסר כיפורים ואי טבול יום אסור טז] למחנה לויה למה לי קרא לרבות במחנה שכינה ומיהו מצי למימר משום כרת איצטריך דאיירי ביה קרא שאין ענוש כרת אלא מחומת העזרה ולפנים ועוד קשה דאי טעמא דרבי יוחנן משום דקסבר דטבול יום דזב לאו כזב דמי והא רבא אית ליה הך דרבי יוחנן בפסחים פרק האשה (דף צב·) ושמעינן ליה לרבא בכריתות פרק שני (דף י·) דמחוסר כיפורים דזב כזב דמי יז] אלא ודאי הא דאמר דטבול יום דזב כזב דמי לאו לענין ביאת מקדש קאמר אלא לענין פסח הבא בטומאה לא יאכלו ממנו זבים וזבות כדפי' לעיל בריש פרק שני (דף יז:) בשם ה"ר חיים ומיהו סוגיא דנזיר (דף מה.) קשה למה שפי' דטבול יום שרי במחנה לויה דמשמע התם דאפי' נאמר דטבול יום דזב לאו כזב דמי אסור ליכנס למחנה לויה דקאמר התם מה אהל מועד מחוסר כיפורים לא עייל אף התם נמי במחנה לויה מחוסר כיפורים לא עייל ומקרא דריש יח] התם דקתני התם בברייתא ובא לפני ה' אל פתח אהל מועד לשער נקנור אימתי הוא בא בזמן שטבל ועשה הערב שמש ונראה דדוקא בטבול יום דזב יט] שלש ראיות שהוא טבול יום ומחוסר כיפורים דאיכא תרתי קאסר במחנה לויה וכי מסיק התם אלא אמר אביי טבול יום דזב לאו כזב דמי ואפי' הכי כיון דמחוסר כיפורים לא עייל כלומר דאיכא תרתי ולאו מלשון כ] זבח דריש דאם כן גבי נזיר דכתיב יביא שתי תורים וגו' הוה לן למידרש הכי כדאמר התם אבל טבול יום דזב בעל שתי ראיות ודבעל קרי שרי דלאו מחוסר כפרה והא דאמר הכא כשראה קרי בו ביום וטבל דנכנס אע"פ שהוא טבול יום וגם מחוסר כיפורים אין אלו שני הדברים על טומאה אחת אלא טבול יום משום קרי ומחוסר כפרה משום צרעתו ולפי' הקונטרס ניחא דנקט בברייתא וראה קרי ולא טמא שרץ ונבילה דטמא שרץ ואפילו טמא מת נכנסין להר הבית כדדרשינן בפסחים פ' אלו דברים (דף סז·) ובסוטה פרק היה נוטל (דף כ:) ויקח משה את עצמות יוסף עמו במחיצתו אבל לפי מה שפירשתי דרבי יוחנן לא פליג כא] אברייתא ולא אסור אלא מדרבנן כולהו· טמאים נמי אסירי כדתנן בפ"ק דכלים החיל מקודש הימנו שאין עובדי כוכבים וטמאי מתים נכנסין לשם וכל שכן בעזרת נשים כדתני התם שאין טבול יום נכנס לשם כב] וכולהו *טבול יום אפילו דטמאי מת דשרץ ונבילה [איירי] דאיירי ביה לעיל ונראה לפרש דלרבותא נקט וראה קרי דאף על גב דמשתלח חוץ לשתי מחנות התירו לו משום פסח: **שחידשו** בה דברים ואמרו טבול יום אל יכנס למחנה לויה · וא"ת מנלן שחידשו מטבול יום אימא שחידשו ממת ויש לומר דמשמע דלא חידשו אלא על חצר וחצר היינו עזרת נשים כדמוכח ביחזקאל (מ) ואילו מת וטמא מת מלינו דאסורין אפילו בחיל: **א"ל** מטונך · פירוש ממלאך שבאת להכביד עלי אכביד עליך דאדרבה משם סייעתא לדברי כג] דשאני מצורע וכו' מדנקט וראה קרי בו ביום משמע דדוקא בו ביום דיצא בשעת היתר דצרעת ואיכא למימר מתוך שהותר לצרעתו הותר לקירויו אבל כד] מאתמול לא ואי ביאה במקצת לא שמה ביאה אפי' מאתמול נמי והשתא אתי שפיר הא דאמר בפ"ק דיבמות (דף ח·) מי לא מודה עולא שאם ראה קרי בליל כה] (שלישי) [שמיני] שאינו מכניס ידיו שלא יצא בשעה שהיא ראויה להביא קרבן מנא ליה דמודה עולא אלא מדנקט בו ביום דייק דטעמא דעולא משום דהואיל והותר לצרעתו הותר לקירויו ובענין זה יש לפרש מטונך דפ' הזרוע והלחיים (חולין דף קלב.) דקאמר התם עולא יהיב מתנתא לכהנתא אלמא דקסבר עולא כהן ואפילו כהנת כו] והכתיב וכל מנחת כהן כליל תהיה ואמר ליה רבי מטונך אהרן ובניו כתובים בפרשה כלומר משם אכביד עליך

שהיא

עין משפט נר מצוה

י א מיי' פ"ג מהלכות ביאת מקדש הלכה יח:

יא ב מיי' פ"ו מהלכות קרבן פסח הלכה ה:

יב ג מיי' פ"ג מהלכות ביאת מקדש הל' ו:

שיטה מקובצת

א] ה' בן הבקר לפני ה' ולא : ב] לפני ה'· ס"א שיהא שוחט ובן הבקר לפני ה':ג] לא תגע ואל המקדש לא תבא וגו': ד] מוטב יבא עשה שיש בו כרת וידחה עשה שאין בו כרת· פרש"י שאין ענוש כרת אלא מן החומה ולפנים משמע (הכי) [הכא] דטבול יום דקרי כקרי דמי וקשה טובא חדא דאיך פליג ר"י על ההיא ברייתא [ועל מתני' דתמיד] דתני אירע קרי לאחד מהם הולך וטובל במסיבה ההולכת תחת הבירה וירד וטבל וישב לו אצל אחיו הכהנים במדורות בית המוקד ומדורות בית המוקד היתה חציה בקדש וחציה בחול אלמא בעל קרי דזב לאו כזב דמי דאי כזב דמי היאך יכול לישב אצל אחיו לכך נראה דר"י אתא לפרושי הברייתא ועתה ניחא האי דתמיד דכיון דליכא אלא טומאה דרבנן לא הזקיקוהו חכמים לצאת וה"ק יבא עשה כו' שאין בו כרת אלא איסור מדרבנן משום דלאו כזב דמי' מהר"פ : ה] החדשה שחדשו בה דברים ואמרו (והשאר נמחק) : ו] דמי וה"ה לטבול יום דקרי' גליון ואין להקשות לפירוש הקונטרס דבפרק שלשה מינין אמרינן טמא יהיה לרבות טבול יום עוד טומאתו בו לרבות מחוסר כפורים ואי טבול יום אסור במחנה לויה למה צריך לרבות טבול יום במחנה שכינה [מיהו אפשר לומר] דאיצטרך משום כרת דאין כרת אלא מחומת עזרה ולפנים מיהו קשה אי טבול יום דזב כזב דמי א"כ לאו נמי איכא ולא יטמאו את מחניהם כמו שהקשו בתוספות ועוד מאי קאמר רבא יבא עשה שיש בו כרת כו' תיפוק ליה הואיל והותר לצרעתו הותר נמי לקירויו אלא ע"כ אינו עשה גמור ורבי יוחנן מפרש הברייתא כדפי' לעיל ויבא עשה כו' לאו דוקא אלא כלו' לא העמידו דבריהם במקום כרת· ע"כ : ז] תיבות ושוחט בסכין ארוכה נמחק: ח] מעייל ידיה לעזרה: ט] שבאת להכביד עלי : י] ביאה במקצת: יא] הותרו אף לזיבתן:יב] גמור התירה עליו תורה : יג] מותר ותנן נמי במס' תמיד : יד] דתמיד אבל דוחק הוא לומר דפליגא הך ברייתא אמתניתין דתמיד וכלים : טו] היא ס"א וקי"ל כמ"ד לאו כזב דמי ותיבת לאו נמחק : טז] אסור במחנה לויה כו' מצי למימר דמשום כרת : יז] דמי וכ"ש טבול יום : יח] דריש ליה התם : יט] דזב בעל שלש : כ] מלשון ובא דריש: כא] אברייתא ס"א אלא קמפרש אליבא דברייתא דאפילו עשה אין בו ומדרבנן מיירי כולהו כו' : כב] לשם ובכולהו טבולי יום קאמר אפילו : כג] לדברי דביאה במקצת שמה ביאה דדוקא משום דהואיל דהותר לצרעתי הותר לקירויו וא"ת מנא ליה האי דיוקא וי"ל מדקתני וראה קרי כו' לשון מהר"פ : כד] אבל בלילה או מאתמול : כה] בליל שמיני שאינו מכניס ידיו לבהונות שלא יצא כו' דייק עילא דטעמא משום : כו] כהנת איתיביה רבה לעולא מנחת כהנת נאכלת והכתיב :

קירא

מסורת הש"ס

[יומא לא.]

פסחים לב. יבמות ז.

רש"ק מ"ו

הוריות ה: ע"ש יבמות ז: ע"ש פסחים לב. ע"ש

כלים פ"א מ"ח

נ"ל לפני

[ר"ה ד: חולין קלב.]

נ"ל לא אישתרו

נ"א שמאים נ"ק

הגהות הב"ח

(א) גמ' ידיה לבהונות : (ב) שם זיבה לא אישתראי דלמא כצ"ל ותיבות אמר ליה נמחק: (ג) שם אמר ליה אין אמר ליה ואכתי:

גליון הש"ס

גמ' אף ביאה במקצת · עיין לקמן דף לג ע"א תוס' ד"ה מכניסו : שם במקצת שמה ביאה· עיין שבועות דף יז ע"א תוס' ד"ה תלה ·

[32b] but *'before the Lord'* is written in connection with 'laying' too?—He can project his hands within and lay [them on the bullock]. Then in the case of *shechitah* too, he can make a long knife and slaughter?—This agrees with Simeon the Temanite. For it was taught: *And he shall kill the bullock before the Lord*: the *bullock* [must be] before the Lord, but the slaughterer need not be before the Lord. Simeon the Temanite said: Whence do we know that the slaughterer's hands must be on the inner side of the slaughtered? From the text, *And he shall slaughter the bullock before the Lord*: he that slaughters the bullock [must be] before the Lord.[3]

'Ulla said in the name of Resh Laḳish: If an unclean person projects his hands within, he is flagellated, because it says, *She shall touch no hallowed things, nor come into the sanctuary*:[4] entry is assimilated to contact. As partial contact ranks as contact,[5] so partial entry is designated entry. R. Hoshaia raised an objection to 'Ulla: If a leper whose eighth day fell on the eve of Passover[6] and who had a nocturnal discharge on that day,[7] and performed immersion,[8]—
a the Sages said: Though any other *ṭebul yom*[1] may not enter [the Levitical camp], this one does enter:[2] it is preferable that an affirmative precept which involves *kareth*[3] should come and override an affirmative precept which does not involve *kareth*.[4] Now R. Joḥanan said: By the law of the Torah[5] there is not even an affirmative precept in connection therewith, for it is said, *And Jehoshaphat stood in the congregation of Judah and Jerusalem, in the house of the Lord, before the new court*.[6] What does *'the new court'* mean? That they introduced a new law there and ruled: A *ṭebul yom* must not enter the Levitical camp.[7] Now if you say that partial entry is called entry, how can he insert his hands for [the sprinkling of his] thumbs; in both cases there is an affirmative precept involving *kareth*?[8]—From your very refutation[9] [I can answer you], he replied: A leper is different. Since he was permitted in respect of his leprosy,[10] he was permitted in respect of his nocturnal discharge. R. Joseph observed: 'Ulla holds [that] if the majority were *zabin* and they became unclean through the dead, since they are permitted in respect of their defilement, they are permitted in respect of their *zibah*.[11] Said Abaye to him, How can you compare? Uncleanness
b was permitted, but *zibah* was not permitted![1] Perhaps this is what you meant: If the majority are unclean through the dead and they become *zabin*, since they are permitted in respect of their uncleanness they are permitted in respect of their *zibah*?—Yes, he replied. Said he to him: Yet they are still not alike. [In the case of] a leper it is permitted,[2] [and] since it is permitted [in respect of leprosy], it is permitted [in respect of his nocturnal discharge]. But defilement is [merely] superseded: in respect of one[3] it was superseded, [while] in respect of the other [*zibah*] it was not superseded?—Said Raba to him: On the contrary, the logic is the reverse: [In the case of] a leper it is permitted: then it is permitted in respect of the one and not permitted in respect of the other. But uncleanness is superseded: What does it matter then whether it is superseded

(3) Reading *we-shoḥeṭ*, and the slaughterer, for *we-shaḥaṭ*, and he shall slaughter. Thus he holds that the slaughterer must be inside too. (4) Lev. XII, 4. (5) Since normally a man does not touch a thing with his whole body. (6) When a leper was healed from his leprosy he waited seven days, performing immersion on the seventh, and brought his sacrifices on the eighth (v. Lev. XIV, 9 f). When he brought these he was still not permitted to enter the Temple court ('the camp of the *Shechinah*'—divine Presence) but stood at the east gate ('the gate of Nicanor'), whose sanctity was lower (it was regarded as 'the Levitical camp'), while the priest, standing inside the Temple court, applied the blood and the oil to the thumb and the great toe of the leper (ibid. 14 f). (7) Before he had offered his sacrifices. One who suffered such a discharge might not enter even the Levitical camp. (8) Again. Though he had performed immersion the previous day, that was on account of his leprosy, whereas now he performs it on account of his discharge.

a (1) V. Glos. (2) For his purification rites. (3) *Sc.* the Passover-offering. He went through his purification rites so that he might eat of the Passover-offering in the evening, the eating of which is enjoined by an affirmative precept. (4) *Sc.* that a *ṭebul yom* must not enter the Levitical camp. That is derived in Naz. 45*a* from, *he shall be unclean; his uncleanness is yet upon him* (Num. XIX, 13); since this is an *affirmative* statement, the injunction likewise counts as an affirmative precept. Its violation does not involve *kareth*. (5) The Pentateuch. (6) II Chron. XX, 5. (7) Since this was an innovation, it is only Rabbinical, and as seen *supra* it was waived for the sake of the Passover-offering. (8) An unclean person may not enter the Temple court on pain of *kareth*. (9) Lit., 'burden'. (10) This is obvious, as Scripture ordains it, and it cannot be done in any other way but by inserting his hands (or thumbs) into the Temple court. (11) For *zab* (pl. *zabim*, *zabin*), *zibah* v. Glos. If the majority of the community are unclean on the eve of Passover through the dead, they are permitted to offer the Passover-offering, as this uncleanness is inoperative (or superseded) in such circumstances. But if they are unclean as *zabin*, they may not offer. Now, if they were thus unclean, and then became unclean through the dead too, since they are permitted in respect of the latter, they are also permitted in respect of the former. This follows from 'Ulla's answer.

b (1) Though the uncleanness through the dead is permitted, yet since it came *after zibah* it cannot render that permitted too, for if it did it would create the absurd position that whereas *zibah* alone is not permitted, yet when defilement through the dead is *added* to it, it is permitted. (2) To project his hands into the Temple court. (3) *Sc.* defilement through the dead.

in one instance or whether it is superseded in two instances? [33a] This proves that both[4] hold that uncleanness is [merely] superseded in the case of a community.[5]

Shall we say that the following supports him:[6] In all cases of laying [hands] I apply [the norm], *shechitah* must immediately follow laying, except this one,[7] which took place at the Nicanor Gate, because the leper might not enter therein[8] until the blood of his sin-offering and his guilt-offering was sprinkled on his account.[9] Now, if you say that partial entry is *not* designated entry, let him project his hands [into the Temple court] and lay [them on the sacrifice]?[10]—Said R. Joseph: This is in accordance with R. Jose son of R. Judah, who maintained: The north is at a distance [from
a the entrance].[1] Then let a small gate be made?[2]—Abaye and Raba both quoted [in reply]: *All this [do I give thee] in writing, as the Lord hath made me wise by His hand upon me, even all the works of this pattern.*[3] Others state [that] R. Joseph said: When one lays [hands], he must project his head and the greater part [of his body into the Temple court].[4] What is the reason?—We require [him to lay hands with] all his strength; therefore it cannot be done [otherwise].

What does [the Tanna] hold?[5] If he holds that the laying [hands on] the guilt-offering of a leper is a Scriptural requirement, and that [the law that] *shechitah* must immediately follow laying is Scriptural, then let him [the leper] enter [the Temple court] and lay [hands], since the Divine Law ordained it?—Said R. Adda b. Mattenah: It is a preventive measure, lest he prolong his route.[6] Others state [that] R. Adda b. Mattenah said: Laying of [hands on] the guilt-offering of a leper is Scriptural, but [that] *shechitah* must immediately follow laying is not Scriptural.[7]

An objection is raised: *And he shall lay [his hands...] and he shall kill:*[8] As 'laying' must be [done] by clean [persons only], so must *shechitah* be [done] by clean [persons only]. If, however, you say that it is not Scriptural, then it can be [done] by unclean persons too?[9]—Rather, reverse it: Laying of [hands on] the guilt-offering of a leper is *not* Scriptural, while [the law that] *shechitah* must immediately follow laying is Scriptural.

(4) Abaye and Raba. (5) V. *supra* 32b n. a 11, and Yoma 6b. (6) 'Ulla, that partial entry is designated entry. (7) Laying of hands on the leper's guilt-offering. (8) Into the Temple court. (9) Hence the animal was brought to the Nicanor Gate, which had intentionally been left unsanctified to enable the leper to stand there, and he laid hands upon it; then it was led to the Temple court and slaughtered, and so these two actions had to be separated by a short interval. (10) So here too *shechitah* could *immediately* follow laying.
a (1) *Sc.* of the Temple court. V. *supra* 20a. The sacrifices of the leper had to be slaughtered at the north side of the altar, which was more than 22 cubits from the main entrance of the Temple court. Hence he could not possibly reach it from outside. (2) On the north wall of the Temple court facing the altar, whereby the animal could be slaughtered immediately after his laying on of hands. (3) I Chron. XXVIII, 19. Thus the Temple was designed by divine guidance, and nothing might be added to it. (4) So that it would not be partial entry but complete entry, which is forbidden to the leper. (5) When he rules that *shechitah* must always immediately follow laying save in the case of a leper. (6) Lit., 'take many steps'—into the Temple court—more than is necessary for laying hands. This would not be covered by the Scriptural dispensation. (7) Hence we cannot permit him to enter the Temple court. (8) Lev. I, 4. (9) Viz., by laying hands *outside* the Temple court, and then the sacrifice is led in and slaughtered.

מכלל דתרוייהו סבירא להו *א*טומאה דחויה היא בצבור לימא מסייע ליה *כל ב'הסמיכות שהיו שם קורא א] *עליהן אני תכף לסמיכה שחיטה ג'חוץ מזו שהיתה בשער נקנור שאין מצורע יכול ליכנס לשם עד שמזין עליו מדם חטאתו ומדם אשמו ואי אמרת ביאה במקצת לא שמה ביאה ליעייל ידיה ולסמוך אמר רב יוסף הא מני *ר' יוסי ברבי יהודה היא דאמר מרחק צפון וליעבד פישפש אביי ורבא דאמרי תרוייהו °הכל בכתב מיד ה' עלי השכיל (את) כל מלאכת התבנית איכא דאמרי אמר רב יוסף כל הסומך ראשו ורובו מכנים מאי טעמא ד'כל כחו בעינן הלכך לא אפשר מאי קסבר אי קסבר סמיכת אשם מצורע דאורייתא *ותכף לסמיכה שחיטה דאורייתא ליעול ולסמוך להדיא דרחמנא אמר אמר רב אדא בר מתנה גזירה שמא ירבה בפסיעות איכא דאמרי אמר רב אדא בר מתנה סמיכת אשם מצורע דאורייתא ותכף לסמיכה שחיטה לאו דאורייתא מיתיבי *וסמך ושחט מה סמיכה בטהורין אף שחיטה בטהורין ב] ואי אמרת לאו דאורייתא בטמאין נמי משכחת לה אלא איפוך סמיכת אשם מצורע לאו דאורייתא ותכף לסמיכה שחיטה דאורייתא רבינא

(דה"א כח)

רש"י

*ג] [טומאה] דחויה היא· כלומר בקושי נדחית אלא דיחוי בעלמא על ידי כשיאות עון שהלין מרלה ולא בהיתר גמור ד] לטומאת מת אידחי ולא לטומאת זיבה: דתרוייהו· אביי ורבא סבירא להו טומאה דחויה היא בצבור וכ"מ למיהוי (א) מאן דאמר בפ"ק דיומא (דף ו:) דאמר הותרה היא בציבור יחיד במקום רבים: לימא מסייע ליה· לעולא דאמר ביאה במקצת שמה ביאה: תכף לסמיכה שחיטה· כדכתיב וסמך ושחט: חוץ מזו· של אשם מצורע: שהיתה בשער נקנור· הוא שער ה] המזרחי כדתנן בשקלים (פ"ו מ"ג) שבמזרח שער נקנור וחלל ו] שער לא נתקדש בקדושת העזרה כדאמרי' בכילד צולין (פסחים פה:) לפי שהמצורע עומד שם ומכניס ידיו ז] לעזרה ושם מוליאין לו את האשם וסומך עליו וחוזר ומכניסו למקום שחיטתו ושוחטו מפני שאין ח] מצורע יכול ליכנס בעזרה ולסמוך: עד שמזין עליו מדם חטאתו· לא עליו ממש קאמר שאין נותנין על בהונות אלא מדם האשם אלא שזורקין בשבילו דם חטאתו ודם אשמו: ליעייל ידיה· (ב) לתוך הפתח ולסמוך ולישחטיה אלל הפתח דהא כל הפתחים שהיו שם רחבן עשר אמות וחמש מהן בלפון וחמש מהן בדרום שהפתח מכוון כנגד פתחו של היכל באמצע העזרה ויכול לשחוט ט] לפני לפונו של פתח דהוה ליה לפון וקס"ד י] רבי היא דאמר כל לפון העזרה כשר יא] לשחיט' קדשים ואף לפון שבמקום דריסת רגלי כהנים וישראל כדאמר יב] לעיל: מרחק לפון· לפון הכשר יג] (מהן) לשחיטת קדשי קדשים רחוק מן הפתח יותר מכ"ב אמה מקום דריסת ישראל ומקום דריסת כהנים דכל אחת מהן י"א אמה במסכת מדות (פ"ה) [וכר"י ברבי יהודה] דאמר (יומא דף לו·) איזהו לפון מקיר מזבח ועד כותל העזרה כנגד לפונו של מזבח ותו לא הילכך לריך להחזירו בלפון המזבח וליכא תכף לסמיכה שחיטה: הכי גרסינן וליעבד פישפש· ופירושו פתח קטן כדתנן במסכת שקלים שבמזרח יד] בשער נקנור ושני פשפשין היו לו אחד מימינו ואחד משמאלו והן מחשבון טו] פתחים שהיו משתחוים כנגד הפתחים והכא פרכינן וניעביד פתח קטן בכותל לפוני של עזרה כנגד המזבח ויעמוד מלורע בחללו ויכנים ידו ויסמוך אי לאו דביאה במקלת שמה ביאה: הכל בכתב· כך אמר דוד כל פתח העזרה ומדותיה ובנין כל הבית נמסר לי מיד ה' ואין להוסיף על החשבון טז] וביאה במקלת לא שמה (ג) ביאה: אמר רב יוסף· לעולם רבי היא ודקאמרת ליעול וליסמוך כל הסומך כו': מאי קסבר· האי תנא דאמר כל הסמיכות לריכות תכף לסמיכה שחיטה חוץ מזו: ליעול וליסמוך יז] בהדיא· דרחמנא אמר לו שיכנס ויסמוך: שמא ירבה בפסיעות· לאחר שסמך אם יכנס פסיעה לגד פנים יותר משהיה לריך נמלא ענוש כרת: סמיכת אשם מלורע דאורייתא· כשאר אשמות דגמרינן להו סמיכה מהיקשא דכחטאת כאשם בפ"ק (לעיל יא·):(ד) תכף לסמיכה שחיטה לאו דאורייתא· דלא משמע ליה וסמך ושחט במקום יח]*שסומך ישחוט: מיתיבי וסמך ושחט· האי דסמכינהו קרא להיקשא סמכינהו כדאמרי' מה סמיכה בטהורים כו' י ט] וסמיכה דפשיטא לן בה משום דכתיב לפני ה' בשחיטה דלריכה שתהא לפנים ומשום דתכף לסמיכה שחיטה לריך שיכנס הסומך לפנים ולעמוד טמא מבחוץ ולסמוך בפנים אי אפשר כדאמרן לעיל שראשו ורובו מכנים: ואי אמרת לאו דאורייתא·היכי פשיטא ליה סמיכה בטהורין: בטמאין נמי איתא·שסומך בחוץ ומכניסה טהור לפנים ושוחט: סמיכת אשם מלורע לאו דאורייתא· קסבר שאינו בכלל כ] אשמות שהרי אינו בא אלא להכשיר: רבינא

תוספות

שהיא ראייה לדברי כא] מדלא שנה התנא חילוק זכרים מנקבות היכא דכתיב כהן סתם כגון גבי מתנות כהונה אלא גבי מנחה דכתיב אהרן ובניו שמע מינה היכא דכתיב כהן סתם לא שנא כהן ולא שנא כהנת ואם תאמר ואי מטעם הואיל והותר לצרעתו הותר לקריו למה לי יבא עשה שיש בו כרת וידחה עשה שאין בו כרת בלאו הכי נמי כב] ויש לומר כג] דעל מחנה לויה שנכנס טבול יום שבבעל קרי הוצרך לומר עשה דפסח דבכרת דחי עשה וכו' דטבול יום כד] אינו נכנס אי מן התורה אי טבול יום דזב כזב דמי אי מדרבנן מגזירת יהושפט והתם לא שייך למימר מתוך שהותר לצרעתו שהרי בשמיני קאי ואינו אלא מחוסר כפורים דלא נאסר מעולם במחנה לויה ומה שייך שם לומר שהותר אבל על מחנה שכינה שמכנים ידיו לבהונות והוא טבול יום של קרי על זה קאמר מתוך שהותר מחוסר כיפורים של מצורע דבעלמא אסור בעזרת שכינה והכא כה] הותר הותר נמי לטבול יום דקרויו כו]:

הגה"ה מכלל דתרוייהו סבירא להו טומאה דחויה היא בציבור· והא דאמר רב תחליפא משמיה דרבא זאת אומרת הותרה היא בציבור בפ"ק דיומא(דף ו:) זאת אומרת ולא סבירא ליה*:

וליעבד פשפש כז] הכל בכתב כו'· והא דמוסיפים על העיר ועל העזרות *היינו היכא דאיכא למימר קרא אשכחו ודרוש כי ההיא דסוכה(דף נא:) ומיהו קשה דהכא נמי אין לך קרא גדול מזה דניעביד פשפש לקיים מצות סמיכה דרחמנא אמר וסמך כח] ולמאי דמסיק דסמיכת אשם מצורע לאו דאורייתא ניחא אבל לטעמא דשמא ירבה בפסיעות קשה דניעבד פשפש דליכא למיחש ומיהו כט] דשמא ירבה בפסיעות גזירה דרבנן בעלמא היא וקרי כאן הכל בכתב והא דאמר בריש כיסוי הדם (חולין פג:) דכיסוי הדם אינו נוהג במוקדשין משום דלא איפשר דהיכי ליעביד לבטליה קא מוסיף אבניין וכתיב הכל בכתב אין זה חשוב כמו קרא דכיון דלא כתב בהדיא בקרא שינהוג כיסוי הדם במוקדשין:

ל] **ניעול** וניסמוך· כיון דלא איפשר בענין אחר ולא מקיימין סמיכה בטהרה *)ולא דמי לשאר [טמאים] שמשלחין קרבנותיהם ולא אמרינן ניעול וניסמוך דמקיימא סמיכה דידהו בטהרה: **סמיכת** אשם מצורע לאו דאורייתא לא] ·ואמרינן *אקפו ידייכו דלא תיהוי עבודה בקדשים ומתוך הך שמעתא אתי שפיר הא לב] דאמר בריש התערובת (לקמן דף עו.) גבי ספק מצורע שמביא אשמו ולוגו עמו ואומר אם מצורע הוא זה אשמו כו' ואותו אשם טעון סמיכה לג] ובהונות והשתא למה לי למיתני סמיכה בין יהא בין לא יהא [אשם] בעי סמיכה אלא משום דסמיכת אשם מצורע לאו דאורייתא לד] וקאתי לאשמועינן דטעון סמיכה (דאורייתא) משום ספיקא דשלמים וכן לעיל בריש מכילתין (דף ד:) גבי אשם דפריך מה לשלמים שכן טעונין סמיכה משום אשם מצורע נקט סמיכה ולא כפי' הקונטרס דלא גרים סמיכה כדפרישית בפ"ק והא דתנן בפ' כל התדיר (לקמן צ:) כל אשמות לה] באין בני שתי שנים ובכסף שקלים חוץ מאשם נזיר ואשם מצורע לא מני למיתני כל אשמות טעונין סמיכה חוץ מאשם נזיר ואשם מצורע כיון דמדרבנן מיהא טעון סמיכה והא דתנן בפ' כל המנחות באות (מנחות דף סא·) רבי שמעון אומר שלשה מינים טעונין שלש מצות שתים בכל אחד ואחד והשלישית אין בהן אשם מצורע טעון סמיכה ותנופה חי ואין בו תנופה שחוט לאו משום שתהא סמיכה דאורייתא והא דפריך בגמ' ויהא אשם מצורע טעון תנופה שחוט מקל וחומר ומה זבחי שלמי יחיד שאין טעונין תנופה חיים טעונין לו] תנופה כו' *לא שייך למיפרך מה לשלמי יחיד שכן טעונין סמיכה·דאורייתא כיון דמתנופה אתנופה עביד קל וחומר ומיהו קשה דפריך התם ויהא שלמי ציבור טעונין סמיכה לז] מקל וחומר ומה שלמי יחיד שאין טעונין תנופה חיים טעונין סמיכה מקל וחומר כו' אמאי לא קאמר אשם מצורע יוכיח שטעון תנופה מחיים ואין טעון סמיכה ובתורת כהנים בפרשת לו את אהרן עביד נמי קל וחומר כי האי גוונא א)וקאמר אשם מצורע יוכיח ודבר תימה הוא ב)אמאי לח]: **איפוך** סמיכת אשם מצורע לאו דאורייתא· לט] לעיל בפ"ק (דף יא:) ילפינן שאר אשמות מדכתיב כחטאת וכאשם מה חטאת טעון סמיכה אף אשם טעון סמיכה ואם כן מ] קשה אפילו אשם מצורע נמי ומה שפירש בקונטרס דקסבר אינו בכלל שאר אשמות משום דאינו בא אלא להכשיר קשה הא אמרינן פרק קמא דיבמות

א) נ"א ולא קאמר ב) גירסת הצ"ק אמאי סמיכת אשם לאו דאורייתא דהא לעיל פ"ק ט' והד"א *) [עי' לעיל כח: וברמב"ם פ"ג מהלכות ביאת מקדש]

מסורת הש"ס

ג] עייך לדף לג

פסחים עז. עט. פ. יומא ו: ז: מו: *תוספתא דנגעים פ"ח ע"ש

[לעיל כ. יומא לו.]

[ברכות מז. ביצה כ. מנחות לג.]

[לעיל לג.]

הגהות הב"ח

(א) רש"י ד"ה דתרוייהו וכו' למאן דאמר בפרק שני דף עז דאמר: (ב) ד"ה ליעייל ידיה לתוך העזרה לפנים מן הפתח ולסמוך וכו' לעיל ל"ב דף יד: (ג) ד"ה הכל וכו' ביאה הס"ד ואח"כ מ"ה א"ד אמר רב יוסף: (ד) ד"ה ותיכף לסמיכה וכו' במקום שסומך ישחוט והאי דסמכינהו קרא להיקשא סמכינהו כדאמרינן בהקומץ הס"ד ואח"כ מ"ה מה סמיכה וכ"ב וע"ש בפרק הקומץ דיש שם היקש אחר:

שסמך ישחוט והאי דסמכינהו קרא להיקשא סמכינהו כדאמרינן הס"ד צ"ק

עין משפט נר מצוה

יג א מיי' פ"ד מהלכות ביאת מקדש הלכה טו:

יד ב מיי' פ"ג מהלכות מעשה הקרבנות הל' יב:

טו ג מיי' פ"ד מהל' מחוסרי כפרה הל' ב ועי' בכ"מ:

[נ"ל אני עליהן]

טז ד מיי' פ"ג מהל' מעשה"ק הל' יא יג:

[וע"ע תוס' יומא ו: ד"ה אמר וכו' שהאריכו בסוגיא הכא]

[סנהדרין ב.]

שיטה מקובצת

ומה"ד אמר רב יוסף לעולם רבי היא וביאה במקצת לא שמה ביאה ודקאמרת: יז] ולסמוך להדיא אות ב' נמחק: יח] במקום שסמך ישחוט והאי דאסמכינהו קרא כו' והד"א והשאר נמחק: יט] כו' הס"ד ומה"ד מיתיבי וסמך ושחט מה סמיכה כו' (ס"א מיתיבי וסמך ושחט מה סמיכה בטהורין) אף שחיטה בטהורין פי' דכתיב ושחט בן הבקר לפני ה' ותיכף לסמיכה שחיטה א"כ צריך הסומך לעמוד בפנים דלעמוד מבחוץ ולסמוך בפנים אי אפשר דהא צריך שיהיה הסומך ראשו ורובו בפנים ואי אמרת כו': כ] ככלל שאר אשמות: כא] לדברי כי לא שנה: כב] נמי שהרי גבי (מנחות) [מחנה שכינה] נמי הותר לצרעתו וי"ל דאי לאו משום פסח שיש בו כרת לא הוי שרי ליה מטעם הותר וריב"א פי' דלא שייך לומר הותר לצרעתו רק במקום [שהוא אסור גם] עתה דהיינו דוקא לגבי עזרה שמכנים ידיו לבהונות וכל מחוסר כפורים אסור ליכנס לעזרה והתורה התירתו ליכנס לעזרה בשמיני שלו לצורך כפרתו [ולכך שייך לומר מתוך שהותר] לצרעתו ליכנס לצורך (היתר) כפרת צרעתו אבל מחנה לויה מה שייך לומר הואיל והותר לצרעתו והלא משמיני והלאה מותר ליכנס לשם משהעריב שמשו דכל מחוסר כפורים מותר ליכנס במחנה לויה אפי' (בא) [בלא] צורך הבאת קרבנותיו דכי כתיב טומאתו בו לרבות מחוסר כפורים במחנה שכינה כתיב ולכך הוצרך לומר יבא עשה דפסח לגבי מחנה לויה וטעמא דאישתראי גבי מחנה שכינה דהיינו העזרה כדפי' · לשון מהר"ם: כג] וי"ל ס"א דאפילו הכי לא הוי שרינן אלא בע"פ ולא בשאר ימות השנה · גליון: כד] יום דאינו נכנס מן תיבת אי נמחק: כה] והכא מותר הותר נמי: כו] דקירויו ע"כ: כז] פשפש כו' הכל: כח] וסמך ושחט ולמאי: כט] ומיהו כיון דשמא: ל] מה"ד ליעול ולסמוך כיון כו' אחר דלא מקיימא ·סמיכה כו' ולא דמי לשאר טמאים שמשלחין: לא] דאורייתא והיינו בהקפת יד כדאמרינן בפרק אין דורשין (דף טז ע"ב) אמרינן להו אקפו: לב] הא דאמרינן בריש: לג] סמיכה ונסכים כו' ס"א בהונות והשתא: לד] דאורייתא נקט וקאתי: לה] אשמות שבתורה באין בני שתים ותיבות שתי שנים נמחק: לו] תנופה שחוטין כו': לז] סמיכה ומה כו' ותיבות מקל וחומר נמחק: לח] אמאי אמרינן סמיכת אשם כו' והד"א: לט] דאורייתא דלעיל בפ"ק: מ] תיבת קשה נמחק:

שיטה מקובצת

א] קורא אני בהן תיכף תיבת עליהן נמחק: ב] ואי אמרת לאו דאורייתא כו' לפרש"י דלא ידעינן סמיכה בטהורים רק (מטמא) [מטעמא] דשחיטה כדפי' דבעינן תיכף לסמיכה שחיטה וכיון דתיכף לסמיכה [שחיטה] לאו דאורייתא א"כ פריך שפיר דבטמאין נמי משכחת לה שיעשה סמיכה (בעזרה) [חוץ לעזרה] וישחוט בעזרה אבל לפי' דלעיל דבסמיכה כתיב לפני ה' איך משכחת לה (בטהורים) [בטמאים] ואומר ריב"א דהך מסקנא אתיא כמ"ד ביאה במקצת לא שמה ביאה והלכך פריך שפיר בטמאים נמי משכחת לה דאי משום לפני ה' אפשר דמעייל ידיה וסמיך אלא ש"מ דתיכף לסמיכה שחיטה דאורייתא היא וא"כ בעינן סמיכה (לפני ה')[בטהורין] וכמו כן שחיטה וא"ת בשחיטה נמי ליעול ידיה וישחוט וי"ל דקסבר מרחק צפון ולא סגי דליעול ידיה א) לישחוט ממש לפני ה' וכמו כן בעינן לסמיכה אי תכף לסמיכה שחיטה דאורייתא אבל אי לאו דאורייתא היא בטמאים נמי משכחת לה כדפי' · מהר"פ: ג] טומאה דחויה היא·כלומר בקושי היא נדחית: ד] גמור דקא אידחי לטומאת: ה] שער העזרה המזרחי: ו] וחלל השער לא: ז] ידיו לבהונות: ח] שאין המצורע יכול: ט] לשחוט ס"א באמצע צפוני: י] וקס"ד דרבי היא: יא] לשחיטת ס"א קדשי קדשים ואף שלא כנגד המזבח במקום דריסת: יב] כדאמר בפרקין דלעיל הס"ד: יג] תיבת מהן נמחק: יד] שבמזרח שער אות ב' נמחק: טו] מחשבון הפתחים שהיו: טז] החשבון הס"ד

א) נראה דצ"ל אלא צריך לשחוט ממש לפני ה' וכמו כן וכו' ·

גליון הש"ס תוס' ד"ה סמיכת וכו' לא שייך למיפרך מה לשלמי יחיד שכן טעונים סמיכה · קשה לי הא בזה י"ל שלמי צבור יוכיחו דאין טעונים סמיכה ומכל מקום טעון תנופה שחוט · גם מ"ש אח"כ ומיהו קשה וכו' אמאי לא קאמר אשם מצורע יוכיח והא י"ל מה לאשם מצורע דאין טעון תנופה שחוט משא"כ שלמי צבור דטעונים תנופה שחוט · וגם הא יש לפרוך הק"ו הכי מה שלמי יחיד דלא טעון תנופה רק פעם אחד צריך סמיכה שלמי צבור דטעון ב' פעמים תנופה לכ"ש דטעונים סמיכה וליכא יוכיח כלל מאשם מצורע דהא התם לא טעון תנופה ב' פעמים :

הרוא

רבינא אמר לענין מלקות איתמר כי אתא רבין אמר רבי אבהו לענין טמא שנגע בקודש איתמר דאיתמר טמא שנגע בקודש ריש לקיש אמר לוקה רבי יוחנן אמר אינו לוקה ריש לקיש אמר לוקה °בכל קודש לא תגע ורבי יוחנן אמר אינו לוקה א] ההוא בתרומה כתיב וריש לקיש האי קרא להכי הוא דאתא האי מיבעי ליה אזהרה לאוכל בשר קודש *דאיתמר אזהרה לאוכל בשר קודש מנין ריש לקיש אמר בכל קודש לא תגע רבי יוחנן אמר תני ברדלא אתיא טומאתו טומאתו מביאת מקדש מה להלן ענש והזהיר אף כאן ענש והזהיר טמא שנגע בקודש מדאפקה רחמנא בלשון נגיעה אזהרה לאוכל מדאיתקש קודש למקדש *תניא כוותיה דריש לקיש ^יבכל קודש לא תגע אזהרה לאוכל אתה אומר אזהרה לאוכל או אינו אלא לנוגע תלמוד לומר בכל קודש לא תגע ואל המקדש לא תבא מקיש קודש למקדש מה מקדש דבר שיש בו

נטילת

תורה אור: ויקרא יב

רבינא אמר · הא דאמר עולא לעיל משמיה דריש לקיש בביאה ב] מקלת: לענין מלקות אמרה · כדקאמר. לוקה בהדיא אבל לא לענין כרת דתותביה ג] מצורע שראה קרי דכי איתקש ביאה לנגיעה לאזהרה איתקש כדכתיב לא תבא אבל לעונש לא איתקש דאין עונש בנגיעה: לטמא שנגע בקדש איתמר · לא יליף ריש לקיש מלקות מהאי קרא אלא לטמא שנגע בקדש ולא איירי בביאת מקדש כלל: בתרומה כתיב · כדמוכח סיפיה דקרא עד מלאת ימי טהרה שיעריב שמשה שהיא טבולת יום ארוך שטובלת בשביעי לנידתה וכל ימי טוהר שלה [הרי] היא כטבולת יום ד] וביום מ' ואחד מביאה קרבנה ומדכתיב לא תגע עד מלאת ה] אבל משימלאו ימיה תגע ואפי' מחוסרת כפרה ע"כ בתרומה כתיב דלענין קדש עד שתביא כפרתה והכי מוקמינן להאי קרא ביבמות בהערל וכיון דבתרומה כתיב לא ילפינן מלקות דקדש ו] ואפילו בק"ו דאין מזהירין מן הדין: לאוכל בשר קדש · בטומאת הגוף: בכל קדש לא תגע · ודרשינן לקמן אזהרה לאוכל: טומאתו טומאתו · כתיב ז] בכרת באוכל קדש בטומאת הגוף וטומאתו עליו וכתיב בביאת מקדש עוד טומאתו בו מה ביאת מקדש איכא אזהרה ולא יטמאו את מחניהם אף טומאת הגוף דאוכל קודש תיפוק ליה אזהרה מהכא: ומשני טמא שנגע נפקא לן מדאפקיה בלשון נגיעה: אזהרה לאוכל · עיקר קרא ח] מידריש מדאיתקש קדש למקדש בהאי קרא ודרשינן מה ביאת מקדש דבר שיש בו כרת אף אזהרת קודש דבר שיש בו כרת והיינו אכילה דאילו בנגיעה לא אשכחן כרת ומיהו אזהרה לנוגע נפקא לן מיניה מדאפקיה בלשון נגיעה: תניא כוותיה דריש לקיש · דאזהרה לאוכל קדש מהכא:

נטילת

דיבמות (דף ז') ולקמן בריש איזהו מקומן (דף מט') לפי שילא אשם מצורע לידון בדבר החדש בבהן יד ובבהן רגל יכול לא יהא טעון מתן דמים ואימורים לגבי מזבח ת"ל כחטאת ט] *כאשם הוא לכהן מה חטאת טעונה וכו' ואם כן נימא י] מה חטאת טעונה סמיכה ומתן דמים ואימורים לגבי מזבח אף אשם כו':

לענין מלקות איתמר · פירש בקונטרס אבל לא לענין כרת דתותביה יא] מצורע שראה קרי והקשה ה"ר חיים דהכתי איכא לאקשויי דאין עשה יב] דוחה לא תעשה ועשה לאו יג] *דנגיעה במקצת וטמא יהיה לרבות טבול יום ועוד קשיא ליה אפילו לאו גרידא היכי דחי ליה הא בעידנא דמיעקר לאו לא מיקיים עשה יד] ויש לומר דעשה שיש בו כרת חמור *ודחי טו] להו כדאשכחן בפרק תמיד נשחט (פסחים נט') דעשה שיש בו כרת דוחה עשה דהשלמה אע"ג דבעלמא אין עשה דוחה עשה ואם תאמר והלא גבי עשה דמצורע דתמיד משום שלום בית ודחי עשה אפילו הכי לא דחי לא תעשה בהדי עשה כדקאמר גבי שילוח הקן (חולין קמא·) לא צריכא טז] שנטל' ע"מ לשלחה דלאו ליכא וי"ל דעשה דמצורע אף ע"ג דחמיר כיון דליכא כרת לא דחי לתרוייהו אבל בפסח איכא *כרת יז] הכי גרסינן רבי יוחנן אומר אינו לוקה גבי תומרות דתרומה דקאמר שכן מחפ"ז הוה מלי למיחשב נמי נגיעת קודש דלוקה בתרומה ולא בקודש לרבי יוחנן ועוד יש תומרות הרבה כדפירש' ביבמות: **ההוא** בתרומה כתיב · הקשה ה"ר חיים מכל מקום נילקי בקודש כדאשכחן בפ"ק דכריתות (דף ד:) דאוכל חלב המוקדשין לוקה שלש משום וכל זר לא יאכל קודש אע"ג דבתרומה כתיב כיון דכתיב לשון קודש יח] ותירץ דהתם איכא מעילה שהוא נהגה ילפי' חט חט מתרומה כדאמר גבי הזיד יט] במעילה ובכל דוכתא ילפינן מעילה חט חט מתרומה אבל לענין שאר לאוין לא ילפינן ללקות על קודש כמו על תרומה כ] דהטאה בשגגה במעילה כתיב ובנוגע בקודש ליכא מעילה וה"ר יעקב דאורלינ"ש לא גריס וכל זר לא יאכל קודש אלא וזר לא יאכל כי קודש הם [דכתיב גבי קודש עצמה ומתרומה לא ילפינן]*:

***אזהרה** לאוכל בשר קודש מנין · תימה תיפוק ליה מלא תוכל לאכול בשעריך כי היכי דנפקא לן בפ' הערל (יבמות דף עג:) מעשר וביכורים דאוכלן בטומאת עצמן לוקה מדכתיב לא תוכל לאכול בשעריך ולהלן הוא אומר בשעריך תאכלנו הטמא והטהור יחדו יאכלנו דאפי' טמא וטהור אוכלין בקערה אחת וקאמר רחמנא כא] לך *בשעריך תאכלנו הכא לא תוכל לאכול ובין בטומאת הגוף ובין בטומאת עצמן איירי קרא ובההוא שמעתא גופה קשה דקאמר גבי מעשר וביכורים טומאת הגוף בהדיא כתיב ביה לא יאכל מן הקדשים כי אם רחץ ואמאי איצטריך והלא מהאי קרא תיפוק לן תרוייהו טומאת הגוף וטומאת בשר ויש מפרש דלא מצי לאפוקי מהאי קרא אלא טומאה הנוהגת במעשר כב] דכתיבי בקרא הילכך צריך קרא בטבול יום שמותר במעשר שמוזהר על אכילת קדשים וקשה מדאמרינן בפרק כל שעה (פסחים כד·) והבשר אשר יגע בכל טמא לא יאכל למה לי מלא תוכל לאכול בשעריך נפקא הא לא נפקא לן מהתם אלא טומאה הנוהגת במעשר ואיצטריך והבשר לטמאים דטהורים במעשר ושמא קרא דלא תוכל הוה מוקמינא כג] לדווקא בטמא האוכל דחמיר טפי אי לאו דכתביה קרא בעלמא ואזהרה לטומאת בשר לא הוה ידענא:

תניא כוותיה דריש לקיש בכל קדש לא תגע · תימה דהכא משמע דהך ברייתא מוקמא להאי קרא בקודש ולא בתרומה ובפ' הערל (יבמות עה·) אמרינן ואיבעית אימא נגיעה דתרומה מהכא נפקא דתניא בכל קדש לא תגע ומייתי הך ברייתא ויש לומר דהתם קאי אקראי דנגיעה דמעשר ותרומה כד] דלעיל מיניה מקשי ואיפוך אנא צריך לחלק בין נגיעה לאכילה דתרומה ולהכי מייתי ראייה מהך ברייתא דגבי קודש נגיעה כאכילה והוא הדין בתרומה ועוד קשיא דבההיא שמעתא דהתם ובפרק קמא דשבועות (דף ז') אמרינן בכל קודש לא תגע לרבות את התרומה וברייתא היא בתורת כהנים ובאכילה דתרומה מיירי כדמוכח שמעתא דהתם דקאי אהא דקאמר אי סלקא דעתך לתרומה גיורת ושפחה בטות מיכל תרומה נינהו ואי במגע נינהו הא ודאי בנות מגע נינהו אלא באכילה מיירי והשתא ההיא דרשא כמאן לא כריש לקיש כה] דמוקי ליה לאזהרה לטמא שאכל את הקדש מדאיתקש קודש למקדש ומדאפקיה כו] בלשון נגיעה אפקיה לאזהרה לנוגע בקודש ומרבויא דבכל אזהרה לאוכל לפני זריקה אבל כז] לתרומה לא מוקי ליה כלל אלא נפקא ליה כח] לאזהרה לאוכל תרומה מאיש איש ורבי יוחנן מוקי לא תגע אזהרה לנוגע בתרומה אבל לאוכל לא מוקי ליה ותירץ ה"ר אפרים האי דמוקי ליה ביבמות [דף עה. ושם ד"ה והכתיב] אזהר' לאוכל תרומה היינו למאן דמוקי קרא דאיש איש מזרע אהרן בזב בעל שלש ראיות ולא יאכל עד אשר יטהר עד דמייתי כפרה ולקודש כדקאמר התם ואם כן אזהרה לאוכל תרומה מנא ליה אלא מבכל קודש לא תגע אע"ג דהתם פריך לתנא דמוקי ליה בזב בעל שתי ראיות מכל מקום פריך שפיר דהא איכא מאן דמוקי ליה בתרומה אע"ג דגיורת ושפחה לאו בנות מיכל תרומה נינהו אף על גב דבאכילת קדשים מגרכינן תרי קראי חד בזב וחד ביולדת כט] [גבי תרומה לא] צריכי כיון דחזינן ככר באכילת קודש דזב ויולדת שוין ה"ג גבי אכילת תרומה ועוד יש לומר דבתרומה דלא תליא בכפרה לא בעי תרי קראי לזב ויולדת אלא דווקא *למקדש שצריך להמתין הכפרה:

והבשר

יח א מיי' פי"ח מהל' פסה"מ הלכה יב:

יט ב מיי' שם הלכה יג:

נ"ל כאשם

ס"א דביאה

[עי' היטב תוס' חולין עת. ד"ה מנין וכו']

גי' הל"ק כרת הס"ד ואח"כ מה"ד הכי גרסינן

[עיין לעיל דף טו ע"ב ד"ה אלא למעוטי]

ע' פתס נ"ק

ז"ק

מכות יד: ע"ש

שם ויבמות עה.

ז"ק [ועי' בתוס' מסכת מכות יד: דמקרע בע"ה]

ר"א לקודש נ"ב

שיטה מקובצת

א] ההוא בתרומה פ"ה כו' והקשה הר"ר חיים כו' וי"ל כו' עד נהנה וילפינן חט חט מתרומה כדאמרינן בעלמא אבל בנגיעה לא ילפינן דליכא מעילה וי"ס דלא גרסי שם [אלא] וזר לא יאכל (קדש שנאמר) כי קדש [שנאמר] גבי קדש אבל קרא דהכא משמע בתרומה כדכתיב עד מלאת ימי טהרה ואי בקדש אפילו לאחר מלאת לא כדפי' רש"י עד שתביא כפרתה והקדוש [ר"ש] מדריוש פי' דההיא בתרומה ליפסל תרומה בנגיעתה הוא דאתא דודאי בנגיעת תרומה ליכא מלקות ולפסול קודש לא איצטריך דאפילו לאחר מלאות נמי פסלה וניחא הכל: ב] במקצת הס"ד: ג] דתותביה ממצורע שראה: ד] יום ארוך: ה] מלאת משמע אבל: ו] דקדש מיניה ואפילו: ז] תיבת בכרת נמחק: ח] קרא ביה מידריש: ט] כחטאת האשם הוא: י] נימא נמי מה: יא] דתותביה ממצורע שראה: יב] עשה דפסח דוחה: יג] לאו דואל המקדש לא תבא אי ביאה במקצת שמה ביאה ועשה דהבא וטמא יהיה: יד] ויש לומר כו' ועי"ל דכי היכא דלא איתרבאי ביאה במקצת לענין כרת כמו כן לא איתרבאי ביאה במקצת לענין עשה דטמא יהיה דכי היכי דלא איתרבאי לענין כרת לא איתרבאי לענין עשה' מהר"ש: טו] ודחי לאו ועשה כדאשכחן: טז] צריכא דעבר ושקליה לאם דלאו ליכא ועשה הוא דאיכא וי"ל: יז] כרת עכ"ה ותיבות הכי גרסינן נמחק: יח] קודש ולא אמרינן אין מזהירין מן הדין ותירץ: יט] הזיד ס"פ הנשרפין ובפרק כל שעה (פסחים דף לג:): כ] שתיבת דחטאה כו' עד תיבת וה"ר יעקב כו' נמחק: כא] רחמנא ההיא דאמרי התם לך: כב] הנוהגת במעשר' ס"א בכל הנהו דכתיבי: כג] מוקמינא דוקא בטמא: כד] ותרומה דלמה דמקשה ואיפוך · ותיבות דלעיל מיניה מקשי ל"ש נמחק: כה] ולא כר"ש דר"ל מוקי ליה אזהרה לטמא: כו] ומדאפקיה ללא תגע בלשון נגיעה אפיק לאזהרה: כז] אבל אזהרה לאוכל תרומה לא: כח] ליה מאיש איש מזרע אהרן ותיבות לאזהרה לאוכל ביולדת גבי תרומה לא צריך כיון:

לוקה

a [33b] Rabina said: It was stated[1] [only] in respect of flagellation.[2] When Rabin came, he said in the name of R. Abbahu: It was stated in respect of an unclean person who touched sacred flesh.[3] For it was stated: If an unclean person touches sacred flesh, Resh Lakish maintains: He is flagellated; R. Joḥanan said: He is not flagellated. Resh Lakish maintained [that] he is flagellated, [because it is written] *She shall touch no hallowed thing.*[4] But R. Joḥanan maintains that he is not flagellated, [for] that [text] is written in reference to *terumah.*[5] Now [does] Resh Lakish [maintain that] this text comes for this purpose? [surely] it is required as a forewarning against eating sacred flesh?[6] For it was stated: Whence do we derive a forewarning against eating sacred flesh? Resh Lakish says: [From the text,] *'She shall touch no hallowed thing'*. R. Joḥanan said, Bardela taught: It is derived from the expression 'his uncleanness' occurring here and in reference to [an unclean person's] entry into the sanctuary:[7] as there [Scripture] prescribes the penalty and gives a forewarning,[8] so here too [Scripture] prescribes the penalty and implies a forewarning![9]—[That] an unclean person who touched sacred flesh [is flagellated follows] from the fact that b the Divine Law expressed this in terms of touching;[1] while a forewarning to one who eats [sacred flesh while unclean follows] from the assimilation of sacred flesh to the sanctuary.[2]

It was taught in accordance with Resh Lakish: *'She shall touch no hallowed thing'*: [this is] a forewarning in respect of eating. You say [that it is] a forewarning in respect of eating; yet perhaps it is not so, but rather in respect of touching? Therefore the text states, *'She shall touch no hallowed thing, nor come into the sanctuary'*: the *hallowed thing'* [sacred flesh] is assimilated to the *sanctuary*. As [the offence in connection with] the sanctuary is one which involves

a (1) That partial entry is designated entry. (2) As 'Ulla explicitly states. But it was not stated in respect of *kareth*, and therefore you cannot raise an objection from the law of a leper, who had a nocturnal issue where the penalty involved is *kareth*. (3) And not in respect of partial entry at all—*contra* 'Ulla. (4) Lev. XII, 4. '*She*' is a woman in childbirth, who is unclean, and she is forbidden to touch it by a negative command, which is punishable by flagellation. (5) But not to sacrifices. And although sacrifices are more sacred than *terumah*, for contact with which flagellation is incurred, we do not deduce *a fortiori* that the same punishment is incurred for touching sacred flesh, as flagellation is not imposed as a result of an *a fortiori* deduction. (6) In a state of bodily uncleanness. (7) Eating sacred flesh whilst unclean (Lev. VII, 20): *But the soul that eateth of the flesh of the sacrifice of peace-offerings, that pertain unto the Lord, having his uncleanness upon him, that soul shall be cut off from his people* (i.e., *kareth*). Entering the sanctuary whilst unclean (Num. XIX, 13): *Whosoever toucheth the dead, even the body of any man that is dead, and purifieth not himself—he hath defiled the tabernacle of the Lord—that soul shall be cut off from Israel; because the water of sprinkling was not dashed against him, he shall be unclean; his uncleanness is yet upon him.* (8) The forewarning is in Num. V, 3: *That they* (the unclean) *defile not their camp.* (9) Thus Resh Lakish utilises the text for a different purpose.

b (1) Since Scripture actually writes, *She shall* touch *no hallowed thing*. (2) Scripture writes, *She shall touch no hallowed thing, nor come into the sanctuary*. Thus the two, being brought together in this way, are assimilated to each other. Hence this deduction is made: as the forewarning in respect of the sanctuary involves *kareth*, so the forewarning in respect of the '*hallowed thing*' i.e., sacred flesh, is in respect of an action which involves *kareth*, viz., *eating* sacred flesh whilst unclean, for we do not find that an unclean person who *touches* sacred flesh incurs *kareth*. Nevertheless, since Scripture does use the expression '*touch*', a forewarning in respect of touching too must be understood from this text.

[34a] the death penalty,[3] so the offence in connection with the hallowed thing is one which involves the death penalty. Now, if this treats of touching, is then the death penalty involved?[4] Hence it must treat of eating.

Yet it is still required in respect of an unclean person who ate the sacred flesh before the sprinkling [of the blood]? For it was stated: If an unclean person ate the sacred flesh before the sprinkling of the blood, Resh Laḳish maintained that he is flagellated; while R. Joḥanan ruled that he is not flagellated. Resh Laḳish maintained [that] he is flagellated [for it is written,] *'She shall touch no hallowed thing'*, no distinction being drawn whether it is before sprinkling or after sprinkling. While R. Joḥanan ruled [that] he is not flagellated, as Bardela taught: 'It is derived from the recurring expression, *'his uncleanness'*, and that is written after the sprinkling'![5] — If so,[6] let Scripture say, '[She shall not touch] a hallowed thing'; why
a state *no hallowed thing?*[1] Hence two things may be inferred from it.

The [above] text [stated]: 'If an unclean person ate sacred flesh before sprinkling, Resh Laḳish maintained: He is flagellated: while R. Joḥanan ruled: He is not flagellated.' Abaye said: This controversy applies only to bodily uncleanness; but where the *flesh* is unclean, all rule that he is flagellated, because a Master said:[2] *And the flesh [that toucheth any unclean thing shall not be eaten]*[3] is to include wood and frankincense; though these are not edible, yet Scripture includes them.[4] Raba said: The controversy is in respect of bodily uncleanness, but where the flesh is unclean[5] all agree that he is *not* flagellated. What is the reason? — Since we cannot apply to him the text, *Having his uncleanness upon him, that soul shall be cut off*,[6] you cannot apply to him the text, *And the flesh that toucheth any unclean thing shall not be eaten*. But a Master said, *And the flesh* includes the wood and the frankincense? — That is where they were sanctified in a vessel,[7] so that they become as though all their *mattirin*[8] had been performed. For we learnt: All which have *mattirin* [involve a penalty through defilement] once their *mattirin* have been offered;[9] whatever has no *mattirin* [involves a penalty through defilement] when it has been sanctified in a [service] vessel.[10]

b It was stated: If one brings up the limbs of an unclean animal[1] on the altar, Resh Laḳish maintained: He is flagellated; R. Joḥanan said: He is not flagellated. 'Resh Laḳish maintained [that] he is flagellated', [for Scripture implies,] Only a clean animal [may be offered], but not an unclean one,[2] and one is flagellated on account of a negative injunction which is inferred from an affirmative precept. 'R. Joḥanan said, He is not flagellated', because one is not flagellated on account of a negative injunction which is inferred from an affirmative precept.

R. Jeremiah raised an objection: *That may ye eat*,[3] but not an unclean animal; and a negative injunction which is inferred from an affirmative precept ranks as an *affirmative* precept?[4] — Said R. Jacob to R. Jeremiah b. Taḥlifa: I will explain it to you: There is no disagreement at all about the limbs of an unclean [domesticated] animal; they disagree about a beast [of chase],[5] and it was thus stated: 'R. Joḥanan said: He transgresses an affirmative precept. While Resh Laḳish said: He does not transgress anything.' 'R. Joḥanan said, He transgresses an affirmative precept', [for Scripture says,] [*Ye shall bring your offering*] *of the cattle* [behemah]: [this implies] only of the cattle, but not of the beast [of chase]; while Resh Laḳish said, He does not transgress anything, [for] that [text] intimates that it is meritorious.[6]

Raba raised an objection: If it were said, '[*When any man of you bringeth*] *an offering to the Lord*,' cattle [*behemah*], I would agree that *ḥayyah* [beast of chase] is included in *behemah*, as in the verse, *These are the animals* [behemah] *which ye may eat: the ox, the sheep, and the*
c *goat, the hart and the gazelle and the roebuck* etc.[1] Therefore the text states, *'even of the herd or of the flock'*: of the herd or of the flock have I prescribed unto thee, but not a beast of chase [*ḥayyah*]. You might think [that] one must not bring [a *ḥayyah*], yet if one did bring [it] it is valid: for to what is this like? To a disciple whom his master bade, 'Bring me wheat' and he brought him wheat and barley, where he is not regarded as having flouted his orders, but as having added thereto[2] — and it is valid; therefore the text states, *'even of the herd or of the flock'*: of the herd and of the flock have I prescribed unto thee, but not a beast. To what is this like? To a disciple whom his master bade, 'Bring me naught but wheat' and he brought him wheat and barley. He is not regarded as having added to his words,

(3) I.e., *kareth*.
(4) Surely not! (5) For the forewarning is learned from the penalty, and the penalty of *kareth* is only incurred *after* the sprinkling, v. Men. 25*b*. — Returning to our subject, we see that Resh Laḳish utilises the text for a different purpose. (6) That the text is required for this purpose only.

a (1) Expressed in Heb. by the addition of *be-kol*, ('all' or 'every'); the emphasis implies an additional teaching. (2) Emended text (BaḤ). (3) Lev. VII, 19. (4) The exegesis is to shew that these can become unclean like an edible (though usually only an edible or a utensil can be defiled), and then the same law applies to them as to food. Now, flesh before sprinkling cannot be worse than these; if these involve flagellation, surely flesh before sprinkling does likewise. (5) *Var. lec.*: The controversy is in respect of the uncleanness of the flesh, but in the case of bodily uncleanness etc. (Sh. M.). (6) Ibid. 20. The text refers to *bodily* uncleanness, which supports the *var. lec.* — *Kareth* is not incurred before the sprinkling of the blood (*supra* n. 5). (7) The wood was removed from the altar in a service vessel, and the frankincense was sanctified in a censer. These, as the Talmud explains, are then in the same position as though all their ritual had been performed, and therefore are analogous to flesh *after* sprinkling. (8) V. Glos. (9) E.g., flesh, whose *mattirin* is the blood which by being sprinkled on the altar permits the flesh to be eaten. (10) V. Me'il. 10*a*.

b (1) E.g., of horses or camels. (2) In the verse, *Ye shall bring your offering of the cattle, even of the herd or of the flock* (Lev. I, 2.). Thus Scripture specifies clean animals. (3) Lev. XI, 3. (4) And but for the special negative injunction which follows in the Scriptural text it would involve no flagellation. (5) Animals are technically divided into *behemah* (domesticated animal) and *ḥayyah* (wild beast, lit., 'living thing'). The former includes dogs, horses and camels; the latter includes the hart, deer and roebuck. (6) To offer sacrifices of the cattle, whereas offering a beast of chase is voluntary and permissive. Nevertheless, though we have no affirmative precept forbidding it, anything unclean of either species may certainly not be offered, v. Men. 6*a*.

c (1) Deut. XIV, 4f. The last three belong to the class of *ḥayyah*. (2) And here too, since one need not offer a sacrifice *at all*, when one offers a *ḥayyah* he is as though adding to God's words.

נטילת נשמה אף קודש דבר שיש בו נטילת נשמה ואי בנוגע נטילת נשמה מי איכא אלא באכילה ואכתי מיבעי ליה לטמא שאכל בשר קודש לפני זריקה דאתמר טמא שאכל בשר קודש לפני זריקה ריש לקיש אמר לוקה ורבי יוחנן אמר אינו לוקה ריש לקיש אמר לוקה בכל קודש לא תגע לא שנא לפני זריקה ולא שנא לאחר זריקה רבי יוחנן אמר אינו לוקה א] כדתני ברדלא אתיא טומאתו טומאתו וכי כתב ההוא לאחר זריקה אם כן לימא קרא בקודש מאי בכל קודש ש"מ תרתי גופא טמא שאכל בשר קודש לפני זריקה ר"ל אמר לוקה רבי יוחנן אמר אינו לוקה אמר אביי מחלוקת בטומאת הגוף אבל בטומאת בשר דברי הכל לוקה דאמר (א) קרא °והבשר לרבות עצים ולבונה דלאו בני אכילה נינהו ואפילו הכי רבינהו קרא ורבא אמר מחלוקת ב] בטומאת הגוף אבל בטומאת בשר דברי הכל אינו לוקה מאי טעמא כיון דלא קרינא ביה °וטומאתו עליו ונכרתה לא קרינא ביה °והבשר אשר יגע בכל טמא לא יאכל *והאמר מר והבשר לרבות עצים ולבונה הכא במאי עסקינן כגון שקדשו בכלי דנעשה כמי שקרבו כל מתיריו *דתנן כל שיש לו מתירים משקרבו מתיריו כל שאין לו מתירין משקדש בכלי איתמר המעלה אברי בהמה טמאה ע"ג המזבח ריש לקיש אמר לוקה רבי יוחנן אמר אינו לוקה ריש לקיש אמר לוקה טהורה אין טמאה לא ולאו הבא מכלל עשה לוקין עליו ורבי יוחנן אמר אין לוקין עליו לאו הבא מכלל עשה ג] אין לוקין עליו מותיב רבי ירמיה °*אותה תאכלו ולא בהמה טמאה *ולאו הבא מכלל עשה א"ל רבי יעקב לרבי ירמיה בר תחליפא אסברא לך באברי בהמה טמאה דכולי עלמא לא פליגי כי פליגי בחיה והכי איתמר רבי יוחנן אמר עובר בעשה ריש לקיש אמר אינו עובר בולא כלום רבי יוחנן אמר עובר בעשה בהמה אין חיה לא ריש לקיש אמר אינו עובר ד] עליו בולא כלום ההוא למצוה מותיב רבא אילו נאמר °קרבן לה' בהמה הייתי אומר חיה בכלל בהמה כענין שנאמר °זאת הבהמה אשר תאכלו שור שה כשבים ושה עזים איל וצבי וגו' תלמוד לומר °בקר וצאן בקר וצאן אמרתי לך ולא חיה יכול לא יביא ואם הביא כשר הא למה זה דומה לתלמיד שאמר לו רבו הבא לי חטים והביא לו חטים ושעורים ה] שאינו כמעביר על דבריו אלא מוסיף על דבריו וכשר תלמוד לומר בקר וצאן בקר וצאן אמרתי לך ולא חיה הא למה זה דומה לתלמיד שאמר לו רבו אל תביא לי אלא חיטין והביא לו חיטין ושעורים שאינו כמוסיף על דבריו אלא כמעביר על דבריו ופסול

נטילת נשמה · כרת: ואכתי מיבעי ליה כו' · וכיון דלאחר זריקה נפקא לן ו] מיניה היכי יליף מיניה תרתי: אתיא טומאתו טומאתו · אזהרת טמא שלא יאכל קדש אלמא אזהרתו מעונשו ילפא ועונשו לאחר זריקה הוא ולא לפני זריקה כדקתני בגמ' דהקומץ רבה (מנחות כה:) יכול יהו חייבין עליו משום טומאה לפני זריקת דמים תלמוד לומר כל טהור יאכל בשר והנפש אשר תאכל בשר וגו' (ויקרא ז) הניתר לטהורים חייבין עליו משום טומאה שאין ניתר לטהורים אין חייבים עליו משום טומאה: אם כן · דלאוכל לאחר זריקה ז] אתא קרא לכתוב בקדש ואנא אמינא לאחר זריקה הוא דומיא דעונש: מחלוקת בטומאת הגוף · בההוא קאמר ר' יוחנן אינו לוקה דנפקא ליה אזהרה מעונש: אבל טומאת בשר · טהור שאכל את הטמא דאזהרה דידיה בהדיא ח] כתיבי והבשר אשר יגע בכל טמא לא יאכל (שם) דברי הכל לוקה: דאמר מר והבשר · יתירא דכתיב בסיפיה והבשר כל טהור וגו': לרבות עצים ולבונה · לטומאת עצמן דחיבת הקדש מכשרתם לשוינהו אוכלא ואע"ג דהני לאו בני אכילה נינהו ובשר לפני זריקה לא גרע מינייהו: ה"ג ורבא אמר ט] בטומאת הגוף אבל טומאת בשר איתקיש לעונש דסמיך לי' והנפש אשר תאכל בשר י] דאוקימנא בלאחר (ב) *(זריקת בשר): שקדשו בכלי · עצים שחתה אותן במחתת כלי שרת מעל המזבח עם גחלים ולבונה שקידשה בבזיכין דאפי' כרת בטומאת הגוף נמי אית בהו: דתנן · לקמן בפרק בית שמאי (דף מג.) גבי טומאת הגוף: כל שיש לו מתירין · המתירין אותו באכילה חייבין עליו משום טומאה משקרבו מתיריו ושאין לו מתירין משקדש בכלי: בהמה טמאה · סוסים וגמלים: יא] טהורים אין · מן הבקר ומן הצאן תקריבו: אותה תאכלו · מפרסת פרסה ומעלת גרה: ולאו הבא מכלל עשה · כך *שנויה בתוך יב] הברייתא ומסקינן בלא תעשה מניין תלמוד לומר אך את זה לא תאכלו אלמא מדאיצטריך לא תעשה אחריה לאו אזהרה הוא: דכ"ע ל"פ · דעשה הוא דאיכא ותו לא: כי פליגי בחיה · ולא לענין מלקות אלא לעשה יג] ואימור נמי איפוך דרבי יוחנן לריש לקיש °והכי הוה שמיע ליה לרבי יעקב: ההוא למצוה · בהמה מצוה להקריב וחיה רשות ומיהו טמאה ודאי לא דכתיב ממשקה ישראל מן המותר לישראל בפרק קמא דמנחות (דף ו.) גבי טריפה: אילו נאמר קרבן לה' מן הבהמה · ולא פירש בקר וצאן: הייתי אומר כו' · כענין שנאמר זאת הבהמה וכתיב בתריה איל וצבי: (ג) תרי בקר וצאן כתיבי התם מן הבקר ומן הצאן תקריבו והדר כתיב אם עולה קרבנו מן הבקר ואם מן הצאן קרבנו מן הכשבים:
פסול

והבשר לרבות עצים ולבונה · מהכא נפקא לן דחיבת הקודש מכשרת ומקשים הא דאמר בפ' קמא דפסחים (דף טז.) משקי בי יד] מדבחיא דכן כגון יין ושמן אמאי ליתכשרו בחיבת הקודש כמו עצים ולבונה וי"ל דחיבת הקודש מהניא לשווי אוכל *מוכשר מידי דדמי לאוכל כגון עצים ולבונה שהוא דבר עב וקשה כעין אוכל אבל לשווי המשקה כאוכל מוכשר לא מהניא חיבת הקודש ואם תאמר הא דאמר בפ' כל שעה (פסחים כד:) והבשר אשר יגע בכל טמא לא יאכל למה לי אם אינו ענין לגופו דנפקא ליה מלא תוכל לאכול בשעריך תנהו ענין לכל איסורין שבתורה הא איצטריך לגופיה דלקי אעצים ולבונה ויש לומר כיון דאיתרבאי עצים ולבונה מייתורא דוהבשר ממילא טו] אשמעינן דלקי מלא תוכל לאכול בשעריך ודברי תימה הוא מנלן דאתא לרבות עצים ולבונה דילמא דווקא לבשר קאתי דמהניא ליה חיבת הקדש ולא טז] בעיא הכשר: ואפי' הכי רבינהו קרא · משמע שהיא דרשא גמורה ולא אסמכתא וכן משמע בפרק שני דחולין (דף לו:) חיבת הקודש דאורייתא ולא כפירוש הקונט' דלקמן בסוף פ' בית שמאי (דף מו:) דקאמר והאמר מר והבשר לרבות עצים ולבונה ומשני לפסולא בעלמא ופי' בקונטרס מדרבנן וכן בפסחים בפרק כל שעה (דף לד:) דקרי ליה מעלה פירש בקונטרס מעלה דרבנן ואי אפשר לומר כן דהכי נמי הביא כפרתו אוכל בקדשים קאמר התם מעלה יז] דאורייתא הוא דמקראי נפקא לן בפ' הערל (יבמות עד:) והא דקאמר לקמן פסולא בעלמא היינו דליכא מלקות אלא איסור *דאורייתא וצריך לדקדק אי אתיא מילתא יח] דאביי דהכא כהני תרי לישני דלקמן פרק ב"ש (דף מו:): שקדש בכלי · תימה מה קידוש כלי יש בעצים דאי מה שמבקעין אותו בקורדום כשהיו מתליעים אותו הא קורדום אינו כלי שרת כדמשמע בתוספתא כדתניא השואל קורדום של הקדש בקע בו ובא חבירו ובקע בו כולן מעלו נתנה לחבירו וחבירו לחבירו הראשון מעל והשני לא מעל ובעולה אינו כן נתנה לחבירו וחבירו לחבירו כולן מעלו ובקונטרס פירש דמיירי הכא בעצים שחתה יט] במחתת כלי שרת מעל המזבח עם גחלים ואין משמע דבמס' תמיד (דף כח:) משמע שהיה חותה מן המאוכלות הפנימיות כ] ומיהו י"ל לא בתרומת הדשן מיירי אלא ביוה"כ שחותה גחלים לקטרת ונראה דקידוש כלי דעצים היינו כא] *דמשכי לגיזרין אע"ג דקורדום לאו כלי שרת הוא כדאמר בפרק י"ב דמנחות (דף קא.) עצים כמה דלא *משכי לגיזרין לא מיתכשרי והא דאמר בהקומץ רבה (שם כא.) יצאו עצים שאין מקבלים טומאה היינו קודם קידוש כלי א): אותה תאכלו · כב] אסיפא סמיך ב) דקתני בתורת כהנים אין לי אלא בעשה בלא תעשה מנין: שאינו כמעביר על דבריו · אע"פ שאין זה מביא אלא חיה לבדה כיון דמרצונו מביא הקרבן אין זה מעביר שהרי תלה בדעתו: אלא כמעביר על דבריו · ל"ע במעילה (דף כ:) ובפ' אלמנה ניזונת (כתובות נח:) גבי זבן לי ליתכא ואזיל וזבן ליה טורתא:
פסול

א) [וע"ע תוספות מנחות קא. ד"ה אע"ג] ב) [ועי' מכות יח: וצ"ע]

עין משפט נר מצוה

יט א ב מיי' פי"ח מהל' פסה"מ הלכה יב:

מוכשר וכן לקמן ז"ק

כ ג מיי' פ"ו מהלכות איסורי מזבח הל' ט:

כא ד מיי' פי"ח מהל' פסה"מ הלכה טו:

כב ה ו מיי' פ"ה מהל' איסורי מזבח הל' ו [דלוקה ועיין כ"מ מפרש טעמו דהא דמסיק הש"ס דכ"ע לא פליגי היינו דכ"ע ס"ל דלוקה ודלא כפרש"י ע"ש]:

כג ז מיי' פ"א מהלכות מעה"ק הלכה א:

[וע"ע תוספו' פסחים יט. ד"ה אלמא ותוס' חגיגה כג: ד"ה והא ותוספות מנחות כח. ד"ה יצאו ותוס' חולין לה. ד"ה אין]

[פסחים מח: יבמות נד: נו: סח. עג: חולין פח.]

שיטה מקובצת

א] לוקה רבי יוחנן לטעמיה. דאמר דתני ברדלא: ב] ס"א בטומאת בשר אבל בטומאת הגוף ד"ה אינו לוקה מאי טעמא כו': ג] אינו לוקה עליו: ד] אינו עובר ולאו כלום· הקשה בקונטרס בהמה טמאה נמי ותירץ א) וקשה דחיה טהורה נמי מי גרע ממפריש נקבה לעולה דאמרינן לקמן דהויא כבעלת מום ובבעלת מום יש שני לאוין משום בל תקריבו ומשום בל תשחטו וי"ל דדוקא בנקבה לעולה דהויא מין הקרבה כמו בעל מום אבל חיה דלאו בת הקרבה היא כמו חולין לא שייך בה לאוין כמו בבעל מום וגם לא הוי מקריב חולין לעזרה כיון שאינם ראוים לזובח בקירוב מקום במקדש דחולין בעזרה נפקא לן מוכי ירחק ממך המקום וזבחת: ההוא למצוה· פרש"י להקדים בהמה לחיה דבהמה מצוה וחיה רשות ולא רצה לפרש למצוה שמצוה לכתחלה להביא בהמה ולא חיה דא"כ היינו עשה ממש ומה שמהפך האמוראים הכי הוי שמיע ליה לרבי יעקב מקבלה וכיוצא בזה אשכחן בכמה מקומות: ה] שאינו כמעביר על דבריו אלא מוסיף על דבריו · וא"ת הא אין הנדון דומה לראיה שאינו מביא רק חיה לבדה והוי כמעביר שאין מביא מה שאמר לו רבו וי"ל דאם נצטוה להביא קרבן הדין עמך שהיה כמעביר [על דבריו] אבל הוא מביא מרצונו וברעתו תלה ולא הוי העברה: ו] לנ(ב) אלא מיניה: ז] זריקה לחודא אתא: ח] בהדיא כתיב והבשר: ט] אמר מחלוקת בטומאת הגוף אבל בטומאת בשר ד"ה אינו לוקה בטומאת הגוף הוא דאמר ריש לקיש לוקה דנפקא ליה מבכל קודש לא תגע אבל: י] בשר וכו' דאוקימנא לאחר זריקה הס"ד: יא] מה"ד טהורה אין: יב] בתוך המשנה ומסקינן בברייתא אין לי אלא בעשה בלא: יג] לעשה ואמוראי נמי איפוך דר"י לדריש לקיש: יד] בי מטבחיא: טו] ממילא שמעינן דלקי: טז] ולא בעי הכשר: יז] מעלה ומדאורייתא: יח] דאביי ס"א דרבא: יט] שחתה במחתה שהיא כלי שרת כו' ואין משמע כן דבמס': כ] הפנימיות ולא היה חותה עצים כלל ומיהו לא בתרומת: כא] היינו דמשפי להו כו' לאו כלי שרת הוא מ"מ חתוכו ותיקונו חשיב להו כלי שרת כדאמר בפרק המנחות והנסכים (דף קא ע"א) עצים כמה דלא משפי להו: כב] תאכלו ולא בהמה טמאה ולאו הבא מכלל עשה עשה' פ"ה שכך לשון המשנה ומסיים עוד בה לא תעשה מנין ת"ל אך את זה כו' ולא דק שהרי בהך ברייתא אינו כן בת"כ והכי איתא התם ולא בהמה טמאה אין לי אלא בעשה בלא תעשה מנין כו' והתלמוד הביא בקיצור ע"כ תוס' מהר"פ זצ"ל · ורבנן

א) נראה דצ"ל ותירץ משום דכתיב ממשקה ישראל וכו' · ומיהו עדיין קשה · ב) נראה דגרס כרש"י לאחר זריקה לא נפקא לן אלא מיניה וכו'.

חולין לז: [לקמן מו: פסחים כד: לה.]

מעילה י.

[מכות יח: ע"ש]

הגהות הב"ח

(א) גמ' דברי הכל לוקה דאמר מר והבשר: (ב) רש"י ד"ה ס"א ורבא וכו' בלאחר זריקה הס"ד ותיבת בשר נמחק: (ג) ד"ה וצבי כו' הס"ד ואח"כ מ"ה ת"ל בקר וצאן פרי בקר:

גליון הש"ס

רש"י ד"ה כי פליגי כחיה וכו' והכי הוה שמיע ליה. וכה שבת דף טו ע"א ד"ה דף כד ע"א:

ופסול תיובתא דריש לקיש תיובתא: וכולן שקיבלו כו': *בעא מיניה ריש לקיש מרבי יוחנן פסול מהו שיעשה שירים אמר ליה *אין (א) עושה שירים אלא חוץ לזמנו וחוץ למקומו הואיל ומרצה לפיגולו רב זביד מתני הכי בעא מיניה ריש לקיש מרבי יוחנן כוס פסול מהו שיעשה שירים אמר ליה פסול גופיה מאי סבירא לך אי פסול משוי שירים כוס פסול נמי משוי שירים אי פסול לא משוי שירים כוס פסול נמי לא משוי שירים רב ירמיה מדיפתי מתני הכי בעא מיניה אביי (מרבא) [מרבה] כוס מהו *שיעשה את חבירו דחוי או שירים אמר ליה פלוגתא דרבי אלעזר ברבי שמעון ורבנן א] *דתניא למעלה הוא אומר °את דמו ישפך למטה הוא אומר °ואת כל דמה ישפך מנין ב]לחטאת שקיבל דמה בארבעה כוסות ונתן מתנה אחת מזה ומתנה אחת מזה שכולן נשפכין ליסוד תלמוד לומר ואת כל דמה ישפך יכול נתן ארבע מתנות מכוס אחד יהו כולן נשפכין ליסוד תלמוד לומר ואת דמו הא כיצד הוא נשפך ליסוד והן נשפכין לאמה רבי אלעזר ברבי שמעון אומר מנין לחטאת שקיבל דמה בארבעה כוסות ונתן ד' מתנות מכוס אחד שכולן נשפכין ליסוד תלמוד לומר ואת כל דמה ישפך והכתיב ואת דמו ישפך א"ר אשי ההוא למעוטי שירים שבצואר בהמה: קיבל הכשר ונתן לפסול כו': וצריכא דאי אשמעינן פסול הוה אמינא מאי פסול טמא ג]דחזי לעבודת ציבור אבל שמאל לא ואי אשמעינן שמאל דאית ליה הכשירא ביום הכיפורים אבל כלי חול לא ואי אשמעינן כלי חול משום דחזו לקדושינהו אבל הנך אימא לא צריכא ולידהוי ג] ליה דחוי אמר ליה רבינא לרב אשי הכי אמר רב ירמיה מדיפתי משמיה דרבא הא מני *חנן המצרי הוא דלית ליה דחויין דתניא חנן המצרי אומר אפי' דם בכוס מביא חבירו ומזווג לו *רב אשי אמר כל שבידו לא הוי דחוי אמר רב שייא כוותיה דרב אשי מסתברא מאן שמעת ליה דאית ליה דחויין רבי יהודה *דתנן ועוד אמר רבי יהודה נשפך הדם ימות המשתלח מת המשתלח ישפך הדם ושמעינן ליה דאמר כל שבידו לא הוי דחוי *דתניא רבי יהודה אומר כוס אחד היה ממלא מדם התערובת וזורקו זריקה אחת כנגד היסוד ש"מ כל שבידו לא הוי דחוי ש"מ גופא תניא רבי יהודה אומר כוס אחד היה ממלא מדם התערובת שאם ישפך אחד מהם נמצא שהוא מכשירו אמרו לו לרבי יהודה והלא לא נתקבל בכלי מנא ידעי אלא שמא לא נתקבל בכלי אמר להן

אף

תורה אור: ויקרא ד, שם

פסול מהו שיעשה שירים · מי שהוא פסול לעבודה: מהו שיעשה שיריים · אם קבל וזרק מהו שיחזור הכשר ויקבל ויזרוק ויכשר הקרבן מי אמרינן כיון דזרק פסול שוייה לדם שבצואר ד] שיריים ותו לא מיחזי לזריקה או דלמא לא אלימא זריקת פסול לשוייה לדם שבצואר בהמה שירים ויחזור הכשר ויקבל: אין לך זריקה פסולה שעושה את השאר שירים · אלא זריקה במחשבת חוץ לזמנו וחוץ למקומו: הואיל ומרצה לפיגולו · הואיל והויא זריקה מן התורה למיקבעיה ה] פיגול ופסול: כוס פסול · כגון שילא מהו שיעשה לדם שבצואר ו]שירים אם זרקו כהן כשר לזה ולא יהא תקנה לקרבן שיחזור ויקבל: פסול גופיה מאי סבירא לך · אדם פסול שזרק מאי סבירא לך בשירים שבצואר בהמה דלא קמיבעיא לך: כוס מהו שיעשה את חבירו דחוי או שירים · כגון חטאת שקבל דמה בשני כוסות ונתן כל מתנותיו מאחד מהן חבירו שירים הוא ונשפך ליסוד ז] דכתיב ואת כל הדם ישפך וגו' (ויקרא ד): או דחוי הוא · ח] דחייה בידים שלא ניתן ממנו על הקרנות וישפך לאמה שבעזרה המוליכה דמים לנחל קדרון: למעלה · בפרשה הוא אומר בשעיר נשיא בשירי הדם ואת דמו ישפך ולא כתיב כל דמו: למטה · בחטאת יחיד הוא אומר ואת כל דמה ישפך: והן נשפכין לאמה · דכוס עושה את חבירו דחוי: למעוטי שירים שבצואר בהמה · שהן נעשין שירים על ידי הדם ט] הנתקבל וישפכו לאמה: וצריכא · לאשמועינן י] דאית להו תקנה בחזרה: דחזי לעבודת ציבור · כגון טמא דחזי יא] לכתחלה בציבור הלכך גבי יחיד איכא תקנתא בחזרה: ביום הכיפורים · נטל את המחתה בימינו ואת הכף בשמאלו: וניהוי דחוי · דהא נראה ונדחה ואמאי אית ליה תקנתא בחזרה: אפילו דם · שעיר הנעשה בפנים: בכוס · ומת המשתלח לא נדחה הדם אלא מביא שעיר אחר ומזווג יב] להדם וכשר הדם למתנותיו וזה ישתלח ולשון אפילו דנקט משום דשלשה מחלוקות בדבר איכא למאן דאמר אפילו בעלי חיים נדחים דקתני ואם משהגריל מת אחד מהן יביא שנים ויגריל עליהם כבתחילה והנשאר ידחה ואיכא למאן דאמר מביא חבירו שלא בהגרלה דבעלי חיים אין נדחין והגרלה לא מעכבא אבל דם בכוס ומת המשתלח ישפך הדם דשוטין נדחין ואין חוזרין ונראין ואתא חנן המצרי למימר אפילו דם בכוס יג] מזווג ליה אחר: שבידו · לתקן להחזיר כי הנך דמתניתין אבל ההוא דמשתלח אין בידו מי יימר דיהבי ליה אחריני: ימות המשתלח · דאידחי ליה ויביא שנים אחרים: מדם יד]התערובת · של פסחים: זורקו זריקה אחת · כדין פסח: כנגד היסוד · לאפוקי קרן דרומית מזרחית כדאמרי' לקמן *שאם נשפך דמו של אחד מהן על ידי שהן רבים ונבהלים לעשות נמצא כוס זה מכשירו שהרי טו]כולם מעורבים בו ואי משום דאיערוב בדם התמצית אמרינן לקמן רבי יהודה לטעמיה דאמר אין דם מבטל דם ולא אמרינן אידחי ליה בהתערבו הואיל ובידו לאוספו: והלא · זה שנשפך: לא נתקבל בכלי · טז]היאך יהיה כשר הא קיימא לן נשפך מן הצואר על הרצפה ואספו פסול: מנא ידעי · רבנן שלא נתקבל והלא לא מעשה היא אלא סברא היא בעלמא דחיים לשמא נשפך דמו של אחד מהן: שמא לא נתקבל · ונמצא זורק דם פסול:

אף

פסול מהו שיעשה שירים · יז] לדם שבצואר בהמה ולא יהיה עוד תקנה או יחזור הכשר ויקבל ויזרוק בפסול שקבל לא מיבעיא יח] דהתנן יחזור הכשר ויקבל אלא בפסול שזרק מיבעיא ליה כדפירש בקונטרס וממתני' ליכא למידק קבלו אין זרק לא דאיכא לדחויי כדאמרינן בפירקין דלעיל לא תימא זרקו לא אלא אימא שחטו לא יט] *ומיהו למאן דאמר שלא במקומו כמקומו דמי מוכח לעיל דהוא הדין *בזרק הפסול שיחזור הכשר ויקבל וה"ר אפרים מפרש דהך בעיא כ] אמתני' דכל הפסולין שעלו לא ירדו קאי דלכתחלה לא יעלו וקמיבעיא כא] אם זרק פסול מהו שיעשה שירים להיות נשפכין לכתחלה ליסוד כמו בכל שירי הדם או לא ואסור לזורקם לכתחלה וישפכו לאמה וקשה לפי' זה דהוה ליה למימר מהו שיעשה שירים או דחוי כדקאמר באידך בעיא כוס מהו שיעשה את חבירו שירים או דחוי ועוד אמרינן בהדיא בריש מסכת מעילה(דף ה.) גבי חטאת פסולה אין דמה טעון כיבוס הא קמ"ל דאע"ג דקיבל פסול וזרק וקבל כשר וזרק לאו כלום כב] (פסול) מאי טעמא שירים נינהו ופריך והא בעי מיניה ר"ל מר' יוחנן פסול מהו שיעשה שירים כג] וא"ל אין עושה שירים כי אם חוץ לזמנו כד] מאי לאו אבל שאר פסולין אינן עושים שירים ומאי קשיא ליה הא מודה ריש לקיש דלכל כה] היותר שירים הוי אבל מיבעיא ליה דשמא אפילו דחוי הוי ואם כן ממה נפשך אין טעון כיבוס ול"נ דלא קשיא מידי דאי שירים הוי א"כ הוי כשאר דמים כשרין שהשירים נשפכין ליסוד אבל שירים דקאמר התם דאין דמה טעון כיבוס היינו שירים ופסול אבל קשה כו] (בסיפא) דקאמר מאי לאו בר משאר פסולין ומאי פריך אי שאר פסולין אינן עושים שירים א"כ ליהוי דחוי וכל שכן דאין דמה טעון כיבוס אבל לפי' רש"י אתי שפיר דאי אינו עושה שירים יחזור הכשר ויקבל והוי דם כשר וטעון כיבוס · ברו"ך:

למעוטי שירים שבצואר בהמה · כז] והא דאמר (לעיל כה·) דצריך שיקבל כל דמו של פר הייני למצוה:

ולהוי דחוי · כח] תימה אם נתן לפסול מה בכך מעשה אילטבא הוא מי גרע מנתן על האבן שהרי לא פריך הכי אמתניתין דאמר פרק הוציאו לו (יומא נג:) דקתני יצא והניחו על כן הזהב שבהיכל ועוד תיקשי ליה קרא דמייתי לעיל בפרק קמא (דף יד·) ויזרקו הכהנים כט] (את הדם) ונראה דהא דפריך וליהוי דחוי לא קאי אנתן לפסול דאין זה אלא מעשה אילטבא בעלמא אלא פריך אנתן לכלי חול ואנשפך מן הכלי על הרצפה:

כל שבידו לא הוי דחוי · ל] *ענפיו מרובין מעליו דסוכה (דף נג·) אין זה בידו כיון דאין ממעטין ביום טוב וגבי כסוי הדם (חולין דף פז.) דקרי ליה דחוי כשכיסהו הרוח ונתגלה כיון דאין מלוה לבטל הדחוי לא] לא חשיב בידו ולא דמי להכא דמלוה לאוספו והפריש קרבן והמיר דת דלעיל לב] בפרק קמא (דף יב:) אין זה קרוי בידו כיון דאין דעתו לחזור*:

אין

עין משפט נר מצוה

כד א מיי' פ"א מהלכות פסה"מ הלכה כח:

כה ב מיי' פ"ב מהלכות פסה"מ הלכה כא:

שיטה מקובצת

א]ורבנן היא דתניא למעלה הוא אומר ואת דמו: ב] פמא · ס"א הנך פסולים דחזי כו' דחזי לעבודת צבור · ואע"ג דהאי טעמא מסיק במעילה דארבה עושה שיריים שאני הכא שלא עשה כלום והרי מעשה איצטבא הוא ושייך לומר איפכא: ג] וליהוי דחוי ותיבת ליה נמחק: ד] שבצואר הבהמה שירים: ה] בפיגול ופסול: ו] שבצואר בהמה שירים: ז] ליסוד כדכתיב ואת: ח]דדחיה בידים שלא נתן: ט]הדם שנתקבל וישפכו לאמה: י] לאשמועינן בכולהו דאית: יא] דחזי לעבודה לכתחלה: יב] ומזווג לו וכשר: יג] בכוס מביא חבירו ומזווג לו ויהיה כשר הדם הס"ד: יד]מדם התערובות: טו] שהרי מכולם מעורבים: טז] והיאך כשר ותיבת יהיה נמחק: יז] שירים' פ"ה כו' ולא רצה לפרש בקבלת פסול ולא זרק דהא תנן בהדיא יחזור הכשר ויקבל וליכא למדחי דהתם משום פסול מחשבה דמחשבה לא פסלא אלא בראוי לעבודה וא"ת זרק נמי תפשום מדתנן קבלו כו': יח] מיבעיא ליה דהתנן יחזור כו' בפסול שקבל חרק מיבעיא: יט] לא וכיון דשחיטה כשרה בפסולין מתניא מחשבתו: כ]בעיא קמייתא אמתני': כא] וקמיבעיא ליה אם זרק פסול כו' שיריים מותר הדם להיות נשפכין: כב] כלום הוא מ"מ: כג] מתיבת וא"ל כו' עד תיבות ומאי קשיא ליה מוקף בשני חצאי לבנה: כד] לזמנו כו' מאי לאו אבל ס"א אפי' שאר פסולים ומאי קשיא: כה] דלכל הפחות שיריים הוי: כו]בסיפא' ס"א מספרים דקאמרי כו': כז] בחמה' אם לא נתקבל כל הדם שלא יהיה השירים הנשאר בצואר הבהמה לשפוך ליסוד אלא ישפוך לאמה: כח] דחוי · פ"ה דהא נראה ונדחה הוא משמע דאכולהו פריך ותימה: כט] הכהנים מידם תיבות את הדם נמחק: ל] דחוי וענפיו מרובים מעליו דהדם דמס' סוכה דפסול דאמר דהיכא דאשחור מע"ש הוי דחוי מעיקרא אע"ג דבידו לתקנו איגזו: לא]הדידהי דאיומצוה לגלותו · לשון תר"ם: לב] דפרק קמא כו' בידו אע"ג דבידו לעשות תשובה כיודאין: [נ"ל מנכיון]

[ועיין היטב תוס' סוכה כג: ד"ה נקטם ותוספות לקמן נט: ד"ס עד]

מסורת הש"ס

מעילה ה:

[יומא מ: לקמן קיב. תמורה כב:]

יומא מב:

יומא סב: תמורה ה: [לקמן עד. מנחות נט:]

[מנחות מעז ע"ש]

יומא סב. [מנחות נט:]

פסחים סה. ע"ש [תוספתא שם פ"ד לקמן פ. ע"ש מנחות נט:]

לקמן

הגהות הב"ח

(א) גמ' אמר ליה אין לך זריקה עושה שיריים:

גליון הש"ס

תוס' ד"ה פסול וכו' ומיהו למ"ד שלא במקומו. לעיל טו ע"ב: באר"ד בזרק הפסול שיחזור הכשר ויקבל · עי' לקמן דף נב ע"א תוס' ד"ה ושקיבלו:

but as having flouted them, [34*b*]—and it [the sacrifice] is invalid. This refutation of Resh Lakish is indeed a refutation.

AND IF ANY OF THESE RECEIVED etc. Resh Lakish asked R. Johanan: Does an unfit person render [the blood in the throat] a residue?[3]—Said he to him: There is no case of sprinkling rendering [the remaining blood] a residue,[4] save [where it is done with the illegal intention of] after time or without bounds, since it counts[5] in respect of *piggul*.[6] R. Zebid recited it thus: Resh Lakish asked R. Johanan: Does an unfit goblet [of blood] render [the remainder] a residue?[7]—Said he to him: What is your opinion about an unfit person himself? If an unfit person renders [the blood] a residue, then an unfit goblet too renders [the blood] a residue; if an unfit person does not render a residue, an unfit goblet too does not render a residue. R. Jeremiah of Difti recited it thus: Abaye asked a Rabbah: Does one goblet render another rejected or a residue?[1]—Said he to him: It is the subject of a controversy between R. Eleazar son of R. Simeon and the Rabbis. For it was taught: Above it is stated, *And the* [*remaining*] *blood thereof shall he pour out* [*at the base of the altar*]; while below it is stated, *And* all *the* [*remaining*] *blood thereof shall he pour out* [*at the base of the altar*]:[2] How do we know that, if [the priest] received the blood of the sin-offering in four goblets and made one application [of blood] from each,[3] all [the rest] are poured out at the base [of the altar]? From the text, *And* all *the* [*remaining*] *blood thereof shall he pour out* [*at the base of the altar*]. You might think that, if he made the four applications from *one* goblet, all [the rest] are to be poured out at the base: therefore the text states, *And the* [*remaining*] *blood thereof* [etc].[4] How is this to be understood? [The remaining blood of] that [goblet] is poured out at the base,[5] but they [the other goblets] are poured out into the duct.[6] R. Eleazar son of R. Simeon said: Whence do we know that, if [the priest] received the blood of the sin-offering in four goblets and made the four applications from one goblet, *all* are poured out at the base? From the text, *And* all *the* [*remaining*] *blood thereof shall he pour out* [*at the base of the altar*]. Yet surely it is written, '*And the remaining blood thereof shall he pour out* etc.'?—Said R. Ashi: That is to exclude the residue [of the blood left] in the throat of the animal

IF THE FIT PERSON RECEIVED [THE BLOOD] AND GAVE b [IT] TO AN UNFIT ONE etc. Now, all these are necessary:[1] For if we were informed about an unfit person, I would say, what is an unfit person? An unclean [priest] who is eligible for public service;[2] but the left [hand] is not so.[3] And if we were informed about the left hand, that is because it is fit on the Day of Atonement,[4] but a secular [non-sacred] vessel is not so. While if we were informed about secular vessels, that is because they are eligible for sanctification; but as for the others, I would say that it is not so. Thus they are all necessary.

Now, let it be regarded as rejection?[5]—Said Rabina to R. Ashi: Thus said R. Jeremiah of Difti in Raba's name: This is in accordance with Ḥanan the Egyptian, who does not accept the law of rejection.[6] For it was taught: Ḥanan the Egyptian said: Even if the blood is in the cup he brings its companion and pairs it.[7] R. Ashi answered: When it lies in one's power [to rectify] the matter, it does not constitute rejection.[8] R. Shaya observed: Reason supports R. Ashi. [For] whom do you know to accept the law of rejection? R. Judah, as we learnt: Even more did R. Judah say: If the blood [of the he-goat to be sacrificed] was spilt, the [he-goat] which was to be sent away must perish;[9] if the [he-goat] which was to be sent away perished, the blood [of the other] must c be poured out.[1] Yet we know him to rule that where it lies in one's power [to rectify the matter] there is no rejection. For it was taught, R. Judah said: He [the priest] used to fill a goblet with the mingled blood[2] and sprinkled it once against the base [of the altar].[3] This proves that where it lies in one's own hands, there is no rejection. This proves it.

[To turn to] the main text: 'It was taught, R. Judah said: He [the priest] used to fill a goblet with the mingled blood, so that should the blood of one of them be spilt, the result is that this renders it valid. Said they to R. Judah: But surely it [the mingled blood] had not been received in a vessel?' How do they know?[4]—Rather [they said to him]: Perhaps it was not caught in a vessel?[5]

(3) If he sprinkles the blood, can a fit person make the sacrifice valid by catching more blood from the animal's throat and sprinkling it? Or do we say, Once the unfit person has *sprinkled* the blood, what still remains in the throat is regarded as the residue of the blood, which cannot be used for sprinkling, and therefore the sacrifice is invalid? (The Mishnah speaks only of receiving the blood, not of sprinkling.) (4) Emended text (BaḤ). (5) Lit., 'propitiates'. (6) Since such sprinkling counts as sprinkling to render the sacrifice *piggul*, it also counts to render the rest of the blood a residue. But no other illegal sprinkling renders the remainder of the blood a residue. (7) If the goblet containing the blood to be sprinkled was taken outside the Temple court, whereby it becomes unfit, and it was then sprinkled, does it render the remainder in the throat a residue?

a (1) E.g., if the blood of a sin-offering was received in two goblets, and all the sprinklings were performed out of one, is the blood in the other regarded as the residue, which must be poured out at the foot of the altar (cf. Lev. IV, 7: *and all the remaining blood of the bullock shall he pour out at the base of the altar*)? Or do we say that by not using it he intentionally, as it were, rejected it, and therefore it is simply poured out into the duct or sewer in the Temple court which discharged its contents into the stream of Kidron? (2) Lev. IV, 25. 30. (3) Four applications of blood were made on the horns of the altar. (4) But not *all*, which apparently contradicts the other text. (5) Since it is the residue of what was actually sprinkled. (6) Because one goblet renders another rejected.

b (1) V. Mishnah. (2) When the whole community is unclean, including the priests, they sacrifice the Passover-offering in that state. (3) Therefore, if the priest transferred the blood into his left hand, it should be permanently invalid. (4) The High Priest took the censer in his right hand and the spoon in his left. (5) The blood was fit in the first place, but by taking it in the wrong hand or in a secular vessel it was rejected, and therefore should no more be fit. (6) Viz., that once rejected it remains permanently so. (7) Two he-goats were taken on the day of Atonement, one of which was sacrificed as a sin-offering, and the other was sent away into the wilderness (the 'scapegoat'), the function of each being decided by lot. The blood of the former was received in a cup or basin and sprinkled on the altar. Now, if the scapegoat died before the blood of the other was sprinkled, Ḥanan rules that we do not say that the blood is thereby rejected, and *two* other goats must be brought, but only one more is brought and paired up with the one already slaughtered. For other views that the blood is thereby rejected permanently (the two goats being interdependent) v. Mishnah Yoma 62*a*. (8) Here it lies in his power to rectify the matter by transferring the blood. (9) But not sent to Azazel, because the two are interdependent, and since a new animal must be brought for the first, as its blood was spilt before sprinkling, a new *pair* must be brought.

c (1) And likewise two fresh animals brought. Thus in each case one is rejected because of the other, and remains so permanently. (2) Of many Passover-offerings. Lit., 'the blood of those which were mixed'. (3) In case the blood of one of them would be spilt, this would make it valid. (4) This is an interjection: how do the Rabbis, who raise this objection, know that it was not caught in a vessel? (5) But poured straight from the animal's throat on to the ground. Rashi (in Pes. 65*a*): in that case sprinkling is of no avail. Tosaf.: sprinkling, if already performed, is efficacious, but such blood must not be taken up to the altar in the first place.

I too, he answered them, [35a] spoke only of that which was received in a vessel. And how does he himself know that?—The priests are careful; but as they work quickly [the blood] may be spilt.

But the draining-blood[6] is mixed with it?[7]—R. Judah is consistent with his view, for he maintained: The draining-blood is called blood.[8] For it was taught: The draining-blood is subject to a 'warning;'[9] R. Judah said: It is subject
a to *kareth*.[1] But surely R. Eleazar said: R. Judah agrees in respect to atonement, that it does not make atonement, because it is said, ***For it is the blood that maketh atonement by reason of the life:***[2] blood wherewith life departs is called blood;[3] blood wherewith life does not depart is not called blood?—Rather [reply]:[4] R. Judah is consistent with his view, for he maintained: Blood cannot nullify [other] blood.[5]

R. Judah said to them [the Sages]: On your view,[6] why did they stop up [the holes in] the Temple court?[7]—Said they to him: It is praiseworthy for the sons of Aaron [the priests] to walk in blood up to their ankles. But blood constitutes an interposition?[8] —It was moist, and did not constitute an interposition. For it was taught: Blood, ink, honey, and milk, if dry, interpose; if moist, they do not interpose.[9] But their garments become [blood-] stained, whereas it was taught: If his garments were soiled and he performed the service, his service is unfit? And should you answer that they raised their garments,[10] surely it was taught: [*And the priest shall put on*] *his linen measure*:[11] [that means] that it must not be [too] short nor too long?[12]—[They raised them] at the carrying of the limbs to the [altar] ascent, which was not a service.[13] Was it not? Surely it was taught: ***And the priest shall offer the whole, and burn it on the altar***:[14] this refers to the carrying of the limbs to the ascent?—Rather, [they raised them] at the carrying of the wood to the [altar] pile, which was not a service. Nevertheless, how
b could they walk at the service?[1]—They walked on balconies.[2]

MISHNAH. IF ONE SLAUGHTERS THE SACRIFICE [INTENDING] TO EAT WHAT IS NOT NORMALLY EATEN, OR TO BURN [ON THE ALTAR] WHAT IS NOT NORMALLY BURNT, IT IS VALID; BUT R. ELIEZER INVALIDATES [THE SACRIFICE].[3] [IF HE SLAUGHTERS IT INTENDING] TO EAT WHAT IS NORMALLY EATEN AND TO BURN WHAT IS NORMALLY BURNT, [BUT] LESS THAN THE SIZE OF AN OLIVE, IT IS VALID. TO EAT HALF AS MUCH AS AN OLIVE AND TO BURN HALF AS MUCH AS AN OLIVE, IT IS VALID, BECAUSE [INTENTIONS CONCERNING] EATING AND BURNING DO NOT COMBINE.[4] IF ONE SLAUGHTERS THE SACRIFICE [INTENDING] TO EAT AS MUCH AS AN OLIVE OF THE SKIN, OR OF THE JUICE, OR OF THE JELLY,[5] OR OF THE OFFAL, OR OF THE BONES, OR OF THE TENDONS, OR OF THE HORNS, OR OF THE HOOFS, EITHER AFTER TIME OR OUT OF BOUNDS, IT IS VALID, AND ONE IS NOT CULPABLE ON THEIR ACCOUNT IN RESPECT OF PIGGUL, NOTHAR, OR UNCLEANNESS.[6] IF ONE SLAUGHTERS SACRED ANIMALS[7] [INTENDING] TO EAT THE FETUS OR THE AFTERBIRTH WITHOUT, HE DOES NOT RENDER PIGGUL. IF ONE WRINGS [THE NECKS OF] DOVES, [INTENDING] TO EAT THEIR EGGS WITHOUT, HE DOES NOT RENDER [THEM] PIGGUL. ONE IS NOT CULPABLE ON ACCOUNT OF THE MILK OF SACRED ANIMALS OR THE EGGS OF DOVES IN RESPECT OF PIGGUL, NOTHAR, OR UNCLEANNESS.

GEMARA. R. Eleazar said: If [the priest] expressed a *piggul*
c intention in respect of the sacrifice, the fetus [too] becomes *piggul*;[1] [if he expresses a *piggul* intention] in connection with the fetus, the sacrifice does not become *piggul*.[2] If he expresses a *piggul* intention in respect of the offal, the crop becomes *piggul*; in respect of the crop, the offal does not become *piggul*.[3] If he expresses a *piggul* intention in respect of *emurim*,[4] the bullocks become *piggul*; in respect of the bullocks,[5] the *emurim* do not become *piggul*.[6] Shall we say that the following supports him:[7] And both agree that if he expressed an intention [of *piggul*] in connection with the eating of the bullocks and their burning, he has done nothing?[8] Surely then, if however he expressed an intention concerning the skin etc., he is not liable, since we do not designate his action eating, as these are not eaten. (7) I.e., sacrifices. The Heb. (*mukdashin*) always refers to females.

(6) *Tamẓith* denotes the last blood which slowly drains off the animal, contrad. to the life-blood, which gushes forth in a stream. (7) Whereas 'life-blood' is required for sprinkling. (8) For the purposes of sprinkling. (9) This is a technical designation for a negative injunction whose violation is punished by lashes. But it involves no *kareth*, as does the consuming of the life-blood (v. Lev. XVII, 10f).

a (1) Just like life-blood. Hence it is also the same in respect to sprinkling. (2) Lev. XVII, 11. (3) And makes atonement. (4) To the objection, 'But the draining-blood is mixed with it'. (5) And there is certainly at least a little of the life-blood in this goblet of mixed blood, and that is sufficient for atonement. (6) That they did not fill a goblet of mixed blood. (7) On the eve of Passover they stopped up the holes through which the blood of the sacrifices passed out to the stream of Kidron. (8) Between the pavement and their feet, whereas they had to stand actually on the pavement itself, *supra* 15*b*. (9) When a person takes a ritual bath (*tebillah*), nothing must interpose between the water and his skin; if something does interpose, it invalidates the bath. (10) I.e., they were short and did not reach down to the blood. (11) E.V. garment, Lev. VI, 3. (12) But reach exactly to the ground. (13) And only then was it praiseworthy for the priests to walk up to their ankles in blood. (14) Lev. I, 13.

b (1) *Sc.* of the sprinkling of the blood. (2) Projecting boards alongside the walls. (3) V. *supra* 28*a*. (4) The whole Mishnah refers to intentions of eating and/or burning after time or out of bounds. (5) The sediments of boiled meat coagulated. (6) If the sacrifice became *piggul*, *nothar*, or unclean, and a priest ate of

c (1) And he who eats the fetus incurs *kareth*, as for eating *piggul*. (2) He holds that the fetus is an intregral part of the sacrifice, being regarded, as it were, as a limb of its mother. Nevertheless, this intention does not render the sacrifice *piggul*, because it is not usually eaten. The fetus itself too does not become *piggul*, in accordance with the Mishnah. (3) The offal is edible, but not the crop. Therefore an intention in respect of the latter is not efficacious; but an intention in respect of the former makes the whole *piggul*, including the crop. (4) If he slaughtered the bullocks which are burnt intending to burn the *emurim* on the altar after time. (5) Intending to eat of their flesh after time. (6) Because it is the intention to eat what is not usually eaten. The bullocks themselves do certainly not become *piggul*. (7) In his view that a thing can become *piggul* through something else, e.g., the fetus, the crop, and the flesh of the bullocks, though it cannot be the vehicle of rendering the sacrifice *piggul*. (8) 'Both' refers to R. Simeon and the Rabbis, v. *infra* 43*a*. The present reference is to the bullocks which were to be burnt without, and they agree that if the priest expressed an intention during one of the blood services to eat of the bullocks on the morrow or to burn them as required in the ash-house on the morrow, his intention is of no effect, because his intention to eat does not count, since this is not normally eaten and his intention with regard to the burning does not count either, for only an intention that the altar should *consume* (expressing it so, but not 'burn') counts.

תורה אור

אף אני לא אמרתי אלא כשנתקבל בכלי והוא גופיה מנא ידע *כהנים זריזין [א] ועבדין הייא ומשתפכין והלא דם התמצית מעורב בו רבי יהודה לטעמיה דאמר דם התמצית קרי דם דתניא *[א]דם התמצית באזהרה רבי יהודה אומר בכרת *והאמר ר' אלעזר [ב]מודה רבי יהודה לענין כפרה שאינו מכפר שנאמר °(כי *הדם הוא [ג] הנפש) דם שהנפש יוצאה בו קרוי דם שאין הנפש יוצאה בו אין קרוי דם אלא *רבי יהודה לטעמיה דאמר אין דם מבטל דם *אמר להם רבי יהודה לדבריכם למה פוקקין העזרה אמרו לו שבח הוא לבני אהרן שיהלכו עד ארכובותיהן בדם והא [ד] דם הוי חציצה לה הוא ולא הוי חציצה *דתנן *[ב]הדם והדיו והדבש והחלב יבישין חוצצין לחין אין חוצצין והא קא מיתווסי מאניידו *ותנן *היו בגדיו מטושטשין ועבד עבודתו פסולה וכי תימא דמדלו להו *והתניא °מדו [ג]כמדתו שלא יחסר ושלא יותיר בהולכת אברים לכבש דלאו עבודה היא אלא *והתניא °והקריב הכהן את הכל [ה] זו הולכת אברים לכבש אלא בהולכת עצים למערכה דלאו עבודה היא ולעבודה היכי אזלי אאיצטבי: **מתני'** *[ד]השוחט את הזבח לאכול דבר שאין דרכו לאכול ולהקטיר דבר שאין דרכו להקטיר כשר ורבי אליעזר פוסל לאכול דבר שדרכו [ה]לאכול ולהקטיר דבר שדרכו להקטיר פחות מכזית כשר *[ו]לאכול כחצי זית [ו] ולהקטיר כחצי זית כשר שאין אכילה והקטרה מצטרפין [ז]השוחט את הזבח לאכול כזית מן העור ומן הרוטב ומן הקיפה ומן האלל ומן העצמות ומן הגידין ומן הקרנים ומן הטלפים חוץ לזמנו וחוץ למקומו כשר [ח]ואין חייבין עליהן משום פיגול ונותר וטמא השוחט את המוקדשין [ט]לאכול שליל או שיליא בחוץ לא פיגל המולק את התורין [ז] [י]לאכול ביציהן בחוץ לא פיגל חלב מוקדשין [כ]וביצי תורין אין חייבין עליהן משום פיגול ונותר וטמא: **גמ'** אמר רבי אלעזר [ח] [ל]פיגל בזבח נתפגל השליל בשליל לא נתפגל הזבח [ט] פיגל באלל נתפגלה מוראה במוראה לא נתפגל אלל פיגל באימורין נתפגלו פרים בפרים לא נתפגלו אימורים לימא מסייע ליה *ושוים [מ]שאם חישב באכילת פרים ובשריפתן לא עשה ולא כלום מאי לאו הא חישב באימורים נתפגלו פרים לא

הא

רש"י

אף אני לא אמרתי · שיאסף אלא בנתקבל בכלי: והוא גופיה · רבי יהודה מנא ידע שנתקבל בכלי: זריזין הן · ומקבלי [י] לכולהו: הייא · מהרה: באזהרה · ה' לאוין כתיבי בדם חד לדם התמצית כדאמרינן בכריתות בפ"ק (דף ד:): ר' יהודה אומר בכרת · התם יליף טעמא: אין דם מבטל דם · דמין במינו לרבי יהודה לא בטיל ולקמן תנן לה בפ' כל הזבחים שנתערבו (דף עח.): למה פוקקין את העזרה · [יא] ערבי פסחים שלא יצאו הדמים דרך אמה לנחל קדרון: והא קא הויא חציצה · בין רגליהם לרצפה וכהן עומד על גבי כלים כו' פסול (לעיל דף טו:): היו בגדיו מטושטשין [יב] · לעיל בפרק ב' תניא לה: בהולכת אברים לכבש · הא דקתני שבח הוא לבני אהרן כו' בהולכת אברים קאמר ולקמן פריך ובהולכת דם היכי אזלי: אאיצטבי · איצטבאות גבוהין היו שם בנין אבנים ואינן הולכין דמן הרצפה הן: **מתני'** לאכול דבר שאין דרכו לאכול · חוץ למקומו או חוץ לזמנו: קיפה · מפרש בהעור והרוטב (חולין דף קכ·) תבלין ודקדקת הבשר השוכנת בשולי קדרה: האלל · גיד הלואר שהוא קשה ואין ראוי לאכילה: ואין חייבין עליהן משום פיגול · אם היה הזבח פגול שחישב על בשרו או על אימוריו חוץ לזמנו ונתפגל האוכל מאלו פטור: וטמא · אם אכל בטומאת הגוף מאחת מאלה [יג] *הזבח כשר: את המוקדשין · כל היכא דנקיט האי לישנא מיירי בנקבות: לאכול שליל · שבמעיה: לא פיגל · את הזבח דלאו גופיה דזיבחא הוא: חלב המוקדשין · חלב שבדדיה: אין חייבין עליהן משום פיגול · אם פיגל בזבח ואכל מחלבה לא מחייב כרת דלאו זיבחא הוא: **גמ'** פיגל בזבח · שחטו ע"מ לאכול או להקטיר חוץ לזמנו: נתפגל השליל · האוכל מהשליל חייב: בשליל · ששחט את הזבח ע"מ לאכול מן השליל חוץ לזמנו: לא נתפגל הזבח · קסבר רבי אלעזר שליל גופיה דזיבחא [יד] הויא דעובר ירך אמו הוא ומיהו אין מחשבתו מפגלת הזבח דדבר שאין דרכו לאכול הוא דרובא דאינשי לא אכלי ליה ושליל עצמו (א) לא נתפגל מדקתני מתני' לאכול שליל או שליא בחוץ לא פיגל: אלל · של עוף ראוי לאכילה הוא דרכיך: מוראה · לא חזי לאכילה דפירשא בעלמא הוא הלכך מחשבה דידה לא מפגלא ומיהו היכא דנתפגל העוף ע"י דבר אחר כיון דאיכא אינשי דאכלי חייב עליו כרת: פיגל באימורין · שחט פרים הנשרפים ע"מ להקטיר אימוריהן חוץ לזמנן: נתפגלו פרים · והאוכל מבשרן חייב: חישב בפרים · ששחט ע"מ לאכול מבשרן חוץ לזמנו: לא נתפגלו אימורי' · להתחייב כרת האוכל מכליות או מיותרת הכבד שלהם וכל שכן דלא נתפגלו פרים עצמן שהרי חישב לאכול דבר שאין דרכו לאכול ואיידי דנקט פיגל באימורין נקט נמי לא נתפגלו אימורין: לימא מסייע ליה · לר' אלעזר דאמר מתפגל ואע"פ שאין מפגל כגון שליל ומוראה ובשר הפרים: ושוין · ר"ש וחכמים שנחלקו בפ' ב"ש (לקמן מג·) דרבנן אמרי פיגול נוהג בפרים הנשרפים ור"ש אמר כל שאינו על מזבח החיצון [טו] אין חייבין עליו משום פיגול ושוין שאם חישב באחת מעבודות הדם לאכול מן הפרים למחר או לשורפן בבית הדשן כהילכתו למחר לא עשה כלום דמחשבת אכילה לא מהניא בהו דדבר שאין דרכו לאכול הוא ומחשבת שריפה *)נמי לא דאמחשבת אכילת מזבח קפיד רחמנא אבל שריפה לאו לשון אכילה הוא ואע"ג דאמרן בפירקין דלעיל חישב שתאכלנו אש למחר פיגול ה"מ דחשיב בלשון אכילה כדאוקי התם: מאי לאו · הא דפליגי רבנן דאמרי פיגול נוהג בהם בבשר דפרים עצמו קאמר דאם חישב באימורין להקטירם למחר דחשיב כי אורחייהו (ב) [טז] ואכילת מזבח נתפגל בשר הפרים ליענש כרת על אכילתו:

*) נ"ל נמי לא מהניא בהו דאמחשבת נ"ק

אימורים

תוספות

אין דם מבטל דם · ודם התמצית זרק ליה לשם מים כרבי אליעזר דפ' התערובות (לקמן דף עז·) דאית ליה רואין אי נמי סבר לה כרבי אליעזר דאמר *נתערב בדם התמצית כשר: והתניא מדו כמדתו [יז] · הך פירכא איצטריך דמ"ד אבנט מיגז גייז לעיל בפרק שני (דף יח.): פיגל בזבח נתפגל שליל · כיון דאיכא אינשי דאכלי ליה חייב כרת דירך אמו [יח] *הוא כו' שאין דרכו לאכול כו' כך פי' בקונטרס וכענין זה [יט] גבי מוראה דלא חזיא לאכילה דפירשא בעלמא היא הלכך מחשבה דידה לא מיפגלא ומיהו היכא דנתפגל העוף ע"י דבר אחר כיון דאיכא אינשי דאכלי חייב עליו כרת וכם דחק בחנם דאפילו חזיא כשאר בשר אינה מפגלת את העוף דמוראה [כ] אבית הדשן ואין בה לא אכילת אדם ולא אכילת מזבח והיינו טעמא דחישב בפרים לא נתפגלו אימורים אבל בשליל לא אפשר לומר כך דאע"ג דבפ' כילד מערימין (תמורה דף כה:) גבי שוחט את החטאת ונמצא בה בן ארבעה חי תני חדא נאכל לכל אדם ובכל מקום ולעולם וא"כ הייתי יכול לומר דהיינו טעמא דלא פסלא ביה מחשבה משום דלאו גופיה דזיבחא הוא אבל ע"כ ר"א סבירא ליה דגופה דזיבחא הוא דהא אמר פיגל בזבח נתפגל שליל וסבר לה כאידך ברייתא דתניא התם דאין נאכל אלא לזכרי כהונה [כא] ליום ולילה לפנים מן הקלעים והתם נמי משני להו הלכך צריך לפרש הטעם כמו שפי' בקונט' ויש דוחקים כאן [כב] לפרש משום דדרשינן בתורת כהנים בפרשת צו גבי נותר הזבח פרט לשליל ולשליא *ועל כרחין שייך נותר בשליל כדאיתא בתמורה בפרק כילד מערימין (גם זה שם) גבי שליל שבחטאת דאין נאכל אלא ליום ולילה הילכך אם אינו ענין לנותר תנהו ענין למחשבת נותר ואין נראה פירוש זה דמנא ליה לתנא הא דלמא איצטריך לגופיה למעוטי שליא [כג] מנותר ונראה דמדין שריפה קממעט שליל ושליא דשריפה כתיבא [כד] בקרא: פיגל באלל נתפגלה מוראה · בפ' העור והרוטב [כה] (חולין דף קכא·) מודו כו"ע דפלטתו סכין היינו אלל *בההוא מיירי הכא [כו] *ודעולה איירי שקודר להסיר המוראה בנוצה דאי אפשר שלא יקח מן הושט עם המוראה: באכילת פרים ובשריפתן לא עשה ולא כלום · דמחשבת אכילה לא מהניא בהו דדבר שאין דרכו לאכול הוא ומחשבת שרפה נמי לא דאמחשבת אכילת מזבח קפיד רחמנא אבל שרפה לאו לשון אכילה הוא ואע"ג דאמרינן בפירקין לעיל (דף לא·) חישב שתאכלהו אש למחר [כז] הני מילי דחישב בלשון אכילה כדאוקימנא התם כך פירש בקונטרס ובחנם דחק דלעיל מיירי במידי דראוי לאכילת אדם ומחשב שתאכלהו האש דהוי פיגול אבל האי לא שייך ביה לא אכילת אדם ולא אכילת מזבח:

וה"מ

עין משפט נר מצוה

[לקמן פח.]

נ"ל הוא ומיהו אין מחשבתו מפגלת הזבח דדבר שאין דרכו לאכול הוא כן פי' כו' נ"ק

כו א מיי' פי"ז מהלכות מאכלות אסורות הלכה ד:

כז ב מיי' פ"ב מהלכות מקוואות הל' ב סמג לאוין קיא טוש"ע י"ד סי' קלח סעיף טו:

[פסחים סה:] תוספתא דפסחים פ"ד

כח ג מיי' פ"ח מהל' כלי המקדש הל' ד:

כט ד מיי' פי"ד מהל' פסה"מ הל' ח:

ל ה ו מיי' שם הל' י:

לא ז מיי' שם הל' ז:

לב ח מיי' פי"ח מהל' פסה"מ הלכה כב:

לג ט י מיי' פי"ד שם הלכה ז:

לד כ מיי' פי"ח שם הלכה כב:

לה ל מיי' שם הל' כג · וע"ש בכ"מ:

לו מ מיי' שם פרק יד הלכה ח:

[נ"ל ונעשה]

נ"א ובעולה שקודר להסיר כו' נ"ק

מסורת הש"ס

[שבת כ. וש"נ]

[תוספתא פ"ב דכריתות] פסחים סה. חולין עד: כריתות ה:

[כריתות כב. פסחים סה. ע"ש]

נ"ל כי הדם הוא בנפש יכפר ויקרא יז

דברים יב

[לקמן נו. עח. עט. פסחים סה: מנחות כב. חולין פז: נדה עא:]

[נ"ל דתניא]

מנחות כא. שבת קכ: פסחים סה: [תוס' מקוואות פ"ו]

[נ"ל והתניא]

פסחים סה: לעיל יח.

יומא כג:

ויקרא ו

נ"ל בזבח

יומא כד. לעיל ד: וש"נ

ויקרא א

לעיל כח: לא:

[לעיל כו: לקמן סט. מנחות יב: יז.]

[לקמן קד:]

הגהות הב"ח

(א) רש"י ד"ה לא נתפגל וכו' ושליל עצמו נמי לא: (ב) ד"ה מאי לאו וכו' כי אורחייהו באכילת:

גליון הש"ס

תוס' ד"ה פיגל בזבח וכו' וע"כ שייך נותר בשליל · קשה לי הא להדיא קתני בברייתא דשמעתין ואין חייבים עליהם משום נותר והרמב"ם פסק דחייב משום נותר · ומצאתי במרכבת המשנה דהירך דסבירא ליה להרמב"ם דכמה דאמר רבא אף אנן נמי תנינא וכו' הא שליל ושליא חייבים · ה"ס דחייב משום נותר וטמא · ומוכח דמתני' פליג אברייתא · אבל תוס' בשמעתין ד"ה הא שליל לא פ"כ · גם אם נימא כך למאי הוצרך לדחוק ברייתא דת"כ הא י"ל דהך ברייתא סברה כתנאי וברייתא דסוגיין דאין חייבים משום נותר · וגם פשטא דדברי תוס' דא"א לומר כלל דליכא חיוב בנותר · ולא הזכירו כלל מברייתא דסוגיין וצ"ע:

שיטה מקובצת

א] זריזין הן אי זריזין הן אשתפוכי נמי לא משתפיך אגב דזריזין עבדין: ב] רבי אלעזר משום רבי יוחנן מודה: ג] הוא בנפש יכפר דם שהנפש: ד] והא קא הוי חציצה: ה]הכל והקטיר המזבחה זו: ו] לאכול כחצי זית·עיין רש"י ריש פ' הקומץ רבה: ז] התורין בפנים לאכול: ח] פיגל בזבח נתפגל השליל [בשליל לא נתפגל הזבח] (ואע"ג דרובא דאינשי לא קא אכלי ליה (מ"מ) [מש"ה] הוי ליה כמחשב בדבר שאין דרכו לאכול כפ"ה והדין עמו שכך צריך לפרש גבי פיגל במוראה ולא כמו שפי' בקונטרס במתני' דמש"ה אם פיגל בשליא לא נתפגל הזבח משום דלאו גופיה דזבח הוא: ט] פיגל באלל נתפגל מוראה · וא"ת הא אלל עצמו לא נתפגל והאוכלו אינו חייב כרת וי"ל כדפי' הקונטרס דהכא איירי באלל של עוף דרכיך טפי וכדנקט מוראה אבל פיגל במוראה לא נתפגלו האלל ולא שאר העוף ואפילו בחטאת העוף דאכלי כהני (מוראה) ואיכא אינשי דאכלי לי' כדפי' גבי שליל אבל בעולת העוף אפי' תהיה המוראה ראויה לאכול לא פיגל דהא אין בה לא אכילת אדם ולא אכילת המזבח ולבית הדשן אזלי: י] הן' ומקבלי להו לכולהו: יא] העזרה' בערבי פסחים שלא יצא הדמים דרך האמה: יב] מטושטשין כו' לעיל: יג] מאלה בזבח כשר: יד] דזיבחא הוא דעובר: טו] החיצון כשלמים אין. טז] אורחייהו באכילת המזבח נתפגל כו' על אכילתו אלמא בבשר פרים אע"פ שאינו מפגל מתפגל ע"י מחשבת אימורים והיינו כר' אלעזר דאמר פיגל כו': יז] כמדתו' וא"ת ודילמא דעביד להו ע"י אבנט וי"ל הך כו': יח] אמו ונפא דזיבחא הוא ומ"מ פיגל בשליל לא נתפגל זבח כיון דרובא דאינשי לא אכלי ליה הוי כמחשב בדבר שאין דרכו לאכול כך: יט] זה פירש גבי: כ] דמוראה לבית אות א' נמחק: כא] כהונה ואינה נאכלת אלא ליום ולילה: כב] כאן הטעם דפיגל בשליל לא נתפגל הזבח לפרש: כג] שליא ושליל מנותר: כד] כתיבא בההוא קרא הס"ד: כה] והרוטב אמרינן מודו: כו] ובעולה מיירי אות ד' נמחק: כז] למחר דהוי פיגול הני מילי:

מגו

הא חישב באימורין נתפגלו אימורין עצמן : *ת"ש *פרים הנשרפים ושעירים הנשרפים מועלין בהן משהוקדשו נשחטו הוכשרו ליפסל בטבול יום ובמחוסר כיפורים ובלינה מאי לאו לינת בשר וש"מ א] מגו דפסלה בלינה פסלה בה מחשבה לא לינת אימורים הא מדקתני סיפא כולן *מועלין בהן על בית הדשן עד שיותך הבשר מכלל דרישא לינת בשר מידי איריא הא כדאיתא והא כדאיתא רישא אימורים וסיפא בשר מותיב (רבא) [רבה] ואלו שאין מפגלין ואין מתפגלין ב] צמר שבראשי כבשים ושער שבזקן תיישים והעור והרוטב והקיפה והאלל והמוראה והעצמות והגידין והקרנים והטלפים והשליל והשיליא וחלב המוקדשין וביצי תורין ג] [כולן] לא מפגלין ולא מתפגלין ואין חייבין עליהן משום פיגול נותר וטמא והמעלה מהן בחוץ פטור מאי לאו לא מפגלין הזבח ולא מתפגלין מחמת זבח לא לא מפגלין את הזבח ולא מתפגלין מחמת עצמן א"ה הא דקתני סיפא כולן לא מפגלין ולא מתפגלין הא תו למה לי ולטעמיך אין חייבין עליו משום פיגול הא תו למה לי אלא איידי דבעי למיתנא נותר וטמא תנא פיגול הכא נמי איידי דבעי למיתני המעלה מהן בחוץ תנא נמי וכולן לא מפגלין ולא מתפגלין ד] רבא אמר אף אנן נמי תנינא השוחט את המוקדשים לאכול שליל או שיליא בחוץ לא פיגל והמולק את התורים לאכול ביציהם בחוץ לא פיגל והדר תני חלב המוקדשין וביצי תורים אין חייב עליהן משום פיגול נותר וטמא הא שליל ושיליא חייבים אלא לאו ש"מ כאן מחמת הזבח כאן מחמת עצמן ש"מ : *תנן התם ובעלי מומין ר"ע מכשיר בבעלי מומים א"ר חייא בר אבא *א"ר יוחנן לא הכשיר ר"ע אלא בדוקין שבעין הואיל וכשירים בעופות והוא שקדם הקדישה את מומה ה] *(א"ר חייא בר אבא) ומודה רבי עקיבא בעולת נקבה דכמאן דקדם מומה להקדישה דמי מתיב רבי זירא המעלה מהן בחוץ פטור הא מאימן חייב והיכי משכחת לה בעולת נקבה אי אמרת בשלמא קסבר רבי עקיבא עולת נקבה אם עלתה לא תרד הא מני ר"ע היא אלא אי אמרת אם עלתה תרד הא מני אימא המעלה מהן בחוץ פטור הא מאימורי אימן חייב והא מהן קתני ואימן דומיא דידהו אלא אימא המעלה מאימוריהן בחוץ פטור הא מאימורי אימן חייב :

מתני' שחטו על מנת להניח את דמו או אימוריו למחר או להוציאן לחוץ *רבי יהודה פוסל *וחכמים מכשירין ע"מ ליתנן על גבי הכבש שלא כנגד היסוד וליתן את הניתנים למטה למעלן ואת הניתנים למעלן למטה ואת הניתנים בפנים

אימורין עצמן · יותרת הכבד והכליות אבל לא בשר שאין מתפגל בדבר שהוא גופו ו] [של] זבח אלא דבר המפגל דכיון דלא חשיב אכילה לענין פיגול לא חשיב נמי אכילה לענין איפגולי : הוכשרו · *נתקנו ז] לקבוע פסולין הללו : בטבול יום ובמחוסר כיפורים · אם נגעו בהן : ח] מדפסלה לינה· פסלה נמי מחשבת לינה : מאי לאו לינת בשר · קתני שאם לן נפסל וה"ה למחשבת לינה שפוסלת בבשר והכי נמי דהיכא דחישב אבשר עצמו לא תדוק מינה דהא מחשבה בדבר שדרכו לאכול בעי וברייתא לעיל נמי תניא בהדיא ושוין שאם חישב ט] לאכול פרים לא עשה כלום אפילו לפסול מיהו הא דייקינן מינה דמחשבת לינת י] אימורים מפגלת הבשר כרבי אלעזר : לא לינת אימורים · *דקתני דפסלה האימורים נפסלים בלינה קתני ודכוותה *פשוט מינה דמחשבת לינת אימורים מפגלת באימורין : עד שיתיך יא] את הבשר · גרסינן במס' מעילה ול"ג משיותך דא"כ הוה ליה דבר שנעשית מצותו ואין מועלין בו אבל עד שיתיך דאכתי אית בהו צורך עבודת גבוה קרי יב] בהו מקדשי ה' : ולא מתפגלין · לקמיה מפרש ליה : צמר שבראשי כבשים ושער שבזקן תישים · איצטריך לאשמועינן דלא מהניא מחשבה בהו משום דעור הראש קרב עם הראש שאינו בכלל הפשט כדתניא בהשוחט (חולין דף כז·) מנין לרבות הראש שכבר הותז ומהניא ביה מחשבת הקטרה בהנך מיהא לא מהניא מחשבה אם חישב להקטיר למחר דלאו דרכו להקטיר הוא דגבי אם עלו ירדו קא תני להו בפ' המזבח יג] (לקמן דף פה:) : והמוראה · של עוף והאלל של בהמה והעובר ל"ג דהיינו שליל : וחלב המוקדשין · חלב שבדדי נקבה : הכי גרסי' יד] לברייתא הכא ובתוספתא כך שנוייה כולן לא מפגלין ולא מתפגלין ואין חייבין עליהן משום פיגול נותר וטמא והמעלה מהן בחוץ פטור ה"נ לגירסא דגמ' מאי לאו לא מפגלין את הזבח ולא מתפגלין מחמת הזבח לא לא מפגלין את הזבח ולא מתפגלים מחמת עצמן אי הכי הא דקתני סיפא כולן לא מפגלים ולא מתפגלין הא תו למה לי וליטעמיך אין חייבין עליהן משום פיגול תו למה לי אלא איידי דבעי למיתני נותר וטמא תנא פגול ה"נ איידי דבעי למיתני המעלה מהן כו' · אין חייבין עליהן משום פיגול אם טו] חישב בזבח פיגול ואכל מאלו והמעלה מהן בחוץ פטור דאין ראויין לפתח אהל מועד [וה"פ] מאי לאו אין מפגלין את הזבח אם זרק ע"מ לאכול או להקטיר מאלו חוץ לזמנם הזבח כשר : ולא מתפגלין מחמת הזבח · אם חישב לאכול מבשר הזבח או להקטיר טז] (*מחמת)אימורין חוץ לזמנו ולא נתפגלו אלו ליענש באכילתו כרת ותיובתא דר"א דהכא שליל ומוראה תנן : מחמת עצמן · אם זרק ע"מ לאכול לאלו חוץ לזמנו אין מתפגלין שאין מחשבתו מחשבה : הא תו למה לי · לאו לאיתויי דאף מחמת זבח אין מתפגלין : וליטעמיך אין חייבין עליהם משום פיגול · פעם שלישית למה לי למיתני הא מאי תיתי לאשמועינן לדידך אלא על כרחך משנה (א) יז] לאו דוקא אלא אגררא דטמא ונותר נסבה לרבי אלעזר נמי משנה שניה לא תיקשי דאגררא דהמעלה מהן בחוץ נסבה : אף אנן נמי תנינא · כרבי אלעזר דשליל ושיליא מתפגלין ולא מפגלין : לא פיגל · משמע לא את עצמן ולא את הזבח : הא שליל ושיליא חייבין · עליהן משום פיגול אלמא מתורת מפגל אפקעינהו מתורת מתפגל לא אפקעינהו : מחמת זבח · מתפגלין מחמת מחשבת עצמן לא מתפגלין : תנן התם · גבי אם עלו לא ירדו בפרק המזבח יח] : מכשיר · אם עלו שלא ירדו : וכשרין בעופות · לכתחילה שאין פוסל בהן אלא חסרון אבר כגון יבש גפה נסמית עינה *(ויצאת) או נקטעה רגלה משום הקריבהו נא לפחתך כדמפרש בבכורות : דוקין · טיילא בלע"ז לשון או דק (ויקרא כא) כמו הנוטה כדוק (ישעיה מ) [אבל] דוקין שבעין לא פסלי בהו ואע"ג דמום גמור הוא לא נאמרו מומין אלא בבהמה דכתיב תמים זכר בבקר בכשבים ובעזים (ויקרא כב) מיניה דרשי' (מנחות דף כה·) תמות וזכרות בבהמה ואין תמות וזכרות בעופות הואיל וכשרין בעופות לכתחלה בבהמה אם עלו לא ירדו : והוא שקדם הקדשן את מומן · אבל קדם מומן את הקדשן לא חלה עליהן קדושת מזבח מעולם אלא קדושת דמים ואין המזבח מקדש פסולין אלא שנראו לו כדמפרש בפ' המזבח : ומודה ר"ע בעולת בהמה נקבה · שתרד ואע"פ שכשרה בעופות לכתחילה מ"ט דכמאן דקדם מומה להקדישה הוא שאין לך מום בעולה גדול מזה דכל עולה זכר הוא : המעלה מהן בחוץ · בברייתא דלעיל תנן לה וקתני בה שליל ומעלה מהן משמע מבשרו פטור דלאו גופיה דזיבחא הוא ולא חזי להקרבה כדתניא בבהמה המקשה (חולין דף עד·) מה יותרת כבד וכליות האמורים באשם מולא מכלל שליל אף כל מולא מכלל שליל : הא מבשר אימן חייב : והיכי משכחת לה בעולת נקבה · דאילו בשלמים המעלה מבשר בחוץ פטור דלא מתקבל בפנים הוא כדתנן בפרק בתרא (לקמן דף קיב:) המעלה מבשר חטאת כו' : הא מני ר"ע היא · דכיון דבפנים אם עלתה לא תרד מיחייב עלה בחוץ : הכי גרסינן אימא המעלה מהן בחוץ פטור הא מאימורי אימן חייב והא מהן קתני ואימן דומיא דידהו אימא המעלה מאימוריהן בחוץ פטור הא מאימורי אימן חייב · לא תימא הא מאימן חייב אלא אימא הא אימורי אימן חייב ובשלמים או בחטאת עסקינן שאין נקבות : והא מהן קתני · דמשמע מבשרן ואימן דומיא דידהו ודייקינן מינה הא מאימן חייב ע"כ דומיא דידה דייקינן מן הבשר ע"כ בעולה קאי : מתני' רבי יהודה פוסל · אף על פי שאין כאן לא אכילה ולא הקטרה ובגמרא מפרש טעמא : שלא כנגד היסוד · או על המזבח שלא כנגד היסוד :

גמ'

וש"מ מיגו דפסלה בה לינה פסלה בה מחשבה · תימה דליסני יט] כדמשני לקמן פרק טבול יום (דף קד:) דלמא מחשבה לא פסלה לינה פסלה וי"ל משום דלא בעי למפשט הא דבעי ר' ירמיה פ' טבול יום לינה מהו שתועיל בפרים הנשרפים כ] ועוד י"ל דקסבר הש"ס דאי לינה מועלת מועיל כא] פיגול לענין דאם פיגל באימורים פיגל הבשר לכל הפחות : *לאכול שליל או שיליא בחוץ לא פיגל · הוא הדין למחר : הא שליל ושליא חייבין אלא ש"מ כאן מחמת זבח כו' · וא"ת אכתי נותר וטמא קשיא דמשמע הכא כב] (דוקא) [דיוקא] דאשליל ושיליא חייבין משום נותר וטמא וברייתא דלעיל קתני ואין חייבין עליהם משום פיגול ונותר וטמא וי"ל דלעולם אין חייבין אשליל ושיליא משום נותר וטמא והאי כג] (דשירייה)[דשיירינהו] משום פיגול : אלא בדוקין שבעין הואיל וכשרים בעופות · לאו דוקא דוקין שבעין דה"ה שאר מומין שאינן מחוסרי אבר כדאמר בפרק קמא דקדושין (דף כד:) דוקא יבש גפה כד] ונסמית עינה *אי נמי שאר מומין פסלי מדרבנן ומה שפי' בקונטרס דמחוסר אבר פסול בעוף משום הקריבהו נא לפחתך בחנם פירש דבהדיא דריש לה בקדושין (ג"ז שם) מדכתיב מן העוף ולא כל העוף :

תרי

לז א ב מיי' פ"ב מהל' מעילה הלכה ד: לח ג מיי' פי"ח מהל' פסה"מ הל' ת:

[עיין למשנה דלעיל פ"א]

[ע' תוס' לקמן עז: ד"ה בדוקין]

פ"א נתקנו לידי פסולין

מעילה ט· לקמן קה·

לקמן פד·

לקמן פה· ע"ש

[שם ליתא]

[לעיל מ·]

הגהות הב"ח (א) רש"י ד"ה וליטעמיך וכו' משנה שלישית לאו דוקא:

שיטה מקובצת
א] מגו דפסלה בה לינה פסלה בה מחשבה · פי' אם חישב לינה באימורים פסל נמי הבשר עצמה דמחשבה בדבר שדרכו לאכול בעינן (וחישבת) [ומחשבה] באכילת פרים ובשריפתן לאו כלום היא אלא ש"מ דלענין לינת אימורין קאמר דמפגלין הבשר · מהר"ש : ב] צמר שבראשי כבשים איצטריך לאשמועינן דלא מהני בה מחשבה ואע"ג דעור הראש קרב עם הראש שאינו בכלל הפשטה אפ"ה לא מהני בה מחשבה משום דלא קרינא ביה בצמר אכילת מזבח לפי (שהוא) [שהשער] בטל אגב הראש · מהר"ש : ג] תורין כולן לא : ד] מתפגלין אמר רבא : ה] תיבות א"ר חייא בר אבא נמחק : ו] גופו של זבח אלא דבר המפגל אבל פרים עצמן כיון דלא חשיב : ז] נתקנו לידי קבול פסולין : ח] בחן חס"ד ומה"ד בלינה מדפסלה לינה : ט] באכילת פרים : י] תיבת אימורים נמחק : יא] תיבת את נמחק : יב] קרי ביה מקדשי : יג] המזבח מקדש : יד] גרסי' לה לברייתא הכא ובתוספתא כך היא שנויה : טו] אם פיגל בזבח ואכל : טז] להקטיר מאימוריו חוץ לזמנו : יז] משנה שלישית לאו : יח] המזבח מקדש : יט] דלשני ליה כדמשני : כ] י"ל כו' ועוד י"ל דלקמן ר"ל דלינה פסלא בבשר ומחשבה לא פסלא כשחשב בבשר עצמו אבל כשחשב באימורים דין הוא שיועיל לפגל הבשר כיון דשייכא לינה בבשר' מתוס' הרא"ש ז"ל: כא] מועיל נמי פיגול : כב] הכא מהאי דיוקא : כג] והאי דשיירינהו משום דשייר פיגול דשייך בהו פיגול משום זבח וטמא משום דבנותר איכא מיעוטא הזבח כדפי' לעיל ופיגול וטמא ילפי' מנותר אבל חישב בזבח לא ילפינן מנותר לטעופי סברת לאכילת שליל ושליא ופשיטא דבלאו מיעוטא יש לחלק בין נותר לפיגול מידי דהוי אפרים דאמר לעיל פיגל באימורים כו' · מהר"ש : כד] גפה ונקטעה רגלה ונסמית עינה : תיבת

emurim, the bullocks become *piggul*?—No: [35*b*] [deduce thus:] but if he expressed an intention concerning the *emurim*, the *emurim* themselves become *piggul*.[9]

Come and hear: The bullocks which are to be burnt and the he-goats which are to be burnt are subject to [the law of] sacrilege from the time they are consecrated.[10] Having been slaughtered, they are ready to become unfit through [the touch of] a *ṭebul yom*
a and one who lacks atonement,[1] and through being kept overnight [*linah*]. Surely that means, through the flesh being kept overnight; and you may infer from this [that] since being kept overnight renders it unfit, an [illegitimate] intention renders it unfit![2]—No: it refers to keeping the *emurim* overnight.[3] But since the second clause teaches: You trespass in the case of all when they are in the ash-house[4] until the flesh is dissolved, it follows that the first clause treats of keeping the flesh overnight?—What reason have you for supposing this: each refers to its particular case; the first clause treats of *emurim*, and the second of the flesh.

Rabbah objected: The following neither render nor are rendered *piggul*:[5] the wool on the head of lambs, and the hair of he-goats' beards, and the skin, the juice, the jelly, the offal, the crop, the bones, the tendons, the horns, the hoofs, the fetus, the after-birth, the milk of consecrated animals, and the eggs of doves; all of these neither render nor are rendered *piggul*, and one is not liable on their account in respect of *piggul*, *nothar* and uncleanness, and one who carries them up without is not liable. Does this not mean: They do not render the sacrifice *piggul*, and they are not rendered *piggul* through the sacrifice?—No: They do not render the sacrifice *piggul*, and they are not rendered *piggul* through themselves.[6] If so, when the sequel teaches, They neither render nor are rendered
b *piggul*, why this repetition?[1]—Yet [even] on your view, [when he teaches,] One is not liable on their account for *piggul*, why this repetition?[2] But [you must answer that] because he wishes to teach [about] *nothar* and defilement, he also teaches about *piggul*. So now too[3] [you can answer], Because he wishes to teach [about] one who carries them without, he also teaches: And all these neither render nor* are rendered *piggul*.

Raba said: We too learnt thus:[4] IF ONE SLAUGHTERS SACRED ANIMALS [INTENDING] TO EAT THE FETUS OR THE AFTER-BIRTH WITHOUT, HE DOES NOT RENDER PIGGUL. IF ONE WRINGS THE NECKS OF DOVES, [INTENDING] TO EAT THEIR EGGS WITHOUT, HE DOES NOT RENDER PIGGUL. Yet then he learns: ONE IS NOT CULPABLE ON ACCOUNT OF THE MILK OF SACRED ANIMALS OR THE EGGS OF DOVES IN RESPECT OF PIGGUL, NOTHAR, OR UNCLEANNESS. Hence [it follows that] one is culpable on account of the fetus and the after-birth?[5] Hence you must surely infer from this that in the one case it means through the sacrifice;[6] in the other, through themselves. This proves it.

We learnt elsewhere: And blemished animals;[7] R. Akiba declares blemished animals fit.[8] R. Ḥiyya b. Abba declared in R. Joḥanan's name: R. Akiba declares [them] fit only in the case of cataracts in the eye, since such are fit in the case of birds,[9] and provided that their consecration [for a sacrifice] preceded their blemish; and R. Akiba admits that a female burnt-offering must be [taken down], because that is tantamount to the blemish preceding its consecration.[10]

c R. Zera objected: 'One who offers them up without is not liable;'[1] but [if one offers up the flesh] of the mother, one is liable; and how is that possible? In the case of a female burnt-offering.[2] Now, it is well if you say that R. Akiba holds that if a female burnt-offering goes up, it does not come down: then this is in accordance with R. Akiba.[3] But if you say that [even] if it went up, it goes down, in accordance with whom is this?—Say: He who offers up [the flesh] of them without is exempt, hence [he who offers up] of the *emurim* of the mother, is liable. But he teaches, 'of them', and the mother is analogous to them?[4]—Rather say: He who offers up of their *emurim* without is exempt; hence [he who offers up] of their *mother's emurim* is liable.

MISHNAH. IF HE SLAUGHTERED IT WITH THE INTENTION[5] OF LEAVING ITS BLOOD OR ITS EMURIM FOR THE MORROW, OR OF CARRYING THEM WITHOUT, R. JUDAH DISQUALIFIES [IT], BUT THE SAGES DECLARE IT FIT. [IF HE SLAUGHTERED IT] WITH THE INTENTION OF SPRINKLING [THE BLOOD] ON THE ASCENT, [OR ON THE ALTAR] BUT NOT OVER AGAINST ITS BASE; OR OF APPLYING BELOW [THE LINE[6]] WHAT SHOULD BE APPLIED ABOVE, OR ABOVE WHAT SHOULD BE APPLIED BELOW, OR WITHOUT WHAT SHOULD BE APPLIED WITHIN,

(9) But not the flesh. (10) One must not misappropriate a consecrated animal (or anything set apart for sacred purposes, e.g., money consecrated to Temple use) for secular use, and if one does, he becomes liable to a trespass-offering (*me'ilah*).

a (1) These defile its flesh, but do not make it unclean to enable it to communicate uncleanness to others, but only unfit. On lacking atonement v. *supra* 15*b* n.a2; on unfitness and uncleanness v. p. 155, nn. 3 and 4. (2) Now, that cannot mean an illegitimate intention to eat the flesh on the morrow (which is tantamount to an intention to keep it overnight), for it has already been stated that this is of no account. Hence it must mean that an illegitimate intention to burn the *emurim* on the morrow renders the *flesh piggul*, which supports R. Eleazar. (3) And you may infer that an intention to keep the *emurim* overnight renders the *emurim piggul*, but not the flesh. (4) Where the flesh is burnt. (5) An illegitimate intention in respect of them does not render the sacrifice *piggul*, nor do they become *piggul* themselves, as the Talmud proceeds to explain. (6) A *piggul* intention in respect of themselves does not make them *piggul*.

b (1) The same is taught at the beginning. (2) Obviously, if they cannot become *piggul*, there can be no liability for same. Thus this is certainly a repetition, on any interpretation. (3) On my interpretation. (4) That the fetus and the placenta are rendered but do not render *piggul*. (5) Which apparently contradicts the first clause. (6) They can be rendered *piggul* through the rest of the sacrifice. (7) If a blemished animal is taken up on to the altar, it must be taken down again; v. *infra* 84*a*. (8) If taken up on to the altar, they are not taken down again. (9) This blemish does not disqualify a bird at all, which is unfit only when it lacks a limb. (10) An animal burnt-offering must be a male (Lev. I, 3). If a female is offered, it must be taken down, although a bird burnt-offering may be of any gender, because there can be no greater blemish than the forbidden sex.

c (1) V. Baraitha *supra*; 'them' includes the fetus. (2) For one who offers up the flesh of a peace-offering without is not liable (v. *infra* 112*b*).—A *female* must be meant since the fetus is discussed. (3) Since it does not come down within, it involves liability without, the two being interdependent (v. *infra* 112*a*). (4) '*Of them*' means of course of their flesh, and so the deduction in respect of the mother must also refer to the mother's flesh. (5) Lit., 'on condition'. (6) Running along the middle of the altar.

*See Corrigenda.

[36*a*] OR WITHIN WHAT SHOULD BE APPLIED WITHOUT; [OR WITH THE INTENTION] THAT UNCLEAN [PERSONS] SHOULD CONSUME IT, [OR] THAT UNCLEAN [PRIESTS] SHOULD OFFER IT;[7] [OR] THAT UNCIRCUMCISED [PERSONS] SHOULD EAT IT, [OR] THAT UNCIRCUMCISED PERSONS SHOULD OFFER IT; [OR WITH THE INTENTION] OF BREAKING THE BONES OF THE PASSOVER-OFFERING, OR EATING THEREOF HALF-ROAST;[8] OR OF MINGLING THE BLOOD WITH THE BLOOD OF INVALID [SACRIFICES], IT IS VALID, BECAUSE AN [ILLEGITIMATE] INTENTION DOES NOT DISQUALIFY [A SACRIFICE] SAVE WHERE IT REFERS TO AFTER TIME OR WITHOUT BOUNDS, AND [IN THE CASE OF] A PASSOVER-OFFERING AND A SIN-OFFERING, [THE INTENTION TO SLAUGHTER THEM] FOR A DIFFERENT PURPOSE.

GEMARA. What is R. Judah's reason?—Said R. Eleazar, Two texts are written in reference to *nothar*. One text says, *And ye shall*
a *let nothing of it remain until the morning*,[1] and another text says, *He shall not leave any of it until the morning*.[2] Since one is superfluous in respect of [actual] leaving, apply it to the *intention* of leaving it.[3]

Now [does] R. Judah [hold] that this text comes for this purpose? Surely it is required for what was taught: '*And the flesh of the sacrifice of his peace-offerings for thanksgiving* [*shall be eaten on the day of his offering: he shall not leave any of it until the morning*]': we have thus learnt that the thanks-offering is eaten a day and a night. How do we know [the same of] an exchange, an offspring, or a substitute?[4]—From the text, 'And *the flesh*'.[5] How do we know [the same of] a sin-offering and a guilt-offering?—Because it says, '[*And the flesh of*] *the sacrifice* [etc]'.[6] And whence do we know to include a nazirite's peace-offering[7] and the peace-offerings of the Passover-offering?[8] From the text, '*his peace-offerings*'. Whence do we know [the same of] the loaves of the thanks-offering and a
b nazirite's loaves and the wafers?[1] Because '*his offering*' is written; [and] to all of these I apply [the injunction], '*he shall not leave any of it until the morning*'![2]—If so,[3] let Scripture write, '*lo tothiru*';[4] why [write] '*lo yaniaḥ*'? [To teach that] since it is superfluous in respect of actual leaving, apply it to the *intention* of leaving.

Granted that this [reason] is satisfactory in respect of [the intention] to leave [the blood or the *emurim*], what can you say about [the intention] to carry [them] out? Moreover R. Judah's reason is based on logic.[5] For it was taught: R. Judah said to them [the Sages]: Do you not admit that if he left it [the blood or the *emurim*] for the morrow, [the sacrifice] is invalid? So also if he *intended* to leave it for the morrow, it is invalid! (And do you not admit that if he carried them without, it is invalid? So also if he intended to carry them without, it is invalid.)[6]—Rather, R. Judah's reason is based on logic.

Now, let R. Judah disagree in the other cases too?[7]—In which case should he disagree? In the case of [intending] to break the bones of a Passover-offering and eating thereof half-roast! does then the sacrifice itself become invalid?[8] [In the case of] the intention that unclean [persons] should eat it or that unclean [persons] should offer it! does then the sacrifice itself become invalid? [In the case of] the intention that uncircumcised persons should eat it or uncircumcised persons should offer it! is then the sacrifice itself invalidated?

Another version:[9] Does it entirely depend on him?[10] [As for the intention] to mingle its blood with the blood of invalid [sacrifices], R. Judah is consistent with his view, for he maintains that blood
c does not nullify [other] blood.[1] [As for the intention] to apply below what should be applied above, and above [what should be applied] below,—R. Judah is consistent with his view, for he maintains: Even what is not its place is also called its place.[2] Then let him disagree where he applied without what should be applied within, or within, what should be applied without?—R. Judah holds: We require a place which has a threefold function, [viz.,] in respect of the blood, the flesh, and the *emurim*.[3]

Does then R. Judah accept that view? Surely it was taught: R. Judah said: [Scripture states, *Thou shalt not sacrifice unto the Lord thy God an ox, or a sheep, wherein is a blemish, even any*] *evil thing*:[4] here [Scripture] extends the law to a sin-offering which one slaughtered on the south [side of the Temple court], or a sin-offering whose blood entered within [the inner sanctum], [teaching that] it is invalid?[5]—But does then R. Judah not accept [this interpretation of] 'third'?[3] Surely we learnt: R. Judah said: If one carried [the blood] within in ignorance, it is valid;[6] hence if [one did this] deliberately, it is invalid, and we have explained this as meaning where he made atonement.[7] Now if in that case, where he has actually carried it within, if he made atonement [therewith] it does [invalidate the sacrifice], but if he did not make atonement, it does not: how much the more so here, where he has merely *intended*?[8]—There is a controversy of two Tannaim as to R. Judah's view.

Now, does R. Judah hold that when one slaughters a sin-offering

(7) I.e., the blood or the *emurim*.
(8) Both of which are forbidden, Ex. XII, 9, 46.
a (1) Ex. XII, 10. (2) Lev. VII, 15. The first refers to the Passover-offering, the second to the thanks-offering. Both were peace-offerings, and therefore it need be stated for one only, and the other would follow. (3) Thus Scripture forbids the intention, and therefore the intention disqualifies. (4) The text has the plural.—If the animal originally set aside for the offering is lost, and another consecrated in its stead, and then the first is found, the second is called the exchange. 'Offspring': if the consecrated animal lambed or calved before it was sacrificed. For 'substitute' v. *supra* 5*b* n.b 8. All three are sacrificed as thanks-offerings. (5) '*And*' is an extension. (6) '*The sacrifice*' is superfluous, for Scripture could say, And the flesh of his peace-offerings. Hence it is understood to include these other sacrifices. (7) V. Num. VI, 14f. This, like an ordinary thanks-offering, was accompanied by loaves of bread. (8) Rashi: the festival sacrifices (*ḥagigah*) which accompanied the Passover-offering on the eve of Passover. Tosaf. (*supra* 9*a*): a Passover remainder, i.e., an animal consecrated as a Passover-offering but not sacrificed as such.

b (1) The Heb. denotes two different kinds of loaves. (2) Thus R. Judah utilises the verse for a different purpose! (3) If this is the *only* purpose of the text. (4) 'Ye shall not let any remain'. *Tothiru* (fr. *hothir*) is the verb used in Ex. XII, 10, and we would expect the same here. (5) Not a Scriptural exegesis. (6) Bracketed addition a *var. lec.* (7) Enumerated in the Mishnah. (8) Even if he actually breaks the bones or eats of it half-roast. Surely not, and so the intention does not invalidate it either. (9) Other reasons why R. Judah does not dispute the other cases of the Mishnah. (10) When he intends that unclean or uncircumcised should partake thereof or offer it up, he may not find such to carry out his intention. Hence his intention does not count.

c (1) *Supra* 35*a*. Hence even if he did it, it would not invalidate the sacrifice. (2) V. *supra* 27*a*. (3) V. *supra* 29*a*. (4) Deut. XVII, 1. (5) Though this carrying without bounds is not in respect of a place that has that threefold function. (6) V. *infra* 82*a*. (7) The mere carrying of the blood into the inner sanctum, even deliberately, does not invalidate the sacrifice, but only its actual sprinkling (called 'making atonement') on the inner altar. (8) The intention alone certainly does not disqualify it, and the reason must be because R. Judah accepts the interpretation of 'third' given *supra* 29*a*.

בפנים בחוץ ואת הניתנין בחוץ בפנים שיאכלוהו טמאים שיקריבוהו טמאים *שיאכלוהו ערלים ושיקריבוהו ערלים לשבר עצמות הפסח לאכול הימנו נא ולערב דמו בדם הפסולים [א]כשר שאין מחשבה פוסלת אלא בחוץ לזמנו וחוץ למקומו [ב]והפסח והחטאת שלא לשמן: **גמ'** מ"ט דרבי יהודה אמר רבי אלעזר תרי קראי כתיבי בנותר כתוב אחד אומר °לא תותירו ממנו עד בקר וכתוב אחד אומר °לא יניח ממנו עד בקר אם אינו ענין להניח תנהו לענין מחשבת הינוח ורבי יהודה האי קרא להכי הוא דאתא האי מיבעי ליה לכדתניא °ובשר זבח תודת שלמיו [ג]למדנו לתודה שנאכלת ליום ולילה חליפין [ד]וולדות [ה]תמורות מנין ת"ל ובשר *[ו]חטאת ואשם מנין ת"ל זבח א] ומנין לרבות [ז]שלמי נזיר *[ח]ושלמי פסח ב] ת"ל שלמיו לחמי תודה וחלות ורקיקים שבנזיר מנין ת"ל קרבנו כולן קורא אני בהן לא יניח ג] א"כ [ט]לימא קרא ד] לא תותירו מאי לא יניח אם אינו ענין להינוח תנהו ענין למחשבת הינוח התינח להניח להוציא מאי איכא למימר ועוד טעמא דר' יהודה סברא הוא דתניא *אמר להם רבי יהודה ה] אי אתם מודים שאם הניחו למחר שהוא פסול אף חישב להניחו ו] למחר פסול* אלא טעמא דרבי יהודה סברא הוא וניפלוג נמי ר"י בכולהו בהי ניפלוג בשובר עצמות הפסח ולאכול ממנו נא זיבחא גופיה מי מיפסיל ע"מ שיאכלוהו טמאים ושיקריבוהו טמאים זיבחא גופיה מי מיפסיל שיאכלוהו ערלים ושיקריבוהו ערלים זיבחא גופיה מי מיפסיל לישנא אחרינא כל כמיניה לערב(א)ז] דמו בדם הפסולין *רבי יהודה לטעמיה דאמר אין דם מבטל דם ליתן את הניתנין למעלה למטה למטה למעלה ח] *רבי יהודה לטעמיה דאמר שלא למקומו נמי מקומו קרינא ביה ט] וליפלוג בניתנין בפנים שנתנן בחוץ והניתנין בחוץ שנתנן בפנים קסבר רבי יהודה בעינן *מקום שיהא משולש בדם בבשר ובאימורין ומי אית ליה לרבי יהודה האי סברא והתניא רבי יהודה אומר °דבר רע ריבה כאן חטאת ששחטה בדרום וחטאת שנכנס דמה לפנים פסולה *ולית י] לרבי יהודה שלישי *והתנן אמר רבי יהודה הכנים בשוגג כשר הא במזיד פסול וקי"ל בשכיפר השתא ומה התם יא] עיילי עיילא אי כיפר אין אי לא כיפר לא הכא דחשיב חשובי לא כל שכן תרי תנאי ואליבא דרבי יהודה וסבר ר' יהודה חטאת ששחטה בדרום יב]

יהא

רש"י

גמ' תרי קראי כתיבי בנותר · חד בפסח וחד בתודה : חליפין · מפריש תודתו ואבדה והפריש אחרת תחתיה ונמצאת הראשונה הויא שניה חליפי תודה וקריבה : וולדות יג] תמורה · ולד תודה ותמורת תודה וכולן קריבין כדאמרי' בבכורות (דף יד:) רק קדשיך אשר יהיו לך אלו התמורות אשר יהיה לך אלו הוולדות בכולן אני קורא בהן תשא ובאת וגו' : ת"ל ובשר · דהוה ליה למכתב ותודתו ביומו יאכל הוה ליה יד] קרא יתירא לדרשא : שלמי נזיר · איל נזיר הטעון לחם כמותה : ושלמי פסח · חגיגת ארבעה עשר אבל שלמים בעלמא לא מצי לרבויי דהא כתיב בהדיא בהו שני ימים ביום זבחכם יאכל וממחרת : ה"ג א"כ לימא קרא לא תותירו · כדכתיב בכל שאר הנותרים לשון נותר: ועוד טעמא דר' יהודה ע"כ סברא הוא · ולא מריבוי דקרא אלא ס"ל דהואיל ומיפסיל בהולאה ובהינוח מיפסיל נמי במחשבת הולאה והינוח : שאם הניח למחר שהוא פסול · דדם נפסל בשקיעת חמה טו] : ונפלוג נמי ר' יהודה בכולהו · הואיל וטעמא מהאי סברא הוא נפלוג בכולהו הנך דמתני' דקתני כשר ומשנינן בהי מינייהו נפלוג : מי קא מיפסיל · אם היה שובר את העלמות או אוכל נא: שיקריבוהו טמאים מי קמיפסיל · טז] והאי יקריבוהו באימורין קאמר דומיא דיאכלוהו בבשר *וכן אם יאכלו טמאים או ערלים זבח שנזרק דמו כהלכתו מי פסיל הקרבן למפרע מלרלות: ה"ג לישנא אחרינא כל כמיניה · מי ישמע לו להקריבו בפסול הכהנים טמאים לא ישמעו לו וכן הערלים להקריב למזבח בעבירה או לאכול קדש בעבירה הלכך אין מחשבתו מחשבה בדבר התלוי באחרים : לערב (ג) דמן בדם כו' · כולי האי משיויא כלומר ואי איפליג בלערב דמה כו' אין דם מבטל דם וכיון דעירוב לא פסיל מחשבת עירוב [נמי] לא פסיל : ליתן את הניתנין כו' · (ג) ליפלוג יז] במחשבה שלא במקומו : ר' יהודה לטעמיה · דאמר אפילו יהביה חוץ למקומו לא מיפסיל זיבחא מלרלות דשלא במקומו כמקומו דמי בפ"ב (לעיל כז.) דאוקימנא מתניתין דחישב ליתן את הניתנין למטה למעלה כו' דס"ל לתנא דשלא במקומו כמקומו דמי יח] דמסקנא מידי דהוה אמחשבת הינוח ואליבא דר' יהודה : (ד) ולפלוג בליתן את הניתנין בפנים בחוץ · יט] והניתנין בחוץ שחשב ליתן בפנים קא מקשי דהתם ודאי אי הוה יהיב חטאת החיצונה בפנים מיפסלא דכתיב וכל חטאת אשר יובא וגו' (ויקרא ו) : קסבר רבי יהודה · מחשבה ליתן את הניתנין בחוץ בפנים לא פסלא דגבי מחשבת חוץ כ] *לזמנו כתוב שלישי ודרשינן שיהא אותו חוץ משולש בדם ובשר ואימורין דהייט חוץ לעזרה ממש שבשעת היתר הבמות נשתלש בכל אלה כא] הלכך גזירת הכתוב דפסול חוץ למקומו אבל להכניסו לפנים לאו מחשבה היא: דבר רע · לא תזבח לה' אלהיך שור ושה אשר יהיה בו מום וגו' ריבה כאן אזהרה שלא ישחוט החטאת בדרום: וחטאת שנכנס דמה לפנים כו'· כלומר כב] לא תזבחט ע"מ להכניס דמה לפנים ולאו בהכנסה ממש קמזהר ליה אלא במחשבת הכנסה דהא בזביחה קאי וקא קרי ליה דבר רע אלמא מיפסיל : הכנים בשוגג כשר · בפרק כל הזבחים שנתערבו וקיימא לן התם בגמרא בשלהי פירקין דהא דדייקינן הא מזיד פסול בשכיפר בשנתן ממש על כג] מזבח הפנימי הוא דקפסיל רבי יהודה ולא מיפסל בהכנסה : והשתא ומה ט' ·

תוספות

כד] **תרי** קראי כתיבי בנותר · חד בפסח וחד בתודה ותימה דדריש בלא"ה ליט כה] דמפסח היכי ילפי' שאר נותר : **שלמי** פסח · פירשתי בפ"ק סמוך כו] לתחילתו (לעיל ט·) **שיאכלוהו** טמאים ויקריבוהו טמאים זיבחא גופיה מי מיפסיל · פי' בקונט' דהאי יקריבוהו באימורין קאמר ולא בדם דומיא דיאכלוהו כז] בבשר דאם אכלו טמאין או ערלים זבח שנזרק דמו כהלכתו מי מפסיל קרבן כח] מלרלות וא"ת חישב להניח אימורים למחר או כט] בחוץ אמאי פסול הלא אם הניח אימורים עד למחר או בחוץ כיון שנזרק דמו כהלכתו לא נפסל קרבן מלרלות וי"ל דלא דמי דלהניח אימורין למחר אי עביד ל] *במחשבתו מיפסיל כוליה קרבן בקדשים הנאכלים ליום ולילה דכיון דהוו אימורין בעין כל כמה דלא מיקטרי לא משתרי בשר באכילה וכי מטי למחר מפסיל בשר משום נותר אבל שיקריבוהו טמאים לא מיפסיל בשר חדא דהקריבוהו טמאין אם עלו לא ירדו ועוד נטמאו אימורים או אבדו משתרי בשר באכילה כיון דנזרק הדם כהלכתו לא] אכתי קשה מלהוציאו לחוץ אי קאי אאימורין אמאי פסיל ר' יהודה הלא אם עשה כן לא נמנע הדם בכך מלרלות וגם בשר מישתרי באכילה דכיון שהוציא אימורים בחוץ הוה ליה כנטמאו אימורים או אבדו לב] והבשר שרי לאכול ואי לא קאי להוציאו רק אדם אתי שפיר לג] הכי : **קסבר** ר' יהודה בעינן מקום שיהא משולש בדם ובבשר ובאימורין · תימה למאי דלא ידע טעמא דמקום משולש תיקשי ליה לרבנן אמאי לא חשיב [הניתנין בחוץ בפנים] חוץ למקומו דמהאי טעמא ממעטינן ליה בפירקין דלעיל ולקמן בפ' התערובות (דף פב:) וי"ל דס"ד דרבי יהודה הוא דלא בעי לד] משום דמסקינן טעמא מסברא : **ומי** אית ליה לרבי יהודה כו' · צריך ליישב סוגיא זו לכל הלשונות שפי' בפירקין דלעיל (דף כט·) מקום משולש : **וחטאת** שנכנס דמה לפנים פסולה · פי' בקונטרס שלא תזבחנה ע"מ להכניס דמה לפנים ולא בהכנסה ממש קמזהר ליה אלא במחשבת הכנסה דהא בזביחה קאי וקא קרי ליה דבר רע אלמא מיפסיל ועוד יש לפרש דדבר רע משמע ליה לה] ע"י דבור דהייט מחשבה ולאו הכנסה ממש : **וקי"ל** בשכיפר · וא"ת למ"ד שלא במקומו לאו כמקומו דמי אמאי פסיל רחמנא טפי בחטאות משאר קרבנות לו] וי"ל דבשאר דמים כשנתן ממש על הפרכת ובין הבדים איכא למימר דיאספגו לז] *ואם יש עוד דם יזרוק במקומו וכשר ובחטאת אין תקנה לדם *הנשאר א"נ תנא דסבר לאו כמקומו דמי יסבור בחטאת דפסול אף בלא כיפר · ברו"ך : **הכא** דחשובי חשיב לא כל שכן · תימה א"כ בטלה תורת פיגול דזרק מקצת דם בחוץ או אוכל כזית בחוץ לא מיפסיל ומחשב לח] מחשבה פוסל הכי נמי נהי דמכנים בלא מכפר לא מיפסיל מחשב *)להכנים ולכפר לט] פוסל וי"ל דבר רע משמע דבר שהוא רע במקום אחר מ] דהוא בכיפר זה אסרתי במחשבה בשעת זביחה הכא דחישב לא כל שכן דכשר דאפילו חישב ליתן בפנים על מזבח הזהב על מנת להתכפר כשר כיון דבמחשבה לא שייכא כפרה כלל אבל נתינה ממש ראויה לכפר בשום מקום : דאיכא למשמע מיניה דכל שכן דמחשבת הכנסה לא פסיל :

*) נ"א להכנים בלא מכפר נ"ק

שיאכלוהו

יהא

[לעיל לא.]

[נ"א מחשבת אכילה]

מז א מיי' פי"ד מהל' פסה"מ הלכה ט:

מח ב מיי' פי"ח מהל' פסה"מ הלכה יט:

מט ג מיי' שם הל' יח:

א ד ה מיי' פ"ב מהל' פסה"מ הלכה א:

ב ו מיי' פי"ז מהלכות פסה"מ הל' א:

ג ז מיי' פ"ב שם הל' ג:

ד ח מיי' פי"ז שם הל' א:

נ"א כיון דמכשרי אף בחטאת · ויליף לקמן מוכפר אע"ס כו' · צ"ק

גי' ל"ק והו"א שעשאן הכתוב כו'

ס"א ל"ג

סנהדרין ד. פסחים סט:

תורה אור

יהא חייב א] והתניא רבי יהודה אומר יכול חטאת ששחטה בדרום יהא חייב ת"ל °לא תזבח לה' אלהיך שור ושה וגו' כל דבר רע על ב] דבר רע אתה מחייבו ואי אתה מחייבו על חטאת ששחטה בדרום תרי תנאי אליבא דרבי יהודה אמר ג] רבי אבא ומודה רבי יהודה שחזר וקובעו לפיגול ד] אמר רבא תדע דפיגול לפני זריקה לא כלום הוא ואתיא זריקה וקבעה לה בפיגול ולא היא התם הוא חדא מחשבה היא הכא תרי מחשבות איתיביה רב הונא ה] לרבי אבא *ליתן את הניתנין למעלה למטה למעלה לאלתר כשר חזר וחישב חוץ למקומו פסול ואין בו כרת חוץ לזמנו פיגול וחייבין עליו כרת למחר פסול חזר וחישב בין חוץ לזמנו בין חוץ למקומו פסול ואין בו כרת תיובתא ו] דרבי אבא תיובתא אמר רב חסדא אמר רבינא בר סילא *חישב שיאכלוהו טמאים למחר חייב אמר רבא תדע דבשר לפני זריקה לא חזי וכי מחשב ביה מיפסיל ולא היא התם זריק ומיחזי הכא לא מיחזי כלל אמר רב חסדא *מרגלא בפומיה דרב דימי בר חיננא ^בשר פסח שלא הוצלה ולחמי תודה שלא הורמו חייבין עליהן משום טומאה אמר רבא תדע *דתניא °אשר לה' ^לרבות אימורי קדשים קלים לטומאה אלמא אע"ג דלאו בני אכילה נינהו חייבין עליהן משום טומאה הכא נמי אע"ג דלאו בני אכילה נינהו חייבין עליהן משום טומאה ולא היא התם אימורי קדשים קלים חזו לגבוה לאפוקי בשר פסח שלא הוצלה ולחמי תודה שלא הורמו דלא חזו לא לגבוה ולא להדיוט (א) ז] (לישנא אחרינא הא אימורין לא חזו ולא היא הנך חזו למילתייהו והני לא חזו כלל) :

דברים יז · ויקרא ז · דברים יב

הדרן עלך כל הפסולין

בית שמאי אומרים *^כל הניתנין על מזבח החיצון שנתן ח] במתנה אחת כיפר ובחטאת שתי מתנות ובית הלל אומרים ^אף חטאת שנתנה מתנה אחת כיפר ^לפיכך אם נתן את הראשונה כתיקנה ואת השניה חוץ לזמנה כיפר ואם נתן את הראשונה חוץ לזמנה ואת השניה חוץ למקומה פיגול וחייבין עליו כרת ^כל הניתנין על המזבח הפנימי ט] שאם חיסר אחת מן המתנות כאילו לא כיפר לפיכך ^נתן כולן כתיקנן ואחת שלא כתיקנה פסולה ואין בו כרת :

גמ' תנו רבנן *מנין לניתנין על מזבח החיצון שנתנן י] במתנה אחת שכיפר תלמוד לומר °ודם זבחיך ישפך והאי להכי הוא דאתא האי מיבעי ליה לכדתניא מנין

שיאכלוהו טמאים · לא דמי לאכילת כלבים *דבטמאים מיפסיל קודם אכילה משעת נגיעה ואפי' תחב לו חבירו מ"מ בהך כב] *(מחשבה אכילת) דבר אחר גורם לו שבלא אכילה יכול לפוסלו בנגיעה : **בשר** פסח שלא הוצלה · הא דתניא בהקומץ רבה (מנחות דף כה:) דשאין ניתר לטהורים אין חייבין עליו משום טומאה הייט בדבר שצריך היתר מזבח כגון בשר שנטמא לפני זריקה ולא דמי לבשר פסח שלא הוצלה ולחמי תודה שלא הורמו וצריך לדקדק דהכא דרשינן אשר לה' לרבות אימורי קדשים קלים לטומאה והתם מוקמינן ליה לרבות לן ויוצא :

הדרן עלך כל הפסולין

מנין לניתנין על מזבח החיצון שנתנן מתנה אחת כיפר כו' · לכאורה אתיא כבית שמאי דבית הלל כג] *כיון דמכשרי בחטאת לקמן וכפר אע"פ שלא נתן אלא אחד לא צריך קרא לשאר קרבנות וכן משמע בסוף שמעתין דקאמר וכל הנך תנאי דמפקי ליה להאי ודם זבחיך ישפך לדרשא אחרינא כל הניתנין על מזבח החיצון שנתנן במתנה אחת שכיפר מנא להו סברי לה כבית הלל דאמרי אף חטאת שנתנה במתנה אחת כיפר וילפי כולהו מחטאת ונראה דאתיא אפי' כב"ה וקסבר האי תנא דלא ילפינן מחטאת משום דשתי מתנות שהן ארבע דשאר קרבנות ילפי' בפ' איזהו מקומן (לקמן דף נג:) מדכתיב סביב כד] *והוה אמינא שתים עשאן הכתוב כמתנה אחת ולא כיפר אי נמי משום דטובא סביב כתיבי כה] ושנה לעכב ולקמן נמי אמרי' וכפר וכפר וכפר מפני הדין כו' מה דמים האמורים למטה שנתנן מתנה אחת כיפר אף דמים שלמעלה כן

יהא חייב · מלקות : **דבר** רע · מום בגלוי שהוא מגונה קרי דבר רע בבכורות בפרק על אלו מומין (דף לז.) : **ומודה** רבי יהודה · בחישב על מנת יא] להניח (ב) שחזר וקובעו לפיגול אם חזר וחישב בעבודה שניה על מנת לאכול חוץ לזמנו ולא אמרי' כבר נפסל במחשבת הינוח : **אמר** רבא תדע · דמחשבת הינוח לרבי יהודה לאו כמחשבת חוץ למקומו ושלא לשמו היא לאפוקי מידי פיגול דהא פיגול דשוחט על מנת לזרוק את דמו למחר לפני זריקה לאו כלום היא ואין המחשבה מועלת עד שיזרק הדם היום דבעינן יב] קרב כל מתיריו ומיהו מחשבה קמייתא מחשבת הינוח הוי וכי זריק ליה אתיא זריקה יג] וקבעי ליה (ג) ולא אמרי' הואיל ומעיקרא פיגול לא חיילא איפסיל ליה במחשבת הינוח וכי זריק ליה או בפיגול או בשתיקה לא ליחול פיגול : **התם** חד מחשבה · דלא שינה יד] מחשבתו הראשונה והיא היתה לשם פיגול : **תרי** מחשבות · והאחד שם פסול לה ולא שם פיגול : **כשר** · כדאמרינן במתני' לדברי הכל : **למחר** פסול · חישב ליתן למחר את הניתנין למטה למעלן ואוקי בפרק שני משום מחשבת הינוח כרבי יהודה ולא משום מחשבת נתינת מחר דא"כ פיגול מיבעיא ליה טו] אלמא לא הוי פיגול דזריקה דלא כשר באכילה לא אתיא לידי פיגול וקתני חזר וחישב בו אלמא לא מיקבע תו טז] פיגול : **חישב** שיאכלוהו טמאים למחר · פיגול ולא אמרינן לאו מחשבה היא דאכילת טמאים לא חזיא והוי כמחשב מחשבת פסול : **תדע** · דמחשבת אכילת פסול לא מפקא מידי פגול בר יז] מחשבת חוץ למקומו (ולזמנו) דהא בשר לפני זריקה לא חזי לאכילה וכי מחשב ביה בשחיטה ע"מ לאוכלה למחר מפגיל יח] דהשתא אכילה פסולה היא בלא שום פיגול : **התם** זריק ומיחזי · ואשתכח דלמחר אי לאו משום פיגול הוה יט] חזיא לאכילה : **שלא** הורמה · ד' חלות הנתרמות לכהן מארבעה מינין שבה דכתיב והקריב ממנו אחד מכל קרבן תרומה וגו' (ויקרא ז) : **משום** טומאה · אם אכלן בטומאת הגוף ואע"ג דקי"ל* כ] שאין ניתר לטהורים אין חייבין עליו משום טומאה האי כיון דאיזרק דם ניתר לטהורין קרינן ביה ואע"ג דאין פסח נאכל אלא צלי וחלות התודה עד שיורמו : **ה"ג** אשר לה' לרבות אימורי קדשים קלים לטומאה · והנפש אשר תאכל מבשר זבח השלמים אשר לה' : **לטומאה** · להתחייב כרת האוכלן בטומאת הגוף דאשר לה' יתירא הוא למידרש ביה דבר שהוא עולה לגבוה :

הדרן עלך כל הפסולין

בית שמאי אומרים · מתנה אחת · זריקה אחת כיפר אע"פ שרובן טעונים שתי מתנות שהן ארבע : **ובחטאת** שתי מתנות · מתנות ארבע ממש ובגמרא יליף טעמא : **לפיכך** · חטאת וכל הזבחים לבית הלל ולבית שמאי שאר זבחים חוץ מחטאת : **נתן** את הראשונה כתקנה · בשתיקה ואת השניה במחשבת אכילת בשר חוץ לזמנו כיפר וכשר הקרבן שכבר ניתר הקרבן ליקרב על ידי מתנה ראשונה ואין השניה מתרת את הבשר לפיכך אינה מפגלת : **פיגול** וחייבין עליו כרת · שאין מחשבת חוץ למקומו דשניה מוליאתו מידי פיגול שכבר הוקבע בראשונה שכבר קרבו כל מתיריו : **שחסר** אחת מכל המתנות לא כיפר · כדיליף בברייתא בגמרא : **לפיכך** · הואיל וכולן מתירות אין זו מתרת בלא זו ואין זו מפגלת בלא זו ואם נתן כולן כתקנן בשתיקה ואחת שלא כתקנה כגון שנתנה במחשבת חוץ למקומו או חוץ לזמנו פסול שלא ניתר בראשונות ואין בו כרת שאין האחרונה מפגלתו דקסבר אין מפגלין בחצי מתיר :

גמ' ישפך · שפיכה אחת משמע כא] דלא כתיב סביב דילפינן מיניה שתי מתנות שהן ארבע בפרק איזהו מקומן :

לעיל כו:[שם איתא חישב ליתן כו']

[עי' פירש"י בסנהדרין נ: ד"ה תרגלא]

פסחים כה: [ע.] כריתות כג:

[פסחים לד: מנחות כה:]

[מנחות מד:]

הגהות הב"ח

(א) גמ' לישנא אחרינא ולא שיא הני אימורים חזו למילתייהו הני לא חזו כלל כצ"ל : (ב) רש"י ד"ה ומודה וכו' על מנת להניח את דמו או אבריו שחוזר וקובעו : (ג) ד"ה אמר רבא וכו' וקבעי ליה בפיגול ולא :

שיטה מקובצת

א] והתניא בספרי בפרשת שופטים מייתי קצת בע"א (ותיבת חייב נמחק): ב] על כל דבר : ג] אמר רבא ומודה ר"י : ד] אמר רבא תדע כו' · תימה א"כ אפי' במחשבת חוץ למקומו ושלא לשמו בפסח וחטאת לא תוציא מפיגול מטעמיה דרבא ואי משום דגלי קרא לא יערב בו מחשבות אחרות א"כ אפי' מחשבת הינוח נמי וי"ל דהא דקאמר הכא שהוקבעו לפיגול לא קאי לכולהו מחשבות דלעיל במתני' אלא אלהניח דמו למחר כיון שחזר וחשב לזרקו למחר אין זה עירוב מחשבות אלא עירוב מחשבתו ראשונה דלהניח ולזרוק דמו קאמר וקצת קשה דמשמע דקאי אכוליה מתני' גם אלהוציאו [לחוץ או להניחו] למחר (בחוץ) כמו שהזכיר בקונטרס לכך נראה למהר"פ דהא דגלי דעירוב מחשבות מוציא מידי פיגול היינו דוקא במחשבות הכתובות בפסוק דהיינו חוץ למקומו או שלא לשמו אבל מחשבת הינוח דמיפסלא מסברא לא וא"ת א"כ אמאי איצטריך להאי תדע דקאמר רבא וי"ל שלא תלמוד אותו פסול מחשבת הינוח משאר עבודות דכתיב בקראי ועוד שלא תאמר כהרצאת כשר : ה] הונא לרבא : ו] תיובתא דרבא : ז] מכאן ועד סוף הפרק נמחק : ח] החיצון שנתן מתנה : ט] הפנימי שחיסר אחת מן המתנות לא כפר : י] שנתנן מתנה אחת : יא] מנת להוציאו לחוץ או להניחו למחר שחוזר : יב] דבעינן קרבו כל : יג] וזריקה וקבעא : יד] שינה ממחשבתו : טו] ליה אלא לא הוי פיגול דזריקה דלא שריא בשר באכילה לא מייתי לידי : טז] תו בפיגול הס"ד : יז] בר ממחשבת חוץ למקומו : יח] מפגיל אע"ג דהשתא : יט] הוה חזי לאכילה : כ] שאם אין ניתר : כא] משמע מדלא כתיב : כב] בהך מחשבת אכילה דבר : כג] כיון דמכשרי בחטאת ומכפר אע"פ ומתיבת ומכפר עד תיבת לא בס"א אינו : כד] והו"א שעשאן מתנה אחת לא כיפר : כה] כתיבי דשנה לעכב ולקמן נמי אמרי' לב"ה וכפר :

a in the south [36b] he is liable?[1] Surely it was taught, R. Judah said: You might think that if one slaughters a sin-offering in the south he is liable; therefore Scripture states, *'Thou shalt not sacrifice unto the Lord thy God an ox, or a sheep wherein is a blemish, even any evil thing'*: You can declare him liable for any evil thing,[2] but you cannot make him liable for slaughtering a sin-offering in the south? —There is a controversy of two Tannaim as to R. Judah's view.

R. Abba[3] said: Yet R. Judah admits that he [the priest] can subsequently render it *piggul*.[4] Said Raba: This is the proof, viz.: [a] *piggul* [intention made] before the sprinkling is nothing, yet the sprinkling comes and brands it as *piggul*.[5] Yet that is not so: there there was only one intention:[6] here there are *two* intentions.[7]

R. Huna raised an objection to R. Abba: [If the priest intended] applying [the blood] which should be applied above [the line] below [it], [or what should be applied] below, above, immediately, it is valid. If he subsequently intended [to consume it] without bounds, it is invalid, but does *not* involve *kareth*: [if he intended consuming it] after time, it is unfit, and one is liable to *kareth* on its account. [If he intended sprinkling the blood in the wrong place] on the morrow, it is unfit; if he subsequently intended [to consume it] without bounds or after time, it is unfit, and does not involve b *kareth*.[1] This refutation of R. Abba is indeed a refutation.

R. Ḥisda said in the name of Rabina b. Sila: If he intended that unclean [persons] should eat it on the morrow,[2] he is liable.[3] Said Raba: This is the proof, viz., before sprinkling the flesh is not fit [for eating], and yet when he declares a [*piggul*] intention it becomes unfit.[4] Yet it is not so: there he will sprinkle [the blood] and [the flesh] will be fit; here [the unclean] are not fit at all.

R. Ḥisda said: R. Dimi b. Ḥinena was wont to say: One is liable for uncleanness in respect of unroast flesh of a Passover-offering and loaves of a thanks-offering of which no separation [for the priest] was made.[5] Raba said, This is the proof, viz.: It was taught, [*But the soul that eateth of the flesh of the sacrifice of peace-offerings,*] *that pertain unto the Lord* [*having his uncleanness upon him, that soul shall be cut off from his people*]:[6] this includes the *emurim* of lesser sacrifices in respect of uncleanness.[7] This proves that though they are not fit for eating at all, one is liable for uncleanness on their account. So here too, though they are not fit for eating, one is liable for uncleanness on their account. Yet it is not so: there the *emurim* of lesser sacrifices are fit for the Most-High;[8] which excludes unroasted flesh of the Passover-offering and the loaves of the thanks-offering of which no separation was made, which are fit neither for the Most-High nor for man. (Another version: Now the *emurim* are not fit!—Yet it is not so: these *emurim* are fit for their purpose, c whereas these are not fit at all.)[1]

CHAPTER IV

MISHNAH. BETH SHAMMAI MAINTAIN: WITH REGARD TO ANY [BLOOD] WHICH IS TO BE SPRINKLED ON THE OUTER ALTAR, IF [THE PRIEST] APPLIED [IT] WITH ONE SPRINKLING, d HE HAS MADE ATONEMENT.[1] BUT IN THE CASE OF A SIN-OFFERING TWO APPLICATIONS [ARE INDISPENSABLE]; BUT BETH HILLEL RULE: IN THE CASE OF THE SIN-OFFERING TOO, IF [THE PRIEST] APPLIED IT WITH A SINGLE APPLICATION, HE HAS MADE ATONEMENT. THEREFORE IF HE MADE THE FIRST APPLICATION IN THE PROPER MANNER AND THE SECOND [WITH THE INTENTION TO EAT THE FLESH] AFTER TIME, HE HAS ATONED.[2] AND IF HE MADE THE FIRST APPLICATION [WITH THE INTENTION TO EAT THE FLESH] AFTER TIME AND THE SECOND WITHOUT BOUNDS, IT IS PIGGUL AND INVOLVES KARETH.[3] WITH REGARD TO ANY [BLOOD] WHICH IS SPRINKLED ON THE INNER ALTAR, IF [THE PRIEST] OMITTED ONE OF THE APPLICATIONS, HE HAS NOT ATONED; THEREFORE IF HE APPLIED ALL IN THE PROPER MANNER BUT ONE IN AN IMPROPER MANNER,[4] IT [THE SACRIFICE] IS INVALID, BUT DOES NOT INVOLVE KARETH.[5]

GEMARA. Our Rabbis taught: How do we know that if [the priest] made one application in the case of those [bloods] which are to be sprinkled on the outer altar, he has made atonement? e From the text, *And the blood of thy sacrifices shall be poured out.*[1] Now, is this text required for that purpose? Surely it is needed for what

a (1) To flagellation, the usual punishment for violating a negative command. This follows since R. Judah includes slaughtering a sin-offering in the south in the Scriptural injunction quoted above. (2) In Bek. 37a this is held to mean a patent blemish. (3) Sh. M. emends: Raba. (4) Where he intended leaving the blood for the morrow or carrying it without. Although R. Judah holds that he thereby disqualifies the sacrifice, yet if he intended at a subsequent service to eat the flesh after time, he renders it *piggul*. This is so in spite of the fact that generally speaking a *piggul* intention is operative only when there is no other disqualification, such as intending to eat it without bounds. (5) Raba proves that the intention to leave the blood until the morrow is not the same as the intention to eat the flesh without bounds, which makes *piggul* impossible. For if, *before* sprinkling, the priest declares his intention of sprinkling the blood on the morrow, it does not render the sacrifice *piggul*, it being axiomatic that a sacrifice is not rendered *piggul* unless the *mattirin* (q.v.Glos.) have been properly offered. Nevertheless, if he subsequently sprinkles the blood properly, his previously declared intention is retrospectively valid and renders the sacrifice valid. Now, this intention was in effect an intention to leave the blood until the morrow, which in R. Judah's view disqualifies the sacrifice (though not rendering it *piggul*). This proves that we do not say, Since it did not become *piggul* at the outset it is disqualified through the intention of leaving the blood, and it cannot subsequently become *piggul*. (6) Viz., to *sprinkle* the blood on the morrow, which is a *piggul* intention. (7) Viz., first to *leave* the blood until the morrow, which disqualifies but does not render *piggul*, and then to eat the flesh after time.

b (1) V. *supra* 26b for notes. The last clause definitely contradicts R. Abba.
c (2) Which is after time. (3) On account of *piggul*. We do not say that this is not an efficacious intention in respect of *piggul* since the unclean may not eat of it at *any* time. (4) As *piggul*. This case is analogous. (5) A thanks-offering was accompanied by forty loaves, four of which were taken off for the priest. Before that was done, the loaves might not be eaten; similarly, a Passover-offering might be eaten roast only. Nevertheless, an unclean person who partakes of them is liable on account of his defilement, though they could not be eaten even by a clean person. (6) Lev. VII, 20. (7) Though the lesser sacrifices were eaten by their owners, the *emurim* were burnt on the altar and thus 'pertained unto the Lord', and Scripture teaches that an unclean priest who eats these *emurim* incurs *kareth*. (8) Viz., to be burnt on the altar.
d (1) The bracketed addition is omitted in some MSS.
(1) The sacrifice is valid, though in the first place two applications are required. (2) Since the first alone sufficed.—According to Beth Shammi this holds good of all sacrifices except a sin-offering, and according to Beth Hillel that too is not excepted. (3) The second intention does not neutralise the first. (4) I.e. with wrongful intention. (5) Since one application is insufficient to make the sacrifice fit; — he holds that a sacrifice cannot be made *piggul* through a service which is incomplete in itself to make the sacrifice fit.
e (1) Deut. XII, 27.—This implies a single pouring out.

was taught: [37a] Whence do we know that all blood must be poured out at the base [of the altar]?[2] From the text, *And the blood of thy sacrifices shall be poured out against the altar*!—He[3] deduces that from Rabbi's [inference]. For it was taught: Rabbi said: [Scripture writes,] *And the rest of the blood shall be drained out* [*at the base of the altar*].[4] Now, '*of the blood*' need not be stated;[5] why then is it stated? Because we have learnt only that that blood which requires four applications must be poured out at the base;[6] whence do we know it of other blood? From the text, '*And the rest of the blood shall be drained out* [*at the base of the altar*]'.[7]

Yet still, does it come for this purpose? It is required for what was taught: How do we know that if [the priest] poured out [the blood] which should be sprinkled,[8] he has fulfilled [his obligation]?[9] From the text, *And the blood of thy sacrifices shall be poured out.*[10]—He holds as R. Akiba who maintained: Pouring is not included in sprinkling, nor is sprinkling included in pouring.[11] For we learnt: If he recited the blessing for the Passover-offering, he thereby exempts the [festival] sacrifice; but if he recited the blessing for the sacrifice, he does not exempt the Passover-offering. This is the view of R. Ishmael. R. Akiba said: The former does not exempt the latter, nor does the latter exempt the former.[12]

Yet still, is it required for this purpose? [Surely] it is needed for what was taught, [viz.]: R. Ishmael said: From the text, *But the firstling of an ox, or the firstling of a sheep, or the firstling of a goat* [*thou shalt not redeem; they are holy: thou shalt dash their blood against the*
a *altar, and shalt make their fat smoke for an offering made by fire*],[1] we learn that a firstling must have its blood and its *emurim* presented at the altar. Whence do we know [it of] the tithe and the Passover-offering? Because it says, '*And the blood of thy sacrifices shall be poured out*'?—He agrees with R. Jose the Galilean. For it was taught: R. Jose the Galilean said: [*Thou shalt dash their blood against the altar, and shalt make their fat smoke*]:[2] not 'its blood' is said, but 'their *blood*'; not 'its fat' is said, but 'their fat'.[3] This teaches concerning the firstling, the tithe [of animals], and the Passover-offering, that their blood and *emurim* must be presented at the altar.[4]

Now, does R. Ishmael utilise this text for both purposes?[5]—
b There is a controversy of two Tannaim as to R. Ishmael's view.[1]

As for R. Ishmael, who makes the whole verse refer to a firstling, it is well: hence it is written, *And the flesh of them shall be thine.*[2] But according to R. Jose the Galilean, who makes it refer to the tithe and the Passover-offering too, [surely] the tithe and the Passover-offering are eaten by their owners; what then is the meaning of '*And the flesh of them shall be thine*'?—[The plural intimates,]

(2) If any blood is left over after the regulation sprinkling.—This is stated explicitly of the sin-offering only (Lev. IV, 18), and the Talmud now wishes to extend it to other sacrifices too. (3) The author of the first deduction. (4) Lev. V, 9. (5) It is understood from the general context. (6) Viz., the sin-offering. (7) The two lines that follow in the original are a mere repetition, and are deleted by Sh. M. (8) Some blood requires sprinkling (*zeriḳah*), i.e., from the distance: other requires pouring out (*shefikah*), i.e., the priest must stand at the side of the altar and pour the blood out. (9) The sacrifice is valid. (10) The plural indicates *all* sacrifices, even those for which *zeriḳah* is prescribed. (11) Therefore where Scripture prescribes sprinkling, the sacrifice is not valid if the blood is merely poured out at the base. Hence he rejects the above interpretation, and so utilises the text for the purpose originally stated. (12) In Pes. 121a it is explained that in R. Ishmael's opinion sprinkling (*zeriḳah*) is included in pouring (*shefikah*), but pouring is not included in sprinkling; whereas R. Akiba holds that neither is included in the other. Thus (as explained by Rashbam a.l.): Both R. Ishmael and R. Akiba hold that the blood of the Passover-offering must be poured out, i.e., the priest must stand quite close to the altar and gently pour the blood on to its base. But the blood of the festival-offering (*ḥagigah*) requires sprinkling, i.e., from a distance and with some force. Now R. Ishmael holds that if the latter is poured out instead of sprinkled, the obligation of sprinkling has nevertheless been discharged. Consequently, the blessing for the Passover-offering includes that of the festival-offering, since in both the blood may be poured on to the base of the altar. But if the blood of the Passover-offering is sprinkled, the obligation has not been discharged: consequently the blessing for the festival-offering, whose blood is normally sprinkled, does not exempt the Passover-offering. By the same reasoning we infer that in R. Akiba's view neither includes the other.

a (1) Num. XVIII, 17. (2) Ibid. (3) Though the passage treats of the firstling only. The *plural* possessive suffix indicates that other sacrifices too are included in this law. (4) These are the only sacrifices in connection with which it is not mentioned elsewhere, hence the plural is applied to them. (5) Lit., 'for this purpose and for that purpose'. Surely not! The reference is to '*and the blood of thy sacrifices thou shalt pour out*', from which he learns that if the priest pours out blood which really should be sprinkled, he discharges his obligation. The author of that cannot be R. Akiba, for if it is, why does the blessing for the Passover-offering not exempt that of the festival sacrifice, since, as shewn *supra*, one is dependent on the other? Hence the author must be R. Ishmael; but he also interprets the same verse as intimating that the blood of the Passover-offering is to be *poured*, not sprinkled.

b (1) Rashi: He who learns from this text that the blood of the Passover-offering is poured out, rejects the ruling that the benediction for the Passover-offering exempts that for the festival-offering, and holds that R. Ishmael does *not* disagree with R. Akiba on this matter, for now we cannot learn from the text that what should be sprinkled is also valid if poured out. He however who maintains that they do disagree, holds that the blood of the Passover must be sprinkled, not poured out, like a peace-offering. Nevertheless, the Passover-offering is the principal one, while the festival-offering is only subsidiary to it; therefore the benediction for the former exempts that of the latter, but not *vice versa*. Tosaf. strongly criticises this explanation, and offers others, none of which, however, are quite free from objections. (2) Num. XVIII, 18.—'*Thine*' means the priest's, to whom the firstling belongs. The plural '*them*' is then understood to mean the ox, sheep, and goat, enumerated in the preceding verse.

מנין לכל הדמים שטעונים [א] מתן דם ליסוד ת"ל ודם זבחיך ישפך נפקא ליה מדרבי דתניא רבי אומר °והנשאר בדם ימצה שאין ת"ל בדם [ב] ומה ת"ל בדם לפי שלא למדנו אלא לניתנין מתן ד' שטעונין מתן דמים ליסוד שאר דמים מנין ת"ל [ג] והנשאר בדם ימצה שאין ת"ל בדם ומה ת"ל בדם לימד על כל הדמים שטעונין מתן דמים ליסוד ואכתי להכי הוא דאתא מיבעי ליה *לכדתניא מנין לניתנין בזריקה שנתנן [ד] בשפיכה *יצא ת"ל ודם זבחיך ישפך סבר לה כר' עקיבא דאמר *לא זריקה בכלל שפיכה ולא שפיכה בכלל זריקה דתנן *ברך ברכת הפסח פטר את של זבח של זבח לא פטר את הפסח דברי רבי ישמעאל רבי עקיבא אומר [א] לא זו פוטרת זו ולא זו פוטרת זו אכתי להכי הוא דאתא מיבעי ליה לכדתניא ר' ישמעאל אומר מתוך שנאמר °אך בכור שור או בכור כשב או בכור עז וגו' למדנו לבכור שטעון מתן דמים ואימורים לגבי מזבח מעשר ופסח מנין תלמוד לומר ודם זבחיך ישפך סבר לה כר' יוסי הגלילי *דתניא רבי יוסי הגלילי אומר דמו לא נאמר אלא דמם חלבו לא נאמר אלא חלבם לימד על בכור מעשר ופסח [ה] שטעון מתן דמים ואימורין לגבי מזבח [ו] ורבי ישמעאל האי קרא מפיק ליה להכי ומפיק ליה להכי תרי תנאי אליבא דרבי ישמעאל בשלמא לרבי ישמעאל דמוקים [ז] לה כוליה בבכור היינו דכתיב °ובשרם יהיה לך אלא לרבי יוסי (א) דמוקי ליה נמי במעשר ופסח מעשר ופסח בעלים אכלי ליה מאי ובשרם יהיה לך אחד תם ואחד בעל מום לימד

ויקרא ה | במדבר יח | שם

מנין · שכל הדמים של כל הקרבנות שטעונים מתן דם ליסוד אם נשאר מן הדם בכלי לאחר שזורק שתי מתנותיו שצריך לשופכו ליסוד ואע"פ שלא נאמר שפיכת שיריים אלא בחטאת : והנשאר בדם וגו' · בחטאת העוף כתיב והנשאר ימצה הוה ליה למכתב : ומה תלמוד לומר בדם כו' אלא על הניתנין מתן ארבע · היינו חטאת שטעונה ארבע מתנות על ארבע קרנות ובחטאת כתיבי שיריים לשפיכה : לימד על כל הדמים · שנשאר בהן כלום לאחר עיקר זריקתן שישפך הנשאר ליסוד : מנין לניתנין בזריקה · כל הדמים ח] שכתב בהן זריקה כגון עולה ושלמים ואשם דכתיב בהו וזרקו ובכור דכתיב ביה ואת דמם תזרוק (במדבר יח) וכל זריקה מרחוק משמע שזורק מן הכלי למזבח למרחוק : שפיכה · עומד אצל היסוד ושופך : ודם זבחיך ישפך · כל זבחים במשמע: בירך ברכת הפסח פטר את של זבח · חגיגת ארבעה עשר שבאה עם הפסח כשהחבורה מרובה ושנינו בתוספתא דפסחים על הפסח הוא אומר ברוך אשר קדשנו במצותיו וצונו לאכול ט] הפסח ועל הזבח הוא אומר אשר קדשנו במצותיו וצונו לאכול את הזבח ואם בירך על הפסח פטר את הזבח : י] על הזבח לא פטר את הפסח · וקס"ד ובפסחים נמי הכי מפרש דקסבר רבי ישמעאל זריקה בכלל שפיכה יא] כדאמר לעיל מנין לניתנין בזריקה *הניתנין בשפיכה יצא הלכך מתן דם שלמים שכתב בה זריקה בכלל מתן דם פסח שכתב בה שפיכה כדאמרינן לקמן וכי בירך על הפסח פטר את הזבח שהזבח בכלל פסח אבל בירך על הזבח לא פטר את הפסח שלא מצינו לניתנין בשפיכה שכשרין בזריקה הלכך אין פסח בכלל שלמים : ר' עקיבא אומר אין זו פוטרת את זו · דלית ליה יב] לניתנין בזריקה שנתנן בשפיכה יצא דהא דפסח בשפיכה מודם זבחיך ישפך נפקא לן לקמן ותרתי לא דרשת מיניה ולקמן פריך לרבי ישמעאל היכי יג] דרשת ליה להכי ולהכי ותנא דברייתא קמייתא סבר לה כרבי עקיבא בהא דאין זריקה בכלל שפיכה אבל בפסח בשפיכה לא סבירא ליה כוותיה דהא לא מייתר ליה קרא דמיבעיא ליה לכל הניתנין יד] במזבח החיצון שנתנן במתנה אחת כיפר והכי אמרינן בשמעתין : סבר לה כרבי יוסי הגלילי · דאמר פסח בזריקה ונפקא ליה (ב) מואת דמם טו] דלא כתיב דמו דליקו אבכור לחודיה : ור' ישמעאל האי קרא · ודם זבחיך ישפך: מפיק ליה להכי ולהכי · בתמיה דריש ליה לניתנין בזריקה שנתנן בשפיכה דעל כרחך כר"ע לא אתיא דאם כן אמאי אין פסח פוטר את הזבח הואיל ושלמים בכלל פסח ואי נמי סבירא ליה לר' עקיבא פסח בזריקה כר' יוסי הגלילי כל שכן דשניהם פוטרין זה את זה וקדריש טז] להו תו לפסח דבשפיכה: תרי תנאי אליבא דר' ישמעאל · דמאן דיליף ליה לפסח בשפיכה לית ליה פסח פוטר את הזבח ולא פליג רבי ישמעאל אדר' עקיבא בהאי יז] כיון דפסח בשפיכה מהאי קרא יליף תו לית לן למילף מינה ניתנין בזריקה כשרים בשפיכה ומאן דאית ליה פלוגתא לית ליה פסח בשפיכה אלא בזריקה כשלמים ומיהו פסח עיקר וזבח טפל לו הלכך אין זבח פוטרו לפסח אבל פסח פוטר את הזבח ובפסחים ירושלמי האי טעמא יח] אמר בה: בשלמא רבי ישמעאל · דמפיק מתן פסח מדם זבחיך ישפך והאי לשון רבים דדמם וחלבם כוליה בבכור מוקי לה יט] ובשור וכשב ועז הוא דנקט לשון רבים *והאי נמי דקאי לשון רבים דבשרם יהיה לך דסמיך ליה אבכור שור ובכור כשב ובכור עז : אלא לרבי יוסי הגלילי · דאית ליה כ] בכור לשון יחיד וקרא דנקט לשון רבים משום מעשר ופסח נקט לה ומעשר ופסח פשיטא לן שאינה מתנה לכהן אלא בעלים אכלי ליה : מאי ובשרם · דקא"ל רחמנא לאהרן: ומשני אחד תם ואחד בעל מום · כלומר לעולם לשון רבים דנקט קרא קמא לאו אמיני כא] דבכורות קאי דכולן בלשון חד בכור מפיק להו ודמם כב] וחלבם לרבות מעשר ופסח ולשון רבים דבשרם אבכור קאי ולא אשלשת מיני בכור דקרא דתימא דחלבם ודמם נמי עלייהו קאי אלא אבכור דחד מינא נמי שייך למימר ובשרם אתם ובעל מום :

תורה אור

כן ולמטה מנא לן אם לא מודם זבחיך ישפך אלמא דבית הלל נמי דרשי ליה ומיהו יש לדחות כג] ונראה לי (תוספת) דשאר זבחים כד] ידע מדלא שנה בהן לעכב אבל חטאת לא נכשיר מטעמא דלא שנה אלא פשיטא ליה כה] דגמר חטאת חיצון מחטאת פנימי לעכב אי לא אשכחן בעלמא דמלינן למיגמר מיניה כו] דמתנה אחת כיפר א"כ על כרחך לב"ש בעי הכא מנין דנגמר מחטאת דבעי שתי מתנות אע"ג דחטאת חמירא גילוי מילתא היא ללמוד סתום מן המפורש דאי לבית הלל מאי בעי מנין הא לא שנה לעכב ומהאי טעמא לא מצי למיבעי יהא כז] כשרה בדיעבד בולא כלום דכפרה בכדי לא אשכחן*: ברו"ך ע"כ :

מתן דם ליסוד ת"ל ודם זבחיך ישפך · אע"ג דלא כתיב יסוד מליט שיריים שנשפכין ליסוד דכתיב בחטאת ואת דמה ישפך אל יסוד המזבח : **תרי** תנאי ואליבא דרבי ישמעאל · דמאן דיליף ליה לפסח בשפיכה לית ליה פסח פוטר את הזבח ולא פליג ר' ישמעאל אדרבי עקיבא כח] דכיון דפסח בשפיכה מהאי קרא תו לית לן למילף מיניה כט] ניתנין בזריקה כשרין בשפיכה ומאן דאית ליה פלוגתא לית ליה פסח בשפיכה אלא בזריקה כשלמים ומיהו פסח עיקר וזבח טפל לו הלכך אין זבח פוטר לפסח אבל פסח פוטר זבח ובפסחים ירושלמי האי טעמא ל] אמר בה כך פי' בקונט' ויש תימה מסוגיא דסוף ע"פ (פסחים קכא·) גבי בירך ברכת הפסח פטר את של זבח דקאמר עלה כשתימצי לומר לדברי ר' ישמעאל זריקה בכלל שפיכה ולא שפיכה בכלל זריקה ולדברי ר' עקיבא לא שפיכה בכלל זריקה ולא זריקה בכלל שפיכה אלמא ר' ישמעאל אית ליה תרתי דפסח לא] בשפיכה וזריקה בכלל שפיכה ועוד קשה לפירוש הקונטרס לב] מסוגיא דשמעתין דקאמר לעיל סבר לה כר' עקיבא ולא סבר לה כוותיה לגמרי דרבי עקיבא סבירא ליה דפסח בשפיכה ותנא דברייתא סבר לג] בזריקה [א] ועוד מאי לד] האי דפריק סבר כר"ע דאמר פסח בשפיכה הלא מאן דאמר פסח בשפיכה הייט מדם זבחיך ישפך דתניא ר' ישמעאל אומר כו' אם כן לא אייתר קרא למתנה אחת כיפר ע"כ לה] ועוד קשה דאמר בפסחים פרק האשה (דף סח:) גבי חמשה שנתערבו עורות פסחיהם והא שלמים בזריקה ופסח בשפיכה ומשני מאי נפקא מינה והתניא מנין לניתנין בזריקה שנתנן בשפיכה שילא אלמא אית ליה תרתי דפסח בשפיכה וניתנין בזריקה שנתנן בשפיכה שילא ועוד מדקתני בברייתא מנין לניתנין בזריקה כו' מכלל דאיכא שפיכה ואי פסח בזריקה אם כן כולהו בזריקה לו] [ב] נינהו לז] [ועוד קשה הא אמרי' בספרי ר' יאשיה אומר קודש הם למה נאמר להביא את המעשר ואת הפסח שיטעו שפיכה אחת שלא שמענו להם בכל התורה כולה] ורבי יצחק אומר אין צריך שהרי כבר נאמר ודם זבחיך ישפך להביא את המעשר ואת הפסח שיטעו שפיכה ומה תלמוד לומר קודש הם להביא את המעשר לח] שיטעון הקטר חלבים שלא מצינו בכל התורה כולה משמע דרבי יאשיה שפיכה לט] דרבי יצחק קאמר ואע"ג דדריש ליה מקרא דכתיב גבי בכור מ] בזריקה דלמא מדאתו מריבויא ולא כתבינהו בהדיא מא] קדריש וכי פריך [התם אבא חנן למה נאמר ומה שאר קדשים שלא הושוו במתן דמים הייט] דאתא למעוטי חטאת דבאצבע ונראה דרבי ישמעאל (דפסחים) קסבר דפסח בשפיכה מקרא אחרינא ולא מדם זבחיך וכי פריך הכא [ג] האי מיבעי ליה לכדתניא רבי ישמעאל אומר מתוך מב] הוה מצי למימר דקסבר פסח בשפיכה מקרא אחרינא ולא מדם זבחיך אלא משום דאשכח ברייתא דרבי יוסי הגלילי נקטה ורבינו שמואל בשם רבינו שלמה פי' בענין אחר האי דערבי פסחים (דף קכא·) כשתימצי לומר לדברי רבי ישמעאל זריקה בכלל שפיכה כלומר מתוך דברי רבי ישמעאל תוכל לימד

פסחים קכ. | [פסחים קכא.] | שם | פסחים סד: לקמן נו: | [ל"ל שנתנן] | שם

ה א מיי' פ"ב מהלכות פסה"מ הלכה ג :
[א מיי' פ"ח מהלכות חמץ ומצה הלכה ז] :
ו ב מיי' פ"ה מהלכות מעה"ק הלכה יח :
ז ג מיי' שם הלכה יח :
[ועי' תוספות סנהדרין די ד"ה כל]

שיטה מקובצת

א] מתן · עיין תוס' ד"ה [תן יסוד למזבח של עילה] (דף כ"א ע"ב): ב] ת"ל בדם אלא והנשאר ימצה: ג] שאר דמים מנין ת"ל בדם לימד (והשאר ל"ש) : ד] בשפיכה שיצא ת"ל כו' ישפך עיין [תוס'] סנהדרין (דף ד ע"א) [ד"ה כל] : ה] שטעונין מתן : ו] ורבי ישמעאל האי קרא כו' פי' הקונטרס ר"י דריש מיניה לניתנים בזריקה שניתנין בשפיכה כדאיתא בברייתא דלעיל דע"כ כר"י אתיא דאל"כ אמאן תרמיה דע"כ כר"ע כו' ולא נהירא משום דלא אתיא כר"ע נימא דאתיא כר"י דלמא לא אתיא לא כמר ולא כמר אלא תנא אחרינא הוא לכך נראה דהכי פריך כיון דדריש פסח בשפיכה מדם זבחיך ישפך ושמעינן ליה לר"י דא"ר בירך על של פסח פטר של זבח וא"כ סבר דניתנין בזריקה שנתנן בשפיכה יצא דאם לא יצא היכא פטר את הזבח והלא פסח בשפיכה וזבח בזריקה אלא ודאי ס"ל דיצא וא"כ היכא מפיק תרוייהו מדם זבחיך : ז] דמוקי ליה: ח] הדמים שכתוב : ט] לאכול את הפסח : י] מה"ד ואם בירך על חובה : יא] כדאמרינן לעיל מנין לניתנין בזריקה שנתנן בשפיכה שיצא הלכך מתן דם זבח שהוא שלמים שכתוב בו זריקה בכלל מתן דם פסח שכתוב בו שפיכה : יב] ניתנין בזריקה : יג] היכי דריש ליה להכי ולהכי כו' סבר ליה כר"ע כו' אבל בפסח · ס"א פליג עליה דר"ע דשפיכה לר"ע בפסח נפקא ליה מדם זבחיך ישפך ותנא דברייתא מפיק ליה מדם זבחיך לכל הניתנין כו' : יד] הניתנין על מזבח החיצון שנתנן מתנה אחת : טו] דמם תזרוק דלא : טז] וקדריש ליה: יז] בהאי דכיון דפסח : יח] טעמא אמרי בה : יט] לה ואשור וכשב ועז כו' רבים הייט דקאי נמי לשון רבים : כ] ליה דבכור לשון : כא] אמיני בכורות וקרא קאי : כב] וחלבם לעולם לרבות : כג] מתיבות ונראה לי עד סוף הדבור מוקף בחצי לבנה ותיבת

ותיבת תוספות נמחק: כד] זבחים ידעינו מסוגיא: כה] ליה דנגמר חטאת: כו] מיניה דבמתנה אחת: כז] יהא כשר בדיעבד: כח] עקיבא בהא דכיון: כט] מינית דניתנין: ל] טעמא אמרי בה כך פירש בקונטרס משמע דמאן דאית ליה הפסח פוטר של זבח לית ליה דפסח בשפיכה ומאן דאית ליה פסח בשפיכה לית ליה שניתנים בזריקה שניתנין בשפיכה יצא ויש : לא] בשפיכה ס"א וניתנים בזריקה שנתנם בשפיכה יצא ועוד דוחק לפרש דפי' דתנא דברייתא דלעיל ס"ל כר"ע כו' : לב] מסתיא ס"א דמסתברא דשמעתין וכו' למימר כר"ע משמע דמברייתא דפסח בשפיכה הלא מ"ד פסח כו' : לג] ע' בחשמונות בסוף המסכת: לד] מאי סבר הא דפריק דאי סברותו ומתיבות ועוד כו' עד תיבות אחת כיפר בס"א אינו : לה] ע"כ חגה : לו] נינהו אם לא נאמר דאתי למעוטי חטאת דבאצבע לכך נראה דודאי מאן דאית ליה פסח בשפיכה סבר שפיר בניתנין בזריקה שנתנן בשפיכה יצא ופסח בשפיכה לאו מודם וזבחיך מפיק ליה אלא מקודש הם מפיק ליה כדדרש בספרי ר' יאשיה אומר קודש הם למה נאמר להביא את המעשר ואת הפסח שטעונין שפיכה אחת שלא שמענו להן בכל התורה כולה: ס"א אם לא נאמר דאתאי למעוטי חטאת דבאצבע ונראה דרבי ישמעאל דפסחים כו' ע' ובחיך · הגה קריבה ואיכא מאן דדריש מקודש הם דאמרינן בספרי ר' יאשיה כו' עד כל התורה כולה בחדיא קדריש עכ"ה וכי פריך הכא האי מבעיא ליה כו': לז] מתיבת ועוד קשה עד אומר ל"ש · לח] להביא את המעשר ואת הפסח הקטר : לט] שפיכה קאמר דומיא : מ] בכור מא] קדריש א"נ בכור נמי בשפיכה וזריקה האמורה בבכור למעוטי שלא יהא כחטאת איתא בתוספתא דזבחים דבכור נמי בשפיכה ואין נראה זה הפירוש ודוחק גדול הוא לומר מדרשא שלא הביאו התלמוד ומתיבת וכי עד תיבת ונראה נמחק [והגה שהגיה מהרש"ק ל"ש]:

הגהות צ"ק [א] כ"ח וא"כ מאי סבר לה דפריק דהא כר"ע וכו' וגי' צ"ק בזריקה דהאי כר"ע וכו' : [ב] צ"ל נינהו ודוחק לומר דאתא למעוטי חטאת דבאצבע · תורת חיים : [ג] ור"י האי קרא מפיק ליה כר' האי מצי לפרש :

הגהות הב"ח (א) גמ' אלא לרבי יוסי הגלילי דמוקי : (ב) רש"י ד"ה סבר וכו' מואת דמם :

*לימד אעל בכור בעל מום שניתן לכהן *שלא מצינו לו בכל התורה כולה ורבי ישמעאל נפקא ליה מלך יהיה דסיפא בשלמא לר' יוסי הגלילי דמוקי ליה נמי במעשר ופסח היינו דכתיב °לא תפדה (כי) קדש הם הם קריבין ואין תמורתן קריבה (א) א] דתנן *תמורת בבכור ומעשר הן גוולדן וולד ולדן עד סוף כל העולם הרי הן כבכור ומעשר ויאכלו במומן לבעלים ותנן *אמר רבי יהושע שמעתי שתמורת פסח קריבה ותמורת פסח אינה קריבה ואין לי לפרש אלא לרבי ישמעאל דמוקי ליה כוליה בבכור מעשר ופסח דלא קריבה תמורתן מנא ליה מעשר גמר *עברה עברה מבכור פסח בהדיא כתב ביה כשב מה ת"ל אם כשב דלרבות תמורת הפסח אחר הפסח שתקרב שלמים יכול אף לפני הפסח כן ב] ת"ל הוא וכל הנך תנאי דמפקי ליה להאי דם זבחיך ישפך לדרשא אחרינא האי כל הניתנין על מזבח החיצון שנתנן מתנה אחת שכיפר מנא להו ג] סברי להו כבית הלל דאמרי אף חטאת שנתנה מתנה אחת כיפר וילפינן כולהו מחטאת: והחטאת שתי מתנות: *אמר רב הונא מ"ט דב"ש °קרנות קרנות קרנות הרי כאן שש ארבעה למצוה ושתים לעכב ובית הלל קרנת קרנת קרנות הרי כאן ארבע שלש למצוה ואחת לעכב ואימא כולהו למצוה כפרה בכדי לא אשכחן ואיבעית אימא היינו טעמא דבית הלל אהני מקרא ואהני מסורת אהני מקרא לטפויי חדא ואהני מסורת לבצורי חדא אלא מעתה °לטטפת °לטטפת °לטוטפות *הרי כאן ארבע אהני (ב) קרא ואהני מסורת חמשה בתי בעי למיעבד סבר לה כר' עקיבא דאמר טט בכתפי שתים פת באפריקי שתים אלא מעתה °בסכת בסכת בסוכות אהני מקרא ואהני מסורת חמשא דפנתא בעי למיעבד

התם

לימד על בכור בעל מום שניתן לכהן שלא מצינו לו ד] מקום אחר בכל התורה כולה · ודמן וחלבן ליכא לאוקומי בחד בכור דבעל מום לא קרב: דסיפיה · וכשוק הימין לך יהיה: היינו דכתיב קדש הם כו' ותנן כו' · כלומר היינו דקודש הם ממעט נמי תמורת מעשר ופסח מהקרבה וניליף ה] מינה טעמא דהנך ב' משניות דתנן בהו דלא קרבי (וולדן): כבכור ומעשר · דאין נפדין במום לחול קדושה על המעות ומיהו ו] לא כבכור ומעשר לקרב אלא יאכלו בעלים במום: ותנן נמי · בפסחים דתמורת פסח לא קריבה: ואין לי לפרש · הי קריבה והי לא קריבה וקיימא לן דתמורה שהמיר בו אחר הפסח קריבה דתמורת שלמים היא ושהמיר בו קודם זמנו לא קרבה דתמורת הפסח היא: עברה עברה · כל אשר יעבור תחת השבט במעשר והעברת כל פטר בבכור: אם כשב · בשלמים כתיב: שקריבה שלמים · שהרי מותר ז] נעשה שלמים משעבר זמנו: הוא · זבח פסח הוא הוא קרב ואין תמורתו קריבה: אף חטאת כו' · וילפינן לה מקראי בשמעתין ח] והדר ילפינן כולהו זבחים מחטאת: קרנת קרנת קרנות · שלש פרשיות נאמרו בחטאות החיצונות בויקרא אחת בשעיר נשיא וב' בחטאת יחיד אחת בכשבה ואחת בשעירה בשתים כתיב על קרנת חסר והאחת מלא וב"ש אית להו יש אם למקרא הרי כאן שש ואין במזבח אלא ארבע ט] והשתים יתירות לא נאמרו אלא ששנה עליה הכתוב לעכב ארבע נאמרו למצוה שמצוה בארבע מתנות ושתים נשנו מהן לעכב: וב"ה · סברי יש אם למסורת הלכך הרי י] ד' ג' מהן למצוה נאמרו שמצוה לכתחילה ליתן אף עליהן והאחת מעכבת כדמפרש ואזיל: ואימא כולהו למצוה · ואין כאן יא] אחת לעכב שהרי לא שנה באחת מהן: בכדי · בלא מתן דמים: אהני יב] קרא · דמשמע שש: ואהני מסורת · דמשמע ארבע הלכך טפי חדא אמסורת ובציר חדא ממקרא והוו להו חמש נמצא ששנה באחת: לטטפת לטטפת לטוטפות · דילפינן מינה ארבע בתים לתפילין ואנן בכולהו לטוטפות קרינן יג] נמי אהני קרא כו': סברי ב"ה כרבי עקיבא · דיליף לה מקרא אחרינא: כתפי · שם מקום:

התם

תוכל לדקדק דזריקה בכלל שפיכה דכיון דקאמר דבירך על הפסח פטר את הזבח אם כן סבירא ליה דמתנותיהם שוין ואף פסח בזריקה והא דזבח לא פטר פסח משום יד] דזבח טפל לו וכיון דפסח בזריקה אם כן אייתר ליה דם זבחיך ישפך טו] ומצי למידרש מיניה לומר דזריקה בכלל שפיכה ולא גרים ולא שפיכה בכלל זריקה דלהאי תנא דרבי ישמעאל כולהו בזריקה ולדברי ר"ע טז] דלא זה פוטר את זה אם כן אין מתנותיהם שוות דפסח בשפיכה מקרא ודם זבחיך ישפך ואם כן לא זריקה בכלל שפיכה ולא שפיכה בכלל זריקה דהא ודם זבחיך אילטריך ליה לדידיה לומר דפסח בשפיכה ולהאי פירושא קשה מכל מקום מההיא דהאשה (פסחים דף פט·) ועוד מנא ליה לרבי ישמעאל דזריקה בכלל שפיכה משום דמייתר ודם זבחיך ישפך דלמא אתא לכל הניתנין על מזבח החיצון שנתנן במתנה אחת כיפר וה"ר חיי"ם אומ"ר דבספרי"ם ישני"ם גרסינן כשתימצי לומר לדברי רבי ישמעאל זריקה בכלל שפיכה ושפיכה בכלל זריקה דהכל אחד דכל הקרבנות בזריקה לרבי ישמעאל ואין לחוש אם בזריקה אם בשפיכה והיינו כשיטת רבינו שמואל וכל מה שהקשיתי עליו קשה גם לפי' זה ולכולהו ליכא קשה אי פסח בשפיכה (לרבי עקיבא) אם כן דריש· לקרא יז] דדמו כרבי ישמעאל *ובשרם דהנך (קאמר) כרבי ישמעאל ואחד תם ואחד בעל מום נפקא ליה יח] מיהיה לך ולקמן בסוף איזהו מקומן (דף נז·) פליג רבי עקיבא ארבי ישמעאל ומוקי לה לקרא דובשרם אחד תם ואחד בעל מום כרבי יוסי הגלילי דהכא: **אחד** תם ואחד בעל מום · אע"ג יט] דיהיו לך כחזה התנופה ושוק התרומה מוקמינן ליה בסוף איזהו מקומן (שם) ובבכורות (כז:) בבכור תם רישיה דקרא דבשרם לשון רבים נקט משום בעל מום: **שלא** מצינו כ] לו בכל התורה כולה · פירש בקונט' שלא מצינו לו קרא אחר בכל התורה כולה ונראה לפרש שלא מצינו בכל התורה כענין זה דשאר פסולי המוקדשין אינו מתנה לכהן אלא פודהו ומקריב אחר תחתיו וזה מתנה לכהן ואוכלו במומו כא] כי האי גוונא בפ' שתי מדות (מנחות נא:) שלא מצינו בכל התורה שיהא טפל חמור מן העיקר גבי כב] את הכבש זו עולת יולדת האחד זה האחד עשר של מעשר א): **קודש** הם הם קריבין ואין תמורתן קריבה · תימה דבפ"ק דתמורה (דף ה:) בין אביי ורבא מוקמי הם *לבכור ומעשר שנתערבו כג] בכל העולין שקריבין לגבי מזבח ואין תמורתן קריבה נפקא להו מדכתיב לה' הוא קרב ואין תמורתו קריבה ועוד קשה דאביי גופיה דריש ליה התם בפ"ק אלו קדשים (תמורה כא·) מקרא דהכא מדכתיב קודש הם: **שמעתי** שתמורת פסח קריבה ותמורת פסח אינה קריבה · מפרש התם כד] בפסח שנמצא קודם שחיטה ירעה וכן תמורתו *משום פסח עצמו דלא קרב לא קרבה תמורתו ועוד איכא כה] למאן דאמר התם דנמצא קודם שחיטה והמיר בו אחר שחיטה תמורתו קריבה שלמים אע"פ שהפסח רועה ואע"ג דדרשינן הוא קרב ואין תמורתו קריבה הכי קאמר הוא קרב כלומר פסח כו] קרב ואין תמורתו קריבה כשהוא מימר בפסח *דחזי ללישנא קמא דרבה דבפרק מי שהיה טמא (פסחים צו:) אפילו המיר בו לאחר שחיטה וללישנא בתרא היכא דהמיר קודם שחיטה וההוא לישנא לא קאי דאיתותב התם וקצת קשה הא דדרשינן קודש הם אבכור מעשר ופסח הם קריבים ואין תמורתן קריבה דלא הוי מעין אחד דגבי פסח אם המיר בפסח עצמו שקרב לשם פסח תמורתו נמי קריבה דאם איתא דלא קרב אמאי איתותב התם לשון שני של רבה לימא דברייתא בהכי מיירי ועוד דרשינן התם אם כשב לרבות פסח שעברה שנתו ושלמים הבאים מחמת פסח לכל מצות שלמים ופירש התם בקונט' שלמים הבאין מחמת פסח דהיינו תמורת הפסח עצמו ובענין אחר לא מיתוקם כדפרישית לעיל פ"ק (דף ט·) ובכל מקום שהפסח קרב או לשם פסח או לשם שלמים גם התמורה קריבה כיון דלא אתיא מכח קדושה דחויה ול"ע אם יכול להקריב התמורה לשם פסח קודם שחיטה דשמא יש לדרוש הוא קרב לשם פסח ואין תמורתו קריבה לשם פסח אבל לשם שלמים קרבה כשקרב הוא לשם פסח: **הרי** כאן שש · וא"ת בחמש סגי דלאחת לא איצטריך דכפרה בכדי לא אשכחן וי"ל דדילמא ב"ש לית ליה האי טעמא: **לטוטפות** ואמר רבינו תם דבספרים מדוייקים לא כתיב לטוטפות כלל בוי"ו לבסוף כז] אלא וי"ו דולטטפת דריש ואפילו למאן דלא דריש וי"ו וי"ו למ"ד דריש כדאמר גבי והנותר פ' הערל (יבמות עב:) ויש מפרשים דלטוטפת מלא בוי"ו דוי"ו דבין שני הטיתין דריש וקסבר גורעין ומוסיפין ודורשין ואומר רבינו תם דלא אמרינן גורעין ומוסיפין ודורשין באמצע התיבה אלא בתחלת התיבה או בסוף כדאשכחן בפרק הזהב (ב"מ דף נד:) גבי וחמישיתו וגבי דם מהפך יקבלנו ב) וגבי ונתתם את נחלתו לשארו בית טוחלין (ב"ב דף קיא:)*: **טט** בכתפי שתים · וא"ת א"כ ליבעי תרי סרי בתי כח] וי"ל כיון דמנין הוא איך הוו להו כפרשה שנאמרה ונשנית ולא דמו לקרנות שאין המנין כתוב בפירוש וה"ר יהודה מקורבי"ל מפרש דחד טטפת לגופיה ואיך תרתי אתו ג) למנין כט] בתים בלשון כתפי ובל' אפריקי*: **אלא** מעתה בסכת כו' ל] במס' סוכה (דף ו:) דדרשינן לדפנות וכן בפ' המביא (ביצה ל:) גבי אין נוטלים עצים מן הסוכה אסרינן נמי מן הדפנות מדכתיב חג הסוכות דכשם שחל שם שמים על לא] החגיגה כך חל על הסוכה ותימה דגבי אין מסככין בדבר המקבל טומאה וגבי העשה ולא מן העשוי לא לב] דרשינן לדפנות:

התם

א) [וע"ע תוס' בכורות כח· ד"ה שלא] ב) [לעיל כה·] ג) נ"א למנין ד' בתים נ"ק

ח א מיי' פ"א מהלכות בכורות הלכה ג:
ט ב מיי' פ"ג מהלכות תמורה הלכה ג:
י ג מיי' פ"ד שם הלכה ו:
[לקמן מ: בכורות כח.]
יא ד מיי' פ"ד מהלכות קרבן פסח הלכה ו:

ס"א לכ"ע
נ"א ובשרם עליהו דהנך בכורות קאמר כר"י וכו'

[שבת פג: וש"נ]
תמורה כא·
פסחים צז
[לעיל ס. מעילה יג: תמורה יט.]
סנהדרין ד.
סנהדרין ד: מנחות לד:

נ"א לדרשא אחריתי אביי מוקי הס בחייתן יז: ורבא מוקי לבכור כו' ועיין נ"ק
ע' נ"ק שמהפך הגירס' של תוס' בשם תוס' בשנים ועי' בשוי"א דהתם בפסחים שם
נ"א מיהו
[וע"ע תוס' סנהדרין ד: ד"ה וא"ת וה"ר יהודה]
[וע"ע שם בסנהדרין ומנחות לד: ד"ה]

הגהות הב"ח
(א) גמ' ואין תמורתן קריבה ותנן: (ב) שם אהני מקרא:

שיטה מקובצת
א] קריבה ותנן אות ד' נמחק: ב] ת"ל הוא האי דרשא גמורה היא אבל אם כבש לרבות תמורת פסח אחר הפסח שקרב שלמים אסמכתא בעלמא היא כדאמרינן בפ' מי שהיה טמא דאם כבש בא לרבות עברה שנתו: ג] סברי להו כב"ה וקשה דאטו אותם תנאי דנפקי ניתנים במתנה אחת כיפר אידם וזבחיך שבקי ב"ה ועבדי כב"ש וי"ל דאתיא שפיר כב"ה נמי למידרש מודם וזבחיך [כל הניתנין על מזבח החיצון] שנתנן מתנה אחת כיפר בשאר קרבנות דהוי שונה הכתוב לעכב הלכך הו"א אע"ג דבחטאת במתנה אחת כיפר מ"מ שאר קרבנות דכתיב טובא סביב בפרשה ליבעי שתי מתנות שהן ד' לעכב לכך איצטריך ודם זבחיך ישפך · ת' מהר"פ והן כתובין בדפוס [כד"ה מנין למעלה דף לו ע"ב בריש הפרק]: ד] לו מקרא אחר בכל התורה כולה שבבכור בעל מום לאו קרב ודמן והלבן ליכא לאוקמי אלא אחד בכור דבעל: ה] מינה טעמא דהנך כו' קרב תמורתן וולדן הס"ד: ו] ומיהו לאו כבכור: ז] מותר הפסח נעשה: ח] והדר ילפי כולהו מקראי: ט] ארבע קרנות והשתים: י] הרי זו ד': יא] כאן אפילו אחת: יב] אהני מקרא דמשמע: יג] קרינן נימא נמי כו' סברי לה ב"ה: יד] משום דפסח עיקר והזבח טפל: טו] תיבות ומצי למידרש מיניה נמחק: טז] מתיבות דלא זה כו' עד תיבת לא זריקה בס"א אינו: יז] דקרא דדמם ובשרם דהנך בבכורות כר"י: יח] ליה מלך יהיה ולקמן כו' פליג ר"ע אדרבי ישמעאל: יט] אע"ג דכחזה התנופה ושוק הימין מוקמינן: כ] מקרא אחר בא התירה וקשה דהא בכל התלמוד לא אשכחן כי האי לישנא ובכל מקום שמרבינן שום דבר מקרא יכול לומר שלא מצינו כו' לכך נראה לפרש: כא] במומו וכי האי גוונא אשכחן בפ': כב] גבי לכבש דמן בכל העולין הקריבין לגבי מזבח כו' נפקא להו מדכתיב לה': כד] התם בפסחים הפסח שנמצא כו' ירעה כו' וכן תמורתו משום דהואיל והוא עצמו לא קרב לא: כה] איכא לישנא דאמר ותיבת לאו ל"ש: כו] פסח כשר קרב ואין כו' בפסח דחוי ללישנא קמא: כז] לבסוף בין פא לתיו: כח] בתי דשלשה טוטפת כתיבי: כט] למנין ד' בתים: ל] כו' הבא דרשינן ותיבות במס' סוכה ואות ד' נמחק: לא] דכשם שחל שם שמים על [סככו] כך חל על הדפנות ותימה: לב] דרשינן ס"א לא היישינן:

whether it be whole or blemished, [37b] thus intimating that a blemished firstling is given to a priest, for which [teaching] we do not find [any other text] in the whole Torah.[3] And R. Ishmael?[4]—He deduces it from *'it shall be thine'*, [written] at the end [of the verse].[5]

It is well according to R. Jose the Galilean, who makes it refer to the tithe and the Passover-offering too: hence it is written, *Thou shalt not redeem; they are holy*,[6] [which intimates] *'they'* are offered, but their substitutes are not offered.[7] And we learnt [even so]. The substitutes of a firstling or tithe—they themselves, their young, and the young of their young *ad infinitum* are as the firstling or tithe [respectively], and are eaten, when blemished, by their
a owners.[1] And we [also] learnt: R. Joshua said: I have heard [from my teachers] that the substitute of a Passover-offering is offered,[2] and that the substitute of a Passover-offering is not offered,[3] and I cannot explain it.[4] But according to R. Ishmael who makes the whole of it refer to a firstling, whence does he know that the substitute of tithe and the Passover-offering are not offered?—As for tithe, he learns similarity of law with a firstling from the fact that 'passing' is written in both cases.[5] As for the Passover-offering, [consider:] 'lamb' is explicitly written in connection with it; why then does Scripture write, *If he bring a lamb for his offering?*[6] To include the substitute of a Passover-offering after Passover, [intimating] that it is sacrificed as a peace-offering. You might think that it is likewise so before Passover, therefore Scripture writes, *It [is the sacrifice of the Lord's Passover]*.[7]

Now, all these Tannaim who utilise this [text], *'the blood of thy sacrifices shall be poured out'*, for a different exegesis, how do they know this [law of the Mishnah that] WITH REGARD TO ANY [BLOOD] WHICH IS SPRINKLED ON THE OUTER ALTAR, IF [THE PRIEST] APPLIED [IT] WITH ONE SPRINKLING, HE HAS MADE ATONEMENT?—They hold as Beth Hillel who maintained: WITH REGARD TO THE SIN-OFFERING TOO, IF [THE PRIEST] APPLIED IT WITH A SINGLE APPLICATION, HE HAS MADE
b ATONEMENT; and we learn all the others from the sin-offering.[1]

BUT IN THE CASE OF A SIN-OFFERING TWO APPLICATIONS [ARE INDISPENSABLE]. R. Ḥuna said, What is Beth Shammai's reason?—The plural form *ḳarnoth* [horns] is written three times, denoting six [applications], [thus intimating that] four are prescribed while two [at least] are essential. But Beth Hillel [argue]: [The written forms are] *ḳarnath* [singular] twice, and *ḳarnoth* [plural] once,[2] which denotes four, implying that three [applications] are prescribed, while [only] one is essential. Yet say, that all are [only] prescribed?[3]—We find no atonement without rite. Alternatively, this is Beth Hillel's reason: Both *miḳra* [the version as read] and *masoreth* [the version as traditionally written] are effective: the *miḳra* is effective in adding one [application], while the *masoreth* is effective in subtracting one.[4]

If so, [when Scripture writes] *leṭoṭafath, leṭoṭafath, leṭoṭafoth*,[5] which denotes four [compartments], [you can likewise argue that] both the *miḳra* and the *masoreth* are effective: then five com-
c partments should be necessary?—He[1] holds as R. Akiba, who said: *Ṭot* means two in Katpi,[2] and *foth* means two in Afriki.[3]

[Again] if so [when Scripture writes], *ba-sukkath, ba-sukkath, ba-sukkoth*,[4] [you may argue that] both the *miḳra* and the *masoreth* are effective: then one should have five walls [for the tabernacle

(3) The point of the question and answer is this: *'Them'* obviously cannot mean the tithe and the Passover-offering, as R. Jose explains the plural in v. 17, since these belong to the owner. Nor can the plural here refer, in his view, to the ox, sheep, and goat, for in that case he could explain 'their *blood*' and 'their *fat*' similarly. Hence the difficulty, why is the plural used? The answer is, to intimate two *categories* of firstlings, whole and blemished. (4) Whence does he know this? (5) This repetition is to include the blemished firstling. (6) Ibid. (7) If one declares another animal a substitute for them, they are not offered, contrary to the general rule that the substitute is offered (together with the original) in exactly the same way as the original.

a (1) But not sacrificed while they are whole. (2) As a peace-offering, after Passover.—This is where the original is available for Passover. (3) As a peace-offering, but must graze until it is blemished, when it is redeemed. (4) For the explanation v. Pes. 96b. (5) V. *supra* 9a. (6) Lev. III, 7.—Scripture prescribes a lamb for a Passover-offering (Ex. XII, 5) which was in the nature of a peace-offering. Why then must Scripture also inform us that a lamb might be brought for a peace-offering? (The Talmud does not quote the exact wording, as *keseb* is not written in connection with the Passover-offering, but a lamb is prescribed, though a slightly different word (*kebes*) is used.) (7) Ex. XII, 27.—*'It'* (Heb. *hu*) is emphatic, and teaches that only the original animal dedicated for a Passover-offering is to be sacrificed, but not its substitute which is kept until after Passover. An animal would be proposed as a substitute if the first one was lost, and is subject to the laws stated here if the first one is refound in time to be sacrificed for its original purpose. If the first is not found until after the second has been offered, it becomes a 'Passover remainder', and is sacrificed as a peace-offering after the festival.

b (1) The case of the sin-offering itself is learnt *infra*. (2) The reference is to Lev. IV, 25, 30, 34 q.v. The traditional reading in all cases is *ḳarnoth* horns, but it is actually written *ḳarnath* (קרנת singular) twice. Beth Shammai make the reading decisive, while Beth Hillel follow the written forms. (3) In the first place, but are not essential, since Scripture does not repeat any of them to intimate that they are indispensable. (4) Since the *miḳra* implies six while the *masoreth* implies four, the implication of *both* is five; but as there are only *four* horns on the altar, the fifth must be regarded as a reiteration of one application, and hence it (i.e., one application) becomes indispensable; v. Sanh. (Sonc. ed.) 4b. q.v. notes. (5) Frontlets. V. Ex. XIII, 16; Deut. VI, 8, XI, 18:—*and it shall be . . . for frontlets between thine eyes*. This is the law of *tefillin* (v. Glos.); the word is *written* twice defectively and once *plene* (in our version it is written only once defectively), but read *plene* in every case. From the two defective and one *plene* forms the Rabbis learnt that the *tefillin* of the head must consist of four compartments.

c (1) The author of this interpretation of *ḳarnoth*. (2) Perhaps the Coptic language. (3) The language of N. Africa or Phrygia in Asia Minor. Hence the word *toṭafoth* itself implies four, without recourse to its repetition. (4) 'In booths': *Ye shall dwell in booths seven days* etc. (Lev. XXIII, 42-43). Here too it is written twice defectively and once *plene*, and the Rabbis learn that the number of walls required by a booth is four, in the same way that they learn that the *tefillin* must have four compartments.

booth]? [38a]—There, subtract one text[5] for the command itself,[6] and one for the covering,[7] so three are left. Then the [Mosaic] *halachah*[8] comes and diminishes the third [wall], fixing it at a hand-breadth.[9]

If so, [when Scripture states] *Then she shall be unclean two weeks* [*shebu'ayim*],[10] *shib'im* [seventy] [is actually written],[11] then [argue,] the *miḳra* and the *masoreth* are both effective, and so she should have to spend forty-two days [in uncleanness]?[12]—There it is different, because it is written, *as in her menstrual state.*[13]

Now the Tanna [of the following Baraitha] adduces it [Beth Hillel's ruling] as follows: *We-kipper* [and he shall make atonement] is stated three times,[14] on account of the analogy [which might otherwise be drawn].[15] But surely we have an analogy to this effect:[16]
a blood is prescribed below [the red line],[1] and blood is prescribed above: as with the blood which is prescribed below, if one made a single application, he effects atonement;[2] so with the blood which is prescribed above, if one makes a single application, he makes atonement. Or you may reason in this direction: Blood is prescribed within,[3] and blood is prescribed without: as in the case of blood prescribed within, if [the priest] omits a single application his action is ineffective;[4] so in the case of the blood prescribed without, if he omits a single application his action is null. Then let us see to which it is comparable: You can draw an analogy between sacrifices offered on the outer altar,[5] but you cannot draw an analogy between [sacrifices offered on] the outer altar and [those offered on] the inner altar. Or, you might argue to the contrary: You may draw an analogy between sin-offerings whose blood is sprinkled on four horns [of the altar],[6] and let not the outer altar prove it,[7] which is not a sin-offering nor [is its blood sprinkled on the] four horns.[8] Therefore Scripture states *'we-kipper'* three times, on account of the analogy [which might otherwise be drawn], [teaching]: *'and he shall make atonement'* even though he sprinkled [the blood] only three times; *'and he shall make atonement'* even though he sprinkled [it] only twice; *'and he shall make atonement'* even though he sprinkled it but once.

But this is required for its own purpose?[9]—Said Raba b. Adda: Mari explained it to me: Scripture says, *and he shall make atonement*
b ... *and he shall be forgiven*: atonement and forgiveness are identical.[1]

Yet say [that] *'and he shall make atonement'* [intimates] even if he made only three applications above [the red line] and one below; *'and he shall make atonement'* even if he made only two applications above and two below; *'and he shall make atonement'* even if he did not apply [the blood] above but only below?[2]—Said R. Adda b. Isaac: If so, you annul the law of horns.[3] But if the Divine Law has ordained [it so], let them be annulled?—Said Raba: What thing is it that requires three? Surely the horns.[4] Yet say, *'and he shall make atonement'* [teaches] even if he made only one application above and three below?—We do not find blood [applied] half above and half below. Do we not? Surely we learnt: He sprinkled thereof[5] once above and seven below?—That was done as *maẓlif* [one swinging a whip].[6] What is a *maẓlif*?—Rab Judah showed it by imitating the movements of a whipper. [Again, we learnt:]

(5) I.e., one of the five implied by the text. (6) There must be at least one to state the law of sitting in booths. (7) The booth must have a covering, which is governed by laws of its own. (8) A law traditionally imputed to Moses at Sinai, but not stated in the Pentateuch. (9) There was a Mosaic tradition that however many walls the *sukkah* required, one of these need be no more than a handbreadth in width. (10) Lev. XII, 5. (11) Though vocalized *shebu'ayim*. (12) This figure is arrived at by taking a point midway between fourteen (days) and seventy. (13) Ibid. E.V. *as in her impurity*. The menstrual state lasts seven days, hence the word must be understood as read, two weeks, which is fairly close to the menstrual state. But forty-two days of uncleanness bear no similarity at all to the menstrual state. (14) In connection with the sprinkling of the blood of sin-offerings. Lev. IV, 26, 31, 35. (15) That the omission of a single application invalidates the offering. (16) I.e. to prove that the omission of any application does not invalidate the offering. Wherefore then is there any need of a verse to intimate this law?

a (1) Which encompassed the altar at the middle of its height.—The blood of burnt-, peace- and tresspass-offerings was sprinkled below it, *infra* 53a. (2) As deduced *supra* 36b, 37a. (3) I.e., to be sprinkled on the inner altar. Viz.: the blood of sacrifices offered on the Day of Atonement, and the sacrifices brought by the High Priest and the community for having sinned through ignorance. (4) He does not make atonement. (5) Lit., 'you judge without from without.' (6) Lit., 'you judge a sin-offering and four horns from a sin-offering and four horns.' (7) I.e., the burnt-offering, whose blood was sprinkled on the outer altar. (8) Consequently, by this analogy one might deduce that the omission of an application invalidates the sin-offering. (9) Surely in each of the three cases referred to (*supra* n. 14). Scripture must state *'and he shall make atonement'* to teach that each sin is atoned for by its respective sin-offering.

b (1) Hence *'and he shall make atonement'* is superfluous. (2) Whence then is it known that atonement is effected even if no application at all was made? (3) Whereas Scripture states that the blood must be applied on the horns of the altar, which of course were above the red line. (4) Each *'we-kipper'* makes one horn less necessary. Hence the threefold repetition diminishes them by three, leaving sprinkling on one essential; for in order to render effective the application of all the four below the line four texts would be required. (5) Of the blood of the bullock sacrificed on the Day of Atonement. (6) He did not aim above or below, but made the movement of swinging a whip.

יב א ב מיי' פ"ג מהל' עבודת יוה"כ הל"ה:

התם (א) חד קרא א] כוליה לגופיה וחד לסככה אתאי הלכתא וגרעתה לשלישית ואוקימתה ויקרא יב אטפח אלא מעתה °וטמאה שבועים שבעים אהני קרא ואהני מסורת ארבעים ותרין בעיא שם למיתב שאני התם דכתי' °כנדתה ותנא מייתי שם ד לה מהכא *°וכפר וכפר וכפר מפני הדין ב] שיכול והלא דין הוא נאמרו דמים למטה ונאמרו דמים למעלה מה ג] מתן דמים האמורים למטה שנתנן במתנה אחת כיפר אף דמים האמורים למעלה שנתנן במתנה אחת כיפר או כלך לדרך זו נאמרו דמים בפנים ונאמרו דמים בחוץ מה דמים האמורים בפנים חיסר אחת מן המתנות לא עשה ולא כלום אף דמים האמורין בחוץ חיסר אחת מן המתנות לא עשה ולא כלום נראה למי דומה דנין חוץ מחוץ ואין דנין חוץ ד] מבפנים או כלך לדרך זו דנין חטאת וארבע קרנות מחטאת וארבע קרנות ואל יוכיח חוץ שאין חטאת וארבע קרנות תלמוד לומר *וכפר וכפר וכפר (מפני הדין) וכפר אע"פ נ"ג שלא נתן אלא שלש וכפר אע"פ שלא נתן אלא שתים וכפר אע"פ שלא נתן אלא אחת והאי מיבעי ליה לגופיה אמר רבא בר אדא מרי אסברה לי אמר קרא וכפר ונסלח זו היא כפרה זו היא סליחה אימא וכפר אע"פ שלא נתן אלא שלש למעלה ואחת למטה וכפר אע"פ שלא נתן אלא שתים למטה ושתים למעלה וכפר אע"פ שלא נתן למעלה אלא למטה אמר רב אדא בר יצחק א"כ ביטלת תורת ארבע קרנות ואי רחמנא אמר ליבטלון אמר *רבא איזהו דבר שצריך שלש הוי אומר אלו קרנות ה] אימא וכפר אע"פ שלא נתן אלא ו] אחת למעלה ושלש למטה לא מצינו דמים שחציין למעלה וחציין למטה ולא והתנן **הזה ממנו אחת למעלה ושבע למטה (ב) ז] כמצליף מאי כמצליף מחוי רב יהודה כמנגדנא יומא נג: *ב הזה על טהרו של מזבח שבע פעמים מאי

וליתנה

רש"י

התם דל חד (ג) לגופיה. פש להו ארבע: וחד לסכך. מאחר שהתחיל לפרש ח] תבניתה פירש סכך עם דפנותיה פשו תלת: אתאי הילכתא. שנאמרה למשה מסיני וגרעתה לשלישית כך נאמרה הלכה שהשלישית דייה בטפח היינו דתנן שתים כהלכתן שלישית אפי' טפח: וטמאה שבועים שבעים. כתיב נימא נמי אהני מסורת לטפויי פלגא דתוספ' שבעים *על שבועיים ואהני מקרא לבצורי פלגא נמצאת מוסיף על שבועי' כ"ח חלין של נ"ו ט] בעי' למיתב. ימי טומאה יולדת נקבה: שאני התם דכתיב כנדתה. משמע שלא ירד הכתוב למנין ימים אלא למנין שבועות שהנדה שבוע אחת והיולדת שבועים שאם אתה אומר שבעים הפלגת מתורת נדה הרבה אבל כשאתה אומר שבועים קרבת' לתורת נדה: ותנא. י] דמתני' לא מייתי להא דב"ה כרב הונא אלא מהכא: וכפר וכפר וכפר. בשעיר נשיא ושעירה יא] וכשבה שכולן על המזבח החיצון: מפני הדין. יב] שחוזר אלילה ומלמד על החטאת החיצונה שכל מתנותיה מעכבות לכך נאמרו אלו להכשיר אם חיסר: והלא דין הוא. יג] להכשירה במתנה אחת וקרא למה לי: נאמרו דמים למטה. מחוט הסיקרא כל הדמים חוץ מחטאת ונאמרו דמים למעלה מחוט הסיקרא חטאת מה יד] תחתונים כפר במתנה אחת *דכתיב ודם זבחיך ישפך ומיהו חטאת מהאי קרא לא יליף דלא טו] שייכי ביה לשון שפיכה כי אם זריקה שהיא במתנת אצבע אלא בבנין אב למד מן התחתונים דאף הוא כפר במתנה אחת: בפנים. בחטאות הפנימיות: בחוץ. בחטאות החיצונות: לא עשה ולא כלום. בפירקין ילפינן לה: חוץ מחוץ. חטאת מעולה: דנין חטאת. החיצונה שהיא חטאת וכתיב בה ארבע קרנות כמו שאמרנו למעלה קרנת קרנות קרנות מחטאת הפנימית שהיא חטאת ונאמרו בה ארבע קרנות כדלקמן למעלה הוא אומר קרן קרנות בפר כהן משיח הרי שתים למטה הוא אומר בפר העדה קרן קרנות טז] ארבע: ולא יוכיח חוץ. דשאר *דמים יז] חוץ ולא נאמר בהן קרנות: מיבעי ליה לגופיה. בכל חד וחד ללמדך שכפר על החטא: אימא וכפר כו'. אבל למיעקרינהו לגמרי לא: א"כ. דדרשינן כפר אע"פ שנתנן כולן למטה מן החוט: בטלת תורת קרנות. הכתובים בחטאת ועל חנם כתיב בה קרנות דהיינו למעלה: ופרכינן ואי יח] דרחמנא אמר. דליבטלון בדיעבד מוכפר ליבטלון וכי כתבינהו למצוה כתבינהו: איזהו דבר שצריך שלשה. וכפר הוי אומר אלו קרנות וכדאמרינן דכל חד וחד מיעט יט] חדא קרן וקם ליה אקרן אחת לעכב דאי כדקאמרת לאשמועינן דאי יהיב כולהו למטה כשר כ] (למטה) ארבע וכפר הוה ליה למיכתב להכשיר ארבע המתנות למטה: ואימא וכפר אף ע"פ שלא נתן אלא אחת למעלה ושלש למטן. ולהכי לא כתיבי ארבעה משום דחדא מיהא כא] (לא) מעכבא בלמעלה ותלת איתכשרי למטה אבל למיעקרינהו לא: הזה ממנו. מדם פר יום הכפורים בסדר יומא: אחת למעלה ושבע למטה. כדכתיב על פני הכפרת קדמה ולפני הכפרת יזה שבע פעמים (ויקרא טז) וקא ס"ד אחת מחצי עביו של כפרת ולמעלה ושבע מחציה ולמטה: ומשני ההוא כמצליף. כדמפרש ואזיל: כמנגדנא. כאדם המכה מלקות ארבעים ברצועה כב] זו למטה מזו בסמוך ולא שכיון אחת מחציו ולמעלה והשאר מחציו ולמטה והא דקתני כאחת חלוקה מהשבע כג] לענין לידוד ידו קתני כדמפרש התם כשהוא מזה למעלה מלדד ידו למטה וכשהוא מזה למטה מלדד ידו למעלה: כזה על טהרו. והתנן התם הזה על טהרו של מזבח הפנימי כדכתיב והזה עליו מן הדם וגו' (גם זה שם):

תוספות

התם כד] חד קרא כוליה לגופיה. לא דמי לקרנות דדרשינן תחילות דקרנות משמע מניינא אבל סוכות לא משמע מניין דפנות אלא משמע שתי סוכות הלכך אין לנו לדרוש תחילות ול"ע גבי אלהים (סנהדרין דף ג:) דמשמע נמי מניין ולא דרשינן תחילות:

ארבעין ותרתין. אלי שבעים ואלי ארבעה עשר:

כה] דכתיב כנדתה. פי' כשיעור נדתה יש לך להוסיף אנקבה יותר מן הזכר כו] ובפ' קמא דסנהדרין (דף ד.) לא מייתי ליה להאי כנדתה:

דנין חטאת וארבע קרנות. תימה דאפילו חוץ מפנים בעי למילף משום חטאת וארבע קרנות כל שכן פנים מבפנים ולקמן מצריך קרא לכל הפנימים דמעכבי ולא ילפי מהדדי *דדריש לפר זה כז] הפר כהן המשיח להקישו לפר העלם דבר של ציבור לומר דמעכבי וביום הכפורים צריך קרא:

וכפר אע"פ שלא נתן למעלה אלא למטה. תימה אמאי איפסיק מסדר שהתחיל לדרוש דהוה ליה למימר וכפר אע"פ שלא נתן כח] למעלה אלא אחת ושלש למטה וי"ל דלא משמע ליה לדרוש שיעשה למטה אלא בהכשר דמים הניתנין למטה ושתים למעלה וב' למטה דקאמר היינו שיעשה למטה כט] אחת שהיא שתים וכן וכפר אע"פ שנתן כולן למטה היינו כדין שאר דמים הניתנין *למטה אבל אי אמרת אחת למעלה ושלש למטה הוי למטה אחת שהיא שתים ואחת שהיא אחת ל] פוסל והיינו תרי שינויי שרובה למטה וגם האחת אינו כמשפט דמים של מטה אבל שלש למעלה ואחת למטה אע"פ שאותה אחת אינו כמשפט אין קפידא כיון שהרוב למעלה ע"כ ומשני רבא איזהו דבר שצריך שלש וכפר הוי אומר לא] זה קרנות פירוש דלדידך בתרי וכפר סגי דכיון דלא בעינן קרא לאחת למעלה ושלש למטה לפי שאינו כדין דמים הניתנין למטה אם כן שלש למעלה ואחת למטה נמי אע"ג דרובן למעלה לא ליבעי קרא דאין זה כדין לב] הניתנין למטה שכל הניתנין למטה ממתנות ארבע הויא אחת שהיא שתים ופריך ואימא וכפר אע"פ שלא נתן אלא אחת למעלה ושלש למטה לג] ולא כולן למטה ולא אחוש בסברא זו דטוב להכשיר אחת למעלה לד] מכולן למטה: (הגה"ה תוספת ודברי רש"י יש לה] לפרש דסבירא ליה כיון דוכפר שלישי אתי לשלש למטה כיון דהרוב למטה כשר הוא הדין כולן למטה ומשני איזהו דבר שצריך שלש וכפר כו' ולדבריך ארבע וכפר היה לו ליכתוב והוא הדין שלך אינו טוב והדר פריך ודילמא שלש למטה דוקא כשר ולא כולן מיהו לישנא דצריך שלש דמשמע ולדבריך אינו צריך שלש לו] משמע כפי' התוס'. ע"כ הגה"ה) וצריך לדקדק אמאי לא דרשינן להני לז] וכפר אע"פ שלא נתן לקרנות כלומר בחודה וכפר אע"פ שלא נתן באצבע וכפר אע"פ שלא נתן ארבע מתנות אלא שתים שהן ד' לח] וזה אין להקשות דהכא דרשינן וכפר לגמרי ואפילו בשר שרי באכילה ולעיל בפרק שני (דף כו:) דרשינן לכפרה נתתיו ולא לדבר אחר ויש לחלק בין לכפר בין לוכפר:

לט] כמצליף. תימה ומאי ס"ד דמקשה הא בהדיא קתני הכי בסיפא ביומא פ' הוציאו לו (דף נג:) דתנן לא היה מתכוין להזות לא למעלה ולא למטה אלא כמצליף וי"ל שבא לתרץ דהאי כמצליף כמנגדנא והכל במקום אחד וכמו שמפורש בערוך מ] כמנגדנא שמרים ידו ואינו מכה עד שיורד ירושלמי מצליף מא] *כמטברר פי' בערוך שמטה ידו עד טיבורו:

מאי לאו אפלגיה דמזבח. ואם כן מצינו דמים חציין למעלה וחציין למטה דמתחלה נתן מב] אקרנות ואחר כך לחצי המזבח. תוספות. ורש"י מפרש בע"א:

ג"י ס"ק דדריש לפר זה פר יוה"כ כאשר עשה לפר זה פר כהן משוח להקישו כו' לומר דמעכבו וצריך קרא לס"ק. ועיין סנהדרין דף ד ע"ב ד"ה דנין דמתמלתו קושיא זו:

למטה שנים שהן ד' אבל כו' נ"ק

נ"י הנ"ק על שבועים דסוי נ"ו ואהכי כו'

[סנהדרין ה. כל סעיין]

סנהדרין ד:

ס"א רב

יומא נג. נג:

נ"ל דמים שאינם חטאת ולא נאמר כו' נ"ק

הגהות הב"ח

(א) גמ' התם דל חד קרא כוליה לגופיה וחד לסכך פשו תלת אתאי הלכתא וכו' אהני מקרא: (ב) שם ושבע למטה ההוא כמצליף: (ג) רש"י ד"ה התם דל חד קרא לגופיה:

גליון הש"ס

רש"י ד"ה נאמרו דמים וכו' דכתיב ודם זבחיך. עיין לעיל דף לו ע"ב תוס' ד"ה מנין: נ"ג

שיטה מקובצת

א] התם דל חד קרא לגופיה וחד לסכך אתאי: ב] תיבת שיכול נמחק: ג] תיבת מתן נמחק: ד] חוץ מפנים אות ב' נמחק: ה] ואימא וכפר וכו'. וא"ת לעיל מעיקרא נמי למה לא קאמר כמו שאמר השתא ודילג באמצע שהיה לו לפרש ולדרוש וכפר אע"פ שלא נתן אלא אחת למעלה וכו' וי"ל דאין סברא שיכפר אלא בהכשר דמים הניתנים למטה ובכאן נמי אם נתנם למטה אחת שהן שתים כיפר אבל ג' למטה דהיינו אחת שהיא אחת ואחת שהיא שתים לא כיפר שלא מצינו בזה הכשר דמים וקאמר א"כ בטלת ד' קרנות כך כתוב בכל הספרים ונראה דה"פ כיון שבאת לדרוש כך אע"פ שלא נתן כולן אלא למטה א"כ על תנם כתיב ד' מתנות על ד' קרנות שהרי אינו נותן אפי' אחת על הקרנות רק כולו למטה אבל למאי דדרשינן אע"פ שלא נתן אלא אחת למעלה לא ביטלת תורת ד' קרנות שהרי צריך מתנה אחת בדיעבד על א' מד' קרנות ועל איזה מד' קרנות שיתן מתנה אחת כיפר ומשני איזה דבר שצריך ג' ופ"ה כדפי' דאי אתא לומר שאם נתנן כולן למטה כשר א"כ ארבע וכפר [הוה ליה למכתב] כו' וקשה דא"כ הול"ל איזה דבר שאינו צריך אלא ג' ועוד דהא לא שייך לדרוש קרא להכשיר אחת למעלה ת' למטה כדפי' ולהכי לא כתיב ד' וכפר א) וכו' עד מכולן למטה לבטל כל הקרנות והשתא צריכי ג' וכפר כי טוב יותר לומר כן מלמטה ג' מתנות משלא יעשה כלל מיהו קשה קצת מאי ס"ד סברת המקשה שלא היה מצריך קרא למעט אחת למעלה וג' למטה והיה מצריך קרא למעט ג' למעלה ואחת למטה הלא לא מצינו אחת למטה בהכשר דמים כמו ג' למטה ואמר מורי שי' דהוי סובר דאחת למטה הוי שפיר בהכשר דמים הניתנים למטה כגון בכור ומעשר ופסח שניתנים במתנה אחת למטה ומ"מ שפיר קאמר רבא איזה דבר הצריך ג' כדפי' דלדידך לא איצטריך כי אם שתים דמהאי טעמא דלא איצטריך קרא למעט ג' למטה לא יצטרך קרא למעט אחת למטה ואע"ג דאשכחן בבכור ומעשר ופסח שניתנים במתנה אחת למטה מ"מ לא דמי דהתם ליכא בשום מקום רק מתנה אחת למטה אבל כה"ג שטעונין ד' מתנות דג' למעלה ואחת למטה לא אשכחן ועי"ל דסברת המקשה בג' למעלה ואחת למטה כיון שרובן למעלה שפיר טפי: ו] אלא ג' למעלה ואחת למטה וכפר אע"פ שלא נתן אלא שתים למעלה ושתים למטה וכפר אע"פ שלא נתן אלא אחת: ז] למטה ההוא כמצליף ותיבות מאי כמצליף בס"א אינו: ח] לפרש בתבניתה כו' פשו להו תלת הס"ד כו' מסיני ע"פ במחיצות דקי"ל שיעורין חציצין ומחיצות הל"מ וגרעתה: ט] ארבעים ושתים בעינן למיתב: י] ותנא דמתניתא לא: יא] ובכבשה שכולן: יב] הדין שחוזר כו' החטאות החיצונות שכל: יג] הוא. להכשיר: יד] מה דמים התחתונים כפר: טו] דלא שייכא: טז] קרנות הרי כאן ארבע: יז] דמים שאינן חטאת ולא נאמר: יח] רחמנא אמר: יט] מיעט חד קרן: כ] תיבת למטה נמחק: כא] מיהא מעכבא בלמעלה ותלת מיתכשרי למטה: כב] ברצועה עד טבורו זו למטה כו' מחציו עובי הכפורת ולמעלה: כג] מהשבע לא קאי אענין מקום הזאות אלא קאי אאצבע לענין: כד] התם דל חד [קרא] לגופיה: כה] מה"ד שאני התם דכתיב כנדתה פ"ה משמע כו' ודוחק א"א ה"פ פי' כשיעור: כו] הזכר דהיינו ז' ימים: כז] זה פר כהן כו' דמעכבי ופר יום הכפורים נמי צריך קרא: כח] נתן אלא אחת למעלה ושלש: כט] למטה שתי מתנות שהן ארבע א"נ א': ל] אחת תוס' ותיבת פוסל ל"ש ונמחק: לא] אומר אלו קרנות: לב] כדין דמים הניתנין: לג] ושלש למטה כלומר ולא אחוש לסברא ותיבות ולא כולן למטה נמחק: לד] למעלה ושלש למטה מכולן: לה] יש לתרץ אמאי הפסיק מסדר שהתחיל דס"ל: לו] שלשה כי אם שתים משמע כפי' ראשון ס"א התוס': לז] וכפר הכי וכפר אע"פ: לח] תיבת וזה נמחק: לט] מה"ד ההוא כמצליף: מ] בערוך וזה לשונו כמנגדנא: מא] ג) כמטבריה פי' מטה ותיבות (כמטברר) בערוך ל"ש: מב] נתן ד' מתנות על ארבע קרנות ואח"כ נתן שבע על חצי המזבח:

א) [מראה דחסר כאן וצ"ל לכן נראה לפרש דרבא ה"ק דלדידך בתרי וכפר סגי וכו' (וכמ"ש בתוס' ד"ה וכפר) עד וכולן למטה והשתא צריכי כו' משלא יעשה כלל לבטל כל הקרנות. מיהו כו']: ב] לפנינו בירושלמי איתא כמטווד:
הת"ג בס"מ שהוא שתי תיבות כמטווד ורד [וכ"ה בכתובות דף עב: במווה ורד ועי"ש ברש"י]

א] מאי לאו אפלגיה דמזבח כדאמרי אינשי *טהר טיהרא (א) דיומא ב] אמר רבא בר שילא לא אגילוייה דכתיב °וכעצם השמים לטוהר והאיכא שירים שירים לא מעכבי והאיכא שירים הפנימים דאיכא ג] דמ"ד מעכבי בחד מקום קאמרינן: תניא רבי אליעזר בן יעקב אומר בית שמאי אומרים שתי מתנות שבחטאת ואחת שבכל הזבחים מתירות ומפגלות בית הלל אומרים אחת שבחטאת ואחת שבכל הזבחים *מתרת ומפגלת *מתקיף לה רב אושעיא אם כן ליתנייה גבי קולי בית שמאי וחומרי בית הלל אמר ליה רבא כי איתשיל להתירא איתשיל דהוו להו בית שמאי לחומרא: אמר רבי יוחנן שלש מתנות שבחטאות אינן באות בלילה ובאות לאחר מיתה והמעלה מהן בחוץ חייב אמר רב פפא יש מהן ד] כתחלתו ויש מהן כסופו חו"ץ ולילה זרות וכלי שרת קרן ואצבע כיבוס ושירים כתחלתן מיתה לא שריא ולא מפגלא ולא עיילא לגואי כסופן אמר רב פפא מנא אמינא לה *דתנן ניתז מן הצואר על הבגד אינו טעון כיבוס מן הקרן ומן היסוד אינו טעון כיבוס הא מן הראוי לקרן טעון כיבוס וליטעמיך מן היסוד ה] אינו טעון כיבוס הא מן הראוי ליסוד טעון כיבוס °אשר יזה כתיב *פרט לזה שכבר הוזה הא מני רבי נחמיה *דתנן רבי נחמיה אומר שירי הדם שהקריבן בחוץ חייב אימר דשמעת ליה לר' נחמיה לענין העלאה מידי דהוי אאיברים ופדרים לענין כיבוס מי שמעת ליה אין

והתניא

תורה אור: שמות כד | ויקרא ו

רש"י

מאי לאו אפלגיה דמזבח. כנגד חצי גובהו ואי אפשר לגמלא שלא יהא מקצתם למעלה ומקצתם למטה: טיהרא. צהרים ו]: לא אגילוייה דמזבח. על ז] גגו של מזבח שהיה מטהרו תחילה מדשן שעליו ומגלה את גגו ועל ח] שמטהרו ומייפהו קרי ליה טהרו כדכתיב *וטהרו: והא איכא שירים. שנשפכים ליסוד ועיקר המתנות למעלה: שירים לא מעכבי. כפרה ותנן בדמים המעכבים קאמרינן דלא מליא חליין למעלה וחליין למטה: דאיכא למ"ד מעכבי. לקמן באיזהו מקומן (דף נב.) ועיקר המתנות בקרנות הפנימי דהיינו למעלה והשירים ביסוד מזבח החיצון דהיינו למטה: בחד מקום. במזבח אחד: שתי מתנות שבחטאת מתירות. כל זמן שלא ט] ניתן שתים לא הותרו אימורין להקטרה ולא הבשר לאכילה: ומפגלות. אם נתן שתיהן במחשבת פיגול אבל אחת בשתיקה ואחת במחשבה לא פיגל שאין מפגלין בחצי מתיר: לתנייה. להך פלוגתא בעדיות גבי קולי בית שמאי שכולן נסדרו במסכת עדיות והא נמי קולי ב"ש הוא דלב"ש לא פיגל אלא אם כן חישב בשתיהן ולבית הלל פיגל באחת מהן: כי איתשיל. י] משנה (ב) בבית המדרש תחילה ונחלקו עליה בית שמאי וב"ה: להיתירא איתשיל. לענין היתר הבשר והאימורין נשאלה שעמד השואל ושאל נתן מתנה אחת בחטאת ונשפך הדם הותרו האימורין והבשר או לא הותרו עמדו בית שמאי ופסלו עמדו ב"ה והכשירו דהוו להו ב"ש (ג) חומרא ומינה גמרינן דכיון דאיכה מתרת לבדה איכה מפגלת: אמר רבי יוחנן שלש מתנות. יא] אחרות שבחטאת אין באות בלילה ואע"פ שאינן מעכבים ולאו זריקה גמורה היא מיהו דם נפסל בשקיעת החמה כדלקמן* ואין מעלין יב] לגבי מזבח לכתחילה: באות לאחר מיתה. אם נתן מתנה ראשונה ומתו בעליה כבר כפר בראשונה ואין שם חטאת גמורה על הדם עוד לפסול משום חטאת שמתו בעליה: יש מהן כתחלתו יג]. יש מדברים שבתורת דמים שהשלש מתנות כמתנה *ראשונה ויש דברים שהן בתורת שירי הדם: חוץ. *)הזורק אותן בחוץ חייב שהרי ראויים לפנים בתורת זריקה גמורה ואסור ליתנן בלילה דנפסלו מלזרוק והא זריקה היא וזר חייב עליהן מיתה בפנים וטעונות כלי שרת יד] ומתנה (ד) אצבע וכיבוס אם ניתז מדם החטאת על הבגד לאחר שנתן טו] במתנה אחת טעון כיבוס כדכתיב ואשר יזה מדמה וגו' כאילו ניתז קודם לכן אבל אם נתן כל מתנותיה ואח"כ ניתז מן השירים אין טעון כיבוס כדאמרינן בשמעתין אשר יזה פרט לזה שכבר הוזה: שירים. חטאת שקיבל דמה בארבע כוסות ונתן מתנה אחת *מכל אחד כולן נעשו שירים ליספך ליסוד אף הג' טז] שירים שלהן כמו *הראשונים: כתחלתו. כמתנה הראשונה: מיתה. באות לאחר מיתה כדאמר לעיל: לא שריא. בשר שכבר הותר: ולא מפגלא. אם נתן הראשונה בשתיקה והשלש במחשבה לא פיגל וכשר כדתנן במתני': ולא עיילא יז]. אין להם תורת פסול כניסת פנים שאם נתן מתנה אחת בחוץ והכניס השאר יח] להיכל לא נפסל משום חטאת שנכנס דמה לפנים דכתיב לכפר בקודש (ויקרא ו) בראוי לכפרה הכתוב מדבר: כסופן. יט] כשירים: מנא אמינא לה. דטעונה כיבוס: ניתז מן הצואר על הבגד אין טעון כיבוס. כדאמרינן בפרק דם חטאת (לקמן דף צג.) אשר יזה בראוי להזאה יצא זה שלא נתקבל בכלי: מן הקרן. משנגע בקרן המזבח ניתז על הבגד: או מן היסוד. משנשפכו שירים ליסוד ניתז מן היסוד לבגד: אין טעון כיבוס. כדאמרינן אשר יזה פרט לזה שכבר הוזה: הא מן הראוי לקרן. כל דהו ואפילו שלש מתנות שבחטאות טעון כיבוס: הא מן הראוי ליסוד. כגון שירי הדם הראויין ליספך ליסוד: טעון כיבוס. בתמיה: הא מני ר' נחמיה היא כ] כו'. הא מילתא הש"ס קאמר לה ומסקנא דקושיין היא לאפוקי מדרב פפא כלומר מהא לא איריא טעמא דידך דהא כא] רבי נחמיה היא דאפילו בשירים נמי טעון כיבוס: שירי הדם. אף של חטאות החיצונות שהקריבן בחוץ חייב אלמא דם כב] קחשיב להו: מידי דהוי אאיברים. דלאו דמים נינהו כג] המעלן בחוץ חייב משום דחזו לפנים:

דמים

*) אחד מהן הזורק אותה כו' כצ"ל ז"ק

תוספות

וליתנייה גבי קולי בית שמאי. פי' רש"י דסבר דשתי מתנות מפגלות ולא אחת דאין מפגלים בחצי מתיר כד] וא"ת אימא מפגלות היינו באחת מהן ולבית הלל בראשונה דווקא ולכולהו מפגלין בחצי מתיר כה] וא"כ אף בפיגול זימנין דהוי חומרא לב"ש אם נתן ראשונה כתיקנה ושניה חוץ לזמנה הוי פיגול ולב"ה אינו פיגול כדאמר במתני' כו] *ונ"ל מדקאמרי בית הלל ראשונה מפגלת מכלל דלב"ש לא מפגלא כז] *דהוה ליה למימר בראשונה ולא בשניה ותו י"ל דומיא דמתירות דהיינו דשתיהן דווקא הוי מפגלות וה"ר יצחק כח] כתב דכן מוכח בתוספתא בהדיא א"ר אלעזר בן יעקב דבר זה כט] מקולי בית שמאי ומחומרי בית הלל שתי מתנות שבחטאת מכשירות ומפגלות כיצד אחת שלא ל] בזמנה ונשפך הדם פסול ואין בו כרת דברי ב"ש ובית הלל אומרים פיגול ויש בו כרת אלמא באחת אין בו פיגול לב"ש לא] ומשמע משום דנשפך הדם ולא קרבו כל מתיריו אבל אם לא נשפך הדם ונתן השניה כתיקנה הוי פיגול דמפגלי' בחצי מתיר ולא כפי' רש"י ולבית הלל פיגל דקרבו כל מתיריו או שמא אפי' לא נשפך ונתן השני' כתיקנה נמי אינו פיגול לב"ש דאין מפגלין בחצי מתיר ונשפך דקתני משום בית הלל אשמועינן דהיינו קרבו כל מתיריו השתא ממה נפשך *בין סברי בית שמאי מפגלין בחצי מתיר לב] הוו לקולא אכתי קשיא לי למה תירץ כי איתשיל בהתירא איתשל אפי' כי איתשיל בפיגול הוי בית שמאי לחומרא היכא דלא נשפך ונתן לג] ראשונה כתיקנה והשניה בפיגול דמפגלין בחצי מתיר *וליכא למימר דנשפך דווקא האי מקולי ב"ש דלמה ליה למימר בעדיות קולא דנשפך כיון דבלא נשפך הוי חומרא ויש לומר דהאי גוונא אינו שנוי לא במשנה ולא בברייתא בפירוש אבל לישנא דברייתא בנשפך הוי לקולא לבית שמאי לכך פריך ליתני' בעדיות לד]:

הגה"ה הא מני רבי נחמיה היא דאמר שירים. לה] ולפירוש הקונטרס שנדחה סייעתא דרב פפא לו] קשה דהוה ליה למימר אלא ולפום ריהטא שיטיה הוא אליבא דרב פפא והיינו טעמא דכיון דאשכחן לרבי נחמיה דטעון כיבוס היכא דחייב בחוץ לז] לרב פפא נמי כיון דחייב בחוץ בג' מתנות שבחטאת הוא הדין דטעון כיבוס לח] *דכיבוס וחיוב חוץ חדא מילתא היא *)דפשיטא שעל זה לא הוצרך ראייה לט] ופריך אימר דשמעת ליה לר' נחמיה לענין העלאה כו' לענין כיבוס מי שמעת ליה ואם כן לא דייקינן הא מן הראוי ליסוד והוא הדין דלא תידוק הא מן הראוי לקרן ומשני אין והתניא כו' וכולה סוגיא לקיומי סייעתא דרב פפא עד לבסוף דמשני אלא כי תניא ההיא בדמים הפנימים דנדחו דבריו (תוספות) ומיהו מ] כל זה אמר רב פפא לקיים דבריו בחטאות הפנימיות ולהכי מחשבה מועלת בהן ומיירי בשירים כדמשמע לישנא דברייתא דנשפכים ליסוד ולא בשלש מתנות דכיון דאיירי בפנימיות כך שוה כמו מתנה ראשונה כיון דכל ארבע מעכבות לכולי עלמא ולא הוי קרי להו נשפכין ליסוד ובסיפא לא מצי לפלוגי בדמים החיצונים דרבי נחמיה היא דחייב בשיריהם בחוץ ואם כן לא מצי למיתני תלתא פטור מא]:

הגה"ה ויש מב] מפרש הא מני רבי נחמיה היא כו'. ואתיא סיפא דהא מן הראוי ליסוד כמו רבי נחמיה ורישא דהא מן הראוי לקרן כרבנן ואשכחן כי האי גוונא בפ' שתי הלחם (מנחות דף מה.) מג] דתנא ואפייתו בפנים אלמא תנור מקדש ואין דוחות את השבת איפסלי להו בלינה וכן ברייתא דריש טבול יום (לקמן דף ק:) דיום שמועה כיום קבורה וכו'. ושקיל וטרי עד אלא כי תניא ההיא בשלש מתנות שבחטאת מד] וגרס אלא בספרים מדוייקים והאי סייעתא דרב פפא מהך ברייתא ולא מקמייתא ולפי שיטה זו יש ליישב כולה סוגיא ובקונטרס פירש כולה שמעתא בע"א:

*) נ"א דפשיטא שחייב בחוץ על זה כו'

הא

עין משפט נר מצוה

יג א מיי' פ"ב מהלכות פסולי המוקדשין הלכה א:
יד ב מיי' פי"ח שם ה"א:
טו ג מיי' פ"ד מהלכות מעשה הקרבנות הלכה א:
טז ד מיי' פי"ז שם הי"ג:
יז ה מיי' פ"ח מהלכות מעשה הקרבנות ה"ו:
יח ו מיי' שם הלכה ז:

נ"א וכ"ל מדלא קאמרי ז"ק
דא"כ ה"ל למימר ז"ק
נ"א אפי'
גי' ז"ק וליכא דנשפך כו' ולמה ליה למימר
וחיוב חוץ וטעון כיבוס דחדא היא מלתא דפשיטא היא וע"ז כו' ז"ק

מסורת הש"ס

למוסר ז"ק
יומא נח. נט.
[יומא ס. חולין נב: קנ. בכורות לז: ערכין כו:]
לקמן נב.
[לקמן נב. מעילה ט.]
לקמן קי: קיב.
[דף מ:]
נ"א ראשונה ויש מהן כסופו ויש דברים שה'
צ"ל מאחד
הראשונים ז"ק

הגהות הב"ח

(א) גמ' טהר טיהרא והוי פלגים דיומא: (ב) רש"י ד"ה כי אתשיל משנה זו בכנסת: (ג) ד"ה להיתירא וכו' לחומרא: (ד) ד"ה מן הזורק וכו' ומתנת קרן ואצבע וכו' כיבוס:

שיטה מקובצת

א] מאי לאו אפלגיה דמזבח. פ"ה כנגד כו' וקשה כיון דאינו מכוין היינו כמנגדנא לכך נראה לר' חיים כהן דפריך משום שכבר נתן ד' מתנות על ד' קרנות למעלה ואח"כ נתן שבע על חצי המזבח דהיינו למטה ומשני לא אטהרו ר"ל על גילוייא והכל היה למעלה על הקרנות ועל גב מזבח וקרו ליה טהרו על שהיה מטהרו ומייפהו תחלה מהדשן שעליו: ב] דיומא ותרי פלגא: ג] דאיכא למ"ד: ד] מהן כתחלתן ויש מהן כסופן: ה] היסוד נמי מן היסוד הוא דאינו טעון כיבוס: ו] צהרים דהוא חצי היום הס"ד: ז] על גילוי גגו: ח] ועל שם שמטהרו: ט] שלא נתן שתים: י] איתשיל מתנה אחת בבהמ"ד: יא] מתנות אחרונות שבחטאת: יב] מעלין פסולין לגבי מזבח: יג] כתחלתן. יש דברים: יד] ומתנת אצבע: טו] שנתן מתנה: טז] כוסות של שלש מתנות אחרונות יש להן שיריים כמו הראשונים הס"ד ומת"ד כתחלתן. כלומר דינן כמתנה: יז] עיילי לגואי: יח] השאר בהיכל: יט] כסופן דינן כשיריים: כ] היא. כולה הא מלתא: כא] דהא סני ר' נחמיה כו' נמי אית ליה כיבוס הס"ד: כב] דם גמור קחשיב: כג] נינהו והמעלן כו' לפנים הס"ד ומת"ד אין והתניא: כד] מתיר וב"ה סברי דקמייתא חשיבא שפיר מתיר שלם: כה] מתיר ס"א והוי נמי ב"ש לחומרא דלב"ש ב' מתנות מפגלות זו או זו ולב"ה כו': כו] במתני' ונ"ל מדקאמרי ב"ה אחת שבחטאת מפגלת דהיינו ראשונה: כז] מפגלא אותה אחת דאל"כ הוה ליה למימר אין מתיר ומפגל אלא בראשונה: כח] יצחק מצא בתוספתא ותיבות כתב דכן מוכח ל"ש: כט] זה אחד מקולי: ל] שלא לזמנו: לא] הוי משום תיבת ומשמע ל"ש: לב] מתיר בין לא סברי הוו: לג] ונתן מתן ראשונה כו' בחצי מתיר ולימא דנשפך: לד] בעדיות ע"כ: לה] שיריים פי' הקונטרס: לו] פפא ומסקנא דקושיא היא לאפוקי מדרב פפא וה"ק אלא כלומר לא איירי בטעמא דידך דהא סני ר' נחמיה היא כלומר דמחייב בחוץ בשיריים וה"ה נמי בג' מתנות שבחטאת שטעון כבוס אבל לרבנן דלא מחייב בשיריים משום חוץ ה"ה נמי דאינו טעון כבוס בג' מתנות ולא תפשום מידי לרבנן ולא נהירא דא"כ הל"ל אלא ועוד דבסמוך מייתי למלתיה לרב פפא דקאמר לא שריא ולא מפגלא כסופן ועוד דלפום רהיטא משמע דשנויא הוא לרב פפא לכך נראה דשנויא הוא וה"ק הא סני ר' נחמיה היא וכי היכא דאשכחן כיבוס כו': לז] בחוץ לרבנן נמי ותיבת לרב פפא ל"ש תמחק: לח] כיבוס דטעון כיבוס וחיוב: [לט] ראייה דמהא לא פליגי רבנן עליה דר' נחמיה: מ] ומיהו נ"ל דגם זה אמר ר"פ לקיים דבריו בדמים הפנימים ולהכי מחשבה מועלת כו' דברייתא נשפכין יסוד ולא: מא] פטור ע"כ: מב] ויש מפרשי': מג] מדתנא ואפייתו: מד] שבחטאת וגרסי' אלא:

He[7] besprinkled the surface[8] of the altar seven times. [38b] Surely that means on the [upper] half of the altar, as people say, The noon-light shines, and so it is midday?[9]—Said Raba b. Shila, No: [it means] on the [altar's] top surface [cleared] from ashes, for it is written, *and the like of the very heaven for clearness.*[10] But there is the remainder [of the blood]?[11]—The [pouring out of] the re-
a mainder [at the altar's base] is not essential.[1] But there is the remainder of inner sin-offerings,[2] which, according to one view is essential?[3]—We mean in one and the same place.[4]

It was taught: R. Eliezer b. Jacob said: Beth Shammai maintain [that] two applications in the case of the sin-offering and one in the case of all [other] sacrifices permit [them for consumption] and may render them *piggul*;[5] Beth Hillel rule: One application [only] in the case of a sin-offering and one in the case of all [other] sacrifices permit [them for consumption] and may render them *piggul*. To this R. Oshaia demurred: If so, this [controversy] should be recited among the lenient rulings of Beth Shammai and the stricter rulings of Beth Hillel?[6]—Said Raba to him: When the question was [first] asked, it was whether [the sacrifice] was permitted,[7] so that Beth Shammai were stricter.

R. Joḥanan said: The three [final] applications of sin-offerings may not be made at night, and are made after [the owners'] death, while he who presents them without the Temple court is culpable.[8]

R. Papa said: In some respects [they are] as the first blood,
b while in others they are as the last:[1] [In respect of sprinkling them] without [the Temple court], at night, *zaruth*,[2] [the requirement of] a service-vessel, [sprinkling on] the horn, [with] the finger, washing,[3] and residue,[4] they are as the first blood. [In respect of] death, not permitting [the flesh], not rendering [it] *piggul*, and not entering within, they are as the last blood.[5]

R. Papa said: How do I know it?[6]—Because we learnt: If [the blood] spurted [direct] from the [animal's] throat on to the [priest's] garment, it does not need washing; from the horn or from the base [of the altar], it does not need washing. Hence, [if some] of [the blood] which was *fit* for the horn [spurted on the garment], it does need washing.[7] Then on your reasoning [you may argue, 'If it spurted] from the base, it does not need washing; hence if
c some [of the blood] which was fit for the base[1] [spurted on the garment], it does need washing? [Yet surely] it is written, *And if aught of the blood which is to be sprinkled* [spurt] *upon any garment, thou shalt wash that whereon it was sprinkled in a holy place,*[2] which excludes this [residue], as the [blood] has already been sprinkled? [Hence you must say that] this is in accordance with R. Nehemiah, for we learnt: R. Nehemiah said: If one presented the residue of the blood without [the Temple court], he is liable.[3] But granted that you know R. Nehemiah [to rule thus] in respect of presenting [the blood without the Temple court], by analogy with the limbs and the fat pieces,[4] do you [however] know him [to rule thus] in

(7) The High Priest, during the Atonement Day Service. (8) Lit., 'the pure' (golden front). (9) This is to shew that the root *ṭahor* (pure) denotes half, as it is used for midday (actually, because then the sun shines in all its clarity and purity). And in this case it was hardly possible to avoid some of the blood falling below the line. (10) Ex. XXIV, 10—Heb. *lo-ṭohar*. This gives the word its usual meaning, and here it is interpreted, the cleared surface (on top). (11) Which is poured out at the base of the altar. Thus part of the blood is applied above, and part is applied below.

a (1) But we find no case of the *essential* sprinkling being partly above and partly below. (2) I.e., the remainder which is poured out on the base of the outer altar, v. *infra* 47a. (3) V. *infra* 52a. Thus the blood itself is applied on the upper part of the inner altar, while another portion of it, the remainder, is poured out at the base of the outer altar. (4) There is no instance of the blood being poured partly above and partly below on the *same* altar. (5) Only if a *piggul* intention is expressed during *both* applications does the sin-offering become *piggul*. For since both are essential, each sprinkling is only half a *mattir* (q.v. Glos.), through which one cannot render a sacrifice *piggul*. (6) In the numerous controversies between these two schools Beth Shammai generally holds the stricter, Beth Hillel the more lenient view; the exceptions are enumerated in the Tractate 'Eduyyoth, and the present controversy is not included. But in fact here too Beth Hillel are more severe, in that they rule that a *piggul* intention expressed during one application only renders the sin-offering *piggul*. (7) If one application only was made. (8) Though the first application is sufficient, the other three are not essential, and so might not be regarded as real sprinklings at all; nevertheless, they must not be done at night, in accordance with the general law that the blood must not be kept until the night. Again, if the owner of the sacrifice dies before its blood is sprinkled, the blood cannot be sprinkled and the sacrifice is burnt. But if the owner dies after the first application, which in itself rendered the sacrifice valid, the other three applications are made. And similarly since the sprinkling of these is deemed a valid sacrificial service, to sprinkle them without is to incur guilt.

b (1) Lit., 'some of them are as the beginning, and some of them are as the end.'—The three final applications are governed in some respects by the laws appertaining to the first application; while in others they are regarded simply as the pouring out of the remainder of the blood. (2) The ineligibility of a lay-Israelite (a non-priest, Heb. *zar*) to perform the sprinkling. (3) If blood spurts on the priest's vestment after the first application, it must be washed in a holy place, just as if it had spurted *before* the first application. But if it spurts on to it after the four applications before the pouring out of the residue, it need not be so washed, as is shewn *infra*. (4) If the blood of the sin-offering was received in four cups, and one application is made from each, the remaining blood in each counts as the residue, which is to be poured out at the base. (5) (i) The three applications are made even after the owner's death, just as the residue would be poured out after all the applications. (ii) They do not permit the flesh, since this was permitted by the first application. (iii) If the first application was made in silence, and these with a *piggul* intention, they do not render the sacrifice *piggul*. Finally, (iv) if the first application was properly made, on the outer altar, and the blood for these applications was taken within, into the *hekal* (q.v. Glos.), the sacrifice does not become invalid, as it would be if the blood for the *first* application were so treated. For Scripture says, *And no sin-offering, whereof any of the blood is brought into the tent of meeting* (i.e. the inner sanctum, corresponding to the *hekal*) to make atonement *in the holy place, shall be eaten; it shall be burnt with fire* (Lev. VI, 23). With the first application, however, atonement is made, and so this blood is not brought '*to make atonement*'. — In all these respects the blood for the three applications is regarded as the residue, just as that which remains after *all* the applications. (6) Referring to the requirement of washing in n. 3. (7) The blood which is fit for the horn is that which is to be sprinkled upon it, even in the last three applications.

c (1) I.e., the residue. (2) Lev., VI, 20. E.V. *and when there is sprinkled of the blood thereof upon any garment* etc. (3) Even in the case of the sin-offerings of the outer altar. Thus R. Nehemiah regards this as blood, and therefore it bears that status in respect to washing too. Hence this does not support R. Papa, as it is an individual view. The others, however, who rule that there is no liability, will also hold that no washing is required. (4) Liability is incurred for presenting these outside the Temple court; though they are not blood. Hence the same may hold good of the residue, even if it should not bear the status of blood.

respect of washing?—Yes, [39a] and [so] it was taught: The bloods which require the base[5] necessitate washing, and an [illegitimate] intention in connection with same is effective, and one who presents thereof without [the Temple court] is liable. The blood, however, which is poured out into the duct[6] does not necessitate washing, and an [illegitimate] intention in connection with same is not effective, and one who presents thereof without is exempt [from punishment]. Now, whom do you know to rule that one who presents thereof without is liable? R. Nehemiah: and he [also] rules [that] it necessitates washing and [that] an [illegitimate] intention in connection with the same is effective. But it was taught: [The pouring out of] the residue and the burning of the limbs [on the altar], which are not indispensable for atonement, are excepted, in that an [illegitimate] intention in connection with
a same is of no effect?[1]—That[2] was taught in reference to the [last] three applications of a sin-offering. If so, [why does it say] 'which requires the base?' [Surely] it is sprinkled on the horn [of the altar]?—Say, which is required for the base.[3] But then, what of 'And an [illegitimate] intention in connection with same is effective'? Surely you said, 'It does not permit [the flesh], it does not render [it] *piggul*, and does not enter within, as the last blood'?—Rather that [Baraitha] was taught in respect of the blood of the inner [sacrifices].[4] But in the case of the blood of outer [sacrifices] what [will you say]? he is exempt?[5] Then instead of teaching [about] the blood which is poured out into the duct, let [the Tanna] teach a distinction in that very case. [Thus:] This is said only of the blood of inner [sacrifices], but in the case of the outer sacrifices, he is exempt?—This is in accordance with R. Nehemiah, who maintained [that] one who presents the residue of the blood[6] without is liable, and so he [the Tanna] could not enumerate three instances of exemption corresponding to three instances of liability.[7]

Rabina said, 'From the horn' is meant literally, but 'from the base' means, from that which is fit for the base.[8] Said R. Taḥlifa b. Gaza to Rabina: Perhaps both mean [the blood] that is fit
b [etc.]?[1]—How is that possible: seeing that you say that [even the blood] fit for the horn [does] not [necessitate washing], need one speak about the blood fit for the base? Hence 'from the horn' is meant literally, while 'from the base' means from that which is fit for the base.

ALL [BLOOD] WHICH IS SPRINKLED ON THE INNER ALTAR etc. Our Rabbis taught: *Thus shall he do [with the bullock]; as he did [with the bullock of the sin-offering, so shall he do with this]*:[2] Why is this stated? As a repetition of the [law of sprinkling], to teach that if [the priest] omitted one of the applications, he has done nothing.[3] I know this only of the seven applications,[4] which are indispensable in all cases; whence do we know [it] of the four applications? From the text, *'So shall he do with this'*.[5] *'With the bullock'* means the bullock

(5) I.e., the residue which must be poured out at the base. (6) Blood which had become unfit was poured into a duct in the Temple court, whence it flowed out into the stream of Kidron.

a (1) Cf. *supra* 13a bottom. (2) *Sc.* the ruling that an illegitimate intention is effective. (3) The ultimate residue is poured out at the base. (4) It refers indeed, as hitherto assumed, to the *residue*, not to the three applications, but to the residue of sin-offerings presented at the *inner* altar, and in accordance with the view that that is indispensable (*infra* 52a); consequently it can render the sacrifice *piggul*. (5) For presenting it without the Temple court. (6) Even of the outer sin-offerings. (7) The Baraitha enumerates three instances of liability and three of exemption (i.e., three instances where the residue bears the full status of blood, and three where it does not). But if the Tanna drew a distinction between the residue of *inner* sacrifices and that of *outer* sacrifices respectively, he could not maintain that parallelism. (8) He refers to the Mishnah quoted *supra* 38b. For if it is meant literally, it is superfluous: seeing that the blood which spurts from the horn does not necessitate washing, it is surely obvious that that which spurts from the base does not necessitate washing.—Thus he answers the objection 'then on your reasoning' etc., which was raised against R. Papa's proof.

b (1) Which interpretation, implying that there is blood fit for the horn, i.e., the three last applications, and yet it does not necessitate washing, would refute R. Papa! (2) Lev. IV, 20. This treats of the sin-offering brought when the whole congregation sins, which was offered on the inner altar. The verse itself is apparently superfluous, since all its rites are described in detail. (3) The sacrifice is invalid. (4) Before the veil of the ark. (5) This is yet another repetition. Since its implication of indispensability is not required in respect of the seven applications, it is transferred to the four applications on the altar.

תורה אור

והתניא דמים הטעונין יסוד טעונין כיבוס ומחשבה מועלת בהן והמעלה מהן בחוץ חייב ודמים הנשפכין לאמה אין טעונין כיבוס ואין מחשבה מועלת בהן והמעלה מהן בחוץ פטור מאן שמעת ליה דאמר מעלה מהן בחוץ חייב רבי נחמיה א] היא וקאמר טעון כיבוס ומחשבה מועלת בהן והתניא °יצאו שירים והקטרת אימורין שאין מעכבין את הכפרה שאין מחשבה מועלת בהן ב] כי תניא ההיא בשלש מתנות שבחטאת אי הכי טעונין יסוד לקרן אזלי אימא ניטענין יסוד ומחשבה מועלת בהן האמרת לא שרי' ולא מפגלא ולא עיילא לגואי כסופן אלא ג] כי תניא ההיא בדמים הפנימים אבל בדמים החיצונים מאי פטור אדתני דמים הנשפכין לאמה ליפלוג וליתני בדידה במה דברים אמורים בדמים הפנימים אבל בדמים החיצונים פטור ד] הא מני *רבי נחמיה היא דאמר שירי הדם שהקריבן בחוץ חייב ולא מתני ליה תלתא פטורי לבהדי תלתא חיובי רבינא אמר מן הקרן ה] ממש מן היסוד מן הראוי ליסוד אמר ליה רב תחליפא בר גזא לרבינא אימא אידי ואידי ראוי ו] הוא האי מאי השתא ראוי לקרן אמרת לא ראוי ליסוד מיבעיא אלא מן הקרן מן הקרן ממש מן היסוד מן הראוי ליסוד : כל הניתנין על מזבח הפנימי כו': ת״ר ז] *°ועשה כאשר עשה מה ח] בא ללמוד לכפול בהזאתו ולמד שאם חיסר אחת מכל המתנות לא עשה ולא כלום אין לי אלא מתן שבע ט] שמעכבות בכל מקום מתן ד' מניין ת״ל כן יעשה לפר זה פר יום הכפורים כאשר

[דף לח.] ויקרא ד

ס"י *[והתניא. בניחותא]: דמים הטעונין יסוד. היינו שירים י] שטעון שפיכת יסוד : יא] מחשבה מועלת בהן. אם חישב בשפיכתן על מנת לאכול בשר למחר ולקמן רמינן עלה : ודמים הנשפכין לאמה. שנפסלו ושופכין אותו לסילון שבעזרה יב] המוליא לנחל קדרון: כי תניא ההיא. דמחשבה מועלת בהן : בשלש מתנות כו'. וכולה חדא מלתא היא דמסקנא דקושיא היא ולאו שינויא יג] כלומר לא תשמע מיניה דשירים טעון כיבוס ואפי' לר' נחמיה דהך ברייתא יד] בשלשה מתנות שבחטאות: נטענין יסוד. מלות טעינת יסוד עליהם ששופך שיריהם ליסוד: ה״ג אלא כי תניא ההיא בדמים הפנימיים. ולעולם בשירים וכמ״ד לקמן שירים הפנימים מעכבי הילכך חשיבי לפגלטו] לענין חוץ ולענין כיבוס: ור' נחמיה היא דאמר. אף שירים החיצונים שהקריבן בחוץ חייב ומשום הכי לא מצי לפלוגי בדידה: דלא מתני ליה תלתא פטורי. בחיצונים : לבהדי תלתא חיובי. דתנא בפנימיות דבשלמא בכיבוס ובמחשבה מצי לפלוגי אבל בהעלאת חוץ לא מצי למיתנייה : רבינא אמר. הא דפרכת לעיל וליטעמיך מן היסוד הוא דאין טעון כיבוס הא מן הראוי ליסוד כו' לאו פירכא היא דמן הקרן מן הקרן ממש קאמר הא מן הראוי לקרן כגון טז] שלש מתנות שבחטאת טעון כיבוס כדרב פפא והא דתנן בהו מן היסוד לאו מן היסוד ממש דתידוק מינה הא מן הראוי ליסוד טעון כיבוס ותקשה לך אלא מן הראוי ליסוד קאמר ואשמעינן דמשכלתה זריקה אין השירים טעון כיבוס דאילו מן היסוד ממש לא איצטריכא ליה דהשתא מן הקרן אמרת לא מן היסוד מיבעי : ואימא אידי ואידי ראוי. וקמ״ל דיש לך ראוי לקרן ואין טעון כיבוס ואיזה זה יז] שלשה מתנות שבחטאת : ראוי לקרן אמרת לא. משנתן מתנה ראשונה ממעטת לכוליה דם מכיבוס : ראוי ליסוד . דכבר נגמרו מתנותיו מיבעיא ליה למיתני בתמיה הא מקמייתא אידחי ליה מכיבוס: אלא ודאי מן הקרן קרן ממש. אבל הראוי לקרן כל זמן שלא גמר מתנותיו טעון כיבוס והדר אשמעינן דמן הראוי ליסוד אין טעון כיבוס ולמעוטי שירים דאי מן היסוד ממש לא איצטריכא ליה : ועשה כאשר עשה. בפר העלם דבר (א) לאחר שפי' בו כל מתנות דמו שנה לכתוב ועשה לפר כאשר עשה לפר החטאת וגו' ומקרא שאינו צריך הוא שהרי כל עבודותיו נתפרשו יח] חוץ מיותרת הכבד ושתי הכליות שהוא צריך ללמוד מפר כהן משיח האמור למעלה הימנו והא ליכא למימר דלהכי הדר ואקשינהו להא מלתא דהאי קרא כתיב ביה כפרה וכפר עליהם וגו' ואימורין לא מעכבי כפרה אלא כולה לדרשא וסרסהו יט] דע״כ לא מצי למימר כדכתיב כאשר עשה לדם הפר דמשמע מאחרינא יליף דלא חסר מידי דניבעי למילפיה אלא ועשה כאשר עשה לכפול באזהרת הזאות שלו והכי משמע כ] כאשר עשה (לו) כאשר כתבתי לך כל עשיותיו ושנה עליהם לעכב שאם חיסר כו' כן שמעתי במנחות: מתן שבע. על הפרכת שמעכבות בכל מקום לקמן מפרש: מתן ארבע. שאין מעכבות בחטאת החיצונה כדאמרינן לעיל מניין שמעכבות בקרנות הפנימי ולקמן פריך למה לי קרא (ב) האי כפילא כא] ועשה כאשר עשה נמי עלייהו קאי דהא איננו נמי בהדיא כתיבו : תלמוד לומר כן יעשה לו. חזר וכפל ואם אינו לענין מתן שבע תנהו לענין מתן ארבע : לפר זה פר יום הכפורים. להשוותו לפר העלם דבר ולקמיה מפרש למאי הילכתא :

[לעיל לח:]

מנחות כז.

הא מני רבי נחמיה היא . דאמר שירי הדם שהקריבן בחוץ חייב ולא מיתני כב] תלתא פטורי בהדי תלתא חיובי כולה סוגיא דשמעתא משמע דרבי נחמיה מיירי בדמים החיצונים כג] והקשה הרב רבי יעקב מאורליינ״ש דלקמן בסוף השוחט והמעלה (דף קיא.) אמרינן והשתא דאמר רב אדא בר אהבה מחלוקת בשירים הפנימים אבל בשירים החיצוני' דברי הכל אין מעכבין כד] וכי קאמר ר' נחמיה בשירים הפנימים ועוד קשה דקאמר*) [א״ר יוחנן] ר' נחמיה כדברי האומר שירים מעכבין והכא אשכחן כה] חיצונים דמקריבן בחוץ חייב ואינן מעכבין דקאמר הכא לר' נחמיה בדמים החיצונים תרי פטורי וחד חיובא וכיון דאין מחשבה מועלת בהן ואין טעונין כיבוס א״כ לא מעכבי ועוד דאי שירים הניתנין ליסוד בדמים החיצונים מעכבי א״כ מליתו דמים חליין למטה וחליין למעלה ובחד מקום לא אשכחן כדאמר לעיל* [דף לח.] ועוד מי עדיפי משלש מתנות שבחטאת ועוד אמרינן בסוף השוחט והמעלה (לקמן דף קיב.) גבי חטאת שקיבל דמה בשתי כוסות דמוקי לה כר' נחמיה משל למה״ד כו' ומוקי לה בשעיר נשיא אלמא כו] ר״נ בחיצונות איירי דומיא דשעיר נשיא מיהו הא לא קשיא אע״ג דהמשל איירי בשעיר נשיא מ״מ רישא לא הוי בשעיר נשיא כז] ול״נ סוגיא דשמעתא אתיא דלא כר' יוחנן וברייתא לא קשיא לר' יוחנן דהא דלא מפליג כח] בדידיה משום דכולה בפנימים קמיירי (תוס') ויש לפרש א״ר יוחנן ר' נחמיה כמ״ד שירים הפנימיים מעכבי ואילו היה עושה אותה בחוץ חייב א״כ יש לחייב אף בחיצונים אע״ג דלא מעכבי דגמרי' מאיברים ופדרים ואי פרכת מה לאיברים ופדרים שכן תחילת עבודה שירייס כט] פנימיים יוכיחו ואי פרכת מה לשירייס הפנימיים שכן מעכבין איברים ופדרים יוכיחו ול״ע דהא שירייס הפנימיים קורא אותן תחילת עבודה לקמן ל] (הגהה) ר״ת השיב לו לא] דאמת הוא דר' נחמיה אף בשירים (ג) החיצונים מיירי מדקתני שירי הדם סתמא ל״ש פנימים ול״ש חיצונים והכי פי' דשמעתא דסוף השוחט והמעלה (ג״ז שם) והשתא דא״ר אדא בר אהבה מחלוקת בשירים הפנימים אבל חיצונים דברי הכל לא מעכבי וכי קאמר ר' לב] *יהודה בשירים הפנימים פירוש כי קאמר דשירים מעכבי לג] מוכלה מכפר היינו בשירים הפנימים וכי תניא ההיא בשירים החיצונים פי' ההיא דר' נחמיה ור' עקיבא בשירים החיצונים כל זה מדברי רב אדא ולדבריו דרבי עקיבא לד] הש״ס קאמר דמה שאמר ר״ע שירי הדם שירי מצוה הן משמע ל״ש פנימים ולא שנא חיצונים לא קשיא לרב אדא דר״ע לדברי עצמו השיב לה] לך דפליג אדר' *יהודה ואית ליה שירים אין מעכבים אפי' בפנימים ורבי נחמיה ס״ל לעולם דפנימים מעכבין ושירים חיצונים אין מעכבין לו] אפ״ה חייבין בחוץ ור' יוחנן היה סובר דאף חיצונים מעכבין לר' נחמיה ובזה לא היה מוקשה דמלא שום תנא דסבר חיצונים מעכבים דודאי איכא שום תנא דאית לז] ליה האי סברא דחיצונים מעכבין אלא בזה איתותב לח] דרבי נחמיה הוה ס״ל דחיצונים מעכבין וטעמא דר' נחמיה דמחייב בחוץ משום עיכובא הוא דהא ודאי ליתיה וק' לפר״ת דע״כ ליכא שום תנא שיאמר שירים החיצונים מעכבין כדפרישי' דלא מליתו דמים שחליין למטה וחליין למעלה ועוד דלא אפשר לומר לט] כן לר' נחמיה שירים החיצונים מעכבין כדמוכח בסוף הוציאו לו (יומא דף ס.) דפליגי ר' יהודה ור' נחמיה בדברים הנעשין בבגדי לבן בחוץ דלרבי יהודה לא מעכבי ולרבי נחמיה מעכבי דמפרש ר' יוחנן דשניהם מקרא אחד דרשו והיתה זאת לכם וגו' וכתיב זאת וכתיב אחת לר' יהודה חד למעוטי בגדי לבן בחוץ וחד למעוטי בגדי זהב בחוץ ולרבי נחמיה חד למעוטי בגדי זהב וחד למעוטי שירים דלא מעכבי מ] והתם פריך [שפיר] דרבי יוחנן אדרבי יוחנן מההיא דלקמן דקאמר ר' יוחנן דתני ר' נחמיה לדברי האומר שירים מעכבין מא] קשיא : **ועשה** מב] לפר כאשר עשה פי' בקונט' בפר העלם דבר של צבור כתיב ומקרא שאינו צריך הוא שהרי כל עבודותיו נתפרשו בו חוץ מיותרת הכבד ושתי הכליות שהוא צריך ללמוד מפר כהן המשיח האמור למעלה הימנו

*) דקאמר ר' יוחנן התם ר' נחמיה כו'. נ״ק

הגהות הב״ח
(א) רש״י ד״ה ועשה וכו' דבר כתיב לאחר: (ב) ד״ה מתן ד' וכו' למה לי קרא הא האי: (ג) תום' ד״ה הא מני וכו' ור״ת השיב וכו' בחיצונים מיירי. נ״ב ועי' בפירש״י בע״ב ד״ה שפיכת שיריים :

גליון הש״ס
גמ' יצאו שירים והקטרת אימורין . לעיל דף יג ע״א :

א] תיבת היא נמחק : ב] כי תניא ההיא . פי' דמחשבה מועלת בהן בג' מתנות ואפי' כרבנן אתיא וסייעתא היא לרב פפא דלדברי הכל מוכח בהדיא דבג' מתנות טעון כיבוס (כי תניא ההיא בדמים הפנימים) כו' : ג] כי תניא ההיא בדמים הפנימים. ולעולם אימא לך בשירים כמאן דאמר לקמן שירים הפנימים מעכבין הלכך חשיבי לפגל ולענין חוץ ולענין כיבוס אבל לעולם לא איפשיטא ליה כרב פפא בדמים החיצונים : ד] הא מני ר' נחמיה היא. והשתא ניחא דראוי ליסוד טעון כיבוס ומ״מ מן הקרן אין טעון כיבוס אפי' לר' נחמיה שכבר נעשה מצוהו אבל שירים אין מצותו נעשית עד שישפכנו ליסוד. מהר״פ: ה] הקרן מן הקרן ממש: ו] תיבת הוא נמחק : ז] ועשה כאשר עשה. פ״ה דמקרא שאינו צריך עד דהא כפרה כתיב בהאי קרא ואימורים לא מעכבי כפרה ואע״ג דמוכח לקמן דיותרת הכבד ושתי הכליות אתיא מהך היקשא מ״מ ע״כ לאו לענין יותרת הכבד ושתי הכליות לחוד אתא כיון דוכפר כתיב משמע דאיתקש גם לענין כפרה והיינו דקאמר מה ת״ל לענין כפרה אלא ש״מ לכפול בהזאות לומר שאם [חיסר] אחת מן כולם לא עשה ולא כלום. לפום רהיטא משמע דה״פ להכי אקשי לפר כהן משיח לכולהו עשיות ועבודות. שכתובות בהדיא בפר העלם גופיה לכפול בהזאות שהרי שינה הכתוב בהן וה״ק קרא ועשה לפר זה דהעלם כאשר עשה לפר דכהן משיח וכן משמע קצת בפ״ג דמנחות [אבל קשה] דא״כ איצטריך לפר שני דכתיב כאשר עשה לפר להאי היקשא דלכפול בהזאות ובסמוך מפרש תלמודא לפר זה פר כהן המשיח למאי הלכתא לעכב ונראה לעכב כפרה [יליף] מדאיתקש לפר העלם כדפי' בקונטרס בסמוך וגם דומיא דלעכב דיוה״כ והשתא בלאו עיכובא בגופיה דפר כהן משיח איצטריך לפר [זה] הפר כהן משיח כדי לכפול בהזאות בפר העלם דבר כדפי' לכך נראה כפ״ה דועשה כאשר עשה לחוד (בא) [בלא] שום לפר ילפינן לכפול בהזאות דכוליה קרא אפר העלם קאי וה״ק ועשה לפר כלומר ועשה לו להאי פר העלם כאשר כתבתי כבר עשיותיו הרי שכפל בהזאות בפר העלם בלא שום היקש דפר כהן [משיח] והלכך אייתרי להו תרי לפר פר ראשון ליוה״כ ופר שני דכאשר לפר זה פר כהן המשיח לעכב בפר כהן משיח גופיה מהיקשא דפר העלם דהא להיקש ולכפול בהזאות לא איצטריך כדפי' וכן לפר ראשון לא איצטריך לגופיה דפר העלם דהא בפר העלם איירי קרא ומועשה לחוד ידעינן דאפר העלם קאי הלכך אייתר ליה לפר הראשון לפר יוה״כ . מ״מ קשה לפ״ה דמפירושו משמע מדבעי תלמודא כאשר עשה מה ת״ל דאי מצינא לאוקמי הך היקשא גופיה לעבודת הדם לא הוי מוקמינן ליה לכפול בהזאות וקשה דהא לר״ש איצטריך בסמוך הך היקשא לעבודת הדם למתן ארבע וא״כ לדידיה מנ״ל לכפול בהזאות לכך נראה ועשה כאשר עשה משמע דלכפול כל מה שבענין כי נמי איצטריך לעבודת הדם נמי משמע ועשה כאשר עשה דקאמר אכולהו עשיות ועבודות שנאמרו בפר כהן משיח והוי כאילו כתוב בהדיא ועשה ככל עשיותיו ולהכי קאמר מה ת״ל הרי עיקר העבודות מפורשות בהדיא לפר העלם . ויש לקיים פ״ה מ״מ ולא קשה מההיא דר״ש בסמוך משום דגבי מתן ארבע כי היכי דצריך ללמוד פר העלם מפר כהן משיח ה״נ צריך ללמוד פר כהן משיח מפר העלם לגבי מתן ארבע דאידי ואידי קרנות כתיב בהו דלא משמע כי אם שתי קרנות הלכך ליכא [לאוקמי הך] היקשא דועשה כאשר עשה לגבי האי מלתא דמתן ד' לחוד דהאי לישנא דועשה כאשר עשה משמע שעיקר ההיקש ללמוד מפר כהן משיח ולא ללמוד פר כהן משיח מפר העלם אבל לגבי יותרת ושתי הכליות שפר העלם למד מפר כהן משיח ואינו מלמד הוי משמע שפיר ההיקשא להכי אי לאו דבהאי קרא כתיב כפרה ואימורים לא מעכבא כפרה [אלא] אכתי אימא דהיקשא דועשה כאשר עשה לאת בדם וטבילה אתיא שפר העלם למד מפר כהן המשיח ואינו מלמד כדפי' בקונטרס לקמן בסוף שמעתין ומידי דכפרה הוא שפיר בשלמא לפיר״ת דלקמן ניחא שפי' דאת בדם וטבילה כתיבי בפר העלם כמו בפר כהן משיח אבל לפ״ה דלקמן קשה לפי שיטת הקונטרס דהכא וי״ל דמ״מ ליכא לאוקמי היקשא דועשה כאשר עשה לדאת בדם וטבילה שהרי ועשה כאשר עשה משמע עיקר עשיה ואת בדם וטבילה אינו עיקר עשיה כי אם פירוש ההזאות איך יעשה אותם : ח] מה תלמוד לומר לכפול בהזאות ללמד שאם : ט] שבע שמעכבת : י] שיריים שטעונין : יא] מה״ד ומחשבה : יב] שבעזרה המוציאן : יג] שנויא היא כלומר לא תשמע מינה : יד] ברייתא בשלש : טו] לפגל ולענין חוץ : טז] כגון שלש מתנות כו' כיבוס כרב פפא והא דתנן בהו ומן : יז] שלש מתנות : יח] נתפרשו בפר העלם כמו בפר כהן משיח תוך:יט] וסרסהו על כרחך דלא מצי כו' עשה לפר דמשמע דמאחרינא יליף הוא דלא:כ] משמע ועשה לו כאשר כתבתי כו': כא] כפילא דועשה:כב] מיתני ליה תלתא פטורי כו' דשמעתא מוכחא דר״נ:כג] והקשה. עיין בתוס' יומא (דף ס' ע״ב) : כד] מעכבין כי קאמר כו' דקאמר ר' יוחנן דקסבר ר' נחמיה : כה] אשכחן דמקריב בחוץ : כו] אלמא בחיצונים מיירי ואפ״ה מוקי לה כר' נחמיה . ס״א כרבנן אע״ג כו' ומתיבת בחיצוניות עד תיבת אע״ג ל״ש : כז] נשיא וסוגיא דשמעתין צ״ל דאתיא : כח] בדידה משום כו' תוס' ובשם רבינו יצחק מצאתי כתוב ויש לפרש כו' נחמיה כדברי האומר שיריים מעכבי וכיון דפנימים מעכבי ואלו כו' : כט] שיריים הפנימים : ל] לקמן בפ' השוחט והמעלה : לא] לו בסנגון [זה] והא לך פירושו דאמת : לב] ר' נחמיה דשיריים הפנימים : לג] דוכלה כפר : לד] עקיבא קאמר תלמודא דמה שאמר כו' מצות הם דמשמע : לה] השיב לו : לו] ואפ״ה חייב אכולן בחוץ כו' לא היה מוקשה דמצי לאשכוחי שום תנא : לז] ליה . עיין בתוס' ע״ב בדף זה : לח] איתותב דהוא סבר דרבי נחמיה : לט] לר' נחמיה דשיריים תיבת כן נמחק : מ] מעכבי ואע״ג דהתם : מא] מעכבין ומסיק קשיא מ״מ רב אדא שלא היה צריך לכך מי ידחקנו לומר דשיריים הפנימים מעכבי לר' נחמיה : מב] ועשה כאשר עשה ותיבת לפר נמחק :

°כאשר עשה לפר זה פר כהן משיח החטאת א] אלו שעירי עבודת כוכבים ב] יכול שאני מרבה אף שעירי הרגלים ושעירי ראשי הדשים תלמוד לומר לו ומה ראית לרבות את אלו ולהוציא את אלו אחר שריבה הכתוב ומיעט מרבה אני את אלו שמכפרין על עבירת מצוה ידועה ומוציא אני אלו שאין מכפרין על עבירת מצוה ידועה וכפר אף על פי שלא סמך ג] ונסלח אף על פי שלא נתן שירים ומה ראית לפסול בהזאות ולהכשיר בסמיכה ושירים אמרת פוסל ד] בהזאות שמעכבות בכל מקום ומכשיר אני בסמיכה ושירים שאין מעכבות בכל מקום

אמר

תורה אור ויקרא ד

כאשר עשה ה] (לדם) לפר. לאו כאשר עשה קדריש שהרי כבר סירשו ודרשו אלא לפר קדריש: זה פר כהן משיח. האמור בפרשה העליונה ולא נכפל לכך חזר והקישן יחד (א) ו] שלימד עיכוב חיסור מתטתיו מזה: אלו שעירי עבודת כוכבים. להביאן בדין פר העלם דבר ליטעון הזיה על הפרוכת ועל מזבח הזהב ולישרף חוץ לשלש מחנות לפי שבמקומו לא נתפרשו הלכותיו בפרשת שלח לך: יכול שאני מרבה שעירי הרגלים וראשי חדשים. להיות פנימים ונשרפין: ת"ל כן יעשה לו. לזה ולא לאחר: מרבה אני שעירי עבודת כוכבים. לתורת פר העלם דבר: שמכפרין על עבירת מצוה ידועה. כמותו שכניהם באין על חטא ז] הידוע ומוציא אני של רגלים שלא היו שוין לו שהרי אין דומין לו בכפרתו שאלו באין על טומאת מקדש וקדשיו שאין בה ידיעה לא בתחלה ולא בסוף שנטמא ונכנס למקדש ואינו מכיר ולא הודע לו לא טומאתו ולא כניסתו כדאמרינן בשבועות (דף ג.): וכפר. וכפר מכל מקום: אע"פ שלא סמכו. עליו זקנים: ונסלח אע"פ שלא נתן שירים. ליסוד מזבח החיצון דלא תימא הואיל וכתיבא ח] בה בהדיא כפילה דועשה כאשר עשה נמי עלייהו קאי הילכך מעטינהו קרא: שמעכבות בכל מקום. כדמפרש לקמיה בפרה ובנגעים: סמיכה לא מעכבא בעלמא. כדאמרינן בפרק קמא וסמך ונרצה וכי סמיכה מכפרת וכו': שפיכת שירים לא מעכבא. בחטאת החיצונה (ב) לדברי הכל:

בפרה

הימנו והא ליכא למימר דלהכי הדר ואקשינהו להא מילתא דהא קרא כפרה כתיב ביה וכפר עליהם ואימורין לא מעכבי כפרה משמע לפי' דאי הוה מליט לאוקומי לעבודת דם לא הוה ט] מוקמינא ליה לכפול בהזאות וקשה לר' שמעון בסמוך קמיבעי למימר דאילטריך י] כן יעשה למתן ארבע (אפ"ה מאי נמי לכפול בהזאה דועשה לכפול כל מה דאמר בענין אתא) דלא כתב מתן ד' בהעלם דבר ומקרנות דכהן משיח למד ואם כן אימא אילטריך ועשה כאשר עשה למתן ד' *וא"כ מנא ליה לכפול בהזאות לכך נראה דועשה יא] לכפול לכל מה שאמור בענין אתיא וא"ת א"כ מאי נמי קאי אמתן ד' לכפול בהזאות דועשה לכפול כל מה דאמר בענין אתיא וי"ל יב] דועשה לא משמע להוסיף בפר העלם שתי מתנות הכתובות בכהן משיח דאין ניכר שיהא חסר שום הזאה אלא הנך שתים דפר העלם היינו אותן שתים דמשיח וקשה דילמא ועשה כאשר עשה אתי לאת בדם וטבילה דלא כתיב בפר העלם וכתיב בפר כהן לפירוש רש"י יג] ולא לכפול בהזאות וי"ל דאת בדם וטבילה אין זה חסרון עבודה אלא תיקון עבודה ולא שייך בהו ועשה כאשר עשה. ברו"ך: *לפר זה פר יום הכפורים. יד] לקמן אמר לא נצרכא אלא לאת בדם וטבילה אבל לעכב לא אילטריך דחוקה כתיבא ביה טו] וגם וכלה וכפר דרשינן מיניה אם כלה כפר ותימה ולמה ליה ועשה לכפול בהזאות תיפוק לי מדאיתקש לפר יום הכפורים טז] ועוד קשה דלרבי יהודה דריש לקמן וכלה מכפר אם כלה כיפר ואם לא כלה לא כיפר לומר דמתנות יום הכפורים מעכבות תיפוק לי מהיקישא דפר העלם דבר ומיהו לההוא לישנא דאמר בפרק איזהו מקומן (לקמן דף נב:) ופרק הוציאו לו (יומא דף ס:) דלרבי יהודה שירים מעכבים ניחא אבל יז] להאי דאמר משמעות דורשין איכא בינייהו ושירים לא מעכבי לרבי יהודה קשה דלעכב בהזאות לא צריך וכלה מכפר דמפר העלם נפקא ויש לומר דאילטריך וכלה לשבע הזאות שעל טהרו דליתנהו בפר העלם יח] (תוספות עד ושעירי ראשי חדשים) ואם תאמר היא גופה נילף בפר העלם דבר בהיקישא וכ"ת דפר יום הכפורים הוא דאיתקש לפר העלם דבר ולא פר העלם לפר יום הכפורים הא ליתא יט] דהא ילפינן יותרת ושתי הכליות בפר העלם מפר כהן משיח דאתו מייתורא דהאי קרא וכן לר"ש בסמוך ילפינן ארבע מתנות בהעלם מכהן משיח הכי נמי נילף עיכובא בהעלם מפר יום הכפורים כ] הילכך נראה לי ועשה דאתי לעיכובא ללמד בכהן משיח ושעירי עבודת כוכבים דכתיבי בהאי קרא מייתורא לומר דמתנותיהם מעכבי דקרבנות דאתי מריבויא דהאי קרא לא כא] ילפינן זה מזה אבל לפירוש רש"י דלקמן אינו יכול להיות תירוץ זה דפירש את בדם לא כתב בהעלם כי אם בכהן משיח וילפינן יום הכפורים ממשיח וכיון דקרבנות דאתו מריבויא כב] גמרינן מהדדי אם כן ליפתוק מועשה וניגמר עיכובא *מכולהו מפר יום הכפורים °מיהו פרש"י אין נראה לר"ת כדמפרש לקמן. ברו"ך. ועוד נ"ל דודאי פר העלם לא ילפינן עיכובא מפר יום הכפורים שהרי אותן פרשיות רחוקות זו מזו אבל פר העלם מפר כהן משיח ילפינן שפיר ליותרת ולשתי הכליות למתן ארבע שסמוכות הפרשיות זו אצל זו. ברוך. לפירוש זה ניחא דלהכי לא ילפינן שבע על טהרו מפר יום הכפורים לפי שהפרשיות רחוקות זו מזו אבל להכי מהני לפר דמיותר למידרש כג] יום הכפורים דילפינן ביה דינין של העלם ולפירוש רש"י נמי דילפינן פר העלם שפיר מפר כהן משיח הא דלא ילפינן שבע דעל טהרו ושמונה דעל הפרכת בפר העלם מפר יום הכפורים היינו טעמא כיון דכתיב ביה והזה שבע כד] על הפרכת וגם ונתן על קרנות אם הוספת לא נתקיים הפסוק ונראה הפסוק שקר אבל ארבע דילפינן בקרנות ממשיח משום דקרנות משמע שפיר טובא לכל הקרנות אחת דהיינו ארבע ובשעירי עבודת כוכבים דיליף משל העלם ויהבינן שבע דעל הפרכת מהיקשא וכן שעירי הרגלים אי לאו מיעוטא משום דלא נכתב בהו כלל עבודת דם אלא כתובין כתם וא"כ אין זה סתירת פסוק ובאימורין דכתיב כל חלבו ואנן מוסיפין יותרת ושתי כליות משום דליכא שום הקטרה בלא יותרת ושתי הכליות. ברו"ך: **ושעירי** ראשי חדשים. ואם תאמר והיאך יכול לרבותו והלא חטאת דראש חדש נאכל היה כדכתיב דרש דרש משה והנה שורף ויש לומר שעל זה הוא בא לדקדק דנידרוש משה מהכא שיהא בשריפה כפנימים: **וכפר** אע"פ שלא סמך. אע"ג דלא מעכבא בעלמא הוה אמינא דמעכבא הכא כדפי' בקונטרס משום דועשה כאשר עשה עלייהו כה] קאי ומיהו להקטרת אימורים לא אילטריך דלא מעכבי בשום מקום דאחר שהוכשר יחזור ויפסל ולא דמי לסמיכה דהויא קודם עבודת הדם ושיריים נמי עבודת הדם נינהו ומעכבי לכמה תנאי: **ונסלח** אע"פ שלא נתן שירים. וא"ת תיפוק לי מהא דדרשינן בפרק איזהו מקומן (לקמן דף נב:) בפר כהן משיח ואת כל הדם ישפך נתקו הכתוב ועשאו שירי מצוה לומר שירים אין מעכבין וה"נ נדרוש ישפך דפר העלם ויש לומר דהני מילי בפר כהן משיח כו] כדפרישית לקמן בקונטרס דדריש מדשינה בהילוך לשונו שבכל העבודות של כהן משיח כתיב ולקח והזה ונתן וכאן לא כתיב ושפך את דמו (על) [אל] יסוד אלא כז] בכתם ישפך שינה במשמעו לנתקן אבל הכא בפר העלם לא שינה הכתוב דהא כתב נמי יתן להכי אילטריך ונסלח מדאיתקש פר כהן משיח לפר העלם לא מצי למילף התם דלא מעכבי כיון דשינה עליו הכתוב כדקאמרת התם ק"ו לפר כהן משיח מעתה יכול יעכבו דמאי דכתב בגופיה הוי כאילו שנה לעכב כיון דאפילו לא הוה כתב אתי מק"ו כח] וקשיא לי דונסלח בפר העלם למה לי נילף מכהן משיח דשירים לא מעכבי וכי תימא לא ילפינן קולות הא ילפינן בסמוך אמין דלא חיין. ברו"ך: **ומכשיר** אני בסמיכה ושירים שאין מעכבין בכל מקום. דלכל הפחות כט] חטאות החיצונות מודו כולי עלמא דשירים לא מעכבי אבל להזאות לא אשכחן בשום מקום שלא יעכבו ולפירוש רבינו תם דאיכא תנא דאמר שירים החיצונים מעכבי קשה לההוא תנא מנא לן לפסול בהזאות ולהכשיר בשירים ושמא לא דריש ונסלח תדע דלמאן דאמר נמי שירים הפנימים מעכבי על כרחין בכל פנימים קאמר מדקאמר מחלוקת בשירים הפנימים אבל בשירים החיצונים כו' ולא קאמר מחלוקת בשירים דיוה"כ אבל בשאר פנימים לא מעכבי:

מתן

שיטה מקובצת

א] החטאת אלו שעירי עבודת כוכבים. פי' שיהיו פנימים ונשרפים דחטאת בא לרבות חטאות אחרות של צבור שיהו כאלו: ב] יכול שאני מרבה כו'. דכיון שבא לרבות נרבה אף את אלו דנרבה כל חטאות צבור. ותימה היכי ס"ד לרבות שעירי ר"ח הא כתיב ואת שעיר החטאת דרוש דרש משה וגו' מדוע לא אכלתם אלמא שעירי ר"ח נאכלים דבשעירי ר"ח מיירי מדהשיב לו אהרן אם שמעת בקדשי שעה לא שמעת בקדשי דורות ר"ל דעל [זה] בא לדקדק הכא שהיה לו למשה לדרוש (מחטאת) [מהחטאת] שיהו שעירי ר"ח נשרפים ולמה כעס אשר שרפוה ודוחק הוא ונראה דעיקר קושיא דהכא אשעירי רגלים הוא ושעירי ר"ח אגב גררא נקטי ומיהו קשה לרבינו נתנאל דאכתי קשה דהיכי מצינו לרבויי שיהיו פנימיים הא כתיב גבי מזבח הפנימי וכפר אהרן על קרנותיו אחת בשנה כלומר כפרה זו לא תהא אלא אחת בשנה ואילו שעירי רגלים שיהו פנימיים נמצא מזבח הפנימי מכפר כמה פעמים בשנה דנהי דבלאו הכי איכא פר כהן משיח ופר העלם ושעירי עבודת כוכבים התם על חטא באים ואינם קבועים אבל שעירי הרגלים קבועים הן. לכך נראה להר"ר נתנאל דה"ק יכול שאני מרבה אף שעירי הרגלים ושעירי ר"ח שיהו מתנותיו מעכבות ולעולם לא יהו פנימים ונשרפים אלא על מזבח החיצון ונאכלים. ומיהו קשה דא"כ אמאי איצטריך ליה"ר בסמוך מרבה אני את אלו שהן מכפרים על עבירות מצות ידועות כו' לימא מרבה אני את אלו שכן פנימים ונשרפים כמו פר כהן ומשיח ופר העלם משא"כ בשעירי הרגלים ובשעירי ר"ח וי"ם דעדיפא מיניה פריך וגם זה דוחק. לכך נראה דלעולם לענין (שהיו) [שיהו] פנימים ונשרפין בעי לרבוייהו ומ"מ לא קשה אחת בשנה דכתיב גבי מזבח הפנימי דהתם לא בעי למעט שאר קרבנות ממזבח הפנימי אלא בא להשמיענו דשעיר הפנימי דיוה"כ כפרה אחד מכפר ואינו מכפר ב' כפרות כדדריש מיניה בפ"ק דשבועות גבי טומאת מקדש וקדשיו ותדע דאחת בשנה לא בא לטעם קרבנות אחרים דהא למ"ד אין מערבין לקרנות אלא נותן מדם הפר לבדו על הקרנות וכן מדם השעיר לבדו א"כ שתים בשנה הן אלא ע"כ כדפי': ג] ונסלח אע"פ שלא נתן שירים. תימה היכי

רפ"ק מ"ז

ומה"ל לכפול בהזאות וי"ל דמסתברא דועשה לכפול בהזאות אתי ומאי נמי קאי אמתן ארבע לכפול בהזאות דועשה לכפול כל מה שאמור בענין אתי אבל [אין] לומר דועשה [אתי] למתן ד' [אתי] דועשה לא משמע להוסיף בפר העלם על כ' מתנות הכתובות כו' בכ"י וכ"ה כס"י נ"ק

שייך לע"א

הגהות הב"ח

(א) רש"י ד"ה זה פר וכו' יחד ללמד עיכוב: (ב) ד"ה שפיכת וכו' לדברי הכל. נ"ב עיין בתוס' ד"ה לא מני בקושי' מהר"ם מלובלין ובכתן ד"ה ומכשיר אני בסמיכה ושירים:

בכולהו נ"ק

גליון הש"ס

תוס' ד"ה לפר וכו' ומיהו פרש"י אין נראה לר"ת. עיין לקמן דף מ ע"ב תוס' ד"ה אלו ואלו:

דריש מתנסלה הא מבעיא ליה לגופיה דכה"ג אמר לעיל גבי חטאות חיצונות דדריש מתנה אחת מוכפר ונסלח מוקי ליה לגופיה ואומר הר"ר חיים בר שניאור דאה"נ דונסלח לגופיה ומכיפר דרשינן ב' דרשות אע"פ שלא סמך ואע"פ שלא נתן שיריים כיון דלא מעכבי כפרה תרוייהו מחד קרא נפקא וכן משמע בסמוך דקאמר סד"א מידי דהוי אסמיכה ושירי הדם כו' והשתא אי לא נפקא לן מחד קרא אלא חדא דרשא א"כ מתן ד' סליה דלא מעכבי הא ליכא אלא תרי קראי וכיפר ונסלח חד לשיריים וחד לסמיכה אלא ודאי דמחד קרא ילפינן שפיר תרתי או תלתא דרשות כדפי': ד] פוסל אני: ה] תיבת לדם נמחק: ו] יחד שילמד: ז] ידוע ומוציא אני של כו' שלא יהו שוין: ח] וכתיבא ביה בהדיא: ט] הוה מוקמינן: י] דאיצטריך ועשה כאשר עשה למתן ארבע א"כ מנ"ל לכפול בהזאות הא לא כתיב מתן ארבע בפר העלם ומקרנות דפר כהן משיח כו' והשאר נמחק: יא] דועשה משמע לכפול לכל מה שאמור בענין אתא הלכך כי נמי איצטריך לעבודת דם מ"מ משמע ועשה כאשר עשה דקאי נמי אכולהו עשיות ועבודות שנאמרו בפר כהן משיח והרי כאילו כתיב בהדיא ועשה ככל עשיות ולהכי קאמר מה ת"ל הרי עיקר העבודות מפורשות בהדיא בפר העלם דבר מתו' מהר"פ ז"ל. מתיבת וא"ת עד תיבת וי"ל נמחק: יב] וי"ל לפי' רש"י דועשה: יג] רש"י אבל לפי' ר"ת דלקמן ניחא שפי' ראת בדם וטבילה כתיבי בפר העלם כמו בפר כהן משיח. מהר"פ ז"ל: יד] לקמן מפרש לא: טו] תיבות וגם כלה וכפר דרשינן מיניה אם כלה כפר נמחק: טז] הכפורים דכתיב ביה חוקה ועוד: יז] אבל למאן דאמר משמעות: יח] העלם סידור אכתי קשה היא גופה כו' והשאר נמחק: יט] ליתא. [תוס' עד ושעירי ראשי חדשים] דהא: כ] הלכך נ"ל דועשה אתי. ומתיבת הלכך כו' עד תיבת הא דלא מוקף חצי לבנה: כא] לא ילפי זה מזה: כב] דקרבנות דאתו מריבויא גמרי: כג] למדרש זה פר יוה"כ: כד] שבע פעמים לפני ה' את פני הפרכת גם ויתן על קרנות כו' לא תקיים הפסוק: כה] עלייהו נמי קאי ומיהו כו' מקום דכי לאחר שהוכשר: כו] כדפריש לקמן: כז] אל יסוד אלא הדם ישפך: כח] מתיבת וקשיא עד סוף הדבור מוקף חצי לבנה: כט] הפחות בהזאות:

of the Day of Atonement.[6] [39b] '*As he did with the bullock*' refers to the bullock of the anointed priest;[7] '*the sin-offering*' refers to the goats of idolatry.[8] You might think that I include the festival goats and new-moon goats.[9] Therefore Scripture states, '[*So shall he do*] *with this*'.[10] And what [reason] do you see for including the former and excluding the latter? Since the Writ intimates extension and intimates limitation, I include the former, which make atonement for the known transgression of a precept: while I exclude the latter, which do not make atonement for the known transgression of a precept.[a1] *And* [*the priest*] *shall make atonement*[2]—even though he had not laid hands [on the bullock]: *and it shall be forgiven to them*[3]—even though he had not poured out the residue.[4] And what [reason] do you see for invalidating [the sacrifice] in the case of sprinklings and validating [it] in the case of laying on [of hands] and the residue?[5] You can answer: I invalidate in the case of sprinklings, as they are indispensable elsewhere:[6] while I validate in the case of laying on [of hands] and the residue, which are not indispensable in all [other] cases.

(6) Teaching that its laws are the same as those which govern that bullock brought for the whole congregation's sin. (7) Which is treated of in the previous section (Lev. IV, 3 *seq.*). This thus becomes a repetition, with the same implication that there too all the blood applications are essential. (8) I.e., which were brought to atone for idolatry; v. Num. XV, 27 *seq.* which is applied to this case. The details of their rites are not explained there; by making the present text refer to them, we learn that their rites are the same as those prescribed here. (9) To teach that their rites too are the same. (10) But not with other sacrifices.

a (1) The festival and new-moon sin-offerings made atonement for the inadvertent defiling of the Temple, of which the offender would not know at all (v. Shebu. 2*a*). (2) Num. XV, 28. (3) Ibid. (4) Of the blood, on the outer altar. (5) Why interpret the verse so that an omission of one of the sprinklings invalidates the sacrifice, while the omission of laying hands or pouring out the residue at the base of the outer altar, leaves it valid? Perhaps you should reverse it. (6) Lit., 'in all places.'—The allusion is explained anon.

[40a] The Master said: 'I know [it] only of the seven applications which are indispensable elsewhere.' Where?—Said R. Papa: In the case of the [red] heifer and leprosy.[7]

'How do we know [it] of the four applications? Because it is written, *so shall he do*'. Why do the seven applications differ? [Presumably] because they are prescribed and reiterated? Then the four applications too are prescribed and reiterated?[8]—Said R. Jeremiah: This is necessary only according to R. Simeon. For it was taught: In the upper section *'horns'* is written, [where] horn [would suffice] [which implies] two, and in the lower section *'horns'* is written [instead of] horn, which implies four: this is R. Simeon's view.[9] R. Judah said: It is unnecessary, [for] surely it says, [*which*] a *is in the tent of meeting,*[1] [intimating,] upon all which is mentioned in the tent of meeting.[2]

Now, how does R. Judah employ [the text], *so shall he do?*[3]—He requires it for what was taught: As we have not learnt about laying on [of hands] and the residue of the blood in the case of the bullock of the Day of Atonement,[4] whence [then] do we know it? From the text, *So shall he do.*[5] But have we not learnt [it] of the bullock of the Day of Atonement? Surely you said, '"*with the bullock*" refers to the bullock of Atonement Day.'[6]—It is necessary: You might think that it applies only to a service which is indispensable for atonement;[7] but as for a service which is not indispensable for atonement, I would agree that it is not so.[8] Hence he informs us [otherwise].

Now, how does R. Simeon employ this [phrase] *'in the tent of meeting'*?—He utilises it [as teaching] that if the ceiling of the *hekal* was broken, [the priest] did not sprinkle.[9] And the other?[10]—[He deduces it] from *'which is'*.[11] And the other?[12]—He does not interpret *'which is'* [as having a particular significance].

Abaye said: According to R. Judah too [the text] is required. You might think that it is analogous to laying [hands] and [pouring out] the residue of the blood, which are not indispensable in spite of being prescribed and reiterated; so you might argue that the four applications too are indispensable. Hence [the text] informs us [that it is not so].

[The Master said:] '"*With the bullock*" refers to the bullock of the Day of Atonement.' In respect of which law? if [to intimate] that [the four applications] are essential, it is obvious, [since] b *'statute'* is written in connection with it?[1]—Said R. Naḥman b. Isaac: This is necessary only on R. Judah's view, for he maintained: *'Statute'* is written only in reference to the rites performed in the white vestments, within [the inner Sanctuary], [and it teaches] that if one rite was [wrongly] performed before another, [the High Priest] has done nothing;[2] but as for the rites performed in the white vestments without, if not performed in correct order,[3] what he has done is done.[4] Then I might argue, since their [prescribed] order is not indispensable, the sprinklings too are not indispensable. Hence [the text] informs us [otherwise].

To this R. Papa demurred: Can you say so?[5] Surely it was taught: *And he shall make an end of atoning for the holy place,* [*and the tent of meeting, and the altar*]:[6] if he atoned,[7] he made an end;[8] while if he did not atone, he did not make an end: this is R. Akiba's view. Said R. Judah to him: Why should we not interpret: If he made an end, he atoned, while if he did not make an end, he did not atone?[9] c Rather said R. Papa: It[1] is required only in respect of [deductions from] the *eth* and [those relating to] the blood and the dipping.[2] *'Eth'*: R. Aḥa b. Jacob said: That is required only to teach that

(7) The red heifer: *This is the* statute (ḥukkath) *of the law . . . And Eleazar . . . shall . . . sprinkle of her blood toward the front of the tent of meeting seven times* (Num. XIX, 2-4). Leprosy: *This* shall be *the law of the leper in the day of his cleansing . . . And the priest . . . shall sprinkle of the oil with his finger seven times before the Lord* (Lev. XIV. 2, 16). It is a general principle that where a law is designated *'statute'* or introduced by *'shall be'*, denoting emphasis, it is indispensable. (8) Why is an additional text required to shew that all the four applications are essential? The reiteration of the seven applications (according to the present exegesis) is *pari passu* a reiteration of the four. (9) The upper and the lower sections are Lev. IV, 1-12, and Lev. IV, 13-21, dealing with the bullock of the anointed priest and the bullock of the whole congregation respectively. In the upper section: *And the priest shall put of the blood upon the* horns *of the altar* (v. 7). In the lower section: *And he shall put of the blood upon the* horns *of the altar which is before the Lord* (v. 18). The plural implies two in each case, and then by analogy the provisions of each are transferred to the other too, which gives the four horns for each. But this transference is made only because we have the repetition, which is thus necessary in R. Simeon's view.

a (1) Lev. IV, 7, 18. (2) I.e., upon all the horns which Scripture prescribed for the altar in the tent of meeting. (3) Why this repetition? (4) I.e., that laying hands and pouring out the residue at the altar's base are necessary. These are not prescribed in Lev. XVI, which treats of the Day of Atonement ritual. (5) An extension which intimates that the bullock of the Day of Atonement requires these, since *'with the bullock'* has been interpreted as referring to it. (6) Which exegesis automatically teaches that the provisions of the passage, including the two under discussion, apply to it; what need then of the further words, *'so shall he do'*? (7) Only those services are included, since Scripture adds, *And the priest shall make atonement for them.* (8) Such are not included in the extension implied in the text.—Laying hands and pouring out the residue at the altar's base are not essential for atonement. (9) Because it is no longer the 'tent' (of meeting). (10) R. Judah; whence does he know this? (11) Which he regards as superfluous. (12) R. Simeon: how does he interpret *'which is'*?

b (1) Lev. XVI, 29: *And it shall be a* statute *for ever unto you*—which implies that all the prescribed rites are essential! (2) His service is invalid. (3) Lit., 'one before the other.' (4) It is valid; v. Yoma 60a. (5) That R. Judah learns the indispensable character of the four sprinklings from the present text. (6) Lev. XVI, 20. (7) I.e., if he performed the rites which are essential for atonement in other cases, e.g., the four sprinklings on the altar and the seven sprinklings before the veil. (8) He could end his service there, even if he did not pour out the residue of the blood at the base of the outer altar. (9) I.e., the service is valid and atonement is made only if he made an end, having performed *all* the prescribed rites (v. Yoma 60b). Thus it is from this text that R. Judah deduces the indispensability of the prescribed rites, including the four applications.

c (1) The text *'with the bullock'*. (2) In connection with the anointed priest's bullock it is written: *And the priest shall dip* (eth) *his finger in the blood, and sprinkle of the blood seven times before the Lord* (Lev. IV, 6). *'Eth'*, which is the sign of the accusative, which is treated as an extension, as well as the phrases *'he shall dip'* and *'in the blood'* teach the number of additional laws about the sprinkling and dipping as anon. Through the present exegesis, that *'with the bullock'* applies to the Atonement Day bullock, Scripture assimilates it to the bullock of the anointed priest, and so teaches that what is deduced from the *'eth'* applies to this too.

תורה אור

אמר מר אין לי אלא מתן שבע שמעכבות בכל מקום היכא אמר רב פפא בפרה ובנגעים מתן ארבע מנין ת"ל כן יעשה מ"ש מתן ז' דכתיבן וכפילן מתן ד' נמי כתיבן וכפילן א"ר ירמיה לא נצרכא אלא לר"ש דתניא למעלה אומר א] קרן קרנות שתים למטה הוא אומר קרן קרנות ארבע דברי ר"ש ר' יהודה אומר אינו צריך הרי הוא אומר באהל מועד על כל האמור באהל מועד ורבי יהודה כן יעשה מאי עביד ליה מיבעי ליה לכדתניא לפי שלא למדנו לפר יוה"כ לסמיכה ושירי הדם מנין ת"ל כן יעשה ולפר יוה"כ לא למדנו הא אמרת לפר זה ב] *יוה"כ איצטריך סד"א הני מילי עבודה דמעכבא כפרה אבל עבודה דלא מעכבא כפרה אימא לא קמ"ל ור"ש האי באהל מועד מאי עביד ליה ג] באהל מועד מבעי ליה שאם נפחתה ד] תקרה של היכל לא היה מזה ואידך מאשר *ואידך *אשר לא דריש אביי אמר לר' יהודה נמי איצטריך סד"א מידי דהוה אסמיכה ושירי הדם דאע"ג דכתיבן וכפילן לא מעכבא מתן ארבע נמי לא ה] תתעכב קמ"ל לפר זה פר יום הכפורים למאי הילכתא אי לעכב פשיטא חוקה כתיבה ביה אמר רב נחמן בר יצחק לא נצרכא אלא לרבי יהודה *דאמר כי כתיבה °חוקה אדברים הנעשים בבגדי לבן בפנים שאם הקדים מעשה לחבירו לא עשה ולא כלום אבל דברים הנעשים בבגדי לבן בחוץ הקדים מעשה לחבירו מה שעשה עשוי אימא מדכסידרן לא מעכבי הזאות נמי לא מעכבי קמ"ל מתקיף לה רב פפא ומי מצית אמרת הכי *והתניא °וכלה מכפר את הקודש ו] אם כיפר כילה ואם לא כיפר לא כילה דברי *ר"ע א"ל רבי יהודה מפני מה לא נאמר אם כילה כיפר ואם לא כילה לא כיפר ז] אמר רב פפא לא נצרכא אלא לאת *דם ובטבילה את אמר רב אחא בר יעקב לא נצרכא ח] *להכשיר

אמין

רש"י

בפרה. והזה אל נכח פני אהל מועד וגו' וכתב חוקה לעיכובא: בנגעים. בלוג שמן של מלורע והזה מן השמן באלבעו וגו' וכתיב זאת תהיה תורת המלורע (ויקרא יד) וכל הוייה ט] עיכובא: דכתיבן. בהדיא: וכפילן. ועשה כאשר עשה: מתן ארבע נמי כתיבן בהדיא וכפילן. דועשה כאשר עשה אכולה מילתא קאי ומהיכא תיתי למעוטינהו: לא נצרכא אלא לר"ש. י] דאמר לא כתיב יא] ביה אלא שתים ושתים אחרות בהיקשא דהאי קרא איתקוש פר כהן משיח ופר העלם דבר כדאמרן לפר זה פר כהן משיח הילכך אי לא דהדר כפלינהו לא הוו כפולין: למעלה. בפר כהן משיח: למטה. בפר העלם: קרן קרנות. מדמלי למיכתב קרן וכתב קרנות יב] הויא שתים דאית ליה לר"ש יש אם למקרא וחוזרים ומלמדים זה מזה בהיקש: הרי הוא יג] אומר. בשניהם על קרנות מזבח קטרת סמים אשר לפני ה' אשר באהל מועד והאי באהל מועד יתירא הוא דהא כתיב אשר לפני ה' יד] ולמדך על כל הקרנות שבתוך ההיכל צריך ליתן: סמיכה ושפיכת שירים לא נאמרו בפרשת אחרי מות: ת"ל כן יעשה. לרבות פר יוה"כ לסמיכה ושירים דהא פר יוה"כ בהאי קרא כתיב כדאמר לפר זה טו] *יוה"כ: והאמרת לפר כו'. וכיון דאיתקש להאי איתרבו להו סמיכה ושירים בהיקשא ולמה לי תו כן יעשה: ס"ד אמינא. כי איתקש לעבודה דמעכבא כפרה הוא דאיתקש כדכתיב וכפר בהאי קרא ולרבויי בי' את בדם וטבילה כדמפרש לקמן: נפחתה. תקרת עלייתו וגגו תו לאו אהל הוא: מאשר. נפקא ליה ארבע קרנות מאשר דמלי למכתב אשר לפני ה' באהל מועד למה לי טז] [למיהדר] למיכתב אשני אלא על כל הקרנות אשר באהל* דהאי אשר בתרא משום מזבח לא אילטריך למיכתביה: לר' יהודה נמי. אע"ג דכתיבי מתן ארבע בהדיא וכפילן בועשה כאשר עשה: אילטריך. כן יעשה לרבויינהו יז] שיעכבו: סד"א מידי דהוה אסמיכה ושירי הדם. דפר העלם גופיה דכתיבן וכפילן ולא מעכבי כדאוקימנא עילוייהו מיעוטא דוכפר ונסלח משום טעם דאין מעכבות בכ"מ: מתן ארבע. שאין מעכבות בחטאת החילונה נמי לא ליעכבו דנימעטו נמי מוכפר ונסלח: קמ"ל. יח] (דלענין סמיכה ושירים שאין מעכבין בכ"מ קא חשיב להו כפרה) דאילו סמיכה ושירים אפילו עקרינהו לגמרי לא מעכבי ואילו מתן ארבע חדא מינייהו יט] מעכב בחטאת החילונה הילכך מייתינן לכולהו לעיכובא מוכן יעשה: למאי הילכתא לעכב. דהא לא כתיבן וכפילן ביה ואילטריך כ] לאקשויי: פשיטא. [לא] גרסינן גבי פר יוה"כ: לעכב. שיהו כל המתנות מעכבות: חוקה כתיב. בסוף פרשת אחרי מות והיתה זאת לכם לחוקת עולם וגו': לרבי יהודה. בפ' הוציאו לו (יומא דף ס.): דאמר דברים הנעשין בבגדי לבן מבפנים. כא] מתנות וקטרת שעל בין הבדים: הקדים מעשה כב] לחבירו לא עשה ולא כלום. דחוקה עלייהו כתיב: אבל דברים הנעשין בבגדי לבן מבחוץ. כגון מתנות פר ושעיר שעל הפרכת: הקדים שעיר לפר מה שעשה עשוי. דחוקה לאו עלייהו כתיב והתם מפרש כג] טעמייהו: אימא מדכסדרן לא מעכבי. אלמא חוקה לאו עלייהו קיימא מנין הזאות גופייהו נמי לא ליעכב אם חסר מהן: קמ"ל. היקשא דהכא: ומי מצית אמרת הכי. דלר' יהודה עיכובא מהכא יליף: וכלה מכפר. קרא יתירא הוא דלא הוה ליה למיכתב אלא והקריב את השעיר החי: אם כיפר. כפרה המעכבת בשאר מקומות כגון כד] מתנת דמים מתן שבע ומתן ד': כילה. אע"פ שלא שפך שיריים ליסוד מזבח חיצון: מפני מה לא נדרוש. המקרא כסדר מכתבו ונאמר אם כילה הכל אפילו שפיכת שירים כיפר: ואם לא כילה לא כיפר. והכי מפרש בסדר יומא דשיריים מעכבין איכא בינייהו אלמא עיכוב לר' יהודה מהכא נפקא: לא נצרכא. האי דמקיש פר יוה"כ לפר העלם דבר ולפר כהן משיח: אלא לאת בדם וטבילה. דפר כהן משיח כתיב וטבל הכהן את אלבעו בדם ואי קשיא בהאי קרא

תוספות

מתן ארבע נמי כתיבן וכפילן אמר רבי ירמיה לא נצרכה כו'. תימה כיון דכתיבן וכפילן תליא מילתא אמאי תלי כה] רבי טעמא דברייתא במה שמעכבות בכל מקום ויש לומר דלא תימא דנילף מתן ארבע ממתן שבע וא"ת מתן שתים לכל הפחות כתיבן וכפילן ואפילו לר"ש ואם כן נילף איך שתים מינייהו כו] (תוספת) נראה לי דאחת *דכתיבה בעלמא כז] ומינה לא נילף ומן השניה דכתיבה לא נילף השתים הנוספות דתרתי מחדא לא ילפינן ע"כ: **לא** נצרכה אלא לר"ש דתניא כו'. פירש בקונטרס דר"ש אית ליה יש אם למקרא וכן ודאי שמעינן ליה בפ"ק דסנהדרין (דף ד.) גבי בסכת בסכת והא דשמעינן כח] בפ"ק דקדושין (דף יח:) דדריש תרווייהו יש אם למקרא ולמסורת גבי בבגדו בה משום דהתם אפשר לקיים שניהם אבל כאן אי אפשר לדרוש שניהם אבל לר"ע קשה דלא דריש התם תרווייהו ובפ' כל שעה (פסחים דף לו.) גבי על לחם עוני דריש מקרא ומסורת ובפ' לולב הגזול (סוכה דף לד:) תנן נמי ר"ע אומר כשם שלולב אחד ואתרוג אחד כו' ודריש בגמ'* לולב אחד מדכתיב כפת וי"ל דנהי דר"ע ס"ל מקרא כט] (ומסורת) עיקר מ"מ לדרשא פורתא דרשינן ליה למסורת ומיהו קשה מר"ש דהכא סבירא ליה יש אם למקרא ובסוף כילד צולין (פסחים דף פו:) גבי בבית אחד יאכל קסבר יש אם למסורת והיא *דיותן דומיא דכי יתן *ועובד דומיא דעבד *ישמע ישמיע *ולא תשא ולא תשיא אומר ר"ת דבהנהו כ"ע מודו שהמקרא והמסורת שניהם ל] משמעותם א' ולא שייכי לפלוגתא לא] (בין מקרא למסורת דשניהם משמעות אחד ולא שייכי לפלוגתא) דמקרא ומסורת*: **למטה** הוא אומר קרן קרנות ארבע דברי ר"ש. וא"ת כיון לב] דהוקשו בזו ובזו גבי הזאות נמי א"כ ליבעי ארביסר לג] וי"ל דלא דמי דמתן ד' אשכחן אבל הזאות ארביסר לא אשכחן בשום מקום לד] (תוספת) ועוד י"ל דקרנות טובא נמי משמע ואם נאמר ארבע אין זה סתירת הפסוק אבל גבי הזאות כתיב והזה שבע ולא יותר:

לסמיכה ושירי הדם. בפ' איזהו מקומן (לקמן דף נב.) דריש מדכתיב הפר [לימד] על פר יוה"כ שטעון מתן דמים ליסוד ותימה להוות תנא סמיכה מנא ליה וי"ל דבתורת כהנים דריש מדכתיב וסמך על ראש הפר לרבית פר יוה"כ לסמיכה:*) ואפי' נפקא ליה להוות תנא מהיקשא דהכא יותרת ושתי הכליות אע"ג דלא מעכבי כפרה מ"מ שירים לא נפקי דגריעי כדאמר בסוף השוחט והמעלה (לקמן דף קיא.) דאימורים תחילת עבודה ושיריים סוף עבודה: **אשר** לא דריש. לעיל פירשתי בריש פ"ב (דף יח: ד"ה ואידך:) **אביי** אמר לרבי יהודה נמי אילטריך. תימה הא שמעינן ליה לרבי יהודה דשיריים הפנימים מעכבי לה] לחד אמורא בפרק איזהו מקומן (לקמן דף נב:) ובפרק הוציאו לו (יומא דף ס:) והך ברייתא קתני ונסלח אע"פ שלא נתן שיריים לו] על כרחין דלא טותיה וכיון דשיריים מעכבין כל שכן מתן ארבע וכי תימא דהני מילי בשיריים דיוה"כ דגלי קרא וכלה מכפר לא משמע הכי כדפרישית לז] מדלא קאמר מחלוקת בשיריים של יוה"כ אלא מפליג בין פנימים לחיצונים ובשום מקום לא מליט שמחלק בפנימים ועוד קשה הא דקאמר לעיל סד"א הני מילי עבודה דמעכבא כפרה כו' הא על כרחין שיריים לרבי יהודה מעכבי כפרה ונראה דהך סוגיא אתא כריב"ל דאמר משמעות דורשין איכא בינייהו ולית ליה לר' יהודה שיריים מעכבין ור' יוחנן דאית ליה לר' יהודה שיריים מעכבי אילטריך וכן יעשה לסמיכה לבד: **אמר** רב נחמן בר יצחק לא נצרכה אלא לרבי יהודה. כאביי ס"ל דלר' ירמיה לח] לעיל לא מיתוקמא כר' יהודה דר' יהודה דריש כן יעשה לסמיכה ושיריים והך ברייתא מוקמא ליה למתן ארבע: **לא** נצרכה אלא לאת בדם ובטבילה. פי' בקונטרס דלא כתיב בדם בפר העלם אלא בפר כהן משיח כתיב וילפינן מיניה פר יוה"כ לט] דאיתקש בהאי

*) ג"י הל"ק לסמיכה סס"ד ואח"כ מה"ד ה"מ עבודה כו' אע"ג דנפקא ליה להוות הנא כו'

שיטה מקובצת

א] קרן קרנות כו'. וא"ת כיון דהטעם משום דלא כפילן א"כ אמאי תלי טעמא בברייתא משום דמתן ד' אינו מעכב בשום מקום וי"ל דאיצטריך ההוא טעמא דלא תימא דנילף מתן ד' ממתן ז'. [אא"ה הוא לשון התוס' ד"ה מתן ד']: ב] זהפר יוה"כ: ג] ליה מבע"ל ותיבות באהל מועד נמחק: ד] תקרת ס"א א) תקרי: ה] לא תעכב קמ"ל אמר מר לפר זה פר כהן משיח למאי הלכתא לעכב. לפר: ו] הקודש את אהל מועד ואת המזבח אם: ז] כיפר שאם חיסר אחת מכל המתנות לא עשה ולא כלום אלא אמר ר"פ ל"נ אלא לאת בדם ובטבילה: ח] נצרכא אלא להכשיר: ט] הוויה לעיכובא: י] לר"ש ולדידיה לא כפילן כדמסיק ואויל דלא כתיב ביה אלא קרנות דהוו שתים ושתים אחרות בהיקשא קא אתי דאיתקש פר כהן משיח לפר העלם דבר כו'. כך היא נוסחת רש"י של הר"פ: יא] כתיב בהדיא ביה אלא כו' דהאי קרא אתי דאיתקש פר: יב] קרנות הרי שתים: יג] הוא אומר בשניהם: יד] ה' אלא ללמדך על כל: טו] זה פר יוה"פ: טז] למהדר ולמכתב: יז] שיעכבו הס"ד: יח] קמ"ל דמתן

[ע' תוס' לעיל יח: ד"ה ואידך]

תוספתא דיומא פ"ג [יומא לט: ס.]

[סוכה לג.]

[לעיל יח: מנחות מג:]

קדושין נט: *פסחים ט.

סנהדרין ז: *שם.

[וע' היטב תוס' סנהדרין ד. ד"ה כולהו ותוס' סוכה ו: ד"ה ור"ש]

עין משפט: יט א מיי' פ"ה מהל' יוה"כ הל' כג: כ ב מיי' שם הל"א:

גליון: נ"ל פר יוה"כ; פר יוה"כ נ"ק; מועד אתי אשר בתרא דמשום מזבח נ"ק; [ילקוט אי' דברי רבי יהודה אמר לו ר' נחמיה מפני מה כו']; [נ"ל בדם ובטבילה]; [נ"ל אלא להכשיר]; כתיבה בעלמא ומינה לא נילף למתן השתיר כצ"ל נ"ק

ד' לגבי סמיכה ושיריים מעכבות בכל מקום ותיבות דלענין סמיכה ושיריים שאין מעכבין קא חשיב להו כפרה נמחק: יט] מינייהו מיהת מעכבא: כ] ואיצטריך לאקשי הס"ד ומה"ד פשיטא לא: כא] מבפנים.כגון קטרת ומתנות של כב] הקדים מעשה שעיר: כג] מפרש טעמיה הס"ד: כד] מתנת הדמים: כה] תיבת רבי נמחק: כו] מתיבת תוספת עד סוף הדבור מוקף בחצי לבנה: כז] בעלמא מינה: כח] דשמעינן ליה בפ"ק: כט] תיבת ומסורת נמחק: ל] שנים שוים משמעותם: לא] מתיבת בין עד תיבת לפלוגתא נמחק: לב] כיון דמוקמי שבצ בזו גבי הזאות נמי נימא הכי [א"כ]: לג] ארביסר הזיות וי"ל: לד] מקום. לשון מהר"ם וא ת לר"ש מתן ארבע לשעירי עכו"ם מעלה אי ספר העלם הוא גופיה למד בהיקש מפר כהן משיח ואינו חוזר ומלמד בהיקש וי"ל דלמד לענין שתי קרנות דכתיב בגופיה דפר העלם למד נמי גם לענין ד' דהוי הימנו ודבר אחר דלא הוי היקש וא"ת התינח למ"ד לא דהוי היקש אלא לא מ"ד הוי היקש מאי איכא למימר וי"ל דלמ"ד דהוי היקש יליף ליה מלפר זה פר העלם דקאמר ת"ק דתנא דבי ר' ישמעאל לענין יותרת ושתי כליות למהוי כמאי דכתיב בגופיה וה"ה לענין [מתן] ד' מיהו קשה דא"כ כי קאמר רב פפא לקמן משום דבעי אגמורי פר העלם לשעירי עכו"ם לענין יותרת הכבד כו' אמאי לא קאמר נמי לענין קרנות וי"ל משום דיותרת ושתי כליות פסיקא ליה גם לר' יהודה אבל קרן קרנות לא איצטריך לר' יהודה: לה] תיבות לחד אמורא נמחק: לו] שיריים ואיצטריך כן יעשה למתן ארבע על כרחין דלא כוותי' דכיון: לז] כדפרישית לעיל: לח] ירמיה דלעיל: לט] יוה"כ דאיתקש:

א) אולי צ"ל ס"א הקירוי.

אמין

עין משפט נר מצוה

כא א מיי' פ"ה מהל' מעשה קרבנות הל"ט:

כב ב מיי' פ"ה מהל' עבודת יוה"כ הל' כד:

א] אמין שבאצבע בדם *שיהא *בדם שיעור טבילה מעיקרא וטבל ולא מספג *ואיצטריך למכתב ב] בדם דאי כתב רחמנא וטבל הוה אמינא אע"ג דליכא שיעור טבילה מעיקרא כתב רחמנא בדם ואי כתב רחמנא בדם ה"א אפי' מספג כתב רחמנא וטבל מזבח קטרת ג] סמים למה לי *שאם לא נתחנך המזבח בקטורת הסמים לא היה מזה תניא כוותיה דרב פפא ועשה כאשר עשה מה ת"ל לפר לרבות פר יום הכפורים לכל ד] מה שאמור בענין דברי *רבי (א) א"ר ישמעאל ק"ו ומה במקום שלא ה] הושוה קרבן לקרבן השוה מעשים למעשים מקום שהשוה קרבן לקרבן אינו דין שישוה מעשה למעשה ו] אלא מה ת"ל לפר זה פר העלם דבר של צבור לפר זה פר כהן משיח אמר מר ומה במקום שלא הושוה קרבן לקרבן מאי לא הושוה קרבן לקרבן אילימא פר יוה"כ ושעיר יום הכפורים איכא למיפרך מה להנך שכן נכנס דמם לפניי ולפנים אלא פר העלם דבר של צבור ושעירי עבודת כוכבים איכא למיפרך ז] מה להנך שכן מכפרין על עבירות מצוה ידועה אלא פר העלם דבר של צבור ושעיר של יום הכפורים והכי קאמר ח] ומה במקום שלא הושוו קרבן לקרבן דהאי פר והאי שעיר ט] הושוו מעשים למעשים למאי דכתב בהו מקום שהושוה קרבן לקרבן דהאי פר והאי פר אינו דין שהושוו

רש"י

קרא פר יום הכפורים לפר העלם הוא דאיתקש דבדידיה קא מישתעי קרא ובפר העלם לא כתיב את בדם וטבילה י] הא אמרן כאשר עשה לפר זה פר כהן משיח אלמא לפר כהן משיח נמי איתקוש ובפר יום הכפורים לא כתיב את ולא כתיב טבילה ולא כתיב בדם דהכי כתיב ולקח מדם הפר יא] באצבעו ואקשינ' להאי ללמד הימנו הילכות ריבוייא של את והילכות בדם וטבילה כדמפרש: [להכשיר אמין.] תמן תנינן (חולין נה:) היא האם היא טרפחת היא שלפוחית וכל שלפוחית היא ושיא"ה כעין אותה של דג כדאמרינן במסכת ע"ז* בשליפוחה גבי עוברי דגים ואם של בהמה כולה עשויה אבעבועות תשובת מורי: את להכשיר אמין שבאצבע. שאם עלתה לו אם באצבע שקורין ושיא"ה כמו ניטלה האם דאלו טריפות (חולין ד' נד.) לא הויא חלילה דאיתרבי מאת אצבעו את הטפל לאצבעו: בדם שיהא בדם שיעור טבילה מעיקרא גרסינן. משעת קבלה ראשונה למעוטי קבל פחות מכדי טבילה (ב) יב] בכלי זה ופחות מכדי טבילה בכלי זה ועירבן והכי מפרש לה במנחות (דף ז:) ולקמן בפרק דם חטאת (דף לג:) ויליף מבדם מדקרינן וטבל יג] בדם ולא קרינן בדם משמע בדם שהיה כבר משעה ראשונה: מספג. מקנח בדופני הכלי כן שמעתי במנחות: הכי גרסינן הוה אמינא אף על גב דליכא שיעור טבילה מעיקרא. אלא שיהא בו עכשיו: אפילו מספג. דאשיעורא בעלמא הוא דקפיד קרא: מזבח קטרת הסמים למה לי. השתא דדרשת אשר באהל מועד על כל האמור כו' מזבח קטרת הסמים מאי דרשת ביה יד] דהאי יתירא דהא כתיב אשר לפני ה': שאם לא נתחנך כו'. אם אירע פר העלם בעוד המזבח חדש שלא הקטירו עליו קטרת מעולם: תניא כוותיה דרב פפא. דהיקשא לאת בדם וטבילה אתא טו]: לכל האמור בענין. הכל בכלל טז] את בדם וטבילה: קל וחומר. כלומר אין צריך להביא פר יום הכפורים לכאן דמקל וחומר נפקא שכל דרכי פר יז] העלם בו: ומה במקום שלא הושוה קרבן לקרבן. שאין הבהמות ממין אחד ולקמן מפרש מאי היא: הושוו מעשים למעשים. מעשה עבודותיהן שוין של זה לשל זה: מקום שהשוה קרבן לקרבן. כגון פר יום הכפורים ופר העלם ששניהם מין אחד אינו דין שיהא עבודותיהן שוות לעבודות שהצריך הכתוב לשניהן כגון הזאות שבהיכל ושבמזבח יח] יהו מעשי עבודותיהן שוין לאת בדם וטבילה: אלא מה תלמוד לומר לפר זה פר העלם. ולקמן פריך מאי קאמר הא קרא בדידיה קאי: לפר. כאשר עשה לפר זה פר כהן משיח בא להקישו לזה יט] לפוסלו בחיסור מתנות כדפרישית לעיל דבפר כהן משיח לא נכפלו וצריך ללמוד מזה: אילימא דפר ושעיר של יום הכפורים. שלא הושוו הבהמות שזה פר וזה שעיר השוו מעשים של זה למעשים של זה שכל עבודותיהן שוות מקום שהושוו קרבן לקרבן כגון פר כ] כהן משיח ופר יוה"כ דשניהן מין אחד אינו דין כו': מה לפר ושעיר של יוה"כ. דין הוא שישוו מעשה עבודותיהן שהרי נכנס דם שניהם לפני ולפנים ואין חילוק ביניהם תאמר שישוו פר [א] העלם ופר יום הכפורים בעבודות האמורות בהן שלא השוו בכניסה לפני ולפנים שזה נכנס וזה לא נכנס: אלא פר העלם ושעירי עבודת כוכבים. שהושוו מעשיהם דאמרן לעיל החטאת לרבות שעירי עבודת כוכבים ואף על פי שלא הושוו קרבן לקרבן דהאי פר והאי שעיר: שכן שניהם מכפרין על עבירות מצוה ידועה. לפיכך הושוו מעשיהם תאמר שישוו כא] מעשה פר [ב] העלם ומעשה פר יום הכפורים שכן לא הושוו בכפרתן שזה מכפר על עבירת מצוה שאינה ידועה וזה מכפר על ידועה כדאמר בשבועות (דף ב.) על שיש בה ידיעה בתחילה ואין בה ידיעה לבסוף שכשנטמא ידע שנטמא ונעלמה ממנו טומאה ונכנס למקדש ושוב לא נודעה לו כניסתו שעיר הנעשה בפנים על ישראל ופר על כהנים תולה עד שיוודע לו ויביא בעולה ויורד:

הושוו

תוספות

קרא וקשה לרביט תם דאמר בשמעתא דאיצטריך לפר זה פר העלם דבר לאגמורי יותרת הכבד ושתי הכליות לשעירי עבודת כוכבים דלא ליהוי דבר הבא מן ההיקש חוזר ומלמד בהיקש ואי כב] איתקש כל הנהו דכתיבי בהאי קרא אהדדי אם כן שעירי כג] עבודת כוכבים גופייהו דדרשינן מהחטאת נילף מפר כהן משיח גופיה דמפורשים בגופיה יותרת הכבד ושתי כליות כד] [ג] וגם תרווייהו שעירי עבודת כוכבים וכהן משיח דכתיבי בהאי קרא מריבויא וכן בפרק איזהו מקומן (לקמן דף מח:) דאיצטריך כאשר יורם למילף יותרת בשעירי עבודת כוכבים שלא תאמר דפר העלם הוי דבר הבא מן ההיקש וכן נמי אמרינן בשמעתין סד"א הני מילי הזאות דכתיבי בגופיה אבל יותרת ושתי הכליות דלא כתיבן בגופיה אימא לא ואי הוקשו לפר כהן משיח הא כתיבי בגופיה כמו בפר יום הכפורים בדם כה] ובטבילה כן פי' רביט יצחק בר' אברהם זצ"ל ומיהו יש ליישב לפירוש הקונטרס דלא דמי דפשטא דקרא ועשה לפר כאשר עשה לפר החטאת מקיש פר ראשון לפר אחרון דהייט פר יום הכפורים לפר כהן משיח אבל לפר החטאת כו] דמוקמה בפר כהן משיח ובשעירי עבודת כוכבים אין נחשב היקש כלל ומיהו קשה את בדם וטבילה בשעירי עבודת כוכבים [ד] מנין דמפר העלם לא הוי כמאן דכתיב בגופיה כמו ביותרת דבסמוך הניחא לרבי ישמעאל אלא לרבי דדריש לפר זה פר יוה"כ מנא ליה דבשלמא יותרת לא קשיא דנפקא ליה מכאשר יורם כדאיתא בפ' איזהו מקומן (ג"ז שם) דאייתר בפר כהן משיח למיהוי כמאן דכתיב בגופיה דפר העלם אבל בדם וטבילה לא שייך ביה ונראה לר"ת כז] דלא איתקוש כולהו אהדדי אלא כולהו איתקש לפר העלם ופר העלם הוקש לפר כהן משיח ובפר העלם דלא כתיב ביה בדם הא כתיב ביה וטבל אצבעו מן הדם דמשמע שפיר שיהא בו שיעור טבילה מעיקרא כמו בדם והא דנקט בדם לפי שהוא תחילה בפרשה בפר כהן משיח וכי תימא הא איצטריך להא דמסקינן בפ"ק דמנחות (דף ז:) ולקמן בפרק דם חטאת (דף לג:) כח] מן הדם שבענין לא [ה] מוטבל בדם דריש אלא מן והזה מן הדם כט] באצבעו דכתיב בפר כהן משיח בתר וטבל תדע דהא מפרש ל] למעוטי משיריים שבאצבע שלא יזה פעם שניה ומה ענין זה גבי וטבל ואם תאמר ובחטאות החיצונות מנא לן את בדם וטבילה הלא אפילו פנימי מפנימי לא יליף אלא בהיקש ובפ"ק דמנחות (דף ז:) משמע דאיתיה בכל חטאות דקאמר דקומץ איט קדוש לחלאין משום דילפינן מדם כל שכן דאית לן למילף דם מדם ולפי' רביט תם ניחא דבחטאות החיצונות כתיב מן הדם דהוי כמו בדם וכתיב בהו ולקח דדרשינן שיעור לקיחה כי היכי דדרשינן וטבל שיעור טבילה ואת להכשיר אמין שבאצבע ילפינן מקל וחומר חיצונות מפנימיות ומיהו צריך לדקדק מכל מקום היכי ילפינן קומץ מדם דאפילו דם מדם לא יליף: (תוספת) וקשה דבפר העלם לא כתיב את וא"כ להכשיר אמין מנא ליה בפר יום הכפורים ובמסורת כתב קדמאה לא] את תניינא לא כתב את וכן כתב רביט סעדיה בקרא דמן הדם לא כתיב את: *לאת בדם וטבילה. הוה מצי למימר נמי לאהל מועד לכדאמרן לעיל שאם נפחתה תקרה כו' ולקטורת סמים לכדאמר בסמוך שאם לא נתחנך המזבח ט': **תניא** כוותיה דרב פפא כו'. משמע ליה דהא דקתני בברייתא לכל מה שאמור בענין דלאת בדם וטבילה קאמר דאי לא אתיא אלא לעכב לא הוה ליה למימר לכל מה שאמור בענין וליותרת ושתי הכליות ליכא למימר דהא בעבודת דם הוקשו ולשירים נמי לא קאמר [ו] דרבי נפקא ליה מקרא אחרינא לקמן בפרק איזהו מקומן (דף נב.) ועוד ק"ו דרבי ישמעאל ומה במקום שלא הושוו לא שייך אלא גבי את בדם וטבילה: **ומה** במקום שלא הושוה קרבן לקרבן כו'. ולקמן בפרק איזהו מקומן (גם זה שם) יליף רבי ישמעאל מתן דם ליסוד בפר יום הכפורים מקל וחומר ומה אם מי שאין נכנס דמו לפנים טובה טעון יסוד ההוא ק"ו לא הוה מצי למימר הכא משום את דהוי קולא להכשיר אמין שבאצבע והאי ק"ו דהכא לא מצי למימר התם דלא ילפינן מהאי ק"ו דבר חדש ליתן האמור של זה בזה דהא חזינן דחלוקין בכמה דברים ולא ילפינן מהאי דינא אלא דלמאי דכתב בהו צריך שיהא זה כזה דבאותו ענין שיעשה הזאות של זה יעשה הזאות של זה והייט לאת בדם וטבילה תדע מדלא פליג רבי ישמעאל אלפר זה פר כהן משיח לעכב דלמה לי תיפוק לי מהאי קל וחומר ומה במקום שלא הושוה קרבן לקרבן בפר העלם ושעירי עבודת כוכבים הושוו מעשים למעשים דמעכבי מקום שהושוה קרבן לקרבן לא כל שכן דמעכבי ומיהו יש לדחות דמה להנך שכן הושוו בציבור:

הושוו

כח] הדם מן הדם שבענין התם לא מוטבל הכהן אצבעו מן הדם דרש: כט] תיבת באצבעו נמחק: ל] מפרש התם למעוטי שיריים: לא] קדמאה כתיב את:

שתהא זו כוו ונילוא מילתיה בעלמא.ע"כ:ט] הושוו מעשים למעשים למאי דכתיב בהם. כלומר אע"ג דריבה הזאות בשעיר יוה"כ יותר מפר העלם בין הבדים ואף בפרכת איכא ריבוי שהרי יש שמנה הזאות בשעיר יוה"כ ובפר העלם

[לקמן לג. מנחות ז:]

[דף מ:]

[גי' סילקוט ר"ע]

הגהות צ"ק [א] צ"ל מפום : [ב] צ"ל משום : [ג] דגם כו' כתיבי בהאי קרא כו' : [ד] מנין למילף מפר העלם וליהוי כמאן דכתיב כו' כצ"ל : [ה] מוטבל אצבעו מן הדם דריש אלא מן והזה מן הדם דכתיב בפר כו' : [ו] צ"ל דרבי עקיבא :

הגהות הב"ח (א) גמ' לכל מה שאמור בענין דברי רבי. נ"ב כצ"ל ול"ג רבי עקיבא כן משמע בתוספות וכן מוכח בד"ה תניא כותיה במה שאמרו דאי לא אתיא אלא לעכב כו' ואי ר"ע הוא למה צריך קרא לעכב והתניא וכולה מכפר הא כולה כיפר דברי ר"ע וק"ל וכ"כ להדיא בדף מא תוס' ד"ה ואתא ליה בעיר כו' וכן בתוספות בדף זה ד"ה לא נצרכה וכן בכמה מקומות : (ב) רש"י ד"ה בדם וכו' מכדי טבילה אצבע בכלי זה ופחות מכדי טבילה אצבע בכלי זה וכו' בדם ולא קרינן בדם משמע בדם :

[40b] if there is a wart on the finger it is fit.[3] *'In the blood'* [teaches] that there must be sufficient blood for dipping at the outset.[4] *'And he shall dip'* [teaches] but not sponge up.[5] Now it is necessary to write both *'and he shall dip'* and *'in the blood'*.[6] For if the Divine Law wrote, *'and he shall dip'* [only], I would say, even where there is insufficient for dipping in the first place; therefore the Divine Law wrote, *'in the blood'*. And if the Divine Law wrote *'in the blood'* [only], I would say [that] he may even sponge it up; therefore the Divine Law wrote, *'and he shall dip'*.

What is the purpose of *the altar of sweet incense?*[7]—[To teach] that if the altar had not been consecrated by sweet incense, [the priest] did not sprinkle.[8]

It was taught in accordance with R. Papa: *'Thus shall he do . . . as he did'*: why does Scripture say, *'with the bullock'*?—To include the bullock of the Day of Atonement in respect of all that is prescribed in this passage: that is Rabbi's view.[9] Said R. Ishmael: It follows *a fortiori*:[10] if rites [of diverse sacrifices] were assimilated
a to each other even where the sacrifices are not the same,[1] surely rites are assimilated to each other where the sacrifices are the same.[2] What then does Scripture intimate by [the phrase] *'with the bullock'*? This refers to the bullock brought for the community's unwitting transgression; while [the other] *'with the bullock'*[3] refers to the bullock of the anointed priest.[4]

The Master said: 'If where the sacrifices are not assimilated to each other'. To what does 'the sacrifices are not assimilated to each other' allude? Shall we say, to the bullock of the Day of Atonement and the goat of the Day of Atonement?[5] Then [the argument] can be refuted: as for these, [their rites are similar] because their blood enters the innermost sanctum![6] Rather, it alludes to the community's bullock for unwitting transgression and the goats [sacrificed] on account of idolatry.[7] But [here too the argument] can be refuted: As for these, [their rites are the same] because they make atonement for the violation of a known precept?[8] Rather, it alludes to the community's bullock for unwitting transgression and the he-goat of the Day of Atonement, and this is what he means: If where the sacrifices are not the same, since one is a bullock and the other is a goat, yet the rites are alike as far as what is prescribed in their case is concerned,[9] then where the sacrifices are the same, this one being a bullock and the other being a bullock, it is

(3) That is learnt from the *eth*: though the blood is taken up by the wart, yet it is fit. (4) Sufficient must be caught in *one* vessel at the outset; but the blood must not be received in two vessels and poured together to make enough for that purpose. (5) By wiping round the sides of the utensil. (6) Emended text (Sh. M.) (7) Ibid. 7. Seeing that *'in the tent of meeting'* has been interpreted as intimating everything which was in the tent of meeting, why specify *'the altar of sweet incense'*? (8) If this bullock was offered at a new altar, upon which incense had never yet been burnt, the priest did not sprinkle. (9) Yalkut reads: that is R. Akiba's view. (10) No text is necessary for this.

a (1) Even where the sacrifices differed in certain respects. (2) E.g., the Day of Atonement bullock and that brought for the sin of the whole community. These are similar, since they both belong to the same category. (3) The phrase is repeated in the verse, q.v. (4) Teaching that the same law applies to this as to the former, viz., that if one of the sprinklings is omitted, the sacrifice is invalid. (5) These are not the same, being different animals, yet their rites of sprinkling etc. are the same. (6) But the blood of the community's bullock did not enter the innermost sanctum. (7) Whose rites are the same, as stated *supra*. (8) V. Shebu. 2*a*. (9) In the matter of sprinkling, which Scripture prescribes for both, they are alike. Both are sprinkled with the finger, on the horns of the altar, and before the veil. Thus they are alike in essence, notwithstanding that the blood of one entered the inner sanctum while that of the other did not, and one requires eight sprinklings as against the other's seven.

surely logical [41a] that their rites shall be alike.[10] Then the [rites of the] Day of Atonement bullock are learnt from [those of] the bullock of the anointed priest, [insofar as the latter are deduced] from
a *'eth'*, *'in the blood'* and the mention of dipping.[1] And [the rites of] the goat of the Day of Atonement are also learnt from [those of] the goats brought on account of idolatry, *a fortiori*.[2] But can that which is learnt through a *hekkesh* then in turn teach *a fortiori*?[3]—Said R. Papa: The Tanna of the School of R. Ishmael holds [that] that which is learnt through a *hekkesh* can in turn teach *a fortiori*.

"*With the bullock*" refers to the community's bullock for unwitting transgression.' But that is written in the very text?[4]—Said R. Papa: Because he wishes that the community's bullock for unwitting transgression shall teach that the goats for idolatry require [the burning of] the lobe [above the liver] and the two kidneys [on the altar]; yet that is not prescribed in the actual passage on the community's bullock for unwitting transgress, but is learnt through a *hekkesh*; therefore *'with the bullock'* is needed, to make it as though it were prescribed in the actual text, and thus it should not be a case of what is learnt through a *hekkesh* in turn teaching through a *hekkesh*.[5]

It was taught in accordance with R. Papa: *'Thus shall he do [with the bullock] as he did'*: why does Scripture [further] state, *with the bullock?* Because it is said, *And they have brought their offering, an offering made by fire unto the Lord, [and their sin-offering before the*
b *Lord, for their error]*.[1] Now, *'their sin-offering'* refers to the he-goats for idolatry, while *'their error'* alludes to the community's bullock for unwitting transgression. [Hence when the text says] *'their sin-offering . . . for their error'*, the Torah intimates: Behold, you must treat their sin-offering as their [offering for] error.[2] But whence have you learned [the law in the case of] their [offering for] error? Was it not through a *hekkesh*?[3] Can then that which is learnt through a *hekkesh* in turn teach through a *hekkesh*? Therefore the text states, '*[As he did] with the bullock*', which refers to the community's bullock for transgression; while [the other] *'with the bullock'* alludes to the anointed priest's bullock.

The Master said: ' "*Their sin-offering*" refers to the he-goats for idolatry.' Deduce this[4] from the earlier verse,[5] for a master said, ' "*The sin-offering*" is to include the he-goats of idolatry'?[6]—Said R. Papa, It is necessary. I might argue that [the force of this extension] applies only to the sprinklings,[7] which are prescribed

(10) Such as the sprinklings before the veil and on the golden altar.
a (1) V. *supra* 40a. (2) If where the sacrifices are not the same, viz., the community's bullock for unwitting transgression and the goat of the Day of Atonement, the rites prescribed for both are alike, since Scripture does not explicitly say that those which they have in common, e.g., the sprinklings in the *hekal*, are different; then where the sacrifices are the same, e.g. the goat of the Day of Atonement and the goats of idolatry, their rites are surely alike. (3) As here. For the rites of the anointed priest's bullock, insofar as these are deduced from *'eth'*, *'in the blood'* and the mention of dipping, are transferred to the goats for idolatry only by a *hekkesh* (q.v. Glos.); then we make them in turn teach *a fortiori* that the same applies to the goats of the Day of Atonement. (4) The whole passage deals with this. (5) It is stated *infra* that the lobe above the liver and the two kidneys of the goats of idolatry are burnt on the altar, and that this is learnt through a *hekkesh* from the community's bullock of unwitting transgression. But there too Scripture does not explicitly state the law, which is learnt through a *hekkesh* from the anointed priest's bullock, where it is explicitly prescribed, and in the case of sacrifices it is stated *infra* 49b that what is learnt through a *hekkesh* cannot in turn teach through a *hekkesh*. Now, here we have in any case a *hekkesh* between the community's bullock and the anointed priest's bullock, since *'as he did with the bullock'* has been interpreted as referring to the anointed priest's bullock, while the whole passage in which it occurs treats of the community's bullock. Hence when Scripture further reiterates this *hekkesh* by saying, *'thus shall he do with the bullock'*, which being superfluous is made to refer to the community's bullock, the effect of this repeated *hekkesh* is to make it as though the burning of the lobe and the kidneys were not derived through a *hekkesh* but explicitly prescribed. Hence one can no longer object that what is learnt through a *hekkesh* cannot teach through a *hekkesh*.
b (1) Num. XV, 25. (2) Viz., that the lobe and the kidneys of the former, as of the latter, must be burnt on the altar. This is a *hekkesh* deduction. (3) V. *supra* n. a 5. (4) That the lobe and kidneys of these must be burnt on the altar. (5) *Sc.* Lev. VII, 19 which is now being discussed. (6) *Supra* 39b. By this inclusion its rites are brought into line with those of the other sacrifices alluded to in that verse, and hence include the burning of the lobe and the kidneys on the altar. (7) Teaching that the blood of the he-goats must be sprinkled in the same way as that of the community's bullock.

תורה אור

שהושוו מעשים למעשים [א] ואתא ליה פר יוה"כ (נמי) לאת בדם וטבילה מפר כהן משיח [ב] ואתי ליה שעיר יוה"כ *משעירי עבודת כוכבים מק"ו וכי דבר הלמד בהיקש חוזר ומלמד בק"ו אמר רב פפא קסבר תנא דבי רבי ישמעאל *דבר הלמד בהיקש חוזר ומלמד בק"ו לפר זה פר העלם דבר של צבור הא [ג] בציבור גופיה כתיב אמר רב פפא משום דבעי אגמורי פר העלם דבר של צבור ביותרת ושתי כליות לשעירי עבודת כוכבים ופר העלם דבר של צבור בגופיה לא כתיב בהיקשא אתי °איצטריך [ד] לפר למיהוי כמאן דכתיב ביה בגופיה ולא ליהוי דבר הלמד בהיקש חוזר ומלמד בהיקש תניא כוותיה דרב פפא ועשה כאשר עשה מה ת"ל לפר במדבר טו לפי שנאמר °והם הביאו את קרבנם אשה לה' [ה] וגו' חטאתם אלו שעירי עבודת כוכבים שגגתם זה פר העלם דבר של צבור חטאתם על שגגתם אמרה תורה חטאתם הרי היא לך כשגגתם [ו] שגגתם מהיכן למדת לא בהיקשא וכי *דבר הלמד בהיקש חוזר ומלמד בהיקש [ז] ת"ל לפר זה פר העלם דבר של צבור לפר זה פר כהן משיח אמר מר חטאתם אלו שעירי עבודת כוכבים תיפוק ליה מקרא קמא דאמר מר החטאת [ח] לרבות שעירי עבודת כוכבים אמר רב פפא איצטריך סלקא דעתך אמינא [ט] הני מילי הזאות דכתיבן בגופיה אבל

רש"י

הושוו מעשים למאי דכתיב בהו.[י] שפירש הכתוב בהזאות הכתובות בהן לא שינה את זו מזו אלו על הפרכת ואלו על הפרכת אלו על הקרנות ואלו על הקרנות אלו באצבע ואלו באצבע ואע"ג דלא כתיב ביה בשעיר את בדם וטבילה לא פירש את הכל דהא [יא] במה דפריש לא שני ואם זה נכנס לפנים וזה לא נכנס לפנים וזה טעון שמנה הזאות וזה טעון שבע מיהו למאי דכתיב בהו לא שינה אם ריבה עבודות בזה יותר מזה מכל מקום מעשה [יב] עבודות שהצריך לשניהם לא שינה: מקום שהושוה קרבן לקרבן דהאי פר והאי פר איט דין. שיושוו מעשה עבודות השוות בשניהם כגון הזאות דפרכת ושל מזבח הזהב*: ה"ג ואתא ליה פר יוה"כ לאת בדם וטבילה מפר [יג] משיח. בהאי ק"ו כדאמרן: ואתי ליה שעיר יוה"כ נמי. לאת בדם וטבילה משעירי עבודת כוכבים בק"ו מה במקום שלא הושוה קרבן לקרבן דפר העלם ושעיר של יוה"כ הושוו מעשים המפורשים בשניהם שלא שינה בפי' עבודות השוות בהם כגון הזאות דהיכל מקום שהושוה קרבן לקרבן כגון שעיר יוה"כ ושעירי עבודת כוכבים איט דין שיושוו מעשים למעשים וילמד סתום מן המפורש שעיר של יוה"כ משעירי עבודת כוכבים: וכי דבר הלמד בהיקש. כגון שעירי עבודת כוכבים לא למדנו בהן את בדם וטבילה אלא בהיקשא שהוקשו לפר *כהן משיח וחוזרין ומלמדין את בדם וטבילה על שעיר יוה"כ כדאמר בק"ו: אמר רב פפא. האי לפר דמוקי רבי ישמעאל בפר העלם משום דלקמן בעינן אגמורי פר העלם ביותרת הכבד ושתי הכליות לשעירי עבודת כוכבים בהיקשא דחטאתם על שגגתם ופר העלם דבר בגופיה לא כתיב יותרת ושתי כליות אלא ואת כל חלבו [יד] *יקריב ממנו [ב] ובהיקשא (להאי קרא) גמר להו מפר כהן משיח דכתיבי ביה להכי אילטריך לפר יתירה [טו] לפר העלם לכפול בהיקשא שנייה דהא בלאו הכי איתקש דהאי קרא ביה קאי וכתיב כאשר עשה לפר זה פר כהן משיח וחזר וכפל ועשה לפר זה פר העלם לכפול בהיקשו ללמד ממנו יותרת דליהוי האי היקש שני במקום כתיבה בגופו דלא ניהוי דבר הלמד בהיקש חוזר ומלמד בהיקשא דקיימא לן לקמן באיזהו מקומן (דף מט:) דאין למדין בקדשים למד בהיקשא מן הלמד בהיקש: והם הביאו את קרבנם וגו'. בפרשת קרבנות עבודת כוכבים כתיב בשלח לך ומקרא יתירא הוא לדרשא דמה לו לכתוב זאת ונסלח להם כי שגגה היא והם הביאו את קרבנם לכתוב ונסלח להם ונשתוק אלא משום דבעי לאקושי שעירי עבודת כוכבים דמשתעי ביה קרא לפר העלם להקטרת אימורים [טז] כדכתיב קרבנם אשה לה' הייט אימוריהם ואקיש חטאתם לשגגה: חטאתם אלו שעירי עבודת כוכבים. דעלייהו קאי: שגגתם זה פר העלם. דכתיב ביה (ויקרא ד) ואם כל עדת ישראל ישגו אמרה תורה חטאת דעבודת כוכבי' זו הרי היא [יז] כשאר שגגתם דשאר עבירות לענין אישים: ושגגתם מהיכן למד. הקטרת האישים שלה לא בהיקש מפר כהן משיח בתמיה והיאך חוזר [יח] ולמד בהיקש ת"ל ועשה לפר זה פר העלם חזר וכפל בהיקשן כדאמרן לעיל למיהוי כמאן דכתיב בגופו: תיפוק ליה. יותרת הכבד לשעירי עבודת כוכבים: מקרא קמא. דאקשינן לעיל לפר העלם: דאמר מר החטאת אלו שעירי עבודת כוכבים. למה לי תו הך [יט] דחטאתם על שגגתם: סד"א הני מילי. דאיתרבו שעירי עבודת כוכבים לדין פר העלם להזאות דכתיבן בגופיה בהדיא אבל ליותרת וכליות לא: קמ"ל

תוספות

הושוו מעשים למאי דכתיב בהו. פי' בקונטרס מה שפירש הכתוב בהזאות הכתובות בהן לא שינה את זו מזו ואע"ג נ"א אלו [כ] [ואלו] על הפרכת ואלו [ואלו] על הקרנות ואלו [ואלו] באצבעות ואע"ג דלא כתיב בשעיר את בדם וטבילה אין זה שינוי דאיכא למימר לא פירש הכל דהא במאי דפריש לא שני ואם זה נכנס לפנים וזה לא נכנס וזה טעון שמונה הזאות וזה טעון שבע מיהו למאי דכתיב בהו לא שני ואם ריבה עבודות בזה יותר מבזה מ"מ מעשה עבודות שהצריך לשניהם לא שינה והגיה רבינו שמואל דכל זה לא יתכן דא"כ למה לנו ללמוד פר יוה"כ (הא) משעיר יוה"כ [הא] מההוא טעמא [כא] דנפיק שעיר ליפוק פר ותו מאי האי דאמרינן לקמן ואתא ליה שעיר יוה"כ מה צריך תו בהאי ק"ו הרי כבר למד מפר העלם [כב] וגם לא הוזכר בברייתא דלעיל שנצטרך ללומדו אלא הכי פירושו ומה במקום שלא הושוו קרבן לקרבן דהאי פר העלם והאי שעיר יוה"כ דשני מיני בהמות הן אפילו הכי הושוו מעשים למעשים לאת בדם וטבילה למאי דכתיב בהו כלומר אותן עבודות שכתובות בהן אע"פ שאינן שוות בחשבון דבשעיר יש לפני ולפנים ובהיכל אחת למעלה ושבע למטה מיהו לאת בדם וטבילה הושוו כדיליף לקמן שעיר יוה"כ משעירי עבודת כוכבים בק"ו מקום שהושוו קרבן לקרבן דהאי פר והאי פר כו' וקיימא לן באיזהו מקומן (לקמן דף נ:) דדבר הלמד בקל וחומר חוזר ומלמד בק"ו והייט דמפרש לקמיה ואתא ליה שעיר יוה"כ משעירי עבודת כוכבים כלומר וכבר אתא ליה שעיר יוה"כ ויכול ללמד על פר יוה"כ [כג] כדאמרינן

עד כאן לשוט כד] [ג]: **וקשיא** היכי אתי שעיר יוה"כ משעירי עבודת כוכבים ופר העלם מה להנך שכן מכפרין על [כה] מלוה ידועה ועוד שכתוב בספרים מפר יוה"כ ושעירי עבודת כוכבים [כו] ועל זה קשה היכי אתי בק"ו ראשון פר יוה"כ משעיר יוה"כ לאת בדם וטבילה הלא שעיר יוה"כ [ד] גופיה לא [כז] קמה לו לאת בדם וטבילה בק"ו אחרון אלא מפר יוה"כ והוא גופיה מנא ליה [כח] ונראה לפרש ק"ו ראשון כמו רש"י ומה במקום שלא הושוו קרבן לקרבן פר העלם ושעיר יוה"כ הושוו מעשים למאי דכתיב בהו השתא לא קאמר דהושוו לאת בדם וטבילה דאכתי לא קמה לו בשעיר יוה"כ אלא הושוו שניהם על הפרכת ועל מזבח הזהב מקום שהושוו קרבן לקרבן איט דין שיושוו למאי דכתיב בהו אפילו לאת בדם וטבילה וכן הוי ק"ו דשעיר יוה"כ וצריך לדקדק אי שייך למימר דיו בהאי ק"ו דמה בפר העלם לא הוי את בדם וטבילה אלא בשבע הזאות אף פר יוה"כ כן אבל הזאה שמינית לא ולהאי פירושא אתי שפיר דרבי חולק על קל וחומר זה שאינו פשוט דתחילת דינו דפר העלם דבר ושעיר יוה"כ בק"ו ראשון דהושוו מעשים לא הוי מאת בדם וטבילה ולא תיקשי לרבי שעיר יוה"כ מנא ליה את בדם וטבילה כיון דלית ליה האי קל וחומר [כט] כיון דלרבי כתיב לפר [למידרש ביה] פר יוה"כ לאת בדם וטבילה א"כ אתיא ליה שעיר יוה"כ בק"ו גמור מפר יוה"כ ושעירי עבודת כוכבים דלא אשווה קרבן לקרבן והושוו מעשים לאת בדם וטבילה כל שכן שעירי [ה] (עבודת כוכבים ושעירי) יוה"כ ע"כ. בר"ק: **ואתא** ליה פר של יום הכפורים לאת בדם וטבילה מפר העלם של צבור. בקונטרס גרים מפר כהן משיח כי היכי דלא ליהוי למד מלמד: **ואתא** ליה שעיר של יוה"כ משעירי עבודת כוכבים מק"ו. ואם תאמר [א] רבי דלית ליה האי ק"ו מהיכא יליף [ל] ליה וכי תימא משום דאיתקש פר ושעיר של יוה"כ אהדדי

[לא] דבקרא לא אשכחן הך היקשא ותו דא"כ לר' ישמעאל נמי תיפוק לי מהיקשא דהכא [ו] ותו מנא ליה הכא ובאיזהו מקומן (לקמן ד' נ.) לר' ישמעאל דדבר הלמד בהיקש חוזר ומלמד בקל וחומר אימא איפכא דדבר הלמד בקל וחומר חוזר ומלמד בהיקשא דפר של יום הכפורים דאתי בק"ו מפר כהן משיח חוזר ומלמד על שעיר בהיקש ובפרק איזהו מקומן (גם זה שם:) משמע דקודם יש לנו לומר דדבר הלמד בקל וחומר חוזר ומלמד בהיקש ממה שנאמר דבר הלמד בהיקש חוזר ומלמד בקל וחומר [לב] שעיר של יום הכפורים משעירי עבודת כוכבים דלעיל דרשינן החטאת אלו שעירי עבודת כוכבים אבל שעיר של יום הכפורים לא אתיא מהחטאת כי היכי דלא מוקמי ליה בשעירי רגלים כדאמר לעיל:

אבל

[...] שעירי עכו"ם מריבוי דהחטאת וא"ת והא לענין את בדם וטבילה נמי ילפינן בשעירי עכו"ם מפר העלם בהך דשאני את בדם וטבילה לא כתיב בגופיה דפר העלם לפי' רש"י כי אם מהיקש דפר כהן משיח וי"ל [...]בילה דאינו ריבויי חדש כי אם דין הזאות ופירושן ולכך אתי מהחטאת אע"ג דלא כתיב בגופיה ומאי טעמא נמי לא חשיב היקש מן ההיקש אף למ"ד הימנו ודבר אחר הוי היקש כדפי' לעיל אבל [...] תוספת דבר חדש ולכך לא יליף מהחטאת כיון דלא כתיב בגופיה וא"ת אמאי לא קאמר [...] מהחטאת הו"א ה"מ לענין עבודות מעכבות הכפרה אבל עבודות דלא מעכבות הכפרה כגון [הקטרת יותרת] וב' הכליות לא דכל הקטרה אינה מעכבת וכה"ג אמרינן לעיל גבי סמיכה ושיריים [...] יעשה ולא נפיק מהיקשא קמא דלפר זה פר יוה"כ אע"ג דסמיכה ושיריים כתיב בגופיה ותירץ [...]קא שיריים דהוי סוף העבודה וסמיכה דאינה עבודה לא נפיק מהיקש קמייתא אבל הקטרת [...]הקטרה חשיבא תחלת עבודה כדאיתא בפ' השוחט והמעלה אתיא שפיר מהיקש קמייתא אי [...] בגופיה ועוד י"ל דהכא לר"ש איצטריך לומר טעמא דלא כתיב בגופיה ולא טעמא דמעכב [...]כן יעשה למתן ד' ולא לסמיכה ושיריים כדאיתא לעיל ואיכא למימר דהיינו משום דלר"ש אתו [...]קשא קמייתא ואע"ג דלא מעכבא כפרה אך קצת קשה ולר"ש נמי [י"ל] דמפיק סמיכה מוסמך ידו על [...]זאת כל הדם הפר ישפך כמו תניא תנא דפרק איזהו מקומן מיהו איכא למימר לר"ש דכולה [...]יתא נפקא: י] בהו מה שפירש: יא] דהא במאי דפריש: יב] מעשה העבודות שהצריך: יג] מפר כהן

בתחילת דינא וי"ל דא"כ הוי מיפרך קו"ח דהוא לענין פרכת ואצבע לא מצפרך פר יוה"כ ללמוד מפר העלם דהא בגופיה דיוה"כ כתיב וא"ת והתניא לר' טרפון דלית ליה דיו היכא דמיפרך קו"ח [illegible] אלא לרבנן [illegible] [illegible]

שיטה מקובצת

משיב"ד] חלבו ירים ממנו ובהיקשא דהאי קרא: טו] יתירה בפר העלם כו' דהא קרא ביה קאי: טז] אימורים. דיותרת וב' הכליות דבהקטרה ע"כ איירי קרא כדכתיב קרבנם אשה לה' דהיינו אימוריהם: יז] כשגגתם דשאר: יח] חוזר ומלמד: יט] הך היקשא: כ] אלו על הפרכת ואלו על הפרכת אלו על הקרנות ואלו על הקרנות אלו באצבעו ואלו באצבעו: כא] עי' בהשמטות בסוף המסכת: כב] העלם שעירי יוה"כ: כג] יוה"כ משעירי עכו"ם: כד] עכ"ל לשון הר"פ וקשיא לפרשב"ם א"כ בפ' איזהו מקומן דמבעיא לן מעיקרא אי דבר הלמד בקו"ח (א') חוזר ומלמד בקו"ח אי לא ופשיט ליה התם מכח סברא הוה לו לפשוט האבעיא מברייתא זו כי היכא דפשיט התם מכח ברייתא דדבר הלמד בהיקש חוזר ומלמד בק"ו וע"ק דע"כ צ"ל לפי שיטתו דקו"ח שני דגבי שעיר יוה"כ פשוט יותר מקו"ח ראשון מדסמיך בקו"ח ראשון על קו"ח שני כדפי' ואמאי הא בקו"ח שני איכא לאקשויי כמו בקו"ח ראשון דהיכא פשיט ליה במלמדין השוואת את בדם וטבילה דליכא למימר דשני המלמדין דקו"ח שני הוי שעירי עכו"ם ופר העלם דכתיב בהו את בדם וטבילה דהא איכא למיפרך שכן מכפרין על מצות ידועה כמו גבי קו"ח ראשון אלא ע"כ היינו משעיר עכו"ם ופר יוה"כ ואימא היא גופיה (קשה) [היקשא] כמו גבי קו"ח ראשון שתרי בפר יוה"כ גופיה לא כתיב את בדם וטבילה וליכא למימר דמ"מ פשיט ליה את בדם וטבילה בפר יוה"כ מכח קו"ח ראשון א"א לומר כן לפרשב"ם דאדרבה קו"ח ראשון נאמר מכח קו"ח שני כדפי' לכך נראה לפרש דהשוות מעשים למעשים דקאמר בתחילת דינא לגבי המלמדים דהיינו פר העלם ושעירי יוה"כ לעולם לאו לענין את בדם וטבילה קאמר דהא אכתי לא קיימא לן בשעיר יוה"כ עד קו"ח אחרון אלא השוה מעשים למעשים ממה שהשוה הכתוב בפירוש קאמר דהיינו לענין פרכת ומתן קרנות ואצבע כדפי' הקונטרס אלו בפרכת ואלו בפרכת ומ"מ שפיר קאמר בסוף דינא מקום שהשוות קרבן לקרבן דהאי פר והאי פר אינו דין שהשוות מעשים למעשים לגמרי גם לענין את בדם וטבילה אע"ג דהתשואה זו אינו במלמדים דתחילת דינא ודכוותיה אשכחן בפ' כיצד הרגל במילתיה דר' טרפון דיליף קרן בחצר הניזק להשוותם לשן בחצר הניזק לענין נזק שלם אע"ג דתחילת דינא במלמד היינו קרן ברה"ר ליכא נזק שלם כי אם חצי נזק וא"ת א"כ נימא דיו ולתחילת דינא מה תחילת דינא פר העלם ושעיר לא השוה מעשים למעשים כי אם פרכת ואצבע אותה השואה דוקא שישנו במלמדים [...] יוה"כ ללמוד מפר העלם דהא [...] קו"ח דשן וקרן בפ' כיצד הרגל [...]שאני הכא דאין קו"ח זה לרבות [...]שה בזה הילכך אפי' רבנן מודו [...]ים ולא דמי להחיא קו"ח דשן [...]חדש דהא ברה"ר קרן חצי נזק [...]יה"כ והלא לא הוזכר בברייתא [...]ללמוד את בדם וטבילה בשעיר [...] שעיר יוה"כ יוכיח שהשוות [...] בדם וטבילה אם לא היינו דנין [...]מר דשעיר יוה"כ יוכיח כדפי' [...]ש ותולך. כך נראה למורי ז"ל: [...] ונראה עד סוף הדבור מוקף [...] ליה ל"ש ונמחק: לא] אהדדי [...]ת לרבי שעיר:

כ"א נמי

[לקמן מט: נ.]

ע"כ שייך לעמוד הקודם

גליון הש"ס

גמ' איצטריך לפר למהוי כמאן דכתיב. עי' יומא דף מד ע"ב תוס' ד"ה אפילו כפרה:

שיטה מקובצת

א] (אלא מפר העלם פר יוה"כ) [ואתי ליה פ' יוה"כ מפר העלם] בקונטרס גרים מפר כהן משיח דאי מפר העלם היא גופיה אתיא מהיקש' מפר כהן משיח והוי דבר הלמד בהיקש חוזר ומלמד [...] ואע"כ [...] היה לו להוכיח מכאן: ב] דבר הלמד בהיקש חוזר ומלמד בק"ו [...] ק"ח ראשון ולמה [...] עד בסמוך בק"ו שני ולפי' ר"ת ניחא שפיר [...] פר העלם [...] כתיב את בדם וטבילה: ג] עיין בהשמטות בסוף המסכת: ג] הא בגופיה כתיב ותיבת בציבור נמחק: ד] איצטריך לפר למהוי כו' וא"ת ורבי דדריש לפר זה פר יוה"כ א"כ יותרת הכבד וב' הכליות למהוי כמאי דכתיב בגופיה בפר העלם לאגמורי מיניה לשעירי עכו"ם מנלן וי"ל דנפקא לן מאשר יורם דכתיב לגבי פר כהן משיח דמייתר ואם אינו ענין לפר כהן משיח תנהו לענין פר העלם [...] דכתיב בגופיה כדאיתא באיזהו מקומן [...] וי"ל דדריש לפר זה [...] פר העלם למהוי כמאי דכתי' בגופיה [...] כאשר יורם למה לי וי"ל [...] כדדריש בפ' כל הבשר מה פר כהן משיח יש בו מעילה לאימורים אף [...] מכל חלב לרבות אימורי קדשים קלים למעילה: ה] לה' וחטאתם לפני ה' על שגגתם חטאתם אלו: ו] כשגגתם. ושגגתם נמחק: ז] בהיקש אלא ת"ל: ח] החטאת אלו שעירי ותיבת לרבות נמחק: ט] הני מילי הזאות דכתיבן בגופיה הוא דיליף

א) [שבת כ"ז ונ"ק אלא לע דכה"ג כתנו תוס' לעיל ה. ד"ה הא אמר כו' ועוד ז: ד"ה מה שלמים וכו' וא"ש בלי שום [...]

הגהות צ"ק [א] דהא במה דפריש: [ב] והיקשא גמר להו מפר כהן משיח דכתיבי ביה בהאי קרא להכי איצטריך כו': [ג] הל"א: [ד] [illegible]

צ"ל מייתר

כג א מיי' פט"ז מהל' פסה"מ הל"ז :

מסורת הש"ס · תורה אור

א] **אבל** יותרת ושתי כליות דלא כתיבן בגופיה אימא לא קא משמע לן : אמר ליה רב הונא בריה דרב נתן לרב פפא והא תנא ב] פר יוה"כ לכל מה שאמר בענין קאמר תנאי היא תנא דבי רב מרבי הכי תנא דבי רבי ישמעאל לא מרבי הכי תנא דבי רבי ישמעאל מפני מה נאמרו יותרת ושתי כליות בפר כהן משיח ולא נאמרו בפר העלם דבר של צבור משל למלך בשר ודם ג] שזעם על אוהבו ומיעט בסרחונו מפני חיבתו ותנא דבי רבי ישמעאל מפני מה נאמרה °פרוכת הקדש (ויקרא ד) בפר כהן משיח ולא נאמר בפר העלם דבר של צבור משל למלך בשר ודם שסרחה עליו מדינה אם מיעוטה סרחה פמליא שלו מתקיימת אם רובה סרחה אין פמליא שלו מתקיימת : לפיכך אם נתן כולן כתיקנן כו' : תנן התם *פיגל בקומץ ולא בלבונה ולא בקומץ רבי מאיר אומר פיגול וחייבין עליו כרת וחכמים אומרים °אין בו כרת עד שיפגל בכל המתיר א"ר שמעון בן לקיש לא תימא טעמא דר' מאיר ד] דקסבר מפגלין בחצי מתיר אלא הכא במאי עסקינן כגון שנתן את הקומץ במחשבה והלבונה בשתיקה קסבר כל העושה על דעת ראשונה הוא עושה ממאי ה] מדקתני לפיכך אם נתן כולן כתיקנן ואחת שלא כתיקנה פסול ואין בו כרת הא אחת שלא כתיקנה וכולן כתיקנן פיגול מני אילימא רבנן הא אמרי רבנן אין מפגלין בחצי מתיר אלא רבי מאיר ואי טעמא דרבי מאיר משום דמפגלין בחצי מתיר הוא אפילו כדקתני נמי ו] לאו משום דקסבר °כל העושה על דעת ראשונה הוא עושה אמר רבי שמואל בר יצחק לעולם רבנן היא ומאי כתיקנן כתיקנן לפיגול והא מדקתני לפיכך אם נתן כולן כתיקנן ואחת שלא *כתיקנן (צ"ל כתיקנה) פסול ואין בו כרת מכלל דתיקנה להכשירה הוא דאתא אמר רבא מאי שלא כתיקנה חוץ למקומו רב אשי אמר שלא לשמו מכלל דכי לא עביד לה חוץ למקומו ושלא לשמו מחייב איידי דתנא רישא פיגול וחייבין עליו כרת תנא נמי סיפא פסול ואין בו כרת : מיתיבי *) במה דברים אמורים בדמים הניתנין על מזבח החיצון אבל

*) שם עו. [תוספתא דזבחים פ"ד]

אבל יותרת ושתי הכליות דלא כתיבן בגופיה אימא לא. תימה הא אמרת לפר *מייתי להכי למיהוי כמאן דכתב בגופיה לאגמורי לשעירי עבודת כוכבים ושמא אי לאו הך היקשא דחטאתם על שגגתם לא הוה דרישנא ליה הכי : **והא** תנא לרבות פר יוה"כ לכל האמור בענין קאמר . פירש בקונטרס אלמא כולה מילתא יליף מיניה ואפילו עיכובא ואת אמרת לאת בדם וטבילה כו] גרידא וקשה לרב פפא דלעיל דלא פי' דאתא לעיכובא ומשני תנאי היא וא"ת ולהאי תנא דיליף עיכובא בהיקשא שבע על טהרו כז] ביוה"כ מנא ליה עיכובא דליתנהו בפר העלם ובפר כהן משיח וי"ל דהיא גופיה ילפינן בהיקש מה התם לא חלקת בהזאותיה אף ביוה"כ לא תחלוק (תוספת) ותימה דלעיל הביא הברייתא לסיועיה לרב פפא והשתא פריך מינה ותו מאי פריך על רב פפא דלא מוקי לה לעיכובא כח] אלא עיכובא ביוה"כ מחוקה נפקא או מוכלה מכפר כדפריך לעיל כט] וי"ל דפריך הכי לכל האמור בענין משמע אפי' ליותרת ושתי הכליות משום דכתיב כאשר יורם בפר כהן משיח דאם אינו ענין לגופיה תנהו ענין בפר העלם כדדרשינן בפרק איזהו מקומן (לקמן דף מט:) ודרשינן לפר זה פר של יוה"כ בין לאת בדם וטבילה בין ליותרת ושתי הכליות מחד היקשא ל] הוא הדין לרבי ישמעאל דדריש לפר זה פר העלם ליותרת [ושתי] כליות ולא דריש כאשר יורם דלא צריך אלא חד היקשא לא] דחטאת לרבות שעירי עבודת כוכבים וא"כ חטאתם על שגגתם למה לי לב] א) וגבי שעירי עבודת כוכבים אמאי מצרכי תרי היקישי ומשני תנאי היא והשתא להאי תנא לג] אתא ליה יותרת ושתי הכליות בפר יוה"כ מדתניא בתורת כהנים כל חלב לד] פר החטאת פר לרבות פר יום הכפורים ליותרת ושתי הכליות יש לתמוה דבכוליה הש"ס לה] נקיט שעירי עבודת כוכבים בלשון רבים ופר העלם בלשון יחיד דמאי שנא והא מאן דאית ליה בהוריות (דף ה.) שעיר לכל שבט ושבט אית ליה נמי פר לכל שבט ושבט :

ממאי מדקתני כו'. בכוליה שמעתא משמע דאע"ג דאין מפגלין בחצי מתיר פסול מיהא הוי ותימה דבפ' תמיד נשחט (פסחים דף סא.) גבי שחטו למולים ולערלים כו' ומוקי לה (שם סג.) בשוחט סימן ראשון למולים כו' ור"מ לטעמיה דאמר מפגלין בחצי מתיר משמע התם דלרבנן הוי כשר גמור ויש לומר דהא דפסלי הכא היינו משום דאיכא למיגזר לו] כדאי' בפ"ב דמנחות (דף יד:) דרבנן גזרי קומץ אטו קומץ דמנחת חוטא לבונה אטו לבונה הבאה בבזיכין אבל התם לא שייך למיגזר סימן א' אטו שני סימנין :

א) גי' צ"ק גבי שעירי עבודת כוכבים ואמאי מצרכי

קמ"ל. ז] דחטאתם על שגגתם דלענין אשה לה' נמי איתקוש : והא תנא לרבות פר יוה"כ לכל ח] הענין קאמר . אלמא כולה מילתא יליף מינה ואפילו עיכובא ואת אמרת לאת בדם וטבילה : תנאי היא ט] תנא דבי רב מרבי הכי . כל א) ת"ר קרי תנא דבי רב ההיא מתני' קמייתא לא מרבי ליה אלא לאת בדם וטבילה ועיכובא נפקא ליה מחוקה ולרבי יהודה מאם כלה כפר : ותנא דבי רבי ישמעאל . הך תנא בתרא דאמר לכל האמור בענין י] מתניתין דבי רבי ישמעאל היא שנשנית ונסדרה בבית מדרשו של ר' ישמעאל וסידרו בה יא] תנאים הרבה כמו שסידרו רבי חייא ור' אושעיא : על אוהבו . ליבור : מיעט בסרחונו . קילר בדברים : מפני מה נאמרה פרכת הקדש . גרס יב] בפר כהן משיח כתיב את פני פרכת הקדש ובפר העדה כתיב את פני הפרכת : פמליא שלו . כניסת חבורת עלתו יג] והמסכימים לדעתו אשר דברי סתרו אליהם ואם רובה סרחה אין פמליא שלו קיימת הרי הוא מסולק מחיבתם ומכניסתם במקלת ואין לבו גם בהן כבראשונה ה"נ כיון דרוב ליבור יד] [סרחה] כביכול אין כאן קדושה : פיגל בקומץ ולא בלבונה . בהקטרת המנחה שני מתירין יש הקומץ והלבונה ואם הקטיר את האחד במחשבת פיגול והאחד בשתיקה : ר"מ אומר פיגול . כדמפרש טעמא לקמן : כגון שנתן את הקומץ במחשבה . תחילה ואחר כך הלבונה בשתיקה וה"ה אם נתן לבונה במחשבה תחילה ואחר כך קומץ בשתיקה וטעמא משום דעל דעת ראשונה עשה ונמלא מפגל בכל המתיר ורבנן סברי על דעת ראשונה לא אמרינן אלא אם כן אמר אף בשני וכל מחשבה דקדשים מוליא בפה טו] הוא אבל ראשונה בשתיקה ושניה במחשבה דאין כאן אלא מחשבת חצי מתיר טז] [מודה ר"מ] דלא פיגל אלא פסל : מדקתני . מתניתין : לפיכך אם נתן כולן כתקנן . וקס"ד יז] היינו שתיקה : ואחת שלא כתקנה . במחשבת חוץ לזמנו : פסול ואין בו כרת . שלא חישב אלא בחצי מתיר דכולן מעכבות בו וכולן מתירות ואין פיגול עד שיפגל בכולן : הא אחת שלא כתיקנה . הראשונה במחשבה והשאר בשתיקה פיגול דאמרינן על דעת הראשונה עשה והוה לי' מחשבה בכוליה מתיר : הא אמרינן אין מפגלין בחצי מתיר . כדקתני בהדיא עד שיפגל בכל המתיר ואפי' ראשונה במחשבה ושניה בשתיקה משמע אלמא לית להו על דעת יח] ראשונה עשה : אפילו כדקתני נמי . ראשונה בשתיקה ואחרונה במחשבה ליהוי פיגול יט] ב) אלמא מדשני ליה בין ראשונה בשתיקה לראשונה במחשבה שמע מינה טעמא משום דעשה על דעת הראשונה הוא : כתיקנה לפיגול . הראשונות כ] במחשבות דחוץ לזמנו ואשמעינן דלא אמרינן על דעת הראשונה עשה : והא מדקתני ואחת שלא כתקנה . ולא קתני כולן כתיקנן חוץ מאחת מהן או ואחת בשתיקה שמע מינה כתקנן דאמר כא] להכשירו הוא דאי במחשבה ולפיגול היכי מקרי לה להך דשתיקה שלא כתיקנה הא לא חשיב בה מידי ולא קילקל מחשבתו ראשונה דניקרייה שלא כתיקנה לפיגול : אמר רבא . לעולם כתקנה לפיגול ורבנן היא ולר"מ לא תשמע מינה מידי ושלא כתקנה דאחרונה נמי שלא כתקנה לפיגול קאמר וכגון שנתנו במחשבת חוץ למקומו המוליאה מידי פיגול : ורב אשי אמר מחשבה שלא לשמו . נמי קרי שלא כתקנה לפיגול דהא חטאת היא ומחשבה שלא לשמו פוסלת בה ומוליאה מידי פיגול : ה"ג מכלל דכי לא עביד לה חוץ למקומו ושלא לשמו מיחייב . מדלא קרי לה תנא פסול אלא בשחישב שלא כתיקנה ואוקימנא בשלא לשמו או חוץ למקומו מכלל דכי לא עביד לה הכי אלא בשתיקה דחייב כלומר הוי פיגול לחייב על אכילתו כרת אלמא על דעת ראשונה כב] עשה א"כ לאו כרבנן מלית לאוקמי : ה"ג איידי דתני רישא פיגול וחייבין עליו כרת תנא סיפא כג] פסול ואין בו כרת . ולא גרסינן אלא כלומר לעולם כתקנן לפיגול ושלא כתיקנה חוץ למקומו וה"ה נמי דאם נתן בשתיקה לא פיגל והאי דנקט שלא כתקנה איידי דתנא רישא בחילופא נתן את הראשונה חוץ לזמנה ואת השניה חוץ למקומו פיגול וחייבין עליו כרת כד] ודוקא נקט חוץ למקומו לאשמועינן רבותא דלא תימא מחשבה שניה חוץ למקומו ומפקא לה מידי פיגול משום דהוקבע בפיגול ראשונה אחת מתרת ומפגל בהן תני נמי סיפא פסול כה] דכ"ג אתיא מחשבה שניה ומפקא ליה מידי פיגול אע"ג דלא צריך למתניה דהא בלאו הכי נמי לא הוה מיקבע כו] בדמים : בדמים . בתוספתא דזבחים היא בד"א דכמתנה אחת פיגל : החיצונים שמתנה אחת מתרת ומפגלת בהן :

א) צ"ל קי"ב . ב) צ"ל אלא לאו מדשני כו' צ"ק

שיטה מקובצת

א] אבל יותרת ושתי כליות כו' וא"ת והא דרשינן לפר זה פר העלם למהוי כמאן דכתי' בגופיה וי"ל דנהי דהוי כמאי דכתיב בגופיה לענין דלא הוי היקש מן ההיקש מ"מ אמת הוא דלא כתיב בגופיה בהדיא מידי דהוי לאידך תנא דנפיק ליה מכאשר יורם באם אינו ענין כו' למהוי כמאי דכתיב בגופיה דלא להוי היקש מן ההיקש ואעפ"כ חשיב ליה לא כתיב בגופיה לענין דלא אתי מהחטאת כדפי' בסמוך והא תנא לפר לכל האמור בענין וכדמפורש בתוס' מיהו מ"מ קשה דהיכא קאמר אבל יותרת ושתי הכליות דלא כתיב בגופיה אימא דלא יליף שעירי עכו"ם מפר העלם מהיקשא קמייתא דחטאת א"כ לפר זה פר העלם למה לי הא כל עיקר לא בא אלא משום יותרת וב' הכליות למהוי כמאי דכתיב בגופיה לאגמורי לשעירי עכו"ם וכיון דסוף סוף לא יליף משום דלא כתיב בגופיה בהדיא א"כ לפר זה פר העלם למה לי וי"ל דאה"נ קאמר דאי לאו היקשא שניה דחטאתם על שגגתם הו"א כיון דלא כתיב בגופיה לא יליף מהיקשא קמייתא ולפר זה פר העלם לא הוי דרשינן ליה אלא הוי דרשינן לפר זה פר יוה"כ : ב] והא תנא לרבות פר כו' פ"ה אלמא כו' עד (דברי רבי) [דבי רב מרבי] ולפי שיטתו צריך לומר דההוא תנא דיליף גם עיכובא מלפר לכל האמור בענין ס"ל כרבי יהודה דחוקה לא נאמרה אלא בדברים הנעשים בבגדי לבן לפני ולפנים הילכך לא יליף עיכובא מחוקה [מדברים] [בדברים] הנעשים בהיכל וכ"ת תיפוק ליה עיכובא מהכא דנפקא ליה לר' יהודה דהיינו מכלה מכפר וי"ל דבהדוא לא ס"ל כר"א אלא סבר לה כר"ע דדריש יכפר כילה ואיכא למימר אם כיפר כפר כפרה במקום אחר בחיצוניות היינו מתנה אחת הילכך לא שמעינן מיניה עיכובא לכולהו מתנות כדפי' בקונטרס לקמן גבי מילתיה דר"ע בפרק איזהו מקומן כך שיטת הקונטרס . וקשה חדא דלשמעתין בעלמא שום תנא שיאמר דלא ילפינן עיכובא ביוה"כ בין מחוקה בין מוכלה וכיפר . ועוד קשה דלעיל מידחקינן לרב פפא לעיל לאוקמי לפר זה לפר יוה"כ ולענין את בדם וטבילה ולא לענין לעכב הברייתא דהכא ולמה לא לרבי דריש עיכובא מוכלה וכיפר ומה בכך אכתי יש מינה ענינא עדיין לענין לעכב וכאותו

קאמר דהיינו לענין יותרת וב' הכליות ואע"ג דלא כתיב בגופיה דפר העלם בהדיא דנהי דמכאשר יורם איתרבי באם אינו ענין כדפי' לעיל כי היכי דלא להוי היקש מן ההיקש מ"מ הא לא כתיב בהדיא בגופיה דיותר אין לו להחשיבו כתוב בגופו מייתור דכאשר יורם ספי מייתור דלפר זה פר העלם אלמא מחדא היקשא דלפר זה פר יוה"כ ילפינן פר יוה"כ מפר העלם אף מידי דלא כתיב בהדיא ומינה נשמע לאידך תנא דדריש לפר זה פר העלם דשמעינן (יותר) [יותרת ושתי הכליות] בשעירי עכו"ם מחדא היקשא מהיקשא קמייתא דחטאת והדרי קושיא לדוכתיה למה לי שנגתם על חטאתם דנהי דהוי מוקמינן דפליגי (מדרשה) [בדרשה] דלפר דמר מוקי בפר יוה"כ ומכאשר יורם דריש דלא להוי היקש מן ההיקש ומר דריש לפר זה פר העלם דלא להוי היקש מן ההיקש מ"מ (מסברא) [בסברא] זו אי מהניא היקשא קמייתא גם במידי דלא כתיב בגופיה בהדיא מסתמא לא פליגי אהדדי כך סובר המקשה ומשני תנאי היא ובהא גופיה פליגי ותנא דבי רב קורא תנא דספרי דחטאתם על שנגתם וא"ת ולתנא דלפר זה פר העלם מגליה בפר יוה"כ ליותרת וב' הכליות וי"ל מדרשה דת"כ ואת כל חלב פר החטאת גבי פר כהן משיח לרבות פר יוה"כ ליותרת ושתי הכליות מייתורא דפר ובמקום אחר הארכתי והר"ם פי' דקאי למיפרך אהא דקאמר דאיצטריך לפר זה פר העלם למהוי כמאי דכתיב בגופיה והיינו הקושיא שהקשו בתוס' לעיל ולרבי דדריש לפר זה פר יוה"כ א"כ יותרת וב' הכליות למהוי כמאי דכתיב בגופיה מגליה ומשני תנאי היא האי תנא ספיק ליה מכאשר יורם ובתוס' רבינו אליהו נמצא גירסא והא תנא החטאת אלו שעירי עכו"ם לרבות לכל האמור בענין דמשמע דאף ליותרת וב' הכליות והשתא ניחא . מהר"ם : ג] ודם שכעס על אוהבו : ד] מאיר משום דקסבר : ה] עיין בהשמטות בסוף המסכת : ו] נמי אלא לאו משום : ז] קמ"ל הטאתם : ח] לכל האמור בענין : ט] היא האי תנא : י] בענין מתניתא דבי רבי : יא] בה דברי : יב] דבפר כהן : יג] עצתו המסכימים לדעתו אשר דברי פתריו : יד] צבור חטאו : טו] בפה עי' תו' לעיל ב' ע"א [ד"ה כל בסופו ודף ד' ע"ב ד"ה מחשבה] (כ"א א' הוא ט"ס) : טז] מתיר לא פיגל לר"מ אלא פסול : יז] וקס"ד דהיינו : יח] ראשונה עושה : יט] פיגול אלא לאו מדשני ליה כו' שמע מינה טעמיה משום דעושה ע"ד הראשונה עושה : כ] הראשונות במחשבת דחוץ לזמנו ואחת שלא כתקנה לפיגול אלא בשתיקה פסול ואין בו כרת : כא] דאמר להכשירה : כב] דאשר עושה א"כ : כג] לאוקמי גליון אלא כו' ר"ם והחשם מינה טעמא דר"א משום דעל דעת

ראשונה הוא עושה : כג] ספא נמי פסול כו' פיגול ולא אמרינן על דעת הראשונה עושה דרבנן הוא [והאי תקיעם] : כד] דדוקא נקט כו' דהוקבע כו' : כה] בכולה כו' קמאי פסול בראשונה שמתנה : כו] לאו דוקא דכי אמרינן על דעת ראשונה לרבנן : כז] נראה ושקלי אצל בדם וטבילה לחד כשיקה משום דלא ושני הקשים תנא דבי רב היינו [תנא מתניתא] כו' ותנא דבי ר"י היינו אותה ברייתא דדריש לכל האמור בענין שבידורה תלמידים [בפירוש] דבפי' מה שחכ התלמידים לדברי ר"י דברי רבי וגוריי וקשה לו"ת נסתק : משום ויותר דלפר זה פר העלם ועל זה פריך והא תנא לפר זה פר העלם אתא ואוקמינן לעיל : [ל] היקשא תוספת : [לא] היקשא דחטאת : [לב] היקשא דהחטאות : [לג] תנא לפר זה פר העלם אתא : [לד] לפ"ח חלב לרבות פר יוה"כ והשאר נמחק : [לה] הש"ס עי' תו' מנחות (ד' נב ע"א) ד"ה פר העלם : [לו] למיגזר כדאמרי' בפ"ב ר'

תנא שלישי הכך ברייתא דלכל האמור בענין דלא דריש עיכובא לא [מחוקה ולא] מוכלה מכפר כדפ"ה ועוד קשה דלשאי מאת' ברייתא עצמה דלכל האמור בענין מייתי מייתא דפר פא' השתא מקשי מינה ועוד דלמה דמתין מלהקשות הך קושיא עד השתא הוה ליה למיפרך לעיל כיון [דלעיל] קאי כדפ"ה [דאדלעיל] כך נראה לר"י דאדסליק מינה קאי שאמר רב פפא בסמוך לעיל דמהקישא קמייתא דועשה לפר כאשר עשה לפר החטאת אלו שעירי עכו"ם לא נפקא לן יותרת וב' הכליות דלא כתיבן בגופיה בהדיא ואע"ג דלא הוי היקש מן ההיקש משום דיותר דלפר זה היה פר העלם ועל זה פריך והא תנא לפר זה פר העלם אתא ואיך יליף דאוקימנא לענין את בדם וטבילה מדמהדר ליה קו"ח [קרבן לקרבן השוה] [מדמקום] שלא הושוה [כך] לשעשים כו' כדפי' מ"מ לישנא דלכל האמור בענין משמע שכולה מילתא הנאמר בכאן ולא נאמרה כלל ביוה"כ

גליון הש"ס גמ' כל העושה ע"ד הראשונה. לעיל דף ב ע"ב שבת דף צ"א :

in that very passage; [41b] but [as for the burning of] the lobe and the two kidneys, which are not prescribed in that passage, I would say [that it is] not [intimated]. Therefore the text informs us [that it is not so].

R. Huna the son of R. Nathan said to R. Papa: But surely the Tanna states, '"*with the bullock*" includes the bullock of the Day of
a Atonement in respect of *everything* which is prescribed in the text'?[1] —It is a controversy of Tannaim. The Tanna of the Academy[2] includes it in this way, while the Tanna of the School of R. Ishmael includes it in that way.

The School of R. Ishmael taught: Why are the lobe and the two kidneys mentioned in connection with the anointed priest's bullock, but not in connection with the community's bullock for unwitting transgression? It may be compared to a king of flesh and blood who was angry with his friend, but spoke little of his offence, out of his love for him.[3]

The School of R. Ishmael also taught: Why is the '*veil of the sanctuary*' mentioned in connection with the anointed priest's bullock, but not in connection with the community's bullock of unwitting transgression?[4] It may be compared to a king of flesh and blood against whom a province sinned. If a minority offended, his retainers remain [with them], but if the majority offend, his retainers do not remain [with them].[5]

THEREFORE, IF HE APPLIED ALL CORRECTLY, AND ONE INCORRECTLY, IT [THE SACRIFICE] IS INVALID, BUT DOES NOT INVOLVE KARETH. We learnt elsewhere: If [the priest] made a *piggul* intention at the [burning of the] fistful [of flour] but not at [the burning of the] incense,[6] [or] at the frankincense but not at the fistful, R. Meir says that it is *piggul*, and one is liable to
b *kareth* on its account;[1] but the Sages maintain: It does not involve *kareth* unless [the priest] makes a *piggul* intention for the whole *mattir*. R. Simeon b. Laḳish commented: Do not say that R. Meir's reason is because he holds that you can make a [sacrifice] *piggul* in half a *mattir*. Rather the circumstances here are that [the priest] presented the fistful [on the altar] with a [*piggul*] intention, and the frankincense in silence. He [R. Meir] holds [that] when one does [a thing], he does it with his first intention.[2] How do you know it?—Because [the Tanna] teaches: THEREFORE IF HE APPLIED ALL CORRECTLY, AND ONE INCORRECTLY, IT [THE SACRIFICE] IS INVALID, BUT DOES NOT INVOLVE KARETH. Hence [if he applies] one correctly and all [the others] incorrectly, it is *piggul*. With whom does this agree? If with the Rabbis? Surely the Rabbis say [that] you cannot make *piggul* at half a *mattir*? Hence it must be R. Meir; now if R. Meir's reason is that you can make *piggul* at half a *mattir*, then even in the conditions which he teaches it is still *piggul*.[3] Hence it must surely be because he holds that when one does [a thing], he does it with his first intention. Said R. Samuel b. Isaac: In truth it agrees with the Rabbis, and what is meant by CORRECTLY? In the proper manner for *piggul*.[4] But since [the Tanna] teaches: THEREFORE, IF HE APPLIED ALL CORRECTLY, AND ONE INCORRECTLY, IT [THE SACRIFICE] IS UNFIT, BUT DOES NOT INVOLVE KARETH, it follows that INCORRECTLY means [in a manner] to make it fit?[5]—Said Raba: What does INCORRECTLY mean?—[With an intention of eating it] without bounds. R. Ashi said: [It means] under a different designation. Hence it[6] follows that if [the priest] did not do it [with an intention of consuming it] without bounds or under a different designation,
c one is liable?[1]—Because the first clause teaches, IT IS PIGGUL, AND ONE IS LIABLE TO KARETH ON ITS ACCOUNT, the second clause too teaches, IT IS UNFIT, AND DOES NOT INVOLVE KARETH.[2]

An objection is raised: When is this said?[3] In the case of blood

a (1) Which implies that even the sprinklings are indispensable, whereas you say (*supra* 40a bottom) that only those laws which are deduced from '*eth*' etc. are learnt in this way. (2) This is the meaning of *Be Rab* as used here, and it refers to the anonymous statement introduced by 'Our Rabbis taught'. (3) In the same way God treats the community's offence more shortly, and leaves a number of details to be deduced rather than state them explicitly. (4) Lev. IV, 6, speaking of the former, states, *And the priest . . . shall sprinkle of the blood . . . in front of the veil of the sanctuary*. But in IV, 17, which treats of the latter, Scripture merely mentions '*the veil*' not the veil of the sanctuary. (5) To shew his resentment he withdraws them. Thus where the whole community sins God, as it were, withdraws His holiness, and there is no sanctuary left. (6) The burning of these two permits the meal-offering to be eaten. The two rites together therefore constitute the *mattir* (q.v. Glos.), and each is only half a *mattir*.

b (1) If one eats of the offering. (2) Hence his silence here is the equivalent of a *piggul* intention. (3) Even if the first application is made in silence and the others with a *piggul* intention, it should be *piggul*. (4) In a manner which will render it *piggul*. Thus: the first application with a *piggul* intention, and the others in silence. (5) For silence could not be called 'INCORRECTLY'. (6) And since it is a sin-offering, it becomes invalidated (v. *supra* 2a) and consequently is not rendered *piggul*.

c (1) I.e., if the second application was made in silence, it is *piggul*, which shews that we regard the second action as done with the same intention as the first. But that is R. Meir's view, not the Rabbis. (2) CORRECTLY does mean in a proper manner for *piggul* whilst INCORRECTLY means with the intention of consuming it without bounds. Actually then even if he made the second sprinkling in silence it would not be *piggul*, but INCORRECTLY is taught for the sake of parallelism. For in the first clause, dealing with the outer sacrifices, he teaches IF HE APPLIED THE FIRST WITH THE INTENTION OF CONSUMING IT AFTER TIME, AND THE SECOND WITH THE INTENTION OF CONSUMING IT WITHOUT BOUNDS, IT IS PIGGUL AND INVOLVES KARETH. There, this second intention is particularly stated in order to teach that it does not nullify the first and free it from *piggul*, because since a single application permits it, a single application makes it *piggul*. For that reason he teaches in the second clause, dealing with the inner sacrifices, that here the second intention does nullify the first and free it from *piggul*, though this in truth need not be taught, since in any case, even if he remained silent at the second application, it would not be *piggul*, as the Rabbis do not hold that he makes the second application with the same intention as the first. (3) That the sacrifice becomes *piggul* through one application.

that is presented on the outer altar. [42a] But in the case of blood presented on the inner altar, e.g., the forty three [applications] of the Day of Atonement,[4] the eleven of the anointed priest's bullock, and the eleven of the community's bullock of unwitting transgression,[5] if he [the priest] declared a *piggul* intention whether at the first, the second, or the third,[6] R. Meir maintains [that] it is *piggul* and involves *kareth;* while the Sages say: It does not involve *kareth* unless [the priest] declares a *piggul* intention at the whole *mattir*. Incidentally he teaches, 'if [the priest] declared a *piggul* intention whether at the first, at the second, or the third,' and yet
a [R. Meir] disagrees?[1]—Said R. Isaac b. Abin: The circumstances here are e.g. that he declared a *piggul* intention at the *shechitah*, this being one *mattir*.[2] If so, what is the reason of the Rabbis?—Said Raba: Who are the Sages [in this passage]? R. Eleazar.[3] For we learnt: [With regard to] the fistful [of flour], the frankincense, the incense, the priest's meal-offering, the anointed priest's meal-offering, and the meal-offering of the libations, if [the priest] presented as much as an olive of one of these without [the Temple court], he is liable. But R. Eleazar[3] exempts [him] unless he offers the whole [without].[4] But surely Raba said: Yet R. Eleazar admits in the case of blood, for we learnt: R. Eleazar and R. Simeon maintain: From where he left off there he recommences![5]—Rather said Raba: It [the Baraitha] means e.g. where he declared a *piggul* intention at the first [applications], was silent at the second, and again declared a *piggul* intention at the third.[6] Now we might argue, If you claim that he acts with his original intention, why should he repeat his *piggul* intention at the third [applications]? Therefore he informs us [that we do not argue so].

To this R. Ashi demurred: Does he then teach [that] he was silent? Rather said R. Ashi: The circumstances here are e.g., that he declared a *piggul* intention at the first, second, and third. You might argue, If you think that whatever one does, one does with the first intention, why must he repeat his *piggul* declaration at each

(4) One application of the blood of the bullock above the red line and seven below (v. *supra* 38a bottom), and similarly with the blood of the he-goat, which gives sixteen. There were similar applications on the veil of the sanctuary, making thirty two. Further, four applications of the blood of both mixed together, on the four horns of the altar, and seven applications on the top of the altar, giving a total of forty-three. (5) Seven on the veil and four on the altar. (6) The first, second and third are the applications in the innermost sanctuary, on the veil, and on the golden altar respectively.

a (1) Thus, if he declared this intention at the second application only, though not at the first, it is still *piggul*, though here he was certainly not continuing his first intention. Hence he must hold that one *can* render a sacrifice *piggul* at a portion of the *mattir*, which contradicts R. Simeon b. Laḳish. (2) Rashi: After the first blood applications the blood was accidentally spilt. A second animal is slaughtered, and the sprinkling is *continued*, starting with the second applications on the veil. Only here does R. Meir rule that it is *piggul*, since *shechitah* is a service complete in itself. Rashbam: At the *shechitah* the priest declared his intention to make the second blood applications after time. This explanation saves the introduction of a second animal. (3) Emended text (Sh. M.); cur. edd. R. Eliezer. (4) Thus even when he actually presents it without the Temple court, R. Eleazar holds that he is not liable, since it was done with a portion of the *mattir* only, which proves that it does not count as a service unless he completes the whole service. So here too, although *shechitah* is a service complete in itself, yet since this particular *shechitah* was merely to make up another *shechitah* (rendered necessary through the spilling of the blood), it is incomplete, and cannot render the sacrifice *piggul*. (5) V. *infra* 110a and *b*.—Since he recommences from where he left off (where the blood was spilt; v. n. 2), this shews that what he did do is a complete service; hence it can become *piggul* thereby. This refutes Raba's explanation that the Sages in the Baraitha quoted *supra* are R. Eleazar. (6) Only then does R. Meir rule it to be *piggul*, as he holds that the second applications in silence were made with the same intention as the first. So that 'whether at the . . . second or third' means whether he was silent at the third and declared a *piggul* intention at the second, or *vice versa*. But in both cases he had declared a *piggul* intention at the first.

אבל דמים הניתנין על המזבח הפנימי כגון ארבעים ושלש של יום הכיפורים ואחד עשר של פר כהן משיח ואחד עשר של פר העלם דבר של ציבור פיגל בין בראשונה ובין בשניה ובין בשלישית רבי מאיר אומר פיגול וחייבין עליו כרת וחכמים אומרים *אין בו כרת עד שיפגל בכל המתיר קתני מיהא פיגל בין בראשונה בין בשניה בין בשלישית ופליג אמר רב יצחק בר אבין הכא במאי עסקינן כגון שפיגל בשחיטה דחד מתיר הוא אי הכי מאי טעמא דרבנן אמר רבא *מאן חכמים רבי א] אליעזר היא *דתנן *הקומץ והלבונה והקטורת ומנחת כהנים ומנחת כהן משיח ומנחת נסכים שהקריב מאחת מהן כזית בחוץ חייב ור' אליעזר פוטר עד שיקריב את כולן והאמר רבא *ומודה רבי אליעזר בדמים דתנן *רבי אליעזר ור' שמעון אומרים ממקום שפסק משם הוא מתחיל אלא *אמר רבא כגון שפיגל בראשונה ושתק בשניה וחזר ופיגל בשלישית מה"ד ב] אי ס"ד על דעת ראשונה הוא ג] מיהדר פיגולי בשלישית למה לי קמ"ל מתקיף לה רב אשי מידי שתק קתני אלא אמר רב אשי הכא במאי עסקינן כגון שפיגל בראשונה ובשניה ובשלישית מהו דתימא אי ס"ד כל העושה על דעת ראשונה הוא עושה מהדר פיגולי בכל חדא וחדא למה לי קא משמע לן

והא

אבל בדמים הפנימים כגון ארבעים ושלש של יום הכיפורים. אחת למעלה ושבע למטה על בין הבדים מדם הפר וכנגדן מדם השעיר הרי ט"ז וכנגדן על הפרכת הרי ל"ב וארבע על קרנות מזבח הפנימי משניהם כאחד מעורבין כדכתיב (ונתן)[ולקח] מדם הפר ומדם השעיר (ויקרא טז) שיהו מעורבין הרי ל"ו ושבע הזאות על טהרו הרי מ"ג : ד] פיגל בין בראשונה. במתנות שלפני ולפנים : בין בשניה. על הפרכת : בין בשלישית. על מזבח הזהב : קתני מיהא בין בשניה. דמשמע לא בראשונה: ופליג. ה] וקאמר ר"מ פיגול ואין כאן משום דעת ראשונה אלא דקסבר מפגלין בחצי מתיר ותיובתא דר"ל : כגון שפיגל בשחיטה. הא דקאמר ר"מ פיגל בשניה פיגול כגון שנשפך הדם לאחר שגמר מתנות שבפנים וקי"ל בסדר יומא (דף ס.) יביא אחר ויתחיל ו] בהיכל וכששחט את השני פיגל בשחיטתו וקאמר ר"מ דההוא פר הוי פיגול שהרי פיגל בו בעבודה שלמה ז]: רבי ח] אליעזר היא. דאפילו בהעלאת חוץ פוטר ט] *בשני מתירין אלמא לאו עבודה היא כלל עד שיגמור כל העבודה ואע"ג דהקטרת כזית הוה הקטרה כדקתני התם וכולן שהקריבן בפנים ושייר מהן כזית והקריבו בחוץ חייב אפילו לר' אליעזר מיהו היכא דלא גמר עבודה הוא לא חשיב לה לחיובי עליה בחוץ י] ה"נ אע"ג דשחיטה עבודה שלמה היא כיון שאין העבודה נגמרה יא] בשעיר זה לבדו שאינו בא אלא להשלים יב] ועבודה אחת היא שנעשית בשתים ושלש שחיטות אין השחיטה יג] חשובות לפגל : והא אמר רבא. לקמן בפ' השוחט (דף קי.) דקתני הזורק מקצת דמים בחוץ חייב ולא פליג רבי אליעזר ואמר רבא עלה בגמרא מודה רבי אליעזר בדמים שאם יד] נותן במתנה אחת מחטאות הפנימיות חוץ לעזרה חייב ואע"פ שכולן עבודה אחת הן לעכב ואיכא למימר דאין כאן אלא חצי העבודה דומיא דקומץ או לבונה חייב הואיל וכנגדה לפני ולפנים מתקבלת היא שאם נתן מתנה אחת בפנים ונשפך הדם מביא דם אחר ומתחיל ממקום שפסק לר' אליעזר : דתנן ר' אליעזר ור' שמעון. טו] פליגי אתנא קמא דאמר נתן מקצת מתנות שבפנים ונשפך הדם יביא דם אחר ויתחיל בתחילה הואיל ולא גמר אותה כפרה ר' אליעזר ור' שמעון [אומרים] כו' אלמא עבודה היא ואי פיגול לחיוב חוץ קא מדמית לא מיבעיא בשחיטה טז] דהוה פיגול אלא אפילו פיגל במתנה אחת לר' אליעזר פיגול היא : אלא אמר רבא. לעולם בשפיגל בהזאות ודקשיא לך קתני פיגל בשניה או בשלישית וקס"ד דבראשונה שתק וקאמר ר' מאיר פיגול יז] *הוא דהכא במאי עסקינן כגון שפיגל בראשונה ושתק בשניה וחזר ופיגל בשלישית ולעולם טעמא דר"מ משום דקסבר שתיקה השניה על דעת מחשבה הראשונה נעשית כר"ל: ה"ג מה"ד אמרינן אי ס"ד כל העושה על דעת הראשונה עושה מיהדר פיגולי בשלישית למה לי קמ"ל. כלומר יח] והאי דנקט חזר ופיגל בשלישית רבותא אשמעינן דאע"ג דחזר ופיגל בשלישית אמרינן דשתיקה שניה נמי על דעת מחשבה קמייתא יהבה : דמהו דתימא. אי על דעת ראשונה הואי שתיקה שניה אמאי לא עבד נמי שלישית בשתיקה : קמ"ל. דלא אמרינן הכי וגירסא הכתוב בספרים יט] (ואי אמרינן אי ס"ד כו' לא שייך למיגרס הכא הכי דהא מהדרינן לתרוצה אליבא דריש לקיש דאמר טעם דר"מ משום דעת ראשונה הוא ואם תאמר האי כ] אם ס"ד אליבא דרבנן נקט למימר טעמא דרבנן משום הכי הוא לאו מילתא הוא דהא לריש לקיש אליבא (*דרב) אפילו לא חזר ופיגל בשלישית לית להו לרבנן על דעת ראשונה עושה ובמנחות (דף טז.) הוא דגרסינן לה הכי דהתם לרב אותיבנא מהא מתני' דאוקי פלוגתייהו בנותן ראשונה בשתיקה ושניה במחשבה ובמפגלים בחצי מתיר פליגי אבל בנותן ראשונה במחשבה ושניה בשתיקה אפילו רבנן מודו דפיגל דאמרינן על דעת ראשונה עשה ואותיבנא מהא דקתני בין בראשונה ומשמע לא בשניה וקאמרי רבנן לא פיגל ושני רבא כא] *אליבייהו כגון שחזר ופיגל בשלישית דאמרינן אי ס"ד על דעת ראשונה : אלא אמר רב אשי כו'. בהא נמי גרס מאי דתימא כב] אי ס"ד כו' קמ"ל וגירסא שבספרים דלא גרסינן מהו דתימא במנחות (שם) איתא ולא שייך למיגרס הכא הכי : אלא אמר רב אשי. כגון שפיגל והוציא פיגול בשפתיו בראשונה ובשניה ובשלישית כג] וברביעית לא פיגל כדקתני בהדיא כד] בין בראשונה כו' ולא קתני רביעית ובהזאות של טהרו שתיק ולעולם טעמא דר"מ משום כה] דעת ראשונה הוא ורבותא אשמעינן דאע"פ שלא שתק אלא בזו אמרינן על דעת ראשונה עשה דמהו דתימא אי ס"ד על דעת הראשונה עושה למה לא שתק בשניה ובשלישית ויעשה על דעת ראשונה קא משמע לן דלא אמרינן הכי ועוד לא גרסינן :

והא

כגון שפיגל בשחיטה דהוי מתיר אחד. פירש רבינו שמואל בשעת שחיטה חישב ע"מ ליתן מתנות שבפנים חוץ לזמנו או מתנות ההיכל או מתנות דמזבח והיינו פיגל בין בראשונה בין בשניה בין בשלישית כמו שוחט שלמים ע"מ לזרוק חוץ לזמנו או ע"מ להקטיר גרידא דהאי פיגול לכ"ע כיון דכל השחיטה הויא בפיגול [ופריך] א"ה מאי טעמא דרבנן דאפילו לשפוך שיריים למחר קיימא לן (לקמן דף מד:). דהאי פיגול *מאן חכמים ר' כו] אליעזר היא דכיון דלר' אליעזר *לא מיחייב במתנה אחת בחוץ הכי נמי אי פיגל לא הוי פיגול כז] ומיהו לא יתכן לפרש כן דלפירוש זה אי אפשר ליישב כלל במה דברים אמורים בדמים הנתנין על כח] המזבח ופירוש הקונטרס עיקר : מאן חכמים רבי אליעזר היא. *ואמרינן דבעי עבודה טפי לפיגול דנימא כט] כמ"ד דמחייב לא הוי דהא מחייב כזית קומץ בחוץ ואילו פיגול אפילו בקומץ שלם לא הוי פיגול אם לא פיגל בלבונה ומדרבי אליעזר לתודיה מייתי ראיה [דפוטר] גבי חוץ כ"ש דלא הוי פיגול ולמאי דמסיק דמודה ר' אליעזר בדמים לא כמו שפי' בקונטרס דמחייב במקצת דמים בחוץ מכלל דהוי פיגול דאין זה ראיה כדפרישית ולא אתי אלא לדחות הא דשנינו הא מני רבי אליעזר היא : כגון שפיגל בראשונה ובשניה ובשלישית. פירש בקונטרס וברביעית לא פיגל וקשה רביעית מאן דכר שמיה ובפ' שני דמנחות (דף טז.*) פי' בקונטרס שפיגל בראשונה ובשניה ושתק בשלישית וא"ת א"כ קשיא מידי שתק קתני כדאקשי לעיל ושמא לעיל דשתק באמצעית הוה ליה לפרושי טפי כיון דראשונה ושלישית במחשבה ושניה בשתיקה ולהאי פירושא חשיב כל הזאות דמזבח הזהב אחת שבע דטהרו וארבע דקרנות וכן משמע בפרק הוציאו לו (יומא דף סא.) דתניא וכפר את ל] הקודש זו לפני ולפנים ואת אהל מועד זה היכל ואת המזבח כמשמעו ולא קתני כלל על טהרו משמע דחשיב דמזבח לא] כפרה אחת *כדקאמר מיכן אמרו עד גמר מתנות שבהיכל ונשפך הדם יביא אחר ויתחיל לב] בתחילה אבל לא קתני גמר לקרנות ונשפך הדם שיביא אחריו ויתחיל בטהרו *דכולהו חשיבי כאחת וקשה דלקמן [קאמר] משכחת לה בד' פרים וד' שעירים פירוש חד אהזאות דבין הבדים וחד אהזאות דפרכת וחד אהזאות דקרנות וחד אטהרו אלמא לא חשיבי לג] כחדא הזאות דקרנות ודטהרו ושמא פר רביעי דלקמן לאו משום דעל טהרו אלא סבירא ליה דשיריים מעכבין והוי חד בשביל שירים ולפירוש זה נוכל לגרוס לד] כגון שפיגל בראשונה ובשניה ובשלישית וכן בספר רבינו גרשום כאן ובהקומץ זוטא (מנחות דף טז.) חשיב חצי מתיר משום דאיכא עדיין שיריים דמעכבי וא"ת והא בעל כרחין סבר האי תנא שיריים לא מעכבי מדלא חשיב אלא מ"ג דההוא דסבר שיריים מעכבי חשיב חדא טפי כדמוכח בסמוך וי"ל דאע"ג דשיריים מעכבי לא חשיב האי תנא אלא הזאות :

כי

כד א מיי' פי"ח מהל' פסה"מ הלכה ו :

כה ב מיי' פי"ט מהל' מעה"ק הלכה ח ט :

כו ג מיי' פ"ה מהלכות יוה"כ הל' ה וכת"ק דפליג עליה שם

[עירובין ס. וש"נ]

מנחות יב: לקמן קט'

ג"א כתוי מתיר ז"ק [לקמן קי:]

[יומא ס. לקמן קי: ושם ליתא אליעזר וכצ"ל גם כאן]

נפי' לא היא כי

גי' הב"ח אליבא דרבנן

צ"ל אליביה

ז"ל ומשני מאן ז"ק

כ"א לא מחייב בכזית אחת בחוץ הכי נמי לענין פיגול לא כו' ז"ק

[מנחות טז. כל הענין]

[שם ד"ה כגון]

כ"ל ועוד דקאמר התם

משמע ז"ק

שיטה מקובצת

א] ר' אלעזר וכן צ"ל לקמן : ב] מה"ד אמרינן אי : ג] הוא עושה מיהדר על פיגול בשלישית : ד] מ"ג הס"ד ומה"ד ואחד עשר של פר כהן משיח כו' היינו ז' הזאות שעל הפרכת וארבע על קרנות מזבח הזהב הס"ד : ה] ופליג ר"מ וקאמר פיגול : ו] בהיכל. מה שפ"ה מתחיל בתחילה בהיכל לכך פי' [כן] שאם היה מתחיל בתחילה פר קמא כמאן דליתא דמי ולמה הזכיר ראשונה ושניה ושלישית. ומיהו קשה לפי' הקונטרס שפי' פיגל בשחיטה דפר שהרי פיגל בראשון משמע דפיגל בהזאות ולא בשחיטה ועוד מאי קמדמי לקומץ שאני קומץ דמיעוטו מעכב רובו אבל כל שחיטה ושחיטה הוי דבר בפני עצמו ופרשב"ם פיגל בשחיטה על מנת שיזה דמו הראשונים או השניים למחר דהוי ליה מפגל בעסק שלם וה"ק הא מני ר"א היא דפטר א) בהקומץ בחוץ עד שהקטיר את כולן משום דמיעוטו מעכב את רובו וה"ה אם פיגל בעסק מתיר שלם כמו בקמיצה ע"מ להקטיר כזית מן הקומץ דלא פיגל עד שיחשוב בכולן ומייתי הר"ם ראיה במנחות [דף יב:] דמייתי מילתיה דר' אלעזר על משנה דהקומץ ע"מ להקטיר כזית חוץ לזמנו וקאמר דלר' אלעזר לא פיגל עד שיפגל בכולן וה"נ במחשב ע"מ לזרוק אחד מן הדמים למחר דאין זה פיגול כיון דמעכבות זו את זו ואי לא דחשיב (בהו) [בכולהו] לא מהני מחשבה : ז] שלימה ס"א ולהכי פריך נשפך דאם לא נשפך למה יביא אחר : ח] ר' אלעזר וכצ"ל בכל העמוד : ט] פוטר בחצי מתיר ותיבת בשני ל"ש : י] בחוץ עד שיגמור כל העבודה : יא] בשעיר . ס"א בפר : יב] להשלים עבודה : יג] חשובה לפגל הס"ד : יד] שאם נתן מתנה : טו] ופליגי את"ק : טז] דהוי פיגול : יז] לא היא : יח] כלומר האי : יט] בספרים דאמרינן אי ס"ד : כ] האי אי ס"ד אליבא כו' למימר דטעמא דרבנן : כא] רבא אליבא דרב כגן : כב] דתימא אמרינן אי : כג] וברביעית . ס"א דהיינו בהזאות לא פיגל בין בראשונה : כד] בהדיא פיגל שהרי שתק : כה] משום דעל דעת ראשונה הוא עושה : כו] ר' אלעזר וכצ"ל בכל העמוד : כז] פיגול תוספת : כח] על מזבח החיצון ופי' הקונטרס עיקר ע"כ תוספת : כט] דנימא למ"ד בחוץ חייב לא הוי פיגול דהא : ל] את מקדש הקודש : לא] כפרה. ס"א מתנה אחת עוד קאמר התם מיכן אמרו עד כו' : לב] ויתחיל במתנות המזבח נתן מקצת מתנות מזבח תשפך הדם מביא אחר ויתחיל בתחלה אבל לא קתני גמר לקרנות ונשפך כו' ויתחיל מטהרו דכלהו כו' קאמר משכחת לה : לג] חשיבי כאחד : לד] לגרוס בכאן כגון כו' וכן כתוב בספר רבינו גרשום כו' וחשיב חצי מתיר :

א) נראה דצ"ל דפטר גבי קומץ אם הקטיר כזית ממנו בחוץ עד שהקטיר וכו' .

שוחט או מקבל נמי יומא כו' דכי חשיב בשחיטה או בקבלה כו' נ"ק

כז א מיי' פי"ט מהל' מעה"ק הל' יב ופ"ד מהלכות עבודת יוה"כ הלכה ג:

כח ב מיי' פי"ג מהל' פסה"מ הלכה ו:

כט ג מיי' פט"ז מהל' פסה"מ הלכה ז:

ל ד מיי' פי"ח מהלכות פסה"מ הלכה ח:

כי מדי בהיכל מיא בעלמא קמדי. הקשה בקונטרס כה] בהקומץ *ושוחט נמי נימא דלא מיפגל דכי חשיב בקבלה איפסיל וכי זריק מיא בעלמא זריק ותירץ דהתם גזירת הכתוב הוא ובהקומץ זוטא (מנחות דף טז:) תירץ דאותה עבודה שפיגל בה נעשית כולה בקדושתה שוחט ע"מ לזרוק או להקטיר וכן מקבל ע"מ לזרוק או להקטיר אבל הנך הזאות כולהו חדא עבודה היא ולא קרבו כו] מתירין העבודה בקדושתן כז] וקשה דכי פיגל בהזאות של בין הבדים אינך דהיכל מים ניהו אבל בהזאה ראשונה של בדים לא פריך דשאר הזאות של בדים מיא כח] דיש לומר יפגל באחרונה או כיון דחד מקום הוי אין בכך כלום [כמו שאפרש] בסמוך אי נמי י"ל דניחא ליה דלא הוו של בין הבדים מיא משום דלא נגמר הפיגול עד שיזרוק כל הזאות של בין הבדים אבל אותן של היכל לא תליא בהו גמר הפיגול כיון שאם נשפך הדם מביא פר אחר ויתחיל בהיכל ולא בין הבדים וכן ההזאות של מזבח הזהב לא תלו בהזאות של היכל למיגמר בהו פיגול של היכל ולרבנן לא פריך דכיון דאין מפגלין בחצי מתיר וצריך לפגל כל ההזאות אם כן לא נגמר הפיגול עד שפיגל בכולן מתחלת בין הבדים עד גמר של טהרו ומשני בד' פרים כדי לחשב ולפגל בכל המקומות קאמר ארבעה וה"ה בפר ראשון של בין הבדים ונשפך הדם והביא פר שני ועשה כט] (פר שני) ממנו של היכל ושל מזבח בשתיקה דהוי פיגול לר' מאיר. ברוך. וקשה דאם כן פיגל בקומץ ולא בלבונה לרבי מאיר ליפרוך אמאי הוי פיגול בחצי מתיר ל] *)והך עבודה לא נעשית בקדושתה וכי מקטר ללבונה עפרא בעלמא מקטר וכי תימא משום דהוו שני מינים אכתי קשה משני בזיכין אם לא נחלק לא] כיון דבעו שני כלים דהוו כשני מינים והוי פיגול ורבינו תם מפרש דבחד מקום פשיטא ליה דלא אמרינן מיא בעלמא הוא דקמדי לב] תחילת עבודה בגמר עבודה והכי גזירת הכתוב אבל בשני מקומות בהכי לא איירי קרא ומיא בעלמא קמדי: **משכחת** לה בד' פרים. וא"ת אכתי הזאות שבפנים היכי משכחת ליה פיגול בפר אחד מכיון שהזה לג] בראשונה במחשבה אידך מיא בעלמא קמדי ולרבינו תם אתי שפיר דחד מקום הוא ויש לומר כגון שפיגל בהזאה אחרונה של בין הבדים: **הא** כמאן דאמר שירים מעכבין. ל"ע פ' איזהו מקומן (לקמן דף נב:) דקאמר רמי בר חמא האי תנא סבר שירים מעכבי ומייתי מברייתא ודחי לה והוה מצי לאתויי הך ועוד מברייתא דלעיל (דף לט.) דדמים הטעונין יסוד טעונין כיבוס ומחשבה פוסלת בהן ומוקמינן לה בשירים וכמאן דאמר דמעכבי:

הקומץ. הקשה בקונטרס בהקומץ זוטא (מנחות דף יד.) למה לי לד] דאין לו מתירין אלא הוא עצמו מתיר אחרים כדאיתא בגמ' תיפוק לי דבלאו הכי נמי פשיטא דקומץ לא מיחייב עליה משום פיגול דהא אי אכיל מיניה פקע פיגולו ממנו שהרי לא קרב מתיר כמצותו ותירץ כגון שהוצתה האור ברובו דחשיב כמאן דקרב המתיר כדקאמר בהקומץ רבה (שם דף כו:) מאימתי מתיר שירים באכילה משהוצת האור ברובו וקשה לפירושו דאי הוצת האור ברובו א"כ פקע פיגולו ממנו כדאמר שלא בגמ' (דף מג.) דאם ירדו נמי יעלו והוא הדין אפילו מאכילה כדמשמע בכריתות פרק אמרו לו (דף יד. ושם) וי"ל לה]דמיירי שחציו העלה ע"ג מזבח וחציו לא העלה דעל ההוא דלארעא לא פקע פיגולו ממנו וחייב עליו אי לאו משום דהוא גופיה מתיר הוא והא דאמר בגמ' לגבי קומץ לו] דפיגול שהעלהו דפלגא מחית אארעא ופלגיה מסקיה אמערכה ומשלה בו האור פקע פיגולו ומסקינן ליה לכתחילה ובפ' אמרו לו (גם זה שם) מתירו ליה לאכילה לז] מיירי כשהיה כבר על המזבח ההוא פלגא דמחית אארעא אבל היכי דלא עלה למזבח מעולם לא כדמוכח בכריתות (גם זה שם) דפותו קלא לח] דחוץ למזבח לא מסקינן ליה והוה ליה פיגול אע"ג דרובא דאבר אמזבח אם איתא דלא הלכו באברים אחר הרוב וכל שכן קומץ דמיפרת דלא מסקינן לט] ומיהו *)פי' בקונטרס *דבגמרא משמע דאפילו לא עלה אמזבח מסקינן ליה לכתחילה ולא דמיא להאי דכריתות כמו שמפרש ר"ת שהקומץ כולו חשוב אזכרה אחת וההוא פלגא דעל המזבח משיך ליה לפלגא דאארעא דאי לאו הכי הוה ההוא דעל המזבח קומץ שחסר וירד וא"כ כיון דמשיך ליה פקע פיגולו ממנו אבל פלגא דהוא עצמו שלא אוקטרו אימוריו כשר אע"ג דמעיקרא סלקא דעתך דקומץ מ] גרע משום דמיפרת ומפרש ר"ת דטעמא דקומץ לאו משום דהוא מתיר אלא משום דלא שייך ביה הרצאה מא] דאי אכלו ולא העלהו אם כן לא קרבו מתיריו ואי העלה חציו פקע פיגולו אפילו מסליה מההוא דלארעא והא דקאמר בגמרא ומוציא אני את הקומץ בהדי הנהו

*) נפי' בקונטרס כו' כצ"ל נ"ק

והא בין בין קתני קשיא *אמר מר רבי מאיר אומר פיגול וחייבין עליו כרת מכדי כרת לא מיחייב עד שיקרבו כל מתיריו דאמר מר *כהרצאת כשר כך הרצאת פסול מה הרצאת כשר עד שיקרבו כל מתיריו אף הרצאת פסול עד שיקרבו כל מתיריו והא כיון דחשיב ביה א] בפנים פסולה כמאן דלא אדי דמי כי הדר מדי בהיכל ב] מיא בעלמא הוא דקא אדי אמר רבה משכחת לה ג] בארבעה פרים ובד' שעירים ד] רבא אמר אפילו תימא בפר אחד ושעיר אחד לפיגולו מרצה ארבעים ושלש והא תניא ארבעים ושבע הא כמאן דאמר *מערבין לקרנות והא כמאן דאמר אין מערבין לקרנות והא תניא *ארבעים ושמונה הא כמאן דאמר *שירים מעכבין הא כמאן דאמר אין שירים מעכבין: מיתיבי *במה דברים אמורים בקמיצה במתן כלי ובהילוך אבל בא לו להקטרה נתן את הקומץ במחשבה ואת הלבונה בשתיקה או שנתן את הקומץ בשתיקה ואת הלבונה במחשבה רבי מאיר אומר פיגול וחייבין עליו כרת וחכמים אומרים אין בו כרת עד שיפגל בכל המתיר קתני מיהא את הקומץ בשתיקה ואת הלבונה במחשבה ה] ופליג אימא כבר נתן את הלבונה במחשבה חדא דהיינו (א) רישא ועוד הא תניא ואחר כך קשיא:

מתני' דא)ואלו *דברים שאין חייבין עליהם משום פיגול ו] הקומץ ז] והקטרת והלבונה (מנחות יד.)

א) [במשנה שבמשניות איתא אלו]

כי הדר מדי בהיכל מיא בעלמא קמדי. והא בין בין קתני. דמשמע או בזו או בזו: אמר מר כו'. אמאן דמהדר לאוקומי טעמא דר"מ משום מפגלין בחצי מתיר קפריך נהי נמי דבעלמא בקומץ ולבונה איכא למימר מפגלין בחצי מתיר אלא בחצי זריקה היכי אמר ר' מאיר פיגל: מכדי כרת לא מיחייב ח] (הא וכו') עד שיקרבו כל מתיריו. שתיכלנה עבודותיו: דאמר מר בפ' שני (לעיל דף כח:): כי הדר מדי בהיכל מיא בעלמא קא מדי. וגמלא שלא ט] זרק דמו דהא מתנה אחת מהן מעכבת דבשלמא מפגל בשחיטה אע"ג דפסליה והדר זרק ליה או במחשבה או בשתיקה כיון דפיגל י] *בעבודה ושוב לא הוציא בו מחשבת פסול אחר אע"פ שזריקת דמו יא] דם פסול הוא כיון דרבי רחמנא פיגול בשחיטה כדאמרן בפרק ראשון (לעיל יג:) בדברים המביאים לידי אכילה הכתוב מדבר ע"כ בהכי אמר רחמנא יב] לפגול וזריקה זו כמו שהיא מרצה לפיגולו וכן לרבנן דבעו מחשבה בכוליה זריקה ולמאן דמוקי נמי יג] טעם דר"מ משום דעת ראשונה ופיגל בכל העבודה בכה"ג אמר רחמנא לפגול דלא משכחת יד] לפגול בזריקה אלא בהכי אלא למ"ד טעמא משום חצי מתיר אין כאן זריקה כיון דלא גמרה טו] מחשבת פיגול ועשה סופה לדעת כשרה וזיל הכא חצי עבודה היא וזיל הכא חצי עבודה היא: משכחת לה. הא דקאמר ר"מ פיגול: בארבעה פרים. פיגל בין הבדים בכל מתנותיו ונשפך הדם ושחט אחר והזה על הפרכת ואחד טז] על הקרנות ואחד לטיהרו של מזבח וכיון דקיימא לן בסדר יומא (דף ס.) יז] כולהו כפרה בפני עצמו ואי עבדינהו כהלכתן מתכפרה עבודה בהכי אפילו לרבנן דפליגי עלייהו דר' שמעון ור' אלעזר בנשפך הדם באמצע מתנות בהא מודו דאין צריך לחזור ולהזות במקום שגמר כל הזאותיו בדאמרינן התם הלכך הכא נמי פיגל שהרי קרבו מתיריו של כל אחד ונגמרה העבודה בחבירו אבל בפר אחד מודה ר"מ דלא פיגל משום דלא גמר זריקה מעולם: לפיגולו מרצה. כי היכי דאם חשב בשחיטה קרי לה יח] לזריקה דם הפסול הזה קרבו מתיריו לרצות לפיגולו כי חשיב ליה (ב) בחצי זריקה נמי ושתק בחציה כל זמן שלא עירב במחשבה אחרת הוי ריצוי (ג) לפיגול: הא כמ"ד כו'. פלוגתא דר' יאשיה ור' יונתן היא (יומא דף נז:) במתן הקרנות יט] ולקח מדם הפר ומדם השעיר חד אומר שיהו מעורבין וחד אומר מזה בפני עצמו ומזה בפני עצמו: והא. דקתני ארבעים ושבע כמ"ד אין מערבין את הדמים *למתן כ] קרנות (והוו תמני): שירים. שפיכת שירים ופלוגתא דר' עקיבא ור' יהודה היא לעיל (דף מ.) כא] אם כלה כפר כו': בד"א כו'. בתוספתא דמנחות קתני לה בד"א שהמנחה נפגלה בעבודה אחת בקמיצה או במתן כלי ובהילוך שאין שם אלא עבודת מתיר אחד שאין קמיצה ומתן כלי *בלבונה והילוך במנחות (דף טז.) מפרש ליה דלא שייך בלבונה: בא לו להקטרה. שהיא עבודת שני מתיריו נתן כו' אלמא אפילו ראשונה בשתיקה ושניה במחשבה קאמר ר' מאיר פיגל אלמא כב] מפגלין בחצי מתיר ותיובתא דר"ל: אימא וכבר נתן לבונה במחשבה. הלכך שניה שבשתיקה על דעת ראשונה עושה: כג] דהיינו קמייתא. דראשון במחשבה הא תנא ליה נתן את הקומץ במחשבה ואת הלבונה בשתיקה למה לי למיהדר למיתני כד] או את הקומץ בשתיקה וכבר נתנה לבונה במחשבה מה לי להקדים קומץ מה לי לבונה: ועוד הא תניא. בברייתא אחריתי או שנתן את הקומץ בשתיקה ואחר כך נתן לבונה במחשבה קשיא: **מתני'** אלו דברים שאין חייבין עליהן. כרת באכילתן משום פיגול: הקומץ. אם קמץ לאכול שירים למחר ונתפגלה המנחה אין האוכל את הקומץ בכרת שאין הפיגול חל אלא על דבר שיש לו מתירין אחרים והקומץ אין אחר מתירו כי הוא מתיר את המנחה וכן לבונה וכן כולם:

מנחת

שיטה מקובצת

א] בפנים פסליה ותיבות כמאן דלא אדי דמי בס"א אינו אבל בספרים שונים ישנם: ב] מיא בעלמא כו'. פ"ה בשלמא מפגל בשחיטה כו' עד מרצה לפיגולו וכן לרבנן ניחא דאינו מפגל עד לבסוף א"כ בשעת הזאה לא הוי פיגול אלא לר"מ דאמר מפגלין בחצי מתיר א"כ מיד כשפיגל גמר פיגולו והשאר מיא בעלמא קא מדי דבשלמא (כמו כן לר"מ) אי טעמא [לר"מ] משום עושה על דעת הראשונה ופיגל בכל העבודה בכה"ג אמר רחמנא ליפגל דלא משכחת פיגול אלא בהכי אלא למ"ד טעמא משום חצי מתיר מיא בעלמא קא מדי כך היא שיטת הקונטרס וא"ת כל פיגול הכי הוי א"כ לא נמצא פיגול לר"מ דכי חשיב בהו נפגל אף בשחיטה או בקומץ וכי הדר זריק מיא בעלמא קא מדי וי"ל דלא אמרינן מיא בעלמא קא מדי אלא בעבודה אחת הואיל ואירע בו פסול אבל בשתי עבודות לא אמרי' מיא בעלמא קא מדי והזאות כולהו עבודה אחת נינהו מיהו קשה דאמרינן לעיל בפרק ב' וכן בפ"ק דמעילה גבי פלוגתא דר"י דאמר אם מחשבת הזמן קודם למחשבת המקום ומפרש אילפא מחלוקת בעבודה אחת כעין שתי עבודות כגון ששחט סימן אחד בחוץ לזמנו ושני בחוץ למקומו כו' ותירץ הר"ם דסבר אילפא דפיגול הוא מרצה כרבא ור"ת פי' דלא אמרינן מיא בעלמא מדי אלא בשתי מקומות כגון שחשב בפנים ומזה בהיכל דכיון שנסתלק מבפנים נגמרה מחשבתו והשתא ניחא דבשחיטה לא גמר עד לבסוף: ג] בארבעה פרים כו'. פ"ה ששוחט פר או שעיר והזה בפנים ופיגל באחרונה ונשפך הדם ומביא אחר ופיגל נמי באחרונה דהיכל ונשפך ושחט שלישית. והזה על הקרנות בשתיקה. והאי דנקט הקונטרס פירו קודם לקרנות לא דק דקרנות קודם וי"ל דטהרו עשה בשתיקה ומיהו קשה א) דפי' דשלישית בא בין קרנות לשבע שעל טהרו (דאמר) [דהא אמרינן] נשפך הדם בין קרנות לשבע דטהרו או באמצע חוזר ומתחיל בראש [אא"ה שם לא נמצא זה"ל כ"א נתן מקצת מתנות שבמזבח ונשפך בו' עכ"ה] וי"ל דפיגל בסוף שביעי דטהרו והרביעי בא לשירים

[מנחות טז:]
[לעיל כח: [מנחות טז:]
בעבודה אחת נ"ק
[מנחות טז: לקמן פלו יומא מז:]
[לקמן נב: קיא. מנחות טו: יומא סז:] תוספתא דמנחות פ"ה
[מנחות טז. ע"ש בתוס']
פ' נ"ק
נ"ל וסילוק לבונה נ"ק
נ"ב מג ע"ב נ"ה

הגהות הב"ח

(א) גמ' חדא דהיינו קמייתא ועוד: (ב) רש"י ד"ה לפיגולו מרצה וכו' כי חשיב ליה נמי בחצי זריקה ושתק וכו' לפיגול כמ"ד מ"ה והא דקתני וכו' תמניא ספ"ד ואחר כך ד"ס הא כמ"ד:

*) נ"א הא מד עבודה כו' ור"ש מפרש כו' הוא דקמדי כמו מתחלת עבודה נגמר פסולו דמהני פיגול נ"ק

דסבר שירים מעכבי וא"ת ממה הוו שירים וי"ל דהיה נותן מתנה אחת על טהרו לעשותה שיריים וצריך לומר דפיגל באחרונה דאל"כ השאר מיא בעלמא קא מדי והאי דנקט בכל אחד נשפך הדם רבותא (דשינוי) [נ"ל דצ"ל שבבי פי' שהולך בדרכי לבו עיין ערוך ערך שב] עסקינן דפיגל הרבה פעמים: ד] רבא. ס"א אביי: ה] במחשבה ופליג: ו] הקומץ. וא"ת תאי קומץ היכי מיירי אי קודם הקטרה אכתי לא קרבו מתיריו ולא אמרינן פיגול עד שיקרבו מתיריו אפילו שיריים ואי לאחר הקטרה ג) הלא הוא עצמו הוא המתיר ובקונטרס תירץ (וכו') וקשה כו' וי"ל דלעולם איירי קודם הקטרה וכגון שנתקדשה בכלי כדאמרינן במנחות דדבר שאין לו מתירין משקדשו בכלי הלכך אי לאו דהוא עצמו המתיר הו"א דהוא פיגול משקדשו בכלי: ז] והלבונה והקטרת: ח] האוכלו עד שיקרבו כל מתיריו שתכלנה כל הזריקה הס"ד: ט] שלא נזרק דמו כו' אחת מעכבת בחן דבשלמא: י] בעבודה אחת ושוב: יא] תיבת דם נמחק: יב] רחמנא לפגל: יג] נמי טעמא דר"מ: יד] משכחת פגול בזריקה כו' למ"ד טעמיה משום: טו] גמרה במחשבת פיגול: טז] ואחר לקרנות ואחד: יז] דכולן כפרה בפני עצמן כו' כהלכתן הוה מתכשרא עבודה כו' דפליגי אדר"ש ור' אלעזר לעיל בנשפך הדם באמצע המתנות בהא מודו כו' הכא נמי הוי פיגול שהרי קרבו כו' דלא נגמרה זריקה מעולם: יח] לה לזריקת דם כו' כי חשב בחצי זריקה: יט] הקרנות דכתיב בהו ולקח כו' חד אמר שיהו מעורבין וחד אמר מזה: כ] למתן הקרנות וחוו להו תמניא הס"ד: כא] לעיל דאמר אם כלה: כב] אלמא קסבר ר"מ מפגלין: כג] מה"ד דהיינו רישא דראשון: כד] למיתני תו שנתן את הקומץ בשתיקה כו' מה לי הקדים קומץ מה לי הקדים לבונה הס"ד: כה] בקונטרס קומץ ושוחט נמי: כו] קרבו מתירו העבודה: כז] וקשה דכי פריך פיגל כו' מתיבת וקשה עד דהוי פיגול לר"מ מוקף בחצי לבנה: כח] מיא וי"ל דפיגל באחרונה כו' אין בכך כלום כדמפרש ר"ת בסמוך: כט] תיבות פר שני נמחק: ל] מתיר הא חך עבודה: לא] נחלק דכיון דבעו שני כלים הוי פיגול משום דהוי כשני מינים ורבינו: לב] דקמדי דתחילת עבודה: לג] שהזה הראשונה: לד] לי טעמא דאין: לה] וי"ל דפלגא דקומץ אחית אארעא ופלגא אסקיה במחשבת פיגול ומשלה בו האור ומתיבת דמיירי עד תיבת לא העלוהו ס"ד ל"ש: לו] קומץ פיגול דפלגא מחית אארעא ופלגא אחית: לז] לאכילה היינו כשהיה: לח] קצת דאבר דחוץ: לט] מסקינן ליה ומיהו מתוך פי' הקונטרס דבגמ' משמע כו' שמפרש רבינו תם שהקומץ כולו חשיב אזכרה אחת מישפה מעכב את רובה והדא: מ] גרעי מאבר משום דמפרת [לעולא] אבל הקמ"ל היפך הסברא [דמעיקרא] וה"ק קמ"ל אדרבה דקומץ פקע כולה אבל אבר לא [פקע] אלא פלגא דמשלה בו האור. לשון מהר"פ: מא] הרצאה תוספות דאי אכלו כו' מתירין ואי דאי העלה חציו כו' מההוא דארעא ע"כ והא דקאמר:

א) נראה דצ"ל ומיהו קשה מהא דפי' דרביעית בא בין קרנות לשבע על טהרו דהא אמרינן ביומא פא. נשפך הדם וכו' . ג) לשון זה אינו מובן ונראה דצ"ל במנחות י"ד ע"א לשון זה פ"ש.

one? Therefore he informs us [that we do not argue so]. [42*b*]
a But he teaches, 'whether ... or'?[1] That is indeed a difficulty.

The Master said: 'R. Meir said, It is *piggul*, and involves *kareth*'.[2] But consider: one is not liable to *kareth*[3] until all the *mattirin* are offered, for a master said: As the acceptance of the valid, so is the acceptance of the invalid. As the acceptance of the valid necessitates that all its *mattirin* be presented, so does the acceptance of the invalid necessitate that all its *mattirin* be presented.[4] Now here he has [already] invalidated it [the sacrifice] by declaring an [illegitimate] intention within, so that it is as though he had not sprinkled [the blood] at all;[5] when therefore he sprinkles again in the *hekal*, he is merely sprinkling water?[6]—Said Rabbah: It is possible in the case of four bullocks and four he-goats.[7] Raba said: You may even say [that R. Meir rules thus] in the case of one bullock and one he-goat: it [the sprinkling] is efficacious in respect of its *piggul*
b status.[1]

[Do you say that there are] forty-three [sprinklings]?[2] Surely it was taught [that there are] forty-seven?—The former agrees with the view that you mingle [the blood of the bullock and of the he-goat] for [sprinkling on] the horns; while the latter agrees with the view that you do not mingle [them] for [sprinkling on] the horns.[3] But it was taught [that] forty-eight [are required]?—One agrees with the view that [the pouring out of] the residue [at the base of the altar] is indispensable;[4] while the other agrees with the view that the residue is not indispensable.[5]

An objection is raised: When is this said?[6] In [the case of] the taking of the fistful, the placing in the vessel, and the carriage.[7] But when he comes to the burning [of the fistful and the frankincense], if he presents the fistful with a [*piggul*] intention and the frankincense in silence; or if he presents the fistful in silence and the frankincense with a [*piggul*] intention,—R. Meir declares it *piggul*, and it involves *kareth*; while the Sages rule: It does not involve *kareth* unless he declares a *piggul* intention in respect of the whole *mattir*. Now he teaches incidentally, [If he presents] 'the fistful in silence and the frankincense with a [*piggul*] intention', and yet they
c disagree![1]—Say 'having already presented the frankincense with a [*piggul*] intention'. One [objection] is that that is the first clause. Moreover, it was indeed taught,[2] 'and *after* that.'[3] That is indeed a difficulty.

MISHNAH. THESE ARE THE THINGS FOR WHICH ONE IS NOT LIABLE ON ACCOUNT OF PIGGUL: THE FISTFUL, THE

a (1) Implying alternatives: *either* at one *or* at the other. (2) V. *supra* 42*a*. (3) For eating thereof. (4) V. *supra* 28*b*. (5) *Var. lec.* omits 'then ... at all'. (6) This is a difficulty on the view that R. Meir's reason is that one can make a sacrifice *piggul* at half a *mattir*. Granted that this is possible in the case of the fistful and the frankincense of a meal-offering, it is surely impossible in the case of sprinkling, for the reason stated.—'He is merely sprinkling water' means that his sprinkling of the blood is just as though he were sprinkling water, since the sacrifice is already invalid. (7) He declared a *piggul* intention during all the applications of the blood between the staves; then the blood was spilt, so that another animal was slaughtered. He sprinkled its blood on the veil (he would start there, and not repeat the first sprinklings between the staves; V. *supra a*) and the blood was again spilt. The same happened with the applications on the horns of the altar, and the same with the sprinklings on the top. Here then all the *mattirin* have been presented, and each counts as a real sprinkling because it is the blood of a different animal; consequently the first is *piggul*, while the same would hold good if he declared his *piggul* intention in connection with any of the other animals.

b (1) If the priest declares a *piggul* intention at the slaughtering, though he thereby invalidates the sacrifice, yet the following sprinklings are counted as the presenting of its *mattirin*. Thus they are obviously efficacious to stamp the animal as *piggul*, for otherwise an animal could not become *piggul* at slaughtering, whereas it is deduced *supra* 13*a* that it does. In the same way then R. Meir holds that when some of the sprinklings are done with a *piggul* intention, the subsequent sprinklings count as the presenting of the *mattirin*, so as to make the sacrifice *piggul*. (2) *Supra a* top. (3) But each is sprinkled separately, which gives an additional four, bringing up the number to forty-seven. (4) Hence it is regarded as another sprinkling. (5) V. *supra* 40*b*. (6) That a meal-offering becomes *piggul* at one service. (7) Where each service consists of a single act.

c (1) R. Meir maintains that it is *piggul*. Here his second act was not done with the same intention as the first, since he was silent at the first. Hence R. Meir's reason must be because he holds that one can make the sacrifice *piggul* during half a *mattir*. (2) In another Baraitha. (3) He presented the frankincense with a *piggul* intention.

INCENSE, THE FRANKINCENSE, [43a] THE PRIESTS' MEAL-OFFERING, THE ANOINTED PRIEST'S MEAL-OFFERING, THE BLOOD, AND THE DRINK-OFFERINGS THAT ARE BROUGHT SEPARATELY: THAT IS THE VIEW OF R. MEIR. THE SAGES MAINTAIN: ALSO THOSE THAT ARE BROUGHT WITH AN ANIMAL [SACRIFICE].[4] A LEPER'S LOG[5] OF OIL,[6] R. SIMEON MAINTAINED, DOES NOT INVOLVE LIABILITY ON ACCOUNT OF
a PIGGUL;[1] WHILE R. MEIR RULES: IT INVOLVES LIABILITY ON ACCOUNT OF PIGGUL, BECAUSE THE BLOOD OF THE GUILT-OFFERING MAKES IT PERMITTED.[2] AND WHATEVER HAS AUGHT THAT MAKES IT PERMITTED,[3] WHETHER FOR MAN OR FOR THE ALTAR, INVOLVES LIABILITY ON ACCOUNT OF PIGGUL. [THE SPRINKLING OF] THE BLOOD OF THE BURNT-OFFERING PERMITS ITS FLESH FOR [BURNING ON] THE ALTAR, AND ITS SKIN TO THE PRIESTS. THE BLOOD OF THE BURNT-OFFERING OF A BIRD PERMITS ITS FLESH TO THE ALTAR. THE BLOOD OF THE SIN-OFFERING OF A BIRD PERMITS ITS FLESH TO THE PRIESTS. THE BLOOD OF THE BULLOCKS THAT ARE BURNT AND THE GOATS THAT ARE BURNT PERMITS THEIR EMURIM TO BE OFFERED [ON THE ALTAR]. R. SIMEON SAID: WHATEVER IS NOT [SPRINKLED] ON THE OUTER ALTAR, AS THE PEACE-OFFERING,[4] DOES NOT INVOLVE LIABILITY ON ACCOUNT OF PIGGUL.

GEMARA. 'Ulla said: If the fistful [of the meal-offering], which is *piggul*, is presented on the altar, its *piggul* status leaves it:[5] seeing that it reduces others to [the state of] *piggul*, how much the more so itself. What does he mean?[6]—This is what he means: if it is unacceptable,[7] how can it reduce others to [the state of] *piggul*?[8]

b What does he inform us?[1] If that it does not involve liability for *piggul*, surely we have learnt it: THESE ARE THE THINGS FOR WHICH ONE IS NOT LIABLE ON ACCOUNT OF PIGGUL: THE FISTFUL, THE INCENSE, THE FRANKINCENSE, THE PRIESTS' MEAL-OFFERING, THE ANOINTED PRIEST'S MEAL-OFFERING, AND THE BLOOD?—Rather, [he informs us] that if it ascended [the altar], it does not descend.[2] But we have learnt it: [Flesh] that is kept overnight, or that goes out [of its permitted boundaries], or which is unclean, or which was slaughtered [with the intention of being consumed] after time or without bounds, if it ascended [the altar], does not descend?[3]—Rather, [he informs us] that if it was taken down [from the altar],[4] it must be taken up [again]. But surely we have learnt:[5] Just as it does not descend once it had ascended, so it does not ascend after having descended![6]—That ['Ulla's teaching] is only when the fire [of the altar] has taken hold of it.[7] But this too 'Ulla has already stated once? For 'Ulla said: They learnt this only where the fire had not taken hold of it; but if the fire had taken hold of it, it must go up [again]!—

(4) If the sacrifice is made *piggul* and one eats these things enumerated here, he is not liable to *piggul*. E.g., if the priest took off the fistful with the intention of eating the remainder on the morrow, he thereby renders the whole sacrifice *piggul*; nevertheless he incurs no liability for eating the fistful itself. For *piggul* applies only to that which is permitted through something else (e.g., the *rest* of the meal-offering is ordinarily permitted for consumption through the taking of the fistful), whereas the fistful is not permitted through anything else. The same applies to the incense, the frankincense, and the others enumerated in the Mishnah.—Votive meal-offerings brought by ordinary priests and the statutory bi-daily offerings of the anointed priest (v. Lev. VI, 13 *seq*.) were wholly burnt on the altar without the rite of taking the fistful; thus they were not permitted by anything else. Drink-offerings could be brought separately or as an accompaniment to animal sacrifices. R. Meir rules that whether they are brought entirely by themselves, nothing else having been vowed, or they are brought actually as an addition to an animal sacrifice, but on the following day, they do not involve liability for *piggul*, because in that case they are not permitted through something else (the sacrificing of the animal), but through themselves. If however they are brought at the same time as the animal, they are permitted through the sacrificing of same, and therefore involve *kareth*. The Sages however maintain that even then we do not regard them as permitted through the animal sacrifice, since they could have been presented separately on the morrow. (5) A liquid measure = 549.391338 cu. centimeters (J.E. art. 'Weight—Measures', Vol. XII. pp. 483[2] and 490, Table). (6) Lev. XIV, 10, 15-18. The residue of this was consumed.

a (1) If the priest rendered the guilt-offering which it accompanied *piggul*, one is not liable to *kareth* for consuming the oil. Though the efficacy of the oil rite is dependent on the prior application of the blood of the guilt-offering on the leper, nor may it be consumed unless the blood of the offering was duly sprinkled; nevertheless since the oil can be brought ten days after the offering, it is not regarded as permitted for consumption through it, and therefore does not involve *kareth* on account of *piggul* even when the oil is brought on the same day. (2) Where it is brought on the same day, to which case R. Meir refers. (3) As explained in *supra* n. 4. (4) Where the law of *piggul* is stated. (5) The Talmud explains this anon. (6) This reason is apparently why it should *retain* its status as *piggul*. (7) If it is not fit for burning on the altar because it is *piggul*. (8) And so, if one burns the fistful with the intention of consuming the remainder on the morrow, how can the meal-offering become *piggul* if we do not regard the burning of the fistful as a valid act, seeing that a sacrifice cannot become *piggul* unless its *mattirin* are offered (*supra* 42*b*)? Hence we must say that the fistful loses its *piggul* status, so that by its burning on the altar the *mattirin* are duly offered, and for that reason the remainder becomes *piggul*. This is then what he means: seeing that it is acceptable (a valid service) in point of making the rest fit to be *piggul*, it is surely acceptable in respect of itself!

b (1) In respect of what law does it lose its *piggul* status? (2) It loses its *piggul* status insofar that once it is taken up on to the altar it remains there, and we do not remove it as *piggul*. (3) And this includes an instance of *piggul*. (4) After having been placed on it. (5) Emended text (Sh. M). (6) Though it should not have been taken down in the first place. (7) Then, even if it is taken down, it must be taken up again. Whereas the Baraitha refers to a case where the fire had not yet taken hold of it.

לא א ב מיי' פי"ח מהלכות פסה"מ הל' ח:
לב ג מיי' שם הלכה ז:

ומנחת כהנים ומנחת כהן משיח והדם והנסכים הבאין בפני עצמן דברי רבי מאיר וחכמים אומרים אף הבאין עם הבהמה לוג שמן של מצורע ר' שמעון אומר אין חייבין עליו משום פיגול ורבי מאיר אומר חייבין עליו משום פיגול שדם האשם מתירו *וכל שיש לו מתירין בין לאדם בין למזבח חייבין עליו משום פיגול העולה דמה מתיר את בשרה למזבח ועורה לכהנים עולת העוף דמה מתיר את בשרה למזבח חטאת העוף דמה מתיר את בשרה לכהנים פרים הנשרפים ושעירים הנשרפים דמן מתיר את אימוריהן ליקרב *ר' שמעון אומר כל שאינו על המזבח החיצון כשלמים אין חייבין עליו משום פיגול:

גמ' אמר עולא *קומץ פיגול שהעלו על גבי המזבח פקע פיגולו ממנו אם אחרים מביא לידי פיגול הוא עצמו לא כל שכן מאי קאמר הכי קאמר אם אינו מתקבל היאך מביא אחרים לידי פיגול מאי קא משמע לן אי דאין חייבין עליו משום פיגול תנינא אלו דברים שאין חייבין עליהם משום פיגול הקומץ א] והקטרת והלבונה ומנחת כהנים ומנחת כהן משיח ב] ומנחת נסכים והדם אלא דאם עלו לא ירדו תנינא ג] *הלן והיוצא והטמא ושנשחט חוץ לזמנו וחוץ למקומו ד] אם עלו לא ירדו ואלא דאם ירדו ה] יעלו הא נמי תנינא *כשם שאם עלו לא ירדו כך אם ירדו לא יעלו לא צריכא שמשלה בהן ו] האור הא נמי אמרה עולא חדא זימנא *דאמר עולא לא שנו אלא שלא משלה בהן ז] האור אבל משלה בהן האור יעלו מהו דתימא הני מילי אבר

רש"י

מנחת נדבת כהנים · שלה כליל ואינה נקמלת הלכך אין אחר מתירה: וכן מנחת כהן משיח · חביתי כהן גדול שמקריב בכל יום מחציתה בבקר ומחציתה בערב (ויקרא ו): ומנחת נסכים לא גרסי' דהא מיפלג פליגי בה ח] ונתן חילוק בין באה עם הזבח לבאה בפני עצמו: והדם · הוא המתיר: והנסכים הבאין בפני עצמן · בין ט] שהתנדבן בפני עצמן כדאמר במנחות (דף קד:) מתנדב אדם מנחת נסכים בין שבאו בגלל זבח אלא שהביא י] היום זבחו ונסכיו למחר דאמר מר מנחתם ונסכיהם אף למחר אבל אם הביאן עם זבחו ופיגל בזבח נתפגלו הנסכים: וחכמים אומרים אף הבאים עם הבהמה · דכיון דיכול להקריב נסכים למחר נמצא שאין הזבח מתירן ליקרב אלא הן מתירין את עצמן: לוג שמן של מצורע · שיריו נאכלין כדיליף בפירקין לקמן (דף מד:): אין חייבין עליו משום פיגול · אם פיגל באשם לא יא] נפגל הלוג ואע"פ שהלוג תלוי באשם כדכתיב על מקום דם האשם (ויקרא יד) ואם לא נתן מדם האשם תחילה אין נתינת השמן כלום אפילו הכי כיון דאדם מביא אשמו עכשיו ולוגו עד עשרה ימים נמצא שאין האשם מתירו וכיון דאין לו מתירין אין חייבין עליו משום פיגול: ר"מ אומר· לוג הבא עם האשם בו ביום חייבין עליו משום פיגול אם פיגל באשם: בין לאדם בין למזבח · או לזה או לזה: דמה מתיר בשרה למזבח · דכתיב (שם א) וזרקו והדר וערכו: ועורה לכהנים · יב] עור העולה אשר הקריבו אין לו אלא לאחר זריקה: חטאת העוף ס' · בגמ' מפרש מנין דנאכל לכהנים: דמן מתיר יג] אימוריהן ליקרב· לפיכך פיגל באימורים בשעת עבודת הדם נתפגלו *פרים: ר' שמעון · אפרים הנשרפין פליג: כל שאין מתן דמו על המזבח החיצון כשלמים · יד] שפיגול כתיב בהו (ויקרא ז) אין חייבין עליו משום פיגול: גמ' פקע פיגולו ממנו · לקמן מפרש למאי הלכתא פקע: מאי קאמר · טו] קבעי למימר פקע פיגולו ממנו וגסיב טעמא דבא לידי פיגול: אם אינו מתקבל · בהקטרה: היאך מביא אחרים לידי פיגול · טז] המקטיר קומץ על מנת שיאכל שירים למחר היאך מנחה מתפגלת אם אין הקטרתו יז] הקטרה והכי קאמר הוא עצמו לא כל שכן שיתקבל אחרי שמתקבל לרצות אחרים לפיגולו: מאי קא משמע לן · למאי מיבעי ליה הא יח] פקע פיגולו: אי · למימרא דאם אכל ממנו יט] אחרי שעלה אין חייבין עליו כרת: כ] תנינן · דבלאו עלה נמי אין חייבין עליו: אלא · להכי אהני פקיעה דכיון שעלה לא ירד: תנינא ושנשחט חוץ לזמנו · דהיינו פיגול: הלן · בשר הלן: אלא · אהני פקיעה שאם ירד לאחר שהעלוהו (לא) יחזור ויעלה: תנינא · כא] *בלאו הכי: לא צריכא · הא דעולא אלא שמשלה בו האור ואשמעינן דנעשה לחמו של מזבח ואפי' כב] ירדו יעלו וההיא דקתני לא יעלו בשלא משלה בו האור: לא שנו · דאם ירדו הנך פסולין משעלו לא יעלה: (בחד אבר

דלא גרסינן מנחת נסכים משום דפליגי בה בסיפא דהך משנה דקתני והנסכים הבאים בפני עצמן דברי רבי מאיר וחכמים אומרים אף הבאין עם הבהמה ובפני עצמן דקאמר היינו *כגון שהתנדב נסכים נג] כדאמר גבי מתנדב אדם מנחת נסכים בכל יום בין הבאין עם הבהמה כגון שהביא זבחו היום ונסכים מכאן ועד עשרה ימים ומיהו יש ליישב גירסת הספרים דמנחת נסכים מיירי במתנדב מנחת נסכים בכל יום וההיא בבאין בפני עצמן מיירי במביא זבחו היום ונסכים ביום מחר אבל קשה שלא היה לו להפסיק בדם והוה ליה למיתני הכי והדם ומנחת נסכים ונסכים הבאין בפני עצמם ושמא איידי דתנא מנחת כהנים ומנחת כהן משיח תנא נמי מנחת נסכים: ולוג שמן של מצורע· נראה דרבי שמעון דהכא הוא רבנן דלעיל גבי נסכים וקשה אמאי לא עירב דתרוייהו חד טעמא הוא*: נאמר

תוספות

הגהו דאין לו כג] מתירין כדי נסבה וקשה התינח קומץ אלא לבונה ומנחת כהנים תיפוק לי משום דאין בהם הרצאה ועוד דגבי דם כד] קאמר בפירוש משום מתיר והיכי משכחת לה דמחייב משום פיגול דאי אכיל ליה קודם שעשה מתנות אם כן ליכא הרצאה ואי מן הדם הנשאר במזרק לאחר שעשה מתנות ההוא לאו מתיר הוא ואם מאותו *שזרק על המזבח הא פקע פיגול ממנו ושמא לא שייך למימר גבי דם פקע פיגולו כי אם גבי הקטרה דוקא שנעשה לחמו של מזבח ותימה הוא כה] אם לא יתחייב בשירי הדם משום פיגול הא יש להם מתירין שהמתנות מתירות לשפיכות שיריים *למזבח כמו שמתירות את האימורים ושמא כו] *כמו מתחילה כל טיפה וטיפה ראויה לזריקה חשיב כוליה דם מתיר ונראה לפרש דהיינו טעמא דקומץ וכולהו דאי הוי בני חובא הוי דינן משקדש בכלי וקידוש כלי הייט הרצאה כז] דידיה *כיון דאינהו גופייהו מתיר אחד כדאמר לעיל (דף לד·) גבי טומאה יש לו מתירין משיקרבו מתירין אין לו מתירין משיקדש בכלי:

והלבונה · ואם תאמר והרי לבונה הקומץ מתירה כח] ואף על פי שיכול להקטירה קודם הקומץ כדאמר בהקומץ זוטא (מנחות סז:) מכל מקום קודם הקמילה ודאי נראה דאין להקטירה ויש לומר דמכל מקום לא הויא לבונה דומיא דשלמים דלבונה היא גופה מתיר שמתרת שירים לאכילה ועיקר פיגול ילפינן כט] משלמים ואע"ג דשייך פיגול באימורים וכמה דלא מיקטרי אימורים כהנים לא מצי אכלי מכל מקום לא חשיבי מתיר כיון דאם נטמאו או אבדו שרי בשר באכילה ועוד יש לומר דלבונה אין לה מתיר בעבודת המזבח ולא הויא דומיא דשלמים שעבודת המזבח מתירן כגון זריקת הדם *ואם תאמר אמאי לא חשיב הכא עצים כי היכי דחשיב לבונה אע"ג דלא חזיא לאכילה דאי הוה להו מתירין היה חייב עליהם משום פיגול כמו שחייבין עליהם משום טומאה אבל אין להם מתירין והן עצמן מתירין ויש לומר דלא שייך למיתני עצים דהיכי דמי אי כגון מתנדב עצים ל] לרבי דאמר בהקומץ רבה (מנחות כ:) דטעונים קמיצה והגשה הוי דינם כמנחה ופטור על הקומץ וחייב על השירים ואי בעצים דמערכה לא שייך בהו מחשבה דאי במחשב בשעת הולכה ע"מ להקטירו למחר לא] *היו הולכת עצים למערכה לכולי עלמא לאו עבודה היא ומיהו לחריפי דפומבדיתא בסוף הקומץ זוטא (שם דף יז·) משכחת לה בהקטיר שומשום על מנת להקטיר שומשום למחר דהקטרה מפגלת הקטרה ושמא אע"ג דחייבין על העצים משום טומאה אין חייבין עליהם משום פיגול דלאו קרבן גמור הם לרבנן דפליגי עליה דרבי בפרק הקומץ רבה (שם כ:) דלא בעו מליחה דמכשירי קרבן הם לב] *דלא קרבן ומיהו קשה דמאי שנא פיגול מטומאה דאי משום דילפינן (לעיל דף כח:) פיגול משלמים טומאה נמי כתיב בשלמים (ויקרא ז) ועוד דפיגול אתי לקמן (דף מה.) עון עון מנותר ונותר חילול חילול מטומאה: מנחת נסכים · פי' בקונטרס

[יומא ס. לקמן מו. חולין קיז:]
נעיל יד. לקמן מו: שבועות ז.
תמורה ג: [כריתות יד.]
לקמן סד.
לקמן סד.
באימורין צ"ק
לקמן סה:
רש"ק מ"ו
בין צ"ק
[סתייע כתב ישוב על זה]

שמשם צ"ק
ליסוד צ"ק
כיון שמתחלה כו' צ"ק
וכיון דאינהו גופייהו מתירין אחרים לא מהני קידוש בכלי כדאמרינן גבי טומאה כו' צ"ק
[וע"ע תוס' מנחות יד. ד"ה והלבונה]
צ"ל הא צ"ק
צ"ל ולא צ"ק

שיטה מקובצת

א] הקומץ והלבונה והקטרת: ב] תיבות ומנחת נסכים נמחק: ג] תנינא ואלו אם עלו לא ירדו הלן: ד] תיבות אם עלו לא ירדו נמחק: ה] ירדו דלא יעלו תנינא ותיבות הא נמי נמחק ובס"י איתא תיבת נמי: ו] בהן את האור: ז] בהן את האור אבל משלה בהן את האור: ח] בה ונותן חילוק: ט] שהתנדבו: י] זבחו היום ונסכיו למחר כו' ונסכיהם אפילו למחר: יא] לא נתפגל: יב] לכהנים· דכתיב עור העולה אשר הקריב: יג] דמן מתיר את אימוריהן ליקרב לפיכך כו' בשעת זריקת הדם נתפגלו: יד] כשלמים· שהפיגול כתוב בהן: טו] קאמר דבעי למימר: טז] פיגול והמקטיר: יז] אם אין הקטרתו של קומץ הקטרה והא בעינן קרבו מתירין אלא ודאי קרבו מתיריו קרינן ביה דפקע פיגולא ממנו ולכן קבע השירים בפיגול והכי קאמר: יח] הא פקיעת פיגול הס"ד: יט] ממנו אחר שעלה: כ] מה"ד תנינא: כא] תנינא דלאו: כב] ואפילו ירד יעלה והתניא כו' משעלו לא יעלו הס"ד ותיבת בחד נמחק: כג] מתירין א) ס"א לא גרסינן ובת"כ ליתא א"נ כדי: כד] דקאמר בפירוש משום כו' שעשה המתנות א"כ: כה] אמאי לא יתחייב: כו] כיון שמתחלה: כז] הרצאה דידהו כיון דאינהו גופייהו אין להם מתיר אחד כדאמר לעיל ולהלן (דף מה ע"ב) גבי: כח] מתירה להקטרה: כט] ילפינן מבשר שלמים והתם לא הוי מתיר לאחר ואע"ג כו' באימורים ואע"ג דמתיר הבשר דכל כמה דלא מצי אכלי בשר מכל מקום: ל] עצים ולרבי: לא] למחר הא הולכת עצים: לב] הם ולא קרבן: לג] נסכים כדאמרינן מתנדב אדם:

א) ר"ל דסס"א גרסי בתוס' אחר תיבת מתירין לא גרסינן ובתו"כ ליתא א"נ כדי נסבה [ומיהו בתו"כ שלפנינו בס' לו איתא את הך מן וצ"ע]·

גליון הש"ס מתני' רש"א כל שאינו· עיין לקמן דף מה ע"ב תוספות ד"ה אבל:

עין משפט
נר מצוה

לג א מיי' פ"ג מהל' פסולי המוקדשין הלכה י:

לד ב ג מיי' פי"ח מהלכות פסה"מ הלכה כא:

[עיין לעיל טו: תוספות ד"ה אלא למעוטי]

לה ד מיי' שם הלכה יג:

מסורת הש"ס

אבר דמחבר איכא יג]למ"ד כיון דמשלה האור במקצתו נקלט כולו בקדושה: אבל קומץ דמיפרת · אימא במאי יד] דמשלה מקומץ משלה אידך כדקאי קמ"ל דכוליה כחד אבר דמי: הלכך · כיון טו] דמחשבת ליה מחובר אפי' לא העלהו אלא חציו ומשלה בו האור נקלט אף זה שעל הקרקע טז] ומעלה דהא כי אסקיה לכוליה נמי לא היה לו להעלותו אם ירד אלא משום ההוא שמשלה בו האור וקאמרת דאם ירד השאר יעלה אלמא אהני לכוליה ואע"ג דמיפרת הלכך לא שנא עלה כולו ולא שנא לא עלה אלא מקצתו: פקע איסורן מהן· איסור פיגול לכדאמרן שאם (א)ירד תורה אור יעלה ואיסור נותר וטמא נמי להכי יז]

אבר דמחבר אבל קומץ דמיפרת אימא לא קמ"ל אמר רב אחאי הלכך [א]האי קומץ פיגול דפלגיה מחית אארעא ופלגיה אסקיה אמערכה ומשלה בו [א] האור מסיקנא ליה לכוליה לכתחלה: אמר רבי יצחק אמר רבי יוחנן [ב] [ב]הפיגול והנותר והטמא שהעלן לגבי מזבח פקע איסור מהן אמר רב חסדא מרי דיכי [ג] מזבח מקוה טהרה אמר רבי זירא [ג]שמשלה בהן האור מתיב ר' יצחק בר ביסנא אחרים אומרים °וטומאתו עליו מי שטומאה פורחת ממנו יצא בשר שאין טומאה פורחת ממנו ואם איתא הרי טומאה פורחת ממנו על ידי האור אמר רבא על ידי מקוה קאמרינן מידי מקוה כתיב אלא אמר רב פפא בבשר שלמים עסקינן דלא חזי להקרבה רבינא אמר [ד] וטומאתו עליו מי שטומאה פורחת ממנו כשהוא שלם יצא בשר [ה] דבר שאין טומאה פורחת כשהוא שלם אלא כשהוא חסר: גופא [ד]וטומאתו עליו בטומאת הגוף הכתוב מדבר [ו] אתה אומר בטומאת הגוף או אינו אלא בטומאת בשר נאמר כאן [ז] טומאתו ונאמר להלן טומאתו (עליו) [*בו] מה להלן בטומאת הגוף הכתוב מדבר אף כאן בטומאת הגוף הכתוב מדבר ר' [ח] יוסי אומר הואיל ונאמרו קדשים בלשון רבים ונאמרה טומאה בלשון יחיד בטומאת הגוף הכתוב מדבר רבי אומר ואכל בטומאת הגוף הכתוב מדבר אחרים [ט] אמרו וטומאתו עליו מי שטומאה פורחת ממנו יצא בשר שאין טומאה פורחת ממנו אמר מר רבי אומר ואכל בטומאת הגוף הכתוב מדבר מאי משמע אמר רבא כל קרא דלא מפרש ליה רב יצחק בר אבודימי וכל מתניתא דלא מפרשא לה [י] רב זעירי לא מיפרשא הכי אמר ר' יצחק בר אבודימי הואיל ופתח הכתוב בלשון נקבה וסיים בלשון נקבה ולשון זכר באמצע בטומאת הגוף הכתוב מדבר מתניתא דתניא אם נאמרו קלות למה נאמרו חמורות ואם נאמר חמורות למה נאמר קלות אם נאמר קלות ולא חמורות הייתי אומר על הקלות בלאו ועל החמורות במיתה לכך נאמר חמורות ואם נאמר חמורות ולא נאמרו קלות הייתי אומר על החמורות יהא חייב ועל הקלות יהא פטור לכך נאמר קלות מאי קלות ומאי חמורות אילימא קלות מעשר חמורות תרומה הייתי אומר במיתה השתא נמי הא במיתה [יא][ותו]ואי לא נאמר הייתי אומר במיתה דיו לבא מן הדין להיות כנדון אלא קלות טומאת שרץ חמורות טומאת מת ובמאי אי בתרומה אידי ואידי [יב] הוא במיתה ותו לכך נאמרו המורות דבלאו הא במיתה היא (ואי לא נאמר הייתי אומר במיתה דיו לבא מן הדין להיות כנדון) ואי באכילת מעשר
אם

[פקע] שלא יתחייב האוכלו מידי: מרי דיכי · בעל השמועה יח] הזאת: מזבח מקוה טהרה הוא · לטהר את הטומאה משום דהעלוהו: וטומאתו עליו כו'·לקמן מייתינלה במתניתין(ב) למימרא דבטומאת הגוף יט] מדבר והאי קרא קאי (ויקרא ז) והנפש אשר תאכל בשר מזבח השלמים אשר לה' וטומאתו עליו יכול טומאת הבשר דנימא דהאי עליו אבשר קאי ונימא דטהור שאכל את הטמא חייב ת"ל וטומאתו עליו משמע שעדיין היא עליו ביכולין ליטהר הכתוב מדבר וזהו הגוף שטומאה פורחת ממנו על ידי טבילה ואם איתא דבשר קדשים יכול ליטהר על ידי מזבח מהיכא ילפי אחרים כ]דלא בבשר משתעי קרא הרי טומאה פורחת ממנו: בבשר שלמים עסקינן · דקרא בשלמים כתיב דאינו ראוי למזבח ואינ מפריח כא] מטומאתו: רבינא אמר · אף כב] אברין הראויין למזבח כתיבי הכא דכתיב (שם) אשר לה' לרבות האימורים ואפילו הכי לא תקשה דשפיר ילפינן מיניה דטומאה לאו עלייהו קאי מדכתיב וטומאתו עליו דמשמע בראוי להפריח טומאתו כשהוא שלם כעין שקיבלה כג] עליו בעיניה משמע: בטומאת הגוף הכתוב מדבר· שהרי עוסק בה והולך דכתיב (שם) כל טהור יאכל בשר וסמיך ליה והנפש אשר תאכל בשר וגו' אע"פ שהתחיל להזכיר הגוף בלשון נקבה והנפש אשר תאכל וכתיב וטומאתו עליו לשון זכר דמשמע דקאי אבשר כד] בטומאת הגוף דבר ולא בטומאת בשר: או אינו אלא בטומאת בשר · דהא עליו לשון זכר הוא והאוכל הוזכר בלשון נקבה: הכי גרסינן כה]טומאתו טומאתו לג"ש · ויליף מביאת מקדש דכתיב ביה עוד טומאתו בו (במדבר יט): הכי גרסי' נאמר כאן טומאתו ונאמר להלן טומאתו: הואיל ונאמרו קדשים בלשון רבים· שלמים לכון רבים הן וטומאה בלשון יחיד דכתיב וטומאתו עליו ולא כתיב וטומאתם עליהם: רבי אומר ואכל בטומאת הגוף הכתוב מדבר· מקרא שלאחריו יוכיח על זה דכתיב בתריה (ויקרא ז) נפש כי תגע בכל טמא וגו' ואכל מבשר זבח השלמים וגו' ולקמיה מפרש היכי משמע ליה מואכל דקרא בתרא הוכחה על כו] ראשון שבטומאת הגוף הכתוב מדבר: וטומאתו עליו · משמע שעדיין לא נטהר ממנו במי שטומאתו פורחת ממנו הכתוב מדבר דאי בבשר לעולם כז] הוא עליו: מאי משמע · מקרא דבתריה דקמא בטומאת הגוף דלמא בתרא בטומאת הגוף כח] כדכתיב נפש אשר תגע בכל טמא וקמא בטומאת בשר מדלא כתיב וטומאתה עליה דמיסתמע דאוהנפש אשר תאכל בשר קאי: וכל מתניתא דלא מפרש לה זעירי · לקמיה מפרש מאי היא: הואיל ופתח הכתוב השני בלשון נקבה וסיים בלשון נקבה ולשון זכר באמצע · דכתיב (שם) נפש כי תגע בכל טמא ואכל מבשר זבח השלמים ונכרתה הנפש וגו' ולא כתיב ואכלה מבשר זבח כט] הוי אף הראשון אל תתמה עליו אם פתח וסיים בלשון נקבה ולשון זכר באמצע אף [על פי כן] בטומאת הגוף הכתוב מדבר ומסתברא הכי שהרי בטומאת הגוף היה עוסק והולך וכבר פסק מלדבר בטומאת בשר דהכי כתיב קרא (שם) והבשר אשר יגע בכל טמא לא יאכל הרי טומאת בשר והבשר כל טהור יאכל בשר פסק מטומאת בשר והתחיל בטומאת הגוף וסמיך ליה והנפש אשר תאכל וגו' ומשום דהזכיר הכתוב את האוכלו בלשון נקבה וכתב וטומאתו עליו בלשון זכר הייתו סבורים שבטומאת בשר מדבר עכשיו ל] מקרא השני יוכיח שאף הוא בלשון הזה מדבר ואי קשיא שני כריתות בטומאת הגוף למה שלש כריתות הן בטומאת הגוף לא] ולקמיה מפרש בהאי פירקין (דף מו.) למאי איצטריכו: מתניתא · לב] דלא מפרש לה זעירי מאי היא איזה *משנה לא פירש יפה: אם נאמרו קלות · לענין אכילת קדשים בטומאת הגוף שנויה בת"כ לקמיה מפרש לג] ואזיל מאי קלות ומאי המורות ומאי הייתי אומר: אי נימא קלות מעשר המורות תרומה · שנאמרו שניהם בפרשה אחת (ויקרא כב) ולא יאכל מן הקדשים כי אם רחץ בשרו במים ואוקימנא ליה במעשר במסכת יבמות (דף עד:) דכתיב כי אם רחץ הא אם רחץ יאכל ואף על פי שלא העריב שמשו הרי טמא שאכל מעשר בלאו וכתיב ובא השמש וטהר ואחר יאכל מן הקדשים ואוקימנא בתרומה וכתיב בההוא ענינא אבל תרומה ומתו בו כי וגו' וקאמר התנא *אם נאמר מעשר לד] מה שאמור בו ולא נאמר תרומה הייתי אומר במיתה אבל השתא דנאמרו אינו במיתה בתמיה והא מיתה כתיבא ביה: ותו אם לא נאמרו הייתי אומר במיתה · בתמיה מהיכא תיתי לי לה] בה מיתה הא לא מייתינן לה אלא בקל וחומר ממעשר ודיו לבא מן הדין להיות כנדון מה מעשר בלאו ולא במיתה אף תרומה בלאו ולא במיתה: אלא קלות והמורות דקאמר · אטומאה קאי דכתיב התם טומאת מת וטומאת שרץ דכתיב (ויקרא כב) והנוגע בכל טמא נפש [וגו'] לו] או איש אשר יגע בכל שרץ דכתיב בתרווייהו אכילת מעשר ותרומה ועונשן וקאמר אם נאמרה טמא שרץ ולא נאמרה טומאת מת כו' ובמאי לז] ועל איזו אכילה אי בתרומה על שתיהן הטומאות הוא באכילת תרומה במיתה ומאי על הקלות בלאו דקתני:
ואם

שיטה מקובצת
א] בו את האור מסקינא: ב] הפיגול והנותר והטמא כו' · וא"ת טעמא מאי בנותר וטמא בשלמא בקומץ דהוי מתיר משום (דעולה) [טעמא דעולא] דלעיל דאם אחרים כו' אבל האי טעמא לא שייך בנותר וטמא [אפי' אי אמרינן] דמשמע אף באימורים וי"ל משום תעשו לחמו של מזבח ולא נהירא דא"כ לעיל אמאי קאמר עולא בקומץ (נמי) דטעמא משום דאחרים מביא כו' (אבל האי) [דהאי] טעמא לא שייך בנותר וטמא דמשמע דמיירי אף באברים וי"ל (ה כ א) [דאין הכי] נמי [דקאי] האי [טעמא] משום אם אחרים כו' מיהו כיון דגלי בקומץ מהאי [טעם דאם משלה בו את] האור מפקיע הפיגול גלי בכל שאר איסורים: ג] דיכי וכי מזבח מקוה טהרה הוא אר"ז שמשלה בהן את האור: ד] אמר אף אימורים במשמע וטומאתו: ה] יצא בשר שאין טומאה פורחת ממנו כשהוא שלם: ו] הגוף הכתוב מדבר אי אתה: ז] כאן · ס"י וטומאתו עליו ונאמר להלן עוד טומאתו בו אמור עליהם לדורותיכם כל איש אשר יקריב מכל זרעכם אל (הקודש) [הקדשים] אשר (יקריבו) [יקדישו] בני ישראל (אל ה') [לה'] וטומאתו עליו: ח] ר' אחיא אומר הואיל ונאמרו קדשים בלשון רבים פ"ה שלמים קשה דהוי ליה למימר הואיל ונאמרו שלמים בלשון רבים · ועוד קשה דבלשון יחיד לא היה יכול לומר אלא בלשון שלמים וא"כ משמע דאף שלמים הוא לשון יחיד ועוד קשה דמאי קאמר וכתיב וטומאתו עליו בלשון יחיד עליהם מבעיא ליה היאך יכול לומר עליהם הא אבשר זבח קאי דבלשון יחיד משמע לכך נראה כגי' הספרים ונאמר להלן כל איש אשר (יקריב) [יקרב] כו' והתם ע"כ בטומאת הגוף איירי דאי אבשר הוי ליה למימר עליהם כי היכי דכתיב קדשים והשתא שפיר יליף ר' אחיא מדכתיב אל הקדשים ולא כתיב אל הקודש אשר יקדישו אלא [לשון רבים] וסיפא לא נקט עליהם ש"מ בטומאת הגוף מיירי וכמו דכאן קאי אטומאת הגוף ה"נ בשלמים קאי אטומאת הגוף: ט] אחרים אומרים: י] לה זעירא ותיבת רב נמחק:

[כ"ה בב"ח וכצ"ל כנראה מפרש"י]

הגהות הב"ח
(א) רש"י ד"ה פקע איסורן וכו' ירד יעלה · נ"ב פי' אבל לענין זה לא פקע איסורו [שאם אכלו לאחר] שהעלו חייב והיינו לדבר מדפי' במתניתין דחשיב דם וקומץ שאין בהם משום פיגול משום דאיהו גופיה מתיר תיפוק ליה דלא שייך [ביה פיגול דאי] הלכך קודש שהעלו הרי לא קרב כמתיר כמאותו ו לאחר [שהעלו הרי פקע] איסורו מהן אלא ודאי דלא פקע איסורו מהן שאם ירדו יעלו וזה הכריח לרש"י לפרש כן: (ב) ד"ה וטומאתו וכו' במתניתין וכצ"ל למימרא:

נ"ל ברייתא

נ"א אם נאמר מעשר שאמור בו לאו ולא נאמר כו' נ"ק

יא] במיתה ותו' ס"י א)ותו לכך נאמרו חמורות דבלאו הא במיתה הוא: נאמר חמורות הייתי אומר: יב] אידי ואידי הא במיתה הוא [ותו] לכך נאמרו חמורות כו' הוא ואי מעשר והשאר נמחק: יג] איכא למימר כיון דמשלה האור במקצתו נקלט כולה בקדושה: יד] דמשלה משלה תיבת מקומץ נמחק: טו] כיון דהשבת ליה: טז] הקרקע ויעלה דהא: יז] וטמא להכי נמי ושלא: יח] השמועה הלזו הס"ד: יט] הגוף הכתוב מדבר וזהו טומאת הגוף ואהא: כ] דלאו בבשר: כא] ואין מפריח טומאתו: כב] אף אאברין: כג] שקיבלה דעליו: כד] אבשר אפ"ה בטומאת: כה] גרסינן ת"ל טומאתו: כו] על הראשון: כז] לעולם היא: כח] הגוף קאי כדכתיב נפש כי תגע בכל טמא וכו' דמשתמע מיניה דאוהנפש אשר: כט] זבח א"כ לא חש הכתוב לשונו אף על הראשון אל תתמה כו' באמצע דאף הוא בטומאת הגוף: ל] עכשיו המקרא ז: לא] הגוף ולקמן בפירקין מפרש ותיבת בהאי נמחק: לב] מתניתא דמפרש ליה זעירי מאי היא איזה ברייתא פירש יפה הס"ד: לג] מפ"ש לה ואזיל: לד] מעשר כמה שאמור בו ולא כו': לה] תיבת בה נמחק לו] נפש וגו' או איש אשר יגע בכל שרץ כתיב בתרייהו אכילת מעשר: לז] ובמאי על איזו אכילה אי בתרומה על שתי הטומאות:

א) נראה דצ"ל לכך נאמרו חמורות דבלאו הא במיתה הוא ותו ואי לא נאמרו חמורות הייתי אומר ור"ל דהס"י לא גרסי כלל בההוא להשתא נמי הא במיתה ·

You might think that this holds good only of [43b] a limb, which is all one; but as for the fistful, which is divisible, I would say [that it is] not [so].[8] Therefore he informs us [otherwise]. R. Aḥai said: Therefore, when half of the fistful, which is *piggul*, is lying on the ground, and half has been taken up on the wood-pile [on the altar], and the fire has taken hold of it, we must take up the whole of it, even at the very outset.

R. Isaac said in R. Joḥanan's name: If *piggul, nothar*, or unclean [flesh] is taken up to the altar, their forbidden status leaves them. Said R. Ḥisda: O author of this [statement]! Is then the altar a ritual bath of purification!—Said R. Zera: [This law applies] where
a the fire has taken hold of it.[1]

R. Isaac b. Bisna objected: Others[2] say: [When Scripture writes, *But the soul that eateth of the flesh of the sacrifice of peace-offerings* . . .] *having his uncleanness upon him* [*that soul shall be cut off from his people*],[3] [it implies] one whose uncleanness can leave him, thus excluding flesh, whose uncleanness cannot leave it.[4] But if this is correct,[5] surely the uncleanness does leave it, through the fire?—Said Raba: We mean, through a *mikweh*.[6] Is then a *mikweh* written [in the text]?—Rather said R. Papa: We are dealing with the flesh of peace-offerings, which is not eligible for presenting [on the altar].[7] Rabina said: '*Having his uncleanness upon him*' implies, one whose uncleanness leaves him while he is yet whole; thus flesh is excluded, because uncleanness does not leave it while it is whole, but only when it is defective.[8]

[To turn to] the main text: '*Having his uncleanness upon him*': Scripture speaks of uncleanness of the person. You say, Scripture speaks of uncleanness of the person: yet perhaps it is not so, but rather of uncleanness of the flesh? Here '*having his uncleanness* [*upon him*]' is said; while elsewhere it says, *his uncleanness is yet upon him*:[9] as there Scripture speaks of uncleanness of the person, so here too Scripture speaks of uncleanness of the person. R. Jose said: Since the '*holy things*' are mentioned, in the plural, whilst '*uncleanness*' is stated in the singular, Scripture must refer to uncleanness of
b the person.[1] Rabbi said: '*And eat*' [shews that] Scripture speaks of uncleanness of the person.[2] Others say: '*Having his uncleanness upon him*' [implies] one whose uncleanness leaves him, thus excluding flesh, whose uncleanness cannot leave it.

A Master said: 'Rabbi said: "*And eat*" [shews that] Scripture speaks of uncleanness of the person.' How does this imply it?[3]—Said Raba, Every text which R. Isaac b. Abudimi, and every Mathnitha [Baraitha] which Ze'iri did not explain, are not explained. Thus did R. Isaac b. Abudimi say: Since the Writ commences in the feminine form and ends in the feminine, while [it employs] the masculine form in the middle, the Writ must speak of uncleanness of the person.[4]

c 'A Mathnitha'?[1]—For it was taught: If the lighter ones were stated, why were the more stringent ones stated; and if the more stringent ones were stated, why were the lighter ones stated?[2] If the lighter ones were stated and not the more stringent ones, I would say: The lighter ones involve a negative injunction,[3] and the more stringent ones involve death;[4] therefore the more stringent ones are stated.[5] While if the more stringent were stated and not the lighter, I would say: The stringent ones involve culpability, but the lighter ones do not involve culpability at all; therefore the lighter ones are stated.

Now, what are the lighter ones and the more stringent ones? Shall we say [that] the lighter ones are the tithe, and the more stringent ones are *terumah*?[6] [Can you then say,] 'I would say: The more stringent ones involve death'? Surely now it too involves death![7] Moreover, if it were *not* stated, would I say that it involves death? Surely it is sufficient for the conclusion to be as its premise?[8] Again if 'the lighter ones' mean uncleanness of a reptile, and 'the
d more stringent ones' uncleanness of a corpse,[1] to what then [does it refer]?[2] If to *terumah*? both involve death![3] Moreover, [can you say,] 'Therefore the more stringent ones are stated, [to teach] that they involve a negative injunction [only]?' but surely it in-

(8) Only the flour which has actually been burnt through must be taken up again, but not the rest.

a (1) Then it belongs, as it were, to the altar. (2) This usually refers to R. Meir; Hor. 13b. (3) Lev. VII, 20. (4) The Heb. *we-ṭumatho 'alaw* might mean, *having its uncleanness upon it*, and thus imply that a *clean* person who partakes of the unclean *flesh* of a sacrifice incurs *kareth*. It is explained, however, that the phrase implies that the uncleanness is in force only now and that it can be raised; hence it must refer to the *person*, not to the flesh, which once unclean can never become clean again. (5) That when unclean flesh is carried up to the altar and the fire takes hold of it, it loses its forbidden status. (6) V. Glos. (7) But is eaten; hence it can never become clean. (8) I.e., when the fire has already partially destroyed it. (9) Num. XIX, 13. Emended text.

b (1) Sh. M.: Scripture writes, *Whosoever . . . approacheth unto the holy things . . . having* his uncleanness *upon* him, *that soul shall be cut off from before Me* (Lev. XXII, 3). Now there it cannot refer to the sacrifices, for in that case the plural, having *their* uncleanness upon *them* would be required. Hence it must refer to the person, and therefore the same is assumed here. (2) Ibid. VII, 21. The verse reads: *And when any one shall touch any unclean thing* . . . and eat *of the flesh of the sacrifice of peace-offerings*. That verse obviously refers to uncleanness of the person, and thus it illumines the previous verse (v. 20), shewing that that too refers to the same. (3) That the previous verse too refers to the same. Perhaps the previous verse treats of uncleanness of the flesh. (4) The second verse (v. 21) writes: *And when any one* (Heb. *nefesh*, lit. 'soul', fem.) shall touch (Heb. *tiga'*, fem.) *any unclean thing . . . and eat* (*we-akal*, masc. instead of *we-aklah*, fem.) *of the flesh of the sacrifice of peace-offerings, that soul shall be cut off* (*we-nikrethah*, fem.). The preceding verse (v. 20) runs: *But the soul* (fem.) *that eateth* (fem.) *of the flesh* (masc.) . . . *having his* (or *its*) *uncleanness upon him* (or *it*) masc.), *that soul shall be cut off* (fem.) Since the suffixes of '*uncleanness*' and '*upon*' are masc., it might be assumed that they refer to '*flesh*' which is masc. But when we see the same change of gender in the following verse, though that obviously refers to the uncleanness of the person, it is reasonable to say the same here. For Scripture has already treated of uncleanness of the flesh earlier in the section: *And the flesh that toucheth any unclean thing, shall not be eaten; it shall be burnt with fire* (v. 19). It continues with, *And as for the flesh, any one that is clean may eat thereof*, which indicates that *unclean* flesh is no longer being dealt with. Hence when it proceeds, *But the soul that eateth . . . having his uncleanness upon him*, it is logical to assume that uncleanness of the person is referred to, in spite of the change of gender.

c (1) Which *mathnitha* required Ze'iri's explanation? (2) This treats of the interdict of eating sacred food while personally unclean. By 'lighter' and 'more stringent' are meant food of lighter and of more stringent sanctities respectively. The Talmud explains anon which these are. (3) Which is punishable by flagellation. (4) At the hands of heaven. (5) To shew that these too involve a negative injunction only. (6) V. Lev. XXII, 6f: *The soul that toucheth any such* (unclean reptiles etc.) *shall be unclean until the even, and shall not eat of the holy things, unless he bathe his flesh in water. And when the sun is down, he shall be clean; and afterwards he may eat of the holy things*. These two verses are apparently contradictory, for the first implies that he may eat of the '*holy things*' immediately after a ritual bath, even before sunset, while the second teaches that even after the ritual bath he must wait until sunset. Therefore the Rabbis (in Yeb. 74b) made the first refer to tithe, whose sanctity is lighter, and the second to *terumah*, whose sanctity is more stringent. Its greater stringency lies in the fact that a *zar* (a lay Israelite) may not partake of *terumah*, whereas he may partake of tithe. Scripture then goes on to say in v. 9: *They* (i.e., the priests) *shall therefore keep My charge, lest they bear sin for it, and die therein, if they profane it*. This is understood to mean that an unclean priest eating *terumah* is liable to death (v. n. 4.). (7) Scripture does in fact teach that for partaking of *terumah* whilst unclean one is liable to death. (8) This is a general principle: when one thing is learnt from another, *a fortiori* or *a minori*, it cannot go further than its premise. Now, if *terumah* were not stated, it could be learnt from tithe, *a minori*. But it could not involve a greater punishment than tithe, which is subject to a negative injunction only.

d (1) I.e., 'lighter' and 'more stringent' apply not to the '*holy things*' (the sacred food) but to the source of the priest's defilement. Both are enumerated in that passage, viz.: *And whoso toucheth any one that is unclean by the dead . . . or whosoever toucheth any swarming thing* (i.e., a reptile) Lev. XXII, 4-5. (2) To the eating of which sacred food? (3) Whether a priest is unclean in the one way or the other, he is liable to death for eating *terumah*.

volves death? Whilst if it refers to the eating of tithe, [44a] [can you say,] 'If the more stringent ones were not stated, I would say that the more stringent ones involve death'?[4] but surely it would be derived from the uncleanness of a reptile, and it is sufficient for the conclusion to be as the premise![5] — Said Ze'iri: The 'lighter ones' are uncleanness of a reptile, while 'the more stringent ones' are uncleanness through a corpse, and this is what [the Tanna] means: If uncleanness of a reptile were stated, and tithe and *terumah* were enumerated, but uncleanness of a corpse were not stated, I would say: The lighter [defilement] involves a negative injunction in respect of the lighter ['*holy things*'], and death in respect of the more stringent.[6] And since the lighter [defilement] involves death in respect of the more stringent ['*holy things*'], the more stringent [defilement] too involves death in respect of the lighter ['*holy things*']. Therefore the more stringent [defilement] is stated.

WHATEVER HAS AUGHT THAT MAKES IT PERMITTED, WHETHER FOR MAN OR FOR THE ALTAR, INVOLVES LIABILITY ON ACCOUNT OF PIGGUL. Our Rabbis taught: . . . Or perhaps it includes only that which is similar to a peace-offering: as a peace-offering is distinguished in that it is eaten two days and one night, so all that may be eaten two days and one night [are included].[7] How do we know that that which is eaten a day and a night [only, is also included]? Because Scripture saith, [*And if any*] *of the flesh* a [*of the sacrifice of his peace-offerings* etc.],[1] [which includes] all whose remainder is eaten.[2] How do we know [that] a burnt-offering, whose remainder is not eaten, [is included]? Because Scripture says '*the sacrifice*'.[3] Whence do we know to include the bird-offerings and meal-offerings, until I can include a leper's *log* of oil? From the text, '*which they hallow unto Me*': *nothar* is then learned from uncleanness, because 'profanation' is written in connection with both; and *piggul* is learned from *nothar*, because '*iniquity*' is written in connection with both.[4] Now, since it [Scripture] ultimately includes all things, why then are peace-offerings specified? To teach you: as a peace-offering is distinguished in that it has something which permits it both for man and for the altar, so everything which has something which permits it both for man and for the altar involves liability on account of *piggul*. [The sprinkling of] the blood of a burnt-offering permits its flesh for [burning on] the altar, and its skin to the priests. The blood of a bird burnt-offering permits its flesh for the altar. The blood of a bird sin-offering permits its flesh to the priests. The blood of the bullocks that are burnt and the goats that are burnt permits their *emurim* to be offered [on the altar]. And I exclude the fistful, the frankincense, the

(4) I.e., for eating tithe while unclean through a corpse one is liable to death. (5) Hence as a negative injunction only is involved in eating tithe whilst unclean through a reptile, so it is likewise in eating tithe while unclean through the dead. (6) As Scripture states. (7) The law of *piggul* is stated in Scripture in reference to a peace-offering only. The present quotation, which is fragmentary, commences thus: You might think that only a peace-offering involves liability for *piggul;* how do we know that other sacrifices too are included in this law? Because Scripture says in reference to uncleanness: *Speak unto Aaron and to his sons, that they separate themselves from the holy things of the children of Israel, which they hallow unto Me, and that they profane not My holy name* (Lev. XXII, 2). This applies to all sacrifices, since the peace-offering is not specified, and an analogy is drawn anon between defilement and *piggul*, and thus other sacrifices too are included in the law of *piggul*. The passage then proceeds as in the text: perhaps only these sacrifices which are similar to a peace-offering are included etc., but not such sacrifices e.g., a sin-offering, or a thanks-offering, which are eaten only on the day they are sacrificed and the night following.

a (1) Lev. VII, 18. This treats of *piggul*. '*Of the flesh*' is superfluous, since Scripture could say, And if any of his peace-offerings, etc.; hence it is treated as an extension. (2) The remainder after the fats etc. are burnt on the altar. (3) In the text just quoted. That too is superfluous, and therefore extends the law to every sacrifice. (4) Uncleanness, as quoted *supra* n. 7; *nothar: But every one that eateth it shall bear his* iniquity, *because he hath* profaned *the holy thing* (same root as 'hallow') *of the Lord* (Lev. XIX, 8). As the interdict of defilement applies to all sacrifices, so does that of *nothar*. Then the scope of *piggul* is learnt from *nothar*, because '*iniquity*' is written in connection with both: *nothar*, in the text just quoted; *piggul: it shall be an abhorred thing* (piggul), *and the soul that eateth of it shall bear his* iniquity (Lev. VII, 18): as the interdict of *nothar* applies to all sacrifices, so does that of *piggul*.

◁ *For the continuation of the English translation of this page see overleaf.*

אם לא נאמרו חמורות הייתי אומר על החמורות במיתה הא מטומאת שרץ קאתיא ודיו לבא מן הדין להיות כנדון אמר זעירי קלות טומאת שרץ חמורות טומאת מת והכי קאמר אילו נאמר טומאת שרץ ונאמר מעשר ותרומה ולא נאמרה טומאת מת הייתי אומר א] [קלות] על הקלות בלאו ועל החמורות במיתה ומדקלות על החמורות במיתה חמורות ב] נמי על הקלות במיתה לכך נאמרו חמורות: *כל שיש לו מתירין בין לאדם בין למזבח חייבין עליו משום פיגול: תנו רבנן או אינו מביא אלא כיוצא בשלמים מה שלמים מיוחדים נאכלין לשני ימים ולילה אחד אף כל נאכל לשני ימים ולילה אחד נאכל ליום ולילה מנין תלמוד לומר מבשר כל ג] ששירין נאכלין עולה שאין שיריה נאכלין מנין תלמוד לומר זבח מנין לרבות העופות והמנחות עד שאני מרבה לוג שמן של מצורע תלמוד לומר °אשר הם מקדישים לי °ואתי נותר חילול מטומאה ואתי פיגול עון עון מנותר ומאחר שסופו לרבות כל דבר למה נאמר שלמים מעתה לומר לך מה שלמים מיוחדים שיש להן מתירין בין לאדם בין למזבח ד] אף כל שיש לו מתירין בין לאדם בין למזבח חייבין עליהן משום ה] פיגול: העולה דמה מתיר את בשרה למזבח ועורה לכהנים עולת העוף דמה מתיר את בשרה למזבח חטאת העוף דמה מתיר את בשרה לכהנים פרים הנשרפים ושעירים הנשרפים דמם מתיר את אימוריהן ליקרב: ומוציא אני את הקומץ ואת הלבונה והקטרת ו] ומנחת כהנים ומנחת כהן משיח ומנחת נסכים והדם ר"ש אומר מה שלמים מיוחדין ז] *שיש בו על מזבח החיצון וחייבין עליו אף כל שישנן על מזבח החיצון חייבין עליו משום פיגול יצאו פרים הנשרפים ושעירים הנשרפים הואיל ח] שאין על מזבח החיצון כשלמים אין חייבין עליו משום פיגול [אמר מר] כיוצא בשלמים מאי ניהו בכור דנאכל לשני ימים ולילה אחד במאי אתי אי במה מצינו איכא למיפרך מה לשלמים ט] שהן טעונין סמיכה ונסכים ותנופת חזה ושוק אלא °מאם האכל יאכל הני תרי כללי דסמיכי אהדדי נינהו אמר *רבא *כדאמרי במערבא כל מקום שאתה מוצא שני כללות הסמוכים זה לזה הטל פרט ביניהם ודונם בכלל ופרט: עד שאני מרבה לוג שמן של מצורע: הא מני רבי מאיר היא דתניא *לוג שמן של מצורע חייבין עליו משום פיגול דברי רבי מאיר אימא סיפא ומוציא אני מנחת נסכים והדם אתאן לרבנן *דתניא נסכי בהמה חייבין עליהן משום פיגול מפני שדם הזבח מתירן ליקרב דברי רבי מאיר אמרו לו והלא *אדם מביא י] את זבחו היום א)ונסכין מיכן עד עשרה ימים אמר להן אף אני לא אמרתי אלא בבאין עם הזבח אמר רב יוסף הא מני רבי היא דאמר לוג שמן של מצורע מתנותיו שרו ליה ומדמתנותיו שרו ליה מתנותיו מפגלי ליה דתניא ב)לוג שמן של מצורע מועלין בו עד שיזרוק הדם נזרק הדם לא נהנין ולא מועלין רבי אומר מועלין יא] עד שיתן מתנותיו ושוין ג)שאסור באכילה עד שיתן מתן שבע ומתן בהונות אמרוה קמיה דרבי ירמיה אמר ג)גברא רבא כרב יוסף לימא כי הא מילתא

הדרי

א) [ע' תוס' ר"ה ל: ד"ה ונתקלקלו] ב) [לקמן ק: כתובות מג.]

רש"י

ואם לא נאמרו הייתי אומר כו' ל"ג הכא דליכא למיפרך דיו דהא קלות נמי במיתה: ואי באכילת מעשר. קאמר דאם לא נאמרו חמורות הייתי אומר על טומאת שרץ בלאו יב] על טומאת מת במיתה לכך נאמרו טומאת מת חמורות ונאמר בהו לאו דלא תימא בהו מיתה (א) במעשר ואם לא נאמרו יג] *קלות הייתי אומר על החמורות במיתה הא מטומאת שרץ הוא דאתיא בק"ו: ודיו לבא מן הדין להיות כנדון. ולא אמינא בה מיתה אלא לאו: והכי קאמר אילו נאמר טומאת שרץ ונאמר מעשר. בלאו כדאיתא ותרומה במיתה כדאיתא ולא נאמר טומאת מת הייתי אומר קלות על הקלות בלאו יד] בטומאת קלה דשרץ על אכילת קלות כגון מעשר יהא בלאו כדאיתא וקלות על החמורות במיתה וטומאת שרץ על אכילות החמורות כגון תרומה במיתה כדאיתא ומינה הוה גמרינן דמה שרץ קלות על החמורות במיתה אף חמורות טו] *על קלות נמי במיתה דמה לי טומאה חמורה ואכילה קלה מה לי אכילה חמורה וטומאה קלה טז] (וטומאת המת על אכילת מעשר תהא במיתה) לכך נאמרו חמורות טומאת המת יז] על אכילת מעשר שלא תהא במיתה ופירש בה לאו ולא במיתה לומר לך שהיא באזהרה: או אינו מביא כו'. רישא דברייתא בת"כ לענין פיגול קתני יכול לא יהא חייב אלא על השלמים בלבד ת"ל לענין טומאה וינזרו מקדשי ולקמן יליף נותר חילול מטומאה ופיגול בעון עון מנותר: או אינו. מרבה אלא כיוצא בשלמים שהרי כלל ופרט יח] אמור כאן כדמפרש לקמן ונימא מה הפרט מפורש נאכלין לשני ימים כו': ת"ל מבשר. ריבויא הוא דכתיב גבי פיגול (ויקרא ז) מבשר זבח השלמים ועלה קאי והנפש האוכלת ממנו עונה תשא: עד שאני מרבה. כלומר אחרי יט] שאני מרבה ארבה עמהם אף לוג שמן של מצורע אם פיגל בדם האשם נתפגל הלוג: תלמוד לומר. לענין טומאה אשר הם מקדישים גבי וינזרו כתיב ואתי נותר חילול מטומאה מה טומאה הכל בכלל אף נותר הכל בכלל בנותר כתיב כי את קודש ה' חילל (ויקרא יט) ובטומאה כתיב וינזרו ולא יחללו (שם כב) והדר אתי פיגול עון עון מנותר: אף כל שיש לו מתירין. או לאדם או למזבח ועולה ילפא *)מאימורי שלמים וכן אימורי כל הקדשים כ] ובשר כל הקדשים הנאכלין ילפי מבשר שלמים שאין לו מתירין אלא לאדם וחייבין עליו: כיוצא בשלמים מאי ניהו. דקתני לעיל או אינו מביא כו' אלא כא](ב)כיוצא: האכל. כלל מבשר שלמים פרט יאכל חזר וכלל: הני תרי כללי דסמיכי כב] נינהו. שלא נכתב הפרט אלא בסוף: הטל פרט ביניהם. כג] הכתוב אחריהם הטל ביניהם ודונם כו' הלכך אי לאו דרבי רחמנא מבשר כד] תחילה הוה דיינינן ליה במה הפרט מפורש כו': חייבין עליו משום פיגול. אם בא עם האשם ופיגל באשם ואף על גב שאם כה] היה רוצה יכול להביאו מכאן ועד עשרה ימים כדלקמן אית ליה לרבי מאיר דכי הביאו עם האשם דם האשם הוא המתירו למתן בהונות ושיריו לאכילה ששירי הלוג נאכלין כדאמרינן במעשה דלקמן: אמר רב יוסף כו] רבי היא כו'. וסבר לה כרבנן דהואיל ואפשר להביא נסכים לאחר זמן אין דם הזבח מפגלן ואפילו הביאן עמו ולוג שמן נמי הא דקתני כז] נמי פיגול לא שיהא דם האשם מפגלו אלא מתנות שמן עצמו שמזה ממנו שבע הזאות בפנים הם מפגלין אותו אם הזה על מנת לאכול שיריו חוץ לזמנו והוא נאכל ליום ולילה כדמרבינן ליה לקמן עם שאר קדשי קדשים: ומדשמעינן ליה לרבי כח] דאמר לוג שמן של מצורע מתנותיו שרו ליה. לכהנים דאמר אף על פי שנזרק דם האשם יש מעילה בשמן עד שיתן שבע הזאות של צרכי גבוה הלכך מתנותיו מפגלין ליה שהן כט] מתירין: ולא נהנין. מדרבנן עד שיתן מתנותיו ל]: ולא מועלין. דקסבר דם האשם מתירו לכהנים וכל שיש בו שעת היתר לכהנים אין בו מעילה: רבי לא] אומר מועלין בו עד שיתן שבע הזאות של גבוה. אבל מתן בהונות דלאו צורך גבוה הוא ודאי לא פליג רבי: ושוין. שאפילו נתן מתנות גבוה אסור הוא לב] מדרבנן עד שיתן אף מתן בהונות: אמרוה. רבנן להא דרב יוסף:

*) [נ"א מאימורי שלמים לפי שאין להם מתירין אלא למזבח]

הכא

תוספות

נאכל ליום ולילה מנין. לקמן בסוף דם חטאת (דף לח.) דרשינן מהיקישא דזאת התורה מה שלמים מפגלין כו' ונראה דהאי תנא לית ליה ההוא היקישא דאי אית ליה לא היה צריך לכל הנך ייתורים: ואתי נותר חילול מטומאה ואתי פיגול עון עון מנותר. מכאן לג] הוה מצי למידק לקמן (דף נ:) דדבר הלמד בגזירה שוה חוזר ומלמד בגזירה שוה: כיוצא בשלמים מאי ניהו בכור. משמע דבכור דמי לשלמים טפי משאר קדשים ובעלמא אינו כן לד] דאמר מנחות (דף לא:) מה שלמים באין בנדר ונדבה אף כל בא בנדר ונדבה לה]: אלא מאם האכל יאכל. ואע"ג דאמרינן לעיל בסוף פרק שני (דף כח:) בשתי אכילות הכתוב מדבר תרתי שמע מינה מדלא כתיב האכל האכל או יאכל יאכל כדאמר בריש הקומץ רבה (מנחות דף יז:) ומיהו רבי אליעזר דמוקי לה התם בדרשא אחרינא נפקא ליה הך דרשא מקרא אחרינא *וכרבא דמפרש לעיל בסוף פרק שני (דף כח:) כולהו מקרא לו] (אחרינא) [אריכא] ודריש מבשר זבח שלמיו מה שלמים מפגלין ומתפגלין כו' לא כמו שפירש שם בקונטרס מדכתיב זבח שלמים לז] דמשמע דמקיש זבח לשלמים אלא אהך ברייתא סמיך והקשה ה"ר חיים אמאי שביק לשון הברייתא דהוה ליה למימר מה שלמים מיוחדים שיש להם מתירין בין לאדם בין למזבח ועוד דמליסנא דמפגל ומתפגלין לא *ממעיט דם דדם מפגל ומתפגל כדתניא בתוספתא דזריקה מפגלת ומתפגלת שהדם מפגל הבשר ומתפגלת על ידי זריקה אם זרק על מנת לשפוך שיריים למחר: ודונם בכלל ופרט. ומ"מ צריכי ייתורי דלעיל דמכלל ופרט לא מרבי אלא הדומה לפרט בכל צדדין: סד"א

עין משפט נר מצוה

לו א מיי' פ"ח מהלכות מחוסרי כפרה הל' ד

לז ב מיי' פ"ב מהלכות מעילה הלכה ו:

לח ג מיי' פ"ד מהל' מחוסרי כפרה הל' ג

מסורת הש"ס

ז"ל אלא קלות וגו' הנ"ק כלום במקום תיבת קלות

חולין קיח:

טומאת מת על קלות מעשר נמי נ"ק

נ"ק מ"ז

ויקרא כב

ורבא נ"ק

ממעיט נ"ק

ז"ל שישנו על כו'

נ"ק

שם

חולין סו: נ"ק סד: בכורות נא. ע"ש שבועות ח.

תוספתא רפ"ה מנחות פז:

ז"ל רבינא

הגהות הב"ח

(א) רש"י ד"ה ואי באכילת וכו' דלא תימא בהו מיתה אף במעשר ואם לא נאמרו כלום הייתי: (ב) ד"ה כיוצא וכו' כיוצא הס"ד ואח"כ מ"ה הני תרי וכו' בסוף הס"ד ואח"כ מ"ה הטל וכו' ביניהם הס"ד ואח"כ מ"ה האכל כלל וכו' וכלל הס"ד ואח"כ מ"ה ודונם כו' הילכך:

גליון הש"ס

גמ' ואתי נותר חילול. ע"ל דף כו ע"א תוס' ד"ה ע"ג:

[מנחות טו: ע"ש מיהו גם במשנה דלעיל דף מג. תנן לוג שמן של מצורע וכו' וכרי מאיר אומר חייבין עליו משום פיגול ואולי יש לגרוס הכא דתנן לוג שמן וכו' והש"ס קיצר לישנא דמתניתין כמו בכמה שאר דוכתי כמ"ש תוס' סוכה ב. ד"ה בית וכ"כ עוד שם יג. ד"ה ובהן וכן שבועות דף יט: ד"ה שבועות דדרך הש"ס לקצר המשנה שהביא וכ"כ עוד לעיל כד: ד"ה והרי]

שיטה מקובצת

א] אומר קלות על הקלות בלאו ועל החמורות: ב] חמורות על הקלות נמי במיתה לכך: ג] כל ששירין נאכלין: ד] למזבח. ס"י חייבין עליהן משום פיגול אף: ה] פיגול ... ו] והקטרת ומנחת כהנים ומנחת כהן משיח ונסכים ותיבת ומנחת נמחק: ז] מיוחדין שישנו על מזבח החיצון וחייבין עליהן אף כל שישנו: ח] הואיל שאינן על מזבח כו' אין חייבין עליהן משום פיגול ס"א אמר מר כיוצא: ט] לשלמים שכן טעונין סמיכה: י] מביא זבחו היום ונסכיו מיכן עד י' ימים: יא] מועלין בו עד: יב] בלאו ועל טומאת: יג] כלום הייתי אומר כו' הוא דהוה אתי' בק"ו: יד] בלאו טומאת קלה: טו] חמורות דהיינו טומאת מת על מעשר קלות: טז] וטומאה קלה לכך נאמרו כו' והשאר נמחק: יז] המת חמורות על אכילת מעשר ופירש בה לאו ולא מיתה לומר לך שהיא באזהרה בלבד הס"ד: יח] ופרט וכלל אמור: יט] אחרי. ס"י שהתחלתי לרבות ארבה כו': כ] הקדשים מאימורי שלמים ילפי שאין להם מתירין אלא למזבח ואתרבו בשר כל הקדשים שהן הנאכלים: כא] אלא מאם האכל ותיבת כיוצא נמחק: כב] דסמיכי אהדדי נינהו: כג] ביניהם הפרט הכתוב: כד] מבשר הוה דיינינן ליה כו' מפורש כו' ולא הוי אתי אלא בכור הס"ד: כה] שאם רצה היה יכול להביא כו' דם האשם מתירו למתן בהונות ושיריו לאכילה דשירי הלוג נאכלין: כו] יוסף הא מני רבי: כז] דקתני פיגול: כח] לרבי לוג ותיבת דאמר נמחק: כט] שהן מתיריו הס"ד: ל] שיתן מתנותיו שבע הס"ד: לא] רבי. גליון דמודה הוא דכיון שניתנו ממנו המתנות שהן צורך גבוה שוב אין מועלין בהן אע"פ שלא ניתן ממנו לבהונות. ע"כ: לב] הוא באכילה מדרבנן: לג] מכאן הוי מצי למיפרך לקמן כן הוא בס"א: לד] כן וי"ל דהכא איירי לגבי אכילה להכי מרבינן (הדמים) [הדומים] לאכילה. ת' מהר"פ ז"ל: לה] ונדבה לאפוקי בכור: לו] מקרא אריכא ודריש מבשר זבח: לז] שלמים דריש משמע דמקיש:

Continuation of translation from previous page as indicated by ◁

incense, the priests' meal-offering, the anointed priest's meal-offering, and the blood. R. Simeon said: As a peace-offering is distinguished in that it comes on the outer altar [for sprinkling], and it involves liability; so all that come on the outer altar involve liability on account of *piggul;* thus the bullocks which are burnt and the goats which are burnt are excluded; since they do not come on the outer altar, like the peace-offering, they do not involve liability.

The Master said: 'That which is similar to a peace-offering'. What [sacrifice] is it? The firstling, which is eaten two days and one night! But how is this learnt? If by analogy? it can be refuted: as for a peace-offering, [it is subject to the law of *piggul*] because it requires laying [of hands], [the accompaniment of] drink-offerings b [libations], and the waving of the breast and the shoulder?[1] Again if [it is learnt] from [the text], *And if there be at all eaten* [*any of the flesh of the sacrifice of his peace-offerings on the third day . . . it shall be an abhorred thing*] [*piggul*],[2] these are two generalisations which immediately follow each other?[3]—Said Raba: It is as they say in the West:[4] Wherever you find two generalisations close to each other, insert the specific proposition between them, and interpret them as a case of a generalisation followed by a specific proposition c [and followed again by a generalisation].[1]

'Until I include a leper's *log* of oil'. With whom does that agree? With R. Meir. For it was taught: A leper's *log* of oil involves liability on account of *piggul:* that is the opinion of R. Meir. Then consider the next clause: And I exclude the meal-offering of libations and the blood. This agrees with the Rabbis. For it was taught: The drink-offering which accompanies an animal [sacrifice] involves liability on account of *piggul,* because the blood of the sacrifice permits it to be offered [on the altar]: that is R. Meir's view. Said they to him: But a man can bring his sacrifice to-day and the drink-offering even ten days later! I too, he answered them, ruled [thus] only when they come together with the sacrifice!—Said R. Joseph: The author of this is Rabbi, who maintained [that] the applications of the leper's *log* of oil permit it,[2] and since its sprinklings permit it, its sprinklings render it *piggul.* For it was taught: You commit trespass in respect of a leper's *log* of oil until the blood is sprinkled; once the blood is sprinkled, you may not use it, and you do not commit trespass. Rabbi said: You commit trespass until its sprinklings are made. And both agree that it may not be eaten until its seven sprinklings and the applications on the thumbs are made.[3]

This was reported before R. Jeremiah, [whereupon] he exclaimed,

b (1) Whereas a firstling does not require these. (2) Lev. VII, 18. The E.V. has been slightly departed from so as to follow the exact order of the Hebrew, which comes under discussion. The Heb. for '*be at all eaten*' is *heakel yeakel,* i.e., the infinitive of the verb followed by the finite form, which is the usual mode of expression. The Talmud now interprets the two forms as two generalisations (anything which is eaten), while '*peace-offerings*' is a specific proposition. In that case it is a rule of exegesis that the generalisation includes everything which is similar in its general features (even if not in every detail) to the specific proposition. Hence the firstling is included, as generally speaking it is similar to the peace-offering, in spite of differing from it in several details. (3) Whereas the exegetical rule applies to two generalisations which are separated by the specific proposition. (4) *Sc.* Palestine, which lay to the west of Babylon.

c (1) Hence the firstling would be included, but not sacrifices which are eaten one day only, since these differ even in the general features (the difference in length of time allowed for eating is an important one). Therefore recourse must be had to the other texts. (2) V. Lev. XIV, 16 *seq.* Now, Rabbi agrees with the Rabbis that since the drink-offering can be brought after the animal sacrifice which it accompanies, the blood of the sacrifice cannot render it *piggul.* And when the Baraitha teaches that the *log* of oil can be *piggul,* it does not mean that the blood of the guilt-offering which the leper brings renders it *piggul,* but the sprinklings of the oil itself do effect this: i.e., if he sprinkles the oil with the intention of consuming the remainder after time. (3) On trespass v. *supra* 35*b* n.10. Now, the *log* of oil may not be consumed until the blood is sprinkled; therefore until then it is sacred, and if one does consume it, he commits trespass. When the blood has been sprinkled, the oil is Scripturally permitted to the priests, and this Tanna holds that whatever is permitted to the priests does not involve trespass even for a *zar* (lay Israelite). Nevertheless, by Rabbinical law its consumption is forbidden until the seven sprinklings of the oil. Rabbi holds that it is even *Scripturally* forbidden until then, and therefore it still involves trespass. But they both agree that it is forbidden by Rabbinical law until *all* its sprinklings have been made.—From this passage we see that Rabbi holds that the oil is permitted for consumption not by the blood of the sacrifice, but by its own sprinklings.

אם לא נאמרו חמורות הייתי אומר על החמורות במיתה הא מטומאת שרץ קאתיא ודיו לבא מן הדין להיות כנדון אמר זעירי קלות טומאת שרץ חמורות טומאת מת והכי קאמר אילו נאמר טומאת שרץ ונאמר מעשר ותרומה ולא נאמרה טומאת מת הייתי אומר א] [קלות] על הקלות בלאו ועל החמורות במיתה ומדקלות על החמורות במיתה חמורות ב] נמי על הקלות במיתה לכך נאמרו חמורות: *כל שיש לו מתירין בין לאדם בין למזבח חייבין עליו משום פיגול: תנו רבנן או אינו מביא אלא כיוצא בשלמים מה שלמים מיוחדים נאכלין לשני ימים ולילה אחד אף כל נאכל לשני ימים ולילה אחד נאכל ליום ולילה מנין תלמוד לומר מבשר כל ג] ששירין נאכלין עולה שאין שיריה נאכלין מנין תלמוד לומר זבח מנין לרבות העופות והמנחות עד שאני מרבה לוג שמן של מצורע תלמוד לומר °אשר הם מקדישים לי °ואתי נותר חילול מטומאה ואתי פיגול עון עון מנותר ומאחר שסופו לרבות כל דבר למה נאמר שלמים מעתה לומר לך מה שלמים מיוחדים שיש להן מתירין בין לאדם בין למזבח ד] אף כל שיש לו מתירין בין לאדם בין למזבח חייבין עליהן משום ה] פיגול: העולה דמה מתיר את בשרה למזבח ועורה לכהנים עולת העוף דמה מתיר את בשרה למזבח חטאת העוף דמה מתיר את בשרה לכהנים פרים הנשרפים ושעירים הנשרפים דמם מתיר את אימוריהן ליקרב: ומוציא אני את הקומץ ואת הלבונה והקטרת ו] ומנחת כהנים ומנחת כהן משיח ומנחת נסכים והדם ר"ש אומר מה שלמים מיוחדין ז] *שיש בו על מזבח החיצון וחייבין עליו אף כל שישנן על מזבח החיצון חייבין עליו משום פיגול יצאו פרים הנשרפים ושעירים הנשרפים הואיל ח] שאין על מזבח החיצון כשלמים אין חייבין עליו משום פיגול [אמר מר] כיוצא בשלמים מאי ניהו בכור דנאכל לשני ימים ולילה אחד במאי אתי אי במה מצינו איכא למיפרך מה לשלמים ט] שהן טעונין סמיכה ונסכים ותנופת חזה ושוק אלא °מאם האכל יאכל הני תרי כללי דסמיכי אהדדי נינהו אמר *רבא *כדאמרי במערבא כל מקום שאתה מוצא שני כללות הסמוכים זה לזה הטל פרט ביניהם ודונם בכלל ופרט: עד שאני מרבה לוג שמן של מצורע: הא מני רבי מאיר היא דתניא *לוג שמן של מצורע חייבין עליו משום פיגול דברי רבי מאיר אימא סיפא ומוציא אני מנחת נסכים והדם אתאן לרבנן *דתניא נסכי בהמה חייבין עליהן משום פיגול מפני שדם הזבח מתירן ליקרב דברי רבי מאיר אמרו לו והלא *אדם מביא י] את זבחו היום א)ונסכין מיכן עד עשרה ימים אמר להן אף אני לא אמרתי אלא בבאין עם הזבח אמר רב יוסף הא מני רבי היא דאמר לוג שמן של מצורע מתנותיו שרו ליה ומדמתנותיו שרו ליה מתנותיו מפגלי ליה דתניא ב)לוג שמן של מצורע מועלין בו עד שיזרוק הדם נזרק הדם לא נהנין ולא מועלין רבי אומר מועלין יא] עד שיתן מתנותיו ושוין ג)שאסור באכילה עד שיתן מתן שבע ומתן בהונות אמרוה קמיה דרבי ירמיה אמר ג)גברא רבא כרב יוסף לימא כי הא מילתא

הרי

א) [ע' תוס' ר"ה ל: ד"ה והתקלקלו] ב) [לקמן ק: כתובות מג.]

ואם לא נאמרו הייתי אומר כו' ל"ג הכא דליכא למיפרך דיו דהא קלות נמי במיתה: ואי באכילת מעשר. קאמר דאם לא נאמרו חמורות הייתי אומר על טומאת שרץ בלאו יב] על טומאת מת במיתה לכך נאמרו טומאת מת חמורות ונאמר בהו לאו דלא תימא בהו מיתה (א) במעשר ואם לא נאמרו יג] *קלות הייתי אומר על החמורות במיתה הא מטומאת שרץ הוא דאתיא בק"ו: ודיו לבא מן הדין להיות כנדון. ולא אמינא בה מיתה אלא לאו: והכי קאמר אילו נאמר טומאת שרץ ונאמר מעשר. בלאו כדאיתא ותרומה במיתה כדאיתא ולא נאמר טומאת מת הייתי אומר קלות על הקלות בלאו יד] בטומאת קלה דשרץ על אכילת קלות כגון מעשר יהא בלאו כדאיתא וקלות על החמורות במיתה וטומאת שרץ על אכילות החמורות כגון תרומה במיתה כדאיתא ומינה הוה גמרינן דמה שרץ קלות על החמורות במיתה אף חמורות טו] *על קלות נמי במיתה דמה לי טומאה חמורה ואכילה קלה מה לי אכילה חמורה וטומאה קלה טז] (וטומאת המת על אכילת מעשר תהא במיתה) לכך נאמרו חמורות טומאת המת יז] על אכילת מעשר שלא תהא במיתה ופירש בה לאו ולא במיתה לומר לך שהיא באזהרה: או אינו מביא כו'. רישא דברייתא בת"כ לענין פיגול קתני יכול לא יהא חייב אלא על השלמים בלבד ת"ל לענין טומאה ויגזרו מקדשי ולקמן יליף נותר חילול מטומאה ופיגול בעון עון מנותר: או אינו. מרבה אלא כיוצא בשלמים שהרי כלל ופרט יח] אמור כאן כדמפרש לקמן ונימא מה הפרט מפורש נאכלין לשני ימים כו': ת"ל מבשר. ריבויא הוא דכתיב גבי פיגול (ויקרא ז) מבשר זבח השלמים ועלה קאי והנפש האוכלת ממנו עונה תשא: עד שאני מרבה. כלומר אחרי יט] שאני מרבה ארבה עמהם אף לוג שמן של מצורע אם פיגל בדם האשם נתפגל הלוג: תלמוד לומר. לענין טומאה אשר הם מקדישים גבי ויגזרו כתיב ואתי נותר חילול חילול מטומאה מה טומאה הכל בכלל אף נותר הכל בכלל בנותר כתיב כי את קודש ה' חילל (ויקרא יט) ובטומאה כתיב ויגזרו ולא יחללו (שם כב) והדר אתי פיגול עון עון מנותר: אף כל שיש לו מתירין. או לאדם או למזבח ועולה ילפא *)מאימורי שלמים וכן אימורי כל הקדשים כ] ובשר כל הקדשים הנאכלין ילפי מבשר שלמים שאין לו מתירין אלא לאדם וחייבין עליו: כיוצא בשלמים מאי ניהו. דקתני לעיל או אינו מביא כו' אלא כא] (ב)כיוצא: האכל. כלל מבשר שלמים פרט יאכל חזר וכלל: הני תרי כללי דסמיכי כב] נינהו. שלא נכתב הפרט אלא בסוף: הטל פרט ביניהם. כג] הכתוב אחריהם הטל ביניהם ודונם כו' הלכך אי לאו דרבי רחמנא מבשר כד] תחילה הוה דיינינן ליה במה הפרט מפורש כו': חייבין עליו משום פיגול. אם בא עם האשם ופיגל באשם ואף על גב שאם כה] היה רוצה יכול להביאו מכאן ועד עשרה ימים כדלקמן אית ליה לרבי מאיר דכי הביאו עם האשם דם האשם הוא המתירו למתן בהונות ושיריו לאכילה שירי הלוג נאכלין כדאמרינן בשמעתא דלקמן: אמר רב יוסף כו] רבי היא כו'. וסבר לה כרבנן דהואיל ואפשר להביא נסכים לאחר זמן אין דם הזבח מפגלן ואפילו הביאן עמו ולוג שמן נמי הא דקתני כז] נמי פיגול לא שיהא דם האשם מפגלו אלא מתנות שמן עלמו שמזה ממנו שבע הזאות בפנים הם מפגלין אותו אם הזה על מנת לאכול שיריו חוץ לזמנו והוא נאכל ליום ולילה כדמרבינן ליה לקמן עם שאר קדשי קדשים: ומדשמעינן ליה לרבי כח] דאמר לוג שמן של מצורע מתנותיו שרו ליה. לכהנים דאמר אף על פי שנזרק דם האשם יש מעילה בשמן עד שיתן שבע הזאות של נרכי גבוה הלכך מתנותיו מפגלין ליה שהן כט] מתירין: ולא נהנין. מדרבנן עד שיתן מתנותיו ל]: ולא מועלין. דקסבר דם האשם מתירו לכהנים וכל שיש בו שעת היתר לכהנים אין בו מעילה: רבי לא] אומר מועלין בו עד שיתן שבע הזאות של גבוה. אבל מתן בהונות דלאו לורך גבוה הוא ודאי לא פליג רבי: ושוין. שאפילו נתן מתנות גבוה אסור הוא לב] מדרבנן עד שיתן אף מתן בהונות: אמרוה. רבנן להא דרב יוסף:

*) [נ"א מאימורי שלמים לפי שאין להם מתירין אלא למזבח]

הבא

נאכל ליום ולילה מנין. לקמן בסוף דם חטאת (דף צח.) דרשינן מהיקישא דזאת התורה מה שלמים מפגלין כו' ונראה דהאי תנא לית ליה ההוא היקישא דאי אית ליה לא היה צריך לכל הנך ייתורים: **ואתי** נותר חילול חילול מטומאה ואתי פיגול עון עון מנותר. מכאן לג] הוה מצי למידק לקמן (דף נ:) דדבר הלמד בגזירה שוה חוזר ומלמד בגזירה שוה: **כיוצא** בשלמים מאי ניהו בכור. משמע דבכור דמי לשלמים טפי משאר קדשים ובעלמא איתו כן לד] דאמר מנחות (דף פג:) מה שלמים באין בנדר ונדבה אף כל בא בנדר ונדבה לה]: **אלא** מאם האכל יאכל. ואע"ג דאמרינן לעיל בסוף פרק שני (דף כח:) בשתי אכילות הכתוב מדבר תרתי שמע מינה מדלא כתיב האכל האכל או יאכל יאכל כדאמר בריש הקומץ רבה (מנחות דף יז:) ומיהו רבי אליעזר דמוקי לה התם בדרשא אחרינא נפקא ליה הך דרשא מקרא אחרינא *וכרבא דמפרש לעיל בסוף פרק שני (דף כח:) כולהו מקרא לו] (אחרינא) [אריכא] ודריש מבשר זבח שלמיו מה שלמים מפגלין ומתפגלין כו' לא כמו שפירש שם בקונטרס מדכתיב זבח שלמים לז] דמשמע דמקיש זבח לשלמים אלא אהך ברייתא סמיך והקשה ה"ר חיים אמאי שביק לשון הברייתא דהוה ליה למימר מה שלמים מיוחדים שיש להם מתירין בין לאדם בין למזבח ועוד דמלישנא דמפגל ומתפגלין לא *ממעיט דם דדם מפגל ומתפגל כדתניא בתוספתא דזריקה מפגלת ומתפגלת שהדם מפגל הבשר ומתפגלת על ידי זריקה אם זרק על מנת לשפוך שיריים למחר: **ודונם** בכלל ופרט. ומ"מ צריכי ייתורי דלעיל דמכלל ופרט לא מרבי אלא הדומה לפרט בכל לדדין: סד"א

לו א מיי' פי"ח מהל' פסולי המוקדשין הל' ה:

לז ב מיי' פ"ב מהל' מעילה הלכה י:

לח ג מיי' פ"ד מהל' מחוסרי כפרה הל' ג:

צ"ל אלא קלות וגו' הס"ד כלום במקום תיבת קלות

חולין קיז:

טומאת מת על קלות מעשר נמי צ"ק

צ"ק מ"ז

ורבא צ"ק

ממעטינן צ"ק

צ"ל שישנו על כו'

צ"ק

חולין סו: ב"ק סג: בכורות נא. ע"ש שבועות ה.

תוספתא רפ"ה מנחות

צ"ל רבינא

הגהות הב"ח

(א) רש"י ד"ה ואי באכילת וכו' דלא תימא בהו מיתה אף במעשר ואם לא נאמרו כלום הייתי: (ב) ד"ה כיוצא וכו' כיוצא בס"ד ואח"כ מ"ס הני תרי וכו' בסוף הס"ד ואח"כ מ"ס הטל וכו' ביניהם הס"ד ואח"כ מ"ס האכל כלל וכו' וכלל הס"ד ואח"כ מ"ס ודונם כו' הולכך:

גליון הש"ס

גמ' ואתי נותר חילול. ע"ל דף כו ע"א תוס' ד"ה סיג:

[מנחות טו: ע"ש מיהו גם משנה לעיל דף מג. הכן לוג שמן של מצורע וכו' דברי מאיר חייבין עליו משום פיגול ואולי יש לגרוס הכא הכן לוג וכו' ותוס' ד"ה עוד שם ה. ד"ה ובכן וכ"כ עוד שבועות יט: ד"ה שבועות ע"ש ועי' עוד לעיל כה: ד"ה והרי]

שיטה מקובצת

א] אומר קלות על הקלות בלאו וקלות על החמורות: ב] חמורות על הקלות נמי במיתה לכך: ג] כל ששיריו נאכלין: ד] למזבח. מ"י וחייבין עליהן משום פיגול אף: ה] פיגול מרבה אני חטאת העוף שיש לו מתירין לאדם מרבה אני פרים הנשרפים ושעירים הנשרפים שיש להם מתירין למזבח ומוציא כו' כל זה מצאתי בס"א והיא נוסחא אמתית ולא גרס כלל העולה כו': ו] והקטרת ומנחת נסכים ומנחת כהנים ומנחת כהן משיח ונסכים ותיבת ומנחת נמחק: ז] מיוחדין שישנו על מזבח החיצון וחייבין עליהן אף כל שישנו: ח] הואיל שאינן על מזבח כו' אין חייבין עליהן משום פיגול ס"א אמר מר כיוצא: ט] לשלמים שכן טעונין סמיכה: י] מביא זבחו היום ונסכיו מכאן עד י' ימים: יא] מועלין בו עד: יב] בלאו ועל טומאת: יג] כלום הייתי אומר כו' הוא דהוה אתי' בק"ו: יד] בלאו טומאת קלה: טו] חמורות דהיינו טומאת מת על מעשר קלות: טז] וטומאה קלה לכך נאמרו כו' והשאר נמחק: יז] המת החמורות על אכילת מעשר ופירש בה לאו ולא מיתה לומר לך שהיא באזהרה בלבד הס"ד: יח] ופרט וכלל אמור: יט] אחרי. ס"י שהתחלתי לרבות ארבה כו': כ] הקדשים מאימורי שלמים ילפי שאין להם מתירין אלא למזבח ואתרבו בשר כל הקדשים שהן הנאכלים: כא] אלא מאם האכל ותיבת כיוצא נמחק: כב] דסמיכי אהדדי נינהו: כג] ביניהם הפרט הכתוב: כד] מבשר הוה דיינינן ליה כו' מפורש כו' ילא הוי אתי אלא בכור הס"ד: כה] שאם רצה היה יכול להביא כו' דם האשם מתירו למתן בהונות ושיריו לאכילה דשירי הלוג נאכלין: כו] יוסף הא מני רבי: כז] דקתני פיגול: כח] לרבי לוג ותיבת דאמר נמחק: כט] שהן מתירין הס"ד: ל] שיתן מתנותיו שבע הס"ד: לא] רבי. גליון דמודה הוא דכיון שניתנו ממנו המתנות שהן צורך גבוה שוב אין מועלין בהן אע"פ שלא ניתן ממנו לבהונות. ע"כ: לב] הוא באכילה מדרבנן: לג] מכאן הוי מצי למיפרך לקמן כן הוא בס"א: לד] כן וי"ל דהכא איירי לגבי אכילה להכי מרבינן (הדמים) [הדומים] לאכילה. ת' מהר"פ ז"ל: לה] ונדבה לאפוקי בכור: לו] מקרא אריכא ודריש מבשר זבח: לז] שלמים דריש משמע דמקיש:

הרי לוג א] [הבא] בפני עצמו דלכ"ע מתנותיו שרו ליה ולא מפגלין ליה דתניא *לוג שמן של מצורע חייבין עליו משום פיגול מפני שדם מתירו לבהונות דברי ר"מ אמרו לו לר"מ והלא אדם מביא. אשמו עכשיו ב] ולוג מיכן ועד עשרה ימים אמר להן אף אני לא אמרתי אלא בבא עם האשם אלא א"ר ירמיה לעולם ר"מ היא וסמי מיכן נסכים ג] אמר אביי לעולם לא תסמי ותנא לוג הבא עם האשם והוא הדין לנסכים הבאין עם הזבח והדר תנא נסכים הבאין בפני עצמן והוא הדין ללוג הבא בפני עצמו: חטאת העוף דמה מתיר את בשרה לכהנים: מנא הני מילי *דתני לוי °כל קרבנם לרבות לוג שמן של מצורע סלקא דעתך אמינא מן האש ד] כתב רחמנא והאי לאו מותר מן האש הוא קמ"ל: °לכל מנחתם *לרבות מנחת עומר ומנחת הקנאות סלקא דעתך אמינא °ואכלו אותם אשר כפר בהם ומנחת העומר להתיר אתיא ומנחת קנאות לברר עון קאתיא קמ"ל: ולכל חטאתם לרבות *חטאת העוף סלקא דעתך אמינא נבילה היא: ה] לכל אשמם לרבות אשם נזיר ואשם מצורע סלקא דעתך אמינא להכשיר קאתו קמ"ל אשם מצורע בהדיא כתיב ביה ו] אלא לרבות אשם נזיר כאשם מצורע: אשר ישיבו *זה גזל הגר לך הוא ז] שלך יהיה אפילו לקדש בו את האשה *תניא ר' אלעזר אומר משום רבי יוסי ח] *הגלילי פיגל בדבר הנעשה בחוץ פיגל בדבר הנעשה בפנים לא פיגל כיצד היה עומד בחוץ ואמר הריני שוחט להזות מדמו למחר לא פיגל שמחשבה בחוץ בדבר הנעשה בפנים ט] לא פיגל היה עומד בפנים ואמר הריני מזה על מנת י] להקטיר אימורים ולשפוך שירים למחר לא פיגל שמחשבה בפנים בדבר הנעשה בחוץ יא] אבל היה עומד בחוץ ואמר הריני שוחט לשפוך שירים למחר או להקטיר אימורים למחר פיגל שמחשבה בחוץ בדבר הנעשה בחוץ א"ר יהושע בן לוי מאי קרא °כאשר יורם משור זבח השלמים *וכי מה למדנו יב] משור זבח השלמים מעתה אלא מקיש פר כהן משיח לשור זבח השלמים מה שור זבח השלמים עד שיהו יג] מעשיו ומחשבותיו על מזבח החיצון אף פר כהן משיח עד שיהו מחשבותיו ומעשיו על המזבח החיצון אמר רב נחמן אמר רבה בר אבוה אמר רב הלכה כרבי אלעזר שאמר משום רבי יוסי אמר יד] *רבא הלכתא

רש"י

הבא בפני עצמו. מצורע שהביא אשמו היום ולוגו לאחר עשרה ימים דלכ"ע מתנותיו שריין ליה באכילה דהואיל ולא קדש בכלי כשנזרק דם האשם לאו שיריים דידיה הוא טו] ולא שרי ליה ואפ"ה לא מפגלין ליה לדברי הכל דאין בו משום פיגול כדקתני אף אני לא אמרתי כו' הלכך בא עם האשם נמי אע"ג דלרבי מתנותיו שריין ליה לא מפגלים ליה שאין מפגל אלא דם או קומץ את שיריו משום דאיתקש מנחה לזבחים: ותנא. רישא: לוג הבא עם האשם. שדם האשם מפגלו ואע"פ שהיה טז] לו להביאו לאחר עשרה ימים וממנו אתה למד דה"ה לנסכים הבאים עם הזבח שדם הזבח מפגלן ואע"פ שבידו להביאן לאחר זמן: ותנא סיפא נסכים הבאים בפני עצמן. כדקתני לה דומיא דקטרת ולבונה ומנחת כהנים שאין להן מתירין וקאמר דאין מתפגלין אם הקריב מקצתן ע"מ פיגול וה"ה ללוג הבא בפני עצמו: מנהני מילי. דחטאת העוף נאכלת יז]: כל קרבנם. גבי סדר מתנות כהונה יח] שנאמר לאהרן על הסדר בפרשת קרח וזה יהיה לך מקדש הקדשים מן האש וגו' וכתיב בתריה בקדש הקדשים תאכלנו וקדריש להו הכא כל כל דכולהו: לרבות לוג שמן. שאף הוא נאכל שהרי קרוי קרבן דכתיב (ויקרא יד) והקריב אותו לאשם ואת לוג השמן אלמא הוא נמי בכלל והקריב והיינו קרבן כ"ש במנחות (דף עג.): ס"ד (א) כו'. כלומר האי דאיצטריך כל יט] קרא לרבויי ולא נפקא ליה מקרבנו: סד"א מן האש כתיב. כ] הנותר מן האש ומזה לא עלה לאשים כלל: ואכלו אותם אשר כופר בהם. דבר שיש בו כפרה נאכל ושאין בו כפרה אינו נאכל: להתיר אתיא. חדש במדינה: נבילה היא. לפי שנמלקה: לרבות אשם נזיר. נזיר שנטמא במת מביא אשם כשטהר מטומאתו ומכשירו להתחיל ולמנות נזירות טהרה והימים הראשונים (ב) יפלו *ולרבות שיהא נאכל דאי לא כא] כתיב לכל לא מרבינן להו דכתיב אשר כופר בהם והני להכשיר אתו זה להכשירו בקדשים וזה להתחיל נזירות כב] טהרה: אשם מצורע בהדיא כתיב ביה. דנאכל כג] כי כחטאת האשם הוא (ויקרא יד) ומיהו נהי דאשמם כתיב הכא לסדר בפרשה כל עשרים וארבע מתנות כהונה אלא כל למה: אשר ישיבו זה גזל הגר. דכתיב כד] (במדבר ה) האשם המושב לה' לכהן ותניא (ב"ק דף קי.) אשם זה קרן המושב זה חומש או אינו אלא זה אשם ממש כשהוא אומר מלבד איל הכפורים כה] (*הרי אמור אלא) אשם זה קרן שהגוזל את חבירו ונשבע לו ואח"כ הודה משלם קרן וחומש לבעלים ואשם למזבח כדכתיב בפרשת ויקרא והיה כי יחטא ואשם וגו' ואם מת נותן ליורשיו ואם גר היה ומת כו] ואין לו יורשין להחזירו להם נתנן הכתוב לכהן ופרשת גזל הגר אמורה בפרשת נשא אם אין לאיש גואל להשיב האשם וגו' וכי יש לך אדם בישראל שאין לו גואל אלא כז] זה גזל הגר. גזל הגר בהדיא כתיב ביה לא גרסינן דהא חטאות ואשמות ושאר האמורים בפרשה בהדיא כתיב כל אחד ואחד במקומו וסידרן לו הכתוב לאהרן כאן מפני מחלוקתו של קרח שערער עליו על הכהונה משל הדיוט אמר כח] לטובתו נשברה רגל פרתו: *לך הוא ולבניך. שיהו ככנסים של חולין שאין בו שום קדושה דממון בעלים הוא ואגזל לחודיה קאי האי לך הוא והאי דכתיב בתריה בקדש הקדשים תאכלנו אשארא קאי דהוו מידי דאכילה: תניא אמר ר' אלעזר כו'. אפרים הגרפים דאיפליגו בה במתני' קאי: פיגל בדבר הנעשה בחוץ. העבודה שהיה עובד במחשבה והאכילה שחישב עליה אם מעבה עזרה הם פיגל ואם מעשה היכל הם לא פיגל ולקמן יליף טעמא מקראי: כט] שוחט. שהרי שחיטתה בעזרה הוא וכל חוץ דהכא עזרה הוא: להזות דמו למחר. הרי חישב על אכילת מזבח *של פנים הריני מזה על הפרכת או על המזבח הפנימי שזו היא זריקתן ל] המפגל: על מנת לשפוך שירים. שהרי זו אכילת מזבח החיצון דמהניא ביה מחשבה: (ג) לא פיגל. מפני שמחשבה היתה בשעת עבודת פנים: כאשר יורם. בפר כהן משיח כתיב בהפרשת אימוריו: *מה למדנו לו. משלמים לענין אימורים הרי אף לא] בזה כולן מפורשים חלב וכליות ויותרת אלא לא בא היקש הזה אלא ללמד על הפיגול שהוא למד בכל הקדשים משלמים ובא ללמדך על אלו שאין פיגול נוהג בהן אלא כשלמים מה שלמים אין פיגולן אלא על לב] מעשי עבודה חיצונית ומחשבת אכילות חיצונות שוחט או מקבל או מוליך או זורק ע"מ לאכול בשר לג] לשפוך שיריים או להקטיר אימוריו חוץ לזמנו אף כאן עד שיחשב בעבודות *על אכילת חוץ: מחשבותיו. מחשבת אכילתו: ומעשיו. עבודה שהוא עובד ומחשב. הלכתא

תוספות

סד"א מן האש כו'. תימה לד] לא לכתוב מן האש ולא בעי לכל: זה גזל הגר. דאע"ג דמכפר לא הוה אמינא דליהוי לכהן אלא מידי לה] דמותר למזבח ולא ממונא ובספרים ישנים גרים גזל הגר בהדיא כתיב ביה בפרשת נשא דכתיב לכהן לו יהיה ובקונטרס לא גרים ליה משום דחטאות ואשמות ושאר לו] אימורים בפרשה בהדיא כתיבי כל אחד ואחד במקומו וסדרן לו הכתוב לאהרן כאן מפני מחלוקתו *של קרח לז]:

ואפילו לקדש בו את האשה. בפ' התכלת (מנחות דף מה:) אמרינן גבי שתי הלחם דעצרת ורבי עקיבא מי כתיב קודש יהיו לה' ולכהן לה' לכהן כתיב כדרב הונא דאמר רב הונא קנאו השם ונתנו לכהן ופי' שם בקונטרס דמשלחן גבוה קא זכו ועיקר מילתיה דרב הונא אגזל הגר איתמר בפ' הגוזל עצים (ב"ק דף קט:) לח] ולא מצינו דברי רב הונא לשם אלא ברייתא היא התם בשילהי פירקין ובמסכת ערכין בשילהי המקדיש שדהו (דף כח:) האשם המושב לה' לכהן קנאו השם ונתנו לכהן שבאותו המשמר *ונראה דלא גרסינן לט] פרק התכלת כדרב הונא אלא הכי גרסינן לה' לכהן קנאו השם ונתנו לכהן ומיהו לא מצי לפרש לכהן שבאותו משמר כי היא דגזל הגר דהתם שהרי ברגל היו כל המשמרות שוות כדדרשינן בפ' בתרא דסוכה (דף נה:) מדכתיב ובא בכל אות נפשו ושרת אלא כמו שפי' בקונטרס לענין דמשלחן גבוה קא זכו ומיהו מ] משמע מתוך דבריו דגזל הגר משלחן גבוה קא זכו *אי אפשר לומר כן דהא אמרינן הכא לך הוא ולבניך אפילו לקדש בו את האשה ובקדושין (דף נב:) אמר במקדש בחלקו בין בקדשי קדשים בין בקדשים קלים אינה מקודשת משום דמשלחן גבוה קא זכו וצ"ל דשאני הכא דגלי קרא לך ולבניך ויש תימה מא] (לך) לה' בגזל הגר למה לי *דלגבי מאי נפקא מינה דקנאו השם למימר דמשלחן גבוה קא זכו:

בדבר הנעשה בפנים לא פיגל. והא דאמר בהניזקין (גיטין דף נד:) כהן גדול ביום הכיפורים יוכיח דכי אמר פיגול מהימן נהי דפיגול לא הוי פסול מיהא הוי מק"ו וכדאמר לעיל ספ"ק (דף יד.) מודה היה רבי שמעון לפסול מק"ו ימה שלא לשמו כו' וה"ר חיים מפ' דההוא פיגול מיירי בפסול שלא לשמו ולא משמע כן דשלא לשמן לא קרי ליה פיגול כדאמר לעיל ספ"ק (דף יג.) דיקא נמי דקתני שהזבח נפסל ולא קתני שהזבח מתפגל:

וכי מה למדנו משור זבח השלמים מעתה. נראה דלית ליה הא דדרשינן בפרק איזהו מקומן (לקמן דף מט:) מכאשר יורם דאיצטריך ליותרת ושתי הכליות *)לפר יום הכיפורים ומקרא אחרינא נפקא ליה להאי תנא: הלכתא

*) נ"א לפר העלם דבר של צבור ומקרא כו' נ"ק

עין משפט נר מצוה

לט א מיי' פי"ח מהל' פסה"מ הלכה ח:

מ ב מיי' פ"ד מהלכות מחוסרי כפרה הל' ב:

[וע' בתוס' דמנחות שהקשו דלפ"ז מאי פריך אשם מצורע בהדיא כתיב ביה וע"ש וברש"י כאן]

מא ג מיי' פ"ז מהלכות תמידין ומוספין הלכה יב:

מב ד מיי' פ"ג מהלכות סוטה הלכה טו:

מג ה מיי' פ"ז מהלכות מעה"ק הלכה ז:

מד ו מיי' פ"ט מהלכות מעה"ק הלכה א:

מה ז מיי' שם הל' ב:

מו ח מיי' פ"ח מהלכות גזילה הלכה ה:

[ע"ש בתוס' מנחות שכתבו בענין אחר]

מז ט מיי' פי"ח מהל' פסה"מ הלכה ז:

ואי נ"ק

נ"ק מ"ז

נ"ל דלגבי גזל סגר נ"ק

מסורת הש"ס

[מנחות טו: תוספתא פ"ט]

מנחות נח. עג. [ע"ש כמה שינויים]

[מנחות עג.]

שם

[שם פ"ט]

מנחות יד. [תוספתא פ"ט]

ע"ש מתוס' דזבחים יד. ד"ה מודה וכו' ותוס' מנחות יד. ד"ה פיגל כו' ותוס' גיטין נד: ד"ה דכי מוכח דל"ג הגלילי וכן במנחות ליתא וכן לקמן בסמוך הלכה כר"א משום רבי יוסי ליתא הגלילי

חולין קז. ע"ש

נ"ל סוי אומר אשם זה כו' נ"ק

[לפ"ד התוס' ד"ה הלכתא] נ"ל רב יוסף וכן גי' נ"ק

עיין נ"ק

של פנים הס"ד והא"ח מ"ס הריני מזה נ"ק

וכי מה נ"ק

חוץ על נ"ק

תורה אור

במדבר יח | שם | שמות כט | ויקרא ד

הגהות הב"ח

(א) רש"י ד"ה ס"ד כלומר כצ"ל והיבת כו' נמחק: (ב) ד"ה לרבות אשם נזיר וכו' יפלו הס"ד ואח"כ מ"ה אשם מצורע בהדיא וכו' אלא כל למה לרבות שיהא נאכל דאי וכו' נזירות בטהרה הס"ד ואח"כ מ"ה אשר ישיבו: (ג) ד"ה לא פיגל צ"ל קודם ד"ה (המפגל) על מנת:

שיטה מקובצת

א] לוג הבא בפני: ב] עכשיו ולוגו: ג] נסכים אביי אמר: ד] האש אמר רחמנא: ה] היא ולכל: ו] ביה. ס"י כי כחטאת האשם הוא לכם אלא: ז] הוא ולבניך שלך הוא ולבניך יהיה (תיבת שלך נמחק) לקדש בו את האשה וא"ת והא כתיב בתריה בקודש קדשים תאכלנו וי"ל דאשאר מתנות קאי דהוי מידי דאכילה: ח] תיבת הגלילי נמחק: ט] תיבות לא פיגל נמחק: י] על מנת לשפוך שירים למחר כו' והשאר נמחק: יא] תיבת אבל נמחק: יב] למדנו. ס"י לפר כהן משיח משור: יג] שיהו מחשבותיו ומעשיו על מזבח החיצון: יד] אמר רב יוסף ותיבת רבא נמחק: טו] הוא. ס"א ולא שרי הדם לשיריים אלא מתנותיו שרו ליה: טז] שהיה יכול להביאו: יז] נאכלת לאחר שנמלקה ואינו נבילה: יח] כהונה שנאמרו לאהרן על הסדר בפרשת ויקח קרח: יט] כל לרבויי ולא נפקא ליה מקרבנם הס"ד: כ] כתיב דמשמע הנותר מן האשים ומזה לא עלה לאשים כלום הס"ד: כא] לא הוה כתיב לכל לא הוה מרבינן להו: כב] נזירות בטהרה הס"ד: כג] דנאכל דכתיב כי כחטאת האשם הוא לכהן ומיהו נהי דאשמם דכתיב הכא לסדר כו' למה לי הס"ד: כד] דכתיב ביה האשם: כה] הכפורים הרי אשם זה (ותיבות הרי אמור אלא ל"ש) קרן וכך הוא הענין שהגוזל את חבירו: כו] ומת שאין לו: כז] זה הגר תיבת גזל נמחק: כח] לטובתי נשברה רגל פרתי: כט] מה"ד הריני שוחט ששחיטתן בעזרה: ל] וזריקתן המפגלת: לא] אף ביה כולן תיבת בזה נמחק: לב] על ידי מעשה: לג] בשר או לשפוך שיריים כו' בעבודות חוץ על אכילת חוץ: לד] כו' תימה דלא מייתי מתניתא מן האש כתיב כ"כ בס"י: לה] *) מיד דנותר למזבח: לו] ושאר האמורים: לז] קרח. וא"ת מאי קאמר לעיל לכל חטאתם לרבות כו' נימא דנשנית מפני מחלוקתו של קרח אע"פ שאינו צריך וי"ל דנהי דנתפרשה פעם אחרת מ"מ איצטריך לומר מה היה צריך לומר ייתור דנאכל מאחר שאני יכול לשמוע ממקום אחר. ה' מהר"פ: לח] עצים ע"ב ולא: לט] גרסינן בפרק: מ] ומיהו מה שמשמע: מא] תימה לה' לכהן בגזל הגר ותיבת לך נמחק:

*) נראה דצ"ל מידי דנותר מן המזבח.

That a great man like R. Joseph should say such a thing! [44*b*] Lo, a all agree that when the *log* comes separately,[1] its sprinklings permit it, and yet they do not render it *piggul*. For it was taught, A leper's *log* of oil involves liability on account of *piggul*, because the blood permits it for [sprinkling on] the thumbs: that is R. Meir's view. Said they to R. Meir: But a man can bring his guilt-offering now, and his *log* even ten days later! I too, he answered them, ruled [thus] only when it comes with the guilt-offering!—Rather said R. Jeremiah: In truth it agrees with R. Meir, but delete '*drink-offerings*' from this passage. Abaye said: After all, you need not delete [it]. But he [first] teaches about the *log* which comes with the guilt-offering,[2] and the same applies to the drink-offering which comes with the sacrifice. And then he teaches about the drink-offering which comes separately,[3] and the same applies to the *log* which comes separately.

THE BLOOD OF THE BIRD SIN-OFFERING PERMITS ITS FLESH TO THE PRIESTS. Whence do we know it?[4]—For Levi taught: [*This shall be thine*—the priest's— . . .] *every offering of theirs:*[5] that is to include a leper's *log* of oil. I might think that the Divine Law wrote, *reserved from the fire,*[6] whereas this is not reserved from the fire;[7] therefore it informs us [that it is not so]. *Even every meal-offering of theirs*[8] includes the meal-offering of the '*omer*[9] and the meal-offering of jealousy.[10] I might think [that it is written,] *And they shall eat these things wherewith atonement was made,*[11] [whereas] the meal-offering of the '*omer* comes to permit [the new corn], while the meal-offering of jealousy comes to establish guilt; therefore [the b text] informs us [that it is not so]. *And every sin-offering of theirs*[1] includes the sin-offering of a bird. I might think that it is *nebelah;*[2] therefore [the text] informs us [that it is not so]. *And every guilt-offering of theirs*[1] includes a nazirite's guilt-offering and a leper's guilt-offering. I might think that these come to qualify [them];[3] therefore [the text] informs us [that it is not so]. But it is explicitly written that a leper's guilt-offering [is eaten]?[4]—Rather, it is to include a nazirite's guilt-offering, [teaching that it is like] a leper's guilt-offering. *Which they may render*[5] includes what is taken by robbery from a proselyte.[6] *Shall be for thee:*[5] it shall be thine even for betrothing a woman.[7]

It was taught, R. Eleazar said on the authority of R. Jose the Galilean:[8] If [the priest] declared a *piggul* intention in respect of a rite which is performed without,[9] he renders it *piggul;* in respect of a rite which is performed within,[10] he does not render it *piggul*. How so? If he stood without and declared, 'Lo, I slaughter [this sacrifice intending] to sprinkle its blood to-morrow,' he does not render it *piggul,* because it is an intention [expressed] without concerning a rite which is performed within.[11] If he stood within and declared, 'Lo, I sprinkle [the blood], intending to burn the c *emurim* and pour out the residue[1] to-morrow,' he does not render it *piggul,* because it is an intention [expressed] within concerning a rite which is performed without. If he stood without and declared, 'Lo, I slaughter [this sacrifice intending] to pour out the residue to-morrow', or 'to burn the *emurim* to-morrow,' he renders it *piggul,* because it is an intention [expressed] without concerning a rite which is performed without. R. Joshua b. Levi said: Which text [teaches this]? *As is taken from the ox of the sacrifice of peace-offerings.*[2] What then do we learn from the ox of the sacrifice of peace-offerings?[3] [Scripture] however likens the anointed priest's bullock to the ox of the sacrifice of peace-offerings: as the ox of the sacrifice of peace-offerings [does not become *piggul*] unless its rites and its intentions are [done] on the outer altar,[4] so the anointed priest's bullock [does not become *piggul*] unless its intentions and its rites are [done] in connection with the outer altar. R. Naḥman said in Rabbah b. Abbuha's name in Rab's name: The *halachah* is

a (1) I.e., when the leper brings it some days after his guilt-offering. (2) That the blood of the guilt-offering can render it *piggul,* though he could have brought the *log* later. (3) That this *cannot* become *piggul*. (4) That its flesh may be eaten. (5) Num. XVIII, 9. (6) Ibid. (7) No portion of it was burnt at all. (8) Ibid. (9) V. Glos., and Lev. XXIII, 10-14. (10) V. Num. V, 12-15. (11) Ex. XXIX, 33.

b (1) Num. XVIII, 9. (2) V. Glos. The bird-offering was killed by wringing its neck (Lev. I, 14-15), whereas ordinary *shechitah* (ritual killing) consists of cutting the windpipe and the gullet.—*Nebelah* of course may not be eaten. (3) A nazirite's guilt-offering qualifies him to recommence his naziriteship after becoming unclean, while a leper's guilt-offering qualifies him to partake of holy food (v. Num. VI, 9-12, Lev. XIV, where the whole ceremony of purification is described). Thus they do not come to make atonement. (4) Lev. XIV, 13: *for as the sin-offering is the priest's, so is the guilt-offering*. (5) Num. XVIII, 9. (6) If a man robs a proselyte, commits perjury in denying it, and then confesses, he must return what he robbed to the proselyte, plus a fifth, and also bring a guilt-offering. But if the proselyte died in the meantime and left no heirs, the principal and the fifth belong to the priest (v. B.Ḳ. 110*a*), and this is taught by the present exegesis. (7) Which was done with money or its value.—This last refers only to the robbery of a proselyte. (8) Sh. M. deletes 'the Galilean'. (9) I.e., in the Temple court. (10) In the *hekal*. (11) This passage deals with the bullocks and he-goats which were burnt, about which there is a controversy in the Mishnah. Their blood was sprinkled on the inner altar in the *hekal*.

c (1) Both were done at the outer altar. (2) Lev. IV, 10. This refers to the anointed priest's bullock, which was burnt. After describing its rites, including the removal of the fat, Scripture proceeds, (This shall be) *as* (the fat which) *is taken* etc. (3) The rites of removing the fat etc. are exactly described: what then does Scripture teach? (4) I.e., unless the intention to perform its rites or to eat the flesh after time is expressed in connection with and during the performance of a rite on the outer altar—since all its rites were on the outer altar.

as R. Eleazar's ruling in the name of R. Jose. Said Raba: [45a] [Do we need] a *halachah* [for the days of] the Messiah?[5]—Abaye answered: If so, we should not study the whole of 'The slaughtering of sacrifices'?[6] Yet we say, study and receive reward;[7] so in this case too, study and receive reward. [He replied] This is what I mean: Why [state] a *halachah*?[8] Another version: He replied, I mean, [Why state the] *halachah*?[9]

a *MISHNAH.* THE SACRIFICES OF HEATHENS[1] DO NOT INVOLVE LIABILITY ON ACCOUNT OF PIGGUL, NOTHAR, OR DEFILEMENT, AND IF [A PRIEST] SLAUGHTERS THEM WITHOUT [THE TEMPLE], HE IS NOT LIABLE: THAT IS R. SIMEON'S VIEW. BUT R. JOSE DECLARES HIM LIABLE.

GEMARA. Our Rabbis taught: You may neither benefit from the sacrifices of heathens,[2] nor do you commit trespass;[3] and they do not involve liability on account of *piggul, nothar* or defilement. And they [the heathens] cannot effect substitution;[4] and they cannot bring drink-offerings,[5] but their [animal] sacrifices require drink-offerings [to accompany them]: that is the view of R. Simeon.[6] Said R. Jose: I hold that a stringent view should be taken on all these matters,[7] because it is said of them, [*Any man . . . that bringeth his offering . . .*] *unto the Lord*.[8] This applies only to sacrifices of the altar;[9] but in the case of objects sacred to the Temple repair,[10] one does commit trespass. 'You may neither benefit nor do you commit trespass:' You may not benefit by Rabbinical law. 'Nor do you commit trespass,' because in respect of the trespass-offering identity of law is derived from the fact that *'sin'* is written here and in the case of *terumah:*[11] while in respect to *terumah 'the children of Israel'* is written,[12] [which intimates,] but not [those of] heathens.

'And they do not involve liability on account of *piggul, nothar* or defilement.' What is the reason?—Because the scope of *piggul* is derived from *nothar*, since *'iniquity'* is written in connection with both, and the scope of *nothar* is derived from defilement, because *'profanation'* is written in connection with both; while in respect to b defilement *'the children of Israel'* is written,[1] [which intimates,] but not [those of] heathens.

'And they cannot effect substitution.' What is the reason?—Because substitution is assimilated to the tithe of cattle,[2] and cattle tithe is assimilated to corn tithe,[3] while *'the children of Israel'* is written in connection with corn tithe,[4] [which intimates,] but not that of heathens. Can then that which is learnt through a *hekkesh* in turn teach through a *hekkesh*?[5]—Corn tithe is *ḥullin*.[6] That is well on the view that the *teacher* is the determining factor; but on the view that the *taught* is the determining factor, what can be said?[7]—Rather, cattle tithe is an obligation for which there is no fixed time, and as it is an obligation for which there is no fixed time, it is brought by Israelites, but not by heathens.[8]

'And they cannot bring drink-offerings.' Our Rabbis taught: [Scripture saith,] [*All that are*] *home-born* [*shall do these things after* c *this manner:*][1] the home-born can bring drink-offerings but a heathen cannot bring drink-offerings. You might think then that his burnt-offering does not require a drink-offering;[2] therefore Scripture teaches, *Thus* [*shall be done for each bullock* etc.].[3]

'Said R. Jose: I hold that a stringent view should be taken on all these matters. This applies only to sacrifices of the altar etc.' What is the reason?—He holds that when [the scope of] trespass is derived from *terumah*, because *'sin'* is written in connection with both, [it applies only to that which is] like *terumah*, whose holiness is intrinsic;[4] but not to the sanctity of the Temple repair, which is [but] monetary sanctity.[5]

Our Rabbis taught: If blood was defiled, and [the priest]

(5) Since the Temple no longer stands there is no practical utility in this ruling, which can become effective only in the days of the Messiah, when the Temple is rebuilt. (6) I.e., the present Tractate. (7) Learning for its own sake is meritorious. (8) While it is right to study the subject, the fixing of a *halachah* is unnecessary. (9) Why state the accepted practice when sacrifices are obsolete? Apart from the slight verbal variants in the two versions as indicated by the square brackets, in the first version the Aramaic *hilketha* is used, in the second the Hebrew *halachah* is used.

a (1) Their votive offerings to the Temple. (2) Before the blood is sprinkled, just as is the case of all sacrifices. (3) V. *supra* 35b n. 10. (4) V. *supra* 5b n. b 8. If the owner is a heathen, he cannot effect substitution in the sense of making the second animal holy. (5) Unless they accompany an animal sacrifice. Whereas Israelites can do so (Men. 104b). (6) Possibly 'that ... R. Simeon' should be deleted. (7) The sacrifices of heathens should be treated as stringently as those of Israelites. (8) Lev. XXII, 18. In Ḥul. 13b this verse is made to include the sacrifices of heathens; thus these too are *'unto the Lord'* just as those of Israelites, and therefore they must be treated with equal severity. (9) I.e., unblemished animals, which will be sacrificed on the altar. (10) This is the technical designation of anything which is dedicated to the Temple, whether it be a blemished animal which cannot be sacrificed or any other object; it is then used for some Temple purpose. (11) Trespass: *If a soul commit a trespass, and* sin *through ignorance in the holy things of the Lord* (Lev. V, 15); *terumah: Lest they bear* sin *for it* (Ibid. XXII, 9). (12) Ibid. 15: *And they shall not profane the holy things of the children of Israel.*

b (1) Lev. XXII, 2: *Speak unto Aaron and to his sons, that they separate themselves* (when unclean) *from the holy things of the children of Israel.* (2) Ibid. XXVII, 32f: *And all the tithe of the herd or the flock ... the tenth shall be holy unto the Lord. He shall not ... change it* etc. Thus substitution of sacrifices in general, to which the second verse refers, is made part of the law of substitution of tithe. (3) Deut. XIV, 22: *Thou shalt surely tithe all the increase of thy seed.* The emphatic *'thou shalt surely tithe'* is expressed in Heb. as usual by the repetition of the verb; this repetition is Talmudically interpreted as referring to two tithes, cattle-tithe and corn-tithe. Thus they are assimilated to each other by being included in the same text. (4) Num. XVIII, 26: *When ye take of the children of Israel the tithe which I have given you.* (5) It is only by analogy with corn-tithe that we learn that the law of cattle does not operate in respect of the cattle of heathens. Can that in turn teach that the law of substitution does not operate in respect of heathens' sacrifices? (6) And only in the case of holy things is this exegesis not permitted. (7) The 'teacher' is corn-tithe, which throws light on 'cattle-tithe', which is the 'taught'. Here the 'teacher' is *ḥullin*, whereas the 'taught' is holy: if the 'teacher' is the determining factor, then the 'teacher' is indeed *ḥullin* and the exegesis is permitted; but if the 'taught' is the determining factor, then the 'taught' is holy, and so that exegesis is not allowable. (8) As they can bring only votive offerings.—They do not bring obligatory offerings for which there is a fixed time either e.g., the festival peace-offerings. Nevertheless this is not mentioned, since they can bring peace-offerings in general; but the law of cattle-tithe does not apply to them at all.

c (1) Num. XV, 13. *'These things'* refers to the rites enumerated in the preceding passage, which includes the bringing of drink-offerings. (2) To accompany it, as does the burnt-offering of an Israelite. (3) Ibid. 11. Thus Scripture makes the sacrifice, not the donor, the determining factor. (4) *Terumah* itself is holy and must be treated as such, similarly the sacrifices of the altar. (5) When an object is dedicated to the Temple repair fund, that object itself is sacred only in so far that it must be redeemed and the redemption money expended on sacred purposes. But when it is redeemed it loses its sanctity.

*See Corrigenda.

*הלכתא למשיחא א"ל אביי אלא מעתה כל שחיטת קדשים לא לתני הלכתא למשיחא הוא אלא *דרוש וקבל שכר ה"נ דרוש וקבל שכר הכי קאמינא לך הלכתא למה לי לישנא אחרינא א"ל הלכה קאמינא: **מתני'** *קדשי עובדי כוכבים אין חייבין עליהן משום פיגול נותר וטמא והשוחטן א] בחוץ פטור דברי *רבי שמעון °רבי יוסי ב מחייב: **גמ'** *ת"ר קדשי עובדי כוכבים ג לא נהנין ולא מועלין ואין חייבין עליהן משום פיגול נותר וטמא ד ואין עושין תמורה ה ואין מביאין נסכים אבל ב] קרבנן °טעון נסכים דברי רבי שמעון ג] אמר רבי יוסי רואה אני בכולן להחמיר שנאמר בהן לה' בד"א בקדשי מזבח אבל בקדשי בדק הבית ד] מועלין בהן: *לא נהנין ולא מועלין: לא נהנין מדרבנן ולא מועלין *דגמר מעילה חטא חטא מתרומה (א) ה] °דבתרומה כתיב בני ישראל ולא עובדי כוכבים: ואין חייבין ו] עליו משום פיגול נותר וטמא: מ"ט דאתי פיגול עון עון מנותר ואתי נותר חילול חילול מטומאה ובטומאה כתיב (ב) ז] בני ישראל ולא עובדי כוכבים: ואין עושין תמורה: מאי טעמא דאיתקש תמורה למעשר בהמה ומעשר בהמה איתקש למעשר דגן ובמעשר דגן כתיב בני ישראל ולא עובדי כוכבים *וכי דבר הלמד בהיקש חוזר ומלמד בהיקש *מעשר דגן חולין הוא הניחא למאן דאמר *בתר מלמד אזלינן אלא למ"ד בתר למד אזלינן מאי איכא למימר אלא מעשר בהמה חובה שאין ח] קבוע לה זמן הוא וחובה שאין ט] לה זמן קבוע ישראל מייתו עובדי כוכבים לא מייתו: ואין מביאין נסכים: *תנו רבנן °אזרח אזרח י] *מביא נסכים ואין העובד כוכבים מביא נסכים יכול לא תהא עולתו טעונה נסכים ת"ל ככה: אמר רבי יוסי רואה אני בכולן יא] להחמיר בד"א בקדשי מזבח כו': מ"ט קסבר כי גמרה מעילה חטא חטא מתרומה דומיא דתרומה דקדישא קדושת הגוף אבל קדושת בדק הבית דקדושת דמים לא *ת"ר ידם שנטמא וזרקו בשוגג הורצה

במזיד

רש"י

הלכתא למשיחא · הרי קבע לנו הלכה הצריכה לנו לימות המשיח כשיבנה בית המקדש ועכשיו לא הוצרכנו לה: א"ל הלכה קאמינא · האי דמיתמהנא יב] קביעות הלכה הוא דמיתמהנא דמיגרס בעינן מיתני משניות ומחלוקת הלכות עבודה לפי שתורה היא ודרוש וקבל שכר אבל קיבוע הלכה אינה אלא להורות הלכה למעשה ועכשיו אינו נוהג: מתני' קדשי עובדי כוכבים כו' · מפרש בגמ' וכשהתנדבום לגבוה קאמר: גמ' ת"ר כו' · מפרשה לקמיה: ואין מביאין נסכים · בפני עצמם בלא זבח כישראל שמתנדבין יין כדתנן במנחות (דף קד:): בכולן אני רואה · בכל הדברים הללו אני רואה בקדשי עובדי כוכבים להחמיר כבקדשי ישראל: שנאמר בהם לה' · דכתיב איש איש מבית ישראל וגו' (ויקרא כב) ודרשינן בהכל שוחטין (חולין יג:) איש מה ת"ל איש איש לרבות את העובדי כוכבים שנודרים נדרים ונדבות כישראל: במה דברים אמורים · דאין מועלין בהן אתאן לת"ק: אבל בקדשי בדק הבית · עובד כוכבים שהתפיס יג] לבדק הבית: מועלין בו · ולקמן מפרש טעמא: דגמרינן מעילה חטא חטא מתרומה · כתיב במעילה וחטאה בשגגה (ויקרא ה) וכתיב בתרומה ולא ישאו עליו חטא (שם כב) ובתרומה כתיב בתריה דהאי קרא ולא יחללו את קדשי בני ישראל: יד] *דבתרומה כתיב בני ישראל · וינזרו מקדשי בני ישראל (שם כב): תמורה · בהמה: למעשר בהמה · דכתיב במעשר והיה הוא ותמורתו (שם כז): ומעשר בהמה למעשר דגן · עשר תעשר ואמר מר בבכורות (דף נג:) בשני מעשרות הכתוב מדבר אחד מעשר בהמה ואחד מעשר דגן: דבר הלמד · טו] מעשר בהמה הלמוד בהיקש שלא יהא נוהג בעובדי כוכבים חוזר ומלמד על התמורה בהיקש: מעשר דגן חולין הוא · ובכל התורה למדין למד מן הלמד חוץ מן הקדשים כדאמר באיזהו מקומן (לקמן מט:): הניחא למאן דאמר בתר מלמד אזלינן · דהאי מלמד חולין אף על גב דלמד קדש למדים בו הלמד מן הלמד ופלוגתייהו באיזהו מקומן (שם): עובדי כוכבים לא מייתו · דלא איתרבו עובדי כוכבים אלא לנדרים ונדבות כדכתיב בקרא לכל נדריהם וגו' (ויקרא כב) וה"ה נמי דלא מייתו חובה הקבוע טז] להם זמן כגון עולת ראייה ושלמי חגיגה אלא לא פסיקא ליה הואיל ומביאין עולה ושלמי נדבה אבל מעשר יז] חטאת ואשם לא שייך בהו כלל: אזרח · בפרשת נסכים כתיב בשלח לך כל האזרח יעשה ככה ומינה ילפינן לקמן בפרק כל התדיר (דף נא:) אזרח מלמד שמתנדבים נסכים יח] ומביא בפני עצמן נדבה: ת"ל ככה · יעשה לשור יט] שאחר שחובה תלויה בקרבן ל"ש ישראל ול"ש עובד כוכבים הלכך שלח דמי נסכיה יקרבו משלו ואם לאו כ] מקריבים משל ציבור שתנאי ב"ד הוא במסכת שקלים (דף יח:): מ"ט כו' · אמילתיה דר"ש קאי אמעילה דקאמר אבל קדשי בדק הבית דעובדי כוכבים מועלין: וכי גמרה מעילה מתרומה · למעוטי עובדי כוכבים דומיא דתרומה קדשי מזבח הוא כא] דגמרה דקדים גופייהו כתרומה שאינן נפדין:

במזיד

תוספות

הלכתא למשיחא · הא דלא פריך הכי גבי הלכה כר' יוסי האי גוונא פריך בריש ד' מיתות (סנהדרין נא:) ותימה דבריש עשרה יוחסין (קדושין עב:) *א"ר יהודה אמר רב הלכה כרבי יוסי דעתידין ממזרין ליטהר כב] ושמא נפקא מינה עכשיו שלא להרחיק משפחות שאינן ידועות ובקדושין (שם) פירשתי *במאי פליגי רבי יוסי ורבנן בממזר ידוע או בשאין ידוע ובפ"ק דיומא (דף יג.) דפסיק כר' יוסי כג] ראשון חוזר לעבודתו ושני אינו ראוי כו' נפקא מינה עכשיו בנשיא או ראש ישיבה או פרנס שנתמנה על הציבור ועבר מחמת אונס ועבר האונס ובפרק אלו דברים (פסחים סט:) דפסיק הלכה כר"ע דכל מלאכה שאפשר לעשותה מערב שבת אינה דוחה את השבת לענין פסח נפקא מינה בזמן הזה לענין מילה ואע"ג דגבי מילה נמי פסיק הכי בהדיא (בשבת קלג.) מ"מ לאשמועי' פסקא דמילה פסק נמי גבי פסח הכי ובפ"ק דתענית (דף ד:) דפסיק רבי אלעזר הלכה כר"ג דאמר בשבעה במרחשון ומוקי לה התם בזמן שבית המקדש קיים נפקא מינה גם בזמן הזה לבני בבל דאית להו פירי בדברא כדקאמר התם הא לן והא להו ומיהו בסוף התכלת (מנחות נב:) קשה דפסיק רבי יוחנן כאבא יוסי בן דוסתאי גבי חביתי כ"ג וכר"א דרב יוסף דוקא כד] דאית ליה הכא ובסנהדרין (דף נא:) דאין לפסוק הלכתא למשיחא וה"ר חיים מפרש דלא פריך הלכתא למשיחא אלא היכא דאיכא תרתי שהוא למשיחא וגם עושה איסור כה] דליכא נפקותא בהלכתא אלא על ידי איסור לא שייך לפסוק למשיחא*:

והשוחטן בחוץ פטור דברי ר' שמעון · בגמרא לא תני בברייתא שוחט בחוץ והכא לא תני תמורה ונסכים דתני בברייתא וזה תימה וא"ת אי ר"ש ס"ל *כרבי כו] אליעזר דאמר פרק ואלו מנחות (דף עג:) דאין עובדי כוכבים מביאין אלא עולות א"כ מאי איריא קדשי עובדי כוכבים דאין חייבין עליהם משום פיגול נותר וטמא אפי' דישראל נמי דהא שמעינן ליה לר"ש בסוף דם שחיטה (כריתות כג:) דאין פיגול בעולין ואין נותר בעולין וצ"ל דסבר לה כר' יוסי הגלילי דמביאין אפילו שלמים ועוד י"ל דבכריתות (דף יג: ודף כג:) מוכח דטעמא דר"ש משום דאין איסור חל על איסור וקדשי עובדי כוכבים שרו מדאורייתא כדתניא בגמרא לא נהנין מדרבנן ולא מועלין דגמר חטא חטא מתרומה כז]:

רואה אני בכולן להחמיר שנאמר בהן לה' · פי' בקרא דאיש איש דמרבינן עובדי כוכבים שנודרין כתיב לה' למימר *שעובדי כוכבים הם בכלל קדשי ה' משמע הכא דאיכא מעילה דאורייתא בקדשי מזבח וקשה דלא כח] איפריך מהכא לר' ינאי דאמר בפ' קדשי מזבח (דף טו.) במעילה דאין חייבין מעילה אלא על קדשי בדק הבית כדפריך התם כט] ומשני כולהו מדרבנן ועוד תנן פ' אמרו לו (כריתות יג:) יש אוכל אכילה אחת וחייב עליה ארבע חטאות ואשם אחד ותו דשילהי כל הבשר (חולין דף קיז.) אמר ר' ינאי גופיה כאשר יורם וגו' מה פר כהן משיח יש בו מעילה אף שלמים יש בהן מעילה ותו דשילהי תמורה (דף לג:) א"ר ינאי גופיה אין מעילה מפורשת מן התורה אלא בעולה בלבד שנאמר לה' קדשים המיוחדים לה' וי"ל אסמכתא נינהו ועוד י"ל דר' ינאי לא איירי אלא בדבר הניתר לטהורים אבל באימורים ועולה דהמעילה לא פקעה פשיטא דאיכא מעילה דאורייתא וקשה לי על זה אמאי לא משני במעילה הכי דכי פריך מטובא ל] ולישני באימורים:

ואין עושין תמורה דאיתקש למעשר בהמה · בפרק קמא דתמורה (דף ג.) דריש מדכתיב בריש ענייני דבר אל בני ישראל איש כי יפליא וגו'*:

ומעשר בהמה למעשר דגן · בבכורות לא] (דף נג:) אמרינן לא איתקש אלא לענין שנה:

דומיא דתרומה דקדישא קדושת הגוף · וא"ת אזהרה לנהנה מקדשי בדק הבית מנין דתנן אלו הן הלוקין (מכות יג.) וחשיב הקדש שלא נפדה משמע דבר שיש לו פדיון והיינו קדשי בדה"ב הא לא ידעינן אזהרה במעילה אלא מגזירה שוה דחטא חטא מתרומה פ' הנשרפין (סנהדרין פד.) והאי תנא לא יליף אלא דומיא דתרומה וי"ל דהקדש שלא נפדה לא מיירי בבדק הבית אלא בקדשי המזבח שהוממו דכיון דמעיקרא הוה בהו מעילה בשביל שהוממו לא פקעה המעילה ולכתי קשה

עין משפט נר מצוה

מח א מיי' פי"ח מהל' פסה"מ הלכה כד:
מט ב מיי' פי"ט מהל' פסה"מ הלכה טו:
נ ג מיי' פ"ה מהלכות מעילה הלכה טו:
נא ד מיי' פ"א מהלכות תמורה הלכה ו:
נב ה מיי' פ"ג מהלכות מעשה הקרבנות הל' ה ועיין בכ"מ:
נג ו מיי' פ"א מהלכות פסה"מ הלכה לד:

[שם איתא אמר ר"י אמר שמואל]
[לא נמצא שם בקדושין]
[בקצת נוסחאות ובמשנה שבמשניות איתא רבי מאיר]
[דאי יהיו כולם לזיקים כ"א בתי"ט ביומא ועי' תוספות יומא יג. ד"ה הלכה וכו' ומש שנרשם שם בגליון]
נ"א רבי עקיבא
[נ"א מקדשי עובדי כוכבים טו']

מסורת הש"ס

סנהדרין נא:
[סוטה מד. סנהדרין שם ונא.]
תמורה ב: ערכין ה: [תוספתא פ"ט]
[תמורה ג.]
[פסחים לג. קדושין מב: סנהדרין פד. תמורה שם מעילה יח:]
נ"א ובטומאה נ"ק
[לקמן מט. מכות יט.]
[לקמן מט. תמורה כא:]
[מכות יט: ע"ש לקמן מט: תמורה כב: ע"ש]
[נ"ל דתניא]
[תמורה ג. מנחות עג:]
יומא ג. מנחות כס. יבמות כד. גיטין כד. פסחים סח: ע:
[ועי' היטב תוס' תמורה ד"ה ומעשר דגן]

הגהות הב"ח

(א) גמ' ובתרומה כתיב בני ישראל ולא עובדי כוכבים: ר"ב עי' לעיל דף מו ע"ב בתוספות ד"ה אלא למעוטי ס':

שיטה מקובצת

א] בחוץ פטור · אמר הר"ם דכי היכי דדרשינן בשחוטי חוץ בני ישראל מצוין על שחוטי חוץ ולא עובדי כוכבים ה"נ נדרוש גבי הקרבן דדוקא קרבן של בני ישראל חייבין על שחוטי חוץ ולא בקרבן של עובדי כוכבים' מהר"פ: ב] אבל קרבנן טעון נסכים ואם שלח הנסכים יהיה משלו ואם לאו משל צבור' מהר"פ: ג] דברי רבי שמעון בספרי כת"י אין כתוב בברייתא זו דברי ר' שמעון וכן נראה מדברי התוס' ד"ה דומיא דתרומה דקאמרי שם וי"ל דלרבנן אפילו בדק הבית כו' ובזה יתיישב מה שפסק הרמב"ם בספי"ח מהל' פה"מ קדשי עובדי כוכבים אין חייבין עליהן משום פיגול נותר וטמא דלא כרבי יוסי ובהל' מעה"ק פסק כר' יוסי בשחטן בחוץ) אבל ברש"י גרים דברי ר"ש: ד] הבית מודה ר"ש שמועלין בהן כך יש בס"י ורש"י לא גרים כן: ה] ובתרומה: ו] חייבין עליהן: ז] בני ישראל ולא עובדי כוכבים' וא"ת (משמע הכא)(הכא משמע) דדרשינן ולא יחללו אפוטאת הגוף והא דרשינן לעיל בפרק קבלה אזהרת או אטמא ששימש וי"ל דנפקא לן חילול חילול שיש בסיפא דקרא [בני ישראל] דכתיב [אשר יקדישו] בני ישראל וא"ת והלא לא כתיב שם חילול וי"ל דקרא (נמי קאי) דחילול קאי נמי אסיפא דקרא דבני ישראל' מהר"פ ז"ל: ח] שאין לו זמן קבוע וא"ת אמאי צריך להזכיר משום דאין קבוע להם זמן הלא הם אין מביאין [אפילו] קרבן הקבוע להם זמן כגון עולת ראייה ושלמי חגיגה וי"ל דס"מ מביאין חדושה להם בשמייתו כגון שלמי נדבה או עולת נדבת משא"כ בשאר שאין קבוע להם זמן ולכך הזכיר משום דאין קבוע להם זמן משום דפסיקא ליה' מהר"פ ז"ל: ט] שאין לו אות ה' נמחק: י] אזרח מביא נסכים (עיין מנחות דף עג ע"ב) בחידושי שכתבתי: יא] להחמיר כו' בד"א בס"י יש אמר ר' יוסי כו' מ"ט לה' כתיב בהו במד"א בקדשי כו' קסבר כו' ורש"י לא גרים כן: יב] דמיתמהנא אקביעות הלכה: יג] שהתפיס מנה לבדק: יד] ישראל ובטומאה כתיב: טו] הלמד בהיקש מעשר בהמה הלמוד בהיקש מדנן שלא יהא: טז] הקבוע לה זמן: יז] מעשר חוטאת: יח] נסכים בכל יום ודוקא אזרח ולא עובד כוכבים הס"ד ומה"ד ומביא נסכים: יט] לשור מאחר שחובה: כ] לאו קרבים משל: כא] הוא דקדיש תיבת דגמרה נמחק: כב] לישהר ולא פריך הלכתא למשיחא: כג] יוסי דאמר: כד] דוקא הוא דאית: כה] איסור כיון דליכא: כו] עקיבא תיבת אליעזר נמחק: כז] מתרומה וא"ת הא דתנן לקמן נוטה ר' שמעון בדבר שדרכו לאכול חייב אבל העצים והלבונה [כו'] [וא"ת בתוספות נמחק (סוף דברי התוס')] מחיבת אבל בע"ב לדבור בפ"ע שלא במקומו והוא שייך לכאן כי הוא דבור אחד עכ"ה: כח] דלא פריך מהכא: כט] התם טובא ומשני: ל] מטובא לישני ואות ו' נמחק: לא] בבכורות (עי' תוס' בכורות נג. ע"א ד"ה ע"א):
א) נ"ל דלפי גי' הכ"ל א"ש דברי הרמב"ם דגבי פיגול נותר וטמא פסק דלא כר"י משום דהתם פליג עליה ת"ק והלכה כת"ק נגד ר"י משא"כ בשחוטי חוץ דסליג עם ר"ש פסק כר"ש · ובעובדי

גליון הש"ס מתני' ר"י מחייב · עיין לקמן דף קטו ע"ב תוס' ד"ה אסור ומנחות דף קט ע"ב תוס' ד"ה וסתם: גמ' טעון נסכים דר"ש · בתשובת מוס' בגלגל הסכמי סימן א' דף ט ע"ג כתב בכל ספרי מדויקי ודוקני אשר מצאתי כתיב ג"כ דר"ש וכ"נ מדברי התוספות בל"ל · שם דבתרומה כתיב בני ישראל · עיין קדושין דף מה ע"ב תוספות ד"ה והכהנים:

עין משפט נר מצוה

נד א מיי' פ"ח מהל' פסה"מ הלכה יז:

נה ב מיי' שם הל' כב:

במזיד לא הורצה בד"א ביחיד אבל בציבור בין בשוגג בין במזיד הורצה א]*ובעובדי כוכבי' בין בשוגג ובין במזיד לא הורצה אמרוה רבנן קמיה דרב פפא ב] כמאן דלא כרבי יוסי דאי רבי יוסי האמר בכולן אני רואה להחמיר אמר להו רב פפא אפי' תימא רבי יוסי שאני התם דאמר קרא להם ולא לעובדי כוכבים אמר ליה רב הונא בריה דרב נתן לרב פפא אלא מעתה °אשר הם מקדישים ה"נ הם ולא עובדי כוכבים אלא אמר רב אשי אמר קרא °לרצון להם ועובדי כוכבים לאו בני הרצאה נינהו: **מתני'** ג] דברים שאין חייבים עליהם משום פיגול *חייבין עליהן משום נותר ומשום טמא חוץ מן הדם ד] ר' שמעון מחייב *בדבר שדרכן לאכול אבל העצים והלבונה והקטורת אין חייבין עליו משום טומאה: **גמ'** ת"ר *יכול לא יהו חייבין משום טומאה אלא על דבר שיש לו מתירין בין לאדם בין למזבח ודין הוא ומה פיגול שהוא בקביעה ובידיעה אחת ולא הותר מכללו אין חייבין עליו אלא על דבר שיש לו מתירין בין לאדם בין למזבח טומאה שהיא בעולה ויורד ובשתי ידיעות והותרה מכללה אינו דין שאינו חייב אלא על דבר שיש לו מתירין בין לאדם בין למזבח ה] ת"ל °אשר הם מקדישים לי יכול מיד ת"ל °יקרב ו] אמר ר"א וכי יש נוגע שהוא חייב אלא מה ת"ל יקרב בהוכשר [בשר] ליקרב הכתוב מדבר הא כיצד יש לו מתירין משיקרבו מתירין ז] אין לו מתירין משיקדש בכלי אשכחן טומאה נותר מנלן אתי חילול חילול מטומאה ח] ולילף עון עון מפיגול מסתברא מטומאה הוי ליה למילף ט] שכן גז"ל סימן אדרבה מפיגול הוה ליה למילף שכן *נותר ציץ טהור בזמן קרב והני נפישן אלא מדתני לוי דתני לוי מנין שאף בפסול זמן הכתוב מדבר ת"ל *°ולא יחללו את *(קדשי בני ישראל) בשני

תורה אור: ויקרא כב · שמות כח · ויקרא כב · שם

רש"י

במזיד לא הורצה · קנסא דרבנן הוא ולא שיבא אחר דא"כ נמצאו ב"ד מתנין לעקור דבר מן התורה ולהביא חולין לעזרה אלא לא הורצה להתיר בשר באכילה] אבל בעלים נתכפרו והכי אמר לה *שמואל במס' יבמות (דף צ.):יא] [כמאן]· הא דקתני דעובדי כוכבים לא הורצה דלא כר' יוסי: אלא מעתה אשר הם מקדישים לי · דכתיב גבי ויזרו : הכי נמי הם ולא עובדי כוכבים · ותימא דקדשי עובדי כוכבים אין חייבין עליהם משום טומאה לר' יוסי והא (א) קאמר בכולן אני רואה להחמיר : לרצון להם · גבי ציץ כתיב : לאו בני הרצאה · להקב"ה הם שאינו מתרצה להם : **מתני'** דברים שאין חייבין עליהם משום פיגול· כגון הקומץ והקטרת וכל השנויים במשנתינו : חייבין עליהן משום טומאה · כרת האוכלן בטומאת הגוף ועל שגגתם חטאת כדיליף בגמרא : חוץ מן הדם· דאימעוט בהדיא כדאמר בגמ' : ה"ג נומי ר"ש בדבר שדרכו לאכול חייב וכך שמעתי מבית יב] מדרשו של רבינו יעקב ול"נ שכך פירש ר' משולם בר קלונימוס גאון *בשעת מיתתו נומי ר"ש כמו אמר (ב) ר"ש ובספרים היה כתוב הדם יג] *ועמו: בדבר שדרכו לאכול· שדרך בני אדם יד] לאכול ואף על פי שזה מן הנקטרים כגון קומץ ומנחת כהנים ודומין לה : אבל לבונה ועצים וקטרת אין חייבין עליהם משום טומאה · ורבנן פליגי עלה כדמרבינן להו טו] מכל הבשר יתירא לרבות עצים ולבונה : **גמ'** ומה פיגול · *האוכל פיגול בשוגג : שהוא בקבוע · חטאתו קבוע לעני כלעשיר כשבה או שעירה : ובידיעה אחת · שאינו צריך ידיעה בתחלה טז] שאכל בשוגג וידע שאכל : ולא הותר מכללו · אצל ציבור : שהיא בעולה ויורד · לעשיר בהמה ובדלות שתי תורים ובדלי דלות עשירית האיפה גבי שמיעת קול בויקרא (ה) : ובשתי ידיעות · כשמא וידע שנטמא ונעלמה ממנו טומאה ואכל את הקודש ולא ידע ומשאכל ידע אבל יז]שיש בה ידיעה בסוף ואין בה ידיעה בתחלה שלפני אכילתו לא ידע מעולם בטומאה זו פטור והכי גמרי' לה בשבועות (דף ד·) : והותרה מכללה · טומאת הגוף הותרה אצל ציבור בפסח דתנן (פסחים דף עו:) הפסח שבא בטומאה נאכל בטומאה : ת"ל אשר הם מקדישים · ריבה כל המוקדשים וגבי ויזרו כתיב : יכול מיד · יח] משהוקדשו מתחייב עליו מיד אם אכלו בטומאה : ת"ל אשר יקרב · מכל זרעכם ר"א מפרש לה ואזיל: וכי יש נוגע חייב · והלא אינו חייב אלא אם כן אכל כדכתיב יט] (ויקרא כב) איש איש מזרע אהרן וגו' : בהוכשר ליקרב · ואקדשים קאי והכי קאמר אשר יקריב קדשים ואח"כ יאכלם כ]וטומאה עליו כדמפרש אכילה בקרא דבתריה:יש לו מתירין· כגון אימורים ובשר שהדם מתירן ושירי מנחות שהקומץ מתירן משיקרבו מתיריו ושאין לו מתירין כגון מנחת כהנים וכהן משיח ונסכים משיקדשו בכלי שהוא המכשירן לאכילה האמורה בהן:נותר מנלן· דחייב כא](כהן)עליו אף על דבר שאין לו מתירין כדקתני מתני' דברים שאין חייבין עליהן משום פיגול חייבין עליהן משום נותר : שכן גז"ל כב]סימן· נותר וטומאה פסול הגוף ופיגול פסול מחשבה כג] נותר וטומאה אין זריקת הדם מביאתן לידי כד]פסולן ופיגול זריקת הדם קובעתו בפסול נותר וטמא נאמר בהן חילול* : שכן הותר ציץ טהור בזמן קרב והני נפישן · נותר ופיגול לא הותרו מכללן כטומאה ואין הציץ מרצה עלייהו כטומאה ואע"ג דבטומאת הגוף כה] קאמינא שאין הציץ מרצה עליה שם טומאה מיהת נרצית בציץ · טהור · שניהן טהורין ושניהן נפסלין בזמן זה בנותר חוץ לזמן וזה במחשבת זמן ושניהן פסולין בקרב לאפוקי טומאת הגוף שפסולן *במקריב: מנין שאף בפסול זמן הכתוב מדבר · האי קרא דויזרו : ולא יחללו · דכתיב גבי טומאה : בשני

תוספות

קשה מהא דילפינן בפרק כו] בתרא דמעילה (דף יח:) חטא חטא מתרומה לענין פגם והנאה כז] *במעילה במחובר לקרקע ומחובר הייתו קדושת דמים ולא גמרי מתרומה וי"ל דהכא דוקא הוא דבעינן דומיא דתרומה משום דכתיב לה' לרבויי כח] דלא גמרינן אלא דומיא דתרומה דקדושת הגוף כט] עוד יש לומר דלרבנן אפי' בדק הבית גמרינן מתרומה למעט עובדי כוכבים ל] *בד"א ר' יוסי קאמר ליה ולא גמר בדק הבית מתרומה וכן נראה מדמייתי הש"ס ר' יוסי אומר בכולן אני רואה להחמיר וכו' ומפרש מ"ט דומיא דתרומה דקדושת הגוף וה"ק שכל קדשי עובדי כוכבים אני רואה להחמיר משום פיגול נותר וטמא אבל מאי דאמריתו אין מועלין הני מילי בקדשי המזבח דגמרינן מתרומה לא] *(ואהני לינא) דלא גמרינן מתרומה אלא מידי דדמיא לה אבל בדק הבית דלא דמי לה מועלין כך פירש רבינו והקשה לו בנו ה"ר אלחנן דבפ"ק דערכין (דף ה:) אמר *אביי וערכו נגנז ופריך א"כ לא ימעטו בו אלמה תניא אבל קדשי בדק הבית מועלין ולישני ההיא ר' יוסי אבל לרבנן אין מועלין וי"ל דשפיר משני התם וכ"ז הגיה רבינו: **אבל** העצים והלבונה והקטרת אין בהם משום טומאה· לב] ואם תאמר מאי איריא משום דאין נאכלין תיפוק ליה דאין איסור טומאה חל עליהם דהא יש בהן מעילה ורבי שמעון היא דאמר (כריתות כג:) אין פיגול בעולין ואין נותר בעולין לפי שאין איסור חל על איסור ועוד חטאות הפנימיות אמאי צריך למעוטינהו מפיגול לר' שמעון ואמאי חייבין עליהם משום נותר וטמא והא אית בהו מעילה ואין איסור חל על איסור ומיהו בזה יש לומר דמשכחת לה לאחר שניתך הבשר ועדיין ראויה לאכילה דתנן במעילה (דף ט.) דמועלין בהן עד שיתוך הבשר לג] ומ"מ קשה מפיגול שהרי פקע פיגולו מכי משלה בו האור אבל מעצים קשה דיש בהן מעילה לעולם וי"ל דתנא דר' שמעון דהכא סבר ליה כההוא תנא דרבי שמעון דאמר התם יש פיגול בעולין ויש נותר בעולין ועוד י"ל דמשכחת לה בבת אחת כגון שהביא שתי שערות אחר כך לד] כדאשכחן ביבמות פרק ד' אחין (דף לג·) וקשה קצת הא דאמר פ' דם שחיטה (כריתות כג:) למאן דאמר אין איסור חל על איסור כל חלב מאי עביד ליה ומוקי לה בוולדי קדשים לוקמי בהביא שתי שערות אחר כך דהוה ליה בת אחת ומיהו בלאו הכי שפיר קמשני וזה אין להקשות למ"ד אין איסור חל על איסור בקדשים *נ"ל קרא בדם למעוטי מותר וטמא דהא איצטריך להביא שתי שערות אחר כך דהוי כבת אחת כדפרישנא ומיהו למאי דבעי למימרא בפ' ד' אחין (יבמות לג·) דר' שמעון אפי' בת אחת לית ליה קשה: **תלמוד** לומר אשר הם מקדישים לי· גבי טמא כתיב ומרבי הכא מיניה כל דבר והא דמייתי ליה בברייתא דלעיל גבי פיגול *הייתו לה] דשייך טומאה בעופות ומנחות והדר אתי נותר חילול חילול מטומאה ופיגול עון עון מנותר לו] ולאחר שריבה הכתוב כל דבר מטומאה חוזר וממעט בפיגול מכלל ופרט וכלל: **יש** לו מתירין משיקרבו מתירין· מכל טהור יאכל בשר דרשינן ליה בהקומץ רבה (מנחות כה:) *ובסמוך* לז] : **שכן** גזל · פירש"י למ"ד *הייתו חילול חילול וקשה על זה בתר הכי דפריך אדרבה מפיגול נילף שכן הותר וכו' אמאי לא אמר גם כן שכן עון מעון ופר"ח למ"ד דגזל הייתו כולו פיגול שייך בכל הקרבן אבל נותר וטומאה שייכי בחתיכה אחת : הכי

מסורת הש"ס

נ"ל ר' יוסי ב"ח נ"ק · [לעיל עו: מנחות סה.] · שבועות ז. · [וכ"כ תוס' במנחות קב: ד"ה בתחלה ע"ש] · וטמי נ"ק · שהוא בקביעה האוכל פיגול בשוגג שהוא בקבוע חטאתו כו' נ"ל וכ"ס נס"י · נ"א סותר כיון נ"ק · [נ"ל שם קדשי אשר הם מקדישים לי] · ופיגול לא נאמר בו חילול הס"ד נ"ק · נמקריבו נ"ק

באכילה וממעט מחובר לקרקע וממחובר הייתו קדושת דמים וגמרינן מתרומה נ"ק · ובד"א נ"ק · נ"א והודו לי וגי' יאהני לה' · נ"ל אביי · [מעילה י: ע"ש] · נ"א כיון דשייך כו' סתר אתי נ"ק · אפרש הס"ד נ"ק · *דגזל הייתו נ"ק

הגהות הב"ח

(א) רש"י ד"ה ה"נ הם ולא עובדי כוכבים וכו' והא קאמר נ"ב ע"ל ר"פ כל הזבחים דף טו ע"ב דגמ' מוכית להדיא כאופן אחר וע"ש בתוס' ד"ה אלא למעוטי וכו' : (ב) ד"ה ה"ג נומי ר"ש וכו' כמו אמר ר"ש נ"ב וכ"כ בחולין דף ע ע"ב להדיא :

שיטה מקובצת

א] ובעובדי כוכבים עי' רש"י לעיל (דף עו ע"ב): ב] פפא הא דלא כרבי יוסי כו' האמר בכולן רואה אני: ג] אף דברים: ד] הדם נומי ר' שמעון בדבר שדרכו לאכול חייב אבל העצים והלבונה כו' אין חייבין עליהן משום : ה] תלמוד לומר אשר הם מקדישים לי וא"ת מה צריך לרבות מבשר זבח נילף הכל מאשר הם מקדישים וי"ל דאי לאו קרא דבשר זבח דגלי דלא נלמד בכלל ופרט וכלל לא הייתי דורש חילול חילול לג"ש לסתור כלל ופרט וכלל ולא הייתי מרבה כי אם (הדמי) [הדומה] לפרט אבל השתא דקרא גופיה מפקיה מדין כלל ופרט וכלל מרבינן כל דאית ליה לרבויי : ו] א"ר אלעזר וכי יש נוגע שהוא חייב א"ת אה"נ ותירץ בקונטרס מדכתיב איש איש וגו' ואכל מן הקדשים · מהר"פ : ז] אין לו מתירין כו' וא"ת ולמה לי האי קרא תיפוק ליה מהתם דאמרינן כל טהור יאכל בשר ודרשינן הניתר לטהורים חייבין עליו משום טומאה ושאין ניתר לטהורים אין חייבין עליו משום טומאה וי"ל דהא דדרשינן הכא מיירי באכילת גבוה והתם מיירי באכילת הדיוט ולא למילף זה מזה · מהר"פ : ח] ולילף עון עון מפיגול · תימה הלא היכא דאיכא לאקושי להומרא ולקולא להומרא מקשינן וכי מקשינן לפיגול הוי לקולא וי"ל דסמיך אהא דפריך אדרבה פיגול עדיפא ליה : ט] שכן גזל פ"ה למד נותר וטומאה נאמר בהן חילול כו' ולא נהירא לחשב הג"ש עצמה דא"כ פיגול נמי נחשוב ג"ש דעון ופר"ח דהלמד היינו כולן דכשמפגל מקצתו מתפגל כל הקרבן אבל נותר וטמא לא הוי בכל הקרבן אלא דוקא ההוא אבר שניתותר או שנטמא אבל גוף הקרבן לא נפסל בהכי מהר"פ: י] באכילה קאמר אבל : יא] תיבת כמאן ל"ש ונמחק ומה"ד הא דקתני בעובדי כוכבים: יב] מדרשו של רבינו יעקב מ"כ ותיבת ול"נ נמחק (עי' תוספות מנחות דף קב ע"ב) ד"ה בתחלה : יג] הדם ונומי : יד] אדם לאוכלו : טו] להו מן הבשר יתירא : טז] בתחלה אלא : יז] אבל יש בה : יח] מיד משהקדישו יתחייב עליו : יט] כדכתיב בתריה איש איש מזרע אהרן ואכל מן הקדשים וגו' והאי קרא משמע באכילה הס"ד : כ] יאכלם וטומאתו עליו : כא] תיבת כהן נמחק : כב] גזל גימ"ל ותיבת סימן ל"ש : כג] מחשבה ודין נותר : כד] לידי פיגול וזריקת כו' בפסול למד נותר וטמא נאמר בהם חילול ופיגול לא נאמר בו חילול הס"ד : כה] הגוף קיימינן ותיבת קאמינא נמחק : כו] בפ' חמישי דמעילה : כז] ונהנה ובמחובר ותיבת במעילה נמחק : כח] לרבויי ולא גמרינן : כט] מתיבת עוד כו' עד תיבת אחת בסוף העמוד מוקף בהצאי לבנה : ל] ובד"א : לא] ואהני לה' דלא גמרינן : לב] תיבות ואם תאמר נמחק [אא"ה כל דבור זה הוא שייך לעמוד א' בסוף ד"ה והשוהמן] : לג] הבשר תוספות ומכל מקום קשה לי כו' בו האור ומעצים קשה דיש כו' : לד] כך תוספות כדאשכחן : לה] היינו ס"א דלא מחייבינן אלא בדבר שיש לו מתירין היינו כדמפרש ואפילו נותר אתיא כו' : לו] מנותר לאחר שריבה : לז] ובסמוך אפרש הס"ד :

גליון הש"ס תוס' ד"ה אבל וכו' למ"ל קרא בדם למעוטי מותר וטמא וכו' · ק"ל הא תוספות כתבו כמה פעמים דדם שבשלו אינו שבר עליו עיין חולין דף קטו ע"א א"כ צריך קרא לבשלו הדם דפקע איסור דם ממכל מקום אינו חייב משום נותר וטמא : ד"ה יש לו מתירין וכו' ובסמוך דף טו ע"ב ד"ה אחת פירשתי כנ"ל :

sprinkled it unwittingly, it [the sacrifice] is accepted; [45b] if deliberately, it is not accepted.[6] This was said only of a private sacrifice, but a public sacrifice, whether done unwittingly or deliberately, is accepted. But a heathen ['s sacrifice], whether it is done unwittingly or deliberately, is not accepted. Now, the Rabbis stated the following in R. Papa's presence: With whom does this agree? Not with R. Jose, for if [it agrees with] R. Jose, surely he said: I hold that a stringent view should be taken on all these matters?[7] Said R. Papa to them: You may even say [that it agrees with] R. Jose: there it is different, because Scripture says,
a [*that it may be accepted*] *for them* [*before the Lord*]:[1] for them, but not for heathens. Said R. Huna the son of R. Nathan to R. Papa: If so, [when Scripture says,] [*Speak unto Aaron and to his sons, that they separate themselves from the holy things of the children of Israel*] *which they hallow unto Me*,[2] does that also mean: They, but not heathens?[3] —Rather said R. Ashi: Scripture says, *'that it may be accepted for them'*, whilst heathens are not subject to 'acceptance'.

MISHNAH. THE THINGS WHICH DO NOT INVOLVE LIABILITY ON ACCOUNT OF PIGGUL,[4] INVOLVE LIABILITY ON ACCOUNT OF NOTHAR AND DEFILEMENT EXCEPT BLOOD. R. SIMEON DECLARES ONE LIABLE IN RESPECT OF ANYTHING WHICH IS NORMALLY EATEN, BUT THE WOOD, THE FRANKINCENSE AND THE INCENSE DO NOT INVOLVE LIABILITY ON ACCOUNT OF DEFILEMENT.

GEMARA. Our Rabbis taught: You might think that liability on account of defilement is incurred only in respect of that which has *mattirin* both for man and for the altar;[5] and that is logical: If liability on account of *piggul* is incurred only in respect of that which has *mattirin* both for man and for the altar, though it is fixed [invariable], and [is incurred] in one state of awareness, and was never permitted contrary to its general prohibition;[6] then surely it is logical that defilement involves liability only in respect of that which has *mattirin* both for man and for the altar, seeing that it
b requires a variable burnt-offering,[1] two states of awareness,[2] and is [sometimes] permitted in opposition to its general prohibition. Therefore Scripture wrote, [*Speak unto Aaron and to his sons, that they separate themselves from the holy things of the children of Israel,*] *which they hallow unto Me*.[3] You might think [that liability is involved] immediately;[4] therefore Scripture teaches, [*Whoever he be . . .*] *that approacheth* [*unto the holy things . . . having his uncleanness upon him, that soul shall be cut off from before Me*].[5] Now R. Eleazar said: Is then one who [merely] *touches* [the holy things] liable?[6] Why does it say *'that approacheth'*?[7] [To teach that] the Writ speaks of flesh which was made fit to be offered.[8] How so? If it has *mattirin*, [culpability is incurred] only when the *mattirin* have been offered; if it has no *mattirin*, [culpability is incurred] as soon as it is sanctified in a [sacred] vessel.

We have thus found [it of] defilement. How do we know [it of] *nothar*?[9]—Identity of law with defilement is learnt from the fact that 'profanation' is written in both. Yet let us learn identity of law from *piggul*, because *'iniquity'* is written in connection with both?—Reason asserts that we should learn it from uncleanness, because [they are alike in respect of] *GeZeL*, [this being a]
c mnemonic.[1] On the contrary, one should learn it from *piggul*, because [it resembles it in the following points:] permissibility, the headplate, cleanness, time, that which is offered; and these are more numerous?[2]—Rather, it [is derived] from Levi's teaching. For Levi taught: How do we know that the Writ speaks of time disqualification too?[3] Because it says, *That they profane not* [*My*

(6) Lit., 'made acceptable'. The language is Biblical, cf. Lev. I, 4: *and it shall be accepted for him to make atonement for him*—i.e., the sacrifice effects its purpose. By Biblical law it is accepted in both cases, but the Rabbis penalized the priests by not permitting the flesh to be eaten when it was done deliberately. (7) Thus he regards the heathen's sacrifice the same as an Israelite's sacrifice; then here too the same law should apply to both.

a (1) Ex. XXVIII, 38. The passage refers to the wearing of the headplate by the High Priest, and teaches (according to the Talmudic interpretation) that in virtue of this wearing sacrifices are accepted, i.e., valid, even when the blood is defiled. (2) Lev. XXII, 2. (3) I.e., that unclean priests need not separate themselves from the sacrifices of heathens.—Surely R. Jose said that he takes a stringent view in all these matters? (4) As enumerated in the Mishnah 42b *seq*. (5) V. notes on Mishnah 42b. (6) The sin-offering for eating *piggul* is fixed, and is the same for rich and poor alike—a lamb or a she-goat. It is incurred in one state of awareness, i.e., to be liable it is not necessary that one should know at first that it is *piggul*, then forget and eat it, and then become aware of it again, as it is in the case of defilement (v. note 2, p. 230). If only one ate it unwittingly, not having known at all that it was unclean, and then become aware of it, there is culpability. Again, the prohibition of *piggul* is never raised, even if all the sacrifices of the whole community had been rendered *piggul*, whereas in the case of uncleanness, if the whole community was in a state of uncleanness, the Passover-offering is brought and is eaten in that same state too.

b (1) A wealthy man offers an animal-sacrifice; a poor man two doves; and a very poor man offers the tenth of an ephah of meal. (2) For one to be culpable he must have known at first that it was unclean, then forgotten and eaten it, and then learn of its uncleanness again (Shebu. 4a). (3) Lev. XXII, 2. The passage refers to uncleanness, and *'which they hallow unto Me'* is an extension (being superfluous in itself), and therefore includes *all* hallowed things. (4) As soon as it is dedicated liability is incurred for eating it in an unclean state. (5) Ibid. 3. (6) Surely not, for culpability is incurred only for eating (as in v. 4.)! (7) Which implies mere touch. (8) 'Offered' is the same root as 'approacheth'; (9) That there is liability even where there are no *mattirin*.

c (1) G = *Guf* (body); Z = *Zeriḳah* (sprinkling); and L = *ḥiLlul*. *Nothar* and defilement are both intrinsic (i.e., bodily) disqualifications in the flesh, whereas *piggul* is disqualification through intention. *Nothar* and defilement do not disqualify through the sprinkling of the blood, whereas *piggul* does. And finally, *ḥillul* (profanation) is written in connection with *nothar* and defilement, but not in connection with *piggul*. (2) (i) *Nothar* and *piggul* are never permitted in opposition to the general interdict, whereas defilement is. (ii) The headplate does not propitiate for these, though it does in the case of defilement (v. *supra a* bottom and note a.l.). (Though we are now discussing the uncleanness of the *person*, whereas the headplate propitiates only if the *blood* of the sacrifice is unclean, nevertheless it is true to say that the headplate does propitiate in a case of uncleanness.) (iii) *Nothar* and *piggul* are both clean. (iv) Both are disqualified through the time element, *nothar* because it was left until after the proper time, *piggul* because of an illegitimate intention in respect of after time. Finally, (v) they are both disqualifications in respect of the sacrifice, which is offered; whereas defilement is a disqualification of the priest, who *offers* it. (3) Such as *nothar*.

holy name]:[4] [46*a*] the Writ speaks of two modes of profanation, viz., the disqualification of *nothar* and the disqualification of defilement.[5]

EXCEPT BLOOD etc. Whence do we know it?—Said 'Ulla, Scripture saith, [*For the life of the flesh is in the blood;*] *and I have given it to you* [*upon the altar to make atonement for your souls*]:[6] [this teaches,] it is yours.[7] The school of R. Ishmael taught: '*To make atonement*' [implies] but not for trespass. R. Joḥanan said: Scripture saith, *it is* [which intimates,] it is before atonement as after atonement: a as there is no trespass after atonement,[1] so there is no trespass before atonement. Say, it is after atonement as before atonement: as it involves trespass before atonement,[2] so it involves trespass after atonement?—Nothing involves trespass once its function is performed. Does it not? But lo, there are the separated ashes?[3]—That is because the separated ashes and the priestly vestments[4] are [taught in] two texts which come for the same purpose,[5] and wherever two texts come for the same purpose, they do not illumine [other cases].[6] That is well according to the Rabbis who maintain that, [*And Aaron ... shall put off the linen garments ...*] *and shall leave them there*[7] teaches that they must be stored away.[8] But what can be said on the view of R. Dosa, who maintained [that] they are permitted to an ordinary priest, only that he [the High Priest] does not use them on another Day of Atonement?—Because the separated ashes and the beheaded heifer[9] are [taught in] two texts which come for the same purpose, and wherever two texts come for the same purpose, they do not illumine [other cases]. That is well on the view that they do not illumine; but what can be said on the view that they do illumine?—Two limitations are written:[10] b here is written, [*over the heifer*] *whose neck was broken;*[1] while there it says, [*And he shall take up the ashes ...*] *and he shall put* them [*beside the altar*].[2] Now, why do I need three texts in connection with blood?[3]—One excludes it from trespass, another from *nothar*, and a third from defilement.[4] But no text is required for *piggul*, for we learnt: Whatever has *mattirin*, whether for man or for the altar, involves liability on account of *piggul;* whereas blood is itself a *mattir*.

R. Joḥanan said: For what purpose is *kareth* stated three times

(4) Lev. XXII, 2.
(5) The two profanations are deduced from the fact that Scripture employs a longer form, *yeḥallelu* (profane) instead of *yeḥallu*. (6) *For it is*—hu—*the blood that maketh atonement by reason of the life*. (Lev. XVII, 11). (7) 'Ulla said this in reference to trespass: 'it is yours' means that in respect of trespass it is treated as secular, and so involves no offering for misappropriation. The deductions by the school of R. Ishmael and R. Joḥanan which follow, point to the same conclusion. Thus we have three texts shewing that blood does not involve trespass; since three are unnecessary for this purpose, they are ultimately employed to teach that blood does not involve liability in respect of *nothar*, trespass, and defilement.

a (1) After the blood has been sprinkled and atonement thereby made, there is no trespass in putting it to secular use, since it is no longer required for a sacred purpose. (2) This would have to be assumed in default of a text to the contrary. R. Joḥanan of course does not deduce the contrary from the other texts. (3) A shovelful of ashes was removed every day from the altar and placed at the east side of the altar, where they might not be used, though their function had already been performed, but left to become absorbed in their place. (4) The four additional vestments worn by the High Priest when he entered the Holy of Holies on the Day of Atonement. On leaving it he removed them, and they might not be put to secular use. Both these cases are deduced from Scriptural texts. (5) In both trespass is involved *after* their function has been fulfilled. (6) For if they were to serve as an illustration for others, one only need be stated, and the other, together with other cases, would follow. (7) Lev. XVI, 23. (8) And not used. Thus there are two such instances. (9) V. Deut. XXI, 9. The Rabbis deduce from the superfluous '*there*' in the passage, *and shall break the heifer's neck* there *in the valley* (v. 4), that the heifer must be buried there and not put to any use. (10) Sh. M. deletes 'two'.

b (1) Deut. XXI v. 6; lit. 'the broken-necked'. The deduction is from the article '*the*': only this animal whose function has been performed may still not be used, but no other similar sacred animal, i.e., one whose function has been performed, may not be used. (2) Lev. VI, 3. Here too '*them*' implies, only these ashes may not be used in such a case, but other sacred things may be used after their function has been performed. (3) To shew that blood does not involve trespass. This is the completion of the answer to the question, 'How do we know that blood does not create liability for *nothar*' etc., as explained *supra* n. 7. (4) I.e., that blood does not involve culpability on account of these.

נו א מיי' פ"ח מהל' כלי המקדש הל' ס:

בשני חילולין הכתוב מדבר אחד פסול נותר ואחד פסול טומאה: חוץ מן הדם כו': מנא הני מילי *אמר עולא אמר קרא °ואני נתתיו לכם א] שלכם יהא דבי רבי ישמעאל תנא אמר קרא °לכפר לכפרה נתתיו ולא למעילה רבי יוחנן אמר אמר קרא °הוא לפני כפרה כלאחר כפרה מה אחר כפרה אין בו מעילה אף לפני כפרה אין בו מעילה אימא לאחר כפרה כלפני כפרה מה לפני כפרה יש בו מעילה אף לאחר כפרה יש בו מעילה אין לך דבר שנעשית מצותו ומועלין בו ולא והרי תרומת הדשן משום דהוי תרומת הדשן ובגדי כהונה שני כתובין הבאין כאחד *וכל שני כתובים הבאין כאחד אין מלמדין הניחא *לרבנן דאמרי °והניחם שם מלמד *שטעונין גניזה אלא לרבי דוסא דאמר מותרות הן לכהן הדיוט ובלבד שלא ישתמש בהן ליה"כ אחר מאי איכא למימר משום דהוי תרומת הדשן ועגלה ערופה שני כתובין הבאין כאחד וכל שני כתובין הבאין כאחד אין מלמדין הניחא למאן דאמר אין מלמדין אלא למאן דאמר מלמדין מאי איכא למימר ב] תרי מיעוטי כתיבי הכא כתיב °הערופה והתם כתיב °ושמו ותלתא קראי בדם למה לי ג] למעוטי ממעילה מנותר ומטומאה אבל פיגול לא צריך קרא דתנן *כל שיש לו מתירין בין לאדם בין למזבח חייבין עליו משום פיגול ודם ד] גופיה מתיר הוא אמר רבי יוחנן *שלשה כריתות בשלמים למה

אחת

רש"י

בשני חילולים · מדלא כתיב ויכזרו ולא ה] יחללו: אחד פסול נותר · דאשכחן ביה חילול דכתיב (ויקרא יט) כי את קדש ה' חילל ואתרוייהו קאי אשר הם מקדישים דמרבינן מיניה כל המוקדשים: מנא הני מילי · דדם אין חייבין עליו משום נותר אם שגג בו בדם ונותר אינו חייב שתים אלא אחת וכן אם ו] אכלן בטומאת הגוף אינו חייב שתים: אמר עולא אמר קרא כו' · הא דעולא לאו הכא איתמר אלא גבי מעילה איתמר במס' מעילה (דף יא·) דקתני אין מועלין בדמים והכא ז] ה"ק מנא הני מילי דמתניתין אמר עולא גבי מעילה אמר קרא לכם ותנא דבי רבי ישמעאל לכפר כו' ור' יוחנן אמר הוא ומסקנא תלתא קראי חד למעוטי מנותר וחד למעוטי ח] ממעילה וחד למעוטי מטומאה: ואני נתתיו לכם שלכם יהא · כחולין שלכם שאין בהן מעילה: לכפר · ואני נתתיו לכם על המזבח לכפר (ויקרא יז) לכפרה נתתיו בתורת קדשים ולא למעול בו לענין מעילה אין בו דין קדשים: הוא · *דמו בנפשו הוא בהווייתו יהא: הוא לפני כפרה כו' מה לאחר כפרה אין בו מעילה · דפשיטא לן כיון דנעשית מצותו אין מועלין בו דכיון דלית ביה תו צורך גבוה לא קרינן ביה קדשי ה': אין לך דבר כו' · הלכך ע"כ לא תדרשיה הכי אלא איפכא: והרי תרומת הדשן · בכל יום חותה במחתה ותורם את הדשן מלא המחתה ממנה ונותן במזרחו של כבש כדכתיב ושמו משמע ט] שם גניזתן ושם נבלע במקומן אלמא אסור בהנאה: ובגדי כהונה · ארבעה בגדים שכהן גדול נכנס בהן לפני ולפנים ביוה"כ שאסור להשתמש י] בו עוד דכתיב ופשט את בגדי הבד וגו' והניחם שם ודרשינן מלמד שטעונין גניזה: פלוגתא דרבנן ורבי דוסא במס' יומא מייתי לה: לרבי דוסא דאמר כשרין הן לכהן [הדיוט] · לעבוד *בהן במקדש כל ימות השנה: ועגלה ערופה · דכתיב וערפו שם (דברים כא) והאי שם קרא יתירא הוא לומר יא] שתהא שם קבורתה: אין מלמדין · וכיון דלא ילפינן יב] ולא מייתי ראיה מינייהו האי קרא נמי הוא"ל ואיכא למדרשיה איפכא לא תדרשיה הכי: *מיעוטי כתיבי · לומר שאין למדין מהן: הערופה · זו ולא אחרת כזו: ושמו · מדהוה ליה למכתב ושם וכתיב ושמו לזה ולא לאחר: תלתא קראי · לכם לכפר הוא: למעוטי מנותר · לכם יג] כשאר חולין ולא כקדשים לכפר לכפרה נתתיו כקדשים ולא לדבר אחר כקדשים אלא כחולין ולא יד] יתחייבו עליו משום טומאה *והוא למעוטי ממעילה כדאמרן: שלשה כריתות · אמור אליהם לדורותיכם וגו' (ויקרא כב) והנפש אשר תאכל בשר וגו' (שם ז) נפש כי תגע בכל טו] טומאת אדם וגו' (שם):

אחת

תוספות

טז] **הכי** גרסינן בשני חילולין · הכתוב מדבר אחד פסול נותר · תימה לי לעיל גבי קדשי עובדי כוכבים אתי נותר חילול חילול מטומאה הלא חילול יז] טומאה נמי בנותר איירי ועוד תימה דבפ' הנשרפין (סנהדרין דף פג·) משמע דלא כתיב בנותר חילול דרבים והכא משכחת לה מדתני יח] ולעיל בריש פרק שני (דף טו:) פירשתי:

הוא לפני כפרה כלאחר כפרה · הקשה ר"ת דבמעילה פרק יט] [ולד] חטאת (דף יב:) אמרינן המקיז דם לבהמת קדשים מועלין בו אלמא יש מעילה בדם ותירץ דהתם כ] מחיים דלא שייכא כפרה אבל לאחר שחיטה אף לפני כפרה אין מועלין וא"ת דהתם כא] תני (דף יב·) ומייתי בפרק כל שעה דם בתחילה אין מועלין בו יצא לנחל קדרון מועלין וי"ל דמעילה דהתם דרבנן וא"ת א"כ בריש מעילה (דף ב:) דדחיק לאשכוחי מי איכא מעילה דרבנן לייתי מהך משנה ועוד קשה בסוף תמורה (דף לג:) גבי מקדיש עולה לבדק הבית דקאמר שמועלין בה שתי מעילות ופריך אי מדרבנן אמאי ב' מעילות כב] מאי קשה הא איכא מעילה דדם שהיא דרבנן וכן בקדשים שמתו בריש מעילה (דף ב·) וי"ל דהתם שיש מעילה דאורייתא משום כג] עולה בדילי מיניה ובדם דליכא מעילה דאורייתא כד] לא בדילי מיניה תקינו רבנן מעילה ובריש מעילה אקדשים ששחטן בדרום כה] קאי דכמאן דחנקינון דמי ועל כה"ג דחיק לאתויי ראיה דתקון רבנן מעילה אע"ג דבדילי מינייהו (כמו) במתו ומייתי כו] מרבי יוחנן דקדשים שמתו וה"ר חיים היה מפרש דיוצא לנחל קדרון מועלין כז] דאורייתא שב"ד מקדשין אותו שלא יהנו ממנו בלא פדיון ודוחק הוא ועוד אכתי אמאי לא מייתי כח] בריש מעילה מההיא דסוף התכלת (מנחות דף נב·) גבי אפר פרה דאמר שתי תקנות הוו מעיקרא תקינו בה מעילה ואין לומר דמעיקרא נמי היתה מעילה דאורייתא דתקון שיהיו ב"ד מקדשין אותו א"כ היאך היו מזין ועוד דבמעילה בריש ולד חטאת (דף יב·) דאמר רבי יוחנן קדשים שמתו יצאו מידי מעילה דבר תורה אבל מדרבנן איכא מעילה ופריך מי איכא מידי דמעיקרא לית ביה מעילה ולבסוף אית ביה מעילה *ולא והרי דם דתנן בתחילתו כו' ואי מעילה דנחל קדרון שבית דין מקדשין אותו מאי קושיא: **אין** לך דבר שנעשית מצותו ומועלין בו · וא"ת אדרבה לא נמעט לפני כפרה דאין לך [דבר] שלא נעשית מצותו שלא ימעלו ואע"ג דאיכא קדשים קלים היינו משום דלא איקרו קדשי ה'. וי"ל דאשכחן טובא כט] דכותה דאין מועלין עד שעת מצותן תרומת הדשן ועגלה ערופה עד אחר ירידתה: **ולא** והרי תרומת הדשן · והא דתנן במעילה פ' ולד חטאת (דף יא:) דישון מזבח הפנימי והמנורה לא נהנין ולא מועלין היינו ל] מזבח הזהב מן הקטרת שנשרף עליו והכא מזבח החיצון שהיה חותה מלא המחתה מן המאוכלות הפנימיות ונותן במזרחו של כבש ומיהו בגמ' משמע התם דאף בחיצון אין מועלין דקאמר בשלמא מזבח החיצון דכתיב ביה ושמו אלא פנימי מנא לן משמע דמושמו דריש דאין מועלין ובשמעתא אדרבה מושמו משמע ליה דמועלין וי"ל דמתני' דהתם משמע לא] דלא מועלין בדישון הפנימי שהדישון מוליאו מידי מעילה אבל קודם דישון מועלין א"כ איכא מלוה לדשן ועל זה קאמר בשלמא חיצון דכתיב ושמו ולכך מלוה לדשן לב] *מ"מ אף לאחר הרמה איכא מעילה כדדרשינן בסוף תמורה (דף לד·) ושמו בנחת ושמו כולו ושמו שלא יפזר אלא פנימי מנא לן דמלוה לדשן שאתה אומר לג] שהדשן מוליאו מידי מעילה ומשני דאמר קרא והסיר את מוראתו והשליך אל מקום הדשן ובפ' שני *דיומא בירושלמי משמע כן קלא דבעי ברישא מנלן דעבדינן דישון כלל בפנימי והדר בעי מנלן שהדישון לד] אסור בהנאה ואם תאמר מוראה ונוצה ימעלו עד שיעשו מצותן שיושלכו אצל מזבח כדישון מזבח הפנימי ובתמורה (לג"ש) אמרינן עולת העוף שנתמלה דמה מוראה ונוצה יצאו מידי מעילה *וי"ל שאני דישון מזבח הפנימי דהייתו מצותו אבל עולת העוף עבודת דם מתיר מוראה ונוצה וא"ת *בקדושין (דף נה·) דאמר אין מועל אחר מועל אלא בהמה וכלי שרת הא איכא תרומת הדשן דלא נפיק לחולין ע"י מעילה כדמוכח בסוף תמורה וי"ל דהוי בכלל בהמה דהיינו כמו אימורים דלא נפיק לחולין: **משום** דהוי תרומת הדשן ובגדי כהונה שני כתובין הבאין כאחד · במעילה פ' ולד חטאת (דף יא:) מאריך יותר ומסקנא כדהכא: **עגלה** ערופה · פי' רש"י מוערפו שם כ"ל בפ"ק דכריתות (דף ו·) והאי דכ"ל בפ' אין מעמידין (ע"ז דף כט:) לה] מדכתיב בה כפרה כקדשים י"ל דשם לריך לאסור לאחר עריפה שלא נומר אין לך דבר שנעשית מצותו ומועלין בו*: **תרי** מיעוטי כתיבי · קשיא דבחד סגי וכן גבי העזים בפרק כל הבשר (חולין דף קיג:)*: **חד** למעוטי מנותר וחד למעוטי מטומאה · תימה לנותר וטומאה סגי בחד מיעוט דילפינן מהדדי חילול חילול °ואף לקולא כדלעיל גבי קדשי עובדי כוכבים וי"ל לו] דמוקמינא מיעוטא בנותר דוקא אבל משום טומאה הוה חייב כי היכי דאין לו מתירין כגון קומץ ומנחת כהנים אע"ג דאין בהן פיגול יש בהן איסור טומאה דמרבינן מאשר הם מקדישים הכי הוה מרבינן נמי לגבי דם:

אחת

מסורת הש"ס

[מעילה יא. חולין קיז.] · יומא נט:

לעיל מג. וש"נ

שבועות ז. [ושם איתא ר' אבהו]

[כהן ל"ק]

תרי מיעוטי ל"ק

הוא ל"ק

ומ"מ ל"ק

ד"ה התמורה

[ועי' בתוספות דיומא נט ע"ב ד"ה מהרל"י בענין אחר משנה במעילה יב:]

[ועי' תוספות קדושין נו: ד"ה כסכה]

[וציין תוספת פסחים כו. ד"ה כתיב ותוס' מעילה יא. ד"ה תרי וביאור היטב ביומא ס. ד"ה תרי ע"ש אבל בחולין קיג. ד"ה עזים ודף קיז: ד"ה הרי הניתו בהימה]

פסחים כו. יומא יב: כד. ס. כריתות ג. חולין קיז. מעילה יא:

גליון הש"ס

תוס' ד"ה חד וכו' ואף לקולא וכו' · עי' קדושין נ ע"א תוס' ד"ה ואסא וצ"ע:

[קדושין כד. וש"נ]

רש"י ד"ה הוא [ת"ל כי הדם הוא בנפש יכפר]

שיטה מקובצת

א] לכם לכם שלכם: ב] למימר מעוטי ותיבת תרי נמחק: ג] לי חד למעוטי מנותר וחד למעוטי מטומאה וחד למעוטי ממעילה · תימה למה לי תרי מיעוטא [בנותר וטומאה] בחדא סגי דילפינן מהדדי בג"ש חילול חילול אף לקולא כדלעיל וי"ל דאי (לאו) [לא] כתיב אלא חדא מיעוטא הוי מוקמינן ליה אנותר וטומאה לא הוי ילפינן מיניה דהוי מרבינן ליה מאשר הם מקדישים לי' מהר"פ: ד] ודם הוא גופיה: ה] ולא יחללו הס"ד: ו] אכלו בטומאת [illegible] ז] והכא ס"א נמי אמרי' מנא הני מילי כו': ח] למעוטי מטומאה וחד למעוטי ממעילה: ט] משמע ששם גניזתו ושם נבלע במקומו אלמא: י] בהן עוד: יא] שם תהא קבורתה: יב] ילפינן מינייהו ולא: יג] כשאר · ס"א בשר חולין: יד] ולא שיתחייבו עליו: טו] בכל טמא בטומאת אדם: טז] מה"ד הצ"ה בשני ותיבות הכי גרסינן נמחק: יז] חילול דטומאה נמי: יח] מדתני לוי: יט] פרק ולד חטאת: כ] דהתם מיירי מחיים: כא] דהתם תנן ומייתי לה בפ' כל שעה: כב] מאי קשיא הא: כג] עולה בדילי אינשי מיניה כבר אבל (הכי) בשור דליכא · ס"א עולה אין לחכמים לתקן מעילה כיון דבלאו הכי בדילי ומשני ראוי למעול שתי מעילות (בבשר אינה מעילה דאורייתא משום עולה) [ותקון רבנן]

מעילה אעור משום דליכא מעילה מדאורייתא אלא בבשר א"כ לא] ותיבת ובדם ל"ש ונמחק: כד] דאורייתא א"כ לא: כה] קאמר דכמאן דחנקינו דמי: כו] ומייתי מדר' יוחנן: כז] מועלין בו מדאורייתא: כח] מייתי ראיה: כט] טובא [דכוותה] הוא דאין מועלין: ל] היינו דמזבח הזהב כו' והכא במזבח החיצון שהיה כו' דאף בדחיצון אין מועלין כו': לא] משמע דאין מועלין תיבת דלא נמחק: לב] לדשן ומ"מ אף: לג] [illegible] לד] שהדישון בפנימי אסור · וא"ת א"כ מוראה ונוצה ימעלו בהם עד שיעשו כו' הפנימי ובסוף התמורה אמרי' דעולת העוף [illegible] עבודת הדם מתיר מוראה ונוצה [illegible] כו' דלא נפקא לחולין הס"ד: לה] מעמידין כפרה כתיב בה כקדשים י"ל כו' לאחר עריפה דלא נימא אין לך דבר: לו] וי"ל דהוה מוקמינא מיעוטא [illegible] הוה אמינא חייב כי היכי:

נז א מיי' פי"ח מהל' פסה"מ הל' טו:
נח ב מיי' פ"ח מהל' טומאת אוכלין הל"ט ופ"ז מהלכות אסורי מזבח הלכה ח:
נט ג מיי' פ"ד מהל' מעה"ק הל' יא:
ס ד מיי' פ"ו מהלכות מעה"ק הלכה ד:
סא ה מיי' פט"ו מהל' פסה"מ הל' ד:

לעיל מג. [וש"נ]

גי' צ"ק או לן ויולא להכי איצטריך יקרב ליש לו מתירין משיקרבו מתירין ועוד איצטריך כו'

אחת לכלל ואחת לפרט ואחת לדברים שאינן נאכלין ולרבי שמעון דאמר דברים שאין נאכלין אין חייבין עליהם משום טומאה לאיתויי מאי לאיתויי *חטאות הפנימיות ס"ד אמינא הואיל *ואמר רבי שמעון כל שאינו על מזבח החיצון כשלמים אין חייבין עליו משום פיגול א] משום טומאה נמי לא ליחייב קמ"ל: גומי ר' שמעון ב] מחייב את שדרכו לאכול כו': איתמר רבי יוחנן וריש לקיש רבי אלעזר ורבי יוסי ברבי חנינא חד מהאי ג] זוזא וחד מהאי זוזא חד אמר מחלוקת בטומאת בשר אבל בטומאת הגוף דברי הכל אינו לוקה וחד אמר כמחלוקת בזו כך מחלוקת בזו ד] מאי טעמא כיון דקרינא ביה °והבשר אשר יגע בכל טמא קרינן ביה °וטומאתו עליו רב טביומי מתני הכי רב כהנא מתני ה] הכי חד מהאי זוזא וחד מהאי זוזא אסיפא חד אמר מחלוקת בטומאת הגוף אבל בטומאת בשר דברי הכל לוקה וחד אמר כמחלוקת בזו כך מחלוקת בזו אמר רבא מסתברא כמ"ד כמחלוקת בזו כך מחלוקת בזו מאי טעמא כיון דלא קרינא ביה וטומאתו עליו ונכרתה לא קרינן ביה והבשר אשר יגע בכל טמא לא יאכל *והאמר מר והבשר °לרבות עצים ו] ולבונה לפוסלה בעלמא:

מתני' *לשם ששה דברים הזבח נזבח °לשם זבח לשם זובח לשם השם לשם אשים לשם ריח לשם ניחוח והחטאת והאשם לשם חטא אמר רבי יוסי ז] אף מי שלא היה בלבו לשם אחד מכל אלו כשר שהוא תנאי בית דין שאין המחשבה הולכת אלא אחר העובד:

גמ' אמר רב יהודה אמר רב עולה לשם עולה לאפוקי לשם שלמים דלא אשים לשם אשים לאפוקי כבבא דלא ריח לשם ריח לאפוקי אברים שצלאן והעלן דלא *דאמר רב יהודה אמר רב °אברים שצלאן והעלן אין בהן משום ריח ניחוח לשם הנחת רוח לה' לשם מי שאמר והיה העולם אמר רב יהודה אמר רב °חטאת ששחטה לשם עולה פסולה לשם חולין כשרה אמר ר' ח] אלעזר מ"ט דרב °ולא יחללו את קדשי בני ישראל קדשים מחללין קדשים ואין חולין מחללין קדשים: מתיב רבה אמר רבי יוסי ט] אף מי שלא היה בלבו לשם אחד מכל אלו כשר שהוא תנאי ב"ד טעמא שלא היה בלבו כלל הא היה בלבו לשם חולין פסול א"ל אביי י] דלמא לא היה כלל כשר ומרצה הא היה בלבו לשם חולין כשר ואינו מרצה א"ר יא] אלעזר חטאת ששחטה לשם חולין פסולה כדבעא מיניה שמואל מרב הונא מנין

אחת לכלל ואחת לפרט · לאו כלל ופרט ממש כד] דמרוחקים זה מזה הן אלא דבר שהיה בכלל ויצא מן הכלל ללמד על הכלל כולו יצא כדדרשינן כה] עלה בפ"ק דיבמות (דף ז׳) ומרבינן כל קדשי מזבח וממעטינן קדשי בדק הבית וא"ת כו] קדשי בדק הבית נמי תיפוק לי מיקרב דדרשי' בכשר ליקרב וי"ל דהוה אמינא כי בעינן כז] כשר ליקרב הני מילי בקדשי מזבח וא"ת הא דאמר בהקומץ רבה (מנחות דף כה:) כל טהור יאכל בשר הניתר לטהורים חייבין עליו משום טומאה כו' למעוטי בשר לפני זריקה תיפוק ליה מיקרב דדרשינן לעיל כח] בכשר ליקרב הא כילד יש לו מתירין משיקרבו מתירין כו' וי"ל דצריכי דאי כתב רחמנא כל טהור ולא כתב יקרב הוה אמינא דקודם זריקה חשיב ניתר לטהורים כיון דיכול לזרוק לכתחילה ולא הוה ממעטי' אלא טמא לפני זריקה *לן ויולא ועוד איצטריך יקרב לאין לו מתירין משיקדש בכלי ואי כתב רחמנא יקרב ולא כתב כל טהור הוה אמינא אפילו פיגולין ונותרות ולא הוה אמינא מזבח השלמים מיעוט אי לאו קרא דניתר לטהורים: אבל בטומאת הגוף דברי הכל אינו לוקה · וא"ת והא אמרינן לעיל שלש כריתות בשלמים חד לדברים שאינן נאכלין כט] לכל הפחות תפשוט דר' יוחנן דאמר כמחלוקת בזו כך מחלוקת בזו ל] ועוד תניא במעילה (דף י׳) גבי לבונה וחייבים עליה משום פיגול ונותר וטמא וי"ל דדוקא מלקות קאמר דאינו לוקה דלא איתרבו אלא לענין כרת ומיהו לא משמע הכי מדקאמר כיון דקרינן ביה והבשר אשר יגע קרינן ביה וטומאתו עליו משמע דאיירי נמי לענין כרת:

מחלוקת בטומאת בשר · הך פלוגתא דהכא בין ללישנא קמא בין ללישנא בתרא לא שייכא לפלוגתא דרבי יוחנן ור"ל דטמא שאכל בשר קדש לפני זריקה בפ' כל הפסולין (לעיל דף לד׳) ובין לאביי ובין לרבא דהתם יש לייסב · וק"ל: מנין

אחת לכלל ואחת לפרט · לדרוש דבר שהיה בכלל ויצא מן הכלל ללמד לא ללמד על עצמו יצא אלא ללמד על הכלל כולו יצא יב] והנפש אשר תאכל בשר [מזבח השלמים] (ויקרא ז) והלא שלמים בכלל כל *הקדשים היו ולמה יצאו להקיש אליהם ולומר לך מה שלמים מיוחדים קדשי מזבח אף כל קדשי מזבח (בכלל כל הקדשים אל הקדשים אשר יקדישו בני ישראל יג] וטומאתו עליו (שם כב) כל הקדשים בכלל): לדברים שאינן נאכלין · כגון עצים ולבונה שאינן ראויים לאכילה אם אכל מהם בטומאת הגוף חייב כרבנן דמתניתין: ולר"ש · דמתני': חד מהאי יד] זוזא · אמרי חדא מילתא ואינך תרי חדא מילתא: חד אמר · חד מהאי טו] זוזא אמר מחלוקת שנחלקו חכמים על רבי שמעון שחייב: בטומאת בשר · אם אכלן לעצים ולבונה טמאין לוקה משום לאו דוהבשר אשר יגע בכל טמא וגו' (ויקרא ז) דאמר מר (חולין דף לו:) והבשר יתירא לרבות עצים ולבונה: אבל בטומאת הגוף · והן טהורים דברי הכל אינו לוקה דלא איתרבו בה: הכי גרסינן כיון דקרינן ביה והבשר אשר יגע וגו' קרינא ביה וטומאתו עליו ונכרתה · כלומר כיון דבטומאת בשר אמרי רבנן לוקה אעצים ולבונה בטומאת הגוף נמי אית להו דלוקה דהא גבי הדדי כתיבי: אסיפא · אמילתיה דר"ש והכי אמרינן מחלוקת דרבי שמעון אדרבנן דלא לקי בטומאת הגוף דלא רבי רחמנא אבל בטומאת עצמן דרבינהו קרא דברי הכל לוקה: כיון דלא קרינן בהו · בעצים ולבונה לרבי שמעון וטומאתו עליו דטומאת הגוף לא קרינן בהו והבשר אשר יגע וגו': לפסולא בעלמא · ומעלה דרבנן היא וקרא אסמכתא טז] בעלמא הוא והכי אמרי' בפסחים (דף כד:) דאין לוקין עליו: מתני' לשם זבח · לאפוקי שנוי קדש כגון לשם זבח אחר: לשם זובח · לאפוקי שנוי בעלים והא ילפינן להו מקראי בפ"ק (לעיל ד:): לשם אשים לשם ריח · בגמרא מפרש לאפוקי מאי ויליף לה מקרא: לשם חטא · לשם חטאו שהוא מביאו עליו: אף מי שלא היה בלבו כו' · ששחט סתם כשר: שהוא תנאי בית דין · יז] שישחט סתם כדאמרן בפ"ק (לעיל ב:) יח] התנו בית דין דלא לימא לשמו דלמא אתי למימר שלא לשמו: שאין המחשבה הולכת אלא אחר העובד · הלכך אי הוה יט] שלא לשמו אע"ג דבעלים אמרי לשמו לאו מידי הוא דלאו בדידהו תליא מילתא דכתיב המקריב אותו לא יחשב (ויקרא ז): גמ' עולה לשם עולה כו' · קרא קדריש עולה אשה ריח ניחוח לה' (ויקרא א) ואע"ג דלאו בשחיטה כתיב אשכחן ליה בשלמים גבי זביחה והקריב מזבח השלמים אשה לה' (שם ג) שתהא זביחה לשם שלמים לשם אשים לשם כ] שם והאי דנקט הכא קרא דעולה משום דכתיבי כולהו גביה וגבי שלמים לא כתיב בההוא קרא לריח ניחוח: לאפוקי כבבא · ע"מ לעשותו חתיכות לצלות בגחלים קרבונייא"ש בלע"ז ודוגמתו בעירובין כא] (דף כט:) ונייתי *הוגנא דערבתא וכביב וניכול: כב] אין בהם משום ריח · דכיון דצלאן תחילה חוץ למערכה תו לא מסקי ריחא: הנחת רוח · נחת רוח לפני הקדוש ברוך הוא שאמר ונעשה רצונו: ולא יחללו · אין דבר אחר מחלל את קדשים אלא מי מחללו קדשים מחללין קדשים כדנפקא לן (לעיל ה׳) דבמחשבה שלא לשמו מתחללים מושחט אותה לחטאת: טעמא דלא היה בלבו כלל · ששחטו סתם וממילא קרב לשמו: הא לשם חולין כשר ואינו מרצה · וכי אמר רב נמי כשרה ואינה מרצה קאמר: לשם חולין · שיודע שהיא חטאת ושחט לשם חולין כשרה כדאמרן שאין חולין מחללין קדשים: משום חולין · כסבור כג] שהם חולין פסולה דהיינו מתעסק בדברים אחרים ואינו עסוק בקדשים: מתעסק

גי' צ"ק הקדשים היו אל הקדשים אשר יקדישו בני ישראל וטומאתו עליו כל הקדשים בכלל ולמה יצאו כו' צ"ק בשם ס"י ונמחק מן בכלל עד הקדשים בכלל

חולין לו: וש"נ
לעיל ב:
מנחות כה.
לעיל ג.

שיטה מקובצת

א] משום טומאה נמי לא ליחייב וקשה דמשמע דהא בהא תליא והרי מנחת נסכים וכו' דאין חייב (עליו) [עליהן] משום פיגול וחייב עליו משום טומאה לכך נראה (דפריך) [דה"פ] משום דאמר שלמים יצא מן הכלל ללמד על טומאה וסד"א דכי היכי דלר"ש דריש משלמים דלגבי פיגול דוקא בדבר שהוא על מזבח החיצון כשלמים חייבין עליו משום פיגול ה"נ נימא דר"ש דריש משלמים דגבי טומאה דוקא דבר שהוא על מזבח החיצון כשלמים חייבין עליו משום טומאה קמ"ל · מהר"פ ז"ל: ב] תיבת מחייב נמחק: ג] מהאי זווא וחד מהאי זווא: ד] מחלוקת בזו אמר רבא מסתברא כמ"ד כמחלוקת בזו כך מחלוקת בזו מאי: ה] כהנא מתני חד ותיבת הכי נמחק: ו] ולבונה לפסולא בעלמא פ"ה ומעלה דרבנן הוא וקרא אסמכתא בעלמא הוא וקשה דבחולין מוכח דעושה שני ואם כן דאורייתא הוא וי"ל לפסולא בעלמא ולא ללקות עליו ולעולם דאורייתא הוא · מהר"פ ז"ל: ז] יוסי שמעתי שאף מי: ח] אלעאי תיבת אלעזר נמחק: ט] יוסי שמעתי שאף מי: י] דילמא לא היה בלבו כלל כשר ומרצה תימה מנ"ל למידק הכי הא איכא מחשבות כמו לשם ריח ניחוח לא מצינא למידק הכי הא לשם חולין אינה מרצה דפשיטא דמחשבת חולין לא פסלא באימורין דהן עצמן שלא הקטירו אימוריו כשר וי"ל דמ"מ משמע ליה מדנקט שלא היה בלבו דלגבי היכא דמצינו למידק דייקינן וא"ת מנ"ל למידק והכי מסילתיה דר"י אדרבה לישנא דר"י משמע לא מבעיא היה בלבו לשם אלו דכשר (אלא) [אבל] למידק הא היה בלבו לשם חולין כשר היכי משמע כלל וצ"ע: יא] אלעאי תיבת אלעזר נמחק: יב] יצא כיצד והנפש אשר תאכל בשר תנ' והלא: יג] ישראל לה' וטומאתו: יד] חד מהאי זווא וחד מהאי זווא: טו] זווא אמר כו' שמעון לומר שחייב הס"ד: טז] אסמכתא עיין לעיל (דף לד ע"א) בתוס' ד"ה ואפי': יז] דין שישחוט: יח] אתנו ב"ד: יט] הוה אמר שלא: כ] לשם השם והאי דנקט כו' קרא ריח ניחוח הס"ד: כא] בעירובין בבבל מערבין (דף כט ע"ב) ונייתי סווינא דערבתא: כב] וניכול הס"ד מה"ד דלא כלומר שצריך שיניחנו במזבח עד שיצלאנו האש לגמרי ולא יורידנו משנצלה מעט הס"ד: כג] כסבור שהיא חולין פסולה: כד] ממש דהא הפרט בשלמים כתיב וכלל בפרשת אמור וא"כ הוי פרט וכלל ואיתרבי כל מילי אלא כיון דמרוחקים זה מזה אין דנין אותו בפרט וכלל אלא דרשינן כדבר שהיה: כה] כדדרשינן בפ"ק דיבמות שלמים בכלל כל הקדשים היו ולמה יצאו לומר לך מה שלמים קדשי מזבח אף כל קדשי כו':כו] וא"ת למה לי למעוטי קדשי בדה"ב תיפוק לי מדכתיב כל איש אשר יקרב דדרשינן לעיל בהוכשר ליקרב: כז] הוכשר ליקרב ה"מ בקדשי מזבח וכן הא דדרשינן לעיל באינו ניתר לטהורים אינו חייבין עליו משום טומאה והר"ר יעקב מקינון פי' דהא דקים לן לעיל (דכאשר) [דאשר] יקרב בהוכשר ליקרב קאמר ולא בנגע ממש היינו מכח האי פרט דשלמים שיצא מן הכלל ללמד כו' ובשלמים כתיב בהדיא אכילה ומינייהו שמעינן דבכלל הקדשים נמי לא מיחייב אלא דוקא באכילה והלכך ע"כ אשר יקרב לאו בנוגע קאמר אבל בקונטרס פי' משום דבההוא עניינא כתיב אכילה דחק את עצמו מאד דההוא במעשר כתיב דסגי להו בטבילה בלא הערב שמש ושמא הקונטרס ר"ל דגילוי מילתא הוא' לשון מהר"פ: כח] לעיל בהוכשר: כט] נאכלין וטומאת הגוף הוא לכל הפחות תפשוט דר' יוחנן הוא דאמר: ל] בזו ותו היכא מצינו לאוקמא מתניתין בטומאת בשר דהא לעיל פירשנו מקרא דוינזרו דמשמע דמיירי בטומאת הגוף וי"ל דדוקא למלקות קאמר דאינו לוקה דנהי דאיתרבי לכרת למלקות לא איתרבי ומתניתין ה"ק ר"ש אומר בדבר שדרכו לאכול חייב לא שנא בטומאת הגוף בכרת ולא שנא בטומאת בשר בלאו אבל עצים ולבונה אינו חייב ושוה כו' עד כרת דוטומאתו עליו כתיב גבי כרת וי"ל דה"נ לא קאמר לענין כרת אלא לענין מלקות קאמר דומיא דבבשר ליכא [כרת] ות"ק כיון דקרינא ביה והבשר [אשר יגע בכל טמא] דמיירי לענין מלקות דבבשר משום טומאת בשר] קרינן ביה וטומאתו עליו להתחייב במלקות · לשון הר"פ:

לרשתכם

in connection with peace-offerings?[5] [46b] One to serve as a generalization, the second as a particularization,[6] and the third [is required] in respect of things which are not eaten.[7] And according to R. Simeon who maintained that the things which cannot be eaten do not involve liability on account of uncleanness, what does it include?—It includes the inner sin-offerings. You might think that since R. Simeon said, Whatever does not come on the outer altar, like peace-offerings, does not involve liability on account of *piggul*, then it does not involve liability on account of uncleanness either. Hence [Scripture] informs us [that it is not so].

Said R. Simeon: That which is normally eaten etc.[8] It was stated, R. Joḥanan and Resh Lakish, R. Eleazar and R. Jose son of R. Ḥanina [are the pairs concerned in the following discussion], one of the former pair and one of the latter pair: One maintained: The a controversy [in the Mishnah] refers to uncleanness of the flesh;[1] but in the case of personal uncleanness all agree that [the offender] is not flagellated. But the other maintained: As there is a controversy in the one case, so is there in the other. [Raba said, Logic supports the view that as there is a controversy in the one case, so is there in the other.][2] What is the reason?—Since the text, *And the flesh that toucheth any unclean thing*[3] is applicable to it, then the text *having his uncleanness upon him*[4] is applicable to it too.[5] That is how R. Ṭabyomi recited [this discussion]. R. Kahana recited [the views of] one of the former pair and one of the latter pair as referring to the final clause:[6] One maintained: The controversy refers to personal uncleanness, but in the case of uncleanness of flesh all agree that he is flagellated. While the other maintained: As there is a controversy in the one case, so is there in the other. Raba said, Logic supports the view that as there is a controversy in the one case, so is there in the other. What is the reason?—Since the text, '*Having his uncleanness upon him*', is not applicable to it,[7] the text, '*And the flesh that toucheth any unclean thing*' is not applicable to it. But surely a master said: 'And *the flesh*' is to include the wood and the frankincense?[8]—That is a mere disqualification.[9]

MISHNAH. THE SACRIFICE IS SLAUGHTERED FOR THE SAKE OF SIX THINGS: FOR THE SAKE OF THE SACRIFICE, FOR THE SAKE OF THE SACRIFICER, FOR THE SAKE OF THE [DIVINE] NAME, FOR THE SAKE OF FIRE-OFFERINGS, FOR THE SAKE OF A SAVOUR, FOR THE SAKE OF PLEASING, AND A SIN-OFFERING AND A GUILT-OFFERING FOR THE SAKE OF SIN. R. JOSE SAID: EVEN IF ONE DID NOT HAVE ANY OF THESE PURPOSES IN HIS HEART, IT IS VALID, BECAUSE IT IS A REGULATION OF THE BETH DIN, SINCE THE INTENTION IS DETER- b MINED ONLY BY THE CELEBRANT.[1]

GEMARA. Rab Judah said in Rab's name: [Scripture says, *It is a burnt-offering, an offering made by fire, of pleasing savour unto the Lord*].[2] '*A burnt-offering*' [intimates that it must be slaughtered] for the sake of a burnt-offering, excluding [where it is slaughtered] for the sake of a peace-offering, in which case it does not [acquit the owner of his obligation]. '*An offering made by fire*' [intimates that] it must be for the sake of an offering made by fire, excluding the charring of the meat,[3] which is not [valid]. '*Savour*' [intimates that] it must be for the sake of a savour: this excludes the roasting of limbs [elsewhere] and bringing them up [on the altar], which is not [valid].[4] For Rab Judah said in Rab's name: If one roasted limbs and took them up on to the altar, they do not fulfil the requirements of '*savour*'. '*Pleasing*' [intimates that] it must be for the sake of pleasing the Lord, for the sake of Him who spoke and called the world into existence.

Rab Judah said in Rab's name: If one slaughtered a sin-offering under the designation of a burnt-offering, it is invalid; [if one slaughtered it] under the designation of *ḥullin*, it is valid. R. Eleazar[5] said: What is Rab's reason?—*And they shall not profane the holy things of the children of Israel*:[6] 'holy things' profane 'holy things', but *ḥullin* does not profane holy things.[7]

Rabbah raised an objection: R. JOSE SAID: EVEN IF ONE DID NOT HAVE ANY OF THESE PURPOSES IN HIS HEART, IT IS VALID, BECAUSE IT IS A REGULATION OF THE BETH DIN. Thus it is only because he had no [purpose] in his heart at all; hence, if he c intended it[1] for the sake of *ḥullin*, it is invalid?—Said Abaye to him: Perhaps [this deduction is to be made]: if he had no intention at all, it is valid and propitiates, while if he intended it for the sake of *ḥullin* it is valid but does not propitiate.[2]

R. Eleazar said: If one slaughters a sin-offering for the sake of *ḥullin*,[3] it is valid; [if one slaughtered it] as *ḥullin*,[4] it is invalid.[5]

(5) V. Lev. VII, 20, 21; XXII, 3. (6) When anything is included in a generalization, and is then made the subject of a particularization, it throws light not only upon itself but upon everything included in the generalization. Now Lev. XXII, 3 (q.v.) is a generalization, including all '*holy things*' and thus the peace-offering too. The latter is therefore singled out in Lev. VII, 20 to teach that as peace-offerings are of the '*holy things*' of the altar, so does the '*holy things*' in XXII, 3 also mean those belonging to the altar, *sc.* sacrifices. (7) E.g., the wood used on the altar and the frankincense. If one nevertheless ate these whilst unclean, he incurs *kareth*. (8) As in the Mishnah, 45*b*, with slight variation. V. Rashi on the Mishnah.

a (1) Hence of the wood and incense. (2) Bracketed passage added by Sh. M. (3) Lev. VII, 19. (4) Ibid. 20. (5) I.e., if the first text applies to wood and frankincense, then the second does too. (6) I.e., to R. Simeon's exemption from liability. (7) In the Rabbis' view.—Before he said, '*is applicable to it*', as he referred to R. Simeon's view. (8) *Supra* 34*a*. (9) The law disqualifying unclean wood and frankincense is only Rabbinical, this Biblical interpretation being a mere support.

b (1) The priest who performs the service, and not the owner of the sacrifice. If the former intended it for a different purpose, it counts as a sacrifice so offered, notwithstanding that the owner intended it for its rightful purpose.—V. *supra* 2*b* for notes. (2) Lev. I, 13. (3) I.e., the intention to make roast pieces of flesh. (4) Since the '*savour*' is then not made on the altar. (5) Sh. M.: Elai. (6) Lev. XXII, 15. (7) Cf. *supra* 3*a*, 5*a*.

c (1) Lit. 'if he had in his heart.' (2) The owner is not acquitted of his obligation; cf. *supra* 2*a*. (3) I.e., he knew that it was a sin-offering, and yet slaughtered it for the sake of *ḥullin*. (4) Thinking that it was *ḥullin*. (5) Since in his mind he was not engaged with sacrifices at all.

This is as the question which Samuel asked R. Huna: [47a] How do we know that when one is unaware engaged in sacrifices,[6] it [the sacrifice] is invalid? Because it says, *And he shall kill the bullock before the Lord,*[7] [which intimates] that the killing must be for the sake of the bullock.[8] We know this,[9] said he to him, [but] how do we know that [awareness] is indispensable?[10] *Ye shall slaughter it with your will,*[11] said he, [which teaches,] slaughter it with your knowledge.[12]

SINCE THE INTENTION IS DETERMINED ONLY BY THE CELEBRANT. Our Mishnah does not agree with the following Tanna. For it was taught, R. Eleazar son of R. Jose said: I have heard that the *owner* [of the sacrifice] renders [it] *piggul!*[13] Raba said: What is R. Eleazar son of R. Jose's reason? Because Scripture says, *Then shall he that offereth [his offering] present [unto the Lord* etc.][14]

Abaye said: R. Eleazar son of R. Jose, R. Eliezer, and R. Simeon b. Eleazar all hold that when one expresses an intention while another
a performs the act,[1] it is an [effective] intention. R. Eleazar son of R. Jose: this [view] that we have stated.[2] R. Eliezer: as we learnt: If one slaughters for a heathen, his *shechitah* is fit; but R. Eliezer declares it unfit.[3] R. Simeon b. Eleazar: as it was taught: R. Simeon b. Eleazar stated a general rule: That which is not fit to put away, and such is not [generally] put away, yet it did become fit to a certain person[4] and he did put it away, and then another came and carried it out, the latter is rendered liable through the former's intention.[5]

Now, both of them[6] agree with R. Eleazar son of R. Jose: if we say [thus] without, is there a question about within?[7] R. Eleazar son of R. Jose does not agree with the other two: perhaps he ruled thus only [in reference to] within, but not [in reference to] without.[8] R. Simeon b. Eleazar agrees with R. Eliezer: if we say [thus] in connection with the Sabbath, is there a question about idolatry?[9] R. Eleazar does not agree with R. Simeon b. Eleazar: perhaps you rule thus only in connection with idolatry, because it is similar to 'within';[10] but in the case of the Sabbath, the Torah interdicted only a considered labour.[11]

CHAPTER V

MISHNAH. WHICH IS THE PLACE [FOR THE RITES] OF SACRIFICES? THE SLAUGHTERING OF SACRIFICES OF THE HIGHER SANCTITY IS AT THE NORTH [SIDE OF THE ALTAR]. THE SLAUGHTERING OF THE BULLOCK AND THE HE-GOAT OF THE DAY OF ATONEMENT IS [DONE] AT THE NORTH, AND THE RECEPTION OF THEIR BLOOD IS [PERFORMED] WITH SERVICE VESSELS AT THE NORTH, AND THEIR BLOOD REQUIRES SPRINKLING BETWEEN THE STAVES [OF THE ARK], ON THE VEIL, AND ON THE GOLDEN ALTAR; [THE OMISSION OF] A SINGLE APPLICATION OF THESE INVALIDATES [THE CEREMONY]. THE RESIDUE OF THE BLOOD HE [THE PRIEST] POURED OUT ON THE WESTERN BASE OF THE OUTER ALTAR, BUT IF HE DID NOT POUR IT OUT, HE DID NOT INVALIDATE [THE SACRIFICE].
b AS FOR THE BULLOCKS WHICH WERE BURNT[1] AND THE HE-GOATS WHICH WERE BURNT,[2] THEIR SLAUGHTERING IS [DONE] AT THE NORTH, AND THE RECEPTION OF THEIR BLOOD IS [DONE] AT THE NORTH, AND THEIR BLOOD REQUIRES SPRINKLING BETWEEN THE STAVES [OF THE ARK], ON THE

(6) He slaughters a sacrifice, but without such intention. (7) Lev. I, 5. (8) I.e., he must intend to kill a *sacred* animal as a sacrifice. (9) Lit. 'this is in our hands'. (10) In the sense that the sacrifice is otherwise invalid. The text quoted may merely teach that intention is required, but not that the sacrifice is invalid in default thereof. (11) Lev. XIX, 5. This is the literal translation. E.V.: *Ye shall offer it that ye may be accepted.* (12) With the knowledge that it is a sacrifice. Thus this refutes the teaching of Lev. I, 5, and it shews that such awareness is indispensable. (13) While the *priest* was performing its rites. (14) Num. XV, 4. Lit. translation. Thus the owner is called 'he that offereth', and so is included in the text, *neither shall it be imputed unto him that offereth it: it shall be an abhorred thing* (piggul)—Lev. VII, 18: hence he can render the sacrifice *piggul*.

a (1) Concerning which the intention is expressed. (2) His ruling *supra*. (3) The animal belonged to a heathen, and it is assumed that a heathen tacitly intends his animal to be slaughtered in honour of his deity, which makes it unfit for food. R. Eleazar maintains that it is unfit even though the *act* of *shechitah* is performed by a Jew, while the intention is performed by the heathen. (4) He found a use for it. (5) The passage refers to the Sabbath. V. Shab. 75b, 76a. (6) R. Eliezer and R. Simeon b. Eleazar. (7) Surely not. 'Within' means in the Temple; 'without', outside the Temple. Now, R. Eliezer and R. Simeon b. Eleazar stated their views in reference to a heathen and the Sabbath respectively (cases 'without' the Temple), and though the law of intention is not written in connection with these at all, they hold that where one man performs an act, another man's intention in reference thereto is effective. Then they will certainly hold the same in reference to sacrifices, where the disqualification of an illegal intention is actually written. (8) By the same argument as in the preceding note. (9) Surely not. Idolatrous acts of sacrifice involve culpability only when they are of the same nature as the acts performed in true sacrifice (Sanh. 60b). Hence it is natural that in respect to intention too they are similar. (10) As in preceding note. (11) I.e., culpability is involved only when one performs a real labour, and which he (or people in general) consider as such. Here, however, his action would not normally be considered carrying, and *another* man's intention cannot make it so.

b (1) *Sc.* the bullocks brought as sin-offerings when either the whole community or the anointed priest sinned. These were not eaten by the priests but burnt without Jerusalem (Lev. IV, 12, 21; Yoma 68a). (2) *Sc.* the he-goats brought for the sin of idolatory.

גמרא

*מנין למתעסק בקדשים שהוא פסול שנאמר °ושחט את בן הבקר לפני ה' עד ^אשתהא שחיטה לשם בן בקר א"ל זו בידינו היא לעכב מנין א"ל °לרצונכם תזבחהו לדעתכם א] זביחו: ^בשאין המחשבה הולכת אלא אחר העובד: מתני' דלא כי האי תנא דתניא *א"ר אלעזר ברבי יוסי שמעתי שהבעלים מפגלין אמר רבא מ"ט דרבי אלעזר ברבי יוסי דאמר קרא והקריב המקריב אמר אביי רבי אלעזר ברבי יוסי ורבי אליעזר ור"ש בן אלעזר כולהו סבירא להו זה מחשב וזה עובד הויא מחשבה רבי אלעזר ברבי יוסי הא דאמרן רבי אליעזר דתנן *^גהשוחט לעובד כוכבים שחיטתו כשרה ורבי אליעזר פוסל ר"ש בן אלעזר ב] *דתנן *כלל אמר רבי שמעון בן אלעזר כל שאין כשר להצניע ואין מצניעין כמוהו. הוכשר לזה והצניעו ובא אחר והוציאו נתחייב זה במחשבה של זה ג] תרוייהו אית להו דרבי אלעזר ברבי יוסי השתא בחוץ אמרינן בפנים מיבעיא רבי אלעזר ברבי יוסי לית ד] להו דתרוייהו דלמא בפנים הוא (א) דאמרינן בחוץ לא אמרינן ר"ש בן אלעזר אית ליה דר' אליעזר השתא בשבת אמרינן בעבודת כוכבים מיבעיא רבי אליעזר לית ליה דרבי שמעון בן אלעזר דלמא בעבודת כוכבים הוא דאמרת כעין ה] בפנים אבל *שבת מלאכת מחשבת אסרה תורה:

הדרן עלך בית שמאי

איזהו מקומן של זבחים קדשי קדשים ^ושחיטתן בצפון פר ושעיר של יום הכיפורים שחיטתן בצפון ^זוקיבול דמן בכלי שרת בצפון ^חודמן טעון הזיה על בין הבדים ועל הפרוכת ועל מזבח הזהב ו] מתנה אחת מהן מעכבת שירי הדם היה שופך על יסוד מערבי של מזבח החיצון ואם לא נתן לא עכב: ^טפרים הנשרפים ושעירים הנשרפים שחיטתן בצפון וקיבול דמן בכלי שרת בצפון ודמן טעון הזיה על הפרוכת ועל מזבח הזהב מתנה

רש"י

למתעסק בקדשים · שוחט קדשים ולא בכוונה אלא כמתעסק בדברים אחרים: בידינו הוא · ראיה ז] זאת כבר ידעט אותה ומיהו מצוה הוא דנפקא לן ולא עיכוב: שמעתי שהבעלים מפגלין · בעבודת הכהן אם קיבל הכהן בשתיקה וחשבו הבעלים עליה על פיגול הוי פיגול: והקריב המקריב · קרבנו בפרשת נסכים כתיב והקריב המקריב קרבנו לה' (במדבר טו) אלמא ח] מקריב קרבנו קרי ליה הלכך הוו להו בכלל המקריב לא יחשב: ורבי אליעזר פוסל · התם מפרש בהדיא שהתם מחשבת עובד כוכבים לעבודת כוכבים ואע"ג ט] דלא איהו שחיט לה פסול: שאין כשר להצניע · במסכת שבת כגון דם נדה או איסור י] (או) הנאה: ואין מצניעין כמוהו · שכשר הוא להצניעו אם היה יא] שיעורו אבל שיעורו של זה מועט הוא ואין אדם חושבו להצניעו: ובא אחר והוציאו · בשבת לרה"ר חייב דחשיב מלאכה מפני מחשבתו של זה שהוכשר לו והצניעו: ותרוייהו · רבי אליעזר ור"ש בן אלעזר: השתא בחוץ · בעבודת כוכבים ושבת דלא כתיבא בהו מחשבה בהדיא אמרינן זה מחשב וזה עושה יב] הוי מחשבה: בפנים · בקרבנות דמחשבה בהו כתיבא מיבעיא: בפנים הוא דאמר · משום דעיקר יג] מחשבות בקרבנות כתיבא: אבל בחוץ · כגון עבודת כוכבים ושבת לא: בעבודת כוכבים מיבעיא · דעבודת כוכבים דומיא דעבודת פנים חייב בה רחמנא כדאמרי' בארבע מיתות (סנהדרין ס:) זובח לאלהים יחרם בלתי לה' יד] עבודות הראויות למקום חייב בהו בעבודת כוכבים בין שדרכה בכך בין שאין דרכה בכך הלכך לענין מחשבה נמי איכא למיגמרה מבפנים: מלאכת מחשבת אסרה תורה · שנסמכה טו] שבת לפרשת המשכן בויקהל ומלאכת מחשבת שהעושה אותה מתכוין למלאכה גמורה אלא ששגג בשבת או סבור שמלאכה זו מותרת *וזה שיעור זה חשוב בעיניו אינו מתכוין למלאכה:

הדרן עלך בית שמאי

קדשי קדשים · כולן בכלל חטאות ואשמות ועולה ושלמי ציבור ומיהו משום דחלוקין במתן דמים או טז] בהקטרתן הדר תני להו כל חד וחד באפי נפשיה לפרש הלכותיהן: שחיטתן בצפון · ובגמ' מפרש מ"ט לא תנא וקבול דמן ומ"ש דתנן חטאות הפנימיות ברישא: פר ושעיר של יום הכפורים כו' · בגמ' יליף טעמא מנא לן דשחיטתן וקיבול דמן יז] בכלי שרת בצפון: בכלי שרת · דכתיב יח] בעולה בסיני וישם באגנות (שמות כד) וממנה למדו כל הזבחים בהיקש ליטעון כלי: הזיה על בין הבדים · עומד בין שני בדי ארון ומזה אחת למעלה וז' למטה כנגד יט] עובייה של כפרת ולא היו נוגעים בה: ועל הפרכת · כדכתיב וכן יעשה לאהל מועד (ויקרא טז): ועל מזבח הזהב · כדכתיב ויצא אל המזבח וגו' באחרי מות: מתנה אחת מהן מעכבת · כדאמרי' בפ' בית שמאי (לעיל דף לו:): שירי הדם היה שופך על יסוד כו' · יליף בגמ': ואם לא נתן · שירים הללו ליסוד לא עיכב הכפרה ובגמ' יליף לה בברייתא יכול יעכבנו כו': פרים הנשרפים · פר העלם ופר כהן משיח שאין נאכלין לכהנים אלא נשרפין חוץ לירושלים כדכתיב בהו אל שפך הדשן ישרף (ויקרא ד) וילפינן בסדר יומא (דף סח·) שהוא חוץ לירושלים: ושעירים הנשרפים · שעירי עבודת כוכבים שהוקשו לפר העלם לכל דבריהם בפרק בית שמאי (שם): הזיה על הפרוכת · כתיב בהו אבל בין הבדים לא כתיב בהו כדכתיב בפר יום הכפורים והזה באצבעו על פני הכפרת וגו' (ויקרא טז): מתנה

תוספות

מנין למתעסק בקדשים שהוא פסול · פ"ק דחולין (דף יג·) פירש בקונטרס כגון מתעסק בסכינו להגביהו כ] [או] לזורקו וקשה דכה"ג אפילו בחולין פסול לרבנן דפליגי עליה דרבי נתן ובעו כוונה ואפי' מתכוין לחתיכה כגון זרק סכין לנועצה בכותל דחשיב מתכוין לחתיכה כדמוכח פ"ב דחולין (דף לא:) אפ"ה פסלי רבנן עד שיתכוין לחתיכת כא] סימנין אף על גב דאינו מתכוין לשחיטה להתיר בשר ואמאי מכשרי כדקאמר התם ורבנן נהי דלא בעו כוונה לזביחה לחתיכה מיהא בעינן פירוש לחתיכת סימנין אבל חתיכה אחרת לא דזרק סכין לנועצה בכותל מתכוין לחתיכה הוא ופסלי רבנן ונראה האי מתעסק דקדשים היינו מתכוין לחתיכת סימנין ולא לשם זביחה דבחולין כשר ובקדשים פסול ועוד יש מתעסק אחר כגון משום חולין כב] דהיינו כסבור שהן חולין וכולהו מושחט את בן הבקר נפקי:

הדרן עלך בית שמאי

איזהו מקומן: קדשי קדשים שחיטתן בצפון · ה"ר אפרים היה מדקדק מכאן דלא בעינן כג] סכין בשחיטה מדלא קתני שחיטתן בכלי שרת בצפון כדקתני גבי קבלה וקיבול דמן בכלי שרת בצפון ומתוך כך אתיא שפיר הא דאמר בפ"ק דחולין (דף ג·) כגון שבדק קרומית של קנה ושחט בה כד] דלא בעי כלי שרת כה] וכן משמע קצת בפסחים פ' אלו דברים (דף סו·) שהיה כל אחד מביא סכינו מתוך ביתו כו] ואי אפשר לומר קודם קדשה התודה (מנחות פב:) ובסוף דם חטאת (לקמן צז:) דריש מדכתיב ויקח את המאכלת דעולה טעונה כלי [א] וילפינן כז] מיניה כולהו ובסוטה פרק היה מביא (דף יד:) משמע דסכין כח] מקדש ליה לדם ועוד בריש התודה (מנחות עח:) איכא למ"ד סכין אלימא מכלי שרת דאף על גב דלית לה תוך מקדשא והיא קרומית של קנה איכא למימר שתקנה ועשאה כלי וכר' יוסי בר' יהודה דאמר בפרק היה מביא (סוטה יד:) דעושין כלי שרת דעץ והיא דאלו דברים (פסחי' סו.) [ב] אימר כל אחד הקדיש סכינו בערב שבת והאי דלא תנן הכא כט] שחיטתן בכלי שרת בצפון כדתנן בקבלה לא דמי דבקבלה נמי לא הזכיר הכלי אלא משום דבעי שיהא גם הכלי בצפון ל] לאפוקי אם הבהמה בצפון והכלי בדרום והדם מקלח בתוכו תדע דבכל הגהו דבעו צפון קתני לא] שחיטה כו' וקיבול דמן בכלי שרת בצפון וגבי קדשים קלים שחיטתן בכל מקום בעזרה לא קתני וקיבול דמן בכלי שרת אע"ג דבעי קבלה בכלי שרת וכן לעיל פרק שני (דף כו·) דתניא קדשים קלים שחיטתן בפנים וקבול דמן בכלי שרת בפנים אתא לאשמועינן שצריך שיהא הכלי בפנים לאפוקי אם רוב הכלי בחוץ [ג] ומיעוטה בפנים אע"פ שאין הדם בפנים נפסל ביוצא דמקבל במיעוט שבפנים אי נמי משום דאיכא אסם מורע שמתקבל ביד אילטריך למיתני

עין משפט נר מצוה

סב א מיי' פ"א מהל' פסה"מ הלכה ג:

סג ב מיי' פי"ד מהל' פסה"מ הלכה א:

סד ג מיי' פ"ב מהל' שחיטה הלכה כב סמג עשין סג טוש"ע י"ד סימן ד סעיף ג:

א ד מיי' פ"ה מהלכות מעה"ק הלכה ב:

ב ה מיי' שם הל' א:

ג ו מיי' שם הלכה יב ופ"ד מהלכות עבד יוה"כ הלכה ב:

ד ז מיי' פ"ה מהלכות מעה"ק הלכה יג:

מסורת הש"ס

חולין יג. לא: מנחות קי. | [חולין לח:] | נ"ב | חולין לח: | צ"ל דתניא | שבת עו. לא. | [בילה יג. חגיגה י: ב"ק כו: ס. סנהדרין סב. כריתות יט:] | ס"א וזה שאין שיעור זה חשוב

הגהות הב"ח

(א) גמ' בפנים הוא דאמר בחוץ לא אמר ר"ש:

שיטה מקובצת

א] לדעתכם זבחו אות י' נמחק: ב] דתניא כלל: ג] זה ותרוייהו: ד] לית ליה: ה] כעין פנים: ו] מתנה אחת מהן מעכבת · הקשה הר"ר אליעזר מטוריש פתח בהזאות וסיים במתנות וי"ל דלרבותא נקט לא מבעיא הזאות דמעכבות בכל מקום שהן אפילו כמזבח החיצון כגון בפרה ובנגעים כדאמר לעיל אפילו מתנות שאין מעכבות על מזבח החיצון דאם נתנם במתנה אחת יצא מ"מ מעכבות על מזבח הפנימי וכן משמע בגמ' דצריך קרא גם לארבע מתנות: ז] ראיה זו כבר ידענו כו' דנפקא לן מינה ולא עיכוב: ח] אלמא בעלים קרי ליה מקריב הלכך הוו להו: ט] דלאו איהו שחיט ליה פסול: י] תיבת או ל"ש ונמחק: יא] היה בו שיעור אבל: יב] עושה הויא מחשבה: יג] דעיקר מחשבה בקרבנות: יד] לה' לבדו: טו] שנסמכה פרשת שבת לפרשת מלאכת המשכן בויקהל ומאי מלאכת מחשבת: טז] או בהקטרת אימוריהן הדר: יז] דמן בצפון ותיבות בכלי שרת נמחק: יח] דכתיב בעולת סיני וישם: יט] כנגד עוביו של כפורת ולא היו נוגעים בו הס"ד: כ] בסכינו להגביהו ולזורקו וקשה כו' דר' נתן בפ"ק דחולין ובעו כוונה: כא] סימנין אבל מתכוון לחתיכת סימנין אע"ג ס"א אפילו לא נתכוון לשחיטה כיון דנתכוון לחתיכת סימנין מכשרי רבנן כדמוכח בפ"ב דחולין דקאמר ורבנן נמי נהי כו': כב] משום חולין דהכא דפסלוהו דהיינו קסבר שהן חולין דפסול משום מתעסק וכולהו: כג] בשחיטה סכין כלי שרת מדלא: כד] בה ואע"ג דמיירי שתקנה ועשה כלי דודאי כלי בעינן כדמוכח בבמה הזכתי מ"מ לא משתמע שתהא כלי שרת שהרי אין עושין כלי שרת של עץ · מהר"פ: כה] (שרת שהרי אין עושין כלי שרת עץ) ואפ"ה שוחטין בקרומית: כו] ביתו מי שפסחו טלה תוחב לו בצוארו ומי שפסחו גדי תוחב לו בין קרניו: כז] וילפינן כולהו מעולה ובסוטה: כח] מקדשא ליה לדם כו' למ"ד דסכין מקדשא אלימא מכלי שרת דאע"ג דלית ליה תוך מקדשא וההיא דקרומית של קנה כו' כלי שרת וכרבי יוסי: כט] הכא דשחיטתן בכלי שרת בצפון משום דפשיטא ליה דכל העבודה בעינן כלי שרת וכ"ת למה תנן וקבול דמן בכלי שרת לא דמי [דלא תני] אלא משום דבעי שיהא הכלי שרת כולה בצפון לאפוקי דאי הוי רובא בדרום ומיעוטו בצפון אע"פ שהוא מקבל באותו מיעוט שבצפון מ"מ [כשהוא מקבל] הדם בכלי בטל אגב רוב הכלי שבדרום דאגד כלי שמיה אגד ולא הוי קבלה בצפון אבל בשעת שחיטה אינו צריך להיות הסכין כולו בצפון דהא אפילו אם הסכין רובו בדרום רק ששוחט במיעוט הסכין שבצפון כשרה וגם א) הבהמה בטלה אגב הסכין והרי יש שחיטה בצפון מיהו אמת דלא בעינן כלי שרת וראיה מתוספתא דמנחות כו' ואינו רוצה לומר [דאינה טעונה] כלי ממש שהרי בעולה [טעון כלי] מויקח [את] המאכלת אלא דאינה טעונה כלי שרת קאמר [וקשה] למורי דמאי [שנא] שחיטה משאר עבודות וכ"ת משום דכשרה בזר הרי בלילה כשרה בזר וטעונה כלי שרת ותירץ דבלילה דאינה כי אם בקדשים אע"ג דכשרה בזר היא כשאר קדשים לענין כלי שרת אבל שחיטה הואיל ושייכא בחולין כמו בקדשים ולכך אע"פ שהצריך כלי לא בעינן כלי שרת וא"ת כיון דגלי קרא בשחיטה דבעי כלי מויקח את המאכלת א"כ מנין לנו לומר (שיהא) [שלא יהא] אותו כלי כלי שרת מידי דהוי [אקבלה] דבעינן כלי שרת משום דגלי קרא וישם באגנות בעולת סיני וי"ל דודאי מוישם באגנות נפקי לן כלי לאפוקי שלא יקבל ביד אבל שיהיה כלי שרת דהיינו שהוקדש בכלי לאו מהתם נפקא אלא מדכתיב ועשית מזרקותיו גבי כלי המזבח שנעשו מתרומת המשכן אבל שחיטה מי כתיב ועשית סכיניו הלכך לא בעיא כלי שרת בשחיטה ומיהו הכיסא של מנחות צריכה להיות כלי שרת מדכתיב גבי מזרקות שניהם מלאים סולת למנחה אלמא היו נותנים המנחה במזרקות שהיו כלי שרת כדפי' כיון שהם כתובים גבי כלי המזבח כך נראה למורי הר"פ: ל] לאפוקי כו' בתוכו וא"ת כיון שאין הכלי בצפון תיפוק ליה משום דבעינן קבלה בצפון וכיון שהכלי בדרום א"כ הויא הקבלה עצמה בדרום וי"ל דאתי למעוטי היכא דרוב הכלי בדרום ומיעוטו בצפון וקיבל במיעוטו שבצפון אפ"ה פסול כיון שרוב הכלי בדרום ובגמרא איכא תרי קראי חד למקבל וחד לכלי שרת כלומר דקבלה עצמה טעונה צפון והשתא אי הוי תני וקיבול דמן בצפון ה"א כיון שמקבל במיעוט כלי שבצפון דסגי בכך לכך תני כלי שרת בצפון לומר לך דבעינן רוב הכלי בצפון שהדם מתקבל בתוכו ולכן שדינן ליה בתר רוב הכלי אבל גבי סכין לא שייך למימר האי טעמא ותדע דכל החדוש דקתני וקיבול דמן בכלי שרת בצפון משום הכי הוא דהא גבי קדשים קלים [לא תני וקבול דמן בכלי שרת] וכן משמע התם דקאמר סכין מקדשא ליה לצואר בהמה אלמא משמע דכלי שרת הוא ויש להיות דלעולם הסכין אינו כלי שרת והא דקאמר התם סכין מקדשא ליה לשחיטה אינו רוצה לומר שהוא כלי שרת אלא משום שהוא ראוי לשחוט וכן משמע בפרק התודה דלא בעינן כלי שרת לשחיטה דקאמר גבי סכין ועדיפא מכלי שרת דאף על גב דלית ליה תוך מקדשא ואי הוי כלי שרת הו"ל ועדיפא משאר כלי שרת אבל ר"ל עדיפא מכלי שרת ממש דהואיל והצריך הכתוב כלי לשחיטה ואף על גב דלית ליה תוך · לשון תוספות אחרות מתלמיד מהר"פ ז"ל: לא] תיבות שחיטה כו' נמחק:

א) נראה דצ"ל וגם הסכין בטל אגב הבהמה

הגהות צ"ק [א] נ"א וילפינן כולהו מעולה: [ב] נ"א יש לומר דכל אחד כו': [ג] ומיעוטה בפנים ומקבל הדם במיעוט שבפנים אף על פי שאין הדם בפנים נפסל ביוצא א"כ כו' וכן הוא בתוספות חולין דף ג ע"א וע"ש:

ה א מיי' פ"ו מהלכות מעה"ק הלכה ו ופ"ד מהלכות פסה"מ הל' ב:

ו ב ג ד מיי' פ"ד מהל' מחוסרי כפרה הל' ב:

תורה אור

מתנה אחת מהן מעכבת שירי הדם היה שופך על יסוד מערבי של מזבח החיצון ואם לא נתן לא עיכב א]*אלו ואלו נשרפין אבית הדשן: גמ' וניתני נמי וקיבול דמן בכלי שרת בצפון כיון דאיכא אשם מצורע דקיבול דמו ביד הוא שיריה ולא והא קתני ב] לה לקמן אשם נזיר ואשם מצורע שחיטתן בצפון וקבול דמן בכלי שרת בצפון ג] מעיקרא סבר קיבול דמו ביד הוא שיריה וכיון ד] דלא סגי ליה אלא בכלי הדר תנייה *דתניא °ולקח (ויקרא יד) יכול בכלי ת"ל ונתן מה נתינה בעצמו של כהן אף לקיחה בעצמו של כהן יכול אף למזבח כן ת"ל °כי כחטאת האשם (שם) הוא מה חטאת טעונה כלי אף אשם טעון כלי נמצאת אתה אומר *אשם מצורע שני כהנים מקבלין את דמו אחד ביד ואחד בכלי זה שקיבלו בכלי בא לו ה]אצל מזבח וזה שקיבלו ביד בא לו אצל מצורע:
פר

יומא סא: · תוספתא דנגעים פ"ח

מתנה אחת מהן מעכבת · כדאמרן בפ' בית שמאי (לעיל לט.) מועשה ו] כאשר עשה: אלו ואלו · של יום הכפורים ושאר הנשרפין: נשרפין אבית הדשן · למקום שמוציאין שם את הדשן של מזבח החיצון דכתיב ביה והוציא את הדשן אל מחוץ למחנה (ויקרא ו) ובפרים הנשרפים כתיב אל שפך הדשן (שם ד) ושל יום הכפורים ז] הקישו לפר העלם כדאמרינן בפרק ב"ש (לעיל לט:) לפר זה פר יום הכפורים: גמ' וניתני נמי ברישא · גבי סתם ח] של קדשי קדשים וקבול דמן כי היכי דתנא שחיטתן: אשם מצורע קיבול דמו ביד · כדיליף לקמן שמקבל דמו לתוך כפו: שייריה · משום דלא פסיקא ליה למיתנייה בהדי כללי דשאר קדשים שכל קבול דמן בכלי: וכיון דלא סגי ליה נמי · בלא קבלת כלי כדיליף לקמן שני כהנים מקבלין את דמו אחד ביד ואחד בכלי הדר תנייה בהדיא ולא כללו: ולקח · באשם מצורע כתיב ולקח הכהן מדם האשם ונתן על תנוך וגו' (ויקרא יד) מה נתינה בעצמו של כהן באצבעו דכתיב אצבע גבי שמן ויליף דם מיניה: יכול אף למזבח · דם אשם מצורע הנזרק למזבח דמרבינן ליה לקמן בדין מתן דמים ואימורין למזבח ואע"ג דלאו בגופיה כתיבא: כי כחטאת האשם הוא ט]· באשם מצורע כתיב כדין חטאת דין אשם זה בעבודת הכהן מה חטאת טעונה כלי בקבלת דמה דילפינן לקיחה לקיחה בתורת כהנים כתיב בחטאת ולקח הכהן מדם החטאת (ויקרא ד) וכתיב בעולת סיני ויקח משה חצי הדם וישם באגנות (שמות כד) אף אשם זה טעון כלי אף על פי שאמרנו בו קבלה ביד:
בעולה

למיתני בכולהו קדשים וקיבול דמן בכלי שרת י] בצפון ומיהו יש לדקדק מהא בתוספתא דמנחות חומר בקמילה מבשחיטה שהקמילה טעונה כלי והשחיטה אינה טעונה כלי יא] אלא אפי' קרומית של קנה ועל כרחיך לא קאמר דלא תבעי כלי כלל דהא אמרינן מה עולה טעונה כלי כו' אלא דלא בעי כלי שרת קאמר ומיהו יש לפרש דלא חיישינן לכלי יפה קאמר יב] דלא פסלה קרומית של קנה משום הקריבהו נא לפחתך כדפריך הש"ס בסוטה פרק היה מביא (דף יד:) גבי כפיפה מצרית דדורון הוא שדרך להביא בכלי נאה אבל בשחיטה לא חיישינן אי נמי כפיפה מצרית מכוערת יותר מקרומית של קנה: אלו ואלו נשרפין אבית הדשן · פירש בקונטרס דפר יום הכיפורים אתי מהיקישא דפר העלם כדאמר בפרק בית שמאי (לעיל לט:) לפר זה פר יום הכיפורים ואם תאמר והא אין דבר הלמד בהיקש חוזר ומלמד בהיקש ופר העלם בגופיה לא כתיב ביה אל בית הדשן ומפר כהן המשיח אתי דכתיב בפר העלם (ויקרא ד) כאשר שרף את הפר הראשון והיינו היקש כמו ושחט החטאת במקום העולה דקרי ליה היקש לקמן (דף מח.) ולפירש"י דפרק בית שמאי (לעיל מ.) דילפינן פר יום הכיפורים לאו בדם וטבילה מפר כהן משיח אם כן יג] *נימא דמליט למילף נמי שריפת בית הדשן אבל לפר"ת דהתם קשיא ויש לומר דאיכא תרי היקישי בפר העלם ועשה כאשר עשה לפר דדרשינן מיניה פרק בית שמאי (גם זה שם) זה פר כהן משיח בין לעכב בהזאות *כמשיח בין לאגמורי יותרת ושתי הכליות בפר העלם ממשיח הוא הדין דניגמר לענין שריפה פר העלם ממשיח וכי הדר וכתב בפר העלם יד] וכאשר שרף (הילכך) הוה ליה כמאן דכתיב בגופיה ועוד יש לומר הא דנשרפין חוץ לג' מחנות יליף לקמן בסוף טבול יום (דף קה:) מדכתיב תלת אל מחוץ טו] למחנה *שלישית אי כתב בכולהו ואין זה אלא כגילוי מילתא בעלמא דמחוץ למחנה דכתב בכל חד וחד טז] במתנה שלישית קאמר הילכך אתי שפיר פר יום הכיפורים מפר העלם ואייתר לו התם יז] מחוץ למחנה דכתיב בפר יום הכיפורים לרבנן טומר לך כיון שילא מחוץ למחנה אחת השורפו מטמא בגדים ולרבי שמעון לג"ש ללמד יח] מפרה מה כאן שלשה מחנות אף להלן שלשה מחנות מה להלן למזרחה של ירושלים אף כאן למזרחה של ירושלים ומיהו בית הדשן ודאי קשה דנהי דשלשה מחנות הוי כמאן דכתיב בגופיה דאפשר חוץ לג' מחנות שלא במקום דשן ואם כן הא דבעי מקום דשן הוי דבר הלמד בהיקש ואינו חוזר ומלמד בהיקש ושמא גם זה חשוב גילוי מילתא בעלמא היא דכל הנשרפין חוץ לשלש מחנות נשרפין במקום הדשן *(אחר) השתא אתי שפיר שעיר יוה"כ דלא איתקש לפר העלם אי נמי כולהו ילפינן בית הדשן בג"ש דמחוץ למחנה מכהן משיח כ] ואין לפרש דאתי מריבויא דחטאת חטאת דכתיב בפר ושעיר של יום הכפורים דדרשינן לקמן בסוף התערובת (דף פב.) ואת פר החטאת ואת שעיר החטאת יוציא אל מחוץ למחנה ושרפו מה ת"ל חטאת חטאת שיכול כא] דאין לי דמטמא בגדים ונשרפין בבית הדשן אלא אלו בלבד מנין לרבות פר כהן משיח ופר העלם דבר של ציבור ושעירי עבודת כוכבים ת"ל חטאת חטאת דברי רבי יהודה דעל כרחין נשרפין אבית הדשן כדי נסבה דהא עיקר על שפך הדשן בפר כהן משיח כתיב אלא משום מטמא בגדים נקט דלא כתיב בהו וכן כב] מוכיח דר' מאיר כג] פליג עליה וקאמר אינו צריך הרי הוא אומר לכפר ליכפר לימד על כל המתכפרים בפנים שטורפן מטמא בגדים ושמא כי היכי דיליף מריבויא דחטאת חטאת טומאת בגדים בכולהו מפר ושעיר של יום הכפורים הכי נמי הוה יליף מינייהו מההוא ריבויא גופיה בית הדשן *מפר ושעיר של יום הכפורים: מה נתינה בעצמו של כהן · פי' בקונטרס מדכתיב אצבע גבי שמן ויליף דם כד] מינייהו ותימה א"כ הוי היקשא מבנין אב ולקמן (דף נא.) מיבעיא לן אי דבר הלמד בבנין אב חוזר ומלמד בהיקש *ונראה לי לקיחה מנתינה נמי הוי בנין אב *ולפינן מנתינה דידיה ולא מנתינה דשאר קרבנות ולקמן אמרינן דילפינן שפיר בנין אב מבנין אב · ברו"ך: אף לקיחה ולקח כה] מדם האשם בעצמו של כהן · תימה דגבי חטאת נמי כתיב (ויקרא ד) ולקח ונתן ולא אמר מה נתינה בעצמו של כהן אף לקיחה בעצמו של כהן ושמא הכא דריש משום דמייתר דכתיב במצורע (שם יד) עשיר ועני ואע"ג דבתורת כהנים דריש מקמאי אבתרא סמיך ונראה לי דבחטאת כתיב ולקח מדם החטאת באצבעו ונתן אם כן לאו בידו מקבל דבאצבע לא אפשר לקבל אלא על כרחין בכלי קאמר ואצבעו הייט דעביד כו] און לשפת מזרק כדאמר לעיל פרק שני (דף כד:) אבל באשם לא כתיב באצבע ומשום דלא כימא ולקח באצבעו הייט וטבל דוקא ולא איירי בקבלה להכי איצטריך לגזירה שוה דגמרינן מויקח חצי הדם וישם באגנות בת"כ · ברו"ך: מה חטאת טעונה כלי כו' · פירש בקונטרס דילפינן לקיחה לקיחה בתורת כהנים כתיב בחטאת ולקח כז] הכהן מדם החטאת וכתיב בעולת סיני ויקח משה חצי הדם וישם באגנות ותימה הוה ליה דבר הלמד בגזירה שוה כח] חוזר ומלמד בהיקשא דכחטאת האשם ובעיא היא לקמן (דף נ:) ולא איפשיטא למאן דאמר בתר מלמד כט] אזלינן ומיהו בתגם פירש בקונטרס דילפינן לקיחה לקיחה דלקמן בסוף דם חטאת (דף צז:) משמע דאתיא בהיקשא דזאת התורה מזבחי שלמי ציבור דקאמר מה עולה טעונה כלי אף כל טעון כלי מאי כלי אילימא מזרק בזבחי שלמי ציבור נמי כתיב ויקח משה חצי הדם וישם באגנות פירוש וכיון דהדר איתקש טולהו לשלמים דכתיב בהאי קרא וילפינן מיניה התם מה שלמים מפגלין ומתפגלין כלי נמי תילף משלמים דהתם נמי שלמים הוו בסיני ומיהו מכל מקום קשה עדיין דהוה ליה דבר הלמד בהיקש ואינו חוזר ומלמד בהיקש יש לומר דבההיא היקשא דזאת התורה כתב נמי אשם ואיתקש *כמו של שלמים וכל אשמות בכלל אפילו אשם מצורע אלא דהוה אמינא דמעטיה קרא מקבלת כלי ל] *ודרשיה ביד דבעצמו של כהן הלכך אתא כחטאת האשם לגלויי דלא בא הכתוב להוציאו מקבלת כלי לגמרי לא] וקשה גזירה שוה דלקיחה מסיני למה לי ליגמר טולהו משלמים יש לומר דחטאת ילפינן משלמים לקבלת כלי מהיקשא וגזירה שוה דלקיחה לקיחה *איצטריך למיהוי כמאן דכתיב בגופיה דחטאת והדר ילפינן אשם מחטאת בהיקשא דכחטאת האשם לב] ולא גמרינן מעיקרא אשם משלמים בהיקשא דזאת התורה כדילפינן לענין פיגול דאם כן גזרה שוה דלקיחה לקיחה למה *[לי]:
איידי

יומא סא: (margin) · כ"א כמשיח בפר העלם בין כו' נ"ק · ז"ק מ"ז · כ"א ושלישית לא כתב בכולהו ואין זה אלא גילוי כו' נ"ק · אחר והשתא נ"ק · כסר נ"ק · [עיין ביומא דף סא ע"ב דמהרי"ו בע"א] *דילפינן נ"ק · נמי לשלמים נ"ק · מדרשא דותנו דבעצמו נ"ק · ועי' נ"ק ורש"ק [וע"ע תוס' יומא סא: ד"ה זה חטאת]

גליון הש"ס
תוס' ד"ה מה חטאת וכו' אצטריך למהוי כמאן דכתיב בגופיה · ועיין דאמרינן לעיל מח ע"א:

שיטה מקובצת
א] אלו ואלו כו' פ"ה בפר כהן משיח כתיב בהדיא בית הדשן ופר העלם איתקש לפר כהן משיח ושעירי עבודת כוכבים הוקשו לפר העלם וכן פר יוה"כ אתי מהיקשא דפר העלם וקשה דבפר העלם גופיה לא כתיב כו' א) וי"ל דבפר העלם איכא תרי היקישא דכתיב ועשה כאשר עשה ושרף כאשר שרף הלכך הוי כאילו כתיב בגופיה ומיהו קשה שעיר יוה"כ מהיכא אתא אי משום דאיתקש לפר יוה"כ הא פר יוה"כ גופיה בהיקשא אתא לכך נראה דאין זה אלא גלוי מלתא בעלמא דכל הנשרפין יהיו נשרפין בבית הדשן שהרי שריפה חוץ לג' מחנות כתיב בגופייהו רק צריכין ללמוד שנשרפין אבית הדשן וכל בית הדשן הרי חוץ לשלש מחנות כדילפינן בפ' טבול יום תלוי מלתא ילפינן מדבר הלמד בהיקש · לשון מהר"פ: ב] תיבת לה נמחק: ג] מעיקרא סבר כו' וא"ת וכי התנא לא היה יודע מסקנא דברייתא וי"ל דה"פ סברתו היתה מעיקרא דלא תני בכלל שאר קדשים משום דאשם מצורע מקצת קבלתו ביד ושאר קדשים כל קבול דמן בכלי והלכך שיריה: ד] וכיון דהוא דלא: ס] לו וזרקו על המזבח תיבת אצל נמחק: ו] מועשה לפר: ז] הכפורים הוקשו לפר: ח] סתם כל קדשי קדשים: ט] והוא לכהן באשם: י] תיבת בצפון נמחק ומיהו יש לדקדק מהא דאמרינן בתוספתא: יא] כלי אלמא אפילו: יב] קאמר ולא פסלה: יג] כן ניחא דמצינו: יד] העלם כאשר שרף: טו] למחנה חד בפר כהן משיח וחד בפר העלם וחד בדישן דלא איצטריכי כולהו דהא לאקשי ליתן מחנה שלישית איכתיבו כולהו ואין זה: טז] וחד למחנה שלישית: יז] התם נמי מחוץ: יח] ללמד על חפרה מה כאן חוץ לשלשה מחנות אף להלן חוץ לשלשה מחנות ומה להלן: יט] הדשן מיהא לא כתיב בגופיה דאי אפשר חוץ לג' מחנות כו' דבעי במקום דשן תני כו' נשרפין במקום אחר' תוס' השתא' ותי' הדשן נמחק ומתיבת השתא עד תיבת ואין לפרש מוקף בח"ל: כ] משיח ע"כ · ואין: כא] שיכול אין לי: כב] וכן ס"א וכי מוכיח: כג] מאיר דפליג: כד] דם מיניה: כה] ולקח הכהן מדם: כו] דעביד ליה און לשפת מורק כדאמרינן לעיל בפרק: כז] ולקח אהרן מדם ותיבת הכהן נמחק: כח] שוה והוזר ומלמד: כט] אזלינן ועוד קשה למה לי לאקשי חטאת לאשם תיפוק ליה כדאמר לקמן דזאת התורה כו' ושלמים הוו בסיני כדאמר לקמן מה עולה טעונה כלי אף כל כו' ופריך מאי כלי אילימא מזרק בזבחי שלמי צבור כתיב ויקח משה וגו' פי' והוקשו לשלמים וא"כ ה"נ אשם תיפוק ליה מהיקשא דאשם וי"ל דקושיא שניה מתרץ לראשונה דודאי מהיא דלקמן לא הייתי יודע אשם מצורע דהואיל ויצא מכלל שאר אשמות לידון בעצמו של כהן להכי אתי היקשא דחטאת כאשם להחזירו לכלל שאר אשמות להטעינו כלי דלא הוי השתא חוזר ומלמד בהיקשא דאין זה רק גלוי מלתא בעלמא לומר גם זה לא יצא מהיקשא לגמרי משלמים לומר דלא צריך כלי רק לחזאת מצורע אבל לשלם מתנות מזבח צריך קבלה בכלי כמו בשאר אשמות ומיהו קשה למה לי ג"ש דקיחה קיחה לחטאת תיפוק ליה מהיקשא דשלמים ואמר מורי דהר"א כיון דחטאת יצא מן הכלל דמתן דמו באצבע ושאר כל הקרבנות בכלי ה"ה לענין קבלה דלא הוי כשאר קרבנות קמ"ל ג"ש דקיחה קיחה אבל אכתי קשה למה לי להקיש אשם מצורע לחטאת תיפוק ליה כמו כן מקיחה קיחה דסיני דבאשם גופיה כתיב קיחה ותירץ דהר"א דאתא קרא וליסקא מג"ש דמקשינן לקיחה לנתינה שיהא בעצמו של כהן ה"ה לענין מזבח קמ"ל ס"א וי"ל דכיון דאיכא היקשא דלקיחה ונתינה הייתי אומר דלכל הקבלה איתקש דבעינן בעצמו של כהן אבל השתא מהדרינה (מבחטאת כאשם) [מכחטאת האשם] לכלל שאר אשמות א"כ נוקי היקשא דלקיחה לנתינה לענין הזאות מצורע דוקא ע"כ כתוב בס"א וא"ת גבי חטאת נמי נימא דאיתקש לקיחה לנתינה דכתיב ולקח הכהן מדם החטאת באצבעו ונתן על קרנות המזבח והנתינה דחטאת היא באצבע וי"ל דהתם גבי חטאת הפסיק הענין שלא להקיש לקיחה לנתינה · והעתקתי לשון מהר"פ ז"ל: ל] כלי מדרשה דבעצמו: לא] לגמרי תוספות וקשה: לב] האשם ומכל מקום קשה אמאי לא גמרינן מעיקרא כו' למה ע"כ הס"ד:

א) עיין בתוספות ד"ה אלו ·

דאתיא

VEIL, AND ON THE GOLDEN ALTAR; [47b] [THE OMISSION OF] A SINGLE ONE OF THESE APPLICATIONS INVALIDATES [THE SACRIFICE]. THE RESIDUE OF THE BLOOD HE [THE PRIEST] POURED OUT ON THE WESTERN BASE OF THE ALTAR; BUT IF HE DID NOT POUR IT OUT, HE DID NOT INVALIDATE [THE SACRIFICE]. BOTH OF THESE[3] WERE BURNT AT THE ASHPIT.[4]

GEMARA. Yet let him [the Tanna] also teach [in the very first clause]. And the reception of their blood is [done] in a service
a vessel at the north?—Since there is the leper's guilt-offering,[1] whose blood is received in the hand, he omits it. Is it then not [received in a vessel]? Surely he teaches later on: As for a nazirite's guilt-offering and a leper's guilt-offering, their slaughtering is at the north, and the reception of their blood is [done] with a service vessel at the north?[2]—At first he thought that the blood was received in the hand, [and so] he omitted it.[3] But when he saw that it cannot be done adequately without a vessel [also being used], he re-included it. For it was taught: *And the priest shall take [of the blood of the guilt-offering]*:[4] You might think, with a vessel; but Scripture adds, *and the priest shall put it* [etc.]:[5] as the putting must be by the very priest himself, so the taking must be by the very priest himself. You might think that it is likewise for the altar:[6] Therefore Scripture states, *For as the sin-offering so is the guilt-offering*:[7] as the sin-offering requires a vessel [for the reception of the blood], so does the guilt-offering require a vessel. Thus you must conclude that two priests received the blood of a leper's guilt-offering, one in his hand and the other in a vessel. He who received it in a vessel went to the altar, and he who received it in his hand went to the leper.

(3) The sin-offerings of the Day of Atonement and the other sin-offerings which were burnt. (4) The place where the ashes of the outer altar were deposited.

a (1) A sacrifice of higher sanctity. (2) *Infra* 54b. (3) The mention of the reception of the blood in the introductory clause. (4) Lev. XIV, 14. (5) Ibid. (6) That the blood which is sprinkled on the altar too is not received in a vessel. (7) Ibid. 13. This rendering follows the exact order of the Hebrew.

[48a] AS FOR THE BULLOCK AND THE HE-GOAT OF THE DAY OF ATONEMENT etc. Consider: the north [side of the altar] is written in connection with the burnt-offering, then let him teach [about] the burnt-offering first?[8]—Because this is deduced about the sin-offering by exegesis, he cherishes it more.[9] Then let him teach the outer sin-offerings [first]?[10]—Because the blood of these [which he does enumerate] enters the inner sanctuary, he cherishes it more.[11]

Now, where is the north written in connection with the burnt-
a offering?—*And he shall kill it on the side of the altar* northward.[1] We have thus found [it of] the flocks;[2] how do we know [it of] the herd?—Scripture saith, And [*we*] *if his offering be of the flock:*[3] the *waw* [and] continues[4] the preceding section, so that the [subject] above may be deduced from [that]below.[5] That is well on the view that you can learn[6] [the subject above from that below]; but on the view that you cannot learn [it thus], what can be said? For it was taught: *And if any one sin* etc.;[7] this teaches that one is liable to a guilt-offering of suspense on account of doubtful trespass:[8] that is R. Akiba's ruling. But the Sages exempt [him]. Surely then they disagree in this: one master holds that we learn [the subject above from that below],[9] while the other master holds that we do not learn it?—Said R. Papa: All agree that we do learn [thus], but this is the Rabbis' reason:[10] *mizwoth*[11] is employed here, and *mizwoth* is employed in connection with the sin-offering of forbidden fat:[12] as there it means a law whose deliberate infringement entails *kareth*
b and its unwitting infringement entails a sin-offering, so here too[1] [it is entailed only by] that whose deliberate infringement entails *kareth*, while its unwitting infringement involves a sin-offering.[2] And R. Akiba?[3]—As there it is fixed, so here it is fixed, thus excluding the sin-offering for the defilement of the sanctuary and its sacred objects [sacrifices], which is variable.[4] And the Rabbis?[5] —There is no semi *gezerah shawah*.[6] But R. Akiba too [surely admits that] there is no semi *gezerah shawah*?—That indeed is so; here, however, they differ in this: R. Akiba holds: '*And if a soul*' is written, and the *waw* indicates conjunction with the preceding subject.[7] But [according to] the Rabbis too, surely it is written, *And if a soul?*[8] Shall we say that they differ in this: one master holds that a *hekkesh* is stronger; while the other master holds that a *gezerah shawah* is stronger?[9]—No: all agree that the *gezerah shawah* is stronger, but the Rabbis can answer you: the subject below is learnt from that above, that the guilt-offering must be [two] silver shekels in value,[10] so that you should not say: Surely the doubt cannot be more stringent than the certainty: as the certainty [of sin] requires a sin-offering [even] a sixth [of a *zuz* in value], so
c [for] the doubt a guilt-offering of a sixth [of a *zuz*] is sufficient.[1] Now, how does R. Akiba know this?—He deduces it from [the text,] *And this is the law of the guilt-offering*,[2] [which intimates that] there is one law for all guilt-offerings. That is well on the view that '*law*' can be [so] interpreted; but on the view that '*law*' cannot be so interpreted, whence does he derive [it]?—He derives [it] from the repetition of '*according to thy valuation.*'[3] [But] what can be said of the guilt-offering of a maidservant promised in marriage,[4] where 'according to thy valuation' is not written?—He derives [it from] the repetition of '*with the ram.*'[5]

How do we know that a sin-offering requires the north?—Because it is written, *And he shall kill the sin-offering in the place of the burnt-offering.*[6] We have found [it of] slaughtering: how do we know [it of] receiving?—Because it is written, *And the priest shall take of the blood of the sin-offering.*[7] How do we know that the receiver himself [must stand in the north]?[8]—The text says, '*And he shall take*', [which intimates,] he shall [be]take himself [to the place where the blood is received].[9] We have thus found [it as] a regulation; how do we know that it is indispensable?[10]—Another text is written, *And he shall kill it for a sin-offering in the place where they kill the burnt-offering*;[11] and it was taught: Where is the burnt-offering slaughtered? in the north: so this too[12] is [slaughtered] in the

(8) V. *infra* 53b. (9) I.e., the Tanna is more desirous of teaching the results of exegesis than what Scripture states explicitly, and therefore he gives them preference. (10) V. *infra* 52b. (11) It is more important in his eyes, and hence he teaches it first.
a (1) Lev. I, 11. (2) To which the text refers. (3) Ibid. 10; *and* is expressed by the letter *waw* in Heb., punctuated *we*. (4) Lit., 'adds to'. (5) When a passage commences with '*and*', this conjunction links it with the previous portion, and a law stated in one applies to the other too. Here the subject above is the burnt-offering of the herd, and the subject below is that of the flock. (6) By means of a conjunction *waw*. (7) Lev. V, 17. (8) V. Mishnah *infra* 54b. Now, the subject immediately preceding deals with the guilt-offering for putting sacred things to secular use (vv. 14-16), when the offender learns that he has definitely sinned. If one is in doubt whether he has offended, this text teaches that he must bring a guilt-offering of suspense (i.e., doubt). The doubt arises thus: Two things lie before a man, one of which he puts to secular use. Subsequently he learns that one of these was sacred, and he does not know which. (9) *And if any one sin* introduces the law of the guilt-offering of suspense for doubtful sin. By learning the subject above from it, it follows that this is entailed by doubtful trespass too. (10) For not doing so here. (11) Lit. '*commandments*': *and if any one sin, and do any of the mizwoth* (E.V. things) *which the Lord hath commanded not to be done* etc. (12) Lev. IV, 27. Forbidden fat is not mentioned there, but 'a sin-offering of forbidden fat' is the usual designation in the Talmud for an ordinary sin-offering. The reason is because *Ye shall eat neither fat nor blood* (Lev. III, 17) is followed by Ch. IV, which deals with sin-offerings (Rashi in Soṭ. 15a). Asheri (in Ned. 4a) explains the reason because the most usual form of sinning thus is eating forbidden fat through having it in the house.
b (1) *Sc.* the guilt-offering of suspense. (2) I.e., a guilt-offering of suspense is brought only when one is in doubt whether he has committed an offence, which, if certainly committed, entails *kareth* or a sin-offering. But the secular misuse of sacred property does not involve a sin-offering, consequently one is not liable to a guilt-offering for doubtful trespass. (3) How does he interpret this *gezerah shawah*? (4) Lit., 'ascends (in value) and descends'.—The ordinary sin-offering is fixed and the same for rich and poor alike. This *gezerah shawah* then teaches that a guilt-offering of suspense is incurred only for the doubtful violation of a law which, if definitely violated, involves a fixed sin-offering. But if one is doubtful whether he entered the Temple whilst unclean, he does not bring a guilt-offering of suspense, because if he were certain he would only be liable to a *variable* sacrifice (v. Lev. V, 1-10). (5) What is their view on this? (6) A *gezerah shawah* shews similarity in *all* respects, not in some only. (7) As above. (8) And it was stated above that all agree that the subject above is learnt from that below. (9) The *hekkesh* or analogy arises from the *waw*, which couples both subjects. Thus apparently the Rabbis give preference to the *gezerah shawah*, while R. Akiba gives preference to the *hekkesh* (only one can be employed here, since they yield apparently contradictory results). (10) The earlier passage reads: *then he shall bring . . . according to thy valuations in silver by shekels . . . a guilt-offering* (v. 15), which the Rabbis interpret as meaning not less than two shekels. The analogy therefore teaches that the guilt-offering of suspense in v. 18 must also have that value.
c (1) Hence the *hekkesh* teaches otherwise. (2) Lev. VII, 1. (3) Heb. בערכך. It is repeated in Lev. V, 15 and Lev. V, 18, and this furnishes a *gezerah shawah*, which teaches that they must be of equal value in both cases. (4) Ibid. XIX, 20-22. (5) Ibid. V, 16 and XIX, 22. (6) Ibid. IV, 24. (7) Ibid 25. This is connected with the immediately preceding words, '*in the place where they kill the burnt-offering.*'—'*Take*' means to receive the blood. (8) And not in the south and stretch out his hand to the north. (A line—imaginary—demarcated the north and the south, and so it would be possible to stand on one side of the line—south—and receive the blood on the other—the north.) (9) I.e., the north. (10) That the sacrifice is invalid otherwise. (11) Ibid. 33. This treats of a lamb brought by a prince (ruler) as a sin-offering. (12) *Sc.* the sin-offering.

ז א מיי' פ"ט מהלכות שגגות הלכה יא:

פר ושעיר של יום הכיפורים כו': מכדי צפון בעולה כתיב ניתני עולה ברישא חטאת אידי א] *דאתי מדרשא חביבא ליה וניתני חטאות החיצונות ב] איידי דנכנס דמן לפני ולפנים חביבא ליה וצפונה בעולה היכא כתיבא °ושחט אותו על ירך המזבח צפונה אשכחן בן צאן בן בקר מנא לן אמר קרא ואם מן הצאן *וי"ו מוסיף על ענין ראשון וילמד עליון מתחתון הניחא למ"ד מלמדין ג] אלא למ"ד אין מלמדין מאי איכא למימר *דתניא °ואם נפש וגו' לחייב על ספק מעילות אשם תלוי דברי רבי עקיבא וחכמים *פוטרין מאי לאו בהא קא מיפלגי ד] מר סבר למידין ומר סבר אין למידין אמר רב פפא דכולי עלמא למידין והיינו טעמא דרבנן נאמר כאן מצות ונאמר *בחטאת חלב מצות מה להלן דבר שחייבין על זדונו כרת ועל שגגתו חטאת אף כאן שחייבין על זדונו כרת ועל שגגתו חטאת ורבי עקיבא מה להלן ה] בקבועה אף כאן בקבועה לאפוקי חטאת דטומאת מקדש וקדשיו דעולה ויורד הוא ורבנן *אין גזירה שוה למחצה ו] ור"ע נמי אין גזירה שוה למחצה אין הכי נמי והכא בהא קמיפלגי ר"ע סבר ואם נפש כתיב *וי"ו מוסיף על ענין ראשון ורבנן נמי הכתיב ואם נפש לימא בהא קמיפלגי *דמר סבר *) היקש עדיף ומר סבר גזירה שוה עדיף לא דכ"ע דהיקש עדיף ז] ואמרי לך רבנן תחתון הוא דגמר מעליון לאשם בכסף שקלים שלא תאמר לא יהא ספיקו חמור מודאו מה ודאו חטאת בת דנקא אף ספיקו אשם בר דנקא ורבי עקיבא ח] הא סברא מנא ליה נפקא ליה °מזאת תורת האשם תורה אחת לכל האשמות תינח מאן דאית ליה תורת ט] מאן דלית ליה תורת מהיכא גמר גמר °בערכך בערכך תינח היכא דכתיב בערכך אשם שפחה חרופה דלא כתיב ביה בערכך מאי איכא למימר גמר באיל באיל: י] חטאת מנא לן דבעיא צפון דכתיב °ושחט את החטאת במקום העולה אשכחן שחיטה יא] קבלה מנא לן דכתיב °ולקח הכהן מדם החטאת מקבל עצמו מנא לן אמר קרא ולקח לו יב] יקח אשכחן למצוה לעכב מנין קרא אחרינא כתיב °ושחט אותו במקום אשר ישחט את העולה ותניא יג] *היכן עולה נשחטה בצפון אף זה בצפון וכי

*) [עי' פירשו בתוספות ברכות כ' ד"ה אלא]

רש"י

בעולה כתיב · גבי עולת צאן בויקרא ושחט אותו על ירך המזבח צפונה: מדרשא · מהיקשא דכתיב במקום אשר תשחט העולה (ויקרא ד): עליון · פרשת בן בקר למעלה מפרשת בן צאן: הניחא למאן דאמר למדין · עליון מתחתון על ידי וי"ו המוסיף: ואם נפש · גבי אשם תלוי כתיב בויקרא ואם נפש כי תחטא וגו' ולמעלה הימנה פרשת מעילה ודאית שידע לאחר זמן שנהנה מן ההקדש בשוגג יד] וחייבין עליה אשם ודאי: על ספק מעילות · הקדש וחולין לפניו ונהנה מאחד מהם כסבור שניהם חולין ועכשיו אינו יודע מאיזה מהן נהנה מביא אשם תלוי להגן טו] מן היסורין עד שיודע לו שודאי מעל ומביא אשם ודאי וגם הוא איל בכסף שקלים: למדין · עליון מתחתון פרשת הקדש מפרשת אשם תלוי שתחתיה למימרא דהנאה מן ההקדש נמי מייתי אשם תלוי על ספיקו: נאמר מצות · באשם תלוי ועשתה אחת מכל מצות (ויקרא ה) וכן בחטאת: מה חטאת · באה על שגגת זדון כרת כדילפינן בהוריות (דף ח·) אף אשם תלוי על ספק דבר שזדונו כרת ושגגתו חטאת: ורבי עקיבא · גמר לה להך גזירה שוה הכי מה חטאת טז] קרבן קבוע לעני כעשיר אף אשם תלוי אינו בא אלא על ספק חטאת קבוע: לאפוקי · ספק נכנס טמא למקדש ספק לא נכנס הואיל וודאי בעולה ויורד אין מביא על ספיקו אשם תלוי: אין גז"ש למחצה · וכי היכי יז] דגמרינן לה לגבי הא מילתא גמור מיניה נמי דאינו בא אלא על ספק כרת: ואמרי לך רבנן · היקש להכי אתא יח] תחתון הוא דגמר מעליון לקנות אשם בשתי סלעים דגבי אשם מעילות כתיב בערכך כסף שקלים וגמר אשם תלוי מיניה שלא תאמר לא יהא ספיקו של כרת חמור מודאו: דנקא · יט] שתות כלומר מעה כסף שהוא שתות של דינר ולאו דווקא נקט אלא כ] דמים קלים בעלמא שלא ניתן לה קצבה: תינח מאן דאית ליה תורת · בשמעתא קמייתא דמנחות (דף ג:): בערכך בערכך · באשם תלוי ובאשם גזילות כתיב בערכך לאשם וגמרינן מערכך דאשם מעילות דכתיב ביה בערכך כסף שקלים: גמר באיל באיל · *כתיב ביה כא] באיל האשם ובחד מהנך נמי כתיב באיל האשם ואשם נזיר ואשם מצורע כב] נמי לא מרבינן משום דכתיב כבש בן שנה ומדאיל שהוא בן שתי שנים בא בשתי סלעים כבש בן שנה בא בסלע כולה כג] שמעתין בכריתות (דף כב:): את החטאת · יתירא הוא דהא בחטאת קאי והוה ליה למכתב ושחט אותה למה לי את החטאת בנין אב כד] לכל ששמו חטאת ששטון צפון דלא תימא דווקא שעירת יחיד דכתיב גביה: ולקח הכהן · בתר ושחט כתיב בחטאת יחיד ומשמע כה] במקום העולה נמי ילקח והך לקיחה קבלה דגמר בג"ש בת"כ נאמר כאן לקיחה ונאמר להלן לקיחה ויקח משה חצי הדם וישם באגנת (שמות כד): מקבל עצמו · שצריך לעמוד בצפון ולא יעמוד בדרום ויושיט ידו כו] בצפון סמוך לו אצל אמצע עזרה שהדרום והצפון נחלקו שם וקיבל מנלן דהא אמר לקמן אם עמד בדרום וקיבל בצפון פסול: ולקח לו כז] יקח · פרסיה למפרע ודרשה את עצמו יקח למקום הדם: קרא אחרינא כתיב · דדריש ליה תנא לעיכובא כדתניא ושחט אותו וגו' בשעיר נשיא כתיב: אף זה בצפון · האי קרא מגמר עליה: וכי

[יבמות ג: וש"נ] [יבמות פ: וש"נ] [כריתות כב (ושם כל הסוגיא ע"ש)] [מנחות ד'] [גיטין מא:] [מנחות סה:]

נ"ל ואשם מעילות כתיב ביה חי' נ"ק

תוספות

אידי [דאתי מדרשא] חביבא ליה · ואם תאמר אם כן ליתני עולה לבסוף כדפריך בשמעתא קמייתא דיבמות (דף ג·) גבי אחות אשה ויש לומר איידי כט] דאתיא עולה בציבור תניא בהדי חטאות דאתות בציבור והדר תניא אשם דאינו אלא ביחיד:

אשכחן בן צאן בן בקר מנלן · תימה דלעיל פרק כל הפסולין (דף לב:) דרשינן בן הבקר לפני ה' ואין השוחט לפני ה' ולא אמרינן בן צאן מנין ולכמה דרשות לא מצרכינן תרי קראי לבן בקר ולבן ל] צאן ושמא אהך דרשא לא] הוי"ו מוסף סמיך אי נמי משום דבבן צאן כתיב אותו למעוטי אילטריך הכא לרבויי מיהו בהסיא דבן הבקר לפני ה' לב] וסמיכה והפשט ניחא דלא קאמר בן צאן מנין דפשיטא דילפינן תחתון מעליון אבל עליון מתחתון ס"ד דלא יליף:

מה להלן דבר שחייבין על זדונו כרת · ואם תאמר היכי יליף מגזירה שוה מצות מצות הא חטאת חלב גופה בהיקשא ילפא לג] כדאמר *הוקשה כל התורה לעבודת כוכבים וי"ל דכי האי גוונא לא חשיב למד בהיקש אינו חוזר ומלמד *בהיקש כיון דאי לאו היקשא הוה מוקמינא ליה בכל דבר ולא אתא היקשא אלא לד] למימר דלא איירי אלא בדבר שיש בו כרת:

דכולי עלמא היקשא עדיפא · וא"ת והאמרינן פ' השולח (גיטין דף מא:) דכ"ע גזירה שוה עדיפא לה] וי"ל הא דקאמר דכ"ע היקש עדיף הייט לענין א) דטוב לנו לעשות הגז"ש למחצה ממה שנבטל ההיקש לגמרי אבל התם דמקיש או תופסה דהייט שטר להפדה לא נפדתה דהייט כסף לומר משחרר חצי עבדו בשטר מועיל כמו בכסף וקאמר גזירה שוה דלה לה מאשה עדיפא מה אשה חליה לא מועיל והתם לא נתבטל ההיקש דשמא צריך לו] למילי אוחרי ועוד י"ל דשטר בשפחה כנענית *לא קמ"ל אלא בגזירה שוה דלה לה מאשה לכך קאמר דגזירה שוה עדיפא דטוב לעשות גזירה שוה דתהוי שטר בשפחה כמו גם דאשה שלא להועיל חליה מלעשותו כמו כסף שסמוך לו והפדה דהא מגט אשה נפקא שטר שחרור ועיקר · ברוך:

וחטאת בת דנקא · פי' בקונטרס לאו דווקא אלא דמים קלים שלא ניתן קצבה והדין עמו דבהדיא איתא בפ' בתרא דכריתות (דף כז·) גבי מפני מה לא נתנה תורה שיעור במחוסרי כפרה ופריך אלא מעתה חטאת חלב תהא לה קצבה וא"ת הא בפ' מחוסרי כפרה (כריתות דף י:) משמע דהוי בסלע גבי האומר הרי עלי בסלע למזבח יביא כבש שאין לך דבר שקרב בסלע אלא כבש והאי סלע הייט בלא נסכים דקאמר דחס רחמנא עליה למיהוי [חד] משיתסר בעשירות וי"ל דהתם למצוה מן המובחר ב):

תינח למאן דאית ליה זאת תורת · פלוגתא בשמעתא קמייתא במנחות (דף ג:) והכי נמי הוה מצי למיבעי לרבנן מנא להו אשם בכסף שקלים בכל אשמות כיון דלית להו זאת תורת:

גמר בערכך בערכך · וא"ת רבנן לח] אי אית להו גזירה שוה דבערכך בערכך א"כ [ואם] נפש למה לי ואי לית להו א"כ אשם לט] גזילות בכסף שקלים מנא להו ואומר ר"ת דאע"ג דאית להו מ] אילטריך ואם נפש שלא יהא ספיקו חמור מודאו דכי האי גוונא אמר פ' דם שחיטה (כריתות כב:) ורבנן אע"ג דכתיב זאת תורת אילטריך ואם נפש ט' דאי מתורה אחת הני מילי לשאר אשמות אבל אשם תלוי לא יהא חמור ספיקו מודאו וא"ת לרבנן מגזירה שוה דבערכך נמי נילף אשם תלוי בספק מעילות וי"ל דבערכך לא משמע מא] להקיש אלא לענין כסף שקלים ומהאי טעמא נמי אילטריך לר"ע ואם נפש לספק מב] מעילות:

אשם שפחה חרופה מג] באיל איל · ובתורת כהנים יליף אשם שפחה לכסף שקלים מגזירה שוה אשם אשם *יכול אף אשם נזיר ומצורע ט' ת"ל הוא והייט טעמא דממעט אשם נזיר ומצורע טפי משאר אשמות משום דבהון כבש שהוא בן שנה כדפירש רש"י:

א) [וע"ע תוס' ברכות כ' ד"ה אלא ותוס' יבמות נט: ד"ה דומיא] ב) [ועי' ביאור בילקוט תוס' מנחות קז: ד"ה כבש ותוס' כריתות י: ד"ה מכלל]

נ"ל ומסיים ישל שאני מרנה אף אשם נזיר כו' נ"ק

שיטה מקובצת

א] דאתיא מדרשא: ב] החיצונות ברישא איידי דהני נכנס דמן: ג] מלמדין עליון מתחתון אלא למ"ד אין למדין מאי: ד] מיפלגי דמר סבר: ה] להלן קבועה אף כאן קבועה: ו] למחצה לימא בהא קא מיפלגי דמר סבר יש ג"ש למחצה ומר סבר אין ג"ש למחצה דכ"ע אין ג"ש למחצה והיינו טעמא דר"ע דכתיב ואם נפש ורבנן הכתיב ואם נפש כו' והשאר נמחק: ז] עדיף · נ"א לעולם אימא לך (דמ"ס) [דכו"ע] דהיקש נמי עדיף ואמרי לך כו' כך כתוב בספרי כתיבת יד: ח] עקיבא האי סברא מנא ליה תימה מאי קשיא תרתי שמעית מיניה כמו שסבר ילמוד עליון מתחתון כמו כן סבר ילמוד תחתון מעליון דאין (ג"ש) [היקש] למחצה וי"ל דאי הוי צריך היקשא לאשם בכסף שקלים הוי ליה לדרוש הג"ש לגמרי והיקשא הוי מוקי לתחתון לענין אשם בכסף שקלים ולא עליון מתחתון משום דלעולם יש לנו לומר דאין ג"ש למחצה יותר מאין היקשא למחצה והאיל ואיכא למימר ההיקש איצטריך לתחתון מעליון ולא (לענין) [לעליון] מתחתון כדפי' לשון תוס' אחרות וי"ל דהסברא שלא (תהא) [יהא] ספיקו חמור מודאי עדיפא כל כך שאם ... טעם ... תחתון ... מוקי ... לדרוש ... ילמוד ... [תחתון מעליון]: ט] עי' בהשמטות בסוף המסכת: י] ... בסוף המסכת: יא] עי' בהשמטות בסוף המסכת: יב] לו ... נמחק: יג] תניא ... ישחט ... נשחטה בצפון ... עולה ...: יד] וחייבין עליו אשם: טו] להגן עליו מן: טז] חטאת חלב קרבן: יז] היכא דגמרינן לה גבי האי מילתא גמרינן מיניה ... דתתתון ...: יח] תיבת שתות נמחק: כ] אלא כלומר דמים: כא] ביה בשפחה חרופה באיל האשם ובאשם מעילות נמי תיבת נמחק: כב] תיבת נמי נמחק: כג] כולה שמעתין בכריתות: כד] אב הוא לכל: כה] ומשמע דאבמקום העולה נמי קאי והך לקיחה קבלה היא דגמר לה בג"ש בת"כ: כו] ידו לצפון סמוך לו אצל אמצע העזרה שהדרום והצפון נחלק שם ויקבל מנלן

דרשו אמרי' לקמן: כו] קח פרסהו למפרע כו' יקח ויקרב למקום הדם: כח] איידי דאתי מדרשא חביבא: כט] איידי דעולה אתיא בצבור: ל] צאן וי"ל דמבעיא ליה הכא טפי משום דבן בקר הוי ליה למכתביה דכתיב ברישא לשון מהר"פ: לא] דרשא דוי"ו מוסף סמיך: לב] דסמיכה והפשט ניחא דלא כו' דפשיטא דוי"ו מוסיף וילפינן תחתון: לג] ילפא כדאמרינן בפ"ק דיבמות הוקשה: לד] אלא למעט ולמימר: לה] עי' בהשמטות בסוף המסכת: לו] צריך למילתא אחרי ועוד י"ל כו' לא קי"ל אלא כו' דטוב לנו לעשות הג"ש ותיתי שטר בשפחה כמו גט באשה שלא להועיל בחציה מלעשותה: לז] למהוי חד משיתסר: לח] רבנן מאי סברי אי אית להו כו' א"כ ואם נפש למ"ל ואי כו': לט] גזילות ואשם שפחה בכסף שקלים מנא להו ואומר ר"ת דלעולם אית להו ג"ש דערכך ומ"מ הו"א שלא יהא ספיקו חמור מודאי ספיק ליה מג"ש לכך איצטריך היקשא לאשם בכסף שקלים וא"ת כיון דאית להו ג"ש דערכך ליחייבו (ר"ע) על ספק מעילות אשם תלוי מג"ש דערכך דאין ג"ש למחצה וי"ל דג"ש דערכך לא הוי אלא לענין שוויין של כבש שכן משמעות של בערכך דבעינן שיהא שוה בכסף שקלים ועי"ל דלרבנן לית להו ג"ש דערכך וכ"ת אשם גזילות ואשם שפחה חרופה מנא להו י"ל כדדרשינן בת"כ דכתיב גבי אשם תלוי אשם הוא אשום אשם לה' לרבות אשם גזילות ואשם שפחה בכסף שקלים יכול אף אשם כו' עד שנה אבל אשם שפחה ואשם גזילות מרבינן משום דבאין בן שתי שנים דומיא דאשם תלוי דכתיב בהו איל כמו באשם תלוי מיהו ואם נפש איצטריך לרבות אשם תלוי גופו דהא אשם דמרבינן מיניה אשם שפחה ואשם גזילות גבי אשם תלוי כתיב הלכך איצטריך ואם נפש ללמוד אשם תלוי והנך דאיתרבו מייתורא דאשם הוא לא הוי למד מן הלמד דאם נפש אכולהו קאי ולא כפי' רש"י שפי' בחומש דלענין ב' שנים אמר אשם אשם לה' יכול שאני מרבה אשם נזיר ואשם מצורע לשתי שנים ת"ל הוא ולא נהירא דהא באשם גזילות ואשם שפחה כתיב בהדיא באיל (מאשם) [האשם] וא"כ בלא ריבוייא דאשם ידעינן ב' שנים ת"כ באשם נזיר ואשם מצורע כתיב בהדיא בן שנתו ולמה לי הוא ולכך נראה כפי' ת"כ לשון מהר"פ: מ] להו ג"ש איצטריך ואם נפש כו' האי נוטא אמרי' פרק דם שחיטה כו' דאי מזאת תורת הו"א הני מילי לשאר אשמות: מא] משמע לפרש תיבת להקיש נמחק: מב] מעילות א"כ לעולם רבנן לא דרשי בערכך ושאר אשמות נפקא להו מקרא אחרינא ובת"כ יליף לה כו' ולא גרים שפחה כו': מג] חרופה גמר באיל ובת"כ יליף אשם שפחה חרופה ואשם גזילות לכסף שקלים כו' כדפירש רש"י ע"כ הס"ד:

עין משפט
נר מצוה

ח א מיי׳ פ״ה מהלכות מעשה קרבנות הלכה ג:

נ״ל קרא נ״ק

נ״א דקדושין דליף ק״ו ומה נ״ק

ט ב מיי׳ פ״א מהלכות פסולי המוקדשין הלכה ט:

בכל הזבחים דינן בכהן וכו׳ ועוד נ״ל כיון וכו׳ נ״ק

י ג מיי׳ שם הלכה ח:

[ועי׳ תוס׳ קדושין נו: ד״ה ומה]

תורה אור

*וכי מכאן אתה למד והלא *כבר נאמר °במקום אשר תשחט העולה תשחט החטאת (ויקרא ו) הא למה יצא לקבוע לו מקום שאם לא שחטה בצפון פסול אתה אומר לכך יצא או אינו אלא שזה טעון צפון ואין אחר טעון צפון תלמוד לומר ושחט את החטאת במקום העולה זה בנה אב לכל חטאות שיהו טעונות צפון אשכחן שעיר נשיא בין למצוה בין לעכב שאר חטאות נמי אשכחן למצוה לעכב מנא לן דכתיב בכשבה וכתיב בשעירה א] אלא אותו למה לי מיבעי ליה לכדתניא *אותו בצפון ואין שעיר נחשון בצפון ב] ותניא *°וסמך ידו על ראש השעיר (שם ד) לרבות שעיר נחשון לסמיכה דברי ר׳ יהודה ר׳ שמעון אומר ג] לרבות שעירי עבודת כוכבים לסמיכה ס״ד אמינא הואיל ואיתרבו לסמיכה איתרבו נמי לצפון קא משמע לן מתקיף לה רבינא הניחא לר׳ יהודה ד] לר״ש מאי איכא למימר א״ל מר זוטרא בריה דרב ה] טבי לרבינא ולר׳ יהודה מי ניחא למאי דאיתרבי איתרבי ומאי דלא איתרבי לא איתרבי וכי תימא אי לא מעטיה קרא הוה אמינא תיתי בבנין אב אם כן סמיכה גופה תיתי מבנין אב אלא ו] מדורות לא גמרי׳ ה״נ מדורות לא גמרינן ואלא אותו בצפון ואין שוחט בצפון שוחט מדרבי אחיא נפקא דתניא *ר׳ אחיא אומר °ושחט אותו על ירך המזבח צפונה (שם א) מה תלמוד לומר לפי שמצינו ז] עומד בצפון ומקבל בצפון ואם עמד בדרום וקיבל בצפון פסול יכול אף זה כן ת״ל אותו אותו בצפון ואין השוחט בצפון אלא אותו בצפון ואין בן עוף בצפון ח] דתניא יכול יהא בן עוף טעון צפון ודין הוא ומה בן צאן שלא קבע לו כהן קבע לו צפון בן עוף שקבע לו כהן אינו דין שיקבע לו צפון ת״ל אותו מה לבן צאן שכן קבע לו כלי אלא אותו בצפון ט] ואין פסח בצפון דתניא ר׳ אליעזר בן יעקב אומר יכול יהא פסח טעון צפון ודין הוא ומה עולה שכן לא קבע לו זמן לשחיטתו קבע לו צפון פסח שקבע לו זמן לשחיטתו אינו דין שיקבע לו צפון ת״ל אותו *מה לעולה שכן כליל מחטאת *מה לחטאת שכן מכפרת על חייבי כריתות מאשם מה לאשם שכן קדשי קדשים י] מכולן נמי שכן קדשי קדשים לעולם כדאמרן מעיקרא אותו בצפון ואין שוחט בצפון ודקשיא לך מדרבי אחיא נפקא לן לאו למעוטי שוחט בצפון אלא אין שוחט בצפון אבל מקבל בצפון מקבל יא] מלקח ולקח נפקא לקח ולקח לא משמע ליה אשכחן שחיטה בעולה יב] למצוה קבלה נמי למצוה אשכחן שחיטה וקבלה לעכב מנלן אמר רב אדא בר אהבה ואיתימא רבה בר שילא ק״ו ומה חטאת הבאה מכח עולה מעכבת עולה שבאה חטאת מכחה אינו דין שמעכבת מה לחטאת שכן מכפרת על חייבי כריתות אמר רבינא הא קשיא ליה לרב אדא בר אהבה °כלום מצינו *טפל חמור מן העיקר אמר ליה מר זוטרא בריה דרב מרי לרבינא ולא

והרי

וכי מכאן · יג] צריך ללמד לזה בפני עצמו והלא כל החטאות בכלל תורת החטאת במקום אשר תשחט העולה וגו׳: יד] לקבוע · לשנות עליו לעכב קיבועו בכך: או אינו · בא לעכב אלא לכתוב בו אותו דהוי מיעוטא וללמד זה בצפון ואין שעיר אחר בצפון כגון שעירי יוה״כ ושעירי עבודת כוכבים ושל מוספי המועדות ומה אני מקיים תשחט החטאת בשאר בהמות חוץ משעירים דאותו כתיב למעוטינהו: תלמוד לומר · בשעירת יחיד (ויקרא ד) ושחט את החטאת דהוה ליה למכתב ושחט אותה בנין אב הוא לכל טו] חטאות ועיכובא מיהא לא נפקא לן מיניה דאיכא למימר למצוה איצטריך ולהביא שעירי חטאות דלא למעוטינהו מאותו דשעיר נשיא ולקמן פריך ואלא אותו למה לי: שאר חטאות נמי למצוה · אשכחן מתשחט החטאת: דכתיב בכשבה וכתיב בשעירה · טז] בכולם כתיב במקום אשר ישחט העולה וסגי ליה בשעירה ותילף מיניה כשבה למצוה וכי הדר כתביה בכשבה תנהו לענין לפנימיות ולשעירי הרגלים לעיכובא: ואין שעיר נחשון · שעירי חנוכת הנשיאים שלא באו על חטא: *לכדתניא · דאיתרבי לסמיכה וס״ד לרבויי נמי לשחיטה בצפון להכי כתיב אותו למעוטי: על ראש השעיר · בשעיר נשיא כתיב והוה ליה למכתב על ראשו: לרבות שעירי עבודת כוכבים לסמיכה · משום דמעטינהו ר׳ יהודה יז] לסמיכה במס׳ מנחות (דף צב.) *מהאי דשעיר המשתלח דכתיב וסמך אהרן את שתי ידיו על ראש השעיר החי (ויקרא טז) החי טעון סמיכה ואין שעירי עבודת כוכבים טעונין סמיכה ור״ש דרש החי טעון סמיכה באהרן ואין שעיר עבודת כוכבים טעון סמיכה באהרן אלא בזקני העדה ומרבי ליה מהכא: הניחא לרבי יהודה · דמרבי ליה לסמיכה איצטריך למעוטי יח] צפון: למאי דלא איתרבי לא איתרבי · דהא רבויא גבי סמיכה כתיב וצפון מהיכא תיתי: הכי גרסינן להך סוגיא במנחות (דף נה:) וכי תימא אי לא מעטיה קרא הוה אמינא תיתי בבנין אב א״כ סמיכה גופה לשתוק קרא מיניה ותיתי מבנין אב: בבנין אב · מושחט את החטאת: סמיכה גופה נמי תיתי מבנין אב · דכתיב וסמך יט] על ראש החטאת ומצי למכתב על ראשו (א) אלא בנין אב הוא לכל ששמו חטאת שיטען סמיכה: אלא כ] כו׳ · מסקנא דקושיא היא סמיכה מאי טעמא איצטריך לרבויי משום דאי לא רבייה לא הוה גמרינן קדשי שעה בבנין אב מקדשי דורות הכי נמי כא] משחיטת צפון למה לי אותו למעוטי כל כמה דלא לימא קרא לא גמרי בבנין אב: ולא שוחט בצפון · אין צריך שיעמוד בצפון שאם רצה עומד בדרום אצל צפון ויושיט ידו בצפון וישחוט: לפי שמצינו שהמקבל כו׳ · כב] מלקח ולקח כדלעיל: ה״ג אלא אותו בצפון ואין בן עוף בצפון דתניא יכול יהא בן עוף טעון צפון ודין הוא כו׳ ת״ל אותו מה לבן צאן כו׳: ואין בן עוף · מליקת תורין ובני יונה: שלא קבע לו כהן · דשחיטה בזר כשרה: בן עוף כג] קבע לו כהן · [דכתיב והקריבו הכהן אל המזבח ומלק את ראשו וגו׳ (ויקרא א)]: שכן קבע לו כלי · סכין לשחיטה מויקח את המאכלת (לקמן דף צז:) והתם עולה הואי וכן מזרק לקבל תאמר בבן עוף שנמלק בצפורן: ולא פסח בצפון · דלא כד] תתייה בקל וחומר הואיל וקבע זמן לשחיטתו בין הערבים יקבע לו מקום נמי לצפון: מדרבי אליעזר בן יעקב נפקא לא גרס אלא הכי גרסינן ולא פסח בצפון דתניא רבי אליעזר בן יעקב אומר כו׳ וכן מצאתיה בספרים הראשונים: אינו דין שיקבע לו צפון תלמוד לומר אותו גרסינן: מחטאת · אי לאו דמעטיה הוה מייתינן ליה מחטאת שאינה כליל וטעונה צפון: מכולהו נמי כה] שכן קדשי קדשים · כלומר ואי בעי לאהויי נמי מכולהו במה הצד איכא למיפרכיה להא פירכא שכן קדשי קדשים: לאו למעוטי שוחט בצפון · אותו דגבי שעיר לאו למעוטי שוחט בצפון קאמרי דודאי מאותו דרבי אחיא נפקא כו] אלא לרבויא מדוקיא דמיעוטא דשוחט בצפון דמקבל בצפון דהכי דרשינן אותו בצפון ואין שוחט בצפון אבל מקבל בצפון: קבלה נמי אשכחן · כדאמרן אבל מקבל בצפון: כז] הא קשיא ליה · כלומר מהאי כח] טעם דייק קל וחומר דידיה: טפל חמור מן העיקר · למד חמור מן המלמד כגון חטאת שבאה מכח עולה דעיקר צפון בעולה כתיב:

והרי

הגה״ה אותו בצפון ולא שוחט בצפון · תימה ל״ל קרא הא אפילו לפני ה׳ לא בעי כדדרשינן לעיל בריש כל הפסולין (דף לב:) בן הבקר לפני ה׳ ולא שוחט לפני ה׳ ויש לומר דהכא סובר כר״ש התימני דדריש התם כט] האי *כתוב בענין אחר:

מה לבן צאן שכן קבע לו כלי · ותימה דלא פריך הכי בפ״ק *דקדושין (דף נז:) ל] ומה בן צאן שלא קבע לו כהן לשחיטתו קבע לו כהן להזאתו בן עוף שקבע לו כהן במליקתו אינו דין שיקבע לו כהן בהזאתו ויש לומר דהתם *דכל דיש בכהן לא שייך למיפרך מכלי לא] ול״נ כיון דהדין הוי מהזאה לא שייך למיפרך מכלי דשחיטה וא״ת וליעביד הכא קל וחומר ממקום ומה בן צאן שלא קבע לו מזבח בשחיטתו קבע לו מקום לצפון לב] בן עוף שקבע לו מזבח במליקתו כדדרשינן (לקמן דף סה.) מה הקטרה בראשו של מזבח אף מליקה אינו דין שיקבע לו לצפון וזה אין לומר לג] דסד״א דבן עוף כיון דחטאת קרייה רחמנא ליבעי צפון לד] דזאת תורת החטאת דשמא דזאת תורת לא הוי אלא לנשחטות*: אלא אין שוחט בצפון אבל מקבל בצפון · תימה הא נמי מדרבי אחיא נפקא מדאיצטריך למעוטי שוחט מכלל דמקבל בצפון דאי לא דמקבל בצפון למה לי קרא למעוטי שוחט כדקאמר רבי אחיא לפי שמצינו שמקבל בצפון יכול אף זה כן ושמא רבי אחיא דריש ולקח לו יקח אבל אנן לא דרשינן ליה: קבלה נמי למצוה אשכחן · פי׳ בקונט׳ כדאמר אבל מקבל בצפון וקשה דמאותו דכתיב גבי עולה דרשינן ולא שוחט בצפון ומאותו דכתיב גבי חטאת דרשינן אבל מקבל בצפון וא״כ מקבל למצוה בעולה מנא לן וגבי אשם צריכי תרי קראי למצוה לקבלה ומקבל ועוד לה] עיכובא במקבל בחטאת מנא לן דלא מצינו ששנה אלא על השחיטה ועל הקבלה אבל לא על המקבל וי״ל *מכיון דאשכחן למצוה מקבל כקבלה ה״ה לעכב וכי האי גוונא אמרינן בפ״ק (לעיל ד׳.) נאמרה זביחה בחטאת ונאמרה זביחה בשלמים מה התם לא חלקת כו׳:

והרי

שיטה מקובצת

א] עי׳ בהשמטות בסוף המסכת: ב] בצפון דתניא: ג] עי׳ בהשמטות בסוף המסכת: ד] עי׳ השמטות בסוף המסכת: ה] דרב מרי לרבינא כו׳ למאי דלא אתרבי: ו] אלא שעה מדורות לא גמרי הכי נמי שעה מדורות לא גמרינן ואלא אותו למה לי לכדתניא אותו בצפון ולא שוחט בצפון: ז] שמצינו שמקבל עומד: ח] בצפון ס״ד דא תיתי בק״ו מבן צאן דתניא מנחות דף נ״ו ובקדושין דף ל״ו: ט] בצפון ולא פסח בצפון דתניא כו׳ ומה עולה שלא קבע לו זמן: י] קדשים מכולהו נמי לא שכן כו׳ בצפון ולא שוחט בצפון ודקשיא לך כו׳ נפקא לן ס״י הא קמ״ל שוחט לא בעי צפון אבל מקבל בעי צפון: יא] מקבל מולקח לו קח נפקא ולקח לו קח לא כו׳ וא״ת עיכובא במקבל מנלן בשלמא למאן דדריש מולקח לו קח א״כ שנה הכתוב בפרשיות דחטאת גבי צפון אבל למאן דלא דריש ליה מקבל עצמו בצפון מנלן וי״ל דמה עצמה לא חלקת בה בין למצוה בין לעכב אף מקבל עצמו לא חלקת בו בין למצוה בין לעכב: יב] בעולה בצפון למצוה קבלה נמי אשכחן למצוה ס״ה כו׳ וקשה דהא הך דרשא לא גבי עולה היא אלא גבי חטאת היא מאותו דשעיר נשיא דהא אותו דעולה מוקמינן ליה לכדרבי אחיא לומר דאין שוחט בצפון וא״כ קבלה בעצמה מנלן לא למקבל עצמו ולא לקבלה ועוד דבקבלה עצמה לא אשכחן בשום מקום בעולה רק בשחיטה ובמקבל וקבלה דהכא משמע קבלה עצמה ולקמן משמע דבעינן [תרי] קראי באשם חד למקבל וחד לקבלה וא״כ כיון דלא דרשינן ולקח (ולקח) [לו קח] מנ״ל קבלה בעולה וי״ל כיון דגבי ושחט את החטאת במקום העולה כתיב ולקח הכהן מדם החטאת דמשמע שבא לומר דבמקום שחיטה וקבלה דעולה תהא שחיטה וקבלה דחטאת אלמא קבלה דעולה במקום שחיטה דעולה דמשמע דקרא אתא לומר דשחיטה דחטאת במקום שחיטה דעולה וקבלה דחטאת במקום קבלה דעולה וקבלה דחטאת בצפון מדכתיב ולקח הכהן ושחט דמשמע דתרוייהו הוו במקום העולה ולקח קאי נמי אמקום עולה דה״ק ושחט את החטאת במקום העולה וגם ולקח נמי תהיה במקום העולה ומורי תירץ דבעולה כתיב בפרשה העליונה בבן בקר ושחט לפני ה׳ דהיינו צפון דיליף עליון מתחתון וכתב בתריה והקריבו זה קבלת הדם אלמא ש״מ דקבלה במקום שחיטה לשון מהר״פ: יג] מכאן אני צריך ללמוד לזה בפני עצמו והלא בכלל (א) החטאות כלל תורת החטאת: יד] לקובעו ולשנות לעכב: טו] לכל ששמו חטאת: טז] בשעירה בכולהו כתיב במקום אשר ישחט את העולה וסגי ליה כו׳ תנהו ענין לפנימיות: יז] יהודה מסמיכה: יח] למעוטי מצפון הס״ד: יט] וסמך את ידו על ראש: כ] אלא שעה מדורות: כא] נמי שחיטת צפון למ״ל אותו למעוטי וכל כמה דלא לימא קרא לא הוה גמרי ליה בבנין אב: כב] כו׳ מולקח לו קח כדלעיל: כג] עוף שקבע: כד] דלא תיתי: כה] נמי לא שכן: כו] נפקא לן אלא לרבויא כו׳ דמקבל הוי בצפון: כז] בצפון הס״ד ומה״ד מה חטאת הבאה מכח עולה מעכבת בין בשחיטה בין בקבלה בשחיטה כדאמרן לעיל וקבלה נמי דכל היכא דכתיבא שחיטה בחטאת בצפון כתיב בתריה ולקח הכהן וילפינן מינה קבלה הס״ד: כח] מהאי טעמא קא דאין קו״ח דידיה: כט] התם הכתוב בענין אחר: ל] דקדושין דאמרינן התם ומה: לא] מכלי תוס׳ ול״נ כיון כו׳ מכלי דשחיטה ע״כ וא״ת: לב] צפון ולא הוה שייך הכא לפרוכי מכלי כיון דכל דינו גמר מיניה ממקום וזה אין להקשות ולומר דבן: לג] תיבת דסד״א ל״ש תמחק: לד] צפון מזאת תורת החטאה כו׳ אלא בנשחטות הס״ד: לה] ועוד תימה עיכובא:

א) אולי צ״ל והלא בכלל כל החטאות הוא · דכתיב במקום כו׳

מסורת הש״ס

מנחות יב

[מנחות נה:]

[שם ולב:]

[נ״ל ותניא]

בס״י מסתי

[מנחות ער]

[לקמן סג. מנחות נה]

[שם]

[לקמן צז: כריתות יד: מנחות נא:]

הגהות הב״ח

(א) רש״י ד״ה סמיכה גופה וכו׳ על ראשו ובנין אב כצ״ל ותיבת אלא נמחק:

גליון הש״ס

גמ׳ כלום מצינו טפל חמור · עי׳ ב״ק דף קא ע״א תוד״ה לא:

north. [48*b*] Do you then learn it from this verse? Is it not already stated, *In the place where the burnt-offering is killed shall the sin-offering* a *be killed?*[1] why then has this[2] been singled out? To fix the place for it, so that if one did not slaughter it in the north, it is invalid.[3] You say it has been singled out for this purpose, yet perhaps it is not so, but rather [to teach] that this one [alone] requires the north,[4] but no other requires the north? Therefore it states, *'And he shall kill the sin-offering in the place of the burnt-offering,'* thus constituting a general law in respect of all sin-offerings that they require the north. We have thus found [it true of] a prince's sin-offering, that it is both a recommendation and indispensable; we have also found it as a recommendation in the case of other sin-offerings; how do we know that it is indispensable [for other sin-offerings]?—Because it is written in reference to both the lamb[5] and the she-goat.[6]

Then what is the purpose of *'it'*?[7]—That is required for what was taught: *'It'* [is slaughtered] on the north, but Nahshon's goat was not [slaughtered] in the north.[8] And it was taught: *And he shall lay his hand upon the head of the goat*[9] includes Nahshon's goat, in respect of laying [hands]: that is R. Judah's view. R. Simeon said: It includes the goats brought on account of idolatry, in respect of laying [hands]. You might argue, Since they are included in respect of laying [hands], they are included in respect of the north. Hence we are informed [otherwise].

To this Rabina demurred: That is well on R. Judah's view; but what can be said on R. Simeon's?[10]—Said Mar Zuṭra son of R. Mari to Rabina: And is it well on R. Judah's view? [surely], where it is included, it is included, and where it is not included, it is not b included?[1] And should you say, Had Scripture not excluded it, [its inclusion] would be inferred by analogy: if so, let laying [hands] itself be inferred by analogy? But [you must answer that] a temporary [sacrifice] can not be inferred from a permanent one,[2] so here too,[3] a temporary [sacrifice] cannot be inferred from a permanent one?[4]—Rather [it teaches this]: *'It'* [is slaughtered in the north], but the slaughterer need not be in the north.[5] But [the law concerning] the slaughterer is deduced by R. Aḥia's [exegesis]? For it was taught, R. Aḥia said: *And he shall kill it on the side of the altar northward'*: why is this stated? Because we find that the receiving priest must stand in the north and receive [the blood] in the north, while if he stood in the south and received [the blood] in the north it is invalid. You might think that this [slaughtering] is likewise. Therefore Scripture states, '[*And he shall kill*] *it*', [intimating that] *'it'* must be in the north, but the slaughterer need not be in the north!—Rather [it teaches this]: *'It'* [must be killed] in the north, but a bird does not need the north.[6] For it was taught: You might think that a bird-offering needs the north, and this is indeed logical: If [Scripture] prescribed north for a lamb, though it did not prescribe a priest for it,[7] is it not logical that it should prescribe north for a bird, seeing that it did prescribe a priest for it? Therefore *'it'* is stated.[8] [No:] as for a lamb, the reason is because [Scripture] prescribed a utensil for it![9]—Rather, [it teaches this]: *'It'* [must be killed] in the north, but the Passover-offering [need] not [be slaughtered] in the north. For it was taught, R. Eliezer b. Jacob said: You might think that a Passover-offering needs the north, and this is indeed logical: if [Scripture] prescribed the north for a burnt-offering, though it did not prescribe a fixed season for its slaughtering; is it not logical that it should prescribe the north for a Passover-offering, seeing that it did prescribe a fixed season for its slaughtering? Therefore *'it'* is stated. [No:] as for a burnt-offering, the reason is because it is altogether burnt. [Then learn it] c from a sin-offering.[1] As for a sin-offering, the reason is because it makes atonement for those who are liable to *kareth*! [Then learn it] from a guilt-offering. [No:] as for a guilt-offering, the reason is because it is a most sacred sacrifice! [And you] cannot [learn it] from all these[2] likewise, because they are most sacred sacrifices! —After all, it is as we said originally: *'It'* [must be] in the north, but the slaughterer need not be in the north, and as to your difficulty, 'That is deduced from R. Aḥia's exegesis', [the answer is that] it does not [really] exclude the slaughterer from the north,[3] but [is meant thus]: The slaughterer need not be in the north, [whence it follows that] the *receiver* must be in the north. 'The receiver'? Surely that is deduced from *'and he shall take,'* [which we interpret] let him [be]take himself [to the north]?—He does not interpret *'and he shall take'* as meaning 'let him [be]take himself.'[4]

We have thus found a recommendation that slaughtering a burnt-offering must be in the north, and a [similar] recommendation about receiving; how do we know that [the north] is indispensable in the case of slaughtering and receiving?[5]—Said R. Adda b. Ahabah,—others state, Rabbah b. Shila: [It is deduced] *a fortiori:* If it is indispensable in the case of a sin-offering, which is [only] learnt from a burnt-offering,[6] surely it is logical that it is indispensable in the case of a burnt-offering, from which a sin-offering is learnt. [No:] As for a sin-offering, the reason is because it makes atonement for those who are liable to *kareth!* Said Rabina: This is d R. Adda's difficulty:[1] Do we ever find the secondary more stringent than the primary?[2] Said Mar Zuṭra son of R. Mari to Rabina:

a (1) Lev. VI, 18. This applies to *all* sin-offerings. (2) The sin-offering brought by a prince. (3) The repetition teaches this. (4) *Sc.* that mentioned in Lev. IV, 33. (5) Ibid. (6) Ibid. 29. (7) In verse 33 quoted *supra:* 'it' implies limitation, whereas *all* sin-offerings have been included. (8) I.e., the sin-offerings brought at the consecration of the altar, which were not on account of sin at all; v. Num. VII, 12 *seq.* (9) Lev. IV, 24. This refers to the prince's goat: instead of '*head of the goat*', Scripture could say, '*its head*'; the longer form is regarded as an extension. (10) He does *not* include it in respect of laying hands: then a text is not required to shew that north does not apply to it.

b (1) No text is necessary for this. (2) Lit. (text as emended by Sh. M.) 'you do not learn the hour from generations'—You could not learn that Nahshon's goat required laying hands, by analogy with an ordinary sin-offering, because the former was a special *ad hoc* offering, whereas the ordinary sin-offering was for all time. (3) In respect of north. (4) So that in any case there is no reason for thinking that Nahshon's sin-offering required the north; why then is a text needed to exclude it? (5) He can stand in the south near the boundary line, stretch out his hand, and slaughter it in the north. (6) When its neck is wrung. (7) It may be slaughtered by a *zar*. (8) As a limitation. (9) It must be slaughtered with a knife, whereas a bird merely has its neck wrung. Hence again there is no reason for thinking that a bird requires north, and therefore no need for a limitation.

c (1) Which is not altogether burnt, yet requires the north. (2) *Sc.* the burnt-offering, guilt-offering and sin-offering. (3) For that is arrived at by R. Aḥia's exegesis. (4) Text as emended by Sh. M. (5) In the sense that the sacrifice is otherwise invalid. (6) Lit., 'which comes from the strength of a burnt-offering'.

d (1) In spite of the refutation, he employs this *a fortiori* argument on account of the following difficulty. (2) Although a sin-offering makes atonement for those liable to *kareth*, here it is only secondary to a burnt-offering, since '*north*' is written primarily in connection with the latter.

Do we not? [49a] Yet there is the [second] tithe, which itself can be redeemed, and yet what is purchased with the [redemption] money of tithe cannot be redeemed. For we learnt: If that which was purchased with the [redemption] money of the [second] tithe became defiled, it must be redeemed. R. Judah said: It must be buried![3]—There the sanctity is not strong enough to take hold of its redemption.[4]

Yet there is the case of a substitute: whereas [sacrificial] sanctity does not fall upon an animal with a permanent blemish, it [substitution] does fall upon an animal with a permanent blemish?[5]—[The sanctity of] a substitute is derived from a consecreated animal, while [that of] a consecreated animal comes from *ḥullin*.[6]

Yet there is a Passover-offering, which itself does not require laying [of hands], drink-offerings, and the waving of the breast a and the shoulder; whereas its remainder[1] does require laying [of hands], drink-offerings, and the waving of the breast and the shoulder?—A Passover remainder[2] during the rest of the year is a peace-offering.[3]

Alternatively,[4] Scripture says, the *burnt-offering*, [which intimates,] it must be in its [appointed] place.[5]

How do we know that a guilt-offering requires the north?—Because it is written, *In the place where they kill the burnt-offering shall they kill the guilt-offering*.[6] We have thus found [it of] slaughtering; how do we know [it of] receiving?—[Because it is written,] *And the blood thereof shall be dashed* etc.[7] [which teaches that] the receiving of its blood too must be in the north.[8] How do we know [that] the receiver himself [must stand in the north]?—*'And its blood'* [is written where] *'its blood'* [alone] would suffice.[9] We have thus found it as a recommendation: how do we know that it is indispensable?—Another text is written, *And he shall kill the he-lamb [in the place where they kill the sin-offering and the burnt-offering]*.[10]

Now, does that come for the present purpose? Surely it is required for what was taught: If anything was included in a general proposition, and was then singled out for a new law, you cannot restore it to [the terms of] its general proposition, unless the Writ explicitly restores it to [the terms of] its general proposition. How so? [Scripture saith,] *And he shall kill the he-lamb in the place where they kill the sin-offering and the guilt-offering, in the place of the sanctuary; for as the sin-offering so is the guilt-offering: it is the priest's; it is most holy*. Now, *'as the sin-offering so is the guilt-offering'* need not b be said.[1] Why then is *'as the sin-offering so is the guilt-offering'* said? Because a leper's guilt-offering was singled out and made subject to a new law, viz., that in respect of the thumb of the hand, the big toe of the foot, and the right ear,[2] you might think that it does not require the presentation of [its] blood and *emurim* at the altar; therefore Scripture says, *'as the sin-offering so is the guilt-offering'*: as the sin-offering requires the presentation of [its] blood and *emurim* at the altar, so does a leper's guilt-offering require the presentation of blood and *emurim* at the altar?[3]—If so,[4] let it be written in the latter [passage][5] and not in the former. Now, that is well if we hold that when anything is made the subject of a new

(3) Second tithe was a tithe of the produce which was to be taken to Jerusalem and eaten there by its owner. If it was too burdensome, he could redeem it, take the redemption money to Jerusalem, and expend it there (Deut. XIV, 22-27).—Thus according to R. Judah what was brought with the redemption money is stricter than the original tithe, for the original could be redeemed, whereas this cannot. (4) An object must possess a certain degree of sanctity before it can be transferred to something else, whereas the sanctity of this is too light to permit such transfer. Hence R. Judah's ruling, though strict, arises out of the *lesser*, not the greater, sanctity of what is brought. (5) If a man dedicates a blemished animal for a sacrifice, it merely receives monetary sanctity, and can be redeemed, whereupon it becomes *ḥullin* (q.v. Glos.) entirely, and may be put to any use, including shearing and labour. But if a man declares a blemished animal a substitute for a consecrated animal, it becomes holy, and must be redeemed, but when redeemed it may not be kept for shearing or service, but must be eaten (this is also the law where an animal *without* a blemish is dedicated for a sacrifice and then receives a blemish). Thus the sanctity of the substitute is greater than that of the original. (6) A substitute receives sanctity because *another* animal has already been sanctified, whereas the originally consecrated animal receives it direct from *ḥullin*.

a (1) V. *supra* 37*b*, n. a 7. (2) Emended text (Sh. M.) (3) And not a Passover-offering at all. Hence it is a different sacrifice and naturally governed by different laws. (4) In reply to the question whence do we know that the north is indispensable in the case of a burnt-offering. (5) The north is not only prescribed, but is also essential. (6) Lev. VII, 1. (7) Ibid. 2. (8) Sh. M.: The *waw* ('and') joins the sentence to the preceding verse, and so the regulation concerning the place of killing applies to the receiving of the blood too. This second verse must be applied to receiving and not to sprinkling, since the blood was not sprinkled at the north. (9) Rashi: the deduction is made from the *eth* (sign of the accusative) before *'its blood'*, which could be omitted. This is therefore regarded as extending the law to the receiver. (10) Lev. XIV, 13. This treats of a leper's guilt-offering. The repetition of place shews that it is indispensable.

b (1) For if it is to teach that it is slaughtered in the north, that follows from the first half of the verse. While if it teaches that the sprinkling of its blood and its consumption are the same as those of the sin-offering, that too is superfluous, since it is already covered by the general regulations prescribed for all guilt-offerings in Lev. VII, 1-10. (2) V. Ibid. XIV, 14 *seq*. These rites are absent in the case of other guilt-offerings. (3) This is the example: since a leper's guilt-offering was singled out for special treatment, the general laws of guilt-offerings could not apply to it without a text specifically intimating that they do.—Thus the text is utilised for this purpose, and not to teach that the north is indispensable. (4) That that is its only purpose. (5) In the passage on leprosy.

גמרא

א] והרי מעשר דהוא נפדה ואילו לקוח בכסף מעשר אינו נפדה דתנן *הלקוח בכסף מעשר שנטמא יפדה ר' יהודה אומר יקבר ב] (נטמא אין לא נטמא לא) התם לא אלימא קדושתיה למיתפס פדיוניה והרי תמורה דאילו *קדשים לא חיילי על בעל מום קבוע ואילו איהי חיילא תמורה מכח קדשים קא אתיא וקדשים מכח חולין קאתי הרי פסח דהוא אינו טעון סמיכה ונסכים ותנופת חזה ושוק ואילו מותר דידיה טעון סמיכה ונסכים ותנופת חזה ושוק ג] פסח בשאר ימות השנה שלמים הוא ואיבע"ת אימא אמר קרא העולה ד] במקומה תהא אשם מנלן דבעי צפון

(ויקרא ו) דכתיב °במקום אשר ישחטו את העולה ישחטו את האשם אשכחן שחיטה קבלה מנא לן ה] ואת דמו יזרוק קבול דמו נמי בצפון מקבל עצמו מנא לן דמו ואת דמו אשכחן למצוה לעכב ו] מנא לן קרא אחרינא כתיב

(שם יד) °ושחט את הכבש ז] והאי להכי הוא דאתא האי מיבעי ליה לכדתניא *דבר שהיה בכלל ויצא לידון בדבר החדש אי אתה ח] רשאי להחזירו לכללו עד שיחזירנו הכתוב לכללו בפירוש כיצד °ושחט את הכבש במקום (שם) אשר ישחט את החטאת ואת העולה במקום הקדש כי כחטאת ט] האשם הוא וגו' י] שאין ת"ל כחטאת האשם מה ת"ל כחטאת האשם לפי שיצא אשם מצורע לידון בדבר החדש בבוהן יד ובוהן רגל ואזן ימנית יכול לא יהא טעון מתן דמים ואימורין לגבי מזבח תלמוד לומר כחטאת האשם הוא מה חטאת טעונה מתן דמים ואימורין לגבי מזבח יא] אף אשם מצורע טעון מתן דמים ואימורין לגבי מזבח אם כן נכתוב בהאי ולא נכתוב בהאי הניחא אי סבירא לן יצא לידון בדבר החדש איהו הוא דלא גמר מכללו

אבל

רש"י

והרי מעשר שני דהוא נפדה · אפי' בירושלים אם נטמא כדילפינן (ב"מ דף נג:) מלא תוכל שאתו ואין שאת אלא אכילה שנאמר וישא משאות : אינו נפדה · אליבא דר' יהודה אלמא איכא טפל חמור מעיקר : התם משום דלא אלים · ולא חומרא הוא : קדשים לא חיילי יב] (עליה) · תחילת הקדש אינו חל על בעל מום קבוע ליקדש קדושת הגוף אלא קדושת דמים בעלמא ויוצאין לחולין גמורין בפדיון ואפילו ליגזז וליעבד כדתניא יג] פרק הוציאו לו בסדר יומא (דף ס:) חומר בתמורה שהתמורה חלה על בעל מום קבוע ואין יוצא לחולין ליגזז וליעבד מה שאין כן בזבח דגבי תמורה כתיב טוב ברע יד] השוה בעל מום לתם לענין תמורה על כולם נאמר והיה הוא ותמורתו יהיה קדש אבל זבח ראשון אם קדם הקדישו את מומו קדוש קדושת הגוף ואינו יוצא לחולין ליגזז *וליעבד טו] כדתנן בבכורות (דף יד·) כל הקדשים שקדם מומן להקדישן טז] נפדה ויליף לה מקראי : קדשים מכח חולין קאתו · לא חלה עליהם קדושה קודמת אבל תמורה באה מכח קדושה קודמת הלכך לאו טפל חמור מן העיקר הוא דהא חומרא דעיקר הוא : שלמים הוא · ולא מותר פסח מיקרי למיחשביה טפל: ואיבעית אימא · עיכובא דעולה מהכא : דכתיב במקום יז] כו' העולה· חזר ושנה לימד מקום שקבעתו לעולה לעולם הוא מקומה: ישחטו את האשם ואת דמו · במקום שחיטתו תהא קבלת דמו : דמו ואת דמו · מדמלי למיכתב ישחטו את האשם ודמו יזרוק וכתיב ואת דמו את לרבות את המקבל : ושחט את הכבש וגו' · באשם מצורע כתיב שנה הכתוב עליו לעכב : לכדתניא כו' · דצריך להחזירו לכללו הלכך לענין שחיטת צפון נמי בעי להחזירו דאי לא הדר כתביה בגוויה כי היכי דאהדריה למתן דמו הוה אמינא לא ליבעי צפון : אי אתה יכול להחזירו לכללו · שיהא עוד כשאר הכלל : שילא אשם מצורע · מכלל וזאת תורת האשם דהוה כתב בכולהו ואת דמו יזרוק על *המזבח יח] אף כאן לשחיטת צפון נמי להחזירו הוא דשנה עליה : לכתוב · שחיטת צפון באשם מצורע ולא נכתוב גבי זאת תורת האשם ונגמר כללו מיניה יט] ומדכתביה הכא והכא לעיכובא הוא :

אבל

תוספות

והרי מעשר דהוא נפדה · אפילו בירושלים אם נטמא כדילפינן מלא תוכל שאתו ואין שאת אלא אכילה ואילו לקוח בכסף מעשר שני אינו נפדה אליבא דר' יהודה כ] אלמא איכא טפל חמור מעיקר כך פי' בקונטרס ובספרי פרשת עשר תעשר מפרש טעמא דרבי יהודה משום דכתיב [הכסף] כסף ראשון ולא כסף שני והא דאמר בריש הזהב (ב"מ דף מה·) גבי סלעין ייגרין דכסף כסף ריבה יש לחלק בזה שנגמר כאן פדיונו לגמרי *וקנה כא] פדיונו מעשר ואם היה טהור לא היה נפדה ותנן במסכת מעשר שני פ' שלישי (מ"י) אמרו לו לר' יהודה מה אם מעשר שני עצמו שנטמא הרי הוא נפדה הלקוח בכסף מעשר שנטמא אינו דין שיפדה אמר להם לא אם אמרתם במעשר שני עצמו שכן נפדה טהור ברחוק מקום תאמרו בלקוח בכסף מעשר שאינו נפדה טהור ברחוק מקום ואית ספרים דגרסי הכא נטמא אין לא נטמא לא ומייתי ראייה מרבנן דטפל חמור מעיקר פירוש נטמא נפדה לרבנן לא נטמא אינו נפדה אפי' חוץ לירושלים אע"פ שמעשר עצמו נפדה והייט חוץ לירושלים דבירושלים אין מעשר טהור נפדה ובתוספתא דמעשר שני משמע כפי' הקונטרס דעל מילתא דר' יהודה כב] פרכינן האי לישנא שעושה טפל חמור מן העיקר והכי איתא התם הלקוח בכסף מעשר כו' אמרו לו לרבי יהודה תחמיר בטפילה יותר מן העיקר כג] ולגירסת הספרים לא נטמא לא ומוכיח דרבנן נמי סברי טפל חמור מן העיקר גבי מעשר טהור חוץ לירושלים כד] קשה *) דאי פרכי רבנן לר' יהודה תיקשי להו לדידהו כיון דקורא טפל חמור מן העיקר האי דלקוח טהור אינו נפדה ומעשר כה] עצמו נפדה אבל לגירסת הקונטרס ניחא דאיכא למימר דהאי לא מיקרי טפל חמור מן העיקר דמעשר עצמו טהור נפדה ברחוק מקום כדי *לפדות בדמים בירושלים בקר ולאן יין ושכר כדכתיב ונתת הכסף בכל אשר תאוה נפשך אבל אם לקח פירות בו חוץ לירושלים כדי לאוכלם בירושלים לא יפדה כמו שלא היה פודה מה שהיה לוקח בירושלים ולגירסת הספרים כו] לא נטמא לא קשה לפירוש הקונטרס דפרק הזהב (ב"מ דף נה:) גבי מחללין אותו כסף על נחשת נחשת על הפירות ויחזור ויפדה את הפירות כז] וחכמים אומרים יעלו פירות ויאכלו בירושלים ופי' בקונטרס וחכמים אומרים לא הזקיקוהו לחזור לחללם כמו ת"ק אלא אם רצה יעלה פירות עצמו דהקלו בו משמע מתוך פירושו דר"מ מחמיר דלא שרי נחשת על הפירות אא"כ יחזור ויפדה את הפירות ויעלה הכסף לירושלים והכא משמע שזו היא קולא כשחוזר ופודה את הפירות ומשמע דאפילו איסורא איכא למאי דגרסי' לא נטמא לא דאינו נפדה טהור ברחוק מקום ומשנה שלימה היא במסכת כח] מעשרות (פ"ג מ"י) ושם הארכתי בפרק הזהב (ב"מ דף נה: ד"ה ויחזור) : **פסח** בשאר ימות השנה שלמים הוא· וא"ת הרי אחד עשר כט] שטפל חמור מן העיקר כדאמרינן בפ' שתי מדות (מנחות נא:) האחד זה אחד עשר שלא מצינו לו בכל התורה טפל חמור מן העיקר וי"ל כדמשני הכא מותר הפסח שלמים הוי ה"נ אחד עשר שלמים הוי דכל דיני שלמים עליו כדמשמע בבכורות (דף סא·) ל] *מדמצריך קרא דמותר הפסח נמי בעי קרא כדדרשינן פרק קמא (לעיל ט·) אם כשב להביא פסח שעברה שנתו ושלמים הבאין מחמת פסח לכל מנות שלמים שיטעט סמיכה ונסכים ותנופת חזה ושוק והא דקרי ליה לא] טפל לאו דווקא : **לעכב** מנא לן דכתיב ושחט את הכבש · למקבל לא ידעינן עיכובא* · **לפי** שילא אשם מצורע לידון בדבר החדש כו' · מה שחטאת לב] מצורע טעונה נסכים ושאר חטאות אין טעונין לא חשיב דבר חדש וכן אוב וידעוני שיש כרת מה שאין כן בשאר מכשפים מדלא תני בל"ו כריתות ואפ"ה גמרינן סקילה מאוב וידעוני בשאר מכשפים פרק קמא דיבמות (דף ד·) ופרק ארבע מיתות (סנהדרין דף סז:) ולא מקרי כרת דכתיב באוב וידעוני דבר החדש היכי גמר מינייהו סקילה למ"ד לג] כללו לא גמר מיניה וזה הקשה ה"ר יעקב מאורלינ"ש אלא *לא קרוי דבר חדש אלא כשסותר כללו כי הכא דשאר אשמות כל הדם למזבח ואשם מצורע לד] הדם ממנו לבהונות וכגון אשת אח בפרק קמא דיבמות (דף ז·) שנאסרו כל העריות וזו הותרה וזהו דבר החדש שסותר כללו אבל מה שחטאת לה] מצורע טעונה נסכים אינו סותר מכללו אלא תוספת הוא על הקרבן וא"ת למאן דאמר כללו גמר מיניה יהיו כל אשמות טעונין מתן בהונות ונילפו נמי כולהו עריות מאשת אח וי"ל דלא גמר מיניה אלא מידי דלא חידש בו כגון שחיטת צפון אבל החידוש לא גמר מיניה כדפירש בקונטרס דא"כ לא היה עוד כאן דבר חדש ועוד דאם כן היה יוצא לידון בדבר החדש כיוצא בו ללמד על הכלל כולו : **נכתוב** בהאי ולא נכתוב בהאי לו] · תימה ושאר אשמות היכי ילפי מאשם מצורע מה לאשם מצורע שכן בא להתיר :

*) נ"א דאדפרכי רבנן לר"י כו' כצ"ל נ"ק

אי

עין משפט נר מצוה

יא א מיי' פ"ב מהלכות מעשר שני הלכה א ג:

נ"ק

יב ב מיי' פ"ג מהלכות פסולי המוקדשין הלכה ה:

ג"א וקנה פירות במעשר שני ואם היה כו' כצ"ל נ"ק ופי' בכ"מ בתוס' ע"ע

יג ג מיי' פ"ג מהלכות מעשה הקרבנות הלכה ו' :

יד ד מיי' שם פ"ס הלכה ג :

מסורת הש"ס

פסחים לח: ב"מ נג: מעשר שני פ"ג מ"י סדרין קנ'

תמורה טז:

ג"י כל"ק וליעבד אבל קדם מומן להקדישן דאין קדושת הגוף עליהם אלא קדושת דמים כדתנן כו' כצ"ל וכ"ה בס"י

יבמות ד

גי' כל"ק המזבח הס"ד ואח"כ מה"ד א"כ דלשחיטת צפון כו' עליה לכתוב כו' כצ"ל

ג"י כל"ק ואם דמצריך קרא מותר הפסח נמי כו'

עי' רש"ק וגי"ק

גליון הש"ס

תוס' ד"ה לפי וכו' לא קרוי דבר חדש. עי' לקמן מ ע"ב תוס' ד"ה ס"ג וכשנאמרו :

שיטה מקובצת

א] עי' בהשמטות בסוף המסכת : ב] תיבות נטמא אין לא נטמא לא נמחק : ג] ושוק מותר פסח : ד] העולה העולה במקומה: ה] מנא לן ת"ל ואת דמו' וי"ו מוסף על ענין ראשון במקום שחיטתו תהא קבלת דמו וע"כ משום קבלה אתיא דלא אתיא בשביל זריקה דזריקה אינה בצפון · לשון הר"פ ומשמע שהוא לשון רש"י שלו : ו] לעכב מנלן · וא"ת מאי בעי כיון דאקיש אשם לעולה א"כ אף לעכב אקשינן דאין היקש למחצה ועיכובא דעולה ידעינן מהעולה במקומה תהא וכן קשה למה לי דשנה הכתוב בחטאת לעכב (בחטאת) תיפוק ליה מדאיתקש לעולה ובעולה כתיב עיכובא מהעולה במקומה תהא וי"ל דודאי אי הוי ההיקש כתיבא בלשון [זה] החטאת כעולה וכן גבי אשם הוי כתיב האשם כעולה אז הוי משמע דאיתקש חטאת לעולה לגמרי גם לעכב וכן אשם לעולה גם לעכב אבל השתא דכתיב במקום אשר ישחטו העולה ישחטו את האשם אינו מקיש לגמרי האשם לעולה אלא למאי דכתיב בפסוק בהדיא דהיינו ישחטו דמשמע למצוה ולא לעכב וכן גבי חטאת דכתיב במקום העולה תשחט את החטאת ומשמע תשחט למצוה דוקא קאמר וסברא הוא דלא עדיף חך דהקישו לשחיטה דעולה מאילו הוה כתיב צפון באשם פעם אחת בהדיא דהות למצוה ולא לעכב · כך נראה למורי מהר"פ ז"ל : ז] הכבש במקום אשר ישחט את החטאת ואת העולה: ח] יכול להחזירו לכללו : ט] כחטאת · גליון כלומר כדין חטאת הוא אשם זה ובאשם מצורע כתיב ע"כ : י] שאין ת"ל כחטאת האשם' גליון דאם לשחיטה בצפון הרי כבר נאמר ושחט את הכבש במקום אשר ישחט את העולה ואם למתן דמים ואכילתו הרי כל אשמות בכלל וזאת תורת האשם וכתיב בכלותו דם תורק על המזבח ומה ת"ל כחטאת כו' ע"כ : יא] אף אשם מצורע כו' אלמא דצריך קרא להחזירו לכללו משום מתן דמים ואימורים כמו כן איצטריך ושחט את הכבש שכתוב באשם מצורע להחזירו לכלל שאר אשמות לצפון וא"כ הק"ל עיכובא מנ"ל ומשני א"כ נכתוב בהא פי' צפון באשם מצורע ולא לכתוב בשאר אשמות צפון ולא נכתוב זאת תורת האשם ונגמור כולו מיניה ומדכתביה הכא והכא ש"מ לעיכובא הוא דכתביה כפ"ה ותימה דהיכא גמר שאר אשמות מאשם מצורע אשם מצורע גופיה מה קשא הוא דאתיא והויא ג"ש מן ההיקש ואיכא מ"ד דבר הבא בהיקש אינו חוזר ומלמד בג"ש ועוד נמי איכא למיפרך מה לאשם מצורע שכן בא להתיר א"נ שכן עמו דמים אחרים וי"ל דלמ"ד דגמרי כללו מיניה סבירא ליה דהוי דבר שבכלל ויצא מן הכלל (ס"א ללמד לא על עצמו יצא אלא כו' וגבי האי מדה לא פרכינן מידי כמו בשאר למודים שבתורה) לדברים שאינה חידוש והוי אחת מן המדות השוות שבתורה וכיון דהוי מדה שוה שבתורה ליכא למיפרך עליה מידי : טעון גליון פי' ואי לאו דאהדריה קרא הוי אמינא למאי דנפק נפק דהיינו בבהן יד ורגל ולמאי דלא נפק לא נפק ואין טעון מתן דמים ואימורים ע"כ : יב] חיילי וכו' תחלת ותיבת עליה נמחק : יג] כדתניא בפרק הוציאו לו כו' שהתמורה חלה על בעל מום : יד] ברע וגו' השוה : טו] וליעבד ואם קדם מומו להקדישו אינו קדוש קדושת הגוף ויוצא לחולין לינזז וליעבד כדתנן : טז] להקדישן נפדים ויליף : יז] תיבת כו' ל"ש ונמחק : יח] המזבח הס"ד ומה"ד א"כ דשחיטת צפון : יט] מיניה בדין לא ללמד על עצמו יצא אלא ללמד על הכלל כולו יצא : כ] יהודה עיין בפ"ג דמע"ש באות' משנה בהר"ש : כא] פירות ממעות מעשר ותיבת פדיונו נמחק : כב] פרכי רבנן האי לישנא : כג] העיקר א"ל מצינו שהתמורה חמורה מן העיקר ולגירסת הספרים (תוס') [דגרסי] לא : כד] לירושלם ע"כ קשה דאפרכי רבנן : כה] ומעשר טהור : כו] תיבות לא ניטמא לא נמחק : כז] הפירות דברי ר"מ וחכמים אומרים: כח] בסמ' מעשר שני אות ו' ת' נמחק : כט] עשר · שקראו עשירי דטעון שקראו אינו טעון נסכים והרי מצינו שטפל: ל] בבכורות מיהו צריך קרא דמותר הפסח(לא) ליה התם : לב] שחטאת ואשם מצורע טעונין נסכים דשאר חטאות ואשמות אין טעונין כו' וידעוני שיש בהם כרת משא"כ דלא תנן בכלל ל"ו כריתות : לג] למ"ד כללו לא גמר מיניה זה פי' ה"ר יעקב : לד] מצורע ניתן ממנו לבהונות : לה] שחטאת ואשם מצורע טעונים נסכים אינו סותר כללו אלא : לו] בהאי פי' ולא לכתוב צפון בשאר אשמות ונילף מאשם מצורע דהא סבירי ליה השתא דכללו גמיר מיניה כדקאמר בסמוך אלא להכי כתביה בשאר אשמות לעכב הכא והכא :

עין משפט נר מצוה

מסורת הש"ס

אבל כללו גמר מיניה א] (לצפון) שפיר אלא אי סבירא לן דלא הוא גמר מכללו ולא כללו גמר מיניה האי לגופיה איצטריך ב] כיון דאהדריה אהדריה אמר ליה מר זוטרא בריה דרב מרי לרבינא אימא ג] כי אהדריה קרא לגבי מתן דמים ואימורין דבעי כהונה אבל שחיטה דלא בעיא כהונה לא ד] מיבעי צפון א"כ נימא קרא כי כחטאת הוא מאי כחטאת האשם כשאר אשמות יהיה למה לי לאקשויי לחטאת למה לי לאקשויי לעולה אמר רבינא איצטריך אי אקשיה לחטאת ולא אקשיה לעולה הוה אמינא ה] חטאת מהיכן למדה מעולה דבר הלמד בהיקש חוזר ומלמד בהיקש א"ל מר זוטרא בריה דרב מרי לרבינא וניקשיה לעולה ולא ניקשיה ו] לחטאת הוה אמינא *דבר הלמד בהיקש חוזר ומלמד בהיקש וכי ז] תימא ניקשי אקושי לחטאת ניחא ליה דמקיש ליה לעיקר ולא נקיש ליה לטפל להכי אקשיה לחטאת ואקשיה לעולה למימר דבר הלמד בהיקש ח] שאינו חוזר ומלמד בהיקש רבא אמר מהכא דכתיב °כאשר יורם משור זבח השלמים למאי [ויקרא ד] הלכתא אי ליותרת הכבד ושתי הכליות בגופיה כתיב ט] (אמר רב פפא) משום דבעי אגמורי יותרת הכבד ושתי הכליות י] מפר העלם דבר של צבור לשעירי עבודת כוכבים יא] בגופיה לא כתיב ומפר כהן משיח הוא דגמר להכי איצטריך כאשר יורם דניהוי כמאן דכתב בגופיה °ולא ניהוי דבר הלמד בהיקש חוזר ומלמד בהיקש אמר ליה רב פפא לרבא וליכתביה בגופיה ולא נקיש אי כתב בגופיה ולא אקיש הוה אמינא *דבר הלמד בהיקש חוזר ומלמד בהיקש וכי תימא נקשי אקושי ניחא ליה דכתביה בגופיה מדאקיש ליה אקושי להכי כתביה ואקשיה למימרא דבר הלמד בהיקש אין חוזר ומלמד בהיקש: (היק"ש וגזיר"ה שו"ה ק"ל וחומ"ר יב] סימן): דבר הלמד בהיקש אין חוזר ומלמד *מהיקש אי מדרבא אי מדרבינא דבר הלמד בהיקש מהו שילמד בגזירה שוה תא שמע *רבי נתן בן אבטולמוס אומר *מנין לפריחה בבגדים שהיא טהורה נאמר קרחת וגבחת בבגדים ונאמר קרחת וגבחת באדם מה להלן פרח בכולו טהור אף כאן פרח בכולו טהור והתם מנא לן דכתיב °מראשו ועד רגליו ואיתקש ראשו לרגל מה להלן יג] כולו הפך לבן [שם יג] פרח בכולו טהור אף כאן כולו הפך לבן פרח בכולו טהור *אמר ר' יוחנן בכל התורה כולה יד] למידין למד מלמד חוץ מן הקדשים שאין דנין למד מלמד טו] דאם כן לא יאמר צפונה באשם ותיתי בג"ש טז] דקדשי קדשים מחטאות °לאו למימרא דדבר הלמד בהיקש אין חוזר ומלמד בגזירה שוה ודלמא משום דאיכא למיפרך מה לחטאת שכן מכפרת על חייבי כריתות יז] קדשי קדשים יתירי כתיבי: *דבר הלמד מהיקש חוזר ומלמד בקל וחומר מדרבנא

אבל כללו גמר מיניה · מידי דלא חידש בו כגון שחיטת לפון אי הוה כתיבא ביה ולא הוה כתיבא בשאר אשמות גמרי ליה שאר אשמות מיניה יח] דלא חידוש הוא אלא יצא מן הכלל הוא ולמד על דבר שלא נאמר בכלל (א) והיכי יט] יצא לידון בדבר החדש כגון מתן דמים שבזה למזבח ובזה שינה ואומר לבהונות: כיון דאהדריה כ] כו' · וכתיב כי כחטאת האשם הוא כדין חטאת כך דין אשם כא]: אהדריה · לכללו בין למתן דמים בין לשחיטת לפון ולא היה לריך לכתוב בו שחיטת לפון אלא לעיכובא: דבעי כהונה · שאינה כשירה בזר אבל כב] למידה דשחיטה דלאו עבודת כהן היא לא אהדריה דהא בחזרתו כתיב כחטאת האשם הוא לכהן לענין עבודות שבכהן: א"כ נימא קרא כי כחטאת הוא · לכהן: כשאר אשמות יהיה · הלכך לענין לפון נמי אהדריה וכי כתיב כג] ביה שחיטה בלפון דקרא לעיכובא אתא ושאר אשמות נמי מיניה ילפינן לעיכובא: למה לי לאקשויי בשחיטתו לחטאת ולעולה · דכתיב במקום אשר ישחטו את החטאת ואת העולה: מהיכן כד] למדו · לשחיטת לפון: אי אקשיה לעולה ולא אקשיה לחטאת הוה אמינא · בעלמא דבר הלמד בהיקש חוזר ומלמד בהיקש: וכי תימא · אם איתא דחוזר ומלמד בהיקש נקשיה לחטאת ולא לעולה משנינן לך ניחא ליה לאקשויי לעיקר כו': למימרא · מדאיצטריך למיהדר כה] ואקושי לעולה ש"מ דבר הלמד בהיקש אין חוזר ומלמד בהיקש ומהכא נפקא לן בכל דוכתא: כאשר יורם · באימורי פר כהן משיח כתיב: משום דבעי אגמורי יותרת הכבד ושתי כליות כו' · שהיה לריך ללמד מפר העלם תורת כו] אימוריהן לשעירי עבודת כוכבים דאיתקוש אהדדי לענין הקטרת אימורין כדאמרינן בפ' ב"ש (לעיל מא·) אשה לה' וחטאתם על שגגתם ופר העלם דבר בגופיה לא כתיב יותרת וכליות ומפר כהן משיח גמר בהיקש כדאמרן בפ' בית שמאי (שם לט:) ועשה לפר כאשר עשה לפר זה פר כהן משיח אקשינהו להדדי: להכי איצטריך כאשר יורם · בפר כהן משיח ואם איט ענין לו תנהו לענין פר העלם דניהוי כמאן דכתיבי בפר העלם גופיה דלא ליהוי דבר הלמד בהיקש חוזר ומלמד בהיקש ואי קשיא הא נפקא לן הך דרשה מועשה לפר זה פר העלם דבר כדאמרן בפרק ב"ש (ב) (לעיל מא·) ה"מ לתנא דבי ר' ישמעאל דאמר לפר זה פר העלם אבל לתנא דבי רב דאמר ועשה לפר זה פר יום הכיפורים איצטריך כאשר יורם להך דרשה: ונכתביה בגופיה · דפר העלם בהדיא ולא ליקשיה לפר כהן משיח הואיל וסוף סוף כז] טרח וכתב כאשר יורם יתירא להכי: הוה אמינא דבר הלמד בהיקש חוזר ומלמד בהיקש · בעלמא דלא הוה ילפינן מהכא מידי: דבר הלמד בהיקש כו' · משום דבעי למיבעי בעיא עלה הדר נקיט לה: אי מדרבא · מכאשר יורם: אי מדרבינא · מאשם מלורע דאילטריך לאקושי לחטאת ולעולה: לפריחה · אם פרחה הלרעת בכל הבגד: מה להלן פרח כח] בכולה טהור · כדכתיב אם פרוח תפרח וגו' (ויקרא יג): והתם · גבי קרחת וגבחת דאדם מנלן דטהורה פריחה דאילו פריחה כי כתיבא בנגע עור בשר כתיב ואילו קרחת וגבחת כתיבי גבי נתקין למקום שער דראש וזקן שאין סימניהן שוין לנגעי עור בשר שזה בשער לבן וזה בשער לחוב: ואיתקש ראשו · נתקי הראש: אף כאן כו' · אלמא נתקין בהיקשא ילפינן להו וחוזרין ומלמדין כט] על הבגדים בג"ש: א"ר יוחנן · מהכא לא תיתי ראייה דלאו קדשים הוא דאף היקש מלמד בהיקש ל] חוץ מקדשים ותדע לך שהמדה הזאת שהבאתה אינה למידה בקדשים: דא"כ הוא · דדבר הלמד בהיקש חוזר ולמד בג"ש: לא יאמר לפון באשם ותיתי בג"ש · דנאמר לא] קדשי קדשים בחטאת ונאמר קדשי קדשים באשם: קדשי קדשים יתירי כתיבי · בהו והוה ליה גזירה שוה מופנה משני לדדין ואין משיבין עליה גבי חטאת כתיב תשחט החטאת קדש קדשים הוא ובאשם כתיב זאת תורת האשם קדש קדשים הוא ובתרווייהו כתיב בויקח קרח לכל חטאתם ולכל אשמם אשר ישיבו לי קדש קדשים לך לב]: מדתנא

אי אקשיה לעולה ולא אקשיה לחטאת · תימה לג] לא לכתוב את החטאת ואי דבר הלמד בהיקש חוזר ומלמד בהיקש אמאי אקשיה לעולה כלל תיפוק ליה לד] *מחטאת האשם דמה חטאת לפון מעכב אף אשם כן וי"ל דאי לא כתב לפון לא הוה אמינא לה] הא הדרה קרא לשחיטת לפון למידי דלא בעיא כהונה והאשם לא דרשינן ליה כלל דהא לא כתב כאשם דהוה משמע כשאר אשם דעלמא ללפון יהא זה אבל האשם משמע האשם זה יהא כחטאת למתן דמים לו] למזבח וכן *יש להקשות אי דבר הלמד בהיקש חוזר ומלמד בהיקש לא נכתוב לפון כלל ותיתי לז] [באשמות] מכחטאת וכאשם כי היכי דילפינן מיניה סמיכה בפרק קמא (לעיל יא·) *ועוד נילף שאר אשמות מאשם מלורע ואשם מלורע מהיקשא דכחטאת וי"ל דלא הוה אמינא דאהדריה קרא לשחיטת לפון ולא הוה דרשינן לח] כאשם כשאר אשם (כיון דלא כתב כאשם) כיון דלא כתב לפון בהדיא בשאר אשמות: [צ"ל מ"ז]

כאשר יורם למאי הלכתא · תימה הא איצטריך לכדדרשינן בסוף כל הבשר (חולין דף קיז·) זה בא ללמד ונמצא למד מה פר כהן משיח יש בו מעילה אף שור זבח השלמים יש בו מעילה וי"ל דמאי לאקשויי לזבח השלמים ולא ליכתוב כאשר יורם לט] דכאשר יורם משמע דאתא לרבויי הרמה אחרת אי נמי ההיא דכל הבשר (שם) כתנא דבי רבי ישמעאל דנפקא ליה דרשא דהכא מועשה לפר זה פר העלם מ] כדאמר פרק בית שמאי (לעיל דף מא·) אבל לתנא דבי רב דאמר ועשה לפר זה פר יום הכיפורים איצטריך כאשר יורם (*להך דרשא): [צ"ל ת"י] [עי' בתוס' חולין קיז· ד"ה למר ר"י דמתמלי בעזרי אמר]

ונכתביה בגופיה · תימה כדאמר פרק ב"ש (נס זה שם:) משל למלך בשר ודם מא] שסרחה עליו מדינה ומיעט בסרחונם מפני מב] חיבתן וי"ל דבשביל חיבתן לא היה לו לגלגל אלו דרשות למילף מהיקשא ומ"מ ילפינן מיניה מג] חיבתן מדלא אשמעינן בדוכתא אחרינא דבר הלמד מהיקש אינו חוזר ומלמד בהיקש:

קדשי קדשים יתירי כתיבי. תימה כיון דילפינן גזרה שוה מהדדי למה לן היקשות דלעיל מד] בחטאת ואשם: לא

[לקמן נס. נז. לעיל מח. יומא נז. מנחות כח. עת. פכ:]

[יומא ס.]

[צ"ל בהיקש]

[סנהדרין פו: [נדה יט. ושם איתא ר' יונתן וכ"א בילקוט]

[שבועות י. תמורה כה:]

[לעיל מח.]

ט א מיי' פ"ב מהלכות טומאת צרעת הלכה ח:

צ"ל מכחטאת ל"ק

ג"י הל"ק אין להקשות ש' ותיתי מכחטאת כאשם

נ"א

ג"י ל"ק ונילף שאר כו' די"ל דלא

שיטה מקובצת

א] תיבת לצפון נמחק: ב] איצטריך והאי לגופיה איצטריך כיון: ג] עי' בהשמטות בסוף המסכת: ד] לא תיבעי · ס"א לא אהדריה א"כ כו': ה] עי' בהשמטות בסוף המסכת: ו] עי' בהשמטות בסוף המסכת: ז] תימא א"כ ניקשי כו' דמקיש לעיקר תיבת ליה ל"ש ונמחק: ח] בהיקש אינו חוזר ומלמד בהיקש רבא אמר דבר הלמד בהיקש אינו חוזר ומלמד בהיקש מהכא: ט] כתיב אלא משום ותיבות אמר רב פפא נמחק: י] הכליות כו' · ואע"ג דלעיל נפקא לן יותרת ושתי הכליות לשעירי ע"ז מלפר י"ל היינו לתנא דבי ר' ישמעאל אבל הכא איירי אליבא דרבי · מהר"פ: יא] כוכבים ופר העלם דבר של צבור בגופיה לא כתיב: יב] וחומר ובנין אב סימן: יג] מה להלן פרח בכולו טהור אף כאן פרח בכולו טהור: יד] כולה דנין למד מלמד: טו] דאם כן כו' א) מטילתיה דר' יוחנן בא להוכיח שמדה שהביא למעלה אינה נוהגת בקדשים · ת"א: טז] בקודש קדשים מחטאת לאו · ס"י למאי הלכתא כתביה רחמנא לאו: יז] קדש קדשים יתירא כתיבי·תימה כיון דאיכא ג"ש וילפינן מהדדי למה לן היקשות דלעיל דכחטאת האשם דכתיב גבי מצורע להחזירו לכללו תיפוק ליה מקדש הקדשים דהא כתיב קרש קדשים גבי אשם מצורע ונילף ליה בג"ש דקדש קדשים מחטאת להחזירו לכללו להטעינו מתן דמים ואימורים וי"ל דכיון שיצא אשם מצורע מן הכלל לידון בדבר החדש אי אתה יכול להחזירו לכללו בפירוש מכח הך ג"ש דקדש קדשים לא הוי חזרה בפירוש אפי' את"ל דג"ש חשיבא כמו היקש מ"מ האי ג"ש דקדש קדשים איצטריך ימילי אחרינא [ולא להחזירו לכללו] לקמן לגבי פגימת המזבח דקאמר אשכחן שירי מנחה קדשי קדשים מנין ת"ל קדש קדשים ולכך לא הוי חזרה בפירוש מכח [הך] ג"ש אבל היקש דכחטאת האשם כולו להחזירו הוא דאתא ולכך חשיבא חזרה בפירוש · ומיהו קשה לעיל בפ"ק למה לי היקשא דכחטאת האשם גבי סתם אשם תיפוק ליה מג"ש דקדש קדשים לומר דטעון סמיכה לרבנן דר' אליעזר ולר"א לשלא לשמו ואמר מורי דשמא ג"ש לא ניתנה לדרוש רק גבי שחיטה משום דקדש קדשים דכתיב בין בסתם אשם בין באשם מצורע גבי שחיטה הוא דכתיב אבל מכחטאת האשם דכתיב גבי סתם אשם דרשינן שפיר מיניה סמיכה דלגמרי מקיש הכתוב אשם לחטאת בהך היקשא כדכתיב כחטאת כאשם תורה אחת לכם ועוד יש לומר דגבי סמיכה כתיב קרבנו דהוי מיעוט והוה מוקמינן ג"ש לדברים אחרים אבל השתא דאיתור היקשא לסמיכה מוקמינן (ג"ש) קרבנו לדרשא אחריתי וכן לר' אליעזר צריך היקש לשלא לשמו לאפוקי מהך היקשא דשלמים דזאת התורה: יח] מיניה דלאו חידוש: יט] והיכא דמי צא: כ] דאהדריה וכתב כי כחטאת: כא] אשם זה הס"ד: כב] אבל לגבי שחיטה דלאו: כג] כתיב שחיטה בצפון ריש"א דקרא וה"בת בית נמחק: כד] מהיכן למדה: כה] ולאקשי לשלה: כו] תורת אימורין לשעירי כו' דאתקיש להדדי לענין הקטרת אימורין כו' שנגתם חטאתם הרי לך כשגגתם ופר העלם: כז] סוף חזר ופרח: כח] פרח בכולו טהר·: כט] ומלמדין בג"ש על הבגדים הס"ד: ל] בהיקש בכל התורה חוץ: לא] קדש קדשים בחטאת ונאמר קדש קדשים באשם הס"ד ומה"ד קדש קדשים יתירי: לב] לך הוא הס"ד: לג] תימה אי דבר הלמד כו' והשאר נמחק: לד] ליה מכחטאת האשם: לה] האי דהדריה קרא למידי דלא בעיא כהונה והאשם כשאר אשמות יהא לא הוה דרשינן ליה כלל תום': לו] דמים ואימורין למזבח וכן יש להקשות ע"כ וא"ת אכתי אי דבר: לז] ותיתי מכחטאת האשם: לח] דרשינן האשם כשאר אשם יהא כיון: לט] יורם אלא כאשר יוזבח השלמים דכאשר: מ] כדאמרי' פרק: מא] ידע שזעם על אוהבו ומיעט בסרחונו: מב] מפני חיבתו: מג] מיניה חיבתו וליכא למימר דכוליה להכי הוא דאתא לאשמעינן דדבר הבא בהיקש כו': מד] כחטאת האשם הס"ד:

א) נראה דל"ל ממילתיה דר"י כוא וכא לטוכיח וכו'.

הגהות הב"ח

(א) רש"י ד"ה אבל כללו וכו' ולהיכי יצא: (ב) ד"ה להכי איצטריך וכו' בפ' ב"ש תינח לתנא דבי ר' ישמעאל:

גליון הש"ס

גמ' ולא ניהוי דבר הלמד בהיקש · ע"ל נז ע"ב תוד"ה ואב"א: שם לאו למימרא דדבר הלמד כו'. עי' לעיל דף מח ע"א תוד"ס מס לנלן:

law, it cannot be learnt from its general law, [49b] but its general law can be learnt from it: then it is correct.[6] But if we hold that neither can it be learnt from the general proposition, nor can the
a general proposition be learnt from it, then this [law][1] is required for its own purpose?[2]—Since [Scripture] restored it, it restored it.[3]

Mar Zuṭra son of R. Mari said to Rabina: Yet say, When Scripture restored it [to the general proposition] [it was only] in respect of the presentation of the blood and *emurim*, since this requires priesthood;[4] but slaughtering, which does not require priesthood, does not require the north [either]?[5]—If so, let Scripture say, 'for it is as the sin-offering': why [state], *'for as the sin-offering so is the guilt-offering'*?[6] [To teach:] Let it be like the other guilt-offerings.[7]

Why must it be likened to both a sin-offering and a guilt-offering?—Said Rabina, It is necessary: if it were likened to a sin-offering and were not likened to a guilt-offering I would say, Whence did we learn [that] a sin-offering [is slaughtered in the north]? from a burnt-offering: thus that which is learnt through a *hekkesh* in turn teaches through a *hekkesh*.[8] Mar Zuṭra the son of R. Mari said to Rabina: Then let it be likened to a burnt-offering and not likened to a sin-offering?—Then I would say, [that elsewhere] that
b which is learnt through a *hekkesh* in turn teaches through a *hekkesh*;[1] and if you object, Then let it be likened to a sin-offering,[2] [I could reply:] It [Scripture] prefers to liken it to the principal rather than to the secondary.[3] Therefore it likened it to a sin-offering and it likened it to a burnt-offering, thus intimating that that which is learnt through a *hekkesh* does *not* in turn teach through a *hekkesh*.

Raba said: [It[4] is learnt] from the following, for it is written, *As is taken off from the ox of the sacrifice of peace-offerings*.[5] For what purpose [is this written]? if for the lobe of the liver and the two kidneys,[6] [surely] that is written in the body of the text![7] But because [Scripture] wishes to intimate that [the burning of] the lobe of the liver and the two kidneys of the he-goats [brought as sin-offerings] for idolatry shall be learnt by analogy from the community's bullock [for a sin-offering on account] of [sinning in] unawareness,[8] whereas this law is not explicitly stated in the passage on the bullock of unawareness, but is learnt from the anointed priest's bullock:[9] therefore *'as is taken off'* is required, so that it might count as written in that very passage[10] and not as something

(6) The general law is that stated in VII, 1-10, while a leper's guilt-offering is singled out for a new law not in harmony with the general law, for whereas the blood of an ordinary guilt-offering is sprinkled on the altar, the blood of this is applied to the right thumb, right ear, and the great toe of the right foot. Now, if it were not stated in the general regulations on the guilt-offerings that it must be slaughtered in the north, but were stated here, this would come not under the preceding but under the following rule: if anything is included in a general proposition and is then singled out to teach a special regulation, this applies not only to the case where it is stated, but to the whole. Thus a leper's guilt-offering is included in the general guilt-offerings dealt with in VII, 1-10; when it is singled out here for slaughtering in the north, that applies to *all* guilt-offerings, and not only to itself. (The other rule with which we are now dealing holds good only when the new law is not in harmony with the general one, as explained at the beginning of the note.) Hence on this view it need not be stated in VII, 1-10 that it is killed in the north, as this would follow from XIV, 14 *seq.*; its repetition teaches that the north is indispensable.

a (1) In VII, 1-10, that it is killed in the north. (2) That it is killed in the north, for on the present view we could not learn *all* guilt-offerings from a leper's guilt-offering, even in respect of a law which is not in disharmony (*sc.* slaughtering in the north), since the latter is made the subject of one law which is in disharmony (*sc.* sprinkling on the right thumb etc.). (3) Scripture restored a leper's guilt-offering to the general rule by saying, *for as the sin-offering so is the guilt-offering*, whence we know that it must be slaughtered in the north. *'And he shall kill the he-lamb in the place where they kill the sin-offering and the burnt-offering'* (*sc.* in the north), written in the same verse, is thus mere repetition, and so teaches that the north is indispensable. (4) It must be done by a priest. Hence the restoration to the general proposition shews that its *emurim* and some of the blood must be presented at the altar, in addition to its being applied to the right thumb etc. (5) But for *'and he shall kill'* etc. In that case it is not a repetition, and does not teach that it is indispensable. (6) Why mention the guilt-offering, seeing that the whole passage deals with it? (7) *Sc.* that it must be slaughtered in the north. Hence *'and he shall kill'* etc. is a repetition. (8) Therefore Scripture adds the burnt-offering, to shew that that is not so.

b (1) I.e., there would be nothing in this text to shew the contrary. (2) Which would *positively* prove it. (3) The burnt-offering is the principal source of the law, since it is there that the north is specified, whereas the sin-offering is only a secondary source, since it is derived from the former. (4) That a thing derived through a *hekkesh* cannot in turn teach through a *hekkesh*. (5) Lev. IV, 10. This refers to the burning of the *emurim* of the anointed priest's bullock for a sin-offering. (6) To intimate that these are burnt on the altar, as in the case of a peace-offering. (7) It is explicitly stated in v. 9. (8) As stated *supra* 41a. (9) As stated *supra* 39b. (10) *Sc.* dealing with the bullock of unawareness. It is so regarded because it is superfluous where it stands.

◁ *For the continuation of the English translation of this page see overleaf*

תורה אור

אבל כללו גמר מיניה א] (לצפון) שפיר אלא אי סבירא לן דלא הוא גמר מכללו ולא כללו גמר מיניה האי לגופיה איצטריך ב] כיון דאהדריה אהדריה אמר ליה מר זוטרא בריה דרב מרי לרבינא אימא ג] כי אהדריה קרא לגבי מתן דמים ואימורין דבעי כהונה אבל שחיטה דלא בעיא כהונה לא ד] מיבעי צפון א"כ נימא קרא כי כחטאת הוא מאי כחטאת האשם כשאר אשמות יהיה למה לי לאקשויי לחטאת למה לי לאקשויי לעולה אמר רבינא איצטריך אי אקשיה לחטאת ולא אקשיה לעולה הוה אמינא ה] חטאת מהיכן למדה מעולה דבר הלמד בהיקש חוזר ומלמד בהיקש א"ל מר זוטרא בריה דרב מרי לרבינא וניקשיה לעולה ולא ניקשיה ו] לחטאת הוה אמינא *דבר הלמד בהיקש חוזר ומלמד בהיקש וכי ז] תימא ניקשי אקושי לחטאת ניחא ליה דמקיש ליה לעיקר ולא נקיש ליה לטפל להכי אקשיה לחטאת ואקשיה לעולה למימר דבר הלמד בהיקש ח] שאינו חוזר ומלמד בהיקש רבא אמר מהכא דכתיב °כאשר יורם משור זבח השלמים למאי הלכתא אי ליותרת הכבד ושתי הכליות בגופיה כתיב ט] (אמר רב פפא) משום דבעי אגמורי יותרת הכבד ושתי הכליות י] מפר העלם דבר של צבור לשעירי עבודת כוכבים יא] בגופיה לא כתיב ומפר כהן משיח הוא דגמר להכי איצטריך כאשר יורם דנידוי כמאן דכתב בגופיה °ולא נידוי דבר הלמד בהיקש חוזר ומלמד בהיקש אמר ליה רב פפא לרבא וליכתביה בגופיה ולא נקיש אי כתב בגופיה ולא אקיש הוה אמינא *דבר הלמד בהיקש חוזר ומלמד בהיקש וכי תימא נקשי אקושי ניחא ליה דכתביה בגופיה מדאקיש ליה אקושי להכי כתביה ואקשיה למימרא דבר הלמד בהיקש אין חוזר ומלמד בהיקש: (היק"ש וגזיר"ה ש"ה ק"ל וחומ"ר יב] סימן): דבר הלמד בהיקש אין חוזר ומלמד *מהיקש אי מדרבא אי מדרבינא דבר הלמד בהיקש מהו שילמד בגזירה שוה תא שמע *רבי נתן בן אבטולמוס אומר °מנין לפריחה בבגדים שהיא טהורה נאמר קרחת וגבחת בבגדים ונאמר קרחת וגבחת באדם מה להלן פרח בכולו טהור אף כאן פרח בכולו טהור והתם מנא לן דכתיב °מראשו ועד רגליו ואיתקש ראשו לרגל מה להלן יג] כולו הפך לבן פרח בכולו טהור אף כאן כולו הפך לבן פרח בכולו טהור *אמר ר' יוחנן בכל התורה כולה יד] למידין למד מלמד חוץ מן הקדשים שאין דנין למד מלמד טו] דאם כן לא יאמר צפונה באשם ותיתי בג"ש טז] דקדשי קדשים מחטאות °לאו למימרא דדבר הלמד בהיקש אין חוזר ומלמד בגזירה שוה ודלמא משום דאיכא למיפרך מה לחטאת שכן מכפרת על חייבי כריתות יז] קדשי קדשים יתירי כתיבי: *דבר הלמד מהיקש חוזר ומלמד בקל וחומר מדתנא

ויקרא ד

שם יג

אבל כללו גמר מיניה · מידי דלא חידש בו כגון שחיטת לפון אי הוה כתיבא ביה ולא הוה כתיבא בשאר אשמות גמרי ליה שאר אשמות מיניה יח] דלא חידוש הוא אלא יצא מן הכלל הוא ולמד על דבר שלא נאמר בכלל (א) והיכי יט] יצא לידון בדבר החדש כגון מתן דמים שבזה למזבח ובזה שינה ואומר לבהונות: כיון דאהדריה כ] כו' · וכתיב כי כחטאת האשם הוא כדין חטאת כך דין אשם כא]: אהדריה · לכללו בין למתן דמים בין לשחיטת לפון ולא היה לריך לכתוב בו שחיטת לפון אלא לעיכובא: דבעי כהונה · שאינה כשירה בזר אבל כב] למידה דשחיטה דלאו עבודת כהן היא לא אהדריה דהא בחזרתו כתיב כחטאת האשם הוא לכהן לענין עבודות שבכהן: א"כ נימא קרא כי כחטאת הוא · לכהן: כשאר אשמות יהיה · הלכך לענין לפון נמי אהדריה וכי כתיב כג] ביה שחיטה בלפון דקרא לעיכובא אתא ושאר אשמות נמי מיניה ילפינן לעיכובא: למה לי לאקשויי בשחיטתו לחטאת ולעולה · דכתיב במקום אשר ישחטו את החטאת ואת העולה: מהיכן כד] למדו · לשחיטת לפון: אי אקשיה לעולה ולא אקשיה לחטאת הוה אמינא · בעלמא דבר הלמד בהיקש חוזר ומלמד בהיקש: וכי תימא · אם איתא דחוזר ומלמד בהיקש נקשיה לחטאת ולא לעולה משנינן לך ניחא ליה לאקשויי לעיקר כו': למימרא · מדאיצטריך למיהדר כה] ואקושי לעולה ש"מ דבר הלמד בהיקש אין חוזר ומלמד בהיקש ומהכא נפקא לן בכל דוכתא: כאשר יורם · באימורי פר כהן משיח כתיב: משום דבעי אגמורי יותרת הכבד ושתי כליות כו' · שהיה לריך ללמד מפר העלם תורת כו] אימוריהן לשעירי עבודת כוכבים דאיתקוש אהדדי לענין הקטרת אימורין כדאמרינן בפ' ב"ש (לעיל מא:) אשה לה' וחטאתם על שגגתם ופר העלם דבר בגופיה לא כתיב יותרת וכליות ומפר כהן משיח גמר בהיקש כדאמרן בפ' בית שמאי (שם לט:) ועשה לפר כאשר עשה לפר זה פר כהן משיח אקשינהו להדדי: להכי איצטריך כאשר יורם · בפר כהן משיח ואם איני ענין לו תנהו לענין פר העלם דניהוי כמאן דכתיבי בפר העלם גופיה דלא ליהוי דבר הלמד בהיקש חוזר ומלמד בהיקש ואי קשיא הא נפקא לן קך דרשה מועשה לפר זה פר העלם דבר כדאמרן בפרק ב"ש (ב) (לעיל מא:) ה"מ לתנא דבי ר' ישמעאל דאמר לפר זה פר העלם אבל לתנא דבי רב דאמר ועשה לפר זה פר יום הכיפורים איצטריך כאשר יורם להך דרשה: ונכתביה בגופיה · דפר העלם בהדיא ולא ליקשיה לפר כהן משיח הואיל וסוף סוף כז] טרח וכתב כאשר יורם יתירא להכי: הוה אמינא דבר הלמד בהיקש חוזר ומלמד בהיקש · בעלמא דלא הוה ילפינן מהכא מידי:

דבר הלמד בהיקש כו' · משום דבעי למיבעי בעיא עלה הדר נקיט לה: אי מדרבא · מכאשר יורס: אי מדרבינא · מאשם מצורע דאיצטריך לאקושי לחטאת ולעולה: לפריחה · אם פרחה הצרעת בכל הבגד: מה להלן פרח כח] בכולה טהור · כדכתיב אם פרוח תפרח וגו' (ויקרא יג): והתם · גבי קרחת וגבחת דאדם מנלן דטהורה פריחה דאילו פריחה כי כתיבא בנגע עור בשר כתיב ואילו קרחת וגבחת כתיבי גבי נתקין למקום שער דראש וזקן שאין סימניהן שוין לנגעי עור בשר שזה בשער לבן וזה בשער להוב: ואיתקש ראשו · נתקי הראש: אף כאן כו' · אלמא נתקין בהיקשא ילפינן להו וחוזרין ומלמדין כט] על הבגדים בג"ש: א"ר יוחנן · מהכא לא תיתי ראייה דלאו קדשים הוא דאף היקש מלמד בהיקש ל] חוץ מקדשים ותדע לך שהמדה הזאת שהבאתה אינה למידה בקדשים: דא"כ הוא · דדבר הלמד בהיקש חוזר ולמד בג"ש: לא יאמר לפון באשם ותיתי בג"ש · דנאמר לא] קדשי קדשים בחטאת ונאמר קדשי קדשים באשם: קדשי קדשים יתירי כתיבי · בהו והוה ליה גזירה שוה מופנה משני לדדין ואין משיבין עליה גבי חטאת כתיב תשחט החטאת קדש קדשים הוא ובאשם כתיב וזאת תורת האשם קדש קדשים הוא ובתרווייהו כתיב בויקח קרא לכל חטאתם ולכל אשמם אשר ישיבו לי קדש קדשים לך לב]:
מדתנא

אי אקשיה לעולה ולא אקשיה לחטאת · תימה לג] לא לכתוב את החטאת ואי דבר הלמד בהיקש חוזר ומלמד בהיקש אמאי אקשיה לעולה כלל תיפוק ליה לד] *מחטאת האשם דמה חטאת לפון מעכב אף אשם כן וי"ל דאי לא כתב לפון לא הוה אמינא לה] הא הדרה קרא לשחיטת לפון למידי דלא בעיא כהונה והאשם לא דרשינן ליה כלל דהא לא כתב כאשם דשוה משמע כשאר אשם דעלמא ללפון יהא זה אבל האשם משמע האשם זה יהא כחטאת למתן דמים לו] למזבח וכן *יש להקשות אי דבר הלמד בהיקש חוזר ומלמד בהיקש לא נכתוב לפון כלל ותיתי לז] [באשמות] מכחטאת וכאשם כי היכי דילפינן מיניה סמיכה בפרק קמא (לעיל יא·) *ועוד נילף שאר אשמות מאשם מצורע ואשם מצורע מהיקשא דכחטאת וי"ל דלא הוה אמינא דאהדריה קרא לשחיטת לפון ולא הוה דרשינן לח] כאשם כשאר אשם (כיון דלא כתב כאשם) כיון דלא כתב לפון בהדיא בשאר אשמות:

כאשר יורם למאי הלכתא · תימה הא איצטריך לכדדרשינן בסוף כל הבשר (חולין דף קיז·) זה בא ללמד ונמצא למד מה פר כהן משיח יש בו מעילה אף שור זבח השלמים יש בו מעילה וי"ל דמאי לאקשויי לזבח השלמים ולא ליכתוב כאשר יורם לט] דכאשר יורם משמע דאתא לרבויי הרמה אחרת אי נמי ההיא דכל הבשר (שם) כתנא דבי רבי ישמעאל דנפקא ליה דרשא דהכא מועשה לפר זה פר העלם מ] כדאמר פרק בית שמאי (לעיל דף מא·) אבל לתנא דבי רב דאמר ועשה לפר זה פר יום הכיפורים איצטריך כאשר יורם (*להך דרשא):

ונכתביה בגופיה · תימה כדאמר פרק ב"ש (גס זה שם:) משל למלך בשר ודם מא] שסרחה עליו מדינה ומיעט בסרחונם מפני מב] חיבתן וי"ל דבשביל חיבתן לא היה לו לגלגל אלו דרשות למילף מהיקשא ומ"מ ילפינן מיניה מג] חיבתן מדלא אשמעינן בדוכתא אחרינא דבר הלמד מהיקש אינו חוזר ומלמד בהיקש:

קדשי קדשים יתירי כתיבי. תימה כיון דילפינן גזרה שוה מהדדי למה לן היקשות דלעיל מד] בחטאת ואשם:
לא

צ"ל מכחטאת צ"ק

מו א מיי' פ"ב מהלכות טומאת צרעת הלכה ח:

ג"י צ"ק אין לוקשות ס' ועיני מכחטאת כאשם

נ"א

ג"י צ"ק ונילף שאר כו' די"ל דלא

[לקמן נס. נז. לעיל מח. יומא נ. מנחות כח. עח. סב:]

יומא ה:

[צ"ל בהיקש]

סנהדרין פו: [נדה יט. ושם איתא ר' יונתן וכ"ה בילקוט]

שבועות י. תמורה כח:

[לעיל מח.]

הגהות הב"ח

(א) רש"י ד"ה אבל כללו וכו' ונלפיכי ילא: (ב) ד"ה להכי איצטריך וכו' כפ' ב"ש תיבת לתנא דבי ר' ישמעאל:

גליון הש"ס

גמ' ולא ניהוי דבר הלמד בהיקש. ע' נז ע"ב תוד"ה ולכ"א: שם לאו למימרא דדבר הלמד כו'. עי' לעיל דף מח ע"א תוד"ס מה לכהן:

שיטה מקובצת

א] תיבת לצפון נמחק: ב] איצטריך והאי לגופיה איצטריך כיון: ג] עי' בהשמטות בסוף המסכת: ד] לא תיבעי · ס"א לא אהדריה א"כ כו': ה] עי' בהשמטות בסוף המסכת: ו] עי' בהשמטות בסוף המסכת: ז] תימא א"כ ניקשי כו' דמקיש לעיקר תיבת ליה ל"ש ונמחק: ח] בהיקש אינו חוזר ומלמד בהיקש רבא אמר דבר הלמד בהיקש אינו חוזר ומלמד בהיקש מהכא: ט] כתיב אלא משום ותיבות אמר רב פפא נמחק: י] הכליות כו' · ואע"ג דלעיל נפקא לן יותרת ושתי הכליות לשעירי ע"ז מלפר י"ל היינו לתנא דבי ר' ישמעאל אבל הכא איירי אליבא דרבי · מהר"פ: יא] כוכבים ופר העלם דבר של צבור בגופיה לא כתיב: יב] וחומר ובנין אב סימן: יג] מה להלן פרח בכולו טהור אף כאן פרח בכולו טהור: יד] כולה דנין למד מלמד: טו] דאם כן כו' א) מטילתיה דר' יוחנן בא להוכיח שמדה שהביא למעלה אינה נוהגת בקדשים · ת"א: טז] בקודש קדשים מחטאת לאו · ס"י למאי הלכתא כתביה רחמנא לאו: יז] קדש קדשים יתירא כתיבי·תימה כיון דאיכא ג"ש וילפינן מהדדי למה לן היקשות דלעיל דכחטאת האשם דכתיב גבי מצורע להחזירו לכללו תיפוק ליה מקדש הקדשים דהא כתיב קדש קדשים גבי אשם מצורע ונילף ליה בג"ש דקדש קדשים מחטאת להחזירו לכללו להטעינו מתן דמים ואימורים וי"ל דכיון שיצא אשם מצורע מן הכלל לידון בדבר החדש אי אתה יכול להחזירו לכללו בפירוש מכח הך ג"ש דקדש קדשים לא הוי חזרה בפירוש אפי' את"ל דג"ש חשיבא כמו היקש מ"מ האי ג"ש דקדש קדשים איצטריך למילי אחרינא [ולא להחזירו לכללו] לקמן לגבי פנימת המזבח דקאמר אשכחן שירי מנחה קדשי קדשים מנין ת"ל קדש קדשים ולכך לא הוי חזרה בפירוש מכח [הך] ג"ש אבל היקש דכחטאת האשם כולו להחזירו הוא דאתא ולכך חשיבא חזרה בפירוש · ומיהו קשה לעיל בפ"ק למה לי היקשא דכחטאת האשם גבי סתם אשם תיפוק ליה מג"ש דקדש קדשים לומר דטעון סמיכה לרבנן דר' אליעזר ולר"א לשלא לשמו ואמר מורי דשמא ג"ש לא ניתנה לדרוש רק גבי שחיטה משום דקדש קדשים דכתיב בין בסתם אשם בין באשם מצורע גבי שחיטה הוא דכתיב אבל בחטאת האשם דכתיב גבי סתם אשם דרשינן שפיר מיניה סמיכה דלגמרי מקיש הכתוב אשם לחטאת בהך היקשא כדכתיב כחטאת האשם תורה אחת לכם ועוד יש לומר דגבי סמיכה כתיב קרבנו דהוי מיעוט והוה מוקמינן ג"ש לדברים אחרים אבל השתא דאייתור היקשא לסמיכה מוקמינן (ג"ש) קרבנו לדרשא אחריתי וכן לר' אליעזר צריך היקש לשלא לשמו לאפוקי מהך היקשא דשלמים דזאת התורה: יח] מיניה דלאו חידוש: יט] והיכא דמי צא: כ] דאהדריה וכתב כי כחטאת: כא] אשם זה הס"ד: כב] אבל לגבי שחיטה דלאו: כג] כתיב שחיטה בצפון ריישא דקרא והיבת ביה נמחק: כד] מהיכן למדה: כה] ולאקשי לשלה: כו] תורת אימורין לשעירי כו' דאתקש להדדי לענין הקטרת אימורין כו' שגגתם חטאתם הרי לך כשגגתם ופר העלם: כז] סוף חזר וטרח: כח] פרח בכולו טהו': כט] ומלמדין בג"ש על הבגדים הס"ד: ל] בהיקש בכל התורה חוץ: לא] קדש קדשים בחטאת ונאמר קדש קדשים באשם הס"ד ומה"ד קדש קדשים יתירי: לב] לך הוא הס"ד: לג] תימה אי דבר הלמד כו' והשאר נמחק: לד] ליה מכחטאת האשם: לה] האי דהדריה קרא למידי דלא בעיא כהונה והאשם כשאר אשמות יהא לא הוה דרשינן ליה כלל תוס': לו] דמים ואימורין למזבח וכן יש להקשות ע"כ וא"ת אכתי אי דבר: לז] ותיתי מכחטאת האשם: לח] דרשינן האשם כשאר אשם יהא כיון: לט] יורם אלא כאשר יזבח השלמים דכאשר: מ] כדאמרי' פרק: מא] ידע שזעם על אוהבו ומיעט בסרחונו: מב] מפני חיבתו: מג] מיניה חיבתו וליכא למימר דכוליה להכי הוא דאתא לאשמעינן דדבר הבא בהיקש כו': מד] כחטאת האשם הס"ד ·

א) נראה דצ"ל ממילתיה דר"י הוא ובא להוכיח וכו' ·

Continuation of translation from previous page as indicated by ◁

which is learnt through a *hekkesh* and then in turn teaches through a *hekkesh*.[11] Said R. Papa to Raba: Then let [Scripture] write it in its own context,[12] and not assimilate [it to the anointed priest's bullock]?[13]—If [Scripture] wrote it in its own context, and did not teach it by assimilation, I would say, That which is learnt through c a *hekkesh* can in turn teach through a *hekkesh*;[1] and if you object, Then let Scripture assimilate it?[2] [I could answer that Scripture] prefers to write it [explicitly] in its own context rather than to teach it through a *hekkesh*. Therefore [Scripture] wrote it[3] and assimilated it, in order to teach that that which is learnt through a *hekkesh* does not in turn teach through a *hekkesh*.

(Mnemonic: *Hekkesh and gezerah shawah; kal wa-homer.*)[4] [It is agreed that] that which is learnt through a *hekkesh* does not in turn teach through a *hekkesh*, [this being learnt] either by Raba's or by Rabina's [exegesis]. Can that which is learnt through a *hekkesh* teach through a *gezerah shawah*?[5]—Come and hear: R. Nathan b. Abtolemos said: Whence do we know that a spreading outbreak [of leprosy] in garments [covering the whole] is clean? *Karahath* [baldness of the back of the head] and *gabbahath* [baldness of the front] are mentioned in connection with garments, and also in connection with man:[6] just as in the latter, if [the plague] spread over the whole skin, he is clean;[7] so in the former too, if it spread over the whole [garment], it is clean. And how do we know it there?[8] Because it is written, [*And if the leprosy ... cover all the skin ...*] *from his head even to his feet*,[9] and [thereby] his head[10] is assimilated [through a *hekkesh*] to his feet:[11] as there, when it is all turned white, having broken out all over him, he is clean; so here too, when it d breaks out all over him,[1] he is clean.[2] Said R. Johanan:[3] In the whole Torah we rule that whatever is learnt can teach, save in the case of sacrifices, where we do not rule that whatever is learnt can teach. For if it were so [that we did rule thus], let 'northward' not be said in connection with a guilt-offering, and it could be inferred from sin-offerings by the *gezerah shawah* of '*it is most holy*'.[4] Surely then its purpose is to teach that that which is learnt by a *hekkesh* does not in turn teach through a *gezerah shawah*.[5] But perhaps [we do not learn it there] because one can refute it: as for a sin-offering, [it requires north] because it makes atonement for those who are liable to *kareth*?—A superfluous '*most holy*' is written.[6]

That which is learnt through a *hekkesh* teaches in turn by a *kal*

(11) Which therefore shews that such is inadmissible. (12) *Sc.* in the section on the bullock of unawareness. (13) Since an extra text is required in any case, let it be written explicitly in its own context.

c (1) I.e., it would be possible to say so. (2) Let Scripture teach it through a *hekkesh*, without writing it explicitly. (3) In the passage dealing with the anointed priest. (4) V. *supra* 7b n. b 6. (5) Thus: The law, which is stated in A, is applied to B by a *hekkesh*; can that then be applied to C, because there is a *gezerah shawah* between B and C? Similarly in the other cases that follow. (6) Leprosy in man: Lev. XIII, 42f; in garments: ibid. 55. In connection with garments, *karahath* denotes leprosy on the inside (right) of the cloth; *gabbahath* on the front or outside thereof. (7) Ibid. 12-13. (8) That a *karahath* or *gabbahath* which spreads and covers the whole head is clean? For Lev. XIII, 12-13 refers to leprosy of the skin, not of the head; moreover, they differ in their symptoms. For the symptom of leprosy of the skin is that the hair turns white (ibid. v. 3, 12), whereas that of a *karahath* or *gabbahath* is that the hair turns yellow or reddish-white (ibid. 30, 42). (9) Ibid 12. (10) I.e., the leprosy of his head, such as a scale, or *karahath* or *gabbahath*. (11) I.e., to the rest of the body.

d (1) I.e., over his whole head or beard.—Emended text (Sh. M). (2) Thus we first learn by a *hekkesh* that a *karahath* or *gabbahath* in human beings covering the whole head is clean, and then that same law is applied to garments by a *gezerah shawah*. (3) In rebutting this proof. (4) Which is stated of both the sin-offering (Lev. VI, 18) and the guilt-offering (VII, 1). (5) For in fact the rule that what is learnt by a *hekkesh* cannot in turn teach by a *hekkesh* applies to sacrifices only, and it is now shewn that it cannot teach in turn through a *gezerah shawah* either. Whereas the passage quoted referred to a different subject, viz., leprosy, and there what is learnt through a *hekkesh* can teach in turn even through a *hekkesh*. (6) In Num. XVIII, 9. Since this is superfluous, a *gezerah shawah* could be learnt even though the guilt-offering is dissimilar from the sin-offering. The fact that we do not do so proves that what is learnt by a *hekkesh* does not, in the case of sacrifices, teach in turn by a *gezerah shawah*.

wa-ḥomer.[7] [50a] [This follows] from what the school of R. Ishmael taught.[8]

That which is learnt through a *hekkesh*, can it teach through a *binyan ab?*[9]—Said R. Jeremiah: Let 'northward' not be written in connection with a guilt-offering, and it could be inferred from a sin-offering by a *binyan ab.*[10] For what purpose then is it written? Surely to intimate that that which is learnt through a *hekkesh* cannot in turn teach through a *binyan ab*. Yet according to your
a reasoning, let it be inferred from a burnt-offering by a *binyan ab?*[1] Why then is it not so inferred? Because you can refute it: as for a burnt-offering, [it requires the north] because it is altogether burnt. So in the case of a sin-offering too, you can refute it: as for a sin-offering, [it requires the north] because it makes atonement for those who are liable to *kareth!*

One cannot be learnt from one; [but] let one be learnt from [the other] two?[2]—From which could it be derived? [Will you say,] Let the Divine Law not write it in the case of a burnt-offering, and it could be derived from a sin-offering and a guilt-offering; [then you can argue,] as for these, [they require the north] because they make atonement. Let not the Divine Law write it in respect of a sin-offering, and let it be derived from the others; [then you can argue,] as for those, the reason is because they are males.[3] Let not the Divine Law write it in connection with a guilt-offering and let it be derived from the others; [then you can argue,] the reason is because they operate in the case of a community as in the case of an individual.[4]

That which is learnt by a *gezerah shawah*, can it in turn teach through a *hekkesh?*—Said R. Papa, It was taught: *And this is the law of the sacrifice of peace-offerings . . . if he offers it for a thanksgiving:*[5] [from this] we learn that a thanksgiving can be brought from tithe,[6] since we find that a peace-offering can be brought from tithe.[7] And how do we know [this of] a peace-offering itself?—Because *'there'* is written in each case.[8] Said Mar Zuṭra the son of
b R. Mari to Rabina: But corn tithe is merely *ḥullin?*[1]—Said he to him: Who says[2] that which is learnt must be holy, and that which teaches must be holy?[3]

Can that which is learnt by a *gezerah shawah* teach by a *gezerah shawah?*—Said Rami b. Ḥama, It was taught: *Of fine flour soaked* [murbeketh]:[4] this teaches that the *rebukah* [soaked cake][5] must be of fine flour [*soleth*].[6] How do we know [the same of] *ḥalloth?*[7] Because *ḥalloth* is stated in both places.[8] How do we know it of *rekikin* [thin wafers]? Because *mazzoth* [unleavened bread] is written in connection with each.[9] Said Rabina to him: How do you know that he learns [the *gezerah shawah* of] *mazzoth, mazzth*, from *ḥalloth;* perhaps he learns it from oven-baked [cakes]?[10]—Rather said Raba: It was taught: *And its inwards, and its dung, [even the whole bullock] shall he carry forth [without the camp]:*[11] this teaches that he carries it forth whole.[12] You might think that he *burns* it whole; [but] *'its head and its legs'* is stated here, and *'its head and its legs'* is stated elsewhere:[13] as there it means after cutting up,[14] so here too it means after cutting up. If so, as there it is after the flaying [of the skin],[15] so here too it means after the flaying? Therefore it says, *'and its inwards and its dung'*. How does this teach [the reverse]?—Said R.
c Papa: Just as its dung is within it,[1] so must its flesh be within its skin. And it was [further] taught, Rabbi said: Skin and flesh and

(7) V. Glos. (8) V. *supra* 41a. (9) Analogy. This differs from a *hekkesh*, in that in a *hekkesh* Scripture intimates that there is a certain similarity between two subjects, whereas in a *binyan ab* (q.v. Glos.) the analogy is drawn from an inherent similarity between two subjects. (10) For these are analogous, since both are brought on account of sin.

a (1) For there it is *explicitly* stated, and the intermediate *hekkesh* is not required at all. (2) Let Scripture intimate that the north is required for two of these, and the third could then be deduced from it. (3) Whereas a sin-offering is a female. (4) Burnt-offerings and sin-offerings might be brought on behalf of the whole community, as public sacrifices, just as by an individual. But a guilt-offering could only be brought by an individual.—This whole passage is a digression. (5) Lev. VII, 11f. (6) A man can vow a thanksgiving and stipulate that he will purchase it with the redemption money of second tithe (v. *supra* 49a n.3). (7) And the thanksgiving is included therein by a *hekkesh*. (8) In connection with both a peace-offering and second tithe. Peace-offering: *And thou shalt sacrifice peace-offerings, and shalt eat* there (Deut. XXVII, 7); Tithe: *And thou shalt eat before the Lord thy God, in the place which He shall choose to cause His name to dwell* there, *the tithe of thy corn*—etc. Deut. XIV, 23. Thus the peace-offering is learnt by a *gezerah shawah*, and that is transferred to the thanksgiving by a *hekkesh*.

b (1) V. Glos. Whereas the question is about cattle tithe, which is holy. (2) The translation here is a paraphrase, and conveys the general sense. (3) I.e., it is unnecessary for both to be holy, but only one. We wish to learn about a peace-offering, and that indeed is holy. (4) Lev. VII, 12. (5) I.e., a cake made of flour that is first boiled. This is the Talmudic interpretation of *murbeketh*. (6) As opposed to *kemaḥ*, a coarse meal. (7) These are ordinary unleavened cakes. (8) Rebukah: *and ḥalloth* (E.V. *cakes*) *mingled with oil, of fine flour soaked;* ḥalloth (one of the three kinds of unleavened bread brought with a thanksgiving): *then he shall offer unleavened* (*mazzoth*) *cakes* (ḥalloth) *mingled with oil* (Ibid.) The word *ḥalloth* in both places shews that both must be of fine meal. (9) For *ḥalloth* v. preceding note; *rekikin: and unleavened wafers* (*rekike*—construct form of *rekikin*—*mazzoth*). Thus we first learn by a *gezerah shawah* that *ḥalloth* must be of fine flour, and then by a further *gezerah shawah* we learn from *ḥalloth* that *rekikin* too must be of fine flour. (10) Lev. II, 4: *And when thou bringest a meal-offering baked in an oven, it shall be unleavened cakes* (*ḥalloth mazzoth*) *of fine flour*. Thus it can be learnt direct, without any intermediate *gezerah shawah*. (11) Ibid. IV, 11f. (12) For if it were cut up, how could he carry them out at once, which the text implies? (13) Ibid. I, 8-9; 12-13. (14) Since *'the pieces'* are mentioned. (15) This being explicitly ordered (I, 6).

c (1) For it would be repulsive to take it out and burn it separately.

טז א מיי' פט"ו מהל' מעשה"ק הל' יז:

יז ב מיי' פ"ז מהל' מעשר שני הל' יב:

יח ג ד ה מיי' פ"ה מהל' מעשה הקרבנות הלכה ג:

ג"י ל"ק כדפירש פי' אלו דברים ופ"ש דף סו ע"א

תורה אור

מדתנא דבי ר' ישמעאל דבר הלמד בהיקש מהו שילמד בבנין אב אמר רבי ירמיה לא לכתוב צפונה באשם ותיתי מבנין אב א] מחטאת למאי הלכתא כתביה לאו למימרא דדבר הלמד בהיקש אין חוזר ומלמד בבנין אב וליטעמיך תיתי מבנין אב מעולה ב] מאי טעמא לא אתי משום דאיכא למיפרך מה לעולה שכן כליל חטאת נמי איכא למיפרך מה לחטאת שכן מכפרת על חייבי כריתות חדא מחדא לא אתיא תיתי ג]חדא מתרתי מהי תיתי לא נכתוב רחמנא ד] עולה ותיתי מחטאת ואשם מה להנך שכן מכפרין לא נכתוב רחמנא בחטאת ותיתי מהנך מה להנך שכן זכרים לא נכתוב באשם ותיתי מהנך מה להנך שכן ישנן בציבור כביחיד דבר הלמד בגז"ש מהו °שילמד בהיקש אמר רב פפא ה] °וזאת תורת זבח השלמים [וגו'] אם על תודה (ויקרא ז) אלמדנו לתודה שבא מן המעשר *מדאשכחן בשלמים דאתו ממעשר שלמים גופייהו מנא לן דכתיב °שם °שם (דברים כז, יד) א"ל מר זוטרא בריה דרב מרי לרבינא *מעשר דגן חולין בעלמא הוא א"ל (א) אמר אמרה °למד קדש ומלמד קדש דבר הלמד בג"ש °מהו שילמד בג"ש אמר רמי בר חמא תניא °סלת מרבכת (ויקרא ז) למדנו ילרבוכה שבאה סולת חלות ו] מניין ת"ל יחלות חלות הרקיקין מניין ת"ל מצות מצות אמר ליה רבינא ממאי דמצות מצות מחלות גמר דלמא ממאפה תנור גמר אלא אמר רבא *תניא °וקרבו ופרשו והוציא (שם ד) מלמד שמוציאו שלם יכול ישרפנו שלם נאמר כאן ז] °ראשו וכרעיו ונאמר להלן °ראשו וכרעיו (שם א) מה להלן ע"י ניתוח אף כאן על ידי ניתוח אי מה להלן בהפשט אף כאן ח] נמי בהפשט תלמוד לומר וקרבו ופרשו מאי תלמודא א"ר פפא כשם שפרשו בקרבו כך בשרו בעורו ותניא *רבי אומר נאמר כאן עור ובשר [ופרש] ונאמר

רש"י

מדתני דבי רבי ישמעאל. בפרק ב"ש (לעיל דף מא.) ומה במקום שלא הושוו קרבן לקרבן ט] ואוקימנא התם דקסבר ר' ישמעאל דבר הלמד בהיקש חוזר ומלמד בקל וחומר: בבנין אב. מה מליט י] וכולן שאילות הללו בקדשים נשאלו וארבעה שאילות בכל מדה ומדה כגון דבר הלמד בהיקש מהו שילמד בהיקש ובגזרה שוה ובקל וחומר ובבנין אב ודבר הלמד בגזרה שוה מהו שילמד בהיקש ובג"ש וק"ו ובבנין אב ודבר הלמד יא] בבנין אב מהו שילמד בכולן: וליטעמיך. אי משום הא כתביה לייתי מעולה דכתיב בה בהדיא: שכן מכפרת כו'. ואין לך לפרש יב] שאילתייהו מכאן: מחדא לא אתיא כו'. יג]מילתא באפיה נפשה היא ולאו למיפשט בעיין: עולה לגבי חטאת ואשם לא חשיבה כפרת עשה דידיה כפרה: למדנו לתודה. מכאן בהיקש משלמים שבאה מן המעשר אם פירש בשעת נדרו ע"מ להביאה ממעות מע"ש: שם שם. בשלמים כתיב (דברים כז) וזבחת שלמים ואכלת שם ובמעשר כתיב (שם יד) ואכלת לפני ה' אלהיך במקום אשר יבחר לשכן שמו שם מעשר דגנך תירושך ויצהרך ובכורות: חולין הוא. ואנן בקדשים קמיבעיא לן: אמר אמרה. יד] האמור למד קדש ומלמד קדש בתמיה וכי שניהן צריכין שיהו טו] בקדשים הואיל ולמד קדש כגון שלמים שפיר מיפשט בעיין דבתר למד אזלינן ומר זוטרא סבר בתר מלמד טז]אזלינן והיינו דאמרינן בעלמא (לעיל דף מה. ולקמן דף ס:) הניחא למ"ד בתר למד אזלינן: למדנו יז] רבוכה. חלות מבושלות במים תחילה שבתודה שבאה סולת ולא קמח: חלות שבתודה מניין. שלשה מינין מלה יש בה חלות רקיקין רבוכה חלות שבה מניין שהן סולת: ת"ל חלות חלות. נאמר בחלות חלות ונאמר ברבוכה חלות: מצות מצות. נאמר ברקיקין מצות ונאמר בחלות מצות וילפינן רקיקין מחלות וחלות יח]למדו מרבוכה ושניהם בגז"ש: וממאי. דרקיקין דתודה מצות מצות מחלות דתודה גמרי: דלמא ממצות דכתיב גבי רקיקין יט] מנחת מאפה גמרי. והתם סלת בהדיא כתיב סלת חלות מצות בלולות בשמן ורקיקי מצות משוחים בשמן (ויקרא ב): כ]מלמד שמוציא את כל הפר שלם. דאי במנתח היאך כא] הכל יוציא בהוצאה אחת הנתחים וקרבו ופרשו: נאמר כאן כב] ראשו וכרעיו. על ראשו ועל כרעיו (שם ד): ונאמר להלן ראשו וכרעיו. *בעולת בן נאן כתיב וערך הכהן את הראש וכתיב וקרבו וכרעיו ירחץכג] (שם א): מה להלן ע"י ניתוח. היה מקטירו דניתוח כתיב ביה: אף שריפה של זה ע"י ניתוח. ובפר כהן משיח קאי: כשם שפרשו בקרבו כו'. דאיתקש שריפת עורו ובשרו לשריפת קרבו ופרשו: מה פרשו בקרבו. דדבר מגונה הוא להוציאו ולשורפו בעין: ונאמר

תוספות

לא נכתוב רחמנא בעולה ותיתי מחטאת ואשם כד]. פי' ולכתוב בהדיא לפון בחטאת ואשם ואם תאמר ולכתוב בזבחי שלמי לבור ונילף עולה מינייהו וי"ל דאיכא למיפרך דמה לזבחי שלמי ליבור שכן זמן קבוע ועוד דחטאת לא אתי כה]מיניה שכן זכרים ואשם שכן איט בליבור וא"ת למהלי לאקושי לקמן (דף נה.) זבחי שלמי ליבור לעולה תיפוק לי בבנין אב וכי תימא לאשמועי' שהם קדשי קדשים כעולה הוי מצי למילף מדאיתקש לחטאת כו] וי"ל דאיכא למיפרך שכן תדיר *כדמפרש בפרק תמיד נשחט (פסחים דף סה.) אי נמי מה לאשם שלמים שכן אינן טעונין לפון וא"ת בפ"ק דשבועות (דף ח. ושם) דיליף שעיר דר"ח משעיר חיצון דאינו מכפר אלא על טומאת מקדש וקדשיו דקאמר הואיל וזה בא לזמן קבוע ושעיר הנעשה בחוץ קאמר כדפירש התם בקונטרס דאי מפנימי כז] הוה ליה למיפרך שכן נכנס דמה. לפני ולפנים ועוד דאדרבה נילף משעיר המשתלח דמכפר בשאר עבירות אבל השתא אי מחיצון גמר ניחא דדמו אהדדי טפי משעיר המשתלח והשתא אי מחיצון גמר א"כ תפשוט דדבר הלמד בהיקש חוזר ומלמד בבנין אב דחיצון גופיה לא ידענא אלא מהיקשא דפנימי וי"ל דהא אמרינן התם דגילוי מילתא בעלמא הוא וא"ת והיכי גמר בפ"ב דבילה (דף כ.) סמיכה בשלמי חובה בבנין אב כח] (משלמי נדבה) [מעולת חובה] והא עולת חובה מכמשפט ילפא דהיינו היקש וי"ל דקושיא בעלמא הוא דפריך התם ממאי דבית הלל כו' דלמא מעולת חובה גמרי כלומר אם תימלי לומר דדבר הלמד בהיקש חוזר ומלמד בבנין אב ועו"ק כט] בהקומץ רבה (מנחות דף כא:) נאמר הבא מנחה והבא מלח ונאמר הבא מנחה והבא עלים מה עלים משל ליבור אף מלח משל ליבור ועלים גופייהו לא ידעינן אלא מדאיתקש למזבח דכתיב (ויקרא א) על העלים אשר על האש אשר על המזבח מה מזבח משל ליבור וכו': אם על תודה כו'. הקשה ה"ר יעקב מאורליינ"ש בפרק דם חטאת (לקמן דף לח.) ובפ' התודה (מנחות דף פג.) דאמר מה חטאת אינה באה אלא מן החולין למה לי הא שלמים ותודה שני כתובין הבאין כאחד ואין מלמדין עוד קשה היכי יליף התם מחטאת כיון דאיכא שלמים ותודה דבאין מן המעשר דלא ילפינן בהיקשא דזאת התורה אלא דבר שיכול לנהוג בכל הנזכרים בפסוק דמהאי טעמא מיבעי לן קרא בפ"ב דבילה (דף כ.) ל] עולת חובה טעונה סמיכה ולא ילפינן *מהיקשא דזאת התורה משום דסמיכה לא בעי בכולהו דבכור ומעשר לא בעו סמיכה כדתנן פרק שתי מדות (מנחות דף צג.) וי"ל דכל חובה מקשינן לחטאת מה חטאת דבר שבחובה ואינו בא אלא מן החולין לא] כדמוכח בפרק התודה (שם דף פג.) ול"ע מנחת נדבה דאינה באה אלא מן החולין מנ"ל וא"ת בפ"ק דחגיגה (דף ח.) דדריש מסת מלמד שאדם מביא חגיגתו מן החולין למה לי הלא חובה היא ותיפוק לי מהיקש וי"ל משום דקאמר התם דחגיגה באה נמי מן המעשר אילטריך מסת למימר דאינה באה הכל מן המעשר אלא מן החולין ומן המעשר מתרווייהו אי נמי משום דכתיב כאשר יברכך בסיפיה דקרא סלקא דעתך דאתיא לב] ממעשר להכי אילטריך מסת: אמר אמרה. לג] ורבינו שמואל מפרש אימר אמרת שמא אתה רוצה לומר שנכנס בעינן קדש ורבינו תם גרים אמי אמרה ואמי שם חכם לד] וביבמות פרק הערל (דף פ.) היינו דשמעינן ליה לאמי כל שמעתי אמו לקוי ובכתובות (דף מד:) לה] אמר רבא תני אמי בתולת ישראל ולא בתולת גרים וא"ת דלמר זוטרא לא איפשיטא בעיא ובסוף אלו מנחות (מנחות עו.) אמרינן לחמי תודה ונזירות באות עשר עשר לחמי תודה בהדיא כתיב בהן פירוש דכתיב ממנו אחד מכל קרבן תרומה לה' ואמר בפרק התודה (שם דף עז:) נאמר כאן תרומה ונאמר להלן בתרומת מעשר תרומה מה להלן אחד מעשרה אף כאן אחד מעשרה ונזירות מהיקש דאמר מר על זבח תודת שלמיו לרבות שלמי נזיר פי' לכל דין לחמי תודה לעשרה קבין ירושלמית וחצי לוג שמן ושיהו באות י' אלמא דין דתודה אתיא בג"ש חוזרת ומלמדת בהיקש לו] *ותו בההיא שמעתא לעיל ילפינן דכל המנחות באות עשר בבנין אב מלחמי תודה דאתיא בג"ש מתרומת מעשר ואם כן תפשוט דדבר הלמד בג"ש חוזר ומלמד בבנין אב ובההיא שמעתא גופה פריך התם אי ס"ל דדבר הלמד בג"ש חוזר ומלמד בבנין אב נילף מחביתין וי"ל דתרומת מעשר דהתם חולין הוא כדקאמר הכא מעשר דגן חולין הוא ומיהו הך קשיא לז] לרבינא דס"ל הכא בתר למד אזלינן ובסמוך אמרינן תיקו ודוחק לומר דלרבינא איפשטא ליה כמו כן בעיא דלקמן מההיא דמנחות: מה להלן ע"י ניתוח שלא בהפשט. ואם תאמר היכי יליף מהכא דדבר הלמד בג"ש חוזר ומלמד בג"ש דילפינן פר יום הכפורים בנתוח שלא בהפשט מפר כהן משיח וניתוח בפר כהן משיח גמרינן מעולה הלא כה"ג אפילו למד בהיקש חוזר ומלמד בהיקש לח] כיון דהוי הימנו ודבר אחר לט] דשלא בהפשט בפר כהן משיח מדאיתקש עור ובשר לפרש יליף כדפירש בקונטרס *ודבר הלמד בהיקש אינו חוזר ומלמד בגזירה שוה ושמא אין זה היקש אלא גילוי מילתא בעלמא וי"ל דשלא בהפשט

שיטה מקובצת

א] מחטאת למאי הלכתא כתביה רחמנא כו'. תימה דהיכא בעי למילף לענין בנין אב הא איצטריך לאשמועינן דדבר הלמד בהיקש אינו חוזר ומלמד בג"ש כדקאמר לעיל ולעולם חוזר ומלמד בבנין אב וי"ל דמ"מ שפיר מוכח דאי סובר חוזר ומלמד בבנין אב א"כ לשתוק מצפונה דאשם דאין לו לכתבו שלא לצורך ובמקום אחר ישמיענו דאין היקש חוזר ומלמד. והקשה הר"ם היכא מוכח זה דלמא ניחא ליה למיכתביה בגופה מדמקיש ליה אקשי דהא קאמר לעיל כי האי סברא דבשלמא לעיל גבי לא לכתוב צפון באשם ותיתי בקדשי קדשים מחטאת ליכא למיפרך הכי דהא ג"ש חשיבא כתיב בגופיה כמו היקש דכתיב במקום אשר (תשחט) [ישחטו את העולה (תשחט)][ישחטו את] האשם אבל הכא גבי בנין אב קשיא דודאי היקש חשיב כתיב בגופיה יותר מבנין אב ותירץ דדוקא היינו קודם שידענו שהקדשים חלוקים מן החולין לענין למד מלמד אז דחינו לעיל בסברא קלה כדי להשוותו לחולין אבל מאחר שלמדנו שההיקש מהיקש נשתנה מחולין אז יש לקיים המדות ולא לדחות בסברא קלה. מהר"פ: ב] מעולה אלא מעולה מאי: ג] תיבת הדא נמחק: ד] רחמנא בעולה ותיתי: ה] א"ר פפא תניא וזאת תורת זבח השלמים וגו' אם על תודה יקריבנו למדנו לתודה שהיא באה מן המעשר כו' ממעשר ושלמים גופייהו מנא ליה: ו] חלות שבתודה מנין ת"ל חלות חלות. ס"י לג"ש מה חלות האמורות ברבוכה סולת אף חלות האמורות בכולן סולת והלא רקיקין לא נאמר בהן סולת מנין שיהו סולת ת"ל מצות מצות מה מצות האמורות בכולן סולת אף מצות האמורות בכאן סולת: ז] ראש וכרעים תאמר להלן ראש וכרעים: ח] תיבת נמי נמחק: ט] לקרבן כו' ואוקימנא התם דקסבר תנא דבי רבי ישמעאל: י] מציט וכל שאילות הללו: יא] הלמד בק"ו מהו שילמד בהיקש ובג"ש ובק"ו ובבנין אב ודבר הלמד בבנין אב וכו': יב] שאלתינו: יג] כו'. אי דבר הלמד בהיקש

מנחות פג.

[לעיל מה. לקמן ס: מכות יג. תמורה כח.]

הגהות הב"ח

(א) גמ' אמר ליה אמר אמרה. נ"ב עי' זה בתוס' דף מא ע"א:

[יומא סח.]

[שם סו.]

עי' רש"י יומא סח. ד"ה ונאמר להלן וגו'

גליון הש"ס

גמ' מהו שילמד בהיקש. עי' לעיל דף יא ע"א תוס' ד"ה בא: שם למד קדש. עי' לקמן דף סה ע"ב: שם מהו שילמד בג"ש. עי' לעיל דף מד ע"א תוס' ד"ה ולחם: רש"י ד"ה ונאמר להלן כו' בעולה כו'. עי' בתשובת חכם צבי סי' יג: תוס' ד"ה אמר וכו'. עי' לקמן דף נו ע"ב תוס' ד"ה פיים:

ד"ה ודבר הלמד כו' וגי' צ"ק ולא סוי דבר הלמד בהיקש אינו חוזר ומלמד בגזירה שוה דשמא אין כו'

חוזר ומלמד בבנין אב תיתי הדא בבנין אב מתרתי דהדא כתיבא והדא ילפא בהיקשא הס"ד ואח"כ מה"ד שכן מכפרת. עולה לגבי: יד] אמר אמרה: אמר האומר למד: טו] שיהו קדשים: טז] מלמד נמי אזלינן: יז] למדנו לרבוכה. שבתודה חלות מבושלות במים תחלה שבאה ותיבת שבתודה נמחק: יח] וחלות למדנו: יט] רקיקין דמנחת מאפה: כ] בשמן הס"ד ומה"ד והוציא משמע ההוצאה אחת הס"ד ומה"ד מלמד: כא] היאך יוציא הכל בהוצאה: כב] כאן ראש וכרעים: כג] ירחץ וגו': כד] מחטאת ואשם. פי' ולכתוב כו' ואשם דאל"כ לא ידעינן ליה בחטאת ואשם גופיה דלא כתיב צפון אלא בעולה וא"ת: כה] אתי מינייהו שכן: כו] לחטאת לקמן וי"ל: כז] מפנימי גמר הוה ליה: כח] בבנין אב מעולת חובה ועולת חובה מכמשפט כו' והשאר נמחק: כט] ועוד קשה דאמרינן בהקומץ: ל] דעולת חובה: לא] החולין אף כל דבר שבחובה אינו בא אלא מן החולין ושלמים מתודה ... עלי אין באין אלא מן החולין כדמוכח: לב] דאתיא מן המעשר להכי: לג] אמר אמרה. רש"י גרים אמר אמרה כלומר שלא היו יודעים שם החכם שאמרה ולכך אמר אמרה. ורבינו שמואל גרים ... מפרש נמחק: לד] חכם כמו דאמר ביבמות כו' ליה לאמי ס"א זו אינו משנה (פי' כי שם גרסי' רב אמי): לה] ובכתובות *) היינו דשמענא לאמי בתולה בתולת (הבתולות) [ישראל כו'] וא"ת: לו] בהיקש על ... : לז] קשיא בתרייתא קשה לרבינא: לח] כיון שניתן לדרוש לענין שלא בהפשט ואינו בא בג"ש בפר כהן משיח אתי ניתוח בהדי אגב גררא [והוי הימנו]: לט] אחר ועוד קשה דשלא:

*) ושם בכתובות הגי' ממאי מדתני אמי בתולת ישראל ולא בתולת גרים כמ"ש בתוס' כאן וגי' רבינו ז"ל בזה צ"ע

ונאמר להלן עור ובשר ופרש א] מה להלן ע"י ניתוח שלא בהפשט אף כאן ע"י ניתוח שלא בהפשט. דבר הלמד בגזירה שוה מהו שילמד בק"ו ק"ו ומה היקש שאינו מלמד ב] בהיקש אי מדרבא אי מדרבינא מלמד בקל וחומר מדתנא דבי רבי ישמעאל גז"ש המלמדת בהיקש מדרב פפא אינו דין שתלמד בק"ו הניחא למאן דאית ליה דרב פפא אלא למאן דלית ליה דרב פפא מאי איכא למימר אלא קל וחומר ומה היקש שאין מלמד בהיקש אי מדרבא אי מדרבינא מלמד בק"ו מדתנא דבי רבי ישמעאל ג] גזירה שוה המלמדת בגז"ש חבירתה *מדרמי בר חמא אינו דין שתלמד בק"ו *דבר הלמד בגז"ש מהו שילמד בבנין אב תיקו. דבר הלמד בקל וחומר מהו שילמד בהיקש ק"ו ומה גזירה שוה שאינה למדה ד] בהיקשא מדר' יוחנן מלמד בהיקש מדרב פפא קל וחומר הלמד מהיקש מדתנא דבי ר' ישמעאל אינו דין שילמד בהיקש הניחא למאן דאית ליה דרב פפא אלא למאן דלית ליה דרב פפא °מאי איכא למימר תיקו. דבר הלמד בקל וחומר מהו שילמד בגזירה שוה קל וחומר ומה גזירה שוה שאינה למידה בהיקשא מדרבי יוחנן מלמד בגזירה שוה ה] מדרמי בר חמא קל וחומר הלמד בהיקש מדתנא דבי רבי ישמעאל אינו דין ו] שתלמד בגז"ש. *דבר הלמד בקל וחומר מהו שילמד בקל וחומר ק"ו ומה גזירה שוה שאינה למידה בהיקש מדר' יוחנן ז] מלמד בק"ו כדאמרן ק"ו הלמד מהיקש מדתנא דבי רבי ישמעאל אינו דין שילמד בקל וחומר וזהו ק"ו בן ק"ו ח] בן בנו של ק"ו הוא אלא ק"ו ומה היקש שאינו למד בהיקש אי מדרבא אי מדרבינא מלמד בק"ו מדתנא דבי רבי ישמעאל ק"ו הלמד מהיקש מדתני דבי רבי ישמעאל אינו דין שילמד בק"ו וזהו ק"ו בן קל וחומר. דבר הלמד בקל וחומר מהו שילמד בבנין אב אמר רבי ירמיה תא שמע *מלק ונמצאת טריפה ר"מ אומר אינה מטמאה בבית הבליעה רבי יהודה אומר *מטמאה בבית הבליעה אמר ר' מאיר קל וחומר ומה נבלת בהמה שמטמאה במגע ובמשא שחיטתה מטהרת טריפתה מטומאתה נבילת עוף שאין מטמא במגע ובמשא אינו דין שתהא שחיטתה מטהרת טריפתה מטומאתה מה מצינו בשחיטה שמכשרתה באכילה

מטהרת

ונאמר להלן. בפר כהן משיח (ויקרא ד) ונאמר כאן בפר ושעיר של יום הכיפורים (שם טז) ואת פר החטאת ואת שעיר החטאת וגו' ואת עורותם ואת בשרם ואת פרשם: מה להלן. בפר כהן משיח: ע"י ניתוח. דילפינן מג"ש מעולה: ק"ו. כלומר מק"ו נלמד לפרש לך שאלה זו: ה"ג ומה היקש שאינו מלמד בהיקש כו'. ול"ג למד: ג"ש המלמדת בהיקש גרסי' ולא גרסי' למדה: מדרב פפא. וזאת תורת זבח השלמים כו' דפשט רב פפא ט] מיניה לגזירה שוה חוזרת ומלמדת בהיקש: הניחא למאן דאית ליה דרב פפא. דאמר בתר למד אזלינן: אלא למאן דאמר. בתר מלמד אזלינן לא אשכחן גז"ש חוזרת ומלמדת בהיקש דהתם מעשר י] חולין הוא המלמדה: בגז"ש חבירתה. מה שאין היקש עושה כן בהיקש חבירו: מדרמי בר חמא. סלת מורבכת חלות: שאינה למידה מן ההיקש גרסי': מדר' יוחנן. לא יאמר לפונה באשם משם למדנו שאין דבר הלמד בהיקש מלמד בגז"ש: שאינה למידה בהיקש. כלומר מן ההיקש: יא] מלמד בק"ו. כדאמר לעיל מק"ו ומה היקש שאינו למד מן ההיקש מלמד בק"ו גז"ש המלמדת מגז"ש חבירתה מדרמי בר חמא וכו': וזהו ק"ו בן קל וחומר. ק"ו זה שאנו מביאין כאן לדורשו בתורה ללמד ק"ו מק"ו אנו למידין אותו מדבר שאף הוא לא למדנוהו אלא בק"ו דהא מייתי לה מגז"ש המלמדת בק"ו והיא גופא לא ידעינן לה אלא ע"י ק"ו דבק"ו ילפינן לעיל: ופרכינן בן בנו של ק"ו הוא. שאפי' היינו למידין אותו מדבר שלא למדנוהו ע"י ק"ו יב] הוא היה עצמו בן ק"ו שהרי בק"ו אנו למדין אותו כדאמרן לעיל יג] בק"ו ומה גז"ש כו' עכשיו שאף גז"ש שאנו למידין אותו ממנו לדורשה בתורה אף היא לא למדה שתלמד בק"ו אלא מק"ו נמצא שאתה מביא מדת קלוחומר בתורה מכח שני קלין וחמורין והו"ל בנו של ק"ו ובן בנו של ק"ו ודלמא כולי האי לית לן למילף ומיזל: אלא. לא תרביה מגזירה שוה המלמדת בק"ו דהיא גופה מק"ו אתיא לן אלא יליף ליה מהיקש המלמד בק"ו דנפקא לן ממתניתא דתני דבי רבי ישמעאל דגמרא גמר לה דדבר יד] המלמד בהיקש חוזר ומלמד בקל וחומר והשתא לא הוי אלא קל וחומר בן קל וחומר כי איכך לעיל דגזירה שוה מלמדת בקל וחומר מקל וחומר: מטמאה בבית הבליעה. כדין נבלת עוף טהור דאין מליקת טריפה בקדשים מטהרת מידי נבלה והוא הדין נמי לשוחט עוף חולין טריפה מטמאה לרבי יהודה. שלשמחלוקת בדבר לר"מ אחת שחיטת טו] עוף של חולין ואחת מליקה בקדשים מטהרות טריפתן מידי נבילה ולר' יהודה זו וזו אינה מטהרת ולר' יוסי שחיטה מטהרת ולא מליקה וכן טז] מפרש במסכת טהרות בפרק שלש עשרה דברים: שחיטתה מטהרת טריפתה מטומאתה. כדאמרינן בהעור והרוטב (חולין דף קכח:) וכי ימות מן הבהמה וגו' מקצת בהמה מטמאה ומקצת בהמה אינה מטמאה ואיזו זו טריפה ששחטה: נבלת עוף יז] אינו מטמא במגע ובמשא. מבחוץ דכתיב (ויקרא כב) לטמאה בה אין לך אלא האמור בה אכילה ולא מגע ומשא: אינו דין שתהא שחיטתה מטהרת טריפתה מטומאתה. והשתא דקי"ל שחיטה דמטהרת בחולין מק"ו הדרא ומיגמרא אמליקה דקדשים בבנין אב: מה מצינו בשחיטה שמכשרת. יח] לאכול בחולין ומטהרת טריפתה מטומאתה אף מליקה כו':

הכי

בהפשט נקט אגב אורחיה ולא צריך למילף יט] למגופיה דפר יום הכפורים שמעינן דכתיב (ויקרא טז) ושרפו באש את עורותם ואת בשרם ואת פרשם דאיתקש עורם ובשרם לפרשם:

אלא למאן דל"ל דרב פפא מאי איכא למימר. °ורב אדא בר אהבה דיליף לעיל לפון דמעכב בעולה מק"ו מחטאת והדר יליף אשם מדאיתקש לעולה כ] היינו למצוה דלמצוה בעולה כתיב *ומיהא מדאיתקש תרי זימני אעולה הוא דילפינן עיכובא באשם וא"ת דבפ' אמר להם הממונה (יומא דף לב.) משמע דקידוש ידים ורגלים הבא בק"ו חוזר ומלמד בהיקש דקאמר ר"ש בן אלעזר ק"ו ומה במקום שאין טעון טבילה טעון קידוש מקום שטעון טבילה אינו דין שטעון קידוש כו' והדר קאמר מקיש פשיטה ללבישה מה לבישה טעון קידוש אף פשיטה טעון קידוש וי"ל דהאי לא איקרי קדשים אלא גוף הקרבן דוקא:

בן בנו של ק"ו הוא. כא] וכולי האי לית לן למילף ולמיזל וקשה כיון דק"ו כב] הוא אמאי לא נילף שפיר כל כמה דמצינן למילף כי היכי דילפינן בג"ש אפילו הן מאה ויש לפרש כג] בן בנו של ק"ו הוא משום דמעיקרא הוא דמבעיא ליה אי דבר הלמד בק"ו *חוזר ומלמד בג"ש היאך בא להוכיח מדהוו בק"ו בג"ש שמלמדה בק"ו ע"י ק"ו א"כ אתה רוצה לדון ק"ו ע"י ק"ו מדבר הבא בקל וחומר הלא זאת היא שאלתך שאתה מסופק בה:

רבי יהודה אומר מטמאה בגדים בבית הבליעה. פי' בקונטרס דבמס' טהרות (פ"א) משמע דלר"מ אחת שחיטה בעוף של חולין ואחת מליקה בקדשים מטהרות טרפותן מידי נבילה ולרבי יהודה זו וזו אינה מטהרת וא"ת דבפרק אלו טריפות (חולין דף נו.) אמרינן רבי יהודה בדיק בידא ור' נחמיה בדיק במחטא וא"ל מאן דבדיק במחטא למאן דבדיק בידא עד מתי אתה מאכיל נבילות לישראל נבילות ס"ד הא שחוטות נינהו מאי קשיא לרבי יהודה ודאי נבילות הויין כדמשמע הכא דשחיטת עוף אינה מטהרת וי"ל דלא הו"ל למיפרך אליבא דרבי יהודה כיון דרבנן פליגי עליה:

מה נבלת בהמה שמטמאה במגע ובמשא כו'. תימה מה לנבלת בהמה שאינה מטמאה כד] בבית הבליעה וי"ל דעיקר טעמא דר"מ מהיקשא דזאת תורת הבהמה והעוף כדלקמן פ' חטאת העוף (דף סט:) כדפי' בקונט':

מה מצינו בשחיטה של עוף שמכשרתה באכילה וכו'. ודאי ולא היא תרוייהו משחיטת חולין גמרי פי' מליקת קדשים במה מצינו משחיטת עוף שאינה כי אם בחולין ושחיטת עוף של חולין בק"ו משחיטת בהמה חולין ותימה היאך גמר מליקת עוף משחיטת עוף מה לשחיטה שכן מכשרת בחולין ועוד קשה דמנא ליה דמליקת עוף משחיטת עוף גמר כה] דלמא משחיטה דבהמה גמר ונראה לי דאם כן הוה גמר בק"ו כדגמר שחיטת עוף והיינו טעמא

דלא

יט א מיי' פ"ז מהל' פסולי המוקדשין הלכה ג:

גי' נ"ק ומהא דאיתקש תרי זימנין לעולה הוא כו'

גי' נ"ק אי מדרמי בר חמא אי מרבא אינו דין

חוזר ומלמד בק"ו היאך בא להוכיח דהוו בק"ו כו' נ"ק

[מנחות עו.]

עי' רש"ק

לקמן דף סט.

גליון הש"ס

גמ' מאי איכא למימר תיקו. עיין לקמן דף נה ע"א תוס' ד"ה מה עולה: תוס' ד"ה אלא וכו' ורב אדא בר אהבה. עי' לקמן דף נה ע"א תוס' ד"ה מה עולה:

שיטה מקובצת

א] מה להלן כו' שלא בהפשט אלמא דדבר הלמד בג"ש חוזר ומלמד בג"ש [דבר כו']. וא"ת דהיכי יליף מהכא לדבר הלמד בג"ש כו' דלמא דשאני הכא משום דניתן לדרוש לענין שלא בהפשט דאינו בא מג"ש בפר כהן משיח אתי ניתוח בהדי אגב גררא דהוי הימנו ודבר אחר ומלמדים הימנו ועוד קשה דשלא בהפשט גופיה היכא יליף בג"ש בפר יוה"כ מפר כהן משיח [הא] בפר כהן משיח גופיה לא כתיב הפשט בהדיא אלא ילפינן ליה בהיקש עור ובשר לקרבו ופרשו והיאך חוזר ומלמד בג"ש וי"ל דקושיא חדא מתרצה לחברתה דמדחזינן דילפינן מיניה שלא בהפשט אע"ג דהתם מהיקשא הוא דאתא א"כ ש"מ דדבר הלמד בג"ש חוזר ומלמד בג"ש והוי ניתוח כמו דכתיב בגופיה לגבי הכי ונילף בג"ש לפר ושעיר יוה"כ מפר כהן משיח וכיון דילפינן מיניה ניתוח מהשתא נילף נמי שלא בהפשט מהתם דהוי הימנו ודבר אחר. ס"א וי"ל קושיא חדא מתרצה לחברתה דאדרבה לגבי שלא בהפשט הימנו ודבר אחר הוא דלא מצי למילף שלא בהפשט אלא עם ניתוח דילפינן ניתוח בג"ש מעולה הלכך כי הדר יליף ניתוח בפר יוה"כ בג"ש דדבר הלמד בג"ש חוזר ומלמד בג"ש יליף עמו הפשט והוי הימנו ודבר אחר ולא הוי היקש חוזר ומלמד בג"ש ועי"ל דשלא בהפשט לא ילפינן מפר כהן משיח אלא בגופייהו כתיב את עורותם כו' ואיתקש בשרם לפירשם ואע"ג (דכתיב) [דלא כתיב] קרבם מ"מ נימא מה פירשם אינו שורפם בפני עצמה בלא קרבם אף בשרם שורפם בעורם והא דקאמר שלא בהפשט אגב ניתוח נקט לה. לשון תוס' מהר"פ: ב] מלמד מן ההיקש אי כו': ג] ג"ש המלמדת בג"ש חבירתה כו'. פ"ה מה שאין ההיקש עושה כו' וא"ת הא לא משום יפוי כח דמלמד הוא דג"ש מלמדת בג"ש אלא משום כח נלמד דלמד בקל ומש"ה לא תהא מלמד בקל ותדע דכמו דאין היקש מלמד בהיקש כמו כן ג"ש אינה מלמדת בהיקש אע"ג דג"ש מלמדת בג"ש אלמא לא משום כח הנלמד הוא וי"ל דק"ו דעביד הוי אף מג"ש וה"ק ומה היקש שאינו מלמד לא בהיקש חבירו ולא בג"ש מלמד בק"ו ג"ש שמלמדת בג"ש חבירתה אע"פ שאינה מלמדת בהיקש אינו דין שתלמוד בק"ו כיון שהיא עושה מה שאין היקש עושה שמלמדת בג"ש ואע"ג דאינה מלמדת בהיקש כמו כן היקש אינו מלמד בהיקש: ד] שאינה למדה מן ההיקש מדר' יוחנן [כו' ק"ו] הלמד בהיקש: ה] בגז"ש חבירתה מדרמי: ו] דין שילמד: ז] מלמדת בק"ו מדתרביצא. ה"ג מלמדת בק"ו מדתרביצא היינו הא דאמרי' לעיל דבר הלמד בג"ש מהו שילמד בק"ו מה היקש שאינה למד מן ההיקש מלמד בק"ו ג"ש המלמדת בג"ש חבירתה מדרמי בר חמא (כולה) [כו'] ולפי שלא הוזכר בה שם חכם אלא מפי כל החבורה נזרקה קרי לה לישנא דתרביצא בית המדרש שמרביצין בו תורה. תיבת כדאמרן נמחק: ח] בן בנו של ק"ו הוא אלא בן ק"ו. נ"ל דה"פ כלומר אתה רוצה להוכיח דבר זה בק"ו מג"ש שמלמדת בק"ו והיא גופה שמלמדת בק"ו לא ידעת רק מכח ק"ו דלעיל. וא"כ אין לפשוט משם שהרי מזה אתה מסופק בתחלת דינך ועל זה אני דנין אם דבר הלמד בק"ו אם חוזר ומלמד בק"ו וכיון שאתה עושה ק"ו מאותה מדה מג"ש שמלמדת בק"ו שזה הדבר עצמו אתה למד לעיל בק"ו א"כ כל עיקר דינך בדבר הלמד בק"ו שחוזר ומלמד בק"ו ואם אינו מלמד בק"ו א"כ אין להוציא בפה אותו ק"ו שבא מג"ש המלמדת בהיקש. לשון מהר"פ: ט] מינה דג"ש: י] מעשר דמחולין הוא: יא] מדבור המתחיל מלמד בק"ו כו' עד סה"ד נמחק: יב] ק"ו הואי הוא עצמו: יג] לעיל ק"ו ומה ג"ש כו' ממנו לדרוש מדה זו בתורה: יד] דדבר הלמד בהיקש: טו] אחת שחיטת העוף: טז] מפורש במס': יז] עוף טהור אינו: יח] שמכשרת לאכילה בחולין ומטהרת מליקה כו' לקמן בפ' חטאת העוף מייתי לה ופריך בגמ' ור"מ לית ליה דיו: יט] למילף בפר יוה"כ מפר כהן משיח דמגופיה: כ] לעולה מצינו למימר דס"ל כרב פפא א"נ לא דמי דלמצוה. ותיבות היינו למצוה נמחק: כא] הוא. פ"ה שאפי' כו' עד כולי האי: כב] דק"ו מלמד על ק"ו אמאי לא נילף: כג] לפרש דקשיא ליה בן בנו כו' דמעיקרא הוא מבעיא ליה אי דבר כו' חוזר ומלמד בק"ו והוא בא כו'. ס"א וא"כ היאך בא [אא"ה לפ"ז צריך למחוק תיבת והוא עכ"ה]: כד] מטמא בגדים בבית הבליעה ועוד קשה דמנא ליה *)כו' בחולין לכך נראה דעיקר טעמא דר"מ הן דשחיטה הן דמליקת העוף מטהרת היינו משום דאיתקש לבהמה מקרא דזאת תורת הבהמה ואין משיבין על ההיקש ומ"מ שפיר שמעינן מהכא דדבר המלמד בג"ש חוזר ומלמד בבנין אב דמדנקט הכא בברייתא מק"ו ולא נקט עיקר טעמא משום היקשא דמוזאת תורת ש"מ דבעלמא בקדשים אמרי' דדבר הלמד בק"ו חוזר ומלמד בבנין אב דהכא נמי הייתי אומר כך אי לאו משום דאיכא פירכא כו'. עכ"ל הר"פ: כה] גמר ושחיטת עוף משחיטת בהמה דלמא מליקת עוף משחיטת בהמה גמר דכך חשיבא מליקת עוף בקדשים כשחיטת בהמה בחולין ונראה וכו'. ובתוס' מהר"פ תירץ כדלעיל דעיקר טעמא משום היקש זאת תורת כו':

*) [נ"ל דמכ"ל דמליקת עוף משחיטת עוף גמר ושחיטת עוף משחיטת בהמה דלמא מליקת ע"פ משחיטת בהמה גמר דכך חשיבא מליקת עוף בקדשים כשחיטת בהמה בחולין] (ועי' בתוס' בסמוך ד"ה מה ובהגהות רביני בא"ח כ"ה בס)

dung are mentioned here, [50*b*] and skin and flesh and dung are mentioned elsewhere:[2] as there [it was burnt after] being cut up, but without flaying, so here too [it is burnt after being] cut up, but without flaying.[3]

Can that which is learnt by a *gezerah shawah* teach in turn by a *kal wa-ḥomer?*—[It can, and we learn this by a] *kal wa-ḥomer:* If [that which is learnt by] a *hekkesh,* which cannot teach by a *hekkesh,* as follows from either Raba's or Rabina's [proof], can teach by a *kal wa-ḥomer,* which follows from what the school of R. Ishmael taught; then [what is learnt through] a *gezerah shawah,* which can [in turn] teach by a *hekkesh,* as follows from R. Papa, can surely teach [in turn] by a *kal wa-ḥomer*! That is well according to him who accepts R. Papa's teaching; but what can be said on the view that rejects R. Papa's teaching?—Rather [this is the] *kal wa-ḥomer:* if [what is learnt by] a *hekkesh,* which cannot [in turn] teach by a *hekkesh,* as follows either from Raba or from Rabina, can teach [in turn] by a *kal wa-ḥomer,* which follows from what the school of R. Ishmael taught; then a *gezerah shawah,* which does teach by a *gezerah shawah* like itself, which follows from Rami b. Ḥama, can surely teach through a *kal wa-ḥomer.*

Can that which is learnt by a *gezerah shawah* subsequently teach by a *binyan ab?*—The question stands.

Can that which is learnt by a *kal wa-ḥomer* teach in turn by a *hekkesh?*—[Yes, and we learn this by a] *kal wa-ḥomer:* if a *gezerah shawah,* which cannot be learnt from a *hekkesh,* as follows from R. Joḥanan's [dictum], can nevertheless teach by a *hekkesh,* in accordance with R. Papa; then a *kal wa-ḥomer,* which can be learnt from a *hekkesh,* in accordance with the school of R. Ishmael, can surely teach by a *hekkesh*! That is well on the view that accepts R. Papa's [dictum], but what can be said on the view that rejects R. Papa's [dictum]? Then the question stands.

Can that which is learnt by a *kal wa-ḥomer* teach in turn by a *gezerah shawah?*—[Yes, for this follows by a] *kal wa-ḥomer:* if a *gezerah shawah,* which cannot be learnt from a *hekkesh,* in accordance with R. Joḥanan, can teach by a *gezerah shawah,* in accordance with Rami b. Ḥama; then is it not logical that a *kal wa-ḥomer,* which can be learnt by a *hekkesh,* in accordance with the school of R. Ishmael, can teach by a *gezerah shawah?*

Can that which is learnt by a *kal wa-ḥomer* teach in turn by a *kal wa-ḥomer?*—[Yes, for this follows from a] *kal wa-ḥomer:* if a *gezerah shawah,* which cannot be learnt by a *hekkesh,* in accordance with R. Joḥanan, can teach by a *kal wa-ḥomer,* as we have [just] said; then a *kal wa-ḥomer* which can be learnt from a *hekkesh,* in accordance with the school of R. Ishmael, is it not logical that it can teach by a *kal wa-ḥomer?* And this is a *kal wa-ḥomer* derived from a *kal*
a *waḥomer.*[1] Surely this is a secondary derivation from a *kal wa-ḥomer?*[2]—Rather, [argue thus: Yes, and this follows from a] *kal wa-ḥomer:* if a *hekkesh* which cannot be learnt through a *hekkesh,* in accordance with either Raba or Rabina, can teach by a *kal wa-ḥomer,* in accordance with the school of R. Ishmael;[3] then a *kal wa-ḥomer,* which is learnt through a *hekkesh,* in accordance with the school of R. Ishmael, can surely teach through a *kal wa-ḥomer*! And this is a *kal wa-ḥomer* derived from a *kal wa-ḥomer.*

Can that which is learnt by a *kal wa-ḥomer* teach in turn through a *binyan ab?*—Said R. Jeremiah, Come and hear: If one nipped the neck [of a bird sacrifice] and it was found to be a *terefah,* R. Meir said: It does not defile in the gullet; R. Judah said: It does defile in
b the gullet.[1] Said R. Meir: It is a *kal wa-ḥomer:* if the *shechitah* of an animal cleanses it, even when *terefah,* from its uncleanness,[2] yet when it is *nebelah* it defiles through contact or carriage; is it not logical that *shechitah* cleanses a bird, when *terefah,* from its uncleanness, seeing that when it is *nebelah* it does *not* defile through touch or carriage? Now, as we have found that *shechitah* which

(2) In reference to the anointed priest's bullock. By 'here' he means in connection with the bullock and the he-goat of the Day of Atonement. (3) Thus the result of one *gezerah shawah* is transferred by another *gezerah shawah.*

a (1) Lit., 'a *kal wa-ḥomer* the son of a *kal wa-ḥomer*'. Thus a *kal wa-ḥomer* is based on the fact that a *gezerah shawah* teaches through a *kal wa-ḥomer,* and that itself is learnt only through a *kal wa-ḥomer.* (2) Lit., 'the grandson of a *kal wa-ḥomer*'. Thus: A, which is learnt through a *kal wa-ḥomer,* teaches B by means of a *kal wa-ḥomer;* that it does so is learnt from the fact C. Now, even if C were directly stated, B would still be the derivative (lit., 'son') of the first *kal wa-ḥomer.* Since however C itself is known only through a *kal wa-ḥomer,* B becomes the secondary derivative (lit., 'grandson'). That is so in the present case. Possibly, however, this is straining the powers of a *kal wa-ḥomer* too far, and is inadmissible, in which case the problem remains unanswered. (3) This itself is not the result of a *kal wa-ḥomer,* but a tradition.

b (1) A bird sin-offering was not slaughtered by the usual ritual method (*shechitah*), but had its neck nipped. If an ordinary bird of *hullin,* or any animal, is killed by any method other than *shechitah,* it becomes *nebelah* (carrion). The term *terefah* is applied to a bird or an animal which was ritually slaughtered, but which was found to be suffering from a disease or other physical defect which renders it forbidden as food. Now when a clean animal, i.e. one permitted for food, becomes *nebelah,* it defiles any person who touches it or even carries it without actually touching it. A clean bird which becomes *nebelah* does not defile thus, but only the person who eats it, i.e., when it enters his gullet. In the present instance the bird's neck was nipped; had it been *hullin,* it would have become *nebelah,* and defiled accordingly. When it is found to be *terefah* the sacrifice cannot be proceeded with, as the bird is unfit. R. Judah holds that it is the same, therefore, as *hullin,* and defiles as such. R. Meir, however, holds that since it was intended for a sacrifice when its neck was nipped, this was its correct method of slaughter, and so it does not defile. (2) As is shewn in Ḥul. 128*b*—Through the *shechitah* it is freed from the uncleanness of *nebelah.*

makes it [a bird of *ḥullin*] fit for eating, [51*a*] cleanses it, when *terefah*, from its uncleanness; so nipping [the neck], which makes it [a bird sacrifice] fit for eating, cleanses it, when *terefah*, from its uncleanness.[3] R. Jose said: It is sufficient that it be like the *nebelah* of a clean [i.e., edible] animal, which is cleansed by *shechitah*, but not by nipping its neck.[4] Yet that is not so: even granted there that it is so, yet it is deduced from the *shechitah* of *ḥullin*.[5]

Can that which is learnt by a *binyan ab* teach by a *hekkesh* or by a *gezerah shawah* or by a *kal wa-ḥomer* or by a *binyan ab*?—Solve one [of the questions] from the following: Why did they say that if the
a blood is kept overnight [on the altar] it is fit?[1] Because if the *emurim* are kept overnight they are fit.[2] Why are the *emurim* fit if kept overnight? Because the flesh is fit if kept overnight.[3] [Flesh that] goes out?[4] Because [flesh that] goes out is fit at the high place [*bamah*].[5] Unclean [flesh]? Because it was permitted in public service.[6] [The *emurim* of a burnt-offering intended to be burnt] after time? Because it propitiates in respect of its *piggul* status.[7] [The *emurim* of a burnt-offering intended to be burnt] out of bounds? Because it was likened to [the intention to burn it] after time. Where unfit [persons] received [the blood] and sprinkled it—in the case of those unfit persons who are eligible for public service.[8] Can you then argue from what is its proper way to that where the same is not the proper way?[9]—The Tanna relies on the extension indicated by *This is the law of the burnt-offering*.[10]

THE RESIDUE OF THE BLOOD etc. What is the reason?—Scripture saith, [*And all the remaining blood of the bullock shall he pour out*] *at the base of the altar of burnt-offering* [*which is at the door of the tent*
b *of meeting*];[1] [this intimates]: the one which you first meet.[2]

Our Rabbis taught: '*At the base of the altar of burnt-offering*', but not at the base of the inner altar; '*at the base of the altar of burnt-offering*': the inner altar itself has no base; '*at the base of the altar of burnt-offering*': apply [the laws of] the base to the altar of burnt-offering.[3] Yet perhaps that is not so; rather [it intimates]: let there be a base to the altar of burnt-offering?[4]—Said R. Ishmael [This would follow] *a fortiori*: if the residue [of the blood of the sin-offering], which does not make atonement, requires the base;
c then surely the sprinkling itself of the [blood of the] burnt-offering,[1] which makes atonement, requires the base![2] Said R. Akiba [too: This would follow] *a fortiori*: if the residue, which does not make atonement and does not come for atonement, requires the base; is it not logical that the sprinkling itself of the [blood of the] burnt-offering, which makes atonement and comes for atonement, requires the base? If so, why does Scripture state, '*at the base of the altar of burnt-offering*'? To teach: apply [the laws of] the base to the altar of burnt-offering.

The Master said: '*At the base of the altar of burnt-offering*, but not at the base of the inner altar.' Surely that is required for its own purpose?[3]—That is learnt from, *which is at the door of the tent of meeting*.[4]

(3) This argument is a *binyan ab*. Thus what was learnt by a *kal wa-ḥomer* then teaches through a *binyan ab*. (4) Since the argument is alternately based on an animal, the bird sacrifice cannot be clean where the animal would not be. (5) The Talmud rejects R. Jeremiah's proof. Firstly, because R. Meir does not really learn it by a *binyan ab*, as might appear here, but from *hekkesh*, as stated *infra* 69*b* q.v. Yet even granted that he does learn it by a *binyan ab*, the premise (i.e., the teacher) is *ḥullin*, and if R. Papa's view is rejected even when what is to be learnt is sacred, nothing can be proved from the present instance (Rashi. Other commentaries explain differently).

a (1) I.e., if it was taken up on the the altar it is not taken down. (2) Likewise in the same sense. Similarly the other cases mentioned. (3) As two days were allowed for the eating of peace-offerings. Thus *emurim* are learnt by a *binyan ab* from the flesh, and these in turn teach by a *binyan ab* in respect of the blood. (4) Why does such flesh not descend if this is taken up on the altar? (5) Where sacrifices were offered before the building of the Temple (v. *supra* 16*a* n. a 1.). (6) V. *supra* 16*b* n. a 7. (7) The sprinkling of the blood is effective (technically 'propitiates') in making it *piggul* and involving *kareth*, just as though all its *mattirin* had been offered (v. *supra* 28*b* n. a 1.). The *emurim* of *piggul* do not descend, once they ascended. (8) E.g., an unclean priest, who is fit when the sacrifice is brought in uncleanness.—Only then does the blood not descend, once it ascended. This is apparently the meaning of the text, but in that case the question is left unanswered. Possibly, however, the second half is the answer; thus: Why does the blood not descend when unfit persons received or sprinkled it? Because it does not descend in the case of those unfit persons who are eligible for public service, i.e., unclean priests when the community is unclean. (9) E.g., you argue that the *emurim* if kept overnight do not descend because the flesh if kept overnight is fit. But the flesh *may* be kept overnight, whereas the *emurim* may not. Similarly, when the Temple stood the flesh might not be taken out; whereas there were no boundaries at all in the case of the *bamah*. (10) Lev. VI, 2. The verse teaches that all the burnt-offerings (i.e., even when they have the defects mentioned in the text) have one law, and do not descend once they have ascended. The arguments given are mere supports, though strictly speaking they cannot be sustained.

b (1) Lev. IV, 7. (2) As you enter from the door. This was the western base. (3) The Bible contains five sections dealing with the sin-offering (Lev. IV), viz.: (i) The sin-offering of the anointed priest (vv. 1-12); (ii) that of the whole congregation (13-22); (iii) that of a ruler (22-26); (iv) the female goat of a common layman (27-32); and (v) the lamb of a common layman (32-35). The first two were offered on the inner altar; the other three on the outer. Again, in reference to the first three Scripture states that the residue of the blood shall be poured out '*at the base of the altar of burnt-offering*' (vv. 7, 18 and 25), whereas in connection with the remaining two the '*base of the altar*' alone is mentioned. Here the Rabbis explain why Scripture specifies the altar of the burnt-offering in the first three. The first teaches that the residue is poured out at the base of the *outer* altar (i.e., the altar of burnt-offering), but not at the base of the inner altar, notwithstanding that the blood was sprinkled on the horns of the inner altar. The second is superfluous, since it is assimilated to the first (v. 20). Hence it teaches that only the outer altar was provided with a special base, but not the inner altar. The third too is superfluous, because firstly, if the residue of the blood of the *inner* sin-offerings is poured out at the base of the *outer* altar, obviously the blood of the *outer* sin-offerings will not be poured out at the base of the inner altar; and secondly, we have already learnt that the inner altar was not provided with a special base. Hence it intimates that the residue of the blood of *all* sacrifices whose blood is sprinkled on the altar of burnt-offering must be poured out at its base. (4) Perhaps it does not teach anything concerning the *residue* of the blood, but that the two sprinklings of the blood of the burnt-offering must be made over against that part of the altar which had a special base; this would exclude the south-east horn, which had no base (v. *infra* 53*b*).

c (1) Lit., 'the beginning of the burnt-offering'. (2) I.e., it must be sprinkled on the horns provided with a base, as in the preceding note. The rendering is not quite literal. Thus a special text would not be required, if its teaching were only as suggested. (3) Viz., that the residue is to be poured out at the base of the outer altar; nevertheless, if he wishes to pour it out at the base of the inner altar, he should certainly be permitted, since this is more sacred. Though it has been deduced that the inner altar had no special base at all, that is only on the assumption that all three are superfluous; but if the first is required for the purpose of stating the law, then the *second* is required for the present limitation, and the third as in the text, leaving nothing to shew that the inner altar was not provided with a base. (4) Which shews that the *outer* altar is meant; hence '*of burnt-offering*' is superfluous.

תורה אור

מטהרת טריפתה מטומאתה אף מליקה שמכשרתה באכילה תטהר טריפתה מטומאתה ר' יוסי אומר דיה כנבלת בהמה טהורה ששחיטתה מטהרתה ולא מליקתה א] ולא היא התם תיהוי היא משחיטה דחולין ב] קאתיין. דבר הלמד בבנין אב מהו שילמד בהיקש ובג"ש ובק"ו ובבנין אב פשוט מהא חדא *מפני מה אמרו לן בדם כשר שהרי לן באימורין כשר ג] לן באימורין כשר שהרי לן בבשר כשר *יוצא הואיל ויוצא כשר בבמה טמא הואיל והותר בעבודת ציבור חוץ לזמנו הואיל ומרצה לפיגולו חוץ למקומו הואיל והוקש לחוץ לזמנו שקיבלו פסולין וזרקו ד]דמן בהנך פסולין דחזו לעבודת ציבור *וכי דנין דבר שלא בהכשירו מדבר שבהכשירו תנא ה] *מזאת תורת העולה ריבה סמיך ליה: שירי הדם כו': מאי טעמא ו] אמר קרא ויקרא ד °אל יסוד מזבח העולה אשר פתח אהל מועד ז] *ההוא דפגע ברישא ת"ר ח] אל יסוד מזבח העולה ולא יסוד מזבח הפנימי אל יסוד מזבח העולה אין לו יסוד לפנימי עצמו אל יסוד מזבח העולה תן יסוד למזבח של עולה או אינו אלא ט] מזבחה של עולה יהא ליסוד אמר ר' ישמעאל קל וחומר מה שיריים שאין מכפרין טעונין יסוד תחלת עולה שמכפרת אינו דין שטעונה יסוד אמר רבי עקיבא מה שיריים שאין מכפרין ואין באין לכפרה י] טעונה יסוד תחלת עולה שמכפרת ובאה לכפרה אינו דין שטעונה יסוד יא] א"כ מה ת"ל אל יסוד מזבח העולה תן יסוד למזבחה של עולה אמר מר אל יסוד מזבח (א) יב] ולא יסוד מזבח הפנימי הא מיבעי ליה לגופיה °מאשר פתח אהל מועד נפקא אל יסוד מזבח העולה שם

תן

הכי גרסי' ולא היא התם תיהוי יג] משחיטה דחולין קאתיא. והכי פירושו התם עיקר טעמא דר"מ לא יליף בבנין אב אלא מהיקש דזאת תורת הבהמה והעוף כדלקמן בפרק חטאת העוף (דף סט:) יד] אמרינן ר"מ קרא אשכח ודרש ואי נמי תיהוי דגמר לה בבנין אב כדקתני במתני' לא מיפשטא בעיין דהא ר"מ מליקה בקדשים משחיטה דחולין גמר טו] הוה ליה מלמד דחולין ולמאן דלית ליה דרב פפא אף על גב דלמד קדש לאו ראייה היא: פשוט מהא. מתני' חדא מהנך בעיא: מפני מה אמרו. לקמן היא בפ' המזבח [מקדש] (דף פד:) לרבי יהודה דדריש זאת היא העולה הרי אלו מיעוטין פרט לנשחטה בלילה ושנשפך דמה ושילא דמה חוץ לקלעים ופריך מה ראה להוציא את אלו ולהכשיר את השאר: מפני מה אמרו לן בדם כשר. שאם עלה לא ירד שהרי טז] כשר באימורין אם לנו אימורין ועלו למזבח לא ירדו: ולן באימורין יז] למה כשר שהרי לן בבשר כשר. גמור מן התורה שזמן אכילת שלמים שני ימים אלמא אימורין גמרי *בבנין אב יח] על הדם: טמא. איברי עולה טמאין מפני מה אם עלו לא ירדו: הואיל ומרצה לפיגולו. הואיל וחשובה הרצאה דמו לחייב עליו משום פיגול כמו שקרבו מתיריו בהכשר לפיכך אימורי פיגול שעלו לא ירדו: שקבלו פסולין. יט] אם זרקו את דמו מפני מה אם עלו הדם או האימורין לא ירדו: בהנך פסולין. מכשירים דחזו לעבודת צבור כגון כהן טמא: וכי דנין דבר כו'. דקא ילפת כ] באימורין שלא בהכשירם מגלן *בבשר דהכשירו בכך וזו היא מלותו ותו היכי יליף יוצא במקדש מיוצא בבמה שכולו יוצא הוא שאין שם קלעים אלא ע"פ השדה: זאת תורת העולה. תורה אחת לכל העולין כא] אם עלו לא ירדו כדכתיב על מוקדה כל הלילה וכל ראיות הללו משום דממעט מזאת היא העולה תלתא פסולי מייתי מהנך מאי שנא הני מהני *והעיקר מקרא ואסמכתא בעלמא הוא: מאי טעמא. אל יסוד מערב כב] הוא דכתיב בפר כהן משיח (ויקרא ד) אל יסוד מזבח העולה אשר פתח אהל מועד יסוד שכנגד הפתח וזו היא מערבו של מזבח שהוא כנגד פתח ההיכל ולקמן בברייתא (דף נג.) נפקא לן פר יום הכפורים מריבויא דהפר שטעון מתן דם ליסוד כג] *בפר כהן משיח ובשעיר כתיב (ויקרא טז) ועשה את דמו כאשר עשה לדם הפר: אל יסוד מזבח העולה. חמש פרשיות הן בחטאת של פר כד] משיח ושל *העלם שהן פנימיות ושל שעיר נשיא ושל כבשת יחיד ושל שעירת יחיד שהן חיצוניות. בשתים הפנימיות ובשעיר נשיא כתיב בשפיכת שיריהן אל יסוד מזבח העולה. בשתים החיצונות כתיב אל יסוד כה] מזבח סתמא וקדרים תנא תלתא אל *)מזבח העולה למה פירש הכתוב וה"ג לה בת"כ אל יסוד מזבח העולה של פר כהן משיח ולא יסוד מזבח הפנימי אל יסוד מזבח העולה של פר העדה שאין ת"ל **)אין לו יסוד לפנימי עצמו. כשהוא אומר אל יסוד מזבח העולה בשעיר נשיא שאין תלמוד לומר כו] שאם את שיריו לא קיבל מזבח הפנימי שירי מזבח החיצון יקבל. דבר אחר וכי יש לו יסוד לפנימי עצמו אם כן מה תלמוד לומר אל יסוד מזבח העולה תן יסוד למזבחה של עולה והכא נמי כז] בעינן תלתא למיגרס והכי גרסי' ופירושו אל יסוד מזבח העולה האמור בפר כהן משיח ולא יסוד מזבח הפנימי שלא תאמר במקום מתן כח] הקרנות שם יהיו שפיכת שיריו: אל יסוד מזבח העולה. האמור בפר כט] העדה דלא צריך תו דהא איתקוש להדדי אלא ללמוד בא שאפילו יסוד אין לו לפנימי והכי מידריש הואיל ומיותר לדרשא יסוד יהיה למזבח העולה ולא לפנימי: אל יסוד מזבח העולה. האמור בשעיר נשיא שאין ת"ל כדמפרש בת"כ בהדיא מתרי טעמי [חדא דהא] שירי דמים של ל] עצמן של פנימי כגון בפר משיח ועדה לא קיבל הפנימי כדאמרן שיריו של חיצון יקבל בתמיה ועוד למדנו שאין לו יסוד ולקמן (דף נג.) נמי הכי פרשינן לה בשמעתין אם כן מה תלמוד לומר אל יסוד מזבח העולה תן יסוד למזבחה של עולה תן תורת לא] שפיכת שירים יסוד להלכות מזבחה של עולה שיהא המזבח טעון בעולה ובכל דמים הניתנין עליו שפיכת שירים אל היסוד אם נשאר בכלי כלום כשזורק ממנו שתי זריקות לשתי קרנות ישפכנו ליסוד ומשום דבעולה לא כתיב שפיכת שירים אילטריך למילף מהכא: או אינו בא ללמד כלום על שפיכת שירים של עולה ושל שאר דמים אלא בא ללמד על לב] הלכות המזבח במתן דנה של עולה שיתן שתי מתנותיה כנגד היסוד ולמעוטי קרן מזרחית דרומית שאין לו יסוד כדאמרינן בהאי פירקין לג] (דף נג:): אמר רבי ישמעאל מקל וחומר. נפקא לן הא ולא בעי קרא: מה שירים של חטאת שאין מכפרין טעונין יסוד כו'. ורבי עקיבא גמר לה להא קל וחומר הכי ומה שירים כו' ולקמיה מפרש מאי בינייהו לד] כו': האי מיבעיא ליה לגופיה. שישפכם ליסוד מזבח החיצון ומיהו כל שכן אם רצה יתנם על הפנימי דמהיכא יליף מיעוטא ואי קשיא הא ילפינן מברייתא דאין לו יסוד לגמרי ההוא מייתורא דקרא ואי דרשת קמא לגופיה ותנייתא למיעוטא תו לא מייתר שני להכי אלא מקרא שלישי ותו לית לך דרשא שלישי: מאשר פתח אהל מועד נפקא. דהיינו חיצון והוה מלי למיכתב אל יסוד המזבח אשר פתח אהל מועד מזבח העולה למה לי למיעוטא:

*) אל יסוד נמחק צ"ק **) אלא ללמד שאין יסוד. כ"ה בתו"כ

הכי

דלא גמר דאיכא תרי שיטיי מליקה משחיטה ועוף מבהמה. ברו"ך. ועוד קשה היכי דייק דדבר הלמד בק"ו חוזר ומלמד בבנין אב אימא דשחיטת עוף אתיא בבנין אב משחיטת בהמה ודבר הלמד בבנין אב חוזר ומלמד בבנין אב לה] כדמסקא בשמעתא ונראה דלישנא דמתני' קדייק דפשיטא דעיקר טעמו של ר"מ מהיקשא דזאת לו] התורה כדלקמן ופשיטא ליה דבמה מלינו מעוף יליף דאי מבהמה למה לי לאיתויי בק"ו: **פשוט** מהא חדא לז]. תימה דתרתי תפשוט דכיון דמלמד בבנין אב חבירו אם כן מלמד בק"ו לח] ומה היקש שאינו מלמד בהיקש *אי מדרבינא מלמד בק"ו מדתנא דבי רבי ישמעאל בנין אב המלמד בבנין אב חבירו אינו דין שילמד בק"ו וכה"ג עביד ק"ו לעיל לט]: **מפני** מה אמרו לן בדם כשר. תימה היכי דייק מהכא דבנין אב חוזר ומלמד בבנין אב דילמא לן הדם לאחר שקיעת החמה יליף מלן דאימורין דלא פסילי בשקיעת החמה אלא בעמוד השחר והדר יליף לן דאימורין הנפסלים בעמוד השחר דאם עלו לא ירדו מלן בשר ויש לומר דפשיטא ליה דאע"ג דיליף באימורים שלא מ] הכשירו מהכשירו דבשר דם המתיר עדיף ולא ילפינן דם שלא בהכשירו מהכשירו תדע מדלא ילפינן מעיקרא לן דם מלן בשר*: **אשר** פתח אהל מועד. יסוד שכנגד הפתח וזהו מערבו של מזבח מא] *שיהו כנגד פתח ההיכל כך פי' בקונטרס ולא גריסמה שכתוב בספרים ההוא דפגע ברישא משום דמשמע מטעם שאין מעבירין על המלות ולא מן הפסוק פתח אהל מועד והא גבי חטאת איכא דאמרי שירי הדם על יסוד מערבי לקמן (דף נג.) ואמר טעמא ילמוד סתום מן המפורש מחטאת פנימי משמע דמפורש בהדיא ועוד דאית דאמרי על יסוד דרומי וקאמר ילמוד ירידתו מן הכבש מב] בסמוך לו ליציאתו מן ההיכל בסמוך לו מהיכן פשוט לו זה יותר מזה והלא בתרווייהו שייך טעמא דאין מעבירין על המלות ועוד אמרינן לקמן (דף נח:) מג] *על קדשי קדשים שיריים בהדיא כתיב בהו אשר פתח אהל מועד ומיהו הא גופא קשיא דלמה לי קרא דפתח אהל מועד תיפוק לי דאין מעבירין על המלות כדאשכחן טעם זה בפ"ק דיומא (דף טו:) דפריך מאי שנא דיהיב מזרחה לפונה ברישא *וגבי דישון מזבח פנימי והמנורה אמר דישון מזבח קודם משום דאין מעבירין *וכן עבורי דרעא אטוטפתא אסור ויש לומר דלא שייך אין מעבירין על המלות אלא כשיש שתי מלות לפניו כגון דישון מזבח פנימית ומנורה או כגון מלות קרנות שאינו יודע מהיכן יתחיל אבל לקבוע מקום אשפיכת שירים לא קבעינן מהאי טעמא אי לאו דגלי קרא בהדיא*):

*) ועי' תוס' במנחות סד: ד"ה אב"א ותוס' במגילה ו: ד"ה מסתבר

תן

[x] דלמא לן בדם מלן דבשר יליף וי"ל דכולי האי לא הוי יליף לן דדם שלא בהכשירו מלן דבשר דהכשר בשלמים לשני ימים ולילה אחת ואע"ג דילפינן אימורים מבשר משום דאימורים בשר נינהו דם שלא בהכשר מיוצא דבמה דהכשר גמור וי"ל דשאני התם דדם מדם יליף אבל דם מבשר מהכשר גמור ודאי לא יליף וא"ת תרתי מצי למיפשט דכיון דבנין אב יליף בבנין אב א"כ נימא מלמד בהיקש כו' וי"ל דמנלן דהמלמד גורם שתאמר כמו כן יועיל ללמד על ק"ו דלמא הנלמד בקל נלמד וליכא למימר דמן הכל עושה הק"ו ונאמר בהיקש שאינו מלמד לא על היקש ולא על פשט לעיל אי היקש מלמד בבנין אב. הר"פ: ו] דכתיב אל. (עיין נהשמטה בסוף המס'): ז] מועד פתח תיבות ההוא דפגע ברישא נמחק: ח] תנו [רבנן] הראב"ד גרים גירסא אחרת בת"כ ופי' אחת כו' יהא יסוד: י] לכפרה טעונים יסוד: יא] יסוד הא מה אני מקיים אל יתיבות א"כ מה ת"ל העולה ולא: יג] תיהוי היא משחיטת דחולין כו' לא בבנין אב יליף לה אלא מהיקש כו': יד] דאמרי' היא דתמר לה: טו] הוה ליה מלמד חולין ולמאן דל"ל דר"פ דאע"ג דלמד קדש לאו ראיה היא. זה של כת"י וכתוב תוס' (לפני) [על] זה ואני אומר דאפי' לרב פפא ראיה היא ושפיר מיפשטי בעיין

כח] מתן דם הקרנות שם כו' שיריו וא"כ יש לנו לומר שיהא שפיכת שיריים של פנימיות לכך אהא לומר שיהא על יסוד מזבח העולה: כט] בפר העלם דלא צריך תו דהא משיח אלא ללמד בא שאפי': ל] דמים של פנימי עצמו כגון דפר משיח ועדה כו' ועוד יסוד כו' הכי מפרשי' לה: לא] תורת יסוד דהיינו שפיכת שיריים למזבח של עולה: לב] לג] פירקין. גליון דליכא למימר לכל הדמים של מזבח העולה להטעינך תהלהן יסוד דהא לקרנות: לד] תיבת כו' נמחק: לה] בבנין אב כדמשמע בשמעתא ונראה דמלישנא דמתניתין הבהמה והעוף כדלקמן: לז] הדא. פי' בתרייתא דדבר הלמד בבנין אב*) כו': לח] בק"ו מק"ו ומה אי מדרבא: לט] לעיל בגז"ש המלמדת בג"ש חבירתה י"ל דלמאי דפי' לעיל ניחא דהתם הדין אבל הכא אינו יכול לעשות ק"ו בתחלת הדין מבנין אב עצמו ותאמר דהיקש אינו מלמד מבעיא לן לעיל ולא אפשים. לישנא הר"פ: מ] שלא בהכשירו מהכשירו כו' ולא ילפינן דם מאימורים שלא בהכשירו מהכשירו ודם מבשר תדע מדלא: מא] מזבח שהוא כנגד: מב] הכבש מיציאתו מן ההיכל בסמוך לו אף ירידתו מן הכבש בסמוך לו מהיכן כו': מג] לקמן בריש קדשי קדשים שירים:

*) [נ"ל בבנין אב חוזר ומלמד בבנין אב. תימה כו']

שיטה מקובצת

הגהות הב"ח

תן יסוד למזבח של עולה דאי סלקא דעתך כדכתיב הני למה לי א] קרא לשירים שירים הא בראי עביד להו וכי תימא ג] דאפיך מיפך דבראי

הכי גרסינן אל יסוד מזבח העולה תן יסוד למזבחה של עולה ג] ואי סלקא דעתך כדכתיב הני למה לי *[קרא לשיריים] שירים הא בראי עביד להו וכי תימא דאפיך מיפך דבראי

תן ד] לה יסוד למזבח של עולה . פירש בקונטרס כל דמים הניתנין על מזבח החיצון טעון שפיכת שירים ליסוד ומשום דבעולה לא כתיבא שפיכת שירים ליסוד איצטריך למילף הכא או אינו מדבר כלל בשירים אלא למזבחה של עולה יהא ה] ליסוד לתחילת דמים שיהו מתנות של כל הזבחים כנגד היסוד אמר רבי ישמעאל ו] כו' וקרא לא איצטריך לתחילת מתנות כנגד היסוד דמקל וחומר דשירים של חטאת אתו אלא אלא על כרחיך להצריך שירים ליסוד לכל הזבחים אתי קרא כך פירש בקונטרס וקשה דלעיל בפרק ב"ש (דף לז.) נפקא לן מקראי אחריני מדם זבחיך ישפך ולרבי מבדם ועפי הוה ליה לאיתויי הך דרשה ז] *דלעיל על רבי עקיבא ורבי ישמעאל דפליגי שהרי אית להו הך דרשה וקרא דלעיל *)מייתי לרבי ישמעאל ורבי עקיבא דהכא ועוד קשה דלקמן בסוף פירקין (דף נו:) ילפינן דגואי לבראי ודבראי לגואי הא אין לו יסוד לפנימי עצמו או יסוד בתחילת מתנות בכור מעשר ופסח בגזירה שוה דזריקה זריקה מעולה ולמה לי תיפוק לי בקל וחומר דרבי ישמעאל ורבי עקיבא דהכא ומה שירים שאין מכפרין כו' כי היכי דילפינן מהאי קל וחומר עולה ושלמים וכי תימא משום דשייכי בכפרה יותר מבכור שהוא בא חובה נילף בקל וחומר כי האי גוונא ומה שירים שאין מעכבין טעונין יסוד תחילת *עולה שמעכבת אינו דין שטעונה יסוד ועוד שירים טעונין יסוד מהאי קרא או מקרא דלעיל התחילתן לא כל שכן ועוד דקאמר אתיא זריקה מעולה אמאי נקט עולה טפי משלמים או שאר קרבנות הלא כולהו מקל וחומר דהכא אתו והוה ליה למימר אתיא זריקה זריקה משאר קרבנות ועוד דקאמר התם ועולה גופא מנא לן דכתיב אל יסוד מזבח העולה הא תחילת מתנות מקל וחומר ח] וקרא אתי לשירים ליסוד ובקונטרס דחק לקמן ופירש דכדי נסבה ועוד קשה היכי עביד קל וחומר משירים נימא חטאת תוכיח ט] שמכפרת ואינה טעונה יסוד אף אני אביא כל תחילת דמים מחטאת י] ויש לומר לפי שהיא על ארבע קרנות וליכא למימר יסוד בכולהו ועוד אמרינן לקמן בפירקין (דף נג:) נאמר סביב בחטאת ונאמר סביב בעולה ופריך אי מה חטאת ארבע מתנות על ארבע קרנות אף עולה טעונה כו' יא] (והא) אמרת עולה טעונה יסוד מהיכן פשוט לו בעולה טפי מבחטאת הא בחטאת נמי איכא ק"ו דעולה ועוד עולת העוף שהיתה נעשית על קרן מזרחית דרומית כדלקמן (שם) אמאי לא תהא טעונה יסוד מקל וחומר ומה שירים דחטאת העוף שאין מכפרין טעונין יסוד תחילת עולה שמכפרת אינו דין שטעונה יסוד ומפרש רבינו חיים דמקרא דהכא ליכא למילף שפיכת שירים יב] לדמים החיצונים אלא לעולה דווקא כדמפרש בקרא וקרא דודם זבחיך ישפך (דברים יב) לא אתא אלא לנאכלין דכתיב בסיפיה והבשר תאכל וכן והנשאר בדם כתיב בחטאת העוף הנאכלת *וקרא דאל יסוד מזבח אתא לאשמועינן בעולה שיש לו תורת יסוד יג] (או אינו כו') כלומר תחילת מתנותיה של עולה יהא כנגד היסוד ומסיק מי כתיב אל יסוד העולה דמשמע תחילת דמים יסוד מזבח העולה כתיב דמשמע שירים והדר אמר דדילמא כתיב מזבח דלא תימא אזקיפה דיסוד אלא אגגו ועל זה קאמר רבי ישמעאל דמקל וחומר אתי דכיון דכתיב ביה יסוד בפירוש מקל וחומר ידענא דהוי אגגו ואם כן על כרחין לשירים של עולה דליהוי איסוד קאתי יד] ומהשתא אתיא תחילת עולה בקל וחומר משירים דידיה אבל משירים של חטאת לא עבדינן קל וחומר *בתחילת דמים בקרבן אחר כי אם על שירים של אותו קרבן עצמו גמרינן תחילה מתנותיו ושאר קרבנות דלא כתיב בהו יסוד אתו בג"ש זריקה זריקה מעולה כמו בכור ומעשר והא דבעי לקמן (דף נז.) אבכור כנגד היסוד מנא לן משום דעליה קאי אי נמי לאחר שפירש כל הקרבנות קבעי כנגד היסוד מנא לן טו] וקאתיא זריקה זריקה מעולה אכולהו אבל מקל וחומר (דחטאת) לא אתי כיון דלא כתיב ביה יסוד בפירוש דהאי קל וחומר לא אתי אלא לגלויי דיסוד דקאמר אגגו קאמר ולא שייך למימר חטאת תוכיח אהאי קל וחומר ומיהו קשה לתנא דבריש בית שמאי (לעיל דף לז.) דדריש טז] שפיכה במעשר ופסח מודם זבחיך ישפך מנא ליה יסוד הא לא כתיב בהו זריקה *ואכתי קשה לי כי היכי דילפינן תחילת עולה מקל וחומר דשירים דידיה הכי נמי נילף שאר קרבנות לתחילת דמים משירים דידהו דאתי מודם זבחיך ולמה לי לקמן למילף בכור ומעשר בגזירה שוה מעולה ותו דלקמן דקאמר ועולה גופה מנא לן דכתיב אל יסוד מזבח העולה קשה כמו לפירוש רש"י וגם אינו מתורץ אמרת עולה טעונה יסוד מהיכא פשוט לו יותר מחטאת ויש ליישב פירוש זה דתחילת עולה כנגד יסוד לא גמר כלל מקל וחומר אפילו משירים יז] דידיה אלא מקרא דאל יסוד מזבח העולה ידעינן תחילת דמים ליסוד ומזבח דמיותר לגג לא איצטריך דמקל וחומר אתי אם כן דרשינן מיניה לשירים ליסוד אבל קל וחומר לא אתי כלל אלא לגגו היכא דכתיב יסוד השתא אתי הכל שפיר אך קשה קצת דדרשינן מן הפסוק תרתי מילי תחילת דמים ומיתורא דמזבח דרשינן שירים יח] ואימא לשירים לחודא אתי ויש לומר דקודם יש לי להעמיד פשטא דקרא דתחילת מתנות והייתור לשירים . יט] ברוך . ויש עוד לפרש בע"א תן יסוד למזבח של עולה שכל תחילת מתן דמים שעל מזבח העולה יהיו כנגד היסוד בר מחטאת דכתיב כ] בהדיא קרנות דגזירת הכתוב הוא או אינו אלא מזבח של עולה יהא ליסוד כלומר דווקא דעולה ולא דשאר קרבנות ופריך מי כתיב כא] ליסוד העולה דמשמע עולה דווקא מזבח העולה כתיב דמשמע כל דמים של מזבח העולה הדר קאמר דילמא כתיב מזבח העולה משום גג יסוד ועלה קאמר רבי ישמעאל גג אתי בקל וחומר והאי קל וחומר לא אתי אלא לגלויי דיסוד דקאמר קרא אגגו קאמר ולא שייך למימר חטאת תוכיח ומסיק תן יסוד למזבח של עולה והא דצריך לקמן גזירה שוה דזריקה זריקה משום דתחילת מתן דמים ליסוד מדרשא כב] למזבחה של עולה לא ידעינן אלא דומיא דעולה שהן דורון ומכפר לאפוקי בכור ומעשר ופסח אי נמי דומיא דעולה דשתי מתנות שהן ארבע ואפילו ילפינן שירים דידהו ליסוד מודם זבחיך ישפך או מדרבי מכל מקום תחילת דמים לא ידעינן בקל וחומר כג] משירים לא אתו דאיכא למימר חטאת תוכיח ולקמן דקאמר אמרת עולה טעונה יסוד משום דעיקר קרא בעולה כתיב ואם תאמר אכתי כד] לא דרשינן מתן דמים ליסוד מזבח למעשר ופסח מודם זבחיך ישפך הא לא כתיב בהו זריקה ומנא לן כה] יסוד וכי תימא מבנין אב דבכור אם כן תיפשוט דדבר הלמד בגזירה שוה חוזר ומלמד בבנין אב ויש לומר כיון דגלי לן קרא גזירה שוה כו] במתנת בכור אם כן תן יסוד למזבחה של עולה בכל דמים איירי אפילו באותן שבמתנה אחת כז] *איתנהו כמעשר ופסח ומיהו עולת העוף לא אתיא דלא מיירי קרא אלא בנזבחים ואם תאמר דלקמן (דף נג:) מפרש דקרן דרומית מזרחית לא היה לה יסוד לפי שלא כח] היה בחלקו של טורף והרצועה יוצאה מחלקו של יהודה ונכנסת לחלקו של בנימין למאן דאמר ירושלים לא נתחלקה כט] (*היכי גמרינן מהתיא) ברייתא דרצועה כדמוכח בפ"ק דיומא (דף יב.) דאם כן לכוליה מזבח היה לו יסוד מזבח ואם כן כל הני קראי למה לי ל] הא אין מזבח בלא יסוד כדאמר לקמן פרק קדשי קדשים (דף סב.) דכבש ויסוד וריבוע מעכבין ושמא אפי' למאן דאמר לא נתחלקה הכי לא] גמרינן דלא היה לו יסוד וצריך לדקדק לקמן*) דבעי למימר רבי יהודה אף בדמים שיכול לזרוק על הרצפה מאי עביד להו להני קראי דמוכחי דעולה טעונה יסוד וגג יסוד לב] ויש לומר דקודם דקדיש דוד הרצפה או אם נעקרה הרצפה סמוך למזבח או לא קדיש עד ארעית תהומא : *הכי גרסינן מאשר פתח אהל מועד נפקא. ואף על גב דדרשינן ליה ליסוד מערבי תרתי שמע מינה לג] :

*) נ"א לייתי אר' ישמעאל כו'

*) [דף ס.]

[גי' צ"ק לעיל על ר' ישמעאל דפליגי שהרי איתא ליה הך דרשא וקרא דלעיל לייתי על ר"ע דהכא]. ונ"א על הך דרשא דלעיל ר"ע

גי' צ"ק קרא לשירים הא בראי כו' וכ"ת דכי אפיך

נ"א עולין

נ"ל ופריך או אינו אלא מזבחה של עולה תהא ליסוד וקרא דאל יסוד מזבח כו' [תורת יסוד כלומר]

תחלת דמים דקרבן אחר כי אם משירים של כו' צ"ק

צ"ק מ"ז

ועוד קשה צ"ק

נ"ל וכיוצ מעשר ופסח

נ"א ופליג אהכיא ברייתא [כו' א"כ] וגי' צ"ק לא גמרינן כהכיא ברייתא כו' א"כ לכוליה כו' יסוד וא"כ

[שייך לע"א]

שיטה מקובצת

א] למה לי לשירים הא. תיבות קרא שירים נמחק: ב] וכי תימא.ס"י אי לא כתיב בעולה אלא אל יסוד המזבח סתמא הו"א דנפיך מיפך : ג] עולה דאי ס"ד כדכתיב הני למה לי לשירים הא בראי עביד להו וכ"ת דנפיך מיפך : ד] תן יסוד תיבת לה נמחק: ה] יהא יסוד אות ל' נמחק : ו] ישמעאל קרא לא איצטריך : ז] דרשא לעיל על כו' שהרי הכא אית להו הך דרשא ואקראי . נ"א וקראי דלעיל מייתרי לדרבי ישמעאל כו' : ח] מק"ו אתי וקרא: ט] שמכפרת. ס"א שמעכבת: י] מחטאת תוס' ויש לומר כו' בכולהו ע"כ ועוד אמרי': יא] תיבת והא נמחק : יב] שירים לכל דמים החיצונים : יג] תורת יסוד וה"ק תן יסוד למזבח של עולה כלומר לזריקת עולה שעל המזבח כדכתיב וזרקו על המזבח תן לו יסוד שישפוך שירים ליסוד או אינו אלא למזבחה של עולה תהא יסוד כלומר כו' ס"א ופריך או אינו כו' כלומר : יד] קאתי והשתא אתיא כו' משירים דידה . תוס' אבל משירים כו' בתחלת דמים לקרבן אחר כי אם משירים של אותו קרבן כו' מתנותיו ע"כ ושאר : טו] מנא לן וקאמר אתיא זריקה : טז] דדריש מתן דמים ואימורין במעשר ופסח מודם כו' מק"ז דשירים דידה ה"נ : יז] משירים דידה אלא מקרא דאל יסוד העולה תיבת מזבח נמחק : יח] ואימא לשירים לחודה אתי נ"א שירים אל יסוד אתי : יט] תיבת ברוך נמחק : כ] דכתיב ביה בהדיא ד' קרנות : כא] כתיב אל יסוד העולה : כב] מדרשא דלמזבחה של עולה כו' שהוא דורון ומכפר תיבת שהן נמחק : כג] בק"ו דתחלת דמים משידים לא אתו : כד] אכתי תנא דדריש מתן . תיבות לא דרשינן נמחק : כה] ומנא לן כנגד יסוד : כו] נז"ש במתנות בכור : כז] ואתי מעשר . תיבת ואיתנהו נמחק : כח] שלא היתה בחלקו של טורף דרצועה יוצאה : כט] לא נתחלקה פליג אהאיא ברייתא דרצועה יוצאה כדמוכח כו' : ל] למה לי לאשמועינן דעולה טעונה יסוד הא : לא] הכי גמירי : לב] יסוד . תוס' וי"ל דקודם כו' למזבח אי לא קדוש עד ארעית תהומא . ע"כ : לג] ש"מ דש"מ אין מקרא יוצא מידי פשוטו דמשמע דהו מזבח החיצון וליכא למימר דכולה להכי הוא דאתא ומנלן יסוד מערבי די"ל דא"כ לכתוב אשר לפני אהל מועד או אשר בחצר מאי ת"ל פתח ש"מ ליסוד מערבי כדאמרי' לקמן . הר"פ :

'At the base of the altar of burnt-offering: [51*b*] apply [the laws of] the base to the altar of burnt-offering.' For if you think that it is [meant literally] as written, why do I need a text in respect of the residue, seeing that [the pouring out of] the residue was performed without?[5] And should you say [that but for the text, I would

(5) On the outer altar as is expressly prescribed in connection with the two inner sacrifices *'at the entrance of the tent of meeting'*, verses 7 and 8. Obviously then the residue of the blood too would be poured out at the base of the same.

argue] that it is indeed reversed: [52a] [the residue of] the inner [offerings] on the outer [altar], and [that of] the outer [offerings] on the inner [altar];[6] surely the inner altar had no base![7]

'Yet perhaps that is not so; rather [it intimates]: let there be a base to the altar of burnt-offering! But is it written, 'at the base of the burnt-offering'? surely it is written, *'at the base of the altar of* a *burnt-offering!'*[1]—If 'at the base of the burnt-offering' were written, I would say [that it means] on the vertical [wall] of the base;[2] now that it is written, *at the base of the* altar *of burnt-offering*, it denotes on the roof [top] of the base.[3] [Thereupon] R. Ishmael said: For the roof of the base, why do I need a text? [this would follow] *a fortiori:* if the residue [of the blood of the sin-offering], which does not make atonement, requires the roof; then the sprinkling itself of [the blood of] the burnt-offering, which makes atonement, is it not logical that it requires the roof [of the base]? Said R. Akiba: If the residue [of the blood of the sin-offering], which does not make atonement and does not come for atonement, requires the roof of the base, is it not logical that the sprinkling itself of [the blood of] the burnt-offering, which makes atonement and comes for atonement, requires the roof of the altar? If so, why does Scripture state, *'at the base of the altar of burnt-offering'*? To teach: apply [the laws of] the base to the altar of burnt-offering.

Wherein do they differ?[4]—Said R. Adda b. Ahabah: They disagree as to whether [the pouring out of] the residue is indispensable. One master holds: It is indispensable, while the other master holds: It is not indispensable.[5] R. Papa said: All agree that the residue is not indispensable, but here they disagree as to whether the draining out of [the blood of] the bird sin-offering is b indispensable or not:[1] one master holds that it is indispensable, while the other master holds that it is not indispensable.

It was taught in accordance with R. Papa: *And all the remaining blood of the bullock shall he pour out at the base of the altar:*[2] Why is *'the bullock'* stated?[3] It teaches that the Day of Atonement bullock must have its blood poured out at the base:[4] that is the view of R. Akiba.[5] Said R. Ishmael: [This is inferred] *a fortiori:* if that whose blood does not enter within as a statutory obligation[6] needs the base, that whose blood enters within as a statutory obligation,[7] is it not logical that it needs the base? Said R. Akiba: If that whose blood does not enter the innermost sanctuary[8] either as a statutory obligation or as a regulation needs the base, that whose blood enters the innermost sanctuary as a statutory obligation, is it not logical that it needs the base? You might think that it is indispensable for it:[9] therefore it states, *And he shall make an end of atoning*,[10] which teaches, All the atoning services are [now] complete:[11] these are the words of R. Ishmael. Now an *a fortiori* argument can be made in respect of the anointed priest's bullock: If that whose blood does not enter within either as a statutory obligation or as a regulation,[12] needs the base; that whose blood enters within both as a statutory obligation and as a regulation,[13] is it not logical that it needs the base?[14] You might think that it is indispensable for it; therefore Scripture says, *'And all the remaining blood of the bullock shall he pour out'*: the Writ trans- c mutes it into the remainder of a precept,[1] to teach you that [the pouring out of] the residue is not indispensable.[2]

Now, does R. Ishmael hold that the draining of [the blood of] the bird sin-offering is indispensable? Surely the school of R. Ishmael taught: *'And the rest of the blood shall be drained out'*: that

(6) I.e., the residue of the blood of the inner sin-offerings is to be poured out at the base of the outer altar, and *vice versa*. (7) Hence it must be interpreted as stated.

a (1) If it intimated that the sprinkling itself must be performed on that part of the altar which has a base (v. *supra* 51a n.b4), it could not refer to sin-offerings, whose blood was sprinkled on *all* the horns of the altar, including the south-east. Hence it would have to refer to the burnt-offering alone; but in that case Scripture should write, at the base of the burnt-offering, which would intimate that the blood of the burnt-offering must be sprinkled over against the base. The word *'altar'* then becomes redundant. (2) The base was a cubit high, the altar then being recessed one cubit; thus the base had a vertical wall of a cubit, and a top surface (roof) of a cubit. (3) Which is hard by the altar itself. (4) R. Ishmael and R. Akiba. (5) R. Akiba holds the latter view; hence he emphasises that it does not come for atonement.

b (1) V. Lev. V, 9: *and the rest of the blood shall be drained out at the base of the altar.* (2) Lev. IV, 7. The text refers to the anointed priest's sin-offering. (3) It is apparently superfluous, since the whole passage deals with it. (4) *'The bullock'*, being superfluous, extends this law to another bullock. (5) Emended text. Cur. edd. Rabbi. (6) *Sc.* the anointed priest's bullock of sin-offering. Its blood is sprinkled on the inner altar, where it is sacrificed, but there is no statutory obligation for the offering at all, as he need not have sinned. (7) The Day of Atonement bullock is a statutory offering, whether the High Priest had sinned or not. (8) The Holy of Holies. (9) *Sc.* the pouring out of the blood of the Day of Atonement bullock at the base. (10) Lev. XVI, 20. (11) I.e., all the services indispensable to atonement have by now been enumerated, and the pouring out of the blood at the base is not one of them. (12) E.g., the blood of the ruler's he-goat or of a common layman's sin-offering: both were slaughtered at the *outer* altar, and their blood was poured out there. (13) Viz., the blood of the anointed priest's bullock. Rashi proposes the deletion of 'a statutory obligation', since it has just been stated that it is not one. If it is retained, we must explain that it is called a statutory obligation only by comparison with the blood of other sin-offerings, which does not enter within at all. (14) Since it can be inferred thus, the explicit Scriptural law to that effect is apparently superfluous, and so might be interpreted as teaching that it is indispensable. Therefore he proceeds to shew that it is not indispensable.

c (1) Scripture changed the form of expression here: for the other services (*sc.* the carrying and sprinkling) are ordered thus: and he shall take . . . and he shall sprinkle etc. The different grammatical form in this case shews that this pouring out is, as it were, not an integral part of the rite, but the remaining portion of it, which should be done, yet is not indispensable. (2) And since this is given as R. Ishmael's view, it supports R. Papa's thesis *supra*.

דבראי לגואי ודגואי לבראי הא אין לו יסוד לפנימי עצמו או אינו אלא מזבח של עולה יהא א] ליסוד מי כתיב אל יסוד העולה ב] אל יסוד מזבח העולה כתיב אי הוה כתיב אל יסוד העולה הוה אמינא ג] בזקיפה אל יסוד השתא דכתיב אל יסוד מזבח העולה אגגו דיסוד ד] א"ר ישמעאל גג יסוד למה לי קרא ק"ו הוא ומה ה] שירי חטאת שאינה מכפרת טעונה גג יסוד תחלת עולה שמכפרת אינו דין שטעונה גג יסוד אמר רבי עקיבא ומה ו] שירי חטאת שאין מכפרין ואין באין לכפר טעונה גג יסוד תחלת עולה שמכפרת ובאה לכפר אינו דין שטעונה גג יסוד אם כן מה ת"ל אל יסוד מזבח העולה תן יסוד למזבח של עולה מאי בינייהו אמר רב אדא בר אהבה שירים מעכבים איכא בינייהו מר סבר מעכבי ומר סבר לא מעכבי *רב פפא אמר דכולי עלמא בשירים אין מעכבים והכא במיצוי חטאת ז] העוף מעכב קא מיפלגי מר סבר מעכב ומר סבר לא מעכב תניא כוותיה דרב פפא °ואת כל ח] (*הדם) [הפר] ישפך מה ת"ל הפר לימד על פר יום הכיפורים שטעון מתן דמים ליסוד דברי *רבי אמר רבי ישמעאל קל וחומר ט] ומה אם מי שאין נכנס דמו י] לפנים חובה טעון יסוד מי שנכנס דמו לפנים חובה אינו דין שטעון יסוד אמר רבי עקיבא ומה מי שאין דמו נכנס לפני ולפנים יא] בין לחובה בין למצוה טעון יסוד מי שנכנס דמו חובה לפני ולפנים אינו דין שטעון יסוד יכול יב] יעכבנו ת"ל °וכלה מכפר את הקדש שלמו כל הכפרות כולן דברי רבי ישמעאל קל וחומר לפר כהן משיח (משעיר נשיא) מעתה ומה מי שאין נכנס דמו לפנים לא חובה ולא מצוה טעון יסוד מי שנכנס דמו לפנים בין לחובה בין למצוה אינו דין שטעון יסוד יכול יעכבנו תלמוד לומר ואת כל (*הדם) [הפר] ישפך נתקו הכתוב יד] לעשה ועשאו שירי מצוה לומר לך שירים אין מעכבין וסבר רבי ישמעאל מיצוי חטאת העוף מעכב והתנא דבי רבי ישמעאל °והנשאר בדם ימצה טו] והנשאר ימצה ושאינו

[מעילה ט.] [צ"ל ר"ע וכ"ה בילקוט] [בס"י ליתא]

תורה אור: ויקרא ד · שם טז · שם ה

או אינו טז] כו' (א) . ואי ס"ד לגופיה אתא הכי למה לי מה בא ללמדנו לשירים יז] אשר ישפך שיריו למזבח החיצון פשיטא דעליו ישפכם דהא תחילת מתנותיו בחוץ נעשו וכי תימא אי (לא) כתיב אל יסוד מזבח יח] סתמא הוה אמינא כפיך מיפך שירי הדם הפנימיים הצריך הכתוב לשפוך בחוץ ומהם אתה לומד שירי החיצון יתננו לפנימי הא אין לו יסוד לפנימי עצמו הילכך על כרחך תן יסוד למזבח של עולה קאמר יט] : מי כתיב אל יסוד העולה אל יסוד מזבח העולה כתיב . בשלמא אי דרשת ליה ליתן תורת שפיכת שיריים לכל דמים החיצונים שפיר כתיב מזבח העולה ליתן תורת יסוד למזבח העולה לכל דמים הנזרקים עליו אלא אי לתחילת כ] דמים קא דרשת ליה תו ליכא למימר ליתן תורה כנגד היסוד למזבח העולה לכל דמיו דהא כא] חטאת טעונה מתן על ארבע קרנות וקרן דרומית מזרחית בכלל ועל כרחך אעולה לחודיה תדרשיה הוה ליה למיכתב אל יסוד העולה שהאה העולה כנגד היסוד מזבח העולה מאי היא : כב] בזקיפה דיסוד . שיזרוק תחילת מתנות העולה בעליית אמה שמן הארץ עד הכניסה שהיא כנוס אמה דכולה ההוא אמה בין בגובהה בין בכניסה יסוד מיקרייא השתא דכתיב אל יסוד המזבח יסוד שהוא דומה למזבח דהיינו גג של יסוד : כג] שיריים מעכבין איכא בינייהו . ר' ישמעאל סבר כפרה הוא דלא מכפרי אבל עכובי מעכבי רבי עקיבא דמוסיף ואין באין לכפרה אשמעינן דאין מתן דמים של כד] מתנות תלוי בהן דלא מעכבי להו שיריים להזאות: דכולי עלמא שיריים כה] לא מעכבי . בחטאות ואפי' פנימיות והנך שיריים דאיפלוג בהו ר' ישמעאל ור' עקיבא במילוי חטאת העוף כו] שהוא שירי הזאתו דכתיב והזה מדם החטאת על קיר המזבח והנשאר בדם וגו' (ויקרא ה): תניא כוותיה דרב פפא כז]. דאית ליה לר' ישמעאל נמי לא מעכבי שיריים : ואת כל דם הפר . בכהן משיח כתיב ואת כל הדם ישפוך היה יכול לכתוב מה ת"ל הפר כו': א"ר ישמעאל כו' . לא לחלוק הוא בא אלא ללמד שאין שיריים מעכבין בו והכי קאמר פר יוה"כ מק"ו הוא בא וכתבו הכתוב יכול לעכב כתבו לך ת"ל וכלה מכפר כו' מסקנא דמילתא דרבי ישמעאל כח] אתיא : מי שאין נכנס דמו לפנים חובה . כגון פר כהן משיח כט] שכניסת דמו לפנים אינה חובה קבועה שלא היה מצוה לחטוא ולהביא חטאת : טעון יסוד . שפיכת שיריים : מי שנכנס דמו לפנים חובה . פר יום הכפורים שהוא חובה קבועה בכל שנה ורבי עקיבא בא להוסיף על דבריו עד שאתה לומדו מהיכל שדם פר נכנס לו מצוה לא ולמדו מלפני ולפנים שאינו נכנס לו לא לחובה ולא למצוה וזה נכנס לו אפילו לחובה אינו דין ל] שיטעון : יכול יעכבנו . דניהוי כמי ששנה עליו הכתוב לעכב שהרי לא הוצרך לכתוב וכתבו : תלמוד לומר . באחרי מות וכלה מכפר שלמו כל הכפרות כולן בעבודות הללו האמורות בענין ושפיכת שיריים לא נאמרו שם : קל וחומר לפר כהן משיח מעתה . מאחר שבאנו לכלל קל וחומר לא] יש לנו לדרוש קל וחומר כיוצא בו ולומר ששיריים מעכבין בפר כהן משיח מריבוי הכתוב שהרי בקל וחומר היה למד לשפיכת שיריים משעיר נשיא יכול יעכבנו מעתה תלמוד לומר לב] וכלה : ומה מי שאין נכנס דמו לפנים . כגון שעיר נשיא וחטאת יחיד שאין נכנסים להיכל לא חובה ולא מצוה טעונין יסוד פר משיח שנכנס דמו לפנים מצוה אינו דין שטעון יסוד נראה בעיני דלא גרסינן בהאי מסקנא בין לחובה בין למצוה אלא למצוה גרידתא ואי גרסינן לה לא תיקשה אדתנא ברישא על דם פר משיח שאינו נכנס לפנים חובה וכאן הוא שונה בין חובה בין מצוה לגבי פר יום הכפורים לא הוי כניסת פר לג] משיח חובה שאינו חובה כמותו אבל לגבי שעיר נשיא דלא עייל ליה כלל קרי לה לכניסת פר משיח חובה ובמסכת סוטה (דף מד:) אמרינן כהאי גוונא מצוה לגבי רשות חובה קרי ליה : יכול יעכבנו . מעתה דניהוי כמי ששנה עליו לעכב : ת"ל ואת כל דם הפר וגו' נתקו הכתוב . מסדר שאר העבודות ועשאו שירי מצוה ששנה בהילוך לשונו לד] שכל העבודות כתיב ולקח והזה ונתן על קרנות וכאן לא כתיב לה] ושפך דמו אל יסוד אלא שנה במשמעה לנתקו מכלל שאר העבודות לומר שאינה חובה לו] כמו אותם לעכב :

דבראי לגואי . וא"ת הא אמר ר' עקיבא לקמן (דף פא:) דכל דמים שהכנים לפנים פסולין וי"ל דשירים אין מכפרין לרבי' עקיבא ולא קרינן בהו לכפר בקודש : **גג** יסוד למה לי קרא ק"ו לז] . הקשה ה"ר חיים לקמן פרק התערובת (דף פא.) אמרינן גבי דם חטאת שנתערב בדם עולה דפליגי רבי אליעזר ורבנן אמר אביי לא שנו אלא תחילת חטאת ועולה אבל סוף חטאת ותחילת עולה דברי הכל מקום עולה מקום שירים פירוש דאם נתערבו שירי חטאת בתחילת עולה לכולי עלמא יתנם למטה מן החוט דמקום תחילת מתן עולה כשר לשירי חטאת ויזרקם לקיר המזבח ומאליהם שותתין ליסוד ואין כאן שנוי מקום א"ל רב יוסף הכי אמר רב יהודה שיריים צריכין אילטבא פירוש שישפכם על גג היסוד ממש העשוי כאילטבא ולא יזרקם לקיר הזקוף כמשפט עולה דמשמע דעולה אינה טעונה גג יסוד וי"ל דהאי דבעינן הכא בתחילת עולה גג יסוד לא אתא אלא למעוטי אמה לח] אדמה התחתונה של מזבח שמן הארץ עד הכניסה אבל קיר הזקוף של מעלה לט] עד היסוד פשיטא דעדיף מ] (בעולה) מגג יסוד ממש דחודה עדיף משום דבעינן שתי מתנות שהן ארבע : **לימד** על פר יוה"כ שטעון מתן דמים ליסוד . לעיל פרק בית שמאי (דף מ:) גבי ועשה לפר כאשר עשה דריש סמיכה ושירי הדם בפר יוה"כ ותימא להאי *תנא סמיכה מנא ליה ושם פירשנו : **ומה** מי שאין נכנס דמו לפנים חובה . תימה מה לפר כהן משיח שכן מכפר על עבירת מצוה ידועה כדפריך לעיל פ' בית שמאי (דף מ:) מא] וי"ל דסמיך אהאי דאתי בקל וחומר משעירי רגלים ושעירי ראשי חדשים דדבר הלמד בהיקש חוזר ומלמד בק"ו : **יכול** יעכבנו מב] . דלית לן למימר טרח וכתב לה קרא כל כמה דאיכא למידרש :

ז"ק מ"ז · ז"ל דם · ג"י' הכ"ק תנא דסכא סמיכה כו'

כא א מיי' פ"ה מהל' מעה"ק הל"ו :
כב ב מיי' שם פי"ט הלכה ד :
כג ג מיי' שם פ"ז הלכה ז :
כד ד מיי' פ"ד מהל' עיוה"כ הל"ב :

הגהות הב"ח
(א) רש"י ד"ה או אינו וכו' וה"ס ואי ס"ד כצ"ל והד"א עם דיבור הקודם :

שיטה מקובצת
א] יהא יסוד מי כתיב : ב] עי' בהשמטות בסוף המסכת : ג] אמינא אזקיפה דיסוד השתא דכתיב אל יסוד המזבח משמע יסוד שהוא דומה למזבח דהיינו גג של יסוד . ואזקיפה דמזבח דממעט הכא היינו שלא יזרוק תחילת מתנות העולה בעליית אמה שמן הארץ עד הכניסה כו' עד יסוד מקרייא אבל הזקיפה שהיא מן הגג עד חוט הסיקרא לא ממעט דאדרבה דהא מוכח לקמן [בפ' התערובת] דשם מקום מתנות העולה ולא על גג יסוד ממש . תו"א : ד] אמר ר' ישמעאל (על) גג היסוד כו' . לעיל פ"ה דעיקר היסוד בתחילת [מתן] דם העולה ילפינן מקו"ח דהטאת וגג יסוד [ג"כ] נפקא לן מהאי קו"ח וכאן לא פי' כלום וקשה לפ"ה כיון דעיקר יסוד מחטאת יליף איכא למיפרך חטאת תוכיח ששיריה ליסוד ואין תחילת דמה ליסוד רק על הקרנות ונראה להר"ר חיים כו' ומיהו אכתי למסקנא כו' ותירץ כו' מ"מ קשה לפי' הר"ר חיים דמשמע דתחילת דמו דעולה נפקא לן מקו"ח ולקמן מייתי אל יסוד מזבח העולה לתחילת דמו לכך נראה לריב"א דבין תחילת דם ובין שירים נפקא דטעונים יסוד מפשטיה דקרא כדמוכח לקמן וקו"ח לא איצטריך כי אם לגג יסוד ותלמודא לא דייק כו' תוס' אחרות: ה] ומה שירים שאינן מכפרים טעונים גג : ו] ומה שירים שאין מכפרין ואין באין לכפרה טעונין גג יסוד כו' ובאה לכפרה אינו דין שטעונה גג יסוד ומה ת"ל אל יסוד : ז] חטאת העוף לקמן דף ס"ה ע"ב: ח] ואת כל דם הפר כו'. פ"ה דהפר מיותר דה"מ למיכתב כו' וא"ת תיפוק ליה מדאתקיש לפר העלם ובפר העלם כתיב יסוד וי"ל דלא איתקש אלא לעבודות המעכבות כפרה כדאמר בפ' ב"ש וא"ת מ"מ תיפוק לי מוכן יעשה דיליף מיניה שירים התם וי"ל דדריש ליה לקרנות וא"ת א"כ דוכן יעשה אתא לקרנות סמיכה בפר יוה"כ מנלן דלא איתקש לפר העלם אלא לעבודות המעכבות הכפרה וי"ל דמדכתיב וסמך ידו על ראש הפר בפר כהן משיח דהוי ליה למיכתב וסמך ידו על ראשו מה ת"ל לפר לרבות פר יוה"כ לסמיכה וא"ת יותרת וב' הכליות בפר יוה"כ מנ"ל [וי"ל] מכל חלב פר החטאת לרבות פר יוה"כ אבל בהיקש לא ידעינן אלא העבודות האמורו' בענין: ט] ומה מי שאין נכנס כו' תימה אמאי לא מייתי קו"ח דפרק ב"ש ומה במקום שלא השוה כו' וי"ל דמהאי קו"ח לא מצי למילף הכא דבר חדש דלא משמע מהתם אלא דבר המפורש בהם ומהאי דהכא חשיב ספי למילף דבר חדש וא"ת מ"מ האי קו"ח אמאי לא מייתי התם וי"ל דמהאי קו"ח לא משמע כי אם חומרא ולעיל בעי למילף נמי קולא להכשיר אמ"ן שבאצבע : י] דמו חובה לפנים טעון יסוד מי שנכנס דמו חובה לפנים אינו דין שטעון יסוד : יא] ולפנים לא לחובה ולא למצוה טעון יסוד מי שנכנס דמו לפני ולפנים בין לחובה ובין למצוה אינו דין : יב] יעכבנו עיין רש"י לעיל (דף יג ע"א) ובתוס' (דף לט ע"ב) : יג] כל דם הפר ישפך נתקו הכתוב פי' דלא כתיב [illegible]

שיטה מקובצת
דדרשינן לעיל בפר העלם דשירים אין מעכבין והרי איתקש פר כהן משיח לפר העלם וי"ל כיון דאיכא הכא קו"ח וגם פסוק הוא דשינה הכתוב לעכב קמ"ל ישפך נתקו [הכתוב וכו'] וא"ת א"כ קשה איפכא למה לי ונסלה לעיל בפר העלם דשירים אין מעכבין תיפוק ליה מהכא כיון דאיתקשו וי"ל דלא הוקשו אלא להקל ולא להחמיר כלומר לריבוי עבודות ולא למעט וא"ת והא איתקש לעיל להכשיר אמ"ן שבאצבע היינו להקל וי"ל דהיינו דוקא לתיקון עבודו' המפורשות בו בכבר ולא לדבר חדש כמו שירים : יד] תיבת לעשה נמחק : טו] ימצה הנשאר ימצה : טז] כו' ס"א כמו אמר מר הוא זה ופרושי קא מפרש אמאי קאמרינן תן יסוד למזבח של עולה משום דאי כו' דאי ס"ד דהכתוב לגופיה אתא [שכל] שיריה [יתן] ליסוד ובשעיר נשיא משתעי קרא הני למה לי : מה בא זה ללמדנו אי : יז] לשירים שישפך שיריו למזבח : יח] מזבח העולה אלא אל יסוד מזבח : יט] קאמר וכדי לגלות לשירי הדם של כל הזבחים שישפוך שיהו' הדם ליסוד : כ] לתחילת מתן דמים : כא] דהא איכא חטאת שטעונה מתן על ארבע כו' מזרחית בכלל שלא היה לו יסוד ועל כרחך : כב] מה"ד אוקיפה דיסוד : כג] יסוד הס"ד ומה"ד שאינן מכפרין טעונין גג יסוד דכתיב בהו אל יסוד המזבח דמשמע' גג הס"ד : כד] של הזאות תלוי בהן כו' : כה] שירים . בחטאת לא מעכבי ואפי' דפנימיות ותיבת בחטאות נמחק : כו] העוף קאמר שהוא : כז] פפא דאמר דלר' ישמעאל ותיבות דאית ליה נמי נמחק : כח] ישמעאל להא אתיא : כט] פר כהן משיח נכנס דמו לפני : ל] דין שטעון יסוד הס"ד : לא] וחומר וזה יש : לב] ת"ל כו' : לג] פר כהן משיח : לד] לשונו שבכל העבודות : לה] ישפך את דמו אל : לו] חובה כמותם לעכב הס"ד : לז] ק"ו הוא הקשה : לח] תיבת אדמה נמחק : לט] תיבת עד נמחק : מ] דעדיף לעולה אות ב' נמחק : מא] שמאי וי"ל דאין זה פירכא דצד חומרא אלא פירכא דהשוואות . מהר"ם : מב] יעכבנו כו' ה"ד דהאי ק"ו מצוה ועיכובא מפשטיה דקרא דאל יסוד מזבח העולה שהרי ליכא לאוקמי לה קרא כיון דאיכא לאוקמי בעיכובא מפשטיה דקרא . מהר"ם .

א) נראה דצ"ל אע"פ שנכנס דמו לפנים חובה דהא מיירי בפר כהן משיח ובפר יוה"כ .

עין משפט נר מצוה

כה א מיי' פ"כ מהל' פסה"מ הל"ח:

כו ב ג מיי' שם הל"ח:

כז ד מיי' שם הל"ג:

כח ה מיי' פ"ה מהל' מעה"ק הל"ז:

גמרא

ושאינו נשאר לא ימצה תרי תנאי ואליבא דר' ישמעאל אמר רמי בר חמא האי תנא סבר שירים מעכבי דתניא °הכהן המחטא אותה (ויקרא ו) אותה שניתן דמה למעלה ולא אותה שניתן דמה למטה אמרת וכי מאין באתה מכלל שנאמר °ודם זבחיך ישפך על מזבח וגו' (דברים יב) אלמדנו לניתנין במתן ארבע שאם נתנן במתנה אחת כיפר יכול אף הניתנין למעלה שנתנן למטה כיפר ודין הוא נאמרו דמים א] למעלה ונאמרו דמים למטן ב] מה דמים האמורים למטן בשנתנן למעלן לא כיפר אף דמים האמורים למעלן גאם ג] נתן למטה לא כיפר לא אם אמרת ד] בתחתונים שניתנין בנתינה למעלה שאין סופן למעלן לא כיפר תאמר בעליונים שנתנן למטה *שיש מהן קרב למטה דמים (שיריים) הפנימיים יוכיחו *שיש מהן קרב בחוץ ואם נתנן בתחלה בחוץ לא כיפר לא אם אמרת בדמים הפנימיים שאין מזבח הפנימי ממרקן תאמר בעליונים שהרי קרנות ממרקות אותן ה] אם נתנן למטה כשרים ת"ל אותה אותה שניתן ו] דמים למעלה ולא שניתן דמה למטה מאי שאין מזבח הפנימי ממרקן לאו ז] אלו שיריים א"ל רבא אי הכי תיתי בק"ו מה שיריים הפנימיים שסופן חובה בחוץ עשאן בתחלה בחוץ לא כיפר הניתנין למעלה שאין סופן חובה למטה ועשאן בתחלה למטה אינו דין שלא כיפר אלא אין מזבח הפנימי ממרקן בלבד אלא פרוכת ח] *תנו רבנן °וכלה מכפר אם כיפר כלה ואם לא כיפר לא כלה *דברי (ויקרא טז) ר' עקיבא אמר לו רבי יהודה מפני מה לא נאמר אם כלה כיפר אם לא כלה לא כיפר *שאם חיסר אחת מכל המתנות דלא עשה ולא כלום *מאי בינייהו רבי יוחנן ורבי יהושע בן לוי חד אמר משמעות דורשין איכא בינייהו וחד אמר *שיריים ט] מעכבין איכא בינייהו תסתיים דר' יהושע בן לוי הוא דאמר שיריים דמעכבי דא"ר יהושע בן לוי לדברי האומר שיריים מעכבין מביא פר אחד ומתחיל בתחלה בפנים אטו ר' יוחנן לית ליה הא סברא והאמר ר' יוחנן *תנא ר' נחמיה כדברי האומר שירים מעכבין אלא כדברי האומר ולאו י] להני תנאי הכא נמי כדברי האומר ולאו להני תנאי: **מתני'** חטאות הצבור והיחיד אלו הן חטאות הצבור שעירי ראשי חדשים ושל מועדות שחיטתן בצפון וקיבול דמן בכלי שרת בצפון הודמן טעון ארבע מתנות על ארבע קרנות כיצד

עלה

רש"י

ושאינו נשאר. כלומר אם יצא כל הדם בהזאה אין צריך מילוי: האי תנא סבר שיריים מעכבין גרסינן: המחטא אותה יא]. הזורק את דמה ובכללה דזאת תורת החטאת כתיב אותה מיעוטא היא אם *מחטא את דמה כהלכתו שכתבתי לך יב] *בה קרנות דהיינו למעלה הוא דהואי חיטוי ונאכלת אי לא לא: וכי מאין באת. להכשיר שנזקקת להביא מקרא לפסול: ישפך. יג] שפיכה אחת ונאמר והבשר תאכל: נאמרו דמים למטה. מחוט הסיקרא בחטאת העוף והזה מדם החטאת (ויקרא ה) ודרשינן ליה לקמן (דף סד:) זה קיר התחתון: ונאמר דמים למעלה. בחטאת בהמה: מה דמים האמורים למטה שנתנן למעלה לא כיפר. דהא כתיב בהזאתו חטאת היא שאם שינה בה פסול דהכי אמרינן לקמן (דף סו.) עשאה למעלה כמעשה כולן פסול: שכן סופן למטה. שיריים ניתנין ליסוד: שסופן לחוץ. שפיכת שיריהם: ואם עשאן בתחילה בחוץ לא כפר. דעיכובא כתיב בהו *כדרבינא מועשה כאשר עשה: שאין מזבח הפנימי ממרקן. שאין שם גמר מתן דמים שעודן צריכין עבודה יד] אחת הילכך חמירי ולקמן מפרש ואזיל מאי היא: תאמר בניתנין למעלה טו] בקרנות שממרקות אותו. שהוא גמר מתן דמיהם לעכב דהא לכולי עלמא שיריים החיצונים לא מעכבי הילכך לא חמירי טז] ויכשרו למטן להכי איצטריך אותה: מאי שכן אין מזבח הפנימי ממרק אותו יז] [לאו]. דשפיכת שיריים מעכבי בהו: אמר ליה רבא. לרמי בר חמא: אי הכי. דשיריים יח] מבחוץ מעכבי בהו כל שכן דאתיא מקל וחומר ולא בעי קרא: ומה דמים הפנימיים שסוף שיריהם חובה לחוץ לעכב עשאן בתחילה בחוץ כו': הכי גרסינן אלא אין מזבח הפנימי ממרקן בלבד אלא פרכת. דדמן טעון תחילת הזייה על הפרוכת יט] הואיל וטעונין שתי עבודות בפנים חמירי לעכב מלעשות' בחוץ תאמר בניתנין למעלן שכן קרנות ממרקות את עבודותיהן העליונות ואין טעונין שתי עבודות כ] אבל בשיריים לא קאמר דליעכבו: ה"ג ת"ר וכלה מכפר וגו'. ולקמיה מפרש מאי קאמרי ומאי בינייהו: מפני מה לא נאמר. מפני מה לא נדרשנו כסדר מכתבו: משמעות דורשין כו'. כא] תרווייהו ללמד על המתנות שמעכבות קאמרי אלא מר משמע ליה הכי ומר משמע ליה הכי רבי עקיבא משמע ליה כב] מדסיפא לרישא מדריש בכפרה דהיינו במתנות תלויה השלמה ושיריים לא מעכבי ור' יהודה נמי שיריים לא מעכבי אית ליה וה"ק מ"ט תדרשיה הכי דהשתא לא שמעינן כג] מינה שכל מתנותיו מעכבות דאיכא למימר בכפרת מתנה אחת קאמר דומיא דחטאות החיצונות אלא דרוש הכי אם כלה הכל כמה כד] שכתב הוא דכיפר ואם לא כלה כל מה שבענין לא כיפר ולמדנו שאם חיסר אחת מן המתנות לא עשה כלום ושיריים לא מעכבי שאינן אמורין בענין זה דגבי פר כהן משיח הוא דאיתרבי פר יום הכיפורים לשיריים (א) ולרבי יהודה איצטריך למילף עיכוב מתנות מהכא משום כה] דאמר כי כתיבא חוקה בדברים הנעשין בבגדי לבן לפני ולפנים הוא דכתיב: שיריים מעכבי איכא בינייהו. ולרבי עקיבא לא מעכבי וה"ק אם כיפר מה שאמור בענין כלה דכתיב חוקה לעיכובא אבל שיריים שאינה אמור בענין לא מעכבי ואתא רבי יהודה למימר כו] כלה כל צורכי עבודותיו ואף המלמדין לו ממקום אחר כיפר ואם לא כלה לא כיפר שאם חיסר אחת מכל המתנות כו' ואפילו כז] במתן יסוד משמע: לדברי האומר שיריים מעכבי כו'. אם גמר כח] מתנות כולן ונשפך הדם מביא פר אחר ומתחיל (ב) בהיכל כדי שיהו לו שיריים דאע"ג דאמרי' גמר מתנות כט] מבפנים ונשפך הדם מביא פר אחר ויתחיל בפרכת גמר מתנות שעל הפרכת ונשפך הדם יביא פר אחר ויתחיל במזבח ואין צריך להתחיל עבודה שהשלים שכולן כפרה ל] בפני עצמן לדברי האומר שיריים מעכבין *ולא אמרי' אם גמר מתנות מזבח הפנימי ונשפך הדם יביא אחר וישפוך על יסוד החיצון דאם כן לאו היינו שיריים אלא במזבח יתחיל שיעשו שיריים וישפכם בחוץ אלמא לרבי יהושע בן לוי איכא למאן דאמר שיריים מעכבין: אטו ר' יוחנן מי לית ליה הך סברא. דאיכא למאן דאמר שיריים מעכבין: והא אמר רבי יוחנן. לא] בפרק השוחט (לקמן דף קיא.): תנא רבי נחמיה כדברי האומר כו'. דקתני רבי נחמיה אומר שירי הדם לב] שהקריבו בחוץ חייב ואמר רבי יוחנן עלה תנא רבי נחמיה למילתיה כדברי האומר שיריים מעכבין אלמא לרבי יוחנן נמי איכא דאית ליה הכי אלא מאי לג] משני עלה דרבי יוחנן כי מוקמן לה כר' יהושע בן לוי מבעית לשנויי אדרבי יוחנן לדברי האומר דקאמר אתנאי אחרים קאי ולא אהני תנאי דלעיל קאי לד] ארבי יהודה ורבי עקיבא הכא נמי איכא למימר דרבי יוחנן הוא דאמר שיריים מעכבים איכא בינייהו והא דקאמר רבי יהושע בן לוי לדברי האומר לאו אהני תנאי קאי: **מתני'** אלו הן חטאות ציבור. שאט צריכים להזכירם שהרי הפנימיות פר העדה ושעירי עבודת כוכבים כבר נשנו: שעירי ראשי חדשים ושל מועדות. שהן על מזבח החיצון: שחיטתן בצפון. שהרי למדנו בבנין אב לכל לה] חטאות: ארבע מתנות כו'. כדילפינן מקרנות קרנות בפרק בית שמאי (לעיל דף לז:):

עלה

תוספות

אותה שנתן דמה למעלה ולא אותה שנתן דמה למטה. וא"ת א"כ היכי פריך לעיל בריש בית שמאי (דף לח.) אימא וכפר אע"פ שלא נתן למעלה אלא למטה נו] וי"ל דהוה דריש אותה לדרשא אחריתי כדדריש לעיל בפ"ק (דף י:) אותה נז] למעלה ולא אחרת למעלה א"כ הוה מפרש אותה יאכלנה אבל למטה לא יאכלנה ולעולם כיפר ולא שייכא כאן נח] דההיא דשמואל (לעיל ד' כו:) דכיון שהגיע דם למזבח נתכפר: **מה** דמים האמורים למטה אם נתן למעלה לא כיפר. פירש בקונט' דבחטאת העוף כתיב היא שאם שינה בה פסלה ותימה הא נט] בבהמה נמי כתיב היא ונימא כמו כן שאם שינה בה פסלה: **תאמר** בניתנין למעלה שסופן למטה. תימה מ] מעולת העוף שסופן למטה ותנן לקמן בפ' חטאת העוף (דף ס.) עשאה למטה כמעשה כולן מא] פסולה ומיהו היא גופה לא ידעינן מנא לן:

כוליה

מסורת הש"ס

נ"ל חטאת נ"ק

נ"ל בה'

כ"א שכן סופן למטה

כ"א שסופן להיות בחוץ

נ"ל וכדרבינן נ"ס

יומא ס: ולעיל מ.

[בילקוט איתא דברי ר' יהודה אמר לו ר' נחמיה מפני מה וכו']

סנהדרין ד:

[יומא ס:]

[מנחות עז:]

[לעיל מב: לקמן קיא. מנחות עז: יומא ס:]

נ"ל לא

הגהות הב"ח

(א) רש"י ד"ה משמעות דורשין וכו' פר יוה"כ לשיריים הס"ד ואח"כ מ"ה שיריים מעכבי וכו' מכל המתנות כו' ולר' יהודה איצטריך למילף וכו' לפני ולפנים הוא דכתיב ואפי' במתן יסוד משמע: (ב) ד"ה לדברי האומר וכו' ומתחיל במזבח כדי שיהו לו שיריים:

שיטה מקובצת

א] דמים למטה ונאמרו דמים למעלה: ב] מה דמים האמורים למטה. פ"ה בחטאת העוף כתיב היא ותימה כו' ועוד קשה מאי קאמר שכמו שמתנה אחת כיפר כך הייתי אומר בניתנין למעלה שנתנן למטה כיפר וכי מה ענין זה לזה לכך נראה לריב"א דה"פ וכי מאין באתה מודם זבחיך ישפך דמשמע במתנה אחת בשפיכה אחת וה"ה דמשתעי קרא בכל הזבחים אפי' בחטאת וכתיב ביה ישפך דהיינו משמע למטה דשפיכה על היסוד דלשון שפיכה משמע ששופך על גבי דבר אחר היינו על גבי יסוד והיינו למטה ומחמת האי קרא הייתי אומר שנתנו למטה כיפר ולא משום שנדמה זה לנתינה במתנה אחת על כן איצטריך אותה למעלה ולא למטה והדר ואומר דין הוא כלומר שיהא פסול בלא פסוק מטעם דנאמרו דמים כו' נתנו למעלה לא כיפר לא מפני מיעוט הוא אלא מסברא כיון ששינה את מקומו אף דמים האמורים כו' ומורי אמר דלא קשה מידי לפירש"י מהיא דשעיר נשיא דאותה הא כתיב קודם מתן דמים ולא שייך לומר שאם שינה קודם מתן דמים פסול דלא משתעי בענין דם אבל היא דחטאת העוף כתיב גבי מתן דם. מהר"פ: ג] אם נתנן: ד] לא אם אמרת בניתנין למטה שכן אין סופן למעלה תאמר בניתנין למעלה שכן סופן למטה דמים הפנימים יוכיחו שסופן לחוץ ואם נתנן כו' והשאר נמחק: ה] אותן הואיל וקרנות ממרקין אותן אם: ו] שניתן דמיה למעלה: ז] לאו אלא שירים א"ל רבא כו' בק"ו ומה שירים הפנימים: ח] פרוכת. ס"א כדתנו רבנן: ט] שירים מעכבי איכא בינייהו: י] ולאו אהני תנאי כו' האומר ולאו אהני תנאי: יא] אותה בחטאת בהמה כתיב כך גירסת מהר"פ: יב] לך בארבע קרנות: יג] ישפך בשפיכה אחת: יד] עבודה אחרת: טו] שכן קרנות ממרקות אותו: טז] חמירי ויוכשרו למטן: יז] ממרק אותן לאו אלא שירים. כלומר דשירים ממרקין אותן אלמא דשפיכת שירים: יח] שבחוץ מעכבי בהו בדמים הפנימים כל שכן: יט] והואיל וטעונין: כ] עבודות למעלה: כא] ותרויהו. גירסת רש"י דמהר"פ ותרויהו אית להו דשירים לא מעכבי וסברי שכל המתנות מעכבות אלא מר משמע [ליה] מתנות שהשלמה תלויה בהם אם כיפר כילה אע"פ שלא [עשה] שירים דשירים [לא] מעכבי ור' יהודה נמי [לא מעכבי] לשירים ור"ע למילף עיכובא הכא לא איצטריך [דהא] כתיב חוקה לעיכובא [ור"י] לטעמיה דאמר כי כתיב חוקה כו': כב] מסיפא לרישא מידריש וה"ק בכפרת דהיינו: כג] שמעינן מיניה שכל כו' למימר דכפרה מתנה אחת: כד] כמה שאמר בענין הוא דכיפר: כה] משום דסבר כי כתיבא: כו] למימר אם כילה: כז] ואפילו מתן יסוד במשמע: כח] גמר המתנות כולן: כט] מתנות שבפנים: ל] כפרה כפרה בפני עצמו לדברי כו' מעכבין לא אמרינן אם גמר כו' על יסוד מזבח החיצון דא"כ לאו כו' במזבח שבהיכל יתחיל כדי שיעשו השאר שירים וישפכם: לא] יוחנן לקמן בפ' השורפ: לב] שהקריבן בחוץ: לג] מאי תשני עלה דר"י כו' כריב"ל מבעיא לן לשנויי אדר"י: לד] קאי דהיינו ר"י ור"ע: לה] לכל החטאות הס"ד: לו] למטה והא ממעט מאותה: לז] אותה דמה למעלה: לח] כאן ההיא דשמואל דכיון שהגיע דם לאויר מזבח נתכפר בבעלים הס"ד: לט] בחטאת בהמה בשעיר נשיא נמי כתיב: מ] תימה ולילף מעולת העוף שסופה למטה: מא] פסולה וי"ל דחטאת העוף נמי לא ידעינן רק מקרא דהכא דאותה דגבי חטאת בהמה וכיון דגלי גלי. מהר"פ:

יסוד

which is left must be drained out, [52b] but what is not left is not drained out?[3]—There is a controversy of two Tannaim as to R. Ishmael's opinion.

Rami b. Ḥama said: The following Tanna holds that [the pouring out of] the residue is indispensable. For it was taught: [*This is the law of the sin-offering* . . .] *the priest that offereth it for sin* [*shall eat it*]:[4] [this teaches,] only that [sin-offering] whose blood was sprinkled above [the red line],[5] but not that whose blood was applied below.[6] Say: whence did you come [to this]?[7] From the implication of what is said, *And the blood of thy sacrifices shall be poured out* [. . . *and thou shalt eat the flesh*],[8] we learn that if [the blood of] those [sacrifices] which need four applications was presented with one application
a [only], it has made atonement;[1] you might therefore think that also if the blood which should be sprinkled above [the red line] was sprinkled below, it makes atonement. And it is [indeed] logical: Blood is prescribed above,[2] and blood is prescribed below:[3] as the blood which is prescribed below does not atone if it is sprinkled above,[4] so also the blood which is prescribed above does not atone if it is sprinkled below. No: if you say [thus] in the case of the blood which should be sprinkled below, that is because it will not eventually [be applied] above;[5] will you say the same of the blood which should be sprinkled above, seeing that it will eventually [find its way] below?[6] Let the inner blood[7] prove it, which will eventually come without,[8] and yet if he applied it in the first place without, he did not make atonement. No: if you speak of the inner blood, that is because the inner altar does not complete it.[9] Will you say thus of the upper [blood], where the horns complete it?[10] [and] since the horns complete it, if he sprinkled it below, it is fit.[11] Therefore it says, '[*The priest that offereth*] it [*for a sin-offering*]': that whose blood was sprinkled above, but not that whose blood was sprinkled below. Now, what is the meaning of 'because the inner altar does not complete it'? Surely it must refer to the residue [of the blood]![12] Said Raba to him: If so, you could infer it *a minori*: if the blood of the inner sacrifices,[13] of which eventually the residue is obligatory without,[14] yet if presented without in the first place, he does not make atonement; then the blood which is to be sprinkled above, and
b is not eventually obligatory below,[1] is it not logical that if he applied it at the outset below he does not make atonement?[2]—Rather [the meaning is this]: Not the altar alone completes it, but also the veil[3].

Our Rabbis taught: '*And he shall make an end of atoning*': if he atoned, he made an end, while if he did not atone, he did not make an end: this is R. Akiba's view. Said R. Judah to him: why should we not interpret: If he made an end, he atoned, while if he did not make an end, he did not atone, which thus intimates that if he omitted one of the sprinklings his service is ineffective?[4] Wherein do they differ?—R. Joḥanan and R. Joshua b. Levi [disagree]. One maintains: They differ on the mode of interpretation.[5] The other maintains: They differ as to whether the [pouring out of the] residue is indispensable.[6] It may be proved that it was R. Joshua b. Levi who maintained that [the pouring out of] the residue is indispensable. For R. Joshua b. Levi said: On the view that the residue is indispensable, he brings another bullock and commences within.[7] But does R. Joḥanan not hold this view?[8] Surely R. Joḥanan said: R. Nehemiah taught in accordance with the view that the
c residue is indispensable?[1] But you must say 'In accordance with the view', but not that of these Tannaim.[2] Then here too,[3] 'on the view' does not refer to that of these Tannaim.

MISHNAH. PUBLIC AND PRIVATE SIN-OFFERINGS (THESE ARE THE PUBLIC SIN-OFFERINGS:[4] THE HE-GOATS OF NEW MOONS AND FESTIVALS) ARE SLAUGHTERED IN THE NORTH, AND THEIR BLOOD IS RECEIVED IN A SERVICE VESSEL IN THE NORTH, AND THEIR BLOOD REQUIRES FOUR APPLICATIONS

(3) I.e., *all* the blood may be used in sprinkling, so that nothing is left for draining. Hence draining cannot be essential and indispensable. (4) Lev. VI, 18, 19. '*Offereth it for sin*,' Heb. *ha-mehatte*, is understood to mean, who correctly performs all the rites (sprinkling) appertaining to a sin-offering; only then may he eat it. (5) As is necessary for a sin-offering, V. *supra* 10a n.c 1. (6) The flesh may not be eaten. (7) Why would you think that the flesh *may* be eaten even if the blood was not properly sprinkled, that you need a text to shew that it may not? (8) Deut. XII, 27.

a (1) Because '*shall be poured out*' implies a single act. (2) Viz., that of an animal sin-offering. (3) That of a bird sin-offering; v. *infra* 64b. (4) V. *infra* 66a. (5) Hence when he sprinkles it above he is definitely performing it incorrectly. (6) I.e. the residue. Hence when he sprinkles it below the line, he is only applying it where it would eventually come, and so he may make atonement. —Emended text (Sh. M). (7) I.e., the blood of the inner sacrifices. (8) The residue is poured out at the base of the *outer* altar.—Emended text. (9) After the blood has been sprinkled on the inner altar there still remains an indispensable service to be performed. (10) No indispensable rite remains to be performed after the blood was sprinkled on the horns of the altar. (11) So we might argue. (12) Viz., that its pouring out at the base of the altar is indispensable. This proves Rami b. Ḥama's assertion. (13) I.e., the residue of the blood which is sprinkled on the inner altar. (14) On the present hypothesis, and indispensable. The text is emended on the basis of Rashi.

b (1) Though the blood will be poured out below, this is not essential for the efficacy of the sacrifice. (2) The sacrifice is invalid, and the flesh may not be eaten. Why then is a Scriptural text necessary? Hence the premise of this argument, that the pouring out of the residue is essential, must be false! (3) The blood must be sprinkled on the veil too. (4) Lit., 'he has done nothing'.—For notes v. *supra* 40a. (5) But not in law. Both hold that all the four applications are indispensable, and that the pouring out of the residue is not indispensable. R. Akiba holds that the conclusion (atoning) illumines the beginning (make an end), whence we learn that the completion depends on atonement, i.e., on the four applications. R. Judah however maintains that 'atoning' might merely mean a single application, therefore (to avoid this conclusion) the interpretation must be reversed, and the beginning made to illumine the end: only when he quite makes an end, having completed the four applications, does he atone. (6) R. Akiba holds that it is not indispensable, and he interprets it thus: if he made atonement, i.e., performed all the rites for atonement as prescribed in that passage, he made an end. Thus the pouring out of the residue, which is not mentioned there, is not essential. R. Judah however interprets: Only when he made an end of *all* the rites, including those prescribed elsewhere (viz., the pouring out of the residue), did he make atonement. (7) If the residue of the blood was spilt after the four applications, another bullock must be slaughtered, and its blood first sprinkled within, and then the residue poured out at the base of the outer altar. But he cannot simply pour out *all* the blood at the base, for then it is not a residue, whereas a residue is indispensable.—Thus R. Joshua b. Levi holds that there is a view that the pouring out of the residue is indispensable. (8) That there is a teacher who maintains that it is indispensable.

c (1) V. *supra* 42b. (2) Viz., R. Akiba and R. Judah. (3) In the case of R. Joshua b. Levi. (4) Which need special mention here, for several have already been taught in the preceding Mishnah (*supra* 47a).

ON THE FOUR HORNS. HOW WAS IT DONE? [53a] HE WENT UP THE ASCENT, TURNED TO THE SURROUNDING BALCONY,[5] AND PASSED ON [SUCCESSIVELY] TO THE SOUTH-EAST, THE NORTH-EAST, THE NORTH-WEST, AND THE SOUTH-WEST CORNERS. THE RESIDUE OF THE BLOOD HE POURED OUT AT THE SOUTHERN BASE. THEY WERE EATEN WITHIN THE HANGINGS,[6] BY MALE PRIESTS, PREPARED IN ANY FASHION,[7] THE SAME DAY AND NIGHT, UNTIL MIDNIGHT.

GEMARA. How did he do it?[8]—R. Joḥanan and R. Eleazar [disagree]. One maintained: He applied it within a cubit in either direction.[9] The other maintained: He applied it[10] with a downward movement on the edge of the horn. On the view of R. Eleazar son of R. Simeon who said that its [blood] is applied essentially
a on the very horn [of the altar],[1] there is no dispute at all.[2] They differ on Rabbi's view:[3] One master holds that a cubit in either direction is also against the horn; while the other master holds: Only at the edge, and no further.

An objection is raised: How was the blood of the public and the private sin-offerings applied? He went up the ascent, turned to the surrounding balcony, and passed on to the south-east horn, where he dipped his right finger—i.e., the index finger of his right hand—into the blood in the bowl, and supported it with his thumb on this side and his little finger on the other,[4] and applied it with a downward movement against the *edge* of the horn until all the blood on his finger was gone, and thus [he did] at every horn?—This is what he means: Its regulation is [that it be applied] at the edge; yet if he applies it within a cubit in either direction, we have no objection.[5]

What was [this allusion to] Rabbi and R. Eleazar son of R. Simeon?—As it was taught: The upper blood is applied above the scarlet line, and the lower blood is applied below the scarlet line: that is Rabbi's view. R. Eleazar son of R. Simeon said: This holds good only of a burnt-offering of a bird; but in the case of an animal sin-offering, its [blood] is applied essentially on the very horn.[6] R. Abbahu said: What is Rabbi's reason? Because it is written, *And the altar shall be four cubits; and from the altar and upward there shall be four horns.*[7] Now, was the altar [only] four cubits?[8]—Said R. Adda b. Ahaba: [It means,] And the place of the horns was four [cubits].[9] Did the horns occupy four cubits?[10]—Say rather: The limits of the horns were four [cubits].[11]

We learnt elsewhere: A scarlet line encompassed it about the middle, to distinguish between the upper and the lower bloods. Whence do we know it?—Said R. Aḥa b. R. Ḳaṭṭina, Because it it
b said: *That the net may reach halfway up the altar:*[1] thus the Torah prescribed a barrier to distinguish between the upper and the lower bloods.

THE RESIDUE OF THE BLOOD etc. Our Rabbis taught: *At the base of the altar*[2] means the southern base. You say, the southern base; yet perhaps it is not so, but rather the western base, and the undefined is learnt from the defined?[3] You can answer: We infer his coming down the ascent from his exit from the *hekal:* as his exit from the *hekal* was to the nearest side, so his coming down the ascent was to the nearest side.[4]

It was taught, R. Ishmael said: In both cases[5] the *western* base [is meant]. R. Simeon b. Yoḥai said: In both cases the *southern* base [is meant]. As for him who maintains that both [were poured out] at the western base, it is well: he holds that the undefined is learnt from the defined.[6] But what is his reason who holds that the *southern* base [is meant] in both cases?—Said R. Assi: This Tanna maintains that the whole altar stood in the north.[7] Another

(5) *Sobeb*, a terrace or balcony which ran round the altar. He had to stand on the balcony because he applied the blood with his finger on the horns of the altar. For other sacrifices he stood on the pavement and dashed the blood from the vessel on to the altar. (6) In the Tabernacle. These hangings corresponded to the walls of the Temple court. (7) Roast or boiled. (8) The application on the horn. (9) He stood e.g. at the south-east corner and applied the blood either in the direction of south or east, but within a cubit from the actual corner; similarly with the other corners. (10) Lit., performed the rites of the sin-offering; cf. *supra* 52b n. 4, for this expression.

a (1) *Infra*. (2) The edge is certainly unnecessary, since anywhere within a cubit from the angle is the horn. (3) Who holds that the blood may be applied above the line even not against the horn, v. *infra*. (4) Like a balanced load. The reading adopted is that of Sh. M. Cur. edd. read: 'with his thumb above and his little finger below'—a rather difficult procedure. (5) As this counts as an extension of the edge. (6) V. *supra* 10a. (7) Ezek. XLIII, 15. (8) It was much larger. (9) I.e., the horns occupied four cubits of the altar, since each was a cubit in length and breadth. (10) Since each was a cubit in length, actually only *two* cubits of the length or the breadth of the altar were occupied by the horns. (11) A distance of four cubits *below* the horns, i.e., as far down as the scarlet line, still ranked as the horns. Therefore Rabbi says that the upper blood, i.e., the blood which is sprinkled on the horn, can be sprinkled anywhere above the scarlet line.

b (1) Ex. XXVII, 5. (2) Lev. IV, 30. (3) Of the blood of the *inner* sin-offering it is said, *at the base of the altar of burnt-offering, which is at the door of the tent of meeting* (ibid., 7). Now, as one entered from the door he came first to the *western* base: this is therefore regarded as defined, and the question is: Why not learn v. 30, where it is undefined, from v. 7, where it is defined? (4) When he left the *hekal* with the residue of the *inner* blood, he poured it out at the *western* base, this being nearest to him. So also when he came down the ascent with the residue of the outer blood, after having applied the blood on the south-west corner he poured it out at the *southern* base, this being nearest to him. (5) *Sc.* the inner and the outer sin-offerings. (6) As in n. 3. (7) I.e., to the north of the door of the *hekal*, and no part of the altar actually stood in front of the door; then the immediate side would be the southern. It may also mean that it stood in the north of the Temple court, five cubits of it facing the door, and one of these five cubits was the southern base, which one would face as he came out of the door.

עלה בכבש ופנה לסובב . מפני שדמה ניתן למעלה על הקרנות ובאצבע צריך לעמוד על גבי סובב אבל בכל שאר הדמים שהן התחתונים מן החוט סו] ולמטה ובקרן זוית המזבח עומד על הרצפה וזורק מן הכלי למזבח וכל מקום שיגיע למזבח כשר : ובא לו לקרן דרומית מזרחית . שבה הוא פוגע ראשון כדקיימא לן לקמן (דף סב:) כל פינות שאתה פונה יהו דרך ימין והכבש בדרום וכשעולה בו ופניו למזבח הוי ימינו סז] למזרח ובא לימינו למזרח ובא לאותו קרן והולך ומקיף בסובב דרך ימין ופניו למזבח מן הדרום למזרח וממזרח לצפון ומצפון למערב דהיינו דרך ימין : על יסוד יז] דרומית . בגמרא יליף לה : לפנים מן הקלעים . לפי שבמשכן היו קלעים היקף לחצר אהל מועד ובמקום הקלעים היתה חומת העזרה *יח] בבית שלמה או בית עולמים ובחטאת כתיבא יט] בחצר אהל מועד במקום קדוש תאכל כ] (ויקרא ו) : לזכרי כהונה . דכתיב הכהן המחטא אותה כא] (שם) לאפוקי נשים שאינן ראויות לחיטוי ובויקח כב] קרח גבי חטאת ואשם ומנחה כתיב כל זכר יאכל אותו : בכל מאכל . משום דקתני בפסח ואינו נאכל אלא צלי לקמן (דף נו:) כג] תני בכולהו ובכל מאכל : ליום ולילה . כדילפינן בפ' שלישי (לעיל דף לו.) ובשר זבח תודת שלמיו כד] למדנו שנאכלת ליום אחד חטאת ואשם מנין תלמוד לומר זבח וכקדשים לילה הולך אחר היום דכתיב לא יניח ממנו עד בקר (ויקרא ז) : עד חצות . סייג עשו חכמים לתורה להרחיק אדם מעבירת כרת כדתנן בברכות בפרק קמא (דף ב.) כל הנאכלין ליום אחד מצותן כו' : גמ' היכי עביד . מתנת אצבע בקרן : אמה אילך כה] . כשהוא עומד אצל זוית המזבח נותן בתוך אמה של מקצוע לאיזה רוח שירצה או לדרום או למזרח בקרן דרומית מזרחית וכן בכל קרן : מחטא ויורד . לשון הכתוב הכהן המחטא אותה (ויקרא ו) : אליבא דרבי אלעזר כו] . לקמן מייתי פלוגתייהו : היא עצמה . כלומר כל עצמה ועיקר מצותה אינו אלא שם : דכ"ע לא פליגי . דלא בעינן כז] חודה דקרן כתיב ואמה על אמה ברום אמה הנתון בראש המזבח בכל זוית וזוית בכל מקום שבה קרוי קרן : כי פליגי אליבא דרבי . דמכשר לה מחוט הסיקרא ולמעלה ואע"ג כח] דלא בקרן : מר סבר . כי היכי דקרן הויא אמה על אמה אף כל שתחתיו כנגדו הוי קרן : ומר סבר . *כיון דקרא לאו אקרנות ממש קפיד בשאר המזבח לא שייך לשון קרן אלא בחודה של זוית : המיומנת שבימין . אצבע הרגילה כט] למלאכה ולא שאר אצבעות מוכנות להושיט ולטבל היינו שאצל גודל מיומנת אמגט"ר בלע"ז : וחומר ל] בגודלו ובאצבע קטנה . מושך את הדם שבאצבע כלפי למטה שיפול כולו למזבח : חומר . לשון נחמרו בני מעיה (חולין דף נד.) דוריי"ר בלע"ז : ומחטא . זריקת חטאת קרוי חיטוי כמו הכהן המחטא אותה : כנגד חודה לא] . רבי היא דמכשר למטה מן הקרן להכי תנא לה בחודה : בד"א . דדמים העליונים כשירין למעלה מן החוט מיד : בעולת העוף . שנעשית למעלה כדאמרינן בפרק קדשי קדשים (לקמן דף סד:) : אבל חטאת בהמה . דכתיב בה קרן בהדיא אינה נעשית כו' : והראל . מזבח : ארבע אמות הוא דהואי . בתמיה וכי אין גובהו או רוחבו אלא ארבע אמות : מקום קרנות ארבע . כלומר הקרנות תופסין ארבע אמות במזבח דכל קרן אמה על אמה : ומקום קרנות ארבע הויא . בתמיה והרי אין הקרנות אוכלין במזבח אלא שתי אמות מן המזרח למערב ושתים מן הדרום לצפון היינו שתים על שתים : אלא . על כרחך ה"ק קרא רשות קרנות ארבע כלומר שם *רשות הקרנות תופסת למטה מהן ארבע אמות דהיינו עד החוט דכוליה לב] הוי קרן : הרשת . כעין ציור מצוירת בקליעה ושל נחשת לג] הויא בתחתיו של מזבח עשוי כנפה וגבוה עד חציו של מזבח : התורה נתנה מחילה . מדקפיד אחצי מזבח : אל יסוד המזבח . האמור בחטאת החיצונה : או אינו אלא יסוד מערבי . כדאשכחן בפנימיות לעיל אשר פתח אהל מועד וילמד סתום מן המפורש : ילמד ירידתו מן הכבש . בחיצונות שירי הדם בידו מיציאתו מן ההיכל לד] [ושיריים הפנימיים בידו מה יציאתו מן ההיכל] ביסוד מערבי שהוא סמוך לו : אף ירידתו מן הכבש . נשפכין ליסוד דרומי שהוא סמוך לו : זה וזה . חיצונים והפנימים : סתום . החיצונים : מפורש . פנימים שכתוב בהן יסוד מערבי דכתיב אשר פתח אהל מועד : לה] מ"ט . הא כתיב בפנימיים אל יסוד אשר פתח אהל מועד : קסבר כוליה מזבח בצפון פתח ההיכל קאי . לו] ואין המזבח לפני הפתח כלום אלא אמה של יסוד דרומי או נמי בצפון העזרה קאי והוו חמש אמותיו כנגד הפתח *ואמה אחת מהן יסוד דרומי אישתכח דכי נפיק מן הפתח רואה יסוד דרומי לפניו מכוון באמצע הפתח ואית דגרס כוליה פתח בדרום מזבח קאי והיא היא כל פתח ההיכל לדרומו של מזבח הוא :

תנא

"עלה בכבש ופנה לסובב ובא לו לקרן דרומית מזרחית מזרחית צפונית צפונית מערבית מערבית דרומית [ב]שירי הדם היה שופך על [א] יסוד דרומית ונאכלין [ג]לפנים מן הקלעים לזכרי כהונה בכל מאכל ליום ולילה עד חצות : גמ' היכי עביד רבי יוחנן ורבי אלעזר חד אמר נותן אמה אילך ואמה אילך וחד אמר מחטא ויורד כנגד חודו של קרן אליבא דרבי אלעזר בר"ש דאמר היא עצמה אינה נעשית אלא בגופה של קרן דכולי עלמא לא פליגי כי פליגי אליבא דרבי מר סבר אמה אילך ואמה אילך כנגד [ב] קרן הוא ומר סבר כנגד חודה אין טפי לא מיתיבי חטאת הציבור והיחיד [ג] כיצד מתן דמן היה עולה לכבש ופנה לסובב ובא לו לקרן דרומית מזרחית [ד]וטובל באצבעו הימנית המיומנת שבימין מן הדם שבמזרק [ד] וחומר בגודלו מלמעלה ובאצבעו קטנה מלמטה ומחטא ויורד כנגד חודה של קרן עד [ה] שמכלה כל הדם שבאצבע וכן כל קרן וקרן הכי קאמר [ה]מצוה בחודה אי עבד אמה אילך ואמה אילך לית לן בה : מאי רבי ומאי רבי אלעזר בר' שמעון *דתניא דמים העליונים ניתנין מחוט הסיקרא ולמעלה דמים התחתונים ניתנין מחוט הסיקרא ולמטן דברי רבי רבי אלעזר ברבי שמעון אומר במה דברים אמורין בעולת העוף אבל בחטאת בהמה היא עצמה אין נעשית אלא על גופה של קרן אמר רבי אבהו מאי טעמא דרבי דכתיב °והראל ארבע [ו] אמות ומהראל ולמעלה וגו' ארבע אמות הוא דהויא אמר רב אדא בר אהבה [ז] ומקום קרנות ארבע מקום קרנות ד' הויא אלא אימא רשות קרנות ד' : *תנן התם [ו]חוט של סיקרא חוגרו באמצע להבדיל בין דמים העליונים לדמים התחתונים מנא הני מילי אמר רב [ח] אחא בר רב קטינא שנאמר °והיתה הרשת עד חצי המזבח התורה נתנה מחיצה להבדיל בין דמים העליונים לדמים התחתונים : שירי הדם כו' : *ת"ר אל יסוד מזבח זה יסוד דרומי אתה אומר זה יסוד דרומי או אינו אלא יסוד [ט] מערבי וילמד סתום מן המפורש אמרת ילמד ירידתו מן הכבש [י] *ליציאתו מן ההיכל מה יציאתו מן ההיכל בסמוך לו °אף ירידתו מן הכבש בסמוך לו : *תניא רבי ישמעאל אומר זה וזה יסוד מערבי ר' שמעון בן יוחאי אומר זה וזה יסוד דרומי בשלמא למאן דאמר [יא] יסוד מערבי קסבר ילמד סתום מן המפורש אלא למאן דאמר [יב] יסוד דרומי מ"ט א"ר אסי קסבר האי תנא [יג] *כוליה מזבח בצפון קאי [יד] ל"א כוליה פתח בדרום קאי

יחזקאל מג | שמות כז

כוליה מזבח בצפון קאי . פירש בקונטרס בצפון פתח ההיכל קאי ואין מן המזבח לפני פתח ההיכל כלום אלא אמה של יסוד דרומית א"נ בצפון העזרה קאי *והוו חמש כנגד הפתח ואחת מהן יסוד דרומי אישתכח דכי נפיק מן לז] הפתח יסוד דרומי לפניו מכוון באמצע הפתח ולשון זה אחרון נראה דלקמן פרק קדשי קדשים (דף נח.) מוכח דלמאן דאמר כוליה מזבח בצפון קאי לח] *האי חמש אמות כנגד הפתח דהא תנן (תמיד דף כט.) מערכה שניה של קטרת היה משוך מן הקרן כלפי צפון ארבע אמות מוקי לה כרבי יוסי דבעי לפני הפתח וקסבר כוליה מזבח בצפון קאי : וסימניך

עין משפט נר מצוה

כט א ב מיי' פ"ה מהל' מעשה"ק הל"י :

נ"ל והוו חמש אמותיו כנגד הפתח ואחת מהן כו' נ"ק

ל ג מיי' שם פ"ז הלכה א :

נ"ל האי חמש כו' דהא דתנן כו' נ"ק

לא ד ה מיי' שם פ"ה הל"ז :

לב ו מיי' פ"ב מהל' בית הבחירה הל"ע :

מסורת הש"ס

בבית עולמים ובחטאת כו' נ"ק

לעיל י:

מנחות פ"ט מ"א [בכורות יג מנחות מז]

יומא נח.

נ"ל מיציאתו

תוספתא דיומא פ"ב ע"ש

[לקמן סג:]

כ"א כיון דקרא אקרנות כו'

גליון הש"ס

גמ' אף ירידתו . ע"ל דף פא ע"א תוד"ה אבל

הגהות נ"ק

ו' אחת מהן נ"ק

שיטה מקובצת

א] יסוד דרומי : ב] קרן נמי קרן הוא כו' מיתיבי . חטאות הצבור : ג] כיצד סדר מתן כו' לכבש ופונה לסובב : ד] וחומר . ס"א וסומך ס"א וחומר בגודלו מכאן ובאצבעו מכאן והרמב"ם ז"ל גריס כן בפ"ה מהלכות מעשה הקרבנות אלא שהוא כתב שם וסומך באצבעו הגדולה מכאן ובגודל מכאן וצ"ע : ה] שיכלה כל כו' מצוה מחודה : ו] אמות ומהריאל ולמעלה הקרנות ארבע : ז] מקום קרנות ארבע ומקום קרנות : ח] רב חנא בר תיבת אחא נמחק : ט] מערבי וילמוד סתום : י] הכבש מיציאתו מן : יא] דאמר זה וזה יסוד : יב] דאמר זה וזה יסוד [דרומי] מ"ט אמר רב אשי : יג] כוליה מזבח בצפון קאי פ"ה ואית דגרסי כו' וקשה לפי זה דלקמן בפ' קדשי קדשים מוכח דלמאן דאמר כוליה מזבח בצפון קאי הוי חמש אמות דרומית כנגד הפתח כו' לכך נראה כלשון אחר שבקונטרס דכוליה מזבח בצפון קאי וצפון העזרה מתחיל באמצע הפתח שהוא רחב עשר אמות נמצא ה' אמות דרומית של מזבח כנגד הפתח ואחת מהן יסוד דרומית וא"כ כשיוצא מן הפתח רואה יסוד דרומי לפניו מכוון כנגד אמצע הפתח ורגילות של אדם לצאת באמצע הפתח ודוחק הוא וכי לעולם הוא יוצא באמצע הפתח ועוד קשה מנלן דאותה אמה היא יסוד לפי שהיא כנגד הפתח אימא דגם ד' אמות מערבית שכנגד הפתח הוו יסוד דאי משום שכל יסוד מערבי לא היה כנגד הפתח מה בכך הלא כי נמי מזבח ממוצע היה מנלן דיסוד מערבי כולו מיקרי כנגד הפתח והלא אורכו ל"ב אמות ורוחב חלל הפתח עשר אמות נמצא דעשר אמות הוו כנגד הפתח ועוד נשאר י"א אמות מכאן וי"א אמות מכאן שלא כנגד הפתח ומ"מ מיקרי כולו יסוד כנגד הפתח משום דמקצתו ככולו ואמר מורי דלמ"ד בצפון קאי איכא לאוקמי פתח אהל מועד ברוח דרומי שכל יסוד שלו כנגד הפתח דאמה דרומית של כל רוח דרומית הוי כנגד הפתח ועוד דלא הוי יסוד לרוח דרומית רק אמה ראשונה של צד מערב כדאמר לקמן והילכך לא מיקרי רוח מערבי כנגד הפתח כיון שאין יסוד שלו כנגד הפתח אבל למ"ד דמזבח ממוצע באמצע הפתח שפיר מיקרי רוח מערבית שכנגד הפתח לפי שלא היה לו שום רוח אחר כנגד והפתח רק רוח מערבי שבאמצעיתו הוא עשר אמות כנגד הפתח כל רוחב הפתח : ס"א ודוחק הוא כו' וא"כ מנלן דיסוד דרומי מיקרי פתח אהל מועד לכן נראה דיסוד דרומי מיקרי יותר פתח אהל מועד מיסוד מערבי לפי שכולו כנגד הפתח אבל יסוד מערבי אינו כנגד הפתח כי אם ה' אמות וכ"ת א"כ כי נמי מזבח ממוצע מנלן דיסוד מערבי כולו מיקרי יסוד שכנגד הפתח והרי אורך היסוד של מערבי אורכו ל"ב אמות וחלל פתח ההיכל הוי עשר אמות נמצא יסוד המזבח מערבי עודף לכל צד על חלל הפתח י"א אמות אלא ודאי אמרינן מקצתו ככולו כי נמי כולו בצפון קאי מקצת יסוד מערבי ככולו וי"ל דודאי כי קאי באמצע העזרה הוי מקצתו ככולו לפי שלא היה רוח אחר של מזבח אפי' מקצתו כנגד הפתח אבל כי קאי בצפון א"כ רוח דרומי מיקרי פתח אהל מועד לפי שהוא כולו כנגד הפתח ולא מערבי שאינו כנגד הפתח כי אם מקצתו כך נראה למורי . מהר"ם : יד] תיבות ל"א בדרום קאי נמחק : טו] ולמטה עומד על הרצפה אצל זוית המזבח : טז] למזרח ופונה לימינו למזרח ובא לו לאותו קרן : יז] דרומי : יח] בבית עולמים תיבות בחצר אהל מועד או בית נמחק : יט] א) תיבות שלמה או בית נמחק : כ] תאכל בחצר אהל מועד : כא] אותה וגו' לאפוקי : כב] קרח כתיב גבי כו' ומנחה כל זכר : כג] תנא ואות י' נמחק : כד] למדנו לתודה שנאכלת : כה] אילך ואמה אילך כשרוא : כו] דר' אלעזר כו' לקמן : כז] חודה משום דקרן : כח] ואע"ג דלאו בקרן : כט] למלאכה בלא שאר אצבעות כלומר מוכנות להרשים ולטבל והיינו : ל] בגודלו למעלה ובאצבע הקטנה מושך כו' כלפי מטה : לא] חודה של קרן רבי כו' להכי לא תנא בחודה : לב] הויא דקרן : לג] הויא בתחתיתו : לד] ההיכל ושירים הפנימים בידו מה יציאתו מן ההיכל ביסוד : לה] מ"ט דהא כתיב בפנימים אל יסוד מזבח העולה אשר : לו] ואין מן המזבח כו' אמותיו של מזבח כנגד הפתח ואחת מהן יסוד דרומי וצפון העזרה מתחיל באמצע הפתח ההיכל שהיה רחב הפתח י' אמות ואשתכח דכי נפיק מן הפתח ס"א ורגילות לצאת באמצע הפתח ומש"ה קרי פתח אהל מועד אמה של יסוד דרומי טפי מד' אמות הנשארות ואית : לז] הפתח רואה יסוד : לח] קאי הוו חמש :

תיבת

נו] נראה דס"ס נפל בכאן וצ"ל ובחטאת כתיבא במקום קדוש תאכל בחצר אהל מועד הס"ד ואח"כ מתחיל אות כ' אותה וגו' .

לג א מיי' פ"ה מהל' מעה"ק הל"ו :
לד ב מיי' שם הל"א :
גברי לגברא נ"ק
לה ג מיי' פ"ה שם הלכה ו :
לו ד מיי' פ"ב מהל' בית הבחירה הל"י :

תנא דבי ר' ישמעאל *כרבי שמעון בן יוחי א] אומרים זה וזה יסוד מערבי וסימניך *משכו גברי לגברא : **מתני'** העולה קדשי קדשים שחיטתה בצפון וקיבול דמה בכלי שרת בצפון [א]ודמה טעון שתי מתנות שהן ארבע [ב]וטעונה הפשט וניתוח וכליל לאשים : **גמ'** עולה מ"ט ב] תני ליה קדשי קדשים משום דלא כתיב בה (לה') קדשי קדשים היא : ודמה טעון שתי מתנות : היכי ג] עביד אמר רב נותן וחוזר ונותן ושמואל אמר מתנה ד] אחת [ג]כמין גמא נותן ה] כתנאי יכול יזרקנו זריקה אחת ת"ל סביב אי סביב יכול יקיפנו כחוט ת"ל וזרקו הא ו] כיצד כמין גמא (*ודמה טעון) שתי מתנות שהן ארבע *ר' ישמעאל אומר נאמר כאן סביב ונאמר להלן °סביב מה להלן פיסוק וארבע מתנות אף כאן פיסוק וארבע מתנות אי מה להלן ארבע מתנות על ארבע קרנות אף כאן ארבע מתנות על ארבע קרנות אמרת עולה טעונה יסוד [ד]וקרן מזרחית דרומית לא היה לה יסוד מ"ט אמר ר' אלעזר *לפי שלא היתה בחלקו של טורף דאמר רב שמואל בר רב יצחק מזבח אוכל בחלקו של יהודה אמה *אמר רבי לוי בר חמא *אמר רבי חמא ברבי חנינא רצועה היתה יוצאה מחלקו של יהודה ונכנסה בחלקו של ז] בנימין והיה בנימין הצדיק מצטער עליה בכל יום לנוטלה שנאמר

חופף

ויקרא ח

רש"י

ח] היו שונין כרבי שמעון בן יוחי זה וזה יסוד מערבי תלמידי רבי ישמעאל היו שונין משנה ששנית בבית מדרשו של רבי שמעון דזה וזה יסוד ט] מערבי כרבי ישמעאל: וסימניך. שלא תחליף הגירסא לומר זה וזה דרומי : משכו גברי לגברא . תלמידי ר' ישמעאל שהן מרובין משכו את ר"ש לומר כדברי רבן : **מתני'** העולה קדשי קדשים . היא ליפסל ביוצא ובטבול יום ובמחוסר כפורים ומועלין בה י] : שתי מתנות . בקרן מזרחית צפונית ובקרן מערבית דרומית שכנגדה באלכסון והכי תנן במסכת תמיד (דף ל:) בא לו לקרן מזרחית צפונית נותן מזרחית צפונית מערבית דרומית נותן מערבית דרומית וטעמא משום דקרן מזרחית דרומית לא היה לה יסוד כדאמרינן בשמעתין ועולה טעונה יא] תורת מתן דמה כנגד היסוד וכדדרשינן לעיל (דף נג.) מק"ו משירי חטאת הילכך בעי יב] [הנך] תרתי דאמרן : שתי מתנות שהן ד' . בעינן כדי שיהא מתן הדם בד' רוחות המזבח והא לא משכחת לה אלא בשתי קרנות העומדות יג] [זו] באלכסונה של זו דאי בשתים שברוח אחת לא הוי דם אלא בג' רוחות של מזבח ולא קרינן ביה סביב : שהן ארבע . בגמ' מפרש היכי עביד : **גמ'** מאי טעמא תני בה קדשי קדשים . מאי דלא תני גבי חטאות ואשמות דהוו נמי קדשי קדשים : ומשני משום דלא כתיב בה . איצטריך לאשמועינן דאפ"ה קדשי קדשים היא דהא כולה לגבוה ואין לך קדשי קדשים כזה ובקדשים קלים גופייהו מאי דאזיל מינייהו לגבוה קדשי קדשים הוא כדתנן לקמן יד] בפ' התדיר (דף פט.) מעשר קודם לעופות מפני שהוא מין זבח ויש בו קדשי קדשים דמו ואימוריו : היכי עביד . דנעשים השתים טו] שהן ארבע : נותן וחוזר ונותן . זורק מן הכלי ולמזבח ברוח זו של קרן וכן ברוח השניה של קרן וכן לקרן שכנגדה באלכסון ונמצא מן הדם לד' רוחות של מזבח מתנה לכל רוח : כמין גמא . זורק טז] נגד הפינה מן הכלי והדם מתפשט לשתי רוחות הפינה והרי הוא כמין גאם אות יונית עשויה ככף יז] פשוטה (א) : וזרקו את הדם על המזבח סביב . בעולה כתיב וכן כתיב בשלמים ואשם : ת"ל וזרקו . ואין זריקה אלא מרחוק ובחוט אי אפשר להקיף אלא באצבע ובנגיעה : ודמה טעון כו' . כמין גמא ובשתי קרנות שבאלכסון דאיכא סביב לארבע רוחות המזבח ובזריקה : ונאמר להלן סביב . יח] בחטאות המלואין בלו את אהרן : מה להלן פיסוק ד' מתנות . ד' נפסקות זו מזו דהא על ארבע קרנות נותן : אף כאן . אע"פ *שבשתי קרנות יט] פיסוק בעינן והיינו כדרב נותן וחוזר ונותן : עולה טעונה יסוד . תחילת כ] מתנותיה צריכה נגד היסוד שיהא יסוד המזבח תחת מקום מתנה ומקל וחומר אייתינה לעיל בפירקין (דף נג.) : לא היה לה יסוד . לקמיה מפרש היכי דמי הילכך בקרן מזרחית צפונית היה מתחיל : כא] מאי טעם . לא היה לה יסוד : טורף . בנימין דכתיב ביה זאב יטרף (בראשית מט) כב] שנתנבא יעקב עליו בבקר יאכל עד (שם) באחסנתיה תיתבני מדבחא ואותה הקרן לא היתה בחלקו כדמפרש ואזיל : דאמר רב שמואל בר רב יצחק מזבח היה כג] אוכל בחלקו של יהודה אמה . אמה במזרחו אמה בדרומו על כל האורך בעובי אמה אלא שלא היתה אמה כד] שבמזרח על פני כל המזרח שכשמגיע לקרן מזרחית צפונית היתה כלה בסמוך כה] לקרן אמה וכן אצילת האמה הדרומית לא היתה מהלכת על פני כל הדרום שכשמגעת לקרן דרומית מערבית כלה כו] בסמוך לקרן אמה כדתנן לקמן (דף נד.) היסוד מהלך על פני כל הצפון ועל פני כל המערב אוכל במזרח אמה אחת ובדרום אמה אחת נמצא יסוד לג' קרנות כזה : רצועה היתה יוצאה מחלקו של יהודה . לדרומו של מזבח שחלקו של יהודה כז] היתה במזרח כדתניא (יומא דף יב.) מה היה בחלקו של יהודה הר הבית (בכניסתו) והלשכות שבו והעזרות עזרת נשים כולה כח] (ועזרת) ושנים ועשרים אמה של מקום דריסת רגלי הכהנים ומקום דריסת רגלי ישראל מיקרו עזרות נמצא חלקו של יהודה במזרח המזבח ובצדו [לדרום] והמזבח אוכל בחלקו אמה במזרח כט] מלבד אמה של קרן מזרחית צפונית ל] היתה כולה חלקו של יהודה שהיתה אותה אמה ברחוק מן הקרן אמה והרצועה היתה יוצאה בדרום למזבח ונכנסת בחלקו של בנימין שממקום הדריסה לא] ולמעלה היה חלקו של בנימין אלא שרצועה זו היתה ליהודה באה בתוך חלקו של בנימין בדרומו של מזבח ומזבח אוכל בה אמה והיא לב] אמה שהיא כניסת היסוד ראוי להיות בה כדאמר מר (מדות פרק ג מ"א) עלה אמה וכנס אמה זהו יסוד כל אורך כותל מזרחי בעובי אמה היה אוכל חלקו של יהודה וכן כותל דרומי לבד אמה סמוך לקרן דרומית מערבית לג] :

חופף

תוספות

וסימניך משכינהו גברי לגברא . פירש בקונטרס תלמידי רבי ישמעאל שהם מרובים משכו את רבי שמעון לומר כדברי רבם ותימה דלקמן פרק בתרא (דף קיט:) אמרינן וסימניך משכינהו *גברא לגברי דר' שמעון דאמר זו וזו ירושלים משכינהו (ב) לרבי ישמעאל והשתא מה סימניך הוא זה כיון דפעמים אמרינן איפכא ונראה כדגרסינן בספרים ישנים וזה וזה יסוד דרומי וסימניך משכינהו גברי לגברא רבי שמעון בן יוחי קרי גברי לפי שנזכר שמו ושם אביו ור' ישמעאל שהוא יחידי קרי גברא וגרסינן נמי פרק בתרא (שם) וסימניך משכינהו גברי לגברא וכן בערוך בערך משך :

העולה קדשי קדשים כו' . תימה לד] דלא תני שפיכות שיריים בעולה והלא כל הדמים טעונין יסוד לה] *כדדרשינן העולה למזבח של עולה לפירוש הקונטרס ובריש בית שמאי (לעיל דף לז.) אמרינן מנין לכל הדמים שטעונין מתן דמים ליסוד ועוד דבמסכת תמיד (דף ל:) תנן שירי הדם היה שופך על יסוד דרומי לו] ותירץ ה"ר משה מפונטייז"א משום דעולה בזריקת כלי וזימנין דלית בה שירים לז] *בחטאת דבאצבע אי אפשר בלא שיריים ולא נהירא דכולה שמעתא מוכחת דמלוה במתן שיריים לח] וה"ר יעקב מאורלייינ"ש פירש דכיון לט] דשמעי' תנא דפנימיים ביסוד מערבי מ] וגם התחיל בחיצונים למיתני יסוד דרומי הוא הדין בכולהו ואע"ג דקתני בכל פנימיים הייטו משום דהתחיל בפנימיים וצריך למיתני בחיצונים ואין רוצה להפסיק :

קדשי קדשים . פי' בקונטרס ליפסל ביוצא ובטבול יום מא] ומועלין בה ולא היה לו לפרש לענין טבול יום ומחוסר כפורים שזה הדין נוהג בכל קדשים אפילו קלים אבל יוצא ומעילה ניחא דקדשים קלים לא (מבטלי) מיפסלי ביוצא ואין בהן מעילה מב] : **משום** דלא כתיב בה קדשי קדשים . תימה מג] ומהאי טעמא הוה ליה למימר גבי זבחי שלמי צבור דהא לא כתב בהו קדשי קדשים וילפינן להו לקמן (דף נה.) מדאיתקש לעולה מה עולה קדשי קדשים : **נאמר** כאן סביב כו' . הא דאיצטריך לעיל לאקושי חטאת לעולה לענין צפון משום דמהך גזירה שוה דסביב ליכא למילף דלא שייכא אלא לענין מתנות דהא חטאת שנכנס דמה לפנים פסולה ודמה טעון כיבוס מה שאין כן בעולה :

מה להלן פיסוק מתנות כו' . תימה כי היכי דדרשינן בפרק קמא (לעיל ד' י:) אותה דמה למעלה ולא אחרת דמה למעלה הכא נמי נימא אותה בפיסוק מתנות ולא אחרת בפיסוק מתנות מד] :

ואי

הוא נתן פיסוק כו' כדרב דאמר נותן וחוזר ונותן : כ] תחילת מתנותיה צריך כנגד היסוד שיהא יסוד למזבח תחת מקום המתנה בקל וחומר אייתינא לה לעיל : כא] מאי טעמא אות מ' נמחק : כב] שנתנבא עליו יעקב בבקר כו' באחסנתא יתבני : כג] אוכל כלומר תופס בחלקו כו' במזרחו ואמה בדרומו : כד] אמה למזרח על : כה] בסמוך אמה לקרן : כו] כלה סמוך לקרן : כז] יהודה היה במזרח : כח] כולה עזרת ישראל שנים ועשרים אמה של עזרה מקום דריסת רגלי ישראל ומקום דריסת רגלי כהנים מיקרו : כט] במזרח אלא שלצד קרן תיבות מלבד אמה של נמחק : ל] היה כלה חלקו של יהודה אותה אות ו' ותיבת שהיתה נמחק : לא] הדריסה ולמערב היה תיבת ולמעלה נמחק : לב] אמה שהיה כניסת : לג] מערבית ולבד אמה סמוך לקרן מזרחית צפונית : לד] תימה אמאי לא תני : לה] כדדרשינן לעיל תן יסוד למזבחות תיבת העולה נמחק : לו] תירץ הר"ר מאורליינ"ש דלא רצה לשנות בכל קרבן וכ"ת למה פירש אותן בחטאת י"ל דהוצרך לפרש פנימיות וחיצוניות אבל לאחר דגלי באחד מתן גלי בכל מקום : לז] שירים אבל בחטאת : לח] שירים ליזהר בזריקה שישאר מן הדם ותירץ הר"ר מאורליינ"ש דלא חשש התנא לאשמועינן שירים בכולו דאטו כי רוכלא ליזל ולחשוב ותני ליה פנימיות וחיצוניות לאפוקי מט"ד זו או זו יסוד דרומי או זו ודתני בכל הפנימים זה לפי שרוצה לשנותו בחיצוניות ולא רצה להפסיק ובתר דתנייה ליסוד דרומי בחיצוניות חד זימנא לא חש לשנותו עוד והר"ם תירץ דתנא ושייר ובתמיד תנא מה ששייר הכא זריקה שלא פירש כאן ובתמיד מפרש דהיינו קרן מזרחית צפונית ומערבית דרומית . לשון מהר"ם : לט] דאשמועינן תנא כו' מערבי וחיצוניות לא חש תו למיתני (דכל) [דאטו] כרוכלא ליחשוב לכל החיצונים לאפוקי מט"ד כולהו ביסוד מערבי או כולהו ביסוד דרומי : מ] מתיבת תם עד תיבת ואף בס"א אינו : מא] יום ובמחוסר כפורים ומועלין : מב] מעילה וקדשי קדשים מועלין בהן בין לפני זריקת דמים ובין לאחר ואפי' מחיים ושייך איסור יוצא אף בירושלים : מג] תימא דמהאי טעמא : מד] מתנות ונראה דאתיא גז"ש ומפקא ליה ממיעוט ומוקמינן ליה למיעוט דאין אחרת למעלה :

א) נראה דצ"ל כמין גמא כפנאי ותיבות נותן נמחק . ב) נראה דהך תיבת נותן נמחק שייך (לאות ד' : ג) וכן הגי' ביומא דף יב ע"א . ד) סדכר צ"ע דגי' רש"י כוודאי דזה וזה יסוד מערבי ועי' בתוס' ד"ה וסימנך ולפי דעים יש כבלא.

שיטה מקובצת

א] תיבת אומרים נמחק: ב] תני ביה קדשי קדשים משום דלא כתיב בה קדשי ותי' לה' נמחק תימה א"כ למה לא תני כמו כן אצל זבחי שלמי צבור ולקמן ילפינן להו מהיקשא דעולה וי"ל כיון דתני בעולה לא צריך למיתני בזבחי שלמי צבור דהא מהיקשא דעולה ילפינן אבל גבי עולה דלא כתיב בה רק דידעינן מסברא כדפ"ה לפי שכולה כליל הילכך צריך למיתני בה קדשי קדשים : ג] עביד רב אמר נותן : ד] אחת נותן כמין א) : ה] כתנאי. וזרקו את הדם וגו' יכול ב) תיבת נותן נמחק: ו] כיצד דמה טעון שתי: ז] בנימין ג) ס"א ובה היה מזבח בנוי : ח] ישמעאל בדבי ר' שמעון : ט] וזה יסוד ד) דרומי : י] בה גליון פי' בין לפני זריקה בין לאחר זריקה ובקדשי' קלים ליכא מעילה אלא באימורים לפני זריקה . ע"כ : יא] טעונה תחילת מתן בעי הנך תרתי : יב] העומדות זו באלכסונה: יג] בפרק כל התדיר : יד] השתים ארבע ותיבת שהן נמחק: טו] זרק כנגד הפינה : טז] פשוטה שלנו : יז] סביב בחטאת אות ר' נמחק : יח] קרנות

הגהות הב"ח

(א) רש"י ד"ה כמין גמא וכו' פשוטה הס"ד ואח"כ מ"ה סביב וזרקו : (ב) תוס' ד"ה וסימניך וכו' משכינהו לתלמידי ר' ישמעאל :

נ"א כדדרשינן לעיל מתן יסוד למזבח של עולה
נ"א אבל בחטאת דבאצבע כו' נ"ק
[ע' תוס' יומא יב. ד"ה ירושלים ותוס' מגילה כו. ד"ה ולעמנה]
[ביומא יב. איתא דתניא וכו' בריית' ועי' תוס' לעיל נג:]

[צ"ל כרבי]
[לקמן קיט: יומא סג.]
רש"ק מ"ו
[כתיב ליתא]
[לעיל י: לקמן לה:]
יומא יב. מגילה כו. לקמן קיח: [אדר"נ פל"ה וע"ש בפי' בנין יהושע הטעם על לפיכך ובילקוט הכתובה דף ש"ל ס"ד]
[צ"ל שבשתי]

a version: The whole entrance stood to the south.[1] [53b] The school of R. Ishmael taught in R. Simeon b. Yoḥai's ruling: In both cases the *western* base is meant;[2] and your token is:[3] Men pulled a man.[4]

MISHNAH. THE BURNT-OFFERING IS A SACRIFICE OF HIGHER SANCTITY. IT IS SLAUGHTERED IN THE NORTH, AND ITS BLOOD IS RECEIVED IN A SERVICE VESSEL IN THE NORTH; AND ITS BLOOD REQUIRES TWO APPLICATIONS, WHICH ARE FOUR.[5] IT HAD TO BE FLAYED, DISMEMBERED, AND COMPLETELY CONSUMED BY THE FIRE.

GEMARA. Why does he teach that the burnt-offering is a sacrifice of higher sanctity?[6]—Because 'it is most holy' is not written in its case.[7]

AND ITS BLOOD REQUIRES TWO APPLICATIONS [WHICH ARE FOUR]. How did he do it?—Rab said: He applied [the blood] and applied [it] again.[8] Samuel said: He made a single application in the shape of a Greek Gamma.[9]

This is a controversy of Tannaim: [*And the priests . . . shall dash the blood round about the altar*]:[10] You might think that he sprinkles it with a single sprinkling; therefore Scripture states, *'round about'*. If *'round about'*, you might think that he must encompass it [with blood] like a thread; therefore Scripture states, *'And they shall* b *dash'*.[1] How then [is it done]? Its blood requires two applications in the shape of a Greek Gamma, which constitute four. R. Ishmael said: *'Round about'* is said here, and *'round about'* is said elsewhere:[2] as there it means four separate applications,[3] so here too it means *four* separate applications. If so, just as there [it means] four applications on the *four* horns, so here too it means four applications on the *four* horns?—You can answer: The burnt-offering needs the base,[4] whereas the south-east horn had no base. What was the reason?—Said R. Eleazar: Because it was not in the portion of the 'ravener'.[5] For R. Samuel son of R. Isaac said: The altar occupied a cubit in Judah's portion.[6] R. Levi b. Ḥama said in R. Ḥama son of R. Ḥanina's name: A strip issued from Judah's portion and entered Benjamin's portion,[7] whereat the righteous Benjamin

a (1) Of the altar. This is the same as the preceding. (2) Not *southern*, as above. (3) To remember this. (4) The school of R. Ishmael, representing many *men*, pulled the one man, R. Simeon b. Yoḥai, to the view of their master, R. Ishmael. (5) The blood is sprinkled on the north-west and the south-west horns. The blood was not applied exactly on the edge, but spread further, so that all the *four* sides of the altar received some of it. (6) Which he does not teach of sin-offerings and guilt-offerings, though they too are likewise. (7) As it is of the others (v. Lev. VI, 18; VII, 1). Nevertheless the Tanna informs us that it is most holy, since it is altogether burnt. For those parts even of sacrifices of lesser sanctity which were burnt on the altar ranked as most holy. (8) He applied it twice on each horn, one on each side of it. (9) He dashed the blood against the edge and it spread on either side, forming an angle. (10) Lev. I, 5.

b (1) Which implies, from a distance, whereas to encompass it he would have to apply the blood directly with his finger round the sides of the altar. (2) In reference to Aaron's sin-offering of consecration, Lev. VIII, 15. (3) Lit., 'a separation and four applications'.—The applications had to be separate, since they were made on the *four* horns. (4) Its blood must be sprinkled on the horns over against the base. (5) *Sc.* Benjamin; cf. Gen. XLIX, 27: *Benjamin is a wolf that raveneth.* (6) I.e., the width of one cubit along the eastern and the southern sides of the altar, but not reaching right to the ends thereof. Hence the south-east horn was in Judah's portion, and this was not provided with a base. (7) And on this strip was situated part of the Temple, including a portion of the altar.

grieved every day, wishing to possess it,[8] as it is said [54a] *Yearning for Him all day.*[9] Therefore was Benjamin privileged to become a host to the Holy One, blessed be He, as it is said: *And He dwelleth between his shoulders.*[10]

An objection is raised: How was the burnt-offering of a bird sacrificed? He [the priest] pinched off its head close by its neck and divided it,[11] and drained out its blood on the wall of the altar.[12] Now if you say that it had no base, did he simply apply it in the
a air?[1]—Said R. Naḥman b. Isaac: Perhaps they thus stipulated that the air-space should count as Benjamin's and the soil as Judah's.[2]

What does 'it had no base' mean?—Rab said: In the construction.[3] R. Levi said: In respect of blood.[4] Now Rab interpreted [the text just quoted]:[5] In his [Benjamin's] heritage shall the altar be built.[6] While Levi interpreted it: In his heritage shall the sanctuary be built, which means, a place sanctified for [the reception of] blood.[7]

Come and hear: The base ran along the whole of the north and the west sides, and extended one cubit into the south and one cubit into the east?—By 'extended' is meant in respect of blood.[8]

Come and hear: The altar was thirty-two [cubits] by thirty-two?[9]—This was the side length.[10]

Come and hear: Thus it was found that it overhung a cubit over the base and a cubit over the balcony?[11]—Say: a cubit corresponding to the base area and a cubit of the balcony.[12]

Come and hear: For Levi taught: How did they build the altar? They brought a frame thirty-two [cubits] square and one cubit
b deep; and they brought round smooth stones[1] of all sizes;[2] then they brought plaster, molten lead and pitch, melted them down and poured them in; and this was the place of the base. Then they brought a frame thirty cubits square and five cubits deep, and they brought smooth stones etc. [and this was the place of the balcony]. Then they brought a frame twenty-eight cubits square, and three cubits deep; and they brought smooth stones etc., and this was the place of the [wood] pile.[3] Then they brought a frame one cubit square, and they brought smooth round stones, of all sizes, and pitch and molten lead, melted them down, and poured them in, and this formed the horn; and similarly for each horn.[4] And

(8) To have the honour that the whole Temple and everything in it might be in his portion. (9) Deut. XXXIII, 12. E.V.: *He* (*sc.* God) *covereth him* (Benjamin) *all day.* (10) Ibid. The significance of this is explained anon. (11) By pinching through both organs, the windpipe and the gullet. In the case of a *sin*-offering of a bird only one organ was pinched. (12) And this was done on the south-east horn; v. *infra* 64a.

a (1) I.e., the blood would simply fall to the earth. Surely that was not permitted! (2) Possibly there was a little ledge on that side, more than three hand-breadths from the ground, where it would not count as belonging to Judah, and on this ledge the blood fell and was thus sacred. Nevertheless, this ledge could not count as a base, where blood actually had to be poured out on the base. (3) The base, which was a separate structure, did not reach under the south-eastern horn. (4) The base did run along the whole length of the eastern side of the altar, but blood was not poured out nor applied in Judah's portion. (5) '*And he dwelleth between his shoulders.*' (6) Hence the base, which was the understructure and foundation of the altar, was omitted from that side which belonged to Judah. (7) There was a base under the south-east horn, but it was not sanctified for the purpose, since it was not in Benjamin's portion. (8) The blood could be poured out there, yet there was no actual construction. (9) This implies that it was of equal length on all sides, whereas according to Rab it was a cubit short on the east and the south. (10) Only the north and west sides were of this length; the other two sides were each a cubit less. (11) V. *infra* 62b. This refers to the ascent, which joined the altar from the south, and thus implies that there was the base on the south. (12) I.e., the cubit which would have been occupied by the base, had there been one on the south side.

b (1) The original implies fresh from the ground. (2) Lit., 'both large and small'. (3) I.e., the top of the altar, where the wood for the fire was placed. (4) Thus the base consisted of a complete square, which implies the inclusion of the south and the east sides too!

חופף עליו כל היום *לפיכך זכה בנימין הצדיק ונעשה אושפיזכן להקב"ה שנאמר °ובין כתפיו שכן מיתיבי *עולת העוף "כיצד היתה נעשית היה מולק את ראשה ממול עורפה ומבדיל וממצה א] דמה על קיר המזבח ואי אמרת לא היה לה יסוד באוירא בעלמא הוא דקא עביד אמר רב נחמן בר יצחק אימר כך התנו אוירא דבנימין קרקע דיהודה מאי לא הוה לה יסוד רב אמר בבנין לוי אמר בדמים רב מתרגם באחסנתיה יתבני מדבחא ב] לוי מתרגם באחסנתיה יתבני מקדשא מקום מקודש לדמים תא שמע *"היסוד היה מהלך על פני כל הצפון ועל פני כל המערב אוכל בדרום אמה אחת ובמזרח אמה אחת מאי אוכל נמי בדמים תא שמע *"המזבח היה שלשים ושתים על שלשים ושתים הבא במאי עסקינן מן הצד ת"ש *נמצא פורח (א) אמה על יסוד ואמה על סובב אימא כנגד אמה יסוד ג] ועל אמה סובב : תא שמע דתני לוי כיצד בונין את המזבח "מביאין מלבן שהוא שלשים ושתים על שלשים ושתים וגובהו אמה ומביא ד] חלוקי אבנים מפולמות בין גדולות בין קטנות ומביא סיד וקוניא וזפת וממחה ושופך *וזה הוא ה] מקום יסוד וחוזר ומביא מלבן שהוא שלשים ו] אמה על שלשים אמה וגובהו חמש אמות ומביא חלוקי אבנים כו' *) וחוזר ומביא (ב) מלבן שהוא כ"ח על כ"ח אמות וגובהו ג' אמות ומביא חלוקי כו' והוא מקום המערכה וחוזר ומביא מלבן שהוא אמה על אמה ומביא חלוקי אבנים מפולמות בין גדולות בין קטנות ומביא זפת וקוניא וממחה ושופך וזהו קרן וכן לכל קרן וקרן ז] וכי תימא

*) וזהו סובב וחוזר כו' נ"ק

דגייז

רש"י

חופף. כמו נזיר חופף ומפספס (שבת דף נ:) דפרוטי"ר דגרנטו"ר בלע"ז כאדם המחשב ודואג : ומבדיל. בשתי סימנין ולא כחטאת שהיא בסימן אחד ולקמן יליף לה בפרק קדשי קדשים (דף סה.) : וממצה מדמה ח]. *(ומקיף מחבר כמו אין מקיפין שתי חביות (ביצה דף לב:)) דוחק בית מליקתו לקיר תורה אור והוא מתמלה ע"י ט] דוחקו בקיר ולקמן אמרינן שעל קרן מזרחית דרומית י] היא נעשית ואי אין לה יסוד נמצא כשהוא מולקה באויר היא נמלקת והדם טפל לארץ לאיבוד וא"ת יא] טפל על הסובב שהרי למעלה היא נעשית הא קתני התם עשאה למטה מרגליו אפי' אמה אחת כשרה דלא קפיד אלא אלמעלה מן החוט : באוירא בעלמא קעביד. בתמיה : אימר כך וכו'. ואיכא למימר למעלה מג' דלאו קרקע הוא עשוי כמין בליטה קטנה כנגד אותה הקרן לקבל בה דם עולת העוף שלא יפול לארץ וקיר מזבח מיקרי אבל יסוד לא מיקרי להכשיר הקרן למתן דמים הצריכין ליתן כנגד היסוד שאין יסוד אלא המיוסד בארץ : רב אמר בבנין. בקרן דרומית מערבית בנו היסוד אמה באורך הדרום וחדלו להם כל הדרום וכל המזרח עד אמה סמוך לקרן לפונית מזרחית כדאמרן (לקמן) אוכל במזרח אמה ובדרום אמה : לוי יב] אומר בדמים. יסוד היה על פני כל המזרח אבל לא נותנין דמים בחלקו של יהודה : יתבני מדבחא. בניינא גופיה משמע : יג] אוכל. תופס : במזרח אמה אחת. ובמקצוע לפונית מזרחית משוך לצד מזרח אמה ולא יותר כמו שציירתי למעלה קשיא ללוי דהא יד] בניינא משמע : על שלשים ושתים. קשיא לרב דמשמע ריבוע היה: מן הצד. לאו טו] בארבעת רבעין קחשיב אלא מצד לפון היה ל"ב אבל מזרח ודרום לא היה אלא ל"א על ל"א דקרן דרומית מזרחית חסרה לה אמה לדרום ואמה למזרח : נמצא פורח על אמה יסוד ועל אמה סובב. טז] ולקמן הוא בפרק קדשי קדשים (דף סב:) דרמינן מתניתין אהדדי דתנן חדא כבש היה לדרומו של מזבח אורך ל"ב והמזבח ל"ב הרי אורך המזבח והכבש ס"ד וכי מני להו אהדדי תנן הכבש והמזבח ס"ב יז] והא שיתין וארבע הוי תפסין בקרקע העזרה והתם לגבי תפיסת הקרקע קא מני להו ומשנינן נמצא שראש הכבש פורח ועולה על שתי אמות של כניסת היסוד יח] וסובב ונמצא שתי אמות העליונות נבלעות בל"ב של מזבח מדקתני פורח על אמה של יסוד מכלל יט] דאיכא כניסת כ] היסוד לדרום קשיא לרב דאמר דאוכל במזרח אמה אחת ובדרום אמה אחת דקתני ותו לא בבנין קאמר והכבש בדרום הוא ויש תחתיו כניסת יסוד כא] המזבח : אימא כנגד אמה יסוד. כנגד מקום שהכניסה ראויה להיות ולא שהיתה שם ומיהו שתי אמות נבלעות לתוך ל"ב של מזבח שהיה נכנס לתוך כב] הפנימי שכנגד בליטה שהיסוד התחיל בה לאכול בה בדרום אמה אחת : מלבן. כג] הוא דפוס מרובע עשוי מארבע קרשים וכל אחת כד] ארוכה ל"ב כעין אנשטר"א שעושין לכירים ורוחב הקרש אמה והוא גובהו של מלבן כה] ממלאו אבנים וסיד וזפת וקוניא עד שמשווהו לגובה המלבן : מפולמות. לחות : קוניא. כו] ניתוך אבר כעין שעושין לצפוי כלי חרס שקורין פולמי"ר : וממחה. אישפרידיי"ר בלע"ז ושופך כז] בתוך המלבן על אבנים ונדבקים יחד על ידי אלו וזה היסוד הראשון שגינו בו עלה אמה : וחוזר ומביא כו'. ומושיבו על זה וממלאו נמצאת כניסת אמה זה (ג) יסוד בולט אמה כח] זה סובב : וחוזר ומביא כו'. וזהו סובב על זה היה כהן מהלך כדמפרש ואזיל שהמלבן השלישי שהושיבו על זה קצר ממנו שתי אמות על שתי אמות נמצא האמצעי בולט מתחת העליון אמה בכל לד : מקום המערכה. כלומר ראש המזבח : וחוזר ומביא מלבן של אמה כו'. ומושיבו בזוית המזבח מלמעלה קתני מיהא מלבן התחתון של ל"ב על ל"ב אלמא יסוד בולט בו מד' רוחותיו :

דגייז

תוספות

ואי אמרת לא היה לו יסוד באוירא בעלמא קעביד. בתמיה דלקמן (דף סד:) אמרי' שעל קרן מזרחית דרומית היא נעשית ואי אין לה יסוד נמצא כשהוא מולקה באויר היא נמלקת והדם טפל לארץ לאיבוד ואם תאמר טפל הוא על הסובב שהרי למעלה היא נעשית הא קתני התם עשאה למטה מרגליו ואפילו אמה אחת כשרה דלא קפיד אלא למעלה מן החוט כך פירש בקונטרס ונראה שלא היה כתוב בהך ברייתא שירי הדם היה שופך ליסוד מדלא מדקדק בקונטרס אלא מהא שהדם הולך לאיבוד וקשה דאם כן הוה ליה לאקשויי ממתני' דקדשי קדשי' (שם סד:) דתנן בא לו לקרן דרומית מזרחית היה מולק ראשה כו' וברוב ספרים גורסין כאן שירי הדם היה שופך ליסוד ומפרש ה"ר חיים דודאי גרסי' ליה ומכח זה פריך דעל כרחין לאותו קרן שמולק שם היה שופך שירי הדם כט] קרי לה יסוד מדלא קתני שהיה הולך לקרן דרומית מערבית שהיה בו יסוד לשפוך שירים ועוד דלקמן פ' קדשי קדשים (נס זה שם.) מפרש שעושה אותה באותו קרן לפי שהוא קרוב לבית הדשן ויכול לזרוק משם מוראה ונוצה ואם היה זקוק לילך לקרן אחר לשפוך שירים מה היה מרויח כיון שהיה צריך לחזור ואין לומר דלאחר זריקת מוראה ונוצה היה הולך לשפוך שירים דאם היה מאחר כל כך היה דם כלה אלא על כרחין במקומו היה שופך ליסוד ולכך פריך ואי אמרת לא היה לה יסוד באוירא בעלמא קעביד ומשני אימר כן התנו אוירא דבנימין ועשו כמין בליטה ועל אותה בליטה היה שופך שירים ומיהו קשה דאי חשיב יסוד לענין שאר דמים נמי יחשב יסוד וי"ל דלא חשיב יסוד אלא לענין דמים הניתנין למעלה מחוט הסיקרא אבל לענין דמים הניתנין למטה אי מכשרת ליה להוא קרן זימנין דאתי למיתב תחת אותה בליטה ונמצא נותן תחת היסוד אבל דמים העליונים לעולם הם למעלה מן הבליטה ומיהו קשה דאם כן היכי ממעט הכא עולה דלא ל] הוה ארבע קרנות *בחטאת משום דטעונה יסוד *לענין דמים העליונים ונראה לרבינו תם דלא גרסינן שירי הדם היה שופך ליסוד דשופך משמע מן הכלי מדלא תני מתמצה ליסוד כדקתני גבי חטאת העוף לא] ועוד דבמתני' דלקמן פרק קדשי קדשים (דף סד:) קתני בחטאת העוף שירי הדם ובעולת העוף לא תני משמע דלית ליה שירים והא דמרבינן לעיל שירים בכל הקרבנות הייט לב] לבד מעולת העוף וכיון דנעשית מלותו מה לנו במה שהדם נופל אחר כך לארץ והולך לאיבוד דכל דמים נמי לאחר שנשפכו ליסוד הולכין לאיבוד אחרי כן ועוד כשמתרץ כך התנו אוירא ופירש בקונטרס שהיה עושה כמין בליטה במזבח לקבל דמים היה לו להש"ס לפרש זה ונראה לר"ת דפריך ממליקה עצמה דבעי בראשו של מזבח דומיא דהקטרה כדלקמן ואי עביד ליה באויר דיהודה אם כן לג] איכה עולה לקדשי מזבח ומשני דאוירא דבנימין וקדיש האויר בקדושת מזבח ואף על גב דהקטרה באויר אי אפשר לא חיים אלא בהא דליהוי קדושת מזבח ומיהו למאן דאמר (לקמן דף סה.) אין עושין מערכה על גבי סובב נראה דמליקה נמי לא מהניא התם אף על גב דקדוש בקדושת מזבח והכא איירי למאן דאמר עושין מערכה על גבי סובב :

רב אמר בבנין. אף על גב דלמטה לא הוי רבוע למעלה במקום המערכה הוי רבוע וקשה קצת *) לישנא דמתני' לרב דתנן במסכת יומא (דף יב.) דרצועה יוצאה מחלקו של יהודה ונכנסת לחלקו של בנימין ובה מזבח בנוי משמע שהיה בה מבנין :

מפולמות. לד] כגון דגים מפולמין פרק אין צדין (ביצה כד:) :

*) נ"ל לישנא דמתניתא לרב דתניא

דגייז

עין משפט נר מצוה

לז א מיי' פ"ו מהלכות מעה"ק הלכה כ :

לח ב מיי' פ"ב מהל' בית הבחירה הל' י :

לט ג מיי' שם הל' ה :

מ ד מיי' שם הלכה טז :

מסורת הש"ס

ש"ך כמוסי' לקמן דף סה:

[סוטה לז.]

לקמן סד.

מדות פ"ג מ"א

שם [מנחות לז:]

לקמן סב:

נ"ק מ"ו

נ"א זהו יסוד וחוזר ומביא מלבן שהוא ל' אמות ושני ספחים על ל' אמות ושני ספחים וגובהו ה' כו' וזהו סובב וחוזר ומביא מלבן של כ"ח אמות וד' ספחים על כ"ח אמות וד' ספחים וגובהו ג' כו'

הגהות הב"ח

(א) גמ' נמצא פורח על אמה יסוד ועל אמה סובב: (ב) שם ומביא מלבן כ"ב ועיין בסוכה דף מה ע"א : (ג) רש"י ד"ה וחוזר ומביא כו' ומושיבו וכו' יסוד הס"ד ותיבות בולט אמה זה סובב נמחק:

שיטה מקובצת

א] וממצה מדמה על קיר המזבח נטל את הראש ומקיף בית מליקתו למזבח ואי : ב] מדבחא מקום דמים לוי : ג] יסוד וכנגד אמה [סובב] : ד] ומביא חלקי אבנים : ה] תיבת מקום נמחק : ו] שלשים ושני טפחים על שלשים ושני טפחים וגבהו חמש אמות ומביא חלקי אבנים מפולמות וכו' וממחה ושופך וחוזר ומביא מלבן של עשרים ושמונה אמות וד' טפחים על שמונה ועשרים וד' טפחים וגבהו שלש ומביא חלקי כו' וממחה ושופך וזהו מקום מערכה וחוזר ומביא מלבן כו' ומביא חלקי אבנים : ז] תיבות וכי תימא ל"ש ונמחק : ח] מדמה א) כו' ומקיף : ט] ע"י שדוחקו בקיר : י] היתה נעשית אות א' נמחק : יא] וא"ת הוא נופל : יב] לוי אמ' : יג] משמע הס"ד ומה"ד מקום המקודש לדמים פירוש היסוד היה בכל המזבח אך הדמים אין ניתנין רק בחלקו של בנימין הס"ד ומה"ד אוכל. תופס במזרח אמה אחת דבמקצוע צפונית: יד] דהא בבניינא משמע : טו] בארבעת רבעיו קחשיב אלא כו' היה ל"ב ומצד מערב ל"ב אבל מזרח: טז] לקמן הוא : יז] ס"ב ופריך והא שתין וארבע הוי תפס בקרקע : יח] היסוד והסובב ונמצא ב' אמות העליונות של כבש נבלעות בל"ב: יט] מכלל ס"א מכלל דאיכא כניסת יסוד בדרום שהרי הכבש בדרום היה וקשיא לרב דאמר בבנין כלומר שברוח דרומית וברוח מזרח לא היה שם יסוד בנוי והכא משמע שהיה שם בנוי : כ] כניסת יסוד : כא] יסוד במזבח הס"ד : כב] שהיה נכנס לתוך הפנימה שכנגד בל"ב שהיסוד התחיל לאכול בה בדרום : כג] תיבת הוא נמחק : כד] ארכה ל"ב : כה] מלבן וממלאו : כו] קוניא. אבר ניתוך כעין כו' שקורין פולמ"ה הס"ד : כז] ושופך לתוך המלבן על האבנים ונדבקין יחד על ידי אלו וזה הוא היסוד : כח] אמה זו סביב : כט] תיבות קרי לה נמחק : ל] דלא הויא מארבע קרנות כחטאת משום דטעונה יסוד הא חשבא ליה יסוד לענין דמים : לא] העוף ועולת העוף : לב] היינו ס"א דוקא בבהמה דכתיב בקרא : לג] כן חול הוא לענין קדושת מזבח ותיבות אינה עולה לקדשי נמחק : לד] מפולמות. לצורת כמו דגים מפולמים :

א) נראה דצ"ל מדמה כו' נטל את הראש ומקיף בית מליקתו מקיף מחבר וכו'.

עין משפט נר מצוה

כא א מיי' פ"א מהל' בית הבחירה הל' טו:
כב ב מיי' שם הל' ח:
כג ג מיי' פ"ב מהל' מעשה"ק הל' ג:
כד ד מיי' שם הל' ו:
כה ה ו מיי' פ"ט מהל' מעשה"ק הלכה א ופ"י שם הל' ג:
כו ז מיי' שם פ"י הל' י:
ז"ק
כז ח מיי' שם הל' ז:
כח ט מיי' שם הל' ח:
נ"ל שמביא בפ"ק כו'

גמרא

דגייז ליה אבנים שלמות כתיב "דמחית מידי מתותיה ושקיל ליה דאי לא תימא הכי הא א] דאמר רב כהנא "אבנים של קרנות חלולות היו דכתיב °ומלאו כמזרק כזויות מזבח הכא נמי אבנים שלמות אמר רחמנא אלא דמחית מידי מתותיה ושקיל ליה ה"נ דמחית מידי מתותיה ושקיל ליה דרש רבא מאי דכתיב °וילך *דוד ושמואל וישבו בנויות ברמה וכי מה ענין נויות אצל רמה אלא שהיו יושבין ברמה ועוסקין בנויו של עולם אמרי כתיב °וקמת ועלית אל המקום *מלמד שבית המקדש גבוה מכל ארץ ישראל וארץ ישראל גבוהה מכל ארצות לא הוו ידעי ב] דוכתיה היכא אייתו ספר יהושע בכולהו ג] כתיב °וירד ועלה הגבול ותאר הגבול בשבט בנימין ועלה כתיב וירד לא כתיב אמרי ש"מ הכא הוא מקומו סבור למבנייה בעין עיטם דמדלי אמרי ד] ניתתי ביה *קליל כדכתיב °ובין כתפיו שכן ה] ואיבעית אימא גמירי דסנהדרין בחלקו דיהודה ושכינה בחלקו דבנימין ואי מדלינן ליה מתפליג טובא מוטב דניתתי ביה פורתא כדכתיב ובין כתפיו שכן ועל דבר זה נתקנא דואג האדומי בדוד כדכתיב °כי קנאת ביתך אכלתני וכתיב °זכור ה' לדוד את כל ענותו אשר נשבע לה' וגו' אם אבא ו] באהל ביתי אם אתן שנת לעיני לעפעפי תנומה עד אמצא מקום לה' וגו' הנה שמענוה באפרתה מצאנוה בשדה יער באפרתה *זה יהושע דקאתי מאפרים מצאנוה בשדה יער זה בנימין דכתיב °בנימין זאב יטרף: **מתני'** זבחי שלמי צבור "ואשמות אלו הן אשמות אשם גזילות אשם מעילות אשם שפחה חרופה אשם נזיר אשם מצורע אשם תלוי שחיטתן בצפון וקיבול דמן בכלי שרת בצפון "ודמן טעון שתי מתנות שהן ארבע "ונאכלין לפנים מן הקלעים "לזכרי כהונה "לכל מאכל "ליום ולילה "עד חצות:

גמ'

תורה אור

זכריה ט; ש"א יט; דברים יז; יהושע יח; דברים לג; תהלים סט; שם קלב; בראשית מט

רש"י

דגייז ליה. אחר שיבש סתר הבנין מעל חלקו של יהודה: ופרכינן והא אבנים שלמות כתיב. שיהא חלק ולא פגימות ואי אפשר לסתירה להיות חלקה: דמחית מידי מתותיה. כלומר במקומו על (כנגד) חלקו של יהודה הניח עץ ז] ארוך ועוביו כעובי המלבן וחלק [והניח] בתוך המלבן ולא יכול להדביק עם חלוקי האבנים ע"י שפיכת המיחוי של סיד וקוניא ולכשיבש קלת נטלו ונשאר מקומו חלק: קרנות של מזבח חלולות היו. נקבים נקבים עמוקים ח] בארבעתן שיפול דם החטאת ויבלע לתוכו: כמזרק כזוית מזבח. אלמא בית קיבול יש ט] כמזרקים: דמחית מידי מתותיה. מקלות וקסמין י] [דקים] נתן בין חלוקי האבנים וכשיבש הוציאם ונשארו מקומות בנקבים יא] חלוקים ולא הוצרך לפגום בפגימות לנקבים: יב] *שהן יושבים ברמה. בעירו של שמואל: נויו של עולם. למצוא מקום לבית הבחירה מן התורה: ועלית. יג] בכל שעריך קרי עלייה ומשם לבית המקדש מלמד שבית המקדש היה גבוה מכל ארץ ישראל: וארץ ישראל גבוהה מכל הארצות. לא מיבעיא לן הכא ולאו מהכא נפקא לן אלא מקרא אחרינא דכתיב (ירמיה טז וכג) לא יאמר עוד חי וגו' כי אם חי ה' אשר העלה ואשר הביא את בני ישראל מארץ צפון ומכל יד] המקומות אשר הדחתים שם וגו': דוכתיה. מקומו היכן מקום הגבוה בא"י בגבול מי הוא: אייתו ספר יהושע. לבדוק בגבולי השבטים ולא טו] פירשו שם באחד מכל השבטים פיאות גבוליהם לארבע רוחותיהם חוץ משבט יהודה ובנימין שנתפרשו שם כל הגבולים מסובבין טז] ברוחותיה ומקצועותיה גבול יהודה לדרומה של ארץ ישראל וארץ אדום גבולו לדרום על פני כולו ואורך גבול יהודה מן המזרח למערב על פני אורך כל גבולה של א"י ים המלח למזרח וים הגדול למערב והן מן גבולי ארץ ישראל בפרשת אלה מסעי וגבול צפוני של יז] ארץ יהודה לא היה מכוון לארכו אלא התחיל למזרח מן הירדן ועולה למערב ומרחיב יח] מאמצעו ופונה באלכסון לצפון ועולה *מדביר ומרחיב לצד צפון אל יט] הכתף היבוסי היא ירושלים ומשהתחיל מן המזרח *מונה והולך עד ירושלים: כתיב ועלה הגבול ולא כתיב וירד. ועוד כתיב כ] בעלייה אחת מירושלים (א) עד ראש ההר על פני גיא בן הינום ומשם עד הים שהוא לרוח מערב כתיב ותאר הגבול וירד הגבול: *ולא כתיב ועלה. ונחלת בנימין בצפונה של נחלת יהודה וגבול נגב לבנימין הוא גבול צפונה ליהודה אלא שאין אורך נחלת בנימין מן המזרח ועד הים אלא עד ירושלים ועד ההר אשר על כא] גיא בן הינום ועד קרית *יערים: *) כתיב ועלה ותאר ולא כתיב וירד. ותאר אינה לא עליה ולא ירידה למדנו שראש ההר אשר על כב] גיא בן הינום הוא גבוה מן הכל ולמעלה מירושלים דמירושלים ולשם כתיב ועלה: סבור למיבנייה בעין עיטם. נראה בעיני שהוא מעין מי נפתוח האמור שם אחר עליית ההר אשר על פני גיא בן הינום אשר לא נכתב ירידה בינתיים: ניתתי ביה קליל. נעשה אותו נמוך מעט ונבנהו בירושלים שהיא למטה כדכתיב כתפיו ולא כתיב כג] ראשו: *ואיכא דאמרי. האי דלא כד] בנאה בעין עיטם משום דרחיק שם נחלת בנימין מנחלת יהודה יותר משיעור הר הבית ואפשר לסמוך לשכת הגזית לעזרה ואנן בעינן סנהדרין בעזרה דכתיב וקמת ועלית וגו' וצריכה להיות בחלקו של יהודה כדמפרש ואזיל גמירי סנהדרין בחלקו של יהודה כדכתיב (בראשית מט) ומחוקק מבין רגליו: את כל ענותו. אשר עינה את עצמו לעסוק ולדעת ונשבע ונדר אם אבא באהל וגו': **מתני'** זבחי שלמי צבור. כבשי עצרת: אשם גזילות. האמור בשבועת הפקדון (ויקרא ה): אשם מעילות. הנהנה מן הקדש: אשם שפחה חרופה. הבא על שפחה כנענית המיועדת לעבד עברי: אשם נזיר. שנטמא במת דכתיב ביה והזיר לה' את ימי נזרו וגו' (במדבר ו): אשם תלוי. ספק שגג בכרת ספק לא חטא והוא כתוב בויקרא גבי אשם מעילות אשם ודאי ל"ג שכל אלו שהוזכרו אשמות ודאין הן חוץ מאשם תלוי: שתי מתנות שהן ארבע. דבאשם נמי כה] בעינן זריקת סביב דכתיב במקום אשר ישחטו וגו' (ויקרא ז): ונאכלין לפנים מן הקלעים. דכתיב באשם בויקרא קרא לכל אשמם וגו' בקדש הקדשים תאכלנו וגו'. וזבחי שלמי צבור בגמרא מפרש מנא ליה:

גמ'

תוספות

דגייז ליה. תימה מעיקרא ליעבד מלבן בענין זה: אבנים שלמות כו'. תימה דהוה ליה לאקשויי לא תניף עליהם ברזל אמר רחמנא ויש לומר שהש"ס קיצר כאן ורוצה לומר כמו שמדקדק הש"ס במסכת ע"ז פרק רבי ישמעאל (דף נב:) גבי אבני מזבח ששקצום אנשי יון ליתברינהו אבנים שלמות אמר רחמנא ליגסרינהו לא תניף עליהם ברזל כתיב ואם תאמר וליעביד על ידי שמיר דבבית שני הוה שמיר כדמוכח בסוטה פרק עגלה ערופה (דף מח.) דקתני משמתו נביאים הראשונים בטלו אורים ותומים כו] [והיינו בית ראשון] משחרב בית המקדש בטל השמיר והיינו בית שני דאי בית ראשון ליערבינהו וליתנינהו דמשמתו נביאים הראשונים היינו חורבן הבית כדתניא בגמרא משחרב בית המקדש בטלו אורים ותומים והיינו בית ראשון דחמשה דברים חסר בית שני מבית ראשון כדאיתא ביומא (דף כא:) ובטל השמיר היינו לאחר בית שני וכן הא דקאמר רבן שמעון בן גמליאל התם משחרב בית המקדש ניטל טעם כז] פירות ומסתמא בבית שני שחרב בימיו איירי תדע דאשכחן בבית שני שהיו פירותיהם מתברכים בימי שמעון בן שטח שנעשו חיטין ככליות של שור הגדול (תענית דף כג.) ועוד יש להביא ראיה דהוה שמיר בבית שני מעובדא דדמא בן נתינה *שמו דפרק קמא דקדושין (דף לא.) ובפרק שני דמסכת ע"ז (דף כג:) שבקשו ממנו חכמי ישראל אבנים לאפוד ואבני אפוד בעו שמיר כח] כדמוכח פרק עגלה ערופה (סוטה דף מח:) מדכתיב במלואותם ואפי' רבי יהודה דפליג עליה ואמר שמיר שבו בנה שלמה את בית המקדש מודה דאבני אפוד נמי בעו שמיר כדמוכח פרק מי שאחזו (גיטין דף סח.) גבי בנין בית המקדש שעשה שלמה דקאמר היכי נעביד איכא שמיר דאייתי משה לאבני אפוד והיא על כרחין רבי יהודה היא דלר' נחמיה לא הוה בעי שמיר למקדש ועובדא כט] דבן נתינה בבית שני דקאמר הדר לשנה אחרת נולדה לו פרה אדומה בעדרו ושבע פרות היו הראשונה עשה משה שניה עשה עזרא כדתנן במסכת פרה (פ"ג מ"ה) וכמו כן קשה בפרק רבי ישמעאל במסכת ע"ז (דף נב:) אמאי גנזו בית חשמונאי אבני מזבח ששקצום אנשי יון כיון דאפשר על ידי שמיר ויש לומר דשמיר אין עושה אותן שלמות שלא תחגור בה הציפורן ופרק קמא דחולין (דף יח.) אמרינן וכמה כדי פגימת המזבח כדי שתחגור בה צפורן ומיהו קשה ל] בית המקדש כתיב אבן שלמה מסע נבנה וקאמר רבי יהודה דהוה שמיר לבית המקדש *): **ומלאו** כמזרק כזוית מזבח. הוה מצי לאתויי מתני' דמסכת מדות (פ"ג מ"ב) ובקרן מערבית דרומית היו שני נקבים כמין שני חוטמין דקין לא] א)שהדמים היו נתונים על יסוד דרומית יורדין בהן ומתערבין באמה ויוצאין לנחל קדרון אלא ניחא ליה לאיתויי דרב כהנא משום לב] קרא ובקונטרס פירש שהנקבים היו בד' קרנות שיפול דם חטאת לתוכן ויבלע ותימה לפירושו שלא היו המתנות למעלה אלא כנגד חודה מבחוץ:

זבחי

א) נ"ל שהדמים שהיו נתונים על יסוד מערבי ועל יסוד דרומי יורדין כו' נ"ק

*) [וע"ע תוס' סוכה מט. ד"ה שכל ותוס' מס' ע"ז כג: ד"ה בקשו ותוס' גיטין סח. ד"ה איכא ותוס' חולין יח. ד"ה וכמה]

מסורת הש"ס

ז"ק
נ"ל הרא
סנהדרין סז. [קדושין סט.]
שהיו ז"ק
[תרגום יונתן של יוקח נא מעט מים קליל מיא]
מדברה ז"ק
ומונה והולך עד ירושלים כתב ועלה והד"א ז"ק
ולא כתב ועלה סר והד"א ז"ק
יערים כתב ועלה והד"א ז"ק
*) עיין חלופי גרסאות
ואיכא דאמרי האי ז"ק

הגהות הב"ח

(א) רש"י ד"ה כתיב ועלה וכו' ועוד כתיב עליה אחת מירושלים אל ראש ההר אשר על פני:

[גי' הערוך ערך נגס זה ספר יהושע ע"ש פי' נכון]

שיטה מקובצת

א] דאמר רב כהנא קרנות של מזבח חלולות היו (תיבת אבנים נמחק) ר"מ קרנות המזבח חלולות היו כדתנן במס' מדות בקרן מערבית דרומית היו שני נקבים כמין שני חוטמין דקין שהדמים הניתנים על יסוד מערבי ועל יסוד דרומי יורדין בהם ומתערבים באמה ויוצאין לנחל קדרון: ב] מקומו היכא ותיבת דוכתיה נמחק: ג] בכולהו שבטים וירד הגבול ותאר הגבול ובשבט בנימין כתיב ועלה פי' מעין עיטם ואילך לדרום היא גבול שאר שבטים וכל הצפון עד עין עיטם גבול בנימין ובאותו גבולים שמעין עיטם ואילך לדרום כתיב וירד ובגבול בנימין שבצפון עד עין עיטם כתיב ועלה נמצא שעין עיטם גבוה מכולם ועין עיטם זה מי נפתוח לשון רש"י בנוסחאות מהר"פ: ד] ניתתי. גליון כמו תייתי ניהלי האמור לעיל (דף יט ע"א): ה] שכן ואיכא דאמרי גמירי: ו] באהל ביתי אם אתן שנת לעיני וא"ת והיאך היה נודר כך הלא אמרי' בנדרים הנודר שלא לישן שלשה ימים סכין אותו וישן לאחר ויש לפרש דקאי אאהל ביתי וה"ק אם אתן שנת לעיני באהל ביתי אבל לא היה נודר שלא לישן כלל: ז] עץ גדול וארוך ועוביו: ח] עמוקים היו בארבעתן שיפול דם החטאת ויבלע: ט] יש להם כמזרקים: י] קסמין חלקים: יא] בנקבים חלולים ולא הוצרך לפגום בהם פגימות לנקבם הס"ד: יב] מה"ד שהיו יושבין: יג] ועלית מכל שעריך קרי עליה משם לבית המקדש: יד] ומכל הארצות אשר הדיחם שמה תו' הס"ד ומה"ד מקומו היכא מקום הגבוה מכל א"י בגבול מי הוא: טו] פירש שם: טז] מסובבין ברוחותיהם ומקצועותיהם גבול: יז] תיבת ארץ מוקף בחצאי לבנה: יח] ומרחיב ס"א מתחיל מקרוב לאמצע לפנות לצד צפון ומרחיב ועולה אל כתף היבוסי היא ירושלים: יט] אל כתף היבוסי היא ירושלים כו' המזרח מרחיב והולך עד: כ] ועוד כתיב בו עלייה אחת מירושלים להר אשר על פני גיא בן הינום ועד קרית יערים: כא] על פני גיא כו' יערים והיינו דקאמר הכא דבכולהו כתיב וירד הגבול ותאר הגבול ובשבט בנימין ועלה כתיב וירד לא כתיב וה"פ בכל תחומי יהודה הנזכרים בצפון שהם מגבלות נחלת בנימין ולהלן לצפון ולצד מערב וסמוכים לצד דרומי של שאר שבטים כתיב בהו וירד הגבול ותאר ולא כתיב ועלה וכל מה שבגבול צפוני של יהודה סמוך לנחלת בנימין מן המזרח עד קרית יערים כתיב ועלה וכו' והד"א: כב] על פני גיא בן הינום הוא הגבוה מן הכל והוא למעלה מירושלים: כג] כתיב בראשו הס"ד: כד] דלא בנה בעין: כה] נמי כתיב זריקה סביב בצו את אהרן במקום אשר: כו] תיבות והיינו בית ראשון נמחק: כז] טעם. ס"א ביאה וניתנה לעוברי עבירה ומסתמא בבית שני שחרב בימיו איירי תדע דקאמר נמי ניטלה ברכה מן הפירות ואשכחנא: כח] כדאמר ר' נחמיה פרק ותיבת כדמוכח נמחק: כט] ועובדא דדמא בן נתינה בבית שני הוה דקאמר התם לשנה אחרת: ל] קשה דבבית המקדש: לא] שהדמים הניתנים על יסוד דרומית הם יורדין בהן: לב] משום דמייתי קרא ובקונטרס פירש כו' חטאת ויבלע לתוכו ותימה:

should you answer [54b] that he [subsequently] cut it away,[5] [surely] *'unhewn* [whole] *stones'* are prescribed![6]—They placed a plank there, and then removed it.[7] For if you will not say thus, when R. Kahana said: The horns[8] were hollow, for it is written, *And they shall be filled like the basins, like the horns of the altar,*[9] here too [you may object that] the Divine Law prescribed *'whole stones'*?[10] But [you must answer] that something was [first] placed there[11] and then removed; so here too, planks were [first] placed there and then removed.

Raba lectured: What is meant by the verse, [*And he asked and said: 'Where are Samuel and David?'*] *And one said: 'Behold, they are at Naioth in Ramah'*:[12] What connection then has Naioth with Ramah? It means, however, that they sat at Ramah and were engaged with
a the glory [beauty] of the world.[1] Said they, It is written, *Then shalt thou arise, and ascend unto the place* [*which the Lord thy God shall choose*]:[2] this teaches that the Temple was higher than the whole of Eretz Israel,[3] while Eretz Israel is higher than all other countries. They did not know where that place was. Thereupon they brought the Book of Joshua.[4] In the case of all [tribal territories] it is written, *'And the border went down' 'and the border went up' 'and the border passed along'*,[5] whereas in reference to the tribe of Benjamin *'and it went up'* is written, but not *'and it went down'*.[6] Said they: This proves that this is its site. They intended building it at the well of Etam, which is raised, but [then] they said: Let us build it slightly lower,[7] as it is written, *And He dwelleth between his shoulders.*[8] Alternatively,[9] there was a tradition that the Sanhedrin[10] should have its *locale* in Judah's portion, while the Divine Presence[11] was to be in Benjamin's portion. If then we build it in the highest spot,[12] [said they,] there will be a considerable distance between them. Better then that we build it slightly lower, as it is written: *'And He dwelleth between his shoulders'*. And for this Doeg the Edomite envied David,[13] as it is written, *Because envy on account of Thy house hath eaten me up.*[14] And it is written, *Lord, remember unto David all his affliction; how he swore unto the Lord, and vowed unto the Mighty One of Jacob: 'Surely I will not come into the tent of my house, nor go up into the bed that is spread for me; I will not give sleep to mine eyes, nor slumber to mine eyelids; until I find out a place for the Lord, a dwelling-place for the Mighty One of Jacob. Lo, we heard of it as being in Ephrath; we found it in*
b *the field of the forest.'*[1] *'In Ephrath'* means in the Book of Joshua,[2] who [Joshua] was descended from Ephraim. *'In the field of the forest'* alludes to [the territory of] Benjamin, as it is written, *Benjamin is a wolf that raveneth.*[3]

MISHNAH. THE PEACE-OFFERINGS OF THE CONGREGATION[4] AND THE GUILT-OFFERINGS (THESE ARE THE GUILT-OFFERINGS: THE GUILT-OFFERING FOR ROBBERY;[5] FOR TRESPASS;[6] FOR A BETROTHED BONDMAID;[7] A NAZIRITE'S GUILT-OFFERING;[8] A LEPER'S GUILT-OFFERING;[9] AND THE GUILT-OFFERING OF SUSPENSE)[10] ARE SLAUGHTERED IN THE NORTH, AND THEIR BLOOD IS RECEIVED IN A SERVICE VESSEL IN THE NORTH, AND THEIR BLOOD REQUIRES TWO SPRINKLINGS, WHICH CONSTITUTE FOUR. AND THEY ARE EATEN WITHIN THE HANGINGS,[11] BY MALE PRIESTS, PREPARED IN ANY MANNER, A DAY AND A NIGHT, UNTIL MIDNIGHT.

(5) After the base was built, a cubit was cut away on the south side. (6) Deut. XXVII, 6. Cutting away from the base would inevitably cut into the stones, so that they would not be whole. (7) In the first mould planks were placed on the south and the east sides, a cubit from the edge, so that when the stones etc. were poured in, these strips would be left empty; subsequently they were removed. (8) So emended by Sh. M. (9) Zech. IX, 15.—That implies that the horns were hollowed out to form a receptable. (10) Whereas if the horns were hollowed or perforated after they were made, the stones would have to be cut into. (11) Thin laths formed the hollow or channels before the stones etc. were poured into it, and these were not filled in. (12) I Sam. XIX, 22.

a (1) Connecting Naioth with *na'eh*, beautiful, glorious. The reference is to the Temple—they sought to determine its exact site. (2) Deut. XVII, 8. (3) Since one had to *'ascend'* to it from wherever he might be. (4) To study the topography of Eretz Israel. (5) Cf. Josh. XV—XVIII. (6) The border of other tribes ran in a southerly direction from the well of Etam, and the north as far as the well of Etam constituted Benjamin's boundary. Now, the boundaries of other tribes as they proceeded south *from* the well of Etam are described as going down, whereas the boundary of Benjamin as it proceeded *to* the well of Etam is described as going up. Hence the well of Etam must have been the highest spot of all. Rashi identifies the well of Etam with *'the waters of Nephtoah'* (ibid. XVIII, 15.) V. also *J.E.* art. 'Etam'. (7) *Sc.* in Jerusalem. (8) Deut. XXXIII, 12. *'Shoulders'* but not 'head' implies that it should not be at the very highest point. (9) An alternative reason why they did not build it at the well of Etam. (10) The Supreme Court of seventy-one; v. Sanh. *2a*. Its seat was in a special chamber ('Chamber of Hewn Stone') in the Temple court. (11) The Temple. (12) Lit., 'if we raise it'. (13) I.e., because David had thus decided the site of the Temple. (14) Ps. LXIX, 10. E.V., *'zeal for Thy house* etc.'

b (1) Ps. CXXXII, 2-6. (2) Emended text (Aruk). (3) Gen. XLIX, 27. Being a 'wolf', he would naturally be found in the forest (4) The lambs offered on Pentecost, Lev. XXIII, 19. (5) V. Lev. V, 20-25. (6) V. *supra* 35*b* n. 10.; ibid 15 f. (7) V. ibid. XIX, 20 seq. (8) A nazirite who became defiled through a corpse, v. Num. VI, 9 seq. (9) At his purification, v. Lev. XIV, 12. (10) V. *supra* 48*a* n. a 8. (11) V. *supra* 53*a* n. 6.

[55a] *GEMARA.* How do we know that it requires the north?—As Raba son of R. Ḥanan[12] recited before Raba: *And ye shall offer one he-goat for a sin-offering, [and two he-lambs of the first year for a sacrifice of peace-offerings]:*[13] as a sin-offering requires the north, so [must] the peace-offerings of the congregation [be slaughtered] in the north. Said Raba to him: Now, whence do we learn this about a sin-offering? From a burnt-offering. Can then that which is learnt

a through a *hekkesh* teach in turn through a *hekkesh?*[1]—Rather, [said Raba], It follows from what R. Mari the son of R. Kahana recited: [*Ye shall blow with the trumpets*] *over your burnt-offerings, and over the sacrifices of your peace-offerings:*[2] as a burnt-offering was a sacrifice of higher sanctity, so were the public peace-offerings sacrifices of higher sanctity; as a burnt-offering [was slaughtered] in the north, so were the public peace-offerings [slaughtered] in the north.

Now, what is the purpose of the first *hekkesh?*[3]—[To teach that it is] like a sin-offering: as a sin-offering is eaten by male priests only, so are public peace-offerings [eaten] by male priests [only]. Said Abaye to him [Raba]: If so, when it is written in connection with a nazirite's ram: *And he shall present his offering unto the Lord, one he-lamb of the first year without blemish for a burnt-offering, and one ewe-lamb of the first year without blemish for a sin-offering, and one ram without blemish for a peace-offering:*[4] will you say that here too the Divine Law assimilated it to a sin-offering: as a sin-offering may be eaten by male priests only, so the nazirite's ram may be eaten by male priests only?—How compare: There, since it is written, *And the priest shall take the shoulder of the ram when it is sodden,* [. . . . *this is holy, for the priest*][5] it follows that the whole of it is eaten by its owner. But at least the shoulder that is sodden should be eaten by male priests only?—That is a difficulty. Alternatively [you can answer]: It[6] is called *'holy'*, but not 'most holy'.[7] Then in respect of which law is it assimilated?[8]—Said Raba: [To teach] that if he shaves himself after one [sacrifice] of the three, he fulfils his duty.[9]

MISHNAH. THE THANKS-OFFERING AND THE NAZIRITE'S RAM ARE SACRIFICES OF LESSER SANCTITY. THEY ARE SLAUGHTERED ANYWHERE IN THE TEMPLE COURT, AND THEIR BLOOD REQUIRES TWO SPRINKLINGS, WHICH CONSTITUTE FOUR; AND THEY ARE EATEN IN ANY PART OF THE

b CITY, BY ANY PERSON,[1] PREPARED IN ANY MANNER, THE SAME DAY AND THE NIGHT FOLLOWING, UNTIL MIDNIGHT. THE PARTS THEREOF WHICH ARE SEPARATED[2] ARE GOVERNED BY THE SAME LAW, SAVE THAT THESE ARE EATEN [ONLY] BY THE PRIESTS, THEIR WIVES, THEIR CHILDREN AND THEIR SLAVES.

GEMARA. Our Rabbis taught: *And the breast of waving and the thigh of heaving shall ye eat in a clean place:*[3] Said R. Nehemiah: Did they then eat the earlier [sacrifices][4] in uncleanness? Rather, 'clean' implies that it is [partially] unclean:[5] [thus it means,] clean from the defilement of a leper, but unclean with the uncleanness of a *zab*, and which place is that? The camp of the Israelites.[6] Yet say [that it means] clean from the defilement of a *zab*, yet unclean with the defilement of the dead, and which [place] is that? The Levitical camp?[7]—Said Abaye, Scripture saith, *And ye shall eat it* [the meal-

c offering] *in a holy place:*[1] *'it'* [must be eaten] in a holy place, but another [need] not [be eaten] in a holy place, thus withdrawing it from the Camp of the Divine Presence into the Levitical Camp.[2] Then *'in a clean place'* is written, which withdraws it into the camp of the Israelites. Raba said: *'It'* [must be eaten] in a holy place but another [need] not [be eaten] in a holy place, withdraws it altogether;[3] then the Divine Law wrote *'in a clean place'*, [thereby] bringing it into the Israelites' camp.[4] Yet say that it brought it into the *Levitical* camp?[5]—We bring it back into one [camp], not into two. If so, [you can] also [argue in respect of] withdrawing: we withdraw it from one, but not from two?[6] Moreover, it is written, *Thou mayest not eat within they gates* etc?[7] Rather, it clearly must be explained as Abaye.

MISHNAH. THE PEACE-OFFERING IS A SACRIFICE OF LESSER SANCTITY. IT MAY BE SLAIN IN ANY PART OF THE TEMPLE COURT, AND ITS BLOOD REQUIRES TWO SPRINKLINGS, WHICH CONSTITUTE FOUR; AND IT MAY BE EATEN IN ANY PART OF THE CITY, BY ANY PERSON, PREPARED IN ANY WAY, DURING TWO DAYS AND ONE NIGHT. THE PARTS THEREOF WHICH ARE SEPARATED ARE SIMILAR, SAVE THAT THESE ARE EATEN BY PRIESTS, THEIR WIVES, THEIR SONS, AND THEIR SLAVES.

GEMARA. Our Rabbis taught: *And he shall kill it at the door of the tent of meeting . . . and he shall kill it before the tent of meeting . . . and he shall kill it before the tent of meeting:*[8] this teaches that all sides [of the Temple court] are fit in the case of sacrifices of lesser

d sanctity,[1] and the north [side] *a fortiori:* if sacrifices of higher sanctity, which were not made fit [for slaughtering] on all sides, are fit on the north; is it not logical that sacrifices of lesser sanctity, which are fit on all sides, are fit in the north?[2] R. Eliezer said: The Writ comes specifically to declare the north fit.[3] For you might say, is not [the reverse] logical: If sacrifices of lesser sanctity, which are fit on all sides, yet their place is not fit for sacrifices of higher sanctity;[4] then sacrifices of higher sanctity, which are permitted in the north only, is it not logical that their [particular] place is not permitted for sacrifices of lesser sanctity? Therefore

(12) Emended text (Sh. M.) (13) Lev. XXIII, 19.

a (1) Surely not. V. *supra* 48*a*, 49*b*. (2) Num. X, 10. It must mean the peace-offerings of the congregation, since private peace-offerings did not require the blowing of trumpets. (3) Where it is assimilated to a sin-offering. (4) Num. VI, 14. (5) Ibid. 19, 20. (6) The shoulder that is sodden. (7) Therefore it cannot be like the sin-offering, which is 'most holy'. (8) *Sc.* the nazirite's ram to a sin-offering. (9) At the termination of his vow a nazirite must bring three sacrifices, viz., a burnt-offering, a sin-offering, and a peace-offering. Yet if he brings only one and shaves, the prohibitions of a nazirite, such as drinking wine, are lifted, because it is written, *And* after that *the nazirite may drink wine* (v. 20), *'after that'* meaning, according to the Rabbis, after he brings his peace-offering. Then the sin-offering is assimilated to the peace-offering to shew that the same applies to the former too.

b (1) I.e., even by a *zar*. (2) In the case of the thanks-offering, the thigh and breast, and four loaves out of the forty by which it is accompanied. In the case of the nazirite's ram, likewise the thigh and the breast, the boiled shoulder, one unleavened loaf and one unleavened wafer. (3) Lev. X, 14. (4) Those enumerated earlier in this passage, which treats of Aaron's consecration. (5) Since Scripture writes *'in a* clean *place* instead of *in a* holy *place,'* as in the preceding verse. (6) Three 'camps' of lessening degrees of sanctity were recognised in the Wilderness: (i) The camp of the Divine Presence,—the Tabernacle; (ii) the camp of the Levites—literally the Levitical camp which immediately surrounded the Tabernacle; and (iii) the camp of the Israelites, likewise literally, each tribe within the camp of his standard, v. Num. II. To these three corresponded the Temple, the Temple Mount, and the city of Jerusalem respectively. A leper was expelled from all three, a *zab* was not permitted in the first two, and permitted in the third. Hence this text teaches that it might be eaten anywhere in Jerusalem. (7) Where a corpse might be taken. So that the flesh of this sacrifice may be eaten in the Temple Mount only, but not anywhere in Jerusalem.

c (1) Lev. X, 13. (2) Emended text (Sh. M.). (3) This would imply that it need not even be eaten in the third camp, hence even *outside* Jerusalem. (4) Hence it must be eaten within the walls of Jerusalem. (5) Teaching that it must be eaten in the Temple Mount. (6) When Scripture implies that it is not bound to be eaten in a particular place, say that one camp (that of the Divine Presence) is excluded, but not two. (7) Deut. XII, 17. *'Within thy gates'* means in the cities outside Jerusalem. (8) Lev. III, 2, 8, 13. The three texts refer to the different animals brought as peace-offerings.

d (1) As *'before'* implies on any side. (2) Thus in the view of this Tanna no text is necessary to shew that it can be slain in the north. (3) Otherwise we would not know it. (4) The latter cannot be slaughtered in any part of the Temple.

תורה אור

גמ' מנא לן דבעי צפון דתני א] רבה בר רב חנן קמיה דרבא °ועשיתם שעיר עזים אחד לחטאת ג] מה חטאת בצפון אף ^א^שלמי צבור בצפון אמר ליה רבא °וכי חטאת מהיכן למדה מעולה ג] *דבר הלמד בהיקש חוזר ומלמד בהיקש אלא ד] *מדתני רב מרי בריה דרב כהנא °על עולותיכם ועל זבחי שלמיכם מה עולה קדשי קדשים אף זבחי שלמי צבור קדשי קדשים מה עולה בצפון אף זבחי שלמי צבור בצפון ה] אלא היקשא קמא למאי אתא כי חטאת מה חטאת אינה נאכלת אלא לזכרי כהונה ^ב^אף זבחי שלמי צבור ו] לזכרי כהונה אמר ליה אביי אי ז] הכי גבי איל נזיר דכתיב °והקריב את קרבנו לה' כבש בן שנתו תמים אחד לעולה וכבשה אחת בת שנתה ח] [תמימה] לחטאת ואיל אחד [תמים] לשלמים הכי נמי נימא ט] דהקיש הכתוב לחטאת מה חטאת אינה נאכלת אלא לזכרי כהונה אף איל נזיר נמי אינו נאכל אלא לזכרי כהונה הכי השתא התם כיון דכתיב °ולקח הכהן את הזרוע בשלה מן האיל ^ג^מכלל דכוליה בעלים אכלי ליה ^ד^זרוע בשלה מיהא לא י] ליתאכיל אלא לזכרי כהונה קשיא ואיבעית אימא יא] קדשי אקרי קדשי קדשים לא יב] איקרו ואלא למאי הלכתא איתקש אמר *רבא *^ה^שאם גלח על אחד יג] משלשתן יצא:

מתני' התודה ואיל נזיר קדשים קלים שחיטתן ^ו^בכל מקום בעזרה ^ז^ודמן טעון שתי מתנות שהן ארבע ^ח^ונאכלין בכל העיר לכל אדם בכל מאכל ליום ולילה עד חצות המורם מהם כיוצא בהן אלא ^ט^שהמורם נאכל לכהנים לנשיהם ולבניהם ולעבדיהם:

גמ' ת"ר יד] °את חזה התנופה ואת שוק התרומה תאכלו במקום טהור אמר רבי נחמיה וכי ראשונים בטומאה אכלום אלא טהור מכלל שהוא טמא טהור מטומאת מצורע וטמא מטומאת זב ואיזה זה ^י^זה מחנה ישראל ואימא טהור מטומאת זב וטמא מטומאת מת ואיזה זה זה מחנה לויה אמר אביי אמר קרא °ואכלתם אותה במקום קדוש אותה במקום קדוש ולא אחרת במקום קדוש אפקה טו] למחנה לויה הדר כתיב במקום טהור אפקה למחנה ישראל רבא אמר אותה במקום קדוש ולא אחרת במקום קדוש אפקה לגמרי הדר כתב טז] רחמנא תאכלו במקום טהור עיילא למחנה ישראל ואימא עיילא למחנה לויה לחדא מעיילינן לתרתי לא מעיילינן אי הכי אפוקי נמי *לחדא מפקינן מתרתי לא מפקינן ועוד °לא תוכל לאכול בשעריך כתיב אלא מחוורתא כדאביי:

מתני' *שלמים קדשים קלים שחיטתן בכל מקום בעזרה ודמן טעון שתי מתנות שהן ארבע ונאכלין בכל העיר לכל אדם בכל מאכל לשני ימים ולילה אחד המורם מהם כיוצא בהם אלא שהמורם נאכל לכהנים לנשיהם ולבניהם ולעבדיהם:

גמ' ת"ר °ושחטו פתח אהל מועד °ושחט אותו לפני אהל מועד °ושחט אותו לפני אהל מועד להכשיר את כל הרוחות ^°^בקדשים קלים יז] ק"ו לצפון ומה קדשי קדשים שלא הוכשרו בכל הרוחות הוכשרו בצפון קדשים קלים שהוכשרו בכל הרוחות אינו דין שהוכשרו בצפון רבי אליעזר אומר לא יח] נאמר הכתוב אלא להכשיר צפון שיכול והלא דין הוא ומה קדשים קלים שהוכשרו בכל הרוחות לא הוכשר מקומן אצל קדשי קדשים קדשי קדשים שלא הוכשרו אלא בצפון אינו דין שלא הוכשר מקומן אצל קדשים קלים ת"ל יט] אהל מועד במאי

רש"י

גמ' ועשיתם שעיר עזים וגו'. גבי שתי הלחם וכבשי עצרת כ) כתיב וסיפיה דקרא ושני כבשים וגו': ועל זבחי שלמיכם וגו'. על כרחך בשלמי צבור כתיב שאין קרבן יחיד טעון כלי שיר שאין אומרים שיר על קרבן יחיד כדאמר בערכין (דף י:): קדשי קדשים. כא] נפסלים בטבול יום ובינה (ובלינה): היקשא קמא. דאיתקש לחטאת: ה"ג מה חטאת כב] כו': כיון דכתיב ולקח הכהן את הזרוע. סיפיה דקרא קדש הוא לכהן ש"מ השאר לבעלים כג]: *קדש איקראי. זרוע בשלה ומדלא כתיב קדשי קדשים ש"מ לא איתקוש לחטאת להכי דתיהוי (א) עלי' *תומרא דקדש קדשים דבהדיא מעטיה כד] מדכתיב קדש ולא כתיב קדשים וגבי שלמי צבור אע"ג דכתיב בהו כה] נמי קדש יהיו לה' לכהן (ויקרא כג) ולא כתיב קדשי קדשים כיון דכתיב לה' לאו למעוטיה כו] הוא מהיקשא דאיכא למימר כמאן דכתיב קדשי קדשים דמי: אלא למאי הלכתא איתקש. איל נזיר לחטאת: שאם גילח על אחת משלשתן יצא. וחטאת הוא דילפא משלמים מה איל נזיר אם הביאו יחידי בלא חטאת ועולה יצא דכתיב (במדבר ו) ואחר ישתה הנזיר יין ואמר מר בספרי כז] אחר מעשה יחידי והיינו שלמים שעיקר תגלחתו של נזיר תלויה בשלמיו שהרי כח] הוזקקו לו לשלח שערו תחת הדוד כדכתיב (שם) על האש אשר תחת זבח השלמים ותניא בספרי כט] וגלח הנזיר פתח אהל מועד בשלמים הכתוב מדבר כלומר גילוחו של נזיר ע"י דבר שנאמר בו ושחט פתח אהל מועד והיינו שלמים בויקרא או אינו אלא כמשמעו שיגלח פתח אהל מועד ממש אם אמרת כן דרך בזיון כו': **מתני'** קדשים קלים. אין ל] (לך) מועלין בהן: בכל מקום. אין טעונין צפון: ונאכלין בכל העיר. בגמ' מפרש: לכל אדם. לזרים: ליום ולילה. בתודה כתיב ביום קרבנו יאכל לא יניח ממנו עד בוקר ותניא תודת שלמיו לרבות שלמי נזיר: המורם מהן. מן התודה *חזה ושוק כשאר שלמים דהא איתקש לשלמים כדאמרן זבח השלמים אם על תודה (ויקרא ז) וארבע חלות מד' מינין שבה כדכתיב אחד מכל קרבן וגו' לכהן הזורק וגו' (שם) ומורם מאיל נזיר זרוע בשלה וחזה ושוק נמי ביה כתיבי וחלת מצה אחת ורקיק מצה אחד כיוצא בהן ונאכלין בכל העיר ליום ולילה: אלא. שאינו לבעלים אלא לכהנים: ולנשיהם. כדכתיב (ויקרא י) ואת חזה התנופה וגו' אתה ובניך ובנותיך: **גמ'** תאכלו במקום טהור. בפרשת ויהי ביום השמיני כתיב: וכי הראשונים בטומאה אכלום. קרבנות הראשונים שנאמרו תחילה בענין כגון שעירים ומנחה: טהור מכלל שהוא טמא. מדלא כתיב קדש ש"מ טהור במקצת קאמר ולא מן הכל הא כיצד במחנה הטהור מטומאת מצורע שאין מצורע נכנס לו וטמא מטומאת זב שהזבין נכנסין שם ואיזה זה זה מחנה ישראל במדבר כל דגל בתוך אסיפת דגלו ובית עולמים תוך ירושלים דאמרינן בפסחים (דף סז.) מצורע משתלח חוץ לג' מחנות זב נכנס למחנה ישראל אבל לא למחנה לויה והוא במדבר חניית הלוים סביב למשכן העדות בבית עולמים הר הבית וטמא מת מותר ליכנס במחנה לויה שנאמר ויקח משה את עצמות יוסף עמו (שמות יג) עמו במחיצתו: אותה. במנחה כתיב בההוא עניינא: ואין אחרת. ואין לחמי תודה במקום קדוש: אפקה. ממחנה שכינה שקרבה בתוכה למחנה לויה הדר כתיב במקום טהור להקל ולומר טהרה כל דהו לא] דלא איצטריך פשיטא דבטומאה ממש לא אכלי לה: אפקה לגמרי. ואפי' חוץ לחומה (ב) במשמע (בשעריך) חוץ לירושלים: ועוד לא תוכל לאכול בשעריך כתיב. והיכי אמרינן לב] אפקיה לגמרי: **מתני'** בכל מקום. אף בדרום ובגמרא יליף לה: בכל העיר. כדאמרן לעיל בחזה ושוק דשלמי: לשני ימים ולילה אחד. דהכי כתיב בהו ובגמרא מייתי לה: **גמ'** ושחטו כו'. לג] כל שלש פרשיות בשלמים חדא בבן בקר וחדא לד] בבן כשב וחדא בעז בקמייתא כתיב ושחטו פתח אהל מועד ובתרתי כתיב לפני אהל מועד: להכשיר לה] כל הרוחות שבעזרה. דלפני משמע כל שלפני ההיכל ושבצדדין לקמיה יליף לו] ומפרש לה: קל וחומר לצפון. לירך מזבח צפוני הקבוע לעולה ולקדשי קדשים ומשום פלוגתא דפליג רבי אליעזר עלה ואמר צפון איצטריך קרא בהדיא לרבויי לשחיטת קדשים קלים איצטריך לת"ק למימר האי קל וחומר לצפון: לז] לא בא אחד מן הכתובין הללו אלא להכשיר צפון. לח] לקמיה מפרש מאי פלוגתייהו: שיכול והלא דין הוא. שלא יהא צפון בכלל לפני אהל מועד להכשירו לשחיטת שלמים: לא הוכשר מקומן. שלשה הרוחות הכשירות להם לא הוכשרו לשחיטת קדשי קדשים לט]: במאי

תוספות

זבחי שלמי צבור מנא לן. לעיל (דף נ. ד"ה לא) פירשנו אמאי לא אתי בבנין אב: **מה** חטאת בצפון כו'. ולענין מתנות ליכא מ] לאקשויי לחטאת כדדרשינן לעיל פרק קמא (דף י:) אותה דמה למעלה ואין אחרת דמה למעלה: **מה** עולה בצפון. וא"ת עיכובא מנא לן דבעולה לא ידעינן עיכובא אלא מק"ו דחטאת כדקאמר רב אדא בר אהבה לעיל (דף מח:) שלא יהא טפל חמור מן העיקר ודבר הלמד בקל וחומר אינו חוזר ומלמד בהיקש (לעיל נ:) אם לא נאמר *דס"ל כרב פפא מא]: **אלא** היקשא קמא למאי אתא. לא מצי למימר לענין ארבע מתנות על ארבע קרנות כדפרי' מב] וכי תימא לענין פיסוק מתנות דנותן וחוזר ונותן כדקאמר רבי ישמעאל בעולה לעיל מג] (דף נג:) כיון דאיתקש נמי לעולה אין לו לשנות מעולה: **מה** חטאת אינה נאכלת אלא לזכרי כהונה. תימה דלקמן פ' דם חטאת (דף צז:) ופ' התודה (מנחות דף פב:) נפקא לן מקרא *אחרינא וא"ת כיון דאיתקש לחטאת אם כן יפסלו שלא לשמה כחטאת ולרבנן דדרשי בפ"ק (לעיל דף י:) אותה מד] ניחא אבל לר' אליעזר קשה וצריך לדקדק בפ' התכלת (מנחות דף מח:) דגמר שלמי חובה משלמי נדבה ולא מקשינן לחטאת: **שאם** גלח על אחת משלשתן יצא. תימה דצריך קרא בנזיר מה] *המשלח שערו תחת הדוד של חטאת תיפוק לי מהך היקשא: שלמים

עין משפט נר מצוה

מט א מיי' פ"ט מהל' מעה"ק הל' ג:
נ ב מיי' שם פ"י הל' ג:
נא ג ד מיי' פ"ט שם הל' יא:
נב ה מיי' פ"ח מהל' נזיר הלכה ג:
נג ו מיי' פ"ט מהל' מעה"ק הלכה ג:
נד ז מיי' שם הל' ו:
נה ח מיי' פ"י שם הלכה ה:
נו ט מיי' שם הל' ד:
נז י מיי' שם הלכה ה:

[ועי' תוס' לקמן נז: ד"ה מה מנחה]

שיטה מקובצת

א] דתני רבא בר רב חנן: ב] לחטאת הקישו הכתוב לחטאת מה חטאת בצפון אף זבחי שלמי: ג] מעולה וכי דבר: ד] אלא אמר רבא מדתני: ה] בצפון ואלא היקשא קמא למה לי אמר רבא מה חטאת כו' והשאר נמחק: ו] צבור אינם נאכלין אלא לזכרי כהונה: ז] עי' בהשמטות בסוף המסכת: ח] שנתה תמימה לחטאת ואיל אחד תמים: ט] נימא דהיקשו הכתוב: י] לא ניתכול אות ל' ואות א' ל"ש: יא] קדשי איקרי. פ"ה גבי שלמי צבור כיון דכתיב לה' כמאן דכתיב קדש קדשים דמי וקשה א"כ למה לי היקשא דשלמי צבור לעולה לומר דהוי קדשי קדשים תיפוק ליה משום דכתיב לה' ותירץ מורי דלא מהני לה' אלא לומר דלא אתא קודש ומפיק להו מהיקשא ולעשותו קדשי קדשים על ידי היקשא. תו' מהר"פ: יב] לא איקרי ואלא כו' אמר רבינא תיבת רבא ל"ש: יג] משלשתן. (מנחות דף ה ע"א) ועיקר (המשנה) [במשנה] (נזיר דף מס ע"א): יד] ת"ר ואת חזה: טו] אפקה ממחנה שכינה למחנה: טז] כתב במקום טהור ותיבות רחמנא תאכלו נמחק: יז] קלים וק"ו: יח] לא בא הכתוב תיבת נאמר נמחק: יט] לומר ושחטו פתח אהל מועד לפני אהל מועד לפני אהל מועד: כ] כתוב וסיפא דקרא ושני כבשים וגו' לזבח שלמים הס"ד: כא] ליפסל בטבול יום: כב] חטאת [אינה] נאכלת כו': כג] לבעלים ואקשינן זרוע בשלה לא יאכל אלא לזכרי כהונה ואנן תנן המורם מהן כיוצא בהן אלא כו' קשיא הס"ד ומה"ד קדש איקרו זרוע בשלה קדש בלחוד איקרו ומדלא כתיב ק"ק ש"מ דלא איתקש לחטאת: כד] מעטיה קרא: כה] תיבת נמי נמחק: כו] למעוטי מהיקשא הוא: כז] בספרי (נזיר דף מו ע"א): כח] שהרי הוקקו לו להגיחם ולשלח שערו: כט] בספרי (נזיר דף מה ע"א): ל] תיבת לך נמחק: לא] דהו דאי להתיר לא איצטריך: לב] אמרי' אפקה: לג] תיבת כל נמחק: לד] וודאי בכשב ותיבת בבן נמחק: לה] להכשיר את כל: לו] יליף לה ומפרש הס"ד: לז] לצפון הס"ד ומה"ד לא בא הכתוב אלא להכשיר צפון. לא בא כו': לח] צפון ולקמיה: לט] קדשים ת"ל אהל מועד כו' ות"ק לית ליה ק"ו דר' אליעזר דמה לקדשי קדשים שהם הסורים ולכך לא הוכשרו בהן שאר הרוחות: מ] לאקשי: מא] פפא דאמר חוזר ומלמד בהיקש וללישנא דהעולה במקומה תהא ניחא דעיכוב בגופיה כתיב והאיל ואיתקש בהיקש גמור איתקש אף לעיכובא ושאני לעיל דלא כתיב אלא ושחט אותה כדפי' לעיל דאינו היקש גמור אלא למצוה. מהר"ם: מב] תיבות וכי תימא נמחק: מג] לעיל דכיון דאיתקש: מד] אותה דהפאת למעט כל שאר קדשים מפסול שלא לשמו ניחא ילר"א דלא דריש אותה אה"נ דסבר דשלמי צבור פסולין שלא לשמן והה"נ איכא תנא בפ' התכלת דפסיל שלמי צבור שלא לשמן והשתא מוקמינן ליה כר"א. מהר"ם: מה] בנזיר דמשלח:

מסורת הש"ס

קדשי איקרי ל"ק
[לעיל מט: וש"נ]
[ערכין יא: ע"ש בתוס']
כל הזמרא ל"ק
נ"א רבינא
[נזיר דף מה. וש"נ]
נ"א חזה ושוק שניתן לכהנים כשאר שלמים דהא איתקש תודה לשלמים כדאמרן ואלא הורת זבח השלמים כו'
*מנחות ג.

הגהות הב"ח

(א) רש"י ד"ה קדש וכו' דתיהוי לה תומרא: (ב) ד"ה אפקה לגמרי וכו' במשמע הס"ד ואח"כ מ"ה ועוד לא תוכל לאכול בשעריך כתיב ובשעריך חוץ לירושלים והיכי אמרי':

גליון הש"ס

גמ' וכי חטאת מהיכן למדה. ע"ל דף נז ע"ב תד"ה ואכ"א: שם בקדשים קלים ק"ו לצפון. ע"ל דף נח ע"א תוד"ה כולו: תוס' ד"ה מה עולה וכו' דס"ל כר"פ. לעיל דף נ ע"ב וע' תוס' שם ד"ה אלא:

עין משפט נר מצוה

פח א ב ג מיי' פ"ה מהל' מעשה הקרבנות הל' ה'

פט ד מיי' פ"ז מהל' בית הבחירה הל' כב

במאי קא מיפלגי תנא קמא סבר תלתא קראי כתיבי חד לגופיה דניבעי פתח אהל מועד וחד להכשיר צדדין א] וחד לפסול צידי צדדין וצפון לא איצטריך קרא ור' אליעזר סבר חד לגופיה דניבעי פתח אהל מועד וחד להכשיר צפון וחד להכשיר צדדין וצידי צדדין לא איצטריך קרא מאי שנא הכא ג] דכתיב פתח אהל מועד ומאי שנא התם דכתיב לפני אהל מועד קמ"ל כדרב יהודה אמר שמואל *דאמר רב יהודה אמר שמואל שלמים ששחטן קודם שיפתחו דלתות ההיכל פסולין שנאמר °ושחטו פתח אהל מועד בזמן שהוא פתוח ולא בזמן שהוא נעול ג] איתמר נמי אמר מר עוקבא בר חמא אמר רבי יוסי ברבי חנינא שלמים ששחטן קודם שיפתחו דלתות ההיכל פסולין שנאמר ושחטו פתח אהל מועד בזמן ד] שפתח ההיכל פתוח ולא בזמן שהוא נעול במערבא מתני הכי אמר רב ה] יעקב בר אחא אמר רב אשי שלמים ששחטן קודם שיפתחו דלתות ההיכל פסולים ו] *ובמשכן קודם שיעמידו לוים את המשכן ולאחר שיפרקו לוים את המשכן פסולים פשיטא מוגף כנעול דמי וילון מאי א"ר זירא ז] הוא עצמו אין נעשה אלא כפתח ח] פתוח גובהה מאי ת"ש דתניא *ר' יוסי בר' יהודה אומר שני פשפשין היו בבית החליפות ט] וגובהן שמנה כדי להכשיר את העזרה כולה לאכילת קדשי קדשים ולשחיטת קדשים קלים מאי לאו דאיכא קמייהו [א] שמנה לא י] דגבהו נינהו שמונה מיתיבי *כל השערים שהיו שם גובהן עשרים אמה ורוחבן עשר אמה פשפשין שאני והאיכא צדדין יא] דמעייל להו בקרן זוית אחורי בית הכפורת מאי תא שמע דאמר רמי בר רב יהודה אמר רב לול קטן היה אחורי בית הכפורת יב] גבוה שמונה אמות כדי להכשיר את העזרה לאכילת קדשי קדשים ולשחיטת קדשים קלים יג] והיינו דכתי' °שנים לפר בר *מאי לפר בר אמר רבה בר רב שילא כמאן דאמר כלפי יד] בר א"ר יהודה אמר שמואל אין חייבין משום טומאה אלא על

אורך

ויקרא ג | דה"א כו

שלמים ששחטן קודם פתיחת ההיכל. מפורש בפ"ק דעירובין (דף ב.) ובפ' התכלת (מנחות דף מט:): הוא עצמו אין נעשה אלא כפתח פתוח. [ד] שהוילון כח] משמשת עשוי לצניעות בעלמא שלא יסתכלו בהיכל בשעת שחיטה דאי משום לאחר שחיטה סגי יכולין כט] לסגור הדלתות: גובהה מאי. תימה אי גובהה פשיט הפסק א"כ כנגד המזבח יפסל שמפסיק ל] ואין לומר משום דרואה פתח מלמעלה למזבח דהא סלקא דעתך השתא דגובהה שמנה מפסיק דליכא למימר משום דגובהה שמנה היה סותם כל הפתח דהא סבור שהיה הפתח גובה עשרים אמה כדפריך בסמוך [ה] ול"ע דביומא פ"ק (דף טז:) לא] גבי כהן השורף פרה שהיה כותל מזרחי נמוך שיוכל לראות פתח אהל מועד וקאמר התם דדרך פנגא אמתא עילאה היה יכול לראות ושמא היינו דוקא לב] הזאה שהיתה מעומד אבל שחיטה [ו] היתה מיושב ואכתי תיקשי מכנגד המזבח אמאי כשר לשחוט כדאמר כל העזרה כולה כשרה לשחיטה: שני פשפשין היו בבית החליפות. במסכת מדות (דף לה:) לג] דאולם עודף עליו חמש עשרה אמה מן הצפון וחמש עשרה אמה מן הדרום והוא היה נקרא בית החליפות והיו לו שני פשפשין להכשיר את כל העזרה דאותו חלל עד כותל מערבי קרוי עזרה ולא כמו שפי' בקונטרס לד] שהכל קרוי בית החליפות עד כותל מערבי לה] ובפרק הניזקין (גיטין נו:) גבי כהן גדול ביוה"כ דקאמר דחזיוה בפשפש ופי' בקונטרס דשני פשפשין היו לו] *באותם החליפות ותימה גדול [ז] פירושו דדרך פשפשין לא היה יכול לראות לז] כלל ופי' רבינו ריב"א דחזיוה' דרך פשפש שיעשו פשפשין לראות אם פיגל ואם לאו וגם זה קשה דלעיל פרק כל הפסולין (דף לג.) פריך וניעביד פשפש לח] הכל בכתב מיד ה' עלי השכיל ומפרש ה"ר יעקב מאורלינ"ש דההוא פשפש היינו דרך הלול שאחורי בית הכפרת שיראה משם לט] דרך בית קדש הקדשים ובהיכל יכול לראות דרך פתח הגדול לאולם: שנים [ח] לפר. גבי שומרין מייתי להאי קרא בפ"ק דתמיד (דף כז.) תימה לי אחורי הכפרת היאך יכול לשחוט הא אינו יכול לראות שם פתח אהל מועד דרך מ] חלון דלפר בר דהא איכא שני פרכות בין היכל ובין קדשי הקדשים ובפרכת לא היה שום פתח אלא אחת פרופה מן הדרום ואחת מן הצפון ויש לומר דהלול קרי פתח ורואה בו קדשי קדשים דלא גרע מאהל מועד כמו אחורי בית החליפות שהיו פשפשין וקרויין פתח וע"י כן כשר לשחוט עד כותל מערבי לפי שרואה בהן האולם שקרוי אהל מועד למאן דאמ' א) קדושת היכל ואולם חדא מילתא ב) ולא נ"ל דבשלמא שני פשפשין דבית החליפות הוו שני פתחים קטנים ומשמשין כניסה ויציאה ומיקרו פתח אבל מא] לפר בר חלון קטן ולא פתח מקרי ובסוף התערובות (לקמן פב:) קרי ליה דרך משופש ולא מיקרי ביאה דרך שם ואי הוה נקב בפתחו של היכל לא היה יכול לשחוט אם היה הפתח נעול על סמך אותו נקב קטן. ברו"ך:

א) [לעיל יד.] ב) כ"א הגהה ולא נ"ל כו'

קדשי

במאי קמיפלגי. מאי קמרבי ת"ק בחד מהנך קראי דמייתי לצפון מק"ו דהא רבי אליעזר למימר לא תרבייה מיניה דקרא לצפון אילטריך: דניבעי פתח אהל מועד. כדאמרי' לקמן שאם אין שם פתח טו] [כגון] קודם שיפתחו הדלתות וקודם שיעמידו הלוים את המשכן ולאחר שפירקוהו לא היה שוחט: וחד להכשיר לדדין. כל רוחב העזרה דלא תימא כנגד הפתח דוקא להכי הדר כתב לפני ולא כתיב פתח וכל האויר בכלל לפני דלא כתיב כנגד: וחד לפסול לידי לדדין. כגון לשכות ואפילו תוכן קדש פסולות לשחיטה כדלקמן דלא תימא מדפתח לאו דוקא לפני נמי לאו דוקא אלא שיהא אהל טז] נטוי להכי הדר כתיב לפני למימרא דדוקא הוא ולא לשכות: יז] צפון לא אילטריך קרא. דמק"ו קאתי: וחד להכשיר צפון. דק"ו מעוטי ממעיט ליה לאידך גיסא וק"ו דרבנן לא דריש דאיכא למימר *להאי קבע צפון ולהאי שאר רוחות דמאי קדושתיה דצפון מדרום אלא דקביעת מקום בעלמא הוא: ולידי לדדין. לפסול לא אילטריך קרא (א) אחרינא יח]: [ב] לפני. כתיב בקרא קמא: בזמן שהוא פתוח. לשון פתח אינו אלא החלל והפותח והנועל קרוי דלת: מוגף. סגור ולא נעול כמו הגפת דלתות (ערכין דף יא:): וילון. פרוש כנגד הפתח מי הוי כנעול או לא: הוא עצמו. וילון עצמו אינו חשוב אלא כפתח פתוח דלצניעותא בעלמא עביד: גובהה. כגון תל או עץ מוטל כנגד הפתח מפסיק בין פתח לשחיטה [והפתח פתוח מאי]: שני פשפשין היו בבית החליפות. (עודף) שהאולם עודף על רוחב ההיכל לצפון ולדרום ט"ו אמה לכל צד וארכו יט] למזרח מן המערב אינו אלא י"א אמות *ובכותל המערבי של אותו עודף היו חלונות לגנוז סכינין מבחוץ ולכן קרוי החלל כנגדו עד כותל מערבי של העזרה בית החליפות ובאותן שני כתלים היו שני פתחים קטנים והכי נמי תניא לה בתוספתא בהדיא ר' יוסי בר' יהודה אומר שני פשפשין היו בבית החליפות ופתוחין למערב וקסבר אולם נמי קרוי אהל מועד: להכשיר את כל העזרה. את כל שאר העזרה שאינו בכלל לפני אהל מועד על ידי פתח ראשון והוו לידי לדדין כגון מכנגד (זויות) כותל האולם ולמערב בצפון ובדרום כ] לבית החליפות ובית החליפות עצמו ואלו שני פשפשין מכשירין כל בית החליפות לארכו ולרחבו דקרינן מהשתא לפני ולקמן פריך הא איכא לדדין: לאכילת קדשי קדשים. קס"ד השתא דלאכילה נמי בעיא כא] פנים ולקמן אמרינן סמי מכאן אכילה: ה"ג מאי לאו דאיכא קמייהו גובהה שמנה. שהיה כנגדן תל גבוה שמנה וש"מ גובהה לא פסיל: לא דגביהי אינהו שמנה. גובהן של פתחים ח' אמות: פשפשין שאני. שהן פתחים קטנים ואין משמשין כניסה ויציאה אלא לאכשורי כב] בשמא בעלמא: והא איכא לדדין. היינו אויר שבין כותל אולם לכותל העזרה לדרום ולצפון דהוו להו אחורי אותם פתחים ולא הוו לפני כג]: דפתח להו בקרן זוית. של אולם מקצת הפתח פונה לצפון ומקצתו למערב וכן בדרום: אחורי בית הכפרת. אחת עשרה אמה היה אויר כד] [ג] עד חומת העזרה למערב כזה*: מאי. במאי מתכשר לשחיטה דקאמר כל העזרה כשרה: לול. כמין חלון פתוח מן התא שאחורי בית הכפרת לאויר העזרה: והיינו דכתיב שנים לפר בר. כה] (בספר עזרא) (ד"ה א כו) משתעי במספר כו] השומרים שהעמידו במקדש לכל הפתחין וקאמר שני שומרים העמידו לבר והיינו לאותו לול: כמאן דאמר כלפי לבר גרסינן. כלפי חוץ אחורי כל כותלי ההיכל כז] וקדשי קדשים: אין חייבין משום טומאה. הנכנס טמא להר הבית אינו חייב אלא אם כן נכנס לתוך היקף חלל העזרה והוא

היה

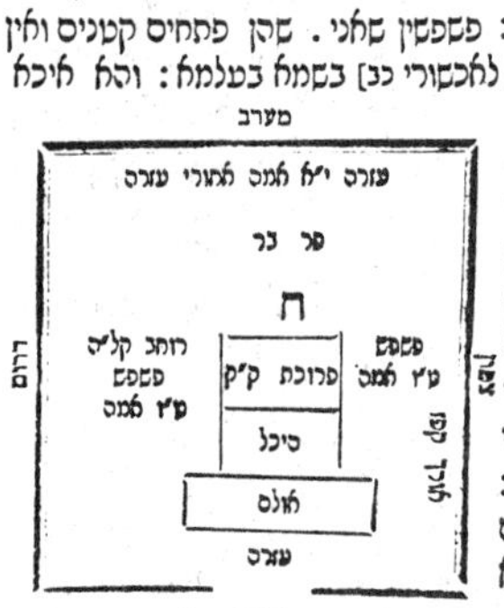

מסורת הש"ס

עירובין ב. יומא [illegible]

דהא דקבע להאי לפון ולהאי שאר רוחות משום קדושתיה דלפון מדרום ולא קביעות מקום בעלמא הוא ז"ק

[ע' תוס' מנחות מט. ד"ה מר אמר]

[לקמן ט.]

ז"ק מ"ז

(מנחות לה) יומא [illegible] מדות פ"ד מ"ז ע"ש *כ"א ובכותל המזרחי

שיטה מקובצת

א] וחד לפסול צידי צדדין. פ"ח דס"ד דמדפתח אהל מועד לאו דוקא כו' ...

ג] שלא יהא דבר קודם תמיד של שחר ת"ל העולה עולה ראשונה ר"ל דהיינו למצוה אבל פסול ליכא : ד] בזמן שפתוח ולא בזמן : ה] רב אחא בר יעקב אמר : ו] פסולים שנאמר ושחטו פתח אהל מועד בזמן שפתוח ולא בזמן שהוא נעול תנ"ה שלמים ששחטן קודם שיפתחו דלתות היכל פסולים שנאמר ושחטו פתח אהל מועד בזמן שפתוח ולא בזמן שהוא נעול וכן במשכן עד שלא העמידו הלוים את המשכן ולאחר שפירקו לוים : ז] הוא עצמו כו' פי' הוילון אינו נעשה אלא כפתח פתוח כפתח בכף כך פי' הקונטרס הוא עצמו דינו כפתח פתוח ותימה דמנין לו זה הלא על זה היה שואל ועוד דהל"ל הרי הוא כפתח פתוח לכן נ"ל דה"ג אינו נעשה אלא בפתח בבית כלומר עיקר הוילון לצורך פתיחת הפתח נתקן להיות שם בשעת שחיטה לצניעות משום דאז הפתח צריך להיות פתוח דאילו לאחר שחיטה אינה צריכה אילון דנגפו הדלתות מתו' מהר"ם וצ"ל : ח] פתוח ס"א הוה גובהה מאי תימה כיון דמכשירינן כל העזרה א"כ גם מזרחו של מזבח כשר ואמאי והלא מפסיק גובהו של מזבח בין שחיטה לפתח ואומר מורי

כד] אויר מחוצת היכל עד : כה] לפר בר בד"ה ותיבות ובספר עזרא נמחק : כו] במספר השוערים ... שני שוערים העמידו לפר בר והיינו לאותו : כז] ההיכל וקדש הקדשים הס"ד : ... נמחק : כט] להגיף הדלתות ותיבת לסגור ל"ש : ל] שמפסיק ומדמכשרינן כל העזרה א"כ ... כשר ואמאי ואין : לא] פ"ק אמרינן גבי : לב] דוקא ההזאה : לג] מידות אמרינן דאי... ס"א דכל העזרה קרי ליה בית החליפות עד כותל מערבי של העזרה : לה] מערבי ... לו] פשפשין היו בבית החליפות : לז] לראות בהיכל ותיבת כלל נמחק : לח] פשפש ומש... דרך נמחק : מ] הלול לפרבר תיבת חלון נמחק : מא] אבל פרבר . אות ל' ...

א) אולי צ"ל עד למימרא דוקא הוה ולא לשכות והכן נראה (ומר וכו'). ב) נראה דצ"ל שכנגד כותל ההיכל מכ' רוחותיו. ג) עי' תוס' עירובין דף ב' ד"ה שלמים מה שהעיר עוד בזה.

הגהות צ"ק

הגהות הב"ח (א) רש"י ד"ה ולידי לדדין וכו' אחרינא דלפני דכתיב בקרא קמא משמע לדדין ולא לידי לדדין :

'the tent of meeting' is stated.[5] [55*b*] Wherein do they differ?—The first Tanna holds, Three texts are written:[6] one is for its own purpose, to intimate that the door of the tent of meeting is required;[7] the second is to permit the sides;[8] and the third is to invalidate the sides of the sides;[9] while no text is necessary for the north. Whereas R. Eliezer holds: One is for its own purpose, to intimate that the door of the tent of meeting is required; the second is to permit the north; and the third is to permit the sides; but no text is required in respect of the sides of the sides.

Why is *'the* door *of the tent of meeting'* written in one case, whereas 'before *the tent of meeting'* is written in the others?—We are thereby informed of Rab Judah's teaching in Samuel's name. For Rab Judah said in Samuel's name: If a peace-offering is slaughtered before the doors of the *hekal* are opened, it is invalid, for it is said, *'And he shall kill it at the* entrance [opening] *of the tent of meeting':* when it is open, but not when it is shut. It was stated likewise: Mar 'Ukba b. Ḥama said in R. Jose son of R. Ḥanina's name: If one slaughtered a peace-offering before the doors of the *hekal* were opened, it is invalid, because it is said, *'And he shall kill it at the* entrance [opening] *of the tent of meeting':* when it is open, and not when it is shut. In the West [Palestine] they recited it thus: R. Aḥa b. Jacob said in R. Ashi's name: If a peace-offering is slaughtered before the doors of the *hekal* are opened, it is invalid; in the
a Tabernacle,[1] [if it is slaughtered] before the Levites set up the Tabernacle or after the Levites take down the Tabernacle, it is invalid.

It is obvious that if it is shut, it is as though it were locked.[2] What if a curtain [shuts it off]?—Said R. Zera: That itself is made only for an open door.[3]

What of an elevation?[4]—Come and hear: For it was taught, R. Jose b. R. Judah said: There were two wickets in the knives' recess and their elevation was eight cubits, in order that the whole of the Temple court might be made fit for the consumption of sacrifices of higher sanctity and the slaughtering of sacrifices of lower sanctity.[5] Does this not mean that [an elevation] eight [cubits high] stood before them [these wickets]?[6]—No: it means that they [themselves][7] were eight cubits high.

An objection is raised: All the gates there were twenty cubits high and ten cubits wide?[8]—The wickets were different.[9] But there were the sides?[10]—They were built at the corners.[11]

What about the space behind the place of the Mercy Seat
b [*kapporeth*]?[1]—Come and hear, for Rami son of Rab Judah said in Rab's name: There was a small passage way behind the place of the Mercy Seat, in order to make the whole Temple court fit for the consumption of most holy sacrifices and the slaughtering of minor sacrifices, and there were two such,[2] and thus it is written, *And two le-par bar.*[3] What does *le-par bar* mean?—Said Rabbah son of R. Shila: As one says, facing without [*ke-lappe le-bar*].

Rab Judah said in Samuel's name: Liability for uncleanness[4] is

(5) Implying *any* part of same. (6) The *'tent of meeting'* is repeated three times. (7) I.e., as stated *infra*, the animal may be slain only when this door is open. (8) One is not limited to the space directly in front of the door. (9) I.e., chambers opening into the Temple court. These, even if sanctified, are unfit.

a (1) When there was no door, but only an opening. (2) The sacrifice then is certainly invalid. (3) The curtain is hung there only because the door of the *hekal* is open and it is indecorous for the priests to look into the *hekal* while they are engaged on the sacrifice. Hence it counts as open, and the sacrifice is valid (*Sh. Mek.*). (4) I.e., a raised construction, e.g., a beam or a board which shuts off the door while it is actually open. (5) The *ulam* (v. Glos.) overlapped the *hekal* by 11 cubits on each side. Now, the sacrifices had to be slain in front of the *hekal*, corresponding to *'before the tent of meeting'*, and this would apparently not include the area directly in front of the overlap, in which there was a special recess for the knives. By means of wickets set in the *ulam* on either side the whole of the area facing the *ulam*, including the overlap, was thus made fit. (6) Which proves that such leaves it technically open. (7) The entrances to the wickets. (8) Consequently the reference must be to the construction before the wickets. (9) Since their purpose was only symbolic. (10) Of the *ulam*, on the north and the south beyond the wickets. The area in front of these would not be made fit by the wickets. (11) Diagonally, so that the space opposite them, viz., up to the north and the south walls of the Temple court, would still be technically *'before the door'*.

b (1) A space of eleven cubits between it and the western wall of the court (v. Mid. V, I); was that fit too? (2) Emended text. (3) E.V. 'at the precinct'. I. Chron. XXVI, 18. The M.T. reads this as one word: *parbar*. (4) I.e., for entering the precincts of the Temple court in an unclean state.

incurred [56*a*] only in respect of [an area] a hundred and eighty-seven cubits in length by a hundred and thirty-five in breadth. A Tanna recited before R. Naḥman: The whole Temple court was a hundred and eighty-seven cubits in length by a hundred and thirty-five in breadth. Said he to him, Thus did my father say: Within such an area the priests entered, consumed the most holy and slaughtered the minor sacrifices there, and were liable for uncleanness. What does this exclude? Shall we say that it excludes the windows, doors and the thickness of the wall? Surely we learnt: The windows and the thickness of the wall are as within?[5]—Rather, it is to exclude the chambers.[6] But if they are built on non-sacred ground and open into sacred ground, surely we learnt: Their inside is holy?—That is by Rabbinical law [only]. And not by Scriptural law? Surely it was taught: How do we know that the priests may enter the chambers which are built on non-sacred ground and open into sacred ground, eat there the most holy sacrifices and the residue of the meal-offering?[7] Because it says, *In the court of the tent of meeting they shall eat it:*[8] Scripture permitted many courts for eating![9]—Said Raba: Eating is different.[10] But are they not [holy] in respect of uncleanness? Surely it was taught: The chambers built on non-sacred ground: priests may enter therein and eat there the most holy sacrifices; you may not slaughter
a minor sacrifices there,[1] and they involve culpability on account of uncleanness?—Did you not say, you may *not* slaughter?[2] then learn too, and they do *not* involve culpability.[3] [No:] as for [saying] you may *not* slaughter, it is well, [the reason being that] it [slaughtering] must be opposite the door, which it is not [in these chambers]. But why [should you learn] 'and they do *not* involve culpability'?—Yet on your view, [consider: when you say,] you may *not* slaughter, are we not discussing a case where the *shechitah* is opposite the entrance,[4] for if it is not, why is it necessary [to teach it]? Hence [you must admit that] although he would slaughter opposite the entrance, yet he teaches, 'You may not slaughter', because they are not sanctified. Then learn also, They do *not* involve culpability.

Now, do we not require the consumption to be facing the entrance? Surely R. Jose son of R. Ḥanina taught: There were two wickets in the knives' recess, and their elevation was eight cubits, in order to make the Temple court fit for the eating of most sacred sacrifices and the slaughtering of minor sacrifices?—Said Rabina: Delete 'eating' from this passage. But it is written, *Boil the flesh at the door of the tent of meeting, and* there *eat it?*[5] Temporary sacrifices are different.[6]

R. Isaac b. Abudimi said: How do we know that the blood is invalidated by sunset?[7] Because it says, *It shall be eaten on the day that he offereth his slaughtering:*[8] on the day that you slaughter, you can offer; on the day that you do *not* slaughter, you cannot offer.[9]

(5) Sacred; hence these cannot be excluded. (6) Flanking the Temple court. (7) What is left after the fistful is separated and burnt on the altar. (8) Lev. VI, 9. (9) These correspond to the chambers under discussion. Since the most holy sacrifices may be eaten there, they must be sacred by Biblical law too. (10) Eating is permitted *because* Scripture intimated it so.

a (1) As these are the 'sides of the sides' (v. *supra* 53*b*), and not '*before the tent of meeting*'. (2) Which proves that they are *not* holy. (3) The text must be so amended. (4) I.e., that the door of this chamber faces that of the knives' recess, so that when both are open it is technically '*at the door of the tent of meeting*', and yet you may not slaughter there. (5) Lev. VIII, 31. (6) These sacrifices were not statutory ones, but specially commanded for the consecration of Aaron. They are not subject to the ordinary laws. (7) It is unfit for sprinkling on the morrow. (8) Ibid. VII, 16. Lit., translation. E.V.: *his sacrifice*. (9) *Sc.* on the morrow. 'Offering' is essentially sprinkling.

קדשי שעה שאני · טז] דתלאו הכתוב באהל מועד דכתיב (ויקרא ח) ומפתח אהל מועד לא תצאו שבעת ימים :

מנין לדם שנפסל בשקיעת החמה · פירש בקונטרס דלא מהגיא ליה הלנה בראש המזבח לאכשורי למחר לזריקה ותימה הניחא למאן דאמר *אין לינה מועלת בראשו של מזבח אלא למאן דאמר מועלת למה לי קרא בלילה אין יכול לזרוק דביום צוותו כתיב (שם ז) ולמחר מיפסיל בעמוד השחר כאימורים וכי תימא דאיצטריך קרא משום אימורין דקיימא לן (לקמן דף פד.) אם עלו לא ירדו וקמ"ל בדם דירדו ואליבא דמאן אי לר"ג האמר לקמן פרק המזבח מקדש (דף פג.) דלא ירד אף בדם ואי לרבי יהושע הא אמר דאין המזבח מקדש פסולין שלא ירדו אלא בהקטרה ואם כן קרא דהכא למה לי ויש לומר דאיצטריך קרא לפסול דם בלינה משום דהוה אמינא דלא מיפסיל כי היכי דאין חייבין עליו משום פיגול ונותר ומיהו אין טעם זה נכון והרי עלים ולבונה לר' שמעון (לעיל דף מו:) דאין חייבין עליהם משום נותר ומיפסלי בלינה היכא דקדשו בכלי ועוד דהוה ליה למימר מנין לדם שנפסל בלינה ויש לפרש שקיעת החמה היינו תחילת שקיעה קודם לאת הכוכבים יז] כדאמר דמשקיעת החמה ועד לאת הכוכבים ד' מילין בפרק מי שהיה טמא (פסחים צד·) וחשוב יום לענין יח] שמלותן ביום ומפסוק מיותר ממעט ליה הכא מביום הקריבו יט] ובכל דוכתא חשוב יום עד לאת הכוכבים כדאמר אף על פי שאין ראיה לדבר זכר לדבר ואנחנו עושים במלאכה וחציים מחזיקים ברמחים מעלות השחר ועד לאת הכוכבים ואומר והיה לנו הלילה משמר והיום מלאכה בפ"ב דמגילה (דף כ:) והשתא לא הוי כמו שקיעת החמה דמסכת תענית (דף יב·) כ] כל תענית שלא שקעה עליו חמה אינו תענית וקבלה בידינו בלאת הכוכבים ובמי שהיה טמא (פסחים דף צג:) נמי הכי משמע דנפסל הדם בשקיעת החמה שקודם לאת הכוכבים ארבע מילין דחשיב דרך רחוקה מן המודיעים משום דלא מטי לירושלים עד תחילת שקיעת החמה דקעבר כא] עליה זמן שחיטת הפסח (ואין) לדחות ההיא דמי שהיה טמא רבנן עבוד הרחקה כדי שלא יבא לידי הלנת דם וכדי לזרוס בפסח והעמידו דבריהם במקום כרת והאי דלא חשיב ליה בפסחים בהדי איך בפ' האשה (דף צב·) ה"נ לא חשיב חתיכת יבלתו והבאתו מחוץ לתחום דלא חשיב אלא דברים של חידוש והא דאמר בשמעתא כב] דנאכלין ליום אחד מחשבים בדמו משתשקע החמה היינו תחילת שקיעה כג] ומדאורייתא ולא לאת הכוכבים דומיא כד] דאימורין ובשר דחשיב לקמן בהדי דם ומשתשקע החמה דלקמן לא הוי כמו משתשקע החמה כה] בעלמא דרגיל רבינו תם לפרש דשקיעה דווקא משמע תחילת שקיעה אבל משתשקע משמע סוף שקיעה משום דקשה ליה דבסוף פרק במה מדליקין (שבת דף לד:) כו] משמע משקיעת חמה עד לילה תלתא ריבעי מיל ובפרק מי שהיה טמא (פסחים דף צד.) משמע דמשתשקע החמה עד לאת הכוכבים ארבע מילין וחשיב ליה במדידת היום כז] *דמפרש רבינו תם דמשקיעה משמע תחילת שקיעה שהחמה מתחלת ליכנס בעובי הרקיע *ואתי שפיר דאיידי דבסמוך קתני גבי כח] בשר קדשים קלים ובבשרם משתשקע החמה של יום שני דהיינו על כרחך לאת הכוכבים תני נמי האי לישנא גבי דם אף על גב שחלוקין זה מזה :
[ועיין תום' שבת לה· ד"ה תרי תילתי מיל ותום' פסחים צד. ד"ה ר' יהודה ותום' מנחות כ: ד"ה נפסל]:

אור

תורה אור

אורך מאה ושמונים ושבע על רוחב מאה ושלשים וחמש תני תנא קמיה דרב נחמן *כל העזרה היתה קפ"ז על רוחב קל"ה אמר ליה הכי אמר א] לי אבא כגוזזה כהנים נכנסין לשם ואוכלין שם קדשי קדשים ושוחטין שם קדשים קלים וחייבין משום טומאה למעוטי מאי אילימא למעוטי חלונות דלתות ועובי החומה תנינא *ב]החלונות ועובי החומה כלפנים ואלא למעוטי לשכות ג] ואי בנויות בחול ופתוחות לקדש *והתנן ד]תוכן קודש מדרבנן ודאורייתא לא והתניא ג] ה]לשכות בנויות בחול ופתוחות לקדש מנין שהכהנים נכנסין לשם ואוכלין שם קדשי קדשים ושירי מנחה תלמוד לומר (ויקרא ו) בחצר אהל מועד יאכלוה התורה ריבתה חצירות הרבה ד] אצל אכילה אתת אמר רבא ו]לאכילה שאני אבל לענין טומאה לא והתניא *לשכות הבנויות לחול ופתוחות לקודש כהנים נכנסין לשם ואוכלין שם קדשי קדשים ואין שוחטין שם קדשים קלים וחייבין משום טומאה לאו אמרת ז]אין שוחטין תני נמי אין חייבין בשלמא אין שוחטין בעינא כנגד הפתח וליכא אלא אין חייבין אמאי וליטעמיך אין שוחטין מי לא עסקינן ה] דאיכא שחיטה כנגד הפתח דאי ליכא למאי איצטריך אלא אף על גב *דקא שחיט כנגד הפתח תני אין שוחטין משום דלא ו] קדיש תני נמי אין חייבין ולאכילה לא בעינן כנגד הפתח והתניא *רבי יוסי ברבי יהודה אומר שני פשפשין היו בבית החליפות גובהן שמונה ז]כדי להכשיר את העזרה לאכילת קדשי קדשים ולשחיטת קדשים קלים אמר רבינא סמי מכאן אכילה והכתיב (שם ח) °בשלו את הבשר פתח אהל מועד ושם תאכלו אותו קדשי שעה שאני : אמר רב יצחק בר אבודימי ח]מנין ח]לדם *שנפסל בשקיעת החמה שנאמר (שם ז) °ביום הקריבו את זבחו יאכל ביום שאתה זובח אתה מקריב ביום שאי אתה זובח אי אתה מקריב האי מיבעי ליה לגופיה

היה אורך קפ"ז על רוחב קל"ה כדתנן במסכת מדות (דף נ"ה) : למעוטי הנכנס ללשכות הבנויות תולה לו ופתוחות לתוכו שלא נתקדשו בקדושת עזרה בשירי מנחה ובשר של פגעים ובאמורים ותומים שמקדשים בהן את העזרה ובהליכה סביב כדאמרינן בשבועות (דף יד) : ה"ג תני תנא קמיה דרב נחמן כל העזרה היתה אורך קפ"ז על רוחב קל"ה אמר ליה הכי אמר לי אבא כו' : ואוכלין שם קדשי קדשים · *דהכי הוא ט] דהוה קדושה בקדושת חצר אהל מועד לאכילת קדשי קדשים וטפי מהכי לא קדיש עזרה והוא חלל כל העזרה ובתוכו היכל ואולם ובית קדשי הקדשים והתא לאחורי בית הכפורת וי"א אמה אויר מאחוריו : ושוחטין שם קדשים קלים *גרסינן י] וחייבין עליו משום טומאה : החלונות · עובי חלל החלונות שבחומות העזרה סביב מבפנים ועובי החומה בראשה למעלה : תנינא · דקדישי והיכי מצי למעוטינהו : ה"ג אלא למעוטי לשכות אי דבנויות בחול ופתוחות לקדש יא] : שהכהנים נכנסין לשם ואוכלין שם קדשי קדשים ושירי מנחה תלמוד לומר בחצר אהל מועד ס' יזל"ג ושוחטין שם קדשים קלים הכא וגם שאר לשון הכתוב בספרים שבוש הוא וכן הגהתי מספרו של רבינו : הא אנן תנן תוכן קדש · וליחייב עלייהו משום טומאה : מדרבנן · מצות חכמים היא שלא יכנסו להן בטומאה אבל כרת וקרבן ליכא : והתניא מנין ללשכות כו' ומדמרבינן להו לענין אכילה ש"מ קדושתם הן מן התורה דאי מדרבנן וקרא אסמכתא הוא היאך הקילו חכמים יב] לעקור דבר ולהכשיר מקום חול לאכילת קדשי קדשים : חצרות הרבה · במקום קדוש בחצר אהל מועד : לאכילה שאני · דרבי בה קרא חצרות הרבה : ואין שוחטין שם קדשים קלים · דהא בעינן לפני אהל מועד למעוטי כדי לדדין : לאו אמרת · דקתני בה אין שוחטין אלמא לאו קדישי תני נמי אין חייבין משום טומאה : מי לא עסקינן יג] דאיכא שחיטה כנגד הפתח · כשהיה פתחו מכוון כנגד פתחי בית החליפות : קדשי שעה שאני · גזירת הכתוב היתה במילואים אבל קדשי דורות איתרבו כדאמר התורה ריבתה חצרות הרבה : ביום שאתה זובח אתה מקריב ביום שאי אתה זובח אי אתה מקריב · הכי גרסינן לה בכולה סוגיא יד] כך מצאתי מוגה והכי פירושה ביום הקריבו את זבחו שתהא הקרבה וזביחה ביום אחד ולא מהגיא ליה הלנה בראש המזבח לאכשורי טו] לזריקה למחר :

לגופיה

מסורת הש"ס: מדות למעוטי וכד"א נ"ק | דעד הכי ס' החצר אהל נ"ק | פסחים פה: | נ"א גרסינן הס"ד ומה"ד למעוטי מאי חייבין עליו כו' | תוספתא דמעשר שני פ"א ע"ש | דשחיטה כנגד נ"ק | [לעיל נה:] | [מנחות כ:] | נ"ל ומפרש ר"ת | נ"ל ואפשר דאיידי כו' ובמנחות שם כתבו נע"א

עין משפט נר מצוה:
ס א מיי' פ"ה מהלכות בית הבחירה הלכה ד :
[לקמן פו.]
סא ב מיי' פ"ו מהל' בית הבחירה הלכה ט ופ"י מהלכות מעה"ק הלכה ה :
סב ג ד ה ו מיי' פ"ו מהל' בית הבחירה הלכה ח :
סג ז מיי' פ"א מהל' פסה"מ הלכה לג ופ"ד מהלכות מעה"ק הלכה א :
פסחים פו. מעשר שני פ"ג מ"ח יומא כה.

שיטה מקובצת
א] אמר אבא כגון זו כהנים אוכלין שם קדשי קדשים כו' וחייבין עליהן משום טומאה כו' למעוטי חלונות ועובי החומה : ב] לשכות אי דבנויות: ג] והתניא מנין ללשכות בנויות כו' לקדש שהכהנים נכנסין : ד] חצרות הרבה לאכילה אמר רבא לאכילה שאני וטומאה לא והא אנן תנן תוכן קדש מדרבנן ודאורייתא לא והתניא מנין ללשכות הבנויות בחול ופתוחות לקדש שהכהנים נכנסים לשם: ה] עסקינן דקא שחיט כנגד הפתח דאי שלא כנגד הפתח למאי אצטריך: ו] דלא קדשי תני : ז] גובהן שמונה להכשיר את כל העזרה כולה לאכילת: ח] מנין לדם שנפסל בשקיעת החמה · וא"ת ותיפוק ליה משום דאינו ראוי לכפרה רק באותו יום דהא בלילה אינו ראוי לזריקה משום דכתיב ביום צוותו ואם למחר הרי הוא נפסל בלינה בעמוד השחר בלא טעמא דשקיעת החמה ופ"ה דבעי היכא שהעלתהו מיד אחר שקיעת החמה קודם עמוד השחר בראשו של מזבח דלינה אינה מועלת בו וקשה הגירסא למ"ד אין לינה (פוסלת) [מועלת] בראשו של מזבח אלא למ"ד מועלת מאי איכא למימר ופר"ת דמיירי הכא בתחלת שקיעה ואע"ג דמתחלת שקיעה ועד צאת הכוכבים ד' מילין הוא ואכתי יממא אפ"ה נפסל מתחלת שקיעת החמה מקרא דביום הקריבו דאם [אינו] ענין ללילה דמביום צוותו נפקא תנהו ענין לתחלת שקיעת החמה.

מהר"ם : ס] הוא דהיא קדוש אות ה' ה' נמחק: י] גרסי' הס"ד ומה"ד למעוטי מאי דאין חייבין עליו: יא] לקדש והא אנן תנן תוכן קדש מדרבנן ומדאורייתא לא והתניא מנין ללשכות הבנוית בחול ופתוחות לקדש שהכהנים : יב] חכמים על דבר תורה להכשיר מקום חול : יג] עסקינן דקא שחיט כנגד : יד] סוגיא וכך מצאתי מוגה והכי פירושא : טו] לאכשורי זריקה למחר : טז] שאני · תימה כיון דתרווייהו נאכלים בעזרה כדמייתי לעיל תלמודא מתאכלו במקום טהור תרווייהו נמי לשוו לפתח אהל מועד ועוד דבשום מקום לא אמרינן קדשי שעה שאני להחמיר אלא להקל וי"ל דה"ק שאני קדשי שעה דהיינו מילואים דגזירת הכתוב בכל מקום באהל מועד שנאמר ומפתח אהל מועד לא תצאו שבעת ימים אבל קדשי דורות איתרבו כדאמרן התורה ריבתה חצרות הרבה · מהר"פ : יז] הכוכבים כדאמרינן : יח] לענין ביום צוותו ומפסוק כו' תיבת שמצוותן נמחק : יט] הקריבו דאם אינו ענין ללילה דמביום צוותו נפקא תנהו לענין לתחילת שקיעת החמה : כ] דאמרינן כל : כא] תיבת עליה נמחק : כב] דאמר בשמעתא משום דנאכלין : כג] תיבת ומדאורייתא נמחק : כד] דומיא דבשר דחשיב לקמן : כה] החמה דבעלמא : כו] מדליקין פליגי אי משקיעת החמה עד לילה (תרי) [תלתא] ריבעי אי לא ובפרק מי שהיה טמא : כז] היום ומפרש ר"ת : כח] תיבת בשר נמחק :

האידנא

סד א מיי' פי"ח מהל' פסה"מ הלכה י :

סה ב מיי' פ"י מהלכות מעה"ק הלכה ו :

סו ג מיי' פי"ט מהלכות פסה"מ הלכה ד :

סז ד מיי' פ"ט מהלכות מעה"ק הלכה יא :

סח ה מיי' פ"ט שם הלכה כה :

סט ו מיי' פ"י שם הלכה ה :

ע ז מיי' פ"ח מהלכות קרבן פסח הלכה א :

עא ח מיי' שם הל' יד:

עב ט מיי' שם פ"ב הלכה א :

עג י מיי' שם פ"ח הלכה ד :

לגופיה אם כן נימא קרא ביום זבחו יאכל הקריבו למה לי ש"מ ביום שאתה זובח אתה מקריב ביום שאי אתה זובח אי אתה מקריב ודילמא ה"ק רחמנא אי קריב דם האידנא א] ניתאכיל בשר האידנא ולמחר אי קריב דם למחר ב] ניתאכיל בשר למחר וליומא אוחרא אם כן נימא קרא ביום הקריבו יאכל זבחו למה לי שמע מינה ביום שאתה זובח אתה מקריבו ביום שאי אתה זובח אי אתה מקריבו: איתמר המחשב לאור שלישי חזקיה אמר כשר רבי יוחנן אמר פסול חזקיה אמר כשר דהא לא אינתיק לשריפה רבי יוחנן אמר פסול דהא אידחי ליה מאכילה האוכל לאור שלישי חזקיה אמר פטור ג] דלא אינתיק לשריפה רבי יוחנן אמר חייב דהא אידחי לי' מאכילה תניא כוותיה דרבי יוחנן ד] *קדשים הנאכלין ליום אחד °מחשבין בדמן משתשקע החמה ובבשרן ובאימוריהן משיעלה עמוד השחר ה] קדשים הנאכלין לשני ימים ולילה אחת מחשבין בדמן משתשקע החמה ובאימוריהן משיעלה עמוד השחר ו] ובבשרן משתשקע החמה של שני ימים: ת"ר יכול *יהו נאכלין לאור שלישי ודין הוא זבחים נאכלין ליום אחד וזבחים נאכלין לשני ימים ז] מה זבחים הנאכלין ליום אחד לילה אחריהן אף זבחים הנאכלין לשני ימים ח] לילה אחריהן תלמוד לומר °והנותר עד יום *בעוד יום הוא נאכל ואינו נאכל לאור שלישי יכול ישרף מיד ודין הוא זבחים נאכלין ליום אחד וזבחים נאכלין לשני ימים מה זבחים הנאכלין ליום אחד תיכף לאכילה שריפה אף זבחים הנאכלין לשני ימים תיכף לאכילה שריפה ת"ל °ביום השלישי באש ישרף *ביום אתה שורפו ואי אתה שורפו בלילה: מתני' הבכור והמעשר והפסח קדשים קלים שחיטתן בכל מקום בעזרה *ודמן טעון מתנה אחת ובלבד שיתן כנגד היסוד שינה באכילתן *הבכור נאכל לכהנים והמעשר לכל אדם ט] *ונאכלין בכל העיר בכל מאכל לשני ימים ולילה אחד *הפסח אינו נאכל אלא בלילה *ואינו נאכל אלא עד חצות *ואינו נאכל אלא למנויו *ואינו נאכל אלא צלי: גמ' מאן תנא אמר רב חסדא ר' יוסי הגלילי היא דתניא *ר' יוסי הגלילי אומר י] חלבו לא נאמר אלא חלבם דמו לא נאמר אלא דמם לימד על בכור ומעשר ופסח שטעונין מתן דמים ואימורין לגבי מזבח כנגד היסוד מנא לן א"ר *אליעזר אתיא זריקה זריקה מעולה ועולה

ויקרא יט · שם

רש"י

לגופיה · ללמד יא] זמן אכילת שלמים ביום זביחתו וממחרת : ה"ג א"כ נימא קרא ביום זבחו יאכל הקריבו למה לי ש"מ ביום שאתה זובח אתה מקריב כו' : דלמא הכי קאמר רחמנא כו' · ה"ג אם כן נימא קרא יב] וביום הקריבו יאכל זבחו למה לי ש"מ ביום שאתה זובח אתה מקריב כך הגהתי מספרו של רבי : ודלמא הכי קאמר רחמנא כו' · דלא תלה רחמנא זמן אכילה בזביחה אלא בזריקה לאוכלו ביום זריקתו וממחרת: המחשב לאור שלישי · יג] בשחיטת שלמים על מנת לאכול מן הבשר לאור שלישי ליל שני לזביחה יד] : כשר · דלא הוי חוץ לזמנו : דלא אינתיק ליה · מזמנו לגמרי ולהיות זמן שריפתו עכשיו עד לפרא כדתני' לקמן בשמעתין : האוכל לאור שלישי · מבשר קרבן כשר : פטור · מקרבן שגגת טהר: לא אינתיק לשריפה · הלכך לאו נותר הוא : מחשבין בדמן משתשקע החמה טו] · אם שחט על מנת לזרוק דמן משתשקע החמה פיגול ובאכילת בשר ובהקטרת אימוריהם אם חישב בשחיטה על מנת לאכול מבשרן או להקטיר מאימוריהן משיעלה עמוד השחר פיגול דהייני חוץ לזמן דידהו : ה"ג והנאכלין לשני ימים ולילה אחד מחשבין בדמן משתשקע החמה ובאימורין משיעלה עמוד השחר ובבשרן משתשקע החמה של שני ימים· והיינו לאור שלישי כר' יוחנן לענין דם ואימורין קדשי קדשים וקדשים קלים שוין דדם ואימורין לעולם קדשי קדשים הם : לילה אחריהם · דכתיב בתודה (ויקרא ז) לא יניח ממנו עד בקר טז] [הא] כל הלילה נאכל אף כאן בשלמים תהא לילה אחר יום המחרת : עד יום · גבי אכילה כתיב בקדושים תהיו ביום זבחכם יאכל וממחרת והנותר עד יום בעוד שהוא יום תאכלנו: יכול ישרף מיד · לאור שלישי הואיל ועבר זמן אכילתו : מה להלן · בנאכלין ליום אחד תיכף לאכילה שריפה דכתיב גבי מילואים ואם יותר מבשר המילואים וגו' יז] בצו את אהרן כתיב ובהאי קרא לא כתיב אכילה אלא שריפה ולהכי לא כתיב עד יום אלא ביום : מתני' והמעשר · מעשר בהמה : מתנה אחת · דלא כתיב בהו סביב אלא ואת דמם תזרוק כתיב בבכור והנך נמי יח] מהכא ילפינן כדאמרינן בגמ' : כנגד היסוד · במקום שיש יסוד תחתיו למעוטי מזרח ודרום: שינה באכילתן · אע"פ שהשוה הכתוב את מתן דמם שינה באכילתן זה מזה : הבכור נאכל לכהנים · כדכתיב ובשרם יהיה לך (במדבר יח) : והמעשר לכל אדם · שלא מצינו יט] לו בתורה שינתן לכהן : ונאכלין בכל העיר בכל מאכל גרס ולא גרסי' לכל אדם דהא קתני בכור כ] לכהנים : בכל העיר · כדכתיב והבאתם שמה עולותיכם וזבחיכם ואת מעשרותיכם (דברים יב) ותניא בספרי ר' עקיבא אומר בשתי מעשרות הכתוב מדבר אחד מעשר בהמה ואחד מעשר דגן וכתיב (א) בההוא קרא ובכורות בקרכם וצאנכם ומדלא קבע כא] בהו מחיצה שמע מינה בכל העיר נאכלין : לשני ימים ולילה אחד · בבכור יליף לה בגמ' מעשר לא ידענא מהיכא : אלא בלילה · כדכתיב בלילה הזה (שמות יב) : ואינו נאכל אלא עד חצות · בגמ' יליף לה : למנויו · שנמנו בדמי לקיחתו כדכתיב לפי אכלו תכוסו (שם) : גמ' מאן תנא · מעשר ופסח בזריקה כב] מדמשוי מתן דמים בכור ומעשר ופסח דקתני שינה באכילתן מכלל דמתן דמים לא שינה ובבכור כתיב ואת דמם תזרוק (במדבר יח) : דמו לא נאמר · אך בכור שור וגו' אבל לר' ישמעאל פסח בשפיכה דנפקא ליה מתן דמים לפסח מודם זבחיך ישפך (דברים יב) :

תוספות

אור לשלישי גרס כמו אור לי"ד דלאור שלישי משמע לילה שאחר שלישי כמו לאור עיבורו דבשמעתא קמייתא דפסחים (דף ב:): ת"ל עד יום · פי' בקונטרס ביום זבחכם יאכל וממחרת והנותר עד יום השלישי בעוד שהוא יום תאכלנו וקשה דהנותר הפסיק הענין וה"ר חיים מפרש עד יום השלישי ולא יום השלישי בכלל א"כ אינו נאכל בליל שלישי : ונאכלין בכל העיר · פירש בקונטרס כדכתיב בפרשת ראה אנכי והבאתם שמה עולותיכם וזבחיכם ואת מעשרותיכם ותניא בספרי רבי עקיבא אומר בשתי מעשרות הכתוב מדבר אחד מעשר בהמה ואחד מעשר דגן וכתיב בההוא קרא ובכורות בקרכם וצאנכם ומדלא קבע בהו מחיצה שמע מינה דנאכלין בכל העיר ותימה גדול לפי' דהא כתיבי נמי התם כג] חטאות ואשמות דבעו קלעים והכי תניא בספרי מעשרותיכם ר"ע אומר בשתי מעשרות הכתוב מדבר אחד מעשר דגן ואחד מעשר בהמה ותרומת ידכם אלו הביכורים כענין שנאמר ולקח הכהן הטנא מידך ובכורות זה הבכור בקרכם וצאנכם אלו חטאות ואשמות ואכלתם שם לפני ה' אלהיכם כד] אלו המחיצה *ויש לתמוה אמאי לא בעי בכור ומעשר מחיצה כיון דכתיב בהו לפני ה' כמו שחיטה דדרשינן (לעיל דף לב·) לפני ה' בעזרה ועוד *אמרינן בתמורה בסוף אלו קדשים (דף כא:) אם ללמוד על הבכור שנאכל לפנים כה] (מן הקלעים) מן החומה אינו צריך שהרי כבר נאמר לפני ה' אלהיך תאכלנו וא"כ ליבעי לפנים מן הקלעים כשחיטה ונראה דנפקא לן מדכתיב לא תוכל לאכול בשעריך מעשר דגנך וגו' ובכורות בקרכם וצאנכם דמשמע בשעריך הוא דלא תוכל לאכול הא בירושלים אכול ומעשר בהמה גמר העברה העברה מבכור ומיהו קשה דבההוא קרא נמי הא כתיבי חטאות ואשמות כדדרשינן בפ' בתרא דמכות (דף יז.) בקרך וצאנך אלו חטאות ואשמות ונראה לפרש דנפקא לן מדמקשינן בגמ' לחזה ושוק של שלמים כו] הנאכלין לשני ימים והוא הדין לענין שנאכלין בכל העיר ותודה ואיל נזיר ושלמים נפקא לן מקרא דחזה ושוק של מילואים : לשני ימים · פי' בקונט' בבכור יליף לה בגמ' מעשר לא ידענא מהיכא ושוב כז] הגיה דיליף העברה העברה מבכור ותימה א"כ תפשוט מהכא דדבר הלמד בהיקש חוזר ומלמד בגז"ש כח] ולעיל אמרינן דאינו חוזר ומלמד בגז"ש מדרבי יוחנן כט] ונראה דמעשר יליף משלמים בבנין אב מה שלמים קדשים קלים אף מעשר קדשים קלים דבכור נמי הוה אתי משלמים אי לאו משום דמתנה לכהן וא"כ מעשר דלא הוי מתנה לכהן משלמים אתי : הפסח אינו נאכל כו' · תימה ליתני נמי דאינו נאכל אלא על מצות ומרורים ותירץ ה"ר חיים דלא חשיב אלא דבר שכנגדו ל] בקדשים והוא חלוק מהם דשאר קדשים נאכלין ביום ובלילה לא] עד היום ולכל אדם בכל מאכל ופסח אינו נאכל אלא בלילה עד חצות ולמנויו וצלי אי נמי לא תנא מצות ומרורים דאין מעכבין א"כ לאו מצוה דגופיה לב] :

למה

מסורת הש"ס

פסחים ג. [ע"ש כמה שינויים]

לעיל לז. פסחים פה:

[נ"ל אלעזר]

הגהות הב"ח

(א) רש"י ד"ה בכל העיר וכו' וכתיב נ"כ בההוא קרא:

גליון הש"ס

גמ' מחשבין בדמן משתשקע החמה· עיין לעיל דף כט ע"א תוס' ד"ה למקום :

נ"א וגם יש לתמוה אמאי כו' נ"ק

גי' הנ"ק ועוד דבתמורה בסוף אלו קדשים רא ללמד על הבכור שנאכל לפנים מן החומה משום שנאמר פני ה' תאכלנו וא"כ ליבעי לפנים כו' כצ"ל

שיטה מקובצת

א] האידנא אכול בשר: ב] למחר אכול בשר : ג] פטור רבי יוחנן אמר חייב חזקיה אמר פטור דלא : ד] זבחים הנאכלין· תיבת קדשים נמחק : ה] עמוד השחר והנאכלין לשני ימים ולילה : ו] ובבשרן משתשקע החמה של שני (תיבת ימים נמחק)· פי' דאז הוי לילה דכל זמן שהוא יום כשר לאכילה כדקאמר בסמוך בעוד שהוא יום הוא נאכל וקשה לפר"ת דעד צאת הכוכבים לא הוי לילה ולא משקיעת החמה ופר"ת דמשתשקע החמה דהכא היינו מסוף שקיעה והוא זמן צאת הכוכבים מרשני בלישניה דהכא קאמר משתשקע החמה ולעיל גבי דם קאמר בשקיעת החמה ואע"ג דגם הכא גבי דם נקט נמי משתשקע החמה והוא ר"ל תחלת שקיעה כדפי' גבי דם וי"ל דאגב דנקט משתשקע דמשמע סוף שקיעה גבי בשר נקטיה נמי להאי לישנא גבי דם וא"ת והיאך נפסל דם במחשבת שקיעה והלא בעינן מקום זמן משולש לפסול גם בשר ואימורים ועדיין ליכא פסול לא באימורים ולא בבשר וי"ל דהאי תנא לא בעי זמן משולש· מהר"ם : ז] ימים ולילה אחת : ח] ימים ולילה אחת לילה אחריהן ת"ל והנותר· ס"א יאכל עד יום: ת"ל כו' עד יום ·

[עי'] פ"ה וקשה שהרי כתיב והנותר בפסוק דהיינו שנפסל ונעשה נותר וי"ל דהאי והנותר לא נפסל קאמר אלא נותר שלא אכל ביום הראשון כמצותו דעיקר מצוה לאכלו ביום הראשון אע"פ שנאכלים א) ליום ולילה וכן נמי אשכחן שמיקרי נותר אף על פי שעדיין כשר הוא לאכילה דכתיב והנותר ממנו יאכל ובפ"ק דפסחים פירשתי· תוס' מהר"ם : ט] תאכלין בכל העיר כו' ג) ודבר תימה כו' עד ונראה דנפקא לן בכור מהיקשא דתודה ומעשר מבנין אב דשלמים כמו לענין ב' ימים ושלמים ותודה נפקא לן דנאכלין בכל העיר משום דכתיב תאכלו במקום טהור כדדרשינן לעיל ומאד תימה הוא אי אתי בהיקש לענין מקום אכילתן אמאי לא מפרש ליה תלמודא כמו לענין ב' ימים אלא ודאי ש"מ דלענין מקום אכילתן לא הוצרך התלמוד לפרש דזיל קרי בי רב הוא כדפי' הקונט' וליכא [למימר] דתלמודא נקט לפרש לענין ב' ימים ומילא שמעינן לענין לכל העיר דאדרבה דהוי ליה לפרושי לענין בכל העיר השני קודם במשנה לכך נראה לריב"א דאע"ג דקרא איירי לענין הבאת מקום מ"מ לענין אכילה לא איירי לגבי חטאות ואשמות ותדע דהא גבי אכילה כתיב ואכלתם לפני ה' אתה וביתכם דהיינו נשים ואלו חטאות ואשמות אינן נאכלין אלא לזכרי כהונה (כאן שייך סג"ה ז) [ס"א אלא ש"מ דאכילה לא קאי אכולהו ולא נכתבו בהאי קרא חטאות ואשמה לענין מקום אכילה אלא לענין הבאת מקום שיחד להם בשעת איסור הבמות להביאם שמה בבית הבחירה דלא נפקא לן מבחצר אהל מועד יאכלוה דה"א דהיינו דוקא כשנשחטה בעזרה אז תאכל בחצר אהל מועד אבל אם היה שוחט בחוץ הייתי אומר דאינו צריך להביאו לאהל מועד לאכול שם לכך נכתבו כאן חטאות ואשמות ואל תתמה אם (לאו) האי ואכלתם לאו אכולהו עניינא קאי דהכי נמי לא קאי אעולותיכם דעולה אין בה אכילה אבל קשה כו' עכ"ה] · וקרא דהבאתם שמה איירי בשני דברים לענין הבאת מקום דכתיב אשר יבחר לאיסור במות ולענין אכילה דכתיב ואכלתם מיהו קשה דהא כתיב גבי אכילה לפני ה' ואימא דהיינו העזרה דומיא דלפני ה' דלגבי שחיטה וי"ל דשאני שחיטה דכתיב בה אהל מועד וא"כ לפני ה' דקאמר היינו העזרה אבל הכא לא כתיב אהל מועד : י] אומר דמו לא נאמר אלא דמם חלבו לא נאמר אלא חלבם לימד: יא] ללמד על זמן אכילת שלמים שהוא ביום זביחתן : יב] קרא ביום הקריבו : יג] שלישי חשב בשוחטת : יד] לזביחה דהיינו ליל שמחרת שלישי כמו אור לי"ד הס"ד : טו] החמה כלומר מחשבת חוץ לזמן זריקת דמן משתשקע החמה הוא אם: טז] בקר הא כל : יז] וגו' הס"ד ומה"ד ביום השלישי וגו' בצו : יח] נמי מהתם ותיבת מהכא נמחק : יט] תיבת לו נמחק : כ] בכור נאכל לכהנים : כא] קבע להו : כב] בזריקה שמשוי מתן דמים כו' מכלל דבמתן דם לא שינה כו' תזרוק (דמו יזרוק) ואיכא תנא דסבר לעיל דפסח ומעשר בשפיכה לכך בעי מאן תנא דסבר בזריקה· גירסת רש"י של מהר"ם : כג] התם בקרכם וצאנכם דהיינו חטאות: כד] אלהיכם במחיצה תיבת אלו ואות ה' נמחק: כה] תיבות מן הקלעים נמחק: כו] שלמים שנאכלין לשני ימים כו' לענין דנאכלין בכל העיר : כז] ושוב פירש בתשובה תיבת הג"ה נמחק : כח] בג"ש למאן דאמר לקמן היכנו ודבר אחר הוי היקש ולעיל : כט] יוחנן ועוד דלעיל אצטריך ודם זבחיך ישפך למתן דם פסח ומעשר והשתא במעשר למה לי קרא תיפוק ליה מג"ש דהעברה העברה אלא ודאי העברה לא ניתן לידרש לדברים הנוהגים לאחר שחיטתו אלא בדברים הנוהגים בחייתו ונראה דמעשר ילפינן משלמים מה שלמים קדשים קלים כו' ונאכלים כו' אף מעשר כו' ולא מצי למיפרך כמו לעיל דבכור מתנה לכהן כו' לשון מהר"פ: ל] שכנגדו בשאר קדשים: לא] ובלילה כל היום תיבת עד נמחק: לב] דגופיה ולא תנא אלא מצוה שבגוף הפסח הס"ד:

א) נראה דצ"ל אע"פ שנאכלים לשני ימים וכן נמי וכו' וכ"כ גם הרמב"ן בפי' החומש בפ' צו על קרא ביום זבחכם יאכל וגו' · ב) נראה דצ"ל עי' תוס' ד"ה ונאכלין כו' · ותימה גדולה לפי' כו' עד ונראה לפרש דנפקא לן וכו' ולי נראה דנפקא לן כו' ·

a But this text is needed [56b] for its own purpose?[1]—If so, let Scripture say, 'It shall be eaten on the day of its slaughtering': what is the purpose of *'that he offereth'*? Infer from it: on the day that you slaughter, you can offer; on the day that you do not slaughter, you cannot offer. Yet perhaps this is what the Divine Law means: If he [the priest] presents the blood on the same day, you may eat the flesh on the same day and on the next; while if he presents the blood on the morrow, you may eat the flesh on the morrow and on the day after?—If so, let Scripture write, 'It shall be eaten on the day that he offereth'; what is the purpose of *'his slaughtering'*? Infer from it: On the day that you slaughter, you can offer: on the day that you do not slaughter, you cannot offer.

It was stated: If one intends [eating the flesh] on the evening of the third day,[2] Hezekiah said: It [the sacrifice] is fit; R. Joḥanan said: It is unfit. Hezekiah said: It is fit, seeing that it was not yet relegated to the fire.[3] R. Joḥanan said: It is unfit, seeing that it is rejected from eating.[4]

If one eats [the flesh] on the evening of the third day, Hezekiah maintained: He is exempt,[5] seeing that it was not yet relegated to the fire; R. Joḥanan maintained, He is culpable, seeing that it was rejected from eating. It was taught in accordance with R. Joḥanan: With regard to sacrifices which are eaten on the same day [only], an intention is effective in respect of their blood from sunset, and in respect of their flesh and their *emurim*, from dawn.[6] But as to sacrifices which are eaten two days and one night, an intention is effective in respect of their blood from sunset; in respect of their *emurim*, from dawn; and in respect of their flesh, from sunset on the second day.[7]

Our Rabbis taught: You might think that they [peace-offerings] may be eaten on the evening of the third day, and this is indeed logical. Some sacrifices are eaten on the same day, and others are eaten during two days; as those sacrifices which are eaten on the
b same day [only], the night follows them;[1] so also the sacrifices which are eaten during two days, the night follows them. Therefore it says, *And if aught remain until the third day:*[2] while it is yet day it may be eaten, but it may not be eaten on the evening of the third day. You might think that it is burnt immediately,[3] and this is logical: some sacrifices are eaten on the same day, and others are eaten during two days: as the sacrifices which are eaten on the same day, burning immediately follows eating;[4] so the sacrifices which are eaten during two days, burning immediately follows eating. Therefore it says, *'On the third* day *it shall be burnt with fire'*: you must burn it by day, but you must not burn it at night.

MISHNAH. THE FIRSTLING, TITHE[5] AND PASSOVER-OFFERING ARE SACRIFICES OF LESSER SANCTITY. THEY ARE SLAUGHTERED IN ANY PART OF THE TEMPLE COURT, AND THEIR BLOOD REQUIRES ONE SPRINKLING, PROVIDED THAT IT IS APPLIED OVER AGAINST THE BASE.[6] THEY DIFFERED IN THEIR CONSUMPTION [AS FOLLOWS]: THE FIRSTLING WAS EATEN BY PRIESTS [ONLY], WHILE THE TITHE MIGHT BE EATEN BY ANY MAN. AND THEY WERE EATEN IN ANY PART OF THE CITY, PREPARED IN ANY MANNER, DURING TWO DAYS AND ONE NIGHT. THE PASSOVER-OFFERING MIGHT BE EATEN ONLY AT NIGHT, ONLY UNTIL MIDNIGHT, AND IT MIGHT BE EATEN ONLY BY THOSE REGISTERED FOR IT,[7] AND IT MIGHT BE EATEN ONLY ROASTED.

c *GEMARA.* Which Tanna [rules thus]?[1]—Said R. Ḥisda, It is R. Jose the Galilean. For it was taught, R. Jose the Galilean said: Not 'its blood' is said, but 'their *blood*'; not 'its fat' is said, but 'their *fat*': this teaches concerning the firstling, tithe, and the Passover-offering, that their blood and *emurim* must be presented at the altar.[2]

How do we know [that it must be sprinkled] over against the base?—Said R. Eleazar: The meaning of 'sprinkling'[3] is learned

a (1) To teach that a peace-offering is eaten on the day it is slaughtered and on the next day. (2) The evening preceding the third day, i.e., after the two days permitted for its eating. (3) If it remains until the evening of the third day it does not become *nothar*, to require burning, but only if it remains until the morning (v.v. 17). Hence the intention to eat it then, expressed at the sacrificing, does not invalidate it. (4) It may not be eaten after the two days. (5) From the penalty for eating *nothar*. (6) If he intended sprinkling their blood after sunset, or eating their flesh or burning their *emurim* after the dawn of the morrow, his intention makes the sacrifice unfit. (7) I.e., the evening of the third day.

b (1) I.e., they are eaten on the night following. (2) Lev. XIX, 6. (3) At the end of the second day, after sunset. (4) From the moment that it may no longer be eaten, it is to be burnt. (5) *Sc.* of cattle; v. Lev. XXVII, 32. (6) On a part of the altar which has a base under it. This excludes the east and south (v. *supra* 53b). (7) By people who had previously registered themselves for that particular animal.

c (1) The Mishnah enumerates the differences in their mode of consumption only. Whence it follows that they are alike in respect of sprinkling and presentation of *emurim*. Whose view is this? (2) V. *supra* 37a for notes. (3) Written in connection with the firstling and tithe.

from a burnt-offering. [57a] And how do we know it of a burnt-offering itself?—Because it is written, *At the base of the altar of the burnt-offering:*[4] this proves that the statutory burnt-offering requires [sprinkling at] the base.[5] If so, just as there two applications which constitute four [are required], so here too, two applications which constitute four [are required]?[6]—Said Abaye: Why must *'round about'* be written in connection with both a burnt-offering and a sin-offering?[7] That there might be two verses with the same teaching, and two verses with the same teaching do not illumine [other cases].[8] That is well on the view that they do not illumine; but on the view that they do illumine, what can be said?—The guilt-offering is a third,[9] and three certainly do not illumine.

THE FIRSTLING IS EATEN BY PRIESTS. Our Rabbis taught, How do we know that a firstling is eaten during two days and one night? Because it is said, *And the flesh of them shall be thine, as the wave-breast and as the right thigh:*[10] the Writ assimilated it to the
a breast and the thigh of a peace-offering:[1] as a peace-offering might be eaten during two days and one night, so may the firstling be eaten during two days and one night. And this question was asked of the Sages in the vineyard of Yabneh:[2] For how long may a firstling be eaten? Whereupon R. Tarfon replied: During two days and one night. Now a certain disciple was present, who had come to the Beth Hammedrash for the first time, by the name of R. Jose the Galilean. Master, said he to him, whence do you know this? My son, replied he, a peace-offering is a sacrifice of lesser sanctity, and a firstling is a sacrifice of lesser sanctity: as a peace-offering is eaten during two days and one night, so a firstling is eaten during two days and one night. Master, he objected, a firstling is the priest's due, and a sin-offering and a guilt-offering are the priest's dues;[3] [then let us argue,] as a sin-offering and a guilt-offering [may be eaten] during one day and one night, so a firstling [may be eaten] one day and one night? Said he to him: Let us compare the two objects, and then deduce one from the other:[4] as a peace-offering does *not* come on account of sin, so a firstling does *not* come on account of sin; [hence,] as a peace-offering is eaten two days and one night, so is a firstling eaten two days and one night. Master, he objected, Let us compare the two objects, and then deduce one from the other: a[5] sin-offering and a guilt-offering are priestly dues, and a firstling is a priestly due; as[5] a sin-offering and a guilt-offering cannot be brought as a vow or a freewill-offering,[6] so a firstling cannot be a vow or a freewill-offering:[7] [hence,] as a sin-offering and a guilt-offering are eaten one day and one night, so may a firstling be eaten one day and one night? R. Akiba then leaped [into the debate], and R. Tarfon withdrew. Said he [R. Akiba] to him, Behold, it says, *'And the flesh of them shall be thine* [etc.]': the Writ assimilated them to the breast and thigh of a peace-offering: as a peace-offering is eaten two days and one night, so a firstling is eaten two days and one night. Said he to him: You have likened it to the breast and thigh of a peace-offering, but I might liken it to the breast and thigh of a thanksoffering: as a thanksoffering is eaten one day and one night, so a firstling is eaten one day and one
b night. Lo, he replied, it says, *it shall be thine.*[1] Now, *'it shall be thine'* need not be stated; why then is it said? The Writ thereby prolonged the existence of a firstling.[2] When this discussion was reported to R. Ishmael, he said to them [those who reported it]: Go forth and say to Akiba, You have erred.[3] Whence do we learn this of the thanksoffering?[4] From a peace-offering.[5] Can then that which is learnt through a *hekkesh* teach in turn by a *hekkesh?*[6] Hence you must determine it not by the second version but by the first version.[7] Now, how does R. Ishmael employ this phrase, *'it shall be thine'?*[8]—It teaches that a blemished firstling is given to the priest, for which teaching we do not find [any other text] in the whole Torah. And R. Akiba?[9]—He learns it from *'their flesh'*, [which intimates,] whether it be whole or blemished. And R. Ishmael?[10]—It means, the flesh of these firstlings.

Wherein do they differ?[11]—One master holds: [That which is inferred] from the subject itself and another does constitute a *hekkesh;* while the other master holds: It does not constitute a
c *hekkesh.*[1] On the view that it does not constitute a *hekkesh,* it is well: hence it is written, *And so shall he do for the tent of meeting,*[2] which [intimates]: As he sprinkles the blood of the bullock in the Holy of Holies once upward and seven times downward, so must he sprinkle in the *hekal;* and as he sprinkles the blood of the he-goat in the Holy of Holies once upward and seven times downward, so must he sprinkle in the Hekal. But on the view that it does constitute a *hekkesh,* what can be said?[3]—The localities only are deduced from

(4) Lev. IV, 7. (5) For in fact the altar was not used for the burnt-offering exclusively, the very sentence quoted treating of a sin-offering. Hence the verse must mean, at the base of the altar, as is done with a burnt-offering. (6) Whereas the Mishnah says otherwise. (7) Burnt-offering, Lev. I, 5: *And he shall dash the blood* round about *against the altar;* sin-offering, VIII, 15: *And when it was slain, Moses took the blood, and put it upon the horns of the altar* round about *with his finger. 'Round about'* implies on all four sides. Now, this could be said with reference to a burnt-offering only, and the other would be deduced from it. (8) Hence the *number* of applications required by a firstling etc. cannot be deduced from a burnt-offering. (9) Where *'round about'* is said, Lev. VII, 2. (10) Num. XVIII, 18. The text refers to firstlings.
a (1) Since it was the breast and the thigh of a peace-offering which belonged to the priest. (2) The famous town to the north-west of Jerusalem, seat of R. Joḥanan b. Zakkai's academy and Sanhedrin after the destruction of the Temple. (3) Whereas a peace-offering belongs to its owner. (4) I.e., let us first see to which the firstling is similar, and then learn from it. (5) The words: 'a sin-offering . . . as' are best omitted with Ms. M. (6) V. *supra* 2*b*, n. 6. These sacrifices can be brought only when one has incurred them. (7) It must actually be a firstling.
b (1) Num. XVIII, 18. This reiterates the first half of the verse. (2) It is correct to liken it to a thanksoffering rather than to a peace-offering, since we cannot permit a longer time for its consumption than the *minimum* of which we are certain. But the reiteration, *'it is thine'*, implies that it is thine for a longer time than you might otherwise think, and so it is permitted for *two* days, like a peace-offering. (3) By likening it to the thanksoffering in the first place. (4) That its breast and thigh belong to the priest. This is not stated explicitly. (5) By means of a *hekkesh*. (6) Surely not (v. *supra* 49*b*). Hence the thanksoffering in this case cannot throw light on the firstling. (7) You must compare it in the first instance to a peace-offering, not to a thanksoffering. (8) Why is it repeated? (9) Whence does he know this? (10) How does he explain the plural *'their'*? V. *supra* 37*a*, *b* for notes. (11) It is a definite rule that what is learnt through a *hekkesh* does *not* teach through a *hekkesh*. Why then does R. Akiba adopt this exegesis here?
c (1) Now, that a thanksoffering is eaten one day and one night is not inferred by a *hekkesh* but stated explicitly, Lev. VII, 15, while that its breast and thigh belong to the priest is inferred by a *hekkesh*. R. Ishmael holds that the fact that the priest may eat the breast and the thigh during one day and one night only must be regarded as an inference by a *hekkesh*, and therefore it cannot become the basis for another *hekkesh* (viz., as to the time permitted for the consumption of a firstling). R. Akiba however maintains that since the time permitted for the thanksoffering is explicitly stated, we do not regard the time allowed for the breast and thigh as the result of a *hekkesh;* hence it can become the basis for another *hekkesh*. (2) Lev. XVI, 16. (3) The passage treats of the ritual of the Day of Atonement. Scripture writes, *And he shall take of the blood of the bullock, and sprinkle with his finger upon the ark-cover on the east; and before the ark-cover shall he sprinkle of the blood with his finger seven times* (ibid. 14). *'Upon'* and *'before'* are understood to mean upward and downward respectively: thus, while it is explicitly stated that it is sprinkled seven times downwards, the number of upward sprinklings is not stated, and this is learnt by analogy (*hekkesh*) from the he-goat, where it says, *And sprinkle it* (otho) *upon the ark-cover, and before the ark-cover* (v. 15). There 'it' (*otho*) is held to indicate one sprinkling, while the number of downward sprinklings is not stated. The present text, *and do with his* (*sc.* the he-goat's) *blood as he did with the blood of the bullock*, teaches that both are sprinkled once upward and seven times downward, since an analogy is drawn between them. Now, each is written partly explicitly and partly inferred by a *hekkesh*, and then the same is applied to the *hekal* by means of a *hekkesh*. Now, if what is inferred partly from the subject itself and partly from another subject does *not* constitute a *hekkesh*, then the sprinklings in the *hekal* can rightly be inferred by a *hekkesh* from those in the Holy of Holies. But if it does, such inference is disallowed, since what is learnt by a *hekkesh* cannot teach by a *hekkesh*.

ועולה גופה מנלן א] דכתיב °אל יסוד מזבח העולה ב]למד על עולת חובה שטעונה יסוד אי מה להלן ג] שתי מתנות שהן ארבע אף כאן שתי מתנות שהן ארבע אמר אביי ד]למה לי למכתב °סביב בעולה סביב בחטאת *הוו שני כתובין הבאין כאחד *וכל שני כתובין הבאין כאחד אין מלמדין הניחא למ"ד אין מלמדין אלא למ"ד מלמדין מאי איכא למימר הוי ה]אשם שלשה ושלשה ודאי אין מלמדין:

ו]הבכור נאכל לכהנים: ת"ר מנין לבכור שנאכל לשני ימים ולילה ז] שנאמר °ובשרם יהיה לך כחזה התנופה וכשוק הימין הקישו הכתוב לחזה ושוק של שלמים מה שלמים נאכלין לשני ימים ולילה אחד אף בכור נאכל לשני ימים ולילה אחד וזו שאלה נשאלה לפני חכמים בכרם ביבנה בכור לכמה נאכל נענה ר"ט ואמר לשני ימים ולילה אחד היה שם תלמיד אחד שבא לבית המדרש ח] לפני חכמים תחלה ור' יוסי הגלילי שמו אמר לו רבי מנין לך אמר לו בני שלמים קדשים קלים ובכור קדשים קלים מה שלמים נאכלין לשני ימים ולילה אחד אף בכור נאכל לשני ימים ולילה אחד אמר לו רבי בכור מתנה לכהן וחטאת ואשם מתנה לכהן מה חטאת ואשם ליום ולילה אף בכור ליום ולילה אמר לו ט] נדון דבר מ(תוך) דבר ונלמד דבר מ(תוך) דבר מה שלמים אין באין על חטא אף בכור אינו בא על חטא מה שלמים נאכלים לשני ימים ולילה אחד אף בכור נאכל לשני ימים ולילה אחד אמר לו רבי נדון דבר מדבר י] ילמד דבר מדבר חטאת ואשם מתנה לכהן יא] ובכור מתנה לכהן מה חטאת ואשם אין באין בנדר ונדבה אף בכור אינו בנדר ונדבה מה חטאת ואשם נאכלין ליום יב] אחד אף בכור נאכל ליום אחד קפץ ר"ע ונסתלק ר"ט אמר לו הרי הוא אומר *ובשרם יהיה לך יג] הקישן הכתוב לחזה ושוק של שלמים מה שלמים נאכלין לשני ימים ולילה אחד אף בכור נאכל לשני ימים ולילה אחד אמר לו יד] היקשתו לחזה ושוק של שלמים ואני מקישו לחזה ושוק של תודה מה תודה נאכלת ליום ולילה אף בכור נאכל ליום ולילה אמר לו הרי הוא אומר ובשרם יהיה לך שאין ת"ל טו] לך יהיה ומה ת"ל לך יהיה *הוסיף הכתוב הויה אחרת בבכור וכשנאמרו דברים לפני ר' ישמעאל אמר להן *צאו ואמרו לו טז]לר"ע טעיתה תודה מהיכן למדה משלמים [וכי] דבר הלמד בהיקש *חוזר ומלמד יז] בהיקש הא אין עליך לידון בלשון אחרון אלא בלשון ראשון ור' ישמעאל האי לך יהיה מאי עביד ליה *לימד על בכור בעל מום שהוא מתנה לכהן *שלא מצינו בכל התורה יח] ור"ע יליף ליה מבשרם חד תם וחד בעל מום ור' ישמעאל מבשרם דהנך בכורות קאמר במאי קמיפלגי מ"ס *הימנו ודבר אחר הוי היקש ומ"ס לא הוי היקש בשלמא למ"ד לא הוי היקש היינו דכתיב °וכן יעשה לאהל מועד *כשם שמזה לפני ולפנים אחת למעלה ושבע למטה מדם הפר כך [א]מזה בהיכל וכשם שלפני ולפנים אחת למעלה ושבע למטה מדם השעיר כך [ב]מזה בהיכל אלא למ"ד הוי היקש מאי איכא למימר יט] *מקומות הוא דגמרי מהדדי

תורה אור: ויקרא ד · שם א · במדבר יח · ויקרא טז

רש"י

ועולה גופה מנלן · כדי נסבה דהא מק"ו ילפינן לעיל בפירקין (דף נג·) והאי קרא לדרשא אחרינא כ] אוקימנא וקילור דברים הוא דנקט לה מקרא דהי לאו ק"ו הוה ילפיק לה כא] מינה: אי מה כו' אף כאן· *דבשר זריקה זריקה מעולה ילפינן מה להלן ד' מתנות שתים שהן ארבע: כתיב בחטאת · במילואים ובעולה מסביב שמעינן ביה ד' מתנות כב] שסובב בדמה *רוחות המזבח: אין מלמדין · ואע"ג דהכא לאו בבנין אב אנו באין ללמוד אשמעינן אביי דשני כתובין הבאין כאחד אין מלמדין אפי' בג"ש אותו דבר שנכתב בשניהן: ובשרם יהיה לך · בבכור כתיב: לחזה ושוק של שלמים · ולקמיה פריך כג] לשל תודה אקשינן: בכרם · ת"ח יושבין שורות ככרם כך מפורש בברכות ירושלמי: שבא לבית המדרש תחלה · היא היתה תחילת ביאתו לפניהם ביבנה: וחטאת ואשם מתנה לכהן · אבל שלמים לבעלים: נדון דבר מדבר· כלומר שכמותו ודומה לו: אין באין על חטא · כחטאת ואשם: אינו בא בנדר ובנדבה · לאפוקי שלמים דבאין בנדר ובנדבה: ונסתלק · נשתתק: הקישו הכתוב·ואין משיבין על ההיקש: הוסיף לך הכתוב כו' · כלומר מודה אני לדבריך שלחזה ושוק של תודה כד] צריכין אנו להקישו דתפסת מועט תפסת מיהו מהדר הכתוב בסיפיה דקרא לך יהיה דלא איצטריך דהא כתיב ברישיה יהיה לך הוסיף לו הכתוב הויה אחרת כמו זו הבאה לו בהיקש: ה"ג וכשנאמרו דברים לפני ר' ישמעאל אמר להם לאו ואמרו לו כה] לר"ע טעית תודה מהיכן למדה משלמים כו] ודבר הלמד בהיקש חוזר ומלמד בהיקש אין עליך כו' · טעיתה במה שחזרת בך מהיקש שלמים ואתה מקישו לתודה דלא למדו הכתוב אלא משלמים דאי מתודה חזה ושוק לא כתיב בה אלא מדאיתקש תודה לשלמים כפקא לן בה חזה ושוק בת"כ דתניא לפי שיצאה תודה לידון בדבר החדש שטעונה לחם יכול אין לך בה אלא חידושה כז] ת"ל תורת זבח השלמים אם על תודה מה שלמים טעונים סמיכה ונסכים ותנופת חזה ושוק אף תודה כו': ודבר הלמד בהיקש כח] יחזור וילמד על הבכור בהיקש · ליאכל ליום ולילה: אין עליך לדונו בלשון אחרון · להקישה לחזה ושוק של תודה: אלא בלשון ראשון · לשל שלמים: שלא מצינו · ללמדו בכל התורה כולה אלא מכאן: דהנך בכורות · בכור שור בכור כשב בכור עז כט] וכל לשון רבים דקרא עלייהו קאי לר' ישמעאל וה"נ אמרינן גבי ואת דמם ואת חלבם לר' ישמעאל בפרק ב"ש (לעיל לז:): במאי קמיפלגי · רבי ישמעאל ור"ע דע"כ אין היקש חוזר מלמד בהיקש ור"ע מ"ט גמיר לה: הימנו ודבר אחר · אכילת חזה ושוק של תודה ליום ולילה הימנו ודבר אחר *העמידוה קלת המלמד כתב בה דכתיב בתודה יום ולילה וקלת היא למדה ממקום אחר ל] מאי היא חזה ושוק דלא כתיב בה: רבי ישמעאל סבר היקש הוא · כמלת מה שחזה ושוק לא] נאכלין ליום ולילה מן ההיקש למד · ור"ע סבר הואיל ויום ולילה בתודה כתיב אע"ג דחזה ושוק למדה לב] בהיקש לא הויא זמן אכילת חזה ושוק של תודה דבר הלמד בהיקש: כשם שמזה לפני ולפנים כו' · ולפני ולפנים גופיה אחת למעלה ושבע למטה בפר ושעיר בהימנו ודבר אחר גמר לג] דבפנים למעלה בפר לא כתיב ביה מגיילא דכתיב (ויקרא טז) והזה באצבעו על פני הכפרת וקדמה ולפני הכפרת יזה שבע פעמים לד] ושבע למטה הוא דכתיבא ביה ובשעיר חטאת למעלה הוא דכתיבא והזה אותו על הכפרת ולפני הכפרת אותו חדא משמע לה] ולפני הכפרת לא כתיב שבע וגמירי בהיקשא מהדדי דכתיב ועשה את דמו כאשר עשה לדם הפר אלמא עבודת פר ושעיר בפנים לו] בהימנו ודבר אחר ילפינן דמקלת עבודה כל אחד כתובה בו ומקלתה למד מחבירו והדר מיגמר היכל מפנים בהיקשא דכן יעשה לאוהל מועד אלמא הימנו ודבר אחר לא כהיקשא חשיב לה: אלא למ"ד הוי היקש · היכי הדר היכל וגמר מיניה בהיקשא: מקומות הוא דגמירי מהדדי · ואין זה לז] חוזר ומלמד בהיקש דבהיקש קמא בהמות איתקוש ובהיקשא בתרא מקומות איתקוש אבל גבי תודה ובכור *חזה ושוק של תודה לח] הוקשה לבכור והיא עצמה למדה משלמים בהיקש: ה"ג

תוספות

למה לי למכתב סביב בעולה סביב בחטאת הוו שני כתובים · לט] סביב בעולה איצטריך לכדאמר לעיל יכול יזרקנו זריקה אחת ת"ל סביב אלא סביב דחטאת קאמר נ"ל דארבע קרנות כתיב ביה מ] ומיהו לרבי ישמעאל קשה דאיצטריך לגזירה שוה דיליף מיניה פיסוק ד' מתנות בעולה כדאמר לעיל ועוד למ"ד לעיל (דף נג·) בחטאת טתן אמה אילך ואמה אילך איצטריך בחטאת סביב לגופיה שלא תאמר דסגי בשתי מתנות *ברוחב אחת בשתי קרנות ושמא סביב דעולה הוא *דמייתי דטובא סביב כתיב בעולה בפרשת ויקרא מא] ועוד דעולה אתיא זריקה זריקה משלמים: ואני מקישו לחזה ושוק של תודה · משום דלחומרא מקשינן: וכי דבר הלמד בהיקש חוזר ומלמד בהיקש · תימה ונקשיה לחזה ושוק של איל נזיר דכתיב בהדיא ונאכל ליום ולילה כדמרבינן לעיל מב] *בפ"ק (דף ד) ובפרק כל הפסולין (דף לו·) מג] וכ"ת דהאי דמרבינן מבשר זבח תודת שלמיו חשיב הקישא מד] א"כ היכי יליף לה לעיל מחטאת ואשם דילפינן *מההוא קרא ולעיל (דף כ·) איבעיא לן אי דבר הלמד בהיקש חוזר ומלמד בבנין אב ולא איפשיטא ויש לומר דמסתברא לאקושי לתודה שטוהגת בכל בהמה מה] *בבכור ולא לאיל נזיר דאינו טהג אלא באיל א"נ בשוק הימין כתב *ותודה ילפי' משלמים דכתיב בהו ימין אבל איל נזיר לא כתיב ביה ימין: ואיבעית

[פסחים סה. ע"ש] [עי' תוס' פסחים סד: ד"ה אתיא] [בכורות כז:] [שם כח.] [יומא עה. ע"ש] [לעיל מט: וש"נ] [בכורות כז: לעיל לז:] [שבת סג: וש"נ] [מנחות פח. יומא נז.] [יומא נז.] [שם]

ג"ו כיון דנכתב בכור ז"ק · גי' בל"ק ד' רוחות שמזבח · צ"ל הוא קלת התלמוד כצ"ל וכן קלת שלמים ז"ק · גי' ז"ק מה ושוק של בכור הוקש לתודה והיא כו' כצ"ל

עין משפט נר מצוה

עד א ב מיי' פ"ה מהלכות מעה"ק הל' יב וא"ג מהלכות עיה"כ הלכה ס:

צ"ל ברוחב ז"ק · גי' הל"ק דמייתר · [קדושין כד. וש"נ] · מה שנרשם כאן בפ"ק דמרבי' שלמי נזיר ליתא ועי' לעיל דף ד ע"א וצ"ל כדמרבינן לעיל בפ' כל הפסולין ז"ק · צ"ל נמי מהאי קרא · צ"ל כבכור · צ"ל כבכור ותודה ז"ק

שיטה מקובצת

א] דכתיב אל יסוד כו' פ"ה דכדי נסבא כו' היינו לשיטתו דלעיל אבל לפי' ריב"א אתי שפיר · ואע"ג דאוקימנא לעיל בשירים בעולה לפי' רבינו חיים מ"מ [אמרינן נמי] בתחלת עולה דהוא פשטיה דקרא לפי' ריב"א ולפירוש רבינו חיים וא"ת אכתי תחלת דמים דכל הקרבנות כנגד היסוד מנלן לפי' רבינו חיים דלא [אתא] קרא דאל יסוד העולה רק בעולה וי"ל דילפינן להו נמי בג"ש דזריקה מעולה כמו בכור ומעשר ה"ה נמי לכל הקרבנות אלא משום דהוי קבעי על הבכור אי נמי א) לאחר שפי' כל הקרבנות קבעי הכא כנגד היסוד מנלן ואכולהו קרבנות קאי וא"ת ולמאן דדריש בכור ומעשר מדם ובחיך ישפך לומר דהם בשפיכה שהם כנגד היסוד מנליה כיון דלא שייך ג"ש דזריקה ואין סברא לומר דפליג בהא דהא לא אשכחן שום תנא דפליג אלא בשפיכה אבל כנגד היסוד לא אשכחן שום תנא דפליג ועוד דמתני' דקתני כנגד היסוד מסברא אתי ככולי עלמא ותירץ ריב"א דיסוד גופיה נפקא משפך דלשון שפיכה משמע ששופך על גבי דבר אחר והיינו על גבי היסוד דהוינו דבר חלק אבל מאן דיליף להו מאת דמם תזרוק לא הוי ידעינן כנגד היסוד אלא מג"ש דזריקה · תו' מהר"פ: ב] על תיבות למד על עולת שטעונה יסוד נרשם מלמעלה קו להורות שאין זה מדברי התלמוד (ותיבת חובה נמחק): ג] להלן ארבע מתנות אף כאן ארבע מתנות (על תיבות שהן ארבע נרשם קו): ד] למה לי למכתב סביב בעולה כו' תימה והלא אינם שוין דעולה היינו ב' מתנות כו' ועוד דהיא לחטאת למטה וחטאת למעלה אלא אחטאת קאמר כו' לשון מהר"ש: ה] אשם שלשה·תימה דלא מצינו לפילף אשם מעולה דאיכא למיפרך מה לעולה שכן כליל וי"ל דבאשם נמי כתיב זריקה וילפינן בג"ש מעולה שטעונה יסוד לתחלת דמו וה"ה דהס"ל הוי שלמים נ' כתובים הבאים[כאחד]דנאמר בהם זריקה וסביב ו] ונאכלים בכל העיר וכו'ת"ר מנין:ז] וליה אחת שנאמר :ח] תיבות לפני חכמים נמחק :ט] א"ל בני נדון דבר מדבר ונלמד דבר מדבר שלמים קדשים קלים ואין באין על חטא ובכור קדשים קלים ואינו בא על חטא : י] ונלמד דבר : יא] מתנה לכהן ואינן באים בנדר ונדבה ובכור מתנה לכהן ואין בא בנדר ונדבה מתיבות מה חטאת כו' עד תיבת ונדבה נמחק:יב] ליום ולילה אחד אף בכור נאכל ליום ולילה אחד :יג] לך וגו' הקישן : יד] לו אתה היקשתו : טו] ת"ל יהיה לך ומה ת"ל יהיה לך הוסיף:טז] לו לעקיבא : יז] בהיקש · וא"ת ולילף בכור בהיקשא דחזה ושוק דאיל נזיר דכתיב בגופיה זמן אכילתו כדדרשינן מזבח תודת שלמיו לרבות שלמי נזיר לעיל וליכא למימר דנם זה חשיב היקש דאיתקש לתודה ואע"ג דאיכא יתורא דא"כ חטאת ואשם נמי לא נפקא אלא מהאי קרא וכיון דחשיב היקש הוכא ילפינן בכור לעיל מבנין אב דחטאת ואשם והלא דבר הלמד בהיקש אינו חוזר וטלמד בבנין אב ולעיל לא איפשט לן וי"ל דמחזה ושוק דאיל נזיר לא מצי יליף משום דהתם יש זרוע בשלה שגם הוא מתנה לכהן ובהאי קרא דבכור לא כתיב כי אם חזה ושוק דמשמע דמקיש בכור לחזה ושוק נרידא דליכא בהדיה דבר אחר שיהא מתנה לכהן · לשון מהר"פ :יח] התורה כולה ור"ע יליף ליה מובשרם כו' ורבי ישמעאל ובשרם דהנך:יט] מקומות הוא כו' דבהיקש קמא איתקש פר ושעיר ובהיקש בתרא אקשינן היכל לבין הבדים הלכך היקשא בתרא לא הוי מעין היקשא קמא :כ] אחרינא אוקימנא : כא] לה תלמודא מהכא כ) כלומר אי דבכור והד"א : כב] מתנות שיסבב בדמה ארבע רוחות : כג] צריך דלמא לחזה ושוק של תודה: כד] תודה הוקש תיבות צריכין אנו להקישו נמחק : כה] לו לעקיבא טעית : כו] משלמים דבר הלמד את ו' נמחק : כז] חידושה בלבד ת"ל וזאת תורת זבח השלמים וגו' : כח] בהיקש היאך חוזר ומלמד על הבכור : כט] עז דכתיבי בקרא וכל לשון רבים דקרא לר' ישמעאל עלייהו קאי והכי נמי : ל] אחר דלא כתיב בה חזה ושוק הס"ד : לא] ושוק של תודה נאכלין ליום כו' למד הלכך אינה חוזרת ומלמדת בהיקש הס"ד : לב] למדה בה בהיקש : לג] נמר דלמעלה ותיבת דבפנים נמחק : לד] פעמים שבע למטה כו' ובשעיר אתת למעלה בלחוד כתיבא והזה אותו: לה] משמע ושבע למטה לא כתיב ונמירי תיבות ולפני הכפורת נמחק : לו] בפנים בהיקש בהימנו ודבר אחר ילפינן דמקצת עבודות כל אחד ואחד כתובות בו ומקצתו הוא למד מחבירו והדר מינמר פנים אהיכל בהיקשא דכן כו' לא היקשא חשיב ליה הס"ד : לז] זה קרוי חוזר : לח] תודה עצמה הוקשה : לט] דאסביב דעולה לא קאי דאיצטריך לאתויי לכדאמר : מ] ביה ואם אינו ענין לגופיה תנהו ענין לעולה והוי ב' כתובים בעולה ואין מלמדין יפיה לר"י קשה דאצטריך סביב לגזירה : מא] עיין בהשמטות בסוף המסכת : מב] לעיל בפרק כל הפסולין ותיבות בפ"ק נמחק : מג] ואין לומר דהאי תיבות וכ"ת ל"ש : מד] היקשא דא"כ : מה] כבכור ולא לאיל נזיר שאינו נוהג :

א) אולי צ"ל לאחר שפירש דבכור ומעשר ופסח טעונין מתן דמים ואימורין ככל הקרבנות קבעי ככה וכו' . ב) נראה דצ"ל מהכא כס"ד ומס"ד אי מה כו' אף כאן כלומר אי דבכור כו'.

ואיבעית

עה א מיי' פ"ח מהל' תמידין ומוספין הלכה ד :

א] ואיבעית אימא חוץ מפנים בחד זימנא גמיר בשלמא למ"ד (א) ב] *הוי היקש היינו דכתיב °ממושבותיכם תביאו לחם תנופה *שאין ת"ל תביאו מה ת"ל תביאו כל שאתה מביא ממקום ג] (למקום) אחר הרי הוא כזה מה להלן עשרון לחלה אף כאן עשרון לחלה אי מה להלן שני עשרונים אף כאן שני עשרונים ת"ל תהיינה ד] ולמדנו *עשרה לחמץ עשרה למצה מנין ת"ל °על חלת לחם חמץ ה] נגד חמץ הבא מצה אלא למאן דאמר ו](ב) (*לא) הוי היקש מאי איכא למימר תביאו ז] יתירא היא : הפסח אינו נאכל : מאן תנא *אמר רב יוסף רבי אלעזר בן עזריה היא דתניא רבי אלעזר ח] [בן עזריה] אומר נאמר כאן °בלילה [הזה] ונאמר להלן °ועברתי בארץ מצרים בלילה הזה מה להלן עד חצות אף כאן עד חצות א"ל ר"ע והלא כבר נאמר ואכלתם אותו בחפזון עד שעת חפזון א"כ מה ת"ל בלילה הזה שיכול יהא ככל הקדשים הנאכלים ביום ת"ל בלילה ט] יהא נאכל ואינו נאכל ביום א"ל אביי וממאי דרבי אלעזר ב"ע ודאורייתא דלמא דרבנן י] ולהרחיק מן העבירה א"כ מאי אלא יא] עד חצות [אלא]כי התם מה התם דאורייתא אף כאן נמי דאוריית':

תורה אור: ויקרא כג · ויקרא ז · שמות יב · שם

הדרן עלך איזהו מקומן

ה"ג ואיבעית אימא חוץ מפנים בחד זימנא גמיר · והכי איתא בסדר יומא בפרק הוציאו לו (דף נז:) כלומר נהי נמי דהיקש מקומות כהיקש בהמות הואיל והיקש יב] לורך פנים הוא אפ"ה לא דמי להההיא דלעיל דאיכו היכל כולה מילתא בעי למילף מפנים ואיידי דניתן היקש לידרש בדברים המפורשים בפנים יג] כמו למטה בפר ולמעלה בשעיר נדרש יד] ולמד בבת אחת ובא אף מה שלמד בפנים בהיקש עמו וגבי היקש *דלעיל נמי אם טו] כתוב *בתודה והוקש בכור לתודה (ג) ללמוד לו חזה ושוק ולמדתה בהיקש אי הוי טז] הוקש בכור לתודה עצמה והיה למד ממנה תנופת חזה ושוק ואכילת יום ולילה יז] דמתוך שיכולה ללמוד עליו זמן לאכילה שהוא כתוב בה מלמדת נמי עליו תנופת חזה ושוק יח] אבל השתא לתודה עצמה לא הקישה הכתוב אלא לחזה ושוק שבתודה ובתודה עצמה לא למדתה אלא בהיקש: היינו דכתיב ממושבותיכם וגו' · גבי שתי הלחם דעלרת יט] כתיב והולרכנו במסכת מנחות (דף עז:) ללמוד מהם כמה עשרונות יש בלחמי תודה ובגופה נכתב י' חלות בכל מין אבל לא נתפרש מכמה היא החלה ומייתי לה לחלות חמץ שבתודה כ] משתי הלחם שאף הן חמץ והכתוב הקיש כל הבאות של חמץ כא] שיהיו שוות ומקרא יתירא דתביאו ילפי' לה דלא אילטריך דכתיב והקרבתם מנחה חדשה ממושבותיכם כב] תביאו לחם תנופה ולא אילטריך תביאו מה ת"ל תביאו כל חמץ שאתה מביא ממקום אחר יהא כזה עשרון לחלה כדכתיב שתים שני עשרונים : אי מה כג] להלן · אלו שני *עשרונים אף אלו כל י' חלות שבה שני עשרונים: ת"ל תהיינה · התם מפרש מאי כד] למודה בפ' התודה : למדנו עשרה · עשרונות לחמץ דהא י' חלות למודות בה בג"ש מתרומת מעשר מה תרומת מעשר אחד מעשר אף תרומת תודה והקריב ממנו אחד מכל קרבן מכל מין תרומה לה' אחד מעשר הרי י' חלות ובהיקש כה] תביאו למדנו שהחלה עשרון הרי למדנו י' עשרונות לחמץ כו] הימנו ודבר אחר י' חלות למדנו בהן כבר ובהיקש הן למידות עשרון לחלה : עשרה עשרון לשלשת מינין שבמלה מנין : ת"ל על חלת לחם חמץ · מנה הכתוב מינין שבמלה וכתב אחריהן על חלת לחם חמץ הרי היקש אלמא חמץ שלמדנו בו עשרה עשרונות בהימנו ודבר אחר חוזר ומלמד על המלה בהיקש עשרה עשרונות: תביאו רבויא הוא · לרבות חמץ שבתודה שכל שתים כז] שבו יהו שתים עשרונים והוי כמאן דכתיב כח] בגופיה בלחמי תודה ולאו משתי הלחם גמרי כט] והיכי דמי דליהוי הימנו ודבר אחר כגון אי איתקוש חמץ דתודה לשתי הלחם בקרא אחרינא דלא מפרש ל] בה עשרון לחלה וילפינן תודה משתי הלחם בהיקש לעשרון לחלה ובדידיה כתיבי עשר חלות : מאן תנא · דאינו נאכל אלא עד חלות : עד שעת חפזון · שהם נחפזים ללכת והייט לאור הבוקר כדכתיב (שמות יב) ואתם לא תלאו איש מפתח ביתו עד בקר : יכול יהא נאכל כשאר כל הקדשים · ביום זביחתו קודם שתחשך יתחיל לאוכלו אם ירלה ת"ל כו' : להרחיק את האדם · כדתנן בכולהו עד חלות : א"כ מאי אלא · ליתני ונאכל עד חלות כדתנא בכולהו : כי התם · דומיא דלילה ומטייו וצלי תנייה דהוו דאורייתא איבעית אימא לא גרסינן וה"ג א"כ מאי אלא כי התם מה התם דאורייתא כו' :

הדרן עלך איזהו מקמן

ואיבעית אימא חוץ מפנים בחדא זימנא גמיר · פירש בקונטרס דכולה מילתא דהיכל בעי למילף מפנים ואיידי דניתן היקש לדרוש בדברים המפורשים בפנים כגון למטה בפר ולמעלה בשעיר נדרוש ולמד בבת אחת אף הלמד בפנים בהיקש עמו וגבי היקש דלעיל נמי אם הייט לריכין ללמוד לבכור תנופת חזה ושוק וזמן אכילה והוקש בכור לתודה עצמה ללמוד שתיהן ממנה מתוך שתודה מלמדת עליו זמן אכילה דכתיב בה מלמדת עליו נמי חזה ושוק שלמדתו בהיקש משלמים אבל עכשיו שלא הוקש לתודה אלא לחזה ושוק לא] וללמוד ממנו זמן אכילה לבדו אם אתה אומר לחזה ושוק של תודה הקישו הכתוב לב] בו עצמו לא למדו בתודה אלא בהיקש ע"כ לשון הקונט' וקשה לפירושו מהא דאמר לעיל (דף מט:) דיותרת ושתי הכליות דעבודת כוכבים הוי דבר הלמד בהיקש ואינו חוזר ומלמד בהיקש *אע"ג לג] דכתיבא ההיא היקשא לדברים דכתיבי בפר העלם גופיה כגון הזאות וכמה דברים ולא אמרי' בחד זימנא גמיר ועוד אמרי' לעיל (דף נה·) דלא ילפינן זבחי שלמי ליבור לגפן מחטאת משום דהוי דבר הבא בהיקש ואינו חוזר ומלמד בהיקש *אף על גב דלריכא ההיא לד] וילפינן בהיקשא לה] [*דנאכל לזכרי כהונה] ותי' ר"י דמאחת למעלה דכתיב בשעיר יליף מבחוץ בין בפר בין בשעיר לו] דהכי משמע וכן יעשה בחוץ בין בפר בין בשעיר וכן *בשבע דלמטה דכתיבי בפר בפנים ילפינן (בין) בחוץ בין לז] בפר [בין] בשעיר כלומר בכל הבהמות ורבינו חננאל פירש בפרק הוליאו לו (יומא נז·) בחדא זימנא גמיר דכי גמרינן שיהיו כל עשיותיו שוות בין בפנים בין בחוץ שכל הזאות שיעשו מהם בכל מקום שיהיו שוות ואית ספרים דגרסי חוץ ופנים בחד זימנא גמר* : **היינו** דכתיב ממושבותיכם תביאו · גבי שתי הלחם כתיב וילפינן מינה חלות חמץ לח] *לתודה דמה כאן בשתי הלחם עשרון לחלה אף כאן חמץ שבתודה עשרון לחלה ומנין חלות שבתודה ילפינן דהוו עשר בג"ש דתרומה תרומה מתרומת מעשר אלמא איכא י' עשרונות לי' חלות של חמץ והדר ילפינן לט] מיניה מחמץ דכנגד חמץ הבא מלה והוו נמי י' עשרונות לג' מינים של מלה דהיינו מ] ג' עשרון ושליש *לכל מין חלה וחלה של מלה ואע"ג דמנין של חלות לאו בגופיה דחמץ כתיב חשיב ליה מא] *בחמץ כדפירש בקונטרס °משום דדבר הלמד בג"ש חוזר ומלמד בהיקש א"נ משום דתרומת מעשר חולין הוא א"נ משום דפריך בפ' התודה (מנחות עז:) ולימא ב' עשרונותיו לא כשתי הלחם וקאמר ת"ל תהיינה וגרסי' התם מאי תלמודא אמר ר' ילחק בר אבדימי תהיינה כתיב *עשרה עשרונות דבר הכתוב ומריבוי ב' יודין דריש דחד יו"ד מב] יתיר משמע עשרה ומסתברא דהאי יו"ד דתהיינה אלחמי תודה קאי דאי אשתי הלחם שתים שתי עשרונים כתיב והיינו הימנו ודבר אחר ד' עשרונות בדידיה כתיב דתהיינה מג] משמע י' חלות ועשרון מתביאו קא יליף ובלשון אחרון פירש בקונט' במנחות (גז"ש) ואית ספרים דגרסי התם אמר רב ילחק בר אבדימי תהיינה כתיב ותו לא ול"ג עשר עשרונות דבר הכתוב ודריש משום דתהיינה מיעוטא הוא דמשמע הני דוקא שני עשרונים ולא אחר שני עשרונות וכ"כ דיו"ד לא מד] *מייתינן למידרש דכמו שיאמר מתעשה לשון יחיד תעשינה לשון רבים כך יאמר מתהיה תהיינה יו"ד אחת של עיקר ויו"ד אחת של שימוש ואם תאמר ומג"ש דתרומת מעשר היכי יליף לי' חלות דלמא עביד חדא חלה מה] אחת גדולה ויטול הימנה פרוסה לתרומה וי"ל דהא אמרינן (פסחים דף לז:) אחד שלא יטול פרוסה ועוד דרשינן התם שיהו כל הקרבנות שוין אלמא דבעי להנך חלות דליהוו *כחלות של תרומה : **להרחיק** מן העבירה · לנאכלין לשני ימים ולילה אחד לא עשו חכמים הרחקה עד חלות דניכר הוא מתי יהיה שקיעת החמה אבל בלילה אינו ניכר מו] : **ואיבעית** אימא כי התם כו' · בקונטרס לא גרס ואיבעית אימא ויש לפרש דדייק מדלא קתני עד חלות לבסוף ותני ליה באמלע ש"מ דהאי דאורייתא כמו לילה ומטייו וצלי ויש לדקדק דהלכה כר' אלעזר בן עזריה דסתם לן תנא סוטיה במתני' ובערבי פסחים (פסחים קכ:) ובפ"ק דברכות (דף ט·) ולריך ליזהר אמלה משום דקאמר רבא בסוף ערבי פסחים אכל מלה אחר חלות לרבי אלעזר בן עזריה לא יצא ידי חובתו [ועיין תוספות פסחים קכ: ד"ה אמר רבא ותוספות מגילה כא· ד"ה לאיתויי] : הדרן עלך איזהו מקמן

[מנחות עז: סג:]

אע"ג דגמרינן בההיא היקשא לדברים כו' נ"ק

אע"ג דזכרי כהונה ילפינן בההיא היקשא ותירץ ר"י כו' נ"ק

משבע נ"ק

[ועי' תוס' יומא נז. ד"ה חוץ מפנים] שבתודה נ"ק

לכל מין ומין של מלה כו' נ"ק

כמאן דכתיב בגופיה דחמץ כדפי' כו' נ"ק

ולאימא עשרה קפיזי ומשני כשעשרות דיבר הכתוב נ"ק

מיותר נ"ק

שיטה מקובצת

א] ואיבעית אימא חוץ מפנים כו' פרש"י דכיון שצריך ללמוד מבין הבדים דבר שנכתב בגופו בהיקשא ילפינן נמי דבר שלא נכתב בגופו דאתי מהיקשא דהיכל גמרינן בחדא זימנא אבל לעיל לא צריך ללמוד א) מתודה אלא ליום ולילה וזה לא נכתב בתודה אלא מהיקשא אתי ודוקא אם היינו צריכים ללמוד בבכור (דתנופת וחזה) [תנופת חזה] ושוק וזמן אכילה והוקש בכור לתודה עצמה [היינו יכולים] ללמוד שתיהן ממנה שהתודה שמלמדת עליו זמן אכילתה הכתוב בה מלמדת עליו נמי חזה ושוק שלמדתו מהיקש משלמים ולא נהירא דכיון דאפילו למ"ד הימנו ודבר אחר הוי היקש לא חשיב היקש בבה"ג כדפי' א"כ אמאי אצטריך לעיל לפר לפר העלם לאגמורי ליותרת הכבד ושתי הכליות לשעירי עבודת כוכבים והא איצטריך היקשא להזאות דכתיב בגופיה דפר העלם ודברים אחרים ולא אמרינן בחדא זימנא גמר לכך נראה דה"ש חוץ מפנים כו' דילפינן אהל מועד מבין הבדים בין לפר [בין] לשעירים כמה שכתוב בהדיא בתרוייהו בפנים דהיינו אחת למעלה בשעיר ושבע למטה בפר ועל זה קאמר וכן יעשה לפר ושעיר הנעשים באהל מועד כמו שמצינו מפורש (בהיכל) [בפנים] בשעירים דהיינו שבע למטה ואחת למעלה ולא ילפינן פר מפר ושעיר משעיר אלא ילפינן פר חיצון משעיר ופר דפנים וכן ילפינן שעיר דחיצון מפר ושעיר דפנים מכל אחד ילפינן מה שכתוב בו בפירוש · תוספות מהר"ם

ב] דאמר לא הוי : ג] ממקום אחר יהא כזה ותיבות למקום הרי הוא נמחק : ד] תהיינה למדנו את י' נמחק : ה] חמץ כנגד חמץ : ו] דאמר הוי תיבת לא נמחק : ז] תביאו ריבויא תיבות יתירא היא נמחק : ח] אלעזר בן עזריה אומר כו' בלילה הזה : ט] בלילה הוא נאכל תיבת יהא נמחק : י] להרחיק את האדם מן : יא] על תיבות עד חצות נרשם עליו קו : יב] והיקש בהמות הואיל צורך : יג] בפנים כגון למטה תיבת כמו נמחק : יד] נדרש ונלמד בבת : טו] אם היינו צריכים ללמוד בבכור תנופת חזה ושוק וזמן אכילה מתיבת כתוב עד תיבת הוי הוקש בכור נמחק : טז] והוקש בכור : יז] ולילה מתוך שיכולים ללמוד עליו זמן אכילה שהוא : יח] ושוק שלמדתו משלמים אבל השתא שלא הוקש לתודה אלא לחזה ושוק ללמוד הימנו זמן אכילה לבדו אם אתה אומר לחזה ושוק של תודה הקישן הכתוב הלא הן עצמן לא למדו בתודה אלא בהיקש חמיד : יט] דעצרת דהוא חמץ כתיב והצרכנו : כ] שבתודה בהיקש משתי : כא] חמץ יהיו שוות את י' ל"ש : כב] ממושבותיכם לחם תיבת תביאו נמחק : כג] מה אלו על תיבת להלן נרשם עליו מלמעלה קו : כד] מאי תלמודא : כה] ובהיקש דתביאו : כו] לחמץ בהימנו ודבר אחר המנין של חלות למדין שלא בהיקש והוי כהימנו דקי"ל דבר הלמד בג"ש חוזר ומלמד בהיקש ומדות החלות הוי דבר אחר שלמדנום בהיקש משתי הלחם (גירסת רש"י של הר"ש ז"ל) [כך] וזה אנו קורין הימנו דבר אחר שחלות מצה למדין מחמץ שהן עשרה ודבר זה למדנו בחמץ מג"ש והוי כמאן דכתיב בגופיה דמיא וזה קרוי הימנו ודבר אחר קרוי והן עשרון דדבר זה למדנו בחמץ (מסברא) (מתביאו) דכתיב גבי שתי הלחם (ע"כ): כז] שתים שבה : כח] בגופייהו דלחמי תודה : כט] נמרי דהא בההוא קרא דכתיב עשרון לחלה כתיב ריבויא לתודה והיכי : ל] מפרש ביה תיבת בה נמחק : לא] ושוק לבדו תיבות וללמוד ממנו וזמן אכילה נמחק : לב] הכתוב הוא עצמו : לג] אע"ג דצריכא ההיא תיבת דכתיבא נמחק : לד] ההיא ילפותא למילף שהן קדשי קדשים ונאכלים לזכרי כהונה דכתיב בגופיה ור"י פי' דמאחת למעלה דכתיב בשעיר בפנים ילפינן : לה] בהיקשא דוכן יעשה בין בפנים בין בחוץ מתיבת דנאכל עד תיבת בין בפר נמחק : לו] בשעיר וכן משבע דלמטה ומתיבת דהכי עד תיבת (דכתיב) [וכן] נמחק (ס"א דהכי משמע ליה וכן יעשה באהל מועד בשתי בהמות כמו שעשה אותו למעלה בשעיר וכן כאשר עשה בפר בפנים למטה יעשה לשני הבהמות באהל מועד ור"ה כו') : לז] בין בחוץ בין בפנים בין בפר : לח] חמץ שבתודה דמה : לט] ילפינן מצה מחמץ דכנגד : מ] דהיינו שלש עשרון לכל חלה וחלה : מא] ליה הימנו כדפי' תיבת בחמץ נמחק : מב] תיבת יתיר ל"ש : מג] דתהיינה דמשמע י' חלות אתביאו קאי ובלשון : מד] לא מייתרא למידרש : מה] תיבת אחת נמחק : מו] עיין בהשמטות בסוף המסכת.

א] נראה דל"ל לא צריך ללמוד משום השוק אלא לתודה וחזה ושוק לא נכתב וכו'.

ר"א לא הוי דלעיל נמי לא הוי הוקש בכור כו' ונשאר נמחק נ"ק *נ"ל תודה ככ"ק ועיין בחילופי גרסאות

ר"א נ"ק

פסחים קכ: ברכות ט: [מגילה כא.]

ר"א עשרונות ותו לא אף כאן כל כו' נ"ק

הגהות הב"ח

(א) גמ' בשלמא למ"ד לא הוי היקש: (ב) שם אלא למ"ד הוי היקש: (ג) רש"י ד"ה ס"א ואיבעית אימא וכו' אם כתוב בתודה עצמה והיה למד כצ"ל ותיבות ללמוד לו חזה ושוק ולמדתה בהיקש אי הוי הוקש בכור לתודה נמחק:

גליון הש"ס

תוס' ד"ה היינו וכו' משום דדבר הלמד בג"ש חוזר ומלמד בהיקש · עיין לעיל דף נ ע"ב תוס' ד"ה אמר · וצ"ע:

דליהוו כל מה כחלות כו' נ"ק

one another.[4] [57b] Alternatively, [the sprinklings] without [in the Hekal] are *directly* inferred from [those] within [the Holy of Holies].[5]

a On the view that it does not[1] constitute a *hekkesh*, it is well: hence it is written, *Ye shall bring out of your dwellings* [*two*] *wave-loaves* [*of two tenth parts of an ephah* etc]:[2] Now, *'ye shall bring'* need not be said;[3] what then does *'ye shall bring'* teach? Whatever you bring on another occasion[4] must be like this: as here a tenth [of an ephah] is used for *ḥallah*, so there[5] too a tenth is required for *ḥallah*. If so, as here two tenths are required, so there too two tenths are required? Therefore Scripture states, *they shall be* [*of fine flour*].[6] We have thus learnt ten [tenths] for leavened [loaves]. Whence do we know ten [tenths] for unleavened loaves? Because it says, *With cakes of leavened bread* [*he shall present his offering with the sacrifice of his peace-offerings for thanksgiving*][7] [which intimates,] Bring an equal quantity of unleavened as of leavened.[8] But on the view that it constitutes a *hekkesh*, what can be said?[9]—*'Ye shall bring'* is superfluous.[10]

THE PASSOVER-OFFERING IS EATEN ONLY [etc]. Which Tanna [rules thus]?—Said R. Joseph, It is R. Eleazar b. 'Azariah. For it was taught, R. Eleazar b. 'Azariah said, [*And they shall eat*
b *the flesh*] *in the night*[1] is stated here, whilst elsewhere it is stated, *For I will go through the land of Egypt in that night:*[2] just as there it means by midnight, so here too it means by midnight. Said R. Akiba to him: Yet surely it is already stated, [*and ye shall eat it*] *in haste*,[3] [implying] until the time of haste?[4] If so, what is taught by *'in that night'*? You might think that it is like all [other] sacrifices, which are eaten by day: therefore it is stated *'in* [*that*] *night'*: it is eaten by night, but it may not be eaten by day. Said Abaye to him [R. Joseph]: How do you know that [the author of our Mishnah is] R. Eleazar b. 'Azariah, while [the law is] Biblical. Perhaps the law is Rabbinical only, [the reason being] to prevent transgression?[5] —If so, why state, ONLY UNTIL MIDNIGHT?[6] But it means, It is as the other laws;[7] as those are Biblical, so is this Biblical.[8]

(4) This is not a case of what is learnt by a *hekkesh* teaching through a *hekkesh*, since the first refers to the *animals*, whereas the second refers to the *localities*. (5) And not *via* the animals at all.
a (1) Emended text (BaḤ, Sh. M.). (2) Lev. XXIII, 17. (3) The text could read: *And ye shall present a new offering unto the Lord* (v. 16) *out of your dwellings* etc. (4) Lit., 'from another place'. (5) Lit., 'as there ... so here.' The *ḥallah* (unleavened loaf) brought on another occasion (v. n. 4) is referred to as 'here', as that is the actual subject being discussed. (6) Ibid. For the interpretation of this v. Men. 78*a* top. (7) Lev. VII, 13. (8) The preceding verses read: *Then he shall offer ... unleavened cakes mingled with oil, and unleavened wafers spread with oil, and cakes mingled with oil.* When this is followed by *'With cakes of leavened bread'* etc, it yields a *hekkesh*, whence we learn that the weight of the former must be the same as that of the latter. (9) The wave-loaves brought on Pentecost were made of a tenth of an ephah of flour, and they were leavened. Now, the thanksoffering was accompanied by four kinds of loaves; v. Lev. VII, 12-14. These included a set of leavened loaves (the other three kinds were unleavened), but neither the actual number of each kind nor their weight is stated. By means of a *gezerah shawah* the Talmud deduces that there were the loaves of each kind, and from the superfluous *'ye shall bring'* it infers that the leavened loaves were each to be made of a tenth of an ephah (these are those brought 'on another occasion'), just like the two wave-loaves, so that ten tenths were required for all. Thus the *number* is not deduced by a *hekkesh* but by a *gezarah shawah*, which is regarded as being explicitly stated in the subject itself, while the *weight* is learned by a *hekkesh* (the superfluous *'ye shall bring'*). Then the Talmud infers by another *hekkesh* that the weight of the unleavened loaves is the same (v. preceding note). The difficulty then is the same as the preceding on the number of sprinklings (v. p. 287, n. 3). (10) Hence the fact that the loaves of the thanks-offering require a tenth of an ephah each is not regarded as an inference by a *hekkesh*, but as though it were explicitly stated.
b (1) Ex. XII, 8. (2) Ibid. 12. (3) Ibid, 11. (4) I.e., when they had to make haste to leave Egypt, which was in the morning. (5) Possibly this Tanna holds that by Scriptural law it may be eaten until morning, yet he gives the limit of midnight so as to make sure that one will not transgress by eating it in the morning. (6) He should state, And it is eaten until midnight. (7) Lit., 'as there'. *Sc.* that it may only be eaten roast and by registered persons. (8) Hence its author must be R. Eleazar b. 'Azariah.

CHAPTER VI

MISHNAH. [58*a*] IF SACRIFICES OF HIGHER SANCTITY ARE SLAUGHTERED ON THE TOP OF THE ALTAR, R. JOSE SAID: [THEY ARE] AS THOUGH THEY WERE SLAUGHTERED IN THE a NORTH;[1] R. JOSE SON OF R. JUDAH SAID: FROM THE MIDDLE OF THE ALTAR SOUTHWARD IS AS SOUTH, FROM THE MIDDLE OF THE ALTAR NORTHWARD IS AS THE NORTH.

GEMARA. R. Assi said in R. Joḥanan's name: R. Jose maintained that the whole of the altar stood in the north.[2] What then does AS THOUGH [etc.] mean? You might think that we require [them to be slaughtered] *on the* side [*of the altar*],[3] which they were not. Hence he informs us [that it is not so]. Said R. Zera to R. Assi: If so, will you indeed say that R. Jose son of R. Judah holds that [the altar] is half in the north and half in the south?[4] And should you answer, That indeed is so; surely it was you who said in R. Joḥanan's name: R. Jose son of R. Judah admits that if he slaughtered them in a corresponding position on the ground,[5] they are unfit?—Said he to him, This is what R. Joḥanan said: Both of them inferred [their views] from the same text:[6] *And thou shalt sacrifice thereon thy burnt-offerings, and thy peace-offerings:*[7] R. Jose holds: The whole of it [the altar] is fit for [the slaughtering of] the burnt-offering,[8] and the whole of it is fit for peace-offerings. While R. Jose son of R. Judah holds: Divide it: half of it is for a burnt-offering, and half for a peace-offering. For if you think that the whole of it is fit for a burnt-offering, then seeing that the whole of it is fit for a burnt-offering, need it be said that the whole of it is fit for a peace-b offering. And the other?[1]—It is necessary:[2] You might think that only a burnt-offering [is fit if slaughtered on the top of the altar], since its room is cramped.[3] But as for peace-offerings, whose room is not cramped,[4] I would say that it is not so. Hence [the text] informs us [otherwise].

The [above] text [stated]: 'R. Assi said in R. Joḥanan's name: R. Jose son of R. Judah admits that if he slaughtered them in a corresponding position on the ground, they are unfit.' R. Aḥa of Difti asked Rabina: What does 'in a corresponding position on the ground' mean?[5] Shall we say, on the cubit of the base or the cubit of the terrace:[6] surely that is the altar itself? Moreover, what does 'on the ground' mean?[7] And if you say that he made a cavity in the ground[8] and slaughtered therein: would that be a [proper altar]? Surely it was taught: *An altar of earth thou shalt make unto Me:*[9] [this teaches] that it must be joined to the earth, that it must not be built over cavities or on rocks?—It means that he shortened it.[10]

c R. Zera said: Is it possible that this statement of R. Joḥanan[1] is correct, and yet we have not learnt it in the Mishnah?[2] So he went out, searched, and found it. For we learnt: They selected from there[3] sound fig-tree wood[4] to arrange the second pile for incense[5] by the south-west horn at a distance of four cubits from it northward; [sufficient wood was taken to make] about five *se'ahs* of coals,[6] and on the Sabbath, about eight *se'ahs*, because they placed there the two censers of frankincense for the shew-bread.[7] And what is the

a (1) Hence valid. (2) *Supra* 53*a*. (3) Lev. I, 11. (4) R. Zera assumed that R. Assi's statement was inferred from the Mishnah: since R. Jose rules that if it is slaughtered *anywhere* on the top of the altar, it is as though it is slaughtered in the north, it follows that the whole of the altar is in the north. But if this inference is correct, a similar deduction can be made with respect to R. Jose b. R. Judah. (5) This will be explained anon. (6) I.e., R. Joḥanan did not base his statement on the Mishnah, but on the Scriptural interpretation of these Rabbis. (7) Ex. XX, 21. (8) Hence the whole of the altar is in the north, since a burnt-offering must be slaughtered in the north (Lev. I, 11).

b (1) How does he rebut this argument? (2) To state that the whole of it is fit for a peace-offering. (3) As it must be slaughtered in the north, there may not be enough room when there are many sacrifices; hence Scripture permitted the top of the altar too. (4) They can be slaughtered anywhere in the Temple court. (5) It cannot mean on the pavement at the side of the altar, for then there would be no difficulty on R. Assi's view. For even if the whole altar stood in the north, yet if one slaughtered on the west or east of it at some distance from the actual side, it would still be unfit, because it must be killed between the north side of the altar and the opposite wall of the Temple court; therefore this could not prove that R. Jose did not hold that half the altar was in the north and half in the south. Hence it must apparently mean, on the ground of the altar itself. Now, how is this possible? (6) The altar was recessed a cubit for the base and a cubit for the terrace (v. *supra* 54*a*). (7) The top of the base or the terrace is not 'on the ground'. (8) Under the altar. (9) Ex. XX, 21. (10) It was decided to shorten the altar, and the northern half of it was thus left clear. Although it is still the side, the offerings slaughtered there are unfit, which proves that he holds that the altar is in the south, as there is no other reason for its unfitness.

c (1) That R. Jose holds that the whole altar stood in the north. (2) There must be some hint of it in the Mishnah. (3) The wood-shed, in which the wood for the altar was kept. (4) Not worm-eaten. (5) At the side of the large wood-pile, on which the offerings were burnt, a smaller pile was made, whence three *kabs* of burning coals were taken every morning and evening for the inner altar, on which the incense was burnt. (6) So that it should be easy to take the necessary quantity of live coals from it for the inner altar. (7) This frankincense was burnt on the Sabbath, and on the *outer* altar, on this special pile. Therefore more coals were required (as the other incense still had to be burnt on the inner altar). V. Tam. II, 5.

קדשי קדשים ששחטן בראש המזבח רבי יוסי אומר *כאילו נשחטו בצפון ר' יוסי בר' יהודה אומר מחצי המזבח ולדרום כדרום מחצי המזבח ולצפון כצפון: **גמ'** אמר רב אסי א"ר יוחנן *אומר היה ר' יוסי כוליה מזבח בצפון קאי ומאי כאילו מהו דתימא בעינן על ירך א] וליכא קמ"ל אמר ליה רבי זירא לרב אסי ב] אלא מעתה לר' יוסי ברבי יהודה הכי נמי ג] דחציו בצפון וחציו בדרום וכי תימא הכי נמי ד] והא את הוא דאמרת משמיה דרבי יוחנן מודי רבי יוסי בר"י שאם שחטן ה] כנגדן בקרקע פסולה אמר ליה הכי קאמר רבי יוחנן שניהם מקרא אחד דרשו (שמות כ) °וזבחת עליו את עולותיך ואת שלמיך ר' יוסי סבר כולו לעולה וכולו לשלמים ו] ורבי יוסי בר' יהודה סבר ז] חציו לעולה וחציו לשלמים דאי ס"ד כולו לעולה כשר השתא כולו לעולה כשר כולו לשלמים מיבעיא ואידך איצטריך ס"ד אמינא עולה הוא דדחיק ח] ליה מקום אבל שלמים דלא דחיק ליה מקום אימא לא קמ"ל גופא אמר רב אסי אמר רבי יוחנן מודי רבי יוסי ברבי יהודה שאם שחטן ט] כנגדן בקרקע פסולות אמר ליה רב אחא מדיפתי לרבינא מאי כנגדן בקרקע י] אילימא אמה יסוד אמה סובב האי גופיה יא] מזבח הוא ועוד מאי כנגדן בקרקע וכ"ת דעביד מחילות בקרקע ושחיט בהו וכי האי גוונא מי הוי מזבח והתניא (שם) °מזבח אדמה תעשה לי *שיהא מחובר יב] מאדמה שלא יבננו לא על גבי מחילות ולא על גבי כיפין לא צריכא יג] דבצריה בצורי אמר רבי זירא אפשר איתא להא דרבי יוחנן ולא תנינא לה במתני' נפק דק ואשכח *דתנן [ג]בירדו משם עצי תאינה יפים לסדר מערכה שניה של קטרת כנגד קרן מערבית דרומית משוך מן הקרן כלפי צפון ארבע אמות באומד חמש סאין גחלים ובשבת באומד שמונה סאין גחלים ששם היו נותנין שני בזיכי לבונה של לחם הפנים ומאי סימנא רבי יוסי היא דתניא
רבי

רש"י

קדשי קדשים. כאילו נשחטו בצפון. בגמ' יליף טעמא: **גמ'** אמר רבי יוחנן אומר היה כו'. גמרא גמיר לה רבי יוחנן: מאי כאילו. הא ודאי בצפון נשחט: אלא מעתה כו'. קס"ד דרבי זירא דממתני' גמיר לה רבי יוחנן להא יד] דאומר היה רבי יוסי: מודה רבי יוסי ברבי יהודה. אע"פ שמכשיר טו] למזבח מחציו לצפון מודה הוא שאם שחטו כנגד אותו מקום מתחתיהם בקרקע טז] פסולות ולקמיה מפרש היאך יכול לשחוט תחת המזבח: א"ל. רב אסי הכי אמר ר' יוחנן כו' כלומר אומר היה רבי יוסי דקאמר ר' יוחנן לעיל לאו ממתני' גמר אלא הכי גמר לה מרבותיו ומתניתין לאו במקום מזבח פליגי דנימא רבי יוסי [א] כולה בצפון ור' יוסי בר' יהודה נימא חציו צפון אלא יז] מדרשא דקרא: ה"ג כולו לעולה וכולו לשלמים. כולו ראוי לשחיטת עולה דקדושת צפון עליו מגזירת הכתוב וכולו ראוי לשלמים שהשלמים כשירין אף בצפון מק"ו בפירקין דלעיל (דף נה.): דדחיק לה מקום. שמקומן קטן ודחוק שאין כשר לה אלא צפון ופעמים שהעולות מרובות וצר להם המקום יח] והכשיר להן הכתוב ראש המזבח: מאי כנגדן בקרקע. הא ליכא לפרושי כנגדן ברצפה למזרח המזבח ובמערבו יט] דאם כן לא הוה קשיא כ] מילתא לרב אסי לעיל דמהכא ליכא למילף דלית ליה לרבי יוסי ברבי יהודה חצי המזבח עומד בצפון כא] דאפילו הוא צפון נמי פסיל ליה לרבי יוסי [ברבי יהודה] ואפילו סמוך לכותל העזרה צפוני פוסל אם משוך מכנגד זוית המזבח צפונה למזרח או למערב דדייקינן על ירך כדאמר בפ"ב (לעיל כו.) איזהו צפון מקיר מזבח צפוני עד כותל עזרה צפונית כנגד המזבח כולו אבל משוך מכנגד המזבח לא הלכך על כרחך האי כנגדו דילפינן מינה דמקום המזבח לאו צפון הוא כב] תחתיו קאמר ומאי היא: אי נימא. אם שחטן על כניסת הסובב והיסוד האי לאו כנגדן הוא אלא מזבח ממש ומכשר בה רבי יוסי בר' יהודה כדקתני מחצי המזבח לצפון כג]: כיפין. אולמים ארקמלו"ש: דבצריה בצורי. אם כד] נמלך לקצר את המזבח ונשאר מחצה של צפון פנוי ושחט שם פסולות ואע"ג דירך הוא פסיל ליה אלמא סבירא ליה בדרום עזרה הוא דאי לא אמאי פסיל ליה: אפשר איתא להא דר' יוחנן. דאמר אומר היה רבי יוסי כוליה מזבח בצפון קאי ולא תנינא לה שום רמז במשנה בששה סדרים: דק ואשכח. במסכת תמיד: בירדו משם. מדיר העצים: עצי תאנה יפין. בשל תאנה היו רגילין וטעם אגדה הוא שבו היתה תקנה לאדם הראשון כה] ויעשו להם חגורות: מערכה שניה של קטרת. אצל מערכה גדולה היו מסדרין מערכה קטנה ליטול ממנה גחלים להכנים על מזבח הפנימי שלשה קבין לכל בקר וערב להקטיר עליהם כו] קטרת ובמסכת יומא בפרק טרף בקלפי (דף מה:) בסופיה ילפינן מקרא דעל מזבח החיצון צריך להיות מערכה לכך: כנגד כז] מערבית דרומית. של מזבח ומשוך לצד צפון להרחיקו מן הקרן ד' אמות וטעם מפרש לקמיה מאי שנא הקרן זה ומ"מ מושכו הימנה ולצפון ד' אמות: משוך מן הקרן כלפי צפון ארבע אמות גרס. וכן מצאתי בסדר המשנה כח] במשנת תמיד: באומד חמש סאין גחלים. לפי אומד ה' סאין גחלים היו נותנין שם עצים כך כט] שיעורו לחתות בתוכו בראש המזבח [ב] שהוא חלק מחתה של סאה לר' יוסי דאמר בסדר יומא (דף מג:) בכל יום חותה בשל סאה ומערה בתוך ג' קבין: בשבת היו מסדרין שם לפי אומד ח' סאין. לפי שצריך להקטיר הבזיכין על מזבח החיצון שעל מזבח הפנימי אין הקטר אלא ל] של קטרת שחרית וערבית כדכתיב לא תעלו עליו קטרת זרה וגו' (שמות ל): ומאי סימנא. מהו [ג] הסימן לא] שהוקבע להם למערכה שניה ולהקטרת הבזיכין קרן מערבית דרומית ומשוך ארבע אמות מן הקרן ולצפון:

א) נ"א מן ונראה לי עד סה"ד שייך לסוף דף סג ע"ב ב) נ"א אכתי טוב אמינא לצד דרום כו' הקישא לחטאת ליסוד מוכח דהוי מערב כיון דכתיב כו' וע' בתוס' מנחות סא ע"ב

תוספות

קדשי קדשים ששחטן בראש המזבח. מדאורייתא שוחט לכתחלה כדדרשינן לב] מוזבחת עליו ושמא הא דנקט דיעבד מדרבנן שלא תרבין גללים: **כולן** לשלמים. ואע"ג דקסבר ליה כולו מזבח בצפון קאי לג] אפילו הכי איצטריך לן לעיל קרא להכשיר לצפון לשלמים דמהכא לא נפקא דעל לד] המזבח גזירת הכתוב הוא כי היכי דמכשר רבי יוסי ברבי יהודה מחציו ולצפון לעולה אע"ג דכנגדן בקרקע פסולות דדרום הוא אלא דעל המזבח גזירת הכתוב: **משוך** מן הקרן כלפי צפון ארבע אמות. בכולה שמעתא משמע דגחלים דיום הכפורים צריך ליקח כנגד הפתח וצריך לומר דהיינו לכתחילה אבל דיעבד כשר אפילו דהאי גיסא ודהאי גיסא כדאמר בפרק טרף בקלפי (יומא מה: מו. ע"ש ד"ה אבל) ואיצטריך מעל המזבח ואיצטריך מלפני ה' לה] וא"ת מהיכא תיתי עיכובא דאיצטריך קרא לאכשורי בדיעבד אין זה בדברים הנעשים בבגדי [ד] לבן לא בפנים ולא בחוץ ובין לרבי יהודה ובין לרבי נחמיה *ליכא עיכובא וי"ל דאיצטריך משום דלורך פנים כפנים דמי לו] כקטורת שחפנה קודם שחיטת הפר שלא עשה ולא כלום [ה] דחוקה כתיב בה (ויקרא טז) דלורך פנים כפנים דמי וא"ת הכא משמע דלא מקרי לפני ה' אלא במערב וכן גבי נר מערבי בפ' שתי הלחם (מנחות דף נח:) ואילו בסוף כל המנחות [באות מלה] (שם סא.) אמרינן לפני ה' במזרח גבי תנופת לוג שמן של מצורע ואשמו וכן גבי שחיטה כתיב לפני ה' ושריא בכל מקום בעזרה וי"ל דשחיטה ותנופת לוג אשם כתיב לפני ה' למעוטי בחוץ דתנופת אשם מחיים אבל גבי גחלים כתיב (ויקרא טז) מעל המזבח ונרות היו בהיכל אם כן לפני ה' למה לי לז] לאו משום דבעינן במערב ומיהו קשה דבההוא שמעתא דכל המנחות באות מלה (גם זה שם) פריך עלה והאמרת במערב לפני ה' פי' גבי הגשת מנחה בפירקין ובריש הקומץ רבה (מנחות דף יט:) ומשני הני מילי מנחות דאיקרי חטאת וחטאת טעונה יסוד וקרן דרומית מזרחית לא היה לה יסוד אבל הכא לפני ה' קרינא ביה משמע דאי לא בעיא יסוד הוה מכשרנא קרן דרומית מזרחית להגשה ואע"ג דכתיב לפני [ו] ה' א) ונראה לי ברו"ך דאי לא כתיב לפני ה' בהגשת מנחה אע"ג דכתיב בה אל פני המזבח דהיינו דרום וגם איתקש לחטאת העוף ליסוד ב) אכתי לח] אמינא לצד דרום באמה של יסוד רחוק מקרן מערבי אבל קשה לט] בלא היקשא לחטאת מ] בעינן ליסוד מערב כיון דכתיב לפני ה' נגלות מערב כמו גבי גחלי יום הכיפורים וגם כתיב פני המזבח דמשמע דרום וכן איתא לקמן בפירקין (דף סג:). ברו"ך:
רבי

עין משפט נר מצוה

א א מיי' פ"ג מהלכות פסה"מ הלכה ה:

ב ב מיי' פ"ב מהלכות בית הבחירה הל' יג ופ"ב שם הלכה טז:

ג ג מיי' פ"ב מהלכות תמידין ומוספין הלכה ח:

מסורת הש"ס

א) לעיל ס. [לקמן סג:] ב) [לקמן סא:] ג) תמיד כט. ד) [יומא ס.]

גליון הש"ס

תוס' ד"ה כולו לשלמים כו' אצטריך לן לעיל. דף נה ע"א:

שיטה מקובצת

א] וליכא. ואם תאמר ואימא אה"נ דבפרק (קבלה) [כ' דף כו.] מוכח דבעינן על ירך לעכב וי"ל דהתם היינו לענין אויר דתלה ושחט לגבי הכי הוי דוקא על ירך אבל כאן לאו באויר שחיט ועי"ל דה"ק קמ"ל דעל ירך מיקרי: ב] אלא מעתה לר"י בר יהודה ה"נ. (פי' משמע) דחציו בצפון [כו'] והא את כו'. וא"ת ותקשי דא"כ הל"ל כאילו בצפון לר"י [בר"י] כמו לת"ק משום מהו דתימא בעינן על ירך וליכא קמ"ל וי"ל דאה"נ אלא סמיך אהא דקאמר ת"ק כבר כאלו ולפיכך לא חש ר"י [בר"י] למימר כאלו ועוד נראה למהר"ם דדוקא לת"ק דמכשיר בכוליה מזבח אפילו לצד דרום אפילו לצד הכבש שנקרא פני המזבח שייך למתני כאלו משום דאין זה על ירך על אותו צד שבדרום ומ"מ מכשרינן משום דצפון הוא ולפיכך שייך למימר כאלו אבל לר"י בר"י דאמר מחציו ולצפון כצפון הא ודאי דבאותו חצי נקרא ירך כדמוכח לקמן דלצד הכבש הוי פני המזבח ולאידך צד מיקרי ירך: ג] נמי חציו ואות ד' נמחק: ד] והא את הוא דאמרת כו'. וא"ת דלמא משום הכי פסיל כנגד צפון משום דאזיל לטעמיה דאמר בפ' קבלה איזה צפון מקיר המזבח צפוני ועד כותל העזרה צפוני וכנגד כל המזבח כולו אלמא דאפילו סמוך לכותל העזרה צפוני פסול אם משוך מכנגד זוית המזבח למזרח או למערב ולכך פסול מכנגד המזבח ברצפה במזרחו או במערבו דהיינו כנגד חצי המזבח דמצד צפון וי"ל דהא דקאמר כנגדן בקרקע פסולה אינו רוצה לומר על הרצפה אלא כנגדן מתחתיהן כדמפרש בסמוך: ה] שחטן כנגדו בקרקע פסולים א"ל הכי אמר ר' יוחנן שניהם מקרא אחד דרשו. וא"ת כיון שאמת הוא דבצפון קאי א"כ למה לי וזבחת עליו לומר כולו לעולה וי"ל דמשום דמ"מ ס"ד למיפסליה משום דאין זה על ירך: ו] ורבי יוסי בר יהודה חלקיהו חציו כו'. פי' אע"ג דבדרום קאי כוליה מ"מ גזירת הכתוב היא אבל תימה למה לי קרא לחציו לשלמים דאפילו יהיה דרום מה בכך הרי דרום כשר לשלמים וי"ל דכיון דרבייה לעולה הו"א לעולה דוקא ולא לשלמים ולכך הוצרך להכשיר לשלמים: ז] סבר חלקיהו חציו: ח] לה מקום אבל כו' דלא דחיק להו מקום: ט] שחטן כנגדו בקרקע פסולים א"ל: י] אילימא אמה יסוד ואמה כו'. פ"ה דליכא לאוקמי כנגדן בקרקע כו' אלא ע"כ כנגדן מתחתיו ובמאי אי באמה יסוד כו' האי גופיה דמזבח הוא ותימה דמשמע דאי לאו גופיה דמזבח ניחא ומי ניחא אכתי היכי מוכח דקסבר דלאו בצפון קאי מדפסיל באמה יסוד ואמה סובב הא כי נמי בצפון קאי מ"מ ראוי לפסול באמת יסוד משום דאין זה על ירך המזבח כיון דלא חשיב כגוף המזבח דדוקא לעיל בראש המזבח בחציו לצפון הוי ממש על ירך המזבח וי"ל דלמאי דפי' לעיל ניחא דר"י בר"י סמוך אכאלו דקאמר ת"ק וא"כ מעל ירך לא ממעט בי אם אויר כדפי' לעיל אבל גבי המזבח וכן מחילות חשיב שפיר על ירך כיון שאינו באויר: יא] דמזבח הוא ועוד מאי בקרקע ותיבת כנגדן נרשם עליו קו: יב] מחובר באדמה שלא: יג] דבצרי בצורי: יד] להא *אמר אומר היה: טו] שמכשיר בראש המזבח מחציו: טז] פסולים ולקמיה: יז] אלא בדרשא דקרא: יח] לפיכך הכשיר להן: יט] ובמערבו וטעמא משום דלא מכשיר צפון אלא מכותל המזבח צפונה עד כותל העזרה צפוני כנגד המזבח לבד כדאיתא לעיל פ' שני: כ] תיבת מילתא נמחק: כא] דאפילו היה כולו בצפון פסיל ליה רבי יוסי ברבי יהודה דאפילו סמוך לכותל העזרה הצפוני פוסל אם משך קמעא מכנגד זוית המזבח למזרח של מזבח. או כו' ועל תיבת צפונה נרשם קו למעלה: כב] הוא בקרקע תחתיו: כג] לצפון כצפון הס"ד: כד] נמלכו לקצר את המזבח כדאמר לקמן ונשאר מחציו של צפון פנוי כו' פסיל ליה כוליה בדרום אלמא: כה] הראשון שנאמר ויעשו: כו] עליהם הקטרת ובמסכת כו' צריך לעשות המערכה לכך: כז] כנגד קרן מערבית דרומית של מזבח החיצון משוך לצד צפון כו' מאי שנא האי קרן ותיבת זה ל"ש: כח] המשנה במס' תמיד ותיבת במשנת נמחק: כט] כך שיעור: ל] אלא לקטורת ותי' של נמחק: לא] הסימן הזה שהוקבע: לב] כדדרשינן בגמרא מוזבחת: לג] קאי וכשרה לשלמים אפילו: לד] דעל ראש המזבח: לה] וא"ת מהיכא כו' דאיצטריך התם קרא לאכשורי אין זה מדברים הנעשים: לו] דמי. פ"א דהוא בשביל הקטורת: לז] לי אי לאו: לח] אכתי אמינא אות ע' ל"ש: לט] בלא. גליון פי' למה לי היקשא דהמצאת לומר דמנחה טעונה יסוד תיפוק לי יסוד מלפני ה' דהוי בקרן מערבית דרומית ששם היה יסוד: מ] להמצאת ליסוד מערב ידענא כיון:

הגהות צ"ק [א] כולו: [ב] נ"ל שהיה לוקח: [ג] סימנא שהוקבע כו': [ד] לבן בפנים וליכא עיכובא לר' יהודה כנ"ל כו': [ה] אע"ג דלא כתיב בה חוקה דלורך פנים כו': [ו] ה' א"נ לפני ה' למה לי ונראה:

תורה אור

רבי יוסי אומר זה סימן א] כל הניטל בפנים לינתן בחוץ אינו נותן אלא בסמוך שאין לפנים *וכל הניטל בחוץ לינתן לפנים אינו ניטל אלא בסמוך שאין לפנים כל הניטל בפנים לינתן בחוץ מאי ניהו אילימא שירים בהדיא כתיב בהו °אל יסוד מזבח העולה אשר פתח אהל מועד ותו כל הניטל בחוץ לינתן בפנים מאי ניהו אילימא גחלים של יום הכיפורים בהדיא כתיב בהו °ולקח מלא המחתה גחלי אש ב] וגו' אלא כל הניטל בפנים לינתן בחוץ שני בזיכי לבונה של לחם הפנים דגמרי משירים הניטל בחוץ לינתן בפנים גחלים דכל יומא ויומא דגמרן מגחלים של יום הכפורים ומאי קסבר אי קסבר כוליה מזבח בדרום קאי עשרים ושבע בעי למיתי ואי נמי קסבר *קדושת היכל ואולם חדא היא עשרים ותרתי בעי ג] מיתי ואי קסבר חציו בצפון וחציו בדרום חד סרי בעי למיתי ד] ואלא קסבר קדושת היכל ואולם חדא ה] מילתא היא שית בעי למיתי אלא לאו משום דקסבר כוליה מזבח בצפון קאי והני ארבע אמות אמה יסוד ואמה סובב ואמה מקום קרנות ואמה מקום רגלי הכהנים דכי ו] מסגו לקמיה טפי תו ליכא פתח אמר רב אדא בר אהבה הא מני רבי יהודה היא *דתניא ר"י אומר מזבח ממוצע ועומד באמצע העזרה ז] ושלשים ושתים אמות היו לו עשר אמות כנגד פתחו של היכל ח] אחת עשרה אמה מיכן ואחת עשרה אמה מיכן נמצא מזבח מכוון כנגד היכל ט] סוף סוף לרבי יהודה חד סרי בעי למיתי ואי קסבר י] קדושת היכל ואולם חדא יא] מילתא היא שית בעי למיתי מי סברת הני ארבע אמות בהדי אמה יסוד ואמה סובב ארבע אמות בר מאמה יסוד ואמה סובב ונוקמה כרבי יוסי ובממוצע משום דרבי יהודה שמענא ליה ממוצע בהדיא ורב שרביא אמר הא מני רבי יוסי הגלילי היא דתניא רבי יוסי הגלילי אומר מתוך שנאמר °ונתת את הכיור בין אהל מועד (א) וגומר יב] °ואת מזבח

ויקרא ד | שם | שם | שמות מ | שם

רבי יוסי היא. וא"ת מי מצית מוקמת לה כר"י הא תנן בסוף מסכת תמיד (דף לג.) עירן לתוך של זהב ונתפזר ממנה קב גחלים ולרבי יוסי היה מתפזר יותר כדתנן פרק טרף בקלפי (יומא דף מג:) רבי יוסי אומר בכל יום היה חותה בשל סאה ומערה לשל שלשת קבין וי"ל נהי דהא דלא כרבי יוסי הך כרבי יוסי אתיא שפיר ולא דמי להא דדייקינן בפ"ק דיומא (דף מז:) ואי ס"ד מדות רבי יהודה היא כו': קדושת היכל ואולם חדא היא. וש"ס מסופק בכל מקום לעיל ספ"ק (דף יז.) וביומא פ' טרף בקלפי (דף מד:) ובריש עירובין (דף ג.): הא מני ר' יוסי הגלילי היא. הוה מצי למימר רבי אלעזר היא דאמר לקמן בפירקין (דף סא:) דקסבר כוליה מזבח בצפון קאי וא"ת דמשמע הכא דמאן דלית ליה כוליה מזבח בצפון קאי הוי כיור בין אהל מועד ובין המזבח ובתוספתא פרק קמא דכלים נכנסים בין האולם ולמזבח שלא רחוץ ידים ורגלים וחכמים אומרים אין נכנסין °ושמא סבר לה כרבי מאיר דאמר נכנסין:

פנוי

רבי יוסי היא לדתניא רבי יוסי אומר זה סימן. בידך כל הניטל מבפנים לינתן בחוץ ולקמיה מפרש מאי ניהו: אינו נותן אלא בסמוך שאין לפנים. אינו ניתן בחוץ על המזבח החיצון אלא בסמוך לצד פנים שאין במזבח החיצון מקום הסמוך לפנים יותר ממנו: וכל הניטל מעל מזבח החיצון ליתן בפנים אינו ניטל אלא ממקום שהוא סמוך לפנים. שאין מקום בכל מזבח החיצון סמוך ממנו: כל הניטל בפנים לינתן בחוץ מאי ניהו אי נימא שירי הדם. דחטאות הפנימיות ל"ל לרבי יוסי לשוייה בהו כללא: הא בהדיא כתיב בהו. דניתנין ביסוד שכנגד הפתח דכתיב ישפך אל יסוד מזבח העולה אשר פתח: ותו כל הניטל בחוץ לינתן בפנים מאי ניהו אי נימא גחלים של יום הכיפורים. שמכניסין במחתה לפני ולפנים להקטיר בהן מלא חפניו קטרת סמים דקה דאף הם ניטלין ממזבח החיצון כדכתיב מעל המזבח מלפני ה' מצד המערב ודרשינן ביומא (דף מה:) איזהו מזבח שמקצתו לפני ה' ואין כולו לפני ה' זהו מזבח החיצון ויהיב לו בה רבי יוסי כללא וסימנא דאין ניטל אלא ממקום שאין סמוך הימנו יג] ולפנים: בהדיא כתיב בהו. מלפני ה' דהיינו לצד פנים: אלא כל הניטל בפנים לינתן בחוץ שני בזיכי לבונה. הניטלין בשבת מן השלחן לינתן על מזבח החיצון ואשמעינן ר' יוסי שניתנין כנגד הפתח דגמרי משירים הפנימיים: והניטל בחוץ לינתן בפנים גחלים דכל יד] יום. הניטלין ממערכה שניה של קטורת לינתן על מזבח הפנימי ואשמעינן רבי יוסי דניטלין מכנגד הפתח דגמרי מגחלים של יוה"כ שקבע להן טו] כנגד הפתח לנטילתן והיינו סימנא דתנא תנא במסכת תמיד למערכה שניה טז] שהיא לנטילת גחלים ולהקטרת בזיכין שתהא בקרן דרומית מערבית ומשוכה לצפון ארבע אמות שתהא מכוונת כנגד הפתח ומיכה פשטינן יז] דלר' יוסי כוליה מזבח בצפון קאי: ומאי קסבר. יח] שקבע למשיכת המערכה מן הקרן ד' אמות: אי קסבר כוליה מזבח בדרום עזרה קאי. ומשיכת ד' יט] האמות לקרבה כנגד הפתח הוא בא: כ"ז אמות בעי למיתי. כ] ולמשוך מקרן מערבית דרומית ולצפון וחוץ לאותן כ"ז אמות סידור המערכה שהרי הפתח באמצע העזרה היה ועשרה אמות רוחבו כא] וחמש בצפון וה' בדרום וכיון שהמזבח בדרום נמצא שאין ממנו לפני הפתח אלא ה' אמות (ב) לפוניות שלו שכלה כנגד אמצע הפתח כשאתרו לו מל"ב [אמות] שלו כ"ז ואת כולן אתה צריך למשוך המערכה מכנגד כב] קרן יסוד המזבח הדרומי ולצפון קודם שהגיע לפתח: וא"נ קסבר קדושת היכל ואולם חדא היא. כג] ומשהגיע כנגד פתח האולם קרינן לפני ה' ופתח האולם עודף לכל רוח על פתח ההיכל ה' אמות לכל צד שהיה רחבו כ' אמות כדתנן במסכת מדות (דף לו.) כ"ב בעי מייתי: ואי נמי קסבר חציו של מזבח בצפון וחציו בדרום. ובא למושכה עד כנגד כד] ההיכל: חד סרי בעי מייתי. שהרי ט"ז אמותיו בדרום נמצאו מהן י"א [אמות] כה] מזוית דרומית של פתח ולדרום: ואי נמי קדושת היכל ואולם חדא היא שית מיהא בעי למיתי. אלא על כרחך לא משכחת לה שתהא משיכת ד' אמות הללו לקרב כנגד הפתח אלא נתן לך מדה כו] בשיעור שלא תמשכנה יותר מכאן שכל מה שאתה יכול לקרבה אצל קרן דרומית הוי מקרבה ובכך אתה מכוונה כנגד הפתח וד' אמות הללו ע"כ הוא מושכה לצפון לפי שאין לו מקום לסדר עליהן כז] וקסבר כוליה בצפון קאי ואין ממנו לפני הפתח אלא חמשה (ג) דרומיות ומהן אמה יסוד ואמה סובב ואמה מקום הקרן ואמה הילוך לכהנים המסדרין את המערכה ומקיפין בין קרן למערכה ואין לו מקום לסדר ולימדך שיסדר הולה להן מיד כדי שתהא אמה מן המערכה כנגד הפתח דכי מסגי לצפון טפי תו ליכא פתח: אמר רב אדא בר אהבה. לעולם לא תידוק מינה לרבי יוסי כח] בצפון קאי אלא (אימא) רבי יהודה היא דאמר חציו בצפון וחציו בדרום עשר אמות אמצעיות שלו היו כנגד פתחו של היכל וי"א אמות כט] מזוית היכל ולצפון וכנגדן לדרום נמצא מכוון כנגד רוחב חללו של היכל *ועובי כתליו שההיכל חללו כ' אמה ועובי ל] של כותל ו' אמות והכי תנן לה במסכת מדות (דף לז.): סוף סוף לא]. כדאקשינן לעיל: בר מאמה יסוד ואמה סובב. ולמטה ברחש המזבח קחשיב לב] להן ונמצא לפני הפתח שהרי נמשך ו' אמות ולא הוזכרו ד' אמות אלו אלא לקרבן לפתח דבציר מהכי לאו כנגד הפתח הוא: ונוקמה כר' יוסי לג] *באמצע. למה לך למשקלה מרבי יוסי דשמעת ליה דאמר אין ניתנין אלא בסמוך שאין לפנים מכדי לד] *להיסתר דוקיא דרבי זירא קא אתית דבעי למידק לה] מיניה לרבי יוסי דכוליה מזבח בצפון קאי אימא הכי לעולם קסבר חציו בדרום וחציו בצפון ומי סברת בהדי אמה יסוד כו': ומשני לרבי יהודה שמעינן לה ממוצע בהדיא. ואי משום דאיירי רבי יוסי בניטלין בפנים וניתנין בחוץ וניטלין בחוץ וניתנין בפנים הא כולי עלמא אית להו: ורב שרביא אמר. ד' אמות דקתני בהדי אמה יסוד ואמה סובב קאמר ודוק מינה כדקאמרת לו] דמזבח בצפון קאי ומיהו לרבי יוחנן לא תסייעיה מינה דנימא רבי יוסי בן חלפתא היא משום דשמעינן ליה דאיירי בניטלין וניתנין דההוא לכולי עלמא אית להו והא דתמיד כרבי יוסי הגלילי מוקמינן לז] דשמעינן ליה דאמר מזבח בצפון קאי אבל לרבי יוסי סתמא דהוא רבי יוסי בן חלפתא דלא שמעת ליה דאמר לא תוקמה דדלמא כרבי יהודה ס"ל: מתוך שנאמר. בכיור בין אהל מועד ובין המזבח וכתוב אחד אומר לח] מזבח

כל נ"ק | [לעיל יח. וש"נ] | יומא מה. | נ"ק | נ"ק מ"ז | כ"א ועבי של כל כותל נ"ק | ובממוצע נ"ק | לסתור נ"ק

הגהות הב"ח

(א) גמ' את הכיור בין אהל מועד וגו' וכתוב אחד אומר ואת מזבח העולה: (ב) רש"י ד"ה כ"ז אמות וכו' נמצא שאין ממנו לפני הפתח אלא ה' אמות דרומיות שלו כצ"ל ועל תיבת ממנו נ"ב ר"ל ממזבח ועל תיבת שלו נ"ב ר"ל של מזבח: (ג) ד"ה וא"נ וכו' חמשה דרומיות נ"ב ר"ל של מזבח:

גליון הש"ס

תום' ד"ה הא וכו' ושמא ס"ל כר"מ כו'. ק"ל הא ר' יוסי ס"ל במתנתין דכוליה מזבח בצפון ואפ"ה ס"ל במתני' ספ"א דכלים דאין נכנסין שלא רחוץ בין אולם ולמזבח וצ"ע:

שיטה מקובצת

א] סימן בידך כל הניטל כו' אינו ניתן אלא: ב] מעל המזבח מלפני ה' ותיבת וגו' נמחק: ג] בעי למיתי ואי: ד] למיתי וא"נ קסבר תיבת ואלא נמחק: ה] תיבת מילתא נמחק: ו] דכי מסגי לקמיה: ז] העזרה עשר ועל תיבות ושלשים ושתים אמות היו לו נרשם קו: ח] היכל ואחת: ט] היכל וכתליו סוף: י] קסבר נמי קדושת: יא] תיבת מילתא נמחק: יב] וגו' וכתי' א] את אות ו' נמחק: יג] הימנו לפנים הס"ד: יד] דכל יומא ויומא הניטלין: טו] להן מקום כנגד: טז] למערכה שניה להקטרת בזיכין והשאר נמחק: יז] פשטינן לר' יוסי דכוליה מזבח: יח] קסבר שהצריך משיכת המערכה מן הקרן ד' אמות לצפון הס"ד: יט] ד' האמות נרשם נקודה על ה' מלמעלה: כ] למיתי ולהמשיך מקרן: כא] רוחבו חמש בצפון וחמש בדרום וכיון שכל המזבח בדרום נמצא שאין ממנו כנגד הפתח אלא ה' אמות צפוניות שלו שהרי כלה הוא כנגד כו': כב] מכנגד זוית יסוד ותיבת קרן נמחק: כג] היא ומשהגיע כנגד פתח האולם כו' עודף על רוחב פתח ההיכל ה' אמות לכל צד שהרי רחבו כ' אמות אות ת' ותיבת לכל נמחק: כד] כנגד פתח ההיכל: כה] ממזוות דרומית: כו] מידה לשיעור: כז] עליהן. דקסבר כוליה מזבח בצפ | קאי ואין ממנו כנגד הפתח אלא חמשה אמות דרומית ומהן אמה כו' מקום הקרנות ואמה למקום הילוך רגלי כהנים המסדרין את כו' בין הקרן למערכה ואין לו שום מקום כנגד הפתח אלא אמה אחת ולימדך שעל אותה אמה יתחיל המערכה שהיא משוכה מן הקרן ארבע אמות ולא יתרחק מן הקרן יותר דכי מסגי כו' ומתיבת שיסדר כו' עד תיבת הפתח נמחק: כח] יוסי דמזבח בצפון קאי אלא ר"י ותיבת אימא נמחק: כט] אמות ממזוות: ל] של כל כותל: לא] סוף כו' כדאקשי: לב] להו אבל מן היסוד שש אמות הוא נמשך ותיבו' ונמצא לפני הפתח שהרי נמחק: לג] יוסי בממוצע. כלומר למה לך (למתוקמא)[לאוקמי'] דלא כר' יוסי דשמענא ליה דאמר כל הניטל בפנים כו' כיון דלא באתה [רק] לדחות סייעתא דר"י מהכא דליכא למידק לר' יוסי דכוליה מזבח בצפון קאי א"כ כי אוקמת כר"י ובממוצע תוכל לומר דקסבר חציו בצפון וחציו בדרום ומשני משום דר' יהודה כו' ואע"ג דר' יוסי איירי בניטלים כו' נימא דלכ"ע אית להו האי סברא דרבי יוסי דר' יוסי אמרה אליבא דכ"ע: ורב שרביא אמר כו' כלומר הא ודאי דדייקינן מיניה דכוליה מזבח בצפון קאי ור' יוסי דאיירי בניטלים בפנים אינו שונה אותה ברייתא ולא הוי סייעתא לר' יוחנן אלא לר' יוסי הגלילי היא דסבר דכל הניטלים דכ"ע אית להו. נוסחאת רש"י של מהר"פ: לד] מכדי לאפוקי מדוקיא דר' זירא: לה] מינה לר': לו] כדקאמרת דכוליה מזבח: לז] מוקמינן ליה דשמעינן: לח] אומר את:

א) ר"ל קרא דונתת את מזבח העולה לפני פתח משכן אהל מועד (שמות מ' פסוק ו') וברש"י העתיק קרא דפסוק כ"ט שם.

token?[8]—This agrees with R. Jose. For it was taught: [58*b*] R. Jose said: This is the token: whatever is taken [from] within to be placed without,[9] is placed as near as possible [to the inner altar]; and whatever is taken from without to be placed within, is taken from as near as possible [to the inner altar]. 'Whatever is taken [from] within to be placed without': What is it? If we say, the residue [of the blood], surely it is distinctly written thereof, [*And all the remaining blood of the bullock shall he pour out*] *at the base of the altar of burnt-offering, which is at the door of the tent of meeting*?[10] Further, as to 'whatever is taken without to be placed within', what is it? If we say, the coals of the Day of Atonement, surely it is explicitly written thereof, *And he shall take a censer full of coals of fire from off the altar before the Lord*?[11] Rather, 'whatever is taken within to be placed without' means the two censers of the frankincense for the
a shewbread,[1] which we infer from the residue [of the blood];[2] and 'Whatever is taken without to be placed within' is the coals of every day,[3] which are inferred from the coals of the Day of Atonement. Now, what does he hold?[4] If he holds [that] the whole altar is in the south, he would have to carry it twenty-seven [cubits from the horn]?[5] And even if he holds that the sanctity of the *hekal* and that of the *ulam* are one,[6] yet he would have to carry it down twenty-two cubits?[7] And if he holds that it was half in the north and half in the south, he would have to bring it down eleven cubits?[8] And even if he holds that the sanctity of the *hekal* and that of the *ulam* are one, he would have to bring it down six cubits?[9] Hence it must surely be that he holds that the whole altar was in the north, and these four cubits are as follows: one cubit for the base, one for the terrace, one for the horns, and one for the feet of the priests; for should one go further than this, there would no more be the door.[10] Said R. Adda b. Ahabah:[11] This is in accordance with R. Judah. For it was taught, R. Judah said: The altar stood in the middle of the Temple court.[12] Now, it was thirty-two cubits [square], [of which] ten cubits faced the door of the *hekal*, and [it extended] eleven cubits on either side [thereof]. Thus the altar was exactly opposite the *hekal*. Yet even so, according to R. Judah he would have to bring it down eleven cubits? And even if he held that the sanctity of the *hekal* and that of the *ulam* are one, he would still have to bring it down six cubits?—Do you think that these four cubits include the cubit of the base and the cubit of the terrace? [No:] they are exclusive of the cubit of the base and the cubit of the terrace. Now, let us make this agree with R. Jose, and
b [assume] that [he too holds that] it stood in the centre?[1]—Because we know definitely that R. Judah holds that it stood in the middle.[2]

R. Sherabia said: This is in accordance with R. Jose the Galilean. For it was taught: R. Jose the Galilean said: Since it says, *And thou shalt set the laver between the tent of meeting and the altar*,[3] while another

(8) By which sign did the Sages rule that this second pile was in that particular spot? (9) From the inner altar on to the outer altar. (10) Lev. IV, 7. That *is* the nearest point to the inner altar. Why then must R. Jose give a general rule for this, when it is explicitly stated? (11) Ibid. XVI, 12. '*Before the Lord*' implies near the inner sanctum.

a (1) They were taken on the Sabbath from the Table, which was within. (2) They must be placed (presented) on the side facing the door, which is the nearest point. (3) Which are taken from the second pile and placed on the inner altar. R. Jose thus teaches that they are taken from the side facing the door. (4) When he states that this second pile is arranged four cubits from the horn northwards. (5) The width of the door was ten cubits, five of which were in the north and five in the south, while the altar was thirty-two square. Now, deducting the five cubits which the door passed into the north, the nearest point to the door would thus be twenty-seven cubits from the opposite horn. (6) *Supra* 14*a*. (7) For then, as soon as he reaches a point opposite the door of the *ulam* he is '*before the Lord*'. As the door of the *ulam* was five cubits wider than that of the *hekal* on both sides (i.e., ten wider in all), five cubits can be deducted from the preceding calculation. (8) For then there will be sixteen cubits in the south. The figure eleven is arrived at by deducting the five of the door from these sixteen. (9) Deducting a further five cubits (cf. n. 5.) from the eleven. (10) I.e., it would carry it beyond the line of the door. Thus we have a Mishnah in support of R. Joḥanan's statement regarding R. Jose. (11) To refute this proof. (12) I.e., half in the north and half in the south.

b (1) Why insist that the author is R. Judah? (2) Whilst we do not know R. Jose's opinion. (3) Ex. XL, 7.

verse states, [*And thou shalt set*] [59a] *the altar of burnt-offering* [*before the door of the tabernacle of the tent of meeting*],[4] [it follows that] the altar was at the door of the tent of meeting, while the laver was not at the door of the tent of meeting. Where then was it [the laver] placed? Between the *ulam* and the altar, slightly toward the south. Now what does he hold? If he holds that the whole altar stood in the south, let it be placed southward from the wall of the *hekal*, [for that would be] between the *ulam* and the altar? And even if he holds that the sanctity of the *ulam* and that of the *hekal* are one, let it be placed southward from the wall of the *ulam*, [for that would still be as] between the *ulam* and the altar? Or if he holds that half was in the north and half in the south, let it be placed southward from the wall of the *hekal*, between the *ulam* and the altar? And even if he holds that the sanctity of the *ulam* and that of the *hekal* are one, let it be placed southward from the wall of the *ulam*, this being between the *ulam* and the altar? Hence it must surely be that he[5] holds that the whole altar stood in the north. Then let it be placed between the altar and the *hekal* northward?—He holds that the sanctity of the *hekal* and *ulam* is identical.[6] Then let it be placed northward from the wall of the *ulam*, when it would be between the *ulam* and the altar?—Scripture saith, *northward*, which means that a the north must be free from vessels.[1]

Which Tanna disagrees with R. Jose the Galilean?[2]—R. Eleazar b. Jacob. For it was taught: R. Eleazar b. Jacob said: '*Northward*' [intimates] that the north must be free from everything, even from the altar.

Rab said, If the altar was damaged, all sacrifices slaughtered there are unfit. We have a text to this effect, but have forgotten it. When R. Kahana went up,[3] he found R. Simeon b. Rabbi teaching in R. Ishmael b. R. Jose's name: How do we know that all the sacrifices slaughtered at a damaged altar are unfit? Because it is said, *And thou shalt sacrifice thereon thy burnt-offerings and thy peace-offerings*:[4] now, do you then sacrifice *on* it?[5] Rather, [it means:] when it is whole, and not when it is defective. Said he: That is the text which eluded Rab. But R. Joḥanan maintained: In both cases they are unfit.[6] Wherein do they disagree?—Rab holds: Live animals cannot be [permanently] rejected; while R. Joḥanan holds: Live animals can be [permanently] rejected.[7]

An objection is raised. All the sacred animals which were before the altar was built,[8] and then the altar was built, are unfit.[9] [Now before] it was built, they were rejected *ab initio?*[10]—[Say] rather: before it was razed.[11] '[Before] it was razed?' But they [the animals] would be too old![12] Rather [it means] [the animals which were consecrated] before the altar was damaged, and then the altar was b damaged, are unfit![1]—Now, did you not emend it? Then read, which were *slaughtered*.[2] But surely R. Giddal said in Rab's name: If the altar was removed [from its place], the incense was burnt on its [the altar's] site?[3]—Even as Raba said, R. Judah agrees in respect of the blood,[4] so here too, Rab agrees in respect of the blood.[5]

What [statement of] R. Judah [is referred to]?—It was taught: *The same day did the king hallow the middle of the court that was before the house of the Lord . . . because the brazen altar that was before the Lord was too little to receive the burnt-offering, and the meal-offering and the fat of the peace-offerings*:[6] this is meant literally:[7] these

(4) Ibid. 6. (5) R. Jose the Galilean. (6) So Rashi. The reading varies in different texts, v. Sh. M.

a (1) And the laver is a vessel. (2) Maintaining that the whole of it was in the south. (3) To Eretz Israel. (4) Ex. XX, 21. (5) Surely not. The sacrifice was slaughtered *at the side* of the altar. (6) All animals in a state of consecration while the altar was damaged are unfit, whether slaughtered while it was actually damaged, or after it was repaired. (7) V. *supra* 12*a*. When the altar became damaged these animals were rejected, since they could not be sacrificed then. The controversy is whether this rejection is permanent or not. (8) The altar in the second Temple. (9) I.e., if they were consecrated before the altar was actually built. (10) At the very moment that they were consecrated they were unfit, since there was as yet no altar, and in this case there is a view that the animals do not become permanently rejected, v. Ḳid. 7*a*. (11) I.e., the animals consecrated before the altar in the first Temple was destroyed might not be offered when that in the second was built. (12) By the time that that in the second was built.

b (1) Even if slaughtered after it is repaired. This contradicts Rab who declares fit sacrifices offered after the altar had been repaired. (2) Since you must emend the text in any case, emend it to: all the animals which were *slaughtered* while the altar was damaged. (3) This refers to the *inner* altar, and it is assumed that the same applies to the outer altar. When it is removed it is as damaged, and so Rab is self-contradictory. (4) The sprinkling of the blood requires an altar. (5) His ruling applies only to incense, but he agrees that the blood must be sprinkled on a whole altar. (6) I Kings VIII, 64. (7) Lit., 'the words are as written'.—I.e., Solomon sanctified the whole of the pavement to serve as an altar, to permit the burning of the limbs, etc., upon it.

מזבח העולה וגו' מזבח בפתח אהל מועד ולא כיור בפתח אהל מועד היכן היה נותנו *בין האולם ולמזבח משוך קימעא כלפי הדרום מאי קסבר אי קסבר א] כוליה מזבח בדרום קאי נוקמיה מכותל היכל ולדרום (א) בין אולם למזבח ואי נמי קסבר *קדושת היכל ואולם חדא היא נוקמיה מכותל אולם ולדרום ב] כבין אולם למזבח אי נמי קסבר חציו בצפון וחציו בדרום נוקמיה מכותל היכל ולדרום בין אולם ג] ולמזבח ואי נמי קסבר קדושת האולם והיכל חדא היא נוקמיה מכותל אולם ולדרום ד] בין אולם ולמזבח אלא לאו משום דקסבר כוליה מזבח בצפון ה] *כי נמי מוקמת לה מכותל היכל ולצפון ה"ל בין אולם ולמזבח ונוקמה מכותל אולם ולצפון ו] כבין אולם ולמזבח אמר קרא צפונה שיהא ז] צפון פנוי מכלים מאן תנא דפליג עליה דר' יוסי הגלילי ר"א בן יעקב היא דתניא ח] *ר"א בן יעקב אומר צפונה שיהא צפון פנוי מכלום ואפילו מן המזבח אמר רב מזבח שנפגם כל הקדשים שנשחטו שם פסולין *מקרא ט] הוא בידינו ושכחנוהו כי סליק °רב כהנא אשכחיה לר"ש ברבי דקאמר משום ר' ישמעאל בר' יוסי מנין למזבח שנפגם שכל הקדשים שנשחטו שם פסולין שנאמר °וזבחת עליו את עולותיך ואת שלמיך וכי עליו אתה זובח אלא י] כשהוא שלם ולא כשהוא חסר אמר היינו קרא דאישתמיט ליה לרב ורבי יוחנן אמר אחד זה ואחד זה פסולין במאי פליגי *רב סבר בעלי חיים אינן נדחים ור' יוחנן סבר *בעלי חיים נידחין מיתיבי כל הקדשים שהיו עד שלא נבנה המזבח ואח"כ נבנה המזבח פסולין נבנה דהויין מעיקרא נינהו אלא עד שלא נהרס יא] המזבח נהרס הא איזקן להו אלא *עד שלא נפגם המזבח יב] ואחר כך נפגם המזבח פסולין ולא תרוצי קא מתרצת יג] אימא שנשחטו והאמר רב גידל אמר רב מזבח שנעקר מקטירין קטרת במקומו כדאמר רבא יד] *מודה היה ר' יהודה בדמים הכא נמי מודה רב בדמים מאי ר' יהודה דתניא °ביום ההוא קידש המלך טו] את תוך החצר וגו' כי מזבח (*שעשה משה) קטן מהכיל דברים ככתבן דברי רבי יהודה א"ל רבי יוסי והלא

תורה אור: שמות כ; מ"א ח

רש"י

מזבח העולה שם פתח טז] אוהל מועד ואין כיור מפסיק בינתיים למדת משני המקראות הללו שצריך ליתנו כל מה שיכול לקרבו באויר שבין מזבח לאהל מועד ובלבד שלא יהא מפסיק בין מזבח ולפתח: היכן היה נתון משוך קימעא. מזוית המזבח ולדרום נמצא שאינו כנגד המזבח כלל אלא כבין אהל מועד ולמזבח: ה"ג יז] בת"כ ובמס' מדות ומדמצריך ליה רבי יוסי הגלילי למשכו מכנגד המזבח ולדרום (ב) והוא אינו צריך להרחיקו אלא מבין המזבח ולפתח פשוט מיניה דכוליה מזבח בצפון קאי ולפיכך על כרחו הוא מושכו מכנגד המזבח כולו שאם נתנו כלל כנגד המזבח א"א שלא יפסיק בינו ולפתח כדמפרש ואזיל: דמאי קסבר. שלא קיים את המקרא שכתב בין אהל מועד ובין המזבח והוא מושכו קימעא: אי כוליה בדרום. הרבה מן המזבח יש בדרום כנגד יח] היכל שלא כנגד הפתח והיה לו לתתו שם: נוקמיה מכותל היכל ולדרום. כלומר משמתחיל כותל פתח ההיכל ליתנם לדרום דהיינו בין פתח האולם ולמזבח וכנגד יט] ההיכל שפתח האולם עודף על של היכל ה' אמות כ] לדרום: וא"כ סבר קדושת אולם והיכל חדא היא. ופתח אולם כפתח היכל והוצרך למושכו אף מכנגד פתחו של אולם: נוקמיה מסתימת כותל אולם ולדרום. דה"ל אכתי כבין האולם ולמזבח דכיון דכותל אולם ככותל היכל קרי ביה בין אהל מועד ולמזבח ומקיימי קראי שפיר: ואי נמי קסבר חציו בצפון כו'. יש לו ס"ז אמה בדרום לא מהן ה' אמות של פתח עדיין יש לו מקום י"א אמה לתתו שם מכותל מזוזת היכל כא] דרום: וא"כ קסבר קדושת אולם והיכל חדא היא. והוצרך למושכו אף מכנגד פתח אולם נוקמיה ממקום סתימת פתח אולם ולדרום כב] כבין האולם ולמזבח דעדיין יש שם מקום ו' אמות: אלא לאו משום דקסבר כוליה מזבח בצפון. קאי ודרומו של מזבח *כולה לפני הפתח ואם היה נותנו כנגד המזבח כלל נמצא מפסיק בין מזבח כג] לפתח: ונוקמיה בין המזבח והיכל בצפון. *בסתימת כותל ההיכל כד] במזוזת צפונית ולצפון: קסבר קדושת היכל כו'. ואינו רשאי להפסיק בין פתח אולם ולמזבח וכי מוקמת ליה מכותל היכל ולצפון ה"ל מפסיק בין אולם ולמזבח: שיהא פנוי מכלים. גרס הכא וכיור כלי הוא: (ג) לפונה. מדהוה ליה למיכתב על ירך המזבח לפון וכתיב לפונה לדהשא אתא: מאן תנא דפליג כו'. ואומר כוליה בדרום קאי: בדר"א גרסינן פנוי מכלום: *שנשחטו שם. בעזרה: כשהוא שלם. והאי עליו בגינו ובשבילו קאמר: אחד זה ואחד זה. בין שנשחטו בשעת כה] פגימתן בין שנשחטו אחר תיקונו פסולין כל הקדשים שהיו קדושין באותה שעה לפי שנראו ונדחו וקסבר בעלי חיים נדחין כשחוטין: עד שלא נבנה. משמע קודם כו] שלא בנאוהו בני הגולה: דהויין מעיקרא הן. שכשהוקדשו לא נראו שמע מיניה דחוי מעיקרו הוי דחוי ותקשה למאן דאמר לא הוי דחוי: נהרס. משמע בימי כז] נבוכד נצר היו: כח] אזקין להו. עד שלא נבנה בית שני ופשיטא דפסולין דגבי מומין קתני כט] להו בבכורות (דף מא.) הזקן והחולה והמזוהם: מזבח שנעקר. במזבח פנימי קמיירי וקא סלקא דעתך הוא הדין לחיצון קשיא דרב אדרב דאמר לעיל כל הקדשים שנשחטו שם פסולין: מודה רבי יהודה בדמים. דבעינן מזבח: דברים ככתבן. שקדש את הרצפה כולה לשם מזבח להקטיר עליה לפי שהיה המזבח קטן מהכיל עולות ושלמים שהקריבו לחנוכת המזבח ואמרינן לקמן ל] לרבי יהודה הכי משמע קרא כי מזבח אבנים אשר תחת מזבח הנחושת קטן היה: אמר לו רבי יוסי והלא כבר נאמר. במזבח לא] שעשה משה במדבר שהיה בנוב וגבעון:

אלא

תוספות

פנוי מכלים. אע"פ שמזבח שעשה משה לג] (אינו פנוי) *[כלי] היה כדאמר דנין כלי מכלי ואין דנין כלי מבנין משאר כלים קאמר דלפונה *אמזבח קאי ואע"פ שהיה בצפון ננסין וקלונסות ושולחנות מסתמא הא דאמרה תורה פנוי מכלום משום שחיטה הוא והני לצורך שחיטה נינהו: שיהא לצפון פנוי מכלים. אפילו מן המזבח צריך לדקדק במתני' דמדות (דף לג) שלא תקשה דרבי אליעזר בן יעקב ס"ל הכא כוליה מזבח בדרום קאי ובפ"ק דיומא (דף טז.) מוקמינן מתני' דמדות כר"א בן יעקב: וכי עליו אתה זובח. אע"ג דלעיל דרשינן עליו ממש הכא דייק משום דוזבחת עליו לג] משמע שמצוה לזבוח עליו וכן לקמן (דף ס.) גבי ואכלוה מצות אצל המזבח לד] משמע שמצוה אלא כשהוא שלם ולא כשהוא חסר: עד שלא נבנה המזבח. דהויין מעיקרא הן לה] אלא עד שלא נפגם ונפגם ומשני לא תרוצי מתרצא לה. ותימה דא"כ משמע דפירכא קמייתא דהויין מעיקרא הוו ואפילו לר' יוחנן ואמאי והא ר' יוחנן סבר גבי בהמה של ב' שותפין (קדושין דף ז.) דחוי מעיקרא הוי דחוי ועוד תקשי ליה ממתני' דמי שהיה טמא (פסחים דף צז:) המפריש נקבה לפסחו דקאמר דחוי מעיקרו הוי דחוי ויש לומר דהתם אין בידו לתקן מיקרי דחוי כדפרישית פ"ק (לעיל דף יב:*) אבל הכא בידו לתקן *המזבח לו] ולכך משמע ליה הכא דכ"ע לא הוי דחוי מידי לז] דהוה אמחוסר זמן בגופו ובבעלים כגון יולדת זב ומצורע שהפרישו קרבנם קודם זמנם ה"נ מפריש קרבנו להקריב לכשיבנה בהמ"ק לח] והוי כמחוסר זמן ולא חשיב נדחה וכן מוכח לקמן פ"ב (דף קיד.) דחובות שהקדישן בגלגל לגבי שילה היו מחוסר זמן וקרבי בשילה דלא אמרינן דהויין הן וקשה לי דבפ"ק (לעיל דף יב.) פריך לבן בתירא פסח היכי משכחת לה אי *אפרשי' בצפרא דהוי מעיקרא הוא שאינו ראוי לשלמים לבן בתירא הואיל לט] ומקצתו הוא ראוי לפסח בחצות מה בכך כיון דבידו להשהותו עד חצות למה לא יהא כשר כמו *מקדיש אותו לאחר שחיטת בנו שראוי למחר ומקדיש בגלגל חובות שכשרין בשילה. ברו"ך. וא"ת אכתי כיון דהוי כמחוסר זמן כי ליכא מזבח דפריך דהויין מעיקרא הן אמאי אמר ר' יוחנן בפ' השוחט והמעלה (לקמן דף קז:) דהמעלה בזמן הזה בחוץ חייב דקדושה ראשונה קידשה לעתיד לבא הא אינו ראוי לפתח אהל ותנן נמי פרק בתרא (לקמן דף קיב:) אותו ואת בנו ומחוסר זמן בחוץ אינו אפילו בלא תעשה לרבנן ואם כן לרבי יוחנן אמאי מחייב משום שחוטי חוץ ותו הא עדיפא מינה אמרינן ביומא פרק שני שעירי (דף סא.) דשלמים ששחטן *קודם פתיחת דלתות

ההיכל

*) בחוץ קודם נ"ק

עין משפט נר מצוה

גי' רש"ק. וגי' נ"ק אינו פנוי היה וקראו כלי כדאמרינן ולא למזבח קאמר נ"ק

ד א מיי' פ"א מהלכות בית הבחירה הל' ו:

ה ב מיי' פ"ב מהלכות פסה"מ הלכה כב:

ו ג מיי' שם הלכה כג וסמ"ג מהל' מעשה הקרבנות הלכה ד:

ז ד מיי' פ"ג מהלכות פסה"מ הלכה כד:

ח ה מיי' פ"ג מהלכות תמידין ומוספין הל' ב:

[ד"ס ושי"מ]

נ"א המזבח ויהא נראה כשהמזבח יהא בנוי ולכך משמע כו' וכן הוא בש"מ ועי' נ"ק

[לקמן עג: יומא סד. פסחי' עג. קדושין ז:]

דאפרשיה סאידנא דחוי כו' נ"ק

שיטה מקובצת

א] כוליה מזבח בדרום קאי. ה"ה דהוי מצי למבעי אי בדרום קאי מאי משוך קימעא הא צריך למשוך כל הדרום ולכל הפחות ה' אמות כנגד הפתח דהא בעינן ולא כיור בפתח אהל מועד: ב] ולדרום כבין אולם: ג] למזבח ואי נמי קסבר קדושת היכל ואולם: ד] ולדרום כבין: ה] בצפון קאי ונוקמיה מכותל היכל ולצפון קסבר קדושת היכל ואולם חדא הוא וכי נמי ס"א כי נמי מוקמת לה מכותל היכל ולדרום הוי ליה בין האולם ולמזבח ונוקמיה מכותל היכל ולצפון בין אהל מועד ולמזבח ואי נמי קסבר קדושת היכל ואולם חדא היא נוקמיה מכותל אולם ולצפון כבין אולם ולמזבח אמר קרא כו' אבל גירסת רש"י אינו כן: ו] ולצפון כבין אולם: ז] צפונה שיהא פנוי מכלום. וא"ת א"כ למה לי להזכיר הברייתא ואת מזבח העולה שם פתח אוהל מועד לומר דאין כיור פתח אהל מועד תיפוק א) ליה משום דאם יעמוד [הכיור] בין המזבח לפתח אהל מועד לצפון הואיל דבעינן צפון דכוליה מזבח בצפון קאי ובעינן צפון פנוי מכלום וליכא וי"ל דאי לאו דמפסיק הוה מעמידו שפיר בין ההיכל ובין המזבח תוך חלל פתח האולם דלא מקרי צפון כדקאמר לעיל דאפילו בית החליפות לא מקרי צפון ולכן מייתי מקרא דאת מזבח העולה כו' דמשמע דבעינן שלא יהא כיור מפסיק בין מזבח לפתח אהל מועד. מהר"ם: ח] ר"א בן יעקב אומר צפונה כו'. תימה דבמס' מדות תנן הכיור היה בין האולם ולמזבח משוך כלפי דרום ואמרינן ביומא מאן תנא מדות ראב"י והכא אית ליה לראב"י דמזבח לאו בצפון קאי וא"כ היכא אתיא ההיא דמדות כותיה דהא לכאורה סבר ההיא דמדות דמזבח בצפון קאי כדדייקינן בהך דר"י הגלילי וי"ל דההיא דמדות איכא למימר דר"ל משוך מן הדרום ה' אמות ממזבח בכותל ההיכל לדרום וקסבר כוליה מזבח בדרום קאי אבל הכא דקתני משוך קימעא ליכא לפרושי הכי במשוך מכנגד הפתח דוקא קאמר ולעולם הוי בין המזבח לכותל ההיכל דא"כ אמאי נקט קימעא אפילו טובא נמי יכול למשכו מכנגד הפתח דאכתי נשאר הרבה מן המזבח לקיומי ונתת את הכיור בין אהל מועד ובין המזבח אלא ודאי משוך קימעא דקאמר משוך ב) מכנגד הפתח קאמר ולכך דוקא קימעא לפי שצריך לקרבו כל מה שנוכל נגד אויר שבין המזבח להיכל ולאולם כדי לקיים בין אהל [מועד] ומזבח ואת"ל שאין להרחיקו מן הכותל כל כך מ"מ לא סגי בקימעא דכיון דאפתח קאי צריך שיהא משוך מתחילת המזבח ה' אמות כשיעור הפתח: ט] מקרא היה בידינו: י] אלא עליו כשהוא: יא] המזבח ואח"כ נהרס המזבח פסולים נהרס (נ"א היכא אסקא להו אלא עד שלא נהרס המזבח ונבנה): יב] המזבח ונפגם ואחר כך נתקן תיבת נפגם נמחק: יג] מתרצת תני נמי שנשחטו ותיבת אימא נמחק: יד] רבא מודי רבי יהודה בדמים הכי נמי מודי רב: טו] המלך את תוך החצר וגו' כי מזבח הנחשת אשר לפני ה' קטן מהכיל: טז] שם פתח משכן אהל: יז] ה"ג לה בת"כ ובמס' מדות ומדאצטריך ליה ריה"ג למושכו מכנגד המזבח: יח] כנגד כותל היכל: יט] וכנגד כותל ההיכל: כ] אמות לכל צד הס"ד: כא] ולדרום הס"ד: כב] ולדרום בין: כג] מזבח ולפתח הס"ד: כד] ההיכל אמזוזת צפונית: כה] בשעה פגימתו: כו] קודם שבנוהו בני תיבת שלא נמחק: כז] נבוכדנצר תיבה אחת: כח] הא אזקין להו עד שנבנה בית שני: כט] תיבת להו נמחק: ל] לקמן דלר"י: לא] במזבח הנחשת שעשה משה במדבר שהיה בבמה (נ"א בנוב וגבעון): לב] משה כלי היה (תיבות אינו פנוי נמחק) כדאמרי' לקמן דנין כלי כו' מבנין הכא פנוים משאר כלים: לג] משמע. ס"א דוקא עליו: לד] המזבח וכי אצל המזבח אוכלים כלומר דוקא ולא במקום אחר [אלא כו'] ותיבות משמע שמצוה נמחק: לה] מתיבת אלא עד תיבת וא"ת אכתי מוקף בחצאי לבנה: לו] ולכך יהא נראה כשהמזבח יהא בנוי ומתוקן ולכך משמע: לז] מידי (דלא) דהוי אמחוסר זמן בין בגופו בין בבעלים דכי מצו חזו הדרי כשרין כגון: לח] בית המקדש הוי כמחוסר זמן: לט] הואיל והוא ראוי ותיבת ומקצתו נמחק:

א) נראה דצ"ל משום דאם יעמוד הכיור בין המזבח כנגד פתח אוהל מועד ע"כ צריך להעמידו בצפון העזרה דהא כוליה מזבח וכו'. ב) נראה דצ"ל משוך מכנגד המזבח קאמר.

מסורת הש"ס

תמיד פ"ג מ"ז

[לעיל יז. וש"נ]

[יומא נז.]

[ע"ש נב:]

[לעיל יב. פסחים עג. יומא סד. קדושין ז: כריתות כז. תמורה כ: לקמן עג:] כלה נ"ק

[פי' תוס' מנחות נט: ד"ה כל שכיון]

מסתימת נ"ק

[לקמן ס.]

נ"ב ונרושת אשר לפני ה'

הגהות הב"ח

(א) גמ' מכותל היכל ולדרום דהיינו בין: (ב) רש"י ד"ה ה"ג וכו' ולדרום והוא אינו צריך: (ג) ד"ה לפונה נ"ל קודם ד"ה שיהא פנוי:

נ"א ונוקמיה בין היכל ולצפון קסבר קדושת היכל ואולם חדא כי נמי כו'

גליון הש"ס

גמ' רב כהנא אשכחיה. עיין גיטין דף סד ע"ב תוס' ד"ה ר"א:

עי' רש"ק שכתב שד"ה שנשחטו כו' עד מלת כשהוא שלם ובעל פנים מאירות בשיטה והוכיח מתוך סוגיות גירסת הש"ס הכא

וכ"ש זה דמחוסרי מעשה גדול ועוד כו' נ"ק

ט א מיי' פ"ב מהלכות בית הבחירה הל' ה :

תורה אור

והלא כבר נאמר °אלף עולות יעלה שלמה על המזבח ההוא א] ואילו בבית עולמים הוא אומר °ויזבח שלמה את זבח השלמים אשר זבח לה' בקר עשרים ושנים אלף וכשאתה מגיע לחשבון עולות ולמנין אמות זה גדול מזה אלא מהו קטן מהכיל כאדם האומר לחבירו פלוני ננס הוא ופסול לעבודה ור' יהודה שפיר קאמר ר' יוסי ר' יהודה לטעמיה דאמר מזבח שעשה משה גדול היה דתניא °חמש אמות אורך וחמש אמות רוחב דברים ככתבן דברי ר' יוסי ר' יהודה אומר נאמר כאן °רבוע ונאמר להלן °רבוע מה להלן מאמצעיתו היה מודד אף כאן מאמצעיתו היה מודד והתם מנלן דכתיב *°והאריאל שתים עשרה ב] אמה לכל רוח *או אינו אלא י"ב על י"ב כשהוא אומר אל ארבעת רבעיו מלמד שמאמצע הוא מודד ג] ור' יוסי כי גמר גזירה שוה בגובהה הוא דגמיר דתניא °ושלש אמות קומתו דברים ככתבן דברי רבי יהודה רבי יוסי אומר נאמר כאן °רבוע ונאמר להלן רבוע מה להלן גובהו פי שנים כארכו אף כאן פי שנים כארכו אמר ליה רבי יהודה *(והלא כבר נאמר ד] *ואת החצר מאה אמה וקומה חמש אמות וגו') אפשר כהן עומד ע"ג המזבח ועבודה בידו וכל העם רואין אותו מבחוץ אמר לו ר' יוסי והלא כבר נאמר °ואת קלעי החצר ואת מסך ה] שער החצר אשר על המשכן ועל המזבח ו] *אמה משכן י' אמות אף מזבח י' אמות ואומר °קלעים חמש עשרה אמה

מ"א ג / שם ח / שמות כז / שם / יחזקאל מג / שם / שמות כז / שם / במדבר ד / שמות לח

רש"י

אלף עולות יעלה שלמה וגו' וכשאתה מגיע לחשבון עולות ז] ולמנין אמות. שהיה מזבח אבנים של שלמה עודף עליו זה של שלמה גדול משל משה לפי צורך העולות שהרי מזבח של משה כתיב ביה ה' אמות אורך וה' אמות רוחב לא מהם מקום הקרנות אמה לכל צד ומקום הילוך רגלי הכהנים אמה לפנים מן הקרנות סביב ח] המערכה נמצא מקום המערכה אמה על אמה הכי אמרינן לקמן בפירקין (דף סב.) יסוד וסובב לא היו ממעטין בארכו ורחבו לפי ט] שמקיפין ובולטין סביביו מעשה רשת נחושת והוא היה סובבו ובמזבח שעשה שלמה היה מקום המערכה *כ' על כ' לרבי יוסי כדתנן במסכת מדות י] (דף לה:) חלקהו לכ' רצועות כל אחת ואחת ברוחב אמה ואורך עשרים הרי ד' מאות יא] אורך ברוחב אמה ואין לך אמה על אמה שאינה מחזקת לבער אלף יב] ליום שהיתה אש של שמים ממהרת לאכול הרי ד' מאות אלף: אלא מהו אומר קטן מהכיל. לאו במזבח אבנים קאמר ומשום יג] ההוא יומא אלא למזבח הנחשת קאמר ובא לפוסלו לעולם יד] שסילקו ומה שתלה הכתוב קטנו בעולות של אותו היום לישנא מעליא נקט: כאדם שאומר לחבירו. באדם שנפסל: ננס פלוני. לישנא מעליא ולא אמר נפסל פלוני: טו] ונפסל. לעבודה. לאו טז] מסקנא דאדם אומר אלא רבי יוסי קאמר לה ואותו פלוני פסול לעבודה והוא קורא לו ננס: שפיר קא"ר יוסי. ול"ל לקדושי רצפה: מזבח של משה גדול היה. וכשאתה מגיע לחשבון עולות ומנין אמות שבשניהם נמצא של שלמה קטן לפי הצורך: ונאמר להלן רבוע. בשל יחזקאל שנתנבא על בית שני או על העתיד רבוע אל ארבעת רבעיו: מה להלן. מדה האמורה בו מאמצעיתו הוא מודד כדמפרש ואזיל: אף כאן מודד ה' על ה' מאמצעיתו. לכל רוח נמצא י' על י' לא מהן אמה מכאן ואמה מכאן לקרנות וכן למקום הילוך הרי ו' על ו' מקום המערכה ושל שלמה כ' על כ' מקום המערכה עשה ממנו ג' רצועות של ו' יז] רוחב נשארו שתי אמות בארך עשרים חלוק ג' הרצועות יח] לרחבו [לחתיכות רבועות של שש שש] תמצא בכל אחת ג' חתיכות רבועות של שש שש הרי תשע ועוד נשארו בכל אחת ב' אמות בארך ששה יט] קרבם זו אצל זו הרי ו' על ו' הרי עשר חתיכות רבועות ועוד צרף הרצועה הארוכה עשרים ורחבה ב' ותמצא ו' על ו' הרי י"א כ] וב' אמות על ב' אמות נמצא של משה אחד מי"א כשל שלמה ומגיע לחשבון י"א אלפים עולות ותו לא כא] ובחנוכתו כתיב בקר כ"ב אלף וצאן כב] *כ"ב אלף: והאריאל. מקום מערכה של מזבח: שתים עשרה. אל ארבעת רבעיו מלמד שמאמצעיתו מודד: ורבי יוסי. דאמר דברים ככתבן: כי גמיר ג"ש. דרבוע רבוע בגובהה הוא דגמר ולאו מרבוע דיחזקאל אלא מרבוע דכתיב במזבח הפנימי כג] דתניא וג' אמות קומתו כו' (שמות כז) כד] ובמזבח הנחשת כתיב: ונאמר להלן רבוע. במזבח הזהב אמה ארכו ואמה רחבו רבוע ואמתים קומתו (שם ל): אף כאן גובהו פי שנים כארכו. הרי י' אמות *ובסיפא מפרש ר' יוסי מאי וג' קומתו: והלא כבר נאמר וקומה ה' אמות. דאין גובה היקף הקלעים של חצר אלא ה' אמות: אפשר כן. שיהא כהן בראש המזבח ועבודה בידו כו': מה משכן. צריך כה] קלעים לחצר סביביו מוקף גובה י' אמות דהא הכי הוה גובהה דכתיב (שם כו) י' אמות אורך הקרש: אף מזבח. צריך כו] היקף לכדי י' אמות: ואומר קלעים ט"ו אמה

תוספות

היכל פטור דאינו ראוי לפתח אהל מועד *דמחוסרי מעשה וכ"ש זה ועוד אמרינן בפ"ק דמס' ע"ז (דף יג:) דאם הקדיש והחרים והעריך בזמן הזה בהמה תעקר דהיינו נועל דלת בפניה והיא מתה מאליה כדאיתא התם ופריך וניסחטינהו מישחט ופי' בקונטרס משום שחוטי חוץ לא מחייב דמיירי בקדשי בדק הבית דאין חייבין משום שחוטי חוץ כדמוכח לקמן (דף קיג:) ובפרק שני שעירי (יומא דף סג:) וקשה דאי בקדשי בדק הבית כז] מאי פריך וניסוייה גיסטרא כח] ומשני מפני שנראה כמטיל מום בקדשים כט] וליכא למימר דיש איסור מטיל מום אף בבהמה תמימה לקדשי בדק הבית כדאמר המתפיס תמימים לבדק הבית אינן יוצאין מידי מזבח לעולם דהיינו מדרבנן משום קנס כדמוכח פרק המנחות והנסכים (מנחות קא.) דקאמר משום דלא שכיחי תמימים תקנו שיהיו למזבח לכך נראה דמיירי בקדשי מזבח ולא מחייבי משום שחוטי חוץ משום דאינו ראוי לפתח אהל מועד או משום דהוי דחוי או משום דמחוסר זמן ודוחק לומר דההיא דמס' ע"ז כמ"ד סותרו הבמות דהא סתם מתניתין לקמן (דף קיב:) דירושלים אין אחריה היתר ובפ"ק דמגילה (דף י.) פריך מינה *לר' יוחנן דאמר שמעתי שמקריבין בבית חוניו ונראה לתרץ דר' יוחנן דמחייב לקמן מעלה בחוץ מיירי בהעלאת קטרת דלא מחוסר מעשה כדאמר בשמעתין מזבח שנעקר מקטירין קטרת במקומו א"נ בהעלאת מנחה שקמצה בכלי שרת בפנים ל] אע"פ שאין בית דאזבחים דוקא בעי מזבח כדכתיב וזבחת עליו וניחא השתא הא דנקט ר' יוחנן מעלה בזמן הזה ולא נקט שוחט בזמן הזה ואין לתרץ דר' יוחנן כרבי יהודה *דשרי להקטיר ברצפת העזרה דלא מיסתבר דלישרי רבי יהודה בשעה שהמזבח פגום אלא בשעה שהמזבח כשר ועוד יש לתרץ דלקמן ר' יוחנן מיירי כשבנה המזבח במקומו והעלה בחוץ כיון דקדשי לעתיד לבא לא] *וההיא דפ"ק דע"ז (דף יג:) יש להקשות בקדשי בדק הבית אמאי נועל דלת בפניה לרבא ונשחטיה או נשוייה גיסטרא אלא פי' רבינו הקדוש דמדרבנן אסור להטיל בהם מום גזירה אטו קדשי מזבח כדאמר בראשית הגז (חולין דף קלה.) דקדשי בדק הבית אסורין בגיזה ועבודה גזירה אטו קדשי מזבח וא"כ יש ליישב פי' רש"י דפריך בקדשי בדק הבית ונשחטיה משחט ונשוייה גסטרא ומשני נראה כמטיל מום דאסור גזרה אטו קדשי מזבח וא"ת מאי טעמא פטרינן שלמים ששחטן לב] קודם פתיחת דלתות ההיכל לג] בחוץ *(לעיל דף נה:) והלא בפנים כי האי גוונא אם עלו לא ירדו לפי מה שפי' הקונטרס לקמן לד] קודם שיעמידו לוים את המשכן ולאחר שפרקו לוים את המשכן דשלמים דוקא בעי פתיחת דלתות ההיכל ולא שאר קדשים וכיון דשאר קדשים כשרין א"כ שלמים נמי אם עלו לא ירדו וחייב בחוץ כמו הלן והיוצא ושנשחט חוץ לזמנו וחוץ למקומו דחייב עליהן בחוץ הואיל ומתקבל בפנים וי"ל דהתם מיירי בהעלאה דכיון שהשחיטה נעשית בפנים כהלכתה מיחייב בהעלאה כיון דמתקבל בפנים אבל הכא דאין השחיטה כהלכתה לא ואפילו אם תימצי לומר דפסח והחטאת ששחטן שלא לשמן בחוץ חייב הבהמה ראויה לפנים לכתחילה אבל אלו קדשים אינן ראויין לפנים לכתחילה: *הא אזקינן להו. וגבי מומין תנן בבכורות (דף מא.) הזקן והא דאמר *(באלה הדברים רבה) חיים כלכם היום קל וחומר מפרים שהתנדבו הנשיאים לשאת הארון במדבר שחיו עד שלמה שהקריבן לגבוה הוראת שעה היתה: והלא כבר נאמר אלף עולות יעלה שלמה. וא"ת מנא ליה דאמזבח הנחשת לה] קאמר הא ג' מזבחות הוו כדאמר לקמן (דף סא:) של נוב ושל גבעון וגדול היה וי"ל דסמיך אקרא (דה"ב ג א) דכתיב בהדיא על מזבח הנחשת שעשה בצלאל :- *מה משכן עשר אמות. תימה כיון דאיכא היקשא גזירה שוה דרבוע למה לי לו]: ואומר קלעים ט"ו אמה אל הכתף. פי' בקונטרס וקס"ד בגובה קאמר וה"ה לכל החצר וקשה לר"ת היכי מצי למימר דאגובה קאי והא מוכח קרא בהדיא דברחבה מיירי דקחשיב מעיקרא החצר לפאת לז] ים חמשים אמה ואחר כך מפרש חמש עשרה אמה קלעים לכתף שאצל השער ולכתף השנית חמש עשרה קלעים ואחר כך לשער החצר מסך עשרים

*) [צ"ל במדבר רבה סדר נשא פ' יב]

מסורת הש"ס

ואלו ההוא בבית נ"ק / עיין רש"ק / נ"א יפול / נ"א ארך החצר מאה באמה וקומה חמש אמות אשר כו' בפ"ל נ"ק / [שבת נב.] / נ"ל מאה וכו' אלף / נ"א ולקמן נ"ק / ועיין רש"ק וגי"ק

[מנחות נג:] / [צ"ל לר' יוחנן ופ"ש] / [אחד עשר תיבות סלנו ליתא בילקוט] / ס"ל דשרי נ"ק / עיין נ"ק שמחסך הגי' כאן / [בדף נט ליתא אבל הוא מסומל דמימרא דרב יהודה אמר שמואל ביומא דף סג.]

שיטה מקובצת

א] ההוא ובבית עולמים ואילו ל"ש : ב] י"ב ארך בי"ב רחב רבוע אל ארבעת רבעיו והריאל שתים עשרה לכל ותיבת אמה נמחק: ג] מודד י"ב אמה לכל רוח : ד] נאמר ארך החצר מאה באמה וגו' וקומה ה' אמות אשר : ה] מסך פתח השער : ו] המזבח סביב מה : ז] עולות של חנוכת המזבח: ח] סביב מן המערכה : ט] לפי שבולטין חוצה לו ומקיפין ובולטין סביביו: י] סדות והוא שנאמר בדברי הימים ויעש שלמה מזבח נחשת כ' אמה ארכו וכו' אמה רחבו ושל אבנים היה ולפי שהיה לעולה תחת מזבח הנחשת של משה קרא לו מזבח הנחשת ועשרים על עשרים דקרא אמקום [המערכה] קאי כמו והריאל שתים עשרה ארך בשתים עשרה רחב דאמקום מערכה קאמר במזבח בית שני חלק עשרים על עשרים לארכו לכ' רצועות ותיבת חלקוהו נמחק : יא] מאות אמות ארך : יב] אלף עולות ליום : יג] ומשום קרבנות דההוא יומא אלא למזבח הנחשת דמשה קאמר : יד] שסילקו . ס"א וקראו שם פסול כאדם שאומר לחבירו על כהן ננס הוא ופסול לעבודה וסילקו וגנזו ועשה חילופו מזבח אבנים והוא שנאמר קדש את תוך החצר להציב בו בנין אבנים למזבח כי שם עשה את העולת כי מזבח של משה ננס ופסול לפי שלא היה ראוי לרוב עולות של אותו היום וזה שנאמר בדברי הימים כי מזבח הנחשת של משה שעשה שלמה תחתיו מזבח אחר קטן מהכיל (שפיר) : טו] מה"ד ופסול לעבודה : טז] לעבודה לאו ס"א אינו ר"ל דאדם אומר לחבירו פלוני ננס ופסול לעבודה אלא ופסול לעבודה ר"י קאמר לה : יז] ו' ו' רוחב : יח] הרצועות . (ס"א לרחבן תמצא בכל אחת שלש חתיכות רבועות של שש שש) לרחב' לחתיכות רבועות של שש שש תמצא שלש בכל אחת הרי תיבות ג' חתיכות רבועות של שש שש נמחק : יט] ששה יצרף שלש חתיכות הקטנים ותמצא חתיכה רבוע ו' כו' ותיבות קרבם ע אצל זו הרי נמחק : כ] י"א רצועות שש על שש וב' : כא] לא כיון דשל משה אלף ותו לא ובחנוכתו : כב] וצאן מאה ועשרים אלף : כג] הפנימי דמשה : כד] במזבח הנחשת : כה] צריך קלעי החצר שסביביו גבוה י' ותיבת מוקף נמחק : כו] צריך להיות מוקף קלעים גובה עשר ותיבות היקף לכדי נמחק : כז] הבית כי פריך תיבת מאי ל"ש : כח] מאי משני מפני אות ו' נמחק : כט] מתיבת וליכא כו' עד תיבות לכך נראה מוקף בחצאי לבנה : ל] בפנים דמקריבין אע"פ : לא] לבא ובההיא מתיבת וההיא עד ותיבת ואת מ"ם מוקף ח"ל : לב] ששחטן בחוץ קודם : לג] תיבת בחוץ נמחק : לד] לקמן גבי קודם : לה] הנחשת קריב ליה שלא היה מקום המערכה אלא אמה דלמא מזבח דנוב וגבעון קאמר דהיה גדול יותר כדאמרינן לקמן ג' מזבחות היו שם בנוב וגבעון וי"ל כו'. מהר"ב : לו] לי תיפוק ליה מהיקשא דהכא וי"ל דאי לאו ג"ש לא הוה דרשינן הך היקשא לסתור משמעות הפסוק שכתוב בהדיא ג' אמות קומתו א"נ הך היקשא לאו אגובה דמזבח קאי אלא אגובה דקלעים כרפ"ה ובא לתרץ קושייתו של רבי יהודה שהקשה מן הפסוק דכתיב גבי קלעים וקאמר ה' אמות לפיכך בא לתרץ ולומר דמה משכן עשר אמות אף קלעים שהוא סביב המזבח עשר אמות ולפיכך לא היה נראה הכהן מבחוץ . מהר"פ : לז] לפאת קדמה מזרחה רחב חמשים אמה :

are the words of R. Judah. Said R. Jose to him: [59b] But surely it is said, *A thousand burnt-offerings did Solomon offer upon that altar,*[8] while of the Eternal House[9] it is said, *And Solomon offered for the sacrifice of peace-offerings, which he offered unto the Lord, two and twenty thousand oxen,*[10] and when you calculate the number of burnt-offerings and the number of cubits, the latter was larger than the former?[11] Rather, what does *'was too little to receive'* mean? As one says to his neighbours, 'So-and-so is a dwarf', when he is unfit
a for [sacrificial] service.[1] But R. Jose says well to R. Judah?[2]—R. Judah is consistent with his view, for he maintained that the altar made by Moses was large. For it was taught: [*And thou shalt make the altar of acacia wood,*] *five cubits long, and five cubits broad;* [*the altar shall be square*]:[3] this is meant literally: these are the words of R. Jose. R. Judah said: *'Square'* is stated here, and *'square'* is stated elsewhere:[4] as there it was measured from the centre, so here it was measured from the centre. And how do we know [that it was so] there?—Because it is written, *And the hearth*[5] *shall be twelve cubits long by twelve cubits broad, square.* You might think that it was only twelve cubits square; when, however, it says, *to*[6] *the four sides thereof,* it teaches that the measurement was taken from the middle.[7] And R. Jose?[8]—The *gezerah shawah* refers to the *height* [of the altar]. For it was taught: *And the height thereof shall be three cubits:*[9] this is meant literally: these are the words of R. Judah. R. Jose said: *'Square'* is stated here, and *'square'* is stated elsewhere:[10] as there its height was twice its length, so here too [its height was] twice its length.[11] Said R. Judah to him: Is it possible that the priest stood on the altar, performing the service, whilst all the people saw him from without?[12] Said R. Jose to him: But surely it is stated, *And the hangings of the court, and the screen for the door of the gate of the court, which is by the tabernacle and by the altar round about,*[13] [which teaches that] as the tabernacle was ten cubits [high], so was the altar ten cubits [high]; and it says, *The hangings for the one side*

(8) Ibid. III, 4. The altar referred to is the brazen one made in the days of Moses (cf. II Chron. I, 6). (9) The Temple. (10) Ibid. VIII, 63. (11) Moses' altar was five cubits square. From these a cubit must be deducted on all sides for the horns, and a further cubit on all sides for the terrace where the priests walked. This left only one cubit square for the actual burning. Whereas in Solomon's altar the actual place for burning was twenty cubits square, according to R. Jose, which means four hundred times as large. If then the smaller altar could cope with a thousand animals, this larger one was surely more than enough for the number offered that day. Hence *'was too little to receive'* etc. cannot be meant literally.

a (1) I.e., instead of saying directly that for some reason he is unfit, he uses a euphemism and calls him a dwarf. Similarly here, the altar had become unfit for service, and that is delicately stated by saying that it was too small. (2) His argument is sound. How then does R. Judah rebut it? (3) Ex. XXVII, 1. (4) Ezek. XLIII, 16, q.v. It is quoted in the text. (5) I.e., the actual portion of the altar for burning. (6) Lit. translation, not *in* as E.V. (7) Interpreting *'to'* as intimating that from one particular point there were twelve cubits in all directions, hence from the centre. Accordingly, Moses' altar was *ten* cubits square, not five, and when the two cubits on all sides are deducted (*supra* n. 11) it was still six as against Solomon's twenty cubits square. The latter therefore would not be large enough for the extra work it had to do. (8) How does he rebut this reasoning? (9) Ex. ibid. (10) In reference to the golden altar, Ex. XXX, 2: *a cubit shall be the length thereof, and a cubit the breadth thereof; square shall it be; and two cubits shall be the height thereof.* (11) Hence, ten cubits. (12) As would be the case if the altar were ten cubits high; this would not be seemly.—The text is emended in accordance with the Yalkut. (13) Num. IV, 26.

Novellae of Hagaon Rabbi Moshe Feinstein o.b.m.

Zebahim

59b Tos. s.v. הא The Tosafists' question how the bulls consecrated by the princes of the tribes to carry the Tabernacle were sacrificed in King Solomon's time apparently presents no difficulty, since there is no intrinsic disqualification of a sacrifice because of age, only because it weakens and old age is obvious, bearing an analogy to a sick animal, which is disqualified because of its weakness. See Rambam *Hilchoth Biath Mikdash* 7:12, where he explains that an aged priest is disqualified for the performance of the sacrificial service for this reason, and the same applies to sacrificial animals. Should a priest be as strong in his old age as he was in his youth, however, he is qualified to perform the sacrificial service although he is advanced in age. This is stated explicitly in *Hullin* 24, that a priest is qualified until he totters from old age. In fact, we find that all the high priests were blessed with longevity. See *Yoma* 9, that according to Riva in Tos. in the first temple there were but eight high priests, and according to the other Tosafists, there were nine, and according to one interpretation, there were eighteen high priests from Phinehas on. Moreover, it is stated explicitly in II Chron. xxiv. 15 that Jehoiada the high priest lived for one hundred thirty years. Also, in the second temple, Johanan the high priest served for eighty years. He was surely over one hundred years old. Hence, it is obvious that the disqualification of age is not due to years but to weakness. Likewise, in sacrificial animals, age disqualifies them for the same reason, since Rambam explains that this old age disqualifies because of weakness both in man and in animals. Also, the wording of the Gemara (Bekhoroth 41), which deals with animals, states that we would think that an aged animal is disqualified because it does not recover its health. It is obvious, therefore, that the aged animal is analogous to the sick one, and because of this the Gemara found it necessary to explain why the Mishnah stated both. Accordingly, the bulls that the princes donated, which lived until Solomon's time, since G-d granted them strength in their old age as in their youth, as the Midrash (*Numbers Rabbah* 12:18) states explicitly concerning the bulls, that they did not develop blemishes, they did not age, they did not sustain organic disorders, and they did not break any limbs, were not disqualified and it is totally unnecessary to say that this was a timely decision. This requires much deliberation.

In the same para. that the princes donated to carry the ark in the desert. This is a typographical error, because the ark was not permitted to carry on wagons but only on the shoulders. Instead, the reading should be: to carry the tabernacle.

a *were fifteen cubits.*[1] [60a] What then is the meaning of '*And the height five cubits*'?[2] From the [upper] edge of the altar to the top [of the hangings]. And what does '*and the height thereof shall be three cubits*' mean? From the edge of the terrace to the top [of the altar]. And R. Judah?[3]—He relates the *gezerah shawah* to the breadth. Now according to R. Judah, surely the priest could be seen?—Granted that the priest could be seen, the service [sacrifice] in his hand could not be seen.

As for R. Judah, it is well: hence it is written, [*did the king*] *hallow.*[4] But according to R. Jose, what is the meaning of '*did hallow* [*the middle of the court*]?'[5]—[He hallowed it] to set up the altar therein.[6]

As for R. Jose, it is well: hence it is written, '[*was*] *little*'.[7] But according to R. Judah, what is meant by '*little*'?[8]—This is what it means: The altar of stones which Solomon made instead of the brazen altar was too small.

Wherein do they differ?[9]—One master holds: You learn without from without,[10] but you do not learn without from within.[11] While the other master holds: You learn a utensil from a utensil, but you do not learn a vessel from an edifice.[12]

b Raba said: R. Judah admits in respect of the blood.[1] For it was taught, R. Judah said: He used to fill a goblet with the mingled blood, so that should the blood of one of them be spilt, it is found that this renders it fit.[2] But if you think that R. Judah holds that the whole of the Temple court was sanctified,[3] the precept has been already performed.[4]—[No:] perhaps that is because he holds that we require pouring out with man's force?[5]—If so, let us take it and pour it out in its place.[6] [No:] perhaps [that cannot be done] because he holds that the precept must be performed in the most fitting way.[7]

R. Eleazar said: If the altar was damaged, you cannot eat the remainder of the meal-offering on account of it, because it is said, *And eat it without leaven beside the altar.*[8] Now did they eat it then beside the altar?[9] Rather [it means]: when it is whole, and not when it is damaged.

We have found [it true of] the residue of the meal-offering. How do we know [it of] sacrifices of higher sanctity?—The implication of 'holy' [*ḳodesh*] is learnt by a *gezerah shawah.*[10] Whence do we know [it of] sacrifices of lesser sanctity?—Said Abaye: It is derived by R. Jose's exegesis. For it was taught: R. Jose stated

a (1) Ex. XXXVIII, 14. Rashi: it is now understood that they were fifteen cubits in height. Tosaf. objects that the whole context refers to the *width*, and accordingly emends: 'and the hangings were fifteen cubits,' omitting 'and it says' and '*for one side*', this being a statement by R. Jose on their height, not a Biblical quotation. (2) Ibid. XXVII, 18. (3) How does he rebut this? (4) He hallowed the pavement to serve as an altar. (5) In which respect did he hallow it? (6) For this purpose itself the pavement had to be hallowed. (7) Not, '*was* too *little*', as E.V. R. Jose understands the verse (I Kings VIII, 64) to mean that Solomon set up an altar of stones, because the brazen altar was unfit, and euphemistically called 'small'. (8) Since according to him even the stone altar was not large enough, why state that '*the* brazen *altar . . . was too little*'? (9) *Sc.* R. Jose who learns the *gezerah shawah* of '*square*' from the golden altar, and R. Judah who learns it from Ezekiel. (10) The brazen altar and the Temple court were both 'without', i.e., not in the inner sanctum. (11) Viz., from the golden altar, which was in the inner sanctum. (12) Both the brazen altar and the golden altar were technically utensils, whereas Ezekiel's stone altar was a constructed edifice.

b (1) That the blood could not be sprinkled on the pavement. He sanctified the pavement only in respect of the burning of the fats and the limbs. (2) V. *supra* 34*b*. (3) Even for the sprinkling of the blood. (4) The very act of spilling constitutes sprinkling. (5) I.e., intentionally done, and not accidently spilt. (6) As soon as the blood is received in a vessel, let it be poured out there and then. (7) Which is to sprinkle the blood actually on the altar. Yet possibly, if he did *intentionally* pour it out on the ground, the rite would be valid. (8) Lev. X, 12. (9) It might be eaten *anywhere* in the Temple court. (10) Lit., we learn 'holy', 'holy' (Emended text—Sh. M.).—The present text states, *for it is most holy*, and so the same law is applied to sacrifices of higher sanctity, which are likewise so designated, e.g., Lev. VI, 18.

אמה אל הכתף ומה ת"ל א] °ה' אמות משפת מזבח ולמעלה ומה ת"ל °ושלש אמות קומתו משפת סובב ולמעלה ור' יהודה כי גמיר גזירה שוה ברחבה הוא דגמיר ב] ולרבי יהודה הא קא מיתחזי כהן נהי דכהן מיתחזי עבודה דבידו לא מיתחזי בשלמא לרבי יהודה היינו דכתיב °קידש אלא לרבי יוסי מאי קידש להעמיד בה מזבח בשלמא לרבי יוסי היינו דכתיב קטן אלא לרבי יהודה מאי קטן הכי קאמר מזבח אבנים שעשה שלמה תחת מזבח הנחשת קטן הוה במאי פליגי מר סבר דנין חוץ מחוץ ואין דנין חוץ מפנים ומר סבר דנין כלי מכלי ואין דנין כלי מבנין אמר רבא מודה רבי יהודה בדמים דתניא *רבי יהודה אומר כוס אחד היה ממלא מדם התערובות ושופכו על גבי מזבח שאם ישפך דמו של אחת מהן נמצא זה מכשירו ואי סלקא דעתך סבר רבי יהודה כולה עזרה מיקדשא הא איתעבידא ליה מצוותיה ודלמא משום דקסבר שפיכה מכח האדם בעינן אם כן נשקליה ונשפיך ליה אדוכתיה ודלמא משום דבעינן מצוה מן המובחר ג] אמר רבי אלעזר *מזבח שנפגם אין אוכלין °בגינו שירי מנחה שנאמר °ואכלוה מצות אצל המזבח וכי אצל המזבח אכלוה אלא בזמן שהוא שלם ולא בזמן שהוא חסר אשכחן שירי מנחה ׳קדשי קדשים מנלן ד] ת"ל קדש קדשים ׳קדשים קלים ה] מנין אמר אביי אתיא מדרשא דר' יוסי דתניא *ר' יוסי אומר ג' דברים משום ג'

אמה אל הכתף · אלא השער *וקס"ד בגובהה קאמר וה"ה לכל החלר : משפת מזבח ולמעלה · למעלה מן המזבח היה גובהן ה' אמות: משפת סובב ולמעלה · עד מקום הקרנות ולמטה הימנו ו' אמות וגובה הקרן אמה: ור' יהודה · ו] אומר דברים ככתבן כי גמיר ג"ש ז] דרבוע רבוע ברחבה דגמיר למימר דמאמלעיתו תורה אור מודד וממזבח דיחזקאל ח] וכדלעיל: ולרבי יהודה · נהי נמי דדברים ככתבן הא קא מיתחזי כהן דהא גובהו שלש וקלעים אינן אלא חמש והוא מלמו ג' אמות נמלא ראשו למעלה מן הקלעים: בשלמא לרבי יהודה היינו דכתיב קידש· המלך ט] את [תוך החלר] וגו' שהולרכה כל הרלפה לקדשה לשם מזבח וקדושתה בשירי מנחה ובשיר כדאמרי' בשבועות (דף יד·) : מאי קידש · את תוך החלר : ומשני קדשו לשם עזרה להעמיד בו מזבח אבנים : בשלמא לר' יוסי · דאמר של שלמה גדול ושל משה קטן : היינו דכתיב קטן · אמזבח הנחשת והכי קאמר העמיד מזבח אבנים כי מזבח הנחשת קטן י] : אלא לרבי יהודה· דאמר כולה רלפה קידש יא]דמזבח שלמה לא יכול להכיל העולה: מאי קטן· דכתיב אמזבח הנחשת הא דשלמה גופיה קטן הוה: הכי קאמר כו'· ומשום דקאי במקום מזבח הנחשת וחילופו הוא קרי ליה מזבח הנחשת ובדברי הימים (ב ד) קרי ליה הכי בהדיא ויעש (המלך) מזבח נחשת כ' אמה ארכו וכ' אמה רחבו ואמקום המערכה קאי : במאי קמיפלגי · ר' יוסי דגמיר רבוע רבוע ממזבח הזהב ורבי יהודה דגמיר לה משל יחזקאל : כלי מכלי · מזבח הנחשת יב] והזהב כלים הם : מודה ר' יהודה בדמים · דאע"ג דאמר רבי יהודה כל העזרה מקודשת הני מילי להקטיר חלבים אבל לזריקת דמים לא: מדם התערובת · של פסחים מעל הרלפה: בגינו · בשבילו : וכי אלל המזבח אכלוה · והלא כל העזרה כשרה לכך דכתיב במנחה יג] מלות תאכל במקום קדוש (ויקרא ו) : קדש קדשים · בג"ש דקדש קדשים ילפי מהדדי : משום ג'

עשרים אמה יד] ובשמעתא קמייתא דעירובין (דף ב:) קשה טפי דפריך בין לרבנן בין לר' יהודה לילפו מפתח שער החלר ופי' שם בקונטרס שני לשונות ופי' בלשון שני דפריך טו] שיחשב פתח ברחב עשרים ומשני פתח שער החלר איקרי פתח סתמא לא איקרי ואיבעית אימא כי כתיב חמש עשרה (א) בגובהה כתיב והכתיב וקומה ה' אמות ההוא משפת מזבח ולמעלה ופי' שם בקונטרס דהייט כר' יוסי דשמעתין וזו היא תימה דלא מלינן למימר חמש עשרה אמה בגובה כתיב אלא ברחבה כדפרישית ועוד קשה דאי מרחבה פריך התם הוה ליה למימר הכי אלא הא דתנן הרחב מעשר אמות ימעט נילף מפתח שער החלר כיון דעד השתא איירי בגובהה ועוד לר' יהודה אמאי הולרך להקשות מפתח החלר מפתח*פתח אולם דקאי ביה הוה ליה לאקשויי ז"ק ועוד מאי קושיא מפתח טז] החלר התנן יש לו לורת הפתח א"ל למעט וחלר לורת הפתח הוה ליה שהיו העמודים משני לדדים וכלונסות על גביהן שהקלעים תלויין בהן [א] ומיהו בסמוך יז](ב)(קשה)כי פריך ור' יהודה מפתחו של אולם גמר והתנן וכו' לא משני שאני פתחו של אולם דה"ל לורת הפתח יח] [ובע"כ ל"ל] דכיון דאליבא דרב קיימא לא משני הכי דאיהו תני במתני' לריך למעט כדאמר התם* ומהאי טעמא יט] פריך [שפיר] השתא ועוד (ג)דשער חלר לא ה"ל לורת הפתח שהכלונסות היו על הווין שקבועין בעמודין מבחוץ ואמרינן התם בפ"ק (דף יא·) לורת הפתח שעשאה מן הלד לא עשה כלום ומפרש כ] רביט דמגובהה פריך התם דלא יחשב פתח ביתר מה' אמות כא] ומסתברא היא לן טפי למילף מפתח החלר ממאי דנילף מפתח ההיכל דפתח כב] המשכן על כרחין שלא כדין איקרי פתח כג] אהל מועד וחידוש הוא דלא הוו ליה גיפופי שהיה פרוך לפניו במלואו הלכך פתח ההיכל שהיה במקומו דלמא שלא כדין נמי איקרי פתח ובתר הכי גרס איבעית אימא קלעים ט"ו אמה כד] וכי כתיב וקומה ברוחב ה' אמות משפת קלעים ולמעלה והכא שיטיא כרבי יוסי דהכא ול"ג ט"ו אמה בגובהה הוא דכתיב וגם לא גרס אל הכתף דלא קאי אחמש עשרה דכתיב בקרא דההוא לא מיתוקמא אלא ברחבה אלא פירוש הוא כלומר הקלעים היו גבוהין חמש עשרה שלא יראו עבודה שבידו כרבי יוסי דאמר מזבח י' אמות והאי דכתיב בקלעים וקומה ה' אמות ודאי משפת מזבח ולמעלה והאי קרא דמייתי וקומה ברוחב ה' אמות (הייט) להוכיח גובה פתח כ' אמה כה] הייט ההוא דכתיב גבי מסך בסוף ויקהל ומפרש דמשפת קלעים ולמעלה קאמר שהקלעים היו גבוהין סביב החלר לפון ודרום ומערב וכן ללד המזרח כו] [שכמו] שהקלעים היו ט"ו רוחב מימין הפתח וכן משמאל הפתח כמו כן היו גבוהין ט"ו אמה ועל מסך הפתח כתיב רוחב כ' אמה וקומה ה' אמות ברוחב לעומת קלעי החלר פירוש שהמסך כל רוחב כ' היה גבוה ה' אמות מאחר קלעי החלר אשתכח המסך גבוה כ' וזו היא כז] אמת גובהו של פתח והיא שיטיא בתרא ליתיה אלא לרבנן דהא לרבי יהודה לא מתוקם כלל ואע"ג דקאי התם לשנויי לרבנן ולרבי יהודה שיטיא קמא יתיישב לרבי יהודה דשנינן פתח סתמא לא איקרי דהכי נמי לא מיתוקם ההוא שיטיא כרבי יוסי דהכא אלא כרבי יהודה והכא בשמעתין דפליג עליה גרסי' מה משכן י' אמות אף מזבח י' אמות קלעים ט"ו ולא גרסינן כח] נמי אל הכתף דלאו קרא מייתי ובברייתא דמלאכת המשכן לא גרסינן כלל קלעים ט"ו במילתא דר' יוסי ופירושא בעלמא הוא כלומר הקלעים היו גבוהין ט"ו אמה שלא יראה כהן ועבודה בידו ומה ת"ל ה' אמות משפת מזבח כו' ור"ת מפרש בספר הישר דלשמואל עלמו פריך נילף מפתח שער החלר כט] מנא ליה דו שחטו פתח אהל מועד אפתח היכל קאי ואי אפשר לומר כן כלל כדמוכחי כמה קראי בפרשת אלה פקודי ובשאר מקומות וקלת קשה לפירוש ל] ר"ת דפריך מגובה חמש דמאי משני פתח שער איקרי פתח סתמא לא איקרי כיון דנקרא שער כ"ש דאיקרי פתח דפתח קטן משער עוד נילף מפתח עזרה שנקרא פתח (ביחזקאל מא) והיה גובהו עשרים* : **הכי** קאמר מזבח אבנים שעשה שלמה תחת מזבח הנחשת · תימה דבפ' במה בהמה (שבת דף נה·) אמרינן ויעמוד אלל מזבח הנחשת מזבח הנחשת מי הוה אמר להן הקב"ה התחילו ממקום שאומרים שירה לפני בכלי נחשת ואמאי לא אמר כי הכא וי"ל דהתם מה לו להזכיר מזבח הנחשת כלל : **מודה** רבי יהודה בדמים · תימה מאי קס"ד מעיקרא והא קרן לא] ורבוע יסוד* מעכבין* : **קדשים** קלים מנין · תימה דלא יליף מהיקשא מזאת התורה : **אתיא** מדרשא דרבי יוסי · תימה ל"ל ג"ש דקדש קדשים לב] ועוד*) לג] [קדשים קלים] גופה נילף ממעשר וכי תימא מה למעשר שכן טעון וידוי וכסף ולורה בכור יוכיח ועוד דבהאי קרא דמייתי דמקיש מעשר לבכור נמי כתיב חטאת ואשם דתניא בספרי פרשת ראה אוכל בקרקס ונאכלס אלו חטאות ואשמות וכן בקרא דלא תוכל לאכול בשעריך דריש פרק בתרא דמכות (דף יז·) בקרך ולאנך לד] אלו חטאות ואשמות :

*) נ"א ועוד כיון גופס וקאי אשירי מנחה וגי' הנ"ק וכ"כ בעל פנים מאירות דה"ג [תימה] דקדשי קדשים גופיה נילף ממעשר וכו' והשאר נמחק

מאי

עין משפט נר מצוה

י א ב ג מיי' פ"ג מהל' פסה"מ הל' כב כג:

שיטה מקובצת

א] [וקומה] חמש אמות (מקומתו) משפת : ב] דגמיר לה ולד"י . ג] המובחר · ה"ה דהמ"ל משום דבעינן יסוד : ד] מנלן אתיא קדש קדש · תיבות ת"ל נמחק: ה] קלים מנלן אמר תיבת מנין נמחק : ו] יהודה· דאמר דברים: ז] ג"ש דרבוע רביע ברחבה הוא דגמר : ח] דיחזקאל גמיר לה וכדלעיל : ט] תיבות את תוך החצר ל"ש : י] קטן: נגם היה הס"ד . יא] קידש דאף מזבח של שלמה : יב] הנחשר ומזבח הזהב כלים הם : יג] במנחה בחצר אהל מועד יאכלוה הס"ד ומה"ד קדש קדש · בג"ש דקדש קדש ילפי מהדדי הס"ד ותיבות מצות תאכל משום נמחק: יד] אמה ועוד דהו"ל לר"י למימר ההוא ברחבה הוא דכתיב · ר"פ : טו] דפריך ארחבה שיחשב : טז] מפתח שער החצר : יז] בסמוך קשה כי פריך כו' והתנן כו' ואמאי לא משני : יח] הפתח וי"ל דכיון : יט] טעמא נמי פריך : כ] ומפרש רבינו (תם) [אא"ה נ"ל שצ"ל רבינו חננאל א) ועי' לקמן בסוף הדבור עכ"ה] דאגובהה אות מ נמחק : כא] אמות דמסתברא : כב] דפתח אהל מועד על כרחין : כג] פתח וחידוש כו' תיבות אהל מועד נמחק : כד] אמה גובהה וכי : כה] אמה והיינו ההוא : כו] המזרח מימין תיבות [שכמו] שהקלעים היו ט"ו רוחב נמחק : כז] היא מדת גובהו תיבת אמת נמחק : כח] ולא גרסינן ואומר ול"ג נמי : כט] החצר ומנא ליה : ל] לפירוש רבינו דפריך' תיבת ר"ת נרשם עליו ק (ועיין למעלה באות כ') ועי' בספר הישר סי' רפו: לא] קרן וכבש ורבוע יסוד שמעכבין הס"ד : לב] קדשים · ס"א הא כתיב בהאי קרא דמייתי והבאתם שמה וגו' ועוד: לג] קדשי קדשים גופית תיבת קלים נמחק : לד] וצאנך' ולמאי דפי' ריב"א לעיל (דף ס ע"א) דאכילה לא קיימי אחטאות ואשמות דכתיב אתם ובתיכם ניחא · מהר"פ :

א) וכ"כ בלאמת כפי' סר"מ למסכת עירובין (דף ב ע"ב) שנדפס לפנים בש"ס שם :

מסורת הש"ס

וקסבר ז"ק

ז"ק

פסחים סה. [לעיל לד: ע"ש מנחות נס: ע"ש תוספתא פסחים פ"ד]

[תוס' סנהדרין פ"ג מכות יס. תמורה כא.]

[וע"ע תוספות עירובין ב: ד"ה בין ד"ס ואב"א]

ז"ל יסוד כתיב שמעכבין רש"ק

*[ועי' תוס' לעיל נא: ד"ה מן ה]

הגהות הב"ח

(א) תוס' ד"ה ולומר קלעים וכו' חמש עשרה אמה בגובהה וכו' : (ב) בא"ד ומיהו בסמוך נמי קשה כי פריך וכו' והתנן וכו' אמאי לא משני וכו' לורת הפתח אלא ז"ל דכיון : (ג) בא"ד ועוד י"ל דשער החלר :

גליון הש"ס

גמ' אין אוכלין בגינו שירי מנחה · ולאחר שחזר ונבנה עי' תוס' בב"מ דף נג ע"ב ד"ה לא פליג :

הגהות צ"ק [א] [ומיהו הא לא קשיא דכיון דאליבא דרב קיימא דאיהו הני במתני' לריך למעט אע"ג (דאין) [דיש] לו לורת הפתח כדאמר התם ומהאי טעמא כי פריך בסמוך ור"י מפתחו של אולם ומר שאני פתחו של אולם דה"ל לורת הפתח כיון דאליבא דרב קיימא לא משני הכי ועוד דשער כו' כנ"ל :]

ג' זקנים א] וזה אחד מהן *רבי ישמעאל אומר *יכול יעלה אדם מעשר שני לירושלים ויאכלנו בזמן הזה ודין הוא בכור טעון הבאת מקום ומעשר טעון הבאת מקום מה בכור אינו אלא בפני הבית אף מעשר אינו אלא בפני הבית מה לבכור שכן טעון מתן דמים ואימורים לגבי מזבח ביכורים יוכיחו מה לביכורים שכן טעונין הנחה ת"ל *°והבאתם שמה עולותיכם וגו' מקיש מעשר לבכור מה בכור אינו אלא בפני הבית אף מעשר אינו אלא בפני הבית ונִיהדר דינא וניתי במה הצד משום דאיכא למיפרך מה להצד השוה שבהן שכן יש בהן צד מזבח ב] מאי קסבר אי קסבר *קדושה ראשונה קידשה לשעתה וקידשה לעתיד לבא אפילו בכור נמי ג] ואי קסבר לא קידשה לעתיד לבא ד] אפילו בכור נמי תיבעי אמר רבינא לעולם קסבר לא קידשה והכא במאי עסקינן בבכור שנזרק דמו קודם חורבן הבית וחרב הבית ועדיין בשרו קיים ואיתקש בשרו לדמו מה דמו במזבח אף בשרו במזבח ואתי מעשר ויליף מבכור *וכי דבר הלמד בהיקש חוזר ומלמד בהיקש מעשר דגן חולין הוא הניחא למ"ד *בתר למד אזלינן אלא למ"ד בתר מלמד אזלינן מאי איכא למימר דם ובשר חדא מילתא היא כי סליקרבין אמרה לשמעתא קמיה דרבי ירמיה אמר *בבלאי טפשאי אמטול דיתבי בארעא חשוכא אמרי שמעתא דמחשכא לא שמיע להו הא *דתניא בשעת סילוק מסעות קדשים נפסלין וזבים ומצורעים משתלחים חוץ למחיצה ותניא אידך בשני מקומות קדשים נאכלים ה] מאי לאו ו] הא בקדשי קדשים הא בקדשים קלים אמר רבינא ז] אידי ואידי בקדשים קלים ולא קשיא הא

רש"י

ג' זקנים · דבר אחד מפי כל זקן וזקן: ר' ישמעאל אומר כו' · זו היא אחת מהן: יכול יעלה אדם מעשר שני · דקסבר קדושת הארץ לא בטלה וצריכה הפרשת מעשרות מן התורה ח] וקאמר יכול יאכלנו עכשיו בירושלים בלא פדיון: ת"ל וכו' · ולקמיה פריך מאי שנא בכור דפשיטא ליה ומאי שנא מעשר דמיבעיא ליה: שכן טעון מתן דמים · הלכך צריך בית ומזבח: בכורים יוכיחו · שאין טעונין מתן דמים וצריכין בית כדכתיב ט] לפני מזבח (דברים כו): שכן טעון הנחה · הלכך בעו בית דהוזקקו למזבח לכך: ת"ל כו' · ולקמיה פריך וליהדר דינא וליתי במה הצד: צד מזבח · זה למתן דמים ואלו להנחה: מאי קסבר · האי תנא דפשיט ליה בכור י] ממעשר: אי קסבר קדושה ראשונה של בית קדשה לשעתה וקדשה לעתיד לבא · כי היכי דס"ל בקדושת הארץ וקמיבעי ליה מי קרינא ביה לפני אלהיך או לא וקפשיט מעשר מבכור: אפילו בכור נמי · אפילו בכור יקריב ויאכל דהא מאן דאית ליה קדשה לעתיד לבא אית ליה שמקריבין אע"פ שאין בית כדאמרינן במגילה יא] (דף י·): ה"ג ואי קסבר לא קדשה אפי' בכור נמי תיבעי · ואי קסבר קדושת בית בטלה יב] לה ומיבעי *לה במעשר הואיל ואינו צריך לבית מי מיתאכיל בירושלים ולפני ה' קרינא ביה או לא: אפילו בכור כה"ג נמי תיבעי ליה · כגון יג] *שקרבו דמיו ואימוריו וחרב הבית ובשרו קיים מהו שיאכלוהו: אמר רבינא לעולם קסבר לא קדשה · והכא דקפשיט ליה מעשר מבכור בבכור שאינו צריך לבית דומיא דמעשר יד] קפשיט ליה דפשיטא ליה גביה דלא *מיתכיל: דאיתקש בשרו לדמו · טו] ואת דמם תזרק ואת חלבם תקטיר ובשרם יהיה לך (במדבר יח) ויליף מיניה בשעה שאתה ראוי לזרוק את הדם אתה אוכל את הבשר ולא אחר שנהרס המזבח: וכי · בשר הלמד בהיקש מן הדם חוזר ומלמד בהיקש על המעשר טז]: לשמעתא · הא דאביי דאמר קדשים קלים נפסלין בפגימת המזבח ומייתי לה מדרשא דרבי יוסי: בשעת סילוק המסעות · כשמורידין את המשכן ומסלקין את המזבחות בעת המסעות במדבר: קדשים נפסלים · בשר קדשי קדשים *וקא סלקא יז] דעתך מפני סילוק המזבח הוא מדקתני וזבין ומצורעין משתלחין שאין מצורע נכנס לדגלי השבטים ולא זב למחנה לוים כשנושאי הארון כדאמרינן לקמן (דף סא:) אע"פ שנכנס אהל מועד הוא אלמא נפסלין דקאמר לאו משום דמיפסלי ביוצא הוא דהא אהל מועד חשיב ליה יח]: ותניא אידך גרים: בשני מקומות יט] נאכלין · חד במקומן במחנות האמורות בהן כשהמשכן במקומו וחד בכל מקום שיהא שם דרך הליכתן משנסעו וקשיין אהדדי: מאי לאו · קמייתא בקדשי קדשים והא בקדשים קלים: הכי גרסינן מאי לאו הא בקדשי קדשים הא בקדשים קלים: אידי ואידי קדשים קלים ולא קשיא · קמייתא רבי

תוספות

מאי קסבר האי תנא · דפשיטא ליה בכור טפי ממעשר אי קסבר קדשה לעתיד לבא בקדושת הארץ וקמבעיא ליה אי קרינא ביה לפני ה' אי לא אפי' בכור נמי יקרב ויאכל דמאן דאית ליה קדשה קסבר דמקריבין אע"פ שאין בית כדאיתא פ"ק דמגילה (דף י·) ואי קסבר לא קדשה דבטלה קדושת כ] *הארץ ומבעיא ליה במעשר משום דאינו צריך לבית כא] ומיתאכיל בירושלים אי קרינא ביה לפני ה' אי לא אפי' בכור נמי תיבעי היכא דהוי כעין מעשר כגון בכי ה"ג שאינו צריך לבית שקרבו דמיו ואימוריו וחרב הבית ובשרו קיים מהו שיאכלוהו ומסיק דקסבר לא קידשה והא דפשיטא ליה בבכור משום דאיתקש בשרו לדמו ולא אכיל בשר אלא בשעה הראויה לזריקת דם ולא משנהרס זו היא גירסת הקונטרס ופירושו ואם תאמר אי קסבר לא קדשה היכי משכחת מעשר שני דאורייתא כיון דבטלה קדושת הארץ כב] וי"ל דאי קסבר לא קידשה מוקמינן ליה למעשר שגדל בפני הבית כמו שפירש בקונטרס כג] [גבי] בכור שקרבו דמו ואימוריו וחרב הבית ובשרו קיים א"נ אפי' קסבר לא קדשה הני מילי קדושת הבית אבל קדושת הארץ לא בטלה ונתחייבו בתרומות ומעשרות כדאשכחנא (לקמן דף קיב:) כשחרב שילה שבטלה קדושת הבית ולא בטלה קדושת הארץ וא"ת כיון דלא קידשה והותרו הבמות כד] יהא נאכל בכל ערי ישראל לספרים דגרסי' לקמן בפ' בתרא (דף קיב:) באו לנוב וגבעון הותרו הבמות מעשר נאכל בכל ערי ישראל וי"ל דלפי אותה גירסא לא מתוקם הכא אלא במעשר שגדל לפני הבית והוזקק להבאת מקום כה] ואינו נאכל בכל ערי ישראל וקשה לפירוש הקונטרס מאי דוחקיה דרבינא לומר לא קדשה ופליג אכוליה הש"ס דקים לן ירושלים אין אחריה היתר כדתנן בפרק בתרא (נט זה שם) לימא דלעולם קסבר קדשה כו] ובכור שנזרק דמו ונפגם המזבח דאין בשרו נאכל בפגימת המזבח ומיהו מצי למימר דלישנא דברייתא קשיתיה דקתני מה בכור אינו אלא בפני הבית דמשמע בית ממש צריך ואי קדשה למה לי בית הלא מקריבין אע"פ שאין בית ואין צריך רק מזבח משום דאיתקש בשרו לדמו אבל ה"ה דלעולם מצי סבר קדשה דכיון דנזרק דמו ואח"כ חרב אין אוכלין בשרו משום דאיתקש לדמו *מיהו האי בפני הבית היינו בפני מזבח ולאו בית ממש קאמר אבל קשה מאי קאמר אפילו בכור נמי תיבעי ולא*) תבעי מעשר אדרבה כיון דלא קדשה פשיטא כז] לא קרינא ביה לפני ה' דמחילה לאכול דאורייתא ועוד דבכור פשיטא דמפסיל ביוצא כשחרב הבית ונפלו מחיצות כיון דלא קדשה ומה צריך כלל כח] היקישא דבשר ודסוכי תימה כשחרב הבית ונהרס המזבח אבל חומות ירושלים כט] קיימת ולא בטלה קדושתה לענין קדשים קלים ומעשר שני זהו תימה לומר דהא ירושלים לא נתקדשה אלא בשביל הבית ואיך יתכן שקדושת הבית תבטל וקדושת ירושלים קיימא לכך נראה כמו גירסת הספרים אי קסבר קדשה אפילו בכור נמי ואי קסבר לא קדשה אפילו מעשר נמי אמר רבינא לעולם קסבר קדשה וכו' והכי פריך אפילו בכור נמי משכחת לה בלא חומות ירושלים ובלא חומת עזרה כמו שפירש בקונטרס דמקריבים אע"פ שאין בית כלומר יבנה המזבח ויזרוק הדם ויאכל הבשר אבל בלא מזבח פשיטא ליה דאינו יכול להקריב כדאמרי' לעיל (דף נט·) מודה רב בדמים אע"פ שהבית קיים וכל שכן בזמן הזה ואי קסבר לא קדשה קדושת הבית לבטלת המזבח וכל שכן קדושת ירושלים אבל קדושת הארץ קיימת להתחייב בתרומה ומעשר כמו בנוב וגבעון אפילו מעשר יהא ל] פסול פשיטא דאין לו היתר בירושלים ולא גרסינן לקמן פ' בתרא (דף קיב:) מעשר שני נאכל בכל ערי ישראל ואי גרסינן ליה צריך לומר דהכי פריך אפילו מעשר **) שני יהא פשיטא דאין חייב להעלותו ואמאי קאמרת יכול יעלה אדם למשמע

*) נ"ל מיבעיא ז"ק **) מעשר יהא כו'

יא א מיי' פ"ז מהלכות בית הבחירה הל' טו ופסק דלאוכלין שם ע"ש:

תורה אור

°דברים יב

שיטה מקובצת

גליון הש"ס

three laws on the authority of [60b] three elders, and the following is one of them: R. Ishmael said: You might think that a man can take up second tithe[11] to Jerusalem and consume it[12] there nowadays,[13] and that would be logical: a firstling must be brought to
a the 'Place',[1] and tithe must be brought to the 'Place': as [the law of] firstling operates only whilst the Temple stands, so [the law of] tithe is valid only whilst the Temple stands. [No:] as for a firstling, the reason is because its blood and *emurim* must be presented at the altar![2] Let first-fruits prove it.[3] As for first-fruits, the reason is because they must be placed [before the altar]![4] Therefore it states, *And thither shall ye bring your burnt-offerings . . . and your tithes . . . and the firstlings of your herd and of your flock:*[5] this assimilates tithe to firstling: as [the law of] firstling is valid only whilst the Temple stands, so is tithe valid only whilst the Temple stands. Yet let us revert to the argument and learn it from the common characteristic?[6]—Because that can be refuted: the feature common to both is that each is connected with the altar.[7]

What does he hold?[8] If he holds that the first sanctity hallowed it for the nonce and for the future,[9] then even a firstling too [is thus]?[10] While if he holds that it did not hallow it for the future; there should be a question even about a firstling too?—Said Rabina: In truth he holds that it did not hallow it [for all time], but here we discuss a firstling whose blood was sprinkled before the Temple was destroyed, then the Temple was destroyed, and we still have
b its flesh.[1] Now its flesh is likened to its blood:[2] as its blood requires the altar, so does its flesh require the altar.[3] Then tithe comes and is learnt from a firstling.[4] But can then that which is derived by a *hekkesh* teach in turn by a *hekkesh*?—The tithe of corn is merely *hullin*. That is well on the view that the taught is the determining factor; but on the view that the teacher is the determining factor, what can be said?[5]—Blood and flesh are the same thing.[6]

When Rabin went up,[7] he reported this teaching[8] in R. Jeremiah's presence, whereupon he observed: The Babylonians are fools. Because they dwell in a land of darkness[9] they engage in dark discussions.[10] Have they not heard what was taught: During the dismantling [of the Tabernacle] on their travels,[11] sacrifices became unfit,[12] and *zabin* and lepers were sent out of their precincts.[13] Whereas another [Baraitha] taught: Sacrifices might be eaten in two places.[14] Surely then, the former refers to sacrifices of higher
c sanctity, and the latter to sacrifices of lesser sanctity?[1]—Said Rabina: Both refer to sacrifices of lesser sanctity, yet there is no

(11) V. *supra* 49a n. 3. (12) Instead of redeeming it. (13) I.e., after the destruction of the Temple.—He holds that the sanctity of Eretz Israel was not annulled thereby, and so one must still set aside tithes.

a (1) The 'Place' *par excellence*—Jerusalem. (2) Hence the law does not operate without a Temple and altar. But that would not apply to tithe. (3) Which were brought only whilst the Temple stood, as it says, *And he shall set it down before the altar of the Lord thy God* (Deut. XXVI, 4) which implies that there must be an altar, though there was no blood or *emurim* to be presented thereat. (4) Hence at this stage there are no grounds for supposing that the law of tithe is valid only when the Temple is standing. (5) Deut. XII, 6. (6) Why is the foregoing *hekkesh* necessary? Though it cannot be learnt from *either* firstling *or* first-fruits, it could be learnt from their common feature, which is that both must be brought to Jerusalem and both are in force only as long as the Temple stands. Hence the same applies to second tithe, which shows this feature. (7) The blood and *emurim* of a firstling must be presented at the altar, and first-fruits must be placed before the altar. But tithe is not connected with the altar in any way. (8) When he assumes that the law is certain and obvious in respect of firstling, but not in respect of tithe. (9) I.e., that the sanctity of the Temple was for all time, even after its destruction. (10) Rashi: even a firstling should be brought to Jerusalem and eaten there, for on the view that its sanctity was for all time it was to be offered even after the Temple's destruction.

b (1) Which no longer needs the altar; nevertheless it may not be eaten. (2) Num. XVIII, 17f: *Thou shalt dash their blood against the altar,-and shalt make their fat smoke for an offering made by fire . . . and the flesh of them shall be thine.* These, being written together, are assimilated to one another. (3) In the sense that it may not be eaten when there is no longer an altar. (4) That the same applies to it. (5) For notes v. *supra* 45a. (6) They are both parts of the same offering. Hence, when we say that the flesh requires the altar, just as the blood, this is not regarded as the result of a *hekkesh*, but as though the Biblical teaching concerning the blood naturally refers to the flesh too. (7) To Palestine. Rabin and R. Dimi were two Rabbis who travelled backwards and forwards between Palestine and Babylon, acting as intellectual links between the academies of both. (8) Viz., Abaye's statement that sacrifices become unfit through the altar being damaged, and its inference by R. Jose's exegesis. (9) Babylonia is possibly so called on account of the Parsees (fireworshippers), who forbade the Jews to have any light in their dwellings on their (the Parsees') festivals. (10) They discuss laws without knowing their true meaning or derive them incorrectly. (11) When the Tabernacle was dismantled and taken apart, which was when the Israelites were actually travelling. (12) The flesh of sacrifices of higher sanctity might not be eaten, even if their blood had been sprinkled before the dismantling. (13) The precincts which were permitted to them whilst the Israelites were encamped. Thus *zabin* were sent out of the Levitical camp, and lepers out of the camp of the Israelites (v. *supra* 55a n.b6). (14) (i) Within their normally permitted boundaries, when the Tabernacle was up; and (ii) in any place, when they were actually travelling. This contradicts the former teaching.

c (1) The latter may be eaten even when the Tabernacle is dismantled. At that time there would be no altar either, and that is certainly no better than when the altar stands but is damaged. This proves that sacrifices of lesser sanctity may be eaten when the altar is damaged, and thus contradicts Abaye. Therefore R. Jeremiah called Abaye's teaching 'dark', i.e., incorrect.

difficulty: [61a] The former agrees with R. Ishmael,[2] the latter with the Rabbis.[3] Alternatively, both treat of sacrifices of higher sanctity; but what does 'in two places' mean? Before the Levites

(2) Who assimilates the flesh to the blood; hence it may not be eaten. (3) Who do not assimilate the flesh to the blood.

הא רבי ישמעאל הא רבנן ואיבעית אימא הא והא בקדשי קדשים ומאי בשני מקומות קודם שיעמידו לוים את המשכן ולאחר

ר' ישמעאל · דיליף בשר מדם א] בתרייתא רבנן : **ואיבעית אימא** · בתרייתא נמי בקדשי קדשים : **ושני מקומות** · לאו לאחר שנכנסו דנסתלק המזבח קאמר אלא חד מינייהו כדאיתא בעוד ב] המשכן נטוי כמשפטו · וחד לאחר שפירקו קרשים וקלעי החצר ועדיין המזבח במקומו וקודם שיעמידו לוים את ג] משכן דנקט הכא לאו דוקא נקט חדא דלא *משכח לה שהרי קודם שיסעו בני קהת נושאי המזבחות היו חונין בני גרשון ומררי נושאי המשכן ומקימין אותו ובנסיעתם היו מורידין את המשכן תחילה *ונושאין בני גרשון ומררי אחר *דגל ד] אחד ובני קהת אחרי שני דגלים כדי שיהו קודמין בני גרשון בחנייתן ומעמידין את המשכן לפני בוא בני קהת כדכתיב אחר מסע דגל בני יהודה והורד המשכן וגו' (במדבר י) ואחר שני דגלים כתיב (שם) ונסעו הקהתים נושאי המקדש דהיינו ארון ומזבחות וכלי השרת והקימו בני גרשון את המשכן עד בואם של בני קהת ה] ועוד אי בשינו את הסדר מוקמת לה היכי שחטי קרבנות קודם שיעמידו משכן הא אמר באיזהו מקומן (לעיל דף נה:) ו] בשלמים ששחטן קודם שיעמידו לוים כו' פסולין ואי ז] גרסת לה מוקי לה בשינו את הסדר וההוא דאיזהו מקומן שלמים דוקא קאמר משום דכתיב בהו (ויקרא ג) ושחטו פתח אהל מועד ולא יליף שאר קדשים מינייהו :

מהו

דמשמע דמספקא ליה אי חייב להעלותו לירושלים או לא כיון דלא קידשה יהא נאכל בכל ערי ישראל כדתנן לקמן (שם) ואמאי צריך לאקושי לבכור דמה בכור אינו מעלהו אף מעשר אינו מעלהו אמר רבינא לעולם קסבר קדשה ולא מיירי כלל בחובת העלאה אלא אם יכול לאוכלו בזמן הזה או לא וילפינן אכילת מעשר מאכילת בכור דמה אכילת בכור בעיא מזבח משום דאיתקש בשרו לדמו אף אכילת מעשר בעיא מזבח ואין שום מעשר נאכל בזמן הזה ואית ספרים דגרסי אי לא קדשה אפילו מעשר נמי לא וה"פ אפילו מעשר נמי לא יהא נאכל כלומר דמדקבעית במעשר בזמן הזה *א"כ במעשר שהוזקק להבאת מקום ח] קבעי' אבל לאחר חורבן ההוא שמא לא נתחייב כלל במעשר כיון דלא קדשה ואפילו נתחייב במעשר כמו בנוב וגבעון מ"מ פשיטא דנאכל בכל ערי ישראל לפי הגירסא דלקמן כדפרישית אלא כי קבעי באותו שגדל בפני הבית וחרב הבית ט] והוא פשיטא דאינו נאכל אמר רבינא לעולם קסבר קדשה ובבכור שנזרק דמו קודם חורבן הבית עסקינן וחרב הבית ועדיין בשרו קיים ואיתקש בשרו לדמו וא"ת והא כתיב (במדבר יח) ואת דמם תזרוק ואת חלבם תקטיר אלמא איתקש י] בההוא קרא להקטרת חלב ואמרי' לעיל* דמזבח שנעקר מקטירין קטורת במקומו וה"ה אימורין וי"ל דקולא וחומרא לחומרא מקשינן ומקשינן בשרו יא] לדמו והשתא מהך דרשא יליף לכל הקדשים דאם נפגם המזבח אין נאכלין וא"ת לפי גירסא זו דגרס קדשה קשיא דר' ישמעאל אדר' ישמעאל דלקמן פ' בתרא (דף קיט·) תניא רבי ישמעאל אומר זה וזה מנוחה ונחלה שילה ופי' בקונטרס דבקדושת ירושלים גופה ס"ל דלא קדשה ויש אחריה *היתר מדלא קרי ליה נחלה כדאיתא בפ"ק דמגילה (דף י·) שמעתי שמקריבין בבית חוניו בזמן הזה ואוקמינן כרבי ישמעאל מיהו בזה לא דק בפירושו דההיא דמגילה (גז"ש) רבי ישמעאל ברבי יוסי וההיא דלקמן רבי ישמעאל בן אלישע בר פלוגתיה דר"ע אבל מ"מ על כרחין *קסבר לא קדשה דכיון דמוקי קרא דנחלה בשילה א"כ מנא ליה דירושלים אין אחריה היתר וי"ל דשמא נפקא ליה מקרא אחרינא והרב רבי חיים מפרש דרבי ישמעאל סבר קדשה והאי דקאמר זה וזה שילה אתא לאשמועינן דשילה אין אחריה היתר דלא כמ"ד יש אחריה היתר והיינו משום דדריש מנוחה זו שילה נחלה זו ירושלים ומדחלקו קדריש ליתן היתר בין זו לזו ופליג אמתני' דקתני שילה יש אחריה היתר דתנן (לקמן דף קיב:) באו לנוב וגבעון כו' ואין נראה כלל שהרי יב] מוכיחים דבנוב וגבעון הותרו הבמות גבי שמואל והוא יברך את הזבח (שמואל א ט) וגם קרי ליה בפסוק במה אבל אחר ירושלים לכולי עלמא לא הותרו הבמות ואפי' מאן דאית ליה לא קדשה מני סבר דאין אחריה היתר וכן משמע פ"ק דמגילה (גז"ש) א"ר יצחק שמעתי שמקריבין בבית חוניו בזמן הזה וקאמר דהדר ביה מהא דתניא ירושלים אין אחריה היתר ואמאי הדר ביה הא קאמר התם כתנאי אי קדשה לעתיד לבא אי לא קדשה ומעיקרא מאי סבר ולבסוף מאי סבר אלא ודאי מעיקרא סבר דלמ"ד לא קדשה הותרו הבמות והדר ביה ממתניתין דמגילה וממתניתין דלקמן בפ' בתרא (דף קיב:) דירושלים אין אחריה היתר דמשמע לכולי עלמא אפילו למ"ד לא קדשה ותנאי דמייתי התם בקדשה ולא קדשה לא קאי אדרבי יצחק אלא ריהטא דהש"ס הוא משום יג] *דאיירי קדושה ראשונה קדשה לשעתה וקדשה לעתיד לבא דנקיט כתנאי ומייתי פלוגתא דבתי ערי חומה דדמי לקדושת הארץ דמשווי להו *אהדדי ובפ"ב דערכין (דף לב:) גבי מקיש ביאתם בימי עזרא לביאתם בימי יהושע וכמה תנאי היה יכול להביא דאיכא דאית ליה לא קדשה ואיכא דאית ליה קדשה ור"מ בפ"ק דחולין (דף ו:) קסבר לא קדשה גבי בית שאן ורבי ישמעאל דהכא ורבי יוסי דסדר עולם בפרק הערל (יבמות דף פב:) יד] וא"ת ומנא ליה לקמן דרבי יוחנן סבר קדשה משום דמחייב מעלה בזמן הזה לעולם אימא לך דסבר לא קדשה אפ"ה אין אחריה היתר כדפי' וי"ל דאי לא קדשה לא מחייב טו] דאינו ראוי לפתח אהל מועד דנדחו לגמרי אבל אי קדשה לא נדחו דיכול לבנות מזבח במקומו ויקריב עליו או מיירי ר' יוחנן בקטרת דלא בעי מזבח כדפי' לעיל ואין להקשות לפי' הקונטרס דגרס הכא לא קדשה ובסוף הערל (גז"ש) שמעינן לרבי יוסי דקדשה בברייתא דסדר עולם טז] ויש חילוק כדפי' לעיל דאפילו בטלה קדושת הבית קדושת הארץ לא בטלה כדאשכחן בנוב וגבעון א"כ תני ולא סבר ליה כדבעי למימר פרק יוצא דופן (נדה דף מו:) א"כ הא דידיה הא דרביה דהכא משמיה דרבי ישמעאל וא"ת למאי דגרס קדשה הא ר"ל ס"ל אליבא דרבי יוסי (יבמות דף פב.) תרומה בזמן הזה דרבנן וי"ל כדפרישית לעיל דאפשר אפילו לא בטלה קדושת הבית קדושת הארץ בטלה ותדע דרבי יהושע שמעי' ליה יז] עיגול בעיגולין עולה בפ"ק דביצה (דף ד·) ובסוף הערל (יבמות דף פא·) מוכח לר"ל יח] למ"ד עולה קסבר תרומה בזמן הזה דרבנן ושמעינן ליה לרבי יהושע בכמה דוכתי דאמר שמעתי שמקריבים אע"פ שאין בית יט] *ותימה הוא לומר שקדושת הבית קיימת להקריב קרבן בלא במה ולא יתחייב בתרומה אבל לעיל דאמר איפכא אתי שפיר כמו בנוב וגבעון והכא י"ל דרבי יוסי משום רבי ישמעאל קאמר ולא ס"ל ומר' יהושע י"ל *דסבר דאינו מקדש אלא ו' דברים בלבד לכן יעלו העיגולין ור"א דמספקא ליה בפרק ידיעות הטומאה (שבועות דף טז·) ובפ"ק דמגילה (דף י·) אי סבר קדשה או לא קדשה ושמעי' ליה בפ"ק דחגיגה (דף ג:) גבי עמון ומואב מעשרין מעשר עני בשביעית דקסבר לא קדשה ומיהו אין ראיה משום דהגיבה כרכים לאו מדברי ר"א כ] כדפרישית פ"ק דיבמות (דף טז· ד"ה עמון) וליתיה כא] במסכת ידים (פ"ד מ"ג) : *

קדשים נפסלין · פי' בקונטרס קס"ד מפני סילוק המזבח הוא מדקתני זבין ומצורעין משתלחין שאין מצורע נכנס לדגלי השבטים ולא זב למחנה הלוים נושאי ארון כדאמר לקמן אע"פ שנסע אהל מועד אלמא נפסלין דקאמר לאו משום דמפסלי ביוצא הוא דהא אהל מועד חשיב ליה וא"ת כב] דלמאי דמוקי לה השתא בקדשי קדשים אפילו בלא סילוק מזבח אלא סילוק קלעי החצר לחוד נפסלין קדשי קדשים ביוצא דבהדיא מוכח בפ' שתי הלחם (מנחות דף צה·) דבשעת כג] מסעות אין קרוי מחנה שכינה קיים ולחם הפנים ושאר קדשי קדשים מיפסלי ביוצא דנסע אהל מועד הוא לאו דוקא לענין מחנה שכינה אבל לגבי קדשים קלים והאי לא מיפסלי ביוצא משום מסע המחנות דלענין מחנה ישראל ומחנה לויה אע"פ שנסע אהל מועד הוא דמחניהם קיימים בדגלי השבטים כדמוכח לקמן פ' בתרא (דף קטז:) ולכך זבין ומצורעין משתלחין וקדשים קלים אין נפסלין ביוצא ואתקפתא הוי מדקתני נאכלין בשני מקומות דמיירי בקדשים קלים ואע"פ שאין מזבח במקומו :

הא ר' ישמעאל והא רבנן · היינו תנאי דפליגי עליה דר' ישמעאל בתמורה פרק ואלו קדשים (דף כא·) ודרשי' ליה לקרא בע"א :

קודם שיעמידו המשכן · פרש"י לאו דוקא קודם אלא לאחר שהעמידו הכל המשכן והמזבח דאין לפרש ממש קודם שהעמידו המשכן כיון שכבר העמידו המזבח במקומו אוכלין קדשי קדשים הלא תחילה נוסעין בני גרשון ומעמידין המשכן ואח"כ בני קהת מעמידין המזבח ואם שינו הסדר והעמידו המזבח תחילה היאך שחטו קדשים קודם העמדת המשכן הא אמרן (יומא דף סב:) שלמים ששחטן קודם פתיחת ההיכל פסולין וי"ל שלמים דוקא כתיב בהו ושחטו פתח אהל מועד כל זה פי' רש"י וק"ל (ברו"ך) הא תנן גבי תמיד (תמיד דף ל:) לא היה שוחט עד ששמע שער הגדול שנפתח אלמא ילפינן שאר קרבנות שאין שוחטין משלמים ואין נראה לומר דהיינו מדרבנן דהא בהיקשא דזאת התורה נילף לפסולא משלמים וגם אין לומר בשלמים גופייהו אינו פוסל רק מדרבנן דלא שנה הכתוב לעכב דהא אמרי' פ' שני שעירי (יומא דף סב:) דשלמים ששחטן בחוץ קודם פתיחת דלתות ההיכל פטור אלמא מן התורה אינו ראוי לפתח אהל מועד דפסול דרבנן חייב בחוץ ואפילו בפסול דאורייתא חייב בחוץ היכא דאם עלו לא ירדו כדמוכח פרק השוחט והמעלה (לקמן קט·) וזהו הוכחה דשאר קדשים נמי פסולין בפנים קודם פתיחת דלתות ההיכל דאי כשירין א"כ בשלמים אם עלו לא ירדו דקרוי פסולו בקודש היכא דאית ליה הכשירא בעלמא א"כ הוא דבשלמים *אם עלו לא ירדו אמאי פטור בחוץ אלא ודאי בשאר קדשים נמי פסולין אם לא תאמר כיון דלא נפתחו קודם השחיטה דלתות ההיכל חשיב שוחט שלמים שלא במקומן וירדו אע"ג דשאר קדשים אין נפסלין מן התורה ודמי לקדשי קדשים ששחטן בדרום בפ"ק דמעילה (דף ג·) דכמאן דחנקינהו דמו וירדו [לרבי יהודה] אע"ג דקדשים קלים שחיטתן כד] בדרום כשירין אבל לר"ש לא ירדו כדאיתא התם א"כ ההיא דשני שעירי דפטר בחוץ כרבי יהודה *וגם אין לומר דקודם שפירקו המשכן כלל שחטו וזרקו את הדם ואחרי כן פירקוהו ושינו הסדר בשעת חנייה והעמידו המזבח וקלעי החצר תחילה וקאמר בשמעתא דקודם שיעמידו קרשי המשכן יאכלו קדשי קדשים הלא מיד שפירקוהו נפסלו ביוצא הקדשים ולא אמרינן נסע אהל מועד הוא לגבי מחנה שכינה אלא ודאי קודם שהעמידו לאו דוקא אלא העמידו הכל וחידושא הוי אלאחר שפירקו כדקאמר קמ"ל אע"פ דנסע אהל מועד הוא ואע"פ שנפרק המשכן כיון שקלעי החצר והמזבח במקומן · ברו"ך :

ולאחר

מסורת הש"ס

גי' הל"ק משכחת לה שיהא המזבח מונח קודם שעמדת המשכן שהרי כו' כצ"ל

צ"ל ונוסעין דגל ראשון כו' אחרי דגל שני כדי צ"ק

היתר כדאמרינן בפ"ק צ"ק

גי' הצ"ק קסבר לא קדשה מדלא קרי ליה נחלה ועוד דכיון דמוקי כו'

דאיירי דנקט קדושה ראשונה קדשה לשעתה ולא קדשה לעתיד לבא נקיט כתנאי כו' כצ"ל *אהדדי בפ"ב צ"ק

[ועי' בתוס' יבמות פא. ד"ה שאני שונה כו' דהו סברא זו ע"ש]

עיין לעיל דף ס ע"ב

[דף נט.]

במעשר כאן סוה אם הוזקק להבאת מקום מאי קבעית אי דגדל לאחר החורבן הוא כו' צ"ק

גליון הש"ס

תוס' ד"ה (בעמוד הקודם) מאי וכו' ותימה הוא לומר שקדושת הבית קיימת· עי' לקמן דף סב ע"א תוס' ד"ה ואחד : תוס' ד"ה קודם וכו' אם עלו לא ירדו אמאי פטור בחוץ· עי' לעיל דף נט ע"א תוס' ד"ה עד : בא"ד וגם אין לומר דקודם שפירקו וכו' נפסלו ביוצא הק"ק"ל הא גם בקדשים קלים כה"ג פסול מאכילה כיון דבעת סילוק מסעות הוי פגם מזבח ואידחי מאכילה ואינו חוזר ונראה כמ"ש תוס' בדיבור הסמוך בד"ה ולאחר וכד"ה אע"פ:

שיטה מקובצת

א] מדם וא"כ בשעת סילוק המחנות כיון שאי אפשר לזרוק את הדם אין הבשר נאכל בתרייתא רבנן דלא ילפי בשר מדם הס"ד : ב] בעוד שהמשכן נטוי : ג] המשכן דנקט הכא לאו דוקא נקט אלא אידי דנקט לאחר שיפרקו נקט [נמי קודם שיעמידו] דלא משכחת לה שיהא המזבח מונח קודם העמדת המשכן שהרי קודם : ד] דגל ראשון ובני קהת אחרי דגל שני כדי : ה] קהת ואי בששינו ותיבת ועוד נמחק : ו] מקומן שלמים ששחטן כו' פסולין ואי כששחטו כבר משעת נסיעה והביאו עמם הבשר א"כ מיפסלא להו ביוצא : ז] ואי גרסת' ס"א ואם תמצ' לומר קודם שיעמידו הלוים את המשכן דוקא קאמר מוקמינן כו' : ח] קבעית דההוא דגדל לאחר ותיבת אבל נמחק : ט] הבית והתיא פשיטא : י] איתקש נמי : יא] לדמו וא"ת הואיל ומוקי ליה בבכור שנזרק דמו א"כ היכא קאמר בברייתא בכורים יוכיחו והא בכורים דהוי כה"ג דמעשר שנזרעו קודם תחורבן ולא מחוסר רק אכילה דהיינו כשהניחו לפני המזבח קודם חורבן הבית אז ודאי נאכלים שפיר לאחר חורבן הבית וכמו שאין אתה למד מעשר מבכור רק בדמי ליה דלא מיחסר רק אכילה כמו כן אין לעשות יוכיח מבכורים רק בדדמי ליה דלא מיחסר רק אכילה וי"ל דדוקא גבי היקשא דבכור ומעשר איכא למימר דלא איתקש אלא לבכור דכוותיה אבל שייך שפיר לומר ביכורים יוכיחו אף מאותם שלא הניחם קודם חורבן הבית כיון שבבנין הבית היה למד· כך נראה למהר"ם תו' סהר"פ : יב] שהרי קראי מוכיחים : יג] דאיירי בקדושה ראשונה כו' לבא הוא דנקט כתנאי כו' דבתי ערי חומה ולאו משום דדמיא ליה דיש חילוק בין קדושת בית לבתי ערי חומה אבל ודאי קדושת .בתי ערי חומה דמיא לקדושת את ד' נמחק : יד] הערל קסבר קדשה ולקמן נמי בפרק השוחט והמעלה גבי פלוגתא דר"י ור"ל דהמעלה בזמן הזה מייתי פלוגתא דר"א ור"י דמקריבין אע"פ שאין בית ולא מייתי דר"מ דבית שאן ור' ישמעאל דהכא ור' יוסי דסדר עולם וא"ת ומנא ליה לקמן בפרק השוחט והמעלה דר' : טו] מחייב כרת דאינו : טז] עולם דיש חילוק : יז] לית דעיגול בעיגולין : יח] דמ"ד עולה : יט] מתיבת ותימה עד תיבת ור"א דמספקא ליה מוקף בה"ל : כ] ר"א הוא כדפי' : כא] וליתיה במילתיה במס' : כב] וא"א לומר כן דלמאי : כג] דבשעת סילוק מסעות אין מחנה שכינה : כד] שחיטתן כשרין בדרום אבל :

סדו

יב א מיי' פ"ב מהלכות בית הבחירה הל' ה:

יג ב מיי' שם פ"א הלכה יג ופ"ב שם הלכה טז:

ולאחר שיפרקו הלוים את המשכן · אבל המזבח וקלעי החצר במקומן אבל נסע מכל וכל אין מחנה שכינה קיים לגבי קדשי קדשים כדפרי' ולחם הפנים נפסל ביוצא כדאמר התם במסולק מסידור השלחן דכ"ע לא פליגי דנפסל ביוצא ועוד דאי כ] נפרק מכל וכל תיפוק לי דמיפסל מטעם פגימת המזבח וא"ת ובמנחות (דף נה:) אמאי תלי טעמא ביוצא בלחם הפנים תיפוק לי משום פגימת המזבח כא] ואי חזרו והעמידו בו ביום ואז יאכלוהו הא כיון שנדחה אינו חוזר ונראה לאכול וכ"ת חד מתרי טעמי נקט א"כ היכי דייק התם ש"מ יש סילוק מסעות בלילה דאי ס"ד ביום מאי איריא משום יוצא תיפוק לי דאיפסול ליה בלינה וי"ל דודאי סילוק מסעות פוסל או משום יוצא או משום פגימת המזבח והתם דייק אם היה נפסל משום לינה קודם סילוק נמצא דלא היה המסע פוסל: **אע"פ** שנסע אהל מועד הוא · וא"ת בפ' שתי הלחם (מנחות דף נה.) כב] דמעיקרא פליגי בלחם הפנים במסולק אם נפסל במסעות דמ"ד אינו נפסל דרש מדכתיב ונסע אהל מועד אע"פ שנסע אהל מועד הוא אפילו למחנה שכינה ואידך ההוא לדגלים אתא אמאי לא משני דאיצטריך לדרשא דהכא או *למחנה ישראל ו'קיים כדאמר פ' בתרא (לקמן קיז:) ותירץ ה"ר חיים דלפי סברתו קמהדר ליה דס"ל דלא צריך קרא לדרשא דהכא ולדרשא דפ' בתרא כיון דאית ליה דאפי' כי ליכא לא מזבח ולא קלעים אפי' לחם הפנים שהוא קדשי קדשים לא מיפסיל דקריגא ביה מחנה שכינה קיים ולכך משני דלדגלים הוא דאתא וא"ת היכי תיסק אדעתא למימר התם דמסולק כשר ביוצא מ"מ הא מסולק מיפסיל בפגימת מזבח וכי תימא כשחזרו והעמידו המשכן בו ביום ואיך יאכלוהו הא כיון דנדחה שוב אינו חוזר ונראה וי"ל דלא קיימא ההיא מסקנא א"נ אפי' בשעת שנשאו בכתף מזבח הוא *כיון דאמר אע"פ שנסע אהל מועד הוא: **ארבע** אמות מן הדרום וד' אמות מן המערב · כך גירסת הקונטרס וקשה לר"ת כג] דא"כ היה המזבח *ד' אמות בחלקו של יהודה דמסתמא בבית ראשון לא היה יסוד לקרן דרומית מזרחית לפי שלא היה בחלקו של טורף כדאמר פ' איזהו מקומן (לעיל נג:) ואם בבית שני הוסיפו בדרום א"כ בט בחלקו של יהודה וגרס ר"ת מן הצפון מן המערב והכי תנן במס' מדות (פ"ג מ"א) וקשה דהא מסקי' הכא דמשום שיתין הוסיפו שיהא הבור כד] קלוט מתוך המזבח ושיתין בדרום היו כדתנן בפירקין (לקמן סד.) בג' דברים היתה קרן מערבית דרומית משמשת למעלה ניסוך המים והיין *ועוד תנן במסכת מדות (פ"ג מ"ג) מקום היה שם אמה על אמה וטבלא של שיש עליה שבה יורדין לשיתין ומליע למידחק ברוח מערבית היה נגד קרן דרומית אבל קשה עוד תניא במעילה פרק ולד חטאת (דף יא:) ומייתי לה בסוכה פרק לולב כה] (דף מח:) לול קטן היה בלד מערבו של כבש אחד לשבעים שנה פרחי כהונה יורדין לשם ומביאין משם יין קרוש לכך נראה כגירסת הספרים דגרסי דרום ומערב ובבית ראשון היה להם יסוד לדרום שהיה משוך בחלקו של טורף תוך מרוח מזרחית שלא נשתנה שהיה בלא יסוד (עד) חלקו של יהודה כמו בבית שני וקראי דממעטי בפרק איזהו מקומן (לעיל דף נג:) קרן שאין לה יסוד משום בית שני נאמרו אי נמי אף בבית ראשון לא חשיב קרן דרומית קרן כיון דלא הוה ליה יסוד משני צדדין כגון בלד מזרח אי נמי לפי שהיה עתיד להיות בלא יסוד בבית שני לא היו טותנין דמים בו כמו במזבח של משה לפי שהיה עתיד להיות בלא יסוד בבית עולמים :

ולא

נ"ל למחנה ישראל ולקדשים קלים כדאמרינן בפ"ב כו' נ"ק

נ"ל כמאן

אמה מערכה בחלקו כו' נ"ק

תורה אור

ולאחר שיפרקו הלוים את המשכן א] *מהו דתימא איפסיל להו ביוצא קא משמע לן *ואימא הכי נמי אמר קרא °ונסע אהל מועד *אף על פי שנסע אהל מועד הוא אמר רב ב] הונא אמר רב מזבח של שילה של אבנים היה ג] *דתניא ר"א בן יעקב אומר מה תלמוד לומר °אבנים °אבנים °אבנים שלש פעמים אחד של שילה ואחד של נוב וגבעון ובית עולמים מתיב רב ד] אחא בר אמי *אש שירדה מן השמים בימי משה לא נסתלקה מעל מזבח הנחושת אלא בימי שלמה ואש שירדה בימי שלמה לא נסתלקה עד שבא מנשה וסילקה ואם איתא מעיקרא הוא דאיסתלק ה] ליה הוא דאמר כרבי נתן דתניא רבי נתן אומר מזבח של שילה של נחושת ו] היה חלול ומלא אבנים ר"נ בר יצחק אמר מאי לא נסתלקה לא נסתלקה ז] לבטלה מאי היא רבנן אמרי שביבא הוה משדרא רב פפא אמר אושפיזא הוה נקט ח] וזימנין הכא וזימנין הכא תנן התם *וכשעלו *בני הגולה הוסיפו עליו ד' אמות מן הדרום וד' אמות מן המערב כמין גמא מאי טעמא אמר רב יוסף משום דלא ט] ספק אמר ליה אביי השתא מקדש ראשון דכתיב ביה °יהודה וישראל רבים כחול אשר על (שפת) הים י] ספק מקדש שני דכתיב ביה °כל הקהל כאחד ארבע רבוא לא יא] ספק א"ל התם אש של שמים מסייעתן הכא אין אש של שמים מסייעתן כי אתא רבין אמר ר"ש בן פזי יב] משום בר קפרא שיתין הוסיפו מעיקרא סבור מזבח אדמה שהוא אטום באדמה ולבסוף סבור שתיה כאכילה ומאי מזבח אדמה *שהוא מחובר באדמה שלא °יבננו לא ע"ג כיפים

ולא

במדבר י · שמות כ · דברים כז · מלכים א ד · עזרא ב

מהו דתימא כו' · כלומר ולא אכילה משנעקר המזבח אתא לאשמועינן אלא אכילת קדשי קדשים בלא קלעים אתא לאשמועינן דלא תימא כיון שנסתלקו קלעים יש כאן פסול יוצא : יג] אבנים ג"פ · אם מזבח אבנים וגו' מזבח אבנים לא תניף [וגו'] אבנים שלמות תבנה וגו' : טב וגבעון · חד חשיב להו דשניהם במה ואינן קדושים : לא נסתלקה · שבשעת המסעות כופין עליו פסכתר ומניחין אותה במקומה : אלא בימי שלמה · שנסתלקה משם למזבח אבנים שעשה שלמה : עד שבא מנשה וסילקה גרס : ואם איתא מעיקרא הוא דאיסתלק · משהוקם המשכן בשילה קובעו מזבח אבנים הוזקקה להסתלק ממזבח של נחשת : הוא דאמר · רב הונא דאמר כרבי נתן והא דלא אמרי' הוא דאמר כר"א בן יעקב משום דר' נתן הוא דשמעי' ליה בהדיא יד] מעשה היה כך אבל מדר"א בן יעקב לא שמעינן אלא דהוכשר בשל אבנים : לא נסתלקה לבטלה · שתהא בטילה ממזבח הנחושת לגמרי : שביבא הוה משדרא · כשהיו מקטירין על של אבנים היו זיקים ולהבות יוצאות מאש שמים שעל מזבח הנחשת של משה שאף הוא מונח שם : תנן התם · במסכת מדות ר' יוסי אומר בתחילה בימי שלמה לא היה *אלא כ"ח (א) כונס ועולה יסוד וסובב ומקום קרנות ומקום הילוך עד שהיה מקום המערכה כ' על כ' וכשעלו בני הגולה הוסיפו עליו כו' נמצא יסודו ל"ב על ל"ב ומקום מערכתו כ"ד על כ"ד : גמא · גימל יוונית עשויה כמין כף פשוטה שלנו טו] כדפרישית דרום ומערב : הכא · במקדש שני אין אש של שמים מסייעתן כדילפינן בפ"ק דיומא (דף כא:) וארצה בו ואכבד מתוסר ה' אלו ה' דברים שחסר מקדש שני ואש אחד מהן ואמרינן התם מיהוי הוה סיועי לא מסייעא : טז] שיתין הוסיפו · קרן מערבית דרומית הוסיפו למשכה לדרום ולמערב יז] ששם היו מנסכין נסכים כדאמרינן יח] (התם) במתני' דלקמן (דף סא.) ובימי שלמה היה כמין בור כרוי אצל המזבח באותה זוית לירד הנסכים בתוכו וורדין מן המזבח יט] ולרצפה ושותתין שם *והסקלטו אותו הבור לתוך המזבח ועשו נקבים כנגדן בראש המזבח לירד הנסכים שם: אטום באדמה · שלא יהא חלול: שתיה כאכילה · מה אכילה מתעכלת במזבח אף שתיה תבלע במזבח:

אמר

[לקמן קטז:]

שם

[שם מנחות לה:]

[נ"ל תניא נמי הכי וכ"ה בילקוט פרשת יתרו רמז ש"ן]

סדר עולם פרק טו

הגהות הב"ח

(א) רש"י ד"ה תנן התם וכו' לא היה אלא כ"ח וכונס אמה יסוד כו' ופינה ועולה נמחק:

נ"א אלא כ"ח על כ"ח וכונס ועולה כו' נ"ק

מדות לג: [פ"ג מ"א]

[לעיל נח.]

נ"א והם סוסיהו במכון עד שהיה אותו הבור קולט לתוך המזבח וסתמו הנקבים כנגדו כו'

נ"א והכי תנן במס' מדות למסס כרינסס באותו הקרן מקום היה כו' נ"ק

שיטה מקובצת

א] מהו דתימא כו' פ"ה שפרקו המשכן הקרשים והיריעות והמזבח קיים וזה לפי שיטתו דלעיל דאינו נפסל אפילו כי הסיר הקלעים וקשה והיכי קאמר אע"פ שנסע אהל מועד הוא ולא נפסל ביוצא [הוא] אין לך יוצא גדול מזה כיון דמותר קלעים הוא אלא יש לפרש לאחר שפרקו הקרשים אבל הקלעים עומדים במקומן וא"ת מאי קמ"ל פשיטא דלא מיפסל משום יוצא הואיל והקלעים קיימין וי"ל כיון דאין הקלעים אלא מחמת המשכן שבתוכן א"כ משנסתלק קדושת המשכן בטלה קדושת קלעים ושייך משום יוצא קמ"ל אף על פי שנסע אה"מ הוא הקלעים כיון שלא נסתלקו והיא דשתי הלחם מיירי שנסתלקו הקלעים דמיפסלי משום יוצא · תוס' מהר"ם : ב] רב הונא אמר רב ותיבת ותנא נמחק : ג] והת' תניא ר"א את ד' נמחק ס"א תניא נמי הכי כו': ד] רב אחדבויי בר אמי תיבת אחא נמחק : ה] דאסתלק לה : ו] היה חלל וכמו כן במדבר נמי היו ממלאין אותו בחנייתן והאש של שמים היה מונח על השפת וכשהיו נושאין אותו היו כופין עליו פסכתר כדי שלא ישרוף את הבגדים שהיו משימין על האש כשמביאין המזבח ממקום למקום · תו"א : ז] לבטלה והיכי הוי רבנן ותיבות מאי היא נמחק: ח] והוה נקים ומצנין הכא: ט] דלא ספיק: י] הים ספק מקדש : יא] לא ספיק א"ל: יב] תיבות משום בר קפרא נמחק: יג] תיבת אבנים נמחק : יד] בהדיא דאמר מעשה : טו] שלנו כדמפרש דרום : טז] מה"ד משום שיתין : יז] ולמערב כדאמרי' ששם : יח] תיבת התם נמחק : יט] המזבח לרצפה ושותתין שם ובני הגולה הוסיפו בבנין עד שהיה אותו הבור קולט לתוך המזבח ופתחו נקבים כנגדו : כ] דאי נסע ותיבת נפרק ל"ש : כא] מתיבת ואי עד תיבת וכ"ת חד מוקף בח"ל : כב] דפליגי בלחם תיבת דמעיקרא נמחק : כג] דא"כ' נ"א דע"כ אותן ד' אמות שהוסיפו בדרום היה בחלקו של טורף דאי בחלקו של יהודה לא תוכשר למזבח ולעיל אמרי' שלא היה לו יסוד בבית ראשון מן הדרום לפי שלא היה בחלקו של טורף לכך נראה דגרסי' מן הצפון כו' אלא לכך נראה כגירסת רש"י דרום ומערב והגיע עד חלקו של יהודה שבבית ראשון והיה לו יסוד לרוח דרומית אבל במזרח לא היה לו יסוד לפי שהיה בחלקו של יהודה וכן מוכח לעיל הלשון דקאמר המזבח אוכל בחלקו של יהודה אמה ולא קאמר אמה מכאן ואמה מכאן משמע דוקא לצד אחד הדרים לצד מזרח אבל בקרן דרומית היה בחלקו של טורף ומ"מ בקרן דרומית מזרחית לא היה בו יסוד לפי שלא היה ראוי אותו קרן למתן דמים משום דבעינן בדם שיהא משפשף מכאן ומכאן על היסוד משני צדדין של הקרן והכא לא היה יסוד באותו קרן של צד מזרח לפי שהיה אוכל בחלקו של יהודה ולא היה יסוד בדרומי כי אם אמה אחת בקרן דרומית מערבית · תוס' מהר"ם : כד] הבור קולט בתוך המזבח : כה] לולב וערבה לול :

set up the Tabernacle [61b] and after the Levites dismantled the Tabernacle.[4] You might argue that [in the latter case the flesh] became unfit through having gone out [of bounds].[5] Therefore he informs us [otherwise]. Yet say that that is indeed so?—Scripture saith, *Then the tent of meeting shall set forward:*[6] even when it has set forward[7] it is 'the tent of meeting.'[8]

R. Ḥisda[9] said in Rab's name: The altar at Shiloh was of stones. For it was taught, R. Eleazar b. Jacob said: Why is '*stones*' stated three times?[10] One refers to that of Shiloh, another to that of Nob and Gibeon, and the third to that of the Eternal House.[11] R. Aḥa b. Ammi raised an objection: The fire which descended from heaven in the days of Moses[12] did not depart from the brazen altar until
a the days of Solomon.[1] And the fire which descended in the days of Solomon[2] did not depart until Manasseh came and removed it. Now if this is correct,[3] it should have departed earlier?[4]—He [R. Ḥisda in Rab's name] made his statement in accordance with R. Nathan. For it was taught, R. Nathan said: The altar at Shiloh was of brass; it was hollow, and filled with stones.[5] R. Naḥman b. Isaac said: What does 'it did not depart' mean? It did not depart [disappear] into nothingness.[6] How was it?—The Rabbis said: It sent forth sparks.[7] R. Papa said: It took up its abode now here, now there.

We learnt elsewhere: And when the Children of the Exile went up [to Eretz Israel],[8] they added thereto[9] four cubits on the south and four cubits on the west, like a [Greek] gamma.[10] What is the reason?—Said R. Joseph: Because it [the first] was not sufficient. Said Abaye to him: If it was sufficient for the first Temple, when it is written, *Judah and Israel were many, as the sand which is by the sea* [*shore*] *in multitude;*[11] would it be insufficient for the second Temple, whereof it is written, *The whole congregation together was forty and two thousand* [etc.]?[12]—There [in the first Temple] the heavenly fire assisted them;[13] here [in the second Temple] it did not assist them.

When Rabin came [from Palestine], he said in the name of R.
b Simeon b. Pazzi: They added the pits [to its structure].[1] At first they had thought that an '*altar of earth*' meant that it was to be closed in with earth.[2] But subsequently they held that drinking must be like eating,[3] and what does '*an altar of earth*' mean? that it

(4) 'Before the Levites set up the Tabernacle' cannot be understood literally, but means whilst the Tabernacle was standing, this phrase merely being used in contrast to the second half. Thus the two places are: (i) within the normal precincts of the Tabernacle (within the 'hangings'—v. *supra* 53a n. 6) whilst it stood; and (ii) likewise within the normal precincts, but after the Tabernacle had been dismantled. The *altar*, however, was still standing. (5) I.e. when the Tabernacle is dismantled, and the hangings are no longer there, the flesh should be regarded as having gone out of bounds, and so disqualified. (6) Num. II, 17. (7) Hence dismantled. (8) It still retains its sanctity, in the sense that the flesh is not regarded as having gone out of bounds. (9) Emended text (Sh. M). Cur. edd. Huna. (10) Ex. XX, 22: *And if thou make Me an altar of stone, thou shalt not build it of hewn* stones; Deut XXVII, 5-6: *And there shalt thou build . . . an altar of* stones . . . *Thou shalt build the altar of the Lord thy God of unhewn* stones. (11) The Temple at Jerusalem. (12) V. Lev. IX, 24.
a (1) Rashi: A pot was placed over it when they travelled, and the fire remained in its place. When Solomon built the Temple, this fire left the brazen altar and moved to the stone altar in the Temple. (2) This same fire. (3) That the altar at Shiloh was of stone. (4) As soon as the stone altar was built at Shiloh, the fire should have departed from Moses' brazen altar. (5) The answer is not clear. Presumably it means that it was Moses' brazen altar except that the hollow was filled with stones instead of earth. (6) Lit., 'in vain,' 'for no purpose.' Until Solomon built the Temple the fire did not completely depart from Moses' altar which was still in existence, for though it did move to the altar at Shiloh, some of it nevertheless remained on that of Moses. (7) When the fat, etc., was burnt on the stone altar, sparks and flames shot out from the heavenly fire on the brazen altar, which was was there too, on to the stone altar. (8) I.e., when the Jews returned from Babylon. (9) To the altar. (10) The altar in the first Temple was twenty-eight cubits square overall, whilst that of the second Temple was thirty-two cubits. The addition would thus be a strip four cubits broad in triangular shape, like a Greek gamma thus: ⌝ (11) I Kings IV, 20. The bracketed word '*shore*', not in the M.T., is found in some old Hebrew MSS. (12) Ezra II, 64. (13) To burn the sacrifices quickly.
b (1) In Solomon's Temple there was a pit near the south-west of the altar, into which the altar libations were directly poured. But in the second Temple the altar was extended on the south and the west, so that the place of the pit was incorporated in it, and over against this extension on top of the altar they made holes for the libations to flow into the pit below. (2) Not hollow or perforated in any way. (3) As 'eating' (the consumption of the flesh) was on top of the altar itself, so must 'drinking' (the libations) be on top of the altar itself.

should be attached to the earth, not built on rocks [62*a*] or over cellars.[4]

R. Joseph said: Is that not which was taught: *And they set the altar upon its bases,*[5] [which means] that they attained to its final measurements?[6] But surely it is written, *And all this* [do I give thee] *in writing, as the Lord hath made me wise by His hand upon me, even all works of this pattern?*[7] Rather said R. Joseph: They found a text and interpreted it:[8] *Then David said: This is the house of the Lord God, and this is the altar of burnt-offering for Israel:*[9] [this intimated that the altar was] like the house: as the house was sixty cubits [in length], so were there sixty cubits for the altar.[10]

a As for the Temple, it is well, for its outline was distinguishable;[1] but how did they know [the site of] the altar?—Said R. Eleazar: They saw [in a vision] the altar built, and Michael the great prince standing and offering upon it. While R. Isaac Nappaḥa[2] said: They saw Isaac's ashes lying in that place.[3] R. Samuel b. Naḥman said: From [the site of] the whole House they smelt the odour of incense, while from there [the site of the altar] they smelt the odour of limbs.

Rabbah b. Ḥanah said in R. Joḥanan's name: Three prophets[4] went up with them from the Exile: one testified to them about [the dimensions of] the altar; another testified to them about the site of the altar; and the third testified to them that they could sacrifice even though there was no Temple.[5] In a Baraitha it was taught, R. Eleazar b. Jacob said: Three prophets went up with them from the Exile: one who testified to them about [the dimensions of] the altar and the site of the altar; another who testified to them that they could sacrifice even though there was no Temple; and a third who testified to them that the Torah should be written in Assyrian characters.[6]

Our Rabbis taught: The horn, the ascent, the base and squareness are indispensable; the measurements of its length, breadth and height are not indispensable. How do we know it?—Said R. Huna, Scripture saith, 'The *altar*', and wherever 'the *altar*' is said it is indispensable.[7] If so, are the laver, according to Rabbi, and the terrace, according to R. Jose son of R. Judah, also indispensable, because it is written, *And thou shalt put it under the* karkob [*ledge*]
b *round* the *altar beneath,*[1] and it was taught: What was the *karkob?* Rabbi said: It was the laver; R. Jose son of R. Judah said: It was the terrace![2]—Yes [it is indeed so], for it was taught: On that day[3] the horn of the altar was damaged, and they brought a lump of salt and stopped it up. Not because it was [now] fit for service, but that it should not appear damaged, for every altar which lacks[4] a horn, ascent, base and squareness is invalid. R. Jose son of R. Judah said: The same applies to the terrace.

Our Rabbis taught: What was the *karkob?* [A strip] between one horn and another horn a cubit [in breadth], where the priests walked. Did then the priests walk between one horn and another?—Rather say: and there was [a strip of] a cubit where the priests walked.[5] But it is written, *Under the* karkob *round it beneath, reaching halfway up!*[6]—Said R. Naḥman b. Isaac: There were two, one for ornamental purposes, and the other for the priests, that they should not slip.[7]

'The measurements of its length, breadth, and height are not indispensable.' Said R. Mani: Provided that it is not smaller than the altar made by Moses. And how much is that?—Said R. Joseph: One cubit [square]. They ridiculed him: [quoting the text, *And thou shalt make the altar . . .*] *five cubits long, and five cubits broad!*[8]—Said Abaye to him: Perhaps the master meant the place of the pile?[9]—The master [*sc.* yourself], who is a great man, knows what I

(4) But that did not exclude the possibility of its being hollow. (5) Ezra III, 3. (6) R. Joseph had once fallen sick, and on his recovery it was found that he had forgotten many of his earlier teachings and traditions. Here he states that his assertion that because the heavenly fire helped them a larger altar was unnecessary was incorrect, the real reason being as he proceeds to explain.—*'They attained its final measurements'* means that it was revealed to the builders of the second altar (the 'Men of the Great Assembly') exactly which site was sacred for the altar, this knowledge having been withheld from Solomon when he built the first altar. (7) I Chron. XXVIII, 19. *'All this'* refers to the plans of the first Temple with all its appurtenances. Thus it had all been divinely revealed to Solomon too, which contradicts the former statement. (8) The Men of the Great Assembly were guided by a text in their decision to enlarge the altar. (9) Ibid. XXII, 1. (10) An area of sixty cubits square was sacred for the altar, and they might build it anywhere within that. Nevertheless, they did not need it so large, and therefore they enlarged it merely according to their requirements.

a (1) They could easily ascertain, from a study of the ruins, what had been sanctified for each part of the Temple. (2) Or, the smith. (3) According to legend Isaac was bound, and the substitute ram sacrificed, on the very site of the altar, and the ashes were still there. (4) Haggai, Zechariah, and Malachi. (5) Because the sanctity of the Temple had hallowed the spot for all time. (6) I.e., the square form of Hebrew now in use. V. Sanh. (Sonc. ed.) 21*b* notes. (7) The def. art. implies that only when it is exactly as specified (in the place where the def. art. is used) is it an altar. The horns: *the horns of* the *altar* (Lev. IV, 18); the base: *the base of* the *altar* (ibid. 30); squareness: the *altar shall be four square* (Ex. XXVII, 1); the ascent: *in front of* the *altar* (Lev. VI, 7), *'in front'* being the ascent to the altar.

b (1) Ex. XXVII, 5. (2) Thus 'the *altar*' is written in connection with these. (3) When 'a certain man' poured out the water of libation over his feet; v. Suk. 48*b*. (4) This includes the case where they are damaged. (5) There was a kind of trench between the *ma'arakah*, i.e., the place on the altar where the sacrifices etc. were burnt, and the edge of the altar. This trench was two cubits wide, including one cubit between the horns and one cubit where the priests walked (Rashi, as emended by Sh. M.). (6) Ibid. XXXVIII, 4. Scripture states that the network grating around the sides of the altar was under the *karkob*. This implies that the *karkob* was on the wall of the altar; for if it was on the top surface, a grating on the sides could not be described as *under* it. (7) There was an ornamental ledge on the side of the altar, and a trench on the top, to provide a firm foothold for the priests. (8) Ex. XXVII, 1. (9) Where the sacrifice was burnt. For of the five cubits two cubits had to be deducted on all sides for the strip between the horns and the pathway for the priests, leaving an area of one cubit square for the place of the pile.

תורה אור

ולא על גבי מחילות אמר רב יוסף לאו היינו דתניא °ויכינו (את) המזבח על מכונותיו שהגיעו לסוף מדותיו והכתיב °הכל בכתב מיד ה' עלי השכיל אלא אמר רב יוסף קרא אשכח ודרש °ויאמר דויד זה הוא בית ה' האלהים וזה מזבח ב] לעולה לישראל כי בית מה בית ששים אמה אף מזבח ששים אמה בשלמא בית מינכרא צורתו אלא מזבח מנא ידעי אמר רבי אלעזר ראו מזבח בנוי ומיכאל ג] השר הגדול עומד ומקריב עליו ור' יצחק נפחא אמר אפרו של יצחק ראו שמונח באותו מקום ד] ור' שמואל בר נחמני אמר מכל הבית כולו הריחו ריח קטרת משם הריחו ריח אברים אמר רבה בר בר חנה א"ר יוחנן *[א]שלשה נביאים עלו עמהם מן הגולה אחד שהעיד להם על המזבח ואחד שהעיד להם על מקום המזבח ואחד שהעיד להם *שמקריבין אף על פי שאין בית במתניתא תנא ר"א בן יעקב אומר שלשה נביאים עלו עמהן מן הגולה אחד שהעיד להם על המזבח ועל מקום המזבח ואחד שהעיד להם שמקריבין אף על פי שאין בית ואחד שהעיד ,להם על התורה שתכתב אשורית ת"ר *[ב]קרן וכבש ויסוד וריבוע מעכבין מדת ארכו ומדת רחבו ומדת קומתו אין מעכבין מנה"מ אמר רב הונא אמר קרא °המזבח כל מקום שנאמר המזבח לעכב אלא מעתה כיור לרבי וסובב לרבי יוסי ברבי יהודה הכי נמי דמעכב דכתי' °ונתתה אותה תחת כרכוב המזבח מלמטה ותניא איזהו כרכוב רבי אומר זה כיור רבי יוסי ברבי יהודה אומר זה הסובב אין *דתניא אותו היום נפגמה קרן מזבח והביאו בול של מלח וסתמוהו ה] ולא מפני שכשר לעבודה אלא שלא יראה מזבח פגום [ג]שכל מזבח שאין לו קרן וכבש ויסוד וריבוע פסול רבי יוסי ברבי יהודה אומר אף הסובב ת"ר איזהו כרכוב בין קרן לקרן מקום הילוך רגלי הכהנים אמה אטו הכהנים בין קרן לקרן הוו אזלי אלא אימא [ד]ומקום הילוך רגלי הכהנים אמה והכתיב °תחת כרכובו מלמטה עד חציו אמר רב נחמן בר יצחק תרי הוו חד לנוי וחד לכהנים דלא נשתרקו מדת ארכו ומדת רחבו ומדת קומתו אין מעכבין א"ד מני [ה]ובלבד שלא יפחתנו ממזבח שעשה משה וכמה אמר רב יוסף אמה ו] מחכו עליה °חמש אמות ארך וחמש אמות רוחב רבוע יהיה המזבח אמר ליה אביי דלמא [ו]מקום מערכה קאמר מר א"ל *מר דגברא רבה הוא ידע מאי קאמינא קרי עלידהו

בני

רש"י

אמר רב יוסף לאו היינו דתניא כו' · רב יוסף חלה ונעקר למודו ופעמים שאמר דבר ונזכר ששנה היפך וחוזר בו (נדרים דף מא·) והכא הכי אמר היכי ז] אמרינן לעיל משום אש של שמים מסייעתן לא הוצרכו ליותר : לאו היינו דתניא · שאנשי כנסת הגדולה הגיעו לסוף מדותיו להם נגלה ח] מקום המקודש למזבח מה שלא נגלה לשלמה : והכתיב הכל בכתב · שכל מקומות הקדושות ומדותיהן נכתבו לדוד אלמא במקדש ראשון נמי הא' דלא עשאוהו גדול לאו משום דלא נגלה לשלמה המקום במדותיו : אלא אמר רב יוסף קרא ט] אשכח ודרש · שנאמר לדוד ששים אמה במקום המזבח ושלמה לא הבין לדרשו והם דרשוהו והוסיפו עליו לפי הצורך להם ולששים אמה לא הוצרכו י] דאמרינן לקמן מדת ארכו ורחבו וקומתו אין מעכבין : מה בית ס' אמה · כדכתיב (מלכים א ו) ששים אמה ארכו אף מזבח עד ששים אמה יא] ראוי לו ומקודש המקום אם ירצו : בשלמא בית · ידעו אנשי כנסת הגדולה מה קדוש לעזרה ומה קדוש להיכל : שניכרים צורתו · יסודות החומות : מנא ידעי · מקומו היכא : שלשה נביאים · חגי זכריה ומלאכי : אחד העיד להם על המזבח · יב] שיש לו מקום להוסיף עד ששים אמה : על מקום המזבח · היכן היה : שמקריבין אע"פ שאין בית· דקדושת הבית קדשה לשעתה וקדשה לעתיד לבא : שתכתב אשורית · שמתחילה ניתנה להם בכתב עברי יג] כתב ליבונאה כדאמר בסנהדרין (דף כא:) : וריבוע · אם אין המזבח מרובע : יד] שכל מקום שנאמר המזבח לעכב · דהמזבח משמע כשהוא כן הוא דמיקרי מזבח ואי לא לא ובקרן כתיב (ויקרא ד) קרנות המזבח וביסוד כתיב (שם) אל יסוד המזבח ובכבש כתיב אל פני המזבח (שם ו) והוא הכבש שהוא פניו של מזבח שעולים לו דרך שם כי היכי דחשיב צד מזרחית פני אהל מועד מחמת שהפתח שם ובריבוע כתיב (שמות כז) רבוע יהיה המזבח : אלא מעתה כיור לרבי כו' · דכתיב בהו המזבח הכי נמי דמעכבי לרבי אם לא עשה ציורים של פרחים וציצים וקלעים סביב למזבח כמו סידו וכיורו* : זה כיור · ציורים סביב למעלה מאמצעו : אותו היום · שנסך כהן צדוקי מי החג על רגליו ורגמוהו כל העם כדאמרינן בסוכה (דף מח:) : בול של מלח · מלא אגרוף של מלח שמעתי : לא שכשר טו] לעבודה · המזבח כל זמן שהקרן פגום כדמסיים ואזיל שכל מזבח שאין לו כו' : אף הסובב · ומדרבי יוסי ברבי יהודה נשמע לרבי דכיור מעכב : איזהו כרכוב · טז] וקס"ד אכרכוב דקרא קאי כרכוב לשון היקף תרגום עגולה כדאמרינן בהכל שוחטין (חולין דף כה·) כל שעתיד לגרר לכרכב : בין קרן לקרן · אמה רוחב שכנגד בין יז] קרנות היתה עמוקה ובולטת גובה מעט היה סביב לה בשפת המזבח : מקום הילוך רגלי הכהנים אמה · השתא משמע יח] והיא היתה אמה של מקום הילוך : אטו כהנים בין קרן לקרן הוו אזלי · והלא כשיגיעו לקרן הקרן מעכבן יט] מהיקף : אלא ה"ק בין קרן לקרן ומקום הילוך רגלי הכהנים · כ] כמין חריץ עמוק ממקום המערכה *משפת המזבח סביב ומקיף את מקום המערכה ורחבו של חריץ שני אמות אמה של בין הקרנות ואמה של מקום הילוך : והכתיב · גבי מכבר מעשה רשת נחשת שנתנוהו תחת כרכבו מלמטה עד חציו כא] הקיפוהו למזבח מאמצעו ולמעלה לבוש כמין היקף של כברה והוא עשוי נקבים נקבים ככברה כב] ורשת של דגים ומגיע למעלה עד מתחת לכרכוב אלמא בקיר כג] מזבח סביב הוה דאי בראש המזבח היכי קרי למכבר האתון סביב הקיר תחת כרכובו : תרי הוו · שני סובבין הוו לו למזבח שעשה משה : חד לנוי וחד לכהנים דלא נשתרקו · סביב הקיר משעלה שש אמות גובה לרבי יוסי דאמר לעיל (דף נט:) י' אמות גובהו היה היקף כד] *הבליטה קטנה תוגרתו סביב לנוי והוא סובב וכיור דאפליגו ביה רבי ור' יוסי בר' יהודה לעיל ומתחת לאותו סובב נתנו המכבר ורחבו מגיע למטה עד חצי המזבח והוא היה סימן להבדיל בין הדמים העליונים לדמים התחתונים *כדאמרינן באיזהו מקומן (לעיל דף ע·) מהאי קרא התורה נתנה מחילה כו' : וחד לכהנים דלא נשתרקו · ולמעלה בראש המזבח העמיקו *סובב כמין חריץ עמוק דבר מועט להיות להם שפתו היקף מעקה קטן סביב שלא יחליקו : דלמא מקום מערכה קאמר · דהוי אמה כה] שבין הקרנות ומקום הילוך ממעטין בו אמתים לכל צד פש ליה אמה על אמה :

בני

תוספות

ולא על גבי מחילות · בור של שיתין לא היה חשוב מחילה כיון דהוא צורך מזבח : אף מזבח ששים אמה · והא דאמר (בסוף) [בריש] כיסוי הדם (חולין דף פג:) קמוסיף כו] אבניין הייני כשהיה המזבח עד ששים כז] א"נ מגובה פריך התם אי נמי פריך קמוסיף שלא יהא רבוע שעל כל מליקת עוף אין יכולת לתת עפר בכל סביביו כדי לרבעו כמשפטו : אחד שהעיד להם על המזבח · תימה כח] קרא כתיב ביחזקאל (מג) *והאריאל שתים עשרה אמות אלמא מקום המערכה כ"ד על כ"ד ומהאי קרא דרשינן במתני' דמדות כט] (פ"ג מ"א) וי"ל דאי לאו עדות הייני מפרשי' עם מקום קרנות שלא לשנות ממזבח שלמה ל] : ואחד שמקריבין אע"פ שאין בית· דקדושת בית קידשה לשעתה ולעתיד ולא דמי לקדושת הארץ דקי"ל דבטלה כדמוכח בפ"ק דחולין (ז:) גבי בית שאן שיש חילוק ביניהם כדפרישית לעיל (סא. ד"ה מאי) : מדת ארכו ומדת רחבו אין מעכבין · והא דכתיב הכל בכתב מיד ה' עלי השכיל ומיירי אף גבי מזבח כדאיתא פרק כיסוי הדם (חולין פג:) דמה בית ששים אף מזבח ששים היינו שיהא קדוש עד ששים אם ירצו להרחיבו ולא שיהא חובה לעשות כן :

באמה

עין משפט נר מצוה

יד א מיי' פ"ב מהל' בית הבחירה הל' ד:

ז"ק

טו ב ג מיי' שם הל' יז:

טז ד מיי' שם הלכה ז:

יז ה ו מיי' שם הל' יח:

ג' כצ"ק והאריאל שתים עשרה אמות ומהאי קרא דרשינן במתניתין דמדות שמן האמצעי הוא מודד י"ב אמה לכל רוח אלמא מקום המערכה כ"ד על כ"ד וא"כ עדותן ל"ל וי"ל כו' כצ"ל

שיטה מקובצת

א] אשכחו ודרוש ויאמר: ב] (מזבח לעולה לישראל): ג] שר הגדול: ד] מקום ר' שמואל אות ו' נמחק : ה] וסתמוהו לא מפני אות ו' נמחק: ו] אמה אחיכו עליה : ז] היכי אמרי לעיל משום ראש של שמים: ח] נגלה המקום: ט] קרא אשכחו ודרוש : י] ואמרינן לקמן : יא] אמה יש לו מקום ראוי ומקודש אם ירצו הס"ד : יב] המזבח שמקומו מקודש עד ששים אמה הס"ד : יג] עברי שהוא כתב : יד] מה"ד כל מקום : טו] שכשר המזבח לעבודה כל: טז] כרכוב קס"ד אכרכוב דקרא קאי וכרכוב לשון : יז] בין הקרנות היתה עמוקה חרוצה ובליטת גובה : יח] משמע דהיא היתה אמה : יט] מעכבן מלהקיף המזבח הס"ד ומה"ד אלא: כ] הכהנים אמה היה יותר כמין חריץ ממקום המערכה עד שפת המזבח סביב : כא] חציו והקיפוהו למזבח : כב] ככברה כרשת של : כג] המזבח סביב היה כרכוב דאי : כד] היקף בליטה קטנה הוגרתו סביב ולנוי והוה: כה] אמה על אמה שבין הקרנות ומקום הילוך : כו] אבנין ומאי קפידא יש אם הוסיף והלא מוסיפין עד כ' אמה : כז] ששים וקא מוסיף עליו כל שעה בכבשי א"נ : כח] תימה כו' קרא כתיב עשרה אמה על י"ב אמה וא"ת לשון הכתוב עשרה אורך בשתים עשרה רוחב עכ"ל: כט] דמדות דהיה המזבח ל"ב על ל"ב ואם כן מה היו צריכים לעדות הנביא וי"ל : ל] שלמה שהיה מקום המערכה שלו כ' על כ' :

בליטה קטנה והוגרתו כו' מלמטה עד חציו ז"ק

כדדרשינן ז"ק

סביב ז"ק

מסורת הש"ס

[לקמן קה: מגילה י. שבועות טז. עדיות פ"ח משנה ו]

[לקמן קח. קכ.]

סוכה מח: [תוספתא שם פרק ג ע"ש]

[כתובות כ: ע' תוספות ערכין ה. ד"ה וכא]

[ע"ז מז:]

כ"ה עד שפת המזבח וגי' ז"ק לשפת המזבח

°בני קטורה בני אחתיה דרבי טרפון הוו יתבי קמיה דרבי א] טרפון פתח ואמר °ויוסף אברהם ויקח אשה ושמה יוחני אמרי ליה קטורה כתיב קרי עלידהם בני קטורה אמר ב] אביי בר הונא אמר רב חמא בר גוריא ג] *גזירין שעשה משה אורכן אמה ורוחבן אמה ועוביין כמחק גודש סאה אמר רבי ירמיה באמה ד] גדומה אמר רב יוסף ולאו היינו דתניא °על העצים אשר על האש אשר על המזבח שלא יהו עצים יוצאין מן המזבח כלום תנן התם *כבש היה לדרומה של מזבח אורך שלשים ושתים על רוחב שש עשרה מנא ה"מ אמר רב הונא אמר קרא °ושחט אותו על ירך המזבח צפונה שיהא ירך בצפון ופניו בדרום אימא ירך בצפון ופניו בצפון אמר רבא רמי גברא אאפיה א"ל אביי אדרבה *תריץ ואותיב גברא א"ל °רבוע כתיב ה] והא מיבעי ליה דמרבע רבועי מי כתיב מרובע וליטעמיך מי כתיב רבוץ ו] א"ל רבוע כתיב דמשמע הכי ומשמע הכי ותנא מייתי לה מהכא דתניא רבי יהודה אומר ז] °ומעלותיהו פנות קדים *כל פינות שאתה פונה לא יהו אלא דרך ימין למזרח ואימא ח] שמאל למזרח לא ס"ד *דתני רמי בר (*יחזקיה) ים שעשה שלמה °עומד על שנים עשר ט](עמודים) בקר שלשה פונים צפונה ושלשה פונים ימה ושלשה פונים נגבה ושלשה פונים י] מזרחה כל פינות שאתה פונה לא יהו אלא דרך ימין למזרח ההוא מיבעי ליה לגופיה א"כ פונים פונים למה לי שאל רבי שמעון בן יוסי בן לקוניא את ר' יוסי אומר היה ר"ש בן יוחי *אויר יש בין כבש למזבח אמר לו ואתה אי אתה אומר כן והלא כבר נאמר °ועשית עולותיך הבשר והדם מה דם בזריקה אף בשר בזריקה אמר לו שאני אומר עומד בצד מערכה וזורק א"ל כשהוא זורק למערכה דלוקה הוא זורק או למערכה שאינה דלוקה הוא זורק הוי אומר למערכה דלוקה הוא *זורק התם משום דלא אפשר יא] רב פפא אמר כי דם מה דם אויר קרקע מפסיקו אף בשר אויר קרקע מפסיקו אמר רב יהודה ישני כבשים קטנים יוצאין מן הכבש יב] שבהן פונים ליסוד ולסובב ומובדלין מן המזבח מלא נימא משום שנאמר סביב יג] ורבי אבהו אמר רבוע ואיצטריך למכתב סביב ואיצטריך למכתב רבוע דאי כתב רחמנא סביב הוה אמינא דעגיל מעגל כתב רחמנא רבוע ואי כתב רחמנא רבוע הוה אמינא דאריך וקטין כתב רחמנא סביב תנן התם *הכבש והמזבח ששים ושתים הני שיתין יד] וארבעה הוו *נמצא פורח אמה על טו] יסוד ואמה על סובב אמר

רש"י

בני קטורה · בני אברהם אתם אבל לא כזרע יצחק ויעקב: הכי גרסינן הוו יתבי קמיה דרבי טרפון · ולא הוו אמרי מידי: פתח ואמר · כדי שידברו: יוחני · מילתא בעלמא הוא דקאמר כדי לפתוח פיהם: בני קטורה · אינם יודעין לדבר בהלכה: גזירין · שני גזרי עצים לריך תורה אור לסדר בראש טז] המזבח המערכה לתמיד של שחר בכהן אחד יז] ולתמיד של בין הערבים בשני כהנים כדקיימא לן בסדר יומא (דף כו:): אמה ארכו ואמה רחבו · כמידת מקום המערכה: באמה גדומה · קצרה שלא יצאו חוץ למערכה ויעכבו הכהנים מלהקיף: לאו היינו דתניא כו' · ואמה גדומה למה לי אלא אמה מצומצמת: מנהני מילי · שהכבש בדרום: ירך · רגליים ופניו בדרום כאדם השוכב אפרקדן ורגליו לצפון כמלא ראשו ופניו לדרום: אימא ירך בצפון ופניו בצפון · כאדם היושב זקוף: רמי גברא אאפיה · שיכר באדם השוכב אפרקדן: אדרבה תריץ ואותיב גברא · זקפוהו והשיבוהו וכמלא ראשו ורגליו לרוח אחת: רבוע כתיב · דרבוע באדם רובץ ומושכב שיער הכתוב: והאי רבוע מיבעי ליה דמרבע ריבועי · שיהא מרובע ולא עגול: יח] ה"ג רבוע כתיב דמשמע הכי ומשמע הכי · הלכך תרווייהו יליף מיניה: ותנא דברייתא מייתי לה להא יט] דאייתי רב הונא מירך המזבח מייתי תנא מהכא: כ] ומעלותיהו פנות קדים כל פינות שאתה פונה יהו דרך ימין למזרח · האי קרא במזבח כתיב ביחזקאל וקאמר כא] *שתמיד כבש מעלותיו ברוח הראויה לפנות הימנה למזרח ותהא אותו הפנייה לימין ואין לך רוח ראויה לכך אלא דרום: ופרכינן ואימא דרך שמאל למזרח· נהי דפנות קדים כתיב בקרא אבל דרך ימין לא כתיב ביה כב] העמידהו בצפון וכשתגיע לראש המזבח פנה אל קרן מזרחית צפונית כג] ודרך שמאל: לא ס"ד· שיהו פונים לשמאל אלא כד] דרך ימין: לא יהו אלא דרך ימין·כי מניא דקרא דקאזיל דרך ימין מצפון למערב וממערב לדרום וכשאתה מקיף שום דבר ופניך אליו ואתה סובבו מצפון למערב לימינך אתה הולך: למזרח· מהאי קרא לא נפקא לן כה] *ומהכא נפקא לן דרך ימין ומקרא דלעיל דכתיב כו] קדים שמעינן למזרח דלא תימא דרך ימין למערב ויהא כבש בצפון: מיבעיא ליה לגופיה· להודיעך מושב הים היאך ומנין לך ללמוד הימנו לפינות המקדש בצורכי עבודה: אויר יש בין כבש למזבח · שלא היה ראש הכבש נוגע במזבח אלא אויר מעט מפסיק בינתיים: ה"ג אמר לו ואתה אי אתה אומר כן: מה דם · עולה כז] שעומד בארץ וזורק מן הכלי כדכתיב וזרקו אף בשר בזריקה אלמא אויר יש ומחמת האויר כח] *הוא צריך זריקה שעומד בכבש וזורק אל עבר האויר למערכה: אמר לו שאני אומר כט] זורק עומד בצד המערכה · בראש המזבח וזורק ל] ולהכי אתא קרא: אמר לו כשהוא זורק למערכה דלוקה הוא זורק כו' · כלומר משום הא למה לי קרא פשיטא דעל כרחו הוא זורקו שהרי אין יכול לסדר סביב על ראשי העצים שאין המערכה דלוקה שם אלא הימנו והלאה מקום שהמערכה דולקת והתם משום דלא אפשר הוא לא] *דע"כ כי אתא קרא לאשמועינן אתא דיש אויר בין כבש למזבח: רב פפא אמר · לא מיית אמרת דהיקש לב] לאשמועינן אתא דעומד בצד המערכה וזורק דהפסקה אויר רצפה בעינן כי דם: מה דם אויר קרקע · הרצפה מפסיק בינו למזבח אף בשר כו' : שני כבשים קטנים יוצאין מן הכבש כו' · אותו שפונין בו לסובב לג] יוצא במזרחו של כבש לימין ויוצא ומתחיל בשפולו של כבש ונמשך ועולה באלכסון עד שמגיע לסובב והפונה ליסוד יוצא למערבו לד] להוליך בו שירים של חטאת *שיורד מן המזבח פונה לשמאלו ליסוד דרומי ומתחיל לצאת בשיפולו של כבש רחוק מן המזבח כדי שיהא נוח לשפע ולירד ליסוד: משום שנאמר סביב · שיהא היקף למזבח כל דהו ואי הוו מחוברין שוב אין לה] היקף אפילו בחוט אין אדם יכול לסובבו : רבי אבהו אמר רבוע · ואי מחוברין לא הוי בניינו מרובע : ואיצטריך למיכתב סביב ואיצטריך למיכתב רבוע · ואף על גב דאפקינהו לתרווייהו להך דרשא שלא יהא בנין אחר מחובר לו : דעגיל מעגל · ולא יהא לו זויות : דאריך וקטין · ארכו יותר על רחבו וזויות יהא לו : כתב רחמנא סביב · שיהו כל סביביו שוין : שיתין וארבע הוו · דהא תנן לעיל אורך הכבש ל"ב אמה וכן המזבח : ומשני נמצא שראש הכבש פורח ועולה על כניסת היסוד והסובב · ומגיע לראש המזבח נמלאו שתי אמות העליונות שלו מובלעים *בשתי אמות לו] : ה"ג

תוספות

באמה גדומה · חסירה ובערוך *פירש גרומה ברי"ש כמו נותן לו את גירומיו לז] (ב"ב פח:) ורב יוסף פריך ממתניתא שלא יהו לח] *עצים יוצאים : אויר קרקע מפסיקו · *קרקע לאו דוקא לט] שהיה פורח אמה על יסוד ואמה על סובב ובלאו קרא היה צריך אויר משום שנאמר סביב כדבסמוך אלא דסגי במשהו אבל הכא בעינן אויר גדול וניכר שהוא לצורך אויר : דאריך וקטין · והא דכתיב חמש אמות אורך וחמש אמות רוחב למצוה והאי קרא לעכב ומיהו קשה דלעכב מהמזבח נפקא מ] : שיתין וד' הוו · *הייט כלוי דאמר לעיל (דף נד·) בדמיםוגקיט כוותיה משום תרגום דידן דמתרגמינן באחסנתיה יתבני מקדשא אבל לרב דלא הוה ליה יסוד בבנין הוה ליה מזבח מן הצפון ולדרום ל"א וכבש ל"ב הרי ס"ג ה"ל לשנויי שהיה פורח על הסובב אמה :

שיטה מקובצת

א] טרפון ולא הוו אמרי מידי פתח : ב] רבי אבין בר תיבת אביי נמחק: ג] גזירין שעשה משה אורכן אמה כו' · ואם תאמר והלא מקום המערכה לא היתה כי אם אמה על אמה וא"כ גיזרין מכסין כולה והיאך היו משימין הקיסמין וי"ל דהיו מניחין אותן על צידיהן והיו נותנין קיסמין בינתים להבעירם : ד] גדומה · פ"ה קצרה כמו גדמת ופריך [רב יוסף] דתניא ואם כן מצומצמת היו יכולים לעשות ואמאי עשו אותה קצרה · וקצת קשה דמשמע דפריך מפשטיה דקרא · לכך נראה כגירסת הערוך גרומה מלשון נותן לו את גירומיו דהיינו יתר על [המשקל] כלומר אמה גדולה והשתא פריך שפיר מההיא דשלא יהיו העצים יוצאים מן המזבח ·ואמה מצומצמת הוי ליה למעבד : ה] כתיב האי רבוע מיבעי תיבת והא ל"ש ונמחק : ו] רבוץ אלא רבוע תיבת א"ל ל"ש: ז] ומעלתהו פנות : ח] ואימא דרך שמאל למזרח כו' בר יחזקאל תיבת יחזקיה נמחק : ט] תיבת עמודים נמחק : י] ושלשה פונים קדמה כו' למזרח לא נפקא לן מהאי קרא אלא דרך ימין נפקא לן מהאי קרא וכ"ת דרך ימין למערב ויהא הכבש בצפון הא כתיב באידך קרא דלעיל פנות קדים תיבת מזרחה נמחק : יא] אפשר הוא רב : יב] שבהן פונים ליסוד פי' בטערבה של כבש היה כבש קטן שבו פונין ליסיד וא"ת למה לי כבש קטן ירד למטה על הרצפה וישפוך שירים על היסוד וי"ל שמא יקרוש הדם אם יאחר כל כך : יג] סביב רבי ואות י' נמחק : יד] עיין בהשמטות בסוף המסכת : טו] על היסוד ואמה על הסובב: טז] תיבת המזבח נמחק : יז] אחד ותמיד של : יח] (א"ל) ה"ג אלא רבוע : יט] להא מילתיה דאייתי רב הונא דכבש בדרום מירך המזבח מהכא הס"ד ותיבות מייתי תנא נמחק : כ] ומעלתהו : כא] וקאמר שתעמיד כבש שיהו' מעלותיו ותיבת שתמיד נמחק : כב] ביה הלכך העמידהו : כג] צפונית דרך שמאל : כד] אלא לימין הס"ד : כה] לן אלא מהכא נפקא : כו] דכתיב פנות קדים שמעינן שיהיו הפניות של מזבח למזרח : כז] עולה בזריקה שעומד : כח] האויר הוזקק לזריקה שעומד כו' ותיבת הוא נמחק ותיבת צריך ל"ש : כט] אומר עומד תיבת זורק ל"ש : ל] וזורק וגזירת הכתוב הוא הס"ד : לא] היא אלא ע"כ כי : לב] דהיקש אתא לאשמועינן דעומד וכו' וזורק דהפסקת אויר רצפה : לג] לסובב יוצא במזרחו של כבש בימין ומתחיל ויוצא בשפולו : לד] למערבו להוריד בו שירי דם הפאת כשיורד מן המזבח : לה] אין לו היקף : לו] אמות של מזבח הס ד : לז] גירומיו כלומר גדולה ורב : לח] ממתניתא שלא יהו עצים : לט] דוקא (עיין בתוס' דף פז ע"ב) שהרי היה פורח על אמה יסוד ועל אמה סובב אלא ר"ל אויר בעלמא מפסיקו וא"ת ולמה לי היקש לכך הא כתיב סביב לומר שיהא ריבוע ויכולים להקיף בחוט וי"ל דר"ל אויר גדול וכו' · מהר"ם : מ] נפקא וי"ל דהו"א דוקא של משה צריך ארכו כרחבו אבל במקדש לא לכך צריך רבוע כזה :

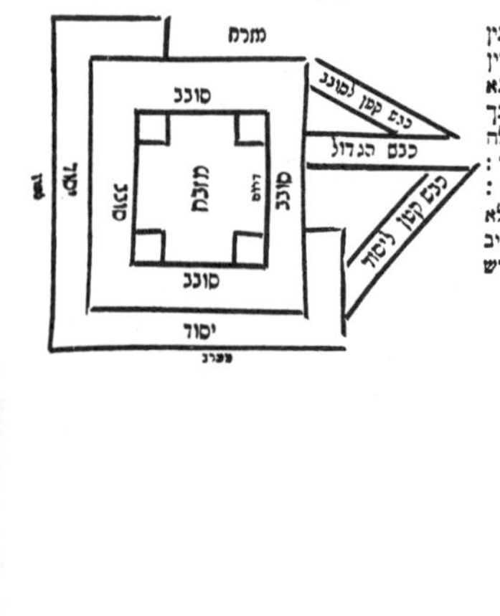

גליון הש"ס תוס' ד"ה אויר וכו' קרקע לאו דווקא · עיין לקמן דף פז ע"ב תוספות ד"ה אויר :

עין משפט נר מצוה

[ערך רגם פי' ע"ש]
[נ"ל עצים]
יח א מיי' פ"ו מהלכות איסורי מזבח הל' ג:
יט ב מיי' פ"ב מהלכות בית הבחירה הל' יג:
כ ג מיי' פ"ו מהלכות מעה"ק הלכה יא :
כא ד מיי' פ"ב מהל' בית הבחירה הלכה יג :
כב ה מיי' פ"ו מהלכות מעה"ק הלכה ד :
כג ו מיי' פ"ב מהלכות בית הבחירה הלכה יד :
כד ז מיי' שם הלכה יג :

מסורת הש"ס

מדות פ"ג מ"ג
[תרגום של בשלוש ובמישור בשלמא ובתלתותא עי' ערוך ערך תרן]
סוטה טו: (סוכה מח) יומא טו: יז: מה. נח.
[נ"ל יחזקאל]
יומא נח:
נ"ק מ"ז
פסחים לד. עז: לקמן קד.
נ"ל שתעמיד נ"ק
זורקו והתם נ"ק
מדות פ"ה מ"א
לעיל נד.
דמהכא נ"ק
הוא זורק נ"ק
וע"כ נ"ק
נ"ל כשיורד נ"ק
בל"ב אמות של מזבח נ"ק

a meant, he replied. Then he dubbed them[1] [62b] *'the children of Keturah'*.[2]

The sons of R. Tarfon's sister were sitting before R. Tarfon.[3] Thereupon he quoted: *And Abraham took another wife, and her name was* Joḥani.[4] Said they to him: *'Keturah'* is written. Then he dubbed them *'the children of Keturah'*.[5]

R. Abin[6] b. Huna said in R. Ḥama b. Guria's name: The logs which Moses made[7] were a cubit long and a cubit broad, and their thickness was that of the instrument for levelling off the top of a *se'ah*.[8] R. Jeremiah observed: [It was measured] with a stumped cubit.[9] Said R. Joseph: Is not that which was taught: *Upon the wood that is on the fire which is upon the altar:*[10] [this intimates] that the wood must not project at all beyond the altar?[11]

We learnt elsewhere: There was an ascent at the south [side] of the altar, thirty-two [cubits] in length by sixteen cubits in breadth. Whence do we know it?[12]—Said R. Huna: Scripture saith, *And he shall kill it on the side of the altar northward*·[13] [this intimates] that the side must be in the north and the front in the south.[14]
b Yet say: the side in the north and the face in the north?[1]—Said Raba: Throw a man on his face.[2] Said Abaye to him: On the contrary, let the man sit upright?—It is written, [*The altar shall be*] rabua'.[3] But surely that is required [to teach] that it must be square? —Is then *meruba'* written?[4] And on your reasoning, is then *rabuz* written?[5] Rather, *rabua'* is written, which implies both.[6]

Now, a Tanna infers it from the following. For it was taught, R. Judah said: *And the steps thereof shall look toward the east:*[7] every turning which you take must be rightward to the east.[8] Yet say: must be *leftward* to the east?[9]—You cannot think so. For Rami b. Ezekiel recited: The sea which Solomon made *'stood upon twelve oxen, three looking toward the north, and three looking toward the west, and three looking toward the south, and three looking toward the east:*[10] [this teaches that] every turning which you take must be to the right, eastward.[11] But that is required for its own purpose[12]—If so, why must *'looking toward'* be repeated?[13]

R. Simeon b. Jose b. Laḳunia asked R. Jose: Did R. Simeon b. Yoḥai maintain that there was a space between the ascent and the altar?[14]—And do you not maintain so? he replied. Surely it is said, *And thou shalt offer thy burnt-offerings, the flesh and the blood:*[15] [this intimates that] just as the blood requires throwing,[16] so does the flesh require throwing?[17] I assert that he stood at the side of the
c place of the *pile* and threw it, he answered.[1] Said he to him: When he threw, did he throw on to a burning pile or on to a pile that was not burning? Surely on to a burning pile, and there it would be impossible [to do otherwise].[2] R. Papa said: [It must be] like the blood. Just as [in the case of the] blood, the air-space above the *pavement* interposed, so [in the case of the] flesh, the air-space above the *pavement* interposed.[3]

Rab Judah said: Two small stairways branched off from the [major] ascent, by which one turned to the base and to the terrace, and these were separated from the altar by a hairsbreadth, because *'round about'* is said.[4] Whilst R. Abbahu quoted *rabua'* [*foursquare*].[5] Now, both *'round about'* and *'rabua''* must be written. For if the Divine Law wrote *'round about'* [only], I would say that it can be circular; therefore the Divine Law wrote *rabua'*. Whilst if the Divine Law wrote *rabua'* [only], I would say that it could be long and narrow;[6] hence the Divine Law wrote *'round about'*.[7]

We learnt elsewhere: The ascent and the altar were sixty-two [cubits]. But they were sixty-four?[8]—Hence it is found that it overhung a cubit of the base and a cubit of the balcony.[9]

a (1) Who had ridiculed him. (2) Gen. XXV, 4. You are indeed Abraham's descendants, but not his true *Jewish* descendants through Isaac and Jacob. (3) In silence. So he misquoted a verse in order to evoke a comment. (4) Ibid. 1. The last word of course is wrong. (5) Rashi: ignoramuses, who could not discuss *halachah*. (6) Emended text (Sh. M.). Cur. edd. Abaye. (7) Two logs were placed on the altar fire pile for the morning *tamid* (q.v. Glos.) and the evening *tamid;* v. Yoma 26b. (8) A *se'ah* was a measure. In buying and selling corn this measure was filled, and the top or pile was levelled down by a stick, called a 'strike'.—Sh. M. observes that as the place of the pile itself on Moses' altar was only one cubit square, these logs must have been stood *endways* upon it, with wood chips between to assist the fire to catch on. (9) I.e., rather shorter than a cubit. 'Aruch reads *gerumah* instead of *gedumah*, which reverses the meaning: with a generous cubit, i.e., slightly *more* than a cubit. This makes the difficulty that follows more plausible. (10) Lev. I, 8. (11) I.e. beyond the place of the pile. Rashi: why then must it be a stumped cubit; it could be exactly a cubit? Tosaf. and Sh. M.: how then can it be a 'generous' cubit?—The objection remains unanswered. (12) That it had to be on the south side. (13) Ibid. 11. (14) *Yerek*, translated *'side'* literally means 'thigh', hence the legs. Thus the altar must be like a man lying with his legs stretched northward and his face in the south. The side of the altar having this ascent would naturally be the front.

b (1) Like a man sitting upright. (2) It must be like a man lying face downward—hence the face in the opposite direction to the legs. (3) E.V. 'foursquare'. Ex. XXVII, 1. He connects *rabua'* with *raba'*, to lie down, and interprets: the altar shall be like a man lying down. (4) Which definitely means square and nothing else. (5) Which equally means lying down and nothing else. (6) Square and lying down. (7) Ezek. XLIII, 17. (8) The text refers to the altar, and is interpreted to mean that the altar must be so constructed that when the priest, standing by the altar, has to turn round the side, he will turn right, and go eastward. That is possible only if the ascent is at the *south*. (9) Which would necessitate the ascent on the *north*. (10) II. Chron. IV, 4. (11) Since the order here is first north and then west, and when a man is facing the north, he must turn *right* in order to go to the west. (12) To describe the position of the oxen. (13) In each case. The word literally means 'turning toward', and the repetition is interpreted as in the text. (14) The ascent did not come right up to the altar, but left a gap between. (15) Deut. XII, 27. (16) I.e., dashing against the altar. (17) On to the altar. Consequently, a priest standing at the top of the ascent could not *place* the flesh on the altar, but had to throw it, which implies that there was a gap.

c (1) This would not necessitate a gap. (2) Since the wood was burning, the priest obviously could not go right up to it, but had to stand at a distance and throw it. But in that case, since it was impossible to do otherwise, no text would be required. Hence the text must teach that there was a gap between the *ascent* and the altar, not that there was one between the *priest* and the pile. (3) Which would not be the case if he stood at the side of the pile. (4) Which implies that it must be possible to encompass the altar itself, even if only by drawing a thread about it. But if the ascent actually joined the altar, this could not be done. (5) Which likewise implies that the altar stood, unattached, as a square edifice. (6) I.e., I could translate *rabua'* = *rectangular*, but not necessarily square. (7) Implying that all its sides must be equal. (8) Since each was thirty-two. (9) Cf. *supra* 54a.

[63a] Rami b. Ḥama said: All the ascents had a gradient of one cubit in three,[10] except the ascent of the altar, which [rose one cubit] in three and a half cubits and a finger and a third, counting the little fingers.[11]

MISHNAH. THE FISTFULS OF MEAL-OFFERINGS WERE TAKEN IN ANY PART OF THE TEMPLE COURT, AND THEY [THE MEAL-OFFERINGS] WERE EATEN WITHIN THE HANGINGS, BY MALE PRIESTS, PREPARED IN ANY MANNER, ON THE SAME DAY AND NIGHT, UNTIL MIDNIGHT.

GEMARA. R. Eleazar said: If the fistful of a meal-offering was taken in the *hekal*, it [the ceremony] is valid, for thus we find it in
a the removal of the censers.[1] R. Jeremiah raised an objection: *And he shall take thence*[2] [*his fistful*]:[3] [that means] from the place where the feet of the *zar* stand.[4] Ben Bathyra said: How do we know that if [the priest] took the fistful with his left [hand], he must return [the fistful] and take it with his right [hand]? Because it says, '*thence*', [which means,] from the place whence he had already taken a fistful?[5] Some state that he [R. Jeremiah] raised the objection, and answered it himself; others state, R. Jacob[6] answered R. Jeremiah: Bar Taḥlifa has explained it: Its purpose is only to declare the *whole* of the Temple court fit.[7] I might argue: Since a burnt-offering is a most holy sacrifice, and a meal-offering is most holy: as a burnt-offering requires the north, so does a meal-offering require the north. [Therefore the text informs us otherwise.] As
b for a burnt-offering, the reason is because it is altogether burnt?[1]—[Then learn it] from a sin-offering.[2] As for a sin-offering, the reason is because it atones for those who are liable to *kareth*?—[Then learn it] from a guilt-offering. As for a guilt-offering, the reason is because it is a blood sacrifice. And as for all these too, the reason is because they are blood sacrifices?[3]—Rather, [the text] is necessary. I might think, since it is written, *And he shall bring it unto the altar* . . .[4] *and he shall take up therefrom his fistful:*[5] as it must be brought near to the south-west horn,[6] so must the fistful be taken by the south-west horn. Hence [the text] informs us [that it is not so].

R. Joḥanan said: If a peace-offering is slaughtered in the *hekal*, it is fit, because it is said, *And he shall kill it at the door of the tent of meeting*,[7] and the adjunct cannot be stricter than the principal.[8] An objection is raised: R. Joḥanan b. Bathyra said: How do we know that if heathens surrounded the whole of the Temple court,[9] the priests enter the *hekal* and eat there the most holy sacrifices and the remainder of the meal-offering?[10] Because it says, *In a most holy place*[11] *shalt thou eat thereof*.[12] Yet why [is this text necessary]? Let us quote, *In the court of the tent of meeting shall they eat it*,[13] and the adjunct cannot be stricter than the principal?[14]—How compare: there [that we are dealing with] service, we say, Let the adjunct not be stricter than the principal, since a man can perform a service in the presence of his master. [But as for] eating, since a man cannot
c eat in the presence of his master,[1] we do not say, Let the adjunct not be stricter than the principal.

MISHNAH. THE SIN-OFFERING OF A BIRD WAS SACRIFICED[2] BY THE SOUTH-WEST HORN. NOW, IT WAS FIT [IF DONE] IN ANY PLACE, BUT THIS WAS ITS [PARTICULAR] PLACE.[3] THAT HORN SERVED FOR THREE THINGS BELOW, AND THREE THINGS ABOVE.[4] BELOW: FOR THE SIN-OFFERING OF THE BIRD, FOR THE PRESENTING [OF MEAL-OFFERINGS],[5] AND FOR THE RESIDUE OF THE BLOOD.[6] ABOVE: FOR THE POURING OUT OF WINE AND WATER, AND FOR THE BURNT-OFFERING OF A BIRD WHEN THE EAST WAS TOO MUCH OCCUPIED.[7] ALL WHO ASCENDED THE ALTAR ASCENDED BY THE RIGHT,

(10) They rose one cubit in every three. (11) Of which six go to a *tefah* (handbreadth).—As heavy limbs of animals had to be carried up on it, it had an easier gradient, nine cubits in thirty-two, which works out as in the text. (The translation adopts the marginal reading.)

a (1) Twelve loaves, called Shewbread, were placed on the Table in the *hekal*, accompanied by censers of frankincense (v. Lev. XXIV, 5 *seq*.). When the censers were removed (a week after they were placed there), the Shewbread might be eaten by the priests. Thus the removing of the censers corresponded to the taking of the fistful, which likewise rendered the rest permitted; hence, as the former was done in the *hekal*, so was the latter valid if done in the *hekal*. (2) E.V. *thereout*, but the Talmud understands the word to bear a local meaning. (3) Lev. II, 2. (4) The verse commences: *And he* (*sc*. the *zar*) *shall bring it to Aaron's sons the priests;* and continues, *And he* (*sc*. the priest) *shall take thence* etc. Hence '*thence*' is interpreted, from the place where the *zar* is standing. This is now assumed to exclude the *ulam* and the *hekal*, where a *zar* might not enter. (5) Thus it intimates that it is sometimes necessary to take the fistful *twice*, which is only possible in this case. (6) Marginal emendation. (7) 'From the place where the feet of the *zar* stand' teaches that the whole of the Temple court is fit for the ceremony, and all the more the *hekal* and the court of the priests, seeing that this was a priestly ceremony.

b (1) But a meal-offering is not, and so there is no reason for supposing that it requires the north. What then is the need for a text to teach that it does not? (2) Which is not altogether burnt, and yet requires the north. (3) I.e., this reason would suffice apart from the others already stated. (4) Lev. II, 8. (5) Ibid. VI, 8. (6) As is deduced *infra*. (7) Ibid. III, 2. (8) Since it must be killed at *the door of the tent of meeting*, the tent of meeting (corresponding to the *hekal*) is obviously the principal place for it, while the Temple court is but an adjunct thereto. (9) Shooting arrows and hurling missiles into it. (10) Emended text (Sh. M.). (11) Implying the *hekal*. (12) Num. XVIII, 10. (13) Lev. VI, 9. (14) By the same argument as above: the '*court*' is an adjunct to the '*tent of meeting*' (the *hekal*); if it can be eaten in the former place, it can surely be eaten in the latter.

c (1) Eating is for one's own benefit, and it may therefore be disrespectful to do it in the master's (here, God's) presence.—The *hekal*, being more sacred than the Temple court, is referred to as 'in the Master's presence'. (2) Lit., 'made'. The Mishnah does not say 'slaughtered', as it was not slaughtered but had its neck nipped. (3) The Gemara discusses what this means. (4) 'Below' and 'above' refer to the scarlet line which encompassed the altar. (5) Before their fistfuls were taken they were presented ('brought near') at this horn. (6) Of the outer sin-offerings. These were sprinkled there. (7) Its proper place was at the south-east horn, but if many animal burnt-offerings were being sacrificed there, this was offered at the south-west horn, above the line.

אמר רמי בר חמא א] (א) °כל כבשי כבשים שלש אמות לאמה ב] חוץ מכבשו של מזבח שהיה שלש אמות ומחצה ואצבע ושליש אצבע *בזכרותא: **מתני'** ג] מנחות היו נקמצות *בכל מקום בעזרה ונאכלות לפנים מן הקלעים לזכרי כהונה בכל מאכל ליום ולילה עד חצות: **גמ'** *א"ר אלעזר מנחה ד] שנקמצה בהיכל כשירה שכן מצינו בסילוק בזיכין מתיב רבי ירמיה °וקמץ משם ממקום שרגלי הזר עומדות בן בתירא אומר מנין שאם קמץ בשמאל ה] שיחזיר ויקמוץ בימין ת"ל משם ממקום שקמץ כבר איכא דאמרי הוא מותיב לה והוא מפרק לה איכא דאמרי א"ל ר' ו] *עקיבא לר' ירמיה בר תחליפא אסברא לך לא נצרכא אלא להכשיר כל העזרה כולה סלקא דעתך אמינא הואיל ועולה קדשי קדשים ומנחה קדשי קדשים מה עולה טעונה צפון אף מנחה טעונה צפון *מה לעולה שכן כליל מחטאת מה לחטאת שכן מכפרת על חייבי כריתות מאשם מה לאשם שכן מיני דמים מכולהו ז] מה לכולהו שכן מיני דמים אלא איצטריך סד"א הואיל וכתיב °והגישה אל המזבח °והרים ממנו בקומצו מה הגשה בקרן מערבית דרומית אף קמיצה בקרן מערבית דרומית קא משמע לן אמר רבי יוחנן *שלמים ששחטן בהיכל כשרים שנאמר °ושחטו (אותו) פתח אהל מועד ולא יהא *טפל חמור מן העיקר מיתיבי *רבי ח] יוחנן בן בתירה אומר מנין שאם הקיפו עובדי כוכבים את כל העזרה [י] שהכהנים נכנסין ט] לשם ואוכלין שם קדשי קדשים ת"ל °בקדש הקדשים תאכלנו ואמאי נימא בחצר אהל מועד יאכלוה ולא יהא טפל חמור מן העיקר הכי השתא התם עבודה דאדם עובד במקום רבו אמרינן לא יהא טפל חמור מן העיקר אכילה דאין אדם אוכל במקום רבו י] לא יהא טפל חמור מן העיקר לא אמרינן: **מתני'** חטאת העוף היתה נעשית °על קרן יא] דרומית מערבית *°ובכל מקום היתה כשירה אלא זה היתה מקומה °ושלשה דברים היתה אותה קרן משמשת מלמטה ושלשה מלמעלה מלמטה חטאת העוף והגשות ושירי הדם ומלמעלן ניסוך היין והמים ועולת העוף כשהיא רבה במזרח *°כל העולין למזבח עולין דרך ימין

ומקיפין

רש"י

ה"ג אמר רמי בר חמא כל כבשי כבשים שלש אמות לאמה חוץ מכבשו של מזבח שהיה ג' אמות ומחצה ואצבע ושליש אצבע· כל כבשים גדולים וקטנים שהיו שם היה להן שיפוע שלש אמות לאמה גובה חוץ מכבש הגדול של מזבח שעולין בו במשא איברים כבידים והוא חלק לרידשיא משופע ביותר וטוח לעלות לכך *האריכוהו ל"ב שיפוע לט' אמות יב] הרי לכל אמה שלש אמות ומחצה ואצבע ושליש אצבע כשתתן לכל אמה שלש ומחצה הרי ל' ואחת ומחצה תן עוד ט' אצבעות וט' שלישי אצבע הרי י"ב אצבעות שהן ג' טפחים והן חצי אמה יג]: **מתני'** היו נקמצות בכל מקום · ואין יד] טעונין צפון: לפנים מן הקלעים לזכרי כהונה · דכתיב לכל קרבנם ולכל מנחתם ולכל חטאתם וגו' וסמיך ליה בקדש הקדשים תאכלנו כל זכר יאכל אותו (במדבר יח): ליום ולילה עד חצות · דילפינן *ממנחת לחמי תודה: **גמ'** שכן מצינו בסילוק בזיכין · שהן אזכרה למנחת לחם הפנים כדכתיב והיתה ללחם לאזכרה (ויקרא כד) ומתירין את הלחם טו] וסילוקן מעל שלחן הפנים שבהיכל במקום קמילה דמנחות הנקמצות: ממקום שרגלי הזר עומדות טז] · לעיל קאי והביא הזר אל בני אהרן הכהנים וקמץ משם מלא קומצו משמע ממקום שהבעלים עומדין שם וקס"ד השתא יז] לאסור בין האולם קאתי שאין זר נכנס לשם: שיחזיר · הקומץ לתוך השירים ולא אמרי' כבר נפסלה: לאו נצרכא · יח] הא ממקום רגלי הזר דקאמר: אלא להכשיר · דלא ליבעי על ירך המזבח לפונה אלא כל מקום דריסת רגלי ישראל כשר לקמילה וכל שכן עזרת כהנים והיכל: שכן כליל · והיכי הוה ילפינן מיניה וקרא למעוטי למה לי: מחטאת · אי לאו דמיעטה הוה ילפינן לה מחטאת: ופרכינן מה לחטאת שכן מכפרת כו': ה"ג מה לאשם שכן מיני דמים: מכולהו · יט] בעיא למגמריה במיהדר דינא ותיתי במה הצד: מה הגשה בקרן מערבית דרומית · קודם קמילתה כ] מגיעתה בהוך כליה לקרן מערבית דרומית של מזבח כדלקמן: שנאמר ושחטו פתח אהל מועד וכו' · אלמא מדתלה הכשר עזרה לשלמים בפתח אהל מועד שמע מינה אהל מועד עיקר ועזרה טפל: ולא יהיה טפל חמור מן העיקר · דכיון דטפל חזי לאו כ"ש עיקר: הקיפו עובדי כוכבים · למלחמה ויורים חיצים ואבני בליסטראות לתוך העזרה: בקדש הקדשים · היכל במשמע: ואמאי · אם איתא דאמרי' לא יהא טפל חמור מן העיקר למה לי למיכתב האי קרא לאכשורי היכל לאכילת כא] קדשים הא כתיב בהו בחצר אהל מועד *ונימא לא יהא טפל חמור מן העיקר: אכילה דאין אדם אוכל במקום רבו · דזילותא דרביה היא לעשות כב] צרכי עבד לפניו לא יהא טפל חמור ליכא למימר דלאו חומרא היא אלא קולא וכן הדין שיהא טפל כג] *חמור מן העיקר: **מתני'** חטאת העוף היתה נעשית כו' · בגמ' יליף כד] מנא ליה: בכל מקום היתה כשירה כו' · בגמ' פריך מאי קאמר: מלמטה · למטה מן החוט: חטאת* · כה] יליף בגמרא שהיא למטה: הגשות · של מנחות קודם קמילתן כדכתיב והגישה ובגמ' יליף הא קרן מנא ליה: ושירי הדם · של חטאות החיצונות ובגמ' מפרש לה: ניסוך המים והיין · שםם היו כו] שיתין ואי אפשר לנסך כי אם שם: ועולת העוף כשהיא רבה במזרח · דעיקר מקומן בקרן דרומית מזרחית כדמפרש טעמא בגמרא מפני שקרובה לבית הדשן לזרוק שם מוראה ונוצה כדכתיב והשליך אותה וגו' אל מקום הדשן (ויקרא א) וכשהיא רבה שם שיש כהנים הרבה באותו הקרן עסוקין בעולות ואין לזה מקום בסובב לעמוד שהעולה נעשית למעלה בא לו לקרן מערבית דרומית שאף היא סמוכה לבית הדשן מאחר שתי הקרנות שבית הדשן סמוך לכבש היה במזרחו של כבש ולדרומו של מזבח:

ויורדין

תוספות

כל כבשי כבשים שלש אמות לאמה · כז] למ"ד (לעיל דף נח:) כוליה מזבח כח] בדרום קאי יש תימה על מזבח הנחשת למ"ד גובהו עשר כט] לא משכחת לכל היותר כי אם כ' אמות לט' אמות דחצר שלפני המשכן חמשים אמה כ"ה אמות חצי החצר וה' אמות מקום מזבח פש ליה כ' אמה עד כותל דרומי כי מטי כבש עד הכותל לא משכחת לאמה אלא שתי אמות וטפח ואצבע ושליש אצבע והוה ליה הילוך על ידי הדחק כדמוכח בשבת (דף ק·) ובעירובין (דף נח:) במתלקט עשרה מתוך ארבע דהוי רשות היחיד ולמ"ד דמזבח רחב עשר אמות לא הוו אלא ט"ו אמה עד הכותל ל] ורבי יוסי דאמר לעיל (דף נט:) מזבח גבוה עשר אמות ורחב חמש לטעמיה דאמר כוליה מזבח בצפון קאי והיה משוך כל כך לצד צפון עד דמשתיירי ל"ב אמה לכבש ומיהו א"כ לא היה כלל מן המזבח לפני פתח המשכן אי מזבח משוך יותר מכ"ה אמה דמסתמא משכן הוה כמו בית עולמים דגלוי יום הכיפורים צריך לפני ה' ולרבי יהודה דאמר עשר רחבו יש לומר דלדידיה שלש אמות קומתו ולא יותר כדתניא לעיל (דף נט:):

חוץ מכבשו של מזבח שהיה שלש אמות ומחצה ואצבע ושליש אצבע *בזכרותא · זו היא גירסת הקונטרס לא] ומכוון חשבון לט' אמות של מזבח ורבותיו גורסים ג' אמות ומחצה וחצי טפח ואצבע ושליש אצבע לב] בזכרותו ופירש בקונטרס לחשבון זה לא היה ראש הכבש שוה לראש המזבח אלא נמוך ממנו רביע אמה דלחשבון גובה ט' יש לכבש יותר מל"ב אמה ולא דק בקונטרס דאין *גבוה אלא חומש אמה חסר משהו והקשה בקונטרס הרי אמרה תורה לא תעלה במעלות על מזבחי *ותירץ רבי נתן מדודיא דבפרק שתי הלחם (מנחות נז:*) אמרינן דאמה של לג] [יסוד] גובה באמה בת חמשה לד] ולפירוש הקונטרס [קשה] דנמצא ראש הכבש גבוה מראשו של מזבח ומיהו אין לחוש אי נמי לפירוש הקונטרס לה] אמות של כבש לפי אמות של מזבח לו]:

שבן מליט בסילוק בזיכין · ולא שייך למימר כאן טעם אחר לז] ולא יהא טפל חמור מן העיקר כדקאמר בשלמים דשלמים תלאן הכתוב בפתח אהל מועד לח] ואם תאמר ל"ל טעמא דבזיכין אמאי ס"ד למיפסל לפי מה שפירש בקונטרס לעיל ספ"ק (דף יד·) מודה ר"ש בחטאות הפנימיות דעבודה שאין יכול לבטלה משום דלאו אורח ארעא לשחוט בהיכל דמשמע דאי לאו הכי היה יכול לשחוט בהיכל אע"ג דחטאת בעי' צפון ואם כן קמילה תתכשר וי"ל דסלקא דעתך לפסול לט] דדרשינן מקום שרגלי הזר עומדות להכשיר כל מקום שזר יכול לעמוד דה"א לפסולי היכל קאתי שאין זר יכול לעמוד שם סלקא דעתך אמינא מ] אף מנחה טעונה צפון לכך אתא קרא דממקום שרגלי הזר עומדות להכשיר כל מקום שזר יכול לעמוד אפי' בדרום אבל אין לפרש דדריש דרום מטעם דאין זר יכול לעמוד בצפון חדא דלעיל בפרק ב' (דף כ·) מוסיף מא] אף מקום דריסת רגלי ישראל דחשוב לפון ועוד אפי' למ"ד מרחק לפון לא מסתבר שיהא זר אסור בצפון כנגד המזבח אלא מב] מדרבנן מעלה בעלמא:

עין משפט נר מצוה

כה א ב מיי' פי"ב מהלכות מעש"ק הלכה יב:

כו ג מיי' שם הלכה ו ופי"ג שם הלכה יב:

כז ד מיי' פ"ב מהלכות מעש"ק הלכה ד: [ד] מיי' פ"י מהלכות מעש"ק דין ג:

כח ה מיי' פ"ז מהל' מעש"ק הלכה ו:

כט ו מיי' שם הל' ט:

ל ז מיי' שם הלכה י:

לא ח מיי' שם הלכה יא:

מסורת הש"ס

עי' תוספ' גרסאות · נ"ל בזוכרתא [ועי' מ"ש תוס' מנחות מח: ד"ה ארבעם] · [מנחות ת.] · [וע"ע רש"י מנחות יא: ד"ה למגמר וכ"ע] · [לעיל מח:] · מנחות ת: · [לעיל מח: וש"נ] · [מנחות ת: ע"ש ושם איתא רבי יהודה בן בתירה ובספרים שלנו מאתי מתיב רבי יוחנן] · [עי' לקמן סו: מנחות כ:] · סוכה מח: · יאכלנה נ"ק · נ"א קל · העוף נ"ק

רש"ק גרס יעקב [וכ"א מנחות ת:] · נ"א בזוכרתא · נ"ל נמוך נ"ק · [ושם ד"ה אל תיק]

תורה אור

ויקרא ב · שם ו · שם ג · במדבר יח

שיטה מקובצת

א] כל כבשי כבשים כו' · משמע דכל כבש דינו להיות כך ותימה דלמ"ד דכוליה מזבח בדרום העזרה קאי א"כ המזבח היה עומד באמצע חצר המשכן שהיתה חמשים על חמשים א"כ א)חצי העזרה לא היתה כי אם כ"ה אמה ולמ"ד שהמזבח גבוה עשר והמזבח היה רוחב ה' אמות וא"כ כי מטי הכבש עד כותל העזרה לא היה הכבש [אורך כי אם עשרים] אמה והמזבח היה גבוה ט' אמות מבלי מקום הקרנות ולחשבון ג' אמות לאמה היה לו לכבש להיות אורך כ"ז אמות וצריך להיות כל הכבש בדרום כדנפקא לן לעיל מירך המזבח צפונה ואפילו להילוך אינו ראוי הואיל ואינו מתלקט כו' וי"ל דר' יוסי [הוא] דאמר גבהו ט' אמה (פי' מבלי מקום הקרנות' עכ"ה) ור' יוסי לטעמיה דאמר כוליה מזבח בצפון קאי מיהו אכתי קשה דלא נשאר מן החצר לכבש רק כ"ה אמה וי"ל שהיה המזבח משוך לצד צפון כל כך שלא היה מן המזבח לפני אהל מועד רק ג' אמות ונשאר מן החצר כ"ז אמות לכבש דהיינו ג' אמות לאמה ודי בכך לפי שלא היה קבוע כל כך אבל ליכא למימר שלא היה כלל מן המזבח לפני המשכן דהא כתיב פתח אהל מועד: ב] עיין בהשמטות בסוף המסכת: ג] מתני' המנחות היו: ד] מנחה שקמצה: ה] שיחזיר' ס"א שהוא מחזיר ויחזור ויקמוץ: ו] ר' יעקב ותיבת עקיבא נמחק: ז] מכולהו' ס"א מכולהו נמי שכן כו': ח] רבי יהודה תיבת יוחנן נמחק: ט] נכנסין להיכל ואוכלין שם קדשי קדשים ושירי מנחה ת"ל בקדש: י] רבו · ס"י טעמא דאהדריה קרא הא לא אהדריה קרא לא כו': יא] קרן מערבית דרומית: יב] אמות גבה הרי: יג] עי' בהשמטות בסוף המסכת: יד] ואין טעונות צפון: טו] הלחם כקומץ שמתיר את השירים וסילוקן מעל השולחן במקום ותיבות הפנים שבהיכל נמחק: טז] עומדות דעל מקום הזר קאי קרא דכתיב והביא: יז] השתא למעוטי היכל ואולם קאתי: יח] האי ממקום שרגלי הזר עומדות דקאמר: יט] מכולהו ואי מכולהו בעי: כ] קמיצתה מגיעה בכלי לקרן מערבית: כא] לאכילת קדשי קדשים: כב] לעשות עבדו צרכיו לפניו: כג] טפל קל מן העיקר: כד] תיבת מנא נמחק: כה] חטאת העוף יליף: כו] היו השיתין: כז] לאמה · משמע שכל כבש דינו להיות כך א"כ למ"ד: כח] מזבח לדרום העזרה קאי: כט] עשר ורחבו חמש לא משכחת כו' לט' אמות דגובה המזבח מלבד הקרנות שהיו אמה דחצר: ל] ושמא ר' יוסי אות ו' נמחק: לא] ומכוון החשבון לט': לב] בזכרותו פי' בשפוע בעובי הגודל והא דנקט בזכרותו כדי ליישב החשבון מצומצם ד' אצבעות לטפח משום דבפתם אצבעות הוי הטפח ששה אצבעות ופי': לג] של גובה יסוד באמה: לד] חמשה ס"א א"כ המזבח היה גבוה ט' אמות פחות טפח ואדרבה לגירסת רש"י קשה מהתם דנמצא כו': לה] הקונטרס יש ליישב דאמות של: לו] מזבח ושל מטה בת חמשה לשיעור יסוד ואינך בבת חמשה: לז] דלא יהא טפל חמור מן העיקר החצר מן האהל כדקאמר: לח] מועד אם כן עשה הפסוק הפתח טפל לאהל אבל הכא לא הזכיר אהל כלל אלא החצר וא"ת: לט] לפסול הוא דדרשינן ממקום שרגלי הזר עומדות דה"א לפסול ההיכל קאתי כו' והשאר נמחק: מ] אמינא הואיל ועולה טעונה צפון אף: מא] מוסיף רבי אף: מב] אלא מעלה מדרבנן בעלמא:

א) נ"ל א"כ חצי החצר וכו' עד כותל דרומי לא היה וכו' ·

הגהות הב"ח (א) גמרא כל כבשי כבשים · נ"ב כאן יש לתמוה טובא ופלא דארכו של הכבש היה ל"ב אמה ובמקום יסוד וסובב כ"א ובמידות קחשיב רחבו של עזרה מקום הכבש ל"ב אמה וזה א"א לפי החשבון שאמרו חכמים כל אמתא בריבוע אמתא ותרי חומשי באלכסונא לפי זה החשבון יגיע ארכו של כבש לשלשים [והשאר חסר]:

גליון הש"ס גמ' כל כבשי כבשים · עיין תשובת מעיל צדקה סימן כח: תוס' ד"ה חוץ וכו' ותירץ ר' נתן וכו' · עיין בתשובת מהר"ם בר ברוך דפוס פראג סימן רל"ט ועיין בערוך ערך כבש · ועיין מנחות דף מא ע"ב תוספות ד"ה ר' נגול:

לב א מיי' [illegible] הלכה יב :

לג ב מיי' פ"ה שם הלכה ט :

ומקיפין ויורדין דרך שמאל חוץ מן העולה לג' א] אלו שהיו עולין ויורדין על העקב :

גמ' מנא ה"מ ב] א"ר *יהושע אמר קרא °לא ישים עליה שמן ולא יתן עליה לבונה כי חטאת היא חטאת קרויה מנחה ומנחה קרויה חטאת מה חטאת טעונה צפון אף מנחה טעונה צפון ומה מנחה בקרן מערבית דרומית ג] אף חטאת בקרן מערבית דרומית ומנחה גופה מנלן ד] *דתניא °לפני ה' יכול במערב ת"ל °אל פני המזבח אי אל פני המזבח יכול בדרום ת"ל לפני ה' הא כיצד *מגישה בקרן מערבית דרומית כנגד חודה של קרן ודיו ר"א אומר יכול יגישנה למערבה של קרן או לדרומה של קרן אמרת *כל מקום שאתה מוצא שני מקראות אחד מקיים עצמו ומקיים חבירו ואחד מקיים עצמו ומבטל חבירו מניחין זה שמקיים עצמו ומבטל חבירו ותופשין ה] את שמקיים עצמו ומקיים חבירו ו] *כשאתה אומר (א) אל פני ה' במערב ז] היכן קיימת אל פני המזבח וכשאתה אומר אל פני המזבח בדרום קיימת לפני ה' ח] בדרום היכן קיימת אמר רב אשי קסבר האי תנא *כוליה מזבח בצפון קאי : בכל מקום היתה כשירה[וכו'] : מאי קאמר אמר רב אשי ה"ק בכל מקום היתה כשירה למליקתה אלא זה היה מקומה להזאתה תנינא להא דת"ר ט] *מלקה בכל מקום במזבח כשירה °היזה דמה בכל מקום כשירה י] היזה ולא מיצה כשירה ובלבד שיתן מחוט הסיקרא ולמטה מדם הנפש מאי קאמר ה"ק מלקה בכל מקום במזבח כשירה מיצה דמה בכ"מ במזבח כשירה

שאם

תורה אור: ויקרא ה · שם ו · שם

רש"י

ומקיפין דרך שמאל · מקיפים את המזבח בשביל צורכי עבודה או למתן דמי חטאת או סידור המערכה או היפוך איברים בצינורא ויורדין במערבו של כבש שהוא שמאל יא] לעולים במזבח בעלייתן : לג' דברים אלו · הנעשים בקרן מערבית דרומית נסכים ועולת העוף יב] כשהוא עולה למזבח פונה לשמאל באותה הקרן וכשגמר חוזר על העקב דרך עלייתו ובגמ' פריך הא בעינן דרך ימין ולג' דברים הנעשים בה למטן אינו עולה ואינו מקיף אלא עומד על הרצפה יג] בקרקע : גמ' מנא הני מילי · דחטאת העוף בקרן מערבית דרומית : לא ישים עליה וגו' · במנחת חוטא כתיב הבאה תחת חטאת העוף בדלי דלות וקרייה רחמנא חטאת יד] ואשמעינן נמי שהחטאת קרויה מנחה דהכי משמע נמי כי החטאת נהפכה להיות מנחה : מה חטאת טעונה צפון · יודע אני שגירסא זו טו] שיבוש שהרי לא חטאת העוף ולא מנחה טעון צפון וא"ת מנחת חוטא חלוקה מן השאר ולחטאת בהמה מקיש לה הוה ליה למיתני במתניתין דקתני לעיל המנחות נקמצות בכל מקום בעזרה חוץ ממנחת חוטא ועוד היאך אפשר חטאת העוף טז] שבאת תחת חטאת בהמה אינה טעונה צפון שהרי נעשית בקרן מערבית דרומית יז] ובמנחה הבאה תחת העוף הטעון צפון וגירסא אחרינא גרסי' בה ואיני יודע אמיתה ונראה בעיני מה חטאת פסולה שלא לשמה אף מנחה פסולה שלא לשמה וה"נ ילפינן לה בפ"ק דמנחות (דף ד.) : ומה מנחה · טעונה הגשה בקרן מערבית דרומית אף חטאת העוף עבודתה בקרן מערבית דרומית והזאת דמה היא עיקר עבודתה : לפני ה' · הקרב אותה בני אהרן לפני ה' היינו שמגיעה למזבח : אל פני המזבח · דרום ששם הכבש : ודיו · במסכת סוטה בפ"ב מפרש מאי יח] דיו וקאמר שאינו צריך להגיע גופה למזבח אלא הכלי : רבי אליעזר אומר · מאחר שפרט לך הכתוב בהגשתה שתי רוחות יכול לאיזה מהן שירצה ה"נ יכול יגישנה למערבה יט] או לדרומה של קרן : כוליה מזבח בצפון קאי · כמאן דרומו של מזבח כלה לנגד הפתח וקרינן נמי בצד דרומו לפני ה' : בכל מקום היתה כשירה למליקתה · בין למעלה בין למטה דכי ילפינן למטה בחטאת העוף כ] בהזאה הוא דילפינן לקמן בשמעתין והזה מדם החטאת על קיר ואמר מר זה קיר התחתון וקרן מערבית דרומית נמי כא] בהזאה הוא דילפינן דהא מהגשה דמנחה יליף והגשתה

תוספות

כב] ויורדין על העקב · לאו משום שלא ירבה בהילוך בחנם דאם כן כשהיה בקרן דרומית מזרחית נמי אלא היינו טעמא דהכא חזרתו על העקב הויא לה דרך ימין :

מנחה קרויה חטאת וחטאת קרויה מנחה · תימה דהוה לן למימר מנחה קרויה חטאת ואין חטאת קרויה מנחה כדאמרינן פ"ק (לעיל ז:) תודה קרויה שלמים ואין שלמים קרויין תודה ובמנחות פרק התודה (דף פ:) לחם איקרי תודה תודה לא איקרי לחם וי"ל כג] דודאי לא מיקרי שם אחד לענין לשמה דפ"ק ולענין ניתותרו המצות דפרק התודה אבל הכא דמהיקשא קדריש דמנחה וחטאת איתקוש ודאי להדדי איכא לאקושינהו שפיר כד] :

מה חטאת טעונה צפון · פירש בקונטרס דגירסא זו משובשת היא שהרי לא חטאת העוף טעונה צפון כדאמר ולא בן עוף בצפון ולא מנחה טעונה צפון וא"ת מנחת כה] *חטאת חלוקה משאר מנחות ולחטאת בהמה מקיש לה הוה ליה למיתני במתניתין לעיל דקתני כל המנחות נקמצות בכל מקום בעזרה חוץ ממנחת כו] חוטא ועוד *אפשר חטאת העוף הבאה בדלות תחת חטאת בהמה אינה טעונה צפון שהרי נעשית בקרן מערבית דרומית ומנחה הבאה תחת חטאת העוף תטען צפון כז] וגירסא אחרינא גרסינן בה ואיני יודע אמיתה ונראה בעיני מה חטאת פסולה שלא לשמה אף מנחה פסולה שלא לשמה וה"נ ילפינן לה בפ"ק [דמנחות] ע"כ לשון הקונטרס וקשה לפירושו כח] דודאי מעיקרא אמרי' בפ"ק דמנחות (דף ד.) בשלמא מנחת חוטא חטאת קרייה רחמנא אבל מנחת קנאות מנלן אבל במסקנא אמרינן אלא מנחת חוטא ומנחת קנאות דפסולות שלא לשמן מנלן חטאת טעמא מאי דכתיב בה היא ה"נא כתיב בהו היא כט] ועוד קשה לגירסת הספרים דבפרק איזהו מקומן (לעיל מח:) מוכח דחטאת הטעונה צפון כעולה הוי היקש אם כן היכי אתיא מנחה והדר ילפינן מחטאה. וכי דבר הלמד בהיקש חוזר ומלמד בהיקש ועוד כמו שהקשה בקונטרס דחמירא לא הויא מנחה מחטאת העוף דאתיא במקומה ואינה טעונה צפון מיהו י"ל הרי בתורת כהנים ילפינן דחטאת העוף פסולה שלא לשמה מן הפסוק ולא ילפינן ממנחת חוטא דמפיק פסול מקרא אחרינא ויש לדחות מיהו אמת דמנחה לא בעיא צפון ל] אלא הגשה בקרן מערבית דרומית כדבסמוך לא] (ואי) והקמילה אינה טעונה צפון אפי' מנחת חוטא נמי כדמוכח בתוספתא דמנחות פ"ק חומר בשחיטה שטעונה צפון מה שאינכן בקמילה וכי תימא היינו במנחת נדבה אבל במנחת חוטא טעונה צפון מכל מקום אינו חומר לב] *בשחיטה לגמרי שהרי בשחיטה נמי ליתא בצפון לג] בקלים מיהו י"ל דכללא בקדשי קדשים הוי דומיא דמנחה וזהו דוחק ועוד דתני בסיפא חומר בקמילה מבמליקה שהקמילה דוחה שבת וטומאה וליתני שהקמילה טעונה צפון ולא מליקה אף על גב דיש קמילה דלא בעיא צפון כגון מנחת נדבה כמו כן אינה דוחה שבת מיהו נ"ל לדחות דה"נ לא מיירי במנחת חוטא דהא אינה דוחה שבת אלא מיירי במנחת העומר ומנחת תמיד שהן בציבור והן ודאי לא בעו צפון אבל מנחת חוטא לד] בעי' צפון דאיתקש לחטאת בהמה שבאה חליפתה בעשירות · ברו"ך : והרב רבי חיים גרים מה חטאת העוף טעונה יסוד דכתיב והנשאר בדם ימצה אל יסוד המזבח אף מנחה טעונה הגשה כנגד היסוד לה] והכי מוכח פרק כל המנחות באות מצה (מנחות דף סא·) [גבי] ואלו טעונות תנופה לוג שמן של מצורע ואשמו [דאמרינן התם] לפני ה' במזרח והאמרת לפני ה' במערב פירוש בהך לו] שמעתיה ומשני ה"מ מנחה דאיקרי חטאת וחטאת טעונה יסוד וקרן דרומית מזרחית לא היה לה יסוד אבל הכא לפני ה' קרינא ביה והשתא כולה בדרום ליכא למימר משום יסוד וכולה במערב נמי לא משום דכתיב (ויקרא ו) אל פני המזבח דהיינו דרום מכל מקום אילטריך לפני ה' דלא תימא אל פני המזבח גזירת הכתוב הוא אף על גב דלית ליה יסוד ובריש פירקין *פירשתי מה שהקשה דגבי גחלים דיום הכיפורים קרי לפני ה' במערב דוקא וא"ת ושאר מנחות מנלן וכי תימא מדאיתקוש כל המנחות לחטאת ואשם בפרשת צו וילפינן משירי הדם שטעונין יסוד אם כן מנחת חוטא לז] תיפוק לי מהתם ועוד מנלן דמקשינן לשירים לקשינהו לתחילת דמים לח] ולא בעי יסוד כחטאת ויש לומר דכתיב לפני ה' במנחת חוטא ובכל המנחות נמי כתיב לפני ה' כי היכי דהאי לפני ה' כנגד היסוד [האי נמי כנגד היסוד לט] ולא ג"ש ממש [היא] דדבר הלמד בהיקש מבעיא לן אי חוזר ומלמד בג"ש אי לא אלא גלוי מילתא בעלמא הוא מ] *ור"ת גרים מה חטאת טעונה ימין אף מנחה כן והיינו דלא כר"ש דאמר לעיל (דף כה·) בא לעובדה בכלי עובדה בשמאל אי נמי אפילו כרבי שמעון וכגון שבא לעובדה ביד דאמר עובדה בימין כחטאת : מא] הגה"ה

אף חטאת בקרן מערבית דרומית · תימה דלא ילפינן מינה מליקה ושמא לא ילפינן אלא מידי דאשכחן דבעי מזבח כמנחה וכן פירש בקונטרס בסמוך :

בדרום קיימת א) עולה · ב) על כרחך רבי אליעזר אית ליה ההיא מב] דמה חטאת טעונה יסוד דאי לאו הכי מנא ליה דאמר מערבית ותימה אם כן לפני ה' למה לי דרומית נפקא לן מאל פני המזבח ומערבית מדבעיא יסוד :

שאם

א) כו' נ"ק ב) עיין רש"ק

מסורת הש"ס

[ג"ר' סילקוס ר' אלעזר]

מנחות יט: סא. סוטה יד:

מנחות יט: סוטה יד:

לעיל נג. נח. סוטה יד:

[לקמן סו. סח.] מנחות כ:

רש"ק כשחיטה

נ"ק

[דף מג. ד"ה משון]

[צ"ל חוטא]

צ"ל היאך

[צ"ל שכשאתה אומר לפני ה' במערב בטלת אל פני המזבח בדרום וכשאתה אומר אל פני המזבח בדרום קיימת לפני ה' במערב והיכן קיימת א"ר אשי כו' וכן היא הגירסא במנחות ובסוטה]

הגהות הב"ח

(א) גמ' כשאתה אומר לפני ה' כצ"ל ותיבת אל נמחק :

גליון הש"ס

תוס' ד"ה מה וכו' ור"ת גרים מה חטאת טעונה ימין אף מנחה כן · פי' לעיל דף כד ע"ב יד יד לקמיצה וצ"ע

שיטה מקובצת

א] לג' דברים אלו שהיו עולין וחוזרין על העקב: ב] עיין בהשמטות בסוף המסכת : ג] אף חטאת בקרן מערבית דרומית פי' הזאה דחטאת אבל לא יליף מליקה דחטאת משום דלא דמי להגשה כדפ"ה לקמן דבבהמה איכא נגיעה ממש מן הדם במזבח דומיא דהגשה דמגיע המנחה למזבח ועוד דמשמע שבא להקיש עיקר עבודתה והיינו הזאת דמה : ד] דתניא לפני ה' יכול במערב · וא"ת והא האי קרא במנחת נדבה כתיב דאית בה שמן ולבונה ואילו מנחת חוטא לית בה שמן ולבונה וי"ל דבפרשת ויקרא כתיב והבאתה את המנחה והגישה' את המנחה קרא יתירא דהוי מצי למכתב והבאתה לבד וכתיב את המנחה לרבות כל המנחות אפי' מנחת חוטא להגשה לעיכוב מקום · וא"ת א"כ לפי' רבינו חיים למה לי היקשא דלעיל למנחת חוטא לומר שטעונה הגשה כנגד היסוד תיפוק לי מרבא דטעונה הגשה כנגד קרן מערבית דרומית שיש לה יסוד וי"ל דהו"א דמגיש' אצל הקרן מלמעלה קמ"ל היקשא למנחת [חוטא] שמגישה מלמטה אצל היסוד אבל קשה למה לי לפני ה' תיפוק לי מהיקשא דלעיל דבדרום ליכא לאוקמי דהא לא היה לו יסוד בדרום וא"כ צריך להגישה בקרן מערבית דרומית דהוי פני המזבח וגם איכא יסוד וא"כ למה לי לפני ה' וי"ל דהו"א דמגישה באמה אחת שבדרום אצל המערב ששם היה יסוד קמ"ל לפני ה' לומר שמגישה כנגד חודה של קרן אבל אכתי קשה בשאר מנחות מנ"ל שמגישן אצל היסוד מלמטה אימא דמגישן מלמעלה אצל הקרן הואיל דמהיקשא דמנחה לחטאת לא נפקא לן רק מנחת חוטא וי"ל דבמנחת חוטא כתיב לפני ה' וכן במנחת נדבה וא"כ כי היכי דלפני ה' דגבי מנחת חוטא היינו למטה מן היסוד כמו כן לפני ה' דכתיב במנחת נדבה ר"ל כלמטה ומיהו ריב"א דקדק ולא מצא במנחת חוטא לפני ה' (ס"א לכך פי' דכך צ"ל מדקאמר הכא דלפני ה' דנדבה חשבינן כאלו כתיב במנחת חוטא דאמנחת חוטא נמי קאי מייתורא דהמנחה כדפי' וע"כ הוי פי' דלפני ה' דמנחת חוטא יסוד מדאיתקש לחטאת א"כ כי נמי קאי אנדבה כפשטיה לא ישתנה פירושו דאתרוייהו קאי) אלא י"ל כיון דכתיב לפני ה' במנחת נדבה מרבינן מנחת חוטא מייתורא מאת המנחה להגשה לעיכוב מקום כדפי' א"כ סברא הוא דכמו דבמנחת חוטא ר"ל ליסוד כמו כן במנחת נדבה ר"ל ליסוד דהואיל דקאי אתרוייהו לא ישתנה פירושו : ה] ותופשין זה שמקיים תיבת את נמחק : ו] עיין בהשמטות בסוף המסכת : ז] כמערב בטלת אל פני המזבח בדרום ותיבת היכן קיימת נמחק : ח] במערב היכן תיבת בדרום נמחק : ט] מליקה בכל : י] תיבות הזה ולא מיצה כשרה נמחק : יא] שמאל העולים למזבח בעלייתן : יב] שכשעולה למזבח פונה לסבב לשמאלו ותיבות כשהוא עולה ל"ש : יג] תיבת בקרקע נמחק : יד] חטאת מינה שמעינן

נמי כו' דהכי נמי משמע כי החטאת : טו] זו משובשת שהרי לא כו' ולא מנחה שטעון צפון : טז] העוף הבאה בדלות תחת חטאת : יז] ומנחה הבאה : יח] מאי ודיו דקאמר שאינו צריך להגיע המנחה גופה : יט] למערבה של קרן או : כ] העוף בהזאה הוא : כא] נמי להוצאה הוא דילפינן דהא כי גמר מהגשה דמנחה הזאה הוא דגמר ותיבת יליף נמחק : כב] מה"ד וחוזרין על העקב : כג] וי"ל דלאו דוקא נקט דודאי : כד] שפיר ודוחק הוא ונראה דבקונטרס דקדק בזה דפי' ושמעינן מינה שהחטאת קרויה מנחה כי חטאת העוף נהפכת לבא תחתיה מנחת חוטא בדלי דלות וא"כ חטאת קרויה מנחה כשהיא פוטר בדלי דלות ממנחת חוטא תחת חטאת העוף · מהר"פ : כה] מנחת חוטא חלוקה : כו] דוטא ועוד דמסתמא אקשינן מנחת חוטא שהיא בדלי דלות לחטאת העוף שלפניו שהיא בדלות ולא להטאת בהמה דעשיר דלפני פניו : כז] עיין בהשמטות בסוף המסכת : כח] לפירושו דא"כ לא ידעינן דמנחת חוטא פסולה שלא לשמה כי אם מהיקשא דחטאת וזה אינו דודאי : כט] היא אלא דמהיא ילפינן ועוד : ל] צפון אי בהגשה הלא היא בקרן תיבת אלא נמחק ול"ש : לא] כדבסמוך ואי הקמיצה : לב] חומר כשחיטה לגמרי : לג] בצפון בקדשים קלים : לד] חוטא שמא בעי : לה] היסוד לאפוקי קרן דרומית מזרחית שאין לו יסוד והכי מוכח כו' באות מצה דתנן ואלו טעונות תנופה כו' ואשמו ואמרינן בגמרא לפני : לו] בהך דשמעתין אוה ה' נמחק : לז] חוטא נמי תיפוק : לח] דמים דלא בעיא : לט] היסוד האי נמי כנגד היסוד ולא ג"ש ממש היא דדבר : מ] מתיבת ור"ת עד סוף הדבור מוקף ח"ל : מא] כחטאת ע"כ הגה"ה : מב] ההיא דרשא דמה חטאת כו' מנא ליה קרן דרומית מערבית ותיבת דאמרת נמחק :

רצשות

[63*b*] THEN THEY WENT ROUND [THE ALTAR][8] AND DESCENDED BY THE LEFT, EXCEPT FOR THESE THREE, WHO ASCENDED AND DESCENDED BY RETRACING THEIR STEPS.[9]

GEMARA. Whence do we know it?—Said R. Joshua, Scripture saith: ***He shall put no oil upon it, neither shall he put any frankincense thereon, for it is a sin-offering:***[10] a sin-offering is designated a meal-offering,[11] and a meal-offering is designated a sin-offering: as a sin-offering requires the north, so does a meal-offering require the
a north;[1] and as a meal-offering [is presented] at the south-west horn, so is a [bird] sin-offering [offered] at the south-west horn.[2]

And how do we know this of the meal-offering itself?—Because it was taught: [*The sons of Aaron shall offer it*] *before the Lord:*[3] You might think, at the west [of the altar];[4] therefore it states, *in* front *of the altar.*[5] If [it is to be] *'in* front *of the altar'*, you might think, in the south; but Scripture says, *'before the Lord'*. How then was it done? He presented it at the south-west horn, opposite the edge of the horn, and that is sufficient. R. Eleazar said: You might think that he presents it on the west of the horn or the south of the horn; but you can rebut [this], [for] wherever you find two texts, one confirming itself and the other, whereas the second confirms itself but annuls the other, you abandon the one which confirms itself and annuls the other, and accept that which confirms itself and the other too. Thus, if you say *'before the Lord'* [means] in the west, how can you confirm *'in* front *of the altar'*? But when you say, *'in* front *of the altar'*, means in the south, you confirm *before the Lord* as meaning the south.[6] But how can you confirm this?—Said R. Ashi: This Tanna holds that the whole altar stood in the north.[7]

NOW, IT WAS FIT [IF DONE] IN ANY PLACE etc. What does this mean?[8]—Said R. Ashi, This is what it means: Any place is fit for its *meliḳah*, but this was the place for its sprinkling. We have thus learnt here what our Rabbis taught: If he nipped it by any part of the altar, it is valid; if he sprinkled its blood on any part [of the altar], it is valid. (If he sprinkled [the blood] but did not
b drain it out, it is valid)[1] provided that he applies some of the life blood[2] below the scarlet line. What does this mean?[3]—This is what he means: If he nipped it by any part of the altar, it is valid;

(8) For whatever they had to do, e.g., sprinkle the blood or arrange the wood pile. (9) By the left. V. Suk. 48*b*. (10) I.e., they returned the same way as they came. (10) Lev. V, 11. This refers to a sinner's meal-offering brought in extreme poverty instead of a bird sin-offering. (11) Since the latter can be a substitute for it.

a (1) Rashi maintains that the text is faulty, because a bird sin-offering did not require the north, nor did a sinner's meal-offering. He conjectures as an emendation: as a (bird) sin-offering is invalid if offered under a different designation, so is a (sinner's) meal-offering invalid in similar circumstances. R. Ḥayyim in Tosaf. emends: as the blood of a bird sin-offering must be poured out at the base, so must a sinner's meal-offering be presented at the base. (2) I.e., its blood is sprinkled there. (3) Lev. VI, 7. This refers to a meal-offering, and *'before the Lord'* means at the altar. (4) Which faced the *hekal*, and so might appropriately be described as *'before the Lord'*. (5) Ibid. *'Front'* is the south, where the ascent ran. (6) For variant reading v. Men. 19*b*. (7) Hence the south of the altar ended opposite the door leading to the *hekal*, and so that too would be called *'before the Lord'*. (8) It cannot be meant as it stands, for if it was fit in any place, why insist on a particular spot?

b (1) Sh. M. deletes the bracketed passage. (2) The first blood which gushes forth. (3) This is apparently self-contradictory, as the first states that it is valid if sprinkled anywhere, and then states that it must be sprinkled below the scarlet line.

if he drained the blood at any part of the altar, it is valid, [64a] for if he sprinkled but did not drain out, it is valid,[4] provided that he applies some of the life blood below the scarlet line.

[THAT HORN SERVED FOR] THREE THINGS etc. FOR THE SIN-OFFERING OF THE BIRD, as we have stated.[5] FOR THE PRESENTING: for it is written, *And he shall bring it near* [i.e., present it] *unto the altar.*[6] FOR THE RESIDUE OF THE BLOOD: for it is written, *And all the remaining blood thereof shall he pour out at the base of the altar.*[7]

ABOVE: FOR THE POURING OF THE WINE AND THE WATER, AND FOR THE BURNT-OFFERING OF A BIRD WHEN THE EAST WAS TOO MUCH OCCUPIED. What is the reason?[8]—R. Joḥanan said: Because it is nearest to the ash deposit.[9] R. Joḥanan said: Come and see how great was the strength of the priests, for no part of birds is lighter than the crop and the feathers, yet sometimes the priest threw them more than thirty cubits.[10] For we learnt: He[11] took a silver pan [brazier] and ascended to the top of the altar, where he parted the coals to either side, [and] shovelled out some of the inner burnt coals; then he descended and reached the pavement. He turned his face toward the north, proceeded to the east of the ascent, a distance of ten cubits. There he heaped up the coals on the pavement three handbreadths away from the slope, at the site where they placed the crop and the feathers and the
a ashes of the inner altar and the candlestick.[1] But this would be more than thirty-one [cubits]?[2]—He does not count the place of the person.[3]

ALL WHO ASCENDED THE ALTAR etc. What is the reason?[4]—Said R. Joḥanan: In the case of libations, lest they become smoke-laden; and as to the burnt-offering of a bird, lest it perish through the smoke.[5] An objection is raised: When he came to make a circuit of the altar,[6] whence did he commence? From the south-east horn, [whence he successively passed to] the north-east, north-west, and south-west, and he was handed the wine to pour it out![7]—

(4) Thus it is valid even if he omits the draining altogether. Therefore it is certainly valid when he drains it anywhere by the altar. (5) *Supra* 63b. (6) Lev. II, 8. It was stated *supra* 63b that this means at the south-west of the altar. (7) Ibid. IV, 30. It is stated *supra* 53a and 54a that this applies to the southern base. (8) This implies that the proper place for the burnt-offering of a bird was the east; what then was the reason for this? (9) The ashes which were placed every morning by the side of the altar, to the east of the ascent. (10) When the bird was sacrificed by the south-west horn, he had to throw the crop and the feathers to the ash deposit, more than thirty cubits away. It requires great strength to throw anything that is very light a great distance. (11) The priest who removed the ashes.

a (1) V. Tam. I, 4. (2) Rashi gives the exact calculation. (3) That itself is responsible for one cubit. (4) Why were these different? (5) Of the burning wood and limbs. Hence the shortest route was taken. (6) This refers to the High Priest, v. Tam. VII, 3. (7) On to the altar. It is now assumed that he is given the wine when he *commences* the circuit, which shews that we are not afraid of the smoke.

שאם היזה ולא מיצה כשירה ובלבד שיתן מחוט הסיקרא ולמטה מדם הנפש: שלשה דברים כו': חטאת העוף הא דאמרן א] הגשות דכתיב °והגישה אל (פני) המזבח ב] שירי הדם דכתיב °ואת כל דם הפר ישפוך אל יסוד המזבח: מלמעלה ניסוך המים והיין ועולת העוף כשהיא רבה במזרח: ג] מ"ט רבי יוחנן אמר ד] מפני שקרובה מבית הדשן אמר רבי יוחנן בא וראה כמה גדול כחן של כהנים שאין לך קל בעופות יותר ממוראה ונוצה פעמים שהכהן זורקן יותר ה] מבשלשים אמה *דתנן אנטל מחתה של כסף ועלה לראש המזבח ופינה את הגחלים אילך ואילך וחתה מן המאוכלות הפנימיות ויורד הגיע לרצפה מחזיר פניו כלפי צפון והולך למזרחו של כבש ו] כעשר אמות צבר את הגחלים על גבי הרצפה רחוק מן הכבש שלשה טפחים מקום שנותנין מוראה ונוצה ודישון מזבח הפנימי והמנורה ז] הני טפי מתלתין וחד הויין מקום ח] גברי לא חשיב: כל העולים למזבח: מ"ט אמר רבי יוחנן נסכים שמא יתעשנו ועולת העוף שמא תמות בעשן ט] ורמינהו *בא לו להקיף את המזבח מאין הוא מתחיל במקרן דרומית מזרחית צפונית צפונית מערבית דרומית י] ונותנין לו יין לנסך גאמר רבי יוחנן

הקפה

(ויקרא ה) (שם ד) (תמיד לג:)

רש"י

והגשתה למזבח הוא דיליף יא] דומיא דהגשה במנחה ומליקה לאו במזבח יב] אלא הזאה ומילוי: *מאי קאמר. קתני הזה דמה בכל מקום ואפילו למעלה מן החוט כשירה והדר יג] תניא ובלבד שיתן מחוט הסיקרא ולמטה והא ליכא למימר דהזה יד] ואח"כ חזר והזה למטה קא טו] מכשרי דהא הזה דמה קתני כל דמה משמע דלא קתני הזה מדמה: מילה דמה. *שהחטאת טעונה מילוי אחר הזאה כדכתיב והנשאר בדם ימצה וגו' (ויקרא ה) שמקיף הגוף למזבח ודוחק בית מליקתו בקיר והדם מתמצה ויורד: בכל מקום כשירה. כדמפרש טעמא דמילוי בחטאת טז] לאו עבודה היא ליפסל בשינוי שאפילו עקר המילוי לגמרי שהזה ולא מילה כשירה כדאמרן באיזהו מקומן (לעיל דף נב.) והנשאר ימצה שאינו נשאר לא ימצה אלמא איכא יז] דסבירא דלא מעכב ומהאי *קרא: ובלבד. יח] שיהא הזאה הנעשית ראשון מחוט הסיקרא ולמטה מדם הנפש: הא דאמרן. דילפינן לעיל מכי חטאת היא האמור במנחה: אל פני המזבח. ודרשינן לעיל דאקרן מערבית דרומית קאי: אל יסוד יט] המזבח. ואמרינן באיזהו מקומן (לעיל דף נג.) ילמד ירידתו מן הכבש בחטאות החיצונות מיציאתו מן ההיכל כ] *בסמוך לו והיינו יסוד דרומי ובכל הדרום אין לך יסוד אלא אמה אחת בקרן מערבית דרומית כדאמרינן (שם דף נד.) אוכל בדרום אמה אחת: מבית הדשן. מקום שנותנין שם בכל בקר תרומת הדשן שכתב בה ושמו אצל המזבח והוא במזרחו של כבש וכתיב גבי מוראה ונוצה (ויקרא א) והשליך אותה אצל המזבח קדמה אל מקום הדשן ולקמן מייתי משנה ממסכת תמיד דבמזרחו של כבש הוה והייט כא] *לקרן דרומית מזרחית: שאין לך קל בעוף. ודבר שהוא קל מאד אין נוח לזורקו למרחוק: פעמים שכהן זורקו כו'. כשהיא רבה במזרח ונעשית בקרן מערבית דרומית צריך לזרוק יותר משלשים אמה: דתנן. במסכת תמיד מי שזכה בתרומת הדשן כב] של מחתה נטל מחתה של כסף ועלה לראש המזבח כו': הגיע לרצפה. לסוף הכבש: מחזיר פניו לצפון. כג] כלפי המזבח והולך למזרחו של כבש ומתקרב למזבח עשר אמות ממקום שכלה הכבש דהייט רחוק כד] מעל ראש המזבח *כ"ב אמה: צבר את הגחלים כו'. אלמא התם הוי בית הדשן וכשהוא עושה עולת העוף בקרן מערבית דרומית צריך לזורקה כה] כל אלכסון של כ"ב על כ"ב שהרי [א] (א) מדרום לצפון אמרנו דאיכא כ"ב וממקום שהוא עומד עד מזרחו של כבש אין פחות *מכ"ב כו] ואפי' הוא מתקרב לכבש כל אמות רוחב הקרן ואין כאן אלא כ"א תן כנגדה אמה מקום מעמדו כז] שהוא מרוחק מן הצפון לדרום לבית הדשן שהוא עומד בראש המזבח ולא בסובב שכשהיא נעשית במזרח עומד בסובב לפי שיש לו כבש קטן במזרח לפנות הימנו לסובב אבל לצד המערב אין לו כח] [כבש] לפנות לסובב וצריך לעלות על ראש המזבח כט] ועומד *בדרומה של קרן והכי תנן במס' סוכה (דף מח.) גבי נסכים עלה ל] ופנה לשמאל ולא תנן בה ופנה לסובב הרי משם ולכבש ה' אמות שהכבש רחב ע"ז באמצע המזבח נמלא ראש המזבח עודף עליו לכל צד ו' אמות הרי כ"ב אמה עם רוחב הקרן ואע"פ שזה נמשך לצד הכבש לא] של קרן הרי נתרחק כנגדה אמה *לדרום נמלא בית הדשן עומד כנגדה באלכסון של כ"ב על כ"ב וכל אמתא בריבוע אמתא ותרי חומשי באלכסונא נמלא תוספת ח' אמות וד' חומשים הרי שלשים אמות וד' טפחים גדולים ובית הדשן היה משוך ממזרחו של כבש שלשה טפחים הרי שלשים וא' אמה וטפח והייטו דפריך לב] טפי (ליה) מתלתין וחדא הויין ומשנינן מקום גברא לא קחשיב לג] [ולא הוי] להו יותר *משלשים: מאי טעמא. העולה לד] אין עולה דרך ימין ויקיף והלא דרך ימין מלוה כדאמרן לעיל: יתעשנו. כשיקיף את המערכה בעשן המערכה וקי"ל במנחות (דף פו:) יין מעושן פסול: בא לו להקיף כו'. משנה היא במסכת תמיד גבי כהן גדול שאינו כשאר כהנים לזכות בפיים לעבודה אחת אלא עובד לה] וגומר בכל חפצו כדתנן במסכת יומא (דף יז:) כהן גדול מקריב חלק בראש אמר עולה זו אני מקריב בזמן שהוא לו] (מקריב) רולה להקטיר מי שזכו בהולכת האיברים מושיטין לו והוא עומד בראש המזבח וזורקן למערכה ולאחר שגמר בא להקיף כו' עד שמגיע לקרן הסיתין וקסלקא דעתך והיין בידו אלמא לא חיישינן לשמא נתעשנו:

הקפה

תוספות

שאם הזה ולא מילה כשירה. הא דלא פריך מהכא במסכת מעילה פרק חטאת העוף (דף ח:) לרב אדא בר אהבה *דאמר לז] דתני רב מילה דמה דמילוי חטאת העוף מעכב דמלי למימר הא מני תנא דבי ר' ישמעאל היא לח] דאמר אינו מעכב לעיל פ' איזהו מקומן (דף נב:) כדאמר תרי תנאי ואליבא דרבי ישמעאל והא דפריך התם* לרב הונא דתני הזה דמילוי אינו מעכב ולא משני דאתא כההוא תנא דאמר אינו מעכב ניחא ליה לשניי טפי לנדדין קתני: הגשות דכתיב והגישה. הוה ליה למימר כדאמרן דמהאי קרא לחודיה לא נפיק: שירי הדם דכתיב. נראה דהיינו שירים החיצונים לט] דבעי קרן *מזרחית דרומית: מ] מפני שקרובה מבית הדשן. תימה ולמה הוא הולך עד הקרן שהיה מרחיק מבית הדשן *ואין לומר משום דכל דמים טעונין קרן דהא אמר לעיל (דף ס.) גבי מודה רבי יהודה בדמים דניסקליה ונשפוך אדוכתיה ואי כל דמים טעונין קרן מאי קשיא ליה: יותר *מל"א אמות. פי' בקונטרס כשהיתה מא] במזרח היה עומד בסובב לפי שבמזרח היה כבש קטן שפנה על סובב אבל במערב לא היה לו כבש לשמאל לפנות בו לסובב וצריך לעלות לראש המזבח ולעמוד בדרומית של קרן והכי תנן במסכת סוכה (דף מח.) גבי נסכים עלה בכבש ופנה לשמאלו ולא תנן בהו ופנה לסובב ונראה דאין משם ראי' שלא היה כבש לסובב מב] במערב אם כן כשהיה נותן ארבע מתנות שבחטאת ותנן פרק איזהו מקומן (לעיל דף נג.) פנה לסובב גבי חטאת וכשהיה מגיע לקרן מערבית דרומית היה צריך לחזור על עקיבו ולכך נראה דהיה מג] שם כבש אבל קשה דלא חשיב ליה לעיל (דף סב:) גבי שני כבשים קטנים יוצאים מן הכבש: מן המאוכלות הפנימיות. אומר ר"ת דגבי גחלים של יום הכפורים* לא גרסינן מן המאוכלות מד] הפנימיות דהכא חשבינן להו דשן וביום הכפורים וכן בקטרת של כל השנה בעינן גחלים דוקא כדאמר התם א) גחלי אם יכול עוממות: צבר את הגחלים. משום דאמר ושמו שלא יפזר: דישון מזבח הפנימי והמנורה. הקשה ריב"א כיון דתרומת הדשן ודישון מזבח הפנימי והמנורה נבלעים במקומן אמאי מועלין בזה יותר מזה דבתרומת הדשן מועלין כדאמר לעיל ס"פ ב"ש (דף מו.) ובדישון מזבח ומנורה תנן במעילה* דלא נהנים ולא מועלים וי"ל דשאני תרומת הדשן דגלי קרא ושמו וכי תימא כיון דנבלעין היכי משכחת בהו מעילה שמא לא היו נבלעין מיד ור"ת אומר דתרומת הדשן לא היה נבלע מדלא חשיב להו ביומא (דף כא.) בהדי אינך דנבלעין מה]ב) דישון מזבח הפנימי והמנורה ואומר ה"ר יוסף טוב דאין זו ראיה דה"נ מו] בת"כ (סדר ויקרא פ' ט) דחשיב ב' [ג] בתי דשנים הן אחד *בדרום דמוראה ונוצה ודישון מזבח הפנימי והמנורה ולא חשיב תרומת הדשן אף על פי שהיתה שם מז] כדתנן בתמיד ג):

א) [פסחים עה:] ב) צ"ל גבי דישון צ"ק ג) [ועי' תוס' יבמות ק. ד"ה והשירים] חטאת

[א] גי' צ"ק ממזרח למערב איכא ס"ז וממקום כו' כל אמה רוחב כו' מעמדו שהיה מרוחק מן דרום ולבית הדשן כו' ועומד במזרחה של קרן כו' לצד הכבש כל אמה של רוחב הקרן כו' אמה מדרום כו' ובית הדשן כו' דפריך טפי: [ב] גי' הצ"ק שני בית הדשנים היו שם א' למזרחו של כבש ואחד למזרח של מזבח זה שבמזרחו של כבש שם היו נותנים מוראת העוף ונוצה ודישון כו' כצ"ל ועיין בילקוט פ' ויקרא רמז תמ"ו

עין משפט נר מצוה

לד א מיי' פ"ב מהל' תמידין ומוספין הל"ב:

דתני מילה דמה ומילוי חטאת כו' צ"ק

לה ב ג מיי' פ"ז מהל' מעשה הקרבנות הל"ב:

[מעילה ט.]

ע' רש"ק וגי' צ"ק מערבית דרומית

ע' רש"ק וצ"ק שנתקש בסכנת דיבור זה

מסורת הש"ס

שייך לע"א

צ"ל כו' צ"ק

יומא מג: תמיד כח:

קרא נשפך צ"ק

גי' הצ"ק מה ילפינן מן ההיכל בסמוך מערבי יסוד לו דהיינו מן הכבש בסמוך לו דהיינו יסוד דרומית ובכל כו' כצ"ל

גי' הצ"ק סמוך לקרן כו'

גי' צ"ק כ' אמה

ס"א מכ"ב שמשם מן הקרן לכבש ורוחב הכבש ט"ז ואפי' כו'

צ"ק

ס"א בצפונה

צ"ל מדרום

צ"א מל"א טפח

הגהות הב"ח

(א) רש"י ד"ה לצד וכו' על כ"ב שהרי מאמון לדרום אמרו דאיכא כ"ב ר"ל מאמון כבש שהוא כוף מזבח לדרום של כבש דהיינו מקום תרומת הדשן:

שיטה מקובצת

א] הגשות דכתיב והגישה. תימה דהוי ליה למימר מקרא דלעיל הקרב אותה [בני אהרן] לפני ה' אל פני המזבח דמינה שמעינן מקום הגשה וי"ל דניחא ליה לאתויי האי קרא משום דמרבינן מיניה כל המנחות אף מנחת חוטא מייתורא דהמנחה אבל עיקר הגשה יליף מההיא דלעיל וריב"א תירץ דמהקרב אותה לא שמעינן הגשה [ממש] אלא הו"א דהויא הזמנה לפני המזבח כמו והקריבו דגבי דם אבל שיגע ממש למזבח לא ילפינן מקרא דהקרב אותה לכך מייתי האי קרא דכתיב ביה הגשה בהדיא : ב] המזבח כדאמרן שירי הדם דכתיב ואת כל הדם ישפוך אל יסוד מזבח העולה : ג] במזרח מדקאמר כשהיא רבה מכלל דמקומה מזרח היא מ"ט אמר ר"י : ד] עי' בהשממות בסוף המסכת : ה] יותר משלשים אמה : ו] כבש עשר אמות : ז] הני ספי מתלתין וחד הוי פי' שהרי עדיין היה ארכו של כבש ממקום בית הדשן עד ראש המזבח כ"ב אמה מדרום לצפון וכן ממזרח למערב ממקום עמידת הכהן שהרי רוחב הכבש י"ו אמה וראש המזבח ממקום עמידת הכהן המולך ו' אמות שהרי היה באמצע המזבח ושתי אמות היה ליסוד ולסובב הרי כ"ב על כ"ב שיצטרך לזרוק המוראה והנוצה אל מקום הדשן באלכסונא וכל אמתא בריבוע אמתא ותרי חומשי באלכסונא וא"כ הוי טפי מל"א דאלכסון של כ' אמות עולה לשמונה וב' אמות הנשארות ד' חומשים ועוד יש ג' טפחים שהיה רחוק בית הדשן מן הכבש לצד מזרח הרי טפי מל"א והקשה בקונטרס הא ליכא רק ה' אמות ממקום מליקת עד הכבש שהרי מתקרב לצד הכבש אמה של קרן וי"ל דתנן כנגדה אמה מקום מעמדו שהרי היה עומד ברוחב דמזבח במקום רגלי הכהנים והלאה לקרן וא"כ יש כ"ב אמות מהקרן שאצל הצפון עד בית הדשן מלבד האלכסון כדפי' אך קשה למה לא היה עומד בסובב בשעת מליקה ויזרוק למטה מן הכבש ולא יעלה כל כך ותירץ בקונטרס דדוקא כשהיה במזרח היה עומד בסובב לפי שהכבש קטן היה במזרח שפונה בו לסובב אבל במערב לא היה בו כבש לשמאל לפנות בו לסובב אכן צריך לעלות לראש המזבח ולעמוד אצל הקרן בצפונו כדפי' לעיל והביא ראיה ממסכת סוכה דתנן גבי נסכים הנעשים במערב עלה לכבש ופנה לשמאלו ולא תני ופנה לסובב אלמא לא היה שום כבש במערב לפנות בו לסובב וקשה לפירושו שהרי כיון שלא היה שום כבש היכי תנן בפרק איזהו מקומן עלה בכבש ופנה לסובב ובא לו לקרן דרומית מזרחית כו' עד מערבית דרומית ושירי הדם היה שופך על יסוד דרומית מערבי ואם אין שם כבש כיצד ירד מן הסובב ליסוד דרומית מערבי ולחזור על עקבו לא אפשר כדקאמר במתני' אלא ודאי ש"מ כשבא בסוף לקרן מערבית דרומית היה יורד מן הסובב בכבש קטן לכבש גדול ומן הגדול יורד ליסוד לשפוך שירי הדם (היה שופך) על יסוד דרומי מערבי ועתה אינו צריך לחזור על עקבו לכך נראה דאה"נ ומההיא דסוכה לא קשה מידי די"ל דשאני ניסוך דלא אפשר לו לעשות בעומדו על הסובב עד ראש הקרן ששם היו הספלים היה גבוה ד' אמות הילכך היה צריך לעשות הניסוך בראש המזבח במקום הילוך רגלי הכהנים אבל ודאי היה שם כבש לשאר עבודות שהיה צריך לעשות שם מעל הסובב ומ"מ פריך שפיר טפי מל"א הויין שהוא זורק אלכסון על כ"ב אם לא היה רוצה לירד על הסובב או פעמים שהיו כל כך הרבה כהנים על הסובב שכל הסובב היה מלא ולא היו יכולים להיות פונה לסובב אלא היה הולך כדרך הילוך הכהנים לצד הקרן ואז זורקה יותר משלשים [ואחד] אבל קשה אם היה בצד מערב ב' כבשים חד ליסוד וחד לסובב ובמזרח היה אחד לסובב א"כ כשהיה פונה לשם להקיף הרי ג' כבשים ולעיל לא חשיב אלא ב' כבשים וי"ל דלא חשיב לעיל רק ב' כבשים לשתי רוחות אבל בכל רוח היה כבשים כל כך שהיו צריכין לו וא"ת למה היה מקרבה לקרן מזרחית יעשה סמוך לכבש מיד ויהיה קרובה יותר לבית הדשן וי"ל דכל דמים טעונין [יסוד] וא"ת א"כ לעיל דפריך נשקליה ונשפוך ארוכתיה לישני ליה הא בעינן קרן וי"ל דעדיפא מיניה קא משני דהא פי' לעיל [דף ס ע"א] דהכי נמי מצי לשנויי משום דבעינן יסוד. מהר"פ : ח] גברא לא קא חשיב ס"י וקאי בקרן מערבית דרומית אות י' נמחק : ט] בעשן מיתיבי בא ותיבת ורמינהו נמחק : י] דרומית נתנו לו תיבת ונותנין נמחק : יא] ע' בהשממות בסוף המסכת : יב] במזבח נגעא אלא בהזאה ומיצוי : יג] והדר תני : יד] דהזה למעלה ואח"כ : טו] קא מכשר דהא הזה דמה כל אות י' ותיבת קתני נמחק : טז] בחטאת העוף לאו : יז] דיליף מהאי קרא דלא מעכב ותיבת דסבירא ואות ו' נמחק : יח] ובלבד שיתן ההזאה הנעשית : יט] יסוד ואמרינן תיבת המזבח נמחק : כ] ההיכל בפנימיות להיות בסמוך : כא] והיינו סמוך לקרן : כב] תיבות של מחתה נמחק : כג] ע' בהשממות בסוף המסכת : כד] רחוק מראש המזבח : כה] לזורקה למוראה ונוצה כל: כו] מכ"ב שש מן הקרן לכבש ורחב הכבש ס"ז אמה ואפי' : כז] מעמדו נמצא שהוא מרוחק מבית הדשן הכ' אמות שהוא עומד והשאר נמחק : כח] לו כבש לפנות: כט] המזבח לעמוד בדרומה תיבת ועומד נמחק : ל] עלה בכבש ופנה לשמאלו ולא תנן כו' הרי משפט הקרן ולכבש ה' אמות : לא] ע' בהשממות בסוף המסכת : לב] דפריך ליה טפי מתלתין : לג] והוי להו טפח יותר משלשים : לד] העולה לג' דברים אלו אין : לה] עובד בכל חפצו : לו] תיבת מקריב נמחק : לז] דאמר רב דתני מיצה : לח] ע' בהשממות [illegible] לט] החיצונים אבל שירים הפנימים הוו במערבית דרומית [illegible] מ] [illegible] כשהיתה נעשית במזרח : מא] ע' בהשממות בסוף המסכת : מב] [illegible] מג] דהיה בו כבש [illegible]

[illegible] ובמסכת תמיד הס"ד

עין משפט
נר מצוה

לו א מיי' פ"ו מהל' מעה"ק הל"ז:
לז ב מיי' שם הל"ז:
לח ג מיי' שם הל"ז:
לט ד מיי' שם הל"ח:
מ ה מיי' פ"ו מהל' מעה"ק הל"כ:
מא ו מיי' שם הל' כא:
מב ז מיי' שם הל' כב:
נ"ל כו' נ"ק
מג ח ט מיי' שם הל"כ:
מד י מיי' פי"ג מהל' פסה"מ הל"ה:
מה כ מיי' פט"ו שם הלכה א:
מו ל מיי' פט"ז שם הלכה א:

תורה אור

א] הקפה ברגל אמר רבא דיקא נמי דקתני ב] נותנין לו יין לנסך ולא קתני אומר לו נסך ש"מ ת"ר כל העולין למזבח עולין דרך ימין ויורדין דרך שמאל עולין דרך מזרח ויורדין דרך מערב חוץ מן ג] העולה לשלשה דברים הללו שעולים דרך מערב ויורדין דרך מערב עולין דרך ימין ויורדין דרך ימין דרך שמאל הוא אמר ד] רבינא תני שמאל רבא אמר מאי ימין ימין דמזבח ומאי שמאל שמאל דגברא וניתני או אידי ואידי דמזבח או אידי ואידי דגברא קשיא: **מתני'** חטאת העוף ה] כיצד היה נעשית (עלה לכבש ופנה לסובב בא לו לקרן דרומית מזרחית) היה מולק את ראשה ממול ערפה ו] ואינו מבדיל ומזה מדמה על קיר המזבח שירי הדם היה מתמצה על היסוד ז] ואין למזבח אלא דמה וכולה לכהנים: **גמ'** ת"ר והזה מדם החטאת ח] מגוף החטאת הא כיצד ט] אוחז בראש ובגוף ומזה על קיר המזבח ולא על קיר הכבש ולא על קיר היכל ולא על קיר אולם ואיזה זה קיר התחתון י] או אינו אלא קיר העליון ודין הוא ומה בהמה שעולתה למטה חטאתה למעלה עוף שעולתו למעלה אינו דין שחטאתו למעלה ת"ל והנשאר בדם ימצה אל יסוד המזבח קיר יא] שהשירין שלו מתמצים ליסוד ואיזה זה קיר התחתון ונעביד מעילאי והדר נעביד מתתאי אמר רבא מי כתיב יב] ימצה ימצה כתיב דממילא משמע אמר רב זוטרא בר טוביה אמר רב כיצד מולקין חטאת העוף אוחז יג] גפיו בשתי אצבעות ושתי רגלים בשתי אצבעות ומותח צוארה על יד] רוחב גודלו ומולקה במתניתא תנא ציפרא מלבר אוחז גפיו בשתי אצבעות ושני רגלים בשתי אצבעות ומותח צוארו על רוחב שתי אצבעותיו ומולק וזו טו] עבודה קשה שבמקדש זו היא ותו לא והאיכא קמיצה וחפינה אלא אימא זו עבודה קשה מעבודות קשות שבמקדש: **מתני'** עולת העוף כיצד טז] נעשית עלה לכבש ופנה לסובב בא לו לקרן דרומית מזרחית היה מולק את ראשה ממול ערפה ומבדיל יז] ומיצה את דמה על קיר המזבח נטל את הראש והקיף בית מליקתו למזבח וספגו במלח וזרקו על גבי האשים בא לו לגוף והסיר את המוראה ואת הנוצה ואת בני המעיים היוצאין יח] עמם והשליכן לבית הדשן שיסע ולא הבדיל ואם הבדיל כשר יט] ספגו במלח וזרקו על גבי האשים לא הסיר המוראה ולא הנוצה כ] ואת בני מעיים היוצאין עמם ולא ספגו במלח כל ששינה בה מאחר שמיצה את דמה כשירה כא] הבדיל בחטאת ולא הבדיל בעולה פסול מיצה כב] את דם הראש ולא מיצה דם הגוף פסולה דם הגוף ולא מיצה דם הראש כשירה חטאת העוף שמלקה שלא לשמה מיצה דמה שלא לשמה כג] לשמה ושלא לשמה או שלא לשמה ולשמה פסול עולת העוף כשירה ובלבד שלא עלתה לבעלים לשם חובה אחד חטאת העוף ואחד עולת העוף שמלקן ושמיצה את דמן לאכול דבר שדרכו לאכול ולהקטיר דבר שדרכו להקטיר חוץ למקומו פסול ואין בו כרת חוץ לזמנו פיגול וחייבין עליו כרת ובלבד שיקריב המתיר כמצותו כיצד קרב המתיר כמצותו מלק בשתיקה ומיצה הדם חוץ לזמנו או שמלק חוץ לזמנו ומיצה הדם בשתיקה או שמלק ומיצה הדם חוץ לזמנו זהו שקרב המתיר כמצותו כיצד לא קרב המתיר כמצותו מלק חוץ למקומו כד] מיצה הדם חוץ לזמנו או שמלק חוץ לזמנו ומיצה הדם חוץ למקומו או שמלק ומיצה הדם חוץ למקומו

חטאת

חטאת העוף כיצד היתה נעשית. משום דדם חטאת קודם לעולה מפרש חטאת תחילה: מגופה של חטאת. מדכתיב והזה מדם החטאת ולא כתיב ולקח דמשמע בכלי:

אוחז בראש ובגוף ומזה. תימה דלא בעי הכא מאי קאמר כדקבעי פ"ק דחולין (דף כב.):

ואיזה זה קיר התחתון. דאי קיר העליון פעמים שהוא מתמלה לסובב אם עושה למעלה מן הסובב דקיר העליון הוי מן החוט עד הקרנות:

קמיצה וחפינה. בכולהו תניא עבודה קשה: והקריבו

הקפה ברגל. ואין היין בידו ולמלוה. בעלמא מפני שכל העולין לשאר דברים פונין לימין ומקיפין וזה כה] להקטיר עולה לפיכך מקיף ובא למקום שמנסכין שם ונותנין לו יין לנסך אבל שאר כהנים כו] שהזוכה בנסכים בפיים לא זכה לעבודה אחרת עולה והיין בידו ופנה לשמאל וחוזר על העקב כדמתני': עולים דרך מזרח. כשהן עולין לכבש במזרחו אצל שפתו עולין שהרי דרך ימין יפנה ולמה לו להאריך הילוס כל רחבו של כבש וכשהוא יורד כז] יורד בשפת מערבו של כבש: ה"ג חוץ מן העולה לג' דברים הללו שעולין דרך מערב ויורדין דרך מערב עולין דרך ימין ויורדין דרך ימין: שמאל הוא. מערבו של כבש כח] שמאל הוי כשהאיש פניו למזבח: מאי ימין. דקתני בסיפא ימין דמזבח שהמזבח פניו לדרום וימינו למערב: ומאי שמאל. דקתני ברישא שמאל דגברא: אידי ואידי. דרישא ודסיפא: **מתני'** ואינו מבדיל. הראש מן הגוף אלא סימן אחד לבדו מולק דכתיב בה ומלק את ראשו ממול ערפו ולא יבדיל (ויקרא ה) ובהכל שוחטין (חולין דף כא:) ילפינן דבסימן אחד הוא: ומזה. אוחז בעוף עצמו ומזה: היה מתמלה. שמקיף כט] ומקרב בית מליקתו למזבח ודוחקו בקיר והדם מתמלה ויורד ליסוד שהרי למטה מן החוט היא נעשית וכניסת הסובב למעלה הימנו: **גמ'** מגוף של חטאת. שלא יזה לא בכלי ולא באצבע אלא אוחז בעוף עצמו ומזה: קיר התחתון. שלמטה מן החוט: בהמה שעולתה למטה. כדאמרן בפ"ק (לעיל דף י:) דכתיב בחטאת בהמה המחטא אותה אותה דמה למעלה ואין אחרת דמה למעלה: חטאתה למעלה. דקרנות כתיבי בה: עוף שעולתו למעלה. כדיליף לקמן בפירקין (דף סה.): שהשיריים שלו. כשמזה הדם שותת ומתמלה ליסוד: ואיזה זה קיר התחתון. ל] פעמים שהוא מתמלה לסובב כשהוא עושהו למעלה מן הסובב דמן החוט עד הקרנות קיר העליון הוא אבל קיר התחתון כולו למטה מן הסובב שהחוט למטה מן הסובב אמה: ונעביד מעילאי. הזאתה יעשה למעלה והדין נותן כדאמרן והדר נעביד מילוי מתתאי כדכתיב: מי כתיב לא] ימלה ימלה כתיב. אי הוה כתיב ימלה הוה משמע שמזהיר את הכהן שיחזור וימלה אחר הזאה השתא דכתיב ימלה משמע נמי לענין הזאה לב] דממילא יהיה דם מלוי אצל היסוד: אוחז שני גפיה בשתי אצבעות. גוף העוף על כפו מבפנים ומכניס שני רגליה בין אצבע קטנה לג] זרת לקמילה ושני גפיה בין אמה לאצבע: ומותח צוארה. גרונה התחתון נ..תח על רוחב החיצון של גודל שמכניס הצואר בין אצבע לגודל כמלא הגרון לצד גודלו ומותחו על גודלו והעורף מלמעלה ומולק: ציפרא מלבר. כמו שאנו לד] עושים על גב היד אלא שהופך פניו של עוף לה] על גב ידו שיהא העורף למעלה: מותח צוארו. הגרון על רוחב הפנימי של שתי אצבעותיו אצבע ואמה: גבי קמילה נמי תניא זו היא עבודה קשה. שצריך למחוק בגודלו מלמעלה ובאצבעו קטנה למטה שלא יהא הקומץ מבורץ וכן בחפינת יום הכפורים נמי תניא זו היא עבודה קשה ותרווייהו בסדר יומא בפרק הוציאו לו (דף מז: ודף מט:): עבודה קשה מעבודות קשות. כלומר אחת מעבודות קשות שבמקדש: **מתני'** עלה בכבש. לפי שנעשית למעלה כדילפינן בגמרא: בא לו לקרן דרומית מזרחית. כדאמרן שקרובה לבית הדשן: ומבדיל. בשני סימנין כדיליף בהכל שוחטין (חולין דף כא:): ערפה. גובה הראש מול ערפה למטה לצד האגפים מול הרואה את העורף: והקיף את בית מליקתו למזבח. סומכו ודוחקו בקיר כדי שיתמלה הדם: ספגו במלח. מקנחו במלח הגמלא בראש המזבח כדכתיב וכל קרבן מנחתך במלח תמלח לו] ואומר בהקומץ רבה (מנחות דף כא:) בג' מקומות המלח נתונה בלישכת המלח ועל גבי הכבש ובראש המזבח: מוראה. זפק: טלה. שטפל העור שכנגד הזפק בטלתה עם הזפק: שיסע. הגוף בין אגפיה: הבדיל בחטאת. במליקתה לז] שמולק שני סימנין או לא הבדיל בעולה שמלקה בסימן אחד: פסול. דכל שינוי שהוא לפני עבודות הדם פסולות ובגמרא מפרש טעמא: מיצה דם כו'. מפרש טעמא בגמרא: לאכול דבר שדרכו לאכול. חטאת העוף: שדרכו להקטיר. עולת העוף: שלא לח] לשמן. אין מוציא עולה מידי פיגול מפני שהיא כשירה בשלא לשמה:

גמ'

ס"א דאי קיר העליון פעמים כו'
*מנחות יח.[יומא מז: מט:]
[לעיל נד. מנחות לב:]
[עי' תוס' לקמן סה: ד"ה כבדיל]
[מגילה ט.]
[עי' תוס' לקמן כה: ד"ה כיצד]
שוחטים נ"ק

הזפק הס"ד ואח"כ ד"ה חטאת העוף שמלקה שלא לשמה אבל עולת העוף שמלקה שלא לשמה אין מוציא עולה מידי פיגול מפני שהיא כשרה כו' שלא לשמה הס"ד וכו"ע ואח"כ ד"ה לאכול דבר שדרכו לאכול חטאת עוף הס"ד ואח"כ ד"ה שדרכו להקטיר עולת העוף הס"ד ל"ק

שיטה מקובצת

א] הקפה ברגל. פ"ה בלא יין וקשה לרש"י א"כ למה היה מקיף יפנה מיד לצד מערב לספלים לנסך ויחזור על העקב כמו שאר כהנים עושין שזוכין בניסוך על ידי פיים וי"ל דלא דמי דאחד משאר כהנים שהיה זוכה בנסכים בפיים לא היה מגיע בחלקו עבודה אחרת אבל כהן הגדול שהיה כמו כן מקטיר היה מקיף בשם שלא כדרכו [לחעלות] אברים שצריך להקטיר ולא נהירא דהתם מוכח דהקף זה אחר כל ההקטרה לכך נראה לרבינו שמשון דלכך היה מקיף להראות שיש לו רשות יותר מלאחרים שהוא בן בית וכן איתא בפרק טרף בקלפי ששאר הכהנים היו עולים ויורדים בשפה של הכבש במזרח או במערב והכהן הגדול באמצע מהאי טעמא להראות שהיה יותר בן בית משאר הכהנים: ב] נתנו לו יין: ג] מן העולים לשלשה: ד] אמר רבא תני שמאל רבינא אמר: ס] כיצד היתה נעשית היה מולק כו' והשאר נמחק: ז] ואינו מבדיל דכיון דהכשר העוף בסימן אחד כל מה שימלוק מכאן ואילך קרוי הבדלה וא"ת א"כ לא היה לו למלוק רק רוב סימן אחד כיון דהכשרו דעוף ברוב סימן אחד וי"ל דאין זה אלא דיעבד אבל לכתחילה בעינן סימן שלם וא"ת כמו כן נמי מוכח בחולין דצריך לשחוט ב' סימנין לכתחילה וי"ל דטעמא לא הוי משום דאין זה אלא דיעבד אלא דמסברא יש לנו לומר כיון שהתחיל למלוק הסימן שימלקנו כולו: ז] היסוד אין למזבח אות ו' נמחק: ח] החטאת מגופו של חטאת: ט] עי' בהשמטות בסוף המסכת: י] התחתון אתה אומר קיר התחתון או: יא] שהשירים שלו מתמצין ליסוד. וא"ת ויעשה למעלה מן החוט באמה שלמטה מן הסובב ומשם ימצה ליסוד ולעולם בקיר העליון הוא וי"ל דא"כ הוי ב' מקומות במזבח דלמטה מן החוט הוי מקום דמים דעולת בהמה ולמעלה מן הסובב עולת העוף ולחטאת בהמה ולמטה מן הסובב באמה שבין הסובב לחוט הסיקרא לחטאת העוף וזה לא יתכן דהואיל חוט הסיקרא מפסיק בין דמים עליונים לתחתונים א"כ משמע דאין בו כי אם שני מקומות לדמים. מהר"פ: יב] כתיב ימצה יִמָּצֵה כתיב ס"א מי כתיב ימציא ימצה כתיב ורש"י לא גרס כן: יג] אוחז שני גפיה בשתי: יד] רוחב גודלו. והעוף אחר ידו ומיעקם צואר העוף על גודלו ובאותו גודל עצמו מולק כי כל העבודות נעשות בימין ולכך היתה עבודה קשה ובמתני' היתה העוף מלבר על גב היד וצואר העוף בין אצבע לגודל ומולק בגודל. תו"א: טו] ומולק וזו היא עבודה: טז] כיצד היתה נעשית: יז] ומצה: יח] היוצאין עמה והשליכן: יט] כשר ספגו במלח: כ] הנוצה ולא את בני המעיים היוצאים עמם ולא ספגן במלח: כא] הבדיל בחטאת ולא הבדיל בעולה פסול פ"ה בפ"ק דחולין דאי דבעינן הבדלה בעולת העוף יליף מולק והקטיר כדמשמע בגמרא אבל בחטאת העוף כתיב לא יבדיל וה"פ לא יבדיל יותר מכשיעור שחיטה והיינו סימן אחד בעוף וא"ת א"כ אם יבדיל [יותר] מרוב סימן אחד תיפסל דהוי יותר משיעור שחיטה וי"ל דמ"מ לכתחילה בעינן (רוב) סימן שלם וא"ת והא מוכח בחולין דלכתחילה בעינן שני סימנים בשחיטת העוף בפרק השוחט דמוקי דיעבד אאחד בעוף משמע הא לכתחילה בעינן שנים אף בעוף לכך נראה דקרא דלא יבדיל קאי אדיעבד דשחיטה ולהכי סגי בחד ומ"מ בעינן סימן שלם ולא סגי ברוב דמסתמא לא הצריך הכתוב לומר דלא יבדיל להפסיק בתוך הסימן אלא לאחר שיסיים סימן שלם דמסברא לא איירי קרא בחצאין: כב] מיצה דם הראש ולא מיצה דם הגוף פסול דם: כג] או לשמה ושלא: כד] למקומו ומיצה הדם:כה] וזה אף הוא להקטיר: כו] כהנים הזוכים בנסכים בפיים ולא זכו לעבודה אחרת עולה בידו ופונה לשמאל והחוזר: כז] יורד היה מוני יורד: כח] כבש הוי שמאל כשהאיש: כט] שמקיף ומקרב בית: ל] התחתון דאי קיר העליון פעמים: לא] כתיב יִמָּצֵה יַמְצֶה כתיב: לב] הזאה שיהא במקום דממילא יהיה הדם מתמצה על היסוד הס"ד: לג] תיבת זרת נמחק: לד] שאנו שוחטין שהעוף על ותיבת עושין נמחק: לה] לצד גב תיבת על נמחק: לו] תמלח וגו' ואמרינן בהקומץ: לז] במליקתה שמלק: לח] שלא לשמה אין ומיצה

Said R. Johanan: [64b] He made the circuit on foot.[8] Raba observed: That indeed may be inferred, for it teaches, 'and he was handed the wine to pour it out', but it does not teach, 'He was told to pour it out'.[9] This proves it.

Our Rabbis taught: All who went up the altar ascended by the right and descended by the left; they ascended by the east and descended by the west,[10] except those who went up for these three things:[11] they ascended by the west and descended by the west, ascended by the right and descended by the right. [You say] 'by the right'; it is by the left?[12]—Said Rabina: Read 'left'.
a Raba said: 'Right'[1] means the right of the *altar*, while 'left'[2] means the left of the *person*.[3] Then let him teach either both with reference to the altar or both with reference to the person? That is indeed a difficulty.

MISHNAH. HOW WAS THE SIN-OFFERING OF A BIRD SACRIFICED?[4] HE PINCHED OFF ITS HEAD CLOSE BY ITS NECK, BUT DID NOT SEVER IT, AND HE SPRINKLED ITS BLOOD ON THE WALL OF THE ALTAR; THE RESIDUE OF THE BLOOD WAS DRAINED OUT ON THE BASE. ONLY THE BLOOD BELONGED TO THE ALTAR, WHILE THE WHOLE OF IT BELONGED TO THE PRIESTS.

GEMARA. Our Rabbis taught: *And he shall sprinkle of the blood of the sin-offering:*[5] [that means] with the body of the sin-offering.[6] How is it done? He [the priest] grasps the head and the body [of the bird] and sprinkles [its blood] on the wall of the altar, but not on the wall of the ascent, nor on the wall of the *hekal*, nor on the wall of the *ulam;* and which [wall] is meant? The lower wall.[7] Yet perhaps it is not so, but rather on the upper wall, and that is indeed logical: if [the blood of] an animal sin-offering is [sprinkled] above, though [that of] an animal burnt-offering is [sprinkled] below: surely [the blood of] a bird sin-offering is [sprinkled] above, seeing that [that of] a bird burnt-offering is [sprinkled] above? Therefore it states, *And the rest of the blood shall be drained out at the base of the altar,*[8] [which intimates that it must be sprinkled on] a wall where the residue will drain down to the base, and which is that? The lower wall.[9] Yet let us [first] perform it above, and then below?[10]—Said Raba: Is then *yamzeh* [he shall drain] written? Surely *yimmazeh* [shall be drained] is written, which implies of its
b own accord.[1]

R. Zutra b. Tobiah said in Rab's name: How is the bird sin-offering pinched off? He grasps its two wings in two fingers, and its two legs in two fingers, stretches its neck over the width of his thumb and pinches it off. In a Baraitha it was taught: The bird is without:[2] he holds its wings in two fingers and its two legs with two fingers, stretches its neck over the width of two fingers, and pinches it off; and this was a difficult rite in the Temple. This and no other? Surely there were *kemizah* and *hafinah?*[3]—Say rather, this was one of the difficult rites in the Temple.

MISHNAH. HOW WAS THE BURNT-OFFERING OF A BIRD SACRIFICED?—HE [THE PRIEST] ASCENDED THE ASCENT AND TURNED TO THE SURROUNDING BALCONY,[4] WHENCE HE MADE HIS WAY TO THE SOUTH-EAST HORN. HE NIPPED ITS HEAD CLOSE BY THE NECK, AND SEVERED IT,[5] AND DRAINED OUT ITS BLOOD ON TO THE WALL OF THE ALTAR. HE TOOK THE HEAD, TURNED THE PART WHERE IT WAS NIPPED TO THE ALTAR,[6] DRIED IT WITH SALT,[7] AND THREW IT ON TO THE [ALTAR-]FIRE.[8] THEN HE CAME TO THE BODY, REMOVED THE CROP, THE FEATHERS,[9] AND THE ENTRAILS THAT CAME FORTH WITH IT,[10] AND THREW THEM ON TO THE ASH DEPOSITORY. HE RENT [THE BODY], BUT DID NOT SEVER IT, YET IF HE DID SEVER IT, IT IS FIT. THEN HE DRIED IT [THE BODY] WITH SALT, AND THREW IT ON TO THE [ALTAR-]FIRE. IF HE DID NOT REMOVE THE CROP OR THE FEATHERS OR THE ENTRAILS WHICH CAME FORTH WITH IT, AND DID NOT DRY IT WITH SALT, OR MADE ANY OTHER DEVIATION THEREIN AFTER HE HAD DRAINED THE BLOOD OUT, IT IS FIT. IF HE SEVERED
c THE SIN-OFFERING[1] OR DID NOT SEVER THE BURNT-OFFERING, IT IS UNFIT. IF HE DRAINED OUT THE BLOOD OF THE HEAD, BUT NOT THE BLOOD OF THE BODY, IT IS UNFIT; THE BLOOD OF THE BODY, BUT NOT THE BLOOD OF THE HEAD, IT IS FIT. IF HE NIPPED A SIN-OFFERING OF A BIRD FOR THE SAKE OF SOMETHING ELSE;[2] IF HE DRAINED OUT ITS BLOOD FOR THE SAKE OF SOMETHING ELSE, OR FOR ITS OWN SAKE AND FOR THE SAKE OF SOMETHING ELSE,[3] OR FOR THE SAKE OF SOMETHING ELSE AND FOR ITS OWN SAKE, IT IS UNFIT. A BURNT-OFFERING OF A BIRD IS FIT [IN SUCH CIRCUMSTANCES], SAVE THAT IT DOES NOT FREE ITS OWNER OF HIS OBLIGATION.[4]

IF A SIN-OFFERING OF A BIRD OR A BURNT-OFFERING OF A BIRD WAS NIPPED OR IF ITS BLOOD WAS DRAINED OUT [WITH THE INTENTION] TO EAT WHAT WAS NORMALLY EATEN OR TO BURN WHAT WAS NORMALLY BURNT WITHOUT BOUNDS, IT IS INVALID, BUT DOES NOT INVOLVE KARETH; AFTER TIME, IT IS PIGGUL AND INVOLVES KARETH, PROVIDED THAT THE MATTIR WAS OFFERED IN ACCORDANCE WITH THE REGULATIONS. HOW DOES HE OFFER THE MATTIR ACCORDING TO REGULATIONS? IF HE NIPPED IT IN SILENCE AND DRAINED THE BLOOD [WITH AN INTENTION OF] AFTER TIME; OR IF HE NIPPED IT [WITH AN INTENTION OF] AFTER TIME AND DRAINED THE BLOOD IN SILENCE; OR IF HE NIPPED IT AND DRAINED THE BLOOD [WITH AN INTENTION OF] AFTER TIME: IN THESE CASES HE OFFERED THE MATTIR ACCORDING TO REGULATION. HOW DOES HE NOT OFFER THE MATTIR ACCORDING TO REGULATION? IF HE NIPPED IT [WITH AN INTENTION OF] WITHOUT BOUNDS AND DRAINED THE BLOOD [WITH AN INTENTION OF] WITHOUT BOUNDS, OR IF HE NIPPED IT [WITH AN INTENTION OF] AFTER TIME AND DRAINED THE BLOOD [WITH AN INTENTION OF] WITHOUT BOUNDS; OR IF HE NIPPED IT AND DRAINED THE BLOOD [WITH AN INTENTION OF] WITHOUT BOUNDS;

(8) He was not given the wine until he completed the circuit, the circuit being made merely to add dignity to the ceremony and to shew that he enjoyed privileges which the other priests lacked (Rashi and Sh. M.). (9) Which would be the case if he already had the wine when he started. (10) They ascended the stairway at its east side, since they would have to turn right, and had they ascended it by the west, they would have to cross the width of the ascent before they could do this. Similarly they descended by the west side of the stairway. (11) Enumerated in the Mishnah. (12) The west of the ascent was on the *left* side of a man facing the altar.

a (1) In the second clause. (2) In the first clause. (3) Standing in front of the altar. (4) Lit., 'made'. V. *supra* 63a n. c 2. (5) Lev. V, 9.—It refers to a bird sin-offering. (6) Not from a vessel. (7) Below the red line. (8) Ibid. (9) For if he sprinkled it on the upper wall, it might drain on to the terrace, not on to the base. (10) I.e., sprinkle the blood on the upper wall, and then drain out the rest on the lower.

b (1) The blood must be so sprinkled that it will then naturally drain down on to the base. (2) It is grasped face-downward to the palm of the hand, so that its nape is uppermost. (3) The taking of the fistful of meal-offerings and the taking of the two hands full of incense on the Day of Atonement. These rites were done in a particular fashion, and both are described as difficult in Yoma 47b and 49b. (4) V. *supra* 53a notes. (5) By nipping both the windpipe and the gullet (Hul. 21b). (6) He pressed it against the wall, to drain out the blood. (7) By rubbing salt on the dripping head until it became dry. (8) Of the burnt-offerings, which were being burnt on the altar. (9) I.e., the skin opposite the crop, together with the feathers on it. (10) *Sc.* with the crop, as he removed this.

c (1) By nipping both organs of the throat. (2) E.g., as a burnt-offering. (3) He nipped it for its own sake and drained it for the sake of something else. (4) V. *supra* 2a.

[65a] IF HE NIPPED A SIN-OFFERING OF A BIRD UNDER A DIFFERENT DESIGNATION AND DRAINED THE BLOOD [WITH AN INTENTION OF] AFTER TIME; OR IF HE NIPPED IT [WITH AN INTENTION OF] AFTER TIME AND DRAINED THE BLOOD UNDER A DIFFERENT DESIGNATION; OR IF HE NIPPED IT AND DRAINED THE BLOOD UNDER A DIFFERENT DESIGNATION: IN THESE CASES HE DID NOT OFFER THE MATTIR ACCORDING TO REGULATION. [IF HE INTENDED] TO EAT AS MUCH AS AN OLIVE WITHOUT BOUNDS [AND] AS MUCH AS AN OLIVE ON THE MORROW, [OR] AS MUCH AS AN OLIVE ON THE MORROW [AND] AS MUCH AS AN OLIVE WITHOUT BOUNDS; HALF AS MUCH AS AN OLIVE WITHOUT BOUNDS [AND] HALF AS MUCH AS AN OLIVE ON THE MORROW; HALF AS MUCH AS AN OLIVE ON THE MORROW [AND] HALF AS MUCH AS AN OLIVE WITHOUT BOUNDS, [THE SACRIFICE] IS UNFIT, AND DOES NOT INVOLVE KARETH. SAID R. JUDAH: THIS IS THE GENERAL RULE: WHERE THE [WRONGFUL] INTENTION OF TIME PRECEDES THAT OF PLACE, [THE SACRIFICE] IS PIGGUL, AND INVOLVES KARETH; BUT IF THE [WRONGFUL] INTENTION OF PLACE PRECEDES THAT OF TIME, IT IS UNFIT AND DOES NOT INVOLVE KARETH. BUT THE SAGES MAINTAIN: IN BOTH CASES [THE SACRIFICE IS] UNFIT AND DOES NOT INVOLVE KARETH. [IF ONE INTENDS] TO EAT HALF AS MUCH AS AN OLIVE [WITHOUT BOUNDS OR AFTER TIME] [AND] TO BURN HALF AS MUCH AS AN OLIVE [SIMILARLY],
a IT IS FIT, FOR EATING AND BURNING DO NOT COMBINE.[1]

GEMARA. Our Rabbis taught: *And* [*the priest*] *shall bring it* [*unto the altar*]:[2] Why is this stated? Because it is said, *Then he shall bring his offering of turtle-doves, or of young pigeons,*[3] you might think that when he vows a bird [as a burnt-offering], he must give not less than two birds; therefore it states, '*And* [*the priest*] *shall bring it*': he can bring even one bird to the altar. Why is '*the priest*'
b stated? To prescribe a priest for it.[1] For you might argue, is not [the reverse] logical? If a priest was not prescribed for a sheep,[2] though north was prescribed for it;[3] is it not logical that a priest is not prescribed for a bird, seeing that [Scripture] did not prescribe north for it? Therefore '*the priest*' is stated, in order to prescribe a priest for it. You might think that he must nip it with a knife, and that is indeed logical: If [Scripture] prescribed a utensil[4] for *shechitah*, though it did not prescribe a priest for it; is it not logical that it prescribed a utensil for nipping, seeing that it prescribed a priest for it? Therefore it states, [*And*] *the priest . . . shall pinch off* [*its head*].[5] Said R. Akiba: Would you then think that a *zar* might approach the altar?[6] Why then is '*the priest*' stated? To teach that the pinching must be done by the very priest himself.[7] You might think that he can pinch it off either above [the red line] or below [it]; therefore it states, '*and pinch off* [*its head*], *and make it smoke* [*on the altar*]:' as *haktarah* [making it smoke] is [done] on the top of the altar, so is pinching [done] on the top of the altar.[8] '*And shall pinch off*': Close by the nape [of the neck]. You say, close by the nape; yet perhaps it is not so, but rather by the throat?[9] It follows by logic: '*and shall pinch off*' is stated here, and '*and shall pinch off*' is stated elsewhere:[10] as there it is close by its neck, so here it is close by its neck. If so, just as there he pinches but does not sever it, so here too he pinches but does not sever it? Therefore it states, '*and shall pinch off* [*its head*], *and make it smoke*': as [in] *haktarah*, the head is by itself and the body is by itself, so [after] pinching, the head is by itself and the body is by itself. And how do we know that the *haktarah* of the head is separate and that of the body is separate? Because it is said, '*And make it smoke*': thus the burning of the body is ordered. How then do I interpret,
c [and the priest] *shall make it smoke upon the altar?*[1] Scripture [here] treats of the burning of the head.[2]

And the blood thereof shall be drained out on the side of the altar,[3] but not on the wall of the ascent, nor on the wall of the *hekal*. And which is it? The upper wall. Yet perhaps it is not so, but rather the lower wall; and that is indeed logical: if [the blood of] an animal burnt-offering is [sprinkled] below, though [that of] an animal sin-offering is [sprinkled] above; surely [the blood of] a burnt-offering of a bird is [sprinkled] below, seeing that [that of] a sin-offering of a bird is [sprinkled] below? Therefore it states, '*and shall pinch off . . . and shall burn . . . and the blood thereof shall be drained out*': now, can you really think that after he has burnt it he returns and drains it?[4] Rather it is to tell you: as *haktarah* is [done] on the top of the altar, so is the draining out on the top of the altar. How did he do this? He ascended the ascent and turned to the terrace, whence he proceeded to the south-east horn. Then he pinched off its head close by the neck, severed it, and drained [some] of its blood on the wall of the altar. If he did it below his feet[5] even a cubit, it is fit.[6] R. Nehemiah and R. Eliezer b. Jacob maintained: It must essentially be done nought elsewhere but on the top of the altar. Wherein do they differ?—Abaye and Raba both said: They differ in respect of building a pyre on the terrace.[7]

THEN HE TOOK THE BODY etc. Our Rabbis taught: *And he shall*
d *take away its crop with the feathers thereof:*[1] that is the crop.[2] You might think that he cuts through with a knife and takes it;[3] therefore it states, '*with the feathers thereof*': [hence] he takes the plumage together with it. Abba Jose b. Ḥanan said: He takes it [the crop] together with the craw.[4] The school of R. Ishmael taught: '*With the feathers thereof*' [means] with its [very] own feathers,[5] [hence] he cuts it [round] with a knife like a skylight.[6]

a (1) V. *supra* 29b for the whole passage. (2) Lev. I, 15. This refers to a bird burnt-offering, and is apparently superfluous, since the preceding verse states, *Then he shall bring his offering* etc. Hence Scripture should continue: 'And the priest shall pinch off its head by the altar.' (3) Ibid. 14.

b (1) Only a priest, and not a *zar*, must nip off its head. (2) A sheep can be slaughtered by a *zar*, and the slaughtering of a sheep corresponds to the nipping of a bird. (3) It must be slaughtered at the north side of the altar. (4) Viz., a knife. (5) The priest himself, without the assistance of a utensil, as R. Akiba explains. (6) For the bird-offering one had actually to ascend the slope of the altar and walk round the terrace (*supra* 64b); that would obviously not be permitted to a *zar*. An animal-offering, however, which could be slaughtered by a *zar*, was killed on the ground, and even at some distance from the altar. (7) Not with a knife. (8) The 'top' here means the upper half, above the red line. (9) The front part of the neck. (10) Lev. V, 8: *and shall pinch off its head close by its neck, but shall not divide it asunder.*

c (1) Lev. I, 17. This apparently a repetition of v. 15. (2) Hence each was separate. (3) Ibid. 15. (4) That is obviously impossible! (5) Stooping down. (6) Because the red line, which demarcated the upper part of the altar from the lower, was a cubit below the terrace. (7) The first Tanna holds that this can be done, therefore the blood can be drained out even below the terrace. But R. Nehemiah and R. Eliezer b. Jacob hold that the *haktarah* must be done on the top of the altar itself; therefore the draining too must be done near there.

d (1) Lev. I, 16. (2) The Talmud translates the less familiar *mur'ah* by the more familiar *zefek*. (3) *Sc.* the crop alone, without the skin and the feathers. (4) The thick muscular stomach of birds. (5) Not more than the feathers opposite the crop. (6) He cuts the skin exactly opposite the crop, and then removes the crop, skin and feathers.

חטאת העוף שמלקו שלא לשמה ומיצה א] הדם חוץ לזמנו או שמלק חוץ לזמנו ומיצה דמו שלא לשמה או שמלק ומיצה הדם שלא לשמה זהו שלא קרב המתיר כמצותו *לאכול *כזית בחוץ כזית למחר כזית למחר כזית בחוץ כחצי זית בחוץ כחצי זית למחר כחצי זית למחר כחצי זית בחוץ פסול ואין בו כרת א"ר יהודה זה הכלל ב אם מחשבת הזמן קדמה למחשבת המקום פיגול וחייבין עליו כרת ואם מחשבת המקום קדמה למחשבת הזמן פסול ואין בו כרת ב] [*וחכ"א זה וזה פסול ואין בו כרת] *ג לאכול כחצי זית ולהקטיר כחצי זית כשר שאין אכילה והקטרה מצטרפין: **גמ'** *ת"ר °והקריבו מה ת"ל לפי שנאמר °והקריב מן התורים או מן בני היונה יכול המתנדב עוף לא יפחות משני פרידין ת"ל והקריבו ד אפילו פרידה אחת יביא אל המזבח מה ת"ל °הכהן לקבוע לו כהן שיכול והלא דין הוא ומה בן צאן שקבע לו צפון לא קבע לו כהן עוף שלא קבע לו צפון אינו דין שלא יקבע לו כהן ת"ל ג] אל הכהן לקבוע לו כהן יכול ימלקנו בסכין ודין הוא ומה אם שחיטה שלא קבע לה כהן קבע לה כלי מליקה שקבע לה כהן אינו דין שיקבע לה כלי ת"ל ד] *°כהן ומלק אמר רבי עקיבא וכי תעלה על דעתך שזר קרב לגבי מזבח אלא מה ת"ל כהן ה שתהא מליקה בעצמו של כהן יכול ימלקנה בין מלמעלה בין מלמטה ת"ל *ומלק והקטיר ו מה הקטרה בראש המזבח אף מליקה בראש המזבח ומלק ה] ז ממול עורף אתה אומר ממול עורף או אינו אלא מן הצואר ו] ודין הוא נאמר כאן ומלק ונאמר להלן °ומלק מה להלן ממול עורף אף כאן ממול עורף אי מה להלן מולק ואינו מבדיל אף כאן מולק ואינו מבדיל ת"ל *ומלק והקטיר ז] מה הקטרה הראש לעצמו והגוף לעצמו ח אף מליקה הראש לעצמו והגוף לעצמו ומנין ט שהקטרת הראש בעצמו והגוף בעצמו שנאמר °והקטיר אותו הרי הקטרת הגוף אמורה הא מה אני מקיים °והקטיר המזבחה בהקטרת הראש הכתוב מדבר °ונמצה דמו כולו ח] אל קיר המזבח ולא על קיר הכבש ולא על קיר ההיכל ט] ואיזה זה י זה קיר העליון או אינו אלא קיר התחתון ודין הוא מה בהמה שחטאתה למעלה עולתה למטה עוף שחטאתו למטה אינו דין י] שעולתו למטה ת"ל ומלק והקטיר ונמצה דמו וכי תעלה על דעתך יא] לאחר שהקטיר חוזר וממצה אלא לומר לך מה הקטרה בראש המזבח אף מיצוי בראש המזבח הא כיצד כ היה עולה בכבש ופונה לסובב ובא לו לקרן דרומית מזרחית היה מולק את ראשה ממול ערפה ומבדיל יב] וממצה דמה על קיר המזבח ל אם עשאה למטה מרגליו אפילו אמה יג] כשירה רבי נחמיה ורבי אליעזר בן יעקב אומרים יד] כל עצמה אין נעשית אלא בראש המזבח מאי בינייהו אביי ורבא דאמרי תרווייהו עושה מערכה ע"ג סובב איכא בינייהו: בא לו לגוף כו': ת"ר °והסיר את מוראתו טו] בנוצתה זו זפק יכול יקדיר בסכין ויטלנו ת"ל בנוצתה טז] נוטל את הנוצה עמה אבא יוסי בן חנן אומר נוטלה ונוטל יז] קורקבנה עמה דבי רבי ישמעאל תנא בנוצתה בנוצה שלה קודרה בסכין כמין ארובה:

שיסע

רש"י

גמ' והקריבו מה תלמוד לומר. בעולת העוף כתיב והקריבו הכהן אל המזבח מה ת"ל הא כתיב והקריב מן התורים וגו' וליכתוב בתריה ומלק הכהן את ראשו על המזבח: פרידין. גוזלות: לקבוע לו כהן. שלא ימלקנו זר: לא קבע לו כהן. דשחיטה בזר כשירה: קבע לה כלי. דנפקא לן מויקח את המאכלת לקמן באידך פירקין (דף לז:): ת"ל כהן ומלק אמר רבי עקיבא כו'. כולה ר' עקיבא קאמר לה: בעצמו של כהן. בצפורנו ולא בסכין: בין יח] למעלה. מן החוט: מן הצואר. מן הגרון: ונאמר להלן. בחטאת [העוף]: והקטיר אותו. *ושסע בכנפיו ולא יבדיל *והקטיר אותו יט] אני יודע מה שנאמרה תחילה ומלק את ראשו והקטיר בהקטרת הראש: דמו כולו. מדלא כתיב ונמצה *מדמו: מאחר שהקטיר הוא ממצה. וא"ת במילוי הגוף לא מקיימא דמו כולו: ה"ג ת"ל ומלק והקטיר ונמצה דמו וכי תעלה על דעתך משהקטיר ממצה אלא לומר לך מה הקטרה בראש המזבח אף המילוי בראש המזבח: ובא לקרן דרומית מזרחית *גרסינן: למטה מרגליו. שהחוט למטה מן הסובב אמה: אלא בראש המזבח. דבעינן והקטיר ונמצה דמו שיהא מילוי בקיר הסמוך למקום הקטרה: מאי בינייהו. כלומר במאי קמיפלגי הא ע"כ לת"ק גופיה אית ליה והקטיר ונמצה דמו דאי לאו ס"ל קיר העליון מנא *ליה: עושה מערכה כו'. לת"ק הרוצה לעשות מערכה על גבי סובב ולהקטיר כ] עושה הילכך מילוי שתחת הסובב סמוך למקום הקטרה כא]: יכול יקדיר את העור בסכין ויטלנו. זפק לבדו בלא עור ובלא נוצה כמו כב] שצולין עוף עושין: ונוטל את קורקבנה. ונוצתה לשון פרש ודבר מאוס הוא כמו (איכה ד) כי נצו גם נעו: בנוצתה שלה. כג] ולא יותר ממה שכנגד הזפק הא

תוספות

והקריבו מה תלמוד לומר. וא"ת דבפ"ק דחולין (דף כא:) דריש כז] לדרשא אחריכא הא איצטריך לכדדרשינן הכא וי"ל דהכא דריש מדסמכיה לתורים ובני יונה ש"מ פרידה אחת והתם דריש *מדסמכיה כח] לוהקטיר ואין לומר דדרשינן תרתי משום וי"ו דוהקריבו דהא בחולין הוא רבי ישמעאל דלא דריש וי"ו פי' אלמנה (יבמות דף סח:)*:

עוף שלא קבע לו לפון אינו דין שלא קבע לו כהן. וא"ת קמילה תוכיח דלא קבע לה לפון וקבע לה כהן כו] ויש לומר מה למנחה שטעונה הגשה ותנופה *וקידוש קומץ כז] וכלי שרת וא"ת כילף מדאיתקש חטאת למנחה כדאמרינן לעיל ונראה דמסתבר ליה דלא תהוי מליקה עבודה יותר משחיטה: **בן** עוף שקבע לו כהן אינו דין שיקבע לו כלי. וא"ת קמילה תוכיח שקבע לה כהן ולא קבע לה כלי כח] וי"ל מה למנחה שכן אינה מיני דמים וא"ת מה לבן צאן שכן מין זבח אבל עוף לא חשיב ליה מין זבח בפ"ק (לעיל דף ח:) וי"ל דהיינו משום דקים לן שהוא ביד אבל כט] אי הוה בכלי הוה חשיב מין זבח וא"ת מה לבן צאן שכן טעון לפון על כן נראה דמעיקרא סמיך אהיקשא דזאת התורה דילפינן מינה מה עולה טעונה כלי דעופות נמי כתיבי בההוא ענייגא מדפריך פ"ק דחולין (דף כב.) ביום מביום צוותו נפקא ובמגילה פרק הקורא למפרע (דף כ:) גבי כל היום כשר למליקה דרשינן בגמרא מביום צוותו:

תלמוד לומר הכהן ומלק ל] בעצמו של כהן. וא"ת ונילף מדאיתקש לעיל חטאת העוף למנחה וי"ל חטאת איתקש עולת העוף לא איתקש ועוד כיון דאיכא לאוקומי *היקש לא מפקא מק"ו דהכא ועוד דאדרבה נקיט בהיקשא דזאת התורה לעולה דבעיא כלי:

וכי תעלה על דעתך שזר קרב למזבח. ואפילו מאן לא] דלית ליה הך סברא גבי הולכת אליתא (יומא דף מה.) משום דהא אפשר דקאי אארעא ועביד במשחא:

אף מליקה בראש מזבח. *חטאת ועולה ילפי מהדדי גבי מול עורף ולענין בעצמו של כהן בג"ש נאמר כאן ומלק ונאמר להלן ומלק אבל להצריך לחטאת מליקה בראש המזבח *כעולה לא ילפינן משום דעולה לא ילפא אלא מהיקשא דהקטרה ודבר הלמד בהיקש אינו חוזר ומלמד בג"ש מדרבי יוחנן כדאמר פרק איזהו מקומן (לעיל דף מט:) וא"ת בפ"ק דקדושין (דף לו.) דאמר דמליקה אינה כשירה בנשים דאיתקש להקטרה ובהקטרה כתיב בני אהרן ולא בנות אהרן תינח מליקה דעולה מליקה דחטאת מנלן דבר הלמד בהיקש אינו חוזר ומלמד בג"ש וי"ל דגלוי מילתא בעלמא הוא כהן ולא כהנת וא"ת ורבי *שמעון דנפקא ליה בפרק קמא דחולין (דף כא:) עולת העוף ממול עורף מהיקשא דכמשפט חטאת העוף ולית ליה ג"ש דהכא א"כ מנא ליה בחטאת העוף דבעינן כהן שתהא בעצמו של כהן וי"ל דחטאת נמי ילפא מעולה מהיקשא דכמשפט: **דמו** טו. נראה דחטאת לא בעי דמו כולו מדלא קתני בה הקיף ביה *מליקה למזבח: **ואם** עשאה למטה מרגליו ואפילו אמה אחת כשירה. אף על גב דכתיב ומלק והקטיר ונמצה לא בעי מקום הקטרה ממש כי היכי דלגבי דם חשיב לב] סמוך לקרן אמה אחת:

הבדיל

מסורת הש"ס

לעיל כט: | מדכתיב ושסע ג"ק | ד"ה והקטיר אותו סס"ד ומה"ד ומה אני מקיים מה שנאמרה כו' | כס"י מיותא כדם | [לעיל נה. וש"נ] | כריתות ס. | ויקרא א | שם | שם | ליה לת"ק ג"ק | וסכין ג"ק | שם | חולין כג. | שם כ | חולין כח: | ויקרא א | שם | שם | נ"ל ישמעאל | מליקתו ג"ק

תורה אור

עין משפט נר מצוה

מז א ב ג מיי' פ"ג מהל' פסה"מ הלכה ג:

גי' שט"ק מדסמכיה לומלק והקטיר כו'

[ועי' תוס' שם ד"ה כמאן כר"ע ובמנחות דף נא: ד"ה וי"ו כו' כתבו דאיכא למ"ד דלגבי דרשי לא דרשו וי"ו ולאיזה דרשה דרשו וי"ו ולפי"ז א"ל נר' נמי הכי]

וקידוש בכלי שרת ג"ק

מח ד מיי' פט"ז מהל' מעה"ק הל"י:

מט ה מיי' שם פ"ו הל' כג:

נ ו ז ח מיי' שם הל' כא:

[נ"ע תכמים סייע ת"ק ועמ"ש לעיל כט: על הגליון]

נא ט מיי' שם הל' כא:

נב י כ מיי' שם הל"ב:

גליון הש"ס

גמ' אם עשאה למטה מרגליו. ע"ל דף סו ע"ב תוספות ד"ה עולת:

כ"א היקש לדרשה אחרינא לא מפקא כו' ג"ק

וחטאת ג"ק

משולה ג"ק

שיטה מקובצת

א] ומיצה דמה חוץ לזמנה או שמלקה חוץ לזמנה ומיצה דמה שלא לשמה או שמלקה ומיצה דמה: ב] כרת וחכ"א זה וזה פסול ואין בו כרת לאכול: ג] תיבת אל נמחק: ד] ת"ל הכהן ומלק. כדמפרש ר"ע שתהא מליקה בעצמו של כהן דר"ע מילתא דת"ק אתא לפרושי אלא דת"ק אית ליה דמשמעות הכהן משמע תרתי שתהא מליקה בעצמו של כהן ולקבוע לו כהן ור"ע אית ליה דהכהן אתא לומר שתהא מליקה בעצמו של כהן אבל לקבוע לו כהן לא איצטריך דסברא הוא בלא פסוק דצריך כהן כדמפרש תלמודא אבל ודאי לא נשמע מרבהן תרתי: ה] ומלק שתהא מליקה ממול: ו] על תיבות ודין הוא נרשם עליו קו: ז] מה הקטרה הראש (בעצמו) [לעצמו] כו'. וא"ת אי מה הקטרה אינה מעכבת אף מליקה אם לא הבדיל בעולה אינה מעכבת וא"כ למה תנן אם לא הבדיל בעולה פסול ותירץ ריב"א דאה"נ נימא מליקה דומיא דהקטרה דאם לא הבדיל אלא בסימן אחד הוי כאילו לא מלק כלל וחיסר מצות מליקה ואז פסול ממילא אבל אם חיסר מצות הקטרה לא מיפסל בהכי אבל קשה דלעיל יליף נמי מה הקטרה בראש המזבח ועוד קשה דאמאי קאמר במתני' דאם שינה פסול נימא דומיא דהקטרה ואם לא הקטיר כשר וי"ל דהתם נמי הויא דומיא דהקטרה ות"ש מה הקטרה אם שינה בה ולא עשאה בראש המזבח חיסר מצות הקטרה והוי כאילו לא הקטיר כלל ואם לא הקטיר כלל פסול אף מליקה אם שינה בה חיסר מצות מליקה כאילו לא מלק כלל ואם לא מלק כלל פסול דאין כאן עבודה כלל: ח] כולו (ס"י אותו בראש ובגוף ומצה בשניהם) על קיר תיבת אל נמחק: ט] ההיכל ולא על קיר האולם ואיזה: י] שתהא עולתו למטה: יא] וכי תעלה על דעתך מאחר שהקטיר כו' וא"ת אה"נ ותמצאות דם העוף קאמר דאכתי לא איירי קרא אלא בהקטרת הראש וי"ל ונמצה דמו משמע ליה כל דמו והא ליכא האיל והקטיר הראש: יב] ומבדיל ס"י ודמה מתמצה על כו': יג] אמה אחת כשרה: יד] היא עצמה אינה נעשית אלא בראש: טו] תיבת בנוצתה נמחק: טז] בנוצתה נוטלה ונוטל: יז] ונוטל את: יח] בין מלמעלה: יט] אותו וגו' הס"ד ומה"ד ומה אני מקיים מה שנאמרה: כ] ולהקטיר בה עושה: כא] הקטרה היא הס"ד: כב] כמו שצולין העוף עושין: כג] שלה שלא יפול יותר ממה שכנגד: כד] דריש. ס"א לומר דחילק הכתוב בין חטאת העוף לעולת העוף א) היינו מהקריב לזה ולא לאחר והכא דריש מדסמכיה והקריבו אל מן התורים: כה] מדסמכי' לומלק ותיבת לוהקטיר נמחק: כו] כהן דכתיב וקמץ הכהן וי"ל מה למנחה שכן טעונה הגשה: כז] בכלי שרת (אות ו' נמחק) לאחר קמיצה מה שאין כן בעוף ועוד אמר ריב"א דמליקה לשחיטה סברא לדמות שכן מיני דמים ולא לקמיצה דמנחה שאינה מיני דמים. תוס' אחרות: כח] כלי שחיה קומץ בידו אף אני אביא מליקה וי"ל דמה למנחה שטעונה הגשה. תוס' אחרות: כט] אבל ס"א כל כמה דלא ידעינן שהוא ביד שפיר מיחשב מין זבח כו': ל] ומלק שתהא מליקה בעצמו: לא] מאן דלית ליה. עי' לעיל בתוס' (דף יד ע"ב) ובתוס' יומא (דף כו ע"א): לב] חשיב קרן סמוך

א) אולי צ"ל וי"ל דהתם הו"מ שמקריב כו'.

עין משפט נר מצוה

סייך למשנה דלעיל סה:

נג א מיי' פ"ז מהל' מעה"ק הל' כג:

נד ב מיי' שם פ"ו הל"ז:

נה ג מיי' שם הל"ו:

[סייך למשנה דלעיל סד:]

מסורת הש"ס

(חולין כא.) [לקמן סו:]

[מעילה ח:]

חולין כא.

תורה אור

שיסע ולא הבדיל: ת"ר ושסע אין א] שיסע אלא ביד וכן הוא אומר וישסעהו כשסע הגדי: לא הסיר את המוראה כו': מתני' דלא כרבי אלעזר בר"ש דתניא *א"ר אלעזר בר"ש שמעתי ב] שמבדילין בחטאת העוף מאי בינייהו אמר רב חסדא ג] מיצוי חטאת העוף מעכב איכא בינייהו ת"ק סבר מיצוי חטאת העוף מעכב וכיון ד] דמצוי דם (א) קעביד מעשה עולה בחטאת העוף ור' אלעזר בר"ש סבר *מיצוי חטאת העוף לא מעכב ה] ומחתך בשר בעלמא הוא רבא אמר שהייה בסימן שני בעולת העוף ו] מעכב איכא בינייהו תנא קמא סבר שהייה בסימן שני בעולת העוף לא ז] מעכב ואע"ג דשהייה קא עביד מעשה עולה בחטאת ורבי אלעזר בר"ש סבר ח] מעכב וכיון דשהייה מחתך בשר בעלמא הוא אביי אמר רוב בשר מעכב איכא בינייהו ובפלוגתא דר' זירא ור' שמואל בר רב יצחק חד אמר שהייה בסימן שני בעולת העוף ט] מעכב איכא בינייהו וחד אמר רוב בשר מעכב איכא בינייהו מכלל דבעינן (ב) י] דרוב בשר בתחילה אין יא] והתניא *כיצד מולקין חטאת העוף חותך שדרה ומפרקת בלא רוב בשר עד שמגיע לוושט או לקנה יב] הגיע לוושט או לקנה חותך סימן אחד או רובו ורוב בשר עמו ובעולה שנים או רוב שנים אמרוה קמיה דרבי ירמיה אמר יג] לא שמיע להו הא דא"ר שמעון בן אליקים משום רבי אלעזר בן פדת משום ר"א בן שמוע אומר היה ר"א בר' שמעון שמעתי בחטאת העוף שמבדילין יד] ומאי לא יבדיל אין

רש"י

הא כיצד קודר את העור סביבות הזפק כמין ארובה ונוטל עם העור שכנגד הזפק עם הזפק אבל בלא קדירה לא שהעור נמשך אחריו ונוטל יותר: וכן הוא אומר. בשמשון והתם מפרש בהדיא דביד הוא: מתני'. דקתני הבדיל במליקת חטאת שמלקה בשני סימנין פסול דלא כרבי אלעזר שמבדילין. שאם הבדיל לא פסל: מאי בינייהו. כלומר במאי קמיפלגי טו]: ת"ק סבר. מילוי טז] בתר הזאה בחטאת העוף מעכב וכיון דבעל כרחו ממלא דם אי אמרת מבדיל קעביד כל מעשה עולה בחטאת מליקה מובדלת ומילוי דעולה *מילוי הוא דעביד בה ולקמן (דף סו.) תנן דחטאת העוף שעשאה כמעשה עולה יז] לשם חטאת פסולה: ור"א בר"ש סבר לא מעכב. הילכך אם רצה להבדיל יבדיל ולא ימלא לאחר הבדלה ולא עבד ליה מעשה עולה ואי משום דשינה בהבדלה כיון דלאו מעשה עולה מצי למימר יח] בה חיתוך בשר בעלמא הוא: ה"ג שהייה בסימן שני בעולת העוף איכא בינייהו. בעולת העוף יט] הצריכו ב' סימנים ושהה שיעור שהייה בין סימן לסימן איכא בינייהו אי פסיל בה כ] בשהייה בין סימן לסימן כבהמה או לא: ת"ק סבר שהייה בסימן שני בעולת העוף לא פסלה. דלא דמי לשחיטת בהמה דטעמא דבהמה כא] בעיא ב' סימנים משום דלא נפקא חיותא בסימן אחד הילכך שם שחיטה על שניהם כב] אבל עוף בסימן אחד פסקא חיותא כג] ועולת העוף מצות הבדלה בעלמא הוא דאיכא עלה אבל שם מליקה אינו אלא על הראשון ולא מהניא שהייה לפסול בשני וחטאת שהבדיל בה אע"ג דבלא שהייה אי אפשר בין סימן לסימן כדתני לקמן במתניתין שבתחילה חותך שדרה ומפרקת בלא רוב בשר הגיע לסימן חותכו ורוב בשר עמו והאי חתיכת רוב בשר כד] אף על גב דאית ביה שיעור שהייה כיון דבעולה שהייה בין סימן לסימן לא פסלה אי כה] עבדיה בחטאת עביד מעשה עולה בחטאת: ור"א בר"ש סבר שהייה בסימן שני בעולת העוף פסלה. הילכך חטאת שהבדיל בה כיון שא"א לה בלא שהייה בין סימן לסימן אין כאן מעשה עולה דבעולה שהייה ליכא ומחתך בשר בעלמא הוא: רוב בשר מעכב איכא בינייהו. ודכולי עלמא שהייה בעולה בסימן שני פסלה והכא בהא פליגי לת"ק חיתוך רוב בשר בחטאת כו] לא מעכב (ג) אי לא מחתיך ליה ואי אמרת מבדיל עביד ליה שני סימנין בלא שהייה ויש כאן מעשה עולה כז] ורבי אלעזר ברבי שמעון סבר רוב בשר בחטאת מעכב כח] וחתיכתו אחר סימן ראשון הוא וכיון דלא סגי בלא שהייה בינתיים אין כאן מעשה עולה: מכלל דבעינן רוב כט] הבשר לכתחילה. מדקמיפלגי בעיכובא מכלל דכולהו מודו לכתחילה בעי לחתוך רוב בשר אחר הסימן: שדרה. חוט השדרה: מפרקת. עצם הצואר: בלא רוב בשר. המקפת סביב כדאמרינן בהכל שוחטין (חולין דף כ:) נשברה מפרקת ורוב בשר עמה נבילה ומטמאה ואפילו מפרכסת הילכך אי הוה חותך רוב בשר קודם הסימן הויא ל] ליה מתה ולא מהניא בה מליקה וסימנין הלכה למשה מסיני הן: שנים או רוב שנים. בהכל שוחטין (שם דף כא.) אמרינן שנים לרבנן רוב שנים לר"א בר"ש והתם פליגי בה בקראי: אמרוה קמיה דר' ירמיה. להך פלוגתא דהנך אמוראי דפליגי בטעמא דר"א ברבי שמעון: אין

תוספות

הבדיל בחטאת ולא הבדיל בעולה פסול. בחטאת ניחא כדדרשינן בת"כ חטאת היא שאם מלקה שלא לשמה פסולה וה"ה דכל שינה בה פסולה אבל בעולה קשה מנלן ועוד דמהקטרה ילפא מה הקטרה הראש בעצמו והגוף בעצמו לא] אף כאן כו' ומה הקטרה אינה מעכבת אף הבדלה אינה מעכבת וכן קשה ממליקת לב] *עוף שעשאה למטה כיון דעשאה למטה מהקטרה ילפא דון מינה ומינה וכי היכי דלא הקטיר למעלה כשר °לא מלק למעלה נמי כשר: *כיצד קרב המתיר. כל הנך משניות דהכא ודפ"ק דמכילתא ודמנחות צריכי לדקדק אמאי צריכי כולהו: קעביד מעשה עולה בחטאת. מה שזה למעלה וזה למטה לא חשיב ליה שינוי: ורבי אלעזר בר"ש סבר מילוי בחטאת לא מעכב. הילכך אם רצה להבדיל יבדיל ולא ימלא אחר הבדלה ולא עביד מעשה עולה לג] ואי משום דשינה *בהבדלה [כיון דלא מילה] כמעשה עולה א"כ כי מבדיל הוי חיתוך בשר בעלמא כך פירש בקונטרס וקשה דבפ"ק דחולין (דף כא:) דדריש רבי אלעזר בר"ש כמשפט חטאת העוף מה להלן כשהוא לד] אוחז הראש בגוף ומזה ויליף מיניה בעולת העוף שאין חותך אלא רוב שנים היכי יליף הא אי בעי מבדיל לגמרי בחטאת והיינו יכולין לפרש כשהוא לה] אוחז הראש בגוף ומזה אם ירצה קאמר *ומדקאמר מה להלן בסימן אחד היינו שאם ירצה לא יחתוך כ"א סימן אחד אבל קשה מברייתא דהתם לעיל לו] דקתני שנים או רוב שנים ומפרש התם שנים לרבנן או רוב שנים לר' אלעזר בר"ש לוקמה כולה כרבי אלעזר בר"ש דאי בעי שנים ואי בעי רוב שנים לז] ובפרק העור והרוטב (שם דף קכג.) נמי גבי טלית שנקרעה רובה שוב אינה חיבור וטהורה ומוקי לה בטלית טבולת יום דכיון דלא חס עלה ואטבלה ליכא למימר דילמא חיים ולא קרע רובה אבל כשאינה טבולת יום גזרינן ופריך אלא מעתה לח] לרבי אלעזר בר"ש ליגזר *) דילמא לא אתי למיעבד *רובא והשתא לט] אי אין אסור לחתוך כל השנים ל"ל למגזר שם כלל דילמא חיים ונראה לפרש כל סוגיא זו בהבדלה שלאחר הזאה אבל קודם הזאה כולי עלמא לא פליגי דפסולה דאמר קרא לא יבדיל ודוקא רבי שמעון בן אליקים דלקמן אית ליה הך סברא לרבי אלעזר בר"ש דיכול להבדיל כל השנים ואפילו קודם הזאה ולית ליה איסור פסול בהבדלה כלל *דהא מפרש לא יבדיל דקרא אין צריך להבדיל וסוגיא דחולין פרק קמא (דף כא:) והיא דהעור והרוטב (שם דף קכג.) דלא כוותיה אלא כרב חסדא ורבה ואביי והכי פירושא דכולה שמעתא מאי בינייהו פי' מאי טעמייהו אמר רב חסדא מילוי חטאת העוף מעכב איכא בינייהו דרבנן סברי מילוי חטאת העוף מעכב וכשהזה עדיין לא נגמרה מצוותה הילכך כשהבדיל סימן שני לאחר הזאה לא חשיב מחתך בשר בעלמא ופסול משום שעשה מעשה עולה בחטאת שיש כאן הבדלה בשנים קודם מילוי כמו בעולה ור"א בר"ש סבר דמילוי אינו מעכב וכבר נגמרה כל מ] מצוותן וכשמבדיל לאחר הזאה אינו אלא מחתך בשר בעלמא והשתא ל"ל מא] דרב חסדא [סבר] דשהייה בסימן שני בעולת העוף לא מעכב דאי מעכב אמאי פסול לרבנן כשהבדיל לאחר הזאה אין כאן מעשה עולה שהרי שהה ואין הכשרה של עולה בכך ואי אפשר לו לעשות הזאה בין מליקת סימן ראשון לסימן שני שלא ישהה ורבה מפרש שהייה בסימן שני בעולת העוף מעכב איכא בינייהו דלרבנן לא מעכב ולרבי אלעזר בר"ש מעכב ואביי מפרש דרוב בשר מעכב איכא בינייהו ורבנן סברי רוב בשר לא מעכב ולכך זימנין דלא חתיך רוב בשר עם סימן הראשון מב] (*מ"מ אסור להבדיל עם סימן הראשון אפילו לאחר ההזאה) גזרינן אטו היכא דלא חתך רוב בשר ור"א ברבי שמעון סבר רוב בשר מעכב ולכך לא פסל דאין כאן מעשה עולה שכבר חתך רוב בשר עם סימן ראשון וכשמבדיל לאחר ההזאה מתה עומד ומבדיל ופסול מג] לאביי דפ"ק דחולין (דף כ:) דפריך תקשי לך עולת העוף דבעיא שני סימנין וכי מתה עומד ומולק ולית ליה טעמא דכדי לקיים מצות הבדלה והדר קאמר אמרוה רבנן קמיה דרבי ירמיה פי' הנך טעמי דרב חסדא ורבה ואביי אמר להו לא שמיעא להו הא דאמר ר"ש בן אליקים משום רבי אלעזר בן פדת אומר היה ר"א ברבי שמעון שמעתי שמבדילין בחטאת העוף ומאי לא יבדיל א"ל להבדיל פי' ולא צריכין לכל הנך טעמי מד] דפריש רב חסדא ורבה ואביי ואף קודם ההזאה מותר להבדיל וא"ת דלדידהו דאסור להבדיל קודם הזאה ואפילו לרבי אלעזר בר"ש א"כ מאי קאמר לעיל מתניתין דלא כר"א בר"ש הא לכאורה מתני' קודם הזאה דומיא דרישא דקתני חטאת העוף כיצד היתה נעשית מלק ראשה ממול ערפה ואין מבדיל ומזה מדמה על

*) נ"ל דילמא לא אתי למיעבד רובא והשתא א"ת בשלמא אסור לחתוך כל השנים פריך שפיר [illegible] כל השנים אלא אי שרי לחתוך כל השנים למה לי למגזר כו'. מתוס' חולין דף כא ע"ב ד"ה ואינו מבדיל

הגהות הב"ח

(א) גמ' וכיון דמצוי דם מעכב קעביד מעשה: (ב) שם מכלל דבעינן רוב בשר בתחילה: (ג) רש"י ד"ה רוב בשר וכו' לא מעכב אע"ג דלא מחתך:

גליון הש"ס

תוס' ד"ה הבדיל כו' לא מלק למעלה נמי כשר. עיין תוס' יומא דף ג ע"ב ד"ה אי מה מילואים:

[65b] HE RENT IT, BUT DID NOT SEVER IT. Our Rabbis taught: *And he shall rend it:*[7] rending is by hand only, and thus it says, *and he rent him as one would have rent a kid.*[8]

IF HE DID NOT REMOVE THE CROP etc. Our Mishnah does not agree with R. Eleazar b. R. Simeon. For it was taught, R. Eleazar son of R. Simeon said: I have heard that one severs the sin-offering of a bird.[9] Wherein do they differ?—Said R. Ḥisda: They disagree as to whether the draining [of the blood] of the bird sin-offering is indispensable. The first Tanna[10] holds that it is indispensable, and since then he must drain out the blood, when he [also] severs [it] he performs the rites of a burnt-offering with the bird sin-offering,[11] whereas R. Eleazar son of R. Simeon holds that the draining out of the bird sin-offering is not indispensable,[12] therefore he is merely cutting flesh.[13] Raba said: They differ about a delay at [the nipping of] the second organ in the case of a bird burnt-offering. The first Tanna holds that it does not invalidate [it], and though he does delay, he performs the rites of a burnt-offering with a sin-offering; whereas R. Eleazar son of R. Simeon holds that it does invalidate [it], and since he delays, he is merely
a cutting flesh.[1] Abaye said: They differ as to whether [the cutting through of] the greater part of the flesh is indispensable. And they [Raba and Abaye] disagree in the same controversy as that of R. Zera and R. Samuel son of R. Isaac: One maintains that they [the first Tanna and R. Eleazar son of R. Simeon] disagree on whether delay at the second organ invalidates; and the other maintains that they disagree as to whether the [cutting of] the greater part of the flesh is indispensable.[2]

Now, this proves that in the first place we require [the cutting of] the greater part of the flesh?[3]—Yes, and it was taught likewise: How is the *meliḳah* of a bird sin-offering performed? He cuts through the spinal column and the nape, without the greater part of the flesh, until he reaches the gullet or the windpipe. When he reaches the gullet or the windpipe he cuts one organ, or the greater part thereof, together with the greater part of the flesh; and in the case
b of a burnt-offering, two [organs] or the greater part thereof.[1]

This was stated before R. Jeremiah.[2] Said he: Have they not heard what R. Simeon b. Eliakim said on the authority of R. Eleazar b. Pedath on the authority of R. Eleazar b. Shammu'a: R. Eleazar son of R. Simeon affirmed: I have heard that a bird sin-offering is severed, and what does *he shall not divide it asunder*[3]

(7) Ibid., 17. (8) Jud. XIV, 6. There, of course, it was done by hand. (9) In the sense that if both organs of the throat are nipped, it is not unfit. Our Mishnah states that it is. (10) The Tanna of our Mishnah. (11) For now the rites do not differ in any way, and it is stated *infra* 66a that such is unfit. Though the blood of the sin-offering is sprinkled *below* and that of the burnt-offering is sprinkled *above* the red line, that is not regarded as a sufficient distinction (Tosaf.). (12) Whereas it is in the case of a burnt-offering. (13) When he nips the second organ. By refraining from draining out the blood after this he makes it clear that he is *not* performing the rites of a burnt-offering.

a (1) The *shechitah* of an animal consists of cutting through both organs of the throat, viz., the windpipe and the gullet; should a delay occur between these two organs, it is invalid, and the animal is *nebelah* (q.v. Glos.). The *shechitah* of a bird (of *ḥullin*) consists of cutting through one organ only (the second is optional), since that is sufficient to kill it. Now, a bird burnt-offering must have both organs pinched (which is the equivalent of cut) through, and this can be done without delay between the organs; but when one nips both organs of a bird sin-offering, delay is inevitable, owing to the particular manner in which the rite must be performed, as stated *infra*. The first Tanna holds that delay between the two organs in the case of a burnt-offering does not invalidate the sacrifice, because the nipping of the second organ is not really part of the *shechitah* at all. Hence when he nips both organs of a sin-offering, he performs the same rite as would be valid in the case of a burnt-offering, and therefore it (the sin-offering) is unfit. R. Eleazar b. R. Simeon holds that delay in the case of a burnt-offering does invalidate the sacrifice, and since delay is *inevitable* in the case of a sin-offering, it is obvious that he is *not* treating it like a burnt-offering. (2) After the priest nips the first organ, he must also cut through the greater part of the flesh that surrounds it (v. *infra*), and this naturally makes a delay before the second organ inevitable. Abaye explains that all hold that a delay at the second organ of a *burnt*-offering invalidates the sacrifice, but they disagree as to whether the cutting through of the flesh in the case of a sin-offering is indispensable. The first Tanna holds that it is not indispensable, hence it is possible to nip both organs without a delay, and so it becomes like the rites of a burnt-offering and is therefore invalid. But R. Eleazar b. R. Simeon holds that this cutting through is indispensable; hence there must be a delay between the organs, and thereby it differs from a burnt-offering. (3) Since they disagree on whether it is indispensable, it follows that it is certainly necessary.

b (1) V. Ḥul. 21a.—By 'cut' is meant with his nail, not with a knife. (2) *Sc.* the controversies of the *amoraim* on the points of difference between the first Tanna and R. Eleazar b. R. Simeon. (3) Lev. I, 17.

mean? [66a] He need not sever it.[4] Said R. Aha the son of Raba to R. Ashi: If so, when it is written in connection with a pit, [*And if a man shall open a pit* . . .] *and not cover it*,[5] does that too mean that he need not cover it?—How compare! There, since it is written, *the owner of the pit shall make it good*,[6] he is [obviously] bound to cover it. But here, consider: it is written, *And* [*the priest*] *shall bring* [*offer*] *it* [*unto the altar*],[7] [whereby] the Writ drew a distinction between a bird sin-offering and a bird burnt-offering. What then is the purpose of '*he shall not divide it asunder*'?[8] Infer from this that he *need* not sever it.[9]

IF HE DRAINED THE BLOOD OF THE BODY. Our Rabbis taught: *A burnt-offering*[10] [teaches that] even if he drained the blood of the body but did not drain the blood of the head [it is still a valid

a burnt-offering].[1] You might think that even if he drained the blood of the head, but not the blood of the body [it is valid]; therefore it states, '*it is*'.[2] How does this imply it?[3]—Said Rabina: It is logical, for most of the blood is found in the body.[4]

CHAPTER VII

b *MISHNAH*. IF A SIN-OFFERING OF A BIRD IS OFFERED[1] BELOW [THE RED LINE] WITH THE RITES OF A SIN-OFFERING[2] [AND] FOR THE SAKE OF A SIN-OFFERING, IT IS FIT. [IF IT IS OFFERED] WITH THE RITES OF A SIN-OFFERING, [BUT] IN THE NAME OF A BURNT-OFFERING; [OR] WITH THE RITES OF A BURNT-OFFERING [AND] IN THE NAME OF A SIN-OFFERING; OR WITH THE RITES OF A BURNT-OFFERING [AND] IN THE NAME OF A BURNT-OFFERING, IT IS UNFIT. IF HE OFFERS IT ABOVE [THE RED LINE], [EVEN] WITH THE RITES OF ANY OF THESE,[3] IT IS UNFIT. IF A BURNT-OFFERING OF A BIRD IS OFFERED ABOVE, WITH THE RITES OF A BURNT-OFFERING [AND] IN THE NAME OF A BURNT-OFFERING, IT IS FIT; WITH THE RITES OF A BURNT-OFFERING [BUT] IN THE NAME OF A SIN-OFFERING, IT IS FIT, BUT DOES NOT FREE ITS OWNER OF HIS OBLIGATION.[4] [IF HE OFFERS IT] WITH THE RITES OF A SIN-OFFERING [AND] IN THE NAME OF A BURNT-OFFERING; [OR] WITH THE RITES OF A SIN-OFFERING [AND] IN THE NAME OF A SIN-OFFERING, IT IS UNFIT. IF HE OFFERS IT BELOW, [EVEN] WITH THE RITES OF ANY OF THESE,[5] IT IS UNFIT.

(4) The foregoing controversies of the *amoraim* assumed that R. Eleazar merely meant that the sacrifice is not unfit if he does sever it, but that nevertheless he may not sever it in the first place. But on the present interpretation he differs from the first Tanna on the very law itself. (5) Ex. XXI, 33. (6) Ibid. 34. (7) Lev. I, 15. This refers to the burnt-offering. (8) In Lev. V, 8, referring to the sin-offering. (9) In Hul. 21a R. Eleazar b. R. Simeon deduces from this '*shall bring it*' that the priest *must* sever the neck of a burnt-offering by nipping both organs; and further, that in this respect Scripture draws a distinction between a burnt-offering and a sin-offering. Now, if '*he shall not divide it asunder*' means that he *may* not sever it, then the distinction would merely justify us in saying that in the case of a burnt-offering he *may* sever it, but not that he *must*. Hence it must mean, he *need* not sever it, and then the distinction shows that he *must* sever a burnt-offering. (10) Lev. I, 17.

a (1) 'A *burnt-offering*' here is superfluous, since the context makes it perfectly clear. Hence it is interpreted to mean that it still counts as such even if something of its rites is omitted. (2) This is emphatic, intimating that it must be done with the proper rites. (3) Perhaps it is the reverse? (4) Hence that it at least must be drained out.

b (1) Lit., 'made'—I.e., its blood is sprinkled. (2) Viz., nipping one organ only, and sprinkling and draining the blood. (3) Enumerated above, i.e., even with the rites and in the name of a sin-offering. (4) V. *supra* 2a. (5) Cf. n. 3.

עין משפט נר מצוה

א א מיי' פ"ז מהלכות פסולי המוקדשין הלכה ו :
ב ב מיי' שם הלכה ה :
ג ג ד מיי' שם הל' ח :
ד ה מיי' שם הלכה ו :

תורה אור

אין צריך להבדיל א"ל רב אחא בריה דרבא לרב אשי א] אלא מעתה גבי בור דכתיב °ולא יכסנו ה"נ דאין צריך לכסות הכי השתא התם כיון דכתיב °בעל הבור ישלם עלויה הוא דרמי לכסויי אבל הכא מכדי כתיב והקריבו חלק הכתוב בין חטאת העוף לעולת העוף ב] לא יבדיל למה לי ש"מ אין צריך להבדיל : מיצה דם הגוף : ת"ר עולה אע"פ שמיצה דם הגוף ולא מיצה דם הראש יכול ג] (א) מיצה דם הראש ולא מיצה דם הגוף ת"ל הוא מאי תלמודא אמר רבינא מסתברא (ב) דרוב דמים בגוף שכיחי :

(שמות כא) (שם)

הדרן עלך קדשי קדשים

חטאת העוף שעשאה למטה כמעשה חטאת לשם חטאת כשירה °כמעשה חטאת לשם עולה כמעשה עולה לשם חטאת כמעשה עולה לשם עולה פסולה °עשאה למעלה כמעשה כולן פסולה עולת העוף שעשאה למעלה כמעשה עולה לשם עולה כשירה °כמעשה עולה לשם חטאת כשירה ובלבד שלא עלתה לבעליה °כמעשה חטאת לשם עולה כמעשה חטאת לשם חטאת פסולה עשאה למטה כמעשה כולן °פסולה ד]:

גמ'

רש"י

אין צריך להבדיל. הילכך אם הבדיל לאו שינוי הוא : מכדי כתיב. בעולת העוף והקריבו ומינה נפקא לן לר"א ברבי שמעון הבדלה בעולת העוף בהכל שוחטין (חולין דף כא.) ולא דרש ומלק והקטיר כדדרשי' לעיל מה הקטרה הראש בעצמו כו' דתישק ליה הבדלה מהתם דהך סברא לית ליה שימלוק את ה] כולן אלא דוקא רוב שנים ויליף לה מקראי ואפילו רבנן דפליגי עליה התם עיקר הבדלה בעולה לא נפקא להו אלא מוהקריבו דמשמע חלק את זה מן החטאת הילכך על כרחך ולא יבדיל האמור בחטאת למה לי. כלומר מאי (ג) ו] קאמר לן שמע מינה א"ל להבדיל קאמר הילכך נפקא לן העולה מוהקריבו דצריך להבדיל ז] דהא חלק ביניהן דאי אזהרה היא בחטאת שלא יבדיל היכי נפקא לן בעולה מוהקריבו דצריך להבדיל ח] אינו מוזהר שלא להבדיל הוא דנפקא לן מחילוקו ולא ט] שטעון הבדלה. ד"א האי למה לי כמו י] מאי היא לשון קצר מדאתא והקריבו לחלק *למדנו הבדלה בעולה שמע מינה ולא יבדיל אין צריך להבדיל קאמר ואשמעי' והקריבו דחלק בעולה דצריך להבדיל (דאי אזהרה היא בחטאת יא] לא שמעי' מוהקריבו אלא דאינו מוזהר מלהבדיל בעולה אבל מצות הבדלה לא נפקא לן) :

*ללמדנו נ"ק

הדרן עלך קדשי קדשים

חטאת העוף. כמעשה חטאת. מליקה בסימן אחד והזאה ומיצוי : כמעשה עולה. בגמרא מפרש דשני במאי : עשאה למעלה כמעשה כולן. כלומר כמעשה אחד מכולן האמורין כאן ואפילו כמעשה חטאת לשם חטאת : כמעשה חטאת. בגמרא מפרש דשני במאי : עשאה למטה כמעשה כולן. כמעשה אחד מכל אלו ואפילו כמעשה עולה לשם עולה יב] :

גמ'

תוספות

קיר המזבח ויש לומר דמשמע ליה דמתני' פוסלת בכל ענין אפי' לאחר הזאה יג] מדקאמר רבי אלעזר בר"ש שמעתי שמבדילין והיינו דוקא לאחר הזאה מכלל דרבנן פליגי עליה ואמרי אין מבדילין אם כן מתני' דלא כוותיה וא"ת יד] ריש פ' חטאת העוף עשאה כמעשה עולה פסולה וקאמר בגמרא דשני במאי אילימא דשני במליקה נימא דלא כר"א בר"ש דאי ר"א בר' שמעון הא אמר שמעתי שמבדילין בחטאת העוף מאי קשיא ליה לרבי אלעזר בר"ש נמי משכחת לה דהבדיל קודם הזאה וי"ל כיון דמוקמינן כמעשה עולה דשני במליקה א"כ מדלא קתני כמעשה עולה קודם הזאה ש"מ דאיירי בין קודם הזאה בין לאחר הזאה ועוד דלר' אלעזר בן פדת ור"ש בן אליקים ורבי ירמיה טו] מכשר רבי אלעזר בר"ש אפילו קודם הזאה דמפרשים לא יבדיל דקרא אין צריך להבדיל ור"ת הגיה בגליון בספרו על מילתא דר"ש בן אליקים ומאי לא יבדיל דמשמע בין בשעת הזאה בין בשעת מילוי אינו צריך להבדיל ואם הבדיל כשר וכ"ש שמתמצה כל הדם ושבקינן לקרא דאיהו דחיק ומוקי אנפשיה דדוקא לא יבדיל בשעת הזאה אבל בשעת מילוי דלדם הוא צריך אי בעי מבדיל אי בעי לא מבדיל עכ"ל משמע שרוצה לפרש דבשעת הזאה אסר קרא ובשעת מילוי בעי למימר קרא דאין צריך ותרווייהו משמעי *מיניה טז] (וש"מ) מדאפקיה קרא בלשון לאו קדריש דבשעת הזאה לא יבדיל ולאסורא אף בשעת מילוי לא אתי קרא דמוהקריבו הוה נפיק יז] דדריש מיניה בחולין (דף כא.) שחילק הכתוב בין חטאת העוף לעולת העוף לכך יש לפרש נמי דאתי קרא למימר דבשעת מילוי אם ירצה לא יבדיל והא דאמר רבי ירמיה לא שמיע להו דמשמע שבא לחלוק על רב חסדא ורבא ואביי היינו משום שבא ר' ירמיה להשמיענו דכשמבדיל לאחר הזאה אין כאן מעשה עולה בחטאת שמצות חטאת נמי כך הוא דקרא אין צריך להבדיל קאמר וא"ת לרב הונא דאמר משמיה דרב במעילה פרק חטאת העוף (דף ח:) דמיצוי חטאת העוף אינו מעכב ולהכי תני במתני' דהתם הוזה דמה אמאי פסלי רבנן כשהבדיל לאחר הזאה הא אין כאן מעשה עולה בחטאת דמחתך בשר בעלמא הוא כדפרישית כיון דכבר נגמרו עבודת הדם דמילוי אינו מעכב ולפי מה שפירשתי ניחא דדילמא רב הונא סבר כר"ש בן אליקים דמוקי פלוגתייהו קודם הזאה אבל לפירוש ר"ת קשה דאפילו לר"ש בן אליקים לא פליגי אלא לאחר הזאה ויש לומר דרב הונא יעמיד מתני' דקתני הבדיל פסול קודם הזאה ואפילו כרבי אלעזר בר"ש וסוגיא דשמעתא דקאמר מתניתין דלא כרבי אלעזר בר"ש אתיא כרב אדא בר אהבה דאמר במעילה* משמיה דרב מילוי חטאת העוף מעכב יח] ורבנן פליגי עליה דר"א בר"ש אפילו לרב הונא מדקאמר רבי אלעזר ברבי שמעון שמעתי שמבדילין משמע דפליגי רבנן עליה ואע"ג דרב הונא סבר מילוי לא מעכב מודה הוא יט] דפליגי רבנן עליה דרבי אלעזר ברבי שמעון *סבר מילוי מעכב וה"נ איכא חד תנא במעילה דסבר הכי ומיהו *)מתני' לא אפשר למימר לרב הונא דסבר מעכב דהא מהדר הש"ס לאוקומי כל סתמי דמתני' כוותיה דאית ליה אינו מעכב וא"ת והא קתני מתני' חטאת העוף שמלקה לשמה ומילה דמה שלא לשמה פסול אלמא דמילוי מעכב ויש לומר דרב הונא לא הוה תני מילה אלא היזה כדתני במתניתין דמעילה הוזה דמה אבל סיפא דמתני' דמייתי התם במעילה כ] אחד חטאת העוף ואחד עולת העוף כא] מלקן ומילה דמן כו' לא מצי לשנויי *דהוא ושהיזה דהא קתני בה נמי עולה והזאה בעולה ליכא לכך צריך לשנויי דלגלדין קתני :

אלא מעתה גבי בור דכתיב ולא יכסנו כו'. מכל לאוין שבתורה כגון לא תחסום לא תאכלו כל נבילה לא תלבש שעטנז לא קשיא ליה למאי כב] כתביה אם לא ללאו אבל הא דמסברא הוה אמינא דמבדיל לפי שצריך לדם אמרינן דכי כתיב לא יבדיל אין צריך להבדיל קאמר וגבי בור נמי מסברא הוה אמינא דחייב לכסותו וכי כתיב לא יכסנו אין צריך לכסותו קאמר :

הדרן עלך קדשי קדשים

חטאת העוף. כמעשה חטאת לשם חטאת כשירה. זו היא מצוותה כג] ואגב אחריני נקטיה : **למעלה** כמעשה כולן פסולה. כד] אף שעשה העבודה כתקנה והיינו באכילה אבל בעלים נתכפרו לשמואל דאמר לעיל פרק ב' (דף כו:) כיון שהגיע דם למזבח נתכפרו בעלים כה] : **למטה** כמעשה כולן פסולה. בסוף פירקין דלעיל (דף סה:) פירשתי דלא ידעינן מנא ליה עיכובא בעולה :

נימא

*) נ"ל ומיהו רבנן דמתני' לא אפשר למימר לר"ה דסברי מעכב כו' נ"ק

*מיניה דמדאפקיה קרא נ"ק

[דף ח:]

נ"ל וסברי מילוי כו' וכן הוא בתוס' חולין דף כח: ד"ה ואינו כו' וע"ש

לשנויי ושהיזה נ"ק

הגהות הב"ח

(א) גמ' יכול אע"פ שמיצה דם הראש : (ב) שם מסתברא רוב כצ"ל ואות ד' נמחק : (ג) רש"י ד"ה מכדי וכו' כלומר מאי קמ"ל :

שיטה מקובצת

א] אלא מעתה גבי בור כו'. וא"ת*) כו' וי"ל דהא דדריש לא יבדיל דאיני צריך להבדיל היינו משום דלדם הוא צריך לעשות ההזאה והמיצוי וא"כ סברא לומר דצריך הבדלה בחטאת יותר מבעולה דבעולה ליכא כי אם מיצוי בלבד ולכך קאמר לא יבדיל דאין צריך להבדיל אבל אם רצה מבדיל ולהכי פריך אלא מעתה כו' דאי כפשוטו לאשמועינן דצריך לכסותו פשיטא דכיון דחפרו צריך לכסותו ומשני הכי השתא כלומר גבי בור כיון דכתיב בעל הבור ישלם אלמא צריך לכסותו ומ"מ כתב ולא יכסנו לספור דברים בעלמא דאם לא כסהו חייב והא דדרשינן לא יבדיל לומר דאינו צריך להבדיל לאו משום דהוי ס"ד מבדיל מסברא כדס"ד אלא משום דמכדי כתיב והקריבו כו' : ב] לא יבדיל למה לי. לפום רהיטא נראה דה"פ כיון דכתיב והקריבו לחלק בענין מליקה א"כ ממילא ידעינן דבחטאת לא יבדיל אלא בסימן אחד אבל לא יבדיל בשני סימנין כענין מליקה דעולה וא"כ על כרחך אתא לא יבדיל לומר דא"צ להבדיל וקשה דאילו לא הוי כתיב לא יבדיל היכא הוי ידעינן בעולה דעביד שני סימנין איפוך אנא ואימא דבחטאת עביד שני סימנין ובעולה סימן אחד ואי משום דדרשינן בעולה ומלק והקטיר מה הקטרה הראש בעצמו וגוף בעצמו וזה אינו דהא לראב"ש קיימינן ובפ"ק דחולין משמע דלראב"ש לית ליה הך היקשא דקאמר התם דבעולה נמי כשהוא אחוז בראש בגוף כו' והיקשא דמליקה להקטרה מוקי לה להקטרה בראשו של מזבח כו' כדקאמר התם לת"ק דברייתא דכמשפט ורש"י דחק ופי' בענין אחר מכדי כתיב בעולה והקריבו וסיניה דריש ראב"ש הבדלה בעולת העוף וא"כ הא דכתיב לא יבדיל בחטאת היינו דא"צ להבדיל קאמר א"כ והקריבו דכתיב לחלק ביניהם לומר דבעולה צריך להבדיל יותר מבחטאת ועביד רוב שנים ומ"מ לא עביד שנים לגמרי והא כמשפט מקיש לענין זו דכשהוא אחוז הראש בגוף (אין) מזה ואי לא יבדיל להזהיר בחטאת מלהבדיל א"כ היכא נפקא בעולה מוהקריבו דצריך להבדיל דלמא לא נפקא לן מיניה אלא שאינו מוזהר מלהבדיל ולא שטעון הבדלה ופליאה גדולה איזו הוכחה היא זו מדקי"ל דבחטאת היא גופיה סנ"ל שמתוך כן אתה דורש דלא יבדיל דאינו צריך להבדיל אימא דבעולה אינו חובה להבדיל ואתא והקריבו לומר דחלק מחטאת דבחטאת אסור להבדיל ובעולה אין אסור להבדיל. וע"ק לפי' לישנא דלמה לי לכך נראה למהר"ם דפי' קמא דפי' לא יבדיל כלומר בלאו הכי נמי ידעינן שפיר דאסור להבדיל מדכתיב והקריבו לומר דחלק מליקה דחטאת ממליקה דעולה ומליקה דעולה בהבדלה היא מהיקשא דהקטרה והא דראב"ש התם דכשאחוז הראש בגוף מזה היינו לבתר דכתיב לא יבדיל וכיון דכתיב לא יבדיל וכמשפט א"כ יש לנו לעשות היקשא לענין דלא יבדיל והיקשא דמליקה להקטרה מוקמינן לה לראשו של מזבח והא דכתיב והקריבו לומר דבעולה לא סגי בסימן אחד אלא בעי רוב שנים אבל הכא מיירי אי לא כתיב לא יבדיל ואז ודאי יש לנו לדרוש היקשא דמלק והקטיר לגמרי אף לענין הראש בעצמו כו' וא"כ מוהקריבו שמעינן דבחטאת אסור להבדיל מדחלק הכתוב בין חטאת העוף לעולת העוף במליקה ואי משום כמשפט מוקמינן ליה לדרשא אחריתי. וקצת קשה למורי דנהי דלא יבדיל לא הוי איצטריך לאיסור הבדלה דחטאת כדפי' מ"מ איצטריך לכתוב לא יבדיל כדי לאקושי (חטאת לעולת העוף) [עולת העוף לחטאת] לאיסור הבדלה כדאמר ראב"ש בחולין מכמשפט דמכח הך היקשא לא דריש ראב"ש היקשא דמליקה להקטרה לענין הראש בעצמו והגוף בעצמו והדרא קושיא לדוכתיה מנ"ל דלא יבדיל דאינו צריך להבדיל קאמר ותירץ דהשתא אית לן למימר א"צ להבדיל דהשתא איצטריך לגופיה דחטאת העוף לומר דלא יבדיל [אין] איסור להבדיל [ולא] לגלות בעולת העוף איסור הבדלה ולא לענין חטאת גופיה : ג] יכול אפי' מיצה : ד] פסולה. וכולן אין מטמאין אבית הבליעה ומועלין בהן חוץ מחטאת העוף שעשאה למטה כמעשה חטאת לשם חטאת : גמ' ומועלין בהן חוץ מחטאת כו'. דחטאת פסולה אין לה היתר לכהנים ועולה אפי' היא כשרה (לאו) בת מעילה היא אבל חטאת העוף שעשאה בהכשר אין מועלין בה דכל שיש לו היתר לכהנים אין מועלין בו : וא"ת ובחטאת העוף ששינה בה אמאי מועלין בה לס"ד במעילה היתר שחיטה שנינו והכא איכא היתר מליקה דהא בגמ' מוקמינן שינוי מקום דגבי חטאת בהזאה וי"ל דדוקא היתר שחיטה מוציאה מידי מעילה משום דלאחר שחיטה הוכשר לקבל דם אבל בעוף דליכא קבלה לא מהני היתר מליקה לאפוקי מידי מעילה : ה] את כולו אלא : ו] מאי קמ"ל אלא ש"מ : ז] להבדיל דמדחלק ביניהן : ח] להבדיל. נוסחאת רש"י מהר"ם גימא הכא דוהקריב חלק לומר דבחטאת מוזהר שלא יבדיל אבל בעולה אינו מוזהר להבדיל אבל דצריך הבדלה לא תיפוק מיניה אלא על כרחך מדנפקא ליה מוהקריב חלק הבדלה בעולת העוף ש"מ ולא יבדיל כו' : ט] שתטעון הבדלה. האי כו'. תיבות ד"א ל"ש ונמחק : י] מאי קאמר ולשון קצר הוא תיבת היא נמחק : יא] בחטאת לומר שלא יבדיל לא : יב] עולה הס"ד ומה"ד וכולן. אע"פ שנפסלו מליקתן מטהרתן מידי נבלה ואין מטמאין בבית הבליעה. כדין נבלת עוף טהור הס"ד ומה"ד ומועלין בהן. ואף בחטאת הואיל ונפסלו ואין בהן שעת היתר לכהנים לא יצא מידי מעילה שבהן הס"ד ומה"ד חוץ מחטאת העוף שעשאה למטה כמעשה חטאת לשם חטאת. דכשרה היא ויש בה שעת היתר לכהנים ושוב אין בה מעילה אפי' לזר הס"ד ומה"ד גמ' : יג] הזאה. ס"א משום דראב"ש אמר שמעתי שמבדילין אמתני' קאמר ובא לחלוק עליה וא"ת : יד] וא"ת לקמן ריש פ' חטאת העוף דתנן עשאה למטה כמעשה עולה כו' : טו] ור' ירמיה פריך שפיר דלדידהו מכשר : טז] ושמא מדאפקיה : יז] נפיק כדדריש : יח] מעכב ואיכא רבנן דפליגי : יט] הוא דאיכא רבנן דפליגי עליה דר"א : כ] במעילה דקתני אחד : כא] העוף שמלקן ושהיזה דמן כו' לא מצי לשנויי דהוה תני ושהיזה תיבת דהוא ל"ש ונמחק : כב] למאי כתבינהו אם לא ללאו אבל האי דמסברא : כג] מצוותה והא דנקט שעשאה בדיעבד אגב אחריני נקטיה : כד] תיבות אף שעשאה העבודה כתקנה נמחק : כה] בעלים. ועי"ל דלא קאמר שמואל אלא בזבחים אבל בעוף לא דקרא דמייתי לעיל גבי זבחים כתיב ואני נתתי לכם על המזבח לכפר הס"ד :

*) [נראה דכוונתו לקושיית התוס' בד"ה אלא. מכל לאוין כו' לא קשיא ליה]

גמ' דשני במאי אילימא דשני במליקה נימא דלא כר' אלעזר בר' שמעון א]*דאמר שמעתי שמבדילין בחטאת העוף ב]ולא אוקימנא דלא כר' אלעזר בר' שמעון ג]לא דשני בהזאה הכי נמי מסתברא מדקתני סיפא עשאה למעלה כמעשה כולן פסולה ואפילו כמעשה חטאת לשם חטאת דשני במאי אילימא דשני במליקה האמר מר ד]מליקה בכל מקום במזבח כשירה אלא לאו דשני בהזאה ומדסיפא בהזאה רישא נמי בהזאה מידי איריא הא כדאיתא והא כדאיתא ה]: עולת העוף כו': דשני במאי אילימא דשני במליקה ו] מדקתני סיפא כולן אין מטמאין בבית הבליעה ומועלין בהן נימא דלא כרבי יהושע דאי כר' יהושע האמר אין מועלין ואלא במיצוי אימא סיפא עולת העוף שעשאה למטה כמעשה חטאת לשם חטאת ר"א אומר מועלין בה ר' יהושע אומר אין מועלין בה דשני במאי אילימא במוצוי אימר דאמר ר' יהושע דשני במליקה במיצוי מי אמר ואלא במליקה רישא וסיפא במליקה ומציעתא במיצוי אין *רישא וסיפא במליקה ומציעתא במיצוי: מתני' ז] *וכולן אין מטמאין בבית הבליעה ומועלים בהן חוץ מחטאת העוף שעשאה למטה כמעשה חטאת לשם חטאת עולת העוף שעשאה למטה כמעשה חטאת לשם חטאת ר"א אומר ח] מועלים בה ר' יהושע אומר אין מועלים בה א"ר אליעזר ומה אם חטאת שאין מועלים בה לשמה כששינה את שמה מועלים בה עולה שמועלים בה לשמה כששינה את שמה אינו דין שימעלו בה א"ל ר' יהושע לא אם אמרת בחטאת ששינה את שמה לשם עולה שכן שינה את שמה לדבר שיש בו מעילה תאמר בעולה ששינה את שמה לשם חטאת שכן שינה את שמה לדבר שאין בו מעילה

אמר

גמ' דשני במאי. אכמעשה עולה לשם חטאת קאי ומיבעי ליה איזה דבר בחטאת עשה כמעשה עולה: אי נימא דשני במליקה. שהבדיל: נימא. הא דקתני פסולה דלא כר"א: ומהדר הש"ס מאי קשיא לך בהאי ודאי פליגי ס] רבנן עליה ולאו מי אוקמה סתמא דפירקין דלעיל דלא כר"א דקתני הבדיל בחטאת פסול: לא. כלומר הך אפי' כר"א: דשני בהזאה. שלא הזה אלא מילה שהמילוי היא י] עבודת העולה: ה"נ מסתברא. דכל שינוי דמתני' בהזאה הוא: דשני במאי. איזהו עבודה יא]למעלה עשה: האמר מר. גבי חטאת העוף בפירקין דלעיל (דף סד:) מליקה בכל מקום *כו' ומדסיפא דאיירי בשינוי למעלה בהזאה איירי רישא נמי יב] דאיירי בשינוי מעשיה בהזאה מיירי: הא כדאיתא והא כדאיתא. כל חדא וחדא יג] במה דהוי שינוי לגביה מיירי רישא דמיירי בשינוי מעשיה איכא למימר דבמליקה נמי איירי סיפא יד] דמעשה דמליקה לא הוי שינוי איתוקם בהזאה: דשני במאי. טו]הני מעשה חטאת דקתני במאי שני: דשני במליקה. שלא הבדיל: טז]מדקתני סיפא. כלומר הא דקתני סיפא כולן מועלין בהן וקאי נמי יז]אעשה כמעשה חטאת לשם חטאת: נימא דלא כרבי יהושע. דאיהו אמר אין מועלין בהן במתניתין: אלא במילוי. ובהא לא פליג ר' יהושע יח]דטעמא כדרב אדא דאמר אומר היה רבי יהושע עולת העוף שעשאה למטה כמעשה חטאת לשם חטאת נמשכת משם עולה ונעשית חטאת העוף והאי טעמא ליכא למימר אלא כדשני במליקה כדמפרש לה רב אשי לקמן משום דעולה צריכה שני סימנין וחטאת כשירה בסימן אחד יט] מליקת עולת העוף למטה ליתא *זה שמולקה למטה ולשם חטאת בסימן ראשון השלים בה כל מעשה החטאת לפיכך יצאתה בה משם עולה ונעשית חטאת והויא חטאת העוף שעשאה למטה כמעשה חטאת לשם חטאת שאין בה מעילה אבל היכא כ]דבמליקה לא שני ומולקה למעלה וכמעשה עולה תו לא כא]נמשכת בשינוי דמילוי שלא מילה אלא היזה כדין חטאת למטה למיהוי חטאת העוף: אימר דא"ר יהושע דשני במליקה. וטעמא כדפרישית: רישא במליקה. משום דבעית לאוקומה כב] דלא כר"א ברבי שמעון כדאיתוקמא כג] סתם באידך פירקין והך סיפא פלוגתא דרבי יהושע ע"כ במליקה: כד] מליעתא במילוי. דתיתוקמא כרבי יהושע משום דר"א שמותי הוא: מתני' כה]וכולן. אע"פ שנפסלו מליקתן מטהרתן מידי נבלה*: ואין מטמאין בבית הבליעה. כדין נבלת עוף טהור: ומועלין בהן. ואף בחטאת הואיל ונפסלו ואין בהן שעת היתר לכהנים לא יצאו מידי מעילה שבהן: חוץ מחטאת העוף שעשאה למטה כמעשה חטאת לשם חטאת. דכשירה היא ויש לה שעת היתר לכהנים ושוב אין בה מעילה אפילו לזר: רבי אליעזר אומר מועלין בה. דהא עולה היא ומי הוציאה ממעילתה שעת היתר לכהנים אין לה: רבי יהושע אומר אין מועלין. דכיון דשינה שמה ומעשיה ומקומה לשם חטאת נעשית חטאת כדמפרש בגמרא: ומה חטאת העוף שאין מועלין כו] לשמה. שהרי נאכלת לכהנים: שינה את שמה. כז] ופסלה ולא באה לכלל היתר מועלין בה דהא רבי יהושע גופיה לא פליג עליה (א): לדבר שיש בו מעילה. לשם עולה:

ששחטן

נימא דלא כר"א בר"ש. לעיל (דף סה: ד"ה ורבי) פירשתי: כח]חטאת העוף כמעשה עולה פסולה דשני במליקה. פי' כט]מלק ב' סימנין והבדיל וכי קאמר שני בהזאה היינו שלא הזה אלא מילה והכל עשה למטה כדין חטאת ולא מצי לפרושי שני במליקה שעשאה למעלה דהא מליקה בכל מקום כשירה ובשני בהזאה ליכא לפרושי ל]*שהזאה למעלה משום דקאי על רישא דקתני עשאה למטה וכן בבא דעולת העוף כמעשה חטאת דקאמר דשני במליקה היינו שלא מלק רק סימן אחד וכי קאמר שני במלוי היינו שלא מילה אלא הזה תחת המילוי והכל למעלה ולא מצי לפרושה דשני במליקה ובתר הכי דשני במילוי וכגון שעשאה למטה כדין חטאת דהא קאי על רישא דקתני עשאה למעלה ובענין זה אתיא כולה בפשיטות: דשני במליקה נימא דלא כרבי יהושע דאמר אין מועלין. לא]תימה לי טעמא דרבי יהושע משום שעשאה למטה ובסימן ראשון נפסלה מעולת העוף וגם הזה למטה כחטאת העוף לכך נמשכה להיות כחטאת כך מפרש רב אשי טעמא לקמן אבל הכא מלק סימן אחד כחטאת למעלה אין זה פסול עולה בסימן ראשון וגם לא הזה (הכא) דהשתא לא נמשכה להיות כחטאת כיון שלא הזה וגם לא נפסל בסימן ראשון ממעשה עולת העוף. ברו"ך: ואלא במילוי. משמע דכל הך בבא דעולה מיירי במילוי *ותימה כמעשה חטאת לב] היכי מיתוקמא דשני במילוי דאי עשה הזאה ואח"כ מילוי אמאי מיפסלא עולה בכך כיון שעושה אח"כ מילוי מדם הנפש ואי משום דדרשינן בסוף פירקין דלעיל (דף סה.) דמו כל דמו וכיון דעבד ליה הזאה ליכא כל דמו במילוי לא מסתבר שאם נשפך מעט לג] מהדם שתפסל בכך וה"נ מ"ש וכי תימא דלא מוקי במילוי אלא היא דכולן מועלין בהן דקאי אפי' עשאה לעולת העוף למטה כמעשה חטאת לשם חטאת אבל הך רישא מיירי דשני במליקה א"כ בלאו הנך דיוקי דקדייק ואזיל הוה מצי לאקשויי *רישא וסיפא במליקה ומליעתא במילוי דבבא דחטאת העוף אוקימנא רישא דשני במליקה וסיפא בהזאה והך בבא דעולה מיתוקמא דשני במליקה כדפרישית ונראה לפרש דלעולם מיירי הך בבא דעולה דשני במילוי וגרעא [מנשפך מעט] משום דמיד כשהזה והגיע דם למזבח נתכפרו בעלים מדשמואל דלעיל פ"ב (דף כו:) והרי נתכפרו בפסול ולא מהני מה שמת מלה אח"כ כיון דכבר נתכפרו ומיהו תימה הוא לומר דנתכפרו כשעשה עבודה שלא כדינה דלא דמי לנתנו על הכבש לד] ועל היסוד שהעבודה כמצותה אלא ששינה מקומו לה]ונראה כפי' הקונט' דכמעשה חטאת היינו שלא עשה מילוי אלא הזאה לו] למ"ד מילוי [בחטאת] לא מעכב ופסולה משום דלא עשה מילוי בעולה זו לז] דליכא לפרושי דשני במילוי שעשה המילוי למטה דהא קאי ארישא ועוד דהיינו סיפא (עשאה למטה) דקתני עשאה למטה כמעשה כולן וה"פ [הקונטרס] לעיל גבי חטאת כמעשה עולה ומפרש דשני בהזאה היינו שלא הזה אלא מילה גרידא ומיהו עדיין מה לו להש"ס לדקדק על בבא זו אלא במילוי דמשמע שאין יכול להקשות בענין אחר רישא וסיפא במליקה ומליעתא במילוי בלאו הכי יכול להקשות דבבא דחטאת אוקימנא רישא במליקה וסיפא בהזאה ופלוגתא דר"א ור' יהושע במליקה ונראה שאין הש"ס מתמיה על סיפא דבבא דחטאת במאי דמיירי דשני בהזאה כיון דלא משכחת בה פסול בשינוי דמליקה דמליקה בכל מקום במזבח כשירה וא"ת אי לא שני אלא במילוי אמאי מועלין בהן למאן דאמר היתר שחיטה שנינו בריש מסכת מעילה (דף ה.) וזה היה לו היתר שחיטה ויצאה מידי מעילה וכן חטאת שעשאה למעלה כמעשה כולן ואפילו כמעשה חטאת לשם חטאת וקתני סיפא דמועלין בה אמאי הרי היה לה שעת הכושר *והיתר מליקה:

והרי

עין משפט נר מצוה

ה א מיי' פ"ז מהלכות פסולי המוקדשין הל' ו ז:

ו ב מיי' שם הלכה א והלכה ט:

ז ג ד ה מיי' פ"ג מהל' מעילה הל' ז:

[נ"ל שהזה]

נ"ל ותימה כמעשה חטאת לשם עולה כמעשה חטאת לשם חטאת היכי מיתוקמא כו'

נ"א רישא ומליעתא במליקה וסיפא במילוי

שיטה מקובצת

א] בר' שמעון דאי ר"א בר"ש האמר שמעתי: ב] העוף ולאו אוקמינא: ג] בר' שמעון ה"נ דלא כראב"ש לא הב"ע דשני: ד] מלקה בכל: ה] כדאיתא רישא במליקה וסיפא בהזאה: ו] במליקה דקתני: ז] מתיבת וכולן כו' עד תיבת עולת העוף נמחק ומקומן לעיל בע"א בסוף המשנה: ח] מועלין בה ר' יהושע אומר אין מועלין בה: ט] פליגי מתני' עליה תיבת רבנן נמחק: י] היא מעבודת: יא] עבודה עשה למעלה: יב] נמי כי איירי בשינוי מעשיה בהזאה איירי הס"ד: יג] במידי דהוי: יד] סיפא דלמעלה במליקה לא הוי שינוי: טו] במאי. האי כמעשה חטאת לשם עולה דקתני מתני' במאי שני: טז] מה"ד דקתני סיפא: יז] נמי אעולה שעשאה למטה כמעשה: יח] יהושע דטעמיה כדרב אדא: יט] אחד ומליקת עולת העוף אינה למטה וזה שמלקה למטה: כ] היכא דלא שני במליקה ומולקה: כא] לא ממשכה: כב] לאוקימה לעיל דלא: כג] סתמא דאידך פירקין: כד] מה"ד ומציעתא במיצוי: כה] מתיבת וכולן כו' עד תיבות ר"א ל"ש ומקומן לעיל בע"א: כו] שאין מועלין בה לשמה: כז] נפסלה: כח] ד"ה חטאת כו' וד"ה דשני במליקה כו' עד ד"ה ואלא מוקף בח"ל: כט] פי' שמלק: ל] לפרושי שהזה למעלה: לא] תימה דהא מוכח לקמן דטעמא דר' יהושע משום דשינה גם במקום שעשאה למטה ואז נמשכת להיות כחטאת אבל היכא דליכא שינוי מקום אלא שינוי מעשה מודה ר' יהושע ותירץ חשר מקוצי דסמיך אסיפא דמתני' דקתני עשאה למטה כמעשה כולן פסולה ואהא קאי וכולן: תו' מהר"פ: תימה לי דטעמא כו': לב] חטאת לשם עולה וכמעשה חטאת לשם חטאת היכי: לג] מעט מן הדם: לד] הכבש שלא כנגד היסוד תיבת ועל נמחק: לה] ונראה לפרש דכמעשה חטאת תיבות כפי' הקונטרס נמחק: לו] הזאה כמ"ד מיצוי: לז] מתיבת דליכא עד תיבת ומיהו מוקף בחצי לבנה ונרשם תוספות:

מסורת הש"ס

לעיל סה:

ט' הס"ד נ"ק

[מעילה ג.]

וזה נ"ק

נבלה ואין הס"ד נ"ק

סיפא נ"ק

הגהות הב"ח

(א) רש"י ד"ה שינה את שמה וכו' לא פליג עליה (דלדבר) [בשינה שמה] לשם עולה יש בו מעילה כצ"ל והד"א:

GEMARA. [66b] Wherein does he deviate?[6] If we say that he deviates in *meliḳah?*[7] Shall we then say that it does not agree with R. Eleazar son of R. Simeon, who said: I have heard that one severs a bird sin-offering?—But have we not explained that it does not agree with R. Eleazar son of R. Simeon?[8]—No:[9] [it means] a that he deviates in the sprinkling.[1] That too is logical, since the sequel teaches, IF HE OFFERS IT ABOVE, EVEN WITH THE RITES OF ANY OF THESE, IT IS UNFIT, [which means] even with the rites of a sin-offering [and] in the name of a sin-offering. Now, wherein does he deviate?[2] If you say that he deviates in *meliḳah*, surely a master said: If he performed its *meliḳah* on any part of the altar, it is fit? Hence it must surely mean that he deviates in sprinkling, and since the second clause means in sprinkling, the first clause too means in sprinkling!—Why interpret it thus? Each is governed by its own circumstances.[3]

IF A BURNT-OFFERING OF A BIRD etc. Wherein does he deviate?[4] If we say, that he deviates in *meliḳah*,[5] then when he [the Tanna] teaches in the sequel:[6] 'All of these do not defile in the gullet,[7] and involve trespass';[8] shall we say that this does not agree with R. Joshua; for if it agreed with R. Joshua, surely he ruled [that] they do not involve trespass?[9]—Rather, [he deviated] in draining [the blood].[10] Then consider the subsequent clause: If one offered a burnt-offering of a bird below [the red line] with the rites of a sin-offering [and] in the name of a sin-offering, R. Eliezer maintains: It involves trespass; R. Joshua said: It does not involve trespass. Now, wherein did he deviate? If we say, in draining; granted that R. Joshua ruled [thus] where he deviated in *meliḳah*, did he rule [thus] in reference to draining?[11] Hence it must mean, in *meliḳah*: then the first and the last clauses refer to *meliḳah*, while the middle clause refers to draining?—Yes: the first and the last clauses refer to *meliḳah*, while the middle clause refers to draining.

b *MISHNAH*. AND ALL OF THESE[1] DO NOT DEFILE IN THE GULLET[2] AND INVOLVE TRESPASS,[3] EXCEPT THE SIN-OFFERING OF A BIRD WHICH WAS OFFERED BELOW [THE RED LINE] WITH THE RITES OF A SIN-OFFERING [AND] IN THE NAME OF A SIN-OFFERING.[4] IF ONE OFFERED THE BURNT-OFFERING OF A BIRD BELOW WITH THE RITES OF A SIN-OFFERING [AND] IN THE NAME OF A SIN-OFFERING, R. ELIEZER MAINTAINED: IT INVOLVES TRESPASS;[5] R. JOSHUA RULED: IT DOES NOT INVOLVE TRESPASS.[6] SAID R. ELIEZER: IF A SIN-OFFERING INVOLVES TRESPASS WHEN [THE PRIEST] DEVIATED IN ITS NAME,[7] THOUGH IT DOES NOT INVOLVE TRESPASS WHEN [IT IS OFFERED] IN ITS OWN NAME, IS IT NOT LOGICAL THAT A BURNT-OFFERING INVOLVES TRESPASS IF HE DEVIATED IN ITS NAME, SEEING THAT IT INVOLVES TRESPASS [WHEN HE OFFERED IT] IN ITS OWN NAME?[8] NO, ANSWERED R. JOSHUA: WHEN YOU SPEAK OF A SIN-OFFERING WHOSE NAME HE ALTERED TO THAT OF A BURNT-OFFERING, [IT INVOLVES TRESPASS] BECAUSE HE CHANGED ITS NAME TO SOMETHING THAT INVOLVES TRESPASS; WILL YOU SAY [THE SAME] OF A BURNT-OFFERING WHOSE NAME HE CHANGED TO THAT OF A SIN-OFFERING, SEEING THAT HE CHANGED ITS NAME TO

(6) When he offers a sin-offering with the rites of a burnt-offering. (7) Nipping both organs, and thus severing it. (8) *Supra* 65b. The same obviously applies here: What then is your difficulty? (9) This Mishnah can be explained as agreeing even with him.

a (1) Instead of first sprinkling some of the blood (v. Lev. V, 9), he drains out the whole of it, thus treating it like a burnt-offering (I, 15). (2) Which rite does he perform above? (3) The sequel, it is true, can only refer to a deviation in sprinkling, yet the first clause can still refer to a deviation in *meliḳah*. (4) When he performs the rites of a sin-offering. (5) He does not sever it. (6) The next Mishnah, which is the sequel to this. (7) V. *supra* 35b n. 10. (8) V. *supra* 50b n. b 1 and note on next Mishnah. (9) If the *meliḳah* is not done properly. (10) There R. Joshua agrees. For R. Joshua's reason, as stated *infra*, will not apply. (11) He did not, as already stated.

b (1) Enumerated in the preceding Mishnah. (2) V. *supra* 50b n. b 1. Though they are unfit, the *meliḳah* frees them from the uncleanness of nebelah. (3) V. *supra* 35b n. 10. If their rites were properly performed, they would no longer involv trespass, since they would be permitted to the priests, which is secular benefit. Since, however, they became unfit, and so were not permitted at any time, they retain the trespass-involving status which they possessed before they were offered. This applies even to a sin-offering, save for the exception which follows. (4) Since that is fit, and there is a time when it is permitted to the priests; hence even a *zar* is not liable to trespass. (5) For it is a burnt-offering, and at no time was it permitted to the priests. (6) For it has become a sin-offering through all these deviations, and is permitted. (7) For it is then unfit and not permitted to the priests. (8) Since a burnt-offering must be altogether burnt, and is not permitted at any time.

SOMETHING WHICH DOES NOT INVOLVE TRESPASS?[9] [67a] SAID R. ELIEZER TO HIM: LET SACRED SACRIFICES WHICH ARE SLAUGHTERED IN THE SOUTH AND IN THE NAME OF LESSER
a SACRIFICES[1] PROVE IT: FOR HE CHANGED THEIR NAME TO SOMETHING WHICH DOES NOT INVOLVE TRESPASS, AND YET THEY INVOLVE TRESPASS.[2] SO ALSO, DO NOT WONDER THAT IN THE CASE OF THE BURNT-OFFERING, ALTHOUGH HE CHANGED ITS NAME TO SOMETHING THAT DOES NOT INVOLVE TRESPASS, IT INVOLVES TRESPASS. NOT SO, REPLIED R. JOSHUA: IF YOU SAY THUS OF MOST SACRED SACRIFICES WHICH ARE SLAUGHTERED IN THE SOUTH AND IN THE NAME OF LESSER SACRIFICES, [THEY INVOLVE TRESPASS] BECAUSE HE CHANGED THEIR NAME TO SOMETHING WHICH IS PARTLY FORBIDDEN AND PARTLY PERMITTED;[3] WILL YOU SAY THE SAME OF A BURNT-OFFERING, WHERE HE CHANGED ITS NAME TO SOMETHING THAT IS ALTOGETHER PERMITTED?[4]

GEMARA. It was taught: R. Eliezer said to R. Joshua: Let a guilt-offering slaughtered in the north as a peace-offering prove it; though he changed its name, it involves trespass.[5] So need you not wonder that a burnt-offering involves trespass even though he changed its name. Said R. Joshua to him: No. If you say thus of a guilt-offering, where he changed its name but not its place,[6] will you say [the same] of a burnt-offering, where he changed its name and its place? Said R. Eliezer to him: Let a guilt-offering slaughtered in the *south* as a peace-offering prove it, where he changed its name and its place, yet it involves trespass. So need you not wonder that a burnt-offering involves trespass even though he changed its name and changed its place. No, replied R. Joshua. If you say [thus] of a guilt-offering, where [though] he changed its name and its place, he did not deviate in its rites; will you say [the same] of a burnt-offering, where he changed its name and its place and its
b rites? Thereupon he was silent. Said Raba: Why was he silent?[1] He could answer him: Let a guilt-offering which one slaughtered in the south, in the name of a peace-offering and with change of owner,[2] prove it, where he changed its name and its place and its rites,[3] and yet it involves trespass. Now, since he did not answer him thus, you may infer that R. Eliezer discerned R. Joshua's reason.[4] For R. Adda b. Ahabah said: R. Joshua maintained: If a bird burnt-offering was offered below with the rites of a sin-offering and in the name of a sin-offering, immediately he nipped one organ thereof it is transmuted into a bird sin-offering.[5] If so, a bird sin-offering which was offered above [the red line] with the rites of a burnt-offering [and] in the name of a burnt-offering, as soon as he nips one organ of it, let it be transmuted through the other organ into a bird burnt-offering? And should you say, That indeed is so,[6] surely R. Joḥanan said in R. Banna'ah's name: That is the tenor of the Mishnah.[7] Does that not mean, That is the tenor of the Mishnah, but no more?[8]—No: [it means,] that is the tenor of the *whole* Mishnah.[9] R. Ashi said: As for a bird burnt-offering offered below with the rites of a sin-offering [and] in the name of a sin-offering, it is well:[10] since the fitness of the latter requires one organ, whereas that of the former requires both organs, while a bird burnt-offering cannot be offered below, immediately he nips one organ, it is transmuted into a bird sin-offering. But when one offers a bird sin-offering above with the rites of a burnt-offering [and] in the name of a burnt-offering, since a master said, *Melikah* is valid wherever it is done, immediately he nips one
c organ, it becomes unfit;[1] when therefore he nips the second organ, how can it be transmuted into a bird burnt-offering?[2]

The [above] text [stated]: 'R. Adda b. Ahabah said: R. Joshua maintained: If a bird burnt-offering was offered below with the rites of a sin-offering [and] in the name of a sin-offering, immediately he nipped one organ thereof, it is transmuted into a bird sin-

(9) Surely not.
a (1) Thus they were treated altogether like lesser sacrifices, both in name and in the place of slaughtering. (2) For since they became unfit through being slaughtered in the south, the subsequent sprinkling does not permit them that they should no longer involve trespass. (3) The flesh is permitted, but the *emurim* are forbidden and involve trespass. (4) No part of a bird sin-offering is forbidden. (5) Rashi: before the sprinkling of the blood, but not after, for then it is eaten by priests. Tosaf.: even *after* the sprinkling, as R. Eliezer holds that a guilt-offering slaughtered under a different designation is unfit and may not be eaten (*supra* 2a). (6) He slaughtered it in the right place.
b (1) Emended text (*Sh. M.*). (2) I.e., in the name of a different person. (3) Change of owner is equivalent to change of rites. (4) Which applies only to a bird burnt-offering. (5) For the latter requires one organ only. Hence immediately one organ is nipped, there is absolutely nothing to distinguish it from a sin-offering, and so it does turn into one before it can become unfit through having its rites incorrectly performed. This reason can only apply to a bird burnt-offering, for animal sacrifices require the cutting of both organs. (6) And it is fit. On this hypothesis the Mishnah which states that it is unfit will not agree with R. Joshua. (7) The Mishnah is to be understood as it is read. (8) I.e., exactly as it reads, viz., that R. Joshua disagrees *only* where stated. (9) That he disagrees in respect of both a burnt-offering and a sin-offering. (10) That R. Joshua disagrees and holds that it is fit.
c (1) For it was *properly* nipped (the wrong place not affecting it) as a sin-offering, but under a different designation, which renders it unfit (*supra* 2a). (2) Hence here R. Joshua *agrees* with the Mishnah.

אמר לו ר' אליעזר והרי קדשי קדשים ששחטן בדרום ושחטן לשם קדשים קלים יוכיחו א] שכן שינה את שמם לדבר שאין בו מעילה *ומועלין בהן אף אתה אל תתמה על העולה ב] אע"פ ששינה שמה לדבר שאין בו מעילה שימעלו בה אמר לו ר' יהושע לא אם אמרת בקדשי קדשים ששחטן בדרום ושחטן לשם קדשים קלים שכן שינה את שמם לדבר שיש בו איסור והיתר תאמר בעולה ששינה את שמה לדבר שכולו היתר: **גמ'** תניא אמר לו ר"א לרבי יהושע אשם ששחטו בצפון לשם שלמים יוכיח ששינה את שמו ומועלין בו ואף אתה אל תתמה על העולה שאע"פ ששינה את שמה שימעלו בה אמר לו רבי יהושע לא אם אמרת באשם ג] שאם שינה את שמו לא שינה את מקומו תאמר בעולה ששינה את שמה ושינה את מקומה אמר לו ר"א אשם ששחטו בדרום לשם שלמים יוכיח ששינה את שמו ושינה את מקומו ומועלין בו אף אתה אל תתמה על העולה שאע"פ ששינה את שמה ושינה את מקומה ד] מועלין בה א"ל ר' יהושע לא אם אמרת באשם ששינה את שמו ושינה את מקומו ולא שינה את מעשיו תאמר בעולה ה] ששינה את שמה ואת מעשיה ושינה את מקומה ו] אמר רבא ונימא ליה אשם ששחטו בדרום לשם שלמים בשינוי בעלים ז] ששינה את שמו ושינה את מקומו ושינה את מעשיו ח] מדלא קאמר ליה הכי שמע מינה נחית רבי אליעזר לטעמיה דרבי יהושע דאמר רב אדא בר אהבה אומר היה רבי יהושע עולת העוף שעשאה למטה כמעשה חטאת לשם חטאת ב)כיון שמלק בה סימן אחד נמשכת ונעשית חטא' העוף ט] אי הכי חטאת העוף נמי שעשאה למעלה כמעשה י] העולה מכי מליק בה סימן אחד יא] תימשך ותהוי עולת העוף וכ"ת ה"נ והא"ר יוחנן משום רבי בנאה כך היא הצעה של משנה מאי לאו כך היא הצעה ותו לא לא כך הצעה של כולה משנה רב אשי אמר בשלמא עולת העוף שעשאה למטה כמעשה חטאת לשם חטאת כיון דהא הכשירה בסימן אחד והא הכשירה בשני סימנין יב] ועולת העוף למטה ליתא כיון דמלק בה סימן אחד נמשכת ונעשית חטאת העוף אלא חטאת העוף יג] כיון *דאמר מר מליקה בכל מקום כשירה מכי מלק בה סימן אחד איפסלא כי הדר מליק באידך סימן היכי ממשכה והויא עולת העוף גופא אמר רב אדא בר אהבה אומר היה רבי יהושע עולת העוף שעשאה למטה כמעשה חטאת לשם חטאת כיון שמלק בה סימן אחד נמשכת ונעשית חטאת העוף

ת"ש

ששחטן בדרום. לשם שלמים יוכיחו ששינה שמם ומעשיהם: לדבר שאין בו מעילה. שקדשים קלים אין בהם מעילה אלא באימורין: ומועלין בהן. מפני שנפסלו בשחיטת דרום ולא הביאתן זריקתן לכלל שעת היתר להוציאן מידי מעילה: איסור. אימוריהן יש בהן מעילה. חטאת העוף כולו היתר: **גמ'** אשם ששחטו בצפון כו' ומועלין בו. לפני זריקה דלאחר זריקה ליכא מעילה שהרי נאכל לכהנים דשלא לשמו לא פסיל ביה: ואף אתה אל תתמה על העולה. עולת העוף קאמר שנחלקו בה דאילו יד] בעולת בהמה ששינה בה לשם חטאת לא פליג דהא שינה שמה לדבר שיש בו מעילה באימורין: שינוי בעלים. בשינוי מעשה חשיב טו] לה: נחית רבי אליעזר. הבין את דברי רבי יהושע שטעמו משום דקסבר נמשכה משם עולה ונעשית חטאת והאי טז] טעם ליכא למימר בשום שינוי שם קרבן אחר אלא בעולת העוף לבדה וכשניהגית לשם חטאת יז] *ומעשיו כדמפרש רב אשי לקמן מפני שחטאת העוף כשירה בסימן א' וכשמלק עולת העוף למטה לשם חטאת ומליקת סימן אחד בעולה יח] לאו כלום היא ובחטאת הוי גמר עבודה מקודם שחל עליה שם פסול עולה משום עשיית מטה חל עליה שם חטאת העוף כשירה ונמשכת ונעשית חטאת העוף: תימשך ותיהוי עולת העוף. ותהא כשירה דקס"ד דקאמר רב אדא לר' יהושע *דחטאת נמי כשירה הויא: וכי תימא. לר' יהושע הכי נמי ומתניתין דקתני פסולה דלא כר' יהושע: והאמר ר' יוחנן כך היא הצעה. של משנתינו: מאי לאו כך היא והו לא. יט] כדגרסינן לה דלא פליג ר' יהושע אלא בעולה שעשאה למטה כמעשה חטאת לשם חטאת: לא. הכי קאמר כך היא הצעתה של כולה משנה דכי היכי דפליג בעולה פליג בחטאת: רב אשי אמר. לעולם לא פליג ולא תיקשה דבשלמא עולת העוף שעשאה למטה כיון דחטאת הכשירה בסימן אחד וגמר כ] עבודתה ממהר להשלים קודם שיחול על זו שם עולה פסולה וזו היא הכשירה בשני סימנין כא] ולפיכך סימן ראשון אינו פוסל בה משום עשיית מטה ועולת העוף למטה ליתא ויש כאן שינוי מעשה עולה והיכר מעשה חטאת מכיון שמלק בה סימן א' ועדיין לא חל עליה שם פסול עולה חל עליה שם חטאת כשירה הילכך נמשכה ויוצאה משם עולה ונעשית חטאת: אלא חטאת. עשאה למעלה כמעשה עולה בשני סימנין ולשם עולה: כיון דאמר מר כב] מליקה בכל מקום במזבח כשירה. משום מליקת מעלה אין כאן שינוי כג] להפקיע ממנה שם חטאת ואין כאן שינוי *השם וכיון דחטאת גמר עבודתה סימן אחד מקודם שיגמור מעשה עולה חל עליה שם חטאת שנמלקה כולה כד] בשלא לשמה ונפסלה משום שלא לשמה וכי הדר מלק אידך סימן להביאה לכלל מעשה עולה היכי מימשכא והויא עולה: נמשכת ונעשית חטאת. לא קסלקא כה] דעתך ואפילו למיסק ליה לשם חובת חטאת קאמר:

והרי קדשי קדשים ששחטן בדרום כו' ט]. משמע דמן התורה מועלים דק"ו דאורייתא הוא ותימה דלא מקשה מהכא לרבה דאמר בריש מעילה קדשי קדשים ששחטן בדרום אין מועלין בהן מן התורה ומאי איצטריך ליה לאקשויי התם חדא מגו חדא וי"ל דלרבה מעילה דר' אליעזר דהכא נמי מדרבנן דעולה שעשאה למטה כשחיטת דרום היא וק"ו דקאמר ר' אליעזר היינו שיש להם לבית דין לתקן מעילה:

לדבר שיש בו איסור והיתר כז]. וא"ת חטאת כח] העוף ששינה את שמה לשם חטאת העוף דיולדת תוכיח ששינה את שמה לדבר שאין בו מעילה ומועלין בה כט] והא פסולה היא כדאמר בפ"ק (דף ט:) לשם חטאת יולדת לשם חטאת נזיר פסולה הני עולות נינהו ומיהו למאי דמסקינן בגמרא דנחית רבי אליעזר לטעמיה דרבי יהושע משום דנמשכת ונעשית חטאת העוף ניחא ועוד י"ל דר' יהושע הוה מצי לאהדורי זאת תורת החטאת תורה אחת לכל החטאות כדקאמר ר"ש בפ"ק דמנחו' (דף ג:) וא"כ אין מועלין בה דהא כשירה הויא: ל] **א"ר** אליעזר אשם ששחטו בצפון לשם שלמים יוכיח דמועלין. לא] תימה לי אימת מועלין אי לאחר זריקה ליכא מעילה דהא מותר באכילה ואי לפני זריקה לב] כפרש"י עולת העוף נמי לפני הזאה ומילוי מודה ר' יהושע דמועלין לג] דאכתי לא נמשכה להיות כחטאת העוף לד] וי"ל דר"א לטעמיה דאמר אשם שלא לשמו פסול כחטאת ומיירי לאחר זריקה. לה] ברו"ך. תימה לי לימא ליה שכן שינה את שמו לדבר האסור ולדבר המותר כדקאמר במתני' וכי פריך בסמוך לימא ליה שינוי בעלים א) לימא ליה הא דפריך במתני'. ברו"ך: **בשינוי** בעלים. ה"נ הוה מצי למימר אשם מצורע שקבל לו] דמו בדרום בכלי לשם שלמים יוכיח שהרי שינה שמו ושינה מקומו ושינה מעשיו דצריך קבלה ביד כדאמר בריש איזהו מקומן (לעיל דף מז:) שני כהנים מקבלין את דמו אחד ביד ואחד בכלי: **חטאת** העוף שעשאה למעלה כו'. משאר קדשי קדשים ששחטן בדרום לשם קדשים קלים לז] לא פריך שימשכו אלא מקינים דאמרי' (יומא דף מא.) אין הקינים מתפרשות אלא או בלקיחת בעלים או בעשיית כהן לח] הילכך תיהני נמי הכא שתימשך: **ועולת** העוף למטה ליתא. מתוך דברי רב אשי משמע דאי היתה למטה אע"פ דהאי בסימן אחד והאי בשני סימנין לא היתה נמשכת ונעשית חטאת העוף ותימה א"כ גבי חטאת העוף כיון דאמר מר מליקה בכל מקום במזבח כשירה למה ליה למימר מכי מלק בה סימן אחד מיפסלא בה לט] ב) האמר כיון דאין בה שינוי מקום אינה יכולה להימשך ועוד קשה דמשמע אם היתה נפסלת למעלה היתה נמשכת לעולה מ] ג) שהרי המקום גורס לה להמשך אם כן גבי עולה למה ליה טעמא דהאי בסימן אחד והאי בשני סימנין מא] ד) היתה נמשכת מחמת המקום ונעשית חטאת העוף ומפרש ה"ר חיים דכלל זה יהא בידך דלעולם אין הקרבן נמשך ליעשות קרבן אחר אלא מחמת שני טעמים שממשיכין אותו לפי שהיו פסולין בראשון וכשרים בשני הילכך גבי עולה צריכין שני טעמים דפסולה למטה וגם הכשרה בשני סימנין וכן חטאת העוף שעשאה למעלה פסולה היתה נמשכת מכח שני טעמים ואם תאמר עולת העוף שעשאה למעלה כמעשה חטאת תימשך ותיהוי חטאת דהא יש כאן שתי פסולות לעולה והכשירן לחטאת שהרי לא הבדיל והזה וי"ל שהמליקה מושכתו ובסימן ראשון ליכא פסול של עולה דנימא שתימשך ותיהוי חטאת והזאה מילתא אחריתי היא:

בתרי

א) גי' הצ"ק ליפרוך נימא ליה כו' ב) נימא כיון כו' צ"ק ג) צ"ל בסיה המקום צ"ק ד) צ"ל תיפוק ליה דהיתה כו' צ"ק

עין משפט נר מצוה

ח א מיי' פ"ג מהלכות מעילה הלכה א:

ט ב מיי' פ"ו מהלכות פסולי המוקדשין הלכה ו:

שיטה מקובצת

א] יוכיחו ששינה את שמם: ב] שאע"פ: ג] באשם ששינה את שמו ולא שינה את מקומו: ד] מקומה שימעלו בה: ה] ששינה את שמה ושינה את מקומה ושינה את מעשיה: ו] מקומה אשתיק אמר רבא אמאי אישתיק ונימא: ז] בעלים יוכיח ששינה: ח] מעשיו ומועלין בו: ט] אי הכי חטאת העוף נמי [כו'] תימשך כו'. הקשה בקונטרס למאי הלכתא תיעשת עולה אי לענין שלא תאכל כמו עולה הלא בלא זה נמי אינה נאכלת דחטאת שלא לשמה פסולה ואי למעילה חטאת שלא לשמה אינה יוצא מידי מעילה ותירץ בקונטרס לענין למיסק לחובה דקס"ד השתא דר' יהושע למיסק לחובה נמי קאמר אבל לפי המסקנא דקאמר לקמן דלמיסק לחובה לא אמר ר' יהושע לא פריך מידי ודוחק לומר כן דלא ידע המסקנא השתא ונראה להר"ם דלענין הקטרה קאמר דאם עלתה לא תרד כמו עולה כמו שאמר ר"י גבי עולה במתני' דאין מועלין שמע מינה דנמשכת להיות חטאת בכל ענין גם לענין הקטרה דאמרי' אם אפי' עלתה תרד כדין חטאת וה"ה לחיפך כדפי': י] כמעשה עולה לשם עולה מכי: יא] אחר באידך סימן תימשך: יב] ועולת העוף למטה ליתא. תימה דבהאי טעמא סגי דמש"ה תהא נמשכת דהמשכה תלויה לגמרי בשינוי מקום אבל גבי חטאת ליכא שינוי מקום וא"כ למה לי תו טעמא דזה בסימן אחד וזה בשני סימנין ואמר רבינו חיים דכלל זה כו' דבעינן ב' פסולים שינוי מקום ושינוי סימן וא"ת א"כ גבי חטאת העוף לימא האי טעמא לחוד דבכל מקום במזבח כשרה ולמה מאריך כל כך מכי מלק סימן אחד מיפסלא דהא כיון שאין בה ב' פסולים אינה נמשכת וי"ל דמ"מ אכתי יש שני פסולים בחטאת מחמת שינוי שעשאה כמעשה עולה דהא שחטה שלא לשמה דהוי פסול בחטאת ועיד דשני סימנין הלכך הוצרך לפרש דפסול ב' סימנין לא חשיב להיות נמשך לעולה משום דמיפסלא בסימן ראשון כדמסיק אבל גבי עולה דכשר שלא לשמה הוצרך לשינוי של סימנין וא"ת היא גופיה טעמא מאי דחטאת מיפסלא בסימן ראשון בשינוי השם אדרבה באותו סימן תמשוך ותהוי עולה ולא תיפסל מחמת שינוי השם וי"ל דכיון דאינה נמשכת

ע"י מפשיו צ"ק

דחטאת כשירה הוי הס"ד צ"ק

לעיל סג: וש"נ

נ"א מקום

רק ע"י שני פסולים א"כ קודם שבא פסול שני שמלק סימן שני כבר נפסלת מחמת חטאת שעשאה שלא לשמה דאכתי שם חטאת עליה והיינו דקאמר מכי מלק סימן אחד מיפסלא לה כלומר ועדיין שם חטאת עליה ולכך נפסלת דאכתי לא בא פסול שני וכאשר בא פסול שני היכא מימשכא והויא עולת העוף. לשון ת' מהר"ם: יג] העוף שעשאה למעלה כמעשה עולה לשם עולה כיון דאמר מר מלקה בכל מקום במזבח כשרה מכי מלק בה הד סימן הוי ליה חטאת העוף דאיפסלא כי הדר: יד] דאלו עולת בהמה ששינה את שמה לשם חטאת לא פליג רבי יהושע דהא: טו] חשיב ליה הס"ד: טז] והאי טעמא ליכא למימר בשינוי שום קרבן אחר: יז] ומעשיה כדמפרש: יח] בעולה אין בו היכר עולה במעשיה ותיבות לאו כלום היא נמחק: יט] ותו לא. אין לך בה מחלוקת אלא אותו ששנינו בתוכה דלא תיבות כדגרסינן לה נמחק: כ] עבודתה מהרה להשלים קודם שיחול עליה שם עולה: כא] סימנין ואין עבודת עולה נכרת בסימן ראשון שבה ועולת כו' ומתיבת ולפיכך עד תיבת ועולת העוף נמחק: כב] מר מלקה: כג] שינוי מעשה להפקיע ממנה כו' ואין כאן אלא שינוי: כד] כולה שלא: כה] קסלקא דעתיה ואפי' למיסק ליה לבעלים לשם חובת: כו] בדרום. תימה למ"ד מאי מועלין בהן מדרבנן תקשי ליה מאי שייך לעשות יוכיח בכאן דפליגי במעילה מן התורה וי"ל דמ"מ מייתי שפיר דאם איתא דעולת העוף נמשכת כששינה כה ונעשית חטאת ואין בה מעילה מן התורה א"כ קדשי קדשים ששחטן בדרום לא היה לנו להחמיר לנהוג בהן מעילה אפי' מדרבנן. תו' אחרות: כז] והיתר תאמר בעולה כו' וא"ת: כח] חטאת בהמה ששחטה לשם חטאת העוף תוכיח ששינה את שמה לדבר שכולו היתר ומועלין בה שהרי פסולה היא כשעשאה שלא לשמה סירו כו' ניחא ודוקא בעוף דליכא אלא סימן אחד כחטאת כדמפרש בגמ' ועי"ל דשמא ר"א דהכא סבר לה כר"ש דאמר בפ"ק דמנחות זאת תורת החטאת תורה אחת לכל החטאות וא"כ כי שחטה לשם חטאת העוף לא מיפסל בהכי. תו' אחרות: כט] בה דהא אות ו' נמחק: ל] סד"ה אמר ר"א עד ד"ה בשינוי מוקף בח"ל: לא] דמועלין. אלמא לא פקע קדושתו תימה: לב] זריקה כדפירש"י: לג] דמועלין דהא דקאמר אין מועלין היינו דוקא לאחר מיצוי מטעם דהיא נמשכת ונעשית חטאת העוף ואין בו מעילה כשעשאה בהכשר וא"כ לאחר עבודת הדם הוא ואז פקע מעילה מחטאת העוף אבל לפני זריקה דאכתי: לד] העוף מודה ר"י וצ"ל דר"א דהכא לטעמיה: לה] זריקה דאף לאחר זריקה אינו מוציא מידי מעילה וא"ת א"כ לימא ליה ר"י לדידי [אשם] כשר שלא לשמו כרבנן דפליג וי"ל משום דהוי מצי למיפרך ליה אף לדברי ר"י חטאת ששחטה בצפון לשם שלמים יוכיחו דבחטאת מודה ר"י דפסול שלא לשמה. (הר"פ): לו] שקיבל כל דמו: לז] קלים ועשו להם כל דין שלמים דאין נמשכין להיות להם דין שלמים דהא מוכח בסמוך דשינוי מקום גורם ההמשכה לא פריך שימשכו אלא מקינים דוקא משום דאמרינן: לח] כהן וכיון דעשיית כהן מהניא בהן הלכך כו' שתימשך אבל בשאר קרבנות לא מהני כלל עשיית כהן כך תירץ רבינו חיים וריב"א תירץ דדוקא בעופות דליכא אלא ב' מיני קרבנות חטאת או עולה שייך טעם המשכה דמיד ששינה מעשה עולה ועשאה מעשה חטאת נמשכת להיות חטאת אבל בבהמה היכא מוכח מתוך מעשיו דתהוי שלמים הרי יש הרבה קרבנות שדומין במעשיהן זה לזה: לט] בה כיון דאבר דאין: מ] לעולה שהיה המקום היבת שהרי ל"ש: מא] סימנין אפי' הוי תרווייהו בשני סימנין היתה כו':

י א מיי' פ"ח מהל' פסולי המוקדשין הלכה ח:
יא ב מיי' שם הל' ו:
יב ג מיי' שם הל' יא:
יג ד מיי' שם פרק י:
יד ה מיי' שם הל' ב:
טו ו מיי' שם הל' ג:

קנים פ"ג מ"ג
ג"ז שם מ"ד
ג"ז שם מ"ו

ת"ש *א חטאת לזו ועולה לזו עשה שתיהן למעלה מחצה כשר ומחצה פסול שתיהן למטה מחצה כשר ומחצה פסול אחת למעלה ואחת למטה שתיהן פסולות שאני אומר חטאת קרבה למעלה ועולה קרבה למטה נהי נמי דעולה קרבה למטה תימשוך ותהוי חטאת העוף אימור דא"ר יהושע בחד גברא א] בתרי גברי מי אמר ת"ש ג] *חטאת ב ועולה וסתומה ומפורשת עשה כולן למעלה מחצה כשר ומחצה פסול כולן למטה מחצה כשר ומחצה פסול ג חציין למעלה וחציין למטה ג] אינה כשירה אלא סתומה ד] ומתחלקת בינידהן ואילו מפורשין לא ואמאי נהי נמי דעולה קרבה למטה תימשוך ותיהוי חטאת העוף וכי תימא הא דלא כר' יהושע ומי מצית אמרת הכי ה] תא שמע *ד האשה שאמרה הרי עלי קן אם אלד זכר ילדה זכר מביאה שתי קינים אחת לנדרה ואחת לחובתה נתנתן לכהן הכהן צריך לעשותן שלש למעלה ואחת למטה לא עשה כן אלא עשה שתים למעלה וב' למטה ולא נמלך צריכה שתביא עוד פרידה אחת ותקריבנה למעלה ממין א' ו] ומשני מינין תביא שתים ה פרשה נדרה ז] [צריכה] להביא עוד ג' פרידין ממין אחד ומב' מינין ח] תביא ד' ו קבעה נדרה צריכה

בתרי גברי מי אמר. תימה היכי ס"ד מעיקרא שתימשך עולת לאה ותיעשה חטאת רחל ושמא ס"ד בשהתנה אם תיפסל לגבי דידה שיועיל לחבירתה אם יוכל ומסיק בתרי גברי מי אמר דלא איירי כלל בהתנו ומיהו לא משמע ליסנא הכי ונראה דמיירי לא] בשחייבין כל אחת חטאת ועולה ונתנו קן אחד לכהן לעשות ממנו חטאת לזו ועולה לזו והוברר איזו לחטאת ואיזו לעולה לב]והכי פריך דנהי דהקרבת עולה למטה תימשך ותהיה חטאת ותפטר מן החטאת שהיא עצמה חייבת ומשני בתרי גברי מי אמר דהיינו תרי גברי דכשנתנו שתיהן לכהן חטאת לרחל ועולה ללאה והכהן טעה לג] להקריב עולת לאה למטה כמעשה חטאת לשם חטאת שהיה סבור שהיא חטאת רחל איך תפטר לאה מחטאת שהיא חייבת משום דנמשכת עולתה ונעשית חטאת הרי לשם רחל עשאה ויש כאן שינוי בעלים וא"ת אמאי לא פריך מרישא דתנן במס' קינים (פ"ג מ"א) אחת לזו ואחת לזו שתים לזו ושתים לזו לח] [ג' לזו] וג' לזו ד) מחצה כשר ומחצה פסול חציו למעלה וחציו למטה את שלמעלה מחצה כשר ומחצה פסול ואת שלמטה מחצה כשר ומחצה פסול פי' כל קן וקן עומד בפני עצמו ולא שעשה מכל אחת חציו למעלה וחציו למטה אלא שלשה קינים שלימים עשה למעלה וג' שלימים עשה למטה והשתא מאותן שלימים שלמעלה אין כשר אלא העולות ומאותן שלמטה החטאות ואי בהנך דלמטה שתים מהן של אשה אחת לא מיפסלי מינייהו אלא פרידה א' דהא מיחייבא ג' חטאות וממשכה עולה ונעשת חטאת ואמאי תני דשלמטה מחצה כשר ומחצה פסול וי"ל דקתני הכי משום דאימר שלשתן של אשה אחת ואגב גררא לט] יפרש סיפא דהך בבא אחת לזו שתים לזו שלש לזו עשר לזו מאה לזו עשה כולן למעלה כו' עד חציה למעלה וחציו למטה המרובה כשר פירוש אותן ארבע נשים של אחת ושל שתים ושל שלש ושל עשר לא יצאו כלל ידי חובתן דאין יודעות אם כל קיניהן למעלה דמתיין חטאות או כל קיניהן למטה דמתיין עולה אבל אותן של מאה מ] אמרינן (קינין פ"ג) יש מהן מ"ב למעלה ומ"ב למטה דבין כולהו מא] קט"ז קינין וכשעשה כ"ח למעלה וכ"ח למטה דל מינייהו ט"ז דמספקא להו בהך נשי פש להו מ"ב ומתכשרי להו לכל הפחות מ"ב חטאות ומ"ב עולות: **חטאת** ועולה. לא הוה צריך למיתני אלא סתומה ומפורשת דבחטאת ועולה אין מרויח כלום:

נתנתן

חטאת לזו ועולה לזו. משנה היא במס' קינין (פ"ג מ"ג) ולקמן אמרינן סתם קינין רבי יהושע היא: חטאת לזו כו'. רחל שהיתה צריכה חטאת ללידתה ועולתה כבר קרבה ולאה היתה צריכה עולה שכבר קרבה חטאתה ולקחו קן בעירוב וקבעו פרידה אחת לחטאת רחל ופרידה אחת לעולת לאה ונתנום לכהן: עשה שתיהן למעלה. לשם עולה: מחצה ס] כשירה ומחצה פסולה. עולה כשירה וחטאת פסולה: תימשך כו'. ותצא ידי חובתה י] ממה נפשך אם חטאתה קרבה למטה הרי טוב ואם לאו הרי עולת חברתה קרבה למטה יא] ונעשית חטאת וחברתה אינה צריכה לה: בתרי גברי מי אמר. היאך קרבנה של זו יעלה לזו שאין לה חלק בו: חטאת ועולה סתומה ומפורשת עשה כולן למעלה מחצה כשר ומחצה פסול כולן למטה מחצה כשר ומחצה פסול חציין למעלה וחציין למטה אין כשר אלא סתומה יב] ומתחלקת ביניהן. ה"ג לה במסכת קינין (שם מ"ד) יג] שתי נשים שלקחו ג' קינין בעירוב זו צריכה עולה וקן שלם יד]א' חטאת וא' עולה דהיינו שתי עולות וחטאת וזו צריכה שתי חטאות ועולה ופירשו אחד מן הקינים טו] פרידה עולה לזו ופרידה חטאת לזו ואחד מן הקינין הניחו סתומה טז] לא פירשו איזה פרידה חטאת ואיזה פרידה עולה והג' פירשו פרידה זו עולה ופרידה זו חטאת אבל שמות בעלים לא נתפרשו הרי חטאת לזו ועולה לזו יז]וקן סתומה וקן מפורשת צריך להקריב ב' הקינים הללו סתם על שתיהן העולות למעלה וחטאות למטה והחטאת יח]לזו והעולה לזו צריך להקריב לשם בעלים ונתנום לכהן: עשה כולן למעלה. כסבור כולן עולות: מחצה כשר ומחצה פסול. כל החטאות פסולות וצריכות להביא כל יט] חטאות שעליהן: כולן למטה. כסבור כולן חטאות: מחצה כשר ומחצה פסול. כל העולות פסולות וצריכות להביא כל עולות שעליהן: חציין למעלה כו'. אין כשר בכולן אלא קן סתומה דהי מינייהו דעבד עולה והי מינייהו דעבד חטאת כשירה דקינין שלא נתפרשו בלקיחת בעלים כ] לא מתפרשות שוב אלא בעשיית כהן כגון דפשיטא ליה דכל קן וקן היה בפני עצמו ומכל כא] קן אחד עשה אחד למעלה ואחד למטה והיא מתחלקת ביניהם הואיל ובעירוב לקחום האחת יוצאה בה ידי חטאת והאחת יוצאה בה ידי עולה ויקחו קן אחד עוד ביניהן ויקריבו בתנאי אם עולה ראשונה לרחל וחטאת ללאה תהא בקן שניה זו עולה ללאה וחטאת לרחל ואם חילוף חילוף ואילו מפורשות לא אית בה כשירה אפילו פרידה: ואמאי. בשלמא חטאת ועולה שהיו מפורשים כג] לשם בעלים לא קשיא לן דהוו להו תרי גברי אלא קן מפורשת שלא היתה מפורשת כג] לשם בעלים אלא איזו פרידה חטאת ואיזו עולה כד] בין שתיהן היה בעירוב אמאי פסולה אותה פרידה שנעשית למטה כמעשה חטאת לשם חטאת נהי נמי דעולה הואי הואיל וקרבה למטה תימשך ותיהוי חטאת ולא יהו צריכות להביא בעירוב אלא עולה אחת ויאמרו אם עולת קן הסתומה לרחל תהא זו ללאה ואם היא ללאה תהא זו לרחל: וכי תימא הא דלא כרבי יהושע ומי מצית אמרת הכי: דקינין לאו רבי יהושע היא: תא שמע. דקינין רבי יהושע דתנן בסיפא דמסכת קינין האשה שאמרה כו' וקתני סיפא אמר רבי יהושע זהו שאמרו כו' אלמא סתמא דקינין רבי יהושע: כה] א) הרי עלי קן כו' ואחת לחובתה. ללידתה: שלש למעלן ואחת למטן. דנדרה שתיהן עולות וחובתה אחת לעולה ואחת לחטאת: עשה שתים למעלה ושתים למטה. כסבור שתי הקינין חובה עליה שמא יולדת בזוב היתה הוזקקה לקן לידה כו] וקן זיבה: ולא נמלך. בא לדעת על מה הביאתן: כז] צריכה שתביא עוד פרידה אחת ותקריבנו למעלה ממין אחד ומשני מינין תביא שתים. כלומר אם הראשונה מין אחד היו שני הקינין כח] תורין או שניהן בני יונה תביא עוד פרידה אחת מאותו המין לעולה ויצאה ידי הכל כט] שמקן שהקריב הכהן ראשון יצאה ידי לידתה שהרי לשם חובה קרב והשני נשאר לנדרה ונפסל גוזל אחד מהן בעשיית מטה והרי זה ל] יהיה תחתיו ואם הראשונה משני מינין היו קן תורים וקן בני יונה לא]ג)תביא שתים תור ובני יונה ויקריב שניהן למעלה משום דמספקא לן איזה קן משנים הראשונים קרב אחרון והוי לנדרה ונפסל ממנו גוזל אחד וצריכה להשלימו מאותו המין דתנן במסכת קינין (פ"ב מ"ה) אין מביאין תור כנגד בן יונה ולא בן יונה כנגד תור: פירשה נדרה. כשנדרה הרי עלי קן פירשה את המין שתביא ואינה יודעת מה פירשה אם תורים אם בני יונה והיא נתנה שני קינין לכהן כדאמרינן ועשה אחת למעלה ואחת למטה צריכה להביא עוד ג' פרידין למעלה ממין אחד לב] ומשני מינין תביא ארבע דכיון שפירשה ואינה יודעת מה פירשה מתחילתה הוזקקה להביא ג' קינין שנים לנדרה אחד מן התורים ואחד מן בני יונה דהא לא ידעה מה נדרה והשלישי לחובתה מאיזה מין שתרצה והיא הביאה שנים וקרב הראשון לחובתה ונשאר השני לנדרה ונפסל הימנו גוזל אחד הילכך אם ממין אחד היו הראשונים צריכה שתביא אחד מאותו המין להשלים הנפסל וקן שלם ממין אחר משום דלא ידעה מה פירשה ואם שני מינין היו צריכה שתביא ד' וכולן עולות משום דמספקא לן איזה מין קרב אחרון שצריכה להשלים מאותו המין גוזל הנפסל ג)ולהביא קן שלם ממין אחר שהרי אינה יודעת אם צריכה תור ושני בני יונה או בן יונה ושתי תורין לפיכך תביא שתי תורין ושני בני יונה ותאמר אחד מאילו שממין הנפסל יהיה תחתיו והשני יהא נדבה וקן השני יהא ספק לג] פירושה: קבעה נדרה. להביאה עם חובתה שאמרה הרי עלי קן להביאו עם חובתי ופירשתו ואינה יודעת מה פירשה כדאמרן והביאה שתי קינין ונתנתן לכהן ועשה כמו שאמרנו: *)צריכה שתביא עוד חמש פרידין למעלה ממין אחד ומשני מינים תביא שש. לד] [דכיון] דקבעה נדרה עם חובתה הוקבע עליה קרבן גדול שלש עולות יחד אם היתה יודעת מה פירשה וזו שלא ידעה מה פירשה

הוזקקה

*) שייך לקמן

יונה וב' תורים לשום ספק פירושה ולכך טוב לה שתביא ד' כאילו לא הביאה כלל כדפי': קבעה נדרה. להביא עם חובתה והביאה ד' ממין אחד צריכה להביא עוד ה' בני יונה לנדרה ועוד א' ממין שהביאה כדי שיהיה ממין חטאת חובתה משום דקבעה עולת חובתה דלקרבן גדול איכוין [צריכה] להביא ג' עולות ביחד דודאי אם עשה הכהן היה די לה בג' פרידין שנים ממין אחד ואחד מאותו המין שהיה קרב עולת חובתה שתי תורין עם חובתה ושתי יונים עם חובתה אבל עתה שנפסל אחד מן הראשונים א"כ לא שנדרה כלל שהרי צריכה להביא ג' עולות ביחד והנה לא קרב למעלה כי אם שנים ולכך ג' ממין אחד וב' ממין אחר כדפי' וריב"א הקשה היאך מביאה חובה אחרת כיון שמחובתה משום דקבעה נדרה להביא עם חובתה מש"ה לא פקעה תורת חובתה שיכולה להפסר ממנה עצמה אלא לפי שקבעה נדרה אתה מחייבה להביאה יחד וא"כ שנפסרת כבר מחובתה השניה כלום דאין חובה אחר חובה. ותירץ מורי דלא קשה מידי דודאי אותו שלישי שמביאה אינה מחובתה בראשונה ומ"מ מביאה חובה אחרת משום דהוי כאילו נדרה בשעת נדרה שאם חובתה שתחזור ותביא ג' עולות לנדרה לקיים קרבן גדול ולעולם אותו שלישי שמביאה אינה

חטאת לשם חטאת ונמשכת להיות חטאת העוף (והחטאת) [וחבירתה כו'] תיבת ונעשית נמחק ונמחק: יב] סתומה והיא מתחלקת ביניהן: יג] קינין וה"פ: יד] שלם דהיינו שני פרידין א': טו] ה... טז] סתומה ולא פירשו: יז] לזו אלו שני קנים הם סתומים ויש לכהן להקריב ב' והשאר נמ... של זו והעולה של זו צריך: יט] להביא כל החטאת: כ] בעלים תלויות בעשיית כהן... והשאר נמחק: כא] תיבת קן נמחק: כב] מפורשים להם שם בעלים: כג] להם בעלים אל... לשם נמחק: כד] עולה ובין שתיהן: כה] תיבות הרי עלי קן כו' נמחק: כו] לידה ולקן... ה"ג צריכה: כח] הקינין החובה והנדבה תורין: כט] הכל שקן שהקריב: ל] זה יהא ת... כלומר אם כו': לא] יונה ואינה יודעת מאיזה מין נעשית חובתה תביא שתים תור ובן יונ... כלומר אם הראשונים מין אחר היו ומשני: לג] ספק פירושי שהרי אינה יודעת מה תביא ל... קבעה נדרה. קבעתו להביאה עם כו' קן כשאלד זכר להביאו עם חובתה ופירשה ואינה יו... דכיון דקבעה: לה] בשחייבת כל: לו] לעולה ולהכי פריך דנהי דקרבה עולה: לז] טעה והקריב... לזו כו' עשה כולן למעלה מחצה. תיבת ג' לזו וג' לזו ל"ש ונמחק: לט] גררא אפרש ד... מס"ג יש מהן תיבת אמרינן ל"ש ונמחק: מא] כולהו הוו קט"ז:
*) [אולי צ"ל ולא מהני פירושה רק לנדרה שלא פירש וכו']

הגהות צ"ק ... צ"ל דליש אחת לנדבתה דאמרה הרי עלי קן הס"ד ואח"כ ד"ה ואחת לחובתה: ב) [נ"ל תביא שתים פרידה אחת תור ופרידה אחת בן יונה]: ג) צ"ל ולהביא קן שלם ממין אחד לא כגי שהרי כו': ד) צ"ל כו' מה"ל:

offering.' [67b] Come and hear: In the case of a sin-offering for one and a burnt-offering for the other,[3] if he [the priest] offered both above [the red line],[4] half is fit and half is unfit;[5] [if he offered] both below, half is fit and half is unfit;[5] [if he offered] one above and one below, both are unfit, for I assume that he offered the sin-offering above and the burnt-offering below.[6] Yet even granted that he did offer the burnt-offering below, let it be transmuted into a bird sin-offering?[7]—Granted that R. Joshua ruled thus in the case of one man, did he rule so in the case of two men?[8]

Come and hear: In the case of a sin-offering and a burnt-offering and an unspecified [sacrifice] and a specified [sacrifice],[9] if he
a [the priest] offered all of them above,[1] half are fit and half are unfit;[2] [if he offered] all of them below, half are fit and half are unfit.[2] [If he offered] half of them above and half of them below, only the undefined [pair] are fit,[3] and they share them.[4] Thus, the defined ones are not [fit]. Yet why so? even granted that he offered the burnt-offering below, let it be transmuted into a sin-offering?[5] And should you answer, This does not agree with R. Joshua—can you say so? Surely we learnt:[6] If a woman declared, I vow a pair of birds if I give birth to a male child,[7] and she bore a male child, she must bring two pairs, one for her vow, and one for her statutory obligation. When she gives them to the priest, the priest must offer three above and one below.[8] If he did not do thus, but offered two above and two below, not having consulted her,[9] she must bring another bird and offer it above, [if both were] of the same species.[10] But if they were of two species,[11] she must bring two [birds].[12] If she defined her vow, she must bring another three birds [and offer them] above [the line], [if both were] of the same species; [if they were] of two species, she must bring four.[13] If she

(3) After birth confinement a woman, if poor, brings two birds for a burnt-offering and a sin-offering (Lev. XII, 8). Now, two women had each brought one bird for a burnt-offering and a sin-offering respectively. Then they bought a brace together, appointed one bird for a sin-offering and one for a burnt-offering, as each required, and gave them to the priest. (4) I.e., as burnt-offerings. (5) What is offered in the right place is fit; the other is unfit. (6) I.e., he may have done so. (7) So that there should be no further liability to a sin-offering. (8) Obviously not. For one woman's burnt-offering cannot acquit the other woman of her liability to a sin-offering. (9) Rashi: Two women, A an B, each owed a bird burnt-offering and a bird sin-offering (e.g., on account of confinement). In addition A owed another bird burnt-offering and B another bird sin-offering (either on account of another confinement or on account of sin. Lev. V, 7—, each having brought so far one sacrifice only). Now, A and B accordingly bought three pairs of birds in conjunction. They took one of the pairs and appointed one bird a burnt-offering for A and one a sin-offering for B. The second pair they left unspecified, not stating which was a burnt-offering and which a sin-offering. The third they did specify, i.e., they appointed one for a burnt-offering and the other for a sin-offering, but did not state the owner of each. V. Ḳin. III, 3.

a (1) As burnt-offerings. (2) Cf. *supra* n. 5. The women still owe the sacrifices which are now unfit. (3) Since the owners did not define them, it depends on the priest. (4) One sacrifice counting to each. V. ibid. 4. (5) For since the owners were not specified, the answer given above obviously no longer applies. (6) Emended text (Sh. M.); cur. edd. 'Come and hear'. (7) In addition to her statutory obligation. (8) A sin-offering cannot be vowed. Hence the additional pair are both burnt-offerings, which makes three in all. These naturally must be offered above the red line. (9) Why she brought two pairs. Thus he thought that *both* pairs were statutory obligations. (10) If both pairs were turtle-doves or young pigeons. (11) One pair were turtle-doves, and the other pair were young pigeons. (12) One bird of one pair has become unfit, and the pair must be completed with a bird of the same species. Since we do not know which bird actually became unfit, she must bring another two, viz., a turtle-dove and a pigeon. (13) When she vowed, she declared which birds she would bring, but subsequently forgot which she had vowed. Hence when she came to fulfil her vow, she needed *two* pairs for the vow alone, viz., a pair of turtle-doves and a pair of pigeons, to cover both contingencies, and in addition one pair of either on account of her statutory obligation, i.e., three pairs in all. She, however, had brought only two pairs of which the first was offered for her statutory obligation, while the second was left for her vow, and of that one bird became unfit. Therefore she now owes one bird of the same species to replace the unfit one, and a pair of the *other* species, in case it was the other species that she had vowed. But if the two pairs which she had brought were of different species, she must now bring *four* birds, all for burnt-offerings, because we do not know which species was offered second for the vow, and it is that species which must be completed. She cannot simply bring a pair of one species, for she does not know whether she owes one turtle-dove and two pigeons, or *vice versa*. Therefore she must bring two turtle-doves and two pigeons and declare: 'Let one of these, of the species which I vowed, replace the one that became unfit, and let the second of that pair be another votive offering. And let the second pair cover the doubt of my definite declaration.'

fixed [the time of] her vow, [68*a*] she must bring another five
birds [to be sacrificed] above, [if she had vowed] of one species; if
a of two, she must bring six.[1] If she gave them to the priest, but
does not know what she gave; and the priest went and offered them,
but he does not know how he offered them, she now requires four
birds on account of her vow and two on account of her statutory
obligation, and one sin-offering. Ben 'Azzai said: Two sin-offerings.
R. Joshua observed: This is the case where they [the Sages] said:
When it is alive it has one voice, and when it is dead, it has seven
b voices![1] —Granted that R. Joshua ruled thus in respect of liberating
it from trespass, did he rule thus in respect of converting it into an
obligatory offering?[2]

MISHNAH. [IN REGARD TO] ALL UNFIT PERSONS WHO
PERFORMED MELIKAH, THE MELIKAH IS INVALID, AND THEY
c [THE SACRIFICES] DO NOT DEFILE IN THE GULLET.[1] IF HE
[THE PRIEST] NIPPED [THEM] WITH HIS LEFT [HAND] OR AT
NIGHT; IF HE SLAUGHTERED ḤULLIN WITHIN[2] OR A SACRI-
FICE WITHOUT [THE TEMPLE COURT], THEY DO NOT DEFILE
IN THE GULLET.[3] IF HE NIPPED WITH A KNIFE; OR IF HE NIPPED

a (1) If she vowed to bring the additional offerings at the same time as her statutory obligation, and then brought two pairs of birds to the priest, who offered them as above, she owes another five or six, as stated. For her vow made her liable to three burnt-offerings *together*, had she remembered what she had vowed. As she did not remember, she required five burnt-offerings in the first place, one for her statutory obligation, and four consisting of a pair of pigeons and a pair of turtle-doves, since she did not know which she owed. Now, what she has already brought does not count, for she does not know these were the birds which she had vowed. Nor can she simply bring another four on account of the vow, since these must be sacrificed at the same time as the statutory offering. Hence she must now bring five, one for the statutory offering and four on account of the vow, whilst the first which was sacrificed as her statutory obligation will count as a votive offering. If, however, she had vowed them of two species, she does not know which species she owes. Therefore she must bring six: viz., two turtle-doves and two pigeons on account of the doubt of what she had specified, and one turtle-dove and one pigeon, because the former had to be offered at the same time as her statutory obligation.

b (1) If she gave the birds to the priest but does not know whether they were turtle-doves or pigeons, or a pair of each, and she does not know how the priest sacrificed them, whether all above or all below or half above and half below, perhaps she did not even fulfil her statutory obligation. For he may have sacrificed *all* above, so that she lacks a sin-offering; or all below, and she lacks a burnt-offering. She must then bring four birds for her vow, since she does not remember which of the two species she specified, and two for her statutory burnt-offering, viz., a turtle-dove and a pigeon, as possibly the first were all offered below, as sin-offerings, and now she requires a burnt-offering of the same species. Or perhaps the first were offered half above and half below, and she has fulfilled her obligation with the first pair offered. But as she had vowed to bring a burnt-offering at the same time and of the same species as the statutory burnt-offering, she must now bring a turtle-dove and a pigeon to cover this doubt. In addition, she must bring one sin-offering of whichever species she wishes, for perhaps the first were all offered below, and this will combine with the bird she brought as her burnt-offering. Though she has already brought the latter, yet the sin-offering need not be of the same species as the *first*, according to the Rabbis who disagree with Ben 'Azzai, for they hold that it all depends on the sin-offering. Therefore, since she must bring two burnt-offerings, as explained, that of the same species as the sin-offering combines with it. But Ben 'Azzai holds that it all depends on the first, i.e., a sin-offering must be brought of the same species as the first burnt-offering which was *correctly* offered for her statutory obligation. Now, perhaps all the first were offered above, in which case she has fulfilled this obligation, and so she must bring a sin-offering of the same species. As, however, she does not know which species this was, she must bring two sin-offerings, one of each. R. Joshua observes that this is similar to what the Rabbis said about a ram, that when it is alive it has one voice only, but when it is dead it has seven: i.e., the two horns are used for two trumpets (bugle-horns); out of the two legs two reed-pipes (flutes) are made; the skin is used for tabrets; the entrails for a lyre, and the guts for harps. In a similar way here too, when she vowed and did not know what she had specified, she merely required four birds and two for her statutory obligation. Whereas now that she has already brought four, she still needs another eight, four on account of her vow and four on account of her obligation; v. Ḳin. III, 6.—Since *R. Joshua* makes this comment, you may infer that he accepts these laws; hence the difficulty of 67*b*. (2) Surely not! This is the answer to the difficulty: The burnt-offering is transmuted only in so far that it no longer involves trespass, but the deviation in its rites cannot turn it into a sin-offering to acquit its owner of his obligation for same.

c (1) V. *supra* 50*b* n.b 1. Although the *meliḳah* is invalid, it frees the birds from uncleanness. The reason is because they became unfit in the sanctuary, and the *meliḳah* is effective in that if they are taken up on to the altar, they are not removed. Therefore the birds are not regarded as *nebelah*. (2) A bird of *ḥullin*, with ritual *shechitah*. (3) Although there must be no *shechitah* (of birds of *ḥullin*) within, or of consecrated birds anywhere at all, yet these do not defile.

צריכה שתביא עוד חמש פרידין למעלה ממין אחד ומב' מינין תביא שש *נתנתן לכהן ואינה יודעת מה נתנה הלך הכהן ועשה ואינו יודע מה עשה צריכה ד' פרידין לנדרה ושתים לחובתה וחטאת אחת בן עזאי אומר ב' חטאות א"ר יהושע זהו שאמרו כשהוא חי קולו אחד וכשהוא מת קולו ז' אימר דא"ר יהושע לאפוקה מידי מעילה למיסק ליה לחובה מי אמר : **מתני'** *ב(כל הפסולין שמלקו מליקתן פסולה ואינו מטמא בבית הבליעה) מלק בשמאל או בלילה גשחט חולין בפנים וקדשים בחוץ אינן מטמאות בבית הבליעה א] *מלק בסכין מלק חולין בפנים וקדשים בחוץ

תורין

רש"י

הוזקקה להביא חמש עולות יחד מתחילתה אחת לחובתה וד' לנדרה ג] וכשהביאה שני קינין אחת לנדרה ואחת לחובתה וממין אחד לא עשתה כלום לנדרה שמא אינו ממין שנדרה ובהשלמת קן שני ממין *אחד לא סגי לה שהרי קובעתו ג] לבא עם מין חובתה וא"ת תביא *קן ממין אחד ופרידה ממין שהביאה שני קינין הראשונים ד] שקרב ממנו עולות חובתה דממ"נ אם תורין נדרה הרי הביאה תורין עם מין שהביאה לחובתה ואם בני יונה נדרה הרי הביאה ב' בני יונה עם מין שקרב ממנו חובתה אם לא נפסל גוזל אחד מן הראשונים ה"נ אבל עכשיו שנפסל אחד מהם אין חבירו עולה לה כלום דג' עולות הוקבעו עליה יחד הילכך אם ב' קינים הראשונים מין אחד היו צריכה שתביא עוד ה' עולות ג' מאותו המין וב' ממין אחר ה] ד' לספק פירושה ואחד לקביעותה שקבעה להביא עולת חובתה עם נדרה וחובתה כבר קרבה ויצאה ידיה אלא שצריכה להביא מאותו המין עם נדרה מפני קביעותה : ואם משני מינין היו תביא שש . שאינה יודעת איזה מין קרב תחילה לחובתה שתביא ו] מאותו המין עם ד' של ספק פירושה לקביעותה הילכך תביא שם שתי תורין ושני בני יונה לספק פירושה ותור *ובני יונה לקביעותה והעוף היתר יהא נדבה : נתנתן לכהן ואין ידוע מה נתנה . אם תורים אם בני יונה ואם קן אחד מזה וקן אחד מזה ז] ואין ידוע מה עשה אם כולן למעלה או כולן למטה או חציין למעלה וחציין למטה כמנהגה שלא יצאת אפי' ח] (ימי לידתה) שמא כולן למעלה ואין כאן חטאת או שמא כולן למטה ואין כאן עולה : צריכה שתביא עוד ד' פרידין לנדרה . לספק פירושה ט] ומשני מינין וב' לעולת חובתה תור ובן יונה שמא הראשונים כולן למטה נעשו ואינה יודעת מאיזה מין והכל הולך אחר החטאת [וצריכה] להביא עולה מאותו מין או שמא הראשונים חציין למעלה וחציין למטה ובקן שקרב ראשון יצאתה ידי חובתה והיא קבעה להביא עולה מאותו המין עם נדרה ואינה יודעת איזה מין היה הילכך תביא עם ספק פירושה תור ובן יונה וממה נפשך אם קן שקרב ראשון תורין היו וקרב מהן עולה למעלה והיא לחובתה הרי היא מביאה עכשיו תור עם נדרה משום קביעותה ואם מבני יונה היה והוקבע עליה להביא בן יונה עם נדרה הרי מביאתו ואם כולן למטה נעשו וצריכה להביא עולתה מאותו המין הרי שתים שהיא מביאה עכשיו לחובתה יעלה לה אחד מהן והשני נדבה : וחטאת י] אחת . תביא מאיזה מין שתרצה משום שמא הראשונים כולן למעלה נעשו והרי יא] לו זוג ממינו לעולה מב' שהביאה חובתה מב' מינין ואע"פ שכבר קרבה עולת חובתה אין צריכה לדקדק להביא חטאת מאותו מין הראשון לרבנן דפליגי עליה דבן עזאי דקסברי הכל הולך אחר חטאת הילכך הואיל ועל כרחה היא מביאה עכשיו ב' עולות תזווג יב] לו אותה שממינו ודייה דהכי תנן פלוגתייהו במסכת קינים (פ"ב מ"ה) שהאשה שהביאה עולתה תור וחטאתה בן יונה תכפול ותביא עולתה בן יונה דהכל הולך אחר חטאת בן עזאי אומר הכל הולך אחר הראשון : בן עזאי אומר ב' חטאות . בן עזאי לטעמיה דאמר הכל הולך אחר הראשון וכיון דאיכא לספוקא שמא הראשונים למעלה נעשו וכבר יצאת ידי עולה צריכה להביא חטאתה מאותו המין והרי אינה יודעת מאיזה מין היה לפיכך תביא שתי חטאות מב' מינין וחטאות הללו אינן נאכלות שהרי על הספק באו ואין מליקתן מליקה להתירן באכילה שמא כבר קרבה חטאתה בראשונות : א"ר יהושע זהו שאמרו כשהוא חי קולו אחד כשהוא מת קולו ז' . התם מפרש לה ובאיל קמיירי דכשהוא חי אין לו אלא קול אחד וכשהוא מת קולו שבעה כיצד קולו שבעה ב' קרניו ב' חצוצרות ב' שוקיו ב' חלילין עורו לתוף מעייו לנבלים בני מעיו לכינורות וה"נ כשנדרה תחלה ואינה יודעת מה פירשה לא יג] צריכה אלא ד' פרידין וב' לחובתה אחת לעולה ואחת לחטאת ועכשיו שהביאה כבר ד' פרידין צריכה להביא יד] ד' לנדרה וד' לחובתה מדאיירי ר' יהושע בהא ש"מ קינין ר' יהושע אמרה וקתני לעיל גבי קן סתומה ומפורשת דאין כשר אלא סתומה ואי אמרת נמשכה ונעשית חטאת העוף תמשך ותהוי חטאת העוף : אימר דאר"י לאפוקה מידי מעילה למיסק ליה לשם חובה מי אמר . שתהא עולה נעשית חטאת בשביל ששינה בה : מתני' כל הפסולין . בגמ' פליגי כל לאיתויי מאי : ואין מטמאין . שמליקתן מטהרתן לפי טו] שנפסל בקדש והני מליקתן שאם עלו לא ירדו הילכך נמי לא הוו נבילה : ה"ג טז] שחט חולין בפנים וקדשים בחוץ אינן מטמאין בבית הבליעה . אף על גב דבפנים אין שחיטה לעוף וכן בעוף קדשים אין שחיטה *בכל מקום אין מטמאין כדיליף בברייתא בגמרא ושחט קדשים בפנים דלא קתני אמרינן בגמ' דאתיא בזה הכלל : מלק בסכין . ומליקה לא הויא דבעצמו של כהן בעינן ושחיטה לא הויא כדאמרינן בהכל שוחטין (חולין דף כ:) מפני שהוא מחליד יז] *מפני שהוא דורס : מלק חולין בפנים וקדשים בחוץ . דלא שייכא מליקה בחולין לא בפנים ולא בחוץ והוא הדין לחולין בחוץ ובגמרא אמרינן דאתיא בזה הכלל :

תוספות

נתנתן לכהן ואינה יודעת מה נתנה . בחנם דחק הקונטרס לאוקמה בשקבעה נדרה עם חובתה דהך בבא מיתוקמא שפיר בשלא קבעה יח] : כשהוא חי קולו אחד כשהוא מת קולו ז' . מפרש במסכת קינין (פ"ג מ"ו) קרניו לחצוצרות משמע דחצוצרות שלא מן הכסף וכן משמע בפרק כל הצלמים (ע"ז דף מז. ושם) דבעי רמי בר חמא המשתחוה לבהמה קרניה מהו לחצוצרות ותימה דבהקומץ רבה (מנחות דף כח.) תניא חצוצרות היתה באה מן העשת של כסף מיהו מההיא לא קשה כולי האי דהתם בשל משה שלא היו כשרות לדורות כדמשמע התם אבל קשה ממסכת תמיד (דף לו) *דתנן ושתי חצוצרות של כסף בידם משמע דאף לדורות בשל כסף ותירץ ר"ת דשני ענייני חצוצרות היו של כהנים בשל כסף ושל לויים בשל קרני בהמה לכלי שיר ועוד י"ל דחצוצרות דקינים ודמסכת ע"ז היינו שופר כדאמר בסוף במה מדליקין (שבת דף לו.) ובפרק לולב הגזול (סוכה דף לד.) דאישתני שמהתייהו חצוצרתא שיפורא שיפורא חצוצרתא ובסוף במה מדליקין (שבת דף לו.) איכא ברייתא שקוראה לחצוצרות שופר ומיהו קשה דבמסכת עבודה זרה איירי במכשירי קרבן כדאמר התם ועל הקרבן לא היו תוקעין בשופר אלא בחצוצרות כדכתיב ותקעתם בחצוצרות על עולותיכם ועל זבחי שלמיכם (במדבר י) : **אימר** דא"ר יהושע (בן לוי) לאפוקה מידי מעילה למיסק ליה לחובה מי אמר . תימה מ"ש זו מזו וי"ל דכי האי גוונא אשכחן פ"ק *דמנחות (דף יב.) דזריקה מועלת ליוצא ושירים שחסרו בין קמילה להקטרה שאסורין באכילה והקטרתן מוציאן מידי מעילה וזריקת פיגול (ר"ל) בפ"ק דמעילה (דף ג:) דמפקא מידי מעילה אע"ג דלא עלה לשם חובה וי"מ דמדאורייתא נמשכה ונעשה חטאת גמורה ותקנתא דרבנן היא דאינו עולה לשם חובה וצ"ל דקסבר ר' יהושע אין שחיטה לעוף מן התורה וחולין בעזרה לאו דאורייתא יט] כדאמר בנזיר (דף כט.) גבי מדיר בנו בנזיר למ"ד כדי לחנכו במצות ואי נמי קסבר חולין בעזרה דאורייתא חיה ועוף לאו דאורייתא כדאשכחן כ] גבי ר"ש בפ' כיסוי הדם (חולין דף פה:) דקסבר דאורייתא ואפ"ה חיה ועוף לאו דאורייתא ולית ליה ההיא דרשה כא] בפ"ב דקדושין (דף נז: נח.) דמרבה בעופות וא"ת למ"ד לאו דאורייתא למאי איצטריך קרא לחטאת העוף באה על הספק דהא ר' יוסי בר חנינא דאמר לאו דאורייתא כדמוכח בנזיר ומצריך קרא לחטאת העוף באה על הספק וי"ל דאתא קרא למימר להביא על הספק כמו בבהמה אשם תלוי :

מלק בשמאל או בלילה אין מטמאין בבית הבליעה . לכאורה כולה מתניתין ר"ש היא דאמר לקמן בפרק המזבח מקדש (דף פד.) שכל שפסולו בקודש אם עלה לא ירד דהא אמרינן בגמרא דמליקה המתרת את האיסור פי' דאם עלה לא ירד אינה מטמאה בבית הבליעה ומליקת לילה לר' יהודה תרד כדאמר בפ' המזבח מקדש (שם) פרט לנשחטה בלילה וכן לעיל דתנן וכולן אין מטמאין בבית הבליעה והיינו *בשחיטת דרום כב] דתרד לר' יהודה כדאמר כג] בשמעתין קמייתא דמעילה (דף ג:) אלא מתניתין ר"ש היא ותימה אי כר' שמעון האמר דמליקת שמאל מליקה גמורה היא למאי דגרס ר"ת לעיל בפ"ב (דף כד:) מלק בשמאל פסול א) ורבי כד] יהודה מכשיר וי"ל דסבר ליה כוותיה בחדא ופליג עליה בחדא א"נ *מודה ר' יהודה בעוף דכל שפסולו בקודש אם עלה לא ירד דהנך תלתא מיעוטי דלקמן בבהמה כתיבי ומיהו על כרחין חד מינייהו בעוף דלא תימא כל פסולי דעוף אם עלה לא ירד : **שחט** חולין בפנים וקדשים בחוץ . בגמ' נפקא לן כה] דמשום שחיטה אינה מטמאה בבית הבליעה אע"ג דאינה מתרת את האיסור : **מלק** בסכין . פירש בקונטרס ב) דמחליד לפי שנועץ ראשו של סכין משום דאינו רוצה לחתוך רוב בשר קודם הסימנין ואי אפשר לומר כן בפ' קמא דחולין (דף כ:) דהתם קרי ליה מחליד אע"ג דסלקא דעתך שחותך רוב בשר והתם פי' בקונטרס דלאחר שנתפרקו פירקי העצם כו] ניגעץ הסכין תחת העצם והויא חלדה ולפי' זה לא איירי בסכין רחבה ונראה דחשיב חלדה לפי ששוחט הסימנין ממטה למעלה ואפילו בסכין רחבה :

א) נ"ל ורבי שמעון מכשיר ב) כרש"י שלפנינו לא נמצא

עין משפט נר מצוה

טז א מיי' פ"ז מהלכות פסה"מ הלכה ג :

יז ב מיי' פ"ז מהל' פסה"מ הל"ח והל"ט :

יח ג מיי' פ"ז מהל' פסה"מ הל"ג ופ"ג מהל' אבות הטומאה הלכה יב :

[פ"ז מ"ג ועי' תוי"ט]

גי' צ"ק דמנחות דבירים שחסרו בין כו' מידי מעילה וזריקה מועלת ליוצא ופיגול כדאמרינן בפ"ק דמעילה כו' ונמחקו לעיל תיבות דזריקה מועלת ליוצא :

מסורת הש"ס

אחר צ"ק

נ"א קן ופרידה ממין אחד

[בקצת נוסחאות גרסי' להך בבא בסיום המשנה]

[חולין כ: כח.]

צ"ל ובן יונה

נ"א ידי חובתה

הכל מקום צ"ק

צ"ל או

שיטה מקובצת

א] מלק בסכין כו'. פ"ה דמליקה דסכין לא מהני לטהר מידי נבילה כדמפרש בסיפא משום דלא הוי פסולו בקודש וא"ת מ"מ יטהר משום שחיטה ונהי דכבר חתך המפרקת מ"מ להוי כשוחט את הטריפה דשחיטה מטהרת מידי נבילה וי"ל דבחולין פ"ק פריך ליה ומשני מפני שהוא מחליד והוי שחיטה פסולה ופ"ה לשם לפי שהסכין נסגר בין פרקי העצם כו' וקשה דמי לא עסקינן שחותך בסכין רחבה שאינו מכוסה לכך פר"י דמשום הכי הויא חלדה לפי שחותך הסימנין לצד המפרקת דהיינו מאחוריהן דהתורה אמרה לשחוט לצד הצואר ומקרי חלדה בין סכין למעלה בין הסימן לאחוריו בין הוא למטה מן הסימנים ולא הקפידה התורה רק שיחתוך הסימן דרך שחיטה לצד הצואר דכששוחט לצד אחר שכנגדו הוי כאילו חתכו מלמטה למעלה וכמו כן אם היה שוחט מצד הצואר אפי' היו הסימנין על גבי הסכין לא הויא חלדה רק בעופא דקליל אמרינן בחולין שמא ידרוס : ב] לנדרה או להביא ששה בשתי פעמים שתי תורים עם עולת חובה ושני בני יונה ופרידה אחת ממין חובתה בקרבן אחד וכשהביאה : ג] קובעתו להביא עם : ד] הראשוני' שכבר קרב ממנו : ה] אחר שתי קינין משתי מינין לספק ותיבת ד' נמחק : ו] שתביא פרידה מאותו המין לקביעותה עם ד' של ספק פירושה הילכך תביא שש כו' ותור ובן יונה לקביעותה : ז] מזה ואינה יודעת מה עשה : ח] אפי' ידי לידתה שמא ותיבת ימי נמחק : ט] פירושה משני מינין : י] וחטאת ס"א ופרידה אחת לחטאתה אע"פ שאינה יודעת מאיזה מין היו הראשונים תביא חטאת אחת ממין שתרצה דאם הראשונים קרבו למעלה ולא יצאת ידי חטאת ולכך תביא חטאת מאחד המינין ותאמר אם זה ממין הראשונים הרי זה בן זוג לעולת חובתי שקרבה כבר ואם מין אחר הוא יזדוג עם פרידת מינו שאני מביאה עמו מן השנים שהם תור ויונה שהיא מביאה באחרונה לספק עולת חובתה ורבנן דפליגי הכא עליה דבן עזאי לטעמייהו דאמרי במס' קינים האשה שהביאה כו' : יא] והרי לה זוג ממינו לעולה אחר מב' שהביאה לחובתה מב' מינין : יב] תזווג לה אותה : יג] לא היתה צריכה אלא ד' פרידין לנדרה ס"א שתים לעולת נדרה וב' לחובתה : יד] להביא עוד שמנה ד' : טו] לפי שנפסלו בקדש [לשון הרב רבינו ר' בצלאל אשכנזי ס"א והיא גירסת רוב הספרים וכן כל מה שיש באלו העשרה דפין שזה אחר זה בדפוס אינו גירסת לשון רש"י ז"ל ולשון רש"י רשמתי בחוץ בשם נוסחאות רש"י כ"י] : טז] ה"ג במתניתין שחט : יז] מחליד ומפני שהוא : יח] עיין בהשמטות בסוף המסכת : יט] דאורייתא כדאמרי' בנזיר בפרק הריני נזיר ושמע חבירו ואמר ואני גבי : כ] כדאשכחן ר"ש תיבת גבי נמחק : כא] דרשה דפ"ב דקדושין דמרבה עופות וא"ת : כב] בשחיטת דרום עיין לעיל בתוס' [דף סו ע"א] בד"ה והרי קדשי קדשים : כג] בשמעתא קמייתא : כד] ור' שמעון מכשיר : כה] לן דשי' אות מ' נמחק : כו] העצם ולפי שאין העצם מתפשט לכאן ולכאן כדרך שאר בית השחיטה אלא עומד במקומו וכשהסכין תחת העצם הויא חלדה ולפי' זה אות ו' נמחק :

נוסחאות רש"י כת"י

מלק בשמאל . דמליקתו פסולה דכתיב בה הכהן וכל מקום שנאמר אצבע וכהונה אינו אלא ימין : או בלילה . דכתיב ביום צותו . וכן גירסת רש"י של מהר"ם : מלק בסכין . ס"א לא מליקה ולא שחיטה היא שהרי בראשו של סכין יסלוק דהא מליקה בציפורן היא ותותך שדרה ומפרקת עד שהוא מגיע לסימן וצריך לעשות ע"י חיתוך קצת שלא יחתוך רוב בשר עד שיגיע לסימן כדאמרן בפירקין דלעיל וכשהוא עושה בסכין אי אפשר אלא בראש הסכין שקורין פונטא ונמצא מחליד כדאיתא בפרק קמא דחולין :

גליון הש"ס

תוד"ה מלק וכו' מודה ר"י בעוף . עיין לקמן דף פד ע"ב תד"ה ומוליא אני בסה"ד . ועי' כריס מעילה תד"ה ורבה :

יט א ב מיי' פ"ז מהל' פסה"מ הל"ב:

תורה אור

*תורין שלא הגיע זמנן ובני יונה שעבר זמנן שיבשה גפה א] שניסמית עינה ושנקטעה רגלה מטמא בבית הבליעה ב] זה הכלל *כל שפסולו בקודש אינו מטמא בבית הבליעה לא היה פסולו בקודש מטמא בבית הבליעה: **גמ'** אמר רב שמאל ולילה אין מטמאין בבית הבליעה זר וסכין מטמאין בבית הבליעה מאי שנא שמאל דאית ליה הכשירה ביוה"כ ולילה אית ליה הכשירה באיברים ופדרים זר נמי אית ליה הכשירה בשחיטה *שחיטה לאו עבודה היא ולא *והא"ר זירא שחיטת פרה בזר פסולה ומחוי רב עלה אלעזר וחוקה שאני *פרה דקדשי בדק הבית היא ולא כל דכן הוא קדשי בדק הבית בעו כהונה קדשי מזבח מיבעיא אמר רב שישא בריה דרב אידי מידי דהוה אמראות נגעים דלאו עבודה היא ובעיא כהונה ג] ונילף מבמה *מבמה לא יליף ולא ד] והתניא *) מנין ליוצא שאם עלה לא ירד שהרי יוצא כשר בבמה ה] תנא °אזאת תורת העולה סמיך ליה ורבי יוחנן אמר זר אין מטמא אבית הבליעה סכין מטמא אבית הבליעה תנן כל הפסולין שמלקו מליקתן פסולה בשלמא לר' יוחנן כל לאיתויי זר אלא לרב כל לאיתויי מאי לאו לאיתויי שמאל ולילה בהדיא קתני תני והדר מפרש תא שמע זה הכלל כל שהיה פסולו בקודש אינו מטמא בגדים אבית הבליעה בשלמא לרבי יוחנן כל לאיתויי זר אלא לרב לאיתויי מאי וליטעמיך

[לעיל יד: וש"נ] מנחות ו: — ויקרא ו

*) לעיל נח. [לקמן סט. פד:] מנחות ו: מח:

רש"י

תורין שלא הגיע זמנן ובני יונה שעבר זמנן. אינן ראויין לקרבן והוו להו כמליקת חולין דתניא בהכל שוחטין (חולין דף כב.) תורין גדולים ולא קטנים בני יונה קטנים ולא גדולים דלא אישתמיט קרא *וכתב מן היונה ומן בני התורים ואימתי תורין כשירין משיזהיבו ואימתי בני יונה פסולין משילהיבו טלה מוזהבת שסביב הצואר: שנסמית עינה. דה"ל מחוסר אבר והקריבהו נא לפחתך וכי אמרינן אין תמות וזכרות בעופות לענין דוקין שבעין הוא דקאמרינן ו]: שפסולה בקדש. שבאה לעזרה בהכשרה ונפסלה: **גמ'** שמאל ולילה. מלק בשמאל או בלילה: זר. והוא הדין לאונן וערל וכל הפסולין: ביום הכפורים. נטל את המחתה בימינו ואת הכף בשמאלו ולילה נמי ז] מאי שנא דאשכחן ליה הכשירה לכתחילה באיברים ופדרים: אלעזר כתיב. בשחיטתה וכתיב חוקה לעכב: דקדשי בדק הבית היא. ועל כרחך אין עבודות שלה חשובות עבודה: ונילף מבמה. שהזר כשר בה למלוק עופות לכתחילה דאין כיהון בבמה כדתנן בפ' בתרא (לקמן דף קיג.) וכיון דאשכחן ליה הכשירה לכתחילה בעלמא יטהר כאן מידי נבילה: מבמה לא ילפינן במקדש. דבמה כחול היא לגבי מקדש: ורבי יוחנן אמר מלק זר אינו מטמא בבית הבליעה. דילפינן מבמה: סכין מטמא. דלא מליקה ולא שחיטה היא ודכוותה לא אשכחן הכשירה: *) לאיתויי שחיטת קדשים בפנים. דלא מטמיא דבמתני' לא תנן לה: כללא דסיפא לאיתויי מליקת חולין בחוץ. דמטמיא

*) עיין לדף שאח"ז

תוספות

ושניסמית עינה. היינו שנחטטה דמחוסר אבר וממעטינן לה בפ"ק דקידושין (דף כד:) מדכתיב מן העוף ולא כל העוף פרט לשיבש גפה ולא כמו שפירש בקונטרס משום הקריבהו נא לפחתך וא"ת ל"ל קרא למחוסר אבר הא אפילו לבני נח אסור כדדרשינן לקמן פ' בתרא (דף קטז.) ופ"ק דע"ז (דף ה:) ח] הבא בהמה שחיין ראשי איברים שלה וי"ל דאי לאו דכתיב קרא בישראל הוה מוקמינן קרא דבני נח לישראל *ולא לבני נח כדאמר בפ' ד' מיתות (סנהדרין דף נט.) כל מצוה שנאמרה לבני נח ולא נשנית בסיני לישראל נאמרה ולא לבני נח א"כ הוה אמינא דכיון דאישתרי בעל מום בעופות לישראל טפי מבהמה *אישתרי אפי' מחוסר אבר א"כ הוה מוקמינן מכל הני דכתיב בבני נח ס] דדוקא בהמה שמליט שנאסר בה מום לישראל א): **אמר** רב שמאל ולילה כו'. כולה הך סוגיא כר"ש כדפרישית במתני' ושמאל ולילה דאין מטמאין י] דאם עלו לא ירדו וזר וסכין דמטמאין יא] [א] (ירדו) לר"ש דכיון דאירע פסול יב] [קודם שחיטה] כמו דחנקינון דמי וירדו דאין פסולן בקודש שלא נתקדש בכלי וכל שפסולו בקודש דלא ירד היינו שאירע פסול משנשחט ונתקדש בקדושת כלי ולא כמו שפי' בקונטרס לקמן בפ' המזבח מקדש (דף פד.) אין פסולו בקודש שאירע פסול קודם ביאתו לעזרה כגון רובע ונרבע דנרבע בעזרה מאי איכא למימר ועוד דשחיטת דרוס ר"ל במעילה דתרד לר"ש ולאו דוקא יג] ר"ש רובע ונרבע דה"ה זר במליקה ובקמילה תרד [ב] דעל יד] כרחיך למאי דבעי למימר רבה דשחיטת דרוס ב) תרד לר"ש ושמאל ולילה דאין מטמאין בבית הבליעה ואם עלו לא ירדו טעמא בכל מקום כדמפרש הכא שמאל דאית ליה הכשר' ביום הכפורים ולילה לאיברים ופדרים ורבי יהודה ממעט לילה אע"ג דאית ליה הכשר' ושמאל נמי טו] ה"ל הכשר' וממעט דאין לומר דלא ממעט אלא ג' דברים משום דתלתא מיעוטי כתיבי דהא מלקה זר ובעל מום תרד לר' יהודה וכן שחיטת דרוס וא"ת ומה בין טז] שחיטת דרוס לרבי יהודה לפסח וחטאת שלא לשמו [ג] דרוס נמי כשר בשאר קדשים וי"ל דדרוס דמי לנשחט בחוץ דתרווייהו יז] פסולי מקום ומהאי טעמא היה רוצה לומר רבה לר"ש דתרד וא"ת דהכא משמע דלרב לא הוי פסול אר כפסול שמאל ובפ"ק דמנחות (דף ו:) מבווה להו לענין אם קמץ יחזיר וי"ל דהתם אין תלוי בהכשר דהא מכשר ר' יהודה בן בתירא בכל הפסולין כולן. הגה"ה נ"ל פירוש דכל שפסולו בקודש היינו כל שפסולו כשר בעלמא בקודש דהא לשון זה תנן לקמן בפ' המזבח מקדש (דף פד.) גבי אם עלו לא ירדו והתם נמי מפרש לכל אותם שלא ירדו היכן כשרים בעלמא ולעיל פ"ה (דף נא.) [ד] מפרש להו לן בדם כשר שהרי לן כשר באימורים וכן כולהו יח] ובשמעתא נמי מפרש מ"ש שמאל דאיתו מטמא דאית ליה הכשיר' ביוה"כ ולילה באיברים ופדרים וזר וסכין מטמאין דלית להו הכשיר' בעלמא ור' יוחנן דאמר מליקת זר אין מטמאה משום דאית ליה הכשירה או בשחיטה או בבמה וכן בהמה בעלת מום דלא תרד לר"ע בדוקין שבעין הואיל וכשר בעופות ולרבנן נמי אי משכחת ליה בבהמה הכשירה לא תרד ולרבי שמעון נמי בעי הכשירה בעלמא דהיינו פסולו בקודש ולהכי תנן גבי אתנן וכלאים ירדו דלית להו הכשירה בעלמא והא דר' יהודה בעצמו אומר מפני מה לן בדם כשר שכשר באימורין [ולן] באימורין [שכשר] בבשר לאורויי דשאר עבודות ילפינן [ה] מלכתחילה או מבמה אבל עבודות דם לא ולהכי קאמר ירדו בג' דמכשירן ר"ש דאיתו חושש [ו] כיון דמשכח הכשירה בשום מקום אבל עבודות דם שפיר יליף ר' יהודה מעבודות דם אפי' מהכשירן ולהכי שלמטה שלמעלה ג) שלמטה שבפנים שבחוץ לא ירד וטריפה [ז] ירד אפי' לר"ש אפי' לר"ע דיליף בהמה מעוף אע"ג דאשכחן הכשירה בעוף טריפה במליקה אם התרץ התם מלוותו בכך הא ילפינן שמאל לא ירד מהכשר דיוה"כ י"ל דהרתי לא ילפי בהמה מעוף וגם שלא בהכשרו ממלוותו בכך אי נמי לא ילפינן פסול של קודם שחיטה כגון טריפה ממליקה שאיט דוגמתו יט] [ח] לא אירע קודם שחיטה וכמדומה לי שכן פירש לנו רבינו הקדוש נ"ע ולא [ט] כמו שבפנים וא"כ אין מטמאין בגדים אבית הבליעה וגם אם עלו לא ירדו [י] הא בהא תליא דהא ליתא דכל שפסולו בקודש גבי תרווייהו תנן לה וברים מעילה (דף ב:) נמי מדמה להו לתרווייהו ושחיטת עוף קדשים בפנים דאמרינן בסמוך אין מטמאין אע"ג דתרד כדמוכח בפרק השוחט והמעלה (לקמן דף קיא.) דפטר ליה אם העלהו אחרי כן בחוץ ואם לא ירדו בפנים היה חייב בחוץ כדאיתא בפ"ב [כ] התם איכא קרא בסמוך למימר אין מטמאין והא דאמרינן בשחיטת דרוס דירדו לרבי יהודה פ"ק דמעילה (דף ג:) אע"ג דאית ליה הכשירה דקדשים קלים ודמים שלמטה למעלה לא ירד אף לר' יהודה מ"מ כיון דשחיטתן למקומן חשיבי כשוחט חוץ והוו כמאן דחנקינהו דמי ומליקת פסול דקאמר בסמוך אין מטמאה [ל] אין כ] נ"ל כפירש"י שפירש בעל מום שכשר לעבודה ואפילו בבמה כא] כדאשכחן (דמוכח) לעיל ריש פ"ב (דף טז.) דפריך מה להצד השוה שבהן שכן לא הותרו בבמה אבל מליקת פסול היינו או אונן או טמא או פסול אחר דאישתרי בעלמא ונשפך דמה מן הצואר דלא ירדו משום דכבר נעשית כל השחיטה כהוגן. ברו"ך: **דאית** ליה הכשירה ביוה"כ. הוה מצי למימר בהולכת אברים אלא כיון דמשכח יוה"כ בעבודה דמעכב כפרה נקטיה: **שחיטה** לאו עבודה היא. פירשתי לעיל בסוף פ"ק (דף יד:): **ונילף** מבמה. פי' כיון דמכשרת לילה אע"ג דאין פסולו בקודש משום דאית ליה הכשירה א"כ זר נמי כיון דאית ליה הכשירה כב] והוה מצי לשנויי דאתיא כמ"ד (לקמן דף סט.) דאין מנחה ועופות בבמה וברייתא דתניא לקמיה כרבי יוחנן לא קשיא לדידיה דאתיא כמ"ד דיש מנחה ושמא משמע ליה דאי ילפא מבמה ילפינן אפי' מנחה ועופות כיון דאיכא הכשירה מיהא לזר: **ובי** תימא מבמה לא יליף והתניא מנין ליוצא כו'. אע"ג דהך ברייתא כר' יהודה בפ' המזבח מקדש (לקמן דף פד:) מ"מ כיון דר' יהודה דמחמיר יליף מבמה כל שכן ר"ש ומשני אזאת תורת העולה סמיך דמרבינן כל דבר שיש לו הכשר אע"ג דלית ליה הכשר אלא בבמה מיהו עבודת הדם לא יליף ר' יהודה כג] דהא ממעט נשחטה בלילה ויצא דמה וכן שחיטת דרוס: **אלא** לרב לאתויי מאי. וליכא למימר לאתויי חוץ לזמנו וחוץ למקומו ושלא לשמו דלא תני במתניתין דהא מקל ותומר אתו דמליקת לילה דלרבי יהודה תרד אינה מטמאה כל שכן הנך דלא תרד לר' יהודה דלא מטמו:

א) [וע"ע תוס' ע"ז דף ה: ד"ה מנין] ב) נ"ל תרד לר"ש לאו דווקא ושמאל וכו' ג) נ"ל למטה כו' בחוץ

מסורת הש"ס

ולכתוב נ"ק

מעילה ג.

יומא מב. ע"ש לעיל יד: ע"ש מנחות ו: ע"ש

[יומא מב. וש"נ]

גליון הש"ס

תוס' ד"ה ושניסמית כו' ולא לבני נח. עיין חולין דף כג ע"א תד"ה תמות:

נ"ל אישתרי אפי' מחוסר אבר והוה מוקמינן כו' ונמחק תיבות אי נמי וכ"ה בתוס' קדושין דף כד ע"ב ד"ה ת"ל נ"ק

נוסחאות רש"י כת"י

מטמא בבית הבליעה. דלא אהני מליקה דידהו למידי שאפילו אם עלו ירדו שאין פסולו בקודש ואמרי' לקמן בפ"ק המזבח מקדש אם עלה ירד וכיון שאין מתרת את האיסור לא מטעים ממשמעו' נבילה וטריפה: פסולו בקודש. כגון קדשים הראויין אבל נפסלו בעבודתיהן: אין מטמאין. דהא אהני מליקה דידהו דאם עלו לא ירדו ונמצא מליקה זו מתרת את האיסור דילפינן בגמ' בברייתא מה טריפה שאינה מתרת כו': גמ' שמאל ולילה אין מטמאין דאם עלו לא ירדו: זר ומליקת סכין מטמאין. דאם עלו ירדו: מ"ש שמאל. דחשיב ליה מליקה המתרת איסור דאם עלו לא ירדו: שחיטה לא עבודה היא. שאף בחולין היא נוהגת: ומחוי רב עלה. למיהב טעמא למילתיה: אלעזר וחוקה. אלעזר כתיב בפרשה ושחט אלעזר וכתיב חוקה בענייני דפרה לעיכובא: ונילף מבמה. נימא מליקת זר אם עלתה לא תרד שהרי הזר כשר בבמה דעבודתה א) בבכורות: וכ"ת לא יליף. התנא עבודת פנים מעבודת במה: שהרי יוצא כשר בבמה. שהרי במת יחיד אף בשדות על הסלעים כדאשכחן בטנוח: תנא אזאת תורת העולה ריבה סמיך. עיקר מילתיה דאמר לא ירד לאו משום דכשר בבמה הוא אלא אקרא סמיך דדרשינן התם בפ' המזבח מקדש תורה אחת לכל העולים שאם עלו לא ירדו דדרשינן התם תורת העולה לרבות וזאת למעט ופרכינן מה ראית לרבות את אלו ולהוציא את אלו מרבה אני את אלו שהיה פסולו בקודש ומוציא אני את אלו שלא היה פסולן בקודש הילכך יוצא פסולו בקודש הוא דהא משבא לקודש נפסל

שיטה מקובצת

א] נפה ושניסמית: ב] זה הכלל כל שהיה פסולו בקודש כו'. פ"ה בעלמא שאירע פסולו לאחר שהובא בעזרה ולא נהירא שהרי מלק בסכין אירע פסולו בעזרה ואפ"ה מטמאינן וכן נמי זר חשיב ליה פסולו בקודש לר' יוחנן בגמרא וכן שמאל ולילה אי לאו משום דאית ליה הכשר ביוה"כ ובאיברים ופדרים כדמוכח בגמרא לכך נראה דפסולו בקודש היינו שיש לפסול הכשר במקום אחר בקודש ומתניתין דהכא לכאורה כר"ש דאית ליה כל שפסולו בקודש אם עלו לא ירדו ולהכי אמר מלק בלילה אין מטמאין לפי שמתרת את האיסור דמשמע בגמרא דבהכי תלי טעמא ואותו טעמא דפסולו בקודש גורם לנו דמתרת את האיסור ואם עלה לא תרד כדתני לקמן וכן כל סוגיא דגמרא כר"ש איירי וא"ת אי מתני' כר"ש היכא מיפסלא מלק בסכין הא אמרינן בפרק קבלה [דף כד ע"ב] דפליג בברייתא ותרים ר"ת מלק כדפי' לעיל וי"ל דמתניתין רבי היא ובלילה סבר כר"ש ולענין מליקה בשמאל סבר לה כרבי יהודה אבל אין לומר דכולה מתני' אתיא כר"י דהא קתני לקמן דלילה תרד והכא קתני דלילה אין מטמא והיינו טעמא משום דמהני שחיטת לילה להכי דלא תרד דאי תרד אמאי אין מטמאין וכן משמע בגמרא דטעמא דלילה אין מטמא היינו משום דלא תרד כדאמר בגמרא והוי מתרת האיסור ור"ל האיסור דלא תרד אלא ודאי צריך לומר דלא אתיא כרבי יהודה: ג] ונילף מבמה. וא"ת והלא איכא מ"ד דאין עוף בבמה וי"ל דמ"מ נילף עוף כבהמה וא"ת ומאיזה עבודה אי משחיטת בהמ' דכשירה בזר בבמה שחיטה לאו עבודה היא ואפי' במקדש כשירה ה"א בזר אבל מליקה הא פסולה הוא בזר וי"ל דמ"מ נילף מליקה דעוף מזריקה דבהמה וזריקה בעיא כהונה כמו מליקה ואפ"ה כשירה בבמה בזר: ד] והתניא מנין ליוצא כו'. וא"ת והלא הך ברייתא מוקמינן לקמן כר' יהודה וכבר פירשתי דמתניתין דלא כר"י וי"ל דמ"מ פריך מכ"ש דתנא דמתניתין מקיל טפי מר"י ולר"י לילה תרד ולתנא דמתני' לא תרד ואפ"ה יליף ר"י מבמה כ"ש ר"ש דמקיל טפי דיליף מבמה: ה] תנא אזאת תורת העולה ריבה סמיך ליה תורה אחת לכל העולין דלא תרד. כלומר יליף יוצא מבמה וא"ת מ"מ גם זה נילף מבמה ויהיה בכלל כל העולים דמיעט דזאת נעמיד בדבר שפסול בבמה לכך נראה דה"פ אזאת תורת סמיך תורה אחת לכל העולים כלומר שפסולו בקודש כדאמר לקמן מרבה אני שפסולו בקודש הילכך דוקא יוצא חשיב פסולו בקודש משום דנפסל אחר שנכשר בעבודה כלומר אחר שהיתה בה עבודה בהכשר אבל מליקה זר דפסול מעיקרא ולא הוקדש בשום עבודה בהכשר ואי משום דאית ליה הכשר בבמה לא יליף והא דנקט לקמן במה בזר כדי נסבא דעיקר טעם הוי כדפי' [זר] אינו מטמא פ"ה הואיל ואית ליה הכשר בבמה וקשה דא"כ בסמוך דקאמר שלא היה פסולו בקודש לאתויי מאי א) ליטא לאתויי בעל מום שאינו כשר בבמה לכך נראה דטעמא דר"י משום דאית ליה הכשר בשחיטה דבעל מום נמי כשר בשחיטה כדתנן כל הפסולים ששחטו שחיטתן כשירה כו' וניטא דשחיטה עבודה לגבי האי: ו] דקאמרי' שאין מומן ניכר הס"ד: ז] תיבות מאי שנא נמחק: ח] דע"ז מכל החי הבא: ט] דוקא בבהמה: י] אם עלו אית ד' ל"ש: יא] ירדו לר"ש: יב] פסול בשחיטה כמאן דחנקינון: יג] דוקא נקט ר"ש: יד] דעל כרחין למאי דבעי למימר רבה דבשחיטת דרוס וכו': טו] נמי הוה ממעט תיבות ה"ל הכשירא ואות ו' נמחק: טז] ומה בין: יז] דתרווייהו הוו פסולי מקום ומהאי טעמא היה רוצה לומר רבה דלר"ש תרד וא"ת דהכא כו': יח] ובשמעתין נמי: יט] דוגמתו שלא אירע: כ] אין נ"ל פירש"י דפי' בעל מום: כא] כדמוכח לעיל ותיבת כדאשכחן נמחק: כב] הכשירא מתכשר ותוה: כג] יהודה מבמה דהא:

ושמאל ולילה כיון דאשכחן להו הכשירא בעבודות אחרות כפסולו בקודש חשיבי אבל מליקת זר כיון דלא אשכחן לה הכשירא בעבודת פנים לאו פסולו בקודש הוא ומטמא:

א) לכאורה נ"ע דהרי בבמת יחיד בשעת היתר הבמות כשר בכל אדם ולא בעי בכור ולא היה עבודה בבכורות רק קודם הקמת המשכן.

א) עי' תוס' לקמן סע ע"א ד"ה וליטעמיך

הגהות צ"ק [א] דירדו: [ב] דב"ב צריך ... [ג] נ"ל דדרוס: [ד] נ"ל לכתחילה מהדדי: [ה] נ"ל נמי מפרש: [ו] הא דמשכח: [ז] דירד: [ח] דלא: [ט] כמותו בפנים וצ"ע: [י] דהא: [כ] הכא: [ל] עיין נ"ק ל"א בזה:

ḤULLIN WITHIN [OR] SACRIFICES WITHOUT; [68b] OR [IF HE SACRIFICED] TURTLE-DOVES BEFORE THEIR TIME OR PIGEONS AFTER THEIR TIME;[4] [OR A BIRD] WHOSE WING WAS WITHERED, [OR] BLIND IN THE EYE, [OR] WHOSE FOOT WAS CUT OFF, —[ALL THESE] DEFILE IN THE GULLET. THIS IS THE GENERAL RULE: ALL WHOSE UNFITNESS [AROSE] IN THE SANCTUARY[5] DO NOT DEFILE IN THE GULLET; IF THEIR UNFITNESS DID NOT ARISE IN THE SANCTUARY, THEY DEFILE IN THE GULLET.

GEMARA. Rab said: [If they were nipped with] the left [hand] or at night, they do not defile in the gullet; [by] a *zar* or [with] a knife, they do defile in the gullet. Why is the left [hand] different; [presumably] because it is fit on the Day of Atonement; and likewise night is fit in respect of [the burning of] the limbs and the fats;[6] then surely a *zar* too is fit for *shechitah*?[7]—*Shechitah* is not a [sacrificial] rite.[8] Is it not? Surely R. Zera said: *Shechitah* of the [red] heifer by a *zar* is invalid, and Rab observed thereon: [The reason is because] '*Eleazar*' and '*statute*' [are written in connection
a with it]?[1]—The [red] heifer is different, because it is of the holy things of the Temple repair. Does it not then follow *a fortiori:* if the holy things of the Temple repair require priesthood, surely the holy objects dedicated to the altar require priesthood?—Said R. Shisha the son of R. Idi: Let it be analogous to the inspection of [leprous] plagues, which is not a rite, and yet requires priesthood.[2] But let us learn it from the high places?[3]—One cannot learn from the high places.[4] Can one not? Surely it was taught: How do we know that if [flesh] which went out ascended [the altar], it does not descend? Because [flesh that] goes out is fit at the high places!—The Tanna relies on the text, *This is the law of the burnt-offering*.[5]

But R. Joḥanan maintained: [If a] *zar* [performed *meliḳah*] it does not defile in the gullet; [if *meliḳah* was done with] a knife, it does defile in the gullet. We learnt: [IN REGARD TO] ALL UNFIT PERSONS WHO PERFORMED MELIḲAH, THE MELIḲAH IS INVALID. As for R. Joḥanan, it is well: ALL includes a *zar;*[6] but according to Rab, what does ALL include?—It is surely to include [*meliḳah* with] the left [hand] and [at] night. [But] the left [hand] and night are explicitly taught?—He [the Tanna] teaches and then explains.[7] Come and hear: THIS IS THE GENERAL RULE: ALL WHOSE UNFITNESS [AROSE] IN THE SANCTUARY DO NOT DEFILE GARMENTS [WHEN THE FLESH OF THE BIRD IS] IN THE GULLET.[8] As for R. Joḥanan, it is well: ALL includes a *zar*. But

(4) Only *fully grown* turtle-doves or *young* pigeons might be sacrificed. Otherwise they are not eligible, and therefore it is as though he nipped *ḥullin*. (5) Birds which were brought to the Temple court fit, and there became unfit. (6) On the Day of Atonement the spoon containing incense was taken with the left hand. The limbs and fats of sacrifices were burnt at night. Thus in two instances the left hand and night are fit for service, and presumably for that reason he rules that even in the present case, though they are not fit, they free them from uncleanness. (7) An animal sacrifice might be slaughtered by a *zar*. (8) Whereas the taking of the spoon and the burning of the limbs are sacrificial rites.

a (1) Cf. Num. XIX, 2. (2) For notes v. *supra* 14*b*. (3) Where a *zar* might perform *meliḳah* (v. *infra* 113*a*). By the same reasoning *meliḳah* by a *zar* even in the Temple should free the bird from defilement. (4) Because by comparison with the Temple they were non-sacred. (5) Lev. VI, 2. For notes v. *supra* 51*a*. He does not really learn it from the high places at all. (6) It is a general principle that 'all' is an extension. (7) First he states the law in general, and then he explains who are meant in the word ALL. (8) 'Garments' is absent in the Mishnah.

according to Rab, what does it include? [69*a*]—Yet even on your view, what does [the clause] IF THEIR UNFITNESS DID NOT ARISE
a IN THE SANCTUARY include?[1] Rather, the first clause includes *shechitah* of [bird] sacrifices within,[2] while the second clause includes *meliḳah* of *ḥullin* without.[3]

It was taught in accordance with R. Joḥanan: If a *zar* nipped it; or if an unfit person nipped it; or [if it was] *piggul, nothar* or [an] unclean [sacrifice],[4] it does not defile in the gullet.[5]

R. Isaac said: I have heard two [laws], one relating to *ḳemiẓah*[6] by a *zar* and the other to *meliḳah* by a *zar:* one descends and the other does not descend, but I do not know which is which.[7] Said Hezekiah: It is logical that [in the case of] *ḳemiẓah* it goes down, while [in the case of] *meliḳah* it does not go down. Why is *meliḳah* different? [presumably] because it was done at the high places?[8] [but] *ḳemiẓah* too was done at the high places? And should you say, There were no meal-offerings at the high places; then there were no bird[-offerings] at the high places [either].[9] For R. Shesheth said: On the view that there were meal-offerings at the high places, there were bird[-offerings] at the high places; on the view that there were no meal-offerings, there were no bird [-offerings]. What is the reason? [*And sacrificed peace-offerings of oxen unto the Lord*]:[10] *offerings* [implies,] but not birds; *offerings* [implies,] but not meal-offerings![11]—Say rather: There was no sanctification of a meal-offering in service vessels at the high places.[12]

IF HE NIPPED [THEM] WITH HIS LEFT [HAND] OR AT NIGHT etc. Our Rabbis taught: You might think that *meliḳah*, which is
b [done] within, defiles garments [when the flesh is] in the gullet;[1] therefore it states, [*And every soul that eateth*] *nebelah* [*that which dieth of itself*] [... *he shall wash his clothes* etc].[2] [But] this too is *nebelah?*[3]—Rather, it states '*terefah*' [*that which is torn of beasts*]:[4] as *terefah* does not permit the forbidden, so everything which does not permit the forbidden [is included]: thus *meliḳah*, which is [performed] within, is excluded: since it permits the forbidden, it does not defile garments [when the flesh is] in the gullet.[5] Hence it includes *meliḳah* (Mnemonic: *ḲeẒ ḤeFeẒ*)[6] of sacrifices without, and *meliḳah* of *ḥullin* both within and without: since they do not permit the forbidden, they defile garments [when the flesh is] in the gullet.

Another [Baraitha] taught: You might think that the *shechitah* of *ḥullin* within and [that of] sacrifices both within and without defile in the gullet: therefore *nebelah* is stated. But this too is '*nebelah*'?[7]—Rather, therefore it states '*terefah*': as *terefah* is the same within and without,[8] so all which are the same within and without [are included in this law]: thus the *shechitah* of *ḥullin* within and [that of] sacrifices within and without is excluded: since these are not the same within as without, they do not defile garments [when the flesh is] in the gullet. As for *ḥullin*, it is well:
c that is not the same within as without;[1] but sacrifices are unfit in both cases?—Said Raba: If *shechitah* without is effective in that it involves *kareth*,[2] shall it not be effective in cleansing it from [the defilement of] *nebelah*?[3] We have thus found [it of *shechitah*] without; how do we know [it of *shechitah*] within?—Because it is not the same within as without.[4] If so, when one performs *meliḳah* on sacrifices without, they too [should] not [defile], since within is not the same as without?[5]—Said R. Shimi b. Ashi: You infer that which does not make it fit from that which does not make it fit,[6] but you do not infer that which does not make it fit from that which does make it fit.[7] Do you not? Surely it was taught: How do we know that [if flesh] which went out ascended [the altar] it does not descend? Because [flesh] that goes out is fit at the high places?—The Tanna relies on the extension intimated in, '*This is the law of the burnt-offering*'[8]

MISHNAH. IF ONE PERFORMED MELIḲAH, AND IT [THE BIRD] WAS FOUND TO BE TEREFAH, R. MEIR SAID: IT DOES

a (1) For the ALL of the first clause applies to that too. (2) That such do not defile. (3) That such do defile. (4) I.e., if the flesh of a bird sacrifice became defiled after it was properly offered up. (5) For only *nebelah* does this.—The ruling thus agrees with R. Joḥanan. (6) V. Glos. (7) Either a bird-offering nipped by a *zar* or a meal-offering whose *ḳemiẓah* was performed by a *zar* does not descend from the altar if it was taken up there. (8) By a *zar*. (9) Hence no *meliḳah*. (10) Ex. XXIV, 5. This was before the erection of the Tabernacle, and so the equivalent of the high places. (11) The Heb. is applicable to animals only. (12) He holds that there were both bird- and meal-offerings at the high places. But whereas *meliḳah* by a *zar* in the Temple can be learnt from that of the high places (in so far, at least, that it does not descend), *ḳemiẓah* can not. For at the high places meal-offerings were not sanctified in service vessels, whereas in the Temple they were. That being so, when *ḳemiẓah* is performed by a *zar* it is unfit to that extent that even if taken up on to the altar, it must be taken down.

b (1) I.e., after *meliḳah* done improperly the flesh defiles. (2) Lev. XVII, 15. (3) Since the *meliḳah* was not properly done and does not permit the eating of the sacrifice, the bird is like any other not killed by *shechitah*, hence *nebelah*. (4) Ibid. (5) The verse quoted is applied to the *nebelah* of a clean bird. *Terefah* is not interpreted literally, for reasons stated anon, but as a definition of *nebelah*, thus: only *nebelah* similar to *terefah* defiles. Now when a bird becomes *terefah*, that fact cannot possibly remove any prohibition to which it was subject. Similarly, only a *nebelah* which cannot remove a prohibition defiles. Now, *meliḳah* should render a bird of *ḥullin nebelah*, but a consecrated bird is thereby relieved of a prohibition, for whilst alive it could not be offered, whereas after *meliḳah* in the sanctuary it can be (i.e., its blood can be sprinkled on the altar, which is the essence of offering). Hence it does not cause the bird to defile garments even when it is improperly done, e.g., at night or with the left hand. (6) A Mnemonic is a phrase consisting of a string of letters or words, as an aid to the memory. Here Ḳ=*Ḳodashim* (sacrifices); Ẓ=*behuẒ* (without); Ḥ=*Ḥullin;* F=*biFenim* (within); Ẓ=*behuẒ*. (7) Since *meliḳah* is required for sacrifices, whilst *ḥullin* may not be slaughtered within at all, the birds so killed are *nebelah!* (8) It is forbidden in both places.

c (1) For *ḥullin* slaughtered without does not defile even when the *shechitah* does not permit it, e.g., if the bird is *terefah*. (2) He who slaughters a sacrificial bird without the Temple incurs *kareth*. This proves that his act does count as *shechitah*. (3) It certainly is. Hence the deduction from the word '*terefah*' is necessary only in respect of *ḥullin*, but not in respect of sacrifices. (4) Sh. M.: Since *shechitah* without involves *kareth*, whilst *shechitah* within does not, although it actually requires *meliḳah*. (5) For *meliḳah* is proper within, but not without. (6) I.e., you infer *shechitah* of sacrifices within from *shechitah* of sacrifices without; similarly, *shechitah* of *ḥullin* within from *shechitah* of *ḥullin*, when same is *terefah*, without. In all these cases *shechitah* does not make the bird permitted. (7) Viz., from *meliḳah* of sacrifices within, which is the proper way. (8) Lev. VI, 2. V. *supra* 51a for notes.

ולישעמיך שלא היה פסולו בקודש לאיתויי מאי אלא רישא א) לאיתויי שחיטת קדשים בפנים סיפא לאיתויי מליקת חולין בחוץ תניא כוותיה דרבי יוחנן מלקה זר מלקה פסול *הפיגול והנותר והטמא אין מטמאין אבית הבליעה א"ר יצחק שמעתי שתים אחת קמיצת זר ואחת מליקת זר אחת תרד ואחת לא תרד ולא ידענא ב) אמר חזקיה מסתברא קמיצה תרד מליקה לא תרד מאי שנא מליקה דישנה בבמה קמיצה נמי ישנה בבמה וכי תימא אין מנחה בבמה אין ג) עופות נמי בבמה דאמר *רב ששת לדברי האומר יש מנחה בבמה יש עופות בבמה לדברי האומר אין מנחה אין עופות *מ"ט זבחים ולא מנחות זבחים ולא עופות אלא אימא אין קידוש ד) בכלי שרת במנחה בבמה: מלק בשמאל או בלילה כו': ת"ר יכול תהא מליקה שהיא לפנים מטמאה בגדים בבית הבליעה תלמוד לומר °נבלה ה) הא נמי נבלה היא אלא ת"ל °טריפה ו) מה טריפה שאין מתרת את האיסור אף כל שאין מתרת את האיסור יצא מליקה שהיא לפנים הואיל והיא מתרת את האיסור אין מטמא בגדים בבית הבליעה ז) הביא א) המולק (ק"צ חפ"צ סימן) קדשים בחוץ ומולק חולין בין מבפנים בין מבחוץ הואיל ואין מתירין את האיסור מטמאין בגדים אבית הבליעה תניא אידך ח) ב) יכול תהא שחיטת חולין לפנים וקדשים בין מבפנים ובין מבחוץ מטמאה אבית הבליעה ת"ל נבלה הא נמי נבלה היא אלא ת"ל טריפה מה טריפה שווה בפנים כבחוץ אף כל ט) שוות בפנים כבחוץ יצא שחיטת חולין בפנים וקדשים בין מבפנים בין מבחוץ הואיל ולא שוו בפנים כבחוץ אין מטמאין בגדים אבית הבליעה בשלמא חולין לא שוו בפנים כבחוץ אלא קדשים אידי ואידי פסולין נינהו אמר רבא אם הועילה לו שחיטת חוץ לחייבו כרת לא תועיל י) לו לטהרה מידי נבילה יא) אשכחן חוץ פנים מנלן הואיל ולא שוו בפנים כבחוץ אי הכי מלק קדשים בחוץ נמי לא יב) דלא שוו בפנים כבחוץ אמר רב שימי בר אשי יג) דנין דבר שלא בהיכשרו מדבר שלא בהיכשרו ואין *דנין דבר שלא בהיכשרו מדבר שבהיכשרו ולא והתניא *מנין ליוצא שאם עלה לא ירד שהרי יוצא כשר בבמה תנא °אזאת תורת העולה ריבה סמיך ליה: **מתני'** *מלק ונמצאת טריפה ר' מאיר אומר אינו מטמא בבית הבליעה

רבי

רש"י

דלא תנן לה במתני': הנותר והטמא. ולא אמרינן נפקי להו מהיתר אכילת קדשים וחל עלייהו איסור נבילה למפרע: דישנה בבמה. בזר: לדברי האומר. בפ' אחרון (לקמן דף קיג.) ר' יהודה אומר אין מנחה בבמה: זבחים. ויזבחו זבחים שלמים בסיני (שמות כד): אין קידוש כלי שרת במנחה בבמה. הילכך לא ילפינן זר במקדש לענין קמילה מזר בבמה דלא דמי הך קמילה להך קמילה דבמקדש הואיל וקידשה בכלי שרת איפסלא בזר: ה"ג בתורת כהנים להך מתני' יכול תהא מליקה שהיא לפנים מטמאה כו': הא נמי נבילה היא. מאן לימא לך דלאו נבילה היא כי דהותרה מליקת חטאת העוף לכהנים מגזירת הכתוב מלכל חטאתם כדאמרן בפרק [בית שמאי] (לעיל דף מד:) עולה שלא הותרה להם תטמא בבית הבליעה: אלא תלמוד לומר טריפה. *ונפש אשר תאכל נבילה וטריפה יד] (ויקרא יז) ובנבלת עוף טהור מיתוקמא קרא בת"כ והאי טריפה קרא יתירא הוא לדרשא כדלקמן שאי אפשר לשומעו כמשמעו טו] שיהא טריפה מטמא בבית הבליעה מחיים אם טריפה חיה *ואם אינה חיה הרי בכלל נבילה והא טז] מתני' לקמיה מיתוקם כר"מ דאית ליה שחיטת עוף טהור מטהרת טריפתו מטומאתו ולא דריש ליה להאי קרא להביא טריפה ששחטה שתטמא הילכך דריש ליה למעוטי מליקה שהיא בפנים ושחיטה שהיא לפנים ומשמע ליה קרא הכי נבילה שהיא כטריפה היא דמטמאה: מה טריפה. אין טריפות המאורע בה מתיר שום איסור שהיה בה מתחילה: אף נבילות. שאין נבילות יז] המאורעת בה מתיר את האיסור יצא נבילות הבא לה ע"י מליקת פנים בהכשר הואיל ומתיר את האיסור שבחייה לא היתה ראויה לקרב לגבוה והותרה במליקה זו: יכול תהא שחיטה שהיא לפנים. ובת"כ גרסי' לה הכי יכול השוחט חולין בפנים וקדשים בין מבפנים בין מבחוץ כו': הא נמי נבילה היא. מי יימר דלאו נבילה היא הואיל ושחיטה בפנים בעוף לא שייכא וכן בקדשים בין בפנים בין בחוץ כו': ת"ל טריפה. כלומר נבילה שהיא כטריפה מטמאה: שוות בפנים כבחוץ. דכאן וכאן היא אסורה: ה"ג יצא השוחט חולין בפנים וקדשים בין בפנים בין בחוץ הואיל ולא שוו בפנים כבחוץ אין מטמאין ולקמן מפרש ואזיל: בשלמא חולין יח] שוותה שחיטתן בפנים כבחוץ. שהרי חולין שחוטין בחוץ אין מטמאין ואפי' יט] שלא בהיכשרו כגון עוף טריפה ששחטה דהא מתניתין לקמן כר"מ דמטהר טריפת העוף שחוטה ומוקי טריפה דכתיב בקרא להך דרשא למעוטי פנים: אידי ואידי. בין בפנים בין בחוץ נבילה זו שוה בהם שאין כאן תורת שחיטה: אמר רבא. שחיטת פנים דחולין הוא דנפקא לן מהך דרשא אבל קדשים לא צריך למילף מינה דממילא נפקא לן דלא מיטמאו עופות קדשים שחוטין בחוץ דאם הועילה שחיטת חוץ לחייבו עליו כרת משום שחוטי חוץ כדמרבינן ליה בפרק השוחט והמעלה (לקמן דף קז.) מאו אשר ישחט לרבות שחיטת עוף אלמא שחיטה כ] היא שמה: לא תועיל. בתמיה: ה"ג אשכחן חוץ פנים מנלן כא]: ומשני הואיל ולא שוות בפנים כבחוץ. דהא אוקימנא דבחוץ לא מטמא ואע"ג דבאכילה אסור בטומאה מיהא לא שוו: אי הכי מלק קדשים. דקתני לעיל מיטמאין: הא לא שוו בחוץ כבפנים. דהא בפנים הכשירו במליקה: דנין דבר שלא בהכשירו. שחיטת קדשים בפנים: מדבר שלא בהכשירו. שחיטת קדשים בחוץ וכן שחיטת חולין בפנים כב] משחיטת חולין טריפה בחוץ: ואין דנין דבר שלא בהכשירו. כגון מליקת קדשים בחוץ: מדבר שבהכשירו. מליקת קדשים בפנים: **מתני'** ר"מ אומר אינה מטמאה. בקל וחומר:

תוספות

ולישעמיך שלא היה פסולו בקודש לאתויי מאי. תימה דילמא לאתויי בעל מום דהא משמע דטעמא דזר לר' יוחנן משום דיליף מבמה ובעל מום לא הותר בבמה כדמוכח לעיל בריש פ"ב (דף טז.) דפריך מה להצד השוה שבהן שכן לא הותר בבמה ואי הוה מפרשינן בטעמא דרבי יוחנן משום דיליף משחיטה אע"ג דלאו עבודה היא הוה ניחא: לאתויי שחיטת קדשים בפנים. ואע"ג דתרד מדתנן פ' השוחט והמעלה (לקמן דף קיא.) שוחט עוף בפנים ומעלהו בחוץ פטור מ"מ אין מטמאה בבית הבליעה דילפינן לקמן מטריפה *ויש לומר לא דמי שוחט עוף בפנים דאינו מטמא היינו טעמא דגם בחוץ אינו מטמא ומטעמא דהועילה השחיטה לחיוב כרת בשביל כך אין לומר דאם עלה בהמה או עוף ששחט חוץ דיקרב אלא פשיטא דירד דמה ענין זה לזה *חיוב כרת לומר לא ירד פשיטא דשוחט בהמה או עוף בחוץ דמשום שחייב כרת לא נאמר דאם עלה לא ירד ולעולם לא נאמר לא ירד אלא היכא שמצינו דוגמתו כשר בפנים וכדריש מעילה (דף ב:) דמשוה להו דכל היכא דאין מטמאין אבית הבליעה הכי נמי לא ירדו היינו דוקא בדבר שיש בפנים כשר כוותייהו. ברו"ך: מליקת זר לא תרד. לרבי שמעון אבל לר' יהודה תרד כמו לילה ויוצא ודרוס דעבודת דם לא יליף ר' יהודה מבמה: אין קידוש כלי שרת במנחה בבמה. תימה כיון דנתקדש בכלי שרת הוא פסולו בקודש קרינא ביה ושמא כיון דתחילת עבודתה ביד ולא נתקדש בכלי שרת בתחילת עבודה לא חשיב פסולו בקודש ולא דמי לשחיטה דסכין מקדשא ליה: יכול תהא שחיטה שהיא לפנים מטמאה בגדים אבית הבליעה כו'. הא דמצריכין הכא קרא לשחיטת עוף קדשים שמטהרת מידי נבילה ולענין איסורי הנאה לא מצריכין קרא לשחיטתה שמטהרת מידי נבילה לא דמי דקדשים אין הכשר אכילתן בשחיטתן אבל איסורי הנאה הכשר אכילתן בשחיטתן אע"ג דהשתא מיהא אין שחיטתם מכשרתן באכילה מ"מ מטהרתן מידי נבילה: ואין דנין דבר שלא בהכשרו מדבר שהוא בהכשרו. *פי' בקונטרס כג] ושחיטת *חולין *) בפנים לאו משחיטת חולין בחוץ ילפינן אלא משחיטת קדשים *בפנים ילפינן ואם תאמר אם כן מליקת חולין בפנים וקדשים בחוץ נילף נמי ממליקת שמאל ולילה דהוי שלא בהכשרו כד] משלא בהכשרו ויש לומר כיון דאם עלה לא ירד הכשרו קרינא ביה כה]:

*) נ"ל בפנים משחיטת חולין טריפה בחוץ ילפינן וא"ת כו' כצ"ל והג"ה שכתוב בצדו אינו מובן נ"ק

א) גי' נ"ק שייך זה לסימן וכצ"ל הביא קדשים בחוץ וחולין בין מבפנים כו' ונמחק תיבת ומולק ב) בס"י איתא יכול תהא שחיטה לפנים מטמאה כו'

עין משפט נר מצוה

כ א מיי' פ"ג מהל' פסה"מ הלכה ט:

כא ב מיי' פ"ב מהל' פסה"מ הל' טו:

כב ג מיי' פ"ג מהל' אבות הטומאה הל"ג:

כג ד מיי' שם הל"ג:

ז"ל ועוד י"ל דלא דמי כו' נ"ק

נ"א חיוב כרת לגלוי ירד לומר דשוחט בהמה או עוף בחוץ דמשום שחייב כרת אם עלה לא ירד ולעולם כו' נ"ק

מסורת הש"ס

[לקמן קיז:]

[עוסה ילקוט פרשת אחרי רמז תקפב מ"ס זבחו זבחי שלמים זבחים ולא עופות זבחים ולא מנחות]

ס"א הרי נבילה אמורה

שיטה מקובצת

א] לאתויי שחיטת קדשים בפנים. וה"ה דהמ"ל לאתויי פיגול ונותר וטמא דאם עלו לא ירדו ואין מטמאין בגדים אבית הבליעה וסיפא לאתויי רובע ונרבע כדפ"ה אלא נקט הדומה למתני' שחיטת קדשים בפנים כעין שחיטת קדשים מבחוץ דקתני במתניתין וכן מליקת חולין מבחוץ כעין מליקת חולין מבפנים: ב] ולא ידענא איזה היא אמר: ג] אין (עוף) [עופות נמי] בבמה. ואת"ל מ"מ ניליף עוף מבהמה כדפי' לע"ל וי"ל דר' יצחק דהכא לית ליה האי סברא אלא אית ליה דעוף מבהמה לא יליף מדלא יליף נמי מנחה מזבח ומשחיטה נמי ליכא למיגמר משום דכשירה בזר כדפי' לעיל לר' יוחנן לפי' שני דאית ליה לר' יצחק דשחיטה לאו עבודה היא מדקאמר קמיצה תרד ולא יליף משחיטה דקמיצה כנגד שחיטה: ד] אין קידוש כלי שרת בבמה. (אות ב' נמחק) כלומר לעולם בין עופות בין מנחה איכא בבמה מיהו [מליקה] דאין צריך קידוש כלי יליף מבמה אבל מנחה דבעי קידוש כלי לא ילפינן זרות דמנחה (מבנים) [מבפנים] מזרות דמנחה שבבמה משום דכיון שקדשה בכלי שרת פסול בה זר אבל בבמה לא היה קידוש כלי שרת כדכתיב אשר ישרתו בקודש כדאמרי' בפ' בתרא: ה] נבילה נבילה: ו] מה טריפה שאין מתרת את האיסור פי' דאם עלתה תרד יצאת מליקה פסולה שהיא לפנים שהיא מתרת את האיסור שאם עלתה לא תרד ולכך לא מטמאת וא"ת לר"מ דאמר מלק ונמצאת טריפה אינה מטמאת וא"כ אית ליה דלא תרד מאי קאמר הכא דטריפה אינה מתרת את האיסור וי"ל דה"ק הכא מה טריפה אין טריפתה מתרת את האיסור כו' יצאת מליקה פסולה כו' כלומר דפסול מליקה (ונבילת) [שהיא נבילה] מתירה לענין דאם עלתה לא תרד משום דחשיב פסולו בקודש כדפי' במתני': ז] הבליעה ב"א המולי"ק ק"ץ סימ"ן אביא מלק קדשים בחוץ וחולין בין מבפנים: ח] תניא אידך כו' כלומר דה"ג אין מתירין דומיא דטריפה דאם עלו ירדו: ט] כל ששוות בפנים: י] תיבת לו נמחק: יא] אשכחן חוץ משום דהועיל לו שחיטת חוץ לחייבו כרת כדמרבינן ליה לקמן: הואיל ולא שוו כו' כלומר כי היכי דאמר בחולין לא שוו משום דבחוץ כשרים הן קדשים נמי אגמירנן לא שוו הואיל דבחוץ יש כרת מה שאין כן בפנים דכמו שבחוץ לא מטמא מבפנים נמי לא מטמא דאי אמרת איטמו לא שוו בפנים כבחוץ: יג] דנין דבר שלא בהיכשר מדבר שלא בהיכשר (אות ו' נמחק) כו' וא"ת א"כ שחיטת חולין בפנים מנלן דלא מטמא אי משחיטת חולין בחוץ הא הוו בהכשירו ואי משחיטת טריפה בחוץ הא נמי בהכשירו לענין לטהרו מידי נבילה וי"ל כדפרש"י דהשתא לא גמרינן להו מחולין בחוץ כדקאמרינן בגמרא אלא משחיטת קדשים בפנים מה קדשים שאין בהם צד שחיטה כו' ומ"מ מצריכינן לטעמא דלא שוה בפנים כבחוץ: יד] וטריפה וגו': טו] כמשמעו שתהא טריפה מטמא בבית הבליעה מחיים אי טריפה היה הרי נבילה אמורה תיבת אם נמחק: טז] מתניתא לקמיה: יז] שאין נבלות המאורע בה כו' יצא נבלות הבא לה: יח] חולין לא שוותה: יט] ואפילו חולין שלא בהיכשר כגון כו' דהא מתניתא מוקמינן לקמן כר"מ: כ] תיבת היא נמחק: כא] מנלן שחיטת פנים דקדשים דאינה מתרת את האיסור מנלן דלא תטמא ומשני והד"א: כב] בפנים ס"א ושחיטת חולין בפנים דאמרן אין מטמאין לאו משחיטת חולין בחוץ גמרי אלא משחיטת קדשים בפנים מה קדשים שאין בהם צד שחיטה לא מטמא ואפי' שלא בהכשירו כ"ש חולין שיש בהם צד שחיטה כ"כ ברש"י כת"י ולא כתוב שם כבעמוד דילפינן משחיטת טריפת חולין: כג] דשחיטת חולין: כד] בהכשירו (וטמא מטמא) [שאינו מטמא בשחיטתה] משלא: כה] ביה כיון שמתרת האיסור הס"ד:

נוסחאות רש"י כת"י

לאתויי מלק חולין בחוץ. דמטמא דלא תנן לה במתני' וה"ה דמצי למימר לאתויי נרבע ומוקצה ונעבד ואתנן ומחיר דמליקתם מטמא שלא [היה] פסולם בקודש והאי דנקט הא משום דתנא מתניתין מלק חולין בפנים וקדשים בחוץ ולא תנא מלק חולין בחוץ: מלקה פסול. כגון בעל מום: הפיגול והנותר והטמא אע"פ שאסורות באכילה ובהקרבה אינן מטמאין בבית הבליעה. ולא אמרינן כל שאינה ראויה לאכילה או להקרבה לא אשתראי מליקה לגבוה ולא יצאה מכלל נבילה שמליקה נבילה היא ומגזירת הכתוב הותרה באכילה בחטאת העוף ולהקרבה בעולה וזו שאינה ראויה לכך הרי היא בטומאה אשמועינן הכא דכיון דפיגול מרצה לפיגולו מהני מליקה לטהר ונותר וטמא בשעת מליקתן ראויין היו ולאחר מכאן נפסלו מליקתן מטהרתן: ואין קידוש כלי שרת במנחה בבמה דבבמה לא הוי כלי שרת כדאמרינן בפרק בתרא אשר ישרתו בם בקודש והילכך לא ילפינן זרות במקדש וכו' א): ה"ג בתורת כהנים הא מתניתא יכול תהא מליקה שהיא בפנים מטמאה בבית הבליעה ובמליקת פסולים כגון בשמאל או בלילה איצטריך ליה דאילו מליקות כשרות בהדיא איתרבו בפרק ב"ש לכל חטאתם לרבות חטאת העוף: הא נמי נבילה היא. כלומר היכי מצית למעוטי מהאי קרא דילמא הא נמי נבילה היא שהרי לא הותרה אלא המליקה מהכשר וכהלכתה להוציאה מכלל נבילות: יצא מליקה שהיא לפנים. ואפי' פסולה הואיל ומתרת את האיסור שאם עלתה לא תרד אינה מטמאה: ה"ג בת"כ יכול השוחט חולין בפנים וקדשים בין מבפנים ובין מבחוץ יטמאו בבית הבליעה כו': ב) ומשני הואיל ולא שוות בפנים כבחוץ מטעמא דכרת דהא אוקימנא כו'. נ"א בס"י כדאמר רבא אם הואיל כו' ואע"ג דשוו לענין אכילה כיון דבחוץ לא מטמא בפנים נמי לא מטמא דאי אמרת מטמא נמצא שלא שוו בפנים כבחוץ:

א) עי' רש"י ד"ה אין קידוש. ב) עי' רש"י ד"ה ומשני.

עין משפט
נר מצוה

כד א מיי' פ"ו מהל' פסה"מ הל"ג:

כה ב מיי' פ"ב מהל' אבות הטומאה הל"ו:

כו ג מיי' פ"ג מהל' אבות הטומאה הל"ד

רבי יהודה אומר *[א]מטמא א"ר מאיר ק"ו אם נבלת בהמה שמטמאה במגע ובמשא שחיטתה מטהרת טריפתה מטומאתה *נבלת העוף שאינו מטמא במגע ובמשא אינו דין שתהא שחיטתו מטהרת טריפתו מטומאתו מה מצינו א] בשחיטתו שהיא מכשרתה לאכילה ומטהרת טריפתו מטומאתו אף מליקתו שהיא מכשרתו באכילה תטהר טריפתו מידי טומאתו ב] רבי יוסי אומר דיה כנבלת בהמה שחיטתה מטהרתה ולא מליקתה: **גמ'** ור"מ לא דריש דיו והא דיו דאורייתא הוא *דתניא מדין קל וחומר כיצד °ויאמר ה' אל משה ואביה ירק ירק בפניה וגו' ק"ו לשכינה ארבעה עשר יום אלא דיו לבא מן הדין להיות כנדון א"ר יוסי ברבי אבין ר"מ קרא אשכח ג] וקדריש °זאת תורת הבהמה והעוף *וכי באיזו תורה שוותה בהמה לעוף ועוף לבהמה בהמה מטמאה במגע ובמשא ד] עוף אינו מטמא במגע ובמשא עוף מטמא בגדים אבית הבליעה בהמה אינה מטמאה בגדים אבית הבליעה אלא לומר לך מה בהמה דבר שמכשירה ה] לאכילה מטהר טריפתה מטומאתה אף עוף דבר שמכשיר באכילה מטהר טריפתו מטומאתו ור' יהודה מ"ט ו] קרא אשכח וקדריש נבלה טריפה אמר רבי יהודה טריפה למה נאמרה ז] אם טריפה חיה הרי נבילה אמורה אם טריפה אינה חיה הרי היא בכלל נבילה אלא להביא טריפה ששחטה שמטמאה אמר ליה רב שיזבי ח] אלא מעתה דכתיב °וחלב נבלה וחלב טרפה התם נמי נימא ט] אם טריפה חיה הרי נבילה אמורה אם טריפה אינה חיה הרי היא בכלל נבילה אלא להביא טריפה ששחטה שחלבה טהור מכלל דהיא מטמאה *והאמר רב יהודה אמר רב ואמרי לה במתניתא תנא °וכי ימות מן הבהמה מקצת בהמה מטמאה מקצת בהמה אינה מטמאה ואיזו זו [ג]זו טריפה ששחטה אלא י] טריפה מיבעי ליה למעוטי טמאה מי שיש במינה טריפה יצתה זו שאין במינה טריפה הכא נמי למעוטי עוף טמא שאין במינו טריפה עוף טמא לר' יהודה מנבילה נפקא ליה דתניא *רבי יהודה אומר יכול תהא נבלת עוף טמא מטמאה בגדים אבית הבליעה [ד]ת"ל °נבלה וטרפה לא יאכל מי שאיסורו משום בל תאכל נבילה יצא זה שאין איסורו משום בל תאכל נבילה אלא משום בל תאכל טמא האי

רבי יהודה אומר מטמא. דלא מהניא מליקה לטריפה וה"ה נמי דבשחיטת חולין טריפה פליג ר' יהודה וכן שנינו במסכת טהרות בפ' י"ג דברים לרבי יהודה אחת מלוקות ואחת שחוטות ולר"מ שתיהן מטהרות ולרבי יוסי שחיטה מטהרת טריפה אבל לא מליקה: ומה בהמה יא] בנבלתה מטמאה במגע ובמשא שחיטתה מטהרת טריפתה מטומאתה. כדילפינן בגמרא מוכי ימות מן הבהמה: עוף שאינו מטמא במגע ובמשא. אלא באכילה ובבית הבליעה כדכתיב (ויקרא כב) לא יאכל לטמאה בה אין לך אלא האמור בה: אינו דין כו'. וכיון דקיי"ל בשחיטה מק"ו ילפינן מליקה דקדשים מינה בבנין אב מה מצינו בשחיטה בחולין שמכשרתה באכילה כשאינה טריפה ומטהרת טריפה מטומאתה: אף מליקה. בקדשים המכשרתה באכילה כשאינה טריפה תטהר: דיה כנבלת בהמה. דהואיל ולא יליף עוף אלא מבהמה לטהר טריפה מטומאתה דיו לבא מן הדין להיות כנדון: **גמ'** מדין ק"ו כיצד. מנין שהתורה ניתנה לידרש ק"ו: הלא תכלם. לשון תימה הוא ולשון ק"ו: אלא דיו לבא מן הדין להיות כנדון. הכתוב לימדך שאינך רשאי להטיל על הבא מן הדין יותר מן הנדון דכתיב תסגר שבעת ימים: עוף אינו מטמא במגע ובמשא. דכתיב לא יאכל לטמאה בה אין לך אלא האמור בה: בהמה אינה מטמאה בבית הבליעה. אם תחב לו חבירו כזית בשר נבילה דתניא במסכת נדה (דף מג:) יכול יהא נבלת בהמה יב] (טמאה) מטמאה בבית הבליעה תלמוד לומר לא יאכל לטמאה בה מי שאין לה טומאה אלא אכילתו יצאתה זו שיש לה טומאה קודם שיאכלנו: דבר יג] שמכשיר. ואפילו מליקת קדשים דאי לשחיטה בק"ו אתיא לן: טריפה למה נאמרה. יד] *אלא ללמדנו בא שמשעת טריפה חלה עליה טומאה אם אכל ממנה מיד או ששחטה ואכל ממנה דאי בטריפה שמתה לאחר שנטרפה קאמר למה נאמרה: אם טריפה חיה. פלוגתא היא באלו טריפות (חולין דף מב.) איכא למ"ד טריפה חיה ואיכא למ"ד אינה חיה אם טריפה חיה ועד שמתה היתה בחזקת חיה: הרי נבילה אמורה. בפסוק טו] כיון שמתה מתנבלת במיתתה ואם טרפה אינה חשובה חיה הרי היא משעה שנטרפה בכלל נבילה: אלא להביא טריפה ששחטה. טז] לאשמעינן טריפה (אינו) חיה ואינו בכלל נבילה ולפיכך הוצרך לומר שטריפתה מביא עליה טומאה יז] זו מיד אם תלש ואכל ממנה בשר אפי' אינו [א]אבר של בשר גידין ועצמות וכיון דשם טריפה מביא לה טומאה מחיים אין שחיטה מועלת בה שאין שחיטה מתרת משום טריפה אלא משום נבילה: חלב נבילה וחלב טריפה יעשה לכל מלאכה. בא הכתוב להשמיענו על חלב נבילה שאינה מטמאה והכי אמרינן בפסחים פ' כל שעה (דף כג.): טריפה למה נאמרה. אם בטריפה שמתה מדבר אם טריפה חשובה חיה הרי נבילה אמורה וזו במיתתה נתנבלה ואם טריפה אינה חיה הרי היא בכלל נבילה יח][ב] מטורפת אלא להביא טריפה ששחטה שחלבה טהור אבל הבשר טמא בתמיה: אלא האי טריפה כו'. מסקנא דקושיא היא כלומר אלא ע"כ האי טריפה לא תדרשיה להכי דמיבעי ליה למעוטי טומאה דאין חלבה טהור וה"נ טריפה דכתיב גבי טומאת בית הבליעה למעוטי עוף טמא דריש ליה ולא טריפה ששחטה: האי

[א]) אבר עם הגידין ועצמות נ"ק [ב]) נ"ל משעה שנטרפה נ"ק

רבי יהודה אומר מטמא בבית הבליעה. תימה אפילו נבילה גמורה יט] לא תטמא לרבי יהודה דלא חייל אאיסור קדשים כדדריש רבי יהודה בגמרא דנבלת עוף טמא אינה מטמאה בגדים אבית הבליעה משום דכתיב נבלה וטרפה לא יאכל לטמאה בה מי שאיסורו משום בל תאכל נבילה יצא זה שאין איסורו משום בל תאכל נבילה אלא משום בל תאכל טמא ובפ' גיד הנשה (חולין דף ק:) דייקינן מינה לר' יהודה דאין איסור חל על איסור גבי רבי יהודה אומר אף בטמאה וי"ל דדוקא עוף טמא שאין במינו משום בל תאכל נבלה קממעט כ] וכן צריך לפרש בגמרא גבי חלב נבלה דלא איצטריך טריפה לאשמועינן דחלב טריפה טהור ולא דרשינן מי שאיסורו משום בל תאכל נבילה יצא טריפה כא] כי היכי דדרשינן גבי טמאה מי שאיסורו משום בל תאכל נבילה יצא בהמה טמאה:

קל וחומר לשכינה ארבעה עשר יום. אומר ר"ת דנקט ארבעה עשר יום משום דאמרינן בפ' המפלת (נדה דף לא.) דשלשה שותפין באדם שהקב"ה נותן בו *עשרה דברים כנגד אביו ואמו והשתא אמרי' דיו כאביו דמיניה ילפינן וה"ר *חיים מפרש דמן הדין הוה ליה למימר ק"ו לשכינה לעולם דחמורה כל כך אלא נקט י"ד כנגד שתי הסגרות דלא מצינו יותר משני הסגרות וכלשון הזה איתא בפרקי דר' אליעזר ק"ו לשכינה שתי הסגרות וקשה דבי"ג יום סגי דיום שביעי עולה לו לכאן ולכאן כדתנן במסכת נגעים (פ"ג מ"ה) אין בשתי הסגרות פחות מי"ג יום וי"ל דלישנא דקרא נקט ארבעה עשר משום דכתיב שבעת ימים בכל הסגר:

וכי באיזו תורה שוותה בהמה לעוף ועוף לבהמה. וא"ת והא איצטריך לכדדרשינן בחולין בריש פ"ב (דף כז:) מה בהמה בשחיטה אף עוף בשחיטה ור"א דריש מה בהמה מן הגואר אף עוף מן הגואר וי"ל כב] דכל מילי דרשינן דהיקשא הוא ואין היקש למחצה: **אי** טריפה חיה. א"כ אינה מטמאה עד לאחר מיתה ואז היא בכלל נבילה ואי טריפה אינה חיה הרי היא בכלל נבילה לא מצינו לפרש לאחר מיתה דמשמע שבא לחדש טומאה טפי אם אינה חיה מאם חיה מהדר ואמר כג] (התם) ואם טריפה אינה חיה הרי היא בכלל נבילה לכך פי' בקונטרס משנטרפה ירדה לה טומאה ומהיכן תלך ממנה ותימה הוא לומר כן דלא מצינו בעלי חיים מטמאין ומילתא דפשיטא בכולי הש"ס דאין טריפה מטמאה מחיים דבסוף פ"ק דחולין (ד' כ:) אמר זעירי נשברה מפרקת ורוב בשר עמה נבלה אבל בלא [א]) בשר לא אע"ג דמלק סימן אחד ומפרקת כדמשמע התם דפריך [ב]) וכי מעתה עומד ומבדיל ור"ת נמי אשכחן פרק אלו טריפות (חולין דף נז:) דאמר טריפה אינה חיה דקאמר סימן לטריפה שלשים יום וקאמר לעיל דמליקתה מטהרת טריפתה מטומאתה ואי טמאה מחיים משעת טריפות היאך תלך הטומאה ממנה ע"י המליקה והרב רבי חיים מפרש דה"ק אי טריפה אינה חיה ומיירי בתלש ממנה בשר חי כד] ואכלו הרי היא בכלל נבילה דבשר הפורש ממנה כפורש מן המתה ומטמא אע"ג שהבהמה עצמה אינה מטמאה לפי שהיא בחייה עתה כה] ויש לפרש אי טריפה חיה כלומר דמיירי בטריפה שעדיין חיה ותלש ממנה כזית כו] בשר ואכלו הרי נבילה דוקא אמורה ולא איירי כלל בפלוגתא דטריפה חיה ואי טריפה אינה חיה כלומר דמיירי בטריפה שאינה חיה שמתה שנתנבלה הרי היא בכלל נבילה ובת"כ גרס אי טריפה אינה מתה והלשון מגומגם קצת דהוה ליה למימר אי בטריפה חיה בב' ועוד הוה כז] למימר הרי היא נבילה: אלא

[א]) נ"ל רוב בשר נ"ק [ב]) נ"ל וכי מתה עומד ומולק נ"ק

יח] נבילה משנטרפה אלא: יט] גמורה של קדשים לא תטמא לר"י דלא חייל איסור נבילה וטומאה אאיסור קדשים: כ] קממעט וכל קדשים יש במינו משום בל תאכל נבילה וכן: כא] טריפה כו' כי: כב] וי"ל דטומאה כתיב בהאי קרא ולענין טומאה במאי שוות ועי"ל דכל: כג] ואמר הכי ואם תיבת התם נמחק: כד] חי ואכל הרי: כה] עתה ועוד יש לפרש: כו] כזית חלב ואכלו תיבת בשר נמחק: כז] הוה ליה למימר: תאכל יעשה לכל מלאכה. בא הכתוב לאשמועינן דחלב נבילה אינו מטמא כנבילה דכתיב יעשה לכל מלאכה אף לשל קודש והכי אמרי' בפסחים בפ' כל שעה: טריפה למה נאמרה. אי בטריפה שמתה מיירי אי אמרינן דטריפה חיה וזו הומתה הרי כבר נבילה אסורה הו נבילה היא: ואם טריפה אינה חיה הרי היא נבילה משעה שנטרפה אלא (על כל פנים) [ע"כ] בטריפה שנשחטה מיירי וקמ"ל דחלבה טהור: מכלל דהיא טמאה. בתמיה והאמר רב יהודה כו': אלא האי טריפה מבעי ליה. כלומר האי וחלב טריפה מבעי ליה למעוטי בהמה טמאה שאין; חלבה טהור אלא טמא כמו הבשר שלה דדרשינן וחלב טריפה מי שיש במינה טריפה יצאת בהמה טמאה שאין במינה טריפה: הכא נמי. האי והנפש אשר תאכל נבילה וטריפה מבעי ליה למעוטי עוף טמא נבלה וטריפה מי שיש במיני טריפה דהיינו עוף טהור נבילה שלו מטמא בגדים בבית הבליעה יצא עוף טמא שאין במיני טריפה ומנ"ל לר"י להביא טריפה ששחטה שתטמא: מנבילה נפקא ליה דלא תטמא טמא וצריך קרא לטהר...

[נ"ל מטמא בבית הבליעה]

טהרות פ"א מ"א

ב"ק כה. כ"ע קיא.

[חולין כז:]

ואם לא ללמדינו בא כו' ואכל ממנה א"כ למה נאמרה דאי בטריפה ט' נ"ק

חולין עד. פה: קכח:

[מ"ז דלא קתני אלא חשעה והלב תמנה והאם ארבעה ועי' תוס' ב"ב קיא. ד"ה קין] [עמ"ש תוס' ב"ב בגס ר' חיים ועי"ק]

נוסחאות
רש"י כת"י

ס"א ה"ג נבילה וטריפה א"ר יהודה טריפה למה נאמרה ול"ג יאכל לטמאה בה דלאו אהאי קרא קאי אלא אוהנפש אשר תאכל נבילה וטריפ' קאי בת"כ ובנבלת עוף טהור משתעי קרא: טריפה למה נאמרה. אם לא ללמוד בא שמשעת טרפותה יורד לה טומאת בית הבליעה ואין שחיטה מטהרתה אם טריפה חיה חשובה כחיה וזו אינה מטמאה אלא לאחר שמתה א"כ נבילה היא והרי כבר נבילה אמורה בפסוק וזו נבילת היא שכבר מתה: ואם טריפה אינה חיה הרי היא בכלל נבילה. משנטרפה ומאז ירדה לה טומאה ומהיכן תלך ממנה: אלא להביא טריפה שנשחטה. שאפילו נאמר טריפה חיה לימדך הכתוב שירדה לה טומאה משנטרפה ושוב אין שחיטתה מטהרת שהשחיטה אינה מקוה טהרה להעלות ממנה טומאה שירדה לה כבר: חלב נבילה וחלב טריפה

שיטה מקובצת

א] בשחיטתה שהיא: ב] רבי יוסי אומר כו'. והשתא איכא ג' מחלוקות בדבר דלר"מ בין שחיטה בין מליקה מטהרת ולר' יהודה בין שחיטה בין מליקה אינה מטהרת דכי היכי דלא מהניא מליקה לטריפה ה"נ לשחיטת עוף חולין טריפה נמי פליג ר' יהודה דאל"כ היינו ר' יוסי ולר' יוסי שחיטה מטהרת ולא מליקה: ג] אשכח ודרש אות ק' נמחק: ד] ובמשא ועוף אינו: ה] שמכשירה באכילה מטהר אות ל' נמחק: ו] מ"ט אמר רבה ר' יהודה קרא אשכח ודרש והנפש אשר תאכל נבילה: ז] אם טריפה חיה כו'. פ"ה דחוק מאד שהרי מחיים לא מצינו שירד לו טומאת נבילות ועי"ק וכי ר' יהודה מסופק במחלוקת האמוראים דפליגי אי טריפה חיה אי לא לכך נראה דה"פ אי טריפה חיה כלומר דמיירי קרא בעודו חיה שתלש ממנה בשר ואכל דמטמא בבית הבליעה הרי נבילה אמורה פירוש ושום טומאה לא שייכא מחיים ואי טריפה אינה חיה כלומר דאיירי קרא שמתה ולאחר טריפתה הרי הוא בכלל נבילה: ח] שיזבי לרבה אלא: ט] נימא טריפה למה נאמרה אם: י] אלא האי טריפה: יא] בהמה שנבלתה מטמאה: יב] תיבת טמאה נמחק: יג] דבר שמכשירה ואפילו מליקת קדשים דאי בשחיטה בק"ו: יד] נאמרה אם לא בא ללמדנו שמשעת (תיבת אלא ל"ש): טו] בפסוק וכיון שמתה נתנבלה במיתתה: טז] ולאשמועינן טריפה חיה תיבת אינו ל"ש: יז] תיבת זו נמחק:

NOT DEFILE IN THE GULLET; [69b] R. JUDAH SAID: IT DOES DEFILE IN THE GULLET. SAID R. MEIR: IT IS A ḲAL WA-ḤOMER: IF THE SHECHITAH OF AN ANIMAL CLEANSES IT, EVEN WHEN TEREFAH, FROM ITS UNCLEANNESS, YET WHEN IT IS NEBELAH IT DEFILES THROUGH CONTACT OR CARRIAGE; IS IT NOT LOGICAL THAT SHECHITAH CLEANSES A BIRD, WHEN TEREFAH FROM ITS UNCLEANNESS, SEEING THAT WHEN IT IS NEBELAH IT DOES NOT DEFILE THROUGH CONTACT OR CARRIAGE? NOW, AS WE HAVE FOUND THAT SHECHITAH, WHICH MAKES IT [A BIRD OF ḤULLIN] FIT FOR EATING, CLEANSES IT WHEN TEREFAH FROM ITS UNCLEANNESS; SO MELIḲAH, WHICH MAKES IT [A BIRD SACRIFICE] FIT FOR EATING, CLEANSES IT WHEN TEREFAH FROM ITS UNCLEANNESS. R. JOSE SAID: IT IS SUFFICIENT FOR IT TO BE LIKE THE NEBELAH OF A CLEAN [PERMITTED] ANIMAL, WHICH IS CLEANSED BY SHECHITAH,
a BUT NOT BY MELIḲAH.[1]

GEMARA. Now, does not R. Meir accept the principle of *dayyo* [it is sufficient]; surely the principle of *dayyo* is biblical? For it was taught: How is a *ḳal wa-ḥomer* applied? *And the Lord said unto Moses: If her father had but spit in her face, should she not hide in shame seven days?*[2] How much more should a divine reproof necessitate [shame for] fourteen days; but it is sufficient for that which is inferred by an argument to be like the premise![3]—Said R. Jose son of R. Abin: R. Meir found a text and interpreted it:[4] *This is the law of the beast and of the bird.*[5] Now, in which law is a beast similar to a bird and a bird to a beast? A beast defiles through contact and carriage, whereas a bird does not defile through contact or carriage; a bird defiles garments [when its flesh] is in the gullet, whereas a beast does not defile garments [when its flesh] is in the gullet. But it is to tell you: as in the case of a beast, that which makes it fit for eating makes it clean when *terefah* from its defilement; so in the case of a bird, that which makes it fit for eating[6] makes it clean when *terefah* from its defilement.

Then what is R. Judah's reason?—Said Rabbah, R. Judah
b found a text, and interpreted it:[1] [*And every soul which eateth*] *nebelah or terefah*[2] [... *he shall wash his clothes* etc.].[3] Said R. Judah: Why is '*terefah*' stated? If '*terefah*' can live, then surely '*nebelah*' is already stated;[4] while if '*terefah*' cannot live, it is included in *nebelah*?[5] Hence it is to include a *terefah* which one slaughtered, [and teaches] that it defiles.

If so, said R. Shisbi to him, when it is written, *And the fat* [ḥeleb] *of nebelah, and the fat of terefah* [*may be used for any other service, but ye shall in no wise eat it*]:[6] there too let us argue: Why is *terefah* stated? If *terefah* can live, then surely *nebelah* is already stated; and if *terefah* cannot live, it is included in *nebelah*? Hence it is to include a *terefah* which one slaughtered, [and teaches] that its *ḥeleb* is clean? Hence it follows that it defiles?[7] But surely Rab Judah said in Rab's name, whilst others say that it was taught in a Baraitha: *And if there die of a beast:*[8] some beasts defile, and some beasts do not. And which is it [that is excluded]? A *terefah* which was slaughtered!—Rather, [this is R. Shizbi's difficulty]: This *terefah*[9] is necessary in order to exclude an unclean animal,[10] [for it intimates:] only that in whose species there is *terefah:* hence this [an unclean animal] is excluded,
c since there is no *terefah* in its species.[1] Then here too[2] [say that] [the inclusion of *terefah*] excludes an unclean [forbidden] bird, since there is no *terefah* in its species?[3]—[The exclusion of] an unclean bird is, in R. Judah's opinion, derived from *nebelah*. For it was taught, R. Judah said: You might think that the *nebelah* of an unclean bird defiles garments [when its flesh] is in the gullet. Therefore it states, *Nebelah or terefah he shall not eat* [*to defile himself therewith*]:[4] only that [defiles] whose interdict is on account of 'do not eat *nebelah*'; hence this [an unclean bird] is excluded, since its interdict is not on account of 'do not eat *nebelah*', but on account

a (1) For notes v. *supra* 50b, 51a. (2) Num. XII, 14. (3) Since you argue from her *father's* reproof, even a Divine reproof does not necessitate a longer period of shame. As Scripture proceeds, '*Let her be shut up without the camp* seven *days*', it is evident that this principle is Scriptural. (4) He accepts the principle of *dayyo*, but his ruling is based on a text, which makes him disregard the principle in this instance. (5) Lev. XI, 46. (6) *Sc. meliḳah*, in the case of a bird sacrifice.
b (1) Emended text (Sh. M.). (2) E.V. *that which dieth of itself, or that which is torn of beasts*. According to the Talmudic interpretation an animal which dies by any method other than the correct ritual one (*shechitah*) is called *nebelah*, even if it is ritually slaughtered, but there is a defect in the *shechitah*. *Terefah* denotes an animal which was properly slaughtered with *shechitah*, but was then found to have been suffering from certain diseases or organic disturbances. These are listed in Ḥul. 42a, where there is a controversy whether a *terefah* could have lived (for more than twelve months) or not. On the view that it could, it is regarded as having been alive until the *shechitah;* on the view that it could not, it is regarded as already dead (technically) even *before* the *shechitah*, in which case it is obviously the same as *nebelah*. (3) Lev. XVII, 15. (4) So that if the *terefah* dies of its disease before it is slaughtered, it is obviously included in *nebelah*. (5) Even whilst alive. So Rashi. Tosaf. and Sh. M. explain differently. (6) Ibid. VII, 24. The Talmud (Pes. 23a) interprets this to mean that the *ḥeleb* of a *nebelah* is clean and does not defile. (7) The Talmud interposes: since R. Shizbi objects thus, it follows that in truth such *ḥeleb* is unclean and defiles. (8) Ibid. XI, 39. Lit. translation. '*Of*' is partitive, and is understood as a limitation. The verse continues: *he that touches the carcass thereof shall be unclean until the evening*. (9) In the verse which he quotes. (10) The *heleb* of an unclean (i.e., forbidden) animal does not defile.
c (1) Only the *ḥeleb* of an animal which can become *terefah* defiles. But an unclean animal, which cannot be eaten in any case, can never become *terefah* in a technical sense, and therefore its *ḥeleb* does not defile. (2) In the verse quoted by R. Judah (the Tanna), not *Rab* Judah, the amora. (3) That is the conclusion of R. Shizbi's objection: Interpret the text thus, and the question returns. What is R. Judah's reason, after R. Meir proves the contrary? (4) Lev. XXII, 8.

of 'do not eat unclean'.[5] [70a] Let this too be derived from, *'And the fat of nebelah'*, [which intimates:] that whose interdict is on account of 'do not eat the *heleb* of *nebelah*;'[6] hence this [the *heleb* of a forbidden animal] is excluded, since its interdict is not on account of 'do not eat the *heleb* of *nebelah*', but on account of uncleanness?[7] —Rather, this *terefah*[8] is required in order to include *hayyah*.[9] I might argue: Only that whose *heleb* is forbidden whilst its flesh is permitted [is included in this law]; hence a *hayyah* is excluded, since its *heleb* and its flesh are permitted.[10] Therefore [the word *terefah*] informs us [that it is not so].[11] Wherein[12] does an unclean [forbidden] animal differ?[13] [Presumably] because its *heleb* is not
a distinct from its flesh?[1] but then the *heleb* of a *hayyah* is not distinct from its flesh?[2] Moreover, surely it is written, *but ye shall in no wise eat it?*[3]—Rather, said Abaye, *Terefah*[4] is needed for its own purpose,[5] lest you argue: Since an unclean [animal] is forbidden whilst yet alive, and a *terefah* is forbidden whilst yet alive:[6] as the *heleb* of an unclean [animal] is unclean [defiles], so is the *heleb* of a *terefah* unclean.[7] If so, this too[8] is required, lest you say: Since an unclean bird may not be eaten, and a *terefah* may not be eaten; as an unclean bird does not defile [garments, when the flesh is in the gullet], so a *terefah* too does not defile? Moreover, can *terefah* really be derived from an unclean animal:[9] an unclean animal enjoyed no period of fitness,[10] whereas a *terefah* enjoyed a period of fitness?[11] And should you answer, what can be said of a *terefah* from birth; yet of its kind this can be said.[12]—Rather said Raba: The Torah ordained, Let the interdict of *nebelah* come and fall upon the interdict of *heleb*; let the interdict of *terefah* come and fall upon the interdict of *heleb*.[13] And both are necessary. For if we were informed [this about] *nebelah*, [I would argue that the reason is] because it defiles;[14] but as for *terefah*, I would say that it does not [fall upon the interdict of *heleb*]. And if we were informed [this about] *terefah*, [I would say that the reason is] because its interdict dates from when it was alive; but as for *nebelah*, I would say that it is not so. Hence [they are both] necessary.

b Now how does R. Meir employ this [word] *terefah?*[1]—He needs it to exclude *shechitah* which is within.[2] And R. Judah?[3]—Another *'terefah'* is written.[4] And R. Meir?[5]—One excludes *shechitah* which is within, and the other excludes an unclean forbidden bird. And R. Judah?[6]—That is derived from *nebelah*.[7] And R. Meir: how does he employ this *'nebelah'*?—[To show that] the standard of eating [is required], viz., as much as an olive.[8] Yet let this be derived from the first text,[9] since the Divine Law expressed it in terms of eating?—One [text] is employed to shew that the standard of eating [is required for defilement], viz., as much as an olive; while the other intimates that this standard of eating must be within the time of eating half [a loaf].[10] I might argue, since this is anomalous,[11] let it defile even when it takes more than the time required for eating half [a loaf].[12] Hence [the text] informs us [otherwise].

Our Rabbis taught: *And the heleb of nebelah, and the heleb of terefah, [may be used for any other service; but ye shall in no wise eat of it]*: Scripture speaks of the *heleb* of a clean [permitted] animal.[13] You say, Scripture speaks of the *heleb* of a clean animal; yet perhaps it is not so, but rather of the *heleb* of an unclean animal? You can answer: [Scripture] declared [an animal] clean on account of its being slaughtered, and declared it clean on account of *heleb*:[14] as when it declared it clean on account of being slaughtered, it referred to a
c clean [permitted], but not an unclean [forbidden] animal;[1] so when it declared it clean on account of *heleb*, it referred to a clean, but not an unclean animal. Or argue in this wise: [Scripture] cleansed from *nebelah*,[2] and it cleansed from *heleb*:[3] as when it cleansed from *nebelah*, it was in the case of unclean, and not in the case of clean;[4] so when it cleansed from *heleb*, [it did so] in the case of unclean,

(5) Hence the former verse is left free for the interpretation stated above. (6) Only that *heleb* does not defile. (7) I.e., the whole animal is forbidden. (8) In the verse quoted by R. Shizbi. (9) A non-domestic animal, e.g., a deer, which may be eaten. The *heleb* of a *hayyah* is permitted; that of a *behemah* (a domestic animal, e.g., a sheep) is forbidden. The discussion hitherto has been about the *heleb* of a *behemah*. (10) Therefore if a *hayyah* becomes *nebelah*, I would think that its *heleb* defiles, just as its flesh. (11) For it teaches that the *heleb* of whatever is liable to become *terefah*, which includes *hayyah*, does not defile when *nebelah*. (12) 'Said he to him' is deleted (Sh. M.). (13) That you do not learn from this text that its *heleb* is clean and does not defile.

a (1) Both are forbidden, and therefore you do not apply this text to it, since that implies that there is a distinction between them. (2) Both being permitted. Hence you should not apply it to *hayyah* either. (3) Lev. VII, 24. From this we infer anon that the *heleb* of a *hayyah* which is *nebelah does* defile. Hence the text cannot apply to it. (4) In the verse quoted by R. Shizbi. (5) To shew that the *heleb* of a *terefah* which died is clean. (6) In the sense that *shechitah* cannot permit it. (7) Hence the text teaches otherwise. (8) *Terefah* in the text quoted by R. Judah. (9) That you need a text to shew that it does not defile. (10) Never at any time might it be eaten. (11) Before it became *terefah*. (12) Though that particular *terefah* was never fit, *terefah* in general was fit at one time. (13) The text teaches that when one eats *heleb* of *nebelah* or *terefah*, he is liable not only on account of *heleb* but also on account of *nebelah* or *terefah*. For otherwise one might argue: since the interdict of *heleb* comes first, the other interdicts cannot apply to it at all. (14) Which *heleb* does not. Hence it is logical that the interdict of *nebelah*, being greater in that respect, falls upon that of *heleb*.

b (1) In the verse quoted by R. Judah. (2) As stated *supra* 69a. (3) How does he know that? (4) *Terefah* is written in Lev. XVII, 15 and XXII, 8. Hence one is used for each. (5) How does he utilise this second *'terefah'*? (6) Whence does he derive the latter? (7) As *supra* 69b bottom. (8) One is not liable for eating *nebelah* unless he eats at least as much as an olive (this is the general standard for all forbidden food). The text intimates that this too is the smallest quantity which defiles. (9) Lev. XVII, 15. (10) One is not liable for eating unless he eats as much as an olive within the normal time for eating half a loaf, which is half a meal (Rashi: half a loaf is the size of four average eggs; Maim.: *three* average eggs). The text teaches that when a man eats the flesh of *nebelah* (of a bird), he does not defile his garments unless he eats as much as an olive within that time. (11) There is no other case in Scripture where an article does not defile through contact, but only when it enters the gullet. (12) Being unique in one respect, it might be unique in another. (13) Teaching that its *heleb* does not defile as *nebelah*. (14) Scripture decreed that when an animal is slaughtered (with *shechitah*) it does not defile; and that the *heleb* of *nebelah* does not defile.

c (1) Even if an unclean animal is ritually slaughtered, it defiles. (2) There is a case where *nebelah* does not defile. (3) *Heleb* does not defile, as stated. (4) An unclean (forbidden) bird does not defile (as *nebelah*) when it is in the gullet, whereas a clean bird does.

האי נמי תיפוק לי °מחלב נבלה מי שאיסורו משום בל תאכל חלב נבלה יצאתה זו שאין איסורה משום בל תאכל א] [חלב נבלה] אלא משום טמא אלא האי טריפה מיבעי ב] לאיתויי חיה סלקא דעתך אמינא מי שחלבה אסור ובשרה מותר יצאת ג] זו שחלבה ובשרה מותר קמ"ל ד] א"ל מאי שנא טמאה דאין חלבה חלוק מבשרה חיה נמי אין חלבה חלוק מבשרה ועוד הכתיב °ואכל לא תאכלוהו אלא אמר אביי טריפה לגופיה איצטריך שלא תאמר הואיל וטמאה אסורה מחיים וטריפה אסורה מחיים מה טמאה חלבה טמא אף טריפה חלבה טמא אי הכי האי נמי מיבעי (א) שלא תאמר הואיל ועוף טמא אסור באכילה וטריפה אסורה באכילה מה עוף טמא אינו מטמא אף טריפה אינה מטמאה ועוד מי איכא למילף טרפה מטמאה טמאה לא היתה לה שעת הכושר טריפה היתה לה שעת הכושר וכי תימא טריפה מבטן מאי איכא למימר במינה מיהא איכא אלא אמר רבא *התורה אמרה יבא איסור נבילה ויחול על איסור חלב יבא איסור טריפה ויחול על איסור חלב וצריכי דאי אשמעינן נבילה משום דמטמיא אבל טריפה אימא לא ואי אשמעינן טריפה משום (ב) דאיסורה מחיים ה] אבל נבילה אימא לא צריכא ור"מ האי טריפה מאי עביד ליה מיבעי ליה למעוטי שחיטה שהיא לפנים ורבי יהודה טריפה אחרינא כתיב ורבי מאיר חד למעוטי שחיטה שהיא לפנים וחד למעוטי עוף טמא ו] ורבי יהודה מנבלה נפקא ליה ורבי מאיר האי נבלה מאי עביד לה לשיעור אכילה בכזית ותיפוק לי מקרא קמא מדאפקיה רחמנא בלשון אכילה חד לשיעור אכילה בכזית וחד לשיעור אכילה בכדי אכילת פרס ס"ד אמינא הואיל וחידוש הוא יותר מכדי אכילת פרס נמי ליטמא קמ"ל ת"ר °וחלב נבלה וחלב טרפה *בחלב בהמה טהורה הכתוב מדבר אתה אומר בחלב בהמה טהורה הכתוב מדבר או אינו אלא בחלב בהמה טמאה אמרת טיהר מכלל שחוטה וטיהר מכלל חלב מה כשטיהר מכלל שחוטה בטהורה ולא בטמאה אף כשטיהר מכלל חלב בטהורה ולא בטמאה או כלך לדרך זו טיהר מכלל נבילה וטיהר מכלל חלב מה כשטיהר מכלל נבילה בטמאה ולא בטהורה אף כשטיהר מכלל חלב בטמאה ולא בטהורה אמרת

כשבא

רש"י

האי נמי תיפוק ליה כו'. חלב טמאה תיפוק ליה נמי דמטמא דמהיכא תיתי לטהרה מהאי קרא דיעשה לכל מלאכה האי לאו א] בטמאה כתיב דהא כתיב [ואכל] לא תאכלוהו לחלב: מי שאיסורו משום אכילת חלב. ובשרה מותר טיהרתי לך יצאת זו שכולה אסורה משום בל תאכל טמא ואכתי אימא טריפה למה נאמרה כו': אלא האי טריפה מיבעי לאיתויי חיה דס"ד מי שחלבה אסור כו' קמ"ל. ה"ג ושינויא הוא לאיתויי חיה טהורה שמתה שחלבה אסור דס"ד ואכל לא תאכלוהו כתיב בהאי קרא מי שחלבו אסור ובשרו מותר טיהרתי לך חלבה מכלל נבילה אבל חיה שחלבה מותר כבשרה לענין נבילה נמי יטמא כבשרה קמ"ל טריפה כל שיש במינו טריפה ואפילו חיה: ופרכינן מ"ש טמאה. דלא נפקא לן לטהר חלבה מהאי קרא דאין חלבה חלוק מבשרה ולא קרינא ח] ואכל לא תאכלוהו לחלב לחודיה שהרי הכל איסור: חיה נמי אין חלבה חלוק מבשרה. לאיסורו ולא קרינא ביה ואכל לא תאכלוהו: ועוד. ממשמעותא דקרא נמי תיקשה לן דלא בחלב חיה קאי דהא כתיב ואכל לא תאכלוהו ולקמן ילפינן מינה בברייתא בשמעתין ט] בחלב חיה נבילה לא טיהר מכלל טומאה: טריפה לגופיה איצטריך. לטהר חלב טריפה שמתה ולעולם טריפה חיה ודקאמרת הרי נבילה אמורה איצטריך סד"א הואיל וטמאה אסורה מחיים וטריפה מחיים אסורה כו': אי הכי. טריפה דכתיב גבי עוף נמי איצטריך לגופיה ולומר עוף י] *שמתה מטמא בבית הבליעה שלא תאמר כו': ועוד. גבי בהמה: מי איכא למילף טריפה מטמאה. דניבעי קרא לטהר: ה"ג אלא אמר רבא כו' התורה אמרה. בא הכתוב לומר לך יבא איסור כו' ומשום אכל לא תאכלוהו דסיפיה דקרא פירש בו נבילה וטריפה לחייב את האוכלו משום חלב ומשום נבילה ומשום טריפה שלא תאמר אין איסור נבילה וטריפה חלין על איסור חלב שקדם לכולם: משום דמטמיא. הילכך אמירא לחול על איסור חלב: ורבי מאיר. דאמר עוף שחיטתו מטהרת טריפתו: האי טריפה. דגבי עוף מאי עביד ליה: למעוטי שחיטה שהיא לפנים. וכדאמרן לעיל (דף סט.) מה טריפה שטוה בפנים כבחוץ אלא השוחט עוף חולין בפנים כו': טריפה אחרינא כתיב. גבי נבילת עוף טהור וכל נפש אשר תאכל נבילה וטריפה באזרח ובגר וכבס *בגדיו (ויקרא יז) וחד יא] לא יאכל נבילה וטריפה לטמאה בה (שם כב): וחד למעוטי עוף טמא. דדרשינן מי שיש במינו טריפה: ורבי יהודה. עוף טמא מקרא יתירא דנבילה לא יאכל נפקא ליה דלא איצטריך אלא לדרוש ולומר מי שאזהרתו משום בל תאכל נבילה יב] יצא זה שאין איסורו משום בל תאכל נבילה אלא משום בל תאכל טמא: ורבי מאיר האי. קרא יתירא דנבילה לא יאכל מיבעיא ליה ללמד טומאתו שאינו מטמא אלא כשיעור איסור אכילתו דהיינו כזית: מקרא קמא. *) והנפש אשר תאכל: בכדי אכילת פרס. שאם שהה באכילת כזית יותר מכדי אכילת פרס הרי היא כשאר אכילות שאין מצטרפין לעונשין ואף זו אין מצטרפת ליטמא בבית הבליעה: דחידוש הוא. שלא מצינו בתורה טומאה כזו שאין לו טומאה מבחוץ יג] ובבית הבליעה באה לו טומאה (ג): הכתוב מדבר. לטהרו מלטמא משום נבילות: יד] טיהר מכלל שחוטה. טיהר מלטמא מטעם שחיטה שהשחיטה מטהרתה: וטיהר מכלל חלב. מטעם חלב טיהר את הנבילה מלטמא שכתב כאן שחלב נבילה טהור: מה כשטיהר. בשר שחוטה מלטמא טהורה טיהר ולא טמאה דטמאה אין שחיטתה מטהרתה דילפינן לה בת"כ מקרא יתירא ולאלה תטמאו כל הנוגע בהם במותם והאי בהם יתירא הוא לומר אע"פ שהן שחוטין ומה אני מקיים במותם ולא בחייהם ובבהמה טמאה כתיב דסמוך ליה כל הבהמה אשר היא מפרסת פרסה (ד) וגו': אף כשטיהר משום חלב. מלטמא בטהורה טיהר ולא בטמאה: ה"ג בתורת כהנים אמרת **) כלך לדרך זו טיהר מכלל נבילה וטיהר מכלל חלב מה כשטיהר מכלל נבילה בטמאה ולא בטהורה אף כשטיהר כו' טיהר בשר נבילה מלטמא ולקמן מפרש לה בנבלת עוף טמא וטיהר מכלל חלב כדאמרן :בטמאה ולא בטהורה. עוף טמא טיהר מלטמא בבית הבליעה ולא עוף טהור: ה"ג

*) נ"ל וכל נפש **) נ"ל או כלך נ"ק

תוספות

אלא לאתויי חיה. טו] כך גרס הקונטרס וקשה דמאי קפריך מ"ש טמאה כו' אדרבה משום דדמי לטמאה איצטריך קרא לאתויי ומאי פריך נמי ואכל לא תאכלוהו אדרבה משום הכי איצטריך קרא טריפה דמשמע כל שיש במינו טריפה חלבה טהור ואפי' חיה ור"ת גרס אלא למעוטי חיה מאי טעמא מי שחלבה אסור וכו' ול"נ סד"א ופריך אמאי איצטריך קרא לומר דחלב חיה טמא מאי שנא טמאה כו' טז] ומיהו קשה דטריפה לא משמע למעוטי אלא לרבויי כל שיש במינה טריפה יז]: מה טמאה חלבה טמא. וכי תימא מה לטמאה שכן אין שחיטתה מטהרתה תאמר לטריפה חיה תוכיח: יבא איסור נבילה ויחול על איסור חלב. תימה *למאן דאית ליה איסור מוסיף למה ליה קראי וכי תימא מהכא יליף בעלמא שאני הכא דאיסור חלב קל הוא דהותר מכללו ולכך אתי איסור נבילה וחייל עליה: ואי אשמעינן טריפה משום דאיסורא מחיים כו'. תימה דבפ"ב דחולין (דף לז:) עביד ק"ו איפכא ומה מחיים אתי איסור טריפה וחייל אאיסור חלב נבילה דלאחר מיתה מבעיא ושם פירשתי: וחד למעוטי עוף טמא. הא דלא נפקא ליה לרבי מאיר מהיכא דנפקא ליה לרבי יהודה משום *דר' מאיר לטעמיה *דאית ליה איסור חל על איסור: ורבי מאיר האי נבילה מאי עביד ליה. וא"ת על כרחיך צריך לכתוב נבילה דאי הוה כתיב טריפה לא יאכל לטמאה בה ולא כתב נבילה אם כן הוה אמינא דטריפה בלא נבילה מטמאה יח] וי"ל כיון דכתיב יט] (ויקרא יז) (והנפש) [וכל נפש] אשר תאכל נבילה וטריפה מה התם נבילה עמה אף כאן נבילה עמה: לשיעור אכילה בכזית. אפשר דרבי יהודה נמי אית ליה ואע"ג דלא מיותר: יצתה חיה שחלבה ובשרה מותר. הא דדחיק בפרק בהמה המקשה (חולין דף ע:) לאשכוחי דנבלת חיה טהורה מטמאה כ] ולא מצי למידרש מהכא דהא חלבה טמא דאי לאו דאשכחן במקום אחר דנבלת חיה מטמאה לא הוה דרשי' הכי: ואפי'

חולין לז. [קב.] | יבמות לד.

הגהות הב"ח

שיטה מקובצת

גליון הש"ס

נוסחאות רש"י כת"י

תורה אור

א] כשבא בדרך זו היא בטהורה כשבא בדרך זו היא בטמאה ג] ת"ל טריפה מי שיש במינה טריפה "אוציא את הטמאה שאין במינה טריפה ולא אוציא את החיה שיש במינה טריפה ת"ל °ואכל לא תאכלוהו מי שחלבה אסור ובשרה מותר ד'יצא חיה שחלבה ובשרה מותר א"ל רב יעקב בר אבא לרבא אלא מעתה נבלת בהמה טהורה הוא דמטמאה נבלת בהמה טמאה לא מטמאה אמר ליה כמה סבי שבישתו בה סיפא אתאן לנבלת עוף טמא אמר רבי יוחנן לא טיהר רבי מאיר אלא בתמימין אבל בבעלי מומין לא ורבי אלעזר אמר אפילו בבעלי מומין איתמר נמי אמר רב ביבי אמר רבי אלעזר מטהר היה רבי מאיר בבעלי מומין ג] ואפילו באווזין ותרנגולין בעי רבי ירמיה ערף עז מהו אווזין ותרנגולין טעמא מאי דמינא דעופות נינהו אבל עז לאו מינא דעגלה נינהו או דילמא מינא דבהמה הוא יתיב רב דימי וקאמר לה להא שמעתא אמר ליה אביי °מכלל דעגלה ערופה טהורה היא א"ל 'אין אמרי דבי רבי ינאי *כפרה כתיב בה כקדשים מתיב רב נתן אבוה דרב הונא *(בר נתן) ואכל לא תאכלוהו אין לי אלא חלב שאסור באכילה ומותר בהנאה חלב של שור הנסקל ועגלה ערופה מנין ת"ל °כל חלב ואי ס"ד עגלה ערופה טהורה היא היא טהורה וחלבה טמא היכא דערף מיערף לא איצטריכא ליה כי איצטריכא 'היכא דשחטה מישחט ותיהני ליה שחיטה לטהרה מידי נבלה לא צריכא שמתה מכלל דמחיים אסורה אין *אמר רבי ינאי גבול שמעתי ושכחתי ונסבין חברייא למימר 'ירידתה לנחל איתן היא אוסרתה:

הדרן עלך חטאת העוף

כל *'הזבחים שנתערבו בחטאות המתות או בשור הנסקל אפילו אחת בריבוא ימותו כולן 'נתערבו בשור שנעבדה בו עבירה או שהמית

ה"ג כשאתה בא בדרך זו היא בטהורה וכשאתה בא בדרך זו היא בטמאה. הילכך מדינא לא נפקא ת"ל טריפה כו': אלא מעתה כו'. אמתני' פריך דקתני מה כשטהר מכלל נבילה בטמאה ולא בטהורה ד]: כמה סבי שבישתו בה. תמיה אני על זקנים מרובין שכמותכם שנשתבשתם בה: סיפא. דקתני טיהר מכלל נבילה: אתאן לנבלת עוף טמא. שטיהרה הכתוב מלטמא בבית הבליעה: לא טיהר רבי מאיר. במליקת טריפה אלא בתמימים דשייכא בהו מליקה: ואפי' באווזים. דלאו בני מזבח הן ובלבד שיהו קדשים בפנים דהא טריפה נמי לא חזיא בתורין ובני יונה וטיהרה הואיל ומליקה הכשר קדשים בפנים היא: ערף עז. על החלל במקום עגלה ערופה: מהו. לר"מ מי אמרינן כי היכי ה] דמטהר מליקת אווזין קדשים בפנים הואיל ומליקת שום עוף בפנים הוא ה"נ (א) עריפה הכשר טהרת עגלה היא מידי נבילה כדאמרי' לקמן: ה"ג אבל עז לאו מינא דעגלה הוא. שזו מין גסה וזו מין דקה: אין לי. שטהור מידי נבילה אלא חלב שאסור באכילה ומותר בהנאה כדכתיב (ויקרא ז) יעשה לכל מלאכה: חלב שור הנסקל ועגלה ערופה. שאסור בהנאה מנין שטהור: ת"ל כל חלב. דסמיך ו] ליה כי כל אוכל חלב ואי ס"ד עגלה ערופה טהורה אילטריך קרא לטהר חלבה וכי היא טהורה וחלבה טמא: להיכא דשחטיה מישחט. משנאסרה בהנאה מחיים כדמפרש לקמיה דמחיים נאסרה: ותיהני לה שחיטתה. אע"פ שאינה מתירתה לא באכילה ולא בהנאה תטהרנה מלטמא דאין לך שחוטה בבהמה טהורה שמטמאה: שמתה. דהשתא בשרה טמאה ואילטריך לטהר חלבה שלא תאמר לא טיהר אלא חלב שאתה קורא בו יעשה לכל מלאכה: מכלל דמחיים אסורה. ואע"פ שלא נערפה מדקתני חלב עגלה ערופה מנין ואוקימתה בשמתה: גבול שמעתי. בהמאימתי ז]: ונסבין חברייא. וסבורין התלמידין מדעתם לומר: ירידתה כו'. ובקידושין יליף לה דנאסרה מחיים:

הדרן עלך חטאת העוף

כל הזבחים. אפילו אחת בריבוא. השתא משמע אחת כשירה ברבוא של חטאות המתות הילכך פריך בגמרא מאי אפילו הא הוו מתות רובא דקתני שנתערבו בחטאות המתות חמש חטאות מתות ח] ניהו *וולד חטאת וחטאת שמתו בעליה ותמורת חטאת ושכיפרו בעליה ושאבדה ושנמצאת בעלת מום: נתערבו. זבחים כשרים בשור שנעבדה בו עבירה אחד באחד ומפרש ואזיל מאי היא כגון שהמית

ואפילו באווזין ותרנגולין. ומתני' דמסכת טהרות(פ"א מ"א)מוכחא קצת דקתני י"ג דברים נאמרו בנבלת עוף טהור וקתני סיפא ר"מ אומר מליקתה ושחיטתה מטהרתה ט] משמע בכל עופות דומיא דרישא ודומיא דשחיטה: אבל עז לאו מינא דעגלה נינהו. אע"פ דאווזין ותרנגולין לאו מינא דתורים ובני יונה ומטהרין לא דמי דהכא עגלה בהמה גסה ועז בהמה דקה אבל בעופות לא שייך למימר מין גסה ודקה אע"ג דמליט בלשון משנה עוף הדק ועוף הגס בפרק אלו טריפות י] (חולין מב.) (*וקשה משילהי אותו ואת בנו) (שם דף פב):

הדרן עלך חטאת העוף

כל הזבחים שנתערבו בחטאות המתות כו'. ואם תאמר תנינא חדא זימנא במס' קינין (פ"ב מ"ג) ואם פרח מבין המתות לכולם הרי כולם ימותו וצריך לעשות נריכותא דבגמרא פריך תנינא חדא זימנא במתני' דכל האסורים לגבי מזבח ומשני נריכא ושמא אי מהתם הוה אמינא ה"מ עופות דהפסד מועט אבל זבחים דהפסידן מרובה אימא לא נפסדינהו *לכולהו:

אפילו אחת בריבוא ימותו כולן. הקשה ה"ר יצחק ברבי מרדכי דבפרק הנשרפין (סנהדרין דף עט:) תנן רוצח שנתערב באחרים כולן פטורין ר' יהודה אומר כונסין אותן לכיפה ומפרש בגמרא בשור שלא נגמר דינו שנתערב בשורים אחרים שנגמר דינן קמיפלגי ופטרי רבנן משום דאין גומרים דינו של שור אלא בפניו והשתא הכא דרובא דהיתירא ופסידא דקדשים אמרינן ימותו כולן התם דרובא דאיסורא יא] והדיוט לא כ"ש ונראה לרבינו יצחק דגרסינן כמו שמצא בספר אחד ישן בשור שלא נגמר דינו שנתערב בשורים אחרים ול"ג שנגמר דינן אלא (איירי) בשורים מעליא עסקינן והשיב לו ר"ת דמתניתין דקתני כולן פטורים משמע שהאחרים בני חיובא ואע"ג דברישא דשמעתין אמרינן מאי אחרים אילימא אחרים כשירין פשיטא ולא פריך פטורים פטור מיבעי ליה התם כיון דמצי למיפרך מגופה לא חש למידק ועוד דריש לקיש אדרבי אבהו קאי דמשני הכא ברוצח שלא נגמר דינו שנתערב ברוצחים אחרים עסקינן ועלה קאי ר"ל ומשני באדם כ"ע לא פליגי דפטירי אלא הכא בשור שלא נגמר דינו כו' ומשמע דההוא עניינא דאוקמה רבי אבהו באדם מוקי לה ריש לקיש *) בשור שנגמר דינו יב] אבל נתערב בשורים יג] מעליא היה אומר ר"ל יד] ניכבשינהו דניידן וכל דפריש מרובא פריש ומתניתין דשילהי מסכת ע"ז (דף עד.) דשור הנסקל טו] אוסר בכל שהוא מיירי בשנסקל דליכא למימר ניכבשינהו ותדע דלא קתני שנגמר דינו ומתני' דהכא דקתני ימותו כולן בנתערב בזבחים מיירי ולגבוה וגזירה שמא יבואו י' כהגים בבת א' (לקמן דף עג:) ומסקי מן הקבוע למזבח אבל בעלמא אמרינן ניכבשינהו דניידן ומטעם זה היה אומר רבינו תם דנראה לו להתיר דרוסת הזאב ברוב למעשים בכל יום דזאבים טורפים וטשאין שה מן העדר ורועה מצילן ושריא להו דאע"ג דבעלי חיים חשיבי וכן רוב עופות דורסין אווזין ותרנגולין ומותרין **) והכא דנתערב ברובא שנגמר דינן דפטרינהו אפילו ניידי ולא אמרינן כל דפריש מרובא פריש לאו פטורין לישתרו בהנאה קאמר אלא פטורין דלא אטרחו בי דינא להורגם דכמיתת בעלים כך מיתת השור ועוד דלא ליתי לאחלופי באדם דאדם

*) גי' הצ"ק בשור לכך נראה כגי' הספרים אבל נתערב כו' **) והתם צ"ק

כח א ב מיי' פ"א מהלכות אבות הטומאה הלכה ה:

כט ג ד מיי' פ"ג מהל' אבות הטומאה הל"ג:

ל ה מיי' פ"י מהל' רוצח הלכה ו:

א ו מיי' פ"ז מהל' פסה"מ הל"א:

ב ז מיי' שם הל"ב:

פי' רש"ק וגי' הצ"ק הכי הוא אלו טריפות הס"ד ואח"כ מה"ד כפרה כתיב בה כו' וקשה משילהי אותו כו' ע"ש

גליון הש"ס

גמ' מכלל דעגלה ערופה טהורה. עיין חולין דף פב ע"א תוס' ד"ה עגלה ומנחות דף קא ע"ב תוס' ד"ה ועגלה:

צ"ל לכולהו ולאי אשמעינן הכא ה"א משום דבהמה חשיבה כ"ש תשיב אבל עוף אימא לא קמ"ל צ"ק

עי' כאן: קדושין מ. חולין יא. [מגילה כא.] כריתות כה.

הגהות הב"ח

(א) רש"י ד"ה מהו לר"מ וכו' וה"נ עריפה הכשר עגלה היא ומטהרת מידי נבלה:

ג"י הצ"ק וולד חטאת ותמורת חטאת וחטאת שמתו בעליה ושכיפרו בעליה ושאבדה ושנמצאת בעלת מום (ועי' במשנה תמורה כא:)

נוסחאות רש"י כת"י

ס"א ואפילו באווזין ותרנגולים. דלא חזו למזבח הואיל ואיכא מליקה בשום עוף דנטרינן טריפה מה

שיטה מקובצת

א] כשאתה בא בדרך: ב] ת"ל טריפה כו'. ואע"ג דלעיל מוקמינן ליה לומר דאיסור טריפה חל על איסור חלב הכא ניחא למסקנא דכתיב ואכול לא תאכלוהו למעוטי חיה והטמאה כדפי' לעיל: ג] ואפילו באווזין ותרנגולין תימה הא ר"מ לא אמר רק בעוף קדשים וי"ם דה"נ איירי כשהוקדשו וקשה דהא לא חזו למזבח ולא חיילא עלייהו קדושת הגוף אלא קדושת דמים לכך נראה דאף בחולין אמר ר"מ דמטהרת מליקה וכן משמע בתוספתא דקתני במילתיה דר"מ גבי עוף טהור דמליקתה ושחיטתה מטהרת טריפת' מטומא' נבילות קתני מליקה דומיא דשחיטה מה שחיטה בין בחולין בין בעוף קדשים כדאמר ליה [רבא] אם הועילה שחיטת חוץ כו' אף מליקה בין בחולין בין בקדשים ומתני' דקתני נקטעה רגלה כו' מטמא בבית הבליעה דלא כר"מ דהא לא גרע מחולין גמורין ומאווזין ותרנגולים והיא גופיה תימה מנ"ל לר' מאיר דמליקה מטהרת בחולין הא טעמיה דר' מאיר דאמר לעיל מהיקשא דזאת תורת הבהמה והעוף מקיש עוף לבהמה מה בהמה דבר המכשירה כו' וא"כ אימא דוקא מליקה בקדשים דהוי דבר המכשירו אבל מליקת חולין לא אע"ג דשחיטה מטהרת טריפתה גם בעוף קדשים אע"ג דלא הוי דבר המכשירו התם היינו טעמא כדאיתא לעיל אם הועילה לו שחיטת חוץ כו' ופנים נמי משום דאין שוה בפנים כבחוץ אבל גבי מליקת חולין לא שייך האי טעמא ופ"ה דדרשינן נמי מה טריפה ששוה בכל פי' בחולין ובקדשים אף נבילה ששות בכל בין בחולין ובין בקדשים יצאת מליקה שאינה מטמאה בקדשים בחולין נמי אינה מטמא וקשה דא"כ הוי המליקה בחולין דבר שלא בהכשירו מקדשים דהוי בהכשירו ולא ילפינן ליה כדקאמר לעיל אע"ג דההיא דלעיל דלא כר"מ מדמטמא מליקת קדשים בחוץ ומליקת חולין מ"מ אין סברא שיחלוק ר"מ (מסברא) [אסברא] ג' דאין דנין שלא בהכשירו מבהכשירו ותדע מדפריך לעיל מההיא דיוצא כשר בבמה וי"ל דהכא שלא בהכשירו משלא בהכשירו הוא דילפינן אליבא דר"מ דאמר מליקת קדשים מטהרת טריפתה מטומאתה אע"ג דטריפה אם עלתה תרד הילכך ילפינן מינה שפיר מליקת טריפה בחולין וההיא דלעיל דלא יליף מליקת קדשים בחוץ מבפנים משום דהוי דבר שלא בהכשירו מדבר שבהכשירו התיא אתיא כמ"ד דאין מליקה מטהר טריפתה מטמאתה גם בקדשים הילכך מליקת קדשים בפנים הוי בהכשירו בלא טריפות ואף שמאל ולילה חשיב ליה בהכשירו כיון דאם עלו לא ירדו מיהו לעיל גבי שחיטת קדשים בפנים ובחוץ [קשה] למה לי טעמא משום אם הועילה לו שחיטה לחייבו כו' תיפוק לי משום כיון דשחיטה מטהרת בחולין מטהרת נמי בקדשים משום מה טריפה ששוה בכל אף נבילה ששוה בכל כדקאמר הכא גבי מליקת חולין ושלא בהכשירו משלא בהכשירו הוא דהא שחיטה מטהרת בחולין גם בטריפה דהוי שלא בהכשירו וי"ל דלר"מ ה"נ וכי איצטריך לעיל טעמא דאם הועילה לו כו' לר' יהודה איצטריך דאמר במתני' דאף שחיטה אינה מטהרת טריפה מטומאתה בעוף כדפ"ה במתני' והילכך ליכא למילף שחיטה בקדשים משחיטה דחולין דא"כ הוי דבר שלא בהכשירו מבהכשירו דהא שחיטת חולין [אינה] מטהרת בטריפה לר' יהודה ואין זה דוחק אי מוקמינן לה כר' יהודה דהא [ברייתא] מיתניא בת"כ וסתם סיפרא ר"י מיהו קשה דלעיל אמר ר"מ טריפה למה לי למעוטי שחיטה שהיא לפנים כלומר דילפינן מה טריפה ששוה בפנים כבחוץ אף נבילה ששוה בפנים כבחוץ לאפוקי שחיטה בפנים שאינו שוה כו' משמע דר"מ גופיה אית ליה האי דרשה ויש לומר דלעולם לית ליה ומ"מ איצטריך טריפה לר"מ למידרש מה טריפה ששוה בכל בחולין ובקדשים אף נבילה ששוה בכל בחולין ובקדשים ומהאי טעמא ידעינן בין שחיטה בעוף קדשים בין מליקה בעוף חולין כדפי' והא דקאמר לעיל לר"מ טריפה למה לי למעוטי שחיטה שהיא לפנים לאו דוקא אלא כלומר טריפה איצטריך לאקושי נבילה לטריפה לר"מ כדאית ליה כדפי' מה טריפה ששוה בכל אף נבילה ששוה בכל כדפ"ה הכא והא דנקט שחיטה שהיא לפנים היינו משום שהזכיר לעיל לר"י הך דרשה דשחיטה שהיא לפנים והיקשא דטריפה נפקא לן תני נמי (איצטריך) לר"מ [איצטריך] טריפה לאקושי נבילה וטריפה לענין שוה בכל כדפי' כל זה דקדק מודי ליישב פ"ה שפירש כאן דיליף נבילה מטריפה מה טריפה ששוה בכל כו' דיליף חולין מקדשים מיהו יש לפרש בע"א דגם לר"מ לא יליף חולין מקדשים לענין מליקה ולא קדשים מחולין לענין שחיטה אע"ג דטריפה הוי שלא בהכשירו כדפי' מ"מ כיון דהכשר קדשים ומצוותן במליקה דוקא ולא בשחיטה הילכך חשיב מליקה בהכשירו גם בטריפה וכן שחיטה בחולין כיון דהיינו דוקא הכשירו ומצותו בכך הילכך חשיב קצת בהכשירו והילכך שפיר איצטריך גם לר"מ גבי שחיטה בקדשים הנך טעמא דלעיל אם הועילה לו שחיטה בחוץ כו' ופנים משום דאינו שוה בפנים כבחוץ דהא ליכא למילף קדשים מחולין וה"ה דלא ילפינן חולין מקדשים לענין מליקה מהאי טעמא כדפי' (וכ"ת) (וא"ת) א"כ מנ"ל לר"מ מליקה בחולין וי"ל כיון דידעינן בשחיטה דמטהרת גם בקדשים משום דאם הועילה כו' ילפינן מינה דמליקה דמליקה מטהרת בחולין גם בקדשים משום אם הועילה כו' (אלא אי אמרת) [כן אמרינן] דמליקה שמכשרת באכילה בשום מקום כגון בחולין שמטהרת טריפה מטומאתה גם בקדשים מצינו דשחיטה מה מצינו בשחיטה שמכשרת באכילה בשום מקום כגון בחולין מטהרת גם בקדשים טריפה מטומאה גם בחולין (מה) (ומה) מצינו דמתני' דקתני במילתיה דר"מ מה מצינו בשחיטה כו' יש לפרש דה"ק כדפי' כך נראה לעורי ת' מהר"ם: ד] בטהורה דמשמע נבילת בהמה טמאה טהורה: ה] דמטהר במליקת: ו] דסמיך ס"א דכתיב לעיל מיניה כל חלב שור וכשב ועז': ז] מאימתי נאסרת הס"ד: ח] מתות וולד חטאת ותמורת חטאת וחטאת שמתו בעליה ושכיפרו בעליה כגון שאבדה ושנמצאת: ט] מטהרתה כו' משמע: י] טריפות לאו משום דשני מינין הן דלעולם לא יהיו שני מינין רק היכא דבלשון מקרא שני מינין הן כגון בקר וצאן: ותיבות וקשה משילהי אותו ואת בנו מוקף בחצי ונכתב מן הצד תוס': יא] דהדיוט לא: יב] דינו לכך נראה כגירסת הספרים אבל נתערב: יג] מעלי' אפי' בנגמר דינו היה: יד] ניכבשינהו דניניידן וכל: טו] תיבות אוסר בכל שהוא נמחק:

not in the case of clean? Thus you must say, [70*b*] when you argue in the one way [the text] applies to clean, whilst when you argue in the other way it applies to unclean. Therefore it says, '*terefah*', [which intimates,] the kind where there is *terefah:* then I might exclude the unclean, since there is no *terefah* in its kind,[5] but I will not exclude *ḥayyah*, since there is *terefah* in its kind. Scripture, however, teaches: '*But ye shall in no wise eat of it*', [intimating that it refers to] that whose *ḥeleb* is forbidden whereas its flesh is permitted; thus *ḥayyah* is excluded, since its *ḥeleb* and its flesh are permitted.

R. Jacob b. Abba said to Raba: If so,[6] is it only the *nebelah* of a clean animal that defiles, whereas the *nebelah* of an unclean animal does not defile?—Said he to him: How many elders [scholars] of you have erred therein![7] the second clause[8] applies to the *nebelah* of an unclean *bird*.

R. Joḥanan said: Only unblemished [birds] did R. Meir declare clean,[9] but not blemished ones. While R. Eleazar maintained: [He ruled thus] even in the case of blemished ones. It was stated likewise: R. Bibi said in R. Eleazar's name: R. Meir declared blemished [birds] clean, even ducks and fowls.[10]

a R. Jeremiah asked: What if one beheaded a goat?[1] What is the reason in the case of ducks and fowls? [Is it] because they are species of birds; but a goat is not of the same species as a heifer.[2] Or perhaps, it is of the species of cattle?[3] R. Dimi sat and recited this discussion. Said Abaye to him: Hence it follows that the beheaded heifer[4] is clean?—Yes, he replied: the School of R. Jannai said: 'Forgiveness'[5] is written in connection therewith, as in the case of sacrifices.[6]

R. Nathan the father of R. Huna objected: '*But ye shall in no wise eat of it*': I know [this law only of] *ḥeleb* which may not be eaten but may be [otherwise] used.[7] How do we know [it of] the *ḥeleb* of the ox that is stoned[8] and the beheaded heifer?—Because it says, *All ḥeleb* [... *ye shall not eat*].[9] But if you think that the beheaded heifer is clean, could it be clean while its *ḥeleb* is unclean?[10]—Where one did indeed behead it, no text is required; it is required only where one slaughtered it.[11] Then let *shechitah* be efficacious in cleansing it from *nebelah*?[12]—The text is necessary only where it died.[13] Hence it follows that it was forbidden whilst yet alive?[14]—Yes.

b R. Jannai observed: I have heard a time limit for it,[1] but have forgotten it; while our colleagues maintain: Its descent to the rugged valley, that renders it forbidden.

CHAPTER VIII

MISHNAH. ALL SACRIFICES WHICH BECAME MIXED UP

c WITH SIN-OFFERINGS THAT MUST BE LEFT TO DIE,[1] OR WITH AN OX THAT IS TO BE STONED,[2] EVEN ONE IN TEN THOUSAND, ALL MUST BE LEFT TO DIE. IF THEY WERE MIXED UP WITH AN OX WITH WHICH TRANSGRESSION HAD BEEN COMMITTED, E.G.[3],

(5) There is no particular interdict of *terefah* since it is forbidden in any case. (6) If you argue, 'as when it cleansed from *nebelah* it was in the case of unclean and not in the case of clean', which implies that the *nebelah* of a forbidden animal is clean. (7) I am astonished that you (and presumably, your colleagues in the Academy—perhaps R. Jacob spoke on their behalf)—should so err. (8) That to which he referred. (9) After *meliḳah*, if they are *terefah*. The reason is because *meliḳah* is applicable to them. (10) Which are not eligible sacrifices at all. For *terefah* too is not fit and yet R. Meir declares it clean.

a (1) V. Deut. XXI, 1-9. Beheading instead of *shechitah* normally renders an animal *nebelah*, so that it defiles, but since it was prescribed for the *heifer*, it presumably does not defile. What, however, if he beheaded a goat instead of a heifer, and for the same purpose: is the goat *nebelah* or not? (2) Hence it will defile.—A heifer is counted amongst the large cattle, while a goat belongs to the small; therefore they are regarded as different species. (3) *Behemah;* v. *supra* 70*a* n. 9. (4) V. Deut. XXI, 1 ff. (5) Ibid. 8. (6) Hence it is treated as such, and does not defile. (7) As Scripture states, *may be used for any other service*. Only such *ḥeleb* does not defile. (8) V. Ex. XXI, 28 f. All benefit of the ox was forbidden. (9) Lev. VII, 23. This ref. adopts Sh. M.'s emendation of Rashi, and is the preceding verse. The marginal ref. is Lev. III, 17, which seems out of place. —'*All*' is an extension and includes the *ḥeleb* of these. (10) Obviously not, and no verse would be necessary to teach it. (11) After becoming forbidden whilst alive through being set aside for this purpose, it was slaughtered (with *shechitah*) instead of beheaded. Then a text is required to shew that its *ḥeleb* does not defile. (12) Though *shechitah* will not permit it, at least it should free it from defilement, since we find no instance of a slaughtered and clean (permitted) animal defiling. (13) This retracts the preceding answer. It had died of itself before it was beheaded. Here its flesh does defile as *nebelah*, and the text teaches that its *ḥeleb* does not defile. (14) Since the question is asked in respect of a heifer which died, it follows that even before it was beheaded, whilst yet alive, all benefit thereof was forbidden, and that is why the question is asked concerning the *ḥeleb*.

b (1) When it becomes forbidden.

c (1) I.e., which for some reason can neither be offered up nor revert to *ḥullin*, so that they must not be put to work, but must be kept until they die. They are as follows: (i) The young of a sin-offering which calved before it was slaughtered. (ii) One whose owner died. (iii) The substitute of a sin-offering (v. p. 22, n. 8). (iv) A sin-offering whose owner had already made atonement. E.g., it was lost, whereupon he dedicated another and sacrificed it, and then the original one was found. And (v) an animal consecrated before it was a year old, but which passed its first year before being sacrificed (Rashi, as marginally emended). In cur. edd. Rashi enumerates an animal found to be blemished after consecration as the fifth. (2) V. Ex. XXI, 28. (3) Lit., 'or'.

[71a] THAT HAD KILLED A MAN ON THE TESTIMONY OF ONE WITNESS OR OF ITS OWNER;[4] A ROBA' OR A NIRBA';[5] OR AN ANIMAL SET ASIDE [FOR AN IDOLATROUS SACRIFICE] OR THAT HAD BEEN WORSHIPPED [AS AN IDOL]; OR THAT WAS [A

(4) So that it cannot be stoned. (5) Animals used bestially: *roba'*, a male with a woman, *nirba'*, a female with a man.

א] *שהמית את האדם ע"פ עד א' או ע"פ הבעלי'
ג] ברובע ונרבע במוקצה ונעבד באתנן ומחיר
בכלאים

שהמית את האדם על פי עד אחד או על פי הבעלים דשור שהמית על פי הבעלים איפטר ליה מסקילה *דמודה בקנס פטור וכן רובע ונרבע ע"פ עד אחד או ע"פ הבעלים דהשתא לאו שור הנסקל הוא וליכא למימר ימותו שהרי מותרין להדיוט אם לא מפני הזבח המעורב בהן ואי אפשר למכור את כולן לנוכרי מין אותה זבח להקריבם שהרי פסולים להקרבה כדאמרינן בתמורה (דף כח.) מן הבהמה להוציא הרובע והנרבע מן הבקר להוציא את הנעבד מן הצאן להוציא את המוקצה ומן הצאן להוציא את הנוגח מוקצה שהקצהו לנורך (תקרובת) עבודת כוכבים ולא* [ז"ל עבדו] הקריבו ונעבד שעשאו עבודת כוכבים והשתחוה לו ואמרינן בפרק כל האסורין במסכת תמורה (דף כט.) דמותרין להדיוט :
כלאים

דאדם כולי עלמא לא פליגי דפטירי תדע דלרבי יהודה אמאי כונסין ג] לכיפה ועביד לצער בעלי חיים ומקלקל אבירו וכיפתו אדרבה ליערפינהו בקופין ולקברינהו אלא ודאי אתי לאחלופי באדם ועבדי היכירא ולרבנן נמי עבדי היכירא דפטרינן להו ולא חיישי' לתקלה אבל במתני' דהכא חיישינן לתקלה דאיכא כמה ספק איסורין לפי שהם מוקדשים כגון *רכב על גבי שור ובא חבירו ורכב וסמיכה על גבי ראש גדי וטלה וחלב מוקדשין *ע"ג מכתו דשרי בשור הנסקל *לפי ד] שאינם דרך הנאתן ועוד דאיכא איסור מעילה דהזיד במעילה במיתה הילכך כולן ימותו ואל תתמה התם כיון דאיסור [ז"ל] הנאה נינהו אמאי לא תקינו בהו רבנן מיתה ויזקיקו להורגן ה] *היכי יזקיקו ב"ד להרוג כל איסורי הנאה הרי האוכל והאי דמוקי לה ר"ל והוא שהמיתו ואסורין בהנאה (סנהדרין דף מו:) ולא תקינו להו מיתה אלא אמרו כל הקודם להורגן זכה ומקשה רבא* ו] היינו דקתני עלה ואפי' אבא חלפתא ביניהם אלא אמר רבא שנים שהיו עומדין ויצא חץ מביניהם ז] פטורין ואפילו אבא חלפתא דלא תלינן ביה שהרג אבל בשוורים אותן שיש לתלות בהן ח] חייבין משום ובערת הרע מקרבך ועוד אומר ר"ת דשור הנסקל אינו נאסר מחיים *ופירש דכולה ההיא שמעתא (ב"ק דף מא.) דממשמע שנאמר סקל יסקל השור איני יודע שהיא נבילה ונבילה אסורה באכילה מוכחת כן וסוגיא דפרק שני דקדושין (דף נו.) ט] הכי פריך כל צפור טהורה תאכלו לרבות המשולחת וזה אשר לא תאכלו מהם לרבות את השחוטה ופריך איפוך אנא ומשני לא מליט בעלי חיים שאסורין י] *שלא יהו מותרין כששוחטן בר מאלו שעומדין ומוקצין למצותן ולכך אין לאסור משולחת לומר דחל עליה איסור לאחר שילוח יא] לאוסרה באכילה כדין שאר עופות טמאין דכתיבי בקרא ופריך (*והרי רובע ונרבע) דאסורין יב] פירוש דמחיים אסורין לשוחטן ולהקריבן לגבוה ומשני הני מילי לגבוה אבל להדיוט שרי והרי רובע ונרבע בעדים דמחיים אסורין פי' דמחיים אסורין לישחט ואם שחטן אסורין אף אני אביא משולחת ומשני רוב בעלי חיים קאמרינן אם כן דאין שור הנסקל נאסר כל זמן שהוא חי שור שלא נגמר דינו שנתערב באחרים שנגמר דינן כולן פטורין דמותרין בגיזה ועבודה ואין כאן עינוי הדין כיון דפטורין מסקילה מיהו לכשישחטו או ימותו יהו אסורין בהנאה והא דאמר בסוף פרק שור שנגח ד' וה' (דף מה. ושם ד"ה מכור) דשור שנגמר דינו מכרו אינו מכור אפילו לרידיא היינו משום דאסור לנטות דינו ומלוה לסוקלו ועוד דאין לו בעלים והלוקח אינו יכול לזכות בו יותר משאר אדם אבל כי לא נגמר דינו מכרו מכור לשחיטה אי נמי לרידיא דמצי לאערוקיה לאגמא וכי שחיט ליה יג] [לאחר שנגמר דינו] אסור באכילה כך נראה לר"ת כמו שפירשנו וקשה דבסוף פרק קמא דערכין (דף ז:) משמע דשור הנסקל נאסר מחיים גבי האשה שמתה נהנין בשערה דמפרש התם זו מיתתה אוסרתה וזו גמר דינה אוסרתה יד] ויש לומר גמר דינה דמחיים גורם לה להיות חל עליה איסור שאסורה אפילו שחטה דעבדה כעין בשר וזו מיתתה אוסרתה אין עליה שום איסור מחיים ויש להביא ראיה דלא נאסר מחיים מהא דתניא בפרק מרובה מדת (ב"ק דף עא.) ובפרק אלו נערות (כתובות דף לג:) טו] (גבי) גנב שור הנסקל וטבחו משלם תשלומי ד' וה' דברי רבי מאיר ואמאי הא ליתא במכירה ושמעינן ליה לריש לקיש בפרק מרובה מדת (ב"ק דף עא.) דכל שישנו בטביחה ישנו במכירה וכל שאינו בטביחה אינו במכירה וה"ה דכל שאינו במכירה אינו בטביחה אבל אי שרי בהנאה ניחא שיכול למוכרו לרכוב עליו עד בית הסקילה או ליהנות בו מעט עד אותה שעה או אם היו בית דין מתעצלין בסקילתו ומיהו מה שאומר ר"ת דאין לו מכר ר"ת דאין לו בעלים זה לא נוכל לקיים ומה שפסק ר"ת בעדר שיש בו שה אחד ספק דרוסה דשרי מטעמא דכל דפריש מרובא פריש לא יתכן דיש לאסור גזירה שמא יקח מן הקבוע אפילו היכא דפריש מאליו רק טז] בדבר שלא נאסר בתערובת כגון ט' חנויות (אחת) מוכרות בשר שחוטה ואחת נבילה (פסחים דף ט:) התם שרינן אי פריש אחת ולא גזרינן שמא יקח מן הקבוע שהרי האיסור ניכר וידוע היכן הוא ולכך שרינן היכא דפריש או כגון דנמצא ביד עובד כוכבים אבל אם נאסר בתערובת ופריש לא אמרינן דפריש מרובא פריש ואם יש בעדר ספק דרוסה אפילו אחד בריבוא כולן ימותו תדע דטבעת של עבודת כוכבים שנתערבה בריבוא כולן אסורות ובפירש אחת מהן פליגי רב ושמואל בגמרא (לקמן דף עד.) אי אוסרת השאר אי לא אבל יז] בההיא גופה אותה שפירשה לא פליגי *וכולי עלמא דאסירא וכל איסורי הנאה שפירשו מתערובתן אסורין ולא אמרינן מרובא פריש וטעמא משום גזירה שמא יקח מן הקבוע ולא שנא חולין ולא שנא קדשים ויש להתיר הבהמה שנשא הזאב והרועה מצילה ונתערבה בעדר משום דאין דרוסה אלא ביד ושמא טרפה בשינים והוה ליה ספק ספיקא וכן הנץ שנושא אווז שמא נושאה בחרטום או בין רגליו ולא הכה ביד מיהו יש ליישב דברי ר"ת דלא דמי לטבעת של עבודת כוכבים דשאני בעלי חיים כיון דאפשר ע"י דנכבשינהו דניידין ואם תאמר אמאי תנן ימותו נימא ירעו עד שיסתאבו ויפדו ואחרי כן נימא כל דפריש מרובא פריש דהשתא להדיוט חזו שהרי כמה קדשים אמרינן בהו ירעו ולא חיישינן לתקלה ובסיפא אמרינן ברובע ונרבע ירעו ולכשיסתאבו יפדם וישחטם ויאכלם מטעם דפריש מרובא פריש ויש לומר דלא עבדינן תקנה ברעייה כיון דלאחר רעייה לא מישתרי נמי אלא מטעם כל דפריש ועוד שאל הרב רבי יצחק מר"ת דקאמר יח] רבי שמעון (סנהדרין דף עט:) הנסקלים בנשרפים ידונו בסקילה שהשריפה חמורה ניזיל בתר רובא להחמיר בדיני נפשות כדאיתא פרק קמא דחולין (דף יא:) דלא חיישינן שמא במקום סייף נקב הוה ותירץ דלא אזלינן בתר רובא להחמיר כיון שנהרג בלאו הכי במיתה אחרת אי נמי לא אזלינן בתר רובא לחייב אותו שהוא ודאי בסקילה ומהאי טעמא לא תקשי לן הא דאמר פרק אלו הן הנשרפין (סנהדרין דף עט:) דאדם רוצח שלא נגמר דינו שנתערב עם אחרים שנגמר דינן כולן פטורים דמשום רובא לא נעביד דבר שהוא שקר ודאי דודאי יש אחד שאינו בר מיתה כלל לפי שלא נגמר דינו ולא דמי לאותו שהרג ודאי אלא דלא ידעינן אי טריפה הוה אי שלם הוה ועוד יש לומר דהוה ליה קבוע וכל קבוע כמחצה על מחצה דמי ופטור מדאורייתא דספק נפשות להקל וכי תימא ניכבשינהו וניזיל כל דפריש אי אתה רשאי למושכן להחמיר עליו יט] ועוד גזירה שמא יקח מן הקבוע והא דפריך מעיקרא כי תני הנשרפים בנסקלים תיפוק לי דרובא נסקלים נינהו הכי פירושא לכל הפחות לא גרע משום דרובא נסקלים* :

על פי עד אחד או על פי הבעלים. פירש בקונטרס דפטר ליה מסקילה משום דמודה בקנס פטור וכן פירש במכות (דף ו.) דאין אדם נהרג על פי עצמו מטעם קנס ונראה דאפי' אמרי שנגמר דינם בבית דין פלוני אין נהרגים על פיהם ואע"ג דכי האי גוונא מחייב בקנס כדמוכח בפרק קמא דמכות (דף ז.) וגבי פלוני רבע שורי בפרק קמא דסנהדרין (דף י.) מפרש משום דאדם קרוב אצל ממונו לא אמרינן ונהרג שורו ולא פלגינן דיבורא אלא הרובע והשור נהרגין ואי קנס מיקרי כי נמי אמת הוא שרבע שורו אמאי נהרג שור על פיו והא מודה בקנס פטור כמו אם אמר גנבתי וטבחתי דפטור מכפל וד' וה' ונראה לי טעמא דאינו נהרג על פי הבעלים אם אין עד אחד עמו כדאיתא פרק כל האסורין (תמורה דף כט.) זה וזה מותרות באכילה מנלן אי ס"ד להדיוט אסירי למה לי למעוטינהו *לרובע ונרבע לגבוה ואע"ג דהתם לא מזכיר ברובע ונרבע על פי הבעלים מכל מקום על כל ענין שפסול גבוה ומותר להדיוט קאי *) מנהני מילי **) . ברוך :

ברובע ונרבע. פירש בקונטרס על פי עד אחד או על פי הבעלים שנאסר לגבוה ולא להדיוט דבשני עדים היה נאסר אפילו להדיוט וכן משמע בריש פ' בתרא דכריתות (ד' כד.) דאמר רבי יוחנן שור הנסקל שהוזמו עדיו כל המחזיק בו זכה אמר רבא מסתברא טעמיה דרבי יוחנן כגון דאמרו ליה נרבע שורו ואי לא ליתסר בהנאה אמאי מייאש הלא העור מותר בהנאה והבשר לכלבים וכן נמי משמע בפרק האיש מקדש (קדושין דף נז:) דפריך והרי רובע ונרבע בעדים דאסירי מחיים להדיוט ואם תאמר ומנלן הא כי כתיב קרא בנוגח כתיב ולא ילפי מהדדי כדאמרינן פרק שור שנגח ד' וה' (ב"ק דף מ:) שיש בנוגח שאין ברובע ויש ברובע שאין בנוגח ושמא איכא שום דרש :
ובטרפה

*) הני מילי ג"ק **) [ועי' תוס' ב"ק מא: ד"ה ע"פ עד]

הב"ח דילפינן נרבע מנוגח דהא יש בנוגח מה שא"כ ברובע ונרבע ופי' ריב"א דמ"מ סברא הוא למילפינהו לענין איסור הנאה כיון דשוין הן לענין איסור סקילה : ג] כונסין אותן לכיפה : ד] שאינו דרך הנאתו : ס] להורגן דהיכי יזקיקו : ו] רבא התם היינו : ז] מביניהם והרג שניהם פטורין : ח] בהן שהרגו חייבין : ט] דקדושין דכל צפור ותיבות הכי פריך נמחק : י] שאסורין פי' שלא : יא] שילוח ולאוסרה באכילה : יב] דאסורין מחיים פי' : יג] ליה לאחר שנגמר דינו אסור : יד] אוסרתה ויש לפרש א גמר דינה אוסרת דמחיים : טו] תיבת גבי נמחק : טז] רק בדניכר שלא תיבת בדבר ל"ש : יז] אבל בהיא גופה אותה שפירשה לא פליגי דכ"ע מודו דאסורה וכו' : יח] דקאמר בפ' הנשרפין ר' שמעון אומר הנסקלים : יט] עליו אלא לחקל עליו ועוד :

שיטה מקובצת

א] שהמית את האדם ע"פ עד אחד או ע"פ הבעלים. דנאסר לגבוה ואינו נאסר להדיוט שאינו נסקל אלא ע"פ שני עדים אבל ע"פ בעלים מודה בקנס הוא ומיפטר ליה מסקילה אבל לגבוה נאסר דקיי"ל מן הצאן להוציא הנוגח. כפ"ה וקשה דלא מצינו בשום מקום שתהא מיתת השור קנס לכך נראה דפטור משום דאדם קרוב אצל ממונו ואפי' אמר דנגמר דינו בב"ד של פלוני דלא שייך מודה בקנס כה"ג ואע"ג דמסקינן בפ"ק דסנהדרין אדם קרוב אצל ממונו לא אמרינן הני מילי לענין מיפלג דיבורא אבל בעלמא אמרינן: ג] ברובע ונרבע. פ"ה ע"פ עד אחד או ע"פ הבעלים דבשני עדים הוי נאסר אף להדיוט כדין שור הנסקל דאסור בהנאה. ותימה מנ"ל משום דשור הנסקל אסור בהנאה נאמר כמו כן דשאר נסקלים אסורים בהנאה דילמא דוקא נוגח אסור בהנאה משום דגבי נוגח כתיב סקל יסקל השור ולא יאכל את בשרו ודרשינן ממשמע שנאמר השור יסקל איני יודע שנבילה היא אלא מלמד שאם שחטו לאחר שנגמר דינו דאסור בהנאה
ובטריפה

ז"ל כמודה בקנס דפטור ז"ק
תוספתא דז"ק [פ"ד קדושין סו. בכורות מא. תמורה כח.]
רש"ק מ"ז
סנהדרין פ.
קדושין נז.
ג"י רש"ק וע"ג ופי' ז"ק
פסחים כד:
ז"ל וכי
ומפירוש ז"ק
ז"ל פי' שלא
ז"ל והרי מוקצה ונעבד ז"ק
ז"ק
ז"ל וכ"ע מודו ז"ק
[ועי' תוס' חולין יא: ד"ה ליתוש ותו' סנהדרין פ: ד"ה הנסקלין]
[רש"ל בספרו יש של שלמה בב"ק פ"ד סי' כ"א מוחק הני ב' תיבות לרובע ונרבע וע"ש שהאריך ורש"ק מקיים ג"י שלפנינו וע"ש]

בכלאים א] ובטריפה ביוצא דופן ירעו עד שיסתאבו וימכרו ויביא בדמי היפה שבהן מאותו המין נתערבו בחולין תמימים ב] ימכרו החולין לצורכי אותו המין ג] קדשים בקדשים מין במינו ד] [זה יקרב לשם מי שהוא וזה יקרב לשם מי שהוא] קדשים בקדשים מין בשאינו מינו ירעו עד שיסתאבו (וימכרו) ויביא בדמי ה] יפה שבהן ממין זה ובדמי היפה שבהן ממין זה ויפסיד המותר מביתו ו] *נתערבו בבכור ובמעשר ירעו עד שיסתאבו ויאכלו כבכור וכמעשר הכל יכולין להתערב ז] חוץ מן החטאת והאשם:

גמ' מאי אפי' ה"ק כל הזבחים שנתערבו בהן ח] חטאות המתות או שור הנסקל אפילו אחד בריבוא ימותו כולן תנינא חדא זימנא *כל האסורין לגבי מזבח אוסרין בכל שהן הרובע והנרבע אמר רב ט] אשי אמריתה לשמעתיה קמיה דרב שימי ואצריכן י] דאי מהתם הוה אמינא הני מילי לגבוה אבל להדיוט אימא לא ואי מהכא ה"א הני הוא דאיסורי הנאה נינהו אבל הני (א) אימא לא צריכי דלאו איסורי הנאה נינהו הא תנא ליה מי קתני א) (בכמה כל שהן התם קתני) וניתני הא ולא בעי הא תקנתא איצטריכא ליה דהדיוט נמי תנא ליה ב) ואלו אסורין ואוסרין בכל שהן יין נסך ועבודת כוכבים

א) רש"ק גירסת רש"י מי קתני בכל שהוא התם קתני ב) תמורה כח. ע"ז עד.

כלאים וטריפה ויוצא דופן. שור או כשב פרט לכלאים כי יולד פרט ליוצא דופן טריפה התם אמרינן *כשהוא אומר מן הבקר למעט שאין ת"ל להוציא את הטריפה ולהדיוט מותרת בהנאה להשליכה לכלבים: ירעו עד שיסתאבו. דמחמת הזבח המעורב בהן נאסרו כולן להדיוט ולחללו על המעות בעודו תם אי אפשר הילכך ירעו עד שיסתאבו ויביא בדמי היפה שבהן מאותו המין ממין הקרבן אם עולה הוא יביא מעות כנגד דמי היפה שבכולן דשמא הזבח הוא היפה ויאמר כל מקום שהוא הזבח יהא מחולל על מעות הללו ויביא מן המעות עולה ואם שלמים שלמים: נתערבו בחולין תמימין. או אחד באחד או זבח אחד בחולין הרבה ימכרו כל החולין לצרכי מין יא] אותו הקרבן [א] ונמצאת הרי כולן קדשים של מין אחד אלא שאין ידוע כל אחד של מי הוא [ב] ויקרבו כולן כל אחד ואחד לשם מי שהוא כדקתני מתני': קדשים בקדשים מין במינו. אלא שבעליהן יב] מוחלקות יקרב כל אחד לשם מי שהוא: מין בשאינו מינו. עולה בשלמים שאין מתן דמן ואימוריהן יג] שוה: וימכרו. כמלאו דמי עולה יד] עולה דמי שלמים שלמים ואינו יודע איזו עולה ואיזו שלמים הילכך יטול מעות [מביתו] כנגד דמי היפה ויאמר כל מקום שהן ממעות עולה יתחללו על אלו טו] [ג] (ואלו מעות כיוצא בהן) לפי שאינו יודע איזו מין היה יפה טז] *[ויביא מעות כיוצא בהן] ויאמר כל מקום שהן מעות שלמים יהו מחוללין על אלו ונמצא מפסיד אותו עודף מביתו ול"נ דלא גרסינן וימכרו אלא ירעו עד שיסתאבו ויביא בדמי היפה כו' ובתחילת חילולן יאמר יז] כל מקום שהיא עולה תהא מחוללת על אלו וכל מקום שהן שלמים יהיו מחוללין על אלו ויביא מאלו עולה ומאלו שלמים ותדע דלא גרסינן ליה דהא יח] נתערבו בבכור ומעשר [ד] דקתני נמי וימכרו אי אפשר דהא תנן במעשר נאמר לא יגאל ואינו נמכר לא חי ולא שחוט לא תם ולא בעל מום וילפינן לה בבכורות (דף לב:) דהאי לא יגאל לא ימכר הוא אלא הכי גרסינן ירעו עד שיסתאבו ויאכלו כמעשר וכבכור: נתערבו. זבחים כגון עולה בבכור או במעשר בהמה שאין תופסין יט] דמיהן בקדושה ולהקריבן אי אפשר שזה כליל וזה נאכל או אפילו הוא שלמים זה טעון מתן ארבע וזה מתן אחת וכן סמיכה ונסכים: ירעו עד שיסתאבו. ויביא מעות כ] בדמי היפה ויאמר כל מקום שהוא הזבח התופס את דמיו יהא מחולל על מעות הללו כמלא חולין מעורב בבכור ומעשר בעלי מומין ויאכלו מעורבים כולן בתורת בכור ומעשר בעלי מומין שלא ישחטו באיטליז ולא ימכרו באיטליז ולא ישקלו בליטרא כדתנן *(מנחות דף עא) כל פסולי מוקדשים הנאתן להקדש לפיכך נשחטין באיטליז לאחר שנפדו ונמכרים באיטליז ונשקלים בליטרא דכמה דמשכיר במכירתן טפי ופריק להו מעיקרא חוץ מן הבכור והמעשר שהנאתן לבעלים שאין מביאין בדמיהן קרבן וא"ת השתא איכא בהאי זבח המעורב פסידא דהקדש דכיון דאין נשקל בליטרא לא טפי ופריק ליה אין ה"נ כא] *אי משום פסידא דידיה לא מזלזלינן בבכור ומעשר נהי דאי לא הוה מערב דליכא זילותא אלא בדידיה מזלזלינן ביה משום דרווחא נמי דידיה הוא אבל באחריני משום איהו לא מזלזלינן: הכל יכולין להתערב. בכל שני מיני קדשים אפשר להו שיהו מעורבין: חוץ מן החטאת והאשם. שאין מתערבין זה בזה לפי שניכרין זה מזה כדמפרש בגמרא:

גמ' מאי אפיט. כל שכן כיון דרובא למיתה ימותו: שנתערבו בהן חטאות המתות. חד דאיסורא כב] ורובא דהתירא: כל האסורין כו'. משנה היא במסכת תמורה: אוסרין בכל שהן. כל המתערבין בהן ואפי' אחד בריבוא: הני מילי לגבוה. כולן המעורבין אסורין לגבוה ומותרין להדיוט ברעייה ובפדייה דלא איירי התם בנתערבו באיסורי הנאה: אבל הכי. דלהדיוט נמי לא חזו כג] לפדייה דהא באיסורי הנאה נתערבו: אימא. ליבטלי איסורי הנאה ברובא שלא ימותו אלא ירעו וימכרו דלא חמיר דין הדיוט כולי האי קמ"ל ימותו: כד] *) אי מהכא. אשמעינן דאפילו קדשים נמי מפסדינן ולא תנא ההיא בתמורה [ה] ה"א הני הוא דמפסדינן משום דאיערוב באיסורי הנאה אבל הנך דתמורה דלא איערוב בהו איסורי הנאה אימא לא לאסרינהו לכולהו אלא ניבטיל ברובא ויקרבו לריכא: אבל הנך דלאו איסורי הנאה נינהו. אימא קיל איסורייהו וניבטלו ברובא ואפילו לגבוה: הא תנא ליה. כה] הנך במתני' דלא בטלי לגבוה דקתני במתניתין נתערבו בשור שנעבדה כו' ולמה לי למהדר ולמיתנייה התם: ומשני מי קתני. במתני' גבי רובע ונרבע בכמה הן אוסרין: כל שהן התם קתני. במסכת תמורה הוא דקתני אוסרין בכל שהן דאי ממתני' דילמא בטלי במאה או במאתים כו] ואחד ברבואה דקתני מתני' לאו עלייהו קאי: וניתני הא דתמורה. ולא ניתני הא דזבחים: תקנתא איצטריכא ליה. דהתם אוסרין בכל שהוא תני ולא תקנתא והכא תנא תקנתא ירעו עד שיסתאבו כו': דהדיוט. נמי תנא במסכת עבודה זרה דאיסורי הנאה לא בטלי ברובא ומיתסרו להדיוט ולמה לי למיתני הכא בחטאות המתות ושור הנסקל: לריכי

*) [ע"ש ברש"י דלא גרס להא]

*) נ"ב שייך האי דיבור אי כו' לקמן עב ע"א קודם ד"ה ופרכינן

ובטריפה. בגמ' דייק האי טריפה היכי דמי אי ידע לה ליזיל וליסקלה ומפרש רבי ירמיה כגון שנתערבה בוולד טריפה ודבי אליעזר היא ורבי ינאי מפרש כגון דאיתערבה נקובת הקוץ בדרוסת הזאב וריש לקיש מפרש כגון דאיערב בנפולה והקשה ה"ר אפרים כיון דלא כז] ידיעה מה מועלת כאן רעייה דלמיכלה א"א משום ספק טריפה ולעובדי כוכבים ולכלבים אי אפשר דאין פודין את הקדשים להאכילן לכלבים כח] ומחיים נמי לא אפשר ליהנות דפסולי המוקדשים אסורים בגיזה ועבודה מיהו למ"ד דאיערב בדרוסה יש לה בדיקה לאחר שחיטה אם האדימה בשר כנגד בני מעיים או כנגד הסימנים דאפי' ודאי דרוסה יש לה בדיקה ולמ"ד דאיערב בנפולה נפולה יש לה בדיקה אבל למ"ד בוולד טריפה קשה ושמא קסבר פודין את הקדשים להאכילן לכלבים כאיכא דאמרי בפרק שני דבכורות (דף טו:) אי נמי כט] *כדאמרינן (פסחים דף*) אין פודין את הקדשים להאכילן לכלבים הני מילי היכא דלא חזו אלא לכלבים כגון קדשים שמתו או נטרפו אבל הני אסורים מחמת טריפות חולין שנתערבו בהן אבל קדשים גופייהו אם היה מכירן דחזו לדידיה שרי להאכילן לעובדי כוכבים ולכלבים ומיהרלא בהכי פירכא אחריתי שהיה מקשה ה"ר אפרים בבכורות פ' כל פסולי המוקדשין (דף לב:) בכור מתיר ר"ע אפי' לעובד כוכבים ולקמן בפ' טבול יום (דף קג:) אמר ר"ע מדבריהם למדנו שהמפשיט את הבכור ונמצא טריפה שיאותו הכהנים בעורו משמע דווקא בעורו אבל בבשרו לא דאסור להאכילו לכלבים ולעובדי כוכבים ולפי מה שפירשתי ניחא דמידי דלא חזי לישראל אסור להאכילו לכלב ולעובדי כוכבים אבל מידי דחזי לישראל כיון שנפדו שרי ליתן לכלב והיינו טעמא דדרשינן ואכלת ולא לכלביך כלומר דבר שאין עומד אלא לכלביך אבל היכא דחזי לדידיה אישתרו לגמרי דאיתקש לצבי ואיל וא"ת בפרק הפרה (ב"ק דף נג:) דפטרינן שור פסולי המוקדשים שנפל לבור משום דכתיב והמת יהיה לו מי שהמת שלו הרי המת שלו כדתנן (לקמן דף קג:) דיאותו הכהנים בעורו ומשום עור לחודיה איצטריך שור ולא אדם דהוה מחייבנא באדם דחשיב המת שלו משום עור דשרי בהנאה מדאורייתא ולא אסור אלא משום גזירה שמא יעשה עורות אביו ואמו שטיחין (חולין דף קכב.) וי"ל דסוגיא דב"ק (דף נג:) אתיא כמסקנא דפרק טבול יום (לקמן ד' קד.) דפסקי' כרבנן *) בשר בקבורה ועור בשריפה:

ויביא בדמי היפה שבהן. פירש"י ויקח מעות כשיעור דמי היפה שבכולן ויאמר כל מקום שהוא הזבח יהא מחולל על מעות הללו משמע לפירושו שהזבח מעורב בריבוא של רובע ונרבע והלשון משמע כן ואי אפשר לומר כן דדומיא דרישא קתני שהנסקל נתערב ברוב זבחים וכן מוכח בגמרא ובדמי היפה שבהן היינו דמי היפה של כל אחד ואחד ומניח הגרוע שבהן שלא יחלל:

לשם מי שהוא. פירש בקונטרס (כדי) כשיקריבנו יאמר הרי הוא לשם בעלים שלו וקשה דהא אמר בריש מכילתין (דף ב:) אתנו בית דין דלא לימא לשמן דילמא אתי למימר שלא לשמן אלא לשם מי שהוא היינו סתמא דסתמא נמי כלשמו דמי: מי קתני בכמה. בפרק כל האסורין (תמורה דף כח.) משני בענין אחר ולא פריך התם וליתני הא ולא בעי הא כדפריך הכא:

דהדיוט נמי תנא ליה ואלו אסורין כו'. מכמה משניות הוה מצי לאתויי ממתני' דאפה בו את הפת במסכת עבודה זרה (דף מט:) וממתני' דערלה (פ"ג מ"ה ו) בערלה וכלאי הכרם: וליבטלו

עין משפט נר מצוה

[לקמן עד:]

ג א מיי' פ"ו מהל' פסה"מ הל"ג:

ד ב מיי' שם הל"ד:

ה ג מיי' שם הלכה ו:

ו ד מיי' שם הל"ד:

ז ה מיי' שם הלט"ז:

ח ו מיי' פט"ו מהל' מאכלות אסורות הלכה ו טוש"ע יו"ד סי' קלד סעיף א:

ט ז מיי' פ"ז מהל' ע"ז הלכה ט סמג לאוין מח טוש"ע יו"ד סי' קמ:

הגהות הב"ח

(א) גמ' אבל הני דלאו איסורי הנאה נינהו אימא לא צריכי הא תנא:

כא כי אמרי'

שיטה מקובצת

א] ובטריפה. הקשה הר"ר אפרים לר' ירמיה דמוקי לה בולד טריפה וכר"א דאמר בחולין דולד טריפה לא יקרב אצל המזבח וה"ה להדיוט נמי אסור כדמוכח בחולין והא דאפלגי בגבוה להודיעך כחן דרבנן דאפי' לגבוה נמי שרי א"כ מאי קאמר במתני' ירעו עד שיסתאבו מה תועלת ברעייה כו' עד לכלבים וא"כ ימותו מבעיא ליה בשלמא למ"ד דאי ערב כו' עד בדיקה לאחר שחיטה ולמכור לישראל לאכול והא דלא בדקינן בקדשים היינו משום דאותם בדיקות הן לאחר שחיטה וכיון דאסור מעיילינן חולין בעזרה אלא למ"ד בוולד טריפה אין פודין את הקדשים להאכילן לכלבים ה"מ היכא דלא ראוי רק לכלבים כגון קדשים שמתו אבל היכא דחזו לדידיה אם היה מכירן שרי להאכיל לעכו"ם או לכלבים והיינו טעמא דדרשינן לך ולא לכלביך כלומר דבר שאינו ראוי אלא לכלבים אבל הכי דחזו (לדמיה) [לדידיה] אשתרו לגמרי דאיתקש לצבי ואיל: לשון תוס' הר"פ ירעו עד שיסתאבו פ"ה שאי אפשר לשחוט אחד מהם בלא מום שמא זהו הזבח והשוחט קדשים בחוץ חייב כרת וא"כ הן פסולין לקרבן אלא ירעו וימכרו ויביא בדמי היפה שבהן מאותו המין אם חטאת חטאת אם עולה עולה ויקח מעות כשיעור דמי היפה שבכולן ויאמר כל מקום שיהיה הזבח יהא מחולל על המעות הללו משמע שפי' מתוך לשונו שפי' כל מקום שיהיה הזבח וגם הלשון דקתני ויביא בדמי היפה שבהן משמע דמיירי הך סיפא בקדשים שנתערבו ברובא פסולים וקשה מסתמא סיפא דומיא דרישא דמפרש בגמרא דשור הנסקל אחד נתערב בכמה קדשים כשרים וה"נ הוי בסיפא בסיפא כדמוכח בגמרא דקאמר כל שהוא התם קתני לכך נראה ויביא בדמי היפה כנגד כל אחד ... מורי מה שפ"ה כן אינו ר"ל שיהיה כן לפי המסקנא אלא ר"ל אי לאו אידך משנה דמייתי הגמרא התם קתני הייתי יכול לפרש מתני' בסיפא דליכא קדשים רק אחד שאת"ל שיש למידק מסתני' ... רישא א"כ מאי קאמר בגמרא כל שהן התם קתני הכא נמי קתני שפיר כל שהן דומיא דרישא ... למידק הכא סיפא דומיא דרישא הוא (ואיסור) [ואימור] אינו שוה ומיהו לפי המסקנא אמת הוא ... דרישא אלא מתני' אין להוכיח כדפי': ג] ימכרו החולין לצרכי אותו המין. ויקרב זה לשם מי

נוסחאות רש"י כת"י

ס"א נתערבו. זבח אחד בחולין. כשרים הרבה: ימכרו החולין לצרכי אותו המין. נמצאו כלם קדשים וממין אחד אלא שאין ידוע מי בעליו של כל אחד ואחד שהרי הראשון שם בעליו עליו ואין ידוע איזהו ותקנתן שנויה במשנתינו: קדשים בקדשים מין במינו. חטאת בחטאת עולה בעולה אלא שהן של בעלים הרבה: יקרב. כל אחד ואחד לשם מי שהוא כשיקריבנו יאמר הרי הוא לשם בעליו ולא יזכיר עליו שם אדם: מין בשאינו מינו. כגון עולה בחטאת: ירעו. שאי אפשר בהקרבה שחלוקין במתן דמן או באכילתן או בהקטרתן שזה כליל וזה נאכל: נתערבו בבכור ומעשר. שאין להן פדיון שתחול קדושתן על דמיהן ויצאו הן לחולין אלא נאכלין בסומן במדינה כולן ירעו עד שיומשו ויאמר כל מקום שהוא הזבח יתחלל על מעות הללו ומותרין באכילה ובלבד שיאכלו בתורת מעשר ובכור שלא ישחטו באיטלו וכו' ודמי הזבח יקחמהן בהמה ויקריבנה ממין הזבח: הכל יכולים להתערב. ס"א כלומר אם נתערבו יש ספק בתערובתו: חוץ מן החטאת והאשם. שאין ספק בתערובתן שהחטא' אינה לעולם איל (כו') [כלל]:

שיטה מקובצת

שהוא: ג] קדשים בקדשים שהם מין אחד רק שחלוקים בשם הבעלים יקרבו כל אחד לשם מי שהוא ולא יאמר כלום דהא סתמא כשר ולא כפ"ה דפי' דאמר הרי הן לשם בעלים שלו דהא אמרינן בפ"ק אתנו ב"ד דלא לימא לשמו כו': ד] במינו זה יקרב לשם מה שהוא וזה יקרב: ה] בדמי היפה שבהן: ו] נתערבו בבכור ומעשר ירעו. ול"נ ימכרו דהא כתיב במעשר לא ימכר אלא ירעו עד שיומשו ואז [בקדשי'] אחרים] יחלו הקדושה על אחרים ויצאו לחולין לגמרי אבל בכור ומעשר צריכין עוד לאוכלן בתורת בכור ומעשר ואינו יכול למוכרם אלא כל תורת בכור ומעשר עליהם שלא לימכר באטלו ושלא לישקל אלא ירעו עד שיומשו ויאמר כל מקום שהוא הזבח יתחלל על מעות הללו ואינם יוצאים לחולין לגמרי שתחול קדושתן שאין להן פדיון אלא נאכלין בסומן: ז] עי' בהשמטות בסוף המסכת: ח] בהן מחטאות המתות: ט] רב כהנא אמריתא להא שמעתיה קמיה דרב שימי בר אשי ואמר צריכין: י] עי' בהשמטות בסוף המסכת: יא] אותו הקרבן היו כולן קדשים: יב] שבעליהן מחולקין: יג] ואימוריהן שוין הס"ד: יד] עולה בעולה דמי שלמים בשלמים ואינו יודע אי אלו עולה ואי אלו שלמים הילכך יטול מעות סביבו כנגד:

טו] אלו ויביא מאלו עולה ויחזור ויביא מעות כיוצא בהן לפי שאינו: טז] תיבות ויביא מעות כיוצא בהן נמחק: יז] יאמר כן כל: יח] דהא גבי נתערבו בבכור ומעשר קתני נמי וימכרו ואי אפשר: יט] תופסין את דמיהן: כ] מעות כדמי היפה: כא] תיבת אי נמחק: כב] בריבוא דהיתרא: כג] חזו בפדיה אות ל' נמחק: כד] ד"ה אי מהכא כו' עד סה"ד ל"ש: כה] ליה הכא במתני' תיבת הנך ל"ש ונמחק: כו] במאתים דאחד אות ו' נמחק: כז] דלא ידיע אות ה' נמחק: כח] לכלבים כדאמרי' בפ' כל שעה דף כט: כט] נמי הא דאמרינן אין פודין:

הגהות צ"ק [א] ונמצאו כולן קדשים: [ב] שהרי זבח א' שם בעליו עליו ואין ידוע איזהו ויקרבו כו': [ג] ויביא מאלו עולה ויחזיר ויביא מעות כיוצא כו': [ד] נ"ל קתני נמי ולמכור במעשר א"א דהא כו': [ה] מדית ס"א הכי כו' דלא איערוב בהו איסורי הנאה אימא קיל איסורייהו ולא לאסרינהו לכולהו אלא ניבטל ברובא ואפי' לגבוה כצ"ל והס"ד ואח"כ מס"ד הא תנא ליה כו':

HARLOT'S] HIRE, OR [A DOG'S] EXCHANGE; [71*b*] OR THAT WAS KILAYIM;[6] OR TEREFAH; OR AN ANIMAL CALVED THROUGH THE CAESAREAN SECTION,[7] THEY MUST GRAZE UNTIL THEY BECOME UNFIT;[8] THEN THEY ARE SOLD, AND ONE BRINGS [A SACRIFICE] OF THE SAME KIND[9] AT THE PRICE OF THE BETTER OF THEM.[10] IF THEY WERE MIXED UP WITH UNBLEM-
a ISHED [ANIMALS] OF ḤULLIN,[1] THE ḤULLIN MUST BE SOLD FOR THE PURPOSE OF THAT KIND.[2] [IF] A SACRIFICE [WAS MIXED UP] WITH A SACRIFICE, BOTH BEING OF THE SAME KIND:[3] THIS ONE MUST BE OFFERED IN THE NAME OF WHOEVER IS ITS OWNER, AND THE OTHER MUST BE OFFERED IN THE NAME OF WHOEVER IS ITS OWNER.[4] [IF] A SACRIFICE [WAS MIXED UP] WITH A SACRIFICE, BOTH BEING OF DIFFERENT KINDS,[5] THEY MUST GRAZE UNTIL THEY BECOME UNFIT,[6] AND THEN ONE PURCHASES AT THE PRICE OF THE BETTER OF THEM [AN ANIMAL] OF EACH KIND,[7] AND BEARS THE LOSS OF THE EXCESS OUT OF HIS OWN POCKET.[8] IF THEY WERE MIXED UP WITH A FIRSTLING OR TITHE, THEY MUST GRAZE UNTIL THEY BECOME UNFIT, AND THEN ARE EATEN AS FIRSTLING OR TITHE.[9] ALL [SACRIFICES] CAN BE MIXED UP, EXCEPT THE SIN-OFFERING AND THE GUILT-OFFERING.[10]

GEMARA. What does EVEN mean?[11]—This is what he means: ALL SACRIFICES with which SIN-OFFERINGS THAT MUST BE LEFT TO DIE, E.G., AN OX THAT MUST BE STONED, BECAME MIXED UP, EVEN ONE IN TEN THOUSAND, MUST BE LEFT TO
b DIE.[1]

[But] we have already learnt it once: *All* which are forbidden to the altar, e.g., a *roba'* and a *nirba'*, render [others] forbidden whatever their number?[2]—Said R. Kahana: I reported this discussion to R. Shimi b. Ashi, and he said to me: They are both necessary.[3] For if [we learnt] from there, I would say, That is only [where they are forbidden] to the altar;[4] but [where they are forbidden] to a layman, it is not [so].[5] While if [we learnt] from here, I would say that [this ruling applies] only to these, which are forbidden for any use; but as for the others, which are not forbidden for general use, it is not [so].[6] Thus they are both necessary.

But surely those which are not interdicted for all use are taught [in this Mishnah]?[7]—Does he teach by what number [they render all forbidden]?[8] Then let him teach the other, and we would not require this one?—He needs the remedy.[9]

But [those which are forbidden] to layman he also teaches; [there:] The following are themselves forbidden, and render [others] forbidden, whatever their number: Wine of *nesek*[10] and [animals

(6) A hybrid, offspring of two heterogeneous animals, e.g., a goat and a sheep. (7) These last two are included, though not implicated in sin, because the same law applies to them. (8) I.e., blemished. (9) As that which had thus been mixed up. (10) None of these are eligible for sacrifices, yet a layman may make use of (though not eat) them; therefore they are not left to perish. At present, however, these animals cannot be used, since one of them is sacred, nor can they be redeemed (i.e., sold, and the money devoted to a sacrifice), for an unblemished consecrated animal cannot be redeemed. Hence they must be allowed to graze until they receive a blemish, when they are sold etc.

a (1) One consecrated animal with either one or many of *ḥullin*. (2) E.g., an animal consecrated for a peace-offering was mixed up with five of *ḥullin*, five of the six must be sold to people who owe a peace-offering. Thus all the six are now sacred and stand for the same purpose. (3) E.g., both are peace-offerings or burnt-offerings, but belong to different owners. (4) Rashi: the priest who offers it must declare, 'Lo, this is for the sake of its owner', without specifying a name. Tosaf. and Sh. M.: the priest says nothing at all about its owner, and then it is *tacitly* understood to be for its owner, whoever he is. (5) E.g., a burnt-offering with a peace-offering. (6) They cannot be offered themselves, because their rites of sprinkling and presenting the *emurim* are dissimilar. (7) One for each sacrifice. (8) The two animals, each of the value of the *better* of the first two, naturally involve a loss. (9) The animals are redeemed, and other sacrifices bought with the redemption money. All those which were mixed up are eaten as firstling or tithe, i.e., they are subject to the same laws as these when blemished, which is that they must not be slaughtered in the public abattoirs (market) nor sold by weight. (10) Because they are distinct, as explained in the Gemara. (11) EVEN ONE IN TEN THOUSAND implies that the unfit are in the majority. But in that case it is *all the more* obvious that they cannot be sacrificed.

b (1) This reverses the numbers. (2) I.e., the smallest number of forbidden animals disqualify even the largest number with which they are mixed up. V. Tem. 28*a*. That is the same as our Mishnah. (3) Emended text (Sh. M.). (4) Lit., 'to the All-high'. (5) All those enumerated there are forbidden to the altar but not for general use, and so they can (and must) be redeemed. Here, however, they are completely forbidden, and cannot be redeemed. I would say therefore that we cannot be so strict as to rule that all must die, but that on the contrary the one (or few) is annulled by the many, and all are permitted. Hence the Mishnah informs us otherwise. (6) This reverses the preceding argument. I would argue that we are stricter here, precisely because the interdict is greater. (7) *Sc.* in the clause, IF THEY BECAME MIXED UP WITH AN OX etc. These are only forbidden as sacrifices, but not for general use. (8) EVEN ONE IN TEN THOUSAND may apply only to what precedes, but not to what follows. Hence the other Mishnah is necessary. (9) The other Mishnah only states that they cannot be sacrificed. Here he teaches what is to be done with them. (10) V. Glos.

of] idolatry?[11] [72a]—They are both necessary: for if [I learnt] from there, I would say, That applies only to *ḥullin;* but as for sacri-
a fices, Let us not cause the loss of all of them.[1] While if [I learnt] from here, I would say, This applies only to sacred animals, because it is repulsive;[2] but as for *ḥullin*, where it is not repulsive, I would say that though they are forbidden for any use, let them be annulled by the majority. Thus [both] are necessary.

Now, let them indeed be annulled by the majority? And should you answer, They are important and cannot be annulled; that is well on the view that we learnt '*whatever* one is wont to count'; but on the view that we learnt '*that* which one is wont to count' what can be said?[3] For we learnt: If a man has bundles of fenugreek

(11) If wine of *nesek* is mixed with other permitted wine, or animals which had been worshipped are mixed up with others, they are all forbidden for any use whatever.

a (1) Since they are of greater (religious) value, let the forbidden animals be annulled by the larger number of consecrated ones. (2) The slightest possibility of sacrificing a forbidden animal, though it be one in a thousand, is repulsive. Therefore they are all forbidden. (3) This is explained anon.

צריכי דאי מהתם א] הוה אמינא להדיוט אבל ב] לגבוה אימא לא נפסדינהו לכולהו ואי מהכא הוה אמינא ג] הני מילי קדשים דמאים אבל חולין דלא מאים אימא *איסורי הנאה ליבטלי ברובא צריכא ד] *וניבטלו ברובא וכי תימא חשיבי ולא בטלי הניחא למאן דאמר כל שדרכו לימנות שנינו ה] אלא למאן דאמר את שדרכו לימנות שנינו מאי איבא למימר דתנן *מי שהיו לו חבילי תילתן של כלאי הכרם ידלקו

רש"י

צריכי דאי מהתם הוה אמינא הני מילי חולין · אבל קדשים אימא ליעביד להו תקנתא דליבטיל איסורי הנאה ברובא ונימא יקרבו כי היכי דלא נפסדינהו לגמרי לכולהו ו]: ופרכינן וניבטיל ברובא · דהא כתיב אחרי רבים להטות: וכי תימא חשיבי · הואיל ודרכן למנות: כל שדרכו לימנות · שיש בני אדם המקפידין במניינם ז] ומוכרין במניינם שנינו דלא בטלי *בסמוך בהך משנה דחבילי תילתן שפיר דהא ח] [בהמות] נמי הרבה בני אדם המקפידין עליהן ומוכרין אותן במנין ואע"פ שיש בני אדם שאין מקפידין כל כך ומוסיפין יתירה או מוכרין העדר יחד: אלא למ"ד את שדרכו לימנות · שדרכו מיוחד לכך שאין לך אדם דמוסיף עליהן יתירה ללוקח ולא מוכר בלא מנין הני אין דרכן מיוחד למנין שיש המוסיפין ט] יתירה או מוכרין העדר בלא מנין: תילתן · מין תבלין *וחבילין חשוב מאד שאף טעם העץ שוה לפרי ובלע"ז פיטגר"ך:

תוספות

וליבטלו ברובא · דמטעם בריה אין לומר דלא בטיל דאע"ג דאבר מן החי חשיב בריה (חולין קב:) איסור תערובת דהכא לאו משום אבר מן החי אלא שלא ישחוט ויאכל משום חטאת המתה ושור הנסקל וכי שחיט ליה אזיל ליה איסור אבר מן החי ואיסור חטאת המתה ושור הנסקל אפי' שלם לא חשיב בריה כמו נבילה וחלב ודם דלא הוי בריה ועוף טהור קטן שלם אם אין בו כזית בשר אין לוקה עליו משום נבילה דלא חשיב בריה דעוף טמא ודאי חשיב בריה דכשאסרו הכתוב אסרו בין גדול בין קטן אע"ג דלית ביה כזית אלא כל שהוא בעלמא וכן גיד הנשה חשיב ליה בריה בפ' גיד הנשה (שם ק.) דכי אמר רחמנא לא תאכל גיד אפילו כל שהוא וכן אבר מן החי חשיב בריה *דטעמא דבריה משום דהוי כאילו פירש בין גדול ובין קטן כדמוכח פ"ג דשבועות (דף כא:) י] דאמר וכי היכן מצינו באוכל כל שהוא שהוא חייב כו' ופריך והרי מפרש ומשני מפרש נמי כבריה דמי והא דאמר בפ' אלו הן הלוקין (מכות יז.) דקאמר ר"ש אף חטה כברייתה ורבנן בריית נשמה חשיבא חטה לא חשיבא דמשמע שהדבר תלוי בנשמה והאיכא גיד הנשה רבנן לדבריו דרבי שמעון קאמרי ליה לדידן טבל לאו בריה הוא דלא דמי למפרש אלא לדידך דמדמית חטה לנמלה לא דמי דנמלה בריית נשמה וחשיבא ואע"ג דרבנן גופייהו לא חיישי בהאי טעמא קאמרי ליה הכי וכהאי גוונא אשכחן לקמן בפירקין (דף עז:) דאמרין באברי בעלי מומין רבי אליעזר אומר יעלו וחכ"א לא יעלו ומפרש טעמא דרבי אליעזר משום דכתיב מום בם הוא דלא ירצו הא ע"י תערובות ירצו והא דקתני רואה אני את בשר בעל מום כאילו הוא עצים לדבריהם דרבנן קאמר להו אע"ג דרבי אליעזר גופיה לא חייש להאי טעמא דעצים*:

אלא למאן דאמר את שדרכו לימנות שנינו מאי איכא למימר · תימה מי גרע שור גדול מאת שדרכו למנות הא אפילו חתיכה בעלמא חשיבא את שדרכו למנות משום דחשובה להתכבד בפני האורחים [כדאמרינן] בפ' גיד הנשה (חולין ק.) וכל הנך י' דברים דחשיבי את שדרכו לכאורה בכולהו לא חשיב כשור הגדול ועוד דבפ' בתרא דע"ז (דף עד.) חשיב שור הנסקל ואמרי' התם האי תנא תרתי אית ליה דבר שבמנין ואיסור הנאה ולא פריך יא] הניחא למאן דאמר כל שדרכו כו' כדפריך הכא ובבילה פ' קמא (דף ג:) ובפ' גיד הנשה (חולין ק.) שמע מינה דלכל הפחות חשיב את שדרכו ועוד מדפריך התם דניתני אגוזי פרך ורימוני באדן ולא פריך מחבילי תלתן משמע דחשיב כששה דברים ונראה לפרש דמשום חטאות המתות פריך הכא למאן דאמר את שדרכו דמשמע אפי' חטאת העוף כדתניא במס' קינים (פ"ב מ"ג) או שפרח מבין המתות ימותו כולן ואע"ג דקתני במתני' זבחים ועוף לאו בכלל זבח הוא מכל מקום מדקתני כל הזבחים משמע אפי' עוף בכלל וא"ת כיון דהני דע"ז כששה דברים חשיבי אם כן יין נסך דקתני התם היינו חביות סתומות והא תנא ליה גבי ששה דברים ולא הוה ליה למיתנייה כי היכי דלא חשיב ככרות של בעל הבית משום דתנא ליה גבי ששה דברים כדמפרש התם ושמא החמירו ביין נסך לאסור אפי' חביות פתוחות משום דחמירא עבודת כוכבים משאר איסורין דמטמאה ותופסת דמיה ועוד נראה דאיצטריך למיתני חביות סתומות משום יב] דיין נסך נפקא לן מדברי קבלה ולא כתיבא איסורה באורייתא ומשמע דהוי כשאר איסורים וס"ד דבטל ועוד אשכחן איסור עבודת כוכבים דקיל לרבי אליעזר דאמר יש פדיון לעבודת כוכבים מה שאין כן בשאר איסורים יג] והשתא אפרש כל הנהו דע"ז היכי חשיבי כששה דברים יין נסך משכחת לה בחביות סתומות עבודת כוכבים בטבעות וכוסות דחשיבי ועורות לבובין כשעשה ממנו כלי נאה אי נמי עבודת כוכבים משום דחשיבא לעובדיה וכן עורות לבובין ואי נמי כדמפרש בירושלמי יין נסך ועבודת כוכבים ועורות לבובים על שם לא ידבק בידך מאומה מן החרם ואיירי אפילו בחביות פתוחות ושמא לא הביא פסוק זה בירושלמי אלא למימרא דמיניה ילפינן איסורי הנאה בהני תלת וציפורי מצורע מיירי בציפור דרור גדולים וחשיבי ושער נזיר בציפרתא כדאי' בסוף תמורה (דף לד.) שעשה טורת ציפור יד] *כבגד מעשה רוקם משער נזיר ויש עוד אחרים משער היתר ופטר חמור ובשר בחלב ועגלה ערופה וחולין שנשחטו בעזרה בחתיכות הראויות להתכבד דעדיפי מאת שדרכו וחשיבי כאגוזי פרך ואע"ג דאיסורי הנאה נינהו חשיב ראוי להתכבד כיון דאי היתה בטילה היתה ראויה להתכבד הלכך לא בטלה והא דאמרי' בסוף הערל (יבמות פא:) דחתיכה של חטאת טמאה במאה של חטאת טהורה תעלה התם אפי' תתבטל לא חשיב ראוי להתכבד בפני אורחים כהנים דאין מחזיקין טובה זה לזה שכולן שוין כדכתיב (ויקרא ז) לכל בני אהרן תהיה איש כאחיו אבל של חטאת בשל חולין *קאמר התם דלא תעלה דלאו דוקא טהורה בשל חולין דהוא הדין טמאה בשל חולין ובקונטרס פירש ביבמות דטמאה בטהורות תעלה משום דלהפסד מרובה חששו אבל טהורה בשל חולין הפסד מועט דחזיא לכהנים וזו תימה דכמה איסורי הנאה לא בטלי ולא חיישינן וא"ת אמאי לא חשיב במסכת ע"ז פרוסה של לחם הפנים וחתיכה של חטאת טמאה וחתיכה של קדשים שמתו וי"ל דבקדשים לא קמיירי ומיהו הוה מצי למתני אברי שעיר המשתלח למאן דאסר ביומא (דף סז.) וחתיכה של עיר הנדחת ושער של מת דאסרינן בפ"ק דערכין (דף ז:) וקצת קשה מירושלמי לפי מה שפירשתי דהנהו דע"ז עדיפי מאת שדרכו דמשמע התם דלא הוו אלא י' דברים את שדרכו והכי איתא התם בפ"ב דמסכת ערלה דר' יוחנן ור"ל איתפלגון חד אמר י' דברים מקדשין דברי רבי מאיר פי' י' דברים השנויים במשנה שכולם את שדרכו טו] *ואחרים אמרו כל הדברים מקדשין דברי רבי מאיר פי' דכל שדרכו למנות שנינו טז] (*ובר) דאותם י' דברים דקאמר רבי יוחנן היינו אותם ששה דברים דקאמרי רבנן וחבילי תלתן הרי ז' ובגד שלבעו בקליפי ערלה ונתערב באחרים ולובע מלא הסיט בקליפי ערלה וארגו בבגד ואינו יודע איזהו דבתרווייהו תנן התם כולן ידלקו דברי ר' מאיר ובגד וסיט *תרי מילי חשיבי וסיט חשיב את שדרכו כדאמר התם בירושלמי ואורג מלא הסיט מלמד הבכור בבגד דקתני התם ידלק הבגד קאמר עלה *בגמ' דאית תנא דתני במשנה דברי ר"מ ואית דלא תני דברי ר"מ מאן דתני דברי רבי מאיר אית ליה י' דברים מקדשים פי' שזו היא העשירית ומאן דלא תני דברי ר"מ מנא ליה י' דברים מקדשין פי' אותן עשרה דברים שאמר ר' יוחנן דמקדשי לר"מ דהוו את שדרכו היכן הם ומשני ר"מ כר"ע שמוסיף אף ככרות של בעל הבית והשתא מאי קא קשיא ליה הא איכא כל הנהו דע"ז דמיקדשי אפי' לרבנן וכ"ש לר"מ ועוד דאמר בפ"ג דבכורות (דף כה:) דגיזי בכור בעל מום שנתערבו בגיזי חולין אוסרין בכל שהן א"כ הוו את שדרכו לר' יוחנן ושמא לא מיירי בירושלמי אלא באותם דברים השנויים במסכת ערלה באותה משנה אבל אכתי איכא טובא וביבמות הארכתי יותר:

*נתערבו באחרות ואחרות באחרות · ר"ת ל"ג בשום מקום ואחרות באחרות בהך משנה ששנויה בסוף מסכת ערלה ובהנהו דמסכת ע"ז בסוף פרק כל הצלמים גבי אפה בו את הפת כו' וגבי בגד שלבעו בקליפי ערלה ובכמה מקומות כיוצא באלו מדפריך לקמן (דף עד.) על שמואל דאסר ספק ספיקא בעבודת כוכבים מברייתא שמתרת *דלא משכח דקאי כשמואל אלא רבי יהודה שאוסר אפילו בשאר איסורין ספק ספיקא כגון רמוני בדן ושמואל סבר לה כוותיה בחדא ופליג עליה בחדא ואי הוה גרסינן הכא ובמסכת ע"ז ואחרות באחרות הוה ליה לאיתויי ראייה לשמואל מהנך משניות ולא היה דוחק להביא מברייתא דרבי יהודה ועוד יש לדקדק מגופה דמתניתין דהתם במסכת ערלה (פ"ג) גבי בגד שלבעו בקליפי ערלה וגבי תבשיל שבשלו בקליפי ערלה והנך דחבילי תלתן קתני נתערבו באחרים וגבי צובע מלא הסיט בקליפי ערלה וארגו בבגד ואינו יודע איזהו וגבי אורג מלא הסיט מלמר בכור בבגד לא קתני נתערבו באחרים והיינו טעמא משום דאם נתערב בשאר בגדים יכול להסיר מכל אחד מלא הסיט ומישתרי מטעם ספק

ספק

כדמשמע בסמוך נ"ק

נ"ל אע"ג דאיסורי הנאה נ"ק

חולין ק.

ביצה ג: יבמות פא. ערלה פ"ג מ"ו

וחשובין מאד שאף נ"ק

רש"י כת"י

צריכא· ס"א דאי מהתם הו"א ה"מ חולין אבל קדשים אימא לעביד להו תקנתא דליבטל איסורא ברובא דהא מדאורייתא כל איסור ברובא בטיל וירעו כו' כי היכי דלא נפסדינהו לגמרי: ה"ג ואי מהכא הו"א לגבוה דמאים אבל להדיוט אימא לא' כלומר אבל מידי דהדיוט כגון חולין דקילא אימא ניבטל ברובא:

נ"ל ואחר אמר כל הדברים כו' נ"ק

בירושלמי נ"ק

שייך לע"ב

נ"ל ולא נ"ק

נ"א וטעמא דבריה משום דהוי כאילו פירש הכתוב שלא תאכל בין גדול ובין קטן כו' שהוא חייב כו' ופריך כו' והרי מפרש פירוש שאמר שבועה שלא אוכל כל שהוא ומשני כו' נ"ק

[וע"ע תוס' חולין צ. ד"ה מאי טעמא]

[בבגד נ"ק וכ"ה בס"י]

דקאמר כו' לאו דוקא נ"ק

נ"ל ומסתברא נ"ק

ג"י נ"ק תרי מילי חשיבי הרי ט' והורג מלא הסיט ט'

שיטה מקובצת

א] הוה אמינא ה"מ [לחולין] (תיבת להדיוט נמחק) דליכא פסידא כלומר דלא חיישינן לפסידא דחולין הואיל דליכא הפסידא דהקדש אבל לגבוה דאיכא הפסידא דהקדש אימא לא כלומר ליבטלו משום הפסידא דקדשים וא"ת אכתי [איך] הוה אמרי' ליבטלו לאו דהוא שמעינן ליה מההיא דתמורה דקתני אוסרין בכל שהוא שאין מועיל ליקרב וא"כ מאי קמ"ל מתני' דהכא אי לענין איסור דהדיוט מההיא דעבודה זרה שמעינן לה ואי משום איסורא דקדשים מההיא דתמורה שמעינן לה וי"ל כדפ"ה דה"ק אימא לא נפסדינהו לכולהו ולעולם לא יקרבו אלא נעשה תקנה לבטל ברוב להתקין איסור דהדיוט ומתוך כך ימתין להדיוט וימכרו כשהוממו ויביאו אחרים לקרבן בדמיהן ויהיו פותרים לימכר להדיוט וע"י כך יהיו דמיהן לגבוה ולא יפסיד ההקדש ומיהו איסור דגבי גבוה אין לו ביטול ולא יקרבו אלא ימכרו להדיוט כדפי' קמ"ל דימותו ואין להן תקנה: ב] ס"י לקדשים אימא תיבת לגבוה: נמחק: ג] הוה אמינא: גירסת ס"י הני דאיסורי הנאה נינהו אבל הנך דלאו איסורי הנאה נינהו אימא לא ואי מהכא הו"א ה"מ קדשים דמאיסא אבל להדיוט אימא אפילו איסורי הנאה ליבטלו ברובא צריכא ומתיבת ה"מ עד תיבת איבטלו נמחק: ד] וניבטלו ברובא · וא"ת והא בריה היא וקי"ל דבריה אינה בטילה מידי דהוי אגיד הנשה ועוף טמא ודג טמא דלא בטיל וי"ל דלא קרינן בריה אלא היכא שהאיסור עליו משעת ברייתו כגון גיד הנשה ועוף טמא ודג טמא דמשעת ברייתן הן נאסרין ולכך בריה הן ולא בטילי אבל הכא גבי שור הנסקל דהאיסור בא עליו אחר ברייתו לא קרינן ליה בריה ולא נהירא שהרי ערלה בטילה באחד ומאתים והוי בריה שהרי האיסור עליה משעת ברייתה לכך נראה דאע"ג דבעלי חיים נינהו מ"מ לא חשיב בריה משום דגבי בריה בעינן ששמו עליו מברייתו ואינו משתנה לעולם אף לאחר מיתה כגון חתיכה דעוף טמא אפילו לאחר מיתה אומרים תן לי חתיכת בשר וכיון דשם בשר עליו אף לאחר מיתה (היינו) [הוי] בריה וכן חתיכת דג טמא וכן גיד שמו גיד בין מחיים בין לאחר מיתה וכן ש"ץ נמי שמו עליו לאחר מיתה אבל הכא בבהמה שמתה אין שמה דמחיים עליה לאחר מיתה אלא נבילה שמה ולכך אמרינן דאינו בריה והטעם היינו משום דבבשר ודג טמא ושרץ איסורייהו אינו על ידי מעשה אלא כך נאסרו בלא שום מעשה כמו שאמר רחמנא ולפיכך אין איסור שמם מפקיע מעליהם כלל אף לאחר מיתה אבל הכא גבי שור הנסקל ואינך דאיסורייהו בא על ידי מעשה הלכך משתנה שמם לאחר מיתה ובמס' חולין הארכתי: ה] עיין בהשמטות בסוף המסכת: ו] לכולהו הס"ד ומה"ד ואי מהכא אשמועינן דאפילו קדשים נמי מפסדינן ולא תנא ההיא דתמורה הס"ד ומה"ד הוה אמינא הני הוא דמפסדינן משום דאיערוב באיסורי הנאה אבל הנך דתמורה דלא איערוב בהו איסורי הנאה אימא לא ליאסרינהו לכולהו אלא ניבטיל ברובא ויקרבו צריכא הס"ד ומה"ד ופרכינן וניבטלו ברובא: ז] במניינם ומוכרין אותה למכור במנין שנינו דלא בטלי בהך משנה דחבילי: ח] בהמות נמי: ט] המוסיפין ללוקח יתירה: י] דשבועות דאמרינן וכו': יא] פריך התם הניחא: יב] משום סתם יינם דרבנן וס"ד דבטל ועוד משום דאשכחן איסור והשאר נמחק: יג] איסורים ולאפוקי מדידיה תנא ליה התם והשתא: יד] צפור בבגד מעשה רוקם: טו] שדרכו ות"ק אמר כל תיבת ואחרים נמחק: טז] שנינו ומסתבר דאותם תיבת ובר נמחק:

י א מיי' פט"ו מהל' מאכלות אסורות הלכה ח:

יא ב מיי' שם הלכה ג טור ש"ע י"ד סי' קי סעיף א:

יב ג שם בהג"ה:

ידלקו נתערבו באחרים א] *(ואחרים באחרים) ב] כולן ידלקו דברי רבי מאיר וחכמים אומרים [א]יעלו באחד ומאתים שהיה רבי מאיר אומר ג] *כל שדרכו למנות מקדש וחכמים אומרים אינו מקדש אלא ששה דברים בלבד רבי עקיבא אומר [ב]שבעה ואלו הן אגוזי פרך ורימוני ד] באדן וחביות סתומות וחילפי תרדין וקילחי כרוב ודלעת יונית ר' עקיבא ה] מוסיף אף ככרות של בעל הבית הראוי לערלה ערלה הראוי לכלאי הכרם כלאי הכרם ואיתמר עלה *רבי יוחנן אמר [ג]את שדרכו למנות שנינו רשב"ל אומר כל שדרכו למנות שנינו הניחא לריש לקיש אלא לרבי יוחנן מאי איכא למימר אמר רב פפא האי תנא דליטרא קציעות הוא דאמר

כל

ידלקו · דכתיב פן תוקדש תוקד אש: באחד ומאתים · זו היא עליית ערלה וכלאי הכרם דתרומה עולה באחד ומאה וכיון שכפל את האיסור שאיסורו איסור הנאה כפל את העלייה הכי תניא לה בספרי *גבי מכל חלבו את מקדשו ממנו דמשתעי בתרומת מעשר שהיא אחד ממאה וקרי ליה מקדשו ומשמע שמקדשו מקדש את המתערבין בו: אינו מקדש · אלא בטל: אלא ששה דברים בלבד · הן שמקדשין את כל המתערבים בהן מתוך שהן גדולים ודמיהן יקרים וחשובין במינן: פרך ובדן · מקומות הן: חילפי ו] תרדין וקלחי כרוב · לשון קלח בירק שלו: ז] כל הראוי לערלה ערלה · *מה שיש ח] באילן מין אילן וראוי לערלה מקדש את עירובו באיסור ערלה:

כל

ספק ספיקא דמותר ומיהו איכא חדא ברייתא בריש מסכת ביצה (דף ג:) דאסרה ספק ספיקא דקתני וספיקה אסור ומוקי לה בספק טריפה וקתני התם נתערבה באלף כולן אסורות ואין לחוש בהא דלא מייתי לקמן כיון דברייתא היא דמאי אולמא מברייתא דרבי יהודה והיא נמי מוקי רב פפא בביצה כרבי יהודה אליבא דרבי יהושע ועדיפא ליה לאתויי ברייתא דמפורש בה רבי יהודה בהדיא ועוד אומר רבינו תם דהא דקתני נתערבה באלף כולן אסורות לא קאי אספיקה אלא אודאה תדע דאפילו רבי יהודה דאסר לקמן ספק ספיקא היינו דוקא ברימוני בדן כדקתני בברייתא רבי יהודה אומר רימוני בדנכו' משמע דוקא *רימוני ט] את שדרכו ועדיף דהוי אחד מששה דברים בהגהו אסר ר' יהודה ספק ספיקא דמאי טעמא נקט רימוני בדן והא אפילו כל שדרכו מקדש לר' יהודה כדמוכח בברייתא דליטרא קציעות וגבי חתיכה בחתיכות דאמר ר' יהודה לא תעלה פ' הערל (יבמות פא:) וחתיכה הוי כל שדרכו כדמוכח התם *דאמר רבי יוחנן והלא חתיכה עולה (למנין) משום דהוי כל שדרכו ואנן את שדרכו בעינן והש"ס דמוקי לה בנימוחה היינו דוקא לריש לקיש ומיהו מצי למימר דנקט רימוני בדן י] לרבי שמעון דפליג עליה דאפילו ברימוני בדן שרי ספק ספיקא ובענין זה צריך לפרש *חדא ברייתא לקמן (דף עד:) דבסתמא דקתני כוס של עבודת כוכבים שנפל לאוצר מלא כוסות כולן אסורות פירש אחד מהן לריבוא ומריבוא לריבוא מותרין דאמאי נקט מריבוא לריבוא הא יא] בפירש אחד מהן לריבוא שרי כ"ש מריבוא לריבוא דהוי ספיקא שלישית אלא נקטיה לאשמועינן דמאן דאסר אסר אפילו בכמה ספיקות וכן צריך לומר בעל כרחין דרימוני בדן לר' יהודה לאו דוקא *ומדתנן במסכת כלים (פי"ז מ"ה) הרימון שאמרו לא גדול ולא קטן אלא בינוני ולמה הוזכרו רימוני בדן שיהו מקדשין כל שהן דברי רבי מאיר רבי יוחנן בן נורי אומר לשער בהן את הכלים רבי עקיבא אומר לכך ולכך הוזכרו לשער בהן את הכלים יב] ושהן מקדשין בכל שהן *רבי יהודה אומר לא הוזכרו רימוני בדן וחצירי גבע אלא שיהו מתעשרין ודאי בכל מקום פירוש יג] *דסתמייהו מבין העובדי כוכבים כך פירש בערוך בערך חצר ומאותה משנה יש לדקדק דסתם רימונים אפילו כל שדרכו לא חשיבי *דלא תקשי דרבי מאיר אדרבי מאיר לריש לקיש דאמר כל שדרכו לימנות שנינו ולרבי יהודה כל הרימונים חשובים כל שדרכו דהא רבי יהודה סבר דליטרא קציעות לא בטלה וקתני לא הוזכרו רימוני בדן לענין קידוש אלמא כל הרימונים מקדשים ושוו לרימוני בדן דאי רימוני ביטנים אינן מקדשין א"כ היה לו להזכירן לענין קידוש כמו רבי מאיר וצריך עיון בירושלמי בפרק בתרא דערלה וכמדומה שיש שם טעות סופר ויש מפרשים דאפילו גרסינן בכל הנך משניות ואחרות באחרות לא מצי לאתויי ראיה דספק ספיקא אסור דדילמא הכי קאמר וכל האחרות באחרות ואין לתמוה מה חידוש הוא לשנות ב' פעמים כיון דקאי אכל האחרות באחרות דאיצטריך ליה לאשמועינן דאע"ג דאיכא תרי רובי דגבי שאר מילי אסרינן חדא רובא ושרינן תרי רובא גבי יוחסין בסוף פ"ק דכתובות (דף טו.) דאמר הולכין אחר רוב העיר והוא דאיכא רוב סיעה בהדיה ואפילו עיר קטנה ואין הולכין אחר רוב עיר גרידתא ואפילו גדולה כאנטוכיא יד] ואחרי רוב סיעה גרידתא*:

כולן ידלקו · ואם תאמר מאי שנא הכא דקתני ידלקו כשנתערבו וכן בכל האיסורין השנויים שם במסכת ערלה (פ"ג) ולא פליג רבי אליעזר דלימא יוליך הנאה לים המלח כמו בס"פ כל הצלמים (ע"ז מט:) לענין עבודת כוכבים *וכוותיה הילכתא כדפסקינן טו] מיהו רבינו שמואל פירש שם דהוא הדין בכל האיסורין אמר רבי אליעזר יוליך הנאה לים המלח ונראה דרבי אליעזר פליג דווקא גבי עבודת כוכבים לפי שתופסת דמיה וכשמוליך הנאה לים המלח נראה כאילו מוליך האיסור ומהאי טעמא הוה אמרינן נמי הכי לענין שביעית גבי הא דתניא בפרק הגוזל עצים (ב"ק קא.) בגד שצבעו בקליפי שביעית ידלק אם היה מתערב באחרים הוה אמרינן יוליך הנאה לים המלח אבל בערלה וכלאים ושער נזיר ופטר חמור וכל שאר איסורים דלא תפסי דמיהם אמרינן לרבי אליעזר ידלק אפילו נתערב ולפי טעם זה טבעת וכוסות דלקמן דמיירי בעבודת כוכבים סגי בהולכת הנאה לים המלח עוד יש לפרש דדוקא בתנור שהסיקו בעצי עבודת כוכבים ואפה בו את הפת ונטל ממנה ככר וארג בה את הבגד אמרי' יוליך הנאה לים המלח כשנתערב לפי שאין ממשות האיסור בעין וההוא גברא דאיתערב ליה חביתא דחמרא כיון *דאי אפשר להנות בהולכת הנאה אלא היתר הנאה שאינה בגוף של עצמו אלא או למכור או ליתן לפועלין אבל שיהנה הוא עצמו לא טז] דאיסורא בשתיה שרי על ידי *ב' זוזי ואם תאמר מאי טעמא לא אמרי' בכל הני דמסכת ערלה ימכרו כולן לעובד כוכבים חוץ מדמי איסור הנאה שבו כדקאמר רבן שמעון בן גמליאל בפרק בתרא דמסכת ע"ז (דף עד:) גבי יין נסך ובירושלמי פריך לה ומשני דחיישינן בכולהו אם ימכרו לעובד כוכבים שמא יחזור העובד כוכבים וימכור לישראל אבל ביין נסך ליכא למיחש וכן בפת ובגד דכל הצלמים (ע"ז מט:) דאע"ג דפת של עובד כוכבים אסור באכילה בהנאה מיהא שרי וחיישינן שמא יקנה ממנו ישראל ויתן לפועליו וחביתא דההוא גברא אם היה רוצה למכור כל יינו יחד ה"ה דהוה מצי למכור חוץ מדמי איסורא שבו וחביות סתומות נמי איכא למיחש שימכרם העובד כוכבים לישראל דמיירי בשמן זית או ביין תפוחים: **ה"ג** אגוזי פרך · על שם שנפרכין כדאמר בפסיקתא בפרשתא דיהודה וישראל רבים אחר פרשת כי תשא על אל גינת אגוז דדרשינן שנמשלו ישראל לאגוז שיש בו שלשה מינין של פרך שנפרך מעצמו:

אף ככרות של בעל הבית · אבל של נחתום לא שהם קטנות והא דמשמע בסוף הערל (יבמות דף פא:) דחתיכה של לחם הפנים בשל חולין לא בטלה שאני לחם הפנים יז] *דסמידא טפי וראוי להתכבד בחתיכה ואפה בו את הפת יח] בפ' כל הצלמים (ע"ז מט:) צריך לאוקמא בככרות של בעל הבית דהא קתני נתערבו באחרים כולן אסורין בהנאה ואפה בו את הפת דתנן במסכת ערלה (פ"ג מ"ה) לא בשל בעל הבית דהא קתני תעלה באחד ומאתים ואי לאו ההיא דמסכת ערלה לא הייתי צריכין לחלק בין לחם הפנים לשאר לחם והוה מצי לאוקמי מתניתין דמסכת ע"ז אפילו בשל נחתום וכדרבי מאיר דלאמר את שדרכו לימנות מקדש או כל שדרכו לריש לקיש אבל מתניתין דמסכת ערלה מוכחא דבסתם פת אפילו לרבי מאיר עולה באחד ומאתים*): **הראוי** לערלה ערלה · בירושלמי מדקדק אמאי לא תנא נמי הראוי לתרומה תרומה דבתרומה נמי כיון דחשיבי לא בטלי ואין עולין באחד ומאה ומשני משום דכולם ראויים לתרומה ולא שייך למיתני האי לישנא ונראה שיש עדיין לתרץ משום דקתני ידלקו ועולין באחד ומאתים ואין דין זה נוהג בתרומה ועוד הוה מצי לשנויי דהאי הנא תרתי אית ליה דבר שבמנין ואיסורי הנאה כדאמרינן במסכת ע"ז (דף עד.) אמתניתין דהתם פרק בתרא:

*)[ועי' היטב תוס' יבמות פא: ד"ה ככרות]

ר"מ

נ"א רימוני בדן שהם את שדרכו כו' נ"ק

נ"א את שדרכו כו' נ"ק

נ"ל דאמר ר"י והלא אני שונה חתיכה בחתיכות עולה משום דהוי כל שדרכו למנות ומשני דאנן את שדרכו שנינו אלא ודאי דבשאר מילי לא אסר ר"י ספק ספיקא והש"ס דמוקי כו' נ"ק

נ"ל הך ברייתא דבסמוך דקתני נ"ק

ובספרים שלפנינו גרסי' ור' יוסי וא"כ אין הוכחת התוספות הוכחה רש"ק

ד' זוזי נ"ק

[עיין מעל"ד בתוס' ד"ה נתערבו כו' שר"ת לא גרס ואחרות באחרות ע"ש]

[עי' תוס' נדה מו. ד"ה אתי וכו' וברש"י שם ד"ה חייבת]

[ביצה ג:]

נ"ל מה שהוא מין אילן כו'

מדתנן נ"ק

דמסתמא באים מבין הכותים נ"ק

נר"מ דלא כו' נ"ק

[ועי' תוס' יבמות פא. ד"ה נתערבו]

נ"ל וכוותיה פסקי' הלכתא התם ומיהו ר"ש כו'

[עי' ביבמות פא: בתוס' ד"ה כולן ידלקו]

[ובתוספות פרק הערל פא: ד"ה ככרות גרס דחמיר טפי ואפשר לומר משום קדושת לחם הפנים חמיר טפי להיות ראוי להתכבד ע"ש ועי' בשו"ת פנים מאירות ח"א שאלה נ"ח]

שיטה מקובצת

א] תיבת ואחרים נמחק ותיבת באחרים ל"ש תמחק: ב] כולן ידלקו' וא"ת אמאי לא אמרינן ימכרו לעובד כוכבים חוץ מדמי האיסור שבו כדאמר רשב"ג בפרק בתרא דעבודת כוכבים ימכרו לעובד כוכבים חוץ מדמי יין נסך שבו וי"ל (דשמא) [דחיישינן שמא] ימכרנו העובד כוכבים לישראל אחר אבל התם גבי יין נסך ליכא למיחש דאין ישראל קונה יין מן העובד כוכבים ומכאן משמע דאם נאסר פת מישראל כגון שאפאו העובד כוכבים ולא הכשיר ישראל את התנור אסור לסוכרו לעובד כוכבים דשמא ימכרנו העובד כוכבים לישראל שאין ישראל אחר מכירו א) ואתי לידי תקלה אבל ישליך אותו למים ואם יש להם נשים עובדות כוכבים רבות שמשרתות בין היהודים (שיכלו) [שיכולים] לאכלו באכילה אחת בלא שהייה יחלקו ביניהם ויאכלו מיד לעיני היהודים ויש מתירין לחותכו (בארבע) חתיכות כדפי' בפסחים *): ג] אומר את שדרכו: ד] באדן · עיין תשובת הרשב"א סימן תשל: ה] ר"ע אומר (תיבת מוסיף נמחק) אף ככרות של בעל הבית אבל של נחתום לא אבל חתיכה של לחם הפנים לא בטלה משום דחמירא טפי: ו] חילפי בתרדין וקלחי בכרוב: ז] תיבת כל נמחק: ח] שיש באילו מין אות ז' נמחק: ט] רימוני בדן שהם את: י] בדן משום ר' שמעון: יא] הא כי פירש אחד: יב] ושיהו מקדשין תיבת ושהן נמחק: יג] דמסתמא באים מבין הכותים: יד] על תיבות ואחרי רוב סיעה גרידתא נכתב עליו קו מלמעלה: טו] כדפסקינן התם: טז] לא דאסורה בשתיה שרי ע"י ארבע זוזי וא"ת: יז] הפנים דחמירא תיבת דסמידא נמחק: יח] הפת דפ' כל הצלמים:

באיזה

*) הנה חדושיו לפסחים לא זכינו לראותו ולפ"ד צריך להיות לחותכו בהרבה חתיכות עיין תו"ח כלל ע"ה דין ד׳ ·

א) ר"ל במקומות שנוהגין היתר בפת עובד כוכבים וכיון שאין הישראל מכיר שהוא פת של ישראל ואפאו עובד כוכבים וסבור שהוא פת של עובד כוכבים גופיה ואתי לידי תקלה ויקח ממנו.

of *kil'ayim*[4] of a vineyard,[5] [72b] they must be burnt.[6] If they were mixed up with others,[7] and those again with others,[8] they must all be burnt: that is the view of R. Meir. But the Sages maintain: They are neutralized in a mixture of two hundred to one. For R. Meir used to say: *Whatever* one is wont to count renders [others] forbidden;[9] while the Sages maintain: Only six things forbid [the whole]—R. Akiba says: Seven—and they are as follows: The nuts of Perek, the pomegranates of Badan,[10] sealed casks [of wine], beetroot tops, cabbage stalks,[11] and Grecian gourds. R. Akiba adds the loaves of a householder.[12] Those which are subject to the
a law of *'orlah*[1] [render the mixture] *'orlah;*[2] and those which are subject to the law of *kil'ayim* of the vineyard, [render the mixture] *kil'ayim* of the vineyard. Now it was stated thereon: R. Joḥanan said: We learnt,[3] *That* which one is wont to count;[4] while Resh Laḳish said: We learnt, *Whatever* one is wont to count.[5] Now, it is well according to Resh Laḳish;[6] but according to R. Joḥanan, what can be said?[7]—Said R. Papa: This Tanna[8] is the Tanna who taught [the Baraitha] concerning the *liṭra* of dried figs, who maintained:

(4) V. Glos.
(5) Cf. Lev. XIX, 19 and Deut. XXII, 9. (6) For they must not be used in any way. Burning is deduced from the word *tiḳdash* (E.V. forfeited) in the latter text, which is read *tuḳad esh*, 'shall be burnt in fire'. (7) *Permitted* bundles of the same. (8) This clause is omitted in 'Orlah III, 6 and Yeb. 81*b*. (9) Lit., 'consecrated.' (10) Perek and Badan are towns in Samaria N.E. of Shechem. In Yeb. 81*b* s.v. פרך Tosaf. renders the former by cracknuts. (11) Beverages were made from these two. (12) In connection with the neutralizing of leavened mixed up with unleavened bread before Passover, when the latter is required for the festival. All these were considered of particular importance, and could not be neutralized. In the last-mentioned a distinction is drawn between home-made loaves and the loaves of a baker, the latter being less important.
a (1) V. Glos. They are the nuts, pomegranates and sealed casks of wine (made of grapes of *'orlah*). (2) The whole comes under the law of *'orlah*. (3) In R. Meir's ruling. (4) Only such objects which are *always* counted cannot be neutralized, but not objects which are sometimes counted and sometimes sold in bulk. (5) Even only occasionally. For further notes v. Yeb. (Sonc. ed.) 81*b*. (6) For animals are sometimes sold singly and sometimes in lots (uncounted save by a general estimate). (7) Let them indeed be neutralized. (8) Of our Mishnah, and the Mishnah cited in the text.

[73a] Whatsoever is numbered [in selling], even [if its prohibition is] Rabbinical, cannot be neutralized, and how much the more when it is Biblical![9] For it was taught: If a *liṭra* of dried figs[10] was pressed on the top of a round jar, and he does not know in which jar it was pressed; or on the top of a cask, and he does not know in which cask; or on top of a 'beehive',[11] and he does not know in which, R. Meir maintains that R. Eliezer said: We regard the upper [layers] as if they are separated, and the lower ones neutralize the upper ones;[12] while R. Joshua ruled: If there were a hundred tops, they neutralize; if not, [all] the tops are forbidden, and the bottom layers[13] are permitted.[14] R. Judah maintained: R. Eliezer said: If there were a hundred tops, they neutralize; if not, [all] the tops are forbidden etc.; while R. Joshua ruled: Even if you have three

a hundred tops, they do not neutralize.[1] If he pressed it[2] in a round jar, and he does not know in which part of the jar he pressed it, whether in the north or in the south, all agree that it is neutralized.[3] R. Ashi said: You may even say [that it agrees with] the Rabbis: Living creatures are important, and cannot be neutralized.

Now, let us detach [them] one by one and say, whatever is detached,[4] is detached from the majority?[5] [You say,] 'detach

(9) As in the instances which we are discussing. (10) Of *terumah* (q.v. Glos.), which may not be eaten by a *zar*. Normally it is neutralized by one hundred times its quantity. By Biblical law *terumah* must be given only of corn, wine, and oil (v. Num. XVIII, 8; Deut. XVIII, 4); the *Rabbis* added fruit. (11) A receptacle of that shape. (12) Though only the *top* layer of each cask etc. is in doubt, for the bottom ones are certainly not *terumah*, we regard the top layers as if they were taken away from their place and dispersed among *all* the layers of *all* the casks. Hence, if there are a hundred layers *in all* against the one in doubt, it is neutralized and all are permitted. (13) I.e., all but the top one. (14) But you cannot count *all* the layers for neutralizing purposes, since they are not in doubt.

a (1) For layers of figs are sold by number. (2) The *liṭra* of figs. (3) Because it may not be a complete layer, and is therefore not sold by number.—Hence our Mishnah agrees with R. Joshua. For further notes v. Bez. (Sonc. ed.) 3*b*ff. (4) Lit., 'separates'. (5) This is a general rule: when one thing is detached from many, we assume that it was detached from what constituted the majority. Here the majority of the animals are fit for sacrifice; as we detach each one, we may assume that it was of the majority, and therefore it can be sacrificed. Only the last two will then remain forbidden.

כל דבר שיש בו מנין כל שדרכו לימנות כגון ליטראות של קציעות שרוב בני אדם אין מוכרין במנין אלא דורסין אותו בעיגול ומוכר כל העיגול יחד הואיל ופעמים שמונין הליטראות לבד למוכרם במנין: ואפילו בדרבנן. במידי דאיסוריה מדרבנן כגון תרומת קציעות לא בטיל הואיל ודרכו לימנות כל כ"ש בדאורייתא כגון פסולי קרבן דמתני': ליטרא קציעות. משקל ליטרא של תאנים יבישות של תרומה שקילעם באיזמל בכלי ששמו מקצוע: שדרסה ע"פ עיגול. שם כלי הוא עגול ודורסין בה קציעות ונדבקין זו בזו ונעשין עיגול כעין גבינה: על פי. דוקא נקט שנראית לעינים: ואין ידוע. איזה פי כלי נאסר ובכל התחתונות ס] פשיטא ליה שאין התרומה מעורבת בהן אלא הפומין ו] לבדם בספק האיסור: רבי מאיר ורבי יהודה פליגי בהא אליבא דר"א ור' יהושע: רואין אותן כאילו הן פרודות. אע"פ שאין כאן ק' פומין של ק' כלים של היתר לבד האיסור לבטל האיסור והתחתונו' אינן בכלל הספק להצטרף עם העליונות לבטלן רואין את כל ליטראות התחתונות והעליונות שבכל הכלים ז] פרודות וזו מעורבת בכולן והתחתונות מצטרפות להעלות את העליונות שבכל פום ופום: ואם לאו הפומין אסורין. שהתחתונות שאינן בכלל הספק אין מעלות ח] הפומין: אפילו יש שם ג' מאות פומין לא יעלו. דכל שדרכו לימנות לא בטיל: דרסה בעיגול ואינו יודע באיזה מקום כו'. שדרסה במקום השולים שהכלי רחב והרבה ליטראות סדורות לרחבו: דברי הכל יעלו. הואיל וליתיה לאיסוריה בעיניה שנדרס ונדבק באחרות מלמעלה ומלמטה ומן הצד אין כאן דבר שבמנין כלל: ה"ג ונמשך *חד וחד מינייהו ונקריב כו'. יטלם אחד אחד וכל חד וחד נימא מרובא הוא: ופרכינן נמשך בתמיה. משמע יקחם אחד אחד מתוך העדר הא הוה לו האיסור קבוע ועומד ביניהם וקיימא לן בסנהדרין (דף עט.) מוארב לו פרעו לזורק אבן לגו

כל

כל דבר שיש בו מנין אפילו בדרבנן לא בטיל וכל שכן בדאורייתא *דתניא *ליטרא קציעות שדרסה על פי עיגול ואינו יודע באיזו עיגול דרסה על פי חבית ואינו יודע באיזו חבית דרסה על פי כוורת ואינו יודע באיזו כוורת דרסה ר"מ אומר ר"א אומר רואין את העליונות כאילו הפרודות והתחתונות מעלות את העליונות ר' יהושע אומר [א]אם יש מאה פומין יעלו ואם לאו הפומין אסורין והשולים מותרין רבי יהודה אומר ר"א אומר אם יש שם ק' פומין יעלו ואם לאו הפומין אסורין וכו' רבי יהושע אומר אפילו יש שם שלשה מאות פומין לא יעלו [ב]דרסה בעיגול ואינו יודע באיזה א] מקום בעיגול דרסה או לצפונה או לדרומה דברי הכל יעלו רב אשי אמר אפי' תימא רבנן [ג]בעלי חיים חשיבי ולא בטלי *ונמשך ב] ונקרב חד מינייהו ונימא ג] *כל דפריש מרובא פריש *נמשך הוה ד] לה קבוע

וכל

ר"מ אומר רבי אליעזר אומר כו'. תימה לר"ל דאמר לעיל גבי חבילי תלתן לר"מ כל שדרכו קשיא דר"מ גופיה קסבר דליטרא קציעות בטלה ט]דאע"ג דהויא כל שדרכו מיהו בפ' הערל (יבמות פא.) משמע דלא אמר ר"ל כל שדרכו מקדש אלא תרומה דאורייתא אבל בתרומה בזמן הזה דהיא מדרבנן לא י] וא"ת אם תרומה בזמן הזה דרבנן א"כ בטלה קדושת הארץ א"כ כלאי הכרם נמי דרבנן ואמאי תני כל שדרכו וי"ל דכלאי הכרם הוא חד דרבנן דאם לא בטלה קדושת הארץ היה דאורייתא' אבל הכא תרתי דרבנן חד דבטלה קדושת הארץ ועוד דתרומת תאנים מדרבנן דלא מיחייב מדאורייתא אלא דגן תירוש ויצהר א"נ דלעיל הכי פירושו שהיה ר"מ אומר כל שדרכו לימנות מקדש מדאורייתא וכיון דבדאורייתא כל שדרכו מקדש דין הוא שיקדש בדרבנן את שדרכו כגון חבילי תלתן של כלאי הכרם א"נ כלאי הכרם כיון שיש בהן איסור הנאה אע"ג דבטלה קדושת הארץ חמור כמו מדאורייתא וא"ת ובפ"ק דמגילה (דף י.) היכי בעי למימר דקסבר ר"א קדושה ראשונה קידשה לשעתה וקידשה לעתיד לבא ועוד דרבי יהושע גופיה קאמר התם בהדיא הכי אלמא קסבר לא בטלה קדושת הארץ *והיכי יא]לרבי יהושע דליטרא קציעות בטלה לר"ל והיינו יכולין לפרש דלר' יהושע קדושת הארץ לא בטלה ומ"מ ליטרא קציעות עולה משום דתרומת תאנים דרבנן דמטעם זה הקילו בה לומר שהתחתונות מעלות את העליונות ואע"פ שלא נתערבו בכל העיגול והא דמשמע בפרק הערל (יבמות פא.) לר"ל דאי תרומה בזמן הזה דאורייתא לא היה עיגול בעיגולין עולה דקאמר ר"ל והלא אני שונה עיגול בעיגולין עולה *אלא תרומה דרבנן ואיזה הוכחה היא והלא ר' יהושע סבר מקריבין אע"פ שאין בית דקדושת הבית לא בטלה וכ"ש קדושת הארץ ואפי' הכי סובר דעיגול עולה ובטל ויש לומר דר' יהושע יסבור דלא מקדש אלא ו' דברים ור"מ דסבר כל שדרכו לא סבר כוותיה בהא א"כ י"ל בדוחק *התם פרק הערל (נז"ש) ה"נ היינו בתרומת ביכורים דהוי דאורייתא בתאנים ומצינו סתם תרומה דאיירי בביכורים דתנן במסכת פרה פ' י"א (מ"ג) דבילה של תרומה שנפלה למי חטאת נטלה ואכלה אם יש כביצה בין טמאה בין טהורה המים טמאים והאוכלה חייב מיתה פי' כשנטלה אדם מיד נטמא גופו מחמת טשא מי חטאת וא"א להיות האוכלה חייב מיתה בסתם תרומה דתרומת פירות דרבנן אם לא נאמר דבתרומת ביכורים מיירי *וה"נ מדקדק ר"ל מהא דעיגול בעיגולין עולה אפילו בביכורים דאורייתא ודוחק הוא זה אלא יש לחלק דלענין קדושה התלויה במחיצות כגון קדושת הבית קאמר ר' יהושע דלא בטלה כדדריש התם במגילה (דף ג:) אשר לו חומה אע"פ שאין לו עכשיו והיה לו קודם לכן וכן צריך לחלק [נמי לעיל] כמו שפירשתי לעיל בפרק קדשי קדשים (דף סא. ד"ה מאי) :**והתחתונות** מעלות את העליונות. אע"פ שאינן בספק דימוע הקילו בתרומת פירות דרבנן והא דתנן במס' תרומות בפ"ד (מ"ח) תאנה לבנה שנפלה לתוך לבנות ושחורות לבנות אסורות השחורות מותרות ואין השחורות מעלות את הלבנות לא דמי דהתם *אינן השחורות ראויות להיות בספק דימוע שלעולם השחורות ניכרות מתוך לבנות: **רבי** יהודה אומר כו'. וא"ת לר' יהודה מאי איריא דבר שבמנין אפילו כל מילי אוסר בכל שהוא דהא שמעי' ליה לר' יהודה לקמן בפירקין דמין במינו לא בטיל ובסיפא נמי דקתני דברי הכל לרבי יהודה יעלו אמאי יעלו וכן לקמן דנקט ר"י רימוני בדן אפילו כל מילי נמי וכן בפ' הנזקין (גיטין נד:) נפלו ונתפלעו בשוגג יעלו דברי רבי יהודה אמאי והא מין במינו לא בטיל לר' יהודה ועוד תנן בפ' טוטל (שבת קמא:) רבי יהודה אומר מעלין את המדומע באחד ומאה *ואומר ר"ת דלא א"ר יהודה מין במינו בכל שהוא אלא בדבר לא דומיא דדם הפר ודם השעיר דיליף מינה לקמן לדבר המתערב הוא והא דאמרי' בסוף בילה (דף לח:) דחיטין בחטין לא בטיל לר' יהודה בקמח מיירי דהוי דבר המתערב תדע דגבי חטין בשעורין קאמר התם דבטל משום דהוי מין בשאינו מינו ואמאי הא מינכרי *מהדדי אלא ודאי בקמח מיירי ולא גרסי' בגיטין נפלו לגת ונתפלעו אלא נפלו ונתפלעו דלא מיירי בלח אלא ביבש ובענין זה מפרש ר"ת הא דא"ר יוחנן בסוף ע"ז (דף עג:) ב' כוסות אחד של חולין ואחד של תרומה שמוזג וערבן זה בזה סלק את מינו כמו שהוא ושאינו מינו רבה עליו ומבטלו יב] וקשיא ליה כיון דתרומה עולה בא' ומאה א"כ מינו נמי יסייע לשאינו מינו לבטל התרומה אלא ש"מ דבמינו במשהו והא דא"ר יוחנן התם (דף עג:) דכל איסורין שבתורה במינו בנותן טעם חוץ מטבל ויין נסך ולא חשיב תרומה משום דבכלל טבל היא דכיון דבחד טעמא הוא דמפרש התם טעמא דטבל דכהיתרו כך איסורו דחיטה אחת פוטרת את הכרי והוא הדין תרומה כעלייתה כך איסורה ובכל דוכתא דתרומה עולה באחד ומאה בדבר יבש ומתני' דהקומץ רבה (מנחות כג.) שתי מנחות שלא נקמצו דלא מבטלי ליה שירים לטיבלא דמוקמינן התם כר' יהודה במנחת סולת איירי יג] שנתערב לגמרי בדבר לח ולא במאפה תנור ומחבת ומרחשת והיא דנבילה בשחוטה יד] בהקומץ רבה (שם כג.) בשנימוחה וה"ר יוסף טוב עלם מפלנ"ל הקשה לר"ת מההיא דפסחים (דף טו.) דחבית של תרומה שנשברה בגת העליונה והתחתונה חולין טמאין דאמרי' התם (דף כא.) דאם נפלה לק' חולין דברי הכל תרד ותטמא אלמא דאפי' לח עולה באחד ומאה טו] ונראה שכמו כן היה יכול להקשות מההיא דשאור של חולין ושל תרומה שנפלו בעיסה דאין לח מתערב יותר ממנו ועוד תניא במסכת תרומה בתוספתא פרק סאה תרומה לוג יין נלול שנפל לתוך ק' לוגין עכורין *וחזר בו ר"ת דודאי אין חילוק בין לח ליבש ותירץ דהא דתרומה עולה בא' ומאה בנפלה לתוך חולין מתוקנין דאי אפשר למבטל דהיינו חולין להיות כבטל דהיינו תרומה והיא דב' כוסות א' של תרומה וא' של חולין שאינן מתוקנין דאפשר להם ליעשות תרומה טז] *קסבר לה ר' יוחנן כמאן דאמר בהקומץ רבה (דף כג:) בתר מבטל אזלינן והוי מין במינו והיא דפסחים (דף כא.) ל"ק *למ"ד בתר בטל אזלי' דמשקין לכי סריחי אין שם משקין עליהן ולא אפשר לה לתרומה שתיעשה חולין וא"ת וטבל במינו במשהו היכי משכחת לה הא א"א למבטל דהיינו החולין שיעשו טבל וי"ל שנפל טבל טבול לתרומה בטבל שאינו טבול לתרומה דהוי מין במינו כיון דשם *טבל עליהם על שניהם א"נ טבל שראה פני הבית בטבל שלא ראה פני הבית א"נ *נפל לתוך חולין מתוקנין ובעודה לתרומה ביד בעלים דאפשר לאיתשולי עלה והשתא דאתינן להכי איכא לאוקומי ההיא דב' כוסות בחולין מתוקנין וכגון דתרומה ביד בעלים וההיא דפסחים בתרומה ביד כהן ועוד י"ל לתירוץ קמא יז] *כר"ת ההיא דפסחים (דף כא.) כר' חייא דאית ליה לר' יהודה נבלה ושחוטה בטלות זו בזו ולהכי חשיב התם מין בשאינו מינו לענין משהו אע"פ שחשובין מין במינו לענין אחד ומאה דלא סגי להו בס' אבל רבי יוחנן דלא כרבי חייא דה"נ מוכח בהקומץ רבה (מנחות כג:) דלאו כ"ע אית להו דר' חייא והיא משנה דאין דם מבטל דם פירש בקונטרס בהקומץ רבה (ג"ז שם) לרב חסדא דאזיל בתר מבטל הויא דלא כרבי חייא ואפילו לרבי חנינא דאזיל בתר בטל נראה דאיכא טובא ההיא דאין רוק מבטל רוק ואין מי רגלים מבטל מי רגלים לקמן בפירקין

וגבי

יג א מיי' פ"ד מהלכות תרומות הלכה ו:

יד ב מיי' שם הלכה ז:

טו ג מיי' פ"ו מהלכות פסה"מ ה"א ופט"ו מהל' מאכלות אסורות ה"ג טוש"ע י"ד סימן קי סעיף א:

תרומות פ"ד מ"י בילם ג:

[יומא פד: וש"נ]

[עי' תוספות חולין צט: ד"ה ספק]

והכא לר"י לליטרא קציעות בטלה לר"מ וסייט בכל נ"ק

אלמא תרומה נ"ק

דהתם בפרק הערל סייעו נ"ק

ומשום הכי נמי מדקדק נ"ק

פלוגתא דר"מ ור"י ליתא במשנה דתרומות אמנם בתוספתא דתרומות פ"ה איתא לכך שפיר איתא דתניא

ג"י הל"ק ונמשך חד חד מינייהו ונקרב ונימא

תר מר נ"ק

אין נ"ק

מהדדי נ"ק

יעלה וחזר נ"ק

וסבר לה נ"ק

אפילו למ"ד נ"ק

טבל על שניהם נ"ק

אפילו נפל נ"ק

דר"ת דהיא דפסחים נ"ק

גליון הש"ס

תוס' ד"ה רבי יהודה אומר וכו' ואומר ר"ת דלא אמר ר' יהודה. עיין לקמן דף עו ע"ב תוס' ד"ה. סא בסס"ד:

שיטה מקובצת

א] באיזה עיגול דרסה דברי הכל יעלו דרסה בעיגול היינו פלוגתייהו אלא אמר רב פפא דרסה בעיגול ואין ידוע היכן דרסה או וכו': ב] ונימשוך חד חד מינייהו וניקרב: ג] כל דפריש מרובא פריש. וא"ת הא אמרינן בעלי חיים חשיבי ולא בטלי וי"ל דהיינו דוקא כי שקלינן כולם או רובם או ודאי לא יועיל המשכה אבל אם משך כל אחד מהם בפני עצמו נימא שפיר כל דפריש מרובא קא פריש: ד] הוה ליה קבוע כו'. בפרק גיד הנשה תנן גיד הנשה (שנתערב) [שנתבשל] עם הגידין בזמן שמכירו בנותן טעם ואם לאו כולן אסורין ופריך בגמ' וליבטל ברובא ומשני בריה חשיבה ולא בטילה ופריך למה לי לשנויי הכי תיפוק ליה משום דגיד הנשה קבוע וכל קבוע כמחצה על מחצה ומשני דאין חשיב מחצה על מחצה רק היכא שידוע האיסור במקום קביעתו כי ההיא דתשע חנויות דהתם של נבילה ידוע ומבורר במקום קביעות והשתא קשה א"כ מאי משני הכא הוי ליה קבוע והלא אין האיסור ידוע ומבורר וי"ל דשאני הכא שיש חשיבות דבעלי חיים ומתוך כך לא בעינן ידוע ומבורר. (וא"ה בספרים שלנו לא נמצא בפ' גיד הנשה לא הקושיא ולא התירוץ אולי היה כך גירסתם עכ"ה): ה] התחתונות פשיטא ליה: ו] הפומין לבדו: ז] הכלים כאילו הן פרודות: ח] אין מעלות את הפומין: ט] בטלה ואע"ג דהויא: י] לא וליטרא קציעות מדרבנן אבל הני דלעיל דאורייתא חמירא ספי ועוד יש לומר דלעיל מיירי אליבא דנפשיה והבא אליבא דרבית. תוס' מהר"פ: יא] והיכי קאמר ר"ם אליבא דר' יהושע: יב] ומבטלו דקשיא ליה: יג] איירי שנתערב לגמרי: יד] בשחוטה דהקומץ רבה: טו] ומאה. ובתוס' מהר"פ תירץ הא דידיה הא דרבית כר"י הלכן דלקמן: טז] תרומה וסבר לה: יז] דר"ת וההיא דפסחים:

ניכבשינהו

וכל קבוע כמחצה על מחצה דמי אלא ניכבשינהו א] דניידי ונימא כל דפריש מרובא פריש אמר רבא ב] (השתא דאמור רבנן לא ניקרב) גזירה שמא יבאו י' כהנים ג] בבת אחת ויקרבו א"ל ההוא מרבנן לרבא *אלא מעתה מגיסא אסירא משום שמא יבאו י' כהנים בבת אחת ויקחו ד] בעשרה כהנים בבת אחת מי אפשר אלא אמר רבא ה] משום קבוע אמר רבא השתא דאמרי רבנן לא נקריב אי ו] נקריב לא מרצי איתיביה רב הונא בר יהודה לרבא *חטאת שנתערבה בעולה ועולה שנתערבה בחטאת אפי' אחת בריבוא ימותו יכולן *במה דברים אמורים בכהן נמלך אבל בכהן שאין נמלך עשאן למעלה מחצה כשר ומחצה פסול למטה מחצה כשר ומחצה פסול אחת למטה ואחת למעלה שניהן פסולות שאני אומר חטאת קריבה למעלה ועולה קריבה למטה ז] *אלא הא כמאן דאמר *בעלי חיים נדחין ח] הא כמאן דאמר יבעלי חיים אינן נידחין הרי שחוטין דלכולי עלמא נידחין ותנן

רש"י

דכל קבוע כמחצה על מחצה דמי: נכבשינהו דניניידו · יכוף אותם שיטולו דלא ליהוי קבוע: אמר רבא גזירה שמא יבאו י' כהנים בבת אחת ויקרבו · קא סלקא דעתך השתא דחייש לשמא אחר שיקחם אחד אחד עד ששחטו י' והם רוב יבואו י' כהנים ויזרקו דמיהן ויקטירו אימוריהן כאחד ואפשר לנמנם והשתא ט] דאשתכח דקריב רובא בבת אחת ואיכא למיחש איסורא ברובא איתיה דבשלמא כי משיך חד חד ומקריב קמא קמא איכא למימר דכל חד דקריב *בהיתר מרובא פריש י] ואיסורי הנהו בהני דפיישי הוא דהוו רובא לגביה אבל השתא דקרבי כי הדדי לא הוו הני דפיישי רובא לגבייהו: אלא מעתה מגיסא אסירא · כלומר וכי מאחר שמשכו ולקחו אחד אחד לבדו ובנידנוד *דכל חד יא] דאמר דמרובא פריש ושחטו וקבל דמו במגים בחזקה שהוא כשר חוזרים ומצטרפין השחוטין להיות רוב ולהיאסר: ומשני משום יב] שמא יבאו י' כהנים בבת אחת ויקחו · מתוך התערובת וכיון דרובא יג] *נכסי כי הדדי איכא למיחש דאיסורא ברובא איתיה: ובבת אחת מי משכחת לה · בשלמא זריקה והקטרה יד] איכא למימר בבת אחת אבל לקיחה כיון דכבשינהו וניידי טו] כלום אפשר לנמנם לקיחתן דלא צריך לרדוף ולהשיג כל אחד: אלא אמר רבא גזירה משום קבוע · דלמא אתי למימסך ולמיסביניהו חד וחד כי לא ניידי דה"ל קבוע וכמחצה על מחצה דמי וליכא למיסמך ולמימר טז] מדרובא פריש: אי מקריב לא מרצי · דאידחי ליה מדרבנן יז] (נ"ל מדאורייתא בשעת קביעותא לא חזו עד דניידי וגזרו ביה רבנן משום קביעותא והוו להו דחויין מן התורה ומתני' אפילו הוכרו לבסוף אסורין הואיל ונדחו ושוב אין חוזר) *ור' אמר לי דהאי קבוע איתו דין מן התורה כמחצה על מחצה אלא א"כ ניכר האיסור כל יח] שהן* (*דמגו דלאחד דמינכר ילפי' לה) ושוב איט חוזר ונראה ואע"פ שהכשרין שבהן ראויין להקרבה הואיל ונדחה מלהקריב לכתחלה מחמת הפסולין המעורבין בהן נדחו לגמרי יט] דהוה להו כפסולין: חטאת שנתערבה בעולה · בעופות כ] קתני דלית להו תקנתא ברעייה שאין פדיון לעוף כדאמרינן במנחות בפרק המנחות והנסכים (דף ק:): מחצה כשר ומחצה פסול · כא] ומביא חטאת ויקריבנה למטה ותיובתא לרבא מהא דקתני מחצה כשר דהא הכא אילו אתי לאימלוכי אמרי' ליה לא תקריב כדקתני ימותו שאין *מכניס לפסול זה בידים מפני תקנת חבירו וכי לא נמלך והקריב קתני דהעשוי כהלכתא כשר וה"נ הכשירין ירצו: הא כמ"ד · פלוגתא כב] רבי יהודה ורבנן היא בסדר יומא (דף סד:): והרי שחוטין לכ"ע · כל הנך דפליגי בבעלי חיים מודו בשחוטין דנידחין: ותנן · במתני' אם קרב הראש כו' אברי בעל מום ואברי עולות תמימות הרבה שנתערבו ר"א אומר אם קודם שנמלך כג] בה הקריב אחד מן הראשים יקרבו כל הראשים ואפי' לכתחלה דתלינן איסורא באותו שקרב ראשון והא הכא דאילו אתי ברישא לאימלוכי א"ל כד] לא תקריב דכתיב ואשה לא תתנו מהם (ויקרא כב) וכי לא אימליך מכשרינן הנך דפרישי ולא אמרי' ידחו: הוא דאמר

תוספות

וגבי דם כסוי (חולין דף פז:) שנתערב בדם בהמה דא"ר יהודה אין דם מבטל דם כולהו א"א לזה להיות כזה אפילו לרבי חנינא דלא דמי לדם קדשים דאפשר להיות כחולין כמו שפי' בקונטרס בהקומץ רבה (מנחות כג:) דכשילין לילה אחת יצא מקדושתו כחולין וטליה סתמא דהש"ס לרב חסדא דלא כרבי חייא דאמר בפ' גיד הנשה (חולין ק:) חתיכה עצמה נעשית נבילה ואוסרת כל החתיכות לרבי יהודה וגבי זרוע בשלה (שם דף לח:) דקאמר לא נצרכא [אלא] לר' יהודה דאמר מין במינו לא בטיל וגבי ציר (שם צט:) דקאמר רבי יהודה שיעורו *במאתים ופריך והא א"ר יהודה מין במינו לא בטל [ומשני שאני כו'] וההיא דצילה דמין במינו לא בטל לר' יהודה ודם תבוסה דאמרינן בנדה (דף עא:) דאין דם מבטל דם לרבי יהודה ואפילו לרבי חנינא ל"ע דנראה שיש מהנך שהבאתי דלא כרבי חייא ועוד יש ליישב תירוץ ר"ת שמחלק בין לח ליבש ולא קשיא ההיא דפסחים (דף כט.) לר' יוחנן דלאו אליבא דכולי עלמא קאמר טבל ויין נסך במשהו דמודה ר' יוחנן *דלרבנן דר' יהודה בנותן טעם אלא רבי יוחנן סבר כה] כדרבנן בשאר איסורים וכר' יהודה בטבל ויין נסך וכן ברייתא דתניא כוותיה דרבי יוחנן והשתא ההיא דפסחים (ג"ז שם) כרבנן דמין במינו בטל כו] *מק"ו ואיכא השתא ג' מחלוקת של תנאים בדבר דהא תניא כוותיה דרבי יוחנן והא דתניא בפרק הנודר מן הירק (נדרים נח.) כלל אמר ר"ש כז] [כל] דבר שיש לו מתירין כו' אמרו לו הרי שביעית שאין לה מתירין ותנן השביעית אוסרת כל שהוא במינו אמר להם לא אמרו שביעית במינו אלא לביעור אבל לאכילה לא ולא מצי למיפרך מטבל ויין נסך דהתם סבירא להו כרבנן דכל איסורין בטילין אפי' במינן כח] וה"ר יצחק הלבן תירץ [הא דידיה] הא דרביה דההיא דלקמן דאין דם מבטל דם רבי יהודה משום רבן גמליאל קאמר לה והכי נמי משני אביי לקמן (דף עט.) (*אם כן) קשה דרבא פליג עליה ויש עוד לפרש ההיא דשני כוסות דהא דאין החולין מסייעין למים לבטל את התרומה לאו משום דמינו במשהו אלא משום דהאי באחד ומאה והאי בששים ולהתבטל בששים קאמר דלא מסייע ליה דכיון דדינו במאה וכגון דליכא מאה בין המים ויין של חולין אבל המים רבין על התרומה ששים דאי לאו אמרינן סלק את מינו כמי שאינו היה נאסר היין של חולין משום דליכא מאה והיה הכל נאסר שאין המים רבים על החולין ועל התרומה בששים: **ונכבשינהו** דנניידן ונימא דכל דפריש מרובא פריש · וכגון שלא בפנינו פירשו ממקום קבוע דאי היתה הפרישה בפנינו היו אסורין כאילו לקחן במקום קביעות וכן מוכח בפרק קמא דפסחים (דף ט:) דתשע צבורין של *חמץ ואחת של *מצה ואתא עכבר ושקל דאמרי' כל קבוע כמחצה על מחצה דמי ובפרק גיד הנשה (חולין צה.) אמרי' גבי תשע חנויות בנמלא הלך אחר הרוב אפילו נמצא ביד עובד כוכבים *והיינו טעמא דגבי צבורין איירי בדשקל עכבר קמן שנולד לנו הספק במקום קביעות ולכך קאמר ונכבשינהו דניידן דכיון שילאו ממקום קיבוען אמרינן מרובא פריש והכי נמי אמרינן בפרק בתרא דיומא (דף פד:) גבי תשעה עכו"ם וישראל אחד ביניהן דבאותה חצר מפקחין ובחצר אחרת אין מפקחין: **אלא** אמר רבא משום קבוע · מדגזור משום קבוע היה נראה דאי שקיל חד מן הקבוע אסור מדאורייתא ולא אמרי' מרובא פריש דכיון דדבר חשוב הוא ולא בטל היכא דה"ל קבוע כמחצה על מחצה דמי אבל א"א לומר כן מדאמר רב בסמוך טבעת של עבודת כוכבים שנתערבה במאה טבעות ונפלה אחת מהן ליס הותרו כולן ומשמע נמי לדידיה דבמתני' [דנתערבו] אחד בריבוא ומית חד מינייהו אמרי' דאיסורא מית והשאר מותרין ואמאי *)אדרבה דהיתר נפל ומית אלא הייט טעמא דהקילו משום דמדאורייתא בטלי ברובא דכל מילי מדאורייתא ברובא בטלי כיון דלא ידיע ואפילו ששה דברים מאחר שנתערב ולא ידיע וכן תרומה בטלה באחד ומאה ולא שייך כל קבוע אלא בדבר הידוע כגון תשע חנויות ותשע צבורין ותשע לפרדעים ותשע עכו"ם שההיתר והאיסור כט] שלהם ידועים במקומם: **במה** דברים אמורים בכהן נמלך כו' · אין משנה זו שנויה כך במסכת קינים אלא פרק אחד הוא שמתחיל כך וקאי אכל מאי דתני לעיל ל]:

*) נ"ל נימא דהיתר נפיל דהיתר מית

עין משפט נר מצוה

טז א מיי' פ"ח מהל' מ"א הל' יא טוש"ע י"ד סימן קי סעיף ג:
יז ב מיי' פ"ח מהלכות פסה"מ הלכה א:
יח ג מיי' פ"ט מהלכות פסה"מ הלכה יז:

נ"ב · נ"ל במאתים ז"ק · קינין פ"א מ"ב · שם פ"ב מ"א · נ"ל דלרבנן בנותן טעם ז"ק · נ"א א"ל וכן גירסת ז"ק [יומא סד: וש"נ] · נ"ל בכל מקום ז"ק · נ"א אבל · [נ"ל מצה] · [נ"ל חמץ] · גי' ז"ק אלא ע"כ היינו טעמא

מסורת הש"ס

נ"ב · בהיתר קרב דמרובה ז"ק נ"א אמר · נ"א דכל חד אמריק דמרובה כו' ז"ק · נ"ל נכסי ז"ק · ס"א נ"ב · *ר"ל פרש לזורק אבן לגו · *נ"ל דמגו דלאחד דילפינן לה לאחד נכרי דמינכר כ"ש וטוב ז"ק · נ"א מקריבין

שיטה מקובצת

א] ניכבשינהו דניניידו תימא כו' וקשה דהא בפ"ק דפסחים גבי ט' צבורין של מצה לא אמרינן כל דפריש כו' כיון דבפנינו פירשו וא"כ מאי פריך הכא הלא כיון דפירש מהקביעות בפנינו לא אמרינן כל דפריש מרובא קא פריש וי"ל דה"ק דניניידינהו שלא בפנינו שנסוג פנינו אחור כדי שלא נראה מהיכן פירש וכן מציע דנכבשינהו ר"ל שנעלים אותם מעינינו כדמתרגמינן ואם העלם יעלימו מיכבש יכבשון· ועוד נראה להשר מקוצי דהא דאמרינן דלא חשיב פירש מרובא היכא דפריש בפנינו מן הקביעות היינו דווקא היכא דהאיסור ידוע ומבורר במקום קביעתו כי ההיא דתשע צבורין דידוע הוא איזה צבור הוא חמץ ולכן היכא דשקיל עכבר בפנינו מאחד מהם ולא ראינו מאיזה צבור לקח לא חשיב פריש מרובא אבל הכא שהאיסור אינו ידוע במקום קביעתו ומשום חשיבות דבעלי חיים מחמרינן לעשותו כידוע הלכך שייך לומר כל דפריש כו' אע"ג דפריש בפנינו וראינו דניידי מקביעות כיון דאינו ידוע ומבורר איסור: ב] תיבות השתא דאמור רבנן לא נקרב נמחק: ג] בבת אחת ויקריבו' פי' ויקריבו הדם והאימורין פריש מרובא כיון דרובא איכא הכא ופריך אלא מעתה מגיסא הוא דאסרה כלומר כיון שפירשו התערובת כל אחד בלבדו ונתבטל איסורן משום דאזלינן בתר הרוב היאך יחזור ויפסל מן המינס מכאן אמר הר"ם דהתיכה שאינה ראויה להתכבד שנתבטלה בשתי חתיכות של היתר שמותר לאוכלן כולן ולבשלם כולם בקדירה אחת דכיון דנתבטל האיסור שוב אינו חוזר ואוסר אע"פ שידוע הוא שהאיסור שם כיון שהתירה התורה איסור ע"י ביטול ברוב הוי ממש כהיתר גמור· ויש שהיו אוסרים מההיא דאמר (בכורות דף כג ע"א) נבלה בשחוטה אינה מטמא במגע ומטמא במשא לפי שבודאי נושא הנבלה ואע"פ שכבר נתבטל הנבילה וא"כ איסור שנתבטל בהיתר יהיה צריך לסלק מן הכל כנגד האיסור שנפל דאם לא יסלקנו א"כ ס"ב יאכל האיסור וכן לא יכול לבשלם כולם בקדירה אחת מהאי טעמא אבל זה אינו כדפי' דכיון דנתבטל הוי כהיתר גמור והיא דנבילה טומאה שאני ·ומשני גזרה שמא יבאו ויקחו בתחלת לקיחתם מן הודר דהשתא רובא פרשי בבת אחת ולא הוי פרוש מרובא: ד] ויקחו בבת אחת תיבות בי' כהנים נמחק: ה] משום קבוע אי שרית ליה ע"י נדנוד אתי למשרי בלא ניידי ולמימר כיון דפרשי מרובא דשרו ואנן קים לן דהוי כקבוע משום חשיבות דבעלי חיים כיון דלא ניידי כדפי' לעיל · תימה הא דתני ובנמצא הלך אחר הרוב לירוש שמא יקח מן הקבוע כי הכא וי"ל דהתם שהאיסור ידוע ומבורר ועוד דהוא איסור דאורייתא לא שייך למיגזר אבל הכא שגם במקום הקביעות האיסור אינו ידוע שייך למיגזר שמא שקיל מספק האיסור במקום הקביעות והתם איסור מיהא מדרבנן לפי שאינו בטל ברוב משום חשיבות דבעלי חיים: ו] עיין בהשמטות בסוף המסכת: ז] למטה א"ל הא וכו': ח] הא כמ"ד בע"ח אינן נדחין · הקשה הר"ר שמואל מאן תני קינין רבי יהושע ואית ליה דתיין דקאמר תמורת פסח קריבה ואינה קריבה ומוקי לה סוף פסח שני (פסחים צו ע"ב) בנמצא קודם שחיטה דאתי שחיטה ודחיא ליה וה"ה לתמורתן אלמא אית ליה בע"ח נידחין ותירץ מורי דההיא חלוק דקודם שחיטה ואחר שחיטה ר"ע הוא דקאמר ליה ולא ר"י והכי תנן בפרק מי שהיה טמא אמר ר"י שמעתי שתמורת פסח קריבה כו' אמר ר"ע אני אפרש כו' והשתא אע"ג דר"ע מפרש לה בבע"ח נידחין איכא למימר דלא קיבלה ר"י מר"ע מדלא השיב לו עקיבא כל הפורש מסך כפורש מחיים כדקאמר ר' טרפון בפ"ק (דף יג ע"א) וה"נ אשכחן בפרק הערל דקאמר שמעתי כו' (כדף עט ע"ב) ואח"כ מפרש ר"א ור"ע [כ"א] כדאית ליה ומוכח התם דר"י לא קבלה ולהכי קאמר ואין לי לפרש דלא מתוקמא לדידיה אותו חילוק דפי' ר"ע בענין דבע"ח נדחין ועי"ל דאפילו קבלה מר"ע מ"מ שמעתי קאמר וליה לא סבירא ליה דה"נ איכא בפ"ק דנדה אמר ר"י שמעתי שהמעמיד בשרף העלין כו' ופי' שם ר"י דשמעתי קאמר וליה לא סבירא ליה כך נראה למורי ז"ל:ט: י] והשתא אשתכח דקריב: י] ואיסורא בהני דפיישי תיבת הנאה נמחק: יא] חד אמרן ביה מרובא: יב] משום דשמא יבאו: יג] דרובא נכסי כי: יד] והקטרה אפשר לצמצם ואיכא למימר: טו] ונידי כולם אי אפשר לצמצם לקיחתן הלא צריך לרדוף ולהשיג את כל אחד הס"ד: טז] מרובא פריש אות ד' נמחק: יז] תיבות נ"ל כו' עד תיבת ילפינן לה בס"א אינו: יח] א) שכן דמגו תיבת שהן ל"ש: יט] לגמרי והוה להו: כ] בעופות קמיירי דלית תיבת דקתני נמחק: כא] פסול ותביא חטאת ויקריבנה למטה: כב] פלוגתא · ס"א רב ורבי יוחנן: כג] שנמלך בא והקריב אחד: כד] א"ל ס"א יצאו לבית השריפה שלא תקריב ספק בעל מום וכי לא אמליך והקריב אחד ויש לתלות האיסור בו מכשרינן אברין הדומין לו ומרצין: כה] סבר כרבנן: כו] בטל בכל מקום ואיכא: כז] ר"ש כל דבר: כח] במינן · חסר כאן עיין בתוספות מנחות (דף כב ע"ב): כט] והאיסור כולם ידועים תיבת שלהם נמחק: ל] לעיל והתלמוד מביא בקצר:

א) נראה דנ"ל ניכר האיסור לכל דמקרא דילפינן קבוע מיירי באחד מינכר

תיבות

[them]'! but that is *ḳabua'* [73*b*] and every [case of] *ḳabua'* is like half and half?[6]—Rather, [the difficulty is this]: Let us force them to scatter and then say, whatever is detached, is detached from the majority?—Said Raba: We fear lest [e.g.] ten priests come at the same time and offer them.[7] One of the Rabbis observed to Raba: If so, is the tray forbidden?[8]—[Rather the reason is] because [we fear] lest [e.g.] ten priests come and *take* them simultaneously.[9] Is that possible?[10]—Rather said Raba: The reason is because of *ḳabua'*.[11]

Raba said: Since the Rabbis ruled that we must not offer them, a if one does offer, it [each animal] does not propitiate.[1] R. Huna b. Judah raised an objection to Raba: If a sin-offering was mixed up with a burnt-offering, or a burnt-offering with a sin-offering,[2] even one in ten thousand, all must die.[3] When is this? If the priest consulted [the authorities].[4] But if the priest did not consult [the authorities], and he sacrificed them [all] above,[5] half are fit and half are unfit;[6] below, half are fit and half are unfit. [If he sacrificed] one above and one below, both are unfit, for I assume [that] the sin-offering was offered above, and the burnt-offering below![7]—Said he to him:[8] This [my ruling] is in accordance with the view that live animals can be [permanently] rejected; the other is in accordance with the view that live animals cannot be [permanently] rejected.[9] But what about slaughtered animals regarding which

(6) This is a general rule in the Talmud: although the majority is always followed, that is only when the minority is not *ḳabua'*, fixed, settled in a certain place; otherwise it is equal to the majority; v. Sanh. (Sonc. ed.) 79*a* n. b 4. Here, the forbidden animal being *ḳabua'*, is therefore equal to the majority. (7) This is now assumed to mean that after they are detached and slaughtered one after the other, ten priests will sprinkle the blood of ten animals or present their *emurim* (these are the essential acts of offering) *simultaneously*. Now, where e.g. the ten constitute the majority, they may therefore be assumed to *include* the forbidden one. (8) After each animal has been slaughtered in the presumption that it is permitted, can they now become forbidden when their *emurim* are on the tray, waiting to be presented at the altar? That is absurd. (9) From the confused herd. (10) Surely not. Since they are scattered, it is impossible for the priests to take them at the identical moment. (11) If we permit this when they are scattered, the priests may come and take them one by one even when they are not scattered, which, as stated above, is forbidden.

a (1) This is a technical expression to denote that the sacrifice is invalid, and the owner still remains liable to his obligation. (2) This refers to birds. These cannot be left until they are blemished, as bird-offerings cannot be redeemed. (3) Since we do not know now how each is to be sacrificed. (4) He asked what he was to do. (5) As burnt-offerings. (6) And if there was one bird of each, he must bring another for a sin-offering; similarly when it is reversed. (7) I.e., this is possible; v. Ḳin. I, 2 and III, 1.—Thus although the priest is forbidden to offer them in the first place, yet if he does, those offered properly are fit. The same then should apply here. (8) Marginal emendation. (9) V. *supra* 59*a* nn. a 7 and a 10.

all agree that they are [permanently] rejected, [74a] yet we learnt, R. Eliezer said: If he offered the head of one of them, all the heads must be offered?[10]—He ruled in accordance with Ḥanan the Egyptian. For it was taught: Ḥanan the Egyptian said: Even if the blood is in the cup, he brings its companion and pairs it.[11]

R. Naḥman said in the name of Rabbah b. Abbuha [in Rab's name]:[12] If a ring of idolatry[13] was mixed up with a hundred rings,
a and one of them fell into the Great Sea,[1] all are permitted, because we say: The one which fell was the one which was forbidden.[2] Raba raised an objection to R. Naḥman: EVEN ONE IN TEN THOUSAND, ALL MUST BE LEFT TO DIE. Yet why so; let us say that the first which dies is the forbidden one? Said he to him: Rab ruled in accordance with R. Eliezer, for we learnt: R. Eliezer said: If he offered the head of one of them, all the heads may be offered.[3] But surely R. Eleazar[4] said: R. Eliezer permitted [them to be offered] only in twos,[5] but not singly?—I also meant in twos,[6] he replied.

Rab said:[7] If a ring of idolatry was mixed up with a hundred rings, and forty of them [were] detached to one place, and sixty to another: if one [was] detached from the forty, it does not forbid [others];[8] if one [was detached] from the sixty, it renders [others] forbidden. Why is one from forty different? [presumably] because we say, The forbidden [article] is among the majority? Then [in the case of] one from sixty too we must say, The forbidden [article] is in the majority?[9]—Rather [this is what he said]: If the forty were all separated to one place, they do not render [others] forbidden;[10] [if] sixty [were detached] to one place, they render [others] forbidden.[11] When I stated this before Samuel, he said to me: Leave idolatry alone, for a doubt therein and a double doubt are for-
b bidden for all time.[1]

An objection is raised: The doubt of idolatry is forbidden, but a double doubt is permitted. How so? If a goblet of idolatry fell into a storeroom filled with goblets, all are forbidden. If one of these was detached and mixed up with ten thousand, and from the ten thousand [one was detached into] ten thousand, they are permitted?[2]—It is a controversy of Tannaim. For it was taught, R. Judah said: Pomegranates of Badan, however small their proportion, render [others] forbidden. How so? If one of them fell into ten thousand, and [one] of the ten thousand into [another] ten thousand, all are forbidden. R. Simeon b. Judah said on R. Simeon's authority: [If it fell] into ten thousand, they are forbidden; but [if one] of the ten thousand [fell] into three, and [one] of the three [fell] among others,[3] they are permitted.[4]

In accordance with whom did Samuel rule? If in accordance with R. Judah, it is forbidden even in the case of other interdicts?[5] If in accordance with R. Simeon, then even in the case of idolatry too [a double doubt] is permitted? And should you say, R. Simeon allows a distinction between idolatry and other interdicts; then when it was taught, 'A doubt of idolatry is forbidden, but a double doubt is permitted,' who is its author? it is neither R. Judah nor R. Simeon?—In truth [the author of this is] R. Simeon, and he
c permits in the case of idolatry too,[1] while Samuel agrees with R. Judah in one matter, but disagrees in another.[2]

The master said: '[If one] of the ten thousand [fell] into three, and [one] of the three [fell] among others, they are permitted.'

(10) V. *infra* 77b. Though had the priest asked, we would have instructed him not to offer any. (11) V. *supra* 34b. (12) Sh. M. deletes 'in Rab's name'. (13) One which adorned an idol; all benefit thereof is forbidden, and it is not neutralized when it is mixed up with any number of others, all of which become forbidden (*supra* 71b).

a (1) Probably the Mediterranean. Of course, the same applies to any place where it is lost. (2) We make this lenient assumption. (3) Thus the first is assumed to have been the forbidden one. (4) The *amora*. (5) Where one is definitely not forbidden, and so we assume the same about the other. (6) The remaining rings must be sold in twos. (7) Marginal emendation: Rab Judah said in Rab's name. (8) If it became mixed up with others. 'Separated' in the whole passage means accidentally. (9) I.e., the remaining fifty nine. (10) If these forty were mixed up with others, because we assume that the forbidden one is in the sixty. If they were not mixed up with others, they would remain forbidden, for the forbidden ring cannot be nullified in the majority, and even R. Eliezer permits a lenient assumption only where an article is lost or destroyed, as where the head of one of them is offered. Nevertheless, when the forty are mixed up with others, all are permitted, because now there is a double doubt concerning each ring: Firstly, the forty may not have contained the forbidden one at all; and secondly, even if they did, each one of the present mixed group may not be of the forty. Hence they are all permitted. (11) Because we assume that the forbidden one is in the majority, and so now there is only a single doubt concerning each ring: whether it is the forbidden one or not. Therefore we must adopt a rigorous ruling.

b (1) No matter how slight the doubt, it is always forbidden. Thus even in the case of forty they render others forbidden. (2) This contradicts Samuel.—It is not clear why this second clause, 'and from the ten thousand into ten thousand' is necessary, for since a double doubt is permitted, when one of the storeroom is mixed up with the *first* ten thousand, the latter should be permitted. Sh. M. suggests that the first ten thousand are permitted, but they may not be all used *simultaneously*, for then we have only a *single* doubt, whether the one from the storeroom was the goblet of idolatry or not. (He rejects the explanation, given by Tosaf. in the next passage, that the second ten thousand is mentioned to shew that he who forbids, forbids even then, as inapplicable here since no view forbidding these is expressed in this Baraitha at all. Nevertheless, it is possible that the Baraitha is a fragment, the other half being lost even in Talmudic times, and so the Talmud cites it as a refutation of Samuel.) (3) Lit., 'into another place'. (4) Rashi: both the first three and the others, because there is a double doubt in connection with both. Tosaf.: the first three may not all be enjoyed simultaneously (v. n. 2.). The number three is discussed anon. (5) Since R. Judah's ruling does not refer particularly to idolatry.

c (1) Emended text (Sh. M.). (2) He agrees that a double doubt of idolatry is forbidden, but does not apply it to other interdicts, as does R. Judah.

ותנן *ר"א אומר אם קרב הראש של אחד מהן יקרבו כל הראשים הוא דאמר כחנן המצרי *דתניא חנן המצרי אומר אפילו דם בכוס מביא חבירו ומזווג לו אמר ר"נ אמר רבה בר אבוה א] אמר רב *טבעת של עבודת כוכבים שנתערבה במאה טבעות ונפלה אחת מהם לים הגדול הותרו כולן דאמרינן הך דנפל ב] היינו דאיסורא איתיביה רבא לרב נחמן אפילו אחת בריבוא ימותו כולן אמאי נימא ג] דמית איסורא מית א"ל רב דאמר כר' אליעזר *דתנן רבי אליעזר אומר אם קרב ד] הראש של אחד מהן יקרבו כל הראשים כולן ה] והא אמר *ר"א לא התיר רבי אליעזר אלא שנים שנים אבל אחד אחד לא א"ל אנא *תרתי ו] קאמינא *אמר רב טבעת של עבודת כוכבים שנתערבה במאה טבעות ופרשו ארבעים למקום אחד וששים למקום אחר פרשה אחת מארבעים אינה אוסרת אחת מששים אוסרת מאי שנא אחת מארבעים דלא דאמרינן איסורא ברובא איתיה אחת מששים נמי אמרינן איסורא ברובא איתיה אלא ז] אם פרשו ארבעים כולן למקום אחד אין אוסרות ששים למקום אחד אוסרות כי אמריתה קמיה דשמואל א"ל הנח לעבודת כוכבים שספיקה וספק ספיקה אסורה ח] עד סוף העולם מיתיבי ספק עבודת כוכבים אסורה וספק ספיקה מותרת כיצד כוס של עבודת כוכבים שנפל לאוצר מלא כוסות כולן אסורין פירש אחד מהן לריבוא ט] ומריבוא לריבוא מותרין תנאי היא *דתניא ר' יהודה אומר רימוני י] באדן אוסרין בכל שהוא כיצד נפל אחד מהן לתוך ריבוא ומריבוא לריבוא אסורין ר"ש בן יהודה אומר משום ר"ש לריבוא אסורין ומריבוא לשלשה ומשלשה למקום אחר מותר שמואל דאמר כמאן אי כרבי יהודה אפילו בשאר איסורים יא] אסור אי כר"ש אפילו בעבודת כוכבים נמי שרי וכי תימא שאני ליה לר"ש בין עבודת כוכבים לשאר איסורים אלא הא דתניא ספק עבודת כוכבים אסורה וספק ספיקה מותרת מני לא רבי יהודה ולא ר' שמעון לעולם רבי שמעון יב] ושמואל סבר לה כר' יהודה בחדא ופליג עליה בחדא אמר מר מריבוא לשלשה ומשלשה למקום אחר מותר

מ"ש

רש"י

דאמר. ר"א כחנן המצרי *ס"ל דאפילו בשחוטין לית ליה דחייה: אפילו דם. שעיר הנעשה בפנים בכוס שכבר נשחט אם מת המשתלח מביא חבירו מן השוק ומזווג לדם ולא אמרינן הואיל ונדחה הדם במיתת חבירו ישפך ויביא שנים ויגריל עליהן ויתכפר בהן: ואמאי ימותו כולן. מכיון שמת אחד מהן ליתלי ביה ונימא דאיסורא מית והנותרים יקרבו: כר"א דאמר *אם קירב כו'. ומתניתין היא אלמא תלינן איסורא בהאי דאזיל: והא אמר ר"א. לקמן בפירקין דלא התיר ר' אליעזר להקריב את הנותרים אלא שנים שנים דודאי חד מינייהו דהיתירא שהרי לא נתערב בהם אלא בעל מום אחד ובכל חד אמרינן מדחבריה לאו דאיסורא היא נמי לאו דאיסורא הוא וההוא דאיסורא אזל ליה בהקרבה ראשונה שקרב אחד מהן אבל אחד ואחד לא יקריבו הראשים דבכל חד מספקינן דלמא דאיסורא הוא דליכא למימר מגו: יג] *טבעת של עבודת כוכבים. שנתקשטה בה עבודת כוכבים: תרתי תרתי קאמינא. שימכור הטבעות שנים שנים: פירשה אחת מארבעים. ונתערבה באחרות יד] אינן נאסרות וכולה מפרש לה ואזיל: מאי שנא אחד מהארבעים. דלא אסרה תערובתה דאמרינן איסורא ברובא איתיה בששים: א' מששים. טו] נימא נמי הך דפריש דהיתירא הוא ואיסורא ברובא איתיה בחמשים ותשע הנותרים: אלא. ה"ק פירשו הארבעים כולם למקום אחד ונתערבו בשאר טבעות אינן אוסרים דאמרינן איסורא בששים איתיה ונהי טז] *דהנך עצמם אם לא נתערבו באחרות אסורות לעולם דאפילו ר' אליעזר לא אמר תולין את האיסור אלא בדבר שאבד כגון שנפלה אחת מהן לים הגדול דומיא דקרב הראש של אחד מהן אבל יז] לא לתלותו בששים ולהתיר את הארבעים יח] דאין ביטול ברוב לעבודת כוכבים והוו כולהו ספק יט] עבודת כוכבים אבל כי נתערבו באחרות הוו להו ספק ספיקא של עבודת כוכבים: פירשו ששים למקום אחד אסורות. דכיון דאיסורא ברובא איתיה הוו כולהו ספק עבודת כוכבים: הנח לעבודת כוכבים. מלהקל בספק ספיקא כשאר איסורין ואפילו פירשו ארבעים למקום אחד כ] אסורות: ה"ג תנאי היא דתניא ר' יהודה אומר רמוני בדן כו'. רמוני בדן אחד משש דברים שאינן בטילים הן הלכך אוסרים בכל כא] שהוא אם של ערלה או של תרומה הן כולן אסורין ואפילו אחרונים: ר"ש אומר לריבוא אסורין. ריבוא הראשון שהאיסור עצמו נפל שם אסור אבל פירש אחד מאותו ריבוא לג' רמונים כב] ומן *השלישי פירש אחד למקום אחר מותר אף הג' אמלעיים דספק ספיקא כג] בטיל: ופרכינן שמואל דאמר. הנח לעבודת כוכבים דמשמע דבשאר איסורין לית ליה ספק ספיקא: כמאן. מהני תנאי סבירא ליה: וכי תימא כד] שני ליה לר"ש. ושמואל כר"ש אמר: *הך דתני. הך מתניתא דאותיבנא מינה לשמואל לעיל מיניה: מאי

תוספות

ותנן ר"א אומר כו'. לא שייך למימר אדפריך מר' אליעזר לסייעיה מדרבנן דאמרו אפילו קרבו כולן חוץ מאחד מהן יצאו לבית השריפה וגבי כוסות ישפך לאמה דלמא דרבנן לאו משום דחייה פסלי אלא מטעם אחרינא כה]:

ונפלה אחת מהן לים הגדול הותרו כולן. משום כו] דמדאורייתא ברובא בטיל כדפירשנו [מש"ה] הקילו כאן ודוקא נפלה ממילא אבל הפילה אפילו שוגג קנסינן אטו מזיד ודוקא לים הגדול שאינה בעין אבל פירשה לא כדמוכח בההיא כז] ופרשו ארבעים למקום אחד דלא מהניא פרישתה להתיר השאר כח] וכן מוכח דקאמר רב דאמר כר"א וגבי אין המדומע מדמע אלא לפי החשבון שמעינן ליה לר"א *בפ"ק דתרומות דאמר היא סאה שנפלה היא סאה שעלתה אבל האחרים לא נתקנו:

רב דאמר כר"א. תימה הא טעמא דר"א משום דכתיב (ויקרא כב) מום בם הוא דלא ירצו הא ע"י תערובת ירצו כדמפרש ביומא פ' שני שעירים (דף סד.) אבל בעלמא לא וי"ל דהא דאיצטריך לן קרא לא לחד בתרי איצטריך דבלאו קרא ברובא בטיל אלא לחד בחד איצטריך והש"ס מייתי ליה לקרא משום דכיון דכל כך התיר הכתוב אין ראוי להחמיר מדרבנן לגבוה:

פירש אחד מהן לריבוא ומריבוא לריבוא מותרין. לא איצטריך מריבוא לריבוא אלא למימר מאן דאסר אסר בכולהו כדפרישית לעיל א"נ משום דיש חילוק בין ריבוא ראשון לריבוא שני דריבוא ראשון אי מתהני מכולהו בבת אחת אסור דקמתהני בחדא ספיקא כיון דבבת אחת מתהני כט] אבל ריבוא שני אפילו נהנה מכולם בבת א' ספק ספיקא הוא ושרי וכן מריבוא לג' ומג' לג' מותר אבל אסור ליהנות מג' הראשונים בבת אחת ומן השניים שרי מהאי טעמא *דפריש ובקונטרס לא פירש כן: יאי

יט א ב ג ד מיי' פ"ז מהל' ע"ז הלכה י טוש"ע י"ד סימן קמ:

כ ה מיי' פט"ז מהל' מאכלות אסורות הל' ד טוש"ע י"ד סימן קי סעיף א:

[יומא סג: לעיל לד: תמורה ו: מנחות נט:]

כא ו מיי' שם הלכה י ע"י בכ"מ טוש"ע שם סעיף ח:

[ת"כ בפ"ט משנה ב]

[לקמן עז: פ.]

נ"א אמר רב יהודה אמר רב

דפרשתי נ"ק

דס"ל נ"ק

לקמן עז:

נ"א אם קירב כו' אלמא תלינן איסורא בהאי דאזיל ומתני' רבנן היא

לקמן עז:

ב"ין קודם ד"ה ואמאי

נמי תרתי נ"ק

דהם עצמם נ"ק

תוספתא דתרומות פ"ה

[נ"ל השלשה]

נ"ל אלא הא דתניא נ"ק

נוסחאות רש"י כת"י

טבעת של עבודת כוכבים. של תקרובת עבודת כוכבים:

שיטה מקובצת

א] תיבות אמר רב ל"ש עיין רשב"א סי' רע"ג: ב] דנפל דאיסורא נפל איתיביה ותיבת היינו נמחק: ג] נימא הך דמית דאיסורא מית א"ל רבה [אא"ה על תיבת רב כתב הרב"א נ"ל רבה עכ"ה]: ד] ראש אחד מהן אות ה' ותיבת של נמחק: ה] כולן אינו: ו] תרתי תרתי קאמינא אמר רב יהודה אמר רב כנ"ל ואח"כ מצאתי מוגה [אא"ה על תיבת רב יהודה כתב הרב"א כנ"ל עכ"ה]: ז] אלא אימא פירשו ותיבת אם נמחק: ח] אסורה ס"א עד סוף כל הדורות: ט] ומריבוא לריבוא מותרין [ס"א כולן מותרין] תימה כיון דתני פירש אחד מהן לריבוא מיד הוי ספק ספיקא ולמה לי תו מריבוא לריבוא ואין לומר דנקיט לאשמועינן דמאן דאסר בריבוא קמא אסר נמי מריבוא לריבוא ולהודיעך כח מאן דאסר כדפ"ה שהרי בהך ברייתא לא הוזכר דברי האוסר כלל וי"ל משום דבריבוא קמא אסור להנות מכולן בבת אחת כו' וכן מריבוא לג' ומג' למקום אחר ג' הראשונות אסור להנות מכולן בבת אחת ולא כפ"ה דפי' דג' הראשונים היתר גמור מכולן ועוד אמר ר"י דדוקא פירשה לריבוא שנתבטלה שם אבל אם פירשה לעצמה לבדה אסור גזירה שמא יקח מן הקבוע. ומכאן קשה לפסק של ר"ת דהתיר היכא שהזאב לקח שה מהעדר [ויש ספק] שמא דרסה והחזירה לעדר ואינו יודע איזה היא והורה ר"ת דנכבשינהו כי היכי דניידי ומותרין כולן משום כל דפריש מרובא קא פריש ולא גזרינן שמא יקח מן הקבוע רק גבי קדשים משום חומרא דקדשים וקשה דהא הכא גבי עבודת כוכבים נמי אסור היכא דפירשה לעצמה כדפי' אלמא בשאר איסורים נמי גזרינן שמא יקח מן הקבוע ואין לומר חומרא דעבודת כוכבים שאני דהא בסמוך מייתי עלה מרימוני בדן וערלה ואין לדחות נמי דדוקא באיסורי הנאה גזרינן שמא יקח מן הקבוע כגון ערלה ועבודת כוכבים אבל טריפה לא דהא עביד בסמוך צריכותא גבי חבית של תרומה דקאמר ואי אשמועינן חבית של תרומה משום דמינכרא נפילתה ולא קאמר משום דתרומה מותרת בהנאה אלמא משמע דאין לחלק בהו וא"כ אין להתיר שה שלקח זאב מן העדר והחזירו וריב"א היה רוצה להתיר מטעם ספק ספיקא ספק אם דרוסת רגל ספק אם דרוסת השן ואפילו את"ל דרוסת הרגל ספק אם זו היא אם לאו אמנם פר"י שאין להתיר מטעם ספק ספיקא אלא היכא דהספקות שוות בתרי ביטולים כגון נתערבו באחרות ואחרות באחרות דכל הספיקות ע"י עירוב אבל הנך ספיקות דזאב ספיקן אינן שוות דספק ראשון אם זו בהמה שנטל הזאב וספק שני אם הוא דרוסת השן אם לאו: תנאי היא. וא"ת אמאי לא מייתי מהא דלעיל נתערבו באחרות ואחרות באחרות כולן ידלקו וי"ל (דל ג) [דאפילו גרסינן] לעיל ואחרות באחרות ר"ל וכולן אחרות באחרות ולפיכך ידלקו דאין כאן ספק ספיקא ואשמועינן דאפילו דנתערבו ונתבטלו אפ"ה ידלקו ולפיכך לא מייתי לה הכא מטעם דאני יכולים לדחותה כדפי': י] רימוני בדן אוסרין בכל שהן כיצד: יא] איסורים נמי אסר אי כר"ש: יב] שמעון ובעבודת כוכבים נמי שרי ושמואל: יג] מתיבת טבעת עד תיבת תרתי נמחק: יד] אינה אוסרת וכולהו מפרש לה: טו] נמי נימא הך: טז] ונהי דהם עצמם: יז] תיבת לא ל"ש ונמחק: יח] הארבעים לא דאין: יט] ספק ראשון של: כ] אחד אסורות נ"ל שצ"ל אסורות [לשון הרב"א]: כא] בכל שהן אם: כב] ומן השלשה פירש: כג] ספיקא מותר הס"ד ותיבת בטיל נמחק: כד] וכי תימא שאני ליה לר"ש ושמואל כר"ש סבירא ליה הס"ד ומה ד אלא הא דתני מתניתא כו' לעיל הס"ד ותיבת מינה נמחק: כה] אחרינא. א"נ ה"מ לכתחלה אבל דיעבד אם עלו לא ירדו כמו שאפרש לקמן הלכך אית להו דאין נדחין: כו] דמדאורייתא חד בתרי בטיל ואין כאן אלא איסור מדרבנן משום דטבעת חשיבי לא בטל. כדפרשנו וכו' ותיבות ברובא בטיל נמחק: כז] בההיא דבסמוך פירשו ארבעים: כח] השאר וטעמא משום דכיון דאפשר לחזור לתערובת גזרינן לפי שישנה בעין שמא תחזור ותתערב לכאן עם התערובות אבל לים הגדול שאינו בעולם כלל שרי השאר וכן מוכח: כט] תיבת אבל ל"ש:

כב א ב מיי' פט"ו מהלכות תרומות הלכה ג :
כג ג ד מיי' שם הל' ג:
כד ה מיי' פ"ט מהל' שחיטה הל' ט סמג עשין סג טוש"ע י"ד סימן נח סעיף ד :
כה ו מיי' שם טוש"ע שם סעיף ו :
כו ז מיי' פ"ו מהלכות פסה"מ הלכה ד :

*מ"ש שלשה דאיכא רובא שנים נמי איכא רובא מאי ג' דקתני תרתי והוא ואיבעית אימא סבר לה א] כר' אליעזר אמר ר"ל ׳חבית של תרומה שנתערבה במאה חביות ב]ונפלה אחת מהן לים ג] המלח הותרו כולן דאמרינן הך דנפל ד]דאיסורא נפל ואיצטריך דר"נ ואיצטריך דר"ל דאי מדר"נ הוה אמינא ה"מ עבודת כוכבים ה] דאין לה מתירין אבל תרומה דיש לה מתירין לא ואי מדר"ל ה"א חבית דמינכרא נפילתה אבל טבעת דלא מינכרא נפילתה ו] לא צריכי אמר רבה לא התיר ר"ל אלא חבית דמינכרא נפילתה ז] אבל ׳תאינה לא ורב יוסף אמר אפילו תאינה כנפילתה כך עלייתה א"ר אלעזר חבית של תרומה ח] שנפלה בק' חביות פותח ט] אחד מהן ונוטל הימנה כדי דימועה ושותה יתיב רב דימי וקאמר לה להא שמעתא א"ל ר"נ גמע וישתי קא חזינא הבא אלא אימא ׳נפתחה אחת מהן נוטל הימנה כדי דימוע ושותה א"ר אושעיא ׳חבית של תרומה שנתערבה במאה וחמשים חביות ונפתחו מאה מהן נוטל י] הימנה כדי דימועה ושותה ושאר יא] אסורין עד שיפתחו לא אמרינן איסורא ברובא איתיה: הרובע והנרבע כו' : בשלמא כולהו לא ידיע אלא האי טריפה היכי דמי אי ידיע ליה ליתי ולישקליה אי לא ידע ליה מנא ידע דאיערב אמרי דבי רבי ינאי הכא במאי עסקינן כגון דאיערב נקובת הקוץ *בדרוסת הזאב ריש לקיש אמר [כגון] דאיערב בנפולה יב] נפולה נמי ליבדקה קסבר *עמדה צריכה מעת לעת הלכה צריכה בדיקה רבי ירמיה אמר כגון דאיעריב בולד טריפה ור' אליעזר היא דאמר *)ולד טריפה לא יקרב לגבי מזבח כולהו כרבי ינאי לא אמרי בין נקובת הקוץ לדרוסת הזאב מידע ידיע האי משיך והאי עגיל כריש לקיש לא אמרי *קסברי ׳עמדה אינה צריכה מעת לעת ׳הלכה אינה צריכה בדיקה כר' ירמיה לא אמרי כרבי אליעזר לא מוקמי : קדשים בקדשים מין במינו כו' : והא בעי סמיכה אמר רב יוסף ׳בקרבן נשים אבל בקרבן אנשים לא איתיביה

*)[בכורות ז. חולין נח. תמורה ל:]

מאי שנא שלשה. והוא רביעי דבטיל בהו : דאיכא רובא. לבטולי : ואי בעית אימא סבר לה כרבי אליעזר. שמואל דאמר ספק ספיקא דעבודת כוכבים אסור יג] דאמר כר"א דתנן במסכת עבודה זרה (דף מט:) נטל הימנה עצים אסורין בהנאה הסיק בהן את התנור חדש יותץ ישן יוצן אפה בו את הפת אסורה בהנאה נתערבה באחרות ואחרות באחרות אסורות בהנאה רבי אליעזר אומר יוליך הנאה לים המלח אלמא אית ליה לר' אליעזר ספק ספיקא בעבודת כוכבים מדקתני ואחרות באחרות. ל"א סבר כר"א אר"ש קאי דאמר מריבוא לג' ותריצנא מאי שלשה דקתני תרי והוא ואי בעית אימא ג' דוקא *ודקאמרינן תיסגי בתרי סבר לה כר' אלעזר דאמר לא התיר ר"א אלא שנים שנים הלכך בעינא דלהוו ד' דלישקלינהו שנים שנים וראשון ישר בעיני : שנתערבה בק' חביות. סתומות ואמרינן לעיל (דף עב:) שהן אחד מו' דברים שאינן בטלין : ואצטריך דר"נ. דאמר לעיל גבי טבעות יד] הכי נמי : תרומה יש לה מתירין. ימכרם כולם לכהנים : חבית. גדולה מקומה ניכר כשהיא נטולה מחברותיה הילכך מינכרא נפילתה ומוכחא מילתא דבה תליא ולא אתי למימר כולהו שרו בלא נפילת טו] האחד לים : אבל טבעת אין מקומה ניכר. ולא מינכרא נפילתה ואתי למישריגהו מעיקרא בלא נפילה: תאינה. קטנה היא ואין מקום חסרונה ניכר : כנפילתה כך עלייתה. כשם שתחילת נפילתה בתוך ההיתר נחשבת בעיניך לאסור את אלו כך כשעלתה מתוכן יחשב בעיניך מקום עלייתה להתיר : בק' חביות סתומות. דלא טז] בטילות : פותח אחד מהן. וכיון דנפתחה יש לה ביטול הלכך נוטל הימנה כדי דימוע אחת ממאה יז] ואחת שבה דהא אחת נתערבה בק' : גמע ושתי קא חזינן הכא. דא"כ דפותח לכתחילה הא דקי"ל חביות סתומות דלא בטלי היכי משכחת לה : נפתחה. בלא מתכוין* יח] : כדי דמועה. אחד מק'* (ג) שבהן והשאר אסורות עד שיפתחו ולא אמרינן יטול אחת מן הק' דאיסורא ברובא איתיה ויהא הכל מותר ויפתח החמשים לכתחילה : לא ידיע. אין פסולן ניכר שיוכל לברר ולהוציא הפסול מביניהם : אלא טריפה אי ידיע ליה. כגון נחתכו רגליה מן הארכובה ולמעלה או ניקב קרום של מוח יט] שטריפתה ניכר : מנא ידע. מעיקרא שזו המעורבת טריפה היתה: נקובת הקוץ. כ] *ואינה נקובה לחלל וכשירה ומום נמי לא הוי דהדר בריא : דרוסת הזאב. טריפה מפני שהארס שורפה ולא כא] ידע בין נקובה לדרוסה : נפולה. מן הגג ואינה יכולה לעמוד ספק טריפה היא ואם שחטה קודם כב] ששהתה מעת לעת טריפה משום ריסוקי אברים ואפילו בדקה ולא מצא בה נקובת ריאה או מעיים ולא פסוקת חוט השדרה כג] *ושום סימן טריפות ואם ששהתה מעת לעת ושחטה צריכה בדיקה מכל סימני טריפות וכיון דאיתחזק בה ספק טריפות אין מכניסין אותה לעזרה לשוחטה משום הקריבהו נא לפחתך : נפולה כד] נבדקת. אם תעמוד ותלך כשירה לגמרי דאיכא למאן דאמר באלו טריפות עמדה אינה צריכה מעת לעת הלכה אינה צריכה בדיקה : קסבר. ר"ל עמדה על רגליה אפילו הכי צריכה מעת לעת ואף אם הלכה צריכה בדיקה לאחר שחיטתה שאין זו בדיקתה : ולד טריפה לא יקרב. בפרק כל האסורים במסכת תמורה (דף ל.) מפרש כה] טעם : דרוסת הזאב משוך. הנקב ואינו עגול שהציפורן קורע ויורד : עמדה. על רגליה אינה צריכה מעת לעת אבל בדיקה בעיא ואם הלכה אף בדיקה אינה צריכה : יקרב. לשם מי שהוא : והא בעיא סמיכה. בבעליו ולא ידיע מנו כו] : אבל קרבן אנשים לא. מתכשר בתערובת בתמיה :

קרבן

ואי בעית אימא סבר לה כר' אליעזר. פי' בקונטרס בלשון ראשון כז] שמואל דאמר לעיל ספק עבודת כוכבים וספק ספיקא אסורין ובשאר אסורין נ"ל דאמר כר"א דאית ליה ספק ספיקא בעבודת כוכבים אסורין דתנן נטל הימנה עצים אסורין בהנאה הסיק בהן את התנור חדש יותץ ישן יוצן אפה בו את הפת אסורה בהנאה נתערבה באחרות ואחרות באחרות דה"ל ספק ספיקא כולן אסורין בהנאה ר"א אומר יוליך הנאה לים המלח אלמא אית ליה לר"א ספק ספיקא בעבודת כוכבים מדבעי פדיון וקשה לר"ת חדא מאי כח] סבר לה כר"א הא רבנן נמי כט] אסרי ודוחק לפרש ל] *דברי ר"א ומחלוקתו קאמר ועוד דר"א בשאר איסורין נמי אסר התם ועוד דהל"ל דתנן ולאתויי מתני' דהתם לא] דכיון שלא הוזכרה בכולה שמעתא ועוד דלעיל פירש דלא גרסינן התם ואחרות באחרות ועוד שכתוב בכל הספרים סבר לה כר"א אליבא דר"א ונראה כלשון אחרון שפירש בקונטרס דר"ש סבר לה כר"א דאמר תולין את האיסור להקל ולומר האיסור הלך לו דאמר אם קרב לב] *הראשון של אחת יקרבו כל הראשים וא"ר אלעזר לא התיר ר"א אלא שנים שנים *הכא נפל איסור לריבוא אסורין שזה ספק ראשון ורימוני באדן לא בטלי מריבוא לג' דה"ל ספק ספיקא לג]דאמר איסורא בריבוא איתיה ואילו ארבעה מותרין וארבעה בעינן כדי שימכרו שנים שנים דאי נפל לד] מב' והוא שלישי נמצא האחד באיסורו כשימכרו השנים וליהנות מכולן בבת אחת פשיטא דאסור כדפרישית לעיל וכן ר' אליעזר דאמר יקרבו הראשים כולן לא להקריב בבת אחת מתיר אלא שנים שנים ונראה דאין הלכה כשמואל לה] אפילו בספק ספיקא בעבודת כוכבים דקיימא לן כרב באיסורי ואפילו ספק ראשון נראה דשרי בהולכת הנאה לים המלח דקי"ל כר"א בפ' כל הצלמים (ע"ז דף מט:) ואפילו לשאר איסורין היה אומר רבינו שמואל שיש להם פדיון כדפרישית לעיל* : דאיערב בולד טריפה ורבי אליעזר היא. אפילו למ"ד היא וולדה נרבעו לא אמרינן היא וולדה נטרפו דעובר יש לו חיות בפני עצמו ואינו נטרף עם האם : האי משוך והאי עגול. וא"ת הא דאמר בפ' אלו טריפות (חולין דף נג:) ספק שוגרא ספק קניא אימר קניא הא אפשר לברר האי משוך והאי עגול וי"ל דה"מ מן הזאב ולמעלה אבל בשוגרא לא ידיע וא"ת א"כ ליסני דאיערב נקובת הקוץ בדרוסת חתול ובגדיים ובטלאים וי"ל דניחא להו לשנויי בכל בהמות והא דלא מסני דאיערב דרוסת הכלב בדרוסת הזאב דלמא אפשר לברר :

והא בעי סמיכה. לא מצי לשנויי בעוף כדמשני בפרק כל הגט (גיטין דף כח:) גבי שולח חטאתו ממדינת הים דפריך והא בעי סמיכה ומשני בחטאת העוף דהכא בזבחים מיירי ועוד דעופות לאו בני רעייה ופדייה נינהו וליכא נמי למימר מין במינו כגון בכור בבכור ומעשר במעשר דמשמע דמיירי בכל קדשים וא"ת ולוקמה ביורש וכרבי יהודה (ערכין דף ב.) דאמר יורש אינו סומך ויש לומר דקתני דומיא דחטאת ואם דאין באין לאחר מיתה וא"ת ולוקמה *)בערל וטמא דמשלחין קרבנותיהן כדאמרינן בפרק תמיד נשחט (פסחים דף סב.) וכ"ת בעוף איירי הא קאמרינן התם דכל הזבחים ערל וטמא משלחין כו' ועוף לאו זבח הוא וכ"ת בבכור ומעשר הא כל הזבחים קאמר וכן קשה בפ' כל הגט (גיטין דף כח:) גבי שולח חטאתו ממדינת הים דפריך והא בעי סמיכה מאי קושיא והא ערל וטמא משלחין קרבנותיהן בלא סמיכה וי"ל ההיא דגיטין כיון שיש עדיין ספק בדבר שצריך להקריב בחזקת שהוא קיים לא היה לנו להתיר מאחר דא"א נמי לקיים מצות סמיכה ומיהו הכא לא יתכן לתרץ כן

*) דהוי כערל וטמא נ"ק

ויש

ע' רש"ק שכתב דהקושיא זו נעלם מן הכ"מ דין י' שכתב וצ"ל כו' ע"ש
נ"ל ודקאמרת
כר"א נ"ק
שראש של אחת מהן נ"ק
והכא נפל איסור לריבוא שזה ספק ראשון ורימוני באדן לא בטלו ומריבוא לג' כו' כצ"ל נ"ק
ע' רש"ק ושנים מאירות
[וע' תוספות חולין נח: סד"ה עמדה דגרסי הכא עמדה אינה צריכה מעת לעת כו']
ואשמועינן אע"ג דבטילה ופשיטא ליה דלא נתערב יין ביין אלא חבית בחביות צריך ליטול מהן כדי דימוע אחד רש"ק
בבשר ואינה נ"ק
וסימן שום טריפות נ"ק

נוסחאות רש"י כת"י
ואב"א כו' אסור ובשאר איסורין כו' מדקתני ס"א מדבעי פדיון לא וכו' : ל"א כו' וראשון ישר בעיני ולשון אחרון שיבוש הוא דהוי מצי ליטלן שלשתן יחד ולמוכרן :

שיטה מקובצת
א] לה ס"א ר"ש כר"א: ב] ונפלה אחת מהן כו' דמדאורייתא נתבטלה במאה אלא רבנן גזרו עליה דכיון דחבית סתומה היא חשיב ולא בטיל והלכך כי נפלה אחת מהן לים הגדול שרינן השאר כדפ' לעיל בטבעת ודוקא סתומות אבל פתוחות נתבטלו במאה דאינם חשובות דבהא לא גזרו רבנן כי אם במידי דחשיב כמו טבעת : ג] לים הגדול תיבת המלח נמחק : ד] דנפל ס"א דתרומה נפל : ה] כוכבים דלית ליה מתירין אבל תרומה דאית לה מתירין אימא לא : ו] נפילתה אימא לא צריכא: ז] אבל תאנה לא ומיירי שנתערבה בפחות ממאה דאי במאה נתבטלה במאה ולא דמי לחבית של תרומה סתומה דחשיבי ולא בטלה אבל תאנה לאו דבר חשיב הוא וה"ה לעיל גבי חבית שנתערב' במאה חביות דה"ה בפחות נמי אמרינן דאם נפלה אחת מהן לים הגדול דמשתרי כמו דאמרינן בתאנה הכא אלא נקט לעיל מאה חביו' להשמיענו חשיבו' דסתומה דאפ"ה לא בטל מדרבנן והכי אשמועינן בתאנה היתר: ח] תרומה שנתערבה תיבת שנפלה נמחק: ט] פותח אחת מהן : י] נוטל מהן כדי תיבת הימנה נמחק: יא] ושאר אסורות עד שיפתחו דעבדינן כאילו החבית של תרומה מעורבת בכל החביות ולא אמרינן איסורא ברובא איתא לאפוקי מרב יהודה אמר רב : יב] נפולה נמי ליבדקה פ"ה אם יכולין כולן להלוך אין כאן טריפה דאיכא מ"ד בפ' אלו טריפות עמדה אינה צריכה מעת לעת הלכה אינה צריכה בדיקה אבל מעמדה לא פריך דאפילו מאן דמכשיר ספי התם ואמר עמדה אינה צריכה מעת לעת מודה דבדיקה מיהא בעי לאחר שחיטה ומספק לא מעיילינן חולין בעזרה כדפ"ה בסמוך ומשני קסבר עמדה צריכה מעת לעת (וכי) [וכו'] והאי שנוייא הוי מהלכה צריך בדיקה ומעמדה ליכא למיפרך כלל כרפ"י דלכ"ע בעי בדיקה אלא אגב דנקט הלכה צריך בדיקה נקיט ליה : יג] אסור ובשאר איסורים לית ליה דאמר : יד] טבעות כה"ג : טו] נפילת האחת לים : טז] דלא בטלי הס"ד : יז] תיבת ואחת נמחק : יח] כתכוין ואשמועינן אע"ג דבטלה ופשיטא ליה דלא נתערב יין ביין אלא בחביות צריך ליטול הימנה כדי דימוע וזה משום גזל השבט הס"ד ומה"ד נוטל כדי : יט] מוח שטריפותה ניכר : כ] הקוץ בבשר ולא לחלל תיבות ואינה נקובה נמחק : כא] ולא ידיע בין : כב] קודם שתשהה מעת לעת : כג] השדרה וסימן שום טריפות : כד] נפולה נמי ליבדקה אם : כה] מפרש טעמא הס"ד : כו] מנו הס"ד ומה"ד בקרבן נשים דלא בעי סמיכה דאמר מר בני ישראל סומכים ולא בנות ישראל סומכות הס"ד : כז] ראשון שבא לתרץ לשמואל בענין אחר שלא יצטרך לומר דסבר ליד כותיה בחדא ופליג עליה בחדא אלא שמואל דשני ליה בין עבודת כוכבים לשאר אסורים כר"א דאית ליה בפרק כל שעה ספק ספיקא אסורין : כח] מאי קאמר סבר : כט] אסרי לשון מהר"פ והלא כ"ש דרבנן דידיה אוסרים יותר דאין לו פדיון ועוד למה המתין עד הכא והפסיק הענין בדברים אחרים לכך נראה פי' ר"ש בע"א דבא להרץ אמאי דסליק מיניה דהקשה תלמודא אמאי נקט ג' דאיכא רובא כו' ומשני סבר לה כר"א דאמר לעיל לא התיר כו' וה"נ לא סגי בתרי והוא דאם ימכור שנים לא ישאר כי אם אחד ובחד לבדו לא שרי ר"א אבל כי איכא שלש והוא הרי ד' יכול למוכרם שנים שנים ומה שהקשה כי נמי איכא תרי והוא אמאי ליכא תקנתא בחד הנשאר הרי יכול למוכרם כל השלשה יחד שלא יהא אחד לבדו לאו פירכא היא דא"כ אם ימכרם יחד לא יוכל ליהנות בבת אחת מכולם דאז ליכא אלא חד ספיקא : ל] לפרש כדר"א ומחלוקתו : לא] דהתם כיון שלא : לב] ערב הראש של אחד מהן יקרבו : לג] כפיקא אמרינן איסורא : לד] נפל לשנים והוא : לה] כשמואל דאסר :

[74b] Why are three different? [presumably] because there is a majority? Then [if it fell] among two, there is also a majority?—What does he mean by 'three'? two together with itself. Alternatively, he agrees with R. Eliezer.[3]

Resh Lakish said: If a cask of *terumah* was mixed up with a hundred casks [of *hullin*], and one of them fell into the Salt Sea,[4] all of them become permitted, for we assume: The one which fell was the forbidden one.[5] Now, the rulings of both R. Naḥman[6] and Resh Lakish are necessary. For if [we learnt] from R. Naḥman's [ruling], I would say: It applies to idolatry only, because it has no remedy to permit it;[7] but in the case of *terumah*, which has a remedy,[8] I would say that it is not so.[9] While if [we learnt] from Resh Lakish, I would say: It applies only to a cask, whose fall is noticeable; but as for a ring, whose fall [loss] is not noticeable, I would say that it is not so.[10] Thus they are both necessary.

Rabbah said: Resh Lakish permitted only a cask, whose fall is
a noticeable, but not a fig.[1] But R. Joseph said: Even a fig: as its fall, so its removal [rise].[2]

R. Eleazar said: If a [closed] cask of *terumah* fell among a hundred casks, he opens one of them, removes therefrom the proportion of the mixture,[3] and drinks [the rest]. R. Dimi sat and reported this ruling. Said R. Naḥman to him: We see here quaffing and drinking![4] Say rather: If one of them was opened,[5] he removes thereof the proportion of the mixture, and drinks.

R. Oshaia said: If a [sealed] cask of *terumah* was mixed up with a hundred and fifty casks, and a hundred of them were opened [accidentally], he removes from them the proportion of the mixture and drinks, but the rest are forbidden until they are opened [accidentally], [for] we do not say, The forbidden article is in the majority.[6]

A ROBA' OR A NIRBA' etc. As for all the others, it is well; [for their disqualification] is not perceptible;[7] but how is this [case of] *terefah* possible? if it is perceptible, let [the priest] come and remove it?[8] whilst if he cannot distinguish it, how does he know that [a *terefah*] was mixed up?[9]—The school of R. Jannai said: The circumstances here are e.g., that [an animal] perforated by a thorn
b was mixed up with one attacked by a wolf.[1] Resh Lakish said: It was mixed up e.g. with a fallen animal. [You say,] 'A fallen animal'? that too can be examined?[2] He holds [that] if it stood up, it needs [observation for] twenty-four hours; if it walked, it needs examination.[3] R. Jeremiah said: E.g., it was mixed up with the young of a *terefah*, this being in accordance with R. Eliezer, who maintained: The young of a *terefah* cannot be offered at the altar.

All these [Rabbis] did not explain it as the school of R. Jannai, [because they hold that] you can distinguish [an animal] perforated by a thorn from one attacked by a wolf, [as the perforation of] the former is elongated, whereas [that of] the latter is round. They did not explain it as Resh Lakish, [for] they hold: If it arose, it does not need twenty-four hours; if it walked, it does not need examination. They did not explain it as R. Jeremiah, because they would not make it agree with R. Eliezer.[4]

[IF] A SACRIFICE [WAS MIXED UP] WITH A SACRIFICE, BOTH BEING OF THE SAME KIND etc. But [the sacrifice] requires laying on [of hands]?[5]—Said R. Joseph: It refers to sacrifices of women.[6]

(3) V. *supra a*, where it is stated that R. Eliezer permits the heads to be offered only in twos. Similarly here, the pomegranates can be used only in twos, and for that reason it must have fallen into at least three, so that there are four in all; otherwise, two could be used, while the third would be forbidden. (Rashi gives two explanations: this is the second, which is adopted by Tosaf. too, though Rashi favours the first.) (4) The Dead Sea. (5) *Sc.* that of *terumah*. (6) V. *supra a:* he gives a similar ruling on a ring of idolatry. (7) In itself; hence it would be too rigorous to say that they remain forbidden. (8) The lot can be sold to a priest, to whom it is permitted. (9) There is no need for this lenient assumption. (10) A cask is a large object, and its loss is noticeable. Hence when the rest are permitted, one can see that it is because one fell out. But a ring is small and its loss out of a large number is not noticeable. Therefore it might be thought that if the rest are permitted, one will not know the reason and believe that they are *all* permitted, even if none fell out.

a (1) Which is small.—Sh. M.: This is only if the fig was mixed up with less than a hundred, as otherwise it is neutralized in any case. But a closed cask is not neutralized by any number (*supra 72b.*). (2) Just as you consider it sufficiently important to render all forbidden when it falls among other figs, so must its removal be considered sufficiently noticeable to render them all permitted. (3) One cask is forbidden, while a hundred are permitted; hence the proportion of the forbidden is 1/101st part; this he must remove, and the rest is permitted, for an open cask *can* be neutralized (Sh. M. reads in Rashi: he must remove 1/100th part, not 1/101st part). (4) If he is permitted to *open* the cask, how is this law, that a sealed cask can never be neutralized, possible? (5) Accidentally. (6) As Rab *supra a*. If we did say thus, we would assume the cask of *terumah* to be in the hundred, so that the other fifty are immediately permitted. (7) Lit., 'known'. Hence they can be mixed up with others. (8) From the other animals.—It is perceptible when it is an *outward* form of *terefah*, e.g., if the skull was perforated. But then it is distinguishable from the other animals. (9) If it is an internal form of *terefah*, so that it is not distinguishable from the others, how indeed does he know that it is *terefah* until it is slaughtered and examined?

b (1) Both show marks of perforation, and so are indistinguishable; but the former is not *terefah* (unless the thorn penetrated right through the flesh into the interior of the animal, which it did not here), whereas the latter is (any animal attacked by a beast of prey is *terefah*). (2) If it can get up and *walk*, it is entirely fit, as there is an opinion that in such a case one need not wait but can slaughter it immediately, and it need not even be examined after slaughter to see if there is a lesion of the vital organs, which would render it *terefah*. Hence it is merely necessary in the present instance to see which animals can walk. (3) If the animal merely succeeded in rising, but could not walk, it must be kept to see if it can live twenty-four hours; if it is slaughtered before, it is *terefah* even if no internal lesion is discovered. But if it succeeded in walking, it can be slaughtered at any time, save that after slaughtering all the vital organs, e.g., the spinal cord, lungs, heart, etc, must be examined for injury (this is not required in the case of an ordinary animal); thus it is considered as a doubtful *terefah* and may not be offered. In this instance all the animals can walk, yet as there remains the doubt, none can be offered. (4) His ruling is generally rejected, v. Shab. (Sonc. ed.) 130b n. a 9. (5) By its owner, whereas he is unknown. (6) Which did not require it.

But not to men's sacrifices? [75a] Abaye raised an objection to him: If an individual's sacrifice was mixed up with an individual's sacrifice, or a congregational sacrifice with a congregational sacrifice, or if an individual's sacrifice and a congregational sacrifice were mixed up, [the priest] must make four applications [of the
a blood] of each [sacrifice];[1] Yet if he made an application of each, he has fulfilled his obligation;[2] and if he made four applications from all,[3] it suffices. When is this said?[4] If they were mixed up alive; but if they were mixed up after being slaughtered,[5] he makes four applications for all of them; yet if he made one application, he fulfilled his duty. Rabbi said: We examine the application: if it contains sufficient for each,[6] it is fit; if not, it is unfit. Now, he teaches about an individual who is similar to the congregation: as the congregation [consists of] men, so the individual [means] a man![7] —Said Raba: And is it reasonable that this is correct [as it stands]? [Surely not,] for he teaches: When is this said? if they were mixed up alive; but not if they were mixed up when slaughtered. But what does it matter whether they are alive or slaughtered?[8] Rather, this is what he means: when is this said? If they were mixed up, when slaughtered, as if they were alive, [viz.,] the goblets [were mixed up]; but where one mingled [the blood in one goblet], [the priest] makes four applications for all of them; yet if he made one application on behalf of all, he has fulfilled his duty.[9]

'Rabbi said: We examine the application: if it contains sufficient for each, it is fit; if not, it is unfit.' Now does Rabbi hold this view?

a (1) Cf. *supra* 52b. (2) Cf. *supra* 36a: whatever is sprinkled on the outer altar, if the priest made one application thereof, he has atoned. (3) Rashi: two for each sacrifice, i.e., four from *one* sacrifice, so that it can be regarded as two for each; similarly according to the explanations of Tosaf. and Sh. M.: this means where *four* sacrifices were mixed up, an individual's with an individual's and a congregational one with a congregational one, so that he makes *one* for each sacrifice. Sh. M. regards this as forced, and proposes an emendation: 'and if he made *two* applications etc'. (4) That in the first place four applications of each are necessary. (5) So that their blood was mixed in one goblet. (6) If he applied enough blood in this one application for two. (7) Not only a woman. (8) Even if they are slaughtered they may still require four applications from each, e.g., if the goblets were mixed up, but all the blood was not in one goblet. (9) Hence the passage refers to *slaughtered* animals, laying of hands having already taken place before they were mixed up.

איתיביה אביי א] קרבן יחיד שנתערב בקרבן יחיד וקרבן ציבור שנתערב בקרבן ציבור וקרבן יחיד וקרבן ציבור שנתערבו זה בזה נותן ד' מתנות מכל אחד ואחד ואם נתן מתנה מכל אחד יצא ואם נתן ב] ארבע מכולן יצא במה דברים אמורים שנתערבו חיין אבל נתערבו שחוטין נותן ארבע מתנות מכולן ואם נתן מתנה אחת מכולן יצא רבי אומר רואין את המתנה אם יש בה כדי לזה וכדי לזה כשרה ואם לאו פסולה קתני יחיד דומיא דציבור מה ציבור גברי אף יחיד גברי ג] אמר רבא ותסברא הא מתרצתא היא דקתני במה דברים אמורים כשנתערבו חיין אבל נתערבו שחוטין לא מה לי חיים מה לי שחוטין אלא הכי קאמר בד"א שנתערבו שחוטין כעין חיים בכוסות אבל בבולל נותן ד' מתנות לכולן ואם נתן מתנה אחת ד] לכולן יצא רבי אומר רואין את המתנה אם יש בה כדי לזה וכדי לזה כשרה ואם לאו פסולה ומי אית ליה לרבי האי סברא והא תניא *אמר רבי לדברי ר"א הזאה

רש"י

קרבן יחיד שנתערב כו' · בכולהו גרסינן קרבן : קרבן יחיד בקרבן ציבור · כגון שעיר נשיא בשעיר הרגלים או עולה בעולה : הכי גרסינן ואם נתן מתנה מכל אחד יצא · כדאמרן בפרק בית שמאי (לעיל דף לו:) כל הניתנין על המזבח החיצון שנתנן במתנה אחת כיפר : ארבע מתנות · שתים מתנות שהן ארבע קאמר : בד"א · דבעינן ארבע מתנות מכל אחד לכתחילה : אבל נתערבו שחוטין · שנבלל דמם בכוס אחד נותן ד' מתנות מכולם יחד שהרי יש כאן משניהם קסבר יש בילה : אף יחיד בגברי · ואע"ג דבעי סמיכה ומדציבור לא מצי לאותביה שאין סמיכה בציבור אלא בחטאות הפנימיו' והכא בפנימיות לא קמיירי מדקתני ה] ארבע מתנות : ותסברא הא מתרצתא היא · והאי חיין דוקא הוא ואנתערבו קודם סמיכה ו] קאי הא קתני אבל שחוטין לא בעי ד' מכל אחד לכתחילה ז] ובשחוטין נמי משכחת לה דבעיא כגון שנתערבו כוסות בכוסות ואין ידוע איזהו של זה ואיזהו של זה ולא נבללו הדמים בכוס אחד : אלא · האי חיין לאו דוקא והכי קאמר בד"א דצריך ארבע מתנות מכל אחד לכתחילה : שנתערבו שחוטין · כוסות בכוסות דהיינו כעין חיין דכל חד לחודיה קאי : אבל בבולל · שני הדמים לתוך כוס אחד נותן ארבע מתנות לכולן והשתא ליכא לאותובי סמיכה דהא לאחר שחיטה וסמיכה נתערבו אבל קודם סמיכה ח] *לא ירצו לדברי הכל : רבי אליעזר · לגבי מי חטאת קאי ומייתינן לה לקמן בפירקין (דף פ·) צלוחית של מי חטאת המוקדשין שנפל לתוכן מים אחרים כל שהוא רבי אליעזר אומר יזה שתי הזאות ולקמן מפרש מילתיה וקאמר רבי לדברי רבי אליעזר הזאה אינה צריכה שיעור אגבא דגברא דאי צריכה שיעור נהי נמי דיש בילה וסמכינן עלה דודאי יש *בכלל הזאה מן המים הכשרים ומצטרפין מה שבראשונה ומה שבשניה מי יימר ט] דמליא שיעורא : הזאה

תוספות

ויש לומר דהכא נמי כיון שיש לו תקנה ברעיה אין לעשות בלא סמיכה דכי האי גוונא מפלגינן נמי לקמן (דף עו·) גבי אשם משום דאית ליה תקנה ברעיה והשתא לא צריכא בההיא דגיטין לטעמא דפרישית דהתם נמי כיון י] דאפשר לקיים מצות סמיכה שיביאנו הוא עצמו אין לו לעשות בלא סמיכה ומיהו קשה מההיא דפסחים פרק האשה (דף פח:) חמשה שנתערבו יא] [עורות] פסחיהן [ונמצא יבלת באחד מהן] דפטורין מלעשות פסח שני אע"פ שהיו יכולין להביא יב] במותר הפסח ולא יעשו סמיכה אפילו הכי פטורין משום דפסח לא בעי סמיכה ומותר הפסח בעי סמיכה ומאי קפידא איכא אם לא יעשו סמיכה הא ערל וטמא משלחין קרבנותיהן וי"ל כיון שהוא ספק דשמא פטור הוא מלעשות פסח לא עשו לו חכמים תקנה כיון דאי אפשר לתקן אם לא יעבור מצות סמיכה מיהו תימה מ"ש מהא דתנן בכריתות בפ' דם שחיטה (דף כג·) ושניהם מביאין חטאת ההת אלמא מייתי קרבן בלא סמיכה כדי ליפטור את עצמו ובנזיר פ' שני נזירים (דף נז·) שמביאין קרבן בתנאי וי"ל דאע"פ שתיקנו חכמים שיביא קרבן מספק בלא סמיכה כדי לפטור מ"מ קרבן אחר שהוא מחוייב סמיכה ודאי כגון מותר הפסח לא התירו לו חכמים להביאו בלא סמיכה כדי לפטור את עצמו ואם תאמר והא דתנן במסכת שקלים ומייתי לה בפרק האיש מקדש (קדושין דף נה·) בהמה שנמצאת בין ירושלים למגדל עדר זכרים עולות נקבות זבחי שלמים והתם הא בעי סמיכה וכ"ת כשמצאום הבעלים ויכולין לסמוך דלא משמע הכי דתניא התם בראשונה היו ממשכנים מוצאיה להביא נסכיה כו' ויש לומר דשאני התם דאין להם תקנה אחרת לאותן קרבנות אלא שיקרבו בלא סמיכה וטוב להקריב בלא סמיכה ממה שנאמר ימותו וכן י"ל ביורש שמקריב קרבן אביו אע"פ שאינו סומך ולא אמרינן הא בעי סמיכה וא"ת הא דאמרינן לקמן (דף עו:) למחר מביא אשמו ולוגו עמו ואותו אשם טעון סמיכה וההיא סמיכה על כרחין היינו בהקפת יד ולא בסמיכה גמורה למ"ד סמיכת אשם מצורע לאו דאורייתא והיכי עביד בלא סמיכה הא בעי סמיכה ובגבולא איירי כדמוכח בתוספתא וי"ל דתקוני גברא שאני כדקאמר נמי התם עלה דההיא והא דאמר פ"ג דמועד קטן (דף טו:) דאבל אינו משלח קרבנותיו משום דכתיב שלמים כשהוא שלם ולא כשהוא חסר אבל אי לאו קרא היה משלח איכא לאוקמא בעוף או בקרבן נשים וכן הא דבעי התם מנודה מהו שישלח קרבנותיו והא דקאמר ת"ש כל אותן שנים שהיו ישראל במדבר מנודים היו ושלחו קרבנותיהם היינו תמידין שבכל יום ואם תאמר הא דתנן בפרק בתרא דמנחות (דף קז·) פירשתי יג] *בן בקר ואיני יודע מה פירשתי מביא פר ועגל וקאמר בגמרא גבי שה לנדבה דאחד מהם לפר [ואחד] לעגל והיכי עביד הכי הא בעי סמיכה וי"ל דהתם בקיץ למזבח איירי שהיא נדבת ציבור ולא בעי סמיכה ומיהו קשה מההיא דכל המנחות באות מצה (מנחות דף סב·) דאמר השולח קרבנותיו ממדינת הים כהן מניף על ידו והיכי עביד הכי והא בעי סמיכה יד] ומדקתני מניף משמע דאיירי בשלמים ובקרבן נשים ליכא לאוקמה דהא תנא ליה רישא והאשה כהן מניף על ידה ודוחק להעמידה בקרבן ערל וטמא והנך קושיות שהקשיתי אינם לפי טעם ראשון שפירשתי לפי שלא חשו על הסמיכה אלא משום שיש עדיין נדנוד אחר דשמא אינו קיים וזה לא שייך אלא בחטאת דאם מתו בעליה למיתה אזלא אבל בשאר קרבנות לא אבל לפי טעם אחרון שפירשתי דכל היכא שיכול לתקן הדבר ולקיים מצות סמיכה אין לו לעשות בלא סמיכה קשה וי"ל דאיירי ביורש כרבי יהודה דאמר יורש אינו סומך והכא דלא משני ביורש משום דדומיא דחטאת קתני כדפרישית וכן בגיטין (דף כח·) השולח חטאתו קתני ויש לתמוה ערל וטמא *מ"ש משלחין קרבנותיהם הא אפשר לערל עד שימול ולטמא עד אשר יטהר ויעשו סמיכה ונראה לומר דבאותם שאין להם תקנה איירי כגון ערל שמתו אחיו מחמת מילה דה"א למולו בשום ענין וטמא כגון זב ומצורע דאין רפואתן תלויה בעצמן אי נמי בקרבן הקבוע להם זמן כגון עולת ראיה וחגיגה טו] (כגון) שהיה עובר עליהם בבל תאחר וא"ת נהי דסמיכה לא מעכבא מ"מ ערל וטמא שאין יכולין לסמוך נימא כל שאינו ראוי לבילה בילה מעכבת בו וכן בההיא דשקלים ודכריתות ודנזיר דכל הני נמי דאין יכולין לסמוך מטעם ספק חשיב שפיר אין ראוין לבילה כדאשכחן בפ' המוכר את הספינה (ב"ב פא:) גבי ביכורים וי"ל דנפקא לן מהא דאמרינן בפ"ג דמועד קטן (דף טו·) וביום בואו אל הקדש אל החצר הפנימית לשרת בקודש יקריב חטאתו זו עשירית האיפה שהכהן מביא בשעה טז] שבא תחילה לעבוד ודריש התם רבי שמעון בבואו יקריב בזמן שראוי לביאה ראוי להקרבה בזמן שאינו ראוי לביאה אינו ראוי להקרבה כגון טמא מת ומצורע משמע דוקא עשירית האיפה אבל שאר קרבנות משלח מיהו אין כל כך ראיה מזה דדלמא הא דמשלח שאר קרבנות היינו בהני דלא בעו סמיכה דומיא דעשירית האיפה ויש לדקדק מהא דדרשינן *בת"כ מזובו ולא מנגעו שמע מינה דטמא משלח קרבנותיו דבהבאת קרבן איירי ועוד יש לדקדק מדממעטינן בפ"ק דחגיגה (דף ד:) טמא מראיה מדכתיב והבאתם שמה כל שישנו בביאה ישנו בהבאה ש"מ דשאר קרבנות משלח ולא חיישינן *לענין סמיכה בראוי לסמיכה ומיהו למ"ד בפ' כל הפסולין (לעיל דף לג·) דטמא בר סמיכה דאפשר דמעייל ידיה וסמיך לא מצי יז] למידק מהני קראי היכא דלא אפשר לסמוך שלא תהא סמיכה מעכבת מטעם דאינו ראוי לבילה ושמא י"ל דלמאן דאית ליה ביאה במקצת לא שמה ביאה קא סבר כל הסומך ראשו ורובו הוא מכניס אי נמי אית ליה דמרחק לפון ומאן דס"ל דלא בעינן ראשו ורובו קא סבר ביאה במקצת שמה ביאה מיהו אכתי קשה אי תיכף לסמיכה שחיטה לאו דאורייתא א"כ *יכולה לסמוך אבראי ויש לומר דבפרק כל הפסולין (שם לג·) מסקינן דתיכף לסמיכה שחיטה דאורייתא* :

ואם נתן ארבע מכולן יצא · *פירש בקונטרס מזה שנים ומזה שנים ותימה דבאחת מזה ואחת מזה סגי ואין לומר דאתיא כבית שמאי (לעיל דף לו:) דאמרי ובחטאת שתי מתנות דהא קתני סיפא ואם נתן מתנה אחת מכולן יצא ויש לומר דקאי על כל ארבע חטאות שנים של יחיד ושנים של ציבור ואתא השתא ארבע כוסות והכי קאמר נתן ד' מתנות יצא דהיינו מתנה אחת מכל אחת ואחת :

הג"ה

שיטה מקובצת

א] קרבן · ס"א כתוב חטאת במקום קרבן חטאת יחיד שנתערב בחטאת צבור וא"ת הא. חטאת יחיד נקבה וחטאת צבור זכר ותירץ בקונטרס דמשכחת לה שעיר נשיא בשעירי רגלים דשניהם זכרים : ב] ואם נתן ד' מתנות מכולן יצא · פ"ת שתי מתנות לכל אחת וקשה דא"כ הוא כב"ש דאמר לעיל כל הניתנים על מזבח החיצון שנתן במתנה אחת כיפר ובחטאת שתי מתנות ועוד דע"כ אתיא כב"ה מדמסיים ואם נתן מתנה אחת מכולן יצא אלמא דבמתנה אחת כשרה אף החטאת כב"ה וי"ל דקאי אארבע מתנות דברייתא יחיד ביחיד וצבור בצבור ודוחק ולכן נראה דגרסינן אם נתן מתנה אחת מכל אחד יצא אי נמי אי נתן שנים מכולן יצא : ג] גברי · וה"ה דבלאו האי דיוקא מצי לאוכחי דהא לא מתוקם אלא בשעיר נשיא כדפירש בקונטרס לעיל : ד] אחת מכולן יצא אות ל' נמחק : ה] מדקתני ואם נתן מתנה אחת יצא ובפנימיות קיי"ל מתנה אחת מהן מעכבת הס"ד ומה"ד ותסברא : ו] קאמר הא : ז] לכתחילה הלא בשחוטין נמי : ח] סמיכת ירצו לדברי ותיבות לא ירצו ל"ש ונמחק : ט] יימר דאיכא שיעורא תיבת דמליא נמחק : י] כיון דיכול לקיים תיבת דאפשר ל"ש : יא] עורות פסחיהן ונמצא יבלת באחד מהן ופטורין : יב] להביא ולהתנות במותר : יג] פירשתי מן הבקר ואיני : יד] דמדקתני מניף : טו] חגיגה או כגון : טז] בשעה שמתחנך לעבודה ותיבות שבא תחילה ל"ש ונמחק : יז] למיגמר מהני תיבת למידק ל"ש :

נוסחאות רש"י כת"י

קרבן חטאת יחיד שנתערב בחטאת יחיד · בכולהו גרסינן חטאת בתוספתא חטאת יחיד וחטאת צבור שנתערבו כגון שעיר נשיא בשעירי רגלים : ואם נתן ארבע מכולן · מזה שנים ומזה שנים יצא דכל הניתנין על מזבח החיצון כו' :

[לקמן פ.]

גי' סל"ק לא יצא כצ"ל וכס"ד ואח"כ מה"ד לדברי ר"א והשאר נמחק

צ"ל בכל

[צ"ל מן]

צ"ל מ"מ

צ"ק מ"ז

[עי' תוספות יבמות קד: ד"ה דאמר]

גי' צ"ק שישנו ראוי לסמיכה

גירסת סל"ק יכול כו'

ליתא בספרי רש"י שלפנינו [גי' בנוסחאות רש"י כת"י]

[ועי' כ"ז בגיטין פרק כל הגט דף כח. בתוספות ד"ה ואם ובמהרש"א שם]

א הזאה כל שהוא מטהרת הזאה אינה צריכה שיעור הזאה מחצה כשר ומחצה פסול לדבריו דר"א קאמר ואיבעית אימא הזאה לחוד ונתינה לחוד: נתערבו בבכור ומעשר כו': אמר רמי בר חמא בכור לב"ש *אין מאכילין לנדות תמורתו מהו ב בכור אינו נפדה תמורתו מהו *ג בכור אינו נשקל בליטרא תמורתו מהו אמר רבא תניא בכור ומעשר משהוממו עושין תמורה ד ותמורתן כיוצא בהן בעי רמי בר חמא התפיס בכור לבדק הבית מהו שישקול בליטרא רווחא דהקדש עדיף או דלמא זילותא דבכור עדיף א"ר יוסי בר זבידא ת"ש נתערבו בבכור ובמעשר ירעו עד שיסתאבו ויאכלו כבכור וכמעשר לאו למימרא דאינו נשקל בליטרא רב הונא ורבי חזקיה תלמידי דרבי ירמיה אמרי מי דמי התם שתי קדושות ושני גופין הכא שתי קדושות וגוף אחד מתקיף לה רבי יוסי בר אבין מה אילו אמר הפדו לי בכור שהתפיסו לבדק הבית כלום שומעין לו א] הפדו רחמנא אמר לא תפדה אלא א"ר אמי ב] כלום ה הקנה זה אלא מה שקנו לו: הכל יכולין להתערב כו': מ"ש חטאת ואשם דהאי זכר והאי נקבה חטאת ועולה נמי ג] *איכא שעיר נשיא *האי שיער והאי צמר פסח ואשם נמי לא מיערב האי בן שנה והאי בן שתי שנים ד] איכא אשם נזיר ואשם מצורע ואיבעית אימא *איכא בן שנה דמיחזי כבן שתי שנים ואיכא בן שתים דמיחזי כבן שנה: **מתני'** *אשם שנתערב בשלמים רבי שמעון אומר שניהם ישחטו בצפון ויאכלו כחמור שבהן אמרו לו *ו אין מביאין קדשים לבית הפסול ז נתערבו התיכות בתתיכות קדשי קדשים בקדשים קלים הנאכלין ליום אחד בנאכלין לשני ימים ולילה יאכלו כחמור שבהן: **גמ'** תני תנא קמיה דרב *שביעית אין לוקחין בדמיה תרומה מפני ה] שממעטין באכילתה אמרוה רבנן קמיה *דרבא הא דלא כר"ש דאי כר"ש האמר *מביאין קדשים לבית הפסול אמר להו אפילו תימרו ר"ש הני מילי ו] *דאיעבד ז] לכתחילה לא ולכתחילה לא איתיביה אביי

וכולן

*הזאה כל שהוא מטהרת · חדא מילתא היא שהזאה כל שהוא מטהרת ולקמן מפרש אמאי יזה שתי הזאות: והזאה מחצה כשר ומחצה פסול · כלומר ולא תימא דהזאה כל שהוא ח] [דמטהרת] (דמועטת) (ומיהו) ט] אם אין עם התערובת פסול אלא אפילו יש עם התערובת פסול כשרה ומחצה לאו דוקא אלא ליכא שיעור [וקס"ד] דהוא הדין למתן דמים: ונתינת דם דמזבח לחוד · צריך שיעור שיראה הדם לשני רוחות הקרן של מזבח: אמר רמי בר חמא פשיטא לי בכור לבית שמאי · אע"פ י] כשהומם ובזמן הזה: אין מאכילין אותו יא] לנדות · דהכי תניא בבכורות בפ' כל יב] פסולין (דף לג.): אינו נשקל בליטרא · אם הכהן מוכר בשרו: אינו נפדה · לצאת מתורת בכורה לחולין ולחול קדושה על המעות: משהוממו · אף משהוממו: התפיס כהן בכור לבדק הבית ·. משהומם: רווחא דהקדש עדיף · וישקל בליטרא כדי שילקחו מכירתו וירבו דמיו דהא קי"ל (בכורות דף לא.) בשאר פסולי המוקדשים בשביל שפדיונו להקדש הקילו עליהן להיות נשחטין באיטליז ונמכרין באיטליז ונשקלין בליטרא כדי שירבה הפודה אותן בדמיהן מתחילה חוץ מן הבכור מפני שהנאת ריבוי דמיו אינה אלא לכהן והאי דהתפיסו לבדק הבית הנאתו להקדש היא: או דלמא · יג] לא דמי התם הנאת ריבוי הדמים אותה קדושה עצמה שמביאין בדמים קרבן כיוצא בו הכא הנאת ריבוי הדמים יד] דקדושה אחרת: לאו למימרא דאין אחד מהן נשקל בליטרא · ואע"ג דאיכא פסידא דהקדש גבי פדיון שאר הזבחים המעורבים שפדיון דמיהם להקדש (פסחים דף לח.) וקאמר דלא מזלזלינן בבכור טו] *משום הני אלמא משום הך נמי לא: התם ב' קדושות וב' גופין · הזבחים שהנאתן להקדש הן קדושה לבדה וגוף לבדו והבכור שדמיו לכהן קדושה לבדה וגוף לבדו הילכך לא מזלזלינן בהך קדושה דהאי *גופיה משום רווחא דקדושה דגופא אחרינא: אבל הכא שתי קדושות הן וגוף אחד · קדושת בכור וקדושת בדק הבית ואיכא למימר הואיל ורווחא דהקדש בהאי גופא הוא ואע"ג דלקדושה אחריתי אזיל מזלזלינן בקדושת בכור דהאי גופא: מתקיף לה רבי יוסי בר אבין · מאי קמיבעיא ליה וכי משום התפסתו מזלזלינן ביה: ומאי אילו אומר הפדו בכור זה · שילא לחולין מקדושתו ליגזז וליעבד כו': שהתפיסו לבדק הבית · וירבו דמיו: כלום שומעין לו · לעבור על דברי תורה: ופרכינן הפדו רחמנא אמר לא תפדה · ועל דבריו אין לעבור אבל לשקול בליטרא אין כאן עבירה על דברי תורה: אלא א"ר אמי · הכי איכא למיפשטא לבעיין: כלום הקנה · הכהן זה לבדק הבית אלא מה שקנו לו טז] (בגופו) בבכור זה וכיון דאללו לא הותר לישקל בליטרא אין יכול להקנות לבדק הבית עודף דמי למלוס משקל הליטרא: שעיר · אין לו צמר אלא שיער אבל אשם איל הוא ויש לו צמר: [אשם נזיר וכו' · באשם מצורע כבש כתיב וסתם כבש בן שנה הוא] : **מתני'** כחמור שבהן · לזכרי כהונה ובעזרה וליום ולילה כדין אשם ובעל השלמים יצא ידי שלמים שהרי כל אחד יקרב למי שהוא: לבית הפסול · שממעט בזמן אכילת שלמים ומביא לידי נותר אלא ירעו וימכרו כדלעיל יז]: יאכלו כחמור שבהן · והא רבנן מודו דליכא הקנאה אחריתי יח]: **גמ'** שביעית אין לוקחין בדמיה תרומה · מפני שממעט בזמן אכילת התרומה ומביאה לידי איסור אכילה שצריכה שתתבער מן העולם קודם שתכלה לחיה שבשדה ותרומה זו מתבואת שאר שני שבוע היתה וזמן אכילתה לעולם דאילו שביעית לאו בת תרומות ומעשרות היא:

וכולן

הג"ה **הזאה** כל שהוא מטהרת · דלא בעיא שיעור אגבא דגברא אבל במנא בעיא שיעור כדאמר בנדה (דף ס:) וביומא (דף יד:): **בכור** אינו נפדה תמורתו מהו · והא דתנן בתמורה בפ' ואלו קדשים (דף כא:) יט] [כל הקדשים] יש להם פדיון ולתמורותיהן פדיון חוץ מן הבכור והמעשר לאו אתמורתן קאי וא"ת ולענין מאי קא מיבעיא ליה אי יש לתמורת בכור פדיון אי לגיזה ועבודה אפילו יש לה פדיון אסורה כשאר פסולי המוקדשין ואי לענין דלא בעי למיתבא לכהן הא תנן בהדיא בתמורה בפ' ואלו קדשים (גז"ש) דנאכלת במומן לבעלים ואי לענין דנאכלת בצלי ובחרדל כדדרשינן למשחה לגדולה הא כיון דלאו מתנות כהונה היא לא שייך בה למשחה ואי לענין לקנות מן המעות קרבן הא אין התמורה עצמה קריבה ואפי' כשהיא תמימה כדאמר ריש ב"ש (לעיל דף לז:) הן קריבין ואין תמורתן קריבה וי"ל דמיבעיא ליה אי חלה קדושה על המעות כשפדאה או לא:

התפיס בכור לבדק הבית מהו שישקול בליטרא · אי האי דאמרי' אינו נשקל בליטרא הוי דרבנן ניחא אבל בהדיא מוכחא בחלק (סנהדרין דף קיב:) ובפ"ק דתמורה (דף ח.) שהוא דאורייתא דדריש בהמתה מי שנאכל בתורת בהמתו יצא בכור ומעשר שאינו נאכל בתורת בהמתו דתנן (בכורות לא.) [כל] הקדשים נשחטים באיטליז ונשקלים בליטרא חוץ מן הבכור והמעשר:

הפדו לי בכור בעל מום · פירש בקונטרס שילא לחולין ליגזז וליעבד כ] וקשה דאפילו בהך פדיון לא נפיק מידי דהוה אשאר פסולי המוקדשים וי"ל דמיירי בבכור בעל מום מעיקרו אי נמי* הוה נפיק לחולין טפי משאר פסולי המוקדשין משום דבשאר פסולי המוקדשין יש בדמיהן צורך גבוה משא"כ בדמי בכור ומעשר:

דהאי צמר והאי שיער · האי דלא חשיב ליה בריש מנחות (דף ג.) מעשיו מוכיחין עליו משום דאמרי' דיכרא אוכמא הוא מ"מ כי דייקינן ביה אפשר לברר:

איכא בן שנה דמיחזי בן שתי שנים · הא דאמרי' בפ' שני דקדושין (דף נה.) גבי בהמה שנמצאת בין ירושלים למגדל עדר דפריך ודלמא חטאת היא כא] [ומשני] חטאת בת שנתה ואשכח בת שתי שנים לאו דוקא בת שתי שנים אלא בת שלש וארבע דמינכר שפיר:

שביעית אין לוקחין בדמיה תרומה מפני שממעט באכילתה · פירש בקונטרס שהתרומה זמן אכילתה לעולם ושביעית זמן אכילתה קודם שתכלה לחיה מן השדה ונמצא זה מביא תרומה לידי ביעור והא דתנן במס' שביעית (פ"ט מ"ח) כב] לאחר ביעור מחלקן שלש סעודות לעניים רבי יוסי אומר אחד עניים ואחד עשירים יאכלו מ"מ ממעט באכילתה לאחר שחילק שלש סעודות ואינו מותר כג] למיחלק וא"ת תרומה קודם לפסח יהא אסור לאכלה משום דקא ממעט באכילתה וי"ל דהכי עדיפא ליה ושרי משום דכתיב (במדבר יח) למשחה ולא דמי למבשל ירק *) בשמן תרומה (לקמן עו:) שהירק מיתקן ע"י השמן ולא השמן ע"י הירק ועוד דעיסה מתחמצת מאיליה ואפילו מערב בה שאור מ"מ בלאו הכי היתה מתחמצת קצת:

*) [נ"ל ירק של שביעית]

אין

שיטה מקובצת

א] הפדו רחמנא אמר לא תפדה · פ"ה אבל דאין נשקלים בליטרא היא דרבנן ולכך מבעיא לן מי שרינן איסור דרבנן משום רווחא דהקדש וקשה דבפ' חלק משמע דהוי מדאורייתא [דדריש] בהמתה כו' והתם ע"כ בבעלי מומין איירי דאי בתמימין משללה ולא שלל שמים נפקא והכי מדקדק תלמודא התם לכך נראה דודאי אסור לשקל בליטרא לכ"ע מדאוריית' אלא שמתחילה היה נראה לו סברא להקל כיון דאיכא רווחא דהקדש ועל זה פריך אי אמר הפדו לי בכור כו' אלמא לא שמעינן ליה להקל מכח סברא גבי פדיון וה"ה לישקול בליטרא דלא מזלזלינן ביה ומתמה תלמודא הפדו רחמנא אמר כו' כלומר האי איסורא בהדיא כתיב וא"כ לא נתירנו מחמת סברא כיון שכתוב בהדיא האיסור לא תפדה אבל איסור דלישקל בליטרא נהי דמדאורייתא הוא מ"מ מסברא הוא דמיתסר שלא לנהוג בו מנהג בזיון וכיון דאין האיסור כתוב בפסוק רק מסברא בעלמא א"כ שמא יש להתירו כמו כן מתוך סברא משום רווחא דהקדש עדיף כדאמר לעיל בבעיין דאתיא סברא ומפקא מסברא וה"ה דהוי מצי לתרוצי הכי מתזבח ולא גיזה דהוי איסור מתוך הפסוק ולא מתוך הסברא אלא דעדיפא מיניה קא משני דאפילו בר פדיון ליתיה כלל אלא תפדה ועוד דלא תפדה כתוב בהדיא טפי מתזבח ולא גיזה: ב] כלום הקנה כו' כלומר מאי טעמא בעית למימר דלישקל בליטרא משום רווחא דהקדש משום דדעת הנודר להכי ולא היא דהא ודאי דעתו לא היה להכי למאי שאינו קנוי לו א"כ לא חל קדושת הקדש על זה ומאי איכפת לך לקיומי תנאה כיון דלא חל מעולם על זה קדושת דמים: ג] נמי האי זכר והאי נקבה איכא שעיר נשיא חטאת ואשם נמי איכא שעיר נשיא האי: ד] שנים הא איכא: ה] מפני שממעט באכילתה: ו] דאיעבד ס"א דאיערוב: ז] אבל לכתחילה: ח] שהוא דמועלת תיבת דמועטת נמחק: ט] תיבת (אם)(ומיהו) ל"ש: י] אע"פ שהומם: יא] אותו אפילו שחטו במומו במדינה הס"ד ומה"ד לנדות: יב] כל פסולי המוקדשים: יג] או דילמא ס"א קדושה דבכור עדיף ולא דמי לשאר קדשים דנשקלים דהתם הנאת: יד] לקדושה אחרת אות ד' נמחק: טו] בבכור משום הכי משום הך קדושה אחריתי הס"ד מתיבת הני עד תיבת התם ל"ש ונמחק: טז] בגוף בכור זה: יז] כדלעיל: קדשי קדשים בקדשי קלים וזמן אכילתו שוה כגון תודה בחטאת ואשם דשניהם שוים ליום ולילה הס"ד: יח] אחריתי דהא התיכות הם הס"ד: יט] קדשים כל הקדשים: כ] וקשה דהא פשיטא דלא שהרי אם היה הבכור בר פדיון כשאר קדשים לא היה מועיל בו פדיון ליגזז וליעבד שהרי שאר פסולי המוקדשים נמי כה"ג אין נפדין להתירם בגיזה ועבודה וי"ל דסברא היה להקל טפי בבכור משאר קדשים לפי שדמי בכור אינו עומד כלל למזבח אבל פסולי המוקדשין דמיהם עומדין למזבח ועל כן אי הוי שייך פדיון לבכור היה יוצא לחולין לגמרי גם ליגזז וליעבד אע"ג דבשאר פסולי המוקדשין אינו כן · תוס' אחרות: כא] היא ומשני: כב] שביעית מי שיש לו פירות שביעית לאחר: כג] מוציא למי לחלק וא"ת:

כז א מיי' פ"א מהלכות פרה הלכה ח:
כח ב מיי' פ"ו מהלכות בכורות הלכה ב:
כט ג מיי' פ"ו מהלכות איסורי מזבח הל' יב:
ל ד מיי' פ"ב מהל' תמורה הלכה ב:
לא ה מיי' פ"ו מהלכות איסורי מזבח הל' יב:
לב ו מיי' פ"ו מהלכות פסה"מ הלכה טו:
לג ז מיי' שם הל' כב:

[מנחות ג.]
אשם נמי איכא שעיר נשיא האי שיער צ"ק
מנחות שם
נ"ל ס"א דנפיק צ"ק

ס"א הזאה כ"ש חדא מילתא הוא שהזאה אין צריכה שיעור
[בכורות לג.] תוספתא דבכורות פ"ג
בכורות לא:

נוסחאות רש"י כת"י
שעיר · אין לו צמר אלא שיער אבל אשם איל הוא ויש לו צמר שאין אשם בא אלא איל: כחמור שבהן כו' · ובעל השלמים יצא ידי (ס"א) [חוב'] נדרו שהרי השלמי' לשמן קרבי ולפי שאין ניכרים אוכלן כחומר אשם ומתן דמים של אשם ושלמים שוה: לבית הפסול שממעט את אכילת שלמים בין באוכליהן בין בזמן אכילתן ומביאן לידי נותר אלא ירעו ויסתאבו וימכרו כדאמרן גבי קדשים בקדשים מין בשאינו מינו:

ס"א משום הך קדושה אחריתי
[פסחים לח:]
[פסחים יג: כריתות יט: בכורות ס: נדה ע:]
נ"ל גופה
תוספתא דשביעית פ"ו ע"ש
[נ"ל דרבה]
[בכורות סא:]
[מנחות קב:]
ס"א

Surely it was taught: Rabbi said: According to R. Eliezer, [75b] sprinkling, no matter how little, cleanses; sprinkling does not require a definite standard; sprinkling [is valid even if the mixture
a is] half fit and half unfit?[1]—He states [the law] according to R. Eliezer.[2] Alternatively, sprinkling [upon a person] is one thing, while a [blood] application is another.[3]

IF THEY WERE MIXED UP WITH A FIRSTLING OR TITHE etc. Rami b. Ḥama said: According to Beth Shammai, a firstling may not be given as food to menstruant women;[4] what about its substitute?[5] A firstling cannot be redeemed;[6] what about its substitute? A firstling cannot be weighed by the pound;[7] what about its substitute?—Said Raba: It was taught: A firstling and tithe, [even] when they became blemished, effect substitution,[8] and their substitute is like themselves.[9]

Rami b. Ḥama asked: If one dedicated a [blemished] firstling for the Temple repair,[10] can it be weighed by the pound?[11] Is the profit of *hekdesh*[12] of greater consideration, or is the degradation of the firstling[13] of greater consideration?—Said R. Jose b. Zebida, Come and hear: IF THEY WERE MIXED UP WITH A FIRSTLING OR TITHE, THEY MUST GRAZE UNTIL THEY BECOME UNFIT, AND THEN THEY ARE EATEN AS FIRSTLING OR TITHE. Surely
b that means that they are not weighed by the pound?[1]—R. Huna and R. Hezekiah, disciples of R. Jeremiah, said: How compare? There you have two sanctities and two bodies,[2] but here you have two sanctities[3] and *one* body.[4] To this R. Jose b. Abin demurred:[5] What if he said, 'Redeem me a firstling'[6] which he had devoted to Temple repair: Would we heed him?[7]—[If he says,] 'Redeem'—[surely] the Divine Law said that it must not be redeemed![8]—Rather said R. Ammi: Did he transmit ought save what he possessed?[9]

ALL [SACRIFICES] CAN BE MIXED UP etc. Why are a sin-offering and a guilt-offering different; [presumably] because one is a male and the other is a female? Then the same applies to a sin-offering and a burnt-offering?—There is the ruler's he-goat.[10] In the case of a guilt-offering too, there is the ruler's he-goat?—One has hair and the other has wool.[11] A Passover-offering and a guilt-offering too cannot be mixed up, for the former is a year old, while the latter is two years old?—There are the nazirite's guilt-offering
c and the leper's guilt-offering.[1] Alternatively, sometimes a year old looks like a two-year old, and sometimes a two-year old looks like a year old.

MISHNAH. IF A GUILT-OFFERING WAS MIXED UP WITH A PEACE-OFFERING, R. SIMEON SAID: THEY MUST BE SLAUGHTERED AT THE NORTH [SIDE OF THE ALTAR][2] AND EATEN IN ACCORDANCE WITH [THE LAWS OF] THE MORE STRINGENT OF THEM.[3] SAID THEY TO HIM: ONE MUST NOT BRING SACRIFICES TO THE PLACE OF UNFITNESS.[4] IF PIECES [OF FLESH] WERE MIXED UP WITH PIECES [OF FLESH], MOST SACRED SACRIFICES WITH LESSER SACRIFICES, [PIECES] THAT ARE EATEN ONE DAY WITH [THOSE] THAT ARE EATEN TWO DAYS AND ONE NIGHT, THEY MUST BE EATEN IN ACCORDANCE WITH [THE LAWS OF] THE MORE STRINGENT OF THEM.[5]

GEMARA. A Tanna recited before Rab: You must not purchase *terumah* with the money of seventh-year produce, because you diminish the time allowed for its consumption.[6] The Rabbis stated in Rabbah's[7] presence: This does not agree with R. Simeon, for if it agreed with R. Simeon, surely he maintained: One may bring sacrifices[8] to the place of unfitness. Said he to them: You
d may say that it agrees even with R. Simeon: That[1] is only when it was done,[2] but not at the very outset.[3] 'But not at the outset'?

a (1) V. *infra* 80a. This refers to the besprinkling of a man defiled through contact with the dead. It is assumed that the same applies to the sprinkling of the blood of a sacrifice, which proves that such does not require a definite quantity at all, and so contradicts Rabbi's present statement. (2) But does not accept it himself. (3) The same law does not apply to both. (4) Bek. 33a. (5) If another animal was proposed as its substitute, whereupon both receive the sanctity of a firstling: does the same law about menstruant women apply? (6) So as to become *ḥullin*, while the redemption-money becomes sacred. (7) When the priest sells it. (8) In the sense that the substitute too is holy. (9) Subject to the same laws. (10) Lit., 'if one caused a firstling to be seized (with sanctity).' On 'Temple repair' v. *supra* 14b n. a 7. (11) Can it be sold by weight, or only by general computation? In the former case a higher price will be obtained, so that the Temple repair will benefit more. (12) V. Glos. (13) It is considered a degradation for a firstling to be treated exactly like *ḥullin* and sold by weight, for which reason it is normally forbidden. When other sacrifices become unfit and are redeemed, they are sold by weight in the public market, thereby fetching a higher price, because the money obtained, which is the redemption money, is used for *hekdesh;* this is not permitted in the case of a firstling, because the money goes to the priest. Here, however, that he dedicated it to *hekdesh*, it may be the same as other sacrifices. On the other hand, in the former instance the money is used for buying other animals for *sacrifices*, whereas here it is used for Temple repair only.

b (1) When they are redeemed. Thus even the other sacrifices, which normally would be sold by the pound, are restricted on account of the firstling. This proves that the degradation of tithe is of greater consideration. (2) The sacrifice and the firstling are two separate animals (bodies) and possess different sanctities; therefore you may not degrade the latter in order to obtain a higher price for the former. (3) Viz., that of a firstling, and that of Temple repair. (4) Since the profit arises in the *same* body, it is possibly permitted, though the profit is utilised for a different purpose. (5) What question is there at all: how can you think that we permit its degradation because it was dedicated? (6) That it might become altogether *ḥullin*, to permit its shearing or being put to the plough etc. (7) Surely not, though the Temple repair would profit thereby. (8) That is forbidden by Biblical law, which obviously cannot be transgressed. But the prohibition of selling by weight is only Rabbinical and therefore it may possibly be waived (Rashi). (9) A man can only give over what he possesses himself. Since the priest could not sell it by weight for his own use, he cannot empower the Temple repair fund to do so. (10) V. Lev. IV, 22f. (11) The guilt-offering is a male *ram*, which has wool. Hence it cannot be mixed up with a he-goat.

c (1) Which are likewise a year old. (2) The side prescribed for the slaughtering of a guilt-offering. Peace-offerings could be slaughtered on any side of the Temple court, *supra* 54b, 55a. (3) I.e., as guilt-offerings, viz., during one day and one night only, within the Temple precincts, and by male priests. For a peace-offering v. *supra* 55a. (4) For one of the sacrifices is a peace-offering, and is fit on the second day; we cannot therefore consign it to the place of unfitness, as is necessary in R. Simeon's ruling. Hence they must be left to graze until blemished. (5) Here the Rabbis agree, as there is no alternative. (6) In the seventh year, when nothing is left for the beasts in the field, this *terumah* will have to be destroyed, whereas if it had not been purchased with the money of seventh-year produce it could always be eaten. (The *terumah* itself was not of seventh-year produce, the latter being exempt from *terumah* or tithe.) (7) Marginal emendation. Cur. edd. Raba's. (8) Or, holy food in general, which includes *terumah*.

d (1) *Sc.* R. Simeon's ruling. (2) As in the Mishnah: Since the animals were mixed up, there is no alternative. (3) There is no need to purchase *terumah* at the outset, when it will have that effect.

Abaye raised an objection to him: [76a] And in all these the priests may deviate in their mode of eating, and eat them roast, stewed, or boiled; and they may season them with condiments of *ḥullin* or *terumah:* that is R. Simeon's ruling![4]—Leave the *terumah* of condiments, he replied, as it is [only] Rabbinical.[5]

He raised an objection: You may not purchase *terumah* with second-tithe money,[6] because you reduce its consumption;[7] but R. Simeon permits it? Thereupon he was silent.

When he [Abaye] came before R. Joseph, he said to him, Why did you not refute him from the following: You may not boil seventh-year vegetables in oil of *terumah,* in order not to bring sacred food[8] to the place of unfitness;[9] but R. Simeon permits it? —Said Abaye to him: Did I not refute him from this law of condiments, and he answered me, 'Leave the *terumah* of condiments, as it is [only] Rabbinical'? So here too [he would answer me]: The *terumah* of vegetables is [only] Rabbinical. If so,[10] he [the Tanna] should teach the reverse, [viz.,] vegetables of *terumah* with seventh-year oil?—And did I not raise the objection to him, and he answered me, It means where they were mixed together?[11] so here too [he could answer me] that they were mixed together.[12] If they were mixed together, what is the reason of the Rabbis?[13]—It is analogous to a guilt-offering and a peace-offering.[14] How compare? there it has
a a remedy, viz., in grazing;[1] whereas here it has no remedy in grazing.[2] This can only be compared to a piece [mixed up] with other pieces, where, since there is no remedy, they are eaten in accordance with [the laws of] the more stringent of them.[3] To this Rabina demurred: How compare? [when] a piece [is mixed up] with [other] pieces, it has no remedy at all; whereas this has a remedy in squeezing out![4] And R. Joseph?[5]—How shall we squeeze it out? If we squeeze it out well, seventh-year produce is spoiled;[6] if we squeeze it a little, then after all it remains mixed up.[7]

He raised an objection to him: R. Simeon said: On the morrow he brings his guilt-offering together with the *log* [of oil] and declares: If this is a leper's [offering], this is his guilt-offering, and this is its

(4) V. *infra* 90b. When he seasons it with *terumah*, he reduces the time for its consumption, as it is now limited to the time in which the sacrifice may be eaten; and yet R. Simeon permits it even at the outset. (5) By Biblical law no *terumah* need be separated at all on condiments. Since it is only Rabbinical, we are not so strict. (6) V. Deut. XIV, 22-26. (7) Before it could be eaten anywhere, whereas now in Jerusalem only. (8) *Sc. terumah.* (9) Cf. *supra* 75b n. c4. (10) If that is why R. Simeon is lenient. (11) The oil and the vegetables were accidentally mixed together. (12) Apparently Abaye answered that he had cited this in refutation of some other ruling (not stated here), and that this had been his reply. Consequently he did not cite it now, as he could give the same reply. (13) In forbidding it. (14) Which must be left to graze until they receive a blemish. So here too, the mixture of oil and vegetables must be left, rather than that we should reduce the time during which the *terumah* may be eaten.

a. (1) The animals will still be eaten, save that we must wait until they are blemished. (2) If they may not be boiled together, the *terumah* is simply wasted altogether. (3) Hence here too let the Rabbis permit them to be boiled together. (4) The oil can be squeezed out of the vegetables. (5) How does he answer this? (6) The action of strong squeezing damages it. (7) You cannot extract all the oil.

*וכולן רשאין א] כהנים לשנות באכילתן לאכלן צלויין שלוקין ומבושלין ולתת לתוכן תבלי חולין ותבלי תרומה דברי ר' ב] *ישמעאל אמר ליה הנח לתרומת תבלין דרבנן איתיביה **[א]אין לוקחין תרומה בכסף מעשר מפני שממעט באכילתה ור' שמעון מתיר אישתיק ליה כי אתא לקמיה דרב יוסף אמר ליה אמאי לא תותביה מהא *[ב]אין מבשלין ירק של שביעית בשמן של תרומה *שלא יביאו ג] קדשים לבית הפסול ור' שמעון מתיר א"ל אביי ולאו מי אותביתיה מהא דתבלין ואמר לי הנח לתרומת תבלין דרבנן ד] הכא נמי (תרומה) תרומת ירק דרבנן אי הכי איפכא מיבעיא ליה למיתני ירק של תרומה בשמן של שביעית ולאו מי אותביתיה ה] ממתני' דמתיר רבי שמעון ואמר לי דאיערב הכא נמי דאיערב אי דאיערב מאי טעמייהו דרבנן מידי דהוה ו] אאשם ושלמים מי דמי התם אית ליה תקנתא ברעייה הא לית ליה תקנתא ברעייה הא לא דמי אלא לחתיכה שבחתיכות דכיון דלית תקנתא דאוכל כחמור שבהן מתקיף לה רבינא מי דמי חתיכה שבחתיכות לית לה תקנתא כלל האי אית ליה תקנתא בסחיטה ורב יוסף היכי נסחוט נסחוט טובא קא מפסיד בשביעית נסחוט פורתא סוף סוף איערובי מיערב איתיביה *רבי שמעון אומר [ג]למחרת מביא אשמו ולוגו עמו ואומר אם של מצורע ז] הרי זה אשמו וזה לוגו ואם

וכולן ח] הכהנים רשאין כו'. משנה היא בפ' כל התדיר (לקמן דף צ:) וגבי קדשים קאי: לשנות באכילתן כגון לאכלן לצויין כו'. ט] *אמר קרא לך נתתים למשחה (במדבר יח) לגדולה כדרך שהמלכים אוכלין: ותבלי תרומה. ואע"ג דקא ממעט בזמן אכילת תרומה: אין לוקחין תרומה. הכהנים בכסף מעשר שני בירושלים: מפני שממעט באכילתה. במקום אכילתה דמעכשיו לא יאכלנה אלא בירושלים: כי אתא. אביי קמיה דרב יוסף: א"ל אמאי לא תותביה. נמי מהא: לבית הפסול. י] כשצריך לאכול השמן בזמן השביעית: ה"נ. דרבנן תרומת ירק: אי הכי. דמשום דרבנן הוא: איפכא מיבעיא ליה למיתני. אין מבשלין ירק של תרומה בשמן שביעית ורבי שמעון מתיר אבל השתא שמן תרומה דאורייתא היא דכתיב (שם) כל חלב יצהר וקא שרי ר"ש: דאיערב. שמן בירק ועל כרחו יבשלם יחד כדמפרש לקמיה דאי אפשר לסוחטו יא] כולו ממנו: הא לא דמי כו'. סיומא דקושיא הוא: חתיכה בחתיכות. מתני' היא וקתני תאכל כחמור שבהן ואפילו לרבנן והכא נמי אי בדאיערב עסקינן לא הוו פליגי רבנן עליה: וקמפסיד בשביעית. ורחמנא אמר לאכלה ולא להפסד: למחרת. בספק מצורע מוחלט וספק אינו מוחלט קאי למחרת ביום השמיני: *שחיטה בצפון ובהונות. כחומר אשם: וסמיכה ונסכים ותנופת חזה ושוק. כחומר שלמים והא

אין לוקחין תרומה בכסף מעשר שני מפני שממעט באכילתה. פי' בקונט' דמתחלה שריא לאונן כדאמר בפ' הערל (יבמות דף עג.) זרות אמרתי לך ולא אנינות והשתא אסירא דמעשר אסור לאונן וגם בעי חומה ותרומה לא בעי חומה יב] ומתוך המשנה משמע שאין הקפידא משום תרומה אלא משום מעשר דמעיקרא שרי לזרים והשתא אסור וגרסי' בסדר המשנה יג] *באכילתן כו' והכי איתא במס' מעשר שני (פ"ג מ"ב) אין לוקחין תרומה בכסף מעשר מפני שהוא ממעט באכילתו ור"ש מתיר אמר להם ר"ש אם הקילו בזבחי שלמים שהוא מביאן לידי פיגול ונותר לא נקל בתרומה יד] מה לי היקל בזבחי שלמים שכן מותרין לזרים נקל בתרומה שהיא אסורה לזרים פירוש אמר ר"ש אם הקלנו ליקח שלמים מכסף מעשר אע"פ שמביא המעשר לידי פסול פיגול ונותר כ"ש שלוקחין תרומה הקלה מכסף מעשר אמרו לו אם לוקחין שלמים שמותרין לזרים כמו מעשר אבל אין לוקחין תרומה שגורם למעשר להיות אסור לזרים: הגה"ה:

*למחרת מביא אשמו ולוגו עמו. פי' בקונט' למחרת יום שמיני טו] ובמנחות טז] (דף קה.) פי' למחרת יום ששים והכל אחד דאספק נזיר טמא וספק מצורע טמא קאי כדמוכח בתוספתא דנזיר פרק בתרא והכי איתא התם ספק נזיר טמא יז] וספק נזיר טהור אבל נזיר ודאי היה ספק מצורע טמא פירוש מוחלט ספק מצורע טהור פי' שטהר כבר אבל מצורע ודאי היה פירוש בחד גברא איירי שיש בו כל ספיקות הללו אוכל בקדשים לאחר ששים ושותה יין ומטמא למתים לאחר מאה ועשרים יום כילד אמרו לו נזיר טמא אתה לא ומנה שבעה הזה ושנה גלח והביא קרבן מנה *שבעה ומבקש לגלח אמרו לו נזיר טהור אתה ואין טהור מגלח פחות משלשים יום לא ומנה עשרים ושלשה יום להשלים שלשים מנה שלשים ומבקש לגלח אמרו לו נזיר טהור אתה ואין נזיר מגלח אלא על הדמים פירוש *שלש בהמות חייב להביא חטאת עולה ושלמים ועל אחת מהן יכול לגלח וחטאת בהמה אינה באה על הספק ושלמי נזיר נמי טעונין תנופה וזה אין יכול להניף מפני שהוא ספק מצורע טמא אבל עולה יכול להביא על תנאי והיינו דקתני כילד הוא עושה מביא עולת בהמה ומתנה עליה ואומר אם טהור אני הרי זו חובה ואם לאו הרי זו נדבה כילד הוא עושה להחמיר עליו מביא פיילי של חרס חדשה יח] ונותנין לתוכה רביעית מים חיים ומביא [שתי] לפורי דרור כדין כל המצורעין ביום תגלחתן וחטאת העוף פירוש כדין נזיר טמא דשמא נזיר טמא הוא ותגלחת זו של טומאה ואינו מתחיל נזירות טהרה עד שיביא חטאתו של טומאה יט] (יש) שחטאתו מעכבתו מלמנות נזירות אבל אשמו אינו מעכבו ומשיגלח תגלחת *טומאה הוא אסור לגלח עד שימנה נזירות טהרה ולהכי צריך להביא חטאת נזירות טומאה למנות נזירות טהרה ולגלח בסופה לטהרת צרעתו והאשם ישהה עד *תגלחת הטומאה שיעשה אחרי טהרתו בודאי מן הצרעת שאותה תעלה לו ודאי לטומאת נזרו כמו שמפורש בסוף הברייתא דימי צרעתו אין עולין לימי נזרו ותגלחת צרעתו אינה עולה לתגלחת נזרו כדאמרי' בפ' מי שאמר הריני נזיר מגלח (נזיר דף יז:) ובפ' ב' נזירים (שם דף ס:) ומה שמביא חטאתו ביום תגלחתו היינו כר' עקיבא דאמר במס' נזיר (דף מז.) אם גילח בשמיני מביא קרבנותיו בו ביום והכא נמי הוי כגילח בשמיני שהרי שוהה תגלחתו ומתנה על חטאתו ואומר אם טמא אני הטאת מחובתי ועולה נדבה פירוש עולה שאמרנו למעלה ואם טהור אני עולה מחובתי וחטאת העוף ספק ומגלח ראשו וזקנו וגבות עיניו כדרך שהמצורעים *מגלחים ומביא עולת בהמה ומתנה עליה כו' ונראה שחסר מן התוספתא וסופר שלשים יום וגרסי' וסופר שלשים יום ומביא עולת בהמה כו' שהרי ספק נזירות טהרה הוא מונה ואינו יכול לגלח תגלחת שניה לצרעתו עד שיזרוק עליו אחד מן הדמים כ] ויביא עולה וחטאת ושלמים *וישהה עד סוף נזירות טהרה שאחר טהרת צרעתו שעולה בודאי ואומר אם טמא אני פירוש אם טמא הייתי בתגלחת ראשונה העולה ראשונה נדבה היתה וזו תהא חובה וחטאת העוף שהבאתי בתגלחת ראשונה מחובתי ואם טהור אני עולה ראשונה חובה וזו נדבה שתגלחת זו של עכשיו אינה כלום וחטאת העוף כא] ספיקו *מגלח ראשו וזקנו וגבות עיניו כדרך מצורעין ותגלחת זו היתה ראויה ליעשות בסוף שבעת ימי ספרו מתגלחת ראשונה אבל לא היה יכול משום דגילוח ספק מצורע אינו דוחה איסור גילוח הנזיר רבי שמעון אומר כב] מחר יביא אשמו ולוג בידו כדין מצורע בשמיני שלו והוא יום ששים ואחד ומתנה עליו לפי שהוא ספק מצורע וחטאת מצורע שמעכבת טהרתו אינו יכול להביא מבהמה שאין חטאת בהמה באה על הספק לפיכך יביא חטאת העוף ואם הוא עשיר יכתוב נכסיו לאחרים ויהא עני ויביא קרבן עני דהיינו עוף ור' שמעון לטעמיה דאמר במס' ערכין (דף יז:) אפי' היה עשיר בשעה שהביא ליפורים או בשעת הבאת אשם והעני הכל הולך אחר חטאת ואפי' לתנאי דפליגי עליה איכא לאוקמא להא דהכא ולפרושי יכתוב נכסיו לאחר מעיקרו ומתנה על חטאת העוף ואומר אם טמא הוא פירוש אם מצורע הוא הרי זו חובתו ואם לאו הרי זו ספיקו ואוכל בקדשים מיד אבל לשתות יין וליטמא למתים אינו יכול שאין ימי נזרו עולין לו *מתוך ימי צרעתו כילד יעשה לדברי בן זומא כג] שאינו מצריך לבקש אחד מן השוק לידור כנגדו בנזיר כמו שמצריך ר' יהושע בפרק שני נזירים (נזיר דף נט:) סופר שלשים יום ומביא עולת בהמה ומגלח פירוש ספק תגלחת טומאה וספק תגלחת טהרה דשמא מצורע היה ונזיר טמא ולא עלו לו אחת מתגלחותיו לנזירותו רק לצרעתו שאין ימי נזרו עולין מתוך ימי צרעתו ולסוף שבעה אחר טהרת ימי צרעתו אינו יכול לגלח דשמא נזיר טהור הוא אבל השתא לא בעי שכבר הזה ושנה ואפי' לסוף שלשים אינו יכול כד] *עד שיזרוק עליו אחד מן הדמים ומביא חטאת העוף משום ספק תגלחת טומאה שאינו יכול להתחיל מנין נזירות טהרה עד שיביא חטאת וכדפרישית ומתנה עליה כתנאי שלמעלה בתגלחת ראשונה וה"ה שיש להתנות שאם אינו נזיר עכשיו כלל שכלתה נזירתו מתגלחת שלמעלה העולה נדבה וחטאת העוף ספיקו אך התנא לא חש לפרש כל זה *סופר שלשים יום ומביא קרבנותיו שלמים ודאי *עולת בהמה ספיקו ומתנה עליה ואומר אם טמא הייתי בתגלחת שלישית העולה ראשונה נדבה

שיטה מקובצת
א] רשאין הכהנים: ב] ר' שמעון תיבת ישמעאל נמחק: ג] תיבת קדשים נמחק: ד] הכי נמי דרבנן (ותיבות תרומה תרומת ירק נמחק). פ"ה דמיירי בתרומת ירק דרבנן ועל זה פריך אי הכי איפכא מבעיא ליה דנהוי מוכח בברייתא דמיירי בתרום' דרבנן וזה דוחק דאיך היה טועה בזה לומר דמיירי בתרומת ירק דרבנן דבברייתא מזכיר בהדיא שמן של תרומה לכך נראה דה"פ ה"נ דרבנן פי' דשמן של תרומה דקתני בברייתא מיירי בשמן שומשמין ואגוזים דתרומה דידהו לא הוי אלא מדרבנן דמדאורייתא לא הויא תרומה אלא שמן של יצהר ועליה פריך אי הכי דמיירי בתרומה דרבנן איפכא מבעיא ליה למימר ירק של תרומה בשמן של שביעית דלא ליתי למטעי כלל בתרומה דאורייתא אלא ש"מ דבתרומה דאורייתא מיירי ומשני דמיירי דאיערב כבר: ה] תיבות ממתני' דמתיר ר"ש ל"ש: ו] אאשם. פי' דאמרי אינהו ירעו דחיישינן להבאת לבית הפסול גליון: ז] מצורע הוא הרי: ח] וכולן רשאין הכהנים כו': ט] כו' דאמר: י] שצריך לאכול השמן בתוך זמן הביעור הס"ד: יא] לסוחטו כו' הס"ד תיבת כולו ממנו נמחק ומה"ד הא: יב] חומה ולא נהירא דאי קאי אתרומה הוי ליה למימר מעשר אין לוקחין בדמיהן תרומה כדלעיל דלעולם מה שאין ממעט באכילתו פתח ברישא ועוד מתוך המשנה כו' אסור לכך נראה דגרסי'

לד א מיי' פ"ג מהלכות מעשר שני הל' יא:
לה ב מיי' פ"ה מהלכות שמיטה ויובל הל' ד:
לו ג מיי' פ"ו מהלכות נזירות הלכה ז:
באכילתו נ"ק
עי' ברמב"ם פ"ו מהל' נזירות וכל"מ ועי' רש"ק

דאמר נ"ק
לקמן צ:
ר"ל שמעון
מעשר שני פ"ג משנה ב
שביעית פ"ח משנה ז [בכורות ס:]
נ"ק מ"ו
שייך לע"ב
נזיר ס. מנחות קה. נדה ע.
שבעה והזה ושנה ומבקש כו' נ"ק
עד שיזרוק הדם עליו דשלש כו' נ"ק
טומאה אסור כו' נ"ק
תגלחת שניה שיעשה נ"ק
גי' הנ"ק מגלחים ואחר גילוח זה כתוב בתוספ' ומביא כו' כצ"ל
משהא נ"ק
ומגלח נ"ק
לו לימי צרעתו נ"ק
לגלח עד נ"ק
וסופר נ"ק
ועולת נ"ק

ואם לאו אשם זה של שלמי נדבה ואותו אשם טעון שחיטה בצפון ומתן בהונות וסמיכה ונסכים ותנופת חזה ושוק ונאכל ליום ולילה *תקוני גברא שאני התינח אשם לוג מאי איכא למימר דאמר לוג זה יהא נדבה ודילמא לאו מצורע הוא ובעי מקמץ דמקמיץ ודילמא מצורע הוא ובעי מתן שבע דיהיב והא חסר ליה דמייתי פורתא ומלי ליה דתנן *[א]חסר הלוג עד שלא יצק ימלאנו והא בעי הקטרה דאקטר ליה אימת אי בתר מתנות שבע הוו להו שיריים שחסרו בין קמיצה להקטרה ואין מקטירין את הקומץ עליהן אי קודם א] מתנות שבע *[ב]כל שממנו לאישים הרי הוא בבל תקטירו אמר רב יהודה בריה דר"ש בן פזי דמסיק להו לשם עצים דתניא* רבי אליעזר אומר [ג]לריח (ויקרא ב) ניחוח אי אתה מעלה אבל אתה מעלה לשם

רש"י

והא הכא דלמא לאו מצורע הוא והוי שלמים וקתני ונאכל ליום ולילה אלמא לכתחלה נמי שרי ר"ש: הא תינח אשם כו'. מלתיה דר"ש קא מפרש ואזיל ולאו לרבא קא מותיב: לוג זה יהא נדבה. אם אינו מצורע דאמרי' לקמן בפ' כל התדיר (דף צא.) מתנדבין שמן בפני עצמו: ובעי מיקמץ. ב] המתנדב שמן קומצו ומקטיר הקומץ ושיריו נאכלין כדיליף ליה מקרבן מנחה (קרבן) מלמד שמתנדבין שמן ג] כמנחה כו': מתן שבע. כדכתיב קרא בלוג של מצורע והזה מן השמן באצבעו [וגו'] (ויקרא יד): והא חסר ליה. ע"י קמיצה ולוג חסר פסול כדכתיב (שם) ולוג שמן: עד שלא יצק. מן הלוג על כפו השמאלית כדכתיב ומן השמן יצק הכהן על כף הכהן השמאלית והזה הכהן באצבעו הימנית מן השמן אשר על כפו השמאלית (שם): והא בעי קומץ הקטרה. דדלמא נדבה הוא: דמקטיר ליה. ושיריים נאכלין ממ"נ אי דמצורע הוא הרי הוא נאכל כדאמרי' בפ' בית שמאי (לעיל דף מד:) לכל קרבנם לרבות לוג שמן של מצורע ואי נדבה הוא הרי הוא כשירי מנחה: אי בתר מתנות שבע. דלמא נדבה הוא וכי יהיב מתן שבע בתר קמיצה הוו להו שיריים שחסרו בין קמיצה להקטרה וקי"ל במנחות בפ"ק (דף ט:) אין מקטירין הקומץ עליהן ד] דכתיב מן המנחה פרט לשחסרה היא כו': ואי קודם מתן שבע. היכי מצי למיתב תו מיניה מתן שבע דלמא נדבה היא והקטרת הקומץ הקטרה והנך הוו להו שיריים וכי הדר מעייל *מידי מינייהו קא עבר משום בל תקטירו כדכתיב (ויקרא ב) כי כל שאור וכל דבש וגו' והאי ממנו יתירא הוא ודרשינן ביה נמי לא תקטירו כל שממנו אשה לה' יש בכלל הזה קדשים ושירי מנחה ולחם הפנים שקרב מהן כבר לאישים האימורים וכן הקומץ וכן הבזיכין קיימי שירים בבל תקטירו והנך הזאות במקום הקטרה קיימי: לשם עצים. דאמר הכי ה] אם מצורע הוא דאין הקטרת הקומץ הקטרה דהא לאו נדבה הואי הרי מזה מאלו שאינן שיריים ואם אינו מצורע והקטרת הקומץ הקטרה ויש ממנו לאישים ואלו שיריים הם ובבל תקטירו הרי הזאות האלו כאילו הם מים שהרי רשאי להעלות שירי מנחה על המזבח: לשם

תוספות

נדבה וזו חובה וחטאת העוף מחובתי ואם טהור אני העולה ראשונה חובה וזו נדבה וחטאת העוף ספיקו וה"ה נמי דמתנה אם כלתה נזירות מתגלחת שניה שתיהן העולות נדבה וחטאת העוף ספק אך לא חש לפרש כל כך ושותה יין ומיטמא למתים ותימה למה לא הזכיר בקרבנות תגלחת רביעית זו *חטאת שהרי ודאי נזיר היה ועדיין לא הביא חטאת בהמה בשום פעם ואם באנו לפרש ריבא דברייתא ספק נזיר טמא וספק אינו נזיר כלל עכשיו אבל נזיר ודאי *היה ולכך לא יביא חטאת בהמה שהרי אינה באה על ספק לא משתמעא הכי דא"כ הו"ל לפרושי בהדיא ועוד א"כ בשלמים הו"ל למיתני תנאי או למיהוי שלמי נדבה או שלמי נזיר לענין מורם מהם דבהאי חזה ושוק ובהאי זרוע בשלה. בד"א בזמן שנדר שלשים יום אבל נדר י"ב חדש אוכל בקדשים לאחר שתי שנים ושותה יין ומיטמא למתים לאחר ד' שנים *באותו ענין ובאותה ו] שאמרנו מגלח לסוף שנה ז] באותה של סוף שלשים באותה תנאי ולבסוף שתי שנים בשניה ולסוף ג' שנים בשלישית ולסוף ארבע ברביעית טמא בספק ומוחלט בודאי אוכל בקדשים לאחר שמונה ימים דתגלחת מצורע ודאי דוחה איסור גילוח דנזיר ומיד *כשיבא לפניו מגלח ראשונה ח] ובשביעית תגלחת שניה ובשמיני מכניס ידיו לבהונות ושותה ביין ומיטמא למתים לאחר שלשים ושבע כך כתוב בתוספתא ונראה דגרס ששים ושבע לפי שיטה שפירשנו. טמא בודאי ומוחלט בספק אוכל בקדשים לאחר שבעה ושלשים יום שותה ביין ומיטמא למתים לאחר שבעים וארבעה יום ט] (טמא בודאי ומוחלט בודאי אוכל בקדשים לאחר שלשים ושבעה יום שותה ביין ומיטמא למתים לאחר ארבעה ושבעים יום) טמא בודאי ומוחלט בודאי אוכל בקדשים לאחר שמונה ימים שותה ביין ומיטמא למתים לאחר ארבעים וארבעה יום:

אשם זו יהא שלמי נדבה. וא"ת והא אמרן לעיל בפ' איזהו מקומן (דף מז:) דאשם מצורע שני כהנים מקבלין את דמו אחד ביד ואחד בכלי ושלמים אמרי' לעיל (דף כה.) דצריך שיקבל בכלי את כל דמו (של פר) וי"ל י] דתקוני גברא שאני: **וסמיכה**. למ"ד (לעיל דף לג.) סמיכת אשם מצורע לאו דאורייתא הוא בהקפת יד ואע"ג דשלמים בעו סמיכה *גמר משום תקוני גברא התירו כדפרישית לעיל ולמאן דאמר דאורייתא הזכיר בחנם סמיכה וכן נסכים דבין אשם *בין שלמים טעונין סמיכה ונסכים: **ונאכל** ליום ולילה. ובתודה דאין נאכלת אלא ליום ולילה אין יכול להתנות משום דבעינן לחם ובלחם אי אפשר לעשות תקנה כדמוכח בפ' התודה (מנחות דף פ:):

לוג מאי איכא למימר. פי' דשמא אינו מצורע והוי חולין בעזרה כיון דעביד מינה עבודה שמזה שבע כנגד פתח אהל מועד ונותן על הבהונות ועל ראש המצורע ותימה ליזיל ליקדיש ליה קדושת דמים על תנאי אם אינו מצורע *דהשתא נמי מייתי פורתא להשלים הלוג וליקדוש ליה קדושת דמים וכי בעי למיכל השיריים פריק להו כדאיתא בסמוך ויש לומר דהכי עדיף טפי לעשות קדושת הגוף בכל מה שיכול *ותימה לי היאך נותן מתן שבע ועל הבהונות מההוא פורתא שקדוש קדושת דמים דשמא אינו מצורע וזורקו לאיבוד שמן הקדש. ברו"ך:

חסר הלוג עד שלא יצק ימלאנו. משנה זו במס' נגעים פ' בתרא (מ"י): **אימת** אי בתר מתנות שבע הוה להו שיריים שחסרו בין קמיצה להקטרה כו'. וא"ת והא ר' יוחנן הוא דאמר בפ"ק דמנחות (דף ט.) דמקטירין קומץ עליהם ואפי' ר"ל דאמר אין מקטירין אליבא דר"א מודה דמקטירין כדאיתא התם וכר' אליעזר משני הכא לבסוף דמסיק לשם עצים ויש לומר אע"ג דמקטירין מ"מ לענין אכילה לא משכחת תקנה דהא אסירי שיריים באכילה כדנפקא ליה התם מוהנותרת ולא הנותרת מן הנותרת:

ואי קודם מתן שבע. דלמא נדבה היא והקטרתו הקטרה והני הוו להו שיריים וכי הדר מעייל מינייהו לפנים להזות קא עבר משום כל שממנו לאישים קיימו שיריים בבל תקטירו והנך הזאות נמי בשמן כהקטרה במזבח בדבר הראוי להקטיר דמי כך פי' בקונטרס והא דמשני דמסיק להו לשם עצים *הוה ליה למינקט דמדי לשם מיא בעלמא ודוחק בקונטרס לפרש [כך] משום לישנא דקרא דאותביה יא] מכל שממנו לאישים הרי הוא בבל תקטירו אפי' בהזאות א"כ קשה הא דאמרי' לקמן (דף פ.) הניתנים במתנה אחת שנתערבו במתן ארבע ר' אליעזר אומר ינתנו במתן ארבע הא כיון יב] דניתן במתנה אחת אידך הוו להו שיריים וקא עבר משום בל תקטירו מיהו יש לומר דר' אליעזר לטעמיה דאית ליה (שם עט:) רואין כאילו הוא מים ועוד כיון דשירי הדם למזבח ליסוד מש"ה כי יהיב ליה למעלה לא עבר בבל תקטירו כיון דבלאו הכי טעונין מזבח ועוד קשה לימא דיהיב מתן שבע ברישא והדר ממלא ליה וקמיץ ואע"ג דאמר ר"ל בפ"ק דמנחות (ג"ז שם) מנחה שחסרה קודם קמיצה לא יביא מתוך ביתו וימלאנה הא איתותב התם ונראה לפרש דמהקטרה ממש פריך דמקטיר מלוג שמן של מצורע חייב כר' עקיבא דאמר בפ' כל המנחות באות מצה (שם דף נח.) כל ששמו קרבן ור' אליעזר פליג עליה ואע"ג דהך סוגיא כר' אליעזר כדמשני דמסיק לשם עצים באידך לא מסתברא כר' אליעזר דשמותי הוא אלא כר' עקיבא ואף על גב דקודם מתן שבע איירי שמו קרבן מיקרי כיון דעתיד להיות קרבן *כמה יג] דמקטיר בשר חטאת קודם זריקת דם דמסתמא חייב ומעיקרא יד] פריך אי לאחר מתן שבע כו' הוי מצי למיפרך נמי מכל שממנו לאישים ובלאו הכי *) טו] שפיר פריך ליה תימה והא קדוש קדושת הגוף דלוג

*) ובלא"ה פריך שפיר הס"ד אח"כ מה"ד דפריך ליה. תימה והא כו' נ"ק

עין משפט נר מצוה

לז א מיי' פ"ט מהל' מחוסרי כפרה הל"ד:

לח ב מיי' פ"ה מהל' איסורי מזבח הל"ה:

חטאת בהמה נ"ק

לט ג מיי' שם הל' ג:

לא היה נ"ק

נ"ל באותו ענין ובאותה שיטה שאמרנו כו' ובאותה תנאי באותה כו' בשלישית ולבסוף ארבע ברביעית נ"ק

כשבא נ"ק וכו' יעב"ץ כשיבא

נ"ק מ"ז

נ"ל גמורה

אשם מצורע בין נ"ק

מה שיכול הס"ד ויק ותימה לי כו' שייך בסוף ד"ה דפריך לי כו' וקאי אפי' אי נ"כ דלקמן. נ"ק

מסורת הש"ס

[מנחות קה:]

נגעים פרק יד משנה י [מנחות ט.]

יומא מז: יבמות ק. סוטה כג. מנחות נח. קו:

יבמות שם סוטה שם [מנחות קו: יומא מז:]

ומדי מינייהו נ"ק

נוסחאות רש"י כת"י

והא הכא כו' שרי ר"ש. תקוני גברא. להתיר לאכול בקדשים: הא תינח כו': מתן שבע. ס"א כנגד בית קדשי הקדשים כדתנן במס' נגעים:

נ"א דהשתא נמי דמייתי פורתא להשלים הלוג מקדיש ליה כו' נ"ק

כמאן דנקיט דמדי נ"ק

וקשה אי כו' נ"ק

כמו דמקטיר בשר חטאת העוף נ"ק

שיטה מקובצת

א] אי קודם מתן שבע כו'. פי' כיון שהקומץ שמפריש מן הלוג עולה לאישים נמצא כל שירי קומץ בבל תקטירו דנפקא לן מהאי קרא דכתיב כל שאור וכל דבש לא תקטירו ממנו כלומר כל שנעשית ממנו עבודה הרי היא בבל תקטירו וכשם שהוא בבל תקטירו כך פסול לעבודה אחרת א"כ היאך מזה מן השיריים ומשני דמסקי לשם עצים ולשם עצים לאו דוקא שהרי איירינן בהזאה כדפי' אלא כלומר מזה לשם מים כמו דאמר ר"א דמסיק להו לשם עצים ועל תנאי אם אינו מצורע וצריך שיאמר הכהן כך כשמזה אם מצורע הוא ואין הקטרתו הקטרה ואלו אינן שיריים הרי הזאת אלו יוכשרו להזאת מצורע ואם אינו מצורע והקטרתו הקטרה ואלו הן שיריים הריני מזה אותן מים בעלמא כמו שאני רשאי להעלות שירי מנחה שהן שיריים ע"ג מזבח לשם עצים כך היא שיטת הקונטרס ולישנא דמסיק לשם עצים קשה לפירושו ועוד תימה כו' לכך נראה דעל הקטרה פריך היכי מקטיר הקומץ אפי' קודם מתן שבע והלא שמא מצורע הוא וטעון מתן דמים לעשות הזאה הריא הזאה (במתן ארבע) [דמתן שבע] כשמנו לאישים נמצא דכל אותו מותר הלוג מן הקומץ הוי שיריים להזאה והוי בבל תקטירו וכל שממנו לאישים לאו דוקא והיאך מקטירין הקומץ ואתיא כר"ע (כו') [דאמר כל ששמו] קרבן כגון לוג שמן של מצורע הוי בבל תקטירו אע"ג דלא הוי ממנו לאישים ואף קודם הזאות עובר משום בל תקטירו והא דפריך אי קודם מתנות שבע אינו ר"ל דלאחר מתנות שבע*) יקשה טפי וא"כ הוי שירי הזאה. אלא ה"פ אי לאחר מתנות שבע אז אית ליה פירכא אחריתי כדפי' מעיקרא דהוו ליה שיריים שחסרו וכ"ש דמצינו למיפרך האי נמי ואי קודם מתנות שבע הא תינח קושיית שיריים שחסרו אבל עדיין תקשי לך הא דאפי' קודם מתנות שבע נמי הרי הוא בבל תקטירו וא"ת והיא גופיה טעמיה מאי למה יקרא הקומץ שירי הזאה כיון שקומץ קודם הזאה וי"ל מידי דהוה אבשר חטאת קודם הקטרת אימורין או קודם זריקת דם ולא נהירא לריב"א דלא דמי לבשר חטאת דהתם א"צ בירור לחלק ומבורר ועומד הוא אבל הכא הזאה אינה מבוררת איזה טיפה היא שהשאר יקרא שיריים עד לאחר מתנות שבע לכך נראה פ"ה עיקר. ומה דקשיא לפ"ה מנלן דהזאות ומתנות חשיבי כהקטרה י"ל דכיון דגלי קרא דאשה לאו דוקא אלא ה"ה כל ששמו קרבן כדקאמר ר"ע בפ' כל המנחות באות מצה כדפי' ומעתה נאמר דה"ה לא תקטירו לאו דוקא וה"ה הזאות ומתנות ואגב אשה נקט תקטירו. והא דקאמר דמסיק להו לשם עצים אגב דאיירי ישנו (בהקטרה בל) [בכל שממנו לאישים הרי הוא בבל] תקטירו נקטיה: ב] מיקמץ דקי"ל בפ' כל התדיר לקמן המתנדב: ג] שמן למנחה כו' הס"ד: ד] עליהן כלומר בשבילם דכתיב: ה] הכי כשמזה אם: ו] ובאותו שיטה שאמרנו: ז] כאותה של סוף שלשים ובאותו תנאי: ח] ראשונה ובשביעי תגלחת: ט] מתיבת טמא בודאי כו' עד תיבת טמא בודאי מוקף בח"ל: י] דמו של פר וי"ל דאין זה אלא למצוה כדאמרי' לעיל והכא משום תקוני גברא התירו הס"ד: יא] דאותביה מבל תקטירו נקט לה ותימה מנ"ל דהזאות ומתנות חשיבי כהקטרה לעבור עליה משום בל תקטירו כל שממנו לאישים דלמא דוקא בבל תקטירו אבל בבל תזה לא ועוד אי שייך: יב] כיון דנתן במתנה: יג] כמה מקטיר אות ד' ל"ש: יד] ומעיקרא דפריך: טו] הכי פריך ליה שפיר הס"ד ומה"ד דפריך ליה. תימה כו' ושייך לדף שאחר זה:

*) [נראה דצ"ל דלאחר מתן שבע ניחא דלאחר מתנת שבע יקשה טפי דא"כ כו']

log [of oil]; [76*b*] and if not, let this guilt-offering be a votive peace-offering.[8] That guilt-offering must be slaughtered in the north, and requires sprinkling on the thumbs,[9] laying [of hands], [the accompaniment of] drink-offerings, and the waving of the breast and the thigh; and it is eaten one day and one night.[10]—A man's repair is different.[11]

That is well of the guilt-offering; what can be said about the *log* [of oil]?[12]—He declares: '[If I was not a leper,] let this *log* be a votive
a gift.'[1] But perhaps he was not a leper, and he must take off a fistful?[2]—He does take off a fistful. But perhaps he was a leper, and he requires seven sprinklings?[3]—He makes them. But it is defective?[4]—He brings a little more and replenishes it. For we learnt: If the *log* became defective before he poured it,[5] he replenishes it. But it [the fistful] must be burnt?—He does burn it [on the altar].[6] When? if after the seven sprinklings, it becomes a residue which was reduced between the taking of the fistful and the burning, and you may then not burn the fistful on its account;[7] while if before the seven sprinklings, [we have the exegetical rule:] Every offering whereof a portion has been consigned to the fire [of the altar] is subject to 'Ye shall not make smoke [burn]'?[8]—Said R. Judah the son of R. Simeon b. Pazzi: He brings it up [on the altar] as mere fuel.[9] For it was taught, R. Eliezer said: '*For a sweet savour*'[10] you

(8) This refers to a case of doubtful leprosy. 'On the morrow' means on the eighth day, the morrow after the final seven days of purification; v. Lev. XIII—XIV. If the man had not actually been a leper he is not liable now to a guilt-offering, and therefore he stipulates that in that event it shall be a votive peace-offering. (9) V. Lev. XIV, 14. (10) Like a guilt-offering. Thus he may reduce the time of its consumption (for it may be a peace-offering, which can be eaten two days) even at the outset! (11) There is no other way by which he can become clean. (12) This is not a refutation of Raba, but a difficulty in R. Simeon's statement. The guilt-offering can be a votive peace-offering, if the man was not a leper; but what about the *log* of oil, to which he is not liable in that case?

a (1) For oil could be brought by itself, without an animal sacrifice. (2) If oil is votively brought, a fistful must be taken off and burnt on the altar; v. *infra* 91*b*. (3) V. Lev. XIV, 16. (4) As a fistful was removed, there is now less than a *log*, and that invalidates the rites. (5) On to his left hand, v. ibid. 15. (6) Then the residue may be consumed in any event. For if he was a leper, it may be consumed, as stated *supra* 44*b*. While if this is a votive offering, it is the same as the residue of any meal-offering, which of course is eaten (v. Lev. II, 3). (7) It may be a votive offering, in which case the sprinklings are not a purification rite but simply a lessening of the oil. Now, the fistful had already been taken, and thus between that act and the burning the residue was reduced, in which case the fistful may not be burnt, v. Men. 9*b*. (8) V. Lev. II, 11. Here too, perhaps it was a votive offering, and so the burning of the fistful is a valid rite, in accordance with Lev. II, 2 q.v. When this burning has once been done, none of the residue may be burnt again on the altar. Now in this instance the sprinklings of the oil are equivalent to the burning on the altar of part of a meal-offering; hence just as that would be forbidden, so are the sprinklings forbidden. (9) Not as a fistful whose burning is a necessary rite. Thus when he sprinkles the oil the priest declares: 'If he was a leper' (so that the burning of the fistful was not a rite and does not count, since it was not a votive offering, for only such requires it), 'this is not a residue, and I sprinkle of the whole, not of the residue. While if he was not a leper' (so that the burning of the fistful was a necessary rite), 'let this not be accounted as ritual sprinkling but as merely pouring water on the altar' (the equivalent of burning the fistful not as a rite, but as though one added fuel to the altar). So Rashi. According to this explanation, the Talmud speaks figuratively: in the difficulty it raises, 'Ye shall not make smoke' means that you must not sprinkle, while 'he brings it up as mere fuel' in the answer means that he simply pours it out as water. This is perhaps forced, while it is questionable whether this sprinkling is the exact equivalent of the ritual burning of the fistful. Tosaf. therefore explains that the passage is meant literally, thus agreeing with R. Akiba who maintained that it is *forbidden* to burn ritually a fistful of the leper's log of oil; hence the difficulty, How can he burn this fistful, in case he *was* a leper? The answer is that he does not burn it ritually, but merely as fuel. (10) Lev. II, 12.

may not take it up [on the altar], but you may take it up [77a]
a for fuel.[1]

But there is the residue which is to be eaten, whereas we have this little more on whose account no fistful was taken?[2]—He redeems it.[3] Where does he redeem it? If within [the Temple court], then he brings *ḥullin* into the Temple court?[4] If without, it becomes unfit through having gone out?[5]—In truth, [he redeems it] within, but it is *ḥullin* automatically.[6]

Yet surely R. Simeon said: You cannot bring oil as a votive offering?—The repair of a man is different.[7]

R. Reḥumi sat before Rabina, and stated in the name of R. Huna
b. Taḥlifa: Yet let him declare:[8] Let this guilt-offering be a suspensive guilt-offering?[9] You may infer from this[10] that the Tanna who disagrees with R. Eliezer and maintains that you cannot bring a suspensive guilt-offering votively is R. Simeon. Said he [Rabina]
b to him [R. Reḥumi] Torah! Torah![1] You have confused lambs with rams![2]

MISHNAH. IF THE LIMBS OF A SIN-OFFERING WERE MIXED UP WITH THOSE OF A BURNT-OFFERING, R. ELIEZER SAID: HE MUST PLACE [THEM ALL] ON THE TOP [OF THE ALTAR], AND I REGARD THE FLESH OF THE SIN-OFFERING ON TOP AS THOUGH IT WERE WOOD.[3] BUT THE SAGES MAINTAIN: THEY MUST BECOME DISFIGURED, AND THEN GO OUT TO THE PLACE OF BURNING.[4]

GEMARA. What is R. Eliezer's reason?—Scripture saith, *But they shall not come up for a sweet savour on the altar*:[5] *'for a sweet savour'* you may not take it up [on the altar], but you may take it up as wood. And the Rabbis?[6]—The Divine Law expressed a limitation [in the word] *'them'*: *'them'* you may not bring up [for a sweet savour] but only as wood; but not anything else.[7] And R. Eliezer?—Only [in respect of] *'them'* have I included the ascent,
c making it like the altar, but not [in respect of] anything else.[1] And the Rabbis?[2]—You may infer both things from it.[3]

Our Mishnah does not agree with the following Tanna. For it was taught: R. Judah said: R. Eliezer and the Sages had no controversy about the limbs of a sin-offering which were mixed up with the limbs of a burnt-offering, [both agreeing] that they must be offered up; [if mixed up] with the limbs of a *roba'* or a *nirba'*,[4] [both agree] that they must not be offered. Wherein do they differ? About the limbs of an unblemished burnt-offering which were mixed up with the limbs of a blemished [one]: there R. Eliezer maintains [that] they must be offered up [on the altar], and I regard the flesh of the blemished animal on top as mere wood; while the Sages say: They must not be offered up.

Now [according to] R. Eliezer, why are *roba'* and *nirba'* different: [presumably] because they are not eligible? A blemished animal

a (1) These things which may not be taken up on the altar for *ritual* burning may be taken up as fuel. (2) It may be a votive offering, of which a fistful must be taken for the altar, and only in virtue thereof is the rest permitted. Here he added a little *after* the fistful was taken, and so it was not permitted thereby. As it is mixed up with the rest, all is forbidden. (3) He declares: 'If he was not a leper, and this log is a votive offering, let the additional oil' (which was not necessary for a votive offering) 'be redeemed by this money.' (4) As soon as he redeems it, it is *ḥullin*, and in the Temple court, whereas *ḥullin* may not be brought into the Temple court. (5) The whole *log*, for it ranks as most holy, which becomes unfit when taken without. (6) He does not actually *bring ḥullin* into the Temple court. (7) It is permitted here, as there is no other way out. (8) If he was not a leper. (9) To atone for a sin doubtfully committed. For R. Eliezer holds that such can be offered *voluntarily*, since every man stands in doubt whether he has sinned or not. This is preferable to declaring it a peace-offering, as the former too may only be eaten one day, and so we would not reduce the time permitted for consumption. (10) Since R. Simeon does *not* adopt this expedient.

b (1) Where is your learning? (2) A leper's guilt-offering must be a year old lamb, whereas a suspensive guilt-offering must be a two year old ram. (3) It cannot be *ritually* burnt, but it can be regarded merely as fuel. (4) They must be kept until they no longer look like flesh and then be taken out and burnt where all unfit flesh is burnt. But they cannot be regarded and treated simply as fuel. (5) Lev. II, 12. As stated *supra* 76b, this means that no sacrifice may be ritually burnt (*haḳtarah*) on the altar after a portion thereof has already been so burnt. (6) How do they rebut this? (7) The two verses (ibid. 11, 12) read: *No meal-offering, which ye shall bring unto the Lord, shall be made with leaven; for all leaven and all honey, ye shall not make smoke* of it *as an offering made by fire unto the Lord* (lit. translation). *As an offering of first-fruits ye may bring* them *unto the Lord; but they shall not come up for a sweet savour on the altar.* Now, as stated *supra* 76b, the first verse is interpreted to mean that the ritual burning on the altar of *anything* whose *haḳtarah* was already done is forbidden. This is learnt from the apparently superfluous *'of it'*, and is made to include sacrifices in general, and not particularly honey or leavened bread. The second verse nevertheless teaches that they can be burnt simply as fuel. The Rabbis hold that *'them'* in the second verse is a limitation: only those things enumerated in the preceding verse, viz., honey and leavened bread may not come up *'for a sweet savour'* yet may come up as fuel; other things, however, which may not come up (as deduced from *'of it'*), may not come up at all.

c (1) From the words, *but they may not come up . . . to* (lit. translation, not *on* as E.V.) *the altar* it is inferred that they may not even be placed on the ascent. R. Eliezer holds that *'them'* teaches that only leavened bread and honey are so forbidden, but nothing else. (2) Whence do they know this? (3) The limitation of *'them'* applies to everything that is implied in that verse; hence, as it teaches that things other than honey or leavened bread may not be brought up even as fuel, so it also teaches that they are *not* included in the interdict of the ascent. (4) V. *supra* 71a.

עין משפט נר מצוה

מ א מיי' פי"ד מהל' מעשה הקרבנות הלכה ח:
מא ב מיי' פ"ז מהל' פסולי המוקדשין הלכה כ:
מב ג מיי' שם פ"ג הל' יח ופ"ה מהל' איסורי מזבח הלכה ד:
מג ד מיי' פ"ו מהל' פסולי המוקדשין הלכה כא:

גמרא (תורה אור)

לשם עצים והא איכא שיריים דבעי א] *מילינהו ואיכא הך פורתא דלא קמיץ עילויה דפריק ליה דפריק ליה היכא ב] אי גוואי קא *מעייל חולין לעזרה אי אבראי איפסיל ליה ביוצא לעולם גוואי וחולין ממילא הויין והא *אמר רבי שמעון אין מתנדבין שמן תקוני גברא שאני יתיב רב רחומי קמיה דרבינא ויתיב וקאמר משמיה דרב הונא בר תחליפא ונימא אשם זה יהא אשם תלוי ש"מ מאן תנא דפליג עליה *דר' אליעזר ג] רבי שמעון הוא דאמר *אין מתנדבין אשם תלוי ד] אמר ליה תורה תורה אימרי בדיכרי מיחלפי לך: **מתני'** *איברי חטאת שנתערבו באיברי עולה ר' אליעזר אומר יתן למעלה ורואה אני את בשר החטאת מלמעלה כאילו הן עצים וחכמים אומרים תעובר צורתן ויצאו לבית השריפה ה]: **גמ'** מ"ט דרבי אליעזר *אמר קרא °ואל המזבח לא יעלו לריח ניחוח ו] לריח ניחוח אי אתה מעלה אבל אתה מעלה לשם עצים ורבנן מיעט רחמנא אותם אותם הוא דאי אתה מעלה אבל אתה מעלה לשם עצים אבל מידי אחרינא לא ורבי אליעזר אותם הוא דרבאי לך כבש כמזבח אבל מידי אחריני לא ורבנן ז] תרתי שמע מינה מתניתין דלא כי האי תנא דתניא אמר רבי יהודה לא נחלקו רבי אליעזר וחכמים על איברי חטאת שנתערבו באיברי עולה שיקרבו ברובע ונרבע שלא יקרבו על מה נחלקו על איברי עולה תמימה שנתערבו באיברי בעלת מום שרבי אליעזר אומר יקרבו ורואה אני ח] *למעלה כאילו הן עצים וחכמים אומרים לא יקרבו ורבי אליעזר מאי שנא רובע ונרבע דלא חזו בעלת מום נמי לא חזי

אמר

(ויקרא ב)

רש"י

לשם עלים. והאי דנקט ט] לישנא דעלים ולא נקט לשם מים משום לישנא דקרא דאותביה מכל תקטירו נקט לה: לריח ניחוח אי אתה מעלה. בתריה דההוא קרא דכל שממנו לאישים כתיב קרבן ראשית תקריבו אותם ואל המזבח לא יעלו לריח ניחוח קרבן ראשית אשאור ודבש הכתוב ברלש המקרא העליון קאי וקאמר יש לך להביא מהן ביכורים מן הדבש ושתי הלחם מהשאור ואל המזבח לא יעלו אכוליה קרא קאי והדרשה דכל תקטירו: שיריים. הך פורתא מה שהוסיף אחר קמילה ודלמא נדבה הוה ולא שרי להו מתנות המצורע אלא קמילה קא שרי להו: דפריק ליה. והאומר אם אינו מצורע י] הלוג נדבה הרי מה שהוספתי שלא לצורך מחולל על מעות הללו דכלי שרת אין מקדשים אלא מדעת וזה לא נתנו לתוך הלוג ע"מ שיקדשנו הלוג אם אינו מצורע לפיכך יש לו פדיון: קא מעייל חולין. כשהוא פודהו ומוליאו לחולין נמצא אותו שמן של חולין בעזרה: אפסיל ליה. כל הלוג ביוצא דהא קדש קדשים הוא כמנחה ואי קשיא למה לי כולי האי דקמיץ ברישא והדר מוסיף עליה ואיכא לאקשויי כל הני ליעבד ברישא כל צרכי מצורע והדר יא] נימלייהו וניקמוץ וניקטר ולא בעי למיפרקיה איכא לתרולי מאחר שהקדישו למזבח אין יכול לשנותו לצרכי מצורע שמא אינו מצורע והלוג של מזבח נמצא מאבד קדשי מזבח בידים הלכך קמיץ ברישא לצורך גבוה ואי נמי מצורע הוא לא מפסיד מידי דהדר ממלי ליה כדאמרן: והאמר רבי שמעון אין מתנדבין שמן. לקמן בפ' כל התדיר (דף צא.) והיכי אמרת לר"ש לוג זה יהא נדבה: ונימא אם אינו מצורע אשם זה יהא אשם תלוי. לכפר על ספק עבירה שבידו כר"א דאמר בכריתות (דף כה.) מתנדב אדם אשם תלוי בכל יום שאין לך אדם שאינו עומד בספק חטא והכי שפיר טפי שזמן אחד לאכילת כל האשמות ולא יב] מביא קדשים לבית הפסול: תורה תורה. כלומר היכן היא תורה של אדם גדול כמותך: אימרי בדיכרי קא מחלפין לך. כבש בן שנתו מיחלף לך באיל בן שתי שנים אשם מצורע כבש בן שנתו הוא והיאך יכול הוא להתנות עליו באשם תלוי שאינו בא אלא איל בן שתי שנים: **מתני'** יתן למעלה. על המזבח: ורואה אני את בשר חטאת. שהוא בבל תקטירו כאילו הן עלים דכיון דלא להקטרה מכוין שרי: ויצאו לבית השריפה. דלית להו רואין וקעבר בכל שממנו לאישים הוא בבל תקטירו שכבר אימוריו קרבו ונעשה הבשר שיריים יג]: **גמ'** ואל המזבח לא יעלו. בתר לא תקטירו ממנו דדרשינן מיניה כל שממנו לאישים כתיב: אותם. ברישא דקרא כתיב קרבן ראשית תקריבו אותם ואשאור ודבש קאי כדפרישית לעיל מה יש לך להביא מהן שתי הלחם מן השאור שהיא ראשית לכל המנחות וביכורים מן הדבש ואל המזבח לא יעלו וגו' אבל אתה מעלה לשם עלים: אבל מידי אחרינא לא. אכל שממנו לאישים דנפיק מסיפיה דקרא קמא לא קאי: ורבי אליעזר. להכי כתיב אותם יד] *למעוטי אשאור ודבש למעוטי שיריים מאזהרת אל המזבח לא יעלו דמרבינן מיניה כבש כמזבח כדתניא בתורת כהנים אין לי אלא מזבח כבש מניין תלמוד לומר אל המזבח: ורבנן תרתי שמעינן מינה. דמיעוטא דאותם אכל מאי דכתיב טו] *בהדא קרא קאי [וכי] היכי דממעט שיריים מאיסורא דריבויא דכבש כמזבח ממעט להו נמי מהיתירא דהעלאה לשם עלים דנפקא מהאי קרא: מתני'. דקתני טז] [דבבשר] חטאת פליגי רבנן וקתני נמי איברים בבעלי מומין לרבי

תוספות

דלוג הוי כלי שרת כדאמרי' בפ"ק דמנחות (דף ז.) ובפ' שתי מדות יז] (שם דף צ.) וי"ל דכלי שרת אין מקדשין אלא מלאין דלא מצטרף להתקדש האי פורתא עם האחר שכבר נתקדש אי נמי האי פורתא מנח ליה בלוג לשם קדושת דמים והשתא משמע הכא דאע"ג דלא קדיש למזבח לא הוי כחולין בעזרה מאחר דקדוש קדושת דמים כדמסיק:

וחולין ממילא הואי. וכי האי גוונא משני בפ' התכלת (שם דף מח.) גבי שחט שני כבשים על ארבע חלות דשתים מהן נאכלות ע"י פדיון וכי האי גוונא משני בפ' המוכר את הספינה (ב"ב דף פא:) גבי ביכורים דמקדיש להו ותימה דבפרק התודה (מנחות דף פ:) גבי תודה שנתערבה בתמורתה ומתה אחת מהן חבירתה אין לה תקנה ופריך ולייתי להם ולימא אי הך *קמייתא תודה היא הא לחמה ואי לא ליפוק לחולין ומשני וכי מכניסין חולין בעזרה והשתא אמאי לא מקדש להו והדר פריק להו וכן בפ' הזרוע (חולין דף קל.) דקאמר טעמא דכתב רחמנא זה הא לאו הכי הוה אמינא חולין חייבין בחזה ושוק הא בעי תנופה היכא ליניפינהו אי אבראי לפני ה' כתיב אי אגואי קמעייל חולין בעזרה אמאי ליקדשינהו והדר ליפרקינהו ומיהו התם ניחא יח] *דמקרא קא דריש וזה לא חייבה תורה אבל עוד קשה בפרק בתרא דמנחות (דף קד:) גבי פירשתי ואיני יודע מה פירשתי יביא מנחה של ששים עשרון דברי חכמים רבי אומר כו' וקאמר* דפליגי במותר להכניס חולין לעזרה דרבי סבר דאסור להכניס חולין לעזרה ואסור לערב חובה בנדבה והשתא ליקדשינהו קדושת דמים והדר לפרקינהו וי"ל דגבי תודה לא בעי למימר דמקדישה ופריק גזירה שמא יאמרו יש פדיון ללחמי תודה וכן בההיא דפ' בתרא יט] (גז"ש) שיש שם שיעור מנחה אתי למימר שיש לה פדיון אבל הכא דליכא שיעורא ידעי דהא דיש לה פדיון משום דאין לה שיעור לכך אין קדוש קדושת הגוף וכן בביכורים ידעי דמשום ספיקא הוא דאין ביכורים נפדין כתרומות ומעשרות דהשתא נמי לאחר פדיון אין נאכלין אלא לכהנים וליכא למיטעי מידי וכן בההיא דהתכלת (שם דף מח.) גבי שחט שני כבשים על ארבע חלות ידעי דלא קדשי אלא שתים ובלחמי תודה דלא קדשי אלא ארבעים ואין להקשות כ] הנך שיריים דהכא דליפרקינהו לשם עלים חדא דרחמנא אמר דליכלינהו למצוה ועוד דלא שרינן לשם עלים אלא בדבר שנתערב במידי דבר הקרבה כגון איברי עולה באיברי חטאת*):

תקוני גברא שאני. תימה אי דאורייתא קאמר ר"ש אין מתנדבין שמן היכי שרי משום תקוני גברא ועוד כיון דאין מתנדבין חולין גמורין הוו:

מאן תנא דפליג עליה דר' אליעזר ר' שמעון הוא. וההוא דקדושין (דף נה.) דבהמה שנמצאת בין ירושלים למגדל עדר דמשמע התם דאי אישתכח בן שתי שנים דאיכא לספוקי באשם לית ליה תקנתא צריך לומר דפליגא אדר' אליעזר דאי מתנדבין לייתי *בהמה וליתני באשם תלוי:

ורבי אליעזר אותם הוא דרבאי לך כבש כמזבח אבל מידי אחריני לא. וא"ת מה סברא היא זו לר' אליעזר כא] דאותם לא קאי אכולהו ולריח ניחוח דבתריה קאי אכולהו אפי' אשיריים ויש לומר משום דלא מסתבר ליה טעמא לר' אליעזר להחמיר בשיריים טפי משאור ודבש ודרשא דכבש כמזבח חומרא היא ולא קאי אלא אשאור ודבש דחמיר:

ורבנן תרתי שמעת מינה. הך סוגיא כרבי אלעזר דאמר בפרק כל המנחות באות מצה (מנחות דף נז:) המעלה מכולן ע"ג הכבש פטור ור' יוחנן מחייב התם והא דקאמר התם ור' יוחנן האי אותם מאי עביד ליה הוה ליה למימר דאיצטריך כב] לכדדרשינן הכא רבנן אבל ניחא ליה לשנויי אפי' כר' אליעזר ועוד בכמה מקומות סוגיא דשמעתא כוותיה לעיל דמשני דמסיק לשם עלים ובפרק *(שני) דמנחות (דף כ.):

*) וע"ע תוס' פסחים סו: ד"ה מכילה ותוס' ב"ב פא: ד"ה ודילמא ותוס' מנחות כח: ד"ה חולין ועוד תוס' שם פ: ד"ה וכי ותוס' חולין קל: ד"ה אי ותוס' תמורה כג: ד"ה אוכלין

הכא

הגהות בגליון

ס"א מיכלינהו
[מנחות מח. וש"נ]
[לקמן נא. מנחות קד:]
[כריתות יח.]
מנחות מח.
[לעיל עו: ע"ש בע"ק]
[נ"ל את בשר בעלת מום למעלה כו' וכן העתיקו תוס' נחולין ע. ד"ה מ"ע]
נ"ל לרבות שאור ודבש ולמעוטי שיריים כו' נ"ך
בהדיא קרא נ"ך
[נ"ל בתרא דמנחות קו:]
נ"ל דקיימא נ"ך
נ"ל דמקרא קריב נ"ך
[שם קו.]

נוסחאות רש"י כת"י

תורה תורה. אתה שאומרים עליך שאתה בקי בתורה:

שיטה מקובצת

א] דבעי מיכלינהו ואיכא הך פורתא דלא קמיץ. וא"ת ולוקמא דעשה הזאה שבע תחלה ואח"כ מילא וקמץ [ואולי] כל הני פירכות דלעיל וי"ל כיון דשמא נדבה הוא א"כ אין לולל בו לכתחלה בלוג ליתן כלום קודם קמיצת הקומץ מאחר דסופו לעשות ממנו עבודת מזבח גנאי הוא אם לא עשה עבודת המזבח ראשונה: ב] אי גוואי קא מעייל חולין בעזרה. וא"ת עד דקשה ליה מפדיון בפנים תקשי ליה דמתחלה הכנסת ההוא פורתא לעזרה כדי למלאות הלוג אחר קמיצה היאך מכנים בעוד שהוא חולין בעזרה וי"ל דמעיקרא מקריש קדושת דמים ולא הוי חולין בעזרה דהכי משני בפ' המוכר [את] הספינה וא"ת אמאי לא מתנה מעיקרא אם אין מצורע דלהוי כל השמן של הלוג (מקדיש) [קדיש] קדושת דמים ודבר הקרב ממנו דהיינו מתנות שבע יזה לשם מים (דהיינו) [דהוא] מותר ודבר הנאכל פריק ואכיל ומאי דוחקיה להתנות בנדבה כל הלוג ויצטרך לדחוק ולומר דאע"ג דלר"ש אין מתנדבין שמן תקוני גברא שאני וגם צריכין להני שינויי דלעיל. ותירץ הר"ר יצחק מנוח דא"כ (אמאי) [איכא] יש פדיון לקרבן שיאמרו מוציאין קדושת הגוף לחולין ע"י פדיון. וא"ת לעיל דקאמר דפריק להו ליחוש שמא יאמרו יש פדיון לקדוש קדושת הגוף וי"ל דודאי משום האי פורתא דמסלא ליה לא אתי למימר דמוציאין קדושת הגוף לחולין ע"י פדיון כיון דאין שיעור קרבן וכן צריך לפרש בפ' בתרא דמנחות: ג] דר' אליעזר ואמר אין תיבות ר"ש הוא ואות ד' נמחק: ד] תלוי ר"ש היא אמר: ה] השריפה איברים באיברי בעלי מומין ר"א אומר אם קרב ראש אחד יקרבו כל הראשים כרעיו של אחד מהן יקרבו כל הכרעים והכ"א אפי' קרבו כולן חוץ מאחד מהן יצא לבית השריפה: ו] לריח ניחוח אי אתה מעלה. פ"ה סמוך לקרא הוא דכי כל שאור. שאור וכל דבש לא תקטירו קרבן ראשית תקריבו ממנו אשה לה' ואל המזבח לא יעלו וגו' ומוסב על מקרא ראשון והכי משמע אותו שאמרתי לך לא תקטירו ממנו פעם שניה לא אמרתי אלא דלא יעלו לריח ניחוח אבל לשם עצים מותר והדקא גבי איברי חטאת שנתערבו אבל גבי ראשים בעי ר"א שיקרב אחד מהן ולא אמרי' דמעלה להו לשם עצים כדקאמר תלמודא וטעמא משום דלא איירי קרא דריח ניחוח בבעלי מומין: ז] תרתי שמעינן מינה. דמאותם נתמעטו שירי [אישים] דלא שייך בהו דין דשאור ודבש בין לענין איסור העלאה דכבש ובין לענין דאין עולין אף לשם עצים דאין סברא למעט להצאין. וא"ת שפיר קאמרי רבנן מאי טעמא דר"א וי"ל (דלר"א) [דר"א] סבר דיותר סברא למעט להצאין מטה שנאמר (דאותם) [דמאותם] נמעים דשאור ודבש אין עולין לכבש כמו שאין עולין לגבי מזבח אבל שירי אישים עולין לכבש והשתא לענין כבש מיקל הכתוב בשירי אישים יותר מבשאור ודבש וגבי מזבח הוי איפכא שנחמיר ספי בשירי אישים תאמר דאין עולין אפי' לשם עצים ושאור ודבש עולין לשם עצים לכך סברא ספי לכל הפחות להשוותם לענין דעולין לשם עצים ומיעט אותם לענין כבש ואין לדרוש איפכא לאיסור העלאה [לשם] עצים דע"כ הוצרכו לאוקמי אותם לענין כבש דסמיך ליה: מתניתין דלא כי האי תנא. ופליג עליה דמתני' בתרתי כדמפרש ואזיל חדא דאמר בברייתא דלא נחלקו באיברי חטאת [כו'] ובמתני' קאמר דפליגי והדא באיברי מום לר"א יקרבו בכל ענין ואפי' לא קריב ראשו של אחד מהן ובמתני' קאמר ר"א אם קריב ראשו של אחד מהן דוקא או אמרינן יקרב השאר והכא קאמר יקרבו בכל ענין וטעמיה כדמסיק ואזיל: ח] אני איברי בעלת מום למעלה: ט] דנקט גבי הוצאת לישנא דמסיק להו לשם עצים ולא נקט לשם כו' נקט ליה הס"ד: י] מצורע והלוג: יא] והדר נמלייה אות ו' נמחק: יב] ולא יביא קדשים אות מ' נמחק: יג] שיריים הס"ד ומה"ד איברים. של עולות הרבה הס"ד ומה"ד באיברי עולת בעלת מום. אם קרב תלינן איסורא ביה הס"ד ומה"ד יצא לבית השריפה דלא תלינן איסורא בקריבין כבר הס"ד ומה"ד גמ' ואל: יד] תיבת למעוטי נמחק: טו] דכתיב בהאי קרא קאי וכי: טז] דקתני דבבשר חטאת פליגי כו' איברין באיברי בעלי מומין: יז] מדות. ותירץ בקונטרס דאין כלי שרת מקדש אלא מדעתו ואין דעתו שיקדש קדושת הגוף ועי"ל דאין חל על פורתא קדושת הגוף לפי שאין באותו פורתא שיעור קרבן ואין כלי שרת מקדש אלא דבר הראוי לקדש כגון לוג שלם. ואע"ג דכי מילאוהו יש בו כשיעור מ"מ אינו מצטרף עם השאר לקדושת הגוף כיון דבאותו שאר לא היה בו כדי שיעור לענין נדבה בלא האי פורתא. מהר"פ: יח] ומיהו התם ניחא דלא חייבה תורה להקדיש מש"ה לא איצטריך קרא אבל עוד קשה: יט] בתרא דמנחות: כ] להקשות דלימא דהנך שיריים דהכא דמסיק להו לשם עצים חדא דרחמנא אמר למצוה ועוד דלא: כא] אליעזר דריבוי דכבש לא קאי תיבת דאותם נמחק: כב] דאיצטריך לכדדרשי הכי:

אמר רב הונא *בדוקין שבעין ואליבא דר' עקיבא דאמר אם עלו לא ירדו אימר דאמר ר' עקיבא דאי עבד לכתחלה מי אמר אמר רב פפא הכא במאי עסקינן כגון שעלו על גבי כבש אי הכי אפי' בעיניהו אלא טעמיה דר' אליעזר מיעט רחמנא מום בם א] הוא דלא ירצו הא ע"י תערובת ירצו ב] ורבנן מום בם הוא דלא ירצו הא עבר ג] מום ירצו ור' אליעזר ד] מבם בהם ורבנן ה] בם בהם לא דרשי אי הכי רואה הא רחמנא אכשריה לדבריהם קאמר להו לדידי רחמנא אכשריה לדידכו אודו לי מיהא בשר בעלת מום כעצים דמי מידי דהוה אבשר חטאת ורבנן הכא מאיסי התם לא מאיסי: **מתני'** *אברין באברין בעלי מומין ר"א אומר *אם קרב ראש אחד מהן יקרבו כל הראשין כרעים של אחד מהן יקרבו כל הכרעים וחכ"א *אפי' קרבו כלם חוץ מאחד מהן יצא לבית השריפה: **גמ'** אמר ר"א *לא הכשיר ר"א אלא שנים שנים אבל אחד אחד לא מתיב ו] ר' ירמיה וחכ"א אפי' קרבו כולן חוץ מאחד מהן יצא לבית השריפה אמר לו ר' ירמיה ברתחליפא *אסברה לך מאי אחד זוג אחד: **מתני'** *דם ב]שנתערב במים אם יש בו מראית דם כשר נתערב ביין ז] רואין אותו כאילו הוא מים נתערב בדם בהמה או בדם החיה רואין אותו כאילו הוא מים רבי

רש"י

לר' אליעזר לא ח] קרב אלא אם כן קרב אחד מהן קודם שנמלך דלאו כי האי תנא: כגון שעלו על הכבש. וכיון דלר"ע לא ירדו מן המזבח הני מעלן לכתחלה מכבש למזבח דקי"ל לקמן (דף פו.) כשם שהמזבח מקדש כך הכבש מקדש: אפי' בעינייהו. שלא נתערבו בתמימים אם עלו בעלי מומין לכבש לר"ע יקרבו: בם. משמע כשהן בפני עצמן: מידי דהוי אבשר חטאת. דמודיתו לי דאם נתערב באיברי עולה יקרב לשם עצים כדאמרן ט]: **מתני'** איברים. של עולות הרבה באיברי עולת בעלת מום אם קרב [א' מהם] תלינן איסורא ביה: יצא לבית השרפה. דלא תלינן איסורא בקריבין כבר: **גמ'** *(לא נחלקו כו'): אלא שנים שנים. זוג זוג יקריבם דאיכא למימר מיגו דהאי לאו דאיסורא הוא י] דהאי נמי לאו איסורא הוא ואיסורא אזיל ליה בההוא דקרב קודם שנמלך אבל אחד אחד דליכא מיגו לא: חוץ מאחד מהן כו'. מכלל דלרבי אליעזר קרב זוג אחד. שני ראשים: **מתני'** שנתערב ביין. שהוא אדום ואין מראה ניכר בו: רואין אותו יין כאילו הוא מים. ואומדין אם היה דם שנתערב כאן ניכר במים הללו כשר לזריקה: בדם הבהמה. של חולין: רואין אותו. של חולין כאילו הוא מים ואומדין אותו אם היה דם הזבח ניכר כשר ואע"פ שהחולין רבין עליו: אין דם מבטל דם. דמין במינו לא בטיל ואפי' טיפה לתוך כלי גדול כשר לזריקה: נתערב בדם

תוספות

הכא בדוקין שבעין ואליבא דר"ע דאמר אם עלו לא ירדו. מילתיה דר"ע בפ' המזבח מקדש (לקמן דף פד.) דתנן ר"ע מכשיר בבעלי מומין ואמר ר' יוחנן בגמ' לא הכשיר ר"ע אלא בדוקין שבעין הואיל וכשרין בעופות דלא פסל בעופות אלא מחוסר אבר כדדרשינן בת"כ ובפ"ק דקדושין (דף כד:) יכול נקטעה רגלה ונשברה גפה ול"ת אמאי לא חשיב נמי ניב שפתים יא] דאמר פ' הניזקין (גיטין דף נו.) דשדא מומא בניב שפתים אתרא דלדידן הוי מומא ולדידהו לא הוי מומא דלא פסול לבני נח אלא מחוסר אבר ושמא בעוף לא שייך ניב שפתים מיהו הכתי קשה דאיכא כמה מומין דלא פסלי ואמאי נקיט דוקין שבעין וכן בגיטין הוה מצי למישדי יב] מומא במקום אחר*:

אי הכי אפי' בעינייהו נמי. תימה דלישני דלדבריהם קאמר להו כדמשני לבסוף: **הא** עבר מום ירצו. אע"ג דדרשינן בבכורות (דף לז.) בכלל ופרט דמום עובר מרצה מום עובר דמוקדשין איצטריך דה"א כיון דנדחה שוב אינו נרצה: *ורבנן בם בהם לא דרשי. משמע דלא דרשינן מיניה תרתי אפי' ר"א לא דריש אלא מדכתיב בהם ולא כתיב בם ותימה דבפ' שני שעירי (יומא דף סד.) דריש רבי יוחנן מבהם ג' דרשות הני הוא דכי עבר מומם ירצו הא שאר דחויין הואיל ונדחו ידחו ועוד דריש בם הוא דלא ירצו הא עבר מומן ירצו ועוד בם הוא דלא ירצו הא ע"י תערובת ירצו ושמא משום דכתיב נמי בם דמייתר ובם ובהם שניהם מיותרין ודרשינן לרבי יוחנן חדא דרש מבם ותרתי מבהם ולרב דרשינן תרתי חדא מבם וחדא מבהם אבל בם בהם לא דריש וכולה סוגיא יג] התם בין לרב בין לר' יוחנן אליבא דר"א ואין לחוש בכך דהכי נמי לעיל (דף עו:) ובפ' בתרא דמנחות (דף קו:) כר"א אי נמי אפי' כרבנן דבין ר"א ובין רבנן דמתני' אית להו דע"י תערובת ירצו והכי פירוש התם בעינייהו הוא דלא ירצו הא ע"י תערובת ירצו דתנן איברים שנתערבו כו' ומשמע מתוך המשנה דמודו רבנן דהנהו דקרבו ועלו למערכה יקרבו דלא ירדו שמעינן מינה דאית להו הך דרשא אלא לכתחלה אסרי מדרבנן דאי לית להו הוה להו יד] *למיסר אפי' אותם *שעלו ירדו כיון דלא בטלי אי לאו משום דשריא תערובת דאורייתא דכיון דאחמור רבנן דלא ליבטלו משום דדרכו למנות *(אית לן למישרי) טו] ע"י ביטולו ברוב בדיעבד משום דעלו והא דקאמר הכא ורבנן בם בהם לא דרשי ולא בעי למימר דרבנן נמי אית להו הך דרשה אלא דלכתחלה אסרי להקריב מדרבנן כי תנאי דמתני' משום דמשמע ליה דלא יקרבו לרבנן מדאורייתא כמו דלא יקרבו דרובע ונרבע דריש דברייתא דאפי' בדיעבד ירדו טז] השתא א"ש דרב ור' יוחנן לא שבקו רבנן ואמרי כר"א ותדע מדמייתי התם מלתא דרבנן דאי אליבא דר' אליעזר קאמרי לא הוה ליה לאיתויי מלתייהו דרבנן ואע"ג דרבנן דברייתא לא דרשי הכי מתני' עיקר *והא דדריש התם יז] *מבם בהם טעמא דר' יוחנן ומתרי בם דריש עבר מומם וע"י תערובת יח] מבם תערובת ועברמומם *מבם בהם ואייתר להם בם יט] דבתרא לכדר' יוחנן כדפרישית לא קשה מידי דלא איכפת ליה להש"ס רק שיוכל לעשות ג' דרשות ולא חש להזכיר דרשא דר' יוחנן אלא הפשוטה יותר וזה אין לפרש דאיברי בעלי מומין בתמימים לא בטלי מן התורה דמאיזה טעם לא בטלו אי משום דאין עולין מבטלין זה את זה הא בעלי מומין לא עולין נינהו ועוד דאפי' עולין נראה דלרבנן מדאורייתא מבטלין זה את זה בדבר שאינו מתערב °כמו מין במינו לר' יהודה שאינו מתערב דלא הוי כדם וסולת בטל *מדאורייתא: **אודו** לי מיהא בשר בעל מום כעצים דמי. אע"ג דר"א גופיה לא חייש להאי טעמא מדמצריך קרא מ"מ תיקשי להו לרבנן והכי אורחיה דהש"ס כדפירשתי בריש פירקין*: **בדם** בהמה או בדם חיה רואין אותו כאילו הוא מים. וא"ת דם בהמה וחיה היכי זריק להו למזבח נהי דאמר רואין כאילו הוא מים ולא מבטל דם אחר מ"מ מים גמורין לא הוי ולא בטל ממנו שם חולין ואפי' למ"ד (נזיר דף כט.) חולין שנשחטו בעזרה לאו דאורייתא היינו שחיטתן אבל להעלותן לגבי המזבח נראה דאסור וי"ל כיון דדם כשר מעורב בו ואין עיקר זריקתן לשם הפסול אלא לשם הכשר שרי אע"ג דבאיברים לא אמר רואין לשם עצים ומיהו בלאו הכי אתי שפיר דבנזיר *פ' ואלו (שם) משמע דלמ"ד לאו דאורייתא אפי' העלאה נמי שרי גבי מדיר בנו בנזיר למ"ד לחנכו במצות *דמביא חטאת העוף דקא סבר חולין בעזרה לאו דאורייתא ושמא סבר לה כר"א דשרי לשם עצים ולשם מים ואפשר דאפי' רבנן מודו דלא אסרי לשם עצים ולשם מים אלא במידי דהקרבה כגון איברי חטאת ואיברי עולה וכן ניתנין למעלה שנתערבו בניתנין למטה ומתן אחת במתן ארבע אבל חולין גמורין שרו לכ"ע לשם עצים ולשם מים וכן נתערב בדם פסול ובדם התמצית וכן מוכיח לקמן (דף עט:) מדרחיק עלה בגמ' במאי פליגי בגוזרין גזירה במקדש ולא קאמר דפליגי ברואה אי כדפליגי בכיפא ולקמן מפרש (ד"ה במאי): **רואין** אותו כאילו הוא מים. הקשה ה"ר שמואל מוורדוס הא דאמרי' בהקומץ רבה (מנחות דף כב.) ולקח מדם הפר ומדם השעיר הדבר ידוע שדם הפר מרובה מדם השעיר *סברי רבנן מכאן לעולין שאין מבטלין זה את זה היכי דריש ליה מיניה כ] הא דלא בטיל היינו משום דאפי' הוי מים היה בו מראית דם וי"ל דפעמים שהוא כל כך רבה דאי הוי דם הפר מים משתנה מראית דם השעיר עד שנעשה דיהה ופסול דאם יש בו מראית דם דקתני היינו מראית דם גמור ולא חזותא בעלמא ועוד י"ל אי לאו משום דאין עולין (אין) מבטלין זה את זה לרבנן או מין במינו לר' יהודה כשמערה טיפה ראשונה הוי ליה בטל ונדחו ומיהו קשה דאיפכא ה"ל למידק דהא אמרי' ביומא (דף נג:) שעירה דם הפר בדם השעיר ובדם שנתערב במים אמר בגמ' לא שנו אלא שנפל מים לתוך דם אבל דם לתוך מים ראשון ראשון בטל הלכך האי דם פר היה לו להתבטל ראשון ראשון בדם השעיר ואפי' מאן דלית ליה ראשון ראשון בטל בפ' בתרא דע"ז (דף עג.) הכא מודה משום דה"ל נראה ונדחה וי"ל דלא אמר ראשון ראשון בטל כשמערה בשפע הרבה יחד כמו שמחלק בע"ז (גז"ש) בין חבית דנפיש עמודיה ללגלור קטן דלא נפיש אפי' למאן דאית ליה ראשון ראשון בטל בחבית ביותר מפי חבית היה מודה דלא בטיל ועוד מי לא עסקינן שמערה דם הפר שבכלי זה ודם השעיר שבכלי זה מכניסם יחד תוך כלי שלישי:

עין משפט נר מצוה

מד א מיי' פ"ו מהל' פסולי המוקדשין הלכה כא:

מה ב מיי' פ"ב שם הלכה כב:

[ועי' תוס' לעיל לה. ד"ה אלא בדוקין וכו' אי נמי שאר מומין וכו']

[לעיל עד.]

גי' בעל פנים מאירות וכ"ג הצ"ק נראה הס"ד ואח"כ ד"ה ורבנן כו'

[לעיל עד. לקמן פ.]

[לקמן פ.]

מנחות כב. חולין פז:

[צ"ל למימר]

כ"א לית לן למיסר

גי' הבעל פנים מאירות והא דדריש התם מה' דבהם כו' והכא דריש מה"א דבהם ועבר מומם מבם דבה"א ואייתר להם בם דבהם לכדר' יוחנן כדמפרש כצ"ל

[ועי' תוס' ערובין לח. ד"ה אי ותוס' חולין נו. ד"ה מ"ט ותוס' לעיל עב. ד"ה וליבטלי]

פ"ד משמע צ"ק

מסורת הש"ס

[בכורות טו.]

שייך לעיל והוא סד"ה מידי דהוי צ"ק

יומא סד. ע"ש

נוסחאו' רש"י כת"י

מתני' איברים. של עולות הרבה באיברי עולת בעלת מום אם קרב ראש של אחד מהן לאחר שנתערב בהן בע"מ בא כהן שאינו יודע מהתערובית והקריב א' מן הראשים יקרבו כל הראשים לכתחלה דתלינן איסורא בהך דקרב והנך כולהו כשרין נינהו: גמ' אלא שנים שנים. זוג זוג יקריבם. ס"א דודאי איכא חד בהאי זוגא דהתירא הוא וניתנה הקרבה זו להקריב משום ההוא דהיתר ואי משום ההוא דאיסורא איכא למיתלי באותו שקרב תחלה: אבל אחד אחד לא. שמא לא ניתנה זו ליקרב דדלמא האי דאיסורא הוא:

שעלו דירדו כו' אי לאו דשריא כו' וכיון דאחמור כו' לית לן למשרי צ"ק

מס' דבהם צ"ק

וסכי צ"ק
מס' דבהם צ"ק

ועי' בתוס' דף עג. ד"ה ר"י דיבש ביבש גם לר"י בטל

דמביא קרבן דקא סבר צ"ק

[שם איתא רבנן סברי]

גליון הש"ס

תוס' ד"ה הא וכו' כמו מין במינו לר"י. ע"ל דף עג ע"א תוס' ד"ה ר"י:

שיטה מקובצת

א] בם מום בם הוא: ב] הא ע"י תערובת ירצו. ונראה דלא איצטריך אלא בתערובת חד בחד או תרי בתרי דלא נתבטל ברוב דאי חד בתרי לא איצטריך קרא לריבויי לומר דמרצה ואין בו איסור אלא מדרבנן דמדאורייתא חד בתרי בטל ובמידי דרבנן לא איצטריך קרא לומר דמרצה: ג] עבר מומם ירצו: ד] מבם. ס"א מום בם בהם כתיב דכתיב כי משחתם בהם מום בם לכלומר והוי תרי מיעוטי. גליון: ה] בם בהם לא דרשי. וא"ת אמאי לא דרשי והלא בהם מיותר דבלא בהם כתיב בם דכתיב כי משחתם בהם מום בם והרי מבם בם דרשו דאם עבר מומם ירצו ומבהם מה ידרשו וי"ל דרבנן דרשי בהם כדר"י דאר"ז בפ' שני שעירים בם הוא דאינו נדחה הא שאר דחויין הואיל ונדחו ידחו. וא"ת ור"א מנ"ל הא וי"ל מדמצי למכתב במקום בהם בם וכתב בהם ש"מ תרתי. אבל רבנן בם בהם לא דרשי כדקאמר הכא וכן מוכח הסוגיא התם. וא"ת ולר"א דמתני' אמאי איצטריך לומר במתני' אם קריב ראשו כו' תיפוק ליה דאפי' לא קריב יקרבו כיון דנתערבו מהאי קרא דדרשינן הא ע"י תערובת ירצו. וכ"ת דתנא דמתני' לית ליה האי סברא הא ליכא למימר הכי דע"כ אית ליה כדמוכח בפ' שני שעירים דהתם רב פליג עליה דר"י ואמר דאף שאר דחויין ירצו ובם דריש דע"י תערובת ירצו כר"א ומייתי התם ר"א דמתני' וי"ל דודאי מה"ת ע"י תערובת יקרבו אפי' לא קריב ראש אחד מהם מיהו מדרבנן אסור אם לא קריב ראש אחד מהם. וא"ת מ"מ רב מנ"ל דר"א דמתני' דריש בם דמייתי מיניה ראיה דלמא כל עיקר טעמא דר"א משום דקריב ראש אחד מהן בלי שום פסוק. וי"ל דא"כ מאי איריא דנקט במתני' בעלי מומין אפי' רובע ונרבע נמי אלא ש"מ דוקא בעלי מומין משום דכתיב בם אבל רובע ונרבע מודה דלא יקרבו. ולפי מה דפי' דאיצטריך טעמא דקריב להפקיע איסורא דרבנן כדפי' לעיל ניחא דמייתי לעיל מלתא [דרב במבעת] עכו"ם דנפל לים הגדול אחד מהן דהותרו כולן. וקאמר רב דאמר כר"א דאמר אם קריב ראש כו' וכי היכי דר"א מתיר השאר כי קריב אחד מהן ה"נ גבי טבעת. וקשה דמאי מייתי דלמא הא דשרי משום דגלי קרא דכתיב בם גבי בעלי מומין והתם ליכא קרא גבי טבעות אבל השתא ניחא דהכא מדאורייתא מותר מחמת קרא בלא קריב ראש של אחד מהם וקריב ראש צריך להתיר איסור דרבנן דוקא. וכן טבעות איסור דאורייתא ליכא דבטל ברוב אע"ג דאיכא חשיבות ונפל אחד לים צריך להפקיע איסורא דרבנן. וא"ת ורב דמייתי התם מר"א וכי עביד כר"א ושביק רבנן שהרי רבנן פליגי עליה במתני' ובברייתא ואמרי דיצא לבית השריפה אלמא לא דרשי בם לומר דע"י תערובת ירצו. וי"ל דגם רבנן דרשי בם לומר דיקרבו מן התורה ונפקא מינה דאם עלו לא ירדו. מיהו מדרבנן אסור להעלותו ואינו מותר אפי' כי קריב ראשו של אחד מהן דאם קריב ראש אחד מהן אינו מעלה ומוריד לרבנן דבהא [פליג לר"א] ותדע דהכי הוא מדאמרי רבנן במתני' אפי' קירבו כולם חוץ מאחד מהן יצא לבית השריפה ולא קאמרי דאם עלו (לא) ירדו אלמא ש"מ דדרשי בם דאם יעלו לא ירדו דאי לא דרשי א"כ הוי בעלי מומין כרובע ונרבע וירדו וליכא למימר דטעמא דמתני' דאם עלו לא ירדו לרבנן משום דמיירי בחד בתרי דבטל מדאורייתא ולפיכך לא ירדו אבל חד בחד תרד דלא דרשי בם לומר דע"י תערובת ירצו שהרי איברים חשיבי משום מנין לר"י דאמר כל שדרכו למנות שנינו או משום עשויה להתכבד ולא בטיל א"כ הוו להו למימר דידרו ואפי' בתרי. ואע"ג דחשיבית מנין וכיבוד הוי מדרבנן מ"מ במידי דחשיב אמרו רבנן דלא בטיל והוי חד בתרי כחד בחד כיון דמדרבנן לא בטיל הוי להו למימר כדאמרי' לעיל בריש פירקין דאמר רבא השתא דאמרי רבנן לא נקריב אי מקריב לא מרצה כמו כן הוי ליה למימר דירדו אי לא דרשי בם אלא ש"מ דגם רבנן דרשי בם לומר דאם עלו לא ירדו. וא"ת א"כ התם יביא ראיה מרבנן וי"ל משום (דלר"א) [דר"א] דרשה יותר בהדיא מיהו בלאו הכי [ניחא] דהא מייתי התם כולה מתני' גם דברי רבנן ומדרבנן נמי מייתי. וא"ת והא משמע לעיל דרבנן לא דרשי בם להתיר תערובת כדקאמר ורבנן כו' הא עבר מומם ירצו. וי"ל דלאו היינו רבנן דמתני' אלא היינו רבנן דברייתא דסבירא להו דאפי' אם עלו ירדו דומיא דלא יקרבו דגבי רובע ונרבע וא"כ ע"כ לית להו דרשה דלהתיר תערובת. מהר"פ: ו] מתיב ר' יעקב לר' ירמיה: ז] רואין אותו כאילו הוא מים *)וא"ת כו' וי"ל כו'. וט"ס מוכח שפיר בדם הפר ובדם השעיר דעולין לא מבטלין זה את זה ואין לרדות משום רואין כי הכא משום דמ"מ משמע דהטיפה ראשונה (לא) הוי ליה בטל ונדחה: ח] לא קרבי אלא: ט] כדאמרן לעיל הס"ד: י] הוא האי נמי אות ד' נמחק: יא] שפתים שאין להם אלא חרטום דאמר: יב] מומא. עי' מס' בכורות דף ל"ו ע"א: יג] סוגיא דהתם בין: יד] להו למימר אפי': טו] לן למישרי ע"י ביטול ברוב: טז] ירדו והשתא ניחא דרב תיבת א"ש ל"ש: יז] התם מה' דבהם טעמא תיבות מבם בהם נמחק: יח] דריש מה' דבהם תערובת ועבר מומם מבם דבהם תיבת מבם קמא נמחק: יט] בם בתרא אות ד' נמחק: כ] מיניה דילמא הא:

*) [כוונתו על דברי קושית התוס' בד"ה רואין הקשה ה"ר שמואל וכו' וי"ל דפעמים וכו' ועוד י"ל דמ"מ מוכח שפיר וכו']

too is not eligible? [77b]—Said R. Huna: It refers to cataracts in the eye, and is in accordance with R. Akiba who maintained that if they ascended [the altar], they do not descend.[5] Granted that R. Akiba ruled thus if it was done; did he rule thus at the very outset?[6]—Said R. Papa: The circumstances here are, e.g., that they went up the ascent. If so, even when they are by themselves [they must be offered]?[7]—Rather, [this is] R. Eliezer's reason: The Divine Law expressed a limitation in, '*There is a blemish* in them; a [*they shall not be accepted:*]'[1] only when there is a blemish *in them* shall they not be accepted, but when they are mixed up they are accepted. And the Rabbis?[2]—Only when the blemish is *in them* shall they not be accepted, but if their blemish has gone they are accepted. And R. Eliezer?[3]—[He derives it] from *bam, bahem.*[4] And the Rabbis?—They attribute no significance to[5] *bam, bahem.* If so, [how can R. Eliezer say,] 'I regard'. Surely the Divine Law declared it fit?[6]—He says this to them on their ruling: In my opinion, the Divine Law declared it fit; but [even] on your view, you should at least admit that the flesh of a blemished animal is like wood, by analogy with the flesh of a sin-offering. And the Rabbis?—Here[7] it is repulsive;[8] there[9] it is not repulsive.

MISHNAH. [IF THE] LIMBS OF BURNT-OFFERINGS [WERE MIXED UP] WITH THE LIMBS OF A BLEMISHED [BURNT-OFFERING], R. ELIEZER SAID: IF [THE PRIEST] OFFERED THE HEAD OF ONE OF THEM, ALL THE HEADS ARE TO BE OFFERED; THE LEGS OF ONE OF THEM, ALL THE LEGS ARE TO BE OFFERED.[10] BUT THE SAGES MAINTAIN: EVEN IF THEY HAD OFFERED ALL EXCEPT ONE OF THEM, IT GOES FORTH TO THE PLACE OF BURNING.

GEMARA. R. Eleazar said: R. Eliezer declared them fit only in twos, but not singly.[11] R. Jacob raised an objection to R. Jeremiah:[12] BUT THE SAGES MAINTAIN: EVEN IF THEY HAD OFFERED ALL EXCEPT ONE OF THEM, IT GOES FORTH TO THE PLACE OF b BURNING?[1]—Said R. Jeremia b. Taḥlifa, I will explain it for you: What does ONE mean? One pair.

MISHNAH. IF THE BLOOD WAS MIXED WITH WATER, IF IT RETAINS THE APPEARANCE OF BLOOD, IT IS FIT.[2] IF IT WAS MIXED WITH WINE, WE REGARD IT AS THOUGH IT WERE WATER.[3] IF IT WAS MIXED WITH THE BLOOD OF A DOMESTIC ANIMAL OR BEAST OF CHASE, WE REGARD IT AS THOUGH IT

(5) V. Bekh. 16a. (6) That they may be taken up—surely not! (7) According to R. Akiba, not only when they are mixed up with unblemished animals.

a (1) Lev. XXII, 25. '*Shall not be accepted*' intimates that they must not be presented on the altar. (2) How do they interpret this? (3) How does he know this? (4) Scripture writes *bam* (in them) instead of *bahem*, as it does in the preceding phrase: '*because their corruption is* bahem (*in them*)'. The change in word suggests a double limitation, and so both are learnt from it. *Var. lec.*: Scripture writes *bam, bahem*, i.e., *two* limiting words. (5) Lit., 'they do not interpret'. (6) If the text teaches that the limbs are fit to be burnt on the altar, how can you regard them as mere wood? (7) In the case of a blemished animal. (8) To burn it on the altar. (9) The flesh of a sin-offering. (10) Burnt on the altar. For I assume that the head or the legs already offered belonged to the blemished animal, and so all the rest are of the unblemished ones; v. *supra* 74a. (11) V. *supra* 74a. (12) Emended text (Sh. M.).

b (1) Hence R. Eliezer must hold that this last one would be offered, which shews that they can be offered singly. (2) For sprinkling. (3) And if the blood would lose its appearance in that quantity of water, it is unfit. Similarly the following clauses.

WERE WATER; [78a] R. JUDAH SAID: BLOOD CANNOT NULLIFY BLOOD.[4] IF IT WAS MIXED WITH THE BLOOD OF UNFIT [ANIMALS],[5] IT MUST BE POURED OUT INTO THE DUCT.[6] [IF IT WAS MIXED] WITH THE DRAINING BLOOD,[7] IT MUST BE POURED OUT INTO THE DUCT; R. ELIEZER DECLARED IT FIT. IF HE [THE PRIEST] DID NOT ASK BUT SPRINKLED IT, IT IS VALID.[8]

GEMARA. R. Ḥiyya b. Abba said in R. Joḥanan s name: We learnt this[9] only if the water fell into the blood; but if the blood fell into the water, each drop is nullified as it falls.[10] R. Papa observed: [But] it is not so in respect to covering, because there is no rejection in precepts.[11]

Resh Laḳish said: If *piggul, nothar* and unclean [flesh] were mixed up together, and one ate them, he is not culpable, [for] it is im-
a possible that one kind should not exceed the other and nullify it.[1] You may infer three things from this. You may infer [i]: Interdicts nullify each other. And you may infer [ii]: [The interdict of] taste in a greater quantity is not Scriptural.[2] And you may infer [iii]: A doubtful warning is not called a warning.

Raba raised an objection: If one made a dough of wheat and rice, if it tastes of corn, it is subject to *ḥallah*.[3] Now that is so even if the greater part is rice?[4]—[That is] by Rabbinical law [only]. If so,
b consider the sequel: A man can fulfil his duty thereby on Passover?[1]

(4) Even if the added blood would cause the original blood to lose its appearance if the former were water, the mixture is still fit for sprinkling. (5) E.g., with the blood of a *roba'* or a *nirba'* (v. *supra* 71a), or the blood of a sacrifice offered with the intention of eating the flesh after time or out of bounds. (6) The duct or sewer in the Temple court which carried off the blood. (7) V. *supra* 35a n. 6. (8) Even according to the first Tanna. (9) That if it retains the appearance of blood it is fit, which implies even where there is more water than blood. (10) Lit., 'the first is nullified'. As each drop of blood falls into the water it is instantaneously nullified, so that even if eventually the mixture looks like blood, it is unfit for sprinkling. (11) When one slaughters a bird or a beast of chase, he must cover its blood (Lev. XVII, 13). Now, even if this blood fell into water, if the whole looks like blood he must cover it, and we do not say that each consecutive drop was nullified. For though the first drop was indeed nullified, yet when so much has fallen in as to make the whole look like blood it regains its identity and combines with the rest, because where precepts are concerned a thing cannot be permanently rejected and made to lose its identity.

a (1) Rashi: if one mixed as much as an olive of two of these (both from Rashi and Tosaf. it appears that 'and unclean flesh' should be deleted), as one chews them together there must be in each piece that he chews rather more of the one kind and less of the other. This lesser part is nullified in the greater and is technically added thereto, whilst the kind which it is, is naturally diminished thereby. This will happen with each piece that he chews, and as it is impossible to equalise them, one of the kinds has less than the standard (as much as an olive is the minimum to involve liability). Now, liability in general is not incurred unless a formal warning, called *hathra'ah*, is first given to the offender; this warning must be couched in precise terms, e.g., 'We warn you that for eating so-and-so you will incur such and such penalty.' In this instance such a precise warning is impossible, for if it is given on account of *piggul*, perhaps liability may be incurred on account of *nothar, piggul* being short of the standard. Hence only a doubtful warning can be given, and such is not accounted a warning. Tosaf. explains differently. (2) If forbidden food is mixed even with a greater quantity of permitted food and communicates its taste to it, the whole is forbidden, (even if the former is subsequently removed). From Resh Laḳish we learn that this interdict is not Scriptural and therefore does not involve flagellation. For if it were Scriptural, then even when one kind exceeds the other, yet since each imparts its taste to the other, there is the forbidden taste in the full standard, and the offender would be culpable. (3) V. Glos. and Num. XV, 20. Only a dough of corn (which includes wheat but not rice) is subject to *ḥallah*. (4) Hence the status conferred by taste is Scriptural, since *ḥallah* is a Scriptural law.

b (1) As much as an olive of unleavened bread must be eaten on the first evening of Passover. This must be made of one of the five species of grain (wheat, barley, rye, oats and spelt), but not of rice. But if this dough counts as a wheat dough only by *Rabbinical* law, how can one fulfil his *Scriptural* obligation with it?

*רבי יהודה אומר אין דם מבטל דם *נתערב בדם פסולין °ישפך לאמה ב]בדם התמצית ישפך לאמה רבי אליעזר מכשיר ג]אם לא נמלך ונתן כשר: **גמ'** *א"ר חייא בר אבא א"ר יוחנן ד]ל"ש אלא שנפלו מים לתוך דם אבל נפל דם לתוך מים ראשון ראשון בטל אמר רב פפא ה]ולענין כיסוי אינו כן לפי שאין דחוי במצות: אמר ר"ל א] *הפיגול והנותר *והטמא שבללן זה בזה ואכלן פטור א"א שלא ירבה מין על חבירו ויבטלנו שמע מינה תלת ש"מ איסורין מבטלין זה את זה °וש"מ נותן טעם ברוב לאו דאורייתא וש"מ התראת ספק לא שמה התראה מתיב רבא *ו]עשה עיסה מן חיטין ומן ב] אורז אם יש בה טעם דגן חייבת בחלה ואע"ג דרובא אורז מדרבנן אי הכי אימא סיפא ג] ז]אדם יוצא בה ידי חובתו בפסח אלא

בדם פסולין. כגון ברובע ונרבע או בנשחט חוץ לזמנו או חוץ למקומו: ישפך לאמה. ואפילו הכשר רבה עליו וכן בדם התמצית ישפך לאמה ואע"פ שדם הנפש רבה עליו ומשום גזירה כדמפרש בגמ': ור"א מכשיר. טעמא מפרש בגמ': אם לא נמלך ונתן כשר. ד] אפילו לת"ק דאפילו לכתחלה אי לאו משום גזירה היה מכשיר: **גמ'** לא שנו. דאם יש בו מראית דם כשר ואע"ג דרובא מים אלא שנפלו מים לתוך דם: ולענין כיסוי. דתנן ביה נמי כה"ג ה] נתערב במים אם יש בו מראית דם חייב לכסות בפ' כיסוי הדם (חולין דף פז.): אינו כן. דאפילו נתן דם לתוך מים אם יש בו מראית דם חייב לכסות ולא אמרינן קמא קמא בטיל ליה: לפי שאין דחוי במצות. דאע"פ שנדחה טפה ראשונה ו] שנפל לתוך המים ולא היה מראיתה ניכר ז] אפ"ה כי הדר נפל טפה שניה חוזרת ראשונה וניעורה להצטרף עמה וכי נפל עד שהפכו מים למראה דם חוזר ונראה לכיסוי ולא אמרינן הואיל ונדחה ידחה דלא שייך דחוי אלא בדבר קדושה: שבללן זה בזה. כזית מזה וכזית מזה ח] ונתן לתוך פיו פטור ממלקות ואפילו התרו בו: אי אפשר שלא ירבה מין על חבירו כו'. כשהוא לועס אותה בפיו נבלל מין לתוך חבירו מיעוטו של זה ברובו של זה ובטל המיעוט ברוב והבטל בכל מין נוסף על המבטל ט] ונקרא בשמו ונגרע ממינו וא"א לכוין שלא יהא ממין האחד בטל בחבירו יותר ממה שבטל ממין חבירו בו ונמצא שאין באותו י] [מין] כשיעור דבצר ליה שיעוריה ולא ידעינן הי מינייהו בצר ליה וכי מתרינן ביה לא ידעינן משום מאי נתרי ביה וצריך להתרות בו משום האיסור הילכך כי מתרו ביה משום פיגול הויא התראת ספק דלמא יא] לא בדידיה תהוי חובא וכן בנותר ואע"ג דבמסקנא ודאי אחד מינייהו עבר בשעת התראה מיהא ספק הוא בכל אחד אם יעבור עליו אם לא והתראת ספק לאו התראה היא: שמע מינה איסורין מבטלין זה את זה. כי היכי דהיתר מבטל איסור ולא אמרינן איסורא לא מבטל איסורא: ושמע מינה נותן טעם ברוב לאו דאורייתא. הא דאמור רבנן בכל יב] דוכתי איסור הנו"ט בהיתר אוסרו ואע"פ שהיתר יג] ברוב לאו דאורייתא הוא ללקות עליו דאי דאורייתא כהי נמי דרבה מין על חבירו מ"מ טעמא יהיב ואיכא טעמא דשיעור שלם וקס"ד השתא דאפילו פיגול ונותר מב' מינים שטעמו של זה ניכר בזה נמי פטור לר"ל כגון האי בשר והאי שירי מנחה: ה"ג עשה עיסתו מן חטין ומן האורז כו'. ואדם יוצא בה ידי חובתו של עשה דקום אכול מצה בפסח ואי נותן טעם ברוב לאו דאורייתא היכי נפיק הא קי"ל (פסחים דף לה.) דאין יוצאין אלא במצה שהיא מחמשת המינין דכתיב לא תאכל עליו חמץ שבעת ימים תאכל עליו מצות (דברים טז) דברים הבאים לידי חימוץ אתה יוצא בהן ידי מצה יצאו אלו שאין באין לידי חימוץ אלא לידי סרחון:
אלא

רבי יהודה אומר אין דם מבטל דם. בהקומץ רבה (מנחות דף כג.) פי' בקונטרס דלרב חסדא דאזיל בתר מבטל הויא דלא כרבי חייא ולעיל פי' בריש פירקין דאפילו לר' חנינא דאזיל בתר בטל *דאיכא כמה משניות וברייתות דלא כר"א: **הפיגול** והנותר כזית מזה וכזית מזה שבללן ואכלן והתרו בו פטור ממלקות א"א שלא ירבה מין על חבירו כו'. כשהוא לועס אותן לתוך פיו נבלל מין לתוך חבירו מיעוטו של זה ברובו של זה ובטל המיעוט ברובו והבטל בכל מין טפל על המבטל והיה כמוהו ונקרא בשמו ונגרע ממינו וא"א לכוין שלא יהא ממין האחד בטל בחבירו יותר ממה שבטל ממין חבירו בו ונמצא שאין באותו יד] [מין] כשיעור דבצר ליה שיעוריה ואכן לא ידעינן הי מינייהו דבצר ליה וכי מתרינן ביה לא ידעינן משום מאי נתרי ביה וצריך להתרות משום האיסור הילכך כי מתרו ביה משום פיגול הויא התראת ספק דלמא לאו בדידיה הוי חיובא וכן בנותר ואע"ג דמסקנא אחד מינייהו עבר בשעת התראה מיהא ספק הוא בכל אחד אם יעבור עליו ואם לאו והתראת ספק לאו התראה היא ע"כ לשון הקונטרס וקשה דאם התרה בשלשתן פשיטא דלוקה אפילו למ"ד (מכות דף טז.) לאו שמה התראה היכן מצינו התראת ספק כה"ג דודאי עבר אלא דלא ידעינן אהי מהני תלת דפיגול ונותר וטמא ואי לא התרו אלא על האחד פשיטא דפטור אפילו למ"ד התראת ספק שמה התראה דאפילו לבסוף שמא אותו שהתרה בו כבר נתבטל דהיכי דמי התראת ספק כגון דלאחר גמר הדבר ודאי שעבר על מה שהתרה אלא דלא ידעינן בשעת התראה אם עובר עבירה בההיא שעתא אם לאו כגון הכה את זה וחזר והכה את זה (יבמות דף קא.) וכן גיד הנשה דלא ידעינן אי דימין אי דשמאל ועוד קשה היכי מיחייב כלל משום חד מינייהו דמיעוט הבטל ברוב לא מצטרף עם הרוב להשלימו לכשיעור דאפילו היתר לא מצטרף לאיסור כ"ש איסור לא מצטרף לאיסור וא"כ אפילו אם תימצא לומר דהתראת ספק שמה התראה הכא פטור דא"א שלא יתערב מכל אחד ואחד משהו בחבירו ובצר ליה שיעורא ועוד קשה אם נפרש פיגול ונותר וטמא שלשתן יחד למה לי למימר א"א שלא ירבה מין על חבירו הא ודאי יש כאן שנים המבטלין את השלישי ואכולהו ליפטר דכל אחד הוי בטל ומבטל ונ"ל לפרש דמיירי כגון דאיכא ב' זיתי פיגול וזית נותר יחד בחתיכה אחת ועוד יש ב' זיתי נותר וזית פיגול בחתיכה אחרת יחד ואכל אחת מן החתיכות והתרו בו אל תאכל פיגול שמא זו היא חתיכה שיש בה רוב נותר ואחרי כן לאחר כדי אכילת פרס או אפילו בתוך כדי אכילת פרס אכל חתיכה שניה והתרו בו אל תאכל פיגול כבראשונה שמא זו היא אותה שיש בה רוב נותר שאוכל באחרונה עתה הוי ממש כמו הכה זה וחזר והכה זה דלמ"ד לאו שמה התראה פטור. ברו"ך. נראה לפרש דבתרי מינייהו קאמר דשקל תרי מהני תלת ובללן זב"ז ואכלן וכגון דשקל ב' זיתים מחד איסורא וד' זיתים מב' איסורין ובללן בקערה אחת ואכלן וא"א שלא יהא רוב מן האחד ומבטל את חבירו הילכך לא ידעינן בהאי איסורא אם יש עליו שם פיגול או שם נותר דאיסורין מבטלין זה את זה טו] לפטור מטעם התראת ספק כגון דאכל בשתי פעמים בכדי אכילת פרס ובאכילה ראשונה התרו בו משום פיגול ובשניה משום נותר א"כ אפילו פחות מכדי אכילת פרס פטור כשאכל בשתי פעמים דכשהתרה בראשונה משום פיגול שמא נותר רבה ולא שפיר מתרי ביה ובשניה כשהתרה משום נותר שמא פיגול רבה ולא שפיר מתרי ביה ואי משום דכבר התרה בו משום פיגול מאכילה ראשונה ואמרינן בקדושין (דף עז.) דבעל חמש אלמנות חייב משום אלמנת ראובן ואלמנת שמעון ובחדא התראה מיירי דאי בשתי התראות אפילו באלמנה אחת נמי חייב דהתראות מחלקות אלמא כיון דעסיק בביאה ומתרה בו בתחילה הוה התראה לכל אחת ואחת וה"נ הרי עסוק כל שעה באכילה ותועיל לו התראה ראשונה לא דמי שאני הכא דנראה כחוזר בו מהתראה ראשונה כשחוזר ומתרה בו משום נותר וכאילו אמר לו לא על פיגול אתה שב אלא על נותר ואם תאמר והא תנן במעילה בפ' קדשי מזבח (דף יז:) הפיגול והנותר אינן מצטרפין זה עם זה מפני שהם ב' שמות ואמר בגמרא ל"ש אלא לטומאת ידים דמדרבנן אבל לענין אכילה מצטרפין דתניא ר"א אומר לא יאכל כי קדש הם כל שבקדש פסול בא הכתוב ליתן לא תעשה על אכילתו וי"ל דהתם בדלא מערב אבל הכא דמערב בטל דאיסורין מבטלין זה את זה א"כ הכא ללקות משום פיגול או נותר קאי אבל התם מיירי לעבור עליו משום כל שבקדש פסול ועוד התם נמי דאיסורא איכא מלקות ליכא לאו שבכללות כדאי' בפסחים (דף כד.): **מתיב** רבא עשה עיסה מן החטין. תימה דלא מקשה ליה °מכל התורה כולה דקי"ל טעם כעיקר: [בס"א מה"ד] **אלא** מין בשאינו מינו בטעמא כו'. תימה דבהקומץ רבה (מנחות דף כג:*) פריך מההיא דתבלה בקלא למ"ד בתר מבטל אזלינן מאי קא מדמי *ההיא דבתר בטל או בתר מבטל אזלינן שהטעם שוה טז] *ההיא דתבלה בקלא שאין הטעם שוה יז] כיון שיש בתבלין טעם מצה ראוי לצאת בו ידי חובתו כדאמרינן הכא אם יש בו טעם דגן חייב בחלה ואדם יוצא בה ידי חובתו בפסח ובכל התורה כולה קי"ל דטעם כעיקר ואין להקשות אהך דשמעתין מהא דאמר בערבי פסחים (פסחים דף קטו.) לא לכרוך איניש מצה ומרור בהדי[הדדי] דלמא אתי מרור דרבנן ומבטל מצה דאורייתא °דהתם תוזק המרירות הוא דמבטל טעם מצה אבל אורז לא מבטל טעם דגן ועוד דהתם כשאוכל כזית מצה דכי מבטל ליה מרור ליכא טעם כזית מצה אבל אם אוכל הרבה שרי:
ונשער

שיטה מקובצת
א] הפיגול והנותר כו'. פ"ה כזית מזה כו' עד שירי מנחה וא"ת [למה הוא פטור] (והא)[דהא] דאמרינן בעלמא טעם כעיקר לאו דאורייתא היינו דוקא כי נבלע בתוך ההיתר שאינו בעין אבל הכא שהוא בעין דאיירינן הכא בבשר קדשים ובשירי מנחה ואמאי כיון שהוא בעין ונותן טעם ויש בו כשיעור לחייב וי"ל כיון דנעשה פירורין ונבלל יחד חשוב כנבלע המיעוט ברוב וא"ת אפילו התראת ספק שמיה התראה יפטר שהרי אין שיעור באחד מהן כיון דאיסורין מבטלין זה את זה שהרי לא היה כי אם שני זיתים זית פיגול וזית נותר וכי נבלל מיעוט של פיגול בנותר חשיב אותו המיעוט כאילו הוא נשרף ונמצא דבציר שיעור כל אחד ואחד וא"כ על איזה מינייהו תוי מחייבת ליה וי"ל דלכך פי' הקונטרס דהבטל נתוסף על המבטל להיות כמוהו ולא חשיב המיעוט כנשרף אלא מיעוט הפיגול שנבלל בנותר חל עליו איסור נותר ומשלים בנותר מה שמחסר ממנו ונבלל בפיגול וכן להפך ולכך אצטריך לומר משום התראת ספק הוא דפטור וא"ת ואמאי פטור הא נחשב כאילו כל אחד שלם וכאילו לא נבלל כלל כיון שוה אחר משלימו ואין כאן התראת ספק וי"ל דודאי אי בשוה נחסר מכל אחד ואחד ונבלל בחבירו אה"נ דחשיבנו משלימו ממה נפשך אבל פי' דאי אפשר שיחסרו בשוה ושמא חסר הפיגול רביע זית ונבלל בנותר ומנותר נחסר חומש זית ונבלל בפיגול וא"כ או הנותר נשלם שיעור ויותר מעט וכנגד אותו יתור נחסר הפיגול משיעורו שהרי רביע שלו אין חומש שבא לו נותר יכול להשלימו וכן להיפך ולכך פטור מטעם התראת ספק וא"ת אכתי מאי איריא דפטור מטעם התראת ספק תיפוק ליה דאפילו אכל כל התערובות בבת אחת והתרו בו משום פיגול או נותר מ"מ שמא ליכא שיעורא מהאי איסור דמתרה בו ושמא הוא אותו שנתערב בו יותר ואין בו כשיעור ואפילו היה יודע מה הוא היה מיפטר וי"ל דמיירי שאכל שנים בבת אחת והתרו בו משום פיגול ומשום נותר בפעם אחת וא"כ ודאי איכא שיעורא מחד מינייהו ומ"מ מיפטר משום התראת ספק דבשעה שמתרה בו משום פיגול ונותר לא ידעו אם על אותו דבר זה הוא שיטת רש"י ולא נהירא חדא דלא מצינו שהאיסור המועט הנבלל ברוב איסור שיפקע שם איסורו מעליו ויחול עליו איסור אחר ועוד קשה אמאי פטור כיון שהזכירו שניהם נותר ופיגול בהתראתם והא לא דמי התראת ספק דהכא להתראת ספק דעלמא דבשלמא גבי ספק (מהן) אחד [איזה מהן] אביו והכה את זה וחזר והכה את זה פטור על כל התראה דשמא אין עובר בה אבל הכא דבשעה שהוא אוכל או מתרה בו על שניהם הא ודאי עובר בשעת התראה אחד מינייהו ויתחייב ממה נפשך על נותר או על פיגול לכך נראה דמיירי שהיה לפניו ב' זיתים מכל אחד ואחד ונבלל וחילקן ואכלן בשתי אכילות זו אחר זו ובשתי אכילות התרו משום איסור אחד על נותר או על פיגול והשתא הוי התראת ספק בכל אכילה שמא באותה אכילה אין בו כשיעור מאותו איסור דשמא מאותו מיעוט [מה] שמתרה בו [נבלל בחבירו] והשתא בכל אכילה מיפטר מטעם התראת ספק לפי שאין ידוע היכן הוא המיעוט והילכך כי מתרה בו באכילה ראשונה משום פיגול שמא בההיא אכילה הנותר רבה על הפיגול ומבטלה כמאן דליתיה וכן כי מתרה בשניה משום פיגול איכא למימר הכי ואע"ג דממה נפשך אחדא מינייהו עבר משום פיגול דאי ראשונה רוב נותר א"כ שניה רוב פיגול ואי שניה רוב נותר א"כ ראשונה רוב פיגול ומשתכח דודאי עבר משום פיגול כדפי' מ"מ כל התראה והתראה בשעתה הויא התראת ספק כדפי' ודמי לההיא דהכה את זה וחזר והכה את זה והשתא ניחא לפי' זה שהמועט מהבטל לגמרי והוי כמאן דליתיה וא"ת אכתי מאי איריא דמיפטר מטעם דמיעוט בטל ברוב תיפוק ליה דאין כאן שיעור ואפילו לא נתבטל מיפטר מטעם התראת ספק כיון דמתרה בו משום איסור אחד בשתי אכילות ואין ידוע באיזה אכילה אוכל כשיעור מאותו איסור שמתרה בו דכיון שאינו אוכל באכילה אחת כי אם שני זיתים משני האיסורים אם הרוב נותר א"כ ליכא כזית מפיגול וכן בשניה וא"כ אפילו אם המיעוט [לא] בטל הויא התראת ספק כדפי' וי"ל דמיירי כגון שאכל אכילה שניה בתוך כדי אכילת פרס (בראשונה) [מראשונה] וא"כ אם לא היה בטל ברוב היה המיעוט שמפיגול באכילה ראשונה מצטרף עם הפיגול שבאכילה (ראשונה) [שניה] ובכזית מפיגול בשתי אכילות היה מתחייב משום פיגול וא"כ אין כאן התראת ספק כיון שחיוב הפיגול התחיל מאכילה הראשונה הוא"ל ואינו בטל ברוב מפיגול היה מתרה בו אבל כי אמרינן דנתבטל המיעוט ברוב א"כ לא שייך שם צירוף ואין מתחיל שום חיוב כלל מהתראתו של פיגול באכילה ראשונה אם הנותר רוב ולהכי הוי התראת ספק כדפי' א"נ י"ל דמשכחת לה דאפילו רחוקים זה מזה יותר מכדי אכילת פרס מ"מ צריך לומר דנתבטל המיעוט ברוב דאם לא נתבטל א"כ יתחייב ממה נפשך באכילה ראשונה או בשניה לפי שיש לפרש דמיירי כגון שיש ג' זיתים מכל אחד ואחד ובלל יחד וחילקן לשתי אכילות דהשתא ממה נפשך יש שיעור מאותו איסור שמתרה בו לכל אכילה דגם במיעוט יש בו כזית כיון דאיכא ג' זיתים מכל אחד ואחד (ואין) [ואם] אין המיעוט בטל א"כ יתחייב עליו אבל השתא דנתבטל מיפטר מטעם התראת ספק ואין ידוע באיזה אכילה היה רוב האיסור שהתרו בו בשם אותו האיסור דהוי המיעוט כמאן דליתיה אך לא נהירא דאפילו בג' זיתים בכל אחד ואחד נמי איכא לספוקי אם באכילת ראשונה היה ב' זיתים וחצי זית מנותר ומפיגול חצי זית ובאכילה שניה ב' זיתים וחצי זית מפיגול וחצי זית נותר או איפכא וא"כ אפילו אין איסורין מבטלין זה את זה מ"מ הויא התראת ספק ע"כ נראה כמו שפי' שאכלו שנית בתוך כדי אכילת פרס לראשונה. מהר"ם: ב] ומן האורז אם: ג] סיפא ואדם יוצא: ד] ואפילו לת"ק: ה] כה"ג שנתערב במים: ו] ראשונה כשנפלה: ז] ניכר ונפטרה מן הכסוי אפ"ה: ח] מזה ונתנן לתוך: ט] המבטל תהיה כמוהו: י] באותו מין: יא] דלמא לאו בדידיה תהוי חיובא אלא באידך וכן: יב] דוכתא דאיסור הנותן: יג] שהיתר רוב אות ב' נמחק: יד] באותו מין כשיעור: טו] זה ופטור מטעם אות ל' נמחק: טז] ההיא דתיבלה: יז] שוה. דכיון שיש

מו א ב ו מיי' פ"ב מהל' פסה"מ הל' כב: [כס"מ איכא]
מז ד מיי' שם הל' כג:
מח ה מיי' פ"ה מהל' שחיטה הל' ו סמג עשין סד טוש"ע י"ד סימן כח סעיף יב:
מט ו מיי' פ"ו מהל' בכורים הל' יא טוש"ע י"ד סימן שכד סעי' ט:
נ ז מיי' פ"ו מהל' חמץ ומצה הל' ה טוש"ע א"ח סי' תנג סעיף ב:
[עי' תוספות יבמות קח. ד"ה הכה]

פסחים סה: [מנחות כג. חולין פז: לעיל לה. לו. לקמן עט. נדה עא:]
[חולין פז:]
[מלת והטמא ליתא בתוס' דהכא ד"ה הפיגול והנותר כזית וכו' וכ"מ מפרש"י דהכא גם בתוס' יבמות קח. ד"ה הכה וכו' וכן עוד בתוס' נדה מו: ד"ה ר"י ור"ל לא העתיקו אלא הפיגול והנותר אמנם ענין והטמא לא נזכר שמה וכן בירושלמי פ"א דחלה ליתא ועדיין בעי להתיישב בדבר הסג"ס]

נוסחאות
רש"י כת"י
לא שנו. דאם יש בו מראית דם כשר ואע"ג דרובא מים: אלא שנפלו מים לתוך דם. דקמא קמא בטל הלכך כל כמה דאיכא מראית דם לא בטיל ליה לדם: אבל נפל דם לתוך מים ראשון ראשון בטל. הדם ומשרבו המים אע"פ שיש לו מראית דם בטל דם:

גליון הש"ס
מתני' ישפך לאמה. עיין מנחות דף מח ע"א תוס' ד"ה חטאת: **גמ'** וש"מ נותן טעם ברוב לאו דאורייתא. ק"ל למ"ש תוספות חולין דף צח בשם הר"י דאורייתא דאף אם טעם כעיקר דאורייתא מ"מ לא לקי דהוי רק עשה וא"כ הכא דמיירי לענין מלקות שפיר אמרינן דבטל ולא נשאר רק עשה דטכ"ע: **תוס'** ד"ה מתיב וכו' מכה"ת כולה דקי"ל טעם כעיקר. ק"ל דמהיכן ה"מ להקשות ולהוכיח דטכ"ע דאורייתא דלמא באמת הוי רק דרבנן וכן ס"ל לרש"י באמת לזה פריך מהא דיוצא ידי חובת מצה מוכח דהוא דאורייתא: **תוס'** ד"ה אלא וכו' דהתם חוזק המרירות. עי' בתוס' פסחים שם ד"ה אבכך אתי מלה ומבטל למרור ועע"ק:

[ועתוס' שם ד"ה אלא במייתב קושיא ע] הכי"א נ"ק לסכיא נ"ק

עין משפט נר מצוה

נא א מיי' פ"ג מהל' מקואות הל' יט:

נב ב ג ד מיי' שם הל' יח:

פ"ה ט' נמי לא נבטל נ"ק

נ"א שלא הזכיר

נ"א רצונו

כמו שהמים נ"ק

גי' הל"ק ומביל הס"ד ואח"כ ד"ה הולכין כו' חציו יין כיון כו' כצ"ל

ונשער מין במינו כמין בשאינו מינו. פי' בקונטרס כיון דהיכא דקיימינן אטעמא כל כמה דיהיב טעמא לא בטל כי ליכא למיקם נמי אמאי מזלזלי באיסורא למיהדר לבטלן נימא רואין אילו היה מין ושאינו מינו *הא יש בו היכר טעמא השתא נמי לא בטיל ואת אמרת מין במינו בטל מן התורה טו] אע"ג דאילו היה אינו מינו היה נותן טעם טז]: הג"ה. ואע"פ *שהזכיר בקונטרס יז] זלזול איסור אינו *רוצה לפרש שמקשה מדרבנן דהא מתניתין דאורייתא היא וכולה שמעתין כן: **לא** רואין לדם כאילו הוא מים. כלומר הדם פסול דמין במינו בטיל ברובא *כגון שהמים פסולין לזריקה: ה"ג **דלי** שיש בו יין לבן וחלב והטבילו הולכין אחר הרוב. לא דמי להא דתנן (שבת דף קכ:) הדיו והחלב לחין אין חוצצין דהכא כיון דהאי דלי יש בו חלב עד רובו לא מתלחלי מיא ולא דמי לחלב דמנח אגבא דמנא או אגבא דגברא ונחית וטביל* הולכין אחר הרוב ואם לא היה חציו כיון שהטבילו ונתמלא ממי מקוה ורבו המים על היין טהור ואם תאמר והא אמרינן (שם דף עז.) כל חמרא דלא דרי על חד תלתא מיא לאו חמרא הוא וכ"ש הכא דאיכא חמרא טובא יח] לא בטל ממנו שם יין ולא מהני ליה השקה דחמרא מזיגא מיקרי כדאמרינן בפ"ק דמכות (דף ג.) וי"ל דהכא מיירי בחמרא מזיגא אי נמי בחמרא דרפי ואין יכול לקבל רוב מים שאין כל הייעות שוין כדאמרינן בפרק המוציא יין (שבת דף עז.) יין יט] השרון לאוד דרפי וכן יש לפרש בסוף הערל (יבמות דף פב:) דאמר נתן סאה ונטל סאה כשר עד רובו ופי' בקונטרס דמיירי במי פירות והשתא אי ביין מיירי אמאי כשר והלא יין גמור הוא לברך בורא פרי הגפן ולכל דבר וביין הוא טובל אלא מיירי בחמרא דרפי ומיהו איכא כ] למימר בשאר מי פירות בר מיין ובפ"ז דמס' מקואות תנינן לה וקאי אשאר משקין ומי פירות והציר והמורייס והתמד כא] א) משום דחמיץ: ב) **דלי** שהוא מלא רוקין גרסינן כאילו לא טבל. שהרוק עב הוא וחוצץ בפני המים ואינו בטל במים ומלא לאו דוקא אלא איידי דבעי למיתני כב] מלא מי רגלים דדוקא הוא לאשמועינן רבותא דלא בעי לבטוליהו דכיון שעברו מי המקוה על פיו ונשקו לאותן שבתוכו נעשו חבור להן וטהר דמי רגלים כג] מים הוא תנא נמי מלא רוקין רואין אותו כאילו הם מים כלומר אע"פ שמראיהן חלוק במקצת ממראה שאר מים אפ"ה כיון דמין מים הם לא בעי רובא לבטולי אלא רואין אותן כו' מלא מי חטאת הואיל והן אב הטומאה וחשיבי משום קדושתייהו לא בטלי אלא ברובא מאן שמעת ליה דאית ליה רואין ר' יהודה וקאמר דהיכא דשוה מראה הבטל למראה המבטל כגון מי חטאת שאין מראיהן חלוק דסגי למיבטל ברובא ולא אמר רואין אותן כאילו הן יין אדום להחמיר: *הא דרביה. הא דתנן לעיל רואין אותן כאילו הן יין אדום דרביה הוא דמחמיר בבטול כי היכי דמחמיר במין במינו כך פירש בקונטרס וקשה לפירושו חדא דמה ענין האי רואין דמי רגלים ליין וחלב דלעיל כד] שאינו מינו לא שייך בהו השקה אבל מי רגלים לדברי רש"י שהם מים גמורים וסלקא להו השקה אם כן מאי רואין שייך בהו וכי משום דנשתנו קצת לא יהא שם מים עליהם ולא תועיל להם השקה דלא דמו למי צבע שבטל מהם תורת מים בפרק קמא דמכות (דף ג:) ועוד בלאו סוגיא דלעיל תקשי ליה רישא לסיפא ועוד מאי קא משני הא דידיה הא דרביה אכתי הך דמי חטאת קשיא רישא לסיפא לסברת הש"ס דאמר דתנא כה] דהנך מי רגלים רואין כאילו הן מים סובר נמי ביין וחלב רואין כאילו הן יין אדום ועל זה פריך אמאי מכשרינן במי חטאת על ידי רוב מי מקוה דבמיעוט מי חטאת נמי הוה לן למימר רואין כאילו הן יין אדום ע"ז לא תירץ כלום דאכתי מי רגלים למי חטאת קשו אהדדי: הג"ה. ועוד אי ההיא דיין לבן וחלב הויא דרביה כי דיהה מראיהן אמאי כשר הא מין במינו לא בטל ומין במינו חשיב ליה כיון דשוין בחזותא ועוד דבההיא הוה ליה לאקשויי מהך ברייתא אמתניתין דקאמר רבי יהודה אין דם מבטל דם דמין במינו לא בטל והא בטלי מי חטאת במים ועוד דמי רגלים מיקרו אינו מינו לגבי מים כדאמרינן בסמוך גבי חרסן של זב: הג"ה ונראה דגרסינן מי רגלים רואין אותן כאילו הן יין וכי האי גוונא תניא בתוספתא דמסכת טהרות בפרק שמתחיל דם טמא מי רגלים שנתערבו ביין רואין אותן כאילו הן מים נתערבו במים רואין אותן כאילו הן יין ג) במים אם בטל מראיהן טהורים ואם לאו טמאים והאי ורמינהו דהכא אמתניתין קאי דקאמר רבי יהודה אין דם מבטל דם והכי פירושו דלי שהוא מלא מי רגלים רואין אותן כאילו הן יין ולא בטלי ברובא מלא מי חטאת עד שירבו המים על מי חטאת שיספוך רובו ולכשיתמלא טהור דלא מהניא להו השקה לטהרם כמו שפירש בקונטרס ואי נמי חומרא בעלמא משום דאין זריעה להקדש כדאמרי' בפרק כל שעה (פסחים דף לד:) וכ"ש למי חטאת דאפילו בגדי אוכלי תרומה מדרס לחטאת (חגיגה דף כ.) אבל היכא דרבו בטלי מהם תורת מי חטאת ונעשו מי מקוה מאן שמעת ליה דאית ליה רואין במין כו] שאינו מינו השוין בחזותא רבי יהודה דקתני בההיא דיין לבן רואין אותו כאילו הוא יין אדום והכי מי רגלים נמי הוי מין בשאינו מינו כדמוכח בסמוך גבי חרסן של זב כז] *וגבי שוין בחזותא וקתני דסגי להו ברובא במי חטאת אלמא דמין במינו בטל לרבי יהודה ומשני הא דידיה הא דרביה מתניתין דרביה דמין במינו לא בטל וברייתא דידיה ומברייתא דלעיל רואין אותן כאילו הן יין אדום אם דיהה מראהו כשר לא הוה מצי לאקשויי אמתניתין אלמא

א) נ"א משהחמיץ ב) עיין בספר פנים מאירות שהאריך בזה הדבור ג) גירסת הר"ש במס' טהרות פ"ד שמביא התוספתא נתערבו במי רגלים אחרים רואין אותן כאילו הן יין במים אם בטל כו' כצ"ל

אלא מין בשאינו מינו בטעמא מין במינו ברובא א] **ונשער מין במינו כמין בשאינו מינו** ג] **דתנן נתערב ביין רואין אותו כאילו הוא מים מאי לאו רואין אותו ליין כאילו הוא מים לא רואין אותו לדם כאילו הוא מים אי הכי בטל מיבעי ליה** ג] **ועוד תניא ר' יהודה אומר רואין אותו כאילו הוא יין אדום** ד] **אם דיהה מראהו כשר ואם לאו פסול תנאי היא דתניא *דלי שיש בו יין לבן או חלב והטבילו *הולכין אחר הרוב ר' יהודה אומר רואין אותו כאילו הוא יין אדום אם דיהה מראהו כשר ואם לאו פסול ורמינהי *דלי שהוא מלא רוקין והטבילו כאילו לא טבל מי רגלים רואין אותו כאילו הן מים מלא מי חטאת עד שירבו המים על מי חטאת** ה] **מאן שמעת ליה דאית ליה רואין רבי יהודה וקתני דסגי ליה ברובא אמר אביי לא קשיא הא**

אלא מין בשאינו מינו. שהטעם ניכר בו בטעמא מחייב ולקי מן התורה וכי אמר ריש לקיש בפיגול ונותר של מין ומינו דליכא למיקם אטעמא ולא תשמע מינה. נותן טעם ברוב לאו דאורייתא: ונשער מין במינו כמין בשאינו מינו. כיון דהיכא דקיימינן אטעמא כל כמה דיהיב טעמא לא בטיל כי ליכא למיקם נמי אמאי מזלזלינן באיסורי למיהדר ולבטלן ברוב נימא רואין אילו היה מין ושאינו מינו *הא יש בו היכר טעמא השתא נמי לא ניבטיל עד דרבה עליו כל כך כשיעור ביטול של מין ושאינו מינו: מאי לאו רואין לאותו יין כאילו מים הוא. ואם מראה דם היה ניכר בהן כשר אלמא אע"ג דמין במינו הוא לענין ביטולא ו] דחזותא לא אמרינן ליבטל ברוב אלא משערינן ליה כמין בשאינו מינו: לא רואין ז] אותו לדם כאילו הוא מים. ופסיל דבטיל ליה ברובא הואיל ובתר חזותא אזלינן והכא ליכא למיקם עליה דמילתא בטיל ברובא: *רבי יהודה אומר רואין אותו כאילו הוא יין אדום. לקמן מייתי לה לכולה משנה: דלי. טמא: שיש בו יין לבן או חלב. שאין מראיהן ניכר בתוך המים: והטבילו. וקאמר ר' יהודה הואיל ואילו יין אדום הוה כל זמן שאדמומית שלו ניכרת לא בטיל במים ואין טבילה עולה לכלי זה אלא אם כן שפך מהן עד שירבו ליכנס לתוכו ממי המקוה כדי להפקיע כל מראה היין הימנו השתא נמי כשהוא לבן רואין אותו כאילו היה אדום אם ח] ממועט כל כך שהמים הנכנסים לתוכו יש בהן שיעור להפקיע מראיו כשר כלומר עלתה לו טבילה ואם לאו פסול אלמא משערין מין במינו כמין בשאינו מינו ולהחמיר דלא ליבטל ברובא כל דהו: תנאי היא. דרבנן פליגי עליה דר' יהודה וכוותייהו קיימינן: והטבילו. ולא ספק מה שבתוכו הולכין אחר הרוב אם לא היה חציו יין כיון שהטבילו ונתמלא ממי המקוה ורבו המים על היין טהור: (כאילו הוא יין. אדום) ט]: דלי שהוא מלא רוקין גרסינן: כאילו לא טבל. שהרוק עב הוא וחוצץ בפני המים ואינו בטל במים ומלא לאו דוקא י] אלא איידי דבעי למיתני *מלא מי רגלים דדוקא הוא דאשמועינן רבותא דלא בעי לבטולינהו דכיון שעברו מי המקוה על פיו ונשקו לאותן שבתוכו נעשו חבור להם וטהר דמי רגלים מין מים הן תני נמי מלא רוקין: רואין יא] אותו כאילו הן מים. כלומר אף על פי שמראיהן חלוק מקצת ממראה שאר מים אפילו הכי כיון דמין מים הן לא בעי רובא לבטולי אלא רואין אותו כו': מלא מי חטאת. הואיל והן אב הטומאה וחשיבי משום קדושתייהו לא בטלין אלא *)ברובא: עד שירבו המים. אין טבילה עולה לכלי עד שישפוך מהם יותר מחציו של כלי כדי שירבו המים הנכנסין על מי חטאת: מאן שמעת ליה יב] [דאמר רואין אותו ר"י]. [דשמעת ליה] דאמר רואין אותו כאילו הוא שנוי ממראה שלו: יג] וקתני. היכא דשוה מראה הבטל למראה המבטל כגון מי חטאת שאין מראיהן חלוק דסגי ליה יד] למבטל ברובא ולא אמרינן רואין אותו כאילו הוא יין אדום להחמיר: הא

*) ברובא עד סד"ה נ"ק

מסורת הש"ס

פ"ה יש נ"ק

תוספתא דמקואות דף פשעו

מקואות פ"י מ"ו ע"ש בהר"ש

עיין חלופי גירסאות שמהפך הדבורים כי הם מסורסים ומהופכים עיין בנ"ק

נ"ק מ"ש

רש"י גורס בגמרא מלא מי רגלים נ"ק

שיטה מקובצת

א] עיין בהשמטות בסוף המסכת: ג] דתנן נתערב ביין רואין אותו כאילו הוא מים וא"ת מאי פריך ממתני' למין במינו דר"ל [מיירי במין במינו] ממש דנהי דמתני' במראיהן שוה מ"מ הוי מין בשאינו מינו והתם לא אמר ר"ל דבטל ברוב דלא איירי אלא במין במינו ממש ותירץ מורי דאסיפא סמיך והוי כמו וכו' ופריך מסיפא דקתני נתערב בדם בהמה דהוי מין במינו ממש ואפ"ה לא בטל ברוב א) ובשיטה תירץ דם דקדשים ודם חולין (מינו מינו) [הוי מין במינו] גמור: ג] ועוד תניא כו'. השתא ודאי קשה מאי פריך לר"ל מהכא הכא ודאי פריך ממין בשאינו מינו יין לבן במים ובהא מודה ר"ל וי"ל דה"פ דודאי לא פריך ליה מר' יהודה אלא מייתי מהכא דר"י קאמר במין (שאינו) [בשאינו] מינו רואין שלא להתבטל וא"כ מר"י נשמע לרבנן דמתני' דאמרו רואין אפילו במין במינו שלא להתבטל (דמזו) [דבזה] לא פליגי אלא במין במינו פליגי דלר"י אינו בטל כלל ולרבנן בטל [אלא] דאמרי רואין והשתא פריך שפיר והדרי קשיא ראשונה שלא תאמר רואין לדם כדמשני לעיל: ד] אדום במים אי דיהה תיבת אם ל"ש: ה] מאן שמעת ליה כו'. וא"ת והא הכא הוי מין במינו ממש מי חטאת במי מקוה אבל לעיל הוי מין בשאינו מינו יין לבן וחלב למקוה ר"ל כיון דמראיהן שוין חשיב לעיל נמי גבי מקוה מין במינו ומשני הא דידיה הא דרביה כלומר דרביה מחמיר במין במינו דלא בטל כלל ה"נ בברייתא דלעיל קאמר דלא סגי ברבייה ומיהו בטל ע"י רואין כיון דאין מין במינו ממש. כך שיטת הקונטרס: מאן שמעת ליה כו' לשיטת הקונטרס קשה טובא חדא דלפי סברת המקשה דמדמה התיא דלעיל יין לבן וחלב במקוה דהוי מין בשאינו מינו למי חטאת דהוי מין במינו ממש א"כ מאי איריא דפריך מהאי ברייתא דלעיל דיין לבן וחלב אהך ברייתא דמי חטאת תקשי ליה ממתני' דקאמר ר"י בהדיא דמין במינו לא בטיל כלל אהך דמי חטאת דקתני בטל ברוב או מההיא דיין לבן וחלב דאמר ר' יהודה רואין אלמא מין במינו בטל מיהא היכא דליכא מראה יין אם היה אדום ובמתני' קתני אין דם מבטל דם כלל ועוד קשה מאי קאמר מאן שמעת כו' היכי מוכח מההיא דמי (חטאת) [רגלים] רואין דאתיא כר"י הא ברואין כזה אפילו רבנן מודו שהרי רש"י פי' דמי רגלים הן כמים ומין מים נינהו ממש לענין השקה והא דלית להו רואין ה"מ ביין וחלב שאינו מינו ממש כמו מקוה כדלעיל בברייתא וא"כ היכי מוכח דר"י היא ועוד דקאמר הא דידיה דמיקל דמין במינו בטל ה"נ דמיקל במי חטאת דסגי ברביה ולא אמרינן רואין משמע דהא בהא תליא רבנן דמתני' יוכיחו דסברי מין במינו בטל ואפ"ה מחמרו ואמרו רואין במתני' דמין במינו ולא מיבטל ברובא לכן נראה כגירסת התוספתא דמי רגלים לאו מינא דמים נינהו ואע"ג דאתו ממים כבר נתעכלו בבני מעיים ופקע מינייהו שם מים ולפי זה מלא מי רגלים לאו דוקא אלא מיירי בחסר ורואין מי רגלים כאילו יין אדום ואם יש מי רגלים כל כך שאם היו יין היו משנין מראית המים טמא דלא מהניא להו השקה דלא מינא דמים נינהו ואם לאו טהור והשתא דייק ליה מאן שמעת ליה כי האי גבי מי רגלים דאית ליה רואין ר"י היא דאמר לעיל גבי יין וחלב רואין כאילו הוא יין אדום וקתני דסגי ברובא במי חטאת דהוי מין במינו ממש אלמא מין במינו בטל לר"י ובמתני' קאמר

שיטה מקובצת

אין דם מבטל דם אלמא מין במינו לא בטל אבל מברייתא דלעיל לא מצי פריך אהך ברייתא דמי חטאת דשאני מי חטאת במי מקוה דהוי מין במינו גמור וכן לא מצי פריך מברייתא דלעיל אמתני' דמשום חומרא דקדשים דחשיבי אין דם מבטל דם אבל ממי חטאת פריך שפיר דגם מי חטאת חשיבי והוי ליה למימר דלא ליבטיל והשתא ניחא דע"כ האי רואין לא הוי כרבנן דברייתא דלעיל דמי רגלים במקוה הוי כיין לבן וחלב במקוה דקאמרי רבנן לעיל דסגי ברובא והכא קאמר דלא סגי ברובא אלא רואין כאילו הוא יין אדום אם בטל מראיתו כדפי' וא"ת אכתי היכי מוכח דר"י הוא משום דקתני רואין דלמא רבנן דמתני' היא דאית להו נמי רואין וי"ל דא"כ מאי איריא מי רגלים דקתני בברייתא רואין לפי שהן במקוה מין בשאינו מינו אפילו מי חטאת במקוה דהוי מין במינו ממש אמרי רבנן רואין במתני' אלא ש"מ ר"י היא דאית ליה (דוקא) רואין [דוקא] במין בשאינו מינו וקשיא דר"י אדר"י דאילו במתניתין הוי מין במינו וקאמר רואין א"נ ה"ק מאן שמעת כו' גבי מקוה ר"י לעיל גבי יין לבן אבל רבנן שמעינן להו רואין גבי דם קדשים ולא גבי מקוה ומשני הא דרביה מתני' דקתני דמין במינו לא בטלי והשתא ניחא דהקושיות והתירוצים בפשיטות והשתא לפי המקשה והמתרץ הא דנקט לעיל מלא לאו דוקא לא גבי רוקין ולא גבי מי רגלים ולמאי דמשני רבא בדלי שתוכו טהור וגבו טמא אז נקט דוקא מלא ובשביל רוקין דאל"כ אלא שהיה חסר ונכנסין בו המים א"כ עלה לו טבילה כיון דהמים עברו על שפתו והכי קי"ל כרבא דאמר דר"י נמי אית ליה דרביה. לשון מהר"ם: ו] ביטולא משום דחזותא דדם ויין חדא הוא והוי כמין במינו והיה ראוי שיהא בטל ברוב: ז] רואין לאותו דם כאילו: ח] אם מועט כל כך שהמים שנכנסין לתוכו: ט] אדום גרסינן דלי: י] דוקא דכיון שהרוק עב חייץ אלא: יא] רואין אותן כאילו: יב] ליה דאית ליה רואין אותו (גרסינן) ר' יהודה היא דשמעינן ליה: יג] שלו וקאמר היכא והד"א ותיבת וקתני ל"ש ונמחק: יד] ליה לבטל אות מ' נמחק: טו] התורה ברובא אף ע"ג: טז] בשאינו מינו ותיבת הגה"ה נמחק: יז] בקונטרס לשון זלזול: יח] טובא דלא בטל: יט] יין השרוני לאוד: כ] איכא לאוקמי בשאר תיבת למימר ל"ש ונמחק: כא] והתמד משהחמיץ הס"ד: כב] למיתני ולא מי אות מ' נמחק: כג] רגלים מין מים: כד] דלעיל דההיא שאינו: כה] דהתנא דתני מי רגלים רואין אותו כאילו תיבת דהנך נמחק: כו] במין בשאינו מינו: כז] זב ושין תיבת וגבי נמחק:

א) נראה דחסר כאן וצ"ל ואפ"ה אכתי הוי מין בשאינו מינו דם קדשים נגד דם חולין ותירץ בביצה דם דקדשים וכו'.

[78b]—Rather, [when] one kind [is mixed] with a different kind, [its status is determined] by taste; [when] one kind [is mixed] with the same kind, [its status is determined] by the greater part.[2]

Yet, [where] one kind [is mixed] with its own kind, let us determine [its status] as though it were one kind with a different kind.[3] For we learnt: IF IT WAS MIXED WITH WINE, WE REGARD IT AS THOUGH IT WERE WATER. Does that not mean [that] we regard the wine as though it were water?[4]—No: [it means that] we regard the *blood* as though it were water.[5] If so, he should state, [The blood] is nullified? Moreover, it was taught, R. Judah said: We regard it as though it were red wine; if its appearance goes faint, it is valid; if not, it is invalid![6]—It is a controversy of Tannaim.[7] For it was taught: If one immerses a pail containing white wine or milk, we decide by the excess. R. Judah said: We regard it as though it were red wine: if its appearance goes faint, it is valid; if not, it is invalid.[8]

But the following contradicts this: If one immersed a pail full of
a saliva, it is as though he had not immersed it.[1] [If it was full of][2] urine, we regard it as though it were water.[3] If it was filled with water of lustration,[4] the water [of the *mikweh*] must exceed the water of lustration.[5] Now, whom do you know to hold [that] 'we regard'? R. Judah;[6] yet he teaches that an excess is sufficient?[7]

(2) Resh Laḳish referred to the latter case. Hence inference [ii] is incorrect. (3) Since an article cannot be nullified where its taste is distinguishable, even though it is the smaller part of the mixture, let us rule likewise even where its taste is not distinguishable because it is of the same kind. (4) And if it would then still look like blood, it is fit. Now, in respect to appearance wine and blood may be regarded as of the same kind: this shews that the lesser is not nullified by the greater, but we regard the mixture as of two *different* kinds. (5) And it is *unfit*, because it is nullified by the greater quantity of water. (6) The passage is quoted in full anon.—This proves definitely that we consider it as a mixture of two *different* kinds. (7) The Sages disagree with R. Judah, and Resh Laḳish accepts their view. (8) An unclean pail containing white wine or milk was immersed in a *mikweh* (ritual bath) for purification, and the water of the *mikweh* naturally filled it. The Sages maintain that if this exceeded the wine or milk (which is not readily distinguishable from the water), the latter is nullified, the whole is regarded as water, and the pail becomes clean. This is similar to the ruling of Resh Laḳish. But R. Judah maintains that we regard it as though it were *red* wine: if there is so little of it that the water of the *mikweh* would make it go faint and lose the appearance of wine, the immersion is valid, and the pail becomes clean; otherwise it is invalid, and the pail remains unclean.

a (1) The saliva is thick and interposes between the water of the *mikweh* and the pail. Hence the immersion is invalid, for there must not be any interposition. (2) The bracketed words are absent from cur. edd., but were apparently contained in Rashi's edition. (3) For it is in fact a kind of water, and immediately it makes contact with the water of the *mikweh*, it becomes part of the *mikweh* itself. For that reason it is not necessary for the water of the *mikweh* to exceed it. (4) Running water mixed with the ashes of the red heifer, used for lustration (v. Num. XIX). Although it cleansed the unclean person upon whom it was sprinkled, it defiled a *clean* person with its touch. (5) He must first pour out some of the water of lustration, so that when the pail is filled with the water of the *mikweh*, the latter exceeds what is left of the former. For although the latter too is water, owing to its sanctity and to its high degree of uncleanness it does not simply become part of the *mikweh*, but must be nullified by an excess. (6) Only he rules that you regard a thing as though it were something else. (7) If the *mikweh* water exceeds the water of lustration, the immersion is valid, and we do not regard the latter as though it were wine, as above.

—Said Abaye: There is no difficulty: [79a] The latter is his own view; the former is his teacher's.[8] For it was taught, R. Judah said on R. Gamaliel's authority: Blood cannot nullify [other] blood;[9] saliva cannot nullify saliva; and urine cannot nullify urine.[10]

Raba said: We are discussing a pail which is clean on the inside and unclean on the outside:[11] by law even a small quantity is sufficient,[12] and it was only the Rabbis who enacted a preventive
a measure,[1] lest one begrudge [the water] and not immerse it.[2] Since then we have an excess [of *miḳweh* water], nothing else is required.[3]

Raba said: The Rabbis have said that taste [is the determining factor]; and the Rabbis have said [that we decide] by the majority; and the Rabbis have said that [we go] by appearance. [When] one kind [is mixed] with a different kind, taste [is the determining factor]. [When] one kind [is mixed] with the same kind, the greater part [determines its status]; and where there is appearance,[4] [we go] by looks.

Now, [Resh Laḳish] disagrees with R. Eleazar. For R. Eleazar said: Just as precepts cannot nullify one another, so can interdicts not nullify one another.[5] Whom do you know to maintain that precepts cannot nullify one another?—It is Hillel. For it was taught: It was related of Hillel the Elder that he used to wrap them[6] together, for it is said, *they shall eat it with unleavened bread and bitter herbs.*[7]

(8) His own view is the lenient one.—The interpretation of this whole passage follows Rashi. Tosaf. urges many objections to this, and gives a different interpretation based on an emended text. (9) In respect to sprinkling; v. *supra* 35a. (10) The saliva and the urine of a *zab* (q.v. Glos.), which are unclean, cannot be nullified by those of a clean person, which are clean, even though the latter exceed the former. This is a stringent view, and the similar stringent view above is likewise his teacher's ruling, not his own. (11) E.g., the outside was defiled through unclean water. Such defilement is Rabbinical only, and leaves the inside clean. (12) Even if a little water enters the pail, it becomes clean, since the inside is clean in any case.—A little must enter, so that we can be sure that it has run over the edge, which is unclean.

a (1) I.e., they ruled that it must be properly immersed, with a considerable quantity of water inside. (2) If he is permitted to immerse the outside only, he may wish to save the water of lustration for further use and not allow even a trickle of *miḳweh* water to enter the pail. (3) Raba explains that R. Judah generally agrees with his teacher's stricter ruling, but that here there is a particular reason for his more lenient ruling. (4) Where taste is irrelevant, as e.g., in the case of a *miḳweh*, as above. (5) One forbidden thing cannot nullify another. Resh Laḳish ruled *supra* 78a that forbidden things do annul one another. (6) *Sc.* unleavened bread and bitter herbs and the paschal meat, the eating of which is obligatory on the first evening of Passover. (7) Num. IX, 11. Thus he does not hold that the taste of one nullifies the other.

Novellae of Hagaon Rabbi Moshe Feinstein o.b.m.

Zebahim

79a Tos. s.v. אמרו If you ask that perhaps he would take a large amount of each one, in which case they would not be nullified. . . . We can apparently solve this difficulty in the following manner: Hillel holds that, according to the Torah, one must eat the unleavened bread, the bitter herbs, and the paschal lamb wrapped together, since he derives this from a verse, and in the verse it is stated without qualification that one must eat them, implying that an olive-sized amount suffices for the unleavened bread, the bitter herbs, and the paschal lamb, and he discharges his duty thereby. We must perforce say that precepts do not nullify each other. Although, after the fact, one discharges his duty even by eating them one after the other, as is stated in the *baraitha* in *Pesahim* 115. from the onset the Torah requires that he eat them wrapped together. Accordingly, since he may eat an olive-sized amount of each one, we must perforce say that precepts do not nullify each other. This is apparently a clear solution to this difficulty. Why the Tosafists do not reply in this manner requires some deliberation.

נג א מיי' פ"ט מהל' מקוואות הל"ט :
נד ב ג מיי' פ"ט מהל' מאכלות אסורות הלכה א סמג לאוין קלט טוש"ע יו"ד סי' צח סעי' א :
נה ד מיי' פ"ו מהל' מקוואות הל"א :
נו ה מיי' פ"ח מהל' [illegible] הל"ב :
נז ו מיי' פ"ח מהל' [illegible] הלכה ו' טוש"ע א"ח סי' תעה סעי' א :

הא דידיה הא דרביה דתניא רבי יהודה אומר משום רבן גמליאל *אין דם מבטל דם אין רוק מבטל רוק ואין מי רגלים מבטלין מי רגלים רבא אמר א] °בדלי שתוכו טהור וגבו טמא עסקינן דמדינא סגי להו בכל דהו ורבנן הוא דגזרו בהו דילמא חיים עלייהו ולא *מבטיל ליה וכיון דאיכא ריבויא לא צריך *אמר רבא אמור רבנן בטעמא ואמור רבנן ברובא ואמור רבנן בחזותא °מין בשאינו מינו בטעמא ב] °מין במינו ברובא °היכא דאיכא חזותא במראה ופליגא דרבי אלעזר דאמר רבי אלעזר °כשם שאין מצות מבטלות זו את זו °כך אין איסורין מבטלין זו את זו מאן שמעת ליה דאמר אין מצות מבטלות זו את זו הלל היא *דתניא אמרו עליו על הלל ג] הזקן °שהיה כורכן בבת אחת ואוכלן משום שנאמר °על מצות ומרורים יאכלוהו

תנו

רש"י

הא דרביה. הא דתנן לעיל רואין אותו כאילו הוא יין אדום דרביה הוא דמחמיר בביטול כי היכי דמחמיר במין ד] ומיט ואמר לא בטיל כלל ומין בשאינו מינו נמי דאית ליה דבטל וקיימא ה] ליה כל זמן שמראה המועט ניכר ברוב לא בטיל מחמיר נמי ואמר דהיכא דמראיהן שוין כגון יין לבן במים דרואין אותו כאילו אדום ולא סגיא ליה ברובא : אין דם מבטל דם. אלא זריקה ואלא כיסוי : ואין רוק. הטהור מבטל רוק הזב : ואין מי רגלים. טהורים מבטלים מי רגלים של זב ו] *ומטמא ואע"פ שרבות הטהורות על הטמאות בכלי : רבא אמר. לעולם חד תנא היא וכרביה ס"ל ז] והא דקאמר ברובא סגי : בדלי שתוכו טהור וגבו טמא. כגון שנטמא גבו בטומאת משקין דרבנן דקי"ל (נדה דף ז:) תוכו אוגנו אזניו וידיו טהורין : דמדינא סגי ליה. בכניסת מים לתוכו כל דהו שתעלה טבילה לשפתו °דהא תוכו אין צריך טבילה : ורבנן הוא דגזור. שיטבלנו יפה דאי אמרת דסגי ליה בטבילת גבו דילמא חיים עלייהו על מי החטאת שלא יתערבו מי המקוה לתוכו ויפסלו ולא מטביל ליה לשפת הכלי לפיכך גזרו עליו להטבילו ולפוסלו וכיון דאיכא ריבוייא תו לא צריך דהא טבילת תוכו חומרא בעלמא הוא : והיכא דאיכא חזותא. מילי דלא תלי בטעמא אלא בחזותא כגון לענין טבילת מקוה בחזותא : ופליגא דרבי אלעזר. הא דריש לקיש דאמר איסורין מבטלין זה את זה : כשם שמצות אין מבטלות זו את זו. כדאמרן לקמן ח] : הלל כורך פסח מצה ומרור בבת אחת. ולא אתי טעם מרור ומבטל לי' לטעם מצה :

חרסן

תוספות

דמין במינו בטל לרבי יהודה דהתם מין בשאינו מינו הוא אע"ג דחשיבי ליה קצת מין במינו לומר דבטל ברוב אי לאו טעמא דרואין כמו מין במינו מ"מ מין במינו גמור לא הוי ומיהו לגירסא זו לא יתכן ליישב הא דנקט מלא רוקין כמו לפירוש הקונטרס דהוה מצי למימר דלי שיש בו רוקין וא"ת ואמאי דוחקיה לשנויי הא דידיה הא דרביה לימא דברייתא כרבנן דמתני' דאית להו רואין ומין במינו בטל ויש לומר דאי כרבנן דמתני' א"כ היה צריך כל כך מי המקוה שאם היו מי חטאת יין אדום הוה דיהה וברייתא קתני דסגיא ברובא וא"ת ולר' יהודה אמאי סגי ליה ברובא נימא רואין וי"ל דלא שמעינן לר' יהודה רואין אלא במין שאינו מינו כגון יין לבן וחלב אבל מין במינו גמור לא שמעינן ליה דאית ליה רואין וצריך לדקדק מ"ש גבי קדשים וטומאה ומקוה אמרינן רואין הכא ובמכות (דף ג:) וגבי איסורא לא אמרינן רואין אלא מין במינו מדאורייתא ברובא וגבי טומאה נמי איכא דוכתא דלא אמרינן רואין וגבי ליר בבכורות בפרק הלוקח בהמה (ד' כג:) ושיליא דלא מטמאה לא במגע ולא במשא ואמר רבי יוחנן* משום ביטול ברוב נגעי בה ואי אפשר לברר טעם אלא היכא דאיתמר איתמר היכא דלא איתמר לא איתמר ועוד צריך לדקדק דפעמים דאמר רואין מן המבטל כגון במתני' דם שנתערב בדם הבהמה נתערב ביין ופעמים מן הבטל גבי דלי ט] יין לבן וחלב פעמים דאמר רואין להחמיר כי ההיא דדלי ופעמים להקל כגון במתני' דמכשרי ליה לזריקה וי"ל י] דבשביל המיעוט שלא יתבטל רואין *המיעוט (או) הרוב בין להקל בין להחמיר :

ה"ג הא דידיה הא דרביה. בכוליה הש"ס דקים לן דר' יהודה ס"ל מין במינו לא בטל הייט מטום דסמכינן °אשיטיה דרבא : רבא אמר בדלי שתוכו טהור כו'. תימה אם כן מלא רוקין אמאי כאילו לא טבל ומלא מי רגלים אמאי רואין כאילו הוא יין ושמא לא קאי רבא אלא אמי חטאת : אמור רבנן בטעמא. ומדלא נקט בששים או במאה משמע דמדאורייתא איירי שהוא בטעמא וכן משמע לעיל דטעם כעיקר דאורייתא דאמר בחורז שיש בו טעם דגן דחייב בחלה ואדם יוצא בה ידי חובתו בפסח וקשה מכאן לפי' הקונטרס דפ' גיד הנשה (חולין דף צח:) גבי לא נצרכה אלא לטעם כעיקר דבקדשים אסור והכא שרי ופירש שם בקונטרס דלהא מילתא יא] *זהו למעוטי שאר קדשים אבל חולין שפיר גמירי מיניה דהא קים לן מאחרי רבים להטות דבטלי ברובא וילפינן מהכא להחמיר דלא ליבטל אלא במאה ולרבא לית ליה טעמא כעיקר בחולין כדמפרש ואזיל מדאורייתא ברובא בטל אלא מדרבנן והכי שמעינן ליה לר' יוחנן במסכת עבודה זרה (דף סו:) כל שטעמו ולא ממשו אין לוקין עליו והא דילפינן ליה בפסחים (דף מד.) מנזיר משרת ליתן טעם כעיקר סבירא להו לאמוראי בתראי דאסמכתא בעלמא הוא ולאו מילף הוא דהוי להו נזיר וגיעולי עובדי כוכבים שני כתובים הבאים כאחד אי נמי גיעולי עובדי כוכבים חידוש הוא כדאמרינן התם ומשרת להיתר מצטרף לאיסור כך פירש בקונטרס ואי אפשר לומר כן כדמוכח בשמעתין ומפרש ר"ת דמין בשאינו מינו מדאורייתא בטעמא דנפקא לן ממשרת ומין במינו ברובא והא דאמר אביי בפרק כל הבשר (חולין דף קח.) ש"מ טעמו ולא ממשו בעלמא דאורייתא דאי ס"ד דרבנן מבשר בחלב מ"ט לא גמרינן דחידוש הוא אי חידוש הוא אע"ג דליכא נותן טעם נמי אמר ליה רבא דרך בישול אסרה תורה פירוש ולעולם דרבנן התם דיחויא בעלמא הוא כלומר דמהכא לא תידוק ובפרק בתרא דע"ז (דף סו:) דא"ר יוחנן טעמו ולא ממשו אסור ואין לוקין עליו היינו במינו דמדאורייתא ברובא בטלי וטעמו וממשו דקאמר התם דלוקין כגון שהאיסור בעין ומכירו וכי קאמר טעמו ולא ממשו דאין לוקין יב] ה"ה דאפי' טעמו וממשו אם אין מכירו אלא נקט טעמו ולא ממשו לרבותא דאפ"ה אסור א"כ טעמו ולא ממשו נקט משום דפסיקא ליה בכל ענין יג] אפילו שלא במינו *הוי טעמו ולא ממשו ואסורין ועוד יש לפרש כולה שלא במינו והיכא דאיכא כזית בכדי אכילת פרס קרי ליה טעמו וממשו והיכא דליכא כזית בכדי אכילת פרס קרי ליה טעמו ולא ממשו וה"ר יוסף דאורליינ"ש היה מפרש דלכך לא נקי' אטעם כעיקר אפי' שלא במינו דרבי יוחנן סבר לה כר"ע דיליף יד] מגיעולי עובדי כוכבים וליכא אלא עשה דהעבירו באש (במדבר לא) דמצריך ליבון והגעלה ור"ת השיב לו דאית לן למימר טו] *אהדריה לאיסוריה כדאשכחן בפרק הלוקח עובר פרתו (בכורות דף טו:) דתנן הגוזז והעובד בהן טז] סופג את הארבעים אע"ג דלא נפקא לן אלא מדכתיב תזבח ולא גיזה אלא היינו טעמא משום דאהדריה לאיסוריה דלא תעבוד ולא תגוז ומיהו לא דמי כל כך להאי דהתם ניחא יז] *דהתם אמר קרא תזבח זביחה התרתי לך בקדשים שהוממו ולא גיזה והא דאמרינן בירושלמי דערלה פרק שני אמר רבי אבהו א"ר יוחנן כל נותני טעמים אין לוקין עליהן חוץ מנותן טעם דנזיר יש לפרש דבהיתר מצטרף לאיסור מיירי דבפרק אלו עוברין (פסחים דף מג:) יח] ובפרק ג' מינים (נזיר דף לה:) קאמר ר' אבהו א"ר יוחנן גופיה כל איסורין שבתורה אין היתר מצטרף לאיסור חוץ מאיסורי נזיר וקרי ליה בירושלמי נותן טעם כעין נזיר שסרה פתו ביין ומיהו סוגיא דירושלמי מוכחא דבנתינת טעם איירי וא"ת אי טעם כעיקר דאורייתא מאי פריך בפרק אלו עוברין (פסחים דף מד.) ובפרק ג' מינים (נזיר דף לז:) גבי שתי קופות אחת של חולין ואחת של תרומה ולפניהם שתי סאין כו' יט] ואי אמרת כזית בכדי אכילת פרס דאורייתא אמאי אמרינן שאני אומר כ] כי אמרינן נמי דכזית בכדי אכילת פרס לאו דאורייתא תיקשי ליה אמאי אמרינן שאני אומר כיון דטעם כעיקר דאורייתא וי"ל דהתם במינו וכן משמע בפרק הערל (יבמות דף פב.) דקאמר ריש לקיש והא שרבו חולין על התרומה ואי במינו ניחא אבל שלא במינו לא שייך רבייה ואם תאמר אם במינו כיון דרבו בטלו להו ברובא אף על גב דאיכא כזית בכדי אכילת פרס ויש לומר דמכל מקום כא] *בכדי אכילת פרס חמיר דלוקה עליו שלא במינו א"כ במינו יש לנו להחמיר דלית לן למימר שאני אומר כיון דלקי שלא במינו דלכל מילתא משוינן להו כי היכי דמצרכי ששים בין במינו בין שלא במינו ומיהו אכתי קשה דהא כב] סתמא דנזיר ופסחים אליבא דרבי יוחנן ורבי יוחנן מוקי לה בפרק הערל (ג"ז שם) אע"פ שלא רבו ואם כן כי נמי אמרת כזית בכדי אכילת פרס לאו דאורייתא תיקשי ליה אמאי אמרינן שאני אומר דכיון דלא רבו ספיקא דאורייתא הוא וי"ל דהמ"ל וליטעמיך וכה"ג איכא טובא *ועוד הארכתי בפרק גיד הנשה (חולין דף צט. ד"ה גני) דגרים ר"ת התם לא נצרכא אלא להיתר מצטרף לאיסור *מין במינו ברובא הייט דלא כתנא דמתניתין דאית ליה רואין אפילו דם בדם : אמרו עליו על הלל שהיה כורכן בבת אחת. בזמן הבית היה שפלשתן דאורייתא *ואם תאמר ומנלן דקסבר אין מצות מבטלות זו את זו דילמא היה לוקח הרבה מכל אחד ואחד דכי האי גוונא לא מבטל כדפרישית לעיל :

שלישי

מסורת הש"ס: פסחים סט: [וש"נ] | צ"ל מבטיל. יעב"ץ | חולין צט. ע"ש | פסחים קטו. | [שם בכורות] | ס"א המיעוט בהרוב

גליון הש"ס

גמ' כשם שאין מצות. עי' מנחות דף כב ע"ב תוס' ד"ה מכאן: רש"י ד"ה דמדינא כו' דהא תוכו א"צ טבילה. עי' חגיגה דף כב ע"ב תוס' ד"ה ואחורים: תוס' ד"ה הא וכו' אשיטיה דרבא. ועיין לעיל עג ע"א תוספות ד"ה ר"י כסבר:

שיטה מקובצת

א] בדלי שתוכו טהור כו'. וא"ת והיכי יכול להיות דגבו טמא ותוכו טהור וי"ל בטומאת משקין דרבנן דקיי"ל תוכו ואוגנו ואזניו וידיו טהורים ומדינא סגי ליה בכניסת המים כל דהו לתוכו שתעלה טבילה על שפתו דהא תוכו אין צריך טבילה ורבנן הוא דגזור שיטבילנו יפה דאי אמרת דסגי בטבילת גבו דילמא חיים עלייהו על מי חטאת שלא יתערבו מי המקוה לתוכו ויפסלו ולא מטביל ליה לשפת הכלי לפיכך גזרו עליו להטבילו ולפוסלו וכיון דאיכא רובו תו לא צריך דהא טבילת תוכו חומרא בעלמא הוא וא"ת א"כ גבי מי רגלים אמאי רואין אותו כאילו הוא יין [הא] התם לא שייך דילמא חיים עלייהו וי"ל דמילי מילי קתני תנבי מי גלגלים ורוקין מיירי שגם תוכו טמא והשתא צריך לומר הא דנקט מלא אגב מי חטאת נקט"ה ואת"ל מאי פסקא וי"ל דע"כ גבי מי חטאת איירי בתוכו טהור סדנתנו לתוכו מי חטאת ואע"ג דמי חטאת שנטמאו מטהרין מ"מ לכתחילה אין לטמאותם [illegible]

[illegible]

א] תנו רבנן *א חרסן של זב וזבה פעם ראשון ושני טמא שלישי טהור במה דברים אמורים שנתן לתוכו מים אבל לא נתן לתוכו מים אפילו עשירי טמא רבי אליעזר בן יעקב אומר ב שלישי אע"פ שלא נתן לתוכו מים טהור *מאן שמעת ליה דאמר מין במינו לא בטיל רבי יהודה ורמינהו *ג פשתן שטוואתו נדה מסיטו טהור ואם היה לח מסיטו טמא משום משקה פיה רבי יהודה אומר אף הרוטבו במים טמא משום משקה פיה ואפילו טובא אמר רב פפא שאני רוק דקריר: נתערב בדם ה פסולין ישפך לאמה: במאי קמיפלגי אמר רב זביד ב] בגוזרין גזירה במקדש קא מיפלגי דמר סבר גוזרין ומר סבר לא גוזרין ג] רב פפא אמר דכולי עלמא גוזרין והכא בדם התמצית מצוי לרבות על דם הנפש קא מיפלגי מר סבר שכיח ומר סבר לא שכיח בשלמא לרב פפא היינו דקתני נתערב בדם הפסולין ישפך לאמה (או) בדם התמצית ישפך לאמה אלא לרב זביד ליערבינהו וליתנינהו קשיא: **מתני'** ד דם ד] תמימים בדם בעלי מומין ישפך לאמה כוס בכוסות רבי אליעזר אומר אם קרב כוס אחד יקרבו כל הכוסות וחכמים אומרים ה אפילו קרבו כולן חוץ מאחד מהן ישפך לאמה הניתנין למטה שנתערבו בניתנין למעלה רבי אליעזר אומר יתן למעלה ורואה אני את התחתונים מלמעלן כאילו הם מים °ויחזור ויתן למטה וחכמים אומרים ו ישפך לאמה ז ואם לא נמלך ונתן כשר

הניתנין

רש"י

חרסן של זב וזבה. עביט של מי רגלים ונשבר וחרסיו בלעו ממי רגלים ה] הזבים והן מטמאין במשא שאע"פ שנבלעו טמאים כדתנן במסכת כלים (פ"ט מ"ה) ומייתי לה בגמרא דנדה* חרסן שבלעו משקין טמאין ונפלו לאויר תנור התנור טמא שסוף משקה לצאת בהיסק התנור: פעם ראשון ושני. כבסו ב' פעמים טמא שעדיין לא פלטו ממי רגלים שבו והן אחד ממעייני הזב: ג' טהור. משנתן לתוכו מים שלשה פעמים טהור שפלטו מי הרגלים הנבלעין בו: אבל לא נתן לתוכו מים. אלא מי רגלים של אדם טהור להוציא את של זב הנבלעים בו טמא דמין במינו לא בטל: ופרכינן מאן שמעת ליה דאמר מין במינו לא בטל רבי יהודה. ושמע מינה מאן ת"ק דרבי אליעזר בן יעקב ר' יהודה היא וקאמר דמשקין הנבלעין בחרס בתלתא זימני פלטי: ורמינהו פשתן שטוואתו נדה מסיטו טהור. שהרי יבש הרוק ומשיבש אינו מטמא כדאמר במסכת נדה* ו] מוכי ירוק כעין רקיקה: ואם היה לח ז] (היה) מסיטו טמא. שהרוק הלח מטמא במשא: ה"ג ר' יהודה אומר אף הרוטבו במים טמא משום משקה פיה. בתוספתא דמסכת טהרות אף המלחלחו במים לאחר שיבש חזר הרוק להיות לח מחמת המים וטמא משום משקה פיה: ואפי' טובא. אפי' כבסו פעמים הרבה קאמר טמא: שאני רוק דקריר. טריסטריט"ש בלע"ז נכנס בפשתן בחזקה וקשה לצאת אבל מי הרגלים לא בליעי בחרס כולי האי: בגוזרין גזירה במקדש פליגי. אם עושין סייג בקדשים להרחיק מן העבירה ולא חיישינן להפסד קדשים שלא יפסיד את אלו בשביל סייג לאחרים קמיפלגי: ת"ק סבר גוזרין. הילכך נתערב דם כשר בדם פסול או בדם התמצית ואף על פי שאין בפסול ולא בתמצית כדי לבטל את הכשר ישפך לאמה גזירה דילמא אתי לאכשורי נמי היכא דיש בדם הפסול או בדם התמצית כדי לבטל את הכשר והאי דלא גזרינן ח]הכא בנתערב בדם הבהמה או בדם החיה משום דחולין בעזרה לא שכיחי אבל פסולין שכיחי וכן תמצית שכיח דרבה על ט]הנפש ורבי אליעזר סבר אין גוזרין חסו חכמים שלא להפסיד קדשים מחמת גזירה הילכך עד שיהא מן הפסול כדי שאילו היו מים לא היה ניכר דם הכשר בו מכשרינן ליה לזריקה: ה"ג רב פפא אמר דכ"ע גוזרין והכא בדם התמצית מצוי כו': דכ"ע גוזרין. דלא חסו להפסד קדשים ובנתערב בדם הפסולין דמילתא דשכיחא הוא י] לא פליג רבי אליעזר אלא בנתערב יא] דם התמצית לחוד פליג ומשום דקא סבר דם התמצית של בהמה אינו מצוי להיות רבה על דם הנפש הילכך אמאי נגזור יב]הוה ליה כנתערב בדם חולין דלא גזרינן ביה מידי משום דלא שכיח. ות"ק סבר פעמים שהוא רבה על דם הנפש הילכך גזרינן ביה היכא דלא רבה אטו היכא דרבה ומיהו אם לא נמלך ונתן כשר דגזירה בעלמא הוא: בשלמא לרב פפא. דאמר לא פליג רבי אליעזר ברישא משום הכי לא עריב ותני להו יג]ישפך דבסיפא פליגי ורישא דברי הכל: אלא לרב זביד ליערבינהו וליתנינהו. נתערב בדם הפסולים או בדם התמצית ישפך לאמה קשיא: **מתני'** דם תמימים בדם בעלי מומין. מילתא דשכיחא היא וישפוך לאמה גזירה שמא יד][לא]ירבה עליו ויכשירוהו: נתערב כוס של דם בעלי מומין בכוסות של כשרין ואינו ניכר: דמים הניתנין למטה. מן החוט שנתערבו בדם חטאת שניתן למעלה: רבי אליעזר אומר יתן למעלה. מתנות חטאת ואף על פי שהתחתונים מעורבין בו הואיל ואינו *מתכוין טו]: התחתונים למעלה. רואה אני אותן כאילו הן מים ומפני שמלוה להקדים עליונים לתחתונים כדאמר בפרק כל התדיר (לקמן דף פט.) שיהו כל החטאות קודמות לעולות: יתן למעלה. תחילה ואח"כ למטה ונתינת מטה תעלה לו לשפיכת שירים של חטאת טז] ולהתחיל מתנות עולה: ישפך לאמה. דלית להו רואין ואין משנין בתחתונים בשביל להכשיר העליונים: ואם לא נמלך ונתן כשר. העליון דהא ניתן ממנו למעלה יז]:

הניתנין

תוספות

שלישי טהור. מכאן מייתי רבינו תם ראיה בפרק שני דמס' ע"ז (דף לג:) גבי כסי פעם ראשון ושני אסור שלישי מותר דמיירי בהדחה לאחר ששתה בו העובד כוכבים דומיא דהך דהכא ולא כמו שפירש רש"י דמיירי בשתה בו העובד כוכבים מתחלתו פעם ראשון ושני קודם ששתה בו ישראל כלל ודוקא כלי חרס הוא דבעי הדחה שלשה פעמים אבל כוסות של עץ או של כסף אפילו בחד זימנא סגי: רבי אליעזר בן יעקב אומר כו'. מכאן ראייה לר"ת דמין במינו בטיל יח] דקיי"ל משנת ר' אליעזר בן יעקב קב ונקי*: אף הרוטבו במים טמא. פירוש מלחלחו במים וא"ת כי לא רוטבו נמי הא תנן בפרק דם נדה (נדה דף נד:) ואם יכולין להשרות ולחזור לכמות שהיו מטמאין לחים ומטמאין יבשים ועוד מאי טעמייהו דרבנן וי"ל יט] *האי דקתני התם וכמה שרייתו בפושרין מעת לעת והכא בדלא הדר מעת לעת הילכך יבש טהור ומיהו נראה דרבי יהודה לאו איבש דרבנן קאי אלא אלא ולאשמועינן דאינו יוצא מטומאה ע"י שרייה אפי' במים טובא וכן משמע בתוספתא דקאמרי כ] רבנן אף זה משנתנו לתוך מים ורבו עליו טהור: במאי קמיפלגי אמר רב זביד בגוזרין גזירה במקדש קמיפלגי. ואם תאמר מאי קשיא ליה במאי קמיפלגי לימא דפליגי ברואה אני דר' אליעזר מכשיר לזרוק משום דאמרינן רואה אני דם הפסולים ודם התמצית כאילו הם מים ורבנן אסרי דלית להו רואה אני ואסור לזרוק דם פסולין למזבח וכי האי גוונא פליגי בסיפא גבי ניתנין למעלה שנתערבו בניתנין למטה והיינו טעמא נמי דמתן אחת במתן ארבע ויש לומר דלא משמע ליה דפליגי בהא מדלא פירש רבי אליעזר דמכשר משום דרואה אני כדמפרש בסיפא אלא ודאי הני רבנן דהכא אית להו רואה אני וטעמייהו משום גוזרין תדע מדאיצטריך למיתני הך בבא כלל והויא דדם בעלי מומין דהשתא בניתנין למעלה ולמטה ששניהם כשירים לא אמרינן רואה אני בדם פסולין מיבעיא ואי משום רבי אליעזר דאפילו בדם פסול אית ליה רואה אני הוה ליה לרבי אליעזר לפרושי בהדיא ועוד נראה כמו שפירש לעיל (דף עז: ד"ה בדם) גבי בדם הבהמה או בדם חיה דבחולין ובפסולין ובתמצית מודו כולי עלמא דשרי לשם מים ולא אסרי אלא במידי דהקרבה כגון ניתנין למעלה בניתנין למטה ומתן אחת במתן ארבע דכיון דשניהם דמים כשירין אין לנו להתיר לשנות בדם כשר לזורקו על המזבח אפילו לשם מים כדי להכשיר את העליונים אבל בחולין ופסולין לא כא] חיישי אי שרי לזורקן לשם מים עם הכשר כיון דיש בילה אם כן על כרחין טעמייהו משום גוזרין כב] אבל בחולין ובדם חיה דלא שכיחי בעזרה לא גזרי: הכי גרסינן דמר סבר גוזרין. אם נפרש דגזרינן היכא דאין בדם הפסולין כדי לבטל הכשר אטו היכא דיש בו כדי לבטל קשה דאם כן ניפלוג רבי יהודה בהא דאמר אין דם מבטל דם וכי האי גוונא פריך לקמן (דף פא:) גבי הניתנין בפנים שנתערבו בניתנין בחוץ וניפלוג נמי רבי אליעזר בהא אלא הכא גזרינן דילמא אתי לאכשורי דם הפסולין לזריקה בעינייהו וכן דם התמצית והך גזירה שייכא אפילו לרבי יהודה כג] וכן פירש בקונטרס לעיל על משנה זו והא דלא גזרינן בדם הבהמה ובדם החיה משום דבההוא לא אתי למיטעי לאכשורי בעיניה ומיהו לרב פפא דאמר בדם התמצית מצוי לרבות על דם הנפש קמיפלגי אי אפשר לומר כן דעל כרחין גזר היכא דלא רבה אטו היכא דרבה והך גזירה ודאי לא שייכא לר' יהודה כד] משום דמינו הוא: רב פפא אמר דכולי עלמא גוזרין. כן כתוב בספרים ור"ת מצא בספר ישן דכולי עלמא אין גוזרין ומפרש אין גוזרין דילמא אתי למיזרקיה בעיניה דבהא לא אתי למיטעי והא דאסרינן בפסולין גזרינן מיעוט אטו רוב ומודה בהא ר"ת משום דשכיחי ופי' זה משובש וסוגיא זו משובשת וגירסת הספרים עיקר: *) אמר לו ר"א הרי הוא עובר על בל תגרע. לא ס"ד דר' אליעזר שיקשה לו ר' יהושע מבל תוסיף משום כה] דרואה אני כאילו הוא מים ור' אליעזר שהשיבו לפי דבריו של רבי יהושע השיבו דלית ליה טעמא כו] רואה אני לשם מים: תנן התם במסכת פרה ללוחית שנפל לתוכו מים כל שהוא כו'. תומרא דמי חטאת הוא דמדאורייתא כז] בטל ברובא:

בשלמא

*) שייך לדף שלאחר זה

עין משפט נר מצוה

נח א ב מיי' פ"ב מהל' מטמאי משכב ומושב הלכה ח:

נט ג מיי' שם הל"ב:

ס ד ה מיי' פ"ו מהל' פסה"מ הל' כג:

סא ו מיי' שם הל"א:

סב ז מיי' שם הל"ב:

[וע' תוס' חולין נז. ד"ה אמר רבא]

ר"ח כא קתני התם כו' נ"ק

מסורת הש"ס

[דף סג:]

תוספתא דטהרות פ"ה

מנחות כב: כג: יבמות פב. חולין לח: נב: ק. *תוספתא דטהרות פ"ד

[דף ס.]

מתכוין התחתונים כו' לשלות יתן הס"ד נ"ק

גליון הש"ס

מתני' ויחזור ויתן למטה. עיין לעיל דף עו ע"ב תוד"ה ולר'

שיטה מקובצת

א] תנן התם חרסין ותיבות תנו רבנן נמחק: ב] בגוזרין כו' לר"א הדאי איצטריך טעמא דאין גוזרין דאי הוי גזור כרבנן א"כ הוי ליה למימר ישפך לאמה אע"ג דאית ליה רואין אבל הא קשיא לרבנן למה לי טעמא דגוזרין [הא] לית להו רואין מידי דהוי אניתנים למעלה שנתערבו בניתנים למטה דהתם לא שייך גזירה ואפ"ה אסרי רבנן משום דלית להו רואין וי"ל דדוקא גבי כשרין שנתערבו בכשר לא אמרינן רואין ואין לזרוק דם הכשר שלא במקום הראוי לו כיון שהוא כשר וקבע לו מקום לזריקתו אין לשנות מקומו כדי להכשיר השני אפי' ע"י רואין אבל הכא שנתערב בפסולים אפי' רבנן מודו דאמרי' רואין אי לא משום גוזרין מידו בדם חולין לא גזרינן כיון דלא שכיח בעזרה כמו דם פסולים ובסיפא דפסול בדיעבד גבי דם בעלי מומין היינו משום דכ"ע מודו משום דמאיסי ע"ל דדוקא בשניהם כשרים ומקמן חלוק חשיבות מצות זריקתן למטה מעכבתן מלומר רואין כאילו הן מים וכן גבי עולה באיברי חטאת חשיבות מצות אכילת דחטאת מעכבת מלומר רואין כאילו איברי חטאת הן עצים להקטירן אבל גבי דם פסולים שאין בהם מצוה לא באכילה ולא בזריקה הילכך אפי' לרבנן אמרי' רואין הילכך הוצרך הטעם לומר לרבנן משום גוזרין ושמא דזהו הטעם שלה לתירוץ ראשון וגבי בעלי מומין אע"ג דלית בהו [חשיבות] מצות מ"מ כיון דמאיסי לא שייך להתיר ע"י רואין: ג] רב פפא אמר כו' וא"ת התינח לרבנן דפסלי כי איכא רוב הפסול או רוב דם התמצית משום דסברי דם מבטל דם אבל לר"י דאמר אין דם מבטל דם א"כ אפי' יש רוב דם התמצית שמעורב בדם הנפש כשר כשזורק התערובת ומאי גוזרין איכא וכי נאמר דשיטה הזאת דלא כר"י וי"ל דתם לר"י גוזרין שמא יתן כולו מדם התמצית וא"ת א"כ אמאי קאמר דם התמצית מצוי לרבות על דם הנפש קמיפלגי והלא טעמא משום דגוזרין אטו כולו לר"י וי"ל דה"ק והכא בדם התמצית מצוי על דם הנפש קמיפלגי מר סבר מצוי וכיון שהוא מצוי יבא להכשיר ברוב דם התמצית כיון שמצוי לרבות ואם נכשיר ע"י רוב אתי להכשיר בעיניה דרובו ככולו ומ"ם לא הוי גזירה לגזירה דכולה גזירה חדא היא וכ... לפרש לעיל גבי גוזרין גזירה במקדש קמיפלגי לרבי יהודה: ד] תיבת תמימים נמחק: ה] תלים הזב והן: ו] נדה וכי ירוק אות ט' נמחק: ז] תיבת חיה נמחק: ח] גזרינן הכי בנתערב אות א' נמחק: ט] על דם הנפש סבר אין גוזרין דחשו חכמים: י] הוא ולא פליג: יא] בנתערב בדם התמצית: יב] דהוה ליה: יג] תיבת ישפך נמחק: יד] שמא ירבה: טו] מתכוין לתת תחתונים למעלה והר"א: טז] חטאת ולתחילת מתנות תיבת נמחק: יז] למעלה דסברי יש בילה ויחזור ויתן למטה הס"ד: יח] בטיל ברובא דאורייתא דקאמר הכא שלישי אע"פ שלא נתן לתוכו מים טהור וקיי"ל אות ד' נמחק: יט] וי"ל הא קתני התם: כ] דקאמרי ליד כא] לא חיישי' אי: כב] גוזרין גזירה במקדש אבל: כג] יהודה דאמר אין דם מבטל דם וכן: כד] יהודה ומר סבר אין גוזרין דמכשיר והא דלא פליג בסיפא בנתערב בדם בעלי מומין בהחיא מודה משום דמאיסי הס"ד דמינו הוא ל"ש ונמחק: כה] משום דס"ל לר"א דרואה כו' מים והא דלא השיב לו ר"א כן לפי שהשיבו ותיבות ור' אליעזר השיבו נמחק: כו] טעמא דרואה אני]: כז] דמדאורייתא מין במינו בטל:

תיבת

[79b] Our Rabbis taught: As to the shard of a *zab* and a *zabah*, the first and second time it is unclean, the third time it is clean. When is that? if one poured water into it; but if one did not pour water into it, it is unclean even the tenth time. R. Eliezer b. Jacob said: At the third time it is clean even if one did not pour water into it.[8] Now, whom do you know to maintain that one kind is not nullified by its own kind? R. Judah.[1] But the following contradicts it: If flax was spun by a *niddah*,[2] he who moves it is clean; but if it is damp, he who moves it is unclean, on account of the fluid of her mouth.[3] R. Judah said: One also who moistens it in water is unclean, on account of the fluid of her mouth,[4] even [if he washes it] many times![5]—Said R. Papa: Saliva is different, because it is incrusted.[6]

IF IT WAS MIXED WITH THE BLOOD OF UNFIT [ANIMALS], IT MUST BE POURED OUT INTO THE DUCT [etc.] Wherein do they differ?—Said R. Zebid: They differ as to whether a preventive measure is enacted in the Temple: one master holds that we enact a preventive measure, while the other master holds that we do not enact a preventive measure.[7] R. Papa said: All agree that we do enact a preventive measure, but here they disagree as to whether it is usual for the draining blood to exceed the life blood: one master holds that it is common, while the other master holds that it is not common.[1] As for R. Papa, it is well: for that reason he teaches, IF IT WAS MIXED WITH THE BLOOD OF UNFIT [ANIMALS], IT MUST BE POURED OUT INTO THE DUCT; WITH THE DRAINING BLOOD, IT MUST BE POURED OUT INTO THE DUCT.[2] But according to R. Zebid, let him [the Tanna] combine them and teach them together?[3]—That indeed is a difficulty.

MISHNAH. [IF] BLOOD OF WHOLE [UNBLEMISHED] ANIMALS [WAS MIXED] WITH BLOOD OF BLEMISHED ANIMALS, IT MUST BE POURED OUT INTO THE DUCT. [IF] A GOBLET [WAS MIXED UP] WITH OTHER GOBLETS,[4] R. ELIEZER SAID: IF HE [THE PRIEST] OFFERED [SPRINKLED] ONE GOBLET, ALL THE GOBLETS ARE OFFERED;[5] BUT THE SAGES MAINTAIN: EVEN IF THEY OFFERED ALL OF THEM SAVE ONE, IT MUST BE POURED OUT INTO THE DUCT. IF [BLOOD] THAT IS SPRINKLED BELOW WAS MIXED WITH BLOOD THAT IS SPRINKLED ABOVE, R. ELIEZER SAID: HE MUST SPRINKLE [IT] ABOVE, AND I REGARD THE LOWER [BLOOD] ABOVE[6] AS THOUGH IT WERE WATER, AND THEN HE SPRINKLES AGAIN BELOW. BUT THE SAGES MAINTAIN: IT MUST BE POURED OUT INTO THE DUCT.[1] YET IF [THE PRIEST] DID NOT ASK BUT SPRINKLED [IT], IT IS

(8) The reference is to an earthen bed-chamber used by a *zab* or *zabah*, which was broken. The shard thereof, having absorbed their urine, contaminates through carriage, i.e., it defiles anyone who carries it even without actually touching it. Now, if one washed it (the pot) once or twice, it still remains unclean, because that does not suffice to expel the urine; but when one washes it a third time, the urine is held to have been washed out, and so it is clean. That however is only when the pot was washed by pouring water into it each time; if, however, not water but the urine of a clean person (which is ritually clean) was poured into it, this does not render it clean, because they are both of the same kind, viz., urine, and one kind cannot nullify the same kind. R. Eliezer b. Jacob holds that it does nullify, and therefore if it was washed three times, even by pouring the urine of a clean person into it, it is clean.

a (1) Hence he must be the author of the first ruling in opposition to R. Eliezer b. Jacob. (2) V. Glos. (3) When flax is spun it is moistened with the moisture or saliva of one's mouth. Now, the saliva of a *niddah* defiles any person who moves it, e.g., when it is on an article, even if he does not touch it; but only as long as it is moist. This explains the passage. (4) As this re-moistens the saliva. (5) For the water does not wash it out. This contradicts his statement *supra* that three washings suffice. (6) It becomes hardened in the flax and is difficult to remove. (7) The first Tanna holds that a preventive measure is enacted in the Temple, though it may cause the loss of sacred flesh. Therefore, when the blood of a fit sacrifice is mixed with that of an unfit sacrifice or with the draining blood, although the latter may be insufficient to nullify the former, it must be poured out (and hence the sacrifice to which it belonged is declared unfit), as a preventive measure, lest one declare it fit even where the latter is sufficient to nullify the former. (Nevertheless, a preventive measure is not enacted where it is mixed with the blood of an animal or beast that is *hullin*, because *hullin* in the Temple court is rare.) R. Eliezer holds that we do not enact a preventive measure, for such would cause the unnecessary loss of sacred flesh. Therefore the mixture is fit for sprinkling unless the unfit blood is so much that if it were water, the fit blood would lose its appearance of blood.

b (1) When it is mixed with the blood of an unfit animal (which may happen quite frequently), all, even R. Eliezer, agree that we enact a preventive measure, and the rule of the first part of the Mishnah applies. They disagree only where it is mixed with the draining blood: here R. Eliezer holds that a preventive measure is not enacted, since it is rare for the draining blood to exceed the life blood. (2) These are taught as separate clauses because R. Eliezer agrees with one and disagrees with the other. (3) As one clause: if it was mixed up with the blood of unfit animals or with the draining blood, it must etc.—Only one clause is necessary, since R. Eliezer disagrees with both. (4) The former containing blood of blemished animals, the latter blood of whole animals. (5) We assume that the first offered was that of the blemished animal, so that the rest are fit. (6) I.e., the blood which should be sprinkled below but was sprinkled above.

c (1) They reject the view that we can regard the lower blood as water, and hold that you cannot deviate in the rites of same (by sprinkling it above) in order to sprinkle the upper blood.

FIT. [80a] [IF BLOOD] WHICH REQUIRES ONE APPLICATION [WAS MIXED] WITH BLOOD [ALSO] REQUIRING ONE APPLICATION,[2] IT [THE MIXTURE] SHOULD BE PRESENTED WITH ONE APPLICATION. [IF BLOOD] WHICH REQUIRES FOUR APPLICATIONS [WAS MIXED] WITH BLOOD REQUIRING FOUR APPLICATIONS,[3] THEY MUST BE PRESENTED WITH FOUR APPLICATIONS. [BLOOD] WHICH REQUIRES FOUR APPLICATIONS WITH THAT WHICH REQUIRES ONE APPLICATION, R. ELIEZER SAID: IT [THE MIXTURE] MUST BE PRESENTED WITH FOUR APPLICATIONS.[4] R. JOSHUA MAINTAINED: IT MUST BE PRESENTED WITH ONE APPLICATION.[5] SAID R. ELIEZER TO HIM: BUT LO, HE TRANSGRESSES THE [INJUNCTION] NOT TO DIMINISH [FROM GOD'S COMMANDMENT]! LO, HE TRANSGRESSES THE INJUNCTION NOT TO ADD [THERETO], R. JOSHUA COUNTERED.[6] THE INJUNCTION NOT TO ADD APPLIES ONLY WHERE IT IS BY ITSELF, REPLIED R. ELIEZER. THE INJUNCTION NOT TO DIMINISH APPLIES ONLY WHERE IT IS BY ITSELF, R. JOSHUA ANSWERED. MOREOVER, SAID R. JOSHUA, WHEN YOU MAKE [FOUR] APPLICATIONS YOU TRANSGRESS THE INJUNCTION NOT TO ADD, AND COMMIT A POSITIVE ACTION WITH YOUR OWN HANDS; WHEREAS WHEN YOU DO NOT MAKE [FOUR] APPLICATIONS YOU TRANSGRESS THE INJUNCTION NOT TO DIMINISH, BUT DO NOT COMMIT A POSITIVE ACTION WITH YOUR OWN HANDS.

GEMARA. R. Eleazar said: R. Eliezer declared them fit only in
a twos, but not singly.[1] R. Dimi raised an objection: BUT THE SAGES MAINTAIN: EVEN IF THEY OFFERED ALL OF THEM SAVE ONE, IT MUST BE POURED OUT INTO THE DUCT.[2] Said R. Jacob to R. Jeremiah b. Taḥlifa: I will explain it to you: What does ONE mean? One pair.

Now, both are necessary.[3] For if it were stated in the former case, I would argue that only there does R. Eliezer rule thus, because his atonement was already made therewith,[4] but in the present instance he agrees with the Rabbis. While if it were stated in the present case, I would argue that only here do the Rabbis rule thus, but in the former instance they agree with R. Eliezer. Hence both are necessary.

We learnt elsewhere: In the case of a flask[5] into which a little water fell,[6] R. Eliezer said: He [the priest] makes two sprinklings;[7] but the Sages disqualify [it]. As for the Rabbis, it is well: They hold that we assume even distribution,[8] and sprinkling requires a [minimum] standard, and sprinklings do not combine.[9] But what does R. Eliezer hold? If he holds that there is no even distribution, what if he does sprinkle twice; perhaps he sprinkles [ordinary] water both times?—Rather, he holds that there is even distribution. Now, if he holds that sprinkling does not require a [minimum] standard, why must he sprinkle *twice?*—Rather, he holds that sprinkling does require a [minimum] standard. And if he holds that sprinklings do not combine, what if he does sprinkle twice? And even if sprinklings do combine, who can say that the standard is made up?—Said Resh Laḳish: In truth he holds that there is even distribution, and sprinkling does require a [minimum] standard; but the case we discuss here is where one [standard
b quantity] was mixed up with another.[1] Raba said: In truth there is even distribution, and sprinkling does not require a standard; but the Rabbis penalised [him] so that he should not benefit thereby.[2] R. Ashi said: There is no even distribution, [therefore] he must sprinkle twice.[3]

An objection is raised: Rabbi said: According to R. Eliezer,[4] the sprinkling of any quantity purifies, sprinkling does not require a standard, sprinkling [is permissible if] half [the water] is fit and

(2) E.g., the blood of a firstling with that of tithe. (3) E.g., the blood of a burnt-offering with that of a peace- or a guilt-offering. (4) And I regard the superfluous three applications in respect of e.g. the firstling as though they were water. (5) Because one must not make more applications than are necessary. On the other hand, even where four are required one suffices (*supra* 36b). (6) V. Deut. IV, 2.

a (1) V. *supra* 74a. Here too, the blood of *two* goblets must be presented each time together. (2) V. *supra* 77b n. b 1. (3) The controversy of R. Eliezer and the Rabbis is taught here and *supra* 77b, q.v. in reference to limbs. (4) The limbs were mixed up *after* the blood was sprinkled. Thus atonement (*sc.* sprinkling) was already made, and therefore R. Eliezer is lenient. (5) Containing water sanctified for lustration; v. Num. XIX, 17 *seq*. (6) Ordinary, unsanctified water. (7) On an unclean person, whereby he becomes clean. (8) Lit., 'there is thorough mixture'—we assume that a mixture is evenly distributed. (9) The unsanctified water is regarded as evenly distributed in the sanctified. Therefore when he sprinkles, it lacks the minimum standard, since part of it is unfit. He cannot remedy this by sprinkling again, for sprinklings do not combine. (It is assumed that one sprinkling could not contain more than the minimum quantity required.)

b (1) Both the unfit and the fit water each contained the minimum standard. Hence when he sprinkles the whole in two applications, he must sprinkle the required amount; v. Parah IX, 1. (2) The Rabbis ordered two sprinklings instead of one so that we should not benefit by the addition of unfit water to be able to use this for more unclean persons than would otherwise have been possible. (3) Sprinkling does not require a minimum standard. Now, in one sprinkling only *all* the water may be the unfit, since there is no even distribution. But in two this is impossible, for only a small quantity fell into it in the first place. (4) That two sprinklings purify.

*הניתנין במתנה אחת שנתערבו בניתנין במתנה אחת ינתנו במתנה אחת א] (מהן) מתן ארבע במתן ארבע ינתנו במתן ארבע מתן ארבע במתנה אחת ר"א ב] אומר ינתנו במתן ארבע ר' יהושע אומר ינתנו בבמתנה אחת אמר לו רבי אליעזר הרי הוא עובר על בל תגרע אמר ג] ליה רבי יהושע הרי הוא עובר על בל תוסיף א"ל רבי אליעזר לא נאמר בל תוסיף אלא כשהוא בעצמו א"ל ר' יהושע לא נאמר בל תגרע אלא כשהוא בעצמו ועוד א"ר יהושע כשנתת עברת על בל תוסיף ועשית מעשה בידך כשלא נתת עברת על בל תגרע ולא עשית מעשה בידך:

גמ' *א"ר אלעזר לא הכשיר ר"א אלא שנים שנים אבל אחד אחד לא מתיב רב דימי וחכמים אומרים אפילו קרבו כולן חוץ מאחד מהן ישפך לאמה אמר ליה רבי יעקב לרבי ירמיה בר תחליפא *אסברא לך מאי אחד זוג אחד וצריכא דאי איתמר בהא בהא קא"ר אליעזר משום דאיתעביד ביה כפרתו אבל בהא אימא מודי להו לרבנן ואי איתמר בהא בהא קאמרי רבנן אבל בהא אימא מודו לרבי אליעזר צריכא תנן התם *צלוחית שנפלו לתוכה מים כל ד] שהו ר"א אומר יזה שתי הזאות וחכמים פוסלין בשלמא ה] רבנן סברי יש בילה *והזאה צריכה שיעור ואין מצטרפין להזאות אלא רבי אליעזר מאי קסבר אי קסבר *אין בילה כי מזה שתי הזאות מאי הוי דילמא תרוייהו מיא קא מזי אלא קא סבר יש בילה ו] אי קסבר *אין הזאה צריכה שיעור למה לי שתי הזאות אלא קסבר הזאה צריכה שיעור ואי קסבר אין מצטרפין להזאות כי מזה שתי הזאות מאי הוי ואי נמי מצטרפין להזאות מי יימר דמלא ליה שיעורא אמר ריש לקיש לעולם יש בילה והזאה צריכה שיעור והכא במאי עסקינן כגון שנתערבו אחת באחת *רבא אמר לעולם יש בילה והזאה אין צריכה שיעור וקנסא ז] דקנסו רבנן כי היכי דלא משתרש ליה רב אשי אמר אין בילה יזה שתי הזאות מיתיבי *רבי אומר לדברי ר"א הזאה כל שהוא מטהרת הזאה אין צריכה שיעור ח] הזאה מחצה כשר ומחצה פסול

רש"י

הניתנין במתנה אחת. כגון דם בכור בבטל בין בכוסות: ינתנו במתנה אחת. קא סלקא ט] דעתך השתא דאמרינן יש בילה וסמכינן עליה שיש במתנה זו משניהם ואם בכוסות יתן מתנה מזה ומתנה מזה: מתן ארבע במתן ארבע. כמו דם עולה בדם שלמים או בדם אשם ששניהם טעונין שתי מתנות שהן ארבע ושניהם תחתונים: מתן ארבע במתן אחת. כגון דם עולה בבכור י] שהן תחתונים: ר' אליעזר אומר ינתנו במתן ארבע. ורואה יא] המתנות היתירות הניתנות מדם הבכור כאילו הן מים ואין זה בל תוסיף: במתנה אחת. משום בל תוסיף וידי עולה יצא דכל הניתנין על מזבח החיצון שנתנן במתנה אחת כיפר: ולא עשית מעשה בידך. ואינו דומה עושה מעשה ליושב ואינו עושה ואיסור בא מאליו: **גמ'** וצריכא. לפלוגי בתרוייהו ר' אליעזר ורבנן בבעלי מומין איברים באיברים וכוסות בכוסות: דאי אשמעינן באיברים. בההיא קאמר ר' אליעזר יקריבו משום דאיתעביד כפרתו בהכשר: אבל גבי כוסות בכוסות יב]. דעיקר בקלקול אימא לא: צלוחית. של מי חטאת המוקדשין שנפל לתוכה מים דעלמא כל שהוא: ר' אליעזר אומר יזה שתי הזאות. הבא להזות מהן על הטמא יזה שתים וטהר: בשלמא רבנן סברי יש בילה. כדתנן במתניתין אם לא נמלך ונתן כשר אלמא סמכינן אבילה *ואמר לא המתערב בלא מתערב בכולו ואין לך טיפה מזה שלא יג] [יהא] בה מחבירו קלא והכא נמי כהי דיש בילה ויש בכל הזאה מן המים *הכשירים: קסברי הזאה צריכה שיעור. ואין כאן שיעור שהרי יש בה מן הפוסלת ואי משום דמזה שתי הזאות קא סברי אין יד] מצטרפין אותו למלאות השניה שיעור החסר בראשונה: אלא ר' אליעזר. דבחדא לא סגיא ליה ובתרתי מכשר: מאי קסבר אי קסבר אין בילה. אין סומכין על כך דזימנין דלא מיבליל בכוליה כי מזה שתי הזאות כו': אלא קסבר יש בילה. אי איפשר שלא טו] יבלול וסמכינן: מי יימר דמלא ליה שיעורא. שמא רוב שתיהן מן השאובין טז] ואין בשתיהן כדי הזאה כשירה: אמר ריש לקיש לעולם קסבר יש בילה. כדשמעינן ליה במתניתין והאי דבעי תרתי משום דהזאה צריכה שיעור יז] ומצטרף להזאות ודקשיא מי יימר דמלא שיעורא: הכא במאי עסקינן כגון שנתערבו אחת באחת. שיעור הזאה מזו ושיעור הזאה מזו ונתערבו הילכך כי מזה שתי הזאות על כרחך מלי ליה שיעורא שהרי לא היו מן הפסולין כאן אלא כדי הזאה אחת והוא הזה שתים ואחת באחת לאו דוקא נקט דאם היו מן הכשירים הרבה כל שכן דכשר כי מזה

תוספות

בשלמא רבנן קסברי יש בילה. פי' אפילו סבירא להו יש בילה מ"מ פסולין דהזאה צריכה שיעור ואין מצטרפין להזאות וה"נ ה"מ למימר אין בילה ואין הזאה צריכה שיעור וכגון שנפלו מים בצלוחית כשיעור מי חטאת ובקונטרס פירש דרבנן סברי יש בילה כדתנן מתני' אם נמלך ונתן כשר אלמא סמכינן אבילה ואמרינן לא המתערב בלא מתערב בכולן ואין לך טיפה מזה שלא יהא [בה] מחבירו קלא וקשה אם כן מאי מספקא ליה לרבי אליעזר לדידי' נמי נידוק ממתניתין דיש בילה דהא מכשר לכתחילה אלא על כרחין ממתניתין ליכא למידק דדילמא כז] בעליונים רובא מכשר רבי אליעזר וכגון שנתן למעלה כשיעור תחתונים ועוד כדמוקי' לקמן לרבנן נמי אם לא נמלך ונתן כשר היינו דמים העליונים מיהו לקמן מוכיח יש בילה מדקתני *והתחתונים עלו לו:

אמר ריש לקיש לעולם קסבר יש בילה והזאה צריכה שיעור ומצטרפין להזאות. פי' בקונט' יש בילה גרסינן כח] בריש לקיש דכיון דאמר הזאה צריכה שיעור מאי דוחקיה למימר דלרבי אליעזר אין בילה לאקשויי מתניתין ולאוקמי מתניתין בשינויי דחיקי כדלקמן ועוד יש לדקדק אי אין בילה למה ליה למימר צריכה שיעור אפי' אין צריכה שיעור נמי:

כגון שנתערב אחת באחת. הקשה ה"ר חיים דביומא (דף יד.) ובנדה [פ"א] (דף ט.) *אמר אפי' למ"ד אין הזאה צריכה שיעור ה"מ אגבא דגברא אבל במנא צריכה שיעור וא"כ כשנתן אחת באחת והזה הזאה ראשונה ליכא בשניה שיעור במנא כט] ותירץ כיון דבתחילת הזאה ראשונה שהיא תחילת טהרתו איכא שיעורא במנא אין בכך כלום שהזאה ראשונה מצטרפת להזאה שניה וכי האי גוונא אמרינן גבי נטילת ידים (חולין דף קז.) דמרביעית נוטלין שנים ובחצי רביעית אין אחד נוטל ועוד י"ל דאחת באחת לאו דוקא כדפי' בקונטרס דאם היה מן הכשירין הרבה כל שכן דכשר דכי מזה שתי הזאות דטופייגא דכשירין מהיכא תיתי למיפסל אלא משום פסולין נקט לה:

רב אשי אמר כל שהוא תנן. ואין בילה וסבר הזאה אין צריכה שיעור ואי יהיב חדא דילמא מן הפסולין הן אבל כי יהיב תרתי אי אפשר דליכא מן הכשירין וקשה דלמא כל שהוא דליכא שיעור הזאה והזאה צריכה שיעור ומצטרפת וסבר יש בילה דהשתא בין שתי הזאות על כרחך איכא שיעור הזאה מן הכשירין דלדבריו נמי היאך יוכל להיות שלא יוכלו לחלוק הכל שהו לשתים. ברו"ך:

ועוד שתי הזאות דטופייגא דכשירין מהיכא תיתי למיפסל אלא משום פסולין נקט לה ויש בילה *גרס בדריש לקיש דכיון דאמר הזאה צריכה שיעור מאי דוחקיה למימר דלר' אליעזר אין בילה לאקשויי מתני' עלה ולאוקמי מתני' בשינויי יח] דחיקא כדלקמן: רבא אמר לעולם יש בילה והזאה אינה צריכה שיעור. ושתי הזאות דקאמר לאו למלויי שיעורא אלא קנסא הוא דלא נשתרש יט] שלא ישתכר בנפילה זו להרבות מימיו במים פסולין: רב אשי אמר כו'. הגירסא כ] הזו משובשת בספרים ונראה בעיני דהכי גרסינן רב אשי אמר מים כל כא] שהוא תנן ואין בילה יזה שתי הזאות וסבירא ליה לרב אשי הזאה אין צריכה שיעור כרבא ומיהו קנסא לית ליה הילכך אי הוה ס"ל כב] יש בילה בחדא הוה סגי ליה ושתי הזאות לר' אליעזר משום דקסבר אין בילה הילכך אי כג] מדי חדא שמא אין כאן מן הכשירין כלום אבל כי מדי תרתי אי אפשר דליכא בחדא מינייהו מן הכשירין (כלום) דהא אין כאן מן הפסולין אלא כל שהוא והיינו טעמא דלא משני *בלישנא דנתערבו אחת באחת דאם כן הוי משמע יש שיעור להזאה ואיהו אין הזאה צריכה שיעור סבירא ליה להכי דק לישנא דמתני' דקתני כל שהוא דאין לך בהזאות פחותה מכאן ואי אפשר שיהו כד] כל הזאות הללו מן הפסולין ואפילו הן קטנות מאד ולקמן מותיב ליה ממתני' כה]: לדברי רבי אליעזר. דמכשיר בשתי הזאות: הזאה כל שהוא *מטהרת. דשמא אין כו] אחת מהן הזאה ברורה שלא יהא בה מן הפסולין אלמא סבירא ליה דהזאה כל שהוא מטהרת והזאה אין צריכה שיעור: והזאה מחצה כשר ומחצה פסול. ולא תימא הזאה כל שהוא היא דכשירה ומיהו לא יהיה עמה תערובת פסול אלא אפילו יש בה תערובת פסול מכשר אלמא טעמא דר' אליעזר דבעי תרתי לאו משום צירוף הוא דצרפו לכשיעור דהא קתני אין צריכה וקשיא לריש לקיש:

ועוד

שיטה מקובצת

א] תיבת מהן נמחק: ב] ר' אליעזר עי' תוס' בכורות (דף ס'): ג] אמר לו רבי יהושע: ד] כל שהן ר"א: ה] בשלמא (לרבנן) [רבנן סברי] יש בילה והזאה צריכה שיעור ואין מצטרפין להזאות ולכן פוסלין. וא"ת ויעשה הזאה אחת גדולה כשיעור שתי הזאות ויהא כשר דהא ודאי יש כאן שיעור מי חטאת וי"ל דגזורי רבנן שמא לא יעשה הזאה גדולה כשיעור שתי הזאות אלא יעשה הזאה אחת כדרכה שיעור הזאה אחת והא דקאמר יש בילה ר"ל אפי' אי סברי יש בילה מ"מ פסלי כדמסיק וכש"כ אי סברי אין בילה דמן הדין פסלי כי שמא הכל מן הפסול: ו] בילה ואי קסבר: ז] וקנסא הוא דקנסו: ח] שיעור והזאה מחצה כשר ומחצה פסול. וא"ת תסגי בחדא וי"ל לרבא מזה השניה משום קנסא ולרב אשי משום דאין בילה אבל לר"ל קשיא דאמר דצריכה שיעור והכא קאמר דאין צריכה שיעור: ט] סלקא דעתיה השתא: י] בבכור ששניהם תחתונים: יא] ורואה אני את המתנות: יב] בכוסות שנתערבו: קודם כפרה דעיקר כפרה בקלקול: יג] שלא יהיה בה מחבירו: יד] אין מצרפין אותו: טו] יבלול בכולו וסמכינן עלה הס"ד: טז] השאובין היה ואין: יז] שיעור ומצרפין להזאות ודקשיא לך מי יימר: יח] בשינויי דחיק כדלקמן: יט] נשתרש ליה שלא: כ] תיבת הזו נמחק: כא] כל שהן תנן: כב] ס"ל לר"א יש: כג] אי וזה מזה חדא תיבת מדי נמחק: כד] שיהו שתי הזאות תיבת כל נמחק: כה] מסתני'. ור"ל לא דייק לישנא דכל שהן לר"א דמוקי לה שנתערב שיעור הזאה סמים פסולים ונקט כל שהן משום רבנן אבל לרבא דייק שפיר כל שהן דלא נתערב רק כל שהו ויש בילה והזאה אין צריכה שיעור קנס קנסו רבנן: כו] אין באחת סתן: כז] עליונים ברובא מכשר: כח] גרסי' בדריש לקיש: כט] בסנא כיון שנתערב אחת באחת ותירץ:

עין משפט נר מצוה

סג א ב מיי' פ"ט מהל' פסולי המוקדשין הל"א:
סד ג מיי' פ"ט מהל' פרה אדומה הל"ג:
סה ד מיי' פ"ו מהל' פרה הלכה ח:

אלו ולא עלו לו ספר ג"ק
אמרינן ג"ק
[ר"ס יג:]

מסורת הש"ס

ר"ה כח: עירובין ק.
[לעיל עד: עה:]
[לעיל עז:]
פרה פ"ט מ"א ומריבין ג"ק
יומא יד. לקמן צג. נדה ט.
הכשירים קסברי סד"א ג"ק
לקמן צג. יומא שם נדה שם
גירסת רבינו שמשון ריש פ"ט דפרה רבה ועיין תוס' ב"ק
לעיל עה. תוספתא דפרה פ"ט
גרסינן ג"ק
בלישנא דאחת באחת ג"ק
ר"ה מסכתא ולא תימא דעתמא דלאין אחד מהן כו' מן הפסולין אלא ס"ל כו'

עין משפט
נר מצוה

סו א מיי' פ"ב מהל' פסס"מ הל"ט:

נ"ל דיוקא צ"ק

ועוד תניא [א] בהדיא הניתנין למעלה שנתערבו בניתנין למטה רבי אליעזר אומר יתן *למעלה [ב] והתחתונים עלו לו ואי אמרת אין בילה אמאי עלו לו דילמא קיהיב עליונים למטה והתחתונים למעלה הכא במאי עסקינן [ג] כגון דאיכא רובא עליונים וקא יהיב למעלה שיעור תחתונים ועוד הא תחתונים עלו לו קתני לשם שירים ת"ש נתן למטה ולא נמלך ר"א אומר יחזור ויתן למעלה והתחתונים עלו לו הכא נמי ברובא עליונים וקא יהיב למעלה שיעור תחתונים ועוד והא תחתונים עלו לו קתני לשם שירים ת"ש [ד] *נתנן למעלה ולא נמלך [אלו ואלו מודים *שיחזור] ויתן למטה ואלו ואלו עלו לו הכא נמי ברובא עליונים וקא יהיב למעלה שיעור תחתונים ועוד [ה] [והא אלו ואלו עלו לו קתני] מי קתני אלו ואלו מודים אלו ואלו עלו לו [ו] קתני סיפא אתאן לרבנן דאמרי יש בילה תא שמע *הניתנין במתנה אחת שנתערבו בניתנין במתנה אחת ינתנו במתנה אחת ואי אמרת אין בילה אמאי ינתנו במתנה אחת [ז] דילמא מהאי קיהיב ומהאילא קיהיב [ח] כגון שנתערבו אחת באחת מתן ארבע במתן ארבע הכא נמי שנתערבו ארבע בארבע מתן ארבע במתנה [ט] *אחת וכי

ועוד תניא הניתנין למעלה כו'. אלמא יש בילה בתוספתא דזבחים איתא והא דלא פריך ממתני' ניחא ליה לאקשויי מברייתא משום כה] *דוקא דתחתונים עלו לו: הכא במאי עסקינן ברובא עליונים וקא יהיב למעלה שיעור דתחתונים ועוד. לא מצי לאוקומא ברובא תחתונים ויהיב למעלה שיעור תחתונים ועוד דאי רובא תחתונים לא היה *אומר רבי אליעזר יתן למעלה: נתן למטה ולא נמלך ר' אליעזר אומר יחזור ט] למעלה. נראה דגרסינן ויחזור ויתן למטה מדמסיק עלו לו לשם שיריים כז] דמה שנתן למטה קודם נתינתו למעלה פשיטא דאין עולה לשם שיריים: *מתן ארבע במתן אחת הייט שתים שהן ארבע כגון עולה או שלמים דלמטה דאי ארבע ממש כגון חטאת אמאי ינתן *מתן אחת לר' יהושע הא רבנן סברי ישפך לאמה לפי שזה למטה וזה למעלה: הג"ה *בל תוסיף מהיכא. תימה לי הלא במתנה אחת של בכור אי אפשר שלא יוכלו לחלק לשתים ואם כן דילמא יהיב מיניה לשתי קרנות דאע"ג דאין בילה זהו שיכול להיות מזה הדם לבדו והוא הדין במתנה אחת יכול להיות בה מדם זה ומדם זה ואי ליכא שיעור נתינה לשתי קרנות דלא היה רישומו ניכר לשתים אם כן היאך הקרבן נאכל דילמא חלקו לשתי קרנות ולא הועיל כלום וי"ל דיש שיעור לשתי קרנות וכיון דאין בילה אין כאן רק ספק בל תוסיף ומשום ספק זה לא יניח קרבנו ואפילו כי הוה נמי דמים כח] מעורבים יחד הוה ספק והכי פריך נהי דנתערב ארבע באחד לא תיקשי מאין בילה אכתי [תיקשי] צ"ק קושיא אחריתי דלא מתרץ דבל תוסיף בודאי ליכא. ברו"ך. ואם תאמר איזה בל תוסיף יש וליהוי מתנה שניה בשביל שיריים של בכור ואי עביד עוד שיריים בשביל עולה אין כט] כלום אלא יעשה ל] שיריים בשביל עולה *) (שתי מתנות שהן ארבע ויש לומר מתנה ראשונה) של עולה נכרת משתי לדדין וזהו בל תוסיף דמתנה של בכור אינה רק מלד אחד אי נמי שיריים הוו באותו קרן של מתנה אחת לא] (ארבע) מתנה שניה שבקרן שני הוי תוספת. הג"ה: הא קתני אלו ואלו עלו לו. וליכא למימר לשם שיריים דאלו ואלו קתני משמע יוצא ידי דמים עליונים וידי דמים תחתונים: כגון שנתערבו אחת באחת. פירש בקונטרס שיעור מתנה מזה ושיעור מתנה מזה ודקתני [ה] ונתן במתנה אחת בשביל כל אחד קא אמר דהייט שתי מתנות דנמלאו שתיהן במזבח ותימה מאי קשיא ליה נימא שנותן כל הדם במתנה אחת דאיכא מתרווייהו ממה נפשך וכי תימא משום דבעי מתנה לשם כל אחד לימא שנותן חצי הדם וחוזר ונותן חצי האחר ולמה ליה למימר כלל אחת באחת וכי תימא דפריך משום דצריך לשייר משני הדמים לשפיכת השיריים ופריך דדילמא מה שנתן היה מאחד מהן והשיריים מן השני דאע"ג דתחילת עולה מקום שיריים מכל מקום לא עשה כעיקר מצוותה אי נמי קסבר תחילת עולה לא מקום שיריים אם כן מאי קא משני שנתערבו לב] בו אחת באחת ועוד (לימא) [למאי] דיהיב (למעלה) שיעור האחד ועוד [ו] אמאי לא פריך מרישא נתערב בדם הפסולין או בדם התמצית דילמא מאי דיהיב מדם הפסולין ושיריים [ז] אלא כיון דשיריים לא מעכבי אין לנו לפסול תערובת משום מצות שיריים ומיהו לקמן משמע שיש לפסול משום שיריים לג] אע"ג דלא מעכבי דקאמר שיריים צריכין אוצבא ונראה לפרש דהכי פריך דילמא מהאי קא יהיב כו' דהכא ליתן לא יתן אלא שתי מתנות אחת משום זה ואחת משום זה ואם נאמר לו שיתן כל הדם לא ישמע לנו ולא דמי לנתערב בדם פסולין דשמא ישמע לנו כיון לד] דידיע דפסול מעורב בו אבל הכא דשניהם כשירין לא ומיהו קשה דאם כן לעיל דקאמר דיהיב למעלה שיעור התחתונים ועוד לא ישמע לנו כיון דשניהם כשרים ועוד יש לומר דלשון מתנה אחת משמע לה] אחת ולא יותר [ח] וכי משני שנתערבו אחת באחת לו] כפרש"י מתנה אחת מכל אחת ולא דמי להאי דלעיל לז] דיתן למעלה ומוקמינן דיהיב למעלה שיעור התחתונים ועוד דסתמא קתני יתן למעלה לח] ולא מפרש כמה וכן בדם הפסולין ובדם התמצית: ה"ג

*) נ"א וי"ל מתנה ראשונה משתי מתנות שהן ארבע של עולה כו'

ועוד תניא. תיובתא לרב אשי דאמר טעמא דבעי תרתי משום דאין בילה הוא י] דשמעינן לרבי אליעזר דאית ליה בילה (אלמא שמעינן) מהנך תרתי מתנייתא דטעמא דר' אליעזר כרבא דבתרא נמי מיתכשר אלמא קשיא הוא: הניתנין למעלה כו'. קא ס"ד דם חטאת בדם עולה יתן למעלה להכשיר חטאת דמטה להקדים עליונים לתחתונים כדאמר לקמן בפרק כל התדיר (דף פט.) ורואה אני את התחתונים למעלה כאילו הן מים ולרבנן ישפך לאמה: והתחתונים עלו לו. כשיחזור ויתן שיריים למטה לשם שיריים. עלו לו ואף למתן דם עולה: ואם אין בילה חטאת אמאי עלתה לו. דלמא לא יהיב למעלה אלא תחתונים: הכא במאי עסקינן כגון דרובא עליונים. וקא יהיב למעלה כל שיעור שיש בו מן התחתונים ועוד דממה נפשך יא] הוא יהיב למעלה מן העליונים ולהכי מוקי לה ברובא עליונים משום דלא מתרץ ליה והתחתונים עלו לו אלא בהכי כדמסיק יב] לה למילתיה: והא תחתונים עלו לו קתני. קס"ד יג] אף בעולה קאמר דעלתה ואי דיהיב למעלה שיעור התחתונים ועוד היכי מיתכשרא עולה דילמא כל מה שהיה בכאן מדם העולה נתן למעלה: ומשני דמאי תחתונים עלו לו דקאמר לשם שיריים. דחטאת קאמר הצריכין לישפך ליסוד יד] וכיון דרובא עליונים כי נתן למעלה כשיעור תחתונים ועוד טו] דאיכא מדם החטאת למעלה ולמטה אפי' כל הניתן למעלה מן העליונים הוא אכתי פש ליה מיניה למטה טז] אבל אי לאו רובא עליונים [תיקשי] צ"ק כיון דיהיב למעלה שיעור תחתונים ועוד כדי להכשיר החטאת תו לא מתרץ ליה התחתונים עלו לו אפילו לשיריים דדילמא כל דם העליונים למעלה ניתן ואין כאן שיריים או שמא כל דם התחתונים למעלה ניתן ואין כאן משל עולה למטה כלום: נתן למטה ולא נמלך. דאי נמלך לרבי אליעזר הוה אמרינן ליה תן למעלה דמצוה להקדים עליונים לתחתונים יז] בפרק כל התדיר (שם) ולרבנן ישפך לאמה: יחזור ויתן למעלה. ושניהם כשרין כדס"ד יח] ולרבנן ישפך לאמה והעולה כשירה יט] דאסור לשנות בתחתון מפני הכשר עליון ולא אמרינן רואין אותו למעלה כאילו הוא מים והכי תניא לה בתוספתא: הכא נמי ברובא עליונים וקא יהיב למעלה שיעור תחתונים ועוד. ועליונים הוא דכשרים ולא תחתונים: ה"ג והא תחתונים עלו לו קתני. כ] ולשון קושיא הוא: ומשני ליה לשם שיריים: נתן למעלה ולא נמלך. מתחילתו דאי נמלך [א] הוה אמרי ליה רבנן ישפך לאמה שלא לשנות בתחתון כא] דכיון דניתן למעלה אפי' חכמים מודו שיחזור ויתן למטה לכתחילה אם בא לימלך דאיט משנה בנתינה זו בעליונים שהרי מה שיש כאן מן העליונים שירים הן דרבנן אית להו בילה וכבר ניתן מן החטאת למעלה ומעתה מצות שיריים ליתן למטה כתחילת עולה: ואלו ואלו עלו לו. ושניהם כשרים: הכא נמי כו'. ולר"א דלית ליה בילה אין כשר אלא חטאת ולרבנן דאית להו בילה שניהם כשירין שהרי יש משניהם למעלה ולמטה: ה"ג מי קתני אלו ואלו מודים אלו ואלו עלו לו קתני סיפא אתאן לרבנן דאמרי יש בילה ת"ש הניתנין כו' ואין כאן הפסק משנה הכתוב בספרים: מי קתני אלו ואלו מודים. שאלו ואלו עלו לו אלו ואלו עלו לו הוא דקתני והך סיפא דקתני ואלו ואלו עלו לו לאו אאלו ואלו מודים קאי אלא רבנן כב] דקאמרי לה דאית להו בילה אבל לרבי אליעזר אין כשר אלא עליון: ינתנו במתנה אחת. ורבי אליעזר [ב] איירי בסיפא ומתני' היא: אחת באחת. שיעור מתנה מזה ושיעור כג] מזה וקתני ינתנו במתנה אחת בשביל כל אחד קאמר דהייט שתי מתנות דנמלאו שתיהן במזבח: ארבע בארבע. שיעור ארבע מתנות בשיעור ארבע מתנות כד] ודקתני ינתנו במתנות ארבע ארבע בשביל זה וארבע בשביל זה: מתן ד' במתן אחת [ג] רבי אליעזר אומר ינתנו במתנת ארבע. שמצוה להקדים מתן ארבע למתן אחת כדאמרינן בכל התדיר (שם) ורואה אני את תוספת מתנות הבכור כאילו הם מים:

וכ"ת

מסורת הש"ס

כא שמעינן צ"ק

נ"ל למעלה ורואה אני את התחתונים כאילו הן מים והתחתונים כו'

גליון הש"ס

גמ' שיחזור ויתן למטה. ע"ל דף ש ע"ב תוס' ד"ה ואי. ולקמן דף פא ע"ב תוס' ד"ה נתן:

[ר"ס כח: ערכין ק.]

נ"א אחת מאי איכא למימר כו'

שיטה מקובצת

א] תיבת בהדיא נמחק: ב] למעלה ורואה אני התחתונים למעלה כאילו דם מים והתחתונים: ג] כגון דאיכא רובא עליונים. ה"ה דמצי למימר חצי מזה וחצי מזה ונתן חציין ועוד דהרי ממה נפשך הגיע העליונים למעלה אך שהיה קשה לן והא תחתונים עלו לו קתני דהשתא לא הוי מצי למימר לשיריים דחטאת כדמשני השתא משום דשמא דם החטאת היתה כולה למעלה אבל השתא דרובא עליונים משני שפיר דדם החטאת מרובה כל כך שמגיע הייתור דחטאת ליותר מעוד כל כך דאכתי יהיה בו שיריים: ד] נתן למעלה ולא נמלך אלו ואלו מודים: ה] והא אלו ואלו עלו לו, קתני. משמע אף לשם תחילת עולה הטעונה יסוד והא דלא משני לשם שיריים ואי משום דקתני עלו לו הא לעיל נמי קתני תחתונים עלו לו ואפ"ה אוקימנא לשיריים משום דאלו ואלו משמע אלו דומיא דאלו תחתונים דומיא דעליונים מה עליונים אותן שנתן למעלה עלו לתחילת מתן דמים אף תחתונים שנתן למטה עלו לתחילת מתן דמים דהיינו תחילת עולה ועי"ל דלא דמי דלעיל [...]

ח] עיין בהשמטות בסוף המסכת: ט] אחת ר"א אומר ינתנו במתן ארבע: י] הוא דהוא שמעינן לרבי אליעזר: [...]

ו] [...] כו' דמסיק ואם נתן מתנה אחת מכולן יצא ומדקאמר רבי רואין את המתנה אם יש בה כדי לזה וכדי לזה מכלל דת"ק סבר אע"פ שאין בה כדי לזה וכדי לזה יצא אלמא יש בילה דאי אין בילה דילמא מהאי [יהיב] ומהאי לא יהיב ועוד אמר מהר"ם דרבנן היינו ר' יהושע מדפריך ר"י הרי הוא עובר על בל תוסיף א"כ קסבר יש בילה כאשר אפרש שם בעזרת האל יתברך: ז] דילמא מהאי קיהיב כו'. תימה דלשני ליה שישפוך כל דם התערובת בבת אחת וי"ל דדייק מדקתני ינתנו במתנה אחת דמשמע כשיעור מתנה אחת ולא כל הדם וא"ת כמו כן לעיל דקאמר דקיהיב למעלה שיעור תחתונים ועוד אימא דוקא שיעור מתנה כדפי' וי"ל דלעיל קתני יתן למעלה סתם כו':

[...] למטה: כז] שיריים דאין עולה לשירים אלא היכא שנתן כבר למעלה אלא ודאי גרסינן [...] עלו לו לשם שיריים דהחטאת בהמה דמה שחזר לבסוף ונתן למטה: כח] דמים רבים מעו[...] כלום: ל] תיבת ארבע נמחק: לא] שנתערבו אחת באחת דילמא דיהיב למעלה שיעור הא[...] הכשר אע"ג: לג] דידוע דדם פסול: לד] משמע שיעור מתנה אחת ולא יותר וכי משני [...] לסימר כפרש"י שיעור מתנה: לו] דלעיל דקאמר יתן למעלה: לז] למעלה סתם ולא מפרש [...] שפיר דקיהיב למעלה שיעור תחתונים ועוד והוי טפי משיעור מתנה:

הגהות צ"ק [א] נ"ל אמרינן ליה לרבנן ישפך לאמה שלא לשנות בתחתונים וכיון דנתן למעלה כו' ולתחילת שלה ס"ד: [ב] ס"א דאיירי בסיפא דמתני' כס"ד: [ג] וקאמר ר"א ינתנו: [ד] אותה שיריים בשביל [...] ארבע וי"ל דמתנה ראשונה של שלה כו' כנ"ל: [ה] ינתנו: [ו] נ"א ועוד ועוד אמאי: [ז] מן הכשירים אלא כו': [ח] נ"ל ומשני:

half is unfit.[5] [80*b*] Moreover, it was explicitly taught: If [blood] which is applied above was mixed with [blood] that is applied below, R. Eliezer said: He must sprinkle [it] above, and the lower [blood] acquits him.[6] But if you say that there is no even distribution, why does it acquit him? perhaps he sprinkled the upper [blood] below and the lower [blood] above?—The case we discuss here is where we have an excess of upper [blood], and he sprinkles above the quantity of the lower [blood] plus a little more.[7] But he teaches that the lower [blood] acquits him?[8]—[It counts] as the residue.[9]

Come and hear: If he [the priest] sprinkled [it][10] without a asking,[1] R. Eliezer said: He must re-sprinkle above, and the lower [blood] acquits him?[2]—Here too the excess was upper [blood], and he sprinkles above the quantity of the lower blood plus a little more. But he teaches that the lower [blood] acquits him?—[It counts] as the residue.

Come and hear: If he sprinkled it above without asking,[3] both[4] agree that he must re-sprinkle below, and *both* [sprinklings] are credited to him![5]—Here too the excess was upper [blood], and he sprinkles above the quantity of the lower blood plus a little more. Yet surely he teaches: *Both* [sprinklings] are credited to him?—Does he then teach, 'Both agree [in this]'? Surely he teaches, 'Both are credited to him', this final clause thus agreeing with the Rabbis [only], who maintain that there is even distribution.

Come and hear: IF [BLOOD] WHICH REQUIRES ONE APPLICATION [WAS MIXED] WITH BLOOD [ALSO] REQUIRING ONE APPLICATION, IT [THE MIXTURE] SHOULD BE PRESENTED WITH ONE APPLICATION. Now, if you say that there is no even distribution, why should it be presented with one application? perhaps he sprinkles [the blood] of one [sacrifice] but not that of the other?[6]—It means, e.g., where one [minimum quantity] was mixed with another [minimum quantity].[7] [BLOOD] WHICH REQUIRES FOUR APPLICATIONS WITH [BLOOD] THAT REQUIRES FOUR APPLICATIONS?[8]—There too it means that [the quantity for] four [applications] was mixed with [the quantity for] four [applications].[9] [BLOOD] WHICH REQUIRES FOUR APPLICATIONS WITH [BLOOD] REQUIRING ONE APPLICATION?[8]

(5) This contradicts Resh Laḳish. (6) When he pours out the residue at the base of the altar, it counts as sprinkling for the burnt-offering. (7) So that *some* of the upper blood must be properly sprinkled above. (8) Whereas *all* the lower blood was perhaps sprinkled above: how then can the *burnt*-offering be made fit thereby? (9) Of the *sin*-offering, which must be poured out at the base. The burnt-offering, however, does not become fit. (10) *Sc.* the mixed blood.

a (1) For had he asked, R. Eliezer holds that he would be bidden to sprinkle above first; v. *infra* 89*a*. (2) Here too it is assumed that both sacrifices are thereby made fit. (3) For had he asked, the Rabbis hold that he would be bidden to pour it out into the duct. (4) The Rabbis and R. Eliezer. (5) Thus *both* sacrifices are fit. (6) And this does agree with R. Eliezer, since the *next* clause contains a controversy of R. Eliezer and the Rabbis. (7) *Sc.* the minimum quantity for sprinkling (one application). When the Mishnah teaches that he must make one application, it means one application on account of *each* separately. (8) The same difficulty arises there too. (9) Here too he must make four applications on behalf of *each* sacrifice.

[81a] And should you answer: Here too it means that [the quantity for] four [applications] was mixed with [the quantity for] one
a [application],[1]—if so: LO HE TRANSGRESSES THE INJUNCTION NOT TO ADD THERETO, R. JOSHUA COUNTERED: Whence have you here the injunction not to add thereto?[2]—Rather said Raba:[3] Where [the blood is] mixed together, they do not disagree; they disagree in respect of the goblets. R. Eliezer holds [the view that] 'we regard' [etc.], while the Rabbis reject [the view that] 'we regard' [etc.].[4]

Now, do they not disagree where [the blood itself] is mingled? Surely it was taught: R. Judah said: R. Eliezer and the Sages did not dispute about the blood of a sin-offering which was mixed with the blood of a burnt-offering, [both agreeing] that it must be offered [sprinkled];[5] [if it was mixed] with the blood of a *roba'* or a *nirba'*,[6] [they agree that] it must not be offered. About what do they disagree? About the blood of an unblemished [animal] which was mixed with the blood of a blemished [animal]; there R. Eliezer maintains that it must be offered, whether [the blood itself is] mingled or whether the goblets [are mixed]; while the Sages say
b that it must not be offered![1]—R. Judah when teaching R. Eliezer's view relates it to both mixing [of the blood itself] and [to that of] the goblets; but the Rabbis[2] hold that they disagree about goblets [only].

Abaye said: They learnt this only of the *beginning* of the sin-offering and the burnt-offering;[3] but as to the end of the sin-offering and the beginning of the burnt-offering,[4] all agree that the place of the burnt-offering is the place of the residue.[5] Said R. Joseph to him: Thus did R. Judah say: The residue requires the projection.[6] And thus said Resh Laḳish:[7] They learnt this only of the beginning of the sin-offering and the burnt-offering; but as to the end of the sin-offering and the beginning of the burnt-offering, all agree that the place of the burnt-offering is the place of the residue. Whereas R. Joḥanan—others say, R. Eleazar—said:
c There is still the controversy.[1]

R. Huna b. Judah raised an objection: *They are holy:*[2] [this teaches] that if it [the blood of a firstling] was mixed with the blood of other sacrifices, it must be offered [sprinkled]. Surely it speaks of the end of a burnt-offering and [the beginning of] a firstling;[3] and this proves that the place of the burnt-offering is the place of the residue?—No: it speaks of the beginning of the burnt-offering and that of the firstling. What then does it inform us?[4] that sacrifices do not nullify one another![5] [Surely] that is deduced from [the text], *And he shall take of the blood of the bullock and of the blood of the goat?*[6]—It is a controversy of Tannaim: one deduces it from this text, and another deduces it from the other text.

Raba raised an objection: *And Aaron's sons, the priests, shall present the blood, and dash the blood* [*round about against the altar*]:[7]

a (1) Emended text (Sh. M.). Thus R. Eliezer means that *four* applications must be made in *addition* to the one, i.e., five in all. (2) Since there is only sufficient for *one* application of the blood of the firstling, he certainly sprinkles the blood of the *burnt*-offering in the other applications, as is actually necessary; thus he does not add thereto. (3) Sh. M. reads: Rabbah. (4) The answers given above are now rejected. When it is taught that the lower blood acquits him, it means both as the residue of the upper blood and as the *sprinklings* of the lower, and the burnt-offering does become fit thereby. Again, when the Mishnah speaks of the mixture, it means even where a *large* quantity is mixed, and not the minimum quantity required. Nevertheless, this does not prove that R. Eliezer holds that there is even distribution, for all these cases refer not to the mixing of the blood (in one goblet) but to the mixing of the *goblets*. Here R. Eliezer rules that *of each goblet* sprinklings must be made above and below, the superfluous sprinklings being regarded as mere water; similarly, if a goblet containing the blood of a firstling is mixed up with another containing the blood of a burnt-offering, four applications must be made from each goblet. The Sages, however, refuse to regard such sprinklings, where they are superfluous, as mere water, and therefore all the blood must be poured out into the duct. (5) For the Sages too accept the view that 'we regard' etc. (In this R. Judah disagrees with the Tanna of our Mishnah.) (6) Cf. *supra* 71a.

b (1) The interdict against sprinkling the blood of a blemished animal is contained in Lev. XXII, 25: *there is a blemish in them; they shall not be accepted for you.* R. Eliezer holds that this applies only where the blood is by itself, but not where it is mixed with that of a sound animal. Now, though R. Judah disagrees with the Tanna of the Mishnah in respect of the scope of the controversy, yet it may be assumed that they both agree that the controversy applies to the mingling of the *blood* as well as that of the goblets. (2) Not the Sages who disagree with R. Eliezer, but the scholars who disagree with R. Judah's interpretation of the controversy; hence the anonymous Tanna of our Mishnah. (An anonymous teacher is often referred to as the Rabbis, because he generally represents the Rabbis in general where an opposing view is recorded in the name of an individual.) (3) The controversy in the Mishnah holds good only at the beginning, i.e., if their blood was mingled *before* the sprinkling. Only then do the Sages disqualify it, as they reject the view that 'we regard' etc. and maintain that we may not sprinkle the blood of the burnt-offering above in order to make the sin-offering fit. (4) Emended text Sh. M. —I.e., if the *residue* of the blood of the sin-offering, *after* it was sprinkled, was mixed with the blood of the burnt-offering *before* it was sprinkled. (5) He sprinkles the blood on the wall of the altar below the scarlet line, and thence it drains down on to the base, whither the residue of the blood of the sin-offering should be poured. Thus this counts for both the initial sprinkling of the burnt-offering and the final pouring out of the residue of the sin-offering. (6) *Sc.* the base, which projected from the altar.—It must not be poured on to the wall of the altar but directly on to the base.—Hence the Sages disagree even if the blood of the sin-offering had already been sprinkled. (7) Emended text.

c (1) Even in the latter instance. (2) Num. XVIII, 17. The whole verse reads: *But the firstling of an ox . . . thou shalt not redeem; they are holy.* These last words are emphatic and imply that they retain their sanctity, and if their blood is mingled with other blood, it must still be offered. According to the Sages this must mean where it is mingled with lower blood, like itself, e.g., with that of a burnt-offering, but not that of a sin-offering. (3) I.e., the blood of a burnt-offering *after* sprinkling was mixed with that of a firstling *before* sprinkling. (The residue of a firstling is not poured out on the base, and sprinkling completes its blood rites.) (4) For in that case the text is apparently superfluous; since both bloods need sprinkling on the lower wall of the altar, it is obvious that they must be sprinkled even when they are mingled. (5) If their blood mingles, even if the blood of one exceeds that of the other, the latter is not nullified. (6) Lev. XVI, 18. Though the former exceeds the latter, it does not nullify it; v. Men. 22a, b. (7) Lev. I, 5.

תורה אור

וכי תימא ה"נ א] בנתערב באחת אי הכי אמר לך רבי יהושע הרי הוא עובר על בל תוסיף הכא בל תוסיף מהיכא אלא אמר ב] רבא בבלול לא פליגי כי פליגי בכוסות לר"א אית ליה רואין לרבנן לית להו רואין ובבלול לא פליגי והתניא א"ר יהודה לא נחלקו ר"א וחכמים על דם חטאת שנתערב בדם עולה שיקרב ברובע ונרבע שלא יקרב על מה נחלקו על דם תמימה שנתערב בדם בעלת מום שר"א אומר יקרב בין בבלול בין בכוסות ג] וחכ"א לא יקרב רבי יהודה אליבא דר"א מתני בין בבלול בין בכוסות ד] ורבנן בכוסות פליגי אמר אביי לא שנו אלא תחלת חטאת ועולה אבל סוף חטאת ה] [ועולה] דברי הכל מקום עולה מקום שיריים ו] א"ל רב יוסף הכי אמר רב יהודה שירים צריכין איצטבא וכן אמר ז] *ר"ש לא שנו אלא תחלת חטאת ועולה אבל סוף חטאת ח] ועולה דברי הכל מקום עולה מקום שירים *א"ר יוחנן ואיתימא רבי אלעזר *עדיין היא מחלוקת ט] מתיב רב הונא בר יהודה קדש הם שאם נתערב בדם קדשים אחרים יקרבו מאי לאו סוף עולה ובכור וש"מ מקום עולה מקום שירים לא תחילת עולה ובכור ומאי קא משמע לן *דאין עולין מבטלים זה את זה האי °מולקח מדם הפר ומדם השעיר נפקא תנאי היא איכא דנפקא ליה מהכא ואיכא °דנפקא ליה מהכא מתיב רבא °והקריבו י] בני אהרן את הדם וזרקו יא] את הדם מה ת"ל

ויקרא טז

שם י

ול"ת ה"נ בנתערב· מתנה אחת מן הבכור בשיעור יב] מתן ד' מתנות מן העולה ודקאמר ינתנו במתן ד' ינתנו חמשתן קאמר שיהו ניתנין ד' מתנות ודאי מן העולה ואחת דרבי יהושע למימר יש בילה ודיו במתנה אחת על שניהן ולא יעבור על בל תוסיף דלית ליה רואין : הכא בל תוסיף מהיכא· הרי אין כאן מן הבכור אלא כדי מתנה יג] : אלא אמר יד] רבא· כל הנך שנויי דשנינן לא טו] תשנין דודאי התחתונים עלו לו דקתני בין לשם שירים בין לתחילת עולה קאמר ומתני' דמתן ד' במתנה אחת בדאיכא טובא מכל חד קאמר ואפ"ה לא תשמע מינה לר"א יש בילה טז] דתקשה לרב אשי דאיכא לשנויי *הא מתני' דלעיל דעליונים ותחתונים ומתני' דמתן ד' במתן אחת לאו בבלול פליגי אלא בתערובת כוסות וקאמר ר"א בעליונים ותחתונים דיתן שניהם למעלה ולמטה ושניהם כשרין ורואה אני את דם יז] (חטאת) למעלה כאילו הוא מים וכן בעולה ובכור נותן ד' מכל כוס וכוס ורואה אני את התוספת כאילו הוא מים יח] (וכן בעולה ובכור) ורבנן לית להו רואין וישפך לאמה ואע"ג דהך פלוגתא יט] בבלול *נמי איכא לאיפלוגי *בהכי כ] ועוד פליגי נמי ביש בילה ואין בילה מיהו הך מתניתא דקתני והתחתונים עלו לו דמשמע יש בילה ומתני' נמי דקתני הרי הוא עובר על בל תוסיף דמשמע כא] דבאיעריב טובא קאי ואפ"ה מכשר משמע דיש בילה וע"כ לאו בבלול קיימי *דלעולם לר"א אין בילה כב] דאי בבלול לא הוה מכשיר ר"א לא בבכור כג] ולא בעולה דדלמא מהאי קא יהיב ומהאי לא קיהיב אלא א"כ נתערבו ד' באחת וכן בעולה כד] *ועולה אלא א"כ נתערבו ד' בד' ולא בחטאת ועולה אלא ברובא עליונים וקיהיב למעלה שיעור תחתונים ועוד וחטאת לבדה תעלה לו ולרבנן ישפך לאמה דלית להו רואין : כה] שיקריב· דרבנן נמי אית להו רואין ומתני' לאו רבי יהודה היא : שר"א אומר כו] יקריב· ואפי' לא קרב אחד מהם דדריש מום בם לא ירצו לכם בעיניה כז] הוא משמע הא ע"י תערובת ירצו בין בבלול כו' ומדר' יהודה נשמע לרבנן דפליגי עליה במתני' כח] ומוקמי פלוגתא ברואין *ואף בחטאת ועולה כט] בין בבלול בין בכוסות קיימי וקתני לר"א התחתונים עלו לו וגבי עולה ובכור נמי מכשיר במתני' אלמא יש בילה : ומשני רבי יהודה אליבא דר"א דמוקי פלוגתא בבעלת מום *דאין כשר לר"א אלא א' ל] ומתני' בין בבלול בין בכוסות ומוקי לה רב אשי לענין בלול כגון דרובא כשר וקיהיב במזבח שיעור בעלת מום ועוד אבל לרבנן דפליגי עליה דר' יהודה לא] ומוקמי' פלוגתא אף בהיכא דשניהם כשרין ומכשר להו לתרווייהו בכוסות פליגי ר"א ורבנן ומש"ה מכשיר רבי אליעזר בתרווייהו דאי בבלול לא הוה מכשר אלא לב] כדאוקימנא לעיל : לא שנו· הך פלוגתא דחטאת ועולה דמתני' דלעיל דאמרי רבנן ישפך לאמה אלא בתחלת חטאת ועולה שנתערבו לפני מתן דמם בההיא פסלי רבנן דלית להו רואין ואסור לשנות את מקומן לתת את העולה למעלה מן החוט מפני הכשר חטאת : אבל סוף חטאת· שנתערב בתחלת עולה שנתערבו לג] (בו) שירי חטאת בתחילת שלה אין כאן מחלוקת ויתנה למטה מן החוט דמקום תחילת מתן שלה כשר לשירי חטאת ויזרקם לקיר המזבח ומאליהן שותתין ליסוד ואין כאן שינוי מקום : צריכין איצטבא· שישפכם על גבי היסוד ממש העשוי כאיצטבא ולא יזרקם לקיר הזקוף כמשפט עולה ובסוף חטאת ועולה נמי לרבנן ישפך לאמה ולקמן מותיב ליה מהא דתניא לעיל נתן למעלה ולא נמלך אלו ואלו מודים שיחזור ויתן למטה : עדיין היא מחלוקת· אף בסוף חטאת ותחילת עולה דלאו חד מקום הוא ולר"א דאית ליה רואין כשר ולרבנן ישפך לאמה : קדש הם· בבכור כתיב ומשמע ליה הם בהוייתן יהו שאם נתערבו בדמים אחרים לא אבדו את שמם ויקרבו ולרבנן מיתוקמא כגון שנתערב בתחתונים כמותו ולא בחטאת לד] ומאי לאו דאיערב בסוף עולה שהוא שירים והולכין למקום שירי חטאת כדאמרן באיזהו מקומן (לעיל נג·) תן יסוד למזבח של עולה וקתני דתחילת בכור כשר בו לכתחלה שמקומו מקום תחילת עולה אלמא מקום תחילת עולה ותחלת בכור הוא מקום כשר לשפיכת שירים לכתחלה : לא תחילת עולה ובכור· דשניהם מקום אחד להם וכיון דלרבנן יש בילה שניהם כשירין : ומאי קא משמע לן· קרא הוא ומקום אחד להן : דאין עולין מבטלין זה את זה· ואפילו אחד מרובה על חבירו לא בטל המועט : האי מולקח מדם הפר ומדם השעיר נפקא לן· במנחות בהקומץ רבה (דף כב.) שמערבין דם פר ודם השעיר לה] [של] יה"כ במתן דם קרנות המזבח הפנימי והדבר ידוע שדם הפר מרובה מדם השעיר מכאן לעולין שאין מבטלין זה את זה : איכא דנפקא ליה כו'· ולקמן מפרש פלוגתא בשמעתא : והקריבו וזרקו מה ת"ל דם דם· גבי עולה קאי בת"כ ושחט את בן הבקר והקריבו בני אהרן הכהנים את הדם לו] [וזרקו את הדם] והקריבו בני אהרן וזרקו אל המזבח היה לו לומר ואין צריך לכתוב דם דמה יש לו לקבל ולזרוק ע"י שחיטה אם לא דם מה ת"ל דם דם : ה"ג מנין אתה אומר נתערב דם עולה בדם עולה דם עולה בדם תמורה דם עולה בדם חולין שיקרבו ת"ל

ה"ג **אבל** סוף חטאת ועולה· במתנה שניה של עולה מיירי שהיא בקרן מערבית דרומית דזה מקום שירים של חטאת אבל במתנה ראשונה של עולה ישפך לאמה לרבנן דאין זה מקום שירים לז] דדם עולה בקרן מזרחית צפונית ושירים בקרן מערבית דרומית לח] מיהו י"ל כיון דיסוד דרומי איתו מן הפסוק אלא מטעמא דבעי' בסמוך לו (לעיל דף נג·) דומיא דשירים פנימיים א"כ אין קפידא אם יתנם במזרחית צפונית להכשיר דם תחלת עולה וכן מוכיח קצת בסמוך גבי נתן למעלה ולא נמלך יחזור ויתן למטה ובעי לאוכוחי דמקום עולה מקום שירים ומשמע שלא נתן עדיין כלל מתנות עולה (*בלבדן) א"כ יפנה דרך שמאל ויתן תחלה בקרן מערבית דרומית שהוא מקום שירים ויתן שירים בשתי קרנות : ה"ג **מאי** קמ"ל· תימה טובא קא משמע לן לט] דיקרבו למר כדאית ליה ב' מתנות שהן ד' ולמר מתן אחד אע"ג דעבר על בל תגרע או בל תוסיף ושמא י"ל כיון דיהיב לשם מים ליכא בל תוסיף וגם לא משום בל תגרע כיון דשב ואל תעשה ומתקן קרבנו ובלא קרא נמי· מ] ברו"ך : **תנאי** היא איכא דנפקא לה מהכא ואיכא דנפקא לה מהכא· תימה למה דוחק לומר תנאי היא דבהקומץ רבה (מנחות כב:) פריך ואימא עד דאיכא מין ומינו ועולין קשיא לימא קרא מא] קדש הם איצטריך דאם איתו ענין למין ומינו ועולין תנהו לענין לעולין לחוד אפילו הוי שלא מינו ועוד קשה דהכא אליבא דר' יוחנן קיימא והתם קאמר מב] רבי יוחנן לההיא דרשה דולקח מדם הפר וע"ק נימא דאיצטריך משום דס"ד שישפך לאמה כדי שלא יעבור על בל תוסיף ועל בל תגרע וע"ק דמאי שנא שנתערבו למטה בלמעלה דמודה ר' יהושע דישפך ואין משנים מג] זה להכשיר זה ומתן אחת במתן ד' משנים ועובר מד] על בל תגרע וכי תימא משום דמתן א' במתן ד' אי אמרת ישפך אין שייך לשלם תחתיהם כגון בכור ומעשר שנפסל אבל עולה וחטאת שנפסל דאפשר לשלם תחתיהם ישפך עולת נדבה מאי איכא למימר ומיהו י"ל דלא דמי דניתנים למעלה בניתנים למטה אין לו לפסול בידים דם שלה להכשיר דם חטאת אבל הכא שאינו פוסלו בידים אלא עומד במקומו מה] שב ואל תעשה שאני ומיהו לר"א קשה דמתנה דחייב ליתן ב' מתנות מו] לבד מתנה אחת ועובר משום בל תוסיף ובניתנין למעלה

סו א מיי' פ"ב מהל' פסה"מ הלכה יא :

כ"א צ"ל כרוך

[צ"ל ר"ש בן לקיש וכ"א בילקוט פרשת אחרי רמז תקעה]

[צ"ל ר' יוחנן ואיתימא ר"א אמר וכ"א בילקוט שם]

רפא דמתני' צ"ק

ר"א סעולם

רש"ק מ"ז ר"א וכן כשעולה ובכור צ"ק

איכא נמי לאיפלוגי בהכי וסליגי נמי ביש בילה צ"ק

ולעולם צ"ק

[מנחות כב: כג. תמורה כו:]

ר"א ומנחים

לף צ"ק

ג"י צ"ק דאין כשר אלא אחד כו' ומוקי לה רב אשי לענין כו'

צ"ק

שיטה מקובצת

א] בנתערב ארבע באחת : ב] אמר רבה אות א' נמחק : ג] בכוסות ורואה אני דם בעלת מום למעלה כאילו הוא מים וחכ"א : ד] בין בבלול בין בכוסות אבל רבנן בכוסות [פליגי]· אף על גב דמתני' לא אתיא כר"י דבמתני' פליגי בעולה ובחטאת (ור"י) [ואליבא דר"י] לא פליגי בעולה וחטאת ועוד דבמתני' משמע דלא פליגי בבעלי מומין אלא לכ"ע ישפך לאמה אף לר"א דמאיסי מ"מ לענין דמיירי בין בבלול כו' אין סברא דמתני' פליג (עליה) [עליו] ומשני דבבלול נמי פליגי (עליה) [עליו] דמתני' לא מיירי אלא בכוסות וא"ת ומ"מ יקשה לרב אשי דאמר לר' אליעזר דאין בילה דלר' יהודה דאמר דמיירי ר"א בבלול א"כ יש בילה והדרי קשיא לדוכתיה וי"ל דמדר' יהודה לא קשיא דמצי למימר דמיירי דאיכא רובא דם תמימה וקא יהיב למזבח שיעור דם בעלת מום ועוד כדמשני לעיל באידך פירכא אבל לרבנן דפליגי עליה דר"י ומוקמי פלוגתייהו אף בהיכא דשניהן שוים ומכשיר להו לתרווייהו בכוסות פליגי ר"א ורבנן ומש"ה מכשיר ר' אליעזר בתרווייהו משום דאית ליה רואין ורואה אני דם חטאת למטה כאילו הוא מים ורבנן לית להו ראין וישפך לאמה אבל מתני' אי איירי בבלול לא מצי לשנויי הכי כדמוכח לעיל מבל תוסיף : ה] חטאת ותחלת עולה דברי הכל : ו] שיריים· עיין בתוס' לעיל (דף נא ע"א) : ז] אמר ריש לקיש לא : ח] חטאת ותחלת עולה דברי הכל : ט] עדיין היא מחלוקת· ולרבנן ישפך לאמה דאין לשנות של תחלת עולה שהוא בזקיפה בשביל הכשר שירים שטעונין איצטבא וכן איפכא אסור : י] תיבות בני אהרן את הדם נמחק : יא] וזרקו מה ת"ל תיבות את הדם נמחק : יב] תיבת מתן נמחק : יג] מתנה אחת הס"ד : יד] אמר רבה : טו] לא תשנינהו דודאי : טז] ותקשה לרב אשי דאיכא לשנויי דמתני' דעליונים ותחתונים כו' : יז] דם עולה תיבת חטאת נמחק : יח] תיבות וכן בעולה ובכור נמחק : יט] תיבת בבלול נמחק : כ] בהכי ולאפלוגי נמי ביש בילה כו' מיהו הנך מתניתא דקתני בהו : כא] דבדאיעריב טובא קאי כו' דמשמע יש בילה : כב] בילה ואי אות ד' נמחק : כג] תיבת ולא נמחק : כד] ושלמים אלא תיבת ועולה נמחק : כה] שיקרב אות י' נמחק : כו] אומר יקרב אות י' נמחק : כז] תיבת הוא נמחק : כח] במתני' ומוקמי' : כט] ועולה דבין בבלול ובין בכוסות : ל] א' מוקי מתני' בין : לא] יהודה ומוקמי' פלוגת' אף : לב] אלא בחד כדאוקימנא : לג] תיבת בו נמחק : לד] בחטאת מאי לאו . לה] השעיר ביום הכפורים למתן קרנות [תיבת של ל"ש] ותיבת דם נמחק : לו] הדם וזרקו את הדם והקריבו בני אהרן וזרקו על המזבח : לז] שיריים דמתנה ראשונה של עולה ותיבת דדם נמחק : לח] דרומית· ומיהו קשה דבפ' איזהו מקומן מוכח דעולה גופיה טעונה גג דיסוד וזקיפה דיסוד לטעוטי וזקיפה דיסוד כדקאמר מ"ד אזקיפה דיסוד קמ"ל אגגו דיסוד ושיריים הוי בזקיפה וי"ל דהא דמטעם התם היינו זקיפה דיסוד למטה מן היסוד כדמשמע לישנא דהתם דקאמר התם זקיפת יסוד דהיינו למטה מן היסוד אבל זקיפת של מעלה מן היסוד אין זה זקיפה דיסוד אלא זקיפה דסובב אלמא דלא מיירי לעיל אלא בזקיפה שלמטה מן היסוד אבל זקיפה שלמעלה מן היסוד מקרי שפיר גג היסוד דהיינו זקיפה דסובב ולא מצית אמרת גג יסוד ממש כיון דכתיב סביב בעולה ולא משכחת סביב בשפיכה על גג היסוד אלא בזריקה בזקיפה כנגד חודו של קרן דהדם מתפזר אילך ואילך· מהר"ם : לט] קמ"ל דאם נתערב בכור בעולה דיקרבו : מ] נמי ובתוס' מהר"ם תירצו ר"ל אי האי דינא ילפינן ליה מקרא א"כ הוי ליה לאתויי האי קרא במתני' גבי מחלוקת דר"א ור"י : מא] דקדש הם : מב] קאמר לה ר' יוחנן והוא דרשא : מג] משנים בזה להכשיר מזה : מד] ועובר משום בל : מה] במקומו דשניהם דשירים ואינו עובר על בל תגרע דשב ואל : מו] מתנות ובכור אינו אלא מתנה אחת :

דם

עין משפט
נר מצוה

סח א מיי' פ"ג מהלכות תמורה הלכה ה:

סט ב ג ד מיי' פ"ב מהלכות פסה"מ הלכה יג:

ע ה מיי' פ"ט מהל' תמידין ומוספין הלכה ט:

למעלה בלמטה לא מכשיר למעלה אלא ע"י רואין לשם מים ומיהו הא נמי חד טעמא הוא דמשום דאית ליה לשם מים הוא דלא עבר משום בל תוסיף ועוד כשעובר על בל תוסיף איט משנה בדם לפסול אבל בניתנין למעלה ולמטה וניתנין בחוץ בניתנין בפנים כולהו משנה בדם לפסול: **מנין** אפי' נתערב באשם כו'. תימה כי היכי דלהאי תנא איצטריך קרא כב] לתודה לעולה ולאשם ולמאן דנפקא ליה כמי מולקח מדם הפר ומדם השעיר דעולין אין מבטלין דלמא ה"מ פר ושעיר שוין לגמרי במתנותיהן מתן אחד במתן ד' מנין או עולה בגאלין וכן למאן דנפקא ליה מקודש הם מנא ליה *נתערב בדם עולה דלמא בקדשים הנאכלין איירי: **ואין** תמורתו קריבה. תימה כיון דתנאי היא אמאי הדר ביה בפ"ק דתמורה (דף ה:) דקאמר כג] ורבא אין ה"נ אלא הם למה לי כו': **הא** אוקימנא ברובא עליונים. פי' בקונטרס והאי דיהיב למטה לשם שירי חטאת הוא דקיהיב אבל עולה לא מתכשרא דהא יהיב למעלה שיעור תחתונים ועוד כד] א"כ מוקמת לה בתערובת חטאת ועולה לא שמעת מינה כה] (לא) מקום עולה מקום שירים דכיון דעולה לא מתכשרא לא זריק להו במקום עולה אלא באיצטבאות וקשה דלרבנן דאמרי יש בילה והויא לה עולה כשרה ויש דם עולה שנשאר למטה וראוי לזריקה: **נתן** בחוץ ואחר כך נתן בפנים כשר. וכגון דיהיב דמים הפנימים בחוץ לשם מים דאי לאו הכי היאך חוזר ונותן בפנים והלא כבר נתכפר לשמואל לפי מה שפירשתי לעיל בפ' שני (כו: ד"ה אמר) דמזבח חיצון לדמים הפנימיים כמקומן דמי ובכי האי גוונא איירי סיפא בפנים ונתן בחוץ שהכנים דמים החיצונים לשם מים וק"ק *אמאי פסול כשמכנים לשם מים דלכפר כתיב כו]:

עכשיו

דנתערב צ"ק

צ"ק ת"ז

[עיין תוס' ריש]

ר"ל מעיקרא דבבלול פליגי ומסקנא כו' צ"ק

תורה אור

*ת"ל דם דם א] שיכול אין לי אלא ב] אלו שנתערבו בתמורתה שאף מחיים תקרב ג] מנין לרבות תודה ושלמים מרבה אני תודה ושלמים שבאין בנדר ונדבה כמותה מנין לרבות את האשם מרבה אני את האשם שטעון מתן ד' ד] כמותו בכור ומעשר ופסח מנין ת"ל דם דם מאי לאו סוף עולה ובכור ושמע מינה מקום עולה מקום שירים לא תחילת עולה ובכור ומאי קמ"ל דאין עולין מבטלין זה את זה מולקח מדם הפר ומדם השעיר נפקא תנאי היא איכא דנפקא ליה מהכא ואיכא דנפקא ליה מהכא והני תנאי מולקח מדם הפר ומדם השעיר לא ילפי קסברי *אין מערבין לקרנות מדם דם. לא ה] יליף דם דם לא משמע להו אלא מקודש הם מאי טעמא לא ילפי קסברי *קודש הם הם קריבין *ואין תמורתן קריבה ואידך נפקא ליה °מאם שור אם שה לה' הוא הוא קרב ואין תמורתו קריבה ת"ש נתן למעלה ולא נמלך אלו ואלו מודים שיחזור ויתן למטה אלו ואלו עולין לו מאי לאו דאיערוב חטאת ועולה וכיון דיהיב ליה למעלה הוו להו שירים וקתני אלו ואלו מודים שיחזור ויתן למטה ושמע מינה מקום עולה מקום שירים כי אתא רב יצחק בר יוסף אמר אמרי במערבא הכא במאי עסקינן כגון דאיערב חטאת החיצונה ו] בשירים א"ל אביי ונימא מר כגון דאיערב בשירים דלמא הא קמ"ל אפילו למ"ד שירים מעכבין חסרו אין מעכבין א"ל רבא תוספאה לרבינא ז] הא אוקימנא ההיא ברובא עליונים וקא יהיב למעלה שיעור תחתונים ועוד [א"ל] ה"מ ח] למאן דאמרו *מעיקרא *אין בילה מסקנא בכוסות פליגי:

ויקרא כז

מתני' הניתנין בפנים שנתערבו בניתנין בחוץ ישפכו לאמה נתן בחוץ וחזר ונתן בפנים כשר בפנים וחזר ונתן בחוץ רבי עקיבא פוסל וחכמים מכשירים *שר"ע אומר כל דמים שנכנסו לכפר בהיכל פסולין וחכמים אומרים חטאת בלבד רבי אליעזר אומר אף האשם שנאמר °כחטאת כאשם: **גמ'** וניפלוג נמי ר"א בהא היכי ליעביד ניתיב בחוץ והדר ניתיב לפנים ט] כשם שמצוה להקדים עליונים לתחתונים כך מצוה להקדים פנים לחוץ וניתיב

שם ויד

ת"ל דם דם שיכול אין לי אלא אלו. יקרבו שאף אם נתערבו מחיים יקרבו מנין אפילו נתערב באשם כו': ת"ל. י] חד מינייהו דריש ומשמע ליה את הדם בכל מקום שהוא שמו עליו ולא בטל: יכול אין לי אלא נתערב באלו. יא] דקא מרבינן מיניה דיקרבו שכן תערובתן ראויה לקרב אפילו נתערבו בהמה בבהמה מחיים דהא עולה בתמורה או בעולה אחרת תנן במתני' קדשים בקדשים מין במינו זה יקרב לשם מי שהוא וזה יקרב לשם מי שהוא וכן יב] בנתערבו בחולין תמימין תנן לעיל (דף עא:) ימכרו החולין לצרכי אותו המין והדר הוו להו קדשים בקדשים מין במינו מנין אפי' נתערב בדם אשם יקרב ואף על פי שאינו מינו ואם נתערב מחיים לא היה קרב כדתנן (שם) קדשים בקדשים מין בשאינו מינו ירעו: אביא את אשר נתערב באשם. מהאי רבויא גופיה ולא בעי קרא אחרינא הואיל ושניהם קדשי קדשים ואע"ג דאם נתערבו מחיים לא קרב התם משום דאית להו תקנתא ברעייה הוא: ת"ל דם דם. להכי איצטריכו דם דם תרי זימני: והני תנאי כו'. לשון בעיא הוא והנך תלתא תנאי דאיפליגו במילף לעולין שאין מבטלין זה את זה מתלתא קראי בשלמא כולהו מולקח מדם הפר ומדם השעיר לא ילפי קסברי תרי תנאי דשמעתין אין מערבין דם פר ושעיר למתן דם קרנות מזבח הפנימי ומאי ולקח מדם הפר ומדם השעיר מזה בפני עצמו ומזה בפני עצמו ופלוגתא דר' יונתן ורבי יאשיה היא במסכת יומא (דף מז:): יג] והאי מדם דם. לא משמע להו לתנא דהקומץ ולתנא דקדש הם אלא מקדש הם כו': ואין תמורתן קריבה. ולא למידרש ביה בהווייתן יהו אתא: נתן למעלה ולא נמלך. מתני' דפליגי ביה ר"א ורבנן בניתנין למעלה שנתערבו בניתנין למטה: מאי לאו פלוגתייהו בחטאת שנתערבה בעולה הוא. כדקס"ד עד השתא וקתני דאפי' לרבנן יחזור ויתן למטה לכתחלה ואף על גב דנתערבו השתא סוף חטאת ועולה וש"מ חד מקום הוא: הכא במאי עסקינן. רישא דפלוגתא יד] למטה לכתחלה כגון דאיערב תחלה חטאת החיצונה בשירי חטאת הפנימית דהיינו שירים סתמא הלכך נתן למעלה ולא נמלך דאי נמלך לרבנן ישפך דהוו להו ניתנים בפנים שחזר ונתן מהם בחוץ בקרנות והוי שלא במקומו אבל מכי נתן למעלה טו] הוו להו שירים ושירים ושניהן ביסוד וכרבי ישמעאל דאמר זה וזה יסוד מערבי או כר"ש דאמר זה וזה יסוד דרומי לעיל (דף נג.): ולימא מר כגון דאיערב חטאת החיצונה בשיריים. כלומר בשירי חיצונה כמותה דהכי שפיר טפי שמקום שיריהן שוה לדברי הכל: דלמא הא קמ"ל. האי דאוקמה אף בשירי פנימית דאפילו למאן דאמר שירים הפנימיים מעכבי ה"מ כי לא יהיב מינייהו מידי אבל חסרו מקלתן לאחר מתן דמים טז] הפנימיים אין החסרון מעכב ושופך הנאר ליסוד דהא הכא חסרו שירים הפנימיים יז] בשנתן דמיהן למעלה ואפ"ה מתכשרי: והא אוקימנא כו'. והא דקא יהיב למטה יח] לשם שירי חטאת הוא דקא יהיב אבל עולה לא מיתכשר דהא יהיב למעלה שיעור תחתונים ועוד יט] *א"כ מוקמת לה בתערובת חטאת ועולה לא ש"מ מקום עולה מקום שירים דכיון דעולה לא מיתכשרא לא זריק להו במקום עולה אלא באיצטבא ומאי דוחקיה לאוקומה בחטאת ושירים: א"ל ה"מ. הנך שינויי דשנינן לעיל למאי דהוה ס"ד מעיקרא דבבלול פליגי והוה מהדרינן אשינויי דחיקי לאוקומי לדרב אשי דאמר לר"א אין בילה דלא תיקשי ליה כ] הך מתנייתא: מסקנא. דשינויין הדרנא בן ואוקימנא לשינוי דפלוגתא דידהו בהך מתני' בתערובת כוסות הוא ומתרווייהו קאמר ר"א דליתיב למעלה ולמטה ושניהן כשירין והיכא דנתן למעלה ולא נמלך דברי הכל יתן למטה ואלו ואלו עלו ואי הוה מוקי לה רב כא] יהודה בחטאת ועולה הוה קשיא ליה: **מתני'** הניתנין בפנים ישפכו לאמה. דלית לן רואין ואסור לשנות בהאו מפני הכשירן של אלו ובגמרא פריך וניפלוג נמי ר"א בהא דהא אית ליה רואין: ר"ע פוסל. בחיצון: וחכמים מכשירין. בכל קרבנות חוץ מחטאת החיצונה דמיפסלא משום וכל חטאת אשר יובא וגו': **גמ'** כשם שמצוה להקדים עליונים לתחתונים. דם חטאת לדם עולה כדאמר בכל התדיר (לקמן דף פט.). כך מצוה להקדים פנים לחוץ. דפנים חשוב:

ניתיב

מסורת הש"ס

עין נתבאר נרפאים

[לעיל עב: תו"ס]

[תמורה ט.]

[לעיל פ.]

[לעיל י: [לקמן נח]]

ול"צ צ"ק

שיטה מקובצת

א] דם דם מנין אתה אומר נתערב דם עולה בדם העולה דם עולה בדם תמורה דם עולה בדם חולין יקרבו ת"ל דם יכול אין לי אלא אלו יקרבו שאף אם נתערבו מחיים יקרבו מנין אפי' נתערב באשם אביא אני את שנתערב באשם שאלו ואלו קדשי קדשים מנין אפילו נתערב בתודה ושלמים אביא אני שנתערב בתודה ובשלמים שאלו ואלו מתן ד' מנין אפילו נתערב בבכור ובפסח ת"ל דם דם כך גירסת רש"י ז"ל תירסת ס"י: ב] אלא עולה שנתערבה בתמורתה: ג] עיין בהשמטות בסוף המס': ד] ד' כמותה: ה] לא ילפי דם: ו] כגון דאיערב חטאת החיצונה תחלתה בשיריים הפנימים' תימה דלוקמא בסוף חטאת ותחלת עולה שנתערבו וינתן למעלה דקאמר בזקיפה שהוא מקום תחלת עולה ויחזור ויתן למטה על גג האיצטבא קאמר שהוא מקום שיריים ואי משום דקאי אניתנין למעלה שנתערבו בניתנים למטה הא נפרש הכי תחלת עולה שהיא למעלה מן היסוד בזקיפה דסובב בסוף החטאת שהיא למטה על גג האיצטבא וי"ל דלמ"ד דניתנים למעלה ממש בקרנות משום דלמעלה מחוט הסיקרא קאמר וא"כ ע"כ היינו תחלת חטאת דאלו סוף (העולת) [הוא עולה] למטה מחוט הסיקרא הוא וכן דכוותיה נתן למעלה אלמעלה מן החוט קאמר וא"כ ע"כ היינו תחלת חטאת ומ"מ יחזור ויתן למטה דקאמר אמקום שירים קאמר דהיינו איצטבא ולא זקיפה מקום עולה אע"ג דגם זקיפה למטה מן החוט הוא מדיהיב טעמא דמודו רבנן דיחזור ויחזיר ויתן למטה משום דנתן כבר למעלה כמשפט תחלת דם החטאת ואז נעשה המותר מדם החטאת שירים דלמטה הוא ולכך יחזור ויתן למטה במקום שירים אלמא יחזור ויתן למטה אמקום שירים קאי: ז] הא אוקימנא [ההיא] ברובא עליונים' פ"ה והא דקא יהיב כו' מתכשרי בהכי דהא יהיב למעלה שיעור תחתונים ועוד ושמא כל דם העולה נתן למעלה וא"כ לא זריק ליה במקום עולה דהיינו בזקיפה אלא באיצטבא שהוא מקום שירים ועלו לו דקתני לשם שירים דחטאת קאמר וא"כ מאי דוחקיה לאוקמי בחטאת ושירים הפנימים שנתערבו וא"ת איך קאמר אלו ואלו [מודים] שיחזור ויתן למטה לכתחלה הא קא משני מקום תחלת עולה דדינה בזקיפה ולעיל פי' דלמ"ד עדיין היא מחלוקת דלרבנן ישפך לאמה דאין לשנות תחלת עולה שהיא בזקיפה בשביל הכשר שירים הטעונים יסוד לכך נראה להשר מקוצי דה"פ שירים צריכות איצטבא ועדיין היא מחלוקת וא"כ לרבנן דלית להו רואין לא ישנה מקום שירים כדי לקיים מצות עולה לזרוק בזקיפה משום דאין זה מקום שירים כלל דאין סוף שירים ראשים לזחול למעלה אלא אדרבה יזרוק הכל באיצטבא במקום שירים דמותר לשנות מקום עולה בשביל מצות שירים גם לרבנן דלית להו רואים וטעמא משום דתחלת עולה שוק בזקיפה של סובב הם שופכים וזוחלים ליסוד למטה מהם וכיון שסופן להיות למטה על היסוד א"כ מותר לשנות מקום תחלת עולה כדי לקיים מצות שירים ואע"ג דמ"מ

שיטה מקובצת

לא יצא ידי עולה דדינה בזריקה בזקיפה ולא בשפיכה ביסוד ואתיא כמ"ד ניתנים בזריקה שנתנם בשפיכה לא יצא דלמ"ד יצא א"כ אצטבא שהיא מקום שירים חזיא נמי למקום הכשר תחלת עולה בדיעבד והא דקאמר לעיל עדיין היא מחלוקת משמע דלרבנן אסור לשנות מקומו של זה בשביל זה הינו שאסור לזרוק התערובת בזקיפה במקום עולה לפי שמשנה מקום שירים ואסור לשנות מקום שירים כדי לקיים מצות עולה לרבנן דלית להו רואין כדפי' וא"ת מאי קאמר הא אוקימנא להתוא ברובא עליונים כו' ועלו לו לשם שירים קאמר אבל עולה לא מיתכשרא אדרבה אסיקנא לעיל דעלו לשם תחלת עולה לרבנן דאמרי יש בילה וי"ל דסוגיא דלעיל אתיא כמ"ד מקום עולה מקום שירים וא"כ לרבנן דאמרי יש בילה אלו ואלו עלו לו דקאמר הוי בין לתחלת עולה בין לשירים דחטאת דהא מקום אחד יש לשניהם ולכך פריך שפיר לעיל והא אלו ואלו עלו לו קתני כדפי' אכן סוגיא דהכא בעי לדחות כדי ליישב דמקום עולה לאו מקום שירים ושירים צריכים איצטבא א"כ ויחזור ויתן למטה למקום שירים קאמר דהיינו על האיצטבא והלכך אלו ואלו עלו לו דקתני גם לרבנן דוקא לשיריים קאמר ולא לתחילת עולה דהא איצטבא שהוא מקום שירים אינו מקום תחלת עולה ולכך פריך הכא והא אוקימנא כו' וא"כ מצינו למדחי דמקום עולה לאו מקום שירים והא ומאי אלו ואלו עלו לו לשם שירים קאמר גם לרבנן דר"א כדפי' ומשני ה"מ למ"ד אין בילה כלו' כשהיינו רוצים להעמיד הברייתות בבלול ואף כמ"ד אין בילה או הוצרכנו להעמיד ברובא עליונים כו' ועלו לו לשם שירים דוקא קאמר ולא לשם תחלת עולה אבל למסקנא בכוסות פליגי ואף כי אין בילה עלו לו גם לשם תחלת עולה ומיהו לפי' שפי' לעיל דדייקי מאלו דומיא דאלו לא מתוקם שפיר: ח] למאי דאמרי: ט] עיין בהשמטות בסוף המסכת: י] ת"ל דם דם חד: יא] באלו הוא דקא: יב] וכן נתערבו בחולין אות ב' נמחק: יג] מת"ד ואי מדם: יד] תיבות למטה לכתחלה נמחק: טו] למעלה משניהם הוו: טז] דמים על מזבח הפנימי אין: יז] הפנימים כשנתן מהן למעלה: יח] למטה מן הדם לשם: יט] ועוד וא"נ מוקמת: כ] ליה הנך מתנייתא הס"ד ומת"ד ומסקנא דשינויין: כא] רב יצחק בחטאת ותיבת יהודה נמחק: כב] קרא לתמורה ועולה ואשם: כג] דקאמר רבא אות ו' נמחק: כד] ועוד וא"צ: כה] תיבת לא נמחק: כו] כתיב' גליון' ר"ל דכיון דאיערב בדמים הפנימים ואינהו אתו לכפר (איכא) ואשר יובא לכפר קרינא בית' ריב"א:

דרן

[81b] why is *'blood'* repeated?[8] For one might think: I only know about a burnt-offering which was mixed up with its substitute,[9] for even [if they were mixed up] whilst alive, they must be offered. Whence do I know to include the thanksoffering and the peace-
a offering?[1] I include the thanksoffering and the peace-offering, because they can be brought as a votive or a freewill-offering,[2] like itself. Whence do I know to include the guilt-offering? I include the guilt-offering which requires four applications, like itself. Whence do I know [to include] a firstling, tithe, and the Passover-offering? Because it says, *blood, blood.*[3] Now surely that speaks of the *end* of the burnt-offering and [the beginning of] the firstling; whence you may infer that the place of the burnt-offering is the place of the residue?—No: it speaks of the *beginning* of the burnt-offering and [that of] the firstling. What then does he inform us? that sacrifices do not nullify one another! [Surely] that is deduced from [the text], *And he shall take of the blood of the bullock and of the blood of the goat?*—It is a controversy of Tannaim: one deduces it from this text, and another deduces it from the other text.

Now, these Tannaim do not learn it from *'and he shall take of the blood of the bullock and of the blood of the goat'*, because they hold, You do not mingle [the blood] for [sprinkling] on the horns.[4] They do not learn it from the repetition of *'blood'*, because they do not attribute any significance to this repetition. But why do they not deduce it from *'they are holy'*?[5]—They hold [that] *'they are holy'* [teaches:] *'they'* are offered, but their substitute is not offered.[6] And the other?[7]—He deduces it from, *Whether it be ox or sheep, it is the Lord's:*[8] *'it'* is offered, but its substitute is not offered.

Come and hear: If [the priest] sprinkled [it][9] above without asking, both agree that he must re-sprinkle [it] below, and both are accounted to him. Now does that not mean that [the blood of] a sin-offering and [that of] a burnt-offering were mixed, in which case as soon as he sprinkles above, it becomes a residue, yet he teaches, 'both agree that he must re-sprinkle [it] below', which proves that the place of the burnt-offering is the place of the residue?
b —When R. Isaac b. Joseph came,[1] he said: In the West[2] they said: The case we are discussing here is where e.g. [the blood of] an outer sin-offering was mixed with the residue of an inner sin-offering.[3] Said Abaye to him: Yet let the master say, 'e.g., where it was mixed with a residue'?[4] Perhaps this is what you would inform us: Even on the view that the residue[5] is indispensable,[6] yet if some of it is lacking it does not matter?[7] Said Raba Tosfa'ah[8] to Rabina: But we have explained that as meaning that the greater part was upper [blood], and he sprinkles above as much as there was of the lower [blood] plus a little more?[9]—That was only, he replied, on the hypothesis first stated that [the Mishnah treats of where the blood itself] was mingled, and in accordance with the thesis that there is no even distribution. But in our final conclusion [we hold that] they disagree where the goblets were mixed up.[10]

MISHNAH. IF [BLOOD] WHICH IS TO BE SPRINKLED WITHIN WAS MIXED WITH [BLOOD] THAT IS TO BE SPRINKLED WITHOUT, IT MUST BE POURED OUT INTO THE DUCT. IF [THE PRIEST] SPRINKLED WITHOUT AND THEN SPRINKLED WITHIN, IT IS VALID. [IF HE SPRINKLED] WITHIN AND THEN RE-SPRINKLED WITHOUT, R. AKIBA DECLARES IT UNFIT, WHILE THE SAGES DECLARE IT FIT. FOR R. AKIBA MAINTAINED: ALL BLOOD WHICH ENTERED THE HEKAL TO MAKE ATONEMENT IS UNFIT; BUT THE SAGES RULE: THE SIN-OFFERING ALONE [IS UNFIT]. R. ELIEZER SAID: THE GUILT-OFFERING TOO, FOR
c IT SAYS, AS IS THE SIN-OFFERING, SO IS THE GUILT-OFFERING.[1]

GEMARA. Now, let R. Eliezer disagree here too?—What should be done? Shall we [first] sprinkle without and then sprinkle within? [that cannot be done], [because] just as the upper [blood] must precede the lower, so must the inner precede the outer.

(8) Rashi reads: How do we know that if the blood of a burnt-offering was mixed with the blood of another burnt-offering, or with the blood of a substitute (v. *supra* 5b n. b 8), or with the blood of *ḥullin*, it must be offered (i.e., sprinkled)? Because it says, *blood, blood* (i.e., this repetition is an extension). I know it only of these, for even if these were mixed up whilst alive they must be offered. How do I know it even when it is mixed with the blood of a guilt-offering? etc. (9) *Sc.* their blood was mixed.—From the verse I know that their blood must still be sprinkled.
a (1) That the blood of a burnt-offering must be sprinkled even if it is mixed with these; similarly the other cases posited. (2) V. *supra* 2b, n. 6. (3) The repetition teaches the inclusion of all these. (4) Of the altar; *supra* 42b. Hence the blood of each must be stated, because they were taken *separately*, not mixed together, and so no inference can be made from the text about nullification. (5) As the first Tanna does. (6) A substitute of a firstling must be redeemed, but cannot be offered. (7) The first Tanna: how does he know this? (8) Lev. XXVII, 26. This refers to a firstling. (9) The mingled blood.
b (1) From Eretz Israel. (2) *Sc.* Palestine, which lies to the west of Babylon. (3) Emended text. After he sprinkles thereof above the red line, *all* the rest is the residue, which must be poured out at the base. (4) Not particularly 'the residue of an *inner* sin-offering'. (5) *Sc.* of the inner sin-offering. (6) It *must* be poured out at the base; otherwise the sacrifice is invalid. (7) It is unnecessary for the *whole* of the residue to be poured out on the base. For here some of the residue will have been *sprinkled* above the line, and yet the sacrifice is valid when the rest is poured out at the base. (8) Perhaps of Thospia. Neub. *Géogr.* p. 332: capital of the Armenian district Thospitis. (9) And he applies it below as the residue of the sin-offering, not as the blood of the burnt-offering, which does *not* become valid. Hence even if it were explained as the mingling of the sin-offering and the burnt-offering, it would not prove that the place of the burnt-offering is the place of the residue, since the burnt-offering does not become fit. Why then must you explain it as meaning that the blood of a *sin*-offering and the residue were mingled? (10) And unless it refers to a sin-offering and residue, this contradicts the opinion that the place of the burnt-offering is *not* the place of the residue.
c (1) Lev. VII, 7. V. *supra* 10b for notes.

[82a] Then let us [first] sprinkle within and then sprinkle without?—Since the sin-offering and the guilt-offering become unfit if their blood enters within, he could not give a general ruling.[2]

FOR R. AKIBA MAINTAINED etc. Rab Judah said in Samuel's name: For example, to what may R. Akiba's ruling be compared? To a disciple who was mixing [wine] for his master with hot water,[3] when he [the master] said to him, Mix me [a drink]. With what?[4] he enquired. Are we not occupied with hot water? he replied; now then [I mean] with either hot or cold.[5] So here too: consider: we are discussing the sin-offering:[6] for what purpose then does the Divine Law write *'sin-offering'*?[7] [To teach:] I do not mean a sin-offering [alone], but all sacrifices.[8] To this R. Huna the son of R. Joshua demurred: Consider: all sacrifices are included in respect of scouring and rinsing; why then does the Divine Law write *'sin-*
a *offering'*?[1] Hence you may infer from this: only the sin-offering, but nothing else. This then can only be compared to a disciple who was mixing [a drink] for his master with either hot or cold water, when he said to him, Mix it for me with hot water only!—Rather, R. Akiba's reason is that 'and every *sin-offering*' is written where '[and] a sin-offering' [would suffice].[2] For it was taught: 'A *sin-offering*': I know [this] only [of] a sin-offering; how do we know [it of] most sacred sacrifices [in general]? Because it says, 'Every *sin-offering*'. How do we know [it of] lesser sacrifices? Because it says, 'And *every sin-offering*': this is the view of R. Akiba. Said R. Jose the Galilean to him: Even if you go on including all day, I will pay no heed to you.[3] Rather: *'a sin-offering'*: I only know [this of] a private sin-offering:[4] whence do we know [it of] a public sin-offering? Because it says, 'Every *sin-offering*'. Again, I know it only of a male sin-offering: whence do I know [it of] a female sin-offering? Because it says, 'And *every*'. It is just the reverse![5]—Rather, this is what he means: I only know [it of] a female sin-offering: whence do I know [it of] a male sin-offering? From the text, *'And every sin-offering'*.

Now, does R. Jose the Galilean hold that this text comes for this purpose? Surely it was taught, R. Jose the Galilean said: The whole passage speaks only of the bullocks which were to be burnt and the he-goats which were to be burnt, and its purpose is [i] to teach that when they are disqualified they must be burnt before the Temple; and [ii] to impose a negative injunction against eating
b them.[1] Said they to him: As to an [outer] sin-offering whose blood entered the innermost [sanctuary], whence do we know [that it is disqualified]? Said he to them: [From the verse,] *Behold, the blood of it was not brought into the sanctuary within?*[2]—He argues on R. Akiba's contention.[3]

MISHNAH. IF THE BLOOD OF A SIN-OFFERING WAS RECEIVED IN TWO GOBLETS AND ONE OF THEM WENT WITHOUT,[4] THE INSIDE ONE IS FIT.[5] IF ONE OF THEM ENTERED WITHIN,[6] R. JOSE THE GALILEAN DECLARES THE OUTER ONE[7] FIT;[8] BUT THE SAGES DISQUALIFY IT. SAID R. JOSE THE GALILEAN: IF THE PLACE WHERE AN INTENTION [DIRECTED TO IT] DISQUALIFIES, [VIZ.,] WITHOUT,[9] YOU DO NOT TREAT WHAT IS LEFT AS WHAT WENT OUT;[9] THEN THE PLACE WHERE AN INTENTION [DIRECTED TO IT] DOES NOT DISQUALIFY, [VIZ.,]
c WITHIN,[1] IS IT NOT LOGICAL THAT WE DO NOT TREAT WHAT IS LEFT[2] AS WHAT ENTERED WITHIN? IF IT ENTERED WITHIN TO MAKE ATONEMENT,[3] EVEN IF HE [THE PRIEST] DID NOT MAKE ATONEMENT,[4] IT IS UNFIT: THESE ARE THE WORDS OF R. ELIEZER. R. SIMEON SAID: [IT IS NOT UNFIT] UNLESS HE MAKES ATONEMENT. R. JUDAH SAID: IF HE TOOK IT IN UNWITTINGLY,[5] IT IS FIT. FOR ALL UNFIT BLOOD WHICH WAS PRESENTED AT THE ALTAR [I.E., SPRINKLED] THE HEADPLATE DOES NOT PROPITIATE,[6] SAVE FOR UNCLEAN [BLOOD], FOR THE HEADPLATE PROPITIATES FOR THAT WHICH IS UNCLEAN, BUT DOES NOT PROPITIATE FOR WHAT GOES OUT.[7]

GEMARA. It was taught, R. Jose the Galilean said: It is a *kal wa-ḥomer:* If the place where an intention [directed to it] disqualifies, [viz.,] without, the blood without does not disqualify that which is within;[8] then the place where an intention [directed to it] does not disqualify, [viz.,] within, is it not logical that the blood within does not disqualify that which is without? Said they to him, Lo, it says, [*And every sin-offering*] *whereof* any *of the blood is brought* [*into the tent of meeting . . . shall be burnt with fire*]:[9] [this implies,] even part of its blood. Said he to them: Then you now have a *kal wa-ḥomer* in respect of [blood] that goes out; if the place where an intention [directed to it] does *not* disqualify [viz.,] within, yet the blood within disqualifies [the blood] without; where intention *does* disqualify, [viz.,] without, is it not logical that the blood without disqualifies [the blood] within? Said they to him: Lo, it says, *whereof* [*any of the blood*] *is brought* [*into* etc.]: that which enters within disqualifies, but that which goes out does not disqualify.
d Now, let intention [to sprinkle] within[1] disqualify, *a fortiori:* if though[2] blood without does not disqualify [the blood] within, yet intention without[3] disqualifies; then seeing that the blood within does disqualify the blood without, is it not logical that intention

(2) That the blood should be sprinkled first within and then without, since this would not apply to these two. Therefore his view is not stated at all. (3) Their wine was too strong to be drunk without dilution. (4) Hot or cold water. (5) As you were actually mixing wine with hot water, I had no need to say anything at all. Therefore when I told you to mix me a drink, I meant that it could be with either hot or cold water (Tosaf.). (6) The whole section in Lev. VI, 19-23 q.v. treats of the sin-offering. (7) Ibid. 23: *And every* sin-offering *whereof any of the blood is brought into the tent of meeting to make atonement in the holy place* (i.e., an outer sin-offering whose blood is sprinkled on the inner altar) *shall not be eaten; it shall be burnt with fire.* (8) Interpreting: And *even* every sin-offering, although some sin-offerings must be brought within, and how much the more other sacrifices!

a (1) Lev. VI, 21 states: *But the earthen vessel wherein it* (*sc.* the sin-offering) *is sodden shall be broken; and if it be sodden in a brazen vessel, it shall be scoured and rinsed in water.* The following verse states '*it is most holy*' from which it is inferred *infra* 96*b* that the law of scouring and rinsing applies to *all* sacrifices. Hence at this stage (v. 22) we are already treating of *all* sacrifices; if then v. 23 is to apply likewise to *all*, Scripture should simply write: And that whereof any of the blood etc. (2) Lit., 'R. Akiba's reason is from sin-offering, and *every* sin-offering.' (3) I reject your view that *'and'* and *'every'* are extensions which include *other kinds* of sacrifices, seeing that the passage speaks of sin-offerings only. (4) For this section is followed by sections on the guilt-offering and the peace- and thanksofferings, which were private sacrifices. (5) The usual sin-offering is a *female*, and no extension is needed to include it.

b (1) This refers to the verse under discussion, which the Rabbis relate to an *outer* sin-offering whose blood was carried into the inner court, thereby disqualifying it. But R. Jose the Galilean relates it to an *inner* sin-offering, e.g., the bullock brought when the entire congregation sins in ignorance (v. Lev. IV, 13 f). Hence he interprets: *And every sin-offering whereof any of the blood is* (rightly) *brought into the tent of meeting* etc. *shall not be eaten.* Now this is superfluous in respect of a valid sacrifice, since it is explicitly stated in IV, 21: *and he shall carry forth the bullock without the camp, and burn it.* Consequently, the verse must mean that if it became unfit through going outside its legitimate boundary or through defilement, it must be burnt in front of the *Birah* (the Temple), and not carried '*without the camp*', i.e., beyond the Temple Mount. Further, this prohibits the eating of its flesh by a *negative* injunction, violation of which involves flagellation (Lev. IV, 21 merely contains an *affirmative* precept, the disregard of which is not punished by flagellation). Thus R. Jose the Galilean does not relate *this* text to outer sin-offerings at all. (2) Lev. X, 18; v. *supra* 10*b*. (3) He personally holds that it refers to *inner* sin-offerings. But he argues that even on R. Akiba's view that it refers to *outer* sin-offerings, the extension of *'and'* and *'every'* must apply to sin-offerings likewise, not to other sacrifices. (4) *Sc.* the Temple court. (5) One can sprinkle the blood in it, and the sacrifice is valid. (6) Into the *hekal*, the inner sanctum. (7) I.e., the one that remained in the Temple court. (8) For sprinkling. (9) An intention at the *shechitah* to sprinkle the blood without the Temple court disqualifies the sacrifice. Yet if one actually carried one goblet without, we do not regard the other goblet as though it too had been carried without, for the first clause states, THE INSIDE ONE IS FIT.

c (1) The intention to sprinkle the blood *within*, in the *hekal*, does not disqualify the sacrifice. (2) V. *supra* n. b 7. (3) If it was carried into the *hekal* for sprinkling. (4) He did not actually sprinkle it. (5) Not knowing that it was forbidden. (6) Make it fit. (7) V. *supra* 23*b*. (8) As in the Mishnah. (9) Lev. VI, 23.

d (1) I.e., the intention to take the blood into the *hekal*. (2) Lit., 'where'. (3) *Sc.* the intention to sprinkle the blood without.

ניתיב לפנים והדר ניתיב לחוץ כיון דאיכא חטאת ואשם דכי נכנס דמן א] פסולין לא פסיקא ליה: שהיה ר"ע אומר [וכו']: אמר רב יהודה אמר שמואל משל ב] למה הדבר דומה לתלמיד שמזג לרבו בחמין ואמר לו מזוג לי אמר לו במה אמר לו לא בחמין אנו עסוקין עכשיו בין בחמין בין בצונן הכא נמי מכדי בחטאת עסקינן ואתי חטאת דכתב רחמנא ל"ל ג] אלא לאו חטאת קאמינא לה אלא כל קדשים מתקיף לה רב הונא בריה דרב יהושע מכדי איתרבו כל קדשים ד] לגבי מזבח לענין מריקה ושטיפה חטאת דכתב רחמנא ל"ל ש"מ חטאת אין מידי אחרינא לא והא לא דמיא אלא לתלמיד שמזג לרבו בין בחמין בין בצונן ה] אמר לו אל תמזוג לי אלא חמין אלא טעמא דר"ע מחטאת וכל חטאת דתניא חטאת אין לי אלא חטאת קדשי קדשים מנין ת"ל °כל חטאת קדשים קלים מנין ו] ת"ל וכל חטאת דברי ר"ע אמר לו רבי יוסי הגלילי *אפילו אתה מרבה כל היום כולו איני שומע לך אלא ז] חטאת אין לי אלא חטאת יחיד חטאת צבור מנין ת"ל כל חטאת ואין לי אלא חטאת זכר חטאת נקבה מנין ח] ת"ל וכל כלפי לייא אלא ה"ק אין לי אלא חטאת נקבה חטאת זכר מנין ת"ל וכל חטאת וסבר רבי יוסי הגלילי האי קרא להכי הוא דאתא *והתניא רבי יוסי הגלילי אומר ט] (לפי שמצינו) כל הענין כולו אינו מדבר אלא בפרים הנשרפים ושעירים הנשרפים לשרוף פסוליהן אבית הבירה ולעמוד בלא תעשה על אכילתו אמרו לו חטאת שנכנס דמה לפני ולפנים מנין אמר להם °הן לא הובא לדבריו דר"ע קאמר:

מתני' חטאת שקבל דמה בשני כוסות יצא אחד מהן לחוץ הפנימי כשר נכנס אחד מהם לפנים ר' יוסי הגלילי מכשיר בחיצון וחכמים פוסלין א"ר יוסי הגלילי מה אם במקום שהמחשבה פוסלת בחוץ לא עשה את המשויר כיוצא מקום שאין המחשבה פוסלת בפנים אינו דין שלא נעשה את המשויר כנכנס נכנס לכפר אע"פ שלא כפר פסול דברי ר"א ר"ש אומר עד שיכפר רבי יהודה אומר אם הכניס שוגג כשר כל הדמים י] פסולין שנתנו ע"ג המזבח לא הרצה הציץ אלא על הטמא שהציץ מרצה על הטמא ואינו מרצה על היוצא:

גמ' תניא א"ר יוסי הגלילי ק"ו ומה במקום שמחשבה פוסלת בחוץ לא פסל דם שבחוץ את שבפנים מקום שאין מחשבה פוסלת בפנים אינו דין שלא יפסול דם שבפנים את שבחוץ א"ל הרי הוא אומר °אשר יובא מדמה אפילו מקצת דמה אמר להם ק"ו ליוצא מעתה ומה במקום שאין מחשבה פוסלת בפנים פוסל דם שבפנים את שבחוץ מקום שמחשבה פוסלת בחוץ אינו דין שיפסול דם שבחוץ את שבפנים אמרו לו הרי הוא אומר אשר יובא הנכנס פוסל ואין היוצא פוסל ותהא מחשבה בפנים פוסלת מקל וחומר ומה במקום שלא פסל דם שבחוץ את שבפנים מחשבה פוסלת בחוץ מקום שפסל דם שבפנים את דם שבחוץ אינו דין שתהא מחשבה פוסלת בפנים הרי הוא אומר °ביום השלישי מקום

רש"י

ניתיב בפנים והדר ניתיב בחוץ · דהא לר"א שאר דמים שנכנסין להיכל כשרין חוץ מחטאת ואשם כדקתני מתני': כיון דאיכא חטאת ואשם · שאם יא] נתערבו דמם בדמים הפנימיים לא מצי למימר יתן בפנים ואח"כ יתן בחוץ משום דמיפסלי חיצונים לא פסיקא ליה ואי"ת ליפסלינהו לחיצונים להכשיר פנימיי' יב] למפסלינהו בידים לא קאמר ר"א ומוטב להמתין עד שקיעת החמה ויפסלו מאליהן ושפכם לאמה: משל דרבי עקיבא · דמשמע ליה שאר כל הדמים בכלל יג] כל חטאת אשר יובא מדמה למה הדבר דומה לתלמיד שמזג לו רבו יין בחמין וכו': לא בחמין אנו עסוקין · וכיון שאני אומר לך מזוג סתם בחמין הייתי אומר לך עכשיו הנני אומר לך בין בחמין בין בצונן כלומר העוסק בדבר אין רגיל להזכירו כשמדבר בו ואם מזכירו בדעתו להוסיף אחרים עמו ואומר אף זה שהייתי עסוק בו יהא בכלל: ה"ג מכדי בחטאת עסקינן ואתי · כולה פרשה: חטאת דכתב רחמנא ל"ל · לכתוב ואם יובא מדמה וגו': אלא ה"ק יד] לאו חטאת לחוד קאמינא · אלא אף חטאת כשאר קדשים אשר יובא וגו' דלא תימא חטאת לא תיפסול שכן מצינו חטאת נכנסת להיכל בחטאות הפנימיות: מכדי איתרבו כל הקדשים · (לעיל) [לקמן] מהאי קרא לענין שיהו טעונים מריקה ושטיפה כלי מתכות שנתבשלו בהן כדילפינן בפרק דם חטאת (לקמן צז:) מקדש קדשים היא וסמיך ליה וכל חטאת אשר יובא ואי שאר קדשים נמי מיפסלי ל"ל למיכתב טו] חטאת ליכתוב ואשר יובא מדמה ש"מ חטאת דוקא קאמר: הא לא דמיא כו' · מסקנא דקושיא היא: אלא חטאת יחיד · דהא טז] כתיב הך פרשת חטאת אצל פרשת אשם ופרשת שלמים ותודה שהן של יז] יחידים: כלפי לייא · סתם חטאת יחיד נקבה היא: להכי הוא דאתא · לחטאת חיצונה שנכנס דמה לפנים: ה"ג כל הענין הזה אינו מדבר כו' · ול"ג לפי שמצינו ואדרבנן פליג בת"כ דמוקמינן ליה ליפסול חטאת החיצונה שנכנס דמה לפנים ואמר להו אין המקרא מדבר אלא בפנימיות שדמם נכנס לפנים *מלוה ואמר קרא שאם אירע בהן פסול ישרפו אבית הבירה בעזרה ולא חוץ לג' מחנות כמלותן יח] כדכתיב בהאי קרא (ויקרא ו) בקדש באש תשרף שתהא שריפתה בקדש וליתן לא תעשה על אכילתן בין כשרין בין פסולין כדכתיב (שם) לא תאכל דבמקומן לא נאמר לאו על אכילתן וכתבו כאן: אמרו לו לדבריך יט] חטאת החיצונית שנכנס דמה לפנים מנין · שנפסלה: אמר להו הן לא הובא את דמה · כתיב גבי שעיר החטאת ששרפו בני אהרן וקאמר להו משה הן לא הובא את דמה הא הובא בדין שרפוה: לדבריו דר"ע · דמוקי ליה בהכי ומרבה והולך שאר קדשי קדשים קאמר דאין לו לרבות בו אלא כ] חטאת: מתני' יצא אחד מהם לחוץ · חוץ לעזרה: הפנימי כשר · ויתן ממנו מתנותיו והקרבן עולה לו: נכנס אחד מהן לפנים · להיכל: מכשיר בחיצון · לתת ממנו מתנותיו והקרבן כשר: וחכמים פוסלין · וטעמייהו מפרש בגמרא: ומה אם במקום שהמחשבה פוסלת בחוץ · כלומר מה בחוץ שהוא מקום שהמחשבה פוסלת בו אם חישב בשחיטה ע"מ לזרוק דמה בחוץ פסול: לא עשה · אלא מוציא מקצת הדם בחוץ: את המשויר · בפנים כיוצא כדאמריתו הפנימי כשר וטעמא ילפינן בגמרא: מקום שאין המחשבה פוסלת בפנים · כלומר היכל שהוא מקום שאין מחשבה פוסלת כא] בפנים שאם שחט ע"מ ליתן את הניתנין בחוץ בפנים כשר כדאמרי' בפרק כל הפסולין (לעיל לו·) אינו דין כו': עד שיכפר · בהיכל: ואין הציץ מרצה על היוצא · דאמרינן בפרק שני (לעיל כג:) הא אינו נושא אלא עון טומאה ואע"ג דפסולין שעלו לא ירדו ארצויי מיהא לא מרצו: גמ' לא פסל דם שבחוץ את דם שבפנים · אם הוציא אחד מן הכוסות השני כשר: מדמה אפילו מקצת · מדלא כתיב את דמה ורבי יוסי הגלילי לטעמיה דאמר האי קרא בחטאות הפנימיות כתיב ופסול דחיצונה שנכנס דמה לפנים מהן לא הובא את דמה והאוא כוליה משמע: ה"ג אמר להן ק"ו ליוצא מעתה · מהשתא דאוקימתון האי קרא להכי: הנכנס פוסל את המשויר ואין היוצא פוסל את המשויר · דמדמה מיעוטא הוא דמה של מזבח ולא דמה של יוצאת: ותהא מחשבה פוסלת כו' · *הש"ס קבעי לה ולא גרס לה בת"כ במילתיה דרבי יוסי הגלילי דהא לדידיה נמי איכא למיבעי: הרי הוא אומר · במחשבת חוץ למקומו שלישי כב] דמוקמינן בפרק ב' (לעיל דף כח:) תניא לענין חוץ למקומו והכי נקיט ליה בלשון שלישי דאין מחשבת מקום פוסלת אלא אם כן משולש בדם ובשר ואימורין כגון חוץ לעזרה שבשעת היתר הבמות מלויין שלשתן בו להפוקי מחשבת כג] הכנסה דלאו מקום בשר ואימורין הוא: *ולא תהא כד] מחשבת חוץ למקומו פוסלת בק"ו ממחשבת הכנסה: פגול זה הוא חוץ למקומו · דאיכא דמפיק כה] לתרוייהו מקרא אריכא דפרשת צו והאי דפרשת קדושים תהיו

תוספות

עכשיו בין בחמין בין בצונן · דמזוג לי לישנא דיתורא הוא דבמזיגה של חמין היו עסוקין ובא לומר ולרבות אפילו צונן: מכדי איתרבו כל הקדשים לענין מריקה ושטיפה · תימה דלמא ר"ע סבר לה כמ"ד לקמן (דף צו:) קדשי קדשים טעונין מריקה ושטיפה ולא קדשים קלים ואתי חטאת לרבות קדשים קלים: ת"ל כל חטאת · ל"ע בריש אלו עוברין (פסחים מג:) דפליגי בדרשה דכל ובבכורות (דף*): אין לי אלא חטאת נקבה חטאת זכר מנין · תימה כיון דכבר ריבה חטאת צבור איתרבי לי' חטאת זכר דאין נקבה בצבור ואי הוה גרסי' איפכא *ניחא כו] תימה לרבי יוסי הגלילי דנפקא ליה מהן לא הובא תיקשי ליה דאין לי אלא חטאת ציבור זכר כגון שעיר דר"ח חטאת יחיד ונקבה מנין כז]: ותהא מחשבה פוסלת בפנים מק"ו · תימה מה לחוץ שכן פסל בו שאר קדשים תאמר בפנים שלא פסל בו אלא חטאת ועוד מה לחוץ שכן פסל בו בשר תאמר בפנים שלא פסל בו אלא דם ועוד מה לחוץ שכן נפסל בכל ענין דם היוצא תאמר בפנים דאין נפסל אלא לכפר: מקום

עין משפט נר מצוה

עא א מיי' פ"ח מהלכות מעה"ק הלכה יד:

עב ב ג מיי' פ"ב מהלכות פסה"מ הלכה טו:

עג ד מיי' שם הלכה טז:

[לד' עי' תוספות נדה עב' ד"ה תלמוד לומר ותוס' מנחות נו: ד"ה אמר ותוס' פסחים מג: ד"ה מאן]

סוס ניחא נ"ק

עד ה מיי' פ"א מהלכות פסה"מ הלכה לד ופ"ד מהלכות ביאת מקדש הלכה ז:

עה ו מיי' פ"א מהלכות פסה"מ הלכה לס:

שיטה מקובצת

א] דמן לפנים פסולין: ב] משל דר"ע למה: ג] ל"ל לאו חטאת קאמינא לך תיבת אלא ל"ש ואות ה' נמחק: ד] תיבות לגבי מזבח נמחק: ה] בצונן ואמר לו אל תמזוג לי אלא בחמין: ו] מנין תימה תיפוק לי דהא איתרבי כל הקדשים למריקה ושטיפה: ז] תיבת חטאת ל"ש: ח] מיין כלפי תיבות ת"ל וכל ל"ש: ט] תיבות לפי שמצינו נמחק: י] הפסולין שניתנו: יא] שאם נתערב דמם: יב] פנימיים דלמיפסלינהו בידים: יג] וכל חטאת: יד] ה"ק לא בחטאת לחוד קאמינא לך אלא: טו] למיכתב וכל חטאת: טז] כתיבא הך: יז] של יחיד הס"ד: יח] כמצותן בכשרות כדכתיב: יט] חטאת החיצונה שנכנס דמה לפנים: כ] אלא חטאות הס"ד: כא] פוסלת בו שאם ותיבת בפנים נמחק: כב] שלישי דאוקימנא בפ"ב: כג] מחשבת היכל דלאו תיבת הכנסה נמחק: כד] מחשבת ס"א מחשבת פוסלת בחוץ כלומר מחשבת חוץ לזמנו או חוץ למקומו לא תהא פוסלת מקל וחומר: כה] דמפיק תרווייהו מקרא אריכא דפרשת צו והוא דפרש' קדושים ותיבת והאי נמחק: כו] ניחא אין לי אלא חטאת נקבה חטאת זכר מנין ת"ל כל חטאת ואין לי אלא חטאת יחיד דביחיד נמי איכא זכר כגון שעיר נשיא חטאת צבור מנין ת"ל וכל חטאת א"נ יש ליישב גירסת רש"י וה"ק חטאת זכר ביחיד מנין דצבור שאני דלא אפשר נקבה בהן: כז] מנין וי"ל מכ"ש דלא מצינו הכשר בפנים ליחיד א):

א) ואף דברו של כה"ג מצינו לו הכשר בפנים י"ל דס"ל לר"י הגלילי כמ"ד ביומא דף נ דמקרי חטאת השותפין ע"ש ·

מנחות פט.

פסחים סג.

נ"ל כמצוותה נ"ק

עיין רש"ק ותוס' ... נרסאות ובספר פנים מאירות

שייך נע"ב

עין משפט
נר מצוה

עז א מיי' פי"א מהל' מעה"ק הלכה ז:

עז ב מיי' שם הלכה ו:

עה ג ד מיי' פ"ו מהלכות תרומות הלכה ה:

עט ה ו מיי' פ"כ מהל' פסה"מ הלכה יד:

[נ"ל לעיל יא. נ"ק]

תורה אור

*מקום שהוא משולש בדם בבשר באימורים ולא תהא מחשבה פוסלת בחוץ מקל וחומר ומה מקום שפסל דם שבפנים את שבחוץ אין מחשבה פוסלת בפנים מקום שלא פסל דם שבחוץ את שבפנים אינו דין שלא יהא פוסל מחשבה בחוץ ת"ל שלישי א] חוץ לזמנו פיגול חוץ למקומו *בשר [היוצא לחוץ פסול] הנכנס לפנים כשר שיהא בדין שפסול ומה במקום שלא פסל דם שבחוץ את שבפנים בשר היוצא לחוץ פסול מקום שפסל דם שבפנים את שבחוץ בשר הנכנס בפנים אינו דין שיפסול הרי הוא אומר מדמה *דמה ולא בשר ק"ו ב] מעתה ומה במקום שפסל דם שבפנים את שבחוץ בשר הנכנס לפנים כשר מקום שלא פסל דם שבחוץ את שבפנים בשר היוצא לחוץ אינו דין שכשר הרי הוא אומר °ובשר בשדה טרפה לא תאכלו *ככיון שיצא בשר חוץ למחיצתו נאסר תנו רבנן פנימה אין לי אלא פנימה היכל מנין ת"ל °אל ג] הקדש פנימה ויאמר קודש ואל יאמר פנימה אמר *רבא בא זה ולימד על זה מידי דהוה אתושב ושכיר דתניא *תושב זה קנוי קנין עולם שכיר זה קנוי קנין שנים יאמר תושב ואל יאמר שכיר ואני אומר קנוי קנין עולם אינו אוכל קנוי קנין שנים לא כ"ש אילו כן הייתי אומר תושב זה קנוי קנין שנים אבל קנוי קנין עולם יהא אוכל בא שכיר ולימד על תושב שזה קנוי קנין עולם וזה קנוי קנין שנים *ואינו אוכל א"ל אביי בשלמא התם תרי גופי נינהו ד] ואע"ג דה"ל לקרא למכתב נרצע לא יאכל ואידך אתי בק"ו *מילתא דאתי בק"ו טרח וכתב לה קרא אלא הכא כיון (דאיכא) דאיפסל בהיכל (הכא) לפני ולפנים מאי בעי אלא אמר אביי לא נצרכא אלא לדרך משופש א"ל רבא והא הבאה כתיב ביה אלא אמר רבא כל מידי דחשיב עליה לפני ולפנים לא מיפסל בהיכל בעי רבא פר העלם דבר של צבור ושעיר עבודת כוכבים שהכניס דמן לפני ולפנים מהו מי אמרי' אל הקודש פנימה כל היכא ה] דקרינן אל הקודש קרינן ליה פנימה כל היכא דלא ו] קרינן אל הקודש לא קרינן פנימה או דלמא שלא במקומן הוא ואם תימצי לומר *שלא *במקומן הוא פר ושעיר של יום הכיפורים שהזה מדמן על הבדים והוציאן להיכל והכניסן מהו מי אמרינן מקומן הוא או דלמא הואיל ונפק נפק ואם תימצי לומר *הואיל ונפק נפק הזה מדמן על הפרכת והוציאן

שמות כב | ויקרא י | ג"ק ה"ג

תהיו מיבעי ליה כדפרישית מקום משולש: בשר היוצא לחוץ פסול. מוטב בשדה נפקא לן לקמן: דמה ולא בשרה. דתרי דמה כתיבי אשר יובא מדמה והן לא הובא את דמה חד למעוטי בשר: ק"ו. לבשר היוצא מעתה שלא יפסל: בשדה. בלא מחילות משמע ודריש ליה לכל הבשר ז] שטעון מחילה טריפה הוא ביוצא ולא תאכל ודם היוצא ק"ו מבשר אתי ועוד נפקא לן מהן לא הובא את דמה אל הקדש פנימה אמר להן שמא הכנסתם לפנים א"ל הן לא הובא את דמה אל הקדש ח] (פנימה) שמא חוץ למחילתה יצתה אמרו לו פנימה היתה הכי דרשינן ליה לקמן בפ' טבול יום (דף קא.) ט]: הן לא הובא וגו' פנימה. אין לי אלא שנכנס דמה לפני ולפנים י]: בא זה ולימד על זה. דאי כתב קדש ולא כתב פנימה הייתי אומר קדש זה לפני ולפנים*: בא פנימה. שהוא מיותר ולימד על קדש שהוא היכל: תושב כהן ושכיר לא יאכל קדש: קנוי קנין עולם. נרצע שמיושב אצלו עד היובל: קנין שנים. עבד עברי שעתיד לצאת בשביעית: אינו אוכל. בתרומה שאין גופו קנוי לכהן: בשלמא התם. איכא למימר בשני מקראות סתומים בא זה ולימד על זה: דתרי גופים נינהו. אין אזהרתו של זה כמשמעו של זה וכל אחד מלמד על עצמו ואי משום דאיכא למפרך נכתוב נרצע בהדיא ולא נבעי שכיר ה"ל שכיר כו' כלומר לאו משום דבמשמעות הוא אלא משום דאתי בק"ו ואיכא לשנויי מילתא דאתיא בק"ו טרח וכתב ליה קרא השתא דסתימי כ"ש דשפיר שנינן בא זה ולימד על זה: אלא הכא. דאזהרת לפני ולפנים בכלל היכל היא דהא לא יכנס לה אלא דרך היכל אין כאן אלא פסול היכל וכיון דמהיכל איפסיל ליה לפני ולפנים מאי בעי הכא למיפסל הרי פסול ועומד והיה לו לפרש היכל ולשתוק שלא ישנה מקרא של חנם שאינו מלמד כלום: לא נצרכא. האי פנימה אלא לדרך משופש שלא כדרכו כגון דרך גגין ועליות בית יא] המקדש בלולין דהשתא הוצרך ללמד על עצמו ואי משום דאתי בק"ו אפ"ה טרח וכתב לה קרא *ומשופש עקום כך יב] שמו במנחות בהקומץ רבה (דף כז:): והא הבאה כתיב. יג] ומשמע דלא מיפסיל אלא דרך הבאה: אלא אמר רבא. לעולם דעייליה דרך פתחים ואשמועי' קרא דהיכא דחשיב עליה מתחילתו להכניסו יד] [לפני] ולפנים ותחילת הבאתו להיכל ע"מ פנים היה לא מיפסיל עד דמטי לפנים ואם החזירו טו] לחוץ כשר: פר העלם דבר. שמצות כפרתו בהיכל והכניסו לפני ולפנים: מהו. מי אמרינן כל היכא דקרינן ביה פסול דאל הקדש כגון בחטאות החיצונות: קרינא ביה פסול דפנימה כו' דהא כי הדדי כתיבי: או דלמא שלא במקומו הוא. והויא הכנסה ומיפסיל: והוליאן להיכל. להזות על הפרכת כמשפטן: מקומן הוא. שהרי הוזקקו לשם תחילתן: או דלמא כיון דנפק בעשיית כל מצותו נפיק ליה לגמרי. והוה ליה שלא מקומו:

והוליאן

מקום משולש. פירשתי לעיל בסוף פ' שני (דף כט. ד"ה למקום): ולא תהא מחשבה פוסלת בחוץ מק"ו. תימה כיון דלא ידע דרשה דשלישי זה חוץ לזמנו ופיגול זה חוץ למקומו בלאו ק"ו נמי לא תהא מחשבה פוסלת וה"ת לא תהא יציאת חוץ פוסלת בלא לכפר ק"ו מבפנים שלא פסל את טז] המשויר וגם יז] חטאת דוקא מק"ו וי"ל כיון דנפקא לן מקרא דבשר נפסל הוא הדין כל דמים: דמה ולא בשרה. *לקמן (דף לג) דרשינן דמה של זו ולא דמה של אחרת וק"ק ל"ל למעוטי בשרה הא לכפר כתיב:

כיון שילא בשר חוץ למחילתו נאסר. פי' בקונטרס ודם היוצא מק"ו מבשר אתי ועוד יח] נפקא לן מהן לא הובא את דמה וגו' אמר יט] שמא הכנסתם את דמה לפנים אמרו הן לא הובא את דמה אל הקדש שמא חוץ למחילתה יצתה אמרו לו פנימה היתה כ] הכי דרשינן ליה לקמן בפרק טבול יום (דף קא.) ולא דק דלקמן דריש מבקדש כא] היתה ול"ע בפ' כילד צולין (פסחים פב.) דדריש לענין בשר היוצא ועוד בפרק בהמה המקשה (חולין סח.) דאיכא תנא דלא דריש התם ובשר בשדה לענין יוצא:

לא נצרכא אלא לדרך משופש. פירש בקונטרס כגון כב] גגין ועליות בית קדשי הקדשים בלולין וקשה דבהקומץ רבה (מנחות דף כז:) דרשי רבנן אל הקדש בלא יבא אבל מבית לפרכת ואל פני הכפרת בלא ימות ופריך לכתוב אל הקדש ומבית לפרכת ולא בעי אל פני הכפרת ומשני למעוטי דרך משופש והשתא ל"ל קרא תיפוק ליה דרך גגין מדכתיב ואל יבא דמשמע דרך ביאה כדממעטינן בפרק ב' דשבועות (דף יז:) טמא שנכנס דרך גגין להיכל ונראה לפרש דבשבועות מיירי כשפיחת את התקרה אבל כג] הכא כשנכנס דרך לול שהיה בעליית בית קדשי קדשים שבו היו משלשלים את האומנים כד] בתיבות דדרך ביאה הוא דלכך נעשה א"נ כמו שפירש בקונטרס במנחות (שם) שחתך החומה לפני ולפנים ועשה פתח בדרום או בצפון ונכנס ולא נכנס בפתח שבמזרח שהיה פניו למערב ועוד פי' בקונטרס התם א"נ נכנס בפתח מזרח ולדד באלכסון כה] *הלכתא בצדדין לא מיחייב דאל פני בעינן שיהו פניו אל פנים מזרחיים של כפורת ועוד יש לפרש דרך משופש כגון דרך לול שהיה אחורי בית הכפורת כדאמר בסוף איזהו מקומן (לעיל דף נה:) שנים לפר בר והקשה ה"ר יעקב דאורלינ"ש ל"ל קרא למעוטי בהקומץ רבה *דרך משופש תיפוק לי מדכתיב ואל יבא כדדייקינן הכא והא הבאה כתיבא בי' ויש לחלק בין הבאת הדם לביאת גוף האדם כו]:

נשרפין

שיטה מקובצת
א] שלישי זהו חוץ לזמנו פיגול זהו: ב] ק"ו לבשר היוצא מעתה: ג] [הקדש] ויאמר (קודש) תיבת פנימה נמחק: ד] נינהו דאי נמי כתב רחמנא יאכל הוהליה שכיר מלת' דאתי בק"ו ומילתא דאתי בק"ו טרח וכתב לה קרא אלא כיון דאיפסלא בהיכל לפני ולפנים מאי בעי: ה] היכא דכתיב ותיבת דקרינן ל"ש ונמחק: ו] דלא כתיב אל ותיבת קרינן ל"ש ונמחק: ז] הבשר הטעון מחיצה ויצא דטריפה הוא ולא תאכל: ח] תיבת פנימה נמחק: ט] מה"ד פנימה: י] ולפנים דהיינו פנימה הס"ד: יא] בית קדשי הקדשים תיבת המקדש נמחק: יב] כך שמעתי תיבת שמו נמחק: יג] כתיב ביה ומשמע: יד] להכניסו לפנים: טו] החזירו מהיכל לחוץ: טז] את החטאת המשויר: יז] תיבת חטאת נמחק: יח] ועוד דנפקא: יט] אמר להם: כ] היתה משמע דאם יצאת לחוץ שפיר עבדו דאשתרוף מפני שהיה נפסל ביוצא והתם מיירי בדם מהר"פ: כא] תיבת היתה נמחק: כב] כגון דרך גגין: כג] אבל במנחות איירי כשנכנס: כד] תיבת בתיבות נמחק: כה] באלכסון והולך בצדדין. כו] האדם דהיינו ביאה ריקנית הס"ד:

נ"ל וסילוק בלדדים כו' נ"ק

[לעיל כט: עי']

ולפנים בא כו' הס"ד נ"ק [לעיל יח:]

[מכות יז: חולין קטז:]

[נ"ל רבה]

קדושין די יבמות מו:

[פסחים יט: וש"נ]

נ"ל משופש משוכב כך שמעתי במנחות פי' נ"ק

מקומן נ"ק

מנחות דף כז: וסס

within disqualifies? Lo, it says: *On the third day:*[4] [82b] [this teaches that the illegitimate intention must refer to] a place with a threefold function, [viz.,] in respect of blood, flesh, and *emurim*.[5]

Now, let an intention concerning without not disqualify [the sacrifice], *a fortiori:* if although the blood within disqualifies [the blood] without, an intention concerning within does not disqualify; then seeing that the blood without does not disqualify [the blood] within, is it not logical that an intention concerning without shall not disqualify? Therefore Scripture writes *'third'*, which means after time; while *piggul* means without bounds.[6]

Flesh which goes without becomes unfit; that which enters within, is fit. Now, logically it might be unfit. For if though the blood without does not disqualify [the blood] within, flesh which goes without becomes unfit; then since blood within does disqualify [blood] without, is it not logical that flesh which enters within shall be disqualified? Lo, it says, *any of* the blood: its blood [disqualifies],[7] but not its flesh. Then in that case you can argue *a fortiori:* if though the blood within disqualifies [the blood] without, flesh that enters within is fit; then since blood without does not disqualify [blood] within, is it not logical that flesh that goes without is fit? Lo, it says, *Therefore ye shall not eat any flesh that is torn of beasts in the field:*[8] once flesh passes without bounds, it is forbidden.[9]

Our Rabbis taught: [*Behold the blood of it was not brought into the sanctuary*] *within:*[10] I only know [it of] within;[11] how do we know
a [it of] the *hekal*? Because it says, *into the sanctuary within*.[1] Then let the *'sanctuary'* be stated, but not *'within'*?—Said Raba: One comes and illumines the other,[2] this being analogous to the case of *toshab* and *sakir*. For it was taught: *Toshab* means one [a Hebrew slave] acquired in perpetuity; *sakir*, one purchased for a period of [six] years.[3] Now, let *toshab* be stated, but not *sakir*, and I would reason: if one acquired in perpetuity may not eat, how much more so one acquired only for a period of [six] years?[4] Were it so, I would say: *Toshab* is one purchased for a limited period, but one acquired in perpetuity may eat. Therefore *sakir* comes and teaches the meaning of *toshab*, that the latter is one purchased in perpetuity, while the former is one purchased for a period of [six] years, and [neither] may eat. Said Abaye to him, As for there, it is well: They are two persons, and though Scripture could write, A [slave] whose ear was bored may not eat,[5] and the other would be inferred *a minori*, yet Scripture [often] takes the trouble to write a thing which is derived *a minori*. But here, since it becomes unfit in the *hekal*, what business has the inner sanctuary?[6]— Rather said Abaye: It is required only [where the priest takes] a circuitous route.[7] Said Raba to him: But 'entering' is written in connection therewith?[8]—Rather said Raba: Whatever [the priest] intends [to carry into] the innermost sanctuary does not become unfit in the *hekal*.[9]

Raba asked: What if [the priest] carried the blood of the congregational bullock for forgetfulness or the he-goat for idolatry into
b the innermost sanctuary?[1] Do we say, [Scripture writes] *'into the sanctuary within'*; wherever we read *'into the sanctuary'* we read *'within'*, and wherever we do not read *'into the sanctuary'*, we do not read *'within'*?[2] Or perhaps, it is not in its place.[3] Now, should you answer that it is not in its place, what if [the priest] sprinkled the blood of the bullock and that of the he-goat of the Day of Atonement on the staves, then carried it out into the *hekal*,[4] and then took it in again?[5] Do we say, It is their place; or perhaps, once it has gone out, it has gone out?[6] Should you answer, Once it has gone out, it has

(4) Lev. VII, 17. (5) V. *supra* 29a. (6) V. *supra* 28a and whole discussion there. (7) When it is brought into the *hekal*. (8) Ex. XXII, 30. (9) *'In the field'* is apparently superfluous. Hence it is interpreted as intimating that when flesh is found beyond its bounds (as a field, which has no barriers), it is a *terefah* (lit., 'torn of the beasts'), and forbidden. (10) Lev. X, 18. (11) I.e., only if the blood is taken into the innermost sanctuary is the sacrifice disqualified.

a (1) The sanctuary corresponds to the *hekal*, which contained the Table and the Candlestick (v. Ex. XXV, 23. 31), and led into the Holy of Holies; cf. *infra* 83a. (2) Only because *'within'* is written do we know that *'sanctuary'* means the *hekal* (for otherwise it is superfluous). But if *'sanctuary'* alone were written, it might mean the innermost sanctuary. (3) The reference is to Lev. XXII, 10: *A* toshab *of a priest, or a* sakir, *shall not eat of the holy thing* (i.e., *terumah*). (4) For the former is more of the priest's chattel (v. ibid. 10) than the latter. (5) V. Ex. XXI, 5 f. (6) For, in order to get into the inner sanctuary it must pass through the *hekal*. (7) E.g. he enters the innermost sanctuary by way of the roof or through upper chambers, avoiding the *hekal* altogether. (8) Which implies that it becomes unfit only if he enters the innermost sanctuary in the usual way. (9) This is intimated when Scripture states both *'sanctuary'* and *'within'*. Hence if he changes his mind after carrying it into the *hekal* and takes it back, it remains fit.

b (1) If the whole congregation sins through having forgotten a law a bullock must be sacrificed; for unwitting idolatry a he-goat is brought. The blood of these must be taken into the *hekal*, but not into the innermost sanctuary. (2) Only where the sacrifice is disqualified when the blood is taken *'into the sanctuary'* (i.e., the *hekal*), it is likewise disqualified when it is taken *'within'* (the innermost shrine), but not otherwise. (3) The text implies that when the blood is taken without bounds the sacrifice is disqualified, and that applies here too. (4) To sprinkle the blood on the veil, as is necessary. (5) Into the innermost shrine: this was no longer necessary. (6) And must not be taken in again.

gone out: What if he sprinkled their blood on the veil, [83a] carried it out to the altar, and then carried it within? Here it is certainly the same place; or perhaps, we designate this carrying [going] out?[7] The questions stand over.

IF IT ENTERED WITHIN TO MAKE ATONEMENT. It was taught, R. Eliezer said: It is stated here, *to make atonement in the holy place;*[8] and it is stated elsewhere, *And there shall be no man in the tent of appointment when he goeth in to make atonement in the holy place:*[9] as
a there it means when he has not yet made atonement,[1] so here too it means when he has not yet made atonement.[2] R. Simeon said: It is stated here, *'to make atonement'*; and it is stated elsewhere, *'And the bullock of the sin-offering, and the goat of the sin-offering, whose blood was brought in to make atonement':*[3] as there it means when he had [already] made atonement,[4] so here it means where he made atonement.[5] Wherein do they differ?—One master holds, You learn without from without,[6] but you do not learn without from within;[7] while the other master holds: You learn an animal from an animal, but you do not learn an animal from man.

R. JUDAH SAID etc. But if [the priest took it in] deliberately, it is disqualified; [when?] if he made atonement, or [even] if he did not make atonement?—Said R. Jeremiah, It was taught:[8] Since it is said, *'And the bullock of the sin-offering, and the goat of the sin-offering, whose blood was brought in to make atonement in the holy place'*; why is it [further] said, *And he that burneth them [shall wash his clothes]*?[9] (You ask, why is it further said, *'And he that burneth them'*? that is required for itself!)[10]—Rather [the question is] why is *'sin-offering,'* repeated? Because we have only learnt that when the bullock and the he-goat of the Day of Atonement are burnt they defile garments; how do we know [the same of] other [sacrifices] which are burnt?—Because *'sin-offering'* is repeated:[11] these are the words of R. Judah. R. Meir said: That [exegesis] is unnecessary.[12] Lo, it says, *'And the bullock of the sin-offering and the he-goat of the sin-offering'*: now, *'to make atonement'* need not be stated;[13] why then is *'to make atonement'*
b stated? It teaches that with all atoning sacrifices,[1] he that burns them [the sacrifices] defiles his garments. Whereas R. Judah does not understand *'to make atonement'* in that way. What is the reason? Surely because he utilises it for a *gezerah shawah.*[2]

CHAPTER IX

MISHNAH. THE ALTAR SANCTIFIES WHATEVER IS ELIGIBLE
c FOR IT.[1] R. JOSHUA SAID: WHATEVER IS ELIGIBLE FOR THE ALTAR FIRE DOES NOT DESCEND [THENCE] ONCE IT ASCENDED, BECAUSE IT IS SAID, THAT IS THE BURNT-OFFERING UPON ITS FIREWOOD:[2] AS THE BURNT-OFFERING, WHICH IS ELIGIBLE FOR THE ALTAR FIRE, DOES NOT DESCEND ONCE IT ASCENDED, SO WHATEVER IS ELIGIBLE FOR THE ALTAR FIRE DOES NOT DESCEND ONCE IT ASCENDED. R. GAMALIEL SAID: WHATEVER IS ELIGIBLE FOR THE ALTAR DOES NOT DESCEND ONCE IT ASCENDED, BECAUSE IT IS SAID: THAT IS THE BURNT-OFFERING UPON ITS FIREWOOD UPON THE ALTAR: AS THE BURNT-OFFERING, WHICH IS ELIGIBLE FOR THE ALTAR, DOES NOT DESCEND ONCE IT ASCENDED, SO WHATEVER IS ELIGIBLE FOR THE ALTAR DOES NOT DESCEND ONCE IT ASCENDED. R. GAMALIEL AND R. JOSHUA DIFFER ONLY IN RESPECT OF THE BLOOD AND LIBATIONS, R. GAMALIEL MAINTAINING THAT THEY MUST NOT DESCEND, WHILE R. JOSHUA MAINTAINS THAT THEY MUST DESCEND.[3] R. SIMEON SAID: IF THE SACRIFICE IS FIT WHILE THE LIBATIONS [WHICH ACCOMPANIED IT] ARE UNFIT; OR IF THE LIBATIONS ARE FIT WHILE THE SACRIFICE IS UNFIT; OR EVEN IF BOTH ARE UNFIT,—THE SACRIFICE MUST NOT DESCEND, WHILE THE LIBATIONS DO DESCEND.[4]

(7) V. Lev. XVI, 18 f: *And he shall go out unto the altar that is before the Lord, and make atonement for it; and shall take of the blood of the bullock, and of the blood of the goat, and put it upon the horns of the altar round about. And he shall sprinkle of the blood upon it with his finger seven times.* According to the Talmud this refers to the *golden* altar which was in the same portion as the veil. Hence *'and he shall go out'* can only mean that he passes beyond the whole altar, i.e., he must not stand on the inner side of the altar, between it and the veil, but on the outer side, between it and the door. In the present instance he carried the blood back on the inner side of the altar; and the question is: as it is in the same portion as the veil, perhaps it does not disqualify it; or do we say that since Scripture designates going to the outer side of the altar 'going out' the inner side is *ipso facto* a separate place and disqualifies it? (8) Lev. VI, 23. (9) Ibid. XVI, 17.

a (1) No man must be there when he is about to make atonement. (2) The flesh is disqualified if the blood is taken into the *hekal* to make atonement, even if atonement was not made, i.e., the blood was not sprinkled there. (3) Lev. XVI, 27. (4) That is evident from the whole passage. (5) Only then is the sacrifice disqualified. (6) Viz., the law about the bullock whose blood must be sprinkled without from the man who is bidden to stay without. (7) From the Day of Atonement sacrifice whose blood is *rightly* brought within. (8) Emended text (Sh. M.). (9) Ibid. 28. (10) To teach that his garments are defiled. (11) The second one being superfluous, it extends the law to all sin-offerings which are burnt. (12) It is implied in the Biblical text itself. (13) We already know from the context that that was its purpose.

b (1) I.e., all those for whom atonement is made. (2) *Sc.* as R. Simeon *supra.* Accordingly, the sacrifice is disqualified only if he did make atonement.

c (1) I.e., anything which was appointed for the altar, even if it subsequently became unfit, is nevertheless sanctified by the altar in the sense that if laid upon it, it must not be removed. (2) Lev. VI, 2. (3) R. Joshua and R. Gamaliel disagree as to the meaning of 'WHATEVER IS ELIGIBLE FOR IT'. R. Joshua holds that it means whatever is eligible *for the altar fire*, i.e., to be burnt on the altar, such as the limbs of a burnt-offering. Blood and libations, however, which are not meant for burning on the altar at all, must be taken down even laid on it. R. Gamaliel maintains that ELIGIBLE means in any capacity, and so if these ascended, they do not descend. (4) R. Simeon agrees with R. Joshua where the libations accompany a sacrifice, and with R. Gamaliel where they come by themselves. His view is discussed below.

והוציאו למזבח והכניסן מהו הכא ודאי חד מקום הוא או א] [דילמא] *יציאה קרינא ביה תיקו: נכנס לכפר: תניא רבי אליעזר אומר נאמר כאן לכפר בקודש ונאמר להלן °וכל אדם לא יהיה באהל מועד בבואו לכפר בקדש מה להלן בשלא כיפר אף כאן בשלא כיפר רבי שמעון אומר נאמר כאן לכפר ונאמר להלן °ואת פר החטאת ואת שעיר החטאת אשר הובא את דמם לכפר מה להלן בשכיפר אף כאן בשכיפר במאי קמיפלגי מ"ס דנין חוץ מחוץ ואין דנין חוץ מבפנים ומ"ס דנין בהמה מבהמה ואין דנין בהמה מאדם: רבי יהודה אומר כו': הא מזיד פסול ב] בשכיפר או בשלא כיפר אמר רבי ירמיה ג] ממשמע שנאמר ואת פר החטאת ואת שעיר החטאת אשר הובא את דמם (אל אהל מועד) לכפר בקודש מה ת"ל °והשורף מה תלמוד לומר והשורף לגופיה איצטריך אלא מה ת"ל חטאת חטאת לפי שלא למדנו אלא לפר ושעיר של יום הכפורים ד] שנשרפין אבית הדשן ה] מטמאין בגדים שאר נשרפין מנין ת"ל חטאת חטאת דברי רבי יהודה רבי מאיר אומר אינו צריך הרי הוא אומר ואת פר החטאת ואת שעיר החטאת שאין תלמוד לומר לכפר מה תלמוד לומר לכפר *לימד על כל המתכפרים שהשורפן מטמא בגדים ורבי יהודה לכפר לא משמע ליה מאי טעמא לאו משום דמיבעיא ליה לגזירה שוה:

הדרן עלך כל הזבחים שנתערבו

המזבח *מקדש ו] [את] הראוי לו רבי יהושע אומר *כל הראוי לאישים אם עלה לא ירד שנאמר °היא העולה על מוקדה מה עולה שהיא ראויה לאישים אם עלתה לא תרד אף כל שהוא ראוי לאישים אם עלה לא ירד רבן גמליאל אומר כל הראוי למזבח אם עלה לא ירד שנאמר היא העולה על מוקדה על המזבח מה עולה שהיא ראויה למזבח אם עלתה לא תרד אף כל דבר שהוא ראוי למזבח אם עלתה לא תרד אין בין דברי רבן גמליאל לדברי רבי יהושע אלא הדם והנסכים שרבן גמליאל אומר לא ירדו ורבי יהושע אומר ירדו רבי שמעון אומר הזבח כשר ז] ונסכים פסולין הנסכים כשירים והזבח פסול אפי' זה וזה פסולין *הזבח לא ירד והנסכים ירדו:

גמ'

והוליכו למזבח. להזות שבע על טיהרו ומתן ד' על קרנותיו כדכתיב ויצא אל המזבח אשר לפני ה' וכפר עליו ותנן זה מזבח הזהב בפרק הוליכו לו (יומא דף נח:) ואמרינן התם דלהכי כתיב ויצא עד דנפיק מכוליה מזבח שלא יעמוד בין המזבח ולפרכת בשעת מתנות המזבח אלא בין המזבח ח] לפתח לצד המזרח: הכא חד מקום הוא. שאין *הפסק ט] (מזבח) בינתים ולא הויא הכנסה שלא במקומה: או דילמא. רחמנא שויה שני מקומות דכתיב ביה יציאה: ה"ג בת"כ רבי אליעזר אומר נאמר כאן לכפר בקדש ונאמר להלן לכפר בקדש מה להלן בשלא כיפר אף כאן בשלא כיפר רבי שמעון אומר נאמר כאן לכפר בקדש ונאמר להלן לכפר בקדש מה להלן בשכיפר אף כאן בשכיפר ר' אליעזר יליף לכפר דאשר יובא מדמה לכפר מוכל אדם לא יהיה באהל מועד בבואו לכפר ומזהיר שפורשין מן ההיכל בשעת הקטרה מה להלן בבואו לכפר משמע מתחילת ביאת המכפר אזהרו חביריו לפרוש הילכך י] כתיב לכפר ועדיין לא כיפר משמע אף יא] אשר יובא מדמה לכפר מתחילת הבאתה ע"מ לכפר משמע שנפסל הילכך אע"פ שלא כיפר: *ונאמר להלן לכפר בקדש. דר' שמעון ואת פר החטאת ואת שעיר החטאת אשר הובא וגו' מה להלן בשכיפר הכתוב מדבר דהא שריפה בתר כפרה היא אף כאן בשכיפר: רבי אליעזר סבר דנין חוץ מחוץ. דם חטאת החיצונה שהכתוב מלמדך שתעמוד בחוץ ולא יכניסוהו לפנים מאדם זה שהכתוב מזהירו שיעמוד בחוץ: ואין דנין חוץ מבפנים. מפר יוה"כ יב] שהבאתה כמצותה לפנים: דנין בהמה מבהמה. חטאת חיצונה מחטאת פנימי: ה"ג [הכניס שוגג כשר] הא מזיד פסול בשכיפר או בשלא כיפר. בשכיפר וכרבי שמעון סבירא ליה או אפי' בשלא כיפר וכרבי אליעזר: ה"ג בתורת כהנים ואת פר החטאת וגו' והשורף אותם וגו' מה ת"ל דמשמע דמיבעי ליה מה ת"ל והשורף הייט דקפריך מה ת"ל הא לגופיה איצטריך ללמדך שהשורפן מטמא בגדים: אלא מה תלמוד לומר. יג] אחטאת חטאת תרי זימני מהדר: ונשרפין אבית הדשן. כדי נסבה דהא עיקר על שפך הדשן ישרף בפר העלם דבר כתיב אלא משום דמטמא בגדים נקט לה דלא כתיב בהו: אינו צריך. ללמד מחטאת חטאת דממשמעותא דקרא נפקא דתלי טעמא דטומאת בגדים משום דהובא את דמה לכפר למדע שכל הפנימים השורפם מטמא בגדים שלא היה לו לכתוב ואשר הובא וגו' אלא ואת פר החטאת ואת שעיר החטאת וגו': מאי טעמא. לא נפקא ליה לר' יהודה מלכפר: לאו משום דמפיק ליה. להאי לכפר לג"ש דרבי שמעון ללמד על דמים החיצונים שנכנס דמם לפנים שאין פסול אלא א"כ כיפר כרבי שמעון ולאו משום דתלי טעמא דשריפה בהובא את יד] דמן הילכך אילטריך חטאת חטאת לרבות שאר הפנימיות:

הדרן עלך כל הזבחים

המזבח מקדש. אפילו דבר פסול שעלה למזבח קדשו המזבח ליעשות לחמו ואין מורידין אותו: את הראוי לו. משהוברר לחלקו ובגמרא מפרש למעוטי קמצים שלא קדשו בכלי לאחר קמילה שלא הוברר לחלק גבוה דאע"ג דקידשה המנחה כולה בכלי אין זה חלק גבוה ברור שאין המנחה קריבה כולה ובקמילה בלא מתן כלי אין זה מבורר למזבח: רבי יהושע אומר כו'. הני תנאי פליגי בפירושא דאת הראוי לו דסתמא דמתניתין טו] רבי סתם מתניתין את הראוי לו למעוטי שאין ראוי לו והדר מפרש ומאי ניהו ראוי לו לרבי יהושע ראוי לאישים שנפסל ולא דם פסול ונסכים פסולין שאינן לאישים ולר"ג כל הראוי למזבח שנפסל אפילו דם ונסכים ואין לך למעט אלא מה שלא נברר לחלק מזבח מעולם ומאי ניהו קמצים שלא קידשו טז] מעולם בכלי: לאישים. לאש: היא העולה על מוקדה. דבר שהוא למוקד *ועולה יז] היא בהוייתן יהא ולא ירד היא משמע בהוייתו תהא מעלתה על מוקדה: אף כל שראוי לאישים. לאפוקי דם ונסכים (פסולים) כדמפרש בסיפא אין בין דברי ר"ג לדברי רבי יהושע אלא הדם והנסכים: רבי שמעון סבירא ליה בנסכים של זבח כרבי יהושע (ובדם) ובנסכים הבאין בפני עצמן כרבן גמליאל ולאו ממוקדה יליף אלא יח] טעמא אחרינא אית ליה כדמפרש בגמרא: אם הזבח כשר והנסכים פסולין. כגון שלנו או נטמאו: או הזבח נפסל והנסכים כשרין. הואיל והם באים בגללו נפסלו עמו ובטלה תורת הקרבה מהן: הזבח לא ירד. דמזבח קדשו והנסכים

נשרפין אבית הדשן. פירש בקונטרס כדי נסבה דעיקר על שפך הדשן ישרף בפר העלם דבר כתיב *ולא דק דלא בפר העלם כתיב אלא בפר כהן משוח מ"מ הדין עמו דכדי נסבה ויש לפרש דהכי קאמר מאותן הנשרפין אבית הדשן לא מליט שמטמא בגדים אלא אלו בלבד מניין לרבות פר כהן משוח כו' *ול"ע אי מהך דרשא כמי נפקא לן שריפת בית הדשן בפר [יום] הכפורים:

הדרן עלך כל הזבחים

המזבח מקדש כו'. רבי יהושע ורבן גמליאל אתו לפרושי רק רישא וכי האי גוונא בחזקת הבתים (ב"ב דף כח.) דרבי ישמעאל ורבי עקיבא קמפרשי בסיפא חזקה דרישא*: **היא** העולה. פירש בקונטרס היא משמע בהוייתה תהא מעלתה על מוקדה וקשה דבגמרא משמע דהיא מיעוטא הוא ולא יט] ריבויא אלא הכא אזאת תורת העולה סמיך:

דהא ר"ג מוסיף עליו על המזבח להוכיח דר"ל ראוי למזבח משמע דכל חד מינייהו לא נחית אלא להוכיח דבריו לר"י ראוי לאישים ולר"ג ראוי למזבח אבל אם עלה לא תרד מסכינן אזאת תורת כרפ'. מהר"ם:

עין משפט נר מצוה

פ א מיי' פ"ב מהל' פסה"מ הל' יד:
פא ב מיי' פ"ה מהל' פרה הלכה ד:
א ג מיי' פ"ג מהל' פסה"מ הל"ג:
ב ד מיי' שם הל"ד:

ועי"ל דף מח ע"ב בתוס' ד"ה אלו ואלו נשרפים כו' וברש"י שם ויפה מדייק רש"י הכא נ"ק ע"ש

[ועיין לעיל דף מח ע"ב ד"ה אלו ואלו כו']

[ועיין תוס' פסחים פג ד"ה ר"ש עוד שם קטז: ד"ה והתם ותוס' מנ"ק כד. ד"ה עזרת ותוס' עירובין מח. ד"ה ר' יוסי]

לא הפסק מזבח בנתים כו' נ"ק

נ"ל ד"ה ור"ש יליף נאמר כאן לכפר בקדש ונאמר להלן ואת פר כו' מה להלן כו' נ"ק

נ"ק

סנהדרין נד.

ועלה בהוויתן תהא ולא ירד נ"ק

נ"ק מ"ז

נ"ק מ"ז

תורה אור: ויקרא טז | שם | שם | ויקרא ו

שיטה מקובצת

א] או דילמא יציאה קרינא: ב] בשכיפר ע' לעיל דף לז ע"א: ג] ירמיה תניא משמע: ד] הכפורים שהשורפו תיבות שנשרפין [אבית הדשן] נמחק: ה] מטמא בגדים ונשרפין אבית הדשן שאר: ו] מקדש את הראוי: ז] כשר והנסכים פסולין: ח] המזבח ולפתח ולצד המזרח הס"ד ומה"ד והכניסן כלומר הכניס בין מזבח לפרכת מהו הס"ד: ט] הפסק מחיצה בנתים ולא הויא הכנסה שניה שלא במקומה: י] תיבת כתיב נמחק: יא] אף כאן אשר: יב] שהבאתו כמצותו לפנים: יג] חטאת חטאת אות א' נמחק: יד] את דמם הילכך: טו] דמתני' דרבי סתם במתני': טז] תיבת מעולם נמחק: יז] ועולה הרי היא בהוייתו ולא תרד היא משמע בהוייתו תהא משתעלה על מוקדה: יח] אלא ר"ש טעמא: יט] ריבויא וגם בכמה מקומות הוי היא מיעוט לכך נראה דאזאת תורת העולה סמיך תורה אחת לכל העולין והא דמ"ית' היא משום דרוצה להוכיח כל הראוי לאישים אבל אם עלתה לא תרד נפקא ליה מזאת תורת העולה ותרע למעים

[עין לעיל במשנה]
ג א מיי' פ"ג מהל' פסה"מ הל"ב :
ד ב מיי' שם הלי"ב :
ה ג מיי' פ"ז מהל' מעה"ק הל"ג :
ו ד מיי' פ"ג מהל' תמידין ומוספין הל"ג :
ז ה מיי' פ"ג מהל' פסה"מ הלכה ג :
ח ו מיי' שם הל' טו :
ט ו מיי' שם הל"ס :

הנסכין כשירין והזבח פסול. אי אפשר להיות נסכין כשירים כז] גמורין כיון דהזבח פסול אלא כלומר כשירין מפסול עצמן: **למעוטי** מאי. אי למעוטי קטרת קאתי הא תנא ליה סיפא וכן רובע ונרבע קתני בסיפא ולא הוה ליה כח] למיתנא ראוי לו אלא המזבח מקדש את הפסולין :

למעוטי קמצים שלא קדשו בכלי. לכאורה כט] אפילו אליבא דר"ש קאי דאמר לקמן (דף פד.) בנשפך דמה דלא ירד חדא דלכולהו תנאי מיבעי ליה לאשכוחי שאין ראוי לו ועוד מדפריך עלה מ"ש מדעולא דההיא דעולא אתיא כר"ש דלרבי יהודה ירדו מדאמר עלה רבי זירא לקמן אף אנן נמי תנינא שנשפך דמה כו' וכי קאמר למעוטי קמצים שלא קדשו בכלי הכי נמי דהוה מצי למימר לרבי יהודה למעוטי אימורי קדשים קלין שהעלן לפני זריקת דמים דירדו אלא משום דאיירי לר' שמעון נקט הכי והקשה ה"ר חיים דהא שמעינן לר' שמעון בהקומץ רבה [יומא מה: פ"ש מנחות כו:] (מנחות דף כו.) דקומץ לא בעי קידוש כלי וצריך לומר על כרחין דהכא אליבא דרבנן נקט דבעו בקומץ קידוש כלי כדקיימא לן בכל דוכתי ולא כרבי שמעון ולרבי שמעון משכחת לה שאין ראוי לו כגון לבונה קודם קמיצת הסולת שהלבונה ניתרת בקמיצת הסולת ועוד נראה דההיא דעולא ככולי עלמא דבכל דוכתי מייתי לה הכא ובפ"ק דמעילה (דף ז:) ועוד מדפריך מאי שנא מדעולא ולא פריך מ"ש ממתני' שנשפך דמה וכן במעילה דמייתי מדעולא ולא מייתי ממתני' דנשפך אע"ג דמייתי דומה לדומה ל] *מתמה משמע דההיא [מ"מ צ"ק] דעולא ככולי עלמא דאפי' ר' יהודה מודה דנעשו לחמו של מזבח ולא דמי לנשפך דמה כיון דאיכא זריקת דמה והא דאמר רבי זירא לקמן אף אנן נמי תנינא *לר"ש מוכח שפיר דנעשה [צ"ל מר"ש משום דלר"ש מוכח צ"ק] לחמו של מזבח ודחי הש"ס דאפילו לרבי שמעון אין כאן ראיה וה"ה דהוה מצי למימר דלר"ש פשיטא וכי איצטריך ליה לעולא לאשמועינן אליבא דר' יהודה :

ההוא לאהדורי פוקעין הוא דאתא . ומהא דדרשינן לקמן ועשית עולותיך הבשר והדם עיכולי עולה אתה מחזיר ואי אתה מחזיר עיכולי גידים ועצמות לא נפקי פוקעין דקסבר האי תנא דלא אמרינן ממילא שמעינן מינה כי היכי לא] דנפקא לן בסמוך מאשר תאכל האש את העולה דדרשינן עיכולי עולה אתה מחזיר ואי אתה מחזיר עיכולי קטרת ומאן דאית ליה ממילא שמעת מינה הכי נמי הוה מצי למדרש פוקעין מועשית ומ"מ *תרוויהו צריכי מאשר תאכל האש לב] דמועשית לא הוה ממעטין קטרת [לתרוייהו צ"ק] כיון דבר הקרבה הוא כמו בשר ודם *ועוד יש לומר דהיינו טעמא דלא נפקא פוקעין מדדרשינן עיכולי עולה אתה מחזיר ואי אתה מחזיר עיכולי גידים ועצמות משום דהוה מוקמינא ליה משפירשו מן המערכה ועודם על גבי המזבח ולא נפלו לארץ אבל נפלו לארץ לג] אפילו עיכולי עולה לא אתה מחזיר: **ואי** אתה מחזיר עיכולי קטרת. עיכולי לבונה לא ממעט דמהדרינן להו כדמוכח בהקומץ רבה (מנחות דף כו:) והיינו טעמא דעל המזבח כל הראוי למזבח החיצון קאמר : **מה** עולה ראויה . וצריך לדקדק בכולה שמעתין דמרבינן כל הקרבנות אע"ג דכתיב עולה : **הוה** אמינא אפילו מחיים . ובדוקין שבעין ואליבא דרבי עקיבא כדאמר לקמן כתב רחמנא עולה שראוי לעלות : (**כל** עולין) אפילו מנחה . תימה דבפרק שתי מדות (מנחות דף צ:*) ממעטים מנחה מנסכים מדכתב עולה ויש לומר דשאני התם דמסתבר עולה דווקא דכולה כליל דדומיא דנסכים דכולה למזבח אי נמי שאני הכא דכתיב כל הנוגע במזבח יקדש דכל משמע לרבויי אי נמי משום דכתיב זאת תורת דריבה תורה אחת לכל העולין : הלן

[כ"א ולאשר תאכל האש לא הוה ממעטינן אלא דליתא על מזבח החיצון אבל עיכולי גידים ועצמות לא] [וכם ד"ה אפילו]

גמ' ראוי לו אין שאין ראוי לו לא למעוטי מאי אמר רב פפא א] למעוטי *קמצין שלא קידשו בכלי מתקיף לה רבינא מאי שנא מדעולא *דאמר עולא ב] *אימורי קדשים קלין שהעלן לפני זריקת ג] דמן לא ירדו נעשו לחמו של מזבח הנך לא מיחסרו מעשה בגופייהו הני מיחסרו מעשה בגופייהו : ר' יהושע אומר כל הראוי לאישים כו' : ורבן גמליאל נמי הכתיב עולה על מוקדה ד] ההוא לאהדורי *פוקעין הוא דאתא ואידך לאהדורי פוקעין מנא ליה נפקא ליה מאשר תאכל האש ואידך ההוא מיבעי ליה ה] לעכולי עולה אתה מחזיר *ואי אתה מחזיר עכולי קטורת דתני *רבי חנינא בר מניומי בר' אליעזר בן יעקב °אשר תאכל האש את העולה ו] על המזבח עכולי עולה אתה מחזיר ואי אתה מחזיר עכולי קטורת ואידך לאו ממילא ש"מ דעכולי עולה מהדרינן : רבן גמליאל אומר כל הראוי כו' : ורבי יהושע נמי הכתיב מזבח ההוא מיבעיא ליה מאי ז] (טעמא) קאמר רחמנא כל הראוי למוקדה מקדש מזבח ואידך מזבח אחרינא כתיב ח] ואידך חד להיכא ט] דהיתה לה שעת הכושר וחד להיכא דלא י] היתה לה שעת הכושר ואידך כיון דפסולין נינהו ורבינהו רחמנא לא שנא היתה לו שעת הכושר לא שנא לא היתה לו שעת הכושר : רבי שמעון אומר הזבח כשר כו' : תניא רבי שמעון אומר עולה מה עולה הבאה בגלל עצמה אף כל הבאין בגלל עצמן יצאו נסכים הבאין בגלל זבח יא] *רבי יוסי הגלילי אומר מתוך שנאמר °כל הנוגע במזבח יקדש שומע אני בין ראוי ובין שאינו ראוי ת"ל °כבשים מה כבשים ראויין אף כל ראוי ר"ע אומר °עולה *מה עולה ראויה אף כל ראויה מאי בינייהו אמר רב אדא בר אהבה עולת העוף פסולה איכא בינייהו מר *מייתי לה מעולה ומר מייתי לה מכבשים ולמאן דמייתי לה מכבשים הכתיב עולה אי כתיב כבשים ולא כתיב עולה יב] ה"א אפילו מחיים כתב רחמנא עולה ולמאן דמייתי ליה מעולה הא כתיב כבשים אי כתיב עולה ולא כתיב כבשים הוה אמינא אפילו מנחה כתב רחמנא כבשים מאי איכא בין הני תנאי להני תנאי דמתניתין אמר רב פפא קמצים שקדשו בכלי איכא בינייהו לתנאי דידן לא ירדו לתנאי דמתניתא *ירדו *(ר"ל אמר) מנחה הבאה בפני עצמה לדברי כולן לא תרד יג] לדברי רבי יוסי הגלילי ור"ע תרד

[שמות כט] [שם] [שם]

והנסכים ירדו. שאין מזבח מקדש פסולין אלא בבאין בגלל עצמן אבל לא הבאין בגלל אחרים כדיליף ר"ש טעמיה בגמרא יד] (מפרש) : **גמ'** למעוטי מאי. טו] שלא נראה למזבח לדברי הכל : אימורי קדשים קלים טז] לפני זריקת דמן . לא הוכרו למזבח שזריקת דמן שלהן קובעתן לחלק גבוה לענין מעילה מה שאין כן בקדשי קדשים שהן מתחילתן לגבוה ואימוריהן יז] *עולין למזבח אבל קדשים קלים אין בהן מעילה אפי' באימוריהן כדתניא בתורת כהנים יח] את קדשי ה' המיוחדים לשם יצאו קדשים קלים אבל לאחר זריקת דמים יש מעילה באימוריהן דנפקא לן יט] מוכל חלב לה' לרבות אימורי קדשים קלים לאחר זריקת דמים למעילה ואפילו הכי קאמר לא ירדו : בגופייהו . כ] *דאיפסולן בדבר אחר הוא : ההוא לאהדורי פוקעין . כא] *דלאו אפסולין קאי אלא אכשרין שפוקעין מן היקידה איסיקלטי"ר וקאמר קרא שיחזירם למוקדה דעל מוקדה משמע מוקד שהיה לה כבר כב] : אשר תאכל האש כו' . קרא יתירא הוא דפשיטא דשן מאשר תאכל האש הוא אלא לדרשא אתא אשר כג] תאכל האש ותפקעם העולה מעל המזבח חזור והעלם על המזבח : לאו ממילא ש"מ כו' . הילכך לא בעי קרא אחרינא : מקדש מזבח . ללמדך כד] טעמא שלא ירד משום קדושת מזבח הוא : מזבח אחרינא כתיב . כל הנוגע במזבח יקדש (שמות כט) : שעת הכושר . להקטרה לפני פסולו כגון לן ויוצא וטמא : לא היתה לו שעת הכושר . נשחט חוץ לזמנו וחוץ למקומו : ת"ל כבשים . כה] וסמיך ליה וזה אשר תעשה על המזבח : ר' עקיבא אומר . עולה בהאי קרא כתיב כו] : מר מייתי לה מעולה . דלא הרד דאף עולת העוף משמע ומר מייתי לה לקידושי פסולין מכבשים בהמה ולא עוף : כתב רחמנא עולה . משראוי לעלות : ה"ג קמצים שקדשו בכלי איכא בינייהו לתנא דידן לא ירדו לתנא דמתניתא ירדו : קמצים שקידשו בכלי . ונפסלו : לתנאי דידן . רבן גמליאל ורבי יהושע לא ירדו דגמרי לה ממוקדה וממזבח והני בני מזבח ומוקדה נינהו עד שלא נפסלו : לתנאי דמתניתא . רבי יוסי הגלילי ורבי עקיבא ירדו דעולה בעינן אבל מנחה תרד :

שיטה מקובצת

א] למעוטי קמצין שלא קידשו בכלי לאחר קמיצתן ואע"ג דהמנחה נתקדשה בביסא דאל"כ חולין גמורין הן ופשיטא דתרד ום"מ אחר שהוברר חלק האישים לא נתקדשה דאותה קדושה שהיה בביסא חלק הכהנים היה מעורב בה ומשום הכי מטעם ליה תנא דמתני' כיון דלא נתקדשה אחרי שהובורר חלק האישים אע"ג דנתקדשה קודם לכן כדפי' וכר"י ראי כר"ש הא לא בעי קידוש קומץ כדאיתא בפ' הקומץ קידשה שלא בכלי שרת פסולה ור' שמעון מכשיר. מהר"פ : ב] אימורי קדשים קלין כו' וקשיא לרב פפא דכי היכי דהקידוש כלי מכשיר הקומץ לקרב כך הזריקה מכשר' האימורי' ליקרב דקודם הזריקה אין בהן מעילה ואפ"ה קאמר לא ירדו וא"ת מאי פריך דילמא ר"ש היא אבל ר"י לית ליה הא דעולא וי"ל דעולא סתמא אמר למילתיה וסתמא דברי הכל הוא וא"ת והיאך אתיא כר"י הא אמר ר"י בהדיא נשפך דמה תרד וי"ל דלא דמי כדאמרי' לקמן התם אם בא לזרוק אינו זורק כלומר אינו יכול לזרוק שהרי נשפך הדם הכא אם בא לזרוק זורק וא"ת ולר"ש מאי מטעם מלישנא דראוי לו דמשמע הא אין ראוי לו תרד י"ל למעוטי לבונה שאינה ניתרת כי אם בקמיצה הסלת ואם עלתה קודם תרד ולא נהדא למורי דא"כ כי היכי דפריך אליבא דר"י [מ"ש מדעולא] כמו כן צריך ליישב (מאי שנא דפריך) אליבא דר"ש וא"כ מאי משני הנך לא מיחסר כו' לבונה נמי לא מיחסר מעשה בגופיה. לכך נראה דלר"ש בא למעט בשר קדשי קדשים ובשר קדשים קלים ואע"ג דבהדיא תני לה במתני' תני והדר מפרש וא"ת א"כ אמאי אמר רב פפא למעוטי קמצים לימא למעוטי הני דמתני' וי"ל דרב פפא רוצה להשמיענו חידוש יותר מבשר קדשי קדשים כו' דהני אינן באים לידי ראויות לעולם אבל קמצים שלא קידשו בכלי סופן באים לידי ראויות ואפ"ה לר"י אין המזבח מקדש ומ"ם לא שביק רב פפא האי למעוטי תני דמתני' לר"ש כדפי' אבל הוא משמיע לנו כל החידוש שיוכל להשמיע וא"ת הא תינח רב פפא אבל מאי בעי תלמודא וכי לא היה יודע דמצי למעוטי תני דמתני' וי"ל דרב פפא עצמו בעי הכי שהיה רחוק לר"י להשמיענו ה] דאם עלו ירדו וכה"ג איתא בפ' לא יחפור ג) ע"ל הא דדייק תלמודא ראוי לו אין הא אין ראוי לו לא זה אינו אליבא דר"ש כי אם להני דאמרי במילתייהו ראוי דמשמע ראוי לו אין הא אין ראוי לו השתא אע"ג דסופו בא לידי ראויות אין המזבח מקדשם ומש"ה דחיק רב פפא למישכח דבר שאינו ראוי השתא וסופו להיות ראוי אבל ר"ש סבר אע"ג דאינו ראוי המזבח מקדשם ותרע מדלא תכיר במילתיה ראוי ולא תלי טעמא אלא דומיא דעולה הבאה בגלל עצמה ומ"מ צריך לדחוק דפליג ארבוותא: ג] זריקת דמם לא: ד] ההוא ע' תוס' לקמן דף קט ע"א: ה] ליה לעיכולי עולה אתה מחזיר כו' מחזיר עיכולי קטרת דתני רב תנינא בר מניומי ברבי ר' אליעזר: ו] תיבות על המזבח נמחק : ז] מאי קאמר רחמנא על מוקדה כל תיבת טעמא ל"ש ונמחק : ח] מזבח אחרינא כתיב כל הנוגע כו' והתם לא כתיב מוקדה : ט] דהיתה לו שעת: י] דלא היה לו שעת : יא] זבח תניא ר' : יב] הוה אמינא אפי' מחיים וא"ת וכי באיזה פסולים מיירי דס"ד דאם עלו מחיים לא ירדו א"ת רובע ונרבע הא אמר במתני' דאפילו לאחר שחיטה ירדו וא"ת לן ויוצא הך פסול לא שייך מחיים וי"ל בבעלי מומין ואליבא דר"ע דמכשיר בבעלי מומין לאחר שחיטה וסר"א דאפי' מחיים לקדשי כתב רחמנא עולה:יג] לדברי. ע' תוס' לקמן דף קח: יד] תיבת מפרש נמחק: טו] מאי ס"א אמר רב פפא למעוטי קמצים כו' דלא נראו למזבח: טז] קלים שהעלן לפני זריקת דמן : יז] עומדין למזבח: יח] תיבת את נמחק : יט] לן מדכתיב וכל חלב : כ] בגופייהו דפסולין מחמת דבר אחר הוא דהיינו וזריקת הדם הס"ד: כא] ולאו אפסולין : כב] כבר נלין קרי ביה על מוקדה ספיק ה"א : כג] יאכל האש : כד] ללמדך דטעמא שלא: כה] כבשים דסמיך : כו] כתיב עולה: כז] גמורין דא"כ אמאי ירדו אלא כיון דהזבח פסול פסולין נ"ב וכשרין דקאמר היינו כשרין כו'. מהר"פ: כח] למיתני : כט] לכאורה משמע דהיינו אפילו : ל] לדומה משמע משום דההיא ותיבת מתמה נמחק : לא] דלא נפקא לן : לב] האש לא הוה ממעטינן גידים ועצמות משום דבני אכילת אש על המזבח נינהו כשהם מחוברים אבל קטרת ממעטינן דעל המזבח כל הראוי למזבח קאמר מועשית עולותיך הבשר והדם לא הוה ממעטינן קטרת : לג] לארץ הו"א אפילו :

א) מלת דל"ל נסמיטו דאף כמקומים שלא קדשו בכלי אם עלו ירדו לר"י . ב) דף כב ע"ב ועי"ש בתוס' ד"ה וכמה

שייך לע"פ
נ"ע שמדין
מעילה ג: לקמן פה.
נ"ל דפסולן מחמת דבר אחר הוא נ"ק
לאו כו' מן המוקדה איסריקלטי"ר בלע"ז וקאמ' קרא שיחזיר למוקדה כו' נ"ק
[סנהדרין לד.]
[נ"ל אמר ריש לקיש]
[יומא מה: פ"ש מנחות כו:]
[מ"מ צ"ק]
[צ"ל מר"ש משום דלר"ש מוכח צ"ק]

GEMARA. [83b] Only what is ELIGIBLE FOR IT, but not what a is not eligible for it; what does this exclude?[1]—Said R. Papa: It excludes 'fistfuls'[2] which were not sanctified in a [service] vessel.[3] To this Rabina demurred: How does this differ from 'Ulla's [ruling]? For 'Ulla said: If the *emurim* of lesser sacrifices were laid [on the altar] before the sprinkling of their blood, they are not removed, [because] they have become the food of the altar![4]—The latter do not themselves lack a rite, while the former themselves lack a rite.[5]

R. JOSHUA SAID: WHATEVER IS ELIGIBLE FOR THE ALTAR FIRE etc. And R. Gamaliel too? Surely it is written, *the burnt-offering upon its* firewood?—That comes to teach that [limbs] which spring off [from the altar] must be replaced.[6] And the other;[7] how does he know that the [limbs] which spring off must be replaced?—He deduces it from *whereto the fire hath consumed.*[8] And the other?[9]—That is required [for teaching]: What was consumed as a burnt-offering you must replace, but you do not replace what was consumed as incense [*ketoreth*]. For R. Ḥanina b. Minyomi the son of R. Eliezer b. Jacob recited: [*And he shall take up the ashes*] *whereto the fire hath consumed the burnt-offering on the altar:* what was consumed as a burnt-offering you replace, but you do not replace what was b consumed as incense. And the other?[1]—Do you then not learn automatically that we replace what was consumed as a burnt-offering?[2]

R. GAMALIEL SAID: WHAT IS ELIGIBLE etc. And R. Joshua too: surely *upon the altar* is written?—He requires that [as follows]: What does the Divine Law say? Whatever is eligible for its firewood, the altar sanctifies.[3] And the other?[4]—Another *'altar'* is written.[5] And the other?[6]—One [is required] where it had a period of fitness,[7] while the other [text] is required where it had no period of fitness.[8] And the other?[9]—Since they are [now] unfit and the Divine Law included them,[10] there is no difference whether they had a period of fitness or did not have a period of fitness.

R. SIMEON SAID: IF THE SACRIFICE IS FIT etc. It was taught, R. Simeon said: [Scripture speaks of] a burnt-offering: as a burnt-offering comes on its own account, so all which come on their own account [are included]:[11] [hence] libations which come on account of a sacrifice are excluded. R. Jose the Galilean said: From the text, '*Whatsoever toucheth the altar shall be holy*', I understand whether it is eligible [for the altar] or not eligible. Therefore Scripture states: [*Now this is what thou shalt offer upon the altar: two*] *lambs:*[12] as lambs are eligible [for the altar], so whatever is eligible [is included]. R. Akiba said: [Scripture states,] *burnt-offering:*[13] as a burnt-offering is eligible [for the altar], so whatever is eligible [is included]. Wherein do they differ?—Said R. Adda b. Ahabah: They differ about a disqualified burnt-offering of a bird: one master deduces c [the law] from *'burnt-offering'*,[1] while the other master deduces it from *'lambs'*.[2] Now, as to the one who deduces it from *'lambs'*, surely *'burnt-offering'* [too] is written?—If *'lambs'* were written while *'burnt-offering'* were not written, I would think [that the law applies] even [if they became disqualified] while yet alive:[3] therefore the Divine Law wrote *'burnt-offering'*.[4] And as to the one who deduces it from *'burnt-offering'*, surely *'lambs'* is written?—If *'burnt-offering'* were written while *'lambs'* were not written, I would think [that the law applies] even [to] a meal-offering.[5] Therefore the Divine Law wrote *'lambs'*.

Wherein do these Tannaim and the Tannaim of our Mishnah differ?—Said R. Papa: They differ in respect of fistfuls which were sanctified in a [service] vessel.[6] According to our Tannaim, they do not descend;[7] while according to the other Tannaim they descend.[8]

Resh Lakish said: With regard to a meal-offering which comes by itself,[9] all[10] of them hold that it does not descend; but according

a (1) On which both R. Joshua and R. Gamaliel will agree. (2) Taken from meal-offerings; v. Lev. II, 2. (3) These are not considered eligible at all, and even if laid on the altar they must be removed. (4) Now, the fistfuls of a meal-offering correspond to the *emurim* of animal sacrifices; and the former are sanctified for the altar by being placed in a service vessel, while the latter are likewise sanctified by the sprinkling of the blood. Hence the same law should apply to both. (5) Nothing more was to be done to the *emurim* themselves, and only the *blood* still required sprinkling. Whereas the fistfuls themselves should first have been placed in a service vessel. (6) Because *'upon its firewood'* implies that whatever has already become as firewood and is feeding the flames of the altar must remain as a burnt-offering; so that if anything springs off it must be put back. (7) R. Joshua. (8) Lev. VI, 3. That is superfluous, as it is obvious that the ashes are the result of the fire. Hence it is interpreted as intimating that whatever once fed the fire belongs to the altar, even if it jumped off. (9) R. Gamaliel; how does he utilise that text?

b (1) R. Joshua; how does he know this? (2) If the text teaches that you must replace whatever sprang off, that obviously includes what was consumed as a burnt-offering. And at the same time, since the whole passage treats of the burnt-offering only, you cannot make it refer to incense. (3) I.e., *'upon the altar'* does not extend the law, as R. Gamaliel maintains, but intimates *why* whatever is eligible for the altar-*fire* must be replaced, viz., because the altar sanctified it. (4) Where does he find the reason? (5) Ex. XXIX, 37: *Whatsoever toucheth the altar shall be holy.* (6) R. Joshua: what need is there of *two* texts? (7) Before it became unfit, e.g., if it was kept overnight, taken out of bounds, or defiled. (8) E.g., if it was slaughtered with an illegitimate intention. (9) R. Gamaliel: whence does he know this? (10) In the law that they must remain on the altar if laid thereon. (11) In the law that if laid on the altar they must remain there. (12) Ex. XXIX, 38. This immediately follows the text quoted. (13) Ibid. 42. Rashi says that it is written in the *present* verse (38). In fact, it is absent in the M.T. in this verse, but found in the Samaritan Text; v. Sanh. (Sonc. ed.) 34a.

c (1) Hence it includes a burnt-offering of a bird too. (2) Hence only *animal* sacrifices are included, but not a burnt-offering of a bird. (3) E.g., if it had a cataract on the eye. (4) Intimating that this law applies only from the time that it was fit to ascend as a burnt-offering (in Heb. *'ascend'*—the altar—and *'burnt-offering'* are the same word viz., *'olah*). Yet the law still applies to *animal* sacrifices only. (5) By interpreting *'olah* that which ascends (v. preceding note), and so including everything that ascends the altar. (6) But were subsequently disqualified. (7) For they infer the law from *'its firewood'* and *'on the altar'* and these fulfil the conditions implied in these words, as they feed the fire and are brought on the altar. (8) As they cannot be included in *'lambs'* or *'burnt-offering'*. (9) It does not accompany an animal sacrifice. (10) I.e., all except those whom he specifies. Similarly the other cases.

to R. Jose the Galilean and R. Akiba [84a] it does descend.[11] With regard to a meal-offering which accompanies a sacrifice, in the view of R. Gamaliel and R. Joshua it does not descend,[12] while in the view of all [the others] it does descend. Libations which a come by themselves,[1] in the view of all of them, descend, but in the view of R. Gamaliel and R. Simeon they do not descend. Libations which come together with a sacrifice, in the view of all of them, descend, and only in the view of R. Gamaliel do they not descend. That is obvious?[2]—He needs [to state this on account of] a meal-offering which comes by itself,[3] and in accordance with Raba. For Raba said: A man can vow a meal-offering of libations every day.[4] Then let [Resh Laḳish] inform us [this law], as Raba?[5] —He needs [to state the law about] libations which come with a sacrifice, where he offers them [the libations] on the morrow or on some other day.[6] I might argue, Since a master said: *And the meal-offerings thereof, and their drink-offerings*[7] [can be brought] at night; *'the meal-offerings thereof and their drink-offerings'* [can be brought] on the morrow,[8] they are as drink-offerings [libations] which are brought by themselves, and R. Simeon admits that they do not descend. Hence he [Resh Laḳish] informs us [that it is not so].

MISHNAH. THE FOLLOWING DO NOT DESCEND ONCE THEY ASCENDED: [FLESH] THAT IS KEPT OVERNIGHT, OR THAT GOES OUT [OF ITS PERMITTED BOUNDARIES], OR WHICH IS UNCLEAN, OR WHICH WAS SLAUGHTERED [WITH THE INTENTION OF CONSUMING SAME] AFTER TIME OR WITHOUT BOUNDS; OR IF UNFIT [PERSONS] RECEIVED AND SPRINKLED ITS BLOOD. R. JUDAH SAID: THAT WHICH WAS SLAUGHTERED AT NIGHT OR WHOSE BLOOD WAS SPILT OR WHOSE BLOOD PASSED WITHOUT THE HANGINGS,[9] IF IT ASCENDED, MUST DESCEND. R. SIMEON SAID: IT DOES NOT DESCEND; BECAUSE R. SIMEON MAINTAINED: IF ITS DISQUALIFICATION AROSE IN b THE SANCTUARY, THE SANCTUARY[1] RECEIVES IT; IF ITS DISQUALIFICATION DID NOT ARISE IN THE SANCTUARY, THE SANCTUARY DOES NOT RECEIVE IT. THE DISQUALIFICATION OF THE FOLLOWING DID NOT ARISE IN THE SANCTUARY: A ROBA' AND NIRBA', ONE SET ASIDE [FOR AN IDOLATROUS SACRIFICE]; AN ANIMAL WORSHIPPED [IDOLATROUSLY]; [A HARLOT'S] HIRE; [A DOG'S] EXCHANGE; KIL'AYIM; TEREFAH; AN ANIMAL CALVED THROUGH THE CAESAREAN SECTION; AND BLEMISHED ANIMALS.[2] R. AKIBA DECLARED BLEMISHED ANIMALS FIT.[3] R. ḤANINA THE SEGAN[4] OF THE PRIESTS SAID: MY FATHER USED TO REPULSE BLEMISHED ANIMALS FROM OFF THE ALTAR. JUST AS THEY DO NOT DESCEND ONCE THEY ASCENDED, SO THEY DO NOT ASCEND IF THEY HAD DESCENDED. AND ALL OF THESE, IF THEY ASCENDED TO THE TOP OF THE ALTAR WHILST ALIVE, MUST DESCEND. IF A BURNT OFFERING WENT UP ALIVE TO THE TOP OF THE ALTAR, IT MUST DESCEND. IF ONE SLAUGHTERED IT ON THE TOP OF THE ALTAR, HE MUST FLAY IT AND DISMEMBER IT WHERE IT LIES.[5]

GEMARA. It was taught, R. Judah said: [*This is the law of the burnt-offering:*] *it is that which goeth up* [*on its firewood upon the altar all night unto the morning*]:[6] here you have three limitations. It excludes [an animal] slaughtered at night; [an animal] whose blood was spilt; and [an animal] whose blood passed out beyound the hangings: if any one of these ascended [the altar], it must descend. R. Simeon said: *'Burnt-offering'*: I only know this of a fit burnt-offering; whence do I know to include one which was slaughtered at night, or whose blood was spilt, or whose blood passed without the hangings, or [the flesh of] which spent the night [away from the altar], or went out, or the unclean, or which was slaughtered [with the intention of burning its flesh] after time or without bounds; or whose blood was received and sprinkled by unfit [persons]; or whose blood was applied below [the scarlet line] when it should be applied above, or above when it should be applied below; or without when it should be applied within, or within when it should be applied without; or a Passover-offering or a sin-offering which one slaughtered for a different purpose: whence do we know [to include all these]? From the phrase, *'the law of the burnt-offering'*, which intimates one law for all burnt-offerings [viz.,] that if they ascended, they do not descend. You might think that I also include a *roba'* and a *nirba'*, one set aside [for an idolatrous sacrifice], or worshipped; a [harlot's] hire or the price [of a dog], or a hybrid, or a *terefah* or an animal calved through the caesarean section. Scripture, however, states: *'it is that.'* And why do you include the

(11) As stated above. (12) Since *'upon its firewood'* and *'on the altar'* are applicable to it.

a (1) E.g., if one vows wine without a sacrifice. (2) All this directly follows from their views stated above. (3) I.e., to teach that a meal-offering can be brought alone. (4) I.e., even without a sacrifice, which naturally would not be vowed so frequently. (5) Explicitly, and not overlay it with all the other rulings. (6) Not at the same time as the animal sacrifice. (7) Num. XXIX, 6 *et passim*. *'Their'* refers to the animal sacrifices. (8) V. *supra* 8a. (9) I.e., outside the Temple court.

b (1) Here the altar. (2) Cf. *supra* 71a and *b*. (3) If they ascend, they do not descend. (4) Chief of the priests and deputy High Priest; v. Sanh. (Sonc. ed.) 19a n. b 1. (5) Lit., 'in its place'. (6) Lev. VI, 2.

תורה אור

תרד מנחה הבאה עם הזבח לדברי ר"ג ורבי יהושע לא תרד לדברי כולן תרד נסכים הבאין בפני עצמן לדברי כולן [א]ירדו לדברי ר"ג ור"ש לא ירדו נסכין הבאין עם הזבח לדברי כולן [ב]ירדו לדברי ר"ג לחודיה לא ירדו פשיטא מנחה הבאה בפני עצמה איצטריכא ליה וכדרבא דאמר רבא *[ג]מתנדב אדם מנחת נסכים בכל יום ונשמעינן כדרבא נסכים הבאים עם הזבח איצטריכא ליה דקא מקרב להו למחר וליומא א] *חרא ס"ד אמינא הואיל *ואמר מר °מנחתם ונסכיהם בלילה מנחתם ונסכיהם למחר כנסכים הבאין בפני עצמן דמו ומודי ר"ש דלא ירדו קמ"ל: **מתני'** *[ד]אלו אם עלו לא ירדו הלן והיוצא והטמא ושנשחט חוץ לזמנו וחוץ למקומו *ושקבלו פסולין וזרקו את דמו רבי יהודה אומר [ה]שנשחט בלילה ב] ונשפך דמה ויצא דמה חוץ לקלעים אם ג] עלתה תרד ר"ש אומר לא תרד *(שהיה ד] פסולו בקדש) שר"ש אומר ה] [ו]כל שפסולו בקדש הקדש מקבלו לא היה פסולו בקדש אין הקדש מקבלו [ז]ואלו שלא היו פסולן בקדש הרובע והנרבע והמוקצה והנעבד והאתנן והמחיר והכלאים והטרפה והיוצא דופן *ובעלי מומין ו] *ר"ע מכשיר בבעלי מומין רבי חנינא סגן הכהנים אומר דוחה היה אבא את בעלי מומין מע"ג המזבח *[ח]כשם שאם עלו לא ירדו כך אם ירדו לא יעלו וכולן שעלו חיים לראש המזבח ירדו [ט]עולה שעלתה חיה לראש המזבח תרד [י]שחטה בראש המזבח יפשיט וינתחה במקומה: **גמ'** תניא *ר' יהודה אומר °זאת היא העולה הרי ז] אלו ג' מיעוטין פרט לשנשחטה בלילה ושנשפך דמה ושיצא דמה חוץ לקלעים שאם עלתה תרד ר"ש אומר עולה אין לי אלא עולה כשרה מנין לרבות שנשחטה בלילה ושנשפך דמה ושיצא דמה חוץ לקלעים והלן והיוצא והטמא ושנשחט חוץ לזמנו וחוץ למקומו ושקבלו פסולין וזרקו את דמו הניתנין למטה שנתנן למעלה ולמעלה שנתנן למטה והניתנין בחוץ שנתנן בפנים ח] בפנים שנתנן בחוץ ופסח וחטאת ששחטן שלא לשמן מנין ת"ל תורת העולה ריבה תורה אחת לכל העולין שאם עלו לא ירדו יכול שאני מרבה הרובע והנרבע והמוקצה והנעבד ואתנן ומחיר וכלאים וטרפה ויוצא דופן ת"ל זאת ומה ראית לרבות את אלו ולהוציא את אלו אחר ט] שריבה הכתוב

(במדבר כט) (ויקרא ו)

*מנחה הבאה. י] *בלולה כולה בגלל עצמה כגון המתנדב מנחת נסכים בלא זבח דאפשר לעשות כן כדלקמן (דף מד:): לדברי כולן. ר"ג ור' יהושע דמתני' דמרבי כל הראוי לאשים ולר"ש נמי דמרבי כל הבא בגלל עצמו אם נפסלה ועלתה לא תרד וכי פליג ר"ש בבאה בגלל זבח: לדברי רבי יוסי הגלילי ור"ע תרד. דהא לא מרבו אלא עולה ודוגמתה מין בהמה ועוף ולא מנחה. הבאה עם הזבח. כלומר בגלל זבח: לדברי כולן תרד. אם פסולה היא תרד לרבי יוסי הגלילי ור"ע ור"ש לדברי ר"ג ורבי יהושע לא תרד דהא יא] *(כתיב) מוקדה ומזבח הוא: נסכים הבאין בפני עצמן. כגון המתנדב יין בלא זבח דתנן במנחות (דף קד:) מתנדבין יין: לדברי כולן. רבי יוסי ור"ע ור' יהושע ירדו לדברי ר"ג ור"ש לא ירדו: ה"ג פשיטא דהכי הוא דלרבי יהושע מידי דבר מוקדה אין דלאו בר מוקדה לא לר"ג כל דבר מזבח ולר"ש בא בגלל עצמו ולתנאי דמתני' מנחה לא: מנחה הבאה בפני עצמה איצטריך ליה. ולאשמועינן דיש מנחת נסכים הבאה בפני עצמה כדרבא: מתנדב אדם מנחת נסכים. בלא זבח ואף על גב שלא אמרה תורה מנחת כליל יב] (הבאה) אלא הבאה בגלל זבח היכא דפריש פריש: ונשמעינן. ר"ל בהדיא כדרבא: נסכים הבאים בגלל זבח אצטריכא ליה. לר"ל לאשמועינן דלר"ש ירדו וכגון דקא מקריב להו למחר וליומא יג] *חרא דקי"ל לעיל (דף מד.) אדם מביא זבחו היום ונסכיו מכאן ועד י' ימים ונפקא לן מהא דאמר מר ומנחתם ונסכיהם יתירי דכתיבי בקרבנות החג להכי כתיבי: **מתני'** הלן. בין דם בין אימורים: רבי יהודה אומר כו'. בהנך תלתא פליג ומודי בשארא וטעמא יליף בגמ': שהיה פסולו בקדש. משבאת לעזרה נפסלה: כל שפסולו בקדש כו'. בגמ' יליף טעמא: מכשיר דאם עלו לא ירדו ובגמ' מוקי לה בדוקין שבעין הואיל וכשרין בעופות לכתחילה: דוחה. ומורידן: כשם שעלו לא ירדו. אכל פסולין דתנן בהו לא ירדו כך אם ירדו לאחר שעלו לא יעלו עוד: **גמ'** זאת היא העולה. זאת מיעוטא והיא מיעוטא וה"א דהעולה מיעוטא דמשמע העולה המיוחדת כשרה ולא פסולה למעוטי יד] פסולין אתו שאפילו עלו ירדו *ולא תימא כל הנוגע במזבח לכל פסולין אתא ומסתבר דהני ממעט שפסולן לפני זריקה ולקמיה מפרש שאר פסולין מנא ליה דלא ירדו טו] ולא ממעט להו מהכא כגון נשחט חוץ לזמנו דפסולו לפני זריקה: תורת העולה. שהיא על מוקדה שתהא שם טז] הלילה עד הבקר ולא תרד: יהודה דלא ממעט אלא הנך ג' ואם תאמר הא ר' יהודה סבר לעיל בפ"ק (דף יד.) רלפה מקדשה כב] ג)במזבח א"כ כולן עלו והיכי משכחת לה פסול בפיגול וטהר וטמא וי"ל כגון שיש הפסק בין הבהמה לרצפת העזרה: **פרט** לנשחטה בלילה. רובע ונרבע לא צריכי מיעוטא לרבי יהודה וכל הני דמרבה ר"ש מרבה נמי רבי יהודה כדלקמן (דף פה:) ומסתבר לרבות כג] הני טפי משום דמשכח להו היכשרא ואם תאמר קדשי קדשים ששחטן בדרום דקאמר בריש מעילה (דף ב:) תרד לר"י הא לית ביה מיעוט רביעי וי"ל משום דדרשינן לעיל בפרק כל הפסולין (דף לו.) כל דבר רע ריבה חטאת ששחטה בדרום כד] (דאם עלו לא ירדו) ושנכנס דמה לפנים ואף על גב דקרא לגלאו שמעינן נמי דאם עלתה תרד א"כ שחט בדרום כעין כה] שחיטת חוץ היא: **הניתנין** למעלה שנתנן למטה כו'. בכל הני מודה רבי יהודה והכי אמרינן לעיל בפרק ב' (דף כז:) קתני מיהא הניתנין למטה שנתנן למעלה ולא פליג רבי יהודה ובפ' כל הפסולין (לעיל דף לו.) נמי אמרינן דלא פסל רבי יהודה במחשבה דלמטה למעלה ולמעלה למטה כי היכי דפסיל במחשבת היטח משום דרבי יהודה לטעמיה דאמר שלא במקומו כבמקומו דמי ותימה דבריש מעילה (דף ב:) משמע דפליג רבי יהודה גבי קדשי קדשים ששחטן בדרום דרבה אמר אם עלו ירדו ורב יוסף

והיוצא. אע"ג דתני אלו תנא ושייר הנך דחשיב בברייתא בגמ' ושמא משום דמהני דהכא שמעינן יז] דכ"ש הנהו ובברייתא נמי בגמ' דהנך דירדו לא חשיב זקן וחולה ומזוהם ונדמה וטומטום ואנדרוגינוס ושמא האי בכלל הנהו דחשיב*: **וחוץ** למקומו. תימה דבפ' התודה (מנחות דף עט.) אמרינן חטאת ששחטה חוץ למקומו רבא אמר תרד כו' ור"ת גורס תודה דאיירי בה התם ומיהו בזה לא הועיל כלום וי"ל דהועיל דשאני תודה דהוי קדשים קלים וליכא מעילה באימורין מקמי זריקה וכי שחיט חוץ למקומו *לא מתירה הזריקה למעילה לכך תרד דהא חסירה זריקה החשובה בה אבל חוץ לזמנו לא ירד משום דמרצה לפיגולו לקובעו בכרת כדאי' במסכת מעילה (דף ג.) גבי מעילה וה"ה באם עלו לא ירדו כי האי גוונא אבל הכא בשמעתין איירי בקדשי קדשים דאיכא מעילה קודם זריקה להכי כי איפסלא בחוץ למקומו לא תרד דבזריקה החסירה אין קפידא דלא מהני מידי וכי האי גוונא מפליג בסמוך (דף פה.) גבי אימורין שהעלן לפני זריקה בין קדשים קלים בין קדשי קדשים וקשה לי פסח שלא לשמו אמאי לא ירד מאי שנא משלא במקומו בתודה דאידי ואידי קדשים קלים ומחשבה פסולה קודם זריקה וי"ל פסול דשלא במקומו חמיר טפי מפסול דשלא לשמו והוי כמו שחטן יח] בדרום בקדשי קדשים דירדו לר' יהודה פ"ק דמעילה (דף ב:) דהיינו נמי חוץ למקומו ובפרק התודה (מנחות דף עט.) נמי מוכח דחוץ למקומו נמי דירד היינו דוקא לר' יהודה אבל לר"ש לא ירדו אי נמי שלא לשמו קיל לפי שכשר בכל הזבחים לבד חטאת ופסח וצריך עיון אי מלי למימר דגבי תודה מיירי יט] דחשיב לאכול הבשר חוץ לירושלים *אין המקום ראוי לשום זבח לכך תרד אבל *חישב לאכול בשר חטאת ואשם חוץ לקלעים או להקטיר אימורי קדשים קלים חוץ לקלעים לא ירד כיון דזה המקום ראוי לקדשים קלים לאכילת שלמים:

הגה"ה ושקבלו פסולין וזרקו דמן. בגמ' (לקמן דף פז:) פליגי ר' יוחנן ור"ל אי מיירי דקבלו וזרקו דתרוייהו נעשו בפסולין וכמו כן מדקדק בריש מעילה (דף ה.): (צ"ל והעלהו)

כל שפסולו בקדש. שאירע לאחר שחיטה *שנתקדש בכלי כדפרישי' לעיל בפ' חטאת העוף (ד' סח: ד"ה אמר): **זאת** היא העולה. זאת תורת העולה היא העולה זאת והיא וה"א דהעולה שני היינו ג' מיעוטין אבל העולה קמא אתא לעולה ראשונה א)כדקאמר רבא בפ' תמיד נשחט (פסחי' דף נח:) ותורת הוי כ] רבוי לרבות איזה פסולין דאם עלו לא ירדו כא] ב)כרבי

א) ראשונה בפ' פינחס כדקאמר כו' לרבות איזה פסולין כו' כר"י צ"ק. ב) נ"א כר"ש. ג) צ"ל כמזבח כו' פסול בכל הנהו וי"ל צ"ק

שיטה מקובצת
א] וליומא אוחרא ס"ד: ב] בלילה ושנשפך דמה ושיצא דמה: ג] עלתה תרד. עי' תוס' לקמן (דף קח): ד] שהיה פסולה בקודש: ה] כל שפסולו בקודש פ"ה לאחר שבא לעזרה ולא נהירא דרובע ונרבע מי לא עסקינן בעזרה נמי ונראה דהיינו שיש לו הכשר במקום אחר וא"ת התינח נשחטה בלילה דיש לה הכשר דכל הלילה כשרה לאיברים ופדרים ויצאה דמה (יוצאה) כשרה בבמה אבל נשפך דמה באיזה מקום יש לה הכשר במקום אחר וי"ל דדוקא גבי שחיטה בלילה צריך שיהא לה הכשר במקום אחר לפי שעדיין לא נעשה בה עמידה בהכשר ואם לא היתה לה הכשר במקום אחר לא היה מכשיר ר"ש אבל נשפך דמה שכבר נשחטה בהכשר כה"ג קרי לה שפיר פסולו בקודש: ו] מומין. לעיל (דף לה ע"ב): ז] הרי אלו ג' מיעוטין. זאת למעוטי נשפך דמה מהיכא ממעים רובע ונרבע וי"ל דנשפך דמה ורובע ונרבע ממעט מחדא מיעוטא דשקולין הן דכי היכי דנשפך דמה אין לו הכשר במקום אחר כמו כן רובע ונרבע אין לו הכשר ע"נ דפי' דנשפך דמה קרי ליה הכשר במקום אחר הואיל והיא אחר שחיטה שנעשית בהכשר היינו לר"ש אבל ר"י לית לי ה האי סברא ושוין שאין להן הכשר במקום אחר: ח] בפנים והניתנין: ט] שריבה ואמר תורת העולה מיעט ואמר זאת: י] הבאה כליל כולה בגלל ותיבת בלולה נמחק: יא] בת מוקדה ותיבת כתיב נמחק: יב] תיבת הבאה נמחק: יג] וליומא אוחרא דקי"ל: יד] למעוטי הני ירדו דלא ממעט: טו] שם כל הלילה: יז] שמעינן להו דכ"ש: יח] שחטן. עי' תוס' (דף סח): יט] מיירי דחשבו לאכול: כ] ריבויא לר' יהודה לאינך פסולין. תיבות לרבות איזה נמחק: כא] ירדו כר"ש תיבת כר"י ל"ש ונמחק: כב] מקדשה כמזבח אות ב' נמחק: כג] לרבות אינך טפי: כד] תיבות דאם עלו לא ירדו נמחק: כה] שחיטה. עיין תוס' (לעיל דף סח):

י א ב מיי' פ"ג מהלכות פסה"מ הלכה יד:
יא ג מיי' פי"ד מהל' מעה"ק הלכה ח:
[וע"ע תוס' יבמות פד: ד"ה אלא לאו ותוס' כתובות כט. סד"ה ועל הכותית ותוס' שבועות לס. ד"ה ואלו נאמרין]
יב ד מיי' פ"ג מהלכות פסה"מ הלכה ז:
צ"ל לא מייתי הזריקה כו' צ"ק ועי' בתוס' מנחות עט. ד"ה והדר
יג ה מיי' שם הלכה ו:
יד ו מיי' שם הל' ח:
טו ז מיי' שם הל' ה
טז ח מיי' שם הל' ח:
יז ט מיי' שם הלכה ד:
יח י מיי' שם הל' ב:
[מוכר בפסחים עג. מנחות עט.]
שאין צ"ק
צ"ל כאן מיירי דחשב צ"ק

שייך לעיל כלומר בגלל עצמה כצ"ל צ"ק
רש"ק פ"ז וג"א בת [מנחות קה: קי.]
אותרא צ"ק
לעיל ח. המובא יד: [תענית ב: מנחות מד: נב.]
לעיל מג.
[לקמן פו:]
[במשנה שבמשניות ליתא]
צ"ק מ"ש
אותרא צ"ק [לעיל לה:]
לעיל מג.
נדה מ. ע"ש לעיל כו: [סוריות ב: ע"ש]
דלא צ"ק
רש"ק פ"ז

הכתוב ומיעט מרבה אני את אלו שהיה פסולן בקדש ומוציא אני את אלו שלא היה פסולן בקודש ורבי יהודה מייתי לה מהכא *מפני מה אמרו לן בדם כשר שהרי לן כשר [לעיל כז.] באימורין לן באימורין כשר שהרי לן כשר בבשר *יוצא שהיוצא כשר בבמה טמא הואיל והותר לעבודת ציבור חוץ לזמנו הואיל ומרצה לפיגולו חוץ למקומו הואיל ואיתקש לחוץ לזמנו שקבלו פסולין וזרקו את דמו בהנך פסולי א] דחזו לעבודת ציבור *וכי דנין דבר שלא בהכשרו מדבר שבהכשרו תנא אזאת תורת העולה ריבה סמיך ליה א"ר יוחנן **השוחט בהמה בלילה בפנים ב] (המעלה בחוץ פטור בחוץ) והעלה בחוץ חייב לא

רש"י:

ור' יהודה מייתי לה. לשאר פסולין מהכא: לן בדם כשר. שאם עלה לא ירד: שהרי לן כשר באימורין. שאם עלו לא ירדו: שהרי לן כשר בבשר. כגון בשר שלמים הנאכלין לשני ימים: יוצא כו'. וביוצא ג] דאימורי עולה ואימורי קדשים אבל יוצא דדם. (א) ד] פוסל רבי יהודה דנפקי לה תלתא פסולי מתלתא מיעוטי ומסתברא למעוטי יוצא *דדם ה] מדנשחט חוץ לזמנו דאשכחן ליה ריצוי אפילו בפנים שמרצה לפיגולו ליענש כרת: דחזו לעבודת ציבור. כגון טמא: דבר שלא בהכשירו. כגון לן באימורין: מדבר שבהכשירו. לן בבשר ויוצא דמקדש מיוצא דבמה שאין שם מחילה: סמיך ליה. לאסמכתא למילתיה: השוחט בהמה בלילה בפנים. והעלה אותה בחוץ חייב משום מעלה בחוץ ואפילו לר' יהודה דאמר אם עלתה בפנים תרד ולא מיבעיא הנך דאם עלו לא ירדו דחייב על העלאתן בחוץ כדאמרינן בפ' השוחט (לקמן דף קיא:) דהא מתקבלין בפנים אלא אפילו הך ו] לר' יהודה חייב: לא

תוספות:

יוסף ז] *לא ירדו וקאמר אליבא דרבי יהודה כ"ע לא פליגי דירדו כי פליגי אליבא דר"ש רב יוסף כר"ש ורבה אמר לך ע"כ לא קאמר ר"ש אלא בניתנין למטה שנתנן למעלה כו' ולעולם בנשחטין בצפון וקבל דמן בצפון ומדנקט למטה שנתנן למעלה משמע דפליגי בה דה"ל למנקט נשחטה בלילה ונשפך דמה ויצא דמה וי"ל דהכי פי' רב יוסף כר"ש דמשמע ליה ניתנין למעלה שנתנן למטה אפילו עולת העוף שמלקה ומילה דמה למטה דהוי כעין שינוי מקום השחיטה קדשי קדשים וקבלת דמן מצפון לדרום ורבה אמר ע"כ לא קאמר ר"ש אלא בזבחים הניתנין למטה שנתנן למעלה ולעולם ח] בשחטה בצפון אבל בעולת העוף שעשאה למטה ובקדשי קדשים ששחטן בדרום מודה ר"ש לרבי יהודה שירדו והא דקאמר לעיל בפרק שני (דף כז:) קתני מיהא הניתנין למטה שנתנן למעלה ולא פליג רבי יהודה אע"ג דלרב יוסף יש במשמע ניתנין למעלה שנתנן למטה אפילו עולת העוף שעשאה למטה דפליג ר' יהודה כיון דמודה בדמי זבחים שייך שפיר לומר דלא פליג ר' יהודה אלא ירדו דניתנין למעלה שנתנן למטה כמו בקבלו פסולין וזרקו את דמן דקאמר בסמוך דלא פליג רבי יהודה אע"ג דלא מודה לר"ש אלא בהנך דחזו לעבודת ציבור ור"ש אפילו בהנך דלא חזו לעבודת ציבור קאמר דלא ירדו דלא גרע משנשפך הדם ונאבד לגמרי דלא ירדו לר"ש ומיהו צריך עיון כי שמא בשנשפך הדם ונאבד קודם קבלה לא יאמר ר"ש לא ירדו בשביל שחיטה לבדה אלא בשנשפך מן הכלי ונאבד אחר קבלה ופסולין דלא חזו לעבודת ציבור דלא אשכחן להו הכשר בשום מקום אם קבלו נמי את הדם לא יאמר ר"ש אם עלו לא ירדו דמשום שחיטה *לבדה שחיטה כשרה לא יחשבו פסולו בקדש כדמשמע בריש מעילה (דף ב: וג.) שאפילו שחט בצפון וקבל בדרום לא היה ט] חושבן רבה פסולו בקדש דקמותיב ליה רב יוסף ממתני' דחטאת העוף (לעיל דף סו:) י] וכולן אין מטמאין בגדים אבית הבליעה בעולת העוף שעשה למטה ולעיל מוקמינן לה בגמ' במילוי ולא במליקה ומייתי מינה ראיה לדרום יא] *וגבי קדשי קדשים דחשיב פסולו בקדש א"כ אע"פ שנעשית המליקה בהכשר יב] שהיה במקום שחיטה לא היה חושבו פסולו בקדש לרבה עד דאותביה רב יוסף אלמא בשחיטה לבדה בהכשר לא חשיב לרבה פסולו בקדש ומיהו יש לדמות פסול מילוי לפסול שחיטה יותר יג] מקבלה כיון שבמילוי הוא ממלה ומוציא הדם מן הגוף כמו שעושה בשחיטה: **ומוציא** אני את אלו שלא היה פסולן בקדש. בריש פרק יוצא דופן (נדה דף מא.) משמע דלא איצטריך יד] האי קרא לנפסלו כשהן חולין אלא לנפסלו לאחר שהוקדשו והשתא רובע ונרבע טו] דיאסרו ניחא אבל מוקצה ונעבד קשה דאין אדם אוסר דבר שאינו שלו וי"ל דאיירי בקדשים קלים ואליבא דר' יוסי הגלילי דאמר ממון בעלים הוא וכן מפרש בפרק בתרא (לקמן דף קיד.) וא"ת אתנן ומחיר אי לאחר שהוקדשו נתן לזונה ובקדשים קלים כרבי יוסי הגלילי הא לא הוי אתנן כדדרשינן בשלהי כל האסורין (תמורה דף ל:) לכל נדר פרט לנדור וי"ל בבהמת קדשים מעוברת ונתן לה העובר וקסבר וולדות קדשים בהווייתן הן קדושים לאחר שילאו לאויר העולם ומ"מ הוי כלאחר שהוקדש כיון דקדיש אגב אימיה וכן בפ' בתרא (לקמן דף קיד.) קרי ליה ראוי לפתח אהל מועד אע"ג דהוי חולין עד שעת יציאתו וכלאים ויוצא דופן בוולדות קדשים והתם בפ' יוצא דופן (נדה דף מא.) פי' בקונטרס דל"ג בהווייתן הן קדושים טז] ולפי מה שפירשתי ניחא וע"כ הא שמעינן לר"ש בסוף דם שחיטה (כריתות דף כג:) דקסבר בהווייתן הן *קדושים יז] מה אמר דאם עלו ירדו וגם משום הך דאתנן ומחיר דשמעתין דלא משכחת לה אלא בוולדות קדשים ובהווייתן הן קדושים אבל קשה כלאים ויוצא דופן היכי משכחת לה דקדושים הוולדות דכיון דלא חזו להקרבה וגם קסבר בהווייתן קדושים לא חל על וולדות קדושה כלל כדתנן פרק כילד מערימין (תמורה דף כד:) רשב"ג אומר ילדה טומטום ואנדרוגינוס אין קדושה יח] [חלה] עליהן *וקסבר בהווייתן [הן] קדושים ולא חלה אפילו קדושת דמים יט] וי"ל דמקדישן בבטן קדושת הפה וקשה על ר"ש דסבר בהווייתן ממתני' דסוף תמורה (דף לג:) כ] אלו הנקברין קדשים שהפילו ובלאו הכי קשה מבשר בחלב דתני בהדייהו דמשמע דלא פליג עלייהו ר"ש אלא על חולין שנשחטו בעזרה *ואילו קדשים שהפילו אין קדושה חלה עליהן כיון דסבר בהווייתן קדושים כמו טומטום ואנדרוגינוס וגם *בשר בחלב אמר ר"ש למותר בהנאה בפ"ק דבכורות (דף י.) א"כ אמאי הוו בקבורה ול"ל דפליג עלייהו ר"ש ולא ליהוו בקבורה א"כ בקדשים שהפילו מודה דבקבורה *דקדושין משום דאי הוו בר קיימא הוו חזו להקרבה להכי לא דמו לטומטום ואנדרוגינוס והכי צריך לפרש שילהי בהמה המקשה (חולין דף עז.) גבי הפילה שליא במוקדשים תקבר ומפרש טעמא משום דרובא בר הקדש הוא וקשיא לר"ת אי סבר וולדות קדשים ממעי אמן קדושין אפילו כולן קדושין ואי סבר בהווייתן קדושין אין חלה קדושה על שום דבר דלא חזי להקרבה כדאמר רשב"ג גבי טומטום ואנדרוגינוס אלא י"ל דנפלים עדיפי כיון דאי הוו בר קיימא הוו חזו להקרבה וחל עלייהו קדושה והייני כא] [דאמר]התם רובא בר מקדש °לאפוקי טומטום ואנדרוגינוס*: הגה"ה יוצא שהרי יוצא כשר בבמה. יוצא דאברי עולה ואימורין קאמר אבל יוצא דדם (ב) פסיל ר' יהודה וא"ת מהאי טעמא נמי כב] ליתכשר יוצא דדם וי"ל דהכשר דם חמור ולא ילפינן מבמה אם לא נמצא לו הכשר בפנים ועוד י"ל דבבמה הוי בהכשרו ואע"ג דבאימורין ילפינן שלא בהכשרו מבהכשרו ע"י ריבוי תורת מיהו בדם המתיר לא ילפינן כדפירשנו לעיל בפ' איזהו מקומן (דף נא. ד"ה מפני) דדייק דבר הלמד בבנין אב חוזר ומלמד בבנין אב מדילפינן לן דמה מלן דאימורין ולן דאימורין מלן דבשר ואמאי נילף דם שנפסל בשקיעת החמה *מאימורין דכשרין דלא מיפסלי אלא בעמוד השחר כג] וכ"ת משום דלן בדם אחר עמוד השחר לא מצי גמר מאימורין מה בכך הא לא מצינו פסול עמוד השחר בדם כלל ועוד כיון שלמדנו דאחר שנפסל לא ירד אין חילוק בין שקיעת החמה לעמוד השחר דאי לא תימא הכי לן בדם שתי *ליעות מנין הא אין כיוצא בו כד] בבשר אלא ודאי לא גמרינן (ג) דם מהכשרו ולהכי חשיב ליה בנין אב מבנין אב דלא מצי למילף אלא מלן דעמוד השחר דאימורין ולהכי נמי לא כייל להו דילמא לן בדם ובאימורין כשר שהרי לן כשר בבשר ולכך נמי אצטריך למימר חוץ למקומו הואיל ואיתקש לחוץ לזמנו דלא מצי למימר הואיל וכשר בבמה וכן קבלו פסולין לא מכשר אלא בהנך דחזו לעבודת ציבור אבל זר לא אף על גב דכשר בבמה ומיהו אשכחן דילפינן (ד) מהכשרו בדם מדם כגון ניתנין למעלה ולמטה לפי שכל אחד כשר בחבירו וגם לא הוצרך כאן לפרש הטעם לפי שהוא פשוט כה] ושלא לשמו דפסח וחטאת שכשר בשאר קרבנות ומיהו קשה דלעיל בפרק חטאת העוף (דף סח:) גבי זר וסכין מטמאין בבית הבליעה פריך דנילף זר מבמה דתניא מנין ליוצא כו' ומאי קושיא הא האי תנא גופיה לא יליף כדפי' דמוקי בחזו לעבודת לבור ולא גמרי נמי דם מבמה ועוד הא דמכשר התם מליקת שמאל משום דאשכחן ליה הכשירא ביוה"כ הא לא ילפינן מבהכשרו וכן *ליגה מאברים ופדרים הא רבי יהודה פסיל ליה הכא וי"ל דלעיל פירשתי דההיא סוגיא כר"ש וכולה מתני' דהתם דמפלגא לענין כו] בליעה (ה) לענין בין פסולו בקדש כר"ש דהכא דברים מעילה מדמי כז] בית הבליעה ואם עלה לא ירד להדדי וה"ק נילף מבמה לר"ש כי היכי דגמר בברייתא פסול *דאימורים לרבי יהודה ומיהו לא לגמרי אתיא כר"ש מדפסלה מליקת שמאל ור"ש מכשר לה לפי גירסת ר"ת דלעיל בפרק שני (דף כד:*) דגרים והא תנן מלק בשמאל כו' *א"כ י"ל דלרבי יהודה לא יעמיד המיעוטין בעוף מיהו לעיל (דף פג:) פסלינן בעוף טפי מבהמה גבי פלוגתא דרבי יוסי הגלילי ור"ע דמה כבשים ראוים כו' ומיהו קשה לרבי יהודה ילא דמה ליתכשר דנילף מיוצא דאימורים ואימורים מבמה כמו לן דדם מאימורים ולן דאימורים מבשר א"כ ילא דאימורים מבשר שלמים דכשרים חוץ לקלעים וממילא שמעת חוץ לירושלים דאין חילוק בין חד פסולא לתרי פסולי כדפירשנו והא דנקט *הכא קרא מבמה ניחא לאשכוחי הכשירא ביוצא דאימורין גופייהו אבל גבי לן דגמר מבשר לא הוה מצי לאשכוחי באימורין לן כח] בבמה דכשר דהא תנן בפ' בתרא (לקמן דף קיג.) הזמן הנותר והטמא שוין בזה ובזה: לא

עין משפט נר מצוה

אמר לא צ"ק

יט א מיי' פי"ח מהל' מעה"ק הלכה יח:

נ"ל לבדו שנעשה בהכשר לא כו' צ"ק

גבי צ"ק

קדושים וגם משום כו' כצ"ל צ"ק

דקסבר בהווייתן הן קדושים כו' צ"ק

והלא קדשים צ"ק

גליון הש"ס

תוס' ד"ה ומוציא וכו' לאפוקי טומטום ואנדרוגינוס. ע' לקמן דף קיד ע"א תו' ד"ה וקסבר: בא"ד אי נמי י"ל דלר"י לא יעמיד המיעוטין. ע"ל דף סח ע"א תוס' ד"ה מלק:

שיטה מקובצת

א] דחזו. עי' תוס' מנחות (דף ו ע"ב): ב] תיבות המעלה בחוץ פטור בחוץ נמחק: ג] וביוצא דאיברי עולה. תיבת דאימורי נמחק: ד] דדם פסיל ר' יהודה דנפקא ליה תלתא: ה] ונשחט חוץ אות מ' ד' נמחק: ו] הך דלר' יהודה תרד חייב: ז] יוסף אמר לא: ח] ולעולם דשחטה בצפון: ט] לא היה חושבו: י] העוף דקתני וכולן: יא] לדרום גבי קדשי: יב] בהכשר שהיא במקום: יג] יותר מלקבלה כיון: יד] תיבת האי ל"ש ונמחק: טו] תיבת דיאסרו ל"ש: טז] קדושים דהא כ"ש למ"ד במעי אמן הן קדושים דאצטריך למעוטי מזאת ויש לפרש דה"ק דאפי' קסבר בהווייתן הן קדושים ניחא דאצטריך קרא למעוטי כיון דהפסול לא בא תחילה אלא בבת אחת אבל לא מצי למימר קסבר במעי אמן הן קדושים דע"כ הא שמעינן וכו':

יז] מה. ס"א ומיהו אמר: יח] אין קדושה חלה עליהן וקאמר דאף על גב דאין קרושה אמן חלה עליהן דקסבר בהווייתן קדושים ולא חלה עליהן אפילו: יט] ר"ל דמקדיש בבטן: כ] תמורה דתנן אלו: כא] והיינו דאמר התם רובא בר מוקדש: כב] נמי דתני ליתכשר. עיין תוס' (מנחות דף ו): כג] ולן בדם אחר עמוד השחר דלא מצי ותיבות וכ"ת משום ואות ד' נמחק: כד] בו כשר בבשר: כה] פשוט וכן שלא לשמו דפסח וחטאת לפי שכשר בשאר: כו] לענין בית הבליעה בין פסולו: כז] סדמי טומאת בית הבליעה ואם עלה לא ירד אהדדי וה"ק: כח] לן כשר בבמה דהא:

מסורת הש"ס

גירסת הצ"ק דדם הס"ד ואח"כ מה"ד לעבודת כו' טמא הס"ד ואח"כ מה"ד חוץ לזמנו כו' כרת הס"ד ותיבת מדנשחט ותיבת דשו יש למחוק

[לעיל סח: סט. מנחות ה: מח:]

[לעיל נא. סט.

לקמן קיא: ע"ש

הגהות הב"ח

(א) רש"י ד"ה יוצא וכו' פסול לר' יהודה וכו' יוצא דדם הס"ד ואח"כ מ"ה ונשחט חוץ: (ב) תום' ד"ה ומוציא וכו' פסול לר' יהודה וכו' ועוד י"ל דפסול דם לא ילפינן מבמה משום דהוי הכשירו בכך ואע"ג דבאימורין ילפינן וכו' מיהו בדם התמור לא ילפינן וכו' דדייק דדבר הלמד: (ג) בא"ד אלא ודאי לא גמרינן פסול דם מהכשרו וכו' ולהכי נמי לא כייל להו דלימא לן בדם: (ד) בא"ד ומיהו אשכחן דילפינן פסול מהכשרו בכך בדם מדם: (ה) בא"ד לענין בליעה בין פסולו כצ"ל ותיבת לענין נמחק:

בבשר צ"ק

גי' הצ"ק דקדושה חלה עליהם משום דאי הוו בר קיימא חזו כו'

[ועיין היטב תוס' חולין עז: ד"ה רובא ותוס' לקמן קיד. ד"ה וקסבר ותו' נדה מא. ד"ה קסבר]

דאם עלו לא ירדו מאימורין צ"ק

ליעות צ"ק

ליגה מאברים צ"ק

גירסת הצ"ק דאימורים מבמה לר"י [ד"ה וכרי]

צ"ל הכא מבמה מייתי ליה צ"ק

former and exclude the latter? Since Scripture includes [84b] and excludes, I include the former, because their disqualification arose in the sanctuary, while I exclude the latter whose disqualification
a did not arise in the sanctuary.[1]

But R. Judah infers [the law] from the following: Why did they say that if blood is kept overnight it is fit? Because if the *emurim* are kept overnight they are fit. Why are the *emurim* fit if they are kept overnight? Because flesh is fit if kept overnight. [Flesh that] goes out? Because [flesh that] goes out is fit at the high place [*bamah*]. Unclean [flesh]? Because it was permitted in public service. [The *emurim* of a sacrifice intended to be burnt] after time? Because it propitiates in respect of its *piggul* status. [The *emurim* of a sacrifice intended to be burnt] out of bounds? Because it was likened to [the intention to burn it] after time. Where unfit [persons] received [the blood] and sprinkled it—in the case of those unfit persons who are eligible for public service. Can you then argue from what is its proper way to that where the same is not the proper way?—The Tanna relies on the extension indicated by, *This is the law of the burnt-offering*.[2]

R. Joḥanan said: If one slaughters an animal at night within[3]

a (1) For notes v. *supra* 27b. (2) Lev. VI, 2. For notes v. *supra* 51a. (3) The Temple court.

and offers it[4] without,[5] he is culpable:[6] [85a] let this not be less
a than slaughtering without and offering up [the limbs without[1]]. R. Ḥiyya b. Abin raised an objection: One who slaughters a bird within and offers it up without is not culpable; if he slaughtered [it] without and offered it up without, he is culpable. Yet let us say: Let it not be less than slaughtering and offering up without?—That is a refutation. Alternatively, The slaughtering of a bird within is mere killing.[2]

'Ulla said: If the *emurim* of lesser sacrifices are laid [on the altar] before their blood is sprinkled, they do not descend, [because] they have become the food of the altar. R. Zera observed, We too learnt [likewise]: THAT ... WHOSE BLOOD WAS SPILT OR WHOSE BLOOD PASSED WITHOUT THE HANGINGS: If you say there that if [the limbs or *emurim*] ascended they do not descend, though if he [the priest] should come to sprinkle, he has nothing to sprinkle;[3] how much more so here, seeing that if he comes to sprinkle, he has what to sprinkle!—[No:] relate this to a most sacred sacrifice.[4] But there is the Passover-offering, which is a lesser sacrifice?[5]—Relate this to [where it is slaughtered] under a different designation.[6]

We learnt: AND ALL OF THESE, IF THEY ASCENDED THE ALTAR WHILST ALIVE, MUST DESCEND. Hence [if they ascended] when slaughtered, they do not descend: surely that is so whether they are most sacred sacrifices or lesser sacrifices?—No: [deduce thus:]
b but if they are slaughtered, some of these must descend,[1] and some do not descend. But he teaches, AND ALL OF THESE.—That refers to whilst alive. That is obvious?[2]—In truth it refers to living animals which have a cataract in the eye, this being in accordance with R. Akiba who maintained that if these ascend they do not descend.[3]

How have you explained it? As referring to unfit [animals]! Then consider the final clause: IF A BURNT-OFFERING WENT UP ALIVE TO THE TOP OF THE ALTAR, IT MUST DESCEND. IF ONE SLAUGHTERED IT ON THE TOP OF THE ALTAR, HE MUST FLAY IT AND DISMEMBER IT WHERE IT LIES. But if it is unfit, can it be flayed and dismembered? Surely the Divine Law said: *And he shall cut it into pieces*,[4] '*it*' [implies] a fit, but not an unfit [animal]?—The final clause refers to a fit [sacrifice]; and what does he [the Tanna] inform us?[5] that flaying and dismembering can be done on top of the altar. Then on the view that flaying and dismembering cannot be done on top of the altar, what can be said?—The case we discuss here is, e.g., where it had a period of fitness and then became disqualified,[6] this agreeing with R. Eleazar son of R. Simeon who maintained: Since the blood was sprinkled and the flesh had become acceptable[7] even for a single hour, he must flay it, and its skin belongs to the priests.[8] If so, when it was taught: 'What does
c he do?[1] He takes down the inwards and washes them', why should he do so?[2]—What then should we do? Offer [i.e. burn] them with their dung? '*Present it now unto thy governor; will he be pleased with thee? or will he accept thy person?*'[3] This is our difficulty: why must he wash them?[4]—So that if another priest chances upon them and does

(4) Lit., 'carries up' (its limbs). (5) The Temple court; he offers it up by laying it on a stone or on an altar-like pile (v. *Sifra* on Lev. XVII, 6). (6) On account of laying limbs sacrificially without, even according to R. Judah who maintained that if it ascended the altar it must still descend. Those which if laid on the altar do not descend certainly render the priest culpable if he lays them without, since these can be received by the altar (v. *infra* 111b).

a (1) Where one is culpable for each act separately. (2) Not ritual slaughtering (*shechitah*), since it requires *meliḳah* (v. Glos.). For that reason he is not culpable. But when he slaughters an animal sacrifice at night, it does count as *shechitah* (since *ḥullin* may be slaughtered at night). (3) Since the blood is spilt. (4) The Mishnah may refer to most sacred sacrifices only, whose *emurim* are *intrinsically* holy even *before* the blood is sprinkled. Possibly, however, the same does not apply to lesser sacrifices, whose *emurim* are sacred only in virtue of the sprinkling of the blood. (5) The Mishnah enumerates this too, and it is now assumed that this law applies even where its blood is spilt. (6) As the Mishnah actually states. It does not apply, however, to the present instance.

b (1) *Sc.* lesser sacrifices. (2) Obviously they cannot remain there but must be brought down and slaughtered, and then they will be taken up again. If then this is not taught for the sake of the inference (viz., that *all* of these, if slaughtered, do *not* descend), it is altogether superfluous. (3) V. *supra* 77b. The Mishnah thus informs us that they must descend, and even if subsequently slaughtered they may not re-ascend. (4) Lev. I, 6. (5) If it is fit, it obviously descends, since it will be taken up again. (6) It refers *indeed* to a *fit* animal which ascended alive, but after it was slaughtered on top of the altar and its blood was sprinkled, it became disqualified; therefore it must be flayed and dismembered on top of the altar, for if it is taken down it may not be taken up again, since it was disqualified. And as to the objection that an unfit animal cannot be flayed, the answer is that it had a period when it was fit for flaying before it became disqualified. (7) This is a technical term denoting that the flesh was now fit for its purpose. (8) Even if it became unfit after the sprinkling of the blood. Though the flesh cannot be burnt on the altar but in the place of burning unfit sacrifices, the skin is not burnt with it but belongs to the priests. So here too, when it is on top of the altar it must likewise be flayed and dismembered.

c (1) In this case where an animal ascended the altar whilst alive and it was slaughtered there. (2) Seeing that they are unfit. For though these unfit animals must not be taken down, yet if they are, they may not be taken up again. (3) Mal. I, 8. This is a protest against offering anything unseemly, and it is most unseemly to offer the inwards uncleaned. (4) Since they must be taken down, after which they cannot go up again, let them be left as they are.

תורה אור

לא תהא פחותה משוחט בחוץ ומעלה בחוץ מתיב רב חייא בר אבין *השוחט עוף בפנים ומעלה בחוץ פטור שחט בחוץ ומעלה בחוץ חייב א] נימא לא תהא פחותה משוחט ומעלה בחוץ *תיובתא איבעית אימא שחיטת העוף בפנים מיקטל קטליה *אמר עולא אימורי קדשים קלים שהעלן לפני זריקת דמן לא ירדו נעשו לחמו של מזבח א"ר זירא אף אנן נמי תנינא שנשפך דמה ושיצא דמה חוץ לקלעים ב] ומה התם דאם בא לזרוק אין לו לזרוק אמרת אם עלו לא ירדו הכא דאם בא לזרוק זורק לא כל שכן תרגמא אקדשי קדשים ג] הרי פסח דקדשים קלים הוא תרגמא ד] בשלא לשמן תנן וכולן שעלו חיין לגבי מזבח ירדו הא שחוטין לא ירדו מאי לאו ל"ש קדשי קדשים לא שנא קדשים קלים לא הא שחוטין מהן ירדו מהן לא ירדו והא כולן קתני כולם אחיין פשיטא לעולם אחיין ובדוקין ה] שבעין *ואליבא דר"ע דאמר אם עלו לא ירדו במאי אוקימתא בפסולין אימא סיפא וכן עולה שעלתה חיה לראש המזבח תרד שחטה בראש המזבח יפשיט וינתח במקומה ואי פסולה בת הפשט ונתוח היא מלאכי א °ונתח אותה אמר רחמנא אותה כשרה ולא פסולה סיפא אתאן לכשרה ומאי קמשמע לן דיש הפשט ונתוח בראש ו] המזבח ז] ולמאן דאמר אין הפשט ונתוח בראש המזבח מאי איכא למימר הכא במאי עסקינן כגון שהיתה לו שעת הכושר ונפסלה ורבי אלעזר ברבי שמעון היא *דאמר כיון שנזרק הדם והורצה בשר שעה אחת יפשיטנה ועורה לכהנים ואלא דקתני כיצד עושה מוריד את הקרבים למטה ומדיחן ח] למה לי היכי נעביד נקרבינהו *בפרתייהו °הקריבהו נא לפחתך הירצך או הישא פניך אנן הכי קאמרינן מדיחן למה לי דאי מיתרמי כהן אחרינא ולא ידע נסקינהו

ואנן

רש"י

לא תהא פחותה משוחט בחוץ ומעלה אותה בחוץ · דקי"ל ט] בהשוחט (לקמן דף קז·) דחייב על שחיטתה ועל עלייתה : השוחט עוף קדשים בפנים והעלהו בחוץ פטור · על העלייתה דאינו מתקבל בפנים אלא מלוק : שחטו בחוץ והעלהו בחוץ חייב · על שתיהן דהשוחט עוף קדשים בחוץ חייב דאיתרבי מאו אשר ישחט בפ' השוחט (שם דף קז·) וכי העלהו בחוץ חייב דמרבינן בהשוחט (שם) לענין העלאת כל הנשחטין י] דכי היכי דחייב על שחיטתן חייב על העלאתן דכתיב ואליהם תאמר לערב פרשיות : ואמאי השוחטו בפנים והעלהו בחוץ פטור נימא לא תהא פחותה כו' : מיקטל קטליה · יא] לא שייכא שחיטה בפנים כלל לא בחולין ולא בקדשים אבל שחיטת לילה שחיטה היא בחולין הלכך בקדשים שחיטה פסולה היא קרויה : שנשפך דמה · לא תרד הבשר אם עלה וקא ס"ד דבאימורי קדשים קלים נמי קאי : ומה · נשפך דמה דהוי עליית בשר לפני זריקה דהא אין כאן זריקה וגריעא משאר עולין לפני זריקה דהתם אם בא לזרוק יש לו מה לזרוק והכא אם בא לזרוק אין לו מה לזרוק ואפ"ה לא תרד וכ"ש יב] היכא דלא נשפך : תרגמא אקדשי קדשים · פירוש המשנה הזאת בקדשי קדשים שקדושת הגוף עליהן לפני זריקה : והרי פסח · שנוי בה דקתני *סיפא והפסח והחטאת כו' וקא ס"ד דאפסולי דקתני ברישא נמי קאי כגון אם נשפך דמו או יצא : תרגמא אשלא לשמו · פסח לא תנא ליה אלא אפסולא דשלא לשמו כדקתני בה ששחטן שלא לשמן יג] : הכי גרסינן תנן וכולן שעלו חיין לגבי מזבח ירדו הא שחוטין לא ירדו מאי לאו לא שנא קדשי קדשים ל"ש קדשים קלים לא הא שחוטין מהן ירדו ומהן לא ירדו והא כולן קתני כולן אחיין פשיטא לעולם אחיין ובדוקין שבעין כו' : תנן וכולן שעלו חיין · קא סלקא יד] דעתך הא כולן אכל קדשים קאמר ואכשרין קאי ולא אפסולין דתני ברישא קאי דלא שייך בהו חיין דבכל הפסולין הנזכרים באם עלו לא ירדו אין בהן פסול מחיים הלכך אכשרין קאי והאי כולן ע"כ טו] כל הקדשים קאמר לא שנא קדשי קדשים ולא שנא קדשים קלים וקאמר הא שחוטין לא ירדו ובלאחר זריקת דמים לא איצטריך טז] לאשמועינן דאמאי ירדו: ומשני לא תימא הא שחוטין כולן לא ירדו אלא אימא הא שחוטין יש מהן ירדו ויש מהן לא ירדו קדשי קדשים לא ירדו קדשים קלים ירדו : והא כולן קתני · מאי לאו יז] אדוקיא דהא שחוטין לא ירדו נמי קאי : יח] כולן משום חיין · נקט לה למימר דירדו דאין מזבח מקדש חיין : פשיטא יט] · דירדו דהא מוחרין ועולין לאחר שחיטה הואיל ובכשרין קיימי : לעולם אחיין · נקט כולן ולאשמועינן דירדו ובדוקין שבעין איצטריך לאשמועינן שפסולין מחיים וכי מחתינן להו תו לא כ] מסקי דקי"ל (לעיל דף פד·) בפסולין כשם שאם עלו לא ירדו כך אם ירדו לא יעלו ואפי' הכי ירדו דאין מזבח מקדש חיים : ואליבא דר"ע · נקט לה דאמר במתניתין בעלי מומין אם עלו לא ירדו ומוקמינן לה לקמן בדוקין שבעין ואשמעינן מתניתין עלו חיים ירדו הא שחוטין לא ירדו : ונתח אותה · אמרינן בתורת כהנים כשרה ולא פסולה שאם נפסלה קודם הפשט שורפה כא] *בעזרה והא נמי בראש המזבח נהי דלא תרד דקדשה מזבח מיהו לא בעי הפשט ונתוח : סיפא דמתני' אתאן כב] לכשרים · והכי קאמר וכן עולה חיה כשרה שעלתה כו' ומאי קא משמע לן פשיטא דתרד דהא הדרא סלקא : ומשני הא קמ"ל דהיכא דשחטה בראש המזבח לא נריך לאחותה ואסוקה ואע"ג דהדר סלקא אלא מפשיטה בראש המזבח : דיש הפשט · בכשרות : אין הפשט · הואיל והדר מלי לאסוקה לאו אורח ארעא להפשיט שם : הכא במאי עסקינן · לעולם כשעלתה כשרה כג] חיה ומששחטה בראש המזבח וזרק דמה נפסלה הלכך יפשיט וינתח במקומה דאי מחית לה תו לא סלקא ודקשיא לך פסולה לאו בת הפשט היא : כגון דהיתה לו שעת כד] הכושר · להפשט קודם פסולה בת הפשט ונתוח היא ואפילו היא למטה והבשר פסול ונשרף וכרבי אלעזר בר"ש דאמר לקמן בפרק טבול יום (דף קד·) כיון שנזרק הדם והורצה בשר שעה אחת להקטיר ונפסלה יפשיטנה ועורה לכהנים ואין עורה נשרף עמה הילכך השתא נמי כי איתא בראש המזבח וקטרת בעיא הפשט ונתוח : עורה לכהנים גרסינן · כדכתיב (ויקרא ז) עור העולה אשר הקריב לכהן : אלא הא דקתני כיצד הוא עושה כו' · בברייתא דזבחים גרסינן ליה גבי עולה שעלתה חיה למזבח ושחטה וקאמר יפשיט וינתח במקומה וקתני סיפא מוריד את הקרביים למטה ומדיחן ואי בפסולה מכי מחית לה תו לא סלקא : ומשני אלא היכי ליעבד ניקרבינהו לקרביים בפרתייהו · בפרש שלהן בתמיה : אנן הכי קאמרינן מדיחן למה לי · הואיל ולא הדרי סלקי : ומשני דאי מתרמי כהן אחרינא דלא ידע · שנפסלה ניסקינהו :

ואנן

תוספות

לא תהא פחותה משוחט בחוץ ומעלה בחוץ · תימה אמאי איתותב הכא לימא אנא דאמרי כרבי שמעון דפ' השוחט והמעלה (לקמן קיא·) דאמר זעירי שחיטת לילה איכא בינייהו דלרבי שמעון חייב וי"ל *דהכא קאמר אפי' לרבי יהודה דאי לרבי שמעון דוקא למה לי טעמא דלא תהא פחותה תיפוק לי משום כה] דראוי להתקבל בפנים וא"ת הא דתניא לקמן בפ' השוחט והמעלה (דף קט·) מנין לרבות פסולין כגון הלן והיוצא כו' ת"ל לא יביאנו לעשות כל המתקבל בפתח אהל מועד חייבין עליו בחוץ ל"ל קרא תיפוק לי דלא תהוי פחותה משוחט בחוץ ומעלה בחוץ וכ"ת דההיא כרבי שמעון דלית ליה האי טעמא א"כ ליתני שחיטת לילה ונשפך דמה ויצא דמה חוץ לקלעים וי"ל דבלן ויוצא וטמא לא שייך לא תהא פחותה משוחט בחוץ :

מקטל קטליה · משום דלא מליט שחיטה בעוף בפנים הלכך ה"ל כהתיז ראשו ולא דמי לשחיטת לילה כו] :

ומאי קמ"ל דיש הפשט ונתוח בראש המזבח הניחא למ"ד כו' · תימה דהך קושיא יכול להקשות בלאו הכי דהיכי דמי אי בפסולים ונתח אותו אמר רחמנא ואי בכשרין הניחא כו' כז] ומפרש ה"ר חיים דאם עלתה בראש המזבח לכ"ע יש הפשט ונתוח וכשהיא למטה פליגי מהו להעלותה ולהפשיטה והכי פירושא בשלמא אי מיירי רישא בכשרין ותיהוי סייעתא לעולא ותנא סיפא לגלויי רישא דבכשרים אף על גב דסיפא לא אשמועינן מידי דלכ"ע יש הפשט ונתוח בראש המזבח ולא תניא אלא לגלויי ארישא אלא אי אמרת רישא בפסולין סיפא במאי אי בפסולין ונתח אותה אמר רחמנא ואי בכשרין מאי קא משמע לן אי קא משמע לן דיש הפשט ונתוח בראש המזבח כלומר אפילו הורידה יעלנה להפשיטה הניחא למאן דאמר כו' :

והוא

שיטה מקובצת

א] חייב ואמאי נימא : ב] ומה התם דאם בא לזרוק כו' · לעיל פי' דעולא אמר לא ירדו אפי' לר"י (והכי)(והכא) משמע לכאורה דאליבא דר"ש קאמר מדפריך ליה מנשפך דמה דאי אליבא דר"י הא אמר אם נשפך דמה ירדו מיהו י"ל דפריך שפיר אליבא דר"י וה"ק מדר"ש נשמע לר"י ואליבא דר"ש פריך שפיר מכ"ש ואף לר"י נמי דעד כאן לא קאמר ר"י ירדו אלא בנשפך דמה אבל היכא דיש בידו לזרוק לא דאין לנו לומר דפליגי אלא במאי דחזינן דפליגי ועוד דלא דמי כלל למתני' דהתם אין בידו לזרוק והכא יש בידו לזרוק ונהי דתלמודא מייתי נשפך דמה היינו משום דבעי למיפרך מכ"ש אליבא דר"ש ומ"מ מיניה נשמע לר"י כדפי' : ג] קדשים והרי פסח : ד] תרגמא אשלא לשמו : ה] שבעין · פי' אבל מתוסר אבר לא וכן כל מום מגונה משום הקריבהו נא לפחתך : ו] המזבח הניחא למ"ד יש הפשט אלא למ"ד אין הפשט בראש המזבח מאי איכא למימר דאיתמר רב פפא ורב שימא בר אשי חד אמר יש הפשט ונתוח בראש המזבח וחד אמר אין הפשט ונתוח בראש המזבח במאי קא מיפלגי מר סבר לשלחן דמי ומר סבר לבית המטבחים דמי הניחא למ"ד יש הפשט ונתוח בראש המזבח אלא : ז] למ"ד אין אות ו' נמחק : ח] ומדיחן והיכי מצי מסיק להו היכי נעביד ותיבות למה לי ל"ש ונמחק : ט] דקי"ל לקמן בהשוחט : י] הנשחטין בחוץ דכי : יא] קטליה דלא שייכא שחיטה בפנים לעוף כלל לא בחולין ולא בקדשים והו"ל כהתיז את ראשו אבל שחיטת כו' בקדשים נמי שחיטה פסולה : יב] וכ"ש הכא דלא : יג] לשמן דהויא ביה זריקה והוכשרו אימורין למזבח ואע"ג דזריקה פסולה הואי להכי מייתא אתני דאם עלו לא ירדו הואיל וברוב זבחים אין פסול שלא לשמו נוהג הס"ד ומה"ד הכי : יד] דעתיה האי כולן : טו] ע"כ אכל הקדשים : טז] איצטריך ליה לאשמועינן : יז] לאו אדיוקא דהא : יח] לא כולן : יט] פשיטא ס"א דמחיים ירדו דאין מזבח מקדש מחיים דאם כשרים הם מה הפסד יש בירידתן הואיל ויכול להעלותן בסוף ואם פסולים הם אינם פסולים אלא ממום או רובע ונרבע או חד מהנך דאין פסולן בקודש וא"כ פשיטא דירדו : כ] לא לסקי דקי"ל דפסולין כשם : כא] שורפה בעזרה והאי נמי דבראש המזבח : כב] אתאן לכשרה : כג] כשרה חיתה ותיבת חיה נמחק : כד] הכשר

להפשיטו: כה] משום דלא ירדו וראוי להתקבל : כו] לילה שהפסול מחמת דבר אחר הוא וחזיא למחר לשחט אבל ליכא לפרש דשחיטת לילה כשרה בחולין שחיטת עוף נמי כשרה בחולין : כז] ומפרש · לשון מהר"פ ומפרש הר"ר חיים דהא דקאמר דאין הפשט ונתוח היינו היכא שירדה למטה ושוב לא יעלנה על המזבח להפשיטה אבל אם שחטה בראש המזבח כ"ע לא פליגי דיפשיטנה במקומה קודם שתרד אם ירצה והשתא ניחא לנופיה דמתני' א"נ דאוקמינא בפסולין וה"פ אא"ב בכשרים מיירי רישא וסיפא ניחא ואע"ג דבהאי דתני סיפא אם עלתה חיה תרד ליכא שום חידוש ולא בהא דקאמר יפשיטנה כיון דבכשרה מיירי דבלא ירדה מיירי כ"מ איכא למימר דתני סיפא לגלויי רישא וברישא איכא חידוש לאשמועינן בין בקדשי קדשים בין בקדשים קלים אלא אי אמרת רישא בפסולים סיפא א"כ בכשרים דאי בפסולים בת הפשט ונתוח היא וא"כ סיפא מאי אתא לאשמועינן דהא לא לגלויי לרישא אתיא אלא ע"כ אתא לאשמועינן דאם שחטה בראש המזבח ואפי' אם ירדה יעלנה ויפשיטנה דאל"כ לא הוי בסיפא שום חידוש ושייך שפיר השתא וניחא :

בעי

מסורת הש"ס

לקמן קיא.

[שבת כ: גיטין כח.]

לעיל פג: [מעילה ז:]

עי' ברמב"ס ועי' ז"ק

נ"א בתוספתא

לקמן קד

[עי' חולין דף יח ע"א ממקמם ליס בפרחה וע"ש ברש"י]

ז"ל בעזרה

כ א מיי' פ"ג מהלכות פסה"מ הלכה יב:

כא ב מיי' פ"ב מהלכות מעילה הלכה ה:

כב ג מיי' פ"ד מהלכות איסורי מזבח הל' ה:

כג ד מיי' פ"ג מהלכות פסה"מ הלכה ט:

כד ה מיי' שם הל' טז:

כה ו מיי' שם ופ"ו מהל' מעה"ק הל' ב:

ואנן ניקו *נעביד להו לכהנים מילתא דאתו בה לידי תקלה אפ"ה עדיפא *שלא יהו קדשי שמים מוטלים כנבילה אמר רבי חייא בר אבא א] בעי רבי יוחנן אימורי קדשים קלים שהעלן לפני זריקת דמן ירדו או לא ירדו א"ל רבי אמי ותיבעי לך מעילה א"ל מעילה לא קמיבעיא לי דזריקה הוא דקבעה להו במעילה כי קמיבעיא ב] ליה ירידה ופשיט לא ירדו ואין בהן מעילה רב נחמן בר יצחק מתני הכי א"ר חייא בר אבא בעי רבי יוחנן אימורי קדשים קלים שהעלן לפני זריקת דמן יש בהן מעילה או לא א"ל רבי אמי ותיבעי לך ירידה א"ל ירידה לא קא מיבעי' לי דנעשו לחמו של מזבח כי קמיבעי' לי מעילה ופשיט הכי "לא ירדו "ואין בהן מעילה: ואלו לא היה ג] פסולן [וכו']: א"ר יוחנן *לא הכשיר ר"ע אלא בדוקין שבעין הואיל וכשרים בעופות והוא שקדם הקדשן את מומן ומודה ר"ע בעולת נקבה דכשקדם מומה להקדשה דמיא בעי רבי ירמיה יש נרבע בעופות או אין נרבע בעופות מי אמר *מן הבהמה להוציא את הרובע ד] והנרבע כל היכא דאיתיה ברובע איתיה בנרבע כל היכא דליתיה ברובע ליתיה בנרבע או דלמא הרי נעבדה בו עבירה אמר רבה ת"ש ר"ע מכשיר בבעלי מומין "ואם איתא נכשיר נמי בנרבע הואיל וכשר בעופות שמע מינה אמר רב נחמן בר יצחק אף אנן נמי תנינא *הנרבע והמוקצה והנעבד ואתנן ומחיר וטומטום ואנדרוגינוס כולן מטמאין בגדים אבית הבליעה ש"מ: רבי חנינא סגן הכהנים כו': מאי קמ"ל איבעית אימא מעשה קמ"ל ואיבעית אימא מאי דוחה כלאחר יד: כשם שאם ה] עלה כו': *אמר עולא "לא שנו אלא שלא משלה בהן האור אבל משלה בהן האור יעלו רב מרי מתני ארישא רב חנינא מסורא מתני אסיפא העצמות והגידין והקרנים והטלפים בזמן שמחוברין יעלו פירשו לא יעלו אמר עולא לא שנו אלא שלא משלה בהן האור אבל משלה בהן האור יעלו מאן דמתני אסיפא ו] כ"ש ארישא ומאן דמתני ארישא אבל אסיפא לאו בני הקטרה נינהו: **מתני'** "ואלו אם עלו ירדו בשר קדשי קדשים ובשר קדשים קלים ומותר העומר ושתי הלחם ולחם הפנים ושירי מנחות ז] והקטורת "הצמר שבראשי כבשים ושער שבזקן תישים והעצמות והגידים והקרנים והטלפים בזמן שהם מחוברים יעלו שנאמר °והקטיר הכהן (ויקרא א) את הכל *פירשו לא יעלו שנאמר °ועשית עולותיך הבשר והדם: **גמ'** *ת"ר (דברים יב) °והקטיר הכהן את הכל המזבחה לרבות העצמות והגידים והקרנים והטלפים (ויקרא א) יכול אפילו פרשו תלמוד לומר ועשית עולותיך הבשר והדם אי בשר ודם יכול

והוא שקדם הקדשן את מומן · שחלה עליהן קדושת מזבח אבל קדם מומן להקדשן לא היו קדשי מזבח מעולם ואפילו בדוקין שבעין אין המזבח מקדשן ותימה דבפ' ב' דבכורות (דף טז·) אמרינן והשוחטן בחוץ פטור רב הונא מתני חייב ומוקי לה בדוקין שבעין ואליבא דרבי עקיבא דאמר אם עלו לא ירדו ולכאורה לא קאי אמתניתין דהתם אלא אברייתא דתניא כוותיה דרב ששת שפירש כללו של דבר לאתויי לשוחט בחוץ דפטור ומיירי דקדם מומן להקדשן ועלה קאמר דרב הונא מתני חייב והשתא אמאי מתני חייב הא אמרינן הכא אפילו בדוקין שבעין ירדו כיון דקדם מומן להקדשן ובלאו הכי קשה דהא בכלל *קתני הרי הן כחולין והיכי מתני חייב ובקונטרס הגיה שם בסיפא דברייתא דקדם הקדשן למומן והשוחט בחוץ פטור ועלה קאי רב הונא ומתני חייב וכן נראה דמייתי בתריה בין לפני פדיון בין לאחר פדיון עושין תמורה דהיינו סיפא דברייתא:

יש נרבע בעופות או אין נרבע בעופות · הא דדרשינן בסוף פרק קמא דחולין (דף כג·) מן התורין למעוטי נרבע היינו כמסקנא דשמעתין אבל אם תמצא לומר דאין נרבע בעופות לא תוקמיה אלא למעוטי מוקצה: **ומותר** העומר · אינו בכלל שירי מנחות דחלוק הוא מהן שבא להתיר מן החדש ומן השעורין יד] שתי הלחם באין חמץ ולחם הפנים אין נקטר בהם אלא שני בזיכי לבונה: מאן

ואנן ניקו כו' · לשון קושיא הוא: לידי תקלה · נהעלות פסולין שירדו: מוטלים כנבלה · הקרבים בפרש שלהן: ותיבעי לך מעילה · אי מהני להו לאיקבעינהו במעילה: לא ירדו · דנעשו לחמו של מזבח ומיהו מעילה לית בהו דלא הוכררו לחלק ראוי לגבוה: תודה אור הואיל וכשרין בעופות · דכתיב (ויקרא כב) תמים זכר בבקר בכשבים תמות וזכרות בבהמה ואין תמות וזכרות בעופות ומיהו מחוסר אבר לא משום הקריבהו נא לפחתך (מלאכי א) *וכן מום מגונה: דוקין · טיל"א לשון הטוטה כדוק שמים (ישעיה מ) והוא לשון דק או תבלול בעינו (ויקרא כא): והוא שקדם הקדשן את מומן · שחלה עליהן קדושת מזבח [קודם] אבל קדם מומן להקדשן לא היו קדשי מזבח מימיהן ואין המזבח מקדשן: ומודה רבי עקיבא בעולת נקבה · שעלתה למזבח תרד ואע"פ שכשרה בעופות דכמאן דקדם מומה להקדשה דמיא דאין לך מום גדול מזה: עוף · לא שייך ביה רובע דאין עוף רובע אשה: ואם איתא · דעוף שנרבע כשר ליכשר ח] לרבי עקיבא נמי בבהמה נרבעת אם עלתה לא תרד הואיל וכשר בעופות לכתחילה: ה"ג אף אנן נמי תנינא הנרבע והמוקצה · ולא גרסינן הרובע דהא בעוף קאי ואין רובע בעוף וקתני דיש נרבע: וטומטום ואנדרוגינוס · ואע"פ שלא נאמר תמות וזכרות בעופות קסבר בריה בפני עצמה היא ואינו ספק זכר ספק נקבה ורבי אליעזר פליג עליה בבכורות (דף מב·) דקתני סיפא רבי אליעזר אומר כל מקום שנאמר זכר ונקבה אתה מוציא טומטום ואנדרוגינוס מביניהם ועוף הואיל ולא נאמר בו זכר ונקבה אי אתה יכול להוציא מביניהן טומטום ואנדרוגינוס: מאי קמ"ל · תנא קמא נמי ירדו קאמר: כלאחר יד · ואין מורידן דרך בזיון בפרהסיא: משלה בהן האור · כל דהו יעלו דנעשו לחמו של אש: ארישא · מתני לה להא דעולא ארישא כדאמרן אפסולין שעלו וירדו דקתני מתניתין לא יעלו: פירשו · שחלצו מן הבשר לפני העלאתן לא יעלו והוא הדין נמי דאם עלו ירדו כדאמר לקמן בברייתא (דף פו·) אליבא דרבי ומוקמינן מתניתין אליביה: כ"ש ארישא · ט] *דאם עולה או אימורים בני הקטרה ניכהו אם לא נפסלו והני כיון דמשלה בהן האור קדשינהו כמה שהן פסולין: אבל עצמות וגידים לאו בני הקטרה ניכהו · דאמרינן לקמן (שם) מועשית עולותיך הבשר והדם הלכך לא שייכא בהו י] משלה אור לקדשינהו: **מתני'** ואלו אם עלו ירדו · ואף על פי שכשרין דלא שייך בהו מזבח כלל יא]: והקטורת · שעלתה על מזבח החיצון דהא לאו ראוי הוא יב]: הצמר שבראשי הכבשים · רישא דבבא אחריתי היא ובהדי עצמות וגידין קתני לה וכמשפטן שבראשי כבשי של עולה שהראש אינו בכלל הפשט וקרב עם עורו כדאמר בשחיטת חולין בפ"ב (כז·) אין לי אלא נתחים שישנן בכלל הפשטה וישנן בכלל הקטרה מנין לרבות את הראש שכבר הותז בשחיטה שאע"פ שאינו בהפשטה ישנו בהקטרה ת"ל כו' ויש למר בגובה יג] ערפו אצל ראשו: וכן שער שבזקן תישים·עולה: גמ'

[פסחים עג:] [שבת קטז:] [ב"ב וכן] [לעיל לס: ע"ש ממנות עט.] [ב"ק מ: בכורות מא. תמורה כח. נדה מא.] יבמות פג: [בכורות מב.] [לעיל ח:] חולין כ. ג"א איברי

נ"ל קתני הרי הן כחולין לכל דבריהם והיכי כו' צ"ק

[נ"ל הכל המזבחה כ"א במשנה שבמשניות]

שיטה מקובצת

א] בעי ר' יוחנן' מכאן יש להוכיח הא דפי' ל"ע"ל דאף לר"י [פריך] דאל"כ הוי ליה למימר לר"י הכי אליבא דר"ש דאמר נשפך דמה לא תרד גבי קדשי קדשים ואימורי קדשים כו': ב] קמיבעיא לי אות ה' נמחק: ג] פסולן וכו': ד] הרובע ונרבע אות ה' נמחק: ה] שאם עלו ואות ה' נמחק: ו] מאן דמתני אסיפא הא דקאמר וכולן שפקעו כו' כ"ש ארישא כך אם ירדו לא יעלו ופ"ה והא דקאמר במתני' לא יחזיר ר"ל אם לא רצה כלומר שאינו צריך והא דקאמר יעלו ר"ל אם רצה ולא נהירא דלא יחזיר משמע בשום ענין אפילו אם רצה לכך נראה לי דלא יחזיר מיירי בצרידי והכא מיירי דעדיין יש בו לחלוחית: ז] והקטורת פי' קטורת על מזבח החיצון הואיל ואין לו שום ראויות עליו וא"ת והרי דמים הניתנים בפנים שנתנן בחוץ או איפכא דאין להם ראויות זה על זה ואמרינן אם עלו לא ירדו וי"ל דמ"מ שם דמים ראוין על מזבח החיצון אבל אין שום קטורת ראוין על מזבח החיצון: ח] ליכשר ר' עקיבא: ט] ארישא דבשר עולה ותיבת דדם ל"ש ונמחק: י] בהו ממשלת האור לקדושינהו: יא] כלל ס"א ומותר העומר כו' כל אלו נאכלים ולא נקטרים: יב] הוא לו הס"ד: יג] בגובה ראשו אצל ערפו: יד] ושתי הלחם:

not know,[5] he will take them up. [85b] And shall we arise and do a thing to priests whereby they may come to a stumbling block?[6]—Even so it is better, that Divine sacrifices should not lie like carrion.[7]

R. Ḥiyya b. Abba said: R. Johanan asked: If the *emurim* of lesser sacrifices were taken up before their blood was sprinkled, must they go down or not? Said R. Ammi to him: Then inquire about a trespass-offering?[8]—I do not ask about a trespass-offering, he replied, because sprinkling alone makes it subject to a trespass-offering; I only ask about [their] going down. And he [eventually] ruled that they do not go down and do not involve trespass.

R. Naḥman b. Isaac recited it thus. R. Ḥiyya b. Abba said, R. Johanan asked: If the *emurim* of lesser sacrifices were taken up before their blood was sprinkled, do they involve a trespass-offering or not? Said R. Ammi to him: Then ask about [their] going down? I do not ask about going down, he replied, because they have become the food of the altar;[9] I ask only about a trespass-offering. And [eventually] he ruled: They do not go down and do not involve trespass.

THE DISQUALIFICATION OF THE FOLLOWING DID NOT ARISE IN THE SANCTUARY etc. R. Johanan said: Only in the case of cataracts in the eye did R. Akiba declare them fit, since such are fit in the case of birds, and provided that their consecration [for a sacrifice] preceded their blemish. And R. Akiba admits in the case of a female burnt-offering [that it must be taken down], because
a that is tantamount to the blemish preceding its consecration.[1]

R. Jeremiah asked: Is *nirba'* [a disqualification] in birds or is *nirba'* no [disqualification] in birds?[2] Do we say: [*Ye shall bring your offering*] of *the cattle*[3] excludes *roba'* and *nirba'*: [hence] whatever is subject to [the disqualification of] *roba'* is subject to [the disqualification of] *nirba'*; and whatever is not subject to *roba'* is not subject to *nirba'*.[4] Or perhaps, sin has been committed with it?[5]—Said Raba, Come and hear: R. AKIBA DECLARED BLEMISHED ANIMALS FIT. Now, if this is correct,[6] let him also declare a *nirba'* fit,[7] since it is fit in the case of birds.[8] Hence infer from this [that it is not fit]. R. Naḥman b. Isaac said: We too have learnt thus: With regard to a *nirba'*, a bird set apart [for an idolatrous sacrifice], a bird worshipped, a [harlot's] hire, the price [of a dog], a *ṭumṭum*[9] and a hermaphrodite, all of these defile garments when they are in the gullet.[10] This proves it.

R. ḤANINA THE SEGAN OF THE PRIESTS. What does he inform us?—I can say that he informs us of the actual fact.[11] Alternatively, what does HE REPULSED mean? Indirectly.[12]

JUST AS THEY DO NOT DESCEND IF THEY ONCE ASCENDED etc. 'Ulla said: They learnt this only where the fire had not taken hold of it; but if the fire had taken hold of it, it must re-ascend.
b R. Mari recited this in connection with the first clause.[1] R. Ḥanina of Sura recited it in connection with the final clause:[2] With regard to the bones, tendons, horns and hoofs, if they are attached [to the animal], they ascend [the altar]; if they are severed [from the animal] they do not ascend.[3] Said 'Ulla: They learnt this only where the fire had not taken hold of them; but if the fire had taken hold of them, they ascend.[4] He who recites it in connection with the final clause [holds that it applies] all the more to the first clause.[5] He however who recites it in connection with the first clause [maintains]: but as for the final clause, those things are not normally burnt [on the altar][6]

MISHNAH THE FOLLOWING IF THEY ASCENDED GO DOWN:[7] THE FLESH OF MOST SACRED SACRIFICES AND THE FLESH OF LESSER SACRIFICES; THE RESIDUE OF THE 'OMER;[8] THE TWO LOAVES;[9] THE SHEWBREAD;[10] THE RESIDUE OF MEAL-OFFERINGS;[11] AND INCENSE.[12] THE WOOL ON THE HEADS OF LAMBS, THE HAIR OF HE-GOATS' BEARDS; THE BONES, TENDONS, HORNS AND HOOFS, IF THEY ARE ATTACHED, GO UP, BECAUSE IT IS SAID, AND THE PRIEST SHALL MAKE THE WHOLE SMOKE ON THE ALTAR;[13] IF THEY ARE SEVERED [FROM THE ANIMAL], THEY DO NOT GO UP, FOR IT IS SAID, AND THOU SHALT OFFER THY BURNT-OFFERINGS, THE FLESH AND THE BLOOD, [UPON THE ALTAR OF THE LORD THY GOD].[14]

GEMARA. Our Rabbis taught: *And the priest shall make* the whole *smoke on the altar:* this includes the bones, tendons, horns and hoofs. You might think, even if they were severed; therefore it states, '*And thou shalt offer thy burnt-offerings*, the flesh and the blood'.

(5) That they are unfit. (6) Surely we may not cause another priest to think that they are fit. (7) Hence they must be washed. (8) If one misappropriates sacred property to secular use he is liable to a trespass-offering. Normally when *emurim* are laid on the altar (*after* the sprinkling of the blood) they become the property of the altar, and anyone thus misappropriating them incurs a trespass-offering. Then let the question be asked: does the law of trespass apply if they were taken up *before* the sprinkling of the blood? (9) V. *supra a.*
a (1) For notes v. *supra* 35b. (2) There is no question about *roba'*, as a male bird does not copulate with a woman. (3) Lev. I, 2. 'Of' (Heb. מ) is partitive, and regarded as a limitation. (4) So that it does not disqualify a bird. (5) Hence it is disqualified. (6) That *nirba'* does not disqualify a bird. (7) *Sc.* an animal, in the sense that it does not descend. (8) Even to sacrifice such in the first place. (9) An animal or bird whose genitals are covered up, so that its sex cannot be determined.—This passage refers to birds. (10) V. *supra* 50b n.b1. This proves that *nirba'* is a disqualification. (11) What happened in such cases. (12) Not openly, as this would seem to degrade sacrifices, but covertly. Lit., 'as with the back of the hand'.
b (1) The present Mishnah, referring to unfit animals. (2) The next Mishnah. (3) And if they did, they must be removed. (4) Even if taken down. (5) Because the first clause deals with things that are normally burnt on the altar. (6) Therefore even if the fire had taken hold of them, they are taken down, since they have no connection with the altar at all. (7) Because they do not belong to the altar at all. (8) The '*omer* (q.v. Glos.) after it was waved; v. Lev. XXIII, 10 *seq.* (9) V. Lev. XXIII, 15 *seq.* (10) V. Ex. XXV, 30. (11) V. Lev. II, 2 *seq.* (12) Which must be burnt on the *inner* altar. (13) Lev. I, 9. (14) Deut. XII, 27.

If [we had only the text] *flesh and blood* [to go by], [86*a*] you might have thought that one *must* remove the tendons and bones and lay [only] flesh on the altar; therefore it says, *'And the priest shall make* the whole *smoke'*. How are these text reconciled? If they are attached, they ascend; if they are severed, even if they are on the top of the altar, they must go down.

Which Tanna do you know to maintain that if they were severed, they must go down? It is Rabbi. For it was taught: *'And the priest shall make* the whole *smoke on the altar'*: this includes the bones, tendons, horns and hoofs, even if they were severed. How do then I interpret, *'And thou shalt offer thy burnt-offerings*, the flesh and the blood'? It is to teach you: Burnt pieces [flesh] of the burnt-offering
a you must replace [on the altar],[1] but you do not replace burnt tendons and bones. Rabbi said: One text states, *'And the priest shall make* the whole *smoke on the altar'*, thus extending [the law], while another text states, *'And thou shalt offer thy burnt-offerings*, the flesh and the blood', thus limiting [it]. How do you reconcile them? If they are attached, they ascend; if they are severed, even if they are on the top of the altar, they descend.

IF THEY ARE SEVERED [FROM THE ANIMAL], THEY DO NOT GO UP etc. R. Zera said: They learnt this only if they were severed downwards;[2] but [if they were severed] upwards,[3] they come nearer to being burnt.[4] Even if they were severed?[5]—Said Rabbah: This is what he means: They learnt this only if they were severed
b after sprinkling;[1] but if they were severed before sprinkling, the sprinkling comes and makes them permitted [for general use], even to make from them a knife handle.[2] He holds as R. Joḥanan said on R. Ishmael's authority: *'It shall be his'* [the priest's] is said of the burnt-offering, and *'it shall be his'* is said of the guilt-offering:[3] as the bones of a guilt-offering are permitted, for even its flesh is permitted to the priests, so are the bones of a burnt-offering permitted. This must be redundant,[4] for if it is not redundant, you can refute [the deduction]: as for a guilt-offering, the reason is because its flesh is permitted.[5] [It is redundant, for] a superfluous *'it shall be his'* is written.[6]

R. Adda b. Ahaba raised an objection: The bones of sacrifices involve trespass[7] before sprinkling, but do not involve trespass after sprinkling; whereas the bones of a burnt-offering always involve trespass?[8]—Say: Whereas those of a burnt-offering, if they were severed before sprinkling, involve trespass until the sprinkling; [if they were severed] after sprinkling, they always involve trespass.[9]

Now he [Rabbah] disagrees with R. Eleazar. For R. Eleazar said: If they were severed before sprinkling, they involve trespass; after sprinkling, one must not use them,[10] but they do not involve trespass.[11]

c *MISHNAH*. AND IF ANY OF THESE[1] SPRANG OFF FROM THE ALTAR[2] THEY ARE NOT REPLACED. SIMILARLY, IF A COAL SPRANG OFF FROM THE ALTAR, IT IS NOT REPLACED. LIMBS THAT SPRANG OFF FROM THE ALTAR: IF BEFORE MIDNIGHT, MUST BE REPLACED, AND INVOLVE TRESPASS; AFTER MIDNIGHT, THEY ARE NOT REPLACED AND DO NOT INVOLVE TRESPASS. JUST AS THE ALTAR SANCTIFIES WHATEVER IS ELIGIBLE FOR IT, SO DOES THE ASCENT SANCTIFY WHATEVER IS ELIGIBLE FOR IT;[3] AND JUST AS THE ALTAR AND THE ASCENT SANCTIFY WHATEVER IS ELIGIBLE FOR THEM, SO DO VESSELS SANCTIFY.[4]

GEMARA. How is it meant? If they have substance,[5] then even after midnight too [let them be returned]; while if they have no substance, even before midnight too [they need] not [be returned]?

a (1) If they sprang off. (2) Away from the burning pile. Then they do not go up, and if they did, they are removed.—They were placed on the altar, of course, whilst attached to the flesh. (3) Springing nearer to the centre of the pile. (4) They are not removed.—This passage is thus apparently based on the Mishnah. Tosaf. however points out that the Mishnah discusses whether they are to be placed on the altar at all, whereas this assumes that it was already there. Accordingly Tosaf. explains that it refers to the Baraitha just quoted, where the first Tanna maintains that the bones etc. are included even if they are severed. (5) The meaning of this is doubtful, and Rashi assumes that there is a lacuna in the text. If the text is correct, the meaning would be: do you say that even if they were severed (upwards) they remain on the altar; surely the Mishnah teaches that only when *attached* do they ascend? Sh. M. quotes a variant reading: It was stated above: this includes the bones etc. even if they were severed. Said Rabbah: They learnt this only etc.

b (1) Then they must descend, nevertheless they are still regarded as sacred, and must be so treated. (2) I.e., they have no sanctity at all. (3) Lev. VII, 7*f*. (4) Lit., 'free', 'disengaged.' The form of exegesis just used, based on the fact that the same words are used of both, is called a *gezerah shawah*, and in such the word used as a basis of deduction must be entirely free for that purpose, being otherwise redundant. (5) Hence its bones are too. Whereas the flesh of a burnt-offering must be burnt on the altar, and so its bones too may be forbidden. (6) Scripture could write, the skin of the burnt-offering... shall be the priest's. (7) V. *supra* 85*b* n. 8. (8) This proves that they are always forbidden. (9) Emended text (Sh.M.). (10) By Rabbinical law. (11) This agrees with R. Ishmael *supra*. When he quotes *'it shall be his'* it must mean after sprinkling, for it is the sprinkling that permits the flesh (and so the bones too, on his view) to the priests.

c (1) The unfit and bones etc. which if laid on the altar must not be removed. (2) Through the heat. (3) If laid on the ascent, it must not be removed. (4) *Sc.* service-vessels—they sanctify what is placed in them. (5) If these limbs are not burnt right through and the flesh is recognisable.

יכול יחלוץ גידין ועצמות ויעלה בשר לגבי מזבח ת"ל והקטיר הכהן את הכל הא כיצד מחוברין יעלו פירשו אפי' הן בראש המזבח ירדו מאן תנא דשמעת ליה דאמר פירשו ירדו [א]רבי היא דתניא °והקטיר הכהן את הכל המזבחה לרבות העצמות והגידין והקרנים והטלפים אפילו פירשו ואלא מה אני מקיים °ועשית עולותיך הבשר והדם לומר לך עיכולי עולה אתה מחזיר ואי אתה מחזיר עיכולי גידין ועצמות רבי אומר כתוב אחד אומר והקטיר הכהן את הכל המזבחה ריבה וכתוב אחד אומר ועשית עולותיך הבשר והדם מיעט הא כיצד מחוברין יעלו פירשו אפי' הן בראש המזבח ירדו: ב] *פירשו לא יעלו [וכו']: אמר רבי זירא לא שנו אלא שפירשו כלפי מטה אבל כלפי מעלה קרובי הוא דאקריבו לעיכול *ואפילו פירשו אמר רבה הכי קאמר לא שנו אלא שפירשו לאחר זריקה אבל פירשו קודם זריקה ג] אתאי זריקה ד]ושריתינהו אפי' למעבד מינייהו קתא דסכיני סבר לה כי הא *דאמר רבי יוחנן משום רבי ישמעאל נאמר °לו יהיה בעולה ונאמר °לו יהיה באשם מה אשם עצמותיו מותרין אף עולה ה] עצמות מותרין מופני דאי לא מופני איכא למיפרך מה לאשם שכן בשרו מותר לו יהיה יתירא כתיב מתיב רב אדא בר אהבה *עצמות קדשים לפני זריקה מועלין בהן *לאחר זריקה אין מועלין בהן ושל עולה מועלין בהן לעולם *אימא ושל עולה פירשו לפני זריקה ו] אין מועלין בהן לאחר זריקה מועלין בהן לעולם ופליגא דר"א ז] דא"ר אלעזר פירשו לפני זריקה מועלין בהם לאחר זריקה לא נהנין ולא מועלין: **מתני'** *וכולן שפקעו מעל גבי המזבח לא יחזיר וכן גחלת שפקעה מעל גבי המזבח לא יחזיר *איברים שפקעו מעל גבי המזבח קודם חצות יחזיר ומועלין בהן לאחר חצות לא יחזיר ואין מועלין בהם כשם שהמזבח מקדש את הראוי לו כך הכבש מקדש ח] כשם שהמזבח והכבש מקדשין את הראוי להן כך הכלים מקדשין: **גמ'** ה"ד אי דאית בהו ממש אפילו לאחר חצות נמי אי ט] דלית בהו ממש אפי' קודם חצות נמי לא לא צריכא בשירי

(ויקרא א) (דברים יב) (ויקרא ז) (שם)

רש"י

גמ' יכול יחלוץ · מלוה מוטלת עליו: מאן שמעת ליה כו' · ומתני' אליביה אתיא: כלפי מטה · דרך ירידה ומתרחקי מן המערכה: כלפי מעלה · לצד המערכה אין זו פרישות אלא קריבה אצל העיכול של אש: ואפי' פירשו · י] נראה בעיני שחסר מן הגירסא ולמאי דגרס ה"פ ואפי' פירשו בתמיה והא מחוברין יעלו הוא דקאמר: לא שנו · דקאמר פירשו ירדו ומיהו איתנהו בכלל קדשים אלא שפירשו לאחר זריקה דכיון דבשעת זריקה מחוברים הוו יא]קובעתן זריקה למזבח וכי פירשו הוו להו קדשים פסולין: אבל פירשו לפני זריקה · דבשעת זריקה לאו בני מזבח היו אתאי זריקה ושריתינהו להדיוט: למיעבד קתא דסכיני · כי היכי דשריא בשר לגבי מזבח דלהכי קאי קשריא נמי עצמות למאי דקיימי והיינו הנאה כהנים כרבי ישמעאל: לו יהיה בעולה · עור העולה אשר הקריב לכהן לו יהיה ונאמר לו יהיה באשם כחטאת כאשם תורה אחת להם הכהן [וגו'] לו יהיה: מה אשם עצמותיו מותרין · שהרי אף בשרו מותר ואי משום נותר דבשריפה לא שייך נותר אלא במידי דבר אכילה כדכתיב (ויקרא ז) והנותר מבשר הזבח וגו': לו יהיה · יתירא הוא דמצי למיכתב עור העולה אשר הקריב לכהן יב] לו יהיה למה לי: עצמות קדשים האכלין · כגון חטאת ואשם מועלין בהן דאין כאן שעת היתר לכהנים: ופליגא דר"א · אדרבה: פירשו לפני זריקה מועלין בהן לעולם · דכיון דפירשו אינהו לאו בני הקטרה נינהו לא אהני להו זריקה ובאיסורייהו קיימי: פירשו לאחר זריקה לא נהנין · מדרבנן ולא מועלין כרבי ישמעאל דגמר מלו יהיה דאשם ואשם פירשו לאחר זריקה הוא דבהדי בשר יג] אישתרו בזריקה לכהנים: **מתני'** וכולן · יד] הנך פסולין שעלו דתנן בהן לא ירדו בין עצמות וגידים שהעלן מחובר ועכלתן האש: שפקעו מעל המזבח · לארץ: לא יחזיר · א"צ להחזיר: קודם חצות יחזיר · בגמרא מפרש טעמא: ומועלין בהן · דאכתי בני מזבח נינהו: ואין מועלין בהן · דכיון דהוו להו כמעוכלין כדמפרש בגמרא הוו להו דבר שנעשית מצותו ואין מועלין בו: **גמ'** טו] אי דלית בהו ממש · שנשרפו כולן טז]:

תוספות

מאן שמעת ליה דאמר פירשו ירדו רבי היא · ופי' רש"י ומתני' אליביה אתיא ור"י פי' כרבנן דוקא היא דמדקתני לא יעלו משמע דאם עלו לא ירדו והא דאמרי רבנן והקטיר לרבות כו' ואפי' פירשו היינו פירשו ועודם על גבי המזבח והא דלא מוקי מיעוטא דועשית עולותיך הבשר והדם בירדו למטה משום דניחא ליה למנקט רבותא דאפי' בעודם ע"ג המזבח ממעט עיכולי גידים וה"ה דממעטי בלא עיכול אם ירדו למטה ופירשו: **עיכולי** עולה אתה מחזיר כו' · ולעיל בריש פירקין (דף פג:) דאיצטריך לרבויי פוקעין מהעולה היינו משום דמהכא לא ידעי אלא בעודם על המזבח אבל למטה לא אי נמי כי היכי דלא נפקא ליה מאשר תאכל האש (ויקרא ו) משום דאיצטריך למעוטי עיכולי קטורת הכי נמי מקרא דהכא כיון דאיצטריך למעוטי עיכולי גידים ולית ליה הא דקאמר לעיל לאו ממילא שמעינן ליה והא דאיצטריך תרי קראי חד למעוטי קטרת וחד למעוטי גידים משום דאי מקרא דאשר תאכל האש לא הוה ממעטי' אלא עיכולי [קטורת] דליתיה על המזבח החיצון אבל עיכולי גידים לא ואי מקרא דהכא לא ממעטי' קטורת דבר הקרבה הוא דומיא דבשר ודם הלכך צריכי: **לא** שנו אלא שפירשו כלפי מטה · פי' לצד חוץ אבל כלפי מעלה פי' לצד המערכה כך גירס' הקונטרס וברייתא קאי ויש ספרים דגרסי פירשו לא יעלו ואמתני' קאי ולא יז] נהירא דמה שייך ביה קריבה לעיכול כיון שהוא למטה בקרקע *ועוד דבתר (א) הכי שקיל וטרי בפירושא דברייתא ומ"מ אפסקיה: **אתיא** זריקה ושריתינהו אפילו למיעבד בהו קתא דסכיני · והא דאמר פ' ראוהו ב"ד (ר"ה דף כח·) שופר של עולה לא יתקע פירש רבינו יח] דאיירי שהפרישו לדמי עולה וכן של שלמים שהפרישו לדמי שלמים ודמי שלמים אין בהם מעילה כדאמרינן בפסחים פר' שני (דף כו:) הכא בבעלי שלמים עסקינן* מיהו לא ידענא מאי טעמא אפקי' ממשמעותיה לאוקומה בדמים דהא איכא לאוקומה בפירש מחיים או פירש קודם זריקה כל זמן שלא נזרק הדם אבל פירש לאחר זריקה לא מצי לאוקומה דבשלמים אין חילוק *ואם זריקה מתרת בפירש מחיים ה"ה יט] במחוסר נמי כמו שמתרת הבשר דמ"מ ואם כן לתקוע נמי שרי · נ"ל: **מה** אשם עצמותיו מותרין · פי' בקונטרס שהרי אף בשרו מותר כל שכן עצמותיו והוא עצמו הקשה על פירוש זה לקמן פרק דם חטאת (דף צח·) כ] דאמר מהיקישא דזאת התורה מה אשם עצמותיו מותרין אף כל עצמותיו מותרין (ולא) ונפיק מלו יהיה (*דעולה) ופירש דמק"ו דבשר לא נפקי עצמות דאיכא למימר דלא התיר הכתוב אלא בשר הראוי לאכילה וא"כ על כרחין הא דפשיטא ליה באשם היינו משום דכתיב לו יהיה והא דנקט אשם טפי מחטאת אע"ג דבההוא קרא נמי כתיב חטאת דכתיב כחטאת כאשם תורה אחת להם לכהן אשר יכפר בו לו יהיה משום דעיקרא דקרא באשם נקטיה ועוד דלו יהיה כתיב לשון יחיד ואיכא לאוקומה באשם דסלק מיניה ומהיקשא דלקמן לא נפקא עולה כיון דאיכא לאוקומה בדברים הנאכלים דומיא דאשם · ומיהו יש להסתפק למה לי ג"ש בעולה הא בגופיה נמי כתיב לו יהיה ומצי לדרוש למישרי עצמות ושמא הוה מוקמינא ליה לדרשא אחריתי: **ופליגא** דר' אלעזר דא"ר אלעזר פירשו לפני זריקה מועלין בהן לעולם · כך גרסת הקונט' ויש ספרים שגורסין מועלין בהם עד זריקה ולהאי גרסא סיפא דמילתא הוא דפליגא דקאמר דלאחר זריקה לא נהנין ולא מועלין וא"ת לרבנן דלית להו דאפי' פירשו יעלו אמאי אין מועלין וי"ל דהיינו פירשו קודם זריקה כא] אבל לאחר זריקה התירתם זריקה אם פירשו אי נמי לפי' ר' יצחק דלעיל אפי' פירשו לאחר זריקה וכגון שפירשו למטה דהא מילתיה דרבנן מיתוקמא בעודם על המזבח כב] וא"ת דבמסכת תרומות (פי"א מ"ה) אמרי' גרעיני תרומה בזמן שמכניסן אסורין השליכן מותרין וכן עצמות קדשים בזמן שמכניסן אסורין השליכן מותרין כג] ופירש רבינו דהתם מיירי בעצמות קדשים הנאכלין דומיא דתרומה ויש עליהם עדיין בשר וקאמר דאם מכניסן ומצניען א"כ הוא מחשבן והאתי שם קדשים עליהן ואסורין אבל משליכן בטל שם אוכל מינייהו וכן גרעיני תרומה מיירי שיש עליהם אוכל ומיפרשא בענין זה: **וכולן** שפקעו מע"ג המזבח כו' · פירש בקונטרס דקאי בין אגידים ועצמות ולפירושו הא דקתני במתני' לא יחזיר ובגמ' אמרינן דמשלה בהם האור יעלו איכא למימר דפקעו דמתני' היינו לאחר שנתעכלו קצת דומיא דאברים שפקעו דמתני' דמוקמינן בגמרא בשירי אבל משלה בהם האור היינו משלה בהם האור פורתא ולא נעשה מצותן ולכך יחזירו ומיהו לפי מה שפירש בקונטרס לא יחזיר אין צריך להחזיר לא קשה מידי דאיכא למימר דיעלו דקאמר היינו אם ירצה אבל אין חובה להעלותם ועוד י"ל דפקעו היינו דפקעו מאליהן וירדו יעלו יש במשמע שהורידן ויש לחלק בין מאליהן לע"י אחרים כעין ההיא דטרף בקלפי (יומא מו:) המוריד גחלת מע"ג המזבח וכבה חייב משום דלא אנתקיה ממצותה אלמא יכול להעלותה וכי פקעה תנן במתניתין דלא יחזיר ואין מועלין בה ואם היינו מפרשים דכולן לא קאי אפסולין לא היינו מתרצים בזה כלום דמכל מקום הוה קשה למאן דמתני לה אסיפא:

עין משפט נר מצוה

כו א מיי' פ"ו מהלכות מעה"ק הלכה ג:
כז ב ג מיי' פ"ב מהל' מעילה הלכה יב:
כח ד ה מיי' פ"ו מהל' מעה"ק הלכה ג.
כט ו מיי' פ"ב מהלכות מעילה הלכה יב:
ל ז ח מיי' פ"ג מהל' פסה"מ הלכה יח:
לא ט מיי' פ"ו מהל' מעה"ק הלכה ג ג

רש"ק גורס אליבא דתוס' פירשו אפי' כו' והוא פיסקא

עיין רש"ק

[וע"ע תוספות בסוכה כו. ד"ה סהולב]

נ"א דאם זריקה מתרת בפירש מחיים ה"ה במחובר נמי כו' צ"ק

שיטה מקובצת

א] רבי היא' פ"ה דקאי נמי אמתני' והאי דקאמר פירשו לא יעלו לאו דוקא דה"נ ר"ל דאם עלו אחר שפירש דירדו ולא נהירא דאדרבה היה לו להשמיענו דירדו דהוי חידוש יותר ומסילא הוי ידעינן דלא יעלו ועוד דבמסכת חולין מייתי לה ולא קאמר הא מני רבי היא אלא (מן) [על] הברייתא לכך נראה דלא קאי אלא על הברייתא אבל מתני' אתיא כרבנן ולא יעלו דוקא אבל אם עלו אפילו אחר שפירשו לא ירדו וא"ת מנא להו לרבנן הני דמתני' דאם פירשו לא יעלו י"ל דנפקא להו מהבשר והדם וא"ת ולמה לי למימר (הני) הבי עיכולי עולה כו' לשמעינן בהני דמתני' דלא יעלו וי"ל דחידוש הוא יותר לומר דאיצ מעלה עיכולי גידים ועצמות אע"פ

מסורת הש"ס

נ"ל פירשו ירדו רש"ק ופי' נ"ק דגרס פירשו אפילו הן בראש המזבח ירדו אר"ז נ"ש כו' מעלה אפילו פירשו קרובי כו' פירשו לא יעלו אמר רבה

לקמן קג:

תוספ' דמעילה פ"א ע"ש

נ"א עד שעת זריקה

נ"א אימא ושל עולה פרשו לפני זריקה מועלין בהן עד שעת זריקה לאחר כו' נ"ק

מעילה ט:

יומא כ.

נ"ל דבאשם וע"ש בדף צח ע"א ברש"י ד"ה אף כל בסוף העמוד ובתוס' ד"ה מה אשם כו'

הגהות הב"ח

(א) תוס' ד"ה לא שנו וכו' ועוד דבתר הכי שקיל נ"ב דברי התוס' אלו קשים הבנה מ"ש דבתר הכי שקיל כו' ומשמע מדבריהם [שאין ר"ל מ"ש] בגמ' ואפי' פירשו אמתניתין דהיינו דואפילו פירשו בלשון קושיא כדפרש"י אלא [היא כמו פיסקא] ואפילו פירשו דקאמרי בברייתא קאי דסברי רבנן אפילו פירשו [יעלו ועל זה] אמר רבה נ"ש דקדישו אלא שפירשו כו' ודלא כפרש"י וכן עיקר דרש"י דחק לפרש פירשו בלשון בתמיה ואינו מוכרח כלל וכן מבואר בילקוט וכן בכסף משנה משמע דלא גריס הכי קאמר אלא ה"ג אמר רבה לא שנו כו' וק"ל:

שכן בראשו של מזבח וא"ת מנלן הא אפיקתיה הבשר והדם לצפר שבראשי הכבשים כו' לומר דפירשו לא יעלו י"ל דתרתי ש"מ דיש לנו להשוות מעוכלין בראשו של מזבח כמו צפר שבראשי הכבשים) למטה וכולהו למטה כלומר קודם שעלו ומורי פי' דקאי נמי למתני' וא"ת אמאי לא קאמר ירדו וי"ל דאגב דקאמר מחוברין כו' קאמר נמי פירשו לא יעלו אבל ה"ה דאם עלו ירדו · מהר"פ: ב] ירדו אמר מר פירשו ירדו אמר ר"ז כו': ג] עיין בהשמטות בסוף המסכת: ד] ושריתינהו' עיין ברש"י במנחות (דף פג ע"א): ה] עולה עצמותיו מותרין וכו': לאחר זריקה כו' לחנם נקט אין מועלין בהן דהדבר פשוט הוא שהרי הבשר מותר אף באכילה אלא אגב דנקט מועלין נקט לאחר זריקה אין מועלין: ו] זריקה מועלין בהן עד שעת זריקה לאחר ותיבת אין נמחק: ז] דר"א' עיין בתוס' בבורות (דף כו): ח] מקדש את הראוי לו כשם: ט] עיין בהשמטות בסוף המסכת: י] ... אמר מר במילתיה דת"ק לרבות עצמות וגידין ואפילו פירשו אמר רבה לא שנו דאמרי רבנן פירשו יעלו אלא כו' ול"ג הכי קאמר: יא] הוו קבעתן זריקה: יב] לכהן יהיה ותיבת לו נמחק ותיבות למה ... מישתרו: יד] בין פסולין ותיבת הנך ל"ש ונמחק: טו] מה"ד אי דאית בהו ממש שבשרן ניכר הס"ד ומה"ד אפילו לאחר הצות נמי דבשר היכי הוי עיכול הס"ד ומה"ד אי דלית: טז] כולן' ס"א אפילו ... לא יחזיר וה"ה דאין מועלין בהן אם פקע למטה דהשתא לא חזי לא לתרומת [הדשן] דלאי דשן הוא ולא (להוצאה) [להקטרה]: יז] נהירא דא"כ מאי קאמר לא שנו כו' לעולם הוא כלפי מטה ועדיין ... יח] דאיירי עיין בתוס' בכורות דף כו): יט] במחובר נמי: כ] הפאת דנמר מהיקשא אות א' נמחק: כא] אבל אם פירשו לאחר זריקה התירתה זריקה לא יעלו אם פירשו: כב] המזבח תימה דבמסכת ... כג] מותרין ובמאי עסקינן אי לפני זריקה כולהו אסירי ואפילו מעילה איכא בקדשי קדשים ואי לאחר זריקה לרבה כולהו שרי ולר"א של עולה כולם אסור ושל אשם והבאת מותרין ופי' רבינו פר"ת

א) נראה דצ"ל כמו צמר שבראשי הכבשים וכו' למטה · כלומר קודם שעלו וכו' ·

בשרירי מנא הני מילי *אמר רב כתוב אחד אומר °כל הלילה והקטיר וכתוב אחד אומר °כל הלילה והרים א] חלקיהו חציו להקטרה וחציו להרמה מתיב רב כהנא **בכל יום ב] תורם את המזבח מקרות הגבר או סמוך לו מלפניו ג] [או] מאחריו ביום הכיפורים בחצות ברגלים באשמורת הראשונה ואי סלקא דעתך מחצות דאורייתא היכי מקדמינן (והיכי מאחרינן אלא) אמר רבי יוחנן ממשמע שנאמר כל הלילה איני יודע שעד הבקר מה תלמוד לומר עד בקר תן בקר לבקרו של לילה הלכך כל יומא מקרות הגבר סגי ביום הכיפורים משום חולשא דכהן גדול מחצות ברגלים דנפישי קרבנות דקדמי אתו ישראל מאשמורת הראשונה כדקתני סיפא לא היתה ד] קריית הגבר מגעת עד שהיתה עזרה מלאה מישראל איתמר פירשו קודם חצות והחזירן אחר חצות רבה אמר חצות

תורה אור: ויקרא ו · שם

בשרירי · קשין שנתקשו מחמת האש ה] שׁשלטה בטלן ושרפו אלא שלא נעשו פחם אלא כעלים יבשים הם מתוכם: מנהני מילי · דבחלות תליא מילתא: כתוב אחד אומר כל הלילה והקטיר · על מוקדה על המזבח כל הלילה עד הבקר דהייט הקטרה: וכתוב אחד אומר כל הלילה · ו] וסמיך ליה והרים את הדשן וע"כ אכל הלילה קאי דהא לא כתיב ולבש הכהן בבקר מדו בד אלא כל הלילה עד הבקר ולבש והרים כך שמעתי בסדר יומא: חליו להקטרה · דלא הוי עיכול אי לאו דשן ממש הוא: וחליו להרמה ז] · אפי' קשין שבהן ראויין להרמה וקרויין דשן ומיהו בשר ממש ליכא למימר דמיקרי דשן: מתיב רב כהנא · אדרב דאמר חליו להרמה דמשמע דקודם חלות לאו שעת הרמה היא אפילו מן הנעשין דשן: היו תורמין · תרומת הדשן מלא ח] מחתה ונותנה במזרחו של כבש: וברגלים מאשמורת הראשונה · ומשום דנפישי קרבנות ונפיש דשן וצריך ט] להעלותן לתפוח שבאמצע המזבח ולסדר את המערכה בלילה שיוכלו לשחוט ולהעלות התמיד בעלות השחר: ה"ג ואי חלות דאורייתא היכי מקדמינן ל"ג *והיכי מאחרינן: א"ר יוחנן גרס ולא גרסינן אלא: ממשמע שנאמר כו' · כלומר קראי כדרב מיתרלי ולאשמועינן דחלות עושה עיכול בשרירי דקודם חלות הן בכלל הקטר ומחלות ואילך ראויין להרמה כדשן מעליא והרמה במעוכלין לגמרי קודם חלות נפקא לן מהאי קרא: ממשמע שנאמר כל הלילה כו' · אם ללמד בא כמשמע כל המקרא שיהא מעלה אברים ומקטירן עד הבקר מכל הלילה נפקא: מת"ל עד בקר · לא נאמר אלא לענין הרמה לומר שתורמין כל הלילה והכי קאמר עד הבקר והרים לפני הבקר והרים ולא נתן שיעור לדבר: תן בקר לבקרו של לילה · בוקרו של לילה עלות השחר בקר אחר תן לו הייט השכמה וכיון דאין זמן לדבר אלא של השכמה הכל לפי צורך השעה יש בידך לעשות הלכך כל יומא בקרות הגבר או סמוך לו לפניו או לאחריו סגי: ביום הכיפורים · שכל העבודה מוטלת על כהן גדול ואיכא חולשא וצריך להקדים יותר: וברגלים מאשמורת הראשונה · כדקתני סיפא דההיא ולא היתה קרות הגבר מגעת ברגלים עד שהיתה עזרה מליאה י] ישראל:

חלות

וחציו להרמה · פירש בקונטרס ושרירי נמי ראויין להרמה מיהו נראה דלאו ראויין להרמה דלאו דשן נינהו אלא חליו להרמה דקאמר לא הרמה ממש אלא כעין הרמה שאין ראויין להקטרה וכן משמע פ' שני דמעילה (דף ט:) דדייקא התם וכן גחלת שפקעה מעל גבי המזבח לא יחזיר הא על גבי המזבח יחזיר ומקשי מינה לרב ומשני שאני גחלת דאית ביה ממשא הלכך יחזיר דלא נעשית מלותו משמע דאין ראוי לתרום מהם דאי ראוי לתרום מהם כשתרמו אמאי יחזיר הרי נעשית מלוותן ומיהו היא גופה לא ידענא מנא ליה דאיירי לאחר תרומת הדשן דמהאי טעמא מקשה לרב *יא] דאמר לאחר תרומת הדשן איירי וכי היכי דמתרלינן ליה לאחר תרומת הדשן לר' יוחנן יתרלה קודם תרומת הדשן לרב דמודה רב דמועלין ונראה בעיני דדומיא דפסולין שפקעו דאיירי בכל ענין *דקתני וכן גחלת שפקעה ומינה נמי דייקא דבגחלת אין חילוק בין קודם חלות לאחר חלות דבכל ענין יב] עיכול דדומיא דפסולין *שברישא קתני דאפילו קודם חלות לא יחזיר ועוד דבסיפא גבי אברים הוא דמפליג אבל בגחלת לא מפליג דעיכול חשיבא ולא שייך לא לשון הקטרה ולא לשון מוקדה דהא יג] *(בכך מיתוקמא) ומ"מ יחזיר דלאו ראויה להרמה היא דלאו דשן היא ולא נעשית מלוותה יד] *על גבי המזבח יחזיר דאכתי לא נגמרה מלוותה וכי פקע לא יחזיר דעל מוקדה על המזבח משמע דדבר שצריך יקידה יהא על המזבח אפילו פקע אבל דבר שאין צריך יקידה לא וא"ת כשמאספין את האפר להעלותו לתפוח אין יכולים להזהר שלא יהו הרבה גחלים על האפר והכא משמע שאסור להוציא הגחלת מן המערכה כדדייק במעילה (ג"ז שם) דיחזיר וכל שכן שאסור להוציא ובמסכת תמיד (דף לג.) נמי משמע שהיה נוטל מן המאוכלות הפנימיות אלמא גחלים היה נוטל וצריך לומר דמאי מן המאוכלות היה נוטל הנהו דלית בהו ממשא וחשיבי אפר אבל גחלת דהכא דמינה דייק במעילה דיחזיר מיירי בגחלת חיה דאית ביה ממשא והא דקאמר במעילה ה"ה דאפילו אפר לאו דליהוי כגחלת ממש אפי' לענין חזרה דגחלת מחזירין לעולם אפילו לאחר תרומת הדשן דאין מעלין אותה לתפוח אבל אפר מעלין לתפוח אלא לענין מעילה הוא דקאמר דהויא כגחלת ואע"פ שלכאורה יש חילוק בין גחלת חיה לשאינה חיה בכלל דשן היא כדתנן נטל מן המאוכלות הפנימיות ומ"מ יש ליישב כפירוש הקונטרס דחליו להרמה הייטו אפילו בשרירי ולענין זה שהרמת הדשן מתירן לאוכפם לתפוח ולא לענין זה שיעשה מהם *תרומה דהא דשן טו] [כתיב והייטו] דאמר רחמנא והרים את הדשן מחלות כדי להתיר אפי' שרירי דמחלות ואילך חשיבי עיכול להקטרה ואם ירצה יאספם לתפוח כדי להוציאם מחוץ למחנה אבל אם רוצה להניחם במקום המערכה כדי למרק מלותם שיהו הם *ראויין עלמם לתרומת הדשן עדיין מלוותם עליהם הלכך יחזיר דמסתבר למימר דעדיין חסר מהם מירוק מלוה כיון שעדיין אין ראויין לתרומת הדשן והשתא ניחא לישנא דחליו להרמה וניחא נמי שבשעה שמאספין את האפר לא היו צריכין להזהר מן הגחלים ואפי' היו לוחשות וקלא היה נראה כן במסכת תמיד פרק ראוהו (דף כח:) דתנן נטלו את המגריפות ואת הצינורות ועלו לראש המזבח האברים והפדרים שלא נתאכלו מבערב סולקין לצדדי המזבח ובתר הכי קתני החלו מסלק באפר על גבי התפוח *וזהו כפי' טז] רש"י שלא היו מסלקין *אותם שלא נתעכלו אבל גחלים עיכול חשיבי ואפילו חיים כדפי' לעיל דאפילו קודם חלות חשיבי עיכול *אם כן לאו בכלל שלא נתעכלו נינהו הלכך נ"ל פירוש הקונטרס עיקר: **אלא** אמר ר' יוחנן · בקונטרס מחק אלא בפירושים הראשונים ופי' דרבי יוחנן מתרץ קראי יז] כרב חליו להקטרה וחליו להרמה ומיהו הייט דוקא בשרירי והאי יח] דקאמר *(דקמדמי) קודם לחלות הייט במעוכלין יט] ומקראי אחרינא נפקא ליה דכתיב עד בקר תן בקר לבוקרו של לילה ומוקמינן ליה בהרמה ומסר המקום הדבר לחכמים להיות *מדמין כל מה שירצו לפי הצורך להם ומיהו קשה לפירוש זה דקרא דעד בקר דכתיב בהקטרה [היכי] מוקמינן ליה בהרמה ועוד דאלא גרסינן בכל הספרים ונראה כגיר' פירושים אחרונים דגרסי אלא ופליג רבי יוחנן אדרב דאמר חליו להרמה דאפילו בדשן המעוכל יפה לא מקדמינן וקאמר רבי יוחנן דכל הלילה קאי אהקטרה וקאי אהרמה דכל הלילה כשר להקטיר כשאין מעוכלין וכל הלילה כשר להרמה אם יש דשן מעוכל וגבי הקטרה כתיב בקר מיותר ליתן בקר לבוקרו של לילה והייט בשרירי דחלות עושה עיכול והכי מידרש קרא תן השכמה אחת לבוקרו של לילה ובוקרו של לילה הוא עמוד השחר ונתן לו הכתוב בקר אחר לומר שאין צריך להקטיר מן כ] השחר ואילך וכיון שלא נתן זמן באותו בקר על כרחך הוא חלות לילה שמעינן דבשרירי תלוי בחלות ובדשן מעוכל דלית ביה משהא כל הלילה והרים אבל אית כא] בהון משהא כל הלילה והקטיר וכך פי' בקונטרס בפ"ק דיומא (דף כ:) ול"ע במגילה (דף כ:) דקאמר כל הלילה כשר להקטרה אמאי לא קאמר נמי להרמה*: **משום** חולשא דכהן גדול מחלות · כאן משמע שעבודת לילה כמו תרומת הדשן וסידור המערכה היו מוטלות עליו והשתא אתי שפיר משום חולשא דכהן גדול שיוכל לנוח אחר תרומת הדשן ולהפסיק כדי לעשות בנחת שחיטת התמיד ועבודת היום אבל אי עבודת לילה בשאר כהנים מאי חולשא איכא וריב"א פירש ביומא (דף כ:) דלא גרס הכא כהן גדול דתרומת הדשן לא הויא בכהן גדול מדלא חשיב טבילת תרומת הדשן בהדי ה' טבילות וי' קידושין שהיה עושה ביום הכפורים ועוד דפיים דתרומת הדשן חשיב בסדר יום הכפורים ואילו היה בכהן גדול למה ליה להזכיר בסדר יום הכפורים *וכן יסד הפייט הוקמו מחלות כב] אפרה לבערה בפיים דשן הבערה ומיהו רביט היה מפרש דאין צריך למוחקו דה"פ משום חולשא דכהן גדול מקדימין תרומת הדשן וסידור המערכה ושריפת אברים שלא נתעכלו מבערב בשאר כהנים כדי שעל ידי כן יהא מזומן כה"ג להתחיל מהבקר כשיעלה עמוד השחר עבודת היום קודם שיהא רעב וחלש*:

אמרי

לב א מיי' פ"ב מהל' תמידין ומוספין הלכה יא:

דאיירי לאחר כו' הדשן וכי כו' נ"ק

דקתני דקתני נ"ק

שבפסולין קתני נ"ק

בכך מיתוקמא וקיימא נ"ק

הלכך ע"ג נ"ק

תרומת הדשן נ"ק

עלמם ראוים נ"ק

עיין מהרש"א במסכת יומא שהגיה כדבריהם שם ועיין רש"ק

יומא כ. · שם

והתוס' ביומא גרס כו' ומפרשים דפריך אכל יום דהא קי"ל דזריזין מקדימין למצות

אלא אברים שלא נתעכלו כו' נ"ק

נ"ל ולא בכלל נ"ק

דקדמינן

נ"ל משכימים

[וביומא כ: סד"ה אלא וכו' כתבו ישוב על זה]

ועיין בזה פלפול ארוך בס"ב דיומא בספר המאור ובמלחמת ה' ע"ש

[וע"ע תוס' יומא כ: ד"ה משום]

שיטה מקובצת

א] והרים הא כיצד חלקהו: ב] היו תורמין את: ג] מלפניו ומאחריו ביום הכפורים מחצות ברגלים מאשמורה הראשונה: ד] היתה קריאת הגבר אות י' נמחק: ה] האש שליחכה האש כל לחותן ושלשה בכולן אלא שלא נעשו פחם: ו] הלילה והרים דסמיך ליה והרים את הדשן: ז] להרמה דאפי' קשין: ח] מלא המחתה: ט] וצריך להעלותו: י] מליאה מישראל הס"ד: יא] לרב דלמא קודם תרומת הדשן איירי: יב] ענין חשיבא עיכול: יג] דהא כבר מתוקדא וקימא: יד] מצוותה הלכך על: טו] דשן כתיב והיינו דקאמר רחמנא והרים וכו' דמחצות ולהלן חשיבי עיכול: טז] כפי' [רש"י] שלא היו מסלקין אלא אותם: יז] קראי כדרב: יח] והאי דקמקדמי לחצות ותיבת דקאמר נמחק ותיבת קודם ל ש: יט] במעוכלין ומקרא אחרינא אות י' נמחק: כ] מן ההשכמה ואילך: כא] אות בהו משמא: כב] מחצות דשן אפרה לנערה תיבת לבערה נמחק: עיכול

—This holds good only [86*b*] of hardened [limbs].[6]

Whence do we know it?[7]—Said Raba: One text states, [*This is the law of the burnt-offering: it is that which goeth up on its firewood upon the altar*] *all night . . . and he shall burn thereon* etc.[8] Whereas another text states, *all night . . . and he shall take up the ashes.*[9] How are these texts reconciled?[10] Divide it [the night]: half is for burning, and half for taking up [the ashes].[11] R. Kahana raised an objection: Every a day he [the priest] takes up [the ashes][1] at cockcrow, or slightly before or slightly after. On the Day of Atonement, [he does this] at midnight; on festivals, at the first watch.[2] If then you maintain that [the altar must be cleared] from midnight [onwards], how may we advance it?—Said R. Joḥanan: From the implication of *'all night'*, do I not know that it is until the morning? Why then is *'unto the morning'* stated? Add another morning to the morning of the night.[3] Therefore every day it is sufficient from cockcrow. On the Day of Atoment [it is done] at midnight, on account of the fatigue[4] of the High Priest.[5] On festivals when there were many sacrifices and so the Israelites came very early, [it was done] at the first watch, as the sequel teaches: and before cockcrow the Temple court was full of Israelites.

It was stated: If they sprang off[6] before midnight and he replaced

(6) The fire had hardened them and completely dried up all their natural moisture, yet had not turned them into charred coals. (7) That the matter depends on midnight. (8) Lev. VI, 2–5. The combination of these texts implies that *'all night'* is meant in respect of burning. (9) Ibid. 3. He assumes that *'and he shall take up the ashes'* also means during the night, (i.e., *'all night'*), since the whole verse reads: *And the priest shall put on his linen garment . . . and he shall take up the ashes:* as it does not say that he must don his linen garment *in the morning*, it is assumed that he did it at night and straightway took up the ashes. Thus this contradicts the implication of the first verse. (10) Emended text (Sh.M.). (11) The first half is for burning, and during this time the flesh is not considered completely consumed unless it has actually been turned into ashes. The second half is for clearing, in the sense that even before the flesh has actually become ashes but has merely reached the stage of hardness it is regarded as ashes. If, however, it still retains the softness of flesh, it is obviously not ashes, and must not be removed.

a (1) A shovelful of ashes which were placed at the east side of the ascent. (2) Yoma 20*a*. The night (roughly from 6 P.M. to 6 A.M.) was divided into three or four watches (the matter is debated in Ber. 3*a*). The end of the first watch would be about 9 or 10 P.M., two or three hours before midnight. (3) The morning of the night is dawn, while the additional morning is any earlier hour when the priests might rise to commence the service, according to the exigencies of the day. Since this is not fixed, it can be put forward or deferred as may be necessary. (4) Lit., 'weakness'. (5) To enable him to rest after it until the morning burnt-offering. This assumes that the High Priest removed the ashes himself. Tosaf. however suggests that it may mean that the ashes were removed (by another priest) earlier to enable the wood pile to be arranged and likewise the other rites to be performed as early as possible, so that the High Priest could sacrifice the daily burnt-offering at dawn, before he was hungry and fatigued. (6) Lit., 'separated'.

them after midnight: Rabbah said: [87a] The second midnight consumes them.[7] R. Ḥisda said: The dawn consumes them. The scholars of the Academy said: What is R. Ḥisda's reason? If midnight, which does not establish *linah*,[8] establishes *'ikul*;[9] then dawn, which establishes *linah*, surely establishes *'ikul*. If they sprang off before midnight and he replaced them after dawn,—Rabbah said: The second midnight consumes them; R. Ḥisda
a said: They never reach *'ikul*.[1] To this R. Joseph demurred: And who is to tell us that midnight establishes *'ikul* [only when they are] on the top of the altar; perhaps it establishes *'ikul* wherever they are? They sent from thence:[2] The law agrees with R. Joseph.[3] It was stated likewise: R. Ḥiyya b. Abba said: If they sprang off before midnight and were replaced after midnight, you may not use them, nor do you commit trespass on their account.[4] Bar Ḳappara taught likewise: If they sprang off before midnight and were replaced after midnight, they are not subject to trespass. R. Papa asked Abaye: Now, since they sent from there [that] the law agrees with R. Joseph, and R. Ḥiyya b. Abba said [the same], and Bar Ḳappara taught likewise, wherein do Rabbah and R. Ḥisda disagree?—In the case of fat [limbs], he answered him.[5]

Raba asked Rabbah: Is *linah* effective [when the limbs are] on the top of the altar, or is it not effective on top of the altar?—What are the circumstances: if we say that they [the limbs] did not descend,[6] surely since you say that even if they were kept overnight in the Temple court they do not descend,[7] can there be a question [when they are kept on] the top of the altar?[8] Rather [the question is] where they descended. Do we liken it to the Table, for we learnt: Even if they[9] are on the Table many days, it does not matter? Or
b perhaps we liken it to the pavement of the Temple court?[1]—Said he to him: *Linah* is not [effective when the flesh is] on the top of the altar. Did he accept [this ruling] from him or did he not accept it from him?—Come and hear. For it was stated: Limbs which spent the night in the Temple court, [the priest] can go on burning them all night;[2] if they were kept overnight on the top of the altar, he can always go on burning them.[3] If they descended: Rabbah said: They re-ascend; Raba said: They do not re-ascend.[4] This proves that he did not accept [the ruling] from him. This proves it.

JUST AS THE ALTAR SANCTIFIES etc. Our Rabbis taught: *Whatsoever touches the altar [shall be holy]*:[5] I know it only of the altar; how do I know [it of] the ascent? Because it says, *the* [eth] *altar*.[6] How do we know [it of] service vessels? Because it says: *Whatsoever toucheth them shall be holy*.[7]

Resh Laḳish asked R. Joḥanan: Do the service vessels sanctify the disqualified?—We have learnt it, he replied: JUST AS THE ALTAR AND THE ASCENT SANCTIFY WHATEVER IS ELIGIBLE FOR THEM, SO DO VESSELS SANCTIFY![8] Said he, My question is whether they can be offered in the first place. But that too we have

(7) They will not be assumed to reach the stage of hardness (v. *supra* 86b) until the following midnight,—unless, of course, they are reduced to ashes before then. (8) The status of flesh that is kept overnight. Midnight does not confer that status, and flesh that falls off after midnight is replaced on the altar. (9) Lit. 'burning,' 'consumption'. If the flesh is hard by midnight (v. *supra* 86b top) it is regarded as consumed, and if it springs off after that it is not replaced.

a (1) Whenever they spring off, until they are actually ashes, they must be replaced, and involve trespass. (2) *Sc.* from Palestine.—The reference is to R. Eleazar (v. Sanh. 17b). (3) His argument is correct.—Actually they did not give a ruling (Tosaf). (4) They need not have been replaced, as they no longer belong to the altar. Hence they do not involve trespass; nevertheless, benefit from them is interdicted by Rabbinical law. (5) Even when they harden they are not regarded as consumed (*'ikul*), because their fat keeps them from becoming ashes. Only then do Rabbah and R. Ḥisda disagree as to their status. But in the case of ordinary flesh they agree that midnight establishes *'ikul*. (6) But remained on the altar, away from the fresh wood pile for the new sacrifices. (7) If placed on the altar after the night passed. (8) Surely they do not descend. (9) The loaves of the Shewbread.

b (1) Hence it becomes unfit. (2) But not after, for *linah* disqualifies them. (3) They are never disqualified as long as they are there. (4) Because *linah* disqualifies them, and so like all disqualified limbs they do not re-ascend once they descended. (5) Ex. XXIX, 37. (6) The reference is probably either to XXIX, 44: *And I will sanctify the tent of meeting, and the altar;* or to XXX, 26–28: *And thou shalt anoint therewith . . . the altar of burnt-offering*. In either case the preceding *eth* (which denotes the acc.) is regarded as an extension, thus including the ascent. (7) Ibid. XXX, 29. '*Them*' refers (among other things) to service vessels, which are spoken of in the preceding verses. (8) The reference being to disqualified sacrificial parts. V. Mishnah notes.

תורה אור

חצות שני עוכלתן רב חסדא אמר עמוד השחר עוכלתן אמרי בי רב מאי טעמא דרב חסדא ומה חצות שאין עושה לינה עושה עיכול עמוד השחר שעושה לינה אינו דין שעושה עיכול פירשו קודם חצות והחזירן לאחר עמוד השחר רבה אמר חצות שני עוכלתן רב חסדא אמר אין בהן עיכול לעולם מתקיף לה רב יוסף ומאן לימא לן דחצות בראש המזבח משויא להו עיכול דילמא כל היכא דמשכחא להו משויא להו עיכול א] שלחו מתם הלכתא כרב יוסף איתמר נמי א"ר חייא בר אבא *פירשו קודם חצות והחזירן אחר חצות לא נהנין ולא מועלין וכן תנא בר קפרא פירשו קודם חצות והחזירן ב] לאחר חצות יוצאין מידי מעילה א"ל רב פפא לאביי וכי מאחר דשלחו מתם הילכתא כרב יוסף וא"ר חייא בר אבא וכן תני בר קפרא רבה ורב חסדא במאי פליגי אמר ליה בשמנים בעא מיניה רבא מרבה °לינה מועלת בראשו של מזבח או אינה מועלת בראשו של מזבח היכי דמי אילימא דלא ירדו השתא לנו בעזרה אמרת דלא ירדו בראשו של מזבח מיבעיא ואלא דירדו לשלחן מדמינן לה דתנן* ג׳אפילו הן על השלחן ימים רבים אין בכך כלום או דילמא לקרקע מדמינן א"ל אין לינה ג] בראשו של מזבח קיבלה מיניה או לא ת"ש דאיתמר איברים שלנו בעזרה מקטר והולך כל הלילה ילן בראשו של מזבח מקטר והולך לעולם ירדו רבה אמר יעלו רבא אמר ד׳לא יעלו ש"מ לא קיבלה מיניה ש"מ: כשם שהמזבח מקדש כו': תנו רבנן °ד] הנוגע במזבח אין לי אלא מזבח כבש מנין ת"ל ה] את המזבח כלי שרת מניין ת"ל °כל הנוגע בהם יקדש *בעא מיניה ר"ל מר"י *כלי שרת מהו שיקדשו את הפסולין א"ל תניתוה כשם שהמזבח והכבש מקדשין את הראוי להן כך כלים מקדשין ו] א"ל לכתחלה ליקרב קמיבעי לי °הא נמי תנינא

שקבלו

שמות כט

שם ל

חצות שני עוכלתן. ו] שיירי דידהו חצות שני של ליל המחרת: שאינו עושה לינה. ז] לאותו שעל הארץ שהרי כל הלילה כשר להעלותן מן הארץ ח] ולמזבח דכתיב לא ילין חלב חגי עד בקר הא כל הלילה ילין: עושה עיכול. לשירי דמערכה: אין בהן עיכול לעולם. וכל ט] שפוקעין יחזיר ומועלין בהן עד שיעשו דשן: כל היכא דמשכחת להו כו'. הלכך פרשו קודם חצות נמי הרי הן עיכול בחצות ואפילו החזירן לאחר חצות*: אין מועלין בהן] ולא צריך *להחזירן ויצאו מידי מעילה גרסי' ולא נהנין מדרבנן: וא"ר חייא בר אבא. נמי כרב יוסף: וכן תני בר קפרא. כרב יוסף: רבה ורב חסדא במאי פליגי. לומר דלא הוי עיכול בחצות: בשמנים. אפילו הוקשו לא הויא עיכול דשומנן מעכבן מליעשות דשן: אילימא דלא ירדו. אותן שמלאן בשחר בראש המזבח שלא במערכה: אלא דירדו. מן המזבח לאחר עמוד השחר מיבעי לך מי הוי כשאר לנים ונפסלים בעמוד השחר ותנן בפסולים כך אם ירדו לא יעלו: או דילמא אין לינה מועלת. ולא נפסלו ויחזור ויעלם: לשלחן מדמינן לה. למזבח שאין לחם הפנים נפסל עליו אם לן בו לאחר זמנו: דתנן אפי' היה על השלחן ימים כו'. במנחות תנן לה סידר את הלחם ואת הבזיכין באחד בשבת והקטיר את הבזיכין יא][בשבת] פסולה לפי שמחוסרים יב] בשבת זמן שצריכין לעמוד עליו שבעת ימים כילד יעשה זה שסידרם באחד בשבת יניחנה לשבת הבאה שאפי' היא כו': או דילמא לקרקע עזרה מדמינן לה. דהא רצפת בנין היא כמותה ולא כלי שרת כשלחן: מקטיר והולך לעולם. דאפילו אמרינן לינה מועלת בראש המזבח מסקינן להו במערכה שהרי פסולין שעלו לא ירדו: רבא אמר לא יעלו. דלינה מועלת והוו להו פסולין וכיון דירדו לא יעלו: את המזבח. ומשחת את המזבח לרבות את הכבש: ה"ג כלי שרת מניין יג] כל הנוגע בהן יקדש: מהו שיקדשו פסולין. הוא יד] סבור לענין פדיון קמיבעיא ליה כגון מנחה טמאה שקדשה בכלי שרת מי קדשה קדושת הגוף ולא נפקא טו] להו לחולין דקדשה כלי אע"פ שהיא טמאה או לא קדשה ותנן* המנחות והנסכים שנטמאו יש [להם] פדיון ואם משקדש בכלי נטמאו אין להם פדיון: א"ל תניתוה. דמקדשין ואין להם פדיון: א"ל לכתחילה ליקרב קמיבעיא לי. ולא לענין פדיון: ושקבלו פסולין וזרקו את דמו. אם עלה הבשר לא ירד: מאי לאו

שקבלו

אמרי בי רב מ"ט דרב חסדא. אע"ג דאמרי בי רב *רב הונא ורב חסדא תלמידו *שמא רב הונא נמי אמרה ופי' טעמו והש"ס קבעיא בלשון זה מ"ט דרב חסדא אי נמי מלינו שרב הונא רגיל לשבח דבריו כדאמר בגיטין (דף ז.) חסדא שמך וחסדאין מילך ובמסכת שבת (פב.) מ"ט לא שכיחת גבי רב חסדא דמחדדן שמעתתיה:

מה חצות שאין עושה לינה כו'. ורבה לטעמיה דאית ליה בסמוך אין לינה מועלת בראשו של מזבח וליח ליה ק"ו דרב חסדא דאיכא למיפרך מה לחצות שכן עושה עיכול בראשו של מזבח דאם פקע לא יחזיר תאמר בעמוד השחר שאין לינה פוסלת בראשו של מזבח כך פי' ה"ר מנחם זצ"ל:

ורב חסדא אמר אין בהם עיכול לעולם. וליכא למימר דעמוד השחר שני יעשה עיכול מק"ו טז] דחצות שהרי אינו עושה לינה אלא לקרבנות היום שלפניו:

הילכתא כרב יוסף. פירוש יפה אמר ואין זה פסק הלכה ולא שייך למיפרך הילכתא למשיחא דהא לבסוף נמי מוכח דלא פליגי עליה וא"כ הלכה למה לי:

לא נהנין. רבינו היה מפרש מן התורה כיון שהם לחמו של מזבח ומ"מ יצא מידי מעילה דכיון דחצות עוכלם נעשית מצוותם ולא חזרה בהם מעילה:

לשלחן מדמינן לה דתנן אפילו היה על השולחן כו'. תימה מנא ליה דלא פסול לאחר שבת כשנסדר כהילכתו יז] וי"ל דדייק יח] מלישנא יתירא דקאמר שאפי' הוא על השולחן כו' דמשמע שבא להוסיף אפי' בענין זה *והא ליתא דהא דוקא משום שנסדר באחד בשבת שלא כהילכתו לא מיפסל כדאיתא יט] שילהי שתי הלחם (מנחות דף ק.) ופרק אמר להם הממונה (יומא דף כט:) *דטעמא דכלי שרת אין מקדשין שלא בזמנו ולא משני התם טעמא דשלחן אינו מקדש ליפסול בלינה כדאמר הכא דבעי למילף מיניה מזבח ול"ע אי מצי למימר דכי נסדר כהילכתו נעשה לחמו של שלחן טפי לא יפסל בלינה זה משמיענו לישנא יתירא דאפילו על השלחן כו' והתם דפריך כיון דלילה אינו מחוסר זמן כ] בי שמשי ליפסול ומשני כיון דנסדר שלא כהלכתו נעשה כמי שסדרו הקוף משמע אם סדרו כהלכתו נפסל בלינה י"ל דאתא למימר דאם נסדר בלילה כיון דלילה אין מחוסר זמן נפסל בלינה אבל נסדר כהלכתו ממש ביום השבת אפילו היה שם ימים רבים אינו נפסל דנעשה לחמו של *מזבח מ"מ תימה למה לא תירץ מתחילה לפי סברתו כי נמי כלי שרת מקדש שלא בזמנו שאני שולחן דאינו נפסל עליו כלל בשום ענין דעל כרחין שום פסוק יש על דבר זה שאינו נפסל אפילו כי נסדר כהלכתו: הגה"ה כבש מנין. וא"ת לרבי יהודה דאמר* עזרה מקדשת כמזבח אמאי איצטריך את לרבויי כבש הא כיון דירד ע"ג רצפה יעלה כ"ש כבש וי"ל דשמא הא דעזרה מקדשת כמזבח הייתו כשירין להקטיר עליה אבל פסולין לא °להכי איצטריך קרא:

כלי שרת מהו שיקדשו את הפסולין. פי' בקונטרס דלענין פדיון בעי א"ל תניתוה כו' א"ל לכתחלה ליקרב קמיבעיא לי כא] ופשיט דמקדש מקבלו פסולין וזרקו את דמו מאי לאו שקבלו פסולין וזרקו פסולין דמשום וזרקו פסולין אם עלו לא ירדו הא אם זרקוהו כשרים לכתחלה יעלו איברים דזריקה מעלייתא היא אף על גב דקבלוהו פסולין דכלי שרת שקבלו בו הדם מקדשת פסולין לכתחלה ליקרב וליזרק כך פירש בקונטרס ותימה לפי' דא"כ תיקשי ליה מתני' הלן והיוצא והטמא שנשחט חוץ לזמנו וחוץ למקומו כו' אם עלו לא ירדו משמע הא לכתחלה לא יעלו ואע"ג דנתקבל הדם בכשרות בכלי שרת דהא לא איירי מידי בנתקבל בפסול ונזרק בפסול *ועוד לן דמה ויצא דמה ונטמא דמה אמאי לא יעלו לר"ש כיון דכלי שרת מקדשין את הפסולין לכתחלה ליקרב וצריך לדחות כל הגי כגון שישנן עתה בכלי חול דהוה ליה כירדו וכן נתערב בדם הפסולין דאמר ישפך לאמה ולא אמרינן דיקרב מיירי בהכי וכן הא דתנן (מנחות דף ק:) המנחות

והנסכים

עין משפט נר מצוה

[סנהדרין יז: וע"ש]

[ועי' תוס' יבמות סג: ושם הניחו קושיא זו בתימה ועיין עוד תוס' סנהדרין יז. ד"ה אגלא]

לג א מיי' פ"ג מהלכות מעילה הלכה יב

לד ב מיי' פ"ה מהלכות תמידין ומוספין הלכה יג:

לה ג ד מיי' פ"ג מהל' פסולי המוקדשין הלכה יא:

לו ה מיי' שם הל' יח יט:

מכאן ועד סה"ד הוא מן הגה"ה. רצ"ק ועי' בתוס' מנחות דף ל

וטעמא דכלי שרת אין מקדשין שלא בזמנו מדלא משני התם כו' עפי ולא יפסל בלינה וזה ט' והתם פריך כיון כו' צ"ק

שיטה מקובצת

א] עיכול ויצאו מידי מעילה ולא נהנין שלהי: ב] אחר חצות: ג] אין לינה מועלת בראשו: ד] ת"ל כל הנוגע: ה] ת"ל בש"ס דפוס ווינציא כתוב אל המזבח והגיה הגאון רב"א לא יעלו. ס"א את המזבח והיא הגירסא הכתובה בש"ס שלנו: ו] מקדשין. את הראוי להן: ו] עוכלתן לשיירי דידהו: ז] לינה לאותן שעל: ח] הארץ למזבח דכתיב: ט] וכל שעה שפוקעין: י] דלא היה צריך להחזירן: יא] הבזיכין בשבת פסולה: יב] תיבת בשבת נמחק: יג] מנין ת"ל כל: יד] הוא סבר לענין: טו] נפקא תו בפדיון

[נ"ל חצות אין מועלי' כו' וכד"א] להחזירן סה"ד ואח"כ מה"ד יצאו כו' כ"ה בש"י

גליון הש"ס

גמ' לינה מועלת. עיין בב"מ דף קי ע"ב תד"ה יצא: תוס' ד"ה כבש וכו' להכי איצטריך קרא. עי' מנחות דף נז ע"ב תוס' ד"ה כבש:

מנחות צ. ק. [יומא כט.]

[מנחות ז.]

[עי' תוס' כריתות כד. ד"ה קסבר]

[מנחות ק:]

לעיל נט.

גי' צ"ק ועוד יצא דמה אמאי תרד לר"י דכיון דר"ש כו' ונמחק השאר. ועי' תוס' מנחות דף ז ע"א ד"ה ואין מקדשין

לחולין: טז] מק"ו דלינה א"כ אם עמוד השחר עושה לינה א"כ נפסלו בעמוד השחר ראשון. מהר"פ: יז] כהלכתו דהתם איירי שנסדר שלא בזמנו כדמוכח בסוף שתי הלחם דקאמר כלי שרת מקדשין שלא בזמנו מתיב ר' זירא כו' וי"ל דממשנה יתירא קדייק דאי לא אתא אלא להוכיח דאין כלי שרת מקדשין שלא בזמנו לא הוי ליה למיתני אלא יניחנה לשבת הבאה מדקאמר אפי' הן על השולחן ימים הרבה משמע דאין נפסלין על השולחן אפי' סידר בזמנן וא"ת א"כ מאי פריך התם ואי ס"ד כלי שרת מקדשין שלא בזמנן ליקדש וליפסל הרי הכא אמר דשולחן מועיל לענין שלא יפסלו בלינה וי"ל דשאני הכא דסדרו בזמנו אבל התם שסדרו שלא בזמנו אין מועיל השולחן להציל מפסול לינה. מהר"פ: יח] דדייק. עי' תוס' מנחות דף צ': יט] בשילהי: כ] זמן כי מטי בי כא] קמיבעיא לי. פי' אם כלי שרת מקדש פסולין ליקרב לכתחלה כאילו עלו על המזבח דקי"ל דלא ירדו או לא ולא לענין פדיון מבעיא לי (א"ל תניתוה) [הא נמי תנינא] שקבלו פסולין וזרקו את דמו כו' ומדקתני שקבלו פסולים והדר זרקו פסולים (דפסולים לכתחלה) [משמע] דלכתחלה לא יעלו וכשרים בדיעבד ודוקא משום דקבלו פסולין וזרקו פסולים דנגמור בפסול איפסיל ליה בשר בזריקת פסולים דלא יעלו לכתחלה אבל אם קבלו פסולים גרידא וזרקו כשרים דזריקה מעליא הוי לפי שקדשו כלי שרת אע"פ שקבלו פסולים אפי' לכתחלה נמי יעלו כאימורים וכמו כן הדם נזרק לכתחלה לפי שקדשו כלי שרת אע"פ שקבלו פסולים וכמו כן כלי שרת מקדש פסולים לכתחלה ליקרב וקשה מדקאמר לכתחלה ליקרב קא מבעיא לי מכלל לכתחלה נמי קא מבעיא ליה ליקרב בדיעבד או לא ולפ"ה לא היה לו לומר אלא ליקרב קא מבעיא לי וע"ק דהכא משמע דר"י אית ליה דכלי שרת מקדשים לכתחלה ובפ"ק דמנחות משמע דסבר אין מקדשים דבעיא מיניה ר"ל כו' ופ"ה התם כגון שנטמאת דקי"ל אם עלתה לא תרד אבל אם נכנסה לכלי אינה בשביל כך קדושה ליקרב לכתחלה למזבח אלמא דפשיטא התם דאין מקדשין והכא פשיט דמקדשין וע"ק מנלן לדמויי פסול דם לפסול איברים דהתם אין הפסול באימורין העולין למזבח ומש"ה אין לאסרו להעלותו לכתחלה בשביל הפסול שבקבלת הדם אבל היכא שהפסול בעולין עצמו אינו דומה להכשירו להעלותו לכתחלה לכן נראה לר"ת דה"פ כלי שרת מהו שיקדשו פסולים לענין דיעבד דאם עלו לא ירדו כגון מנחה שנטמאת ונתנה בכלי שרת ועלתה ע"ג מזבח וא"ת מאי מבעיא ליה פשיטא דאם עלו לא ירדו תיפוק לי דמזבח עצמו מקדש וי"ל דה"מ באיברים דלא מפסיק מנא והכא קא מבעיא ליה היכא דעודם עוד בכלי שרת ע"ג המזבח דהכלי מפסיק בינתים ומשום מזבח לא קדשה ומבעיא ליה דאם כלי שרת מקדשה לענין דאם עלו לא ירדו א"נ מבעיא ליה לענין קמצים פסולים שאין המזבח מקדשם אם לא קדשו כבר בכלי ואם [אין] הכלי מקדשם אין המזבח מועיל להם כלום וא"ת מאי קאמר לכתחלה ליקרב קמבעיא לי פשיטא דלא קדשי לכתחלה דהא אמר לעיל בזבחים נתערב דמם בדם הפסולים ישפוך לאמה מת המשתלח ישפך לאמה נטמא הדם לא יזרוק אלמא כלי שרת אינו מקדש לכתחלה ליקרב דאי מקדש למה ישפכו וי"ל דכל הני דבמתניתין יכול למדחייה דאיירי שעירן בכלי חול דאבדו קדושתן (תניתוה) [הא נמי תנינא] שקבלו פסולים כו' ודוקא קבלו פסולים וזרקו פסולים שכבר נעשית הזריקה מש"ה אם עלו לא ירדו הא אם קבלו פסולים גרידא (ס"א לא שייך דין זה דאם עלו לא ירדו דודאי לא יבאו לידי עלייה דכיון שנתקבל הדם בפסול לא יזרוק אלא ישפוך לאמה אלמא אין כלי שרת מקדש הדם שנתקבל בפסול להעלותו לכתחלה על המזבח וכיון שאין הדם נזרק על גבי המזבח לא יבאו האימורים לידי עלייה). ושוב לא נזרק פשיטא דאפי' עלו ירדו וטעמא משום דאין האימורים נקטרים אא"כ נזרק הדם והשתא לא יעשו הזריקה בפסול שהרי אין מקדשים כלי שרת לכתחלה ליקרב ומש"ה כי קבלו פסולים ולא זרקו ירדו ותפשוט מהכא דאין כלי שרת מקדש לכתחלה ליקרב לא שקבלו פסולים כו' הה"ק קבלו פסולים כלי שרת מקדש הדם ליקרב לכתחלה אבל האימורים לכתחלה לא יעלו ואם עלו לא ירדו אי נמי זרקו פסולים אם עלו אימורים לא ירדו ואין זה [קשה] דקבלו פסולים מקדש ליקרב הדם לכתחלה ובזרקו אינו מקדש המזבח אלא דאם עלו לא ירדו אבל לכתחלה לא יעלו דהא באימורים קיימינן ובאימורים קבלו וזרקו דלכתחלה לא יעלו ואם עלו לא ירדו ותו לא מידי. אלו הקושיות הקשה הר"ר פטר לר"ת והשיב לו כדפירשית. לשון מהר"פ.

*שקיבלו פסולין וזרקו את דמו מאי לאו שקיבלו פסולין וזרקו פסולין לא שקיבלו פסולין א"נ שזרקו פסולין א] אויר מזבח כמזבח דמי או לא ת"ש כשם שהמזבח מקדש כך ב] כבש מקדש ואי אמרת אויר מזבח לאו כמזבח דמי אויר כבש נמי לאו ככבש דמי היכי מסיק ליה מכבש למזבח הוה ליה ירוד דנגד ליה והא אויר יש בין כבש למזבח רובו לכבש ככבש רובו למזבח כמזבח תיפשוט מהא הא דבעי רמי בר חמא יש חיבור ג] לעולין או לא תיפשוט דיש חיבור °הא לא קשיא תיפשוט מתקיף לה רבא בר רב חנן ואי אמרת אויר מזבח כמזבח דמי ד] עולת העוף דפסלה במחשבה היכי משכחת לה הא קלטה מזבח מתקיף לה רב שימי בר אשי אלמה לא משכחת לה כגון דאמר הריני מולקה על מנת להורידה למחר ולהעלותה ולהקטירה הניחא לרבא דאמר לינה מועלת בראש המזבח אלא לרבה דאמר אין לינה מועלת בראש המזבח ליתא למחשבתו לרבה נמי משכחת לה כגון דאמר הריני מולקה על מנת להורידה קודם עמוד השחר ולהעלותה לאחר עמוד השחר להך גיסא מיהא תיפשוט *דאויר מזבח כמזבח דמי דאי ס"ד אויר מזבח לאו כמזבח דמי

חטאת

שקיבלו פסולין והדר זרקו פסולין ולמה לי זרקו מקבלה איפסלה לה אי לאו לאשמועינן טעמא דזרקו פסולין הוא דהוו איברים בתורת אם עלו לא ירדו ולכתחלה לא יעלו *דתפסל בשר בזריקת פסולין הא זרקו כשרין לכתחלה נמי יעלו האיברים דזריקה מעליא הוא ואע"ג דקיבלו פסולין משום ה] דקדשיה כלי שרת ליזרוק לכתחלה: אי נמי שזרקו פסולין. ומשום היא גופא איצטריך לאשמועינן אם עלו איברים לא ירדו ואף על פי שנפסלו בזריקה: אויר המזבח. אם תלה איברים פסולים באויר ראש המזבח כמזבח דמי ולא ירדו: או לאו. כמזבח דמי וירדו: היכי מסיק לה מכבש למזבח. הא כי מגבה ליה באויר הכבש הוה ליה ירוד ותנן כך אם ירדו לא יעלו: ומשני דנגד ליה. גוררן עד המזבח ואינו מגביהן: ופרכינן אויר יש בין כבש למזבח. כדאמרן בפרק קדשי קדשים (לעיל דף סב:) וכי מטי כנגד אותו אויר הוה ליה ירוד: ומשני רובו לכבש ככבש כו'. מה שכנגד ו] אויר שדינן ליה בתר רובא אם רוב האבר בכבש שדינן ליה בתר כבש ואי ז] רובן במזבח שדינן ליה בתר מזבח: יש חבור בעולין. דלא חשבינן להו כמאן דמיפרת ואזלינן בהו בתר רובא או אין חיבור: (א) תפשוט דיש חיבור. דאי אין חיבור קמא קמא דמטא כנגד אויר איפסיל ליה ובכריתות (דף יד*.) גרסינן ליה בלישנא אחרינא תיפשוט דבעי רמי בר חמא הלכו באיברים אחר הרוב או לא הלכו: עולת העוף. שמליקתה בראש המזבח: היכי משכחת לה. דפסל בה מחשבה חוץ לזמנו הא קלטיה אויר המזבח דאי נמי אמרינן לינה מועלת בראש המזבח וקיים זה את מחשבתו ושהה עד למחר והקטירה בת הקטרה היא דהא פסולין שעלו לא ירדו וכיון דבת הקטרה מחר לכתחלה היא אמאי פסלה בה מחשבת הקטרת מחר: אלמה לא. בתמיה (ב) ולא משכחת בה פסול מחשבה והא משכחת כגון שחישב עליה להוריד למחר לאחר שנפסל ולהעלותה ולהקטירה דכיון ח] דאיקיים ליה מחשבתו תו לא סלקא דהא איפסל ליה בלינה השתא נמי אהני בה מחשבה: ופרכינן אאתקפתא דרב שימי: הניחא לרבא דאמר לינה מועלת. איכא ט] לאשכחא בכה"ג: אלא לרבה. אפי' קיימא למחשבתו לא מיפסל וכל שכן דמחשבה לא י]הויא: ומהדרינן לרבה נמי כו' להורידה קודם עמוד השחר וכיון דעמוד השחר *משכחת לה אדלפה פסיל לה בלינה הילכך מהניא לה נמי מחשבה: להך גיסא מיהא תפשוט כו'. רב שימי מסיים ביה באתקפתיה הכי את בעי למילף מיניה אויר מזבח לאו כמזבח דמי לאידך גיסא מצית למיפשט מינה ולמימר דכמזבח דמי דאי לא כמזבח דמי:

חטאת

והנסכים שנטמאו משקדשו בכלי אין להם פדיון דמשמע מקרב לא קרבו יא] *בעורכו לכלי חול איירי וכן היה מקריב מנחת העומר ונטמאת בידו אומר לו הבא אחרת תחתיה בהכי מוקמינן לה מיהו אכתי קשה לפי' דאי מעיקרא ס"ד דלטעון פדיון קבעי אם כן לא הוה ליה למימר לכתחלה ליקרב מיבעיא לי אלא ליקרב מיבעיא לי ומדקאמר לכתחלה ליקרב מיבעיא לי משמע דמעיקרא נמי הוה ידע דליקרב קמיבעיא ליה אלא דמיבעיא ליה בדיעבד ועוד קשה ה"ר פטר לפרש"י יב] שהשיב ר"י דדוקא משום דזרקוהו פסולין אחרי שקבלו פסולין אבל קבלו פסולין וזרקוהו כשרים יעלו יג] תחילה ליקרב איברים דכלי שרת מקדשין לכתחלה ליקרב דבהדיא אמרינן בפ"ק דמנחות (דף ז.) והא בעי מיניה ריש לקיש מרבי יוחנן כלי שרת מהו שיקדשו פסולין לכתחלה ליקרב וא"ל אין מקדשין ומשני אין מקדשין ליקרב אבל מקדשין ליפסל ש"מ דאין מקדשין ליקרב פשיטא ליה הילכך נראה פר"ת שפירש דמעיקרא ס"ד דר' יוחנן דקבעי מיניה אם העלה פסולין לגבי מזבח בכלי שרת ומפסיק הכלי שרת וקמיבעי ליה נהי דאין לומר דלא ירדו מטעם דאויר מזבח כמזבח דמי שהרי תחתית הכלי מפסיק מיהו כלי שרת שמא מתוך קדושתו לא הוי חלילה והוי כאילו הפסולים ע"ג המזבח ממש דלא ירדו או הויא חלילה וירדו אמר ליה תניתוה כשם שהמזבח כו' לענין דאם עלו לא ירדו כך הכלים מקדשין לענין זה יד] (מכאן ואילך לשון ר"ת) א"ל לכתחלה ליקרב קמבעיא לי דסבר ריש לקיש דאיכא לאוקומה מתני' דקתני טו] *הך כלים מקדשים שאם עלו בכלי ע"ג המזבח לא ירד דאין כאן לא קדושת המזבח ולא קדושת אויר הואיל והם בכלי וקבעי שאם לא העלה הקמצין הפסולין בכלי אלא קדשו בכלי מהו שיעלו לכתחלה דכי היכי דמזבח מקדש מה שנגע בו ולא ירדו כך כלי מקדש מה שנגע בו ולא ירדו או לא אא"כ העלהו אמר ליה תניתוה שקבלו פסולין וזרקו את דמו מאי לאו שקבלו פסולין וזרקו פסולין כלומר שקבלו פסולין וזרקו בדיעבד הא אם לא זרקוהו לכתחלה לא יזרוק דהכי מיפרשא מתני' הלן והיוצא כו' שזרקו את הדם בדיעבד לא ירד הא אם לא זרקוהו לא יעלה והא דקאמר וזרקו פסולין פי' דמתני' [כך] הוא ואינו אלא מסיים לשון המשנה ולאו טז] מפסולא קדייק תדע שלא היה לו לומר רק לא שקבלו אי נמי זרקו אלמא דריש לקיש דדחי ליה בפסולין יז] מוקי לה והיינו דאמר בפ"ק דמנחות (ג"ז שם) והא בעי מיניה ריש לקיש(כו') מר' יוחנן כלי שרת מהו שיקדשו פסולין [כו'] ואמר ליה אין מקדשין *עד לא קבלו פסולין ואי נמי זרקו פסולין כלומר שקבלו פסולין אם עלה הבשר לא ירד והדם יעלה ויזרק דכלי שרת מקדשין לכתחלה ליקרב אי נמי אם זרקו פסולין הבשר אם עלה לא ירד והדם לא יתקנח דהא המשנה בכל עניינים אם עלה לא ירד קתני בין חומרא בין קולא *כדמוכח לשון ר"ת וכל מה שפירשתי לפירוש הקונטרס שהעמדתי יח] *בעודן בכלי חול צריך לפרש גם לפי' ר"ת למאי דבעי למימר ר"ל דמקדשין לכתחלה ומה שפי' הדם לא יתקנח אין שייך להזכיר כאן דלאו הייט אם עלו לא ירדו דאפילו מאן דאית ליה גבי דם אם עלו ירדו מודה יט] בדם הנזרק דקלטו מזבח דאי לא הוי אלא לר"ג דוקא א"כ בסמוך דפריך חטאת העוף דפסולה היכי מזה מדמה פירוש לר"ג דאמר אם עלה לא ירד כיון דאויר מזבח לאו כמזבח דמי לעולם הוי ירוד ומאי קושיא אימא הא דקתני אם עלה לא ירד היינו אם זרק לא יקנחט אבל אם עלה בכלי ירד אלא ודאי לא יקנחט הוי לכולי עלמא ואם עלה לא ירד דקאמר הייט אם עלה בכלי לא ירד אלא יזרקט בעל כרחו ובההיא דמנחות (ג"ז שם) דקדק רבינו חיים דקאמר התם אין מקדשין ליקרב אבל מקדשין ליפסל וכי לא היה יודע דמקדשין ליפסל הא מתני' היא בין לפי' הקונטרס בין לפי' ר"ת דתנן כך הכלים מקדשין: **אויר** יש בין כבש למזבח. אבל אי אויר מזבח כמזבח דמו לא קשיא ליה מכי מטי כנגד אויר (לא) הוה ליה ירוד דכנגד אותו אויר יש אמה סובב כ] וסובב חשיב מזבח דאפילו להקטיר עליו איכא מאן דאמר פרק קדשי קדשים (לעיל דף סב:) דמקטירין כא] מיהו אין נראה לרבינו חיים שהרי יש אויר מפסיק יותר מכדי אמה סובב כדי שיהא אויר קרקע כב] מפסיקו כדאמרינן לעיל מה דם אויר קרקע מפסיקו אף בשר אויר קרקע מפסיקו וא"כ אכתי מכי מטי כנגד אויר קרקע ה"ל ירוד: **עולת** העוף דפסלה בה מחשבה. תימה מאי קשיא ליה הא אמרינן בפרק קדשי קדשים (לעיל דף סה.) שאם עשאה למטה מרגליו אפילו אמה אחת כשרה וא"כ אין כאן אויר מזבח ולפירוש הקונטרס שפירש למעלה שהיתה שם בליטה ניחא אי נמי פריך לרבי נחמיה דאמר (לעיל דף סה.) היא עצמה אינה נעשת אלא בגופו של קרן:

חטאת

עין משפט נר מצוה: לו א מיי' פ"ג מהלכות פסה"מ הלכה יב :

נ"ל בעירן נ"ק | רש"ק מ"ז | נ"ל כך הכלים | גי' נ"ק ומשני לא שקיבלו כו' | נ"א כך מוכח

מסורת הש"ם: נ"ל דאיפסל נ"ק | [לעיל סד. | ועיין היטב פירש"י ותוס' שם | [נ"ל משכח]

הגהות הב"ח
(א) רש"י ד"ה תיפשוט נ"ל קודם ד"ה יש חיבור : (ב) שם ד"ה אלמה לא בתמיה אלמה לא משכחת:

גליון הש"ם
גמ' הא לא קשיא תפשוט. שבת דף ג ע"ב :

שיטה מקובצת
א] פסולין אבעיא להו אויר : ב] הכבש מקדש: ג] בעולין אות ל' נמחק: ד] עולת העוף דפסלה במחשבה . (וא"ת) [הקונטרס פי'] מליקה היתה בראשו של מזבח והא קלטה לה מזבח דאויר מזבח כמזבח ואילו היה מקטירו למחר היה כשר וי"ל דלישנא דקלטה משמע דבר הנפסל שהמזבח קלטתו והכא הרי הוא כשרה ממש א"נ (ר"ת אלא נראה) ה"פ [אפי'] אמרת דלינה מועלת בראשו של מזבח מ"מ הא קלטה לה מזבח דהא פסולים שעלו לא ירדו וא"כ למחר נמי בת הקטרה היא . מהר"ם : ה] דקדשו כלי שרת : ו] שכנגד האויר שדינן : ז] ואי רוב אות ו' נמחק : ח] דכיון דאי מקיים ליה : ט] איכא לאשכוחא : י] לא מהניא הס"ד : יא] לא קרבו בעירן לכלי חול : יב] לפרש"י שחשיב לא ירדו דוקא משום ותיבות שהשיב ר"י דדוקא ל"ש : יג] יעלו לכתחלה איברים ליקרב דכלי : יד] תיבות מכאן ואילך לשון ר"ת נמחק : טו] דקתני כך כלים מקדשים שמא מעלו בפלי (ס"א שמשהעלו בכלי) תיבת הך נמחק : טז] ולאו מפסולין קדייק : יז] בפסולין נמי מוקי : יח] שהעמדתי בעירן בכלי תיבת בעודן נמחק : יט] בדם . עי' תוס' מנחות דף ו' : כ] סובב דהכבש היה פורח אמה יסוד ואמה סובב : כא] דמקטירין אבל השתא דלאו כמזבח דמי ע"ס הוי כאויר וכי היכי דאויר סובח לאו כמזבח דמי כמו כן אמה סובב לאו כסובב דמי וא"כ הו"ל ירוד : כב] הקרקע . עיין לעיל בתוס' דף ס"ב :

learnt: [87b] [Or] where unfit [persons] received and sprinkled the blood.[9] Surely that means, where unfit [persons] received *and* sprinkled the blood.[10]—No: [it may mean] that unfit [persons] received it *or* unfit persons sprinkled the blood.[11]

a The scholars asked:[1] Is the air-space above the altar as the altar, or not?[2]—Come and hear: JUST AS THE ALTAR SANCTIFIES SO DOES THE ASCENT SANCTIFY. Now, if you say that the air-space above the altar is not as the altar, then the air-space above the ascent too is not as the ascent; how then can one carry it up from the ascent to the altar, seeing that it is as having descended?[3]—He drags it.[4] But there was a gap between the ascent and the altar?[5]—When the greater part of it [the limb] is nearer the ascent, it is as though it were [on] the ascent, and when the greater part of it is nearer the altar, it is as though it were on the altar. Then from this you can solve Rami b. Ḥama's question, [viz.]: Is there a connective in [limbs which] ascend the altar or not?[6] Solve that there is a connective?[7]—That is no difficulty: Then solve it!

Raba son of R. Ḥanan demurred: If you say that the air-space above the altar is as the altar, how is it possible for a burnt-offering of a bird to be disqualified through an [illegitimate] intention; surely the altar has received it?[8] R. Shimi b. Ashi demurred: Why not? It is possible e.g., where he declared: Behold, I pinch it intending to take it off to-morrow [from the altar], then carry it up

b again and burn it.[1] (That is well according to Raba who maintained [that] *linah* is effective [when the sacrifice is] on top of the altar; but according to Rabbah who held that *linah* is not effective on top of the altar, his intention [certainly] does not count![2]—According to Rabbah too it is possible e.g. if he declared: Behold, I pinch it with the intention of taking it down before dawn and taking it up again after dawn.)[3] At all events, you can solve [the question] in the other direction, viz., that the air-space of the altar *is* as the altar,[4] for should you think that the air-space of an altar is not as the altar,

(9) V. *supra* 84*a*. (10) The 'and' (Heb. ו) being conjunctive. This implies that only then do they not descend once they ascended, which further implies that they may not ascend in the first place. Hence, if unfit persons received the blood (naturally, in a service vessel) whilst *fit* persons sprinkled it, they may ascend (be offered) in the first place, and that must be because the vessels sanctified the blood to permit its sprinkling at the outset. (11) And we are informed that even then the limbs do not descend once they ascended, notwithstanding that they were disqualified by the sprinkling.

a (1) Emended text (Sh.M.). (2) If one suspends disqualified limbs above the altar, is it as though they are on the altar itself and must not be removed, or not? (3) For if it is *not* as the ascent, when he lifts it up to carry to the altar it is as though he had taken it down, and we learnt that if it descended it must not re-ascend. (4) Up to the altar without lifting it up from the ascent. (5) V. *supra* 62*b*. And when the limbs reach the gap, they are as though taken down. (6) If the smaller part of a limb springs off, is it considered as still attached to the whole, and so must be replaced, or not? (7) For otherwise each portion of the limb becomes disqualified as it enters the gap between the altar and the ascent. (8) The neck of a burnt-offering of a bird was pinched (v. Lev. I, 15) on top of the altar, i.e., in the air-space above the altar. Now if the priest actually kept it suspended in the air-space above the altar until the next day it would be fit then for ritual burning, for disqualified sacrifices do not descend once they ascended (i.e., even if *linah* does disqualify when the sacrifice is on the altar). Since then it is *fit* for burning on the morrow, why should the *intention* to burn it on the morrow disqualify it, seeing that at the very moment that it is killed it is as though laid on the altar?

b (1) This would be forbidden, as if it descended it does not re-ascend. Hence the intention too can disqualify it. (2) For even if he kept it until the morrow on the top of the altar it would not be disqualified, so that if he took it down then he would still have to replace it. The *intention* to do this would certainly not disqualify it. (3) If the sacrifice were actually on the ground at dawn it would be disqualified, and so the *intention* too disqualifies it. (4) This is the conclusion of R. Shimi b. Ashi's argument: though R. Ḥanan's reasoning is faulty, yet one can argue in the reverse direction.

[88*a*] how may one sprinkle the blood of a disqualified sin-offering of a bird, as it has the status of having descended,[5] [and] how could one sprinkle the blood of other disqualified [sacrifices]?[6]—He contacts [the blood] [with the wall of the altar].[7] Is that *haza'ah*? it is draining; is that *zeriḳah*? it is pouring out;[8] moreover, is that the way of *haza'ah* and *zeriḳah*?[9]—Said R. Ashi: If he held it on top of the altar, that would indeed be so; the question arises where he [the priest] stands on the ground and suspends it [the blood] on a cane?[10] what then? The question stands over.

MISHNAH. THE VESSELS FOR LIQUIDS SANCTIFY
a LIQUIDS,[1] AND THE MEASURES FOR DRY MATTER SANCTIFY DRY MATTER.[2] A LIQUID VESSEL DOES NOT SANCTIFY DRY MATTER, NOR DOES A DRY [MEASURE] SANCTIFY A LIQUID. IF HOLY VESSELS WERE PERFORATED AND THEY CAN BE USED FOR THE SAME PURPOSE AS WHEN WHOLE, THEY SANCTIFY [WHAT IS PLACED IN THEM]; IF NOT, THEY DO NOT SANCTIFY. AND ALL THESE SANCTIFY ONLY IN THE SANCTUARY.[3]

GEMARA. Samuel said: They learnt [this] only of the measures,[4] but the basins sanctified,[5] for it is said: *Both of them filled with fine flour.*[6] Said R. Aḥa of Difti to Rabina: But that was a moist meal-offering?[7]—He replied, The proof is from the dry parts thereof.[8] Alternatively, a meal-offering is dry in comparison with blood.[9]

Samuel said. The service vessels sanctified only when whole, full,[10] and through the inside.[11] Others state it: They sanctify only when whole, full, and within.[12] Wherein do they differ?—They
b differ in respect of the overflow of measures.[1] In a Baraitha it was taught: They sanctify only when full, whole, through the inside and within. R. Assi said in R. Joḥanan's name: They learnt this[2] only where he [the priest] does not intend to add thereto; but if he intends adding thereto, each portion becomes holy in turn.[3] It was taught likewise: [*Both of them*] *filled* [*with fine flour*]: '*filled*' means complete.[4] Said R. Jose: When is that? When he does not intend to add [thereto]; but if he intends to add [thereto], each portion becomes holy in turn.

A LIQUID VESSEL DOES NOT SANCTIFY etc. Rab—others state R. Assi—said: They do not sanctify to be offered, but they sanctify [it] to be disqualified.[5] Others recite it in connection with the following: You may not bring meal-offerings, drink-offerings, and the meal-offering of an animal [sacrifice], or the first-fruits,[6] from a mixture;[7] and it goes without saying from *'orlah* and *kil'ayim* of the vineyard.[8] If one did bring [such], it is not sanctified. Said Rab—others state, R. Assi—: It is not sanctified to be offered, but it is sanctified to be disqualified.[9]

Our Rabbis taught: When holy vessels are perforated, you may
c not melt them[1] nor melt lead into them.[2] If they were damaged,[3] you may not repair them. If a knife was damaged, you may not smooth out the damage;[4] if it slipped out [of its haft], you may not replace it. Abba Saul said: There was a knife which caused *terefoth*[5] in the Temple, whereupon the priests decided by vote to hide it.

Our Rabbis taught: The priestly garments were not sewn but woven,[6] as it is said, *of woven work.*[7] If soiled, they might not be washed with natron[8] or with ahal.[9] But you may wash them in water?[10]—Said Abaye, This is what he means: If they [merely] needed water,[11] you may wash them [even] with natron or *ahal.*

(5) If one pinched the bird on the altar with an illegitimate intention, it is disqualified; as soon as he lifts it in order to sprinkle the blood, it is as though he had taken it down from the altar, and such may not be taken up again. Hence the blood could not be sprinkled. (6) According to R. Gamaliel who maintains that if the blood of disqualified sacrifices ascended the altar, it must not descend. But sprinkling is done from a distance, so that the blood passes through the air-space of the altar. (7) Not from the distance. (8) *Haza'ah* and *zeriḳah* are two words for sprinkling, the latter denoting a sprinkling with greater force than the former.—If he does not sprinkle the blood from the distance, it is not sprinkling at all. (9) Even if this could be called sprinkling, it is certainly not the manner in which sprinkling is done. (10) The above argument proves nothing. For when the man stands on the altar and holds the blood or the bird in his hand, the air-space is certainly as the altar itself, for the fact that he is standing on it gives the blood etc. the same status as though it were on the altar.

a (1) E.g. the plates and basins for blood, wine and oil. (2) There were two dry measures, an *'issaron* (tenth part of an ephah) and half an *'issaron:* the first was used for measuring all meal-offerings, while the second was used for the High Priest's daily morning and evening meal-offerings (v. Lev. VI, 12 *seq.*).—Rashi and Tosaf. give different reasons why the Mishnah speaks of liquid *vessels* and dry *measures.* (3) The Temple court. (4) Only the liquid *measures,* of which there were seven, do not sanctify dry matter. The reason is because these were only fit for measuring, and had been anointed (whereby they were sanctified) for this purpose only. (5) Though meant primarily for liquids, they could also be used for meal. (6) Num. VII, 13. '*Both*' included a basin, which was normally used for liquids. (7) V. ibid.: *with fine flour mingled with oil for a meal-offering.* (8) Lit., 'it is necessary only for the dry parts'.—Mingling could not be so thorough as to leave no dry parts at all, yet these too were sanctified by the basins. (9) For which the basins were normally used. (10) They must contain as much as is required, e.g., if flour for a meal-offering is placed in them, there must be at least an *'issaron.* (11) But if flour is heaped up on the outside of a service vessel, it is not sanctified. (12) Rashi: in the Temple court.

b (1) When a measure is overfilled, so that there is a brim, the Rabbis disagree as to whether the overflow is sanctified (Men. 90*a*). He who maintains that only the *inside* sanctifies, holds that the overflow is not sanctified. (2) That it sanctifies only when full. (3) Lit., 'the first, the first is holy'. Every little quantity is sanctified as it is poured into the vessel, and it remains sanctified even if it was not full eventually. (4) Containing the necessary measure (v. *supra* n.a10); only then is it sanctified. (5) If meal is placed in a liquid vessel, it is sanctified in so far that if it is then carried out of the Temple court or touched by a *ṭebul yom* (q.v. Glos.), it is disqualified from being used henceforth for a meal-offering. (6) I.e., which accompanied an animal sacrifice or the first-fruits. (7) A mixture of *terumah* and *ḥullin.* (8) V. Glos. and Deut. XXII, 9. A meal-offering or drink-offering can certainly not be brought from these, which are forbidden to all, including priests. But it may not be brought even from a mixture of *terumah* and *ḥullin,* which is permitted to priests, though priests consume the meal-offering, because what is brought must be permitted to all. (9) It does not count simply as *ḥullin* but as sanctified meal which had become unfit, having been sanctified by the service-vessel in which it was placed, and therefore it must be burnt.

c (1) I.e., melt the metal around the hole to close it up. (2) For the same purpose. (3) More extensively. (4) I.e., if the edge is heavily notched it may not be re-ground. (5) It frequently became slightly notched and was inadvertently used, thus making the sacrifices *terefah.*—*Terefoth* is used loosely for *nebeloth.* (6) They were woven directly into garments, not first into cloth and then sewn together. (7) Ex. XXVIII, 32. (8) V. Sanh. (Sonc. ed.) 49*b* n.a5. (9) A substance used as soap.—The reason for all these is that it savours of poverty to repair or cleanse them for Temple use. (10) Surely not; that too savours of poverty and is moreover inefficient. (11) Lit., 'if they were brought to water.'—i.e., they were only slightly soiled.

חטאת העוף פסולה היכי מזה מדמה הוה ליה ירוד שאר פסולים היכי זריק להו מדמה דמגע להו הא הזאה היא מיצוי היא הא זריקה שפיכה היא ועוד א] דרך הזאה בכך דרך זריקה בכך אמר רב אשי אי דנקט להו בראש המזבח ה"נ כי ב] קאמר דתלנהו בקניא מאי תיקו: **מתני'** *כלי הלח מקדשין את הלח ומדות יבש מקדשות את היבש *אין כלי הלח מקדשת את היבש ולא יבש מקדש את הלח: כלי הקודש שניקבו אם עושין בהן מעין מלאכתן שהיו עושין והן שלימים מקדשין ואם לאו אין מקדשין וכולן אין מקדשין אלא בקודש: **גמ'** *אמר שמואל לא שנו אלא מדות אבל מזרקות מקדשין שנאמר °שניהם מלאים סולת א"ל רב אחא מדיפתי לרבינא מנחה לחה היא א"ל לא נצרכה אלא ליבש שבה איבעית אימא מנחה לגבי דם כיבש דמי אמר שמואל כלי שרת אין מקדשין אלא שלימין אין מקדשין אלא מלאין אין מקדשין אלא מתוכן ואמרי לה אין מקדשין אלא שלימין ומלאים ומבפנים מאי בינייהו איכא בינייהו בירוצי מדות במתניתא תנא אין מקדשין אלא שלימין ומלאים ומתוכן ובפנים א"ר אסי א"ר יוחנן לא שנו אלא שאין דעתו להוסיף אבל דעתו להוסיף ראשון ראשון קודש תניא נמי הכי *מלאין אין מלאין אלא שלימין אמר רבי יוסי אימתי בזמן שאין דעתו להוסיף אבל דעתו להוסיף ראשון ראשון קודש: אין כלי הלח מקדש [וכו']: אמר רב ואיתימא רב אסי אין מקדשין ליקרב אבל מקדשין ליפסל ג] איכא דמתני לה אהא *אין °מביאין מנחות ונסכים ומנחת בהמה וביכורים מן המדומע ואין צ"ל מערלה וכלאי הכרם ואם הביא לא קדש אמר רב ואיתימא רב אסי לא קדש ליקרב אבל קדש ליפסל ד] *ת"ר כלי קדש שניקבו אין מתיכין אותן ואין מתיכין לתוכן אבר °נפגמו אין מתקנין אותן סכין שנפגם אין משחיזין את פגימתה נשמטה אין מחזירין אותה אבא שאול אומר סכין מטרפת היתה במקדש ונמנו עליה כהנים וגנזוה ת"ר *בגדי כהונה אין עושין אותם מעשה מחט אלא מעשה אורג שנאמר °מעשה אורג נתגעלו אין מכבסין ה] לא בנתר ולא באהל הא במים מכבסין אמר אביי ה"ק °הוגעו ו] במים מכבסין אותו בנתר ואהל

הוגעו

רש"י

חטאת העוף פסולה. שמלקה בראש המזבח שלא לשמה ז] ופסל דאף על גב ח] דנעשית למטן הא אמר מר לעיל (דף סג:) מלקה בכל מקום במזבח כשרה ולא פסול *מעלה דידיה אלא בהזאה והיכא דמלקה בפסול בראש המזבח וקי"ל בכל הפסולין אם עלו לא ירדו היכי שרי ליה מר להזות מדמה הרי מגביה ומתיז כשאוחז בה ומזה והוה ליה ירוד: שאר פסולים. דמים (א) ט] בבהמה לר"ג דאמר במתני' הדם פסול שעלה לא ירד: היכי זריק. מדמן הרי זריקה מרחוק הוא זורק והוה ליה אויר המזבח: ומשני דמגע להו. לכותל מזבח כשמזה בחטאת העוף וכן בזריקת דם פסול: ופרכינן הא הזאה היא. בתמיה מיצוי הוא ולענין דמים פסולים נמי אי מגע להו י] שפיכה הוי ולא זריקה ועוד וכי דרך הזאה וזריקה בכך אלא לאו משום דאויר מזבח כמזבח דמי: אמר רב אשי. לעולם בעיין מהא לא תפשוט יא] *דהא גברא בראש המזבח קאי ונקיט להו וכה"ג לא מיבעיא לן באויר מזבח לעיל דהנחת גופו בראש המזבח כהנחת קרבן דמי וכי קמבעיא לן כגון דקאי אארעא ותלינהו בקניא באויר המזבח: **מתני'** כלי הלח. קערות ומזרקות לדם ולייך ולשמן: מדות היבש. שתי מדות של יבש היו שם עשרון וחצי עשרון עשרון למדידת כל המנחות וחצי עשרון לחלות בו מנחת חביתי כ"ג יב] מחליתה בבוקר ומחליתה בערב להכי נקט גבי יבש מדות יג] שאין כלים מיוחדים ליבש אלא אלו דכלי שנותנין בו מנחה כלי לא הוא שמזרקות וקערות ראוין לכך: ואין כלי לח מקדשות את היבש. בגמרא מתרגם לה אמדות הלח: שהיו עושין והן שלימים. כשהן שלימים: אלא בקדש. בעזרה: **גמ'** לא שנו. דאין כלי הלח מקדשין את היבש: אלא מדות. ז' מדות הלח שהיו שם הין וחצי הין ושליש ההין וכו' דכיון דהנך לא חזו ליבש *למידי למדוד והן לא נמשחו אלא למדידה לפיכך אין מקדשין אלא ע"י מדידה: אבל מזרקות. אע"ג דכלי הלח נינהו מקדשין יבש דכי היכי דחזו ללח חזו לסלת שהוא יבש: לחה היא. דהא כתיב בלולה בשמן והיכי ילפת מהאי קרא דמקדשין יבש: ליבש שבה. שאי אפשר ליבלל כולה שלא יהו בה קרטין קרטין של יבש שלא נגע בהן השמן וקדשינהו מזרקות (ב) כ"ש: כיבש דמיא. ושפיר תפשוט מינה ליבש גמור: אלא שלימין. לאפוקי נקבו: ואין מקדשין אלא מלאין. כלומר שיהא בהן שיעור שלם הצריך לדבר אם יבש הוא שיהיה שם עשרון שלם למנחה ואם מנחת נסכים היא שניתנה בכלי יהא שם ג' עשרונים לפר ושני עשרונים לאיל אבל אם חסר השיעור אין הכלי מקדשן שאינו ראוי לכלי (ג) כך שמעתי במנחות (דף ח.): אלא בפנים. בעזרה: בירוצי מדות איכא בינייהו. למאן דתני אין מקדשין אלא מתוכן קסבר בירוצי מדות לא נתקדשו אלא מה שבתוך חללו של כלי בירוצי מדות גודשי מדות ופלוגתא היא במנחות בפרק שתי מדות (דף צ.): לא שנו. הא דאמרינן דאין מקדשין אלא מלאים: אלא שאין דעתו להשלים. ולהוסיף עד כשיעור: תניא נמי הכי מלאים. שניהם מלאים סלת: אלא שלימים. *שהיו עשרונים ולוגין שלימים לאפוקי שיעור חסר דלא מקדשי: אבל מקדשין כלי הלח את היבש ליפסל. *שאם יצא חוץ לקלעים או נגע בו טבול יום נפסל דהכי ליה כלי להכשירו ליפסל יד] כדתניא מעילה (דף י.) המנחות מועלין בהן משהוקדשו קדשו בכלי הוכשרו ליפסל בטבול יום ובמחוסר כפורים: מנחות ונסכים ומנחת בהמה מן המדומע. ואע"פ שמותר לכהנים דבעינן מותר לכל ישראל שנאמר (יחזקאל מה) ממשקה ישראל מן המותר לישראל: ואין צ"ל מערלה. שאסורה אף לכהנים: ליפסל. דלא נפקי *לחול וישרפו שקדשם הכלי והא דרב אסי לא מהדר אבכורים אלא אמנחות דבכורים לאו קדושת כלי טו] הוא ומאי ליפסל איכא הא לא קרבו טז]: אין מתיכין אותן. כמו שעושין יז] למדות מעקבות שמתיכין אותן כשיבות הנקב וסתם הנקב: ואין מתיכין לתוכן אבר. לסתום הנקב וכולהו משום דמיחזי כעניות ולאו אורח ארעא: נפגמו. פגימה גדולה שתיקון השחזתה ניכר: סכין מטרפת. שהיתה רכה ליפגם פגימות דקות תמיד ומטרפת את הקדשים: אין עושין אותן מעשה מחט. לאורגן כמין יריעה ולעשותן אחרי לבוש תפור במחט אלא כמין מלבוש אורגין אותן בכליהם: אהל. מין כיבוס הוא שמעביר את הגיעול וכן נתר: הא במים מכבסין. בתמיה כיון דטעמא משום דמיחזי כעניות הוא מה לי נתר מה לי מים הרי נתגעלו וכבסן כל שכן דכי לא מחוור לאו שפיר גריעי ספי:

הוגעו

תוספות

חטאת העוף פסולה היכי מזה מדמה. פירש בקונטרס וקי"ל בכל הפסולין (לעיל דף פד.) *דאם עלו יח] יזרוק הדם לכתחילה וא"ת מנא ליה הא דקודם זריקה קאמר דלא ירדו דילמא היינו לאחר זריקה ויש קצת ראיה ממליקת חטאת העוף דאין מטמא בבית הבליעה שמתרת את האסור ואם אין יכול לזרוק לכתחילה במה מתרת את יט] האכילה דלענין אם זרק את הדם לא יקנחנו לא קאמר דאפי' למאן דאמר תרד לא יקנחנו כדפי' לעיל (דף פז: ד"ה כלי):

מדות היבש. פירש בקונטרס דלהכי קרי ליה ליבש מדה וללח כלי שאין שום *כלי מקדש ליבש אלא שתי מדות עשרון וחצי עשרון ותימה והאיכא בישא פרק הקומץ [רבה] (מנחות דף כד.) והאיכא מחתה לקטורת והאיכא כף והאיכא מכתשת בשבועות (דף יא.) והאיכא בזיכין ושולחן ופי' ר"ת דלהכי קרי לי' ליבש מדה ולא כלי לפי שיבש יכולין למדוד מחוק או גדוש בכל ענין שירצה אבל דבר לח לא שייך מדה גביה שהרי מדת לח אינה שוה דדבר לח אינו יכול להיות גדוש ופעמים שמדת לח זה יתירה מזה כמו מדת יין יתירה ממדת מים לפי שיין עב יותר וכן שמן מיין להכי לא קרי ליה מדה כ]*:

אלא בפנים. פי' בקונטרס בעזרה *ותימה למה שינה לשון המשנה הוה ליה למימר בקדש ומפ' רבינו חיים דמבפנים לכלי קאמר כא] ואתי למעוטי °חקק מושבו מבחוץ*:

מן המדומע. פירש בקונטרס מדומע דתרומה ורבינו חיים פירש מעורב בערלה וכלאי הכרם אבל ערלה וכלאי הכרם לא איצטריך למיתני ופי' הקונטרס ל"ע איך יתיישב ממשקה ישראל כיון דשרי לכהנים ומההיא דחגיגה (דף כד:) דקאמר אם אמר הפרשתי לתוכה רביעית קדש נאמן על התרומה לא שייכא לכאן דהתם לאו מדומע הוי שהרי אין מקדיש הרביעית ואין קורא שם על התרומה בעוד שהיא בחבית אלא יחדה ושמרה בטהרה ליקח ממנה רביעית אחר שיתרום ויעשה אותה [תרומה]:

נשמטה אין מחזירין אותה. לקתה דאין עניות במקום עשירות:

כמחלוקת

עין משפט נר מצוה

נ"ל דאם עלו לא ירדו ויזרוק הדם כו' נ"ק

לח א מיי' פ"ג מהל' פסה"מ הל"ט:

לט ב ג מיי' שם הל"ט

מ ד מיי' שם הל"ט:

מא ה מיי' שם הל"כ:

מב ו מיי' פ"א מהל' כלי המקדש הל"ט:

מג ז ח מיי' פ"ג מהל' פסה"מ הל"כ:

נ"ל כלי במקדש נ"ק

מד ט י מיי' פ"ס מהל' איסורי מזבח הל"ט:

מה כ מיי' פ"א מהל' כלי המקדש הל"ד:

מו ל מיי' שם הל"ט:

[מנחות יט:]

[וע' תוס' מנחות פג ד"ה כלי]

ע' בס' פנים מאירות

[ועיין תוס' פסחים סג: ד"ה מידי דהוי ותוספות יומא מט. ד"ה בעי]

גליון הש"ס

גמ' נפגמו אין מתקנין. עיין שבועות דף יא ע"א תוס' ד"ה מ"מ קשיא: שם הוגעו במים מכבסים. ע' סוטה דף טו ע"ב תוס' ד"ה נתאכמו: רש"י ד"ה אבל מקדשין וכו' שאם יצא. עיין לעיל דף כ ע"ב תוס' ד"ה יצאה: תוס' ד"ה אלא וכו' חקק מושבו מבחוץ. עי' פסחים דף סג ע"ב תוס' ד"ה מידי וסוכה דף ג ע"א תוס' ד"ה ואי:

שיטה מקובצת

א] ועוד וכי דרך: ב] ס"א כי קא מבעיא לן דקאי אארע' ותלינהו: ג] ליפסל. ס"א איכא דמתני לה אסיפא דמתניתין אין מקדשין אלא בקודש אמר רב ואיתימא רב אסי אין מקדשין ליקרב אבל מקדשין ליפסל: ד] ליפסל: כלי קודש שנקבו כו'. ת"ר כלי קודש: ה] מכבסין אותו לא: ו] הוגעו למים מכבסין אותו בנתר ואהל הוגעו לנתר וכו': ז] לשמה ופסלה: ח] גב דלא נעשית למטן הא אמר מר לעיל מליקה בכל מקום כו' מעלה דידיה אלא: ט] דמים דבהמה: י] להו לכותל שפיכה היא ולא זריקה: יא] תפשוט דהכא גברא: יב] כה"ג מחצית בבוקר ומחצית בערב: יג] מדות דאין כלים: יד] ליפסל כדתנן מעילה: טו] כלי אית בהו ומאי: טז] לא קרבי חסד"ד: יז] שעושין ליורות מנוקבות: יח] עלו לא ירדו ויזרוק הדם: יט] את האיסור ותיבת האכילה נמחק: כ] מידה א"נ משום דמלת יש כלים שאינן מדות כגון קערות וכיוצא בהם. מהר"ש: כא] קאמר ולמעוטי מגבו וא"ת היינו מתוכן י"ל דאתא למעוטי כו' תיבת ואתי נמחק:

מסורת הש"ס

ר"ה מעלה גרידא אנא ס'

מנחות ח: יט:

נ"ל דהיכא דגברא בראש המזבח קאי ונקיט להו כה"ג כו' נ"ק

במדבר ז

[מנחות ח.]

תוספתא דמנחות ספ"ח תוספתא דמעילה פ"א

למדוד נ"ק

תוספתא דמנחות ספ"ט

[יומא עב:]

שמות כח

נ"ל שיהיו נ"ק

לחולין נ"ק

הגהות הב"ח

(א) רש"י ד"ה שאר פסולים דמים של בהמה: (ב) ד"ה ליבש וכו' מזרקות קס"ד ותיבת כ"ש נמחק: (ג) ד"ה ואין מקדשין וכו' לכלי קס"ד ותיבות כ"ש במנחות נמחק:

עין משפט נר מצוה

מז א מיי' פ"ח מהל' כלי המקדש הל"ה :
מח ב מיי' שם פ"ט הלכה ג :
מט ג ד מיי' שם הל"ד :

הוגעו לנתר ואהל אף במים אין מכבסים ויש אומרים *אין מכבסין אותן כל עיקר *שאין עניות במקום עשירות : ת"ר מעיל כולו של תכלת היה שנאמר °ויעש את מעיל האפוד כליל תכלת שוליו כיצד א] מביא תכלת וארגמן ותולעת שני שזורין ועושה אותן כמין רימונים שלא פיתחו פיהן וכמין קונאות של ב] קנסות שבראשי תינוקות ומביא שבעים ושנים זגין שבהן שבעים ושנים עינבלין ותולה ג] בהן שלשים וששה בצד זה ושלשים וששה מצד זה רבי ד] דוסא אומר משום רבי יהודה שלשים וששה היו שמונה עשרה מצד זה ושמנה עשרה מצד זה אמר רבי עיניני בר ששון כמחלוקת כאן כך מחלוקת במראות נגעים *דתנן מראות נגעים רבי דוסא בן הרכינס אומר ל"ו עקביא בן מהללאל אומר שבעים ושנים *ואמר רבי עיניני בר ששון °למה נסמכה פרשת קרבנות לפרשת בגדי כהונה לומר לך מה קרבנות מכפרין אף בגדי כהונה מכפרין כתונת מכפרת על שפיכות דם שנאמר °וישחטו שעיר עזים ויטבלו את הכתנת בדם מכנסים ה] מכפרת על גילוי עריות שנאמר °ועשה להם מכנסי בד ו] [לכסות (את) בשר ערוה] מצנפת מכפרת על גסי הרוח מנין אמר רבי חנינא יבא דבר שבגובה ויכפר על גובה אבנט מכפר על הרהור הלב ז] *היכא דאיתיה חושן מכפר על הדינין שנא' °ועשית חושן משפט אפוד מכפר על עבודת כוכבים שנאמר °אין אפוד ותרפים מעיל מכפר על לשון הרע מנין א"ר חנינא יבא דבר שבקול ויכפר על קול הרע ציץ מכפר על עזות פנים בציץ כתיב °והיה על מצח אהרן ובעזות פנים כתיב °ומצח אשה זונה היה לך אינו והא"ר יהושע בן לוי שני דברים לא מצינו להן כפרה בקרבנות ומצינו לו כפרה ממקום אחר ואלו הן שפיכות דמים ולשון הרע שפיכות דמים מעגלה ערופה ולשון הרע מקטרת דתני רב חנניה מנין לקטרת שמכפרת שנאמר °ויתן את הקטרת ויכפר על העם *ותני דבי רבי ישמעאל על מה קטורת מכפרת על לשון הרע יבא דבר שבחשאי ויכפר על מעשה חשאי קשיא לשון הרע אלשון הרע קשיא שפיכות דמים אשפיכות *דמים לא קשיא הא דידיע מאן קטליה הא דלא ידיע מאן קטליה אי דידיע מאן קטליה בר קטלא הוא במזיד ולא אתרו ביה ולשון הרע אלשון הרע נמי לא קשיא הא בצינעא הא בפרהסיא :

הדרן עלך המזבח מקדש

במחלוקת כאן כך מחלוקת במראות נגעים . פר"ת דתני האי בהאי דמשום דמעיל בא לכפר על לשון הרע וכן נגעים באין על לשון הרע כדאמרינן פרק יש בערכין (ערכין דף טז.): **שבעים** ושנים. לא פליג כג] התנא אמתניתין דשבועות (דף ו.) דתנן שתים שהן ארבע דהתם מיירי בנגעים לבנים והכא מיירי בכל מיני נגעים ירקרק ואדמדם ופתוכים ויש להוסיף עוד נגעי בתים ונגעי בגדים : **מכפרים** על שפיכות דמים. מה שמפרשים כד] אהא מיום שחרב בית המקדש אף על פי שבטלו ד' מיתות דין [ארבע] מיתות לא בטלו דלהכי לא נקט מ' שנה קודם שחרב בית המקדש שגלתה סנהדרין דבההיא שעתא אפי' דין ארבע מיתות לא הוה דבגדי כהונה מכפרין ולא נהירא דגבי שמעון בן שטח פריך ליה כה] באחד דיני ממונות (סנהדרין דף לז:) אף על גב דהוו בגדי כהונה *ומיהו הייתי יכול לקיים פירוש זה ולומר דלהכי לא נקט מ' שנה *משום דאיכא דין מיתות דבטלו כגון עריות ועבודת כוכבים שמכפרין עליהם מכנסים ואפוד אבל דין שפיכות דמים לא בטל דכתונת שמכפרת על שפיכות דמים אין מכפרת על ההורג אלא על ישראל שערבין זה בזה דומיא דעגלה ערופה דכתיב (דברים כא) כפר לעמך ישראל ואציבור מכפרת ולא על ההורג וכן משמע הכא דכתונת לא מכפרת אהורג דאי מכפרת מאי פריך הכא מעגלה ערופה והא עגלה ערופה אישראל מכפרה וכן משמע פ' יש בערכין (ערכין דף טז.) דקאמר על ז' דברים נגעים באים וקחשיב שפיכות דמים ולשון הרע ופריך התם ממעיל שמכפר על לשון הרע ומכתנת שמכפר על שפיכות דמים לא פריך מידי משום דלא מכפר אהורג אלא אישראל כדפרישית אבל מלשון הרע כו] דלא מצינו לשניי הכי דמסתמא אין ציבור נענשין על לשון הרע של זה כיון דשמא לא יבא לידי תקלה וכן פירש בקונט' התם ועוד יש מפרשים בההיא דערכין (נז"ש) דלהכי לא פריך מכתנת דנהי דמללת מעונש מיתה מנגעים ויסורין לא מללת ואם תאמר הכא משמע דכתנת מכפרת על דידיע מאן קטליה ובשבועות (דף ח.) מצריך קרא למימר שאין שעיר *המשתלח מכפר על דידיע מאן קטליה ואמאי צריך קרא פשיטא דהא כתנת מכפרת ומיהו יש לפרש דיש חילוק בין ציבור לכל ישראל דכתנת מכפרת אציבור ושעיר *המשתלח על כל ישראל :

[יתכן לאיות מפנימי] [צ"ל מפנימי]

הדרן עלך המזבח מקדש

הוגעו במים . כלומר אם היה גיעולן מועט ולא ח] הזקיקן אלא לכיבוס מים מכבסים אותן אף בנתר ואהל : הוגעו לנתר ואהל . שנתגעלו גיעול רב שהגיעו ליזקק לכיבוס נתר ואהל תו לא מתקן להו כלל : אף במים . לאו לרבותא הוא אלא למימרא דנתר ואהל דנקט לאו לענין כיבוס נקט דהיכא דאסור אסור לגמרי והיכא דשרי שרי לגמרי אלא לענין גיעול נקיט ליה וה"ק נתגעלו אין מכבסין אותן כלל אם הוזקקו לנתר ואהל : נראה בעיני דה"ג שוליו כיצד היה מביא כו' דברימונים נאמרו שלשה צבעים : שלא נפתחו פיהם . דרך רימונים כשעושין באילן אחר גמר בישולן מתפתחין מאליהן כדרך שעושין קליפי אגוזים החיצונות : וכמין קונאות . בוטונ"ש עשויין כמין תיק של נחשת שעושין ט] [בסוף] בית יד הרומח שקורין ארישטייל לשון (שמואל ב כא) ומשקל קינו דישבי בנוב והתינוקות תולין אותו בראשי כובעי נגרים שעושין אותו למלחמתן שקורים הילמ"ש : י] קנסות שבראשי תינוקות . לשון וקלסא דנחשא על רישיה : זגין . אינגלינ"ש : עינבלים . מה שתלוי בתוכן לקשקש ותולה בו אצל הרמון [והוא] פעמון כדכתיב (שמות לט) פעמון ורמון יא] ובתוך הרמונים דקרא לאו בתוך החלל קאמר אלא ביניהם דפעמון אחד בין שני רמונים : מצד זה . מלפניו ומלאחריו : מראות נגעים . לטמא יב] מפתוכין של לבן אדמדם ולבנים של נתקי הראש וזקן ושל נגעי בתים [ובגדים] : למה נסמכה . בצו את אהרן זאת תורת העולה זאת תורת החטאת והאשם וזבח השלמים והדר קח את אהרן ואת הבגדים : ויטבלו את הכתנת . רמז הוא לעתיד יג] שיכפר שפיכת דמים בכתנת טבילה הייט כפרה : לכסות יד] את בשר ערוה . לחפות על גילוי עריות : אהיכא דאיתיה . שהיו חוגרין כנגד אצילי ידיהן דהייט כנגד הלב כדילפינן בפרק שני (לעיל דף יט.) מולא יחגרו ביזע : אין אפוד . נגלה עון תרפים הא יש אפוד אין תרפים כך שמעתי במסכת ערכין (דף טז.) : דבר שבקול . פעמונים שבו טו] (מכפר) : [ויכפר] על העם . במחלוקת קרח שהוא לשון הרע טז] [שנאמר] אתם המיתם וגו' : שבחשאי . שהיה יז] לבדו שם כדתנן פורשין *בין האולם ולמזבח בשעת הקטרה וכל שכן מן ההיכל יח] שנאמר וכל אדם לא יהיה וגו' בסדר יומא (דף מד.) : ידיע מאן קטליה . כתונת מכפרת על הציבור שלא יענשו : בר קטלא הוא . וכל כמה דלא קטליה מיענשי דכתיבים [ולארץ] לא יכופר וגו' (במדבר לה) : ומשני במזיד ולא אתרו ביה. דלאו בר קטלא הוא הילכך ציבור מתכפרי בכתונת והוא כ] נגעים באים עליו כדאמר בערכין כא] : בצינעא . דהוה דבר שבחשאי קטרת מכפרת שהוא מעשה חשאי : בפרהסיא . שהוא דבר שבקול קול כב] פעמונים מכפר עליו :

הדרן עלך המזבח מקדש

[שבת קכ:] מנחות פח.
[כתובות קו: תמיד כט. לח:]
נגעים פ"א משנה ד
ערכין טז. [ע"ש ונס' ברש"י דשם]
[צ"ל אהיכא וכ"ג רש"י אבל באלתות איתא על היכא]
יומא מד. ערכין טז. [צ"ל מנין]
נ"ל דמים שפיכות דמים אשפיכות דמים לא קשיא

[וע"ע תוס' כתובות ל. וכסוטה ח: וכסנהדרין לז: ד"ה מיום]
נ"ל משום דאיכא דין כו'

גליון הש"ס

גמ' למה נסמכה פרשת קרבנות לפרשת בגדי כהונה . בערכין דף ו איתא למה נסמכה פרשת בגדי כהונה לפ' קרבנות וע' ברש"י כאן והתם . ועיין בדרשות הרא"ת פ' תצוה :

שיטה מקובצת

א] כיצד היה מביא : ב] קולסות שבראשי : ג] ותולה בו שלשים ותיבת בהן נמחק : ד] תיבת דוסא נמחק וכ"א ר' דוסא אומר ששה ושלשים היו וכו' תיבות משום ר' יהודה נמחק : ה] מכנסים מכפרים אות ת' נמחק : ו] לכסות בשר ערוה מצנפת ותיבת את ל"ש: ז] אהיכא דאיתיה : ח] ולא הוזקקו אלא : ט] שעושין בסוף בית יד : י] מה"ד קלסות שבראשי : יא] ורמון והא דכתיב וישם פעמונים בתוך הרמונים לאו כו' ותיבת דקרא נמחק : יב] לטמא משנה היא במס' נגעים בפ"ק והני רצאי חשבי בפתוכין של לבן : יג] שכפרת שפיכת תיבת שיכפר ל"ש : יד] תיבת את נמחק : טו] ויכפר על ותיבת מכפר נמחק: טז] דכתיב ביה אתם : יז] שהיה הכהן לבדו : יח] ההיכל דיליף מכל אדם לא יהיה : יט] דכתיב ולארץ לא: כ] והוא כו' . גליון וצ"ע דהא הכא לא קאי אלא אשפיכת דמים ובתוס' כתוב בגליון וז"ל כאן בפרהסיא מעיל ודוקא לציבור אבל איהו לא מכפר ליה אלא בנגעים ושב ורפא לו : כא] בערכין ס"א דנגעים באים על לשון הרע : כב] קול הפעמונים : כג] פליג האי תנא אמתניתין : כד] שמפרשים אהאי דאמרי' מיום: כה] ליה בפ' אחד : כו] לא מצינו דתדירא

[88*b*] If they needed natron or *ahal*, you may not wash them even in water. Others maintain: You may not wash them at all,[12] because there is no poverty in the place of wealth.

Our Rabbis taught: The robe [*me'il*] was entirely of blue,[13] as it is said, *And he made the robe of the ephod of woven work, all of blue*.[14] How were its skirts [made]? Blue [wool], purple wool and crimson thread, twisted together, were brought, and manufactured into the shape of pomegranates whose mouths were not yet opened[15] and in the shape of the cones of the helmets on children's heads. Seventy two bells containing seventy two clappers were brought and hung thereon, thirty six on each side.[16] R. Dosa[17] said on the authority of Rabbi Judah: There were thirty six, eighteen on each side.

R. 'Inyani b. Sason said: As there is a controversy here, so is
a there a controversy in respect to leprous plagues.[1] For we learnt: The appearances of plagues, R. Dosa b. Harkinas said: They are thirty six; Akabia b. Mahalallel said: They are eighteen.[2]

R. 'Inyani b. Sason also said: Why are the sections on sacrifices and the priestly vestments close together?[3] To teach you: as sacrifices make atonement, so do the priestly vestments make atonement. The coat atones for bloodshed, for it is said, *And they killed a he-goat, and dipped the coat in the blood*.[4] The breeches atoned for lewdness, as it is said, *And thou shalt make them linen breeches to cover the flesh of their nakedness*.[5] The mitre made atonement for arrogance. How do we know it?—Said R. Hanina: Let an article placed high up[6] come and atone for an offence of hauteur. The girdle atoned for [impure] meditations of the heart, i.e., where it was placed.[7] The breastplate atoned for [neglect of] civil laws, as it is said, *And thou shalt make a breastplate of judgment*.[8] The ephod atoned for idolatry, as it is said, *Without ephod there are teraphim*.[9] The robe atoned for slander. How do we know it?—Said R. Ḥanina: Let an article of sound[10] come and atone for an offence of sound. The headplate atoned for brazenness: of the headplate it is written, *And it shall be upon Aaron's* forehead,[11] whilst of brazenness it is written, *Yet thou hadst a harlot's* forehead.[12]

But that is not so, for surely R. Joshua b. Levi said: For two things we find no atonement through sacrifices, but find atonement for them through something else,[13] and they are bloodshed and slander. Bloodshed [is atoned for] by the beheaded heifer,[14] while slander [is atoned for] by incense. For R. Ḥanania recited: How do we know that incense atones? Because it is said, *And he put on*
b *the incense, and made atonement for the people*.[1] And the school of R. Ishmael taught [likewise]: For what does incense atone? For slander: let that which is done in secret[2] come and atone for an offence committed in secret.[3] Thus slander contradicts slander, and bloodshed contradicts bloodshed?—There is no difficulty: bloodshed does not contradict bloodshed: In the one case the murderer is known,[4] in the other the murderer is unknown.[5] If the murderer is known, he is liable to death?[6]—It means [where he committed murder] deliberately, but was not warned.[7] Slander too does not contradict slander: Here it was done in secret;[8] there it was done in public.[9]

(12) Even if slightly soiled. (13) *Tekeleth*, wool dyed with a peculiar blue, now no longer obtainable. (14) Ibid. XXXIX, 22. (15) Overripe pomegranates open up slightly. (16) I.e., in front and behind. (17) Sh.M. reads: Rabbi.

a (1) Lit., 'the appearances of plagues'. (2) They disagree as to how many colours render these plagues leprous and unclean. (3) Immediately after discussing the burnt-offering, meal-offering, sin-offering, and peace-offerings (Lev. VII), Scripture speaks of the priestly garments (VIII, 1 *seq*.) (4) Gen. XXXVII, 31. This was a sign that later the coat would make atonement, even as dipping (Heb. *ṭebillah*, in later Hebrew denoting ritual immersion for purification) symbolised atonement. (5) Ex. XXVIII, 42. (6) On top of the head. (7) It was placed at the level of the heart. (8) Ibid., 15. (9) Hos. III, 4. Where there is no ephod, there is the unatoned-for sin of teraphim (idols).—E.V.: *without ephod or teraphim*. (10) *Sc*. the robe, which was fringed with bells. (11) Ex. XXVIII, 38. (12) Jer. III, 3. (13) Lit., 'from another place.' (14) V. Deut. XXI, 1–9.

b (1) Num. XVII, 12. (2) None was present when the incense was offered. (3) Slander is first related in private and then it spreads. (4) Then the coat makes atonement, so that the whole community should not be divinely punished. (5) Then the beheaded heifer makes atonement. (6) And until he is executed the community is not forgiven. (7) On 'warning, (*hathra'ah*) v. *supra* 78*a* n. a 1. He could not be executed in that case. (8) Then the incense atones. (9) Then the robe atones.

CHAPTER X

MISHNAH. [89a] WHATEVER IS MORE CONSTANT THAN ANOTHER TAKES PRECEDENCE OVER THE OTHER. THE DAILY-
a OFFERINGS[1] PRECEDE THE ADDITIONAL OFFERINGS;[2] THE ADDITIONAL OFFERINGS OF THE SABBATH PRECEDE THE ADDITIONAL OFFERINGS OF NEW MOON;[3] THE ADDITIONAL OFFERINGS OF NEW MOON PRECEDE THE ADDITIONAL OFFERINGS OF NEW YEAR; FOR IT IS SAID, [YE SHALL OFFER THESE] BESIDE THE BURNT-OFFERING OF THE MORNING, WHICH IS FOR A CONTINUAL BURNT-OFFERING.[4]

GEMARA. Whence do we know it? [You ask] Whence do we know it: surely he [the Tanna] states the reason, viz., 'BESIDE THE BURNT-OFFERING OF THE MORNING'?—Perhaps only the daily-offerings precede the additional offerings, because they are constant; how do we know that additional-offerings [precede] [less frequent] additional-offerings?[5]—Said R. Elai, Because Scripture states, ***Like these ye shall offer daily, for seven days:***[6] [instead of] 'these', 'like ***these***' [is written].[7] But this is required for its own purpose?[8]—If so,[9] let [Scripture] write, 'These ye shall offer daily'.[10] If it wrote, 'These ye shall offer daily for seven days', I would think
b [that] these [are offered] in the seven days?[1]—'***Daily***' is written.[2] Yet I might still interpret, ***These*** [ye shall offer] ***for*** the ***day,***[3] but on the remaining days I could not know how many?[4]—Scripture says, ***Ye shall offer,*** [which implies] that all your offerings must be alike.[5] Abaye said: [We learn it] from that very text.[6] For if so,[7] let Scripture say ***'beside the burnt-offering of the morning'***, and then be silent; why state, ***which is for a continual burnt-offering?*** To teach that that which is more constant takes precedence.[8]

MISHNAH. WHATEVER IS MORE SACRED THAN ANOTHER PRECEDES THAT OTHER. THE BLOOD OF A SIN-OFFERING PRECEDES THE BLOOD OF A BURNT-OFFERING,[9] BECAUSE IT PROPITIATES.[10] THE LIMBS OF A BURNT-OFFERING PRECEDE THE EMURIM OF A SIN-OFFERING,[11] BECAUSE IT [THE FORMER] IS ENTIRELY FOR [ALTAR] FIRES. A SIN-OFFERING PRECEDES A GUILT-OFFERING, BECAUSE ITS BLOOD IS SPRINKLED ON THE FOUR HORNS AND ON THE BASE.[12] A GUILT-OFFERING PRECEDES A THANKSOFFERING AND A NAZIRITE'S RAM, BECAUSE IT IS A SACRIFICE OF HIGHER SANCTITY. A THANKS-OFFERING AND A NAZIRITE'S RAM PRECEDE A PEACE-OFFERING, BECAUSE THEY ARE EATEN ONE DAY [ONLY] AND REQUIRE [THE ACCOMPANIMENT OF] LOAVES. A PEACE-OFFERING PRECEDES A FIRSTLING, BECAUSE IT REQUIRES FOUR [BLOOD] APPLICATIONS, LAYING [OF HANDS], DRINK-OFFERINGS, AND THE WAVING OF THE BREAST AND THE THIGH. A FIRSTLING PRECEDES TITHE, BECAUSE ITS SANCTITY IS
c FROM THE WOMB,[1] AND IT IS EATEN BY PRIESTS. TITHE PRECEDES BIRD[-OFFERINGS], BECAUSE IT IS A SLAUGHTERED SACRIFICE,[2] AND PART OF IT IS MOST SACRED, [VIZ.,] ITS BLOOD AND EMURIM.[3] BIRDS PRECEDE MEAL-OFFERINGS, BECAUSE THEY ARE BLOOD SACRIFICES. A SINNER'S MEAL-OFFERING PRECEDES A VOTIVE MEAL-OFFERING, BECAUSE IT COMES ON ACCOUNT OF SIN. A SIN-OFFERING OF A BIRD PRECEDES A BURNT-OFFERING OF A BIRD; AND IT IS LIKEWISE WHEN HE DEDICATES THEM.[4]

a (1) Lit., 'continual' offerings—the daily burnt-offerings. (2) Which were sacrificed on Sabbaths, Festivals, and New Moons. (3) When the Sabbath and New Moon concurred, similarly the other cases. (4) Num. XXVIII, 23. '***These***' are the additional festival offerings, whilst '***beside the burnt-offering of the morning***' implies that that had already been offered, having preceded the additional offerings. (5) Since even the more frequent additional offerings are not really constant, perhaps we disregard their greater frequency. (6) Ibid. 24. (7) He interprets: like those which are mentioned in the preceding verse: as in those the more frequent take precedence, so in these (the festival additional-offerings) the more frequent take precedence. (8) To teach that an additional offering must be brought every day of the festival. (9) If that is its only purpose. (10) Not 'like ***these***.'

b (1) I.e., the seven he-lambs specified in Num. XXVIII, 19 are not offered each day but spread over the seven days. (2) Which precludes that interpretation. (3) *Sc.* the first day. (4) If Scripture did not write, ***like*** these. (5) The offerings on each day (including the first) must be the same. Hence '***like***' is unnecessary for that purpose, and so intimates precedence. (6) Cited in the Mishnah. (7) If its teaching applies only to the daily offerings. (8) In all cases. For that reason '***continual***' is emphasized. (9) If both are ready for sprinkling at the same time. (10) It makes atonement where ***kareth*** is involved. (11) For burning. (12) Whereas of the guilt-offering only two applications are made, and not on the horns; nor is the blood poured out on the base (Rashi).

c (1) It is born sacred. (2) Whereas a bird requires ***meliḳah;*** slaughtering is considered higher. (3) Even in lesser sacrifices these possess the same sanctity as the most sacred sacrifices, since they belong to the altar. In the case of a bird only the blood possesses that sanctity, but there are no ***emurim.*** (4) When a man dedicates the two birds (v. Lev. V, 7) he first dedicates the one for sin-offering and then the one for burnt-offering.

כל התדיר

כל התדיר *מחבירו קודם את חבירו *התמידין קודמין למוספין *מוספי שבת קודמין למוספי ר"ח מוספי ר"ח קודמין למוספי ר"ה שנאמר °מלבד עולת הבקר אשר לעולת התמיד תעשו את אלה:

גמ' מנא לן כדקאמר טעמא מלבד עולת הבקר דילמא תמידין הן דקדמו למוספין משום דתדירי מוספין למוספין מנ"ל א"ר אילעא דאמר קרא °כאלה תעשו ליום שבעת ימים אלה כאלה והאי מיבעי ליה לגופיה א"כ ניכתוב אלה תעשו ליום אי כתב אלה תעשו ליום שבעת הימים ה"א אלה לשבעת הימים (אין מידי אחרינא לא) ליום כתיב ואכתי אימא אלה ליום אבל שאר יומי לא ידענא כמה אמר קרא תעשו שיהו כל העשיות שוות *אביי אמר מגופה דקרא אם כן לימא קרא מלבד עולת הבקר ותישתוק אשר לעולת התמיד ל"ל למימר דהך דתדירא א] תיקדום:

מתני' *כל המקודש מחבירו קודם את חבירו *דם החטאת קודם לדם העולה מפני שהוא מרצה איברי עולה קודמין לאימורי חטאת מפני שהוא כליל לאישים ב] חטאת קודמת לאשם מפני שדמה ניתן ג] לד' קרנות על היסוד *אשם קודם לתודה ואיל נזיר מפני שהוא קדשי קדשים תודה ואיל נזיר קודמים לשלמים מפני שהן נאכלין ליום אחד וטעונין לחם *השלמים קודמין לבכור מפני שהן טעונין מתן ד' ד] [וסמיכה] ונסכים ותנופות חזה ושוק הבכור קודם למעשר מפני שקדושתו מרחם ונאכל לכהנים המעשר קודם לעופות מפני שהוא זבח ויש בו ה] קודש קדשים דמו ואימוריו ו] העופות קודמין למנחות מפני שהן מיני דמים *מנחת חוטא קודם למנחת נדבה מפני ז] שהוא בא על חטא ח] *חטאת העוף קודמת לעולת העוף וכן בהקדישה:

גמ'

רש"י

כל התדיר. שבת תדירה מר"ח וכן כולם: מלבד עולת הבקר. ט] העשויה כבר משמע אלמא תמידין קדמי למוספין: **גמ'** משום דתדירי. דתמיד בכל יום הילכך חשיב י] תדירתא דידיה: כאלה תעשו וגו'. בתר ההוא קרא דמלבד עולת הבקר תעשו את אלה כתיב כאלה העשו משמע כסדר תורה אור שאמרתי לך כאלה של מעלה יא] כשם שהתדיר קודם כך סדר המוספין שאם יב] יום שיש ב' מוספין כגון בשבת שבתוך הרגל יהא התדיר קודם: לגופיה. להטעין מוסף לז' הימים דמקרא קמא יום ראשון הוא דנפקא לן: אי כתב אלה כו'. לשון קושיא הוא: אלה לשבעת הימים. אותן שבעה כבשים האמורין בענין יתחלקו לשבעת הימים: אלה ליום. ליום ראשון והדר כתיב ז' ימים יג] אשה ריח ניחוח לה' ולא ידענא כמה להכי איצטריך כאלה דעל כרחך מהשתא תוקים תעשו ליום אשאר יומי: מגופיה דקרא. דמלבד עולת הבקר שמעי' דמוספין תדירין יקדמו: אשר לעולת התמיד ל"ל. פשיטא דעולת הבקר עולת התמיד היא אלא תלה לך טעם הקדמתה בתדירות כדי שתלמוד לשאר תדירין שיקדימו דמשום היא גופא ל"ל לפרושי טעמא: **מתני'** כל המקודש מחבירו. שיש בו לד ריבוי קדושה ממנו: דם חטאת קודם לדם העולה. אם שניהן שחוטין ועומדין ליזרק: שהוא מרצה. מכפר על חייבי כריתות הצריך ריצוי גדול: איברי עולה קודמין. בהקטרתן לאימורי חטאת אם נזרקו דמי שניהן: מפני שהוא יד] כולה כליל. ולד ריבוי קדושה הוא זה למזבח: על ד' קרנות. ואשם ב' מתנות שהן ד' ולא על הקרנות: ועל היסוד. שפיכת שירים ובאשם לא מצינו *שנאמרו: מתן ארבע. ב' מתנות שהן ד' ובכור אינו טו] אלא מתנה אחת ואינו טעון סמיכה ונסכים כדאמרינן במנחות בפ' שתי מדות (דף צ:) כל הקרבנות כו': מפני שהוא מין זבח. זביחת סכין ועוף במליקה וזבחים חשיבי מפני שמלותן מרובה שכל הקרבנות באין מהן: ויש בו קדשי קדשים. לחלק גבוה ב' דברים דמו טז] (ואיבריו) ואימוריו מה שאין כן בחטאת העוף שאין למזבח אלא דמה וכיון דקדמה לחטאת העוף כל שכן לעולת העוף דהא חטאת העוף קודמת לעולת העוף כדקתני ואזיל: שהן מיני דמים. יז] כפרתן מרובה: יח] שהוא בא על חטא. והייני קדושתו דמכפרת: חטאת העוף קודמת לעולת העוף. מקראי נפקא לן בגמרא: וכן בהקדישה. כשהוא יט] מפרש את קינו קורא שם לחטאת תחילה:

תוספות

כל התדיר. שנאמר מלבד עולת הבקר אשר לעולת התמיד. תימה דבפרק תמיד נשחט (פסחים דף נח:) אמרינן מנין שלא יהא דבר קודם לתמיד שנאמר העולה עולה ראשונה ל"ל תיפוק לי מהכא וכי תימא דההוא לנדרים ונדבות והאי למוספין כ] *דמוספין קבוע להם זמן ונדרים ונדבות אפשר בכל יום ותדיר הא בפרק התכלת (מנחות דף מט.) מייתי בהדיא קרא דהעולה אמתני' דהתמידין אין מעכבין את המוספין דקאמר ה"ד אי דאית ליה כא] [ולקדם] והתניא מנין שלא יהא דבר כו' ועוד קשה טפי בסוף הגוזל קמא (ב"ק דף קיא.) דריש מדכתיב מלבד איל הכפורים מכלל דכסף ברישא ופריך אלא מעתה מלבד עולת הבוקר מכלל דמוספין ברישא והתניא מנין שלא יהא דבר כו' הוה ליה למיפרך ממתני' דהכא דאדרבה דדריש מדכתיב מלבד עולת הבוקר מכלל דתמידין קודמין וליכא למימר נמי דאיצטריך קרא דהכא לציבור שאין להם תמידים ומוספין אלא כדי אחד מהם דמתני' לאו בכי האי גוונא איירי דומיא דסיפא דקתני דם חטאת קודם לדם כב] עולה וליכא למימר דחד למצוה וחד לעכב דעיכובא ליכא כג] כדאמר בפ' התכלת (מנחות דף מט.) וי"ל דהעולה עולה ראשונה להקדמת הקטרה דבהקטרה איירי וקרא דהכא להקדמת שחיטה דתעשו את אלה כד] בעשייה דדם [איירי] והשתא ניחא *דמייתי דרבא בפרק התכלת (שם) למימר דאפי' בהקטרה דלא תנן תמיד של שחר קודם א"כ משום דלשון שלא יהא דבר קודם משמע טפי עיכובא אתיא טפי מן משנה והשתא ניחא דלא מייתי בהגוזל קמא (ב"ק דף קיא.) ממתני' לאוכוחי על מלבד איל הכפורים דלא הוי כסף ברישא דלעולם כסף ברישא כיון דכתיב כסף קודם ואחר כך איל אבל הכא איירי בעשיית הדם וה"ק קרא מלבד עולת הבוקר שעשיתם כבר עבודת הדם תעשו את אלה אבל הקטרה דכתיב מקמי קרא דמלבד עולת הבוקר תהיה קודם התמיד דכולהו קראי דקמיה בהקטרה משתעי דהא כתיב בהו אשה ריח ולהכי איצטריך לאתויי מהעולה דאע"ג כה] דהקטרת דמוספין כתיבי מקמי עולת הבקר הקטרת תמיד קודמת להן ה"נ הכא אע"ג דכסף כתיב מקמי מלבד איל הכפורים יכול להיות דאיל קודם מיהו קשה דקראי דקמי מלבד עולת הבוקר בעבודת דם [נמי] איירי כדכתיב לעיל מיניה ושעיר חטאת אחד לכפר עליכם וכפרה בדם היא ועוד אמאי לא גמרינן הקטרה ודם מהדדי ומפרש ה"ר חיים דקרא דהעולה איצטריך לחביתין דמכל התדיר לא אתי דבכל יום איתנהו כתמיד וכן מוכח ביומא בפרק אמר להם הממונה (דף לד.) דקאמר איברים קודמין למנחה דתניא מנין שלא יהא דבר כו' ואמר רבא כו' ובמנחת חביתים איירי דאי במנחת נסכים תיפוק לי מדכתיב עולה ומנחה וקרא דהכא איצטריך ללמד על כל התדירין שקודמין מיהו אין מרויח כלל בזה יותר משאם נאמר דאיצטריך העולה לנדרים ונדבות ויש לתמוה אמאי לא נפקא לן דתמידים קודמין למוספין מדכתיב בתמיד בבקר ויוקדם דבר שנאמר בו בבוקר למוסף כו] שכתב בו ביום דמשמע בעילומו של יום כדדרשינן [התם] (ג"ז שם) ביום לאחר ואמרינן נמי (פסחים דף נח.) מוספין בשש ואז אינו בקר והיינו יכולין לדחוק ולומר דאי לאו קרא דהעולה הייני מאחרין הקטרת תמיד עד אחר הקטרת כז] המוסף כדמשמע בהגוזל קמא (ב"ק ד' קיא.) מדכתיב מלבד ותעשה בבוקר הוה מוקמינא לעבודת הדם אבל עדיין קשה כיון דכתיב העולה לאפוקי מהאי סברא ל"ל קרא דמלבד לאשמועי' דתמידין קודמין למוספין לעבודת הדם תיפוק ליה מדכתיב בתמיד בבוקר ובמוספין ביום: **מנא** לן כדקתני טעמא. הכא ניחא שהטעם מפורש במשנה אבל בשמעתא קמייתא דמגילה (דף ב.) קשה דקאמר מנ"ל כדבעינן למימר קמן חכמים הקילו כו' ומה בכך אטו מש"ה לית ליה למיבעי מנ"ל מאחר שאותו הטעם אינו מפורש במשנה: **אשם** קודם לתודה ואיל נזיר מפני שהוא קדשי קדשים. הא דלא קאמר טעמא מפני שהוא מרצה משום דאיכא אשם נזיר ואשם מצורע דאין באין לכפר אלא להכשיר כדאמר בפ"ק דמנחות (ד' ד:) ומיהו גבי חטאת קאמר טעמא דמרצה אע"ג דאיכא נמי חטאת נזיר וחטאת מצורע דאין באין לכפר אלא להכשיר כדקאמר לעיל בפ"ק (דף ט:) הני עולות ניכהו כח] ויש לומר דלא סגי ליה בטעמא דמרצה משום דתודה ואיל נזיר מקודשין דטעונין לחם כדאמר בגמ': **מעשר** קודם לעופות מפני שהוא מין זבח. ויש בו קדשי קדשים דמו ואימוריו מה שאין כן בחטאת העוף שאין למזבח אלא דמה כט] וכיון דקדמה לחטאת העוף כל שכן לעולת העוף דהא חטאת העוף קודמת לעולת העוף כדקתני ואזיל כך פי"ה בקונטרס ואי טעמא ניחא בדם אבל אימורי מעשר דקדמי לעולת העוף מאי טעמא דאטלה מילתא קאמר דקודמים כדמוכח בגמרא ושמא באימורין סגי בטעמא דמין זבח:

דם

עין משפט נר מצוה

ג"ל וצריכא דמוספין סי' ג"ק

א א ב מיי' פ"ט מהל' תמידין ומוספין הל"ב:

ב ג מיי' שם הל"ט:

ג ד מיי' שם הל"ח:

ד ה מיי' שם הל"י:

ה ו מיי' שם הל"י:

ג"ל דמייתי בפ' התכלת האי קרא דהעולה למימר כו' א"נ משום דס"ד דהמקשה שהוא מעכב הילכך פריך מברייתא' דלשון שלא יהא דבר קודם משמע ספי עיכובא מלישנא דמתניתין והשתא ניחא כו' ג"ק [וכן הוא בתוס' יומא דף לד ע"א ד"ה העולה וע"ש]

מסורת הש"ס

[סוריות יב:]

[עמון כ:]

[שם נח.]

[הוריות יב: פ"ש]

[הוריות שם]

[לעיל יא:]

ג"ל שנאמר כו יסוד ג"ק

גליון הש"ס

בבשנה דם החטאת קודם לדם עולה. עי' לעיל דף ז ע"ב ובתוס' ד"ה ריצה:

שיטה מקובצת

א] דתדירא היא תיקדום: ב] חטאת קודמת לאשם כו' פ"ה ועל היסוד שפיכת שיריים ובאשם לא מצינו שנאמרו וקשה דהא לעיל פרק ב"ש מוכח בהדיא דאשם טעון שפיכת שיריים ליסוד וכ"ת דלא נאמרו ר"ל לא נאמרו בהדיא מה בכך מ"מ איתנהו ביה מה לי אי אתיא מדרשה או דכתיבה ביה בהדיא הא לא קפיד אלא על מאי דיש בזה ספי מבזה לכך נראה דלא יהיב טעמא למילתיה א) אלא (מדמה) [דמה דמדמה] ניתן על הקרנות אבל על היסוד איתיה נמי באשם וא"ת א"כ אמאי אמר על היסוד כיון דאיתיה באשם י"ל דה"ק חטאת מקודשת מאשם מפני שדמה ניתן על הקרנות וג"כ הוא טעון שפיכת שיריים כמו אשם שלא תאמר כשם שחטאת קודם לאשם מפני שדמה ניתן על הקרנות כך נמי אשם מקודש מחטאת מפני שהוא טעון שפיכת שיריים ליסוד לכך קאמר ועל היסוד שטעון שפיכת שיריים על היסוד כמו אשם אבל אין לומר מפני שהוא מרצה כדלעיל גבי עולה מפני שאשם נמי מרצה כך נראה למורי ז"ל: ג] ניתן על ד' קרנות ועל היסוד: ד] ד' וסמיכה ונסכים ותנופת חזה: ה] בו קדשי קדשים: ו] העופות. עי' תוס' מנחות דף סט ע"א: ז] מפני שהיא בא: ח] חטא חטאת בהמה קודם לעולת בהמה חטאת העוף: ט] חבקר עשויה כבר: י] חשיב תדירות דידיה: יא] מעלה שהתדיר ותיבת ששם ל"ש ונמחק: יב] שאם יש שם ב' מוספין: יג] ימים לחם אשה: יד] תיבת כולה נמחק: טו] אינו טעון אלא: טז] תיבת ואיבריו נמחק: יז] דמים ומיני דמים: יח] מה"ד שהיא בא: יט] כשהוא מפריש: כ] למוספין וצריכי דמוספין: כא] וליקדם והתניא: כב] לדם העולה וליכא: כג] ליכא כדאמרי' בפ': כד] בעשיית הדם כתיב והשתא ותיבות דדם איירי ל"ש: כה] דאע"ג דהקטרה דמוספין כתיבי מקמי מלבד עולת: כו] למוסף שכתוב בו: כז] הקטרת דמוסף כדמשמע: כח] נינהו אלא ע"כ שם חטאת מרצה ה"נ שם אשם מרצה וי"ל: כט] דמה וא"ת תינח חטאת העוף עולת העוף מאי איכא למימר דהיא כולה כליל וא"כ למה יקדים מעשר מפני י"ל כיון כו':

א) נראה דר"ל דלא יהיב טעמא למילתיה אלא מה דבחטאת דמה ניתן על הקרנות וכו'.

עין משפט נר מצוה

ו א ב ג מיי' פ"ט מהל' תמידין ומוספין הל"ה:

ד מיי' שם הל"ה.

ח ה מיי' פ"א מהל' פסה"מ הל' לב:

ט ו מיי' שם הל' לג:

י ז מיי' פ"ב מהל' מעילה הלכה א:

מסורת הש"ס

[תוספתא פ"א דפרה]

נ"א משום דדם חטאת עלה וה"ה כו' נ"ק

[ברכות כח. וש"נ ועיין נדרים עב.]

[לקמן קד:]

מעילה ו: [מנחות מח:]

[ופי' תוס' לעיל כו. ד"ה דילמא]

דם חטאת קודם לדם עולה מפני שהוא מרצה. הא דלא קאמר טעמא משום שדמה ניתן על ד' קרנות כדקאמר גבי אשם משום דכיון דדם עולה אתי מכח כליל כדאמר בגמרא לא סגי בטעמא דארבע קרנות: **הכא** בחטאת הלוים עסקינן. והא דקאמר מפני שמרצה בחטאת דעלמא:

דם עולה ואימורי חטאת איזה מהן קודם. לא דמיא לבעיין דלעיל דמיירי במכפר וכליל גופייהו והכא איירי כד] באותו שבא מכח כליל ומכח מכפר: **דם** עולה ודם אשם איזה מהן קודם. דם אשם ואיברי דעולה דם אשם קודם דאשם מכפר כחטאת א"כ פשיטא ליה דאיברי עולה כה] קודמין לדם אשם מפני שהן כליל ולא דמי לאיברי עולה ודם חטאת דחשיב דם חטאת משום דהוי אד' קרנות: **אבל** עולה לא. דעל כרחין למעוטי עולה אתא דאי עולה קודמת לאשם ליתני עולה וכל שכן חטאת דהא דם חטאת קודם לדם עולה: **לימא** מסייע ליה בשר קדשים קלים כו'. תימה דלא מייתי סייעתא מברייתא דלעיל בפ' ב' (דף כו.) דקתני גבי קדשים קלים פרכסה ויצתה לחוץ וחזרה פסולה ואמרי' שלה ש"מ בשר קדשים קלים שיצא לפני זריקת דמים פסולה ומשני דילמא באליה ויותרת הכבד ושתי הכליות*:

והא דקא מפלגי בבשר להודיעך כחו דר"ל. הוה מצי לאיפלוגי באימורין להודיעך כח דהיתירא:

ואין

גמ' מנא הני מילי דת"ר א] *°ופר שני בן בקר תקח לחטאת ב] אם בא ללמד שהן שנים הרי כבר נאמר °ועשה את האחד חטאת ואת האחד עולה מה ת"ל ופר שני בן בקר תקח לחטאת שיכול ג] שיהא חטאת קודמת לכל מעשה עולה ת"ל ופר שני בן בקר תקח לחטאת אי פר שני יכול תהא עולה קודמת לחטאת לכל מעשיה ת"ל ועשה את האחד חטאת ואת האחד עולה הא כיצד דם חטאת קודמת לדם עולה מפני שמרצה: איברי עולה ד]כו' (א) ואמאי מתנה קמייתא דמכפרה תיקדום והנך לא ה] אמר רבינא הכא בחטאת הלוים עסקינן ואע"ג דכי עולה דמי קאמר רחמנא ו] היא תיקדים במערבא אמרי הואיל והתחיל במתנות גומר: איבעיא להו דם חטאת ואיברי עולה איזה מהן קודם דם חטאת קודם מפני שמרצה או דילמא איברי עולה קודמין מפני שהן כליל לאישים ת"ש דם חטאת קודם לדם עולה לדם עולה הוא דקדים לאיברי עולה לא קדים אדרבה מסיפא איברי עולה קודמין לאימורי חטאת לאימורי חטאת הוא דקדים לדם חטאת לא קדים אלא *מהא ליכא למשמע מינה: איבעיא להו דם עולה ואימורי חטאת איזה מהן קודם דם עולה קודם דקאתי מכח כליל או דילמא אימורי חטאת קודמין דקאתי מכח מכפר ת"ש דם חטאת קודם לדם עולה דם חטאת הוא דקדים לדם עולה אבל אימורי חטאת לא אדרבה מסיפא איברי עולה קודמין לאימורי חטאת איברי עולה הוא דקדמי לאימורי חטאת אבל דם עולה לא אלא מהא ליכא למשמע מינה: איבעיא להו דם עולה ודם אשם איזה מהן קודם דם עולה קודם דקאתי מכח כליל או דילמא דם אשם קודם ז] (דקאתי מכח) דמכפר ת"ש דם חטאת קודם לדם עולה אבל דם אשם לא בדין הוא דאיבעי למיתני דם אשם ואיידי דבעא למיתני סיפא איברי עולה קודמין לאימורי חטאת דאי תנא לאימורי אשם ה"א לאימורי אשם הוא דקדמי לאימורי חטאת לא קדמי מש"ה תנא חטאת ת"ש חטאת קודם לאשם חטאת הוא דקדמה ליה לאשם אבל עולה לא מאי לאו דם לא אאימורים דיקא נמי דקתני ח] מפני שדמה ניתן *ש"מ: חטאת קודמת כו': אדרבה אשם קדים שכן יש לו קיצבה אפ"ה ריבוי דמזבח עדיף: אשם קודם לתודה כו': אדרבה התודה ואיל נזיר קדמי שכן טעונין לחם אפ"ה קדשי קדשים עדיפי: תודה ואיל נזיר כו': אדרבה שלמים קדמי שכן ישנן בציבור כביחיד אפילו הכי נאכלין ליום אחד עדיפי איבעיא להו תודה ואיל נזיר איזה מהן קודם תודה קדמה שכן טעונה ד' מיני לחם או דילמא איל נזיר קודם שכן יש עמו דמים אחרים ת"ש זו ט] קודמת לזו שזו טעונה ד' מיני לחם וזו אינה טעונה אלא שני מיני לחם: השלמים קודמין לבכור כו': אדרבה בכור קודם שכן קדושתו מרחם ונאכל לכהנים אפ"ה מצות יתירות עדיפי: הבכור קודם כו': אדרבה מעשר קודם שכן מקדש לפניו ולאחריו אפ"ה קדושה מרחם עדיפא: מעשר קודם לעופות כו': אדרבה עופות קדמי שכן קדשי קדשים אפ"ה מין זבח עדיף אמר רבינא בר שילא אימורי קדשים קלים שיצאו לפני זריקת דמים פסולין ותנא תונא מפני שהוא זבח וישנו קדשי קדשים דמיו י] ואימורין בשלמא אימורין ליתנהו בעופות יא] אלא דם מיהא איתיה אלא לאו יב] קמ"ל אימורין כי דמו מה דמו לפני זריקה אף אימורין קודם זריקה וקא קרי להו קדשי קדשים ומה דמו מיפסל ביוצא אף אימורין מיפסל ביוצא נימא מסייע ליה בשר קדשים קלים שיצא לפני זריקת דמים רבי יוחנן אמר כשר ר"ל אמר פסול רבי יוחנן אמר כשר. יג] הואיל וסופו לצאת ר"ל אמר פסול *עדיין לא הגיע זמנו לצאת ע"כ לא פליגי אלא בבשר אבל באימורין לא הוא הדין דבאימורין נמי פליגי והא דקא מיפלגי בבשר יד] להודיעך כחו דר"ל דאפילו בבשר דסופה לצאת טו] אמר עדיין לא הגיע זמנו לצאת לימא כתנאי *אימורי קדשים קלים שיצאו לפני זריקת דמים ר"א אומר אין מועלין בהן ואין

גמ' מנהני מילי. דדם חטאת קודם לדם עולה ואיברי עולה קודמין לאימורי חטאת: ופר שני בן בקר. בחינוך הלוים כתיב בבהעלותך: טז] כבר נאמר. באותה פרשה ועשה את האחד חטאת רישיה דקרא והלוים יסמכו את ידיהם וגו': יכול תקדום חטאת לעולה לכל מעשיה. כדכתיב ועשה את האחד חטאת ואת האחד עולה: ופר שני. משמע שיהא שני לו: מתנה קמייתא. דחטאת מכפרה ושלמה כפרה בדידה כדאמרן בפרק ב"ש (לעיל דף לח.) וכפר אע"פ שלא יז] ניתן אלא אחת: דכי עולה דמיא. שלא הביאוה על חטא ואפ"ה יח] (חטאת) קודם לעולה *משום דדם חטאת יט] קודם לעולה וה"ה לג' מתנות שבחטאת (ב): אימורי חטאת לא מכפרי. שאין כפרה אלא בדם דם עולה לאו כליל הוא דאין כליל אלא באישים אבל מכח כליל קאתי שהאיברים יהיו כליל: ה"ג או דילמא דם אשם קדים דמכפר: לאימורי חטאת לא קדמי. דחטאת חמורה מאשם כדקתני מתני': שדמה ניתן. אלמא באימורין קאי דאי בדם קאי שהיא ניתנית מיבעי ליה: יש לו קיצבה. לדמיו דכתיב כ] (ויקרא ה) בכסף שקלים אבל חטאת כל (ג) דהו: שלמים ישנן בציבור. כבשי עצרת: דמים אחרים. חטאת ועולה באין עמו חובה: זו קודמת לזו. לעיל מיניה איירי בתודה ואיל נזיר: לפניו ולאחריו. דתנן קרא לתשיעי עשירי ולעשירי תשיעי ולאחד עשר עשירי שלשתן מקודשין וילפינן בבכורות (דף ס:) מקראי: שכן קדשי קדשים. אפילו אכילת אדם שבהן קדשי קדשים הוא: פסולין. ואע"ג דלענין מעילה לפני זריקת דמים לא קדישי לענין איפסולי ביוצא קדשי קדשים נינהו: ותנא תונא. ותנא תנא דידן סייעתא למילתא: אלא דם מיהא איתיה. ולא ה"ל למיתני אלא ואימוריו קדשי קדשים מה שאין כן בעופות אלא להכי נקט דמו בהדי אימוריו לאשמועינן דכי הדדי קדשי בשעה שזה קרוי קדשי קדשים קרוי גם זה קדשי קדשים: ומה דמו מיפסיל ביוצא אף אימוריו כא] מיפסלו ביוצא. דהא קדשי קדשים קרי להו: ה"ג בשר קדשים קלים שיצא לפני זריקת דמים חוץ לקלעים: הואיל וסופו לצאת. שהרי אכילתן בכל העיר: לא הגיע זמנו לצאת. דאכתי לא אישתרי כב] באכילה: ע"כ לא פליגי אלא בבשר. בההוא הוא דמכשר רבי יוחנן משום דסופו לצאת: הוא הדין דבאימורין. מכשר שזריקה עושה אותו קדשי קדשים והאי דפריש כג] משום דסופו לצאת הש"ס קמפרש ליה ולא מילתיה דרבי יוחנן היא: אין מועלין בהן. אפי' לאחר זריקה דלא מהניא בהו זריקה להכי למיקבעינהו במעילה:

ואין

שיטה מקובצת

א] דת"ר א) רבי אומר ופר: ב] לחטאת מה ת"ל אם ללמד: ג] שיכול שתהא חטאת: ד] עולה קודמין לאימורי חטאת מפני שהן כליל לאישים ואימא מתנה כו': ה] לא ניקדמו אמר: ו] רחמנא תיקדום תיבת היא נמחק: ז] קודם דקאתי מכח מכפר כך גירסת כל הספרים אבל רש"י גרים קדים דמכפר: ח] מפני שדמה ניתן ולא קתני מפני שהיא ניתנת פי' אלמא דבאימורים קאי כלומר דהקטרת אימורים קודמ' מפני שדמה ניתן דאי הוה קאי על מתנות הדם הוי ליה למימר מפני שהיא ניתנת דהוה משמע מתנותיה קודמת מפני שהיא ניתנת: ט] זו קודמה לזו: י] דמיו ואימוריו: יא] אלא דם מיהא איתיה פ"ה ולא הו"ל למיתני אלא כו' והקשה מורי לפי' דאע"ג דאיתא בעוף חשיב ליה שלא תאמר דם של עוף קדשי קדשים מה שאין כן במעשר להכי אמר דמו וה"ק משני דברים מקודש שהוא מין זבח ואימוריו קדשי קדשים וגם דמו קדשי קדשים כמו בעוף כדפי' במתניתין גבי על היסוד וי"ל דא"כ הוה ליה למתנייה לבסוף כמו במתני' השתא דתני ליה באמצע ע"כ צריך לומר דהוא כעין אותו שלפניו או שלאחריו וזה אינו יכול להיות א"כ ע"כ בא להשמיענו כדדייק תלמודא שאם אתה ר"ל כדפי' במתניתין גבי על היסוד לא היה לו להפסיק בין שני דברים הללו דליתנהו בעוף ולמיתני זה בנתיים דאיתנהו נמי בעוף ולא הוי ליה למתנייה [אלא] לבסוף כמו במתני' ואז הוה ניחא דלא הוי אלא גמר טעמא כדפי' במתניתין מדלא תני הכי ש"מ כדפי' ומייתי מורי ראיה דכה"ג איתא בסוף פ' איזהו מקומן דקאמר ואי בעית אימא כי התם ופ"ה דל"ג ליה ור"י פי' דיש ליישבו ואיבעית אימא כי התם כלומר מדלא קתני עד חצות לבסוף אלא תנא ליה באמצע ש"מ דהוי דאורייתא כמו לילה ומנויין וצלי דאיירי ביה לפניו ולאחריו והכא דליכא למימר הכי צריך לומר כדפי': יב] לאו הא קמ"ל דאימורין כו': יג] הואיל וסופו לצאת תימה דאמרינן בפ' התכלת אם משנשחטה יצא לחמה הלחם פסול ואמאי נימא כשר הואיל וסופו לצאת וי"ל דמיירי דיצא חוץ לחומת ירושלים: יד] להודיעך כחו דריש לקיש. וה"ה דמצי לאפלוגי באימורים להודיעך כחו דר"י ואע"ג דתלו טעמא בסופו לצאת תלמודא הוא דמפרש הכי מעיקרא והשתא הדר ביה אבל אינו מדברי ר"י: טו] לצאת אמר' עדיין: טז] מה"ד והלא כבר: יז] שלא נתן: יח] ואפ"ה כו' משום ותי' חטאת קודם לעולה ל"ש ונמחק: יט] עלה וה"ה ותי' קודם לעולה ל"ש ונמחק: כ] דכתיב ביה כסף שקלים: כא] אימוריו לפני זריקה מיפסל: כב] אישתרי בשר: כג] דפריש טעמא משום: כד] איירי באתו מכח ואות ו' ותיבת שבא נמחק: כה] עולה לא מבעיא ליה דהיינו בעיא דלעיל דם חטאת ואיברי עולה:

הגהות הב"ח

(א) גמ' כו' מפני שהן כליל ואימא מתנה קמייתא: (ב) רש"י ד"ה דכי עולה וכו' שבחטאת הס"ד ואח"כ מ"ה דקאתי מכח כליל אימורי חטאת: (ג) ד"ה יש לו וכו' כל דהו הס"ד ואח"כ מ"ה ישנן בצבור שלמים:

ולא קתני מפני שהיא ניתנה כצ"ל

גליון הש"ס

גמ' מהא ליכא למשמע מינה. תמוה לי דילמא שניהם שוים ויכול להקדים למי שירצה ואין הדיוקים סותרים אהדדי וצ"ע:

א) יב"ה כתו"כ בפ' ויקרא בפרשה דפר כהן משיח רבי אומר נגה ת"ל.

מא׳

GEMARA. [89b] How do we know these things?—Because our Rabbis taught: *And a second young bullock thou shalt take for a sin-offering:*[5] Now, if this comes to teach that there are two [sacrifices], surely it has already been said, *And offer thou the one for a sin-offering, and the other for a burnt-offering.*[6] What then is taught by, *And* a second *young bullock thou shalt take for a sin-offering?* For one might think that a sin-offering takes precedence over *all* the rites of a burnt-offering,[7] therefore it says, *And* a second *young bullock thou shalt take for a sin-offering.*[8] If [we had only the text] *And* a second *young bullock* [to go by], you might think that a burnt-offering precedes a sin-offering in all its rites: therefore it says, *And offer thou the one for a sin-offering, and the other for a burnt-offering.* How are these [to be reconciled]? The blood of a sin-offering takes precedence over the blood of a burnt-offering [in sprinkling], because it propitiates.[9]

THE LIMBS OF A BURNT-OFFERING etc. Yet why so? say that [only] the first application [of the blood of the sin-offering], which a makes atonement, takes precedence, but not the rest?[1]—Said Rabina: Here we are treating of the Levites' sin-offering, and though it was like a burnt-offering,[2] the Divine Law ordered it to take precedence.[3] In the West [Palestine] they said: Since he commenced the applications [of the sin-offering], he completes [them].

It was asked: Regarding the blood of a sin-offering and the limbs of a burnt-offering, which of them takes precedence? Does the blood of a sin-offering take precedence, because it propitiates; or perhaps the limbs of a burnt-offering take precedence, because they are entirely [destined] for [altar] fires?—Come and hear: THE BLOOD OF A SIN-OFFERING PRECEDES THE BLOOD OF A BURNT-OFFERING; thus only the *blood* of a burnt-offering does it precede, but it does not precede the *limbs* of a burnt-offering. On the contrary, [infer] from the subsequent clause: THE LIMBS OF A BURNT-OFFERING PRECEDE THE EMURIM OF A SIN-OFFERING: thus only the *emurim* of a sin-offering do they precede, but they do not precede the *blood* of a sin-offering. Rather, no inference can be made from this

It was asked: [As to] the blood of a burnt-offering and the *emurim* of a sin-offering, which of these takes precedence? Does the blood of a burnt-offering take precedence, because it comes in virtue of a sacrifice that is altogether burnt; or perhaps the *emurim* of a sin-offering take precedence, because they come in virtue of an atoning [sacrifice]?—Come and hear: THE BLOOD OF A SIN-OFFERING PRECEDES THE BLOOD OF A BURNT-OFFERING; thus, only the *blood* of a sin-offering precedes the blood of a burnt-offering, but the *emurim* of a sin-offering do not. On the contrary, [infer] from the subsequent clause: THE LIMBS OF A BURNT-OFFERING PRECEDE THE EMURIM OF A SIN-OFFERING: thus, only the *limbs* of a burnt-offering precede the *emurim* of a sin-offering, but the *blood* of a burnt-offering does not. Rather, no inference can be made from this.

It was asked: [As to] the blood of a burnt-offering and the blood of a guilt-offering, which takes precedence? Does the blood of a burnt-offering precede, because it comes in virtue of a sacrifice that is altogether burnt; or perhaps the blood of a guilt-offering precedes, because it makes atonement?—Come and hear: THE BLOOD OF A SIN-OFFERING PRECEDES THE BLOOD OF A BURNT-OFFERING; hence the blood of a guilt-offering does not. [No:] by right he [the Tanna] should have taught the blood of a guilt-offering [too], but because he wishes to teach in a later clause: THE LIMBS OF A BURNT-OFFERING PRECEDE THE EMURIM OF A SIN-OFFERING; for if he taught [that they precede] the *emurim* of a guilt-offering, I would argue: only the *emurim* of a guilt-offering do they precede, but they do not precede the *emurim* of a sin-

(5) Num. VIII, 8. This treats of the consecration of the Levites. (6) Ibid. 12. He speaks of it as 'already said' although it comes later. (7) As is implied in v. 13, where sin-offering is mentioned first. (8) Which intimates that it is second to the burnt-offering in the performance of its rites. (9) Whilst the limbs of the burnt-offering are burnt before the *emurim* of a sin-offering.

a (1) For atonement is made with a single application, *supra* 38a. (2) Since it was not on account of sin at all. (3) Hence its precedence does not cease when atonement has been made, since here there was no atonement.

◁ *For the continuation of the English translation of this page see overleaf*

ו א ב ג מיי' פ"ט מהל' המידין ומוספין הל"ה:

ד מיי' שם הל"ה.

ה ה מיי' פ"א מהל' פסה"מ הל' לג:

ט ו מיי' שם הל' לג:

י ז מיי' פ"ב מהל' מעילה הלכה א:

[ופ' היטב תוס' לעיל כו. ד"ה דילמא]

[תוספתא פ"א דפרה]

כ"א משום דשם חטאת עלה וה"ס כו' נ"ק

[ברכות כב. וש"נ ועיין נדרים עב.]

[לקמן קד:]

מעילה ו: [מנחות מח:]

גמ' מנא הני מילי דת"ר א] *ופר שני בן בקר תקח לחטאת ב] אם בא ללמד שהן שנים הרי כבר נאמר °ועשה את האחד חטאת ואת האחד עולה מה ת"ל ופר שני בן בקר תקח לחטאת שיכול ג] שיהא חטאת קודמת לכל מעשה עולה ת"ל ופר שני בן בקר תקח לחטאת אי פר שני יכול תהא עולה קודמת לחטאת לכל מעשיה ת"ל ועשה את האחד חטאת ואת האחד עולה הא כיצד דם חטאת קודמת לדם עולה מפני שמרצה: איברי עולה ד] כו' (א) ואמאי מתנה קמייתא דמכפרה תיקדום והנך לא ה] אמר רבינא הכא בחטאת הלוים עסקינן ואע"ג דכי עולה דמי קאמר רחמנא ו] היא תיקדים במערבא אמרי הואיל והתחיל במתנות גומר: איבעיא להו דם חטאת ואיברי עולה איזה מהן קודם דם חטאת קודם מפני שמרצה או דילמא איברי עולה קודמין מפני שהן כליל לאישים ת"ש דם חטאת קודם לדם עולה לדם עולה הוא דקדים לאיברי עולה לא קדים אדרבה מסיפא איברי עולה קודמין לאימורי חטאת לאימורי חטאת הוא דקדים לדם חטאת לא קדים אלא *מהא ליכא למשמע מינה: איבעיא להו דם עולה ואימורי חטאת איזה מהן קודם דם עולה קודם דקאתי מכח כליל או דילמא אימורי חטאת קודמין דקאתי מכח מכפר ת"ש דם חטאת קודם לדם עולה דם חטאת הוא דקדים לדם עולה אבל אימורי חטאת לא אדרבה מסיפא איברי עולה קודמין לאימורי חטאת איברי עולה הוא דקדמי לאימורי חטאת אבל דם עולה לא אלא מהא ליכא למשמע מינה: איבעיא להו דם עולה ודם אשם איזה מהן קודם דם עולה קודם דקאתי מכח כליל או דילמא דם אשם קודם ז] (דקאתי מכח) דמכפר ת"ש דם חטאת קודם לדם עולה אבל דם אשם לא בדין הוא דאיבעי למיתני דם אשם ואיידי דבעא למיתני סיפא איברי עולה קודמין לאימורי חטאת דאי תנא לאימורי אשם ה"א לאימורי אשם הוא דקדמי לאימורי חטאת לא קדמי מש"ה תנא חטאת ת"ש חטאת קודם לאשם חטאת הוא דקדמה ליה לאשם אבל עולה לא מאי לאו דם לא אאימורים דיקא נמי דקתני ח] מפני שדמה ניתן *ש"מ: חטאת קודמת כו': אדרבה אשם קדים שכן יש לו קיצבה אפ"ה ריבוי דמזבח עדיף: אשם קודם לתודה כו': אדרבה התודה ואיל נזיר קדמי שכן טעונין לחם אפ"ה קדשי קדשים עדיפי: תודה ואיל נזיר כו': אדרבה שלמים קדמי שכן ישנן בציבור כביחיד אפילו הכי נאכלין ליום אחד עדיפי איבעיא להו תודה ואיל נזיר איזה מהן קודם תודה קדמה שכן טעונה ד' מיני לחם או דילמא איל נזיר קודם שכן יש עמו דמים אחרים ת"ש ˚זו ט] קודמת לזו שזו טעונה ד' מיני לחם וזו אינה טעונה אלא שני מיני לחם: השלמים קודמין לבכור כו': אדרבה בכור קודם שכן קדושתו מרחם ונאכל לכהנים אפ"ה מצות יתירות עדיפי: הבכור קודם כו': אדרבה מעשר קודם שכן מקדש לפניו ולאחריו אפ"ה קדושה מרחם עדיפא: מעשר קודם לעופות כו': אדרבה עופות קדמי שכן קדשי קדשים אפ"ה מין זבח עדיף אמר רבינא בר שילא אימורי קדשים קלים שיצאו לפני זריקת דמים פסולין ותנא תונא מפני שהוא זבח וישנו קדשי קדשים דמיו י] ואימורין בשלמא אימורין ליתנהו בעופות יא] אלא דם מיהא איתיה אלא לאו יב] קמ"ל אימורין כי דמו מה דמו לפני זריקה אף אימורין קודם זריקה וקא קרי להו קדשי קדשים ומה דמו מיפסל ביוצא אף אימורין מיפסל ביוצא נימא מסייע ליה בשר קדשים קלים שיצא לפני זריקת דמים רבי יוחנן אמר ˚כשר ר"ל אמר פסול רבי יוחנן אמר כשר. יג] הואיל וסופו לצאת ר"ל אמר פסול *עדיין לא הגיע זמנו לצאת ע"כ לא פליגי אלא בבשר אבל באימורין לא ˚הוא הדין דבאימורין נמי פליגי והא דקא מיפלגי בבשר יד] להודיעך כחו דר"ל דאפילו בשר דסופה לצאת טו] אמר עדיין לא הגיע זמנו לצאת לימא כתנאי *אימורי קדשים קלים שיצאו לפני זריקת דמים ר"א אומר ˚אין מועלין בהן ואין

גמ' מנהני מילי. דדם חטאת קודם לדם עולה ואיברי עולה קודמין לאימורי חטאת: ופר שני בן בקר. בחינוך הלוים כתיב בבהעלותך: טז] כבר נאמר. באותה פרשה ועשה את האחד חטאת רישיה דקרא והלוים יסמכו את ידיהם וגו': יכול תקדום חטאת לעולה לכל מעשיה. כדכתיב ועשה את האחד חטאת ואת האחד עולה: ופר שני. משמע שיהא שני לו: מתנה קמייתא. דחטאת מכפרה ושלמה כפרה בדידה כדאמרן בפרק ב"ש (לעיל דף לח.) וכפר אע"פ שלא יז] ניתן אלא אחת: דכי עולה דמיא. שלא הביאוה על חטא ואפ"ה יח] (חטאת) קודם לעולה *משום דשם חטאת יט] קודם לעולה וה"ה לג' מתנות שבחטאת (ב): אימורי חטאת לא מכפרי. שאין כפרה אלא בדם דם עולה נמי כליל הוא דאין כליל אלא באישים אבל מכח כליל קאתי שהאיברים יהיו כליל: ה"ג או דילמא דם אשם קדים דמכפר: לאימורי חטאת לא קדמי. דחטאת חמורה מאשם כדקתני מתני': שדמה ניתן. אלמא באימורין קאי דאי בדם קאי שהיא ניתנית מיבעי ליה: יש לו קיצבה. לדמיו דכתיב כ] (ויקרא ה) בכסף שקלים אבל חטאת כל (ג) דהו: שלמים ישנן בציבור. כבשי עצרת: דמים אחרים. חטאת ועולה באין עמו חובה: זו קודמת לזו. לעיל מיניה איירי בתודה ואיל נזיר: לפניו ולאחריו. דתנן קרא לתשיעי עשירי ולעשירי תשיעי ולאחד עשר עשירי שלשתן מקודשין וילפינן בבכורות (דף ס:) מקראי: שכן קדשי קדשים. אפילו אכילת אדם שבהן קדשי קדשים הוא: פסולין. ואע"ג דלענין מעילה לפני זריקת דמים לא קדישי לענין איפסולי ביוצא קדשי קדשים נינהו: ותנא תונא. ותנא תנא דידן סייעתא למילתא: אלא דם מיהא איתיה. ולא ה"ל למיתני אלא ואימוריו קדשי קדשים מה שאין כן בעופות אלא להכי נקט דמו בהדי אימוריו לאשמועינן דכי הדדי קדשי בשעה שזה קרוי קדשי קדשים קרוי גם זה קדשי קדשים: ומה דמו מיפסיל ביוצא אף אימוריו כא] מיפסלו ביוצא. דהא קדשי קדשים קרי להו: ה"ג בשר קדשים קלים שיצא לפני זריקת דמים חוץ לקלעים: הואיל וסופו לצאת. שהרי אכילתן בכל העיר: לא הגיע זמנו לצאת. דאכתי לא אישתרי כב] באכילה: ע"כ לא פליגי אלא בבשר. בההוא הוא דמכשר רבי יוחנן משום דסופו לצאת: הוא הדין דבאימורין. מכשר שזריקה עושה אותו קדשי קדשים והאי דפריש כג] משום דסופו לצאת הש"ס קמפרש ליה ולא מילתיה דרבי יוחנן היא: אין מועלין בהן. אפי' לאחר זריקה דלא מהניא בהו זריקה להכי למיקבעינהו במעילה:

ואין

דם חטאת קודם לדם עולה מפני שהוא מרצה. הא דלא קאמר טעמא משום שדמה ניתן על ד' קרנות כדקאמר גבי אשם משום דכיון דדם עולה אתי מכח כליל כדאמר בגמרא לא סגי בטעמא דארבע קרנות: הכא בחטאת הלוים עסקינן. והא דקאמר מפני שמרצה בחטאת דעלמא: דם עולה ואימורי חטאת איזה מהן קודם. לא דמיא לבעיין דלעיל דמיירי במכפר וכליל גופייהו והכא איירי כד] באותו שבא מכח כליל ומכח מכפר: דם עולה ודם אשם איזה מהן קודם. דם אשם ואיברי דעולה דם אשם קודם דאשם מכפר כחטאת א"כ פשיטא ליה דאיברי עולה כה] קודמין לדם אשם מפני שהן כליל ולא דמי לאיברי עולה ודם חטאת דחשיב דם חטאת משום דהוי אד' קרנות: אבל עולה לא. דעל כרחין למעוטי עולה אתא דאי עולה קודמת לאשם ליתני עולה וכל שכן חטאת דהא דם חטאת קודם לדם עולה: לימא מסייע ליה בשר קדשים קלים כו'. תימה דלא מייתי סייעתא מברייתא דלעיל בפ' ב' (דף כו.) דקתני גבי קדשים קלים פרכסה וילתה לחוץ וחזרה פסולה ואמרי' עלה ש"מ בשר קדשים קלים שילא לפני זריקת דמים פסולה ומשני דילמא באליה ויותרת הכבד ושתי הכליות*: והא דקא מיפלגי בבשר להודיעך כחו דר"ל. הוה מצי לאיפלוגי באימורין להודיעך כח דהיתירא:

ואין

הגהות הב"ח

(א) גמ' כו' מפני שהן כליל ואימא מתנה קמייתא: (ב) רש"י ד"ה דכי עולה וכו' שבחטאת הס"ד ואח"כ מ"ה דקאתי מכח כליל אימורי חטאת: (ג) ד"ה יש לו וכו' כל דהו הס"ד ואח"כ מ"ה ישנן בצבור שלמים:

ולא קתני מפני שהיא ניתנה כצ"ל

גליון הש"ס

גמ' מהא ליכא למשמע מינה. תמוה לי דילמא שניהם שוים ויכול להקדים למי שירצה ואין הדיוקים סותרים אהדדי וצ"ע:

שיטה מקובצת

א] דת"ר א) רבי אומר ופר: ב] לחטאת מה ת"ל אם ללמד: ג] שיכול שתהא חטאת: ד] עולה קודמין לאימורי חטאת מפני שהן כליל לאישים ואימא מתנה כו': ה] לא ניקדמו אמר: ו] רחמנא תיקדום תיבת היא נמחק: ז] קודם דקאתי מכח מכפר כך גירסת כל הספרים אבל רש"י גרים קדים דמכפר: ח] מפני שדמה ניתן ולא קתני מפני שהיא ניתנת פי' אלמא דבאימורים קאי כלומר דהקטרת אימורים קודמ' מפני שדמה ניתן דאי הוה קאי על מתנות הדם הוי ליה למימר מפני שהיא ניתנת דהוה משמע מתנותיה קודמת מפני שהיא ניתנת: ט] זו קודמה לזו: י] דמיו ואימוריו: יא] אלא דם מיהא איתיה פ"ה ולא הו"ל למיתני אלא כו' והקשה מורי לפי' דאע"ג דאיתא בעוף חשיב ליה שלא תאמר דם של עוף קדשי קדשים מה שאין כן במעשר להכי אמר דמו וה"ק משני דברים מקודש שהוא מין זבח ואימוריו קדשי קדשים וגם דמו קדשי קדשים כמו בעוף כדפי' במתניתין גבי על היסוד וי"ל דא"כ הוה ליה למתנייה לבסוף כמו במתני' השתא דתני ליה באמצע ע"כ צריך לומר דהוא כעין אותו שלפניו או מלאחריו וזה אינו יכול להיות א"כ ע"כ בא להשמיענו כדדייק תלמודא שאם אתה ר"ל כדפי' במתניתין גבי על היסוד לא היה לו להפסיק בין שני דברים הללו דליתנהו בעוף ולמיתני זה בנתיים דאיתנהו נמי בעוף ולא הוי ליה למתנייה [אלא] לבסוף כמו במתני' ואז הוה ניחא דלא הוי אלא גמר טעמא כדפי' במתניתין מדלא תני הכי ש"מ כדפי' ומייתי מורי ראיה דכה"ג איתא בסוף פ' איזהו מקומן דקאמר ואי בעית אימא כי התם ופ"ה דל"ג ליה ור"י פי' דיש ליישבו ואיבעית אימא כי התם כלומר מדלא קתני עד חצות לבסוף אלא תנא ליה באמצע ש"מ דהוי דאורייתא כמו לילה ומינריו וצלי דאיירי ביה לפניו ולאחריו והכא דליכא למימר הכי צריך לומר כדפי': יב] לאו הא קמ"ל דאימורין כי: יג] הואיל וסופו לצאת תימה דאמרינן בפ' התכלת אם משנשחטה יצא לחמה הלחם פסול ואמאי נימא כשר הואיל וסופו לצאת וי"ל דמיירי דיצא חוץ לחומת ירושלים: יד] להודיעך כחו דריש לקיש. וה"ה דמצי לאפלוגי באימורים להודיעך כחו דר"י ואע"ג דתלו טעמא בסופו לצאת תלמודא הוא דמפרש הכי מעיקרא והשתא הדר ביה אבל אינו מדברי ר"י: טו] לצאת אמר' עדיין: טז] מה"ד והלא כבר: יז] שלא נתן: יח] ואפ"ה כו' משום ותי' חטאת קודם לעולה ל"ש ונמחק: יט] עלה וה"ה ותי' קודם לעולה ל"ש ונמחק: כ] דכתיב ביה כסף שקלים: כא] אימוריו לפני זריקה מיפסל: כב] אישתרי בשר: כג] דפריש טעמא משום: כד] איירי באתו מכח ואות ו' ותיבת שבא נמחק: כה] עולה לא מבעיא ליה דהיינו בעיא דלעיל דם חטאת ואיברי עולה:

מא׳

א) יכ"ה בתו"כ פ' ויקרא בפרשה דפר כהן משיח רבי אומר נגה ת"ל.

Continuation of translation from previous page as indicated by ◁

b offering;[1] for that reason he teaches about a sin-offering [only].

Come and hear: A SIN-OFFERING PRECEDES A GUILT-OFFERING; thus, only a sin-offering precedes a guilt-offering, but a burnt-offering does not. Surely that refers to the blood?—No: it refers to the *emurim*. This may be proved too, for he teaches. BECAUSE ITS BLOOD IS APPLIED, [and does not teach, Because *it* is applied].[2] This proves it.

A SIN-OFFERING PRECEDES etc. On the contrary, a guilt-offering should precede, because it has a fixed value?[3]—Even so, the greater number of altar [rites] is more important.

A GUILT-OFFERING PRECEDES A THANKSOFFERING etc. On the contrary, a thanksoffering and a nazirite's ram should take precedence, since they require loaves?—Even so, sacrifices of higher sanctity are more important.

A THANKSOFFERING AND A NAZIRITE'S RAM etc. On the contrary, a peace-offering should take precedence, since it is congregational as well as private?[4]—Even so, [the fact that] they are eaten for one day only is more weighty.

It was asked: [As to] a thanksoffering and a nazirite's ram, which of these takes precedence? Does a thanksoffering take precedence, c because it requires [the accompaniment of] four kinds of loaves;[1] or perhaps a nazirite's ram takes precedence, because other sacrifices[2] accompany it?[3]—Come and hear: This one precedes the other,[4] because the former requires four kinds of loaves, whereas the latter requires only two kinds of loaves.[5]

A PEACE-OFFERING PRECEDES A FIRSTLING etc. On the contrary, a firstling should take precedence, since its sanctity is from the womb and it is eaten by priests [only]?—Even so, the greater number of rites [connected with a peace-offering] are more important.

A FIRSTLING PRECEDES etc. On the contrary, tithe should take precedence, since it sanctifies what precedes it and what follows it?[6]—Even so, sanctity from the womb is weightier.

TITHE PRECEDES BIRD-OFFERINGS etc. On the contrary, bird-offerings should take precedence, since they are most sacred?—Even so, the species of slaughtering is more important.

Rabina b. Shila said: If the *emurim* of lesser sacrifices are taken out[7] before the sprinkling of the blood, they are disqualified. Now, our Tanna supports this: BECAUSE IT IS A SLAUGHTERED SACRIFICE, AND PART OF IT IS MOST SACRED, [VIZ.,] ITS BLOOD AND EMURIM. As for *emurim*, it is well, [as] these are absent in birds; but blood at all events is present?[8] Surely then he informs us this: *emurim* are like blood: just as blood [is most holy] before sprinkling, so are *emurim* [most holy only] before sprinkling, and [only then] are they designated most sacred; and as blood is disqualified through being taken out, so are *emurim* disqualified through going out. Shall we say that the following supports him: If the flesh of lesser sacrifices was taken out before the sprinkling of the blood, R. Joḥanan says: It is fit; Resh Laḳish maintains: It is disqualified. R. Joḥanan says [that] it is fit, since it must eventually d be carried out [in any case].[1] Resh Laḳish maintains [that] it is disqualified: it was not yet time for it to be carried out. Thus, they disagree only in respect of flesh, but not in respect of *emurim*![2]—[No:] in fact they disagree in respect of *emurim* too, but the reason that they disagree [explicitly] about flesh is to inform you how far Resh Laḳish maintains his view,[3] that even flesh, which will eventually be carried out, he maintains that it was not yet time for it to be carried out.

Shall we say that it is dependent on Tannaim: [With regard to] *emurim* of lesser sacrifices which were taken out before sprinkling:

b (1) Since a sin-offering is more sacred than a guilt-offering. (2) If by SIN-OFFERING he meant the *blood*, he should say, because *it* is applied.—Emended text. (3) Not less than two *shekels*; v. Lev. V, 15: *a ram . . . according to thy valuation in silver by shekels . . . for a guilt-offering*. Shekels implies at least two, whereas a sin-offering may be of any value. (4) Congregational (public) peace-offerings were offered on the Feast of Weeks, v. Lev. XXIII, 19, whereas these others were private sacrifices only.

c (1) V. Lev. VII, 12*f*. (2) Lit., 'blood'. (3) *Sc.* a sin-offering and a burnt-offering. (4) *Sc.* the thanksoffering precedes the nazirite's ram. (5) V. Num. VI, 15. (6) If a man counts his cattle in order to tithe them, and declares the ninth and eleventh each as the tenth, in addition to the real tenth, they are all sanctified. (7) Of the Temple court. (8) Hence blood should not be mentioned, since in this respect birds are the same.

d (1) As it is eaten anywhere in Jerusalem. (2) Presumably R. Joḥanan too agrees that these are disqualified. (3) Lit., 'to inform you the strength of Resh Laḳish'.

R. Eliezer maintains: They do not involve trespass,[4] [90a] and one is not culpable on their account in respect of *piggul*,[5] *nothar*,[6] or uncleanness.[7] R. Akiba maintains: They involve trespass, and one is culpable on their account for *piggul*, *nothar*, and defilement. Surely they disagree where they were taken in again,[8] and they disagree in this: one master [R. Eliezer] holds that they were disqualified by having been taken out, while another master holds that they were not disqualified by being taken out?—Said R. Papa:
a If they were taken in again, none disagree;[1] but here they disagree where they are still without,[2] and they disagree in this: one master holds [that] sprinkling is not effective for what is without,[3] while the other master holds [that] sprinkling is effective for what went out. But surely it was R. Papa who said:[4] If they are still without, none disagree;[5] they disagree only where they were taken in again?—That is only in connection with the Two Loaves, which are not part of the sacrifice itself; but since *emurim* are part of the sacrifice itself, they disagree where they are still without.

BIRD-OFFERINGS PRECEDE etc. On the contrary, meal-offerings should take precedence, since they are both congregational and private?[6]—Even so, the fact that they are blood sacrifices outweighs this.

A SINNER'S MEAL-OFFERING etc. On the contrary, a votive meal-offering should take precedence, since it requires oil and frankincense?—Even so, a sinner's meal-offering, which is brought on account of sin, is more important, since it makes atonement.

It was asked: [As to] the meal-offering of a *soṭah*[7] and a votive meal-offering, which of these takes precedence? Does a votive meal-offering take precedence, because it requires oil and frankincense; or perhaps a *soṭah's* meal-offering takes precedence, because it is brought to investigate sin?—Come and hear: A SINNER'S MEAL-OFFERING PRECEDES A VOTIVE MEAL-OFFERING: thus, only a sinner's meal-offering precedes a votive meal-offering, but a *soṭah's* meal-offering does not!—[No:] does he then teach, because it makes atonement; [surely] he teaches, BECAUSE IT COMES ON ACCOUNT OF SIN, and this one [a *soṭah's* meal-offering] too comes on account of sin.

Come and hear: This one precedes that one, because the former
b is of[1] wheat, while the latter is of barley.[2] Surely that means, a votive meal-offering [precedes] a *soṭah's* meal-offering?—No: [it means that] a sinner's meal-offering [precedes] a *soṭah's* meal-offering. Then infer it from the fact that the former makes atonement while the latter does not make atonement?[3]—What then: [it refers to] a votive meal-offering? Then infer it from the fact that the one [a votive meal-offering] requires oil and frankincense, while the other does not require oil and frankincense? Rather, he states one of two reasons.[4]

A SIN-OFFERING OF A BIRD PRECEDES etc. Whence do we know it?—For our Rabbis taught: *And he shall offer that which is for the sin-offering first*:[5] for what purpose is this stated? If to teach that it comes before the burnt-offering, surely it is already said, *And he shall prepare the second for a burnt-offering*?[6] This, however, furnishes a general rule for *all* sin-offerings, that they take precedence over all burnt-offerings which accompany them, [*sc.*] the bird sin-offering [precedes] the bird burnt-offering, the animal sin-offering [precedes] the animal burnt-offering, and even a bird sin-offering [precedes] an animal burnt-offering.[7] Therefore, [that] a bird sin-offering [precedes] a bird burnt-offering [is inferred from], *And he shall prepare the second for a burnt-offering*. An animal sin-offering [precedes] an animal burnt-offering, because the Divine Law intimated an extension;[8] a bird sin-offering [precedes] an animal burnt-offering, because this is a general rule.[9]

Come and hear: R. Eliezer said: Wherever a sin-offering is exchanged, the sin-offering [of a bird] takes precedence,[10] but
c here[1] the burnt-offering [of a bird] takes precedence.[2] Wherever it comes on account of sin, the sin-offering takes precedence; but here the burnt-offering takes precedence.[3] Wherever both [birds] come instead of one sin-offering, the sin-offering takes precedence; but here that they do not both come on account of one sin-offering,[4] the burnt-offering takes precedence?[5]—Said Raba: Scripture accorded it precedence in respect of designating it.[6]

Come and hear: Bullocks take precedence over rams, rams

(4) V. *supra* 85*b* n. 8.—This is even *after* sprinkling, because sprinkling is now of no avail to make them subject to trespass. (5) Because they are as though blood had not been sprinkled for them, and so all their *mattirin* (q.v. Glos. and *supra* 29*b*, 43*a*) had not been presented. (6) Because *nothar* applies only to what may be eaten within the prescribed period; this, however, may not. (7) I.e., if an unclean person eats them, he is not liable. For only what is permitted to clean persons involves liability on account of personal defilement, but what is not so permitted does not involve liability. Now *emurim* (which are burnt on the altar, and so not permitted even to clean persons) are nevertheless included, as is deduced by Scriptural exegesis, but only on a similar basis to flesh: as flesh involves culpability only *after* sprinkling, so the *emurim*. *Sprinkling*, however, is ineffective in respect of these *emurim*, and therefore they do not involve culpability. (8) Before sprinkling, yet even then R. Eliezer maintains that sprinkling is of no avail, because taking them out had disqualified them.
a (1) Sprinkling is certainly effective. (2) At the time of sprinkling. (3) Lit., 'for what went out'—and is still outside. (4) In connection with the two loaves which were brought on Pentecost, if they were taken out of the Temple court between the slaughtering of the accompanying sacrifice and the sprinkling of its blood. (5) Sprinkling is certainly of no avail. (6) *Sc.* the meal-offerings which accompanied the *'omer* (sheaf of corn) and the Two Loaves; these were congregational (v. Lev. XXIII, 10-21). There were no public offerings of birds. (7) A wife suspected of adultery, v. Num. V, 12-15.

b (1) Lit., 'comes from'. (2) Wheat is superior to barley. (3) Instead of because one is of wheat while the other is of barley. (4) This answer must be given whatever you relate it to, and therefore it may well refer to a votive meal-offering and a sinner's meal-offering. (5) Lev. V, 8. (6) Ibid. 10. (7) E.g. a woman after childbirth, who brings a year-old lamb for a burnt-offering, and a pigeon or a turtle-dove for a sin-offering. (8) By the additional text. (9) I.e., the law thus established applies to *all* sin-offerings and burnt-offerings. (10) Where an animal sin-offering is prescribed in the first place, but Scripture permits it, when one is poor, to be exchanged for two birds of which one is for a sin-offering and one for a burnt-offering (e.g. when an unclean person enters the sanctuary, v. Lev. V, 1 *seq.*), the bird sin-offering takes precedence over the bird burnt-offering.
c (1) In the case of a woman after childbirth to whom 'here' refers in the whole passage. (2) Because she is liable to an animal *burnt-offering*, and in poverty she may bring two birds, one for a burnt-offering and another for a sin-offering, v. Lev. XII, 1 *seq.* (3) As even the sin-offering is not on account of sin. (4) In poverty she substitutes a bird burnt-offering for an animal burnt-offering, as a bird sin-offering was brought in any case, v. ibid. 6-8. (5) This contradicts the Mishnah which teaches that a bird sin-offering takes precedence over an animal burnt-offering, whereas here she brings the animal burnt-offering before the bird sin-offering. (6) One must first designate (i.e. dedicate) the animal (or bird) for the burnt-offering, and then the bird for the sin-offering. But the latter is sacrificed first.

תורה אור

ואין חייבין עליהן משום פיגול נותר וטמא ר"ע אומר מועלין בהן [א]וחייבין עליהן משום פיגול נותר וטמא א] מאי לאו בדהדר עיילינהו פליגי ובהא פליגי דמר סבר מיפסלי ביוצא ומר סבר לא מיפסלי ביוצא אמר רב פפא בדהדר עיילינהו כ"ע לא פליגי [ב]והכא בדאיתנהו אבראי פליגי ובהא פליגי דמר סבר *אין זריקה מועלת ליוצא ומר סבר זריקה מועלת ליוצא והא *רב פפא הוא דאמר בדאיתנהו אבראי כ"ע לא פליגי בדעיילינהו לגוואי פליגי ה"מ גבי [ג]שתי לחם דלאו גופיה דזיבחא ב] אבל אימורין דגופיה דזיבחא הוא בדאיתנהו אבראי פליגי: עופות קודמין כו': אדרבה מנחות קודמות שכן ישנן בצבור כביחיד אפ"ה מיני דמים עדיפי: מנחת חוטא כו': אדרבה מנחת נדבה קודמת שכן טעונה שמן ולבונה אפ"ה ג] מנחת חוטא הבאה על חטא עדיפא דמכפרת איבעיא להו [ד]מנחת סוטה ומנחת נדבה איזו מהן קודמת מנחת נדבה קדמה שכן טעונה שמן ד] (או) ולבונה או דלמא מנחת סוטה קדמה שכן באה לברר עון ת"ש מנחת חוטא קודמת למנחת נדבה מנחת חוטא הוא דקדמה למנחת נדבה הא מנחת סוטה לא מי קתני מפני שהיא מכפרת מפני שהיא באה על חטא קתני והא נמי באה על חטא ת"ש זו קודמת לזו שזו באה מן החיטין וזו באה מן השעורין מאי לאו מנחת נדבה למנחת סוטה לא מנחת חוטא למנחת סוטה תיפוק לי דהא מכפרת והא לא מכפרת ואלא מאי מנחת נדבה תיפוק לי דזו טעונה שמן ולבונה וזו אינה טעונה שמן ולבונה אלא *[ה]חד מתרי טעמי ה] [נקיט]: חטאת העוף קודמת כו': מנא ה"מ דת"ר *°והקריב את אשר לחטאת ראשונה מה ת"ל ו] שאין ת"ל ללמד שתקרב ראשונה הרי כבר נאמר °ואת השני יעשה עולה אלא זה בנה אב לכל חטאות שיקדמו ז] לעולה הבאות עמהן בין חטאת העוף לעולת העוף בין חטאת בהמה לעולת בהמה ואפי' חטאת העוף לעולת בהמה הלכך חטאת העוף לעולת העוף מואת השני חטאת בהמה לעולת בהמה מדרבי ח] רחמנא חטאת העוף לעולת בהמה מזה בנה אב תא שמע ר"א אומר כל מקום שנתחלפה חטאת חטאת קודמת וכאן ט] (ביולדת) עולה קודמת י] כל מקום שבא על חטא חטאת קודמת וכאן עולה קודמת יא] וכל מקום ששנים באים *תחת חטאת חטאת קודמת *וכאן עולה קודמת *) אמר רבא למקראה הקדימה הכתוב: תא שמע פרים [ו]קודמין לאילים ואילים קודמין לכבשים כבשים לשעירים מאי

ויקר' ה
שם

*) ערכין כח.

ואין חייבין עליהן משום פיגול. יב] דהוי להו כמי שלא נזרק עליהן הדם ולא קרבו כל מתיריהן: ומשום נותר. דאין נותר אלא *בבשר יג] באכילה בתוך זמנו כדכתיב (ויקרא יז) ביום זבחכם יאכל וממחרת וגו': ומשום טומאת הגוף. כדאמרי' במנחות (דף כה:) הניתר לטהורין חייבין עליו משום טומאה שאין ניתר לטהורין אין חייבין עליו משום טומאה ואימורין דאיתרבו לטומאה מאשר לה' דומיא דבשר איתרבו דלאחר זריקה הוא דמחייב עלייהו ולא לפני זריקה והני לא אהניא להו זריקה: מאי לאו יד] בהדר עיילינהו. דהוו לגואי בשעת זריקה פליגי ואפי' הכי קאמר ר"א דלא אהניא להו זריקה משום דאיפסילו ביוצא: בדאיתנהו אבראי. בשעת זריקה: והא רב פפא הוא דאמר. במנחות בפרק התכלת (דף מז:) גבי שתי הלחם שילאו בין שחיטה לזריקה דפליגי נמי ר"א ורבי עקיבא: בדאיתנהו אבראי כ"ע לא פליגי. דלא מהניא להו זריקה: דלאו גופיה דזיבחא הוא. דבזריקת כבשים קא מישתרו דלאו גופייהו הוא הלכך כל טו] דאיתנהו אבראי מודה ר"ע דלא מהניא להו זריקה: מנחות ישנן בצבור. מנחת העומר ושתי הלחם. עוף איתו בצבור דתניא (תמורה דף יד) והקריב היחיד מביא עוף ואין צבור מביאין עוף: מנחת חוטא היא דקודמת למנחת נדבה. משום דמכפרת אבל מנחת סוטה לא: והא נמי. דסוטה באה על חטא: והקריב את אשר לחטאת וגו'. בשמיעת הקול כתיב: זה בנה אב. תלה טעם הקדמתו בשביל שם חטאת: חטאת בהמה לעולת בהמה מדרבי רחמנא. דתניא לעיל ופר שני בן בקר וגו': חטאת העוף לעולת בהמה. כגון יולדת עשירה טז] כבש בן שנתו לעולה ובן יונה או תור לחטאת (ויקרא יב): כל מקום שנתחלפה חטאת. והעופות באין תחתיה בדלות כגון במטמא מקדש (ויקרא ה) דעיקרו חטאת בהמה ובדלות נתחלפה שתי תורים: חטאת קודמת. דכתיב לחטאת ראשונה משום דעיקר חטאת הוא: וכאן. ביולדת שהעוף תחת עולה הוא בא והבהמה עיקר היתה עולה קודמת כדכתיב בה אחד לעולה ואחד *לחטאת: וכל מקום ששנים באים תחת אחד חטאת קודמת. כגון במטמא מקדש שתי העופות תחת חטאת אחד הן באין שהרי בעשירות לא היה מחוייב אלא חטאת וכאן ביולדת שאין בא תחת הבהמה אלא עוף העולה דאילו בעשירות נמי הוה מתיא עוף לחטאת עם עולת בהמה: עולה קודמת. אלמא יז] עולה של בהמה יולדת קודמת לחטאת שהרי אף חליפין קודמין לחטאת ומתניתין תנן חטאת העוף קודמת לעולת בהמה: למקראה הקדימה הכתוב. שתהא נקראת בענין תחילה אבל בעבודתן חטאת קודמת וכדאמרן מזה בנה אב: מאי

ואין חייבין עליהן משום פיגול נותר וטמא. האי דאין חייבין משום טומאה נראה דהיינו טעמא כדאמר לעיל בסוף ב"ש (דף מה:) בהוכשר ליקרב וזה אין ראוי ליקרב עד אחר זריקה ובקונטרס פי' טעם אחר: והא רב פפא הוא דאמר בדאיתנהו אבראי דכ"ע ל"פ. מילתיה דרב פפא בפרק התכלת (מנחות דף מז:) גבי שתי הלחם שילאו בין שחיטה לזריקה וס"ד דאין חילוק בין זה לזה: מנא הני מילי דת"ר כו'. לעיל גבי דם חטאת קודם לדם עולה ניחא דבעי קרא אע"ג דמפ' טעמא במתני' משום דאיכא תרי קראי חד דמשמע דחטאת קודמת וחד דמשמע דעולה קודמת אבל הכא קשה ל"ל קרא תיפוק לי משום דחטאת העוף מרצה ושמא כיון דלית בה הקטרה לא מהני בה האי טעמא: חטאת בהמה קודמת לעולת בהמה. וא"ת הא תנא ליה רישא דם חטאת קודם לדם עולה וי"ל דאיצטריך לאשמועי' אפי' בעולה הבאה *לשם חטאת כדקתני וכן בהקדישה: חטאת העוף לעולת בהמה מזה בנה אב. והא דאמרי' בפ' תמיד נשחט (פסחים נט.) זה בנה אב לכל החטאות שיקדמו לעולות וקיימא לן דאפילו' חטאת העוף לעולת בהמה קשה קצת הלשון דמאי קאמר וקיימא לן כו' הא לא יח] משמע מבנין אב טפי אלא הך מילתא לחודה ועוד קשה הא דקאמר לכל החטאות: למקראה הקדימה הכתוב. פירש בקונט' שתהא נקראת בענין תחילה ותימה מה חידוש הוא זה יט] ומפרש ה"ר חיים להקדישה תחילה שיקדים העולה קודם החטאת אבל להקריב חטאת קודמת והא דתנן וכן בהקדישה מתני' לא מיירי ביולדת אע"ג דמשמע קצת דאכל מה דתנן חטאת קודמת לעולה בהקרבה בכל הנהו וכן בהקדישה וקשה לפי' מהא דאמרינן בערכין פרק האומר משקלי עלי (דף כא.) חייבי חטאות אין ממשכנין אותן חייבי עולות ממשכנין אותן ופעמים שחייבי עולות אין ממשכנין אותן ופריך מאי ניהו אי נימא עולת יולדת פי' דא"ל למשכנה משום דאי אפשר לה להביא חטאת עד שתביא עולתה והאמר רבא למקראה הקדימה הכתוב כ] ואי כפירוש ה"ר חיים כיון דצריכה להקדיש עולה קודם לחטאת א"כ א"ל למשכן כא] ועל כרחה תביא שתיהן: מאי

יא א ב מיי' פ"א מהל' פסה"מ הלכה לג:
יב ג מיי' שם פי"ז הל' יט וכרבי עקיבא:
יג ד מיי' פ"ט מהל' תמידין ומוספין הל' י:
יד ה מיי' שם הלכה י:
טו ו מיי' שם הל' ז:

עס חטאת ולשם חטאת נ"ק

נ"א בבשר לאכילה ובס"י איתא בבשר הראוי לאכילה כו'
[מנחות כה:]
[שם מז:]
[לעיל י: יבמות מח: וש"נ]
[פסחים נט. הוריות יג.]
נ"א לחטאת הס"ד ומה"ד כ"מ שבא על חטא כגון שבועת עדות ושבועת ביטוי ושגגת טומאת מקדש וקדשיו שבכולן הקרבן בא לכפר על החטא חטאת קודמת וכאן ביולדת שאינה באה על חטא אלא לטהרה העולה קודמת
נ"א תחת אחד נ"ק
נ"א וכאן שאין ב' באין תחת חטאת אחת עולה קודמת

שיטה מקובצת
א] מאי לאו בדהדר עיילינהו. וקשה היאך ס"ד דבהדר עיילינהו פליגי הרי כמו כן פליגי ברישא בבשר קדשי קדשים שיצא לפני זריקת דמים וצ"ל דבאימורי קדשים קלים פליגי בדהדר עיילינהו: ב] דזיבחא הוא אבל: ג] תיבות מנחת חוטא נמחק: ד] תיבת או נמחק: ה] טעמי נקיט: ו] מה ת"ל אם ללמד שתקרב חטאת. ותיבות שאין ת"ל נמחק: ז] לעולות הבאות: ח] תיבת רחמנא נמחק: ט] וכאן שנתחלפה עולה עולה קודמת תיב' ביולדת ל"ש ונמחק: י] כל.ס"א איתו זה הבבא: יא] קודמת כל: יב] פיגול. דלא קבע להו הך זריקה בפיגול דהוו ולהו: יג] בבש' הראוי לאכילה בתוך: יד] לאו בדהדר עיילינהו: טו] כל כמה דאיתנהו: טז] עשירה שיש לה להביא כבש: יז] אלמא עולת בהמה של יולדת: יח] לא אשמעינן הבנין אב ותיבת משמע ואות מ' נמחק: יט] זה דזיל קרי ביה רב הוא: כ] ואי. לשון מהר"ם ואי כפי' הר"ר חיים מאי פריך הא צריך להקדישה קודם חטאת וא"כ נימא דאין צריך למשכן עולת יולדת לכך נראה להר"ר יחיאל דה"פ למקראה לשון מקרה כלומר אם לא נזדמן לה כי אם פרידה אחת והיא רוצה לעשות ממנה עולתה וכשיזדמן לה מהרית תביא חטאת הרשות בידה ולכך הקדימה הכתוב אבל כשהן באות יחד לעולם חטאת קודמת לה ואפי' כשהיא עשירה שהיא מביאה עולת בהמה וחטאת העוף החטאת קודמת לעולה: כא] למשכן דעל כרחת ·

עין משפט
נר מצוה

טז א ב מיי' פ"ט מהל' תמידין ומוספין הלכה ו:
יז ג ד מיי' שם הל' ח:
יח ה מיי' פ"ד מהל' פסה"מ הל' כג:
נ"ל דקודמת כדאמרינן באלו מציאות כו' צ"ק
יט ו מיי' פ"ט מהל' תמידין ומוספין הלכה יג:
[בקידושין לב. ד"ה רב יהודה אומר פשוטו ע"ש וכן בתוס' ב"מ לג. ד"ה אבידתו ע"ש]
כ ז מיי' שם הלכה יג:
כא ח ט מיי' פ"י מהל' מעה"ק הלכה י:
כב י מיי' פ"ט מהל' תמידין ומוספין הל' ב:
[עיין רש"ק ותוי"ט]
פ"א אכילה
[לעיל ש.]
[ועיין תוס' פסחים לט: ד"ה ולא שלוקין]

מאי לאו דחג ‹א› לא לנדבה פרים קודמין לאילים שכן נתרבו בנסכים ‹ב› וכן אילים לכבשים כבשים לשעירים שכן נתרבו באליה ת"ש *‹א›פר כהן משיח קודם לפר העלם דבר של צבור פר העלם דבר של צבור קודם לפר עבודת כוכבים פר עבודת כוכבים קודם לשעירי עבודת כוכבים ‹ג› דאע"ג דפר עבודת כוכבים עולה ושעירי עבודת כוכבים חטאת ואימא מרישא פר העלם דבר של צבור קודם לפר עבודת כוכבים בחד מינא מיהא לא קאמרינן דחטאת קדמה כי קאמרינן בתרי מיני ‹ד› אשכחן עולה דקדמה לחטאת אמרי במערבא משמיה דרבא בר מרי חטאת עבודת כוכבים חסר א' °לחטת כתיב *רבינא אמר ‹ב›כמשפט (במדבר טו) כתיב בהו השתא דאתית להכי אפילו תימא פרים דחג נמי כמשפטם כתיב בהו: איבעיא להו חטאת העוף ועולת בהמה ומעשר איזו מהן קודם תיקדום חטאת העוף איכא מעשר דקדים לה ליקדים מעשר איכא עולת בהמה דקדמה ליה תיקדום עולת בהמה איכא חטאת העוף דקדמה לה הכא תרגימו מין זבח עדיף במערבא אמרי ‹ג›עיילא בה עולת בהמה בחטאת העוף ואגבהתה ממעשר:

מתני' ‹ד›כל החטאות שבתורה קודמות לאשמות חוץ מאשם מצורע מפני שהוא בא על הכשר ‹ה› *‹ה›כל האשמות שבתורה באין בני שתים ובאין בכסף שקלים חוץ מאשם נזיר ואשם מצורע שהן באין בני שנתן ואין באין בכסף שקלים ‹ו›כשם שקודמין בהקרבתן ‹ו› קודמין באכילתן ‹ז›שלמים של אמש ושלמים ישל ‹ז› יום של אמש קודמין ‹ח› לשל יום שלמים של אמש חטאת ואשם של היום שלמים של אמש קודמין דברי ר"מ וחכ"א חטאת קודמת מפני שהיא קדשי קדשים *(א) ‹ט› ‹ח›וכולן הכהנים רשאין לשנות באכילתן לאכלן צלוין ושלוקין ומבושלין ‹י› לתת לתוכו תבלי חולין ותבלי תרומה דברי ר"ש ר"מ אומר ‹ט›לא יתן לתוכו תבלי תרומה שלא יביא התרומה לידי פסול:

גמ' °איבעיא להו *‹י›תדיר ומקודש איזה מהם קודם תדיר קודם משום דתדיר או דלמא מקודש קדים דקדיש תא שמע *תמידין קודמין למוספין ואף

רש"י

מאי לאו למוספי החג. דשעירים הוי חטאת וכבשים עולה וקתני כבשים קודמין: לא יא] נדבה. ושניהם עולה: וטעמא מאי קדמו פרים לאילים כו' שכן נתרבו בנסכים. פר שלשה עשרונים ואיל שני עשרונים וכבש עשרון: שכן נתרבו באליה. לענין אימוריו ואע"ג דהשתא בעולה קיימינן שכולה כליל מיהו לד ריבוי למזבח אשכחן ביה גבי שלמים וחטאת: פר כהן משיח קודם לפר העלם דבר. מפורש טעם בהוריות פ"ב (דף יג.) כאשר שרף הפר הראשון ראשון יב] יהא לפר העדה לכל מעשיו: פר העלם דבר קודם לפר עבודת כוכבים. שזה חטאת וזה עולה ואמרן לעיל חטאת קודמת: פר עבודת כוכבים קודם לשעיר עבודת כוכבים. אלמא יש עולה קודמת לחטאת: ואימא מרישא. כלומר אדמותבת מסיפא סייען מרישא דקתני פר העלם דבר יג] [קודם] לפר עבודת כוכבים: ומשני יד] לה בחד מינא לא קאמרי'. דהא ודאי ניחא לי דבחד מינא חטאת קדמה: כי אמרי' בתרי מיני. קשיא לן דקאמרת מין קטן של חטאת קודם למין גדול של עולה כדקאמרת ואפי' חטאת העוף לעולת בהמה והא הכא דפר עולה קודם לשעיר חטאת: לחטת כתיב. בפרשת שלח לך טו] והיה אם מעיני העדה נעשתה בשגגה וגו' [וכתיב התם ושעיר אחד לחטת חסר א' לומר שאינו כשאר חטאות שכל חטאת שבתורה הבאה עם עולה חטאת קודמת וזו עולה קודמת]: כמשפט כתיב. בההוא קרא ומנחתו ונסכו כמשפט משמע כמשפט סדר מקראו כך סדר עבודתו ופר ברישא כתיב: אפילו תימא פרים וכבשים דמוספי החג. הך טז] מתניתין דתניא לעיל כבשים קודמין לשעירים לא יז] תקשה דכמשפט כתיב בהו ומשמע כסדר האמור בענין ושעירי' כתובים אחרונים: חטאת העוף ועולת בהמה ומעשר בהמה. שלשתן עומדין: הכא תרגימו. בבבל: מין זבח עדיף. ויקדים מעשר ואח"כ חטאת ועולה דאילו עולת בהמה לא מצי קדמה לחטאת העוף מגזירת הכתוב: עיילא בה חשיבות דעולת בהמה. שבאה עמה והיא חשובה ממעשר שהיא יח] קדש קדשים וכליל ומגזירת הכתוב החטאת קודמת ואף על פי שזו מין זבח: ואגבהתה ממעשר. לבטל חשיבות שם מין זבח שבו דהא בעולה נמי איתיה לאותה חשיבות ובטיל ליה מגזירת הכתוב הלכך יקדים חטאת העוף לעולה ועולה למעשר:

מתני' קודמות לאשמות. אם היה יט] מקריב חטאת ואשם והביאן* חטאת קודמת כדתנן שדמה ניתן על ד' קרנות ועל היסוד: מפני שהוא בא להכשיר את המצורע. לקדשים ולביאת מקדש הלכך חשיבות הוא לגביה שטהרה תלויה בו: ובאין בכסף שקלים. דכתיב (ויקרא ה) בערכך כסף שקלים באשם מעילות ואתי אשם תלוי ואשם גזילות בג"ש בערכך בערכך ואשם שפחה חרופה גמר באיל באיל כדאמר באיזהו מקומן (לעיל דף מח.) חוץ מאשם נזיר דכתיב כ] כבש בן שנתו ומדאיל בן ב' שנים בשתי סלעים כבש בן שנה לאו בשתי סלעים הוא: כך קודמין באכילתן. אכולהו דבני אכילה קאי כגון חטאת לאשם כא] אשם לתודה ותודה לשלמים ושלמים לבכור: שלמים כב] שבאו אמש. לעזרה ושהו עד היום ושחטן: וחטאת ואשם של כג] יום. עומדין להקריב: שלמים של אמש קודמין. דזלזול כד] להשהותן כל כך והואיל ובאו ראשון יקרבו ראשון וכן מפרש בתוספתא דזבחים: ובכולן. בכל הנאכלין רשאין הכהנים לשנות באכילתן כגון לאוכלן צלוין שלוקין ומבושלין: לידי פסול. שטעם קדשים הנעשה היתר אוסרה: גמ' תדיר ומקודש. כגון דם עולת תמיד ודם חטאת כה] עומדין זה תדיר וזה מקודש ממש כדאמרן דם חטאת קודם לדם עולה מפני שהוא מרצה אי נמי עולות מוספי ראש חדש ופר העדה עומדים זה תדיר וזה מקודש:
ואף

תוספות

מאי לאו דחג. תימה מאי קשיא דלמא לא איירי בדם אלא באברי עולה דקודמין לאימורי חטאת כדתנן:

חטאת העוף ועולת בהמה ומעשר איזה מהן קודם. וכעין בעיא זו איכא למיבעי אבדתו ואבדת חבירו וכיבוד אב ואם למ"ד משל בן בפ"ק דקדושין (דף לב.) איזה מהן קודם תקדום אבדתו איכא כיבוד אב ואם [דקודם] למ"ד דמשל בן תקדום כו] אב ואם איכא אבדת חבירו כז] *דאמר באלו מציאות (ב"מ דף לג.) כח] אפילו אמר ליה אביו אל תחזיר כט] לא ישמע לו כו' תקדום אבידת חבירו איכא אבידתו דקודמת לאבידת חבירו*:

תקדום חטאת העוף איכא מעשר דקדים ליה. תימה תקדום חטאת העוף מק"ו ומה עולת בהמה שהיא חמורה וכולה כליל ל] ומין זבח קודמת למעשר חטאת העוף קודם לה מעשר לא] שאינו כליל ועולת בהמה קודמת לו אינו דין שחטאת העוף קודם לה וכי האי ק"ו אמרי' סנהדרין (דף לה:) דרציחה דוחה לב] שבת מק"ו ומה עבודה שדוחה שבת רציחה דוחה אותה שבת שנידחת מפני עבודה אינו דין שתהא רציחה דוחה אותה וי"ל דחידוש הוא הא דחטאת העוף קודם לעולה ולא גמרי' מיניה לג]:

חוץ מאשם מצורע מפני שהוא בא להכשיר. ואם תאמר אדרבה חטאת מצורע עדיף דאכשורי ומכפר וי"ל כיון דמתן בהונות מדם האשם הוא חשיב ליה מכשיר טפי א"נ האי כל חטאות שבתורה דקתני לאו בחטאת הבאה עם האשם קאמר אלא בשאר חטאות:

שלמים של אמש וחטאת ואשם של יום שלמים של אמש קודמין. *פי' בקונטרס דזלזול הוא להשהותם כל כך שצורת הבשר מתקלקלת ועל חנם דחק אלא היינו טעמא דשלמים של אמש אין להם היתר לד] *(אניות) אלא עד הלילה וחטאת ואשם של יום עד הבקר דנאכלין ליום ולילה:

וחכמים אומרים חטאת קודמת. והוא הדין אשם דקדש קדשים:

צלויין שלוקין ומבושלין. אף על גב דקתני שלוקין והדר תני מבושלין מ"מ לה] שליקה הוי טפי מבישול כדמוכח בפרק כל הבשר (חולין דף קיא.) גבי כבד דקאמר שלוקה אוסרת ונאסרת*:

תדיר ומקודש איזה מהן קודם. פירש בקונטרס כגון דם עולת תמיד ודם חטאת וקשה דבריש פירקין פרשינן דמלבד עולת הבוקר בעבודת הדם איירי ונראה כלשון אחר שפי' בקונטרס עולת מוספי ר"ח לו] ופר העדה וא"ת תפשוט ממתניתין דתנא מוספי שבת קודמין למוספי ר"ח לז] דמשמע אפילו עולת מוסף של שבת לחטאת מוסף של שבת ר"ח וי"ל כיון דעולת מוסף דשבת קודמת לעולת מוסף דר"ח משום דתדירה קודמת נמי לחטאת לח] שהשוה הכתוב עולה דמוסף עם החטאת:
תא

מסורת הש"ס

[הוריות יג. ע"ש]
[בהוריות שם איתא רבא]
[כעין זה במנחות מט.]
[לעיל סג.]
כלאחר חטאת כו' צ"ק

הגהות הב"ח

(א) במשנה וכולן הכהנים וכו' צלוין שלוקין כצ"ל ואות ו' נמחק:

גליון הש"ס

מתני' כל האשמות. עיין לעיל דף נג. ע"א תוס' ד"ה סמיכות: גמ' איבעיא להו תדיר ומקודש. עיין ירושלמי פ"ו מ"ז סוף הלכה א':

שיטה מקובצת

א] לא דנדבה פרים: ב] בנסכים אילים לכבשים שכן נתרבו בנסכים כבשים ותיבת וכן ל"ש: ג] ואע"ג דפר: ד] מיני דבתרי מיני מיהא אשכחן: ה] שהוא בא להכשר תיבת על נמחק. אע"ג דחטאת מצורע כמו כן בא להכשיר וגם לכפר מ"מ אינו כל כך עיקר הכשר כמו אשם שהרי מדם האשם היה על נוף המצורע על הבהונות: ו] בהקרבתן כך קודמין: ז] של היום: ח] תיבות לשל יום נמחק: ט] ותכולן הכהנים: י] ומבושלין ולתת לתוכו: יא] לא דנדבה. ושניהם: יב] ראשון שיהא לפר: יג] דבר קודם לפר: יד] ומשני ליה בחד מינא מיהא לא: טו] לך בההוא קרא והיה: טז] הך מתניתא דתניא: יז] לא תיקשי: יח] שהיא קדשי קדשים: יט] היה מתחייב חטאת ואשם והביאן ותיבת מקריב נמחק: כ] דכתיב ביה כבש: כא] לאשם ואשם לתודה: כב] שלמים. ס"א שלמים שקרבו אמש: וחטאת כו' עומדים כו' כ"כ שצורות הבשר מתקלקלת ואע"פ שזמן אכילתן כל היום יקריבו ראשון וכן כו': כג] של היום. עומדין: כד] דזלזול הוא להשהותן: כה] חטאת מוספין שעומדין זה: כו] תקדום כבוד אב: כז] חבירו דאמרי' באלו: כח] יכול אמר לו אבא אל ותיבת אפי' ל"ש: כט] תחזיר ישמע תיבת לא ל"ש ונמחק: ל] כליל וקודמת ותיבות ומין זבח נמחק: לא] מעשר הקל שאינו: לב] דוחה עבודה מק"ו תיבת שבת נמחק: לג] מיניה דהא מין זבח הוא אלא דגזירת הכתוב הוא ולא מחמת חשיבות קודמת וק"ו אינו אלא מכח סברא: לד] היתר אכילה אלא תיבת אניות נמחק: לה] מ"מ שליקה הוי: לו] ר"ח לפר העדה: לז] ר"ח ואע"ג דמוספי שבת כולן עולות ומוספי ר"ח חד חטאת וחד עולה דמשמע כו': לח] לחטאת שעמה שהשוה הכתוב עולת מוסף עם החטאת:

take precedence over lambs, lambs over he-goats. [90b] Does that not refer to those of the Festival?[7]—No: [it means those] of a votive offering:[8] bullocks precede rams, because their drink-offerings are larger;[9] and for the same reason rams [precede] lambs; [while] lambs [precede] he-goats because more [is offered] of them, [viz.,] the fat-tail.[10]

Come and hear: The bullock of the anointed priest precedes the congregation's bullock for inadvertent sin; the congregation's bullock for inadvertent sin precedes the bullock for idolatry; the bullock of idolatry precedes the he-goats of idolatry. [And this is so] notwithstanding that the bullock of idolatry is a burnt-offering, whereas the he-goats of idolatry are sin-offerings? But why not deduce from the first clause: the congregation's bullock for inadver-
a tent sin precedes the bullock of idolatry?[1]—We do not speak [of where both sacrifices are] of one kind: there a sin-offering [certainly] takes precedence. We speak of two kinds,[2] and yet here we find a burnt-offering preceding a sin-offering?—In the West [Palestine] they said in Raba b. Mari's name: The sin-offering of idolatry lacks an *alef*, as *le-ḥaṭṭath* is written.[3] Rabina said: In their case[4] '*according to the ordinance*' is written.[5] Now that you have come to this, you may even say that [the preceding passage refers to] the bullocks of the Festival, [for] '*after their ordinance*' is written in connection with them too.[6]

It was asked: [With regard to] a bird sin-offering, an animal burnt-offering, and tithe, which of these precede?[7] Shall the bird sin-offering come first? there is tithe, which must precede it! Shall tithe come first? there is the animal burnt-offering, which must precede it! Shall the animal burnt-offering come first? there is the bird sin-offering, which must precede it!—Here[8] they held that a slaughtered sacrifice is more important.[9] In the West they said: The superiority of an animal burnt-offering [over tithe] serves the bird sin-offering and advances it over that of tithe.[10]

MISHNAH. ALL SIN-OFFERINGS IN THE TORAH PRE-
b CEDE GUILT-OFFERINGS,[1] EXCEPT A LEPER'S GUILT-OFFERING, BECAUSE IT COMES TO MAKE [A PERSON] FIT.[2] ALL GUILT-OFFERINGS OF THE TORAH MUST BE[3] TWO-YEAR OLDS AND [TWO] SILVER SHEKELS IN VALUE,[4] EXCEPT A NAZIRITE'S GUILT-OFFERING AND A LEPER'S GUILT-OFFERING: THESE MUST BE A YEAR OLD, AND NEED NOT BE [TWO] SILVER SHEKELS IN VALUE.[5] AS THEY TAKE PRECEDENCE IN BEING OFFERED, SO THEY TAKE PRECEDENCE IN BEING EATEN.[6] IN THE CASE OF A PEACE-OFFERING OF YESTERDAY AND A PEACE-OFFERING OF TO-DAY,[7] THAT OF YESTERDAY TAKES PRECEDENCE. IN THE CASE OF A PEACE-OFFERING OF YESTERDAY AND A SIN-OFFERING AND A GUILT-OFFERING OF TO-DAY, YESTERDAY'S PEACE-OFFERING TAKES PRECEDENCE: THAT IS R. MEIR'S RULING. BUT THE SAGES MAINTAIN: THE SIN-OFFERING TAKES PRECEDENCE, BECAUSE IT IS A MOST SACRED SACRIFICE. AND IN ALL OF THESE, THE PRIESTS MAY DEVIATE IN THEIR MODE OF EATING, AND EAT THEM ROAST, STEWED OR BOILED, AND SEASON THEM WITH CONDIMENTS OF ḤULLIN OR OF TERUMAH: SO SAID R. SIMEON. R. MEIR SAID: ONE MAY NOT SEASON THEM WITH CONDIMENTS OF TERUMAH, SO AS NOT TO BRING TERUMAH TO UNFITNESS.[8]

GEMARA. It was asked: That which is more constant and that
c which is more sacred,[1] which takes precedence? Does that which is more constant take precedence, because it is more constant; or does that which is more sacred take precedence, because it is more sacred?—Come and hear: The continual [burnt-]offerings precede

(7) *Sc.* Tabernacles; the he-goats were sin-offerings and the lambs were burnt-offerings, yet the lambs take precedence. (8) And both are burnt-offerings. (9) A bullock requires a drink-offering of three '*esronim* (pl. of '*issaron*, a tenth part of an ephah), a ram one of two, and a lamb one '*issaron*. (10) Which in the case of a lamb is burnt on the altar as *emurim*, but not in the case of a he-goat; cf. Lev. III, 6-10 with 12-15. Though this passage refers to burnt-offerings, which are *entirely* burnt on the altar, yet the reason is valid, because it holds good of sacrifices in general.

a (1) Instead of raising a difficulty from the final clause, cite the first clause to corroborate the Mishnah. (2) Which is what the above-stated principle sets out to establish, that a bird sin-offering takes precedence over an animal burnt-offering. (3) Heb. לחטת instead of לחטאת Num. XV, 24. This teaches that it is an exception and does not precede the burnt-offering. (4) *Sc.* the offerings for idolatry. (5) Ibid. This implies that they must be offered in the same order as they are prescribed, and the burnt-offering is mentioned there first. (6) Ibid. XXIX, 33. There too the burnt-offerings are mentioned first. But in all other cases the sin-offering, even if it is only a bird, precedes. (7) When we have the three together. (8) In Babylon. (9) Therefore tithe comes first, then the bird sin-offering and then the animal burnt-offering. The animal burnt-offering cannot come first, since Scripture expressly stated that it follows the sin-offering. (10) Since the burnt-offering accompanies the sin-offering, the higher importance of the former over tithe, viz., that it is a most sacred sacrifice and is altogether burnt, invests the sin-offering with the same superiority over tithe. Hence the sin-offering must be sacrificed first, then the burnt-offering, and last of all tithe.

b (1) Where a person was liable to both and brought them at the same time. (2) To enter the Temple and partake of sacrifices. This invests it with greater importance. (3) Lit., 'come'. (4) *According to thy valuation in silver by shekels* (Lev. V, 15), denoting at least two, is written in connection with the guilt-offering for trespass; other guilt-offerings are inferred from it, v. *supra* 48a. (5) For both a year-old animal is prescribed (Num. VI, 12; v. Lev. XIV, 10-12). Again, since Scripture decreed that the two-year old ram for the guilt-offerings must be worth two silver *shekels*, a year-old lamb would be worth less. (6) This refers to all sacrifices, those enumerated in the preceding Mishnah too. (7) I.e., the former animal was brought yesterday, but has not yet been offered. Or, one *sacrificed* yesterday and one to-day, but neither has yet been eaten. (8) For should they become *nothar*, the condiments too might not be eaten, even if they could be separated from the flesh, because they absorbed the taste of that flesh, which is now forbidden.

c (1) E.g. if we have the blood of the daily burnt-offering and that of a sin-offering for sprinkling: the daily burnt-offering is more constant, while the sin-offering is more sacred.

the additional offerings. [91a] [Now this is so] notwithstanding that the additional offerings are more sacred![2]—[No:] does then the Sabbath affect the additional offerings and not affect the continual-offerings?[3]

Come and hear: The additional-offerings of the Sabbath precede the additional-offerings of New Moon!—Does then New Moon affect its own additional offerings and not affect the additional offerings of the Sabbath?

Come and hear: The additional offerings of New Moon precede the additional offerings of New Year, although New Year is holier!—Does then New Year affect its own additional offerings and not affect the additional offerings of New Moon?

Come and hear: Another reason: the blessing for wine is constant, while the blessing for the day is not constant, and of that which is constant and that which is not constant, that which is constant comes first.[4] [Now this is so] notwithstanding that the blessing for the day is holier![5]—Does then the Sabbath affect the blessing for the day and not affect the blessing for the wine?[6]

Come and hear, for R. Joḥanan said: The *halachah* is that one must recite the *minḥah* [afternoon] service and then recite the additional
a service.[1] [Although the additional service is more sacred]![2]—Does then the Sabbath affect the additional service and not affect the *minḥah* service?

Come and hear: IN THE CASE OF A PEACE-OFFERING OF YESTERDAY, AND A SIN-OFFERING AND A GUILT-OFFERING OF TO-DAY, YESTERDAY'S PEACE-OFFERING TAKES PRECEDENCE. Hence, if both are of to-day, the sin-offering and the guilt-offering take precedence, although a peace-offering is more constant![3]—Said Raba: You speak of what is common: we ask about what is constant, not about what is more common.[4] Said R. Huna b. Judah to Raba: Is then what is common not [the same as what is] constant?[5] Surely it was taught: I would exclude the Passover-offering, which is not constant, but I would not exclude circumcision, which is constant![6]—What does 'constant' mean? It is more constant in precepts.[7] Alternatively, circumcision is constant in comparison with the Passover-offering.[8]

It was asked: [If one thing is] constant and [another] non-constant, and [the priest] slaughtered the non-constant first, what is the law?[9] Do we say, since he slaughtered it, he must offer [i.e., sprinkle] it [first]; or perhaps he must give it to another to stir the
b blood until he offers the constant, and then offer the non-constant?[1]—Said R. Huna[2] of Sura,[3] Come and hear: IN THE CASE OF A PEACE-OFFERING OF YESTERDAY, AND A SIN-OFFERING AND

(2) For they are brought on Sabbath and Festivals, whereas continual offerings are brought on week-days too. (3) Just as it invests the former with greater sanctity, so it invests the latter too, seeing that we are now treating of the continual offering brought on the Sabbath. (4) This explains why in *Ḳiddush* (Sanctification Benediction, recited at the beginning of every festival) the blessing over wine precedes that over the festival!—*Whenever* wine is drunk a blessing over it is required, whereas the blessing of sanctification is confined to festivals. (5) Since the other is recited on week-days too. (6) The sanctity of the latter too is enhanced when it is recited on the Sabbath or festival.

a (1) V. *supra* 12*a*. (2) Bracketed passage added by Sh.M. (3) They are more common, since they can be brought at any time, whereas a sin-offering and a guilt-offering can be brought only when one is liable to them. (4) A peace-offering is not *legally* more constant than a sin-offering, since one is not obliged to vow a peace-offering. (5) Is not a thing regarded as more constant when it is more common? (6) It is a general rule that one incurs a sin-offering for an inadvertent transgression which if committed deliberately would involve *kareth*. This however refers to *negative* injunctions (hence, sins of commission), not to *positive* commands; therefore, though deliberate neglect of the Passover-offering or circumcision involves *kareth*, unintentional neglect does not involve a sin-offering. In the present passage, however, it is sought to draw a distinction between the Passover-offering and circumcision, on the grounds that the latter is constant. Now actually it is no more constant than the former, since both are obligatory, and it is only more common (since circumcision takes place at any time, while the Passover-offering is sacrificed only for Passover), and yet it is called constant, which shews that the two are identical. (7) It is more emphasized in Scripture, the word '*covenant*' occurring thirteen times in connection with it. (8) For the reason stated in n. 6. But a peace-offering is not so much more common than a sin- or a guilt-offering to rank as constant in comparison with it. (9) Whose blood must be sprinkled first?

b (1) The blood would have to be stirred to keep it from congealing. (2) Sh.M. reads: R. Ḥanina. (3) The great academy town on the river Sura, a branch of the Euphrates; v. Obermeyer *Landschaft*, pp. 283-287.

◁ *For the continuation of the English translation of this page see overleaf.*

ואף ע"ג דמוספין קדישי אטו שבת למוספין א] אהנאי לתמידין לא אהנאי ת"ש *מוספי שבת קודמין למוספי ראש חודש אטו ראש חודש למוספין דידיה אהני למוספי שבת לא אהני תא שמע מוספי ראש חודש קודמין למוספי ראש השנה אע"ג דראש השנה קדשה אטו ראש השנה למוספי דידיה אהני למוספי ראש חודש לא אהני ת"ש ד"א *ברכת היין *תדירה וברכת היום אינה תדירה ותדיר ושאינו תדיר תדיר קודם אע"ג דברכת היום קדישה אטו שבת לברכת היום ב] אהנאי לברכת היין לא אהנאי תא שמע *דאמר רבי יוחנן הלכה [ב]מתפלל אדם של מנחה ואח"כ של מוספין ג] אטו שבת לתפלת מוספין ד] אהנאי לתפלת מנחה לא אהנאי ת"ש שלמים של אמש חטאת ואשם של ה] יום שלמים של אמש קודמין הא אידי ואידי דיום חטאת ואשם קדמי ואע"ג דשלמים תדירי אמר רבא מצוי קאמרת תדיר קמיבעיא לן מצוי לא קמיבעיא לן אמר ליה רב הונא בר יהודה לרבא אטו ו] מצוי לאו תדיר והתניא אוציא את הפסח שאינו תדיר ולא אוציא את המילה שהיא תדירה מאי תדירה תדירה במצות ואיבעית אימא מילה לגבי פסח כי תדיר דמיא איבעיא להו תדיר ושאינו תדיר וקדים ושחט לשאינו תדיר מאי מי אמרינן כיון דשחטיה [ו]מקריב ליה או דלמא יהיב לאחר דממרס בדמו עד דמקריב ליה לתדיר והדר מקריב לשאינו תדיר אמר רב ז] הונא מסורא ת"ש שלמים של אמש חטאת ואשם של ח] יום של אמש קודם לשל יום הא דיום דומיא דאמש וה"ד דקדים שחטיה לשלמים חטאת ואשם קדמי דלמא שלמים דאמש וחטאת ואשם דיום היכי משכחת לה דשחטינהו לתרוייהו ט] אבל לא שחטינהו לתרוייהו תיבעי לך ת"ש ד"א ברכת היין תדירה וברכת היום אינה תדירה ותדיר ושאינו תדיר תדיר קודם ה"נ דכיון י] דאתיין כמאן דשחיטי תרוייהו דמי ת"ש דא"ר יוחנן הלכה מתפלל אדם של מנחה ואח"כ של מוספין ה"נ כיון דמטי זמן תפלת מנחה כמאן דשחיטי תרוייהו דמי אמר ליה רב אחא בריה דרב אשי לרבינא יא] *[ד]שחטו קודם חצות פסול מפני שנאמר בו בין הערבים קודם [ה]לתמיד כשר ויהא ממרס בדמו עד שיזרוק יב] הדם הכא במאי עסקינן כגון דקדים שחטיה לתמיד ברישא אמר ליה רב אחא סבא לרב אשי מתניתין נמי דיקא דקתני עד שיזרק יג] הדם (תמיד) ולא קתני עד שישחוט ויזרק דם ש"מ: ובכולן כהנים רשאין כו': מאי טעמא אמר קרא °למשחה *לגדולה כדרך שהמלכים אוכלין: **מתני'** אמר רבי שמעון אם ראית שמן שהוא מתחלק בעזרה אין יד] צריך לשאול מהו אלא מותר רקיקי [ו]מנחות ישראל [ז]ולוג שמן של מצורע אם ראית שמן שהוא ניתן על גבי האישים אין טו] צריך לשאול מהו אלא מותר [ח]רקיקי מנחת כהנים ומנחת כהן משיח *שאין מתנדבין שמן רבי טרפון אומר °מתנדבין שמן:

גמ'

תורה אור: שמות יב | במדבר יח

רש"י

ואף על גב דמוספין קדישי. טז] מוספין שם שבת עליהן שהם באים חובה לה והתמידין באין אף בחול: לתמידין לא יז] אהנאי. כיון דהאידנא יח] קריבין *אם כן שם שבת עליהם: מוספי ר"ח. מקודשין משל שבת דאיקרי מועד יט]: ד"א כו'. בפסחים תנינן לה דקאמרי ב"ה מברך על היין ואח"כ מברך על היום שהיין גורם לקידוש שתאמר דבר אחר כו': הכי גרסינן כ] דאע"ג דברכת היום קדישה. ששם שבת עליה שחובה לשבת היא באה דאילו ברכת היין אף בחול היא: הלכה מתפלל של מנחה. במסכת ברכות כא] היו לפניו שתי תפלות של מוספין ושל מנחה ופליגי רבי יהודה ורבנן וקא"ר יוחנן הלכה כדברי האומר מתפלל של מנחה ואחר כך מתפלל כו': שלמים של אמש. הא פרישית לה לעיל כב] (גבי במתני'): תדירי. שהן מצויין מתוך שבאין בנדר ובנדבה: מצוי קאמרת. שאין תדירותו חובה אלא שהוא מצוי תמיד יותר מחבירו: הכי גרס *מצוי לאו תדיר הוא בתמיה: אוציא את הפסח שאינו תדיר. בת"כ שנויה גבי חטאת דקתני והרי פסח ומילה כג] ענושין כרת יכול יביא על שגגתן חטאת ת"ל אשר לא תעשינה יצאו. פסח ומילה שהן מצות עשה: אוציא את הפסח שאינו תדיר ולא אוציא את המילה שהיא תדירה. ת"ל אשר לא תעשינה אלמא מצוי תדיר הוא: תדירה במצות. שגורה במצות שנכרתו עליה שלש עשרה בריתות ולווין: כי תדיר דמיא. שמצויה היא כד] הרבה מפסח אבל מצוי דשלמים לגבי מצוי דחטאת לאו כתדירה דמי: הא דיום דומיא דאמש והיכי דמי כגון כה] דשחטו שלמים ברישא כו'. וקא ס"ד ה"ק שלמים שהביאן מאמש ושחטן היום וחטאת ואשם של יום עומדין לישחט שלמים של אמש קודמין ליזרק דאי בשניהם עומדין לישחט לא אמר כו] דקדמו שלמים וטעמא דבאו מאמש הא אידי ואידי כז] דהיום וקדים שחטינהו לשלמים ברישא אמרי' שחיטת חטאת ואשם קדמה לזריקת שלמים אלמא מקודש ושאינו מקודש וקדים שחטיה לשאינו מקודש יהא אחד ממרס בדמו ויזרוק את המקודש וה"ה לתדיר ושאינו תדיר: דלמא שלמים של אמש וחטאת של יום. דאשמעינן של אמש קדמו: היכי דמי דשחטינהו לתרוייהו. אע"ג דשחטיה לחטאת אחר השלמים ושניהן עומדין ליזרק אשמעינן דשלמים של אמש קדמו ודכותיה כח] דייקא מיניה הא אידי ואידי דיום ושחט שלמים ואחר כך חטאת ובא לימלך על הזריקה אמרי' ליה חטאת קדמה: אבל לא שחטיה. לחטאת בתר שלמים ובא לימלך על השחיטה תיבעי לך אי מזלזלינן בשלמים למרס בדמן ולהקדים שחיטת חטאת וזריקתה וכי מיבעיא לן בתדיר ושאינו תדיר כט] *הך מיבעיא לן ששחט את שאינו תדיר והתדיר קיים: ברכת היין תדירה כו' תדיר קודם. ואע"ג דשאינו תדיר קדם ובא שכבר קדש היום ועדיין יין לא בא ל] ודומיא קדים שחטיה לשאינו תדיר ברישא: ומשני ה"נ כיון דאתא השתא יין קמן ומזומן לברכה כמאן דשחיטי תרוייהו לגבי קדשים לא] [דמי] ולא תפשוט מינה לבעיין: ואח"כ מתפלל של מוספין. ואף על גב דזמן מוספין אתא ברישא: שחטו קודם חצות. בפסח קאי: קודם לתמיד. של בין הערבים כשר ואע"פ שלכתחילה מצוה לאחרו כדתניא לעיל (דף יב.) יאוחר דבר שנאמר בו בערב ובין הערבים לדבר שלא נאמר בו אלא בין הערבים בלבד: ויהא אחד ממרס בדמו. אלמא לב] דקדים ושחטיה למאוחר אמרי ליה לשהות את הזריקה ולשחוט את הראוי ליקדם ולזרקו: כגון דקדים שחטיה לתמיד. קודם שבא לימלך ולא נמלך אלא על הזריקה: **מתני'** שהוא מתחלק. לאכילת כהנים: מותר רקיקי מנחת ישראל. למשחה. לך נתתים למשחה מתרגמינן לרבו והיינו לגדולה: מנחת מאפה שבאה חלות לג] ורקיקין חלות בוללן ברקיקין מושחן ואמר רבי שמעון במנחות (דף עה.) מושחן כמין כ"י ושאר השמן נאכל לכהנים: מנחת כהנים. כולה כליל ומותר מנחת כהן משיח לפי ששמנה מרובה שלשה לוגין לעשרון ומתוך שהיא אפויה תחילה אין שמנה נבלע בפיתיה וצריך להקטיר המותר לד] בעצמו: שאין מתנדבין שמן. לפיכך לא יעלה על דעתך שיהא שמן המתחלק *מן הנקטר נדבה:

תוספות

תא שמע מוספי שבת קודמין כו'. בכל הני תא שמע צריך טעם מאי קס"ד מאחר דכבר שני אטו שבת למוספין אהני לתמידין לה] לא אהנאי *וצריך לדקדק בפרק התכלת (מנחות דף מט.) גבי התמידין אין מעכבין את המוספין דאיכא כי הך בעיא דתדיר ומקודש ולא פשיט מיניה מידי דלא מייתי הכא ראיות דהתם והנהו דהכא לא מייתי התם:

דשחטינן לתרוייהו. תימה אם כן ליתני שלמים ושחט קודם לחטאת ואשם והכל ביום אחד שלמים קדימי לזרוק ואמאי נקט של אמש וי"ל דשל אמש נמי שמא הוי כעין של אמש והכל ביום אחד כדאמר בפ' התערובות (לעיל עה.) מאי תיין כעין חיין. ברו"ך:

אמר

מסורת הש"ס

נ"א אף כש שם שבת כו' ש"ק

[לעיל פט.]

ברכות כו: פסחים קיד.

לעיל יב. ברכות כח.

נ"א אגו מצוי כו' ש"ק

פסחים כח.

[לעיל פט. סוטה טו. חולין קלב:]

מנחות קד: [לעיל עז.]

נ"א הכי מיבעיא לן ש"ק

ס"א או

עין משפט נר מצוה

עיין בספר פנים מאירות

כג א מיי' פכ"ט מהל' שבת הל' ז טוש"ע א"ח סימן רעא סעיף י:

כד ב מיי' פ"ג מהל' תפלה הל"א טוש"ע א"ח סימן רפו סעיף ד:

כה ג מיי' פ"ט מהל' תמידין ומוספין הלכה ג:

כו ד ה מיי' פ"א מהל' קרבן פסח הלכה ד:

כז ו מיי' פט"ו מהל' מעה"ק הלכה יד:

כח ז מיי' פ"ד מהל' מחוסרי כפרה הלכה ג:

כט ח מיי' פי"ב מהל' מעה"ק הלכה ט:

ל ט מיי' שם פט"ו הלכה יד:

הג"ה

שיטה מקובצת

א] אהני לתמידין לא אהני: ב] היום אהני לברכת יין לא אהני. ג] מוספין ואף על גב דתפילת מוספין קדישא אטו: ד] מוספין אהני לתפלת מנחה לא אהני: ה] של היום שלמים: ו] אטו תדיר לאו מצוי הוא והתניא: ז] רב הונא תיבת הונא נמחק: ח] של היום שלמים של אמש קודם ותיבות לשל יום נמחק: ט] לתרוייהו ודיום דומיא דאמש נמי דשחטינהו לתרוייהו אבל: י] דכיון דאתא: יא] לרבינא ת"ש שחטו: יב] שיזרק דם התמיד הכא במאי עסקינן דקדים שחיט לתמיד ברישא: יג] שיזרק דם התמיד: יד] אין אתה צריך: טו] קדישי. שהמוספין שם: יז] לא אהני: יח] קרבי אף הם שם שבת: יט] מועד וישבהו שעיר חטאת שמכפר, על טומאת מקדש וקדשיו הס"ד: כ] גרסי' אע"ג דברכת: כא] ברכות [כב] לעיל גבי מתני' הס"ד: כג] ומילה עונשן כרת: כד] היא תמיד: כה] דשחטי לשלמים ברישא כו'. ס"א שלמים של אמש קודמים באכילה הס"ד ומה"ד הא דיום דומיא דאמש והיכי דמי [כו] דשחטינהו לשלמים ברישא חטאת ואשם דיום קדמי. קדמה זריקתם לזריקת שלמים ויאכלו תחילה כמו כן אלמא מקודש ושאינו מקודש וקדים שחטיה לשאינו מקודש יהא אחר ממרס בדמו וישחוט המקודש וה"ה לתדיר ושאינו תדיר הס"ד ומה"ד דלמא לא גרסינן ה"נ שלמים של אמש וחטאת ואשם דיום ה"ד דשחטי' לתרוייהו אבל לא שחטינהו לתרוייהו תיבעי לך'. ושלמים דאמש וחטאת דיום דקתני ע"כ היכי משכחת לה דשחטינהו לתרוייהו דהא לענין אכילה איירי וכי תידוק מינה לענין הקרבה נמי הא דיום דומיא דאמש וה"ד כגון דשחטיה לשלמים ברישא חטאת ואשם קדמי כדשחטינהו להו שחור ושחט את החטאת קודם שבא לימלך על הזריקה דהתם אמרינן ליה דחטאת קדמה דכיון דסוף סוף צריך למרס אחד מן הדמים קדשי קדשים קדמי אבל לא שחטיה לחטאת בתר השחיטה תיבעי אי מזלזלינן בשלמים למרס בדמן כו' (ככתוב לקמן ברש"י ד"ה אבל לא כו'): כו] אמר דניקדמו: כז] ואידי דיום יקדים: כח] ויוק מ'ניה: כט] תיבת הך נמחק: ל] בא ודמיא לקדים שאינו: לא] קדשים דמי ולא תפשוט בעיין מינה הס"ד: לב] אלמא היכא דקדים ושחטיה למאוחר ברישא ובא לימלך אמרי' ליה: לג] חלות או רקיקין: לד] המותר לעצמו הס"ד: לה] לא אהני:

Continuation of translation from previous page as indicated by ◁

A GUILT-OFFERING OF TO-DAY, YESTERDAY'S PEACE-OFFERING TAKES PRECEDENCE. Hence if it were [a peace-offering] of to-day analogous to that of yesterday—and how could that be? if he slaughtered the peace-offering first—[the sprinkling of] the sin-offering and the guilt-offering would take precedence![4]—[No:] perhaps how [is the case of] a peace-offering of yesterday and a sin-offering and a guilt-offering of to-day meant? Where he slaughtered both.[5] Where, however, he did not slaughter both, there you have the question.

Come and hear: Another reason: the blessing for the wine is constant, whereas the blessing for the day is not constant, and of that which is constant and that which is not constant, that which is constant comes first![6]—Here too, since it [the wine] c has arrived,[1] it is analogous to both having been slaughtered.

Come and hear, for R. Joḥanan said: The *halachah* is that one must recite the *minḥah* [afternoon] service and then recite the additional service![2]—Here too, since the time for the *minḥah* service has come, it is as though they were both slaughtered.

R. Aḥa the son of R. Ashi said to Rabina: Come and hear:[3] If he killed it[4] before midday, it is disqualified, because *'at dusk'* is said in connection with it.[5] [If he killed it] before the [evening] *tamid*, it is fit, and one must stir its blood until he sprinkles the blood of the *tamid*![6]—The case we discuss here is where e.g. he first slaughtered the *tamid*.[7] Said R. Aḥa the elder to R. Ashi: The Mishnah too proves that, because it teaches, 'until he sprinkles the blood of the *tamid*,' but it does not teach, until he slaughters [the *tamid*] and sprinkles its blood. This proves it.

AND IN ALL OF THESE, THE PRIESTS MAY DEVIATE etc. What is the reason?—Scripture says, [*Even all the hallowed things . . . unto thee have I given them*] *for a consecrated portion*,[8] which means, as [a symbol of] greatness [so that they can be eaten] just as kings eat.[9]

MISHNAH. R. SIMEON SAID: IF YOU SEE OIL BEING SHARED OUT IN THE TEMPLE COURT,[10] YOU NEED NOT ASK WHAT IT IS, FOR IT IS THE RESIDUE OF THE WAFERS [REḲIḲIM] OF THE ISRAELITE'S MEAL-OFFERINGS,[11] OR OF THE LEPER'S LOG OF OIL.[12] IF YOU SEE OIL BEING POURED ON TO THE FIRES,[13] YOU NEED NOT ASK WHAT IT IS, FOR IT IS THE RESIDUE OF THE OIL OF THE WAFERS OF PRIESTS' MEAL-OFFERINGS, OR OF THE ANOINTED PRIEST'S MEAL-OFFERING; FOR MEN CANNOT d OFFER OIL [ALONE].[1] R. TARFON SAID: OIL CAN BE DONATED [BY ITSELF].

(4) R. Huna understands the Mishnah thus: If a peace-offering was brought yesterday but only killed to-day, while a sin-offering or a guilt-offering brought to-day is still waiting to be slaughtered, the blood of the peace-offering must be sprinkled before the other is slaughtered. For he holds that if the peace-offering too has yet to be slaughtered, the Mishnah would not rule that it takes precedence. Hence by inference, if *both* were brought to-day and the peace-offering was wrongly slaughtered first, the slaughtering of the sin-offering etc. must precede the sprinkling of the peace-offering. This proves that where one sacrifice is more sacred than another, and the latter was slaughtered first, the former must nevertheless be slaughtered, and its blood sprinkled, before that of the less sacred is sprinkled, and presumably the same applies where one sacrifice is more constant than the other. (5) Though he wrongly slaughtered the peace-offering first, yet since it is yesterday's, he must sprinkle its blood first too. From this you could infer that if both were of to-day, he must sprinkle the blood of the sin-offering first. (6) Although the non-constant actually preceded the other, since the sanctity of the day automatically commenced at nightfall. This is analogous to slaughtering the non-constant first; and as here the blessing for the *wine* must be recited first, by analogy the blood of the constant must be sprinkled first.

c (1) We have the wine actually before us. (2) Although the time for the additional service came first; v. *supra* n. b 6: the argument here is similar. (3) Emended text (Sh.M.). (4) The Passover-offering. (5) Ex. XII, 6: *And the whole assembly . . . shall kill it at dusk;* lit., 'between the evenings'. (6) This proves that when one sacrifice is sacrificed earlier than it should be, the sprinkling must nevertheless wait. (7) Before sprinkling the blood of the Passover-offering. (8) Num. XVIII, 8. (9) Hence they can eat it as they like. Cf. *supra* 28a. (10) To the priests, for food. (11) V. Lev. II, 4. The oil was used in smearing the wafers. (12) V. Ibid., XIV, 12 *seq.* (13) I.e., being burnt on the altar. The 'fires' (Heb. *ishim*, pl. of *isheh*, generally rendered, 'an offering made by fire') are those of sacrifices or portions thereof (*sc.* the *emurim*) as they are burnt on the altar.

d (1) Hence this oil must be the residue of oil used in a meal-offering.

תורה אור

ואף ע"ג דמוספין קדישי אטו שבת למוספין א] אהנאי לתמידין לא אהנאי ת"ש *מוספי שבת קודמין למוספי ראש חודש אטו ראש חודש למוספין דידיה אהני למוספי שבת לא אהני תא שמע מוספי ראש חודש קודמין למוספי ראש השנה אע"ג דראש השנה קדשה אטו ראש השנה למוספי דידיה אהני למוספי ראש חודש לא אהני ת"ש ד"א *ברכת היין "תדירה וברכת היום אינה תדירה ותדיר ושאינו תדיר תדיר קודם אע"ג דברכת היום קדישה אטו שבת לברכת היום ב] אהנאי לברכת היין לא אהנאי תא שמע *דאמר רבי יוחנן הלכה "מתפלל אדם של מנחה ואח"כ של מוספין ג] אטו שבת לתפלת מוספין ד] אהנאי לתפלת מנחה לא אהנאי ת"ש שלמים של אמש חטאת ואשם של ה] יום שלמים של אמש קודמין הא אידי ואידי דיום חטאת ואשם קדמי ואע"ג דשלמים תדירי אמר רבא מצוי קאמרת תדיר קמיבעיא לן מצוי לא קמיבעיא לן אמר ליה רב הונא בר יהודה לרבא אטו ו] מצוי לאו תדיר והתניא אוציא את הפסח שאינו תדיר ולא אוציא את המילה שהיא תדירה מאי תדירה תדירה במצות ואיבעית אימא מילה לגבי פסח כי תדיר דמיא איבעיא להו תדיר ושאינו תדיר וקדים ושחט לשאינו תדיר מאי מי אמרינן כיון דשחטיה "מקריב ליה או דלמא יהיב לאחר דממרס בדמו עד דמקריב ליה לתדיר והדר מקריב לשאינו תדיר אמר רב ז] הונא מסורא ת"ש שלמים של אמש חטאת ואשם של ח] יום של אמש קודם לשל יום הא דיום דומיא דאמש וה"ד דקדים שחטיה לשלמים חטאת ואשם קדמי דלמא שלמים דאמש וחטאת ואשם דיום היכי משכחת לה דשחטינהו לתרוייהו ט] אבל לא שחטינהו לתרוייהו תיבעי לך ת"ש ד"א ברכת היין תדירה וברכת היום אינה תדירה ותדיר ושאינו תדיר תדיר קודם ה"נ דכיון י] דאתיין כמאן דשחיטי תרוייהו דמי ת"ש דא"ר יוחנן הלכה מתפלל אדם של מנחה ואח"כ של מוספין ה"נ כיון דמטי זמן תפלת מנחה כמאן דשחיטי תרוייהו דמי אמר ליה רב אחא בריה דרב אשי לרבינא יא] *"שחטו קודם חצות פסול מפני שנאמר בו שמות יב °בין הערבים קודם "לתמיד כשר ויהא ממרס בדמו עד שיזורק יב] הדם הכא במאי עסקינן כגון דקדים שחטיה לתמיד ברישא אמר ליה רב אחא סבא לרב אשי מתניתין נמי דיקא דקתני עד שיזרק יג] הדם (תמיד) ולא קתני עד שישחוט ויזרק דם ש"מ : ובכולן כהנים רשאין כו' : מאי טעמא אמר קרא במדבר יח °למשחה *לגדולה כדרך שהמלכים אוכלין : **מתני'** אמר רבי שמעון אם ראית שמן שהוא מתחלק בעזרה אין יד] צריך לשאול מהו אלא מותר רקיקי "מנחות ישראל "ולוג שמן של מצורע אם ראית שמן שהוא ניתן על גבי האישים אין טו] צריך לשאול מהו אלא מותר "רקיקי מנחת כהנים ומנחת כהן משיח *שאין מתנדבין שמן רבי טרפון אומר "מתנדבין שמן : גמ'

ואף על גב דמוספין קדישי . טז] מוספין שם שבת עליהן שהם באים חובה לה והתמידין באין אף בחול : לתמידין לא יז] אהנאי . כיון דהאידנא יח] קריבין *אם כן שם שבת עליהם : מוספי ר"ח . מקודשין משל שבת דאיקרי מועד יט] : ד"א כו'. בפסחים תנינן לה דקאמרי ב"ה מברך על היין ואח"כ מברך על היום שהיין גורם לקידוש שתאמר דבר אחר כו' : הכי גרסינן כ] דאע"ג דברכת היום קדישה . שהם שבת עליה שחובה לשבת היא באה דאילו ברכת היין אף בחול היא : הלכה מתפלל של מנחה . במסכת ברכות כא] היו לפניו שתי תפלות של מוספין ושל מנחה ופליגי רבי יהודה ורבנן וקא"ר יוחנן הלכה כדברי האומר מתפלל של מנחה ואחר כך מתפלל כו' : שלמים של אמש . הא פרישית לה לעיל כב] (גבי במתני') : תדירי . שהן מצויין מתוך שבאין בנדר ובנדבה : מצוי קאמרת . שאין תדירותו חובה אלא שהוא מצוי תמיד יותר מחבירו : הכי גרס *מצוי לאו תדיר הוא בתמיה : אוציא את הפסח שאינו תדיר . בת"כ שנויה גבי חטאת דקתני והרי פסח ומילה כג] ענושין כרת יכול יביא על שגגתן חטאת ת"ל אשר לא תעשנה יצאו. פסח ומילה שהן מצות עשה : אוציא את הפסח שאינו תדיר ולא אוציא את המילה שהיא תדירה . ת"ל אשר לא תעשנה אלמא מצוי תדיר הוא : תדירה במצות . סדורה במצות שנכרתו עליה שלש עשרה בריתות ולווין : כי תדיר דמיא. שמצויה היא כד] הרבה מפסח אבל מצוי דשלמים לגבי מצוי דחטאת לאו כתדירה דמי : הא דיום דומיא דאמש והיכי דמי כגון כה] דשחטו שלמים ברישא כו'. וקא ס"ד ה"ק שלמים שהביאן מאמש ושחטן היום וחטאת ואשם של יום עומדין לישחט שלמים של אמש קודמין ליזרק דאי בשניהם עומדין לישחט לא אמר כו] דקדמו שלמים וטעמא דבאו מאמש הא אידי ואידי כז] דהיום וקדים שחטינהו לשלמים ברישא אמרי' שחיטת חטאת ואשם קדמה לזריקת שלמים אלמא מקודש ושאינו מקודש וקדים שחטיה לשאינו מקודש יהא אחד ממרס בדמו ויזרוק את המקודש וה"ה לתדיר ושאינו תדיר : דלמא שלמים של אמש וחטאת של יום . דאשמעינן של אמש קדמו : היכי דמי דשחטינהו לתרוייהו . אע"ג דשחטיה לחטאת אחר השלמים ושניהן עומדין ליזרק אשמעינן דשלמים של אמש קדמו ודכותיה כח] דייקא מיניה הא אידי ואידי דיום ושחט שלמים ואחר כך חטאת ובא לימלך על הזריקה אמרי' ליה חטאת קדמה : אבל לא שחטיה . לחטאת בתר שלמים ובא לימלך על השחיטה תיבעי לך אי מזלזלינן בשלמים למרס בדמן ולהקדים שחיטת חטאת וזריקתה וכי מיבעיא לן בתדיר ושאינו תדיר כט] *הך מיבעיא לן ששחט את שאינו תדיר והתדיר קיים : ברכת היין תדירה כו' תדיר קודם . ואע"ג דשאינו תדיר קדם ובא שכבר קדש היום ועדיין יין לא בא ל] ודומיא קדים שחטיה לשאינו תדיר ברישא : ומשני ה"נ כיון דאתא השתא יין קמן ומזומן לברכה כמאן דשחיטי תרוייהו לגבי קדשים לא] [דמי] ולא תפשוט מינה לבעיין : ואח"כ מתפלל של מוספין . ואף על גב דזמן מוספין אתא ברישא : שחטו קודם חצות . בפסח קאי : קודם לתמיד . של בין הערבים כשר ואע"פ שלכתחילה מצוה לאחרו כדתניא לעיל (דף יב.) יאוחר דבר שנאמר בו בערב ובין הערבים לדבר שלא נאמר בו אלא בין הערבים בלבד : ויהא אחד ממרס בדמו . אלמא לב] דקדים ושחטיה למאוחר אמרי ליה לשהות את הזריקה ולשחוט את הראוי ליקדם ולזרקו : כגון דקדים שחטיה לתמיד . קודם שבא לימלך ולא נמלך אלא על הזריקה : למשחה . לך נתתים למשחה מתרגמינן לרבו והיינו לגדולה : **מתני'** שהוא מתחלק . לאכילת כהנים : מותר רקיקי מנחת ישראל . מנחת מאפה שבא חלות לג] ורקיקין חלות בוללן רקיקין מושחן ואמר רבי שמעון במנחות (דף עה.) מושחן כמין כ"י ושאר השמן נאכל לכהנים : מנחת כהנים . כולה כליל ומותר מנחת כהן משיח לפי ששמנה מרובה שלשה לוגין לעשרון ומתוך שהיא אפויה תחילה אין שמנה נבלע בפיתיה וצריך להקטיר המותר לד] בעצמו : שאין מתנדבין שמן . לפיכך לא יעלה על דעתך שיהא שמן המתחלק *מן הנקטר נדבה : גמ'

תא שמע מוספי שבת קודמין כו'. בכל הני תא שמע צריך טעם מאי קס"ד מאחר דכבר שני אטו שבת למוספין אהני לתמידין לה] לא אהגאי *וצריך לדקדק בפרק התכלת (מנחות דף מט.) גבי התמידין אין מעכבין את המוספין דאיכא כי הך בעיא דתדיר ומקודש ולא פשיט מיניה מידי דלא מייתי הכא ראיות דהתם והגהו דהכא לא מייתי התם :

דשחטינן לתרוייהו . תימה אם כן ליתני שלמים ושחט קודם לחטאת ואשם והכל ביום אחד שלמים קדימי לזרוק ואמאי נקט של אמש וי"ל דשל אמש נמי שמא הוי כעין של אמש והכל ביום אחד כדאמר בפ' התערובות (לעיל עה.) מאי אין כעין חיין. ברו"ך : אמר

עין משפט נר מצוה

עיין בספר פנים מאירות

כג א מיי' פכ"ט מהל' שבת הל' ז טוש"ע א"ח סימן רעא סעיף י :

כד ב מיי' פ"ג מהל' תפלה הל' י"א טוש"ע א"ח סימן רפו סעיף ד :

כה ג מיי' פ"ט מהל' תמידין ומוספין הלכה ג :

כו ד ה מיי' פ"א מהל' קרבן פסח הלכה ד :

כז ו מיי' פ"ט מהל' מעה"ק הלכה יד :

כח ז מיי' פ"ד מהל' מחוסרי כפרה הלכה ג :

כט ח מיי' פי"ג מהל' מעה"ק הלכה ט :

ל ט מיי' שם פט"ז הלכה יד :

מסורת הש"ס: צ"ל לא אף הם שם שבת כו' צ"ק | [לעיל פט.] | ברכות כח: פסחים קיד. | לעיל יב. ברכות כח. | צ"ל הנה מצוי כו' צ"ק | פסחים נח. | לעיל פח. סוטה טו. חולין קלב: | מנחות קה: [לעיל עז.] | צ"ל הכי מיבעיא לן צ"ק | ס"א לא | רש"ק פ"ו

שיטה מקובצת

א] אהני לתמידין לא אהני : ב] היום אהני לברכת יין לא אהני . ג] מוספין ואף על גב דתפילת מוספין קדישא אטו : ד] מוספין אהני לתפלת מנחה לא אהני : ה] של היום שלמים : ו] אטו תדיר לאו מצוי הוא והתניא: ז] רב חנינא תיבת הונא נמחק : ח] של היום שלמים של אמש קודם ותיבות לשל יום נמחק : ט] לתרוייהו ודיום דומיא דאמש נמי דשחטינהו לתרוייהו אבל : י] דכיון דאתא : יא] לרבינא ת"ש שחטו : יב] שיזורק דם התמיד הכא במאי עסקינן דקדים שחיט לתמיד ברישא : יג] שיזרק דם התמיד : יד] אין אתה צריך : טו] קדישי. שהמוספין שם : יז] לא אהני : יח] קרבי אף הם שם שבת : יט] מועד ויש בהו שעיר חטאת שמכפר, על טומאת מקדש וקדשיו הס"ד : כ] גרסי' אע"ג דברכת : כא] ברכות אמרינן ודו : כב] לעיל גבי מתני' הס"ד : כג] ומילה עונשן כרת : כד] היא תמיד : כה] דשחטי לשלמים ברישא כו'. ס"א שלמים של אמש קודמים באכילה הס"ד ומה"ד הא דיום דומיא דאמש והיכי דמי כגון דקדים ושחטינהו לשלמים ברישא חטאת ואשם דיום קדמי. קדמה זריקתם לזריקת שלמים ויאכלו תחילה כמו כן אלמא מקודש ושאינו מקודש וקדים שחטיה לשאינו מקודש יהא אחר ממרס בדמו וישחוט וזורק את המקודש וה"ה לתדיר ושאינו תדיר הס"ד ומה"ד דלמא לא גרסינן ה"נ שלמים של אמש וחטאת ואשם דיום ח"ד דשחטי' לתרוייהו אבל לא שחטינהו לתרוייהו תיבעי לך'. ושלמים דאמש וחטאת ואשם דיום קתני ע"כ היכי משכחת לה דשחטינהו לתרוייהו דהא לענין אכילה איירי וכי תידוק מינה לענין הקרבה נמי הא דיום דומיא דאמש וה"ד כגון דשחטיה לשלמים ברישא חטאת ואשם קדמי כדשחטינהו לתרוייהו תידוק לה שחזר ושחט את החטאת קודם שבא לימלך על הזריקה דהתם אמרינן ליה דחטאת קדמה דכיון דסוף סוף צריך למרס אחד מן הדמים קדשי קדשים קדמי אבל לא שחטיה לחטאת בתר שלמים ובא לימלך על השחיטה תיבעי אי מזלזלינן בשלמים למרס בדמן כו' (ככתוב לקמן ברש"י ד"ה אבל לא כו') : כו] אמר דניקדמו : כז] ואידי דיום יקדים : כח] דוק מיניה : כט] תיבת הך נמחק : ל] בא ודמיא לקדים ושחטיה לשאינו : לא] קדשים דמי ולא תפשוט בעיין מינה הס"ד : לב] אלמא היכא דקדים ושחטיה למאוחר ברישא ובא לימלך אמרי' ליה : לג] חלות או רקיקין : לד] המותר לעצמו הס"ד : לה] לא אהני :

עין משפט נר מצוה

לא א ב מיי' פט"ז מהלכות מעשה"ק הלכה יד :

נ"ל דמסקינן

לב ג מיי' פי"ז מהל' מעשה"ק הלכה יד :

לג ד מיי' פ"ב מהל' תמידין הלכה ו :

לד ה מיי' פי"ב מהל' שבת הל' ב טוש"ע א"ח סימן שלד סעיף כז :

גליון הש"ס

גמ' יין כדברי ר"ע. ע' מנחות דף לא ע"ב תוס' ד"ה דמייתי

נ"א דרבנן סברי דון מינה ומינה מה מנחה כו' ושיריו נאכלין ורבי סבר דון מינה ואוקי באתרה מה מנחה כו' אי ממנחה מייתי לה רבי דכ"ע כו' נ"ק

תורה אור

גמ' *אמר שמואל א] לדברי ר"ט *המתנדב שמן קומצו ב] ושיריו נאכלין מאי טעמא ג] אמר קרא קרבן מנחה *מלמד שמתנדבין שמן ד] וכי מנחה מה מנחה *קומצה ושיריה נאכלין אף שמן קומצו ושיריו נאכלין א"ר זירא אף אנן נמי תנינא א"ר שמעון אם ראית שמן שמתחלק בעזרה אי אתה צריך לשאול מהו אלא מותר רקיקי מנחות ישראל ולוג שמן של מצורע שאין מתנדבין ה] מכלל דמ"ד מתנדבין מתחלק אמר ליה אביי אימא סיפא אם ראית שמן שניתן על גבי אישים אי אתה צריך לשאול מהו אלא מותר רקיקי מנחת כהנים ומנחת כהן משיח שאין מתנדבין שמן מכלל דלמ"ד ו] מתנדב כולן לאישים לאביי קשיא רישא לרבי זירא קשיא סיפא בשלמא לרבי זירא רישא בשירים סיפא בקומץ אלא לאביי קשיא תנא רישא אטו סיפא בשלמא סיפא תני משום רישא אלא רישא משום סיפא מי תני אין אמרי במערבא *תנא רישא משום סיפא : *ת"ש °יין כדברי ר"ע ג לספלים שמן כדברי רבי טרפון לאישים מאי לאו מדיין כולו לספלים שמן ז] כולו לאישים מידי איריא הא כדאיתא והא כדאיתא ח] אמר רב פפא כתנאי *ג שמן לא יפחות מלוג רבי אומר שלשת לוגין במאי קמיפלגי אמרוה רבנן קמיה דרב פפא *דון מינה ומינה ט] דון מינה ואוקי באתרה איכא בינייהו *דרבנן סברי י] מה מנחה מתנדבין אף שמן מתנדבין יא] [ומינה מה מנחה לוג שמן אף כאן לוג שמן ומה מנחה קומצה ושיריה נאכלין אף שמן קומצו ושיריו נאכלין ואידך ממנחה מה מנחה מתנדבין אף שמן מתנדבין ואוקי באתרה] כנסכים מה נסכים שלשת לוגין יב] [אף שמן שלש לוגין ומה נסכים כולן לספלין] אף שמן כולן לאישים אמר ליה רב פפא *לאביי אי ממנחה מייתי לה [רבי] דכ"ע דון מינה ומינה אלא רבי מאזרח גמר לה א"ל רב הונא בריה דרב נתן לרב פפא מי מצית אמרת הכי והתניא קרבן מנחה מלמד שמתנדבין שמן וכמה שלשה לוגין ומאן שמעת ליה דאמר שלשה לוגין רבי היא וקא מייתי יג] לה מקרבן א"ל *אי תניא תניא *אמר שמואל המתנדב יין מביא ומזלפו על גבי האישים יד] מ"ט אמר קרא °ויין תקריב לנסך חצי ההין אשה ריח ניחוח לה' (במדבר טו) והא קא מכבי כיבוי במקצת לא שמיה כיבוי איני *והאמר רב נחמן אמר רבה בר אבוה ד המוריד גחלת מעל גבי המזבח וכיבה חייב דליכא אלא האי איבעית אימא כיבוי דמצוה שאני ת"ש דתנא ר"א בן יעקב כלפי שנתנה טו] תורה לתרום יכול יכבה ויתרום *אמרת לא יכבה שאני התם אפשר דיתיב ונטר ת"ש יין כדברי ר"ע לספלים שמן כדברי רבי טרפון לאישים ועוד תניא יין נסך לספלים או אינו אלא לאישים אמרת לא יכבה *לא קשיא הא *רבי יהודה הא ר"ש למימרא דשמואל כר"ש סבירא ליה *והאמר שמואל מכבין ה גחלת של מתכת ברה"ר בשביל שלא יוזקו בה רבים אבל

אמר ליה אי תניא תניא. הא דפליגי רבי ורבנן בסוף כל המנחות באות מצה (מנחות סג.) גבי תנופת זבחי שלמי צבור דילפינן מזבחי שלמי יחיד וקאמר רב פפא דכולי עלמא דון מינה ומינה וההיא מקמי דשמעה לברייתא דהכא לג] *דמפקינן גבי מתנדב שמן דפליגי בדון מינה ומינה ויש לתמוה דבפרק המנחות והנסכים (שם קד:) תנן אמר רבי טרפון מה מצינו ביין שהוא בא חובה לד] בא בנדבה אף שמן שהוא בא חובה בא נדבה למה לי מה מצינו כיון דיליף הכא מקרא מדכתיב קרבן :

המוריד גחלת מעל המזבח וכיבה חייב. וא"ת אמאי חייב הא איתעבידא לה מצותה דהא תנן לה לה] בפרק המזבח מקדש (לעיל פו.) וכן גחלת שפקעה מעל גבי המזבח לא יחזיר ושמא יש חילוק בין הורידה לפקעה לו] וההיא דתנן במסכת תמיד (דף לג.) נתפזר ממנה כקב גחלים מכבדן לאמה ניחא בלאו הכי משום דאינתיק למצוותה כדאמר בשלהי טרף בקלפי (יומא מו:) :

הא רבי יהודה הא רבי שמעון. וא"ת הא שמעינן ליה לר"ע דסבר ליה כר' שמעון בהגוזל בתרא (ב"ק קיג.) דקאמר רבי שמעון משום ר' עקיבא לובש אדם י' כלאים זה על גב זה כדי להעביר כו' ויש לומר דתרי תנאי ואליבא דר"ע : אבל

גמ' אמר שמואל המתנדב שמן טז] לדברי רבי טרפון קומצו. ומקטיר הקומץ ושיריו נאכלים : קרבן מנחה. יז] דמצי למכתב כי תקריב וכתב קרבן יתירא לדרשא : אף אנן נמי תנינא. דנאכל ולא מקטיר ליה יח] כולו : אין אתה צריך לשאול. אם של אלו הוא או של נדבה הוא ויהיב טעמא למילתיה שאין מתנדבין שמן : מכלל דמאן דאמר מתנדבין. איכא לספוקי בנדבה אלמא שמן נדבה מתחלק : בשלמא לר' זירא. דמתרץ למתני' כשמואל רישא דמשמע מתחלק [בשירים] וסיפ' דמשמע נדבה לאישים דאיכא לאוקמא בקומץ : תנא רישא משום סיפא. רישא דתני גבי שמן המתחלק אי אתה צריך לשאול מהו כדי נסבה דאי נמי מתנדבין שמן אינו מתחלק אלא משום דבעי למיתני סיפא אם ראית שמן ניתן על גבי האישים אי אתה צריך יט] לספקה בנדבה שאין מתנדבין שמן דדוקא אשמעינן דאילו למאן דאמר מתנדבין כ] *טתן תנא רישא נמי אם ראית שמן מתחלק : יין כדברי רבי עקיבא. דאמר במסכת מנחות (דף קד:) מתנדבין יין ואין מתנדבין שמן אותו יין לספלים הוא נותן לנסך ולא לזלף על האישים כא] והוא הדין לרבי טרפון כב] ביין אלא משום דאיצטריך כג] שמן למיתני [כדברי] רבי טרפון דלא כד] ליתני לה סתמא דהא לר' עקיבא אין מתנדבין שמן תנא נמי יין כדברי רבי עקיבא : שמן של נדבה כדברי רבי טרפון. דאמר אף מתנדבין שמן לאישים הוא כה] נותן : הא כדאיתא והא כדאיתא. יין כולו לספלים ודקתני בשמן לאישים אקומץ קאי : ה"ג כתנאי שמן לא יפחות מן הלוג רבי אומר שלשת לוגין : בדון מינה כו'. כל דבר שאתה למד מחבירו בג"ש או בהיקש הוי כו] למוד ממנו בכל דבריו : דון מינה ואוקי באתרה. מה שהדבר צריך ללמוד מחבירו שאין יכול ללמוד מגופו ילמד מחבירו ולשאר דברים כז] שיכול ללמד מגופו העמידהו על מקומו : מה מנחה מתנדבין כו'. דעיקר נדבת שמן מקרבן מנחה נפקא לן וסתם מנחה צריכה לוג שמן דכתיב (ויקרא יד) למנחה ולוג שמן : ומה מנחה קומצה כו'. כלומר וכיון דאית ליה לתנא קמא דון מינה ומינה לענין הקטרה נמי דיינינן ומינה מה מנחה קומצה כו' : כנסכים. *דהא שמן של נדבה לא קרב אלא בפני עצמו כיין הבא בפני עצמו הלכך לנסכים דמי וביין פשיטא לן דשלשת לוגין ניינהו כדנפקא לן במנחות (דף עג:) אזרח מלמד שמתנדבין יין : ומה נסכים כולן לספלים. כלומר כח] כיון דרבי אוקי באתרה אית ליה להא נמי אוקי באתרה ומה יין כולו לספלים אף שמן דלאו בר ספלים כולו לאישים וביין פשיטא לן דכולו לספלים ואינו מתחלק לכהנים דהא מאזרח איתרבי דכתיב בנסכים כל האזרח יעשה ככה (במדבר טו) ומנחת נסכים כולה כליל : *רבי מאזרח גמר לה. לנדבת שמן וכי נמי דיינת מינה ומינה שלשת לוגין הן שהוא פחות שבנסכים דנסכים של כבש רביעית ההין יין כתיב בהו (שם) כט] : ומי מצית אמרת הכי. דרבי מאזרח גמר לה : אשה ריח ניחוח. אלמא יש יין שהוא לאישים ואיזה זה יין הבא בפני עצמו דאילו הבא בגלל זבח כתיב הסך נסך שכר (שם כח) לשון שביעה לשון שכרות שיהא נראה על גבי המזבח כשפוקקין את השיתין כדאמרינן במסכת סוכה (דף מט:) : לא שמיה כיבוי. דלא קפיד קרא אלא אש תמיד תוקד על המזבח (ויקרא ו) : כלפי. כלומר הואיל : לתרום. את הדשן : יכול יכבה. אם מצאן כולן לוחשות שאינן מאוכלות : אמרת לא יכבה. אלמא כיבוי דמצוה ל] אסיר : ונטר. וממתין : או אינו אלא לאישים. דהא כתיב אשה ביין : הא רבי יהודה. דאמר (שבת דף קכ:*) דבר שאין מתכוין אסור הוי לא תכבה אפילו בלא מתכוין הלכך עקר ליה למשמעותיה דאשה למדרשיה נחת רוח הוא לפני כאישים והכי מסיק לה לברייתא בספרי : הא רבי שמעון. שמואל כרבי שמעון דכיון דאין מתכוין לכבות אין לא תכבה ראייה לא] עליו לאסור למיעקר משמעותא דאשה משום קושיא דלא תכבה ואם תאמר פסיק רישא ולא ימות הוא אפשר דמזליף ליה בטיפין דקות מאד הלכך אי נמי מכבה בטיפים גסות דבר שאין מתכוין הוא : גחלת של מתכת. לאו בת כיבוי לב] הוא ואיסורא דרבנן הוא דאיכא ובמקום היזק רבים לא גזור רבנן : אבל

מסורת הש"ס

[עיין תוס' סוף פ"ב דמנחות]

[מנחות קו.]

[שם עד:]

נ"ל ניתן ע"ג האישים תנא כו' נ"ק

[שבת ל. וש"נ]

תוספתא דמנחות פי"ב

מנחות קו. [ושם כל הסוגיא בכמה שינויים] [יבמות עח. וש"נ]

[במנחות ליתא]

[שבת קטו. וש"נ]

מנחות עד:

[יומא מו:]

נ"א אמרת לא תכבה שאני כו' וכן לקמן נ"ק

נ"ל דהא שמן של נדבה הבא בפני עצמו כיין הבא כו' נ"ק

עיין רפ"ק [שבת מח. וש"נ]

שם מג.

עיין חלופי גרסאות

[וד' כב. כט: מה. ובשאר דוכתי מנסם עיקר מילתא דר' יהודה גופיה כבר' כג: במשנה ובגמרא]

שיטה מקובצת

א] אמר שמואל (מנחות עד ע"ב) תיבת לדברי נמחק ותיבות ר"ט ל"ש : ב] קומצו ומקטיר ושיריו : ג] טעמא. ס"י דתניא ונפש כי תקריב ותיבות אמר קרא נמחק: ד] וכמנחה מה מנחה : ה] מתנדבין שמן מכלל : ו] דלמ"ד מתנדבין שמן אזיל לאישים ותיבת כולן נמחק : ז] שמן נמי כולו : ח] תיבות אמר רב פפא נמחק : ט] ודון מינה : י] סברי דון מינה ומינה מה דון מינה מה מנחה מתנדבין אף שמן מתנדבין ומינה מה מנחה לוג אף שמן לוג ומה מנחה קמצה ושיריה נאכלין אף שמן קומצו ושיריו נאכלין ורבי סבר דון מינה ואוקי באתרה דון מינה מה : יא] מתנדבין ואוקי באתרה ומתיבת ומינה כו' עד תיבת כנסכים ל"ש ונמחק : יב] אף שמן שלשה לוגין ומה נסכים כולן לספלים אף שמן כולו לאישים אמר להו רב פפא אי ממנחה ילפי לה דכ"ע ל"פ דדון מינה ותיבות לאביי מייתי דון נמחק : יג] מייתי ליה מקרבן : יד] האישים ודוקא נסכים הבאין בפני עצמן אבל נסכים הבאין בגלל הזבח אינו מזלפן דכתיב בהו הסך נסך שכר דמשמע לשון שביעה ושכרות למזבח וזהו כשנתנו לספלים ומאן דלית ליה מזלפו על גבי האישים מפרש להאי קרא נחת רוח לשם כאישים : טו] התורה רשות לתרום : טז] שמן כדברי רבי טרפון : יז] מנחה מדמצי למכתב כי תקריב מנחה וכתב : יח] כולה הס"ד : יט] צריך לספקו בנדבה : כ] מתנדבין ניתן תנא : כא] האישים וטעמא דר' עקיבא מפרש בגמרא והוא : כב] תיבת ביין ל"ש : כג] דאיצטריך למיתני שמן כדברי ר"ט : כד] דלא מיתני ליה : כה] הוא ניתן הס"ד : כו] הוי למד ממנו בכל : כז] שאתה יכול ללמד : כח] כלומר וכיון דרבי : כט] בהו והין י"ב לוגין : ל] דמצוה נמי אסיר : לא] ראייה לאסור עליו למיעקר : לב] כיבוי היא ואיסורא : לג] דהבא דמסקינן גבי. תיבת דמפקינן נמחק : לד] הובה ובא בנדבה : לה] לעיל בפרק : לו] לפקעה דפקעה מאליה חשיבא נעשית מצוותה אבל הורידה לא נעשית מצותו וההיא :

GEMARA. [91*b*] Samuel said: According to R. Tarfon, when a man donates oil [by itself], he removes a fistful, burns it [on the altar], and its residue is eaten. What is the reason?—Scripture saith, [*And when any one bringeth*] *a meal-offering*:[2] this teaches that one can donate oil [by itself],[3] and that it [an offering of oil] is like a meal-offering: as a fistful is taken of a meal-offering and the rest is eaten,[4] so the oil: one takes a fistful off and the rest of it is eaten. R. Zera observed, We too have learnt thus: R. SIMEON SAID: IF YOU SEE OIL BEING SHARED OUT IN THE TEMPLE COURT, YOU NEED NOT ASK WHAT IT IS, FOR IT IS THE RESIDUE OF THE WAFERS [REḲIḲIM] OF THE ISRAELITES' MEAL-OFFERINGS OR OF THE LEPER'S LOG OF OIL . . . FOR MEN CANNOT OFFER OIL [ALONE]: hence it follows that on the view that it can be offered, it can be shared out![5]—Said Abaye to him: Then consider the next clause: IF YOU SEE OIL POURED ON THE FIRES, YOU NEED NOT ASK WHAT IT IS, FOR IT IS THE RESIDUE OF THE WAFERS OF PRIESTS' MEAL-OFFERINGS OR OF THE ANOINTED PRIEST'S MEAL-OFFERING, FOR MEN CANNOT OFFER OIL [ALONE]: hence it follows that on the view that it can be offered, the whole of it is a fire offering. Thus the first clause presents a difficulty on Abaye's view, while the last clause presents a difficulty on R.
a Zera's view. As for R. Zera, it is well: the first clause[1] refers to the residue, while the last clause refers to the fistful. But on Abaye's view there is a difficulty?—The first clause is taught on account of the last clause.[2] As for saying that a second clause it taught on account of a first clause, that is well; but does one teach a first clause on account of a second clause?[3]—Yes: they said in the West [Palestine]: The first clause is taught on account of the second clause.

Come and hear: Wine, in R. Akiba's view, is for the basins; oil, in R. Tarfon's view, is for the fires.[4] Now surely, since the *whole* of the wine is for basins, the *whole* of the oil is for burning?[5]—Why choose to say thus: each is conditioned by its own law.[6]

R. Papa said:[7] This is dependent on Tannaim: [When one donates] oil, he must bring not less than a *log*; Rabbi said: Three *logs*. Wherein do they differ?—The scholars stated before R. Papa: They differ as to whether [we say]: Judge from it and [all] from it; or, judge from it and place the deduction on its own basis.[8] The Rabbis hold: 'Judge from it and [all] from it': as a meal-offering can be donated, so can oil be donated; 'and [all] from it': as a meal-
b offering [requires] a *log* of oil,[1] so here too[2] a *log* of oil [is required]; and as a meal-offering, a fistful thereof is removed, and the rest is eaten, so the oil [alone], a fistful thereof is removed and the rest is eaten. And the other [learns] from a meal-offering: as a meal-offering is donated, so is oil donated; 'but place it on its own basis', viz., it is like a drink-offering [of wine]:[3] as a drink-offering consists of three *logs*,[4] so oil consists of three *logs*; and as the whole of a drink-offering is for basins, so the oil is altogether for the fires. R. Papa observed to Abaye: If Rabbi inferred it from a meal-offering, then all would agree that you judge from it and [all] from it. Rabbi, however, deduces it from *'home-born'*.[5] Said R. Huna the son of R. Nathan to R. Papa: Can you say thus? Surely it was taught: '*A meal-offering*': this teaches that oil [alone] can be donated? And how much? Three *logs*. Now, whom do you know to maintain [that it must be] three *logs*? Rabbi; yet he deduces it from a meal-offering!—If it was taught, it was taught, he replied.[6]

Samuel said: When one donates wine, he brings it and sprinkles it on the fires. What is the reason? Scripture saith, *And thou shalt present for the drink-offering half a hin of wine, for an offering made by fire, of a sweet savour unto the Lord.*[7] But he extinguishes [the fires]?[8]—Partial extinguishing[9] is not called extinguishing. But that is not so, for surely R. Naḥman said in Rabbah b. Abbuha's name: If one removes a coal from the altar and extinguishes it, he is culpable?—That is when there is none but that [coal]. Alternatively, extinguishing as [part of] a religious rite is different.[10]

Come and hear, for R. Eliezer b. Jacob taught: Since Scripture authorised the taking up [of the ashes], you might think that one can extinguish [the embers] and take [them] up; but you must say
c that one may not extinguish![1]—There it is different, for one can sit and wait.[2]

Come and hear: Wine, in R. Akiba's view, is for the bowls; oil, in R. Tarfon's view, is for the fires.[3] Moreover, it was taught: The wine of a drink-offering is for the bowls. Yet perhaps it is not so, but rather for the fires? Say, he must not extinguish![4]—There is no difficulty: One agrees with R. Judah; the other with R. Simeon.[5] Are we to say that Samuel agrees with R. Simeon? Surely Samuel said: One may extinguish a lump of fiery metal in the street, that it

(2) Lev. II,
1. (3) The Heb. is קרבן מנחה of which קרבן (an offering) is superfluous, since מנחה itself denotes the offering, and moreover תקריב, *bringeth*, is of the same root as קרבן and implies it. Hence it is understood to include even an offering of oil alone, without flour. (מנחה, generally rendered *meal*-offering, simply means a gift, of anything, although it is usually applied to offerings of flour.) (4) Ibid. 2*f*. (5) R. Simeon maintains that one need not ask what it is, i.e., whether it is a meal-offering in itself, because such cannot be donated. Hence he who holds that it can be donated maintains that it might happen that such itself is shared out; whence it follows that it is not altogether burnt on the altar.

a (1) Which implies that oil, when donated by itself, is shared out among the priests. (2) For the sake of symmetry and parallelism. The first clause, IF YOU SEE OIL BEING SHARED OUT IN THE TEMPLE COURT, is irrelevant to the controversy as to whether oil can be donated or not, for even if it could be donated, it would still not be shared out to the priests and so this oil, which was being shared out to the priests could only be the residue, as the Mishnah explains, *on all views*. But it is taught merely as a parallel to the second clause referring to a fire-offering, where it is only on the view that oil cannot be donated that one need not doubt, for on the view that oil can be donated, one might doubt what this oil is, since a votive offering of oil too is burnt on the altar. (3) It is logical that when one clause has *already been taught*, a second is added for the sake of parallelism. But is it logical that an *earlier* clause should be added, before there is anything which it can parallel? (4) R. Akiba holds (Men. 104*b*) that wine can be offered by itself, but not oil. When such wine is offered, it is to be put in basins or beakers, as a drink-offering, but it is not sprinkled on the fires. R. Tarfon agrees in this; R. Akiba's name, however, is mentioned in contrast to the next clause, which is only according to R. Tarfon, since R. Akiba holds that oil alone cannot be donated. (5) When such is offered by itself. This contradicts Samuel. (6) Though the *whole* of the wine is for basins, the whole of the oil need not be for burning. (7) Sh.M. deletes this. (8) I.e., whether an analogy must be carried through on all points, so that the case deduced agrees throughout with the case from which the deduction has started; or whether the deduction won by analogy be regulated by the rules of the original case (Jast.).

b (1) V. Lev. XIV, 10. (2) When oil alone is donated. (3) Which is donated by itself. It is more logical to liken it to a drink-offering than to the ordinary meal-offering of which oil is only a part. (4) As deduced in Men. 73*b*. (5) Num. XV, 13; V. Men. 73*b*. (6) I must accept it. (7) Ibid. 10. '*For an offering made by fire*' implies that it is sprinkled on same. (8) Whereas Scripture says, *Fire shall be kept burning on the altar continually; thou shalt not extinguish it* (Lev. VI, 6). (9) This could only extinguish a little. (10) When he sprinkles the wine, he performs a religious rite.

c (1) The *var. lec.* is preferable: say, however, (it is written), *thou shalt not extinguish it*.—Thus one may not extinguish even in the performance of a religious rite. (2) Until they go out. (3) Thus wine is *not* for the fires. (4) Cf. n. 1. (5) These scholars dispute in Shab. 41*b* about an unintentional act on the Sabbath: R. Judah forbids, while R. Simeon permits it. Here too, the extinguishing is unintentional: the Baraithas which rule that the wine may *not* be sprinkled on the fires agree with R. Judah; whereas Samuel agrees with R. Simeon.

should not harm the public,[6] [92a] but not a burning piece of wood.[7] Now if you think that he agrees with R. Simeon, even that of wood too [should be permitted]?[8]—In respect to what is unintentional he holds with R. Simeon; but in the matter of work which is not needed *per se*,[9] he agrees with R. Judah.[10]

R. Huna said: If a drink-offering [of wine] was defiled, one must
a make a separate fire for it[1] and burn it, for it is said, *And every [sin-offering] ... in the holy place ... it shall be burnt with fire.*[2] It was taught likewise: If blood, oil, meal-offerings or drink-offerings were defiled, a separate fire is made for them, and they are burnt. Samuel said to R. Ḥana of Baghdad: Bring me ten people and I will teach you in their presence:[3] If drink-offerings were defiled, one makes a separate fire for them and burns them.

CHAPTER XI

MISHNAH. IF THE BLOOD OF A SIN-OFFERING SPURTED
b ON TO A GARMENT, IT MUST BE WASHED.[1] THOUGH SCRIPTURE SPEAKS ONLY OF [SIN-OFFERINGS] WHICH ARE EATEN, FOR IT IS SAID, IN A HOLY PLACE SHALL IT BE EATEN,[2] YET BOTH THOSE WHICH MAY BE EATEN AND THE INNER [SACRIFICES][3] NECESSITATE WASHING, FOR IT IS SAID, [THIS IS] THE LAW OF THE SIN-OFFERING:[4] THERE IS ONE LAW FOR ALL SIN-OFFERINGS. THE BLOOD OF A DISQUALIFIED SIN-OFFERING DOES NOT NECESSITATE WASHING, WHETHER IT HAD A PERIOD OF FITNESS OR DID NOT HAVE A PERIOD OF FITNESS. WHICH HAD A PERIOD OF FITNESS? ONE [WHOSE BLOOD] WAS KEPT OVERNIGHT, OR WAS DEFILED, OR WAS TAKEN OUT [OF THE TEMPLE COURT]. WHICH DID NOT HAVE A PERIOD OF FITNESS? ONE WHICH WAS SLAUGHTERED [WITH THE INTENTION OF EATING IT][5] AFTER TIME OR WITHOUT BOUNDS; OR WHOSE BLOOD WAS RECEIVED BY UNFIT PERSONS.

GEMARA. IF THE BLOOD OF A SIN-OFFERING SPURTED etc. If there is one law for *all* sin-offerings, even a bird sin-offering too [should be included]. Why then was it taught: You might think that the blood of a bird sin-offering requires washing; therefore it states, *This is [the law of the sin-offering]*?[6]—Said Resh Laḳish on Bar Ḳappara's authority, Scripture saith, *shall [the sin-offering] be slaughtered*:[7] thus the Writ speaks [only] of those which are slaugh-
c tered.[1] Yet say rather that the Writ speaks [only] of those which are *eaten*, as it is written, '*in a holy place shall it be eaten*', but not inner [sin-offerings]?—The Divine Law included [them by writing] '*the law of*'.[2] If so, even a bird sin-offering too [is included]?—The Divine Law expressed a limitation in '*this is*'. And why do you prefer it thus?[3]—It is logical to include *animal* inner sin-offerings, because: it is an animal; it is slaughtered in the north;[4] [its blood is] received

(6) Metal does not really burn, but throws off fiery sparks when hot. The prohibition of extinguishing (on the Sabbath, to which this refers) does not apply in this case by Biblical law at all, save by Rabbinical law; hence where general damage may ensue the Rabbis waived their prohibition. (7) For that is Biblically forbidden. (8) For though he *intentionally* extinguishes it, yet his work is not needed *per se* (v. n. 6.), and R. Simeon permits such. (9) E.g., when one carries out a corpse on Sabbath into the street. He does not really want the corpse in the street, but merely wants it out of the house. Every case of extinguishing except that of a wick to make it easier for subsequent relighting, falls within this category, since with this exception extinguishing is always negative. R. Judah forbids such, and R. Simeon permits it. (10) Hence he permits the unintentional extinguishing on the altar, but forbids the unintentional extinguishing of a burning piece of wood.

a (1) On the pavement of the Temple court; but it must not be taken out. (2) Lev. VI, 23. The accents are disregarded in this rendering. In Pes. 24b the verse is interpreted to mean that all sacrifices which must be eaten in the Temple court when fit, must be burnt in the same place if unfit; and the same applies to this wine. (3) Probably a proverbial expression, denoting emphasis and certainty.

b (1) Lev. VI, 20: *And when there is sprinkled of the blood thereof upon any garment, thou shalt wash that whereon it was sprinkled in a holy place.* (2) Ibid. 19. (3) The sin-offerings slaughtered in the inner sanctuary (*hekal*); these may not be eaten; v. Lev. IV, 1-12; 13-21. (4) Ibid. VI, 18; this is the superscription of the present passage containing this law of washing. (5) Or sprinkling its blood. (6) '*This is*' is a limitation, implying, only what is enumerated in the section. (7) Ibid.

c (1) I.e., with *shechitah*, whereas a bird requires *meliḳah*. (2) One law for all. (3) Why apply the extension to inner sin-offerings and the limitation to birds, and not the reverse? (4) Rashi reads, and BaḤ emends accordingly: it is slaughtered; it requires the north.

אבל לא גחלת של עץ ואי ס"ד כר"ש ס"ל אפילו גחלת של עץ נמי *בדבר שאין מתכוין סברלה כר"ש במלאכה שאינה צריכה לגופה סבר לה כרבי יהודה אמר רב הונא *נסכים שנטמאו עושה להן מערכה בפני עצמן ושורפן משום שנאמר א] °בקודש באש תשרף תניא נמי הכי *הדם והשמן והמנחות והנסכים שנטמאו עושה להן מערכה בפני עצמן ושורפן א"ל שמואל לרב חנא בגדתאה *אייתי לי בי עשרה ואימא לך קמייהו נסכים שנטמאו עושה להן מערכה בפני עצמן ושורפן :

הדרן עלך כל התדיר

דם ב]חטאת שנתז על הבגד הרי זה טעון כיבוס אע"פ שאין הכתוב מדבר אלא בנאכלות שנאמר °במקום קדוש תאכל ג]אחד הנאכלות ואחד הפנימיות טעונות כיבוס שנאמר תורת החטאת תורה אחת לכל ד] החטאות *חטאת פסולה אין דמה טעון כיבוס בין שהיתה לה שעת הכושר ובין שלא היתה לה שעת הכושר איזו היא שהיתה לה שעת הכושר שלנה ושנטמאה ושיצאת ואיזו היא שלא היתה לה שעת הכושר שנשחטה חוץ לזמנה וחוץ למקומה ב] ושקיבלו פסולין (וזרקו) את דמה : **גמ'** דם חטאת ג] (*שמתה) כו' ואי תורה אחת לכל חטאות אפילו חטאת העוף נמי אלמה תניא ה]יכול תהא דם חטאת העוף טעון כיבוס ת"ל °זאת אמר ר"ל משום בר קפרא ו]אמר קרא °תשחט בנשחטות הכתוב מדבר ואימא בנאכלות הכתוב מדבר כדכתיב במקום קדוש תאכל אבל פנימיות לא רבי רחמנא תורת אי הכי אפילו חטאת העוף נמי מיעט רחמנא זאת ומה ראית מסתברא דחטאת ד] [בהמה] פנימיות ה"ל לרבויי שכן בהמה (א) שחיטת צפון וקבלת כלי וקרן

רש"י

אבל לא של עץ · דבת כיבוי הוא ואיסורא דאורייתא הוא ואי כר"ש לא מכבתת כיבוי ה] אלא במתכוין לעשות פחמין בכיבויו וצריך להס דאר"ש מלאכה שאינה צריכה לגופה פטור עליה וכיבוי ו] לאו לצורך גופו הוא *שיהא צריך לו דהלואי שלא בא עליו ודמי למוציא את המת לסלקו מעל פניו דפטור עליה ר"ש במסכת שבת בפרק המצניע (דף צד·) : מערכה · על הרצפה בעזרה ולא יוציאה לחוץ משום שנאמר ז] בקדש באש תשרף בפ' שני דפסחים (דף כד·) דרשינן האי קרא וכל חטאת אשר יובא וגו' ח] ומרבינן מיניה כל פסולי קדשים ט] שפסולתו בעזרה שיהו נשרפים בעזרה כדכתיב בקדש לא תאכל באש תשרף י] ותמיה אני למה שורפן לעצמן ואינו שורפן בבית הדשן שהיה בעזרה שבו שורפין פסולי קדשי קדשים ונראה בעיני יא] שהוא דבר לא שורפן לעצמן שתהא שריפתן ניכרת לעצמן שאם היה שורפן עם בשר אין ניכרין שהרי אין בהן ממש: הדם והשמן גרסי':

הדרן עלך כל התדיר

דם חטאת טעון כיבוס · כדכתיב ואשר יזה מדמה וגו' : במקום קדוש תאכל · בההוא עניינא כתיב : תורת החטאת · רישא דעניינא הוא : פסולה אין יב] טעון דמה כיבוס · דכתיב אשר יזה בראוי להזאה הכתוב מדבר : שעת הכושר · לזריקה : שלנה · לן דמה : ושקבלו פסולין את דמה יג] · גרסי' ולא גרסי' וזרקו דהא אפילו כשרה שנתז יד] (את) מדמה לאחר זריקה על הבגד אין טעון כיבוס כדאמרינן לקמן *פרט לזה שכבר הוזה: **גמ'** תשחט החטאת · בההוא עניגא כתיב בנשחטות ולא בנמלקות: אפילו חטאת העוף נמי · אע"ג דכתיב זאת למעוטא הא פנימיות נמי אימעיטו דבנאכלות הכתוב מדבר וקמרבינן להו מתורת : ומה ראית · לרבות פנימיות מתורת ולמעט עוף מזאת : דחטאת בהמה פנימיות ה"ל לרבויי · כדין החיצונים שכן בהמה כמותה שחיטה כמותה טעונה צפון כמותה וקבלת כלי כמותה וקרנות המזבח כמותה וכנגד חודה של קרן ובאצבע ואישים אימוריהן לאישים אבל עוף אינו בהמה ואינו שחוט ואינו טעון צפון וקבלה ולא קרן שהרי חטאת העוף למטה נעשית ואינו טו] טעונה באצבע בחודה של קרן ואין ממנה לאישים :

יאכלנה

תוספות

אבל לא גחלת של עץ · תימה היכי ס"ד דדבר שאין מתכוין טז] שוה לאינה צריכה לגופה דמה ענין זה לזה ובפ' כירה (שבת מב·) ניחא טפי גבי הא דשרי שמואל אפילו שיעור לצרף דפריך התם כה"ג ומצי למימר דס"ד דלא הוה שרי ר"ש דבר שאין מתכוין לכתחילה אי לאו משום דאית ביה תרתי דהוה נמי מלאכה שאינה צריכה לגופה הלכך רבי יהודה דמחייב באינה צריכה לגופה אוסר באין מתכוין דהא בהא תליא אבל הכא אי אפשר לפרש כן דמייתי לה אההיא דהמתנדב יין מביאו ומזלפו על גבי האישים דלא שייך טעמא דאין צריכה לגופה אלא גבי מלאכות דשבת ובסוף פרק ראשון דחגיגה (דף י·) מייתי לה גבי הלכות שבת כהררים התלוים בשערה וצריך לפרש דמשמע יז] להש"ס דהשתא דכי היכי דמחייב שמואל באינה צריכה יח] לגופה ה"נ יש לו לחייב אין מתכוין כמתכוין : **במלאכה** שאינה צריכה לגופה סבר לה כרבי יהודה · הקשה בהלכות גדולות דבשמעתא קמייתא דשבת (דף ג·) קאמר שמואל כל פטורי דשבת פטור אבל אסור לבר מהני תלת דפטור ומותר הצד צבי והצד נחש ומפיס מורסא פי' דשרו רבנן משום צער יט] דגופא דצד נחש ומפיס מורסא לא מיפטר אלא לר"ש דפטר מלאכה שאינה צריכה לגופה כדאיתא בפ' שמנה שרצים (שבת קז:) ודוחק הוא לתרץ בהלכות גדולות ור"ת תירץ דהא דחשיב לה שמואל כ] [בהדי] פטור ומותר (קאמר) לאו משום דס"ל הכי אלא כלומר מאן דס"ל שהוא פטור קסבר דפטור ומותר כמו שמדקדק שמואל בסוף האורג (שם קז·) דודאי פטור ומותר קאמר מיהו אנן לא קיימא לן כשמואל במלאכה שאינה צריכה לגופה כדאשכחן רבא דהוא בתרא דסבר כר"ש בריש נוטל (שם קמא:) ואמוראי דפרק כל כתבי הקדש (שם קכא:) דאמרי כל המזיקין נהרגין בשבת ואפילו מאן דאסר לא פליג אמהני' דעל עקרב שלא תשוך הלכך מותר להפיס מורסא בשבת להוציא ממנה ליחה :

הדרן עלך כל התדיר

שלנה ושנטמאה · פירוש לן דמה ונטמא דמה ואם תאמר ונטמא מ"ט לא בעי כיבוס הא מדאורייתא זורקו לכתחילה כדאמרינן (פסחים דף פ: *) דם שנטמא וזרקו בשוגג הורצה וי"ל דמיירי כגון שנשבר הציץ או אינו על מצחו למאן דאית ליה [שאינו מרצה] (יומא דף ז:) : **ושקבלו** פסולין וזרקו את דמה · *פירש בקונטרס או זרקו ואע"ג דאפילו כשרה אם ניתז דמה לאחר זריקה אין טעון כיבוס כדאמר לקמן פרט לזה שכבר הוזה איצטריך לאשמועינן בפסולין למימר דדם דחוי הוא ואין הנותר במזרק כשר לזריקה ולא תימא יחזור הכשר ויזרוק °דפסול עושה שירים ול"ע בפ"ק דמעילה (דף ה·) : *) **יכול** תהא דם חטאת העוף טעון כיבוס ת"ל זאת · והוא הדין קדשים קלים מימעטי מזאת ותימה דבסוף פירקין (דף צח·) מרבי מזאת התורה לעולה ולמנחה ולחטאת מה חטאת מתקדשת בבלוע אף כל מתקדש בבלוע והשתא מנ"ל דאתיא היקשא לרבות כל הקדשים כחטאת לענין בלוע ומיעוטא דהכא לענין כיבוס אימא איפכא וי"ל כיון דאשכחן דכל קדשים טעונין מריקה ושטיפה מדאיצטריך אותה למעוטי תרומה סברא הוא לאוקומה היקשא לענין להתקדש בבלוע מאחר דאשכחן דטעונין מריקה ושטיפה מטעם בליעת כלי ומיתרצא נמי בהכי קושיא אחריתי דרבי יהודה מפיק לקמן כל קדשים לענין מריקה ושטיפה מקדש קדשים והשתא ל"ל קרא תיפוק לי מהיקשא דחטאת דכל קדשים טעונין מריקה ושטיפה כחטאת אבל למאי דפרישית ניחא דאי לאו דאשכחן מריקה [ושטיפה] בהדיא הוה מוקמי היקשא לענין כיבוס ומיעוטא דזאת למעוטי מריקה ושטיפה ובלוע :

*) שייך לע"ב

וקרן

עין משפט נר מצוה

לה א מיי' פ"ו מהלכות איסורי מזבח הלכה

א ב מיי' פ"ח מהלכות מעשה הקרבנות הלכה א

ב ג מיי' שם הלכה כ :

ג ד מיי' שם הלכה ג ·

ד ה ו מיי' שם הלכה כ:

שיטה מקובצת

א] שנאמר וכל בקודש : ב] ושקבלו פסולים כו' פ"הא או קתני שקבלו פסולים וזרקו כשרים או זרקו פסולים אבל קבלו כשרים ולא נהירא דא"כ היאך חשיב לא היתה לו שעת הכושר כיון דקבלו כשרים ועוד דבמס' מעילה משמע דחדא קאמר לכך נראה לי דחדא קאמר וה"פ קבלו פסולים וזרקו פסולים משמע דאם קבלו כשרים וזרקו דמה טעון כיבוס דא"כ למה לי זרקו פסולים וקשה דהא כתיב אשר יזה פרט לשכבר הוזה וי"ל דה"ה אם קבלו כשרים וזרקו כשרים דאין דמה טעון כיבוס דהא כתיב אשר יזה והאי דנקט זרקו פסולים לאשמועינן דפסול עושה שיריים דאי לאו הוי תני אלא קבלו פסולים מ"מ הוה מצי למהוי דדמה טעון כיבוס כגון אם היה דם עוד בצוארה דנימא יחזור הכשר ויקבל ואותו הדם הוי בר הזאה להכי תני זרקו פסולים דהשתא אפילו היה דם בצוארה ויחזור הכשר ויקבל לא הוי טעון כיבוס דפסול עושה שיריים · תוס' מהר"פ : ג] חטאת שניתז כו' : ד] דחטאת בהמה : ה] כיבוי מן התורה אלא : ו] וכיבוי זה לאו: ז] שנאמר וכל בקודש : ח] וגו' בקדש לא תאכל באש תשרף ומרבינן : ט] קדשים שמחיצתן בעזרה : י] תשרף תמהני למה שורפן לעצמן: יא] בעיני מפני: יב] אין דמה טעון כיבוס : יג] דמה ס"א או זרקו את דמה ואיצטריך לאשמועינן פסולים ואע"ג דהא אפילו כשרים שניתז דמן לאחר זריקה על הבגד אין טעון כיבוס כדאמרינן לקמן פרט לזה שכבר הוזה איצטריך, לאשמועינן פסולין ולמימר דדם דחוי הוא ואין הנותר במזרק כשר לזריקה ולא תימא יחזור הכשר ויזרוק : יד] תיבת את נמחק : טו] ואינו מתנה באצבע : טז] מתכוין הוי כדבר שאינה צריכה : יז] דמשמע ליה לתלמודא השתא דכי : יח] לגופיה במתכוין ה"נ יש לו : יט] דגופא והשתא כיון דס"ל לשמואל כרבי יהודה דמלאכה שאינה צריכה לגופה חייב עליה מדאורייתא היכי שרו רבנן משום צערא דגופה דצד : כ] שמואל בהדי פטור ומותר ותיבת קאמר נמחק :

מסורת הש"ס

נ"ל שאינו צריך לו דהלואי שלא כבה ודמי כו' צ"ק

[שבת מב.]

תוספתא דתמורה [פ"ד ע"ש]

[יבמות פז. וש"נ]

מעילה ה:

נ"ל אשר יזה פרט כו' צ"ק

[נ"ל שניתז]

ולעיל מח.

פיס לשם גי' אחרת ברש"י רש"ק וגירסת הש"ק הכי פירש בקונטרס דלא גרסינן וזרקו ול"נ דגרסינן או זרקו כו'

הגהות הב"ח

(א) גמ' שכן בהמה כמותה ושחיטה כמותה שחיטת צפון וקבלת צפון כלי וקרן :

גליון הש"ס

תוס' ד"ה ושקבלו כו' דפסול עושה שירים · ע"ל ד' לד ע"ב תוס' ד"ה פסול :

ה א מיי' פ"ב מהלכות פסה"מ הלכה יט :
ו ב מיי' שם הלכה יח :
ז ג מיי' פ"א מהלכות פסה"מ הלכה יא :
ח ד מיי' פ"ב שם הלכה כ :
ט ה מיי' פ"ח מהלכות מעה"ק הלכה ט דלא כר"ע :

וקרן ואצבע וחודה ואישים אדרבה חטאת העוף הוה ליה לרבויי שכן חוץ כמותה ואכילה כמותה הנך נפישין רב יוסף אמר אמר קרא °יאכלנה א] לזו ולא לאחרת (ויקרא ו) בנאכלות מיעט הכתוב ואלא זאת ל"ל אי לאו זאת הוי אמינא יאכלנה אורחיה דקרא ב] קמ"ל רבה אמר אמר קרא °אשר יזה (שם) ג] בהזאות הכתוב מדבר ד] (א) *והתניא אע"פ שאין הכתוב מדבר אלא בנאכלות ה] לענין מריקה ושטיפה אבל לענין כיבוס אשר יזה כתיב אי הכי אחד הנאכלות ואחד הפנימיות אחד הפנימיות ואחד הנאכלות מיבעי ליה תני אחד הפנימיות ואחד הנאכלות אי הכי חטאת העוף נמי מיעט רחמנא זאת אי הכי חיצונה נמי לא ריבה רחמנא תורת ומה ראית מסתברא חטאת בהמה הוה ליה לרבויי שכן בהמה שחיטת צפון וקבלת כלי וקרן ואצבע וחודה ואישים אדרבה חטאת העוף הו"ל לרבויי שכן הזאה כמותה הנך נפישין *בעי רבי אבין °חטאת העוף שהכניס דמה בצוארה בפנים מהו צוארה ככלי שרת דמי ומיפסיל או דלמא *כצואר בהמה ו] מדמה אמר רחמנא ולא בשרה ז] ת"ש °פירכסה ונכנסה לפנים וחזרה כשירה הא הכניסה ח] פסולה וליטעמיך גבי קדשי קדשים דקתני *°פירכסה ויצאה לדרום וחזרה כשרה הא הוציאה ט] פסולה אלא האי יצתה לחוץ איצטריכא ליה ה"נ יצתה לחוץ איצטריכא ליה בעי רבי אבין י] °נשפך על הרצפה ואספה מהו אצרוכיה הוא דלא אצרכיה רחמנא כלי שרת והלכך אוספו וכשר או דלמא מיפסל פסל ביה רחמנא כלי שרת והלכך אוספו ופסול אמר רבא ת"ש יכול יהא דם חטאת העוף טעון כיבוס תלמוד לומר זאת ואי ס"ד מיפסל פסיל ביה רחמנא יא] תיפוק לי דהא אפסיל לה באויר כלי אמר רב הונא בריה דרב יהושע במדביק כלי בצוארה בעא מיניה לוי יב] *ניתז מבגד לבגד מהו °מבגד קמא אידחי ליה לכיבוס או דלמא לא יג] א"ל *זו שאלה טעון כיבוס ממה נפשך אי אוספו וכשר הא כשר ואי אוספו ופסול אנא יד] כרבי עקיבא ס"ל דאמר היתה לו שעת הכושר ונפסלה דמה טעון כיבוס [לעיל לג: ב"ק קטו.]

בעא

וקרן ואצבע וחודה · תימה לו חומרי קחשיב הא לא הוי אליבא דחד תנא דמאן דאית ליה חודה לית ליה קרן כדמוכח לעיל בפרק איזהו מקומן (דף נג·) דפליגי רבי ור"א בר"ש ויש לומר דהכי לג] אמר קרן למאן דאית ליה וחודה למאן דאית ליה °וכן צריך לפרש לעיל בפ"ק לד] (דף י:) והאיכא חודה: **אי** הכי אחד הנאכלות ואחד הפנימיות אחד הפנימיות ואחד הנאכלות מיבעי ליה · שהפשוט יותר יש לו להזכיר תחלה ובפ"ק דסוכה (דף כ·) גרים רש"י במשנה אחת קטנה ואחת גדולה ופריך בגמרא אחת גדולה ואחת קטנה מיבעי ליה דהכי משמע אחת היא הגדולה ואחת היא הקטנה כלומר כמוה היא ואינה חלוקה לדין שני וכן דרך תנאים בכל מקום דההיא דפשיטא ליה תני ברישא ואותו השני כשבא להשמיענו שסוה לו לה] שונה אחריו כדאמר בר"ה (דף כט:) אחד יבנה ואחד כל מקום שיש שם ב"ד ובב"ק (דף כ:) אחד החופר בור ואחד החופר שיח ומערה ובמסכת סוטה (דף מג·) אחד הבונה ואחד הלוקח ואחד היורש ונוטע תנן התם גבי מערכי המלחמה הכי וקשה מההיא דפ' ב' דכתובות (דף כ:) דאחד חדשות ואחד ישנות וישנות פשוט לטומאה יותר מחדשות ובפ' החולץ (יבמות מא·) אחד בתולות ואחד בעולות אלמא דנקט שאינו פשוט תחילה ויש לחלק דהיכא לו] דקאי אקרא *או לז] בפלוגתא דלעיל התם הוא דרגיל למתני לח] הפשוט תחילה והא דתנן (סנהדרין דף לב·) אחד דיני ממונות ואחד דיני נפשות בדרישה ובחקירה אע"ג דקאי אקרא איידי דאיירי *בפרקא דלעיל בדיני ממונות נקט נמי דיני ממונות ברישא וה"ר שמעון הקשה מההיא דמנחות פרק רבי ישמעאל (מנחות סג:) דקתני וחכ"א אחד חול ואחד שבת משלש היה בא וה"ל למיתני שבת ברישא לט] *ובסיפא וחכ"א אחד שבת וא' חול בשלש קופות ובשלש מגלות וה"ל למיקנט חול ברישא* :

מי

יאכלנה לזו ולא לאחרת · יאכלנה חדא משמע לומר באחת מן הנאכלות כתבתי לך הענין הזה ולא בכל הנאכלות טו] נתמעטה חטאת העוף שהוא נאכלת מדברים האמורים בענין טז] ומה אמור בענין כיבוס מריקה ושטיפה: אורחיה דקרא · שכל הענין בלשון זה נאמר תשחט החטאת בבשרה מדמה: רבה אמר · האי פירכא דפרכת דלמא פנימיות נתמעטו ממיעוטא דזאת עיקר כיבוס בפנימיות כתיב דאשר יזה בהזאות הכתוב מדבר והייתו בפנימיות יז] כתיב בהן הזאה על הפרכת אבל בחיצונות אין יח] כתיב הזאה וחיצונות הוא דאיתרבו מתורת: והא תנא דמתני' אע"פ שאין הכתוב מדבר אלא בנאכלות קאמר · אלמא עיקר קרא בחיצונות הוא דכתיב ופנימיות מתורת איתרבו: ה"ק אף על פי שיש דברים בענין שאינו מדבר אלא בנאכלות ומאי ניהו מריקה ושטיפה דההיא דוקא בנאכלות דסמיך ליה כל זכר בכהנים יאכל אותה מיהו לענין כיבוס אחד הנאכלות ואחד הפנימיות והפנימיות עיקר דאשר יזה כתיב בהו וחיצונות מזאת תורת החטאת: אי הכי · דעיקר בפנימיות כתיב אמאי תנא אחד הנאכלות ואחד הפנימיות דמשמע יט] האמורה בנאכלות נוהגת אף בפנימיות דהכי משמע האמור בנאכלות הוא הדין האמור בפנימיות אלמא נאכלות במשמעותא אתו ופנימיות מריבויא: אי הכי חטאת העוף נמי · תיתי ממשמעותא שהרי אף היא מן הניזאות דכתיבוהזה *(מן) החטאתוגו' (ויקרא ה) כ]: חטאת העוף שהכנים דמה בצוארה בפנים · בין מליקה להזייה מהו שתיפסל משום וכל חטאת אשר יובא: ככלי שרת דמי · שהרי לא הוזקקה כא] בקבלת כלי וזהו כלייה ומיפסל בהכנסת הדם שהכניסה בכלי להיכל: או דלמא כו' · וצבהמה שהכניסה לפנים משנשחטה והוליאה וקיבל דמה לא מיפסלא דמדמה אמר רחמנא ולא שהכניסו עם בשרה: פרכסה ונכנסה לפנים · בחטאת העוף קתני לה כב] כשרה וקס"ד משום דמאליה נכנסה ולא הכניסה הוא ע"מ לכפר וקרא כתיב לכפר בקדש: ויצתה לדרום וחזרה · לאו דוקא נקט וחזרה אלא משום דקתני בה (ב) בההיא פרכסה ויצתה לחוץ וחזרה פסולה דדוקא נקט לאשמועינן רבותא דאע"ג דחזרה פסולה נקט נמי גבי כשרה וחזרה: הא הוציאה הוא פסולה · בתמיה וכי יש מחילה בלפון ובדרום ליפסל ביוצא אלא הא דתני פרכסה יצאת לחוץ איצטריכא ליה דקתני בה בההיא פרכסה ויצאת לחוץ לעזרה וחזרה פסולה כג] ואפילו פרכסה ויצאת מאליה דנפסלה ביוצא ובפ' שני (לעיל כו·) מייתי לה בגמרא: ה"נ · דקתני כד] פרכסה גבי עוף משום דההיא נקט לה בלשון כה] פרכסה דקתני בה נמי פרכסה ויצאה לחוץ וחזרה פסולה: נשפך על הרצפה · מצואר העוף: אצרוכי הוא דלא אצרכיה רחמנא כלי שרת · וצואר כו] דידיה הוא במקום כלי שרת *והלכך לאוספו כשר ולהזותו למזבח דה"ל כנשפך מן הכלי על הרצפה ואספו דכשר: או דלמא מיפסל פסיל ביה רחמנא כלי שרת · דדוקא כז] *שייר ולא כתב ביה קבלה משום דבעי להזותו מן העוף עצמו למזבח וכ"ש דרצפה פוסלתו: תיפוק לי · דלא בעי כיבוס בלאו מיעוטא דזאת דהא איפסיל ליה דם מכי מטא לאויר הבגד ואכן ראוי להזאה בעינן ואויר כלי ככלי דמי: במדביק כלי בצוארה · דלא היה על אוירו עד שנגע בו ולהאי אילטריך זאת למעוטי: ניתז מבגד לבגד · בדם בהמה קמיירי: אידחי ליה לכיבוס · וגרע ליה מנשפך מן כח] כלי על הרצפה ואספו ואחר כך ניתז על הבגד דהתם כיון דכשר לזריקה ראוי להזאה קרינא ביה אבל על הבגד דאיזקוקי איזקיק לכיבוס אדחי כט] *מתורת הזאה ולא קרינא ביה ראוי להזאה ולא בעי כיבוס האי אחרון : זו שאלה · בניחותא יפה שאלת ואשיבך עליה: ל] *אוספו וכשר · ואע"ג דאיזדקיק לכיבוס לא בטל מתורת דם כל זמן שלא כיבסו וה"ל כנשפך מן הכלי על הרצפה: הא כשר · וטעון האחרון כיבוס: ואם תימצי לומר שאם אוספו מן הראשון פסול לא] · כדקא ס"ד משום דהוזקק לכיבוס בטיל ליה מתורת דם: אנא לב] כר"ע ס"ל · דאמר לקמן (דף צג·) היתה לה שעת הכושר לזריקה ונפסלה דמה טעון כיבוס והאי הרי מתחילתו בכלי נתקבל והיתה לו שעת הכושר ואח"כ נפסל בנפילתו על בגד ראשון :

ניתז

[צ"ל והתנן]

[לעיל יא·]

הגהות הב"ח
(א) גמ' והא תנא אע"פ:
(ב) רש"י ד"ה ויצאת לדרום וכו' בבבא · נ"ב בקדשי קדשים :

צ"ל מדם

לעיל ט.

גליון הש"ס
תוס' ד"ה וקרן וכו' וכן צריך לפרש · וכן לקמן דף לד ע"ב :

[חסר כאן מי הוא השואל והמשיב ואפשר דצ"ל מרבי ועיין לעיל ל:]

צ"ל והלכך אוספו וכשר להזותו למזבח כו' נ"ק ג"א נוהר

צ"ל מתורת דם כו' נ"ק

צ"ל אי אוספו נ"ק

צ"ל או אפלוגתא כו' נ"ק

צ"ל כצואר בהמה דמי ומדמה אמר רחמנא כו' נ"ק

צ"ל בפרקא דלעיל ברישא דיני ממונות כו' נ"ק

וצ"ע שם לפי הגירסא שלפנינו

[וע"ע תוספות מנחות סג: ד"ה רבי ותוס' פסחים פב. קה: ותוס' כתובות כ: ד"ה אחד ותוס' סוכה כ: ד"ה אחת ותוס' שבת כ: ד"ה אחד מבושל ועיין תוס' קדושין יג· ד"ה כסס]

שיטה מקובצת
א] יאכלנה יאכלנה לזו: ב] דקרא הוא קמ"ל : ג] יזה בניזאות הכתוב: ד] והא תנא אע"פ : ה] בנאכלות קאמר ה"ק אע"פ שאין הכתוב מדבר אלא בנאכלות הני מילי לענין : ו] בהמה דמי ומדמה אמר : ז] בשרה אמר רבה ת"ש : ח] הכניסה הוא פסולה: ט] הוציאה הוא פסולה: י] אבין חטאת העוף שנשפך דמה על הרצפה ואספו מהו: יא] רחמנא כלי שרת תיפוק לי דהא איפסל ליה באויר : יב] לוי מרבי ניתז : יג] דילמא לא שנא : יד] אנא כר' יעקב ס"ל : טו] הנאכלות ונתמעטה חטאת: טז] תיבות ומה אמור בענין נמחק : יז] בפנימיות שכתוב בהן הזאה תיבת כתיב נמחק : יח] אין כתוב בהן הזאה : יט] דמשמע הזאת האמורה : כ] וגו' הס"ד ומה"ד חטאת בהמה הוי ליה לרבויי חיצונות כפנימיות הס"ד ומה"ד חטאת העוף : כא] הוזקקה לקבלת כלי וזהו כלי ומיפסל בהכנסה כדם : כב] לה בתוספתא בזבחים הס"ד ומה"ד כשרה : כג] פסולה דאפילו פירכסה ויצאת מאליה נפסלה ביוצא : כד] דקתני נכנסה גבי תיבת פירכסה נמחק : כה] לשון נכנסה דקתני תיבת פירכסה נמחק : כו] וצואר דידיה הוא במקום כלי שרת והלכך אוספו כשר להזותו למזבח : כז] דדוקא צואר ולא תיבת שייר נמחק : כח] מן הכלי על : כט] אדחי ליה מתורת דם ותיבת הזאה ל"ש : ל] מה"ד אי אוספו : לא] פסול לזריקה כדקא ס"ד דמשום דהוזקק : לב] אנא כר' יעקב ס"ל : לג] דהכי קאמר קרן: לד] בפ"ק דפריך והאיכא: לה] לו הוא שונה: לו] דקאי עיין בתוס' פסחים (דף פ"ב ע"א): לז] אפלוגתא דלעיל : לח] למיתני מה דפשוט: לט] ברישא ובגמרא וחכ"א ותיבת א') ובסיפא ל"ש:

א) לפנינו הגירסא שם בסיפא דמתני' גופא וחכ"א אחד שבת ואחד חול בשלש קופות וכו' וא"ש הגי' בסיפא ואולי דלפני רבינו היה גירסא אחרת במשנה שם וצ"ע .

in a vessel; [92*b*] [its blood is sprinkled on] the horn; with the finger; on the edge [of the horn]; and it is an offering made by fire.[5] On the contrary, include rather the bird sin-offering, because it is an outer [offering], like itself, and is eaten, like itself?—Those [points of similarity] are more.

R. Joseph said, Scripture saith, [*The priest*] . . . *shall eat* it:[6] this one shall he eat, but not another; thus the Writ excluded of those which are eaten.[7] Then what is the purpose of *'this is'*?[8]—If not for *'this is'* I would say that *'shall eat it'* is the style of Scripture;[9] hence this informs us [otherwise][10]

Rabbah said, Scripture saith, *and when there is sprinkled* [yazzeh]: hence the Writ speaks of those which are sprinkled.[11] But surely we learnt: THOUGH SCRIPTURE SPEAKS OF [THE SIN-OFFERINGS] WHICH ARE EATEN?[12]—This is what [the Tanna] means: Although Scripture speaks of [the sin-offerings] which are eaten, that is only
a in respect of scouring and rinsing,[1] but in respect to washing, *'and when there is sprinkled* [yazzeh]' is written.[2] If so, [instead of saying BOTH THOSE WHICH MAY BE EATEN AND THE INNER [SIN-OFFERINGS], he should say, Both the inner [sin-offerings] and those which may be eaten?[3]—Learn, both the inner [sin-offerings] and those which may be eaten.

If so, the bird sin-offering too [is included]?[4]—The Divine Law expressed a limitation in *'this is'*. If so, an outer [sin-offering] too is not [included]?—The Divine Law expressed an extension in *'the law of'*. And why do you prefer it thus?—It is logical to include an animal sin-offering, because: it is an animal; it is slaughtered in the north; [its blood is] received in a vessel; [its blood is sprinkled on] the horn; with the finger; on the edge [of the horn]; and it is an offering made by fire. On the contrary, include the bird sin-offering, since it requires *haza'ah*, like itself?[5]—Those [points of similarity] are more.

R. Abin asked: What if one took the blood of a bird sin-offering within[6] by its neck?[7] Is its neck like a service vessel,[8] and so it [the sacrifice] is disqualified; or perhaps it is like an animal's neck, while the Divine Law said, [*And every sin-offering*], *whereof any of* the blood [*is brought into the tent of meeting . . . shall be burnt with fire*],[9] [implying] of its blood, but not of its flesh![10]—Come and hear: If it [the bird] struggled, entered within[11] and then returned,[12] it is fit. Hence, if,
b however, [the priest] *took* it in, it is disqualified.[1] Then according to your reasoning, when it is taught in connection with most sacred sacrifices, If it struggled and entered the south[2] and then returned, it is fit; [will you infer], but if he [the priest] carried it out [of the north into the south] it is disqualified?[3] Rather, this is required where it went without; so there too, it is required where it went without.[4]

R. Abin asked: What if the blood [of the bird-offering] poured out on to the pavement,[5] and one collected it? [Do we say that] the Divine Law merely did not demand[6] a service vessel,[7] and therefore one collects it and it is fit;[8] or perhaps, in its case the Divine Law actually disqualified a service vessel, and therefore one collects it, but it is disqualified?[9]—Said Raba, Come and hear: You might think that the blood of a bird sin-offering necessitates washing; therefore *'this is'* is stated. Now, if you think that in its case the Divine Law actually disqualified a service vessel, I can infer this since it was disqualified in the air-space of a vessel![10]—Said R. Huna son of Joshua: [The text is necessary] where one presses the garment[11] to its neck.[12]

c Levi asked Rabbi:[1] What if it spurted from one garment on to another garment?[2] [Do we say,] It was rejected from the first garment in respect of washing,[3] or not?—That is indeed a question, he replied. It does need washing, on either alternative: if one can collect [the blood] and it is fit [for sprinkling], then this is fit.[4] While if it is collected and disqualified,[5] I agree with R. Akiba who maintained [that] if it had a period of fitness and was then disqualified, its blood necessitates washing.

(5) I.e , the *emurim* are burnt on the altar. The inner sin-offering has all these in common with the outer, whereas the bird sin-offering is unlike the outer in all these respects. (6) Lev. VI, 19. (7) *'It'* sing., implies that the passage speaks only of *one* of the sin-offerings which may be eaten; hence the bird sin-offering is excluded. (8) Since you already have a limitation in *'it'*. (9) Not a limitation at all. (10) Now that we know from *'this is'* that a limitation is intended, '*shall eat* it' teaches that the limitation concerns those which are eaten. (11) *Haza'ah*, from which *yazzeh* is derived, is written only in connection with the *inner* sin-offerings, but not in connection with the outer sin-offerings, where *zaraḳ* is written (both *haza'ah* and *zeriḳah* denote sprinkling, but the latter implies with more force than the former). Hence the Writ refers *primarily* to *inner* sin-offerings, and it is the *outer* sin-offerings which are included by *'the law of'*, implying one law for all. (12) Which shews that it refers primarily to *outer* sin-offerings.

a (1) V. Lev. VI, 21. (2) Emended text (Sh.M.). (3) The more obvious should be mentioned first, and according to Rabbah that is the *inner* sin-offering. (4) If *yazzeh* shews that inner sin-offerings are primarily meant, the same should apply to a bird sin-offering, as this word is written in connection with it too. (5) *Sc.* like the *inner* sin-offering. (6) Into the *hekal*. (7) Not in a service-vessel; but its neck was taken within and *ipso facto* the blood too. Is the sacrifice disqualified under the law forbidding the blood of an outer sin-offering to be taken within (v. Lev. VI, 23), or not? (8) Since no service vessel is required in its case, the blood being sprinkled straight from the throat, the throat itself may take the place of a service vessel. (9) Ibid., 23. (10) Only when the blood alone is taken in, *sc.* in a service vessel, is the sacrifice disqualified, but not when it is taken in by means of the flesh. (11) Into the *hekal*. (12) I.e., its head was nipped near the *hekal*, and in its death struggles it entered therein.

b (1) This assumes that only when it entered itself is it fit. (2) The south side of the Temple court; it was killed in the north. (3) Surely not, for no barrier divided the north from the south, to disqualify a sacrifice if its blood was carried from one into the other. (4) Do not infer that if one carried it out it is unfit (that is obviously incorrect), but that if it struggled and went *out of the Temple court*, even if it returned, it is disqualified. Similarly, the bird remains fit only if it struggled and entered *within*; but if it struggled *out* of the Temple court, it is disqualified. No deduction, however, is to be made where one *carried* the bird within. (5) Of the Temple court. (6) Lit, 'make it need.' (7) The bird's throat counting as such. (8) Just as when the blood of an animal-offering is spilt from the service vessel in which it was received. (9) For sprinkling, for Scripture insisted that it must be sprinkled direct from the throat. (10) As soon as the blood enters the air-space above the garment it is technically received in a vessel (a garment ranks as a utensil or vessel) and is disqualified for sprinkling. Consequently the garment need not be washed, for only blood fit for sprinkling necessitates washing. What need then is there of a text? (11) Lit., 'vessel.' (12) So that the blood did not enter the air-space above the garment at all. Even then it need not be washed.

c (1) Emended text (Sh.M.). (2) This refers to the blood of an *animal* sin-offering. (3) When it fell on the first garment it became unfit for sprinkling, since it must be washed out, and therefore the second garment does not need washing. (4) Although it should be washed out of the first garment, yet as long as this was not done, it is fit for sprinkling, just as though it had fallen on to the pavement; and so *fit* blood spurted on to the second garment. (5) For further sprinkling.

[93a] Rami b. Ḥama asked R. Ḥisda: What if it spurted on to an unclean garment?[6] R. Huna the son of R. Joshua observed: Since he asks thus, you may infer that he holds that if it had a period of fitness and was disqualified, its blood does not necessitate washing. [Nevertheless his question is:] is that only when they come consecutively, but not when they come simultaneously; or perhaps there is not difference?[7]—He [R. Ḥisda] replied: This is a controversy of R. Eleazar and the Rabbis, in accordance with Rabbah's view, and as explained by Abaye. For it was taught: R. Eleazar said: If the water of lustration[8] was defiled, it cleanses [an unclean person],[9] for lo, we sprinkle [the water of lustration] upon a *niddah*.[10] Now Rabbah observed: R. Eleazar said this in accordance with the thesis of R. Akiba, his teacher, who maintained that when the vessel [containing the water of lustration] is carried over an unclean
a place, it is as though it rested there.[1] For we learnt: If a man stood on the outer side of an oven, and a reptile was in the oven, and he put forth his hand to the window, took a flask, and carried it across the oven,[2] R. Akiba declares it unclean, while the Rabbis declare it clean. Now, they disagree in this: R. Akiba holds that it is as lying,[3] while the Rabbis hold that it is not as lying [thereon]. But Abaye raised an objection: [It was taught:] R. Akiba admits that in the case of sprinkling, if one carried it over an unclean earthen vessel or over an unclean couch or seat, it is clean,[4] for nothing defiles above as below[5] save as much as an olive of a corpse and other things which defile through overshadowing,[6] which includes a leprous stone![7] Rather said Abaye: All agree that it is not as though it lay thereon, but here they differ in this: R. Akiba
b holds that we enact a preventive measure, lest it lay thereon;[1] while the Rabbis hold that we do not enact a preventive measure. But R. Akiba admits in the case of sprinkling,[2] for since it has gone out, it has gone out.[3] Now, wherein do R. Eleazar and the Rabbis disagree?[4]—Said Abaye: They disagree as to whether we draw an analogy between previous defilement and contemporary defilement: one master holds that we draw an analogy,[5] and the other master holds that we do not draw an analogy.[6] Raba said: All hold that we do not draw an analogy; but here they disagree in this: R. Eleazar holds that sprinkling requires a [minimum] standard, and sprinklings combine; while the Rabbis hold that sprinkling does not require a [minimum] standard.[7]

THE BLOOD OF A DISQUALIFIED SIN-OFFERING etc. Our
c Rabbis taught: [*And when there is sprinkled*] *of the blood thereof:*[1] [that means,] of the blood of a fit [sacrifice], but not of the blood of a disqualified [one].[2] R. Akiba[3] said: If it had a period of fitness and was [subsequently] disqualified, its blood necessitates washing; if it did not have a period of fitness and was disqualified *ab initio*, its blood does not necessitate washing. Whereas R. Simeon maintained: In both cases its blood does not necessitate washing. What is R. Simeon's reason?—'*Thereof*' is written,[4] and '*of the blood thereof*' is written:[5] one [excludes] where it had a period of fitness, and the other excludes where it did not have a period of fitness.[6] And R. Akiba?[7]—'*Thereof*' excludes *terumah*.[8] R. Simeon, however, is consistent with his view, for he maintained: Lesser sacrifices do not necessitate scouring and rinsing, and how much the more *terumah*![9]

MISHNAH. IF [BLOOD] SPURTED [DIRECT] FROM THE [ANIMAL'S] THROAT ON TO A GARMENT, IT DOES NOT NECESSITATE WASHING; FROM THE HORN OR FROM THE BASE [OF THE ALTAR], IT DOES NOT NECESSITATE WASHING. IF IT POURED OUT ON TO THE PAVEMENT AND [THE PRIEST] COLLECTED IT, IT[10] DOES NOT NEED WASHING. ONLY BLOOD WHICH WAS RECEIVED IN A VESSEL AND IS FIT FOR SPRINKLING NECESSITATES WASHING.

GEMARA. Our Rabbis taught: You might think that, if [the blood] spurted from the throat on to the garment, it necessitates washing; therefore it states, '*and when there is sprinkled* [etc.]': I ordered thee [to wash the garment] only when [the blood] is fit
d for sprinkling.[1] Another [Baraitha] taught: You might think that, if it spurted from the horn or from the base, it requires washing, therefore it states, '*and when there shall be sprinkled*': that excludes this [blood], which was already sprinkled.

(6) Whereby the blood was defiled, and so disqualified for sprinkling. Do we regard it as though it were defiled *before* it touched the garment, and hence does not necessitate washing; or perhaps the defilement of the blood and the obligation to wash the garment came simultaneously? (7) He asks only if it fell on an unclean garment; hence he holds that if the blood was defiled *before* it fell, thus having been fit and then become disqualified, it certainly does not necessitate washing. But his question is whether that is only where these came consecutively, i.e., first the blood was disqualified and then it spurted on to the garment; or does it hold good even when both are simultaneous? (8) Running water mixed with the ashes of the red heifer; this was sprinkled on a person defiled through the dead as a purificatory rite; v. Num. XIX. (9) Just as though it had not been defiled. (10) If a *niddah* was defiled through the dead, thereby becoming doubly unclean, both as a *niddah* and as one defiled by the dead, we besprinkle her with the water of lustration, while she is *still* a *niddah*, and the subsequent immersion counts for both forms of uncleanness, since we do not find Scripture ordering her first to perform immersion as a *niddah* and then to be besprinkled and repeat her immersion on account of her defilement through the dead. Now, as the water of lustration touches her, it is defiled itself through contact with a *niddah*, and yet it cleanses her. Now the analogy is apparently faulty, for here the defilement of the water and its sprinkling upon the woman are simultaneous, whereas R. Eleazar speaks of a case where the water was defiled first. Rabbah proceeds to explain why R. Eleazar regards it nevertheless as a true analogy.

a . (1) And unclean. (2) An oven stood near a wall, in which was a window with a flask containing water of lustration; inside the oven lay a reptile, which made it unclean. A man, standing on the outer side of the oven, took the flask from the window, and in taking it to himself naturally carried it above the oven, through the air-space. (3) On the oven, and is therefore defiled by it. (4) I.e., if the water of lustration was sprinkled upon an unclean person, and in its passage passed over unclean vessels etc., it remains clean. (5) Nothing defiles anything above, passing through its air-space, as when it is below, actually touching it. (6) Lit. 'tent'. This is a technical expression denoting defilement caused by the defiler being under the same covering (technically called a tent) as the defiled. E.g., everything in a room containing a corpse, or as much as an olive of a corpse, is unclean through being under the same covering as the corpse. (7) All things, both animate and inanimate, smitten with leprosy, defile through overshadowing.—Now, an oven unclean through a reptile does *not* defile through overshadowing. Hence this contradicts Rabbah's statement that R. Akiba holds there too that the air-space above an article defiles the water of lustration just as though it touched it.

b (1) We declare this vessel unclean, lest one think that even if it actually lay on the oven it is still clean. Sh.M. emends: lest one lay it (thereon).—Thus the vessel (and, of course, its contents) are only *Rabbinically* unclean, but clean by Scriptural law. (2) Where not the vessel but the water itself passed through the air-space of something unclean, as it was sprinkled. (3) Since the water leaves the priest's hand as he sprinkles it, we need not fear that he will place the water on the oven. (4) Above, when R. Eleazar draws an analogy with a *niddah*, which the Rabbis reject. (5) *Sc.* R. Eleazar: he draws an analogy with *niddah*, where the defilement is contemporary, i.e., simultaneous (v. *supra* n. 10). (6) Therefore if water of lustration was defiled *before*, it does not cleanse.—Similarly, when blood of an animal sin-offering spurts on to an unclean garment, R. Eleazar will rule that it must be regarded as unclean (hence disqualified for sprinkling) even before it spurted, and therefore the garment need not be washed. The Rabbis, however, who reject this view, will rule that it must be washed. This then is the answer to Rami b. Ḥama's question, *sc.* that it is dependent on Tannaim. (7) V. *supra* 80a. Now, the first sprinkling does not contain the minimum standard, and so does not count as sprinkling; nevertheless it is defiled when it falls on the *niddah*. Hence at the next sprinkling, which is to combine with the first, the first is already unclean. Therefore it is a case of *previous* defilement, and is completely analogous to sprinkling with defiled water of lustration. The Rabbis, however, maintain that sprinkling does not require a minimum standard, and so the first counts as sprinkling; hence defilement and sprinkling are simultaneous, and no inference can be drawn in respect of previous defilement.—The R. Eleazar here is R. Eleazar b. Shammu'a, a disciple of R. Akiba; the R. Eliezer *supra* 80a, who maintains that sprinkling does not require a minimum standard, is R. Eliezer b. Hyrcanus.

c (1) Lev. VI, 20. (2) '*Thereof*' is a limitation. (3) Marginal emendation, R. Jacob. (4) In v. 22, after the law of scouring and rinsing in v. 21: *Every male among the priests may eat thereof*. (5) These are two limitations. (6) Marginal emendation. (7) How does he explain the second limitation? (8) If *terumah* is boiled in a pot, it does not need scouring and rinsing. (9) Hence no limitation is required in respect of *terumah*. (10) The garment on which it fell.

d (1) I.e., received in a vessel.

ניתז על בגד טמא · ונטמא בנגיעתו בו מי הוי דם פסול כאילו נטמא קודם לכן ולא בעי כיבוס או דלמא כיון דבעידנא דנפל עליה אכתי כשר הוה והוי פסול דם וטעינת כיבוס לבגד באין כאחד כדמפרש ואזיל לה רב הונא בריה דרב יהושע : *מדקא מיבעי ליה הכי · מכלל דפשיטא ליה ט] נטמא קודם לכן דלא בעי כיבוס ואע״ג דהיתה לו שעת הכושר ש״מ קסבר כו׳ ומיהו היכא דפסול דם וטבילת בגד באין כאחד מיבעי ליה הכי מי אמרינן ה״מ דפסולה אין דמה טעון כיבוס : בזה אחר זה · שנפסל ואח״כ ניתז : וכדקא מתרץ אביי · למילתיה דרבה דפריש פלוגתייהו דר׳ אלעזר ורבנן : מטהרין · את האדם מטומאת מת כאילו לא נטמא : שהרי נדה · שנטמאה במת מזין עליה לפני טבילת נדתה וטובלת לשתי הטומאות בטבילה אחת שלא מליט בתורה שהוזקקה לטבול לנדתה תחלה ולקבל הזאה י] וטהרה כשתטבול ויש מיכן ראיה למי חטאת שנטמאו קודם הזאתן כדמפרש רבה ואזיל : (א) ואמר רבה· ר׳ אלעזר שמביא ראיה מהזאת נדה שאינו דומה לזו דאינו נדה הזאה וטומאת המים באין כאחד ואין זו ראיה לנטמאו קודם הזייה : אלא שאמרה בשיטת רבי עקיבא רבו · דאמר כל הטומאות מטמאין מי חטאת העוברין על אוירו הלכך נטמאו המים משעברו על אויר הנדה והזאה לא הואי עד שנגעו המים בבשרה : יא] חוץ לתנור · שהיה התנור סמוך לכותל וחלון בכותל ובו לגין והאדם עומד חוץ לתנור כלומר להלן מן התנור שהתנור מפסיק בינו לבין הכותל יב] : העברת כלי · של מי חטאת : והעבירו ע״פ התנור · על אויר פיו שכל תנוריהם פיהם למעלה : יג] ונטל את הלגין · של מי חטאת ובמסכת פרה תנינן לה ומעלה היא למי חטאת : ואיתיביה אביי גרסינן : מודה ר׳ עקיבא · אע״פ שנחלק בלגין של מי חטאת מודה הוא בהזאה שהעבירה כו׳ שהיה מזה על האדם ותנור טמא מפסיקו ועברה ההזאה על פי התנור : יד] [למעלה כלמטה · באוהל כבנגיעה] : ה״ג ושאר כל המאהילים לאיתויי אבן המנוגעת · אלמא בהזאת נדה ליכא למימר לרבי עקיבא משבאה למעלה באויר על הנדה נטמאת : אלא אמר אביי דכ״ע אפילו במי חטאת לאו כמונח דמי · אלא לענין לגין הוא דגזר רבי עקיבא גזירה שמא יניחנה בתוך האויר דרך העברתו אבל בהזאה שאינו מעביר אלא זורקה מודה הוא דטהור דכיון דנפק מידו נפק לגמרי ואין בידו להכניסה לתנור : ורבי אלעזר · דמייתי ראייה למילתיה מהזאת נדה ורבנן דאמרי אינה ראייה : בדנין טומאה קדומה · כגון מי חטאת שנטמאו לפני הזאתן מטומאה שבאותה שעה כגון הזאת נדה שטומאת המים והזאה באין כאחד קמיפלגי : רבי אלעזר סבר דנין ורבנן סברי אין דנין · ולגבי ניתז דם חטאת על בגד טמא דאיבעיא לן לעיל נמי פלוגתא דרבי אלעזר ורבנן הוא דלרבי אלעזר אין טעון כיבוס דטומאה שבשעת נפילה כטומאה שלפני נפילה ולרבנן לא דמו אהדדי והאי דקאמרינן אליבא דרבה טו] וכדמפרק אביי ולא אמרינן אליבא דאביי (ואע״ג) דהא דרבה טז] ליתיה משום דאביי תלמידו הוה ולא נחלק עליו אלא דן לפניו ותירגם הדבר לפניו ואודה לו : דכולי עלמא אין דנין · ורבי אלעזר טומאה קדומה *מטומאה קדומה יליף דרבי אלעזר סבר הזאה צריכה שיעור ומצטרפין להזאות וכי נפלה הזאה קמייתא עלה אכתי לאו הזאה היא לטהרה ואע״ג שנטמאת ההזאה הראשונה כשנגעה בה חוזרת ומצטרפת עם השניה להשלים השיעור אלמא מי חטאת שנטמאו לפני הזאה מטהרין : ורבנן סברי אין הזאה צריך שיעור · ומהזאה קמייתא אסתלקא לה הזאה וליכא למילף מינה טומאה קדומה דהך דגבי נדה טומאה שבאותה שעה היא : *מדמה · מיעוטא היא דמה של זו ולא דמה של אחרת: יז] *) רבי עקיבא ורבי שמעון פליגי בהאי פסולה דמיעט קרא ולפרושי קאתו : כתיב אותה · בתריה דקרא דכיבוס ומריקה ושטיפה כתיב כל זכר בכהנים יאכל אותה (ויקרא ו) : אותה פרט לתרומה · ואמריקה ושטיפה קאי כדאמרינן לקמן בפירקין (דף צז:) : ורבי שמעון לטעמיה · לקמן במתניתין (דף צה:) : מתני׳ ניתז מן הצואר על הבגד כו׳ · כדמפרש טעמא בגמרא : מן הקרן · של מזבח ומן היסוד של שירים יח] ובפרק בית שמאי (לעיל נט.) תרגימנא דמן הקרן מן הקרן ממש ומן היסוד מן הראוי ליסוד דמשניתן מתן דמה אין שירים טעונין כיבוס וטעמא מפרש בגמרא: הכי גרסינן במתניתין נשפך על הרצפה ואספו אין טעון כיבוס ואין טעון כיבוס אלא הדם שנתקבל בכלי כו׳ יט] ובגמרא פריך הא תו למה לי : נשפך על הרצפה · מצואר בהמה : גמ׳ בראוי להזאה · שנתקבל בכלי :
*) [נ״ל ר׳ יעקב ור״ש כמו דאיתא בתוספתא וכ״ה בס״י]

מי חטאת שנטמאו מטהרין · וא״ת א״כ למה גזרו שלא יעביר אדם מי חטאת ואפר חטאת בנהר ובספינה כמעשה שהיה כדאיתא ביבמות פרק האשה שלום (דף קטז: ובחגיגה כג.) וי״ל דהתם קודם קידוש והכא לאחר קידוש *) : *ניתז מן הצואר על הבגד אין טעון כיבוס · מרישא לא שמעינן דהוה אמינא הכא שאני משום דבבת אחת :
*) עיין רש״ק

בעא מיניה רמי בר חמא מרב חסדא ניתז על בגד טמא *מהו אמר רב הונא בריה דרב יהושע מדקמיבעיא ליה הכי ש״מ א] היתה לה שעת הכושר ונפסלה אין דמה טעון כיבוס ה״מ בזה אחר זה אבל בבת אחת לא או דלמא לא שנא א״ל פלוגתא דר״א ורבנן אליבא דרבה וכדקא מתריץ אביי דתניא ר׳ אלעזר אומר מי חטאת שנטמאו מטהרין שהרי ב]נדה מזין עליה ג] ואמר רבה ר״א בשיטת ר״ע רבו אמרה דאמר העברת כלי על גבי מקום טמא כמונח דמי *דתנן היה עומד חוץ לתנור ושרץ בתנור והושיט ידו לחלון ונטל את הלגין והעבירו ע״פ תנור ר״ע מטמא וחכמים ג]מטהרין ובהא פליגי דר׳ עקיבא סבר כמונח דמי ורבנן סברי לאו כמונח דמי ואיתיביה אביי *מודה רבי עקיבא בהזאה שהעבירה על ג] כלי חרס טמא על גבי משכב ומושב טמא שהיא ד]טהורה שאין לך דבר שמטמא למעלה כלמטה אלא כזית מן המת ושאר כל המאהילין לאיתויי אבן המנוגעת אלא אמר אביי דכ״ע לאו כמונח דמי והכא בהא קמיפלגי דרבי עקיבא סבר גזרינן שמא ד] ינוח ורבנן סברי לא גזרינן ומודה רבי עקיבא בהזאה ה] כיון דנפק נפק ורבי אלעזר ורבנן במאי קמיפלגי אמר אביי בדנין טומאה קדומה מטומאה שבאותה שעה קמיפלגי מ״ס דנין ומ״ס אין דנין *רבא אמר דכ״ע אין דנין והכא בהא קמיפלגי *דר״א סבר *הזאה צריכה שיעור ו] ומצטרפין להזאות ורבנן סברי הזאה אין צריכה שיעור : חטאת פסולה כו׳ : ת״ר מדמה מדם כשירה ולא מדם פסולה ז] *ר״ע אומר היתה לה שעת הכושר ונפסלה דמה טעון כיבוס לא היתה לה שעת הכושר ונפסלה אין דמה טעון כיבוס ור״ש אומר ה]אחד זה ואחד זה אין דמה טעון כיבוס מאי טעמא דרבי שמעון כתיב אותה וכתיב מדמה חד להיכא דהיתה לו שעת הכושר *ח] ורבי עקיבא אותה פרט לתרומה ור״ש לטעמיה דאמר *קדשים קלים אין טעונין מריקה ושטיפה וכ״ש תרומה : מתני׳ *ניתז מן הצואר על הבגד אינו טעון כיבוס מן הקרן ומן היסוד אינו טעון כיבוס נשפך על הרצפה ואספו אין טעון כיבוס ו]אין טעון כיבוס אלא דם שנתקבל בכלי וראוי להזאה : גמ׳ ת״ר יכול ניתז מן הצואר על הבגד יהא טעון כיבוס ת״ל אשר יזה לא אמרתי לך אלא בראוי להזאה תניא אידך יכול ניתז מן הקרן ומן היסוד יהא טעון כיבוס ת״ל אשר יזה *פרט לזה שכבר הוזה : נשפך על הרצפה כו׳ :
הא

יב] חבותל הס״ד ומה״ד ונטל את הלגין של מי חטאת בפ׳ פרה תנינן לה ומעלה היא במי חטאת הס״ד ודבור המתחיל העברת כלי של מי חטאת נמחק : יג] כל הדבור ונטל כו׳ עד ד״ה ואותיביה נמחק מכאן וכתוב למעלה : יד] למעלה כלמטה באהל כבנגיעה : טו] וכדמתרץ אביי תיבת וכדמפרק ל״ש : טז] דרבה ליתא : יז] ר׳ יעקב ור״ש : יח] שירים ובפרקי קמאי תרגימנא תיבות ב״ש ל״ש : יט] מתיבת ובגמרא עד תיבת בכלי בסוף השיטה כולה נמחק :

הגהות הב״ח (א) רש״י ד״ה ואמר רבה הד״א עם ד״ה אלא. וכו׳ כשעוברין וכו׳ בבשרה הס״ד ואח״כ מ״ה העברת כלי של מי חטאת הס״ד ואח״כ מ״ה חוץ וכו׳ לבין הכותל הס״ד ואח״כ מ״ה ונטל את הלגין וכו׳ חטאת הס״ד ואח״כ מ״ה והעבירו על פי וכו׳ למעלה הס״ד ואח״כ מ״ה ואותביה :

עין משפט נר מצוה
י א מיי׳ פ״ח מהלכות מעשה הקרבנות הלכה ט :
יא ב מיי׳ פי״ח מהלכות פרה אדומה הלכה ג :
יב ג ד מיי׳ פי״ד מהלכות פרה אדומה הלכה ה :
יג ה מיי׳ פ״ח מהלכות מעה״ק הלכה ג :
יד ו מיי׳ שם הלכה ו :
טו ז מיי׳ שם הלכה ד :

[ובחגיגה כג: ד״ה מת כו׳ כתבו דהיינו דוקא בשאר טומאות אך בטומאת מת נפסלו]
עיין רש״ק
[לעיל פי׳ יומא יד. נדה ס׳:]
[נ״ל ר׳ יעקב וכ״א בתוספתא פ׳ כל התדיר]
נ״א וחד ללא היתה לו שעת הכושר
[לקמן צה: צו: צז׳:]
[לעיל נח.]

מסורת הש״ס
יד ד״ה וד״ה בזה אחר זה הד״א נ״ק
פרה פ״י [מ״ה ע״ש דבמשנה ליתא ושרץ בתנור]
תוספתא דפרה פ״ט ע״ש
[הא דמסיק רבא לעיל פ. דלר״א הזאה אינה צריכה שיעור ר״א דהתם הוא ר׳ אליעזר בן הורקנוס ור״א דהכא הוא רבי אלעזר בן שמוע כדאיתא ביבמות סב: דהיה תלמידו של רבי עקיבא לכך קאמר רבה ר״א בשיטת ר״ע רבו אמרה ושמחתי שמצאתי אח״כ בספ׳ הרא״ד מ״ה פ״ז דעדיות דהכא גרס ר׳ אלעזר בלא יו״ד ולעיל ר׳ אליעזר ביו״ד ע״ש]
[לעיל נח: מעילה ס.]
נ״א מטומאה שבאותה שעה יליף אלא דר״א כו׳
מדמה כו׳ ור׳ עקיבא כו׳ סד״א בנ״ל נ״ק

שיטה מקובצת
א] ש״מ קסבר היתה :
ב] עלי׳ ומהורה ואמר :
ג] על גבי כלי חרס טמא או על גבי :ד] שמא יניח ורבנן : ה] בהזאה דכיון דנפק : ו] שיעור ומצרפין להזאות :
ז] פסולה ר׳ יעקב אומר:
ח] הכושר וחד להיכא דלא היתה לה שעת הכושר(ור״ע)[ור׳ יעקב]:
ט] ליה בנטמא קודם :
י] הזאה ומהורה כשתטבול : יא] בבשרה הס״ד ומה״ד העברת כלי של מי חטאת הס״ד ומה״ד חוץ :

הא תו ל"ל מה טעם קאמר מה טעם נשפך על הרצפה ואספו אין טעון כיבוס לפי שאין טעון כיבוס אלא דם שנתקבל בכלי וראוי להזייה: ראוי להזאה: למעוטי מאי למעוטי קיבל פחות מכדי הזייה בכלי זה ופחות מכדי הזייה בכלי זה דתניא *רבי חלפתא בר שאול א] אומר *קידש פחות מכדי הזייה בכלי זה ופחות מכדי הזייה בכלי זה לא קידש *איבעיא להו בדם מהו הלכתא היא ומהלכתא לא גמרינן או דלמא התם מ"ט דכתיב °וטבל במים ה"נ כתיב °וטבל בדם תא שמע דא"ר זריקא א"ר אלעזר אף בדם לא קידש אמר רבא *תניא וטבל ג ולא *מספג בדם עד שיהא בדם שיעור טבילה ג] מעיקרו מן הדם מן הדם שבענין ואיצטריך למיכתב ג] בדם דאי כתב רחמנא וטבל ה"א אע"פ דליכא שיעור טבילה ד] מעיקרו כתב [רחמנא] בדם ואי כתב רחמנא בדם ה"א אפילו מספג כתב רחמנא וטבל מן הדם שבענין למעוטי מאי אמר רבא ל למעוטי שיריים שבאצבע מסייע לרבי אלעזר דאר"א ג שיריים שבאצבע פסולין א"ל רבין בר רב אדא *לרב (א) אמר תלמידך אמר רב עמרם תנינא היה מזה וניתזה הזאה מידו עד שלא הזה טעון כיבוס משהזה אין טעון כיבוס מאי לאו ה"ק עד שלא גמר מלהזות טעון כיבוס משגמר להזות אין טעון כיבוס לא ה"ק עד שלא יצתה הזאה מידו טעון כיבוס ד משיצתה הזאה מידו אין טעון כיבוס איתיביה אביי *גמר מלהזות מקנח ידו בגופה של פרה גמר אין לא גמר לא א"ל גמר מקנח ידו בגופה של פרה לא גמר מקנח אצבעו בשלמא גמר מקנח ידו ה בגופה של פרה שנאמר °ושרף את הפרה לעיניו אלא אצבעו במאי מקנח *אמר אביי ו בשפת מזרק כדכתיב °כפורי זהב: **מתני'** ז ניתז על העור עד שלא הופשט אינו טעון כיבוס משהופשט טעון כיבוס דברי רבי יהודה רבי אלעזר אומר אף משהופשט *ח אינו טעון כיבוס (ב) ה] אלא מקום הדם ודבר שהוא ראוי לקבל טומאה ט וראוי לכיבוס י אחד הבגד ואחד השק ואחד העור טעונין כיבוס כ והכיבוס במקום קדוש ושבירת כלי חרס במקום קדוש ומריקה ושטיפה בכלי נחושת במקום קדוש ל זה חומר בחטאת מקדשי קדשים: **גמ'** מנהני מילי דת"ר °בגד אין לי אלא בגד מנין לרבות עור משהופשט ת"ל °אשר יזה עליה תכבס יכול שאני מרבה עור עד שלא הופשט תלמוד לומר בגד מה בגד הראוי לקבל טומאה אף כל הראוי לקבל טומאה דברי ר' יהודה רבי אלעזר אומר בגד אין לי אלא בגד מנין לרבות שק
וכל

הא תו למה לי · למיתני אין טעון כיבוס אלא שנתקבל בכלי הא תנא ליה נשפך על הרצפה: קיבל פחות מכדי הזייה בכלי זה · וחזר ועירב: דתני ר' חלפתא · לגבי מי חטאת: קידש · מי חטאת באפר פרה: לא קידש · ו] כדבעי טעמא ואזיל: בדם מאי · גבי חטאת הפנימית קיבל פחות מכדי הזייה כו' וחזר ועירב מי האי קבלה או לא: הלכתא · ז] גבי מי חטאת: ומהלכתא לא גמרינן · מילתא אחריתי דקי"ל שבת (דף קלג·) אין דנין מהלכה: וטבל במים · מדקרינן ח] במים ולא קרינן במים משמע במים הנזכרים למעלה לענין קידוש שיהא ט] בשעת קידוש שיעור טבילה: ה"נ · הא כתיב וטבל הכהן את אצבעו י] בדם שיהא בדם הראשון שיעור טבילה מתחילתו: מספג · מקנח בשולי הכלי או בדופנותיו: שיהא בדם שיעור טבילה מעיקרא · גרסינן כדפרי' בדם הראשון משמע: מן הדם · והזה מן הדם: שבענין · מדם האמור בענין יא] טבילה שהזה ממנה ראשונה יזה את כולן שצריך לחזור ולטבול בו אצבעו על כל הזייה (ג) *טבילה ולמעוטי שירים שבאצבע דהאי מן הדם קרא יתירא הוא דלא צריך למיכתב אלא והזה ז' פעמים: אע"ג דליכא שיעור טבילה מעיקרא · הואיל ואיכא שיעור בשעת טבילה: להכי אילטריך למיכתב בדם · דמשמע בדם שהזכיר לענין קבלה: אמר רב עמרם תנינא · תיובתא לר' אלעזר: היה מזה · בחטאות הפנימיות וניתזה הזאה מידו על הבגד: עד שלא גמר כל ההזאות · טעון כיבוס ואפי' ניתז בין יב] ההזאה להזאה משירים שבאצבע אלמא שירים שבאצבע כשרין דאי פסולין אמאי טעון כיבוס: עד שלא יצתה מידו · משטבל טעון כיבוס משיצתה הזאה מידו לאחר טבילה דהוי להו שירים יג] באצבע אין טעון כיבוס: גמר מלהזות · במס' פרה (פ"ג מ"ט) תנן לה גמר מלהזות ז' הזאות שמזה בהר המשחה כנגד פתחו של היכל כדכתיב (במדבר יט) אל נכח פני אהל מועד: מקנח ידו בגופה של פרה · שאף דמה טעון שריפה כדכתיב את עורה ואת בשרה ואת דמה על פרשה ישרוף: אלא אצבעו · בין הזאה להזאה: במה יקנח · בגופה של פרה לא מצית אמרת שילכלך אצבעו בגוף הפרה וידבקו בו נימין: כפורי זהב · גבי כלי שרת כתיב בספר עזרא והן מזרקין ועל שם שמקנח בו אצבעו קרי להן כפורי לשון וכפר ידיה דנירון קיסר (גיטין דף נו·): **מתני'** עד שלא הופשט אין טעון כיבוס · טעמא מפרש בגמרא דבעינן ראוי לקבל טומאה בלא חסרון מלאכה: אף משהופשט · כל זמן שלא נתקן להיות כלי אין טעון כיבוס דבעינן דבר המקבל טומאה שאין מחוסר אפילו מחשבה: אלא מקום הדם · ולא כל הבגד: ודבר הראוי לקבל טומאה · ואע"פ שמחוסר מחשבה ובלבד שלא יהא מחוסר מלאכה וסתמא כרבי יהודה: וראוי לכיבוס · בגמרא מפרש למעוטי מאי: במקום קדוש · בעזרה: ושבירת כלי חרס · שבישל בה חטאת במקום קדוש ובגמרא יליף לה: זה חומר · *אכיבוס קאי: **גמ'** מה בגד הראוי לקבל טומאה · דאין לך בגד קטן ששמו בגד שאינו ראוי לקבל טומאה אם חישב עליו לכלי כמות שהוא אף כל כו' ועור משהופשט ראוי לקבל טומאה אם חישב עליו יד] לעבדה כמו שהיא אבל כל זמן שלא הופשט אינו ראוי לכלי: אין לי אלא בגד · סתם בגדים שבתורה צמר ופשתים: שק · מטלה של עזים:
וכל

מה טעם קאמר · מתוך התירוץ משמע דהא דקשיא ליה הא תו ל"ל קאי אלפי שאין טעון כיבוס כו' ותימה ונשפך על הרצפה למה לי הא שמעינן לה מניתז מן הצואר: **אלא** אצבעו במאי מקנח · בפ"ק דמנחות (דף ז:) פי' בקונטרס לפי שהיה מזה מדמה בהר המשחה אל נכח פני אהל מועד ופרה לפניו נשרפת לאחר שיורד מן ההר והילך היה יורד בין כל הזאה והזאה מהר המשחה לקנח בגוף הפרה *וקשה מהא דאמר לקמן בריש פרק בתרא (דף קיג·) שחטה שלא כנגד הפתח פסולה שנאמר ושחט והזה מה הזאה כנגד הפתח אף שחיטה כנגד הפתח דמשמע שהיה הכל במקום אחד טו] ונראה כמו שפירש כאן בקונטרס שלא היה יכול לקנח אצבעו בגוף הפרה שלא יתלכלך אצבעו מן הנימין והכי נמי אשכחן דחיישינן לנימין טז] פרק כל כתבי הקדש (שבת קטז:) גבי מפשיטין את הפסח עד החזה*: **מנין** לרבות שק וכל מיני בגדים כו' · מדאוקי ריבויא לשק וכל מיני בגדים · משמע דעור אף משהופשט לא בעי כיבוס לרבי אלעזר וגרסי' במילתיה יכול שאני מרבה את העור משהופשט כדפי' בקונטרס ול"ג עד שלא הופשט דא"כ הוה משמע יז] משהופשט בעי כיבוס וזה אינו דר"א לא יח] מביא אלא שק ומיני בגדים ושמעינן ליה נמי במתני' דאף משהופשט אין טעון כבוס *זה אינו דיוק דאדרבה דעור משהופשט ואינו מחוסר שום דבר לא תיקון ולא מחשבה לקבל טומאה טעון כבוס אפילו לר"א דהא (משהופשט נמי) לא ממעט אלא מטעם דבעינן יט] דבר המקבל טומאה כדאיתא בברייתא אלמא אי מקבל טומאה השתא טעון כיבוס ובסמוך נמי קאמר שלבא שחישב לקלעה איכא בינייהו דלרבי אלעזר לא בעי כיבוס משום יט] דאינו מקבל טומאה עד שיקלענה אבל אם קלעה או לא חישב לקלעה *דהשתא אי מקבל העור טומאה טעון כיבוס והא דמרבי שק ושאר מיני בגדים משום דאפילו הני כ] דאינן בכלל בגד כי אם למר ופשתים כדפרש"י וצריך יתור כא] *לרבות' וה"ה דמההוא יתור נמי אתי עור ואי גרסי' בר"א משהופשט מיירי שעדיין צריך מחשבה קודם שיקבל טומאה כב] *אי צריך שיבטל מחשבתו שחישב העולבא לקלעה וכן פרש"י דהשתא אינו מקבל טומאה כג] לא בעי כיבוס ולרבי יהודה בעי כיבוס כיון דראוי לקבל בלא מעשה ע"י ייחוד כד] *מודי אבל ר"א לא מיירי בעור שצריך תיקון ומעשה קודם שיקבל טומאה דההוא אפי' רבי יהודה מודה דלא בעי כיבוס דהא אינו ראוי לקבל דהא מחוסר מעשה אבל קשה אי גרים משהופשט מאי בעי מאי בינייהו ליבעי פירוש דר"א עור משהופשט דאינו מקבל טומאה השתא אבל ראוי לקבל ע"י מחשבה היכי משכחת לה דאי מחוסר מעשה אפי' רבי יהודה מודה דהא אינו ראוי מיהו הייט נמי מאי בינייהו דקאמר שצריך לעשות הבעיא מכח דברי שניהם ואי גרסינן אף במילתיה דר"א עד שלא הופשט א"ש דבעי מאי בינייהו אבל קשה ממתניתין אי גרים אף משהופשט: הג"ה השתא אפילו גרס משהופשט ע"כ לא פליגי ר"י ור"א אלא דר"י דריש מה בגד ראוי לקבל טומאה ור"א דריש מה בגד מקבל טומאה ומשום הכי ר"י דדריש ראוי מרבה עור משהופשט דראוי לקבל טומאה במחשבה ואין מחוסר מעשה ור"א דדריש מקבל ממעט עור שהופשט אע"ג דראוי משום דבעי דבר המקבל טומאה שאין מחוסר אפילו מחשבה אבל לאחר מחשבה מקבל טומאה בלא שום מעשה דאי מחוסר מעשה אפילו ר"י מודה דלא בעי כיבוס

פז א מיי' פ"ט מהלכות פרה הלכה ג ·
פח ב מיי' פ"ה מהלכות מעה"ק הלכה ט:
פט ג מיי' שם הלכה ח ופ"ג מהלכות פרה הלכה ג:
[ועי' במנחות שם בתוס' דמתרלי קושיא זו]
צ ד מיי' פ"ח מהלכות מעה"ק הלכה ח:
צא ה מיי' פ"ג מהלכות פרה הלכה כ:
צב ו מיי' פ"ה מהל' מעה"ק הלכה ח:
צג ז מיי' שם פ"ח הלכה ה:
[וע' היטב תוס' מנחות ז: ד"ה אלא:]
נ"א תניא נמי הכי וטבל כו'
צד ח ט מיי' שם הלכה ד:
צה י מיי' שם הלכה כ:
צו כ מיי' שם הלכה יא:
צז ל מיי' שם הלכה א:

נ"א אבל זה כו' נ"ק
נ"ל דהשתא מקבל העור כו' נ"ק
נ"א לרבויי נ"ק
נ"א או
נ"ל למודי נ"ק

מנחות ז: [כל הסוגיא כאיתא שייכים]
[ואיבעיא להו ט' וכ"ס שם במנחות]
[שם לעיל ט:]
טבילה הס"ד ואח"כ ד"ה אע"ג דליכא כו' טבילה הס"ד ואח"כ ד"ה למעוטי שיריים שבאצבעו כו' כצ"ל נ"ק
[נ"ל לרבא]
מנחות ז: פרה פ"ג מ"ט
[לעיל כה:] מנחות צא:
[לקמן צה.]
עיין תוי"ט ורש"ק

הגהות הב"ח
(א) גמ' לרב עמרם תלמידי אמר רב עמרם:
(ב) במשנה כיבוס אינו טעון כיבוס אלא מקום:
(ג) רש"י ד"ה שבענין וכו' הזייה טבילה הס"ד ואח"כ מ"ה אף על גב דליכא וכו' לענין קבלה הס"ד ואח"כ מ"ה למעוטי שיריים וכו' פעמים הס"ד ואח"כ מ"ה אמר רב עמרם:

שיטה מקובצת
א] תיבת אומר ל"ש:
ב] טבילה מעיקרא מן:
ג] למכתב וטבל ואיצטריך למכתב בדם:
ד] טבילה מעיקרא כתב רחמנא: ה] כיבוס אינו טעון כיבוס אלא:
ו] קידש כדמפרש טעמא:
ז] הלכתא היא גבי:
ח] במים ולא קרינן במים: ט] שיהא בדם בשעת: י] בדם: יא] בענין שהזה ממנו טבילה ראשונה יזה את: יב] בין הזאה להזאה:
יג] שבאצבע אין: יד] עליו לעוצבא ותיבת לעבדה נמחק: טו] אחד וה"ה לשריפה שהיה שם כמו שפי' כאן בקונטרס נראה שלא היה: טז] לגימין בפ' כל: יז] משמע דמשהופשט: יח] לא מרבה אלא שק: יט] משום דלא מקבל טומאה: כ] הני אינן בכלל: כא] יתור לרבותם וה"ח: כב] טומאה או צריך: כג] טומאה וכ"ה לא: כד] ייחוד סיד ותיבת מודי נמחק:

IF IT POURED OUT ON TO THE PAVEMENT etc. [93b] Why do I need this too?[2]—He states the reason: What is the reason that IF IT POURED OUT ON TO THE PAVEMENT AND [THE PRIEST] COLLECTED IT, IT DOES NOT NEED WASHING?—Because ONLY BLOOD WHICH WAS RECEIVED IN A VESSEL AND IS FIT FOR SPRINKLING NECESSITATES WASHING.

FIT FOR SPRINKLING. What does this exclude?—It excludes the case where one received less than is required for sprinkling in one vessel and less than is required for sprinkling in another vessel.[3] For it was taught: R. Ḥalafta b. Saul said: If he sanctified less than is required for sprinkling in one vessel, and less than is required for sprinkling in another vessel,[4] he has not sanctified it.[5] Now it was asked: How is it with blood? Is it a traditional law,[6] and we cannot learn from a traditional law,[7] or perhaps, what is the reason there? Because it is written, *And a clean person shall take [hyssop,] and dip it in* the *water;*[8] so here too it is written, *And [the priest] shall dip [his finger] in* the *blood?*[9]—Come and hear, for R. Zerika said in R. Eleazar's name: In the case of blood too he does not sanctify it.

Raba said, It was taught: *And [the priest] shall dip:*[10] but not sponge up; *in the blood:*[10] there must be sufficient blood for dipping from the beginning; *[and sprinkle] of the blood:*[10] of the blood specified
a in this passage.[1] Now, it is necessary to write both *'and he shall dip'* and *'in the blood'*.[2] For if the Divine Law wrote *'and he shall dip'* [only], I would say, even where there is insufficient for dipping in the first place; therefore the Divine Law wrote *'in the blood'*. And if the Divine Law wrote *'in the blood'* [only], I would say that he may even sponge it up; therefore the Divine Law wrote, *'and he shall dip'*.[3] What does 'of the blood specified in this passage' exclude?—Said Raba: It excludes the [blood] remaining on his finger.[4] This supports R. Eleazar. For R. Eleazar said: The [blood] remaining on his finger is unfit.

Rabin son of R. Adda said to Raba: Your disciple said in R. Amram's name: It was taught: If [the priest] was sprinkling, and [the blood of] the sprinkling spurted out of his hand,[5] [and this happened] before he had sprinkled, it needs washing; after he had sprinkled, it does not need washing. Surely this is what he means: [If it happened] before he finished sprinkling, it needs washing; after he finished sprinkling, it does not need washing.[6]—No: this is what he means: before the sprinkling had left his hand, it necessitates washing; after it had gone forth from his hand, it does not need washing.[7]

Abaye raised an objection to him: When he finished sprinkling,[8] he wipes his hand on the body of the heifer.[9] Thus, only if he finished, but not if he had not finished![10]—Said he to him: When he finished, he wiped his hand on the body of the heifer; before he finished, he simply wiped his finger. Now, when he finishes, it is well: he wipes his hand on the body of the heifer, as it is said, *And the flesh shall he burn in his sight, [her skin, and her flesh, and her blood . . .*
b *shall be burnt]*.[1] But on what does he wipe his finger?[2]—Said Abaye: On the edge of the bowl, as it is written, *Wipers* [cleansers] *of gold*.[3]

MISHNAH. IF [THE BLOOD] SPURTED ON TO THE SKIN, BEFORE IT WAS FLAYED, IT NEED NOT BE WASHED; [IF IT SPURTED] AFTER IT WAS FLAYED, IT MUST BE WASHED: THESE ARE THE WORDS OF R. JUDAH. R. ELEAZAR SAID: [IT NEED NOT BE WASHED] EVEN [IF IT SPURTED] AFTER IT WAS FLAYED. ONLY THE PLACE OF THE BLOOD NEEDS WASHING.[4] AND WHATEVER IS ELIGIBLE TO CONTRACT UNCLEANNESS,[5] AND IS FIT FOR WASHING, WHETHER A GARMENT, A SACK, OR A HIDE, MUST BE WASHED. THE WASHING MUST BE IN A HOLY PLACE;[6] THE BREAKING OF AN EARTHEN VESSEL MUST BE IN A HOLY PLACE; AND THE SCOURING AND RINSING OF A BRAZEN VESSEL MUST BE IN A HOLY PLACE.[7] IN THIS THE SIN-OFFERING IS MORE STRINGENT THAN [OTHER] SACRIFICES OF HIGHER SANCTITY.

GEMARA. How do we know it?—Because our Rabbis taught: *[And when there is sprinkled of the blood thereof upon] a garment:*[8] I know it only of a garment: whence do I know to include the skin, after it is flayed? Because it says, *thou shalt wash that whereon it was sprinkled.*[9] You might think that I include the skin [even] before it was flayed: therefore it states, *'a garment'*: as a garment is an article eligible to contract uncleanness, so everything that is eligible to contract
c uncleanness [is included]:[1] these are the words of R. Judah. R. Eleazar said: *'A garment'*: I know it only of a garment; whence do I

(2) It is included in the first ruling. (3) Then they were combined in one vessel, and some blood spurted on a garment; that garment does not need washing. Thus the Mishnah means. Only blood which was fit for sprinkling when it was received in a vessel; here, however, it was not fit then. (4) This refers to the water of lustration, which was sanctified for its purpose by being mixed with the ashes of the red heifer. (5) For he must sanctify as much as is required in one vessel. (6) In the case of the water of lustration.—A traditional law is one handed down by tradition, and not learnt directly or by inference from Scripture. (7) In respect of other cases. (8) Num. XIX, 18. The def. art. implies, in the water mentioned above, *sc.* the water sanctified for lustration; conversely it implies that the water when sanctified was sufficient for dipping, i.e., sprinkling. (9) Lev. IV, 6. (10) Ibid.

a (1) This is explained anon. (2) Emended text (Sh.M.). (3) For notes v. *supra* 40b. (4) He must not sprinkle with the blood left on his finger, but must dip his finger into the blood for each of the seven sprinklings. (5) On to a garment.—This refers to inner sin-offerings. (6) That implies that if blood which remained on his finger after one of the sprinklings spurted on to a garment, it must be washed. As a corollary, that remaining blood must be fit for sprinkling, for only such necessitates washing. Hence this contradicts R. Eleazar. (7) I.e., he had dipped his finger into the blood: now, if this blood spurted off his finger *before* he had sprinkled it, it necessitates washing; if after, it does not, precisely because it is then the residue of the blood. (8) The blood of the red heifer; v. Num. XIX, 4. (9) For the blood must be burnt together with the body. (10) Yet if he does not wipe it, he is using this blood for the next sprinkling—there were seven in all.

b (1) Num. XIX, 5. (2) Between the sprinklings. He cannot wipe it on the body, as he would soil his finger through hairs sticking to it. (3) Ezra. I, 10; cf. *supra*. 25a. (4) But not the whole skin. (5) V. discussion *infra*. (6) In the Temple court. (7) V. Lev. VI, 21: *But the earthen vessel wherein it* (*sc.* the flesh of a sin-offering) *is sodden shall be broken; and if it be sodden in a brazen vessel, it shall be scoured, and rinsed in water*. (8) Lev. VI, 20. (9) This is a repetition, and intimates extension.

c (1) After a skin is flayed it can be put to use as it is, without further dressing; therefore if its owner expressly intended to use it thus, it is technically a utensil, and subject to defilement. Before it is flayed, however, it cannot be put to use, and cannot become unclean.

know to include a sack [94a] and all kinds of garments?[2] Because it says, *'thou shalt wash that whereon it was sprinkled'*. You might think that I can include a skin after it was flayed? Therefore it says, *'a garment'*: as a garment is an article which contracts uncleanness, so everything which contracts uncleanness [is included].[3] Wherein do they differ?[4]—Said Abaye: They differ about a cloth less than three [fingerbreadths square].[5] He who says [that it must be] eligible, this too is eligible, for if [its owner] desires, he can intend it [for use]. But he who maintains, anything which contracts uncleanness, this at all events cannot contract uncleanness.[6] Raba said, They disagree over a garment which [its owner] intended to embroider.[7] He who maintains [that it must be] eligible, this too is eligible, for if [its owner] desires, he can abandon his intention. He however who maintains, anything which can contract uncleanness: now at all events it cannot contract uncleanness. Others state,[8] Raba said: They disagree about an [untrimmed] hide which he intended to trim.[9] He who maintains [that it must be] eligible, this too is eligible; he however who maintains, anything which can contract uncleanness, this however cannot contract uncleanness until he trims it. And it was taught even so: R. Simeon b. Menassia
a said: A hide which [its owner] intended trimming is clean[1] until he trims it.

ONLY THE PLACE OF THE BLOOD NEEDS WASHING. How do we know it?—For our Rabbis taught: You might think that if [the blood] spurted on part of the garment, the whole garment must be washed. Therefore it states, *'[thou shalt wash] that whereon it was sprinkled'*: I ordered thee [to wash] only the place of the blood.

WHATEVER IS ELIGIBLE TO CONTRACT UNCLEANNESS. This anonymous teaching agrees with R. Judah.[2] AND FIT FOR WASHING excludes a vessel which requires scraping.[3]

WHETHER A GARMENT, SACKCLOTH, OR HIDE. Are we to say that a skin can be washed? But the following contradicts this: If dirt is upon it, one wipes it off with a rag; if it is of leather [skin], water is poured over it until it disappears.[4]—Said Abaye, There is no difficulty: one agrees with the Rabbis; the other agrees with 'others'.[5] For it was taught: A garment and sackcloth are washed;[6] a vessel and a skin are scraped; others maintain: A garment, sackcloth, and skin are washed; while a vessel is scraped.

With whom does the following statement of R. Ḥiyya b. Ashi agree, [viz.:] I stood many times before Rab, and dabbed his shoes with water?[7] With whom? With the Rabbis.[8]

Raba observed: Does anyone maintain that skin is not washable? Surely it is written, *And the garment, or the warp, or the woof, or whatso-*
b *ever thing* of skin *it be, which thou shalt* wash![1] Rather said Raba: The Scriptural text and our Mishnah refer to soft [skins], whereas they disagree about hard [skins].[2] But surely R. Ḥiyya b. Ashi said: I stood many times before Rab, and dabbed his shoes with water?[3]—They were of hard [leather], and [he acted] in accordance with the Rabbis.

Subsequently Raba said: My statement was incorrect. Are we to say that the text refers [only] to soft [skins]? Does it not refer [even] to foresters' apparel which comes from overseas,[4] yet the Divine Law states that it must be washed?[5] Rather said Raba: Leprosy,[6] since it breaks out in the article itself, moistens it and softens it.[7]

(2) Garments made of any materials. A garment usually was of wool. (3) A garment contracts uncleanness whether its owner intends to use it or not; hence the hide, even after it is flayed, is not included, because it does not contract uncleanness, but can only be *made* to contract uncleanness, by the owner's intention to use it. (4) What garment is merely *eligible* to become unclean, though at present it cannot become unclean? (5) This is the smallest piece which counts technically as a *'garment'*. A smaller piece ranks as a garment only if the owner intends to use it. (6) Without its owner's intention. Hence if the blood spurted on such a cloth, in R. Judah's opinion it must be washed, but not in R. Eleazar's. (7) I.e., even a larger piece of cloth, but which has not yet been used, because its owner had expressed his intention to embroider it first. This counts as unfinished, and hence not a 'garment'; nevertheless, if the owner expressly abandons his intention, it becomes a 'garment'. Thus it is eligible, but cannot contract uncleanness at present. (8) Marginal addition. (9) *'Uẓba* is anything used as a rug or mat or tablecloth; it is generally of hide, but sometimes of cloth. Now, if one intended to use it for such purpose, it *immediately* ranks as a utensil, even before it is trimmed, and hence can be defiled. But if he intended trimming it, it cannot become unclean until he either trims it or abandons his intention.

a (1) I.e., it cannot become unclean. (2) Though its author is not named, we know from the Baraitha that it is R. Judah's view.—When an individual's view is stated anonymously in the Mishnah, it is generally the *halachah*. (3) E.g., a wooden vessel, whence it may be impossible to wash out the blood. This does not need washing at all but scraping. (4) This treats of the Sabbath, when washing garments is forbidden as a prohibited labour. Dirt on a cushion may be wiped off with a cloth, but not with water, as this constitutes washing. Water, however, may be poured over skin, for that is not regarded as washing. Thus skin is not technically subject to washing. (5) 'Others' generally refers to R. Meir; Hor. 13*b*. (6) If the blood of a sin-offering spurts upon them. (7) On the Sabbath. (8) Who hold pouring water over skin (or leather) is not washing.

b (1) Lev. XIII, 58. (2) E.g., leather. (3) It is now assumed that they were of soft leather. (4) It was manufactured of hard leather. (5) Scripture does not limit itself but writes, *or whatsoever thing of skin it be*. (6) To which the passage refers. (7) Any leather garment.—Hence the text refers even to hard leather; our Mishnah refers to soft; while the controversy is in respect of hard.

וכל מיני בגדים תלמוד לומר °אשר עליה תכבס יכול שאני מרבה עור משהופשט ת"ל בגד מה בגד דבר המקבל טומאה אף כל דבר המקבל טומאה מאי בינייהו אמר אביי מטלית פחותה משלש איכא בינייהו מאן דאמר ראוי הא נמי ראוי °דאי א] בעי "חשיב עליה מ"ד דבר המקבל טומאה הא מיהא לאו בת קבולי טומאה היא רבא אמר בגד שחישב עליה ב] לצורה איכא בינייהו מ"ד ראוי הא נמי ראוי דאי ג] בעי מבטיל ליה למחשבתיה מ"ד דבר המקבל טומאה השתא מיהא לאו בת קבולי טומאה היא *רבא אמר עוצבא דחשיב עלה לקצעה איכא בינייהו מ"ד ראוי הא נמי ראויה מאן דאמר דבר המקבל טומאה הא לאו מקבלה טומאה עד דמקצע לה *והתניא רבי שמעון בן מנסיא אומר ב'עוצבא שחשב עליה לקצעה טהורה עד שיקציענה: ד] אין טעון כיבוס כו': מנה"מ דת"ר יכול נתז על מקצת בגד יהא כל הבגד טעון כיבוס ת"ל °אשר יזה ג'לא אמרתי לך אלא מקום דם בלבד: דבר שהוא ראוי לקבל טומאה [וכו']: סתמא כרבי יהודה ה] ראוי לכיבוס ד'למעוטי כלי דבר גרידה הוא: אחד הבגד ואחד השק כו': למימרא דעור בר כיבוס הוא ורמינהו *ה'היתה עליו לשלשת מקנחה בסמרטוט היתה *(על) של עור נותן עליה מים עד שתכלה אמר אביי לא קשיא הא רבנן הא אחרים דתניא הבגד והשק ו] מכבסו הכלי והעור מגררו אחרים אומרים הבגד והשק והעור ז] מכבסו והכלי מגררו כמאן אזלא הא דאמר רב חייא בר אשי זימנין סגיאין הוה קאימנא קמיה דרב ושבשיכי ליה מסאניה במיא כמאן כרבנן אמר רבא ומי איכא למאן דאמר עור לאו בר כיבוס הוא והכתיב °והבגד או השתי או הערב או כל כלי העור אשר תכבס אלא אמר רבא קרא ומתניתין ו'ברכין ח]כי פליגי בקשין והאמר רב חייא זימנין סגיאין הוה קאימנא קמיה דרב ושבשיכי ליה מסאניה במיא בקשין וכרבנן *הדר אמר רבא לאו מילתא היא דאמרי ניקו נימא ליה לקרא דכי ט] כתיבן ברכין כתיבן מי לא עסקינן *)בכלי י]*אבסלגיא הבאים ממדינת הים יא] וקאמר רחמנא ניבעי כיבוס אלא אמר רבא יב] ז'צרעת כיון דמגופיה קא פרחה מחלחלא ליה ומשוי לה רך אמר רבא אי קשיא לי הא קשיא לי יג]

*) חגיגה כו: [וע"ש בתוס' ותוס' מנחות לז. ד"ה כלי]

כרים

רש"י

וכל מיני בגדים. השירים והכלך וסריקין: יכול שאני מרבה עור משהופשט. גרסינן כרבי אלעזר משהופשט מיד בלא שום תיקון: מה בגד המקבל טומאה. דרבי אלעזר גמר בגד דהכא מבגד האמור בשרצים (ויקרא יא) שהוא מקבל טומאה יד] ואינה מחוסר מחשבה: מאי בינייהו. במאי פליגי היכן מצינו בגד הראוי לקבל טומאה ואינה מקבלה (א) טו] ויליף ר' יהודה מיניה: דאי טז][בעי] חשיב עלה. לתקן חלוקו: רבא אמר. בגד גדול נמי משכחת לה דראוי לקבל ואינו מקבל כגון שחישב עליו יז] לציירו במעשה רוקם דכל כמה דלא צייריה יח] או מבטל למחשבתו לאו כלי הוא: דאי יט] בעי מבטל ליה למחשבתו. כ] הא דקיימא לן מחשבה אינה מוציאה מידי מחשבה לענין כא] הוציאו מתורת טומאה תנן לה (כלים פרק כה משנה ט) דמשירדו לטומאתן במחשבה אין מחשבה חוזרת ומוציאתן אבל להורידן לטומאה קי"ל (שם) כל הכלים יורדין לידי טומאתן במחשבה: עוצבא. שטיח לאכול עליו או לשכב עליו ורובן מן העור ויש שעושין מן הבגד וקי"ל שאם חישב עליו לעוצבא אין צריך קילוע דדוייי"ר בלע"ז כב] ליפותו דבלאו קילוע חזי לעוצבא בב"ק מייתי לה בפ' מרובה (דף סו:) אבל היכא דחשיב עליה לקולעה אינה מקבלת טומאה עד שיקלענה כדאמרינן לקמן או יבטל מחשבתו הילכך בגד שעומד לעוצבא וחישב כג] עליה לקולעה הרי ראוי לקבל טומאה דאי בעי מבטל למחשבתיה ואינו מקבל עדיין ובהא פליגי לרבי יהודה כל בגד במשמע ויש בגד שאינו מקבל טומאה אלא ראוי לטומאה ור' אלעזר כבגד האמור בשרצים בעינן: והתניא. בניחותא: עד שיקלענה. או יבטל מחשבתו דקי"ל (שם) כל הכלים יורדין לידי טומאתן במחשבה: דבר גרידה הוא. דאין מכבסים *[אותו] אלא כד]גורדו: היתה עליו לשלשת. במס' שבת תנן לה היתה על הכר של בגד ניעול של רוק או של צואה מקנחו בסמרטוט בשבת ואינו נותן עליה מים לכלותה כה] להעבירה מפני שהוא מכבס וכיבוס אב מלאכה הוא כו] היינו מלבן ואם היתה לשלשת זו על כר של עור נותן עליה מים עד שתכלה בשטיפת מים ומיהו שפשופי בידים לא ומדקתני נותן עליה מים ש"מ אין כיבוס בעור: כז] מכבסו. גבי דם חטאת קאי: מסאניה. בשבת: קרא. כח] גבי נגעים דכתיב (ויקרא יג) כיבוס בעור: ומתני'. דהכא דקתני העור טעון כיבוס: ברכין. ודברי הכל וכי פליגי אחרים ורבנן בקשין: לאו מילתא היא דאמרי. לאוקומי קרא ברכין דהא קרא סתמא כתיב לא שנא רך ולא שנא קשה דמי לא עסקינן דקרא אפילו כט] אכסלגיא קאמר דקשין הן אכסלגיא עור שלוק וקשה: ומשויא ליה רך. הילכך קרא לצרעת אפילו בקשין ומתניתין ברכין ופלוגתא בקשין:

כריס

תוספות

כיבוס דהא אינו ראוי וכל שכן אי גרסינן עד שלא הופשט שיש הוכחה שלאחר הפשט מקבל טומאה בלא שום מעשה עד כאן הגה"ה ותימה ל] בפ' במה טומנין (שבת דף מט:) משמע דאין עור מקבל טומאה עד לאחר עיבוד דתניא עורות בין עבודים בין שאינן עבודים מותר לטלטלן בשבת ולא אמרו עבודים אלא לענין טומאה בלבד ופי' שם בקונטרס דאין עור מקבל טומאה עד לאחר עיבוד ושמא יש לפרש דאחר עיבוד אפילו מחשבה לא בעי אבל קודם עיבוד בעי מחשבה וה"ר חיים מפרש בשם ריב"א דהתם מיירי באותם שעורותיהם כבשרם דתנן בפ' העור והרוטב (חולין דף קכב.) וכולן שעיבדן או שהלך בהן כדי עבודה טהורין וה"ק לא אמרו שיש חילוק בין עבודין לשאין עבודין אלא לענין טומאה ובאותם שעורותיהן כבשרם דקודם עיבוד טמאין בכזית כדין בשר לא]המת ונבלה ושרץ בכעדשה ולאחר עיבוד טהורין עד שיהא בו חמשה על חמשה כדין עור וא"ת דמשמע הכא דעור משהופשט אפילו לא מקבל טומאה במחשבה דהא דומיא דעור שלא הופשט קמרבי דהוי לא ומדחשיב מנא במחשבה לענין טומאה אם כן מותר לטלטלו בשבת כדאשכחן בפרק כל הכלים (שבת דף קכג.) במחט שאינה נקובה בגלמי דכיון דזימנין דמימלך עלה ומשוי לה מנא שרי לטלטלו וקשה מכאן לר"ת דמפרש בבמה טומנין (שם דף מט.) גבי טומנין בשלחין ומטלטלין אותן דמיירי ביבשין אבל לחין לא משום דקשיא ליה ההיא דכל כתבי הקדש (שם דף קטז:) גבי מפשיטין את הפסח עד החזה דקאמר לא נטלטל עור אגב בשר אבל בלא בשר לא וכן בפ"ק דבילה (דף יא:) גבי עור לפני הדורסן דהתירו סופן משום תחילתן קאמר מהו דתימא טעמא דב"ה משום דחזי למזגא עליה ואפילו בעי"ט קמ"ל כו' וי"ל דאע"ג דמקבל טומאה במחשבה לב]*כאן (דלא שכרה) שייחדה לישיבה בעוד שהוא לח אסור לטלטל וכן צ"ל גבי מחט שניטל חררה או עוקצה דאסרינן לטלטלה אע"ג דאם איתקנא למתוח טמאה כדתנן במס' כלים (פרק יג מ"ה) ובקונטרס פי' בפ' כל כתבי הקודש (שבת דף קכ.) דההיא דבמה טומנין דעור בהמה גסה ולפירושו צריך לאוקומה נמי ההיא דבילה בבהמה דקה כי ההיא דכל כתבי דגבי פסח וטעמא דעור בהמה דקה לא חזיא למזגא כולי האי והא דתנן בפרק כל כתבי (שם) פורסין עור של גדי כו' צריך להעמידה לג](כ"ש) כשייחדו לישיבה אי נמי בדליקה התירו טפי כדאמר התם ולפר"ת אתי שפיר דמיירי ביבשין כי ההיא דבמה טומנין (שם דף מט.): מאי בינייהו. פירוש לרבי יהודה על כרחין איירי קרא בבגד דאינו מקבל טומאה אלא דראוי לקבל ולרבי אלעזר איירי קרא בבגד דמקבל טומאה אבל בבגד הראוי ואינו מקבל לא בעי כיבוס והשתא איזה בגד הוא זה לד] הראוי ואינו מקבל ואיכא בינייהו לרבי יהודה בעי כיבוס ולרבי אלעזר לא בעי כיבוס: **לשלשת**. פירש בערוך צואת תרנגולין: **מקנחה** בסמרטוט. אבל ליתן מים אסור משום דשרייתו זהו כיבוסו והא דאמר לה] בפ"ק דבילה (דף יח.) נדה מערמת וטובלת בבגדיה אומר ר"ת דלא חשיב כיבוס משום דהוי דרך לכלוך ויותר מתלכלכים בגדים כשנכנסה בנהר לבושה ממה שמתכבסין וכן תיכי חלילתא דברים במה אשה (שבת דף נז.) לא אסרינן אלא שמא תטלם ותעבירם ארבע אמות בשבת

ברשות

עין משפט נר מצוה

כז א מיי' פכ"ב מהל' כלים הלכה כא:

כח ב מיי' שם פכ"ד הלכה ו:

כט ג ד מיי' פ"ח מהל' מעשה הקרבנות הלכה ד:

ל ה מיי' פכ"ב מהל' שבת הל' יח טוש"ע או"ח סי' שב סעיף ט:

לא ו מיי' פ"ח מהל' מעשה הקרבנות הלכה ג:

לב ז מיי' פי"ג מהל' טומאת צרעת הל"א:

מסורת הש"ס

נ"ל א"ד

תוספתא דכלים פ"ד דב"ב פ"ש

שבת קמב:

[בשבת ליתא]

גי' יעב"ץ

[שבת סב: וש"נ]

הגהות הב"ח

(א) רש"י ד"ה מאי בינייהו וכו' ואינה מקבלה הס"ד והשאר נמחק:

גליון הש"ס

גמ' דאי בעי חשיב עלה. עיין סוכה דף טז ע"א תוס' ד"ה דלא חזי. ונדה דף ס ע"ב תוס' ד"ה במטלניות:

[גי' ערוך בערך אבלוסמוס מי לא עסקינן בכלי אבלוסמוס פי' כלים של עור קשין ועבין וז"ל הרב המוסף בנוסחאות דידן גרסי' אכסלגם ולא יתכן כי אכסלגם בל' יוני מין עץ ופי' אמבולוסמוס בלשון יוני כלים עשויים מחתיכות עורות או בגדים עכ"ל ובדברים אלו מיושב היטב קושיית תוס' בחגיגה כו: ד"ה בכלי וכו' ותוס' מנחות לז. ד"ה כלי כו' גם בשאלתות סי' פ"ח איתא בכלי אבלוסמוס]

שיטה מקובצת

א] דאי מחשיב עליה מ"ד דבר המקבל טומאה השתא מיהא: ב] עליה לציירו איכא: ג] דאי מבטל ליה: ד] אינו טעון: ה] וראוי לכיבוס: ו] מכבסן הכלי והעור מגררן: ז] והעור מכבסן והכלי מגררן: ח] ברכין וכי פליגי בקשין דאמר רב: ט] דכי כתיבא ברכין כתיבא: י] בכלי אבסלגוס. ס"א אבלוסמים: יא] הים דקשין נינהו וקאמר: יב] רבא כיון דצרעת מגופיה קא פרחה: יג] לי דהא כרים: יד] טומאה ואינו מחוסר: טו] מקבלה דקא יליף: טז] דאי מחשב עליה. לתקן: יז] עליו מתחלתו לציירו: יח] על תיבות או מבטל למחשבתו כתוב מן הצד

נ"ל למחוק: יט] תיבת בעי ל"ש: כ] למחשבתו דהא דקימא: כא] לענין להוציאו מתורת: כב] בלע"ז דהיינו ליפותו: כג] וחישב עליו לקוצעה הוי ראוי לקבל טומאה ואי מבטל למחשבתו: כד] גוררו כגון כלי עץ תס"ד ומת"ד היתה: כה] לכלותה ולהעבירה: כו] דהיינו: כז] מה"ד מכבסן. גבי כיבוס דם חטאת: כח] קרא דגבי נגעים: כט] אפי' כלי אכסלגוס: ל] ותימה דבפ' במה: לא] בשר שנתנבלה ודשרץ תיבות הפת ונבילה נמחק: לב] במחשבה כיון דלא שכיח שייחדו לישיבה: לג] תיבת כ"ש נמחק: לד] דראוי ואינו מקבל דאיכא בינייהו: לה] דאמר בפ' שני:

תורה אור

כרים וכסתות דרכין נינהו ותנן היתה א] של עור נותן עליה מים עד שתכלה אלא אמר רבא כל כיבוס דלית ליה כיסכוס לא שמיה כיבוס והא דאמר רב חייא בר אשי זימנין סגיאין הוה קאימנא קמיה דרב ושכשיכי ליה מסאניה במיא *שכשוך אין אבל *כבוס לא אי ב] ברכין וכדברי הכל אי בקשין וכאחרים אי הכי בגד נמי ‌בגד שרייתו זהו כיבוסו ג] [רבא לטעמיה דאמר רבא זרק סודר למים רש"ק חייב [בב] זרק ד] *פשתן למים חייב בשלמא סודר ה] עביד כיבוס] אלא *זרע פשתן מ"ט וכ"ת משום דמקדח אי הכי חיטי ושערי נמי הנך אית להו רירי א"ה שלחים נמי התם קעביד לישה דרש רבא מותר לכבס מנעל בשבת א"ל רב פפא לרבא והא"ר חייא בר אשי זימנין סגיאין הוה קאימנא קמיה דרב ושכשיכי ליה מסאני במיא שכשוך אין אבל כיבוס לא הדר אוקי רבא אמורא עליה ודרש *דברים שאמרתי לפניכם טעות הם בידי ברם כך אמרו שכשוך מותר *כיבוס אסור: הכיבוס במקום קדוש כו': מנא הני מילי דת"ר °תכבס במקום קדוש ו] שבירת כלי ויקרא ו חרם מניין ת"ל °וכלי חרם אשר תבושל בו שם ישבר מריקה ושטיפה בכלי נחשת מנין ת"ל °ואם בכלי נחשת בושלה ומורק ושוטף שם במים: זה חומר בחטאת כו': ותו ליכא והאיכא ז] שנכנס דמה (לפני ו) לפנים בחטאות החיצונו' ח] שאם נכנס דמה (לפני ו) לפנים פסולה כר"ע דאמר כל דמים שנכנסו להיכל לכפר ט] פסולה שכן מכפרין על חייבי כריתות בחטאת דשמיעת הקול י] שכן טעונה ארבע מתנות כר' ישמעאל דאמר *כל דמים טעונין ד' מתנות יא] על ד' קרנות וליטעמיך האיכא קרן (בדם) האיכא אצבע °האיכא חודה אלא *חד מתרי *תלתא חומרי נקט: **מתני'** ‌בגד שיצא חוץ לקלעים נכנס ומכבסו במקום קדוש נטמא חוץ לקלעים קורעו יב] נכנס ומכבסו במקום קדוש ‌כלי חרם שיצא חוץ לקלעים נכנס ושוברו במקום קדוש נטמא חוץ לקלעים נוקבו ונכנס ושוברו במקום קדוש ‌כלי נחשת שיצא חוץ לקלעים נכנס ומורקו ושוטפו במקום קדוש נטמא חוץ לקלעים פוחתו ונכנס ומורקו ושוטפו במקום קדוש: **גמ'** מתקיף לה רבינא קורעו בגד אמר רחמנא יג] ולאו בגד הוא ‌דמשייר ביה כדי מעפורת איני והאמר *רב הונא ל"ש אלא שלא שייר בהכדי מעפורת אבל שייר בהכדי מעפורת חבור הוי מדרבנן

רש"י

כרים וכסתות דרכין נינהו. דאין עושין אותן אלא מעור רך שיהא נוח לישכב עליו: כסכוס. משפשף לזו זה על לזו יד] זה כדרך המכבס בגדים אוחז הבגד בשתי ידיו ומשפשף: לא שמיה כיבוס. הילכך נותן עליו מים עד שתכלה שרי בעור ואפילו רך ולקמן פריך אי הכי בגד נמי כיבוס לא [הוי אלא] על ידי כסכוס: בגד נמי. יתן עליו מים טו] ואמאי תנא מקנחה בסמרטוט: טז] זרע פשתן במים חייב. כדמפרש ואזיל: דמיקדח. צומח במים והויא לה זריעה: הכי גרסינן אי הכי חיטי ושערי נמי הנך אית להו רירא אי הכי שלחים נמי התם קעביד לישה: הנך אית להו רירא. זרע פשתן במים נפקא רירא מיניה ומדבקי אהדדי: אי הכי שלחים נמי. אי משום דמדבקי בריריהו יז] מחייבין להו בשלחים נמי עורות שאינן עבודין ונתנן במים רירא קנפקא מינייהו: ומשני התם. גבי זרע פשתנכי מדבקת ברירא דנפקי מינייהו הוי תולדות לישה אבל שלחים לא שייכא בדיבוקא דידהו ענין לישה: אמר ליה רב פפא. לאחר שישב לו המתורגמן: הדר אוקי. באותה שעה חזר ואמר למתורגמן עמוד והשמע לרבים שאני חוזר בי ממה שדרשתי: וכלי חרס. בתר כיבוס כתיב: והאיכא. אכתי חומר בחטאת שהרי יש בהן יח] דמן נכנס לפנים מה שאין בשאר קדשים: ומשני בחטאות החיצונות קאמרינן: ופרכינן בחטאות החיצונות נמי איכא שאם נכנס דמה לפנים פסולה. דכתיב (ויקרא ו) וכל חטאת אשר יובא: ומשני כרבי עקיבא. סבירא ליה לתנא דידן: דאמר כל דמים כו'. בכל הזבחים שנתערבו (לעיל דף פא:): והאיכא שכן טעונה ארבע מתנות. מפוסקות ושאר קדשים *שתי מתנות שהן ארבע ואין בהן אלא פיסוק שתי מתנות: כר' ישמעאל. דאמר באיזהו מקומן (לעיל דף נג:) כל הדמים טעונין פיסוק ארבע מתנות לד' קרנות: ופרכינן לר' ישמעאל איכא יט] חומר בחטאת שהוא טעון ארבע קרנות: וליטעמיך טובא איכא. שהרי חטאת טעונה קרן ושאר דמים ניתנין למטה מן החוט כ] והיכא שטעונה אצבע ושאר דמים נזרקין מן הכלי מרחוק למזבח וטעונה חודה של קרן מה שאין כן בשאר דמים: **מתני'** בגד. שניתז עליו דם חטאת ויצא חוץ לקלעים: נכנס. לעזרה ומכבסו במקום קדוש: נטמא חוץ לקלעים. לאחר שיצא ואי אפשר להכניס טומאה לעזרה: קורעו. וטהור כא] *מטומאה ומותר להכניסו ונכנס ומכבסו במקום קדוש: נוקבו. לטהרו מטומאתו: פוחתו. דכלי מתכות אינו טהור בנקב כל דהו אלא בנקב גדול: **גמ'** כב] בגד אמר רחמנא. שיהא שם בגד עליו דמשייר ביה. שלא יבדיל את הקרע על פני כולו לחלוק את הבגד לשנים אלא משייר בו כדי רוחב סודר דמטומאתו טהור הואיל ונקרע רובו. וכיון ששייר בו כדי מעפורת ראוי לחברו ושמו עליו ובגד קרינן ביה: והאמר רב הונא. בפרק העור והרוטב (חולין דף קכג:) לא שנו דטלית טמאה שהתחיל בה כג] לקורעו כיון שנקרע רובה טהורה אלא שלא שייר באותה מיעוט כדי מעפורת: אבל שייר בה כדי מעפורת חיבור הוי. ועדיין הוא בטומאתו: מדרבנן

תוספות

ברשות הרבים ולא משום שרייתן זהו כיבוסן דדרך טינוף הוא ומהאי טעמא נמי שרי לקנח ידיו במפה בשבת: **אי** הכי שלחים נמי. ה"ר חיים גריס *שלחים כד]: **אלא** מתרי תלת חומרי נקט. תימה מ"מ קשה זה חומר דמשמע זה חומר ותו לא כדדייקינן בפ' הזהב (ב"מ דף נז:) [גבי] אלו דברים שאין להם אונאה בשלמא הדיוט זה חומר ותו לא אלא הקדש זה חומר ותו לא ומיהו בלאו הכי קשה התם מאי קאמר בשלמא הדיוט זה חומר ותו לא אכתי איכא כה] (בעי) תשלומי כפל דאיתיה בהדיוט וליתיה בהקדש ושומר חנם שנשבע להדיוט ואין נשבע להקדש ואית דלא כו] גרס התם ותו לא והכי פירושא בשלמא בהדיוט שייך למיתני זה חומר לפי שמוטעות חומרות של הדיוט משל הקדש וכשאלה כז] [חומרא] שייך למיתני זה חומר עליה אבל חומרי דהקדש משל הדיוט כפישן ואינו שום חידוש דליתני עלה זה חומר ולפירוש זה ניחא הכא וכן במסכת ערכין בפרק האומר משקלי עלי (דף יט:) דקתני זה חומר בנדרים מבערכין ובגמ' חשיב טפי מברייתא ואי גרסינן ותו לא יש לפרש משום דחומרא כח] באונאה שכיחא אבל חומרא דחיוב ד' וה' וכפל ושבועת שומר חנם ותשלומי שומר שכר לא שכיח כט] האי חומרא בהדיוט אלא הקדש זה חומר ותו לא אכתי איכא טובא דשכיחי ולפירוש זה לא מיתרצא הך דמעתין והיא דערכין*: **לא** שנו אלא שלא שייר בה כדי מעפורת אבל שייר בה כדי מעפורת חיבור. מילתיה דר"ה איתמר בהעור והרוטב (חולין דף קכג:) אההיא דטלית שהתחיל בה לקורעה כיון שנקרע בה רובה שוב אינו חיבור וטהורה ומשמע דטהורה לגמרי ותימה אמאי אינה טמאה מגע מדרס כדאמר בפ' בהמה המקשה (שם דף עב:) שלשה על שלשה שנחלק טהורה מן המדרס אבל טמא מגע מדרס דברי רבי מאיר ומסיק התם בשלש על שלש הבאות מבגד גדול לכולי עלמא בשעת פרישתן מאביהן מקבלות טומאה מאביהן ואפי' מיירי הך דטלית בשלא נטמאה מדרס אלא מגע טומאה בעלמא מ"מ כל כמה דאשתייר בה שלש על שלש שהוא שיעור טומאת מגע לא פקעה מינה טומאת מגע ואי לאו הך דשמעתין הוה מלינן למימר דטהורה דקתני מן המדרס קאמר והא דלא קתני ל] אבל טמא מגע מדרס כדקתני בבהמה המקשה משום דלא נחת להשמיע חידוש של לא] *טהרה אלא קמ"ל אע"ג לב] דטלית גדולה (הרבה יותר) עדיין יותר מג' על ג' אפ"ה טהורה מן המדרס הואיל ולא חזיא למלאכתו ראשונה *) [להתעטף] אבל קשה מהך שמעתא דאי לא פקעה מינה טומאת מגע היאך מכניסו הא אכתי טמא הוא בשעת כיבוסו: דמשייר ביה. מ"מ

*) כ"ה נס"י

עין משפט נר מצוה

ר"ל ירק כרתי דלפירש"י לא מתייבש יפה דלא שייך בעור רירא. רש"ק

נ"ק מ"ז

לג א ב מיי' פכ"ב מהל' שבת הל' יח טוש"ע א"ח סי' שב סעיף ט: [בב] [מיי' פ"ח מהלכות שבת הל' טו טוש"ע א"ח סי' שמ סעיף יב וסי' שלו סעיף יא]:

לד ג מיי' פ"ח מהל' מעשה הקרבנות הלכה יט:

פ"א זרק

לה ד המיי' שם הל' כא:

לו ו מיי' שם הל' יט:

[ועי' תוס' ערכין כ. ד"ה פ"ב חומר]

[לעיל יבמות מח: וש"נ]

נ"ל של טומאה אלא קמ"ל דאע"ג דעדיין הטלית גדולה הרבה יותר מג'. ועיין בר"ש בפ"ט דכלים מ"ח

מסורת הש"ס

[נ"ל כסכוסי וכן איתא בשאלתות פרשת מצורע סי' פ"ח]

[נ"ל זרע פשתן וכ"א בשאלתות שם]

[שבת סג: וש"נ]

[בשאלתות איתא כסכוסי]

נ"ל שני בשתי מהטות נ"ק

[לעיל י: נג.]

נ"ל ותלתא נ"ק

גליון הש"ס

גמ' האיכא חודה. עיין לעיל דף לב ע"ב תוס' ד"ה וקרן:

נ"ל מטומאתו נ"ק

[חולין קכג: ע"ש]

שיטה מקובצת

א] היתה על של עור: ב] אי בעית אימא ברכין וכדברי הכל אי בעית אימא בקשין: ג] ואודא רבא: ד] זרק זרע פשתן: ה] סודר שרייתו זהו כיבוסו אלא תיבת עביד כיבוס ל"ש ונמחק: ו] קדוש למדנו לכיבוס במקום קדוש שבירת: ז] האיכא דנכנס: ח] החיצונות קאמרינן חיצונות נמי שאם: ט] פסולים שכן: י] הקול דשבועת בישוי שכן: יא] מתנות האיכא על וכו' קרן האיכא תיבת בדם נמחק: יב] קורעו ונכנס: יג] רחמנא ולא שירי בגד דמשייר ביה תיבות ולאו הוא נמחק: יד] צדו של זה: טו] מים ובלא כיסכוס ואמאי: טז] זרק זרע: יז] מחייבת להו בשלחים נמי היינו עורות: יח] בהן דדמן נכנס לפנים מה שאין כן בשאר קדשים: יט] איכא נמי דאמר: כ] החוט והא איכא שטעונה: כא] וטהור מטומאתו: כב] מה"ד קורעו. בתמיהה הס"ד ומה"ד בגד: כג] ב, לקורעה כיון: כד] שחלים. פי' והן מין זרעים דאית בהו רירא ולפי' רש"י ז"ל קשה ודקארי לה מאי קארי לה מה ענין שלחים אצל זרעים. מהר"פ ז"ל: כה] איכא כנך תשלומי תיבת בעי נמחק: כו] דלא גרסי התם: כז] וכשמוצא הותרא: כח] דהותרא דאונאה: כט] לא שכיח ולהכי פריך בשלמא הדיוט זה חומר והו לא דליכא דשכיח אלא כו': ל] דלא קתני אחר כך טמא תיבת אבל ל"ש: לא] של טומאה תיבת טהרה נמחק: לב] דטלית גדולה הרבה עדיין יותר מג':

Raba observed: If I have a difficulty, it is this: [94b] Pillows and bolsters are soft, yet we learnt: 'If it is of leather, water is poured over it until it disappears'?[8]—Rather said Raba: All washing without rubbing is not called washing. And as to R. Ḥiyya b. Ashi's statement, I stood many times before Rab and dabbed his shoes with water; dabbing is [permitted], but not rubbing. [Now, our Mishnah treats] either of soft [skins], and it agrees with all; or of hard ones, and it agrees with 'others'. If so, [let water be poured] even [over] a garment too?[9]—In the case of a garment, soaking it [in water] constitutes its washing. Now, Raba is consistent with his view. For Raba said: If one threw a scarf into water, he is culpable;[10] if one threw linseed into water, he is culpable. As for a scarf, it is well, [as] he thereby washes it. But what is the reason in the case of linseed? And should you say, because he causes it to grow;[11] if so, the same applies to wheat and barley too?—This a [linseed] emits mucus.[1] If so, the same applies to [undressed] hides?[2]—There he kneads.[3]

Raba lectured: It is permitted to wash a shoe on the Sabbath. Said R. Papa to Raba. But surely R. Ḥiyya b. Ashi said: I stood many times before Rab, and dabbed his shoes with water for him. Thus, only dabbing [is permitted], but not washing? Subsequently Raba appointed an interpreter before him and lectured:[4] What I told you was an error; but in truth, dabbing is permitted but washing is forbidden.

THE WASHING MUST BE IN A HOLY PLACE, etc. How do we know it?—Because our Rabbis taught: *Thou shalt wash in a holy place:*[5] from this we learn that the washing must be in a holy place.[6] How do we know that earthen vessels must be broken? Because it says, *But the earthen vessel wherein it is sodden shall be broken.*[7] How do we know that brazen vessels must be scoured and rinsed? Because it says, *And if it be sodden in a brazen vessel, it shall be scoured and rinsed in water.*[8]

IN THIS THE SIN-OFFERING IS MORE STRINGENT, etc. And is there nothing else:[9] surely there is the fact that its blood enters within?[10]—This refers to outer sin-offerings.[11] But outer sin-offerings too [have a peculiar stringency, viz.] if their blood entered within, they are disqualified?—This is in accordance with R. Akiba, who maintained: *All* bloods which enter the *hekal* to make atonement are disqualified.[12] Yet there is the fact that they make atonement for those who are liable to *kareth*?—This refers to the sin-offering for b the 'hearing of the voice' or 'oath of utterance'.[1] Yet there is the fact that they require four sprinklings?—This agrees with R. Ishmael who maintained: *All* blood requires four sprinklings. But there is the fact that [the sprinklings must be] on the four horns?—Yet on your reasoning, surely there are the horn, the finger, and the edge?[2] Rather, [the Tanna] mentions one out of two or three stringencies.

MISHNAH. IF A GARMENT[3] WAS CARRIED OUTSIDE THE HANGINGS,[4] IT MUST RE-ENTER, AND IT IS WASHED IN A HOLY PLACE. IF IT WAS DEFILED WITHOUT THE HANGINGS[5] ONE MUST TEAR IT,[6] THEN IT RE-ENTERS, AND IS WASHED IN A HOLY PLACE. IF AN EARTHEN VESSEL WAS CARRIED OUTSIDE THE HANGINGS, IT RE-ENTERS AND IS BROKEN IN A HOLY PLACE. IF IT WAS DEFILED WITHOUT THE HANGINGS, A HOLE IS MADE IN IT, THEN IT RE-ENTERS AND IS BROKEN IN A HOLY PLACE. IF A BRAZEN VESSEL WAS CARRIED OUTSIDE THE HANGINGS, IT RE-ENTERS AND IS SCOURED AND RINSED IN A HOLY PLACE. IF IT WAS DEFILED OUTSIDE THE HANGINGS, IT MUST BE BROKEN THROUGH,[7] THEN IT RE-ENTERS AND IS SCOURED AND RINSED IN A HOLY PLACE.

GEMARA. To this Rabina demurred. [You say,] ONE MUST TEAR IT: Surely the Divine Law speaks of a '*garment*', and this is not a garment?[8]—He leaves enough of it [untorn] to be used as an c apron.[1] But that is not so, for surely R. Huna said: They learnt this[2] only if one did *not* leave enough to be used as an apron [untorn], but if one left enough to be used as an apron, it is [technically]

(8) *Supra* in connection with the Sabbath. (9) Why must the dirt be wiped off only with a rag? (10) For washing on the Sabbath, to which this refers. (11) In the water. Thus it is a form of sowing, and for this he is culpable.

a (1) Thin threads of mucus ooze from these seeds when they are put into water, which fastens them together. (2) From these too a mucus issues in water. (3) When the mucus causes the linseed to stick together, it is a kind of kneading, for which he is culpable. But kneading is inapplicable to hides. (4) The Rabbis gave their public lectures through interpreters (*amora*). (5) Lev. VI, 20. (6) Emended text (Sh.M.). (7) Ibid. 21. (8) Ibid.—In each case the question is: how do we know that these things must be done in a holy place? The answer is, by reading '*in a holy place*' with what *follows*, as well as with what precedes, thus: and in a holy place shall the earthen vessel ... be broken (and) a brazen vessel ... be scoured and rinsed; v. Sifra *a.l.* (9) In which the sin-offering is more stringent. (10) In the inner sanctuary (*hekal*), which feature is absent from other most sacred sacrifices. (11) Whose blood was not taken into the *hekal*. (12) V. *supra* 81*b*.

b (1) V. Lev. V, 1. 4 *seq.*—*Kareth* is not incurred for these even if they are committed deliberately. (2) The blood of the sin-offering must be applied with the finger, on the horn, and on the edge of the horn. In all these too it is more stringent than other most sacred sacrifices. (3) Which needed washing through the blood. (4) I.e., outside the Temple court. (5) In which condition it cannot re-enter, because nothing unclean may be taken into the Temple court. (6) It ceases to be a garment, and thereby ceases to be unclean. (7) I.e., a very large hole made in it. Metal vessels do not lose their uncleanness through a small hole. (8) Scripture orders the *garment* to be washed, which implies that it must be a garment when it is washed.

c (1) He does not tear it right across, but leaves the width of an apron (or duster) untorn. Since the greater part of it is torn it ceases to be unclean; nevertheless, since so much is left untorn, it is still technically a garment. (2) That a garment loses its uncleanness when it is torn.

joined?[3] [95a] That is by Rabbinical law [only].[4]

IF AN EARTHEN VESSEL WAS CARRIED OUTSIDE etc. But the Divine Law spoke of a *'vessel'*, and this is not a vessel?—The hole is only large enough for a little root.[5]

IF A BRAZEN VESSEL ... IT MUST BE BROKEN THROUGH etc. But then it is not a vessel?—He hammers [the hole] together.[6]

Resh Laḳish said: If the [priest's] robe became unclean,[7] one must take it in less than three [fingerbreadths] square at a time, and wash it, because it is said, *That it* [the robe] *be not rent*.[8] R. Adda b. Ahabah objected: Thick [garments] and soft [unwoven garments] are not subject to the law of three [fingerbreadths] square?[9]—They count, because of the parent [piece].[10]

But surely it requires seven substances, for R. Naḥman said in Rabbah b. Abbuha's name: The blood of the sin-offering and the appearance of leprosy require seven substances; whereas it was

(3) And remains unclean. (4) As a preventive measure, lest one does not tear the greater part of it. But Scripturally it is clean, and here the Rabbis waived this measure in order that the precept of washing may be fulfilled. (5) Of a plant to push through. That suffices to make it clean, but not deprive it of the status of a vessel. (6) Having broken it through, whereby it became clean, he then hammers the hole together, which makes it a vessel again. (7) Outside the Temple court. (8) Ex. XXVIII, 32. Hence it cannot be torn, as the Mishnah states. Therefore less than three fingerbreadths square of it must be insinuated into the Temple court at a time, as then it does not count as an unclean garment. (9) They cannot be unclean unless they are three *handbreadths* square. Now, the robe was of *thick* cloth; why then cannot one take in three *handbreadths* square at a time? (10) As they are not separate pieces, but part of the whole robe, even three *fingerbreadths* square counts technically as a garment.

מדרבנן (א) הוא: כלי חרס שיצא כו': ג] כלי אמר רחמנא ולא כלי הוא שניקב בשורש קטן: כלי נחשת ג] [כו'] פוחתו [וכו']: *והא לאו כלי הוא דרציף* ד] מרציף (הוא) אמר ריש לקיש מעיל שניטמא מכניסו בפחות (א) משלש על שלש ומכבסו משום שנא' °לא יקרע מותיב רב אדא בר אהבה ה] *העבין והרכים אין בהן משום שלש על שלש אגב ו] אביהן חשיבי והא בעי שבעת סממנין דא"ר נחמן אמר רבה בר אבוה דם חטאת ומראות נגעים צריכין שבעת סממנין ותניא *אלא שאין מכניסין מי רגלים למקדש וכי

שמות כח

רש"י

מדרבנן. גזירה דילמא לא אתית למיקרע רובה אבל מדאורייתא טהורה ומותר להכניסה משום מלות כיבוס: נראה ז] בעיני שחסר מן הספרים דגבי כלי חרס לא שייך לשניי דמרלף ליה מרלף והאי שיטיא גבי כלי נחשת הוא והכי פריך פוחתו כלי אמר רחמנא והאי לאו כלי הוא בשעת מריקה ושטיפה: ומשני דרלף ליה מרלף. אחר ח] שפוחתו מכין עליו בקורנס ומחברו וחוזר שם כלי עליו וגבי כלי חרס איכא למימר דניקבו דמתניתין *במוליא משקה ליטהר ועדיין כלי הוא לקבל זיתים במס' שבת בפרק המלניע (דף נה:): מעיל. של בגדי כהונה שניתז עליו דם חטאת וילא חוץ לקלעים ונטמא מכנים מקום הדם לפנים: בפחות משלש על שלש. שאינו מכנים שיעור בגד טמא לעזרה לפי שאי אפשר לקורעו ולהכניסו משום שנאמר לא יקרע: העבים. בגד עב: והרכין. פלטר"א שאינו ארוג: אין בהן משום שלש על שלש. דלאו ללבישה חזו ולאו לתקן בהן חלוק אלא ליסב עליו ולריך שלשה על שלשה ומעיל עב הוא כדקי"ל בסדר יומא (דף עא:) חוטן כפול ששה עשר ואפי' שלש על שלש יכנים: אגב אבוהון. כשהוא מחובר בבגד חשוב ג' על ג' דידיה: והא בעי. דם חטאת שבעה סממנים השנויין במס' נדה (דף סא:) לענין כתמים רוק תפל ט] ומי רגלים ונתר ובורית ואהל וקמוניא ואשלג והיכי מעיילינן מ"ר מ"ר לעזרה ואמתני' קפריך: ומראות נגעים. שהזקיק הכתוב נגעי בגדים לכיבוס דכתיב וכבסו את אשר בו הנגע: ותניא. בפיטום הקטרת [כריתות ו:] שאין מכניסין מי רגלים למקדש: הכי

תוספות

מ"מ י"ל דטלית ובגד דשמעתין שאני שהם כלי ושם כלי עליהן וכשנקרעו כיון דאזיל שם כלי מינייהו טהרו לגמרי אבל בבהמה המקשה (חולין דף עב:) מיירי בחתיכת בגד דעלמא ואין שם כלי עליו ולא טהר ממגע מדרס אע"פ שטהור מן המדרס ובפ' העור והרוטב (שם דף קכג:) פי' בקונטרס דההיא דאבל טמא מגע מדרס כשהיה בו ב' טומאות מדרס החמורה ומגע זב והגי החלוקה לבטל המדרס דתו לא חזו ליה ופקא ליה טומאת מגע דחזיא לשלש אצבעות אבל בהעור והרוטב (שם) מיירי דליכא אלא חדא טומאה או מגע זב בלא הסכדה או מגע שרץ ונבלה וחד שמה הוי וכולה טומאה דשלשה על שלשה היא וקריעה מהניא לבטולי שמה מינה ותו לא פש עלה מידי ואין זו שום סברא לחלק בין טומאה אחת לשתי טומאות דכיון שנשאר בטלית שלש על שלש שזהו שיעור טומאת מגע היאך יהיה טהור ובתחילת הסוגיא פי' שם בקונטרס טלית שהתחיל בה לקורעה ולבטלה מתורת טלית מאחר שאין ראוי למלאכה ראשונה ואין שמה עליה מיטהרת אע"פ שיש בשיריס שלש על שלש ועדיין ראויין לקבל טומאה י] טהרו מטומאתן ראשונה דומיא דכלי חרס דשבירתו מטהרתו ושבריו מקבלין טומאה כדאמר באלו טריפות (שם דף נד:) הן וקרקרותיהן ואזן יא] (זו) מסס ראיה דהתם מיירי כשייחד השברים אח"כ אבל בלא ייחוד לא כדפרישית שם *ונראה לפרש דקריעה דבגד וטלית מיירי תרוייהו כשקורע קרעים הרבה ואין בכל אחד רוחב שלשה והכי קאמר טהורה לגמרי אע"ג שעדיין כל הקריעות מחוברין בסופן לאו חיבור הוא כיון שכל קרע *וקרע יב] שקרע עד רובה של טלית (בפחות משלשה על שלשה) הוי כאילו גמר כל אחד ואחד עד סופן וכגון שלא שייר בטלית באותו מיעוט שלא נקרע כדי מעפורת דאם שייר הוי טמא מדרבנן כדמסקינן הכא וזהו תימה מ"מ דלענין טומאה לא מיקרי בגד מן התורה אע"ג דשייר בה כדי מעפורת ולגבי* חטאת מקרי בגד וכמו כן קשה בסמוך גבי כלי חרס שניטמא יג] [טו' טוקבו כו'] [דפריך] כלי אמר רחמנא והאי לאו כלי הוא ומשני דנקיב ליה בכדי שורש קטן והשתא א"כ לאו כלי הוא שהרי מיטהר יד] מטומאתו ונראה לפרש כיון שמועיל לו ייחוד לאותו בגד ששייר בו כדי מעפורת שלא הבדיל הקרעים על פני כולו ולאותו כלי שניקב בשורש קטן שאם היה מיחדו לזיתים או לרימון היה מקבל טומאה מכאן ולהבא חשיב הוא כלי ובגד לענין דם חטאת כיון דאין מחוסר מעשה אלא ייחוד בעלמא והא דקאמר בסמוך גבי כלי נחשת פוחתו כלי אמר רחמנא והאי לאו כלי הוא ומשני דרליף ליה מרליף אין לפרש כמו דלפיכהו מרליף דפ"ק דשבת (דף טז:) *פי' טו] שיתקן הפחיתה שמכה עליו בקורנס ומחברו וחוזר שם כלי עליו דא"כ בגד נמי לישני הכי שחוזר ותפרו לאחר שקרעו אלא ע"כ הוא חשיב בגד חדש וכלי חדש וכאילו אינו ראשון ורליף ליה הייט שהופך לד פנים לצד חוץ ולד חוץ לצד פנים ונעשה תוכו גבו וגבו תוכו ומיטהר בכך מטומאתו וקצת תימה מה שייך טז] באותו שיעור דשורש קטן לענין טהרת כלי שאותו שיעור הוא לענין הכשר זרעים בסוף המלניע (שבת דף נה:) ואם הכלי מיוחד לאוכלין שיעורו בזיתים אבל בשורש קטן לא ואם הוא מיוחד למשקין שיעורו ככונס משקין ובקונטרס פירש דשורש קטן איכא למ"ד שזהו שיעור נקיבתו ליטהר ואי אפשר לומר כן דהא פלוגתא דאמוראי הוא בסוף המלניע (שם דף נה:) דכדי שורש קטן וכדי מוליא רימון ופי' שם בקונטרס דפליגי לענין הכשר זרעים דלענין טומאה משנה היא במסכת כלים (פ"ג) דעשוי לאוכלין שיעורו כזיתים ומשקין ככונס משקה ומיהו גם לאותו פי' קשה דמתני' היא במס' עוקלין (פ"ב מ"י) דלהכשיר זרעים בשורש קטן ומפרש ר"ת דלענין למיד פתיל פליגי ליחשב פתח בסתם כלים אבל לענין טומאה לא פליגי ויש לפרש בדוחק דהאי כלי חרס עשוי לאוכלין ולמשקין שהרי מבשלין בו חטאת ויש בו מרק ולכך שיעורו בשורש קטן ואין עליו לא תורת כלי העשוי למשקין ולא תורת כלי העשוי לאוכלין ולא דמי להא דגרסי' במס' כלים (פ"ג מ"א) העשוי לכך ולכך מטילין אותו לחומרא יז] כזיתים הייט בשעה שמניחים בו משקין יח] אין מניחין בו אוכלין וכשמניחין בו אוכלין אין מניחין בו משקין אלא שמניחין בו אוכלין בפני עצמן ומשקין בפני עצמן אבל הכא בקדירה שמבשלין בה בשר שעשוי להשתמש אוכלין ומשקין על ידי תערובת והא דאין שיעורה ככונס משקה משום דלאכתי ראוי לבשל בה שיכול להניח בשר כנגד הנקב יט] וגם המרק* שהאור מעמיד המרק שלא ילא לכך שיעורה בשורש קטן והאי דלא קאמר בסוף המלניע (שבת דף נה:) שם מדות בכלי חרס משום דמדה זו של שורש קטן קחשיב כ] *(זה) לענין הכשר זרעים ומיהו קשה דבהדיא תנן במס' כלים (פ"ג מ"ב) האלפס והקדירה שיעורן כזיתים ואי הוה אמינא דשיעור זיתים כא] דבעינן מדרבנן הוה ניחא כדקאמר גבי בגד אבל מדאורייתא אם ניקב בשורש קטן טהור:

מעיל שנטמא מכניסו בפחות משלש על שלש ומכבסו. בסוף כירה (שבת דף מז.) גבי בגד עניים משמע מתוך פירוש הקונטרס בשלש על שלש ביד עשיר דלא מקבל טומאה כלל והא דתנן (כלים פרק כז מ"ב) שלש על שלש לטמא מת הייט דוקא בענייס אבל בעשירים בעי שלשה על שלשה וקשה לר"ת מהך דמעיל דפריך עלה רב אדא מההיא דעבין והרכין והשתא למה לי לאקשויי מההיא והא בגדי כהונה בגדי עשירים הם דאין עניות במקום עשירות ושיעורן בשלשה על שלשה ועוד תניא בפ' במה מדליקין (שבת דף כו:) שלש על שלש מכיין ת"ל והבגד והתם לא מפליג בין עניים לעשירים לא בקרא ולא בשמעתא ואומר ר"ת דלענין טומאת מת ושרץ אין חילוק בין עניים לעשירים אלא לענין מדרס איירי התם דבעי שלשה על שלשה לעשירים והייט טעמא דמדרס בייחוד תליא מילתא ואין דרך עשיר לייחד למדרס פחות משלשה על שלשה ואפילו ייחד בטלה דעתו ועוד הביא ר"ת ראיה דבטומאת מדרס הוא דמפלגי בין עניים לעשירים דבמס' כלים (פרק כז מ"ב) תנן דבגד מטמא משום שלשה על שלשה למדרס משום שלש על שלש לטמא מת ובעל כרחין בעשירים איירי דאי בעניים הא תנן בפ' (כח מ"ח) בגדי עניים אע"פ שאין בהם שלשה על שלשה טמאין מדרס ויש משניות שכ' בהן אע"פ שאין בהן שלש על שלש ודומה שהוא טעות סופר*: **מכניסו** פחות משלש. אפילו למאן דאמר בריש כל הפסולין (לעיל דף לב:) ביאה במקצת שמה ביאה שאני בגד הואיל ויכול לחותכו לא חשיב כאילו נכנס טלו: **והא** בעי שבעה סממנין. פי' בקונטרס דאמתניתין פריך וקשה דלעיל הוה ליה לאקשויי ונראה דלריש לקיש דוקא פריך דאיירי בבגדי כהונה בהדיא אבל מתני' איכא לאוקומה בבגדי הדיוט שיכול להעביר ולכבס ע"י לפון אבל מעיל דכהן גדול אינו יכול לכבסו ע"י לפון משום דאמרינן במסכת נדה (דף סב.) כב] דאפילו לבעא נמי מעבר מיהו אמילתא דרבה בר אבוה גופא דקאמר דם חטאת ומראות נגעים לריכין ז' סממנין [נמי] הוה מלי לאקשויי הא אין מכניסין מי רגלים למקדש:

עירה

מסורת הש"ס

נ"ל ככונס משקה נ"ק
[נ"ל דרציף ליה מרציף]
כלים פכ"ח משנה ח
[כריתות ו.]
נ"ל ועוד כ"ל לפרש נ"ק
נ"ל וקרע נקרע עד רובה של טלית בפחות משלש על שלש הוי כו' נ"ק וכ"ה בתוס' חולין דף עג
[נ"ל דם חטאת]
ולא כמו שפירש"י דפי' שיתקן כו' נ"ק
קחשיב שם לענין כו' נ"ק
[אמנם פר"ש מקיים בגי' ע"ש]

הגהות הב"ח

(א) גמ' בפחות משלשה על שלשה כצ"ל וכן בסמוך וכן ברש"י:

עין משפט נר מצוה

לז א ב מיי' פ"ח מהל' מעשה הקרבנות הלכה כא:
לח ג מיי' שם הלכה כ:
לט ד מיי' פכ"ב מהל' כלים הלכה ג:
מ ה מיי' פ"ח מהל' מעשה הקרבנות הל"ג:
[נ"ל כלי אמר רחמנא והא לאו כלי הוא כו' כן גירסת הערוך בערך רטף וכן איתא ברש"י ותוס' והב"ח]
מא ו מיי' פ"ח מהל' טומאת לרעת הל' ס:
מב ז מיי' פ"ח מהל' מעשה הקרבנות הלכה י:
וגם המרק עב והאור כו' נ"ק

שיטה מקובצת

א] תיבת הוא נמחק: ב] כו'. נוקבו כלי אמר רחמנא ולאו כלי הוא. ס"א דרצף ליה מרצף: שניקב. ס"א במוציא משקה: ג] כלי נחשת שיצא פוחתו כלי אמר רחמנא והא. תיבות כו' פותתו כו' ל"ש ונמחק: ד] דרציף ליה מרציף אמר תיבת הוא נמחק: ה] העבים והרכין: ו] אגב אבוהון: ז] נראה. (ס"א ה"ג נקבו כלי אמר רחמנא והאי לאו כלי הוא חס"ד ומה"ד דנקיב ליה בשורש קטן ואיכא למ"ד במס' שבת שזהו שיעור נקיבתו לטהר ומיהו עדיין כלי הוי לקבל זיתים חס"ד ומה"ד פוחתו כלי אמר רחמנא כו' ומשני דרציף ליה מרצף חס"ד ומה"ד מעיל כו'): ח] שפיחתו מקיש עליו תיבת מכין נמחק: ט] תפל ומי גריסין ומי רגלים כו' ובורית וקמוניא כו' תיבת ואהל נמחק: י] טומאה טהורה תיבת טהרו נמחק: יא] ואין מזו שום ראיה: יב] וקרע נקרע עד רובה תיבת שקרע ל"ש ונמחק: יג] שנטמא דפריך נוקבו כלי אמר: יד] מיטהר בכך מטומאתו: טו] שתיקן: טז] אותו שיעור: יז] לחומרא בזיתים דהאיך בשעה תיבת הייט ל"ש: יח] אין. (ס"א א"נ שמניחין): יט] וגם המרק עב והאור מעמיד: כ] קא חשיב ליה לענין תיבת זה נמחק: כא] תיבת דבעינן נמחק: כב] נדה דצפון אפי' צבעא אות ד' נמחק:

עין משפט
נר מצוה

מג א ב מיי' פ"ט מהל' איסורי ביאה הל' לו :
מד ג מיי' פ"ח מהל' מעשה הקרבנות הלכה יא :
[וע"ש תוס' ד"ה אבל נותן]
מה ד מיי' שם הל' ס :
מו ה מיי' שם ב.
מז ו מיי' פי"ב מהל' מעשה הקרבנות הלכה כג :
מח ז מיי' פ"ט מהל' מאכלות אסורות הל' כב טוש"ע יו"ד סי' צא סעיף א :
מט ח מיי' שם טוש"ע שם סעיף ב :
נ ט טוש"ע א"ח סי' תנא סעיף א :
נ"ל נותן
[עי' ת"כ פ' צו פ"ז]

וכי תימא דמבלע להו בהדי שבעה סממנין ומעבר להו לכולהו כחד והתנן *ההעבירן שלא כסדרן או שהעביר שבעתן כאחד לא עשה ולא כלום וכי תימא דמיבלע להו בהדי חד מסממנין והא בצריך לכסכס שלש פעמים בכל אחד ואחד תנן אלא דמבלע להו ברוק תפל דאמר ריש לקיש רוק תפל צריך שיהא עם כל אחד ואחד : **מתני'** גאחד שבישל בו ואחד שעירה לתוכה רותח דאחד קדשי א] הקדשים ואחד קדשים קלים טעונין מריקה ושטיפה *ר"ש אומר קדשים קלים אין טעונין מריקה ושטיפה : **גמ'** ב] ת"ר °אשר תבושל ויקרא ו בו אין לי אלא שבישל בו עירה לתוכו רותח מנין ת"ל ג] ואשר תבושל בו ישבר בעי רמי בר חמא התלאו באויר תנור מהו אבישול ובילוע הוא דקפיד רחמנא או דילמא אבישול בלא בילוע אמר רבא ת"ש אחד שבישל בו ואחד שעירה לתוכו רותח בלוע בלא בישול לא קמיבעיא לן כי קמיבעיא לן בישול בלא בילוע מאי ת"ש *דאמר רב נחמן אמר רבה בר אבוה ותנור של מקדש של מתכת היה ואי ס"ד בישול(א) בלא בלוע ד]לא קפיד ניעביד של חרס כיון דאיכא שירי מנחות דאפייתן בתנור ואיכא בישול ה] ובילוע עבדינן של מתכת *ההוא תנורא דאטחו ו] בה טיחייא אסרה רבה בר אהילאי למיכלה לריפתא לעולם ואפי' במילחא דילמא אתי למיכלה בכותחא מיתיבי *זאין לשין את העיסה בחלב ואם לש כל הפת כולה אסורה מפני הרגל עבירה כיוצא בו חאין *טשין את התנור באליה ואם טש כל הפת כולה אסורה עד שיסיק את התנור תיובתא דרבה בר אהילאי תיובתא אמר ליה רבינא לרב אשי וכי מאחר דאיתותב רבה בר אהילאי אמאי *אמר רב קדירות בפסח ישברו אמר ליה רב מוקי לה ז]ההיא בשל מתכת ואי בעית אימא בתנור של חרס זה הסיקו מבפנים וזה הסיקו מבחוץ ונעביד ח] הסקה מבפנים טחיים עלייהו דמתברי הילכך האי *כוביא הסיקו מבחוץ הוא ואסיר אלא

הכי גרסי' וכי תימא דמיבלע להו בהדי שבעה סממנין ט] ומעבר להו לכולהו כחד : שלא כסדרן. כסדר שהן שנויין במשנה זה אחר זה י] כסדר העברתן : צריך לכסכס. צריך לשפשף הכתם שלשה פעמים בכל אחד והכי אמרינן בנדה : **מתני'** ר"ש אומר קדשים קלים כו'. ובגמ' מפרש טעמא ואם תאמר הרי הבלוע נעשה נותר ופולטו בהיתר לאחר זמן מודי רבי שמעון דבעי הגעלה ברותחין ומתורת מריקה ושטיפה הוא דממעיט ליה כדמתרלינן בגמ' גבי תרומה. ג"א נגרכה לכדאמר מר במים ולא ביין במים ולא במזוג הא אפי' ביין ואפי' במזוג : **גמ'** ה"ג בתורת כהנים עירה לתוכו רותח מניין ת"ל (ב) אשר בו ישבר. מדסמיך ישבר אצל בו ולא כתב אם בכלי חרס תבושל ישבר למידרש אם נבלע בו מ"מ ישבר : תלאו. לשפוד של חטאת ללותו באויר תנור יא]דנתבשל בו אבל לא נבלע בו כלום יב] : מהו. מי הוי יג] צריך תנור שבירה או לא : ואחד שעירה לתוכו. אלמא אחדא קפיד דהא עירה לתוכו בלוע איכא בישול ליכא : בלוע בלא בישול לא מיבעיא לן. דכיון דהאי נותר והתורה העידה על כלי חרס שאינו יוצא מידי יד] דופיו לעולם ובעי שבירה : של מתכת היה. קס"ד מפני שצולין בו טו] שפודי חטאת שלא יטען שבירה : בישול ובלוע. טז] שמן המנחה: טחו ביה טחייה. מין טיגון הוא שעושין מלחם וטשין התנור באליה ואופין את הלחם אחר שטחוהו ובמס' שבת (דף קיט.) כמי אמרינן תלתא שאוי טחיי : לעולם. ואפילו הסיקוהו ואפו בו דקסבר אינו יוצא מידי יז]דופיו : מפני הרגל עבירה. שלא יאכל הפת עם הבשר : אמאי אמר רב כו'. הא אית להו תקנתא בהיסק : מוקים לההיא. דקתני עד שיוסק התנור בשל מתכת: יח]כוביא. רעפים חלולין כמין שפיתת קדירה ופעמים שטחין יט] אותו שמנואופין בו לחם הקרוי טיחיא:

עירה לתוכו רותח מנין ת"ל אשר כ] תבושל בו ישבר. מכאן מדקדק ר"ת דעירוי ככלי ראשון מדחשיב כמבושל ונראה דאדרבה קשה מכאן דהא קרי ליה בסמוך בלוע בלא בישול מיהו י"ל דחשיב ליה בלוע בלא בישול לפי שאינו מתבשל מחמת הכלי דבכלי אחר נתבשל ורבינו שמואל היה מדקדק דעירוי ככלי שני מהא דתנן בפרק כירה (שבת דף מב:)* האילפס והקדירה שהעבירן מרותחין לא יתן לתוכן תבלין דמשמע הא לערות מהם על התבלין שרי ועוד היה מדקדק מהא דקי"ל כשמואל דאמר תתאה גבר דתניא כוותיה בפ' כיצד צולין (פסחים דף עו.) והיה מתיר מתוך כך לערות רותחין מכלי ראשון על התרנגולת כדי למולגה ור"ת אומר דאדרבה דוק מסיפא אבל נותן לתוך הקערה הא לערות מאילפס על התבלין אסור ועוד לדבריו קשה ההיא משנה למ"ד עילאה גבר אלא איידי דתנא רישא המיחם שפינהו לא יתן לתוכו *מים אבל נותן לתוך הכוס תנא סיפא נמי האילפס והקדירה לא יתן לתוכן (מים) [תבלין] אבל נותן לתוך הקערה ובירושלמי משמע דעירוי ככלי ראשון דאמרינן עלה בגמ' מהו ליתן תבלין מלמטה ולערות עליהן מלמעלה רבי יונה אומר עירוי ככלי ראשון חייליה דר' יונה מן הדא וכל כלי חרס אשר תבושל בו ישבר אין לי אלא שבישל בו עירה לתוכו רותח מניין ת"ל ואשר תבושל בו ישבר מ"מ *(וכה אמר הכין) א"ר יוסי כא] תמן כלי חרס בולע תבלין אינו מבשל כב] פירוש כלי חרס בולע טפי משאר כלים איתיב רבי יוסי בר' בון והתני אף *בכלי נחשת כן אית לך למימר כלי נחשת בולע פי' וכי בלע יותר משאר כלים בתמיה השתא מדמי התם כמו שבולע על ידי עירוי כמו כן מבשל ע"י עירוי ש"מ כג]מיתניא כוותיה דרבי יונה אלמא הילכתא כוותיה ואע"ג דקי"ל כוותיה דשמואל דאמר תתאה גבר מודה שמואל דמבשל כדי קליפה דהא ברייתא דמסייע ליה קתני חם לתוך צונן מדיח ופריך הש"ס אדמיקר ליה בלע פירוש קודם שיצטנן חום שלמעלה נבלע ממנו מקצת בהתחון ומשני אימא חם לתוך צונן קולף ועוד מייתי ר"ת ראיה מהא דקאמר בפרק כל שעה (פסחים דף לז:) המעיסה ב"ש פוטרין וב"ה מחייבין החליטה ב"ש מחייבין ובית הלל פוטרין איזו היא המעיסה ואיזו היא החליטה המעיסה קמח על גבי מוגלשין פירוש מוגלשין מים רותחין ופריך מ"ש המעיסה ומאי שנא החליטה ומשני תברא מי ששנה זו לא שנה זו אלמא מאן דפטר מחלה בקמח על גבי מוגלשין משום דלאו לחם הוא כיון שנילוש ברותחין פטר נמי במוגלשין ששפכן על גבי קמח אע"פ שנשפכו לכלי שני אלמא עירוי ככלי ראשון מיהו קשה היכי פטר הא אינו מבשל אלא כדי קליפה לשמואל דאמר תתאה גבר דקי"ל כוותיה וי"ל דמיירי כגון דליכא אלא כדי חיוב חלה מצומצם או מעט יותר דבתר קליפה אין נשאר כשיעור חלה ועוד מביא ר"ת ראיה מהא דאמר בשילהי ע"ז (דף עד:) נטוה ארתחו אלמא עירוי ככלי ראשון דאין יכול להכשירו אלא בעירוי ועוד יש לדקדק דמיירי בעירוי מדתניא התם רבי יוסי אומר הרוצה לטהרן מיד מגעילן ברותחין או חולטן במי זיתים והחלטה כד] אינו אלא עירוי כדמפרש בפסחים (דף לז:) מוגלשין ע"ג קמח מיהו אין ראיה משם לשאר דברים דבכמה דברים מיקל ביין נסך שאין מיקל בשאר איסורין דחולטן במי זיתים משמע אפילו צונן כמו חלטי לה בחלא דכל הבשר (חולין דף קיא.) גבי כבדא וכן עירוי שלשה ימים מעת לעת וניגוב והגהה מגת לגת שכל אלו העניינים לא מהני בשאר איסורים וטעמא משום דביין נסך אין איסור רווח כל אלא שהחמירו בו להרחיקו ואף ר"ת התיר לשפוך רותחין לתוך החבית שהיה בה יין נסך ולהפכם מצד זה לצד זה בתוך החבית אע"פ שכבר היו בכלי שני מיד כה] כששופכן בחבית ולא נפלו על כל צידי החבית אלא מכלי שני שהופכן מצד זה לצד זה ואפילו עירוי מכלי ראשון ליכא ומ"מ עירוי הוא ככלי ראשון לענין שאר איסורין כו] כמה שהוכחתי ומה שכתב בסדר של פסח *המתחיל אדיר דר מתוחים הכנת קערות ומיליהם בכלי שני שימושיהם כשופכין מסיר בהן כך שופכין רותחין עליהן אומר ר"ת דליתיה דכל כלים שבעולם מהגיא שפיכת רותחין

שיטה מקובצת
א] קדשי קדשים אות ה' נמחק : ב] ת"ר. [עי' תשובת] רשב"א סי' אלפים ע"ז וקע"ו : ג] ת"ל אשר בו אות ו' ותיבת תבושל נמחק : ד] בלא בלוע מותר ניעביד נמי של חרס תיבות לא קפיד ל"ש ונמחק: ה] בישול ובלוע עבדינן : ו] דאטחו ביה טחייה : ז] לה להההיא : ח] ונעביד להו הסקה מבפנים חיים עלייהו דלא מיתברן הלכך האי בוכיא הסיקו: ט] סממנין. ול"נ א"נ מעביר. מהר"פ: י] כך סדר העברתן : יא] ונתבשל בו אות ד' נמחק : יב] כלום. פי' מה שנפל מן הבשר בגחלים שיש בתנור הוא נופל ואינו נבלע כלל בתנור : יג] הרי התנור טעון שבירה תיבת צריך ל"ש : יד] מידי דופנו לעולם בעי שבירה : טו] שפודי הפאות : טז] ובלוע משמן : יז] מידי דופנו תס"ד : יח] מה"ד בוכיא רעפים : יט] אותם ואופין בו תיבת שמן נמחק : כ] תיבת תבושל נמחק : כא] תוך כלי תיבת תמן נמחק : כב] מתיבת פי' כו' עד תיבת איתיב ר' יוסי נמחק : כג] ש"מ מדתניא כוותיה : כד] והחלטה היינו עירוי תיבת אינו נמחק ותיבת אלא ל"ש : כה] מיד כששפכן בהבית : כו] איסורין כמו שהוכחתי ומה שכתוב בסדר :

מסורת הש"ס
נדה סב. סנהדרין מט:
[לעיל צג. לקמן צו: צז.]
[לקמן צו.]
[פסחים ל.]
שם וש"נ
[עי' תוס' כ"ב קי. ד"ס נשוט]
פסחים שם
[ג"י סערוך בוביא ובפסחים איתא בוכיא ועי' פרישה ביו"ד סי' לג ס"ק ו]
[ועי' תוס' ע"ז עד: ד"ס דר]

הגהות הב"ח
(א) גמ' ואי ס"ד בישול ובילוע נעביד של חרס : (ב) רש"י ד"ה ה"ג וכו' ת"ל בו כצ"ל ותיבת אשר נמחק :

taught: But that urine may not be taken into the Temple?[11] [95b]
a And should you say that one mixes it in with the seven substances[1] and applies them all at once; surely we learnt: If they were not applied in their order,[2] or if they were all applied simultaneously, it is of no avail? And should you say that he mixes it up in *one* of the substances; but surely we learnt [that] he must rub the stain three times with each [substance]?—Rather, he mixes it up in tasteless saliva, for Resh Laḳish said: There must be tasteless saliva with each one.

MISHNAH. WHETHER ONE BOILED THEREIN OR POURED BOILING [FLESH ETC.] INTO IT, WHETHER MOST SACRED SACRIFICES OR LESSER SACRIFICES, [THE POT] REQUIRES SCOURING AND RINSING. R. SIMEON SAID: LESSER SACRIFICES DO NOT NECESSITATE SCOURING AND RINSING.

GEMARA. Our Rabbis taught: [*But the earthen vessel*] *which it is boiled* in it.[3] I know it only when one boiled [the flesh] therein; how do I know it when one poured boiling [flesh] therein? Because it says, *which* [*it is boiled*] *in it*. [shall be broken].[4]

Rami b. Ḥama asked: What if one suspended [the flesh] in the air-space of an [earthen] oven?[5] Is the Divine Law particular about boiling and absorbing; or perhaps, [it is particular] about boiling [even] without absorbing?[6]—Said Raba, Come and hear: WHETHER ONE BOILED THEREIN OR POURED BOILING [FLESH] INTO
b IT![1]—We do not ask about absorbing without boiling;[2] we ask about boiling without absorbing: what is the law?—Come and hear, for R. Naḥman said in Rabbah b. Abbuha's name: The Temple oven was of metal.[3] Now, if you think that [only] boiling and absorbing [necessitates] breaking, let it be an earthen one?[4]—Since there were the remainders of meal-offerings, which were baked in the oven, so that there is boiling and absorbing,[5] we must make it of metal.

A certain oven was greased with fat. [Thereupon] Raba b. Ahilai forbade for all time[6] the bread [baked therein] to be eaten even with salt, lest one come to eat it with *kutaḥ*.[7] An objection is raised: One must not knead dough with milk, and if he does knead it, the whole loaf is forbidden, because it leads to sin.[8] Similarly, one must not grease an oven with fat, and if he does grease it, all the bread [baked therein] is forbidden until the oven is refired. This is a refutation of Raba b. Ahilai. [It is indeed] a refutation.

Rabina said to R. Ashi: Now since Raba b. Ahilai was refuted, why did Rab say: Pots must be broken on Passover?[9] Rab main-
c tained that there[1] a metal one is meant. Alternatively, it may be an earthen oven: this [the oven] is fired from the inside;[2] while the other [the pot] is fired on the outside. Then let us burn it [the pot] from within?—He would spare it, lest it break [burst].[3] Therefore a tiled pan,[4] since it is burnt from without,[5] is forbidden.[6]

(11) This is a difficulty according to the Mishnah: A garment on which the blood of a sin-offering spurted, as well as a garment which shewed symptoms of leprosy, which must also be washed, needs the application of seven substances to cleanse it, viz., tasteless saliva, the liquid exuded by crushed beans, urine, natron, lye, Cimolean earth, and *ashleg* (v. Sanh. [Sonc. ed.] **49b**). How then can it be washed in the Temple Court, seeing that urine must not be brought there?

a (1) The urine is not brought in separately, but mixed (lit. 'swallowed') with the other substances. Then it is not noticeable, and can be taken into the Temple. (2) As enumerated in *supra* 95a n. 11. (3) Lev. VI, 21. (4) Rashi: *'shall be broken'* coming immediately after *'in it'* indicated that every vessel shall be broken if anything of the sin-offering is absorbed in it, even if it had not actually been boiled in it. If boiling flesh is placed in the vessel, the vessel must absorb some of it. (5) Thus boiling or cooking it. (6) The flesh is thus cooked, but the oven absorbs nothing of it. Does Scripture mean that only a vessel in which it is boiled and which thereby absorbs some of it must be broken; or perhaps it must be broken even when it does not absorb?

b (1) Thus even if one thing only happened to the vessel (i.e., it absorbed but was not used for actual boiling), it must be broken or scoured and rinsed. Presumably boiling without absorbing is the same. (2) That obviously necessitates breaking, since absorption is the principal reason for the whole law. For after the time allowed for the consumption of this flesh, the absorbed matter becomes *nothar* (v. Glos.), which is forbidden, and it will impart its flavour to any other flesh that is subsequently boiled in it, unless it is scoured and rinsed. (Scouring and rinsing are not efficacious for earthen vessels, for which reason they must be broken.) (3) It is assumed that the reason is that it should not have to be broken. (4) For the flesh was not actually placed in the area, but cooked (or roasted) in it on a spit.—Their ovens were open on top. (5) Baking is technically the same as boiling. (6) Even if the oven should be fired and burnt through again. (7) A preserve consisting of sour milk, bread-crusts and salt (Jast.). The bread of course receives the flavour of the fat, and must not be eaten with anything containing milk or a milk product. (8) One might eat it with meat. (9) For we see that greased ovens (these were generally of earth) can be refired and used, the heat expelling the traces of fat. Then let the pots too be subjected to fire, which would likewise expel the absorbed leaven (it was on account of the absorbed leaven that Rab forbade their use on Passover).

c (1) The oven that could be refired. (2) Which is efficacious to expel absorbed matter. (3) Hence if he is told to burn it from within; he will burn it from without and think that enough. (4) A kind of plaque made of tiles and upon which bread was baked. (5) The coals being under it and the bread on top. (6) For use on Passover.

[96a] Then why should the pots in the Temple be broken: let them be returned to the kiln?[7]—Said R. Zera: Because kilns are not permitted in Jerusalem.[8] Abaye retorted: And are then refuse heaps permitted in the Temple court?[9] [Abaye, however,] had overlooked what Shemaiah of Kalnebo[10] recited: The fragments of earthen vessels were swallowed up in their place.[11] Now, when R. Naḥman said in Rabbah b. Abbuha's name, 'The Temple oven was of metal', let it be an earthen one, since it was heated within?[12]—Since the Two Loaves and the Shewbread[13] were baked in the oven and were sanctified in the oven, it became a service vessel, and we

(7) Which would expel what they had absorbed. (8) On account of the smoke. (9) *Sc.* of broken potsherds. (10) Kar-nebo, 'the city of Nebo', conjectured to be Borsippa, Funk, *Monumenta*, I, p. 299. (11) Yoma 21*a*. (12) And thus what it absorbed of the sacrifices would be expelled. (13) V. Lev. XXIII, 15-17; Ex. XXV, 30.

אלא קדירות של מקדש אמאי(*אמר רחמנא) ישברו נהדרינהו לכבשונות א"ר זירא לפי *שאין עושין *כבשונות בירושלים אמר א] אביי וכי עושין אשפתות בעזרה אישתמיטתיה הא דתני ב] *שמעיה בקלנבו *שברי כלי חרס נבלעין במקומן אלא הא *דאמר רב נחמן אמר רבה בר אבוה תנור של מקדש של מתכת הוה נעביד דחרס דהסיקו מבפנים הוא דכיון דאיכא שתי הלחם ולחם הפנים דאפייתן בתנור וקדושתן בתנור הוה ליה כלי שרת ג]וכלי שרת דחרס לא עבדינן ואפילו

אלא קדירות של מקדש אמאי ישברו · הואיל ואית להו תקנתא בליבון הא אוקימנא דטעמא משום בלוע היא ולא אבישול קפיד קרא דנימא גזירת הכתוב היא והני דבמשכן כתיב ישבר לפי שלא היו ג] (לו) קבועין להיום להם כבשונות לצרף כלי חרס אבל במקדש נהדרינהו לכבשונות שהיוצר צורפן בהם ויתלבנו: אין עושים כבשונות בירושלים · משום קוטרא כדאמרינן בבבא קמא (דף פב:): אשפתות · משברי כלי חרס: בקלנבו · שם מקום שנקרא על שם עבודת כוכבים כדכתיב(ישעיה מו) קרס נבו: וקדושתן בתנור · שאין נעשין בכלי שרת לפי שאין טעונין שמן כדאמרינן בפרק שתי הלחם(מנחות נה:) לישתן ועריכתן בחוץ ואפייתן בפנים דתנור מקדש להו: ואפילו

רותחין דעירוי ככלי ראשון וקשה לרבינו שמואל נהי דמהני עירוי רותחין מכלי ראשון לתוך קערות ושאר כלים שדרך לערות בהן היאך יועיל לאותן קערות וכלים שהוכנסו כולן לתוך כלי ראשון ד] ומלואן איסורין מכל נד בכל עודי הכלי לענין שיוכל לחזור ולהכניסן בתוך אילפס וקדירה מרותחין של היתר כיון דקיימא לן כשמואל דאמר תתאה גבר ואינו מבשל אלא כדי קליפה ואם היינו מפרשים דעירוי ככלי ראשון לגמרי ומבשל יותר מכדי קליפה ומאי דאמר שמואל דאינו מבשל אלא בכדי קליפה זה דוקא בשני דברים יבשים שנוגעין זה בזה ואפילו בדבר לח כגון נטף ה]מרוטבו על הסולת שאותו רוטב אינו כנגו עירוי שהרי נפסקה אבל עירוי שאין כח הכלי ראשון נפסק מבשל לגמרי לפי זה יתיישב מה שאומר ר"ת דשופכין רותחין עליהן הוא הכשר גמור אפילו לקערות ו] שנותנן בתוך הסיר והאילפס ולא תקשי כמו מה שפירשתי לעיל דמוגלשין על גבי קמח היכי פטור מחלה והלא אינו מבשל אלא כדי קליפה דאיכא למימר דמבשל לגמרי כדפירשתי מיהו ר"ת לא היה סובר כן מדאיצטריך ליה למימר דעירוי אינו מבשל אלא כדי קליפה משום קושיא דתתאה גבר וא"ת הא דתנן בפ' חבית (שבת דף קמה:) כל שבא בחמין מלפני השבת שורין אותו בחמין בשבת וכל שלא בא בחמין מלפני השבת מדיחין אותו בחמין [בשבת] חוץ ממליח הישן וקולייס האיספנין ואי עירוי ככלי ראשון אמאי מדיחין וי"ל התם בכלי שני מיירי ואפי' הכי מדיחין אין שורין לא משום דמיחזי כמבשל ולא דמי לתבלין דשרי בפרק כירה (שם מב:) ליתן לתוך הקערה או לתוך התמחוי דעשויין למתק את הקדירה ולא מיחזי כמבשל אי נמי לרבותא נקט מדיחין דאפי' הדחה אסור במליח ישן וקולייס האיספנין: *ואם עם כל הפת כולה אסורה · וא"ת מאי שנא מהא דאמרינן בפ' כל הבשר (חולין קיא:) דגים שעלו בקערה מותר לאוכלם בכותח דנותן טעם בר נותן טעם מותר ובשם רש"י פירש ה"ר יהודה חתנו דדוקא עלו שרו ז] הא נתבשלו אסור ובא מעשה לפניו בבילים שנתבשלו בקדירה שבשלו בה חלב ואסר לעשות ח] מולייתא על גבי בשר ואין להביא ראיה לדבריו מקדירה שבישל בה בשר לא יבשל בה חלב ואם בישל בנותן טעם (לקמן ע"ב) דהתם לאו נותן טעם בר נותן טעם הוא שהטעם שני באיסור אבל כאן הטעם שני בהיתר וקודם שיבא לידי איסור נתבטל הטעם בדגים לפי שהוא שני אבל יש לדקדק מלגון שחתכו בסכין של בשר דאסור לאוכלו בכותח (חולין דף קיא:) דאגב חורפיה בלע טפי וחשיב כחד טעמא ולא גרע נתבשל מלגון מיהו לפי לשון אחר שפירש שם בקונטרס ט] היינו טעמא שיש חילוק בין קערה לסכין דסתם קערה מקנחין אותה משומן הקרוש עליה משום מיאוס אבל סכין י] טעמא שהשומן קרוש עליו ואינו ניכר יא] *כשחותך הוי כלונן טעם הבא מן הממש ולפי זה אין ראיה מלגון שחתכו בסכין והך דתנור שטשו באליה נמי מפרש ר"ת דאי אפשר לו לתנור להתקנח יפה ונדבק בו השמנונית והוי בעין עד שיוסק ומיהו יש לדקדק דאפי' נתבשלו שרי מהא דאמר לקמן (דף צז:) דכל יום ויום נעשה גיעול לחבירו ומותר לבשל אידנא שלמים בקדירה שבישל בה שלמים אתמול ולא אמרינן דקממעט באכילת שלמים דהאידנא דטעם שני הוא ונתבטל קודם שיבוא לידי איסור *ואפי' יב] למ"ד דשאני התם שהוא טעם שלישי שיש מים בקדירה שמבשלים בה שלמים מטעם זה נמי יהו מותרין הבילים שנתבשלו בקדירה החולבת לעשות מהם מולייתא בבשר שבתוך המים נתבשלו ועוד דגבי ספוד ואסכלא מייתי בסוף ע"ז (דף עו:) ההיא דכל יום ויום נעשה גיעול לחבירו ומיהו על כרחין אין זו ראיה דלענין חטאת אין שייך לומר כן דבסוף ע"ז (שם) קשרי לבשל חטאת והדר שלמים והרי ממעט באכילתן דמיתסרי לזרים לנשים ולעבדים *ואין נאכלין אלא ליום ולילה גם מיפסלי ביוצא כחטאת ואין שייך כאן להתיר מכח נותן טעם בר נותן טעם כי אם היכא שיש שני טעמי טעם של היתר אבל האחד של איסור לא דהוי כמו קדירה שבישל בה בשר לא יבשל בה חלב תרומה לא יבשל בה חולין ועל כרחין יש לומר שם משום דמין במינו דאורייתא ברובא בטל ובכלי המקדש ברגל אוקמיה אדאורייתא ואע"ג דאסרי לקמן (דף צז:) רקיק שנגע ברקיק וחתיכה בחתיכה גבי כלים אקילו רבנן טפי ותימה אי נתבשלו נמי מותר אמאי אמרו רבנן מזמן אכילה של ראשון טעון מריקה ושטיפה לגבי שלמים דאתמול ושלמים דהאידנא דשניהם היתר דאין סברא לומר גזירת הכתוב היא בדבר שמותר גמור בחולין אפי' מדרבנן · ברו"ך:

אלא קדירות של מקדש אמאי ישברו · תימה מאי קשיא ליה הא טעמא דשבירה לאו משום בליעה הויא אלא גזירת הכתוב אי סבירא ליה דתלאו באויר תנור טעון שבירה אע"ג דליכא אלא בישול בלא בלוע ור"ת היה אומר דכשהוסקו נעשו ככלים חדשים תדע דאמרינן בכולה הש"ס (פסחים ל: ע"ז לג:) התורה העידה על כלי חרס שאינו יוצא מידי דופיו לעולם ואמאי הרי יוצא מידי דופיו ע"י החזרת כבשן אלא ודאי כשהוסקו נעשו ככלים חדשים וחשיבי כלים אחרים דפנים חדשות באו לכאן יג] ואע"ג [דלגבי] טומאה כלי חרס טעון שבירה ואמרינן (כלים פ"ה מ"ז) תנור חולקו לשלשה כדכתיב תנור וכירים יותץ ולא אמרינן אמאי יותץ והלא כשמסיקו לאפות בו זו היא טהרתו דחשיב ככלי אחר וכן תנור שהסיקו בקליפי ערלה דאמרינן (פסחים דף כו:) חדש יותץ אמאי לא דמי כלי חרס לתנור דכיון דתנור תשמישו ע"י היסק לא חשיב פנים חדשות ושמא אף בתנור אם היה מסיקו בפנים ובחוץ כעין תחילת עשייתו כשהיוצר עושהו נותנו בכבשן אפשר שזה היה מועיל מיהו קשה מהא דאמרי' בסוטה פרק היה מביא (דף טו:) גבי פיילי של חרס חדשה (וגבי כלי חרס של מצורע) אמר רבא לא שנו אלא שלא נתאכמו אבל נתאכמו פסולין מ"ט דומיא דמים מה מים שלא נשתנו אף כלי שלא נשתנה בעי רבא נתאכמו והחזירן לכבשן ונתלבנו מהו מי אמרינן כיון דאידחו אידחו או דלמא כיון דהדור הדור ולא פשיט מינה מידי ומאי תיבעי ליה הא אמרינן פנים חדשות באו לכאן וככלי יד]חרס [חדש] דמי ושפיר הוי האי כלי דומיא דמים שלא נשתנו ועוד קשה הא אפי' בחולין קי"ל פסחים (דף ל:) התורה העידה על כלי חרס שאינו יוצא מידי דופיו לעולם מנא לן דמחטאת ליכא למילף דהתם גזירת הכתוב כדפירש אם תמצא לומר דבישול בלא בלוע טו] טעון שבירה ונראה לפרש דמאחר שהתיר הכתוב כלי נחשת במריקה ושטיפה ובכלי חרס לא התיר ש"מ דטעם משום בליעה הוא דזה יוצא מידי דופיו וזה אינו יוצא מידי דופיו ובישול בלא בלוע טעון שבירה בזה סברא לומר לפי שהחמיר בו הכתוב לחושבו כבלוע ודוקא בהגעלה אינו יוצא מידי דופיו אבל בהחזרת כבשונות יוצא וא"ת למה הצריך הכתוב שבירה דלא שייך למימר על הכתוב דלמא חיים ולא שאין עושין כבשונות בירושלים ויש לומר חידוש הוא שהתירו הכתוב בשבירה דהוה אמינא דלא מהגיא שבירה כיון דעדיין טעם חטאת בחרס דצריך שיהא הטעם בטל מן העולם כמו בכלי נחשת שעשו בו מריקה ושטיפה אבל הא פשיטא דר"ש החזרת כבשונות דמהגיא טפי טז] *ולא כספרים דגרסי הכא קדירות של מקדש אמאי אמר רחמנא ישברו ליהדרו לכבשונות דמשמע דפריך אקרא מדקאמר אמאי אמר רחמנא:

הכי גרסינן כיון דאיכא שתי הלחם ולחם הפנים דאפייתן בתנור וקדושתן בתנור · תימה דשבק מנחת מאפה דכתיב בה תנור בהדיא (ויקרא ב) וכי תימא משום דר"ש לא בעי הקדש בתנור כדדריש בסוף כל המנחות באות מצה (מנחות סג·)מדכתיב תנור תנור ב' פעמים אלא שיהא הקדישן לשם תנור א"כ שתי הלחם ולחם הפנים נמי ר"ש לא מפליג כדמוכח התם ודייק לה מדתנן בפרק שתי הלחם (שם נה:) ר"ש אומר לעולם הוי רגיל לומר שתי הלחם ולחם הפנים כשרות בעזרה וכשרות אבי פאגי ויש לומר דלא נקט מנחת מאפה משום דהיא גופה לא ידעינן לרבנן דר"ש אלא משתי הלחם *ולחם יז] הפנימית שהן גמרא כדאמר בריש שתי הלחם (שם צו:) דרבי יהודה ור"ש בגמרא פליגי:

ביסל

[לפרש"י ותוס' ליתא להך שתי תיבות ועיין שאלתות פ' מצות סימן קלז]
*[חגיגה ט. ב"ק פב:]
נ"א רב שמעיה
יומא כח.
[לעיל לה:]
שייך לעיל
נ"ל וכשחותך הוי בלגון טעם כו' נ"ק
נ"ל ואין נאכלין אלא לזכרי כהונה גם מיפסלי כו'
[נ"ל ולחם הפנים]

נ"א ואין לומר דשאני התם כו' נ"ק
נ"א ויש ספרים דגרסי הכי כו' נ"ק

נא א מיי' פ"ז מהל' בית הבחירה הלכה יד:
נב ב מיי' פ"א מהל' בית הבחירה הלכה יח:

שיטה מקובצת

א] אמר ליה אביי: ב] דתני רב שמעיה: ג] תיבת לו נמחק: ד] ומלאין איסורין מכל: ה] נטף (פסחים דף עה): ו] לקערות שניתנו בתוך: ז] שרו אבל נתבשלו ותיבת הא ל"ש: ח] לעשות מהם מולייתא של בשר ותיבות על גבי נמחק: ט] בקונט' דהיינו: י] סכין פעמים שהשומן תיבת טעמא נמחק: יא] ניכר וכשחותך הוי בצנון טעם: יב] ואפילו נאמר דשאני תיבות למ"ד ל"ש ונמחק: יג] לכאן ולענין טומאה תיבות ואע"ג נמחק: יד] וככלי אחר דמי תיבת חרס נמחק ותיבת חדש ל"ש: טו] בלוע דטעון שבירה: טז] טפי דלספרים דגרפי הכא תיבות ולא כספרים ל"ש: יז] ולחם הפנים שהן:

עין משפט נר מצוה

נג א מיי' פ"ח מהל' מעה"ק הלכה יג:

נד ב מיי' פ"ט מהלכות מאכלות אסורות הל' יא טוש"ע י"ד סימן נג:

נה ג ד ה מיי' פט"ו מהלכות תרומות הלכה יט:

נו ו מיי' פ"ח מהלכות מעה"ק הלכה יב:

נז ז מיי' שם הלכה יד:

נח ח מיי' שם הל' יב:

גמרא

ואפי' *ר' יוסי ברבי יהודה לא קאמר אלא דע"ץ אבל דחרס לא רב יצחק[א] בר יהודה הוה רגיל קמיה דרמי בר חמא שבקיה ואזיל[ב] לרב ששת יומא חד פגע ביה אמר ליה אלקפטא נקטן [ג] ריחא אתי לה ליד משום דאזלת לך [ד] לקמיה דרב ששת הוית לך כי רב ששת א"ל לאו משו"ה מר כי בעינא מילתא [ה] פשיט לי מסברא כי משכחנא מתניתא פרכא [ו] לה רב ששת כי בעינא מילתא מיניה פשיט לי ממתניתא דכי נמי משכחת מתניתא ופרכא מתניתא ומתניתא היא אמר ליה בעי [ז] מיני מילתא דאיפשיט לך כי מתניתא בעא מיניה בישל במקצת [ח] כלי טעון מריקה ושטיפה [ט] או אין טעון א"ל אינו טעון מידי דהוה אהזאה והא לא [י] תנא הכי א"ל מסתברא כבגד מה בגד *אינו טעון כיבוס אלא [יא] מקום הדם אף כלי אינו טעון מריקה ושטיפה אלא במקום בישול א"ל מי דמי דם לא מפעפע בישול מפעפע ועוד תניא חומר בהזאה ממריקה ושטיפה וחומר במריקה ושטיפה מבהזאה חומר בהזאה שהזאה ישנה בחטאות החיצונות ובחטאות הפנימיות וישנה לפני זריקה מה שאין כן במריקה ושטיפה חומר במריקה ושטיפה שהמריקה ושטיפה נוהגת בין בקדשי קדשים בין בקדשים קלים *בישל במקצת הכלי טעון מריקה ושטיפה כל הכלי מה שאין כן בהזאה א"ל *אי תניא תניא וטעמא מאי אמר קרא °ואם בכלי נחשת בושלה ואפילו במקצת כלי: אחד קדשי קדשים וכו': ת"ר חטאת אין לי אלא חטאת כל [יב] קדשים מנין ת"ל °קדש קדשים היא יכול שאני מרבה את התרומה ת"ל אותה פרט לתרומה דברי ר' יהודה ר"ש אומר קדשי קדשים טעונין מריקה ושטיפה קדשים קלים אינן טעונין מריקה ושטיפה [יג] דכתיב קדש קדשים קדשי קדשים אין קדשים קלים לא [יד] מ"ט דרבי יהודה מדאיצטריך אותה למעוטי תרומה מכלל דקדשים קלים טעונין מריקה ושטיפה ור"ש אמר לך אותה [טו] כדאמרינן ותרומה לא בעיא [טז] שטיפה ומריקה והתניא *קדרה שבישל בה בשר לא יבשל בה חלב ואם בישל בנותן טעם [יז] תרומה לא יבשל בה חולין ואם בישל בנותן טעם אמר אביי לא צריכא אלא [יח] לדאמר מר בישל במקצת כלי טעון מריקה ושטיפה כל הכלי הא תרומה לא צריך אלא מקום בישול רבא אמר לא צריכא אלא לדאמר מר במים ולא ביין [יט] במזוג הא אפי' ביין ואפי' במזוג רבה בר עולא אמר לא צריכא אלא [כ] לדאמר מר מריקה ושטיפה בצונן הא אפי' בחמין הניחא למ"ד מריקה ושטיפה בצונן אלא למ"ד מריקה בחמין ושטיפה בצונן מאי איכא למימר שטיפה יתירתא: **מתני'** רבי טרפון אומר [כא] *בישל מתחילת הרגל יבשל בו כל הרגל וחכ"א *עד זמן אכילה מריקה ושטיפה מריקה כמריקת הכוס ושטיפה כשטיפת הכוס מריקה* ושטיפה בצונן

השפוד

(ויקרא ו; שם)

תוספות

בישל במקצת כלי טעון מריקה ושטיפה כל הכלי או אינו טעון · תימה מאי קמבעיא ליה ומאי ס"ד דרב יצחק אי כשמקצת כלי על האש שמבשל בו [חם] ושאר הכלי צונן קמבעיא ליה אם כן מאי קאמר בישול מפעפע הא לא מפעפע בכוליה כלי ואי בשכל הכלי חם פשיטא דמפעפע בכוליה ובעי מריקה ושטיפה ואי קמבעיא ליה אי מפעפע בכוליה כלי או לא אם כן בשאר איסורים נמי תיבעי ליה:

חומר במריקה ושטיפה כו' · תימה אמאי לא קאמר שהמריקה ושטיפה היא לאחר זריקה מה שאין כן בהזאה וי"ל דלא חשיב חומרא אלא מה שלפני זריקה קודם כפרה שתלוי בעבודת הדם:

מדאיצטריך אותה למעוטי תרומה כו' · דמקדש קדשים הוה ממעטינא קדשים קלים וכל שכן תרומה *הלכך דרשינן אותה למעוטי תרומה דוקא [מ] ודאי דאין מיעוט אחר מיעוט אלא לרבות:

לא צריכא [מא] מדאמר מר מריקה ושטיפה בצונן · אחר הגעלה הא אפי' בחמין פירוש תרומה סגי בהגעלה ולא בעיא מריקה ושטיפה בצונן ופריך הניחא למאן דאמר מריקה ושטיפה בצונן פירוש אחר הגעלה אלא למ"ד מריקה בחמין ושטיפה בצונן דמריקה היינו הגעלה מאי איכא למימר ומשני שטיפה יתירתא דצריך לעשות בקדשים שטיפה יתירתא אחר הגעלה משא"כ בתרומה [מב] ויש ללמוד מכאן דכלים *האסורין כשמגעילן אין צריך לשוטפן בצונן אחרי כן אף על פי שנוהגין עתה לעשות כן*:

השפוד

נ"ל הלכך כדדרשינן אותה למעוטי תרומה ע"כ דוקא תרומה ולא קדשים קלים דאין מיעוט כו' נ"ק

נ"א הבלועין

[וע"ע בתוס' ע"ז עו. ד"ה מכאן]

נ"א כל

נ"א בחמין

רש"י

ואפי' לרבי יוסי כו' · במסכת סוכה בפרק החליל (דף נ:): אבל דחרס לא · כדאמרינן התם מאי מיעט מיעט חרס: פגע ביה · רמי בר חמא ברב יצחק: אמר ליה · רמי לרב יצחק: [כב] אלקפטין נקטן ריח אתי לה ליד משום דאזלת לך קמיה דרב ששת הוית לך כי רב ששת · משל הוא על גסי הרוח [כג] משתדלין לעמוד במקום גדולים [ואמר] הדוכוס אחזני בידי וריח המלוכה נקלט לתוך [כד] ידי אלקפטא דוכוס במסכת שבועות (דף ו:): א"ל לאו לא לגאוה נתכוונתי: [כה] משכחנא מתניתא · דלא אמרה הכי פרכא [כו] לה למילתיה דמר דשמעתא דאמורא במקום מתניתא ליתא: פשיט [כז] ממתניתא · *שמשניות סדורות בפיו [כח] כדאמרינן בעירובין (דף סז.) רב חסדא *מרתען שיפוותיה ממתנית' דרב ששת *וכי נמי משכחנא כו': דאיפשיט לך כי מתניתא · מסברא איפשוט לך וכי תדוק במתניתא תשכח כוותי: מידי דהוה אהזאה · דם חטאת שניתז על הבגד דתנן במתניתין אין טעון כיבוס אלא מקום הדם: והא לא תניא הכי · [כט] הא לא אשכחן מתניתא דקאי כוותך ואת אמרת דתפשוט כי מתני': [ל] [א"ל] מסתברא כי בגד · דמתניתין היא: מפעפע · מתפשט בכל הכלי: חומר בהזאה (א) מבמריקה כו' · בדם חטאת שניתז על הבגד: מריקה ושטיפה אינה בפנימיות ואינה לפני זריקה · שאין הכתוב מדבר אלא [לא] בנאכלות דסמיך ליה (ויקרא ו) כל זכר בכהנים יאכל אותה: הכי גרסי' בת"כ כל הקדשים מנין ת"ל קדש קדשים היא [לב] וסמיך ליה כל זכר בכהנים יאכל אותה: קדש קדשים היא · ולקמן מפרש דקדש קדשים לאו דוקא מדאיצטריך אותה למעוטי תרומה דאי קדש קדשים דוקא אותה למעוטי מאי אתא[לג] לאו לקדשים קלים איצטריך וכ"ש (ב) לתרומה: אותה · יאכל אותה בתר מריקה ושטיפה כתיב: אותה כדאמרן · אותה כשרה ולא פסולה [לד] דאפקיה ר' שמעון לעיל (דף צג.) חטאת שהיתה לה שעת הכושר ונפסלה: ואם בישל בנ"ט · נאסרין החולין לזרים אלמא בעי הגעלה לפלוט איסור הנבלע בכלי שלא יאסר: אמר אביי · מודינן דהגעלה בעי ולא נצרכא האי דאימעיט מתורת מריקה ושטיפה: [לה] אלא מקום בישול · הא דאמרינן בקדשים צריך מריקה כל הכלי גזירת הכתוב היא בדת מריקה ושטיפה: אלא לכדאמר מר · בתורת כהנים ומורק ושוטף במים ולא ביין כו': במזוג · מים ויין כאחד שני חלקי מים ואחד יין: הא · תרומה אפי' ביין ומזוג דלא קפדינן אלא אהגעלת איסור הנבלע בו [לו]: הכי גרסינן לא נצרכא אלא לכדאמר מר מריקה ושטיפה בצונן הא אפילו בחמין הניחא למאן דאמר מריקה ושטיפה בצונן אלא למאן דאמר מריקה בחמין ושטיפה בצונן מאי איכא למימר שטיפה יתירתא: לא נצרכא אלא לכדאמר מר · לקמן (דף צז.): מריקה ושטיפה בצונן · בר מהגעלת חמין הא דתרומה דאימעיט מתורת מריקה ושטיפה סגי לה בהגעלת חמין לחודייהו: אלא למ"ד מריקה בחמין · והיא הגעלה שלהן מהשתא ממאי אימעיט תרומה: ומשני שטיפה יתירתא · בצונן איכא בקדשים בתר מריקה [לז] דהוא הגעלת חמין ותרומה לא בעי שטיפת צונן: **מתני'** יבשל בו כל הרגל · בלא מריקה ושטיפה ולבסוף הרגל ימרוק וישטוף וטעמא מפרש בגמרא: זמן אכילה כו' · [לח] מפרש בגמרא מאי קאמר: מריקה כמריקת הכוס · מבפנים ככוס של ברכה כדאמרינן בברכות (דף נא.) שטעון הדחה [לט] בפנים ושטיפה מבחוץ:

האסכלה

מסורת הש"ס

[סוכה נ: סוטה יג. מנחות כח:]

[נ"ל שבברייתות]

נ"ל מרתען

נ"ל ואמר לי דתניא כי האי מלתא וכי נמי וכו' נ"ק

[לעיל צג:]

[שבת קטו: וש"נ]

תוספתא דתרומות פ"ח חולין נו. קיא:

[נ"ל אם בישל וכ"א במשנה שבמשניות]

הגהות הב"ח

(א) רש"י ד"ה חומר בהזאה כדם חטאת וכו' שבגד מבמריקה כו': (ב) ד"ה קדש קדשים וכו' וכ"ש לתרומה נ"ב א"כ נ"ל אותה וק"ל:

שיטה מקובצת

א] רב יצחק בריה דרב יהודה הוה: ב] ואזיל קמיה דרב ששת: ג] נקטן ביד ריחא: ד] קמיה דרב: ה] מילתא מיניה פשיט: ו] פרכא ליה רב: ז] בעי מינאי: ח] כליגליון פי' שמקצת האחר הוא חוץ לאש: ט] ושטיפה כל הכלי או: י] לא תניא הכי: יא] אלא במקום הדם: יב] כל הקדשים מנין: יג] ושטיפה מ"ט דרבי יהודה נמחק: יד] תיבות מ"ט דרבי יהודה כתיב קדש: טו] אותה כדאמרן: טז] מריקה ושטיפה והתניא: יז] טעם בישל בה תרומה: יח] אלא לכדאמר מר תיבת בישל עד תיבות במים אין כאן מקומו: יט] במזוג רבא אמר לא צריכא אלא לכדאמר מר בישל במקצת כלי טעון מריקה ושטיפה כל הכלי הא לא צריך רבה: כ] אלא לכדאמר: כא] אומר אם בישל בו מתחלת: כב] מה"ד אלקפטא נקטן ביד ריחא: כג] הרוח המשתדלין (ס"א להיות אצל גדולים): כד] ידו האלקפטא דוכוס: כה] מה"ד כי משכחנא: כו] פרכה ליה למילתיה: כז] פשים לי ממתניתא: כח] בפיו ואמר לי ת"ש דתניא כי הא מילתא: כט] תיבת הא נמחק: ל] א"ל מסתברא: לא] אלא בנאכלים דסמיך: לב] היא דסמיך ליה: לג] אתא לא לקדשים: לד] פסולה ואפקיה רבי: לה] כל הדבור המתחיל אלא מקום כו' עד ושטיפה נמחק ואכ"מ: לו] בו הא לא צריך אלא מקום בישול והא דאמרינן בקדשים צריך מריקה ושטיפה כל הכלי גזירת הכתוב היא בדת מריקה ושטיפה: לז] מריקה דהיא הגעלת: לח] בגמרא מפרש מאי: לט] הדחה מבפנים ושטיפה: מ] דוקא ודמי לאין מיעוט: מא] צריכא כדאמר: מב] ויש ללמוד (עיין תוספות ע"ז דף עו):

רו"ם

do not make earthen service vessels.[14] [96b] And even R. Jose son of R. Judah said only that wooden ones [were permitted], but not earthen ones.[15]

R. Isaac the son of R. Judah used to attend Rami b. Ḥama['s lectures]. He left him and attended R. Shesheth['s lectures]. One day he [Rami b. Ḥama] met him, and observed: The noble[16] has taken us by the hand, and his scent has come into the hand![17] Because a you have gone to R. Shesheth, you are like R. Shesheth![1] That was not the reason, he replied. Whenever I asked a question of you, you answered me from reason, [and] if I found a teaching[2] [to the contrary], it refuted your answer. [But] when I ask a question of R. Shesheth, he answers it from a teaching, so that even if I find a teaching which refutes him, it is one teaching against another.[3] Said he to him: Ask me a question, and I will answer you in accordance with a teaching.[4] [Thereupon] he asked him: If one boiled [the sacrifice] in part of a vessel,[5] does it require scouring and rinsing, or does it not require [them]?[6]—It does not require them, he replied, by analogy with [the] spurting [of blood].[7] But it was not taught so, he protested?[8]—It is logical that it is like a garment, he replied; just as a garment needs washing only in the place of the blood,[9] so a vessel requires scouring and rinsing only in the place of boiling. How can you compare them, he objected: blood does not spread,[10] whereas boiling spreads.[11] Moreover it was taught: [The] spurting [of blood] is more stringent than scouring and rinsing, and scouring and rinsing are more stringent than spurting. Spurting is more stringent, since [the law of] spurting operates in respect to outer sin-offerings and inner sin-offerings, and it operated before sprinkling,[12] which is not so in the case of scouring and rinsing.[13] Scouring and rinsing are more stringent, in that scouring and rinsing are required for most sacred sacrifices and for lesser sacrifices; [again] if one boiled [the flesh] in part of a vessel, the whole vessel requires scouring and rinsing, which is b not so in the case of spurting!—If it was taught, it was taught,[1] he replied. And what is the reason?—Scripture says, *'And if it be boiled in a brazen vessel'*, which means, even in part of a vessel.

WHETHER MOST SACRED SACRIFICES etc. Our Rabbis taught: [Scripture saith] *A sin-offering:*[2] I know it only of a sin-offering; how do I know it of all sacrifices? Because it says, *it is most holy.*[3] You might think that I include *terumah;* therefore it says, *[Every male among the priests may eat] thereof*, which excludes *terumah:*[4] these are the words of R. Judah. R. Simeon said: Most holy sacrifices necessitate scouring and rinsing, [but] lesser sacrifices do not necessitate scouring and rinsing, because it is written, *'It is most holy'*: most holy sacrifices do [necessitate it], but lesser sacrifices do not. What is R. Judah's reason?—Since *'thereof'* is necessary to exclude *terumah*, it follows that lesser sacrifices necessitate scouring and rinsing.[5] And R. Simeon?[6]—He can answer you: *'Thereof'* intimates what we said elsewhere.[7]

Now, does not *terumah* necessitate scouring and rinsing? Surely it was taught: You may not boil milk in a pot in which meat was boiled, and if one did, [the milk is forbidden] if it [the meat] could communicate its flavour [to it].[8] If one boiled *terumah* in it, one must not boil *ḥullin* in it; and if one did, [the *ḥullin* is forbidden] if it [the *terumah*] could communicate flavour [to it]![9]—Said Abaye: c This holds good[1] only in respect of what a master said, [viz.]: If one boiled [flesh] in part of a vessel, the *whole* vessel must be scoured and rinsed; but [in the case of] *terumah* only the part where it was boiled needs [scouring and rinsing]. Raba said: It holds good only in respect of what a master said: *'[It shall be scoured and rinsed] in water'*, but not in wine; *'in water'*, but not in a mixture:[2] this, however,[3] may be [scoured and rinsed] even in wine, even in a mixture. Rabbah b. 'Ulla said: It holds good only in respect of what a master said: The scouring and rinsing must be in cold water;[4] this however is done in hot water.[5] That is well on the view that scouring and rinsing must be done in cold [water]; but on the view that the scouring is in hot water and the rinsing in cold,[6] what can be said?[7]—There is the additional rinsing.[8]

MISHNAH. R. TARFON SAID: IF ONE BOILED [FLESH IN A POT] AT THE BEGINNING OF A FESTIVAL, HE CAN BOIL THEREIN DURING THE WHOLE FESTIVAL;[9] BUT THE SAGES MAINTAIN: UNTIL THE TIME OF EATING, SCOURING AND RINSING.[10] SCOURING [MERIKAH] IS AS THE SCOURING OF A GOBLET;[11] AND RINSING IS AS THE RINSING OF A GOBLET. SCOURING

(14) Offerings such as meal-offerings, loaves etc. were sanctified by being placed in service vessels. The Two Loaves and the Shewbread, however, were not placed in a service vessel, but were kneaded and shaped outside the Temple court, then brought in and baked in the oven. Thus the oven itself sanctified them, and *ipso facto* ranked as a service vessel. (15) V. Suk. 50*b*. (16) The *alkafta* or *arkafta* was a high Persian dignitary, v. Shebu. (Sonc. ed.) 6*b*. (17) A proverbial taunt against those who cultivate high acquaintances, thinking that they are thereby ennobled themselves.

a (1) You think that that will give you his reputation! (2) A Mishnah or Baraitha. (3) A controversy, and I may still adhere to the first. (4) I will base my answer on logic, yet you will find a *mathnitha* to corroborate it. (5) It was boiled with water, and so it could be boiled as it lay only in part of a vessel. Sh.M. explains that the other part of the vessel was not over the fire. (6) *Sc.* the part in which the flesh was not boiled. (7) When the blood spurts on part of a garment, only that part must be washed. (8) We do not find a teaching to corroborate this, whereas you said that your answer could be corroborated. (9) And that is explicitly taught in the Mishnah, *supra* 93*b*. (10) There is no blood at all save where it can actually be seen on the garment. (11) Even the part where the flesh does not lie absorbs some of it. (12) Whether the blood be of an outer or an inner sin-offering, it necessitates the washing of the garment; also it applies to blood that spurts *before* it is sprinkled. (13) Scouring and rinsing are required for outer sin-offerings only, which are eaten, since Scripture continues: *Every male among the priests may eat thereof* (Lev. VI, 22). For the same reason they are necessary only when the flesh is boiled *after* the sprinkling, for if boiled before the blood is sprinkled, it may not be eaten.

b (1) I must accept it. (2) Lev. VI, 18 q.v.; this introduces the law of scouring and rinsing, and therefore whatever this verse includes is included in the law of scouring and rinsing. (3) Ibid. 22. It is explained anon that this includes not only most holy, but also lesser sacrifices. (4) This limitation applies to all the laws of this section, including that of scouring and rinsing. (5) For if they did not, then *terumah*, whose holiness is certainly less than theirs, would obviously not necessitate scouring and rinsing, and the Scriptural limitation would be superfluous. (6) How does he rebut this? (7) That only a fit sacrifice necessitates scouring and rinsing, but not an unfit one; v. *supra* 93*a*. (8) If the pot had absorbed so much of the meat that it now would noticeably impart its flavour to the milk. (9) As in the preceding note. Hence it must be made fit by scalding with boiling water, which expels the absorbed matter (this is called *hage'alah*), as otherwise whatever is subsequently boiled therein is forbidden to lay Israelites. It is assumed that *hage'alah* is the same as scouring and rinsing.

c (1) This statement that *terumah* does not necessitate scouring and rinsing. (2) Of wine and water. (3) *Sc.* a vessel in which *terumah* was boiled. (4) After *hage'alah* (v. *supra* n.b 9) is performed, which must be in boiling water, the vessels must be scoured and rinsed in cold water. (5) I.e., *hage'alah* alone suffices. (6) And that nothing else is required. (7) For scouring in hot water is ordinary *hage'alah*, and *terumah* too necessitates that. (8) Which ordinary *hage'alah* does not require. (9) It need not be scoured and rinsed until the end of the festival. (10) The Gemara explains the meaning of this. (11) I.e., within and without. Grace after meals was recited over a goblet of wine, and this was first washed and rinsed within and without; v. Ber. 51*a*.

AND RINSING ARE DONE IN COLD [WATER].[12] [97a] THE SPIT AND THE GRILLE[13] ARE SCALDED IN HOT WATER.[14]

GEMARA. What is R. Tarfon's reason?—Because Scripture
a saith, *And thou shalt turn in the morning, and go unto thy tents:*[1] the Writ treats the whole [of the festival] as one morning.[2] To this R. Aḥadboi b. Ammi demurred: Is there no *piggul* during a festival, and is there no *nothar* during a festival?[3] And should you say, that indeed is so; surely it was taught, R. Nathan said: R. Tarfon gave this ruling only.[4] Rather, [the reason is] as R. Naḥman said in Rabbah b. Abbuha's name, viz.: Each day effects scalding for the previous one.[5]

BUT THE SAGES MAINTAIN: UNTIL THE TIME OF EATING etc. What does this mean?—Said R. Naḥman in Rabbah b. Abbuhah's name: He must wait as long as [the sacrifice] may be eaten, and then scour and rinse it. Whence do we know this?—Said R. Joḥanan on the authority of Abba Jose b. Abba: It is written, *'It shall be scoured and rinsed'*;[6] and it is written, *'Every male among the priests may eat'*:[7] what does this proximity intimate?[8] He must wait as long as [the sacrifice] may be eaten, and then scour and rinse it.

SCOURING IS AS THE SCOURING OF A GOBLET; RINSING IS AS THE RINSING OF A GOBLET. Our Rabbis taught: Scouring and rinsing are [done] with cold [water]: these are the words of Rabbi; but the Sages maintain: Scouring is with hot [water], and rinsing is with cold. What is the reason of the Rabbis?—It is comparable to the cleansing [*gi'ul*] of heathen [vessels].[9] And Rabbi?[10]—
b He can tell you: I do not speak of *hage'alah* [scalding];[1] I speak of the scouring and rinsing after *hage'alah*. And the Rabbis?—If so,[2] let Scripture write either, 'it shall be well scoured', or, 'well rinsed';[3] why say *'it shall be scoured and rinsed'*?—To inform you [that] scouring is [done] with hot water[4] and rinsing is [done] with cold. And Rabbi?—If Scripture wrote, 'it shall be well scoured', I would say [that it requires] two scourings or two rinsings; therefore *'it shall be scoured and rinsed'* is written to inform you that scouring must be as the scouring of a goblet, rinsing must be as the rinsing of a goblet.[5]

MISHNAH. IF ONE BOILED SACRIFICES AND ḤULLIN IN IT, OR MOST HOLY SACRIFICES AND LESSER SACRIFICES; IF THEY WERE SUFFICIENT TO IMPART THEIR FLAVOUR,[6] THE LESS STRINGENT MUST BE EATEN AS THE MORE STRINGENT OF THEM;[7] BUT THEY DO NOT NECESSITATE SCOURING AND RINSING;[8] AND THEY DO NOT DISQUALIFY BY TOUCH.[9] IF [AN UNFIT] WAFER TOUCHED A [FIT] WAFER,[10] OR AN [UNFIT]
c PIECE OF FLESH TOUCHED A [FIT] PIECE OF FLESH,[1] NOT THE WHOLE WAFER OR THE WHOLE PIECE OF FLESH IS FORBIDDEN; ONLY THE PART THAT ABSORBED [OF THE UNFIT] IS FORBIDDEN.

GEMARA. What does this mean?[2]—This is what it means: If they were sufficient to impart their flavour, the less stringent must be eaten as the more stringent of them, and they require scouring and rinsing,[3] and they disqualify by their touch.[4] If they were insufficient to impart their flavour, the less stringent need not be eaten as the more stringent, and they do not necessitate scouring and rinsing, and do not disqualify by their touch. Granted that they do not require [scouring and rinsing] as for most sacred sacrifices, yet they should require [them] as for lesser sacrifices?—Said Abaye: What does he mean by THEY DO NOT NECESSITATE? [As for] most sacred sacrifices; but they do necessitate [them] as for lesser sacrifices. Raba said: This is in accordance with R. Simeon, who maintained: Lesser sacrifices do not necessitate scouring and rinsing.

As for Raba, it is well: for that reason he [the Tanna] teaches, SACRIFICES AND ḤULLIN, OR MOST SACRED SACRIFICES AND LESSER SACRIFICES.[5] But on Abaye's explanation, why do I need two clauses?[6]—They are necessary. For if he taught SACRIFICES AND ḤULLIN [only] I would say, Only *ḥullin* can nullify sacrifices,[7] as they are not of the same kind; but in the case of MOST SACRED SACRIFICES AND LESSER SACRIFICES, it is not so.[8] And if he taught about MOST SACRED SACRIFICES AND LESSER SACRIFICES only, I would think that only sacrifices are strong enough to nullify other sacrifices; but *ḥullin* I would say is not [strong
d enough].[1] Thus both are necessary.

IF AN [UNFIT] WAFER TOUCHED A [FIT] WAFER etc. Our Rabbis taught: *Whatever shall touch* [... *shall be holy*];[2] you might think, even if it did not absorb; therefore it says, *in the flesh thereof:*[3]

(12) *Var. lec.* scouring is in hot water and rinsing is in cold. (13) On which flesh was roasted. (14) V. n. 5. This makes them fit for further use.

a (1) Deut. XVI, 7. This means that the Israelite could return home on the morning after the festival. (2) I.e., as one day. Since the reason for scouring and rinsing is that what is absorbed of the meat in the pot becomes *nothar*, it follows that it cannot become *nothar* from the beginning until the end of a festival, as it is all counted as one day. (3) If one intends eating the sacrifice after its permitted period of two days, or if flesh is left over after two days, does it not become *piggul* or *nothar*, although it is still the festival? (4) *Sc.* in respect of scouring and rinsing; but he admits that there can be *piggul* and *nothar* during a festival. (5) Many peace-offerings were sacrificed during the festival, and the boiling of each day's sacrifice expels from the pot what it absorbed the previous day, and thus it does not become *nothar*. (6) Lev. VI, 21. (7) Ibid. 22. (8) Lit., 'how is this?'—The second text immediately follows the first. (9) In order to expel what they had absorbed. This requires heat, as Scripture says in this connection: *Every thing that may abide the fire, ye shall make go through the fire, and it shall be clean* (Num. XXXI, 23). (10) Why does he not accept this argument?

b (1) That certainly requires hot water. (2) If Scripture meant that scouring and rinsing must follow *hage'alah*, for scouring is not *hage'alah* itself. (3) Lit., shall be scoured, scoured, or, shall be rinsed, rinsed. For if scouring is not *hage'alah*, it is identical with rinsing (both being in cold water), and Scripture merely means that it must be rinsed twice. Then the same word should be used for each operation. (4) I.e., it is *hage'alah*. (5) I.e., once on the *outside* and once on the *inside*. (6) If the pot had absorbed enough of the former to impart its flavour to the latter; or, if both were boiled together, if the former was sufficient to impart its flavour noticeably to the latter.—If they are both of the same kind, we regard them as though they were two different kinds. (7) If lesser sacrifices and *ḥullin* were boiled, the *ḥullin* must be eaten within the precincts of Jerusalem, and for two days only. If lesser sacrifices and most holy sacrifices were boiled in it, the lesser sacrifices must be eaten in the Temple court, on the same day, and by male priests only. (8) At the end of the shorter period allowed for the consumption of the more stringent, but only at the end of the longer allowed for the less stringent. (9) If the less stringent became disqualified, they do not in turn disqualify any flesh that touches them. (10) Of a meal-offering, v. Lev. II, 4.

c (1) The latter in each case absorbing from the former. (2) Why is it not scoured and rinsed at the end of the period allowed for the more stringent? (3) Accordingly, i.e. at the end of the *shorter* time. (4) If the more stringent were unfit while the less stringent were fit, the less stringent become disqualified too and in turn disqualify others just as the more stringent disqualified. (5) To give an anonymous ruling in accordance with R. Simeon, viz., that lesser sacrifices do necessitate scouring and rinsing. (6) Seeing that the same principle operates in both. (7) When the latter do not communicate their flavour to the former. (8) Even if the former do not impart their flavour to the latter, the whole must be treated with the stringency of the former.

d (1) Even if the sacrifice does not impart its flavour to the *ḥullin*, the whole must be treated with the stringency of the former. (2) Lev. VI, 20. *'Holy'* means that it is subject to the same restrictions as the flesh of the sacrifice. (3) Lit. translation.

*השפוד ״והאסכלא מגעילן בחמין: גמ׳ מאי טעמא דר״ט א] דאמר קרא °ופנית בבקר והלכת לאהלך הכתוב עשאו לכולן בקר אחד מתקיף לה רב אחדבוי בר אמי וכי אין פיגול ברגל ואין נותר ברגל וכי תימא ה״נ והתניא ר׳ נתן אומר לא אמר ר״ט אלא זו בלבד אלא כדר״נ אמר רבה בר אבוה *דאמר ר״נ אמר רבה בר אבוה כל יום ויום נעשה גיעול לחבירו: וחכ״א עד זמן אכילה כו׳: מאי קאמר אמר ר״נ אמר רבה בר אבוה ממתין לה ב] עד זמן אכילה והדר עביד לה מריקה ושטיפה מנהני מילי א״ר יוחנן משום אבא יוסי בן אבא כתיב °ומורק ושוטף וכתיב °כל זכר בכהנים יאכל הא כיצד ממתין לה עד זמן אכילה והדר עביד לה מריקה ושטיפה: מריקה כמריקת הכוס שטיפה כשטיפת הכוס: ת״ד מריקה ושטיפה בצונן דברי רבי וחכמים אומרים ״מריקה בחמין ושטיפה בצונן מ״ט דרבנן מידי דהוה אגיעולי עובדי כוכבים ורבי אמר לך הגעלה לא קאמינא כי קאמינא למריקה ושטיפה דבתר הגעלה ורבנן א״כ לכתוב קרא או מורק מורק או שוטף שוטף מאי ומורק ושוטף ג] ש״מ מריקה בחמין ושטיפה בצונן ורבי אי ד] כתיב ומורק מורק ה״א תרי זימני מורק או תרי זימני שוטף לכך כתיב ומורק ושוטף לומר לך מריקה כמריקת הכוס שטיפה כשטיפת הכוס: מתני׳ *״בישל בו קדשים וחולין או קדשי קדשים וקדשים קלים אם יש בהן בנותן טעם הרי הקלים נאכלין כחמורין ה] שבהן ואינן טעונין מריקה ושטיפה ״ואינן פוסלים במגע ״רקיק שנגע ברקיק ותתיכה בתתיכה לא כל ו] הרקיקין ולא כל התתיכות אסורין אינו אסור אלא במקום שבלע: גמ׳ *מאי קאמר (א) ז] אם יש בהן בנותן טעם הרי הקלין נאכלין כחמורין וטעונין מריקה ושטיפה ופוסלין במגע אין בהן בנותן טעם אין הקלין נאכלין כחמורים ואין טעונין מריקה ושטיפה ואין פוסלין במגע נהי דקדשי קדשים לא בעו קדשים קלים ח] ניבעי אמר אביי ״מאי אין טעונין דקאמר קדשי קדשים אבל קדשים קלים טעונין רבא אמר הא מני ר״ש היא *דאמר קדשים קלים אין טעונין מריקה ושטיפה בשלמא לרבא היינו דקתני ט] או קדשי קדשים וקדשים קלים אלא לאביי תרתי למה לי צריכי דאי תנא קדשים וחולין ה״א חולין הוא ״דמבטלי קדשים דלאו מינייהו אבל קדשי קדשים וקדשים קלים אימא לא ואי תנא קדשי קדשים וקדשים קלים ה״א קדשים הוא דאלימי לבטולי קדשים אבל חולין אימא לא צריכא: רקיק יא] *שהגיע ברקיק כו׳: ת״ר כל אשר יגע יכול אפי׳ שלא בלע ת״ל בבשרה

עד

רש״י

האסכלא · גרדיל״י ותולין עליו צלי ובגמ׳ דמסכת ע״ז פריך הא ליבון בעי : גמ׳ ופנית בבקר · על כרחך בקר של חול קאמר וקרי ליה בקר ראשון : אין פיגול ברגל · אם שחט ע״מ לאכול למחר אינו פיגול: ואין נותר ברגל · אם הותיר בשר חטאת למחר אינו נותר דחד יומא הוא לר״ט : אלא זו בלבד · לענין מריקה ושטיפה יב] לחודה ולא לענין פיגול ונותר ואי טעמיה מהאי קרא הוא אפילו לענין פיגול ונותר נמי : נעשה גיעול לחבירו · מתוך שהשלמים מצויין ברגל אין בלוע שלה נעשה נותר שהרי זמן שלמים לב׳ ימים וכי מבשל ביה שלמים האידנא הדר מבשל ביה שלמים למחר יג] ובולע משלמים שנשחטו ביום המחרת ופולט מה שבלע אתמול ובולע מן האחרונים נמצא שאינו בא לידי נותר *ואם בא לבשל חטאת יד] זהיר לבשל אחריו שלמים בו ביום ופולט את החטאת ובולע את השלמים : הא כיצד · כלומר למה סמכן הכתוב לומר טו] שממתין [עד] זמן אכילה כו׳ : מידי דהוה אגיעולי עובדי כוכבים · דחמין בעינן דכתיב (במדבר לא) כל דבר אשר יבא באש טז]: א״כ · דתרווייהו חדא היא ומריקה לאו היינו הגעלה לכתוב קרא לשון שוה בשניהם : ה״ג ומאי מורק ושוטף ש״מ מריקה בחמין שטיפה בצונן : ורבי · אמר לך מריקה כמריקת הכוס ושטיפה כשטיפת הכוס לכך שינה בלשון שזה מבחוץ וזה מבפנים : מתני׳ הרי הקלים נאכלין כחמורין · לפנים מן הקלעים יז] ליום ולילה : ואין טעונין מריקה ושטיפה · לסוף זמן אכילת חמורים אלא לסוף זמן אכילת קלים ובגמ׳ פריך מאי קאמר הרי יש בהן בנותן טעם ואמר הרי הקלין נאכלין כחמורין(ב): ואין פוסלין במגע · אם נפסלו הקלין ונגע בהן בשר ובלע מהן אין נפסלין ובגמ׳ מפרש לה : רקיק · פסול יח] שהגיע ברקיק כשר ובלע ממנו : גמ׳ וטעונים מריקה ושטיפה · כדין החמורין : ופוסלין במגע · אם היו החמורין פסולין והקלים כשרין נעשו הקלים כחמורין לפסול את הנוגעין בהן כדכתיב (ויקרא ו) כל אשר יגע בבשרה יקדש יט] ואומר לקמן להיות כמוהו שאם פסולה (ג) תפסל : כ] (ואם לא הקלין כו׳) ואין טעונין מריקה · לקמיה פריך ליטעון מיהא כדין קלין לסוף זמן אכילתן: ואין פוסלין במגע · אם היה החמור שנתבשל עם הקלין פסול הואיל ומועט ואין בו בנותן טעם בקלין לא נעשו הקלים כמוהו לפסול את הנוגעין בהן שהרי אף הם לא נפסלו ואיידי דתנא רישא פוסלין נקט סיפא אין פוסלין : נהי דקדשי קדשים לא בעו · כלומר נהי דלא בעו מריקה לסוף זמן אכילת חמורין דהא מועטין ובטלי ניבעי מיהא משום קלים לסוף זמן אכילתן : היינו דתנא או קדשי קדשים וקדשים קלים · לאשמועינן דסתם לן כרבי שמעון דאמר קדשים קלים אין טעונין מריקה ושטיפה : אלא לאביי · דאמר מאי אין טעונין דקאמר כדין חמורין כא] תרתי למה לי למיתנייה כיון דתנא קדשים וחולין ואשמועינן דבטל במיעוטו מה לי הני מה לי הני :

עד

תוספות

השפוד והאסכלא מגעילן בחמין · אית דלא גרסי בחמין משום דבעי רבה למימר בסוף ע״ז (דף עו.) מאי הגעלה דקתני מריקה ושטיפה א״ל אביי מי דמי מריקה ושטיפה בצונן הגעלה בחמין ואי גרסינן במשנה גופה בחמין היכי טעי רבה ונראה דשפיר גרסינן ליה וקסבר רבה מריקה בחמין והא דנקט רבה שטיפה אגב מריקה נקט ושטיפה לאו דוקא והכי קאמר מאי הגעלה בחמין דקאמר היינו מריקה דאיירי בה לעיל דאיכא למ״ד בגמ׳ דמריקה בחמין:

ופנית בבקר · פי׳ בקונטרס על כרחין בקר של חול קאמר וקרי ליה בקר ראשון וקשה דלמא בי״ט וכגון שהלנו בתוך התחום ואפי׳ כב] תימא לומר דבעי ראיית פנים כג] ביום ראשון שמביא קרבנו מ״מ י״ל למחרתו שהוא חה״מ כל ז׳ מנא ליה ונראה לפרש דמשמע ליה כולהו בקר אחד משום דכולהו ז׳ תשלומין דראשון דחגיגה יש לה תשלומים כל ז׳ ומכאן קשה ללשון אחר שפירש בקונטרס בפסחים בפרק מי שהיה טמא (דף צה:) גבי פסח ראשון טעון לינה פסח שני אין טעון לינה דראשון טעון יום אחד והכא מוכח דבעי לינה ז׳ וכן בסוכה בפרק לולב וערבה (דף מז.) דקתני כשם ששבעת ימי החג טעונין קרבן שיר וברכה ולינה כך שמיני טעון קרבן שיר וברכה ולינה *מאי לאו זמן לא ברכת המזון ותפלה ה״נ מסתברא דאי ס״ד זמן זמן כל ז׳ מי איכא משמע דקרבן ולינה ניחא ליה דהוה כל ז׳ ושמא י״ל דה״ה דהוה מצי למיפרך מלינה וליטעמיך ולשיטיה דהתם אתי הכל שפיר דמשני דזמן כל ז׳ משכחת לה אי לא בריך ביומא קמא בריך באידך יומי וכן נמי מצי למימר מלינה דעולת ראייה יש לה תשלומין כל ז׳ ויום הבאת קרבנו טעון לינה ולא יותר כד] (הג״ה) והך דשמעתין נמי מעיקרא ס״ד דהוי כל ז׳ מטעמא דפרישית אבל לא קאי הכי ובספרי מוכח דלא הוי אלא יום אחד דקתני אין לי אלא אלו מנין לרבות המנחות והעופות כו׳ ת״ל ופנית בבקר כל פינות שאתה פונה לא יהו אלא כאלו משמע דלא הויא לינה אלא יום אחד דומיא דשלמים של כל השנה וקשיא לי אי לינה ברגל אינו רק יום א׳ אמאי פסח שני אין טעון לינה מי גרע ממביא עוף או מנחה בחול דטעון לינה יום אחד אבל אי רגל טעון לינה ז׳ אתי שפיר דקמ״ל דפסח שני אין טעון לינה רק יום אחד · ברוך :

ממתין להם כל זמן אכילה והדר עביד מריקה ושטיפה · אין לפרש דמריקה ושטיפה קודם שיעשה נותר כדי שלא יבואו קדשים לבית הפסול דהא משמע הכא דלאחר זמן אכילה עביד מריקה ושטיפה ומיהו יש ספרים דגרסי ממתין להו עד זמן אכילה ועוד יש קצת לדקדק מדקאמר לעיל לרבי טרפון כל יום ויום נעשה גיעול לחבירו ואם קודם כה] שעשה נותר עביד מריקה ושטיפה ה״נ ליעביד דכי בשיל ביה שלמים אתמול כשבא היום והוזקק למריקה ושטיפה אי כו] בשיל ביה שלמים דהאידנא קודם מריקה ושטיפה ליתסרו אלא ודאי לא חייב הכתוב עד אחד שנעשה נותר :

ניתי

מסורת הש״ס

ע״ז עו. · דברים טז · ויקרא ו · ג״ז שם · נ״ל ואם בשיל ביה חטאת האידנא הדר מבשל אחריו שלמים בו ביום כו׳ נ״ק · (מעילה פרק ב) · נ״ל מאי קאמר חסורי מחסרא והכי קתני אם יש בהן כו׳ · [לעיל צג: צו:] · נ״ל שנגע · שם · נ״ל מאי ברכה לאו זמן כו׳ נ״ק

עין משפט נר מצוה

נט א ב מיי׳ פ״ח מהל׳ מעה״ק הלכה יב .
ס ג מיי׳ שם הל׳ יח :
סא ד מיי׳ שם הלכה טז :
סב ה מיי׳ שם הלכה יח :
סג ו מיי׳ שם הלכה יט:

שיטה מקובצת

א] דר״ט אמר ר׳ יצחק דאמר קרא עיין תוס׳ סוכה (דף מז) : ב] לה כל זמן תיבת עד נמחק: ג] ושוטף לומר לך מריקה בחמין תיבת ש״מ ל״ש : ד] אי כתב רחמנא ומורק ומורק הו״א תרתי זימנא במריקה כתב רחמנא ומורק ושוטף לומר כו׳ והשאר ל״ש: ה] תיבת שבהן נמחק: ו] כל הרקיק ולא כל התתיכה אסורין : ז] קאמר ה״ק אם : ח] קלין מיהא ניבעי : ט] דקתני קדשים וחולין או : י] הוא דאלימא לבטולי : יא] רקיק שנגע ברקיק: יב] ושטיפה להודיה ולא : יג] תיבת ובולע ל״ש ונמחק: יד] חטאת יהא זהיר : טו] לומר לך שממתין זמן ותיבת עד נמחק: טז] באש וגו׳ הס״ד : יז] הקלעים וליום ולילה : יח] פסול שנגע ברקיק: יט] יקדש ואמר לקמן יקדש להיות : כ] מה״ד אין הקלין כו׳ : כא] תיבת תרתי ל״ש : כב] ואפילו אם תמצא לומר דבעי : כג] בליל יום ראשון ותיבת ביום נמחק: כד] תיבת הג״ה נמחק : כה] קודם שיעשה נותר : כו] אי דבשיל ביה :

עד שיבלע בבשרה יכול נגע במקצת חתיכה יהא כולו פסול ת"ל יגע הנוגע פסולה א כיצד חותך את מקום שבלע בבשרה ולא בגידין ולא בעצמות ולא בקרנים ולא בטלפים *ב יקדש להיות כמוה הא כיצד אם פסולה היא תפסל [ואם] כשרה היא תאכל כחמור שבה אמאי וניתי עשה ולידחי את לא תעשה אמר רבא אין עושה דוחה את לא תעשה שבמקדש א] שנאמר *°ועצם לא תשברו בו ר"ש בן מנסיא אומר אחד עצם שיש בו מוח ואחד עצם שאין בו מוח אמאי ניתי עשה ולידחי את לא תעשה אלא ב] אין עשה דוחה לא תעשה שבמקדש רב אשי אמר יקדש עשה הוא ג] ואין עשה דוחה את לא תעשה ועשה אשכחן חטאת ד] דמתקדש בבלוע שאר קדשים מנלן *אמר שמואל משום ר"א °ג זאת התורה לעולה ולמנחה ולחטאת ולאשם ולמילואים ולזבח השלמים ה] [לעולה] כי עולה מה עולה טעונה כלי אף כל טעונה כלי מאי כלי אילימא מזרק בשלמי ציבור נמי כתיב בהו °ויקח משה חצי הדם וישם באגנות אלא *ד דסכין ועולה גופה מנלן דכתיב °וישלח אברהם את ידו ויקח את המאכלת והתם עולה הוא דכתיב °ויעלהו לעולה תחת בנו מה מנחה אינה נאכלת אלא לזכרי כהונה אף כל אינם נאכלין אלא לזכרי כהונה מאי היא אי חטאת ואשם בהדיא כתיב בהו °כל זכר בכהנים יאכלנו ואי ו] שלמי ציבור מריבוייא דקרא אתי °בקדש הקדשים תאכלנו כל זכר יאכל אותו ה לימד על שלמי ציבור שאינן נאכלין אלא לזכרי כהונה תנאי היא

איכא

רש"י

עד שיבלע · כגון ז] המהתך שומן חטאת וסך ממנו צלי של שלמים ונבלע בו ומכאן אנו למידים (פסחים מה.) היתר מצטרף לאיסור בקדשים ח] *ואין ללמוד מכאן טעם כעיקר שאין זה טעם אלא ממש : תאכל כחמור שבה · שהרי יש בה עכשיו שני מינין ט] וכחומר שבשניהם תיאכל : תורה אור אמאי · תיפסל משום האי פורתא : ניתי עשה · דואכלו אותם דכשירה : ולידחי לא תעשה · דלא תאכל דפסולה ואע"ג דאיכא לא תעשה באכילת פסולין כדאמרינן בפסחים י] בכל שעה (דף כד·) כל שבקדש פסול בא הכתוב ליתן לא תעשה על אכילתו : ניתי עשה ולידחי · ניתי עשה דאכילת מוח דכתיב ואכלו את הבשר בלילה הזה : זאת התורה · הוקשו כולן זה לזה ללמוד זה על זה יא] לכך הוקשו כולן לעולה דמה עולה טעונה כו' : יב] אי נימא מזרק · לקבלת דם וליף מעולת סיני דכתיב וישלח את נערי בני ישראל וכתיב יג] עולה התם : וישם באגנות · יד] וכיון דהדור איתקוש כולהו לשלמים דכתיב ביה בהאי קרא וילפינן מינה לקמן בשמעתין (דף לח·)

מה

תוספות

*ניתי עשה ולידחי את לא תעשה · לאו את לא תעשה · לאו תאכל כחמור שבה פריך שתיאכל בלילה ולמחר כשלמים דהאידנא דה"ל נותר ואין עשה דוחה את ל"ת שיש בו כרת (יבמות ח.) אלא אם פסולה היא תיפסל קאי דניתי עשה דאכילת קדשים ולידחי לאו דכל שבקדשים פסול בא הכתוב ליתן ל"ת על אכילתו [דקאי] (אי) כמי אשאר פסולין דליכא כרת כגון דנשחטה בלילה ולן דמה וחוץ למקומו (וחוץ לזמנו) וא"ת ומאי קושיא דלמא גזירת הכתוב הוא דאמר קרא יקדש להיות כמוה ויש לומר דקרא איכא לאוקומי בכשרה שתיאכל טו] כחומר *שבה עד הלילה ומיהו קשה דכי הוי לילה *ניתי עשה ונדחה ונראה דקרא איכא לאוקומי בבישול קדשים וחולין כי מתני' *ועוד דאם איתא דהכא לא דחי מאי חזית דילפת מכלאים בציצית דעשה דוחה את לא תעשה אדרבה נילף מהכא דלא דחי : ואחד עצם שאין בו מוח ואמאי ניתי עשה כו' · *בסוף כילד צולין (פסחים פה·) דריש מדכתיב ועצם לא טז] ישברו בו בפסח שני שאין ת"ל שהרי כבר נאמר ככל חוקת הפסח *יעשו אותו אבל אי לאו קרא דפסח שני ה"א ואכלו את הבשר בלילה הזה בבשר שבתוך העצם ומה אני מקיים ועצם לא תשברו בו בעצם שאין בו מוח אבל עצם שיש בו מוח שובר ואוכל דיבא עשה וידחה לא תעשה *והא דפריך הכא ואמאי ניתי עשה כו' הכי פריך כלומר מהכא נגמור דאין עשה דוחה לא תעשה בעלמא כי הכא אלא ודאי במקדש שאני* וצ"ל דהכי פריך ניתי עשה כו' כמו בחולין ונוקי קרא דיקדש אם כשרה תיאכל כחומר שבה דשייך בה כרת אם היא נותר וקמ"ל דהיתר מצטרף לאיסור כדאיתא פרק אלו עוברין (שם מה·) ובפרק ג' מינין (נזיר לז:) ולא נוקים קרא לאם פסולה תיפסל דליכא אלא לאו ומשני גלי קרא גבי קדשים בעצם שיש בו מוח דלא דחי ולכך נילף קדשים מקדשים ולא נילף קדשים מחולין ברו"ך · וא"ת שאני הכא משום דאפשר לקיים שניהם דמנח גומרתא עילוייה ושקיל ליה מוח וי"ל *דרבא הכא לטעמיה דמפרש בסוף כילד צולין (פסחים פד:) גבי אין נימנין על מוח שבקולית דלא אפשר בגומרתא משום פסידא דקדשים א"כ לא מקיים עשה דואכלו את הבשר בלילה הזה דא"א שלא ישרוף הגומרתא מעט מן המוח שבפנים ואפי' אביי שמפרש התם משום פקע לאו משום דס"ל דגומרתא אפשר בלא שריפת מוח אלא קסבר דמשום הפסד קדשים מועט כזה לא חיישינן יז] מיהא אכתי קשה *היכי אתי האי עשה ודחי לא תעשה הא בעידנא דמתעקר לאו דשבירת עצם לא מיקיים עשה דאכילה* : והתם עולה הוא כדכתיב ויעלהו לעולה תחת בנו · תימה דהאי קרא דרשי' ליה לענין חולין בפ"ק דחולין (דף טז.) דאמרינן מנין לשחיטה שהיא בתלוש שנאמר ויקח את המאכלת ואומר ר"ת דגמרי' כמי חולין מדכתיב לשחוט את בנו ולא כתיב לשחוט את העולה אבל כלי לא שייך למילף בחולין אלא בקדשים כשאר עבודות דבעו כלי שרת ומדכתיב ויקח דמשמע דבר תלוש ולא כתיב יח] *סכין דרשינן תלוש בחולין וכלי בקדשים מדהזכיר מאכלת דהוה מצי למכתב ויקח המחתך ואע"ג דהתם בחולין (ג"ז שם) דחי רבי חייא זריזותיה דאברהם קמ"ל הכא לא שייך לדחויי הכי דלענין מה שהביא דבר תלוש ולא סמך על מה שימצא צור וקנה מחובר שייך למימר יט] דכתב קרא לאשמועינן זריזותיה אבל לענין מאכלת שהזכיר למה לי למכתב אי לאו לאשמועינן דעולה טעונה כלי : מה מנחה אינה נאכלת אלא לזכרי כהונה · ופריך בחטאת ואשם נמי *כתיב כל זכר אלא לשלמי ציבור פירש בקונטרס הא דלא ילפינן זכרי כהונה מחטאת ואשם כדילפינן ממנחה משום דכתיב בתרווייהו גבי אכילת זכרים הוא קדש קדשים הוא דמשמע מיעוט הוא ולא אחר וקשה כ] דבפרק איזהו מקומן (לעיל דף נה·) איכא תנא דיליף מהיקשא דחטאת מקרא דכתיב ועשיתם שעיר עזים [אחד] לחטאת ושני כבשים בני שנה לזבח שלמים מה חטאת לזכרי כהונה אף שלמי ציבור לזכרי כהונה כא] *הא לא קשיא מידי דההיא היקשא לא איצטריך למילתא אחריתי כב] ועוד נראה לפרש דהיינו טעמא הכא דהיקשא דחטאת ואשם איכא לאוקומי ל מילתא אחריתי כדמפרש הכא לא מוקמינן לה לאכילת זכרים כג] דכיון דאיתו שוה בכל הנהו דכתיבי בקרא אבל מנחה על כרחין להכי אתיא דלא משכחת למלתא אחריתי : אף כד] שלמי ציבור אין נאכלין אלא לזכרי כהונה · ושלמים דהאי קרא בכבשי עצרת קאי דקדש קדשים נינהו כל הכתובין במקרא זה כה] ונראה דעל כרחין איירי נמי בשלמי נדבה דהא בפ"ק (לעיל דף ה:) נפקא לן מהאי קרא שלא כו] לשמו ועוד בכולהו קרבנות דטעונין כלי מהכא נפקא לן :

בקדש הקדשים תאכלנו כל זכר יאכל אותו וגו' לימד על זבחי שלמי ציבור כו' · האי קרא בפרשת קרח כתיב ואף על גב דזבחי שלמי ציבור לא כתיב התם כיון דכתיב בהאי קרא קדש יהיה לך וגבי כבשי עצרת כתיב בפרשת אמור אל הכהנים קודש יהיו לה' לכהן מסתברא דבדידהו מיירי וכן פירש בקונטרס ועוד כז] ילפינן משום דאיקרו קדש קדשים כדילפינן לעיל בפרק איזהו מקומן (דף נה.) ובפרק שני דערכין (דף יא:) מדכתיב על עולותיכם ועל זבחי שלמיכם מה עולה קדשי קדשים אף זבחי שלמי ציבור קדשי קדשים :

איכא

עין משפט נר מצוה

ועי' בספר קרבן אהרן פרשה נו דף יד ע"א בהגהת הדיבור הזה

סד א מיי' פ"ח מהלכות מעה"ק הל' יז :

סה ב מיי' שם הל' טו :

סו ג מיי' שם הל' טז : רש"ק מ"ז

סז ד מיי' פ"ד מהל' מעה"ק הלכה ז :

נ"א שבהן כגי' ר"ח בפסחים ובחולין וקאי אחטאת של אמש

צ"ל ועוד נ"ל דהכי פריך דאם איתא דהכא כו' צ"ק

סח ה מיי' פי' מהל' מעה"ק הלכה ג :

צ"ל תימה בסוף כילד כו' צ"ק

צ"ל יעשו אותו דמשמע אבל אי לאו כו' צ"ק

[עי' פרש"י לקמן לח. ד"ה אלא סכין]

צ"ל ושמא הא דפריך כו' צ"ק

וגירסת הצ"ק במקדש שאני לפ"ז ועצם לא ישברו בו בפסח שני למה לי וכו' וצ"ל וכ"ה בס"י כ"א מן וצ"ל עד קדשים מחולין מקומו לעיל בד"ה ניתי עשה

מסורת הש"ס

נ"ע הא בהדיא מוכח במסכת נזיר לז: דילפינן מכאן לטעם כעיקר שם רש"י גופיה מקיים גם הגירסא וכ"כ רש"י במס' חולין לט. ובפסחים מה. צ"ק

פסחים מה. נזיר לז: חולין לט.

פסחים פה. ע"ש

מנחות פב:

ויקרא ז

שמות כד

בראשית כב

שם

ויקרא ו

במדבר יח

צ"ל דרבא לטעמיה צ"ק

גי' הצ"ק היכי ס"ד דאתי

[ועי' בפיסקי תוס' סעיף שם ישוב על זה ועיין במל"מ פ"י מהל' ק"פ דין א']

גירסת הצ"ק וסכין

צ"ל בהדיא כתיב כל צ"ק

צ"ל וצ"ל לפרש דהא צ"ק מידי דהיינו טעמא הכא דלא ילפינן מהיקשא דחטאת ואשם דאיכא לאוקמי כו' צ"ק

שיטה מקובצת

א] דתניא ועצם ותיבת שנאמר נמחק : ב] אלא ש"מ אין : ג] הוא הו"ל עשה ולא תעשה ואין : ד] חטאת דמקדשת בבלוע : ה] השלמים לעולה מה עולה: ו] ואי זבחי שלמי : ז] כגון המחה שומן ותיבת המהתך נמחק: ח] ואין· עיין ברש"י בחולין (דף לט) : ט] מינין ולחמור שבשניהם : י] בפרק כל שעה : יא] זה הס"ד ומה"ד לעולה · לכך הוקשו : יב] מה"ד אילימא מזרק: יג] תיבת עולה ל"ש א) : יד] באגנות· בשלמי צבור וכיון כו' : טו] שתאכל כחמור שבה· עיין בתוס' חולין (דף לט) : טז] לא תשברו בו : יז] היישי' ומיהו אכתי : יח] סכין ה"א ויכין : יט] למימר דכתבי' קרא : כ] וקשה דלעיל בפרק איזהו מקומן : כא] מתיבת הא כו' עד תיבות ועוד נראה מוקף בח"ל : כב] ונראה לפרש היינו טעמא הכא כיון דהיקשא : כג] זכרים כיון דאיתו : כד] אף כל אין ותיבות שלמי צבור נמחק : כה] זה כך פירש בקונטרס ונראה : כו] שלא לשמן ועוד דבכולהו קרבנות : כז] ועוד יש לפרש משום ותיבת ילפינן נמחק :

א) נראה דלפי הגהתו ז"ל וכתיב התם וישם באגנות והד"א ומכבסס דבסמוך אות יד לא משמע כן וצ"ע

[97b] [this intimates] that it must absorb [thereof] in its flesh. You might think that if it touched a part of a piece of flesh, the whole of it is unfit. Therefore it says, '[*Whatever*] *shall touch*': only that which touches is unfit. How so? The part which absorbed is cut away. '[*In*] *the flesh thereof*': but not the tendons, bones, horns or hoofs.[4] '*Shall be holy*', to be as itself, so that if it [the sin-offering] is unfit, that [which touches it] becomes unfit; while if it is fit, it may be eaten [only] in accordance with its stringencies. Yet why so?[5] let the positive command[6] come and override the negative injunction![7]—Said Raba, A positive injunction does not override a negative injunction in the Temple. For it was taught: *Neither shall ye break a bone thereof*.[8] R. Simeon b. Menassia said: [This refers to] both a bone which contains marrow and a bone which does not contain marrow. Yet why so? let the positive injunction[9] come and override the negative injunction? Hence you can infer that a positive injunction does not override a negative injunction in the Temple. R. Ashi said: '*Shall be holy*' is a positive injunction: thus there are a positive and a negative injunction,[10] and a positive injunction cannot override a positive and a negative injunction [combined].

a We have thus found that a sin-offering sanctifies[1] [whatever touches it] through absorption; whence do we know it of other sacrifices?—Said Samuel on R. Eleazar's authority: [Scripture saith,] *This is the law of the burnt-offering, of the meal-offering, and of the sin-offering, and of the guilt-offering, and of the consecration-offering, and of the sacrifice of peace-offerings*.[2] '*Of a burnt-offering*': as a burnt-offering requires a utensil,[3] so all require a utensil. What utensil is meant? If we say, a basin?[4] in respect of public peace-offerings too it is written, *And Moses took half of the blood, and put it in basins!*[5] Rather, it means a knife.[6] And how do we know it of a burnt-offering itself?—Because it is written, *And Abraham stretched forth his hand, and took the knife* [*to slay his son*],[7] and there it was a burnt-offering, as it is written, *And offered him up for a burnt-offering in the stead of his son*.[8]

'*Of a meal-offering*': as a meal-offering may be eaten by male priests [only], so all may be eaten by male priests only. Which [are thus inferred]? If the sin-offering and the guilt-offering? [surely] it is explicitly written in connection with them, *Every male among the priests may eat thereof!*[9] If public peace-offerings? that is deduced from a Scriptural extension, [viz.] *In a most holy place shalt thou*[10] *eat thereof; every male may eat* thereof:[11] this teaches that public peace-offerings may be eaten by male priests only!—It is a controversy of Tannaim:

(4) These do not render the flesh that touches them '*holy*'. (5) Why does the flesh of the fit sacrifice become unfit through absorbing of the unfit? (6) Ex. XXIX, 33: *and they shall eat those things wherewith atonement was made* (*sc.* the flesh of the sacrifices). (7) Forbidding the unfit to be eaten, e.g. in Lev. VI, 23 q.v. It is a general principle that a positive injunction overrides a negative injunction when the two are in conflict. (8) Ex. XII, 46. This refers to the Passover-offering. (9) To eat the flesh (which includes marrow), *sc. and they shall eat the flesh in that night* (Ex. XII, 8). (10) Forbidding the flesh which absorbed the taste of the disqualified sacrifice.

a (1) In the sense stated above. (2) Lev. VII, 37. The enumeration of all these together with the single superscription '*this is the law*' teaches that they are all assimilated to one another, and the Talmud proceeds to explain in which respect they are so assimilated. (3) The Heb. *keli* denotes a vessel or a utensil. (4) For receiving the blood; and this teaches that a peace-offering too needs a basin. That a burnt-offering requires a basin is inferred from Ex. XXIV, 5*f*, q.v. (5) Ibid. 6. The blood was that of burnt-offerings and peace-offerings. Hence peace-offerings need not be inferred from burnt-offerings. (6) A burnt-offering must be killed with a knife (a utensil) and not e.g. with a sharp piece of stone (unfashioned into a utensil), and the text intimates that the same applies to the others. (7) Gen. XXII, 10. (8) Ibid 13. (9) Lev. VII, 6. (10) *Sc.* Aaron. (11) Num. XVIII, 10.

[98*a*] one infers it from this verse, and another infers it from the other.

'Of a sin-offering': as a sin-offering sanctifies through absorption,
a so all [sacrifices] sanctify through absorption.[1]

'Of a guilt-offering': as a guilt-offering, the foetus and after-birth inside it are not holy, so all [sacrifices], the foetus and after-birth inside them are not holy.[2] He holds that the young of sacrifices become holy when they come into existence,[3] and that we infer what is possible from what is not possible.[4]

'Of the consecration-offering': as the consecration-offering, the remainder thereof was burnt,[5] and there were no living animals among its remainder;[6] so all [sacrifices], their remainder is burnt, but living animals are not counted as remainder.[7]

'Of the . . . peace-offering': as [parts of] a peace-offering render *piggul*, and [parts] are rendered *piggul*, so [in] all [sacrifices] [where there are parts which] render *piggul* and [parts which] are made *piggul* [the law of *piggul* applies].[8]

It was taught in a Baraitha in R. Akiba's name: *'Of the meal-offering'*: as a meal-offering sanctifies through absorption,[9] so all [sacrifices] sanctify through absorption. Now, it is necessary for
b both *'meal-offering'* and *'sin-offering'* to be written.[1] For if we were informed [this about] a meal-offering, [I might say that was] because it is soft it absorbs; but [as for] a sin-offering, I would say [that it is] not [so]. And if we were informed about a sin-offering, [I might say] that is because it is solid;[2] but a meal-offering I would say is not so. Thus both are necessary.

'Of the sin-offering': as a sin-offering comes of *ḥullin* only, and by day, and [its rites must be performed] with his [the priest's] right hand; so every [sacrifice] comes of *ḥullin* only, by day, and [its rites must be performed] with his right hand. And how do we know it of a sin-offering [itself]?—Said R. Ḥisda, Scripture saith: *And Aaron shall present the bullock of the sin-offering, which is his*:[3] [that intimates that] it must be his,[4] and not the congregation's,[5] nor of tithe.[6] [That its rites must be performed] by day is inferred from: *in* the day *that he commanded* [etc.]?[7]—That is stated unnecessarily. [That its rites must be performed] with his right hand is inferred from Rabbah b. Bar Ḥanah's [exegesis]? For Rabbah b. Bar Ḥanah said in the name of Resh Laḳish: Wherever 'finger' and 'priesthood' are stated, the right hand only [must be used]?[8] That [too] is stated unnecessarily. Alternatively, he agrees with R. Simeon, who maintained: [Where] 'finger' [is stated], priesthood is not required;[9] [but where] 'priesthood' [is stated], 'finger' is required.[10]

'Of the guilt-offering': as the bones of a guilt-offering are permitted, so the bones of every [sacrifice] are permitted.[11]

a (1) This is the answer to the question, how do we know that all sacrifices sanctify through absorption? The rest of the discussion is really irrelevant here. (2) A guilt-offering was a male, and so there could be no foetus or afterbirth inside it to be holy. From this we learn that the foetus and after-birth in female sacrifices, e.g. peace-offerings and sin-offerings, are not holy. If then a foetus was found in a sacrifice after it was slaughtered, its *ḥeleb* (fat) and kidneys are not burnt on the altar as *emurim*, as in the case of the sacrifice itself. (3) I.e., when they are born, but not before. (4) I.e., females from males, though in the latter case the foetus and after-birth are not holy because they do not exist. (5) V. Lev. VIII, 32, which refers to the consecration-offering. (6) The consecration-offering was a public sacrifice, and we do not find that two animals were dedicated for the purpose (v. next note), so that one should be a 'remainder'. Thus only flesh and bread were a remainder, and these alone were burnt. (7) Whatever remains of a sacrifice after the time allowed for its consumption is burnt (as *nothar*). This, however, does not apply to a living remainder. E.g. if a man dedicated an animal for a sacrifice, lost it, dedicated a second, found the first and sacrificed one of them; similarly, if he dedicated two animals in the first instance, so that if one were lost the second would be sacrificed. The other is technically called a remainder, but this remainder is not burnt. (8) V. *supra* 28*b*. (9) For it is written, *whatsoever toucheth them* (*sc.* the meal-offerings) *shall be holy* (Lev. VI, 11).

b (1) The same is written of the sin-offering. (2) Since the flesh is thick, the grease penetrates deeply into it. (3) Lev. XVI, 6. E.V. *which is for himself*. (4) Purchased at his own expense. (5) Not bought with public funds. (6) It must not be an animal of tithe, which is sacred in its own right. Hence it must be *ḥullin*. (7) Lev. VII, 38. This refers to *all* the sacrifices enumerated in the preceding verse; why then derive it from a sin-offering? (8) And 'priesthood' is stated in connection with each of these sacrifices. (9) To shew that the right hand is meant. (10) Both are stated in connection with a sin-offering, but only priesthood is stated in connection with the others. Hence they must be inferred from a sin-offering. (11) *Supra* 86*a*.

איכא דנפקא ליה מהכא ואיכא דנפקא ליה מהכא חטאת מה חטאת (א)[א] מתקדשת בבלוע אף כל מתקדשת בבלוע אשם מה אשם אין שפיר ושליא קדוש בו אף כל אין שפיר ושליא קדוש בו קסבר *ולדות קדשים בהווייתן הן קדושים ודנין *אפשר משאי אפשר מלואים מה מלואים מותריהן בשריפה ואין בעלי חיים במותריהן אף כל מותריהן בשריפה ואין בעלי חיים במותריהן שלמים *מה שלמים מפגלין ומתפגלין אף כל מפגלין ומתפגלין במתניתא תנא משמיה דר"ע *מנחה מה מנחה ג] מתקדשת בבלוע אף כל מתקדשת בבלוע ואיצטריך למכתב מנחה ואיצטריך למכתב חטאת דאי אשמעינן מנחה דאיידי דרכיכא מיבלעא אבל חטאת אימא לא ואי אשמעינן חטאת *משום °דקריר אבל מנחה אימא לא צריכא חטאת *מה חטאת אינה באה אלא מן החולין וביום ובידו הימנית אף כל אינה באה *אלא מן החולין וביום ובידו הימנית *וחטאת מנלן אמר רב חסדא אמר קרא °והקריב אהרן את פר החטאת אשר לו משלו ולא משל ציבור ולא משל מעשר ביום °מביום צוותו נפקא *כדי נסבה בידו הימנית מדרבה בר בר חנה נפקא *דאמר רבה בר בר חנה אמר ר"ל כל מקום שנאמר אצבע וכהונה אינו אלא ימין כדי נסבה ואיבעית אימא סבר לה כר"ש *דאמר אצבע לא בעיא כהונה כהונה בעיא אצבע אשם *מה אשם עצמותיו מותרין אף כל עצמותיו מותרין אמר רבא פשיטא לי

דם

ויקרא טז | שם ז

רש"י

מה שלמים מפגלין ומתפגלין הא נמי תילף משלמים דהתם (ב)נמי שלמים בסיני הוו: *אלא סכין. לשחיטה לאפוקי צור וקנה דכלי שרת בעינן ג]: מאי היא. הי מינייהו יליף ד] לאכול לזכרי כהונה ממנחה: בקדש הקדשים תאכלנו. בויקרא קרא כתיב ה] וקדש יהיה לך דכתיב בסיפיה דקרא יתירא הוא למילף שלמי ציבור ו] וכבשי עצרת דכתיב בהו קדש יהיו לה' לכהן*: מה חטאת מקדש בבלוע כו'. ואף על גב דבמנחה נמי כתיב (ויקרא ו) כל אשר יגע בה יקדש דמקדשת בבלוע אצטריך לאקושינהו לחטאת דממנחה לא מצי ילפי דאיכא למימר לא איתקש למנחה אלא לענין זכרי כהונה אבל לענין בלוע דמנחה דוקא דרכיכא (ג) למיבלע אבל שאר קדשים לא: מה אשם אין שפיר ושליא קדוש. ז] דהא זכר הוא ואין לך לומר בחלב ושתי כליות שלו שאף של שליא שבמעיו משמע אף הבאים נקבות כגון חטאת ושלמים אין שפיר ושליא קדוש בהן ואין חלב ושתי הכליות של שליל שבמעיהן קריבין ומעולה לא ה"ל למילף דכליל היא (ד) ואף כל ח] שאין שפיר ושליא קדוש בו לא מצי למימר דלאו לעולה מדמית להו שהרי אף שאר הבשר אינו קרב ואכילת זכרי כהונה לא יליף מחטאת ואשם כדיליף ממנחה דתקשה לך אמאי אקשינהו למנחה לילפו זבחי שלמי ציבור מאשם וחטאת משום דכתיב בתרווייהו גבי אכילת זכרים הוא ט] קדשי קדשים הוא הלכך מהתם לא מצי ילפי אי לא מהיקשא דמנחה: וולדות בהמות קדשים בהווייתן הן קדושים. כשנולדים הן קדושים ולא במעי אמן *וגמרי מאשם: ודנין אפשר משאי אפשר. נקבות מזכרים ולגמרי לא מצי *למעוטינהו י] מקדשים להקריבם דכתיב רק קדשיך אשר יהיו לך ואמר מר בכורות (דף יד:) רק קדשיך אלו התמורות אשר יהיו לך אלו הוולדות ומאשם גמרינן דבמעי אמן מיהא לא קדשי אלא בהווייתן כדכתיב אשר יהיו: מה מלואים מותריהן בשריפה. ולא היו בעלי חיים במותריהן דמלואים שהרי קרבן צבור היו ולא הופרשו שנים לאחריות וגם לא אבד אחד מהם והפריש אחר תחתיו ונמצא הראשון: אף כל הקדשים יא] מותריהן בשריפה ואין בעלי חיים במותריהן. שאם היו בעלי חיים במותריהן כגון יחיד שהפריש שני קרבנות לאחריות חובתו שאם יאבד האחד יתכפר בשני או אם הפריש קרבן ואבד והפריש אחר תחתיו ונמצא הראשון והקריב את יב] האחד מהן ואת השני נותר אין נותר זה בשריפה כדין נותר של מילואים: יג] מפגלים. את הנסכים שאם חישב בזבח אף הנסכים מפוגלין ומש"ה יליף משלמים דעיקר פיגול יד] כתיב בהו: דקריר. טריסטטרי"ט בלע"ז מתוך שהבשר עב נכנס בתוכו השומן בעומקו: חטאת. באה ביום דכתיב טו] (ביום) בפר יוה"כ (ויקרא טז) כי ביום הזה יכפר עליכם: ובידו הימנית. דכתיב טז] אצבע וכהונה ואמר מר לעיל (דף כד:) כ"מ שנאמר אצבע וכהונה אינו אלא ימין: מדרבה בר בר חנה נפקא כו'. וקס"ד או אצבע או כהונה ואין לך בכל אלו שלא נאמר כהן בהקרבתן: כר"ש. בפ"ב (שם) כהונה בעי אצבע ובחטאת תרווייהו כתיב ולקח הכהן מדם החטאת באצבעו: מה אשם עצמותיו מותרין. לעשות מהן כלים אני שמעתי שהרי נאכל לכהנים ונותר בעצמות לא שייך אלא בדבר הנאכל: אף כל. ואפי' עולה ומיבעי (ה)לי הא נמי מחטאת הוה מצי יז] יליף ונראה בעיני דמלו יהיה יתירא נפקא ליה באשם דכתיב ביה (שם ז) לכהן יח] לו יהיה:

דם

תוספות

איכא דנפקא ליה מהכא כו'. עוד יש תנא שלישי בפרק איזהו מקומן (לעיל דף נה.) דאמר אלא היקישא למאי אתא מה חטאת לזכרי כהונה אף זבחי שלמי ציבור לזכרי כהונה והא דלא מייתי לה הכא משום דסוגיא דשמעתא היא ולא משכח לה ברייתא בהדיא:

מה חטאת מקדשת בבלוע כו'. הא דאמרינן בפרק גיד הנשה (חולין דף צח:) לא נצרכה [אלא] לטעם כעיקר דבקדשים אסור והכא שרי [ופריך] וליגמר מינה גלי רחמנא גבי חטאת כל אשר יגע בבשרה יקדש משמע דפשיטא ליה דשאר קדשים ילפינן מחטאת היינו מהיקשא דהכא:

אף כל אין שפיר ושליא קדוש בו. פירש בקונטרס ואין חלב ושתי כליות של שליל שבמעיה קריבין וקשה דהוה ליה לתנא לפרושי חלב וכליות של שפיר ושליא כמו שילהי בהמה המקשה (חולין דף עה.): הג"ה ועוד דמשמע מתוך פירושו דדוקא חלב ושתי כליות הוא דאין קדושין ליקרב אבל הוולדות גופן קדושין הן וא"א לומר כן דתניא תמורה (דף יא.) השוחט את החטאת ומצא בה בן ד' נאכל לכל אדם ובכל מקום ולעולם ומוקי לה יט] למאן דאית ליה בהווייתן הן קדושין בריש כילד מערימין (שם דף כה:) דהן עצמן חולין במעי אמן ונראה לפרש דלענין חולין גמורין קא יליף דשפיר ושליא הנמצא בבטן חטאת לאחר שחיטה אינן קדושין כלל ומהכא אית ליה ולדות קדשים בהווייתן הן קדושין והא דתניא כ] ברייתא בהמה המקשה (חולין דף עה.) מה חלב ושתי כליות האמורין באשם מולא מכלל שליל אף כל מולא מכלל שליל ההוא תנא סבר במעי אמן קדושין ולכך אילטריך קרא למעוטי חלב ושתי כליות מהקרבה ולפי מה שפירשתי לא אתי שפיר הא דלא יליף מעולה כמו לפי' הקונטרס:

מה שלמים מפגלין כו'. לעיל בסוף פרק ב' (דף כח:) איכא תנא דדריש לה מדכתיב ואם האכל יאכל מבשר זבח שלמיו מה שלמים מפגלים ומתפגלין כו' וכן בפרק ב"ש (לעיל דף מד.) דדריש לה נמי מההוא קרא מה שלמים מיוחדין שיש להם מתירין בין לאדם בין למזבח מפגלין ומתפגלין פי' בקונטרס מפגלין את הנסכים אם חישב בזבח ובחנם דחק דהוה מצי למימר שהדם מפגל את הבשר והבשר עצמו מתפגל:

מה חטאת אינה באה אלא מן החולין כו'. תרתי דריש מחטאת דכבר דרש נמי מה חטאת מקדשת בבלוע:

כדי נסבה ואי בעית אימא סבר לה כר"ש כו'. הכא מסיק להני תרי שינויי אבל בסוף התודה (מנחות דף פג.) משני כדי נסבה לחודיה ובפ"ק דחולין (דף כב.) משני כהונה בעיא אצבע כו' ותו לא *ונראה דלמאן דאמר לעיל (דף נ.) דבר הלמד בג"ש אינו חוזר ומלמד בהיקש נ"ל הכא *(ובפ"ק דחולין) כדי נסבה דאצבע דחטאת גופיה ילפינן בג"ש דמלורע דהייט ימין לעיל בפ' ב' (דף כד:) ובפ"ק דמנחות (דף י.) ואם כן כא] לא מצינו למילף בהיקש שאר קרבנות מחטאת:

מה אשם עצמותיו מותרין כו'. פי' בקונטרס לעשות מהם כלים אני שמעתי באשם פשוט לו שעצמותיו מותרין שהרי נאכל לכהנים ונותר בעצמות לא שייך אלא בדבר הנאכל אף כל ואפילו עולה ומיבעי לי הא נמי מחטאת הוה מצי יליף ונראה בעיני דמלו יהיה יתירא נפקא ליה באשם דכתיב ביה לכהן אשר יכפר בו לו יהיה כך פי' בקונטרס והשתא לפירוש רבותיו דמסברא ידע דעצמות מותרין בכל קדשים הנאכלין ולא אצטריך היקישא אלא להתיר עצמות עולה קשה משלמים או משאר קדשים הנאכלין נילף ולמה איכתוב אשם ועוד דבפרק המזבח מקדש (לעיל דף פו.) דריש מג"ש נאמר באשם לו יהיה ונאמר בעולה לו יהיה וקאמר דמופני מה אשם עצמותיו מותרין אף עולה כו' והשתא תיפוק ליה מהיקשא דהכא ול"ל ג"ש כיון דלא איצטריכא היקישא דהכא אלא לאגמורי בעולה ויש לומר כיון דשאר קרבנות לריכי כל חד למלתיה כדמפרש הכא לא נילף מינייהו דבר אחר שאינו נ"ל בכל הקדשים רק בעולה וכי האי גוונא פירשנו לעיל (דף לז:) גבי מנחה דילפינן מיניה זכרי כהונה ולא ילפינן מחטאתו אשם ולפי' זה האי תנא לית ליה דרשא דשפיר ושליא

עצרת: ז] קדוש בו. דהא: ח] כל אין שפיר: ט] הוא קדש קדשים הוא: י] למעוטינהו מקדושה והקרבה דכתיב רק קדשיך: יא] הקדשים מותר בשרן בשרפה: יב] את אחד מהן: יג] מפגלין ס"א מפגלין את הלחם דהא בכבשי עצרת כתיב שאם חשב בזבח אף הלחם מפוגל אף כל שבא דבר אחר עמו הזבח מפגלו כגון איל נזיר שהוא טעון לחם וכן תודה ומשום הכי יליף משלמים משום דעיקר פיגול בהו כתיבי: יד] פיגול בהו כתיב: טו] תיבת ביום נמחק: טז] דכתיב ביה אצבע: יז] מצי למילף ונראה: יח] לכהן אשר יכפר בו לו יהיה: יט] לה כמאן דאית: כ] דתניא בברייתא בפ' בהמה המקשה: כא] וא"כ היכי מצינו ותיבת לא ל"ש:

עין משפט נר מצוה

סט א מיי' פ"י מהל' מעה"ק הלכה טו:

ע ב מיי' פ"ד מהל' מעה"ק הלכה א:

עא ג מיי' פ"ט מהלכות ביאת מקדש הל' יח:

עב ד מיי' פ"י מהל' מעה"ק הלכה י:

מסורת הש"ס

שייך לעיל | מנחות פג. | ע"ל שייך לעיל | [לקמן קיד. וש"נ] | [סוכה כ: יבמות מו. סח: הוריות ו: מנחות יט. פב. תמורה יז: נדה לז.] | [מנחות פג. לעיל כח.] | מנחות פג. כל הסוגי' | [ע"ש במנחות] | [עי' תוספות לעיל כ. ד"ה אם] | יומא נ: חולין כב. מנחות פג. | [ר"ה ה. וש"נ] | ממאשם ודנין כד"א ל"ק | נ"א למעוטינהו מקודשתן מלהקריב דכתיב כו' ל"ק

חולין פב. לעיל כה. מנחות י פג. | ג"ש שם | [לעיל טו.] | [ועי' תוס' סנהדרין כס. ד"ה ילא] | נ"ל ובסוף התודה

הגהות הב"ח

(א) גמ' מה חטאת מקדשת בבלוע אף כל מקדשת: (ב) רש"י ד"ה (בעמוד הקודם) ויהם כאגנות וכו' לקמן במשתין מה שלמים וכו' תילף משלמים דהתם בסיני שלמים מי הוו הס"ד ואח"כ מ"ה אלא סכין: (ג) ד"ה מה חטאת וכו' מיבלע כצ"ל ואות ל' נמחק: (ד) ד"ה מה אשם וכו' לא ה"ל למילף דכליל היא ולא מצינן למימר אף כל שאין שפיר ושליא קדוש בו דלאו לעולה וכו' גבי אכילת זכרים קדשי קדשים הוא אבל שלמים קדשים קלים היא הילכך מהתם: (ה) ד"ה אף כל ואפילו עולה ומיבעי לן הא מחטאת נמי הוה מצי כ"כ על פשט זה דשמעתין סנ"ל:

גליון הש"ס

גמ' דקריר. לשון זה ג"כ לעיל דף עט ע"ב:

שיטה מקובצת

א] חטאת מקדשת בבלוע אף כל מקדשת בבלוע: ב] מנחה מקדשת בבלוע אף כל מקדשת בבלוע: ג] בעינן הס"ד ומה"ד אף כל אין נאכלים אלא לזכרי כהונה ושלמים. דהאי קרא בכבשי עצרת קאי דקדשי קדשים נינהו ככל הכתובים במקרא זה הס"ד: ד] יליף ליאכל לזכרי: ה] כתיב ואע"ג דזבחי שלמי ציבור לא כתיב התם אפ"ה וקדש: ו] ציבור דהיינו כבשי

עג א מיי' פ"ח מהל' מעה"ק הלכה ט :
עד ב ג מיי' פ"ג מהל' מקואות הלכה ו ז :
א ד מיי' פ"י מהלכות מעה"ק הלכה יט :
ב ה מיי' פ"ב מהלכות שאר אבות הטומאה הלכה טו ופ"ב מהלכות ביאת מקדש הלכה ח :
ג ו מיי' פ"ב מהלכות ביאת מקדש הל' ו :
ד ז מיי' פ"י מהלכות מעה"ק הלכה יט :
ה ח מיי' שם הל' יז ופ"ו מהלכות ביאת מקדש הל' יב ועי' רש"ק :
ו ט מיי' פ"ו מהלכות ביאת מקדש הלכה א :
ז י מיי' פ"י מהלכות מעה"ק הלכה יד :
ח כ מיי' שם הל' כא :

נ"ל דאשם נקטיה נ"ק

גי' נ"ק לו יהיה ולא דרים אלא מיותרא כו' ועיין רש"ק

תורה אור

דם חטאת למטה ודם עולה למעלה טעון כיבוס בעי רבא דם עולה למטה ודם חטאת למעלה מהו משום נוגע הוא והא נוגע או דלמא משום בלוע הוא והא לא בלע א] (הוא) הדר פשטה דאין [א]טעונין כיבוס אמר רבא פשיטא לי דם [ב]על בגדו חוצץ ואם טבח הוא אינו חוצץ רבב על בגדו חוצץ ואם מוכר רבב הוא אינו חוצץ בעי רבא דם ורבב על בגדו מהו אם טבח הוא תיפוק לי משום רבב ואי מוכר רבב הוא תיפוק לי משום דם לא צריכא דעביד הא והא אחדא לא קפיד אתרתי קפיד או דלמא אתרתי נמי לא קפיד [ג]תיקו :

הדרן עלך דם חטאת

טבול [ד]יום ומחוסר כיפורים אינן חולקין בקדשים לאכול לערב אונן ב] (אינו) [ה]נוגע [ו]ואינו מקריב [ז]ואינו חולק לאכול לערב [ח]בעלי מומין בין בעלי מומין ג] עוברין בין בעלי מומין קבועין חולקין ואוכלין [ט]אבל לא מקריבין [י]כל שאינו ראוי לעבודה אינו חולק בבשר [כ]וכל שאין לו בבשר אין לו בעורות אפילו טמא בשעת זריקת דמים וטהור בשעת הקטר חלבים אינו חולק בבשר שנא' ד] °המקריב את דם השלמים ה] [ואת החלב מבני אהרן] לו (יהיה) [תהיה שוק הימין למנה]: ויקרא ז
גמ'

דם חטאת למטה ודם עולה למעלה . נפל דם חטאת תחילה על הבגד וחזר וניתז דם עולה על אותו כתם : טעון כיבוס . דהא דם חטאת נוגע בבגד ובלוע בו : והא נוגע . שדם עולה נבלע בבגד וכשנפל דם חטאת עליו נוגע הוא בבגד אבל אינו נבלע דהא שבע ליה בבלוע דם עולה : חוצץ . לענין טבילה בבגד שנטמא : ואם טבח הוא . שאינו מקפיד בדם שעל בגדו : אינו חוצץ . דחציצה בקפידא תליא ו] : רבב . כל דבר הנתוך כגון שומן וחלב ושעוה : ותיפוק ליה משום רבב . שאינו רגיל בו ומקפיד עליו והוי חציצה : אתרתי קפיד . [ואף על גב] דרגיל בתרווייהו גנאי הוא לו שיראו שניהם על בגדו : או דלמא לא קפיד . הואיל ובשניהם רגיל :

הדרן עלך דם חטאת

טבול יום ומחוסר כיפורים . הואיל ואין ראוין לאכילה ז]: אין חולקין לאכול לערב . לכשיטהרו ובגמרא מפרש טעמא : אונן אינו מקריב . כדאמר בפרק שני (לעיל דף טז.) : בעלי מומין חולקין . טעמא מפרש בגמרא : כל שאינו ראוי לעבודה כו' . בגמרא פריך והרי ח] בעל מום : וטהור בשעת הקטר חלבים . שהוא כל הלילה כגון שטבל וטהר בהערב שמש : **גמ'** *מחטא . זורק את הדם : וכללא הוא . ריש לקיש גופיה [ויליף] ואזיל למילתיה ופריך לקרא עד דממילא מיתוקמא בחטקה משמרה

[שייך לדף צז.]

ושליא דלעיל ומאן דדריש עלמות מותרין מלו יהיה פרק המזבח מקדש (לעיל דף פו.) אית ליה היקישא דאשם לגבי ספיר ושליא ולפרש"י דאמר דבכל הקדשים מן הדין אסורין העלמות דלא התיר הכתוב אלא בשר הראוי לאכילה וגילה לנו באשם לו יהיה דמשמע שריותא נילף כמו כן היתר בכל הקדשים ע"פ זה : הגהה . קשה דבההוא קרא כתיבי חטאת ואשם בפרשת צו את אהרן כחטאת כאשם תורה אחת להם הכהן אשר יכפר בו לו יהיה ולמה נקט אשם וי"ל דעיקר פרשה *באשם ועוד דלו יהיה נכתב ל' יחיד שמא לא קאי רק על האשם דסליק מיניה ולא תקשי ט] (הכי גרסינן) הא דדרשינן לעיל בפרק המזבח מקדש (שם) נאמר לו יהיה בעולה עור העולה אשר הקריב לכהן לו יהיה ונאמר לו יהיה באשם מה אשם עלמותיו מותרין אף עולה עלמותיה מותרין וקאמר התם מופני והשתא למה לי בעולה לו יהיה תיפוק לי מהיקישא דאשם דשמעתין וי"ל דלא גמרינן מהיקישא אלא קרבנות הנאכלין ומ"מ קשה אי ממשמעותא דלו יהיה דאשם דרשינן עלמותיו מותרין וילפינן מיניה שאר קרבנות שלמים חטאת ותודה הלא בעולה נמי כתיב לו יהיה ול"ל גזירה שוה פרק המזבח מקדש (שם) למיגמר מאשם וי"ל דלו יהיה דעולה קאי על העור ולא להתיר עלמות דהכי כתיב קרא עור העולה לו יהיה*: הגהה . לו יהיה י] לא דריש אלא מייתורא ושם פירש בקונטרס דפשיטא ליה באשם יותר מעולה משום דאף בשרו מותר ואי משום נותר דבשריפה לא שייך נותר אלא במידי דבר אכילה כדכתיב והנותר מבשר הזבח וא"כ לא לריכנא למגמר אלא עולה דכליל והיינו כמו שפירש בשמעתין בשם רבותיו : הגה"ה . ובפרק כילד צולין (פסחים דף פג.) מוכח בהדיא כדבריו דאין נותר בעלמות ובמנחות בסוף התודה (דף פג.) פירש בקונטרס דהא דפשיטא ליה באשם יותר משאר קרבנות הנאכלין משום דכתיב באשם הוא לאחר הקטרת אימורין דמשמע הוא אשם ואין עלמותיו אשם ולריך לדקדק ל"ל תרי קראי לעלמות היקישא דהכא יא] דאתי מהוא וגזירה שוה דלו יהיה בפרק המזבח מקדש (לעיל דף פו.) ותו קשה לי דהוא דאשם דרשינן פ"ק (לעיל דף ה:) לאשם שניתק לרעייה מיהו תרי הוא כתיבי באשם בפרשת ויקרא . ברו"ך :

הדרן עלך דם חטאת

טבול יום ומחוסר כיפורים אינם חולקים בקדשים לאכול לערב . משמע הכא דמחוסרי כיפורים שהביאו כפרתן בעו עדיין טבילה והערב שמש וכן משמע פרק בכל מערבין (עירובין דף לב:) דמייתי יב] הא מתניתא האשה שיש עליה לידה או זיבה מביאה מעות ונותנת בשופר וטובלת ואוכלת בקדשים לערב וברים תמיד נשחט (פסחים דף נט.) נמי אמרינן אף מחוסר כפרה בשאר ימות השנה שטובל ואוכל יג] לערב ותימה דתנא פרק חומר בקודש (חגיגה דף כא.) ובשמעתין מייתי לה האונן והמחוסר כיפורים צריכין טבילה לקדש ובשמעתין נמי בגמ' משמע דטבילה דוקא בעי דמייתי ההיא דמחוסר כפרה דחגיגה ופריך בתר הכי טמא שרץ טמא מעליא הוא והערב שמש בעי משמע דעד השתא לא איירי כלל בהערב שמש ועוד אמרינן בפסחים בפ' האשה (דף צ:) שוחטין וזורקין על טבול יום ועל מחוסר כיפורים ואין שוחטין וזורקין על טמא שרץ ופריך מאי שנא טבול יום דחזי לאורתא טמא שרץ נמי חזי לאורתא ומשני מחוסר טבילה וחיישינן דלמא פשע אבל במחוסר כיפורים לא חיישינן כשמסר קינו לב"ד וכדרב שמעיה דאין ב"ד של כהנים מתעללין והשתא מחוסר כיפורים יד] הא בעי טבילה ניחוש דלמא פשע אלא ודאי בטמא שרץ דבעי הערב שמש איכא למיחש דלמא פשע ולא טבל עד לאורתא אבל הא דלא בעי הערב שמש למאי ניחוש ליה אפילו בלילה יכול לטבול ויאכל ועוד אמרינן בפרק שני דבילה (דף יח.) כלי שנטמא באב הטומאה אין מטבילין אותו ביום טוב בולד הטומאה מטבילין אותו בי"ט ואי בטבילה דרבנן בעי הערב שמש אם כן לא יוכל להשתמש בו טו] ביום עד הלילה ולצורך חול הוא מטביל ליה ועוד תנן במס' פרה (פ"א מ"ה) כל הטעון ביאת מים מדברי סופרים מטמא את הקדש ופוסל את התרומה ומותר בחולין ובמעשר לאחר ביאתו הותר בכולן ובהדיא אמרינן בירושלמי במס' תרומות פ' שני נפל דלי לתוך הבור נפלו כליו לתוך הבור מטריס עליהן ומטבילן תרין אמוראין חד אמר באב הטומאה וחד אמר בולד הטומאה מתיב מ"ד בולד הטומאה למ"ד באב הטומאה *אף בחול טז] והא לריך הערב שמש ומשני ברולה להשתמש בהן חולין בטהרה משמע בהדיא דלמ"ד בולד הטומאה ניחא דלא בעי הערב שמש ובירושלמי פ' שני דבילה איכא איפכא מתיב מ"ד באב הטומאה למ"ד בולד הטומאה ואותה גירסא משובשת וההיא דמס' תרומות עיקר ונראה לפרש דהא דקתני הכא במתניתין לערב לאו משום מחוסר כיפורים אלא משום טבול יום ובפ' בכל מערבין (עירובין דף לב.) דנקט לערב לאו משום הערב שמש דאי ידעה שהוקרב קינה ודאי יז] טובלת ואוכלת לאלתר אלא התם הוא מטעם חזקה שאין ב"ד של כהנים *מתעללין עד שילכו כל מעות שבשופר ומטעם זה לא תוכל לאכול כל היום וכי תימא משעה שמתחילין להקריב את התמיד של בין הערבים תהא טובלת ואוכלת הא אפשר להקריב את הקינים לאחר תמיד כיון שאין למזבח אלא דמה כדאמר ברים תמיד נשחט (פסחים דף נט.) ובהמה נמי אמרינן התם מעלה ומליקה וההיא דתמיד נשחט (שם) דמחוסר כיפורים בשאר ימות השנה שטובל ואוכל בקדשים לערב איידי דנקט התם גבי פסח שטובל ואוכל פסחו לערב דפסח אינו נאכל אלא בלילה נקט נמי בההיא לערב והא דאמרינן בפסחים

נ"ל אפילו בחול הא צריך כו' נ"ק

[נ"ל עומדין משם עד שילכו סי' וכ"ה שם]

שיטה מקובצת

א] תיבת הוא נמחק : ב] תיבת אינו נמחק : ג] בין בעלי מומין קבועין בין בעלי מומין עוברין : ד] שנאמר לכהן הזורק את דם השלמים לו יהיה כצ"ל וכן משמע בגמרא (דף קב ע"ב) ואח"כ מצאתי כך בתוס' (דף קג) [בדפוס שלנו כדף לט ע"א] [כפי הנראה דברים אלו מהגאון רב"א זצ"ל] : ה] השלמים ואת החלב מבני אהרן לו יהיה שוק הימין למנה : ו] תליא מילתא הס"ד : ז] הואיל ואין ראוין לאכילה אינן חולקין והד"א : ח] והרי בעלי מומין : ט] תיבות הכי גרסינן נמחק : י] יהיה ולהכי ממשמעות לו לא : יא] תיבות דאתי מהוא נמחק : יב] דמייתי התם מתניתין דהאשה שיש עליה : יג] ואוכל בקדשים לערב ותימה דתנן בפ' חומר בקודש האונן א) תיבות דתנא ובשמעתין מייתי לה נמחק לקדש אבל לא לתרומה ומשמע טבילה אין הערב שמש לא דכה"ג דייק התם גבי כלים הנגמרים בטהרה צריכין טבילה לקדש ובשמעתין מייתי לה כו' : יד] כיפורים נמי הא : טו] בו היום אות ב' נמחק : טז] בחול יהא צריך אות ו' נמחק : יז] ודאי היתה טובלת :

א) מראה דל"ל האונן והמחוסר כיפורים צריכים טבילה לקודש אבל לא לתרומה ומשמע וכו' טבילה לקודש ובשמעתין נמי בגמ' משמע וכו' והתיבות ובשמעתין מייתי לה נמחק .

Raba said: It is clear to me [98b] that if blood of a sin-offering is below and blood of a burnt-offering is above,[12] it requires a washing.[1] Raba asked: What if blood of a burnt-offering is below and blood of a sin-offering is above? [Does a garment need washing] because of contact,[2] and here there is contact;[3] or perhaps the reason is on account of absorption, and here it did not absorb?[4] Subsequently he solved it, that it does not require washing.

Raba said: It is clear to me that blood on his garment interposes, but if [its owner] is a slaughterer, it does not interpose.[5] Grease on a garment interposes, but if [the owner] is a grease merchant, it does not interpose. Raba asked: What if there are blood and grease on a garment? [Why do you ask?] If he is a slaughterer, you can infer [that the immersion is ineffectual] because of the grease; and if he is a grease merchant, you can infer [that it is ineffectual] because of the blood. The question arises only where he is both; [do we say that] he does not object to one, but objects to two; or perhaps he does not object to two either? The question stands over.

(12) First blood of a sin-offering fell on a garment and then blood of a burnt-offering fell upon it.—Only the former necessitates the washing of the garment.

(1) Since the blood of a sin-offering fell actually on the garment and soaked into it. (2) With the blood of a sin-offering. (3) The blood of the burnt-offering soaks into the material, and so the second blood does actually touch the garment. (4) The blood of the sin-offering, for the material is already saturated with the other blood. (5) An unclean garment must be immersed in a ritual bath (*miḳweh*) for purification; the ceremony is called immersion. Now, when immersion is performed, no foreign matter may interpose between the article to be purified and the water. Normally, blood is foreign matter, for a person objects to blood on his garment, and it interposes (rendering immersion ineffectual). A slaughterer, however, does not object to blood on his garment, and so it is not regarded as foreign matter and does not interpose.

CHAPTER XII

MISHNAH. A ṬEBUL YOM[1] AND ONE WHO LACKS ATONEMENT[2] DO NOT SHARE IN SACRIFICES FOR CONSUMPTION IN THE EVENING.[3] AN ONEN[1] MAY HANDLE [SACRED FLESH], BUT MAY NOT OFFER,[4] AND DOES NOT RECEIVE A SHARE FOR CONSUMPTION IN THE EVENING. MEN WITH BLEMISHES, WHETHER PERMANENT OR TRANSIENT, RECEIVE A SHARE AND MAY EAT [OF THE SACRIFICES], BUT MAY NOT OFFER. WHOEVER IS NOT ELIGIBLE FOR SERVICE[5] DOES NOT SHARE IN THE FLESH;[6] AND HE WHO DOES NOT SHARE IN THE FLESH DOES NOT SHARE IN THE HIDES. EVEN IF ONE WAS UNCLEAN WHEN THE BLOOD WAS SPRINKLED BUT CLEAN WHEN THE FATS WERE BURNED [ON THE ALTAR], HE DOES NOT SHARE IN THE FLESH, FOR IT IS SAID: HE AMONG THE SONS OF AARON, THAT OFFERETH THE BLOOD OF THE PEACE-OFFERINGS, AND THE FAT, SHALL HAVE THE RIGHT THIGH FOR A PORTION.[7]

(1) V. Glos. (2) V. *supra* **15b** n. a2. (3) By which time they will be clean. (4) I.e., perform the sacrificial rites, e.g., sprinkling. (5) I.e., to perform the sacrificial rites. (6) The Talmud discusses the obvious contradiction between this and the preceding statements. (7) Lev. VII, 33. Thus he receives a portion only when he can offer both the blood (i.e., perform the sprinkling) and the fat, but not otherwise. Nevertheless, this text seems irrelevant, as it refers to the thigh only. Sh.M. substitutes, *It shall belong to the priest that sprinkleth the blood of the peace-offerings* (ibid. 14).

GEMARA. [99*a*] How do we know it?—Said Resh Laḳish, Because Scripture saith, *The priest that offereth it for sin shall eat it:*[8] the priest who offers for sin[9] may eat; he who does not offer for sin, may not eat. Yet is this a general rule? surely there is the whole ward, which do not offer for sin, yet they eat?[10]—We mean he who is *eligible* to offer for sin. But lo, a minor is not eligible to offer for sin, yet he eats [thereof]?—Rather, what does '*Shall eat it*' mean? He shall receive a share therein: he who is eligible to offer for sin, receives a share; he who is not eligible to offer for
a sin, does not receive a share.[1]

But surely one who is blemished is not eligible to offer for sin, yet he receives a share?—The Divine Law included a blemished [person][in the privilege of sharing], viz., *Every male among the priests, [may eat thereof]*,[2] which includes a [priest] with a blemish.[3] Yet say that '*every male*' includes a *ṭebul yom?*—It is logical to include a blemished [priest], since he may eat. On the contrary, one should include a *ṭebul yom*, since he will be eligible in the evening?[4]—Nevertheless, he is not eligible at present. R. Joseph said:[5] Consider: what does '*shall eat it*' mean? [Surely] shall share therein. Then let the Divine Law write 'shall share therein'? why '*shall eat therein*'? That you may infer: he who is fit to eat, shares [therein]; he who is not fit to eat[6] does not share [in it].[7]

Resh Laḳish asked: Is a share to be given to a blemished [priest] who is unclean? [Do we say,] Since he is not eligible [to perform the service] and yet the Divine Law included him, it makes no difference, for what does it matter whether he is unclean or blemished? Or perhaps, he who is fit to eat [when the sacrifice is offered] receives a share, [while] he who is not fit to eat does not receive a share?—Said Rabbah, Come and hear: A High Priest can offer [a sacrifice] as an *onen*, but he may not eat nor receive a share to eat in the eve-
b ning.[1] This proves that one must be fit to eat [when the sacrifice is offered]. This proves it.[2]

R. Oshaia asked: Is a share of public sacrifices given to an unclean [priest]?[3] Do we say, the Divine Law saith, '*The priest that offereth it for sin [shall eat it]*', and this one too can offer for sin;[4] or perhaps, he who is fit to eat receives a share, he who is not fit to eat does not receive a share?[5]—Said Rabina, Come and hear: A High Priest may offer [sacrifices] as an *onen*, but he may not eat, nor receive a share to eat in the evening. This proves that he must be fit to eat. This proves it.

AN ONEN MAY HANDLE [SACRED FLESH], BUT MAY NOT OFFER etc. An *onen* may handle [sacred flesh]? Surely the following contradicts it: An *onen* and one who lacks atonement need immersion for sacred flesh?[6]—Said R. Ammi in R. Joḥanan's name: There is no difficulty: here [in the Mishnah] he had performed immersion; there, he had not performed immersion. But what even if he did perform immersion: *aninuth*[7] returns to him?[8] for Rabbah son of R. Huna said: If an *onen* performed immersion, his *aninuth* returns to him!—Rather, there is no difficulty: here he dismissed [it] from his mind;[9] in the other case he did not dismiss [it] from his mind. But inattention requires [sprinkling on] the third and the seventh [days]: for R. Justai son of R. Mathun said in R. Joḥanan's name: Inattention[10] requires sprinkling on the third and the seventh [days]![11]—There is no difficulty: In the one case he was careless about defilement of the dead;[12] in the other he was careless about
c defilement by a reptile.[1] Defilement of the dead is genuine defilement and requires sunset?[2] moreover, even *terumah* too [should require immersion]?[3]—Said R. Jeremiah: [This law holds good] when he declares, I was on my guard against anything that would defile me, but not against anything that would disqualify me.[4]

And is there half watchfulness?—Yes, and it was taught even so:

(8) Ibid. VI, 19. (9) I.e., sprinkles the blood and performs the priestly rites. (10) The priests were divided into wards, which officiated in rotation, (v. Glos. s.v. *Mishmar*). Only one of the priests sprinkled the blood of a particular sacrifice, yet the whole of the ward to which he belonged would share it.

a (1) A minor accordingly does not receive a share in his own right, but merely eats of another priest's share.—From this we learn that a *ṭebul yom* and one who lacks atonement do not receive shares. (2) Lev. VI, 22. (3) It is shewn *infra* 102*a* that he is included in respect of *sharing*, for it is *explicitly* stated elsewhere that he may eat, viz., *He* (*sc.* a blemished priest) *may eat the bread of his God, both of the most holy, and of the holy* (ibid. XXI, 22). No extension therefore would be required to shew that he may eat. (4) Even to perform the sacrificial rites. (5) In reply to your question that one should include a *ṭebul yom*. (6) When it is actually offered. (7) Hence it includes a blemished priest, who is fit to eat when it is sacrificed, but not a *ṭebul yom*, who will not be fit until the evening.

b (1) When he ceases to be an *onen*. (2) Hence an unclean blemished priest does not receive a share. (3) The sacrifices having been offered by clean priests. (4) For *public* sacrifices can be offered in uncleanness, if the whole congregation is unclean. Hence, though this priest could not sacrifice just then, yet in general he was eligible for public sacrifices. (5) He is definitely not fit to eat, for a public sacrifice brought in uncleanness may not be eaten. (6) Which they may not handle otherwise. (7) The status of *onen*. (8) Since *aninuth* lasts to the end of the first day. (9) *Sc.* the care not to become unclean. He paid no attention to this, knowing that he could not officiate in any case. (10) To ritual cleanness. (11) From the day that he ceased to be watchful, for he may have been defiled through the dead on that day. Thus mere immersion is insufficient. (12) He did not even take care to avoid that. Then he needs sprinkling on the third and the seventh days.

c (1) But took care not to be defiled by the dead. (2) Even after immersion the priest may not eat flesh of sacrifices until sunset, whereas only immersion is required above. (3) He who is defiled by a reptile may not eat *terumah* without immersion, whereas immersion is required above only for eating sacred flesh (i.e., of sacrifices, whose sanctity is higher than that of *terumah*). (4) 'Defile' means by Scriptural, 'disqualify' by Rabbinical law. The former requires sunset, but the latter requires immersion only. Also, the former disqualifies one in respect of *terumah* too, but not the latter.

משמרה כולה. לא זרקו את הדם אלא אחד זרק ע"י כולן וכולן חולקין ואוכלין: קטן. פסול לעבודה דנפקא לן מאיש מזרעך לדורותם בהכל שוחטין (חולין דף כד:) (ב) בסיפא ובקדשים אוכל דאמרינן במנחות (דף עג.) איש כאחיו איש חולק ואין קטן חולק ומדמעט ליה מחלוקה מכלל דאכיל ועוד כל זכר כתיב: יחלקנה. ומהכא נפקא לן מתני' דקתני טבול יום אינו חולק: כל זכר בכהנים יאכל לרבות בעל מום. ולקמן מוקמינן לה בפרקין (ד' קב.) דלחלוקה רבייה דאי לאכילה לא אצטריך דהא בהדיא כתיב ביה (ויקרא כא) ומן הקדשים יאכל: שכן אוכל. כדכתיב ומן הקדשים יאכל: דלאורתא חזי. לעבודה כגון הקטר חלבים: רב יוסף אמר. לרבות טבול יום לחלוקה לא מצית אמרת ז] הא אוקימנא מאי יאכלנה יחלקנה כו': ראוי לאכילה. בעל מום: כיון דלא חזי. לעבודה ח] לחיטוי ואפילו מקמי טומאה ורחמנא רבייה לחלוקה הלכך מה לי כשהוא בעל מום לחודיה מה לי כשהוא טמא ובעל מום דהא לא קרינא ביה המחטא מעיקרא ופליג השתא נמי ניפלוג: מקריב אונן. דכתיב ביה (שם כא) לאביו ולאמו לא יטמא ומן המקדש לא יצא אינו צריך לצאת מן המקדש ביום מיתת אביו ואמו ט] שעבודתו אינה מחוללת הא אחר הדיוט שלא יצא חילל: ואינו חולק לאכול י] בערב. לכשיפטר מאנינותו אלמא אע"ג דקרינן המחטא אותה לא פליג דעיקר חלוקה באכילה תלי מדאפקה רחמנא בלשון אכילה הלכך אתן דמייתי ראיה מבעל מום קודם טומאה דפליג אע"ג דאין ראוי לחיטוי ומהיא טעמא בעית לרבויי אף לאחר טומאה לאו ראיה היא דבראוי לאכילה תלוי ולא בראוי לחיטוי ובעל מום בלא טומאה ראוי לאכילה הוא: מהו שיחלקו לו. מקרבן ציבור לאכול לערב ובקרבן ציבור שהקריבוהו טהורים קא מיבעיא ליה אי פלגי מיניה להאי טמא הואיל וראוי לחיטוי דקרבן צבור דוחה טומאה: או דלמא ראוי לאכילה בעינן. אבל בהקריבוהו טמאין לא מיבעי לן שהרי אינו נאכל דקי"ל בכילד צולין (פסחים דף עו:) קרבנות ציבור באין בטומאה אבל יא] אין (ג) נאכלין: מתני' דקתני אונן נוגע בשטבל לאנינותו בו ביום. וקא טבילה לא בעיא הערב שמש דמעלה דרבנן בעלמא היא: אונן שטבל. בו ביום דאנינות בליר מחד יומא ליתיה כדכתיב ואחריתה כיום מר במ"ק (דף כא.): ה"ג אלא לא קשיא הא דאסח דעתיה כו'. ההיא דחומר בקדש דמצריך ליה טבילה: בדאסח דעתיה. משמירת גופו מפני שהוא אסור בקדשים לבו ביום: מטמא מת. מטומאת מת: מטמא שרץ. מטומאת שרץ: ועוד לתרומה נמי. ליבעי טבילה אלמה תנן התם צריכין טבילה לקדש אבל לא לתרומה: ה"ג באומר נשמרתי מדבר המטמאני ולא מדבר הפוסלני ומדבר המטמאני טומאה דאורייתא דבעיא הערב שמש: הפוסלני. לאכילת קדשים מדרבנן דלא בעי הערב שמש יב] וכן לגבי תרומה באומר [לא] נשמרתי מדבר הפוסלני בתרומה ושינויא דחיקא הוא ולא מיתוקם במסקנא הכי:

תורה אור

גמ' מנא הני מילי אמר ר"ל דאמר קרא (ויקרא ו) °הכהן המחטא אותה יאכלנה כהן המחטא א] יאכל שאינו מחטא אינו אוכל וכללא הוא והרי משמרה כולה דאין מחטאין ואוכלין ראוי לחיטוי קאמרינן הרי קטן דאינו ראוי לחיטוי ואוכל אלא מאי יאכלנה יחלקנה ראוי לחיטוי חולק שאינו ראוי לחיטוי אינו חולק הרי בעל מום דאינו ראוי לחיטוי וחולק ב בעל מום רחמנא רבייה (שם) °כל זכר בכהנים לרבות בעל מום ואימא כל זכר לרבות טבול יום מסתברא בעל מום ה"ל לרבויי שכן אוכל אדרבה טבול יום הוה ליה לרבויי דלאורתא ב] מיחזא חזי השתא מיהא הא לא חזי רב יוסף אמר מכדי מאי יאכלנה יחלקנה לכתוב רחמנא יחלקנה מאי יאכלנה ש"מ ראוי לאכילה חולק שאינו ראוי לאכילה אינו חולק בעי ר"ל בעל מום והוא טמא מהו שיחלקו לו כיון דלא חזי ורחמנא רבייה לא שנא (א) מה לי טמא מה לי בעל מום או דלמא ראוי לאכילה חולק שאינו ראוי לאכילה אינו חולק אמר רבה ת"ש *ג כהן גדול מקריב אונן ואינו אוכל ואינו חולק לאכול לערב ש"מ ד ראוי לאכילה בעינן ש"מ בעי רב אושעיא טמא בקרבנות ציבור מהו שיחלקו לו מי אמרינן ג] המחטא אמר רחמנא והאי נמי מחטא הוא או דלמא ראוי לאכילה חולק שאין ראוי לאכילה אינו חולק אמר רבינא ת"ש כהן גדול מקריב אונן ואינו אוכל ואינו חולק לאכול לערב ש"מ ה ראוי לאכילה בעינן ש"מ: אונן נוגע ואינו מקריב כו': אונן נוגע ורמינהי *אונן ומחוסר כיפורים ו צריכין טבילה לקודש א"ר אמי א"ר יוחנן לא קשיא כאן בשטבל כאן בשלא טבל וכי טבל מאי הוי הא הדרא עליה אנינות דאמר רבה בר רב הונא אונן שטבל אנינותו חוזרת עליו ד] *ל"ק הא דאסח דעתיה הא דלא אסח דעתיה היסח הדעת ה] שלישי ושביעי בעי *דא"ר יוסטאי ברבי מתון א"ר יוחנן ז היסח הדעת צריך הזאה שלישי ושביעי לא קשיא הא דאסח דעתיה מטמא מת הא דאסח דעתיה מטמא שרץ טמא מעלייא הוא הערב שמש ו] בעי ועוד אפילו תרומה נמי *א"ר ירמיה באומר נשמרתי מדבר המטמאני ולא נשמרתי מדבר הפוסלני ומי איכא נטירותא לפלגא אין והתניא *עודהו הסל על ראשו ומגריפה

בפסחים בפ' אלו דברים (דף ע.) סכין שנמצא בי"ד שוחט בה מיד בי"ג שוחט ומטביל פי' בנמצא חוץ לירושלים דלא גזרו על ספק כלים הנמצאים בירושלים כדאמר בפ"ק דפסחים (דף יט:) ובי"ד שוחט בה מיד דמסתמא הטבילוהו מאתמול כדי שיהא לו הערב שמש ולא חיישינן שמא נטמא בטומאה דרבנן דלא בעי הערב שמש ולא חש להטביל עד י"ד ועדיין לא הטביל היינו משום דכיון דהוזקק להטביל בי"ג משום טומאה דאורייתא לא חיישינן שמא נטמא אחר כך בשום טומאה ועוד כשגזרו על ספק כלים הנמצאים משום חשש טומאה דאורייתא גזרו ולא משום טומאה דרבנן ומיהו יש טומאה דרבנן דבעיא הערב שמש כדאשכחן בפסחים בסוף האשה (דף צב.) כל הפורש מן הערלה כפורש מן הקבר דבעי הזאה שלישי ושביעי וכ"ש הערב שמש והיא דרבי ישמעאל בן קמחית בפרק הוציאו לו (יומא דף מז.) שנתזה צינורא דהגמון על בגדו יג] (צנורא דערבי) ונכנסו אחיו ושימשו תחתיו אע"ג דטומאת עכו"ם דרבנן בעיא הערב שמש וכי ההיא דחומר בקודש (חגיגה דף כג.) דשפופרת שחתכה לחטאת ר' יהושע אומר יטמא ויטביל ופריך דחתכה מאן אי דחתכה חבר ל"ל טבילה ואי דחתכה עם הארץ בהא נימא רבי יהושע יטמא ויטביל משמע בהדיא דטומאת עם הארץ בעיא הערב שמש והיא דכהן יד] השורף את הפרה שהיו אחיו הכהנים סומכין ידיהן עליו כדי לטמאותו לעשות טו] *להכעיס לצדוקים שהיו אומרים במעורבי שמש היתה נעשית ובגדי אוכלי קודש מדרס לחטאת ומשמע דבעי הערב שמש: *אינו חולק בבשר שנאמר המקריב את דם השלמים ואת החלב. ר"ת ל"ג ליה משום דבגמ' (לקמן דף קב:) בדינא דר"א בר"ש דריש ליה מקרא אחרינא מדכתיב הזורק את דם השלמים והאי קרא טז] דמקריב אתא לכהן שאינו מודה בעבודה כדדרשינן בחולין בפ' הזרוע (דף קלג:) כדפירש בקונטרס בגמ' לת"ק דאבא שאול ומיהו י"ל דכולה מילתא דרשינן מקרא דהמקריב דמואת החלב דרשינן כהן שאינו מודה בעבודה יז] *והמקריב דרשינן שיהא טהור בשעת זריקה ושמא הנך תרי קראי צריכי חד לזריקה וחד לקבלה דהמקריב משמע קבלה כדדרשינן בפ"ק (לעיל יג.) והקריבו זו קבלת הדם ומיהו מדקאמר התם בחולין ובהקומץ רבה (מנחות דף יח:) יח] לרבות הקבלות וההזאות משמע דאכתי לא ידעינן קבלה: **והרי** קטן דאין ראוי לחיטוי ואוכל. וא"ת אמאי לא משני קטן רחמנא רבייה כדמשני בתר הכי גבי בעל מום לבתר דמסיק מאי יאכלנה יחלקנה וי"ל כיון דקטן ובעל מום יט] אוכל מאי אתא קרא לאשמועינן א) אי כדרוש שאינו מחטא אינו אוכל אי למעוטי טבול יום ומחוסר כיפורים הא נפקא לן בפ' הערל (יבמות דף עד:) מקרא אחרינא דהביא כפרתו אוכל בקדשים ב) הילכך נדרוש אינו חולק א"כ אי הוה משני רבייה קרא ג) תיקשי ליה אכתי מבעל מום ד) כדפריך בסמוך: כ] **ה"ג** ראוי לחיטוי חולק. ותימה הרי כה"ג אונן וטמא בקרבנות ציבור דראויין לחיטוי ואינם חולקין כדבסמוך וי"ל דעיקר קרא אצטריך לדיוק שאינו ראוי לחיטוי אינו חולק: כא] **ה"ג** הא דאסח דעתיה כו'. היסח הדעת פוסל בקדשים והא דנקט אונן משום דרגיל לאסוחי דעתיה לפי שאינו יכול לאכול: **מדבר** המטמאני. טומאה דאורייתא דבעיא הערב שמש ולא מדבר הפוסלני לאכילת קדשים מדרבנן דלא *בעיא הערב שמש [ה"ג רש"י ונראה דה"ג באומר לא נשמרתי מדבר הפוסלני לקודש אבל נשמרתי מדבר הפוסלני מתרומה] דאונן אסור לאכול קודש ולכך לא שמר עצמו מדבר הפוסלו לקודש ולא נתן לבו שיהא מותר לערב אבל לתרומה מותר אפילו [בו] ביום כדאמרינן זרות אמרתי לך ולא אנינות ולכך שמר עצמו מדבר הפוסלו לתרומה כב] וא"ת מאי ניהו אותה טומאה דקאמר כג] דטמא בה °לקודש אבל לא לתרומה דקתני מתני' דחגיגה (דף כ:) צריכין טבילה לקודש אבל לא לתרומה ומפרש ה"ר חיים כגון דאכל ככר שלישי של תרומה כד] שגופו שני לקדש אבל לא לתרומה כדאמר בפרק שני דחולין (דף לג:) ובסמוך ליכא לפרושי הכי גבי כה] (כלי) [לבי] על הסל ולא על המגריפה טמאה לפסול קודש ואינה פוסלת פירות תרומה שבסל דככר אינו פוסל כלי

א) אי אתא למעוטי שאינו מחטא אינו כו' כצ"ל נ"ק ב) נ"ל הלכך מעני אינו חולק ואכתי תיקשי ליה מבעל מום כדפריך בסמוך ומשני רבייה קרא נ"ק ג) נ"א תיפוק ד) נ"א כדפריש'

עין משפט נר מצוה

ט א מיי' פ"י מהל' מעה"ק הלכה יד:

י ב ג מיי' פ"י מהלכות מעה"ק הלכה כ:

יא ד מיי' שם הל' ח:

יב ה מיי' שם הל' כג:

יג ו מיי' פי"ב מהלכות אבות הטומאה הל' טו:

יד ז מיי' שם:

סיכר נ"ק

[שייך לדף לח ע"ב במתני' נ"ק]

חגיגה כא.

נ"א אבא נ"ק

[יומא ל: ע"ש]

נ"ל והמקריב נ"ק

מסורת הש"ס

תוספתא זבחים פי"א יומא יג: הוריות יב: ב"ק קי. [מ"ק יד:]

חגיגה כ. ע"ש

חגיגה כ. ע"ש תוספתא דטהרות פ"א

הגהות הב"ח

(א) גמ' לא שנא מה לי בעל מום ומה לי בעל מום והוא טמא או דלמא: (ב) רש"י ד"ה קטן וכו' בסופיה וכו' כל זכר כתיב כל זכר בכהנים יאכל הס"ד ואח"כ מ"ה יחלקנה וכו' חולק הס"ד ואח"כ מ"ה לרבות: (ג) ד"ה או דלמא וכו' אין נאכלין הס"ד ואח"כ מ"ה כאן כשטבל מתני' דקתני:

גליון הש"ס

תוס' ד"ה מדבר וכו' לקדש אבל לא לתרומה. עדיין יקשה למ"ד התם בין לקדש בין לתרומה:

שיטה מקובצת

א] אוכל שאינו אות י' נמחק: ב] דלאורת' מיחת חזי תיבת מיחזא נמחק: ג] אמרינן כהן המחטא: ד] עליו אלא ל"ק: ה] הדעת הזאה שלישי: ו] שמש נמי בעי: ז] אמרת דמכדי הא: ח] תיבת לחיטוי נמחק: ט] ואמו ולא יחלל שהעבודה שיעבוד אינה מחוללת הא הדיוט אחר שלא: י] לאכול לערב: יא] אינן נאכלין: יב] שמש אבל לגבי תרומה ליכא למימר דאמר לא נשמרתי מדבר הפוסלני בתרומה דהא אונן מותר הוא בתרומה כדאי' ביבמות הלכך לא אסח דעתיה ושינויא דחיקא: יג] בגדו וצנורא דערבי: יד] דכהן. פי' בפי' המשניות של ר"ש במס' פרה: טו] לעשות היכרא לצדוקים. טז] קרא דהמקריב אתא: יז] ומהמקריב דרשינן: יח] רבה מנין לרבות: יט] ובבעל מום אוכלים מאי: כ] הג"ה תיבת ה"ג נמחק: כא] הג"ה תיבת ה"ג נמחק: כב] לתרומה עכ"ה וא"ת: כג] דקאמר מיטמא בה: כד] תרומה שנעשה גופו שני: כה] גבי לבי על תיבת כלי נמחק:

ומגריפה בתוכו ואמר לבי על הסל ואין לבי על המגריפה [א]הסל טהור והמגריפה טמאה ותטמא מגריפה לסל אין כלי מטמא כלי ותטמא מה שבתוכו אמר רבא *[ב]באומר שמרתיה מדבר המטמאה ולא שמרתיה מדבר הפוסלה איגלגל מילתא ומטאי לקמיה דרבי אבא בר ממל א"ל לא שמיע להו *הא דאמר רבי *יוחנן א"ר [ג]האוכל שלישי של תרומה [א] אסור לאכול ומותר ליגע אלמא באכילה עבוד רבנן מעלה בנגיעה לא עבוד רבנן מעלה [ב] : ואינו חולק לאכול כו' : מיפלג הוא דלא פליג וכי מזמני ליה אכיל ורמינהי *[ד]אונן ([ה]ומחוסר כיפורים) טובל ואוכל את פסחו לערב אבל לא בקדשים אמר רב ירמיה מדיפתי לא קשיא כאן בפסח כאן בשאר ימות השנה בפסח °איידי דאכיל פסח [ו]אכיל נמי [ג] קדשים בשאר ימות השנה *דלא חזי לא חזי ומאי אבל לא בקדשים אבל לא בקדשים של כל השנה [ד] רב אסי אמר ל"ק [ז]כאן שמת לו מת בארבעה עשר וקברו בארבעה עשר כאן שמת לו מת בשלשה עשר וקברו בארבעה עשר [ה] יום קבורה לא *תפיס לילו מדרבנן מאן תנא [ו] *[ח]אנינות לילה מדרבנן ר"ש היא דתניא אנינות לילה מדברי תורה דברי רבי יהודה ר"ש אומר אונן אינו מדברי תורה אלא מדברי סופרים תדע שהרי אמרו *אונן טובל ואוכל את פסחו לערב אבל לא בקדשים וסבר ר"ש אנינות לילה מדרבנן והתניא ר"ש אומר [ט]אונן אינו משלח קרבנותיו מאי לאו [ז] ואפילו בפסח לא לבר מפסח *והתניא ר"ש אומר שלמים כשהוא שלם מביא ואינו מביא כשהוא אונן מנין לרבות את התודה מרבה אני את התודה שכן נאכלת בשמחה כשלמים מנין לרבות את העולה מרבה אני את העולה שכן באה בנדר ובנדבה כשלמים מנין לרבות [ח] [בכור ומעשר ופסח מרבה אני] בכור ומעשר ופסח שכן אינן באין *על חטא מנין לרבות חטאת ואשם ת"ל זבח מנין לרבות העופות והמנחות [י]והיין והעצים והלבונה ת"ל שלמים קרבנו כל קרבנות שהוא מביא כשהוא שלם [ט] מביא ואינו מביא כשהוא אונן קתני מיהא פסח *אמר רב חסדא פסח כדי נסביה רב ששת אמר *מאי פסח שלמי פסח אי הכי היינו שלמים תנא שלמים הבאין מחמת [י] פסח ותנא שלמים הבאין מחמת [יא] עצמן דאי לא תנא שלמים הבאין מחמת פסח סלקא דעתך אמינא *הואיל ומחמת פסח אתי כגופיה דפסח דמי קמ"ל רב מרי אמר לא

מגריפה. כלי ברזל הוא וראשו רחב ומבדילים בו גרוגרות הנדבקות זו בזו : לבי על הסל. לשומרו [יב] מדבר המטמא אב הטומאה שמטמא כלי וכן מטומאות דרבנן המטמאות אותה לטמא חולין ותרומה [יג] מדרבנן ולא מדבר הפוסלה לחולין ולתרומה ומיהו טמאה היא להשתמש בה קדשים : איגלגל מילתא. הא דרמינהו לעיל מתני' דאונן [יד] דאיבעי לך לשנויי עלה הנך שינויי דחיקי : של תרומה. עלמה וכ"ש שלישי של חולין שנעשו על טהרת תרומה : מותר ליגע. בתרומה דאינו נעשה גופו אלא שלישי [טו] כמו המאכל שאכל ואסור לאכול תרומה אבל מותר ליגע אלמא מעלות עבוד רבנן באכילה דליתנהו בנגיעה וגבי אונן נמי הא דתנן אונן צריך טבילה באכילה תנן אבל טוגע אין צריך לטבול : כי מזמני ליה. אם זימנו חבירו כהן לאכול עמו לערב בחלקו בקדשים אוכל : ורמינהו אונן טובל ואוכל פסחו [טז]. משנה היא בפסחים (דף צא:) ולא גרסינן בה מחוסר כיפורים דאינו צריך להמתין לערב אלא מביא כפרתו וטובל ואוכל בקדשים : טובל. כדתנן אונן צריך טבילה לקדש : ואוכל פסחו לערב. אבל לא בקדשים מפרש לה בפסחים (דף צב.) קסבר אנינות לילה דרבנן ואנינות דאורייתא חד יומא הוא כדכתיב ואחריתה כיום מר (עמוס ח) וגבי פסח לא העמידו דבריהם במקום כרת גבי קדשים העמידו דבריהם במקום עשה דאכילת *קדשים [יז] כדאמרינן : כאן בפסח. מתני' דקתני אינו חולק ואי מזמנו ליה [יח] לאכילת קדשים אוכל בלילי פסחים קאי דמגו דשרו [יט] רבנן אכילת פסחים שרו ליה נמי שאר קדשים : והא דקתני אבל לא בקדשים אשאר ימות השנה קאי . [כ] והאי אבל לא בקדשים לאו אלילי פסחים קמהדר ואע"ג דעליה קאי אלא אבל לא בקדשים של כל השנה וה"ק טובל ואוכל פסחו בערב וה"ה לכל הקדשים באותו לילה אבל לא בקדשים של שאר ימות השנה : רב אסי אמר. אידי ואידי בלילי פסחים ולא קשיא הא דפסחים שמת בי"ד וקברו בי"ד הלכך בפסח אוכל אבל לא בקדשים דאנינות לילה דיום מיתה דרבנן : ומתני' כשמת בי"ג וקברו בי"ד. דיום קבורה גופיה דרבנן ולילו לא תפיס אפילו מדרבנן : מאן תנא. דתנא להך דפסחים דאית ליה אנינות ליל [כא] יום מיתה דרבנן:מדברי תורה. לקמן יליף לה רבי יהודה בשמעתין מאנינות דאהרן ובניו : תדע שהרי אונן כו'. ואי דאורייתא פסח נמי לא ליכול : נאכלת בשמחה. יוצא בה ידי חובת שמחה [כב] דכתיב בה שמחה וזבחת שלמים ואכלת שם ושמחת (דברים כו) ותודה שלמים [כג] איקרא : שאינן באין על חטא. הלכך כשלמים דמי : ת"ל זבח. אם זבח שלמים קרבנו : והעצים. המתנדב עצים מביא קרבן עמהן : קתני מיהת פסח. דבשלמא כולהו איכא למימר מדרבנן וקרא אסמכתא בעלמא אלא פסח קשיא אדלעיל דתנא טובל ואוכל פסחו : שלמי פסח. חגיגת י"ד כשהחבורה מרובה : לא

ואי משקין דמטמו כלי גזירה משום משקה זב וזבה א"כ אפילו לתרומה נמי ואי משקין שנגעו לטבול יום דאינו תחלה אלא לקדש כדתנן (פרה פ"ח מ"ז) כל הפוסל התרומה מטמא משקין להיות תחילה חוץ מטבול יום א"כ אפילו קדש נמי לא מטמא רק לפסול כדאיתא במעילה ריש פ' חטאת העוף (דף ח.) וא"כ לא יטמאו המגריפה לפסול קדש דטמאה משמע לעשות פסול אחרי כן מדלא קאמר מגריפה פסולה *דכי [כד] אמרינן פ"ק דפסחים (דף כ.) גבי הבשר טמא למאי אי למנות ראשון ושני בחיבת הקדש תפשוט דבעי ר"ל לריד של מנחות כו' לכך נראה לפרש דמשכחת לה במעת לעת שבנדה דאמרינן פ"ק דנדה (דף ו.) לקודש אבל לא לתרומה א"נ כבגדי [כה] תרומה דמדרס לקודש והא דאמר ולא שמרתיה מדבר הפוסלה אע"פ [כו] שמטמאה לקדש כל דבר שאינו [כז] *(עושה שלישי ועושה) אחרי כן לקדש [כח] קרי פוסלה כמו שלישי של חולין : **ה"ג** ה"נ באכילה עבוד רבנן מעלה. פירש בקונטרס והא דתנן אונן צריך טבילה אאכילה תנן אבל טוגע א"צ לטבול והשתא לא קאי שינויא דרבי יוחנן ונראה דאפשר לקיימו דלעולם מתני' בשטבל והיא דחגיגה בדלא טבל אבל הא דאמר אונן שטבל [כט] דאנינותו חוזרת עליו היינו באכילה ופ"ה עיקר: **אונן** טובל ואוכל פסחו לערב אבל לא בקדשים. משנה היא בפסחים בפרק האשה (דף צא:) ול"ג מחוסר כיפורים דאונן דוקא הוא דלא אכיל בקדשים לערב משום אנינות לילה אבל מחוסר כיפורים כיון שהביא כפרתו וטבל למה לא יאכל : **אמר** רב חסדא פסח כדי נסביה. במסקנא משני [ל] כאן קודם שחטו וזרקו עליו כאן לאחר שחטו וזרקו עליו דההיא [לא] לא יביא פסחו כשמת קודם שחטו וזרקו עליו וההיא דטובל ואוכל לערב כשמת לאחר שחטו וזרקו עליו אבל הנך אמוראי לא בעו לשנויי הכי משום דקסברי אכילה לא מעכבא וכיון דלא מעכבא אמאי דחיא אכילתה אנינות לילה דרבנן טפי משאר קדשים אבל היכא דמת קודם שחטו אף על גב דאכילה לא [לב] מעכבת אי לא שרית לאוכלו לא מייתי ויש לתמוה דמשמע דשרי ר"ש לשחוט ולזרוק אחר שמת לו מת משום דאנינות לילה דרבנן והלא אנינות יום דאורייתא ול"ל אכילה מהכא מ"מ הקרבה ביום אסור [לג] בחטאת עולה ואשם דאסור להביא כשהוא אונן מדכתיב קרבנו כל שמו קרבן וכי תימא משום דאתי עשה דפסח [לד] ודחי עשה דאנינות דכשהוא שלם מביא א) א"כ היכי דייק מינה אנינות לילה מדרבנן אפילו היא דאורייתא דחיא ומתוך פי' הקונטרס משמע דסבר השתא דכולה אסמכתא בעלמא ונראה לפרש כיון דעיקר פסח לא בא אלא לאכילה כדתנן (פסחים דף עו:) פסח הבא בטומאה נאכל בטומאה שעיקרו לא בא אלא לאכילה הלכך לא חיישינן ביה לאנינות [לה] בזמן הקרבה אלא בזמן אכילה ואף על גב דאכילה ב) לא מעכבת :

א) עיין רש"ק ב) נ"א לא מעכב' מ"מ אם לא היה ראוי לאכילה גרע

עין משפט נר מצוה

טו ב מיי' פי"ג מהל' מטמא משכב ומושב הלכה ו :

טז ג מיי' פי"א מהלכות אבות הטומאה הלכה יא :

[צ"ל דכי פ"ג]

יז ד מיי' פ"ו מהלכות קרבן פסח הלכה ט :

יח ה מיי' שם הל' ד :

יט ו ז מיי' שם הל' ט :

כ ח מיי' פ"ב מהלכות ביאת מקדש הל' ט :

כא ט י מיי' שם הל' יא:

נ"א פוסל חולין ופוסל וגירסת הצ"ק עושה שכשיו כלום ועושה אחרי כן לקדש

[פסחים צא:]

מ"ק טו:

מסורת הש"ס

חגיגה כ. [ע"ש]

חולין לג.

נ"א יונתן

רש"ק מ"ז

נ"א דלא חזי לא אכיל

נ"א תפיס לילו אפילו מדרבנן

[ברכות טז: וש"נ]

גי' הצ"ק קדשים עשה כדאמרינן ואכלו אותם אשר כופר בהם וכס"ד כצ"ל

גליון הש"ס

גמ' איידי דאכיל פסח. ע' חגיגה דף כט ע"ב ובתוס' אבן שם ד"ה מדמהימן אפסח :

צ"ל על חטא כשלמים מנין כו' צ"ק

[ר"ס ס. וש"נ]

[שם]

[שם]

שיטה מקובצת

א] תרומה עצמה אסור: ב] מעלה ה"נ באכילה עבוד רבנן מעלה בנגיעה לא עבוד רבנן מעלה : ג] נמי בקדשים בשאר : ד] השנה כולה רב אסי : ה] עשר מת לו מת בארבעה עשר וקברו בי"ד יום מיתה תפיס לילו מדרבנן מת לו מת בי"ג וקברו בי"ד יום קבורה : ו] תנא דאמר אנינות : ז] לאו אפילו בפסח אות ו' נמחק : ח] לרבות בכור ומעשר ופסח מרבה אני בכור : ט] שלם הוא מביא : י] מחמת עצמן ותיבת פסח נמחק: יא] מחמת פסח ותיבות עצמן כו' עד תיבת סלקא נמחק: יב] לשומרו הס"ד ומה"ד מדבר כו': יג] תיבת מדרבנן נמחק: יד] דאונן אהדדי דאיבעי לן לשנויי : טו] שלישי כמות המאכל: טז] פסחו לערב.משנה: יז] תיבת כדאמרינן נמחק: יח] ליה אכיל באכילת קדשים : יט] דשרו ליה רבנן : כ] מתיבת והאי כו' עד תיבות וה"ק טובל בס"א הכל אינו : כא] ליל דיום מיתה : כב] שמחה . ס"א ושלמים כתיב בהו וזבחת כו' : כג] איקרי הס"ד : כד] פסולה דכי האי גוונא אמרינן : כה] בבגדי אוכלי תרומה : כו] אע"פ שמטמאה לקדש ותיבת שמטמאה לקדש נמחק : כז] שאינו מטמא כלים ועושה אחרי תיבות עושה שלישי ל"ש ונמחק : כח] לקדש נקרא פוסלה : כט] שטבל אנינותו : ל] משני רבא כאן : לא] דההיא דלא יביא : לב] לא מעכבא : לג] אסור כחטאת עולה : לד] דפסח דחמיר ודחי : לה] לאנינות לזמן הקרבה אלא לזמן אכילה ואע"ג דאכילה לא מעכבא מכל מקום הנו לאכילה כעי חס"ד :

If the basket was still on his head[5] [99b] and a shovel was in it, and he declared, 'My mind was on the basket[6] but not on the shovel', the basket is clean, but the shovel is unclean. But let the shovel defile the basket?—One utensil cannot defile another. Then let it defile its contents?[7] Said Raba: It means that he declared: 'I guarded it from anything which might defile, but not from anything which might disqualify it.'[8] The matter was eventually reported[9] to R. Abba b. Memmel. Said he to them: Have they not heard what R. Joḥanan[10] said: He who eats *terumah* of the third degree may not eat [*terumah* again], but he may touch [*terumah*]?[11] This proves that the Rabbis raised eating to a high degree[12] but did not raise touch to a high degree.[13]

AND DOES NOT RECEIVE A SHARE FOR CONSUMPTION etc.
a He merely does not receive a share,[1] but may eat if he is invited? Surely the following contradicts it: An *onen* performs immersion and eats his Passover-offering in the evening, but [may] not [partake] of [other] sacrifices?[2]—Said R. Jeremiah of Difti: There is no difficulty: the former means on Passover [itself]; the latter, during the rest of the year. On Passover, since he may eat the Passover-offering, he may also eat other sacrifices; during the rest of the year, when he is not fit [for the former],[3] he is not fit [for the latter]. And what does 'but [may] not [partake] of [other] sacrifices' mean? But [may] not [partake] of [other] sacrifices of the whole year.

R. Assi said, There is no difficulty: In the one case the man died on the fourteenth [of Nisan] and was buried on the fourteenth; in the other [*sc.* our Mishnah], the man died on the thirteenth and was buried on the fourteenth, [for] the day of burial does not embrace the night [that follows] [even] by Rabbinical law.[4]

Which Tanna holds that [the law of] *aninuth* at night is Rabbinical [only]?—R. Simeon. For it was taught: [The law of] *aninuth* at night is Scriptural: these are the words of R. Judah. R. Simeon said: [The law of] *aninuth* at night is not Scriptural but of the rulings of the Scribes.[5] The proof is that they [the Rabbis] said: An *onen* performs immersion and eats his Passover-offering in the evening, but [may] not [partake] of [other] sacrifices.[6] Now, does R. Simeon hold [that the law of] *aninuth* at night is [only] Rabbinical? Surely
b it was taught, R. Simeon said: An *onen* may not send his sacrifices.[1] Now does that mean, even on Passover?—No, except the Passover-offering. But it was taught, R. Simeon said: [The designation] '*Peace-offerings*' [shelamim] [indicates that] a man may bring [it] when he is whole [*shalem*][2] but not when he is an *onen*. How do I know to include the thanksoffering?[3] I include the thanksoffering, because it is eaten with rejoicing, like a peace-offering.[4] How do I know to include a burnt-offering? I include a burnt-offering, because it is brought as a vow or as a freewill-offering, like the peace-offering. How do I know to include a firstling, tithe, and the Passover-offering? I include firstling, tithe, and the Passover-offering because they are not brought on account of sin, like a peace-offering. How do I know to include the sin-offering and the guilt-offering? Because it says, '*sacrifice*'.[5] How do we know to include bird-[offerings], meal-offerings, wine, wood[6] and frankincense? Because it says, '*his offering be shelamim*': all offerings which he brings, he brings when he is whole [*shalem*], but does not bring [them] when he is an *onen*. Thus at all events he includes the Passover-offering?—Said R. Ḥisda: The Passover-offering is mentioned *en courant*.[7] R. Shesheth said: What does the 'Passover-offering' mean? The Passover peace-offerings.[8] If so, it is identical with peace-offerings?—He teaches about peace-offerings which are brought on account of Passover, and he teaches about peace-offerings which are brought independently. For if he did not teach about the peace-offering which is brought on account of Passover,
c I would argue: Since it comes on account of the Passover-offering,[1] it is like the Passover-offering itself. Hence he informs us [that it is not so].

(5) It is not clear to what 'still' refers. It is absent in Tosef. Ṭoh. VIII, whence it is cited in the present passage. (6) To guard it from defilement. (7) *Sc.* the food or eatables in the basket. (8) 'Defile' means to render an object unclean in the sense that it can render another object unclean (or disqualified) in turn; 'disqualify' means to render an object unfit for use on account of uncleanness, but that object cannot disqualify another object in turn; v. Pes. (Sonc. ed.) 14*a* n. a 2, for this and the rest of the passage. (9) Lit., 'the matter was rolled about and reached'. (10) *Var. lec.* Jonathan. (11) His body becomes, as it were, unclean (or disqualified) in the third degree; he may not eat *terumah* again without immersion, nevertheless his touch does not render *terumah* unfit. (12) They demanded a high standard of purity for eating. (13) And so here too, when we learnt that an *onen* needs immersion, it means for eating, but not for touching.

a (1) As a right. (2) An *onen* may not eat the flesh of sacrifices (v. Lev. X, 19*f*). By Scriptural law a man is an *onen* on the *day* of death only, but not at night; the Rabbis, however, extended these restrictions to the night too. As, however, the Passover-offering is a Scriptural obligation, they waived their prohibition in respect of the night, and he may eat thereof. He is not unclean, but requires immersion to emphasize that until evening sacred flesh was forbidden to him, whereas now it is permitted. (3) Obviously, since the Passover-offering can be eaten only on Passover. (4) V. n. 2. That, however, applies only when the person died on the same day too; but if he was merely buried on that day, but died the previous day, there is no *aninuth* at all by night. Accordingly, the passage quoted (from Pes. 91*b*) treats of Passover itself, and not of the rest of the year. (5) I.e., Rabbinical only. On Soferim (scribes) v. Ḳid. (Sonc. ed.) 17*b* n. b 7. (6) Whereas if the interdict were Scriptural, he could not partake of the Passover-offering either.

b (1) To be offered on his account. (2) The very word for peace-offering, *shelamim*, indicates that a man must be whole (*shalem*, sing. of *shelamim*).—The verse discussed is Lev. III, 6: *And if his offering for a sacrifice of peace-offerings* etc. (3) In the same limitation. (4) V. Deut. XXVII, 7: *And thou shalt sacrifice peace-offerings, and shalt eat there; and thou shalt rejoice before the Lord thy God*. This precept to rejoice is fulfilled by the eating of either peace-offerings or thanksofferings, which are called peace-offerings, v. Lev. VII, 11-12. (5) Lit., 'a slaughtering', hence including every slaughtered sacrifice. (A bird was not slaughtered but nipped (*meliḳah*), which explains the question that follows.) (6) One who donated wood brought a sacrifice along with it. (7) Firstling, tithe and the Passover-offering are generally mentioned together, and so it is mentioned here too. But actually it does not apply to the Passover-offering. (8) When a large company shared in the Paschal lamb, an additional peace-offering (called *ḥagigah*) was brought and eaten before the Passover-offering.

c (1) To remedy its inadequateness.

R. Mari said: [100a] There is no difficulty:[2] in the one case the man died on the fourteenth and was buried on the fourteenth; in the other the man died on the thirteenth and was buried on the fourteenth. If the man died on the fourteenth and was buried on the fourteenth, the day of death embraces the night [that follows] by *Scriptural* law;[3] if the man died on the thirteenth and was buried on the fourteenth, [*aninuth* even on] the *day* of burial is [only] Rabbinical,[4] and it embraces the night [that follows only] by Rabbinical law.[5] Said R. Ashi to R. Mari: If so, when it is taught, R. Simeon said to him, The proof is that they [the Rabbis] said: An *onen* performs immersion and eats his Passover-offering in the evening, but [may] not [partake] of [other] sacrifices; let him [R. Judah] answer him: I speak to you of the day of *death*, [when one is an *onen*] by Scriptural law, whereas you tell me about the day of *burial*, [when *aninuth* is only] Rabbinical? That is a difficulty.

Abaye said, There is no difficulty: In the one case he died before midday [of the fourteenth]; in the other he died after midday. [If he died] before midday, when he had [as yet] no obligation of the Passover-offering, *aninuth* falls upon him; [if he died] after midday, when he is subject to the Passover-offering, *aninuth* does not fall upon him.[6] And how do you know that we differentiate between [death] before midday and [death] after midday?—
a Because it was taught: *For her shall he defile himself:*[1] this is obligatory; if he does not wish to, we defile him by force. Now, the wife of Joseph the priest happened to die on the eve of Passover, and he did not wish to defile himself, whereupon his brother priests took a vote and defiled him by force. But the following contradicts it: [*He shall not make himself unclean for his father* . . .] *and for his sister* [*when they die*]:[2] why is this stated?[3] [For this reason:] Behold if he[4] was on his way to slaughter the Passover-offering or to circumcise his son,[5] and he learnt that a near relation of his had died,[6] you might think that he may defile himself; hence you read,[7] '*he shall not make himself unclean*'. You might think that just as he may not defile himself for his sister, so may he not defile himself for an unattended corpse:[8] therefore it states, '*and for his sister*': he may not defile himself for his sister, but he must defile himself for an unattended corpse.[9] Hence you must surely infer that one holds good [where the person died] before midday, and the other where he died after midday.[10] Whence [does this follow]? Perhaps I can argue that in truth both refer to after midday, but one agrees with R. Ishmael and the other with R. Akiba. For it was taught: '*For her shall he defile himself*': this is permissive; these are the words
b of R. Ishmael.[1] R. Akiba said: It is an obligation![2]—You cannot think so, for the first clause of that [Baraitha][3] was taught by R. Akiba. For it was taught, R. Akiba said: [*He shall not come near to a body,* [*to*] *the dead.*[4] '*Body*' refers to strangers;[5] '*dead*' refers to relations. '*For his father*' he may not defile himself, but he must defile himself for an unattended corpse.[6] '*For his mother*': [even] if he was [both] a priest and nazirite, only for his mother he may not defile himself, but he must defile himself for an unattended corpse. '*For his brother*': [even] if he was [both] a High Priest and a nazirite, only for his brother he may not defile himself, but he must defile himself for an unattended corpse. '*And for his sister*': why is this stated? If he was on his way to slaughter his Passover-offering or to circumcise his son, and he learnt that a near relation of his had died, you might think that he may defile himself; hence you read, '*he shall not make himself unclean*'. You might think that just as he may not defile himself for his sister, so he may not defile himself for an unattended corpse; therefore it states, '*and for his sister*': he may not defile himself for his sister, but he must defile himself for an unattended corpse.

(2) R. Simeon is not self-contradictory. (3) Hence he may not eat of the Passover-offering in the evening. (4) He holds that by Scriptural law *aninuth* applies only to the day of death. (5) And this Rabbinical law is waived in favour of the Passover-offering. (6) In both cases the man died on the fourteenth, and R. Simeon holds that the *aninuth* of the following night is Rabbinical. Now, the obligation to sacrifice the Passover-offering commences at midday on the fourteenth. Consequently, if death took place before midday, *aninuth* preceded the obligation, and this prevents the obligation from becoming operative; therefore he does not eat the Passover-offering in the evening. But if the man died *after* midday, this person was already under the obligation, therefore he does eat the Passover-offering in the evening.

a (1) Lev. XXI, 3. This refers to a priest, who may not defile himself for the dead, except for certain near relations, e.g., father and mother etc. '*Her*' means an unmarried sister, and, according to the Rabbis, his wife ('*his kin that is near to him*,' v. 2). (2) Num. VI, 7. This refers to a nazirite. (3) If he may not defile himself even for his parents, it is obvious that he may not defile himself for his sister. (4) *Sc.* one who was both a nazirite and a High Priest. (5) So that he could partake of the Passover-offering, which may not be eaten by a man whose son is uncircumcised. (6) Lit., 'that a dead had died unto him.' (7) Lit., 'say'. (8) Heb., *meth mizwah*, a corpse which it is a duty to bury. If any person, even a High Priest, comes across an unattended corpse, he must defile himself and attend to his burial. (9) Thus it is taught here that he must not defile himself but sacrifice the Passover-offering, whereas the first Baraitha teaches that he must defile himself. An obvious difficulty arises here: the first Baraitha refers to a priest, who *must* defile himself for his near relations, whereas the second treats of a nazirite who is also a High Priest, who may not defile himself even for his relations. Sh.M. quotes a *var. lec.*, according to which this second Baraitha, though interpreting a passage dealing with a nazirite, transfers its teaching to an ordinary priest; in which case there is a definite contradiction between the two. (10) Cf. *supra* n. 6.

b (1) Hence the *obligation* to sacrifice the Passover-offering overrides this permission, and he *may not* defile himself. (2) Yet there may be no difference between death before midday and death after midday. (3) Which forbids him to defile himself. (4) Num. VI, 6. E.V. *to a dead body*. R. Akiba however understands the Hebrew as two substantives. (5) Lit., 'distant ones'. (6) Since '*dead*' refers to relations, v. 7 which enumerates these relations is superfluous; R. Akiba explains that each relation enumerated has a particular teaching.

לא קשיא כאן שמת לו מת בי"ד וקברו בי"ד כאן שמת לו מת בי"ג וקברו בי"ד מת לו מת בי"ד וקברו בי"ד יום מיתה א] תופס לילו מדאורייתא מת לו מת בי"ג וקברו בי"ד יום קבורה מדרבנן אינו ב] תופס לילו אלא מדרבנן א"ל רב אשי לרב מרי ואלא הא דקתני אמר לו ר"ש תדע שהרי אמרו אונן טובל ואוכל את פסחו ג] אבל לא בקדשים נימא ליה ד] קאמינא לך אנא יום מיתה דאורייתא ואמרת לי את יום קבורה דרבנן קשיא אביי אמר לא קשיא *א כאן שמת קודם חצות כאן שמת לאחר חצות קודם חצות דלא איחזי לפסח חיילא עליה אנינות אחר חצות דאיחזי לפסח לא חיילא עליה אנינות ומנא תימרא דשני ה] ליה בין קודם חצות בין לאחר חצות ויקרא כא *דתניא °לה יטמא מצוה ג לא רצה מטמאין אותו על כרחו ומעשה ביוסף הכהן שמתה אשתו בערב הפסח ולא רצה ליטמא ו] ונמנו אחיו הכהנים וטימאוהו בעל כרחו במדבר ו ורמינהי °*ולאחותו מה ת"ל הרי שהלך לשחוט את פסחו ולמול את בנו ושמע שמת לו מת יכול יטמא אמרת שם °לא יטמא יכול כשם ז] שלא יטמא לאחותו כך אין מטמא למת מצוה ת"ל ולאחותו לאחותו הוא דאינו מטמא אבל מטמא ב הוא למת מצוה ח] לאו ש"מ כאן קודם חצות כאן לאחר חצות ממאי דילמא לעולם אימא לך אידי ואידי ט] אחר חצות והא רבי ישמעאל והא ר"ע דתניא *לה יטמא רשות דברי רבי ישמעאל ר"ע אומר חובה לא ס"ד דרישא דההיא ר"ע קתני לה שם דתניא *ר"ע אומר °נפש אלו הקרובים מת אלו הרחוקים לאביו אינו מטמא אבל מטמא הוא למת מצוה לאמו י] היה כהן והוא נזיר לאמו הוא דאינו מטמא אבל מטמא הוא למת מצוה לאחיו שאם היה כ"ג והוא נזיר לאחיו הוא דאינו מטמא אבל מטמא הוא למת מצוה ולאחותו מה ת"ל הרי שהלך לשחוט את פסחו ולמול את בנו ושמע שמת לו מת יכול יטמא אמרת לא יטמא יכול כשם שאין מטמא לאחותו כך אינו מטמא למת מצוה תלמוד לומר ולאחותו יא] לא יטמא אבל יטמא הוא למת מצוה

רבא

רש"י

לא קשיא. דר"ש אדר"ש הא דקתני הכא אונן לא מייתי פסח כשמת יב] וקברו בי"ד דיום מיתה דאורייתא ותפיס לילו מדאורייתא כדיליף ליה רבי יהודה לקמן והא דקתני לעיל אוכל פסחו יג] בשמת בי"ג וקברו בי"ד דיום קבורה גופיה דרבנן ולא תפיס לילו אלא מדרבנן ורומיא דתרתי מתני' קמייתא משני לה רב מרי אידי ואידי יד] יום קבורה וכאן בפסח וכאן בשאר ימות השנה כדשנין לה מעיקרא ומאי אבל לא בקדשים אבל לא בקדשים של כל השנה כולה: הכי גרס לא תפיס לילו עמו אלא מדרבנן: אמינא לך אנינות יום מיתה דאורייתא. דהא מאנינות דאהרן מייתי לה לקמן והתם יום מיתה הואי: ואת מהדרת יום קבורה. דהוא גופיה מדרבנן והתם מודינא: אביי אמר. אידי ואידי ביום מיתה ולעולם אנינות לילה לר"ש דרבנן ודקתני בברייתא פסח אינו בא באנינות כשמת קודם חצות דרחמנא דחייה מהאי קרא דדרשינן כשהוא שלם הוא מביא ולא כשהוא אונן ודקתני בפסחים טובל ואוכל פסחו אלמא מייתי ליה אונן כשמת אחר חצות דקדמה חובת שחיטת פסח לאנינות ותו לא דחיא ליה אנינות מלשלח טו] קרבנו ומיהו על כרחך ש"מ אנינות לילה דרבנן דאי מדאורייתא היא טז] האי לא הוה אכיל נהי דקדמה חובת שחיטה לאנינות אבל חובת אכילה לא קדמה ליה ואכילת פסחים לא מעכבא לאביי יז] אלא משום דאנינות לילה דרבנן והם לא העמידו דבריהם במקום כרת דדילמא ממנע ולא שחיט א"נ כיון דעל יח] כרחך שחטיה לאו אורח ארעא דנימרו ישחטו ע"מ ליפסל הילכך אוכל פסחו אבל לא שאר קדשים אפי' ליל פסח דהעמידו דבריהם במקום עשה ומתני' דדייקינן אי יט] מזמנו ליה אכיל ביום קבורה כדאמר רב אסי לעיל [דמת בי"ג וקברו בי"ד] אפילו מדרבנן לא תפיס לילו: דשני לן. (א) מדאורייתא: ורמינהי כו'. מסקנא דמילתיה הוא דבעי לאתויי מגו רומיא ושינויי: לאחותו מה ת"ל. בנזיר קאי וכיון דכתיב לאביו ולאמו כ] כ"ש לאחותו: אמרת לא יטמא. רישא דברייתא בנזיר קא איירי כדתני לה לקמן בשמעתין וה"ק סיפא הרי שהיה נזיר והוא כ"ג והולך לשחוט את פסחו או למול את בנו ושמע שמת לו מת יכול יטמא אמרת לא יטמא אי משום נזיר אי משום כ"ג אי משום פסח וכ"ש הכא דאיתנהו לכולהו: ולמול את בנו. דמילת זכריו מעכבתו מלאכול כא] פסחו: לאחותו אין מטמא. אלמא אתיא חובה דפסח ואסרה ליה להיטמא ומביא פסח *אונן וקס"ד *דתרווייהו קתני אליבא דר' עקיבא דאמר לה יטמא מצוה והילכך לא מיתוקמא הך בתרייתא אלא בשמת לאחר חצות דאתיא חובת פסח ודחיא למצות טומאה וקמייתא במת קודם חצות דאפקעתיה אנינות מפסח: וממאי. דטעמא דקמייתא משום דקדמה אנינות הוא דתוקמא לר"ש דאמר לעיל (ב) אין מביא פסח אונן במת קודם חצות וכר"ע: דילמא. כב] טעם דר"ע לאו משום קודם חצות הוא והיכא דלא איטמי במת ואפילו כג] קודם חצות בעי למעבד פסח והכא משום דאיטמי הוא ואפילו מת לאחר חצות נמי קאמר ר' עקיבא יטמא משום דקסבר לה יטמא מצוה ואין לה תשלומין הילכך מטמאינן ליה וממילא אזל ליה כרת דה"ל טמא ופסח יש לו תשלומין בשני והך דקתני לא יטמא רבי ישמעאל היא דאמר רשות הילכך כד] לא תדחייה מצות פסח בשביל רשות דטומאה ולעולם בין לרבי ישמעאל בין לר"ע אונן שלא נטמא מביא פסחו ואפילו מת קודם חצות דטעם דהכא לאו משום אנינות הוא כה]: דרישא. דההיא דנזיר ר"ע קתני לה דאומר מצוה הילכך לא מיתרצי אלא משום טעמא דקודם חצות ואחר חצות כו] היכא דמת קודם חצות קדמה לה חובת טומאה לפסח וטמא והוא הדין לאנינות דהא קדמה והיכא דמת לאחר חצות קדמה חובת פסח ומפקע לחובת טומאה והוא הדין לאנינות: נפש. בנזיר כתיב כל ימי הזירו לה' על נפש מת לא יבא וסמיך ליה לאביו ולאמו וגו' וכוליה קרא יתירא הוא דהא כתיב כז] ליה קרובים ורחוקים: נפש אלו הקרובים. לאו ממשמעותא היא דתיקשה לך אם כן למה נאמרו רחוקים דאי לא כתיב תרתי קראי הוה מוקמינן ליה ברחוקים אבל השתא כח] דאיכתיבא תרי קראי נפש קרובים משמע שהן כנפשו: לאביו. מה ת"ל אם ללמד שלא יטמא לו הרי פירש קרובים ורחוקים אלא בא לפרט כט] את מי אסר את הקרובים אבל לא מת מצוה: לאמו. מה תלמוד לומר אם לאסור הרי למדנו אם להתיר מת מצוה הרי למדנו אלא לא הוצרך לנזיר לבדו אלא ללמדך שאם היתה בו עוד קדושה אחרת כגון שהיה כהן ונזיר התרתי לך בו מת מצוה ל] ממיעוט דלאמו דרשינן לאמו לא יטמא אבל מיטמא הוא למ"מ וכן כולם: הרי שהלך לשחוט את פסחו. לא] זה שהיה כ"ג ונזיר וניתוסף בו עוד דבר אחר המעכבו מליטמא שהיה צריך לשחוט את פסחו אף זה לאחותו פטרתי לך בו אבל מיטמא הוא למת מצוה דאם איתו ענין לנזיר לבדו תנהו ענין למי שיש בו כל אלו:

רבא

תוספות

הרי שהיה [צריך] לשחוט את פסחו ולמול את בנו כו'. תימה היכי דייק מהכא דשחיטת פסח דוחה טומאת מתו שאני הכא שהוא כ"ג ונזיר וכי תימא אי לאו דבאפי נפשיה דחיא מתו לא היה צריך קרא למת מצוה דדחיא שלשתן דכיון דכ"ג ונזיר נדחים משום מת מצוה בשביל שהולך עדיין לשחוט את פסחו לא מימנע א"א לומר כן *דהא לכהן הדיוט ונזיר איצטריך קרא אף על גב דכהן הדיוט לחודיה מיטמא למתו ויש פירושים שמוגה בהם משום הך קושיא דלא איירי *הכא בנזיר אלא בהולך לשחוט פסחו לחודיה ולא יתכן כלל דהיינו ברייתא דמייתי בסמוך דמיירי בכהן לב] ונזיר ונראה דדייק משום דקתני הכא אמרת לא יטמא ובכולהו לא קתני הכי לג] משמע לא יטמא משום שחיטת פסחו ולא גרסינן ת"ל לא יטמא ועוד נראה לדקדק אי שחיטת הפסח לחודה לא דחיא טומאת קרובים ה"ל למתנייה ברישא דהולך לשחוט כו' הרי שהיה כ"ג ונזיר והולך לשחוט כו' כמו כהן הדיוט דתני ברישא דמעיקרא תני הקל יותר כי היכי דתני כהן הדיוט לד] קודם לנזיר ואח"כ כ"ג ונזיר: הא רבי ישמעאל הא ר"ע. פי' בקונטרס ואפילו מת לאחר חצות נמי קאמר ר"ע יטמא משום דקסבר לה יטמא מצוה ואין לה תשלומין הילכך מטמאינן ליה וממילא אזל ליה כרת דה"ל טמא דפסח יש לו תשלומין בשני ולא דמי לעשה דהשלמה דאתי עשה דפסח ודחי ליה כדאמר בריש תמיד נשחט (פסחים דף נט. ושם*) אע"פ שיש לה] לו תשלומין בשני: נפש אלו הקרובים מת אלו הרחוקים. בנזיר בפ' כ"ג (דף מח:) גרס איפכא ועיקר ועושה שם [חדא] דרשא מלאביו ולאמו:

אכילת

עין משפט נר מצוה

כב א מיי' פ"ו מהל' קרבן פסח הל"ט:
כג ב מיי' פ"ב מהל' אבל הל' ז:
כד ג מיי' שם פ"ג הל' ח:

[ובתוס' דברכות דחו וה בשם הר"ש מקוצי ע"ש]

גי' הש"ק הכא בכהן ונזיר כו'

[קצרו כאן דבריהם וע"ש בתוס' בפסחים ועי' רש"ק]

נ"א דברייתא דקתני לא רצה מטמאין אותו אליבא כו'

מסורת הש"ס

שמות פ"ד סוטה ג.

מגילה ג: ברכות יט: סנהדרין לה. נזיר מח:

[סוטה ג.]

[נזיר מח:]

גירסת ר"ק באנינות וקס"ד דהכך ברייתות תרוייהו קתני אליבא דר"ע כו' וכ"ה בס"י

הגהות הב"ח

(א) רש"י ד"ה דשני לן בדאורייתא: (ב) ד"ה וממאי וכו' לעיל אונן אין מביא פסח במת:

שיטה מקובצת

א] מיתה תפיס לילו: ב] אינו תפיס לילו: ג] פסחו לערב אבל: ד] אנא קאמינא לך יום: ה] דשני לן בין: ו] ליטמא לה ונמנו: ז] כשם שאינו מטמא לאחותו כך אינו מטמא למת מצוה: ח] מצוה אלא לאו: ט] ואידי לאחר חצות: י] לאמו שאם היה: יא] לאחותו הוא דאינו מטמא אבל מטמא הוא: יב] כשמת בי"ד וקברו בי"ד: יג] פסחו כשמת בי"ג: יד] ואידי ביום קבורה: טו] מלשלח פסחו ומיהו תיבת קרבנו נמחק: טז] היא לא הוה אכיל דנהי דקדמה תיבת האי נמחק: יז] לאביי. ס"א אבל אי סבירא ליה אכילת פסחים מעכבא אז מצי ר"ש למיסבר אנינות לילה דאורייתא ואפ"ה כיון דחל עליו חובת פסח קודם אנינות אכיל פסחו לערב דאי לא אכיל לא מצי להקריב ומיהו אע"ג דלא מעכב אכיל דלא העמידו כו': יח] דעל כרחי' שחיט לאו אורח ארעא דנימרו רבנן ישחטנו: יט] אי מזמני ליה: כ] ולאמו כ"ש ולאחותו ס"א ואמו ואחיו איתנהו לדרשא אחריתי ברישא דברייתא למידרש לאחיו לא יטמא אבל מטמא הוא למת מצוה ולקמן בשמעתין מייתי לה וה"ק סיפא ולאחותו מה ת"ל הרי שהיה הולך כו' כלומר אם אינו ענין לנזיר לא לאיסור אחותו ולא להתיר מת מצוה דהא נפקא לן מרישא דקרא תניהו ענין להולך לשחוט את פסחו ולמול את בנו דמילת זכריו מעכבתו מלאכול פסח הס"ד. ומה"ד אמרת לא יטמא. כי היכא דנזיר אין לו לדחות נזירות מפני טומאת קרוביו כך שוחט פסחו אין לו לדחות פסחו מפני טומאת קרוביו ואינו יכול לפרש אותה בנזיר עצמו ולומר הרי שהיה הולך נזיר זה לשחוט את פסחו דא"כ מאי רומיא דמרמינן לה אדיוסף הכהן דילמא הא דקתני אמרת לא יטמא משום נזירות היא דנזיר אין מטמא לקרובים: הס"ד ומה"ד לאחותו אינו מטמא אלמא אתיא חובה כו': כא] מלאכול פסח הס"ד ומה"ד ולאחותו אין כו' אתיא חובת פסח ואסרה כו' ומביא פסחו אונן: כב] דילמא טעמא דר"ע: כג] ואפילו מת קודם חצות בעי למעבד פסחו דאנינות לא דחיא והכא: כד] הילכך כיון דלאחר חצות הוא וחיילא עליה חובת פסח לא: כה] הוא ובקודם חצות לא מצינן מוקמי' ליה דא"כ אפי' יטמא רשות אמאי לא יטמא אם ירצה הא לא חיילא עליה חובת פסח וכ"ת משום תומרא דפסח א"כ מאי איו"א ערב פסח אפילו ששה ימים קודם פסח נמי דהא הזאה שלישי ושביעי בעי הס"ד: כו] חצות דהיכא דמת קודם חצות קדמה ליה חובת טומאה לפסח ומטמא והוא הדין: כז] תיבת ליה נמחק: כח] השתא דאיכתבו תרי: כט] לפרט דאת מי אסר: ל] מצוה ממיעוטא דלאמו דדרשינן לאמו: לא] פסחו. ס"א ולמול את בנו אם אינו ענין לנזיר תניהו ענין לכל מי שהלך לשחוט את פסחו ולמול את בנו זה כו': לב] בכהן גדול ונזיר: לג] הכי אלמא משמע: לד] כהן הדיוט ונזיר ואח"כ כ"ג ונזיר: לה] שיש לפסח תשלומין בשני תיבת לו נמחק:

א"ל

רבא אמר אידי ואידי אחר חצות ול"ק [א]כאן קודם ששחטו וזרקו עליו כאן לאחר ששחטו וזרקו עליו א"ל רב אדא בר מתנה לרבא אחר ששחטו וזרקו את דמו מה דהוה הוה א"ל רבינא *אכילת פסחים מעכבא מדרבה בר רב הונא א"ל א] ציית מאי דקאמר לך רבך מאי דרבה בר רב הונא *דתניא [ב]יום שמועה כיום קבורה למצות שבעה ושלשים [ג]ולאכילת פסחים כיום ליקוט עצמות אחד זה ואחד זה טובל ואוכל בקדשים לערב הא גופא קשיא אמרת יום שמועה כיום קבורה למצות שבעה ושלשים ולאכילת פסחים כיום ליקוט עצמות מכלל דיום קבורה אפילו לערב נמי לא אכיל והדר תני אחד זה ואחד זה טובל ואוכל בקדשים לערב אמר רב חסדא תנאי היא רבה בר רב הונא אמר ל"ק כאן ששמע שמועה על מתו סמוך לשקיעת החמה וכן שליקטו לו עצמות סמוך לשקיעת החמה וכן שמת לו מת וקברו סמוך לשקיעת החמה וכאן לאחר שקיעת החמה לאחר שקה"ח מאי דהוה הוה אלא ש"מ אכילת פסחים מעכבא רב אשי אמר מאי אחד זה ואחד זה ה"ק אחד יום שמועה ואחד יום ליקוט ג] טובל ואוכל בקדשים לערב והא דרב אשי *בדותא היא מכדי עלה קאי זה וזה מיבעי ליה אלא ש"מ בדותא היא ומאי תנאי דתניא *עד מתי מתאונן עליו כל היום רבי אומר כל זמן [ד]שלא נקבר במאי עסקינן אילימא ביום מיתה מי איכא דלית ליה ג] דיום מיתה דתפיס לילו מדרבנן ותו רבי אומר כל זמן שלא נקבר ד] הא קברו אישתרי ליה ומי איכא דלית ליה *°ואחריתה כיום מר אמר רב ששת איום קבורה קאי מתקיף (א) רב יוסף אלא הא דקתני [ה]השומע על מתו ה] *כמלקט עצמות טובל ואוכל בקדשים לערב מכלל דיום קבורה אפילו לערב נמי לא אכיל הא מני אלא תריץ ו] עד מתי מתאוננין עליו כל אותו היום ולילו רבי אומר כל זמן שלא נקבר [אבל נקבר] בלא לילו אמרוה(ב) קמיה דר' ירמיה אמר *גברא רבה כרב יוסף לימא הכי ז] לימא דרבי לקולא והתניא עד מתי מתאונן עליו כל זמן ח] שאינו נקבר אפילו מכאן ועד עשרה ימים דברי רבי וחכ"א אין מתאונן עליו אלא אותו היום בלבד אלא תריץ הכי עד מתי הוא מתאונן עליו כל אותו היום בלא לילו רבי אומר כל זמן שלא נקבר (ג) ט] ואם נקבר תופס לילו אמרוה קמיה דרבא מדקאמר רבי יום קבורה י] תופס לילו מדרבנן מכלל דיום מיתה תופס לילו מדאורייתא וסבר רבי אנינות לילה דאורייתא והתניא °הן היום אני אסור (ד) ולילה מותר ולדורות בין ביום ובין בלילה אסור דברי רבי יהודה רבי אומר *אנינות לילה אינה מדברי תורה אלא מדברי סופרים לעולם דרבנן היא

וחכמים

רבא אמר כו'. אמילתיה דר"ש קאי לשנויי דר"ש אדר"ש: אידי ואידי לאחר חצות. ואפילו מת לאחר חצות קודם ששחטו עליו אית ליה לר"ש לא יביא את פסחו דרחמנא דחייה כדדריש ואזיל שלמים קרבנו כל קרבנותיו לא יביא אלא כשהוא שלם ודקתני אונן טובל ואוכל יא] פסחו לערב כשמת לאחר ששחטו וזרקו עליו: מאי דהוה הוה. הרי נפטר ואמאי דחייא אכילתו אנינות לילה דרבנן טפי משאר קדשים בשלמא לאביי דמוקי לה בקודם ששחטו וזרקו עליו ובלאחר חצות חובת פסח חלה עליו להביא ואי לא שריא ליה לאוכלו לא מייתי הילכך לא העמידו דבריהם אלא לרבא אמאי לא העמידו הא יב] כבר שחט וזרק: ה"ג א"ל רבינא אכילת פסחים מעכבא מדרבה בר רב הונא. ולקמן מייתינן לה: א"ל רבא לרב אדא ציית מאי דאמר לך רבך. רבינא שמע לו שיפה השיבך על שאילתך ובמסכת שבועות יג] כי האי סוגיא *דרבה ורבינא ורב אדא בפ' ידיעות הטומאה (דף יח.): יום שמועה. ששמע שמת לו מת ובשמועה קרובה שתוך ל' עסקינן: כיום קבורה למצות שבעה ושלשים. מיום שמועה מתחיל למנות ז' לרחיצה ונעילת הסנדל ול' לגיהוץ: ולאכילת פסחים. האי יום שמועה כיום ליקוט עצמות דקיימא לן בפסחים בפרק האשה (דף צב.) השומע על מתו והמלקט עצמות טובל ואוכל בקדשים לערב והוינן בה מלקט עצמות הזאה שלישי וז' בעי ומשנינן אימא שליקטו יד] [לו] אחרים עצמות דאמרינן במו"ק (דף ח.) המלקט עצמות אביו ואמו הרי זה מתאבל עליהם כל היום ואשמועינן בפסחים דלערב מותר בקדשים והכא אשמועינן טו] יום שמועה לענין אכילת פסחים לא כיום קבורה הוא דאילו יום קבורה לא אכיל פסחו לערב ואפילו מת טז] באתמול בי"ג אלא כיום ליקוט עצמות הוי ומותר בכל הקדשים והא דנקט פסחים משום יז] דיום קבורה נקט ליה למימר דביום קבורה אפילו פסח נמי לא: אחד זה ואחד זה. (ה) על כרחך איום קבורה ויום ליקוט קאי וקשיא רישא לסיפא כדלקמן דאי איום שמועה ויום ליקוט לא שייך למיתני אחד זה ואחד זה דכיון דמינייהו סליק זה וזה מיבעי ליה: טובל ואוכל. בקדשים לערב וכ"ש פסחו: (ו) כיום ליקוט עצמות. משמע ולא כיום קבורה דאילו יום קבורה לא אכיל פסחו לערב: תנאי היא. דפליגי בליל יום קבורה שאינה יום מיתה דאיכא למ"ד תפיס לילו מדרבנן וסבר אכילת פסחים לא מעכבא הילכך אפילו פסח לא אכיל ולקמן מייתי להו: רבה בר רב הונא אמר כאן ששמע שמועה או שלקטו לו עצמות או שקבר מתו בי"ד סמוך לשקיעת החמה וכאן לאחר שקיעת החמה. סיפא דקתני בכולהו אוכל קדשים וכ"ש פסחו כשבא עליו אחד מאלו לפני שקיעת החמה דה"ל לערב ליל יום קבורה וליל יח] יום שמועה וליל (פסחים) *ביום ליקוט עצמות וסבר יום קבורה לא תפיס לילו אפילו מדרבנן וכ"ש יום שמועה וליקוט עצמות והא דתני רישא ולאכילת פסחים כיום ליקוט עצמות דאילו יום קבורה לא יט] אבל כשאירע לו אחד מאלו לאחר שקיעת החמה דה"ל לילה זה יום קבורה עצמו ולא ליל יום קבורה אע"ג דאף הוא מדרבנן החמירו ביום קבורה עצמו יותר מיום שמועה וליקוט לאוסרו בפסח אבל ביום ליקוט לא אסרוהו בפסח אלא בשאר קדשים הצריכוהו להמתין כ] עד ערב וה"ק לאכילת פסחים הוי יום שמועה כיום ליקוט ואוכל פסחו ואפי' שמע או ליקט אחר שקיעה דה"ל יום שמועה עצמו ויום ליקוט כא] עצמות. ואפילו הכי שרי מה שאין כן ביום קבורה עצמו דאילו מת לו מת בי"ג וקברו אותו עממים לאחר שקיעה די"ד אסור לאכול בפסח ואע"ג דחלה עליו שמחת הרגל ואינו נוהג אבילות ברגל ה"מ אבילות דמדרבנן היא וכתיב ושמחת בחגך אבל אנינות ליאסר בקדשים חלה עליו ואחד זה ואחד זה (ז) היכא דבאו עליו מבעוד יום אוכל בקדשים לערב כב] דלילו לא תפיס ומיהו ביום אסור בשאר קדשים אפי' כג] יום שמועה וליקוט עצמות בר מפסח כדמפרש טעמא ואזיל: מאי דהוה הוה. ומה לי פסח ומה לי שאר קדשים הא אמרת קדשים אסור ביום ליקוט לבו ביום כדקתני לערב ובפסח אמאי שרית ליה: אכילת פסחים מעכבת. כד] לא העמידו דבריהם במקום כרת ומיהו ביום קבורה העמידו דבריהם משום דרובא קברי ביום מיתה ואתי למישרי יום מיתה עצמו ויש מקומות שהעמידו דבריהם במקום כרת כדאמרינן בפסחים בהאשה (דף צב.): ומאי תנאי. דפליגי ביום קבורה למיתפס לילו מדרבנן דקאמר רב חסדא לעיל תנאי היא: עד מתי מתאונן. ליאסר בקדשים: כל היום. קס"ד בלא לילו: כל זמן שלא נקבר. קא ס"ד לקולא פליג ואמר כה] דכל היום לא מיתסר דמשקברו (ח) הותר מיד: אי נימא ביום מיתה. שקברו ביום שמת: מי איכא דלית ליה כו'. הא בין לר"ש בין לרבי דפליגי עליה דר' יהודה באנינות לילה דיום מיתה מודו כו] מדברי סופרים מיהא אסור: אחריתה כיום מר. *אחריתה של זונה כיום מר שמתאבל ומימר על מתו לפי שסופו למות עליה ויתאבלו כז] עליהן אלמא מרירות יום שלם הוא: איום קבורה. שמת אתמול וקברו היום והכתי לא אסיקנא מילתיה לתנאי דרב חסדא עד סיפא דתרלה ר' ירמיה: הא מני. *) בין לרבי בין לרבנן כח] מותר: כל אותו היום. של קבורה ולילו: רבי אומר כל זמן שלא נקבר. אבל קברו אישתרי ליה בלילה ומיהו ביום ליכא למימר דשרי ליה רבי דאפילו יום כט] דליקוט עצמות אסור כל היום כדאמרת טובל ואוכל לערב: והתניא כו'. אלמא רבי לחומרא אמרה וכיון דליכא לפרושי פלוגתא ל] דרבנן (ט) לאכול בעודו מוטל לפניו וע"כ בליל יום קבורה פליגי דקאמר רבי אפי' קברו לסוף י' ימים מתאונן עליו ליל יום קבורה וחכ"א אינו מתאונן עליו ביום קבורה אלא יום עצמו אבל לא לילו והיינו תנאי דרב חסדא: מדקא"ר יום קבורה. דאיהו גופיה דרבנן תפיס לילו מדרבנן מכלל דיום מיתה דאורייתא: תפיס לילו לא] דאורייתא. דקא סלקא דעתך לא עשו חכמים חיזוק לדבריהם שעיקרו מדבריהם יותר משעשתה תורה לדבריה: הן היום. הן משמע דאלו הקרבנות חלוקין משאר קרבנות שעליהן שמעת לאוכלן באנינות לילה מפני שכולנו אוננין ואין כהן לאוכלן אבל לדורות שיש כהנים לאוכלן בין ביום ובין בלילה אסור: לעולם דרבנן היא. אפילו אנינות לילה דיום מיתה ואפילו הכי יום קבורה דאיהו גופיה מדרבנן לילו נמי לרבי אסור מדרבנן:

וחכמים

*) נ"ל בין לרבי בין לרבנן לילה מותר נ"ק

אכילת פסחים מעכבא. פלוגתא היא בפרק כילד צולין (פסחים דף עח:) דרבי נתן *ורבנן ומשמע מתוך פירוש הקונטרס דסבר לה כמ"ד מעכבא לב] לגבי הא [דאפילו למ"ד לא מעכבא] דבעינן גברא ראוי לאכילה כדמוכח התם אם כן אכילה לג] היא מצוה וסברא הוא שדוחה אנינות דרבנן א"נ כיון דכתיב איש לפי אכלו למצוה דמצוה בדידיה מבאחריני סברא הוא דדחיא אנינות דרבנן ומעכבא דקאמר לאו דוקא:

סמוך לשקיעת החמה. לד] במנחה נקט סמוך נקט נמי הכא סמוך דהוה מצי למימר כאן קודם שקיעה כאן לאחר שקיעה:

ואחריתה כיום מר. פסוק הוא בתרי עשר [עמוס ח']. ושמתיה לאבל יחיד ואחריתה כיום מר ולא כמו שפירש בקונטרס:

וחכמים

גי' הנ"ך ורבנן ומדלא קמי דס"ל כמ"ד מעכבא משמע לגבי הא אפי' למ"ד לא מעכבא דהא מודה דבעינן גברא כו'

כה א מיי' פ"ו מהל' קרבן פסח הל"ט:

כו ב מיי' פ"ז מהל' אבל הל"א טוש"ע יו"ד סי' תב סעי' א:

כז ג מיי' פ"ו מהל' קרבן פסח הל"ט:

כח ד מיי' פ"ב מהל' ביאת המקדש הלכה ט ופ"ד מהל' אבל הל"ו טוש"ע יו"ד סי' שמא סעיף א:

כט ה מיי' פ"ב מהל' ביאת המקדש הל"י:

ל ו מיי' שם הל"ט [וברב אלפס ברכות פ"ב דף יא: יב. וע"ש]:

שיטה מקובצת

א] א"ל רבא ציית: ב] ליקוט עצמות טובל: ג] ליה יום מיתה תפיס לילו: ד] הא קבריה אישתרי אות ו' נמחק: ה] מתו והמלקט עצמות: ו] תריץ הכי עד מתי מתאונן: ז] הכי למימרא דרבי: ח] כל זמן שלא נקבר: ט] תיבות ואם נקבר ל"ש ונמחק: י] קבורה תפיס לילו כו' דיום מיתה תפיס: יא] ואוכל את פסחו: יב] תיבת כבר ל"ש: יג] שבועות גרסינן כי האי סוגיא דרבא ורבינא כו': יד] שליקטו לו: טו] אשמועינן דיום שמועה: טז] מת מאתמול בי"ג: יז] יום קבורה: יח] וליל יום ליקוט תיבת פסחים ואות ב' נמחק: יט] לא אכיל כשאירע: כ] להמתין לערב וה"ק תיבות עד ערב ל"ש: כא] עצמות אפילו הכי אות ו' נמחק: כב] לערב דליל לא תפיס ומיהו בו ביום אסור: כג] אפי' ביום שמועה: כד] מעכבת. דלא העמידו: כה] ואמר רבי דאפילו כל היום: כו] מודו דמדברי סופרים: כז] ויתאבלו עליו אלמא: כח] לרבנן לילה מותר: כט] יום ליקוט עצמות: ל] פלוגתא דתישרו רבנן לאכול בעודו מוטל לפניו ע"כ בליל: לא] לילו מדאורייתא. דקא ס"ד לא עשו חכמים חיזוק לדבר שעיקרו (מדבריהם): לב] מעכבא ודוחק הוא לומר דפליגי אמוראי דשמעתין בהכי ונראה לפרש דאפי' לר' נתן דאמר לא מעכב כיון דמעכבא לגבי הא דבעינן: לג] אכילה חשובה היא וסברא כו' תיבת מצוה ל"ש ונמחק: לד] (א) בחינם נקט סמוך ותיבת במנחה נמחק:

א) נ"ל בחנם נקט סמוך דהוה כו'. תיבות במנחה נקט נמי הכא נמחק.

הגהות הב"ח

(א) גמ' מתקיף לה רב יוסף: (ב) שם אמרוה [רבנן] קמיה דר' ירמיה: (ג) שם תריץ הכי וכו' רבי אומר כל זמן שלא נקבר תופס לילו עמו אמרוה רבנן קמיה דרבא אמר מדקאמר וכו' תופס לילו עמו מדרבנן מכלל דיום מיתה תופס: (ד) שם אני היום אסור ובלילה: (ה) רש"י ד"ה אחד זה וכו' ועל כרחך וכו' רישא לסיפא דאי איום וכו' מיבעי ליה כדלקמן הס"ד: (ו) ד"ה כיום ליקוט כ"ל קודם ד"ה אחד זה: (ז) ד"ה רבה וכו' ואחד זה כ"ב כן ליקוט כן שמועה: (ח) ד"ה כל זמן וכו' דמשקברו מותר מיד: (ט) ד"ה והתניא וכו' פלוגתא דרבנן בעודו כצ"ל ותיבת לאכול נמחק:

תורה אור: עמוס ח; ויקרא י

שמחות פ"ד הלכה ד' ע"ש

[פסחים עח:]

שמחות פי"ב ע"ש

[צ"ל דרבא]

[כ"ה ברותא ערוך ערך בר ד' וע' מ"ש פסחים יא. על הגליון]

מ"ק כא.

גי' הנ"ך והמלקט עצמות

[לעיל מד. כתובות מג.]

[ברכות טז: וש"נ]

[כמ"י יום]

[בכל המקומות שהביא הש"ס כך קרא ברכות טז: ומו"ק כא. סוכה כה: לא פירש רש"י כמו כאן וגם לא נמצא בשום פסוק רק בעמוס ח פ"י כדאיתא בתוס' ד"ה ואחריתה]

[100b] Raba said: Both are meant after midday, yet there is no difficulty: in the one case it was before they had slaughtered [the Passover-offering] and sprinkled [its blood] on his account;[7] in the other it was after they had slaughtered and sprinkled on his account.[8] R. Adda b. Mattenah said to Raba: after they slaughtered and sprinkled on his account, what is done is done![9]—Said Rabina to him: The *eating* of the Passover-offering is indispensable, [which follows] from Rabbah son of R. Huna's [teaching]. Said [Raba] to him: Pay heed to what your master [Rabina] has told you [R.
a Adda b. Mattenah].[1]

What was Rabbah son of R. Huna's [teaching]?—It was taught: The day when one learns [of a near relation's death] is as the day of burial in respect of the laws of seven and thirty [days' mourning];[2] in respect of eating the Passover-offering it is as the day on which the bones [of one's parents] are collected.[3] In both cases[4] he performs immersion and eats [of] sacrifices in the evening. Now this is self-contradictory: You say, the day when one learns is as the day of burial in respect of seven and thirty [days' mourning], but in respect of eating the Passover-offering it is as the day when the bones [of one's parents] are collected; whence it follows that as for the day of *burial*, one may not eat even in the evening; and then you teach, in both cases he performs immersion and eats of sacrifices in the evening?—Said R. Ḥisda: It is a controversy of Tannaim.[5] Rabbah son of R. Huna said: There is no difficulty. In the one case he learnt about his bereavement just before sunset, and similarly the bones of his dead were gathered just before sunset, and similarly his relation died and was buried just before sunset. In the other
b case [these things happened] after sunset.[1] 'After sunset'! but what has been has been![2] Hence you must surely infer from this that the eating of the Passover-offering is indispensable.[3]

R. Ashi said: What does 'both the one and the other' [mean]? It means that both on the day of hearing and on the day of gathering the bones, he performs immersion and eats of the sacrifices in the evening.[4] But this statement of R. Ashi is fiction. Consider: he [the Tanna] is discussing these;[5] then he should say, 'the one and the other.' Hence it surely follows that it is fiction.

Now, what is this controversy of Tannaim?[6]—For it was taught: For how long is he an *onen* on his account?[7] The whole day.[8] Rabbi said: As long as he is not buried.[9] What are we discussing? Shall we say, the day of death? does anyone reject the view that the day of death embraces the night following by Rabbinical law?[10] Moreover, 'Rabbi said: As long as he is not buried'; but if he was buried, he is permitted?[11] Does anyone reject [the implication of] ***And the end thereof as a bitter day?***[12]—Said R. Shesheth: [We are discussing] the day of burial. To this R. Joseph demurred: Then when it is taught, He who learns about his bereavement, and he who gathers bones, performs immersion and eats in the evening; whence it follows that as for the day of burial, he may not even eat in the evening; with
c whom will it agree?[1] Rather, explain it thus: For how long is he an *onen* on his account? The whole of that day[2] and the [following] night. Rabbi said: That is only as long as he was not buried; but if he was buried, [it is the day] without the [following] night. Now, this was reported before R. Jeremiah, whereupon he observed: That a great man like R. Joseph should say thus! Are we to assume then that Rabbi is more lenient? Surely it was taught: How long is he an *onen* on his account? As long as he is not buried, even for ten days: these are the words of Rabbi; but the Sages maintain: He observes *aninuth* on his account only on that day itself! Rather, explain it thus: How long does he observe *aninuth* on his account? The whole of that day without the [following] night. Rabbi maintained: As long as he is not buried, it embraces the [following] night.[3]

Now, it was stated before Raba: Since Rabbi maintained that the day of burial embraces the [following] night by Rabbinical law,[4] it follows that the day of *death* embraces the [following] night by Scriptural law.[5] Does then Rabbi hold that *aninuth* at night is Scriptural? Surely it was taught: *'Behold, this day* [etc].[6] I am forbidden by day yet am permitted at night;[7] but [future] generations will be forbidden both by day and by night':[8] these are the words of R. Judah. Rabbi maintained: *Aninuth* at night is not Scriptural

(7) Then they must not do so, for he has become an *onen* and Scripture disqualified him. (8) The main thing that the Baraitha teaches then is that he partakes thereof in the evening. (9) Why is he permitted to eat thereof in the evening, any more than of other sacrifices, seeing that his *aninuth* exempts him? On Abaye's explanation this difficulty does not arise. For he explains that the person died after midday, but *before* the offering was slaughtered on his behalf. Now, since the obligation to sacrifice preceded his *aninuth* and is therefore still in force, if he is forbidden to eat of it in the evening, he will refrain from sacrificing at all; therefore the Rabbis waived their prohibition. But there is nothing to fear if his relation died *after* the sacrifice was offered, and so he should still be forbidden.

a (1) His answer is correct. (2) One must observe deep mourning for seven days after the burial of a near relation, during which time he must not work, bathe, or wear his shoes. A lighter mourning is observed for thirty days after burial, such as not putting on new garments or attending festivities. If a person learns of such a relation's death within thirty days, he must observe the seven and the thirty days' mourning from the day that he learnt it. (3) A man may eat of the Passover-offering on the evening following the day when his parents' bones were collected; v. Pes. 92a. (4) This can only mean, on the day of burial or on the day that the bones are collected. It cannot mean on the day of hearing and on the day of collecting, for the reason explained anon. (5) The two clauses represent the views of different Tannaim.

b (1) He may eat of sacrifices, and all the more so of the Passover-offering, if his relation died etc. before *sunset*; hence the evening is the night *following* his *aninuth*, and he holds that in this respect the day does not embrace the night following even by Biblical law. He may *not* eat on the evening of burial where he died *after* sunset, so that it is not the evening *following* the day of burial, but the evening of burial itself (the corpse will be buried either that same evening or on the next day). (2) How can you then differentiate between the Passover-offering and other sacrifices, seeing that sacrifices may not be eaten on the day of burial? That certainly should apply to the Passover-offering too. (3) For that reason they permitted it in the evening, because neglect to eat of it entails *kareth* (v. Glos.). (4) But not on the evening after burial. (5) *Sc.* the two mentioned by R. Ashi. (6) To which R. Ḥisda alluded above. (7) To be forbidden to partake of sacrifices. (8) This is now assumed to mean without the night following. (9) V. Sem. IV, 14. (10) Surely not! (11) On the same day. (12) Amos VIII, 10. From this the Rabbis deduce (M. Ḳ. 21a) that the interdict of *aninuth* lasts the whole day of death, even after burial.

c (1) Both Rabbi and the Rabbis hold that the evening is permitted. (2) Of burial. (3) This then is the controversy alluded to by R. Ḥisda. (4) Obviously by Rabbinical law only, for *aninuth* even on the *day* of burial itself is Rabbinical only. (5) Just as *aninuth* on the day of death is Scriptural. (6) Lev. X, 19. Aaron was explaining why he had not eaten of the sin-offering offered on the day of his consecration, viz., because he had lost two sons on that day. (7) Since there were no other priests to eat thereof. (8) Thus *aninuth* on the night following is Scriptural.

but a law of the Scribes!—In truth, it is Rabbinical.[9] [101*a*] but the Sages made their law even stricter than Scripture.[10]

Our Rabbis taught: *'For so I am commanded'; 'as I commanded'; 'as*
a *the Lord hath commanded'*:[1] *'For so I am commanded'* that they should eat it during their bereavement [*aninuth*]; *'As I commanded'*, when it happened;[2] *'As the Lord commanded'*, I did not bid you [to do this] on my own authority. But the following contradicts it: [The sin-offering] was burnt on account of *aninuth*, for which reason it is said, [*And there have befallen me*] *such things as these?*[3]—Said Samuel, There is no difficulty: one agrees with R. Nehemiah, the other with R. Judah and R. Simeon. For it was taught: They burnt it because of *aninuth;* therefore it is stated, *'such things as these'*: these are the words of R. Nehemiah. R. Judah and R. Simeon maintained: It was burnt because of defilement, for if because of bereavement, they should have burnt the three.[4] Another argument: they would have been fit to eat them in the evening.[5] Another argument: surely Phinehas was with them![6] Raba said: Both agree with R. Nehemiah, yet there is no difficulty: one refers to special *ad hoc* sacrifices, and the other to regular sacrifices.[7]

Now, how does R. Nehemiah explain these texts, and how do
b the Rabbis[1] explain these texts?—R. Nehemiah explains it thus: *'Wherefore have ye not eaten* etc?'[2] 'Perhaps', said Moses to Aaron, 'its blood entered the innermost sanctuary?'[3] 'Behold, the blood of it was not brought [into the sanctuary within]', he answered. 'Perhaps it passed without its barrier?'[4] he suggested. 'It was in the sanctuary', he replied. 'And perhaps ye offered it in bereavement, and thus disqualified it?' 'Moses', replied he, 'did *they*, [my sons] offer it: *I* offered it?'[5] Thereupon he exclaimed, *'Behold, the blood of it was not brought within*, and it was *in the sanctuary*,[6] *then ye should certainly have eaten it, as I commanded*, [viz.,] that they should eat it in their bereavement.' Said he to him: *'And there have befallen me such things as these, and if I had eaten the sin-offering to-day, would it have been pleasing in the sight of the Lord?* perhaps you heard thus[7] only about the special sacrifices? For if [you would apply it] to the regular sacrifices, [you may argue] *a minori* from tithe, which is of lesser holiness,[8] [that it is not so]. For if the Torah said of tithe, which is of lesser holiness, *I have not eaten thereof in my mourning*,[9] how much the more does it apply to sacrifices, which are more holy?'[10] Forthwith, *and when Moses heard that, it was pleasing in his sight.*[11] He admitted [his error], and Moses was not ashamed [to excuse himself] by saying, 'I had not heard it', but said, 'I heard it and forgot.'

How do R. Judah and R. Simeon explain these verses?—They explain it thus: *'Wherefore have ye not eaten the sin-offering'*: perhaps the blood entered the innermost sanctuary? *'Behold, the blood of it was not brought into the sanctuary within'*, he replied. Perhaps it passed without its barrier? It was in the sanctuary, was his answer. And perhaps ye offered it in bereavement, and thus disqualified it? Moses, replied he, did they offer it, that bereavement should disqualify? *I* offered it. And perhaps ye were negligent through your grief, and it was defiled? Moses, he exclaimed, am I thus in your eyes, that I would despise Divine sacrifices? *'And there have befallen me such things as these'*, and even many more, yet would I not despise Divine sacrifices. If then, said he, *'behold, the blood of it was not brought within*, and it was *in the sanctuary, then ye should certainly have eaten it, as I commanded'*, [viz.] that they should eat it in their
c bereavement! Perhaps you heard thus only of the night,[1] he suggested; for if [you would apply it to] the day, [you may argue] *a minori* from tithe, which is of lesser holiness, [that it is not so]. For if the Torah said of tithe, which is of lesser holiness, *'I have not eaten thereof in my mourning'*, how much the more does it apply to sacrifices, which are more holy! Forthwith, *'and when Moses heard*

(9) *Sc.* the law of *aninuth* on the night after the day of death. (10) Lit., 'strengthened their words more than did Scripture.' Thus, while Scripture prescribes *aninuth* only on the *day* of death, the Rabbis decreed *aninuth* on the day of burial *and* on the night following.

a (1) Lev. X, 13. 18. 15. The first refers to the meal-offering, the second to the sin-offering, and the third to the peace-offering. These three were brought at the consecration of Aaron and his sons into the priesthood, and Moses ordered them to eat them, adding, *For so I am commanded* etc. (2) *Sc.* the death of Nadab and Abihu. He then told them that they were still to eat the sacrifice. (3) *Sc.* the death of my children. Now, Moses admitted that they had acted rightly (v. 19); evidently then he had *not* been instructed that they were to eat it in bereavement. (4) Three he-goats were sacrificed, yet only one was burnt. (5) R. Simeon holds that *aninuth* does not extend to the following evening by Scriptural law at all. And even R. Judah, who maintains that it does, admits that on that occasion it did not (*supra* 100*b*). (6) He was not an *onen*, and could have eaten it. Hence the sin-offering must have become defiled, and on that account only was it burnt. (7) Lit., 'of the hour . . . of generations'. R. Nehemiah holds that the meal-offering was to be eaten in bereavement, as it is written, *'for so I am commanded'*. Now, that meal-offering was a special sacrifice, and was permitted by a special dispensation. The sin-offering, however, was the ordinary New Moon sin-offering (this happened on New Moon). Moses erroneously thought that what he had been told about the meal-offering also applied to the sin-offering, and was therefore angry that it was burnt. Aaron, however, pointed out that he might have been told only about the *special* meal-offering, and Moses then admitted that he was right.

b (1) *Sc.* R. Judah and R. Simeon. (2) Lev. X, 17. (3) I.e., into the Hekal, in which case you rightly burnt it. (4) I.e., outside the Temple court. (5) He renders v. 19: *And Aaron spoke unto Moses: Behold, have they this day offered their sin-offering* etc.? Surely I offered it, and I, being the High Priest, was permitted to do so. (6) He thus renders v. 18. (7) *Sc.* that I should eat in spite of my bereavement. (8) Lit., 'tithe, which is light'. (9) Deut. XXVI, 14. (10) Lit., 'which is heavier'. Emended text (Sh.M.). (11) Lev. ibid. 20.

c (1) That the sacrifice is to be eaten on the night following the day of death.

*וחכמים עשו חיזוק לדבריהם יותר משל תורה *תנו רבנן °כי כן צויתי כאשר צויתי כאשר צוה ה' כי כן צויתי באנינות יאכלוה כאשר צויתי בשעת מעשה (א) אמר להן כאשר צוה ה' לא מאליי אני אומר ורמינהי מפני אנינות (א) נשרפה לכך נאמר כאלה אמר שמואל לא קשיא הא ב] ר"י הא ר"נ דתניא *מפני אנינות שרפוה לכך נאמר כאלה דברי רבי נחמיה רבי יהודה ור"ש אומרים *מפני טומאה נשרפה שאם אתה אומר מפני אנינות נשרפה היו ג] לשלשתן שישרפוה ד"א היו ראוי לאוכלן לערב ד"א והלא פינחס היה עמהן רבא אמר אידי ואידי רבי נחמיה ולא קשיא כאן בקדשי שעה כאן בקדשי דורות רבי נחמיה היכי מתריץ ד] להני קראי ורבנן היכי מתרצי להו להני קראי רבי נחמיה מתריץ להו הכי מדוע לא אכלתם ה] *אמר לו משה לאהרן שמא נכנס דמה ו] לפני ולפנים אמר לו °הן לא הובא את דמה שמא חוץ למחיצתה יצאת אמר לו בקדש היתה ודלמא באנינות אקריבתוה ופסלתוה אמר לו משה וכי הם הקריבו אני הקרבתי וא"ל הן לא הובא את דמה ובקדש היתה אבול תאכלו אותה כאשר צויתי באנינות יאכלוה אמר לו °ותקראנה אותי כאלה ואכלתי חטאת היום הייטב בעיני ה' שמא לא שמעת אלא בקדשי שעה דאי בקדשי דורות *ק"ו ממעשר הקל ומה מעשר הקל אמרה תורה °לא אכלתי באוני ממנו ז] בקדשי דורות לא כל שכן מיד °וישמע משה וייטב בעיניו הודה ולא בוש ח] משה לומר לא שמעתי אלא אמר שמעתי ושכחתי ור"י ור"ש היכי מתרצי להו ט] הכי מתרצי להו °מדוע לא אכלתם את החטאת י] (ב) במקום [הקודש] שמא נכנס דמה יא] לפני ולפנים אמר לו °הן לא הובא את דמה (אל הקדש פנימה) שמא חוץ יב] למחיצתה יצאת אמר לו יג] הן בקודש היתה ודילמא באנינות אקריבתוה ופסלתוה אמר לו משה הן הקריבוה דפסלה בהו אנינות אני הקרבתיה ודילמא אגב מרדייכו פשעתו בה ואיטמאי אמר לו משה כך אני בעיניך שאני מבזה קדשי שמים ותקראנה אותי כאלה ואפילו אלה וכאלה אין אני מבזה קדשי שמים אמר לו ואי הן לא הובא את דמה ובקודש היתה אבול תאכלו אותה בקודש כאשר צויתי באנינות יאכלוה אמר לו שמא לא שמעת אלא בלילה דאי ביום *ק"ו ממעשר הקל ומה מעשר הקל אמרה תורה °לא אכלתי באוני ממנו קודשי יד] חמור לא כל שכן מיד וישמע משה וייטב

ויקרא י · שם · שם · דברים כו · ויקרא י · שם · שם · דברים כו

רש"י

וחכמים עשו חיזוק לדבריהם יותר. ממה שעשתה תורה לדבריה: כי כן צויתי. טו] במנחות שמיני כתיב קחו את המנחה וגו': טז] באנינות. דנדב ואביהוא: כאשר צויתי. בחטאת דר"ח חדש שנשרפה כתיב הן לא הובא את דמה וגו': בשעת מעשה. כשאירע להם אנינותם אמר להם שלא ימנעו מאכילת קדשים היום ששמע מפי הגבורה שחלוק אנינות היום בקדשים משאר ימים וכשראה שנשרפה אמר להם אכול תאכלו אותה היה *להם לאוכלה כאשר צויתי אתכם בשעת מעשה: כאשר צוה ה'. באכילת חזה ושוק של יז] צבור שקרבו בו ביום נאמר: ולא מאליי אני אומר. לאוכלם באנינות: מפני אנינות נשרפה. לכך נאמר ותקראנה אותי כאלה ומצינו שהודה לו משה כדכתיב וייטב בעיניו ואם מפי הגבורה שמע היתר אנינות לבו ביום למה הודה: מפני אנינות נשרפה. שלא הותרה להם אנינות לבו ביום ולית ליה לרבי נחמיה הך דרשא דבאנינות יאכלוה אלא הכי קאמר יח] לו כי כן צויתי שאף מנחת צבור זו שלא מצינו מנחה קריבה לצבור כיוצא בה נאכלת ועל האנינות לא הוזכר למשה לדרוש ק"ו ממעשר וכשהזכירו אהרן הודה לו: מפני טומאה נשרפה. יט] שנגעה בה טומאה בחטאת של שעיר ר"ח חדש שקרבה (להם) בו ביום שהוקם המשכן בר"ח חדש ניסן והוא היה שמיני למלואים ושלשה שעירים קרבו בו ביום שעיר נחשון ושעיר ר"ח חדש ושעיר שבא לשעה כדכתיב (ויקרא ט) קחו שעיר עזים לחטאת ושל ר"ח חדש נשרפה כדאמרינן לקמן: היה להם לשלשתן. דשלשה שעירים קרבו להם כדלקמן: היה להם לאוכלם לערב. לר' יהודה אע"ג דאמר אנינות לילה דאורייתא מודה הוא דלאותו היום הותרה להן אנינות לילה וכל שכן לר"ש דאף לדורות אינו אלא מדברי סופרים ולקמן מפרש טעם דרבי נחמיה: והלא פינחס היה עמהן. שלא היה אונן ולקמן פריך שפיר קאמרי ליה: אידי ואידי רבי נחמיה. ואית ליה לרבי נחמיה דהותרה אנינות במנחה דכתיב כי כן צויתי ואפי' הכי בשעיר של ר"ח חודש הודה לדברי אהרן ולא קשיא מנחה קדשי שעה כ] היא והוראת שעה היתה בה שתאכל לאוננין אבל שעיר של ר"ח חדש קדשי דורות הן ומשה כשקלף טעה כסבור כיון ששמעתי היתר אנינות במנחה הוא הדין לחטאת ואמר לו אהרן שמא דוקא קדשי שעה שמעת והודה לו: רבי נחמיה. דאמר מפני אנינות נשרפה היכי מתרץ להני קראי דאותה פרשה מאי אמר משה ומאי אהדריה לענין אנינות ומה היה הקלפון ומה היא הודאה: ורבנן. כא] רבי יהודה ורבי שמעון היכי מתרצי להו לענין טומאה: שמא נכנס כב] דמו לפנים. מתשובתו אתה למד שכך אמר להם מתחילה מדקאמר הן לא הובא וגו' פנימה: אמר לו. אהרן למשה: משה הן הקריבו. בתמיה וכי בניי שהם הדיוטים שמשו היום והלא עלי הטלת כל העבודה כדכתיב (שם) קרב אל המזבח ועשה וגו' ואני כהן גדול אני ומקריב אונן: כאשר צויתי. במנחה: קדשי שעה. כגון מנחה שחובת שעה היתה ואינה נוהגת לדורות: מרדייכו. לעריכם: שאני מבזה קדשי שמים. להסיח דעתי מהם אפי' אלה וכאלה אבלות אירעוני אין אני מבזה כו' והיינו דכתיב כאלה ולא כתיב אלה: טומאה

תוספות

וחכמים עשו חיזוק לדבריהם יותר משל תורה. אין פירושו כג] יותר משל תורה דעלמא אלא כלומר חכמים עשו חיזוק לדבריהם יותר ממה שעשתה תורה לדבריה:

ורמינהי מפני אנינות נשרפה. לכך נאמר כאלה פי' בקונטרס שהודה לו משה כדכתיב וייטב בעיניו ואם מפי הגבורה שמע היתר אנינות לבו ביום למה הודה ומשני שמואל דההיא כרבי נחמיה דאמר מפני אנינות נשרפה ולית ליה לרבי נחמיה דרשא דבאנינות יאכלוה אלא הכי אמר להן משה כי כן צויתי שאף מנחת צבור זו שלא מליט מנחה קרבה לצבור כיוצא בה נאכלת ועל האנינות לא הוזכר לו למשה לדרוש קל וחומר ממעשר וכשהזכירו אהרן הודה לו כך פירש בקונטרס ולא מיסתבר ליה לשמואל לשנויי כדרבא אידי ואידי רבי נחמיה כאן בקדשי שעה כאן בקדשי דורות ששמע משה היתר אנינות במנחה שהיא קדשי שעה והיה סבור כמו כן בחטאת דראש חדש שהיא קדשי דורות דאין סברא שיהא משה טועה בין קדשי שעה לקדשי דורות וקשה לשמואל מאי כד] הוה משני רבי נחמיה *מקושיא דר' יהודה אם אתה אומר מפני אנינות נשרפה היה לשלשתן שישרפו ועוד משמע לקמן דיש חילוק לרבי נחמיה בין קדשי שעה לקדשי דורות דקאמר אלא לר' נחמיה מאי היום חובת היום הייטב דורות ונראה לפרש דסלקא דעתך כאשר צויתי דכתיב בשעיר דר"ח חדש לא בעי למימר כאשר צויתי במנחה תעשו את החטאת אלא כאשר אני מלוה עכשיו תאכלו באנינות והיה סבור משה דכמו שהותר כה] קדשי דורות אנינות לילה הוא הדין ביום ובין יום ללילה היה טועה לכך פריך ורמינהי מפני אנינות נשרפה ואם היתה אנינות לילה מותרת אמאי נשרפה היה להם לאכול בלילה ומשני הא רבי נחמיה *הא ר' יהודה כו]:(הג"ה) ההיא דלעיל דהותר אנינות לילה בכל הקדשים לר' יהודה והא דנשרפה שעיר החדש מפני טומאה אבל רבי נחמיה סבר אף לילה נאסר בקדשי דורות בשעיר החדש ולא הותרה אנינות אלא בקדשי שעה אבל משה אמר כאשר צויתי חטאת החדש לאכול באנינות דהיה סבור שהתיר לו בכל הקדשים* כז] (הג"ה) והא דלא משני טולה רבי נחמיה היא כאן בקדשי שעה כאן בקדשי דורות היינו משום דכאשר צויתי בחטאת כתיב דהוי בקדשי דורות ורבא סבירא ליה כאשר צויתי אמנחה קאי ולא אחטאת וה"ק כאשר צויתי במנחה מפי הגבורה כך אני מלוה מעצמי בחטאת והשתא ניחא דלשמואל לא קשיא ליה היה לשלשתן שישרפו דיש חילוק לרבי נחמיה בין קדשי שעה לקדשי דורות:

ומה מעשר הקל כו'. (ג) תימה מה למעשר שכן טעון כסף צורה דכה"ג פריך בפרק אלו הן הלוקין (מכות דף יז:) א):

דאי ביום קל וחומר ממעשר. *תימה בלילה נמי נימא קל וחומר דהא רבי יהודה אית ליה אנינות לילה דאורייתא לדורות:

א) [ועי' ביבמות עג: ד"ה דפסח גופיה וכו' כתבו ישוב נכון על זה]

מסורת הש"ס

[יבמות נו: וש"נ] · יומא כ: · [ר"ל לכם] · [לעיל מו: פסחים פב:] · [לעיל מז.] · פסחים פב. · [אבות דר"נ פרק לז] · אבות דר"נ פל"ז

ל"ל ושני, ועי' מהרש"א

ג"י הנ"ק הא ר"י וס"ק הסיא כו' כנ"ל וכן הוא בס"י

נ"ל כמו באלו הב' והאי דלא וכו' ותיבת הגה"ה נמחק נ"ק

[עיין בר"א מזרחי שהקשה קושית התוס' והניח בצ"ע ע"ש ומהתימה שלא הקשה כן בשם תוס' ועי' בספר קרבן אהרן דף ס ע"ב שהאריך בזה ליישב ג"כ קושייתם ועיין רש"ק ונ"ק]

הגהות הב"ח

(א) גמ' ורמינהו מפני אנינות שרפוה לכך: (ב) שם מדוע לא אכלתם את החטאת שמא כנ"ל ותיבות במקום [הקודש] נמחק: (ג) תוס' ד"ה ומה מעשר וכו' תימה. נ"ב והתוס' בר"פ הערל תירצו קושיא זו ע"ש בד"ה דפסח בד"ע:

שיטה מקובצת

א] תיבות אמר להן נמחק: ב] הא ר' נחמיה הא ר"י ור"ש דתניא: ג] היו להם לשלשתן שישרפוה ד"א היו להם לאוכלן לערב: ד] מתריץ להו להני: ה] אכלתם את החטאת אמר: ו] דמה לפנים אמר תיבת לפני ואות ו' נמחק: ז] ממנו קודש החמור לא כ"ש: ח] הודה ולא בוש לומר לא שמעתי אלא שמעתי ושכחתי: ט] להו להני קראי הכי: י] תיבות במקום הקודש נמחק: יא] דמה לפנים אמר לו: יב] חוץ. עיין בתוס' לעיל דף פב: יג] תיבת הן נמחק: יד] קודש החמור: טו] צויתי. במנחת שמיני: טז] וגו' באנינות. דנדב ואביהוא כתיב כאשר הד"א: יז] של שלמי צבור: יח] קאמר להו כי תיבת לו נמחק: יט] נשרפה שנגע בה: כ] שעה הוא והוראת: כא] ורבנן היינו ר"י: כב] נכנס דמה לפנים: כג] כיותר משל: כד] מאי הוי משני: כה] שהותר לדורות אנינות ותיבת קדשי נמחק: כו] יהודה הג"ה התיא: כז] הקדשים ע"כ הג"ה:

תורה אור

וייטב בעיניו לא בוש משה לומר לא שמעתי אלא שמעתי ושכחתי איבעי להו לשהוייה ולמיכלא א] באורתא טומאה באונס באתה בשלמא לרבנן היינו דכתיב היום אלא לרבי נחמיה מאי היום חובת היום בשלמא לרבי נחמיה היינו דכתיב הן היום אלא לרבנן מאי הן היום ה"ק הן הקריבו אני הקרבתי אמר מר ב] היו לשלשתן שישרפו מאי שלשתן דתניא °ואת שעיר החטאת דרש דרש משה שעיר ויקרא י (א) זו שעיר נחשון חטאת זו חטאת שמיני דרש ג] שעיר של ראש חודש יכול שלשתן נשרפו ת"ל והנה שורף אחד נשרף ולא שלשתן נשרפו דרש דרש שתי דרישות למה אמר להו מפני מה חטאת זו נשרפה ואלו מונחות ואיני יודע איזהו כשהוא אומר °ואותה נתן לכם לשאת את עון העדה ד] הוי שם אומר זה שעיר של ראש חודש שפיר קאמרי ליה רבי נחמיה לטעמיה דאמר קדשי שעה לא פסלה בהו אנינות אמר מר היה ה] לו לאכלה לערב שפיר קאמרי ליה *קסבר אנינות לילה דאורייתא דבר אחר והלא פינחס היה עמהן שפיר קאמרי ליה סבר לה ו] כרבי אלעזר דאר"א א"ר חנינא לא נתכהן פינחס עד שהרגו לזמרי דכתיב °והיתה לו ולזרעו במדבר כה אחריו ברית כהונת עולם רב אשי אמר עד ששם שלום בין השבטים שנאמר °וישמע יהושע כב פינחס הכהן ונשיאי העדה וראשי אלפי ישראל וגו' ואידך נמי והכתיב והיתה לו ולזרעו אחריו כי כתיב ההוא בברכה הוא דכתיב ואידך נמי הא כתיב וישמע פינחס הכהן ההוא ליחס זרעו אחריו ז] אמר רב °משה רבינו כהן גדול ח] וחולק בקדשי שמים היה שנאמר °מאיל ויקרא ח המלואים למשה היה למנה מיתיבי והלא פינחס היה עמהן ואם איתא לימא והלא משה רבינו היה עמהן דילמא שאני משה דטריד בשכינה *דאמר מר משה בהשכמה עלה ובהשכמה ירד מיתיבי °לחם אלהיו מקדשי הקדשים ומן הקדשים יאכל אם נאמרו קדשי קדשים שם כא למה ט] נאמר קדשים קלים ואם נאמרו קדשים קלים למה י] נאמר קדשי קדשים אילו לא נאמר קדשים קלים הייתי אומר קדשי קדשים הוא דאוכל שהרי הותרו לזר ולהן קדשים קלים לא יאכל ואילו לא נאמרו קדשי קדשים הייתי אומר בקדשים קלים יהא אוכל שהן קלים בקדשי קדשים לא יהא אוכל לכך נאמרו קדשי קדשים·ולכך נאמר קדשים קלים קתני מיהא שהרי הותרו לזר ולהן יא] לאו משה אמר רב ששת לא בבמה יב] לזר וכדברי *האומר יש מנחה בבמה מיתיבי מרים מי הסגירה א"ת משה הסגירה משה זר הוא ואין

טומאה באונס. שרצו להשהותה עד הלילה ולאוכלן כולן יחד ונטמאת באונס: בשלמא לרבנן. דאמרי אחד קדשי שעה ואחד קדשי דורות לילה הותר להן ולא יום יג] עד הלילה היו רוצין להשהותה היינו דכתיב ואכלתי חטאת היום אני אונן ואוכל היום חטאת שמא לא שמעת אלא בלילה: אלא לרבי נחמיה. דאמר מה שהותר להם הותר אפי' ביום כגון קדשי שעה ומה שנאסר נאסר אף בלילה: מאי ואכלתי חטאת היום. בלילה נמי קדשי דורות הוו אסירי דהאמר מפני אנינות נשרפה ולא המתינו עד הערב ויאכלוה אלמא קסבר אנינות לילה דאורייתא והכי אמר לקמן: מאי היום חובת היום. כלומר קדשי דורות שהן חובת היום של ר"ח אתה אומר לי לאכול אונן והיינו חטאת היום חטאת הקבוע ליום: בשלמא לרבי נחמיה היינו דכתיב הן היום הקריבו. כלומר קרבן זה לחובת היום קרב וקדשי דורות הוא יד] ואני אוכלן אונן בתמיה שמא לא שמעת אלא בשל שעה: אלא לרבנן. דאמרי שמא לא שמעת אלא בלילה קאמר ליה מאי (ב) טו] *היא דקאמר ליה הן היום הקריבו: הכי קאמר ליה. אמרת טז] דילמא באנינות אקריבתיה וכי הן בניי יז] הדיוטות היום הקריבו שום קרבן אני הקרבתי את הכל: שעיר נחשון. שאותו היום היה ראשון להקרבת נשיאים דתניא בסדר עולם בכ"ג באדר התחילו המלואים וכל שבעת הימים היה משה מעמיד המשכן ומקריב את קרבנותיו בכל בקר ובקר יח] ופרקו ובשמיני העמידו ולא פירקו והוא ראש חדש ניסן ואותו היום נטל עשר עטרות וכו': חטאת שמיני. שבא חובה לשעה דכתיב קחו שעיר עזים לחטאת: שתי דרישות. דרישה יט] לנשרפות דרישה למונחות למה מונחות להמתין לערב ולא נאכלו ביום: ואיני יודע איזו היא. תנא דמתניתא הוא דקמהדר למילתיה: הוי אומר זה שעיר ר"ח. שמכפר על טומאת מקדש וקדשיו כדאמר בשבועות (דף ב.): שפיר קא"ל. לעיל קאי דאמרן לר' נחמיה היה להן לשלשתן שישרפו: קסבר (ג) לילה דאורייתא. ומהכא כ"ל דמותקמא אותי כאלה יליף מפני אנינות נשרפה ומדלא אכלוה לערב נפקא ליה אנינות לילה דאורייתא ור' יהודה לדורות אית ליה אנינות לילה דאורייתא אבל לאותו היום הותרה דדריש היום אני היום אסור ולילה מותר כו': ברית כהונת עולם. תחת אשר קנא אלמא מכאן ואילך הוא: ששם שלום בין השבטים. בימי יהושע כשבט בני גד ובני ראובן שבנו את המזבח בעבר הירדן ובקשו שאר שבטים לעלות עליהם לצבא ושלחו את פנחס לדבר עמהם: וישמע פינחס הכהן. בכל מקום אתה מוצא פינחס בן אלעזר בן אהרן הכהן אין כהונה כתובה אלא באלעזר וכאן כתובה *בפנחס: ההוא. קרא התם בברכה כתיב בשרו שלא תפסוק כהונה מזרעו אבל עדיין לא נתכהן: לייחס זרעו אחריו כ]. [מימי משה נתכהן וכששם שלום נתייחס ליקרא כהן ולייחס זרעו במעלות כהונה להיותם כהנים גדולים שלא הי' כהנים גדולים אלא מפנחס]: למשה היה למנה. לשון חלוקה כא] בכהנים: טריד בשכינה. ולא היה עסוק באכילת קדשים שהדבור טורדו להיות תמיד בהר מבקר ועד ערב: בהשכמה עלה. להר בימי מתן תורה כשהיה עולה ויורד לקדש את העם ולהשיב את דברי העם אל ה' בפרק רבי עקיבא במסכת שבת (דף פו.) אלמא טרוד היה: לחם אלהיו וגו'. בבעל מום כתיב להתירו בקדשים: שהרי הותרו לזר ולהן. קא ס"ד כב] הותר לזר במשה קאמר שאכל חזה ושוק של איל המילואים וקדשי קדשים היה כדכתיב ביה בשלו את הבשר פתח אהל מועד ושם תאכלו אותו ולא נאכל אלא ליום ולילה דכתיב (ד) ואם יותר וגו': בקדשים קלים. בחזה ושוק של שלמי יחיד לא יחלוק עם אחיו שלא מצינו זר ופסול חולק בהן: לאו משה. דהא כג] לאו זר אוכל בקדשים אלא במילואים: לא בבמה קאמר. דהותרו לזר וכדברי האומר בפרק אחרון (דף קיג.) יש מנחה בבמה קטנה ומנחה קדשי קדשים היא ואוכלין שיריה כד] זרים שהיו עובדים בבמה קטנה שהזר עובד שם כדאמר בפרק בתרא אבל קדשים קלים לא יאכל בחזה ושוק של כהנים שהרי לא הותרו לזר דלא אשכחן זר חולק בתורם משלמי יחיד דאילו במקדש נאכל לכהנים ובבמה קטנה לא היה חזה ושוק כה] כדתניא בפרק בתרא חזה ושוק בבמה גדולה ואין חזה ושוק בבמה קטנה והאי דבעי למינקט כדברי האומר יש מנחה בבמה דאי אין מנחה בבמה כו] אין לך עוד קדשי קדשים נאכלין בבמה דאילו חטאת ואשם בבמה לא קרבי דתנן מגילה (דף ט:) כל שאין נידר ונידב אין קרב בבמה אין לך נדר ונדבה בקדשי קדשים אלא עולה ומנחה: ואין

בשלמא לרבי נחמיה היינו דכתיב הן היום הקריבו. כלומר קרבן זה לחובת היום קרב וקדשי דורות הוא ואכלתי חטאת היום בתמיה *לא שמעת אלא בשל שעה אלא לרבנן דאמרי שמא לא שמעת אלא בלילה קאמר ליה מאי (ה) היא דקאמר ליה הן היום הקריבו הכי קאמר ליה אמרת לי דילמא באנינות אקריבתיה וכי הן בניי הדיוטות היום הקריבו שום קרבן אני הקרבתי אותם זו היא גירסת הקונט' ופירושו והשתא לפי זה למ"ד מפני אנינות נשרפה הוי הן היום בניחותא ולמ"ד מפני טומאה הוי בתמיה וקשה דלעיל בריש פ"ב (דף טז.) משמע איפכא ונראה דגרסינן נמי בהך פירקא בתרייתא בשלמא לרבנן היינו דכתיב הן היום כמו בקמייתא ובתרווייהו פריך לר' נחמיה מדכתיב היום כדמפרש בקונט' בקמייתא ומשני הכי קאמר וכי הן כז] הקריבו אני הקרבתי כל הקרבנות שקרבו היום: ההוא בברכה הוא דכתיב. שברכו הקב"ה שיהיה כהן ומיד היה יכול להיות כהן אלא שתחילה צריך להלבישו ולמושחו ולחנכו בחביתין כדין הדיוטות המתחנכים בחביתין כדאמרינן בסוף התכלת (מנחות דף נא:) אבל שמא לא נתרצו לו כל ישראל באותה שעה מפני שהרג נשיא שבט עד ששם שלום בין השבטים בימי יהושע ואז נתרצו לו והלבישוהו *[ומשחוהו] ותנכוהו בחביתין: *ואידך נמי הכתיב וישמע פנחס הכהן ההוא לייחס זרעו אחריו. פי' מימי משה נתכהן וכששם שלום נתייחס ליקרא כהן ולייחס זרעו במעלות כהונה להיותם כהנים גדולים שכן מצינו בדברי הימים (א' ה') שלא היו כהנים גדולים אלא מפנחס ובספרי מפיק ליה מאת בריתי שלום שעמדו ממנו שמונים כהנים בבית ראשון ושלש מאות בבית שני וכולם נמנו בספרי*: אהרן

נ"ל שמא לא

הגהות הב"ח
(א) גמ' שעיר זה שעיר של נחשון החטאת זו חטאת יום שמיני דרש משה זה שעיר של ר"ח: (ב) רש"י ד"ה אלא וכו' מאי האי דקאמר: (ג) ד"ה קסבר אנינות לילה: (ד) ד"ה שהרי וכו' דכתיב והנותר וגו': (ה) תוס' ד"ה בשלמא וכו' מאי האי דקאמר:

כ"ה בס"י

[ע' זה באורך במס' יומא דף ע ע"א בתוס' ד"ה ולא שמשו]

[ע' תוס' יומא ע. ד"ה ולא וכו' שהעתיקו בשם ספרי נוסחא אחרת]

שיטה מקובצת
א] ולמיכלא לאורתא טומאה: ב] היה להם לשלשתן: ג] דרש זה שעיר: ד] העדה איזה היא שנשא עון העדה הוי: ה] היה להם לאכלה: ו] סבר לה כהא דא"ר אילעי דא"ר אילעי אמר רבי חנינא: ז] אחריו הוא דאתא אמר: ח] גדול היה וחולק בקדשי שמים שנאמר: ט] למה נאמרו קדשים: י] למה נאמרו קדשי כו' לא נאמרו: יא] ולהן מאי זר לאו: יב] תיבת לזר נמחק: יג] יום ועד הלילה: יד] הוא ואכלתי חטאת היום בתמיה כלומר לא שמעת וכו' א) ותיבת שמא נמחק: טו] מאי האי דקאמר: טז] אמרת לי דילמא: יז] בניי שהם הדיוטות: יח] ובבקר ומפרקו ובשמיני: יט] דרישה לנשרפת למה נשרפה דרישה: כ] מתיבת מימי כו' עד

נ"ל הן דקאמר נ"ק

לעיל ק.

גליון הש"ס
גמ' משה רבינו כס"א. עי' ע"ז דף לד ע"א תוד"ה כתס:

שבת פו.

לקמן קיג.

בפנחס והטוא קרא סתם כתיבא סס"ד ואח"כ מ"ס בברכה כתיב ברט ס' כצ"ל נ"ק

that, [101*b*] *it was pleasing in his sight'.* He admitted his error, and Moses was not ashamed [to excuse himself] by saying, 'I had not heard it', but, 'I heard it and forgot.' But they should have kept it and eaten it in the evening?—It was accidentally defiled.[2]

As for the Rabbis, it is well: for that reason it is written, '[*and if I had eaten the sin-offering*] *this* day.'[3] But on R. Nehemiah's explanation, why [did he say] '*this* day'?—[He meant that it was] a statutory obligation of the day.[4]

As for R. Nehemiah, it is well: for that reason it is written, '*Behold, this day* [*have they offered* etc.]'[5] But according to the Rabbis, what is [the significance of] '*Behold, this day*'?[6]—This is what he meant: '*Behold, have* they *offered?*' It was *I* who offered.[7]

The Master said: 'Then the three should have been burnt.' What were the three?—For it was taught: '*And Moses diligently inquired for the goat of the sin-offering*':[8] '*Goat*' alludes to Nahshon's
a goat;[1] '*sin-offering*' refers to the sin-offering of the eighth day;[2] '[*Moses*] *inquired*' refers to the goat of New Moon.[3] You might think that the three of them were burnt; therefore it says, '*and, behold,* it was *burnt*': *one* was burnt, but three were not burnt. '*Diligently inquired*': why these two enquiries?[4] He said to them: 'Why is this sin-offering burnt, and these others lying?'[5] Now, I do not know which one [was burnt]. But when it says, '*And He hath given it to you to bear the iniquity of the congregation*',[6] it follows that it was the goat of New Moon.[7]

They said well to him?[8]—R. Nehemiah is consistent with his view, for he maintained [that] bereavement did not disqualify *ad hoc* sacrifices.[9]

The Master said: 'Then they should have eaten it in the evening.' They said well to him?—He holds that [the law of] *aninuth* at night is Scriptural.[10]

'Another argument: surely Phinehas was with them.' They said well to him?—He agrees with R. Eleazar. For R. Eleazar said in R. Ḥanina's name: Phinehas was not elevated to the priesthood until he slew Zimri, for it is written, *And it shall be unto him, and unto his seed after him, the covenant of an everlasting priesthood.*[11] R. Ashi said: Until he made peace between the tribes, for it is said, *And when Phinehas the priest, and the princes of the congregation, even the heads of the thousands of Israel that were with him, heard* etc.[12] And as to the others too, surely it is written, '*And it shall be unto him, and unto*
b *his seed after him*' [etc.]?—That is written as a blessing.[1] And as to the other too, surely it is written, '*And when Phinehas the priest heard*'?—That was to invest his descendants with his rank.[2]

Rab said: Our teacher Moses was a High Priest, and received a share of the holy sacrifices, as it is said, *It was Moses' portion of the ram of consecration.*[3] An objection is raised: 'But was not Phinehas with them?' Now if this is correct, let them argue, But was not our teacher Moses with them? Perhaps Moses was different, because he was engaged by the *Shechinah*,[4] for a master said: Moses ascended early in the morning and descended early in the morning.[5]

An objection is raised: *He may eat the bread of his God, both of the most holy, and of the holy:*[6] if sacrifices of higher sanctity are stated, why are lesser sacrifices stated; and if lesser sacrifices are stated, why are sacrifices of higher sanctity stated? If lesser sacrifices were not stated, I would say, He may eat only of higher sacrifices, because they were permitted to a *zar*[7] and to them,[8] but he may not eat of lesser sacrifices. And if higher sacrifices were not stated I would say: He may eat only of lesser sacrifices, since they are lesser,[9] but not of higher sacrifices. For that reason both higher sacrifices and lesser sacrifices are stated. At all events he [the Tanna] teaches, Because they were permitted to a *zar* and to them: surely that
c means [to] Moses?[1]—Said R. Shesheth: No; it refers to the High Places [*bamah*], this agreeing with the view that a meal-offering could be offered at the High Places.[2]

An objection is raised: Who shut Miriam up?[3] If you say, Moses

(2) But not through negligence. (3) He stressed that it was only during the day that he could not eat it, but he had intended to eat it that night. (4) Could I eat the sin-offering, which is a statutory obligation for this day, and not a special sacrifice? (as *supra a.*) (5) Meaning that it was a statutory and regular offering for that day, and therefore might not be eaten in mourning. (6) It is apparently quite irrelevant. (7) As *supra a.* (8) Lev. X, 16.

a (1) It was the first of Nisan, and the first day of the consecration ceremonies of the Tabernacle, when Nahshon sacrificed a goat on behalf of the tribe of Judah (Num. VII, 12-17; *Seder 'Olam*). (2) Of Aaron's consecration rites. (3) Thus this verse is made to refer to *three* sacrifices, not to one. (4) The emphatic '*diligently*' is expressed in Hebrew, as usual, by the repetition of the verb, and hence understood to mean two enquiries. (5) Waiting for the evening to be eaten: why did you not eat it during the day? (6) Lev. X, 17. (7) Which 'bears the iniquity of the congregation' by atoning for the defilement of the sanctuary and the sacrifices, Shebu. 2*a*. (8) This reverts to the earlier part of the discussion. Surely the argument that all three should have been burnt, if it was on account of their bereavement, is sound! (9) Such as the other two were. (10) Hence they could not eat it in the evening either. (11) Num. XXV, 13. This was spoken after he had slain Zimri: thus only then was the priesthood conferred upon him. (12) Josh. XXII, 30; v. whole chapter for the controversy between the two and a half tribes in Transjordan and the rest of Israel, and how it was settled. This is the first time that Phinehas is spoken of as '*the priest*'; previously he is always referred to as 'Phinehas the son of Eleazar the son of Aaron the priest'. Thus priesthood is ascribed to his forbears, but not to himself.

b (1) He was informed that he would be invested with the priesthood, but it was not conferred upon him until later. (2) Tosaf: a promise that all High Priests would be descended from him. (3) Lev. VIII, 29. (4) V. Glos. (5) During the days preceding Revelation, when he ascended the mountain of Sinai and descended thence to the people. (6) Lev. XXI, 22. This refers to a blemished priest, who may not officiate, yet may partake of the sacrifices. (7) V. Glos. Though normally higher sacrifices might be eaten by male priests only, yet we do find an instance where they were permitted to a *zar;* the instance(s) is discussed anon. But a *zar* was never permitted to eat the priestly portions (viz., the breast and thigh) of lesser sacrifices.—Since then a *zar* may sometimes partake of higher sacrifices, it is logical that a blemished priest may always do so. (8) *Sc.* the priests. (9) Their sanctity is not so great.

c (1) The only instance found of a *zar* eating of higher sacrifices was when Moses received the breast and thigh of the ram of consecration, which was a higher sacrifice. Thus Moses is counted as a *zar*, not as a priest (2) *Infra* 113*a*. The meal-offering was a higher sacrifice, and when offered at the High Places (where a *zar* could officiate), after the handful had been burnt on the altar the remainder might be eaten by a *zar*, whereas in the Temple this belonged to the priests only. (3) As a leper; v. Num. XII, 14 *seq.* Before she could be shut away, the symptoms had to be duly diagnosed as leprous.

shut her up, surely Moses was a *zar*, [102*a*] and a *zar* cannot inspect plagues [of leprosy].[4] If you say that Aaron shut her away, Aaron was a relation, and a relation cannot inspect [leprous] plagues. Rather, the Holy One, blessed be He, bestowed great honour upon Miriam in that moment, and declared, I am a priest: I will shut her away, I will declare her a definite [leper], and I will free her. He teaches at all events, 'Moses was a *zar* and a *zar* cannot inspect plagues'?—Said R. Naḥman b. Isaac: The inspection of leprosy[5] is different, because Aaron and his sons are specified in that section.

An objection is raised: Elisheba[6] had five joys more than the other daughters of Israel:[7] her brother-in-law [Moses] was a king, her husband was a High Priest, her son [Eleazar] was Segan [deputy High Priest], her grandson [Phinehas] was anointed for battle,[8] and her brother [Nahshon] was the prince of his tribe; yet she was bereaved of her two sons. At all events he teaches, Her brother-in-law was a king: thus he was a king, but not a High Priest?—Emend, was *also* a king.

This is dependent on Tannaim: *And the anger of the Lord was kindled against Moses.*[9] R. Joshua b. Ḳarḥah said: A [lasting] effect is recorded of every fierce anger in the Torah,[10] but no [lasting] effect is recorded in this instance. R. Simeon b. Yoḥai said: A [lasting] effect is recorded in this instance too, for it is said, *Is there*
a *not Aaron thy brother the Levite?*[1] Now surely he was a priest? Rather, this is what He meant: I had said that thou wouldst be a priest and he a Levite; now, however, he will be a priest and thou a Levite. The Sages maintain: Moses was invested with priesthood only for the seven days of consecration. Some maintain: Only Moses' descendants were deprived of priesthood,[2] for it is said, *But as for Moses the man of God,* his sons *are named among the tribe of Levi;*[3] and it says, *Moses and Aaron among His priests, and Samuel among them that call upon His name.*[4] Why [add] 'and it says'?[5]—You might argue that [the first proof-text] is written for [future] generations,[6] hence it says, however, *'Moses and Aaron among His priests'.*

Now, is then a [lasting] effect recorded of every fierce anger in the Torah? Surely it is written, *And he went out from Pharoah in hot anger,*[7] and yet he said nothing to him?—Said Resh Laḳish: He slapped him and went out. But did Resh Laḳish say thus? Surely it is written, *And thou shalt stand by the river's brink to meet him,*[8] whereon Resh Laḳish commented: [The Holy One, blessed be He, said to Moses,] He is a king, and thou must show him reverence;[9] while R. Joḥanan maintained: [God said to him:] He is a wicked man, therefore be thou insolent toward him?—Reverse it.[10]

R. Jannai said: Let the awe of kingship always be upon thee, for it is written, *And all these thy servants shall come down unto me,*[11] but he did not say it of [Pharoah] himself.[12] R. Joḥanan said: It may be inferred from the following: *And the hand of the Lord was on Elijah; and he girded up his loins, and ran before Ahab.*[13]

'Ulla said: Moses desired kingship, but He did not grant it to
b him, for it is written, *Draw not nigh halom [hither];*[1] *'halom'* can only mean kingship, as it is said, [*Then David . . . said:*] *'Who am I, O Lord God . . . that Thou hast brought me halom [thus far]?*[2] Raba raised an objection: R. Ishmael said: Her [Elisheba's] brother-in-law [Moses] was a king?—Said Rabbah b. 'Ulla:[3] He ['Ulla] meant, for himself and for his descendants.[4]

Does then *'halom'* refer to [future] generations wherever it is written?[5] Surely it is written in connection with Saul, *Is there yet a man come halom [hither],*[6] yet only he [enjoyed kingship], but not his seed?—If you wish I can answer that there was Ish-bosheth.[7] Alternatively, Saul was different, for it [kingship] did not remain even with him.[8] This agrees with R. Eleazar's dictum in R. Ḥanina's name: When greatness is decreed for a man, it is decreed for him and for his seed unto all generations, for it is said: *He withdraweth not His eyes from the righteous; but with kings upon the throne He setteth them for ever.*[9] But if he becomes arrogant, the Holy One, blessed be He, abases him, for it is said [*And they are exalted . . .*] *And if they be bound in fetters, and be holden in cords of affliction.*[10]

MEN WITH A BLEMISH, WHETHER TRANSIENT. How do we know this?—Because our Rabbis taught: *Every male [may eat of it]:*[11] this includes men with a blemish. In which respect? If in respect of eating, surely it is said elsewhere, *He may eat the bread of his God, both of the most holy, and of the holy?*[12] Hence it means in respect of sharing.[13] Another [Baraitha] taught: *'Every male':* this includes men with a blemish. In which respect? If in respect of eating, surely that is already stated [elsewhere]; if in respect of sharing, surely
c that [too] is already stated?[1] Hence [it is required] in respect of a man blemished from birth.[2] For I might think: I know it only of an unblemished [priest] who became blemished; how do I know it of a man blemished from birth? Therefore it says, *'Every male'.* Another [Baraitha] taught: *'Every male'* includes a man with a blemish. In which respect? If in respect of eating, surely it is already stated; if in respect of sharing, surely it is already stated; if in respect of a man blemished from birth, surely it is already stated? For I might think: I know it only of a man with a permanent blemish; how do I know it of a man with a transient blemish? Therefore it says, *'Every male'.* Surely this should be reversed![3]—Said R. Shesheth: Reverse it. R. Ashi said: After all, do not reverse it, yet it is

(4) V. Lev. XIII, 2. (5) Lit., 'the appearance of plagues'. (6) Aaron's wife. (7) On the day that the Tabernacle was erected. (8) He was anointed as the deputy High Priest to lead in battle. (9) Ex. IV, 14. The reason for God's anger was Moses' extreme reluctance to go to Pharaoh. (10) Wherever it is stated that God's anger was kindled, it left its mark in some way.

a (1) Ex. IV, 14. (2) But he remained a priest all his life. (3) 1 Chron. XXIII, 14. (4) Ps. XCIX, 6. (5) Which implies that the first proof-text is insufficient. (6) The first text deals with the status of the people then living, and for that reason Moses himself is not included. Thus it may not prove that he was a priest. (7) Ex. XI, 8. (8) Ibid. VII, 15. (9) Surely then he would not have slapped him. (10) Resh Laḳish maintained that he was to be insolent toward him, and R. Joḥanan the reverse. (11) Ibid. XI, 8. (12) Out of respect for royalty, though he knew that Pharoah himself would eventually appeal to him (ibid. XII, 30 *seq.*) (13) 1 Kings XVIII, 46. Thus he shewed him respect as a king, in spite of the strong opposition he had always displayed.

b (1) Ex. III, 5. (2) II. Sam. VII, 18. *'Halom' (thus far)* there means the kingship. (3) Emended text (Sh.M.). (4) Moses desired royalty for himself and his descendants, but it was granted only for himself. (5) For according to the answer just given, when God said to Moses, *'Draw not nigh halom'*, He meant that he could not enjoy kingship for future generations. (6) 1. Sam. X, 22. (7) His son, who did succeed him for a time. (8) Even in his own lifetime it was torn from him. But originally it was decreed both for him and for his descendants, and he lost it only through his own instability. (9) Job XXXVI, 7. (10) Ibid. 8. This is their punishment if *'they are exalted'*, i.e., arrogant. (11) Lev. VI, 11, 22; VII, 6. These refer to the meal-offering, the sin-offering, and the guilt-offering respectively. The Talmud now interprets each one. (12) Ibid. XXI, 22. (13) Blemished priests receive a share in their own rights.

c (1) That is deduced from the first *'every male'*. (2) Lit., 'from the beginning'. —Emended text. (3) One would include a non-permanent blemish sooner than a permanent one.

תורה אור

ואין *זר רואה את הנגעים וא"ת אהרן הסגירה
אהרן *קרוב הוא ואין [ב]קרוב רואה את
הנגעים אלא כבוד גדול חלק לה הקב"ה
למרים א] אותה שעה אני כהן ואני מסגירה
אני חולטה ואני פוטרה קתני מיהת משה
זר ואין זר רואה את הנגעים אמר רב נחמן
בר יצחק שאני מראות נגעים דאהרן ובניו
כתובין בפרשה מיתיבי *חמש שמחות
היתה אלישבע יתירה על בנות ישראל
ב] יבמה מלך אישה כהן גדול בנה סגן בן
בנה משוח מלחמה ואחיה נשיא שבט
ואבילה על שני בניה קתני מיהת יבמה מלך
שמות ד מלך אין כ"ג לא אימא אף מלך כתנאי °ויחר אף ה' במשה רבי יהושע
בן קרחה אומר *כל חרון אף שבתורה נאמר בו רושם וזה לא נאמר בו
שם רושם ר"ש בן יוחי אומר אף זה נאמר בו רושם שנאמר °הלא אהרן
אחיך הלוי והלא כהן הוא ג] הכי קאמר אני אמרתי אתה כהן והוא לוי
עכשיו הוא כהן ואתה לוי וחכמים אומרים לא נתכהן משה אלא שבעת
ימי המלואים בלבד ויש אומרים לא פסקה כהונה אלא מזרעו של משה
ד"ה א כג שנאמר °ומשה איש האלהים בניו יקראו על שבט הלוי ואומר °משה
ואהרן בכהניו ושמואל בקוראי שמו מאי ואומר וכי תימא ד] לדורות הוא
דכתיב ואומר משה ואהרן בכהניו וכל חרון אף שבתורה נאמר בו
שמות יא רושם והכתיב °ויצא (משה) מעם פרעה בחרי אף ולא א"ל ולא מידי
שם ז אמר ר"ל סטרו ויצא ומי אמר ר"ל הכי והכתיב °ונצבת לקראתו על
שפת היאור ואמר ר"ל ה] מלך הוא והסביר לו פנים ורבי יוחנן אמר רשע
הוא והעיז פניך בו איפוך *א"ר ינאי לעולם תהא אימת מלכות עליך
שם יא דכתיב °וירדו כל עבדיך אלה אלי ואילו לדידיה לא קאמר ליה רבי יוחנן
מ"א יח אמר מהכא °ויד ה' היתה אל אליהו וישנס מתניו וירץ לפני אחאב אמר עולא
שמות ג בקש משה מלכות ולא נתנו לו דכתיב °אל תקרב הלום ואין הלום אלא
ש"ב ז מלכות שנאמר °מי אנכי ה' אלהים ו] [וגו'] כי הביאתני עד הלום מתיב
רבא רבי ישמעאל אומר יבמה מלך אמר ז] רבא לו ולזרעו קאמר וכל היכא
שמואל א י דכתיב הלום ח] לדורות הוא והא גבי שאול דכתיב °הבא עוד הלום איש ט] הוא
אין זרעו לא איבעית אימא הא הוה איש בשת ואיבעית אימא שאני שאול
דאפי' בגויה לא קאים *כדר' אלעזר אמר רבי חנינא י] בשעה שפוסקים גדולה
איוב לו לאדם פוסקים לו ולזרעו עד סוף כל הדורות שנאמר °לא יגרע מצדיק עיניו
שם ואת מלכים לכסא וגו' ואם הגיס דעתו הקב"ה משפילו שנאמר °ואם אסורים
בזקים ילכדון בחבלי עוני : בעלי מומין בין בעלי מומין כו' : מנא ה"מ דת"ר
ויקר' ו °כל זכר לרבות בעלי מומין למאי אי לאכילה הרי כבר נאמר °לחם אלהיו
מקדשי הקדשים יאכל אלא לחלוקה תניא אידך כל זכר לרבות בעלי מומין
למאי אי לאכילה הרי כבר אמור אי לחלוקה הרי כבר *אמור שיכול אין לי
אלא תם ונעשה בעל מום בעל מום מעיקרו מנין ת"ל כל זכר תניא אידך כל
זכר לרבות בעל מום למאי אי לאכילה הרי כבר אמור ואי לחלוקה הרי
כבר אמור ואי לבעל מום מעיקרו הרי כבר אמור שיכול אין לי אלא בעל
מום קבוע בעל מום עובר מנין ת"ל כל זכר כלפי לייא אמר רב ששת
איפוך רב אשי אמר לעולם לא תיפוך ואיצטריך סלקא דעתך אמינא
כי

ואין זר רואה את הנגעים · דכתיב (ויקרא יג) והובא אל אהרן וגו' : ואין קרוב רואה את הנגעים · כדתניא בסנהדרין (דף לד:) כל ריב וכל נגע מה ריבים שלא בקרובים אף נגעים שלא בקרובים : היתה אלישבע יתירה · ביום שהוקם המשכן קאי בסדר עולם : בנה סגן · אלעזר : בן בנה · פנחס משוח מלחמה כדאשכחן במדין אותם ואת פנחס בן אלעזר הכהן לצבא והוא המדבר אל העם שמע ישראל אתם קרבים היום למלחמה על אויביכם : אחיה · נחשון : כתנאי · אם משה כהן היה : נאמר בו רושם · סימן מה של חרון היה שם פעמים הכאה פעמים נזיפה פעמים קללה וגידוף כגון (שמואל א כ) ויחר אף שאול כתיב בתריה בן נעות המרדות ויחר אף אליהוא (איוב לב) לא רבים יחכמו (שם) ויחר אף יעקב ברחל התחת אלהים (בראשית ל) לשון נזיפה הוא : הלא אהרן אחיך · שהיה ראוי להיות לוי ידעתי כי דבר ידבר הוא ומשם זכה לכהונה : לא נתכהן משה · ולא פסקו לו כהונה מעולם : ויש אומרים · לא פסקה כהונה אלא מזרעו אבל הוא כל ימיו כהן היה ורב דאמר כיש אומרים : בניו יקראו על שבט הלוי · אבל הוא כהן : וכי תימא יא] לדורות הוא דכתיב · לאחר זמן נכתב כשהיו מייחסים את הכהונה ואת הלויה ולהכי נקט בניו יקראו דלא הוה ליה למימר משה יקרא על שבט הלוי שהרי *לא יב] קיים ואין לו לומר אלא על המתייחסים : סטרו · הכהו על לחיו : הסביר לו פנים · והיינו ונצבת לקראתו לפי גדולתו הכון לקראתו : העיז בו פניך · היינו ונצבת לקראתו למלחמה ולדבר עזות : ואילו לדידיה לא קאמר ליה · וירדת אלי והשתחוית לי לאמר וגו' ואע"ג דמסקנא הכי הוה דכתיב (שמות יב) ויקרא למשה ולאהרן לילה ויאמר קומו וגו' : וירץ לפני אחאב · אחאב רוכב והוא רץ לפניו שהיה אחאב יחידי ולאו אורח ארעא : מי אנכי · דוד אמרה : שאני שאול דאפי' בגויה *לא קמא · ומיהו הלום מלכות עולמית הוא וכשפסקו לו לשאול מלכות עולמית פסקו לו אבל הוא גרם לעצמו שתבטל הימנו : כדרבי אלעזר · דאמר אם הגיס כו' ויגבהו ואם אסורים בזקים גבהות לבם גורם להם להיות אסורים בזקים יג] ילכדו בחבלי עוני : כל זכר · קמא במנחה כתיב בנו את אהרן : אם לאכילה · להתירו לאכול מחלק חביריו אם יזמנוהו עמהם אבל הוא לא יחלוק : לחלוקה · ליטול חלק כאחד הכשרים : כל זכר · תנייתא בחטאת כתיב והשלישי באשם וברייתות הללו בת"כ במדרש המקראות: כלפי לייא· בעל מום עובר משמע להתירו טפי מבעל מום קבוע: לא תיפוך· ואיצטריך קרא למידרשיה הכי מהו דתימא קרא קמא קבוע הוא דאכשר דרחמנא יד]חס עליה משום דלית ליה היתירא למחר וליומא אחרינא אבל עובר דאית ליה היתירא למתנת אימא

אהרן קרוב הוא ואין קרוב רואה את הנגעים · פלוגתא היא במסכת נגעים פ"ב (מ"ה) דתנן כל הנגעים אדם רואה חוץ מנגעי עצמו ר"מ אומר אף לא נגעי קרוביו טו] ותנא ברייתא דהכא כרבי מאיר וטעמא דרבי מאיר כדמפרש באחד דיני ממונות* מקיש ריבים לנגעים* מה נגעים ביום אף ריבים ביום ומה ריבים שלא בקרובים אף נגעים שלא בקרובים ורבנן לא מקשי דסברי דיני ממונות בלילה : אני מסגירה אני חולטה אני פוטרה· בספרי תניא אמר אהרן נמלאת מפסיד לאחותנו טז] שאינו יכול להסגירה ולא לטמאה ולא לטהרה יז] לפי *דבריו למדנו שהיה אהרן דורש אין אדם רואה בנגעי קרובו ותימה במה היה מפסידה הא יח] דאין אדם רואה את הנגעים כל שכן שהיתה טהורה : בעל

לא א מיי' פ"ט מהל' טומאת צרעת הל' ב:
לב ב מיי' שם הלכה א ופסק דקרוב רואה:

[סנהדרין לד :]
נ"ל ונגעים לריבים צ"ק
נ"ל לפי דרכנו צ"ק
עיין רש"ק מה שהקשה על רש"י בתומס מסוגיא דהכא
תהלים צט
ויקרא כא
אמור אלא לבעל מום מעיקרא שיכול אין לי כו' כצ"ל צ"ק

נגעים פ"ב מ"ה [ע"ש בר"ש]
סדר עולם פ"ד
[ר"א לא היה קיים]
מנחות לח.
[מגילה יג: ע"ש]
[ר"א לא קיימא]

שיטה מקובצת
א] למרים באותה שעה אמר אני : ב] ישראל ואבל אחד · יבמה : ג] הוא אלא ה"ק ליה אני אמרתי : ד] וכ"ת ההוא לדורות : ה] ר"ל לו הקב"ה למשה מלך : ו] אלהים ומי ביתי כי : ז] אמר רבה בר עולא ותיבת רבא נמחק : ח] הלום עד עולם הוא ותיבת לדורות נמחק : ט] איש והוא : י] חנינא דאמר ר' אלעזר אמר ר' חנינא בשעה : יא] וכ"ת ההוא לדורות הוא : יב] לא היה קיים: יג] בזקים וילכדו : יד] רחמנא דחס עליה : טו] קרוביו ואתא תנא ברייתא דהכא : טז] לאחותנו שאיני יכול : יז] ולפי דרכינו למדנו : יח] הא כיון דאין :

דלא

לג א מיי' פ"י מהלכות מעה"ק הלכה כח:

לד ב מיי' שם הל' כב:

ועי' רש"ק מה שתירץ על קושיא זו ועי' בספר פנים מאירות

לה ג מיי' פ"ג מהלכות ק"ש הל' ד טוש"ע א"ח סימן פה סעיף ב:

בעל מום עובר מנין ת"ל כל זכר · תימה דלמה אילטריך לבעל מום מעיקרו חד לאכילה וחד לחלוקה דאי מחד ה"א דוקא אכילה ולא חלוקה כמו קטן דאוכל ואינו חולק וי"ל כיון דאשכחן תם ונעשה בעל מום דאין חילוק בין אכילה לחלוקה דבסתמא ה"ה לבעל מום מעיקרו *וא"ת דהכא מייתרי ליה הנך תלתא כל זכר דכתיבי במנחה וחטאת ואשם משמע דילפי מהדדי וגבי טבול יום בדינא דר"א בר' שמעון מצריך תלת קראי למנחת ישראל וחטאת וחזה ושוק : **הרי** טמא בקרבנות ציבור דראוי לעבודה ואינו חולק · תימה דפריך מטמא בקרבנות ציבור שהיא בעיא לעיל והוה מצי למיפרך מכהן גדול אונן כח] וראוי לעבודה ואינו חולק דפשיטא לן לעיל בריש פירקין כדתניא בהדיא : **מה** אם דחיתני מחטאת שכן הורע כחי אצל נשיי ועבדיי · תימה אמאי לא קאמר כדקאמר לעיל ומה אם דחיתני מחטאת שכשם שיפה כחי כך יפה כחך תדיחני מחזה ושוק שכשם שהורע כחי כך הורע כחך : **פריך** רב אחאי · בכל מקום לשון מסוה' כדאשכחן בריש כתובות (דף ב:) פשיט רב אחאי ומתוך כך היה אומר רבינו שמואל דהוא רב אחאי שעשה השאלתות שהיה מרבנן סבוראי דבתר רבינא ורב אשי כט] *דהוסיף הוראה וכתבו אחרי כן דבריו ל] בסוף הש"ס ומיהו בההיא דכתובות אשכחן רב אשי דמיירי בתריה*: הגיהה

נ"י דנסוף]

[וע ע תוספות כתובות ב: ד"ה פשיט]

יח] (אימא כי טמא כו') : [הרי] טמא בקרבנות ציבור · אמרן לעיל בריש פירקין (דף צט:) דאין חולק : קטן אינו חולק · דכתיב איש כאחיו ודרשינן יט] ליה במנחות (דף עג·) ובקדושין (דף נג·) איש חולק אפילו בעל מום ואין קטן חולק אפילו תם : הא לא קתני · כ] הא ראוי לאכילה חולק דדייקא לא קתני כא] דתיקשי לך קטן לא תדוק מיניה הכי דהיא גופה אילטריך לאשמועינן דכל שאינו ראוי אינו חולק ולאו כב] דיוקא תני : כדאמרינן מעיקרא · ראוי לעבודה : הא לא קתני · הא ראוי לעבודה חולק דקא דייקת וקשיא לך עלה טמא בקרבנות ציבור לא קתני לה מתניתין ואת לא תיתי מדיוקא דלאשמועינן היא גופה אתאי מתני' ולאו לדיוקא דילה : דאפילו הקטר חלבים נמי בעי · שיהא ראוי להקטיר ות"ק סבר לו תהיה שוק הימין למנה אהמקריב דם השלמים קאי כדאשכחן קרא אחרינא לכהן הזורק את דם השלמים לו יהיה (ויקרא ז) ולא כתיב כג] מקטיר חלבים והכא דכתיב את החלב לא לראוי אתא אלא למודה בעבודות כדדרשינן ליה בשחיטת חולין (דף קלב:) רבי שמעון אומר כל כהן שאינו מודה בעבודה אינו חולק בכהונה שנאמר המקריב את דם השלמים אין לי אלא זריקה מנין לרבות הקטר חלבים ת"ל ואת החלב מנין לרבות שאר כל עבודות ת"ל מבני אהרן עבודה המסורה לבני אהרן כל כהן שאינו מודה בה אינו חולק בכהונה : בעי רב אשי · אליבא דאבא שאול : דנתה · יכול אתה לדון : בא טבול יום ואמר · לחבירו טהור של בית אב שלו : תן לי · כד] בחלק מן המנחה של ישראל ואוכל לערב : א"ל · טהור לטבול יום כלומר כן יש לו להשיבו : ומה אם במקום שיפה כחך בחטאתך · דכהן המחוייב חטאת מביאו ומקריב אפילו במשמר שאינו שלו ועבודתה ועורה שלו כה] בפרק הגוזל בב"ק (דף קט:) מנין לכהן שבא ומקריב קרבנותיו בכל עת ובכל שעה שירצה ת"ל ובא בכל אות נפשו ושרת ומנין שעבודתה ועורה שלו ת"ל ואיש את קדשיו לו יהיו : דחיתיך מחטאת ישראל · דטבול יום אינו חולק בה דכתיב (ויקרא ו) הכהן המחטא אותה יאכלנה ואוקימנא לעיל (דף צט·) יאכלנה: מקום שהורע כחך במנחתך · שאם התנדבת מנחה והקרבת אפילו אתה טהור אי אתה אוכלה כדכתיב כל מנחת כהן כליל וגו' (ויקרא ו) : אינו דין שאדיחך · כל זמן שאתה טבול יום ואינך ראוי להקריב ממנחת ישראל : כך יפה כחך · בחטאתך : לכהן המקריב אותה לו תהיה · במנחה כתיב : ומה במקום כו' · טהור קמהדר ליה לטבול יום הכי שלא יחלוק עמו : *שכשם שהורע כחי · במנחתי כך הורע כחך במנחתך : תן לי מחזה ושוק · חלק כמוך ואוכל לערב : שכן הורע כחי אצל נשיי ועבדיי · אף כשאני טהור שאיני רשאי להאכילה להם : יצא טבול יום · בפחי נפש : קוליו וחומריו · שהיה דורש להגאתו ואומר כו] למה דחיתני כו' : אונן מימינו כו' · שאף הם נדחים מן המקראות הללו שאינן ראויין לעבודה: פריך רב אחאי ולימא · וליתני כז] ר' אלעזר בר' שמעון בהאי דינא : תן לי מבכור ואוכל · לערב אמר לו טהור מה אם במקום כו' : את דמם תזרוק · בבכור כתיב בא זרוק ואכול ואע"ג דאין בכור נאכל במחלוקת שאינו ניתן לאנשי משמר אלא לכל כהן שירצה כתרומה וכפדיון הבכור מיהו תיפוק לן מינה דלא יתנו בכור אלא למי שראוי לעבודה באותה שעה : והיכי עביד הכי · רבי אלעזר ברבי שמעון דאמר האי דינא בבית הכסא : לאונסו · שהיתה שמועתו שגורה בפיו ומהרהר בה על כרחו ודוגמתו שמעתי בקדושין (דף לג·) :

מתני'

תורה אור

כי טמא מה טמא כמה דלא טהור לא אכיל אף האי נמי כמה דלא א] מתקן לא אכיל קא משמע לן : כל שאינו ראוי וכו' : ולא והרי בעל מום דלא ראוי לעבודה וחולק ותו הא ראוי לעבודה חולק הרי טמא בקרבנות ציבור דראוי לעבודה ואינו חולק ראוי לאכילי' קאמר ב] והרי קטן דראוי לאכילה ואינו חולק הא לא קתני השתא דאתית להכי לעולם ג] כדקאמר מעיקרא אי משום טמא טמא לא קתני אי משום בעל מום רחמנא רבייה : אפי' טמא בשעת זריקת דמים וטהור בשעת הקטר חלבים אינו חולק : הא טהור בשעת זריקת דמים וטמא בשעת הקטר חלבים חולק מתניתין דלא כאבא שאול *דתניא אבא שאול אומר °לעולם אינו אוכל עד שיהא טהור משעת זריקה עד שעת הקטר חלבים דאמר קרא °המקריב את דם השלמים ואת החלב דאפי' הקטר חלבים נמי בעי : בעי רב אשי נטמא בינתיים מהו בשעת זריקה ובשעת הקטרה בעינן והאיכא או דלמא עד שיהא טהור משעת זריקה ועד שעת הקטר חלבים ג]תיקו אמר ד] *רבא האי דינא מרבי אלעזר ברבי שמעון גמירנא ה] דאמר בבית הכסא דנתה בא ו] טבול יום ואמר תן לי ז] ממנחה ואוכל אמר לו ומה אם במקום שיפה כחך בחטאתך דחיתיך מחטאת ישראל מקום שהורע כחך במנחתך אינו דין שאדיחך ממנחת ישראל ח] ומה אם דחיתני מחטאת ישראל שכשם שיפה כחי כך יפה כחך תדחני ט] ממנחה שכשם שהורע כחי כך הורע כחך הרי הוא אומר °לכהן המקריב אותה לו תהיה בא הקרב ואכול י] תן לי מחטאת ישראל ואוכל א"ל ומה במקום שהורע כחי במנחתי דחיתיך ממנחת ישראל מקום שיפה כחי בחטאתי אינו דין שאדיחך מחטאת ישראל א"ל ומה אם שדחיתני ממנחת ישראל שכשם שהורע כחך כך הורע כחי תדחני מחטאת ישראל שכשם שיפה כחך כך יפה כחי יא] הרי הוא אומר °הכהן המחטא אותה יאכלנה בא יב] חטא ואכול אמר ליה תן לי מחזה ושוק ואוכל אמר ליה ומה במקום שיפה כחך בחטאתך דחיתיך יג] [מחטאת ישראל] (מחזה ושוק) מקום שהורע כחך בשלמים שאין לך בהן אלא חזה ושוק אינו דין שאדיחך יד] מה אם דחיתני מחטאת טו] שכן הורע כחי אצל נשיי ועבדיי תדחני מחזה וש"ק שכן יפה כחי אצל נשיי ועבדיי טז] הרי הוא אומר °לכהן הזורק את דם השלמים לו יהיה בא זרוק ואכול יצא טבול יום קוליו וחמוריו על ראשו אונן מימינו מחוסר כפרה משמאלו *פריך רב אחאי לימא ליה תן לי מבכור ואוכל משום דא"ל ומה במקום שהורע כחי בחטאת אצל נשיי ועבדיי דחיתיך מחטאת ישראל מקום שיפה כחי בבכור דכוליה דילי יז] היא אינו דין שאדחך ממנו ומה אם דחיתני מחטאת שכשם שהורע כחך כך הורע כחי תדיחני מבכור שכשם שיפה כחך כך יפה כחי הרי הוא אומר °את דמם תזרוק על המזבח ואת חלבם תקטיר ובשרם יהיה לך בא זרוק ואכול ואידך פריך מי כתיב ובשרם לכהן הזורק ובשרם יהיה לך כתיב אפי' לכהן אחר והיכי עביד הכי והאמר *רבה בר בר חנה א"ר יוחנן ג]בכל מקום מותר להרהר חוץ ממרחץ ומבית הכסא לאונסו שאני :

מתני'

ג"ק מ"ג

תוספתא דמנחות פ"ג [ע"ש]

ויקרא ז

מהרש"ק גרס רב

שם

שם ו

גי' רש"ק ומ"ז

שם

[קדושין יג. וש"נ]

במדבר יח

ברכות כד. שבת מ ק. ע"ש מד: קדושין לג.

נ"ל שכשם שהורע כחך במנחתי כך הורע כחי במנחתך נ"ק

שיטה מקובצת

א] דלא מתקן לא : ב] קאמר והא קטן ותיבת והרי ל"ש : ג] כדקאמר' מעיקרא אי משום טמא הא לא קתני ואי משום בעל מום בעל מום רחמנא רבייה : ד] אמר (רבי') [רב] : ה] נמירנא ליה דאמר : ו] בא כהן טבול יום : ז] ממנחת ישראל ואוכל : ח] ישראל א"ל ומה : ט] תדחיני ממנחת ישראל שכשם שהורע כו' כחך א"ל הרי הוא אומר לכהן המקריב : י] ואכול א"ל תן · ס"א א"ל אם לאו תן : יא] כחי א"ל הרי : יב] בא חטא : יג] דחיתך מחטאת ישראל ותיבות מחזה ושוק נמחק : יד] שאדיחך סתן א"ל מה ב
טו] מחטאת ישראל שכן : טז] ועבדיי א"ל הרי : יז] דילי הוא אינו : יח] אימא כי טמא כו' מטא ותיבת הרי ל"ש : יט] תיבת ליה נמחק : כ] לא קתני' האי הא : כא] לא קתני ליה בהדיא דתיקשי לך קטן ולא תדוק
כב] ולאו לדיוקא : כג] כתיב המקטיר החלבים והבא : כד] לי חלק מן אות ב' נמחק : כה] שלו כדאיתא בפ' : כו] ואומר מה אם דחיתני ותיבת למה נמחק : כז] וליתני נמי ר"א : כח] אונן דראוי לעבודה ואינו
כט] אשי דהוו סוף הוראה : ל] בתוך הש"ס :

necessary. For I might argue, [102b] [he is] like an unclean [person]: as an unclean person may not eat so long as he is not clean, so may this man not eat so long as he is not made whole;[4] hence it informs us [otherwise].

WHOEVER IS NOT ELIGIBLE etc. Is he not? surely a [priest] with a blemish is not eligible, yet he receives a share? Moreover [it implies that every] one who is eligible for service receives a share; lo, an unclean [priest] is eligible for the service in public sacrifices, and yet does not receive a share?—He means: who is fit to eat. Lo, a minor is fit to eat, yet does not receive a share?—He does not teach this.[5] Now that you have arrived at this, [you can say,] After all, it is as we first said:[6] if [your difficulty is] on account of an unclean [priest], he does not teach this;[7] and if [your difficulty is] on account of a [priest] with a blemish: a [priest] with a blemish
a was included by the Divine Law.[1]

EVEN IF ONE WAS UNCLEAN WHEN THE BLOOD WAS SPRINKLED BUT CLEAN WHEN THE FATS WERE BURNED, HE DOES NOT RECEIVE A SHARE. Hence, if he was clean when the blood was sprinkled but unclean when the fats were burned, he does receive a share. Our Mishnah does not agree with Abba Saul. For it was taught, Abba Saul said: He never receives a share unless he was clean from the time of the sprinkling of the blood until the time of the burning of the fats [inclusive], because it is said, *He [among the sons of Aaron,] that offereth the blood of the peace-offerings, and the fat, [shall have the right thigh for a portion]*[2] this intimates that even [at] the burning of the fat too [cleanness] is required.

R. Ashi asked: What if he was defiled in between?[3] Do we require him [to be clean] at the sprinkling and at the burning, and [this condition] is fulfilled; or perhaps he must be clean from the time of the sprinkling until the time of the burning of the fats? The question stands over.

Raba[4] said: I have the following discussion as a tradition from R. Eleazar son of R. Simeon, which he stated in a privy. You can argue: If a priest, a *ṭebul yom*, came and demanded: Give me of an Israelite's meal-offering, that I may eat thereof,[5] one [the clean priest] can answer him: If I can repulse you from an Israelite's sin-offering, though you have a valid right[6] to your own sin-offering, surely I can repulse you from an Israelite's meal-offering, seeing that you have no valid right[6] in your own meal-offering.[7] [He can reply:] If you repulse me from an Israelite's sin-offering, that is because just as I have a great privilege, so have you a great pri-
b vilege;[1] will you repulse me from an Israelite's meal-offering, where just as my own rights are weak, so are your rights weak? [He can answer:] Lo, it says, *[And every meal-offering . . .] shall be the priest's that offereth it:*[2] come, offer, and eat.[3]

[If the *ṭebul yom* demands:] Give me [a share] of an Israelite's sin-offering, that I may eat, he can reply: If I can repulse you from an Israelite's meal-offering, though I have no privileges in my own meal-offering, surely I can repulse you from an Israelite's sin-offering, seeing that I have great privileges in my own sin-offering. He can retort: If you can repulse me from an Israelite's meal-offering, where just as you have no privileges so have I no privileges: will you repulse me from an Israelite's sin-offering, where just as you have great privileges, so have I great privileges? He can answer: Lo, it says, *The priest that offereth it for sin shall eat it:*[4] come, offer it for sin, and eat!

If [the *ṭebul yom*] demands: Give me [a share] of the breast and the thigh, that I may eat, he can reply: If I can repulse you from an Israelite's sin-offering, though you have great privileges in your own sin-offering, surely I can repulse you from a peace-offering, where your privileges are weak, since you have rights only to the breast and thigh thereof. He can retort: If you can repulse me from a sin-offering, where my rights are weak in respect of my wives and servants,[5] will you repulse me from the breast and thigh, where my rights are strong in respect of my wives and my slaves?[6] He can answer: Lo, it says, *It shall be the priest's that sprinkleth the blood of the peace-offerings against the altar:*[7] Come, sprinkle and eat. Thus the *ṭebul yom* departs, bearing his arguments on his head,[8] with
c an *onen* on his right and one who lacks atonement on his left.[1]

R. Aḥai raised a difficulty: Let him [the *ṭebul yom*] demand:[2] Give me [a share] of a firstling, that I may eat. Because he [the clean priest] can answer: If I can repulse you from an Israelite's sin-offering, though my own privileges in a sin-offering are weak in respect to my wives and slaves, surely I can repulse you from a firstling, where I enjoy great privileges, as it is altogether mine. [He can answer:] If you have repulsed me from a sin-offering, where just as your privileges are weak so are my privileges weak, will you repulse me from a firstling, where just as your privileges are great, so are mine great? [He can retort:] Lo, it says, *Thou shalt sprinkle their blood against the altar, and shalt make their fat smoke for an offering made by fire . . . and the flesh of them shall be thine:*[3] come, sprinkle, and eat.[4] And the other?[5]—Refute it [thus]: Is it then written, And the flesh of them shall be the priest's who sprinkleth? Surely it is written, *And the flesh of them shall be thine*, which means even another priest's.[6]

Now, how might he [R. Eleazar son of R. Simeon] do this?[7] Surely Rabbah b. Bar Ḥanah said in R. Joḥanan's name: One may meditate [on learning] in all places, except in a bath-house and a privy?—It is different [when it is done] involuntarily.

(4) I would say that Scripture includes only a man with a permanent blemish, because he can never be made whole. But one with a transitory blemish must wait. (5) The Tanna does not in fact teach the converse that all who are fit to eat do share therein. (6) Viz., whoever is not eligible *for the service* (not, not fit to *eat*). (7) The Tanna merely teaches that whoever is not eligible for the service does not receive a share, but not the converse.

a (1) Therefore he is an obvious exception. (2) Lev. VII, 33. (3) And was clean again by the time the fats were burned.—This question is asked on Abba Saul's view. (4) Sh. M. emends: Rab. (5) In the evening. (6) Lit., 'your strength is good . . . your strength is feeble'. (7) A priest liable to a sin-offering, can offer it himself even when his ward (v. *supra* 99a n. 10) is not officiating, and the flesh and hide then belong to him. Nevertheless, when a *ṭebul yom* he has no share in an Israelite's sin-offering (i.e., of course, even when his own ward is officiating). On the other hand, a priest has no share even in his own meal-offering, since a priest's meal-offering is completely burnt (Lev. VI, 16); surely then he has no claim, when a *ṭebul yom*, to an Israelite's meal-offering.

b (1) Just as I can offer my own sin-offering, so can you offer your own; obviously then I cannot claim any greater privileges in an Israelite's sin-offering. (2) Lev. VII, 9. (3) But as you cannot offer, being a *ṭebul yom*, you cannot eat either. (4) Ibid. VI, 19. (5) Even when I am clean and receive a share, my wives and slaves may not eat thereof. (6) They may eat of my share. (7) Ibid. VII, 14. (8) Lit., 'with his leniencies and stringencies on his head'—his arguments have availed him nought, and he retires crestfallen.

c (1) They too can be similarly repulsed. (2) I.e., why did R. Eleazar b. R. Simeon not discuss the case where a *ṭebul yom* demands a share in a firstling? (3) Num. XVIII, 17, 18. This refers to firstlings. (4) Why then did R. Eleazar b. R. Simeon omit this? Actually a firstling was not given to the ward but to any individual priest, to whom the whole of it belonged. R. Aḥai nevertheless suggests that the above argument shews that it cannot be given to a priest (e.g. a *ṭebul yom*) who at the time of giving is not fit to officiate. Since R. Eleazar b. R. Simeon omits this, it follows that he does not accept this view. (5) R. Eleazar b. R. Simeon: why does he reject this argument? (6) '*Thine*' meaning the priesthood's in general. (7) *Sc.* think of all this in a privy.

MISHNAH. [103a] WHENEVER THE ALTAR DOES NOT ACQUIRE ITS FLESH,[8] THE PRIESTS DO NOT ACQUIRE THE SKIN, FOR IT IS SAID, [AND THE PRIEST THAT OFFERETH] ANY MAN'S BURNT-OFFERING [EVEN THE PRIEST SHALL HAVE
a ... THE SKIN]:[1] [THIS MEANS,] A BURNT-OFFERING WHICH COUNTS FOR A MAN.[2] IF A BURNT-OFFERING WAS SLAUGHTERED UNDER A DIFFERENT DESIGNATION, ALTHOUGH IT DOES NOT COUNT FOR ITS OWNER, ITS SKIN BELONGS TO THE PRIESTS. WHETHER [IT BE] A MAN'S BURNT-OFFERING OR A WOMAN'S BURNT-OFFERING, THE SKINS BELONG TO THE PRIESTS. THE SKINS OF LESSER SACRIFICES BELONG TO THEIR OWNERS. THE SKINS OF MOST SACRED SACRIFICES BELONG TO THE PRIEST, [AS CAN BE INFERRED] A MINORI: IF THEY ACQUIRE THE SKIN OF A BURNT-OFFERING, THOUGH THEY DO NOT ACQUIRE ITS FLESH; IS IT NOT LOGICAL THAT THEY ACQUIRE THE SKINS OF MOST SACRED SACRIFICES, WHEN THEY ACQUIRE THEIR FLESH? THE ALTAR DOES NOT REFUTE [THIS ARGUMENT], FOR IT DOES NOT ACQUIRE THE SKIN IN ANY INSTANCE.[3]

GEMARA. Our Rabbis taught: '*Any man's burnt-offering*'; this excludes a burnt-offering of *hekdesh*:[4] these are the words of R. Judah. R. Jose son of R. Judah said: It excludes a proselyte's burnt-offering.[5]

What is meant by, 'This excludes a burnt-offering of *hekdesh*?—Said R. Ḥiyya b. Joseph: It excludes a burnt-offering derived from 'left-overs'.[6] That is well on the view that 'left-overs' were devoted to public sacrifices; but what can be said on the view that 'left-
b overs' were devoted to *private* sacrifices?[1]—As Raba said [elsewhere], '*The* burnt-offering' intimates, the first burnt-offering;[2] so here too, '*the* burnt-offering' intimates, the first burnt-offering.[3]

R. Aibu[4] said in R. Jannai's name: It excludes the case where one dedicates a burnt-offering to the Temple Repair:[5] Now, on the view that the sanctity of Temple Repair seizes [it] by Scriptural law, there can be no question; but even on the view that it does not seize [it] [by Scriptural law], that applies only to the flesh, but it does seize the skin.[6] R. Naḥman in Rabbah b. Abbuha's name also said: It excludes a burnt-offering derived from 'left-overs'. Said R. Hamnuna to R. Naḥman: With whom does that agree?

(8) E.g., if the sacrifice is disqualified before the blood is sprinkled, so that it was never fit for the altar.

a (1) Lev. VII, 8. (2) I.e., its owner has fulfilled his obligation thereby. Only of such does the skin belong to the priest. But if it is disqualified (v. n. 8, p. 496), its owner must bring another. (3) You might say, Let the altar refute this argument, for the altar acquires the flesh of the burnt-offering but not its skin; similarly, then, the priests may acquire the flesh of most sacred sacrifices, but not their skins. This analogy, however, is faulty, for the altar has no right to the skin of any sacrifice, whereas the skins of burnt-offerings belong to priests. (4) V. Glos; the meaning is explained anon. (5) The skins of these do not belong to the priests. (6) When a guilt-offering cannot be sacrificed, e.g., its owner died, it is left to graze until it is blemished. Then it is redeemed, and a burnt-offering is purchased with the redemption-money. This burnt-offering is sacrificed when there is a scarcity of other sacrifices (hence it was known as the sacrifice for 'the altar's summer fruit'), and ranks as a *public* sacrifice; hence it was not '*any man's burnt-offering*', and its skin did not belong to the priests.

b (1) E.g. the heir of the dead man would bring it as a private sacrifice: why then should the skin not belong to the priest? (2) V. Pes. 58*b*. (3) The def. art. in '*the priest shall have the skin of* the *burnt-offering*' intimates that a particular one is meant, viz., an animal consecrated as such in the first place. A 'left-over', however, was originally consecrated for something else. (4) Sh.M. emends: Ila. (5) Lit., 'one causes a burnt-offering to be seized (with sanctity) for the Temple Repair.'—'Temple Repair' is a technical term, denoting a thing dedicated for any Temple use except a sacrifice. This animal itself must be sacrificed. (6) There are two views on the dedication of a sacrifice to Temple Repair (inferred from a discussion in Tem. 32*a* bottom, *b*): (i) This animal is seized with the sanctity of Temple Repair by Scriptural law. Consequently it must be redeemed (the redemption money going to the Temple Repair), and then sacrificed. On this view the skin is certainly not the priest's, for it is not 'the burnt-offering of any man', but one which belongs to Temple Repair. (ii) By Scriptural law this animal cannot be 'seized' with any other sanctity, since it already belongs to God. Yet even this view applies only to the *flesh* of the offering, which belongs to the altar; but as the skin does not belong to the altar in any case, it is 'seized' with the sanctity of Temple Repair, and does not belong to the priest.

◁ *For the continuation of the English translation of this page see overleaf*

מתני' *כל שלא זכה המזבח בבשרה לא זכו כהנים בעורה שנאמר °עולת איש עולה *שעלתה לאיש [ב]עולה שנשחטה שלא לשמה אע"פ שלא עלתה לבעלים עורה לכהנים [ג]אחד עולת האיש ואחד עולת האשה עורותיהן לכהנים [ד]עורות קדשים קלים לבעלים [ה]עורות קדשי קדשים לכהנים קל וחומר ומה אם עולה שלא זכו בבשרה זכו בעורה קדשי קדשים שזכו בבשרה אינו דין שיזכו [א] בעורה אין מזבח יוכיח שאין לו עור בכל מקום: גמ' ת"ר עולת איש [ו]פרט לעולת הקדש דברי ר' יהודה רבי יוסי בר' יהודה אומר פרט לעולת גרים מאי פרט לעולת הקדש אמר רבי חייא בר יוסף פרט לעולה הבאה מן המותרות הניחא למ"ד מותרות לנדבת ציבור אזלי אלא למ"ד מותרות לנדבת יחיד אזלי מאי איכא למימר כדאמר רבא *העולה עולה ראשונה ה"נ העולה עולה ראשונה [ב] רבי אייבו א"ר ינאי פרט למתפים עולה לבדק הבית [ג]לא מיבעיא למ"ד קדשי בדק הבית תפסי מדאורייתא אלא אפילו למ"ד לא תפסי [ד] הני מילי בשר אבל עור תפיס וכן אמר רב נחמן אמר רבה בר אבוה פרט לעולה הבאה מן המותרות א"ל רב המנונא לרב נחמן כמאן כרבי יהודה הא הדר ביה דתניא ששה לנדבה לעולה הבאה מן המותרות שלא יהו [ה] כהנים זכאין בעורה דברי רבי יהודה אמר לו רבי נחמיה ואמרי לה ר"ש אם כן ביטלת מדרשו של [ויקר' ה]יהוידע הכהן *דתניא *זה מדרש דרש יהוידע הכהן °אשם הוא אשם אשם לה' [ז]כל שבא משום חטאת ומשום אשם ילקח [ו] בו עולות הבשר לשם [ח]עורה לכהנים א"ל אלא מר במאי מוקים לה א"ל מוקמינא ליה במקדיש נכסיו וכדרבי יהושע *דתנן המקדיש נכסיו והיו בהן בהמות הראויות לגבי מזבח זכרים ונקבות ר"א אומר [ט]זכרים ימכרו לצורכי עולות [ז] נקבות ימכרו לצורכי זבחי שלמים ודמיהן [ח] יפלו עם שאר נכסים לבדק הבית רבי יהושע אומר זכרים עצמם יקרבו עולות ונקבות ימכרו לצורכי שלמים ויביא בדמיהן עולות ושאר נכסים יפלו לבדק הבית ואפי' לרבי יהושע דאמר אדם חולק הקדישו הני מילי בשר אבל עור תפיס רבי יוסי ברבי יהודה אומר פרט לעולת גרים אמר ליה רב סימאי בר חילקאי לרבינא אטו גר לאו איש הוא אמר ליה פרט לגר שמת ואין לו יורשים תנו רבנן עולת איש אין לי אלא עולת איש [י]עולת [ט] *גרים נשים ועבדים מנין ת"ל עור העולה ריבה אם כן מה תלמוד לומר עולת איש עולה שעלתה לאיש פרט לשנשחטה חוץ לזמנה וחוץ למקומה שלא יהו הכהנים זכאין בעורה יכול שאני *מרבה שנשחטה שלא לשמה הואיל ולא עלתה לבעלים
לא

מתני' כל שלא זכה המזבח בבשרה · כגון שאירע בה פסול קודם זריקה דלא היתה לה שעת היתר למזבח: עורה לכהנים · מקראי איתרבאי בברייתא בגמרא: ואחד עולת האשה · דאיתרבאי נמי מקרא: עורות קדשי קדשים · חטאות ואשמות לכהנים כדמפרש טעמא ואזיל: אין המזבח מוכיח · כלומר ואין לך לומר מזבח יוכיח שזכה בבשר העולה ולא זכה בעורה ואף אתה אל תתמה בקדשי קדשים שאע"פ שזכו כהנים בבשרן לא יזכו בעורן אין זו הוכחה שאין למזבח עור בכל מקום אבל לכהנים מצינו [י] שזכו בעור העולה וקל וחומר שיזכו בעורות קדשי קדשים: גמ' פרט לעולת הקדש · לקמיה מפרש לה: פרט לעולת גרים · לקמיה פריך אטו גר לאו איש הוא: מן המותרות · [יא] דכל אשמות של רעייה כגון תמורת אשם ואשם שמתו בעליו ושכיפרו בעליו באחר דקיימא לן [יב] ירעו וימכרו ויפלו דמיהן לנדבה והוא עולת קיץ המזבח דלאו עולת איש הוא אלא נדבת לבור היא ונסכיה משל לבור ואין בעליו סומך עליה ואינו שוחטה כדתנן בתמורה (דף כ:): הניחא כו' · פלוגתא דרבי [יג] *אליעזר ורבנן היא בתמורה (שם): לנדבת לבור · לקיץ המזבח: לנדבת יחיד בעליו של אשם שניתותר הוא עלמו מביא עולה בדמיו והוא סומך עליה ושוחטה ונסכיה קריבין משלו: כדאמר רבא · (יומא דף לד·) גבי וערך עליה העולה דילפינן מינה מנין שלא יהא דבר קודם לתמיד של שחר ת"ל וערך עליה העולה וגו' ואמרינן מאי תלמודא ואמר רבא העולה משמע העולה ראשונה האמורה בסדר קרבנות היום הכא נמי עור העולה כתיב העולה ראשונה שהופרשה מתחילה לשם עולה ולא הבאה ממותר אשם וממותר חטאת ולקמיה פריך והא קי"ל [יד] עורה לכהנים ממדרש יהוידע הכהן: פרט למתפים עולתו לבדק הבית · שאין עורה לכהנים: ולא מיבעיא וכו' בפ' בתרא דתמורה (דף לג:) דקאמר עולא המתפים עולה לבדק הבית אין בה אלא עיכוב גיזברים בלבד ומותבינן לעולא המתפים עולה לבדק הבית אסור לשוחטה עד שתפדה ומשני עולא האי דמצריך ליה פדיה מדרבנן מכלל [טו] מאן דמותיב בעי למימר דאורייתא ולענין עורה לא מיבעיא למ"ד מדאורייתא תפסה בה קדושת בדק הבית דאין עורה לכהנים אם שחטה עד שלא נפדית דלאו עולת איש הוא אלא עולת הקדש: אלא אפי' למ"ד · מדרבנן בעלמא אבל מדאורייתא לא הני מילי דמדאורייתא לא בשר דשל מזבח הוא ואין קדושה *אלה [טז] עליו שאינו שלו על פיו אבל עור דלאו ממון מזבח הוא וכהנים אכתי לא זכו ביה תפוס: כמאן כרבי יהודה · לקמן מייתי לה דאמר אין עורה לכהנים: הא הדר ביה · דקאמרי ליה אם כן בטלת מדרשו של יהוידע הכהן ולא אהדר להו מידי: ששה לנדבה · בי"ג שופרות שהיו במקדש קמיירי דכתוב עליהן תקלין חדתין [יז] [ותקלין עתיקין] קינין וגוזלי עולה עלים ולבונה וזהב לכפרת וששה לנדבה ומפרש מאי ניהו ששה לנדבה: ה"ג ששה לנדבה לעולה הבאה מן המותרות שאין הכהנים זכאין בעורה [יח]: אשם לה' · אי אפשר [יט] אשם לה' שכבר נאמר אשם לכהן כחטאת כאשם תורה אחת להם וגו' הא כיצד כל דבר הבא ממותר חטאת כגון מפריש מעות לחטאתו וניתותר מהן וממותר אשמות כגון הנך דאזלי לרעייה דקיימא לן (תמורה דף יח.) כל שבחטאת מתה באשם רועה: ילקח בהן כו' · נמצאו שני כתובים [כ] מקויימין אשם לה' בשר לעולה ואשם לכהן העור והיינו דכתיב כסף אשם וכסף חטאות לא יובא וגו': אלא מר במאי [כא] מוקי לה · להא דתני לעיל פרט לעולת הקדש: וכרבי יהושע · דאמר זכרים עלמן יקרבו עולות והך עולת הקדש היא וכדמסיים ואזיל דכי א"ר יהושע דחייל שם מזבח עלייהו מעיקרא אמאי דחזי למזבח קאמר אבל בעור מודה דחייל [כב] עלה קדושת בדק הבית: המקדיש נכסיו · לבדק הבית: הראויות למזבח · תמימים: זכרים ימכרו לצרכי עולות כו' · דקי"ל בתמורה (דף לג:) המתפים תמימים לבדק הבית כשהן נפדין אינן נפדין אלא למזבח שכל הראוי למזבח אינו יוצא מידי מזבח לעולם: זכרים עלמן יקרבו עולות · לשם אותו האיש דקסבר אדם חולק הקדישו ואע"ג [כג] דמקדיש סתמא דעתיה הוה להקריב למזבח הראוי לו: ונקבות ימכרו כו' · אבל הן עלמן לא יקרבו שלמים עד שימכרו דכיון [כד] דמקדיש סתמא הכל הקדיש הראוי למזבח דומיא דבדק הבית שכולו קדוש הלכך לדמי עולה אקדישנהו ובהך עולה דרבי יהושע [כה] זכרים הקריבים עולות קא"ר יהודה לעיל פרט לעולת הקדש: ואפי' לרבי יהושע · כלומר ואע"ג דאמר ר' יהושע אדם חולק הקדישו הראוי למזבח למזבח ושאינו ראוי למזבח יהא לבדק הבית לא שיהו כשאר קדשי מזבח שעורותיהן לכהנים דמודה הוא שהעור נתפס לבדק הבית כשאר נכסים שלו: ואין לו יורשין · דאין לה בעלים: ה"ג עולת איש אין לי אלא עולת איש נשים ועבדים מנין [כו] ת"ל כו': העולה · קרא יתירה הוא דלא איצטריך למכתב אלא העור לכהן אלא לרבות בא: הואיל ולא עלתה לבעלים · ואף על פי שהיא כשרה
לא

הניחא למ"ד מותרות לנדבת ציבור אזלי · תימה לדידיה מ"ש דממעט מותרות טפי מעולת תמיד וי"ל דסברא הוא למעוטי טפי מותרות משום דהוו מעיקרא לאיש: אלא למ"ד לנדבת יחיד מאי איכא למימר · תימה מאי קשיא ליה הא רבי יהודה דממעט הכא עולת הקדש הוא דקאמר בסמוך לנדבת ציבור אזלי דקתני ששה לנדבה ואי לנדבת יחיד לא היה משימה בשופר דקרבן יחיד בעי סמיכה וי"ל דלא שמיע ליה ההיא ברייתא תדע דאי שמיע ליה הא הדר ביה רבי יהודה ממדרשו של יהוידע: לא מיבעיא למ"ד קדשי בדק הבית תפסי מדאורייתא · תימה לדידיה אמאי איצטריך קרא הכא דאם שחט קודם פדייה אין עורה לכהנים פשיטא דקדשי בדק הבית היו בכלל העמדה והערכה: אין לי אלא עולת איש גרים נשים ועבדים מנין · משמע מחד קרא הוה ממעטינן נשים ועבדים ודין הוא דהא ילפינן מהדדי בג"ש דלה לה מאשה והקשה הר"ר חיים דבפרק החובל (ב"ק דף פח.) מצריך תרי קראי גבי עדות חד למעוטי נשים וחד למעוטי עבדים וי"ל דגבי מלות הוא דילפינן מהדדי בג"ש דלה לה אבל גבי עדות לא שייך למילף דאין תלוי בנאמנות שהרי משה ואהרן לא מעידין לא משום דלא מהימני הלכך היכא דגלי גלי*:
ומודה

[פסחים נח: וש"נ]
כ"א שזכה
צ"ל אלעזר
צ"ל דתנן
שקלים פ"ד מ"ז ב"ב קנג. תמורה כ. ודף לה:
ר"א עובדי כוכבים ועי' בכ"מ ועי' רש"ק וצ"ק ובעל פ"מ
צידסם כצ"ק ממעט
צ"ל אלה על דבר שאינו שלו צ"ק

לז א מיי' פ"ה מהלכות מעה"ק הל' כ:
לז ב מיי' פי"ט מהל' פסה"מ הל' ט:
לח ג מיי' פ"ה מהלכות מעה"ק הלכה כא:
לט ד ה מיי' שם הל' יט:
מ ו מיי' שם הל' כא:
מא ז מיי' פ"ה מהל' פסה"מ הל' ט ופ"ד מהל' בקלים הלכה ט:
מב ח מיי' פ"ה מהל' מעה"ק הלכה כא:
מג ט מיי' פ"ה מהל' ערכין הלכה ז:
מד י מיי' פ"ה מהל' מעה"ק הלכה כא:

[וב"ק פח. ד"ה יצא עבד תירצו באופן אחר]
שקלים פ"ו מ"ו [תמורה כג: ע"ש]

שיטה מקובצת
א] שיזכו בעורה אין המזבח מוכיח שאין: ב] ראשונה ר' אילא א"ר ותיבת אייבו ל"ש ונמחק: ג] הבית ולא: ד] תפסי דאורייתא הני: ה] יהו הכהנים זכאין: ו] ילקח בהן עולות הבשר לה' והעורות לכהנים: ז] עולות ונקבות: ח] ודמיהן עם שאר נכסים יפלו לבדק הבית: ט] תיבת גרים נמחק: י] א)מצינו עולת שזכו: יא] המותרות דמי אשמות ותיבת דכל נמחק: יב] דקי"ל בכולן ירעו: יג] אלעזר ורבנן: יד] קי"ל דעורה לכהנים: טו] מכלל דמאן דמותיב: טז] חלה על שאינו: יז] חדתין ועתיקין קינין: יח] בעורה · פי' אלא חוזרין ומוכרין העור ולוקחין בדמיו בהמה לעולה לקיץ המזבח דברי רבי יהודה הס"ד: יט] אפשר לומר אשם: כ] כתובין קיימין אשם לה' בשר עולה ואשם לכהן: כא] במאי מוקים לה: כב] דחייל עליה קדושת: כג] ואע"ג דאקדיש: כד] דכיון דאקדיש סתמא: כה] יהושע של זכרים: כו] תיבות ת"ל נמחק:
א) נראה דצ"ל מצינו עולה שזכו בעורה וקל וחומר וכו'

Continuation of translation from previous page as indicated by ◁

with R. Judah?[7] Surely he retracted [from his view]? For it was taught: Six were for votive [offerings], [viz.,] for burnt-offerings brought from [the proceeds of] left-overs, the skins of which [burnt-offerings] did not belong to the priests:[8] these are the words of R. Judah. Said R. Nehemiah—others say, R. Simeon—to him: If so, you have nullified the teaching of Jehoiada the Priest. For it was c taught:[1] This teaching did Jehoiada the priest expound: *It is a guilt-offering—he oweth a guilt-offering unto the Lord:*[2] whatever comes in virtue of a sin-offering and a guilt-offering,[3] burnt-offerings are purchased therewith: the flesh belongs to the Lord,[4] while the skin belongs to the priests![5]—Said he to him:[6] Then how does the Master explain it?—I explain it as referring to one who dedicates his property [to Temple Repair], he replied, and it is in accordance with R. Joshua. For we learnt: If one dedicates his property, amongst which were animals eligible for the altar, both males and females,—R. Eliezer said: The males must be sold for the purpose of burnt-offerings, and the females must be sold for the purpose of peace-offerings,[7] whilst the money [obtained] for them, together with the rest of the estate, falls to the Temple Repair. R. Joshua said: The males themselves must be offered as burnt-offerings, and the females must be sold for the purpose of peace-offerings, and burnt-offerings be brought with the money [obtained] for them.[8] Now, even R. Joshua who maintains that a man divides his con-d secration,[1] that is only in respect of the flesh,[2] but the skin is seized [with the sanctity of Temple Repair].[3]

'R. Jose son of R. Judah said: It excludes a proselyte's burnt-offering'. Said R. Simai b. Ḥilkai to Rabina: Is then a proselyte not a man?[4]—It excludes, replied he, a proselyte who died without heirs.[5]

Our Rabbis taught: *'Any man's burnt-offering':* I know it only of a *man's* burnt-offering;[6] how do I know it of the burnt-offering of proselytes,[7] women, and slaves? Because it says, *The skin of the* burnt-offering,[8] [which is] an extension. If so, why does it say, *any* man's *burnt-offering?* [It intimates,] a burnt-offering which has freed a man [of his obligation], and [thus] excludes one which was slaughtered [with the intention of sprinkling its blood] after time or without bounds, [teaching] that the priests have no rights in its skin. You might think that I include[9] one which was slaughtered under a different designation, [for] since it does not free its owner,

(7) Who maintains anon that the skin of left-overs is the priest's. (8) There were thirteen horn-shaped receptacles in the Temple for various funds. Six of these were for the purpose stated in the text.

c (1) Marginal emendation: we learnt. (2) Lev. V, 19. E.V. *he is certainly guilty before the Lord.* The present rendering, which gives the sense as it is understood here, viz., that the guilt-offering belongs to the Lord, contradicts Lev. VII, 7 q.v., and the text proceeds to reconcile the two verses. (3) I.e., if the animals so dedicated cannot be offered as such for any reason; thus they are left-overs. They are left to graze until they are blemished, when they are redeemed, and other animals purchased for sacrifices, as explained. (4) It is burnt on the altar. (5) But not to the Lord. Now, R. Judah did not answer this, which shews that he accepted it and retracted from his view. (6) *Sc.* R. Naḥman to R. Hamnuna. (7) If one consecrates an animal fit for the altar to Temple Repair, the animal must be sacrificed. Hence these animals must be sold to those who need them for sacrifices. This selling constitutes redemption, for R. Eliezer holds that everything consecrated for Temple Repair must be redeemed, if it cannot be used itself for that purpose, and the money goes to that fund. (8) R. Joshua holds that when a man consecrates property without defining it, whatever is fit for the altar is meant to be sacrificed itself, and not redeemed. But at the same time, the *whole* of it must be for the altar, just as the *whole* of anything consecrated to Temple Repair belongs to the Temple Repair Fund. Consequently, males are sacrificed as burnt-offerings on behalf of the person who consecrated them, and not sold to another. Females, however, cannot be similarly sacrificed as peace-offerings, since only a portion of peace-offerings belong to the altar. Therefore they are sold for peace-offerings, and with the money males for burnt-offerings are bought, and the rest of the estate falls to Temple Repair.

d (1) I.e., though he does not specify, he intends each thing for whatever it is fit, whether for the Temple Repair Fund or for the altar. (2) I.e., the flesh of the animal belongs to the altar. (3) Since skin could be consecrated to the Temple Repair Fund, it belongs to it now too, and not to the priests. This then is what we exclude above. (4) Surely he is included in, *'any* man's *burnt-offering'?* (5) An ordinary Jew cannot be without an heir, since he must have some relation, however distant. A proselyte, however, loses all relationship with his pre-conversion relations, and so may die without a legal heir. Hence the animal does not belong to *'any man'* when it is sacrificed. (6) That the skin belongs to the priests. (7) Sh.M. (and apparently Rashi) delete 'proselyte.' *Var. lec.* heathens.—Sacrifices were accepted from non-Jews. (8) *'Burnt-offering'* is a repetition in the same verse. (9) Among those whose skin does not belong to the priests. *Var. lec.* exclude—*sc.* from those whose skins belong to the priest—this is preferable.

מתני' ^א^כל שלא זכה המזבח בבשרה לא זכו כהנים בעורה שנאמר °עולת איש עולה *שעלתה לאיש ^ב^עולה שנשחטה שלא לשמה אע"פ שלא עלתה לבעלים עורה לכהנים ^ג^אחד עולת האיש ואחד עולת האשה עורותיהן לכהנים ^ד^עורות קדשים קלים לבעלים ^ה^עורות קדשי קדשים לכהנים קל וחומר ומה אם עולה שלא זכו בבשרה זכו בעורה קדשי קדשים שזכו בבשרה אינו דין שיזכו א] בעורה אין מזבח יוכיח שאין לו עור בכל מקום: גמ' ת"ר עולת איש ^ו^פרט לעולת הקדש דברי ר' יהודה רבי יוסי בר' יהודה אומר פרט לעולת גרים מאי פרט לעולת הקדש אמר רבי חייא בר יוסף פרט לעולה הבאה מן המותרות הניחא למ"ד מותרות לנדבת ציבור אזלי אלא למ"ד מותרות לנדבת יחיד אזלי מאי איכא למימר כדאמר רבא *העולה עולה ראשונה ה"נ העולה עולה ראשונה ב] רבי אייבו א"ר ינאי פרט למתפים עולה לבדק הבית ג] לא מיבעיא למ"ד קדשי בדק הבית תפסי מדאורייתא אלא אפילו למ"ד לא תפסי ד] הני מילי בשר אבל עור תפיס וכן אמר רב נחמן אמר רבה בר אבוה פרט לעולה הבאה מן המותרות א"ל רב המנונא לרב נחמן כמאן כרבי יהודה הא הדר ביה דתניא ששה לנדבה לעולה הבאה מן המותרות שלא יהו ה] כהנים זכאין בעורה דברי רבי יהודה אמר לו רבי נחמיה ואמרי לה ר"ש אם כן ביטלת מדרשו של יהודע הכהן *דתניא *זה מדרש דרש יהוידע הכהן °אשם הוא אשם אשם לה' ^ז^כל שבא משום חטאת ומשום אשם ילקח ו] בו עולות הבשר לשם ^ח^עורה לכהנים א"ל אלא מר במאי מוקים לה א"ל מוקמינא ליה במקדיש נכסיו וכדרבי יהושע *דתנן המקדיש נכסיו והיו בהן בהמות הראויות לגבי מזבח זכרים ונקבות ר"א אומר ^ט^זכרים ימכרו לצורכי עולות ז] נקבות ימכרו לצורכי זבחי שלמים ודמיהן ח] יפלו עם שאר נכסים לבדק הבית רבי יהושע אומר זכרים עצמם יקרבו עולות ונקבות ימכרו לצורכי שלמים ויביא בדמיהן עולות ושאר נכסים יפלו לבדק הבית ואפי' לרבי יהושע דאמר אדם חולק הקדישו הני מילי בשר אבל עור תפיס רבי יוסי ברבי יהודה אומר פרט לעולת גרים אמר ליה רב סימאי בר חילקאי לרבינא אטו גר לאו איש הוא אמר ליה פרט לגר שמת ואין לו יורשים תנו רבנן עולת איש אין לי אלא עולת איש ^י^עולת ט] *גרים נשים ועבדים מנין ת"ל עור העולה ריבה אם כן מה תלמוד לומר עולת איש עולה שעלתה לאיש פרט לשנשחטה חוץ לזמנה וחוץ למקומה שלא יהו הכהנים זכאין בעורה יכול שאני *מרבה שנשחטה שלא לשמה הואיל ולא עלתה לבעלים

לא

רש"י

מתני' כל שלא זכה המזבח בבשרה · כגון שאירע בה פסול קודם זריקה דלא היתה לה שעת היתר למזבח: עורה לכהנים · מקרא איתרבאי בברייתא בגמרא: ואחד עולת האשה · דאיתרבאי נמי מקרא: עורות קדשי קדשים · חטאות ואשמות לכהנים כדמפרש טעמא ואזיל: אין המזבח מוכיח · כלומר ואין לך לומר מזבח יוכיח שזכה בבשר העולה ולא זכה בעורה ואף אתה אל תתמה בקדשי קדשים שאע"פ שזכו כהנים בבשרן לא יזכו בעורן אין זו הוכחה שאין למזבח עור בכל מקום אבל לכהנים מצינו י] שזכו בעור העולה וקל וחומר שיזכו בעורות קדשי קדשים: גמ' פרט לעולת הקדש · לקמיה מפרש לה: פרט לעולת גרים · לקמיה פריך אטו גר לאו איש הוא: מן המותרות · יא] דכל אשמות של רעייה כגון תמורת אשם ואשם שמתו בעליו ושכיפרו בעליו באחר דקיימא לן יב] ירעו וימכרו ויפלו דמיהן לנדבה והוא עולת קיץ המזבח דלאו עולת איש הוא אלא נדבת צבור היא ונסכיה משל צבור ואין בעליו סומך עליה ואינו שוחטה כדתנן בתמורה (דף כ:): הניחא כו' · פלוגתא דרבי יג] *אליעזר ורבנן היא בתמורה (שם): לנדבת צבור · לקיץ המזבח: לנדבת יחיד · בעליו של אשם שניתותר הוא עצמו מביא עולה בדמיו והוא סומך עליה ושוחטה ונסכיה קריבין משלו: כדאמר רבא · (יומא דף לד·) גבי וערך עליה העולה דילפינן מינה מנין שלא יהא דבר קודם לתמיד של שחר ת"ל וערך עליה העולה וגו' ואמרינן מאי תלמודא ואמר רבא העולה משמע העולה ראשונה האמורה בסדר קרבנות היום הכא נמי עור העולה כתיב העולה ראשונה שהופרשה מתחילה לשם עולה ^*^ולא הבאה ממותר אשם וממותר חטאת ולקמיה פריך והא קי"ל יד] עורה לכהנים ממדרש יהוידע הכהן: פרט למתפים עולתו לבדק הבית · שאין עורה לכהנים: ולא מיבעיא וכו' בפ' בתרא דתמורה (דף לג:) דקאמר עולא המתפים עולה לבדק הבית אין בה אלא עיכוב גיזברים בלבד ומותבינן לעולא המתפים עולה לבדק הבית אסור לשוחטה עד שתפדה ומשני עולא האי דמצריך ליה פדיה מדרבנן מכלל טו] מאן דמותיב בעי למימר דאורייתא ולענין עורה לא מיבעיא למ"ד מדאורייתא תפסה בה קדושת בדק הבית דאין עורה לכהנים אם שחטה עד שלא נפדית דלאו עולת איש הוא אלא עולת הקדש: אלא אפי' למ"ד · מדרבנן בעלמא אבל מדאורייתא לא הני מילי דמדאורייתא לא בשר דשל מזבח הוא ואין קדושה *חלה טז] עליו שאינו שלו על פיו אבל עור דלאו ממון מזבח הוא וכהנים אכתי לא זכו ביה תפוס: כמאן כרבי יהודה · לקמן מייתי לה דהאמר אין עורה לכהנים: הא הדר ביה · דקאמרי ליה אם כן בטלת מדרשו של יהוידע הכהן ולא אהדר להו מידי: ששה לנדבה · בי"ג שופרות שהיו במקדש קמיירי דכתוב עליהן תקלין חדתין יז] [ותקלין עתיקין] קינין וגוזלי עולה עצים ולבונה וזהב ·לכפרת וששה לנדבה ומפרש מאי ניהו ששה לנדבה: ה"ג ששה לנדבה לעולה הבאה מן המותרות שאין הכהנים זכאין בעורה יח]: אשם לה' · אי אפשר יט] אשם לה' שכבר נאמר אשם לכהן כחטאת כאשם תורה אחת להם וגו' הא כיצד כל דבר הבא ממותר חטאת כגון מפריש מעות לחטאתו וניתותר מהן וממותר אשמות כגון הנך דאזלי לרעייה דקיימא לן (תמורה דף יח.) כל שבחטאת מתה באשם רועה: ילקח בהן ס' · נמצאו שני כתובים כ] מקויימין אשם לה' בשר לעולה ואשם לכהן העור והיינו דכתיב כסף אשם וכסף חטאות לא יובא וגו': אלא מר במאי כא] מוקי לה · להא דתני לעיל פרט לעולת הקדש: וכרבי יהושע · דאמר זכרים עצמן יקרבו עולות והך עולת הקדש היא וכדמסיים ואזיל דכי א"ר יהושע דחייל שם מזבח עלייהו מעיקרא אמאי דחזי למזבח קאמר אבל בעור מודה דחייל כב] עלה קדושת בדק הבית: המקדיש נכסיו · לבדק הבית: הראויות למזבח · תמימים: זכרים ימכרו לצרכי עולות כו' · דקי"ל בתמורה (דף לג:) המתפים תמימים לבדק הבית כשהן נפדין אינן נפדין אלא למזבח שכל הראוי למזבח אינו יוצא מידי מזבח לעולם: זכרים עצמן יקרבו עולות · לשם אותו האיש דקסבר אדם חולק הקדישו ואע"ג כג] דמקדיש סתמא דעתיה הוה להקריב למזבח הראוי לו: ונקבות ימכרו כו' · אבל הן עצמן לא יקרבו שלמים עד שימכרו דכיון כד] דמקדיש סתמא הכל הקדיש הראוי למזבח דומיא דבדק הבית שכולו קדוש הלכך לדמי עולה אקדישינהו והך עולה דרבי יהושע כה] זכרים הקריבים עולות קא"ר יהודה לעיל פרט לעולת הקדש: ואפי' לרבי יהושע · כלומר ואע"ג דאמר ר' יהושע אדם חולק הקדישו הראוי למזבח למזבח ושאינו ראוי למזבח יהא לבדק הבית לא שיהו כשאר קדשי מזבח שעורותיהן לכהנים דמודה הוא שהעור נתפס לבדק הבית כשאר נכסים שלו: ואין לו יורשין · דאין לה בעלים: ה"ג עולת איש אין לי אלא עולת איש עולת נשים ועבדים מנין כו] ת"ל כו': העולה · קרא יתירא הוא דלא איצטריך למכתב אלא העור לכהן אלא לרבות בא: הואיל ולא עלתה לבעלים · ואף על פי שהיא כשרה

לא

תוספות

הניחא למ"ד מותרות לנדבת ליבור אזלי · תימה לדידיה מ"ש דממעט מותרות טפי מעולת תמיד וי"ל דסברא הוא למעוטי טפי מותרות משום דהיו מעיקרא לאיש: אלא למ"ד לנדבת יחיד מאי איכא למימר · תימה מאי קשיא ליה הא רבי יהודה דממעט הכא עולת הקדש הוא דקאמר בסמוך לנדבת ליבור אזלי דקתני ששה לנדבה ואי לנדבת יחיד לא היה משימה בשופר דקרבן יחיד בעי סמיכה וי"ל דלא שמיע ליה ההיא ברייתא אדע דאי שמיע ליה הא הדר ביה רבי יהודה ממדרשו של יהוידע: לא מיבעיא למ"ד קדשי בדק הבית תפסי מדאורייתא · תימה לדידיה אמאי איצטריך קרא הכא דאם שחט קודם פדייה אין עורה לכהנים פשיטא דקדשי בדק הבית הוו בכלל העמדה והערכה: אין לי אלא עולת איש גרים נשים ועבדים מנין · משמע מחד קרא הוה ממעטינן נשים ועבדים ודין הוא דהא ילפינן מהדדי בג"ש דלה לה מאשה והקשה הר"ר חיים דבפרק החובל (ב"ק דף פח.) מצריך תרי קראי גבי עדות חד למעוטי נשים וחד למעוטי עבדים וי"ל דגבי מצות הוא דילפינן מהדדי בג"ש דלה לה אבל גבי עדות לא שייך למילף דאין תלוי בנאמנות שהרי משה ואהרן לא מעידין לא משום דלא מהימני הלכך היכא דגלי גלי*:

ומודס

עין משפט נר מצוה

לו א מיי' פ"ה מהלכות מעה"ק הל' כ:

לז ב מיי' פי"ט מהל' פסה"מ הל' ט:

לח ג מיי' פ"ה מהלכות מעה"ק הלכה כא:

לט ד ה מיי' שם הל' יט:

מ ו מיי' שם הל' כא:

מא ז מיי' פ"ה מהל' פסה"מ הל' ט ופ"ד מהל' שקלים הלכה ט:

מב ח מיי' פ"ה מהל' מעה"ק הלכה כא:

מג ט מיי' פ"ה מהל' ערכין הלכה ז:

מד י מיי' פ"ה מהל' מעה"ק הלכה כא:

[וב"ק פח. ד"ה יהא עבד תירצו באופן אחר]

שקלים פ"ו מ"ו [תמורה כג: ע"ש]

שיטה מקובצת

א] שיזכו בעורה אין המזבח מוכיח שאין: ב] ראשונה ר' אילא א"ר ותיבת איבו ל"ש ונמחק: ג] הבית ולא: ד] תפסי דאורייתא הני: ה] יהו הכהנים זכאין: ו] ילקח בהן עולות הבשר לה' והעורות לכהנים: ז] עולות ונקבות: ח] ודמיהן עם שאר נכסים יפלו לבדק הבית: ט] תיבת גרים נמחק: י] א]מצינו עולה שזכו: יא] המותרות דמי אשמות ותיבת דכל נמחק: יב] דקי"ל בכולן ירעו: יג] אלעזר ורבנן: יד]קי"ל דעורה לכהנים: טו] מכלל דמאן דמותיב: טז] חלה על שאינו: יז]חדתין ועתיקין קינין: יח] בעורה · פי' אלא חוזרין ומוכרין העור ולוקחין בדמיו בהמה לעולה לקיץ המזבח דברי רבי יהודה תס"ד: יט] אפשר לומר אשם: כ] כתובין קיימין אשם לה' בשר עולה ואשם לכהן: כא] במאי מוקים לה: כב] דחייל עליה קדושה: כג] ואע"ג דאקדיש: כד] דכיון דאקדיש סתמא: כה] יהושע של זכרים: כו] תיבות ת"ל נמחק:

א) נראה דצ"ל מלינו עולה שזכו בעורה וקל וחומר וכו' ·

מסורת הש"ס

נ"א שזכה

[פסחים נח: וש"נ] נ"ל אלעזר

נ"ל דתנן

שקלים פ"ד מ"ז ב"ב קמג. תמורה כ. ודף לא:

נ"ל עובדי כוכבים ועי' בכ"מ ועי' רש"ק וצ"ק ובעל ס"מ

ביומא כ"ק ממעט

נ"ל אלא על דבר שאינו שלו צ"ק

תורה אור

לא יזכו כהנים זכאין בעורה ת"ל עור העולה מ"מ עור העולה אין לי אלא עור העולה עורות קדשי קדשים מנין ת"ל א] עור העולה אשר הקריב יכול שאני מרבה אף קדשים קלים ת"ל עולה מה עולה קדשי קדשים אף כל קדשי קדשים רבי ישמעאל אומר עור העולה אין לי אלא ב] העולה עורות קדשי קדשים מנין ודין הוא ומה עולה שלא זכו בבשרה זכו בעורה קדשי קדשים שזכו בבשרן אינו דין ג] שזכו בעורן מזבח יוכיח שזכה בבשר ולא זכה בעור מה למזבח שכן לא זכה במקצת תאמר בכהנים שזכו במקצת הואיל וזכו במקצת ד] זכו בכוליה רבי אומר כל ה] עצמו לא הוצרכנו אלא לעור העולה בלבד שבכל מקום ו] העור מהלך אחר הבשר *פרים הנשרפין ושעירים הנשרפין ז] ועורותיהן [נשרפין] עמהן חטאת ואשם וזבחי שלמי ציבור מתנה לכהן רצו מפשיטין אותן לא רצו אוכלין אותן ע"ג עורן קדשים קלים לבעלים רצו מפשיטין אותן רצו אוכלין אותן על גב עורן אבל עולה נאמר בה °והפשיט את העולה ונתח אותה לנתחיה יכול לא יזכו הכהנים זכאין בעורה ת"ל °עור העולה אשר הקריב לו יהיה פרט לטבול יום (ומחוסר כיפורים) ואונן שיכול לא יזכו בבשר שהוא לאכילה ח] יזכו בעור שאינו לאכילה ת"ל לו יהיה פרט למחוסר כיפורים וטבול יום ואונן ות"ק נמי תיפוק לי מדינא *מילתא דאתיא בקל וחומר טרח וכתב לה קרא ורבי ישמעאל האי אשר הקריב מאי עביד ליה פרט לטבול יום ומחוסר כיפורים ואונן ותיפוק ליה מלו יהיה רבי ישמעאל לטעמיה *דאמר רבי יוחנן משום רבי ישמעאל נאמר בעולה לו יהיה ונאמר באשם לו יהיה מה להלן עצמותיו מותרין אף כאן עצמותיו מותרין מופני דאי לא מופני איכא למיפרך מה לאשם שכן בשרו מותר לו יהיה קרא יתירא הוא: **מתני'** °כל הקדשים שאירע בהן פסול קודם להפשיטן אין עורותיהן לכהנים לאחר הפשיטן עורותיהן לכהנים *אמר רבי חנינא סגן הכהנים מימי לא ראיתי עור שיוצא לבית השריפה *אמר רבי עקיבא מדבריו למדנו שהמפשיט את הבכור ונמצא טריפה שיאותו הכהנים בעורו ט] וחכמים אומרים אין *לא י] ראינו ראיה אלא °יצא לבית השריפה: **גמ'** כל שלא זכה המזבח בבשרה לא זכו הכהנים בעורה ואע"ג דאפשטיה לעור קודם זריקה מני רבי אלעזר ברבי שמעון היא דאמר אין הדם מרצה על העור בפני עצמו אימא סיפא כל הקדשים שאירע בהן פסול קודם הפשיטן אין עורותיהן לכהנים לאחר הפשיטן עורותיהן לכהנים אתאן לרבי דאמר הדם מרצה על העור בפני עצמו רישא רבי אלעזר ברבי שמעון סיפא רבי אמר אביי מדסיפא רבי היא רישא נמי רבי היא ומודה רבי °שאין הפשט קודם זריקה רבא אמר מדרישא ר"א ברבי שמעון סיפא נמי ר"א בר"ש מאי קודם הפשט ומאי

ויקרא א · שם ז · צ"ק · מנחות ה.

רש"י

לא יזכו בעזרה: אשר הקריב · כל הקרבנות במשמע : שזכה בבשר · באימורים : שכן לא זכה במקצת · עורות שלא מצינו עור למזבח תאמר בכהנים שזכו במקצת בעור העולה : כל יא] עצמו כו' · אין לנו להביא ראיה לשאר עורות מעולה שפרט בה הכתוב לבדה מפני שלא הוצרכנו ללמוד על שאר עורות מה תהא עליהן אלא על של עולה בלבד : ועורותיהן עמהן · כדכתיב ואת הפר ואת עורו וגו': רצו מפשיטין יב] · שהרי לא הצריכו להפשיט ונתנו לכהן כמות שהן כדכתיב כחטאת כאשם תורה אחת וגו': נאמר בה והפשיט · והבשר למזבח ועל העור שהזקיקו להפשיט לא אמור מה תהא עליו ולמזבח אינך יכול להביאו יג] *(זה) דבהדיא פרט לך הקטר באברים מופשטין ולא פרט לך העור עמהן: לו יהיה · רישיה דקרא המקריב את עולת איש ועליה קאי לו יהיה: פרט לאונן כו' · דלא חזי להקרבה : שיכול לא יזכו בבשר · כלומר אע"פ שנתמעטו מלחלוק בבשר יד] מלאכול לערב הוצרכו למעטן מן העורות : שיכול לא יזכו בבשר · מפני שהוא טו] ראוי לאכילה והן אינן ראוים טז] לאכילת היום : מדינא · כי היכי דנפקא ליה לרבי ישמעאל ולמה לי קרא לעורות קדשי קדשים : אשר הקריב · דיליף ת"ק מיניה עורות קדשי קדשים מאי עביד ליה : תיפוק ליה מלו יהיה · כדנפקא ליה לרבי : רבי ישמעאל לטעמיה · דדריש לו יהיה לדרשא אחריתי : קרא יתירא הוא · דמצי למכתב עור העולה אשר הקריב לכהן ולשתוק : **מתני'** אין עורותיהן לכהנים · אלא נשרפים עם עורן: לא ראיתי עור יוצא יז] לשריפה · משהופשט הכי מפרש לה בגמרא : ונמצא טריפה · ואפילו שפסול זה היה בו קודם הפשט הואיל ולא ניכר עד לאחר הפשט יאותו הכהנים בעורו : אין לא *ראיתי ראיה · שמא לא אירע בימיו שימצא טריפה אחר הפשט ואם אירע ושרפוה הוא לא ראה : אלא יצא לבית השריפה · הואיל וקודם הפשט הוה ביה יח]: **גמ'** ה"ג בגמ' כל שלא זכה המזבח בבשרה לא זכו הכהנים בעורה ואע"ג דאפשטיה לעור קודם זריקה ול"ג כל שאין לו בבשר דההיא מאי בעיא לענין דם מרצה על העור הא ההיא בכהן טמא קאמר אלא יט] רישיה דהך דלעיל מהך נקט ואותיב (א) הכי קתני רישא כל שלא זכה המזבח בבשרה כגון שאירע בו פסול קודם זריקה דלא היה כ] לה לבשר שעת היתר למזבח לא זכו הכהנים בעורה ולא פליג בין שהופשט קודם הפסול בין לא הופשט אלמא אע"ג דאפשטיה לעור קודם זריקה ונפסל הבשר ואח"כ זרק קאמר דלא זכו בעורה : מני ר' אלעזר בר' שמעון היא · דאמר לקמן (דף קד·) אין הדם מרצה על עור חלוץ בפני עצמו בלא בשר כגון אם נפסל הבשר ואין הדם מרצה עליו אף העור לא יצא מידי מעילה להיות ניתר לכהנים אחר הפשטן : עורותיהן לכהנים · ואפילו אירע פסול זה קודם זריקה : אתאן לרבי · דפליג עליה דרבי אלעזר לקמן (שם) ואמר הדם מרצה על עור חלוץ בפני עצמו בלא הרצאת בשר : ומודה רבי שאין הפשט קודם זריקה · אע"ג דאמר הדם מרצה על העור בפני עצמו היכא דאיתרמי דאיפשט קודם זריקה מודה הוא שאין כא] כהנים רגילין בכך שאסור לשהות הדם כל כך הלכך כב] נמי דקתני כל שלא זכה המזבח בבשרה לא זכו הכהנים בעורה טעמא משום דפסול דקודם זריקה קודם הפשט הוא כג] ומיהו היכא דאיתרמי דהפשיט קודם זריקה ונפסל אחר הפשט אע"פ שלא זכה מזבח בבשר יזכו הכהנים בעורה ומשנתינו דברה בהוה: קודם שנראו כד] להפשט · קודם זריקה אין עורותיהן לכהנים ואפי' הופשט ואח"כ נפסל וכל שכן כשהוא עם הבשר דאין דם מרצה על העור בלא בשר : לאחר שנראו להפשט · דהיינו לאחר זריקה עורותיהן לכהנים ואפי' עורו עם הבשר כשנפסל כדקאמר רבי אלעזר דכיון שנזרק הדם והורצה בשר שעה אחת יפשיטנו ועורו לכהנים : על העור בפני עצמו · אם הופשט ונפסל הבשר קודם זריקה וזרק הדם הותר העור דקסבר רבי אין עור פסול אלא הנפסל עם הבשר אבל הופשט קודם פסולו אפי' כה] קודם זריקה אתיא זריקה ושריא ליה וכל שכן כו] אחר הפשט ואחר זריקה אבל אם קודם הפשט נפסל ואפילו אחר זריקה הרי הוא כבשר :
רבי

תוספות

ומודה רבי שאין הפשט קודם זריקה · משמע הכא דלכ"ע היכא דעלד פסול קודם הפשט וקודם זריקה אין הדם מרצה על העור ותימה דבסוף הגוזל קמא (ב"ק דף קיא·) כז] אמר גבי נתן אשם ליהויריב וכסף לידעיה דאם קדמו בני יהויריב והקריבו את האשם זכו במה שבידם ופריך למאי חזי אשם פסול הוא אמר רבא לעורו והשתא עורו גופיה הא לא חזי דהיינו קודם הפשט וזריקה דתחלת הבאתו בפסול וי"ל דהתם לאחר שחיטת האשם יכול להביא כסף קודם זריקה קרינא ביה מלבד איל הכפורים אשר יכפר בו כיון דעדיין כח] לא נכפר הלכך לא חשיב פסול דקודם זריקה ומיהו קשה כיון דאיכא הפסול כט] בידם מה לי קודם זריקה ומה לי לאחר זריקה *וי"ל ל] דהוי כמו שנמצא טריפה בבני מעיים לרבי חנינא סגן הכהנים הואיל ולא הוכר פסולו קודם הפשט לרבי וקודם זריקה לרבי אלעזר מרצה על העור *(הג"ה) וקשה דתניא בתוספתא דפסחים הביא את אשמו קודם גזילו לא יהא אחר ממרס בדמו עד שיביא גזילו אלא תעובר צורתו ותצא לבית השריפה אלמא אין תקנה להביא הגזל לא] קודם *שנשחט ואין לומר היינו מדרבנן לב] הא תניא בסיפא גבי מצורע (*לעיל) (*דף ה) הקדיש חטאתו לאשמו לא יהא אחר ממרס בדמו אלא תעובר צורתו ותצא לבית השריפה ומהכא מוכח פ' קמא דמנחות (דף ה·) יש מחוסר זמן לבו ביום ואע"ג דמן התורה פסול צריך עבור צורה כדתניא פרק כיצד צולין (פסחים דף *ס) כל שפסולו בגופו ישרף מיד בדם ובבעלים תעובר צורתו ופסולו בגופו הוי כמו פיגול וטריפה ונבלה אבל הקדמה לא · ברוך :
מאן

עין משפט נר מצוה

מה א מיי' פ"ה מהל' מעשה"ק הלכה יח:

מו ב מיי' שם הל' כ:

מז ג מיי' פ"ו מהלכות בכורות הל' י ופי"ט מהלכות פסה"מ הל' ט:

מח ד מיי' פ"ה מהל' מעשה"ק הל' יח:

מסורת הש"ס / גליון

ג"א עולה ובאימורי קדשי קדשים צ"ק · ס"א דבה כהדיא · רש"ק פ"ג · [פסחים יט: וש"נ] · ראיתי צ"ק · עדיות פ"ב הלכה ב · [כתובות כג.] · ג"א וי"ל מידי דהוי כמו צ"ק · ג"א ס"ג וכ"ל כיון דיכול להביא הכסף קודם זריקה הוי לא הוכר פסולו · ס"א שמרק · [לעיל כט:] · [גי' בכוכון איתא שם לה:] · לעיל פו. · [עי' תוס' לקמן קד: ד"ה היו עקיבא]

הגהות הב"ח

(א) רש"י ד"ה ג' וכו' ואותיב הכי קתני:

שיטה מקובצת

א] תיבות עור העולה נמחק : ב] אלא עור העולה : ג] דין שיזכו בעורן : ד] במקצת יזכו בכולן : ה] כל עצמו לא : ו] עור הולך אחר : ז] הן נשרפין ועורותיהן עמהן : ח] לאכילה אבל יזכו : ט] בעורו · עיין שו"ת מהר"ם בנייר סי' ת"ח ובקלף סי' תע"ב : י] לא ראיתי ראיה : יא] כל עצמו כו' : יב] מפשיטין כו' · שהרי לא הזקיקו להפשיט ונותנן לכהן : יג] להביאו דהא בהדיא פרט לך הקטרה באברים המופשטין ולא פרט לך הכתוב העור עמה : יד] בבשר לאכול : טו] תיבת ראוי נמחק : טז] לאכילה היום : יז] לבית השריפה משהופשט : יח] ביה פסול הס"ד : יט] אלא רישא לו לבשר : כא] שאין הכהנים רגילין : כב] הילכך מתניתין : כג] הוא דסתם זריקה קודם הפשט הוא ומיהו : כד] להפשט דהיינו קודם : כה] אפילו פסולו קודם : כו] וכל שכן אם אירע הפסול ואחר זריקה דהוי עור לכהנים אבל אם קודם: כז] קמא אמרינן : כח] לא כיפר הילכך : כט] הפסול בדם מה לי : ל] וי"ל כגון שנמצא ותיבת דהוי כמו נמחק : לא] הגזל אחר שנשחט ותיבת קודם נמחק

[103b] the skin does not belong to the priests. Therefore it says, *'the skin of the burnt-offering'*, [which implies,] at all events. *'The skin of the burnt-offering'*: I know it only of the skin of a burnt-offering; how do I know it of the skin of most holy sacrifices? Because it
a says, [*'the skin of the burnt-offering*][1] *which he hath offered.'*[2] You might think that I include lesser sacrifices too: therefore it states, *'burnt-offering'*: as a burnt-offering is a most sacred sacrifice, so all most sacred sacrifices [are included].[3] R. Ishmael said: *'The skin of the burnt-offering'*: I know it only of the skin of a burnt-offering. How do I know it of the skin of most sacred sacrifices? It is inferred by logic. If the priests have a right to the skin of a burnt-offering, though they have no right to its flesh, is it not logical that they have a right to the skin of [other] most sacred sacrifices, seeing that they have a right to their flesh? Let the altar refute it, for it has a right to the flesh and has no right to the skin? As for the altar, that is because it has no right to part thereof;[4] but in the case of priests who have a right to part thereof, you must say: since they have a right to part, they have a right to the whole.[5] Rabbi said: The text bears essentially only upon the skin of a burnt-offering.[6] For in every instance the skin follows the flesh. [Thus:] the bullocks that are to be burnt and the goats that are to be burnt are burnt and their skin with them. The sin-offering, guilt-offering, and public peace-offerings are the priestly dues: if they wish, they can flay them; if they do not so desire, they can consume them together with their skin.[7] Lesser sacrifices belong to their owners: if they desire, they can flay them; if they do not desire, they can eat them together with the skin. But of the burnt-offering it is said, *And he shall flay the burnt-offering, and cut it into its pieces.*[8] You might thus think that the priests do not acquire its skin; therefore it states, *'even the priest shall have to himself the skin of the burnt-offering which he hath offered'*; and this excludes a *ṭebul yom*, [one who lacks atonement],[9] and an *onen*. For you might think that these have no right to the flesh, which is eaten, but they have a right to the skin, which
b is not eaten:[1] therefore it states, *it shall be his*:[2] which excludes one who lacks atonement, a *ṭebul yom*, and an *onen*.

Now, let the first Tanna too deduce it by logic?—That which may be inferred *a fortiori*, Scripture takes the trouble of writing it [explicitly]. Now, how does R. Ishmael utilise this text, *'which he hath offered'*?—It excludes a *ṭebul yom*, one who lacks atonement, and an *onen*. But let him deduce that from *'it shall be his'*?—R. Ishmael is consistent with his view. For R. Joḥanan said on R. Ishmael's authority: *'It shall be his'* is said in connection with a burnt-offering, and *'it shall be his'* is said in connection with a guilt-offering: as there its bones are permitted, so here too its bones are permitted. This must be redundant, for if it is not redundant, it can be refuted: as for a guilt-offering, that is because its flesh is permitted! *'It shall be his'* is a superfluous text.[3]

MISHNAH. ALL SACRIFICES WHICH BECAME DISQUALIFIED: [IF THIS HAPPENED] BEFORE THEY WERE FLAYED, THEIR SKINS DO NOT BELONG TO THE PRIESTS.[4] [IF IT OCCURRED] AFTER THEY WERE FLAYED, THEIR SKINS BELONG TO THE PRIESTS. SAID R. ḤANINA THE SEGAN OF THE PRIESTS:[5] NEVER IN MY LIFE HAVE I SEEN SKIN GO OUT TO THE PLACE OF BURNING.[6] R. AKIBA OBSERVED: WE LEARN FROM HIS WORDS THAT IF ONE FLAYS A FIRSTLING AND IT IS FOUND TO BE TEREFAH,[7] THE PRIESTS HAVE A RIGHT TO ITS SKIN. BUT THE SAGES MAINTAIN: 'I HAVE NEVER SEEN' IS NOT PROOF: RATHER, IT [THE SKIN] MUST GO FORTH TO THE PLACE OF BURNING.[8]

GEMARA. [The preceding Mishnah teaches,] Whenever the altar does not acquire the flesh, the priests do not acquire the skin, [which implies,] even though the skin was stripped before the sprinkling [of the blood]. Who is the author of this? R. Eleazar b. R. Simeon, who maintained: The blood does not propitiate on
c behalf of the skin when it is by itself.[1] Then consider the second clause:[2] ALL SACRIFICES WHICH BECAME DISQUALIFIED: [IF THIS HAPPENED] BEFORE THEY WERE FLAYED, THEIR SKINS DO NOT BELONG TO THE PRIESTS; [IF IT OCCURRED] AFTER THEY WERE FLAYED, THEIR SKINS BELONG TO THE PRIESTS: this agrees with Rabbi, who maintained: The blood propitiates on behalf of the skin when it is by itself. Thus the first clause agrees with R. Eleazar b. R. Simeon, while the second clause agrees with Rabbi?—Said Abaye: Since the second clause agrees with Rabbi, the first clause too agrees with Rabbi; Rabbi however admits that flaying is not done before sprinkling.[3] Raba said: Since the first clause agrees with R. Eleazar b. R. Simeon, the second clause too agrees with R. Eleazar b. R. Simeon. What

a (1) Sh.M. deletes this. (2) This is superfluous, and therefore intimates: *all* sacrifices which a priest offers. (3) But not others. (4) As in the Mishnah: in no instance does the skin belong to the altar. (5) To the skin of *all* most sacred sacrifices. (6) And does not apply to or is not needed for any other sacrifices. (7) I.e., the priests are not bound to flay the animals first. Obviously then the skin is theirs together with the flesh, and no text is required in respect of these. (8) Lev. I, 6. Scripture does not state at this stage what is done with the skin. (9) RaSHaK omits bracketed words.

b (1) I.e., while they have no share in the *flesh* of other sacrifices, since they are not eligible to eat it when they are sacrificed, there seems no reason why they should not share in the *skin* of the burnt-offering. (2) The literal translation of the text quoted is, the skin of the burnt-offering which he hath offered is the priest's; it shall be his. *'It shall be his'* is emphatic; implying *his* only, and not any other priest's. (3) *Supra* 86*a* q.v. notes. Thus he utilises *'it shall be his'* for this purpose. (4) But are burnt together with the flesh. (5) V. *supra* 84*a* n.b 4. (6) *Sc.* after it was flayed. (7) Though this disqualification occurred before it was even slaughtered. (8) Since it was disqualified before it was flayed.

c (1) If the flesh becomes disqualified after the animal is flayed, so that the sprinkling does not 'propitiate' on behalf of the flesh, i.e., it does not render the flesh permitted, it does not propitiate on behalf of the skin either, i.e., it does not permit the skin to the priests. (2) *Sc.* the present Mishnah. (3) Though the blood does propitiate on behalf of the skin by itself, he admits that it is very rare for the skin to be by itself when the blood is sprinkled, since the flaying is generally done afterwards, in order not to keep the blood so long. Hence the preceding Mishnah assumes that the skin was not stripped before the sprinkling. If, however, it was, the skin would belong to the priests, notwithstanding that the altar did not acquire its flesh.

however is meant by 'before flaying' [104a] and 'after flaying'?—Before it is eligible for flaying and after it is eligible for flaying [respectively].[4]

What is this allusion to Rabbi and R. Eleazar b. R. Simeon?—It was taught: Rabbi said: The blood propitiates on behalf of the skin by itself. But when it is together with the flesh and a disqualification arises in it, whether before or after the sprinkling, it
a is the same as itself.[1] R. Eleazar b. R. Simeon maintained: The blood does not propitiate on behalf of the skin by itself. And when it is together with the flesh and a disqualification arises in it before sprinkling, it is the same as itself; [if it arises] after the sprinkling, the flesh has been permitted for a short space of time, [and so] it is flayed, and the skin belongs to the priests.[2]

Shall we say that they differ on the same lines as R. Eliezer and R. Joshua? For it was taught: *And thou shalt offer thy burnt-offerings, the flesh and the blood:*[3] R. Joshua said: If there is no blood there is no flesh, and if there is no flesh there is no blood.[4] R. Eliezer said: The blood is [fit] even if there is no flesh, because it is said, *And the blood of thy sacrifices shall be poured out* [*against the altar of the Lord thy God*].[5] If so, why is it stated, *And thou shalt offer thy burnt-offerings, the flesh and the blood?* To teach you: just as the blood requires throwing,[6] so does the flesh require throwing.[7] Thus you learn that there was a space between the ascent and the altar.[8] Shall we say that he who maintains that it propitiates[9] agrees with R. Eliezer,[10] while he who maintains that it does not propitiate agrees with R. Joshua?—About the view of R. Eliezer there is no controversy at all.[11] They disagree in reference to R. Joshua. He who maintains that it does not propitiate holds as R. Joshua. While he who maintains that it does propitiate can tell you: R. Joshua rules thus only there, where there is no loss to the priests.[12] But as for the skin, which would entail a loss to the priests, even R. Joshua admits,[13] by analogy with a *fait accompli*.[14] For
b it was taught: If the flesh was defiled or disqualified,[1] or it passed without the curtains,—R. Eliezer said: He must sprinkle [the blood]; R. Joshua maintained: He must not sprinkle [the blood]. Yet R. Joshua admits that if he does sprinkle [it], it is accepted.[2]

SAID R. ḤANINA THE SEGAN OF THE PRIESTS etc. Did he not? Surely there are the bullocks which are burnt and the goats which are burnt?[3]—We do not speak of [what is burnt] in pursuance of their prescribed rites.[4] But what when [the sacrifice is disqualified] before it is flayed and before sprinkling?[5]—We refer to a *stripped* [skin].[6] But there is [a disqualification] after flaying and before sprinkling, according to R. Eleazar b. R. Simeon who maintained [that] the blood does not propitiate on behalf of the skin by itself?[7]—R. Ḥanina agrees with Rabbi.[8] Alternatively, you may even say that he holds as R. Eliezer b. R. Simeon: Rabbi admits that there was no flaying before sprinkling.[9] But there is [the case] where it is discovered *terefah* in its inwards?[10]—He holds that where it is found *terefah* in its inwards, it [the blood] propitiates. This may be proved too, for it teaches, R. AKIBA OBSERVED: WE LEARN FROM HIS WORDS THAT IF ONE FLAYS A FIRSTLING AND IT IS FOUND TO BE TEREFAH, THE PRIESTS HAVE A RIGHT TO ITS SKIN. This
c proves it. What then does R. Akiba inform us?[1]—He informs us this, [viz.,] that it is so even in the country.[2] R. Ḥiyya b. Abba said in R. Joḥanan's name: The *halachah* is as R. Akiba. But even R. Akiba ruled thus only where an expert had permitted it,[3] but not if an expert had not permitted it. [The Talmud however states:] The law agrees with the view of the Sages: [the flesh is buried and the skin is burnt].[4]

MISHNAH. BULLOCKS WHICH ARE BURNT AND GOATS WHICH ARE BURNT: WHEN THEY ARE BURNT IN PURSUANCE OF THEIR PRESCRIBED RITES, THEY ARE BURNT IN THE ASH DEPOSITORY, AND DEFILE GARMENTS;[5] BUT WHEN THEY ARE NOT BURNT IN PURSUANCE OF THEIR PRESCRIBED RITES,[6] THEY ARE BURNT IN THE PLACE OF THE BIRAH[7] AND DO NOT

(4) I.e., before and after *sprinkling*. If it is disqualified before sprinkling, even after flaying, the skin does not belong to the priests. If it is disqualified after sprinkling, even though it was not yet flayed, the skin belongs to the priests.
a (1) *Sc.* the flesh. (2) Cf. *supra* 85a. (3) Deut. XII, 27. (4) If either is defiled, the other is unfit for its purpose. (5) Ibid. (6) I.e., dashing against the altar. (7) On the altar. (8) V. *supra* 62b. (9) The blood propitiates on behalf of the skin after the flesh is disqualified.—Lit., 'it (the skin) is propitiated'. (10) That the blood is fit (and efficacious) even when there is no flesh. (11) He certainly disagrees with R. Eleazar b. R. Simeon, since he holds that the blood can be sprinkled even if there is no flesh, and therefore it must be efficacious in permitting the skin. (12) R. Joshua rules that if there is no flesh there is no blood only in the sense that the owner is not yet freed from his obligation and must bring another sacrifice. Thus this does not involve the priests in loss. (13) That the sprinkling of the blood makes it available for the priests, since Scripture ordains that the skin belongs to the priest who offers it, and here the priests have offered it. (14) As the text proceeds to explain. Sh.M. emends: with (flesh) that went out.
b (1) By the touch of a *ṭebul yom*. (2) Hence here in the same way the sprinkling permits the skin to the priests. (3) Their skin was burnt too. (4) There the burning of the skin (as of the whole animal) is part of the prescribed rites of that particular sacrifice. R. Ḥanina, however, spoke of sacrifices which were burnt through being disqualified. (5) There all agree that the skin is burnt. (6) Whereas in the case just quoted the animal was burnt without being flayed. (7) So that it must be burnt. (8) That the blood does propitiate in that case. (9) V. *supra* 103b n.c3. R. Eleazar b. R. Simeon would certainly hold the same. Thus though theoretically the skin might be burnt by itself, in practice this never happened. (10) This was disqualified before sprinkling and flaying, and it is now assumed that both Rabbi and R. Eleazar b. R. Simeon agree that the skin is burnt. (As this *terefah* would not be discovered until the skin was stripped, the skin would be burnt by itself.)
c (1) Since R. Ḥanina rules thus of *all* sacrifices, why does R. Akiba tell us this particularly about a firstling? (2) Lit., 'borders'—a technical term for all places outside Jerusalem. When a firstling becomes blemished, it is slaughtered and eaten outside Jerusalem just like *ḥullin*. But Scripture permits nothing else but eating, so that if it dies, the carcass must not be put to any use, but must be buried. If, however, it was found to be *terefah* (and so cannot be eaten), R. Akiba informs us that since this was discovered after it was flayed, the skin is permitted, just as the skin is permitted in similar circumstances in the Temple. (3) Before a blemished firstling might be slaughtered for food it had to be examined by an expert, to make sure that the blemish was a permanent one and had not been deliberately inflicted. (4) Presumably this means that the Talmud rejects the ruling of R. Ḥiyya b. Abba and rules in accordance with the Sages. Consequently, R. Akiba's inference, being based on R. Ḥanina's ruling, is likewise rejected. Hence if a firstling is found *terefah* after it is stripped, the *whole* of it is forbidden. The flesh is buried, not burnt, for only the flesh of sacrifices which had been brought to the Temple court and there disqualified is burnt. Rashi knows no reason why the skin is burnt, and suggests that 'the flesh . . . burnt' should altogether be deleted, and that we simply read: The law agrees with the Sages. (5) The garments of those who burn it, v. Lev. XVI, 28. (6) But because they had been disqualified. (7) Lit., 'the Edifice.' V. Gemara.

ומאי אחר הפשט קודם א] שנראו להפשט אחר שנראו להפשט מאי רבי ומאי רבי אלעזר בר' שמעון דתניא רבי אומר הדם מרצה על העור בפני עצמו וכשהוא עם הבשר נולד בו פסול בין קודם זריקה בין לאחר זריקה הרי הוא כיוצא בו *רבי אלעזר בר"ש אומר אין הדם מרצה על העור בפני עצמו וכשהוא עם הבשר נולד בו פסול קודם זריקה הרי הוא כיוצא בו אחר זריקה הורצה בשר שעה אחת יפשיטנו ועורו לכהנים לימא בדרבי אליעזר ורבי יהושע קמיפלגי ב] °ועשית עולותיך הבשר והדם *רבי יהושע אומר אם אין דם אין בשר אם אין בשר אין דם רבי אליעזר אומר דם אע"פ שאין בשר שנאמר °ודם זבחיך ישפך א"כ מה ת"ל ועשית ג] עולותיך הבשר והדם לומר לך *מה דם בזריקה אף בשר בזריקה הא למדת שריוח יש בין כבש למזבח לימא מ"ד הורצה כר"א ומ"ד לא הורצה כר' יהושע אליבא דר"א כ"ע לא פליגי כי פליגי אליבא דרבי יהושע מ"ד לא הורצה כרבי יהושע מ"ד הורצה אמר לך עד כאן לא קאמר רבי יהושע התם אלא בבשר דליכא פסידא לכהנים אבל עור דאיכא פסידא לכהנים אפילו רבי יהושע מודה מידי דהוה ד] אדיעבד *דתנן *נטמא ה] בשר או נפסל או שיצא חוץ לקלעים ר"א אומר יזרוק רבי יהושע אומר לא יזרוק ומודה רבי יהושע שאם זרק הורצה: א"ר חנינא סגן הכהנים כו': ולא הרי פרים הנשרפים ושעירים הנשרפים למצותן לא קאמרינן ו] הרי קודם הפשט וקודם זריקה חלוץ קאמרינן והאיכא אחר הפשט וקודם זריקה ז] לרבי אלעזר ברבי שמעון דאמר אין הדם מרצה על העור בפני עצמו ח] רבי חנינא כרבי סבירא ליה ואיבעית אימא אפילו ט] תוקמא כרבי אלעזר ברבי שמעון מודה רבי שאין הפשט קודם זריקה והאיכא נמצאת טריפה בבני מעיים קסבר נמצאת טריפה בבני מעיים מרצה דיקא נמי דקתני א"ר עקיבא מדבריו למדנו שהמפשיט את הבכור ונמצא טריפה שיאותו הכהנים בעורו ש"מ ואלא מאי קמ"ל ר"ע הא קמ"ל י] אפילו בגבולין א"ר חייא בר אבא א"ר יוחנן הלכה כר"ע ואף יא] ר"ע לא אמר אלא כשהתירו מומחה אבל לא התירו מומחה לא והלכתא כדברי חכמים (*בשר בקבורה והעור בשריפה): **מתני'** פרים הנשרפים ושעירים הנשרפים בזמן שהן נשרפין כמצותן נשרפים בבית הדשן ומטמאין בגדים ואם אינן נשרפין כמצותן נשרפין בבית הבירה ואינן מטמאין בגדים

הדרן עלך טבול יום

תורה אור: דברים יב

[צ"ל דתניא]

רש"י

רבי אלעזר ברבי שמעון כו' · קסבר בזריקה כשרה תליא היתר העור אבל נפסל בשר קודם זריקה אין העור מותר ואפילו הופשט קודם פסולו: מ"ד · הדם מרצה על העור לאחר שנפסל בשר: כרבי אליעזר · דאמר דם אע"פ שאין בשר: אליבא דר' אליעזר כ"ע לא פליגי · כלומר מילתיה דרבי אלעזר ברבי שמעון דאמר לא הורצה ודאי פלוגתא היא דעל כרחך מודה הוא דאילו רבי אליעזר לא קאי כוותיה דהא קאמר יזרוק לכתחילה אף ע"פ שאין בשר כגון אבד או נשרף אלמא זריקה מעלייתא היא: כי פליגי אליבא דרבי יהושע · כלומר הא דאמר דמ"ד הורצה כר' אליעזר ולא כרבי יהושע ליתא דאפילו אליבא דרבי יהושע אמרה רבי למילתיה: ה"ג עד כאן לא א"ר יהושע אלא בבשר דליכא פסידא לכהנים · ע"כ לא קאמר רבי יהושע אם אין בשר אין דם אלא לענין לעלות קרבן לבעלים לחובה דליכא פסידא לכהנים והתורה אמרה (דברים יב) הבשר והדם: אבל לענין עור דאיכא פסידא דכהנים אפילו רבי יהושע מודה · דלא מפסידנא להו שלא כדין ואם נשרף בשר או אבד קודם זריקה לכתחילה לא יזרוק וליכא פסידא דכהנים שהרי לא קרב הקרבן ואם עבר וזרק הדם הויא זריקה להתיר העור אע"פ שלא עלה לו הקרבן הקרבה הוי וקרינא ביה עור העולה אשר הקריב: מידי דהוה יב] אדיעבד · דקתני אם זרק הורצה הניחא גבי נטמא איכא למימר הציץ מרצה אבל גבי יוצא לא מרצה הציץ וקאמר אם זרק הורצה אלמא יג] *ק"ל היה לו לרבי יהושע בדרשה זו דאם אין בשר אין דם דאם זרק הורצה הלכך גבי אבוד ושרוף נמי אע"ג דבדיעבד נמי פסול כדאמרינן בכילד צולין (פסחים עח:) לענין עור מיהא מודה: למצותן לא קאמר · דהני הכשר מצותן בכך וכי קאמר ר' חנינא בנשרפין מחמת פסולן: והאיכא קודם הפשט וקודם זריקה · דבין לרבי בין לרבי אלעזר ברבי שמעון נשרף לרבי משום דקודם הפשט ולרבי אלעזר משום דקודם זריקה: חלוץ קאמרי' · מימי לא ראיתי עור מופשט יוצא לבית השריפה והנפסל קודם הפשט עורו נשרף בבשרו ואין מפשיטים אותו: והאיכא אחר הפשט קודם זריקה · דלרבי אלעזר ברבי שמעון יד] חלוץ ונשרף הוא: ומשני רבי חנינא כרבי ס"ל · דאמר הדם מרצה על העור: ה"ג ואב"א אפילו תימא כר' אלעזר בר"ש ומודה רבי שאין הפשט קודם זריקה. אפילו תימא רבי חנינא כרבי אלעזר ס"ל ודקא קשיא לך הא איכא אירע בו טו] אחר הפשט קודם זריקה לא איתרמי בימיו דאפילו לרבי דאמר הדם מרצה על העור בפני עצמו מודה הוא דאין הפשט קודם זריקה טז] (ולא הורגלו בכך) וכל שכן לרבי אלעזר ברבי שמעון לא הורגלו בכך: והאיכא נמצאת טריפה בבני מעיים · יז] לא נמצא פסולו עד שהופשט ופסול זה קודם זריקה וקודם הפשט היה בו דקס"ד דבין לרבי ובין לרבי אלעזר נשרף כדאמרן לרבי משום דקודם הפשט ולרבי אלעזר משום קודם זריקה: מרצה · הואיל ולא הוכר פסולו קודם הפשט לרבי וקודם זריקה לרבי אלעזר מרצה על העור והבשר ישרף כשאר פסולי קדשים: אלא מאי קמ"ל רבי עקיבא · כיון דשמעינן לרבי חנינא דאמר בשאר קדשים מרצה למה לי לאשמועינן יח] בכור: דאפילו בגבולין · בכור בעל מום הנשחט יט] בו במדינה על מומו ולא התירו הכתוב אלא באכילה כדכתיב (דברים טו) בשעריך תאכלנו אבל אם מת עורו אסור וטעון קבורה ואשמועינן רבי עקיבא דהיכא דלא ניכר כ] טריפתו עד לאחר הפשט *שראה שחיטתו *) והפשיט עורו כאילו נזרק דמו במקדש ונמצא טריפה לאחר הפשט: בשר בקבורה · כא] דאין מאכילין קדשים לכלבים ושריפה ליכא דאין שריפה בקדשים אלא כב] כשהובאה לעזרה ונפסל לאחר שחיטה: והעור בשריפה · לא ידענא טעמא ונראה בעיני דל"ג כג] האי פירושא *אלא ה"ג והלכה כדברי חכמים ותו לא מידי כד] ותוספתא זו גירסא דתלמידי כה] **) תרביצאי היא וטעו במה ששנינו במתניתין במילתייהו דרבנן כו] לבית השריפה (א) יצא ואני אומר דרבנן לאו אדר"ע קיימי דאיירי בבכור בגבולין אלא אדרבי חנינא קיימי דאיירי בקדשי המקדש: **מתני'** נשרפין בבית הדשן · חוץ לג' מחנות כדיליף לקמן בפירקין: ומטמאין בגדים · כז] לעסוקין בהן כדכתיב (ויקרא טז) והשורף אותם וגו': שלא כמצותן · שנפסלו טעונין שריפה כשאר פסולי קדשים: בבית הבירה · פעמים בעזרה פעמים בהר הבית כדאמרינן בגמרא:

*) נ"ל והפשטת עורו. נ"ק **) פי' בית המדרש [ועיין רש"י במנחות סב:]

תוספות

מאן דאמר לא הורצה כרבי יהושע · תימה היכי מצי סבר כוותיה הא קתני ומודה רבי יהושע דאם זרק הורצה כדבסמוך ונראה לפרש כח] ומ"ד לא הורצה כר' יהושע דגזר נטמא בשר או נפסל דלא יזרוק אטו אבוד ושרוף דליכא בשר כלל דהתם אפילו בדיעבד לא הורצה והכא נמי אין הדם מרצה על העור בפני עצמו אפילו בדיעבד בנטמא גזירה אטו אבוד ושרוף ולא מיירי הכא באבוד ושרוף אלא בנטמא או נפסל ומ"ד הורצה ע"כ לא קאמר רבי יהושע כט] דגזר אטו אבוד ושרוף ולא יזרוק אלא גבי בעלים דליכא פסידא דכהנים שעדיין לא זכו בעורו אבל עור דאיכא פסידא [דכהנים] דכבר זכו כהנים משנזרק הדם התם לא גזרינן אטו אבוד ושרוף מידי דהוה אדיעבד פי' בפסול יוצא וטומאה דדיעבד אם זרק הורצה ולא גזרינן הכא נמי מרצה הדם על העור בפני עצמו ופירוש הקונטרס דחוק: *א"ר עקיבא מדבריו למדנו כו' · משמע דוקא בעורו יאותו הכהנים אבל בבשרו לא דאפילו לעובדי כוכבים אסור והקשה ה"ר אפרים דבפרק כל פסולי המוקדשים (בכורות דף לג:) מתיר רבי עקיבא אפילו לעובדי כוכבים ולעיל פי' בריש פ' *התערובת (דף עח:) אבל לא התירו מומחה לא משמע דוקא משום טריפות הא לאו הכי לא והיינו דלא כר"מ דקניס בפ' (*כל פסולי המוקדשין (דף לג)) ל] בבכור שנשחט שלא על פי מומחה מכאן דקדק בהלכות גדולות דהא דקיימא לן *כרבי מאיר בגזירותיו דוקא בגזירותיו ולא בקנסיו*:

לא

עין משפט נר מצוה

מט א ב ג מיי' פ"א מהלכות פסה"מ הלכה לא:

נ ד ה מיי' פ"ג מהלכות בכורות הלכה י ופ"ש בכ"מ:

נא ו מיי' פ"ז מהלכות מעה"ק הלכה ד:

נב ז מיי' פ"ה מהלכות פרה אדומה הלכה ה:

נג ח מיי' פ"ז מהלכות מעה"ק הלכה ד ופ"ה מהלכות פרה הלכה ד:

[שייך לעיל במשנה קג:]

גירסת הש"ס התערובת הס"ד ואח"כ מה"ד אבל לא התירו

[נ"ל עד כמה בכורות דף כח.]

[עירובין מו.]

[ועי' תוספות יבמות לד: ד"ה מי כו' וכב"ק לב: ד"ה וחכמים וב"מ עב: ד"ה קונסין וב"ב נה: ד"ה וחכמים ובכורות כח: ד"ה ר"מ כו']

מסורת הש"ס

לעיל פס'

תוספתא דזבחים פ"ד פסחים עז:

לעיל סב:

[פסחים לד: עז:] ס"א קל

הגהות הב"ח

(א) רש"י ד"ה והעור כו' לבית השריפה ואני כצ"ל ותיבת יצא נמחק:

[ועי' תוס' לעיל עז: סד"ה ובטנפס ותוס' בכורות לג: ד"ה פסק מתני' מני]

ס"א שרייה

[אבל הרמב"ם גרס לה ומוקי לה בבכור תם ועיין כר"ע ברטנורה וכס"מ שם פ"ג מהלכות בכורה הלכה י וע' רש"ק וצ"ק]

שיטה מקובצת

א] קודם שיראו להפשט: ב] קמיפלגי דתניא ועשית: ג] עולותיך עיין לעיל דף ס"ב ע"ב: ד] דהוה איוצא ותיבת אדיעבד נמחק: ה] נטמא הבשר או שנפסל או: ו] קאמרינן והאיכא קודם ותיבת הרי נמחק: ז] זריקה כר"א בר"ש: ח] עצמו כרבי דאמר הדם מרצה על העור בפני עצמו ותיבות רבי חנינא כרבי ס"ל ל"ש: ט] אפילו תימא כר"א ותיבת תוקמא נמחק: י] קמ"ל דאפי' בגבולין: יא] ואף רבי עקיבא עיין בתוס' בכורות (דף ל"ב ע"ב): יב] דהוה איוצא דקתני גבי יוצא אם ותיבת אדיעבד נמחק: יג] קל היה: יד] שמעון נשרף וחלוץ הוא הס"ד: טו] בו פסול אחר: טז] תיבות ולא הורגלו בכך ל"ש ונמחק: יז] מעים דלא נמצא פסולו כו' בו וקס"ד דבין: יח] לאשמועינן בבכור הס"ד: יט] תיבת בו נמחק: כ] ניכר טריפתו עד לאחר הפשט שראיה שהיטתו והפשיט לעורו כאילו: כא] בקבורה כדין קדשים בחוץ דאין: כב] אלא כשהובאו: כג] דל"נ להאי פירושא: כד] מידי ותוספתא זו אות א' נמחק: כה] דתלמידי דתרביצאי: כו] דרבנן יצא לבית השריפה יאני: כז] בגדים לעוסקים בהן: כח] לפרש מ"ד לא: כט] יהושע גזירה אטו אבוד: ל] המוקדשין בכור אות ב' נמחק:

תורה אור

אהיו *סובלין א] אותו. במוטות (א) יצאו הראשונים חוץ לחומת העזרה והאחרונים לא יצאו הראשונים מטמאין בגדים והאחרונים אינן מטמאין בגדים עד שיצאו יצאו אלו ב] ואלו מטמאין בגדים *רבי שמעון אומר ג] אינן מטמאין עד שיוצת האור ברובן ניתך הבשר אין השורף מטמא בגדים: **גמ'** *מאי בירה אמר רבה בר בר חנה אמר רבי יוחנן מקום יש בהר הבית ובירה שמו ור"ל אמר כל הבית כולו קרוי בירה שנאמר °(ואל) הבירה אשר הכינותי אמר רב נחמן אמר רבה בר אבוה ד] שלשה בבית הדשנין הן בית הדשן גדול היה בעזרה ששם שורפין פסולי קדשי קדשים ואימורי קדשים קלים ופרים הנשרפין ושעירים הנשרפין שאירע בהן פסול קודם זריקה גובית הדשן אחר היה בהר הבית ששם שורפין פרים הנשרפים ושעירים הנשרפים שאירע בהן פסול אחר זריקה ה] וכמצותן חוץ לשלש מחנות תני לוי שלשה בית הדשנין הן בית הדשן גדול היה בעזרה ששם שורפין פסולי קדשי קדשים ואימורי קדשים קלים ופרים הנשרפים ושעירים הנשרפים שאירע בהן פסול בין קודם זריקה בין לאחר זריקה ובית הדשן אחר היה בהר הבית ששם שורפין פרים הנשרפין ושעירים הנשרפין שאירע בהן פסול ביציאתן ו] וכמצותן חוץ לשלש מחנות בעי רבי ז] ירמיה דלינה מהו שתועיל בפרים הנשרפים ובשעירים הנשרפים מי אמרינן כי מהניא לינה בבשר דבר אכילה אבל הני דלאו בני אכילה נינהו לא או דלמא לא שנא אמר רבא הא מילתא איבעיא ליה לאביי ופשטנא ליה מהא הושוין *שאם חישב באכילת פרים ובשריפתן שלא עשה כלום מאי לאו מדמחשבה לא פסלה לינה נמי לא פסלה ח] ודלמא מחשבה הוא דלא פסלה אבל לינה פסלה תא שמע *ופרים הנשרפים ושעירים הנשרפין מועלין בהן משהוקדשו נשחטו הוכשרו ליפסל בטבול יום ובמחוסר כיפורים ובלינה מאי לאו לינת בשר לא לינת אימורין והא מדקתני סיפא זכולן מועלין בהן בבית הדשן עד שיותך הבשר מדסיפא בשר רישא נמי בשר מידי איריא סיפא בשר רישא אימורין תא שמע דתני לוי שאירע בהן פסול ביציאתן מאי לאו ט] לינה °לא פסול טומאה ופסול יציאה בעי ר"א °יציאה חמהו שתועיל בפרים הנשרפים ושעירים הנשרפים מאי קמיבעיא ליה א"ר ירמיה בר אבא (ג) י] אליבא דמ"ד *עדיין לא הגיע זמנו לצאת מי אמרינן ה"מ בשר דאין סופו לצאת יא] חובה אבל הני דסופן לצאת חובה לא או דלמא ה"נ לא הגיע זמנו לצאת ת"ש דתני לוי שאירע יב] בו פסול ביציאתו מאי לאו פסול יציאה לא פסול טומאה ופסול לינה בעי רבי אלעזר פרים הנשרפים ושעירים הנשרפים *יג] שיצא רובו במיעוט אבר מהו הך מיעוטא דאבר בתר רובא שדינן ליה והא לא נפקא ליה או דלמא בתר רובא דבהמה שדינן פשיטא דלא שבקינן רובא דבהמה ואזלינן בתר רובא יד] דאברים אלא טשיצא חציו ברוב אבר האי מיעוטא דאבר בתר

[לעיל לה] [לעיל פט:]

היו סובלין טו] אותו · הנשרפין כמצותן במוטות לקמן יליף לה טז]: הראשונים · בני אדם הטוענין במוט אותן שבראש האחד יוצאים ראשונים: עד שיצאו · האחרונים בגמרא יליף לה. ניתך הבשר · יז] דגמרה שריפתן אין המסייע שוב בהן מטמא בגדים אבל מקמי הכי כל המסייעין בשעת שריפה מטמאין בגדים וכולה יליף יח] בגמרא: **גמ'** ששם שורפים פסולי בשר קדשי קדשים · שתחילת אכילתן בעזרה ופסולי אימורים אפילו של קדשים קלים דהואיל והקטרת הכשירן בעזרה אף שריפת פסוליהן בעזרה כדילפינן בפסחים בפרק כל שעה (דף כד·) מבקדש באש תשרף: קודם זריקה · שלא הגיע יט] זמנו לצאת לפיכך נשרפין בעזרה: אחר זריקה · שהגיע כ] זמנו לצאת לפיכך נשרפין חוץ לעזרה: כא] וכמצותן · וכשהן נשרפין כמצותן שלא אירע בהן שום פסול: נשרפין חוץ לג' מחנות · כדילפינן בפירקין: בין לאחר זריקה · הואיל ועדיין לא יצאו: ביציאתן · לאחר שיצאו: מהו שתועיל · לפוסלן אם לנו: בבשר דבר אכילה · כב] עולה או אימורין שהן *לאכילת מזבח (ג) כג] אבל הני דלשריפה קיימי דלא אשכחן לה אלא או באכילת מזבח כדכתיב (שמות כג) לא ילין חלב חגי וגו' או באכילת אדם כדכתיב (שם יב) לא תותירו וגו': ושוין שאם חישב כו' · ושוין ר"ש וחכמי' שנחלקו בפ"ב שכד] (לעיל מג·) אם פיגול נוהג בחטאות הפנימיות (ד) שאם חישב לאכול מבשר הפרים למחר או אם חישב בשחיטה על מנת לשורפן חוץ לג' מחנות למחר לא עשה כלום דמחשבת אכילה בדבר שדרכו לאכול בעינן והני לאו דרכן לאכול וגבי שריפה נמי אע"ג דכי אורחיה חשיב אכילת מזבח או אכילת אדם בעינן לפגל ומ"ד פיגול נוהג בפנימיים כגון אם חישב על הקטרת אימורים כה] להקריבו למחר: לינה נמי לא פסלה · כו] בבשרו (ה) קס"ד דאי לינה פסלה מחשבת לינה נמי פסלה: לינת אימורין · דבמידי דהקטרה ודאי פסלה לינה: עד שיותך הבשר · דכל זמן שלא נעשית מצותן מועלין בהן: מדסיפא · לענין מעילה בבשר איירי: רישא נמי · לענין לינה כז] לענין בשר קאמר: דתני לוי · במתניתא דלעיל: ופסול יציאה · כגון שיצאו לפני זריקת דמים שעדיין לא הגיע זמנן לצאת כח]: יציאה מהו שתועיל · לפוסלן אם יצאו מן העזרה לפני זריקת דמים: מאי קמיבעיא ליה · אמאי תיפסול הרי סופן לצאת: א"ר ירמיה בר אבא · כי קא מיבעיא ליה אליבא דמאן דפסיל בשר קדשים קלים שיצא לפני זריקת דמים משום דעדיין לא הגיע זמנו לצאת בפרק כל התדיר (לעיל פט:) הכא מאי מי אמרינן הני מילי בבשר קדשים קלים דאין סופן חובה לצאת אבל הני שסופן כט] לצאת חובה לא מיפסלי ביציאתן: לא פסול טומאה ולינה · דקאי הכא ומדחי ליה קאי הכא ומדחי ליה: ל] שיצא רובו · ומיעוט אחד מן האברים משלים לרובא של בהמה ליציאתה: מהו · מי הוי יציאה לא] לטמא את המתעסקין בהוצאת רובן או לב] לא הוי יציאה מי אמרינן שדי מיעוטא דאבר בתר

לא מחשבה הוא דלא פסלה אבל לינה פסלה · תימה דבריש הוציאו לו (יומא דף מח·) בעי רב פפא חישב בחפינת קטרת מהו ת"ש הוסיף רבי עקיבא הקומץ והקטרת כו' מדפסיל *טבול יום פסולה נמי מלינה ומדפסלה לינה פסלה נמי מחשבה ולא דחי כדהכא וי"ל דהתם דבאכילת מזבח מה לי מחשבה מה לי לינה אבל הכא בבשר *פרים הנשרפין וא"ת היכי פסלה מחשבה בקטרת הא תנן לעיל בפרק ב"ש (דף מב:) דקטרת ולבונה אין בהן משום פיגול וי"ל דנהי דכרת ליכא מחשבה מיהא פסלה מידי דהוה אחטאות הפנימיות לרבי שמעון דאמר בפ"ק (לעיל יד·) מודה היה רבי שמעון לפסול מק"ו מפגל לשמו ובקטרת נמי אהני ג"ש דמלא מלא ממנחה והתם הקשה בקונטרס אמאי הוצרך לדקדק מטבול יום הוה ליה לאתויי ממתני' דמעילה (דף י·) דקתני בהדיא הוכשרו ליפסל בטבול יום ובמחוסר כיפורים ובלינה ותירץ רבינו יב"א משום דההיא מיירי בקטרת דכל השנה כדקתני קדשו בכלי וההוא דמיקדש בכלי פסלה ביה לינה אבל התם בקטרת דיום הכיפורים דעיקרה אינה בכלי אלא משום דלא אפשר כדאמר התם לעיל נג] *והא אמרי' דלא מיפסלה בלינה אבל ההיא דרבי עקיבא משמע דמיירי בכל קטרת ועוד י"ל דההיא דמעילה איכא לדחויי מדרבנן *וכן מחייבין עליה משום פיגול וטמא הוה אמינא מכת מרדות כמו *אבל אוכלין טמאין ושתה משקין טמאין ושתה רביעית יין ונכנס למקדש ושהה כדי אכילת פרס חייב דהייטו מדרבנן דפסול לד] גויה [הוי דרבנן] כדאמרינן בפרק בתרא דיומא (דף פ:) אבל ההיא דר' עקיבא פשיטא דאורייתא מדפסל טבול יום ע"י צירוף דאי מדרבנן *לא הוה מחמירין נמי האי פסול על ידי צירוף וא"ת והיכי דייק מדפסיל טבול יום פסלה נמי לינה והא משניתנה במכתשת נפסלת בטבול יום ולינה לא פסלה עד שתנתן במחתה כדאמר פרק קמא דשבועות (דף יא·) וי"ל דהא דנפסלת בטבול יום *הייטו מדרבנן:

לה] **שיצא** רובו במיעוט אבר · פי' בקונטרס דמיבעיא ליה לענין טמא המתעסק בהן וקשה דבסוף כילד צולין (פסחים פה:) אמרינן המוציא בשר פסח מחבורה לחבורה אינו חייב עד שיניח הואיל כתיב ביה כשבת ופריך ממתני' דהכא דהיו סובלין אותו במוטות דקתני ראשונים מטמאין בגדים אחרונים אין מטמאין בגדים עד שיצאו ואף על גב דלא נח ומשני בנגררים ואם כן רובו במיעוט אבר דהכא לא מחייב לענין שבת כיון דאגודו בפנים לא יטמא בגדים ונראה לפרש דמבעיא ליה לענין לשורפו בפנים:

או

עין משפט נר מצוה

נד א מיי' פ"ג מהלכות פרה אדומה הלכה ה:

ג"א טבול יום פסלה נמי לינה כו'

נה ב מיי' פי"ז מהלכות מעשה הקרבנות הלכה ג:

נ"א פרים הנשרפים נהי דלינה פסלה נהו דלמא מחשבה לא פסלה נהו וא"ת כו' נ"ק

נו ג מיי' שם הלכה ד:

נז ד מיי' פי"ט מהלכות פסה"מ הלכה ג ולחומרא:

נח ה מיי' שם פי"ד הלכה ח:

נט ו ז מיי' פ"ב מהלכות מעילה הלכה ד:

ס ח ט מיי' פי"ט מהלכות פסה"מ הלכה ג:

נ"ל והוי

נ"א וכן הא דקתני סיפא ומייבין עליה כו' נ"ק

[כריתות יב:]

נ"ל לא הוי מחמרינן כולי האי לטמאה ע"י צירוף כו' נ"ק

[פי' ההיא דשבועות דמכתשת ועי' בתוספות יומא מח. ד"ה מדפסיל ביתר ביאור]

שיטה מקובצת

א] סובלין אותן: ב] אלו · אלו ואלו: ג] אשר אלו ואלו אינן מטמאין עד שיצת: ד] אבוה אמר רב שלשה בית הדשנין היו בית הדשן: ה] ובמצותן חוץ: ו] ביציאתן ובמצותן: ז] רבי אלעזר לינה ותיבת ירמיה נמחק: ח] פסלה · לא מחשבה ותיבת דלמא נמחק: ט] לאו פסול: י] אבא כי קא מיבעיא ליה אליבא: יא] תיבות חובה ל"ש: יב] שאירע בהן פסול ביציאתן: יג] הנשרפין שיצאו רובן במיעוט: יד] רובא דאבר אלא: טו] סובלין אותן את הנשרפין: טז] לה להוציאן לבית השריפה: יז] דנגמרה שריפתן: יח] יליף לה בגמרא: יט] שלא הגיע זמנן: כ] שהגיע זמנן: כא] מה"ד ובמצותן: כב] אכילה כגון בשר עולה: כג] מזבח או בשר קדשי קדשים שהן לאכילת אדם אבל הני דלשרפה קיימי לא אשכחן לה: כד] ב"ש בפיגול אם נוהג בחטאות הפנימיות: כה] אימורים להקטירו ותיבת להקריבו נמחק: כו] פסלה בבשר דקס"ד דאי לינה: כז] לינה בבשר קאמר ותיבת לענין נמחק: כח] לצאת ופסול קודם זריקה דתני בה דשריפתה בעזרת בשאר פסולים מיירי ולא בפסול יוצא: כט] שסופן חובה לצאת לא: ל] מה"ד שיצאו רובן במיעוט אבר מיעוט אחד: לא] לטמא ס"א אם נטמא שורפו בהר וצית כדתני לוי: לב] או לאו יציאה היא דאמרינן שדי מיעוטא דאבר: לג] לעיל והוי אמרינן תיבת והא נמחק: לד] גזירה מדרבנן כדאמרינן: לה] שיצאו רובן במיעוט:

מסורת הש"ס

פסחים פה:

יומא סו: תוספתא פי"ג

יומא כ:

נ"א לאכילת מזבח או בשר קדשי קדשים שהם אכילת אדם אבל הני כו' דלא אשכחן לינה אלא כו' נ"ק

הגהות הב"ח

(א) במשנה במוטות הראשונים יצאו חוץ לחומת: (ב) גמ' אמר רבי ירמיה בר אבא כי קמיבעיא ליה אליבא דמ"ד: (ג) רש"י ד"ה בבשר דבר וכו' לאכילת מזבח או בשר קדשי קדשים שהן אכילת אדם הס"ד ואח"כ מ"ה אבל הני דלשריפה קיימא לא דלא אשכחן להו לפסול בלינה אלא או: (ד) ד"ה ושוין וכו' הפנימיות שין שאם חישב וכו' על הקטרת אימורין כ"ב דסוף אכילת מזבח: (ה) ד"ה לינה וכו' דקס"ד:

מעילה ט. לעיל נג:

גליון הש"ס

גמ' לא פסול טומאה ופסול יציאה. הא דקיים פסול יציאה דלמ"ד טומאה הותרה בציבור ל"ש טומאה · וקי"ל דאיך נפרש מה דאמר לוי נפסל אחר זריקה שריפתו בעזרה מה פסול מכתחת לה אם אין בו פסול לינה ולא נשאר רק פסול יוצא וממילא הוי נפסל ביציאתו דשריפתו בבירה: שם יציאה מהו שתועיל בפרים. עיין בירושלמי פרק ו דיומא הלכה ו:

חולין ער

DEFILE GARMENTS. [104b] IF THEY WERE CARRYING THEM[8] ON STAVES,[9] [AND] THOSE IN FRONT HAD PASSED WITHOUT THE WALL OF THE TEMPLE COURT WHILE THOSE IN THE REAR HAD NOT [YET] GONE OUT, THOSE IN FRONT DEFILE THEIR GARMENTS, WHILE THOSE IN THE REAR DO NOT DEFILE THEIR GARMENTS, UNTIL THEY GO OUT. WHEN BOTH GO OUT, BOTH DEFILE THEIR GARMENTS. R. SIMEON SAID: THEY DO NOT DEFILE [THEIR GARMENTS] UNTIL THE FIRE IS BURNING IN THE
a GREATER PART OF THEM.[1] WHEN THE FLESH IS DISSOLVED, HE WHO BURNS [IT] DOES NOT DEFILE HIS GARMENTS.[2]

GEMARA. WHAT IS THE BIRAH?—Said Rabbah b. Bar Ḥanah in R. Joḥanan's name: There is a place on the Temple Mount called '*Birah*'. While Resh Laḳish maintained: The whole Temple [House] is called *Birah*, for it is said, *And to build the Birah* [*Temple*], *for which I have made provision.*[3]

R. Naḥman said in Rabbah b. Abbuha's name: There were three ash-pits. There was the large ash-pit in the Temple court: there they burnt most holy sacrifices and *emurim* of lesser sacrifices which had become disqualified, and the bullocks which were burnt and the goats which were burnt, which had become disqualified before sprinkling. There was a second ash-pit on the Temple Mount: there they burnt the bullocks which were burnt and the goats which were burnt, which had become disqualified after sprinkling, while [those which were burnt] in pursuance of their rites, [were burnt] without the three camps.[4] Levi recited: There were three ash-pits. There was the large ash-pit in the Temple court: there they burnt most holy sacrifices and *emurim* of lesser sacrifices which had become disqualified, and the bullocks which were burnt and the goats which were burnt, which had become disqualified either before or after the sprinkling. There was a second ash-pit on the Temple Mount: there they burnt the bullocks which were burnt and the goats which were burnt, which had become disqualified
b after they had gone out,[1] while [those burnt] in pursuance of their prescribed rites, [were burnt] without the three camps.

R. Jeremiah[2] asked: Is *linah*[3] effective in the case of the bullocks which are burnt and the goats which are burnt?[4] Do we say, *linah* is effective only in respect of flesh which can be eaten, but not in respect of these which cannot be eaten; or perhaps there is no difference?—Said Raba: This question was raised by Abaye, and I solved it for him from the following: And both agree that if he expressed an intention [of *piggul*] in connection with the eating of the bullocks and their burning, he has done nothing.[5] Surely then, since intention does not disqualify it, *linah* too does not disqualify it.—[No]: perhaps only intention does not disqualify it, but *linah* does disqualify it.

Come and hear: You trespass in respect of the bullocks which are burnt and the goats which are burnt from the time they are consecrated. Having been slaughtered, they are ready to become unfit through a *ṭebul yom* and one who lacks atonement, and through *linah*.[6] Surely that means, *linah* of the flesh? No, it means *linah* of the *emurim*.[7] But since the second clause teaches, You trespass in the case of all when they are in the ash-pit until the flesh is dissolved, it follows that the first clause treats of *linah* of the flesh?—What reason have you for supposing this? the second clause treats of the flesh, while the first clause treats of *emurim*.

Come and hear, for Levi recited: '... which had become disqualified after they had gone out.' Does that not mean disqualification through *linah*?—No: it means disqualification through defilement or through going out.[8]

R. Eleazar asked: Is going out effective in respect of the bullocks that are burnt and the goats that are burnt?[9] Why does he ask?[10]—Said R. Jeremiah b. Abba: His question is asked on the view that
c 'it is not time yet for them to be carried out' [is a disqualification].[1] Do we say, that applies only to flesh which one is not eventually bound to carry out; but not to these, which must eventually be carried out; or perhaps here too [we argue that] it was not yet time for them to go out?—Come and hear, for Levi recited: 'which had become disqualified after they had gone out'. Does that not mean disqualification through going out?—No: it means disqualification through defilement or *linah*.[2]

R. Eleazar asked: What of the bullocks which were burnt and the goats which were burnt, if the greater part of them went out through the inclusion of the smaller part of a limb?[3] Do we cast this lesser part of the limb after its greater part, and that indeed has not gone out;[4] or perhaps we cast it after the greater part of the animal?—It is obvious that we do not disregard the greater part of the animal and regard the greater part of the limb! Rather [the question arises] where *half* of it went out, through the inclusion of the greater part of the limb. Do we cast this lesser part of the

(8) *Sc.* the bullocks or goats. (9) In order to burn them in pursuance of their rites.

a (1) *Sc.* of the sacrifices. Hence those who leave the animal before the greater part of the carcass is burning, do not defile their garments. (2) If a person comes to engage in its burning when the flesh is already disintegrated through the fire, he does not defile his garments. (3) I. Chron. XXIX, 19. (4) V. p. 276, n. 6. That was the third ash-pit.

b (1) Of the Temple court. (2) Sh.M. reads: Eleazar. (3) V. Glos. (4) Does *linah* disqualify them, as it does other sacrifices? (5) V. *supra* 35a. (6) V. *supra* 35b. (7) Since these require burning on the altar (*haḳtarah*), *linah* certainly disqualifies them. (8) It was carried out before the blood was sprinkled; this disqualifies it. (9) V. preceding note: R. Eleazar asks whether this does disqualify them. (10) Since they must eventually be carried out, why should he think that they are disqualified if this is done before the sprinkling of the blood?

c (1) V. *supra* 89b. (2) The Talmud means that when we ask about going out, we can argue that this may refer to *linah*, and *vice versa*. (3) The greater part of the carcass was carried out, but it was the greater part only because it included the lesser part of a limb, the greater part of which was still within. Rashi: the question is whether that counts as going out, so that the men in front, who had carried that portion out (for the purpose of burning) defile their garments. Tosaf.: the question is whether (assuming that going out disqualifies), this must now be burnt within (v. *supra*). (4) Hence the lesser part itself is regarded as still within, and consequently the greater part of the carcass has *not* gone out.

limb[5] [105a] after its greater part, and that indeed has gone out;[6] or perhaps we cast it after the animal? The question stands over.

Rabbah b. R. Huna recited [this passage] in reference to *men*. Thus: five men were engaged on it,[7] three had gone out and two were left [within]. What [is the law]? Do we follow the majority of those engaged on it;[8] or perhaps we go by the animal? The question stands over.

R. Eleazar asked: What if the bullocks which were burnt and the goats which were burnt were carried out and then brought
a back:[1] do we say, since they [the carcasses] went out, they are unclean; or perhaps, since they returned, they returned?[2]—Said R. Abba b. Memmel, Come and hear: IF THEY WERE CARRYING THEM ON STAVES, AND THOSE IN FRONT HAD PASSED WITHOUT THE WALL OF THE TEMPLE COURT WHILE THOSE IN THE REAR HAD NOT [YET] GONE OUT, THOSE IN FRONT DEFILE THEIR GARMENTS, WHILE THOSE IN THE REAR DO NOT DEFILE THEIR GARMENTS, UNTIL THEY GO OUT. Now, if you should think that as soon as they go out, they [the garments] are defiled, then let those who are within also be defiled?[3] Said Rabina:[4] Now, is that logical?[5] Surely we require, *and after that he may come into the camp*,[6] which is absent. Then in which circumstances does R. Eleazar's question arise?[7]—Where they seized it with crooks.[8]

Our Rabbis taught: The bullocks [which are burnt], the [red] heifer, and the goat that is sent away:[9] he that leads [the last] away, he who burns them, and he who carries [the first-named] out [of the Temple court], defile their garments. They themselves, however, do not defile garments;[10] but they defile foodstuffs and liquids: these are the words of R. Meir. But the Sages maintain: The [red] heifer and the bullocks defile foodstuffs and liquids, [whereas] the goat which is sent away does not defile, because it is alive, and a live thing does not defile foodstuffs and liquids. As for R. Meir, it is well, [as his view] agrees with the teaching of the School of R. Ishmael. For the School of R. Ishmael taught: *Upon any sowing seed*
b *which is to be sown*:[1] as seeds, which will not ultimately defile with stringent uncleanness, require a qualification [*hekhsher*], so all which will not ultimately defile with stringent uncleanness require a qualification. Thus the carcass of a clean bird is excluded: since it will eventually defile with stringent uncleanness, it does not require a qualification.[2] But as for the Rabbis, if they accept the teaching of the school of R. Ishmael, even the goat that is sent away too [should defile]; while if they reject it, how do they know [that] the [red] heifer and the bullocks [defile foodstuffs]?[3] When R. Dimi came,[4] he said: In the West [Palestine] they said: They need a qualification for defilement from a foreign source.[5]

R. Eleazar asked: Can the bullocks which are burnt and the goats which are burnt defile foodstuffs and liquids within [the Temple court] as without?[6] When it lacks going out, is it as
c though it lacks an action,[1] or not? After he asked, he answered it: That which lacks going out is as though it lacked an action.[2]

R. Abba b. Samuel[3] asked R. Ḥiyya b. Abba: According to R. Meir, can as much as an olive of the *nebelah* of a clean bird defile?[4] When it is lying on the ground, there is no question.[5] When one has it in his mouth, there is no question.[6] The question arises when one is holding it in his hand.[7] [Do we say:] Since it was not yet taken [to his mouth], it is as though it lacked an action,[8]

(5) Which remained within. (6) And by adding this lesser part, the *greater* part of the animal has now gone out. (7) In carrying out its carcass. (8) Hence even those within are regarded as without.
a (1) It is assumed that he asked whether the garments of the men who carried it out are defiled. (2) And are regarded as not having gone out at all. (3) For the defilement of garments depends on the going out of the *carcass*, not on that of the men (*infra b*). Hence those within do not defile their garments only because if the carcass is carried back within, even the garments of the men *without* remain clean. (4) Rashi and BAḤ read: Raba. (5) Do you really think that this proof is valid? (6) Lev. XIV, 8. '*After that*' means after he washes his garments, which were unclean. This shews that Scripture speaks of one who is *without* (he cannot come *in* otherwise), and only then does he defile his garments. (7) According to this, it obviously depends on whether the men have gone out. (8) While standing outside, the carcass having been carried out once and taken in again. Are the garments of these men (if they are not the same as those who carried it out the first time) unclean, or not? (9) V. Lev. XVI, 21 *seq*. (10) The carcasses do not defile any garments which they touch.
b (1) Lev. XI, 37. (2) The whole Scriptural passage reads: *And if aught of their carcass* (*sc*. of unclean 'swarming things'—*sheraẓim*) *fall upon any sowing seed which is to be sown, it is clean. But if water be put upon the seed, and aught of their carcass fall thereon, it is unclean unto you*. Thus '*seed*' is a foodstuff which requires a 'qualification' to become unclean, viz., water must first fall upon it, and it must be touched by a *shereẓ* (q.v. Glos.). When it is unclean, it can in turn defile only eatables and liquids, but not human beings or utensils or garments; thus its defilement is said to be light, not stringent. The School of R. Ishmael deduces that only such require a 'qualification' before they defile; but those which will defile human beings etc. do not require any qualification. The carcass (*nebelah*, q.v. Glos.) of a clean bird (i.e., one permitted for food) defiles the garments of the person who eats it; therefore it does not require a 'qualification'. Now, the red heifer, the goat that is sent away, and the bullocks which are burnt, will eventually defile garments; hence they do not need any qualification, and so defile even while they are alive. (3) Seeing that Scripture speaks only of *garments*. (4) V. *supra* 60b n.d 7. (5) The School of R. Ishmael meant that whatever will not eventually defile with stringent defilement needs a qualification from a foreign source, i.e., it must first touch a *shereẓ* or *nebelah*, whereas that which will eventually defile in this manner e.g. the red heifer, need not first touch a *shereẓ* or *nebelah*, but defiles foodstuffs and liquids automatically. Nevertheless, it must be such as is capable of defiling in general, and we find no instance of a living creature defiling. (6) According to the foregoing, they defile foodstuffs because they defile with stringent defilement (*sc*. garments). But that is only when they go out: hence the question whether they defile foodstuffs whilst they are still within, just as when they are without.
c (1) Which is necessary before it can defile. (2) Hence they do not defile foodstuffs within. (3) Sh. M. emends: R. Abba b. Memmel. (4) Foodstuffs and liquids.—There is no question on the view of the Rabbis, as they maintain that before anything can defile it must conform to the general laws which govern it, and as much as an olive of this *nebelah* can defile only when it is in a man's throat. R. Meir, however, holds that whatever can eventually defile with a stringent defilement need not be fit for defilement. Hence on his view the question arises. (5) It certainly does not defile, for it may never reach the stage of stringent defilement, as perhaps none will take it in his mouth. (6) It certainly does defile, for it has already reached that stage. (7) And about to eat it. (8) To render it capable of defilement.

עין משפט נר מצוה

סא א מיי' פי"ט מהל' פסה"מ הלכה ג:
סב ב ג מיי' פ"ה מהלכות פרה אדומה הלכה ה:
סג ד מיי' שם הלכה ז ופ"ו מהלכות אבות הטומאה הלכה טו: [נ"ל מקוה]
סד ה מיי' פ"ג מהלכות אבות הטומאה הלכה ג:
נ"א כגון נ"ק
נ"ל שחזרו כו' נ"ק
סה ו מיי' שם הלכה ג:
סו ז עי' בכ"מ בפ"ה מהלכות פרה הלכה ז:

מסורת הש"ס

נ"ל מ"ז
נ"ל בחלי הפר שבחוץ ילא רוב כו' נ"ק
נ"ל דלא שבקינן נ"ק
תוספתא דפרה פרק ו [וע"ש תוספתא יומא פרק ג]
חולין קכח: כריתות כא. נדה נא:

גמרא

בתר רוב אבר שדינן ליה והא נפק ליה או דלמא בתר בהמה שדינן ליה תיקו רבה בר רב הונא מתני לה בגברי במתעסקין בו חמשה בני אדם ונפקו תלתא ופשו להו תרי מאי בתר רוב מתעסקין אזלינן או [א] בתר בהמה אזלינן *תיקו. בעי רבי אלעזר פרים [ב] ושעירים הנשרפים שיצאו וחזרו מהו מי אמרינן כיון דנפקי [ג] להו איטמו להו או דלמא כיון דהדור הדור אמר ר' אבא בר ממל ת"ש היו סובלין אותן במוטות [ד] הראשונים יצאו חוץ לחומת העזרה והאחרונים לא יצאו הראשונים שיצאו חוץ לחומת העזרה מטמאין בגדים והאחרונים [ה] אין מטמאין בגדים עד שיצאו ואי ס"ד כיון דנפקי להו איטמו הנך דאיכא גואי (א) ליטמא אמר רבינא ותסברא הא בעינא °ואחר יבא אל המחנה וליכא אלא רבי אלעזר היכי בעי לה כגון דנקיטי לה בבקולסי *ת"ר [ו] *פרים ופרה *ושעיר המשתלח השורפן והמוציאן מטמא בגדים והן עצמן [ז] אין מטמאין בגדים אבל מטמאין אוכלין ומשקין דברי ר"מ וחכ"א פרה ופרים מטמאין אוכלין ומשקין שעיר המשתלח אינו מטמא [ח] שהוא חי והחי אינו מטמא אוכלין ומשקין בשלמא לרבי מאיר כדתנא [ט] דבי ר' ישמעאל *דתנא דבי רבי ישמעאל °על כל זרע זרוע מה זרעים שאין סופן ליטמא טומאה חמורה [י] וצריכין הכשר אף כל שאין סופן ליטמא טומאה חמורה צריכין הכשר יצתה נבלת עוף טהור שסופה ליטמא טומאה חמורה *ואין צריכה הכשר אלא לרבנן אי אית להו דתנא דבי רבי ישמעאל אפילו שעיר המשתלח (ב) [יא] אי לית ליה אפי' פרה ופרים מנלן כי אתא רב דימי אמר אמרי במערבא °צריכין הכשר טומאה ממקום אחר בעי רבי אלעזר פרים [יב] ושעירים הנשרפים מהו שיטמאו אוכלין ומשקין בפנים כבחוץ מחוסר יציאה כמחוסר מעשה דמי או לא בתר דבעיא הדר פשטה מחוסר יציאה כמחוסר מעשה דמי בעא מיניה רבי אבא בר [יג] שמואל מרבי חייא בר אבא נבלת עוף טהור לר' מאיר מהו [יד] שיטמא בכזית דמתתא לארעא לא תיבעי לך דנקיט בפומיה לא תיבעי לך כי תיבעי לך דנקיט ליה בידיה מחוסר קריבה כמחוסר מעשה דמי או לא [טו] (בתר דבעיא הדר פשטה) מחוסר

תורה אור: ויקרא יד; שם יא

רש"י

בתר רוב האבר והוה ליה כמאן דלא נפק ואין כאן רוב הבהמה לחוץ ולענין טומאת בגדים מחוץ למחנה בעי [טז] (*האי מיעוטא דאבר שילא לחוץ): אלא שילא חליו של פר ברוב אבר* בחלי הפר [יז] (הג"ה) ילא רוב אחד מן האברים ומיעוטו בחלי הפר שבפנים. האי מיעוטא דאבר שנשאר בפנים בתר רובא דאבר שילא שדינן ליה והוה ליה כמאן דנפק ואשתכח רוב בהמה מבחוץ: או דלמא בתר בהמה. דמיחבר בה והיכא דאיתא שדינן לה (ג) ואע"ג דלאו רובא דבהמה [יח] היא אלא פלגא וליכא למימר כדאמרן לעיל [יט] *שבקינן רובא דבהמה (ד) אפילו הכי כיון דאין האבר נתוק לא אזלינן ביה בתר רובא ולא הויא יליאה ואם נטמא הפר שורפו בפנים: מתני לה. להך בעיא ברובא דמניינא דגברי: שילאו וחזרו מהו. קס"ד לענין טומאת בגדים של אלו שהוליאום קמיבעיא ליה: איטמו להו. בגדיהם: כיון דהדור הדור. והוו להו כמי שלא ילאו: הנך דאיכא גוואי נמי נטמאו. דהא יליאה לענין טומאת בגדים בפרים כתיבא יוליא אל מחוץ למחנה ושרפו וגו' ומיניה ילפינן לקמן בפירקין (דף קה:) לומר לך כיון שילא הפר חוץ למחנה אחת מטמא בגדים אע"פ דלא נפוק גברי נטמאו אלא לאו משום דאמר דאי הדר הדור וכל שכן אלו שמוחזרים ועומדין שהרי לא ילאו: אמר רבא ותסברא. דהך [כ] דקמייתי ראיה מילתא היא: הא בעינן ואחר יבא אל המחנה. אלמא קרא בדנפיק לברא קאי דכל כמה דלא נפק לא קרינא ביה ואחר יבא וכיון דלא קרינא ביה ואחר יבא לא קרינא ביה יכבס בגדיו: ופרכינן אלא ר' אלעזר היכי בעי לה. דכיון דבהכי תליא מילתא מכי נפק קרינא ביה יכבס בגדיו ואי אהדרינהו ואתו אחריני לאפוקינהו אפי' השתא להו מוליאין לא מטמאו הנך בתראי עד דנפקי דהא לא קרינא בהו ואחר יבא: דנקיטי לה בבקולסי. שאחוזים במקלות ועומדין מבחוץ להוליאם לאחר שחזרו וקמיבעיא ליה מי אמרינן כיון שילאו חוץ לעזרה כל העסוקים בהן מכאן ואילך חוץ לעזרה מטמאין בגדים או דלמא כיון דהדור הדור ועד דנפקי לא מטמאו: בקולסי בלשון הש"ס ירושלמי מקל וראיתי דוגמתו (ה) [כא] *בירושלמי תרח נטל בקולסא ותבריטון: השורף פרה אדומה ופרים הנשרפים מטמאין בגדים. פרה בהדיא כתיב בה (במדבר יט) פרים פר כהן משיח ופר העדה (ו) [כב] ופר יום הכיפורים גמרי מקרא יתירא דחטאת חטאת בשילהי כל הזבחים שנתערבו (לעיל פג:) ופר יוה"כ בהדיא כתיב (ויקרא טז): והן אינן מטמאין בגדים. פרה ופרים עלמן אין מטמאין בגדים הנוגעין בהן בלא מתעסקין אבל מטמאין אוכלין ומשקין הנוגעין בהן ולקמן מפרש טעמא: כדתנא דבי ר' ישמעאל מה זרעים שאין סופן לטמא טומאה חמורה. כגון אדם ובגדים: [כג] וצריכין הכשר. דבר המכשירן לקבל טומאה כגון נתינת מים ומגע שרץ: אף כל שאין סופו לטמא כו'. כגון שאר אוכלין אבל הני פרה ופרים ושעיר הואיל וסופן לטמא אדם ובגדים כגון המתעסקין בהן אין צריכין הכשר טומאה הלכך מטמאו מחיים ואע"ג [כד] *דלא איטמויי שאר בעלי חיים דעלמא: אלא לרבנן אי דאית להו דתנא דבי רבי ישמעאל אפי' שעיר המשתלח ואי לית להו דתנא דבי רבי ישמעאל פרה ופרים מנא להו. הרי טהורין הן ולא נאמרה בהן טומאה אלא למתעסקים בהן: אמרי במערבא צריכין הכשר טומאה ממקום אחר. הא דתנא דבי רבי ישמעאל ה"ק כל שאין סופו לטמא טומאה חמורה צריך הכשר טומאה ממקום אחר שיגע בשרץ או בנבלה ולא שיטמאו מאליו אבל מי שסופו לטמא טומאה חמורה אין צריך ליגע בטומאה ומטמא טומאת אוכלין מאליו כגון פרה ופרים אבל חזי לטומאה מיהת בעלמא בעינן ולא בעלי חיים דלא אשכחן בבהמות בעלי חיים מטמאין: מהו שיטמאו בפנים אוכלין ומשקין. הואיל ועדיין לא הגיעו להיות מטמאין טומאה חמורה לא מטמאו טומאה קלה או דלמא הואיל וסופן לטמא לכשילאו מטמאו: נבלת [כה] עוף טהור. מטמאה טומאה חמורה בבית הבליעה בכזית: מהו שיטמא. לרבי מאיר אוכלין ומשקין בכזית לרבנן לא תיבעי לך דאמרי מידי דחזי לטומאה בעינן ובכזית אין *לזו טומאה אלא בבית הבליעה אבל לענין מגע ליכא שיעורא בכזית אלא לרבי מאיר דאמר כל שסופו לטמא טומאה חמורה אין צריך ראויה לטומאה מהו שתטמא בכזית מאליה: דמחתא על ארעא לא תיבעי לך. דלא מיטמאה דהא אכתי לא הוגעה לסוף טומאה חמורה שמא לא תיכנס לבית הבליעה לעולם: דנקט בפומיה לא תיבעי לך. דאם הוו אוכלים אחרים לתוך פיו [כו] מטמאתן דהא הגיעה לטומאה חמורה בהאי שיעורא כי תיבעי לך כו': הכי

תוספות

או דלמא בתר בהמה אזלינן. תימה אם הבהמה בפנים פשיטא דגברי טהורים כדמוכח כולה שמעתין ויש לומר דה"ק בתר בהמה דוקא אזלינן בתר רובא אבל בגברי לא: **או** דלמא כיון דהדור הדור. פי' בקונטרס דמבעיא ליה לענין טומאת בגדים של אלו שהוליאו וקשה אטו מחילות עזרה *מקוה טהרה דכיון שנטמאו מי יטהרם ונראה לפרש דמבעיא ליה לענין הנוגע בפנים דדלמא כיון דילאו בחוץ אע"ג דחזרו הנוגע בפנים טמא ומסיק דמיבעיא ליה [כז] *כיון דנקטי בבקולסי ומיירי בעומד בחוץ ואוחז במקלות להוליאם לאחר *שיחזרו כדפירש בקונטרס. הג"ה:
פרים הנשרפים. שילאו הפרים והאנשים וחזרו הפרים וגברי מהו פשיטא האנשים וגם בגדים שהיו עליהם טמאים ובחזרתן לא נטהרו אלא אם אנשים אחרים נכנסו בעזרה ויתעסקו בהולאתן או הראשונים לבשו בגדים אחרים מי הוו טמאים בעסק זה קודם שילאו חוץ לעזרה כיון שילאו הפרים כבר חשוב כאילו מוליאים אותם מפתח עזרה ולחוץ וקאמר [כח] *מי תלי מילתא בהולאת הפר לבדו אע"פ שלא ילאו האנשים א"כ גבי סובלין אותן במוטות כיון שילא הפר ולכך נטמאו הראשונים אם כן גם דגואי נטמאו ותסברא שיהא תלוי ביליאת הפר לבדו והא בעינן ואחר יבא אל המחנה אלא פשיטא *דבעיא גם שילאו האנשים עם הפרים ולכך דגואי לא מטמאי וגם בבעיא דילך אנשים אחרים שמעולם לא ילאו פשיטא דטהורין או גברי קדמאי אם לבשו בגדים אחרים אלא רבי אלעזר הכי בעי דנקטי בבקולסי שהפרים ילאו *וחזרו [כט] אנשים אחרים ועמדו חוץ לעזרה ומוליאין הפרים שבתוך העזרה במקלות מי אמרינן כיון שהפרים כבר ילאו והאנשים עומדים בחוץ חשוב כאילו מוליאין אותן מפתח עזרה ולחוץ וטמאין או חשוב כאילו לא ילאו הפרים מעולם לחוץ וטהורים אבל אם נכנסו בפנים גברי חדשים או הראשונים בבגדים חדשים כיון שמעולם אלו לא ילאו פשיטא דטהורים אע"פ שילאו כבר הפרים. *מה שבפנים אינו מבואר וזה עיקר. ברוך ד"ד:
מחוסר יליאה כמחוסר מעשה דמי או לא. וא"ת אי מטמאו בפנים אם כן יטמאו את האימורים ויש לומר דמחוסר חתיכה פשיטא דהוי כמחוסר מעשה ולא תטמאו בשעת פרישתן דמיירי בניתוחין *בעל כרחו ובירושלמי

הגהות הב"ח

(א) גמ' הנך דאיכא גואי נמי ליטמא אמר רבא הא בעינא: (ב) שם שעיר המשתלח נמי אי לית להו פרה ופרים מנלן כצ"ל ותיבת אפי' נמחק: (ג) רש"י ד"ה או דלמא וכו' שדינן לה ולאו רובא כצ"ל ותיבת ואע"ג נמחק: (ד) בא"ד אפילו הכי. נ"ב זהו פסק הלכה של רש"י: (ה) ד"ה בקולסי וכו' דוגמתו בירושלמי תרח: (ו) ד"ה השורף וכו' ופר העדה גמרי כצ"ל ותיבות ופר יוה"כ נמחק:

[בב"ר ס"פ נח]

גליון הש"ס

גמ' צריכין הכשר טומאה. עיין בב"ק דף עו ע"א תוס' ד"ה פרה:

הערות גליון

נ"ל אי תלי נ"ק
[עי' תוספות ב"ק ע"ד ד"ה פרה]
נ"ל ושעיר המשתלח השורפן נ"ק
נ"ל דבעיא גם וכו' נ"ק
גי' הש"ק וחזרו ובאו אנשים
נ"ל אין נ"ק
נ"ל ומה שפירשתי דמיבעיא ליה לענין הנוגע בפנים אינו מבואר וזה עיקר הס"ד נ"ק
גירסת הש"ק בכל כוחו
נ"ל דלא מטמאו נ"ק
נ"ל לו נ"ק

שיטה מקובצת

א] או דלמא בתר: ב] פרים הנשרפין ושעירים: ג] תיבת להו נמחק: ד] במוטות יצאו הראשונים חוץ: ה] והאחרונים אינן מטמאין: ו] ת"ר השורף פרה ופרים הנשרפין והמשלח את השעיר והמוציאן מטמאין בגדים כו' והשאר נמחק: ז] עצמן אינן מטמאין: ח] מטמא מפני שהוא חי וכל דבר שהוא חי אינו מטמא: ט] כדתנא עיין תוס' ב"ק דף ע"ז. י] חטי"ה צריכין הכשר אות ו' נמחק: יא] המשתלח נמי ואי לית להו דתנא דבי ר' ישמעאל אפי' פרה ופרים מנא להו כי אתא: יב] פרים הנשרפין ושעירים: יג] בר ממל תיבת שמואל נמחק: יד] מהו שתטמא בכזית: טו] תיבות בתר כו' פשטה נמחק: טז] בעי הס"ד ומה"ד האי: יז] תיבת הג"ה נמחק: יח] הוא אלא: יט] לעיל לא שבקינן: כ] דהך (דקסיית') [ראיה] מילתא היא: כא] דוגמתו באגדה בצלמי: כב] תיבות ופר יום הכיפורים נמחק: כג] צריכין הכשר אות ו' נמחק: כד] דלא חזו לאיטמויי: כה] נבלת דעוף טהור: כו] פיו מטמאן דהא: כז] כגון דנקטי בבקולסי: כח] וקאמר אי אית ליה מילתא ותיבות אי תלי ל"ש: כט] יצאו וחזרו ובאו אנשים:

ט) וכ"ה בתוספתא דפרה פ"ו השורף פרה ופרים והמשלח את השעיר מטמא בגדים ע"ש.

א] *מחוסר קריבה *לאו כמחוסר מעשה דמי איתיביה *שלשה עשר דברים נאמרו בנבלת עוף טהור וזה אחד מהן צריכה מחשבה ואין צריכה הכשר *ומטמא טומאת אוכלין בכביצה מאי לאו ר"מ היא לא רבנן היא ב] והא קתני רישא צריכה מחשבה ואין צריכה הכשר *°ומאן שמעת ליה האי סברא ר"מ ומדרישא ר"מ סיפא נמי ר"מ מידי איריא הא כדאיתא והא כדאיתא והא מדקתני סיפא *שחיטתה ומליקתה מטהרת טריפתה מטומאתה *מאן שמעת ליה האי סברא ר"מ רישא וסיפא רבי מאיר ומציעתא רבנן אין רישא וסיפא רבי מאיר ומציעתא רבנן אמר ליה רב המנונא לרבי זירא *לא תיתיב *אכרעך עד דאמרת לי הא מילתא נבלת עוף טהור לר"מ מונין ג] לה ראשון ושני או אין מונין ד] ראשון ושני א"ל כל היכא דמטמא אדם במגע מונין בו ראשון ושני כל היכא ה] דאין מטמא אדם במגע אין מונין בו ראשון ושני בעא מיניה רבי זירא ו] מרבי אמי בר חייא ואמרי לה מר' אבין בר כהנא הא *דתנן *חיבורי אוכלין ע"י משקין חיבור לטומאה קלה ואין חיבור לטומאה חמורה מונין ז] בו ראשון ושני או אין מונין בו ראשון ושני א"ל כל היכא דמטמא אדם מונין בו ראשון ושני ח] אין מטמא אדם אין מונין בו ראשון ושני:

יצאו אלו ואלו: מה"מ דת"ר *להלן ט] הוא אומר חוץ לג' מחנות כאן למחנה אחת לומר לך כיון שיצא חוץ למחנה אחת מטמא בגדים י] והיא גופה מנלן דת"ר °והוציא את כל הפר אל מחוץ למחנה חוץ לג' מחנות (ויקרא ד) אתה אומר חוץ לג' מחנות או אינו אלא יא] מחנה אחת כשהוא אומר בפר העדה °מחוץ למחנה שאין יב] צריך לומר שהרי (שם) כבר נאמר °כאשר שרף את הפר הראשון (שם) יג] ליתן לו מחנה שניה כשהוא אומר מחוץ למחנה בדשן יד] שאצ"ל שהרי כבר נאמר °על שפך הדשן ישרף טו] ליתן לו מחנה (שם) שלישית ור"ש האי מחוץ למחנה מאי עביד ליה מיבעי ליה לכדתניא רבי אליעזר אומר נאמר כאן טז] חוץ למחנה ונאמר להלן °חוץ למחנה (במדבר יט) *מה להלן חוץ לג' מחנות אף כאן חוץ לג' מחנות ומה להלן למזרחה של ירושלים אף

רש"י

הכי גרסינן אמר ליה מחוסר קריבה לאו כמחוסר מעשה דמי: יז] °צריכה מחשבה · להצטרף פחות מכזית ממנה להשלים פחות מכביצה אוכלין לקבל טומאת אוכלין במגע: ואינה צריכה הכשר · לטמא לא למים ולא למגע שרץ שאליה מטמאה הואיל וסופה לטמא טומאה חמורה: ומטמאה טומאת אוכלין בכביצה · מדקתני צריכה מחשבה ואינה צריכה הכשר אלמא בדנקיט ליה בידיה עסקינן דאי מחתא אארעא אמאי אינה צריכה הכשר ואי דנקט לה בפומיה אמאי צריכה מחשבה אין לך מחשבה גדולה מזו וקתני כביצה אין כזית לא: ה"ג שחיטתה ומליקתה מטהרת טריפתה מטומאתה: האי סברא ר' מאיר · בפרק חטאת העוף (לעיל סט·): נבלת עוף טהור לר' מאיר · דמטמא טומאת אוכלין מאליה בכזית מונין בו ראשון ושני או לא: כל היכא דלא מטמא אדם במגע אין מונין בו ראשון ושני · דגמר משרץ דכתיב ביה מנין ראשון ושני דכתיב (ויקרא יא) כל אשר בתוכו יטמא דהוה ליה הכלי ראשון והאוכל שני ונבלת עוף טהור לא מטמא אדם במגע: חיבורי אוכלין על ידי משקין · חצי זית נבלה מכאן וחצי זית נבלה מכאן ומשקה טופח באמצע ונוגע בשניהם מחברן לטמא אוכלין ומשקין הנוגעים באחד מן החצאין האלו: ואין חיבור לטומאה חמורה · לטמא אדם וכלים וטעמא לא ידענא: ה"ג להלן אתה נותן להם שלש מחנות וכאן מחנה אחת א"כ למה נאמר אל מחוץ למחנה לומר לך כיון שיצא חוץ למחנה אחת מטמאים בגדים והא מתניא בת"כ גבי פר יוה"כ דכתיב (ויקרא טז) ואת פר החטאת ואת שעיר החטאת אשר הובא וגו' וקמתמה תנא יח] ואמר להלן בפר העדה וכאן משיח אתה נותן להם מקום שריפתן חוץ לשלש מחנות כדיליף לקמיה וכאן אתה אומר אל מחוץ למחנה ושרפו דמשמע שורפן חוץ לעזרה מיד בהר הבית והלא אף אלו פנימים ואייתי לשלהוכי הדדי בריבויא דחטאת החטאת בשילהי כל הזבחים ואמר נמי בפ' בית שמאי (לעיל נט·) לפר זה פר יום הכיפורים: אם כן למה נאמר אל מחוץ למחנה · לענין טומאת בגדים דכתיבי בקרא דבתריה קאמר (ויקרא טז) אל מחוץ למחנה והשורף אותם יכבס בגדיו: לומר לך כיון שיצאו חוץ לעזרה · המתעסקין בהן מטמאין בגדים: מחוץ למחנה בדשן · בהוצאת דשן המזבח והוציא את הדשן אל מחוץ למחנה (שם ו): שאין ת"ל · אין מלמד כלום דהא ידענא דאל מחוץ למחנה מוציאין אותו דכתיב בפרים הנשרפים (שם ד) אל שפך הדשן וכתיב בהו אל (א) מחוץ יט]: ור' שמעון · דאמר במתני' אין מטמאין בגדים עד שיוצת האור ברובו האי מחוץ למחנה דכתיב בפר ושעיר של יום הכיפורים מאי עביד ליה: נאמר כאן · בפר יום הכיפורים: ונאמר להלן · בפרה אדומה (במדבר יט) והוציא אותה אל מחוץ: מה כאן · בפרים הנשרפים חוץ לג' מחנות אף *שחיטת פרה אדומה חוץ לג' מחנות: מה להלן · בפרה אדומה במזרחו של ירושלים דכתיב בה והזה אל נכח פני אהל מועד אלמא עומד במזרח ופניו למערב כנגד פתחו של היכל שהוא בכותל מזרחי ופתחו למזרח
אף

תוספות

ובירושלמי גרסינן בסוף פרק שני שעירים רבי אליעזר שאל פרים הנשרפין ושעירים הנשרפים מהו שיטמאו בגדים בלא הכשר ובלא טומאה מפני שסופן לטמאות טומאה חמורה השיב רבי שמואל קפודקיא מעתה יטמאו אימורים אלא כשפרשו ואפילו תימא דלא פירשו כהדא אין מי חטאת מטמאין דבר לחזור ולטמאות ממט:

ומטמא טומאת אוכלין בכביצה · פי' בקונטרס מדקתני צריכה מחשבה ואין צריכה הכשר אלמא בדנקיט ליה בידיה עסקינן דאי מחתא אארעא אמאי אינה צריכה הכשר ואי דנקיט ליה בפומיה אמאי צריכה מחשבה אין לך מחשבה גדולה מזו וקתני כביצה אין כזית לא וקשה כיון דיש בו כביצה אע"ג דמחית אארעא מטמא בלא הכשר משום דסופו לטמא טומאה חמורה ולא דמי למחוסר יציאה דפנים אין ראוי כלל לטמא ומשום הכי לא מבעיא ליה לרבנן בכביצה דנקיט בידיה ונראה לפרש דהיינו טעמא דמשמע ליה דמיירי בנקיט בידיה משום דאז איכא חידוש לאשמועינן דבעי כביצה ולא חשיב כנקיט בפומיה אבל במחית אארעא פשיטא דבעי כביצה (*ופי' הקונטרס יש ליישב כמו שפירשתי לעיל בהגהה וכן עיקר):

ומדסיפא ר"מ רישא נמי ר"מ · הוה מצי למימר וליטעמיך הא קתני מציעתא האוכל אבר מן החי ממנה סופג את הארבעים והיינו דלא כרבי מאיר דקסבר איטו טהג אלא *בטהורה בפרק גיד הנשה (חולין דף קב:) (כדפרישית לעיל):

חיבורי אוכלין ע"י משקין · פי' בקונט' חצי זית נבלה מכאן וחצי זית נבלה מכאן ומשקה טופח באמצע ונוגע בשניהן מחברן לטמא אוכלין ומשקין הנוגעין באחד מן החצאין האלו ואין חיבור לטומאה חמורה לטמא אדם וכלים וטעמא לא ידענא וכענין זה פירש בהקומץ רבה (מנחות דף כד·) גבי צירוף כלי וחיבור מים מהו דפירש התם בקונטרס כלומר חצי עשרון שנטמא בצירוף כלי מהו שמטמא אחר בחיבור מים כגון אם יש שתי חצאי עשרון בכלי ואין נוגעין וחצי עשרון יש *חוץ לכלי השני וחיבור מים כגון ניצוק או צינור מחבר את של חוץ לכלי ואת שבתוך הכלי ונגע טומאה לזה שבכלי שאין נוגע במים ונטמא חבירו משום צירוף כלי מהו שיטמא זה את של חוץ בחיבור מים ודבר תימה הוא לומר שמשקין מחברין אוכלין לקבל טומאה ולטמא אחרים דאפילו עור אין מצרפו כדאיתא בהעור והרוטב (חולין דף קיז:) ועוד שפירש שמחברין ע"י ניצוק והלא אפי' למים עצמן קי"ל *דאין ניצוק חיבור לטומאה וקלא היה נראה לפרש דמיירי בבינמותו ע"י המים ונדבקו יחד ומיהו כעין פירוש הקונטרס יש משנה אחת במסכת טהרות (פ"ח מ"ח) עריבה שהיא קטפרס *וניצוק מלמעלן ומשקה טופח מלמטן וג' חתיכות כביצה אינן מצטרפות וב' מצטרפות ור' יוסי אומר אף שתים אינן מצטרפות אלא א"כ רוצצות משקה ואם היה משקה עומד אפי' כעין החרדל מצטרף ובתוספתא *תניא אתרוג שנפרץ ותחבו בכוש או בקיסם אינו חיבור שאין חיבורי אדם חיבור עיסה שנילושה במי פירות טהורה שאין לך דבר שהוא מחבר את האוכלין אלא שבעה משקין *ודבר תימה הוא אם אין לישת *) פירות מועלת לחבר את הקמח ושמא לשה לאו דוקא אלא אורחא דמילתא נקט [דבר שאדם] לש במי פירות פעמים שמי פירות מחברים שני חצאי זיתים של עיסה במשקים הבאים מזה לזה:

מה כאן חוץ לשלש מחנות ביום הכיפורים כ] אף להלן בפרה אדומה כן · תימה הא בפר יוה"כ לא ידעי' שלש מחנות אלא מהיקשא דלפר זה פר יום הכיפורים בפרק ב"ש (לעיל דף נט·) כדפירש בקונט' ומספקינן אי דבר הלמד בהיקש חוזר ומלמד בג"ש או לא ואפי' תימלי לומר דאתא מריבוי דחטאת דבסוף התערובת (לעיל פג·) ההוא נמי היקשא הוא ושמא ג"ש הוא *ויש לפרש דפרה קדשי בדק הבית היא והשתא נמי אתי שפיר דיליף בג"ש מזרחה של ירושלים אע"ג דשריפת פרה ילפא מהזאתה לקמן בפרק בתרא (דף קיג·):

*) מי פירות · יעב"ץ

הדרן עלך טבול יום

עין משפט נר מצוה

סז א מיי' פ"ג מהלכות אבות הטומאה הלכה יז:
סח ב מיי' שם הלכה יב אבל לא מליקתה:
[נ"ל אמר ליה מחוסר כו']
סט ג מיי' פ"א מהלכות אבות הטומאה הלכה ו:
ע ד שם בכסגות:
עא ה מיי' פ"ה מהלכות פרה הלכה ה:
עב ו מיי' פ"ג מהלכות פרה הלכה ב:
[פי' תוס' מיר כה: כד"ה אמר שמואל וכו' כתבו פירוש על זה]
עיין ש"ק
[נ"ל בנכנסה טהורה]
נ"ל חוץ לכלי וחיבור מים כו' ש"ק
[פרק ה דמכשירין מ"ס כן פ"ח דטהרות מ"ח]
נ"ל וכלקח מלמטן ש"ק
[דשקין פ"א]

מסורת הש"ס

[חולין קכ:]
נדה נ טהרות פ"א משנה א בכורות י·
[צריך עיון רב]
[קושיא בזה תמצא בתוס' חולין קכ: סד"ה ורבי מאיר וע"ש וע"ע תוספות ב"ק עז: ד"ה פרה]
[קדושין לו: וש"נ]
[נ"ל דתניא]
(טהרות פ"ז)
סנהדרין מבי יומא סח·
נ"ל מה כאן חוץ לשלש מחנות אף להלן חוץ לשלש ש"ק
[כס"י שריפת פרה כו']
עיין ש"ק שהאריך
נ"ל ושד יש לפרש כו' ש"ק

הגהות הב"ח

(א) רש"י ד"ה שאין ת"ל מחוץ למחנה כו"ד:

גליון הש"ס

גמ' ומאן שמעת ליה וכו' ר"מ · יש לעיין הא מסקינן לעיל דגם לרבנן סע כתנא דבי ר"י ורק בשעיר המשתלח לא כיון דלא חזי בעלמא לקבל טומאה: רש"י ד"ה צריכה מחשבה להצטרף פחות מכזית · ק"ל אמאי לא כפשוטו דצריך מחשבה דעי"ז יש לו טומאת עצמו לטמא אוכלין ומשקין כיון דסופו לטמא טומאה תמורה · ובנדה באמת לא כתב רש"י כן:

שיטה מקובצת

א] א"ל מחוסר: כ] היא והא מדקתני סיפא שחיטתה ומליקתה מטהרת טריפתה מטומאתה מאן שמעת ליה האי סברא ר' מאיר מדסיפא ר"מ רישא נמי ר"מ מידי איריא סיפא ר"מ רישא רבנן א"ל רב כו' כן גירסת ס"י וכן משמע ברש"י ז"ל והגירסא בעמוד קשה לעמוד עליה: ג] מונין בו ראשון תיבת לה נמחק: ד] מונין בו ראשון: ה] דלא מטמא תיבת דאין נמחק: ו] מר' אבין בר חייא תיבת אמי נמחק: ז] מונין בהן ראשון ושני או אין מונין בהן ראשון ושני: ח] ושני כל היכא דלא מטמא אדם תיבת אין נמחק: ט] להלן אתה נותן להם ג' מחנות וכאן מחנה אחת א"כ למה נאמר מחוץ למחנה לומר לך כיון: י] בגדים אמר מר להלן אתה נותן כו' מנ"ל תיבות והיא גופא נמחק: יא] אלא חוץ למחנה: יב] שאין ת"ל שהרי תיבות צ"ל נמחק: יג] הראשון תן לו: יד] בדשן שאין ת"ל ותיבות שא"צ נמחק: טו] ישרף תן לו: טז] כאן מחוץ למחנה ונאמר להלן מחוץ למחנה מה כאן חוץ לג' מחנות אף להלן חוץ לג' מחנות: יז] צריכה · עיין בתוס' נדה דף נ ברש"י ובתוס': יח] תנא ואומר להלן: יט] מחוץ למחנה הס"ז: כ] הכיפורים · עיין בתוס' יומא (דף ס"ח):

or not? [After he asked, he solved it]:[9] [105*b*] The fact that it was not yet taken [to his mouth] is not as though it lacked an action. He refuted him: Thirteen laws were stated on the *nebelah* of a clean bird, and this is one of them: It needs intention[10] and it does not need a qualification,[11] and as much as an *egg* thereof defiles foodstuffs.[12] Surely this is in accordance with R. Meir?—No: it agrees with the Rabbis. But the first clause teaches, 'it needs intention and it does not need a qualification,' and whom do you know to hold thus? R. Meir. And since the first clause agrees with R. Meir, the second clause agrees with R. Meir?—Why say thus? each is governed by its own conditions.[13] But the final clause teaches, *Shechitah*
a or *melikah* relieves it, when *terefah*, from its uncleanness:[1] now, whom do you know to hold this view? R. Meir. Then the first and the last clauses agree with R. Meir, while the middle clause agrees with the Rabbis?—Yes: the first and the last clauses agree with R. Meir, while the middle clause agrees with the Rabbis.

R. Hamnuna said to R. Zera: Do not sit down on your haunches until you have told me this law:[2] on R. Meir's view do we distinguish first and second [degrees of uncleanness][3] in the *nebelah* of a clean bird, or do we not distinguish first and second [degrees]?—Said he to him: Where a thing defiles a human being by touch, we distinguish first and second [degrees] in it; where it does not defile a human being by touch, we do not distinguish first and second [degrees] in it.[4]

R. Zera asked R. Ammi[5] b. Ḥiyya—others say, R. Abin b. Kahana: As to what was taught, When foodstuffs are joined by means of a liquid, they are united in respect of a light uncleanness, but are not united in respect of stringent defilement:[6] do we distinguish first and second [degrees] in their case, or do we not distinguish first and second [degrees] in their case?—Said he to him: Where a thing defiles a human being, we distinguish first and second [degrees] in it; where it does not defile a human being, we do not distinguish first and second [degrees] in it.

WHEN BOTH GO OUT. How do we know it?—Because our Rabbis taught: Elsewhere without *three* camps is said, whereas here without *one* camp [is prescribed]?[7] It is to teach you: im-
b mediately it has gone forth from the *first* camp, it defiles garments.[1]

And how do we know it in the case of that itself?[2]—Because our Rabbis taught: *Even the whole bullock shall he carry forth without the camp:*[3] [that means,] without the three camps. You say, without the three camps; yet perhaps it is not so, but rather, without one camp?—When it says in connection with the congregational bullock, *without the camp,*[4] which is superfluous, since it states, *as he burned the first bullock,*[5] that prescribes a second camp. When further *'without the camp'* is stated in connection with the ashes,[6] which is superfluous, since it is already stated, *where the ashes are poured out it shall be burnt,*[7] it prescribes a third camp.[8]

Now, how does R. Simeon employ this *'without the camp'*?[9]—He requires it for what was taught: R. Eliezer said: *'Without the camp'* is stated here, and *'without the camp'* is stated elsewhere:[10] as here it means without the three camps, so there it means without the three camps.

(9) Sh.M. deletes bracketed words. Rashi reads: said he to him. (10) Before it can defile foodstuffs, one must intend to eat it, (though such eating is not permissible). (11) For defiling; v. *supra a*. (12) Now, if it is on the ground, it certainly does need qualification, since one may never eat it. On the other hand, if it is in one's mouth, it does not need intention. Hence it must mean that he is holding it in his hand, and yet only as much as an *egg* defiles, but not as much as an olive. (13) One may agree with the Rabbis, and the other with R. Meir.

a (1) I.e., if it is ritually killed with *shechitah* or *melikah*, but found to be *terefah*, it does not defile. (2) I.e., do not sit down at all. (3) V. Pes. (Sonc. ed.) 14*a* n. a 2. (4) Hence we do not count it here. (5) Sh.M. reads: Abin. (6) Rashi: 'If two pieces of *nebelah*, each half an olive in size, are lying apart, but are joined by a liquid, this liquid unites them to enable them to defile any foodstuff which touches one of them, but does not unite them to defile a human being in the same way. I do not know the reason for this differentiation.'—As much as an olive of the *nebelah* of a clean animal (but not of a bird) defiles a man by contact. (7) 'Elsewhere' means in the case of the bullock brought by the anointed priest or that brought when the whole congregation sins in ignorance; these were burnt without the camp (v. Lev. IV, 12, 21), and it is deduced anon that Scripture means without the three camps. Whereas 'here' in reference to the Day of Atonement it is said: *And the bullock of the sin-offering, and the goat of the sin-offering . . . shall be carried forth without the camp, and they shall burn in the fire their skins* etc. (Lev. XVI, 27). This implies that they are burnt immediately they leave the *first* camp. In fact, however, they are all alike, for Lev. XII, 21 is applied to the bullock of the Day of Atonement (v. *supra* 39*a*); hence the text is assumed to convey a different teaching, as the Gemara explains.—On the 'three camps', v. *supra* 55*a* n.b 6.

b (1) *Sc.* of those who are to burn it. But it is not burnt until it has left the three camps. (2) *Sc.* that 'elsewhere' *three* camps are meant. (3) Lev. IV, 12. (4) Ibid. 21. (5) Ibid. That itself implies without the camp. (6) Ibid. VI, 4: *and he shall carry forth the ashes without the camp.* (7) Ibid. IV, 12. This refers to the anointed priest's bullock, which as we already know was burnt without; hence it follows that the place of the ashes was without. (8) Each superfluous *'without the camp'* intimates an additional camp whence it must be carried out. (9) Since he maintains that the garments are not defiled until the fire has caught hold of the greater part of the carcass. (10) In connection with the red heifer, Num. XIX, 3.

three camps; and as there it means on the east of Jerusalem,[11] [106a] so here too it means on the east of Jerusalem.

And according to the Rabbis,[12] where did one burn them?—Even as it was taught: Where were they burnt? On the north of Jerusalem, without the three camps. R. Jose the Galilean said: They are
a burnt in the place of the ashes.[1] Raba observed: Who is the Tanna that disagrees with R. Jose the Galilean?—R. Eliezer b. Jacob. For it was taught: *Where the ashes are poured out it shall be burnt:* [this intimates] that ashes must be there [first]. R. Eliezer b. Jacob said: It intimates that the ground must slope down.[2] Said Abaye to him: Perhaps they disagree whether the ground must slope[3]?

Our Rabbis taught: He who burns [the bullocks] defiles [his] garments, but he who kindles the fire does not defile [his] garments, nor does he who arranges the pile defile [his] garments. And what is the definition of 'he who burns'?—He who assists at the time of the burning. You might think that also he [who assists] when they have already been reduced to ashes defiles [his] garments: therefore it states, [*And he that burneth*] *them* [*shall wash his clothes*]:[4] [when he burns] *them* they defile garments, but when they have become ashes they do not defile garments. R. Simeon said: [When he burns] *them* they defile [his] garments, but when the flesh is disintegrated they do not defile garments. Wherein do they disagree?—Said Raba: They disagree where it [the flesh] is completely charred.[5]

CHAPTER XIII

MISHNAH. HE WHO SLAUGHTERS AND OFFERS UP WITHOUT [THE TEMPLE COURT], IS CULPABLE IN RESPECT OF
b SLAUGHTERING AND IN RESPECT OF OFFERING.[1] R. JOSE THE GALILEAN MAINTAINED: IF HE SLAUGHTERED WITHIN AND OFFERED UP WITHOUT, [HE IS CULPABLE];[2] IF HE SLAUGHTERED WITHOUT AND OFFERED UP WITHOUT, HE IS NOT LIABLE, BECAUSE HE OFFERED UP ONLY THAT WHICH WAS UNFIT.[3] SAID THEY TO HIM: WHEN ONE SLAUGHTERS WITHIN AND OFFERS UP WITHOUT, IMMEDIATELY HE CARRIES IT OUT, HE RENDERS IT UNFIT.[4]

AN UNCLEAN [PERSON] WHO EATS [OF SACRIFICES], WHETHER UNCLEAN SACRIFICES OR CLEAN SACRIFICES, IS CULPABLE. R. JOSE THE GALILEAN SAID: AN UNCLEAN PERSON WHO EATS CLEAN [SACRIFICES] IS CULPABLE, BUT AN UNCLEAN PERSON WHO EATS UNCLEAN [FLESH OF SACRIFICES] IS NOT CULPABLE, BECAUSE HE ATE ONLY THAT WHICH IS UNCLEAN. SAID THEY TO HIM: WHEN AN UNCLEAN PERSON EATS CLEAN [FLESH], IMMEDIATELY HE TOUCHES IT, HE DEFILES IT.[5] A CLEAN PERSON WHO EATS UNCLEAN [FLESH] IS NOT CULPABLE, BECAUSE ONE IS CULPABLE ONLY ON ACCOUNT OF PERSONAL UNCLEANNESS.[6]

GEMARA. As for offering up, it is well: the penalty is written
c and the interdict[1] is written. The penalty, for it is written, *And bringeth it not unto the door of the tent of meeting* [*... even that man shall be cut off from his people*].[2] The interdict, for it is written, *Take heed to thyself that thou offer not thy burnt-offerings* [*in every place that thou seest*],[3] and in accordance with R. Abin's dictum in R. Eleazar's[4] name, viz.: Wherever '*take heed*', '*lest*', or '*not*' is stated, it is nought but a negative command. But as for slaughtering, the penalty, it is true, is stated, for it is written, [*What man soever ... that killeth an ox ...*] *and hath not brought it unto the door of the tent of meeting* [*... shall be cut off from among his people*];[5] but whence [do we derive] the interdict?—Scripture saith, *And they shall no more sacrifice their sacrifices* [*unto the satyrs* etc].[6] That is required for R. Eleazar's dictum, viz.: How do we know that if one sacrifices an animal to Merculis[7] he is liable to punishment? Because it is written, '*And they shall no more sacrifice their sacrifices unto the satyrs*'. Since this is redundant in respect of normal worship, being derived from, *How did these nations serve their gods?*[8] apply it to abnormal worship [as being punishable]![9]—Said Rabbah: Read in this text, *and they shall not sacrifice*, and read in it, *and they shall no more*.[10]

But it is still required for what was taught: Thus far[11] it speaks of sacrifices which one consecrated when *bamoth* were forbidden

(11) Ibid. 4: *And Eleazar ... shall sprinkle of her blood toward the front of the tent of meeting.* The tent of meeting faced east, hence Eleazar would stand still further east and face west. Similarly in the days of the Temple the heifer would be burnt without Jerusalem on the east. (12) Who employ this verse for a different purpose, as above.

a (1) Ashes from the altar must first be placed there, so that they are burnt '*where the ashes are poured out.*'—It follows that the first Tanna does not require this. (2) Lit., 'poured out', it must be a place where the ashes naturally pour down. (3) Possibly R. Eliezer b. Jacob too admits that ashes must first be placed there, but he adds that the place must slope too.—Abaye's suggestion is unrefuted. (4) Lev. XVI, 28. (5) It is then disintegrated, yet not ashes. According to R. Simeon, a person who comes to assist in the burning at this stage does not defile his garments, whereas in the opinion of the Rabbis he does.

b (1) A man who wantonly slaughters or offers up a sacrifice without the Temple (by offering up' is meant e.g. that he burns it on a block of stone—but v. Mishnah infra 108a—as one would burn it on the altar) incurs *kareth*. If he does these in ignorance, being unaware that they are forbidden, he is liable to a separate sin-offering on account of each action, as each counts as a distinct transgression. (2) Bracketed words are added from the separate edition of the Mishnayoth. (3) One is culpable for offering up without only when it was fit to be offered up within. But this was not, on account of having been slaughtered without. (4) Even before he offers it up. Nevertheless he is liable; the same therefore applies when he slaughters without and offers up without. (5) Even before he eats it, yet he is culpable. (6) Cf. *supra* 43a.

c (1) Lit., 'the warning'. (2) Lev. XVII, 9. This refers to sacrifices. (3) Deut. XII, 13: '*Every place that thou seest*' means outside the Temple. Thus one text intimates the penalty and another the interdict. (4) *Var. lec.* Ilai's. (5) Lev. XVII, 3f. (6) Ibid. 7. (7) Mercurius, a Roman divinity, identified with the Greek Hermes; also a statue or a way-mark dedicated to Hermes, the patron deity of the wayfarer. (8) Deut. XII, 30. (9) Hence sacrificing to Merculis, though not its normal worship (its normal worship consisted of throwing stones at it; v. Sanh. 60b), involves guilt.—Thus the text is required for this! (10) I.e., this is really a double injunction, and the first, '*they shall not sacrifice*', interdicts sacrificing without, this being the subject of the whole passage. (11) The passage until this verse, *and they shall no more sacrifice*, i.e., Lev. XVII, 3-6.

השוחט והמעלה

תורה אור

אף כאן למזרחה של ירושלים א] אלא לרבנן היכא שריף להו כדתניא היכן נשרפין לצפון ירושלים חוץ לשלש מחנות רבי יוסי הגלילי אומר אבית הדשן ב] נשרפין אמר רבא מאן תנא דפליג עליה דר' יוסי הגלילי ר' אליעזר בן יעקב ג] היא דתניא °על שפך הדשן (ויקרא ד) ישרף שיהא שם דשן (שיקדים לשם דשן) ר' אליעזר בן יעקב אומר שיהא מקומו משופך אמר ליה אביי ד] דילמא במקומו משופך פליגי תנו רבנן השורף ה] מטמא בגדים ולא המצית את האור ו] מטמא בגדים ולא המסדר את המערכה מטמא בגדים ואיזהו השורף ז] המסייע בשעת שריפה יכול אף משנעשו אפר מטמא בגדים תלמוד לומר אותם אותם מטמאין בגדים ומשנעשין אפר אין מטמאין בגדים *רבי שמעון אומר אותם מטמאין בגדים ניתך הבשר אין מטמאין בגדים מאי בינייהו אמר רבא איכא בינייהו דשוייה חרוכא:

הדרן עלך טבול יום

השוחט והמעלה בחוץ חייב על השחיטה וחייב על העלאה רבי יוסי הגלילי אומר שחט בפנים והעלה בחוץ* שחט בחוץ והעלה בחוץ פטור שלא העלה אלא דבר פסול אמרו לו אף השוחט בפנים ומעלה בחוץ כיון שהוציאו פסלו *הטמא שאכל בין קדש טמא בין קדש טהור חייב רבי יוסי הגלילי אומר טמא שאכל טהור חייב וטמא שאכל טמא פטור שלא אכל אלא דבר טמא אמרו לו אף טמא שאכל את הטהור כיון שנגע בו טמאוהו וטהור שאכל טמא פטור שאינו חייב אלא על טומאת הגוף: **גמ'** בשלמא ח] העלה כתיב עונש וכתיב אזהרה עונש דכתיב °ואל פתח אהל מועד לא (שם יז) הביאו* [דברים יב] אזהרה דכתיב °השמר לך פן תעלה עולותיך וכי הא *דא"ר אבין א"ר *אלעזר כל מקום שנאמר השמר פן ואל אינו אלא לא תעשה אלא שחיטה בשלמא עונש דכתיב °ואל פתח אהל מועד לא הביאו (ויקרא יז) אלא אזהרה מנלן אמר קרא °ולא יזבחו עוד (שם) י] האי מיבעי ליה לכדר"א *דאמר יא] מנין לזובח בהמה למרקולים שהוא חייב דכתיב ולא יזבחו עוד את זבחיהם אם אינו ענין לכדרכה יב] דכתיב °איכה יעבדו (דברים יב) תנהו ענין לשלא כדרכה אמר רבה קרי ביה ולא יזבחו וקרי ביה ולא עוד אכתי מיבעי ליה לכדתניא עד כאן הוא מדבר בקדשים שהקדישן בשעת איסור הבמות והקריבן [נ"ל שענש] בשעת איסור הבמות שהרי

רש"י

אף כאן כו': יג] ורבנן. דמפקי ליה לקרא לטומאת בגדים ולית להו ג"ש: היכא שריף להו. לאיזו רוח של ירושלים: לצפונה של ירושלים. שכל מעשה חטאת בצפון: אבית הדשן. צריך שיקדים לשם דשן יד] מזבח שיהא נקרא קודם לכן מקום שפך הדשן מכלל דלת"ק לא צריך: רבי אליעזר בן יעקב היא. דאמר לא אשמועינן על שפך אלא שיהא מקומו מדרון שיהא דשנו משתפך: ודילמא במקומו משופך הוא דפליגי. ומודה רבי אליעזר בן יעקב שיקדים שם דשן אלא דבעי נמי מקומו משופך (א): השורף. המתעסק בצרכי שריפתן טו] כגון המסייע בשעת שריפה והאי תנא אית ליה כרבי שמעון דאין מטמאין בגדים עד שיוצת בהן האור: דשוייה חרוכא. דהוי ניתך הבשר ואפר מיהא לא טז] הוה לתנא קמא מטמאין עד שיעשו אפר דאותם קרינא בהו אבל אפר לא מיקרי ולרבי (ב) יז] אלעזר ברבי שמעון אין מטמאין בגדים:

הדרן עלך טבול יום

השוחט. קדשים בחוץ יח] והעלה בחוץ. בהעלם אחד: חייב על השחיטה וחייב על העלייה. שהן שני גופי עבירה דתרווייהו כתיבי אשר ישחט ואשר יעלה (ויקרא יז): שלא העלה אלא דבר פסול. ואין מתקבל בפנים בעינן דכתיב ואל פתח אהל מועד לא יביאנו (שם): כיון שהוציאו פסלו. ואפ"ה חייב וה"ה לשוחט בחוץ ומעלה בחוץ: הטמא שאכל כו'. משום דפליגי ר' יוסי הגלילי ורבנן בתרווייהו ודמו הנך פלוגתא להדדי תנינהו גבי הדדי: כיון שנגע בו טמאוהו. ואפ"ה יט] [כי] הדר אכיל ליה מחייב ומה לי נטמא בשר על ידו מה לי נטמא ע"י אחרים: שאינו חייב אלא על טומאת הגוף. כדכתיב וטומאתו עליו ונכרתה ודרשינן בפ' בית שמאי (לעיל דף מג.) בטומאת הגוף הכתוב מדבר מי שטומאה פורחת ממנו: **גמ'** שחיטה והעלאה ב' פרשיות סמוכות זו לזו באחרי מות: אלא אזהרה מנלן. דקא מחייבינן ליה כ] עליה חטאת שאין חטאת באה אלא על לאו וכרת כדתנן (ג) הפסח והמילה מצות עשה ואין חייבין עליהן חטאת במסכת כריתות (דף ב.): למרקולים. אע"פ שעבודתו דרך בזיון לסקלו באבנים וזה עובדו דרך כבוד ולא קרינא ביה איכה יעבדו (ד) ואעשה כן ואפ"ה מניין שהוא חייב: קרי ביה ולא יזבחו וקרי ביה ולא עוד. דהאי לכדרבי אלעזר לכתוב ולא עוד את זבחיהם לשעירים והאי דכתיב ולא יזבחו לאזהרת שחוטי חוץ אתא דסמיך להאי פרשתא: ע"כ. עד המקרא הזה דלא יזבחו כל הענין העליון כא] *שנענש כרת על שחיטת חוץ ועל העלאת חוץ: מדבר בקדשים שהקדישן בשעת איסור הבמות. משהוקם המשכן דאילו הנך דהוקדשו מעיקרא אי לא מרבי להו קרא בהדיא מסתמא לא שמעינן להו:

תוספות

כיון שנגע בו טימאהו. אע"ג דמשכחת לה כשתחב לו חבירו בבית הבליעה סתמא דמילתא מיירי קרא אפילו בנותן לתוך פיו*: **אזהרה** מנלן. פי' בקונטרס דקא מחייבי ליה עלה *[חטאת] שאין חטאת באה אלא על לאו וכרת כדתנן הפסח והמילה מצות עשה ואין חייבין עליהן חטאת במסכת כריתות (דף ב.) וקשה לפי' דבריש אלו הן הלוקין (מכות דף יג:) משמע °דקרבן לא בעי אזהרה דפריך התם ודילמא אזהרה לקרבן הוא דהא פסח ומילה דלית בהו אזהרה לא מייתי קרבן ומשני התם הייט טעמא משום דאיתקוש כל התורה כולה לעבודת כוכבים מה עבודת כוכבים שב ואל תעשה לאפוקי הני דקום עשה נינהו ונראה לפרש דהאי דבעי הכא אזהרה מנא לן היינו משום דחשיב ליה בפרק אלו הן הלוקין (שם.) השוחט והמעלה בחוץ ולאו אמתני'* קאי והאי דקתני בכריתות (דף ב.) הפסח והמילה מצות עשה היינו כלומר דקום עשה נינהו ולהכי לית בהו חטאת ומיהו לקמן בשמעתין משמע דלאפוקי לאו קאתיא דפריך רבא הא דתנן פסח ומילה מצות עשה תיתי בק"ו ממותיר ומה מותיר שלא ענש הזהיר כו' וכן פ' המוצא תפילין (עירובין דף צו.) יצא פסח [ומילה] שהן מצות עשה [ופריך] הא כתיב ושמרת את החוקה וא"ר אילעאי כל מקום שנאמר השמר פן ואל הוי לא תעשה אלמא הוי פירושא יצא פסח [ומילה] שיש בעשה היינו שאינבהן לאו ואזהרה ואין לומר דסוגיא דידן כרבינא דמשני שינויא אחרינא בפרק אלו הן הלוקין (מכות דף יג:) ומצי למימר אליביה דקרבן קבעי אזהרה דמ"מ קשיא דרבא אדרבא דהייט רבא בשמעתין והיא מסקנא דמכות דקרבן לא בעי אזהרה אליבא דרבא ולפירוש הקונטרס נמי קשה קצת דאמאי תלי טעמא דפסח ומילה משום דלית בהו לאו תיפוק ליה משום דלית בהו מעשה דאפילו לר"ע דאמר לא בעי מעשה הא אמר ריש לקיש בריש כריתות (דף ג:) כהי דלא בעי ר"ע מעשה רבה מעשה זוטא בעי מיהו איכא לאוקמה שמעתין כרבי יוחנן דאמר ר"ע לא בעי מעשה כלל ונראה לפרש דלישנא דמתני' קא דייק דקתני פסח ומילה מצות עשה היינו שהם בקום עשה ומשמע נמי הלשון דלית בהו אזהרה כלל:

מניין לזובח בהמה למרקולים שהוא חייב. פי' בקונטרס אע"פ שעבודתו דרך בזיון לסקלו באבנים וזה עובדו דרך כבוד ולא קרינא ביה איכה יעבדו הגוים האלה את אלהיהם ואעשה כן אפ"ה מניין שחייב ונראה דכל הנהו דלאו אורחייהו בזביחה אע"ג דמכובדים נינהו לא נפקא מאיכה יעבדו כדמוכח בפרק ארבע מיתות (סנהדרין דף ס.) דאמר אביי שלש השתחואות בעבודת כוכבים [למה] אחת כדרכה ואחת שלא כדרכה ואחת לחלק ופריך כדרכה מאיכה

עין משפט נר מצוה

[ועי' תוס' חולין קא. ד"ה שפיר ותוס' סנהדרין פג: ד"ה פרט]

עג א מיי' פ"ז מהל' מעשה הקרבנות הלכה ד:

עד ב ג מיי' פ"ה מהל' פרה אדומה הל"ד:

א ד ה מיי' פי"ח מהל' מעשה הקרבנות הל"ה:

ב ו מיי' פי"ח מהלכות פסולי המוקדשין הלכה יג:

ג ז מיי' שם הל' יב:

ד ח ט י' פ"ג מהלכות ע"ז הל' ג:

נ"ל אמתני' דהכא קאי נ"ק

[נ"ל והעלה בחוץ חייב וכ"א במשנה שבמשניות]

הגהות הב"ח

(א) רש"י ד"ה ודלמא וכו' משופך הס"ד ואח"כ מה"ד המסייע כגון המתעסק: (ב) שם ד"ה דשויא וכו' לא מיקרי ולר"ש כצ"ל ותיבת אליעזר ברבי נמחק: (ג) שם ד"ה אלא וכו' כדתנן במס' כריתות הפסח וכו' חטאת הס"ד: (ד) שם ד"ה למרקולים וכו' איכה יעבדו ואפ"ה כצ"ל ותיבות ואעשה כן נמחק:

[נ"ל יביאנו]

עירובין צו: סוטה ה. ע"ז נא: שבועות ד. לו: מכות יג: מנחות לו: לט:

[סנהדרין סא: ע"ז נא.]

גליון הש"ס

תוס' ד"ה אזהרה וכו' דקרבן לא בעי אזהרה. עיין בב"ק דף קה ע"ב תוס' ד"ה מאי לאו ושבועות דף יח ע"ב תוס' ד"ה ל"מ:

שיטה מקובצת

א] ירושלים ולרבנן תיבת אלא נמחק: ב] הדשן הם נשרפין. עי' בכפתור ופרח דף כ"א ע"ב: ג] תי' היא נמחק: ד] אביי ודלמא: ה] השורף והמתעסק בצרכי שריפה מטמא בגדים: ו] תיבות מטמא בגדים נמחק: ז] השורף זה המסייע: ח] בשלמא העלאה כתיב: ט] יביאנו אזהרה תיבת הביאו נמחק: י] עוד את זבחיהם לשעירים האי: יא] דאמר ר"א מנין: יב] לכדרכה דנפקא לן מאיכה יעבדו: יג] מה"ד ולרבנן דמפקי: יד] המזבח שיהא: טו] שריפתן בגוף דכתיב אותם כגון: טז] לא הוי לתנא: יז] תיבות אליעזר ברבי נמחק: יח] בחוץ והמעלה בחוץ: יט] ואפ"ה כי הדר: כ] ליה עלה: כא] שענש כרת:

שהרי עונשן אמור °ואל פתח אהל מועד אזהרה א] דכתיב °השמר לך פן תעלה עולותיך מכאן ואילך ב] בזבחים שהקדישן בשעת היתר הבמות והקריבן בשעת איסור הבמות ג] שנא' °למען אשר יביאו בני ישראל את זבחיהם אשר הם זובחים זבחים שהתרתי לך כבר על פני השדה לומר לך הזובח בשעת איסור הבמות מעלה עליו הכתוב כאילו הקריב על פני השדה °והביאום לה' זו מצות עשה ד] לא תעשה מניין ת"ל °ולא יזבחו עוד יכול יהא ענוש כרת ת"ל °חוקת עולם תהיה זאת להם לדורותם זאת להם ולא אחרת להם אלא אמר (א) ה] (ר' אבין) ק"ו ומה במקום שלא ענש הזהיר מקום שענש אינו דין שהזהיר א"ל רבינא ו] לרב אשי א"כ לא יאמר לאו בחלב ותיתי ק"ו מנבילה מה נבילה שלא ענש הזהיר חלב שענש אינו דין שהזהיר אתא לקמיה דרבא א"ל מנבלה ז] נמי לא אתיא דאיכא למיפרך מה לנבלה שכן מטמא משרצים טמאין מה לשרצים טמאין שמטמאין *במשהו משרצים טהורים מה לשרצים טהורים שאיסורן במשהו מערלה וכלאי הכרם מה לערלה וכלאי הכרם שכן אסורין בהנאה משביעית מה לשביעית שכן תופסת דמיה מתרומה ח] שכן לא הותר מכללה מכולהו נמי שכן לא הותרו מכללן אמר רבא אי קשיא לי הא קשיא לי הא דתנן *פסח ומילה מצות עשה תיתי בק"ו ממותיר מה מותיר שלא ענש הזהיר פסח ומילה שענש אינו דין שהזהיר אמר רב אשי אמריתה לשמעתא קמיה דרב כהנא ואמר לי ממותיר לא אתיא דאיכא למיפרך מה למותיר שכן אין לו תקנה תאמר ט] פסח יש לו תקנה וכי מזהירין מן הדין אפילו למ"ד *עונשין מן הדין אין מזהירין מן הדין אלא *כדרבי יוחנן דאמר י] אתיא הבאה הבאה מה להלן לא ענש אא"כ הזהיר אף כאן לא ענש אא"כ הזהיר

רבא

שהרי עונשן אמור. כלומר דמסתמא בהו משתעי קרא לאסור והרי עונשן אמור כאן: מכאן ואילך כו'. שנאמר למען אשר יביאו וגו' דמדכתיב אשר הם זובחים משמע שהיו עומדים לישחט בבמה ומכאן ואילך והביאום לה' (ב): כזובח בשדה. שלא לשם שמים: (מצות) לא תעשה. בהנך דהוקדשו בשעת היתר מניין: ת"ל ולא יזבחו עוד. משמע מעכשיו אסורין ועד עכשיו יא] מותרין: זאת להם. עונש עשה ולא תעשה: ולא אחרת להם. כרת: מקום שלא ענש. כגון בקדשים שהקדישן בשעת היתר: הזהיר. כדאמרן יב] כאן: יג] שענש. כשהוקדשו בשעת איסור: אינו דין שהזהיר. ולקמן פריך וכי מזהירין מן הדין: משרצים. וא"ת תיתי אזהרה בחלב בק"ו משרצים טמאין כגון שמונה שרצים: במשהו. טומאתן בכעדשה אבל חלב בכזית: משרצים טהורים. שאין מטמאין כגון צפרדע ונמלה: שכן אסורין במשהו. לאכילה בכעדשה כדתניא במעילה בגמרא בפרק קדשי מזבח (דף טז:) ולא תשקצו את נפשותיכם בבהמה ובעוף וגו' פתח הכתוב באכילה וסיים בטומאה לומר לך כשיעור טומאתן של שרצים טמאים שיעור אכילתן של כל השרצים דהא כולהו כייל להו בהאי קרא ובכל אשר תרמוש האדמה וגו' ושיעור טומאתן נפקא לן בהכל חייבים (חגיגה דף יא:) שכן חומט תחילת ברייתו בכעדשה: שכן תופסת את דמיה. באיסורא כדתניא במסכת סוכה (דף מ:) קדש תהיה לכם מה קדש תופס את דמיו אף שביעית תופסת את דמיה: מכללו. חלב הותר מכללו בחיה ובכולהו כמי איכא למיפרך הא פירכא ומש"ה איצטריך אזהרה בחלב: אי קשיא. יד] בהאי דאייתינא אזהרה לשחוטי חוץ בהאי ק"ו הא קשיא לי הא דתנן בפרק קמא דכריתות (דף ב.) דקחשיב ל"ו כריתות להתחייב עליהם חטאת וקתני והפסח והמילה כרת שלהם על מצות עשה היא באה ואין חייבין חטאת על שגגתה דחטאת אינה באה אלא על לאו וכרת כדכתיב אשר לא תעשינה (ויקרא ד): תיתי. בו אזהרה טו] מק"ו ממותיר ממנו עד בוקר: יש לו תקנה. בתשלומי פסח שני: וכי מזהירין מן הדין. לעיל קאי דמייתי אזהרה לשחוטי חוץ מק"ו: אפילו למ"ד. במסכת מכות עונשין מדין ק"ו מודה דאין מזהירין מן הדין דתניא בפ"ק דמכות (דף ה:) איש כי יקח את אחותו וגו' אין לי אלא בת אביו שלא בת אמו בת אמו שלא בת אביו בת אביו ובת אמו מנין תלמוד לומר ערות אחותו גילה והלא קל וחומר הוא למדת שאין עונשין מן הדין וכן לענין אזהרת ערות אחותך בת אביך וגו' אין לי כו' עד שאין מזהירין מן הדין ופליגי תנאי בפ' בתרא ואיכא דדרים להאי אחותו גילה דגבי עונש לדרשא (ג) טז] ועונש דבת אביו ובת אמו קסבר עונשין מן הדין ואילו אחותך היא דגבי אזהרה דילפינן מיניה אין מזהירין מן הדין דלא אפנייה לדרשא אחריתי: אתיא הבאה הבאה. שחיטה מהעלאה כתיב בשחיטה (ויקרא יז) לא הביאו וכתיב בהעלאה (שם) לא יביאנו וגזרה שוה הואיל ומופנה היא לכך הרי היא יז] כמי שמפרש בה ואין זה מן הדין כק"ו שאדם דן מעצמו:

ה"ג

מאיכה יעבדו נפקא אלא אחת לשלא כדרכה ואפילו כלל שעובדין אותה בבזיון כגון פעור ומ"קולים ואחת כדרכה ושלא כדרכה פי' כדרכה בעבודת כבוד אלא שאין דרכה בהשתחואה ואם תאמר מנלן הכא זובח בהמה למרקולים אימא כי אתא קרא למכובדים שאין דרכן בזביחה אבל למבוזין כגון פעור ומרקולים לא וי"ל דגלי ליה בהשתחואה דמכובדים ומבוזין שוין הוא הדין בזביחה ור"ת מפרש דתרי קראי בזביחה כתיבי האי קרא דהכא ולא יזבחו ועוד כתיב זובח לאלהים יחרם דדרשינן בפ' ארבע מיתות (סנהדרין דף סא.) דילתה זביחה ללמד על הכלל לחייב בכל עבודת פנים אפילו בשלא כדרכה וקשה לפי' דמהאי קרא לא שמעינן אלא אזהרה אבל עונש במבוזין מנא לן ועוד תרוייהו למכובדין צריכי חד לעונש וחד לאזהרה ועוד דלא ה"ל לאיתויי איכה יעבדו אלא הוה ליה למימר אם אינו ענין לכדרכה של מכובדין דכתיב זובח לאלהים יחרם תנהו ענין לשלא כדרכה כלומר מבוזין אלא כמו שפירשנו נראה דרבי אלעזר אכל שלא כדרכה אתא לאשמועי' דחייב אלא דנקט מרקולים לרבותא ומהשתחואה נפקא לן דאין חילוק בין מכובדין למבוזין כדפרי' תדע דהא אמר בפרק ד' מיתות (שם דף סד:) ג' כריתות בעבודת כוכבים למה אחת לכדרכה ואחת לשלא כדרכה ואחת למולך ולא מיבעיא לן קרא אחרינא חד למכובדין וחד למבוזין וק"ק הא דפריך בפ' ד' מיתות אימא יצתה השתחואה ללמד על הכלל כולו ודקאמרת זובח למה לי לגופיה דמחשבין מעבודה לעבודה ומתמה עליה הש"ס אלא הא דקאמר רבי אלעזר מניין לזובח בהמה למרקולים כו' מהשתחואה נפקא מאי קושיא דילמא איצטריך לאזהרה במחשב מעבודה לעבודה דהא לעולם הוא כך דלא יזבחו אזהרה לעונש דזובח לאלהים יחרם וי"ל דאם איתא דהשתחואה ללמד על הכלל א"כ לא תעבדם דאוקמינן (סנהדרין דף ס:) למגפף ומנשק הוה מייתר לן לאזהרה *אזביחה דמהשתחואה הוה ילפינן אפילו חיוב מיתה במגפף ומנשק: **אזהרה** מניין ת"ל השמר לך פן תעלה עולותיך. הא דמייתי אזביחה אזהרה דהעלאה אמסקנא סמיך דילפי הבאה הבאה או שם שם אבל לאביי דבסמוך קשה דק"ו הו"ל לאתויי: **מקום** שענש אינו דין שהזהיר. ולא שייך למימר פסח ומילה יוכיחו דאיכא למיפרך שכן קום עשה: **מה** לשרצים טהורים שכן אסורין במשהו. פי' בקונטרס דתניא במסכת מעילה בפרק קדשי מזבח (דף טז:) ולא תשקצו את נפשותיכם בבהמה ובעוף וגו' פתח הכתוב באכילה וסיים בטומאה לומר כשיעור טומאתן של שרצים טמאים שיעור אכילתן של כל השרצים דהא כולהו כייל להו בהאי קרא ובכל אשר תרמוש וגו' ושיעור טומאתן נפקא לן בהכל חייבין (חגיגה דף יא:) שכן חומט תחילת ברייתו בכעדשה עד כאן לשון הקונטרס ואגב חורפיה לא עיין בה ובהדיא מסיק התם דוקא בשרצים טמאים ולא בטהורים דאמרינן במובדלין דיבר הכתוב דכתיב בסיפיה דקרא אשר הבדלתי לכם לטמא ול"ל דכל שהוא דהכא בבריה קמיירי דבכל שהוא מיחייב משום בריה כדאמרינן בפ"ק דחגיגה (דף י.) ובפ' כהן גדול ונזיר (נזיר דף נג.) ובמכות (דף יז.) ובפ' גיד הנשה (חולין דף נו.*): **מכולהו** שכן לא הותר מכללן. תימה נילף בכולהו כרת בק"ו מחלב שהותר מכללו: **תיתי** בק"ו ממותיר. הא דנקט מותיר טפי מגזל וגניבה וכמה לאוין שבתורה משום דמותיר לא עביד מעשה דומיא דפסח ומילה ומש"ה לא נקט כמי הנך דלעיל דאיכא למיפרך שכן יש בהן מעשה:

ה"ג

גי' רש"ק אביי

[עי' תוס' חולין קכ. ד"ה שכן וכו' דמה דאיתא הכא (מה לשרצים טמאים שמטמאין) בכל שהוא לא גרסי' לה וסופרים שבשו משום דבתר הכי קאמר מה לשרצים טהורים שאיסורן במשהו ע"ש ומעתה בהכר דמה דאיתא בפירש"י ד"ה משרצים וכו' וכן בד"ה במשהו וכו' לאו רש"י כתבו אלא תלמיד אח' פי' כן ע"פ הגי' שבשבשו הסופרים ותדע דכך היא דאם מפי רש"י יצאו הדברים תמוה טובא במ"ש ד"ה במשהו כו' אבל חלב בכזית הלא ידענא דחלב אינו מטמא כלל וטהור לגמרי כמבואר הכא דקאמר מה לנבלה שכן מטמא כלומר אבל חלב אינו מטמא וכן נתבאר להדיא בפסחים כג.]

נ"ל אמחשב מעבודה לעבודה דמהשתחואה כו' נ"ק

עירובין נו. כריתות ב.

סנהדרין נד. וש"נ מכות יז:

[בילקוט אחרי רמז תקפ"א הגי' אלא אמר ר"י אתיא]

הגהות הב"ח

(א) גמ' אלא אמר אביי ק"ו. נ"ב כצ"ל וכן איתא בילקוט רמז תקפ"א*) וכן מבואר בתוס' ד"ה אזהרה וכן משמע להדיא מגמ': (ב) רש"י ד"ה מכאן וכו' לה' הס"ד ואח"כ מה"ד כאילו הקריב על פני השדה: (ג) שם ד"ה אפי' למ"ד כו' לדרשא אחריתא ועונש וכו' דילפינן מיניה בת אביו ובת אמו אין מזהירין: *) [לפנינו בילקוט שם איתא ר' אבין]

[וע"ע תוס' יבמות קיד: ד"ה משום ותוס' חולין קכ. ד"ה שכן]

שיטה מקובצת

א] אזהרה מנין דכתיב: ב] ואילך הוא מדבר בזבחים: ג] הבמות שהרי נאמר למען ותיבת שנאמר נמחק: ד] עשה מצות ל"ת: ה] אמר אביי ק"ו ותיבות ר' אבין נמחק: ו] רבינא לאביי א"כ ותיבות לרב אשי נמחק: ז] תיבת נמי נמחק: ח] מתרומה מה לתרומה שכן לא הותר מכולהו מה לכולהו שכן תיבת נמי נמחק: ט] תאמר בפסח שיש לו: י] דאמר ר' יוחנן אתיא: יא] עכשיו היו מותרין: יב] תיבת כאן נמחק: יג] מה"ד מקום שענש: יד] קשיא לי בהא דאייתינן אזהרה: טו] אזהרה בק"ו ואות מ' נמחק: טז] לדרשה אחריתי ועונש: יז] כמו שמפורש בה:

and offered up when *bamoth* were forbidden,[12] [106b] since their penalty is stated, [viz.,] *'and hath not brought it unto the door of the tent of meeting'* [etc.], whilst whence do we know the interdict? *'Take heed to thyself that thou offer not thy burnt-offerings* [etc.].' From
a here onward[1] it speaks of sacrifices which one consecrated when *bamoth* were permitted but offered when they were forbidden, for it is said, *To the end that the children of Israel may bring their sacrifices which they sacrifice*[2] [viz.,] sacrifices which I formerly permitted,—*in the open field*:[2] this teaches you [that] he who sacrifices [slaughters] [at *bamoth*] when *bamoth* are forbidden, the Writ regards him as though he offered in the open field. *'Even that they may bring them unto the Lord'*:[2] this is a positive injunction.[3] Whence have we a negative injunction? From the text, *'And they shall no more sacrifice* [etc.]'[4] You might think that one is punished for it by *kareth;* therefore it states, *This shall be a statute for ever unto them throughout their generations:*[1] *'this'* is their [statute], but nought else is theirs![5]—Rather said R. Abin:[6] [We learn it] *a minori:* if [Scripture] interdicted where it did not punish [with *kareth*];[7] is it not logical that it interdicted where it punished [with *kareth*]?[8] Rabina observed to R. Ashi: If so, let a negative injunction not be stated in connection with *ḥeleb*,[9] and it could be inferred *a minori* from *nebelah*:[9] if [Scripture] interdicted *nebelah,* where it did not punish [with *kareth*]; is it not logical that it interdicted *ḥeleb,* seeing that it did punish [with *kareth*]. Then he came before Raba.[10] Said he to him: It could not be inferred from *nebelah,* because [the argument] can be refuted:
b As for *nebelah,* the reason is because it defiles.[1] [Nor can it be deduced] from unclean *sheraẓim* [reptiles], [because,] As for unclean *sheraẓim,* the reason is because a small portion defiles.[2] [Nor] from clean *sheraẓim*,[3] [because,] As for clean *sheraẓim,* the reason is because [the standard of] their interdict is very small.[4] [Nor] from *'orlah* and *kilayim* of the vineyard, [because,] As for *'orlah* and *kilayim* of the vineyard, that is because all benefit from them is forbidden.[5] [Nor] from *shebi'ith*,[6] [because,] As for *shebi'ith,* that is because it imposes its own status upon the money received for it.[7] [Nor] from *terumah,* [because,] As for *terumah,* that is because it is never exceptionally permitted.[8] [Nor can you deduce it] from all these because they are never permitted exceptionally.

Raba said: If I have a difficulty, it is this: When we learnt, The Passover-offering and circumcision are positive commands,[9] let us infer [a *negative* injunction in their case] from one who leaves [anything] over [of the Passover-offering]:[10] If Scripture interdicted in the case of one who leaves over, though it did not prescribe a penalty, is it not logical that it interdicted in the case of the Passover-offering and circumcision, where it did prescribe a penalty?[11] R. Ashi said: I reported this discussion in R. Kahana's presence, and he told me: [A negative injunction] cannot be inferred from leaving over, because [the argument] can be refuted: as for leaving over,
c that is because it cannot be repaired;[1] will you say [that there is a negative injunction] in the case of a Passover-offering, which can be repaired [if neglected]?[2]

But can you assume an interdict by inferring *a minori?* [For] even on the view that you can *punish* through inferring *a minori,* you cannot assume a formal prohibition by inferring *a minori!*—Rather, it is as R. Joḥanan said [elsewhere]. For R. Joḥanan said: 'Bringing' is inferred from 'bringing':[3] as in the latter case [Scripture] did not prescribe a penalty without formally interdicting, so in the former case [Scripture] did not prescribe a penalty without formally

(12) I.e., after the Tabernacle was erected. If, however, one consecrated an animal before the Tabernacle was erected, when *bamoth* were permitted, there is nothing as yet to shew that he is culpable if he slaughters it at a *bamah after* it is erected.

a (1) From Lev. XVII, 7. (2) Ibid., 5. (3) Though the inference is obviously that they may *not* bring them to the *bamoth* but only *'unto* the Lord' (i.e. at the Tabernacle), yet since it is expressed *affirmatively*, the implied interdict counts as a positive injunction. (4) *'No more'* implies that hitherto it was permitted, but from now onwards it is forbidden. (5) It is subject only to an affirmative and a negative precept, but not to *kareth.*—Thus the negative injunction applies to sacrifices which were consecrated when *bamoth* were permitted, but we have no *explicit* negative injunction in respect of those consecrated when *bamoth* were forbidden. (6) Sh.M. and BaḤ emend: Abaye. (7) *Sc.* where the sacrifice was consecrated when *bamoth* were permitted. As just stated, we have a negative injunction covering that case, but *kareth* is not involved. (8) *Sc.* where the sacrifice was consecrated when *bamoth* were already forbidden. (9) V. Glos. (10) Rabina and R. Ashi were later than Raba. For that reason the text is amended to Abaye (v. n. 6.), Raba's contemporary.

b (1) Whereas *ḥeleb* does not defile. (2) As much as a lentil defiles. (3) Those which do not defile, e.g., a frog or an ant, but which are forbidden as food by a negative interdict. (4) He who eats as much as a lentil is culpable; whereas no penalty is incurred for eating less than an olive size of *ḥeleb.* (5) Whereas *ḥeleb* is only forbidden as *food.* (6) For all these words v. Glos. (7) Lit., 'it seizes its money.'—If *shebi'ith* is sold, the money is forbidden in the same way as itself. That does not apply to *ḥeleb,* however. (8) Lit., 'it is not permitted out of its general (interdict).' *Terumah* is *always* forbidden to unclean priests, whereas some *ḥeleb* is permitted, viz., the *ḥeleb* of a *ḥayyah* (non-domesticated animal, e.g., deer). (9) It is stated in Ker. 2a that one is liable to a sin-offering for the unintentional violation of all *negative* injunctions which if *deliberately* violated involve *kareth.* These two however, though entailing *kareth,* are *positive* precepts, and so their neglect does not necessitate a sin-offering. (10) This is forbidden by a negative injunction: *And ye shall let nothing of it remain until the morning* (Ex. XII, 10). (11) Hence, if such an argument is permissible, they should rank as subject to a *negative* injunction too, viz., not to neglect them.

c (1) Once the flesh is left over, nothing can be done. (2) By bringing an offering on the *Second* Passover (v. Num. IX, 9 *seq.*). Circumcision should be done on the eighth day; yet if not done then, it can be performed at any time subsequently.—Thus so far all the arguments against the assumption of an interdict *a minori* have been rebutted. (3) A *gezerah shawah* between slaughtering and offering up is deduced, based on the fact that 'bringing' is written in connection with both: Slaughtering: *What man soever . . . that* killeth *an ox . . . and hath not* brought *it unto the door of the tent of meeting;* offering up: *Whatsoever man . . . that* offereth up *a burnt-offering or sacrifice, and* bringeth *it not unto the door of the tent of meeting.*—R. Joḥanan stated this exegesis with respect to another question (v. *infra* 107a), but the same applies here.

interdicting. [107*a*] Raba said, It is as R. Jonah['s exegesis]. For R. Jonah said: '*There*' is inferred from '*there*':[4] as in the one case, [Scripture] did not prescribe a penalty without formally prohibiting, so in the other case [Scripture] did not punish without formally prohibiting.[5]

We have [now] found the case of those which should be burnt within, which were offered up without;[6] how do we know the case of those which should be burnt without,[7] which were offered up
a without?[1]—Said R. Kahana: Scripture saith, *And thou shalt say unto them*[2] [which means,] thou shalt say concerning those just mentioned.[3] To this Raba[4] demurred: Is it then written, '*concerning* them': Surely 'unto *them*' is written?[5] Rather, it as the School of R. Ishmael taught: '*And thou shalt say unto them*' combines the sections.[6] R. Johanan said: 'Bringing' is inferred from 'bringing':[7] as there it refers to those [sacrifices] which must be burnt without, so here too it refers to those which must be burnt without. To this R. Bibi demurred: When we learnt, There are thirty-six offences in the Torah which entail *kareth:* surely there are thirty *seven*, for there are offering up [a sacrifice which should be burnt within] and offering up [a sacrifice which should be burnt without]?[8] That is indeed a difficulty.

Now, when we learnt: He who sprinkles some of the blood without, is culpable:[9] how do we know it?[10]—It is inferred from what
b was taught: *Blood shall be imputed* [*unto that man*]:[1] that is to include one who sprinkles [without]: these are the words of R. Ishmael. R. Akiba said: Or *sacrifice*[2] includes sprinkling. And how does R. Ishmael employ this [phrase] '*or sacrifice*'?—To divide.[3] And whence does R. Akiba know to divide?—He infers it from, *and bringeth* it *not* [*unto the door of the tent of meeting*].[4] And R. Ishmael?[5]—He requires that ['*it*'] [for teaching:] One is culpable for [offering up] the whole [animal], but not for [offering up] an incomplete one.[6] And R. Akiba?[7]—He infers it from [the phrase] '*to sacrifice it*'. And R. Ishmael?—One ['*it*'] is in respect of those [sacrifices] which should be burnt within, which were made incomplete and offered up without; the other is in respect of those which should be burnt without, which one made incomplete and offered up without.[8] And it was taught even so: R. Ishmael said: You might think that if one made incomplete and offered up without what should be burnt within, he is culpable; therefore it says, '*to sacrifice* it': one is culpable for [offering up] a whole [animal], but not for [offering up] an incomplete one. And R. Akiba?[9]—He holds that if one made incomplete and offered up without what should be burnt within, he *is* culpable.

And R. Akiba: How does he employ this [phrase], '*blood shall be imputed*'?—It includes the *shechitah* of a bird.[10] And R. Ishmael?—He deduces it from, *or that killeth.*[11] And R. Akiba?—He can answer you: He requires that [to teach]: One is culpable for slaughtering
c [*shechitah*], but not for nipping [*melikah*].[1] And R. Ishmael?—He infers it from, *This is the thing* [*which the Lord hath commanded*].[2] For it was taught: [*What man soever . . .*] *that killeth* [*an ox* etc.]: I know it only of slaughtering an animal; how do I know [that] if one slaughters a bird [he is culpable]? Because it says, *or that killeth.*[3] You might think that I also include one who performs *melikah*, and that is indeed logical: if one is culpable for *shechitah* [of a bird], though this is not its correct rite within; is it not logical that one is culpable for *melikah* [without], seeing that that is its correct rite within? Therefore it states, 'This *is the thing* [etc.]'. And R. Akiba?—He can answer you: that is required for a *gezerah shawah.*[4]

Now, as to what we learnt: He who takes the fistful,[5] and he who receives the blood [of a sacrifice slaughtered without] is not liable: how do we know it? But whence would you infer that he is culpable?[6]—From *shechitah.*[7] As for *shechitah*, the reason may be because it invalidates a Passover-offering [when it is done] on behalf of such who cannot eat it![8]—Then infer it from sprinkling: as for sprinkling, the reason may be because a lay-Israelite is liable

(4) Deut. XII, 14: There *shalt thou* offer up *thy burnt-offerings, and* there *thou shalt* do *all that I command thee*. '*Do*' refers to all rites (including slaughtering) in connection with sacrifices. (5) The 'one case' and 'the other case' are 'offering up' and 'doing' respectively (v. preceding note). (6) *Sc.* those which were slaughtered *within*, so that they should have been burnt (i.e., *haktarah*) within. (7) *Sc.* which were slaughtered *without* so that they could not be burnt within but without. 'Burnt' in this connection does not mean *haktarah*, but the burning of unfit sacrifices.

a (1) That this too makes one liable. For it might be argued that there is no culpability here, since the animal could not be burnt within in any case. (2) Lev. XVII, 8. (3) Lit., 'the near ones'. (Sh.M. reads: the preceding.) Lev. XVII, 3-7 deals with *slaughtering* without: vv. 8*f* treats of *offering up* without, and they commence with, '*And thou shalt say unto them*' which implies, thou shalt say about them just mentioned, *sc.* those who *slaughter* without, that they are also culpable for *offering up* without. (4) Sh.M. reads: Rabbah. (5) I.e., אליהם ('*alehem*), not עליהם ('*alehem*). (6) *Sc.* vv. 3-7 and vv. 8*f*. Hence the provisions of the latter section (*sc.* liability for *offering up* without) apply to those mentioned in the former (viz., those who *slaughter* without).—Though this exegesis too infers the law from the same phrase, the method of interpretation is different and retains the correct rendering of '*alehem*, unto them. (7) V. *supra* 106*b* and n. c 3. Similarly here: as 'bringing' in the former section refers to one who slaughters without, so it does in the latter too. (8) The thirty-six as enumerated include offering up without. Now in answer to the question, since they are all enumerated, why is the number stated? The Talmud says that it teaches that if one committed all of them in a single state of ignorance (not knowing that they are forbidden), he is liable to thirty-six sin-offerings. If, however, culpability for offering up without sacrifices which should be burnt without, is inferred by a *gezerah shawah* from those which should be burnt within, they constitute two *separate* offences and involve *separate* sin-offerings. But in that case they should be enumerated separately there too, and the number given is thirty-*seven*. (9) I.e., even if he made one sprinkling only instead of four. (10) For Scripture speaks only of slaughtering and offering up without, but not of sprinkling.

b (1) Lev. XVII, 4. (2) Ibid. 8; it refers to offering up without, and '*or*' is regarded as an extension. (3) To shew that one is liable for offering up without *either* a burnt-offering *or* any other sacrifice. Without '*or*' you would assume that liability is incurred only for offering up *both*. (4) '*It*' is singular and so implies one. (5) Does he not admit this exegesis? (6) From which part is missing. The exact meaning of 'whole' and 'incomplete' is discussed anon. (7) How does he know this? (8) If '*it*' were written once only, I would say that its implication applies only to those which should be burnt without. But as for those which should be burnt within, he is culpable even if he offers up only part, for when a single limb springs off the altar during the burning (*haktarah*), it must be replaced, which shews that *haktarah* applies even to part. (The general principle is that the performance of a rite without involves liability when it would count as a proper rite within.) (9) Whence does he learn this? (10) Though a bird sacrifice requires *melikah*, not *shechitah*, yet if it is slaughtered without (i.e., with *shechitah*), it involves liability. (11) Ibid., 3.

c (1) Thus both are necessary. For from the first I would conclude that *even shechitah* of a bird involves liability, and all the more *melikah*, since that is the correct way of sacrificing a bird. Hence the second teaches that *only shechitah* involves liability. (2) Lev. XVII, 2. This is the superscription to the whole passage, and is emphatic, implying that the law is exactly as stated. (3) This is superfluous, as Scripture could say, that killeth an ox . . . in the camp or without the camp. (4) V. Ned. 78*a*; B. B. 120*b*. (5) Of a meal-offering, without, and does not burn it. (6) That you seek a text to shew that he is not. (7) By analogy: as *shechitah* is a sacrificial rite and involves culpability if performed without, so it is the same with every sacrificial rite. (8) V. *supra* 4*a*. But that obviously cannot apply to taking the fistful, or to receiving.

רבא אמר כדרבי יונה דאמר רבי יונה "אתיא שם שם מה להלן לא ענש אלא א"כ הזהיר אף כאן לא ענש אלא אם כן הזהיר אשכחן מוקטרי פנים שהעלן א] לחוץ מוקטרי חוץ שהעלן לחוץ מנין אמר רב כהנא אמר קרא °ואליהם תאמר *על ג]הסמוכין תאמר מתקיף לה ג] רבא מי כתיב ועליהם ואליהם כתיב אלא כדתנא דבי ר' ישמעאל ואליהם תאמר לערב פרשיות *ר' יוחנן אמר אתיא הבאה הבאה מה להלן מוקטרי חוץ אף כאן מוקטרי חוץ מתקיף לה רב ביבי ד] הא דתנן *שלשים ושש כריתות בתורה תלתין ושב הויין דאיכא המעלה והמעלה קשיא והדתנן* [ג]הזורק מקצת דמים בחוץ חייב מנלן נפקא ליה מדתניא *°דם יחשב לרבות הזורק דברי רבי ישמעאל ר"ע אומר °או זבח לרבות את הזורק ורבי ישמעאל האי או זבח מאי עביד ליה ה] לחלק ור' עקיבא לחלק מנא ליה נפקא ליה °מלא יביאנו ורבי ישמעאל ההוא מיבעי ליה *[י]על השלם הוא חייב ואינו חייב על החסר ורבי עקיבא נפקא ליה °מלעשות אותו ור' ישמעאל חד למוקטרי פנים שחסרו ו] והעלו בחוץ וחד למוקטרי חוץ שחסרו והעלו בחוץ והא תניא רבי ישמעאל אומר יכול מוקטרי פנים שחסרו ז] והעלו בחוץ חייב [ד]ת"ל לעשות אותו על השלם חייב ואינו חייב על החסר ורבי עקיבא ח] מוקטרי פנים שחסרו והעלו בחוץ חייב ורבי עקיבא האי דם יחשב מאי עביד ליה [ה]לרבות שחיטת העוף ורבי ישמעאל נפקא ליה °מאו אשר ישחט ורבי עקיבא אמר לך ההוא מיבעי ליה על השוחט הוא חייב ט]ולא על המולק ור' ישמעאל נפקא ליה מזה הדבר דתניא אשר ישחט אין לי אלא שוחט בהמה שחט עוף מנ"ל ת"ל או אשר ישחט יכול י] אף המולק ודין הוא מה שחיטה דאין דרך הכשירה בפנים חייב מליקה שדרך הכשירה בפנים אינו דין שהוא חייב ת"ל °זה הדבר ורבי עקיבא אמר לך ההוא מיבעי ליה *לגזירה שוה והא דתנן [ו]הקומץ והמקבל דמים בחוץ פטור מנלן ומהיכא תיתי דחייב תיתי משחיטה *מה לשחיטה [ח]שכן יא] נפסלת שלא לאוכלין בפסח תיתי מזריקה מה לזריקה שבן זר חייב עליה מיתה

תיתי

רש"י

ה"ג דאמר רבי יונה אמר קרא שם תעלה עולותיך ושם תעשה. איתקש שאר עשיות להעלאה מה העלאה לא ענש אלא אם כן הזהיר אף שחיטה לא ענש אלא א"כ הזהיר: אשכחן מוקטרי יב] בפנים שהעלן בחוץ. שחוטי פנים שהיו עומדים להקטירן בפנים יג] והעלו בחוץ חייב כדכתיב בהעלאה (ויקרא יז) ואל פתח אהל מועד לא יביאנו בראויין להביאן לפנים ולהעלותן הכתוב מדבר: מוקטרי חוץ. שחוטי חוץ שעומדין ליקטר בחוץ ולא בפנים: ואליהם תאמר. זהו תחילת פרשת העלאה וסמוכה לפרשת שחוטי חוץ על הראשונים דמשתעי בשחוטי חוץ יד]*שאמר שאם העלו בחוץ חייב ועליהם קרינן: ואליהם כתיב טו]. לשון קושיא הוא: ה"ג אלא כדתנא דבי ר' ישמעאל ואליהם תאמר לערב פרשיות. וי"ו מוסיף על ענין ראשון ומערב הפרשיות לומר שאף שחוטי חוץ שהעלן בחוץ חייב: ל"ו כריתות בתורה. וקחשיב התם המעלה בחוץ והוינן בה מניינא למה לי ואמר רבי יוחנן שאם עשאן כולן בהעלם אחד חייב על כל אחת ואחת הא תרתי נינהו לחובא המעלה איברי פנים והמעלה איברי חוץ דכיון דגמרת להו בהיקשא או בגזירה שוה הוה ליה כל חד וחד גוף עבירה וחייב על כל אחת ואחת אפילו בהעלם אחד וניתני שלשים ושבע והא ליכא לשנויי שם העלאה קתני כי היכי דקא חשיב המחלל את השבת טז] והעובד עבודת כוכבים בחדא ואע"ג דטובא חיובי איכא דהכי שנינו בכריתות ואקשינן עלה (א) שבת יז] ועבודת כוכבים [ומשני] תנא חילוקין שלהן במקומן דתנן במסכת שבת (דף עג.) אבות מלאכות ארבעים חסר אחת ודעבודת כוכבים תניא בסנהדרין (דף ס:) אחד העובד ואחד הזובח ואחד המקטר ואחד המנסך אבל יח] הכא לא תנא בהדיא המעלה איברי פנים והמעלה איברי חוץ ואף על גב דאיכא למשמע מפלוגתא דרבי יוסי הגלילי ורבנן בהדיא מיהא לא תנינהי בתרתי: והא דתנן. לקמן במתניתין (דף קי.) הזורק יט][מקצת] דמים בחוץ שלא נתן ארבע מתנות אלא מתנה אחת חייב דהויא זריקה בפנים דכוותיה דתנן (לעיל דף לו:) כל הניתנין על מזבח החיצון שנתנן במתנה אחת כיפר: מנלן. דאיחייב אזריקת דם בחוץ הא שחיטה והעלאה הוא דכתיבן: דם יחשב דם שפך. לרבות את הזורק והאי כ] קראי בשחוטי חוץ כתיבי: או זבח. כתיב גבי העלאה או לרבות את הזורק: לחלק. דלא תימא עד דמסיק עולה ושלמים: לא יביאנו. משמע חד: ואינו חייב על החסר. לקמן פליגי בה איכא למאן דאמר על אבר חסר ואיכא למאן דאמר על בהמה חסירה עד שיעלה כא] כל הבהמה ואיכא למאן דאמר על הקטרה חסירה כגון פחות מכזית: אותו. שלם משמע: חד למוקטרי פנים כו'. דאי כתב חד הוה אמינא הני מילי מוקטרי חוץ אבל מוקטרי פנים מיחייב דהא מהדרינן פוקעין (ב) דחסרו אלמא הקטרה היא: והא תניא. בניחותא: ור"ע סבר מוקטרי פנים. שחוטי פנים שחסרו כגון פקעו מעל האור והעלן בחוץ חייב דהא מהדרינן פוקעין: ור' ישמעאל נפקא ליה מאו אשר ישחט. אע"ג דאיצטריך מחוץ למחנה כדלקמן אפילו הכי אשר ישחט יתירא הוא דמצי למיכתב כב] אל מחוץ למחנה אייתר ליה אשר ישחט לרבות שחיטת העוף: ההוא מיבעיא ליה כג] השוחט העוף חייב ואינו חייב על המולק. והילכך איצטריכו תרוייהו דאי כתיב אשר ישחט לרבות שחיטת העוף הוה אמינא כל שכן מליקה שהיא דרך הכשירו בפנים להכי כתיב *דם שפך לרבות את העוף והדר כתיב אשר ישחט למעוטי מולק: אין לי אלא שוחט בהמה. כדכתיב אשר ישחט שור או כשב: ומה שחיטה. שאין זה דרך הכשירו של עוף בפנים חייב עליה בחוץ מליקה לא כ"ש: ת"ל זה הדבר. אשר צוה וגו' וסמיך ליה אשר ישחט שחיטה ולא מליקה: לגזירה שוה. מפורשת בית נוחלין (ב"ב דף קכ:) ובנדרים בפרק *בתרא (דף עח.): הקומץ מנחה בחוץ. ולא הקטיר פטור: מנא ליה. דפטור: ופרכינן מהי תיתי לחובא. דאיצטריך קרא למיפטריה: מה לשחיטה שכן פוסלת בפסח ששחטו שלא לאוכלין. כגון לחולה וזקן שאין יכול לאכול כזית כדכתיב (שמות יב) איש לפי אכלו תכוסו תאמר בקומץ מנחה דלא שייך כד] פסול שלא לאוכליו ובקבלה נמי אפילו בפסח לא מיפסלא כדאמרן בפרק תמיד נשחט (פסחים דף סא.) רבי אומר לשון סורסי הוא זה כאדם שאומר כה] כוס לי טלה זה דבשחיטה לתודה הוא דפסלה מחשבת אוכלין: תיתי מזריקה. דלא פסלה שלא לשם אוכלין בפסח ומחייב עלה בחוץ וה"ה לקמילה וקבלה: שכן זר חייב עליה מיתה. מה שאין כן בקמילה וקבלה דבעינן עבודה תמה ולא עבודה שיש אחריה עבודה כדאמרינן פרק בראשונה בסדר יומא (דף כד.) והני תרוייהו יש אחריהן עבודה:

היכי

תוספות

ה"ג **דאמר** רבי יונה. בפ"ק דכריתות (דף ג:) מהיקשא יליף: **הני** תלתין ושב הויין דאיכא המעלה והמעלה. דכיון דגמרת להו בהיקשא או בגזירה שוה הוה ליה כל חד וחד גוף עבירה וחייב על כל אחת ואחת אפי' כו]*בהעלם אחת והשוחט ומעלה נמי דקתני התם בתרתי לא ידעינן בהו תרתי לאוי אלא בגזירה שוה פי' בקונטרס והא ליכא לשנויי שם העלאה קתני כי היכי דקא חשיב המחלל את השבת בחדא ואע"ג דטובא חיובי איכא דהכי שנינן לה בכריתות (דף ג:) דאקשינן עליה שבת ועבודת כוכבים תנא חלוקים שלהן במקומן דתנן במס' שבת (דף עג:) אבות מלאכות מ' חסר אחת ודעבודת כוכבים תנינן בסנהדרין (דף ס:) אחד העובד ואחד הזובח ואחד המקטר ואחד המנסך אבל הני לא תנא הכא בהדיא המעלה איברי פנים והמעלה איברי חוץ ואע"ג דאיכא למשמע מפלוגתא דרבי יוסי הגלילי ורבנן בהדיא מיהא לא תנינהי בתרתי עכ"ל וקשה תימה גבי עבודת כוכבים היכי קאמר התם בפ' קמא דכריתות (דף ג:) דקתני יתהון אבינייהו פירוש במקומן הא ליכא למשמע ממתני' דד' מיתות אלא חיוב חטאת אהנך עבודות אבל חילוק חטאות לא שמעינן מינה: **דאיכא** המעלה והמעלה קשיא. כז] קשה מהא דלא משני ההיא דכריתות (נ"ז שם) כרבי יוסי הגלילי דפטר מוקטרי חוץ: **מאי** עביד ליה לחלק. *תימה דהך סוגיא דלא כרבא אלא כאביי דפ' השואל (ב"מ דף צה:) דסבר לה כרבי יאשיה דפ' ד' מיתות (סנהדרין דף סו:) דבעי קרא לחלק גבי אביו ואמו: **חד** למוקטרי פנים שחסרו וחד למוקטרי חוץ שחסרו. הכא לא שייך למילף מואליהם תאמר או הבאה הבאה משום דבפנים טעמא דמהדרינן פוקעין וחשיבה הקטרה ולא שייך למילף למוקטרי חוץ:

להכי

עין משפט נר מצוה

ה א מיי' פי"ח מהלכות מעשה הקרבנות הל' ה:
ו ב מיי' פי"ט שם הל' ג: [כס"מ אי' בהעלם אחת]
ז ג מיי' שם הלכה יא:
ח ד מיי' שם הל' ט:
ט ה ו מיי' פי"ח שם הלכה יח:
י ז מיי' פי"ט שם הל' ו:
יא ח מיי' פ"ב מהלכות קרבן פסח הל' ג:

ילקוט רמז תקס"ב פרשת אחרי מות השמיט [מהיכת ר"י עד מה להלן ושם סגי' מה להלן בשחוטי חוץ אף כאן בשחוטי חוץ] ועי' רש"ק ול"ק

פיין נ"ק

שיטה מקובצת

א] שהעלן בחוץ מוקטרי חוץ שהעלן בחוץ מנלן אמר כו': ב] על הראשונים תאמר תיבת הסמוכין נמחק: ג] לה רבה מי כתיב ועליהם תאמר ואליהם כתיב ואליהם קרינא אלא כדתנא דבי רבי ישמעאל דתנא רבי ר' ישמעאל ואליהם תאמר: ד] ביבי בר אביי הא: ה] ליה מבעי ליה לחלק: ו] והעלן בחוץ וחד כו' שחסרו והעלן בחוץ: ז] שחסרו והעלן בחוץ יהא חייב: ח] עקיבא סבר מוקטרי פנים שחסרו והעלן בחוץ: ט] חייב ואינו חייב על כו' תיבת ולא נמחק: י] יכול שאני מרבה אף: יא] שכן פוסלת שלא לשום אוכלין בפסח: יב] מוקטרי פנים: יג] בפנים והעלן בחוץ: יד] חוץ תאמר שאם: טו] כתיב ואליהם קרינן: טז] השבת בחדא והעובד: יז] תיבות ועבודת כוכבים נמחק והיבת ומשני ל"ש: יח] אבל הני לא תנא הכא בהדיא: יט] הזורק מקצת דמים: כ] והאי קרא בשחוטי: כא] שיעלה את כל: כב] למיכתב או מחוץ תיבת אל נמחק: כג] ליה על השוחט חייב תיבת העוף נמחק: כד] שייך בה פסול שלא לאוכלין ובקבלה: כה] שאומר לחברו כוס: כו] אפי' בהעלם אחד: כז] תימה סרהא תיבת קשה נמחק:

מסורת הש"ס

[לקמן קיט:]
נ"ל תאמר
כריתות ג.
לקמן ק.
סנהדרין לד: פ"ש
[לקמן קח: קטו:]
נ"ק
[מו"ס עת. כ"ב קכ:]
[לעיל ד.]
נ"ל דם יחשב נ"ק
[נ"ל בפרק [illegible]]

הגהות הב"ח

(א) רש"י ד"ה ל"ו כריתות וכו' ושבת וע"ז תנא. נ"ב זהו תירוץ של רש"י: (ב) שם ד"ה חד למוקטרי וכו' פוקעין שפקעו מעל מזבח דחסרו:

תיתי מבינייא א"כ לא יאמר בזריקה א] ותיתי מבינייא ותיתי משחיטה מה לשחיטה שכן נפסלת שלא לשם אוכלין בפסח תיתי מהעלאה מה להעלאה שכן ישנה במנחה (א) ותיתי מבינייא ב] להכי כתיב קרא למימר °דלא אתא מבינייא *אמר ר' אבהו שחט וזרק ג] לדברי ר' ישמעאל חייב אחת לדברי ר"ע חייב שתים *אביי אמר אפי' [לדברי] ר"ע אינו חייב אלא אחת דאמר קרא שם ד] תעשה הכתוב עשאן לכולן עבודה אחת זרק והעלה לדברי ר' ישמעאל חייב שתים לדברי ר"ע אינו חייב אלא אחת אביי אמר אפי' ה] [לדברי] ר"ע א'חייב שתים להכי פלגינהו קרא °שם תעלה ושם תעשה שחט וזרק והעלה לדברי הכל חייב שתים ת"ר *(במחנה יכול השוחט עולה בדרום יהא חייב ת"ל ו] אל) מחוץ למחנה יכול חוץ לשלש מחנות ז] [ת"ל °או עז במחנה] (מנין אף במחנה לוייה ת"ל במחנה) אי במחנה יכול השוחט עולה בדרום יהא חייב ת"ל או ח] אל מחוץ למחנה מה חוץ למחנה מיוחד שאין ראוי לשחיטת קדשים ולשחיטת כל זבח יצא דרום שאע"פ שאין ראוי לשחיטת קדשי קדשים ראוי לשחיטת קדשים קלים אמר עולא השוחט על גגו של היכל חייב הואיל ואין ראוי לשחיטת כל זבח מתקיף לה רבא א"כ ניכתוב קרא ט] (אל) מחוץ למחנה ולא בעי אל פתח אהל מועד אל פתח אהל מועד ל"ל לאו ג'למעוטי גגו ולרבא א"כ נכתוב אל פתח אהל מועד י] במחנה (ואל) מחוץ למחנה ל"ל לאו לאתויי גגו אמר רב מרי יא] לאיתויי ד'כולה בפנים וצווארה בחוץ [צווארה] בחוץ יב] פשיטא אמאי קפיד רחמנא אשחיטה ושחיטה בחוץ היא אלא לאיתויי ה'כולה בחוץ וצווארה בפנים איתמר המעלה בזמן הזה ר' יוחנן אמר ו'חייב ריש לקיש אמר פטור ר' יוחנן אמר חייב *קדושה ראשונה קידשה לשעתה וקידשה לעתיד לבא ריש לקיש אמר פטור קדושה ראשונה קידשה לשעתה ולא קידשה לעתיד לבא יג] נימא דבפלוגתא דר"א ור' יהושע קמיפלגי *דתנן א"ר אליעזר יד] כשהיו בונין בהיכל היו עושים ז'קלעים בהיכל קלעים בעזרות אלא שבהיכל בונין מבחוץ טו] ובעזרה בונין מבפנים א"ר יהושע שמעתי ח'שהיו *מקריבין אע"פ שאין בית ט'ואוכלים קדשי קדשים אע"פ שאין קלעים קדשים קלים ומעשר שני אע"פ שאין חומה מפני שקדושה ראשונה קידשה לשעתה וקידשה לעתיד לבא לאו מכלל דר"א סבר לא קידשה טז] א"ל רבינא לרב אשי ממאי דלמא דכולי עלמא קדושה ראשונה קידשה לשעתה וקידשה לעתיד לבא ומר מאי דשמיע ליה קאמר ומר מאי דשמיע ליה קאמר וכי תימא קלעים לר' אליעזר למה לי לצניעותא בעלמא איתמר *המעלה יז] ואין בו כזית ועצם משלימו לכזית רבי יוחנן אמר י'חייב ריש לקיש אמר פטור ר' יוחנן אמר חייב חיבורי עולין כעולין דמי ריש לקיש אמר פטור חיבורי עולין לאו כעולין דמו בעי רבא כ'המעלה

ראש

תורה אור

תיתי מבינייא. משחיטה וזריקה דכי פרכת מה לשחיטה שכן פוסלת שלא לשם אוכלין בפסח זריקה תוכיח מה לזריקה שכן זר חייב עליה מיתה שחיטה תוכיח וחזר הדין הצד השוה שבהן שהן עבודה וחייבין עליהן בחוץ אף אני אביא קמילה וקבלה שהן עבודה ויתחייב עליהן בחוץ: אם כן. יח] דמייתי מבינייא לחייב בחוץ על עבודות שאינם מפורשות בפרשה ויש להביאן במה הצד לא יאמר בזריקה ותיתי מבינייא משחיטה והעלאה: ה"ג להכי כתבה קרא דלא אתיא מבינייא. למימר דאע"ג דאתיא מבינייא לא תיתי מבינייא: שחט וזרק בהעלם אחד לר' ישמעאל. דנפקא ליה זריקה מדם *שפך יט] בעונש של שחיטה: אינו חייב אלא אחת. דחד כרת וחד לאו הוא: לר"ע. יט] נפקא ליה מאו זבח דכתיב (ויקרא יז) גבי העלאה: חייב שתים. משום דשמות מוחלקין: שם תעלה ושם תעשה. הזכיר העלאה לבדה והשאר כללן בעשיה אחת למימרא דלא מחייב אכולהו אלא חדא: (ב) פלגינהו קרא. הוציא העלאה מכלל שאר עשיות למימרא דמחייב עלה באפי נפשה ואשארא באפי נפשייהו: שחט וזרק והעלה לד"ה. בין לר' ישמעאל בין לר"ע חייב שתים לר' ישמעאל כיון כ] דכולם בהעלם [אחד] מחייב בהעלאה חדא דאית לה קרא בהדיא ואשחיטה וזריקה חדא דמחד קרא נפקי ולר"ע אשחיטה מיחייב חדא כא] והעלאה וזריקה חדא ובהא לא פליג אביי אדר' אבהו דלאביי נמי לדברי הכל חייב שתים חדא אהעלאה וחדא אשאר עשיות: כב] ת"ר או אשר ישחט מחוץ למחנה יכול עד שישחט חוץ לשלש מחנות. וגילף גז"ש מפרים הנשרפים כדילפינן בהרוגי ב"ד בסנהדרין (דף מב:): ת"ל. ברישיה דקרא או עז במחנה: אי במחנה יכול אף במחנה שכינה. אלא שינה מקום שחיטתו כגון שחט עולה בדרום יהא חייב: ת"ל מחוץ למחנה. דמשמע חוץ לשלש מחנות: מה להלן. מיוחד שאינו ראוי לשחיטת שום זבח אף במחנה כגון במחנה לויה שאינו ראוי לשחיטה כג] לשום זבח: נכתוב קרא במחנה ואל מחוץ למחנה. חוץ למעוטי עולה בדרום ובמחנה לפרושי דלא בעינן חוץ לשלש מחנות ואל פתח אהל מועד לא הביאו למה לי: לאו למעוטי גגו של היכל. דהכי משמע כד] שלא הביאו לפתח אהל מועד יצא זה שהביאו לעזרה: ופרכינן ולרבא. דפטר אגגו דמשמע כה] כל חללה של עזרה קרי אל פתח: ניכתוב אל פתח. למעוטי גגו ולמעוטי עולה בדרום שהרי באו אל פתח וממילא משתמע חיובא במחנה לויה שלא הביאו אל פתח: מחוץ למחנה ובמחנה ל"ל לאו לאיתויי גגו. אתא במחנה והדר אתא מחוץ דלא תימא מבמחנה איתרבי נמי שוחט עולה בדרום ת"ל מחוץ למידרש דבעינן מקום שאינו ראוי לשחיטת שום זבח ואל פתח איצטריך לדרשא אחריתי הראוי לפתח אהל מועד חייבין עליו בחוץ יצאו פרת חטאת וקדשי בדק הבית: כו] (לאו) לאיתויי [כולה] בפנים כו'. לעולם גג היכל לא מיחייב דלא קרינא ביה ואל פתח אהל מועד לא הביאו שהרי הביאו אלא לאיתויי היא בפנים וצוארה בחוץ דלא תימא פתח אהל מועד היא לכך נאמר במחנה לאיתויי לחובא והדר אתא מחוץ דלא תרבי מבמחנה שוחט עולה בדרום כז] ומהו אל פתח אהל מועד לא הביאו שלא הביאו כדרך כח] הבאת קדשי קדשים בלפון תלמוד לומר מחוץ דלא חייב אלא משום חוץ דאינו ראוי לשום זבח יצא זה ואתא אל פתח למעוטי גגו דלא תרבייה כדקאמרת שהוא מקום שאינו ראוי לשחיטת כל זבח דכיון דאשמעינן מחוץ דעולה בדרום פטור שמע מינה אל פתח אהל מועד לא אכדרך הבאתו קפיד אלא אהבאה כל דהו ובלבד שיהא כולו לתוך חלל העזרה: שחיטה בחוץ היא. והרי לא הביאו לבית השחיטה אל פתח ומאל פתח נפקא: המעלה בזמן הזה. בחוץ: וקידשה לעתיד לבא. והיא לה ירושלים בית הבחירה ושעת איסור הבמות היא: כשהיו בונין בהיכל. בימי עזרא: לאו מכלל דר' אליעזר סבר לא קידשה. הלכך עושין קלעים במקום חומה וחזרו וקדשו בקידוש המפורש במסכת שבועות (דף יו.): עלם. אין מלוה להעלותו אם פירש כדאמרן בפרק המזבח מקדש (לעיל דף פה:):

ראש

להכי כתביה קרא דלא תיתי מבינייא. *תימה על סוגיא זו דבפ' בתרא (דף קטו:) דרשינן אשר יעלה עולה מה העולה שהיא גמר עבודה אף כל שהיא גמר עבודה למעוטי קומץ ומקבל והיולק והבולל והפותת והמולח כו': יכול חוץ לשלש מחנות. ונילף גז"ש מפרים הנשרפים כדילפי' בהרוגי ב"ד בפ' נגמר הדין (סנהדרין דף מב:) ואפי' אינה מופנה ילפינן בגילוי מלתא כיון דלא אשכחן מחוץ למחנה אלא חוץ לשלש מחנות:

ולא בעי אל פתח אהל מועד. אע"ג דאיצטריך לקמן (דף קיג:) למעוטי רובע ונרבע ופרת חטאת וקדשי בדק הבית טובא פתח אהל מועד כתיבי:

ה"ג ולרבא נכתוב רחמנא ואל פתח אהל מועד מחוץ למחנה ובמחנה למה לי. וקא קשיא ליה לרבא ל"ל דכתב רחמנא כלל מחוץ למחנה ובמחנה וכן פי' הקונט':

המעלה בזמן הזה. לעיל פירשתי בריש קדשי קדשים (דף ס.) גבי מזבח שנפגם ופירשתי מ"ט [נקט] הכא המעלה ולא נקט השוחט:

ריש לקיש אמר פטור קדושה ראשונה כו'. תימה דלא פריך עליה מהנך משניות דפריך בפ"ק דמגילה (דף י.) אר' יצחק דאמר שמעתי שמקריבין בבית חוניו:

רבי יוחנן אמר חייב חיבורי עולין כעולין דמו. וא"ת למה לי חיבורי הא שמעינן ליה לר' יוחנן דאמר בפ' הקומץ רבה (מנחות דף כו:) יש הקטרה בפחות מכזית וכיון דחשיב הקטרה בפנים מחייב בחוץ כדאמר לקמן (דף קח:) גבי מוקטרי פנים שחסרו דחייבין עליהם בחוץ כיון דבפנים הויא הקטרה דמהדרינן פוקעין וי"ל הא דחשיב ליה לר' יוחנן הקטרה היינו לענין מקטיר לחלאין שמשלים אח"כ ואע"ג דבפרק כל המנחות באות מצה (מנחות דף נח.) חשיב ליה הקטרה גבי שאור ודבש דאמרי' יש קומץ פחות משני זיתים ויש הקטרה פחות מכזית שאני התם דכתיב קרא ועוד דבשאור חוץ מיפטר טפי כדדרשינן הכא על השלם הוא חייב ואינו חייב על החסר ועוד דהא איתקש מחשבות זו לזו אכילת מזבח לאכילת אדם ומדחשב על מנת להקטיר חוץ למקומו לא מיפסלא בפחות מכזית ש"מ דמקטיר בחוץ לא מחייב בפחות מכזית:

שחיטת

עין משפט
נר מצוה

עיין נ"ק

יב א מיי' פי"ט מהל' מעשה הקרבנות הלכה יא ועי' רש"ק:

יג ב ג ד מיי' פי"ח שם הלכה טו:

יד ה מיי' שם פרק י"ט הל' טו:

טו ו מיי' פ"א מהל' בית הבחירה הל"ה:

טז ז מיי' פ"ו שם הלט"ו:

יז ח מיי' פי"ט מהל' מעשה הקרבנות הל' טו ופ"ו מהלכות בית הבחירה הל' טו:

יח ט י מיי' פי"ט מהל' מעשה הקרבנות הלכה י:

שיטה מקובצת

א] מתיבת ותיתי כו' עד תיבת אלא להכי רש"י לא גרים זה וכן בס"י ליתא: ב] אלא להכי כתיב קרא ולא אתיא מבינייא למימר דאע"ג דאתיא מבינייא לא תיתי מבינייא אמר: ג] לר' ישמעאל אינו חייב אלא אחת לר"ע חייב שתים אביי אמר אפי' לר"ע אינו חייב: ד] שם תעלה ושם תעשה כל אשר אנכי מצוך הכתוב עשאן עשיה אחת זרק והעלה לר' ישמעאל חייב שתים לר"ע אינו חייב מ': ה] אפי' לר"ע חייב: ו] ת"ל מחוץ למחנה אי מחוץ למחנה תיבת אל נמחק: ז] תיבות ת"ל או עז במחנה ל"ש ונמחק: ח] או אשר ישחט מחוץ למחנה מה חוץ למחנה מיוחד שאין ראוי לשחיטת כל זבח אף במחנה שאין ראוי לשחיטת כל זבח יצא דרום: ט] קרא במחנה ואל מחוץ: י] מועד ומחוץ למחנה ובמחנה למה לי: יא] מרי לא לאתויי: יב] צוואה בחוץ אמאי קא קפיד תיבת פשיטא ל"ש: יג] לימא דבפלוגתא: יד] אליעזר שמעתי כשהיו: טו] מבחוץ ובעזורות: טז] קידשה לעתיד לבא א"ל: יז] המעלה אבר שאין בו כזית: יח] כן דמייתינן: יט] שפך הכתוב בעונש: יט] דנפקא ליה: כ] כיון דעשה כולם בהעלם אחד מחייב: כא] חדא ואהעלאה וזריקה: כב] מה"ד אי אשר ישחט תיבות ת"ר או נמחק: כג] שום זבח אות ל' נמחק: כד] משמע מי שלא: כה] דמשמע אל פתח כל חללה של עזרה הס"ד ותיבות קרי אל פתח נמחק: כו] מה"ד לא לאתויי היא בפנים: כז] בדרום ומאי אל: כח] כדרך הבאתו:

נ"ק מ"ז

מסורת הש"ס

סנהדרין לה:

שם ע"ש

נ"ל ת"ר או אשר ישחט מחוץ למחנה יכול חוץ כו' נ"ק

ויקרא יז

דברים יב

הגהות הב"ח
(א) גמ' שכן ישנה במנחה. שחיטה תוכיח תיתי מבינייא: (ב) רש"י ד"ה פלגינהו נ"ל קודם ד"ה שם תעלה:

[לעיל ס: מגילה י. מכות יט. שבועות טז. חולין ז. תמורה כא. ערכין לב:]

מגילה י. שבועות טז. עדיות פ"ח מ"ו

[לעיל סב.]

מנחות כג.

גליון הש"ס
גמ' דלא אתא מבינייא. עי' יומא דף סג ע"ב תוס' ד"ה זריקה:

to death on its account![9] [107b]—Infer it from both combined.[10] But if so,[11] let it not be stated in connection with sprinkling, which may be inferred from both [*shechitah* and offering up] combined. [Thus: when you say,] let it be inferred from *shechitah*, [you can argue]: as for *shechitah*, the reason is because it is invalid in the case of the Passover-offering [when done] on behalf of such who cannot eat. Let it be inferred from offering up: As for offering up,
a the reason is because it applies to a meal-offering [too].[1] Then infer it from both combined? Rather, for that reason a text is written [to include sprinkling] to intimate that you may not infer from both combined.[2]

R. Abbahu said: If one slaughtered [a sacrifice] and sprinkled [its blood without]: according to R. Ishmael he is liable to one [sin-offering], [whereas] according to R. Akiba he is liable to two.[3] Abaye said: Even on R. Akiba's view, he is liable to one only, because Scripture saith, *There thou shalt offer up thy burnt-offerings, and there thou shalt* do *all that I command thee:*[4] Scripture thus ranked them as one 'doing' [rite].[5]

If one sprinkled and offered up [without], according to R. Ishmael he is liable to two [sin-offerings], [whereas] according to R. Akiba he is liable to one only.[6] Abaye said: Even on R. Akiba's view he is liable to two, that being the reason that Scripture divided them, [viz.] '*There thou shalt* offer-up . . . *and there thou shalt* do'. If one slaughtered, sprinkled, and offered up, all agree that he is liable to two.

b Our Rabbis taught: [*Or that killeth it*] *without the camp:*[1] You might think [that that means] without the three camps;[2] therefore it states, '. . . *or goat, in the camp.*'[1] If [you thus stress] 'in *the camp*', you might think that [even] one who slaughters a burnt-offering in the south is culpable;[3] therefore it is stated, *or that killeth it* without *the camp:* as '*without the camp*' is distinguished in that it is not eligible for the slaughtering of most sacred sacrifices or for the slaughtering of *any* sacrifice, so 'in *the camp*' means in a place which is not eligible for the slaughtering of *any* sacrifice: hence the south [side of the Temple court] is excluded, for though it is not fit for the slaughtering of most sacred sacrifices, it is eligible for the slaughtering of lesser sacrifices.

'Ulla said: One who slaughters on the roof of the *Hekal* is culpable, since it is not eligible for the slaughtering of any sacrifice. To this Raba demurred: If so, let Scripture write, '*in the camp or* . . . *without the camp*', and '*unto the door of the tent of meeting*' will not be necessary; what is the purpose of '[*and hath not brought it*] *unto the door of the tent of meeting*': surely it is to exclude the roof?[4] Now according to Raba, if that is so,[5] let [Scripture] write, '*unto the door of the tent of meeting*' [only]: what is the purpose of '*in the camp*' and '*without the camp*'?[6] Surely that is to include the roof?[7]—Said R. Mari: No: it includes [the case where] the whole of [the animal] is within, but its throat is without.[8] If its throat is without, it is obvious [that one is culpable]; [for] to what does the Divine Law object? to slaughtering without; and this is slaughtering without! —Rather, it includes [the case where] the whole of the animal is
c without, while its throat is within.[1]

It was stated: One who offers up nowadays,[2] R. Joḥanan maintained: He is culpable;[3] Resh Laḳish said: He is not liable. R. Joḥanan maintained, He is culpable: The first sanctity hallowed it for the nonce and for the future. Resh Laḳish said, He is not liable: the first sanctity hallowed it for the nonce, but did not hallow it for the future.[4]

Shall we say that they differ in the same controversy as that of R. Eliezer and R. Joshua? For we learnt: R. Eliezer said: [I have heard that] when they were building the Temple,[5] they made curtains for the Temple and curtains for the courts;[6] but that they built the Temple [walls] on the *outside* [of these curtains], whereas they built the courts on the *inside* [of these curtains]. R. Joshua said: I have heard that they offered [sacrifices] though there was no Temple; and they ate most sacred sacrifices though there were no curtains, and lesser sacrifices and second tithe though there was no wall,[7] because the first sanctity hallowed it for the nonce and hallowed it for the future.[8] Hence it follows that R. Eliezer holds that it did not hallow it [for the future].[9] Said Rabina to R. Ashi: Whence [does this follow]? Perhaps all agree that the first sanctity hallowed it for the nonce and hallowed it for the future, and one master reported what he had heard, while the other master reported what he had heard. And should you say, What was the purpose of curtains, according to R. Eliezer? Simply for privacy.

It was stated: If one offers up [a limb] less than an olive [in size],[10]
d but the bone makes it up to an olive,[1] R. Joḥanan maintained: He is culpable; Resh Laḳish said: He is not culpable. R. Joḥanan maintained, He is culpable: that which is attached to what ascends [the altar] is as what ascends [in its own right]. Resh Laḳish said, He is not liable: that which is attached to what ascends is not as what ascends.[2]

(9) For performing it. But he is not liable for the other rites. (10) Lit., 'from between them'—*sc. shechitah* and sprinkling, for the refutation that applies to one does not apply to the other. Their only common feature is that they are both sacrificial rites; hence the same law should apply to all other sacrificial rites. (11) That such reasoning is permissible.

a (1) But there is no sprinkling in a meal-offering. (2) Scripture thus intimates that this reasoning is not permissible in the present instance. Hence it is also not permissible in respect of taking the fistful or receiving, and so no text is required to show that these do not involve liability. (3) R. Ishmael infers liability for sprinkling from the phrase, '*blood shall be imputed*'. Now, this is actually written in connection with *slaughtering*: thus we have a single interdict covering both, and the same *kareth* is written in connection with both. Hence when he commits both in one state of ignorance, they rank as *one* offence, and render him liable to *one* sin-offering only. R. Akiba, however, infers it from '*or a sacrifice*', which is written in reference to *offering-up*. Hence slaughtering and sprinkling are separate interdicts and involve separate sin-offerings. (4) Deut. XII, 14. (5) By enumerating '*offer-up*' and '*do*' separately, it follows that Scripture counts offering up as one act, and all other rites which are 'done' as another single act. Hence they involve one offering only. 'Offer up' means to burn on the altar. The other sacrificial rites (do) comprise slaughtering, receiving the blood and carrying it to the altar, and sprinkling. (6) The reasoning is similar to that in n. 3, but reversed.

b (1) Lev. XVII, 3. (2) V. *supra* 55*a* n.b6. Only then is he culpable. (3) Since it should be slaughtered on the north side of the Temple court; *supra* 53*b*. (4) For the text implies, only he who does not bring it to the '*tent of meeting*' (the Temple court) at all is liable, whereas he who slaughters on the roof has brought it. (5) That '*unto the door of the tent of meeting*' implies any part thereof. (6) Scripture should simply say: *What man soever . . . killeth an ox . . . and hath not brought it unto the door of the tent of meeting*. This would shew that killing anywhere *outside* the Temple court makes one liable, while killing anywhere *inside* (e.g. on the roof, or a burnt-offering in the south) does not. (7) As being a place of culpability. (8) Even then one is culpable.

c (1) Even then one is culpable. (2) After the destruction of the Temple, when all offering up is without. (3) If he does it deliberately he incurs *kareth*. (4) V. *supra* 60*b*. On the first view, Jerusalem is still 'the chosen place'; hence the present is technically a time when *bamoth* are forbidden, and so there is culpability. (5) *Sc.* the second Temple, in the days of Ezra. (6) Temporarily, until proper walls should be built. (7) Around Jerusalem. (8) Hence the *sites* were holy for their various purposes, though walls and curtains were lacking. (9) For which reason temporary curtains were necessary to make the site which they enclosed holy. (10) *Sc.* the flesh.

d (1) If a bone springs off the altar while it is being offered *within*, it is not replaced; *supra* 85*b*; v. also *supra* 107*a* n.b 8. (2) Actually, only the flesh ascends, while the bone ascends too merely because it is attached to the flesh. R. Joḥanan, holds that the bone nevertheless counts as something which is itself offered up, and therefore in the present case one is culpable. Resh Laḳish takes the reverse view.

*See Corrigenda.

Raba asked: What if one offers up [108*a*] the head of a pigeon, which is not as much as an olive, but the salt makes it up to an olive? Said Raba of Parzakia[3] to R. Ashi: Is not that the controversy of R. Johanan and Resh Lakish?—[No:] You may ask on R. Johanan's view, and you may ask on the view of Resh Lakish. You may ask on R. Johanan's view: R. Johanan gives his ruling only there, in respect of the bone, which is related to the flesh,[4] but not in the case of salt, which is not related to the flesh; [or perhaps, there is no difference]? You may ask on the view of Resh Lakish: Resh Lakish gives his ruling only there, in respect of the bone, because if it parts from it [the flesh], there is no obligation to take it up [on the altar]; but not here, where if it parts, there is an obligation to take it up;[5] or perhaps, there is no difference? The question stands over.

R. JOSE THE GALILEAN SAID etc. Rabbi answered on behalf of R. Jose the Galilean: As for one who slaughters within and offers up without, the reason is because it had a time of fitness; will you say [the same] when one slaughters without and offers up without, where it never had a period of fitness? R. Eleazar son of R. Simeon answered on behalf of R. Jose the Galilean: As for slaughtering within and offering up without, that is because the sanctuary
a [the altar] receives it;[1] will you say [the same] when one slaughters without and offers up without, where the Sanctuary does not receive it?[2] Wherein do they differ?[3]—Said Ze'iri: They differ in respect of slaughtering at night.[4] Rabbah said: They disagree where one received it [the blood] in a non-sacred vessel.[5]

AN UNCLEAN [PERSON] WHO EATS [OF SACRIFICES], WHETHER UNCLEAN SACRIFICES etc. The Rabbis say well to R. Jose the Galilean?—Said Raba: Where the [priest's] body [first] became unclean, and then the flesh became unclean, none disagree that he is liable, because personal defilement involves *kareth*. They disagree where the flesh [first] became unclean and then the [priest's] body became unclean: the Rabbis hold, We say *miggo* ['since']; whereas R. Jose the Galilean holds: We do not say *miggo*.[6] Now according to R. Jose, granted that we do not say *miggo*, yet let his personal uncleanness, which is graver, come and fall upon the uncleanness of the flesh?[7]—Said R. Ashi: How do you know that personal uncleanness is more stringent? Perhaps uncleanness of the flesh is more stringent, since it cannot be puri-
b fied in a *mikweh*.[1]

MISHNAH. SLAUGHTERING [WITHOUT] IS MORE STRINGENT THAN OFFERING UP [WITHOUT], AND OFFERING UP [IS MORE STRINGENT] THAN SLAUGHTERING. SLAUGHTERING IS MORE STRINGENT, FOR HE WHO SLAUGHTERS [A SACRIFICE] ON BEHALF OF MAN[2] IS CULPABLE, WHEREAS HE WHO OFFERS UP TO A MAN IS NOT CULPABLE.[3] OFFERING UP IS MORE STRINGENT: TWO WHO HOLD A KNIFE AND SLAUGHTER [WITHOUT] ARE NOT CULPABLE, [WHEREAS] IF THEY TAKE HOLD OF A LIMB AND OFFER IT UP, THEY ARE CULPABLE. IF ONE OFFERED UP, THEN OFFERED UP AGAIN, THEN OFFERED UP AGAIN,[4] HE IS CULPABLE IN RESPECT OF EACH [ACT OF] OFFERING UP: THESE ARE THE WORDS OF R. SIMEON. R. JOSE SAID: HE IS LIABLE ONLY TO ONE [SIN-OFFERING]. HE IS LIABLE ONLY WHEN HE OFFERS UP ON THE TOP OF AN ALTAR;[5] R. SIMEON SAID: HE IS LIABLE EVEN IF HE OFFERS UP ON THE TOP OF A ROCK OR A STONE.

GEMARA. Why is offering up to a man [without] different, that it is not culpable? [presumably] because *unto the Lord* is written![6] Then in the case of slaughtering too, surely *'unto the Lord'* is
c written?[1]—There it is different, because Scripture saith, *'What man soever'*.[2] *'What man soever'* is written in connection with offering up too?—That is required for teaching that when two men offer up a limb, they are liable. If so, [say that] here too it is required for teaching that if two men hold the knife and slaughter, they are liable?—There it is different, because Scripture saith, *that [man]*:[3] [this implies,] one, but not two. If so, *'that [man]'* is written in

(3) V. *supra* 10*b*, n. b 5. (4) Lit., 'which is of the kind of the flesh'. (5) If the salt springs off the altar, the piece must be re-salted, because it is written, *neither shalt thou suffer the salt of the covenant of thy God to be lacking* (Lev. II, 13).

a (1) If after being taken out, it is taken in again and offered up on the altar, the altar receives it, and it is not taken down (v. *supra* 84*a*). (2) If it is offered up on the altar after it was slaughtered without, it must be removed. (3) Rabbi and R. Eleazar b. R. Simeon. (4) According to Rabbi, if one slaughtered a sacrifice within at night and then offered it up, he is not liable, since it never had a period of fitness, for a sacrifice slaughtered at night is unfit. According to R. Eliezer, he is culpable, for if it is laid on the altar, it does not descend. (5) The sacrifice is immediately invalid, so it never had a period of fitness; nevertheless, the altar receives it. (6) A clean person who eats unclean flesh is not liable to a sin-offering; an unclean person who eats clean flesh is liable. Now, in the latter case posited by Raba the flesh was already forbidden on account of its own uncleanness. Nevertheless the Rabbis hold that the interdict of personal uncleanness can fall upon the first and be added to it, because it is more comprehensive, as now not only is that piece forbidden to him, but all other pieces, and so we argue: since (*miggo*) he is interdicted in respect of other pieces, he is also interdicted *through his personal uncleanness* in respect of this piece too, though that is forbidden in any case. Consequently he is liable to a sin-offering. R. Jose does not accept this argument of *miggo*, and holds that since the flesh is already forbidden, his own uncleanness does not count at all, and he is not liable. If, however, he became unclean first, he was already forbidden to eat any flesh on pain of a sin-offering, and that interdict is not lessened, to free him from a sin-offering, simply because the flesh too became unclean. (7) As an additional interdict. For even if a more comprehensive interdict does not fall upon a less comprehensive one, that is only where both are of equal gravity. Here, however, personal uncleanness is more stringent, since it involves a sin-offering, whereas the uncleanness of the flesh does not.

b (1) Whereas an unclean priest is cleansed in a *mikweh*. (2) I.e., for lay consumption, not as a sacrifice. (3) On account of offering up without, though this constitutes idolatry and he is culpable on that account. (4) Each time part of the same animal. He offered them up in ignorance, but between each offering he became aware that it was forbidden, and then forgot. (5) I.e., he must first build an altar without and then offer up upon it. (6) Lev. XVII, 8*f*: *Whatsoever man . . . offereth up a burnt-offering . . . and bringeth it not unto the door of the tent of meeting to sacrifice it* unto the Lord, *even that man shall be cut off from his people*. *'Unto the Lord'* shews that Scripture speaks of one who is offering to God, not to man, and only then does he incur *kareth* (or, a sin-offering if he acts in ignorance).

c (1) Ibid. 3*f*: *What man soever . . . killeth an ox . . . and hath not brought it unto the door of the tent of meeting, to present it as an offering* unto the Lord. (2) Heb. *ish ish*, lit., 'a man, a man'. The repetition extends the law even to one who slaughters to a human being. (3) Ibid. *and* that man *shall be cut off from among his people*.

תורה אור

ראש בן יונה שאין בו כזית ומלח משלימו לכזית מהו א"ל רבא מפרזקיא לרב אשי לאו היינו פלוגתייהו דר' יוחנן ור"ל תיבעי לרבי יוחנן ותיבעי לר"ל תיבעי לר' יוחנן ע"כ לא קאמר ר' יוחנן התם אלא עצם דמינא דבשר הוא אבל מלח דלאו מינא דבר יונה הוא לא א] תיבעי לר"ל ע"כ לא קאמר ר"ל התם אלא דאי פריש ב] מינה לאו מצוה לאסוקי אבל הכא דאי פריש ג] מצוה לאסוקי לא או דלמא ל"ש תיקו: ר' יוסי הגלילי אומר כו': השיב רבי תחת רבי יוסי הגלילי מה לשוחט בפנים ומעלה בחוץ ד] שהיתה לו שעת הכושר תאמר בשוחט ה] חוץ ומעלה בחוץ שלא היתה לו שעת הכושר השיב ר"א בר' שמעון תחת ר"י הגלילי מה לשוחט בפנים ומעלה בחוץ שכן קודש מקבלו תאמר בשוחט בחוץ ו] שאין קודש מקבלו מאי בינייהו *אמר זעירי *שחיטת לילה איכא בינייהו *רבה אמר קבלה בכלי חול איכא בינייהו: טמא שאכל בין קודש כו': שפיר קאמרי ליה רבנן לרבי יוסי הגלילי *אמר רבא כל היכא דנטמא ז] טומאת הגוף ואחר כך נטמא בשר דכולי עלמא לא פליגי דחייב שכן טומאת הגוף בכרת כי פליגי בשנטמא בשר ואח"כ נטמא הגוף דרבנן סברי אמרינן מיגו ור' יוסי הגלילי סבר לא אמרינן מיגו ורבי יוסי ח] נהי דמיגו לא אמרינן תיתי טומאת הגוף דחמירא ותחול על טומאת בשר אמר רב אשי ממאי דטומאת הגוף חמורה דלמא טומאת בשר חמורה שכן אין לה טהרה במקוה: **מתני'** חומר בשחיטה מבעלייה ובעלייה מבשחיטה חומר בשחיטה שהשוחט להדיוט חייב והמעלה להדיוט פטור חומר בעלייה שנים *שאחזו בסכין ושחטו פטורים אחזו באבר ט] והעלו חייבין העלה חזר והעלה וחזר והעלה חייב על כל עלייה י] דברי ר"ש ר' יוסי אומר אינו חייב אלא אחת ואינו חייב עד שיעלה לראש המזבח *ר"ש אומר אפילו העלה על הסלע או על האבן חייב: **גמ'** מאי שנא המעלה להדיוט דפטור דכתיב °לה' בשחיטה נמי הכתיב לה' שאני התם דאמר קרא °איש איש גבי העלאה נמי כתיב איש איש יא] °מיבעי ליה *לשנים יב] שהעלו באבר חייבין אי הכי ה"נ מיבעי ליה לשנים שאחזו בסכין ושחטו שחייבין שאני התם דאמר קרא ההוא אחד ולא שנים אי הכי גבי העלאה נמי הא כתיב ההוא יג] מיבעי ליה למעוטי

ויקרא יז / שם

רש"י

ראש יונה. של עולת העוף והעלו בחוץ: מלח אי פריש מלוה לחזור ולמולחו כדכתיב (ויקרא ב) ולא תשבית מלח ברית: שעת הכושר. ליקרב בפנים: שכן קדש מקבלו. אע"פ שהוליאו אם חזר והכניסו והעלהו *לא ירד כדאמרן בהמזבח מקדש (לעיל דף פד.) הלן והיולא כו': שחיטת לילה איכא בינייהו. לרבי שחט בהמה בלילה בפנים והעלה בחוץ פטור שלא היתה לה שעת הכושר דבשחיטתה נפסלה לר"א חייב שהרי הקדש מקבלו שאם עלה לא ירד: רבה אמר קבלה בכלי חול איכא בינייהו. שעת הכושר ליכא קדש מקבלו איכא דכל שפסולו בקדש הקדש מקבלו: כל היכא דנטמא גופו של זה ואח"כ נטמא הבשר. ואפילו ע"י אחרים מודה ר' יוסי הגלילי דחייב כדאמרן מה לי על ידו מה לי ע"י אחרים דטעמא דר' יוסי משום דאין איסור חל על איסור הוא וכאן איסור טומאת הגוף קודם: כי פליגי בשנטמא בשר תחילה. ונאסר על זה משום טומאת בשר שאין חייבין עליו חטאת וכי הדר נטמא הגוף אית ליה לר' יוסי אין איסור טומאת הגוף חל על איסור זה ואע"ג דאיסור כולל הוא דאיכא למימר דמיגו דמיתסר בשאר חתיכות טהורות משום טומאת הגוף נתסר נמי בהך לא אמרינן האי מיגו הלכך אין ראויה מטמא שאכל את הטהור לכאן דהתם טומאת הגוף קדים. ורבנן סברי אמרינן מגו. ואיסור כולל חל על איסור אחר דהא דאמרינן אין איסור חל על איסור באיסורי דעלמא קאמרינן: נהי דלא אמריק מגו. לחול איסור על איסור ואפילו הוא כולל מיהו הני מילי היכא דשניהן שוין *אבל הכא תיתי טומאת הגוף דחמירא ותיחול בכולל על טומאת בשר דקילא דהכי אמרינן בשחיטת חולין בפרק גיד הנשה (דף קא.) דרבי יוסי הגלילי לית ליה איסור חל על איסור אפילו ע"י כולל ובאיסור חמור אית ליה איסור חל על איסור כשהוא איסור כולל גבי אוכל גיד הנשה של עולה דאוקימנא כרבי יוסי הגלילי דקתני חייב שתים: **מתני'** השוחט קדשים בחוץ. לאכילת הדיוט חייב: והמעלה להדיוט פטור. משום העלאת חוץ וחייב משום עובד עבודת כוכבים ואם הזיד בעבודת כוכבים ושגג בהעלאת חוץ אינו מביא יד] על שגגתו חטאת וטעמא מפרש בגמ': שנים שאחזו. בגמרא מפרש לה: העלה וחזר והעלה. מאותה בהמה עצמה ובגמרא מפרש פלוגתייהו: שיעלה לראש המזבח. שיבנה מזבח לשם כך ויעלה וטעמא מפרש בגמ': **גמ'** דכתיב לה'. ואל פתח אהל מועד לא יביאנו לעשות אותו לה' (ויקרא יז) מכלל דבעושה לשם הכתוב מדבר: בשחיטת חוץ נמי כתיב. (שם) ואל פתח אהל מועד לא הביאו להקריב קרבן לה': איש איש. להביא איש ששחט לאיש: שאני התם. בשחיטה לא מצית למדרש איש איש לחייב שנים שאחזו בסכין ושחטו: דהא כתיב ההוא. וקא סלקא דעתך ונכרת האיש ההוא (שם): למעוטי שוגג

תוספות

שחיטת לילה איכא בינייהו. לכאורה רבי ורבי אלעזר בר"ש סברי כר"ש דאמר בפרק המזבח מקדש (לעיל דף פד.) נשחטה בלילה אם עלתה לא תרד דהשתא קדש מקבלו ולא היתה לו שעת הכושר אבל לרבי יהודה דאמר אם עלתה תרד בין לרבי בין לרבי אלעזר בר"ש שחט בלילה בפנים והעלה בחוץ לא מבעיא (ליה) לרבי יוסי הגלילי דפטור אלא אפילו לרבנן נמי פטור כדמוכח בסוף פירקין (לקמן קיא:) גבי הא דתנן ר"ש אומר כל שחייבין עליו בחוץ חייבין על כיולא בו בפנים שהעלה בחוץ ומפרש זעירי גופיה שחיטת בהמה בלילה איכא בינייהו וה"ק השוחט בהמה בלילה בפנים והעלה בחוץ פטור פירוש דאין מתקבל בפנים כר' יהודה דאמר אם עלה (לא) ירד שחט בחוץ והעלה בחוץ חייב אלמא דאפילו לרבנן דמחייבי שוחט בחוץ ומעלה בחוץ מודו בשוחט בלילה בפנים ומעלה בחוץ דפטור לר' יהודה וקלת תימה זעירי ורבה אמאי נקטי הכא שחיטת לילה וקבלה בכלי חול דהייט כמו נשפך דמה דלא הוי אלא לר"ש דלרבי יהודה תרוייהו ירדו הוי להו למימר איכא בינייהו נשחטה חוץ לזמנו וחוץ למקומו דלכולי עלמא לא ירד דהרי קדש מקבלו ולא היתה לו שעת הכושר ושמא אגב דנקטי רבה וזעירי בסוף פירקין (שם) גבי פלוגתא דר"ש ורבנן שחיטת לילה וקבלה בכלי חול נקטי נמי הכא ולריך לדקדק לר' יהודה דאמר (לעיל דף פד.) בילא דמה אם עלה ירד הרי זורק מקלת דמים בחוץ דחייב אע"ג דאין קדש מקבלו ושמא לרבי יהודה לא הוה חייב והא דדרשינן מקרא לרבות הזורק דלמא בשחוטי חוץ ולא בשחוטי פנים מידי דהוה אשחיטת לילה בסוף פירקין אבל לרבי יוסי הגלילי אליבא דרבי יהודה ודאי לא משכחת לה זורק בחוץ דחייב ועוד נראה דהא דמיפטר לר' יהודה משום דאין קדש מקבלו היינו כשאין קדש מקבלו מחמת פסול אחר מלבד פסול זה שילא לחוץ והעלהו וניחא נמי דמתני' מחייב הקומץ והלבונה והקטרת ומנחת כהנים שהעלן בחוץ אף על גב דאמרינן בריש המזבח (לעיל דף פג:) למנחות לר"י הגלילי ירדו וכן נסכים הבאים עם הזבח דאמרינן לדברי כולן ירדו ובריית' דבסמוך (דף קט.) דמרבי פסולין לא חשיב נשחטה בלילה ונשפך דמה שמע מינה דרבי יהודה היא ולא מחייבי אהני משום דירדו ואפילו הכי מחייב אקומץ ומנחת נסכים וניסוך היין והמים והיינו טעמא כדפרישית וקלת קשה דלרבי יהודה אין מתיישב מה שהשיב ר' אלעזר בר"ש תחת ר"י הגלילי דלהכי תיקשי ליה אף הקומץ בפנים והעלה בחוץ כיון שהוליאו פסלו: **רבנן** סברי מיגו. באיסור כולל פליגי כדמפרש בסוף גיד הנשה (חולין דף קא.):

עין משפט נר מצוה

יט א ב מיי' פי"ח מהל' מעה"ק הלכה יז וע"ש בהשג"ד ובכ"מ:

כ ג מיי' פי"ח מהל' מעה"ק הלכה טו:

כא ד מיי' פי"ט שם הלכה א:

כב ה מיי' שם הלכה יב ופי"ח הלכה טו:

כג ו מיי' פי"ט שם הלכה יב:

כד ז מיי' שם הל' יא עי' כ"מ:

כה ח מיי' שם הל' א.

[גי' תוי"ט לשנים שאחזו באבר והעלוהו שחייבין אי הכי ה"נ כו']

מסורת הש"ס

נ"ע לא ירדו כדאמרינן כו' ל"ק

[לקמן קיא:]

[שם ע"ש]

חולין קא. ע"ש

גי' הל"ק אבל הכא שאין שניהם שוין תיתי כו'

קדושין מג.

[לקמן קי.]

גליון הש"ס

גמ' מיבעי ליה לשנים שהעלו. עי' תוספות שור הלכות שחיטה סי' כ ס"ק כב:

שיטה מקובצת

א] לא או דלמא לא שנא תיבעי: ב] פריש מיניה לאו: ג] פריש מיניה מצוה: ד] בחוץ שכן היתה לו: ה] תיבת חוץ ל"ש: ו] בחוץ ומעלה בחוץ שאין: ז] דנטמא הגוף ואח"כ נטמא הבשר: ח] יוסי הגלילי נהי: ט] והעלוהו חייבין העלה וחזר: י] עלייה ועליית חטאת דברי: יא] ההוא מיבעי: יב] לשנים שאחזו באבר והעלוהו שחייבין ה"נ מיבעי ליה לשנים שאחזו בסכין תיבות שהעלו אי הכי ל"ש ונמחק: יג] ההוא ההוא מיבעי: יד] אינו מביא חטאת על שגגתו:

שוגג אנוס ומוטעה. קצת קשה אנוס ל"ל קרא פשיטא דאונס רחמנא פטריה ושמא האי אנוס פרט לאומר מותר ותימה ל"ל קרא למיפטריה מכרת כשהוא שוגג פשיטא בר קרבן הוא וי"ל ס"ד אמינא אי לא מייתי קרבן ליהוי בכרת דהא לאחר הבאת קרבן דוקא כתיב ונסלח לו :

למעוטי שוגג אנוס ומוטעה. דהכי דריש בת"כ כל ההוא דגבי ונכרת כשישנו בהווייתו ובדעתו ולא אנוס ולא שוגג מאליו או מוטעה ע"י אחרים: תרי ההוא כתיבי. דם יחשב לאיש ההוא בשחיטה כתיב (ויקרא יז): אלא לה'. דכתיב גבי שחיטה: ל"ל להוציא שעיר המשתלח.

תורה אור

*למעוטי שוגג אנוס ומוטעה אי הכי הכא נמי מיבעי למעוטי אנוס שוגג ומוטעה תרי ההוא כתיבי ואלא לה' למה לי להוציא שעיר המשתלח: חומר בהעלאה כו': ת"ר (ויקרא יז) איש א] איש מה ת"ל לרבות שנים שאחזו באבר והעלו שחייבין שיכול והלא דין הוא ומה השוחט להדיוט שחייב שנים שאחזו בסכין ושחטו פטורין המעלה להדיוט שפטור אינו דין ששנים שאחזו ב] פטורין ת"ל איש איש דברי ר"ש רבי יוסי אומר ההוא אחד ולא שנים א"כ מה ת"ל איש איש *דברה תורה כלשון בני אדם ור"ש האי ההוא ג] מיבעי ליה למעוטי שוגג אנוס מוטעה ורבי יוסי מהוא ההוא ור"ש הוא ההוא לא דריש ורבי יוסי מדהאי איש איש דברה תורה כלשון בני אדם ד] ההוא איש איש נמי דברה תורה כלשון בני אדם ואלא השוחט להדיוט ה] מנא ליה דחייב נפקא ליה (שם) מדם יחשב לאיש ההוא דם שפך ואפילו השוחט לאיש: העלה וחזר והעלה כו': אמר ר"ל מחלוקת בד' וה' אברים דמר סבר כי כתיב לעשות אותו *על השלם הוא חייב ואינו חייב על החסר אבל בהמה כתיב ומר סבר אכל אבר ואבר כתיב אבל ו] אבר אחד דברי הכל אינו חייב אלא אחת ור' יוחנן אמר מחלוקת באבר אחד דמר סבר מוקטרי פנים שחסרו ז] והעלה בחוץ חייב ומר סבר פטור אבל בד' וה' איברין דברי הכל חייב על כל אבר ואבר ופליגא דעולא דאמר עולא הכל מודים במוקטרי פנים שחסרו והעלו בחוץ שחייב לא נחלקו אלא במוקטרי ח] בחוץ שחסרו והעלו בחוץ דמר סבר פטור ומ"ס חייב איכא דאמרי אמר עולא הכל מודים במוקטרי חוץ שחסרו והעלו בחוץ שהוא פטור לא נחלקו אלא במוקטרי פנים שחסרו והעלו בחוץ דמ"ס פטור ומ"ס חייב ופליגי דאבוה דשמואל אלישנא קמא דעולא דאמר אבוה דשמואל כמאן מהדרינן פוקעין לגבי מזבח כמאן דלא כר' יוסי: ואינו חייב עד שיעלה כו': אמר רב הונא מאי טעמא דרבי יוסי ט] דכתיב (בראשית ח) ויבן נח מזבח לה' א"ר יוחנן מ"ט דר"ש דכתיב (שופטים יג) ויקח מנוח את גדי העזים ואת המנחה ויעל על הצור לה' ואידך נמי יג] והכתיב ויבן מזבח לה' ההוא גובהה בעלמא ואידך נמי הא כתיב ויקח מנוח הוראת שעה היתה ואיבעית אימא ה"ט דר"ש כדתניא ר"ש אומר (ויקרא יז) מזבח פתח אהל מועד ואין מזבח בבמה לפיכך העלה על הסלע או על האבן חייב (א) יצא מיבעי ליה ה"ק לפיכך בשעת איסור הבמות העלה על הסלע או על האבן חייב בעי רבי יוסי בר' חנינא קרן וכבש ויסוד וריבוע מהו שיעכבו בבמה א"ל רבי ירמיה תניא *קרן וכבש וריבוע ויסוד מעכבין בבמה גדולה ואין מעכבין בבמה קטנה:

מתני'

*והמעלה להדיוט פטור. פי' בקונטרס פטור משום העלאת חוץ וחייב משום עובד עבודת כוכבים ואם הזיד בעבודת כוכבים ושגג בהעלאת חוץ אינו מביא על שגגתו חטאת ותימה אמאי יתחייב מעלה לחבירו משום מעלה בחוץ כיון דמזיד בעבודת כוכבים לאו שב מידיעתו הוא דמומר לעבודת כוכבים מומר לכל התורה כולה ונראה דחק עצמו בקונטרס דמעלה לחבירו אין שייך לחייבו משום עבודת כוכבים כיון דאין מתכוין לשם עבודת כוכבים: להוציא שעיר המשתלח. היינו לאחר הגרלה דקודם הגרלה מיחייב אתרוייהו כדמוכח פרק שני שעירי (יומא דף סב:): דברה תורה כלשון בני אדם. בפרק אלו מציאות (ב"מ דף לא:) פירשתי: אבל בהמה כתיב. לפיכך העלה כמה אברים זה אחר זה אינו חייב אלא אחת אקמא *מיחייב דאייתיה לכולה בהמה ואאחריני פטור בכבר חסרה דמה שהעלה הרי הוא כנאבד ומ"ס אכל אבר ואבר אבל אבר אחד שהעלה לחצאין לכ"ע לא מיחייב אלא אחת ומיחייב אזית קמא ורבי יוחנן אמר מחלוקת באבר אחד דמר סבר מוקטרי פנים שחסרו והעלן בחוץ חייב וכי כתיב לעשות אותו אשחוטי חוץ אבל לא אשחוטי פנים דהא מהדרינן פוקעין ומר סבר פטור כר' ישמעאל דלעיל וקסבר דלא מהדרינן פוקעין [אבל בד' וה' אברים חייב על כל אבר] לכ"ע וא"ת מאי טעמא לא מיחייב אכזית שני כהי דלא מהדרינן פוקעין מ"מ אם מחתך אבר אחד לכמה זיתים חייב להעלות את כולן א"כ הקטרה הוא ואמאי לא מיחייב עלה בחוץ וי"ל דהא *מיחייב להקטיר הכל לאו משום דתיהוי חשובה הקטרה בחצי אבר אלא משום דכולה חדא הקטרה היא וכיון שהתחיל בה גומר *אבל אי מהדרי פוקעין שחסרה וקטרה שאר מזה יש ללמוד דחשיבא הקטרה בחצי אבר וכ"כ שיטה זו ובקונטרס פי' בע"א: לא נחלקו אלא במוקטרי חוץ שחסרו והעלן בחוץ מר סבר חייב. פי' בקונטרס וכי כתיב אותו למעוטי פחות מכזית אתא שאין הקטרה שלימה וכדדריש לקמן וא"ת ומאי טעמא בעי קרא למעוטי פחות מכזית היכן מצינו שחייבה תורה בחצי שיעור וחצי זית חצי שיעור הוא דלא מצינו הקטרה להתחייב בפחות מכזית לא לענין מחשבה ושום דבר אלא דוקא גבי שאור ודבש דחייב בפחות מכזית למאן דאית ליה מכח קראי ויש לומר דשמא כיון דמהדרי' פוקעין פחות מכזית הוה אמינא דמחייב בחוץ אי לאו דכתיב אותו: כמאן מהדרינן פוקעין כו'. הא דמיחייבינן ברים פירקין (דף קז.) לר"ע מוקטרי פנים שחסרו והקריבן בחוץ היינו דוקא כגון אימורי או איברי עולה שחסרו דלא מפסלי בהכי אבל מנחה שחסרה וקטרת ולבונה שחסרו דמיפסלי מחמת חסרון פטור כדתנן לקמן (דף קט:) וכולן שחסרו כל שהוא והקריבן בחוץ פטור *וגבי עולה קתני המעלה *(עולת כזית) חייב ומצטרפין לכזית להעלותן בחוץ וליחייב עליהן משום פיגול נותר וטמא (ואימורים ומן האימורין בחוץ חייב) ומשמע בגמרא דבניתותרו מיירי דקתני בברייתא עולה ואימורין אין שלמים ואימוריהן לא

דמשמע הראוי ליקרב לשם חייבין עליו בחוץ ושאינו עומד לשם אין חייבין עליו בחוץ ולקמן בפ' בתרא (דף קיג:) דריש לה תנא דברייתא הכי וגלי בשחיטה והוא הדין להעלאה דהא מיגמר גמירי מהדדי כדאמרן לערב פרשיות בר מהנך תרי חומרי דמתני' דמפרשי קראי בכולהו בין לחיובא בין לפטורא: מה ת"ל איש איש. גבי העלאה: ושחטו פטורין. כדילפינן לעיל דכתיב ההוא: אבל בהמה כתיב. על כל הבהמה הוא חייב ואינו חייב על אבר אחד הלכך כולה חדא העלאה היא: אבל באבר אחד. והקריבו לחצאין לאחר שהקריב שאר האיברים דהאי עליו לבדו אפילו הקריב שלם פטר ליה ר' יוסי או מיירי שפקע מעל האש וחזר והחזירו: דברי הכל העלאה אחת היא. דהא אותו כתיב שלם ולא חסר: ור' יוחנן אמר מחלוקת באבר אחד. ודכולי עלמא אותו אכל אבר ואבר כתיב ומאן דמחייב סבר מוקטרי פנים שחסרו והעלו בחוץ חייב דהא מהדרינן פוקעין למזבח דהוו להו חסר וכי כתיב אותו אמוקטרי חוץ כתיב: ומ"ס פטור. דנפקא ליה מלא יביאנו כר' ישמעאל: לא נחלקו אלא במוקטרי חוץ כו'. מר סבר חייב דכי כתיב אותו למעוטי פחות מכזית אתא שאין הקטרה שלימה וכדדריש ליה לקמן: פוקעין. שפוקעין מעל האש: דלא כר' יוסי. ט] דכיון דבפנים בני הקטרה נינהו ואע"ג דחסרו בחוץ נמי י] מיחייב במוקטרי פנים שחסרו והעלו בחוץ אלמא קסבר אבוה דשמואל דרבי יוסי אמוקטרי פנים שחסרו והעלו בחוץ פליג: ויבן נח מזבח. אלמא יא] אפילו במת יחיד שהיא בחוץ אינה העלאה בלא מזבח: על הצור. בלא בנין מזבח לשם כך וקרי ליה העלאה: גובהה בעלמא. כדרך כל הארץ שיהא נוח להשתמש ולא לחובת מזבח: מזבח פתח אהל מועד כו'. האי קרא דריש ליה ר"ש בת"כ הכי וזרק הכהן את הדם על מזבח ה' פתח אהל מועד ולא מזבח בבמת יחיד בשעת היתר הבמות ובפ' המעלה בחוץ כתיב: ה"ג חייב ולא מיבעי ליה ה"ק לפיכך בשעת איסור הבמות העלה ע"ג הסלע או על גבי האבן חייב: ולא מיבעי ליה. כיון דאמר אין מזבח בבמה בשעת היתר הבמות קאי הילכך ולא מיבעי ליה: ה"ק לפיכך. הואיל ובבמה בשעת היתר הבמות הויא הקטרה בשעת יב] איסורו אם העלו על הסלע חייב: קרן וכבש ויסוד וריבוע. דקי"ל דמעכבי במזבח המשכן בפרק קדשי קדשים (לעיל דף סב.) מהו שיעכבו בבמת יחיד: בבמה גדולה. אף נוב וגבעון שהיו במות ציבור וכל שכן שילה ובית עולמים:

מתני'

עין משפט נר מצוה

כו א מיי' פי"ח מהלכות מעשה הקרבנות הל' יא ופי"ט הלכה ז :

כז ב מיי' שם פי"ט הלכה יא

שייך מעל"ד

כח ג מיי' פי"ט שם הלכה א :

נ"ל מיחייב דעדיין איתא לכולה בהמה כו' נ"ק

נ"ל דמחייב נ"ק

נ"א אבל אי מהדרין פוקעין בחסרה וקטרה עם השאר מזה כו' נ"ק

שיטה מקובצת

א] ת"ר איש מה ת"ל איש איש לרבות: ב] שאחזו באבר והעלוהו שפטורין ת"ל: ג] ההוא מאי עביד ליה מיבעי: ד] הך איש איש דשחיטה נמי ותיבת ההוא נמחק: ה] להדיוט דחייב מנא ליה נפקא ליה: ו] אבל באבר אחד: ז] שחסרו והעלו בחוץ: ח] במוקטרי חוץ: ט] יוסי. דאי כר' יוסי כיון דבפנים: י] נמי ניחייב במוקטרי: יא] תיבת אפילו נמחק: יב] איסורן אם העלו:

נ"ל וגבי עולה קתני עולה ואימוריהן מצטרפין לכזית להעלותן בחוץ ולחייב עליהן משום פיגול נותר וטמא ומשמע בגמרא דבניתותרו מיירי דקתני וכו'

מסורת הש"ס

[קדושין מג.]

[שם יז: וש"נ]

[לעיל קו: לקמן קט:]

הגהות הב"ח

(א) גמ' על האבן חייב ולא מיבעי :

[לעיל סב. לקמן קי.]

נ"א כזית מן העולה ומן האימורין בחוץ

connection with offering up too?—That is required [108b] in order to exclude one who acts in ignorance, under constraint, or in error.[4] If so, there too it is required in order to exclude one who acts in ignorance, under constraint, or in error?—'*That*' is written twice.[5] Then what is the purpose of '*unto the Lord*'?[6]—It is to exclude the goat that is sent away.[7]

OFFERING UP IS MORE STRINGENT etc. Our Rabbis taught: *A man, a man:*[8] why this [repetition]? To include two who take hold of a limb and offer it up, [and it teaches] that they are liable. For I might argue, is not [the reverse] logical: if two who hold a knife and slaughter are not liable, though when one slaughters to a man he is liable; is it not logical that when two take hold [of a limb and offer it up] they are not liable, seeing that one who offers up to a man is not liable? Therefore '*a man, a man*' is stated: these are the words of R. Simeon. R. Jose said: '*That* [*man*]' implies one but no two. If so, why is '*a man, a man*' stated?—[Because] Scripture employs human idiom.[9] And R. Simeon?[10]—He requires that for excluding one who acts in ignorance, under constraint, or in error.
a And R. Jose?[1]—[He infers that] from *ha-hu* [being written instead of] *hu*.[2] And R. Simeon?—He does not attribute any particular significance to[3] *ha-hu* [as opposed to] *hu*.

Now, according to R. Jose, since [in] this '*ish ish*' the Torah employs human idiom, in the other *ish ish* too[4] [we must say that] the Torah employs human idiom; whence then does he know that one who slaughters to a man is liable?—He infers it from, *blood shall be imputed unto that man, he hath shed blood*: [this implies,] even one who slaughters to a man.[5]

IF ONE OFFERED UP, THEN OFFERED UP AGAIN etc. Resh Laḳish said: The controversy is about four or five limbs, one master holds that the text, *to sacrifice* it, [which teaches that] a person is liable on account of a whole, but not on account of an incomplete one, is written in connection with the whole *animal*;[6] the other master holds that it is written in connection with each limb.[7] But in the case of one limb,[8] all agree that he is liable to one [offering] only. But R. Joḥanan maintained: The controversy is about one limb; one master holds that if one offers up without [limbs] which were [first] burnt within and [thus] became incomplete, he is liable;[9] while the other master holds that he is not liable.[10] But in the case of four or five limbs, all agree that he is liable on account of each limb [separately]. Now, this disagrees with 'Ulla. For 'Ulla said: All agree that one is liable if he offers up without [limbs] which were burnt within and [thus] became incomplete. They disagree only where one offers up without [limbs] which were burnt *without* and [thus] became incomplete: there one master holds
b that he is not liable, while the other master holds that he is liable.[1] Others say, 'Ulla said: All agree that one is not liable if he offers up without [limbs] which were burnt without and [thus] became incomplete. They disagree only where one offers up without [limbs] which were burnt within and [thus] became incomplete: one master holds that he is not liable, while the other master holds that he is liable. Now, Samuel's father disagrees with 'Ulla's [view] in its first version. For Samuel's father said: In accordance with whom do we replace on the altar [limbs] that spring off? It is not in accordance with R. Jose.[2]

HE IS LIABLE ONLY WHEN HE OFFERS UP [ON TOP OF AN ALTAR] etc. R. Huna said, What is R. Jose's reason?—Because it is written, *And Noah builded an* altar *unto the Lord*.[3] R. Joḥanan said: What is R. Simeon's reason?—Because it is written, *So Manoah took the kid with the meal-offering, and offered it upon the* rock *unto the Lord*.[4] Now as to the other too, surely it is written, *And Noah builded an* altar *unto the Lord*?—That was merely for its elevation.[5] And as to the other too, surely it is written, *So Manoah took* [etc.]?—That was a temporary dispensation.

Alternatively, this is R. Simeon's reason, [viz.,] as it was taught: R .Simeon said: [There is] *the altar* [*of the Lord*] *at the door of the tent of meeting*,[6] but there is no altar at the *bamah*;[7] therefore if one offered up [without] on a rock or on a stone, he is liable.
c ['He is liable'!] Surely he should say, [he] is excluded?[1]—This is what he means: Therefore if one offers up on a rock or on a stone when *bamoth* are *forbidden*, he is liable.

R. Jose son of R. Ḥanina asked: As to the horn, the ascent, the base and squareness, are these indispensable at the *bamoth*?[2]—Said R. Jeremiah to him. It was taught: The horn, the ascent, the base and squareness were indispensable at the great *bamoth*,[3] but were not indispensable at minor *bamoth*.[4]

(4) 'In error' means when he is led into error by another. (5) *Blood shall be imputed unto* that man ... *and* that man *shall be cut off*. Thus we have two limitations. (6) Written in connection with slaughtering. (7) On the Day of Atonement, Lev. XVI, 21. A man is not liable for slaughtering that without, because '*unto the Lord*' implies that liability is incurred only when it could be sacrificed, and its rites performed, within. (8) V. n. 2. (9) Where this repetition is quite common. (10) Does he not admit the implication of '*that*'?

a (1) Whence does he know this? (2) Both mean 'that'. The longer form implies a further limitation. (3) Lit., 'he does not interpret'. (4) *Sc.* in connection with slaughtering. (5) That is implied in the emphatic '*he hath shed blood*'—no matter to whom. (6) One is liable only when he offers up the whole animal; therefore even if he offered up several limbs, he is liable to one offering only, viz., on account of the first, because the animal was still whole then. (7) One is liable only when he offers up a whole *limb*, but not when he offers up part of a limb. Hence each limb imposes a separate liability. (8) I.e., if a man offered up one limb in several portions consecutively. (9) Because if such a limb springs off the altar, it must be replaced. This shews that it still requires *haḳtarah* after it has become incomplete, therefore when one offers it up without, performing *haḳtarah* there, he is liable. Consequently, each successive offering up of a portion of the same limb entails a separate sacrifice. (10) Save for a whole limb. Therefore when he offers up the limb in several parts, he incurs one offering only.

b (1) The latter holds that '*it*' excludes less than the size of an olive, but not an incomplete limb. (2) For if R. Jose held thus, then since they still require *haḳtarah* within, though when they spring off they are already incomplete, he should also hold that one is liable for offering up without limbs which were incomplete through having been burnt within. This proves that in the opinion of Samuel's father, R. Jose disagrees, and holds that one is *not* liable, even if he offers up without limbs which were incomplete through having been first burnt *within*. (3) Gen. VIII, 20. This proves that only an altar makes the act one of offering up. (4) Judg. XIII, 19. (5) To facilitate the act of offering up, but not because an actual altar was necessary. (6) Lev. XVII, 6. (7) Only at the door of the tent of meeting was a proper altar required. But when *bamoth* were permitted, no proper altar was necessary, and one could sacrifice and offer up on a simple stone.

c (1) 'But there is no altar at a *bamah*', obviously means when this is *permitted*. But one is *not* liable then for offering up without, and so he should have said, this *excludes* (from liability) one who offers up on a rock or on a stone. (2) These were indispensable to the altar in the Tabernacle: v. *supra* 62a. (3) *Sc.* at Nob and Gibeon; these were *public bamoth*. (4) *Sc.* private *bamoth* which individuals built for themselves.

MISHNAH [109*a*]. IF EITHER VALID SACRIFICES OR INVALID SACRIFICES HAD BECOME UNFIT WITHIN, AND ONE OFFERS THEM WITHOUT, HE IS LIABLE.[5] IF ONE OFFERS UP WITHOUT AS MUCH AS AN OLIVE OF A BURNT-OFFERING AND ITS EMURIM [COMBINED],[6] HE IS LIABLE.

GEMARA. Our Rabbis taught: [*Whatsoever man* . . .] *that offereth up a burnt-offering:*[7] I know it only of a burnt-offering; whence do I know to include the *emurim* of a guilt-offering, the *emurim* of a sin-offering, the *emurim* of most sacred sacrifices and the *emurim* of lesser sacrifices?[8] Because it says, '[*or*] *sacrifice*'.[9] Whence do we know to include the fistful, frankincense, incense, the meal-offering of priests, the meal-offering of the anointed priest, and one who makes a libation of three *logs* of wine or of water?[10] Because it says, '*And bringeth it not unto the door of the tent of meeting*':[11] whatever comes to the door of the tent of meeting, you are liable on its account [if it is done] without. Again, I know it only of valid sacrifices; whence do I know to include invalid [ones], e.g., [a sacrifice] that is kept overnight, or that goes out, or is unclean, or which was slaughtered [with the intention of being eaten] after time or without bounds, or whose blood was received and sprinkled by unfit persons; or [whose blood] was sprinkled above when it should have been sprinkled below, or below when it should have been sprinkled above, or within instead of without, or without instead
a of within;[1] or a Passover-offering or a sin-offering which one slaughtered under a different designation?—Because it says, '*And bringeth it not to sacrifice*', [this teaches,] whatever is received at the door of the tent of meeting,[2] you are liable on its account without.

IF ONE OFFERS UP WITHOUT AS MUCH AS AN OLIVE OF A BURNT-OFFERING [AND ITS EMURIM] etc. Only [of] a *burnt-offering* and its *emurim*, but not [of] a *peace*-offering and its *emurim*.[3] We have thus learnt here what our Rabbis taught: A burnt-offering and its *emurim* combine to [make up the standard of] an olive, in respect of offering them up without, and in respect of being liable through them on account of *piggul, nothar*, and defilement.[4] As for offering-up, it is well: only a burnt-offering, because it is altogether burnt [*kalil*],[5] but not a peace-offering. What however is the reason for *piggul, nothar*, and uncleanness? Surely we learnt: All instances of *piggul* combine, and all instances of *nothar* combine:[6] thus the rulings on *piggul* are contradictory, and those on *nothar* are contradictory?—The rulings on *piggul* are not contradictory: one refers to *piggul*, the other refers to the *intention* of *piggul*.[7] Nor are the rulings on *nothar* contradictory: one refers to [actual] *nothar*, the other refers to such which were left over before the blood was
b sprinkled.[1] And who is the author of this?—R. Joshua. For it was taught: R. Joshua said: [In the case of] all the sacrifices of the Torah of which as much as an olive of flesh or an olive of *ḥeleb* remains,

(5) Because if such unfit sacrifices are placed on the altar within they are not removed. (6) E.g. half as much as an olive of each. (7) Lev. XVII, 8. (8) That if one offers up these without, he is liable. (9) Ibid. This is an extension. (10) This is the smallest measure which constitutes a libation. (11) Ibid. 9.

a (1) 'Within' and 'without' here mean on the inner altar and on the outer altar respectively. (2) I.e., whatever is not removed from the altar if placed thereon. (3) The flesh and the *emurim* of a peace-offering do not combine to make up the standard of an olive. (4) This is now assumed to mean that one is liable for eating as much as an olive of the flesh and the *emurim* combined when it is *piggul* or *nothar*, or if he is unclean. (5) Hence no distinction is drawn between the flesh and the *emurim*, and they combine. (6) Now, *piggul* and *nothar* apply both to the flesh and to the *emurim* of a peace-offering (v. *supra* 43*a*): hence the two should combine. (7) If one eats half as much as an olive of the flesh of a peace-offering which is already *piggul* and the same quantity of its *emurim*, he is liable to a sin-offering. If, however, one slaughters a peace-offering with the intention of eating or burning half as much as an olive of the flesh and half as much as an olive of the *emurim* after time, it does not become *piggul*, because the flesh should be eaten and the *emurim* should be burnt, whereas an illegitimate intention of eating or burning renders a sacrifice *piggul* only when it is made in respect of what is eaten or burnt respectively. Such intentions do combine, however, in the case of a burnt-offering, since the whole of it is burnt.

b (1) In the case of ordinary *nothar* the flesh and the *emurim*, even of a peace-offering, combine. It is different, however, in the following instance: The whole of the animal, except half as much as an olive of the flesh and the same of the *emurim*, was lost or destroyed before the sprinkling of the blood. Now, if this happened with a burnt-offering, we would have as much as an olive for the altar's consumption, and therefore the sprinkling is valid to render it *nothar*, in the sense that if it is left until after time and then eaten, it entails liability. In the case of a peace-offering, however, there is only half as much as an olive for the altar's consumption and the same for man's consumption: these do not combine to permit the sprinkling. If one did sprinkle, therefore, the sprinkling is not valid to render it *nothar* in the above sense. The same applies to defilement.

מתני' *אחד קדשים כשרין ואחד קדשים פסולין שהיה פסולן בקודש והקריבן בחוץ חייב *המעלה כזית מן העולה א] ומן האימורין בחוץ חייב: גמ' ת"ר °אשר יעלה עולה ב] או זבח אין לי אלא עולה מנין *לרבות אימורי אשם ואימורי חטאת ואימורי קדשי קדשים ואימורי קדשים קלים ת"ל זבח ג] מנין *לרבות הקומץ והלבונה והקטורת ומנחת כהנים ומנחת כהן משיח והמנסך שלשת לוגין יין ושלשת לוגין מים ת"ל °ואל פתח אהל מועד לא יביאנו כל הבא לפתח אהל מועד חייבין עליו בחוץ ואין לי אלא קדשים כשרים מנין לרבות פסולין *כגון הלן והיוצא והטמא ושנשחט חוץ לזמנו וחוץ למקומו ושקבלו פסולין וזרקו את דמו והניתנין למטה שנתנן למעלה והניתנין למעלה שנתנן למטה והניתנין בחוץ שנתנן בפנים והניתנין בפנים שנתנן בחוץ ופסח וחטאת ד] *שנתנן שלא לשמן מנין ת"ל לא יביאנו לעשות *כל המתקבל בפתח אהל מועד חייבין עליו בחוץ: המעלה כזית מן העולה כו': עולה ואימוריה אין שלמים ואימוריהן לא תנינא להא דת"ר *עולה ואימוריה מצטרפין לכזית להעלותן בחוץ ולחייב עליהן משום פיגול נותר וטמא בשלמא *העלאת עולה דכליל אין שלמים לא אלא פיגול ונותר וטמא מ"ט ה] והא *תנן *כל הפגולין מצטרפין וכל הנותרין מצטרפין קשיא פיגול אפיגול קשיא נותר אנותר פיגול אפיגול לא קשיא כאן בפיגול כאן במחשבת פיגול נותר אנותר לא קשיא כאן בנותר כאן בשניתותרו עד שלא נזרק הדם ומני רבי יהושע היא *דתניא ר' יהושע אומר כל הזבחים שבתורה שנשתייר ו] בהן כזית בשר וכזית

תורה אור: ויקרא יז — שם

רש"י

מתני' ואחד קדשים פסולין שהיה פסולן בקדש. הואיל ובפנים אם עלו לא ירדו מתקבל בפנים קריגא ביה וחייבין עליהן בחוץ כדיליף בגמ': המעלה כזית מן העולה ומאימוריה. חצי זית מזה וחצי זית מזה חייב דעולה כליל: גמ' ואימורי קדשי קדשים. כבשי עצרת: הלבונה. של מנחת נדבה: ומנחת כהנים. שהיא כליל וראויה להעלאה כקומץ מנחת ישראל אבל שירי מנחת ישראל אינו חייב על העלאתם: מנחת כהן משיח. עשירית האיפה שהוא מביא בכל יום: ושלשת לוגין יין. שהוא פחות שבנסכים: ושלשת לוגין מים. בחג קאמר ובמוקדשין לחג שאין העלאת חוץ נוהגת בחולין: מנין לרבות פסולין. הנך דאם עלו לא ירדו דלא מתרבו מלא יביאנו דהא אינם ראויין להביא לכתחילה: ת"ל לעשות. משמע הראויין ז] לעשות אפילו אינו ראוי לבא מחוץ לפנים והני נמי כיון דאם עלו לא ירדו וכהן נזקק להפך בהם בצינורא או להעלותן מראש המזבח למערכה ראויין ליעשות קריגא ביה: שלמים לא. אין בשרן מצטרף עם אימוריהן לכזית העלאת חוץ משום דבשר שלמים לאו בר הקטרה הוא ולא קריגא ביה אל פתח אהל מועד לא יביאנו: ולחייב עליהן משום פיגול ונותר וטמא. קא ס"ד באוכל כזית בשר ואימורין מעולת פיגול או נותר או בטומאת הגוף אכלו: מאי טעמא. לא מצטרף נמי בשר שלמים עם אימוריו לפיגול ונותר וטמא הא בין בבשר בין באימורין שייך פיגול נותר וטמא כדאמר בפ' בית שמאי (לעיל דף מג.) דכל שיש לו מתירין בין לאדם בין למזבח חייבין עליו משום פיגול והרי הדם מתיר את הבשר לאדם ואת האימורין למזבח ותנן נמי התם דברים שאין חייבין עליהם משום פיגול כגון הקומץ והלבונה והקטרת שאין להם מתירין אלא הם עצמן מתירין חייבין עליהן משום נותר ומשום טמא וכל שכן אימורין שהפיגול נוהג בהן ומקראי ילפינן להו: כל הפיגולין מצטרפין. משנה היא במעילה: כאן בפיגול כאן במחשבת פיגול. הא דקתני מצטרפין באוכל פיגול קאמר ולהתחייב חטאת והא דקתני עולה אין שלמים לא במחשבת פיגול שאם שחט או זרק על מנת להקטיר חצי זית בשר עולה וחצי זית מאימורין חוץ לזמנו פיגל אבל בשלמים ח] חישב לאכול או להקטיר חצי זית בשר וחצי זית אימורין לא פיגל שאין מחשבת אכילה בנקטרין ואין מחשבת הקטרה בנאכלין: כאן בנותר כאן בשניתותרו עד שלא נזרק הדם. הא דקתני מצטרפין באוכל נותר קאמר והא דקתני עולה אין שלמים לא בשניתותרו מאיבוד ושריפה כגון אבדו הבשר והאימורין קודם זריקה ונשתייר חצי זית מזה וחצי זית מזה בעולה דכולה כליל הויא זריקת דם זריקה דהא איכא אכילת מזבח וכר' יהושע דאמר בפרק טבול יום (לעיל דף קד.) אם אין בשר אין דם וכיון דזריקה היא (א) חייבין עליו משום נותר אם ניתותרו ואכל ממנו כדאמרן (לעיל דף מה:) דברים שאין חייבין עליהם משום פיגול חייבין ט] משום נותר כגון קומץ שהוא אכילת מזבח כעולה וכל שכן דברים שחייבין עליהן משום פיגול כגון בשר עולה אבל שלמים אין חצי זית מבשרן וחצי זית מאימוריהן מצטרפין להיות שיור לזרוק עליהם את הדם דלא אכילת אדם איכא ולא אכילת מזבח איכא וכיון דלא הויא זריקה אם זרק אין חייבין עליהן משום נותר וטמא דקי"ל (מנחות דף כה:) י] כל הניתר לטהורין חייבין עליו משום טומאה ובפ' ב"ש (לעיל דף מה:) אתי טהר חילול מטומאה ובמס' מעילה (דף ו:) לענין יוצא אמרינן יא] לר"א דאמר אין זריקה מועלת ליוצא אין חייבין עליו משום נותר וטמא: כל הזבחים. בר מעולה: יב] *אין זורק את הדם. דאית ליה לר' יהושע* אם אין בשר אין דם מועשית עולותיך הבשר והדם ובזבחים כתיב (דברים יב) ודם זבחיך ישפך והבשר תאכל הזקיקן הכתוב זה לזה

תוספות

לא ומוקי לה בניתותרו וכר' יהושע וקצת תימה קומץ ולבונה אמאי לא מיחייב עלייהו בחוץ כשחסרו נהי דמיפסלי לכתחילה מ"מ מתקבלין הם בפנים דאם עלו לא ירדו דהוה ליה פסולו בקדש כשחסר בין קמילה להקטרה ולמאן דחשיב במנחות פ' קמא (דף ט:) חסרון כבעל מום ניחא וי"ל דאפילו תמצא לומר דאם עלה לא ירד מ"מ סברא הוא למעוטיה מדכתיב אותו על השלם הוא חייב ואינו חייב על החסר כיון דלכתחילה לא יעלה *וצריך לדקדק אי מהדרינן פוקעין דידהו *ובפרק המזבח מקדש (לעיל דף פג:) איכא כמה קראי לרבן גמליאל מהיא העולה על מוקדה ולאידך מאשר תאכל האש ועוד דדרשינן לעיל (דף פו.) ועשית עולותיך הבשר והדם עיכולי עולה אתה מחזיר ואי אתה מחזיר עיכולי גידין ועצמות *משמע הא בשר דומיא דגידים ועצמות מהדרינן אפילו במקצת ותימה אי פליג עליה רבי יוסי: **ומנחת** כהנים ומנחת כהן משיח. הא דפלגינהו משום דמנחת כהנים באה עשרון ומנחת כהן משיח חצי עשרון ותימה דלא תני מנחת נסכים: **עולה** ואימורין מצטרפין לכזית להעלותן בחוץ ולחייב עליהם משום פיגול נותר וטמא. במסכת מעילה פרק קדשי מזבח (דף טו:) תנן חמשה דברים בעולה מצטרפין זה עם זה הבשר והחלב והסלת והיין והשמן וששה בתודה דאיכא לחם ותימה לענין מאי קאמר אי לענין מעילה הא תנא ליה רישא (שם.) קדשי מזבח מצטרפין זה עם זה למעילה כו' ועוד דתודה אין בה מעילה כי אם לאחר זריקה באימורין אבל בלחם לא ואי *(לא יתחייב) בחוץ הא לא תני במתניתין אלא עולה ואימורין אבל חמשה דברים לא דהא על גב דמיחייבי בחוץ כדדרשינן לעיל מקרא הני מילי בפני עצמן אבל איצטרופי לא ועוד דלא מיחייב בחוץ אלחם שבתודה ועוד חלב ויין היאך מצטרפין והא אין שיעורן שוה שזה בכזית וזה בשלשה לוגין ואי לענין לזרוק עליהן הדם הא אמר ובמנחה אפילו כולה קיימת לא יזרוק ואי לענין מחשבת פיגול אין אכילה והקטרה מצטרפין ונראה דמיירי לענין אכילה דמיחייב האוכל משום פיגול נותר וטמא ואי מרישא דקתני קדשי מזבח מצטרפין הוה אמינא במין אחד קמ"ל אפילו בכמה מינין ועוד תניגהו למעוטי דאין דם חייבין עליו משום פיגול ועוד אשמעינן דחל פיגול אהנך דברים חמשה וששה וצריך לומר דאתיא כר"מ דתנן לעיל בפרק ב"ש (דף מג:) [ואלו] דברים שאין חייבין עליהן משום פיגול מנחת נסכים והנסכים הבאין בפני עצמן דברי ר"מ וחכ"א אף הבאים עם הבהמה ובהקומץ זוטא (מנחות דף טו:) תנן נמי הזבח מפגל את הנסכים *משקדש בכלי דברי ר"מ והא דחלב ויין מצטרפין אע"ג דחלב בכזית ומשקין ברביעית ה"מ בשתיה אבל דרך אכילה שערה פתו ביין שיעורו בכזית וקצת תימה מאי איריא דנקט חמשה דברים בעולה הא בשלמים נמי מצטרפין לחייב משום פיגול ויש לומר דנקט עולה משום דאיירי נמי במעילה אף על גב דבתודה לא איירי במעילה: **כל** הפיגולין מצטרפין. תימה דלא מייתי מרישא דקתני (מעילה דף טו.) קדשי מזבח מצטרפין לפיגול ויש לומר דהוה מוקמינן לה בעולה דהא תני נמי מעילה אבל הך משמע טפי: **וכל** הנותרות מצטרפין. תימה דלא תני כל הטומאות מצטרפין ויש לומר דהוה משמע אפילו שרץ ונבלה ובשר המת והנהו לא מצטרפין כדתנן התם (דף יז:):

כאן — לו

עין משפט נר מצוה

כט א מיי' פי"ט מהל' מעה"ק הלכה ז:

ל ב מיי' שם הל' י:

לא ג ד מיי' שם הל' ג:

לב ה מיי' שם הל' ז.

לג ו מיי' שם הלכה ג:

ע' רש"ק וצ"ק

נ"ל דבפרק צ"ק

לד ז מיי' פי"ח מהל' פסה"מ הלכה יא:

גירסת צ"ק משמע הא דומיא דבשר ודם אפילו במקצת מהדרינן ותימה היכא פליג ר"י

גירסת צ"ק שהתחייב

נ"ל משקדשו

שיטה מקובצת

א] העולה ומאימוריה תיבות ומן האימורין נמחק: ב] תיבות או זבח נמחק: ג] זבח מנין לרבות את הדם ת"ל או זבח מנין: ד] וחטאת ששחטן שלא: ה] מ"ט לא והא: ו] שנשתייר מהן כזית: ז] הראויין ליעשות אפילו: ח] בשלמים אם חישב: ט] חייבין עליהן: י] תיבת כל נמחק: יא] אמרינן נמי לר"א: יב] מה"ד אינו זורק:

מסורת הש"ס

נ"ל ששחטן נ"ק

תוספתא דמעילה פ"א

נ"א להעלותן נ"ק

מעילה טו.

מעילה שם מנחות ע. כו. תוספתא דפסחים פ"ו [פסחים עג. בכורות לג: לעיל כה: תוספתא זבחים פרק ד]

שייך לע"ב ד"ה [לעיל קד.]

הגהות הב"ח

(א) רש"י ד"ה כאן בנותר וכו' דזריקה היא אבל שלמים חייבין:

*וכזית חלב *זורק את הדם חצי זית בשר וחצי זית חלב אינו זורק את הדם *ובעולה חצי זית בשר וחצי זית חלב זורק את הדם מפני שכולה כליל ומנחה אפילו כולה קיימת לא יזרוק מנחה מאי עבידתה אמר רב פפא מנחת נסכים הבאה עם הזבח: **מתני'** *הקומץ והלבונה והקטרת ומנחת כהנים ומנחת כהן משיח ומנחת נסכים א] שהקריב מאחת מהן *כזית בחוץ חייב ר"א פוטר עד שיקריב את כולן *וכולן ב] שהקריב בפנים ושייר מהן כזית והקריבו בחוץ חייב *וכולן שחסרו כל שהו והקריבו בחוץ פטור (א) המקריב קדשים ואימורים בחוץ חייב:

גמ' ת"ר *המקטיר כזית ג] בחוץ חייב חצי פרס בפנים פטור קס"ד מאי פטור פטור זר אמאי ד] הקטרה היא א"ר זירא אמר רב חסדא אמר רב ירמיה בר אבא אמר רב מאי פטור פטור ציבור א"ר זירא אי קשיא לי הא קשיא לי הא דאמר רב עלה בהא אפילו ר' ה] אליעזר מודה דהא ר' אליעזר לאו הקטרה היא קאמר אמר רבה בהקטרה דהיכל דכולי עלמא לא פליגי כי פליגי בהקטרה דפנים דמר סבר °מלא חפניו דוקא ומ"ס מלא חפניו לאו דוקא [ויקרא טז] א"ל אביי והא כי קא כתיבא חוקה בהקטרה דפנים הוא דכתיב אלא אמר אביי בהקטרה ו] *בפנים כ"ע לא פליגי כי פליגי בהקטרה דחוץ מ"ס ילפינן פנים מחוץ ומ"ס לא ילפינן אמר רבא השתא חוץ מחוץ לא ילפי רבנן פנים מחוץ מיבעי מה היא דתניא יכול המעלה פחות מכזית קומץ ופחות מכזית אימורין והמנסך פחות משלשת לוגין יין ז] [פחות] מג' לוגין מים יהא חייב תלמוד לומר לעשות ח] *על השלם חייב ואינו חייב על החסר והא פחות משלשת לוגין דאית בהו כמה זיתים ולא ילפי רבנן חוץ מחוץ אלא אמר רבא כגון דקבעינהו ט] שני חצאי פרס במנא

תורה אור: ויקרא טז

*כאן בשניתותרו [עד] שלא נזרק הדם ומני רבי יהושע. ה"ג לה במעילה בפ' קדשי מזבח (דף טו:) אלא אימא עולה ואימורים מצטרפין זה עם זה לכזית לזרוק עליהם את הדם ומאן קתני לה רבי יהושע וגירסא דמתניתין נמי יש ליישב דהכי נמי קאמר *וקשה לישנא דברייתא דקתני ולחייב עליהם משום פיגול נותר וטמא ויש לפרש דכשניתותרו כזית מעולה ואימורין אשמעינן דזריקה מעלייתא היא לאיחיובי משום פיגול נותר וטמא דקרבו מתיריו קרינא ביה והשתא לא צריכי להא דקאמר הכא פיגול אפיגול לא קשיא כאן בפיגול כאן במחשבת פיגול דבשינויא דניתותרו מתרלי תרוייהו פיגול ונותר ובמסכת מעילה לא גרסינן ליה *ויש מוחקין טמא מן הברייתא משום דמטמא לא משני מידי אבל לפי מה שפירשתי ניחא דכולהו מיתרלי וע"כ גרסינן ליה דאי לא גרסינן ליה הא דקאמר התם במעילה תנינא להא דתנו רבנן מנא ליה הא דקתני בברייתא דמצטרפין לענין אכילה *ואימא פיגול אפיגול לא קשיא כאן בפיגול כאן במחשבת פיגול ונותר אנותר לא קשיא כאן בנותר כאן בשניתותרו דלמא איירי להצטרף לענין להכשיר הקרבן ולזרוק עליהם את הדם אבל לאכילה לא מצטרפין אבל מכיון דתני טמא על כרחין לענין אכילה קאמר דמצטרפין דהיינו תנינא להא דתנו רבנן: **ומר** סבר מלא חפניו לאו דוקא. תימה למה לי למימר לאו דוקא אפילו יהא דוקא הוו מחייבי רבנן אכזית ממנו בחוץ מידי דהוה אקומץ וכמו כן קשה בסמוך למה לי למימר דסברי רבנן קביעות דמנא לאו כלום היא ויש לומר דעד כאן לא מחייבי רבנן בקומץ אלא משום דחשיב להתפגל על מנת להקטיר כזית מקומצה בחוץ הלכך חשיבא נמי הקטרה לחייב אכזית ממנו בחוץ ומנחת כהנים ומנחת כהן משיח אע"ג דלא שייך בהם פיגול כיון דמנחה נינהו ומליטו במנחה דכזית נמי חשיבא הקטרה שם מנחה אחד הוא אבל קטרת לא אשכחן דחשיב הקטרה בכזית דלא שייך ביה פיגול ועוד דהא א"ר יוסי דאין פיגול אלא בדבר שהוא על מזבח החיצון הלכך הא דמחייבי רבנן בקטרת בכזית על כרחין משום דמלא חפניו לאו דוקא וקביעות מנא לאו כלום היא: *דקבעינהו במנא. למאי דאסיקנא (למאי) דקבעינהו במנא הוי' לבונה דמתניתין שיעור שלם ופטור בחוץ לרבי אליעזר הואיל וקבעינהו במנא:

אבל

או כזית חלב. דכתיב וזרק הכהן את הדם וגו' והקטיר החלב אע"פ שאין בשר זורק עליו את הדם והכי מפרש במנחות בהקומץ רבה (דף כו.): *י] ובמנחה מאי עבידתה. מאי זריקת דם איכא במנחה: מנחת נסכים שבאה עם הזבח. ואבד בשר הזבח והמנחה קיימת לא יזרוק את הדם בשבילה דלאו גופא דזביחה הוא: **מתני'** הלבונה. של מנחה: והקטרת. שבכל יום פרס [של] שחרית ופרס של בין הערבים שהקטיר יא] כזית מהן בחוץ חייב קסבר כי כתיב אותו על השלם הוא חייב ואינו חייב על החסר אשיעור הקטרה כתיב והיינו *כזית ורבי יב] אליעזר נמי מדלא פליג ארישא גבי עולה הכי נמי דריש ליה אותו אשיעור הקטרה כרבנן מיהו עולה דלא מיפסלא בחסרון דכל עצמה בדם תלויה כפרתה חייב בכזית אבל בהני פליג דקא סבר קומץ כוליה הייט שיעור הקטרתו אף בפנים דהא מיפסל בחסרון וכן כולם שכולם מתירין הם כל זמן שלא קרבו כולם לא הויא הקטרה לצאת בעלים ידי חובתן ולרבנן בהני נמי הויא הקטרתן בכזית היכא דכוליה קיים ולא חסרו קודם הקטרה ותנן מנחות (דף כו.) הקטיר קומצה פעמים כשירה הילכך הקטרה היא: וכולן שהקריבן בפנים ושייר מהן כו'. חייב שהרי בזה נגמרה הקטרתן ולר' אליעזר נמי כי דריש אותו אשיעור הקטרה דריש ליה ושיעור הקטרה בכזית היכא דבפנים הויא הקטרה גמורה: וכולן שחסרו כל שהוא. קודם הקטרה ע"י איבוד או שריפה נפסלו בחסרונן כדאמר במנחות (דף ט:) מן המנחה פרט לשחסרה היא ושחסר קומצה והאי וכולן לאו אלבונה קאי דהא מיפליג פליגי בה במנחות בפרק קמא (דף יא:) בלבונה שחסרה דלר"ש כשירה אפילו עמדה על קורט אחד ולר' יהודה בשני קרטין ואי אלבונה נמי קאי מיירי שחסרה משיעור הכשרה למר כדאית ליה ולמר כדאית ליה: והקריבו בחוץ פטור. הואיל ואין יג] מתקבלין בפנים: *המעלה קדשים ואימוריהן. שהקריב הבשר והאימורין מחוברין בו חייב משום אימורין: **גמ'** חצי פרס בפנים. לאו דוקא חצי פרס נקט דה"ה לכזית אלא פחות מכשיעור הכשר מלותה נקט: קס"ד מאי פטור פטור זר. דאי לאו בזרות קאמר מאי פטור שייך למימר בפנים ואמאי פטור הא הקטרה היא דהא האי תנא דקמחייב עלה בחוץ: מאי פטור פטור ציבור. דילאו ידי חובתן דכזית הויא הקטרה: בהא אפילו רבי יד] אליעזר מודה. ואע"ג דפליג במתני' אבחוץ מודה הוא להאי תנא בהאי סיפא דפטור ציבור וקשיא לי עלה אמאי מודה והא רבי אליעזר לאו הקטרה היא קאמר מדפטר עלה בחוץ: אמר רבה בהקטרה דהיכל. שבכל יום שלא נאמר בו שיעור והאי פרס שיעור דרבנן הוא מודה רבי טו] אליעזר דבכזית הויא הקטרה לחייב עליה בחוץ ולהוציא ציבור ידי חובתן בפנים *ומתני' כולה רישא וסיפא דברי הכל היא ובהקטרה דהיכל מיירי: כי פליגי. במתני' בהקטרה דיום הכפורים דלפני ולפנים שנאמר בה שיעור (ויקרא טז): מלא חפניו דוקא. ובבת אחת הילכך בחוץ נמי לא מיחייב אלא אשלימה: והא כי כתיבא חוקה בפנים כתיבא. כדכתיב (שם) והיתה (זאת) לכם לחוקת עולם לכפר וגו' דברים שאין נעשין אלא *אחת בשנה וחוקה עיכובא הוא: ה"ג אלא אמר אביי בהקטרה דפנים דכולי עלמא לא פליגי כי פליגי בהקטרה דחוץ. אביי נמי כרבה מתרץ לה דברייתא דמודה בה רבי אליעזר בהקטרה דהיכל ומתניתין בהקטרה דפנים ומיהו לא כטעמא דרבה דאמר לרבנן מלא חפניו לאו דוקא דכולי עלמא מלא חפניו דוקא ובפנים דכ"ע לא פליגי דשלימה בעינן כי פליגי כגון שהקטיר כזית מן הקטרת של חפינת פנים בחוץ מר סבר ילפינן פנים מחוץ ילפינן קטרת של פנים מקטרת של היכל מה הקטרה של היכל טז] בבמה בחוץ בכזית אף הקטרה של פנים חייבין עליה בבמה בכזית ואע"ג דבדוכתה לא הויא הקטרה הואיל ובהיכל הויא הקטרה: ור' אליעזר סבר לא ילפינן פנים מחוץ. הקטרה דהיכל הוא דמיחייב עלה בחוץ בכזית דהא בדוכתה בהכי חשיבא אבל יז] הקטרת פנים לא מיחייב עלה בחוץ בכזית הואיל ובדוכתה לאו הקטרה היא: השתא חוץ מחוץ. כגון ניסוך היין שהוא על המזבח החיצון לא ילפי רבנן מהקטר חלבים שהוא על המזבח החיצון לחייב על פחות משלשה לוגין בחוץ אע"פ שיש שם כמה זיתים וגבי כל הקטרות של מזבח החיצון הקטרה היא הואיל וגבי ניסוך שיעורא אחרינא הוא לא מיחייב עליה אלא בכשיעור: פנים מחוץ. לחייב על קטרת שלפני ולפנים בבמה בחוץ ילפינן מהקטרה דהיכל: פחות מכזית קומץ. על כרחך רבנן היא דאי רבי יח] אליעזר אפילו אכזית לא מיחייב דהא אמר עד שיקריב את כולן: אלא אמר רבא כגון דקבעינהו במנא. לעולם מתניתין וברייתא בהקטרה דהיכל היא הקטרה בדוכתה בכזית ומשום הכי קתני לה בברייתא חייב יט] ור' אליעזר מודה בה כדרב ופלוגתא דמתניתין כגון *דקבעיה(דכולה)שני חצאי פרס במנא

וקסבר

עין משפט נר מצוה

שייך לעיל מעל"ד

לה א ב מיי' פ"א מהל' פסה"מ הלכה ל:

נ"ל וקשה לישנא דברייתא דלא קתני לזרוק עליהם את הדם ולחייב עליהם כו' נ"ק

לו ג ד ה מיי' פי"ט מהל' מעה"ק הל' ח:

לז ו מיי' שם

לח ז מיי' פ"ט מהלכות ביאת מקדש הל' ד:

[לעיל מב. מנחות יב:]

[וע' תוספות מנחות נח: ד"ה ואיכא דאמרי]

קאמר ואימא כו' נ"ק

שיטה מקובצת

א] נסכים שהקטיר ותיבת שהקריב נמחק: ב] וכולן שהקריבן בפנים: ג] כזית קטורת בחוץ: ד] אמאי הא הקטרה היא: ה] ר' אלעזר מודה והא ר' אלעזר לאו: ו] דפנים כ"ע: ז] ופחות מג': ח] לעשות אותו על: ט] תיבות שני חצאי פרס נמחק: י] מה"ד מנחה מאי: יא] שהקטיר מהן כזית בחוץ: יב] ורבי אלעזר: יג] ואין מתקבל בפנים: יד] ר' אלעזר מודה כו' והא ר' אלעזר לאו: טו] רבי אלעזר דבכזית כו' דהיכל קא מיירי הס"ד: טז] היכל חייבין עליהן בבמה: יז] אבל קטורת פנים: יח] רבי אלעזר אפילו: יט] ורבי אלעזר מודה כו' כגון דקבעיה לכולה חצי פרס תיבת שני נמחק:

עיין רש"ק וצ"ק

ס"א וברייתא

מסורת הש"ס

כאן שייך ד"ה אין זורק כו' שמעל"ד נ"ק

נ"ל או כזית

כזית הס"ד ואח"כ מ"ס ור"א פוטר ומדלא פליג ארישא גבי עולה ה"נ דריש וכו' כצ"ל נ"ק

הגהות הב"ח

(א) במשנה בחוץ פטור המעלה קדשים:

[לעיל קו. קח:]

נ"ל המקריב קדשים ואימוריהן כו' נ"ק

נ"ל פעם אחת בשנה ט' נ"ק

גי' נ"ק כגון דקבעי' לכולי פרס במנא

[109b] he sprinkles the blood. [If there remains] half as much as an olive of flesh and half an olive of *ḥeleb*, he must not sprinkle the blood. But in the case of a burnt-offering, even [if there remains] half as much as an olive of flesh and half an olive of *ḥeleb*, he sprinkles the blood, because the whole of it is entirely burnt. While as for a meal-offering, even if the whole of it is in existence, he must not sprinkle [the blood]. What business has a meal-offering [here]?[2] —Said R. Papa: [This refers to] the meal-offering of libations which accompanies the [animal] sacrifice.[3]

MISHNAH. AS FOR THE FISTFUL [OF FLOUR], THE FRANKINCENSE, THE INCENSE, THE PRIESTS' MEAL-OFFERING, THE ANOINTED PRIEST'S MEAL-OFFERING, AND THE MEAL-OFFERING OF LIBATIONS, IF [ONE] PRESENTED AS MUCH AS AN OLIVE OF ONE OF THESE WITHOUT, HE IS LIABLE. BUT
a R. ELEAZAR[1] RULES THAT ONE IS NOT LIABLE UNLESS HE PRESENTS THE WHOLE OF THEM [WITHOUT].[2] IN THE CASE OF ALL OF THESE, IF THEY WERE OFFERED WITHIN, BUT AS MUCH AS AN OLIVE WAS LEFT OVER AND ONE OFFERED IT WITHOUT, HE IS LIABLE.[3] IN THE CASE OF ALL OF THESE, IF THEY BECAME SLIGHTLY INCOMPLETE, AND ONE OFFERED THEM WITHOUT, HE IS NOT LIABLE.[4] ONE WHO OFFERS SACRIFICES TOGETHER WITH THE EMURIM WITHOUT,[5] IS LIABLE.[6]

GEMARA. Our Rabbis taught: If one burns as much as an olive of incense[7] without, he is liable; [if one burns] half a *peras*[8] within he is not liable. Now it was assumed that what does 'not liable' mean? A *zar* is not liable;[9] [then the difficulty arises] why so? Surely it is *haktarah*?[10]—Said R. Zera in R. Ḥisda's name in R. Jeremiah b. Abba's name in Rab's name: What does 'not liable' mean? The *community* is not liable.[11]

R. Zera said: If I have a difficulty, it is this, viz., Rab's statement thereon [that] here even R. Eleazar agrees; but surely R. Eleazar maintains that this does not constitute *haktarah*?[12]—Said Rabbah: In respect of *haktarah* in the *Hekal* none disagree.[13] They disagree
b only in respect of the *haktarah* within:[1] one master holds, *'his hands full'* is particularly meant;[2] while the other master holds [that] *'his hands full'* is not meant particularly. But surely, said Abaye to him, *'statute'* is written in reference to *haktarah* within?[3]—Rather said Abaye: In respect of *haktarah* within, none disagree. They disagree only in respect of *haktarah* without: one master holds [that] we learn within from without; while the other master holds that we do not learn [within from without].[4]

Raba observed: Seeing that the Rabbis do not learn without from without, can there be a question of [learning] within from without?[5] To what is this allusion?[6]—To what was taught: You might think that if one offers up [without] less than an olive of the fistful [of flour] or less than an olive of *emurim*, or if one makes libations of less than three *logs* of wine or less than three *logs* of water, he is liable: therefore it states, *'to sacrifice* [*do*]': one is liable for a complete [standard], but one is not liable for an incomplete one. Now, less than three *logs* nevertheless contains many olives,
c and yet the Rabbis do not learn without from without![1]—Rather said Raba: [The Mishnah applies to] where e.g., one appointed

(2) There is no blood to sprinkle in a meal-offering. (3) If the flesh is lost while the meal-offering is in existence, the blood must not be sprinkled.
a (1) So Sh.M. (2) Because it is not valid *within* unless the whole of it is offered. The Rabbis, however, hold that even if as much as an olive is offered within it is valid, provided that the whole of it was *available* for offering. (3) R. Eleazar agrees here, because this would have completed the offering within and made it valid. (4) Since offering them *within* would not have been valid. (5) I.e., he offers up the flesh, to which is attached the *emurim*. (6) On account of the *emurim*. (7) Emended text (Sh.M.). (8) A *peras* (half a *maneh*) of incense was offered twice daily, morning and evening. 'Half a *peras*' means any quantity less than a *peras*. (9) If a *zar* burns less than a *peras* within he is not liable, though only a priest is permitted to burn it. (10) V. Glos. Even with that quantity; and a *zar* who performs *haktarah* is liable. (11) They have fulfilled their obligation, though it was less than the standard quantity prescribed. (12) Why then is the community quit of its obligation? (13) All agree that the daily *haktarah* in the *Hekal* is fulfilled with as much as an olive, because Scripture does not prescribe a quantity for this, the standard of a *peras* being Rabbinical only. Consequently R. Eleazar admits that if one burns as much as an olive of this without, he is liable; and for the same reason the community is quit of its obligation when as much as an olive is burnt within. Hence the Baraitha, which refers to the daily *haktarah*, agrees with all.
b (1) On the Day of Atonement, which was done in the innermost sanctuary. There a definite quantity is prescribed, viz., *'his hands full'* (Lev. XVI, 12). (2) Not less, and the whole must be taken simultaneously. Hence less does not constitute *haktarah* on that occasion, and if one burns this without, he is not liable. (3) Ibid. 34: *And this shall be an everlasting* statute *unto you, to make atonement . . . once in the year. 'Statute'* intimates that everything which is so designated must be carried out *exactly* as prescribed; further, it applies to all the rites enumerated in the chapter which are performed only *'once in the year'*, and hence includes *haktarah* within. How then can anyone maintain that *'his hands full'* is not meant particularly? (4) Abaye too explains that the Baraitha treats of *haktarah* of the *Hekal*, while the Mishnah treats of *haktarah* within. But his premises and reasoning are different. Thus: all agree that a complete *haktarah*, viz., *'his hands full'* is indispensable within. They disagree where one burnt without the Temple as much as an olive of this incense that should have been burnt within, in the innermost sanctuary. One master holds that we learn within from without, i.e. the incense of the innermost sanctuary from the incense of the *Hekal:* just as one is liable for burning as much as an olive of the latter without, so is one liable for burning as much as an olive of the *former* without, although that same quantity burnt in its rightful place, *sc.* the innermost sanctuary, does not constitute *haktarah*. R. Eleazar, however, holds that we cannot make this inference, precisely because of the difference just noted. Hence when he burns it without he is not liable. (5) Surely they would not make such an inference. (6) Where do we find that they do not learn without from without?
c (1) They do not say that since as much as an olive of *incense* burnt without entails liability, the same measure of wine or water offered as a libation without entails liability, though both of these are 'without', i.e., they are rightly offered on the outer altar. The author of this must be the Rabbis, since R. Eleazar holds that one is not liable even when he burns as much as an olive without. (It should be noted that 'without' in the present passage is used with two different meanings: (i) outside the Temple court altogether, where all offering is forbidden; and (ii) the outer altar in the Temple court, where the daily incense is burnt and the drink-offerings are made.)

it [110a] in a vessel: one master holds that appointing in a vessel is an act that counts, while the other master holds that it is not an act that counts.[2]

Raba said: Now that we have said that there is a view that appointment through a vessel does not count, if one appointed six [*logs*] for a bullock[3] and removed four of them and offered them up without, he is liable, since they are fit for a ram.[4] If one appointed four [*logs*] for a ram and removed three of them and offered them up without, he is liable, since they are fit for a lamb. If they [the three *logs*] were slightly incomplete, he is not liable.[5]

a R. Ashi said: The Rabbis do not learn *nisuk*[1] from *haktarah*, though it is without from without; they do learn *haktarah* from *haktarah*, though it is within from without.[2]

IN THE CASE OF ALL OF THESE, IF THEY BECAME SLIGHTLY INCOMPLETE etc. It was asked: Does incompleteness without count as incompleteness, or does it not count as incompleteness?[3] Do we say, since it went out, it was disqualified; what is the difference then whether there is less or more?[4] Or perhaps, only when it goes out and is wholly existent [does it involve liability], but not when it is not wholly existent?—Said Abaye, Come and hear: R. ELEAZAR RULES THAT ONE IS NOT LIABLE UNLESS HE PRESENTS THE WHOLE OF THEM.[5] Rabbah son of R. Ḥanan objected to Abaye: Does the master solve it from R. Eleazar?[6]—I explicitly heard it from a master, he replied: the Rabbis disagree with R. Eleazar only when the whole of it is available; but if it is incomplete, they agree with him. Surely that means, [even] if it became incomplete without?—No: [only] when it became incomplete within.

Come and hear: IN THE CASE OF ALL OF THESE, IF THEY BECAME SLIGHTLY INCOMPLETE AND ONE OFFERED THEM WITHOUT, HE IS NOT LIABLE: does that not mean [even] where it became incomplete without?—No: [only] when it became incomplete within.

ONE WHO OFFERS SACRIFICES [etc.]. Why so? surely it interposes?[7]—Said Samuel: It means where he turns them over.[8] R. Joḥanan said: You may even say that he does not turn them over, but the author of this is R. Simeon who maintained: Even if one

b offers them up on a rock or on a stone, he is liable.[1] Rab said: One kind is not an interposition for the same kind.[2]

MISHNAH. IF THE FISTFUL OF A MEAL-OFFERING WAS

(2) Both the Mishnah and the Baraitha treat of *haktarah* of the *Hekal*, where Scripture does not prescribe a fixed quantity. Therefore the Baraitha teaches that he is liable, and R. Eleazar agrees, as Rab stated. The controversy in the Mishnah arises where one appointed the whole *peras* that was to be burnt (by Rabbinical law) for its purpose by placing it in a vessel. R. Eleazar holds that this appointment is a substantial act, in the sense that if the priest does not burn it *all* in the *Hekal* it is not *haktarah* and the community is not quit of its obligation. Therefore one is not liable for burning it without unless he burns the whole of it. The Rabbis, however, hold that this appointing does not count at all, and so it is the same as any other incense. (3) I.e., he put six *logs* of wine in a vessel, to be used for the drink-offering which accompanied the sacrifice of a bullock. (4) This measure would suffice for a ram, and so he is culpable. If, however, appointment in a vessel counted as a substantial act, he would not be liable unless he offered up the whole six *logs* without. (5) Because less than three *logs* are not fit for anything within.

a (1) The act of offering libations. (2) R. Ashi defends Abaye's explanation, and rebuts Raba's objection.—The text is emended. (3) If the full standard was taken without (whereby it was immediately disqualified for use within), and then some of it was lost before he offered it up: does it count as incomplete or not? (4) Since it is disqualified in any case, and yet one is liable for offering it without, he may also be liable when it becomes short without. (5) Thus even if it is taken out whole, there is no liability unless it is offered whole. (6) Surely not. For R. Eleazar holds that even if the whole is existent he is not liable unless he offers the whole, whereas the Rabbis hold that if the whole is existent one is liable when he offers as much as an olive. The question is asked on the view of the Rabbis. (7) The flesh interposes between the fire and the *emurim*, and such would not constitute proper offering up within, for the *emurim* must lie directly on the fire. (8) *Sc.* that the *emurim* lie on the fire.

b (1) If even a proper altar is not necessary, it is certainly not necessary for the *emurim* to lie directly on the fire. (2) Flesh is the same kind of matter as *emurim*, and therefore it does not count as an interposition.

◁ *For the continuation of the English translation of this page see overleaf.*

במנא מר סבר קביעות מנא מילתא היא ומר סבר לאו מילתא היא אמר רבא השתא [א] למאן דאמר קביעותא דמנא ולא כלום הוא קבע ששה לפר ומשך מהן ארבעה והקריבן בחוץ חייב [ב] שראויין לאיל קבע ארבעה לאיל ומשך מהן שלשה. והקריבן בחוץ חייב [ג] שראויין לכבש חסרו כל שהוא והקריבן בחוץ פטור רב אשי אמר ניסוך מהקטרה לא ילפי רבנן אף על גב דחוץ מחוץ [ד] לא ילפי הקטרה מהקטרה ילפי *אף על גב [ה] דחוץ מפנים: וכולן [ו] שחסרו: איבעיא להו [א]חסרון דחוץ שמיה חסרון או לא שמיה חסרון מי אמרינן כיון דנפק [ז] איפסלו להו מה לי חסר מה לי *יתר או דילמא יוצא דאיתיה בעיניה אין דליתיה בעיניה לא אמר אביי ת"ש ר' אליעזר פוטר עד שיקריב את כולן אמר ליה רבה בר רב חנן לאביי מדר' אליעזר פשיט מר אמר ליה בפירוש שמיע לי מיניה [ח] דרב עד כאן לא פליגי רבנן עליה דר' [ט] אליעזר אלא דאיתיה בעיניה אבל בחסרון מודו ליה לאו דחסר בחוץ לא דחסר בפנים ת"ש וכולן שחסרו [י] והקריבן בחוץ פטור לאו דחסר בחוץ לא דחסר בפנים: המקריב קדשים: אמאי והאיכא חציצה אמר שמואל כשהפכן ור' יוחנן אמר אפילו תימא שלא הפכן והא מני רבי שמעון היא דאמר *אפילו העלו על הסלע [יא] חייב רב אמר *מין במינו אינו חוצץ: **מתני'** [ב]מנחה שלא נקמצה והקריבה בחוץ פטור [ג]קמצה וחזר קומצה לתוכה [יב] והקריבו בחוץ חייב: **גמ'** [יג] ואמאי ליבטלי שירים לקומץ *אמר רבי זירא נאמרה הקטרה בקומץ ונאמרה הקטרה בשירים מה [יד] הקטרת קומץ אין קומץ מבטל חבירו אף הקטרת שירים אין שירים מבטלין קומץ: **מתני'** *[ד]הקומץ והלבונה שהקריב את אחד מהן בחוץ חייב ר' אליעזר פוטר עד שיקריב את השני [ה]אחד בפנים ואחד בחוץ חייב [ו]שני בזיכי לבונה שהקריב את אחד מהם בחוץ חייב ר' אליעזר פוטר עד שיקריב את השני [ז]אחד בפנים ואחד בחוץ חייב: **גמ'** בעי ר' יצחק נפחא קומץ מהו שיתיר כנגדו בשירים מישרא שרי או [טו] קלושי מיקלש אליבא דמאן אי אליבא *דרבי מאיר דאמר מפגלין בחצי מתיר מישרא שרי אי אליבא דרבנן דאמרי אין מפגלין בחצי מתיר לא מישרא שרי ולא [טז] מקלש קליש אלא אליבא דרבי אליעזר ר"א כרבנן סבירא ליה דאמר אין מפגלין בחצי מתיר (א) אלא אליבא דרבנן דהכא מאי מישרא שרי או [יז] קליש מקלש תיקו: **מתני'** [ח]*הזורק מקצת [יח] דם בחוץ חייב

וקסבר ר"א [יט] [קביעותא] דמנא מילתא הוא הואיל ונתן שני חלאי פרס בכלי [כ] הקטרת היכל קבעיה מנא ואי חסיר כל שהוא מיפסל הילכך בחוץ לא מיחייב עד שיקריב את כולו: ורבנן סברי. קביעותא דמנא לאו כלום היא: קבע ששה לוגין. דהוא חצי ההין לנסכי פר ונתנן בכלי ומשך ארבעה מהן והקריבן בחוץ חייב שהרי ראויין בפנים לאיל: פטור. דבציר משלשת לוגין לא חזו בפנים: רב אשי אמר. לעולם כדתרלה אביי דבהקטרה של פנים בחוץ פליגי ובמילף פנים מחוץ ודקא קשיא לך השתא חוץ מחוץ לא ילפי רבנן כו' לא דמי ניסוך להקטרה דניסוך מהקטרה לא ילפי רבנן ואע"ג דחוץ מחוץ אבל קטרת של פנים מקטרת של היכל ילפי ואע"ג דפנים מחוץ: חסרון דחוץ. הוציאן שלימים לחוץ וחסרו לאיבוד: שמיה חסרון. ואם העלה את המשוייר בחוץ פטור: או לא שמיה חסרון. וחייב לרבנן כאילו כולו קיים: איפסיל [כא] ליה. ואפי' הכי מיחייב עליה בחוץ ומה לי יוצא ומה לי חסרון: עד שיקריב [כב] כולו. אלמא כוליה בעינן: מדרבי [כג] אליעזר פשיט מר. בתמיה רבי אליעזר אפי' בכולו קיים נמי פטר ואנן לרבנן מיבעי לן דמחייבי בכולו קיים ומודו בשחסר בפנים: והאיכא חציצה. שהבשר [כד] אינו ראוי להקטרה חוצץ בין אימורין למערכה ודכוותיה בפנים לאו העלאה היא דרחמנא אמר (ויקרא א) על העצים אשר על האש וקס"ד דמתני' רבי יוסי היא דאמר אינו חייב עד שיעלה לראש המזבח כהקטרת פנים: כשהפכן. החלבים למטה: **מתני'** מנחה שלא נקמצה. לא חזי לפנים הילכך המקריבה בחוץ פטור: קמצה וחזר קומצה לתוכה והקריבה בחוץ חייב. שכיוצא בה בפנים כשירה כדתנן בהקומץ (מנחות דף כג.) נתערב קומצה בשיריה לא יקטיר ואם הקטיר עלתה לבעלים: **גמ'** וניבטלי שירים לקומץ. ברובא והוי כמאן דליתיה ולא ניחייב עליה ובמנחות (דף כג:) נמי פרכינן לה גבי הקטרת פנים: נאמר הקטרה בקומץ. וקמץ והקטיר (ויקרא ב): ונאמר הקטרה בשירים. לא תקטירו ממנו אשה לה' (שם) כל שממנו לאשים הרי הוא בבל תקטירו דהיינו שירים: אין קומץ מבטל קומץ. ואפי' רבה עליו כדאמרינן בהקומץ רבה (מנחות דף כג.) ולקח מדם הפר ומדם השעיר הדבר ידוע שדם הפר מרובה מדם השעיר מכאן לעולין שאין מבטלין זה את זה: **מתני'** הקומץ והלבונה. של מנחת נדבה שניהם מתירין את שיריה לאכילה הילכך רבי אליעזר פוטר דבעי הקטרת כל המתיר: אחד בפנים. תחילה ואחר כך השני בחוץ: חייב. שזה גמר ובו הכל תלוי: שני בזיכי לבונה. מתירין לחם הפנים דכתיב (ויקרא כד) והיתה ללחם לאזכרה ואמרינן נאמר כאן אזכרה ונאמר להלן אזכרה מה להלן קומץ מתיר את השירים אף הלבונה מתרת את הלחם ובשירי מנחה כתיב (ויקרא ו) יאכלו אהרן ובניו קדש קדשים מאשי ה' אין [כה] לנו אלא לאחר מתנות האשים: **גמ'** מהו שיתיר כנגדו בשירים. הקטיר קומץ לבדו על מנת להתיר חצי השירים [כו] ובורר לחלקן מהו לאוכלן: מישרא שרי. פלגא לגמרי: או אקלושי מקליש. לאיסורא דכולהו שירים [כז] וקומץ ולבונה תרווייהו אכולהו שיריים *דמו וכי מקטיר לחד מקליש ליה איסורייהו ומיהו לא אישתרי מידי מינייהו לגמרי: פלוגתא דרבי מאיר ורבנן במנחות בהקומץ זוטא (דף טז.): מפגלין בחצי מתיר. פיגל בקומץ[כח] או בלבונה שהקטיר קומץ ע"מ לאכול זית מן השירים חוץ לזמנו פיגול: מישרא שרי. דאי כי מקטיר ליה בשתיקה לא שרי כזית מינייהו לגמרי היכי הויא מחשבה בההוא זית הא דומיא דזריקה בעינן דשרי לגמרי: לא מישרא שרי כו'. כלומר דילמא לא הא ולא הא והיכי פשיטא ליה לר' יצחק נפחא דלאו הא או הא עביד: אלא אליבא דר"א. קמיבעיא דאמר לא מחייב עלה לחודיה בחוץ ומשום הכי מספקא ליה לרבי יצחק דילמא שרי: ר"א כרבנן ס"ל. ולא שריא ולא מיקלש לשון קושיא הוא אמאי פשיטא ליה אליביה דלאו הא או הא והא ר"א מדקאמר לאו הקטרה הוא כרבנן דפליגי עליה דר"מ סבירא ליה: אלא אליבא דרבנן דהכא. דמחייבי אחד מינייהו אלמא הקטרה היא בפנים וקא מיבעי ליה למאי הילכתא הויא הקטרה למישרי פלגא או לאקלושי והכא ליכא למיפשט מדמחייבי עלה בחוץ ש"מ מישרא שרי דאי נמי לאקלושי אתיא הויא הקטרה לחיובי בחוץ עלה: **מתני'** הזורק מקצת דמים. כגון מתנה אחת ואפילו מחטאות הפנימיות שכל מתנותיהן מעכבות: חייב

אבל בחסרון מודו ליה. ומסיק בחסרו מבפנים ותימה מאי קא משמע לן תנינא לעיל (דף קט:) וכולן שחסרו כל שהוא פ' וכל הפחות היינו חסרו מבפנים: **אמר** שמואל כשהפכן. וכי תימא מאי קמ"ל סד"א דאין דרך הקטרה בכך:

מין במינו אינו חוצץ. והא דאמרינן לעיל (דף טו:) גבי רגל חבירו פסול °אין דרך שירות בכך:

קומץ מהו שיתיר כנגדו בשירים. פירש בקונטרס דהקטיר קומץ לבדו על מנת להתיר חצי השירים ובוררן לחלקן מהו לאוכלן מישרא שרי פלגא לגמרי או אקלושי מקלש לאיסורא דכולהו שירים וקומץ ולבונה תרווייהו אכולהו שירים *דמו וכי מקטיר חד איקליש ליה איסורייהו ומיהו לא אישתרי מידי מינייהו לגמרי עכ"ל והא דתנן בהקומץ רבה (מנחות דף כז.) הקומץ והלבונה מעכבין זה את זה היינו דבעי שיהו שניהם דלא לייתי מנחה בלא לבונה ובעי קמילה ומכל מקום תימה דאפילו למאן דאמר [כט] *מישרא שרי לה היאך מתברר חלקו של קומץ ונראה לפרש דלאו לאשתרויי באכילה קאמר אלא דאי משרא שרי פלגא אידך פלגא באיסור' קיימא ואי אכיל לה לקי כמו אוכל בשר חטאת ואשם קודם זריקה ואי איקלושי מקליש לכולה מנחה לא לקי כלל אי נמי לענין מעילה וכי האי גוונא בנדרים בפרק נערה (דף סח.) בעל מיגז גייז או אקלושי מיקליש כגון דנדרה מן תרין זיתין ושמע ארוס והפר לה ואכלתינון אי אמר מיגז גייז לקיא אי אמר מקלש קליש איסורא בעלמא הוא: **ואי** אליבא דר"מ דאמר מפגלין בחצי מתיר. הך סוגיא דלא כרים לקיש דאמר לעיל בפרק בית שמאי (דף מא:) טעמא דרבי מאיר משום דכל העושה על דעתו ראשונה הוא עושה ול"ע אי שחט סימן אחד *וקבל אחד דמו וזרקו כיון דחשיב חצי מתיר אי אמרינן מישרא שרי ומיהו הא פשיטא אי לא גמר אחר כך שחיטתו לא שרי: ומודה

לט א מיי' פי"ט מהל' מעה"ק הל"ט והדבר ספק:
מ ב ג מיי' שם הל"ס:
מא ד ה ו ז מיי' שם הל"ד:
מב (ז מיי' פס"ז מהל' פסה"מ הל"ח):
מג ח מיי' פי"ט מהל' מעה"ק הל"ג:

נ"ל דמו נ"ק

נ"א יוצא

נ"א יש ברירה היאך מתברר כו' נ"ק וע"ש

הגהות הב"ח
(א) גמ' ר"א כרבנן וכו' חצי מתיר ולא שרי ולא מקלש אלא אליבא דרבנן:

גליון הש"ס
תוס' ד"ה מין וכו' אין דרך שירות בכך. עיין יומא דף נח ע"א:

נ"ל וקבל את דמו נ"ק

שיטה מקובצת
א] השתא דאמרי' למאן: ב] חייב שהרי ראויין לאיל: ג] חייב שהרי ראויין לכבש: ד] תיבות לא ילפי נמחק: ה] אע"ג דפנים מחוץ: ו] שהקריבן כו' ותיבת שחסרו ל"ש: ז] דנפק איפסל להו מה לי פסול יוצא מה לי פסול חסרון או דלמא: ח] מיניה דמר עד כאן ותיבת דרב נמחק: ט] דר' אלעזר וכצ"ל לקמן: י] שחסרו כל שהוא והקריבן: יא] הסלע או על האבן חייב: יב] לתוכה והקריבה בחוץ: יג] וניבטלו שיריים תיבת ואמאי ואות ל' נמחק: יד] מה הקטרה האמורה בקומץ אין קומץ כו' אף הקטרה האמורה בשיריים אין שיריים מבטלין את הקומץ: טו] או אקלושי מיקלש: טז] ולא אקלושי מיקלש: יז] או אקלושי מיקלש: יח] מקצת דמים בחוץ: יט] ר"א קביעותא דמנא: כ] בכלי הקטרת היכל קבעי מנא: כא] איפסל להו ואפי' תיבת ליה נמחק: כב] שיקריב את כולן: כג] מדר' אלעזר וכצ"ל לקמן: כד] שאינו ראוי: כה] אין להם אלא ותיבת לנו נמחק: כו] ובירר לחלקן: כז] שיריים דקומץ ולבונה כו' שיריים דמו וכי: כח] בקומץ ולא בלבנה ותיבת או ל"ש: כט] דאמר יש ברירה האך תיבות משרא שרי לה ל"ש:

[מנחות כג:] [לעיל קח.] [סוכה לז. ע"ש בכורות כט:] [מנחות כג.] [פסחים סא. וש"נ] [לעיל קח.] [מנחות יב: לעיל קי.]

[מהרש"א גורס היה בגמרא ואע"ג דפנים מחוץ ועיין משנה למלך פי"ט מהל' מעה"ק ד"ה ומ"ש. כנראה שגרסתו היתה כמו שהוא לפנינו וע"ש]

Continuation of translation from previous page as indicated by ◁

NOT [YET] TAKEN, AND ONE OFFERED IT WITHOUT, HE IS NOT LIABLE.[3] IF ONE TOOK OFF THE FISTFUL, THEN REPLACED THE FISTFUL WITHIN IT, AND OFFERED IT WITHOUT, HE IS LIABLE.[4]

GEMARA. But why so? let the remainder nullify the fistful?[5]—Said R. Zera: *Haḳtarah* is stated in connection with the fistful, and *haḳtarah* is stated in connection with the remainder:[6] as in the case of the *haḳtarah* stated in connection with the fistful, one fistful does not nullify another;[7] so in the case of *haḳtarah* stated in connection with the remainder, the remainder does not nullify the fistful.

MISHNAH. AS FOR THE FISTFUL AND THE FRANKINCENSE, IF ONE OFFERED ONE OF THEM WITHOUT, HE IS LIABLE; R. ELIEZER RULES THAT HE IS NOT LIABLE UNLESS HE OFFERS THE SECOND [TOO].[8] [IF ONE OFFERED] ONE
c WITHIN AND THE OTHER WITHOUT,[1] HE IS LIABLE.[2] AS FOR THE TWO DISHES OF FRANKINCENSE,[3] IF ONE OFFERED ONE OF THEM WITHOUT, HE IS LIABLE; R. ELIEZER RULES THAT HE IS NOT LIABLE UNLESS HE OFFERS THE SECOND [TOO]. [IF ONE OFFERED] ONE WITHIN AND THE OTHER WITHOUT, HE IS LIABLE.

GEMARA. R. Isaac Nappaḥa[4] asked: Can the fistful permit a proportionate quantity of the remainder?[5] does it [the fistful] indeed permit, or does it merely weaken [the prohibition]?[6]—On whose view [is this question asked]? if on the view of R. Meir, who maintained, You can render a sacrifice *piggul* through half of the *mattir*,[7] it indeed permits it;[8] and if on the view of the Rabbis who maintained that you cannot render a sacrifice *piggul* through half of the *mattir*, it may neither permit nor weaken it?[9]—Rather, [the question is asked] on the view of R. Eliezer.[10] But R. Eliezer agrees with the Rabbis?[11]—Rather, [the question is asked] on the
d view of the Rabbis here:[1] does it permit, or does it weaken?[2] The question stands over.

MISHNAH. IF ONE SPRINKLES PART OF THE BLOOD

(3) Because in that state it is not fit for offering within either. (4) Because in that case, if it is offered within, it is valid; Men. 23*a*. (5) Hence he should not be liable. (6) Lev. II, 2: *And he shall take thereout his handful . . . and . . . shall make (it) smoke (we-hiḳtir)*. Ibid. 11: *No meal-offering . . . shall be made with leaven, for ye shall make no leaven, nor any honey, smoke* (lo taḳtiru) *as an offering made by fire unto the Lord*. This is interpreted to mean that one must not burn (*haḳtarah*) any portion of the meal-offering whereof part is to be *'an offering made by fire;'* hence it applies to the remainder, as part thereof (viz., the fistful) has been taken as *'an offering made by fire'*. (7) Even if it exceeds it. (8) Both must normally be offered before the remainder may be eaten (in the case of a votive meal-offering, to which this refers). Hence the two together are the *mattir* (v. Glos.), and R. Eliezer holds that one is liable only when he offers without the *whole mattir*.

c (1) In this order. (2) Because the second completes it, and had it been offered within, it would have permitted the consumption of the remainder. (3) The burning of which permitted the eating of the Shewbread. (4) Or, the smith. (5) V. *supra* n. b 6. If one burned the fistful alone, stating that this was to permit *part* of the remainder (which he determined beforehand), while the other part was to be permitted by the frankincense, is the first part thus permitted? (6) Does the fistful *completely* permit *part*, in which case this part is now permitted; or does it merely *weaken* the prohibition of the whole, while the frankincense finally removes it? in that case it will still be forbidden. (7) If the priest declares a *piggul* intention at the burning of *either* the fistful *or* the frankincense, the offering is *piggul*. (8) For a sacrifice can be rendered *piggul* only through a rite which *completely* permits it (or at least, a portion thereof), just as sprinkling *completely* permits an animal sacrifice. R. Meir then must certainly hold that the burning of the fistful permits part of the remainder. (9) There is no proof that on their view the burning of the fistful either permits part or even weakens the prohibition of the whole. (10) In our Mishnah: since he rules that one is not liable for burning that alone without, it may be that he holds that it permits part only. (11) *Sc.* those who disagree with R. Meir.—I.e., the same difficulty that arises on the view of the Rabbis, *sc.* that they may hold that it neither permits nor weakens, arises on the view of R. Eliezer.

d (1) In our Mishnah. (2) Since they maintain that one is liable for burning the fistful alone without, they must regard the same within as a proper *haḳtarah*, even without the frankincense. Hence the question, in respect of what is it *haḳtarah*: is it in respect of permitting part, or in respect of weakening the whole?

במנא מר סבר קביעות מנא מילתא היא ומר סבר לאו מילתא היא אמר רבא השתא א] למאן דאמר קביעותא דמנא ולא כלום הוא קבע ששה לפר ומשך מהן ארבעה והקריבן בחוץ חייב ב] שראויין לאיל קבע ארבעה לאיל ומשך מהן שלשה. והקריבן בחוץ חייב ג] שראויין לכבש חסרו כל שהוא והקריבן בחוץ פטור רב אשי אמר ניסוך מהקטרה לא ילפי רבנן אף על גב דחוץ מחוץ ד] לא ילפי הקטרה מהקטרה ילפי *אף על גב ה] דחוץ מפנים: וכולן ו] שחסרו: איבעיא להו [א]חסרון דחוץ שמיה חסרון או לא שמיה חסרון מי אמרינן כיון דנפק ז] איפסלו להו מה לי חסר מה לי *יתר או דילמא יוצא דאיתיה בעיניה אין דליתיה בעיניה לא אמר אביי ת"ש ר' אליעזר פוטר עד שיקריב את כולן אמר ליה רבה בר רב חנן לאביי מדר' אליעזר פשיט מר אמר ליה בפירוש שמיע לי מיניה ח] דרב עד כאן לא פליגי רבנן עליה דר' ט] אליעזר אלא דאיתיה בעיניה אבל בחסרון מודו ליה לאו דחסר בחוץ לא דחסר בפנים ת"ש וכולן שחסרו י] והקריבן בחוץ פטור לאו דחסר בחוץ לא דחסר בפנים: המקריב קדשים: אמאי והאיכא חציצה אמר שמואל כשהפכן ור' יוחנן אמר אפילו תימא שלא הפכן והא מני רבי שמעון היא דאמר *אפילו העלו על הסלע יא] חייב רב אמר *מין במינו אינו חוצץ: **מתני'** [ב]מנחה שלא נקמצה והקריבה בחוץ פטור [ג]קמצה וחזר קומצה לתוכה יב] והקריבו בחוץ חייב: **גמ'** יג] ואמאי ליבטלי שירים לקומץ *אמר רבי זירא נאמרה הקטרה בקומץ ונאמרה הקטרה בשירים מה יד] הקטרת קומץ אין קומץ מבטל חבירו אף הקטרת שירים אין שירים מבטלין קומץ: **מתני'** *[ד]הקומץ והלבונה שהקריב את אחד מהן בחוץ חייב ר' אליעזר פוטר עד שיקריב את השני [ה]אחד בפנים ואחד בחוץ חייב [ו]שני בזיכי לבונה שהקריב את אחד מהם בחוץ חייב ר' אליעזר פוטר עד שיקריב את השני [ז]אחד בפנים ואחד בחוץ חייב: **גמ'** בעי ר' יצחק נפחא קומץ מהו שיתיר כנגדו בשירים מישרא שרי או טו] קלושי מיקלש אליבא דמאן אי אליבא *דרבי מאיר דאמר מפגלין בחצי מתיר מישרא שרי אי אליבא דרבנן דאמרי אין מפגלין בחצי מתיר לא מישרא שרי ולא טז] מקלש קליש אלא אליבא דרבי אליעזר ר"א כרבנן סבירא ליה דאמר אין מפגלין בחצי מתיר (א) אלא אליבא דרבנן דהכא מאי מישרא שרי או יז] קליש מקלש תיקו: **מתני'** [ח]*הזורק מקצת יח] דם בחוץ חייב

וקסבר ר"א יט] [קביעותא] דמנא מילתא הוא הואיל ונתן שני חלאי פרס בכלי כ] הקטרת היכל קבעיה מנא ואי חסיר כל שהוא מיפסל הילכך בחוץ לא מיחייב עד שיקריב את כולו: ורבנן סברי. קביעותא דמנא לאו כלום היא: קבע ששה לוגין. דהוא חצי ההין לנסכי פר ונתנן בכלי ומשך ארבעה מהן והקריבן בחוץ חייב שהרי ראויין בפנים לאיל: פטור. דבציר משלשת לוגין לא חזו בפנים: רב אשי אמר. לעולם כדתרלה אביי דבהקטרה של פנים בחוץ פליגי ובמילף פנים מחוץ ודקא קשיא לך השתא חוץ מחוץ לא ילפי רבנן כו' לא דמי ניסוך להקטרה דניסוך מהקטרה לא ילפי רבנן ואע"ג דחוץ מחוץ אבל קטרת של פנים מקטרת של היכל ילפי ואע"ג דפנים מחוץ: חסרון דחוץ. הוציאן שלימים לחוץ וחסרו לאיבוד: שמיה חסרון. ואם העלה את המשוייר בחוץ פטור: או לא שמיה חסרון. וחייב לרבנן כאילו כולו קיים: איפסיל כא] ליה. ואפי' הכי מיחייב עליה בחוץ ומה לי יוצא ומה לי חסרון: עד שיקריב כב]כולו. אלמא כוליה בעינן: מדרבי כג] אליעזר פשיט מר. בתמיה רבי אליעזר אפי' בכולו קיים נמי פטר ואנן לרבנן מיבעי לן דמחייבי בכולו קיים ומודו בשחסר בפנים: והאיכא חלילה. שהבשר כד] אינו ראוי להקטרה חולץ בין אימורין למערכה ודכוותיה בפנים לאו העלאה היא דרחמנא אמר (ויקרא א) על העלים אשר על האש וקס"ד דמתני' רבי יוסי היא דאמר אינו חייב עד שיעלה לראש המזבח כהקטרת פנים: כשהפכן. החלבים למטה: **מתני'** מנחה שלא נקמצה. לא חזי לפנים הילכך המקריבה בחוץ פטור: קמצה וחזר קומצה לתוכה והקריבה בחוץ חייב. שכיוצא בה בפנים כשירה כדתנן בהקומץ (מנחות דף כג.) נתערב קומצה בשיריה לא יקטיר ואם הקטיר עלתה לבעלים: **גמ'** וניבטלי שירים לקומץ. ברובא והוי כמאן דליתיה ולא ניחייב עליה ובמנחות (דף כג:) כמי פרכינן לה גבי הקטרת פנים: נאמר הקטרה בקומץ. וקמץ והקטיר (ויקרא ב): ונאמר הקטרה בשירים. לא תקטירו ממנו אשה לה' (שם) כל שממנו לאשים הרי הוא בבל תקטירו דהייתו שירים: אין קומץ מבטל קומץ. ואפי' רבה עליו כדאמרינן בהקומץ רבה (מנחות דף כב.) ולקח מדם הפר ומדם השעיר הדבר ידוע שדם הפר מרובה מדם השעיר מכאן לעולין שאין מבטלין זה את זה: **מתני'** הקומץ והלבונה. של מנחת נדבה שניהם מתירין את שיריה לאכילה הילכך רבי אליעזר פוטר דבעי הקטרת כל המתיר: אחד בפנים. תחילה ואחר כך השני בחוץ: חייב. שזה גמר ובו הכל תלוי: שני בזיכי לבונה. מתירין לחם הפנים דכתיב (ויקרא כד) והיתה ללחם לאזכרה ואמרינן נאמר כאן אזכרה ונאמר להלן אזכרה מה להלן קומץ מתיר את השירים אף הלבונה מתרת את הלחם ובשירי מנחה כתיב (ויקרא ו) יאכלו אהרן ובניו קדש קדשים מאשי ה' אין כה] לנו אלא לאחר מתנות האשים: **גמ'** מהו שיתיר כנגדו בשירים. הקטיר קומץ לבדו על מנת להתיר חצי השירים כו] ובורכן לחלקן מהו. לאוכלן: מישרא שרי. פלגא לגמרי: או אקלושי מקלים. לאיסורא דכולהו שירים כז] וקומץ ולבונה תרוייהו אכולהו שיריים *דמו וכי מקטיר לחד מקלים ליה איסורייהו ומיהו לא אישתרי מידי מינייהו לגמרי: פלוגתא דרבי מאיר ורבנן במנחות בהקומץ זוטא (דף טז.): מפגלין בחצי מתיר. פיגל בקומץ כח] או בלבונה שהקטיר קומץ ע"מ לאכול זית מן השירים חוץ לזמנו פיגול: מישרא שרי. דאי כי מקטיר ליה בשתיקה לא שרי כזית מינייהו לגמרי היכי הויא מחשבה בההוא זית הא דומיא דזריקה בעינן דשרי לגמרי: לא מישרא שרי כו'. כלומר דילמא לא הא ולא הא והיכי פשיטא ליה לר' יצחק נפחא דלאו הא או הא עביד: אלא אליבא דר"א. קמיבעיא דאמר לא מחייב עלה לחודיה בחוץ ומשום הכי מספקא ליה לרבי יצחק דילמא שרי: ר"א כרבנן ס"ל. ולא שריא ולא מיקלש לשון קושיא הוא אמאי פשיטא ליה אליביה דלאו הא או הא והא ר"א מדקאמר לאו הקטרה הוא כרבנן דפליגי עליה דר"מ סבירא ליה: אלא אליבא דרבנן דהכא. דמחייבי אחד מינייהו אלמא הקטרה היא בפנים וקא מיבעי ליה למאי הילכתא הויא הקטרה למישרי פלגא או לאקלושי והכא ליכא למיפשט מדמחייבי עלה בחוץ ש"מ מישרא שרי דאי נמי לאקלושי אתיא הויא הקטרה לחובי בחוץ עלה: **מתני'** הזורק מקצת דמים. כגון מתנה אחת ואפילו מחטאות הפנימיות שכל מתנותיהן מעכבות

אבל בחסרון מודו ליה. ומסיק בחסרו מבפנים ותימה מאי קא משמע לן תנינא לעיל (דף קט:) וכולן שחסרו כל שהוא כו' וכל הפחות היינו חסרו מבפנים: **אמר** שמואל כשהפכן. וכי תימא מאי קמ"ל סד"א דאין דרך הקטרה בכך:

מין במינו אינו חוצץ. והא דאמרינן לעיל (דף טו:) גבי רגל חבירו פסול °אין דרך שירות בכך:

קומץ מהו שיתיר כנגדו בשירים. פירש בקונטרס דהקטיר קומץ לבדו על מנת להתיר חצי השירים ובורכן לחלקן מהו לאוכלן מישרא שרי פלגא לגמרי או אקלושי מקלש לאיסורא דכולהו שירים וקומץ ולבונה תרוייהו אכולהו שירים *דמו וכי מקטיר חד איקליש ליה איסורייהו ומיהו לא אישתרי מידי מינייהו לגמרי עכ"ל והא דתנן בהקומץ רבה (מנחות דף כז.) הקומץ והלבונה מעכבין זה את זה היינו דבעי שיהו שניהם דלא לייתי מנחה בלא לבונה ובעי קמילה ומכל מקום תימה דאפילו למאן דאמר כט] *מישרא שרי לה היאך מתברר חלקו של קומץ ונראה לפרש דלאו לאשתרויי באכילה קאמר אלא דאי משרא שרי פלגא אידך פלגא באיסור' קיימא ואי אכיל לה לקי כמו אוכל בשר חטאת ואשם קודם זריקה ואי איקלושי מקליש לכולה מנחה לא לקי כלל אי נמי לענין מעילה וכי האי גוונא בנדרים בפרק נערה (דף סח.) בעל מיגז גייז או אקלושי מיקליש כגון דנדרה מן תרין זיתין ושמע ארוס והפר לה ואכלתינון אי אמר מיגז גייז לקיא אי אמר מקלש קליש איסורא בעלמא הוא: **ואי** אליבא דר"מ דאמר מפגלין בחצי מתיר. הך סוגיא דלא כרים לקיש דאמר לעיל בפרק בית שמאי (דף מא:) טעמא דרבי מאיר משום דכל העושה על דעתו ראשונה הוא עושה ול"ע אי שחט סימן אחד *וקבל אחד דמו וזרקו כיון דחשיב חצי מתיר אי אמרינן מישרא שרי ומיהו הא פשיטא אי לא גמר אחר כך שחיטתו לא שרי:

לט א מיי' פי"ט מהל' מעשה"ק הל"ט והדבר ספק:
מ ב ג מיי' שם הל"ט:
מא ד ה ו ז מיי' שם הל"ד:
מב (ז מיי' פט"ז מהל' פסה"מ הל"ח):
מג ח מיי' פי"ט מהל' מעשה"ק הל"ג:

נ"ל רמו ז"ק

כ"א יוצא

כ"א יש גריסה היאך מתברר כו' ז"ק וע"ש

הגהות הב"ח

(א) גמ' ר"א כרבנן וכו' :חצי מתיר ולא שרי ולא מקלש אלא אליבא דרבנן:

גליון הש"ס

תוס' ד"ה מין וכו' אין דרך שירות בכך. עיין יומא דף נח ע"א:

נ"ל וקבל את דמו ז"ק

שיטה מקובצת

א] השתא דאמרי' למאן: ב] חייב שהרי ראויין לאיל: ג] חייב שהרי ראויין לכבש: ד] תיבות לא ילפי נמחק: ה] אע"ג דפנים מחוץ: ו] שהקריבן כו' ותיבת שחסרו ל"ש: ז] דנפק איפסל להו מה לי פסול יוצא מה לי פסול חסרון או דלמא: ח] מיניה דמר עד כאן ותיבת דרב נמחק: ט] דר' אלעזר וכצ"ל לקמן: י] שחסרו כל שהוא והקריבן: יא] הסלע או על האבן חייב: יב] לתוכה והקריבה בחוץ: יג] וניבטלו שיריים תיבת ואמאי ואות ל' נמחק: יד] מה הקטרה האמורה בקומץ אין קומץ כו' אף הקטרה האמורה בשיריים אין שיריים מבטלין את הקומץ: טו] או אקלושי מיקלש: טז] ולא אקלושי מיקלש: יז] או אקלושי מיקלש: יח] מקצת דמים בחוץ: יט] ר"א קביעותא דמנא: כ] בכלי הקטרת היכל קבעי מנא: כא] איפסל להו ואפי' תיבת ליה נמחק: כב] שיקריב את כולן: כג] מדר' אלעזר וכצ"ל לקמן: כד] שאינו ראוי: כה] אין להם אלא ותיבת לנו נמחק: כו] וביררן לחלקן: כז] שיריים דקומץ ולבונה כו' שיריים דמו וכי: כח] בקומץ ולא בלבונה ותיבת או ל"ש: כט] דאמר יש ברירה היאך תיבות משרא שרי לא ל"ש:

[מרש"י נראה שגרסתו היתה בגמרא ואע"ג דפנים מחוץ ועיין משנה למלך פי"ט מהל' מעה"ק ד"ה ומ"ש. נראה שגרסתו היתה כמו שהוא לפנינו וע"ש]

[לעיל קח.]

[סוכה לז: ע"ש בכורות ט:]

[מנחות כג:]

מנחות יב: לעיל קז.

[פסחים סא. וש"נ]

[לעיל קי.]

חייב ר"א אומר [א]אף *המנסך מי החג בחג בחוץ חייב רבי *נחמיה אומר שירי הדם שהקריבו בחוץ חייב: **גמ'** [ב]אמר רבא ומודה רבי אלעזר בדמים *דתניא *רבי אלעזר ורבי שמעון אומרים ממקום שפסק הוא מתחיל: רבי אלעזר אומר אף המנסך מי החג [בחג בחוץ [א]]: א"ר יוחנן משום רבי *מנחם יודפאה רבי אלעזר בשטת רבי עקיבא רבו אמרה דאמר ניסוך המים דאורייתא דתניא *רבי עקיבא אומר °ונסכיה בשני ניסוכים הכתוב מדבר אחד ניסוך המים ואחד ניסוך היין אמר ליה ריש לקיש לר' יוחנן אי מה להלן שלשת לוגין אף כאן שלשת לוגין והא ר"א מי החג קאמר אי מה להלן בשאר ימות השנה אף כאן בשאר ימות השנה [ור"א] בחג קאמר אישתמיטתיה הא דאמר רבי אסי [ג] *דאמר רבי אסי אמר רבי יוחנן משום רבי נחוניא איש בקעת בית חורתן [ד]עשר נטיעות [ה]ערבה [ו]וניסוך המים הלכה למשה מסיני תנו רבנן [ז]המנסך שלשת לוגין מים בחג בחוץ חייב ר"א (בר"ש) אומר [ג] אם מלאן לשם חג חייב(א) מאי בינייהו אמר רב נחמן בר יצחק ביש שיעור במים קמיפלגי רב פפא אמר בקרבו

במדבר כט לא

רש"י

חייב. לרבנן דלא בעו כולו מתיר ורבי אלעזר נמי מודה בה כדאמרינן בגמרא: מי החג. שהמלאו לשם ניסוך המים בחג הסוכות: שירי הדם. של חטאות הטעונין שפיכה ליסוד [ד] שהקריב בחוץ חייב דקסבר שירים מעכבין הילכך מתקבלים בפנים וזריקה גמורה הן: **גמ'** מודה ר' אלעזר בדמים. ואפי' בחטאות הפנימיות דהא בפנים אם נשפך הדם אחר שנתן מתנה אחת מביא הך דיהבה ומביא פר אחר ומתחיל ממקום שפסק: דתנן כו'. במסכת יומא בהוציאו לו (דף ס.): יודפאה. דמן יודפת*: ניסוך המים דאורייתא. הילכך בחוץ נמי מיחייב עלה: אמר ליה ריש לקיש. אי רבי אלעזר מההוא קרא יליף [ה] ובההוא קרא מים ויין איתקוש אלמא שלשת לוגין בעינן כנסכי יין של עולת התמיד: והא ר' אלעזר מי החג קאמר. ואפילו פחות משלשת לוגין דאיכא למאן דאמר סוכה (דף מח.) בלוג *היה מנסך: בחג קאמר. בלשון קושיא גרסינן ליה: אישתמיטתיה. למנחם יודפאה: הא דא"ר יוחנן כו'. אלמא לכולי עלמא דאורייתא הוא הילכך איכא למ"ד בלוג גמירי לה או אין להם שיעור: [מאי בינייהו]. במאי קמיפלגי ומאי קא אתי רבי אלעזר למימר: ביש שיעור למים. דקאמר תנא קמא המנסך שלשת לוגין חייב והוא הדין [ו] יותר משלשת לוגין דיש בכלל מאתים מנה ואף על גב דמליניהו בכלי גדול קדשינהו כלי דאין שיעור למי החג למעלה ואתא רבי אלעזר למימר והוא שמילאן לשם חג כדרך מילואן דהיינו שלשת לוגין ותו לא כדתנן (שם) צלוחית של זהב מחזקת שלשת לוגין ממלא מן השילוח אבל אי הוי טפי לא קדשינהו כלי דלא חזו ליה דיש שיעור למים ואין כלי שרת מקדשין אלא הראוי להם:

בקרבו

תוספות

ומודה רבי אלעזר בדמים. תימה מאי קמ"ל רבא מתניתין היא דהא תנן רבי אלעזר אומר אף המנסך כו' שמע מינה דמודה ברישא וי"ל דסלקא דעתך דרבי אלעזר קאי אהנהו דלעיל ולא אמקבל דמים ועוד י"ל דמתניתין איכא לאוקומי בדמים החיצונים דבמתנה אחת כיפר ואתא רבא לאשמועינן דאפילו בפנימיים דכל מתנות מעכבות אפ"ה מודה ר"א דחייב על מקבל בחוץ *דתניא ר"א אומר ממקום שפסק הוא מתחיל ולעיל נמי בפרק בית שמאי (דף מב.) דאמר והאמר רבא מודה ר"א בדמים גבי חטאות פנימיות מייתי לה: **אי** מה להלן בשאר ימות השנה אף כאן בשאר ימות השנה. תימה דהא רבי עקיבא מודה דאין ניסוך המים אלא בחג ויש ספרים דגרסי הסך נסך בשני ניסוכים וההוא קרא בתמיד כתיב וליתא דר' נתן גרים הכי בריש מסכת תענית (דף ג.) ואפילו לרבי נתן נמי לא מישתמיט תנא דלימא ניסוך המים כל השנה כולה ואמר רבינו תם דמלא בספרים ישנים אי מה להלן בשאר ימות החג לא דלרבי עקיבא לא רמזה אלא בששי ואמרינן במסכת תענית (שם) אלא הך דתנן ניסוך המים כל שבעה מני אי רבי עקיבא האמר בששי מזכיר תרי יומי הוו ורבי אלעזר בחג קאמר משמע כל ימות החג ונראה שפיר ליישב גרסת הספרים דאף על גב דאין ניסוך המים אלא בחג מכל מקום חייבין עליו בחוץ כל השנה כדאשכחן בשמעתין למאן דאמר קרבו נסכים במדבר דמחייב בלא כלי שרת אע"ג דאין מתקבל בפנים הואיל ובשעת היתר הבמות קריבים בלא קדושת כלי וכדאמרינן לעיל (דף קח:) במעלה על גבי הסלע דמשום דהויא הקטרה בבמת יחיד מחייב עליו בחוץ בשעת איסור הבמות ומיהו לא דמי דאין לך מחוסר זמן גדול מזה וכיון דהשתא לא חזו בפנים היכי מיחייב ואמרינן ביומא בריש פרק שני שעירי (דף סג:) שלמים ששחטן בחוץ קודם שיפתחו דלתות ההיכל פטור מ"ט מחוסר פתיחה כמחוסר *מעשה דמי וא"ת ומאי שנא נסכים בכלי חול מקבלת דם בכלי חול דאמר רבא לעיל דקבלה בכלי חול לרבי פטור ויש לומר דלא דמי לקבלה בכלי חול בפנים חרק בחוץ אין לנו לחייב מחמת דכשר בבמה הואיל וכבר נפסל בפנים ולא דמי לנסכים שמקריבין בחוץ בכלי חול דלא נפסלו בפנים: **אישתמיטתיה** כו'. פי' בקונטרס למנחם יודפאה ותימה דהא רבי יוחנן אמרן לתרוייהו ושמא לבתר הכי שמעה רבי יוחנן *וי"ל דאישתמיטתיה לריש לקיש דאי הוה שמעה לא היה מקשה כלום דהוי מצי לפרושי בשיטת רבי עקיבא רבו אמרה דאמר ניסוך המים דאורייתא ולאו מטעמיה *ולפי זה משמע דאיכא למאן דאמר ניסוך המים דרבנן והוא תימה דאפילו למאן דאמר (מנחות דף קו.) חולין בעזרה לאו דאורייתא שתקנו חכמים לנסך חולין בעזרה *שמא לפי שהוא אז זמן גשמים כדי שיזכרו לפני המקום להברך במי גשמים *וקלא משמע בריש לולב וערבה (סוכה דף מד.) דריש לקיש הוה ידע להא דר' יוחנן דעשר נטיעות ערבה וניסוך המים גבי הא דאמר ריש לקיש התם כהנים בעלי מומין היו נכנסים בין האולם ולמזבח כדי לצאת בערבה ושמא נהי דשמיע ליה ערבה ניסוך המים לא שמיע ליה ומיהו לא יתכן פי' זה לפי' הקונטרס במעילה פרק ולד חטאת (דף יג:) דתנן התם נתנן לצלוחית מועלין בהן אמר ריש לקיש אין מועלין אלא בשלשת לוגין ורבי יוחנן אמר מועלין בכולן ופריך למימרא דקסבר ריש לקיש יש שיעור למים והא תנן רבי אלעזר אומר אף המנסך מי החג בחוץ חייב ואמר רבי יוחנן משום ר' מנחם יודפאה רבי אלעזר בשיטת רבי עקיבא אמרה דדריש ונסכיה אחד נסכי יין ואחד נסכי מים ואמר ליה ריש לקיש אי מה יין שלשת לוגין אף מים נמי שלשת לוגין מכלל דקסבר ריש לקיש אין שיעור למים ומשני לטעמיה דמנחם יודפאה קאמר *ופי' בקונטרס דריש לקיש דאמר יש שיעור למים היינו לטעמיה דמנחם דאמר רבי אלעזר בשיטת רבי עקיבא אבל איהו סבירא ליה כרבי יוחנן רביה דאין שיעור למים ומיהו לא יתכן הוא פי' דמעילה דלמה ליה למימר לטעמא דמנחם יודפאה הוה ליה למימר לטעמיה דרבי עקיבא ורבי אלעזר ור' נתן ונראה לפרש לטעמיה דמנחם יודפאה היינו מה שהקשה אי מה להלן שלשת לוגין דלרבי עקיבא יש שיעור ורבי אלעזר מי החג קאמר אלמא סבירא ליה אין שיעור ולא משום דסבירא ליה כרבי אלעזר דר"ל קסבר יש שיעור אלא לאפוקי ממנחם יודפאה קאתי דאמר רבי אלעזר בשיטת רבי עקיבא:

ביש שיעור במים קא מיפלגי. פירש בקונטרס דקאמר תנא קמא המנסך שלשת לוגין חייב והוא הדין יותר מג' לוגין דיש בכלל מאתים מנה ואע"ג דמליניא בכלי גדול קדשינא כלי דאין שיעור למי החג למעלה ואתא רבי אלעזר למימר והוא שמלאן לשם חג כדרך מילואן דהיינו שלשת לוגין ותו לא כדתנן צלוחית של זהב מחזקת שלשת לוגין ממלא מן השילוח אבל אי הוו טפי לא קדשינהו כלי דלא חזו ליה דיש שיעור נמי התם ואין כלי שרת מקדשין אלא הראויין להן עד כאן לשונו וקשה דהא רבי אלעזר מי החג קאמר לעיל דאין שיעור למים כלל לא למעלה ולא למטה כדמוכחא נמי ההיא דמעילה (שם) ומפרש הר' חיים איפכא דתנא קמא סבר יש שיעור דבעינן שלשת לוגין לא פחות ולא יותר ואתא רבי אלעזר למימר והוא שמלאן לשם חג דקבעינהו מנא דרבי אלעזר לטעמיה דאמר לעיל קביעותא דמנא מילתא הוא אבל לא קבעינהו מנא חייב בפחות משלשת לוגין דאין שיעור למים ור' אלעזר לטעמיה דאמר במתני' מי החג:

בקרבו

עין משפט נר מצוה

מד א מיי' פי"ט מהל' מעה"ק הל"ג:
מה ב מיי' שם ולא פסק כמותו:
מו ג מיי' פ"ג מהל' שמיטה ויובל הל"ב:
מז ד מיי' פ"ז מהל' לולב הל"ב:

צ"ל דתנן

צ"ל דתנן

מח ה מיי' פ"י מהל' תמידין ומוספין הל"ו:
מט ו מיי' פי"ט מהל' מעה"ק הל"ג:

שיטה מקובצת

א] בחוץ חייב. אמר ר"י משום מנחם ותיבת רבי נמחק: ב] אסי אמר ר' יוחנן דאמר: ג] אומר והוא שמלאן לשם חג ותיבת חייב נמחק: ד] ליסוד שהקריבן: ה] יליף לה ובהרוא: ו] ליותר משלשת לוגין:

רש"ק מ"ז

גי' בל"ק ויש מפרשים

צ"ל וקלא קשה דמשמע כו' צ"ק

מסורת הש"ס

מעילה יג:

[לעיל לח: לט. לקמן קיב.]

יומא ס: לעיל מב.

[שם עיר ערכין לג.]

מעילה יג:

תענית ב: שבת קג:

צ"ל היה מנסך כו במוגה צ"ק

תענית ג. ע"ש מו"ק ג: סוכה לד. ע"ש מד.

הגהות הב"ח

(א) גמ' לשם חג חייב במאי קמיפלגי אמר רב נחמן בר יצחק:

מעשה דמי הס"ד והד"א ואי"ת עד סס"ד שייך לקמן דף קיא ע"א כד"ה בקרבו נסכים במדבר. צ"ק

ולפי' זה צ"ק

צ"ל ושמא צ"ק

ובספרים שלנו איתא גם בפי' רש"י כפי' התוס' ופי' התוס' שכתבו כאן בשם רש"י כתבו גם תוס' בשם י"מ וע"ב ועי' רש"ק

WITHOUT,[3] [110b] HE IS LIABLE. R. ELEAZAR SAID: ALSO HE WHO MAKES A LIBATION OF THE WATER OF THE FESTIVAL, ON THE FESTIVAL, WITHOUT, IS LIABLE.[4] R. NEHEMIAH SAID: IF ONE PRESENTED THE RESIDUE OF THE BLOOD[5] WITHOUT, HE IS LIABLE.

GEMARA. Raba said: R. Eleazar too agrees in the case of blood.[6] For we learnt: R. Eleazar and R. Simeon maintained: From where he left off, there he recommences.[7]

R. ELEAZAR SAID: ALSO HE WHO MAKES A LIBATION OF THE WATER OF THE FESTIVAL, ON THE FESTIVAL, WITHOUT, IS LIABLE. R. Joḥanan said on the authority of R. Menahem of Jotapata:[8] R. Eleazar ruled thus in accordance with the thesis of R. Akiba, his teacher, who maintained [that] the pouring of water [on the Feast of Tabernacles] is [required] by Scriptural law. For it was taught: R. Akiba said: *And the drink-offerings thereof*:[9] Scripture speaks of *two* drink-offerings, viz., the libation of water
a and the libation of wine.[1] Said Resh Laḳish to R. Joḥanan: If so, just as there three logs [are required], so here too three *logs* [are required], whereas R. Eleazar speaks of THE WATER OF THE FESTIVAL?[2] [Again,] if so, just as there [there is liability] during the rest of the year, so here too [one should be liable] during the rest of the year, whereas R. Eleazar says [that one is only liable] ON THE FESTIVAL? He, however, had overlooked R. Assi's statement in R. Joḥanan's name. For R. Assi said in the name of R. Joḥanan on the authority of R. Neḥunia of the valley of Beth Hauran:[3] Ten Saplings,[4] the Willow,[5] and the Water Libation are Mosaic laws from Sinai.[6]

Our Rabbis taught: One who makes a libation of three *logs* of water on the Feast [of Tabernacles], without, is liable. R. Eleazar said: If he drew it for the sake of the Feast, he is liable. Wherein do they disagree?—Said R. Naḥman b. Isaac: They disagree as to whether a standard quantity of water is required.[7] R. Papa said:

(3) E.g., he made one application only; this holds good even in the case of the inner sin-offerings, where all the four applications are indispensable. (4) Special water libations on the altar were made during the Feast of Tabernacles. If one makes a libation without of the water specially drawn for this purpose, he is liable. (5) Of these sin-offerings whose blood must be poured out at the base of the altar. (6) He accepts the view in the Mishnah, though he disagrees in the case of frankincense. (7) V. *supra* 42a. If the blood is accidentally spilt after the first application, a second animal is slaughtered, and the sprinkling is *continued*, starting with the second application. Thus the first application was effective, and therefore if it is made without, it entails liability. (8) A fortress in Galilee. (9) Num. XXIX, 31. This refers to the drink-offerings which accompanied the animal sacrifices on Tabernacles. R. Akiba stresses the plural '*offerings*'.

a (1) Hence it is Scriptural, and since it is a Scriptural rite, one is liable for doing it without. (2) If R. Eleazar based his view on R. Akiba's interpretation, then one should argue: since the rite is learnt from the plural form, '*drink-offerings*', the two are alike, and there is no liability for less than three *logs* without. R. Eleazar, however, merely speaks of THE WATER OF THE FESTIVAL, which may, on one view, be one *log* (Suk. 48a).

(3) Or, Beth Haurathan. A town in a valley S.E. of Damascus, and a station for announcing the New Moon; cf. Ezek. XLVII, 18; R.H. 22b. (4) The *whole* of a plantation fifty cubits square, containing at least ten saplings (the definition of 'saplings' is given in Shebi.I.) may be ploughed until the very end of the sixth year (the seventh is the Sabbatical year). In a plantation of older trees tilling must cease at least one month before. (5) The circuits around the altar with a willow during the Feast of Tabernacles. (6) Thus not only R. Akiba, but all the Rabbis agree that the Water Libation is Scriptural. As, however, this is a Mosaic tradition, and not directly indicated in Scripture, one is not bound by the analogy of the Wine Libation; hence three *logs* are not needed.—'*He* overlooked' presumably means Menahem of Jotapata, and though R. Joḥanan cites both statements, the present one may be of later date, when he had rejected Menahem's view (Tosaf.). (7) The first Tanna holds that it is, and so liability is incurred only for three *logs*, *neither more nor less*. R. Eleazar maintains that there is no standard: consequently, this condition of three *logs* holds good only if the water was specially drawn for libations in the vessel used for the purpose, which held three *logs*, whereby the vessel appointed the whole of the three *logs* (cf. *supra* a top). But if the vessel did not thus appoint it, one is liable even for less. (Tosaf. Rashi explains it otherwise.)

[111a] They disagree as to whether libations were offered in the
a wilderness.[1] Rabina said: They disagree as to whether we learn water libation from wine libation.[2]

Our Rabbis taught: One who makes a libation of three *logs* of wine without, is liable. R. Eleazar son of R. Simeon said: Provided that he [first] sanctified them in a [service] vessel. Wherein do they disagree?—Said R. Adda the son of R. Isaac: They differ about
b the overflow of measures.[1] Rabbah the son of Raba[2] said: They disagree as to whether libations were offered at the *bamoth*, and in the controversy of the following Tannaim. For it was taught: A private *bamah* does not require libations: these are the words of Rabbi. But the Sages maintain: It does require libations.[3] Now, these Tannaim [disagree on the same lines] as the following Tannaim. For it was taught: '*When ye are come* [etc.]':[4] Scripture prescribes [the bringing of] libations at the great *bamah*. You say, at the great *bamah*: yet perhaps it is not so, but rather at a minor *bamah*?[5] When it says, *into the land of your habitations, which I give unto you*,[4] surely Scripture speaks of a *bamah* in use by *all* of you: these are the words of R. Ishmael. R. Akiba said: '*When ye are come*' prescribes libations at a minor *bamah*. You say, at a minor *bamah*: yet perhaps it is not so, but rather at the great *bamah*? When it says, '*into the land of your habitations*,' Scripture speaks of a *bamah* in use in *all* your habitations.[6] Now when you analyse the matter, [you find that] on R. Ishmael's view they did not offer libations in the wilderness, while on R. Akiba's they did offer libations in the wilderness.

R. NEHEMIAH SAID: IF ONE PRESENTED THE RESIDUE OF THE BLOOD WITHOUT, HE IS LIABLE. R. Joḥanan said: R. Nehemiah taught in agreement with the view that [the pouring out of] the residue is indispensable.[7] An objection is raised: R. Nehemiah said: If one offered the residue of the blood without, he is liable. Said R. Akiba to him: Surely [the pouring out of] the
c residue of the blood is [but] the remainder of a rite?[1] Let [the burning of] the limbs and the fat-pieces prove it, he replied, which is the remainder of a rite,[2] yet if one offers them up without, he is liable. Not so, said he. If you speak of [the burning of] the limbs and the fat-pieces, that is because it is the beginning of the service; will you say the same of the residue of the blood, which is the end of the service?[3] Now if this is correct,[4] let him answer him: This too is indispensable? That is indeed a refutation! But now that R. Adda b. Ahabah said: The controversy[5] is about the residue of the inner [sin-offering];[6] but all agree that [the pouring out of] the residue of the outer [sin-offering] is not indispensable, [you can answer thus]: R. Nehemiah spoke [in the Mishanah] of the residue of the inner [sin-offering]; whereas that [Baraitha] was taught in connection with the residue of the outer [sin-offerings].[7] If so, let him [R. Nehemiah] answer him: I spoke [only] of the residue of the inner [sin-offerings]?—Rather, he argued on R. Akiba's hypothesis.[8]

MISHNAH. IF ONE NIPS A BIRD[-OFFERING] WITHIN AND OFFERS IT UP WITHOUT, HE IS LIABLE; IF ONE NIPS IT WITHOUT AND OFFERS IT UP WITHOUT, HE IS NOT LIABLE.[9] IF ONE SLAUGHTERS A BIRD WITHIN AND OFFERS IT UP WITHOUT,

a (1) Both agree that no standard is required, and when the Tanna says three *logs* he is not exact, for the same applies even to less. (Tosaf. Rashi reverses it; both agree that there is a definite standard, and liability is incurred only for three, not for more or less.) The first Tanna holds that libations were offered in the wilderness. Now, Scripture states, *When ye are come into the land of your habitations* (*sc.* Eretz Israel) . . . *and will make an offering by fire unto the Lord . . . then shall he that bringeth his offering present unto the Lord . . . wine for the drink-offering* (Num. XV, 2 *seq.*). This implies that libations became obligatory only after they entered Eretz Israel. This cannot mean at the *public bamoth*, since these were the same as the Tabernacle in the wilderness, where libations were already offered. Hence it must mean at *private bamoth*, and in this respect it was a new obligation, since there were no private *bamoth* in the wilderness. At these private *bamoth*, however, there were no service vessels to sanctify the wine before use; hence the wine could not require special sanctification. For that reason the first Tanna maintains that even when private *bamoth* were subsequently forbidden, and wine and water for libations would first be sanctified in service vessels, yet if one made a libation without even of water not specially drawn and sanctified, he was liable, since there had been a time when unsanctified wine was used for libations. R. Eleazar, however, holds that libations were not offered in the wilderness. Hence '*when ye are come*' etc. refers to the Tabernacle at Shiloh, where the wine was first sanctified. Therefore liability is incurred only for wine (or water) specially drawn and sanctified, since we find no instance of unsanctified wine being used. (2) They agree that libations were offered in the wilderness; therefore the text must refer to private *bamoth*, where *unsanctified* wine was used. But this was only in the case of wine; water libations, however, were offered only at the public *bamoth*, and the water was first sanctified. The first Tanna holds that we learn water libation from wine libation: as liability is incurred for offering a libation without even of unsanctified wine, so is it incurred for water not specially drawn. R. Eleazar rejects this analogy and maintains that since only sanctified water was used in libations, liability is incurred only for same.

b (1) The brim that floats above the actual vessel. Both hold that sanctification by a service-vessel is required; the Rabbis maintain that the overflow is sanctified, and therefore even if the three logs consisted of such overflow, one is liable. R. Eleazar holds that the overflow is not sanctified, and liability is incurred only for wine that was sanctified in the vessel itself. (2) Emended text (Sh.M.). Cur. edd. Raba the son of Rabbah. (3) R. Eleazar b. R. Simeon agrees with Rabbi that there were no libations at a private *bamah*, and so we never find them without prior sanctification; the first Tanna agrees with the Sages that libations were offered at a private *bamah*, and these, of course, were not first sanctified. (4) Numb. XV, 2. (5) 'Great' and 'minor' mean public and private respectively. (6) Hence, a private *bamah*. (7) V. *supra* 42*b*. Therefore it is a service and entails liability if done without.

c (1) And is not indispensable (v. *supra* 52*a*); hence it does not entail liability when done without. (2) It is not indispensable, for the sprinkling of the blood alone is indispensable. (3) Surely not. (4) That R. Nehemiah holds that the pouring out of the residue of the blood is indispensable. (5) Whether the pouring out of the residue is indispensable or not. (6) The residue of the blood of sin-offerings which is sprinkled within, in the *Hekal*. (7) R. Nehemiah admits that that is not indispensable; hence one who offers it without is not liable. (8) I maintain that the pouring out of the residue is indispensable. But even if, as you say, it is not, let the burning of the limbs prove that one who offers it without is liable. (9) Once he nips it without it is *nebelah* and not fit for offering up within. He is not liable for nipping it without, as stated *supra* 107*a*.

בקרבו נסכים במדבר א] פליגי רבינא אמר בלמדין ניסוך המים מניסוך היין ב] פליגי ת"ר *המנסך שלשה לוגין יין בחוץ חייב ר' אלעזר בר"ש אומר והוא שקדשן בכלי מאי בינייהו אמר רב אדא ג] בר רב יצחק בירוצי מידות איכא בינייהו ד] רבא בריה דרבה אמר קרבו נסכים בבמה איכא בינייהו ובפלוגתא דהני תנאי דתניא במת יחיד אינה צריכה נסכים דברי רבי וחכ"א טעונה נסכים והני תנאי כהני תנאי דתניא °כי תבאו להטעינה נסכים בבמה גדולה הכתוב מדבר אתה אומר בבמה גדולה או אינו אפי' בבמה קטנה כשהוא אומר ה] °אל ארץ מושבותיכם וגו' אשר אני נותן לכם ו] הרי בבמה הנוהגת לכולכם הכתוב מדבר דברי רבי ישמעאל ר"ע אומר כי תבאו להטעינה נסכים בבמה קטנה הכתוב מדבר אתה אומר לבמה קטנה או אינו אלא לבמה גדולה כשהוא אומר אל ארץ מושבותיכם הרי בבמה הנוהגת בכל מושבות הכתוב מדבר כשתמצא לומר לדברי רבי ישמעאל לא *קרבו נסכים במדבר ולדברי ר"ע קרבו נסכים במדבר: רבי נחמיה אומר שירי הדם שהקריבן בחוץ חייב: א"ר יוחנן ז] [תנא] רבי נחמיה *כדברי האומר (א) שיריים מעכבין מיתיבי רבי נחמיה אומר שירי הדם שהקריבן בחוץ חייב אמר לו ר"ע והלא שירי הדם שירי מצוה הם אמר לו איברין ופדרין יוכיחו שהן שירי מצוה והמקריבן בחוץ חייב אמר לו לא אם אמרת באיברים ופדרים שהן תחלת עבודה תאמר בשירי הדם ח] שאינן תחלת עבודה ואם איתא לימא ליה הני נמי ט] מעכבי תיובתא והשתא דאמר רב אדא בר אהבה מחלוקת בשיריים הפנימיים אבל בשיריים החיצונים דברי הכל לא מעכבי כי קאמר רבי נחמיה בשיריים הפנימים כי תניא ההיא בשיריים החיצונים י] *(ורבי עקיבא לא ידע מאי קאמר רבי נחמיה הוא סבר רבי נחמיה שיריים חיצונים אמר וקא מהדר ליה שיריים החיצונים ורבי נחמיה) לדבריו דר' עקיבא קאמר:

מתני' המולק את העוף בפנים והעלה בחוץ חייב מלק בחוץ והעלה בחוץ פטור *השוחט את העוף בפנים והעלה בחוץ פטור שחט

בקרבו נסכים במדבר קמיפלגי. ותרוייהו אית להו יש שיעור למים יא] וכי מלי טפי לא קדשינהו כלי ותנא קמא דמחייב לא בעי בנסכים קדושת כלי לחייב עליהן בחוץ דקסבר קרבו נסכים באהל מועד שבמדבר כל ארבעים שנה הילכך ביאת הארץ האמורה בפרשת נסכים בשלח לך ללמדו בא שבשבע של כיבוש הארץ ושבע של חילוק הארץ כשהיו בגלגל והותרו הבמות כדתנן בפרק בתרא (לקמן דף קיב:) תהא במה קטנה של כל יחיד טעונה נסכים דמשום במת ליבור לא איצטריך למימר ביאת הארץ דהא מן המדבר נתחייבו בכך וכיון דבמות יחיד טעונין נסכים והתם כלי שרת ליכא כדאמר בפרק בתרא (לקמן דף קיג.) בחוץ נמי מיחייב עלייהו בשעת איסור הבמות בלא קידוש כלי הואיל ובשעת היתר הבמות קריבין בלא קדושת כלי כדאמרן לעיל במעלן על גבי סלע משום דהויא הקרבה בבמת יחיד בשעת היתר הבמות מיחייב עלה בשעת איסור דהא בפנים אם עלה לא ירד כדאמרן לעיל (דף פד:) מנין ליוצא אם עלה לא ירד שהרי יוצא כשר בבמה ור' אלעזר סבר לא קרבו נסכים במדבר וביאת הארץ האמור בנסכים לאחר ירושה וישיבה לאחר שקבעו משכן בשילה יב] הוא דנתחייבו לפיכך הוצרכה ביאת הארץ יג] לכתוב משום שכל ארבעים שנה שבמדבר לא קרבו במשכן ובא הכתוב לחייבו בשילה ובית עולמים יד] ולא בשעת הכיבוש והחילוק בבמות הקטנות הילכך לא קרבו נסכים בבמה קטנה שהיא טו] שלא בכלי שרת ואי אסקינהו בשאין מוקדשין בחוץ לא מיחייב עלייהו והכי נמי אמרינן לקמן דמאן דבעי קדושת כלי בנסכים סבר לא קרבו נסכים במדבר: רבינא אמר בלמדין ניסוך המים כו'. ודכ"ע קרבו נסכים במדבר וביאת הארץ האמור בנסכים לבמה קטנה אתא וקרבו בבמה בלא קידוש כלי ומיהו בניסוך היין אשכחן בניסוך המים לא אשכחן דהא חובת ליבור הן ולא קרבו אלא בבמת ליבור בכלי שרת ובהא פליגי תנא קמא סבר למידין ניסוך המים מניסוך היין לחייב בחוץ ואפי' לא קדשו בכלי ורבי אלעזר סבר אין למידין וניסוך היין הוא דמתחייב בחוץ בלא כלי אבל ניסוך המים קדשו אין לא קדשו לא: מאי בינייהו. במאי פליגי: בירוצי המדות. מה שלף על שפת הכלי ותרוייהו קדושת כלי בעו מיהו רבנן סברי בירוצי מדות של לח נתקדשו ורבי אלעזר סבר לא נתקדשו ותוך כלי בעינן ופלוגתא דתנאי היא במנחות (דף פח.): רבה בריה דרבא אמר. תנא קמא לא בעי קדושת כלי ובקרבו נסכים במדבר קמיפלגי לתנא קמא קרבו לרבי אלעזר בר"ש לא קרבו כדפרישית: ובפלוגתא דהני תנאי. ר"א בר"ש טז] [כרבי] דאמר אין נסכים בבמה קטנה הילכך לא אשכחן ניסוך בלא קידוש כלי ות"ק כרבנן ס"ל דאמרי יש נסכים בבמת יחיד ואשכחן ליה בלא כלי שרת: כי תבאו. בפרשת נסכים כתיב בשלח לך: להטעינה נסכים בבמה גדולה. בא הכתוב ללמדך שלא קרבו נסכים במדבר ומשבאו לארץ נתחייבו בהן ובבמת ליבור ולא בבמת יחיד: או אינו אלא בבמה קטנה. דאילו בבמה גדולה במדבר נמי קרבי ומיהו עד השתא במה קטנה לא הואי דכל מ' שנה נאסרו הבמות משהוקם המשכן וכשנכנסו לארץ הותרו בשנים שכיבשו וחילקו ובא הכתוב להטעינם נסכים לקדשי במת יחיד: כשהוא אומר (ב) אשר אני נותן לכם כו': ורבי עקיבא יז] אומר להטעינה נסכים לבמה קטנה. דאגדולה לא איצטריך דהא במדבר נמי קרבי: או אינו אלא לבמה גדולה. ואשמועינן קרא דלא קרבו נסכים במדבר: בכל מושבות. דהיינו במת יחיד דאילו במת ליבור יח] אינה אלא במקום אחד ור' ישמעאל משמע ליה מושבות לאחר ירושה וישיבה: תנא ר' נחמיה. במתני' כדברי האומר באיזהו מקומן (לעיל דף נג.) שירי הדם מעכבין בחטאת הילכך עבודה היא להתחייב עליה בחוץ כשאר זורק מקצת דמים: שירי מצוה הן. שאין מעכבין את הכפרה כדאמר באיזהו מקומן (שם) יכול יעכבו תלמוד לומר ואת כל הדם נתקו הכתוב ועשאו שירי מצוה: הקטר איברים ופדרים. אין מעכבין את הכפרה דאין כפרה אלא בדם: ואם איתא. דלרבי נחמיה מעכבין נימא ליה הכי נמי (ג) יט] כתחילת עבודה הן כשאר מתנות: מחלוקת. (ד) באיזהו מקומן דעיכוב שירים: בחטאות הפנימיות. כל מתנותיהן מעכבות: וכי תניא ההיא. דאודי ליה רבי נחמיה דשירי מצוה הן בשירים החיצונים ומודה רבי נחמיה בהו דהמקריבן בחוץ פטור: אי הכי. אמאי אהדר ליה הקטר איברים יוכיח נימא ליה כי אמרי כ] בפנימים ולא בחיצונים ואת אמרת לי חיצונים: ה"ג אלא לדבריו דרבי עקיבא קא"ל. לדידי שירים מעכבין לדידך נמי דאמרת שירי מצוה הן הקטר איברים יוכיח:

מתני' מלק בחוץ. נבלה היא שאין מליקה אלא בפנים לפיכך פטור על העלאתו ועל מליקתו נמי פטור כדאמרן בריש פירקין (דף קז.) השוחט ולא המולק: השוחט את העוף בפנים. פסול ושוב אינו ראוי בפנים לפיכך פטור על העלאתו בחוץ ואם תאמר והלא כל העולין בחוץ נפסלין ביציאתן כא] וכל השוחט בחוץ פסול הוא וחייבין על העלאתו התם רחמנא רבייה אבל לענין שאר פסולין מתקבל בפנים בעינן:

בקרבו נסכים במדבר קא מיפלגי. פי' בקונטרס ותרוייהו אית להו יש שיעור למים ואי אפשר לומר כן דר"א על כרחין סבר אין שיעור אלא תרוייהו סברי אין שיעור ושלשת לוגין דתנא קמא לאו דוקא*: **במה** גדולה ובמה קטנה. יש מפרשים דבמה גדולה קרי שעת איסור הבמות ובמה קטנה שעת היתר ופירוש הקונטרס עיקר דתרוייהו היתר הבמות אלא דבמה גדולה היא במת ליבור ובמה קטנה היא במת יחיד ואע"ג דרבי ישמעאל אמר להטעינה נסכים לבמה גדולה ודריש מושבות לאחר ירושה וישיבה כדפירש בקונטרס וכדתניא בספרי ובפרק קמא דקדושין (דף לז.) ואז נאסרו הבמות שבאו לשילה *ומ"מ אף כשהותרו אחרי כן בנוב וגבעון מודה רבי ישמעאל דבמת ליבור טעונה נסכים: **לדברי** רבי ישמעאל לא קרבו נסכים במדבר. בקדושין (ג"ז שם) פירש בקונטרס דלכולי עלמא קרבו בקרבן ליבור ואיני יודע מי הזקיקו לכך ושמא משום דקתני בסיפרי אמר אחד מתלמידי רבי ישמעאל בא הכתוב ללמדך על הנסכים שלא נתחייב יחיד על הנסכים אלא מביאתן לארץ וזה לשון הקונטרס דפירש בקדושין (ג"ז שם) ר' ישמעאל סבר לא קרבו נסכים במדבר ואף על גב דכתיב במילואים וזה אשר תעשה על המזבח וכתיב בה נסכים בעולת תמיד בקרבן ליבור הוא דהוי אבל היחידים לא נתחייבו בנסכים אלא מביאת הארץ לאחר ירושה וישיבה ורבי עקיבא סבר קרבו נסכים ליחיד במדבר: **כי** קאמר רבי נחמיה בשיריים הפנימיים. לעיל בפרק ב"ש (דף נט.) משמע דרבי נחמיה איירי בשיריים החיצונים ושם פירשתי: **וכי** תניא ההיא בשיריים החיצונים. ומה שהשיב לו איברים יוכיחו אע"ג דאיהו גופיה לא חייש בהאי טעמא אורחיה דתנא הכי כדפרישית בפרק התערובת (לעיל דף עז:*): השוחט

[לקמן קיח.] קדושין לז:
יומא מ: [לעיל מב: נג: מנחות טז:]
גירסת רש"י אי הכי נימא ליה כי אמרי אנא בפנימים אלא לדבריו כו'
לעיל פס.
צ"ק

נ א ב מיי' פי"ט מהל' מעש"ק הל"ג ד:
נא ג ד ה מיי' שם פי"ט הל' יח:
עיין צ"ק בשם סי'
צ"ל מ"מ אף פי' צ"ק

הגהות הב"ח
(א) גמ' כדברי האומר שירי הדם מעכבי: (ב) רש"י ד"ה כשהוא אומר אל ארץ מושבותיכם אשר אני: (ג) ד"ה ואם איתא וכו' הכי נמי עבודה כצ"ל ותיבת כתחילת נמחק: (ד) ד"ה מחלוקת דעיכוב שירים באיזהו מקומן בשיריים הפנימיים בחטאות הפנימיות:

[ד"ס אחו]

שיטה מקובצת
א] במדבר קא מיפלגי רבינא אמר: ב] היין קא מיפלגי: ג] אדא בריה דרב יצחק: ד] בינייהו רבה בריה דרבא אמר בקרבו נסכים: ה] תיבות אל ארץ מושבותיכם וגו' נמחק: ו] תיבת הרי נמחק: ז] יוחנן תנא רבי: ח] הדם שהן סוף העבודה ותיבות שאינן תחילת עבודה ל"ש: ט] נמי תחילת עבודה הן ותיבת מעכבי ל"ש: י] החיצונים. אי הכי נימא ליה כי אמרי אנא בפנימים אלא לדבריו ומתיבות ורבי כו' עד תיבת לדבריו בס"א אינה: יא] למים ואין כלי שרת מקדשין אלא הראוי להן: יב] בשילה ובית עולמים הוא דנתחייבו ולא בשעת כיבוש: יג] הארץ לכתוב אות ו' ל"ש: יד] ולא בשעת ותיבת בשנות נמחק: טו] שהיא בלא כלי שרת וכי אסקינהו בשאינו מקודשין בחוץ: טז] בר"ש כרבי דאמר: יז] ור"ע אמר: יח] ציבור לא היתה אלא ותיבת אינה ל"ש יט] נמי תחילת: כ] אמרי אנא בפנימים: כא] ביציאתן וכן השוחט בחוץ פסול הוא וחייבין על העלאתו התם:

עין משפט נר מצוה

נב א מיי׳ פי״ח מהל׳ מעה״ק הל׳ יח :
נג ב ג ד מיי׳ שם פי״ח הלכה יז :
נד ה ו מיי׳ שם הל״ח :
נה ז מיי׳ פי״ט מהל׳ מעה״ק הל״ג :
[עיין לעיל דף סט ע״א תוס׳ ד״ה לאתויי כו׳]

אשחט בחוץ והעלה בחוץ חייב נמצא דרך הכשירו בפנים פטורו בחוץ דרך הכשירו מבחוץ פטורו בפנים ר״ש אומר כל שחייבין עליו בחוץ חייבין על כיוצא בו בפנים שהעלה בחוץ חוץ מן השוחט בפנים ומעלה בחוץ :

גמ׳ האי הכשירו חיובו הוא תני חיובו : ר״ש אומר א] [וכו׳] : אהיכא קאי אילימא ארישא קאי המולק עוף בפנים והעלה בחוץ חייב מלק בחוץ והעלה בחוץ פטור וא״ל ר״ש כי היכי ב] דפנים מיחייב בחוץ נמי מיחייב ג] האי כל שחייבין עליו בחוץ כל שחייבין עליו בפנים מיבעי ליה ד] אלא כי היכי דבחוץ לא מיחייב בפנים נמי לא ה] ליחייב האי כל שאין חייבין עליו בחוץ ו] מיבעי ליה אלא אסיפא קאי השוחט עוף בפנים והעלה בחוץ פטור שחט בחוץ והעלה בחוץ חייב ואמר ליה ר״ש כי היכי דבפנים לא מיחייב בחוץ נמי לא מיחייב ז] האי כל שאין חייבין מיבעי ליה אלא כי היכי דבחוץ מיחייב בפנים נמי מיחייב הא קתני חוץ מן השוחט בפנים והמעלה בחוץ *אמר זעירי שחיטת (א) בהמה בלילה איכא בינייהו והכי קאמר [וכן] בהשוחט ח] *בהמה בפנים בלילה והעלה בחוץ פטור גשחט בחוץ בלילה והעלה בחוץ חייב ר״ש אומר כל שחייבין עליו בחוץ חייבין על כיוצא בו בפנים והעלה בחוץ חוץ מן השוחט עוף בפנים והעלה בחוץ *רבא אמר קבלה בכלי חול איכא בינייהו וה״ק [וכן] דהמקבל בכלי חול בפנים והעלה בחוץ פטור המקבל בכלי חול בחוץ והעלה בחוץ חייב ר״ש אומר כל שחייבין עליו בחוץ חייבין על כיוצא בו בפנים והעלו בחוץ חוץ מן השוחט עוף בפנים ט] והעלו בחוץ השתא דתני אבוה דשמואל בר רב יצחק ההמולק עוף בפנים והעלו בחוץ חייב ומלק בחוץ והעלה בחוץ פטור ור״ש מיחייב י] ר״ש התם קאי ותני כל שחייבין עליו בפנים והעלה בחוץ חייבין עליו בחוץ : **מתני׳** וחטאת שקבל דמה בכוס אחד נתן בחוץ וחזר ונתן בפנים בפנים וחזר ונתן בחוץ חייב שכולו ראוי יא] בפנים קבל דמה בשתי כוסות נתן שניהם בפנים פטור שניהם בחוץ חייב אחד בפנים ואחד בחוץ פטור אחד בחוץ ואחד בפנים חייב על החיצון והפנימי מכפר למה הדבר דומה *למפריש חטאתו ואבדה והפריש אחרת תחתיה ואח״כ נמצאת הראשונה והרי שתיהן עומדות שחט שתיהן בפנים פטור שתיהן בחוץ חייב אחת בפנים ואחת בחוץ פטור אחת בחוץ ואחת בפנים חייב על החיצונה והפנימית מכפרת *כשם שדמה פוטר את בשרה כך היא פוטרת את בשר חבירתה :

גמ׳

השוחט בלילה בהמה כו׳. ואם תאמר שחט בחוץ בלילה והעלה בחוץ אמאי חייב ומאי שנא משלמים ששחטן בחוץ קודם פתיחת דלתות ההיכל דפטור כדאיתא בפרק שני שעירי (יומא דף סג:) ויש לומר דלילה אין מחוסר זמן אבל התם מחוסר מעשה ואם תאמר לר״ש מאי שנא שוחט בהמה בלילה בפנים משוחט עוף בפנים *ויש לומר דשוחט עוף בפנים מקטל קטליה ואם עלה ירד אפי׳ לר״ש אע״ג דלא מטמא בגדים אבית הבליעה שאין שום שחיטה מטמא בגדים אבית הבליעה אפילו טרפה או נרבע אלא שחט בחוץ והעלה בחוץ חייב : דבשחיטת חוץ לא שנא לילה מיום דהא ראוי הוא לבא אל פתח אהל מועד למחר ובהעלאתו נמי חייב דהא כתיב (ויקרא יז) ואליהם תאמר : חייבין על כיוצא יט] בפנים והעלה בחוץ . והשוחט בהמה בלילה בפנים והעלה בחוץ חייב כאילו כ] שוחטה בחוץ דהא בפנים אם עלתה לא תרד אית ליה בפרק המזבח מקדש (שם) דקתני ר״ש אומר עולה אין לי אלא עולה כשירה מנין לרבות שנשחטה בלילה כו׳ : חוץ מן השוחט כא] העוף בפנים והעלה בחוץ . דפנים נמי אם עלה ירד דהא מיקטל קטליה כדאמרי׳ בהמזבח מקדש (לעיל דף פה.) : [וכן] המקבל בכלי חול בפנים והעלה בחוץ פטור . דהא בפנים אם עלה ירד דה״ל כנשפך דמה ורבי יהודה היא דלית ליה אם עלו לא ירדו אלא בלן ויוצא ונשחט חוץ לזמנו וחוץ למקומו ושקיבלו פסולין את דמו בהנך פסולין דחזו לעבודת צבור כדמפרש בהמזבח מקדש (שם דף פד:) : רבי שמעון אומר כו׳ . דהא בפנים נמי אית ליה אם עלתה לא תרד ואפי׳ נשפך דמה כדקתני התם : והשתא דתני אבוה דשמואל . דרבי שמעון מחייב אמלק בחוץ והעלה בחוץ תני במילתיה דר״ש במתני׳ כל שחייבין עליו בפנים כגון המולק בפנים והמעלה בחוץ חייבין עליו בחוץ ודקתני סיפא חוץ מן השוחט בפנים ומעלה בחוץ אדיוקא קאי דאיכא למידק ממילתא דר״ש הא כל שאין חייבין עליו בפנים והעלה בחוץ כגון קדשים פסולין שלא היה פסולן בקדש כגון הרובע והנרבע כו׳ אין חייבין עליהן אם שחטן בחוץ והעלן בחוץ אשחיטתן לא מיחייב דלא קרינא ביה ואל פתח אהל מועד לא הביאו והעלאתן מהיכא תיתי כב] דהא לא קרינא ביה נמי אל פתח אהל מועד לא יביאנו חוץ מן השוחט עוף בפנים והעלו בחוץ שאף על פי שפטור על העלאתו בחוץ חייבין על כיוצא בו בשוחט בחוץ והעלה בחוץ דהא איתרבאי לעיל (דף קז.) שחיטתו מאו אשר ישחט והעלאתו מואליהם תאמר : **מתני׳** נתן בחוץ וחזר ונתן בפנים חייב . כדי נסבה אלא משום סיפא דבעי מיתני בפנים וחזר ונתן בחוץ ואשמעינן דאע״ג דשיריים נינהו מיחייב עלייהו וסתמא כרבי נחמיה : שניהם בחוץ חייב . אחת ואם היתה לו ידיעה בינתיים חייב שתים : אחד בפנים ואח״כ השני בחוץ פטור . ואפילו לרבי נחמיה כדמפרש בגמרא דקסבר כוס אחד עושה את חבירו דחוי הילכך אפילו שיריים לא הוי : והפנימי מכפר . להכשיר הזבח כדאמרן בכל הזבחים שנתערבו (שם דף פב.) דלא עשה את המשוייר כיוצא בו : למה הדבר דומה . בגמרא מפרש למה לי לדמויינהו ומאי גמרי מהדדי : שתיהן בחוץ חייב . על כל אחת ואחת דבשעת שחיטה כל אחת היתה ראויה לפנים : אחת בפנים והשניה כג] בחוץ פטור . דהויא לה חטאת שכיפרו בעליה ולמיתה אזלא ואינה מתקבלת בפנים : חייב על החיצונה . דהא חזיא לפנים דאיזו מהן שירצה יקריב : והפנימית מכפרת . על הבעלים : כשם שדמה פוטר כד] בשרה . מן המעילה דזריקת דם מוציאה בשר קדשי קדשים *מן המעילה דיהא בה שעת היתר לכהנים כך היא פוטרת את בשר חברתה ואע״פ שפסולה ואשמעינן דהיכא דמונח בכוסות וקדם וזרק את דם האחת פוטרת את חברתה מן המעילה משום חטאת שכיפרו בעליה דקיימא לן *חטאות המתות לא נהנין ולא מועלין אבל משום שחוטי חוץ לא איצטריכא ליה דכמאן כה] דקטלינהו דמי ולית בהו מעילה כדאמרינן כו] בשמעתא קמייתא קדשים שמתו יצאו מידי מעילה ואגב גררא נסבה הכא אידי כז] דנקטא משום שחיטת חוץ ובפרק קמא דמעילה (דף ה) נמי קתני לה לטולה :

גמ׳

שחט בחוץ והעלה בחוץ חייב . אף על העלאה שחיטה בחוץ בשוף יב] רבייה רחמנא (ויקרא יז) מאו אשר ישחט* ואהעלאתו נמי אמרינן לקמן (דף קיט:) ואליהם תאמר לערב פרשיות דכל שמתחייב על שחיטתו בחוץ אם חזר והעלן או הוא או אחר חייב : נמלא דרך הכשירו בפנים כו׳ . בגמרא פריך אסיפא דרך הכשירו בחוץ חיובו הוא דעוף קדשים אין לו הכשר בחוץ בשחיטה והכי איבעי למיתני דרך חיובו בחוץ יג] *פטורו בפנים דרך חיובו בפנים פטורו בחוץ כגון שחט בפנים והעלה בחוץ פטור יד] שחט בחוץ והעלה בחוץ חייב מלק בפנים והעלה בחוץ חייב מלק בחוץ והעלה בחוץ פטור נמלא במקום שמתחייב על העלאתו *אם נעשית עבודה הראשונה בפנים כגון במליקת פנים פטור על העלאתו אם נעשית עבודה ראשונה בחוץ ודרך שמתחייב על העלאה אם נעשית העבודה ראשונה בחוץ כגון בשחיטה פטורו בפנים אם נשחט בפנים והעלה בחוץ : ר״ש אומר כל שחייבין עליו בחוץ חייבין על כיוצא [בו] בפנים והעלה בחוץ כו׳ . בגמרא מפרש לה ומיהו הכי משמע כל שחייבין על העלאתו טו] כו׳ אם נעשית עבודתו כולה בחוץ חייבין עליו בנעשית עבודתו ראשונה בפנים ואח״כ טז] העלהו בחוץ חוץ מן השוחט עוף בפנים והעלה בחוץ דפטור ואילו דשחיט בחוץ הוה מתחייב אף בהעלאה :

גמ׳ הכשרו חיובו הוא . דבחוץ מאי הכשר שייך למימר חיובו שייך למימר כדפרישית לעיל : ר״ש אהייא . פליג : בחוץ נמי מיחייב . אם מלקו בחוץ נמי מחייב אהעלאתו בחוץ : שחיטת לילה בבהמה יז] והעלה בחוץ איכא בינייהו . ותסורי מחסרא מתניתין במילתיה דתנא קמא והכי קאמר וכן השוחט בהמה בלילה בפנים והעלה בחוץ פטור דאינה מתקבלת בפנים דכתיב (ויקרא יט) ביום זבחכם ואפי׳ עלתה תרד ורבי יהודה היא דאמר בפרק המזבח יח] (לעיל דף פד.) פרט לנשחטה בלילה :

מסורת הש״ס
[לעיל קז.]
[לעיל קח.]
[לעי׳ ל פד: ע״ש]
[לעיל קח.]
מעילה ו:
[שם]
[מעילה ג.]

ז״ל פטורו בפנים דרך שחיטה דרך חיובו בפנים פטורו בחוץ מליקה כגון שחט כו׳

ג״ ס״א אם נעשית עבודה הראשונה בפנים כגון במליקה פטור על העלאתו אם נעשית המליקה בחוץ ודרך שמתחייב כו׳

מן המעילה דביה בה שעת כו׳ כצ״ל

הגהות הב״ח
(א) גמ׳ אמר זעירי שחיטת לילה בבהמה איכא בינייהו:

שיטה מקובצת
א] אומר אהייא אילימא תיבת כו׳ ל״ש ותיבות אהיכא קאי נמחק : ב] היכי דבפנים : ג] מחייב כל שחייבין עליו בפנים חייבין עליו בחוץ מיבעי : ד] ליה ואלא כי : ה] לא מחייב כל ואות ל׳ ותיבת האי נמחק : ו] בחוץ אין חייבין עליו בפנים מיבעי ליה ואלא : ז] מיחייב . כל שאין חייבין עליו בפנים אין חייבין עליו בחוץ מיבעי ליה ואלא כי : ח] השוחט בלילה בפנים והעלה בחוץ פטור שחט בלילה בחוץ והעלה: ט] והעלה בחוץ והשתא דתני אבוה דרב שמואל המולק אות ו׳ ותיבות בר רב יצחק נמחק : י] תיבות ר׳ שמעון התם קאי נמחק : יא] ראוי לבא בפנים קבל דמו בשני כוסות : יב] רחמנא רבייה מאו : יג] (בחוץ פטורו בפנים אות ו׳ נמחק):יד] תיבות שחט בחוץ והעלה בחוץ חייב ל״ש : טו] תיבת כו׳ נמחק : טז] העלה בחוץ אות ו׳ נמחק : יז] בבהמה בפנים והעלה : יח] המזבח מקדש : יט] כיוצא בו בפנים : כ] כאילו שחטה בחוץ : כא] השוחט עוף בפנים אות ה׳ נמחק: כב] דלא קרינא ותיבת דהא ל״ש : כג] והשניה אחריה בחוץ : כד] פוטר את בשרה : כה] דכמאן דהנקינהו דמי תיבת דקטלינהו ל״ש : כו] כדאמרי׳ במעילה בשמעתא : כז] אידי דנקט שחיטת אות א׳ ותיבת משום נמחק :

a HE IS NOT LIABLE.[1] [111b] IF ONE SLAUGHTERS [IT] WITHOUT AND OFFERS [IT] UP WITHOUT, HE IS LIABLE.[2] THUS ITS PRESCRIBED RITE WITHIN FREES HIM FROM LIABILITY [IF HE DOES IT] WITHOUT, WHILE ITS PRESCRIBED RITE WITHOUT FREES HIM FROM LIABILITY [IF HE DOES IT] WITHIN. R. SIMEON SAID: WHATEVER ENTAILS LIABILITY WITHOUT, ENTAILS IN SIMILAR CIRCUMSTANCES WITHIN WHEN ONE [SUBSEQUENTLY] OFFERS IT UP WITHOUT; EXCEPT WHEN ONE SLAUGHTERS [A BIRD] WITHIN AND OFFERS [IT] UP WITHOUT.[3]

GEMARA. Is this ITS PRESCRIBED RITE? Surely it is its *inculpating* rite?[4]—Learn, its inculpating rite.

R. SIMEON SAID etc. To what does he refer? If we say, to the first clause, [viz.] IF ONE NIPS A BIRD [SACRIFICE] WITHIN AND OFFERS [IT] UP WITHOUT, HE IS LIABLE; IF ONE NIPS [IT] WITHOUT AND OFFERS [IT] UP WITHOUT, HE IS NOT LIABLE; whereon R. Simeon observed [that] just as he is liable [when he nips it] within, so is he liable[5] [when he nips it] without,—then instead of [saying] WHATEVER ENTAILS LIABILITY WITHOUT, he should say, 'whatever entails liability within'? And if [he means:] just as one is not liable [when he nips it] without, so is he not liable [when he nips it] within,—then he should say, Whatever does not entail liability without does not entail liability within?[6] Again if he refers to the second clause: IF ONE SLAUGHTERS A BIRD WITHIN AND OFFERS [IT] UP WITHOUT, HE IS NOT LIABLE; IF ONE SLAUGHTERS [IT] WITHOUT AND OFFERS [IT] UP WITHOUT, HE IS LIABLE; whereon R. Simeon observed: Just as one is not liable [when he slaughters it] within, so is he not liable [when he slaughters it] without,—then he should say, Whatever does not entail liability within does not entail liability without? Or again if [he means], just as he is liable [when he slaughters] without, so is he liable [when he slaughters it] within,— surely he teaches, EXCEPT WHEN ONE SLAUGHTERS [A BIRD] WITHIN

b AND OFFERS [IT] UP WITHOUT?[1]—Said Ze'iri: They disagree about the slaughtering of an animal at night, and this is what [the Mishnah] says: Likewise if one slaughters an animal at night, within, and offers it up without, he is not liable;[2] if one slaughtered [it] at night without and offered [it] up without, he is liable.[3] R. SIMEON SAID: WHATEVER ENTAILS LIABILITY WITHOUT, ENTAILS LIABILITY IN SIMILAR CIRCUMSTANCES WITHIN WHEN ONE [SUBSEQUENTLY] OFFERS [IT] UP WITHOUT,[4] EXCEPT WHEN ONE SLAUGHTERS [A BIRD] WITHIN AND OFFERS [IT] UP WITHOUT. Raba said: They disagree about receiving [the blood] in a non-sacred vessel, and this is what it says: Likewise, if one receives [the blood] in a non-sacred vessel within, and offers it up without, he is not liable;[5] if one receives [the blood] in a non-sacred vessel without and offers [it] up without, he is liable. R. SIMEON SAID: WHATEVER ENTAILS LIABILITY WITHOUT, ENTAILS LIABILITY IN SIMILAR CIRCUMSTANCES WHITHIN WHEN ONE [SUBSEQUENTLY] OFFERS [IT] UP WITHOUT, EXCEPT WHEN ONE SLAUGHTERS [A BIRD] WITHIN AND OFFERS [IT] UP WITHOUT. And now that the father of Samuel son of R. Isaac recited: If one nips a bird within and offers [it] up without, he is liable; if he nips [it] without and offers [it] up without, he is not liable; but R. Simeon rules that he is liable: [you can say that] R. Simeon refers to that case, but read: Whatever entails liability [when it is sacrificed] within and offered up without, entails liability [when it is

c sacrificed] without.[1]

MISHNAH. AS FOR A SIN-OFFERING WHOSE BLOOD WAS RECEIVED IN ONE GOBLET, IF ONE [FIRST] SPRINKLED [THE BLOOD] WITHOUT AND THEN SPRINKLED [IT] WITHIN; [OR] WITHIN AND THEN WITHOUT, HE IS LIABLE, BECAUSE THE WHOLE OF IT WAS ELIGIBLE WITHIN. IF THE BLOOD WAS RECEIVED IN TWO GOBLETS AND ONE SPRINKLED BOTH WITHIN, HE IS NOT LIABLE; BOTH WITHOUT, HE IS LIABLE. [IF HE SPRINKLED] ONE WITHIN AND ONE WITHOUT,[2] HE IS NOT LIABLE; ONE WITHOUT AND ONE WITHIN, HE IS LIABLE ON ACCOUNT OF THE ONE WITHOUT, WHILE THE ONE WITHIN MAKES ATONEMENT.[3] TO WHAT MAY THIS BE COMPARED? TO A MAN WHO SET ASIDE [AN ANIMAL FOR] HIS SIN-OFFERING, THEN IT WAS LOST, AND HE SET ASIDE ANOTHER IN ITS PLACE; THEN THE FIRST WAS FOUND, AND [SO] BOTH ARE PRESENT. IF HE SLAUGHTERED BOTH OF THEM WITHIN, HE IS NOT LIABLE; BOTH OF THEM WITHOUT, HE IS LIABLE. [IF HE SLAUGHTERED] ONE WITHIN AND ONE WITHOUT, HE IS NOT LIABLE;[4] ONE WITHOUT AND ONE WITHIN, HE IS LIABLE ON ACCOUNT OF THE ONE WITHOUT,[5] WHILE THE ONE WITHIN MAKES ATONEMENT. JUST AS THE BLOOD RELIEVES ITS OWN FLESH, SO DOES IT RELIEVE THE FLESH OF ITS COMPANION

d [THE OTHER ANIMAL].[1]

a (1) Because by slaughtering it within, instead of nipping it, he disqualified it, and therefore it could not be offered up within. (2) Both for slaughtering (*supra* 107*a*) and for offering up (*infra* 119*b*). (3) The Gemara discusses the meaning of this. (4) There cannot be a prescribed rite of slaughtering a sacrifice without; rather, this slaughter is the act which inculpates one and makes him liable. (5) For offering it up without. (6) Emended text (Sh.M.).

b (1) Which makes it obvious that he means something else, since this is stated as an exception. (2) This would agree with R. Judah *supra* 84*a*, q.v., that an animal sacrifice slaughtered at night must be removed from the altar even if placed thereon. Hence it was not fit for offering up within, and so does not entail liability when it is offered up without.—Ze'iri assumes a lacuna in the Mishnah. (3) Because in respect of slaughtering without night does not differ from day, since it was eligible to be brought the following day to the '*door of the tent of meeting*'. (4) For he holds that when it is slaughtered within at night it is not removed from the altar (ibid.). (5) Cf. n. 2. The same applies here.

c (1) The exception will then refer to an *inference* that follows from R. Simeon's statement. For one might infer that whatever does not entail liability when it is sacrificed within and offered up without, e.g., if one sacrifices an unfit animal which was disqualified before it came to the Temple—e.g. one with which an unnatural crime had been committed—does not entail liability when sacrificed without and offered up without. An exception to this is the case of a bird; though it does not entail liability when slaughtered within and offered up without, it does entail liability when slaughtered without and offered up without. (2) In that order. (3) I.e., makes the sacrifice valid. (4) For atonement was made with the first, and so the second was not eligible for slaughtering within. For a sin-offering can be brought only when one is liable; after the first was offered, the second was in the position of a sin-offering whose owner dies before it is sacrificed, and is henceforth unfit for sacrificing. (5) Since it was eligible then.

d (1) This refers to where he slaughtered both within. The sprinkling of the blood of the first relieves its flesh from liability to trespass (v. *supra* 85*b* n. 8.); it also relieves the flesh of the second from the same liability, though the second was unfit.

GEMARA. [112*a*] As for [sprinkling the blood] without and then sprinkling [it] within, it is well, because the whole of it was eligible within.[2] But [if he first sprinkled] within and then offered [it] up without, it is [but] the residue?[3]—This agrees with R. Nehemiah, who ruled: If one offers the residue of the blood without, he is liable. If it agrees with R. Nehemiah, consider the sequel: IF THE BLOOD WAS RECEIVED IN TWO GOBLETS: IF ONE SPRINKLED BOTH WITHIN, HE IS NOT LIABLE; BOTH WITHOUT, HE IS LIABLE. [IF HE SPRINKLED] ONE WITHIN AND ONE WITHOUT, HE IS NOT LIABLE. Surely R. Nehemiah maintained [that] if one offers the residue of the blood without, he is liable?—I will answer you: Which Tanna disagrees with R. Eleazar son of R. Simeon [and maintains that] one goblet renders the other rejected? It is R. Nehemiah.[4]

TO WHAT MAY THIS BE COMPARED? TO ONE WHO SETS ASIDE [AN ANIMAL FOR] HIS SIN-OFFERING, THEN IT WAS LOST, AND HE SET ASIDE ANOTHER IN ITS PLACE; THEN THE FIRST WAS FOUND [etc.] What is the purpose of [adding], TO WHAT MAY THIS BE COMPARED?[5]—The author of this is Rabbi, who maintained: If [the first animal] was lost when [the second] was set aside, it must perish.[6] And this is what it means: This is only if [the first] was lost. If, however, one set aside two [animals for]
a sin-offerings as surety,[1] one of these was a burnt-offering from the very outset, in accordance with R. Huna's dictum in Rab's name, viz.: If a guilt-offering was transferred to pasture, and one then slaughtered it without a specified purpose, it is valid as a burnt-offering.[2] How compare: there, a guilt-offering is a male and a burnt-offering is a male; but a sin-offering was a *female*?[3]—Said R. Ḥiyya of Vastania:[4] It refers to a ruler's goat.[5]

CHAPTER XIV

MISHNAH. IF ONE SLAUGHTERED THE COW OF LUSTRA-
b TION[1] OUTSIDE ITS APPOINTED PLACE,[2] AND LIKEWISE IF ONE OFFERED WITHOUT THE SCAPEGOAT,[3] HE IS NOT LIABLE, BECAUSE IT SAYS, AND HATH NOT BROUGHT IT UNTO THE DOOR OF THE TENT OF MEETING,[4] [WHICH INTIMATES THAT FOR] WHATEVER IS NOT ELIGIBLE TO COME TO THE DOOR OF THE TENT OF MEETING, ONE IS NOT LIABLE ON ITS ACCOUNT. [AS FOR] A ROBA', A NIRBA', AN ANIMAL SET ASIDE [FOR AN IDOLATROUS SACRIFICE], AN ANIMAL WORSHIPPED [AS AN IDOL], A [DOG'S] EXCHANGE, [A HARLOT'S] HIRE, KIL'AYIM, A TEREFAH, AN ANIMAL CALVED THROUGH THE CAESAREAN SECTION,[5] IF ONE OFFERED THESE WITHOUT, HE IS NOT LIABLE, BECAUSE IT SAYS, 'BEFORE THE TABERNACLE OF THE LORD': FOR WHATEVER IS NOT ELIGIBLE TO COME BEFORE THE TABERNACLE OF THE LORD, ONE IS NOT LIABLE ON ITS ACCOUNT. [AS FOR] BLEMISHED ANIMALS, WHETHER WITH

(2) When he sprinkled it without. Hence he is liable. (3) Which should not entail liability. (4) Emended text (Sh.M.). For the allusion v. *supra* 34*b*. Hence the blood in the second goblet, according to R. Nehemiah, is not even a residue, and therefore he is not liable. (5) What does this analogy teach, for apparently the point is quite clear without it? (6) Even if it had been found by the time that the second was *sacrificed*. (The Rabbis hold that in the latter case it does not perish, but must be left to graze until it receives a blemish, when it is redeemed, and a burnt-offering is brought for the redemption money. If they did not wait for it to become blemished, but sacrificed it as a burnt-offering, it is valid. Therefore if one sacrificed it without he is liable, in the view of the Rabbis.)

a (1) I.e., *in case* one is lost, the other should be available. (2) V. *supra* 5*b*. The same applies here, and so if one offers it without, he is liable (cf. the view of the Rabbis in n. a 6). (3) Hence it was *not* fit for a burnt-offering. (4) Or, Astunia (in cur. edd. Justinia), near Pumbeditha, v. Obermeyer, *Landschaft*, p. 229. (5) Brought as a sin-offering (v. Lev. IV, 22 *seq.*). This was a male. If he set aside two, and the second is offered without. it entails liability.

b (1) I.e., the red heifer, v. Num. XIX. (2) Lit. 'vat', 'pit'. (3) V. Lev. XVI, 21. (4) Lev. XVII, 4. (5) V. *supra* 71*a* for all these.

גמ' בשלמא בחוץ וחזר ונתן בפנים שכולו ראוי א] להיות בפנים אבל בפנים והעלן בחוץ שיריים נינהו *הא מני רבי נחמיה היא דאמר שירי הדם שהקריבן בחוץ חייב אי רבי נחמיה אימא סיפא קבל דמה בשני כוסות נתן שניהם בפנים פטור שניהם בחוץ חייב אחד בפנים ואחד בחוץ פטור והאמר רבי נחמיה שירי הדם שהקריבן בחוץ חייב ב] סיפא אתאן לתנא קמא דרבי אלעזר ברבי שמעון* דאמר *כוס עושה דחוי לחבירו : למה הדבר דומה למפריש חטאתו ואבדה והפריש אחרת תחתיה ואחר כך נמצאת הראשונה : ג] למה הדבר דומה למה לי הא מני רבי *היא דאמר *אבודה בשעת הפרשה מתה והכי קאמר טעמא דאבדה הא הפריש שתי חטאות לאחריות חדא מינייהו מעיקרא עולה היא וכדרב הונא אמר רב *דאמר רב הונא אמר רב *אשם שניתק לרעייה ושחטו סתם כשר לעולה מי דמי התם אשם זכר ועולה זכר אבל ד] חטאת נקבה היא א"ר חייא מיוסתיניא בשעיר נשיא :

הדרן עלך השוחט והמעלה

פרת *חטאת ה] ששרפה חוץ מגתה וכן שעיר המשתלח ו] שהקריב בחוץ פטור שנאמר °ואל פתח אהל מועד לא הביאו *כל שאין ראוי לבא אל פתח אהל מועד אין חייבין עליו ז] *הרובע והנרבע והמוקצה והנעבד והמחיר ח] [והאתנן] והכלאים והטריפה ויוצא דופן שהקריבן בחוץ פטור שנאמר °לפני משכן ה' *כל שאין ראוי לבא לפני משכן ה' אין חייבין עליו בעלי מומין בין בעלי מומין קבועין בין בעלי

(ויקרא יז · שם)

רש"י

גמ' מאן תנא דפליג עליה דר' אלעזר בר' שמעון · בפרק כל הפסולין (לעיל דף לה:) ואומר כוס עושה חבירו דחוי דקתני חטאת שקבל דמה בארבע כוסות ונתן ארבע מתנות מאחד מהם הוא לבדו נשפך ליסוד והן נשפכין לאמה ורבי אלעזר ב"ר שמעון אמר התם כולן נשפכין ליסוד דקסבר כוס אחד עושה את חבירו שירים : רבי נחמיה הוא · דפליג עליה דאמר הכא קבל דמה בכוס אחד נתן בפנים וחזר ונתן בחוץ חייב דשירים נינהו ושירי הדם ט] שהקריבו בחוץ חייב והיכא דקיבלו בשני כוסות אמר פטור אלמא כוס שני לאו שירים חשיב ליה אלא דחוי י] היה לשפוך לאמה הלכך לא מיחייב עליה בחוץ : (א) מאי למה הדבר דומה · למאי הלכתא דמיגהו ומאי גמר מינה : הא מני רבי היא דאמר · במסכת תמורה (דף כב:) אבודה בשעת הפרשה מתה כחטאת שכיפרו בעליה דקיימא לן (שם דף כא:) דאזלא למיתה אפילו לא היתה ראשונה אבודה בשעה שמתכפר בשניה אלא בשעת הפרשה ומשהפריש זו תחתיה נמצאת קיימא לן בה דאם נתכפר באחת מהן שניה מתה והכי קאמר תנא דמתני' טעמא דאבדה כלומר זו שהופרשה על ידי איבוד חבירתה הוא דכי שוחט אחת מהן בחוץ אחר שקרבה חבירתה יא] פטור דדמיא לכוס דחוי משום דכרבי סבירא ליה דאמר למיתה אזלא אבל המפריש שתי חטאות לאחריות מעיקרא שאם תאבד האחת יתכפר בחבירתה דאפי' רבי מודה יב] בו דמתכפר באחת מהן והשניה תרעה ודמיה לעולת קיץ המזבח וכן לרבנן באבודה בשעת הפרשה דאית להו תרעה בההוא לא אמרינן דאם שחטה בחוץ לשניה דנפטר ואף על גב דלכתחילה לא קרבה היא גופה עולה אלא יג] דמיהן חייב עליה בחוץ דאי אקרבה לדידה גופה עולה בפנים מתקבלת היא : כדרב הונא [א"ר] אשם שניתק לרעייה · כגון תמורת אשם ואשם שמתו בעליו או נתכפרו באחר וקיימא לן (שם דף יח·) כל שבחטאת מתה באשם רועה ונמלך בב"ד ואמרו לו ירעה ושחטו סתם כשר לעולה ודוקא ניתק אבל לא ניתק לא כדאמר בפ"ק (לעיל ד' ה:) הוא בהווייתו יהא : מי דמי · מתני' לדרב הונא לחוובי אחטאת שניה בחוץ מהאי טעמא הא לא חזיא היא גופה לעולה כלל דהא נקבה היא : מיוסתיניא · מקום : בשעיר נשיא · שהפריש שנים לאחריות דהתם זכר הוא :

הדרן עלך השוחט והמעלה

פרת חטאת · חוץ מגתה · בגמרא מפרש היכא : גתה · לשון גת כלומר יד] מקום עמוק : ששחטה חוץ מגתה גרסי' : פטור · ולא אמרינן שוחט קדשים בחוץ טו] שלא במקום מצוה דרחמנא פטריה מואל פתח אהל מועד וגו' הראוי לפתח אהל מועד שחובה עליו להביאו שם דמקפיד קרא לענשו על שלא הביאו ש"מ בעומד להביאו שם משתעי קרא : כל שאינו ראוי · כל שאינו עתיד [לבא] ובגמרא פריך הא שעיר המשתלח עתיד לבא להגריל ולהתוודות : שנאמר לפני משכן · להקריב קרבן לפני משכן אע"פ שכשר לבא הואיל ואינו כשר ליקרב ובגמרא פריך הני נמי תיפוק לי מואל פתח אהל מועד : שעבר בל"ת · הואיל וראוי לבא לאחר זמן כדקתני בסיפא שהיה

פרת חטאת ששחטה חוץ מגתה · ברוב ספרים *גרסינן שארפה והוא הדין בשחיטה דאין חיובי חוץ לא בשחיטה ולא בהעלאה כדמוכח בגמרא ועיקר גת ניתקן לשריפה שהוא כעין גומא כדפירש בערוך ושורפין אותה שם ואוספין אפרה :

תוספות

אלא בפנים וחזר ונתן בחוץ שיריים נינהו · אע"ג דאית לאוקומא בג' מתנות שבחטאת דאמרינן בפ' ב"ש (לעיל דף לח:) דלענין חוץ הוי כתחילתן לא משמע ליה אלא בשיריים דומיא דסיפא דשני כוסות אחד בפנים ואחד בחוץ שלא היה עושה חבירו דחוי אא"כ נתן לכולם : *כשם שדמה פוטר את בשרה מן המעילה דזריקת דם מוציאה בשר קדשי קדשים מן המעילה כך הוא פוטר את בשר חבירתה מן המעילה ופי' בקונטרס משום חטאת שכיפרו בעליה דקי"ל חטאות המתות לא נהנין ולא מועלין וקשה לפירושו דבסוף פרק קמא דמעילה (דף ו:) תנן אמר רבי עקיבא והרי מפריש חטאתו ואבדה והפריש אחרת תחתיה ואחר כך נמצאת הראשונה הרי שניהם עומדים לא כשם שדמה פוטר את בשרה כך פוטר את בשר חבירתה ואמרינן בגמרא *אמר רבי אלעזר לא אמר רבי עקיבא אלא ששחט שניהם בבת אחת רלה מזה זורק רלה מזה זורק אבל בזה אחר זה לא ואי חשיב כחטאות המתות אפילו בזה אחר זה נמי אלא ודאי כיון דנשחטה קודם זריקת דמה של חבירתה שראוי להתכפר לא הויא חטאת המתה והיינו טעמא דיש חילוק בין בת אחת לזה אחר זה דבבת אחת חשיבי תרוייהו כחד גופא ולכך פוטר את בשר חבירתה וכן מוכחת הסוגיא : **הא** מני רבי היא דאמר אבודה בשעת הפרשה מתה · למאן דאמר בפרק ולד חטאת (תמורה דף כג·) דהכל מודים במתכפר בשאינה אבודה דאבודה מתה מיירי הכא בכל ענין דהשניה מתה לרבי ואיכא למאן דאמר התם דבבא לימלך פליגי והיכא דמשך מדעתו אחת מהן והקריב השניה מתה לכולי עלמא דנתכוין לדחותה והיכא דנמלך מודה רבי *דנתכפר באבודה דשאינה אבודה רועה והכא מיירי בשחט שאינה אבודה בפנים ואבודה בחוץ וקשה קצת מאי רבי היא רבנן נמי לא פליגי בהכי : **והכי** קאמר טעמא דאבדה אבל הפריש שתי חטאות לאחריות כו' · משמע היכא דקתני אבדה הוי אבדה דוקא ותימה דבסוף פ"ק דמעילה (דף ז·) תניא אמר רבי שמעון כשהלכתי לכפר (בגא) [פאגי] כו' עד אמר לי בני אתה אומר כן והרי מפריש חטאת ואבדה והפריש אחרת תחתיה כו' ולר"ש על כרחין לא מחלק דרועה לר' שמעון לית ליה כלל כדאיתא בפרק מי שהיה טמא (פסחים דף צז:) ובתמורה פרק *ולד חטאת (תמורה דף י) וי"ל דבמעילה אינו יורד לחידוש זה אלא לאשמועינן דזריקה מועלת ליוצא וחד מינייהו נקט אבל מתני' דהכא לחידוש תנייה דאין זה דמיון כ"כ ולא נקטה אלא לאשמועינן *דרבי היא חדא מינייהו מעיקרא עולה היא ואפילו למ"ד בעי עקירה חסרון עקירה לא שמיה חסרון בהאי דעומד ליעקר ולא דמי להא דאמרינן בפ' בתרא (לקמן דף קיד:) אי הכי לשמו ליחייב הואיל וראוי שלא לשמו ומשני מחוסר עקירה דהתם אינו עומד ליעקר : **בשעיר** נשיא · וא"ת לר"ש חטאת זכר אמאי מתה הא אמרי' בפרק קמא דהוריות (דף ו:) ובפרק שני דתמורה (דף טו:) דחמש חטאות בחד מקום גמירי להו ולא משכחת ולד חטאת בחטאת זכר וי"ל דמתני' דלא כר"ש והא דאמרינן בפ' ולד חטאת (שם דף כג·) גבי שעירי יום הכיפורים והשני ירעה לרבי שמעון ודייקא הא ביחיד מתה לאו בזכר כיוצא בהן אלא בנקבה :

הדרן עלך השוחט והמעלה

שייך למתני' דלעיל

נו א מיי' פ"ד מהלכות פסה"מ הלכה ג:

נז ב מיי' שם הל' טו:

א ג ד מיי' פי"ט מהל' מעה"ק הלכה ז:

ב ה ו מיי' שם ופי"ח הלכה ו:

[יומא נו: לעיל לד: תמורה כב:]

[מעילה ז.]

לעיל ה: [וש"נ]

נ"ל דאם נתכפר באבודה נ"ק

[נ"ל יש נקרבנות טו.]

דרבי היא ס"ס סס"ד ואח"כ מס"ד חדא נ"ק

[לעיל לח: לט. קי.]

נ"א ומאןתנא דפליג עליה דאב"ש ר' נחמיה הוא וכ"ה בס"י נ"ק

[תמורה כב:]

[וכן גי' ערוך ערך גת א']

הגהות הב"ח

(א) רש"י ד"ה למה הדבר דומה למה לי למאי הילכתא :

שיטה מקובצת

א] ראוי לבא בפנים אלא בפנים וחזר ונתן בחוץ שירים נינהו אמרי הא מני : ב] חייב אמרי מאן תנא דפליג עליה דר"א בר"ש כוס עושה חבירו דיחוי ר' נחמיה היא : ג] מאי למה הדבר דומה הא מני ותיבות למה לי נמחק : ד] אבל הכא חטאת :

ה] חטאת ששחטה חוץ ותיבת ששרפה נמחק : ו] המשתלח שהקריבו : ז] הרובע · עי' תוס' תמורה (דף כד) : ח] והמחיר והאתנן והכלאים : ט] שהקריבן בחוץ : י] הוה לשפוך : יא] חבירתה בפנים פטור דדמיא לכוס משום ותיבת דחוי נמחק : יב] בה דמתכפר : יג] אלא דמיה חייב : יד] כלומר א) מקומה ששחטה תיבות מקום עמוק ל"ש : טו] בחוץ הוא שלא :

א) נראה דל"ל חוץ ממקומה ששחטה תוך וכו' תיבות מקום עמוק ל"ש :

בעלי מומין עוברין שהקריבן בחוץ פטור ר"ש אומר בעלי מומין קבועין פטור בעלי מומין עוברין (א) א] חייב בלא תעשה ^א^תורים שלא הגיע זמנן ובני יונה שעבר זמנן שהקריבן בחוץ פטור ר"ש אומר בני יונה שעבר זמנן פטור ותורים שלא הגיע זמנן בלא תעשה *אותו ואת בנו ומחוסר זמן פטור ר"ש אומר הרי זה בלא תעשה ב] *שר"ש אומר כל שהוא ראוי לבא לאחר זמן ה"ז בלא תעשה ואין בו כרת וחכ"א כל שאין בו כרת אין בו לא תעשה *^ב^מחוסר זמן בין בגופו בין בבעליו ג] ^ג^איזהו מחוסר זמן בבעליו הזב והזבה והיולדת והמצורע שהקריבו חטאתם ואשמם בחוץ פטורין עולותיהן ושלמיהן בחוץ חייבין ^ד^המעלה מבשר חטאת מבשר אשם מבשר קדשי קדשים מבשר קדשים קלים ומותר העומר ושתי הלחם ולחם הפנים ושירי מנחות *^ה^והיוצק ד] והפותת והבולל והמולח והמניף והמגיש והמסדר את השולחן והמטיב את הנרות והקומץ והמקבל דמים בחוץ פטור (ב) ^ו^ואין חייבין עליו לא משום זרות ^ז^ולא משום טומאה ולא משום מחוסר בגדים ולא משום [שלא] רחוץ ידים ורגלים עד *שלא הוקם המשכן היו הבמות מותרות ועבודה בבכורות ומשהוקם המשכן נאסרו הבמות ועבודה בכהנים קדשי קדשים נאכלין לפנים מן הקלעים וקדשים קלים בכל מחנה ישראל באו לגלגל הותרו הבמות קדשי קדשים נאכלין לפנים מן הקלעים וקדשים קלים בכל מקום *באו לשילה נאסרו הבמות *ולא היה שם תקרה אלא בית אבנים ה] בלבד מלמטן (ג) והיריעות מלמעלן והיא היתה מנוחה קדשי קדשים נאכלין לפנים מן הקלעים וקדשים קלים ומעשר שני בכל הרואה *באו לנוב וגבעון הותרו הבמות קדשי קדשים נאכלין לפנים מן הקלעים קדשים קלים ו] *בכל ערי ישראל *^ח^באו לירושלים נאסרו הבמות ולא היה להן ז] *היתר והיא היתה נחלה ^ט^קדשי קדשים נאכלין לפנים מן הקלעים ^י^קדשים קלים ומעשר שני לפנים מן החומה כל הקדשים שהקדישן בשעת איסור הבמות והקריבן בשעת איסור הבמות ח] מבחוץ ^כ^הרי אלו בעשה ולא תעשה וחייבין ט] עליו כרת הקדישן בשעת היתר הבמות והקריבן בשעת איסור הבמות בחוץ הרי אלו בעשה ולא תעשה ואין חייבין עליהן כרת הקדישן בשעת איסור הבמות והקריבן בשעת היתר הבמות הרי אלו בעשה ואין בהן לא תעשה ואלו קדשים קרבין במשכן קדשים שהוקדשו למשכן קרבנות ציבור קרבין במשכן וקרבנות היחיד בבמה קרבנות היחיד שהוקדשו למשכן יקריבו במשכן ואם הקריבן בבמה פטור ומה בין במת יחיד לבמת ציבור סמיכה ושחיטת צפון ומתן

(ד) שהיה ר"ש אומר כו' · בגמרא מפרש לא תעשה דידהו : תורין שלא הגיע זמנן · כדתנן י] בחולין (דף כב:) משיזהיבו כשירין ומקמי הכי פסולין דתורין משמע גדולים ולא קטנים בני יונה קטנים משמע ולא גדולים ופסולין מתחילת הציהוב ואילך : בלא תעשה · הואיל וראוין לאחר זמן יש יא] בו לא תעשה לשוחטן בחוץ : מחוסר זמן · שאמרנו פטור בין שהוא מחוסר זמן בגופו בין שהוא מחוסר זמן בבעלים שלא הגיע זמן יב] בעלים להקריב קרבנותיהם : והמצורע לא גרסי' במתני': שהקריבו · בתוך ימי ספרן : ויולדת · בתוך מלאת: ואשמם · בגמרא פריך מאי אשם איכא בהני : פטור · שאין מתקבלין בפנים לא לחובה ולא לנדבה : עולותיהן · דזב וזבה (ה) דעוף ודיולדת בהמה : חייבין · שהרי מתקבלות בפנים נדבה לשמן : ושלמיהן · בגמ' פריך מאי שלמים איכא בהני : קדשי קדשים · כבשי עצרת : ומותר העומר · לאחר קמיצה : היוצק · שמן על המנחה כדכתיב (ויקרא ב) ויצקת וגו': והפותת · מנחת מחבת כדכתיב (שם) פתות אותה פתים : והמגיש · מנחה בחוץ והיא טעונה הגשה בפנים בקרן מערבית דרומית כמשפטה: המטיב את הנרות · מדשן את המנורה בבקר : פטור · טעמא יליף בברייתא בגמ' : אין בהן משום זרות · חיוב מיתה כל הנך הקטרות בדבר שדרכן לאכול לאו הקטרה נינהו וכל הנך עבודות הואיל ויש אחריהן עבודה אין זר חייב עליה מיתה כדאמרינן בפרק בראשונה (יומא דף כד·) עבודת מתנה ולא עבודת סילוק עבודה תמה ולא עבודה שיש אחריה עבודה : ולא משום טומאה · כהן טמא ששימש דאזהרת זרות ושימוש בטומאה מחד קרא נפקי מוינזרו ולא יחללו בכל הזבחים תניא (לעיל יז.) מאי דמחייב אזרות מחייב אשימוש טומאה : ולא משום מחוסר בגדים · דאיכהו נמי כזר בזמן שאין בגדיהן עליהם אין כהונתם עליהם והוו להו זרים הכי נפקא לן בפרק שני (שם יז:) : ולא משום שלא רחוץ ידים ורגלים · גמר חוקה חוקה ממחוסר בגדים התם לענין אחולי עבודה ולענין מיתה נמי אכן גמרינן לה מהתם : ועבודה בבכורות · כדכתיב וישלח את נערי בני ישראל וגו' (שמות כד) : נאסרו הבמות · כדכתיב בשחוטי חוץ : ועבודה בכהנים · כדכתיב קרב אל המזבח : לפנים מן הקלעים · דכתיב בחטאת ואשם ומנחה (ויקרא ו) בחצר אהל מועד : קדשים קלים בכל מחנה ישראל · במות שהן שרויין בדגליהם והא ילפינן יג] באיזהו מקומן (לעיל נה·) מקראי : באו לגלגל · כשעברו את הירדן והוקבע אהל מועד שם שבע שנים שכבשו ושבע שחלקו : הותרו הבמות · כדילפינן לקמן מאיש כל הישר בעיניו : קדשי קדשים יד] הנאכלין לא קרב בבמת יחיד טו] *כל שאין נידר ונידב אין קרב בבמה קטנה ואין מנחה בבמה הלכך עולה הוא דהואי ואין נאכלת וחטאת ואשם בבמת ציבור הוא דקרבי ונאכלין לפנים מן הקלעים : קדשים קלים · כולהו יליף בגמרא דלא כהיני בבמת יחיד: במת ציבור · גלגל נוב וגבעון (ח):

קלים בכל מקום · דכיון שבטלו הדגלים והן היו הולכים בכל הארץ לכבשה ולא היתה חנייתן סביבות המשכן בטלה קדושת מחנה ישראל מעשר שני לא הוזכר כאן לפי שלא נהגו מעשרות עד לאחר ירושה וישיבה : באו לשילה · לאחר *חילוקו מיד קבעוהו בשילה : נאסרו הבמות · כדקתני והיא היתה מנוחה וכתיב כי לא באתם עד עתה וגו' כלומר כשתעברו את הירדן לא טז] תקריבו בבמות ככל אשר אנחנו עושים פה היום שאנו מקריבין במשכן חטאות ואשמות אלא איש כל הישר בעיניו תעשו דהייט נדרים ונדבות שאינן עליכם חובה אלא לפי מה שישר בעיניכם כי בעוד שתכבשו ותחלקו לא באתם עד עתה אל המנוחה יז] ועברתם את הירדן וישבתם בארץ הייט לאחר ירושה וישיבה והיה המקום וגו' השמר לך וגו' הייט איסור הבמות : תקרה · יח] (של) גג של נסרים : ויריעות מלמעלן · בגמרא יליף לה : בכל הרואה · במקום שרואין משם את שילה ובגמרא יליף לה : באו לנוב וגבעון · כשחרבה שילה ונלקח הארון בימי עלי באו לנוב יט] וגבעון כמו שנאמר אין לחם חול [וגו'] כי אם לחם קדש כ] אשר מלפני ה' (שמואל א כא) אלמא שולחן ומזבח התם הוה חרבה נוב בימי שאול באו לגבעון כדכתיב במלכים (א ג) כי (ו) שם הבמה גדולה : הותרו הבמות · יליף בגמרא : קדשים קלים בכל ערי ישראל · דהא בכל מקום שהוא שם עושה במה (ז) ומקריבו : ומעשר שני · פריך בגמרא נסקיה להתם : והיא היתה נחלה · ההיא דכתיב בקרא דמשבאו אל המנוחה ואל הנחלה יאסרו הבמות : לפנים מן החומה · של ירושלים שהיא במקום מחנה ישראל שבמדבר כדכתיב ואכלת שם לפני ה' (דברים יב) : בעשה · והביאום לה' וגו' (ויקרא יז) : ולא תעשה · כדילפי' משם תעלה כא] לשחיטה ואזהרה דהעלאה השמר לך פן תעלה עולותיך וגו' (דברים יב) : וחייבין עליהן כרת · כדכתיב (ויקרא יז) ואל פתח אהל מועד לא הביאו : ואין חייבין עליהן כרת · כדאמרן בהשוחט (לעיל קו:) עד כאן הוא מדבר בקדשים שהקדישן כו' וקתני סיפא יכול יהו חייבין עליהן כרת תלמוד לומר זאת להם ואין אחרת להם : הקדישן בשעת איסור הבמות · מההיא שעתא קרינא בהו והביאום לה' וכיון שהמתין עד שלא כב] יבא לקיימו נתבטל העשה על ידו אבל לאו וכרת ליכא דאזהרה ועונש בשעת הקרבה כתיבי והרי הותרו הבמות : ואלו קדשים קרבין במשכן · קדשים שהוקדשו למשכן בזמן שהיה המשכן בגלגל והותר במה אלו קדשים צריכין להקריבן במשכן ולא יקרבו בבמה אותם שהוקדשו לשם משכן כג] מפרש ואזיל : קרבנות ציבור · סתמן כד] למקדש : קרבנות יחיד · סתמן בבמה : קרבנות יחיד שהוקדשו למשכן · שפירש בשעת הקדישן על מנת להקריבן למשכן : פטור · מאזהרה ומעונש שהרי הותרו הבמות ומיהו אסור לשנות משום כאשר נדרת תשמור ועשית (דברים כג) : ומה בין במת יחיד כו' ·

ג א מיי' פי"ח מהלכות מעשה"ק הלכה ח:
ד ב מיי' שם הלכה ז:
ה ג מיי' שם הלכה ט:
ו ד מיי' שם פרק יט הלכה ד:
ז ה מיי' שם הלכה ו:
ח ו מיי' פ"ט מהלכות ביאת מקדש הלכה ה:
ט ז מיי' שם הלכה י:
י ח מיי' פ"א מהלכות בית הבחירה הלכה ג:
יא ט מיי' פ"ו מהלכות בית הבחירה הל' יא ופ"ג מהלכות מעה"ק הל' ג ופי"א שם הל' ה:
יב י מיי' פ"ו מהלכות בית הבחירה הל' טו ופ"ג שם הלכה יד ופי"ט מהלכות מעה"ק הל' ה:
יג כ מיי' פי"ח מהלכות מעה"ק הלכה ב:

[נ"ל תנוקס]
חולין פב.
[מעילה יב. חולין פא. וכזכר ג"כ תמורה יט:]
יומא סג.
סנהדרין פב: [ופי"ש בתוספות סוטה הירכס]
[בכורות ד:]
מגילה י:
סדר עולם פי"א
[עי' תוס' לקמן קיט. ד"ה באו ותוס' לעיל ס: ד"ה מאי סבר]
נ"א ומעשר שני
מגילה י
[נ"ל עוד היתר קך לזאת במגילה י. וכן במשנה שבמשניות]
נ"ל שבגל נ"מ

הגהות הב"ח

(א) במשנה ר"ש אומר וכו' מומין עוברין עובר בלא תעשה : (ב) שם ואין בהם משום זרות כצ"ל ותיבות חייבין עליו לא נמחק : (ג) שם ויריעות מלמעלן: (ד) רש"י ד"ה (בע"א) עובר וכו' בסיפא שר"ש אומר כצ"ל ותיבת שהיה נמחק : (ה) ד"ה עולותיהן דזב וזבה שוף : (ו) ד"ה באו לנוב וכו' במלכים כי היא הבמה גדולה : (ז) ד"ה קדשים קלים וכו' ומקריב ובגמרא פריך מעשר שני נסקיה להתם כצ"ל וכד"א: (ח) ד"ה במת ציבור וכו' וגבעון הס"ד ואח"כ מ"ה מתן סביב ותיבות מתן סובב נמחק :

שיטה מקובצת

א] עוברין עובר בלא תעשה תיבת חייב נמחק: ב] בלא תעשה שהיה ר"ש אומר : ג] בבעליו ואיזהו מחוסר : ד] והיוצק והבולל והפותת והמולח: ה] תיבת בלבד נמחק : ו] בכלי' עיין לעיל בתוס' (דף ס ע"ב) : ז] להן עוד היתר : ח] הבמות בחוץ : ט] וחייבין עליהן כרת: י] כדתנן בשחיטת חולין משיזהיבו : יא] יש בה : יב] זמן הבעלים להקריב : יג] ילפינן לה באיזהו : יד] קדשי קדשים נאכלין לפנים מן הקלעים · שאין לך קדשי קדשים א) אות ה' נמחק : טו] יחיד דכל שאין : טז] לא תעשון בבמות תיבת תקריבו נמחק : יז] המנוחה אבל ועברתם : יח] תקרה גג של נסרים : יט] תיבת וגבעון נמחק : כ] קדש המוסרים מלפני תיבת אשר נמחק : כא] תעלה ושם תעשה לשחיטה : כב] שלא יכול לקיימו : כג] משכן ומפרש ואזיל : כד] סתמן למשכן הס"ד ותיבת למקדש נמחק :

א) אולי נ"ל שאין לך קדשי קדשים נאכלין שקרבין בבמת יחיד :

PERMANENT BLEMISHES OR [112b] WITH TRANSIENT BLEMISHES, IF ONE OFFERS THEM WITHOUT, HE IS NOT LIABLE. R. SIMEON SAID: [IF ONE OFFERS] ANIMALS WITH PERMANENT BLEMISHES, HE IS NOT LIABLE; [IF ONE OFFERS] ANIMALS WITH TRANSIENT BLEMISHES, HE VIOLATES A NEGATIVE INJUNCTION. [WITH REGARD TO] TURTLEDOVES BEFORE THEIR TIME AND YOUNG PIGEONS AFTER THEIR TIME,[6] IF ONE OFFERED THEM WITHOUT, HE IS NOT LIABLE. R. SIMEON SAID: [IF ONE OFFERS] YOUNG PIGEONS AFTER THEIR TIME, HE IS NOT LIABLE; [IF HE OFFERS] TURTLEDOVES BEFORE THEIR TIME, HE VIOLATES A NEGATIVE INJUNCTION. [ONE WHO OFFERS] AN ANIMAL TOGETHER WITH ITS YOUNG [ON THE SAME DAY], AND [ONE WHO OFFERS] BEFORE TIME, IS
a NOT LIABLE.[1] R. SIMEON SAID: HE TRANSGRESSES A NEGATIVE INJUNCTION. FOR R. SIMEON MAINTAINED: WHATEVER IS ELIGIBLE TO COME LATER INVOLVES A NEGATIVE INJUNCTION, BUT DOES NOT INVOLVE KARETH.[2] BUT THE SAGES MAINTAIN: WHATEVER DOES NOT INVOLVE KARETH DOES NOT INVOLVE A NEGATIVE INJUNCTION. 'BEFORE TIME' APPLIES BOTH TO ITSELF AND TO ITS OWNER.[3] WHAT IS 'BEFORE TIME' AS APPLIED TO ITS OWNER? IF A ZAB OR A ZABAH, A WOMAN AFTER CHILDBIRTH,[4] OR A LEPER,[5] OFFERED THEIR SIN-OFFERING OR THEIR GUILT-OFFERING WITHOUT, THEY ARE NOT LIABLE; [IF THEY OFFERED] THEIR BURNT-OFFERINGS OR THEIR PEACE-OFFERINGS WITHOUT, THEY ARE LIABLE.[6] IF ONE OFFERS UP FLESH OF A SIN-OFFERING, OR FLESH OF A GUILT-OFFERING, OR FLESH OF MOST SACRED SACRIFICES, OR FLESH OF LESSER SACRIFICES, OR THE RESIDUE OF THE 'OMER,[7] OR THE TWO LOAVES, OR THE SHEWBREAD, OR THE REMAINDER OF MEAL-OFFERINGS; OR IF HE POURS [THE OIL ON TO THE MEAL-OFFERING], OR MINGLES [IT WITH FLOUR], OR BREAKS UP [THE MEAL-OFFERING CAKES], OR SALTS [THE MEAL-OFFERING], OR WAVES IT, OR PRESENTS [IT OPPOSITE THE SOUTH-WEST CORNER OF THE ALTAR], OR SETS THE TABLE [WITH THE SHEWBREAD], OR TRIMS THE LAMPS, OR TAKES OFF THE FISTFUL, OR RECEIVES THE BLOOD,—[IF HE DOES ANY OF THESE] WITHOUT, HE IS NOT LIABLE. NOR IS ONE LIABLE ON ACCOUNT OF ANY OF
b THESE ACTS ON ACCOUNT OF ZARUTH,[1] OR UNCLEANNESS, OR LACK OF [PRIESTLY] VESTMENTS,[2] OR THE NON-WASHING OF HANDS AND FEET.[3]

BEFORE THE TABERNACLE WAS SET UP BAMOTH WERE PERMITTED AND THE SERVICE WAS PERFORMED BY THE FIRST-BORN; AFTER THE TABERNACLE WAS SET UP BAMOTH WERE FORBIDDEN AND THE SERVICE WAS PERFORMED BY PRIESTS. MOST SACRED SACRIFICES WERE [THEN] EATEN WITHIN THE CURTAINS, AND LESSER SACRIFICES [WERE EATEN] ANYWHERE IN THE CAMP OF THE ISRAELITES.[4] WHEN THEY CAME TO GILGAL,[5] BAMOTH WERE [AGAIN] PERMITTED: MOST SACRED SACRIFICES WERE EATEN WITHIN THE CURTAINS, AND LESSER SACRIFICES [WERE EATEN] ANYWHERE. WHEN THEY CAME TO SHILOH,[6] BAMOTH WERE [AGAIN] FORBIDDEN. [THE TABERNACLE] THERE HAD NO ROOF, BUT [CONSISTED OF] A STONE EDIFICE CEILED WITH CURTAINS, AND THAT WAS THE 'REST' [ALLUDED TO IN SCRIPTURE]:[7] MOST HOLY SACRIFICES WERE EATEN [THERE] WITHIN THE CURTAINS, AND LESSER SACRIFICES AND SECOND TITHE[8] [WERE EATEN] WHEREVER [SHILOH] COULD BE SEEN. WHEN THEY CAME TO NOB AND TO GIBEON,[9] BAMOTH WERE [AGAIN] PERMITTED: MOST HOLY SACRIFICES WERE EATEN WITHIN THE CURTAINS,
c AND LESSER SACRIFICES [AND SECOND TITHE][1] IN ALL THE CITIES OF ISRAEL. WHEN THEY CAME TO JERUSALEM, BAMOTH WERE FORBIDDEN AND WERE NEVER AGAIN PERMITTED,[2] AND THAT WAS THE 'INHERITANCE'. MOST HOLY SACRIFICES WERE EATEN WITHIN THE CURTAINS,[3] AND LESSER SACRIFICES AND SECOND TITHE WITHIN THE WALL [OF JERUSALEM].

ALL SACRIFICES CONSECRATED WHILE BAMOTH WERE FORBIDDEN AND OFFERED WITHOUT WHILE BAMOTH WERE FORBIDDEN, INVOLVE A POSITIVE AND A NEGATIVE INJUNCTION,[4] AND ONE IS LIABLE TO KARETH ON THEIR ACCOUNT.[5] IF ONE CONSECRATED THEM WHILE BAMOTH WERE PERMITTED, BUT OFFERED THEM WITHOUT WHEN BAMOTH WERE FORBIDDEN, THEY INVOLVE A POSITIVE AND A NEGATIVE INJUNCTION, BUT ONE IS NOT LIABLE TO KARETH ON THEIR ACCOUNT.[6] IF ONE CONSECRATED THEM WHEN BAMOTH WERE FORBIDDEN, AND OFFERED THEM WHEN BAMOTH WERE PERMITTED, THEY INVOLVE A POSITIVE INJUNCTION,[7] BUT THEY DO NOT INVOLVE A NEGATIVE INJUNCTION. THE FOLLOWING SACRIFICES WERE OFFERED IN THE TABERNACLE:[8] SACRIFICES CONSECRATED FOR THE TABERNACLE: PUBLIC SACRIFICES WERE OFFERED IN THE TABERNACLE, AND PRIVATE SACRIFICES WERE OFFERED AT A BAMAH.[9] IF PRIVATE SACRIFICES WERE CONSECRATED FOR THE TABERNACLE, THEY MUST BE OFFERED IN THE TABERNACLE; YET IF ONE OFFERED THEM AT A BAMAH, HE IS NOT LIABLE.

WHEREIN DID THE MINOR BAMAH AND THE GREAT BAMAH DIFFER? [IN RESPECT OF] LAYING [OF HANDS], SLAUGHTER-

(6) Turtledoves may be sacrificed only *after* they reach a certain stage; pigeons, only before. V. Hul. 22a.

a (1) 'Before time' is explained anon. An animal may not be slaughtered together with its young on the same day (cf. Lev. XXII, 28).—In the whole passage the reference is to liability or otherwise for slaughtering without. R. Simeon too means that he has transgressed the negative injunction forbidding the slaughtering of sacrifices without, but is not liable. (2) And therefore if one does it in ignorance, he is not liable to a sin-offering. (3) Whether the animal (or bird) was not yet eligible, or whether its owner was not yet eligible or liable. (4) Before the expiration of forty or eighty days; v. Lev. XII, 1-8. (5) All these, within the period of their counting; v. Lev. XIV, 1-10; XV, 1-15; 25-30. (6) Since these could have been offered as a votive offering within in their name. A sin-offering and a guilt-offering, however, cannot be offered votively. (7) After the fistful is taken.

b (1) I.e., the prohibition of a *zar* (a non-priest) to officiate in the Temple. (2) The priest had to officiate in the special garments prescribed in Ex. XXVIII; if he did not wear them all whilst engaged in any of these, he incurs no liability. (3) V. Ex. XXX, 17-21. (4) V. *supra* 55a n. b 6. (5) After crossing the Jordan and entering the promised land; the Tent of Meeting was then set up at Gilgal, and it remained there during the fourteen years of conquering and allotting the country. (6) After the fourteen years. (7) Deut. XII, 9: *For ye are not as yet come to the* rest *and to the inheritance, which the Lord your God giveth thee.* When they arrived at Shiloh, they had come to that '*rest*'. The significance of this is discussed in the Gemara. (8) Which was to be eaten '*in the place which the Lord thy God shall choose*' (ibid. 18). (9) After Shiloh, the Tabernacle was erected at Nob, and subsequently it was set up at Gibeon.

c (1) 'And second tithe' is a *var. lec.* (2) Even after the destruction of the Temple. (3) In the place corresponding to within the curtains of the Tabernacle, viz., in the Temple court. (4) Lev. XVII, 5: *even that they may bring them unto the Lord;* this is a positive injunction. Deut. XII, 13: *Take heed to thyself that thou offer not thy burnt-offerings in every place that thou seest;* this is the negative injunction, and is understood to apply to *all* sacrifices. (5) Lev. XVII, 4: *And hath not brought it unto the door of the tent of meeting . . . that man shall be cut off among his people.* (6) V. *supra* 106b. (7) Having consecrated them when *bamoth* were forbidden, he was subject to the positive injunction, '*even that they may bring them unto the Lord*', which means to the Tabernacle. By waiting until the Tabernacle was destroyed, which rendered this impossible, he transgressed that injunction. (8) When it was at Gilgal, when *bamoth* too were permitted. (9) If animals were consecrated for public or private sacrifices, and the place was unspecified, it is tacitly assumed that the former were meant for sacrifice in the Tabernacle (public sacrifices could be sacrificed only there), and the latter were meant for *bamoth*.

a ING IN THE NORTH, [113a] SPRINKLING ROUND ABOUT,[1] WAVING AND PRESENTING,[2] (R. JUDAH MAINTAINED: THERE WERE NO MEAL-OFFERINGS AT THE BAMAH), PRIESTHOOD, SACRIFICIAL VESTMENTS, SERVICE VESSELS, A SWEET ODOUR,[3] A LINE OF DEMARCATION FOR [THE SPRINKLING OF] THE BLOOD,[4] AND THE WASHING OF HANDS AND FEET.[5] BUT TIME, NOTHAR AND DEFILEMENT WERE ALIKE IN BOTH.[6]

GEMARA. What does OUTSIDE ITS APPOINTED PLACE mean?—Resh Lakish said: Outside the place which had been examined for it.[7] Said R. Joḥanan to him: But surely the whole of Eretz Israel had been thus examined?[8] Rather said R. Joḥanan: It means, e.g., that one slaughtered it within the wall of Jerusalem.[9] But let him explain it [as meaning] that he slaughtered it without the wall, but not opposite the door [of the *Hekal*], for R. Adda b. Ahabah said: If one did not slaughter it opposite the door [of the *Hekal*], it is disqualified, for it is said, *And he shall slay it . . . and sprinkle* [*of her blood toward the front of the tent of meeting*]:[10] As the sprinkling must be opposite the door, so must its slaughtering be opposite the door? And should you answer that he [R. Joḥanan] does not assimilate [slaughtering to sprinkling], surely it was stated: (If one did not slaughter it opposite the door, R. Joḥanan maintained that it was disqualified, [because it says], *And he shall slay . . . and sprinkle*. Resh Lakish said: It is fit, [because it says,
b *and she shall be brought forth*] *without the camp and he shall slay.*[1] And it was stated likewise:)[2] If one did not burn it opposite the door,—R. Joḥanan said: It is disqualified; R. Oshaia said: It is fit. R. Joḥanan said, 'It is disqualified', [because it says,] and *he shall burn . . . and he shall sprinkle.*[3] R. Oshaia said, 'It is fit', because Scripture saith, *with her dung* [pirshah] *it shall be burnt*: [that means, in] the place that she departs [*poresheth*] to death, there must she be burnt![4]—I will answer you: He [R. Joḥanan] proceeds to a climax:[5] it goes without saying that [if he slaughters it] without the wall [and not opposite the door] [it is disqualified], because he removed it further [from the Sanctuary]. But even [if he slaughtered it] within the wall, so that he brought it nearer, and I might argue that it is fit, he informs us [that it is not].

The master said: 'Said R. Joḥanan to him, But surely the whole of Eretz Israel had been thus examined'. Wherein do they differ?—One master holds that the Flood descended in Eretz Israel;[6] while the other master holds that it did not descend [there]. R. Naḥman b. Isaac observed: Both interpret the same text, [viz.:] *Son of man, say unto her: Thou art a land that is not cleansed, nor rained upon in the day of indignation.*[7] R. Joḥanan holds: Scripture speaks rhetorically:[8] O Eretz Israel, how art thou not clean; did then the rain [flood] descend upon thee in the day of indignation? While Resh Lakish holds that it bears its plain sense: Eretz Israel, thou art not clean, [for] did not the rain descend upon thee in the day of indignation?

Resh Lakish refuted R. Joḥanan: There were courtyards in Jerusalem built on a rock; beneath them was a hollow, on account of
c graves down in the depths.[1] There they brought pregnant women, and women who had given birth, and there they reared their children for [the service of] the [Red] Heifer.[2] And they brought oxen with doors on their backs;[3] the children sat on them and carried stone goblets,[4] which they filled [with water] and then returned to their place![5]—Said R. Huna, the son of R. Joshua: They were especially strict in the case of the [Red] Heifer.

R. Joḥanan refuted Resh Lakish: On one occasion they found [human] bones in the Wood Chamber,[6] and they desired to declare Jerusalem unclean. Whereupon R. Joshua rose to his feet and exclaimed: Is it not a shame and disgrace to us that we declare the city of our fathers unclean! Where are the dead of the Flood, and where are the dead of Nebuchadnezzar?[7] Since he said, 'Where are the dead of the Flood?' he surely meant that they had *not* been there [in Jerusalem]?—Then on your reasoning, had there been none of the slain of Nebuchadnezzar [there]?[8] Rather, they had been, but were removed; so here too[9] they had been [in Eretz Israel], but were cleared away. But if they were removed,

a (1) So that the blood touched the four sides of the altar. (2) *Sc.* the meal-offerings, opposite the south-west corner of the altar. (3) V. *supra 46b.* (4) Whether it was to be sprinkled above or below. (5) All these were required at the public *bamah* but not at a private one. (6) The prohibition of eating the flesh after time and when unclean, or when it had been rendered *piggul* (v. Glos.) through the intention of eating it after time, operated at both. (7) Examined to see that there was no hidden grave under it. Only in such a place might it be slaughtered. (8) V. *infra.* (9) Whereas it was to be slaughtered without, Num. XIX, 3. (10) Ibid. *3f.* This would correspond to opposite the door of the Hekal.

b (1) Which implies anywhere outside the camp. (2) Sh.M. deletes the bracketed passage. (3) Actually the order is reversed: *And Eleazar . . . shall sprinkle of her blood toward the front of the tent of meeting seven times, and he shall burn the heifer.* This proximity denotes assimilation: the blood must be sprinkled and the flesh burnt in the same place.—Thus R. Joḥanan does assimilate two actions stated in proximity, and the same must apply to slaughtering and sprinkling. (Or, he states this explicitly, if the bracketed passage is retained in the text.) (4) I.e., where her last death-struggles take place. In her struggles she may move away from the spot opposite the door of the *Hekal.* (5) Lit., 'he states, "it is not necessary".' (6) So the bones of many dead sunk in the earth; hence it is not purified. (7) Ezek. XXII, 24. (8) Lit., 'indeed wonders.'

c (1) In case there were unknown graves below, the hollow prevented the defilement from striking upward and rendering unclean what was in the courtyard. (2) These children, who would thus be rigidly guarded from defilement, besprinkled the priest who burnt the Red Heifer. (3) These doors likewise interposed between the defilement of a possible lost grave and the children who sat on them. This was done when they left the courtyards and went to the Pool of Siloam to draw water for mixing with the ashes of the Red Heifer. (4) A vessel of stone cannot become unclean. (5) This proves that Eretz Israel was not regarded as clear of lost graves. (6) Where the wood was kept for the altar. (7) They are found elsewhere, but not here. (8) Of course there were, as many were slain when he captured Jerusalem. (9) In respect of the dead of the Flood.

ומתן סביב ותנופה והגשה ר"י אומר *אין מנחה בבמה וכיהון ובגדי שרת וכלי שרת וריח ניחוח ומחיצה לדמים וריחוץ ידים ורגלים אבל הזמן הנותר והטמא שוין בזה ובזה: **גמ'** מאי חוץ מגתה אמר ר"ל חוץ ממקום הבדוק לה אמר לו רבי יוחנן והלא כל א"י בדוקה היא אלא א"ר יוחנן כגון ששחטה לפנים מן [א] חומת ירושלים ולוקמה כגון ששחטה חוץ לחומה שלא כנגד הפתח דאמר רב אדא בר אהבה שחטה שלא כנגד הפתח פסולה שנאמר °ושחט והזה מה הזאתה כנגד הפתח אף °שחיטתה כנגד הפתח וכי תימא דלא מקיש והא אתמר [ב] (שחטה שלא כנגד הפתח רבי יוחנן אמר *פסולה ושחט והזה ר"ל אמר כשרה °אל מחוץ למחנה ושחט ואיתמר נמי) שרפה שלא כנגד הפתח רבי יוחנן אמר פסולה ור' אושעיא אמר כשרה ר' יוחנן אמר פסולה ושרף והזה ורבי אושעיא אמר כשרה [ג] °על פרשה ישרף מקום שפורשת למיתה שםתהא שריפתה אמרי לא מיבעיא קאמר לא מיבעיא חוץ לחומה דרחוקי רחקה אלא אפי' לפנים מן החומה דקרובי קרבה ואימא תתכשר קמ"ל אמר מר אמר לו רבי יוחנן והלא כל א"י בדוקה היא במאי קמיפלגי מר סבר ירד מבול לא"י ומר סבר לא ירד אר"נ בר יצחק ושניהם מקרא אחד דרשו °בן אדם אמר לה את ארץ לא מטוהרה היא לא גושמה ביום זעם רבי יוחנן סבר אתמוהי מתמה קרא [ד] א"י מי לא [ה] מטוהרה את כלום ירדו עליך גשמים ביום זעם ור"ל סבר כפשטיה ארץ לא [ו] מטוהרה את מי לא ירדו עליך גשמים ביום זעם איתיביה ר"ל לר' יוחנן *חצירות היו בירושלים בנויות על [ז] הסלע ותחתיהן חלול מפני קבר התהום ומביאין נשים מעוברות ויולדות ומגדלות שם בניהם לפרה ומביאין שוורים ועל גביהן דלתות ותינוקות יושבין עליהן וכוסות של אבן [ח] בידן ומלאו וישבו במקומן אמר רב הונא בריה דרב יהושע מעלה עשו בפרה איתיבי' רבי יוחנן לריש לקיש [ט] *פעם אחד מצאו עצמות בלשכת דיר העצים ובקשו לגזור טומאה על ירושלים עמד רבי יהושע על רגליו ואמר לא בושה וכלימה היא לנו שנגזור טומאה על עיר אבותינו איה מתי מבול איה מתי נבוכדנצר [י] מדקאמר הכי לאו למימרא דלא הוו ולטעמיך הרוגי נבוכדנצר הכי נמי דלא הוו אלא הוו (א) ופנינהו הכא נמי הוו ופנינהו [יא] ואי אפנו

הא

במדבר יט | רש"ק מ"ז | שם | שם | יחזקאל כב

תורה אור

רש"י

יב] ומתן סובב מתן סביב שתהא נראית המתנה לשתי רוחות המזבח דהיינו ב' מתנות שהן ארבע: תנופה והגשה · דמנחות: אין מנחה בבמה · מפרש בגמ' מנא ליה: וכיהון · כהונה דאפי' זר בבמת יחיד כשר: בגדי שרת · בגדי כהונה: ריח ניחוח · כדאמרינן בפרק בית שמאי (לעיל דף מו:) לשם ששה דברים הזבח נזבח לשם ריח לאפוקי אברים שצלאן והעלן שאין בהם משום ריח ניחוח: ומחיצה לדמים · חוט הסיקרא להבדיל בין דמים העליונים לדמים התחתונים: הזמן · שנפסלין במחשבת חוץ לזמנו וחייבין על קדשים משום נותר וטמא שוין בשתיהם: **גמ'** ממקום הבדוק לה · לשוחטה שם שאין תחתיה קבר התהום: בדוקה היא · לקמן מפרש פלוגתייהו: לפנים מן החומה · של ירושלים דכתיב בה (במדבר יט) והוציא אותה וגו': שלא כנגד הפתח · של היכל: הזאה · יג] מפרש בה אל נכח וגו': ושרף והזה · בתר והזה סמך ושרף: מקום שפורשת למיתה · מקום שנפשה יוצאה בגמר פירכוסה וליציאת נפשה שלא קבע לה הכתוב מקום: לא מיבעיא יד] לחוץ לחומה · שלא כנגד הפתח: דרחוקי רחקה · מכנגד (ב) הקדושה: ר"ל סבר ירד מבול לא"י · ושקעו בה עצמות המתים: ותחתיהן חלול · שאם יש קבר מפסיק החלל ושוב אין טומאה בוקעת למעלה מן החלל אבל טומאה רצוצה בוקעת ועולה עד לרקיע: ומגדלות שם בניהם · לפרה דמשום דמטמאין את הכהן השורף את הפרה מפני הצדוקים עשו בה שאר מעלות הרבה שאין אחיו הכהנים נוגעין בו כל שבעת ימי טו] פרישתו *והוו אלו תינוקות נוגעין בו ומזין עליו: ועל גביהן דלתות · להפסיק בין התינוקות לקרקע שלא יאהילו על קבר התהום בלכתם למלאות מים חיים לקידוש מן השילוח אלמא לאו טולה בדוקה היא: וכוסות של אבן · שכל מעשה פרה בכלי גללים בכלי אבנים שאין מקבלים טומאה כדאמר טעמא במעתא קמייתא דסדר יומא (דף ג:): מעלה עשו בפרה · משום קולא דאקילו בה משום צדוקין שהיו אומרים במעורבי שמש היתה נעשית והיו מטמאין את הכהן ומטבילין אותו ושרפה טבול יום עשו בה מעלות אחרות דלא לזלזלו בה ומיהו אם שחטה במקום שאין בדוק לה לא מיפסלא בהכי דכל א"י בדוקה היא: איה מתי מבול · שנמצאים בשאר מקומות וכאן אינן נמצאין: איה הרוגי נבוכדנצר · שהרג בה *והופטו כולם ואין אחד מצוי בה על כרחיע בדוקה היא:

נהי

תוספות

חוץ ממקום הבדוק לה · קסבר דבעי בדיקה משום דירד מבול לא"י תימה *וכי מדאורייתא בעי בדיקה וי"ל דאיצטריך קרא (שלא) לשרפה במקום טומאה דאסור מדאורייתא דבעי' שחיטה ושריפה במקום טהור כשריפת פרים דאיתקוש אהדדי כדמשמע לעיל בסוף טבול יום (דף קה:) ואם תאמר אמאי לא מיחייב משום חוץ כששחטה חוץ למקומה כיון דתמימה היא וראויה לשאר קרבנות כדאמרינן בפרק שני שעירי (יומא דף סג:) גבי שעירי יום הכפורים ששחטן בחוץ דחייב על שניהם הואיל וראוין לשעיר הנעשה בחוץ ויש לומר דלא דמי דיכול לשוחטם דאין עליהם קריאת שם עד שעת הגרלה ועוד דאין קרבן שתהא פרה זו ראויה דאי לשלמים אין שלמים בציבור ועוד דפרה קדשי בדק הבית היא ואין יכול לשוחטה בקדשי מזבח:

שנאמר ושחט והזה מה הזאה כנגד הפתח וכו' · יש ספרים דגרסי ושרף והזה וכן משמע מדמייתי עלה מפלוגתא דרבי יוחנן ור' אושעיא ומיהו אפי' גרסינן הכא ושחט והזה ניחא דמשמע ליה דאי מקשינן שריפה להזאה ה"ה שחיטה:

אבל לפנים מן החומה דקרובי קרבה אימא תתכשר קא משמע לן · דפסולה משום דבעיא חוץ לשלש מחנות:

לא ירד מבול לא"י · תימה והכתיב (בראשית ז) ויכסו כל ההרים הגבוהים אשר תחת כל השמים ובבראשית *רבה אמרינן דר' ישמעאל ב"ר יוסי ובהמי אחד היו הולכין בדרך פירוש בהמי שומר בהמות אמר להון ההוא כותאה איתו לצליי על טורא גריזים דלא נחית עליה טופנא אמר אותו בהמי לפני ר' ישמעאל בר' יוסי רבי תן לי רשות להשיב לו תשובה א"ל השב א"ל הר גריזים תחת כל השמים הוא א"ל הן ולא כתיב ויכסו כל ההרים הגבוהים אשר תחת כל השמים קרא עליו ולא יהיה בך עקר ועקרה ובבהמתך אפי' הבהמי שבך לא יתעקר מן התשובה ושמא י"ל דויכסו כל ההרים היינו שנלט הגל המבול בכל מקום כדאמרינן לקמן דמתו בהבלא ואותו כותי היה ר"ל שלא היה שם לא הבל ולא שום דבר אי נמי לאותו כותי נתכוונו לדחות בקש וקרא (להכא) ל"ק דבמקום שירד מבול התם קאמר שנתכסו ההרים:

ומביאין נשים עוברות ויולדות שם · אף על פי שהתינוקות טמאין בנדה ויולדות לא היו חוששין אלא לשמרם מטומאת מת דבעי הזאה ומטומאה היוצאה מגופן כגון בעל קרי*:

ועל גביהן דלתות · מאן דאמר בפ' קמא דגיטין (דף ח:) ובנזיר פרק כ"ג (דף נה:) ובפ' בכל מערבין (עירובין דף ל:) ובפ' בתרא דחגיגה (דף כה:) אהל זרוק לא שמיה אהל סבר כר' יהודה דאמר בריש הישן (סוכה דף כא.) לא היו מביאין דלתות אלא שוורים שכריסן רחבה והתם טעמא משום דכתיב קרא (איוב י) ובעצמות וגידים תסוככני אע"ג דבעלמא אהל שאינו עשוי בידי אדם לא שמיה אהל ומיהו רבי יהודה ודאי סבר שמיה אהל דהא קא אמר טעמא מפני שדעתו של תינוק גסה עליו:

ומלאו ועלו וישבו במקומן · קשה תימה מה מועיל בתינוקות דסוף סוף בעינן איש בשעת קידוש שנותנין האפר במים או בשעת הזאה לרבי יהודה או לרבנן כדמוכח *בפרק טרף בקלפי (יומא דף מג:)*:

מעלה עשו בפרה · ר"ל נמי ידע דמעלה עשו אלא דאי לא ירד מבול לא"י אין ראוי לעשות מעלה זו ומיהו קשה דהא מודה רבי יוחנן דמתו בהבלא כדלקמן:

מדקאמר איה מתי מבול מכלל דלא הוו · תימה דלרבי יוחנן גופיה תקשי ליה הכא דמתו בהבלא:

היינו

עין משפט נר מצוה

ג"י ל"ק וכי מדאורייתא בעי בדיקה דאיצטריך קרא לפוטרה וי"ל דכיון דמדאוריית' אסור לשורפה במקום טומאה דבעינן שחיטה כו'

יד א ב מיי' פ"ד מהל' פרה אדומה הל' ה:

טו ג ד מיי' פ"ב מהל' פרה הלכה ז:

שיטה מקובצת

א] מן החומה ולוקמה תיבות חומת ירושלים נמחק: ב] מן תיבת שחטה עד תיבת שרפה רשום עליו קו שהוא נמחק: ג] כשרה אמר קרא על: ד] קרא ארץ אמאי ותיבות א"י מי נמחק: ה] לא מטהורה את: ו] לא טהורה תיבת מטוהרה ל"ש: ז] על גבי סלע: ח] אבן בידם תניא לשילוח ירדו ומלאו עלו וישבו: ט] לקיש מעשה ומצאו: י] מדקאמר איה מתי מבול לאו ותיבת הכי נמחק: יא] תיבות ואי אפנו נמחק: יב] תיבות ומתן סובב נמחק: יג] הזאה מפורש בה אל נוכח פני וגו': יד] מיבעי' חוץ לחומה אות ל' נמחק: טו] ימי פרישותו:

[סדר נח פרשה לג וע"ש כמה וכמה שינויים ועיין עוד בדברים רבה סדר עקב פ"ג בנוסחא אחרת]

תוספתא דעדיות פ"ג

[וע"ע בתוס' סוכה כא.]

[וע"ע בתוס' סוכה כא. בתנו ישוב לפס]

מסורת הש"ס

[עי' תוס' לקמן קיט: ד"ה אין מנחה]

הגהות הב"ח

(א) גמ' אלא הוו והופנו הכא נמי הוו והופנו ואי: (ב) רש"י ד"ה דרחוקי וכו' הקדושה הס"ד ואח"כ מ"ה מ"ס ירד מבול ר"ל סבר:

גליון הש"ס

גמ' שחיטתה כנגד הפתח· עיין לעיל דף לג ע"ב תוס' ד"ה אלא:

ס"א והיו אלו תינוקות ממלאין מי חטאת ומזין עליו

סוכה כא. תוספתא דפרה פ"ג [משנה דפרה פ"ג מ"ב]

סס"ד ואת"ב מס"ד כא איפני כולם ואין כו' כצ"ל נ"ק

ג"י ל"ק בפ' טרף בקלפי וי"ל דמה שהיה יכול לתקן מתקני' משום מעלה דכולה מילתא מעלה בעלמא כדחשי מעלה עשו בפרה ור"ל לקיש נמי ידע כו' וכד"א

עין משפט נר מצוה

טז א מיי' פי"ח מהלכות מעשה"ק הלכה יג:

מסורת הש"ס

תורה אור

א] הא איפני נהי דאיפני מירושלים מכולה א"י לא איפני איכא דאמרי איתיביה ר"ל לרבי יוחנן איה מתי מבול איה מתי נבוכדנאצר מאי לאו מדהני הוו הני נמי הוו מידי איר' הא כדאיתיה והא כדאיתיה איתיביה ב] °מכל אשר בחרבה מתו בשלמא לדידי דאמינא ירד מבול לא"י משום הכי מתו אלא לדידך אמאי מתו ג] משום הבלא כדרב חסדא דאמר רב חסדא *ברותחין קלקלו וברותחין נידונו ד] דכתיב הכא °וישוכו המים וכתיב התם °וחמת המלך שככה איכא דאמרי איתיביה רבי יוחנן לר"ל מכל אשר בחרבה מתו בשלמא לדידי דאמינא לא ירד מבול לא"י ה] משום הכי הוי חרבה אלא לדידך מאי חרבה חרבה שהיתה מעיקרא ואמאי קרי ליה חרבה כדרב חסדא דאמר רב חסדא בדור המבול *לא נגזרה גזרה על דגים שבים שנאמר מכל אשר בחרבה מתו ולא דגים שבים בשלמא למ"ד לא ירד מבול לא"י היינו דקם רימא התם אלא למ"ד ירד רימא היכא קם א"ר ינאי גוריות הכניסו בתיבה *והאמר רבה בר בר חנה לדידי חזי לי אורזילא דרימא בת יומא והוי כהר תבור והר תבור כמה הויא ארבעין פרסי משכא דצואריה תלתא פרסי ו] מרבעתא דרישא פרסא ופלגא רמא ז] *כבא וסכר ירדנא א"ר יוחנן ראשו הכניסו לתיבה והאמר מר מרבעתא דרישא פרסא ופלגא אלא ח] ראש חוטמו הכניסו לתיבה והא א"ר יוחנן לא ירד מבול לא"י לדברי ר"ל קאמר והא קסגיא תיבה אמר ר"ל קרניו קשרו בתיבה *והאמר רב חסדא אנשי דור המבול ברותחין קלקלו וברותחין נידונו ולטעמיך תיבה היכי סגיא ועוד עוג מלך הבשן היכא קאי אלא נס נעשה להם שנצטננו בצידי התיבה ולר"ש ט] [בן לקיש] נהי נמי דירד מבול לא"י והא לא פש י] דאמר ר"ל *למה נקרא שמה מצולה שכל מתי מבול נצתללו יא] שם ורבי יוחנן אמר למה נקרא שמה שנער שכל מתי מבול ננערו שם אי אפשר דלא אידבקו א"ר אבהו למה נקרא שמה שנער שמנערת עשיריה והא קחזינן יב] דהוו תלתא דרי לא משכי א"ר אמי *כל האוכל מעפרה של בבל כאילו אוכל בשר אבותיו תנ"ה כל האוכל מעפרה של בבל כאילו אוכל בשר אבותיו וי"א כאילו אוכל שקצים ורמשים: יג] שעיר המשתלח: *ורמינהי *°או קרבן שומע אני אפילו קדשי בדק הבית שנקראו קרבן שנאמר °ונקרב את קרבן ה' ת"ל ואל פתח אהל מועד לא הביאו מי שראוי לבא יד] באהל מועד יצאו קדשי בדק הבית שאינן ראוין טו] אוציא את אלו שאינן ראוין ולא אוציא את שעיר המשתלח שהוא ראוי לבא אל פתח אהל מועד ת"ל לה' *להוציא שעיר המשתלח שאינו מיוחד לה' לא קשיא כאן קודם הגרלה כאן לאחר הגרלה אחר הגרלה נמי האיכא וידוי אלא אמר רב מני לא קשיא כאן *קודם וידוי כאן לאחר וידוי : הרובע והנרבע: והא נמי תיפוק לי מפתח אהל מועד

בשלמא

נהי דאיפני מירושלים · כולה ר"ל קאמר לה : מהבלא מתו · וקברום הבאים אחריהם בבתי קברות ואין לחוש לכל הארץ אלא לשאר ארצות שהיה שם מבול ונשקעו בטיט : חרבה דמעיקרא · קודם מבול טז] : מכל אשר בחרבה · לאפוקי דגים שבים : יז] דהיינו דקם רימא התם · הראם זכר ונקבה שהוא גדול ואינו יכול ליכנס לתיבה עמדו שם : גוריות · הכניסם לתיבה : אורזילא · הוא ראם דימא שהוא על שפת הים : בר יומא · ביום שנולד : משכא דצוארי' · משך צוארו : בי מרבעתא דרישיה · בי מרבץ של ראשו : רמא יח] כבא וסכר לירדנא · הטיל גלל בירדן וסכר הירדן וסתם הילוך מימיו יט] כבא כמו (עירובין דף כט:) כיבוי דרעותא דניסן : חוטמו · שיוכל להנשם: לא ירד מבול לא"י · ולמה ליה לשנויי הכי· לימא דהתם קם כ"ל דל"ג : והא קא סגיא תיבה · והא התיבה מהלכת על פני המים מגבוה לנמוך נמצא חוטמו נשמטת מן התיבה ומת: ומשני· קרניו קשרו לתיבה : ברותחין נידונו · ונמצא נמלג ברותחין : וליטעמיך תיבה היכי סגיא · והלא זפותה היא מבית ומבחוץ כדכתיב וכפרת אותה וגו' (בראשית ו) וכיון דרותחין הן היאך כ] מהלכת שאין זפתה נפשר : עוג מלך הבשן · דכתיב ביה ויבא הפליט וא"ר יוחנן (נדה דף סא:) זה עוג שפלט מאנשי דור המבול : נס נעשה ונצטננו המים · שבצידי התיבה ושם עמד עוג והראם וגם הזפת לא נפשר והראם לא הוצרך לתיבה ומפני גובהן לא טבעו : הא לא פש · מן המתים שם כלום דאיידי דגבוה היא השפילו המים לבבל שהיא מצולה : למה נקרא שמה מצולה · דכתיב (ישעיה מד) האומר לצולה חרבי: אי אפשר דלא אדביקו · בטיט : שמנערת עשיריה · כא] מפני שאינן מרחמים על הבריות כדאמרינן במסכת ביצה (דף לב:) עשירי בבל יורדי גיהנם הן : כאילו אוכל שקצים ורמשים · של מבול : או קרבן שומע אני כו' · קרבן דכתיב בשחוטי חוץ (ויקרא יז) להקריב קרבן וגו' דריש ליה בת"כ על הקרבן כב] חייב ואינו חייב על השוחט חולין בפנים או קרבן לאו להכי אתא אלא לחייב על קדשי בדק הבית ששחטן בחוץ שאף הן נקראו קרבן כענין שנאמר (במדבר לא) ונקרב את קרבן ה' איש אשר מצא כלי זהב אצעדה וצמיד ואין זה אלא לבדק הבית : שאין ראוין לפתח אהל מועד · אני שמעתי בסדר יומא לפי שסתמן בעלי מומין דקי"ל המתפיס תמימים לבדק הבית עובר בעשה במס' תמורה (דף ז:) אבל לענין הסוגיא אני למד כאן דאפילו תמים נמי קרי אינו ראוי דלא הועתד לבא אל אהל מועד דהא פרת חטאת תמימה היא וקרי לה אינו ראוי : אוציא את אלו שאין עתידין כד] לאהל מועד · ולא אוציא שעיר המשתלח דראוי הוא שהוא תמים דבעינן שיהא ראוי לשם דלא ידעינן הי מתרמי כה] זה שמעתי ולפי סוגיא של שמועה זו משמע דקרי ליה ראוי ועתיד ליכנס משום הגרלה ווידוי : ת"ל לה' · להקריב קרבן לה' המיוחד לה' להוציא שעיר המשתלח שאינו מיוחד לשם : קודם הגרלה · הוי ראוי ועתיד ליכנס משום הגרלה ואי לאו דמעטינן מלה' ה"א לחייב : כו] אחר הגרלה · לא ראוי לבא הוא ומימעיט מאל פתח : הא איכא וידוי · דבעי ליכנס להתוודות עליו : תיפוק לי מאל פתח אהל מועד · דהא לאו ראוין הן לבא לעזרה :

בשלמא

היינו דקם רימא התם · ואע"ג דכל השאר מתו בהבלא מחמת שהיה גדול וגבור לא הזיק לו ההבל : אורזילא דרימא · גר' ר"ת פי' עופר של ראם דעופר האילים מתרגמי' אורזילא דאיילא (שיר ב) ורימא הוא ראם ולא כרבי שמואל דג רם בהמוכר את הספינה (ב"ב דף עג:) אורזילא דימא ומפרש דג של ים ואגב ריהטיה לא דק דהא אמר הכא לא נגזרה גזרה על דגים שבים ואותם בופל"ש שאנו קורין ראם ליתא וחלבם אסור דראם ודאי מין חיה הוא וחלבו מותר כדכתיב אקו ודישון ומתרגמינן יעלא ורימא ובופל"ש שבמקומינו קטנים דאין לומר שהוא מין ראם ויש במינו גדול דא"כ מאי קשיא ליה היכא קם הא לא קשיא ליה *אריה דבי עילאי בפרק אלו טרפות (חולין דף נט:) היכא קם *שהיו אריות אחרים קטנים שיכול להכנים ועוד הא קא חזינן דאותן בופל"ש בני מלאכה נינהו ומושכין בקרון וחורשין בהן וראם לאו בר מלאכה הוא דכתיב התקשר ראם בתלם עבותו אם ישדד עמקים אחריך (איוב לט) : יצאו קדשי בדק הבית · בלשון אחר פי' בקונטרס דממעט אפי' תמימים דהא פרת חטאת תמימה וממעטא משום דאינה ראויה לפתח אהל מועד ונראה דאין זו ראיה דפרת חטאת לא קיימא למזבח *ולאו מתפיס תמימים לבדק הבית *הא אמר בסוף תמורה (דף לג:) דכל הראוי למזבח אינו יוצא מידי מזבח לעולם ונמכרו לצורכי עולות ושלמים וא"ת מאי שנא קדשי בדק הבית תמימים משעירי יוה"כ דאמר בפ' שני שעירי (יומא דף סג:) דחייב על שניהם בחוץ הואיל וראויים לשעיר הנעשה בחוץ וכ"ש הנך דאין יוצאין מידי מזבח וי"ל כיון דעדיין לאו קדשי מזבח נינהו לא חשיבי ראוין לפתח אהל מועד* : כאן קודם הגרלה כו' · בפ' שני שעירי (יומא דף סג:) אמרי' דחייב על שניהם והיינו למסקנא דשמעתין דמשני כאן קודם וידוי וכו' אבל קודם הגרלה חייב דראוי לשעיר הנעשה בחוץ : כאן קודם וידוי כאן לאחר וידוי · ומדפטר קרא קודם וידוי כ"ש לאחר וידוי וכי אצטריך פתח אהל מועד משום פרה ומשום קדשי בדק הבית ומיהו היא גופה תימה אמאי לא ממעטינן מלה' ובפ"ק דתמורה (דף יג·) גרס בכל הספרים ולא אוציא פרת חטאת ושעיר המשתלח שהם ראויין לפתח אהל מועד ת"ל לה' שמיוחדים לה' יצאו אלו שאין מיוחדין לה' ומיהו קדשי בדק הבית שפיר מיקרו מיוחדין לה' דכולם לשמים וע"כ נמי לא גרס פרת חטאת בברייתא' דלא תיקשי מתני' ועוד אצטריך אל פתח אהל מועד למעוטי גגו כדאמרינן לעיל בפ' השוחט והמעלה (דף קז:) :

תנן

מהרי"ב כצ"ל נ"ק

אלא שהיו סי' כצ"ל נ"ק

נ"ב הכי קיימא למזבח כדאמרינן בסוף תמורה כו'

[ופי' תוס' יומא סג: ד"ה וכל שאין]

[שבת קנ: ע"ש דברי ר"ל ור"י נהפך]

[יומא סג: תמורה ו: יג: ושם איתא או קרבן וע"ש ברש"י]

[ר"ש יב. סנהדרין קח:]

סנהדרין קח. קדושין יג.

ב"ב עג: ע"ש

[בב"ב איתא כופתא וע"ש ברשב"ם ותוס' וכן מוכח ברש"י סנהדרין קח: ד"ה בטולה וקצת נ"ע בד"י דסכא]

ר"ס יב. סנהדרין קח:

[שבת קיג:]

[סג' בת"כ קך היא אוציא הקדש בדק הבית שאינו בא אל אהל מועד ולא אוציא רובע ונרבע וכו' ת"ל להקריב הכשרים ליקרב אוציא את אלו שאינם כשרים ליקרב ולא אוציא שעיר המשתלח ת"ל לה' המיוחדים לשם יצאו אלו שאין מיוחדים לשם· והקושיא כמלא שעיר המשתלח לא ממועט מן ואל פתח אהל מועד לא הכיאו רק צריך קרא אחרינא לה' המיוחדים לשם ובמתניתין ממעט שעיר המשתלח מפסוק ואל פתח אהל מועד ועי' רש"י]

שיטה מקובצת

א] תיבות הא איפני נמחק : ב] איתיביה ר"ל לר"י מכל : ג] מתו מהבלא כדרב חסדא תיבת משום נמחק : ד] נידונו ברותחין קלקלו בשכבת זרע וברותחין נידונו כתיב הכא : ה] לא"י אמטול כתיב חרבה דהוי חרבה בעולם אלא לדידך מאי חרבה חרבה דמעיקרא דאמר רב חסדא והשאר נמחק : ו] פרסי בי מרבעתא

דרישא : ז] רמא כבא וסכר תיבת כבא וי"ג כופתא נמחק : ח] תיבת ראש נמחק : ט] שמעון בן לקיש : י] פש תמן מיתא דאמר ר"ל : יא] נצתללו לשם : יב] קחזינן דאיכא עד תלתא ותיבת דהוו נמחק : יג] וכן שעיר המשתלח שעיר המשתלח לאו ראוי לפתח אהל מועד הוא והתניא ותיבת ורמינהי נמחק : יד] לבא לפתח אהל מועד : טו] ראויין לפתח אהל מועד יכול שאני אוציא את אלו ולא אוציא את שעיר המשתלח ת"ל והשאר ל"ש : טז] מבול כלומר כל אשר ביבשה לאפוקי והד"א ותיבות מכל אשר בחרבה ל"ש : יז] מה"ד היינו דקם : יח] רמא כבא וסכריה : יט] כבא כמו כיבוי דרעיתא : כ] היאך היא : כא] עשיריה אין עשיריה מתקיימין מפני : כב] הקרבן הוא חייב : כג] ראוי דאין עתידין לבא : כד] שאין עתידין לבא אל פתח אהל מועד : כה] מתרמי לשם חטאת זה : כו] מה"ד לאחר הגרלה :

הדר

[113*b*] then they were removed![10]—Granted that they had been cleared away from Jerusalem, they had not been cleared away from the whole of Eretz Israel.

Others state, Resh Laḳish refuted R. Joḥanan: 'Where are the dead of the Flood; where are the dead of Nebuchadnezzar?' Surely then, since the latter were [in Eretz Israel], the former
a too were there?—Why say thus? each had its own state.[1]

Resh Laḳish refuted R. Joḥanan: *Whatsoever was in the dry land, died:*[2] according to my opinion that the Flood descended to Eretz Israel, it is well: for that reason they died. But on your view, why did they die?—Because of the heat, in accordance with R. Ḥisda. For R. Ḥisda said: With hot passion they sinned, and by hot water they were punished. [For] here it is written, *And the water cooled;*[3] whilst elsewhere it is said, *Then the king's wrath cooled down.*[4]

Others state, R. Joḥanan refuted Resh Laḳish: *Whatsoever was in the dry land, died.* On my opinion that the Flood did not descend to Eretz Israel, it is well: for that reason is it called dry land. But on your view, what is the meaning of *'dry land'*?—The place which was originally dry land. And why does he specify *'dry land'*?[5]—In accordance with R. Ḥisda. For R. Ḥisda said: In the generation of the Flood the decree [of destruction] was not decreed against the fish in the sea, because it says, '*Whatsoever was in the* dry land *died*', but not the fish in the sea.

On the view that the Flood did not descend there, it is well: thus the *re'em*[6] stayed there. But on the view that it did descend, where did it stay?[7]—Said R. Jannai: They took the young [of the *re'em*] into the Ark. But surely Rabbah b. Bar Ḥanah said: I saw a sea *re'em*, one day old, which was as big as Mount Tabor. And how big is Mount Tabor? Forty parasangs.[8] Its neck, stretched out, was three parasangs; the place where its head rested was a parasang and a half. It cast a ball of excrements and blocked the Jordan!—Said R. Joḥanan: They took its head [only] into the Ark. But a master said: The place where its head rested was three parasangs?—Rather, they took the tip of its nose into the Ark. But surely
b R. Joḥanan said: The Flood did not descend in Eretz Israel?[1]—He explains [it thus] on the view of Resh Laḳish. But the Ark plunged up and down?[2]—Said Resh Laḳish: They tied its horns to the Ark.[3] But surely R. Ḥisda said: The people in the generation of the Flood sinned with hot passion, and with hot water they were punished?[4]—And on your view, how could the Ark travel [at all]?[5] Moreover, how did Og king of Bashan stand?[6] Rather, a miracle was performed for it [the water], and it was cooled at the side of the Ark.

Now according to Resh Laḳish, even granted that the Flood fell upon Eretz Israel, surely, however, none [of the dead] were left there. For Resh Laḳish said: Why was it [Babylon] called *Meẓulah?* Because all the dead of the Flood were dumped [*niẓtallelu*] there? And R. Joḥanan said: Why was it called Shinar? Because all the dead of the Flood were shaken out thither [*nin'aru lesham*]?—Yet it was impossible that some should not have cleaved [remained]. R. Abbahu said: Why was it called Shinar?—Because it shakes out its wealthy men [*mena'ereth 'ashirim*].[7] But we see that there are [wealthy people there]?—They do not last three generations. R. Ammi said: He who eats earth of Babylon is as though he ate the flesh of his ancestors.[8] It has also been learnt likewise: He who eats earth in Babylon is as though he ate the flesh of his ancestors. Some say, It is as though he ate of abominations and creeping things.[9]

THE SCAPEGOAT. [Is it not eligible to come to the door of the tent of meeting?] Surely the following contradicts it: *Or sa-*
c *crifice* [ḳorban]:[1] I might understand even sacred things of the Temple Repair,[2] which are designated *ḳorban,* as it says, *And we have brought the Lord's ḳorban [offering].*[3] Therefore it states, *and bringeth it not unto the door of the tent of meeting:* [the law applies only to] what is eligible to come to the door of the tent of meeting; hence sacred things of Temple Repair, which are not thus eligible,[4] are excluded.[5] I might think that I exclude these, which are not eligible, but I do not exclude the scapegoat that is sent away, which is eligible to come to the door of the tent of meeting:[6] therefore it states, [*to sacrifice it*] *unto the Lord,* which excludes the scapegoat, as that is not dedicated to the Lord?—There is no difficulty: the one means before the casting of lots;[7] the other means after the casting of lots. After the casting of lots too there is still the confession?[8]—Rather, said R. Mani, there is no difficulty: The one means before confession; the other means after confession.

A ROBA' AND A NIRBA'. But this too I may infer from *'unto the*

(10) In any case then Eretz Israel is free from lost graves.

a (1) The latter had been in Eretz Israel, and cleared out, but the former were never there. (2) Gen. VII, 22. (3) Ibid. VIII, 1. E.V. abated. (4) Est. VII, 10. In both cases the root שכך is used, giving them the same meaning, and proving that the water was hot when it descended.—This heat spread to Eretz Israel. (5) Obviously all land where people lived was dry before the Flood. (6) A huge animal, too large to enter the Ark. (7) That it was able to survive the flood. (8) A Persian mile, nearly four English miles.—This passage occurs in a series of 'tall' stories by Rabbah b. Bar Ḥanah related in B. B. 73*a seq.*, which were probably veiled allegories on the political and social conditions of the time.

b (1) Hence he needs no explanation at all. (2) And this would cause the *re'em* to slip out and drown. (3) To secure it. (4) It would have been scalded. (5) Since its seams were caulked with pitch, why did not the pitch dissolve in the hot water and leave the Ark unseaworthy? (6) According to legend he was such a giant that he escaped from the Flood (Nid. 61*b*). Why wasn't he scalded by the hot water? (7) People cannot be wealthy there. (8) Who died there. (9) V. Shab. 113*b*.

c (1) Lev. XVII, 8. (2) V. *supra* 14*a* n. a 7. (3) Num. XXXI, 50. The verse continues: *of jewels of gold, armlets* etc.; hence it obviously refers to sacred things of Temple Repair. (4) Because only blemished animals can be consecrated for Temple Repair, and such are not eligible for a sacrifice. (5) If one slaughtered these without as a sacrifice, he is not culpable. (6) As we do not know which will be sacrificed and which will be sent away, until the lots are cast. (7) To determine which shall be sacrificed and which sent away; V. Lev. XVI, 8. At that stage it is eligible to come to the tent of meeting. (8) Which is made over that goat, v. ibid. 21. That was made within.

door of the tent of meeting'?[9] [114a] As for a *roba'* and a *nirba'*, it is well: it is conceivable [that the other proof-text is required] where one first consecrated them and then bestiality was committed with them.[10] But as for an animal set apart [for idolatrous worship] and an animal worshipped [as an idol], no man can for-
a bid that which does not belong to him?[1]—This refers to lesser sacrifices, and in accordance with R. Jose the Galilean, who maintained that lesser sacrifices are their owner's property.[2] For it was taught: [*If any one sin*] *and commit a trespass against the Lord* [. . . *then he shall bring his guilt-offering*]:[3] this is to include lesser sacrifices, because they are his [the individual's] property:[4] this is the view of R. Jose the Galilean. Therefore [the second proof-text is required for] *roba'* and *nirba'*, because immorality is involved.[5] [It is required for] a [harlot's] hire, the price [of a dog], *kil'ayim*, and a animal calved through the caesarean section, in the case of the young of consecrated animals [sacrifices]; [because] he holds: The offerings of sacred animals are sacred from birth.[6]

BLEMISHED ANIMALS . . . AN ANIMAL TOGETHER WITH ITS
b YOUNG etc. Now, they are all necessary.[1] For if he taught about blemished animals [only], I would say that the reason is that they are repulsive,[2] but as for turtledoves, which are not repulsive, I would say that they agree with R. Simeon. While if he taught about turtledoves, I would say that the reason is because they were not rejected after having been eligible; but as for blemished animals which were eligible but became rejected, I would say that R. Simeon agrees with the Rabbis.[3] And if he taught about these two, I would say that the reason is because their disqualification is intrinsic; but as for an animal and its young, where the disqualification comes from without,[4] I would say that the Rabbis agree with R. Simeon. Thus [all three] are necessary.

FOR R. SIMEON MAINTAINED etc. What is R. Simeon's reason?—Said R. Ela in the name of Resh Lakish: Because Scripture saith, *Ye shall not do after all that we do here this day,* [*every man whatsoever is right in his own eyes*]:[5] Moses spoke thus to Israel: When ye enter the [Promised] Land, ye shall offer votive [sacrifices],[6] but ye shall not offer obligatory offerings. Thus Gilgal in comparison with Shiloh was premature, and Moses said to them, *Ye shall not*

(9) Why does the Mishnah quote a different proof-text here? (10) Now, when it was consecrated, it was fit to come to the door of the tent of meeting and therefore the text, *'and hath not brought it'* etc. may not exclude this case; for the first text might mean that if an animal was eligible when it was consecrated and then one slaughtered it without, he is liable, even if it was not eligible when it was slaughtered; hence the Mishnah quotes the other proof-text, *'to present it as an offering unto the Lord before the Tabernacle of the Lord'*. This definitely excludes whatever is not actually fit to be offered.

a (1) The Mishnah must mean that the animal had been set apart *before* it was consecrated, for once it is consecrated it belongs to God, and it cannot be forbidden by any man's act, viz., dedicating it for an idolatrous sacrifice or worshipping it. But in that case the first proof-text is sufficient. (2) Hence they can be forbidden even after they are consecrated, and the Mishnah treats of such a case. (3) Lev. V, 21. The trespass referred to is false repudiation of liability on oath. (4) If one swears falsely that he did not vow a peace-offering, which is of lesser sanctity, he brings a guilt-offering. Though this law does not apply to sacred property (deduced from, *'and deal falsely with his neighbour'* ibid.), the phrase *'against the Lord'* shews that it does apply nevertheless even where there is an element of sanctity, viz., in the case of lesser sacrifices, and thus teaches that these count as the individual's property. (5) For which reason they are disqualified even if bestiality is committed after they were consecrated. (6) As stated above, the second proof-text is necessary only if the animals were eligible when consecrated, and in these that is possible only in the case of the *young* of consecrated animals, which were disqualified before birth by being promised as a harlot's hire or the exchange of a dog: when one came to sacrifice their mother, they would come *'to the door'* too. It cannot arise in the case of the animals themselves, for if they were consecrated and then given as a harlot's hire, this second act is invalid (Tem. 30*b*) and they remain fit. Whilst if they were first a harlot's hire and then consecrated, the law is deduced from the first proof-text. The same applies to the other cases, viz., *kil'ayim* etc. Again, if these young become sacred even before birth, the act of subsequently giving them as a harlot's hire etc. would not disqualify them, just as it does not disqualify the mother. Therefore he must hold that they are sacred only from birth.—Several words are omitted from the text, in accordance with Rashi and Sh.M.

b (1) The controversy between R. Simeon and the Sages must be taught in all three instances. (2) Therefore the Rabbis hold that he is not liable for slaughtering them without. (3) That he is not liable. (4) It is not intrinsic and only due to an accident of time, viz., that they are both slaughtered on the same day. (5) Deut. XII, 8. (6) Lit., 'which are right (or pleasing) in your eyes'.

בשלמא רובע ונרבע משכחת ליה דאקדשינהו מעיקרא והדר א] רבעו אלא מוקצה ונעבד *אין אדם אוסר דבר שאינו שלו בקדשים קלים *ואליבא דר' יוסי הגלילי דאמר קדשים קלים ממון בעלים ב] הוא *דתניא °ומעלה מעל בה' לרבות קדשים קלים שהן ממונו דברי רבי יוסי הגלילי הלכך רובע ונרבע דבר ערוה ג] מוקצה ונעבד עבודת כוכבים בקדשים קלים אתנן ומחיר כלאים יוצא דופן בולדות קדשים קסבר *ולדי קדשים בהוייתן הן קדושים: בעלי מומין וכו' אותו ואת בנו וכו': וצריכי דאי תנא בעלי מומין משום דמאיסי אבל תורין דלא מאיסי אימא ד] (לא)דמודו ליה לר"ש ואי תנא תורין משום דלא חזי ואידחו אבל בעלי מומין דאיחזו ואידחו אימא ה] (לא) דמודה להו ר"ש לרבנן ואי תנא הני תרתי משום דפסולא דגופייהו אבל אותו ואת בנו דפסולא מעלמא קאתי ו] לה אימא מודו ליה רבנן לר"ש צריכא: שהיה רבי שמעון אומר: מאי טעמא דר"ש אמר רבי אילעא אמר ריש לקיש דאמר קרא °לא תעשון ככל אשר אנחנו עושים פה היום אמר להו משה לישראל כי עייליתו לארץ ישרות תקריבו הובות לא תקריבו וגלגל לגבי שילה מחוסר זמן הוא וקאמר להו משה לא תעשון אמר רבי ירמיה לרבי זירא אי הכי מילקי

(ויקרא ה; דברים יב)

בשלמא רובע ונרבע משכחת לה · דאילטריך למעוטינהו מלהקריב דאקדשינהו והדר נרבעו וכיון דחזו כבר ואידחו ראוייס קרינא בהו שנראו כבר ולא מימעטי מאל פתח דאיכא למימר הכי אמר קרא ואל פתח אהל מועד לא הביאו בשנראה לבא ואחר כך שחטו בחוץ חייב אבל שעיר המשתלח לאחר וידוי [תורה אור] מימעיט מאל פתח שהרי זה הביאו כשנראה לבא ומשילא לאחר וידוי לא נראה לבא: אלא מוקצה ונעבד · על כרחך מקמי דאקדשינהו הוו להו מוקצה ונעבד דאי לבתר דאקדשינהו תו לא מיתסרי בהקצאה ועבודה דאין אדם אוסר דבר שאינו שלו: בה' · וכחש בעמיתו דברים שיש בהם לשם ולעמיתו: לרבות קדשים קלי' · *שהכופר בהן ונשבע והודה חייב עליהם אשם גזילות שהן ממון בעלים דקרינא ביה וכחש בעמיתו: דבר ערוה · ואייל אף על המוקדשים כבר הלכך ממעטי בחוץ מלהקריב קרבן דלאו בני הקרבה נינהו דכתיב (ויקרא כב) כי משחתם בהם וכל מקום שנאמר השחתה אינו אלא דבר ערוה ועבודת כוכבים: נראה לי הכי גרסינן אתנן ומחיר וכלאים ויוצא דופן בולדות קדשים · כלומר הנך דאצרכנו למעוטינהו מלהקריב קרבן ולא נפקי מאל פתח על כרחך בשנראו כבר מיירי לא משכחת ז] אלא בולדות קדשים ואירע להו פסול במעי אמן דנראו לבא אל פתח אהל מועד קודם שנעשו אתנן ומחיר אם בא להקריב את אמן היו כן באין אל פתח דאי בדאקדשינהו לא משכחת לה דאין אתנן ומחיר חל על המוקדשין לפי שאינן שלו ומקרא נפקא לן בתמורה (דף ל:) ואי בדהוו אתנן והדר אקדשינהו מאל פתח נפקי וכן כלאים ויוצא דופן דאי אקדשינהו משנולדו מאל פתח נפקי אלא בולדות קדשים דמעיקרא עם אמן נראו לבא: וקסבר ולדות קדשים בהוייתן הן קדושין · בלידתן מתקדשות הלכך חל אתנן ומחיר עליהן אם נתן לה עובר של ח] מוקדשין באתנן דלא קדיש עד שנולד: בהוייתן ט] (הן) · לשון הוייה נקט בהו משום דמאשר יהיה לך נפקי לן ולדות קדשים ליקרב י] רק קדשיך אשר יהיו לך אלו התמורות אלו הולדות במסכת תמורה (דף יז:): וצריכי · הנך תלת פלוגתא דר' שמעון ורבנן במתני': משום דמאיסי · בעודן במומן פטרי רבנן בחוץ דלא מתקבלין *בפנים: מודו ליה · יא] דהואיל וחזו לאחר זמן קאי בלא תעשה: ובני יונה לא גרסינן: דאיחזו ואידחו · אימא אע"ג דכי עבר מומן ירצו השתא מיהא דהוין נינהו ונפטר בחוץ: לא תעשון כן · בספרי דריש ליה בתחילת ביאת הארץ היום אנו מטלטלין את המשכן ואנו אסורין בבמה ואין אנו מקריבין אלא במשכן לפיכך כל הקרבנות כשרים להקריב משנבוא לארץ י"ד שנים של כיבוש וחילוק אנו מותרין בבמה ושם לא תעשון ככל אשר אנחנו עושים פה יב] להקריב חובות ומה אנו מוהרין בה איש כל הישר בעיניו נדרים ונדבות שאין חובה עליו אלא שישרו בעיניו להתנדב כי לא באתם עד עתה וגו' עד שתבאו אל המנוחה לשילה שאע"פ שנכנסתם לארץ בעברכם את הירדן עדיין לא באתם אל המנוחה: כי עייליתו לארץ · י"ד שנים שתכבשו ותחלקו: ישרות תקריבו: נדרים ונדבות יג] הקרב בבמת ציבור: חובות לא תקריבו · איש איש שבכם לא יקריב שום חובה ואפילו בבמת ציבור עד שתבאו אל המנוחה והקריבום אלמא חובות דגלגל מחוסרי זמן הם עד כי יבא שילה ויקריבום שם וקאמר רחמנא לא תעשון אותם בגלגל ומשמע בין בבמת ציבור בין בבמת יחיד אלמא מחוסר זמן בבמה בלא תעשה: אי הכי · דהנך דגלגל מחוסרי זמן קרית להו: מילקי

אתנן ומחיר יולא דופן וכלאים בוולדות קדשים · אתנן ומחיר לא מיתפסים בקדשים קלים אפילו לרבי יוסי הגלילי דאף על גב דממונו הוי אינו חל עליו כדדרשינן פ' כל האסורין (תמורה ל:) לכל נדר פרט לנדור: וקסבר ולדות קדשים בהוייתן הן קדושים · וא"ת למה לי קרא למעוטי הלא חולין גמורים נינהו ודינם כשאר חולין לישחט בחוץ דאפילו פדיון לא בעו דאין קדושה חלה עליהן כלל כדמוכח בתמורה בפרק כילד מערימין (דף כד:) דתנן אם זכר עולה ואם נקבה זבחי שלמים ופריך בגמ' ל"ל למימר אם נקבה זבחי שלמים נקבה מי קדשה בבכורה ומשני סיפא אתאן לבהמה דהקדש וקתני סיפא ילדה טומטום או אנדרוגינוס רשב"ג אומר אין קדושה חלה עליהן ומפרש בגמ' *משום דסבר בהוייתן הן קדושים ואין קדושה חלה בדבר שאין ראוי ליקרב א"כ הכא נמי לא חיילא אאתנן ומחיר וכלאים ויוצא דופן וי"ל דהא דאמר רשב"ג אין קדושה חלה עליהן היינו קדושת הגוף (לפדות) וליאסר בגיזה ועבודה אבל קדושת דמים איכא ליפדות שלא במום ולכך בעי האי קרא דלא ממעטי מפתח אהל מועד *בקדשי בדק הבית *ולמאן דאמר במעי אמן הן קדושים אפילו קדושת הגוף נחתא עלייהו דתפסתינהו קדושה דאימיה וא"ת למאן דאמר בהוייתן נמי נימא מיגו דנחתא להן קדושת דמים נחתא להן קדושת הגוף כדאמר בתמורה בפרק אלו קדשים (דף יט: ושם) גבי מפריש נקבה לאשם ודוחק לומר רשב"ג סבר לה כרבי שמעון דלית ליה מיגו דאמר תמכר שלא במום ועוד דאי כרבי שמעון אפילו סבר במעי אמן קדושים לא חיילא עליה קדושת הגוף כדמפרש התם רבי שמעון לטעמיה דאמר כל מידי דלא חזי לגופיה לא נחתא ליה קדושת הגוף וגם אין לפרש דשאני מפריש נקבה דחזי לשאר קרבנות ושייך מגו טפי דהא אפילו בטרפה אשכחן דאמרינן מגו בסוף יש בקרבנות (שם דף יז·) ונראה לפרש דהכא מיירי כגון דלאחר שנעשו אתנן ומחיר הקדישן או בעודן במעי אמן או אחר שנולדו דכיון שהקדישן בפירוש חיילא עלייהו קדושה וא"ת ולוקמה נמי הכא כמ"ד במעי אמן הן קדושים וכגון שהקדיש בהמה מעוברת ושייר העובר כר' יוחנן דאמר בפ' כילד מערימין (תמורה כה·) אם שייר משוייר ועשה העובר אתנן ומחיר ואחר כך הקדישן ואע"ג דרבי יוחנן איתותב התם הא לבסוף *מסיק כתנאי ועוד מצי לאוקמה בבהמה של חולין מעוברת ועשה העובר אתנן ומחיר ואחר כך הקדישה וי"ל דניחא ליה לאוקמה בפשיטות כמאן דאמר בהוייתן הן קדושים והקדישן ואח"כ נתעברה ואם תאמר בההיא דכילד מערימין (ג"ז שם) דדייק אשב"ג דסבר בהוייתן הן קדושין מרישא נמי הוה מצי למידק הכי דאם נקבה זבחי שלמים דאוקימנא בבהמה דהקדש ואי במעי אמן הן קדושות לא היה יכול להפקיע קדושת הולד ויש לומר דנטר עד סיפא ומפרש לה וה"ה לרישא ואם תאמר בסוף בהמה המקשה (חולין עז·) דתנן המבכרת שהפילה שליא ישליכנה לכלבים ובמוקדשין תקבר ומפרש בגמ' (שם:) משום דרובא בר מיקדש היא על כרחך מדקאמר תקבר קסבר במעי אמן הן קדושין דאי בהוייתן אמאי תקבר הא לא חיילא קדושה אלא בחזי להקרבה כדפרים ואם כן טולה בר מיקדש היא ואמאי נקט רובא דאפי' אכלאים וכדמה תפסה קדושת אימיה אי במעי אמן הן קדושים כדאשכחן בתמורה בסוף יש בקרבנות (דף יז·) דאמרינן גבי כלאים טומטום ואנדרוגינוס דאי אתה מוצא אלא בולדות קדשים ולכל הפחות איא כמאן דאמר במעי אמן הן קדושים °ויש לומר דנקט רובא ולא כולה משום דאיכא דמות יונה או קלוט לר' שמעון דכיון דלא מיתסרי באכילה לא מיסתבר דתפסינהו קדושת אמן אף על גב דבמעי אמן הן קדושין:

משום דפסולא דגופייהו · בכל דוכתי משמע דפסול הגוף חמיר מפסולא דאתי מעלמא כדאמרינן בפרק קמא (לעיל דף ד·) מה לשינוי קודש שכן פסולו בגופו ובפסחים בסוף אלו דברים (דף עג:) נמי אמרינן כל שפסולו בגופו ישרף מיד* *דהא דמשמע הכא איפכא לאו משום דפסול הגוף קיל אלא הכי קאמר דמום עובר מיד והתורים גדילין לאחר היו ראויין אבל אותו ואת בנו אין הפסול תלוי בגופו שיועיל לו שום תיקון דלכולי יומא לא חזי: אלמא

יז א מיי' פ"ד מהלכות איסורי מזבח הל' ה:

[פסחים ל. ב"ק יב: מו. סנהדרין קיב:]

[שם כס·]

נ"ל כקדשי נ"ק

[עי' בתוספות דתמורה כד: ד"ה קסבר דמתרלו בע"א ע"ש]

[עי' תוס' ב"ק מז. ד"ה מ"מ ותוס' סנהדרין ס: ד"ה שוכר]

והא כצ"ל נ"ק

[עי' תוספות חולין מח. ד"ה כיון]

קדושין נב: ב"ק יב: ב"ב קכג: בכורות נג: תמורה ח.

כ"א שאם כפר בהם

[תמורה יח: כה. מנחות פג. לעיל לח. חולין ל. כריתות כג: נדה מא.]

ליתא בת"ג

גליון הש"ס

תוס' ד"ה וקסבר וכו' וי"ל דנקט רובא · עיין לעיל דף פד ע"ב תוס' ד"ה ומ"מ:

[לפי שיטתם מ ש מ ע שגורסים בפנים אימא מודה ליה ר"ש לרבנן וכ"ה גי' ר"ע נרעזנורה]

שיטה מקובצת

א] והדר רבען אלא: ב] בעלים הן דתניא: ג] תיבות מוקצה ונעבד עבודת כוכבים נמחק ותיבות בקדשים קלים ל"ש: ד] תיבת לא נמחק: ה] תיבת לא נמחק: ו] קאתי להו: ז] משכחת לה אלא: ח] מוקדשים באתננת דלא: ט] תיבת הן נמחק: י] ליקרב דכתיב רק: יא] ליה לר"ש דהואיל: יב] פה היום: יג] ונדבות הקריבו בבמת צבור:

עין משפט
נר מצוה

יח א ב מיי' פ"א מהל' קרבן פסח הל' ג:
צ"ל ומחזיר גרושתו ואנוסתו דלא יוכל כו' צ"ק
יט ג ד מיי' פי"ח מהל' מעה"ק הלכה ט:
כ ה מיי' שם הלכה י:

תורה אור

מילקי נמי לילקי אלמה *אמר רבי זירא הכתוב נתקו לעשה א] הני מילי לרבנן לרבי שמעון הכי נמי רב נחמן בר יצחק אמר פנים דגלגל לגבי שילה כחוץ דמי רבה אמר טעמיה דרבי שמעון *כדתניא רבי שמעון אומר מנין לזובח פסח בבמת יחיד בשעת איסור הבמות שהוא בלא תעשה ת"ל °לא תוכל לזבוח את הפסח (דברים טז) יכול אף בשעת היתר הבמות כן ת"ל באחד שעריך לא אמרתי לך אלא בשעה שכל ישראל נכנסין בשער אחד אימת אי נימא אחר חצות כרת נמי ב] מחייב אלא לאו קודם חצות ג] לעולם לאחר חצות ובשעת היתר הבמות קאי והא בשעת איסור הבמות קאמר איסור במה לו היתר במה לחבירו: מחוסר זמן כו': והני בני אשמות נינהו אמר זעירי תני מצורע בהדייהו: עולותיהן ושלמיהן: והני בני שלמים נינהו אמר רב ששת תני נזיר דזעירי קבעוה תנאי דרב ששת לא קבעוה תנאי א"ר ד] *חלקיה (דבי) רב טובי לא שנו אלא לשמו אבל שלא לשמו חייב הואיל וראוי לשלא לשמו בפנים אי הכי לשמו נמי ניחייב הואיל וראוי לשלא לשמו בפנים (א) ה] בעי עקירה מתקיף לה רב הונא וכי יש לך *דבר שאינו כשר לשמו וכשר שלא לשמו ולא והרי
פסח

מילקי נמי לילקי · השוחט מחוסר זמן ו] דהא משכן דגלגל דהיא במת ציבור פנים הוא שאהל מועד של מדבר היה שם וקאמר רחמנא ביה נמי לא תעשון: אלמה אמר רבי זירא · בפ' אותו ואת בנו (חולין פ:) דקתני קדשים בפנים ז] סופג את הארבעים משום לאו דאותו ואת בנו והוינן בה ונילקי נמי משום לאו דמחוסר זמן דתניא מנין שכל הפסולים שבשור ושבשה שהן בלא ירצה ת"ל ושור ושה שרוע וקלוט ומחוסר זמן פסול הוא ומשני ר' זירא ח] הכא לאו דמחוסר זמן ההכתוב נתקו לעשה דכתיב ביה עשה יתירא כדמפרש התם למימרא שהוציאו ונתקו מכלל לאו דלא קאי עליה (ב) בלאו דשאר פסולין והשתא דאמרת הכא לאו בהדיא כתיב ביה נילקי עליה: (דלמא) ה"מ · דמשני נמי התם דלא לקי לרבנן דפליגי עליה דרבי שמעון דלא דרשי להאי לא תעשה למחוסר זמן דההוא דאותו ואת בנו דשני ר' זירא עלה מיתוקמא התם דלא כר"ש אבל לר' שמעון ה"נ דלקי אלאו דמחוסר זמן בפנים: רב נחמן בר יצחק אמר · לר' שמעון נמי לא לקי אמחוסר (ג) זמן בפנים דגלגל לגבי שילה חוץ הוא לגבי חובות הואיל ט] דאינו כשר להקרבתו הלכך בחוץ הוא דאשכחן ביה לא תעשה משום איסור במה ולא בפנים: בשעת איסור הבמות · קס"ד במדבר ושילה ובית עולמים: אחר חצות · די"ד דמטי זימניה: כרת נמי ניחייב · דהא מתקבל בפנים: קודם חצות · דהוי מחוסר זמן לשמו: בשעת היתר הבמות קאמר · כמו בגלגל ונוב וגבעון דהותרו במות יחיד לעולה ושלמים ואשמעינן קרא דלגבי חובות איכא לא תעשה ולאו משום מחוסר זמן דהא השתא חזו בבמה גדולה: איסור במה לו · לקרבן זה: היתר במה לחבירו · לעולה ושלמים דנדר ונדבה וסיפא ה"ק יכול אף בשעה שהוא מותר בבמה כגון קודם חצות שהוא י] לשלמים *ת"ל כו' בשער אחד בבמה גדולה לשחוט פסחיהם: דזעירי קבעוה תנאי · למיתני במתניתין מצורע בהדיא: דרב ששת לא קבעוה תנאי · ומיהו אנן משנינן לה בגמרא וקבעינן לה בגמ' הכי ככל חסורי מחסרא דהש"ס: רב חלקיה · אאשם קאי ולא אחטאת דאילו חטאת פסולה שלא לשמו בפנים: לא שנו · דפטור בחוץ: אלא לשמו · ואפילו סתמא דבהאי שמא אינו מתקבל עכשיו בפנים: אבל שלא לשמו · כגון לשם עולה ובשם זה הוא ראוי לבא לפנים דכל הזבחים שנזבחו שלא לשמן כשרין חוץ מן הפסח והחטאת: אי הכי כי שחיט ליה לשמו בחוץ נמי ניחייב · דהא ראוי היה לעקור שם זה ממנו ולבא לפנים: מחוסר עקירה · וכל כמה דלא איעקר שם אשם מיניה סתמיה לאו למיעקר קאי ולאו ראוי הוא: וכי יש לך דבר שאינו כשר לשמו · לפנים: וכשר שלא לשמו · *אפי' דקי"ל לעיל (דף ב·) כל הזבחים כשרין שלא לשמן ה"מ היכא דכשרין לשמן אבל מחוסר זמן בבעלים זה שאינו כשר לשמו היאך יוכשר שלא לשמו:
פסח

אלמה אמר רבי זירא הכתוב נתקו לעשה · אין זה כשאר לאו הניתק לעשה דבפ' בתרא דחולין (דף קמא·) ובפ' ב' דמכות (דף יד· טו· טז·) כגון לאו דגזילה ולקט שכחה ופיאה ונותר *ולא יוכל לשלחה כל ימיו דא"כ מאי פריך דללקי משום לאו דלא תעשון והא ניתק לעשה הוא אלא הוי כמו נתקו הכתוב מטומאה חמורה לטומאה קלה דאותו ואת בנו (חולין פ:) דרשינן ולנדר לא ירצה לימד על כל הפסולים שבשור ושה שהם בלא ירצה וכתב רחמנא במחוסר זמן מיום השמיני והלאה ירצה להוציאו מכלל שאר פסולים שהם בלא ירצה ולומר דבהאי ליכא אלא עשה כעין דבר שהיה בכלל ויצא לידון בדבר החדש בסוף פ"ק דתמורה (דף יג:) וכענין זה הוי בדד ישב דמצורע בפ' אלו דברים (פסחים סז·) דאמרי' שהכתוב נתקו לעשה והוציאו מכלל שאר טמאים שהם בלאו דלא יטמאו את מחניהם ולהכי פריך דלילקי משום דמפורש בגופיה לאו בהדיא כדדרשינן מלא תעשון וכן פי' בקונטרס אבל בפרק אותו ואת בנו (חולין פא·) פירש בקונטרס דהוי כשאר לאו הניתק לעשה דעלמא דמיום השמיני והלאה ירצה משמע קודם זמנו לא ירצה והניחהו עד שיעבור זמנו *וקשה מהך דשמעתא וכי תימא דהכי פריך משום דאיכא נמי לאו דלא תעשון לא אמרינן דאתי חד עשה ועקר תרי לאוי כדאמרי' בפ"ק דתמורה (דף ד:) לא דמי דהני מילי התם דסמיכי גבי הדדי הלאוין אצל העשה תדע דהא בפרק ב' דמכות (ד' טו· ושם ד"ה תניא) חשיב לא יטמאו את מחניהם ניתק לעשה אי לאו משום דקדמו עשה אף על גב דאיכא לאו נמי דואל המקדש לא תבא ומיהו התם איכא למימר משום דאיכא תרי עשה דכתיב מחוץ למחנה תשלחום אבל אשכחן גזלה דאיכא תרי לאוי לאו דלא תעשוק ולא תגזול דבפרק המקבל (ב"מ קיא·) אמר רבא זהו עושק זהו גזל וחשבי ליה ניתק לעשה במכות (דף יד:) ובחולין (דף פ:) הלכך צריך לחלק בההיא דתמורה (דף ד:) כדפרישית דלכך סמך שני הלאוין אצל העשה לומר שאין העשה מנתקם: **רב** נחמן בר יצחק אמר פנים דגלגל כו' · שינויא הוא דקמשני (התם) דאפילו לר"ש לא לקי במחוסר זמן בפנים כי אם בחוץ כדפי' בקונטרס ויש גירסא אחרת בספרים לרבי שמעון ה"נ והא גלגל פנים הוא אמר רב נחמן בר יצחק פנים דגלגל כו' *וריש לקיש פריך דנפקא ליה מלא תעשון לאו במחוסר זמן דהאי קרא בגלגל קאי ופנים הוא וכי תימא קל וחומר בחוץ הא אין מזהירין מן הדין ומשני פנים דגלגל לגבי שילה כחוץ דמי: **אלא** לאו קודם חצות · ואע"ג דחזי בפנים שלא לשמו לא מיחייב כרת כיון דמחוסר עקירה ואין עומד האי ליעקר קודם זמנו: **היתר** במה לחבירו · ושעת היתר הבמות דקתני היינו קודם חצות דכשר בבמה שלא לשמו וא"ת דמשמע הכא דתורין שלא הגיע זמנן לרבי שמעון חיילא קדושה עלייהו והשוחטן בחוץ בלאו ובמעילה בפרק ולד חטאת (דף יב·) נמי אמר רבי שמעון דמועלין משום דראוין לאחר זמן ובתמורה בפרק אלו קדשים (דף יט:) גבי אשם בן שתים והביאו בן שנה אמר ר' שמעון דכל עצמן אין קדושים משום דכל מידי דלא חזי ליה לגופיה לא נחתא ליה קדושת הגוף ופריך התם מאי שנא ממחוסר זמן דלא חזי ליה *לגופיה (לא נחתא ליה קדושת הגוף) ואמר ר"ש דקדוש פירוש במתני' דהכא דתנן מחוסר זמן רבי שמעון אומר בלא תעשה ומשני דאיתקוש לבכור דקדוש לפני זמנו וקרב לאחר זמן והשתא תיקשי מחוסר זמן תורין שלא הגיע זמנן מאי טעמא וי"ל דדבר שאינו ראוי לשם קרבן ילפינן ממחוסר זמן שאין ראוי לשום קרבן אבל דבר שראוי לקרבן אחר ולקרבן זה שהוא מקדישו אינו ראוי לא נחתא ליה קדושת הגוף ופסח קודם חצות דקדוש לר' שמעון וכן חטאת ואשם דזב וזבה ויולדת ומצורע דקדושים קודם זמנן כדתנן בפירקין (לעיל קיב·) ולא פליג ר' שמעון ובתורת כהנים בפ' אחרי מות קאמר נמי רבי שמעון והשוחטן בחוץ בלאו הני אין מחוסר זמן בגופן ולא דמי לאשם בן שנה והביאו בן שתים בן שנה דמחוסרי זמן בגופן וא"ת דמחוסר זמן היאך קדוש הא אמרינן לעיל בפ"ק (דף יב·) לילה לקדושה יום להרצאה אבל ביום שביעי לא ובבכורות פרק הלוקח בהמה (דף כא·) קאמר ר"ש מחוסר זמן נכנס לדיר להתעשר יליף מבכור דקדוש לפני זמנו ופריך ודיליף מבכור לילף מקדשים אלמא משמע דקדשים קודם זמנן לא קדשי וי"ל דאסור להקדיש אבל אם הקדישם תוך זמנם קדושין אלא דעבד איסור דרחמנא אמר °מיום השמיני אין הא קודם לכן לא אבל מעשר לרבי שמעון שרי להכניסו תוך זמנו לדיר להתעשר כדיליף התם מעשר העברה העברה מבכור והא דלא ניחא ליה למילף תחת תחת מקדשים דניחא ליה למילף העברה טפי משום דהעברה דתרווייהו מאיתי שמעבירה להקדישה ויש ליתן טעם לרבא דריש תמורה (דף ה:) היאך מחוסר זמן קדוש קדושת הגוף דכל היכא דאמר רחמנא לא תעביד אי עביד לא מהני ושמא לענין זה יליף תחת תחת ממעשר או שמא יש טעם אחר: **דזעירי** קבעוה תנאי · משום דמצורע יש בו טומאה כעין זב וזבה ויולדת אבל נזיר דלא דמי להו שייריה וכן בכריתות בפרק ארבעה מחוסרי כפרה (דף ח:) נמי אשכחן דתני זב וזבה ויולדת ומצורע והתם מפרש מאי טעמא לא תני מצורע ומצורעת כדקתני זב וזבה וניחא השתא לזעירי דבנזיר בלא מצורע סגי דאיכא תרתי בנזיר דנזיר נמי מביא אשם*:
פסח

שיטה מקובצת
א] לעשה דלמא הני מילי לרבנן אבל לרבי: ב] נמי ניחייב אלא: ג] חצות לא לעולם: ד] חלקיה בר טובי תיבות דבי רב נמחק: ה] בפנים מחוסר עקירה תיבת בעי נמחק: ו] זמן בפנים דהא: ז] בפנים השני סופג: ח] ר' זירא הך לאו דמחוסר זמן הכתוב נתקו לעשה: ט] הואיל ואינו כשר להקרבתן הלכך: י] שהוא כשר לשלמים:

עיין צ"ק

צ"ל וריש לקיש כו' צ"ק

צ"ל לגופיה ונחתא ליה קדושת הגוף דאמר ר"ש כו'

[חולין פ:]

פסחים לא. תוספתא פי"ג

הגהות הב"ח
(א) גמ' וראוי לשלא לשמו בפנים (בעי) תא"מ ונ"ב גירסת רש"י מחוסר: (ב) רש"י ד"ה אלמה וכו' דלא קאי עליה לאו כצ"ל ואות ב' נמחק: (ג) ד"ה רב נחמן וכו' זמן הס"ד ואח"כ מ"ה פנים:

[יומא סג.]

[מנחות מז:]

ת"ל כו' הס"ד ואח"כ מ"ה בשער צ"ק

צ"ל אע"פ צ"ק

גליון הש"ס
תום' ד"ה היתר וכו' מיום השמיני אין הא קודם לכן לא · עיין יומא דף סג ע"ב:

עיין רש"ק

do.[7] Said R. Jeremiah to R. Zera: If so,[8] [114*b*] one should even be flagellated too?[1] Why did R. Zera say: Scripture transmuted it into a positive command?[2]—Perhaps that is only according to the Rabbis,[3] but in the view of R. Simeon, that indeed is so.[4] R. Naḥman b. Isaac said: Within, at Gilgal, was like without in comparison with Shiloh.[5]

Rabbah said: R. Simeon's reason is as it was taught: R. Simeon said: How do we know that one who sacrifices his Passover-offering at a private *bamah* when *bamoth* were prohibited, violates a negative command? Because it is said, '*Thou mayest not sacrifice the Passover-offering* [*within one of thy gates*]'.[6] You might think that it is also thus when *bamoth* were permitted;[7] therefore it is stated, '*within one of thy gates*': I have told you [that he violates a negative injunction] only when all Israel enter through one gate.[8] Now when is this thus? if we say, after midday,[9] let him even incur *kareth* too![10] Hence it must surely mean before midday![11]—No: in truth it means *after* midday, but it means when *bamoth* were permitted. But surely he says, 'When *bamoth* were prohibited'?—He means when the *bamah* was forbidden for *that* [sacrifice], but
b permitted for another.[1]

BEFORE TIME etc. Are these then subject to guilt-offerings?—Said Ze'iri: Include a leper amongst them.[2]

THEIR BURNT-OFFERINGS AND THEIR PEACE-OFFERINGS. And are these subject to peace-offerings?—Said R. Shesheth: Learn a nazirite [in the Mishnah]. According to Ze'iri, the Tannaim [explicitly] included it:[3] according to R. Shesheth, the Tannaim did not include it.[4]

R. Ḥilkiah b. Ṭobi said: They learnt it[5] only [when he sacrifices it] for its own sake. But [if he sacrifices it] under a different designation[6] he is culpable, since it is eligible, under a different designation, within.[7] If so, let him also be culpable [when he slaughters it] for its own sake, since it was eligible, under a different designation, within?—It lacks abrogation.[8]

To this R. Huna demurred: Is there anything which [when slaughtered] for its own sake is not fit, yet [when slaughtered]

(7) The Sifre applies the text to their first fourteen years in Eretz Israel, when the Tabernacle was at Gilgal. These years were spent in conquering and sharing the land, and so one could apply to them the words, *for ye are not as yet come to the rest . . . which the Lord your God giveth thee* (ibid. v. 9). This is what Moses said to them: At present, when we are travelling about with the Tabernacle and *bamoth* are forbidden, all sacrifices can be offered. But in the years of conquest and division, before ye are come to the '*rest*', '*Ye shall not do after all that we do here this day,*' viz., offer obligatory offerings, but only '*every man whatsoever is right in his eyes,*' i.e., votive sacrifices. Thus the statutory offerings were premature at Gilgal, (and would have to wait until they came to Shiloh), and Moses forbids their sacrifice at the *bamoth* by a negative injunction. '*Ye shall not do.*' From this R. Simeon infers that the premature sacrifice of all animals at the *bamoth*, i.e., before they become eligible, is forbidden by a negative injunction. (8) That those at Gilgal are premature.

a (1) *Sc.* one who slaughters an animal prematurely within. For the public *bamah* at the Tabernacle of Gilgal, which was the Tent of Meeting of the wilderness, naturally ranked as *within*, yet Scripture said '*Ye shall not do*'.—The transgression of a negative injunction is punished by flagellation. (2) V. Ḥul. 80*b*. If, however, '*Ye shall not do*' applies to such, we have a *negative* command. (3) As they do not relate '*Ye shall not do*' to premature slaughtering. (4) One would be flagellated. (5) It counts as without since obligatory sacrifices might not be offered there. Thus even R. Simeon admits that he is not flagellated, for now we find the negative injunction only in connection with slaughtering without, but not in connection with slaughtering within. (6) Deut. XVI, 5. (7) For even then private *bamoth* were permitted only for votive sacrifices, but not for obligatory sacrifices like the Passover-offering, which were sacrificed at the public *bamoth*. (8) I.e., when there is a central sanctuary; but when *bamoth* were permitted there was no central sanctuary. The verse is understood thus: '*Thou mayest not sacrifice the Passover-offering*' at a private *bamah* when all Israel enter through '*one of the gates*'. (9) On the fourteenth of Nisan. (10) And not merely flagellation, (v. n. 1.), since it can then be received within. (11) When it is premature. Thus a sacrifice slaughtered prematurely without, under its correct designation, entails the violation of a negative prohibition.

b (1) It was forbidden for the Passover-offering, but permitted for a burnt-offering and peace-offering (i.e., votive offerings). This then is what he means: You might think that this is so even when it (the Passover-offering) may be sacrificed at a *bamah*, viz., before midday, when it can be offered as a peace-offering; therefore it says, '*in one of thy gates*'. I have told . . . 'at one gate', viz., at the public *bamah*, to slaughter their Passover-offerings, which is after midday. (2) I.e., 'guilt-offering' is mentioned only in connection with the leper, who is also enumerated. Rashi, in the Mishnah, deletes 'leper'. (3) *Sc.* leper, in the Mishnah. (4) 'Leper' is absent in the version of the Mishnah, nevertheless it must be added, on the assumption that the text of the Mishnah is defective. (5) That when a leper prematurely sacrifices his guilt-offering without he is not culpable. (6) E.g., as a burnt-offering. (7) For all sacrifices slaughtered under a different designation are fit, except the Passover-offering and the sin-offering. (8) Before it can be eligible, its name as a guilt-offering must be abrogated, and as long as this was not done it is not eligible.

under a different designation is fit?[9]—Is there not? Surely [115a] a Passover-offering, though not fit [if slaughtered] during the rest of the year under its own designation, is nevertheless fit [if slaughtered] under a different designation!—A Passover-offering during a the rest of the year is a peace-offering.[1]

Shall we say that the following supports him [R. Ḥilkiah]? [It was taught:] You might think that I also exclude[2] a burnt-offering which is premature in relation to its owner,[3] or a nazirite's guilt-offering and a leper's guilt-offering;[4] therefore it says, *'an ox'*, [implying] in all cases; *'or lamb'*, [implying] in all cases; *'or goat'*, [implying] in all cases. Thus he omits a sin-offering. Now what are we discussing? If we say, [when it is sacrificed] in its time,[5] why particularly a guilt-offering; even a sin-offering too [entails liability]? Hence it must mean [when it is] not [sacrificed] in its proper time; and in which [case]? If we say, [when he sacrifices it] for its own sake, why is he liable for a guilt-offering?[6] Hence it must surely mean [when he sacrifices it] under a different designation![7]—In truth it means in the proper time and under a different designation, and this is in accordance with R. Eliezer, who maintained: We assimilate the guilt-offering to the sin-offering; and he teaches the derived case, and the same law applies to the principal case.[8]

Come and hear: You might think that I include a burnt-offering b which is intrinsically premature[1] and a sin-offering [which is premature] either intrinsically or through its owners;[2] therefore it says, *'And hath not brought it unto the door of the tent of meeting'*: Whatever is not eligible to come to the door of the tent of meeting, you are not liable on its account. But [the Tanna] omits a guilt-offering. Now what are we discussing? If we say, [when it is sacrificed] for its own sake, let him not be liable in the case of a guilt-offering too?[3] Hence it must surely mean [when one does] not [sacrifice it] for its own sake![4]—This agrees with R. Eliezer, who assimilates the guilt-offering to the sin-offering; and he teaches the principal case [the sin-offering], and all the more [does it apply to] the derived case.

Come and hear, for when R. Dimi came,[5] he said: The school of Bar Liwai taught: You might think that I also exclude a burnt-offering which is premature through its owner, and a nazirite's guilt-offering and a leper's guilt-offering [etc.]. Now, he [the Tanna] thus infers that one is liable, but I do not know how he infers it. Said Rabina: [The reference is:] *'an ox'*, in all cases; *'a sheep'*, in all cases; *'a goat'*, in all cases. But he omits a sin-offering. And what are we discussing [etc.]?[6] What difficulty is this?[7] Perhaps [it is to be explained] as you stated [in the previous discussion]?—Said R. Naḥman [b. Isaac]: Because this teaching of the school of Bar Liwai contradicts what Levi taught, viz.: As to a nazirite's guilt-offering and a leper's guilt-offering, if one slaughtered them under a different designation they are valid, but do not free their owners of their obligations. If one slaughtered them before they were due from their owners, or if they were two years old when they were slaughtered, they are unfit.[8] [And R. Dimi answered][9] There is no difficulty: In the one case [he slaughtered it] for its own sake; in c the other it was not [slaughtered] for its own sake.[1]

R. Ashi pointed out a contradiction between our Mishnah and the Baraitha,[2] and he reconciled them; one means [where he slaughters it] for its own sake;[3] the other [where he does] not [slaughter it] for its own sake. Shall we say that this refutes R. Huna?—R. Huna can answer you: The case we discuss here is that of one who set aside two [animals for] guilt-offerings, as security,[4]

(9) For although all sacrifices slaughtered under a different designation are fit, that is surely only when they are fit if slaughtered for their own sake.

a (1) Hence when one slaughters it as such, he is slaughtering it for its own sake. (2) From the implication of the text, *'and hath not brought it unto the door'* etc. (3) E.g. one brought by a leper or a woman after childbirth before they were fit. (4) Disqualified for some other reason.—I might think that these do not entail liability when sacrificed without, since they were not eligible within. (5) And for its own sake. (6) Since it is not eligible within. (7) Thus what is not fit within under its own designation is fit under a different designation. (8) R. Eliezer maintains that a guilt-offering too is disqualified if slaughtered under a different designation, which he infers from the sin-offering (*supra* 10b), which is thus the principal instance of such disqualification. The Baraitha teaches that nevertheless when one slaughters it under a different designation without, he is liable. The reason is because even after he abrogated its name as a guilt-offering, he could still slaughter it within without any specific purpose, when it would count as a valid guilt-offering and free its owner of his obligation. Hence at the time that he slaughtered it without, under a different designation, it was *fit* for slaughtering within. The same law applies to the sin-offering too, this being the leading case of unfitness, as explained. This must be in accordance with R. Eliezer, because the Rabbis maintain that a guilt-offering is *valid* when slaughtered under a different designation. Hence it is fit to be received within, and no special text is necessary for shewing that he is culpable.

b (1) E.g., if one sacrifices it before it is eight days old. (2) E.g. a leper's and a nazirite's sin-offering, sacrificed before it is due.—I might think that if one sacrifices these without, he is liable. (3) Since it is not eligible. (4) Thus this supports R. Ḥilkiah and refutes R. Huna. (5) V. *supra* 10a n. a1. (6) The reasoning then follows as above.—The text is in some disorder, and the emendations of Sh.M. and Margin have been adopted. (7) Why do you cite this to refute R. Huna? (8) Hence, if slaughtered *without* under such conditions, they do not entail liability, in accordance with the general rule that what is unfit within does not entail liability without. Thus it contradicts the earlier teaching. (9) Sh.M. deletes bracketed words.

c (1) The school of Bar Liwai means that he is culpable if he slaughtered it under a different designation; while Levi teaches that they are unfit (and hence entail no liability without) when slaughtered for their own sake. (Accordingly, the two clauses of Levi's teaching do not deal with the same circumstances.) Now, since R. Dimi opposed these two Baraitha's, he must have known that the former too applies where the guilt-offering is slaughtered prematurely, and thus it refutes R. Huna. (R. Huna presumably rejects this reasoning.) (2) Our Mishnah states that one is not liable in the case of a leper's guilt-offering, whereas the Baraitha states that one is. (3) Then he is not liable. (4) In case one is lost, the other should be sacrificed.

פסח בשאר ימות השנה דאינו כשר לשמו וכשר שלא לשמו פסח בשאר ימות השנה שלמים נינהו לימא מסייע ליה יכול שאני מוציא אף א] עולת מחוסר זמן בבעלים ואשם נזיר ואשם מצורע ת"ל °שור מ"מ כשב מ"מ עז מ"מ ואילו חטאת שיירא במאי עסקינן אילימא בזמנו מאי איריא אשם אפילו חטאת נמי אלא שלא ב] לזמנו ובמאי אילימא לשמו אשם אמאי חייב אלא לאו שלא לשמו לעולם בזמנו ושלא לשמו *ורבי ג] אליעזר היאדאמר מקשינן אשם לחטאת ותנא טפל וה"ה עיקר ת"ש *יכול שאני מרבה ד] עולת מחוסר זמן בגופה וחטאת בין בגופה בין בבעלים ת"ל °ואל פתח אהל מועד כל שאינו ראוי לבא בפתח אהל מועד אין חייבין עליהן ואילו אשם שיירא במאי עסקינן אילימא לשמו אשם נמי ליפטריה אלא לאו שלא לשמו ה] לעולם שלא לשמו ור"א היא דמקיש אשם לחטאת תנא עיקר וכ"ש לטפל ת"ש דכי אתא רב דימי אמר תנא דבי ו] ר' ליואי יכול שאני מוציא אף עולת מחוסר זמן בבעלים ז] אשם נזיר ואשם מצורע (מנין ונסיב להו תלמודא לחיובא ולא ידענא מאי היא) מאי תלמודא אמר רבינא שור מכל מקום כשב מכל מקום *עז מכל מקום ח] הא מאי רומיא כדאמרת אמר ר"נ (א) משום [דרמי] דתנא דבי ר' ליואי *) אדתני לוי ט] באשם נזיר ואשם מצורע ששחטן שלא לשמן כשירין ולא עלו לבעלים לשום חובה שחטן מחוסר זמן בבעלים או שהיו בני שתי שנים ושחטן פסולין י] ומשני רב דימי לא קשיא כאן לשמו כאן שלא לשמו רב אשי רמי מתני' אברייתא ומשני כאן לשמו וכאן שלא לשמו לימא תיהוי תיובתיה דרב הונא אמר לך רב הונא הכא במאי עסקינן כגון שהפריש שתי אשמות לאחריות דחד מינייהו יא] מעיקרא עולה היא

כדרב

*) מנחות מה:

תורה אור: ויקרא יז; שם טז

רש"י

פסח בשאר ימות השנה · אינו כשר לשמו דתנן *שחטו קודש חצות פסול שנאמר בין הערבים: שלמים הוא · ואין זה אלא לשמו: לימא מסייע ליה · לרב חלקיה: יכול שאני מוציא · מאל פסח שלא יתחייב בחוץ על עולת מחוסר זמן בבעלים כגון של יולדת ומצורע הואיל ואינה ראויה לבא לפנים למלותה: ואשם נזיר ואשם מצורע · שיש בה פסול ולקמיה מפרש ואזיל מאי פסולה: שור מ"מ כו' · דמצי למימר אשר ישחט במחנה או אשר ישחט מחוץ למחנה ואל פתח וגו' ואנא ידענא דשור או כשב או עז הוא: ואילו חטאת שייריה · ולא רבייה לחיובא: אי נימא בזמנו · ולשמו: מאי איריא · אשם דרבייה חטאת נמי מחייב יב] דלא בעי רבוייא ואפילו אשם דהא חזי בפנים: אלא שלא בזמנו · רבייה לחיובא באשם: אי לשמו אשם אמאי חייב · והא אינו כשר ליקרב יג] ומתני' תנא פטור ואי משום דראוי לשלא לשמו בפני' הא מחוסר עקיר' וכולהו מודו בו אלא לאו שלא לשמו רבי' לחיובא בחוץ כרב חלקיה אלמא דבר שאינו כשר לשמו בפנים כשר לשלא לשמו ומחייב עליה שלא לשמו בחוץ: ה"ג לעולם בזמנו ושלא לשמו א"נ ה"ג לעולם בזמנו ותו לא וממילא אשלא לשמו דאוקימנא קאי יד] ושכתבו בספרים ולשמו (ב) מפרש טועה כתבו ולפום ריהטא משום דפרכינן לעיל אי נימא בזמנו מאי איריא כו' וקא בעי לשנויי לעולם בזמנו ולשמו ודקא קשיא לך אי הכי חטאת נמי אין ה"נ ותנא אשם והוא הדין לחטאת ולאו מילתא היא דא"כ ר"א מאי בעי הכא מכדי ר"א לענין שלא לשמו אקשיה בפ"ק (לעיל י:) בפסול אשם שלא לשמו כחטאת אבל לענין לשמו מאי עיקר ומאי טפל איכא תרווייהו כתיבי להכשיר בפנים וחיוב בחוץ ותו נ"ל לרבויי להאי מסור וכשב ועז הרי כשר ליקרב וכמלותו בפנים הוא שוחטו בחוץ אלא קא משני לעולם בזמנו ושלא לשמו ואיצטריך לרבוייה משום דשלא לשמו פסול הוא: ור"א היא · דמקיש אשם לחטאת דמיפסיל בשלא לשמו בפנים טו] *באשמות דאפ"ה מחייב עלה בחוץ אע"ג דעקר מיניה שם אשם אכתי אי הוה מעייל ליה לפנים הוה כשר למישחטיה סתמא וכשר לשם אשם ועולה (ג) לשם חובה דמשום דיבוריה לא מיעקר שמיה מיניה וכל כמה דלא שחטיה ליה טז] *בעיקרה קאי סתמא לשמו הלכך כי שחיט ליה ראוי לפנים לשמו היה וה"ה דלחטאת שלא לשמו נמי חייב אלא תנא טפל ואשמעינן אע"ג דכה"ג פסול בפנים מיחייב עליה בחוץ וה"ה לעיקר דמ"ש סוף סוף תרווייהו פסילי שלא לשמן ובת"כ קתני בה בהדיא שלא לשמו וע"כ מוקי לה כר"א דאילו לרבנן לא איצטריך ליה לרבויי דהא כי האי גוונא מתקבלת בפנים היא: ת"ש · סייעתא לרב חלקיה ותיובתא דרב הונא: בגופה · כגון תוך שמונה ללידתה: יכול שאני מרבה יז] גרס הכא דרישא דלעיל היא ובתורת כהנים הכי תניא לה הוציא את אלו שאינן מיוחדין לשם ולא הוציא עולה מחוסרת זמן בגופה וחטאת בין בגופה כו' והגרסינן שינו את הלשון יח] וגרסינן הכא יכול שאני מרבה את כו' *לפי שהביאוה יט] בלימודא אחרינא וסברי דסיפא דההיא דלעיל היא: יכול שאני מרבה כ] *) משום מכ"מ אף עולה מחוסר זמן וכו': וחטאת בין בגופה בין בבעלים · כגון של נזיר ומצורע שלא מלאו ימיהם ואילו אשם נזיר ומצורע מחוסרי זמן בבעלים שייריה ולא רבייה לפטורא שמע מינה ס"ל דחייב: ובמאי אי נימא בלשמו אשם נמי ניפטריה · דהא לא חזי: אלא שלא לשמו · הלכך חטאת פטור דלא חזי לפנים ואשם חייב דחזי לפנים ואף על גב דאין כא] ראוי לשמו והיינו כרב חלקיה ודלא כרב הונא: ה"ג הא מני ר"א היא כו' ולא גרסינן לעולם בלשמו: הא מני ר"א היא · כלומר ודאי בשלא לשמו היא כדקאמרת הלכך חטאת פטור דלא חזי בפנים לא בלשמו ולא בשלא לשמו דמחוסר זמן הוא ואשם נמי פטור דלא חזי לפנים לשמו במחוסר זמן ולא לשלא לשמו דר"א קאמר דפסול באשם שלא לשמו והאי דשייריה לאשם לאו דס"ל דחייב אלא כיון דחד טעמא הוא משום דתרווייהו פסולין שלא לשמו בפנים הוא תנא עיקר חטאת דפטור וכ"ש טפל אשם והאי כ"ש גמגום ודוחקיה דרב הונא לאוקמיה כר"א משום סיפא דעל כרחיך כרבי אליעזר מיתוקמא כדפרישנא לעיל ועוד משום דלרבנן כב] לא ילפינן אשם מחטאת ליכא למימר תנא האי והוא הדין להאי ואף על גב דלרבנן נמי קאמר דפטור דאין לך דבר שאינו כשר לשמו וכשר שלא לשמו לא מצי לאוקמא כרבנן דא"כ כג] נשמעינן אשם דפטור דנשמעינן בה תרתי וכ"ש חטאת: ת"ש דכי אתא רב דימי כו' ואילו חטאת שיירא ובמאי כו' · כד] כדאותיבנא (ד) בקמייתא: ומאי קושיא · לסיועה לרב חלקיה דלמא ה"נ כדאמרינן דבזמנו קאי כדאוקמא בקמייתא לעיל ור"א היא: אמר ר"נ בר יצחק · לא מצי לאוקומי להא בזמנו משום דרב דימי קשיא ליה דתני כה] (ליה) בר ליואי אדתני לוי שחטן מחוסר זמן בבעלים פסולין ובחוץ נמי כפטור: ומשני כו] ליה רב דימי · הא דתני חייב שלא לשמו והא דתני פסולין ודכוותיה בחוץ פטור בשחטן לשמו ומדקשיא ליה דתני לוי אבר ליואי ש"מ שמיע ליה לרב דימי דמתני' דבר ליואי נמי במחוסר זמן וקאמר חייב ואע"ג דאינו ראוי לשמו בפנים ראוי לשלא לשמו וסייעתא לרב חלקיה: רב אשי רמי מתני' · דקתני לשמו פטור אברייתא קמייתא דתניא לעיל חייב: ומשני מתני' לשמו וברייתא שלא לשמו · כרב חלקיה: נימא תהוי תיובתיה דרב הונא · כז] מדכי אהא רב דימי כדאמרן דליכא לאוקומא בזמנו מדקשיא ליה תני לוי אדתני בר ליואי: הכא במאי עסקינן · דמחוסר זמן חייב בשלא לשמו: כגון שהפריש שני אשמות לאחריות · שאם יאבד האחד יתכפר בשני ושחט האחד מהם בחוץ קודם זמנו לשם עולה דהאי כיון דסופו לרעיה קאי דאשם שכיפרו בעליו רועה ודמיו לקיץ המזבח בהיא עולה חזי לדוכתיה בפנים אי שחיט לגופיה לעולה:

*) ס"א משר

תוספות

פסח בשאר ימות השנה שלמים הוא · פי' בקונטרס ואין זה אלא לשמו משמע שרוצה לומר דכיון דשלמים הוא כששוחטו לשם שלמים היינו לשמו וא"ת והלא כששחטו לשם עולה או לשם זבח אחר הוי נמי שלמים כדאמרי' בפ"ק (לעיל ח:) לכל דשחיט ליה שלמים ליהוי וי"ל דמ"מ כיון דשלמים הוא הרי הוא כשר לשמו ושלא לשמו כגון לשם שלמים ולשם זבח אחר:

מחוסר זמן בבעלים · אעולה דוקא קאי ולא אאידך:

או שהיו בני שתי שנים ושחטן פסולין · הך ברייתא איתא בפ' התכלת (מנחות מח:) והכא והתם קתני פסולין ועוד תניא התם באידך ברייתא פסולין ותעובר צורתן ויצאו לבית השריפה ותימה דבתמורה בפ' אלו קדשים (דף יט:) תניא אשם בן שנה והביאו בן שתים בן שתים והביאו בן שנה כשרים ולא עלו *לשם בעלים לשם חובה ר"ש אומר כל עצמן אינן קדושים וי"ל דכאן לשמו כאן שלא לשמו כדמשני הכא ומיהו קשה דא"כ קשיא לרב הונא הא איכא האי דפסול לשמו וכשר שלא לשמו ועוד דאי בשלא לשמו מיירי בתמורה ל"ל למיתני ולא עלו לשם חובה הא אפי' במלותו נמי דכיון דשלא לשמו הוא אין עולה לשם חובה:

[נ"ל לבעלים]

עין משפט נר מצוה: כא א מיי' פט"ו מהל' פסה"מ הלכה יא: | כב ב מיי' שם הל' כ:

מסורת הש"ס: פסחים סג. | לעיל ה' מנחות כח. | (יומא סג.) | ס"א אינו | ס"א עז מ"מ ואילו חטאת כו' הא אמאי תרמיה דלמא ה"נ וכדאמרת בקמייתא אמר ר"נ כו' | ס"א ואשמועינן | נ"ל בעקירת שמו עדיין קאי סתמא | נ"ל לפי שהביאו התלמוד אחרונה וסברי דסיפא כו'

שיטה מקובצת

א] אף עולה מחוסר: ב] שלא בזמנו ובמאי: ג] ור' אלעזר אות ו' נמחק: ד] מרבה עולת מחוסר זמן: ה] שלא לשמו הא מני ר' אלעזר היא ותיבות לעולם שלא לשמו ואות ו' נמחק: ו] דבי בר לואי תיבת ר' נמחק: ז] בבעלים ואשם נזיר ואשם מצורע ונסיב לה תלמודא לחיובא ולא ידענא מאי תלמודא אמר רבינא מאי טעמא לא ידעת שור מ"מ והשאר נמחק: ח] מ"מ ומאי קשיא דלמא כדאמרת אמר רב נחמן בר יצחק משום דקשיא ליה דתני דבי בר לואי ותיבות רומיא דרמי ל"ש ונם מה שיש גורסים אמאי תרמיה דבעי למרמי ר' נמחק: ט] לוי דתני לוי אשם: י] תיבות ומשני רב דימי ל"ש: יא] תיבת מעיקרא נמחק: יב] נמי מחייב ואפילו אשם לא בעי רבוייא דהא: יג] ליקרב ובמתני': יד] קאי ושכתוב: טו] בפנים ואשמועינן דאפ"ה: טז] ליה בעקירה קאי: יז] מרבה לא גרס הכא דרישא דההיא דלעיל היא: יח] הלשון וגרסי הכא: יט] שהביאוה בתלמודא אחרונה וסברי תיבת בלימודא ל"ש ותיבת אחרינא נמחק: כ] מרבה משור תיבת משום ל"ש: כא] ראויה לשמו והיינו: כב] דלרבנן דלא ילפי אשם: כג] דא"כ נשמעינה אשם: כד] כדאוקמא ברייתא לעיל ותיבת בקמייתא נמחק: כה] תיבת ליה נמחק: כו] ומשני לה רב דימי: כז] הונא הא דכי אתא מ' נמחק:

הגהות הב"ח

(א) גמ' א"ר נחמן ב"י משום: (ב) רש"י ד"ה ה"ג לעולם וכו' ולשמו מספר טעות כתבו: (ג) ד"ה ור"א היא וכו' ועולה לבעלים לשם חובה: (ד) ד"ה ת"ש וכו' בקמייתא הס"ד ואח"כ מ"ה הא אמאי כו' ומאי קושיא וכו' כדאוקמא בקמייתא לעיל:

תורה אור

כדרב הונא אמר רב דאמר *רב הונא אמר רב אשם שניתק לרעיה ושחטו סתם כשר לעולה: המעלה מבשר חטאת [וכו'] : ת"ר מנין למעלה מבשר חטאת ומבשר אשם ומבשר קדשי קדשים ומבשר קדשים קלים וממותר העומר ושתי הלחם ולחם הפנים ושירי מנחות שפטור ת"ל עולה מה עולה שהיא ראויה להעלאה אף כל שראויה להעלאה מנין שאף היוצק והבולל והפותת והמולח והמניף והמגיש והמסדר השלחן והמטיב את הנרות והקומץ והמקבל א] בחוץ שפטור ת"ל °אשר יעלה עולה או זבח מה העלאה שהיא גמר עבודה אף כל שהוא גמר עבודה: עד שלא הוקם המשכן [וכו']: יתיב רב (א) ב] הונא בר רב קטינא קמיה *דרב חסדא וקא קרי °וישלח את נערי בני ישראל א"ל הכי אמר ר' אסי ג] (קרבו) ופסקו סבר לאותוביה ממתניתין שמעיה דקאמר משמיה דרב אדא בר אהבה *עולה שהקריבו ישראל במדבר אינה טעונה הפשט וניתוח ד] אותביה ברייתא דשויא בכולהו דתני' עד שלא הוקם המשכן ה] הבמות מותרות ועבודה בבכורות והכל כשירין ו] להקריב בהמה חיה ועוף זכרים ונקבות תמימין ובעלי מומין טהורין אבל לא טמאין והכל קרבו עולות ועולה שהקריבו ישראל במדבר טעונה הפשט וניתוח ונכרים בזמן הזה רשאין לעשות כן תנאי היא דתניא °וגם הכהנים הנגשים אל ה' יתקדשו ר' יהושע בן קרחה אומר זו פרישות בכורות רבי אומר זו פרישות נדב ואביהוא בשלמא למ"ד זו פרישות נדב ואביהוא היינו דכתיב °הוא אשר דבר ה' לאמר בקרובי אקדש אלא למ"ד זו פרישות בכורות היכא רמיזא דכתיב °ונועדתי שמה לבני ישראל ונקדש בכבודי אל תקרי בכבודי אלא ז] במכובדיי דבר זה אמר הקב"ה למשה ולא ידעו עד שמתו בני אהרן כיון שמתו בני אהרן אמר לו אהרן אחי לא מתו בניך אלא להקדיש ח] שמו של הקב"ה כיון שידע אהרן שבניו ידועי מקום הן שתק וקבל שכר ט] שנאמר °וידום אהרן וכן *בדוד הוא אומר °דום לה' והתחולל לו *אע"פ שמפיל לך חללים את י] שתוק וכן יא] *בשלמה הוא אומר °עת לחשות ועת לדבר פעמים יב] ששותק ומקבל שכר על השתיקה יג] פעמים מדבר ומקבל שכר על הדבור והיינו דא"ר חייא בר אבא א"ר יוחנן מאי דכתיב °נורא אלהים ממקדשך אל תיקרי ממקדשך אלא ממקודשיך בשעה יד] *שעושה הקב"ה דין בקדושיו מתיירא ומתעלה ומתהלל אלא קשיא עולה תרי תנאי היא *דתניא ר' ישמעאל אומר כללות נאמרו בסיני ופרטות טו] באהל מועד ר"ע אומר כללות ופרטות נאמרו בסיני ונשנו באהל מועד ונשתלשו בערבות מואב אמר מר הכל כשירין להקריב מנא הני מילי אמר רב הונא דאמר קרא °ויבן נח מזבח לה' ויקח מכל הבהמה הטהורה ומכל עוף הטהור *בהמה טז] כמשמעו *חיה בכלל בהמה זכרים

[ויקרא טז] [שמות כד] [ויקרא י] [שמות כט] [תהלים לז] [קהלת ג] [תהלים סח] [בראשית ח]

תוספות

מה העלאה שהיא גמר עבודה כו' · סוגיא זו קשה אההיא דלעיל בריש השוחט (דף קז: ושם) דדרשינן להכי כתב רחמנא או לרבות את הזורק דלא תיתי מבינייא ומשום הכי פטור מקבל בחוץ:
ויתיב וקאמר וישלח וגו' · פירש בקונטרס ויתיב רב חסדא וקאמר *ונראה לפרש דיתיב וקאמר ארב הונא קאי: **א"ל** הכי אמר רב אסי ופסקוהו · פי' כמו שאמרת אמר רב אסי דוישלח היינו עבודה בבכורות אבל חכמים הפסיקוהו ומנעוהו מלומר כן ושני לשונות שבקונטרס עיקר:
רמוז הקב"ה למשה ולא ידעו · פי' ולא ידע במי אבל היה יודע שעתיד הקב"ה לקדש את המשכן באדם גדול דאמרי' במדרש* שאמר לו משה לאהרן הייתי סבור בי או בך:
וקיבל שכר על שתיקתו · תניא בתורת כהנים שבשכר זה נתייחד אליו הדיבור דכתיב בפרשת יין ושכר אל תשת וידבר ה' אל אהרן ולא כתיב אל משה ותימה דבסיפרי דריש בפרשת קרח דכתיב וידבר אל אהרן שומע אני שהדיבור אל אהרן ת"ל כאשר דבר ה' ביד משה לו בפרשת מחתות השרופים הא למדנו שהדיבור למשה שיאמר לאהרן ושמא זה קורא נתייחד הא דכתיב אל אהרן ולא שיאמר לבני ישראל:
כללות נאמרו בסיני כו' · הוה מצי לאיתויי מדר' יוסי הגלילי דאמר בפ"ק דחגיגה (דף ו: ולקמן קכ·) דאין טעונה הפשט וניתוח: ודלמא

רש"י

כדרב הונא אמר רב כו' שניתק לרעייה · שניתק מדין הקרבה ומסרוהו לרועה עד שיסתאב דקי"ל (תמורה דף יח.) כל שבחטאת מתה באשם רועה: עולה · אשר יעלה עולה: גמר עבודה · שאין אחריה עבודה ואיתרבו להו באף כל כגון המנסך ומקטיר קטרת ומקטיר קמצים יז] ומקטיר מנחת כהנים: ויתיב רב חסדא וקאמר וישלח את נערי בני ישראל · נראה בעיני שהספרים חסרים כאן ולא ידעתי מה ואם אין חסרין זהו פירושו יתיב רב חסדא וקאמר להאי קרא וישלח את נערי וגו' ומפרש דאלו הבכורות: א"ל רב הונא הכי אמר רב אסי ופסקו · אותו היום פסקה עבודה מן הבכורות שמסיני נלטוו על הכהונה כדיליף לקמן ושמשו נדב ואביהוא כל אותה שנה ראשונה עד שהוקם המשכן ומתו: לישנא אחרינא הכי אמר רב אסי ופסקיה · צריך להפסיק כאן יח] נגינת טעם המקרא באתנחתא ולא יקרא בטעם פשטא כמו שאנו קורין אותו דכשהוא נקרא בטעם פשטא משמע שקריאת נערי בני ישראל דבק על ויעלו עולות משמע שהם העלום אבל כשאתה קורהו באתנחתא עומדת התיבה לבדה ואינה דבק על ויעלו וי"ל שלא שלחם אלא להביא הקרבנות ולעמוד עליהם ויעלו עולות אותם שכשרים להעלותם דהיינו נדב ואביהוא שמשבאו לסיני הופרשו הכהנים כדיליף לקמן: סבר רב חסדא יט] לאותביה מתני' · דקתני שנהגו עבודה בבכורות עד יום הקמת המשכן: שמעיה · רב חסדא לרב *חנא דיתיב וקאמר תו משמיה דרב אדא כו': כ] איתיביה מברייתא דשויא בכולהו · שתהא שוה להשיב על כל דבריו: עולה שהקריבו ישראל במדבר סיני · קודם מתן תורה וישלח את נערי וגו': והכל כשרין ליקרב · כדמפרש ואזיל בהמה וחיה ועוף כו': והכל קרבו עולות · השתא משמע שלא היו מקריבין אלא עולות ולקמיה פריך עליה: רשאין לעשות כן · דלא נאסרו להן הבמות: יתקדשו · מלעלות ואע"פ שרגילין לגשת אלי ולהעלות העד בהן שלא יעלו בהר: זו פרישת בכורות · הזהיר את הבכורות כא] להפריש מן ההר: זו פרישת נדב ואביהוא · כלומר לא נקראו בכורות כהנים אלא מי הן הכהנים הנגשים שהוזהרו כאן לפרוש מן ההר זה נדב ואביהוא שנעשו כב] בסיני כהנים והן הכהנים הנגשים אל ה' להקריב קרבנות: היינו דכתיב · כשמתו נדב ואביהוא אשר דבר וגו' כדקאמר בסיני (שמות יט) פן יפרוץ (ב) בהם ה' וכיון שלא נזהרו לפרוש מן ההיכל בהקמת המשכן פרץ בהם: אלא למ"ד זו פרישת בכורות היכא רמיזא · ה"ג ולא גרסי' פרישת נדב ואביהוא היכא רמיזא מיתת נדב ואביהוא היכא רמזה למשה קודם לכן דקאמר הוא אשר דבר: ונקדש בכבודי · נאמרה לו למשה ביום שנצטווה על מלאכת המשכן ורמז לו שביום שישרה שכינתו על הבית יתקדש בכב ודיו ולא נרמז להבין מה הוא עד שמתו: אלא כדי להתקדש כבודו של מקום עליהם · להודיע שהוא נורא על יראיו ומיודעיו וזהו הוא אשר דבר אני ביום שנצטוויתי על המשכן ונקדש בכבודי באותם הנכבדים וקרובים לי אקדש: שנאמר וידום אהרן · הרי ששתק וקבל השכר מפרש בב"ר שמתוך כך זכה ונתייחד אליו הדיבור שנאמר אחרי אותו ענין פרשת שתויי יין ולא הוזכר באותו דיבור משה אלא אהרן: נורא אלהים ממקדשך · אלהים זו מדת הדין אימתי הוא נורא ע"י שהוא עושה דין במקודשיו: אלא עולה קשיא · דקתני הכא כג] [דטעונה הפשט] וניתוח: כללות נאמרו בסיני · כגון מזבח אדמה תעשה לי וזבחת עליו וגו' ולא נתפרשו הלכות עולה ושלמים שם: ופרטות באהל מועד · לאחר שהוקם המשכן נאמרה ת"כ למשה ושם נתפרשו והפשיט ונתח (ג) לרבי ישמעאל שמעי' דעולה שהקריבו בסיני לא הוטענה הפשט וניתוח: כד] נשתלשו בערבות מואב · משנה תורה שחזר משה ואמרה להם על הסדר כדכתיב (דברים א) בעבר הירדן בארץ מואב הואיל משה וגו': חיה בכלל בהמה · דכתיב זאת הבהמה אשר תאכלו וגו' וסמיך ליה איל וצבי ויחמור וגו' (שם יד): ה"ג

שיטה מקובצת

א] והמקבל דמים בחוץ: ב] רב חנא בר רב קטינא קמיה דרב חסדא יתיב וקאמר וישלח את: ג] תיבת קרבו נמחק: ד] וניתוח אותביה מברייתא' דשויא: ה] המשכן היו הבמות: ו] כשרין ליקרב אות ה' נמחק: ז] אלא בִּכְבוּדַי דבר זה רמז הקב"ה ואות מ' ל"ש ותיבת אמר נמחק: ח] להקדיש כבודו של מקום עליהם כיון שידע תיבות שמו של הקב"ה הוא טעות הדפוס: ט] שכר על שתיקתו שנאמר: י] את דום תיבת שתוק נמחק: יא] וכן שלמה הוא אומר: יב] פעמים שאדם שותק ומקבל אות ש' נמחק: יג] השתיקה ופעמים שמדבר ומקבל: יד] בשעה שהקב"ה עושה דין בקדושיו: טו] ופרטות נאמרו באהל מועד: טז] בהמה ועוף במשמעו חיה הרי היא בכלל: יז] קמצים של מנחות: יח] כאן טעם נגינת המקרא: יט] לאותובי' מתני': כ] כו' הס"ד ומה"ד עולה ואח"כ מה"ד איתיבי': כא] הבכורות לפרוש מן: כב] כהנים בסיני והן: כג] הכא דטעונה הפשט וניתוח: כד] מה"ד ונשתלשו בערבות:

[שהקב"ה עושה דין במקדשיו כך גירסת סילקוט]

נ"א ולי נראה לפרש כו' נ"ק

[רבה שמיני פרשה יב]

נ"א בהמה ועוף כמשמעו נ"ק

מסורת הש"ס

לעיל ס: קיז. מיר כט: ע"ש מנחות ד. פסחים עג. תמורה יח.

[לפי גי' רש"י ז"ל דר"ח ויתיב רב חסדא וקא קרי]

חגיגה ו: ע"ש תוספתא דפרה פ"ג [לקמן קכ. ע"ש]

[נ"ל חנא]

[גרסת סילקוט ע"י דוד]

גיטין ז. ע"ש
*[גי' סילקוט ע"י שלמה]

חגיגה ו. סוטה לג.

[נדרים פה. וש"נ]

הגהות הב"ח

(א) גמ' יתיב רב חנא בר רב קטינא: (ב) רש"י ד"ה סיני וכו' פן יפרוץ בם ס"א: (ג) ד"ה ופרטות וכו' ונהי דמשמע לרבי ישמעאל דשלם:

so that one of them was a burnt-offering from the outset, [115b] this agreeing with R. Huna's dictum in Rab's name, viz.: If a guilt-offering was transferred to pasture and one then slaughtered it without a specified purpose, it is valid as a burnt-offering.[5]

ONE WHO OFFERS UP THE FLESH OF A SIN-OFFERING [... WITHOUT, IS NOT LIABLE]. Our Rabbis taught: How do we know that he who offers up the flesh of a sin-offering, or the flesh of a guilt-offering, or the flesh of most sacred sacrifices, or the flesh of lesser sacrifices, or the remainder of the *'omer*, or the two loaves, or the Shewbread, or the residue of meal-offerings, [without], is not liable? Because it says, '[*Whatsoever man ... that offereth*] *a burnt-offering*': as a burnt-offering is eligible for offering up,[6] so everything which is eligible for offering up [on the altar a entails liability].[1] How do we know that also he who pours [the oil on the meal-offering], or mingles [it with flour], or breaks up [the meal-offering cakes], or salts [the meal-offering], or waves [it], or presents [it opposite the south-west corner of the altar], or sets the table [with the Shewbread], or trims the lamps, or takes off the fistful, or receives the blood, without, is not liable? Because it says, '*that offereth a burnt-offering or sacrifice*': as offering up completes the service, so everything that completes the service [entails liability].[2]

BEFORE THE TABERNACLE WAS SET UP [etc.] R. Huna[3] son of R. Ḳaṭṭina sat before R. Ḥisda, and recited [the text], *And he sent the young men of the children of Israel, [who offered burnt-offerings, and sacrificed peace-offerings of oxen unto the Lord]*.[4] Said he to him: Thus said R. Assi: And then they ceased.[5] Now, he thought to refute him from our Mishnah, when he heard him teach in R. Adda b. Ahaba's name: The burnt-offering[s] which Israel sacrificed in the wilderness did not require flaying and dismembering; whereupon he refuted him from a Baraitha, which had a bearing upon the whole [of his teaching]. For it was taught: Before the Tabernacle was set up *bamoth* were permitted and the service was performed by the firstborn, and all were eligible to be offered, viz., animals, beasts, birds, male and female, unblemished or blemished; clean, but not unclean;[6] and all offered burnt-offerings, and the burnt-offering[s] which Israel offered in the wilderness required flaying and dismembering; and gentiles are permitted to do thus in these days?[7]—It is a controversy of Tannaim. For it was taught: *And let* b *the priests also, that come near to the Lord, sanctify themselves*:[1] R. Joshua b. Ḳarḥah said: This intimated the separation of the first born.[2] Rabbi said: This intimated the separation of Nadab and Abihu.[3] On the view that this meant the separation of Nadab and Abihu, it is well: hence it is written, *This is that the Lord spoke, saying: 'Through them that are near unto Me I will be sanctified'*.[4] But on the view that it meant the retirement of the firstborn, where was [this warning] indicated?[5] In the text, *And there I will meet with the children of Israel; and [the Tent] shall be sanctified by My glory* [bi-kebodi]:[6] read not *bi-kebodi*, but *bi-kebuday* [My honoured ones]:[7] this the Holy One, blessed be He, said to Moses, but they did not know [its meaning] until the sons of Aaron died.[8] When the sons of Aaron died, he [Moses] said to him: 'Oh my brother! Thy sons died only that the glory of the Holy One, blessed be He, might be sanctified through them'.[9] When Aaron thus perceived that his sons were the honoured ones[10] of the Omnipresent, he was silent, and was rewarded for his silence, as it is said, *And Aaron held his peace*.[11] And thus it says of David, *Be silent before the Lord, and wait patiently [hith-ḥollel] for Him*:[12] though He casts down many slain [*ḥalalim*] of thee, be silent before Him. And thus it was said by Solomon, [*There is ...*] *a time to keep silence, and a time to speak*:[13] sometimes a man is silent and is rewarded for his silence; at others a man speaks and is rewarded for his speaking. And this is what R. Ḥiyya b. Abba said in R. Johanan's name: What is meant by the text, *Awful is God out* c *of thy holy places [mi-miḳdasheka]*?[1] Read not *mi-miḳdasheka* but *mi-meḳuddasheka* [through thy consecrated ones]: when the Holy One, blessed be He, executes judgment on His consecrated ones, He makes Himself feared, exalted, and praised.

[To return to the original discussion:] Yet the burnt-offering is a difficulty?[2]—It is a controversy of two Tannaim. For it was taught, R. Ishmael said: The general laws were stated at Sinai,[3] while the details were stated at the Tent of Meeting.[4] R. Akiba said: The general laws and the details were stated at Sinai, repeated in the Tent of Meeting, and a third time in the plains of Moab.[5]

The master said: 'All were eligible to be offered'. How do we know this?—Said R. Huna, Because Scripture saith: *And Noah builded an altar unto the Lord, and took of every clean animal [behemah] and of every clean fowl, [and offered burnt-offerings on the altar]*.[6] Animal [*behemah*] and fowl [bear] their plain meaning; beast [*ḥayyah*] is

(5) *Supra* 5b, 112a. Hence if he slaughtered one of these without as a burnt-offering (presumably, even before the other had been sacrificed as a guilt-offering), it counts as having been slaughtered for its own sake, and therefore he is liable. (6) The whole of it is offered up on the altar.

a (1) These, however, were eaten and not offered up on the altar. (2) None of these do so, as they are followed by another rite. On the other hand, by the same reasoning he who offers libations or burns incense or the fistful removed from a meal-offering, without, is liable. (3) BaḤ and Sh.M. emend: Ḥana. (4) Ex. XXIV, 5. The '*young men*' were the firstborn, not priests, and the occasion was when Moses built an altar at the foot of Mount Sinai (ibid. v. 4). (5) This was the last time that the firstborn performed the sacrificial service, though it was nearly a year before the Tabernacle was set up. (6) Only clean animals etc., i.e., those which may be eaten, could be offered. (7) Non-Jews might still offer at *bamoth* 'in these days', after the building of the Temple.

b (1) Ex. XIX, 22. This was immediately before Revelation, while the incident cited above took place immediately after Revelation. (2) By '*priests*' the firstborn are meant here, as it was they who '*came near the Lord*' to perform sacrifices, and the verse now separated them and forbade them to approach the mountain. (3) Not the firstborn but actual priests are meant, viz., Nadab and Abihu, who became priests at Sinai.—Thus Rabbi holds that henceforth only the children of Aaron might act as priests, while R. Joshua b. Ḳarḥah maintains that the service was still performed by the firstborn. (4) Lev. X, 3. I.e., God had warned them previously, in the verse under discussion. (5) The *priests* had never been warned. (6) Ex. XXIX, 43. (7) This requires only a change of punctuation. (8) God intimated that when He would '*meet with the children of Israel*', i.e., at the consecration of the Tabernacle, He would be sanctified through His honoured ones (the priests), but they did not understand the allusion. (9) This is what God had meant.—Emended text (Sh.M.). (10) Or, the favoured ones. Lit., 'the known ones'. (11) Lev. X, 3. The reward was that God subsequently spoke specially to him, v. 8. (12) Ps. XXXVII, 7. (13) Ecc. III, 7.

c (1) Ps. LXVIII, 36. (2) For it states that it did require flaying and dismembering. (3) E.g., *an altar of earth thou shalt make unto Me, and shalt sacrifice thereon thy burnt-offerings, and thy peace-offerings* (Ex. XX, 21). (4) E.g., that the burnt-offering was to be flayed and cut up. Hence until the Tent of Meeting was set up, burnt-offerings were not flayed and dismembered. (5) I.e., in Deuteronomy (v. Deut. I, 5). (6) Gen. VIII, 20.

included in animal [*behemah*]. [116*a*] 'Males and females, unblemished and blemished animals': this excludes an animal lacking a limb, which might not [be sacrificed]. For R. Eleazar said: How do we know that [an animal or bird] lacking a limb was forbidden to the children of Noah?[7] Because it says, '*And of every living thing of all flesh*':[8] the Holy One, blessed be He, said to Noah: Bring [into the Ark] animal[s] whose chief limbs are alive.[9] But perhaps that was to exclude a *terefah*?—That is inferred from *to keep seed alive*.[10] That is correct on the view that a *trefah* cannot give birth; but on the view that a *trefah* can give birth, what can be said?—Surely Scripture said, '[*to keep them alive*] *with thee*': [this means] those that
a are like thee.[1] But perhaps Noah himself was *trefah*?[2]—'Whole' [*tamim*] is written of him.[3] Perhaps that means, whole in his ways?[4]—'*Righteous*' is written of him.[5] But perhaps [it means that he was] whole in his ways and righteous in his actions?—If you should think that Noah himself was *trefah*, could the Merciful One say to Noah, Take in [only] such as are like thee, [but] do not take in whole [animals]?[6] Now, since we infer it from '*with thee*', what is the purpose of '*to keep seed alive*'?—You might think that '*with thee*' meant merely for companionship, [so they might be] even aged or castrated. Therefore ['*to keep seed alive*'] informs us [that it is not so].

[The master said:] 'Clean, but not unclean'. Were there then clean and unclean [animals] at that time?[7]—Said R. Samuel b. Naḥmani in R. Jonathan's name: [It means] of those with which no sin had been committed.[8] How did he [Noah] know?[9]—As R. Ḥisda said. For R. Ḥisda said: He led them past the Ark; those which the Ark accepted were certainly clean; those which the Ark rejected were certainly unclean. R. Abbahu said: Scripture saith, '*And they that went in, went in male and female*':[10] [that means,] that they went in of their own accord.[11]

The master said: 'And all offered burnt-offerings'. Only burnt-offerings, but not peace-offerings? Surely it is written, *and sacrificed peace-offerings of oxen?*[12]—Say rather, all offered burnt-offerings and peace-offerings. But it was taught: But not peace-offerings, save only burnt-offerings?—That is in accordance with the view that the Children of Noah did not offer peace-offerings.[13] For it was stated, R. Eleazar and R. Jose b. Ḥanina [disagree]. One maintained: The Children of Noah offered peace-offerings; while the other maintained: They did not. What is the reason for the view that the Children of Noah did offer peace-offerings?—Because it is written, *And Abel, he also brought of the firstlings of his flock*
b *and of the fat* [ḥeleb] *thereof*.[1] What thing is it whose 'fat' [*ḥeleb*] [only] is offered on the altar, but the whole of it is not offered on the altar? Say, that is a peace-offering. What is the reason of the view that the Children of Noah did not offer peace-offerings?—Because it is written, *Awake, O north, and come, thou south*:[2] [this means,] Awake, O people whose rites [were performed] in the north, and come, O people, whose rites [will henceforth be performed] in the north and the south.[3] But as to this master, surely it is written, '*of the fat thereof*'?—That means, of their fat ones.[4] And as to the other master, surely it is written, '*Awake, O north* [etc.]'?—That refers to the ingathering of the exiles.[5]

But surely it is written, *And Moses said: 'Thou must also give into our hands sacrifices* [zebaḥim] *and burnt-offerings, that we may sacrifice unto the Lord our God?*[6]—[He demanded] *zebaḥim* for food and burnt-offerings for sacrifice.[7] But surely it is written, *And Jethro, Moses' father-in-law, took a burnt-offering and sacrifices unto the Lord?*[8]—That was written after the giving of the Torah [Revelation].[9] That is well on the view that Jethro came after Revelation; but on the view that Jethro came before Revelation, what can be said? For it was stated: The sons of R. Ḥiyya and R. Joshua b. Levi [disagree]: one [side] maintains: Jethro came before Revelation; while the other maintains: Jethro came after Revelation!—He who maintains that Jethro came before Revelation holds that the Children of Noah sacrificed peace-offerings.

This is a controversy of Tannaim: *Now Jethro, the priest of Midian,*
c *heard*:[1] what news did he hear that he came and turned a proselyte? R. Joshua said: He heard of the battle with the Amalekites, since this is immediately preceded by,[2] *And Joshua discomfited Amalek and his people with the edge of the sword*.[3] R. Eleazar of Modim[4] said: He heard of the giving of the Torah and came. For when the Torah was given to Israel the sound thereof travelled from one end of the earth to the other, and all the heathen kings were seized with trembling in their palaces, and they uttered song,[5] as it is said, *And in his palace all say: 'Glory'*.[6] They all assembled by the wicked Balaam and asked him: What is this tumultuous noise that we have heard: perhaps a flood is coming upon the world, for it says, *The Lord sat enthroned at the flood?—The Lord sitteth as King for ever*, he replied: the Holy One, blessed be He, has already sworn that He will not bring [another] flood upon the world.[7] Perhaps, they ventured, He will not bring a flood of water, yet He will bring a flood of fire, as it is said, *For by fire will the Lord contend?*[8] He has already sworn that He will not destroy all flesh, he assured them. Then what is the sound of this tumult that we have heard? He has a precious treasure in His storehouse, which was hidden by Him nine hundred and seventy-four generations before the world was created,[9] and He has desired to give it to His children, as it is said, *The Lord will give strength unto His people*.[10] Forthwith they all exclaimed, *The Lord will bless His people with peace*.[10]

R. Eleazar said: He heard about the dividing of the Red Sea, and came, for it is said, *And it came to pass, when all the kings of the Amorites* heard [... *how that the Lord had dried up the waters of the Jordan*
d *before the children of Israel*];[1] and Rahab the harlot too said to Joshua's messengers [spies]: *For we have* heard *how the Lord dried up the water of the Red Sea*.[2] Why is, '*neither was there spirit in them any more*' written in the first text, whereas in the second it says, '*neither did*

(7) As sacrifices. 'Children of Noah' is a technical term denoting all people before the Revelation at Sinai, and all non-Israelites who did not accept the Torah after Revelation. In the present discussion even Israelites technically ranked as Children of Noah, until the laws of sacrifices as stated in Leviticus became operative. (8) Gen. VI, 19. (9) I.e., not missing.—Of these animals Noah subsequently sacrificed. (10) Ibid. VII, 3. A *terefah*, however, cannot give birth, and so cannot keep seed alive.

a (1) Not *trefah*. (2) Perhaps he suffered from a disease or organic disturbance which in the case of an animal would render it *trefah*. (3) Gen. VI, 9. E.V. *whole-hearted*. (4) Modest and patient. (5) Which includes that. (6) That is obviously absurd. (7) Before the Torah was given. (8) Those which had mated only with their kind. (9) Which were clean and which unclean. (10) Ibid. VII, 16. (11) In their respective pairs, seven of the clean and two of the unclean. (12) Ex. XXIV, 5. (13) V. *supra* n. 7, on 'the children of Noah'. But Ex. XXIV, 5 was after Revelation.

b (1) Gen. IV, 4. (2) S. S. IV, 16. (3) The burnt-offering was slaughtered on the north side of the altar; the peace-offering, on any side. He renders: Awake, O nation who hitherto, as Children of Noah, could only sacrifice on the north side of the altar (hence, burnt-offerings) and now, by accepting the Torah, come as a people who can sacrifice in the north and the south.—Cf. Gen. Rab. XXII, 5 (Sonc. ed. p. 183.) (4) *Sc.* the best. (5) It is a summons to the north and the south to bring in their exiles. (6) Ex. X, 25. This was said before Revelation, and since 'burnt-offerings' are specifically mentioned, '*sacrifices*' must mean peace-offerings. (7) The answer renders *zebaḥim* animals for slaughtering, not sacrifices. (8) Ibid. XVIII, 12. (9) Although it is written before.—It is a principle of exegesis that the Torah is not necessarily in chronological order (Pes. 6*b*).

c (1) Ex. XVIII, 1. (2) Lit., 'since it is written at the side thereof'. (3) Ibid. XVII, 13. (4) The native place of the Hasmoneans, fifteen miles N. W. of Jerusalem. (5) Of reverence to God. (6) Ps. XXIX, 9. E.V. '*and in His temple* etc.' (7) For He could only be a King (over His creatures) for ever as long as mankind existed. Hence He could not destroy them. (8) Isa. LXVI, 16. (9) Cf. Gen. Rab. I, 10 (Sonc. ed. p. 10); Cant. Rab. V, 11 (Sonc. ed. p. 243 and n. 3. a.l.). (10) Ps. ibid. 11.—The Torah is the strength of Israel.

d (1) Josh. V, 1. As '*heard*' here refers to the drying up of waters, it has a similar connotation in connection with Jethro. (2) Ibid. II, 10.

ה"ג זכרים ונקבות תמימים ובעלי מומין לאפוקי מחוסר אבר דלא. *ולא (ב) גרסי' תמות וזכרות בבהמות כו' דמאי איריא קודם מתן תורה לאחר הקמת המשכן נמי איתא להא ועוד מדקאמר אבל מחוסר אבר לא מכלל דבעלי מומין לא נפסלו לא בבהמה ולא בעוף: שנאסר לבני נח. להקריב לגבוה: שחיין ראשי איברים. ולמה לי לאזהורי עלייהו אי לאו משום הקרבה שהקריב מהן בצאתו מן התיבה: מלחיות זרע נפקא. דטריפה אינה יולדת: בדומין לך. למעוטי טריפה: תמים בדרכיו. עניו וסבלן: מהו דתימא אתך. לאו למידרש בדומין לך אלא כא] שהודיע שאינו עושה אלא לכבודו להיות לו לצוותא: קמ"ל לחיות זרע. לאו לצוותא בעי להו ומהשתא על כרחך אתך יתירא הוא למידרש ביה בדומין לך: מי הוו. הרי לא נתנה תורה: הבאין מאיליהן. וכל אותן שבאו אל התיבה מאיליהן באו ובהן הכיר אותם שבאו שבעה שבעה ידע שהן טהורין ושבאו שנים שנים שהן טמאין: ויזבחו זבחים שלמים. וסיני קודם הקמת המשכן הוה ולא אמרת דעד [שלא] הוקם המשכן לא קרבו שלמים כלל: *לכל. בין לישראל בין לבני נח קרבו עולות אבל שלמים לא קרבו לבני נח ומשעת מתן תורה שנבחרו ישראל קרבו להם שלמים: כב] תתנער. לשון (שמות יד) וינער ה' את מצרים: שמעשיה בצפון. היינו עולה שטעונה צפון: כג] ותבא. אל מלך המשיח: אומה שמעשיה צפון ודרום. דהיינו ישראל שמקריבין עולות ושלמים: משמניהון דידהו. מן השמנין שבהן ומיהו עולות הוו: בקיבוץ גליות. [וה"ק] עורי רוח צפונית ובואי רוח דרומית לקבץ גליות המפוזרות בכם: זבחים ועולות. זבחים היינו שלמים וקודם מתן תורה כולהו בני נח. ומשני זבחים אינן שלמים אלא לשון שחיטה בעלמא ולאכילה: הניחא למ"ד כו'. פלוגתא לקמן: כתנאי. אי קודם מתן תורה הוה [יתרו] אי לאחר: ובהיכלו כולו אומר כבוד כו'. רישא דקרא קול ה' יחולל אילות ובמתן תורה משתעי ובהיכלו של כל מלך ומלך כולו אומר כבוד להקב"ה: אמר להם וישב ה' מלך לעולם. כבר נשבע שיהא מלך לעולם על בריותיו ולא ישחיתם: תשע מאות ושבעים וארבעה דורות קודם שנברא העולם. וכ"ו מאדם ועד משה רבינו הרי דבר צוה לאלף דור (תהלים קה): עוז. התורה שהיא מעוזן של ישראל: דאפי'

ודילמא למעוטי טריפה. תימה דבפ' שילוח הקן (חולין דף קמ.) [וסס] גבי שתי לפרים חיות דרשי' מינה תרתי שחיין ראשי איברים שלה ולמעוטי טריפה וי"ל דשאני ליפורי מצורע שהוא כעין קרבן ושניהן שוין לענין פסול אבל גבי נח דשאר מומין כשרין הו"ל לאוקמיה למעוטי טריפה דוקא:

אבל למ"ד טריפה יולדת מאי איכא למימר. פי' דלדידיה לא מייתר ליה מכל החי למחוסר אבר ואיצטריך למעוטי טריפה וא"ת כיון דטריפה חיה ויולדת היכי מימעטא מכל החי הא בפ' שילוח הקן (ג"ז שם) לא ממעט מחיות טריפות למ"ד טריפה חיה ויש לומר דשאני הכא דמכל החי מיותר ושפיר משתמע למעוטי טריפה אע"ג דחיה דמשתמע חיות גמורה ומסתבר למעוטי טריפה אע"ג דחיה ויולדת טפי ממחוסרת אבר דמ"מ אין טריפה בריאה נשארת ולא חזיא לקיום העולם טלי האי:

אתך בדומין לך. וא"ת א"כ האי מכל החי למה לי דתרוייהו מאתך נפקא וכי תימא דלמא נח גופיה מחוסר אבר הוה מי קאמר רחמנא דכוותך עייל שלמים לא תעייל *וי"ל דמוקמא קרא בדדמי לטריפה ולא דמי למחוסרת אבר דלענין קיום העולם לא חיישינן:

דילמא נח גופיה טריפה יהוה. וא"ת והלא חי אחרי כן ג' מאות שנה וי"ל דשמא לא היה בכח ובריאות כראוי לו וסוגיין כמ"ד טריפה חיה *ור"ת היה רגיל לחלק בין טריפות דאדם לטריפות דבהמה משום דאדם אית ליה מזלא וקשה דבריש אלו טריפות (חולין דף מג.) מייתי ראיה מאיוב אטריפות דבהמה*: אסור

רש"ק זכרים ונקבות תמימין ובעלי מומין א] (*דאמר מר **תמות וזכרות בבהמה ואין תמות וזכרות בעופות ואיתקש בהמה לעוף תמימין ובעלי מומין) לאפוקי מחוסר אבר דלא ב] א"ר אלעזר *מנין למחוסר אבר שנאסר לבני נח ת"ל °ומכל החי מכל בשר ג] אמרה תורה הבא בהמה שחיין ראשי איברין שלה ודילמא ד] למעוטי טריפה ההוא מלחיות זרע נפקא הניחא *למ"ד טריפה אינה יולדת אלא למ"ד טריפה יולדת מאי איכא למימר האמר קרא אתך בדומין לך ודילמא נח גופיה טריפה הוה תמים כתיב ביה ודילמא תמים בדרכיו צדיק כתיב ביה ודילמא תמים בדרכיו צדיק במעשיו אי סלקא דעתך דנח גופיה טריפה הוה מי קאמר ליה ה] לנח דכוותך עייל שלמים לא תעייל ומאחר דנפקא לן מאתך לחיות זרע למה לי מהו דתימא אתך לצותא בעלמא אפי' זקן אפילו סריס קמשמע לן: ו] טהורין אבל לא טמאין: ומי הוו טמאין וטהורין בההיא שעתא א"ר *שמואל בר נחמני א"ר יונתן *מאותן שלא נעבדה בהן עבירה ז] מנאהוו ידעי כדרב חסדא דאמר רב חסדא העבירן לפני התיבה כל שהתיבה קולטתן בידוע שהוא טהור אין התיבה קולטתן בידוע שהן טמאין רבי אבהו אמר קרא °והבאים זכר ונקבה הבאין מאיליהן אמר מר והכל קרבו עולות עולות אין שלמים לא והא כתיב °ויזבחו זבחים שלמים לה' פרים אלא אימא ח] הכל קרבו עולות [ושלמים והתניא אבל שלמים לא כ"א עולות] עולות אין שלמים לא כמ"ד לא קרבו שלמים ט] בני נח דאיתמר ר"א ור' יוסי בר חנינא חד אמר קרבו [שלמים י] בני נח] וחד אמר לא קרבו מ"ט דמ"ד קרבו שלמים בני נח דכתיב °והבל הביא גם הוא מבכורות צאנו ומחלביהן איזהו דבר שחלבו קרב לגבי מזבח ואין כולו קרב לגבי מזבח הוי אומר זה שלמים מ"ט דמ"ד לא קרבו יא] דכתיב °עורי צפון ובואי תימן יב] תתנער אומה שמעשיה בצפון ותבוא אומה שמעשיה בצפון ובדרום ומר נמי הכתיב ומחלביהן יג] משמניהן [דידהו] ומר נמי הכתיב עורי צפון [ההוא] בקיבוץ גליות הוא דכתיב והא כתיב °ויאמר משה גם אתה תתן בידינו זבחים ועולות ועשינו לה' אלהינו זבחים לאכילה ועולות להקרבה והא כתיב °ויקח יתרו יד] [חותן משה] עולה וזבחים ההוא לאחר מתן תורה הוא דכתיב הניחא *למ"ד [יתרו] אחר מתן תורה היה אלא למ"ד [יתרו] קודם מתן תורה היה מאי איכא למימר דאיתמר *בני ר' חייא ור' יהושע בן לוי חד אמר יתרו קודם מתן תורה היה וחד אמר יתרו אחר מתן תורה היה למ"ד יתרו קודם מתן תורה היה קסבר שלמים הקריבו בני נח כתנאי °וישמע יתרו כהן מדין מה שמועה שמע ובא ונתגייר ר' יהושע אומר מלחמת עמלק שמע (א) שהרי טו] כתיב בצדו °ויחלש יהושע את עמלק ואת עמו לפי חרב ר"א המודעי אומר מתן תורה שמע [ובא] שכשניתנה תורה לישראל היה קולו הולך מסוף העולם ועד סופו וכל [מלכי] עובדי כוכבים אחזתן רעדה בהיכליהן ואמרו שירה שנאמר °ובהיכלו כולו אומר כבוד נתקבצו כולם אצל בלעם הרשע ואמרו לו מה קול ההמון אשר שמענו שמא מבול בא לעולם טז] (אמר להם) °ה' למבול ישב [אמר להם] וישב ה' מלך לעולם *כבר נשבע הקב"ה שאינו מביא מבול לעולם יז] אמרו לו מבול של מים אינו מביא אבל מבול של אש מביא שנא' °כי (הנה) באש ה' נשפט אמר להן כבר **נשבע שאינו** יח] משחית כל בשר ומה קול ההמון הזה ששמענו אמר להם חמדה טובה יש לו בבית גנזיו שהיתה גנוזה אצלו *תתקע"ד דורות קודם שנברא העולם וביקש ליתנה לבניו שנאמר °ה' עוז לעמו יתן יט] [מיד] פתחו כולם ואמרו °ה' יברך את עמו בשלום *)ר"א אומר קריעת ים סוף שמע ובא שנא' °ויהי כשמוע כל מלכי האמורי ואף רחב הזונה אמרה לשלוחי יהושע °כי שמענו את אשר הוביש ה' את מי ים סוף מאי שנא התם כ] **)דאמר(ליה) °ולא היה בם עוד רוח ומ"ש הכא***)דקאמר °ולא קמה עוד רוח באיש

דאפילו

*) כ"א ר"א בן יעקב **)נ"א דכתיב ***)נ"א דכתיב

הגהות הב"ח

(א) גמ' שמע ובא שהרי: (ב) רש"י ד"ה ה"ג זכרים וכו' ולא (אמרי') [גרסי' דאמר מר] תמות וזכרות בבהמות (לאפוקי לא בעופות) כו' דמאי איריא:

שיטה מקובצת

א] מתיבת דאמר כו' עד תיבת לאפוקי נמחק: ב] דלא דאר"א: ג] בשר אמר הקב"ה לנח הבא. תיבות אמרה תורה נמחק: ד] ודילמא ההיא למעוטי: ה] ליה רחמנא לנח: ו] לן. אמר מר טהורין: ז] עבירה. ל"א מאותן שעתידין ליטהר: ח] אימא לכל קרבו עולות ולבני נח עולות אין שלמים לא והשאר נמחק: ט] שלמים לבני נח: י] קרבו שלמים לבני נח ה"ט דמ"ד קרבו שלמים לבני נח: יא] קרבו שלמים לבני נח דכתיב: יב] תימן התנערי: יג] מחלביהן משמני דידהו: יד] יתרו חותן משה עולה וזבחים יתרו לאחר מתן תורה הוה הניחא למ"ד יתרו לאחר מתן תורה הוה אלא למ"ד יתרו קודם מתן תורה הוה מאי כו' קודם מתן תורה הוה וח"א יתרו לאחר מתן תורה הוה ומ"ד יתרו קודם מתן תורה הוה קסבר קרבו שלמים: טו] שהרי כתוב בצידו: טז] לעולם שנאמר ה' למבול ישב אמר להם וישב ה' מלך לעולם: יז] לעולם שנאמר כי מי נח זאת לי אשר נשבעתי אמרו לו שמא מבול של מים כו' שנאמר ה' באש יבא ותיבות כי הנה באש ה' נשפט נמחק: יח] שאינו מביא מבול כל עיקר שנאמר ולא יהיה עוד מבול לשחת כל בשר ואלא מה קול ההמון הזה: יט] יתן מיד פתחו: כ] התם דכתיב ולא היה בהם עוד רוח ומ"ש הכא דכתיב ולא קמה. סוטה דף ל"ד: כא] אלא להודיעו: כב] מה"ד התנערי לשון וינער: כג] ותבוא אל:

כג א מיי' פ"ט מהל' איסורי מזבח הל' ח:

עי' בתוס' מס' ע"ז ו. דמתרצת קושיא זו בענין אחר

עי' בכ"מ בפ"ג מהל' גירושין מה שכתב על הרמב"ם ועי' בכנס"ג ובפ"מ

וע"ע תוס' חולין מב: ד"ה ואמר רב יהודה ותוס' עירובין ז. ד"ה כגון שדרה ומיהו וכו' ותוס' גיטין נז: ד"ה וניקר ותוס' ב"ק נה. ד"ה נעבד ותוס' בכורות לו: ד"ה כחי

עיין נפים מאירות

קדושין כד: מנחות ו. כס. תמורה יד. [חולין כג.]

ע"ז ה: ודף נא. כל הענין

[חולין נז:]

ס"א סכל

[סנהדרין קח: ע"ש]

כ"א מאותן העתידין ליטהר כו' ועי' מהרש"א במ"א שכך סוף גירסא נכונה]

[ע"ז כד.]

נתב רש"י בע"ז מו. ד"ס בני ר"ח. יהודה ותוקים שמן

[סוטה יא. ע"ש]

[תענית יד. שבת פח:]

כד א ב ג מיי' פ"ט מהל' מעשה הקרבנות הלכה טז :
כה ד מיי' פ"ז מהל' איסורי מזבח הל"ג :
כו ה מיי' פ"ז מהל' בית הבחירה הל' יא :

דאפילו אקשויי נמי לא אקשו ומנא ידעה דאמר מר אין לך כל שר ונגיד שלא בא על רחב הזונה אמרו בת י' שנים היתה כשיצאו ישראל ממצרים וזנתה א] [כל] מ' שנה שהיו ישראל במדבר אחר נ' שנה נתגיירה אמרה ב] יהא מחול לי בשכר חבל חלון ופשתים: אמר מר ועובדי כוכבים בזמן הזה רשאין לעשות כן מנא ה"מ דת"ר °דבר אל בני ישראל בני ישראל מצווין על שחוטי חוץ *ואין העובדי כוכבים מצווין על שחוטי חוץ לפיכך כל אחד ואחד בונה לו במה לעצמו ומקריב עליה כל מה שירצה א"ר יעקב בר אחא אמר רב אסי *אסור לסייען ולעשות שליחותן אמר ג] רבה *ולאורינהו [להו] שרי כי הא *דאיפרא הורמיז *אימיה דשבור מלכא שדרה ד] קורבנא לרבא שלחה ליה אסקוה ניהליה לשם שמים *אמר להו לרב ספרא ולרב אחא בר הונא זילו ודברו תרי עולמי גולאי וחזו היכא דמסקא ימא שירטון ושקלו ציבי חדתי ואפיקו נורא ה] ממרא חדתא ואסקוה ניהליה לשם שמים א"ל אביי כמאן כר"א ו] בן שמוע *דתניא ר' אלעזר בן שמוע אומר מה מזבח שלא ישתמש בו הדיוט *אף עצים שלא ישתמש בהן הדיוט והא מודה ר"א בן שמוע בבמה דתניא כתוב אחד אומר °ויתן דוד ז] לארנן במקום שקלי זהב משקל שש מאות וגו' וכתיב °ויקן דוד את הגרן ואת הבקר בכסף שקלים חמשים הא כיצד ח] גובה מכל שבט ושבט חמשים שהן שש מאות רבי אומר משום אבא יוסי בן דוסתאי בקר [*ועצים] ומקום מזבח בנ' וכל הבית ט] כולו בשש מאות ר"א בן שמוע אומר בקר ועצים ומקום מזבח בנ' וכל הבית כולו בשש מאות דכתיב °ויאמר ארונה אל דוד יקח ויעל אדוני המלך [הטוב בעיניו] ראה הבקר לעולה והמוריגים [וכלי הבקר] לעצים ורבא אמר לך התם נמי בחדתי מאי *מוריגים אמר עולא מטה של טורבל מאי מטה של טורבל אמר *אביי עיזא דקרקסא דדיישן י] דישאי אמר אביי מאי קרא °הנה שמתיך למורג חרוץ חדש בעל פיפיות מקרי ליה יא] רבא לבריה ורמי ליה קראי אהדדי כתיב ויתן דוד יב] לארנן וגו' וכתיב ויקן דוד וגו' הא כיצד גובה מכל שבט ושבט חמשים שהן שש מאות ואכתי קשיין יג] אהדדי התם כסף הכא זהב אלא יד] ה"ק גובה כסף במשקל שש מאות זהב: קדשים קלים טו] נאכלים [בכל מחנה ישראל]: אמר רב הונא בכל מקומות ישראל טז] אבל מחנה לא הוי איתיביה יז] ר"נ לרב הונא ומחנות במדבר לא הואי והא תניא *כשם יח] שמחנה במדבר כך מחנה בירושלים מירושלים להר הבית מחנה ישראל מהר הבית לשער נקנור מחנה לויה מבאן ואילך מחנה שכינה והן הן קלעים שבמדבר יט] אלא אימא בכל מקום מחנה ישראל פשיטא מהו דתימא איפסלו ביוצא קמ"ל ואימא ה"נ אמר קרא °ונסע אהל מועד *אע"פ שנסע אהל מועד הוא תניא רשב"י אומר עוד אחרת היתה כ] וחיל עזרת נשים היא ולא היו עונשין עליה ובשילה לא היו אלא שני מחנות בלבד הי מינייהו לא הוה אמר כא] רבה מסתברא דמחנה לויה (א) כב] הואי דאי סלקא דעתך מחנה לויה לא כג] הואי נמצאו

ויקרא יז | דה"א כא | ש"ב כד | שם | ישעיה מא | במדבר ב

תוספות

אסור לסייען ואסור לעשות שליחותן. תימה לר' יוסי דאמר לעיל בפרק ב"ש (דף מה.) דקדשי עובדי כוכבים השוחטן בחוץ חייב לא ה"ל למיתני הכא לשון אסור כדמוכח בריש פ' בתרא דיומא (דף עג:) לד] דחיוב כרת לית ליה למיתני אסור וי"ל דקתני אסור לפי שיש כמה עבודות דלא מיחייב עלייהו בחוץ דאסור לסייען דזריקן אטו עבודה דבת חיובא: כמאן כרבי אלעזר בן שמוע כו'. עיקר מילתיה במנחות בהקומץ רבה (דף כב.): גבה חמשים מכל שבט ושבט שהן שש מאות. הא דכתיב הכא כסף והכא זהב מפרש לקמיה דה"ק גבה כסף שוה נ' שקלים של זהב לכל שבט דהיינו שוה שש מאות זהב לכל השבטים ור"ת אומר שיש במדרש דנתן לו חמשים שקלי זהב דהיינו שש מאות שקלי כסף וקשה דבפ' שור שנגח (ב"ק דף לו.) משמע דדינר של זהב שוה כ"ה של כסף ואומר ר"ת דדינר של זהב עב כפלים משל כסף ותדע מדאמרי' בפ' אלו טריפות (חולין דף נה:) גבי טחול ואי אישתייר ביה כעובי דינר זהב כשירה משמע דמשוה בעוביו משל כסף*: אימא בכל מקומות מחנה ישראל. שאפילו בשעת

רש"י

דאפי' אקשויי. אבל לתשמיש לא אקשו והיא שהיתה יודעת בדבר אמרה לשלוחי יהושע בלשון זה: דאמר מר. במכילתא בפ' יתרו: אמרה כד] ימחל לי בשביל חבל ופשתים וחלון. במכילתא תניא הכי אמרה רבש"ע בג' דברים חטאתי בג' ימחל כה] בחבל ופשתים וחלון שהיו מנאפים עולין אליה בחבלים דרך החלון ויורדים וגם טמנתם בפשתי העץ ובאותן שלשה דברים עצמן זכתה להציל השלוחים: אסור לסייען. בשעת איסור הבמות כגון בזמן הזה דקדושת ירושלים אין אחריה היתר: אורויי להן. היאך יעשו: זילו כו] דברו תרין עולמי גילאי. לכו כז] וקחו שני עובדי כוכבים בחורים בני גיל אחד שכן טוי לדבר: דמסקא ימא שירטון. לימון בלע"ז ומתייבש ונעשה קרקע דבעינן שלא נשתמש הדיוט במזבח: ואייתו ציבי חדתי. שלא נשתמש בהן אדם שלא יהא שברי כלים: ואפקו טרא כח] ממרא חדתא. נ"ל שהוא פויישי"ר של איסתמא אציי"ר בלע"ז שמוציאין בו אש מן האבנים: ה"ג כמאן כר"א בן שמוע דתניא ר"א בן שמוע אומר מה מזבח כו'. ובת"כ היא שנויה בפרשה ראשונה: כתוב אחד אומר. ברייתא זו משובשת בספרים ושנויה היא בספרי בברכת כהנים וכך היא שנויה הא כילד מקום מזבח בחמשים וכל הבית בשש מאות רבי אומר בשם אבא יוסי בן דוסתאי גבה מכל שבט חמשים שהן שש מאות ר"א בן שמוע אומר ויקן דוד את הגורן כדמפרש בענין כט] ויתן דוד לארונה במקום [שקלי] זהב משקל שש מאות אבל הבקר לעולה והמוריגים וכלי הבקר לעצים בכסף שקלים חמשים ל] ויאמר ארונה וגו' (ע"כ הגי') והכי פירושא דקרא ויקן דוד את הגורן ולא פירש במה קנאו שהרי פירשו במקום אחר כבר (דה"א כא) ויתן דוד לארונה במקום וגו' ואת הבקר קנה בכסף שקלים חמשים לא] (זהב): (ב) הא מודה ר' אלעזר בבמה. דקתני המוריגים לקח דוד לעצים כדבר ארונה: משקל שש מאות. לקמיה מפרש כסף שוה משקל שש מאות זהב: מטה של טורבל. כך נקרא במסכת פרה (פי"ב מ"ט): עיזא דקורקסא. כמין עז של עץ ויש בו יתידות חדים לב] [וגם עשוי] חריצים קרני"ש ומוליכו ומביאו על הקשים של דישה לאחר שנידושה ומתחתכין ונעשין תבן: מאי קרא. דהוא עשוי חריצים ומוכן לדוך ולדוק: כסף שש מאות שקלי זהב. וה"ק כסף שוה שקלים חמשים של זהב גבה מכל שבט ושבט: בכל מקומות ישראל. קא סלקא דעתך השתא דאפי' יצא אחד מהן חוץ למחנה ישראל אוכל קדשים קלים שם: שער נקטר. של עזרה לג] היה שער המזרח: והן הן קלעים שבמדבר. לפנים משער נקטר הוה כמקום לפנים מן הקלעים במשכן: אימא בכל מקומות מחנה ישראל. שאפי' בשעת סילוק מסעות אין נפסלים אלא מוליכן עמו ובמקום חנייתן אוכלין במחנה: עוד אחרת היתה. מחנה רביעית חלוקה מהר הבית ומעזרה ולא היו עונשין עליה על הנכנס לה בטומאה במסכת כלים (פ"א מ"ח) מפרש מה היא חלוקתו מהר הבית: דמחנה לויה מיהא הואי. ומחנה ישראל הוא דחסר דאם לא כן דמחנה ישראל הואי ולא מחנה לויה: נמצאו

מסורת הש"ס

ב"ב ח.
נ"א אמר להו רבא
מנחות כב.
ג"ז שם וע"ז כ"ד:
[במנחות שם איתא רב יהודה ובע"ז הוא סתמא ע"ש]
תוספתא דכלים פ"ק
פי' מ"ש רש"י נדה כ: וע"ע תוס' ב"ב ח. ד"ה איפרא ותוס' סנהדרין לט. ד"ה דשולמי
[וע"ע תוס' כתובות לט: ד"ה נתן ובכ"מ מד: ד"ה אלא מכ"ס ובשבועות מה: ד"ה התקבלת]
ועי' רש"א כת"א
לעיל סה: [מנחות לג.]

הגהות הב"ח

(א) גמ' דמחנה לויה מיהא הואי: (ב) רש"י ד"ה הא מודה נ"ל קודם ד"ה כתוב אחד כו' [ושם נ"ל ויתן דוד לארנן] במקום שקלי זהב משקל וכו' בכסף שקלים חמשים שנאמ' (ויקן) [ויאמר] דוד וגו' והכי פירושו דקרא וכו' ולא פי' במה וכו' חמשים כס"ד :

שיטה מקובצת

א] וזנתה כל מ' : ב] אמרה ימחול לי בשביל חבל ופשתים וחלון : ג] אמר רבא אות ה' נמחק : ד] שדרה עגלא תילתא לקמיה דרבא שלחה : ה] נורא מסגנא חדתא תיבת ממרא ל"ש : ו] אלעזר בר שמוע . וכצ"ל לקמן : ז] דוד לארונה תיבת לארנן נמחק : ח] הא כיצד מקים מזבח בחמשים ומה שבנתים נמחק : ט] הבית בשש מאות רבי אומר משום אבא יוסי בן דוסתאי גובה מכל שבט ושבט חמשים שהן שש מאות ר"א בר שמוע אומר ויקן דוד את הגורן כדמפרש בענין ומה מפורש ויתן דוד לארונה במקום זהב משקל שש מאות אבל את הבקר לעולה והמוריגים וכלי הבקר לעצים בכסף שקלים חמשים שנאמר ויאמר ארונה תו' ורבא אמר לך : י] דדיישן דישתאי : יא] ליה רחבה לבריה תיבת רבא נמחק : יב] דוד לארונא תיבת לארנן נמחק : יג] קשיין קראי אהדדי : יד] אלא אימא גובה תיבות ה"ק נמחק : טו] קדשים קלים נאכלים בכל מחנה ישראל : טז] מתיבת אבל עד תיבת ר"נ נמחק : יז] א"ל ר"נ לרב הונא : יח] כשם שהיה מחנות במדבר כך היה מחנה בירושלים : יט] שבמדבר אימא בכל מקומות מחנה ישראל ותיבת אלא נמחק : כ] היתה שם עזרת נשים ולא היו עונשין עליה : כא] אמר אביי תיבת רבה נמחק : כב] לויה מיהא הואי : כג] לא הוה דא"כ נמצאו . תיבת הואי נמחק : כד] אמרה ימחול לי : כה] ימחול לי בחבל : כז] לכו ודברו שני תיבת קחו ל"ש : כח] נורא מסגנא תיבת ממרא ל"ש : כט] בענין ומה מפורש ויתן : ל] חמשים שנאמר ויאמר : לא] חמשים הוא סה"ד ואח"כ מה"ד והב משקל שש מאות לקמיה מפרש כסף שוה משקל שש מאות זהב ואח"כ מה"ד הא : לב] חדים וגם עשוי חריצים : לג] עזרה הוא תיבת היה נמחק : לד] דיומא דבחיוב כרת :

there remain [stand] *any more spirit in any man*? [116b]—[She meant that] they even lost their virility. And how did she know this?—Because, as a master said, There was no prince or ruler who had not possessed Rahab the harlot. It was said: She was ten years old when the Israelites departed from Egypt, and she played the harlot the whole of the forty years spent by the Israelites in the wilderness. At the age of fifty she became a proselyte. Said she: May I be forgiven as a reward for the cord, window, and flax.[3]

The master said: 'And gentiles are permitted to do thus in these days'. How do we know it?—Because our Rabbis taught: *Speak unto the children of Israel*:[4] the children of Israel are enjoined against [sacrifices] slaughtered without, but gentiles are not enjoined against [sacrifices] slaughtered without. Therefore each one may build himself a *bamah* and offer thereon whatever he desires. R. Jacob b. Aḥa said in R. Assi's name: It is forbidden to assist them or act as their agents.[5] Raba observed: Yet we may instruct them.[6] [This happened with] Ifra Hormiz, mother of King Shabur,[7] who sent an offering to Raba, with the request, Offer it up in honour of Heaven. Said Raba to R. Safra and R. Aḥa b. Huna: Go, fetch two young men [non-Jews] of like age, seek a spot where the sea has thrown up alluvial mud,[8] take new [unused] twigs,[9] produce a fire with a new flint, and offer it up in honour of Heaven.[10] Said Abaye to him: In accordance with whom [do you give these instructions]? In accordance with R. Eleazar b. Shammua'? For it was taught, R. Eleazar b. Shammua' said: As the altar must not have been used by a layman [for secular purposes], so the wood must not have been used by a layman. But surely R. Eleazar b.
a Shammua' admits in the case of a *bamah*?[1] For it was taught: One text says, *So David gave to Ornan for the place six hundred shekels of gold by weight*;[2] whereas it is written, *So David bought the threshing-floor and the oxen for fifty shekels of silver*;[3] how can these be reconciled? He collected fifty [*shekels*] from each tribe, which amounted to six hundred [in all]. Rabbi said on the authority of Abba Jose b. Dosethai: [He bought] the oxen, wood, and site of the altar for fifty, and [the site of] the whole Temple for six hundred. R. Eleazar b. Shammua' said: [He bought] the oxen, wood, and site of the altar for fifty, and [the site of] the whole Temple for six hundred,[4] for it is written, *And Araunah said unto David: 'Let my lord the king take and offer up what seemeth good unto him; behold the oxen for the burnt-offering, and the threshing instruments* [morigim] *and the furniture of the oxen for the wood'*.[5] And Raba?—He can answer you: There too they were new.[6]

What are *morigim*?—Said 'Ulla: A bed of *ṭurbel*. What is a bed of *ṭurbel*?—Said Abaye: 'A goat with hooks', with which the threshers thresh.[7] Abaye said: Which text [proves this meaning]? —*Behold, I make thee a new threshing-sledge* [morag] *having sharp*
b *teeth;* [*thou shalt thresh the mountains* etc.].[1]

Raba[2] read out [Scripture] to his son, and opposed texts to each other: It is written: *'So David gave to Ornan* etc.'; whereas it is also written, *'So David bought* etc.' How can these be reconciled? He collected fifty from each tribe, which totalled six hundred. Yet the texts are still contradictory, for there it was silver and here it was gold?—Say rather: He collected silver to the value [weight] of six hundred [shekels of] gold.

LESSER SACRIFICES WERE EATEN ANYWHERE IN THE CAMP OF THE ISRAELITES. R. Huna said: [This means,] wherever the Israelites were, but there was no camp.[3] R. Naḥman refuted R. Huna: Were there no camps in the wilderness? Surely it was taught: Just as there were camps in the wilderness, so there was a camp in Jerusalem. From [the walls of] Jerusalem to the Temple Mount was the camp of the Israelites; from the Temple Mount to the Gate of Nicanor[4] was the Levitical camp; beyond that was the camp of the *Shechinah*, and that corresponded to [the place within] the curtains in the wilderness!—Say rather, wherever the camp of the Israelites was.[5] That is obvious?—You might say, it is disqualified through having gone out. Therefore he informs us [otherwise]. Yet say that it is indeed so?—Scripture saith, *Then the tent of meeting shall set forward*:[6] even when it sets forward, it is still the *'tent of meeting'*.[7]

It was taught, R. Simeon b. Yoḥai said: Yet another place was there, [viz.] the Women's Court,[8] and no penalty was imposed on its account.[9] But at Shiloh there were only two camps. Which was absent?—Said Abaye:[10] It is logical that there was certainly the Levitical camp; for if you should think that there was no Levi-

(3) For hiding them in flax, and then letting them down by a cord through a window (ibid. 6, 15). (4) Lev. XVII, 2. (5) In sacrificing without. (6) How to sacrifice. (7) Of Persia. (8) Which has dried and can be used as an altar. (9) Or, chips. (10) He held that an altar must never have been used for a secular purpose; similarly the wood must not be fragments of utensils, and the flint etc. must likewise never have been used for secular purposes. Hence he told them to seek virgin soil caused by the drying of alluvial mud.—They would then instruct the young men how to offer the sacrifice.

a (1) That the wood may have been used previously for something else. (2) I Chron. XXI, 25. (3) II Sam. XXIV, 24. (4) On the present version the views of R. Eleazar b. Shammua' and Rabbi are identical. Sh.M. emends: 'How can these be reconciled? (He bought) the site of the altar (only) for fifty, and (the site of) the whole Temple for six hundred. Rabbi said on the authority of Abba Jose b. Dostai: He collected fifty *shekels* ... (in all). R. Eleazar b. Shammua' said (continuing as in the text)'. (5) Ibid. 22. Thus he took utensils that had already been used for a secular purpose, and used them as fuel for the altar.—As the Temple was not built until the reign of Solomon, the altar erected here by David was simply a *bamah*. (6) They had never yet been used. (7) 'Goat with hooks' was the name of a threshing sledge. It was a wooden platform (hence 'bed') studded underneath with sharp pieces of flint or with iron teeth (Jast.).

b (1) Isa. XLI, 15. (2) Sh.M. emends: Raḥabah. (3) This is now assumed to mean that one could eat lesser sacrifices even if he went out of the camp of the Israelites. (4) The east gate of the Temple court. (5) If they broke camp and pitched their camp elsewhere, a sacrifice which had been offered at the former site could be eaten in the new site. (6) Num. II, 17. (7) V. *supra* 61b. Hence the camps even in travelling are regarded as camps. (8) This did not have the status either of the Temple Mount or of the Temple court. (9) One was not punished for entering it whilst unclean. (10) Emended text (Sh.M.). Cur. edd. Rabbah.

tical camp, [117a] this would result in *zabin* and the unclean a through the dead being sent out from one camp [only],[1] whereas the Torah said, *That they defile not their camps:*[2] [this intimates,] assign a camp for this one and a camp for that one.[3] Said Raba to him: What then? there was no camp of the Israelites![4] If so, *zabin* and lepers would be sent to the same place, whereas the Torah said, *He* [the leper] *shall dwell alone,*[5] [intimating] that no other unclean person may dwell with him?—Rather, there were all three camps after all; and what is meant by 'there were only two camps'? In respect of reception.[6] Hence it follows that in the wilderness the Levitical camp received [an involuntary homicide]?—Yes: and it was taught even so: *Then I will appoint thee a place [whither he may flee]:*[7] *'thee'* [implies] in thy lifetime;[8] *'thee a place'* [implies] in *thy* place;[9] *'whither he may flee':* this teaches that they banished [a homicide] in the wilderness; whither did they banish him? To the Levitical camp. From this they deduced that if a Levite committed homicide, he was banished from one district to another;[10] and if he fled to his own [juridical] district,[11] his district receives him. Which text [teaches this]?—Said R. Aḥa the son of R. Iḳa: *Because he must remain in his city of refuge:*[12] [this b implies,] in the city which has already provided him with refuge.[1]

WHEN THEY CAME TO GILGAL [etc.]. Our Rabbis taught: Whatever could be vowed or offered as a freewill-offering[2] could be offered at a *bamah;*[3] what could not be vowed or offered as a freewill-offering[4] could not be offered at a *bamah*. A meal-offering and [a sacrifice of] naziriteship[5] were offered at a *bamah*: these are the words of R. Meir. But the Sages maintain: Only peace-offerings and burnt-offerings were sacrificed on behalf of a private individual. R. Judah said: Whatever the community and an individual offered in the Tent of Meeting in the wilderness[6] were offered in the Tent of Meeting at Gilgal.[7] What was the difference between the Tent of Meeting in the wilderness and the Tent of Meeting at Gilgal? [When] the Tent of Meeting in the wilderness [existed], *bamoth* were not permitted; [when] the Tent of Meeting at Gilgal [existed], *bamoth* were permitted, and one could offer on his *bamah* on the top of his roof[8] only burnt-offering[s] and peace-offerings. But the Sages maintain: whatever the community offered in the Tent of Meeting in the wilderness they offered in the Tent of Meeting at Gilgal. In both places[9] only burnt-offering[s] and peace-offerings were offered on behalf of a private individual. R. Simeon said: Even the commu-

a (1) Viz., the camp of the *Shechinah*, since both are permitted in the camp of the Israelites (Pes. 67a). (2) Num. V, 3 q.v.; camp*s*, plural. (3) Each is sent into a different camp: he who is unclean through the dead is expelled from the camp of the *Shechinah* but permitted in the Levitical camp, whereas *zabin* are expelled from the Levitical camp too. (4) So that every place outside the Levitical camp had no status at all, and was simply like a field, whither a leper too might repair. (5) Lev. XIII, 46. (6) An involuntary homicide took refuge in a city specially designated for that purpose (Ex. XXI, 13; Num. XXXV, 9 *seq.*). In the wilderness this function was served by the Levitical camp; when they came to Shiloh, the Levitical camp lost that function. (7) Ex. XXI, 13. (8) *Sc.* in Moses' lifetime; hence, in the wilderness. (9) *'Thy' sc.* Moses'—hence, the Levitical camp. (10) All the forty-eight Levitical cities were cities of refuge. Hence, a Levite who committed involuntary homicide fled from his own city to another Levitical city. (11) Having committed homicide elsewhere. Rashi however reads (and Sh. M. emends): and if he fled *within* his own district; and explains: if he fled from one quarter to another in his own city. (12) Num. XXXV, 28.

b (1) E.g., in the case of a homicide who fled to a city of refuge, and then again committed homicide in that city, he must remain in this same city. The same therefore applies to a Levite living in that city. (2) V. *supra 2b*, n. a 6. (3) I.e., at a private *bamah*, for statutory offerings *were* offered at the public *bamah*. (4) Statutory offerings. (5) These were both votive, since naziriteship itself was the result of a vow. (6) I.e., *all* sacrifices. (7) Which was a public *bamah*. (8) I.e., at a private *bamah*. (9) *Sc.* both at public and at private *bamoth*.

נמצאו זבין וטמאי מתים משתלחין חוץ (במדבר ה) למחנה אחת והתורה אמרה °ולא יטמאו את מחניהם *תן מחנה לזה ומחנה לזה א"ל רבא אלא מאי מחנה ישראל לא הואי א] נמצאו זבין ומצורעין משתלחין ב] למקום אחד והתורה (ויקרא יג) אמרה °בדד ישב *שלא ישב טמא אחר עמו אלא לעולם כולהו תלתא הוו ומאי לא היו אלא שתי מחנות לקליטה מכלל דבמדבר הואי קלטה מחנה לויה אין *והא תניא (שמות כא) °ושמתי לך ג] מקום בחייך *מקום מקומך (שם) °אשר ינוס שמה מלמד שמגלין במדבר להיכן גולין למחנה לויה מכאן אמרו בן לוי *שהרג גולה מפלך לפלך ואם גלה ד] לפלכו פלכו קולטו מאי קרא אמר רב אחא בריה דרב (במדבר לה) איקא °כי בעיר מקלטו ישב עיר שקלטתו כבר: באו לגלגל: ת"ר *כל נידר ונידב ה] היה קרב בבמה שאין נידר ונידב אין קרב בבמה ו] *מנחה ונזירות קריבין בבמה דברי ר"מ וחכ"א לא קרבו ז] יחיד אלא עולות ושלמים בלבד ר' יהודה אומר כל שהצבור והיחיד מקריבין באהל מועד שבמדבר מקריבין באהל מועד שבגלגל מה בין אהל מועד שבמדבר לבין אהל מועד שבגלגל אהל מועד שבמדבר לא היו במות מותרות אהל מועד שבגלגל היו הבמות מותרות ובמתו שבראש גגו לא היה מקריב עליה אלא עולה ושלמים ח] וחכ"א כל שהצבור מקריבין באהל מועד שבמדבר מקריבין באהל מועד שבגלגל וכאן וכאן *לא קרבו [מגילה ט:] יחיד אלא עולה ושלמים בלבד *ר' שמעון אומר אף צבור לא הקריבו אלא פסחים וחובות

רש"י

נמלאו זבין וטמאי מתים משתלחין חוץ למחנה. שכינה לבדה דהא שניהם מותרין במחנה ישראל כדאמרי' בפסחים בפ' אלו דברים (דף סז.): מחניהם. שני מחנות משמע אחת י] לכל זב ואחת לכל טמא נפש אלא ודאי הואי מחנה לויה ומשתלחין טמאי מתים ממחנה שכינה ומותרין במחנה לויה וזבין ובעלי קריין משתלחין חוץ למחנה לויה: אלא מאי מחנה ישראל לא הואי. ומשילא תוך למחנה לויה שוב אין שם יא] קבע מחנה והרי הוא כשדה בעלמא ומותרין מצורעין לישב שם הצריכין להשתלח ממחנה ישראל וישבו עכשיו עם הזבין: א"כ נמצאו זבין ומצורעים. חוץ למחנה לויה בלבד: אלא כולהו הוו. ודקתני לא היו אלא שתי מחנות לענין קליטה הוא דנסתלקה תורת מחנה לויה מלקלוט את ההורגים שוגג: ושמתי לך יב] מקום בחייך. רמז לו הקב"ה למשה במתן תורה שיזכה למצוה זו כדכתיב (דברים ד) אז יבדיל משה שלש ערים בסוף ארבעים שנה: לך מקום. המקום שלך דהיינו מחנה לויה אף הוא נקלט: מכאן אמרו בן לוי. *שהיה דר בערי מקלט שכל ארבעים ושמנה עיירות של לוים ערי מקלט היו כדאמרי' במס' מכות (דף יג.) ואם הרג בשוגג גולה לאחד מערי חביריו דדריש ביה נמי הכי ושמתי לך מקום אף הלוים גולים: ואם גלה בפלכו. עצמו כגון משכונה לשכונה: פלכו קולטו. דומיא דמדבר יג] שהיה מחנה לויה קולטת: כל הנידר והנידב קרב בבמה. קטנה דאילו בבמה גדולה ע"כ קרבו חובת צבור דכתיב ויעשו את הפסח בגלגל אלא בקטנה *ואמר דקרבי נדרים ונדבות ולא חובות ובתורת כהנים תני לה בהדיא לר' מאיר: מנחות ונזירות. נידר ונידב יד] הוא וקרבי: כל שאין נידר ונידב אין קרב בבמה קטנה. כדיליף טעמיה לקמיה שאין יחיד מקריב חובה בשעת היתר הבמות ואפילו בגדולה וצבור בקטנה לא מקרבי טו] כו' אישתכח דאין חובות קריבין בקטנה ואי קשיא לר' מאיר א"כ יחיד לא עשה פסחו בגלגל וקרא כתיב *ויעשו את הפסח (במדבר ט) פסח קרבן צבור קרי ליה דאתי בכנופיא במס' יומא (דף נא.) והכי נמי בדר"ש קתני אף צבור לא הקריבו אלא טז] פסחיהם אלמא קרבן צבור קרי ליה לקמן יז] יליף טעמא דכולהו: לא יח] קרבי כו'. לאפוקי מנחות ונזירות דלא יט] קרבי בבמה קטנה: כל שהצבור והיחיד מקריבין באהל מועד שבמדבר. דהיינו כל הקרבנות כולן נדרים ונדבות וחובות (שקבוע להם זמן) מקריבין באהל מועד שבגלגל דהיא במה גדולה והשתא פליג אדר"מ ואדרבנן דמדקתני כל שהצבור כו' לאשמועינן דאין חילוק כ] באהל מועד שבמדבר לאהל מועד שבגלגל מכלל דשמעינא לר"מ ורבנן דאמרי יש חילוק כא] *ומה חילוקו שאין יחיד מקריב בו חובות וטעמייהו נמי שמעינן לקמן דאפי' בבמה גדולה לא קרבי ליחיד אלא נדרים ונדבות ולר' מאיר מנחות ונזירות בכלל (א): במות מותרות. במות יחיד: ובמתו שבראש הגג. היא במת יחיד: אלא עולה ושלמים. ולא מנחות ונזירות: וכאן וכאן. במת צבור ובמת יחיד לא קרבו בהן ליחיד אלא עולות ושלמים ולקמן פריך הייני תנא קמא דהא חכמים דלעיל נמי הכי אמרי: ר' שמעון פליג אכולהו דכולהו סבירא להו דאין חילוק לצבור בין מדבר לגלגל בבמה גדולה ורבי שמעון אומר אף צבור עצמם לא הקריבו בגדולה יותר מיחיד בקטנה: אלא פסחים כו'. אבל לא פר העלם דבר ושעירי עבודת כוכבים לא קרבו להם בגלגל:

לא

תוספות

בשעת סילוק המסעות אין נפסלין אלא מוליכן עמו ובמקום חנייתן אוכלין במחנה כך פירש בקונטרס ונראה דאף שעת הליכתם שרי כיון דאמרי' לעיל (דף סא.) אע"פ שנכסא אהל מועד הוא ודוקא לקדשים קלים אע"פ שנכסא אהל מועד הוא אבל קדשי קדשים דבעי מחילה כיון דנסתלקו מסעות אין מחנה שכינה קיים ולחם הפנים ושאר קדשי קדשים מיפסלי ביוצא כדמוכח במנחות בפ' שתי הלחם (דף צה.) ולעיל בפ' קדשי קדשים (דף ס:) *דאמר בשני מקומות קדשים נאכלין ומוקי לה בקדשי קדשים ולאחר שיפרקו לוים את המשכן היינו כל זמן שלא נסע מכל וכל דעדיין המזבח וקלעי החצר במקומן וא"ת בריש שתי הלחם (מנחות דף צה.) דפליגי בלחם הפנים אם נפסל במסעות ומפרש דבמסודר כ"ע לא פליגי דלא מיפסיל כי פליגי במסולק מאן דאמר איפו נפסל כדדרשינן דאע"פ שנכסא אהל מועד הוא ואידך ההוא לדגלים הוא דאתא פי' להודיע איזה דגל יסע תחלה והשתא אמאי לא משני דאתא לקדשים קלים ולקדשי קדשים קודם סילוק הקלעים*: **והתורה** אמרה בדד ישב. שלא יהו טמאים אחרים יושבים עמו אע"ג דהך סוגיא לר"ש והך דרשא לר' יהודה דלר"ש דריש ליה מקרא אחרינא בפסחים בריש אלו דברים (דף סז.) ניחא ליה להש"ס לאתויי דרשא הפשוטה והקצרה*: **פלכו** קלטתו. כף דגושה בנחמיה (ג) כמו נסך נסכו: **עיר** שקלטתו כבר. עיקר קרא ברוצח שהרג בעיר מקלטו ותרווייהו תניהו במכות פ"ב (דף יב:) הרג באותה העיר גולה משכונה לשכונה ולוי גולה מעיר לעיר ושמא היינו לכתחלה דבן לוי גולה מעיר לעיר אבל דיעבד הא אמרי' דאם גולה לתוך פלכו פלכו קולטו ומפלך לפלך היינו מעיר לעיר ואם גולה לתוך פלכו כגון משכונה לשכונה וכן משמע פי' הקונטרס אי נמי גם לכתחלה אין זקוק לצאת מן העיר והא דגולה לעיר אחרת כדי להלך כולה ובתחומה דאי בעירו משכונה לשכונה אם חזר לשכונתו יצא חוץ לתחום: **כל** הנידר ונידב קרב בבמה. אפי' מנחות ונזירות קרב בבמה קטנה כדמפרש ושאין נידר ונידב אין קרב בבמה קטנה דאילו לצבור אין מקריבין בקטנה וחובות דיחיד אפי' בגדולה לא קרבי בשעת היתר הבמות לר' מאיר כדמוכח מלתא דר' יהודה כדפי' בקונטרס דמדקאמר ר' יהודה כל שהצבור ויחיד מקריבין כו' מכלל דשמעינהו לר' מאיר ורבנן שיש חילוק וזהו חלוקו שאין יחיד מקריב חובות בגלגל אפי' בבמה גדולה דר' מאיר ורבנן דרשי לא תעשו בגלגל ככל אשר אנחנו עושים פה היום חובות ואפי' בבמה גדולה אלא איש הישר בעיניו יעשה ישרות דהיינו נדבות ור' יהודה סבר דכי כתיב הישר בעיניו קאי דהיא במת יחיד: **רבי** שמעון אומר אף צבור לא הקריבו כו'. פי' בקונטרס ר"ש פליג אכולהו דכולהו סבירא להו דאין חילוק לצבור בין מדבר לגלגל בבמה גדולה ור"ש אומר אף צבור עצמן לא הקריבו בגדולה יותר מיחיד בקטנה אלא פסחים כו'

וחובות

עין משפט נר מצוה

כז א מיי' פ"ז מהלכות רוצח הלכה ה:

מסורת הש"ס

[פסחים סז.]
שם
מכות יב: ע"ש
ס"א לך מקום המקום שלך
מגילה ט:
אע"פ שהיה נ"ק
[תמורה יד:]
קאמר דקרבו נ"ק
[בתוספתא פי"ג הגי' אין היחיד מקריב עליה אלא כו']
[נ"ל ויחנו בני ישראל בגלגל ויעשו את הפסח (יהושע ה)]
דאמרינן נ"ה
[ועיין מה שתירצו תוס' בזבחים סח: ד"ה אע"פ וכו' ובמנחות צה. ד"ה מר וכו' ועי' מ"ש לעיל מח. בתוס' ד"ה ואתא]
[וכ"כ תוס' שבת קכח: ועי' מה שרשמתי שם על לוז]
וזהו חילוקו נ"ק

שיטה מקובצת

א] הואי א"כ נמצאו: ב] משתלחין חוץ למחנה אחת והתורה אמרה בדד ישב לבדו ישב שלא יהא טמאים אחרים יושבים עמו אלא כולהו הוו ומחנה לויה לא הוה קלטה ומאי לא היו: ג] לך בחייך לך מקום במקומך אשר ינוס שמה מלמד שהיו ישראל גולין במדבר להיכן: ד] גלה לתוך פלכו: ה] תיבת היה נמחק: ו] בבמה מנחות ומתיבות מנחות ונזירות קריבין בבמה בס"א אינו אלא רש"י ז"ל מביאו מת"כ וק"ל: ז] קרבו ליחיד אלא: ח] ושלמים בלבד וחכ"א: ט] ליחיד אלא: י] אחת זב ואחת טמא נפש: יא] שם עוד מחנה תיבת קבע נמחק: יב] לך בחייך. תיבת מקום נמחק: יג] דמדבר שהיתה מחנה: יד] הן וקרבי תיבת הוא נמחק: טו] מקרבי כלל אשתכח תיבת כו' נמחק: טז] אלא פסחים אות ה' נמחק: יז] ילפי טעמייהו דכולהו: יח] לא קרבו: יט] קרבו בבמה: כ] בין אהל מועד: כא] חילוק וזהו חילוקן שאין:

הגהות הב"ח

(א) (רש"י ד"ה וכל שהצבור וכו' בכלל מותרות במות יחיד כצ"ל והד"א):

וחובות [א] שקבוע להן זמן מאי טעמא דר"מ דאמר קרא °לא תעשון ככל אשר אנחנו עושים פה היום אמר להן משה לישראל כי עייליתו לארץ ישרות תקריבו חובות לא תקריבו מנחות ונזירות ישרות נינהו ורבנן [ב] אין מנחה בבמה נזירות חובות נינהו אמר שמואל מחלוקת בחטאת ואשם אבל בעולות ושלמים דברי הכל ישרות נינהו וקרבי מותיב רבה *חזה ושוק ותרומת לחמי תודה נוהגין בבמה גדולה ואין נוהגין בבמה קטנה ואילו הזרוע בשלה שיירה אי אמרת בשלמא בעולה ושלמים פליגי הא מני רבנן היא אלא אי אמרת בחטאת ואשם פליגי הא מני אלא אי איתמר הכי איתמר אמר שמואל מחלוקת בעולה ושלמים אבל בחטאת ואשם דברי הכל חובות נינהו ולא קרבי אמר מר וחכמים אומרים כל שהצבור מקריבין באהל וכו' מאי טעמייהו דרבנן אמר קרא *°איש הישר בעיניו יעשה איש ישרות הוא דליקרוב חובות לא ליקרוב וצבור אפי' חובות [ג] ליקרוב

ורבי

תורה אור: דברים יב · שופטים יז

לא תעשון וגו'. לאחר ביאת הארץ משתעי וקאמר לא תעשון כשתבאו בגלגל: ככל אשר אנחנו עושים פה היום. שאנו בין צבור בין יחיד מקריבין חטאות ואשמות ובכור ומעשר שהן חובות שאין קבוע להם זמן וכ"ש חובות הקבוע להם זמן אבל מה אנו עושים שם איש כל הישר בעיניו היחיד לא יקריב שם אלא נדרים ונדבות שישרו בעיניו לנדור ולנדוב עד מתי כי לא באתם וגו' עד שתבאו לשילה: ישרות תקריבו. נדרים ונדבות: חובות לא תקריבו. היחידים דאיש כתיב ולא פליג קרא בין גדולה בין קטנה דליחיד לא קרב אלא נידר ונידב הלכך שאין נידר ונידב אין קרב בבמת יחיד דהא אין קדשי צבור קריבין [ד] כדתנן במתני' (דף קיב:) קרבנות צבור קריבין במשכן קרבנות יחיד קריבין בבמה: מנחות ונזירות ישרות נינהו. דאע"ג דבמלאת נזרו הויין קרבנותיו [ה] חובה עליו מיהא ע"י נדר באו עליו: אין מנחה בבמה. כדאמרי' לקמן זבחים ולא מנחות [דכתיב] למען אשר יביאו בני ישראל וגו' על פני השדה היינו [ו] במות שעת היתר שלהם והביאום לה' אותם שהוקדשו בשעת היתר ולא הספיק להביאם עד שנאסרו כדאמרן בהשוחט לעיל (דף קו:) דפסוק זה בקדשי קדשים שהוקדשו בשעת היתר והקריבום בשעת איסור קאי וזבחו זבחי שלמים ומפרש בת"כ אין לי שקרבו בבמה אלא שלמים דהא אוקימנא בקדשי במה מניין אף עולה ת"ל זבחים יכול אף חטאת ואשם ת"ל אותם ומה ראית אחרי שריבה ומיעט אמרת מה שלמים הבאים בנדר ונדבה אף כל הבא בנדר ונדבה ולר"מ איתרבו נמי מנחות ונזירות ורבנן דייקי זבחים ולא מנחות אלא דבר הזבוח: נזירות חובה היא. דהוא לא התנדב [ז] *[אלו] הקרבנות אלא אסר עצמו ביין ובתגלחת ומאליו נתחייב בקרבנות: מחלוקת. דר"מ ורבנן בנזירות בחטאת ואשם שבה אבל עולות ושלמים דנזיר דברי הכל קרבי: חזה ושוק. המורם משלמים ותודה (א) וארבע חלות המורמות לכהן מארבע מיני חלות שבתודה כדכתיב והקריב ממנו אחד מכל קרבן וגו' (ויקרא ז): ואין נוהגין בבמה קטנה. גרסינן בסוף פירקין (דף קיט:) דכתיב בהו להניף תנופה לה' ולא בבמה ואילו מורם מאיל נזיר דהיינו זרוע בשלה שיירה ולא תנייה שמע מינה לא קרבי שלמי נזיר בבמה דאי הוו קרבי הוה תני דלא נהיג ביה כמי תרומה דידיה (ב): אלא אי אמרת בחטאת ואשם הוא דפליג. אבל שלמי נזיר דברי הכל קרבי הא מני: איש הוא דחובות לא הקריבו. ואפי' בגדולה אבל צבור מקריבים חובות:

ורבי

וחובות הקבוע להם זמן אבל פר העלם דבר ושעירי עבודת כוכבים לא קרבו להם בגלגל עכ"ל ובחנם הזכיר פר העלם דבר ושעירי עבודת כוכבים שהן חטאות שאין קבוע להם זמן דאפי' חטאות הקבוע להם זמן כגון שעירי הרגלים לא קרבו לר"ש כדמסיק לקמן תתרגם מתני' בעולה. (הג"ה וא"כ ביוה"כ לא קרבו צבור באהל מועד* בנוב וגבעון לא פרים ולא שעירים כי אם *תמידים והא דאמרי' בתוספתא ר' יהודה אומר אבשלום נזיר היה שנאמר ויאמר אבשלום אלכה נא ואשלם נדרי אשר נדרתי בחברון כי נדר נדר עבדך בשבתי בגשור והאי קרא בהיותם בגבעון כתיב ומפרש פ"ב דתמורה (דף יד:) שהקריבם בחברון בבמת יחיד דאי הלך בחברון להביא כבשים טובים ולהקריבם בבמה גדולה א"כ מחברון מיבעי ליה והשתא לר' יהודה אי נזירות נידר ונידב הוא אתי שפיר שהקריבן בבמת יחיד בחברון ואי נזירות חובה הוי א"כ הקריבן בגבעון באהל מועד שהיה שם *דלר' יהודה יחיד נמי מלי מקריב חובות בבמה גדולה אף בשעת היתר הבמות ולא דייק בין מחברון ובחברון אבל רבנן דאמרי נזירות חובה הוא ולא קרב יחיד חובות אף בבמת צבור בנוב וגבעון א"כ אבשלום לא נזיר היה והא קרא דאלכה ואשובה ואשלם נדרי מיירי בנדרים ונדבות. הג"ה): *רבי שמעון אומר אף צבור לא הקריבו כו'. לכאורה ר"ש אדרבנן דלעיל מיניה קאי ואינהו סברי כרבנן קמאי דמנחות. ונזירות לא קרבו בבמה דליכא בינייהו אלא נסכים כדמפרש לקמיה ש"מ דלר"ש נמי לא קרבו דהא אפי' בצבור ממעט יותר משאר תנאים ותימה דבפ"ק דמגילה (דף ט:) [במתני' דקתני] אין בין במה גדולה לבמה קטנה אלא פסחים זה הכלל כל הנידר ונידב קרב כו' ומפרש בגמ' כעין פסחים דהיינו חובות הקבוע להם זמן אבל שאין קבוע להם זמן הכא והכא לא קרב ומוקי לה כר"ש אלמא ר"ש תני האי כללא א"כ מנחות ונזירות קרבי לר"ש וכדאמרינן הכא לר"מ דתני האי כללא ואי הוה גרסי' במגילה זה הכלל נידר ונידב בלא כל הוה ניחא ליה דכל דר"מ אתי לרבויי מנחות ונזירות ועוד יש לומר דהא דפשיטא ליה לר"מ דמנחות ונזירות ישרות משום דתניא בת"כ בפרשת אחרי מות מה שלמים מיוחדין שהן נידר ונידב קריבין בבמה אף כל נידר ונידב קרב בבמה אף המנחות והנזירות דברי ר"מ וקלת תימה אי אההיא סמיך דלא מייתי לה ועוד לר"ש דמגילה מי נפקא מנחה מכלל נידר ונידב ונראה ליישב מתניתין דהכי קאמר דאין חילוק בין במה גדולה לבמה קטנה אלא פסחים כל הנידר ונידב הקרב בבמה גדולה קרב בקטנה וכל שאין נידר ונידב* שאין קרב בגדולה אין קרב בקטנה ולא נחת אלא לפרש מה ששותה הגדולה והקטנה אבל *יש נידר ונידב שאין קרב לא בזו ולא בזו כגון מנחות ונזירות אבל לנידר ונידב דר"מ אין לפרש דלא איירי במנחות ונזירות דשפיר מישתמע מלישנא דנידב ועוד דקתני לה בהדיא בת"כ וכן נראה ודאי לפרש דאההיא דתורת כהנים סמיך אע"ג דלא מייתי לה דבתמורה מייתי לה בפ"ב (דף יד:) דאמרי' התם אמר ליה אביי ולימא מר שלמי פסח דאי שלמי נזיר נידר ונידב הוא דהא תניא זה הכלל כל הנידר ונידב קרב בבמת יחיד וכל שאינו נידר ונידב אינו קרב בבמת יחיד ותניא המנחות ונזירות קריבות בבמת יחיד דברי ר"מ משמע דמההיא דייק ולא מלישנא ומאן דלא חשיב התם נזירות נידר ונידב קמשני סמי מכאן נזירות: **ורבנן** מנחות אין מנחה בבמה ליחיד. בין בבמה גדולה בין בבמה קטנה קאמר כדתניא איך רבנן כאן וכאן לא קרבו (נסכים) ליחיד אלא עולה ושלמים בלבד ואמרי' דנסכים איכא בינייהו והו לא וה"ה דעופות נמי לא קרבו לרבנן כדאמרי' בסוף פירקין (דף קיט.) לדברי האומר אין מנחה בבמה אין עופות בבמה מ"ט זבחים ולא עופות זבחים ולא מנחות דאוקימנא שהוא קרא לעיל בריש השוחט (דף קו:) בקדשים שהקדישן בשעת היתר הבמות ותימה *דבסוף פירקין (קיג.) תנן ר' יהודה אומר אין מנחה בבמה והכא קא"ר יהודה כל שהצבור והיחיד מקריבין באהל מועד שבמדבר מקריבין באהל מועד שבגלגל והרי מנחות ועופות דבגלגל כאן וכאן לא קרבו ולא מיסתבר למימר דנהי דלרבנן כאן וכאן לא קרבו לר' יהודה קרבו *בבמה לצבור דמהיכי תיתי הך דרשא למר ולמר ועוד א"כ לקמן הפריך חכמים היינו תנא קמא ומשני קרבו נסכים במדבר איכא בינייהו לימא דמנחה קריבה בבמת צבור איכא בינייהו לרבנן קדמאי קרבה ולבתראי לא קרבה: **מחלוקת** בחטאת ואשם. בחטאת ואשם של נזירות איירי:

ואין נוהגין בבמה קטנה. פי' בקונטרס דכתיב בהו להניף תנופה לה' וא"ת הרי מנחה לת"ק דר' יהודה דמתני' דאיתא בבמה קטנה ואין תנופה והגשה בה וא"כ הך נמי ליהוי בבמה ולא ליבעי תנופה ויש לומר דהני חזה ושוק ותרומת לחמי תודה עיקר מצותן בתנופה הלכך בטלה תנופה בטלי אינהו אבל מנחה עיקר מצותה קמילה והקטרה:

מחלוקת בעולה (ואשם) [ושלמים]. של נזירות קאמר *ותימה דמאן דאמר לא קרבו ואפי' בבמה גדולה היכי משני קרא דאבשלום דכתיב (שמואל ב טו) ואשלם נדרי דליכא למימר בשאר נדרים דבפרק שני דתמורה (דף יד:) משמע דאיירי בקרבן נזירות:

ותתרגם

מועד שבגלגל ונוב נ"ק

דומיא דתמידים נ"ק

ודר"י נ"ק

[איש כל הישר בעיניו (דברים יב) כצ"ל]

שייך לע"א

[לקמן קיט: ע"ש]

נ"ק

אבל מודה ר"ש דיש נ"ק

אע"ש שקרב בבמה גדולה נ"ק

רש"ק מ"ז

נ"ל דמתני' אין נ"ק

נ"ל בבמה נמר

ודה"ס דלעיל לא כתבו כן ועי' תוס' דתמורה דף יד ע"ב ד"ה סמי ותנדב תמים וו

הגהות הב"ח

(א) רש"י ד"ה חזה וכו' ותודה ס"ד ואח"כ מה"ד ותרומת לחמי תודה ארבע: (ב) ד"ה ואין נוהגין וכו' תרומה דידיה בבמת יחיד ס"ס ד:

שיטה מקובצת

א] וחובות הקבוע להן: ב] ורבנן מנחות אין מנחה: ג] חובות נמי ליקריב: ד] קריבין ביה כדתנן: ה] קרבנותיו עליו חובה מיהו: ו] היינו במה בשעת היתר: ז] התנדב את הקרבנות:

nity offered only Passover-offerings [117b] and statutory offerings for which there is a fixed time.

What is R. Meir's reason?—Because Scripture saith, *Ye shall not do after all that we do here this day, [every man whatsoever is right in his eyes]*:[10] Moses spoke thus to Israel: When ye enter the [Promised] Land, ye shall offer votive sacrifices, but ye shall not offer obligatory offerings;[11] [and] meal-offerings and [sacrifices of] naziriteship were votive sacrifices. And the Rabbis?[12]—There were no
a meal-offering[s] at the *bamah* [at all];[1] [and the sacrifices of] naziriteship were obligatory.[2]

Samuel said: They disagree about the sin-offering and the guilt-offering;[3] but all agree that the burnt-offerings and peace-offerings [of a nazirite] are votive sacrifices. Rabbah raised an objection: [The law of] the breast and thigh and the separation of the loaves of the thanksoffering[4] operated at the great [public] *bamah*, but did not operate at a minor [private] *bamah*; but he [the Tanna] omits the sodden shoulder.[5] If you say that they disagree about the burnt-offering and the peace-offering, it is well: this agrees with the Rabbis. But if you maintain that they disagree [only] about the sin-offering and the guilt-offering, who is the author of this? Rather, if stated, it was thus stated: Samuel said: They disagree about the burnt-offering and the peace-offering; but all agree that the sin-offering and the guilt-offering are obligatory, and [so] they were not offered.

The master said: 'But the Sages maintain: Whatever the community offered in the Tent etc.' What is the reason of the Rabbis?—Scripture saith, *Every man whatsoever is right in his eyes*:[6] only a *man* may offer voluntary sacrifices and not obligatory ones; but a

(10) Deut. XII, 8. (11) V. *supra* 114a. (12) How do they refute this argument?

a (1) For only animal sacrifices were permitted there. (2) Since the vow of naziriteship merely meant abstention from wine, grapes, defilement, and cutting the hair. The sacrifices were then *imposed* upon the vower. (3) Which a nazirite brought on the completion of his naziriteship. (4) The breast and thigh of peace-offerings, and four loaves out of the forty which accompanied a thanks-offering, belonged to the priest. (5) Of the nazirite's peace-offering ram, which likewise was a priestly due, Num. VI, 14, 19. This implies that this was not offered at a private *bamah* at all. (6) Deut. XII, 8. This is the marginal emendation. The text quotes Judg. XVII, 6.

community can offer obligatory [sacrifices] too. [118a] And R. Judah?[7]—He can answer you: *'Whatsoever is right'* is written in reference to *'in his eyes'*,[8] but at the great *bamah* one could offer even statutory offerings. But surely *'man'* is written, and does that not intimate that [only] a *man* may offer voluntary but not
a obligatory sacrifices?[1]—*'Man'* is written to intimate that a *zar* is fit.[2] [The fitness of] a *zar* is deduced from, *And the priest shall sprinkle the blood on the altar of the Lord* [*at the door of the tent of meeting*]?[3]—You might say, it requires the sanctification of the firstborn, as originally:[4] hence it [*'man'*] informs us [that it is not so].

The Sages are identical with the first Tanna?[5]—Said R. Papa: They differ as to whether libations were offered in the wilderness.[6]

The master said: 'R. Simeon said etc'. What is R. Simeon's reason?—Because it is written, *And the children of Israel encamped in Gilgal, and they offered the Passover-offering.*[7] Now that is obvious?[8] Surely then this is what [the text] informs us: they offered only obligatory [sacrifices] similar to the Passover-offering,[9] but they did not offer [obligatory sacrifices] which were not like the Passover-offering.[10] And the other?[11]—It is required for R. Joḥanan's dictum. For R. Joḥanan said on R. Bana'ah's authority: An uncircumcised
b person received sprinkling.[1]

A Tanna recited before R. Adda b. Ahabah: The only difference between the great [public] *bamah* and the minor [private] *bamah* was [in respect of] Passover-offerings and obligatory-offerings which have a fixed time. Said he to him: in accordance with whom was this told to you? In accordance with R. Simeon, who maintained: The only difference between the great *bamah* and the minor *bamah* was [in respect of] Passover-offerings and obligatory offerings which have a fixed time; and you must make your teaching refer to a statutory burnt-offering,[2] as there is also a votive burnt-offering.[3] For if you would refer to sin-offerings, is there then a votive sin-offering?[4] Yet let him make it refer to an obligatory meal-offering, since there were *ḥabitin*?[5]—He holds that there were no meal-offering[s] at the *bamah*.

WHEN THEY CAME TO SHILOH etc. Whence do we know it?—Said R. Ḥiyya b. Abba in R. Joḥanan's name: one text says,
c *And she brought him unto the* house *of the Lord in Shiloh;*[1] whereas another text says, *And He forsook the Tabernacle of Shiloh, the* tent *which He had made to dwell among men;* and it also says, *Moreover He abhorred the* tent *of Joseph, and chose not the tribe of Ephraim.*[2] How are these reconciled? It had no roof, but stones below and curtains above.[3]

MOST SACRED SACRIFICES [etc.] Whence do we know it?—Said [R. Eleazar in] R. Oshaia['s name]: Because Scripture saith, *Take heed to thyself that thou offer not thy burnt-offerings in every place that thou seest:*[4] You may not offer *'in every place that thou seest'*, but you may eat [the sacrifice] *'in every place that thou seest'*. Yet say: *'in every place that thou seest'* you may not *offer*,[5] but you may slaughter *'in every place that thou seest'*?—Said R. Jannai: Scripture saith, *There shalt thou offer . . . and there thou shalt sacrifice.*[6] R. Abdimi b.

(7) How does he justify his view that an individual too could offer obligatory sacrifices at the public *bamah*? (8) I.e., in reference to the private *bamah*, which one could erect wherever one chose.

a (1) And if this does not apply to the *public bamah* too, why is *'man'* written? Scripture should simply write, *Whatsoever is right in his eyes*, and since *'in his eyes'* implies a private *bamah*, it is obvious that the limitation applies to an individual only, for the community did not sacrifice at a private *bamah*. Hence *'man'* must teach that this limitation applies to the *public bamah* too. (2) To officiate at a *bamah*. (3) Lev. XVII, 6. The inference is: only *'at the door of the tent of meeting'* must a *priest* sprinkle the blood; but at a *bamah* a *zar* (lay-Israelite) too could officiate. (4) Though priests are not necessary, yet we require the firstborn, who officiated originally. (5) The first Sages (referred to as the first Tanna) say that only peace-offerings and burnt-offerings were offered on behalf of *an individual*, which implies that the community could offer obligatory sacrifices; while the second Sages (referred to as 'the Sages') likewise maintain that whatever the community could offer at the Tent of Meeting in the wilderness, they could offer at the Tent of Meeting at Gilgal (which was a public *bamah*), but that a private individual could offer only peace-offerings and burnt-offerings both at a public and at a private *bamah*. Thus their views are identical. (6) *Supra* 111a, q.v. The first Sages hold that libations were not offered in the wilderness, and therefore they merely teach that peace-offerings and burnt-offerings were permitted at the *bamah*. The second Sages hold that libations were offered in the wilderness, and so they teach: whatever the community *had to offer* in the wilderness, *sc.* libations, they also had to offer at Gilgal. (7) Josh. V, 10. Cur. edd. read: And the children of Israel offered the Passover-offering in Gilgal. (8) That they had to sacrifice the Passover-offering: why then does Scripture state it? (9) I.e., those which must be offered at a fixed time. (10) E.g., sin-offerings. (11) The Rabbis: how do they explain the verse?

b (1) If an uncircumcised person becomes unclean through the dead, he is besprinkled and becomes clean (v. Num. XIX, 17 *seq.*), and may then handle sacrifices. He learns this from the present text, *'and they offered the Passover-offering'*. Now, the majority of them had been uncircumcised in the wilderness (Josh. V, 5): according to the Talmud (Yeb, 71*b*) they were circumcised on the eleventh of Nisan (the first month); many of them were unclean through the dead, their parents having died in the wilderness right up to the time of their crossing the Jordan into Eretz Israel. If they had not been besprinkled whilst yet uncircumcised, they would not be clean, for two sprinklings were necessary, and if the first were on the eleventh, the second would be on the *fifteenth* (v. Num. *a.l.*), whereas they had to sacrifice on the fourteenth. (2) Viz., the daily and additional burnt-offerings (v. Num. XXVIII-XXIX); these are the 'obligatory offerings which have a fixed time' which you mean, but the statutory sin-offerings of festivals could not be offered there. (3) Which could be offered at a private *bamah* only. (4) Surely not. For the passage must mean that apart from Passover-offerings R. Simeon includes only those obligatory offerings of which there were also votive offerings. For if he meant *all* obligatory offerings which have a fixed time, he should simply mention *them*, and not the Passover-offering at all, since that too is an obligatory offering with a fixed time. Hence this is what he means: The only difference between the public and the private *bamoth* was in respect of the Passover-offerings, which were offered at the former but not at all at the latter, while as for other sacrifices which were offered at both, the difference is that at the private *bamah* only votive offerings were offered, whereas at the public *bamah* statutory offerings which have a fixed time were also offered.—The text is emended; v. Marginal Gloss. (5) A sort of cake (v. Lev. VI, 13 *seq.*; the actual word occurs in I Chron. IX, 31 where it is rendered, *things that were baked on griddles*). These were statutory daily offerings, and as there were also votive meal-offerings, these too fulfilled the conditions required by R. Adda b. Ahabah.

c (1) I Sam. I, 24. (2) Ps. LXXVIII, 60, 67. Thus it is called a *'house'* in Samuel, but *'tent'* in Psalms. (3) Thus it partook partly of the nature of a house, and partly of the nature of a tent.—Cur. edd. add: 'And that was the rest': this is deleted by Sh.M. (4) Deut. XII, 13. This means when they will have 'come to the rest' (v. 9), *sc.* Shiloh, and *'in every place that thou seest'* is understood to mean: in every place whence the Tabernacle at Shiloh can be seen. (5) 'Offer' in its limited sense means to burn the *emurim* on the altar. (6) Deut. XII, 14. Lit., 'do' (so E.V.).—Thus it must be 'sacrificed' (slaughtered) and 'offered' in the same place.

ורבי יהודה אמר לך כי כתיב הישר (*בעיניו) הוא דכתיב אבל בבמה גדולה אפילו חובות נמי ליקרוב אלא הא כתיב איש לאו למימרא דאיש ישרות הוא דליקרוב הא חובות לא ליקרוב כי כתיב איש להכשיר את הזר זר °מזרק הכהן את הדם על מזבח ה' נפקא מהו דתימא ליבעי קדוש בכורות כמעיקרא קא משמע לן חכמים היינו תנא קמא אמר רב פפא *קרבו נסכים במדבר איכא בינייהו: אמר מר רבי שמעון אומר וכו': מ"ט דרבי שמעון דכתיב °*ויעשו בני ישראל את הפסח בגלגל פשיטא אלא א] הא קמ"ל דחובות כעין פסח הוא דקרב הא לאו כעין פסח לא קרב ואידך מיבעי ליה לכדרבי יוחנן *דא"ר יוחנן משום רבי בנאה "ערל מקבל הזאה תני תנא קמיה דרב אדא בר אהבה *אין בין במה גדולה לבמה קטנה אלא ב] פסח וחובות הקבוע להן *זמן (א"ל יחיד חובות שקבוע להן זמן מנא ליה א"ל אסמייה) א"ל תתרגם מתניתך בעולת חובה דאיכא עולת נדבה ג] *דאי חטאת יחיד הוא חובות דקביע ליה זמן מי איכא ולוקמה במנחת חובה דהא איכא חביתין קא סבר *אין מנחה בבמה: באו לשילה וכו': מנא הני מילי א"ר חייא בר אבא אמר רבי יוחנן כתוב אחד אומר °ותביאהו בית ה' שילה ד] וכתוב אחד אומר °ויטש (את) משכן שילה ה] אהל שכן באדם וכתיב °וימאס באהל יוסף ובשבט אפרים לא בחר הא כיצד "לא היתה שם תקרה אלא אבנים מלמטן ויריעות ו] מלמעלן והיא היתה מנוחה: קדשי קדשים: מנא הני מילי ז] א"ר אושעיא דאמר קרא °השמר לך פן תעלה עולותיך בכל מקום אשר (אתה) תראה בכל מקום ח] אשר תראה אי אתה מעלה אבל אתה אוכל בכל מקום שאתה רואה אימא בכל מקום שאתה רואה אי אתה מעלה אבל אתה זובח בכל מקום ט] שתראה א"ר ינאי אמר קרא °שם תעלה ושם תעשה רבי אבדימי בר י] חמא אמר קרא

ולו

תורה אור: ויקרא יז | יהושע ה | ש"א א | תהלים עח | שם | שם | דברים יב | שם

רש"י

ורבי יהודה. דאמר יחיד נמי מקריב חובות בגדולה אמר לך כי כתיב הישר דממעט יחיד מהקרבת חובות אבעיניו כתיב יא]: אלא לרבי יהודה הא כתיב איש. ואי לאו למעוטי אף מבמה גדולה אתא למה לי דכתיב איש נכתוב כל הישר בעיניו וכיון דבעיניו היינו יב] קטנה פשיטא דאיש הוא דמימעיט דהא צבור לא מקרבי בה: להכשיר את הזר. לעבודת במה: זר מזרק הכהן נפקא לן. לקמן בפירקין דכתיב (ויקרא יז) וזרק הכהן את הדם על מזבח ה' פתח אהל מועד כהן פתח אהל מועד ואין כהן בבמה אלא אפי' זר ואפי' עבד הכי דריש ליה בתורת כהנים: חכמים היינו תנא קמא. רבנן בתראי היינו רבנן קמאי דהא איכהו נמי הכי אמרי דיחיד לא קרבו אלא עולות ושלמים ולצבור קרבי [נמי חובות] דהא מאיש נפקא להו מיעוטא: קרבו נסכים במדבר איכא בינייהו. לרבנן קמאי לא קרבו נסכים במדבר ועולה ושלמים גרידא בלא נסכים קא גמרי דקרבי בבמה דבמדבר לא קרבי דכי תבאו דפרשת נסכים (במדבר טו) להטעינה נסכים במשכן שילה אתא לאחר ירושה וישיבה כדאמרן בהשוחט (לעיל קיא.) ורבנן בתראי לטפויי אתו מדתנן משנה יתירא כל שהצבור מקריבין באהל מועד שבמדבר מקריבין בגלגל למה להו למיתני הא רבי יהודה נמי בצבור כוותייהו קאמר והכי איבעי להו למימר כאן וכאן לא קרבו ליחיד אלא עולה ושלמים אלא לטפויי אדרבנן קמאי אתו ואמרי כל שהציבור צריכין להקריב (א) מקריבין באהל מועד שבמדבר יג] מקריבין באהל מועד שבגלגל ולטפויי נסכים אתו ולמימר דקרבו במדבר לצבור וליחיד וכן בגלגל(ב) לשתי הבמות ולמאן דאית ליה קרבו במדבר אית ליה דקרבו בבמת יחיד בגלגל דכי תבאו לא אתא אלא להטעינה נסכים לבמה קטנה דהא בגדולה כבר היו קריבין: פשיטא. דבעו למיעבד פסח: ערל. שנטמא במת מקבל הזאה וטהור מטומאת מת ליגע בקדשים ויליף מהכא דכתיב (יהושע ה) ויעשו את הפסח בגלגל דמשמע שעשאוהו כהלכתו במילה בטהרה ורובן ערלים היו במדבר דכתיב (שם) לא מלו ואמרינן ביבמות בעשרה בניסן שעברו את הירדן לא מהול משום חולשא דאורחא אלא בחד סרי הוא דמהול ואשתכח דטמאי מתים שהיו בהם שהרי רובן טמאי מתים היו שמתו אבותיהם כל ארבעים שנה במדבר ונטמאו בהם ואם לא קבלו הזאה ונטהרו בערלותן אין להם שהות להזות משמלו דהא צריך להפריש שלשה ימים בין הזאה להזאה רביעי חמישי וששי וכאן אי לא הזו עד יום אחד עשר בניסן הזאה ראשונה לאחר שמלו תו לא מטי זמן הזאה שניה עד יום חמשה עשר וביבמות איתיה להא דרבי יוחנן בפרק הערל (דף עא:): יד] ותתרגם מתניתך. דקתני חובות הקבוע להם זמן קרבו בגדולה: בעולה. כגון עולות של תמידין ומוספין לצבור קרבו בה טו] [אבל] חטאות הקבוע להם זמן כגון שעירי הרגלים של צבור לא קרבו בה: דאי חובות הקבוע להם זמן בחטאת. דאי בחטאת נמי קאמר: חטאת נדבה מי איכא. ליקרב כיוצא בה בקטנה ועל כרחיך טז] מתניתין קמ"ל דלא קרבו לר"ש בגדולה לבד מפסחים אלא חובות שיש כיוצא בהן נדבה מדקתני אלא פסחים וחובות הקבוע להם זמן ואי ס"ד כל חובות הקבוע להם זמן קאמר פסחים דקתני למה לי הכי הוה ליה למימר אין בין במה גדולה לבמה קטנה אלא חובות הקבוע להם זמן והוו להו פסחים בכלל אלא ה"ק אלא פסחים שקרבו בגדולה ולא קרבו בקטנה כלל ושאר דברים שקרבו כאן וכאן אין חילוק בהן אלא שבזו לא קרבו אלא נדבות ובזו קרבו אף חובות הקבוע להם זמן: ונוקמה נמי במנחה. דמשכחת לה כאן יז] מנחת נדבה בקטנה ובגדולה עודפת מנחת חביתין שהיא יח] חובות הקבוע להן זמן בכל יום: קא סבר רב אדא בר אהבה אין מנחה בבמה. דזבחים כתיב ובשלמי צבור דעצרת ליכא לאוקמה משום דשלמי במה קטנה לא דמי להו שאלו קדשי קדשים ואלו קדשים קלים: מנה"מ. דבית אבנים למטן ויריעות לגג: ויטש משכן שילה אהל שכן באדם: השמר לך. משתבאו אל המנוחה קאי קרא:

ולו

תוספות

ותתרגם מתניתך בעולה. פירוש כגון עולות תמידין ומוספין שיש כיוצא בהם נדבות אבל חטאות הצבור כגון שעירי הרגלים אע"ג דקבוע להם זמן לא קרבו והא מילתא דייק לה מדקתני פסחים דליתני קבוע להם זמן ותו לא והוו להו פסחים בכלל אלא על כרחך מתניתין קמ"ל דלא קרבו לרבי שמעון בגדולה לבד מפסחים אלא שיש כיוצא בהם בבמה והכי קאמר אלא פסחים שקרבו בגדולה לא קרבו בקטנה כלל ושאר דברים שקרבו כאן וכאן אין חילוק בהם אלא שבזה לא הקריבו אלא נדבות ובזה קרבו חובות הקבוע להם זמן כדפירש בקונטרס והכי נמי הוה מצי למידק אברייתא דלעיל דקאמר ר"ש אף לצבור לא הקריבו כו' "ואי משום דלא איירי התם רבי שמעון בחילוק שבין במה גדולה לבמה קטנה כדאיירי הכא מ"מ על חנם הזכיר פסחים דהא הוו בכלל חובות הקבוע להם זמן ותימה מנא ליה לר' שמעון הא מילתא דחטאת דקבוע להם זמן לא קרב דהא לעיל מפרשינן טעמא דרבי שמעון דיליף מפסח גלגל והא ליכא למילף מפסח דפסח נמי אין כיוצא בו נדבה ואי הוה מפרשינן כן דפסח חשיב כיוצא בו נדבה משום דהוי קדשים קלים כעין שלמים הוה ניחא אבל בקונטרס לא פירש כן וע"ק היכי דייק מדקתני פסחים דלמא הא דקתני פסחים משום דעיקר טעמא מפסח יליף וכן בפ"ק דמגילה (דף ט:) תני פסחים לחוד ופריך בגמרא פסחים ותו לא אלא כעין פסחים ע"כ מה שהזכיר פסחים טפי מאידך משום דכולהו מפסח ילפינן לכן נראה לפרש דקא אמר תתרגם מתניתך בעולה היינו משום דכיון דמפסח יליף אית לן למימר מה פסח שקבוע לו זמן וישנו בצבור כביחיד בשעת היתר הבמות לצבור בפסח ראשון ויחיד בפסח שני כדאמרי' פסחים (דף סז.) איש נדחה ואין צבור נדחין אף כל שקבוע להם זמן וישנו בצבור כביחיד בשעת היתר הבמות דהיינו עולות שישנן בצבור בתמידין ומוספין וביחיד בנדבה אבל חטאת לא משכחת ביחיד בשעת היתר הבמות דאפילו בבמה גדולה לא קרבו חובות דיחיד לרבי שמעון כמו לר"מ ורבנן והכי פירושו דשמעתא ותתרגם מתניתך בעולה דאיכא עולת נדבה ונדבות דיחיד קרבו והוי דומיא דפסח דאי בחטאת חטאת נדבה מי איכא דמשכחת ביה חטאת ביחיד דאילו חובות דיחיד לא קרבו לא עולות ולא חטאות ופריך ונוקמה במנחה דאיכא חביתים ומשני אין מנחה בבמה וא"ת ונוקמה בשלמים כגון כבשי עצרת דהא איכא ביה שלמי נדבה וי"ל כדפרש"י דכבשי עצרת קק"ד נינהו ושלמי יחיד קדשים קלים ולא משכחת כיוצא בהן ביחיד:

דאו

[נ"ל אבעיניו] | [לעיל קיא. קידושין לז:] | יבמות עא: | מגילה ט: ע"ש | ס"ל דאי חטאת חטאת נדבה מי איכא | [לעיל קיג.] | רש"ק וכ"ק מ"ז

הגהות הב"ח

(א) רש"י ד"ה קרבו נסכים וכו' כל שהצבור צריכין להקריב באהל מועד כצ"ל ותיבת מקריבין נמחק: (ב) בא"ד וכן בגלגל בשעת הבמות:

עין משפט נר מצוה

כח א מיי' פי"א מהל' פרה אדומה הל' ג:

כט ב מיי' פי"א מהלכות בית הבחירה הל' ב:

ג"א ואע"ג דלא איירי כו' נ"ק

[בקרא כתיב ויחנו בני ישראל בגלגל ויעשו את הפסח]

ס"א זמן א"ל דאמר לך סני רבי שמעון היא דאמר אין בין במה גדולה לבמה קטנה אלא פסח וחובות הקבוע להן זמן ותתרגם מתני' כו' ועיין נ"ק ועיין בספר פנים מאירות

שיטה מקובצת

א] אלא לאו הא: ב] אלא פסחים וחובות הקבוע להן זמן א"ל דאמר לך מני ר' שמעון היא דאמר אין בין במה גדולה לבמה קטנה אלא פסחים וחובות הקבוע להן זמן תתרגם מתניתך א) בעולת נדבה: ג] דאי בחטאת נדבה מי איכא ולוקמה נמי במנחה דהא איכא חביתין והשאר נמחק: ד] שילה אלמא בית הוא: ה] שילה אלמא אהל הוא הא כיצד מלמד שלא היתה שם תקרה והשאר נמחק: ו] מלמעלן: קדשים קלים בכל הרואה ותיבות והיא היתה מנוחה קדשי קדשים נמחק: ז] א"ר אלעזר א"ר אושעיא: ח] מקום שאתה רואה תיבות אשר תראה נמחק ותיבת אתה ל"ש: ט] שאתה רואה תיבת שתראה נמחק: י] בר חמא תיבת חסא נמחק: יא] כתיב אבמה קטנה שהיא לפניו בכל אשר יבחר אבל בגדולה אף היחיד מקריב חובות הס"ד: יב] היינו במה קטנה: יג] שבמדבר ומקריבין באהל: יד] מה"ד תתרגם: טו] בה אבל חטאות: טז] תיבת מתניתין נמחק: יז] כאן וכאן מנחת: יח] שהיא חובה הקבוע:

א) נראה דצ"ל נשלת מנס.

תורה אור

ולו א] תאנת שילה מקום שכל הרואה אותו מתאנח עליו על אכילת קדשים שלו רבי אבהו אמר אמר קרא °בן פרת יוסף בן פרת עלי עין עין שלא רצתה לזון וליהנות מדבר שאינו ב] שלו תזכה ותאכל כמלא עיניה רבי יוסי ברבי חנינא אמר °ורצון שוכני סנה עין שלא רצתה ליהנות מדבר שאינו ג] שלו תזכה ותאכל בין השנואין ד] תנא *רואה שאמרו ה] רואה כולו ולא המפסיק בינו לבינו אמר ליה רבי שמעון בן אליקום לר' אלעזר *אסברא ו] לך כגון בי כנישתא דמעון אמר רב פפא רואה שאמרו לא ז] רואה כולו אלא רואה מקצתו בעי רב פפא עומד ורואה יושב ואינו רואה מאי בעי ר' ירמיה עומד על ח] גבי הנחל ורואה (יושב) בתוך הנחל ואינו רואה מאי תיקו כי אתא רב דימי אמר ט] רבי *בשלשה מקומות שרתה שכינה על ישראל בשילה ונוב וגבעון ובית עולמים ובכולן לא שרתה אלא בחלק בנימין שנאמר °חופף עליו כל היום כל חפיפות לא יהו אלא בחלקו של בנימין י] כי אזיל אביי אמרה קמיה דרב יוסף אמר חד ברא הוה ליה לכייליל ולא מיתקן והכתיב °ויטש (את) משכן שילה יא] וכתיב °וימאס באהל יוסף ובשבט אפרים לא בחר אמר רב אדא יב] מאי קא קשיא ליה דלמא שכינה בחלקבנימין יג] וסנהדרי גדולה בחלק יוסף יד] מדמצינו בבית עולמים דשכינה בחלקו של בנימין וסנהדרין בחלק יהודה אמר ליה הכי השתא התם מיקרבן נחלות גבי הדדי הכא מי מקרבן טו] הכא נמי מקרבן *כדאמר רבי חמא בר' חנינא רצועה היתה יוצאת מחלקו של יהודה ונכנסת לחלקו של בנימין ובה היה מזבח בנוי והיה בנימין הצדיק מצטער עליה לבלעה ה״נ רצועה היתה יוצאת מחלקו של יוסף לחלקו של בנימין והיינו דכתיב °תאנת שילה כתנאי חופף עליו זה מקדש ראשון כל היום זה מקדש שני ובין כתיפיו שכן אלו ימות המשיח רבי אומר חופף עליו זה העולם הזה כל היום אלו ימות המשיח ובין כתיפיו שכן זה העולם הבא *ת״ר ימי אהל מועד שבמדבר ארבעים שנה חסר אחת °ימי אהל מועד שבגלגל ארבע עשרה ז' שכבשו וז' שחלקו ימי אהל מועד שבנוב וגבעון חמשים ושבע נשתיירו לשילה ג' מאות ושבעים חסר אחת ימי אהל מועד שבמדבר ארבעים חסר אחת מנלן דאמר מר *שנה ראשונה עשה משה את המשכן שניה הוקם המשכן ושלח משה מרגלים שבגלגל ארבע עשרה שבע שכבשו ושבע שחלקו מנלן דקאמר כלב °בן ארבעים שנה אנכי בשלוח משה עבד ה' אותי מקדש ברנע לרגל את הארץ ואשיב אותו דבר כאשר עם לבבי וכתיב ועתה הנה אנכי היום בן חמש ושמונים שנה כי עבריה לירדן בר כמה הוי בר שבעין ותמני וקאמר בן חמש ושמונים שנה הרי שבע שכבשו ושבע שחלקו מנלן איבעית אימא מדשבע טז] שכבשו שבע נמי שחלקו ואיבעית אימא מדלא משכחת לה °בארבע עשרה שנה אחר אשר הוכתה העיר: אהל מועד שבנוב וגבעון חמשים ושבע מנ״ל דכתיב °ויהי כהזכירו את ארון האלהים יז] *)ותנא כשמת עלי הכהן חרבה שילה ובאו יח] לנוב כשמת שמואל הרמתי חרבה נוב ובאו לגבעון וכתיב °ויהי מיום שבת הארון בקרית יערים וירבו הימים ויהיו עשרים שנה וינהו כל בית ישראל אחרי ה' הני עשרים שנה יט] עשר שנה *שמלך שמואל בעצמו ושנה שמלך שמואל ושאול ושתים שמלך שאול ושבע כ] דדוד דכתיב

*) סדר עולם פרק יא

ולו תאנת שילה. חפשתיו ולא מצאתיו במקרא אבל מצאתיו *(ועבר) מזרחה תאנת שילה (יהושע טז): תאנת. לשון תאניה ואניה (איכה ב) שהיו מתאנחין ורואין שמשם היו זוכרין אכילת קדשים שהיתה במקום מראיתו: (א) כא] שאינו שלו. אשת אדוניו: בן פרת יוסף. לשון פריה ורביה מקום אכילת קדשים נתרבה לו על ידי העין ושילה בחלקו של יוסף היתה כדכתיב (תהלים עח) וימאס באהל יוסף וגו' כב] אחר ויטש משכן שילה כתיב: ורצון. ע״י רצון שלא רצה ליזון ממה שאינו שלו: בין השנואים. שילה קדשיו נאכלין אף בגבולי שאר שבטים שנאוהו: אסברא (ב) לי. הראני דוגמא לדבר: בי כנישתא דמעון. משם היו רואין את שילה ולא היה דבר מפסיק: לא רואה את כולה. לראות משם את כולה שילה אלא מקצת: חד ברא הוה ליה לכייליל ולא מיתקן. נראה בעיני כי אביו של אביי כייליל שמו: מי מקרבן. שילה וגבול נחלת בנימין: תאנת שילה. על כג] שהיה בנימין מתאונן עליה: העולם הזה. כל מקום ששרתה שכינה ואף שילה וטוב וגבעון: נשתיירו לשילה. מארבע מאות ושמונים מיציאת מצרים לבנין הבית שם״ש: שניה הוקם המשכן. דכתיב ויהי בשנה השנית בחדש הראשון וגו' (שמות מ): וקאמר כלב. בשעת חילוק כשבא לתבוע חברון בן מ' שנה וגו' והיא היתה השנה השניה נתעכבו במדבר עוד שלשים ושמונה שנה נמצא כלב בן ע״ח שנים כשעברו הירדן וקאמר בשעת חילוקה בן חמש ושמונים שנה הרי שבע נשתהו לכיבוש: מדשבע כיבשו שבע חילקו. סברא בעלמא היא: ואיבעית אימא מדלא כד] אשכח י״ד שנה אחר (ג) שהוכתה העיר'. דלא מיתוקם קרא דכתיב ביחזקאל (מ) בארבע עשרה שנה אחר אשר הוכתה העיר בראש השנה כה] שנאמר בעשור לחדש היה דבר ה' אלי וגו' ודרשינן במסכת ערכין כו] (דף יב.) איזה היא שנה שראש השנה בעשור לחדש הוי אומר זה יובל ולא מנו שמיטין ויובלות אלא לאחר ירושה וישיבה וכי אמרת דשנות כיבוש וחילוק י״ד היו ודלית להו ממכין היובלות משכחת לה דחרב הבית בשנת ל״ו ליובל והוה ליה שנת היובל שנת י״ד שנה

אחר כז] שנה שהוכתה העיר ואי לא לא משכחת לה כילד ויהי בשמנים שנה וד' מאות שנה וגו' ויבן הבית לה' לא מהן מ' שהיו במדבר נמצא משבאו לארץ עד שנבנה הבית ארבע מאות וארבעים והבית עמד ד' מאות ועשר הרי ח' מאות וחמשים הרי י״ז יובלות שלימים לא מהן י״ד שכבשו ושחלקו שלא מנו יובלות נמצא בית חרב קודם השלמת היובל י״ד שנה והכי תניא בהדיא בערכין (שם:) י״ז יובלות מנו ישראל משנכנסו לארץ עד שיצאו ואי אתה יכול לומר משנכנסו מנו שאם אתה אומר כן נמצא בית חרב בתחילת היובל ואי אתה מוצא י״ד שנה אחרי אשר הוכתה העיר אלא לא מהן שבע שכבשו ושבע שחלקו ואתה מוצא ארבע עשרה שנה אחר שהוכתה העיר: חרבה נב. ע״י שאול: בקרית יערים. שם נתנוהו לסוף ד' חדשים שעמד בשדה פלשתים שנאמר (שמואל א ה) ותכבד יד ה' אל האשדודים והחזירוהו בעגלה חדשה ונתנוהו שם ועשה שם עשרים שנה עד שהביאו דוד משם בשנה ראשונה שנעשה מלך על כל ישראל שהיא שנה שמינית למלכו על יהודה: הכי גרסינן עשרה דשמואל עצמו. שהיה שופט לבדו משמת עלי עד שמלך שאול ובמסכת תמורה (דף יד: וטו.) ה״ג לה עשר שנים שמלך שמואל לעצמו דאותה שנה ששאלו להם מלך היא שנה עשירית לשמואל הרמתי ושנה אחת מלכו שמואל ושאול יחד שהיה שאול הולך אחר עצת שמואל עד שסרח במעשה אגג וסר שמואל מעליו כדכתיב (שמואל א טו) ולא יסף שמואל לראות את שאול וגו' ומלך עוד שאול שתי שנים והן שכתב במקרא (שם יג) ושתי שנים מלך על ישראל דלא חשיב כח] אותם דמלך שמואל בהדיה והיינו דאמרינן במסכת תענית (דף ה:) מי גרם לשאול שישב בגבעה שתי שנים ומחלה תפלתו של שמואל ברמה דבאי שנה ראשונה סרח ונגזרה עליו מיתה אלא שעמדה לו תפלת שמואל ושבע שמלך דוד בחברון על יהודה ולכשהמליכוהו כל ישראל עליהם הביא את הארון מקרית יערים כט] עיר דוד הרי עשרים: דכתיב

ל א מיי׳ פ״ו מהלכות בית הבחירה הל׳ ב:

[בארבע כן הוא בע״י וע׳ רש״י לקמן קיט. ד״ה טוב ונכשן מלה מהיב לנו]

[ל״ל ע. מגילה כו. יומא יב.]

[תענית כח. סנהדרין סט: ערכין יג.]

סדר עולם פרק יא

יהושע יד

יחזקאל מ

שמואל א ד

שם ז

[תמורה יד: טו.]

ז״ל רואה שאמרו כל שהוא רואה ואין דבר מפסיק בינו לבינו וכן הוא בס״י

הגהות הב״ח

(א) רש״י ד״ה שאינו שלו נ״ב אחר ד״ה בן פרת: (ב) ד״ה אסברא לך הראנו: (ג) ד״ה ואיבעית אימא וכו' אחר אשר הוכתה העיר:

גליון הש״ס

גמ' אסברא לך. ברש״י הגי' אסברא לי. ובסדר הדורות בהקדמה אות ד' כתב שכן עיקר:

שיטה מקובצת

א] ולו. ס״א ועלה הגבול מזרחה תאנת שילה: ב] שאינו שלה תזכה ותאכל בקדשים כמלא עיניה שלה: ג] שאינו שלה: ד] השנואין שלה: ה] שאמרו כל שרואה ואין דבר מפסיק א״ל והשאר נמחק: ו] אסברא לי אמ׳ ליה כגון כו': ז] לא שרואה כולו אלא אפילו מקצתו: ח] על שפת הנחל ורואה בתוך הנחל: ט] אמר בשלשה תיבת רבי נמחק: י] תיבת כי נמחק: יא] משכן שילה וגו' וכתיב: יב] אדא בר מתנה מאי: יג] בנימין וסנהדרין בחלק תיבת גדולה נמחק: יד] יוסף כדרך שמצינו בבית עולמים שכינה בחלק בנימין וסנהדרין בחלק יהודה אמרי הכי השתא: טו] מקרבן אמרי הכא: טז] מדשבע כיבשו שבע חילקו: יז] האלהים וגו' ותנא: יח] ובאו להם לנוב: יט] עשרים שנה אחת עשרה שנה שמלך שמואל בעצמו ותיבות שאול ושמואל ל״ש (רק רש״י ז״ל הוא דגרים הכי עכ״ה): כ] ושבע שמלך דוד בחברון דכתיב: כא] מה״ד שאינה שלה: כב] וגו' בתר ויטוש כו' ותיבת אחר ל״ש: כג] על שם שהיה: כד] מדלא [illegible] שהוכתה העיר מדלא מיתוקם ותיבת שנה נמחק: כה] תיבת שנאמר נמחק: כו] ערכין בפרק שני איזה היא שראש השנה שלה בעשור לחדש: כז] תיבת שנה נמחק: כח] אותו דמלך שמואל: כט] יערים לעיר דוד:

Ḥasa[7] said, Scripture saith, [118*b*] 'And there was Taanath [the lamenting of] Shiloh', which means the place which made whoever saw it mourn for the sacrifices which he ate there.[8] R. Abbahu said: Scripture saith, *Joseph is a fruitful vine, a fruitful vine through the*
a *eye:*[1] [this means,] let the eye which would not feed upon and enjoy that which did not belong to it,[2] be privileged to eat [of sacrifices] as far as it can see. R. Jose son of R. Ḥanina quoted: '*And the desire of him that dwelt in hatred*';[3] [this means,] let the eye that did not desire to enjoy that which did not belong to it, be privileged to eat [sacrifices] among those that hated it.[4]

It was taught: When they said, [As far as the eye could] see, they meant: [from] wherever one could see [the Tabernacle] without anything interposing. R. Simeon b. Eliakim observed to R. Eleazar: Give me an example. Said he to him: E.g., the synagogue of Maon.[5]

R. Papa said: When they said, 'see', they did not mean that one must see the whole of it, but that one must see part of it. R. Papa asked: What of [a place whence] one could see [the Tabernacle] whilst standing, but not when sitting? R. Jeremiah asked: What [of a place where] if one stood on the edge of the valley one could see [it], but when he sat in the valley he could not see [it]? The questions stand over.

When R. Dimi came [from Palestine], he said: The *Shechinah* rested on Israel in three[6] places: in Shiloh, in Nob and Gibeon,[7] and in the Eternal House;[8] and in all of these it rested [on Israel] only in the portion of Benjamin, for it is said, *He covereth him all day*:[9] all 'coverings' will be nought elsewhere but in Benjamin's portion.
b Abaye went and told this to R. Joseph. Said he to him: Kaylil[1] had but one son, and *he* is not '*finished*'.[2] Surely it is written, *And He forsook the tabernacle of Shiloh*; and it is written, *Moreover He abhorred the tent of* Joseph, *and chose not the tribe of* Ephraim?[3]—Said R. Adda [b. Mattenah]: What is his difficulty? perhaps the *Shechinah* was in Benjamin's portion, while the Sanhedrin[4] was in Joseph's portion,[5] as we find in the Eternal House that the *Shechinah* was in Benjamin's portion, whereas the Sanhedrin was in Judah's portion? How compare? replied he. There the territories [of Judah and Benjamin] were contiguous; but were they contiguous here?[6]—They were indeed contiguous, even as R. Ḥama son of R. Ḥanina said:[7] A strip issued from Judah's portion and entered Benjamin's portion, and on this the altar was built. The righteous Benjamin grieved thereat every day, [wishing] to absorb it;[8] so here too a strip issued from Joseph's portion into Benjamin's portion, and that is the meaning of *Taanath-Shiloh*.[9]

This is a controversy of Tannaim: '*He covereth him*'; this alludes to the first Temple; '*all the day*', to the second Temple; '*and He dwelleth between his shoulders*', to the days of the Messiah.[10] Rabbi said: '*He covereth him*', alludes to this world;[11] '*all the day*', to the days of the Messiah; '*and He dwelleth between his shoulders*', to the World to Come.

Our Rabbis taught: The duration of the Tent of Meeting in the wilderness was forty years less one; the duration of the Tent of Meeting at Gilgal was fourteen years, [viz.,] the seven [years] of
c conquest and the seven of division.[1] The duration of the Tent of Meeting at Nob and Gibeon [combined] was fifty-seven years. Thus for Shiloh was left three hundred and seventy less one.

'The duration of the Tent of Meeting in the wilderness was forty less one.' How do we know it?—Because a master said: In the first year[2] Moses made the Tabernacle; in the second the Tabernacle was set up, and Moses sent out the spies.

'That of Gilgal was fourteen years, [viz.,] the seven [years] of conquest and the seven of division.' How do we know it?—Because Caleb said: *Forty years old was I when Moses the servant of the Lord sent me from Kadesh-barnea to spy out the land; and I brought him back word as it was in my heart;* and it is written, *and now, lo, I am this day fourscore and five years old.*[3] How old was he when he crossed the Jordan? Seventy eight years;[4] and he said, '[*I am this day*] *fourscore and five years old*': thus [you have] seven years for the conquest. And how do we know the seven years of division?—I can say, since the conquest took seven [years], the dividing too took seven years. Alternatively, because [otherwise] we cannot explain [the verse] *In the fourteenth year after that the city was smitten.*[5]

'The Tent of Meeting at Nob and Gibeon lasted fifty-seven years.' How do we know it?—Because it is written, *And it came to pass, when he made mention of the ark of God,* [*that he fell from off his*
d *seat . . . and died*].[1] Now it was taught: When Eli the priest died, Shiloh was destroyed and they repaired to Nob; when Samuel the Ramathite died, Nob was destroyed and they went to Gibeon. And it is written, *And it came to pass, from the day that the ark abode in Kiriath-jearim, that the time was long; for it was twenty years; and all the house of Israel yearned after the Lord.*[2] These twenty years [were made up as follows]: Ten years during which Samuel ruled alone,[3] one year that Samuel and Saul ruled [together],[4] two years that Saul

(7) Sh.M. emends: Ḥama. (8) Before the Tabernacle was destroyed. There is no such text in the Bible. Rashi suggests, and Sh.M. cites as a *var. lec.*, Josh. XVI, 6: *And the border turned about eastward unto Taanath-Shiloh.*—He treats *Taanath* as an adjectival substantive, the lamenting of, from *anah* to lament (cf. *ta'aniah* in Isa. XXIX, 2: *and there shall be mourning* (ta'aniah), and explains it as in the text, and thus infers that sacrifices could be eaten wherever the Tabernacle at Shiloh could be seen.

a (1) Gen. XLIX, 22. E.V. by a *fountain.*—Shiloh was in Ephraim's (i.e., Joseph's) territory. (2) Potiphar's wife. (3) Deut. XXXIII, 16. By a play on words סנה is connected with שנאה hatred. E.V.: *And the good will of Him that dwelt in the bush.* The verse refers to Joseph. (4) *Sc.* in the territories surrounding Shiloh, which belonged to the other tribes whose ancestors had hated Joseph.—Presumably 'as far as the eye could see' would embrace the borders of these territories.—This interpretation, of course, is merely aggadic and is not the actual source of the law. (5) In Judea. From there one would have an uninterrupted view of the Tabernacle at Shiloh—The text is emended. (6) Marginal emendation; four. (7) These were two separate places, but they are generally coupled, which probably explains why cur. edd. read 'three', treating these as one. (8) The Temple in Jerusalem. (9) Deut. XXXIII, 12.—This refers to Benjamin.

b (1) Rashi suggests that this was the name of Abaye's father. (2) That one son—Abaye—is but half-baked—he has not mastered his studies. (3) Ps. LXXVIII, 60, 67. The comparison of these two verses shews that the Tabernacle was in Ephraim's portion, not Benjamin's. (4) The religious and civil court; v. Sanh. 2*a*. (5) He assumes that the Sanhedrin had its seat in or by the Tabernacle, and that the verses in Psalms refer to the forsaking by the Divine Presence (*Shechinah*) of this Sanhedrin. (6) Did Joseph (Ephraim) and Benjamin have a common boundary at Shiloh? (7) In reference to the Temple at Jerusalem. (8) V. *supra* 53*b*. (9) Josh. XVI, 6; v. *supra*. He now suggests that it means: (Benjamin's) mourning for Shiloh, that it was in Joseph's territory. (10) On this view only the two Temples were in Benjamin's territory, but not the Tabernacles at Shiloh and elsewhere. (11) *Wherever* the *Shechinah* rested in this world, i.e., in both Temples and in all Tabernacles, it was in Benjamin's territory.

c (1) Dividing the land among the tribes. (2) Of the Exodus. (3) Josh. XIV, 7, 10.—'*This day*' means when they started dividing the country. (4) Since the spies were not sent out at the beginning of the second year, but some months later. (5) Ezek. XL, 1. According to the Talmud ('Ar. 12*a*), this was a jubilee year, while the Release years (*shemittoth*) and Jubilee years did not commence until the land had been divided. The calculation is then as follows: The Temple was built four hundred and eighty years after the Exodus, which was four hundred and forty years after their entry into Eretz Israel. The Temple stood four hundred and ten years, making a total of eight hundred and fifty years from their entry until its destruction, which is thirty-seven Jubilees. Deducting fourteen years for conquest and division, as these did not count for Jubilee, we find that it was destroyed fourteen years before a Jubilee year, and therefore the fourteenth year after its destruction was a Jubilee year. (The Talmud deduces that this was a Jubilee year *independently* of this calculation.)

d (1) I Sam. IV, 18. This refers to Eli the priest. (2) Ibid. VII, 2. The Ark was placed in Kiriath-jearim when it returned from the land of the Philistines, where it had been four months. (3) As judge. (4) I.e., Saul ruled with the advice of Samuel. Sh.M. reads: the *eleven* years that Samuel ruled, and deletes 'one . . . together'.

reigned,[5] and the seven which David reigned [in Hebron], [119a] for it is written, *And the days that David reigned over Israel were forty years: seven years reigned he in Hebron, [and thirty and three years reigned he in Jerusalem]*.[6] Now of Solomon it is written, *And he began to build . . . in the fourth year of his reign*.[7] Thus three hundred and seventy less one was left for Shiloh.[8]

WHEN THEY CAME TO NOB AND GIBEON etc. How do we know it?—Because our Rabbis taught: *For ye are not as yet come to the rest and to the inheritance, [which the Lord your God giveth thee]*:[9] *'to the rest'* alludes to Shiloh, *'inheritance'* alludes to Jerusalem. Why does Scripture separate them?[10] In order to grant permission between one and the other.[11] Resh Lakish said to R. Joḥanan: If so,[12] let
a [the Mishnah] teach second tithe too?[1]—As for tithe, he replied, the implication of *'there'* is derived from *'there'* [written] in connection with the Ark:[2] since there was no Ark [at Nob and Gibeon],[3] there was no tithe either. If so, the Passover-offering and [other] sacrifices are the same, for we learn the meaning of *'there'* [in their case][4] from *'there'* [written] in connection with the Ark: since there was no Ark, these too were not [offered]?—Who has told you [this]? he replied: R. Simeon,[5] who maintained that even the community could only offer Passover-offerings and obligatory offerings which have a fixed time,[6] but obligatory offerings for which there was no fixed time might not be offered at either place. Now, animal tithe is an obligatory offering without a fixed time, and corn tithe is assimilated to animal tithe.

Hence it follows that in R. Judah's view [second tithe] is offered?[7]—Yes. For surely R. Adda b. Mattenah said: Second tithe and animal tithe were eaten in Nob and Gibeon [only], in R. Judah's opinion. Yet surely a *birah* [Divine residence] was required?[8]—Did not R. Joseph recite: There were three Divine
b residences, [viz.,] at Shiloh, [at] Nob and Gibeon,[1] and [at] the Eternal House? He [R. Joseph] recited it, and he explained it: [These were] in respect of second tithe, and in accordance with R. Judah.

WHEN THEY CAME TO JERUSALEM etc. Our Rabbis taught: *For ye are not as yet come to the rest and to the inheritance: 'rest'* alludes to Shiloh; *'inheritance'*, to Jerusalem. And thus it says, *My inheritance is become unto Me as a lion in the forest;* and it says, *Is My inheritance unto Me as a speckled bird of prey?*[2] this is R. Judah's opinion. R. Simeon said: *'Rest'* alludes to Jerusalem; *'inheritance'*, to Shiloh, as it is said, *This is My* resting-place *for ever; here will I dwell, for I have desired it;* and it says, *For the Lord hath chosen* Zion; *He hath* desired *it for His habitation*.[3]

On the view that *'rest'* alludes to Shiloh, it is well: hence it is written, *'to the* rest *and to the* inheritance'.[4] But on the view that *'rest'* alludes to Jerusalem while *'inheritance'* alludes to Shiloh, [Moses] should say, 'to the inheritance and to the rest'?—This is what he said: Not only have ye not reached the *'rest'* [Jerusalem]; you have not even reached the *'inheritance'* [Shiloh].

The school of R. Ishmael taught: Both [words] allude to Shiloh;[5] R. Simeon b. Yoḥai said: Both allude to Jerusalem.[6] It is well on

(5) V. Ibid. XIII, 1. Rashi maintains that the first year, when he ruled with Samuel, is not counted. (6) I Kings II, 11. (7) II Chron. III, 2. The period of Nob and Gibeon is calculated from the time that the Ark was taken to Kiriath-jearim until Solomon began building the Temple. Thus we have 20 and 33 (which he reigned in Jerusalem) and 4 = 57. (8) The Temple was consecrated four hundred and eighty years after the Exodus. The figure three hundred and sixty-nine is arrived at by deducting the forty years in the wilderness, the fourteen at Gilgal, and the fifty-seven of Nob and Gibeon. (9) Deut. XII, 9. (10) Why is each enumerated separately? (11) For the text refers to the permissibility of *bamoth* at Gilgal, and teaches: until when may each man sacrifice what is *'right in his own eyes'* (v. 8—*sc.* at the *bamoth*)? until you come to the rest, i.e., to Shiloh, and then *bamoth* will be forbidden. Now, if they were to remain *permanently* forbidden, Scripture need say nothing more. By adding *'and to the inheritance'* it intimates that when they come to Jerusalem *bamoth* will *again* be forbidden, and thus implies that they were permitted between the destruction of the Tabernacle at Shiloh and the consecration of the Temple in Jerusalem. (12) That the time between—*sc.* when the Tabernacle was at Nob and Gibeon—was completely permitted.

a (1) That it must be eaten at Nob and Gibeon only, seeing that the sanctity of Shiloh was completely departed. (2) Tithe, Deut. XIV, 23: *And thou shalt eat before the Lord thy God, in the place which He shall choose to cause His name to dwell* there, *the* tithe *of thy corn* etc.; Ark, Ex. XL, 3: *And thou shalt put* there *the* ark *of the testimony*. The use of *'there'* in both cases implies that they are connected. (3) But first at Kiriath-jearim and then in the city of David. (4) Deut. XII, 7: *and* there *ye shall eat*—this refers to the sacrifices enumerated in v. 6. (5) The Mishnah which implies that second tithe might be eaten anywhere is in accordance with R. Simeon. (6) For that reason he maintains that firstlings and animal tithes, which did not have a fixed time, were not brought there; and therefore it was unnecessary to bring corn tithe there either, since the two are assimilated. (Though the two are not really alike: whereas the law of firstling and animal tithe was not operative, and these could not be brought at Nob and Gibeon or anywhere else, second tithe *need* not be brought at Nob and Gibeon, but might be eaten anywhere.) (7) I.e., it must be eaten only at Nob and Gibeon. (8) They were to be eaten *'before the Lord your God'*, which implies a structure in the nature of a Temple or Tabernacle.

b (1) Which are counted as one. (2) Jer. XII, 8-9. In both verses *'inheritance'* means Jerusalem. (3) Ps. CXXXII, 14, 13. (4) In correct chronological order. (5) Yet even so, *bamoth* were permitted after the destruction of the Sanctuary at Shiloh, for he holds that they were permitted even after the destruction of the Temple at Jerusalem (cf. Meg. 10a). (6) Hence *bamoth* were not forbidden until the Temple was built.

[א]דכתיב °והימים אשר מלך דוד על ישראל מ' שנה בחברון מלך ז' שנים [א] [וגו'] ובשלמה [ב]כתיב °ויחל לבנותו בשנת ארבע למלכותו *נשתיירו לשילה שלש מאות ושבעים חסר אחת: באו לנוב וגבעון [ב] [וכו']: מנא ה"מ דת"ר °כי לא באתם עד עתה אל המנוחה ואל הנחלה *אל המנוחה זו שילה נחלה זו ירושלי' למה חלקן [ג] כדי ליתן היתר בין זה לזה א"ל ריש לקיש לר' יוחנן (א) [ד] מעשר שני נמי ליתני א"ל מעשר שם שם מארון קא ילפי כיון דארון לא הוה מעשר נמי לא הואי אי הכי פסח וקדשים נמי דשם שם מארון ילפי דכיון דארון לא הוה אינהו נמי לא הוו א"ל [ה] [דאמר לך] הא מני ר"ש היא דאמר אף צבור לא הקריבו אלא פסח וחובות הקבוע להן זמן אבל חובות שאין קבוע להם זמן הבא והכא לא קרב [ו] מעשר בהמה חובות שאין קבוע להן זמן הוא ואיתקש מעשר דגן למעשר בהמה מכלל דלרבי יהודה קרב אין דהאמר רב אדא בר מתנה מעשר שני ומעשר בהמה נאכלין בנוב וגבעון לדברי רבי יהודה והא בעי בירה ולאו תני רב יוסף שלש בירות הן שילה ונוב וגבעון ובית עולמים הוא תני לה והוא אמר לה לאכילת מעשר שני ואליב' דרבי יהודה: באו לירושלים [ז] [וכו']: ת"ר כי לא באתם עד עתה אל המנוחה ואל הנחלה מנוחה זו שילה נחלה זו ירושלים [ח] ואומר °היתה לי נחלתי כאריה ביער ואומר °העיט צבוע נחלתי לי העיט סביב עליה דברי רבי יהודה ר"ש אומר מנוחה זו ירושלים נחלה זו שילה ואומר °זאת מנוחתי עדי עד פה אשב כי אויתיה ואומר °כי בחר ה' בציון אוה למושב לו בשלמא למ"ד מנוחה זו שילה היינו דכתיב אל המנוחה ואל הנחלה אלא למ"ד מנוחה *זו ירושלים נחלה זו שילה אל הנחלה ואל המנוחה מיבעי ליה הכי קאמר לא מיבעיא מנוחה דלא מטיתו אלא אפילו לנחלה נמי לא מטיתו תנא דבי רבי ישמעאל זו וזו שילה רבי שמעון בן יוחי אומר זו וזו ירושלים בשלמא למאן דאמר מנוחה זו שילה

תורה אור: מ"א ב · דברים יב · ירמיה יב · שם · תהלים קלב · שם

רש"י

דכתיב והימים אשר מלך וגו'. *ל"ג שנה הרי כ"ג ולארבע שמלך שלמה לפני בנין הבית ואותה שנה שלמו ארבע מאות ושמונים ליציאת מצרים נשתיירו לשילה שס"ט: מנהני מילי. שהיה היתר לבמות אחר קדושת שילה משחרבה: כי לא באתם. בימי גלגל אל המנוחה וגו': ולמה חלקן. הכתוב לכתוב את שניהם: ליתן היתר במה בין זה לזה. דהא קרא בהיתר במות דגלגל משתעי וקאמר עד מתי אני אומר לכם איש כל הישר בעיניו כי לא באתם עד עתה וגו' אבל לא משבאתם ואי אין היתר בין זו לזו לא ה"ל למיכתב אלא מנוחה ומדכתיב נחלה ש"מ דה"ק לאו אחר קדושת המנוחה תחזרו להיתר הראשון עד בואכם אל הנחלה: אי הכי. דשעת היתר הואי ליתני נמי מעשר שני לנוב וגבעון שהרי [ט] נסתלקו כל קדושת שילה ומאי טעם לא תנן במתני' לאוכלו שם: שם שם. ואכלתם שם (דברים יב) אי נמי *(כי אם) לפני ה' אלהיך (תאכלנו) במקום אשר יבחר לשכן שמו שם (שם יד) ובארון כתיב (שמות מ) [י] [ונתת] שם את הארון וגו': וכיון דארון לא הוה. דכל ימי נוב וגבעון היה הארון בקרית יערים כ' שנה ובעיר דוד עד שנבנה הבית: פסח וקדשים נמי. דהא ואכלתם שם בהו נמי כתיב (דברים יב): מני. הך מתני' דקתני מעשר שני בכל ערי ישראל ולא היה צריך להביאן שם: ר"ש היא. דאמר חובות שאין קבוע להם זמן לא קרבו בנוב וגבעון והיינו בכורות ומעשר בהמה ויליף טעמא כדאמרן לעיל בגלגל וכיון דמעשר בהמה לא הוה התם מעשר דגן נמי לא בעי לאיתויי התם דאיתקוש להדדי דכתיב (שם יד) עשר תעשר ואמרינן בשתי מעשרות הכתוב מדבר במסכת בכורות (דף נג:): ה"ג אבל לר' יהודה ה"נ דאמר רב אדא *בר אהבה מעשר שני נאכל בנוב וגבעון לדברי ר' יהודה: והא בעינן בירה. [יא] דכתיב (דברים יב) לפני ה' אלהיכם: נוב וגבעון. חדא חשיב לה: זו וזו שילה. ואפי' הכי [יב] *יש היתר בתרה דקסבר קדושה ראשונה קדשה לשעתה ולא קדשה לעתיד לבא ובקדושת ירושלים גופה סבירא ליה דיש אחריה היתר כדאמרינן במגילה (דף י.) שמעתי שמקריבין בבית חוניו בזמן הזה ואוקימנא כר' ישמעאל: זו וזו ירושלים. ועד שיבנה הבית לא נאסרו הבמות:

ויהי

תוספות

באו לנוב וגבעון [ט'] קדשים קלים ומעשר שני בכל ערי ישראל. בריש פירקין במתניתין (דף קיב:) פירש בקונטרס דלעיל גבאו גלגל לא הוזכר מעשר שני לפי שלא נהגו מעשרות עד לאחר ירושה וישיבה ותימה דהא פריך הכא בגמרא דמעשר שני נמי נסקיה להתם בנוב וגבעון ומסיק דמתני' ר' שמעון היא דאמר חובות שאין קבוע להם זמן לא קרבו דהיינו בבכור ומעשר בהמה וכיון דמעשר בהמה לא הוה התם מעשר דגן לא בעי לאתויי התם דאיתקוש להדדי והשתא מהאי טעמא דאיתקש למעשר לא יהא נאכל כלל כמו מעשר בהמה *בנוב וגבעון למ"ד לא קרבו חובות והיו צריכין להמתין בבכור ומעשר עד שיומם ונאכלין במומן לבעלים ומעשר שני לא יהא לו תקנה אלא בפדיון ויש ספרים דלא גרסי במתניתין מעשר שני כלל גבי נוב וגבעון ונראה לפרש דלענין הבאה הוא שייך להקיש דאי האי טעון הבאת מקום גם זה יהא טעון הבאת מקום כדקאמר לר' יהודה דאמר חובות קרבו דבנוב וגבעון נאכל גם מעשר שני נאכל שם אבל מה שאין מעשר בהמה קרב לרבי שמעון משום דחובות לא קרבו לענין זה אין שייך להקיש מעשר שני שלא יהא נאכל בכל מקום דהא דאין מעשר בהמה נאכל משום דבעי מתן דמים ואימורים ולא אפשר אבל מעשר שני שרי ומיהו קשה דלעיל בפרק קדשי קדשים (דף ס:) ילפינן מעשר מבכור · דאין נאכל בזמן הזה ויש גירסות בספרים ושם פירשתי *ועוד קשה אי מסכתת מעשר דנאכל בכל ערי ישראל א"כ הא דאמר בפרק כל שעה (פסחים דף לו:) מרבה אני מעשר שיש לו היתר בכל מושבות דאמר ר' אלעזר מנין למעשר שנטמא כו' למה לי דרבי אלעזר הא כיון דבנוב (נאכל) וגבעון נאכל בכל ערי ישראל א"כ יש היתר בכל מושבות כדאמר התם (דף לו:) לקמיה בההוא פירקא גבי חלות תודה ורקיקי נזיר נאכלין בנוב וגבעון וי"ל דאיצטריך התם דרבי אלעזר משום רבי יהודה דאמר בשמעתין שלש בירות הן של שילה ושל נוב וגבעון ושל בית עולמים לאכילת מעשר שני ואליבא דרבי יהודה וא"ת והיכי קאמר התם ומוליא אני בכורים שאין להם היתר בכל מושבות והלא נאכלין בנוב וגבעון בכל ערי ישראל כמעשר שני ויש לומר דבכורים לא אפשר משום דבעו הנחה אצל המזבח *ובנוב וגבעון ממשו לאו התם כדאמרינן לעיל בפרק קדשי קדשים (דף ס:) ובפרק בתרא דמכות (דף יט:) ובתמורה בפרק אלו קדשים (דף כא.) דבכורים אינם אלא בפני הבית משום דבעי הנחה ועוד מידי דהוה אחזה ושוק ותרומת לחמי תודה דאמרי' לעיל (דף קיז:) טוענין בבמה גדולה ואין טוענין בבמה קטנה משום דבעו תנופה ובכורים נמי בעו תנופה דלא דמי למנחה דקרבה בבמה בלא תנופה לרבנן דפליגי עליה דר' יהודה במתניתין בפירקין כדפרישית לעיל דמנחה עיקר מלותה *(סמיכה) והקטרה הלכך משום תנופה לא בטלה אבל הני דעיקר מלותן תנופה בטלה תנופה בטלי אינהו: **הא** מני רבי שמעון היא. הכי נמי מצי למימר רבנן היא דאמרי חובות ליחיד לא קרבו בשעת היתר הבמות אף בבמת צבור וכן רבי מאיר אלא נקט ר' שמעון משום דעביד הך דרשא עשר תעשר בשני מעשרות הכתוב מדבר: הג"ה **ואיתקש** [מעשר] דגן למעשר בהמה. לעיל בפרק קדשי קדשים (דף ס:) נקט היקשא דמעשר לבכור והכא והתם סגי בחדא: **זו** וזו שילה. פירש בקונטרס ואפילו הכי הוי היתר בתרה דקסבר קדושה ראשונה קדשה לשעתה ולא קדשה לעתיד לבא ובקדושת ירושלים גופה סבירא ליה דיש אחריה היתר כדאמרינן במגילה (דף י.) שמעתי שמקריבין בבית חוניו בזמן הזה ואוקימנא כרבי ישמעאל עכ"ל ולא *דק דהתם רבי ישמעאל ב"ר יוסי דהוא בתראה בימי רבי והכא רבי ישמעאל בן אלישע בר פלוגתיה דר' עקיבא רבו של ר' שמעון בן יוחי והואה אסיקנא לעיל לפום חד גירסא דכולי עלמא קידשה ומיהו אי אפשר לומר לדידיה שלא יהא היתר אחר שילה דהא

מגיט

מסורת הש"ס

ג"י הצ"ק ל"ג שנה שמלך על כל ישראל ח' שנים מלך בחברון הרי כ"ג וכו'

כדר עולם פי"א

[מגילה י.]

נ"ל ואכלת

[כפנים איתא בר מתנה]

[מגילה י.]

נ"ל סוס היתר כו' נ"ק

[נ"א סמיכה]

הגהות הב"ח

(א) גמ' א"ל ר"ל לר' יוחנן אי הכי מעשר שני:

גליון הש"ס

תוס' ד"ה זו וכו' ולא דק. עיין לעיל דף ס ע"ב תוס' ד"ה קסבר:

נ"ל בנוב ובגבעון דלא קרבו והיו כו' נ"ק

שיטה מקובצת

א] שנים ובירושלים מלך ל"ג שנים וארבע דשלמה דכתיב: ב] ובגבעון וכו' מנא ה"מ: ג] חלקן הכתוב כדי: ד] יוחנן אי הכי מעשר: ה] א"ל דאמר לך הא מני: ו] קרב ומעשר ברמה: ז] לירושלים כו': ח] ירושלים וכן הוא אומר והיתה: ט] נסתלקה כל: י] כתיב ונתת שם: יא] בירה מקרא דכתיב: יב] הכי הוי היתר:

עיין נ"ק

[ועי' תוס' פסחים לו: ד"ה דאמר ר"א]

תורה אור

שילה נחלה זו ירושלים אי נמי איפכא היינו דכתיב °אל המנוחה ואל הנחלה אלא למאן דאמר זו וזו שילה או זו וזו ירושלים מנוחה *נחלה מיבעי ליה קשיא בשלמא למ"ד זו וזו שילה מנוחה דנחו מכיבוש נחלה א] (זו) דפלגו התם נחלות דכתיב °*ויחלק להם יהושע ויפל להם גורל בשילה על פי ה' אלא למ"ד זו וזו ירושלים בשלמא נחלה נחלת עולמים אלא מנוחה ב] מאי מנוחה מנוחת ארון דכתיב ויהי כנוח הארון בשלמא למ"ד זו וזו ירושלים אבל שילה הוה שריא במות היינו דכתיב °ויקח מנוח את גדי העזים ואת המנחה ויעל על הצור לה' אלא למ"ד זו וזו שילה ובמות הוה אסירן מאי ויקח מנוח הוראת שעה היתה תנא דבי רבי ישמעאל כרבי שמעון בן יוחי דאמר זו וזו ירושלים *וסימניך ג] משכי גברא לגברי: כל הקדשים ד] [וכו']: אמר רב כהנא לא שנו אלא בשחיטה אבל בהעלאה כרת נמי מיחייב מאי טעמא דאמר קרא °ואליהם תאמר על ה] *הסמוכין תאמר מתקיף לה רבה מי כתיב ועליהם תאמר ו] אלידם כתיב (ואלידם קרינן) ועוד תניא ארבעה כללות היה רבי שמעון אומר בקדשים הקדישן בשעת איסור הבמות ושחט והעלה בשעת איסור הבמות בחוץ הרי הן בעשה ולא תעשה ויש בהן כרת הקדישן בשעת היתר הבמות ושחט והעלה בשעת איסור הבמות ז] הרי הן בעשה ולא תעשה ואין בהן כרת הקדישן בשעת איסור הבמות ושחט והעלה בחוץ בשעת היתר הבמות הרי הן בעשה ואין בהן בלא תעשה הקדישן בשעת היתר הבמות ושחט והעלה בשעת היתר הבמות פטור מכלום תיובתא דרב כהנא תיובתא: ואלו קדשים ח] [וכו']: סמיכה דכתיב °לפני ה' וסמך שחיטת צפון דכתיב צפונה לפני ה' מתנות סביב דכתיב °וזרק ט] על המזבח סביב (סביב) תנופה דכתיב °והניף הכהן לפני ה' הגשה דכתיב °והגישה אל המזבח: רבי יהודה אומר אין מנחה בבמה: *אמר רב ששת לדברי האומר י] יש מנחה בבמה יש עופות בבמה לדברי האומר אין מנחה בבמה אין עופות בבמה °זבחים ולא מנחות זבחים ולא עופות וכהן דכתיב °וזרק הכהן בגדי שרת °לשרת בקדש וכלי שרת °אשר ישרתו בם בקודש: לריח ניחוח דכתיב °לריח ניחוח לה': מחיצה יא] *בדמים דכתיב °והיתה הרשת עד חצי המזבח: ריחוץ ידים יב] דכתיב °ובקרבתם אל המזבח ירחצו אמר רמי בר חמא *לא שנו אלא בקדשי במה יג] קטנה והקריבום בבמה קטנה אבל בקדשי במה קטנה דקרבינהו בבמה גדולה יד] יש חיצוי מותיב רבה *חזה ושוק טו] תרומת לחמי תודה נוהגין בקדשי במה גדולה ואין נוהגין בקדשי במה קטנה אימא נוהגין בבמה גדולה ואין נוהגין בבמה קטנה איכא דאמרי אמר רמי בר חמא לא שנו אלא טז] בקדשי במה גדולה והקריבן בבמה גדולה אבל בקדשי במה קטנה אף על גב דקרבינהו בבמה גדולה אין חיצוי יז] לימא מסייע ליה חזה ושוק ותרומת לחמי תודה נוהגין יח] בקדשי במה גדולה ואין נוהגין בקדשי במה קטנה אימא נוהגין בבמה גדולה ואין נוהגין בבמה קטנה ופליגא דרבי אלעזר דאמר רבי אלעזר *עולת במת יחיד שהכניסה בפנים יט] קלטוה מחיצות לכל דבר בעי רבי זירא עולת במת יחיד שהכניסה

מינו אבשלום שהקריב בחברון כדכתיב (שמואל ב טו) אלכה נא ואשלמה את נדרי אשר נדרתי לה' בחברון וכתיב (שם) כי נדר נדר עבדך בשבתי בגשור דאין לומר דהוה מפרש דלא הלך אבשלום אלא להביא כבשים מחברון שהיו שם טובים ולהקריבם בגבעון בבמה גדולה באהל מועד כדבעי למימר בריש פרק שני דתמורה (דף יד.) דהא מסקינן התם על כרחין דלאקרובי בחברון בבמת יחיד אזל דאי להביא מחברון מיבעי ליה ועוד כתיב בשמואל (א ט) כי הוא יברך הזבח ובשאול כתיב (שם יג) הגישו אלי העולה והשלמים ויעל העולה ובסמוך מייתי לה קראי שהקריב בלילה בבמה: **ויהי** כנוח הארון. פירש רש"י פסוק בדברי הימים (ב ו) קומה ה' אלהים לנוחך אתה וארון עוזך והוה מצי להביא פסוק דכתיב ביהושע (ג) והיה כנוח כפות רגלי הכהנים נושאי הארון א"נ (במדבר י) ויהי בנסוע הארון וגו' ובנוחה יאמר וגו': ה"ג **משכינהו** גברא לגברי. פירשתי לעיל בפ' איזהו מקומן (דף נג:) גבי זה וזה יסוד דרומי: לג] **ואליהם** כתיב. והא דאמרן לעיל ואליהם לערב פרשיות היינו שחיטה והעלאה אבל כולי האי לא אמרן לערב היתר הבמות על איסור הבמות: ה"ג **הקדישן** בשעת היתר הבמות ושחט והעלה בשעת היתר הבמות פטור מכלום. וקשה היאך שייך א) למיתני בדבר שמנותו בכך וכי תימא דאיצטריך משום חובות דאין קריבין בבמה או משום קרבנות צבור ואם שחט והעלה בחוץ פטור מכלום הא איכא לאו הבא מכלל עשה ונראה לפרש דמיירי בעולת במת יחיד דאפילו הקדישה על מנת להקריבה ב) בבמה גדולה ואפי' הכניסה בפנים דקלטוה מחילות כדבסמוך אפי' הכי אם חזר והוציאה ושחט והעלה בחוץ פטור מכלום: *__אין__ מנחה בבמה וכיהון ובגדי שרת כו'. מנחה לא הויא דומיא דאינך דמאן *דלית ליה מנחה בבמה היינו דלא קרבה כלל אפילו בבמה גדולה כגון מזבח הנחושת שבנוב' וגבעון וכולהו נהגו דכולי עלמא מודו דבקדשי במה גדולה יש חילוי: **בעי** רב *אדא עולת במת יחיד שהכניסה בפנים וחזר והוציאה לחוץ מהו מי אמרינן כיון דעיילא לה קלטה להו מחילות או דלמא כיון דהדור לאו היינו דרבה ורב יוסף דתנן קדשי קדשים ששחטן בדרום מועלין בהן ואיבעיא להו *מהו שירדו רבה אמר ירדו רב יוסף אמר לא ירדו תיבעי לרבה תיבעי לרב יוסף כך גירסת רש"י ז"ל

א) גירסת הש"ק למיתני פטור מכלום בדבר כו'
ב) נ"ל בבמה גדולה והכניסה בפנים כו' ש"ק

ויהי כנוח הארון. חיפשתיו ולא מצאתיו ואם איט בכתובים יש לי מקרא אחר בדברי הימים (ב ו) בשלמה *קומה ה' אלהים לנוחך אתה וארון עוזך: מנוח. בימי שילה היה שהרי לא חרבה עד שמת עלי: הכי גרסינן תנא דבי ר' ישמעאל כר' שמעון בן יוחי. ברייתא נמצאת בבית מדרשו של ר' כ] שמעון שהיו תלמידי ר' ישמעאל שונים כמותו: משכינהו גברא לגברי. ר' שמעון שהוא יחידי משך את תלמידי ר' ישמעאל להניח דברי רבם שאמר זו וזו שילה: לא שנו. הא דקתני דהקדישן בשעת היתר והקריבם בשעת איסור אין בהם כרת: כא] אלא בשחיטה. כדתניא בהשוחט (לעיל דף קו:) יכול יהא חייבין כב] עליו כרת תלמוד לומר זאת להם ואין אחרת להם: ואליהם תאמר. גבי העלאה כתיב ובתר כג] קרא דאיירי בשוחט קדשים שהקדישן בשעת היתר כד] ושחטן בשעת איסור ולא יזבחו עוד וגו' דאוקימנא בהכי: ושחט והעלה. כה] *אחד שחט והעלה אחד שחט וחבירו העלה אלמא בהעלאה נמי קתני דאין בה כרת: לפני ה' וסמך. לרצונו לפני ה' וסמיך ליה (ויקרא א) וסמך את ידו: לפונה לפני ה' ולא לפונה בבמה והכי דריש ליה נמי בתורת כהנים: על המזבח סביב. ומהכא נפקא לן מתן סובב באיזהו מקומן (לעיל דף נג:) וסיפיה דקרא אשר פתח אהל מועד: נראה בעיני דהכי גרסינן הגשה דכתיב (ויקרא ו) הקרב אותה לפני ה' וגו' ומהאי קרא נפקא לן הגשה בקרן מערבית דרומית במסכת סוטה (דף יד:) ובמנחות כו] (דף יט:): זבחים. כז] (ויזבחו זבחים) שלמים לה' אותם ואוקימנן לעיל (דף קו:) להאי קרא בקדשים שהקדישן בשעת היתר במות וכתיב אותם מיעוטא אלמא זבחים הוא דהוו נהגי בהו ולא עופות ומנחות: וזרק הכהן את הדם על מזבח ה' פתח וגו' (ויקרא יז) ודרשינן ליה בת"כ בפרשת שחוטי חוץ זריקת כהן פתח אהל מועד יוצאין זריקת כהן בבמה אלא אף הזרים והעבדים: ישרתו בם בקדש. היינו משכן: ריח ניחוח. בההוא קרא כח] נמי והקריב החלב לריח ניחוח לה': עד חצי המזבח. מהכא נפקא לן מחיצה לדמים בפרק איזהו מקומן (לעיל דף נג.) וכתיב המזבח היינו מיעוטא בההוא מזבח לחודיה דאיירי בה קרא והיינו מזבח של משכן: לא שנו. דיש מחיצה לדמים בבמה גדולה: אלא קדשים. שהוקדשו כט] לשמו והקריבו בה: אבל קדשים ל] ששחטן לבמה קטנה. והכניסן והקריבן בגדולה אין חיצוי ואם בא ליתן עולה למטה מן החוט יתן: ואין נוהגין בקטנה. דכתיב בהו תנופה לה' מכל מקום בבמה גדולה איתנהו ואפילו בקדשי במה קטנה וה"ה לכולהו: *לא שנו. דיש חיצוי בבמה גדולה אלא בזמן במה גדולה כלומר בשעת איסור הבמות אבל בזמן היתר הבמות אין חילוק בין זו לזו בדבר הקרב בשתיהן הלכך *אפילו לא] גדולה הקריבן לגדולה אין חיצוי:

שהכניסה

א] תיבת זו נמחק: ב] מנוחה אמאי מנוחת ארון דכתיב: ג] וסימניך משכינהו: ד] הקדשים וכו': ה] על הראשונים ותיבת הסמוכין נמחק. ו] ואלהם כתיב ואליהם קרינן: ז] הבמות בחוץ הרי: ח] קדשים וכו' סמיכה: ט] וזורק את הדם על המזבח סביב תנופה: י] האומר אין מנחה בבמה אין עופות בבמה לדברי האומר יש מנחה בבמה יש עופות בבמה מאי טעמא זבחים: יא] מחיצה לדמים: יב] ידים ורגלים דכתיב: יג] במה גדולה והקריבו בבמה גדולה: יד] גדולה אין חיצוי: טו] ושוק ותרומת לחמי תודה נוהגין בבמה גדולה ואין נוהגין בבמה קטנה אימא נוהגין בקדשי במה גדולה ואין נוהגין בקדשי במה קטנה איכא דאמרי: טז] אלא בזמן במה והקריבן: יז] חיצוי מתיב רבה תיבות לימא מסייע נמחק: יח] נוהגין בבמה גדולה ואין נוהגין בבמה קטנה אימא נוהגין בזמן במה גדולה ואין נוהגין בזמן במה קטנה: יט] קלטה לה מחיצות: כ] ר' ישמעאל תיבת שמעון נמחק: כא] כרת כדתניא והד"א תיבות אלא בשחיטה נמחק: כב] חייבין עליה כרת: כג] ובתר האי קרא: כד] היתר במות ושחטן: כה] והעלה אחד שחט והעלה אחד שחט: כו] ובמנחות ובהאי מכילתא בפרק קדשי קדשים (דף סג): כז] זבחים ויזבחו זבחי שלמים: כח] קרא כתיב ותיבת נמי נמחק: כט] שהוקדשו לשמה והקריבו: ל] קדשים שהוקדשו לבמה ותיבת ששחטן נמחק: לא] אפי' קדשי גדולה והקריבו בגדולה אין חיצוי: לב] מהו"ד מי כתיב ועליהם והוא תיבת ואליהם ל"ש ותיבת כתיב נמחק:

שייך לעיל במשנה קיג.

ס"י דמאן דאית ליה אין מנחה כו'

[נגמ' ר' זירא]

נ"ל עלו מהו כו' ש"ק

נ"ל לא שנו אלא בקדשי במה גדולה והקריבו בבמה גדולה אבל בקדשי במה קטנה וקריבינהו בבמה גדולה אין חיצוי מתיב רבה חזה ושוק ותרומות לחמי תודה נוהגים בבמה גדולה ואין נוהגין בבמה קטנה אימא נוהגין בקדשי במה גדולה ואין נוהגין בקדשי במה קטנה איכא דאמרי אמר רמב"ח לא שנו אלא בזמן במה גדולה אבל בזמן במה קטנה אע"ג דקריבינהו בבמה גדולה אין חיצוי מתיב רבה חזה ושוק ותרומות לחמי תודה נוהגין בבמה גדולה ואין נוהגין בבמה קטנה אימא נוהגין בזמן גדולה ואין נוהגין בזמן קטנה ופליגא דר"א

[מקרא זה סוף פסוק בכתובים בתהלים סימן קלב ע"ש ויש להביא ראיה מן פסוק אחר כד"ס א סי' כח גבי דוד כתיב אני עם לבבי גו' בית מנוחה לארון ברית ה' ע"ש]

[נ"ל ונחלה וכ"ה בספ"י]

[ביהושע יח פ"י כתיב וישלך להם יהושע גורל בשילה לפני ה' אבל קרא ויחלק וגו' לא מצאתי]

נ"ל אחד שחט והעלה הוא ואחד שחט כו' ש"ק

[יומא נח.] לעיל נג:

[לעיל קו ע"ש]

[ותבחו זבחי]

[לעיל סט.]

נ"ל מחילה לדמים דכתיב כו' ש"ק

[לעיל קיז: ע"ש]

עיין ש"ק

נ"ל אפילו קדשי גדולה שקריבן בגדולה ש"ק

מעילה ג.

the view that *'rest'* alludes to [119*b*] Shiloh [and] *'inheritance'* to Jerusalem; or the reverse; hence it is written, *'to the rest and to the inheritance'*. But on the view that both allude to Shiloh or both allude to Jerusalem, he should say, 'unto the rest and inheritance'?[7] That is a difficulty.

On the view that both allude to Shiloh it is well: *'rest'* means when they rested from conquest, while [it is called] *'inheritance'* because there they divided their inheritance, as it is said, *And Joshua cast lots for them in Shiloh before the Lord; and there Joshua divided*
a *the land unto the children of Israel according to their divisions.*[1] But on the view that both allude to Jerusalem, *'inheritance'* is well, as it means the eternal inheritance; but why is it called *'rest'*?—It was the place where the Ark rested, as it is written, *Arise, O Lord, unto Thy resting-place, Thou, and the ark of Thy strength.*[2]

On the view that both allude to Jerusalem, but that [during the period of] Shiloh *bamoth* were permitted, it is well; hence it is written, *So Manoah took the kid with the meal-offering, and offered it upon the rock unto the Lord*[3]. But on the view that both allude to Shiloh, and *bamoth* were [then] forbidden, how [say], *'and offered it upon the rock unto the Lord'*?[4]—It was a special dispensation.[5]

The school of R. Ishmael taught as R. Simeon b. Yoḥai, who maintained: Both allude to Jerusalem. And your token is, One man attracted [many] men.[6]

ALL THE SACRIFICES etc. R. Kahana said: They learnt this[7] only of *shechitah*. But for offering up[8] one incurs *kareth* too. What is the reason? Because Scripture saith, *And thou shalt say unto them*[9] [which means,] thou shalt say concerning those just mentioned.[10] To this Rabbah demurred: Is it then written, 'and thou shalt say *concerning* them';[11] surely, *'and thou shalt say* unto *them'* is written?[12] Moreover it was taught: R. Simeon stated four general rules about sacrifices: If he consecrated them when *bamoth* were forbidden and slaughtered and offered [them] up when *bamoth* were forbidden, without, they are subject to a positive and a negative injunction, and entail *kareth*. If he consecrated them when *bamoth* were permitted and slaughtered and offered [them] up when *bamoth* were forbidden, without, they are subject to an affirmative and a negative injunction,
b and do not entail *kareth*.[1] If he consecrated them when *bamoth* were forbidden, and slaughtered and offered them up without when *bamoth* were permitted, they are subject to an affirmative precept,[2] but not to a negative precept. If he consecrated them when *bamoth* were permitted and slaughtered and offered [them] up when *bamoth* were permitted, he is not liable to anything at all.[3]

AND THE FOLLOWING SACRIFICES ... LAYING [OF HANDS] etc. Laying [of hands] [is not practised at a private *bamah*] because it is written ... *before the Lord, and he shall lay his hand.*[4] Slaughtering in the north, because it is written, [*And he shall kill it on the side of the altar*] *northward before the Lord.*[5] [Blood] applications round about [the altar], because it is written, *And he shall sprinkle the blood round about the altar* [*that is at the door of the tent of meeting*].[6] Waving, because it is written, *To wave it for a wave-offering before the Lord.*[7] Presenting, because it is written, *The sons of Aaron shall present it before the Lord, in front of the altar.*[8]

R. JUDAH MAINTAINED: THERE WERE NO MEAL-OFFERINGS AT THE BAMAH. R. Shesheth said: On the view that there were no meal-offerings at the *bamah*, there were no bird [-offerings] [either]; on the view that there were meal-offerings at the *bamah* there were bird [-offerings] [also]. What is the reason?— [*And sacrifice them for*] *sacrifices* [zebaḥim]:[9] *'zebaḥim'*, but not meal-offerings; *'zebaḥim'*, but not bird [-offerings].[10]

PRIESTHOOD, because it is written, *And the priest shall sprinkle*
c *the blood* [*on the altar of the Lord at the door of the tent of meeting*].[1]

PRIESTLY VESTMENTS, because it is written, [*And they*—the priestly vestments—*shall be upon Aaron, and upon his sons* ...] *to minister in the holy place.*[2]

SERVICE VESSELS, because it is written, [*The vessels of ministry*], *wherewith they minister in the sanctuary.*[3]

A SWEET ODOUR, because it is written, *A sweet savour unto the Lord.*[4]

A LINE OF DEMARCATION FOR [THE SPRINKLING OF] THE BLOOD, because it is written, *That the net may reach halfway up* the *altar.*[5]

THE WASHING OF HANDS AND FEET, because it is written, *And when they came near unto* the *altar, they should wash.*[6]

Rami b. Ḥama said: They learnt it[7] only about sacrifices of the great *bamah* which were offered at the great *bamah;* but no demarcation was required for sacrifices of a minor *bamah* which were offered at the great *bamah.*[8] Rabbah raised an objection: [The laws of] the breast and the thigh, and the separation of the loaves of the thanksoffering, operated at the great *bamah*, but did not operate at a minor *bamah*![9]—Say, they are operative in connection with the sacrifices of the great *bamah* and are not operative in connection with the sacrifices of a minor *bamah.*[10]

Others say, Rami b. Ḥama said: They learnt it only when the
d great *bamah* [was essential],[1] but when minor *bamoth* [were permitted], even if one sacrificed at the great *bamah*, there was no demarcation. Rabbah raised an objection: [The laws of] the breast and the thigh and the separation of the loaves of the thanksoffering operated at the great *bamah*, but did not operate at a minor *bamah*?—Say, they operate when the great *bamah* [was essential], but did not operate when minor *bamoth* [were permitted].

Now, he disagrees with R. Eleazar, for R. Eleazar said: If one took a burnt-offering of a minor *bamah* within, its barriers receive it in respect of all things.[2]

R. Zera asked: If one took the burnt-offering of a private *bamah*

(7) Not repeat 'to'.
a (1) Josh. XVIII, 10. Cur. edd. quote the text rather differently. (2) Ps. CXXXII, 8. Cur. edd. quote: And it came to pass when the Ark rested; but there is no such text in the Bible. (3) Judg. XIII, 19. (4) This was simply a *bamah*, which was forbidden. (5) That permitted him on that occasion. (6) R. Simeon b. Yoḥai, an individual, won over the *school* of R. Ishmael to his view. Cf. *supra* 53*b*. (7) That if one consecrated an animal when *bamoth* were permitted and offered it when they were forbidden, he does not incur *kareth*. (8) On the altar, i.e., burning the *emurim*. (9) Lev. XVII, 8. (10) V. *supra* 107*a*. 'Those just mentioned' are those who consecrated the animal when *bamoth* were permitted and sacrificed them without when *bamoth* were forbidden (v. 7 is thus explained). (11) Which would justify this command. (12) In Hebrew the difference is in one letter only.
b (1) This explicitly contradicts R. Kahana. (2) I.e., he has violated an affirmative precept; similarly in the other cases. (3) This last clause is obvious, and probably included merely for the sake of completeness. Tosaf. explains it thus: if one consecrated an animal for a burnt-offering, to be offered at the *public bamah*; even if he took it to the precincts of this *bamah*, and then took it out and sacrificed it at a private *bamah*, he is not liable. (4) Lev. I, 3*f*. *'Before the Lord'* implies at a *public* place of sacrifice; similarly the others. (5) Ibid., 11. (6) Ibid. 5. Hence *'round about'* is required only at *'tent of meeting'*, i.e., at a public altar. (7) Ibid. X, 15. (8) Ibid. VI, 7. This is the reading according to Rashi. (9) Ibid. XVII, 5. (10) *Zebaḥim* denotes sacrifices that are slaughtered (with *shechitah*). If, then, the word excludes meal-offerings, *ipso facto* it excludes bird-offerings, since these were killed with *meliḳah*, not *shechitah*.
c (1) Lev. XVII, 6, excluding then a private *bamah*. (2) Ex. XXVIII, 43. *'In the holy place'* implies a *public* sanctuary, but not a private one. (3) Num. IV, 12. (4) Lev. I, 9. (5) Ex. XXVII, 5. From this verse we learn that a line of demarcation is necessary (*supra* 53*a*); 'the altar' is a limitation, implying only the altar in the Tabernacle, which was a *public* sanctuary. (6) Ex. XL, 32. (7) That a line of demarcation was necessary at the public *bamah*. (8) Emended text (Sh.M. and margin). 'Sacrifices of the great *bamah* ... of a minor *bamah*' means those which were consecrated for sacrifice at a public or at a private *bamah* respectively. 'No demarcation was required'—their blood could be sprinkled above or below the line. (9) *Supra* 117*b*. This implies that these laws operated whenever a sacrifice was offered at a great *bamah*, even if it had been consecrated for the small *bamah*. The same therefore should apply to the other laws which governed the great *bamah*. (10) As explained in n. 8.
d (1) I.e., when private *bamoth* were forbidden. (2) If a burnt-offering which was consecrated for a private *bamah* was carried within the precincts of the public *bamah*, the barriers of the public *bamah* receive it, and all the laws of the public *bamah* apply to it. This proves that even sacrifices consecrated for a private *bamah* are governed by the laws of a public *bamah* in such circumstances. A further corollary is that the laws of the public *bamah* hold good at all times, whether private *bamoth* were permitted or forbidden.—Rashi explains here that R. Eleazar means that he took the burnt-offering within the precincts of the public *bamah after* it was slaughtered. His interpretation in Me'illah 3*a*, however, assumes that it applies before its slaughter too.

[120a] within, and then took it out again, what is the law?[3] do we say, Since it has entered, the barriers [of the public *bamah*] have received it; or perhaps, since it has returned, it has returned?[4]—Is this not the controversy of Rabbah and R. Joseph? For we learnt: If sacrifices of higher sanctity were slaughtered in the south,[5] they are subject to trespass.[6] Now the [scholars] asked: If they ascended [the altar], must they be taken down? Rabbah maintained: They must be taken down; R. Joseph maintained: They must not be taken down![7]—The question arises on both Rabbah's and R. Joseph's views. The question arises on Rabbah's view, [for you can argue:] Rabbah rules thus only in respect of the altar, [for]
a what is eligible for it, it sanctifies,[1] and what is not eligible for it, it does not sanctify;[2] but the barrier may receive it even when it is not eligible for it. Or perhaps, there is no difference? The question arises on R. Joseph's view, [for you may argue:] R. Joseph rules thus only there, since it is one place;[3] but here, that they are two places,[4] it is not so. Or perhaps, there is no difference? The question stands over.

That which is certain to Rabbah in one direction and to R. Joseph in the opposite direction, was a question to R. Jannai. For R. Jannai asked: If the limbs of the burnt-offering of a private *bamah* ascended the altar[5] and were taken down, what is the law? If the fire has not taken hold of them, there is no question;[6] the question arises where the fire had taken hold of them: what then? The question stands over.

It was stated: As for night slaughtering at a private *bamah*, Rab and Samuel [disagree]. One maintains: It is valid; the other maintains: It is invalid.[7] Now, they disagree on R. Eleazar's [difficulty]. For R. Eleazar pointed out a contradiction between texts. It is written, *And he said: 'Ye have dealt treacherously; roll a great stone unto me this* day'.[8] But it is written: *And Saul said: 'Disperse yourselves among the people, and say unto them: Bring me hither every man his ox, and every man his sheep, and slay them here, and eat; and sin not against the Lord in eating with the blood'. And all the people brought every man*
b *his ox with him that* night, *and slew them there.*[1] One master answered: one [text] applies to *hullin*, the other to sacrifices.[2] The other master answered: One refers to the sacrifices of a great *bamah*,[3] the other refers to the sacrifices of a minor *bamah*.

It was stated: As for the burnt-offering of a private *bamah*, Rab maintained: It does not require flaying and dismembering; while R. Joḥanan said: It does require flaying and dismembering. Now, they disagree on R. Jose the Galilean['s dictum]. For it was taught, R. Jose the Galilean said: The burnt-offering[s] which the Israelites sacrificed in the wilderness[4] did not require flaying and dismembering, because flaying and dismembering were required only from [the erection of] the Tent of Meeting and onward. One master holds: From [the erection of] the Tent of Meeting and onward, there was no difference [in this respect] between the great *bamah* and the minor *bamah*; while the other master holds: At the great *bamah*, yes; at the lesser *bamah*, no.

It was taught in accordance with R. Joḥanan: In the [following] matters the great *bamah* differed from the minor *bamah*: Horn, ascent, base, and squareness [were required at] the great *bamah*; but there were no horn, ascent, base and squareness at a minor *bamah*.[5] There were a laver and its base at the great *bamah*, but there were no laver and base at a minor *bamah*. The breast and the thigh were [waved] at the great *bamah*, but there were no breast and thigh at a minor *bamah*. In the [following] matters the great *bamah* and a minor *bamah* were alike: *shechitah* was required at the great *bamah* and at a minor *bamah*; flaying and dismembering were required at the great and at the minor [*bamoth*]. Blood permitted, and rendered *piggul*[6] at the great and at a minor [*bamoth*]. [The laws of] blem-
c ishes and time[1] [operated] at the great and at a minor [*bamah*].

BUT TIME, NOTHAR AND DEFILEMENT WERE ALIKE IN BOTH. Our Rabbis taught: How do we know that time operates at a minor *bamah* as at a great *bamah*? For [you might argue:] the Torah ordered [flesh] that was kept overnight[2] to be burnt, and [flesh] that went out [of its permitted boundaries] to be burnt:[3] just as flesh which went out is fit at a [minor] *bamah*,[4] so [flesh] which was kept overnight is fit at a [minor] *bamah*. But does not

(3) Does the law of a public *bamah* apply to it, so that it must be taken back and have its breast and thigh waved before the altar, or not? Here too Rashi explains that it was taken within after it was slaughtered. (4) And is subject to the laws of a private *bamah* only. (5) Instead of the north. (6) V. *supra* 35*b* n. 10. We do not say that since they were slaughtered in the wrong place, it is as though they were simply killed unritually, when they cease to be subject to trespass. (7) Emended text (Rashi and Sh.M.). Now, Rabbah who says that they must be taken down holds that these are not the same as other sacrifices which were disqualified in the Sanctuary, but as though they were killed unritually. Thus he holds that the barriers have *not* received them. Whereas R. Joseph, who rules that they must be taken down, holds that the barriers have received them.

a (1) So that it must not be removed thence, once it is placed thereon. (2) And since it is as though it were not ritually slaughtered (in his view), it is not eligible for it. (3) It was slaughtered in the Temple court, after all. (4) The public and the private *bamoth*. (5) Of the public *bamah*. Rashi apparently explains that the question refers to a burnt-offering consecrated for sacrifices at a public *bamah*, which was slaughtered at a private *bamah*. (6) They certainly must descend. (7) Rashi reads: Rab says it is valid; Samuel says: It is invalid. (8) I Sam. XIV, 33, q.v. As they were engaged in pursuit of the enemy, this could only have been in the nature of a private *bamah*, and his emphasis on '*this day*' proves that the night was not valid for slaughtering.

b (1) I Sam. XIV, 34. R. Eleazar leaves the difficulty unanswered. (2) The text specifying '*day*' applies to sacrifices, which must be slaughtered by day even at a private *bamah*. (3) These must be sacrificed by day.—He would explain then that when Saul specified day, he referred to those who would wait until they could sacrifice at the public *bamah*. (4) Before the Tabernacle was erected. (5) V. *supra* 62*a*. (6) The sprinkling of the blood permitted the flesh, while a *piggul* intention at the sprinkling rendered the sacrifice *piggul*.

c (1) That a blemish disqualified an animal, and that there was a time limit for the eating of the flesh. (2) I.e., *nothar*, flesh kept after its prescribed period. (3) This is deduced in Pes. 82*a* q.v. (4) Since it had no walls to define its boundaries.

תורה אור

שהכניסה לפנים והוציאה לחוץ מהו מי אמרי' כיון דעיילא קלטה לה מחיצתא או דלמא כיון דהדר הדר א] לאו היינו פלוגתא דרבה ורב יוסף דתנן *קדשי קדשים ששחטן בדרום מועלין בהן ב] (*ואם עלו לא ירדו) *ואיבעיא להו ג] (א) *ירדו מהו שיעלו רבה אמר לא יעלו ורב יוסף אמר יעלו תיבעי לרבה תיבעי לרב יוסף תיבעי לרבה עד כאן לא קאמר רבה אלא במזבח ד] דחזי ליה מקדש דלא חזי לא מקדש אבל מחיצה אע"ג דלא חזי ליה קלטה או דלמא ה] אפי' לרב יוסף עד כאן לא קאמר רב יוסף התם אלא דחד מקום הוא אבל הכא דתרי מקומות נינהו לא או דלמא לא שנא תיקו ו] מילתא דפשיטא ליה לרבה בחד גיסא ולרב יוסף בחד גיסא מיבעי ליה לרבי ינאי דבעי רבי ינאי אברי עולת במת יחיד שעלו למזבח וירדו מהו ז] היכא דלא משלה בהן האור לא תיבעי לך כי תיבעי לך היכא דמשלה בהן האור מאי תיקו איתמר שחיטת לילה בבמת יחיד רב ושמואל *חד אמר כשרה וחד אמר פסולה וקא מיפלגי בדרבי אלעזר דרבי אלעזר רמי קראי אהדדי כתיב °ויאמר בגדתם גלו אלי היום אבן גדולה וכתיב °ויאמר שאול פוצו בעם ואמרתם להם הגישו אלי איש שורו ואיש ח] שיהו ושחטתם בזה ואכלתם ולא תחטאו לה' לאכול על הדם ויגישו כל העם איש שורו בידו הלילה וישחטו שם מר משני כאן בחולין כאן בקדשים ומר משני כאן בקדשי במה גדולה כאן בקדשי במה קטנה איתמר עולת במת יחיד רב אמר אין טעונה הפשט וניתוח ורבי יוחנן אמר טעונה הפשט וניתוח וקא מיפלגי בדר"י הגלילי *דתניא ר"י הגלילי אומר *עולה שהקריבו ישראל במדבר אין טעונה הפשט וניתוח שאין הפשט וניתוח אלא מאהל מועד ואילך מר סבר מאהל מועד ואילך לא שנא במה גדולה ולא שנא במה קטנה ומר סבר בבמה גדולה אין בבמה קטנה לא תניא כותיה דרבי יוחנן דברים שבין במה גדולה לבמה קטנה *קרן וכבש ויסוד וריבוע בבמה גדולה ואין קרן ויסוד וכבש וריבוע בבמה קטנה כיור ט] וכנו בבמה גדולה ואין כיור וכנו בבמה קטנה חזה ושוק בבמה גדולה ואין חזה ושוק בבמה קטנה דברים ששוותה במה גדולה לבמה קטנה שחיטה בבמה גדולה וקטנה הפשט וניתוח בגדולה וקטנה דם מתיר ומפגל בגדולה וקטנה מומין וזמן בגדולה וקטנה: אבל י] (ב) נותר והזמן והטמא שוין בזה ובזה: ת"ר מנין לעשות זמן בבמה קטנה כבמה גדולה יא] (אמרה תורה לן ישרף ופיגול ישרף מה פיגול פסול בבמה אף לן פסול בבמה או כלך לדרך זו) דהא אמרה תורה לן ישרף ויוצא ישרף מה יוצא כשר בבמה אף לן כשר בבמה ולאו ק"ו הוא מעופות מה

ש"א יד | שם

רש"י

שהכניסה · גרס בדרבי אלעזר שהכניסה לאחר ששחטה בחוץ קלטוה מחיצות לכל דבר גרס במסכת מעילה (דף ג.) אלמא אף קדשים שנשחטו בבמה קטנה שהקריבן בגדולה כל דין במה גדולה נוהג בהן ושמעינן מינה נמי דבשעת היתר במה נמי לא נשתנה דין גדולה מהלכתא יב] ששתיהן הלשונות דרמי בר חמא פליגי אדרבי אלעזר: שהכניסה לפנים · אחר ששחטה בחוץ וחזר והוציאה: מהו · מי נהוג בה דין קדשי במה גדולה ליטעון בתרומת חזה ושוק וצריך להחזירה לפנים או לא: ה"ג דתנן קדשי קדשים כו' · ולא גרסינן דאיתמר ולא גרס אם עלו לא ירדו ומשנה היא במסכת מעילה: מועלין בהן · ולא אמרינן כמאן דחנקינון דמי והוי להו כקדשים שמתו דילאו מידי מעילה כדתניא במסכת מעילה: ה"ג *במסכת מעילה והכי נמי גרסינן לה יג] לאו הייט דרבה ורב יוסף דתנן קדשי קדשים ששחטן בדרום מועלין בהם ואיבעיא להו עלו מהו שירדו רבה אמר ירדו ורב יוסף אמר יד] אם עלו לא ירדו רבה אמר ירדו דלא דמו לשאר פסולין שפסולן בקדש אלא כמאן דחנקינון דמי אלמא לרבה לא אמרינן קלוט לרב יוסף אמרינן קלוט: דלא חזי לא מקדש · דתניא בפ' המזבח [מקדש] (לעיל פג:) מתוך שנאמר כל הנוגע במזבח יקדש שומע אני בין ראוי בין שאינו ראוי ת"ל עולה *והני לאו ראוי נינהו טו] דלרבה כמאן דחנקינון דמי: דחד מקום הוא · שהרי בעזרה נשחטו: דבעי רבי ינאי אברי עולת במת יחיד שעלו למזבח מהו שירדו · ה"ג ובמעילה (דף ג:) נמי הכי גרס לה אבל לא ברבי ינאי טז] גרס לה *התם: אברי עולה שנשחטה בבמת יחיד · שלא במקומה הוא לגבי במה גדולה כקדשי קדשים ששחטן בדרום: ה"ג איתמר עולת במת יחיד ששחטה בלילה רב אמר כשר ושמואל אמר פסול וקמיפלגי בהא דרבי אלעזר רמי כתיב גולו אלי היום אבן גדולה בעוד שהוא יום אלמא דלילה פסולה בבמה קטנה והתם במה קטנה הואי שהרי במלחמה היו רודפים אחרי פלשתים וכתיב סיפא דקרא ויגישו כל העם איש שורו בידו הלילה: רב משני כאן בקדשי במה גדולה · שהוקדשו ליקרב בבמה גדולה ואע"ג דאקרבינהו בבמה קטנה בעינן יום: כאן בקדשי במה קטנה · קרבו בלילה: ושמואל משני הא דכתיב יום אקדשים קאי ואפילו בקדשי במה קטנה בעינן יום הא דכתיב לילה בחולין: במדבר · יז] *סיני: מאהל מועד ואילך · ששם נאמר בויקרא: קרן וכבש ויסוד וריבוע · ילפינן להו בפרק קדשי *קדשים (לעיל סב.) ובמזבח של משכן כתיב כיור וכן בין אהל מועד ובין המזבח כתיב ביה (שמות ל): חזה ושוק · תנופה לפני ה' כתיב בהו (ויקרא ז): שחיטה הפשט וניתוח כו' · דלא אשכחן בהו מיעוטא: דם · לזריקה מתיר את הבשר בזריקה ומקמי זריקה אסירא: ומפגל · פיגול נוהג בהן כדיליף לקמן: ומומין · דלא אשכחן דשריניהו בקטנה: וזמן · לאכילה: אבל הזמן והנותר והטמא כו' · סיפא דמתני' היא ולא בברייתא הוא: מנין לעשות זמן · להיות נפסל בנותר: הלן · הייט נותר: והיוצא ישרף · נפקא לן בפסחים (דף פב.) מהן לא הובא את דמה אל הקדש פנימה היתה לפיכך אכל תאכלו אותה הא (ג) אם לא היתה פנימה ראויה היא לישרף: מה יוצא כשר בבמה · קטנה שהרי כשירה בלא מחיצות אף לן כשר ומעתה לא יהא הזמן פוסל דהא אתיא מהאי דינא כדאמרן: ודין הוא · מדרך אחרת שיהא הזמן פוסל בה: ומה

תוספות

אבל בספרים ישנים גרסינן קדשי קדשים ששחטן בדרום מועלין בהן אם עלו לא ירדו ואיבעיא להו ירדו מהו שיעלו רבה אמר לא יעלו רב יוסף אמר יעלו תיבעי לרבה כו' ומיירי במשלה בהן האור להכי לכ"ע אם עלו לא ירדו וגריס מעילה (דף ג:) דאמר רבה אם עלו ירדו מיירי בלא משלה בהן האור ותדע בלא ההיא דמעילה צריך לאוקמא הכא במשלה בהן האור דאי בלא משלה אמאי אמר רב יוסף אם ירדו יעלו הא אמרינן פרק ב"ש (לעיל מג.) כשם שאם עלו לא ירדו כך אם ירדו לא יעלו וכל שכן בשחיטת דרום דגרוע משאר פסולין והכא מיירי בהכניסה חיה וקלטוה כדין במה גדולה להצריך כיור וריחוץ ידים ורגלים מן הכיור ואם היא שלמים בעי תנופת חזה ושוק ולפי גירסא זו גרסינן בסמוך אברי עולת במת יחיד שעלו למזבח של במה גדולה וירדו מהו שיעלו פירוש דכיון דשחטן בחוץ שמא הוי כמו שחטן בדרום *וגם שמא כיון ששחטה בהיתר בחוץ בבמת יחיד שלכך הקדישה תחילה לכולי עלמא היכא דמשלה האור יעלה *אבל ללשון ראשון דמבעיא ליה בלא משלה ומדמי ליה לשחיטת דרום הלא פשיטא אפי' שאר פסולין דלא גריעי כמו שחיטת דרום אם עלו וירדו לא יעלו כדאמר עולא פרק ב"ש (שם) אם לא משלה בהן האור כשם שאם עלו לא ירדו כך אם ירדו לא יעלו *וצריך לומר הא דקאמר מילתא דפשיטא לרבה ורב יוסף מיבעיא ליה לרבי ינאי היינו לאיכא דאמרי:

הדרן עלך פרת חטאת
וסליקא לה מסכת זבחים

מסורת הש"ס

מעילה ג.

[ג' הספרים היא גירסת הרמב"ם ועי' ברש"י גירסא אחרת]

נ"ל במסכת מעילה וה"ג במס' מעילה וה"נ גרסי' הכי לאו היינו כו' מועלין בה ולא אמרי' כמאן דחנקינן דמי והוה ליה קדשים שמתו דילאו מידי מעילה כדתניא במסכת מעילה ואיבעיא להו עלו כו' נ"ק

נ"ל והכנו לאו כו' נ"ק

רא התם אלא רבי אלעזר

נ"ל נסיני נ"ק

הגהות הב"ח

(א) גמ' ואיבעיא להו עלו מהו שירדו רבה אמר: (ב) שם אבל הזמן ונותר וטמא: (ג) רש"י ד"ה והיוצא ישרף וכו' הא אם היתה הובא פנימה ראויה:

עין משפט נר מצוה

לא א מיי' פ"ג מהלכות מעילה הלכה א:

לב ב מיי' פ"ג מהלכות פסה"מ הלכה ז:

מעילה ג:

[עיין תוספות לעיל יד. ד"ה הג"ה חוץ עזרה]

נ"א או שמא כו' נ"ק

נ"ל וללשון ראשון דמיבעיא ליה כו' ול"נ אבל ללשון ראשון נ"ק

לפי גי' רש"י נ"ל רב אמר כשרה ושמואל אמר פסולה

עי' רש"ק

חגיגה ו:

[לעיל קטו:]

[לעיל סב. קח:]

רש"ק מ"ז

נ"ל קדשים הס"ד ואח"כ ד"ה כיור וכנו במזבח של משכן כתיב כיור ובין אהל מועד ובין המזבח כתיב ביה הס"ד וכו' נ"ק

שיטה מקובצת

א] לאו היינו פלוגתא דרבה ורב יוסף וכו' ואיבעיא להו עלו מהו שירדו וכו' פי' אע"ג דפלוגתא דרבה ורב יוסף לאו בהוציאה לחוץ וא"כ הכי בעי למפשט מהתם מ"מ שפיר מצי למיפשט דדוקא התם דלא חזר והוציאה ס"ל לרב יוסף אם עלו לא ירדו אבל הכא דהדר והוציא אפילו רב יוסף מודה דלא קלטוהו מחיצות ולרבה פשיט מכ"ש ומה התם דלא חזר והוציאה ס"ל ירדו כ"ש הכא דאמרינן כיון דהדר הדר א"נ דלרב יוסף פשיט אם בקדשים פסולין דהיינו ששחטן בדרום דהו"ל כמאן דחנקינהו ס"ל דאם עלו לא ירדו כ"ש הכא דקדשים כשרין הן דאמרינן קלטוהו מחיצות ולא מיפסל להו מה שחזר והוציאה לחוץ וכה"ג אפשר דגם רבה מודה דקלטוהו מחיצות ודו"ק: ב] תיבות ואם עלו לא ירדו נמחק: ג] להו עלו מהו שירדו רבה אמר ירדו ורב יוסף אמר לא ירדו: ד] במזבח מאי דחזי ליה מקדש מאי דלא חזי ליה לא מקדש: ה] דלמא לא שנא תיבעי לרב יוסף: ו] מילתא דפשיטא ליה לרבה וכו' מיבעי לר' ינאי הקשו חכמי ישיבה יצ"ו דהיכא קאמר פשיטא לרב יוסף דלא ירדו הא לעיל אמר דבתרי מקומות אפילו לרב יוסף מיבעי והכי תרי מקומות נינהו אברי עולת במת יחיד שעלו למזבח במת גדולה ונראה לפע"ד דמתרצא במאי דכתיבנא אם בקדשים פסולים אמרינן למר כדאית ליה ולמר כדאית ליה כ"ש הכא דקדשים כשרין הן דאפילו רבה מודה דלא ירדו א"נ לעיל ששחטו בחוץ והכניסו לפנים לעזרה דבודאי ממקום הפסול דהיינו מחוץ לעזרה שהוא מקום קדוש תרי מקומות נינהו אבל הכא מבמה קטנה לבמה גדולה כיון דמשם אחד הן תם בהרבה דברים ששוו א לוו כדבסמוך דברים ששותה במה גדולה וכו' כחד מקום דמי ודו"ק: ז] מהו שירדו היכא דמשלה בהן האור לא תיבעי לך כי תיבעי לך היכא דלא משלה בהן האור איכא דאמרי היכא: ח] ואיש שֵׂיהּ: ט] כיור וכן ואות נ' ו' נמחק: י] אבל זמן ונותר וטמא: יא] מתיבת אמרה עד תיבת אמרה בס"י כל זאת אינו אלא כתוב מיד אמרה תורה לן ישרף כו' עד כשר בבמה יכול לא יהא זמן פוסל בה ודין הוא ומה עופות: יב] ושתי הלשונות: יג] לה הכא לאו: יד] תיבות אם עלו נמחק: טו] נינהו לרבה דכמאן: טז] ינאי כו' · פי' דהתם לא מבעיא דבעיא משם ר' ינאי כדהכא וכו' וק"ל: יז] במדבר במדבר סיני:

מה עופות "שאין המום פוסל בהן 'זמן פוסל בהן קדשי במה קטנה שהמום פוסל בהן אינו דין שזמן פוסל בהן מה לעופות שכן 'אין הזר כשר בהן תאמר בבמה קטנה שהזר כשר א)בה לא יהא זמן פסול בה ת"ל °וזאת תורת זבח השלמים לעשות זמן במה קטנה כזמן במה גדולה:

הדרן עלך פרת חטאת וסליקא לה מסכת זבחים

תורה אור: ויקרא ז

ומה עופות שאין המום פוסל בהן · דאמר מר (תמורה דף יז.) אין תמות וזכרות בעופות: זמן פוסל בהן · דהא רבינהו להו גבי פיגול בפ' בית שמאי (לעיל מג.) אלמא פסול בהו זמן: תורת זבח השלמים · תורה אחת לכל השלמים ואפילו לשלמי במה קטנה למה שאמור בענין ומה אמור בתוכו ענין זמן לתודה וזמן לשלמים ומחשבת פיגול והא דאיצטריך לרבוייהו משום דאתי מבנין אב דהכא ישרף והיוצא ישרף דלא יפסול בה זמן לפיכך הוצרך לרבותו: לעשות זמן ב) במה קטנה כזמן במה גדולה · לתודה יום ולילה ולשלמים שני ימים ולילה אחד ונותר כמו מפיגול יליף(שם)מג"ש דעון עון וטמא כמו בההיא פרשתא כתיב (ויקרא ז) והנפש אשר תאכל וגו':

עין משפט נר מצוה

לג א מיי' פ"ג מהל' איסורי מזבח הלכה א:

לד ב מיי' פי"ח מהל' פסה"מ הל' ז:

לה ג מיי' פ"ז מהלכות פסה"מ הלכה א:

שיטה מקובצת

א) כשר בה הואיל והזר כשר בה לא: ב) זמן בבמה קטנה:

הדרן עלך פרת חטאת וסליקא לה מסכת זבח

אחר השלמת המסכת יאמר זה ויועיל לזכרון בעזרת השם יתברך ·

הדרן עלך א) מסכת זבחים והדרך עלן דעתן עלך מסכת זבחים ודעתך עלן לא נתנשי מינך מסכת זבחים ולא תתנשי מינן לא בעלמא הדין ולא בעלמא דאתי: יאמר כן שלש פעמים ואחר כך יאמר

יהי רצון מלפניך יי אלהינו ואלהי אבותינו שתהא תורתך אומנותנו בעולם הזה ותהא עמנו לעולם הבא ב) חנינא בר פפא רמי בר פפא נחמן בר פפא אחאי בר פפא אבא מרי בר פפא רפרם בר פפא רכיש בר פפא סורחב בר פפא אדא בר פפא דרו בר פפא:

הערב נא יי אלהינו את דברי תורתך בפינו ובפיפיות עמך בית ישראל ונהיה כולנו אנחנו וצאצאינו וצאצאי עמך בית ישראל כולנו יודעי שמך ולומדי תורתך: מאויבי תחכמני מצותיך כי לעולם היא לי: יהי לבי תמים בחקיך למען לא אבוש: לעולם לא אשכח פקודיך כי בם חייתני: ברוך אתה יי למדני חקיך: אמן אמן אמן סלה ועד:

מודים אנחנו לפניך יי אלהינו ואלהי אבותינו ששמת חלקנו מיושבי בית המדרש ולא שמת חלקנו מיושבי קרנות שאנו משכימים והם משכימים אנו משכימים לדברי תורה והם משכימים לדברים בטלים אנו עמלים והם עמלים אנו עמלים ומקבלים שכר והם עמלים ואינם מקבלים שכר אנו רצים והם רצים אנו רצים לחיי העולם הבא והם רצים לבאר שחת שנאמר ואתה אלהים תורידם לבאר שחת אנשי דמים ומרמה לא יחצו ימיהם ואני אבטח בך:

יהי רצון מלפניך יי אלהי כשם שעזרתני לסיים מסכת זבחים כן תעזרני להתחיל מסכתות וספרים אחרים ולסיימם ללמוד וללמד לשמור ולעשות ולקיים את כל דברי תלמוד תורתך באהבה וזכות כל התנאים ואמוראים ותלמידי חכמים יעמוד לי ולזרעי שלא תמוש התורה מפי ומפי זרעי וזרע זרעי עד עולם. ויתקיים בי בהתהלכך תנחה אותך בשכבך תשמור עליך והקיצות היא תשיחך: כי בי ירבו ימיך ויוסיפו לך שנות חיים: אורך ימים בימינה בשמאלה עושר וכבוד: ה' עוז לעמו יתן ה' יברך את עמו בשלום:

יתגדל ויתקדש שמיה רבא בעלמא דהוא עתיד לאתחדתא ולאחיא מתיא ולאסקא לחיי עלמא ולמבני קרתא דירושלם ולשכלל היכליה בגוה ולמעקר פולחנא נוכראה מארעא ולאתבא פולחנא דשמיא לאתריה וימליך קודשא בריך הוא במלכותיה ויקריה בחייכון וביומיכון ובחיי דכל בית ישראל בעגלא ובזמן קריב ואמרו אמן: יהא שמיה רבא מברך לעלם ולעלמי עלמיא: יתברך וישתבח ויתפאר ויתרומם ויתנשא. ויתהדר ויתעלה ויתהלל שמיה דקודשא. בריך הוא לעילא מן כל ברכתא ושירתא תושבחתא ונחמתא דאמירן בעלמא ואמרו אמן: על ישראל ועל רבנן ועל תלמידיהון ועל כל תלמידי תלמידיהון ועל כל מאן דעסקין באורייתא. די באתרא הדין ודי בכל אתר ואתר. יהא להון ולכון שלמא רבא חנא וחסדא ורחמי וחיי אריכי ומזוני רויחי ופורקנא מן קדם אבוהון די בשמיא וארעא ואמרו אמן: יהא שלמא רבא מן שמיא וחיים טובים עלינו ועל כל ישראל ואמרו אמן: עושה שלום במרומיו הוא יעשה ברחמיו שלום עלינו ועל כל ישראל ואמרו אמן:

א) פי' הגון על זה תמלא בספר החיים שחיבר אחי הגאון מהר"ל מפראג. בספר זכיות ח"א פ"ג ב) בסיומא וסוף תשובת הרמ"א ז"ל וכן בסוף יש"ש בב"ק כתוב רמזים על הזכרת שמות אלו.

בשם הרב הגאון הגדול המפורסם מהור"ד **נפתלי הירש** נר"ו לקא"ב אב"ד במדינת פפאלץ כפי שנדפס בשמו בקול יהודה ד' הומבורג בשנת תקב"ל

דף יד ע"א **מודה** היה ר"ש לפסול מק"ו · ומה שלא לשמן וכו' · ובתוס' תימה מה שלא לשמן שכן נוהג בד' עבודות כו' · וכה"ג פריך לעיל [מ"ה לחוץ לזמנו שכן כר"ת] חמשה תיבות אלו המצויינים בהלכ' מחקו כל הגהוס' ה"ה בעל תורת חיים ובה"ז ופניס מאירות ובעקבם דרכו מדפיסי ש"ס חדש עם הגהות הגאון מוהר"ש מקראקא אב"ד דק"ק פרנקפורט דמיין · ואין לעיין לעיל דף ד' ע"א דעביד הגמרא פירכא שכן נוהג בד' עבודות ולפע"ד נראה שהתוס' טונו לחזק קושייתם מהא דפריך רבה בר אהילאי לעיל דף י' ע"א מה לחוץ לזמנו שכן כרת· דהגה התוס' כתבו בקידושין דף ה' ע"א בד"ה שאין פודין· ובחולין דף פה ע"א ד"ה מה למילה והעיקר בב"ק דף כה ע"א ד"ה אני לא אדון · שהקשו כיון שאין הפירכא מעין הק"ו נסים הפירכא בתוך הק"ו ותירצו דאין משימין הפירכא בתוך הק"ו רק היכא דהוי רק סברא בעלמא אבל חומרא וקולא דכתיבי כגון הכא פרכינן אע"ג דלא הוי מעין הק"ו· ומביאין שם ראיה מפירכא דרבה בר אהילאי הנ"ל· וכיון דעל קושיית התוס' הכא מה לחוץ לזמנו שכן נוהג בד"ע ג"כ יש לתרץ כיון דאין הפירכא מעין הק"ו נסים הפירכא בתוך הק"ו · לכך מסיימי התוס' וכה"ג פריך לעיל מה לחוץ לזמנו שכן כרת דמוכח מזה דכיון דהתומרא וקולא כתיבי פרכינן אע"ג דלא הוי מעין ק"ו א"כ תימה מה שלא לשמן שכן נוהג בד' עבודות והו"ק ותמלא שאמת כדברי:

[the reverse] follow from birds, *a minori*: [120*b*] if time disqualifies birds, though a blemish does not disqualify them;[5] is it not logical that time should disqualify the sacrifices of a minor *bamah*, seeing that a blemish does disqualify them? As for birds, the reason is because a *zar* is not fit in their case; but in the case of a minor *bamah*, where a *zar* is fit [to officiate], let time not disqualify. Therefore it states, *And this is the law of the sacrifice of peace-offerings*,[6] which makes time at a minor *bamah* the same as time at the great *bamah*.[7]

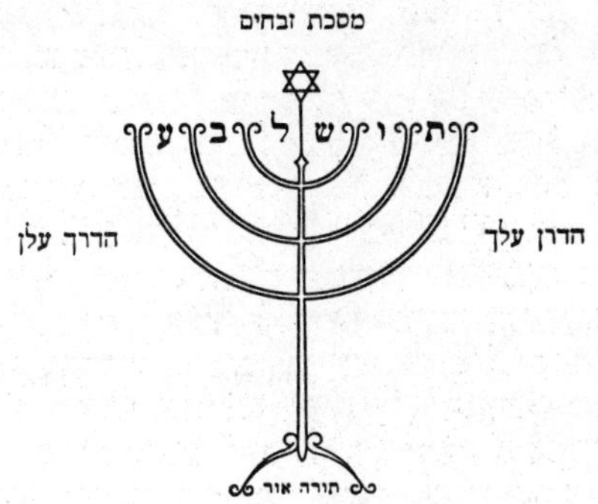

(5) V. *supra* 116*a*. (6) Lev. VII, 11. (7) *Sc*. a disqualification. '*This is the law*' etc. implies that *all* peace-offerings, wherever offered, are governed by the same law in respect of the contents of that passage. That passage (q.v.) deals with time, *piggul*, and defilement.

ABBREVIATIONS

Ab.	Aboth.
Alfasi	R. Isaac b. Jacob Alfasi (1013-1103).
Aruk	Talmudic Dictionary by R. Nathan b. Jeḥiel of Rome (d. 1106).
Asheri	R. Asher b. Jeḥiel (1250-1327).
A.Z.	'Abodah Zarah.
b.	ben, bar: son of.
B.B.	Baba Bathra.
BaḤ.	Bayith Ḥadash, Glosses by R. Joel b. Samuel Sirkes (1561-1640).
Bek.	Bekoroth.
Ber.	Berakoth.
Beẓ.	Beẓah.
Bik.	Bikkurim.
B.Ḳ.	Baba Ḳamma.
B.M.	Baba Meẓi'a.
Cur. ed(d).	Current edition(s).
D.S.	*Diḳduḳe Soferim*, by R. Rabbinowicz.
'Ed.	'Eduyyoth.
E.J.	*Encyclopaedia Judaica.*
E.V.	English Version.
Giṭ.	Giṭṭin.
G.K.	Gesenius-Kautzsch, Hebrew Grammar.
Glos.	Glossary.
Golds.	Translation of the Babylonian Talmud in German by L. Goldschmidt.
Graetz	Graetz, H., *Geschichte der Juden* (4th ed.).
Hag.	Ḥagigah.
Hananel	R. Ḥananel b. Ḥushiel of Kairwan (about 990-1050).
Hor.	Horayoth.
HUCA.	Hebrew Union College Annual.
Jast.	M. Jastrow's Dictionary of the Targumim, the Talmud Bible and Yerushalmi, and the Midrashic Literature.
J.E.	*Jewish Encyclopedia.*
JQR.	*Jewish Quarterly Review.*
J.T.	Jerusalem Talmud.
Keth.	Kethuboth.
Ḳid.	Ḳiddushin.
Maharsha	R. Samuel Eliezer Halevi Edels (1555-1631).
Maim.	Moses Maimonides (1135-1204).
Mak.	Makkoth.
Meg.	Megillah.
Men.	Menaḥoth.
MGWJ.	*Monatsschrift für Geschichte und Wissenschaft des Judentums.*
Mid.	Middoth.
M.Ḳ.	Mo'ed Ḳatan.
MS.M.	Munich Codex of the Talmud.
Ned.	Nedarim.
Nid.	Niddah.
Obermeyer	Obermeyer J., *Die Landschaft Babylonien.*
P.B.	*The authorized Daily Prayer Book*, S. Singer.
Pes.	Pesaḥim.
R.	Rab, Rabban, Rabbenu, Rabbi.
Rashi	Commentary of R. Isaac Yiẓḥaḳi (d. 1105).
REJ.	*Revue des Etudes Juives.*
R.H.	Rosh Hashanah.
R.V.	Revised version of the Bible.
Sanh.	Sanhedrin.
Shab.	Shabbath.
Sheb.	Shebi'ith.
Shebu.	Shebu'oth.
Sheḳ.	Sheḳalim.
Sof.	Soferim.
Sonc. ed.	English Translation of the Babylonian Talmud. Soncino Press, London.
Soṭ.	Soṭah.
Suk.	Sukkah.
Ta'an.	Ta'anith.
T.A.	*Talmudische Archäologie*, by S. Krauss.
Ter.	Terumoth.
T.J.	Talmud Jerusalemi.
Tosaf.	Tosafoth.
Tosef.	Tosefta.
Wilna Gaon	Notes by Elijah of Wilna (1720-1797) in the Wilna editions of the Talmud.
Yeb.	Yebamoth.
Zeb.	Zebaḥim.

TRANSLITERATION OF HEBREW LETTERS

א (in middle of word)	= '
ב	= b
ו	= w
ח	= ḥ
ט	= ṭ
כ	= k
ע	= '
פ	= f
צ	= ẓ
ק	= ḳ
ת	= th

Full particulars regarding the method and scope of the translation are given in the Editor's Introduction.

AGGADAH (Lit., 'tale', 'lesson'); the name given to those sections of Rabbinic literature which contain homiletic expositions of the Bible, stories, legends, folk-lore, anecdotes or maxims. Opposed to *halachah*, q.v.

'AM HA-AREẒ pl. *'amme ha areẓ*, (lit., 'people of the land', 'country people'); the name given in Rabbinic literature to (*a*) a person who through ignorance was careless in the observance of the laws of Levitical purity and of those relating to the priestly and Levitical gifts. In this sense opposed to *ḥaber*, q.v.; (*b*) an illiterate or uncultured man, as opposed to *talmid ḥakam*, q.v.

'AMIDAH (Lit., 'standing'); the Eighteen Benedictions (seven on Sabbaths and Festivals) which the worshipper always recites in a standing posture.

AMORA. 'Speaker', 'interpreter'; originally denoted the interpreter who attended upon the public preacher or lecturer for the purpose of expounding at length and in popular style the heads of the discourse given to him by the latter. Subsequently (pl. Amoraim) the name given to the Rabbinic authorities responsible for the Gemara, as opposed to the Mishnah or Baraitha (v. Tanna).

BAMAH (Lit. 'high place'). The private altar or sanctuary in vogue before the establishment of a central Sanctuary.

BARAITHA (Lit., 'outside'); a teaching or a tradition of the Tannaim that has been excluded from the Mishnah and incorporated in a later collection compiled by R. Ḥiyya and R. Oshaiah, generally introduced by 'Our Rabbis taught', or, 'It has been taught'.

BETH DIN (Lit., 'house of law or judgment'); a gathering of three or more learned men acting as a Jewish court of law.

BETH HAMIDRASH. House of study; the college or academy where the study of the Torah was carried on under the guidance of a Rabbinical authority.

BINYAN AB (Lit., 'constructing of a family'); a norm of interpretation denoting that a certain Biblical passage is regarded as having laid the foundation of a family, because it *is* the *principal passage* from which is derived the explanation to passages which are similar to it.

EMURIM (Lit., 'the consecrated parts'); the parts of a sacrifice which were to be burnt on the altar.

GEMARA (Lit., 'completion' or 'learning'). The traditions, discussions and rulings of the Amoras, based mainly on the Mishnah and forming (*a*) the Babylonian Talmud and (*b*) the Palestinian Talmud.

GEZERAH SHAWAH (Lit., 'equal cut'); the application to one subject of a rule already known to apply to another, on the strength of a common expression used in connection with both in the Scriptures.

HALACHAH (Lit., 'step', 'guidance'), (*a*) the final decision of the Rabbis, whether based on tradition or argument, on disputed rules of conduct; (*b*) those sections of Rabbinic literature which deal with legal questions, as opposed to the *Aggadah*.

ḤALIẒAH (Lit., 'drawing off'); the ceremony of taking off the shoe of the brother of a husband who has died childless. (V. Deut. XXV, 5-9.)

ḤALLAH. The portion of the dough which belongs to the priest (v. Num. XV, 20f); in the Diaspora this is not given to the priest but burnt.

HAḲṬARAH. The burning of sacrificial portions on the altar.

ḤALUẒAH. A woman who has performed *ḥaliẓah* (q.v.).

ḤAYYAH. Beast of chase, e.g. deer, contra. to *behema*, a domesticated animal.

HAZA'AH. The sprinkling of the blood of sacrifices, and of the water of purification, upon the unclean.

HEKAL. The holy temple, especially the hall containing the golden altar etc. in contradistinction to the Holy of Holies.

HEḲDESH. Any object consecrated to the Sanctuary.

HEḲḲESH. Analogy, proving that the law in respect of one thing applies also to another, either because both have some feature in common or there is a Biblical intimation to the effect.

ḤELEB. The portion of the fat of a permitted domestic animal which may not be eaten; in sacrifices that fat was burnt upon the altar.

ḤULLIN (Lit., 'profane'); ordinary unhallowed food, as opposed to *terumah*, q.v.; unconsecrated animals, as opposed to *heḳdesh*, q.v.

ḲAB. Measure of capacity equal to four *logs* or one sixth of a *se'ah*.

ḲAL WA-ḤOMER (Lit., 'light and heavy'); an argument, or proof of a contention, *a minori* or *a fortiori*.

KARETH. 'Cutting off'; divine punishment for a number of sins for which no human penalty is specified. Sudden death is described as '*kareth* of days', premature death at sixty as '*kareth* of years'.

ḲEMIẒAH. The taking of the fistful of flour from the meal-offering.

KIL'AYIM (Lit., 'junction of diverse kinds'); the prohibition either (*a*) of seeds or plants for sowing; (*b*) of animals for propagation; and (*c*) of material containing wool and linen for wearing (v. Lev. XIX, 19, XXII, 9ff).

LINAH. 'Staying overnight'. The disqualification of a holy thing which remained overnight.

LOG. A liquid measure equal to a quarter of a *ḳab* (q.v.), or the space occupied by six eggs, c. 549 cubic centimetres.

MATTIR (pl. MATTIRIN) lit., 'that which renders permissible'. The essential rite of a sacrifice which renders the offering permissible for the altar or for eating.

MELIḲAH (Lit., 'wringing'); the wringing off of the head of the burnt-offering of a bird (v. Lev. I, 15).

MIḲWEH (Lit., 'a gathering [of water]'); a ritual bath containing not less than forty *se'ahs* of water.

MISHMAR (rt. SHaMaR, 'to keep'), a guard of priests and Levites representing one of the eight divisions which carried on the Temple services in rotation. The *mishmar* again was subdivided into smaller groups each being designated *beth ab*.

MISHNAH (rt. SHaNaH, 'to learn', 'to repeat'), (*a*) the collection of the statements, discussions and Biblical interpretations of the Tannaim in the form edited by R. Judah the Patriarch c. 200; (*b*) similar minor collections by previous editors; (*c*) a single clause or paragraph the author of which was a Tanna.

NEBELAH (pl. *nebeloth*); an animal slaughtered in any manner other than that prescribed by Jewish ritual law; the least deviation therefrom, e.g., if the knife has the slightest notch, renders the animal *nebelah*.

NEZEK (YEN NEZEK, Lit. 'wine of libation'); wine forbidden to the Jew because it has been handed by an idolator who may have dedicated it as an offering to his deity.

NIDDAH. A woman in the period of her menstruation.

NOTHAR ('left over'); portions of sacrifices left over after the prescribed time within which they must be eaten.

OMER (Lit., 'sheaf'); the sheaf of barley offered on the sixteenth of Nisan, before which the new cereals of that year were forbidden for use (v. Lev. XXIII, 10).

'ORLAH ('uncircumcised'); applied to newly-planted trees for a period of three years during which their fruits must not be eaten (v. Lev. XIX, 23ff).

PIGGUL (Lit., 'abhorred'); flesh of the sacrifice which the officiating priest has formed the intention of eating at an improper time. V. Lev. VII, 18.

REBI'ITH. A liquid measure, one fourth of a *log*.

SANHEDRIN (συνέδριον); the council of state and supreme tribunal of the Jewish people during the century or more preceding the fall of the Second

Temple. It consisted of seventy-one members, and was presided over by the High Priest. A minor court (for judical purposes only) consisting of twenty-three members was known as the 'Small Sanhedrin'.

SHEBI'ITH. The seventh or Sabbatical year in which cultivation of the land is forbidden. V. Lev. XXV.

SHECHINAH (Lit., 'abiding [of God'] 'Divine presence'); the spirit of the Omnipresent as manifested on earth.

SHECHITAH. Ritual slaughter, without which an animal is not fit for food.

SHEREẒ. Unclean reptile (including rodents).

TALMID ḤAKAM (Lit., 'disciple of the wise'); scholar, student of the Torah.

TALMUD (Lit., 'teaching', 'learning') applies (*a*) to the Gemara (q.v.) or (*b*) generally to the Mishnah and Gemara combined.

TAMID. The continual or daily burnt-offering, sacrificed every morning and evening.

TANNA (Lit., 'one who repeats' or 'teaches'); (*a*) a Rabbi quoted in the Mishnah or Baraitha (q.v.); (*b*) in the Amoraic period, a scholar whose special task was to memorize and recite Baraithas in the presence of expounding teachers.

ṬEBEL. Produce, already at the stage of liability to the levitical and priestly dues (v. *Terumah*), before these have been separated.

ṬEBILLAH. The act of taking a ritual bath in a *mikweh*, q.v.

ṬEBUL YOM (Lit., 'bathed during the day'); a person who has bathed to cleanse himself at the end of the period of his defilement, but who must wait until sunset to regain his ritual purity (Lev. XXII, 7).

TEFILLIN. Phylacteries; small cases containing passages from the Scripture and affixed to the forehead and arm during the recital of morning prayers, in accordance with Deut. VI, 8.

TERUMAH. 'That which is lifted or separated'; the heave-offering given from the yields of the yearly harvests, from certain sacrifices, and from the *shekels* collected in a special chamber in the Temple (*terumath ha-lishkah*). *Terumah gedolah* (great offering): the first levy on the produce of the year given to the priest, (v. Num. XVIII, 8ff). Its quantity varied according to the generosity of the owner, who could give one-fortieth, one-fiftieth, or one-sixtieth of his harvest. *Terumath ma'aser* (heave-offering of the tithe): the heave-offering given to the priest by the Levite from the tithes he receives (v. Num. XVIII, 25ff).

TORAH (Lit., 'teaching', 'learning', 'instruction'); (*a*) the Pentateuch (Written Law); (*b*) the Mishnah (Oral Law); (*c*) the whole body of Jewish religious literature.

TREFA or TEREFA (Lit., 'torn'); (*a*) an animal torn by a wild beast; (*b*) any animal suffering from a serious organic disease, whose meat is forbidden even if it has been ritually slaughtered.

ULAM. The hall or porch leading to the interior of the Temple.

ZAB, (fem. ZABAH). The biblical term for a person who has experienced seminal emission (Lev. XV, 2).

ZAR (Lit., 'stranger'); an Israelite, as opposed to a priest, who may not eat of *terumah* or perform certain acts in connection with sacrifices.

ZIBAH. A flux; gonorrhoea. Also the state of uncleanness of a *Zab*, q.v.

CORRIGENDA

On page 4b note b1 for 'him,' as stated in end of n. 9, p. 14.' read 'him.' V. supra n. a9.'

On page 35b note a1 for 'v.p. 155 nn. 3 and 4.' read V. supra 31a nn. a3 and 4.'

On page 45a lines 19-20 for 'slaughtering of sacrifices?[6] Yet we' read 'slaughtering of sacrifices;[6] they are also only for the Messianic era? Yet we'

On page 48b note b9 for 'its neck wrung. Hence' read 'its neck nipped with the fingernail of his thumb. Hence'

On page 52b note a9 for '(v.p. 287, n. 3),' read '(v. supra 57a n. c3).'

On page 70b note C1 for '(v.p. 22, n. 8).' read '(v. supra 5b n. b8).'

On page 99b line 20 for 'en courant.[7]' read 'incidentally.[7]'

On page 103a note a2 for '(v. n. 8, p. 496),' read '(v. supra 103a n. 8),'

On page 107b line 6 for 'for the nonce' read 'only for the time being'

On page 107b line 7 for 'for the nonce' read 'only for the time being'

On page 107b line 19 for 'for the nonce' read 'only for the time being'

On page 107b line 22 for 'for the nonce' read 'only for the time being'